TEACHER'S EDITION

U.S. HISTORY

AMERICAN STORIES

UNITED STATES

The Space Race

The space race was a competition that started in 1957 between the United States and the Soviet Union to see which nation could make the greatest advances in space travel and technology. In 1961, President John F. Kennedy set a lofty goal: to send American astronauts to the moon.

His dream was realized on July 16, 1969, by the Apollo 11 mission. Astronauts Buzz Aldrin and Neil Armstrong landed a small lunar module on the moon's surface and Armstrong took the first steps. It was an important moment for humankind, for the United States, and for technology—a moment that continues to shape history.

For more information about the space race and the lunar landing, read Lesson 1.2 in Chapter 27 and Lesson 1.3 in Chapter 28.

 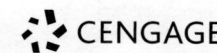

Acknowledgments

Grateful acknowledgment is given to the authors, artists, photographers, museums, publishers, and agents for permission to reprint copyrighted material. Every effort has been made to secure the appropriate permission. If any omissions have been made or if corrections are required, please contact the Publisher.

LEXILE®, LEXILE® FRAMEWORK, LEXILE ANALYZER®, LEXILE ANALYZER® EDITOR ASSISTANT™, LEXILE TITLES DATABASE™, LEXILE CAREER DATABASE™, LEXILE GROWTH PLANNER™, the LEXILE® logo and POWERV™ are trademarks of MetaMetrics, Inc., and are registered in the United States and abroad. The trademarks and names of other companies and products mentioned herein are the property of their respective owners. Copyright © 2017 MetaMetrics, Inc. All rights reserved.

Pre-AP™ is a registered trademark of The College Board and used under agreement.

Credits

Wrap Cover: Mark Summers/National Geographic Learning

Acknowledgments and credits continue on page R89.

For product information and technology assistance, contact us at Customer & Sales Support, 888-915-3276

For permission to use material from this text or product, submit all requests online at **www.cengage.com/permissions**

Further permissions questions can be emailed to **permissionrequest@cengage.com**

National Geographic Learning | Cengage
1 N. State Street, Suite 900
Chicago, IL 60602

Cengage is a leading provider of customized learning solutions with office locations around the globe, including Singapore, the United Kingdom, Australia, Mexico, Brazil, and Japan. Locate your local office at **www.cengage.com/global.**

Visit National Geographic Learning online at **NGL.Cengage.com/school**
Visit our corporate website at **www.cengage.com**

ISBN: 978-133-738-7064

Printed in the the United States of America.
Print Number: 01
Print Year: 2018

NATIONAL GEOGRAPHIC

Senior Consultants

Fredrik Hiebert

Fred Hiebert is National Geographic's Archaeologist-in-Residence. He has led archaeological expeditions at ancient Silk Roads sites across Asia. Hiebert was curator of National Geographic's exhibition "Afghanistan: Hidden Treasures from the National Museum, Kabul," and its most recent exhibition, "The Greeks: Agamemnon to Alexander the Great."

Peggy Altoff

Peggy Altoff's career includes teaching middle school and high school students, supervising teachers, and serving as adjunct university faculty. Altoff served as a state social studies specialist in Maryland and as a K–12 coordinator in Colorado Springs. She is a past president of the National Council for the Social Studies (NCSS) and served on the task force for the 2012 NCSS National Curriculum Standards.

Fritz Fischer

Fritz Fischer is a professor and Director of History Education at the University of Northern Colorado, where he teaches U.S. History and Social Studies Education courses. Fischer is also Chair Emeritus of the Board of Trustees of the National Council for History Education (NCHE), the largest national membership organization focusing on history education at the K–12 level.

Program Consultants

Terence Clark
Director, Shíshálh Archaeological
Research Project
University of Saskatchewan

William Parkinson
Associate Curator of Anthropology,
Field Museum of Natural History
National Geographic Explorer

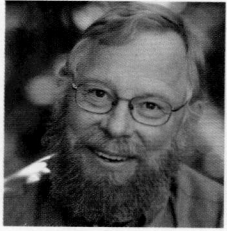

Ken Garrett
National Geographic Photographer

Robert Reid
Travel Writer
National Geographic
Digital Nomad

Kathryn Keane
Vice President, National Geographic
Exhibitions

Andrés Ruzo
Geothermal Scientist
National Geographic Explorer

National Geographic Teacher Reviewers

National Geographic works with teachers at all grade levels from across the country.
The following teachers reviewed chapters in *U.S. History: American Stories*.

Wesley Brown
Ravenscroft School
Raleigh, North Carolina

Karen Davis
St. Joseph School
Conway, Arkansas

Tama Nunnelley
Guntersville Middle School
Guntersville, Alabama

Natalie Wojinski
West Contra Costa USD
Richmond, California

Crystal Culp
McCracken Regional School
Paducah, Kentucky

Jessica Lura
Bullis Charter School
Los Altos, California

Ann Viegut
John Muir Middle School
Wausau, Wisconsin

Gain access to additional National Geographic lesson plans, activities, and educational programs at NatGeoEd.org.

National Geographic Society

The National Geographic Society contributed significantly to *National Geographic U.S. History:
American Stories*. Our collaboration with each of the following has been a pleasure and a privilege:
National Geographic Maps, National Geographic Education and Children's Media, and National
Geographic Missions programs. We thank the Society for its guidance and support.

NATIONAL GEOGRAPHIC

National Geographic Exploration

National Geographic supports the work of a host of anthropologists, archaeologists, adventurers, biologists, educators, writers, and photographers across the world. The individuals below each contributed substantially to *U.S. History: American Stories*.

Jason De Leon

Anthropologist

National Geographic Explorer

Ken Garrett

National Geographic Photographer

Caroline Gerdes

Writer

National Geographic Explorer

Barrington Irving, Jr.

Aviator

National Geographic Explorer

John Kelly

Archaeologist

National Geographic Explorer

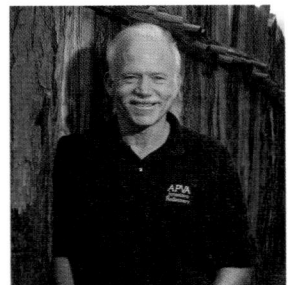

William Kelso

Archaeologist

National Geographic Explorer

Robert Reid

Travel Writer

National Geographic Digital Nomad

Pardis Sabeti

Computational Geneticist

National Geographic Explorer

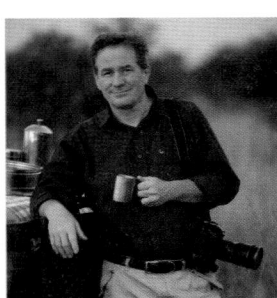

Joel Sartore

National Geographic Photographer

Donald Slater

Educator

National Geographic Explorer

The National Geographic Approach

Most of us recognize that familiar magazine with the yellow border on newsstands and library shelves. You've probably come to expect from *National Geographic* engaging stories on historical and global topics, with interesting photographs. But did you know that the magazine is only one part of an institution that dates back more than 128 years—and today plays an important role in world events?

OUR PURPOSE: The National Geographic Society pushes the boundaries of exploration to further our understanding of our planet and empower us all to generate solutions for a healthier and more sustainable future.

SCIENCE AND EXPLORATION

National Geographic has become one of the largest nonprofit scientific and educational institutions in the world. NatGeo supports thousands of scientists, archaeologists, marine biologists, divers, climbers, photographers, researchers, teachers, oceanographers, geologists, adventurers, physicists, artists, curators, and writers who work on projects that add to the scientific and human record.

THE NATIONAL GEOGRAPHIC LEARNING FRAMEWORK

The Learning Framework defines and shapes National Geographic's philosophy about teaching and learning. The framework is based on the **Attitudes**, **Skills**, and **Knowledge** that embody the Explorer mindset. It covers diverse fields of knowledge and recognizes the core principles established at National Geographic, as well as the values held by families, communities, and cultures. You will see National Geographic Learning Framework activities in each unit of this text.

The chart on the next page outlines the Attitudes, Skills, and Knowledge (A.S.K.) dimensions of the National Geographic Learning Framework as it applies to *American Stories*.

ATTITUDES

Curiosity. An explorer remains curious about how the world works. An explorer is adventurous, seeking out new and challenging experiences.

Responsibility. An explorer has concern for other people, cultures, and the planet. An explorer considers multiple perspectives and respects others regardless of differences.

Empowerment. An explorer acts on curiosity, respect, responsibility, and adventurousness and persists in the face of challenges.

SKILLS

Observation. An explorer notices and documents the world and is able to make sense of those observations.

Communication. An explorer is a storyteller, communicating experiences and ideas effectively through language and media. An explorer has literacy skills, interpreting and creating new understanding from spoken language, writing, and a wide variety of visual and audio media.

Collaboration. An explorer works effectively with others to achieve goals.

NG Learning Framework: Attitudes, Skills, and Knowledge

ATTITUDES Feelings we want students to express and experience during the activity	SKILLS What we want students to do during the activity	KNOWLDEGE The type of content the activity pertains to
Curiosity	Observation	Our Human Story
Responsibility	Communication	Our Living Planet
Empowerment	Collaboration	Critical Species
	Problem Solving	New Frontiers

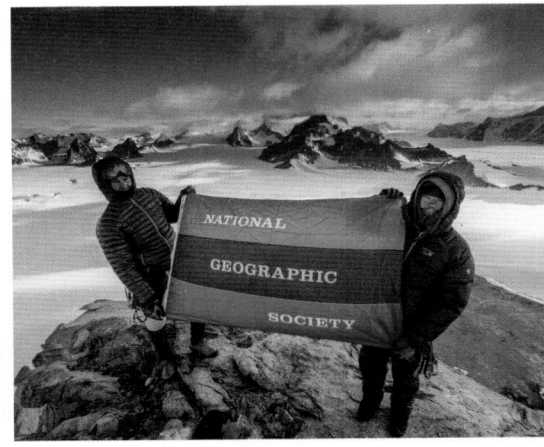

Problem Solving. An explorer is able to generate, evaluate, and implement solutions to problems. An explorer is a capable decision-maker—able to identify alternatives and weigh trade-offs to make a well-reasoned decision.

KNOWLEDGE

In addition to the skills and attitudes of an explorer, people need a certain knowledge set to understand how the world works. National Geographic expresses this critical knowledge through our key focus areas:

Our Human Story. Exploring where we came from, how we live today, and where we may find ourselves tomorrow.

Our Living Planet. Understanding the amazing, intricate, and interconnected systems of the changing planet we live on.

Critical Species. Revealing, celebrating, and helping to protect the amazing and diverse creatures we share our world with.

New Frontiers. Searching every day for the "new" and the "next," using the latest technology and science to go places no one has ever been and find answers no one has ever found.

A Note on National Geographic Style

Throughout the text, you will see the abbreviations B.C. and A.D. As you know, a date followed by B.C. refers to the number of years the date occurred before the birth of Christ. A date preceded by A.D. refers to the number of years the date occurred after the birth of Christ. Many historians use the abbreviations B.C.E. and C.E. for these time periods. B.C.E. stands for "Before the Common Era," and C.E. stands for "Common Era." The National Geographic Society adheres to the practice of using B.C. and A.D., and that is what is used in this text.

NATIONAL GEOGRAPHIC LEARNING
SOCIAL STUDIES CREDO

National Geographic Learning wants students to think about the impact of their choices on themselves and others, to think critically and carefully about ideas and actions, to become lifelong learners and teachers, and to advocate for the greater good as leaders in their communities. NGL follows these guidelines:

1 Our goal is to establish relevance by connecting the physical environment and historical events to students' lives.

2 We view history as the study of identity.

3 We foster the development of empathy, tolerance, and understanding for diverse peoples, cultures, traditions, and ideas.

4 We empower students to explore their interests and strengths, find their own voices, and speak out on their beliefs.

5 We encourage students to become active and responsible citizens on local and national levels and to become global citizens.

6 We believe in the beauty and endurance of the human record and the need to preserve it.

7 We affirm the critical need to care for the planet and all of its inhabitants.

Planning a Museum Visit

As they study history, students learn how and where civilizations developed through the centuries. They learn how to think about the world and discover the ways in which cultures and civilizations are similar—and how they are unique. They come to understand that knowing why a civilization developed can help them interpret the past, analyze the present, and anticipate the future.

By Kathryn Keane, Vice President, Exhibitions, National Geographic Society

To help your students take a trip into the past, to actually immerse themselves in history, take them to a museum. Museums are like time machines. They are the keepers of our shared and collective history. Museums were created to keep track of the most special examples of human-made objects, or **material culture**. Paintings, sculpture, pottery, jewelry, clothing, furniture, cars, toys, weapons, tools, fishing lures—just about anything that humans make is a remarkable historical record of the way we live.

Some examples of material culture are featured in the Curating History lessons in this program. Each lesson features objects drawn from the collection of an important U.S. museum. But what do we learn from this stuff? Why are some things in a museum and others are not?

Generally, museums look for the best artifacts for their collections, the ones that helped define a people or culture. Egyptian sarcophagi, Peruvian face pots, African ceremonial masks, Native American pottery, or Cycladic figurines from the Greek islands are all examples of artifacts that help us better understand those who made them. People from thousands of miles away and hundreds of years ago feel more familiar when you observe that even in the distant past people ate on plates and drank from cups, had rugs on their floors and keys for their doors, and rocked their babies to sleep in wooden cradles. **Material culture** refers to what humans make—but also what makes us human. There is no better way to see this than in a museum. Use the following tips to ensure a positive museum visit for your class.

1. Plan ahead.

Before you visit, talk about the museum and its collection. Most museums have great websites, and many even have their entire collections online. Identify the must-see artifacts and works of art—the more students know ahead of time, the better. Contact the museum to see if a docent or museum educator can accompany your group. Plan travel logistics carefully, building in frequent small breaks, snacks, and so forth.

2. Let the museum help.

Once you arrive, check in with the information desk. Get maps and brochures for your students. If you haven't arranged for a docent or tour guide, ask if one might be available to accompany your class on a tour.

3. Encourage students to read, listen, and learn—and to use their imaginations.

Point out that labels, maps, time lines, videos, and audio tours will give students all the information they need as "context" for the objects. Audio tours are usually narrated by a curator, or expert, and are almost like getting a private tour. Remind students to use an artifact analysis form similar to the one shown in their History Notebook to help them analyze an artifact. Model how to think about the meaning of the objects. Ask students to imagine what it was like to live a long time ago or in a faraway place—or even in the mind of a creative artist. **ASK:** What will students 100 years from now learn about our society in a museum?

4. Dos and don'ts

Remind students to keep their voices down and leave their phones turned off and out of sight. Most important: Don't touch artifacts or lean on cases. Don't take photos unless expressly allowed, and make sure students are careful around fragile or delicate objects.

5. Back in the classroom

Spend some class time reviewing the visit and eliciting students' reactions to what they saw. **ASK:** What did you like best about the museum? What was your favorite artifact? What surprised you the most?

Encourage students to explore the museums in their community and to check out museums when they travel. Museums can become familiar and exciting companions in studying history.

Supporting Young Photographers

Photography as storytelling. For 40 years, I have made photographs for *National Geographic* magazine. Do you have students who are interested in photography? Here are some ideas to discuss with them.

Check out Ken Garrett's photo essay on the Civil War in Chapter 15 of the Student Edition.

By Kenneth Garrett, National Geographic Photographer

Help students understand how to know their subject thoroughly.

To photograph or illustrate a story, they need to think about what they want to communicate. Explain that they can follow the work of key scientists or historians in the field. It is all about being ready to photograph the moment of discovery and then to publish it in the popular media for everyone to see. Without media coverage, many great discoveries lie silent on shelves in storerooms around the world. The process is always the same. Research the subject. Know the people. Know how to be in the right place at the right time.

Help students practice their photographic and storytelling skills.

I have held this advice close to my heart throughout my career—always working to make sure that my photographs have something to say. Assignments that can be accompanied by photographs will give students practice at explaining something with visuals. Obviously, the more practice, the better.

Explain the importance of crafting each image with intent and being prepared.

I was in Guatemala working on a story about remote imaging of Maya cities, and my editor knew there was going to be a planetary alignment of Venus, Jupiter, and Mars directly over a temple in Tikal and that it would not happen again for 200 years. Of course he wanted me to get a photograph of it. I brought a portable spotlight to "paint" the temple with light and made a wonderful photo with the planets aligned over the temple. This is what I call making your own luck—being prepared and ready for what's about to happen.

Talk about customizing lighting and how to make the subject "pop."

If my subject is an artifact in a museum, I study it with a flashlight until I find an angle where it "speaks" to me. Then I create a lighting setup to bring out the personality that I identified with the flashlight. Sometimes I even make the photo by painting the object with the light from the flashlight. Photographs are made up of light, so lighting the subject, whether it is an object, a landscape, or an architectural feature, is most important. The image must pop, and readers must say "wow," or they won't stop to learn. There is simply too much visual competition out there.

Emphasize that students should be adaptable but at the same time unafraid to develop their own vision.

I was trained to be a generalist, flexible, able to adapt to any situation. I was identified as the photographer to send if there was nothing to photograph because I would *find* something to photograph. In today's world, I still believe it is important to be adaptable, but the market is often looking for photographers with an unusual specialty—a way of seeing that translates into your own unique style.

Help students develop a portfolio.

Encourage students to work for the school newspaper or yearbook. Once they have built a portfolio, they can approach local newspapers. Today, with Instagram, Facebook, and other platforms, they can have their photos "out there" as soon as they shoot them. Remind students that the ownership of their photos can be compromised if they are posted online.

Remind students to follow the new technology in photography.

Today's cameras have eliminated much of the technical difficulty of capturing an image. With this new technology come exciting new opportunities to push the envelope— for example, to shoot in virtual darkness, shoot remotely, shoot from a drone, or shoot underwater from a remotely operated submersible. Constantly following the new technology is a requirement of today's photography business.

Caution students to be prepared for the lifestyle of a photographer.

An established photographer has to be prepared to be away from home for weeks or months at a time, living with a subject until just the right situation presents itself: until a rapport is established that allows special access to an event, until a discovery is made, or until a polar bear walks up to the camera!

NatGeo's Digital Nomad Takes on U.S. History—Sort Of

Just what does a so-called Digital Nomad do? Based on what we see of Robert Reid in the *Reid-on-the Road* video series that accompanies *American Stories*, just about anything! Here, Robert shares his thoughts on how travel helps to make history come alive—and connect to students' lives today.

By Robert Reid, National Geographic's Digital Nomad

Every time I travel to a place as National Geographic's Digital Nomad, my first questions are the same: What happened here, what books and movies talk about it, and how can I add an angle to the ongoing story, something that adds to the existing conversation? In short, my focus is looking backward to look forward. I do that by putting history into travel. It's fun and informative. Working on this *American Stories* textbook is the same, but in reverse direction—in trying to show how history is *alive* and accessible, I'm putting it through the filter of travel.

For each of the videos that accompany *American Stories*, we talk with local experts—including those impersonating George Washington, overseeing Motown Records, and digging gold mines—and go up close and personal. The goal is to bring a question or two that, I hope, will resonate with students: Why is the Statue of Liberty the greatest gift of all time?

Why did Pilgrims wear funny hats? What's a hippie? Then I use travel to answer those questions.

And in some cases, I wear three layers of wool to do so. (Watch the videos—you'll get it!)

Perhaps my favorite story about developing the *Reid on the Road* video series was visiting Angel Island in San Francisco Bay. I lived in the city several years ago and had never made it there, nor did I realize that it was, in effect, the Ellis Island of the West Coast. Going there, I interviewed a Chinese American whose father entered the country through Angel Island, and I heard the stories of how immigrants entering the country from the west didn't exactly get the same reception as those entering through New York. I'll not forget it.

The goal, again, is to make a difference in students' understanding of this country—and to show that history isn't relegated to the past but is indeed alive. It moves, it changes. And how we use it is how we go through life. This may sound serious, but it's the first step in our personal chase of understanding. Which means that, like travel itself, it's about as much fun as you can have.

Robert Reid, NG's Digital Nomad, interviews a modern-day George Washington on the banks of the Delaware River.

Why Study U.S. History?

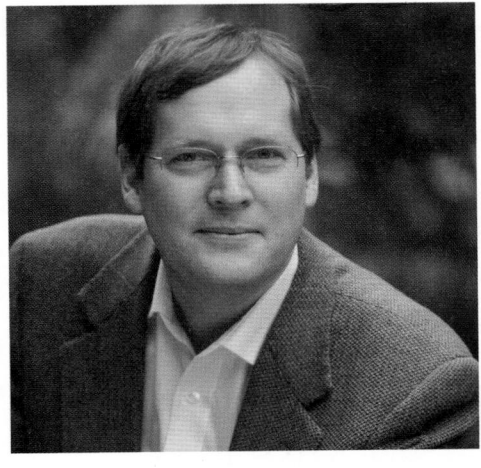

Dr. Fredrik Hiebert
National Geographic
Archaeologist-in-Residence

"Why Study U.S. History?" is a recurring feature in *American Stories*, helping students connect ideas and events from U.S. history to their own lives. Dr. Fred Hiebert, National Geographic's Archaeologist-in-Residence, provides a model for students to tell their own American stories. Have students use their History Notebooks to enhance their content understanding and to record their ideas as they read. "Why Study U.S. History?" encourages students to:

EXPLORE WHAT IT MEANS TO BE AN AMERICAN

With *American Stories*, the emphasis is on making individual meaning from the content rather than memorizing facts and dates. Content breadth and depth is still important, of course—but it's not very meaningful if students don't see the relevance and know how to apply history's lessons to their daily lives.

In "Why Study U.S. History?," Fred Hiebert introduces a **Framework for U.S. History** as one way to guide students' reading. He makes it clear from the beginning—students reading *American Stories* will be challenged to think about what it means to be an American today.

They should be asking themselves and each other these questions:

• What people and places are part of my American experience?

• How is my American experience similar to or different from others my age?

• What do I want my friends and family to know about my American experience?

Be sure to show the "Why Study U.S. History?" videos that accompany *American Stories*. And refer students to the "Why Study U.S. History?" pages in their History Notebooks.

TELL THEIR AMERICAN STORIES

In the introduction to "Why Study U.S. History?" Fred Hiebert begins to tell his own American story. He models for students ways to think about how their personal lives intersect with the larger community—and how an American identity can take shape.

UNDERSTAND THE ROLE OF THE UNITED STATES IN THE WORLD

In the final "Why Study U.S. History?" students focus on the California-Pacific Exposition in San Diego, an event that brought worldwide attention to the state and city. Remind students to use the pages in their History Notebooks to write about their American story.

EXAMPLE

Historical Thinking in the Middle School Classroom

Professor Fritz Fischer's understanding of what historical thinking looks like in the middle school classroom has proved to be a powerful foundation for *American Stories*. Here, he explains the ways historical thinking is supported in the chapters and lessons in this program.

By Fritz Fischer, Professor of History and History Education, University of Northern Colorado

The old-fashioned middle school history classes many adults remember too often devolved into a boring recitation of names, dates, and facts. Teachers merely presented facts in a stand-and-deliver lecture format, expecting students to regurgitate these facts on multiple-choice exams. Students were confronted with a blizzard of detail and often struggled to learn the content, only to forget what they learned in rushed bouts of memorization.

Ironically, historians themselves do not learn history in this way. History is about questions, not answers. To study history is to learn how to inquire. To understand the past, we first need to question the past. We learn how to gather and sift evidence from the past in order to answer these questions. Then we take this evidence and fashion it into an argument, or a logical story, about what happened. These are the basic processes in what historians and history educators now refer to as **historical thinking**.

The purpose of historical thinking is not to create a world of little historians. Rather, by teaching students to utilize the skills, concepts, and understandings central to historical thinking, we teach them how to better navigate their own lives. These abilities will help students gather and sift information in our current world. Recent studies have shown that a wide range of Americans, from middle schoolers to adults, have tremendous difficulty separating fact from fiction, real news from fake news, and accurate information from propaganda. Historical thinking is a critical antidote to these problems.

American Stories utilizes the skills, concepts, and understandings of historical thinking as a central organizational principle. Students will encounter a Historical Thinking section at the end of each lesson. These sections include a wide variety of tasks, all of which are important in building the capabilities of historical thinking in students. Here are some examples of the historical thinking exercises from *American Stories*:

Reading Check Many historical thinking tasks overlap with literacy skills, and reading is no exception. History is a literary discipline, and history teachers must be literacy teachers, helping students become proficient at reading and writing.

Compare and Contrast Historical understanding requires students to be able to differentiate among various examples, ideas, and events.

Interpret Visuals Historical evidence comes in many forms, and often it is not written down. Paintings, photographs, and artifacts are important historical evidence. Yet their significance and connection to other historical evidence is not always clear, and students need practice in interpreting this evidence.

Analyze Cause and Effect This is one of the most basic requirements of historical thinking. As we all know, history is not a haphazard collection of unconnected events.

Make Inferences We need to look beyond the words in a document and try to connect them with the context of the times. Another way of stating this is that students need to learn to read between the lines to understand the subtext of a document.

Synthesize and Draw Conclusions Students need to be encouraged to put information together and develop their own interpretations of ideas and events based on the evidence they have encountered.

This is merely an introductory list and, as you will see in the program materials, not exhaustive.

Perhaps the most exciting historical thinking exercises in *American Stories* are the Document-Based Questions, or DBQ, in each chapter. Fundamental to the concept of historical thinking is the understanding and use of *primary sources*, the building blocks of history. They are the documents and artifacts from the past, words spoken and artifacts fashioned by historical actors. Students need to be challenged to work to understand and then interpret these sources. Yet individual sources are insufficient to provide such an interpretation. Students need to learn how to examine a variety of sources with differing viewpoints if they are to have any chance of understanding the "truth" about the past. The DBQs in *American Stories* include three to five important sources for students to examine and think about as they create their own interpretations of the past.

I often encounter teachers who want to learn more about historical thinking and how they can integrate these ideas into their method of telling the American story. One idea is to get connected to organizations where history teaching and historical thinking are discussed on a regular basis.

For much of my career, I have been intimately connected with the National Council for History Education (NCHE), an organization designed to bring together K–12 history teachers, university historians, and public historians on an equal playing field. These groups have much to teach each other about how to think historically and how students learn this method of thinking. NCHE annual conferences, the NCHE newsletter *History Matters!* and NCHE professional development workshops provide just such platforms.

There are also plenty of free resources online that provide more information and ideas for teachers about historical thinking. NCHE has a website (*nche.net*) that provides a "Blueprint for Student Learning in History" as well as an outline of "History's Habits of Mind," among other important resources.

The Stanford History Education Group has a brilliant website (*sheg.stanford.edu*) including lesson ideas and assessments all centered on historical thinking.

In the first decade of the 21st century, the federal government funded the Teaching American History Grant Program, which created an extraordinary free website at *teachinghistory.org*. This site includes valuable videos explaining historical thinking at all levels and also has links to hundreds of different lessons connected to historical thinking.

Basing classroom activities on historical thinking means creating an active, inquiry-based classroom. Students should be consistently questioning the past, questioning the teacher, and questioning each other. They should constantly be engaging and manipulating historical sources and creating interpretations about how these sources fit together. Finally, students should learn how to argue about their interpretations in a thoughtful and civil way. There is no better way to engage and excite a group of 8th graders than by creating such a historical thinking–based classroom.

For more on historical thinking in the classroom:

nche.net

sheg.stanford.edu

teachinghistory.org

Active Learning in the History Classroom

Easily influenced by peers and distracted by text messaging and social media, middle school learners can be challenging. A class of middle school students is a highly diverse group of learners with myriad personalities and learning styles—what's the best way to reach them?

By Peggy Altoff, Senior Consultant, former teacher and past president of NCSS

As you know from experience, a middle school teacher must be fully prepared to engage students each day and flexible enough to change plans at a moment's notice with the shifting classroom dynamic. National Geographic's U.S. History program, *American Stories*, contains a wealth of teaching options that are perfect for the active teacher—and active students.

VARIETY AND FLEXIBILITY

An expansive repertoire of proven strategies and appropriate activities provides the best preparation for each day's teaching. The structure of the Student Edition in this program is specifically designed to provide options that engage students in meaningful learning activities. The two-page format of each lesson in a chapter allows for several approaches, including

- selecting lessons and sections that are most appropriate for any given class of learners;
- focusing on one lesson each day to provide a depth of content knowledge;
- using cooperative learning activities that allow students to teach and learn from each other.

In a cooperative learning activity, for example, students can participate in a Jigsaw strategy, in which groups of students become "experts" on one lesson in a chapter. Next, all expert groups switch into new groups with each new group having one expert on each lesson. Each expert is then responsible for teaching the others in the group about the lesson. (See **Cooperative Learning Strategies** in this Teacher's Edition for a complete explanation of the Jigsaw strategy.)

Another cooperative learning possibility involves breaking a lesson into segments by subheading. Most of the lessons in the Student Edition have two subheadings. This makes it easy for students to work in pairs, with each student reading and learning about information in one segment and then sharing and discussing with the other.

You may also consider having students work in pairs or small groups to discuss a **Historical Thinking** question, a **Critical Viewing** question, or other text-based features. Experience suggests that each grouping strategy requires practice with students so that they can meet teacher expectations for appropriate conduct while acquiring knowledge of the content presented.

Student Edition activities are intended to address a variety of learning styles. The **Reading Strategy** at the beginning of each chapter provides students with a plan to organize and analyze what they are about to read. The **Historical Thinking** questions at the end of each lesson provide skill practice with interpreting maps, analyzing visuals, sequencing events, and so on that can be completed individually, in small groups, or as a class. **Chapter Reviews** include an activity that requires students to demonstrate what they have learned through writing. A **Unit Wrap-Up** at the end of each unit offers students insight into the work of archaeologists, scientists, writers, and other experts. It also includes a **Unit Inquiry** project that asks students to present what they've learned using many different formats, including writing, video, and multimedia.

COMPONENTS FOR THE TEACHER

The Teacher's Edition of *American Stories* presents many possibilities for active learning and student engagement. The **Cooperative Learning Strategies** section offers a preview of the types of strategies located throughout the Teacher's Edition with a clear explanation of how to implement each one. For the highly experienced teacher, this may offer a review of practical procedures. Those new to the profession will probably want to return to these pages frequently to plan new experiences for students.

The **Chapter Planner** in the Teacher's Edition provides an overview of the lesson support in, each chapter and lists such tools as **Reading and Note-Taking**, **Vocabulary Practice**, **Social Studies Skills Lessons**, **Section Quizzes**, and **Formal Assessment Tests**. The **Strategies for Differentiation** section that opens each Teacher's Edition chapter offers ideas that engage different groups of students under the headings Striving Readers, Inclusion, English Language Learners, Gifted & Talented, and Pre-AP.

You can decide how to apply each of these strategies to individual learners.

For daily planning, refer to each lesson's **Plan**, **Teach**, and **Differentiate** sections. The Teach section includes discussion questions and activities that help students summarize and analyze the lesson. It also contains an **Active Options** component that especially engages students with **Critical Viewing**, **National Geographic Learning Framework**, and (my personal favorite) **On Your Feet** activities. We know that middle school students are constantly moving and doing, and this feature provides ways to channel that bounding energy meaningfully.

Think carefully about how to select the options that are appropriate for your

students. For me, Rule No. 1 in working with middle school students has always been to start simple and move toward the complex. It may not be a good idea, for example, to try to implement all of the available strategies and activities in one lesson. Start with those that make the most sense to you and gradually experiment with others. Inform students when you attempt a new strategy or activity and get their feedback on ways to improve it the next time. The activities and strategies in this program are not meant to provide a recipe for success. Instead, they form a menu of options that support daily decision-making based on your own abilities and preferences and those of your students.

EXAMPLE TEACHER'S EDITION LESSON ALIGNED WITH STUDENT EDITION LESSON 3.3 IN CHAPTER 2

Striking images, graphics, and detailed maps engage and inform students.

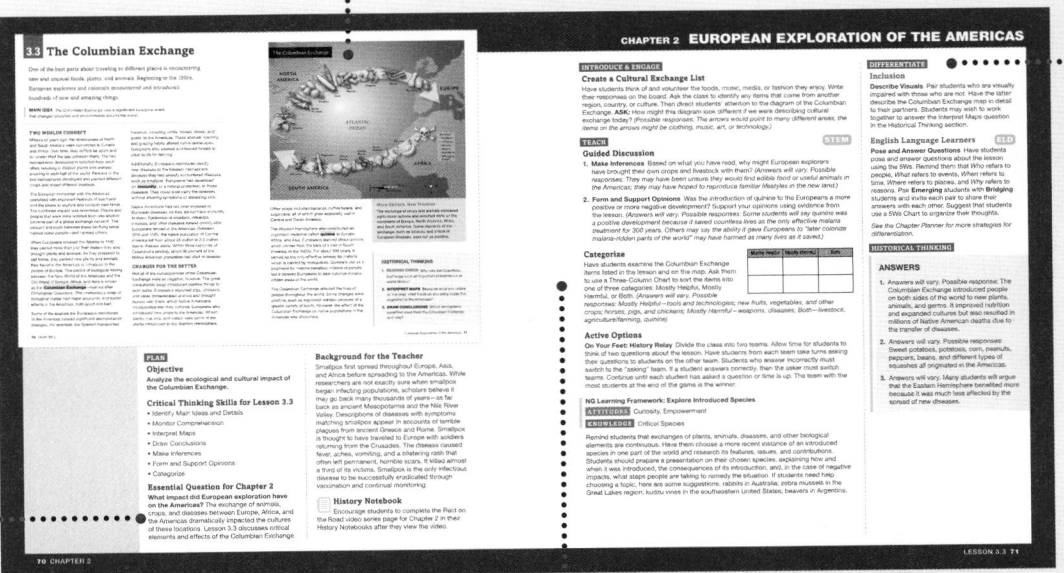

Each lesson offers two Differentiate options for instruction.

The Plan section helps teachers prepare to teach lessons.

The Introduce & Engage and Teach sections provide multiple access points for teaching content.

Project-Based Learning

Project-based learning is integral to successful history–social studies instruction. Well-designed projects allow students to

- explore a topic in depth;

- hone their skills in research, analysis, and critical thinking;

- work collaboratively with others toward a shared goal—an ability that is highly valued in both academic circles and the professional marketplace;

- become engaged and enthusiastic about a social studies topic;

- exercise creative control over their final product.

In addition, teachers may use projects to assess both students' grasp of content and their progress in developing collaboration and critical thinking skills.

The best projects not only allow students to express themselves creatively but also guide them through a rigorous, structured process of inquiry and research.

The best projects also ask students to create an end product that can be shared with their classmates. This project read-out can become part of each student's creative portfolio.

THE NATURE OF INQUIRY

The National Council for the Social Studies (NCSS) details the process of inquiry in the College, Career, and Civic Life Framework for Social Studies State Standards, or C3 Framework. The document proposes an Inquiry Arc that enumerates four dimensions of the process:

1. **Developing Questions and Planning Inquiries** Teachers or students generate a compelling question to guide research and supporting questions to help in seeking out specific evidence. The Essential Question at the beginning of each chapter in *American Stories* is designed to spark inquiry-style thinking in students as they move through the text.

EXAMPLES

ESSENTIAL QUESTION
How did early settlers cope with challenges as they established the first 13 colonies?

ESSENTIAL QUESTION
In what ways did Thomas Jefferson's policies change the country?

2. **Applying Disciplinary Concepts and Tools** Students determine which disciplines—economics, civics, geography, or history—relate to their guiding and follow-up questions. The tools and concepts from these disciplines will enable them to seek out and analyze evidence.

3. **Evaluating Sources and Using Evidence** Students conduct their research, determine which sources are both useful and reliable, and locate relevant evidence they can use for claims and counterclaims.

4. **Communicating Conclusions and Taking Informed Action** Students shape and present their final projects, which may take a wide variety of forms, such as traditional essays, multimedia presentations, performance pieces, or virtual museum galleries. When a project relates to a present-day issue, students may also follow up on their conclusions by taking constructive action within the school or in the wider community.

Of necessity, some projects during the school year will be smaller in scope and may not emphasize all four dimensions of the Inquiry Arc. For example, the inquiry question may be determined in advance by the teacher, or students may be directed to use the textbook or other preselected sources for their research. Similarly, students' choices of methods for communicating their conclusions may be limited to a few options that take less time to produce.

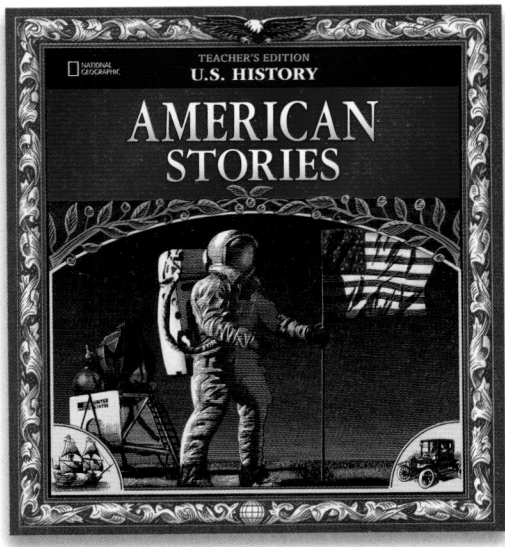

American Stories offers a variety of options for inquiry and project-based learning:

- The History Notebook contains four long-term **Projects for Inquiry-Based Learning** that can be completed over a semester or a school year. Over the course of the projects, students conduct research and synthesize information from multiple sources to answer questions on broader themes.

- At the end of each unit, a **Unit Inquiry** challenges students with open-ended questions and guides them to gather evidence from the text, synthesize a response, and present their conclusion to the class in a creative, engaging format.

  For example, the Unit Inquiry for Unit 3 in *American Stories* asks students to prepare an argument for or against declaring independence from Britain and to be prepared to present both sides to the class.

  Students use a T-chart to record risks and benefits of independence and shape an argument that they present through a speech to the class or in a classroom debate.

You may choose to expand the scope of the Unit Inquiry by having students conduct independent research using other sources or explicitly apply concepts from more than one discipline in their presentations. Alternatively, you might choose to limit the scope of the project by limiting students' options for presenting their projects.

- The National Geographic Learning Framework activities at the end of each unit also offer multiple opportunities for inquiry and creative thought. Depending on students' needs, you might select an activity and explicitly guide the class through the four dimensions of the Inquiry Arc to complete it, or you might have students complete the activities independently or in small groups.

RESEARCH SKILLS

Developing good research skills benefits students both inside and outside the classroom. Learning how to locate and evaluate information helps them improve the critical thinking skills they need not only to make and support an argument within a social studies project but also to make well-considered decisions in their everyday lives. Students can hone their research skills through instruction, guidance, and a great deal of practice.

Before launching the first inquiry project, make sure students understand the differences between quantitative and qualitative research:

quantitative research: "hard evidence"—numbers, facts, and figures that can support an assertion

qualitative research: opinions from scholars, scientists, and other experts; firsthand accounts of events; information that provides insights into reasons or motivations

You might also explain that quantitative research answers *who, what, where,* and *when* questions. Qualitative research helps answer *why* and *how* questions.

Social studies inquiry projects should incorporate both types of research. Often, it is qualitative research that enables students to form hypotheses or outline their arguments. Both qualitative and quantitative research can be used to support claims and counterclaims.

Teachers should provide examples of sources students can use to conduct both types of research. For example, government websites, scientific articles, newspaper articles, and encyclopedia entries can be mined for quantitative information.

Qualitative information can be found in firsthand accounts of historical events and analyses of those events written by scholars. Of course, many sources contain both types of information, and students might benefit from an activity in which they review an article to distinguish the qualitative and quantitative information it contains.

Similarly, at the beginning of the year, teachers should provide numerous examples of both reliable and unreliable sources and clearly explain the characteristics of each. You might also provide a list of approved sources for students to use or have students submit their sources before they proceed to gather evidence. As students gain confidence and skill, you can gradually release to them the responsibility for finding and evaluating sources.

Cross-Disciplinary Teaching

American Stories includes numerous features to support students' reading development, including explicit vocabulary instruction, text within the Lexile band recommended by the Common Core State Standards, and differentiation notes in the Teacher's Edition to help teachers scaffold comprehension for striving readers.

Vocabulary support begins in the Student Edition, with each chapter's key vocabulary and important terms and names listed in the chapter introduction. Striving readers will benefit from the highlighting that calls out these terms in the lessons themselves, signaling their critical role in enhancing comprehension of content area text.

At the beginning of the year, you can identify striving readers in the class and provide ongoing support, such as additional vocabulary help and small-group time during which students can ask questions. Advanced readers can be offered activities from the Teacher's Edition differentiation notes for gifted and talented and pre-AP students.

The digital Vocabulary Practice page for each section of the Student Edition (example below) reinforces students' understanding of social studies terms.

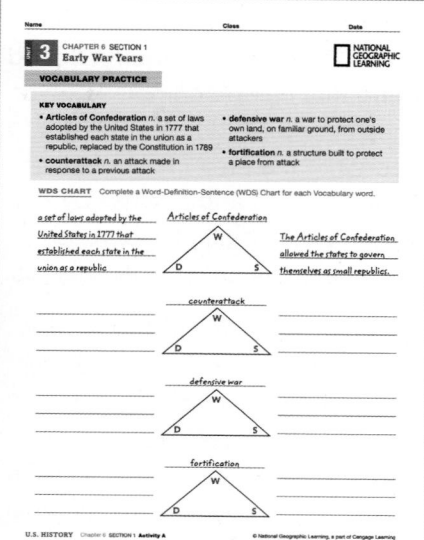

EXAMPLE VOCABULARY TREATMENT IN CHAPTER 6 INTRODUCTION AND LESSON 1.1

Chapter-level vocabulary lists alert students to watch for important terms and names as they read.

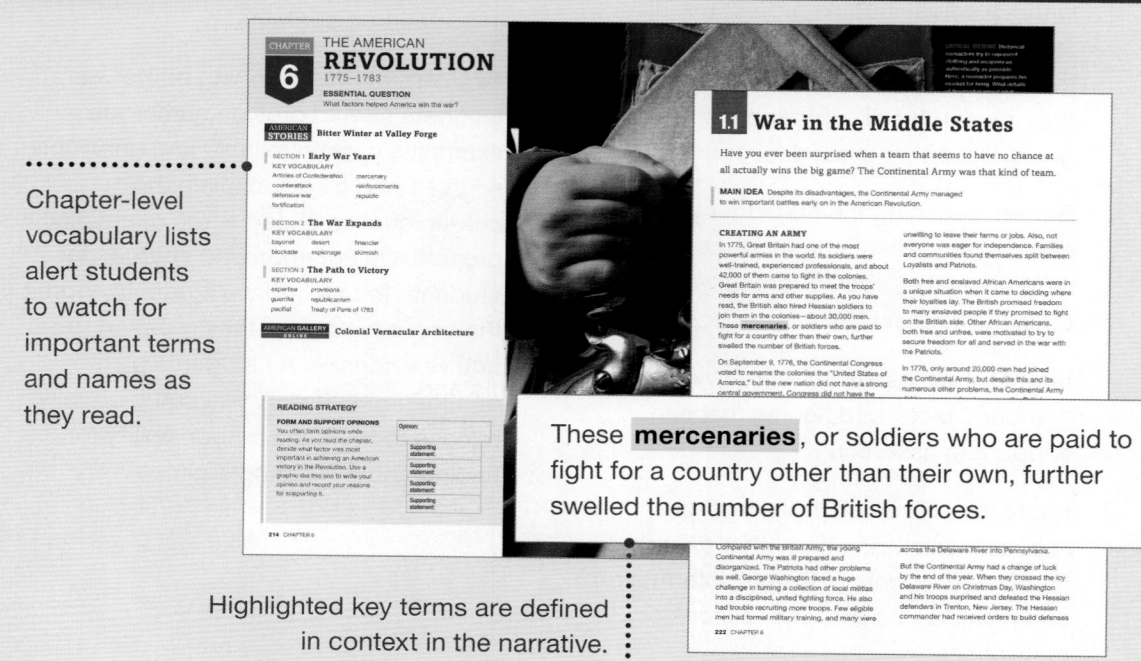

These **mercenaries**, or soldiers who are paid to fight for a country other than their own, further swelled the number of British forces.

Highlighted key terms are defined in context in the narrative.

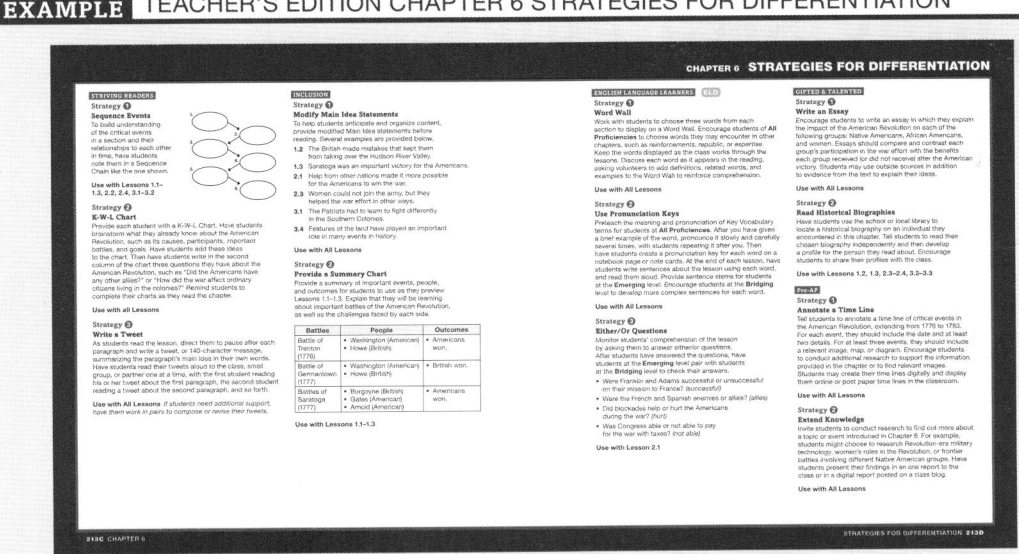

Pages 213C–213D in this Teacher's Edition

This Teacher's Edition also provides differentiation activities to customize instruction for ELs at the Emerging, Expanding, and Bridging levels. To support ELD, teachers should establish ongoing routines, such as previewing the lessons to identify language that may be challenging to ELs and providing specific help with these passages, working with small groups of ELs, and occasionally pairing ELs with more proficient readers.

You might also collaborate with the ELD teacher to incorporate content or language from the current *American Stories* lesson. Where possible, it is valuable to encourage ELs to share the connections they can make between social studies content and their own experiences or home culture. This practice creates speaking opportunities for ELs and allows them to experience the rewards of making a unique and useful contribution to the classroom conversation.

IN THE CONTENT AREAS

STEM History–social studies topics often lend themselves to cross-disciplinary lessons with STEM concepts. Annotations throughout this Teacher's Edition highlight opportunities to connect to STEM instruction. You can also encourage students to look for such connections on their own and point them out to the class.

Geography An obvious cross-disciplinary connection for history students is geography. *American Stories* leverages National Geographic assets to include Geography in History and Geology in History lessons in selected chapters. The approach is always on how geography can enhance our understanding of historical decisions and events.

The National Geographic maps in this program are created using real-time data as appropriate and are geared toward a student audience. An online National Geographic Atlas furnishes ample support for both history and geography.

In addition, a Geography Handbook in the reference section of the text provides support and practice for analyzing maps and covers common geographic concepts.

EXAMPLE ELL STRATEGIES

ENGLISH LANGUAGE LEARNERS

Strategy ❶

Use Paired Reading

To help students with comprehension, pair **Expanding** and **Bridging** students to read passages from the text aloud:

1. Partner 1 reads a passage; Partner 2 retells the passage in his or her own words.
2. Partner 2 reads a different passage; Partner 1 retells it.
3. Pairs repeat the whole exercise, switching roles.

Use with All Lessons

Page 295D in this Teacher's Edition

ENGLISH LANGUAGE LEARNERS

Strategy ❶

Pair Partners for Dictation

After reading a lesson, direct students to write in their own words a sentence telling an important idea from the reading. Pair students and let them take turns dictating their sentences to each other. Then allow them to work together to check spelling and accuracy.

Use with All Lessons *You may wish to pair students at the **Emerging** level with those at the **Bridging** level.*

Page 379D in this Teacher's Edition

Cooperative Learning Strategies

Cooperative learning strategies transform today's classroom diversity into a vital resource for promoting students' acquisition of both challenging academic content and language. These strategies promote active engagement and social motivation for all students.

STRUCTURE & GRAPHIC	DESCRIPTION	BENEFITS & PURPOSES
CORNERS A strongly agree B disagree C agree D strongly disagree	• Corners of the classroom are designated for focused discussion of four aspects of a topic. • Students individually think and write about the topic for a short time. • Students group into the corner of their choice and discuss the topic. • At least one student from each corner shares about the corner discussion.	• By "voting" with their feet, students literally take a position about a topic. • Focused discussion develops deeper thought about a topic. • Students experience many valid points of view about a topic.
FISHBOWL 	• Part of the class sits in a close circle facing inward; the other part of the class sits in a larger circle around them. • Students on the inside discuss a topic while those outside listen for new information and/or evaluate the discussion according to pre-established criteria. • Groups reverse positions.	• Focused listening enhances knowledge acquisition and listening skills. • Peer evaluation supports development of specific discussion skills. • Identification of criteria for evaluation promotes self-monitoring.
INSIDE-OUTSIDE CIRCLE 	• Students stand in concentric circles facing each other. • Students in the outside circle ask questions; those inside answer. • On a signal, students rotate to create new partnerships. • On another signal, students trade inside/outside roles.	• Talking one-on-one with a variety of partners gives risk-free practice in speaking skills. • Interactions can be structured to focus on specific speaking skills. • Students practice both speaking and active listening.
JIGSAW Expert Group 1 · A's Expert Group 2 · B's Expert Group 3 · C's Expert Group 4 · D's	• Group students evenly into "expert" groups. • Expert groups study one topic or aspect of a topic in depth. • Regroup students so that each new group has at least one member from each expert group. • Experts report on their study. Other students learn from the experts.	• Becoming an expert provides in-depth understanding in one aspect of study. • Learning from peers provides breadth of understanding of overarching concepts.

STRUCTURE & GRAPHIC	DESCRIPTION	BENEFITS & PURPOSES
NUMBERED HEADS 	• Students number off within each group. • Teacher prompts or gives a directive. • Students think individually about the topic. • Groups discuss the topic so that any member of the group can report for the group. • Teacher calls a number and the student with that number reports for the group.	• Group discussion of topics provides each student with language and concept understanding. • Random recitation provides an opportunity for evaluation of both individual and group progress.
ROUNDTABLE 	• Seat students around a table in groups of four. • Teacher asks a question with many possible answers. • Each student around the table answers the question a different way.	• Encouraging elaboration creates appreciation for diversity of opinion and thought. • Eliciting multiple answers enhances language fluency.
TEAM WORD WEBBING 	• Provide each team with a single large piece of paper. Give each student a different colored marker. • Teacher assigns a topic for a word web. • Each student adds to the part of the web nearest to him or her. • On a signal, students rotate the paper and each student adds to the nearest part again.	• Individual input to a group product ensures participation by all students. • Shifting points of view support both broad and in-depth understanding of concepts.
THINK, PAIR, SHARE 	• Students think about a topic suggested by the teacher. • Pairs discuss the topic. • Students individually share information with the class.	• The opportunity for self-talk during the individual think time allows the student to formulate thoughts before speaking. • Discussion with a partner reduces performance anxiety and enhances understanding.
THREE-STEP INTERVIEW 	• Students form pairs. • Student A interviews Student B about a topic. • Partners reverse roles. • Student A shares with the class information from Student B; then Student B shares information from Student A.	• Interviewing supports language acquisition by providing scripts for expression. • Responding provides opportunities for structured self-expression.

Assessment in *American Stories*

American Stories provides opportunities for two main types of assessment: formative and summative.

- **Formative assessment** is assessment *for* learning. Its focus is to assist in immediate learning, it is delivered from teacher to individual students, and it takes place during instruction or in the sequence of lessons.

- **Summative assessment** is assessment *of* learning. Its focus is to measure students' progress and inform future teaching or to evaluate educational programs. Summative assessment takes place at the end of a unit, semester, or course.

Some tests or projects may serve both a formative and a summative purpose. Effective use of both formative and summative assessment enables you to create a positive feedback loop in which you can use assessment results to differentiate instruction or determine which content or skills need to be retaught and then customize future assessments to gauge learning of new and retaught material.

It is important, too, to engage in a variety of assessment modes. Some students may better demonstrate their understanding through performance assessments, such as discussions, debates, or presentations. Others may be more accurately assessed using pencil-and-paper tests and writing assignments. Students should have chances to demonstrate their knowledge through both individual and cooperative assessments.

The activities and tests in *American Stories* offer a generous variety of opportunities for both formative and summative assessment in numerous modes. The following assessments, with examples, will enable you to support and measure learning at the lesson, chapter, and unit levels.

Historical Thinking Each lesson in the Student Edition ends with questions that assess students' understanding of the lesson's content and their ability to analyze it. You can use this quick formative assessment to help students develop their critical thinking skills and to determine whether any concepts need to be reinforced or retaught.

The skill head on each question reflects the support for historical thinking offered in *American Stories*. Practice with these social studies skills supports student comprehension and enables students to improve their writing about history.

EXAMPLE

HISTORICAL THINKING

1. **READING CHECK** How was the Continental Navy able to hold its own against Britain's Royal Navy?

2. **ANALYZE CAUSE AND EFFECT** How were France and Spain affected by the war at sea?

3. **MAKE INFERENCES** What do you think James Forten hoped to gain by fighting to uphold the American principles of freedom?

Guided Discussions and Active Options For each lesson, this Teacher's Edition provides Guided Discussion questions and an On Your Feet activity that requires students to engage physically by moving in the classroom and to perform collaborative activities, such as fishbowl conversations, interviews, and inside-outside circles. By observing students and providing feedback, you can use these activities for formative assessment of content mastery, critical thinking skills, and discussion skills.

EXAMPLE

Guided Discussion

1. **Summarize** What factors accounted for the Pilgrims' survival upon arriving in America? *(The Pilgrims planned how to govern themselves and kept the group together. After the first winter killed half of the group, the Pilgrims made friends with the Pawtuxet, who helped the Pilgrims grow crops.)*

2. **Evaluate** Why were the Mayflower Compact and the Fundamental Orders of Connecticut significant to the development of self-government in the colonies? *(Both documents were created by the colonists and provided rules and plans for governing the colonies. These documents were not imposed by the king of England nor subject to England's laws. In addition, the Fundamental Orders established a General Assembly that included representatives from towns and did not limit voting to church members.)*

Guided Discussion questions like those above provide additional material for classroom interaction. These questions can be discussed as a whole class, used for small group work, or assigned as homework.

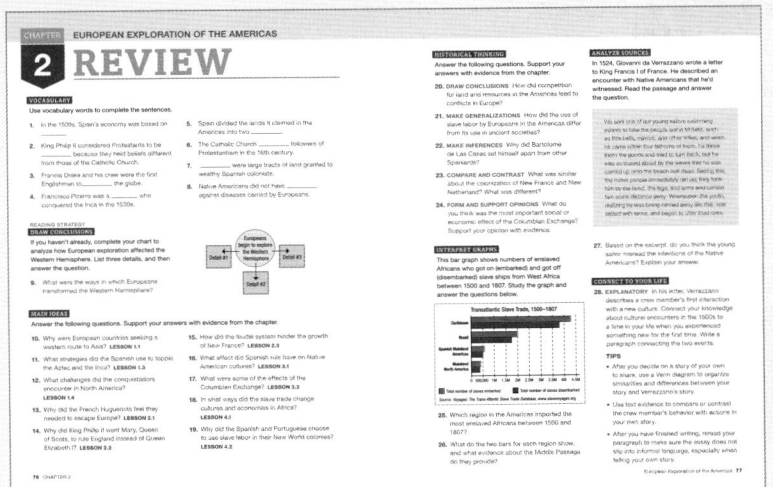

Chapter Review Each chapter concludes with a review that includes a short vocabulary test and a series of constructed response items that require students to restate the main ideas in the chapter, engage in historical thinking, interpret a visual, analyze a primary source, and write a brief essay connecting the chapter topic to their lives. This summative assessment allows you to measure students' progress and give feedback in the form of a chapter grade.

Unit Test At the end of each unit, a summative assessment evaluates students' grasp of the main ideas and overarching themes of the unit. As in the chapter review, students answer historical thinking questions, interpret visuals, and analyze a primary source. In the extended response, students engage in comparative thinking as they compare two eras or themes in history.

Gradebook The electronic Gradebook function in MindTap allows teachers to track and analyze an individual student's progress with ease. You can view the class's grades for each activity, click on a grade to view assignment details such as score and student answers, view the scores for each individual student, and categorize assignments for purposes such as applying weighting for different assessments. Students may also view their assignments, due dates, and scores. This accurate and flexible grading tool helps teachers create the assessment feedback loop that benefits all students.

Projects At the end of each unit, a Unit Inquiry and two National Geographic Learning Framework activities can be used as summative performance assessments. Teachers may use these projects to assess students' research and presentation skills as well as their content knowledge. In addition, four **Projects for Inquiry-Based Learning** in the History Notebook can be used for both formative and summative assessment. Over the course of these long-term projects, you will have frequent opportunities to provide ongoing assessment and feedback to students, and the end products can be assessed to measure student learning.

EXAMPLES

Propose a New Invention

ATTITUDES Responsibility, Empowerment

SKILL Problem-Solving

Part of being a good citizen is taking care of the people and environment around you. The men and women who innovated new technologies in the early republic were all trying to solve some sort of problem or make a process more efficient. Using evidence from the reading, develop a proposal for a new invention. Define the problem that you are solving and how your invention would benefit your community or even the world. Consider including illustrations of your invention. Present your proposal to the class as if you were presenting to a panel of financial backers.

Write a Campaign Speech

SKILLS Collaboration, Communication

KNOWLEDGE Our Human Story

Political campaigns have been a part of American democracy since it began. Effective campaigns and their candidates have to deliver a clear message to potential voters if they want to win elections. Work with a small team of classmates to write a campaign speech about an important issue during the early republic. Use evidence from the reading to define your issue, craft your message, and select the candidate who would best deliver the speech. Present your team's speech and be prepared to listen to other teams' speeches.

The National Geographic Learning Framework activities help students understand the attitudes, skills, and knowledge that are involved in living the life of an Explorer. You will find additional explanation about the Learning Framework in this Teacher's Edition and at the National Geographic website under "Education."

MindTap for *American Stories*

MindTap is a personalized learning experience with relevant assignments that guide students to analyze, apply, and improve thinking. Teachers can measure skills and impact outcomes with ease.

EXAMPLE MINDTAP HOME PAGE

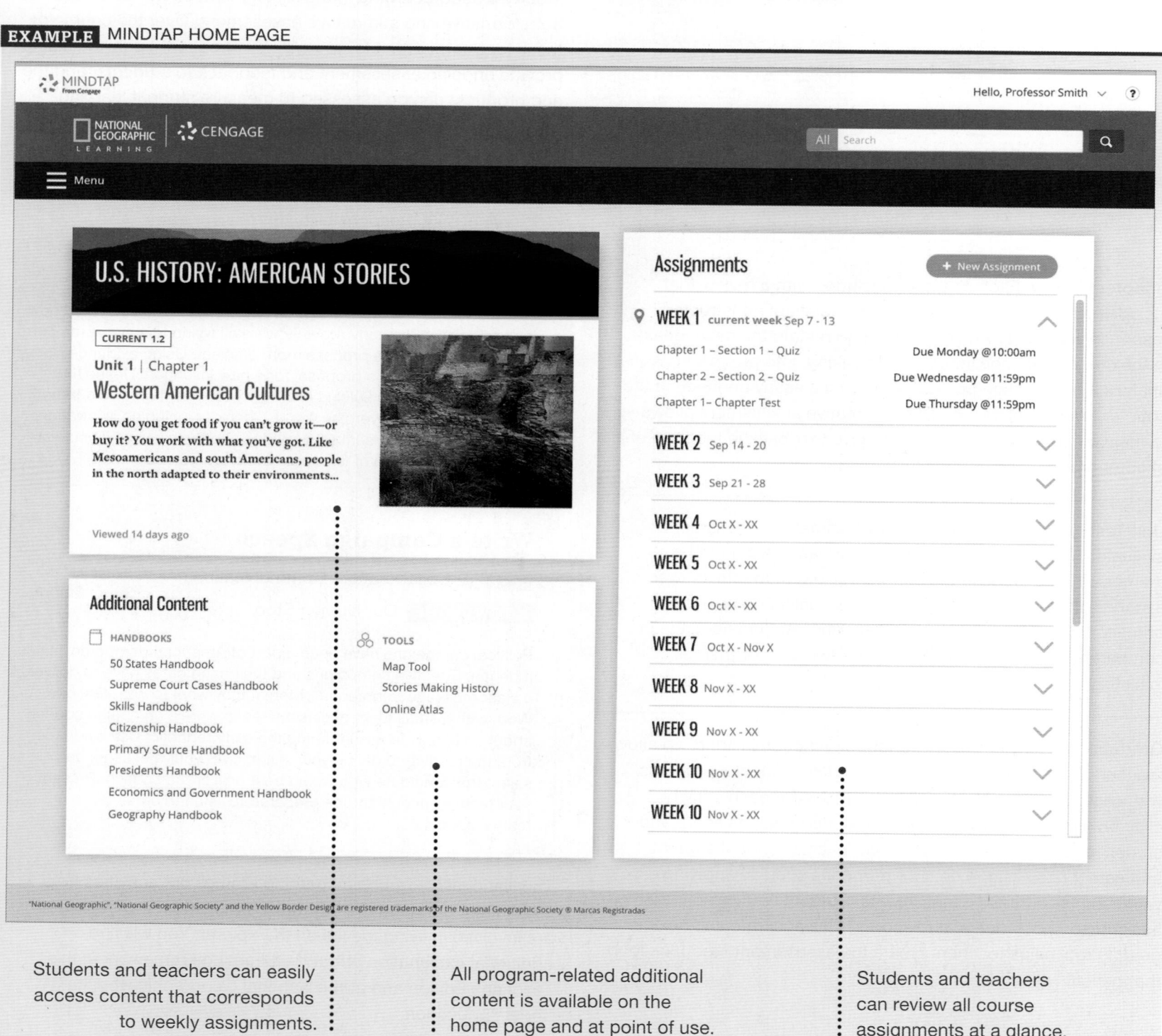

Students and teachers can easily access content that corresponds to weekly assignments.

All program-related additional content is available on the home page and at point of use.

Students and teachers can review all course assignments at a glance.

DIGITAL EXPERIENCE

The Student and Teacher eEditions provide enhancements and extra features not found in the print editions.

eReader

- The responsive page layout adjusts to students' screen or browser size.

- Clickable vocabulary words link to definition pop-ups.

- The Modified Text feature provides lesson content at a lower reading level.

- Additional features allow students to take notes, highlight text, and bookmark important content.

Student Tools

- Resources appear at the book, unit, chapter, and lesson level.

- Students can bookmark useful resources for easy access.

- eAssessment provides immediate feedback.

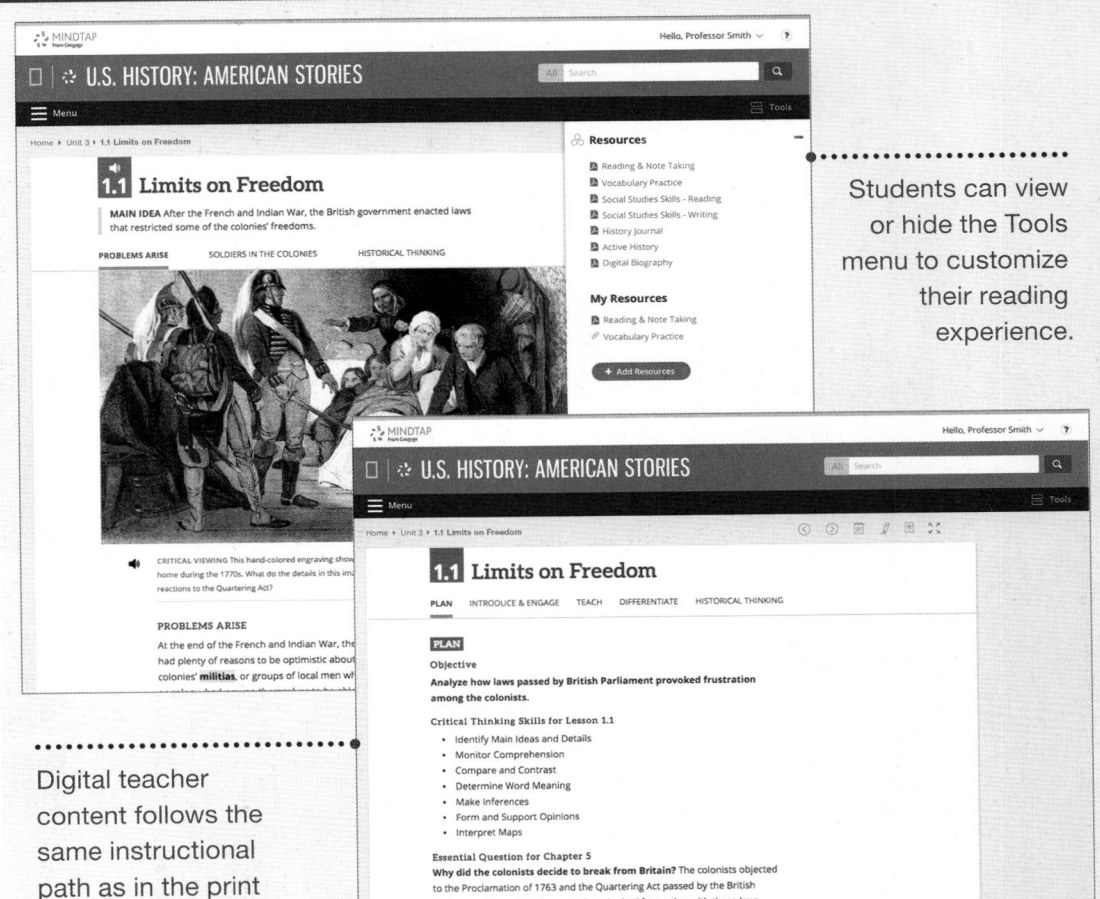

Students can view or hide the Tools menu to customize their reading experience.

Digital teacher content follows the same instructional path as in the print Teacher's Edition.

CLASS MANAGEMENT AND METRICS

A series of tools provides teachers with flexibility and support.

Teacher Dashboard

- Assignments can be customized to control student access to content.

- Student progress can be tracked in the Gradebook.

- A series of reports allow teachers to measure student progress.

- A correlations tool allows teachers to search content by content standard.

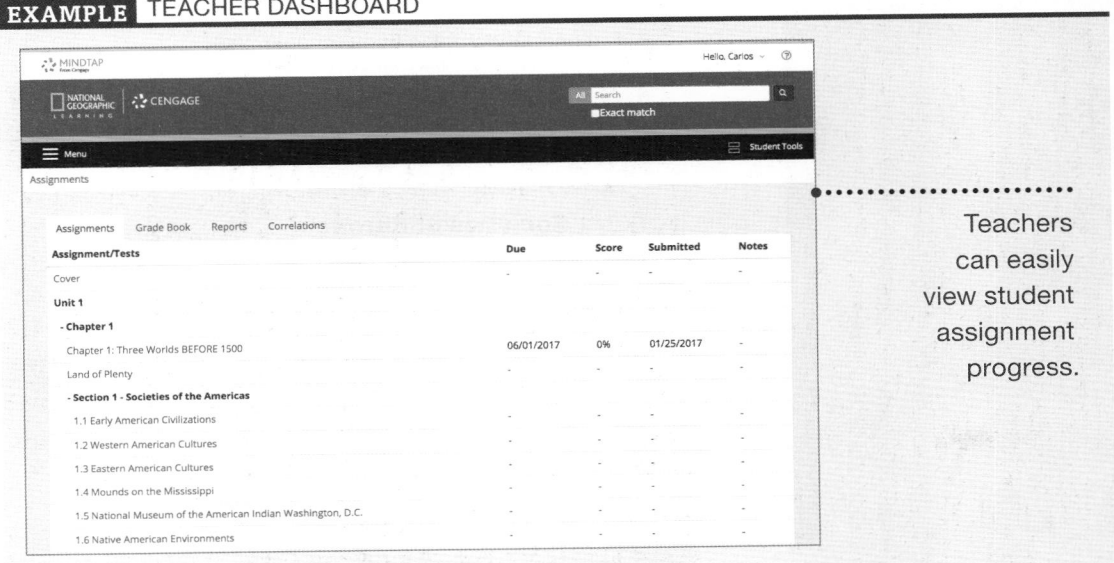

Teachers can easily view student assignment progress.

UNIT 1
EARLY ENCOUNTERS

(Beginnings–1650)

UNIT 2
ENGLISH SETTLEMENT
(1585–1763)

UNIT 3
A NEW
NATION
(1763–1791)

UNIT 4
THE EARLY REPUBLIC (1789–1844)

UNIT 5
PUSHING NATIONAL BOUNDARIES
(1821–1860)

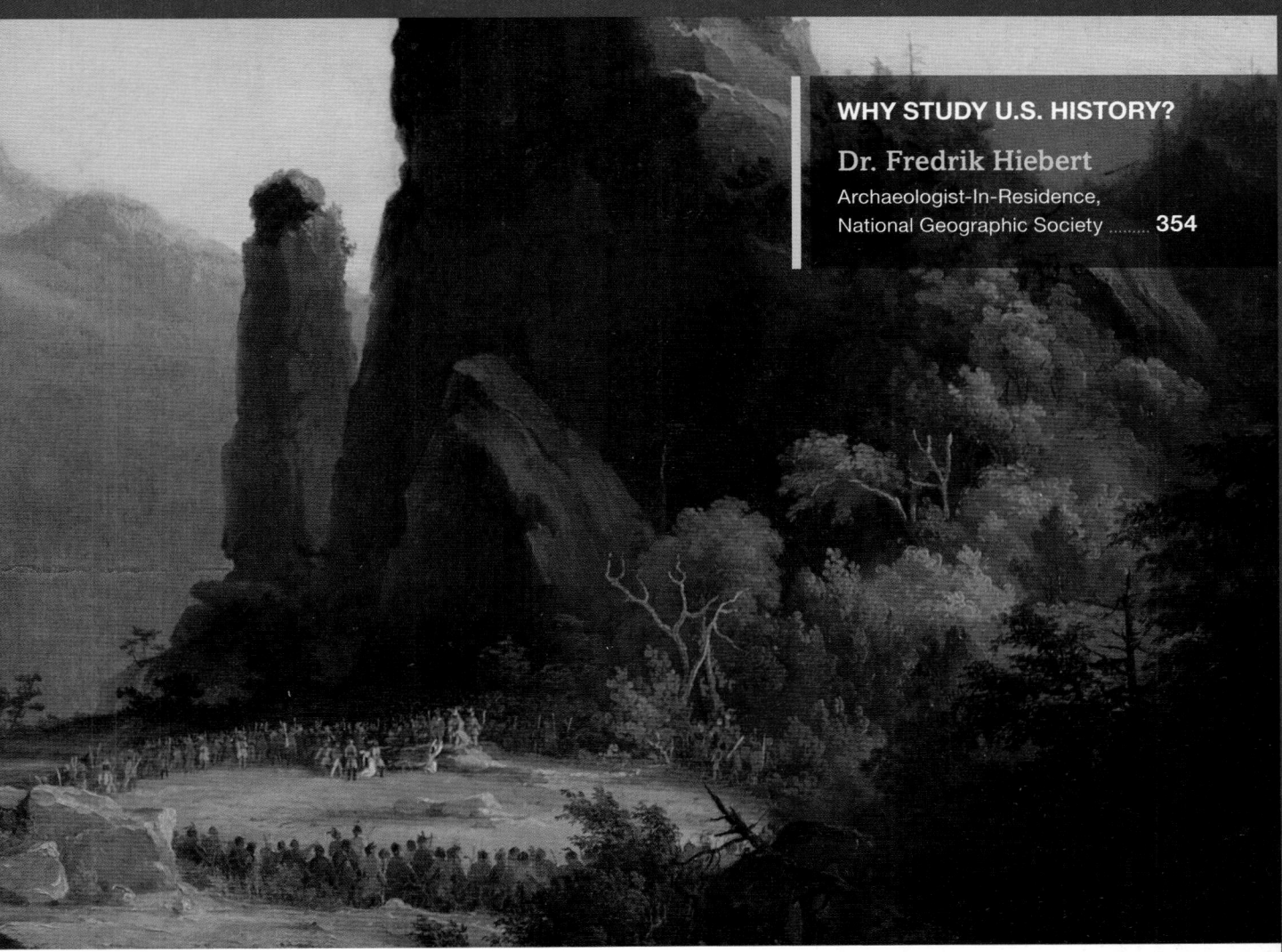

UNIT 6
CIVIL WAR AND RECONSTRUCTION
(1846–1877)

UNIT 7
AMERICA ON THE MOVE
(1860–1920)

UNIT 8
TWENTIETH-CENTURY
CRISES
(1914–1945)

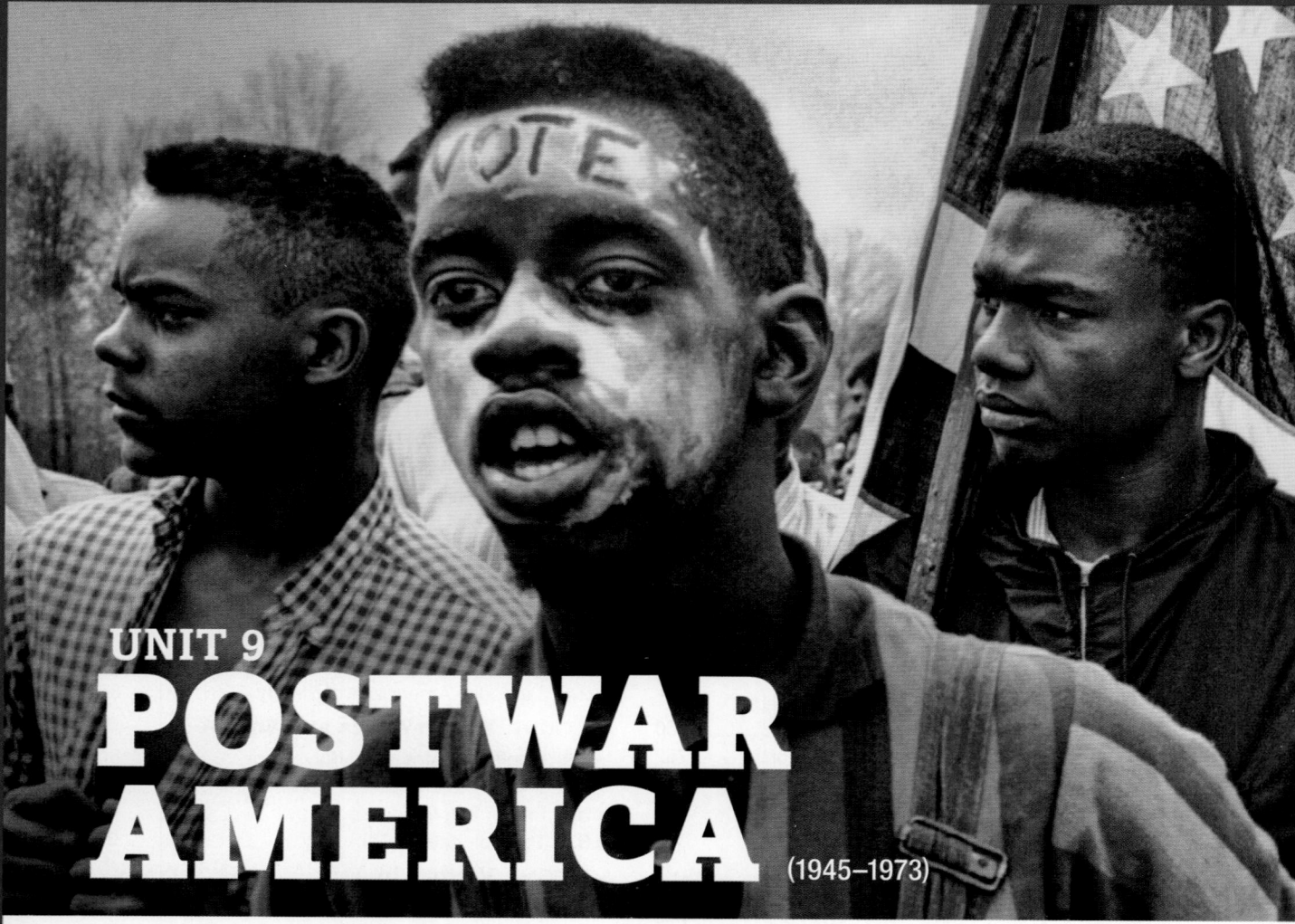

UNIT 9
POSTWAR AMERICA
(1945–1973)

UNIT 10
AMERICA IN A CHANGING WORLD

(1969–Present)

National Geographic Features

Maps

National Geographic Explorer Barrington Irving, Jr.

National Geographic Explorers

Curating History

Valley Forge National Historical Park, Pennsylvania

Student Handbooks

Geography in History

Geology in History

American Voices Biographies

American Places

Special Features

The Mississippi River

Objectives

- **Identify four general categories of U.S. history.**
- **Explore the concept of identity and how identity is shaped by historical events.**
- **Discuss details of one American's personal story.**
- **Consider what it means to be an American.**

Critical Thinking Skills for "Why Study U.S. History?"

- Make Connections
- Draw Conclusions
- Integrate Visuals
- Analyze Cause and Effect

Background for the Teacher

"Why Study U.S. History?" is a feature that appears three times in this book to help students gain a deeper understanding of their relationship with history.

On these first pages, Fred Hiebert, National Geographic's Archaeologist-in-Residence, invites students to consider what it means to be an American by exploring how historical events shape people's identities. He introduces the concept by relating how historical events have shaped his own family history and sense of identity. Use Hiebert's story to interest students and to generate discussion before they write from a personal perspective about identity and what it means to be an American.

Why Study U.S. History?

I'm Fred Hiebert, National Geographic's Archaeologist-in-Residence. Like you, I live in the United States. But my work takes me all over the world, and that gives me a chance to view the United States from a global perspective. I think a lot about what it means to be an American.

The history of the United States is a chronicle of different regions that today are pulled together on a cultural basis. In the early years, our identity as a nation was defined on a military or political basis— and we're still struggling with those differences.

As we look back on U.S. history, we'll consider the role of justice and American values in giving people an opportunity to make a life for themselves and to move between these regions. One of our freedoms is the ability to move across the country and experience different ideas about what it means to be American.

HISTORY NOTEBOOK

Find "Why Study U.S. History?" in your History Notebook. The questions and activities will help you begin to find meaning in what you're reading. Use the notebook to record your ideas and questions as you read.

What makes the history of the United States special?

U.S. history is a microcosm of world history; think of it as a mini-world history. It includes the history of our natural resources and how they've been conserved— or not. It involves the defense of our nation and the United States' role in the world. U.S. history examines our collective identity as American citizens or people who call this country home. And on a personal level, U.S. history explores how our identity has been shaped by critical events from the past and the key women and men who brought them about.

Has anyone ever said to you, "Who *are* you?" What did that person mean by asking that? How did you respond? And how does that question relate to U.S. history?

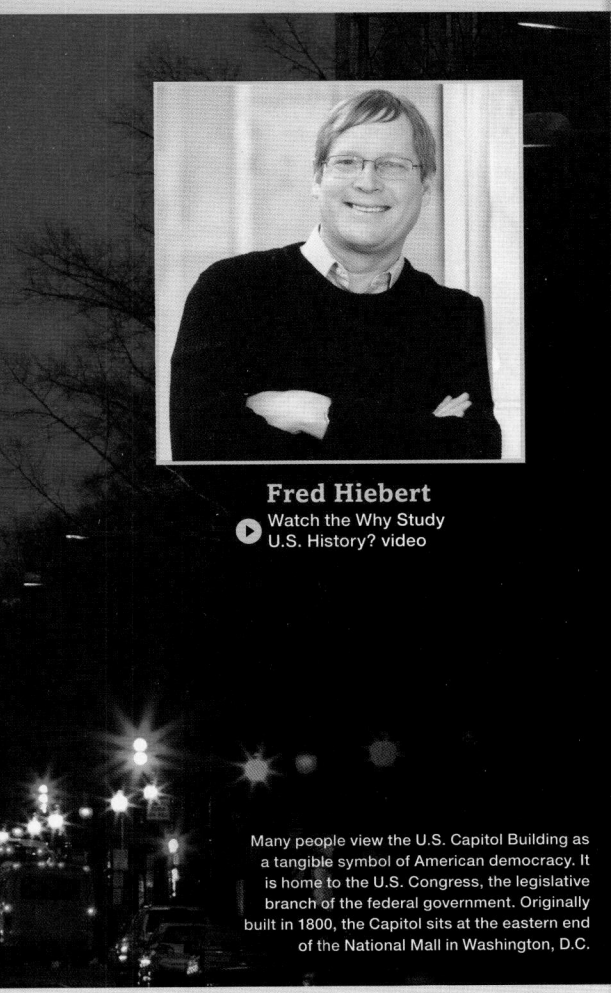

Fred Hiebert

▶ Watch the Why Study U.S. History? video

Many people view the U.S. Capitol Building as a tangible symbol of American democracy. It is home to the U.S. Congress, the legislative branch of the federal government. Originally built in 1800, the Capitol sits at the eastern end of the National Mall in Washington, D.C.

The fact is your life today is the result of events and ideas that make up the history of the United States. We study history to learn how we became who we are at this place and at this time, which helps us actually answer that question for ourselves.

History really can tell you something about yourself and your identity.

Think about ways in which you are unique: What factors affect your personal identity, your home, your family, your community, your country? How can you shape who you are and who you want to be?

National Geographic Framework for U.S. History

The **Framework for U.S. History** can help you use your text to explore these questions—and to start a dialogue with your classmates about the history and culture of the United States. Your *American Stories* textbook divides history into these general categories:

UNITS 1 AND 2
Core Populations

The United States is made up of indigenous peoples as well as people from other lands, other traditions, and other cultures, including north Asian, Scandinavian, Spanish, English, French, and African.

UNITS 3, 4, AND 5
Primary Development of the American Republic

The early American republic unifies as a new nation and begins to develop a national identity. Americans act on a spirit of boundless possibility as they push westward and stretch national borders.

UNITS 6 AND 7
Second Stage of National Development

The young country endures deep political and philosophical divisions that result in the Civil War. Postwar changes lead to new freedoms for formerly enslaved people and make Americans more mobile than ever before. The building of the Panama Canal brings economic excitement, but optimism is overshadowed by political uncertainty in Europe and the ways conflict and war might affect the United States.

UNITS 8, 9, AND 10
Modern America Emerges

On the world's stage, the United States faces international conflict. At home, social changes divide and unite, reshaping American culture. How our country's leaders deal with these issues impacts what the nation will become.

1

Explore Identity

Draw a Word Web on the board and write *identity* in the center. **ASK:** What does *identity* mean when talking about people? *(Possible response: who someone is and/or what someone is or does)* Ask students to provide examples and add them to the spokes of the web. *(Answers will vary. Possible responses:* student, teacher, daughter, son, brother, sister, American) If students do not mention *American*, add it to the web. Tell students that they are going to explore the concept of identity and what it means to be an American.

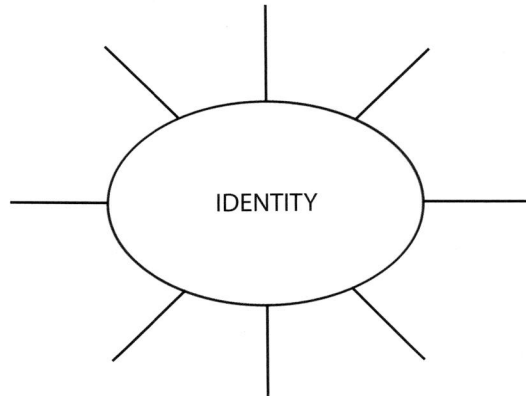

Activate Prior Knowledge

ASK: What makes the history of the United States special? Why would personal freedom, the promise of justice for all, and an open society make U.S. history special? *(Possible response: Not all societies enjoy these traits.)* As a class, discuss what these traits mean in practical terms.

Preview the Framework for U.S. History

Direct students' attention to the four general categories used to divide history in *American Stories*: Core Populations (Units 1–2), Primary Development of the American Republic (Units 3–5), Second Stage of National Development (Units 6–7), and Modern America Emerges (Units 8–10). Call on volunteers to read the synopsis beneath each heading aloud. Invite students to predict how these categories might relate to the ideas of a national identity and to a personal identity.

Guided Discussion

1. **Integrate Visuals** Based on the text and the visuals, what can you conclude about when and why Hiebert's great-great-grandparents homesteaded in Kansas? *(Possible response: The text states that Hiebert's great-great-grandparents were invited to homestead in Kansas in order to grow a new strain of wheat that was planted in the fall and harvested in the spring—that is, winter wheat. The envelope commemorating the centennial of hard winter wheat in Kansas suggests that Hiebert's great-great-grandparents homesteaded in the late 1800s, since Hiebert says that they planted a new strain of wheat. Additional evidence appears in the photograph of Hiebert's grandmother in 1912, indicating that enough time had passed to create a second-generation farm.)*

2. **Analyze Cause and Effect** What historical events led the family of Hiebert's father to move to California? *(Possible response: The family moved to California because of the Dust Bowl and the Great Depression.)*

Active Option

NG Learning Framework: Research Winter Wheat

SKILL Collaboration

KNOWLEDGE Our Human Story

Have groups research the role of Mennonites in introducing hard winter wheat to Kansas. Assign each group one of the following questions:

- Who were the Mennonites?
- Why did the Mennonites settle in Kansas?
- What prior connection did the Mennonites have to hard winter wheat?

Ask groups to collaborate by sharing their findings with the class.

WHY STUDY U.S. HISTORY?

To explore what it means to be an American

U.S. history is full of stories. Some of those stories may seem a little slow-moving, but others couldn't be more exciting. You live in the United States, and whether you are a citizen or not, those stories belong to you and to all of us—and you have your own story to tell. Use Fred Hiebert's personal story below as a model for capturing your own story about life in this country.

FRED'S AMERICAN STORY

My great-great-grandparents were invited to homestead in the Great Plains region of Kansas and raise a new strain of wheat that is planted in the fall and harvested in the spring. This type of wheat revolutionized farming in this country.

Both my mom's and dad's families came from the same Kansas community. Their way of life was disrupted by the Great Depression of 1929, a financial low point in American history during which many farmers found themselves greatly in debt.

Fred's grandmother, Helen Hiebert, is shown here on her father's farm about 1912, bringing lunch to harvesters.

This postage stamp—shown here on its first day of issue in 1974—celebrates the centennial of the introduction of winter wheat to the Great Plains, where it became an important commercial crop. Winter wheat usually produces higher crop yields than other types of wheat. This intersection between the lives of individual Americans like Fred Hiebert's grandparents and the development of the United States into a major economic force still happens today in large and small ways across the country.

My parents' families lived in the Dust Bowl, the area within the Great Plains of the Midwest where extended drought and soil erosion sometimes made farming impossible. That forced my dad's family to move to Nebraska and later to California.

My mom's family stayed in Kansas, and my parents met at a local college before World War II. During the war, my dad got interested in health care and, like his brothers and sisters, went to college. Eventually they settled in cities from Bakersfield, California, to Chicago, Illinois. I was born in Washington, D.C., while my dad was interning in a hospital, and I grew up in Michigan.

For the last 18 years, my hometown has been in Haverford Township, Pennsylvania, close to Philadelphia. I'm connected by train service to New York City and Washington, D.C., where my office at the National Geographic Society is located. Today, from my suburban hometown I am linked to the world through internet, telephone, and a close airport, making me a "global citizen."

As You Read

We all have our own stories about life in the United States. The important thing is to share our experiences and be good listeners, showing respect and tolerance for the storytellers.

In your History Notebook, write a paragraph on what the term *identity* means to you. Think about how the events you read about might connect to your own life and how these events helped shape the community and country you live in today. And finally, think about how you might answer this question:

What does it mean to be an American?

English Language Learners

Explore the 5Ws Explain to students that reporters use the questions *Who? What? Where? When?* and *Why?* to guide their reporting and that students can use the same questions to understand the information in Hiebert's story. Pair students at the **Emerging** level of proficiency with English-proficient students to work on answering the following questions:

- **Who** are the people Hiebert discusses? *(his great-great-grandparents, grandparents, parents, and himself)*
- **What** historical events does he describe? *(homesteading the Great Plains, the Dust Bowl, the Great Depression, World War II)*
- **Where** have Hiebert and his family lived? *(Kansas; Nebraska; California, including Bakersfield; Chicago, Illinois; Washington, D.C.; Michigan; and Haverford Township, Pennsylvania)*
- **When** does Hiebert's family story begin? *(in the late 1800s)*
- **Why** is Hiebert's story presented? *(to model how to capture a personal story about life in the United States)*

Gifted & Talented

Create a Multimedia Presentation Instruct students to create a short multimedia presentation about the Dust Bowl in Kansas using photos, spoken words, and written text. Encourage students to focus their presentation on how conditions affected the lives of farm families—thus providing context for understanding Hiebert's family story. Invite students to share their presentations with the class.

Objectives

- **Explore the climate, landscape, and plant and animal life of the North American continent and the ways they have changed over time.**
- **Identify characteristics of the Pleistocene epoch.**
- **Understand how human populations settled North America.**
- **Analyze the causes and effects of the Agricultural Revolution on humans and on the North American continent.**
- **Analyze artifacts that represent North American cultures in the era before European exploration.**

Critical Thinking Skills for "The Story of a Continent"

- Interpret Time Lines
- Make Connections
- Draw Conclusions
- Make Inferences
- Determine Chronology
- Make Generalizations
- Analyze Visuals
- Compare and Contrast
- Analyze Cause and Effect
- Form and Support Opinions

Background for the Teacher

The Story of a Continent feature provides students with a brief history of the North American continent's climate, geography, and inhabitants from the Pleistocene epoch through the era just prior to European exploration. Using maps, time lines, illustrations, and artifacts, students will analyze how changes in climate and technology affected human migration to North America and the development of human cultures on the continent.

Use this introductory feature to help build students' knowledge of North America as it existed before European explorers began to arrive. This knowledge will help students make connections as they go on to read about the drastic ways in which exploration and colonization, the founding of the United States, and the nation's expansion and growth shaped North America's geography and cultures.

History Notebook

Encourage students to complete the pages for The Story of a Continent in their History Notebooks as they read.

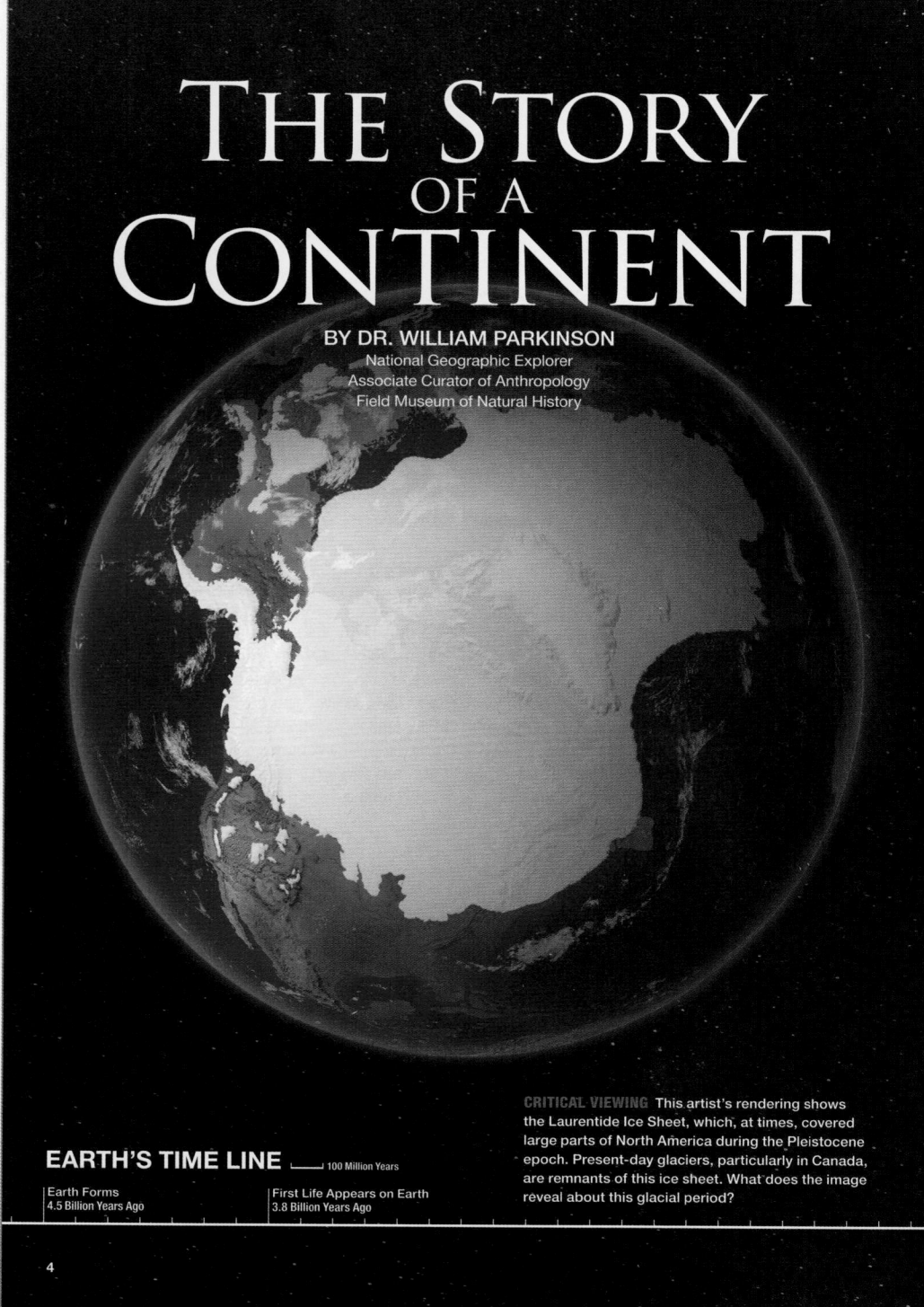

THE STORY OF A CONTINENT

BY DR. WILLIAM PARKINSON
National Geographic Explorer
Associate Curator of Anthropology
Field Museum of Natural History

CRITICAL VIEWING This artist's rendering shows the Laurentide Ice Sheet, which, at times, covered large parts of North America during the Pleistocene epoch. Present-day glaciers, particularly in Canada, are remnants of this ice sheet. What does the image reveal about this glacial period?

EARTH'S TIME LINE ⌊⎯⎯⎯⌋ 100 Million Years

Earth Forms	First Life Appears on Earth
4.5 Billion Years Ago	3.8 Billion Years Ago

4

Close your eyes for a minute. Try to imagine the United States without any of the familiar trappings of 21st-century life—no smartphones, hoverboards, or tablets. No iTunes, YouTube, or video games.

Imagine moving from place to place without paved roads to follow—in fact, with no roads at all, and no wheeled vehicles or even horses to carry you. Instead of strip malls, fast-food chains, and electric streetlights, there are lush, dark forests, pristine rivers and streams, and abundant plant and animal life as far as your eye can see.

Take a deep breath—you're in for an adventure. Travel back to the earliest history of North America, from the beginnings of civilization and even further back to a time when mammoths and mastodons, saber-toothed cats, and giant ground sloths roamed the lands of North America. It was a time when your own species, *Homo sapiens*, evolved and spread throughout the world.

This is the moment in a play just before the main curtain rises on North America—a continent with a story much longer than you may think.

GEOLOGY AND LANDSCAPE

North America is geologically dramatic. It features towering mountains, vast deserts, sandy beaches, and rolling hills. But the landscape that Europeans like Christopher Columbus encountered when they arrived in the "New World" just a few hundred years ago was profoundly different from the world that the earliest humans experienced when they first came to North America.

Let's go way back in time. The first modern humans arrived in North America at the end of a period geologists refer to as the **Pleistocene epoch** (PLEIS-toh-seen EH-puhk). The Pleistocene lasted over 2 million years. During this period, the climate and ecology of North America was completely different from the climate and ecology of today. It included supersized animals and plants that no longer exist. During the Pleistocene epoch, modern humans across the world honed their skills in hunting, created early artwork, developed fire, and began to use language.

Many people think the climate during the Pleistocene was always cold. In fact, there were dramatic fluctuations in temperature over relatively short periods of time. At some points, the climate during the Pleistocene was about the same as it is today. During **glacial periods**, or **ice ages**, when glaciers expanded across Earth's surface, the global average annual temperature was significantly colder.

There were more than 20 cycles of glacial periods during the Pleistocene epoch. The movement of ice and water during these cycles changed the landscape and shorelines of the continents drastically, especially around the edges of the Arctic Circle and in present-day Europe, Asia, and North America.

INTRODUCE & ENGAGE

Quickwrite About Migration

Give students a few minutes to write about what they think of when they hear the word *migration*. Questions for students to consider might include the following: Who or what migrates? Why do migrations take place? How do migrations change populations and places? Have any migrations affected my life or my family's life—and, if so, how? Invite volunteers to share their responses with the class. Explain that in this feature students will learn about the factors that prompted early human migration to North America and the kind of continent people found when they arrived.

Interpret Time Lines

Take a class vote on the following question: Is 75,000 years a long time? Then direct students' attention to Earth's Time Line, which runs across the bottom of these pages. **ASK:** How much of this time line represents modern human existence? *(Human existence occupies a small part of the time line; it is represented by the small part of the red sliver near the end of the time line.)* How many years does that small part of the red sliver represent? *(75,000 years)* Discuss how students' perceptions of that time frame have or have not shifted, now that they have examined the time line. **ASK:** What does this time line suggest about the subjects we often study when we study history? *(Possible response: When we study human history and events, we typically focus on a small fraction of Earth's history.)* Explain that in this feature students will learn about some of the major changes that took place within that red sliver.

CRITICAL VIEWING Possible response: The artist's rendering reveals that major land masses that are currently separated by oceans were once connected by the ice sheet. It also suggests that the climate for that half of the world must have been much colder than it is now to allow such a massive ice sheet to exist.

◄ 2.6 MILLION YEARS AGO

TODAY ►

PLEISTOCENE EPOCH ⌊____⌋ 100 Thousand Years
2.6 Million to 11,700 Years Ago

People Arrive in North America 18–12,000 Years Ago

Modern Humans Evolve 75,000 Years Ago

HOLOCENE EPOCH
11,700 Years Ago to Today

North America Splits from Pangea
200 Million Years Ago

TODAY ►

Early Humans

Modern humans followed a long line of hominid ancestors, and even lived alongside one of them: the Neanderthal, or *Homo neanderthalensis*. Students may be familiar with Neanderthals, in particular the pop culture image of the "caveman," with its somewhat derogatory associations. Explain that many scientists believe that Neanderthals actually would have been much like modern humans, although somewhat shorter and stronger, with differently shaped skulls—but similarly sized brains.

Archaeological evidence shows that, like the earliest modern humans, Neanderthals hunted and gathered, made and used tools, and produced some forms of art. Some scientists even think the genetic evidence found in Neanderthal remains suggests that modern humans and Neanderthals interbred, though other evidence suggests that if this did occur, it would have been rare. In either case, the traits of modern humans won out, and Neanderthals eventually became extinct.

Enormous Animals

About 11,000 years ago, the large mammals that had characterized the Pleistocene epoch in North America and elsewhere began to go extinct relatively quickly. Some scientists connect this extinction event to the spread of early modern humans: As increasing numbers of humans became more effective at hunting, they began to wipe out the smaller animals that large mammals relied on for food—in addition to hunting the larger mammals themselves.

Other scientists think that climate fluctuations at the end of the Pleistocene, which led to warmer temperatures, higher sea levels, and changes in plant life, may have had a more devastating effect on these species. Most scientists agree that both human development and climate had some impact on the level of extinction.

While humans and these large mammals coexisted, however, the mammals seem to have played a significant role in early human life. Woolly mammoths, bison, and bears appear in many early cave paintings and carvings. In fact, they appear in these paintings more frequently than other types of animals, including human beings.

BRIDGING THE CONTINENTS

In Europe, Asia, and Africa, modern humans evolved between 75,000 and 35,000 years ago—long before they arrived in North America. By the end of the Pleistocene, about 12,000 years ago, the only surviving hominid species was modern humans.

Scientists love debates, and one of the biggest debates in archaeology centers around the arrival of the earliest modern humans in North America. We know that when the Pleistocene ended, there were modern human societies living throughout the continent. The debate revolves around pinpointing when during the Pleistocene the first people migrated to the Americas and whether they came by boat or walked. Could people have *walked* from Europe and Asia to the Americas? Yes! But the continents are separated by oceans!

Remember during the Pleistocene, there were glacial periods when ice sheets covered the continents. The oceans contained less water, and the coastlines of the continents were much larger. After the last major glacial period, about 20,000 years ago, the two ice sheets that covered northern North America began to melt. North America was temporarily connected to Asia by a large stretch of land between modern-day Alaska and Siberia that scientists call the **Bering Land Bridge**. About 11,000 to 12,000 years ago, the land bridge disappeared as the ice melted, the oceans filled with the water, and the coastlines receded.

A paleontological team led by the University of Michigan recovered this mastodon skull and more than 60 percent of the animal's skeleton in October 2016. Mastodons are extinct relatives of the elephant.

MAN   ELEPHANT   MAMMOTH   MASTODON

ENORMOUS ANIMALS

About 12,000 years ago, we entered the Holocene (HO-luh-seen) epoch, which we are still in today. Many animals that lived during the Pleistocene went extinct around the beginning of the Holocene. This included many species of large animals, or **megafauna**, such as mammoths, mastodons, and saber-toothed cats. Along with other oversize animals, like giant sloths, giant beavers, and American lions, horses also lived in North America until the end of the Pleistocene. Horses were then reintroduced by Europeans a few hundred years ago. They became a critical aspect of Native American culture, especially on the Great Plains. This was the incredible environment the earliest humans encountered when they first arrived in North America at the end of the Pleistocene.

THE GREAT DEBATE

Until recently, scientists believed that the earliest people—**hunter-gatherers**—arrived in the Americas just before the land bridge disappeared. They specialized in hunting large herd animals that migrated back and forth across the continent. Archaeologists call them the Clovis Culture, based on a kind of stone tool—a Clovis point—that people made at that time.

But there is growing evidence that other groups may have reached the Americas before the Clovis Culture. Sites in Chile and Pennsylvania suggest that there was a pre-Clovis occupation of North America, and some scientists even speculate that people may have arrived by boats earlier in the Pleistocene, perhaps from Europe rather than Asia.

By the end of the Pleistocene, the climate began to stabilize, and modern humans spread throughout the Americas. They were specialized, mobile hunters and gatherers like their contemporaries elsewhere in the world, and they used the same technology—Clovis points—to hunt. These points have been found throughout North America, and similar ones have appeared as far south as Venezuela. People began to settle in different regions of the North American continent. These regions can be distinguished according to the specialized stone tools that were made and used in the Holocene.

CLOVIS POINT DISCOVERIES

Coastline at 75 m below current sea level	Glacial ice 12,000 years before present
	Glacial ice 13,000 years before present

CLOVIS POINT DISTRIBUTION

1–4   5–12   13–24   25–54   88–142

No sites reported finding 55–87 Clovis points.

0   250   500 Miles
0   250   500 Kilometers

Clovis Point
Carbon dating of points like the one above indicates the Clovis Culture dates to around 11,500 years ago—a time archaeologists call the Paleoindian period. Examine the proportional symbol map to see where points have been found.

Guided Discussion

1. **Make Inferences** What factors might have encouraged early hunter-gatherers to move across the Bering Land Bridge? *(Because the climate at that time was cold, they may have been traveling in search of warmer temperatures, animals for hunting, or edible plants. They may have been following herds of animals that also migrated across the land bridge.)*

2. **Determine Chronology** How has the interpretation of when and how humans arrived in North America changed as scientists have uncovered new information about early human cultures? *(Some scientists argue that certain sites in Chile and Pennsylvania show evidence of people who arrived in North America before the Clovis people and who may have traveled there from Europe instead of across the Bering Land Bridge.)*

More Information

The Folsom Culture Another early human culture that developed shortly after the Clovis Culture was the Folsom Culture. As they have with the Clovis Culture, archaeologists identify this group by the artifacts left behind: knives, points (typically shorter and wider than Clovis points), and other tools. Folsom artifacts, however, are not as widespread as their Clovis counterparts; they appear to be concentrated in the Great Plains region. The Folsom seem to have primarily hunted bison, whereas the earlier Clovis people hunted mammoths. **ASK:** Why do you think the Folsom Culture differed in these ways from the Clovis? *(Possible responses: The Folsom Culture followed the Clovis, and mammoths were beginning to go extinct at this time. The Folsom may have hunted bison because mammoths were scarce. They may have changed their weapon points to be more effective on new animals. Changes in climate may have made it less necessary for the Folsom to spread out in search of food, so they stayed in one region.)*

Corn Evolves

Evidence from caves in southern Mexico suggests that ancient forms of corn quickly began evolving in ways that brought them closer to our modern corn plants. Nonetheless, the kernels they produced probably had a much lower nutritional value. Archaeologists and paleobotanists, or scientists who study plant fossils, have also looked for evidence that indicates how people would have eaten this corn. Tool artifacts suggest that some of it was ground up for cooking, but it may also have been eaten as a kind of popcorn.

Point out that not all paleobotanists agree about the evolution of the corn plant. While many theorize that it evolved from teosinte, some argue that corn may have had a different wild ancestor that we have not yet found. Have students examine the side-by-side depictions of modern corn and teosinte. **ASK:** What details in these diagrams suggest that the plants are related? *(Possible responses: The teosinte kernel is much smaller and darker, but its shape is similar to that of modern corn kernels. The diagrams also shows that the plants produce similar stalks, leaves, and ears.)*

THE SPREAD OF CORN

Possible response: Corn took thousands of years to travel from Mexico into the greater Southwest and almost a thousand years more to spread to the East Coast. That time frame makes sense given that people would have traveled largely on foot and would not have had any means of communicating with distant groups. In addition, corn's more rapid spread in the East might have been related to the fact that people there were already skilled farmers in communities that could begin using the corn right away.

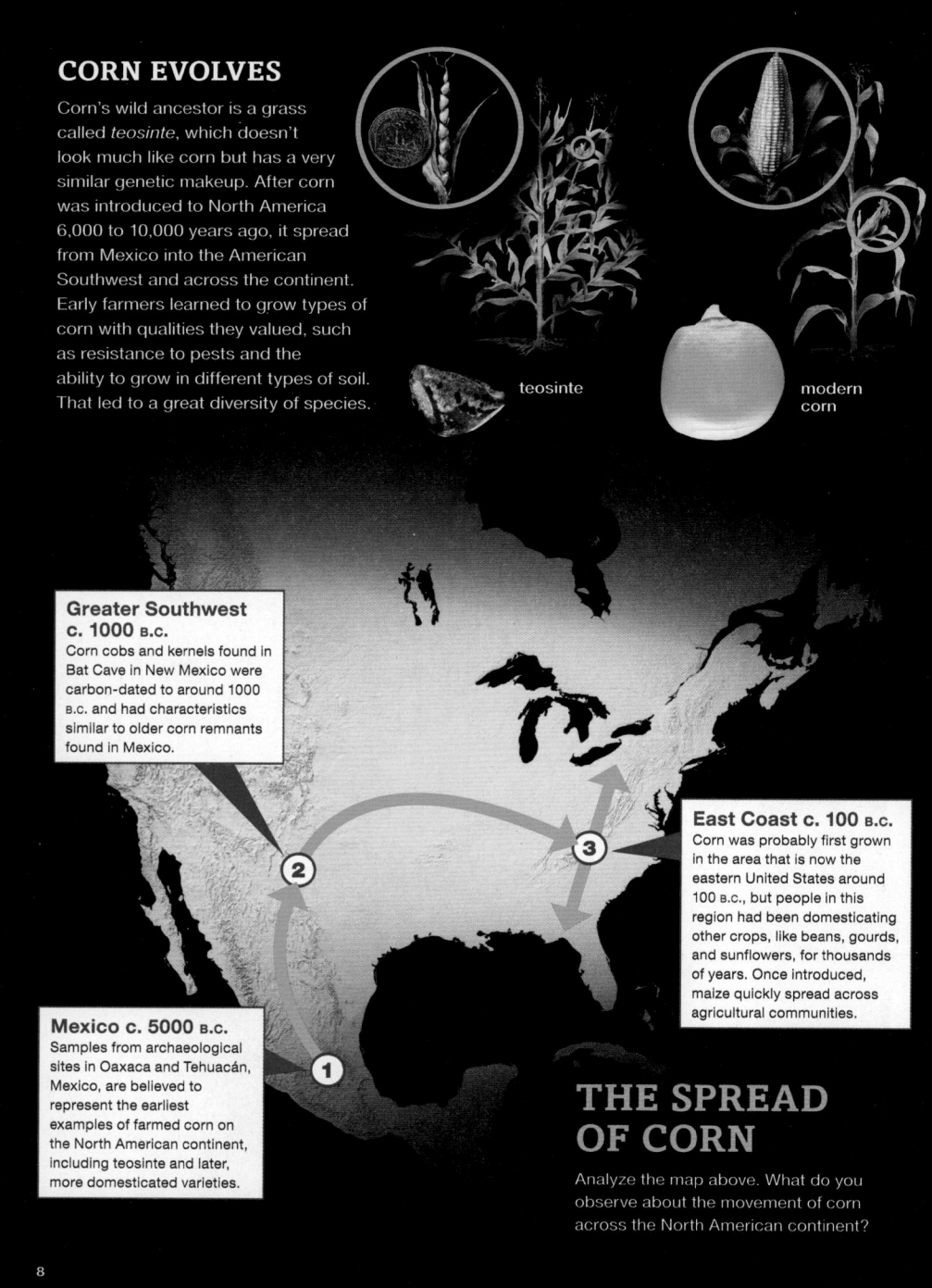

CORN EVOLVES

Corn's wild ancestor is a grass called *teosinte*, which doesn't look much like corn but has a very similar genetic makeup. After corn was introduced to North America 6,000 to 10,000 years ago, it spread from Mexico into the American Southwest and across the continent. Early farmers learned to grow types of corn with qualities they valued, such as resistance to pests and the ability to grow in different types of soil. That led to a great diversity of species.

teosinte

modern corn

Greater Southwest c. 1000 B.C.
Corn cobs and kernels found in Bat Cave in New Mexico were carbon-dated to around 1000 B.C. and had characteristics similar to older corn remnants found in Mexico.

East Coast c. 100 B.C.
Corn was probably first grown in the area that is now the eastern United States around 100 B.C., but people in this region had been domesticating other crops, like beans, gourds, and sunflowers, for thousands of years. Once introduced, maize quickly spread across agricultural communities.

Mexico c. 5000 B.C.
Samples from archaeological sites in Oaxaca and Tehuacán, Mexico, are believed to represent the earliest examples of farmed corn on the North American continent, including teosinte and later, more domesticated varieties.

THE SPREAD OF CORN

Analyze the map above. What do you observe about the movement of corn across the North American continent?

8

THE AGRICULTURAL REVOLUTION

For several thousand years during the Holocene, people continued to live in small groups and move frequently throughout the year. Everything changed when some groups of mobile hunters and gatherers started to experiment with planting their own crops. This transition from relying on gathering wild plants and hunting animals to planting crops and raising animals is called the **Agricultural Revolution**.

The practice of bringing plants and animals under human control is called **domestication**. Almost all the foods we eat today are domesticated instead of wild. This means that they have been modified from their wild forms and are to some extent reliant upon humans for their existence. Corn, for example, is the domesticated form of a plant called *teosinte* (TAY-oh-SIN-tay), and cows are the domestic form of a wild herd animal called an *aurochs* (OR-auks). Domestication had a dramatic impact on society. Once people settled down and became reliant upon domestic plants and animals, human life transformed.

This c. 1250 cedar mask was discovered in Fulton, Illinois, and provides evidence of Mississippian cultures outside of Cahokia.

Out of all the plants domesticated in North America thousands of years ago, the real game changer was corn. The hunters and gatherers who began experimenting with the domestication of corn had no idea of the impact their little experiment would have on the world in the years to come. Corn is now grown almost everywhere in the world and tied to almost everything Americans eat. It's even used to make toothpaste and gasoline. But the biggest impact corn had in North America was its unparalleled ability to feed large populations.

SETTLING DOWN

It took a while for corn to be adopted and widely used in North America. In eastern North America, for example, it wasn't a major part of the human diet until about 1,000 years ago. Growing crops like corn and remaining in one location allowed social groups to grow larger and develop more complex political systems. In some places, these groups built massive cities and had extensive trade networks that moved goods across the continent.

One of these cities was located in present-day Illinois along the Mississippi River near the modern town of St. Louis, Missouri. Founded around A.D. 800, Cahokia would come to be the capital of a large community called a **chiefdom**. By A.D. 1250, Cahokia was a thriving community. This large city controlled a massive geographic area at the confluence of three rivers (the Missouri, Illinois, and Mississippi), and at its height may have had a population of about 15,000 people. It is considered the most sophisticated prehistoric native civilization north of Mexico.

The fertile soil of Cahokia was easy to farm and well suited to growing corn. As a result, people farmed more and hunted less. And archaeological evidence unearthed from the site indicates the people of Cahokia ate well.

Although Cahokia and other similar sites in the southeastern United States were heavily dependent upon domestic crops like corn, communities in other parts of North America were not. They continued to hunt and gather wild resources as a major part of their diet.

Active Options

On Your Feet: Word Chain Gather students into three lines. Give the first student in each line a piece of paper with one of these terms from the text: *Agricultural Revolution, corn, Cahokia*. That student adds a word that relates to the original term. Students pass the paper from person to person in the line, each one adding a word or phrase associated with the previously written word or phrase. When all students have participated, ask a volunteer from each line to read off the Word Chain. Ask the rest of the class to listen for any words or phrases that were used in more than one chain or any that may not connect logically.

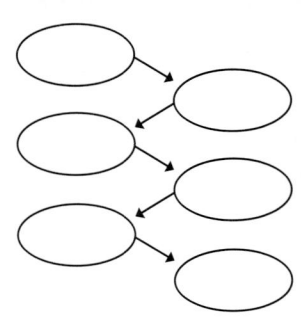

NG Learning Framework: Follow the Foods

SKILLS Observation, Communication

KNOWLEDGE Our Living Planet

Provide pairs or small groups of students with maps of the world, or display a large blank map on a wall or board. Ask students to choose a plant or an animal that is part of their regular diet. Then, have them use library and online resources to identify the origin of their chosen food and to trace how it has spread over time. Students will then record this path on their own map or the class map. Encourage them to include relevant images and dates or time lines along with their maps. After all pairs or groups have presented their findings to the class, discuss ways in which the spread of these foods might have combined with other events to create new patterns in human behavior or society.

Guided Discussion

1. **Make Generalizations** What do the artifacts from early North American cultures suggest about the people who made them? *(Answers will vary. Possible responses: The artifacts suggest the importance of wildlife to early North American cultures. The quality of the works suggests that the cultures valued art.)*

2. **Compare and Contrast** In what general ways was the human, cultural, and political landscape of the "New World" similar to and different from the landscape of North America today? Explain. *(Answers will vary. Possible response: In both eras, diverse people populated the continent, with different traditions, languages, and cultures. Today, however, the continent is divided into just a few political regions rather than many.)*

More Information

The Ancient Pueblo Direct students' attention to the photograph of ancient Pueblo cliff dwellings at Mesa Verde National Park. **ASK:** What inferences can you make about the people who built these dwellings? *(Answers will vary. Possible response: The people were skilled at using the landscape to its advantage, and it was centralized or "urban" in its approach to dwellings.)*

Explain that the buildings shown were built during a later phase of ancient Pueblo civilization called Pueblo III. Earlier groups lived first as nomadic hunter-gatherers, then dwelled in caves and covered pits, and later settled in small villages or large communities. The cliff dwellings were remarkable achievements. Their construction was high quality and durable, and because they were accessible only by ladder, they were easily defended against attack. Even so, archaeological evidence suggests that a drought forced the ancient Pueblo to abandon these communities. Later ancient Pueblo dwellings were less well constructed. **ASK:** What does a decline in building quality suggest about ancient Pueblo communities that followed the cliff dwellers? *(Answers will vary. Possible response: People built in a hurry or did not have enough resources.)*

THINK ABOUT IT

Answers will vary. Possible response: The emergence of art across so many cultures suggests that early humans were similar in many ways to modern ones. It may be that early humans developed at a similar pace and in similar ways despite being geographically distant from one another.

A CULTURAL MOSAIC

Before the 1500s, the Americas, Europe, and Africa had been isolated from one another. But as Europeans began looking beyond their shores for riches and resources, Africa's mighty empires wanted to show their strength. Both continents were on a collision course with the Americas, but the Europeans got there first.

When the Europeans arrived in the "New World," they experienced a mosaic of diverse cultures and landscapes. From the hierarchical chiefdoms of Florida to the more mobile, less hierarchical groups of the Great Basin, the cultures of North America made up a patchwork quilt of societies with distinct languages, economic practices, political systems, and traditions as varied as the landscape.

This bird-shaped tobacco pipe was found in Canada in the Pacific Northwest region of North America.

Groups such as the Chumash, who settled along the California coastline, fished from canoe-like boats made of rushes.

Chumash fishing hook, carved from a shell

As you read in Why Study U.S. History, everyone has a personal American story to tell, and those stories often reflect the diversity of our cultural mosaic. That diversity is one of the best things about life in the United States. It's not always easy to build consensus or get everyone "on the same page," but that's what's exciting. With so many opinions and perspectives and our dogged American drive, we have the potential to develop amazingly creative solutions to 21st-century issues.

Believed to be 1,000 years old, the Pilling Figurines from the Fremont group in Utah were named for the rancher who discovered them in 1950.

So raise the curtain on this incredibly rich and varied landscape, well equipped to sustain and nurture the promise of a unique new country and a vibrant people. The action and the drama are just about to begin.

THINK ABOUT IT

What does the fact that these diverse cultures all expressed themselves through art suggest about early humans?

Like other groups in the Southwest, the Hohokam of southern Arizona frequently painted birds on items, such as the pot from which this shard came.

NORTHWEST

PLATEAU

BASIN

CALIFORNIA

SOUTHWEST

In the Woodlands culture, a bird stone like this one found in Jefferson County, New York, was used to properly weight a throwing stick, or atlatl.

This hand made by a Hopewell artist from the Ohio River Valley was cut from a type of soft rock called mica.

These ear spools, which were carved from shells and worn in large holes in the earlobes, were unearthed from an Oklahoma mound.

Carved from wood and bone, this Mississippian mask fuses a human face with deer antlers and dates to between 800 and 1500.

The ruins of more than 600 cliff dwellings where the ancient Pueblo lived between 500 and c. 1300 can be seen at Mesa Verde National Park in Colorado.

ARCTIC

SUBARCTIC

PLAINS

NORTHEAST

SOUTHEAST

The Story of a Continent 11

Striving Readers

Complete Time Lines Have students work in pairs to complete a time line of important events and civilizations as they read The Story of a Continent. Then ask them to trade with another pair to check their work and to use peer input to revise their time lines if necessary.

Gifted & Talented

Create a "Time Travel" Brochure Instruct students to select one of the civilizations mentioned in The Story of a Continent and use library and online resources to research its location, art, economy, architecture, and other important characteristics. Students should then synthesize this information into a travel brochure, encouraging people to travel through time to visit the civilization.

See the Chapter Planner for more strategies for differentiation.

HISTORICAL THINKING

Ask and have students answer the following questions.

1. **READING CHECK** What was Earth's climate like during the Pleistocene epoch?

2. **ANALYZE CAUSE AND EFFECT** What effect did the birth and spread of agriculture have on the development of early human societies?

3. **FORM AND SUPPORT OPINIONS** What was the most important factor in the human settlement of the North American continent, and why?

ANSWERS

1. During the Pleistocene epoch, Earth's climate fluctuated between glacial periods (or ice ages) and periods of climate similar to what we know today. At the end of the Pleistocene, the climate stabilized at warmer temperatures.

2. The birth and spread of agriculture allowed humans to stay in one place and feed larger populations than hunting and gathering had permitted. As a result, villages developed, followed eventually by large communities.

3. Answers will vary.

Pueblo Petroglyphs

These Pueblo petroglyphs are located in the Galisteo Basin. Most of the more than 1800 petroglyphs are concentrated on sheer cliffs. Archaeologists believe these petroglyphs were not randomly placed, but deliberately carved in relationship to one another, the landscape, and the horizon. While many petroglyph meanings are obscure, archaeologists have made breakthroughs to understand that an interpretation for some encompasses the Pueblo Kachina (katsina) religion, tribal societal structure, battles, and entry and exodus of tribes into the area. These carvings offer a window into the past.

Point out to students some of the possible challenges in creating these works. For example, artisans carrying carving tools would have had to scale the cliffs, either from below or above, using ropes or ladders and their own climbing skills. **ASK:** Why would the Native Americans have chosen this location for their works, despite the difficulties involved? *(Answers will vary. Possible responses: The works would have been visible from far away, telling anyone who saw them that people lived there. Positioning the works high on a cliff wall suggests loftiness of purpose, such as depicting a belief system.)*

Have students study the photograph. **ASK:** What familiar shapes or figures do you see in the carvings? *(Answers will vary. Possible responses: Shapes and figures include birds, a round shape that might represent the sun, a snake, a person with a feathered headdress, and a mask or sun with rays or arrows extending from it.)* **ASK:** Do you think these petroglyphs were the work of a single craftsman or many? Why? *(Answers will vary. Possible responses: Based on the size of the work, it probably took many craftsmen to carve the images. Different styles—either rounded or angular—suggest the work of different artists.)*

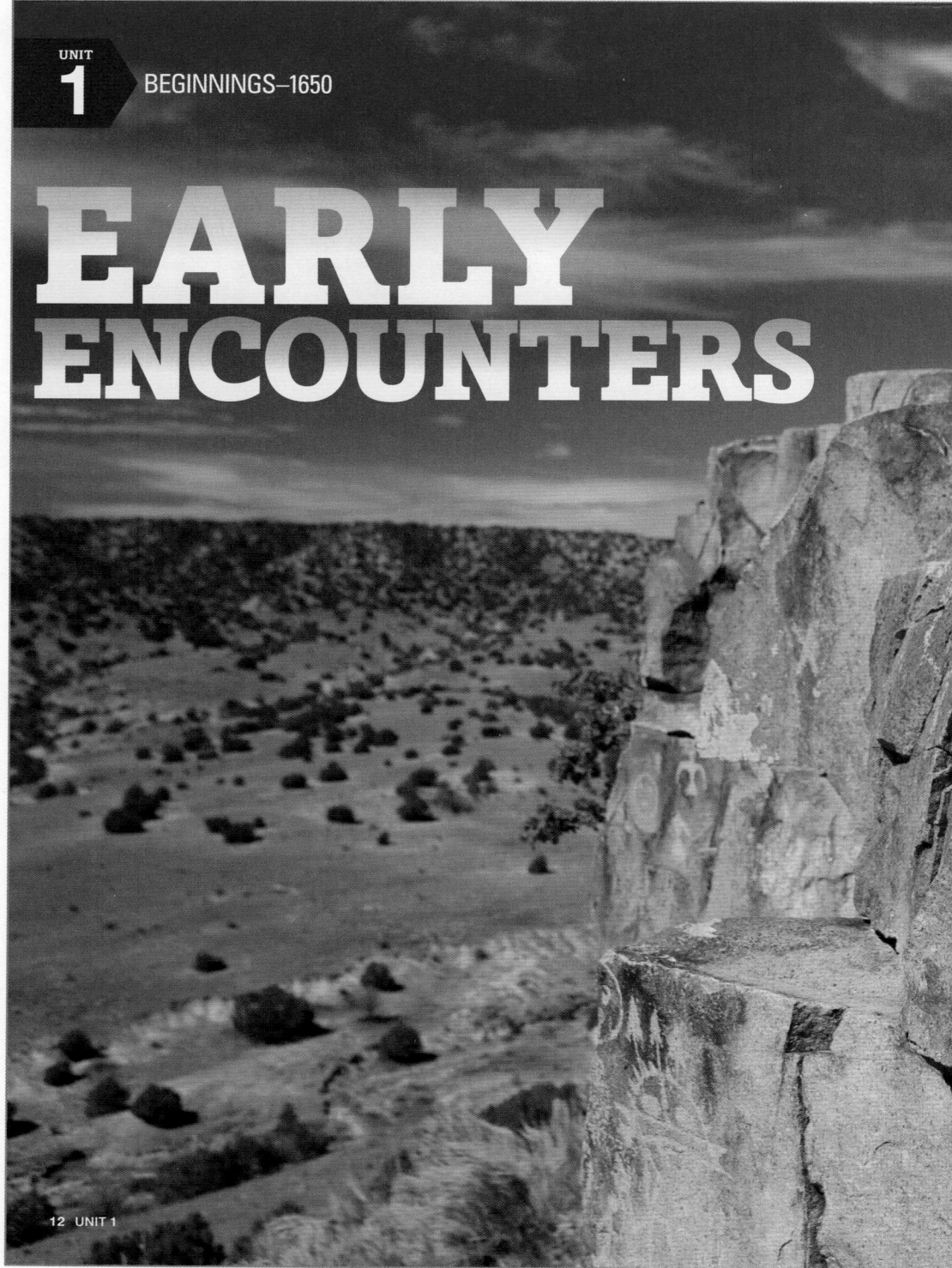

UNIT **1** BEGINNINGS—1650

EARLY ENCOUNTERS

12 UNIT 1

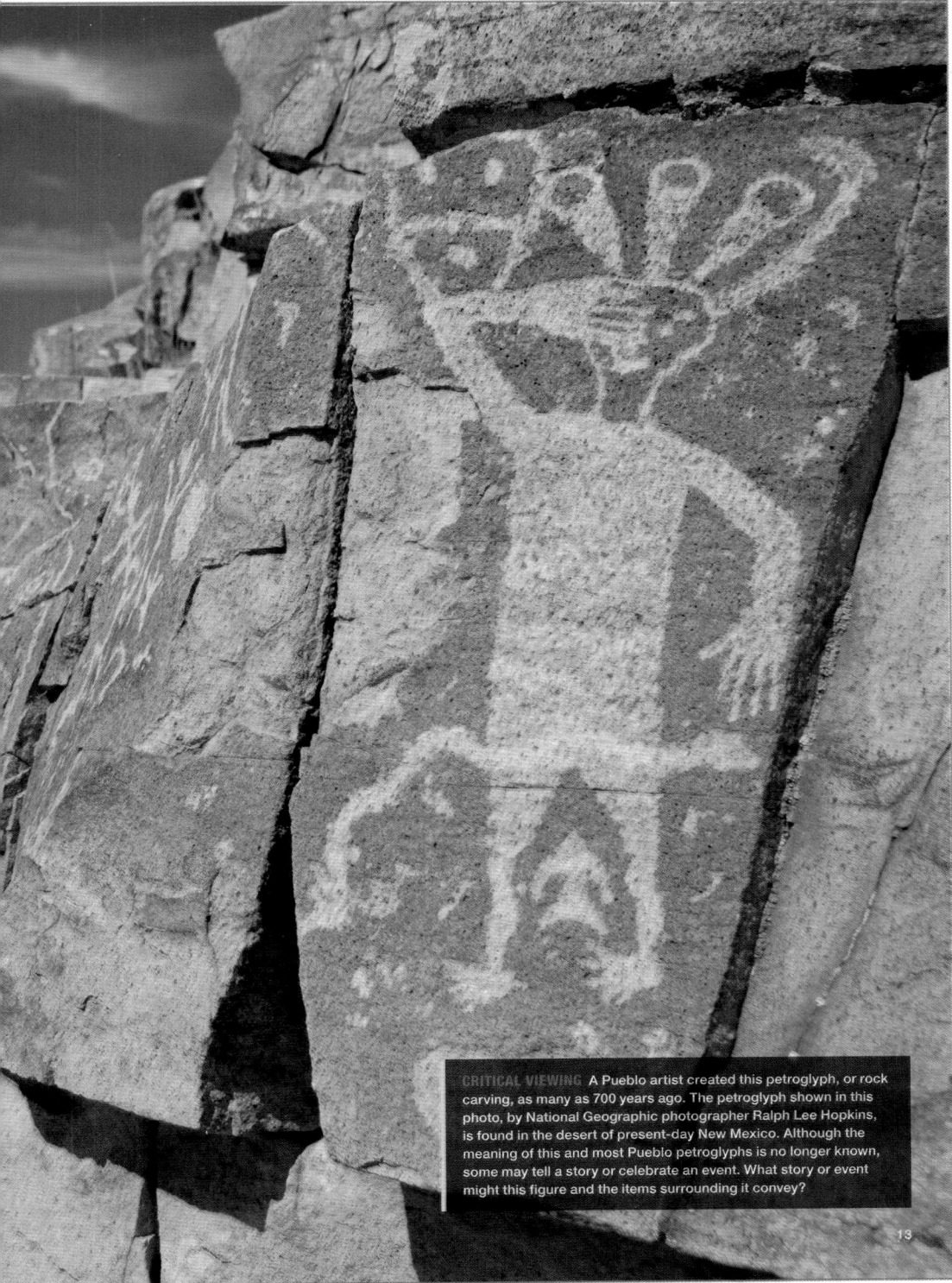

CRITICAL VIEWING A Pueblo artist created this petroglyph, or rock carving, as many as 700 years ago. The petroglyph shown in this photo, by National Geographic photographer Ralph Lee Hopkins, is found in the desert of present-day New Mexico. Although the meaning of this and most Pueblo petroglyphs is no longer known, some may tell a story or celebrate an event. What story or event might this figure and the items surrounding it convey?

13

NATIONAL GEOGRAPHIC PHOTOGRAPHER
Ralph Lee Hopkins

Based in New Mexico, Ralph Lee Hopkins is a professional landscape photographer with a background in geology. He has created a plethora of photographic studies of the Galisteo Basin and Puebloan petroglyphs, and his appreciation of nature is clearly shown in his photographs. In addition to his work for *National Geographic* magazine, Hopkins has co-written two geology-based guidebooks, *Hiking Colorado's Geology* and *Hiking the Southwest's Geology*. He is also a contributing photographer for many other magazines. In recent years, Hopkins has shifted his focus to Baja California, the Galápagos Islands, and Ecuador, where he documents the impact of human development and efforts at environmental conservation.

CRITICAL VIEWING Answers will vary. Possible response: The larger figure could represent a priest, a god in the form of a bird, or a powerful leader. The smaller petroglyph could represent a warrior or subject. The surrounding images could be weapons, tools, shields, or ceremonial objects. The carving could represent a battle in which a Pueblo group successfully defended its valley.

1200 Africa:
The Rise of Mali

In 1203, amidst struggles over power in the failing empire of Ghana, the Susu took over the former Ghanaian capital. The Malinke people of the Kangaba state in West Africa, who had long played a role in the Ghanaian gold trade, were unhappy with the Susu chief, Sumanguru, and promptly revolted. The Malinke leader Sundiata defeated the Susu in 1230. It was a final blow for both the Susu and for Ghana, which was absorbed into Mali. Sundiata was an expansionist who aimed to control the regions surrounding Mali. Mansa Musa, a descendant of Sundiata, came to power in 1307, and Mali became one of the largest empires in the world.

As with Ghana, much of Mali's wealth came from gold. On a visit to Cairo, Egypt, Mansa Musa allegedly spent enough gold to affect the Egyptian gold market for more than a dozen years. **ASK:** What might have been the purpose of spending so much gold in Cairo? *(Possible response: Mansa Musa may have wanted to persuade Egypt to join in trade with Mali.)* In addition to trade, Mansa Musa devoted his wealth to advancing Mali's culture. He brought scholars to his cities, supported artists, and commissioned mosques to serve as centers of learning. **ASK:** Why might an emperor seek cultural advancements? *(Possible responses: An emperor might want to promote his ideals about learning among his people, build the empire's reputation as a cultural center, or create a legacy.)*

Time Travel

Throughout the text, students will see the abbreviations B.C. and A.D. A date followed by B.C. refers to the number of years the date occurred before the birth of Christ. A date preceded by A.D. refers to the number of years the date occurred after the birth of Christ. Many historians also use the abbreviations B.C.E. and C.E. for these time periods. However, B.C.E. stands for "Before the Common Era," and C.E. stands for "Common Era."

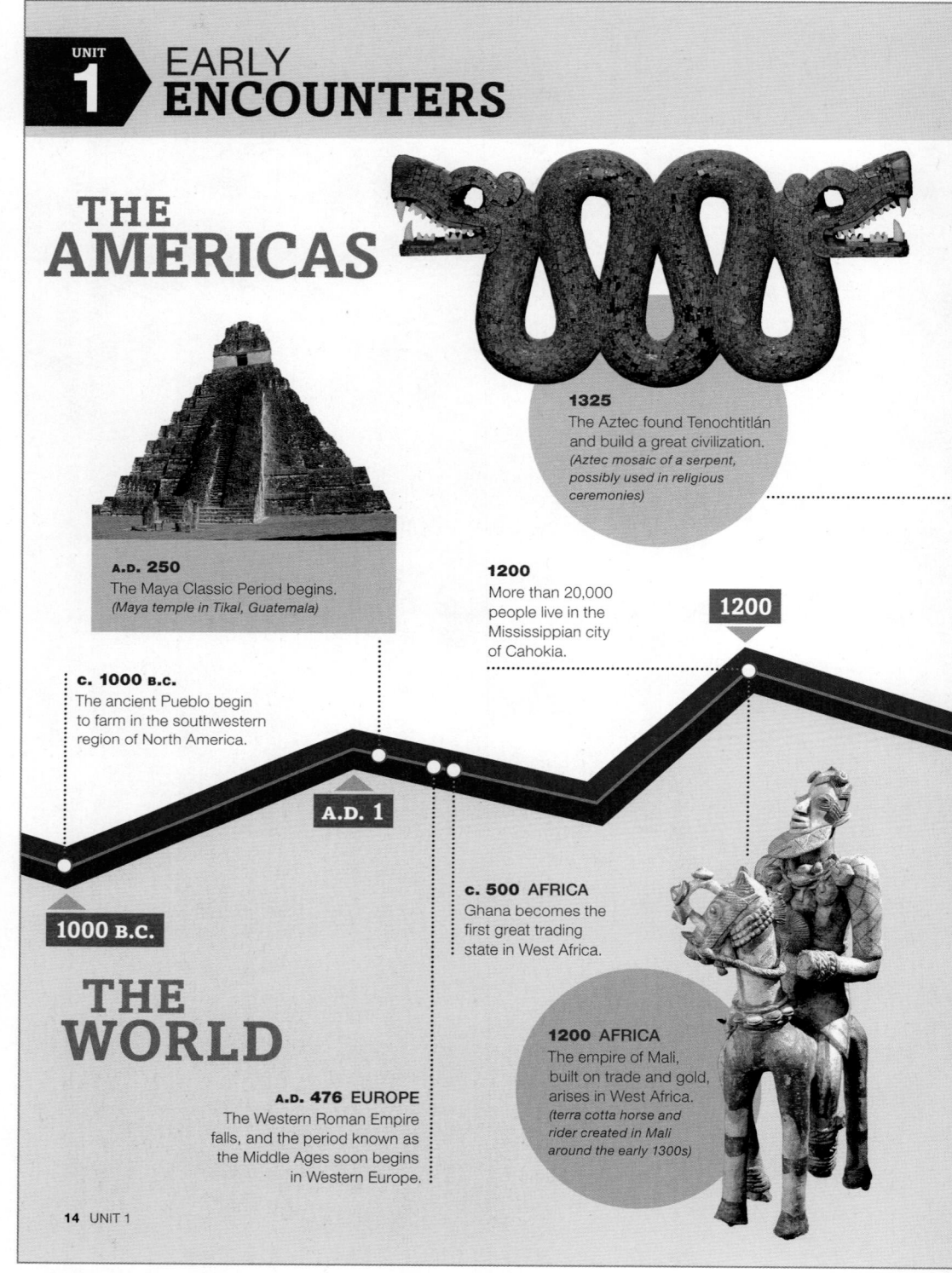

UNIT 1

EARLY ENCOUNTERS

THE AMERICAS

A.D. 250
The Maya Classic Period begins.
(Maya temple in Tikal, Guatemala)

1325
The Aztec found Tenochtitlán and build a great civilization.
(Aztec mosaic of a serpent, possibly used in religious ceremonies)

1200
More than 20,000 people live in the Mississippian city of Cahokia.

1200

c. 1000 B.C.
The ancient Pueblo begin to farm in the southwestern region of North America.

A.D. 1

c. 500 AFRICA
Ghana becomes the first great trading state in West Africa.

1000 B.C.

THE WORLD

A.D. 476 EUROPE
The Western Roman Empire falls, and the period known as the Middle Ages soon begins in Western Europe.

1200 AFRICA
The empire of Mali, built on trade and gold, arises in West Africa.
(terra cotta horse and rider created in Mali around the early 1300s)

HISTORICAL THINKING: DETERMINE CHRONOLOGY

What activities were undertaken throughout much of the world beginning in the 1400s?

1450
The Inca build Machu Picchu in the Andes Mountains. *(golden Inca artifact)*

1519
Hernán Cortés leads the invasion of Mexico and conquers the Aztec.

1492
Columbus makes the first of several voyages to the Americas.

t' Fort nieûw Amsterdam op de Manhatans

1626
The Dutch buy Manhattan Island from Native Americans and found New Amsterdam (present-day New York City) on the site. *(fine art image of the New Amsterdam settlement)*

1400

1800

1405 ASIA
Zheng He begins the first of seven voyages from China, exploring Asia and Africa.

1650 AFRICA
More than 40 trading posts on Africa's west coast send slaves to the New World.

1300 EUROPE
The Renaissance begins in Europe. *(Renaissance artist Leonardo da Vinci's painting, the Mona Lisa)*

Early Encounters **15**

INTRODUCE TIME LINE EVENT

1405 Asia:
Zheng He and the Seven Voyages

In the early 1400s, the Chinese emperor appointed a young man named Zheng He as commander in chief of a massive armada of 62 ships. Zheng He's official mission was to explore the oceans, as well as the lands of Asia and Africa. His unofficial mission was to advertise the incredible might of China's naval forces far and wide.

As commander of the armada, Zheng He made a total of seven journeys between 1405 and his death in 1433. In his first three expeditions, he reached Siam (now Thailand), the coast of India, Sumatra, and the Persian Gulf. Later expeditions took him as far as the eastern coast of Africa. Along the way, he sent smaller missions to destinations such as Egypt and Mecca. He also brought foreign emissaries to China and inspired Chinese emigration. However, unlike the European explorers, Zheng He did not use his voyages to establish colonies or expand the empire. **ASK:** Why might China have chosen Zheng He's travels to be expeditions instead of opportunities to claim land to build colonies? *(Possible responses: The Chinese may have believed they had enough land and wealth; they were tired of a ravaged economy due to war; they may have considered it more beneficial to build peaceful relationships with other lands; they did not want the trouble of managing colonies.)*

HISTORICAL THINKING: DETERMINE CHRONOLOGY

Answer: Beginning in the 1400s, many countries began crossing oceans and other great distances to explore, conquer, lay claim to land, and trade with far away lands. In Mexico, the Inca built the citadel of Machu Picchu. Later, in the 1600s, Native Americans sold Manhattan Island to the Dutch, and Africa began the slave trade with Europe and the New World.

UNIT INTRODUCTION

UNIT TIME LINE

UNIT WRAP-UP

NATIONAL GEOGRAPHIC | CONNECTION

National Geographic Magazine Adapted Articles
- "First Americans"
- "Scurvy Struck Columbus's Crew" ONLINE

Unit 1 Inquiry: Establish an Empire

NG Learning Framework Activities
- Create a Map
- Think Like an Archaeologist

Unit 1 Formal Assessment

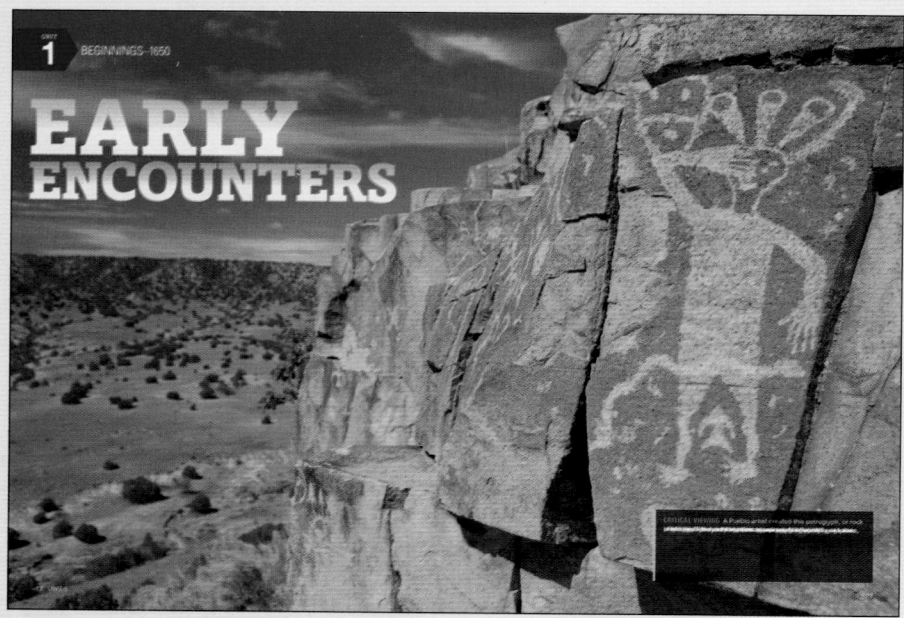

CHAPTER 1 RESOURCES

Available at NGLSync.Cengage.com

TEACHER RESOURCES & ASSESSMENT

Reading and Note-Taking

Vocabulary Practice

Document-Based Question Template

Social Studies Skills Lessons
- Reading: Compare and Contrast
- Writing: Write an Argument

Formal Assessment
- Chapter 1 Pretest
- Chapter 1 Tests A & B
- Section Quizzes

Chapter 1 Answer Key

ExamView®
One-time Download

STUDENT DIGITAL RESOURCES

- **eEdition** (English)
- **eEdition** (Spanish)
- **Handbooks**

- **Online Atlas**
- **American Gallery Online**
- **History Notebook**

- **American Voices (Biographies)**
- **Active History**
- **Projects for Inquiry-Based Learning**

Chapter 1 Spanish Resources are available at NGLSync.Cengage.com.

AMERICAN STORIES | Land of Plenty

- Primary Sources
- On Your Feet: Narrate a Place
- **NG Learning Framework:** Learn About Wildlife

SECTION 1 RESOURCES
SOCIETIES OF THE AMERICAS

LESSON 1.1
Early American Civilizations

- On Your Feet: Jigsaw
- **NG Learning Framework:** Research Mesoamerican Achievements

LESSON 1.2
Western American Cultures

- On Your Feet: Choose Your Home
- **NG Learning Framework:** Explore Native American Cultures

LESSON 1.3
Eastern American Cultures

- On Your Feet: Team Word Webbing
- **NG Learning Framework:** Analyze Environmental Concepts

LESSON 1.4
NATIONAL GEOGRAPHIC EXPLORER
JOHN KELLY
Mounds on the Mississippi

- Active History: Think Like an Archaeologist

AMERICAN **GALLERY** ONLINE Cahokia: A Native American City

LESSON 1.5
CURATING HISTORY
National Museum of the American Indian, Washington, D.C.

- On Your Feet: Sort the Artifacts

LESSON 1.6
GEOGRAPHY IN HISTORY
Native American Environments

- On Your Feet: Fishbowl
- **NG Learning Framework:** Determine the Effects of Geography

SECTION 2 RESOURCES
SOCIETIES OF EUROPE

LESSON 2.1
The Middle Ages

- On Your Feet: Create a Concept Web
- **NG Learning Framework:** Write a Diary Entry

LESSON 2.2
Renaissance and Reformation

- On Your Feet: Inside-Outside Circle
- **NG Learning Framework:** Learn More About Gutenberg's Printing Press

LESSON 2.3
Trade Expands

- On Your Feet: Question and Answer
- **NG Learning Framework:** Research Caravels

SECTION 3 RESOURCES
SOCIETIES OF WEST AFRICA

LESSON 3.1
The Kingdom of Ghana

- On Your Feet: Stage a Quiz Show
- **NG Learning Framework:** Explore Modern Trans-Saharan Trade

LESSON 3.2
Mali and Songhai

- On Your Feet: Fishbowl
- **NG Learning Framework:** Compare Mali and Songhai

LESSON 3.3
DOCUMENT-BASED QUESTION
Impressions of Mali

- On Your Feet: Host a DBQ Roundtable

CHAPTER 1 REVIEW

Strategy ❶
Preview the Text

Work with students to preview lessons in this chapter. For each lesson, guide them to read the lesson titles, lesson introductions, Main Idea statements, captions, and lesson headings. Then tell them to list the information they expect to find in the text. Instruct students to read a lesson and discuss with a partner what they learned and whether or not it matched their list.

Use with All Lessons

Strategy ❷
Play Vocabulary Tic-Tac-Toe

Write nine Key Vocabulary words on a tic-tac-toe grid on the board. Position the words on the grid so that an X or O can be written below each word. Player A chooses a word. If the player correctly pronounces, defines, and uses the word in a sentence, he or she can put an X or O in the insert box in that square. Play alternates until one person has a row of Xs or Os.

Use with All Lessons *This game can also be played using teams. Divide the class into two teams, Team A and Team B, and alternate play until one team has a row of Xs or Os.*

Strategy ❸
Use a Word Splash

Present the words on the board in a random "splash" arrangement, and ask students to choose three pairs of words that are related to each other. Have students use this sentence starter to write how each pair of words is related.

_____ and _____ are related because . . .

Use with Lesson 1.2

Strategy ❶
Provide Terms and Names on Audio

Decide which of the terms and names are important for mastery and have a volunteer record the pronunciations and a short sentence defining each word. Encourage students to listen to the recording as often as necessary.

Use with All Lessons *You might also use the recordings to quiz students on their mastery of the terms. Play one definition at a time from the recording and ask students to identify the term or name described.*

Strategy ❷
Modify Main Idea Statements

Provide these modifications of the Main Idea statements at the beginning of each lesson:

1.1 Civilizations arose in Mesoamerica and South America.

1.2 Environmental factors influenced cultures in western North America.

1.3 Stable farming societies developed in eastern North America.

1.4 Archaeologist John Kelly studies mounds to learn about Cahokia.

1.6 Geography shaped how Native American cultures developed.

2.1 Western Europe changed during the Middle Ages.

2.2 The Renaissance and Reformation led to new ideas.

2.3 European trade expanded in the 1400s.

3.1 Trade helped to create the kingdom of Ghana and to spread Islam.

3.2 Mali and Songhai were wealthy trading kingdoms.

Use with Lessons 1.1–1.4, 1.6, 2.1–2.3, and 3.1–3.2

ENGLISH LANGUAGE LEARNERS ELD

Strategy 1
PREP Before Reading

Have students use the PREP strategy to prepare for reading. Write this acrostic on the board:

PREP   **P**review title.
Read Main Idea statement.
Examine visuals.
Predict what you will learn.

Have students write their prediction and share it with a partner. After reading, ask students to write a sentence that begins with "I also learned . . ."

Use with All Lessons, All Levels *Encourage students at the Emerging level to ask questions if they have trouble writing a prediction. Students at the Bridging level might want to help students at the Emerging and Expanding levels with their "I also learned..." sentences.*

Strategy 2
Create a Word Web

To activate prior knowledge and build vocabulary, work with students at **All Proficiencies** to create two Word Webs, one for the word *Renaissance* and one for the word *Reformation*, before beginning Lesson 2.2.

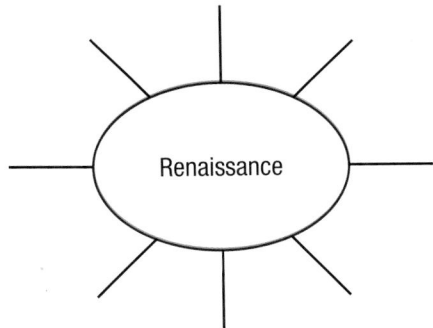

Use with Lesson 2.2 *Ask students at the Emerging level to name related words. Ask students at the Expanding level to tell how the words relate to the topic. Students at the Bridging level can write sentences using the words.*

Strategy 3
Set Up a Word Wall

Pair students at the **Emerging** and **Expanding** levels. Tell them to choose three words from each section. Ask students at the **Bridging** level to sort the words to avoid duplicates, ask for new words if necessary, and display them. Define and discuss each word as it comes up in reading. Students can add words and examples to develop understanding.

Use with All Lessons, All Levels

GIFTED & TALENTED

Strategy 1
Create a Fan Zine

Tell students to select an individual discussed in the chapter and then create a comic or zine based on that individual. Encourage students to use both visuals and text, quotations from or about the individual, and examples illustrating that individual's ideas.

Use with Lessons 1.4, 2.2–2.3, and 3.2–3.3

Strategy 2
Sketch a Flip Chart

Tell students that all the civilizations and cultures in this chapter are distinctive, both in their histories and in their artisanship. Ask them to create flip charts by sketching a symbol for each culture group. Tell them not to label their symbols. Then ask them to make a review game out of their flip charts, quizzing classmates on which symbol goes with what culture.

Use with All Lessons

Pre-AP

Strategy 1
Write a Summary

Remind students of the Essential Question introduced at the beginning of the chapter: How were early civilizations in the Americas, Africa, and Europe both similar and different? Tell students to review all the lessons and identify characteristics of the cultures. Then have students write a chapter summary essay using the examples they identified to answer the Essential Question.

Use with All Lessons

Strategy 2
Create a Travel Brochure

Have students imagine that they are members of one of the cultures discussed in the chapter. Tell students to work in pairs to design a travel brochure to encourage people to visit the culture they select. Direct students to include factual information about their culture, important sites, and major events.

Use with All Lessons

THREE WORLDS
BEFORE 1500

ESSENTIAL QUESTION
How were early civilizations in the Americas, Africa, and Europe both similar and different?

AMERICAN STORIES Land of Plenty

SECTION 1 **Societies of the Americas**
KEY VOCABULARY

civilization	irrigation	physical geography
domesticate	kayak	potlatch
geographic perspective	matrilineal	slash-and-burn agriculture
human geography	migrate	tepee
Iroquois League		tundra

SECTION 2 **Societies of Europe**
KEY VOCABULARY

caravel	manor system	Protestant
feudalism	navigation	serf
hierarchy	printing press	vassal
humanism	profit	

SECTION 3 **Societies of West Africa**
KEY VOCABULARY

caravan	oasis	steppe
convert	pilgrimage	trans-Saharan

AMERICAN GALLERY
ONLINE Cahokia: A Native American City

READING STRATEGY

COMPARE AND CONTRAST
To compare and contrast, note similarities and differences between two or more people, places, events, or things. As you read, use a graphic organizer like this one to compare and contrast the societies discussed.

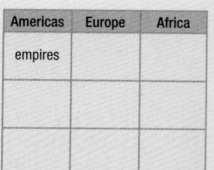

Americas	Europe	Africa
empires		

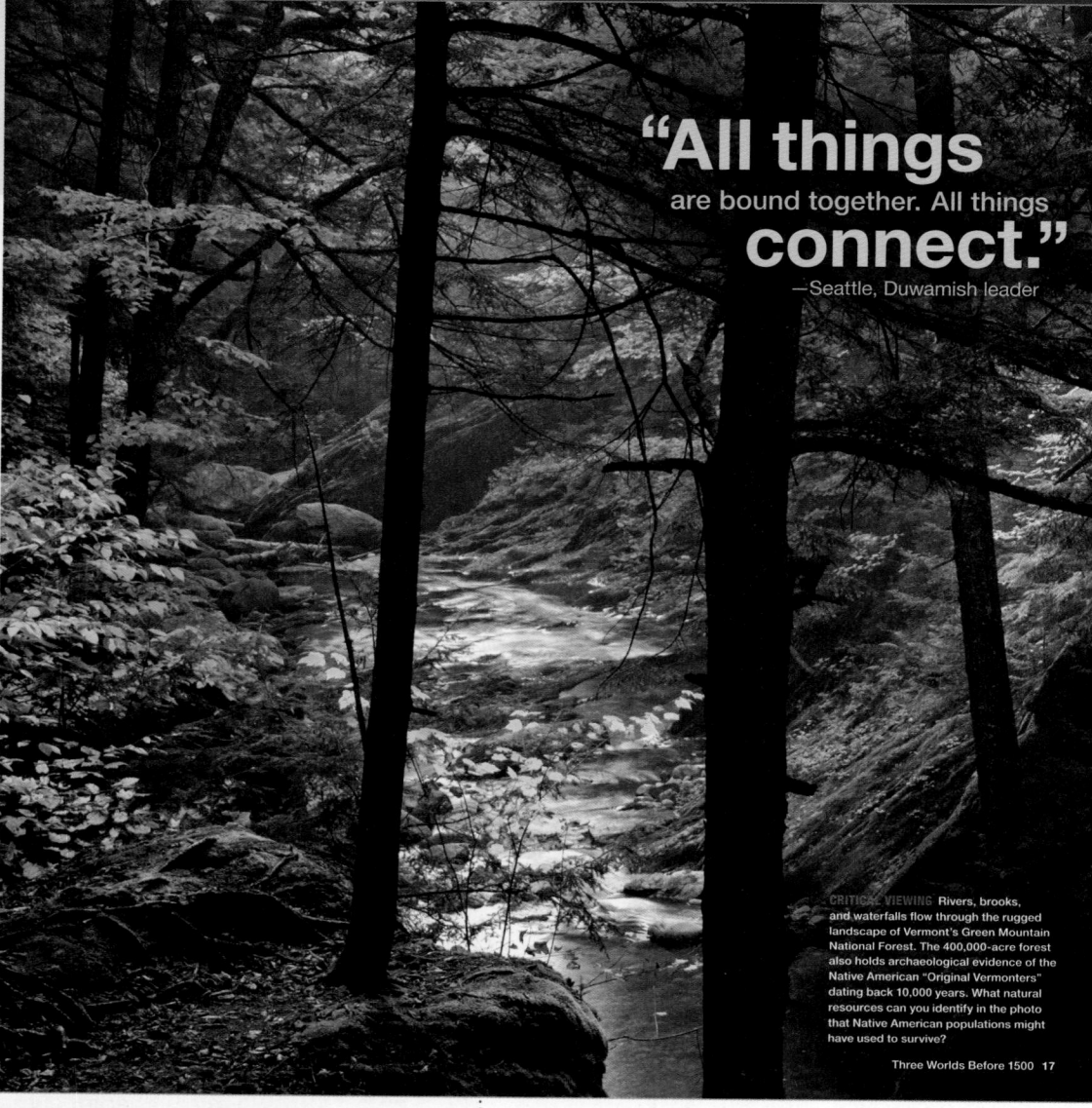

"All things
are bound together. All things
connect."
—Seattle, Duwamish leader

CRITICAL VIEWING Rivers, brooks, and waterfalls flow through the rugged landscape of Vermont's Green Mountain National Forest. The 400,000-acre forest also holds archaeological evidence of the Native American "Original Vermonters" dating back 10,000 years. What natural resources can you identify in the photo that Native American populations might have used to survive?

INTRODUCE THE PHOTOGRAPH

Green Mountain National Forest

Have students study the photograph of Green Mountain National Forest in Vermont. Discuss the natural resources evident in the photo, such as water, trees, and rocks, and what resources are likely there but not evident, such as fish, animals, nuts, and berries. Then draw attention to the Seattle quote. **ASK:** How do you think the quote applies to the photo? *(Answers will vary. Possible response: Everything in a forest ecosystem is connected. The health of the plants and animals depends on the health of the air, water, and soil. People need to protect the resources of the forest if they want to maintain them for future use.)* Tell students that one of the things they will learn in this chapter is how Native Americans adapted to their environments and created rich cultures before the arrival of Europeans.

For Chapter 1 Spanish Resources, visit the Resources Menu. Chapter 1 Resources are available at NGLSync.Cengage.com.

Share Background

The area that is now the Green Mountain National Forest is the traditional homeland of the Abenaki, an Algonquian-speaking tribe, and their ancient ancestors. In 1932, the federal government established the Green Mountain National Forest to repair the environmental damage that resulted from intensive logging in the 1800s. Today, much of the terrain has been returned to its natural state without sacrificing Green Mountain's status as a working forest.

CRITICAL VIEWING Answers will vary. Possible response: Native Americans would have used the brook for fishing and its water for drinking. They would have hunted in the forest for animals as a source of food, hides, and bones; foraged for nuts, berries, and edible plants; and used trees, bark, and bones for building materials and to make tools.

INTRODUCE THE ESSENTIAL QUESTION

How were early civilizations in the Americas, Africa, and Europe both similar and different?

Brainstorming Activity: Characteristics of Civilizations Invite students to brainstorm different characteristics of civilizations. Record students' responses in a Concept Cluster about civilizations. If students need help getting started, encourage them to think about these questions:

- Where do people live?
- What makes people feel safe?
- How do people get food?
- How does work get done?
- What do people believe in?
- How do groups interact with each other?

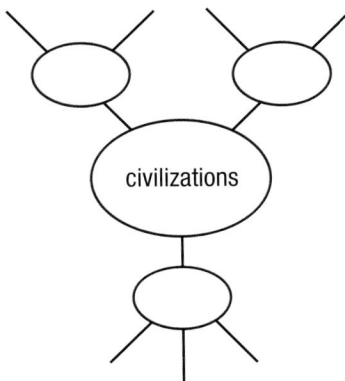

INTRODUCE CHAPTER VOCABULARY

Word Webs

Tell students to complete a Word Web for Key Vocabulary words as they read the chapter. Ask them to write each word in the center of an oval. Tell them to look through the chapter to find examples, characteristics, and descriptive words that may be associated with the vocabulary word. At the end of the chapter, ask students what they learned about each word. Model an example for students on the board, using the graphic organizer below.

INTRODUCE THE READING STRATEGY

COMPARE AND CONTRAST

Remind students that when they compare and contrast, they are looking for similarities and differences between two or more people, places, events, or things. Point out that, in this chapter, they will be noting similarities and differences between the cultural traits and practices of civilizations in the Americas, Europe, and Africa before 1500. Model completing the first row of the Compare-and-Contrast Chart. Point out the headings: "Americas," "Europe," and "Africa." Tell students that "empires" refers to the political organization of civilizations in the Americas. Encourage students to refer to and complete their charts as they read.

Americas	Europe	Africa
empires		

KEY DATES FOR CHAPTER 1

1200–400 B.C.	Olmec civilization prospers in Mesoamerica
A.D. 100–800	Moche civilization thrives in South America
A.D. 500–1450	Europe experiences the Middle Ages
c. 700	Mississippian culture spreads
1300s	Renaissance begins in Europe
1324	Mansa Musa makes pilgrimage to Mecca
early 1400s	Henry the Navigator establishes school in Portugal
mid-1400s	Johann Gutenberg invents printing press
1591	Morocco invades Songhai

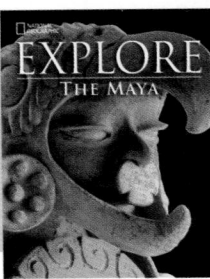

For more on civilizations in the Americas, see *EXPLORE THE MAYA*.

STEM

Objectives

- **Learn about North America's vast natural resources.**
- **Analyze the relationship between people, the environment, and natural resources.**
- **Consider the concept of plenty and what it meant to the first people who lived in North America.**
- **Study a primary source: *The Religion of the Kwakiutl Indians.***

Critical Thinking Skills for "Land of Plenty"

- Make Connections
- Draw Conclusions
- Identify Main Ideas and Details
- Analyze Environmental Concepts
- Form and Support Opinions
- Identify Problems and Solutions
- Analyze Cause and Effect

Background for the Teacher

This American Story introduces the concept of plenty and the relationship between the environment and natural resources. Historians and archaeologists suggest that early people crossed into the Americas by way of land bridges from Asia between 15,000 and 20,000 years ago, migrating as they followed herds of animals they hunted for food. This high-interest story focuses specifically on the Northwest Coast and how the people who lived there balanced the use of natural resources with respect for the land.

This chapter describes the early societies of the Americas, Europe during the Middle Ages, and West Africa and how major civilizations struggled with the concept of plenty, shifting the balance from cultural sharing to conflict.

History Notebook

Encourage students to complete the American Story pages for Chapter 1 in their History Notebooks as they read.

Note to the Teacher

Use this American Story as a teaser for content students will encounter in Chapter 1.

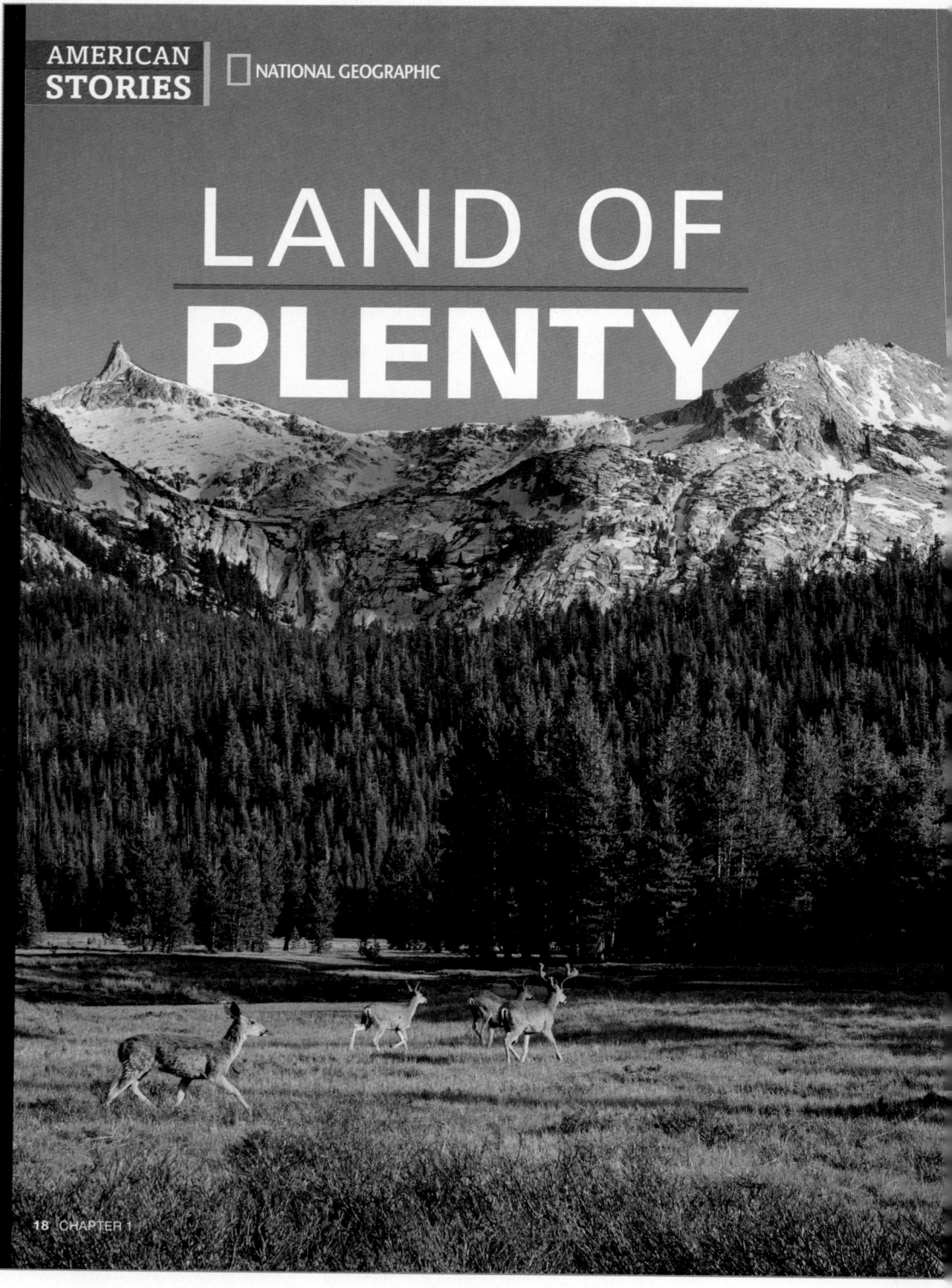

AMERICAN STORIES | NATIONAL GEOGRAPHIC

LAND OF PLENTY

18 CHAPTER 1

CRITICAL VIEWING Deer run through Tuolumne Meadows in California's Yosemite National Park. What details in this photo represent North America as a "land of plenty"?

BY DR. TERENCE CLARK
Director, Shíshálh Archaeological Research Project, University of Saskatchewan

What does *plenty* mean to you? For the first people who lived in North America, the concept of plenty revolved around food. Hunting, gathering, and growing food took up a lot of their time. Lucky for them, they lived in a Land of Plenty.

As you have just read, North America is one of the most geographically varied places in the world. It has towering mountain ranges, wide, grassy plains, rocky coasts, and gentle valleys. Networks of powerful rivers support rich soil. Countless species thrive in every part of the continent. For thousands of years, North America's varied environments have provided people, both ancient and modern, with lush natural resources. Whether bison on the Great Plains, berries from a rain forest, elk in the Rocky Mountains, or fish along the coasts, the first residents had plenty to eat.

In addition, Native Americans across the continent developed ways to produce even more food. In the southwestern deserts, they raised crops like corn, beans, and squash. In the eastern woodlands, they devised a slash-and-burn method to create land on which to farm. Native Americans knew a great deal about the world around them, and they understood the delicate balance of taking from nature in moderation and with respect.

How might the concept of plenty have defined people who lived in North America in the past?

Observe and Discuss

Ask students to select an item found in the classroom and state what natural resources went into its creation. Resources might include wood, fibers, stone, metals, and/or oil. **ASK:** Where did the natural resources used to make the item come from? Nearby? Another state? Another country? *(Answers will vary.)* Encourage students to think about the natural resources in their community. **ASK:** How might your life be different if everything you used were produced only with natural resources from nearby? *(Answers will vary.)* Tell students they are going to read an American Story about several early North American cultures and how they thrived because of the resources in their region.

Survey and Write

Survey students to assess their experience with growing vegetables or farmers' markets. Discuss kinds of foods produced in home gardens or found in local markets. **ASK:** Is there enough variety of regional foods to sustain your community? If not, what additional foods might your community need to survive? *(Answers will vary.)* Tell students to spend two minutes writing their thoughts. Invite volunteers to share what they have written. Explain that early North American people, such as those who lived on the Northwest Coast, were sustained by the foods available in their region and did not have access to foods from far away.

CRITICAL VIEWING Answers will vary. Possible response: There are many deer, and the vast grassland provides food for the deer. The mountains covered in snow contribute to streams and rivers, providing water. There are also plenty of trees, which can provide homes for animals and wood for humans.

Who Lived Where?

Several major groups lived in the Northwest Coast region. The Chinook lived in the present-day states of Oregon and Washington, from the mouth of the Columbia River to The Dalles, a section of the river with strong rapids. The Kwakiutl lived along waterways in present-day British Columbia, Canada, between the mainland and Vancouver Island. The Tlingit lived farther north than any of the other early Northwest Coast people, making their homes along the coast and on the islands of southern Alaska. The Haida lived on a string of islands along northwest British Columbia and southeastern Alaska. If time permits, encourage students to consult a map in the classroom or online to identify the areas in which these people lived and still live.

A Closer Look at Totem Poles

Northwest Coast people created totem poles from wood, and many tribes still create them. Different types include memorial poles, created when a new person or family moves into a house to honor the past owner and acknowledge the new one. Some totem poles serve as grave markers. House posts and portal poles are totems used in house construction. House posts support roofs, and portal poles have an opening that serves as an entry to the house. To show ownership of the waterfront, welcoming poles are set near the edge of a body of water. Mortuary poles contain the remains of those who have died.

CULTURES OF THE NORTHWEST COAST

Let's take a look at one region in particular—the Pacific Northwest—that demonstrates the powerful relationship between Native Americans and the natural world. The Pacific Northwest is a geographic and cultural area that stretches from what is now northern California to present-day Alaska. It includes coastal areas, inland forests, and several mountain ranges. It is also where the massive Columbia River flows through the Cascade Mountains and into the Pacific Ocean.

One unique feature of the Pacific Northwest is its temperate rain forests, which are characterized by heavy rainfall—as much as 14 feet per year—and by moderate temperatures. These rain forests are also home to some of the biggest trees in the world, including Sitka spruce, giant sequoia, and Douglas fir. These trees can grow to more than 250 feet tall and live for hundreds of years.

The first people who lived in the Pacific Northwest developed distinctive cultures, including the Kwakiutl (kwak-ee-YOU-tuhl), the Tlingit (KLING-kit), the Haida (HIGH-dah), the Chinook (SHIH-nuhk), and many others.

Because they lived among giant trees, these cultures mastered skills in woodworking. They built huge cedar plank houses, some large enough for hundreds of people. They also carved sturdy and seaworthy boats out of enormous tree trunks.

Northwest Coast people used woodworking in other ways, too. Intricately carved and painted totem poles towered over villages. Totems demonstrated village or family identities and indicated families' positions in the tribal social structure. They incorporated colorful representations of Pacific Northwest wildlife, including bears, ravens, whales, and eagles, as well as human figures and supernatural spirits. Totems functioned as collective histories, and the stories they told have been passed down among the generations.

Woodcarving also played a role in Northwest Coast ceremonies. Several ceremonies marked important times of the year or life events, and others reinforced social ties. Shamans, or people who were believed to be able to help others communicate with the spirit world, guided the carving of masks used during some ceremonies.

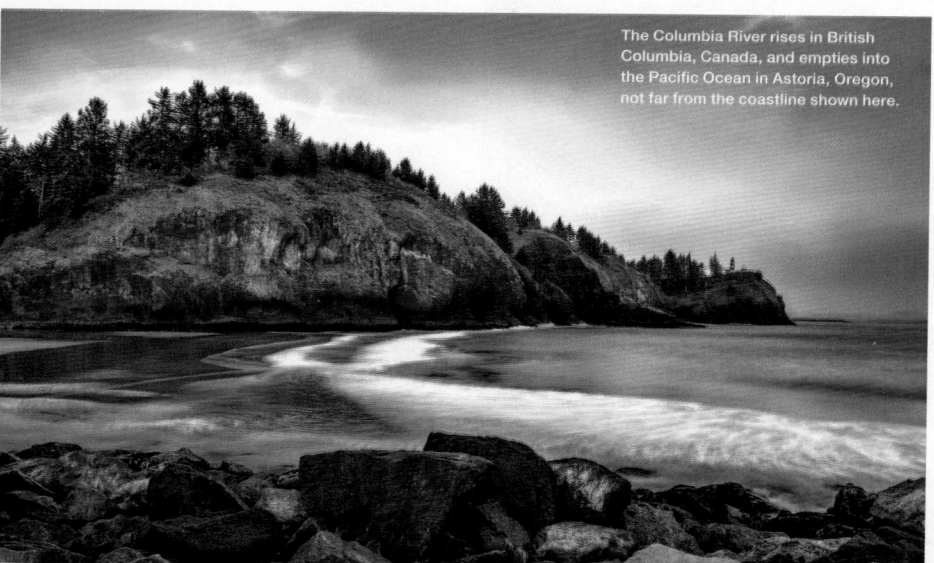

The Columbia River rises in British Columbia, Canada, and empties into the Pacific Ocean in Astoria, Oregon, not far from the coastline shown here.

OCEANS, FORESTS, AND RIVERS

Unlike groups in many other areas of North America, the coastal people of the Pacific Northwest did not farm to obtain food. Instead, they relied on the plentiful natural resources available to them. The many rivers that flow into the Pacific Ocean nourished the land and provided a welcome habitat for hundreds of species of plants and animals.

Perhaps the most important of these was the salmon. Since the earliest days of North America, five species of salmon born in rivers and lakes have traveled downstream to live their adult lives in the ocean. They only return to fresh water to spawn, or reproduce, and die. These spawning events, when millions of fish return to the streams and lakes where they were born, are some of the greatest migrations on Earth.

For early Northwest Coast people, abundant and predictable salmon migrations, or runs, provided the backbone of their traditional economies. The spring salmon runs in April and May were, and continue to be, incredibly important in providing food for Northwest Coast people. After a long winter of subsisting on dried foods—including smoked and dried salmon—spring was a time of plenty as fresh foods returned to the menu. Historically, the coming of the salmon often saved tribes from starvation as their winter supplies dwindled.

In addition to salmon, Northwest Coast people harvested a variety of shellfish, including clams, cockles, mussels, and oysters. They also hunted many land animals and birds, gathered a wide variety of plants and berries, and even hunted whales in some areas.

A UNIQUE WORLDVIEW

Northwest Coast people saw themselves as an important part of their environment. Respect for the natural world was at the core of their worldview. They believed the plants and animals around them were as important as their human neighbors. How does this compare with the view people today have about the relationship between humans and nature?

Northwest Coast cultures also believed that many animals possessed human-like abilities. Some could even change into human form and take on traits such as anger if they were not treated with respect. If someone didn't hunt or fish in a respectful way, the animal might tell its kin to refuse to be caught in the future. All this added up to one clear point: survival required living in balance with animals and plants and respecting the natural world. Living a balanced life would ensure that food would be available year after year. Not doing so would bring dire consequences to the tribe.

Northwest Coast people adapted to and were shaped by their environments. In what ways does your environment shape who you are?

Northwest Coast totem poles are truly distinctive, with bright colors, detailed carving, and graphic patterns. What animals can you see on this totem?

Guided Discussion

1. **Identify Main Ideas and Details** In what ways were the ocean and rivers important to the people of the Northwest Coast? *(Since the people did not farm for food, water was a major source of food, providing fish, particularly salmon.)*

2. **Analyze Environmental Concepts** How might the lives of the people of the Northwest Coast have changed if disease had affected and killed most of the trees of the region? Ask students to support their answers with evidence from the text. *(Possible response: The people might have had to migrate somewhere else where trees were abundant or, less likely, they would have sought other natural resources to replace wood.)*

Active Options

On Your Feet: Narrate a Place Ask students to consider the connection of the early people of the Northwest Coast to the land. Explain that whether students live in a city, a suburb, small town, or out in the country, they are connected to their environments in basic ways. First, as a class, have students discuss how they depend on their environment and the resources found there. Then ask students to think about where they live and how their connection to that place is part of their identity. Ask students to work in pairs or small groups to describe their environment via short skits in which group members represent different features of their environments.

NG Learning Framework: Learn About Wildlife

SKILL Collaboration

KNOWLEDGE Critical Species

Encourage students to find out more about animals of the Northwest Coast. Tell students to work in pairs, assigning tasks and sharing the work equally, and use online research to learn about elk, moose, mountain sheep, salmon, or another animal they may discover that lives in the region. Ask them to consider the following: lifespan, habitat, food, adaptations, and their young. Call on pairs to present their findings to the class. Encourage students to include a minimum of two visuals in their oral report.

Guided Discussion

1. **Form and Support Opinions** Do you think it is important for traditions to be passed on to younger generations? Why or why not? Support your opinion with evidence from the text. *(Answers will vary.)*

2. **Identify Problems and Solutions** What happened to the salmon stocks during the 20th century, and how did Lummi efforts help correct this problem? *(Large commercial fisheries depleted the salmon stocks, and development, overfishing, and pollution damaged the rivers and streams where salmon migrated to spawn. The Lummi brought back the First Salmon ceremony and reclaimed salmon spawning habitats in order to restore them to their natural state.)*

Analyze Primary Sources

Ask a volunteer to read the excerpt from *The Religion of the Kwakiutl Indians* aloud. Ask students to identify specific words that refer to the King of the Salmon. *(Swimmer, friend, Supernatural One, Long-Life-Giver)* **ASK:** Why does the blessing use these words? *(The words express what is important to the Kwakiutl about the salmon, that it is their friend from the river who nourishes their bodies and their spirits.)* Why might the blessing address the King of Salmon directly? *(Answers will vary. Possible response: The blessing speaks to the salmon itself and shows respect. If the blessing were not directed to the King of the Salmon, it might feel less personal and less appreciative toward the salmon.)*

WRITE ABOUT HISTORY

Explore Natural Resources This American Story explains how North America provides the resources necessary for people to survive and thrive. To help students make connections between the American Story and their own lives, have them write an informational essay on how the first people of the land cared for the natural resources and how people today also strive to protect the resources necessary for human survival. Students may choose to focus on one or more resources: water, soil, forests, animals, fossil fuels, or air. Students can conduct online research or use other source materials for important facts to include in their essays.

AMERICAN STORIES

KING OF THE SALMON

Northwest Coast cultures performed special ceremonies to honor nature and to show respect for the plants and animals that kept them alive. One of the most important of these was the First Salmon ceremony. After a grueling winter of cold rain, with little access to fresh foods, spring brought new hope and abundance. People anxiously awaited the arrival of the salmon to usher in a season of plenty.

The first salmon to return to the river was called the King of the Salmon. People believed that as the leader, the King of the Salmon had the power to encourage other salmon to come and be caught or to scare away the other fish. If he was not treated with respect, the entire salmon run could be affected. To welcome the King of the Salmon, shamans conducted the First Salmon ceremony. Whole communities gathered to pay respect.

Although the First Salmon ceremony varied among different groups, three steps (described at right) characterize this ritual, which is still performed today. Once the ceremony is complete, the salmon fishing season is declared officially open and everyone can begin catching fish for food.

Students at the Lummi Nation School in Bellingham, Washington, prepare to bring in the First Salmon at their annual celebration of this traditional ceremony.

1. **Catching and welcoming the salmon**
   The chief selects a fisherman to catch the King of the Salmon. Once caught, tribal members carry it to the chief on a bed made of cedar.

2. **Cleaning, cooking, and eating the fish**
   Cooks delicately remove the meat from the fish. The head, entrails, and bones are set aside. Then community members eat the fish.

3. **Returning the remains to the water**
   Tribal members place the remains, which are considered sacred, in a cedar basket with its head facing upstream, pointing the way home. Then the salmon is released back into the water, where it is believed it will become whole again to continue its journey.

A master of ceremony named La-mos lifts the King of the Salmon to the sky as part of the Lummi Nation's First Salmon ceremony in May 2010.

This Tlingit wood rattle carved in the shape of a salmon is an excellent example of Northwest Coast art. It has bold shapes and colors and takes the form of wildlife native to the region.

CULTURAL REVIVAL

When European settlers arrived in the region in the early 1800s, two different worldviews came into contact with one another. In many cases, this contact led to changes among native traditions and practices.

Missionaries introduced Christianity and pressured native people to change their traditions. Europeans frowned on native beliefs that elevated the natural world to the level of humans, so they halted some ceremonies and declared others illegal. Along with ceremonies and religious beliefs, Europeans also replaced native foods with Western ones. Over time, Northwest Coast people began to shift away from traditional practices and focused on trade with the newcomers. By the late 1800s, the First Salmon ceremony began to die out.

During the 20th century, large commercial fisheries depleted salmon stocks all along the Pacific Coast. Development, overfishing, and pollution endangered the rivers and streams where the salmon migrated to spawn. According to the Native American worldview, this lack of respect for nature led to negative consequences, which included much smaller salmon runs than had been historically known.

In the 1970s, the Lummi people of Puget Sound, near Seattle, Washington, decided to bring back the First Salmon ceremony. They had never lost their belief in the importance of the plants and animals around them. And they felt the ceremony could help the salmon and the Lummi people.

In addition to reviving the First Salmon ceremony, the Lummi have also reclaimed salmon spawning habitats. They have restored streams to their natural state, ensuring the vital environment that salmon need to reproduce. The Lummi's efforts are paying off. Growing numbers of salmon are returning to their territory, and the Lummi are able to teach their children about the importance of respecting nature.

THINK ABOUT IT

The Lummi revived a ceremony to reinforce their connection to the natural world. What kinds of ceremonies or celebrations do you participate in that reinforce beliefs in your family and community?

A CEREMONIAL BLESSING

After the King of the Salmon is caught, cleaned, and cooked, it is ready to be eaten—after a blessing.

Among the Kwakiutl, this blessing is recited to honor the First Salmon. It has likely been handed down from generation to generation of Kwakiutl and is delivered before the salmon can be enjoyed. From this primary source, what can you conclude about how the Kwakiutl viewed their relationship with the King of the Salmon?

PRIMARY SOURCE

We have come to meet alive, Swimmer.
Do not feel wrong about what I have done to you,
friend Swimmer, for that is the reason why you come
that I may spear you, that I may eat you,
Supernatural One, you, Long-Life-Giver,
you, Swimmer.
Now protect us, (me) and my wife, that we may keep
well, that nothing may be difficult for us.

Source: from *The Religion of the Kwakiutl Indians*, by Frank Boas, New York: Columbia University Press, 1930, p. 207

English Language Learners

Pose and Answer Questions Ask pairs at the **Bridging** level to read the American Story. Instruct them to pause after each paragraph and ask one another *who, what, when, where,* or *why* questions about what they have just read. Suggest students use a 5Ws Chart to help organize their questions and answers.

Striving Readers

Record and Compare Facts After they read each section, ask students to write at least three facts they can recall. Allow pairs to compare and check their facts and combine them into one list. If the classroom dynamic is amenable, suggest a competition among pairs about which one can produce the longest list.

THINK ABOUT IT

Students may list holiday celebrations, birthdays, and anniversaries acknowledging family and community milestones and passages.

See the Chapter Planner for more strategies for differentiation.

HISTORICAL THINKING

Ask and have students answer the following questions.

1. **READING CHECK** In what ways did the Northeast Coast prove to be a land of plenty?

2. **MAKE PREDICTIONS** Based on the American Story you just read, how do you predict the topics will relate to Chapter 1?

3. **ANALYZE CAUSE AND EFFECT** How did the arrival of European settlers change the lives of the people of the Northwest Coast?

ANSWERS

1. The Northeast Coast is a region with giant trees, heavy rainfall, rivers, a moderate temperature, and plenty of fish.

2. Answers will vary.

3. Europeans introduced Christianity and pressured native people to change traditions. Native people began to replace native foods with western ones, trade with settlers, and move away from their cultural practices.

1.1 Early American Civilizations

The Americas were never a blank slate, waiting for someone to "discover" them. People began arriving in the region about 20,000 years ago. Over time, they developed cultures that would influence all of the Americas and the world.

MAIN IDEA Civilizations emerged and thrived in Mesoamerica and South America for thousands of years.

MESOAMERICA

Long before 1492, great **civilizations**, or complex societies, arose in the Americas. The earliest of these civilizations began in **Mesoamerica**, which stretches from southern Mexico into part of Central America. Mesoamerica's landscape consists of two main areas: highlands and lowlands. The highlands lie between the mountains of the Sierra Madre (see-AIR-uh MAH-dray), a mountain system in Mexico. The lowlands are found along the coast of the Gulf of Mexico and in the jungles of the Yucatán (yoo-kuh-TAN) Peninsula. Both areas provided fertile land for agriculture.

The fertile land allowed several civilizations to develop in Mesoamerica. The **Olmec, Maya,** and **Aztec** thrived at different times from around 1200 B.C. to about A.D. 1520. The oldest civilization, the Olmec society, settled along present-day Mexico's Gulf Coast. The Maya, who were influenced by Olmec culture, mainly lived in parts of the countries we now call Mexico, Guatemala, and Belize. The Aztec were the last of the major Mesoamerican civilizations, establishing their empire in central and southern Mexico.

SOUTH AMERICA

To the south of Mesoamerica lies South America, a continent twice the size of the United States. South America contains coastal plains, dry forests and deserts, and vast river basins covered by dense rain forests and grasslands. The Andes Mountains rise along the continent over a distance of about 5,500 miles, extending from the northwestern coast all the way down to the southern tip. The mountains divide the Pacific coast from the continent's interior and separated the early civilizations in lands that are now the countries of Peru, Bolivia, Argentina, and Chile.

The **Moche** (MOH-chay) and the **Inca** were two of the most important early civilizations. The Moche lived on the arid northern coast of present-day Peru between about A.D. 100 and 800. They developed a complex **irrigation** system that channeled water to their crops. The rise of the Inca started in the 12th century. They established a capital city in Cusco (KOOS-koh), Peru, and later built the complex and mysterious city of Machu Picchu (MAH-choo PEE-choo) high in the Andes Mountains.

Moche Metalworking
The Moche were known for their vibrant murals, fine pottery, and advanced metalwork. Gold monkey-head beads, like this one, were often buried with members of the Moche nobility.

HISTORICAL THINKING

1. **READING CHECK** Which three civilizations developed in Mesoamerica?

2. **COMPARE AND CONTRAST** How were the highlands and lowlands of Mesoamerica similar?

3. **INTERPRET MAPS** How do you think the Andes Mountains benefited both the Moche and the Inca?

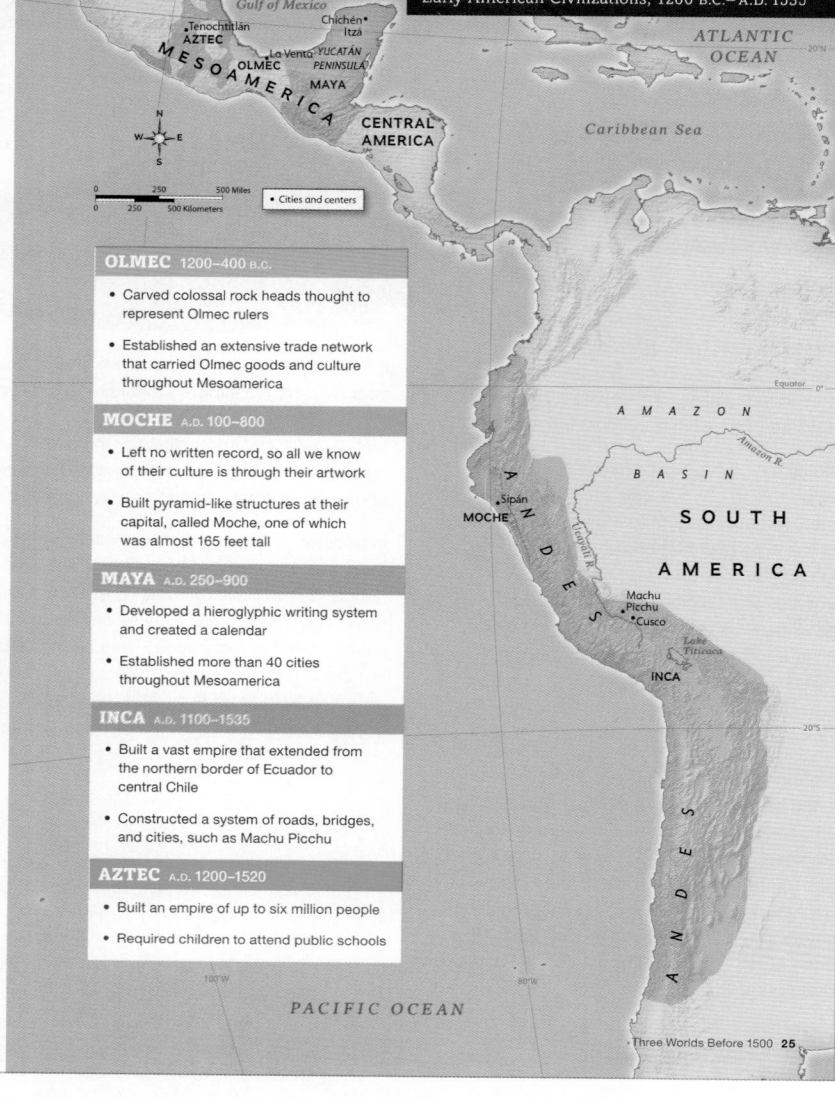

Early American Civilizations, 1200 B.C.– A.D. 1535

OLMEC 1200–400 B.C.
- Carved colossal rock heads thought to represent Olmec rulers
- Established an extensive trade network that carried Olmec goods and culture throughout Mesoamerica

MOCHE A.D. 100–800
- Left no written record, so all we know of their culture is through their artwork
- Built pyramid-like structures at their capital, called Moche, one of which was almost 165 feet tall

MAYA A.D. 250–900
- Developed a hieroglyphic writing system and created a calendar
- Established more than 40 cities throughout Mesoamerica

INCA A.D. 1100–1535
- Built a vast empire that extended from the northern border of Ecuador to central Chile
- Constructed a system of roads, bridges, and cities, such as Machu Picchu

AZTEC A.D. 1200–1520
- Built an empire of up to six million people
- Required children to attend public schools

PLAN

Objective

Learn about and distinguish the Olmec, Maya, Aztec, Moche, and Inca civilizations.

Critical Thinking Skills for Lesson 1.1
- Identify Main Ideas and Details
- Monitor Comprehension
- Compare and Contrast
- Interpret Maps
- Identify
- Describe

Essential Question for Chapter 1

How were early civilizations in the Americas, Africa, and Europe both similar and different?
Geographic factors helped shape early civilizations in Mesoamerica and South America. Lesson 1.1 describes how these factors played a role in the emergence of five key civilizations.

Background for the Teacher

Similar to European feudal society and later Mesoamerican societies, Olmec society was hierarchical. Rulers and religious leaders were at the top. Farmers and laborers were at the bottom. In the middle were artisans and the traders who spread Olmec goods and culture.

Many archaeologists consider the Olmec, with their monumental art and architecture, the "mother culture" of Mesoamerica. The Olmec built San Lorenzo, La Venta, and Tres Zapotes as gathering places for religious, political, and economic activities. These ceremonial centers were likely the first cities in Mesoamerica. Archaeologists believe that San Lorenzo had roads paved in stone and drainage and water-storage systems. The Olmec may have been the first Mesoamericans to develop a writing system, a number system, and a calendar.

Preview with Vocabulary

Draw an Idea Web on the board and write the Key Vocabulary word *civilization* in the center square. Ask students to volunteer what comes to mind when they hear the word *civilization* and add their ideas to the web. Then tell them that Mesoamerica and South America were home to several early civilizations, most notably the Olmec, Maya, Aztec, Moche, and Inca.

TEACH
Guided Discussion

1. **Identify** Where are the highlands and lowlands of Mesoamerica located? *(The highlands are located among the Sierra Madre mountains in Mexico. The lowlands are located along the coast of the Gulf of Mexico and in the jungles of the Yucatán Peninsula.)*

2. **Describe** What are the geographic features of South America? *(South America has coastal plains, dry forests and deserts, and vast river basins covered by dense rain forests and grasslands. The Andes Mountains extend for about 5,500 miles along the northwestern coast all the way down to the southern tip. The mountains divide the Pacific coast from the continent's interior.)*

Interpret Maps

Direct students' attention to the map of early American civilizations. Ask them to explain the relationship between the map and the chart. *(Students may explain the correlation between the chart colors and map colors and that the chart provides the time periods for the development of each civilization shown on the map.)* **ASK:** How would you describe the location of the Mesoamerican civilizations in relation to each other? *(The Olmec, Maya, and Aztec civilizations developed very close to each other.)* How would you describe the location of the South American civilizations? *(They developed along the Pacific coast and in the Andes Mountains.)* Which civilization created the largest empire? *(Inca)* How does the chart contribute to your understanding of the Inca? *(Possible response: The chart describes how far the empire extended—from the northern border of Ecuador to central Chile. It also indicates that the Inca built roads, bridges, and cities such as Machu Picchu.)*

Active Options

On Your Feet: Jigsaw Invite students to divide into five "expert" groups and assign one of the civilizations covered in the lesson to each group. Encourage them to research their civilization on the Internet, taking notes and gathering facts not covered in the lesson. Then reshuffle students so that each new group has at least one member from each expert group. Invite experts to report on their civilization to the rest of their new group.

NG Learning Framework: Research Mesoamerican Achievements

ATTITUDE Curiosity

KNOWLEDGE Our Human Story

Encourage groups of students to research Mesoamerican achievements in astronomy, mathematics, and the development of the calendar. Have each group select one topic and find three facts about it to share with the class. Then have groups take turns presenting their sets of facts to the class.

DIFFERENTIATE
Striving Readers

Take Notes Have students take notes as they read the lesson by completing a chart like the one shown below. Allow students to compare their completed charts in small groups and make any necessary corrections. Then call on volunteers to use their charts to summarize what they know about early Mesoamerican and South American civilizations.

	Location	Characteristics
Olmec		
Moche		
Maya		
Inca		
Aztec		

English Language Learners ELD

Read in Pairs Partner students at the **Emerging** level with English-proficient students and have them read the lesson together. Instruct the native speakers to pause whenever they encounter a word or sentence construction that is confusing to their partners. Suggest that the native speakers point out context clues to help their partners understand the meanings of unfamiliar terms. Encourage English language learners to restate sentences in their own words.

See the Chapter Planner for more strategies for differentiation.

HISTORICAL THINKING

ANSWERS

1. The Olmec, Maya, and Aztec civilizations developed in Mesoamerica.

2. The highlands and lowlands had fertile land for agriculture.

3. Possible response: The Moche likely used stream water from the mountains to irrigate crops. The mountains would have provided building materials for Inca cities and isolation and some protection from enemies.

1.2 Western American Cultures

How do you get food if you can't grow it—or buy it? You work with what you've got. Like the Mesoamericans and South Americans, people in the north adapted to their environments.

MAIN IDEA A variety of environments, characterized by climate and landforms, influenced the development of western North American cultures.

THE FAR NORTH AND PACIFIC COAST

South America and Mesoamerica weren't the only places where civilizations developed in the Western Hemisphere. In the extreme northwest of North America, several Native American groups flourished in particularly harsh climates. The Aleut (a-lee-OOT) lived on the cold, nearly treeless islands off the coast of what is now Alaska. The Inuit (IH-noo-wit) lived on the flat, frozen Arctic **tundra** of present-day Alaska and northwestern Canada. Since the weather did not favor growing crops, the groups fished and hunted sea mammals for food. They used **kayaks**, light boats made of wood and seal or walrus hides.

Farther to the south, a number of tribes lived in the evergreen forests that swept down the coast from present-day British Columbia to Oregon. Groups such as the Kwakiutl (kwah-kee-YOO-tuhl) and Haida (HI-duh) hunted and fished, and the ocean provided plenty of food. The abundance of trees made wood the preferred material for houses, boats, and household goods. The Kwakiutl also hosted **potlatches**, feasts where families gave gifts to guests to show social rank and wealth.

Even farther down the coast, in what is now California, the Pomo lived as hunter-gatherers. The Pomo didn't need to farm because the streams were full of fish, and plenty of edible wild plants, nuts, and berries grew on the land. The Pomo had a unique religion. Worshippers dressed as animal spirits and other beings to sing, dance, and distribute gifts.

THE DESERTS AND PLAINS

Like the people of the North and the West, Native Americans living in the Southwest and Great Plains had to adapt to special climates and conditions. In the arid American Southwest, the **ancient Pueblo** (PWAY-bloh) and the **Hohokam** (ho-ho-KOM) thrived during the time of the Maya. In fact, Mesoamerican culture heavily influenced these groups. Not only did the Hohokam trade with Mesoamericans, they also **domesticated**, or grew, similar crops for food. They irrigated their crops in the dry climate. The Hohokam grew cotton, squash, beans, and maize, or corn, by digging canals from their fields to nearby rivers. Having extra food allowed the population to grow.

Around A.D. 1000, both the Hohokam and the ancient Pueblo built large adobe (uh-DOH-bee) homes made of sun-dried clay and straw bricks. These dwellings were similar to apartment buildings with multiple floors. For example, Pueblo Bonito, pictured to the left, once had as many as five floors and at least 600 rooms.

The ancient Pueblo were once referred to as the Anasazi, a name given them by the Navajo. In the 1990s, descendants of the ancient Pueblo protested the use of the term, pointing out that it means "enemy ancestor." Today many historians use the term "ancient Pueblo."

Northeast of the Hohokam, the Great Plains tribes experienced a very different way of life. Vast grasslands stretched from the Mississippi River to the Rocky Mountains. Native Americans who lived in the eastern part of the Great Plains, such as the Mandan and Pawnee, lived the settled lives of farmers, building villages of earthen lodges. In the western grasslands, the Blackfoot and other tribes like them **migrated**, or moved from place to place, hunting herds of bison (also commonly called buffalo) and other game for food and clothing. **Tepees**, or tents made of bison hides, served as their portable homes.

At this time, tribes herded bison on foot. They steered the animals over cliffs or into corrals where men could kill them with arrows. Nonetheless, Plains Indian tribes considered the bison sacred. They used every part of the animal: meat for food, skin and fur for clothes and tepees, and bones for tools and crafts.

Early North American Civilizations, c. 1400

- Arctic
- California
- Great Basin
- Great Plains
- Northeast
- Northwest Coast
- Plateau
- Southeast
- Southwest
- Subarctic

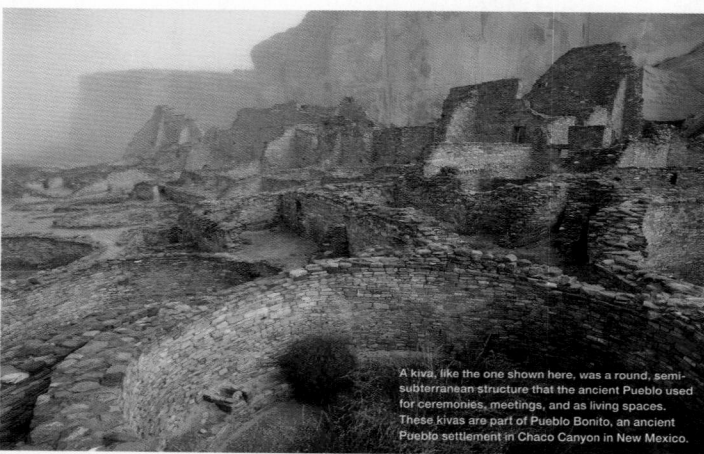

A kiva, like the one shown here, was a round, semi-subterranean structure that the ancient Pueblo used for ceremonies, meetings, and as living spaces. These kivas are part of Pueblo Bonito, an ancient Pueblo settlement in Chaco Canyon in New Mexico.

HISTORICAL THINKING

1. **READING CHECK** How did the tribes of northern and western North America adapt to their environments?

2. **COMPARE AND CONTRAST** How did lifestyles differ among Great Plains tribes?

3. **DRAW CONCLUSIONS** What can you conclude about similarities between the Maya culture and those of the ancient Pueblo and the Hohokam?

Three Worlds Before 1500 **27**

Objective
Learn how native groups of the North, Pacific Coast, Southwest, and Great Plains emerged in western North America.

Critical Thinking Skills for Lesson 1.2
- Identify Main Ideas and Details
- Monitor Comprehension
- Analyze Environmental Concepts
- Draw Conclusions
- Make Inferences

Essential Question for Chapter 1
How were early civilizations in the Americas, Africa, and Europe both similar and different?
Geographic factors also played major roles in shaping the lives and cultures of Native Americans in western North America. Lesson 1.2 describes how coastal and inland cultures thrived.

Background for the Teacher
The Pomo are expert basket makers. They use variations of two basic methods. One involves weaving two or more horizontal strands through vertical strands, much like weaving cloth. The second involves stitching together long coils of plant material, such as reeds, grasses, roots, and bark. Pomo basket makers use beads, shells, feathers, and dyes found in their environment to decorate their work. The Pomo also use basket-making skills to create cooking pots, trays, hats, cradles, fish traps, and boats. Today, Pomo baskets are considered works of art.

Activate Prior Knowledge

Draw a large Word Web on the board with *Western North America* in the center. Display a map of North America, and point out the far north, Northwest Coast, Great Plains, and Southwest. Ask students what they know about the climate and geography of western North America. Write students' descriptive phrases on the spokes of the web.

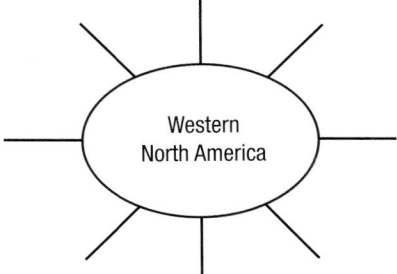

Western North America

TEACH

Guided Discussion

1. **Make Inferences** What do kayaks and potlatches tell you about the environments of the Aleut and Inuit in the far north and the Kwakiutl in coastal areas farther south? *(Possible response: The Aleut and Inuit used hides from sea mammals to make kayaks. Kayaks provided the means to reach sea mammals and move items along coast. The potlatch shows that food and materials were abundant in coastal areas.)*

2. **Analyze Environmental Concepts** What practices by the Hohokam and Blackfoot show that they adapted well to their environments? *(The Hohokam adapted to a dry climate by digging canals to rivers to irrigate their crops and using adobe—sun-dried clay and straw bricks—to build their homes. The Blackfoot used portable tepees, allowing them to migrate as they followed herds of bison.)*

More Information

Pueblo Bonito The ancient Pueblo built Pueblo Bonito in stages between A.D. 850 and 1150. The pueblo provided living quarters and served as a ceremonial, political, and trading center. It was designed in a "D," or semicircular shape, and oriented in relation to solar, lunar, and cardinal directions. Although only the foundation remains today, archaeologists believe that the structure ranged from one to five stories, with two plazas in the center. At its height, Pueblo Bonito was probably home to around 1,000 people.

Active Options

On Your Feet: Choose Your Home Label the four corners of the room: Far North, Pacific Coast, Deserts, Plains. Tell students to study the photo, map, and text and think about what each region had to offer its inhabitants in terms of geography, climate, and resources. Have students imagine living in the different regions. Then have them choose which area they would have preferred to live by going to that corner of the room. Finally, ask the groups in each corner to explain their choices.

NG Learning Framework: Explore Native American Cultures

SKILL Collaboration

KNOWLEDGE Our Human Story

Have students select something about one of the groups that they would like to know about in depth. For example, students might be interested in Inuit kayaks or Blackfoot tepees. Have students work in pairs to research their topic, making sure that they share the work equally. Ask pairs to prepare an oral report that gives details about their topic. Encourage students to share their reports with the class.

DIFFERENTIATE

Inclusion

Clarify Text Have visually-impaired students work with sighted partners. As they listen to an audio recording of the text, have the visually impaired students indicate if there are words or passages they do not understand. Their partners can clarify meaning by repeating passages, emphasizing context clues, and paraphrasing.

Pre-AP

Compare Across Regions Encourage students to compare Native American groups across regions. Have students make a chart with categories such as physical geography, food sources, and shelter. Tell them to conduct research to supplement the information in the text. Then have students present their findings about Native American groups across regions to the class.

See the Chapter Planner for more strategies for differentiation.

HISTORICAL THINKING

ANSWERS

1. Aleut and Inuit made kayaks from hides and wood and fished. People of the Northwest Coast made wood houses and boats and fished. The Pomo hunted and fished and gathered plants, nuts, and berries.

2. Possible response: Native Americans in the eastern part of the Great Plains lived a settled life as farmers, while those in the western grasslands moved from place to place.

3. Possible response: The Maya, ancient Pueblo, and Hohokam built large, multilevel apartment-style dwellings from adobe. The ancient Pueblo and Hohokam lived around the time of the Maya, had similar farming practices, and traded with Mesoamericans.

You climb to the top of the tower at Serpent Mound in southern Ohio and look down at the amazing sight below. It really does appear to be a gigantic, grass-covered snake slithering across the landscape with an egg or a jewel in its mouth. How did it get here? Who made it, and when?

MAIN IDEA Native Americans in eastern North America established stable agricultural societies and specialized burial and religious practices.

Ancient Mounds
Serpent Mound in Adams County, Ohio, resembles a writhing snake. The mound stretches more than 1,300 feet. It is estimated to be between 1,000 and 2,000 years old.

28 CHAPTER 1

THE MOUND BUILDERS

Serpent Mound and other mounds like it began dotting the North American landscape around 1000 B.C. The people who created these structures are known as the **Mound Builders**. They lived in the river valleys of the Midwest and eastern United States. These earthen mounds came in different shapes and sizes and served a variety of purposes. Some housed the dead, and others served as temples.

The Adena and Hopewell were two cultures that built mounds. Both groups lived chiefly in the southern part of present-day Ohio, where Serpent Mound is located. They also settled in the region we now call Indiana, Kentucky, West Virginia, Michigan, Wisconsin, and Pennsylvania. Both groups were primarily hunter-gatherers, though the Hopewell farmed as well. Studies of the Hopewell Mound Group have determined that their mounds served as ancient burial sites.

A couple of hundred years after the Hopewell culture died out, the Mississippians emerged. Beginning in about A.D. 700, this group spread across North America from present-day Georgia to Minnesota. The Mississippians topped their mounds with grand temples or chiefs' residences. Cahokia (kuh-HO-kee-yuh), a grouping of mounds located in Illinois, served as the culture's capital. At the Cahokia Mounds site, Monks Mound stands nearly 100 feet high. Its base is larger than that of the Great Pyramid of Giza in Egypt.

Unlike the hunter-gatherer cultures of the Adena and Hopewell, the Mississippians were largely agricultural. For food, they planted crops such as corn, beans, and squash. Having a large and dependable harvest helped them feed a large population. Cahokia alone may have housed as many as 15,000 people.

PEOPLE OF THE WOODLANDS

Just as the Mississippians depended on farming for their livelihoods, so too did the tribes who lived after them in the woodlands of eastern and southeastern North America.

The mild climate of the Southeast made it an ideal place to grow crops. The Chickasaw and Choctaw of present-day Mississippi and Alabama grew corn, beans, and pumpkins. Women planted and harvested the crops. They also cooked, cared for the children, and made baskets, clothes, and other goods. Men cleared the land, constructed buildings, hunted, served as warriors, and engaged in trade. Both the Chickasaw and Choctaw societies were **matrilineal**, meaning they traced their family lines through their mothers.

Agriculture was so important to these groups that one of their religious ceremonies was a Green Corn festival. The festival was held each summer as the corn began to ripen. Over a series of days, people fasted, feasted, danced, played games, and prayed.

The region in which the Eastern Woodlands people lived was heavily wooded, which explains its name. The tribes of the Eastern Woodlands practiced a technique known as **slash-and-burn agriculture**. This method involved cutting down and burning trees to clear land, and it supported the groups' pattern of moving frequently. Their farms were not permanent.

Two groups, named for the languages they spoke, lived in the Eastern Woodlands: the Algonquian (al-GAHN-kwee-uhn) and the Iroquois (EER-uh-kwoy). The Algonquian lived along the Atlantic coast. The Iroquois primarily lived in the central part of present-day New York State. In Algonquian groups, men were the heads of households, but Iroquois society was matrilineal, and women shared political power with men. Five Iroquois-speaking nations banded together to form the **Iroquois League**: the Mohawk, Oneida, Onondaga, Cayuga (kah-YOO-guh), and Seneca. This brought long-lasting peace among them. The Iroquois nations still exist to this day.

HISTORICAL THINKING

1. **READING CHECK** How did farming help maintain a large population in Cahokia?

2. **IDENTIFY PROBLEMS AND SOLUTIONS** How did the Eastern Woodlands people solve the problem of growing food in forests?

3. **MAKE INFERENCES** Why would the mild climate of the Southeast have made it an ideal place to grow crops?

Three Worlds Before 1500 **29**

PLAN

Objective
Learn about practices, beliefs, and societies of Mound Builders and Eastern Woodlands tribes.

Critical Thinking Skills for Lesson 1.3
- Identify Main Ideas and Details
- Monitor Comprehension
- Identify Problems and Solutions
- Analyze Environmental Concepts
- Compare and Contrast
- Categorize
- Analyze Visuals

Essential Question for Chapter 1
How were early civilizations in the Americas, Africa, and Europe both similar and different?
Cultivation of crops was crucial to civilizations examined in earlier lessons. Lesson 1.3 explores how agriculture affected the growth of Native American societies in eastern North America.

Background for the Teacher
In the 1880s, Frederick W. Putnam excavated part of the Great Serpent Mound and, finding no Adena artifacts, credited its creation to the Adena because of the existence of nearby Adena burials. Archaeologists accepted this interpretation until the 1990s, when samples from undisturbed areas of the mound yielded radiocarbon dates of around A.D. 1070—long after the end of the Adena culture. Some archaeologists used this new information to suggest that the Mississippian people created the mound. The discovery of Mississippian ruins near the mound added support for this theory, as did the widespread use of rattlesnake imagery in Mississippian culture. But the issue was far from settled. In 2014, new radiocarbon testing dated the mound to around 300 B.C., once again suggesting that the Adena were responsible for its creation.

Preview with the Photograph

Have students look at the photograph of the Great Serpent Mound as you read the introduction to the lesson aloud. Ask students to think about why it might be difficult to know who built the mound, why they built it, and why the answers might change as archaeologists learn more about the mound. After students have time to think about the topic, tell them to share their ideas with the class. Use information in Background for the Teacher to help students understand how interpretations of history are subject to change as new information is uncovered.

TEACH

Guided Discussion

1. **Compare and Contrast** In what ways were the Mississippians similar to and different from the Adena and Hopewell? *(Like the Adena and Hopewell, the Mississippians built mounds, some for burials. However, the Mississippians topped their huge mounds with grand temples or chiefs' residences. The Mississippians were largely agricultural, supporting large populations. The Adena and Hopewell were mostly hunter-gatherers.)*

2. **Categorize** If you were going to sort the groups discussed in this lesson into the categories of hunter-gatherers, farmers, Mound Builders, and matrilineal societies, which cultures would you place in each category? *(hunter-gathers: Adena and Hopewell; farmers: Hopewell, Mississippians, Chickasaw, Choctaw, Algonquian, Iroquois; Mound Builders: Adena, Hopewell, Mississippian; matrilineal: Chickasaw, Choctaw, Iroquois)*

Analyze Visuals

Have students examine the photograph of the Great Serpent Mound. **ASK:** In what way does the mound look like a "slithering" snake? *(Like a snake's body, the mound consists of curved S shapes.)* Why might the mound have been challenging to create? *(Possible response: Because it is so large, it would have been difficult to design and judge the overall size and effect and would have required many people to complete.)*

Active Options

On Your Feet: Team Word Webbing Invite students to gather in small groups and provide each group with a single large piece of paper. Give each student a different colored marker. Ask students to use a Word Web to brainstorm the words and phrases that come to mind when they hear the phrase *Mound Builders.* Each student should add to the part of the web closest to him or her. After a minute, signal to the groups to rotate their paper and have students add to the nearest part again.

NG Learning Framework: Analyze Environmental Concepts

SKILLS Observation, Collaboration

KNOWLEDGE Our Living Planet

Have students revisit Lesson 1.3 for information about why Native Americans were able to establish stable agricultural societies. Ask pairs to create a list of observations about how the geography of eastern North America affected farming and how Native Americans figured out ways to farm successfully. Once they have completed their list of observations, each pair should exchange lists with another pair and discuss the new list.

English Language Learners   ELD

Use Sentence Strips Choose a paragraph from the lesson and make sentence strips out of it. Read the paragraph aloud and ask students at all proficiency levels to follow along in their books. Then have students close their books and give them the set of sentence strips. Ask students at the **Emerging** level to put the strips in order and then read the paragraph aloud. Pair students at the **Expanding** and **Bridging** levels and ask them to order the strips correctly and then write a summary of the paragraph in their own words.

Gifted & Talented

Draw Parallels to Today Invite students to research the use of slash-and-burn agriculture in Central America, Mexico, and other places today. Tell them to list ways in which the techniques used by the tribes of the Eastern Woodlands were similar and different. Then ask students to write an expository text describing why the slash-and-burn agriculture practiced by the Eastern Woodlands tribes was less environmentally destructive than similar practices used in modern agriculture.

See the Chapter Planner for more strategies for differentiation.

HISTORICAL THINKING

ANSWERS

1. Farming provided a dependable food source that could support a large population.

2. The Eastern Woodlands tribes practiced slash-and-burn agriculture, which means they cut down and burned the trees to clear the land for planting. When they moved, they simply cleared new land.

3. Possible response: A mild climate is characterized by warm, dry summers and short, rainy winters. These conditions would have allowed farmers in the Southeast to grow many crops, which would have thrived.

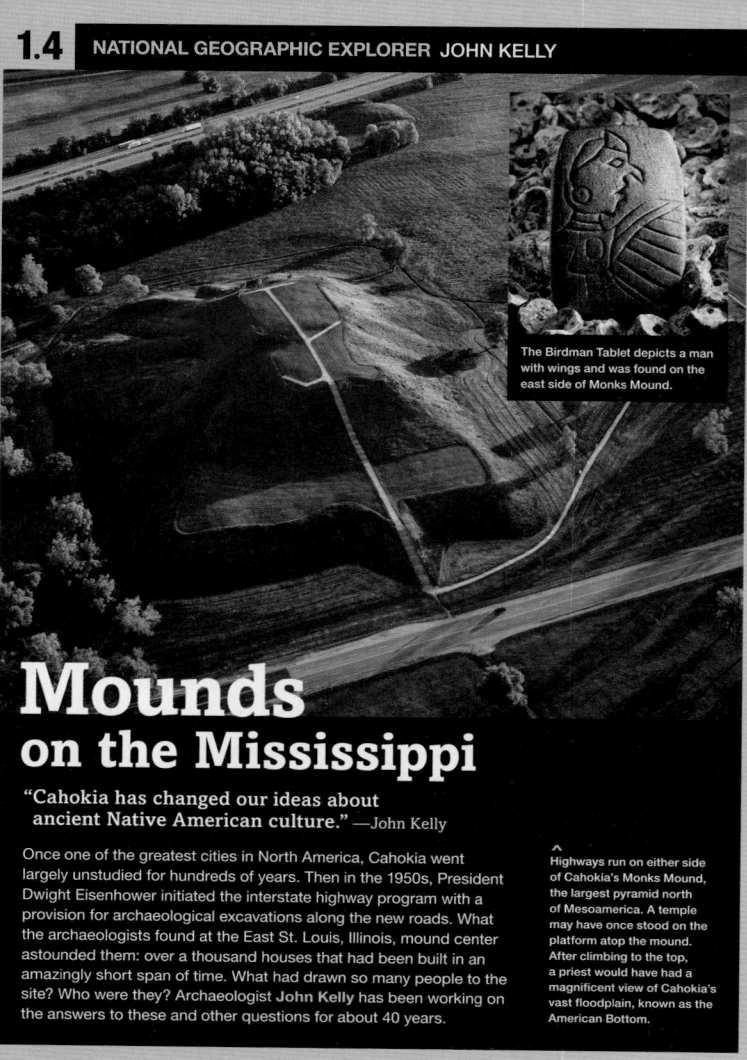

The Birdman Tablet depicts a man with wings and was found on the east side of Monks Mound.

Mounds
on the Mississippi

"Cahokia has changed our ideas about ancient Native American culture." —John Kelly

Once one of the greatest cities in North America, Cahokia went largely unstudied for hundreds of years. Then in the 1950s, President Dwight Eisenhower initiated the interstate highway program with a provision for archaeological excavations along the new roads. What the archaeologists found at the East St. Louis, Illinois, mound center astounded them: over a thousand houses that had been built in an amazingly short span of time. What had drawn so many people to the site? Who were they? Archaeologist **John Kelly** has been working on the answers to these and other questions for about 40 years.

^ Highways run on either side of Cahokia's Monks Mound, the largest pyramid north of Mesoamerica. A temple may have once stood on the platform atop the mound. After climbing to the top, a priest would have had a magnificent view of Cahokia's vast floodplain, known as the American Bottom.

MAIN IDEA Archaeologist John Kelly's excavations of the Cahokia Mounds have provided insight into the city's culture and its rise and fall.

Kelly (center) works with students at the site of Cahokia's Mound 34. They are actually standing underneath the mound, which was removed. Artifacts suggest that a special society of hunters or warriors may have used the building that stood on top of the mound. Monks Mound rises in the background.

CITY OF MYSTERY

National Geographic Explorer John Kelly has his work cut out for him. We know very little about Cahokia. The people who lived there didn't have a written language. We don't even know what they called themselves or the city they lived in. Cahokia was the name of people who lived briefly on the site in the 1700s, long after the city had disappeared. Archaeologists have pieced together what evidence they've found to expand our understanding of Cahokia. But as Kelly admits, "People still aren't really sure what it was."

According to Kelly, one thing we do know is that people had been living in Cahokia for years. The area was easy to reach along the Missouri, Illinois, and Mississippi rivers, and the land was good for growing a variety of crops, including corn. But why did the population swell from about 7,000 to 15,000 people between 1000 and 1100? One surprising theory states that people arrived after an extremely bright star called a supernova appeared around this time.

For whatever reason, people arrived in Cahokia in large numbers to build a ritual city with houses, farmland, and great plazas for religious celebrations. Above all—literally—they built the mounds. Monks Mound was the tallest. Named for the French monks who once lived in its shadow, the mound rose 100 feet in the center of the city. Laborers toiled on it for about 25 years using only baskets and stone hoes.

RISE AND FALL

Over time, the Cahokians built at least 110 other mounds. Some of these were used as burial sites. Archaeologists working at one called Mound 72 unearthed the remains of a man surrounded by ornaments and weapons. They also discovered the bodies of men and young women buried with and near him. Some were likely human sacrifices.

Kelly has spent much of his time investigating a mound that wasn't used for burials: Mound 34. Actually, his research takes him underneath the mound. The Cahokians constructed a building on top of the mound's platform, but other buildings and a copper workshop stood beneath the mound. According to Kelly, the buildings may have been placed there and covered with earth to represent the view of the world as existing in three layers: the beneath world with Earth Mother, this world, and the upper world. As Kelly says, "We focus on the mounds, but the history's really about the building that was there before the mound!"

Around the end of the 1100s, a different kind of construction began in Cahokia. Walls were erected around the city, possibly as protection against attack. But by then, the population had already begun to dwindle and the city to decline. Some say climate change or disease may have led to the fall of Cahokia. Kelly says that a massive flood may have covered the city and caused the people to leave for a brief time. Over a century later, a long drought may have led to the eventual abandonment. What we do know is that, for some reason, by the late 1300s, the residents had left the city. Cahokia remains mysterious to the end.

HISTORICAL THINKING

1. **READING CHECK** What did the Cahokians build in their city?

2. **ANALYZE CAUSE AND EFFECT** Why did Cahokia decline?

Objective

Learn what John Kelly's work has revealed about the North American city of Cahokia.

Critical Thinking Skills for Lesson 1.4

- Identify Main Ideas and Details
- Monitor Comprehension
- Analyze Cause and Effect
- Form and Support Opinions
- Make Generalizations

Essential Question for Chapter 1

How were early civilizations in the Americas, Africa, and Europe both similar and different?
The Mississippians were successful farmers. As a result, they had sufficient food to support a city with a large population. Lesson 1.4 explores archaeological evidence and theories about the rise and fall of the city of Cahokia.

Background for the Teacher

Cahokia Mounds is one of several sites John Kelly has investigated on the American Bottom, the archaeologically rich floodplain of the Mississippi River. Excavating these sites helps Kelly gain insight into how and why communities formed, organized, and eventually dispersed and whether factors such as kinship and ritual may have played a role. Cahokia, for example, once contained thousands of thatched-roof houses organized into neighborhoods. While many of the mounds at Cahokia and in nearby areas have been destroyed over the years, many are preserved as the Cahokia Mounds State Historic Site. The mounds were designated a UNESCO World Heritage site in 1982.

History Notebook

Encourage students to complete the Explorer and American Gallery pages for Chapter 1 in their History Notebooks as they read.

K-W-L Chart

Provide each student with a K-W-L Chart. Have students brainstorm what they know about the Mound Builders from Lesson 1.3, particularly the Mississippians. Then ask them to write questions they would like to have answered as they study the lesson. Allow time at the end of the lesson for students to fill in what they have learned.

K What Do I Know?	W What Do I Want To Learn?	L What Did I Learn?

TEACH STEM

Guided Discussion

1. **Form and Support Opinions** Do you think Cahokia is a "city of mystery"? Cite evidence to support your opinion. *(Answers will vary. Possible response: Cahokia is a "city of mystery." Archaeologists know very little about Cahokia since the people did not have a written language. They don't know what the people called themselves or their city, why the population swelled and then declined, why the people built a wall around the city, or why the people abandoned the city.)*

2. **Make Generalizations** Why is John Kelly so interested in Mound 34? *(Kelly thinks the mound and the buildings that once stood above and below it represented the Cahokians' view of the world as existing in three layers.)*

More Information

Supernovas and Cahokia In the summer of 1054, a supernova (visible today as the Crab Nebula) appeared in the sky as a bright star near Earth's moon. For 23 days, the star shown so brightly that it could be seen during the daytime. At night, it remained bright for nearly two years. Some archaeologists believe that the Cahokians took this supernova as a sign to create a planned community on a large scale. Other archaeologists suggest the Cahokians might have been inspired by contact with Mesoamericans, since there are parallels between Mississippian and Mesoamerican cultures, including human sacrifice and a similar views of the cosmos.

Active Options

Active History: Think Like an Archaeologist Extend the lesson by using either the PDF or Whiteboard version of the activity. These activities take a deeper look at a topic from, or related to, the lesson. Explore the activities as a class, turn them into group assignments, or even assign them individually.

AMERICAN GALLERY ONLINE **Cahokia: A Native American City** Invite students to explore the American Gallery. Have them select one of the images and do additional research to learn more about it. Ask questions that will inspire additional inquiry about the chosen image, such as: What is this? Where and when was this created? By whom? Why was it created? What is it made of? Why does it belong in this chapter? What else would you like to know about it?

DIFFERENTIATE

Striving Readers

Use Reciprocal Teaching Have partners take turns reading each paragraph of the lesson aloud. At the end of the paragraph, the reading student should ask the listening student questions about the paragraph. Students may ask their partners to state the main idea, identify important details that support the main idea, or summarize the paragraph in their own words. Then have students work together to answer the Historical Thinking questions.

Gifted & Talented

Design a Website Have students work in small groups to design the home page for a website about Cahokia. The page should include visuals and text introducing Cahokia to the online audience, as well as a menu with titles for supporting pages that they would want to include if they were creating the entire site. Invite each group to share their home page with the class and discuss the thinking behind their home page design.

See the Chapter Planner for more strategies for differentiation.

HISTORICAL THINKING

ANSWERS

1. The Cahokians built an urban trading center with houses, farmland, and a great plaza for religious celebrations. They also built mounds, including the huge Monks Mound. Many of the mounds were burial sites. On some mounds, the Cahokians constructed buildings on platforms. They also built walls around the city, possibly for protection.

2. No one knows for certain why Cahokia declined. Some archaeologists suggest that climate change or disease may have led to the fall of Cahokia. John Kelly says that a massive flood covered the mounds and caused the people to leave.

1.5 National Museum of the American Indian Washington, D.C.

The National Museum of the American Indian (NMAI) is located in Washington, D.C., on the National Mall. The museum and its grounds were designed with the help of tribes and communities from across the hemisphere to share the sense and spirit of Native Americans with its many visitors. NMAI has a tremendous collection of Native American arts and artifacts—over 800,000 items representing more than 1,200 cultures throughout the Americas and over 12,000 years of history. Visitors experience everything from ancient tools and weapons to modern Native American art, cultural and religious artifacts, and everyday items. Which of the items below were used for everyday activities and which ones served a different purpose?

Chief of the Undersea Mask
This colorful carved wood mask is made of western red cedar. It represents the chief of the undersea kingdom. He is believed to live in a copper home under the ocean, guarded by sea monsters. Ceremonial masks like this one usually depict characters from family histories or from the supernatural. This mask was carved by a master carver from the New Vancouver Tribe in western Canada in the late 1800s or early 1900s.

The U-shaped designs that surround the face represent the scales of a fish or a sea creature. They may have been added to the mask later by a second artist.

Tlingit Canoe Paddles
These Tlingit paddles date to the early 1900s. The Tlingit are indigenous people of the Pacific Northwest in North America, where fish are abundant. For the Tlingit, canoes and paddles are tools necessary for survival.

Odawa Moccasins
This pair of beaded Odawa (Ottawa) moccasins was purchased by a trader at Crown Point, Indiana, a fur trade depot. The moccasins feature folded-down silk cuffs decorated with small beads arranged in dashed lines, a pattern often found on this type of Odawa moccasins. Silk teardrops and diamond shapes also decorate the moccasins and are outlined with even smaller white glass beads.

What do you observe about the craftsmanship of these Odawa moccasins?

"We seek to bring the Native voice into **every school, every library, every university,** indeed, every home."

—Kevin Gover (Pawnee)
Director, National Museum of the American Indian

The paddles are made of yellow cedar and ornately painted with a wolf design.

PLAN

Objective
Identify artifacts relating to Native Americans.

Critical Thinking Skills for Lesson 1.5
- Make Connections
- Analyze Visuals
- Describe
- Draw Conclusions

Essential Question for Chapter 1
How were early civilizations in the Americas, Africa, and Europe both similar and different?
Artifacts reveal the cultural beliefs and practices of the people who created them. Lesson 1.5 shows several Native American artifacts from the collections of the National Museum of the American Indian and explains their origin and significance.

Background for the Teacher
The Chief of the Undersea mask depicts Kumugwé, a name that means "wealthy." This potlatch dance mask might have been worn by a dancer who moved slowly like a wave in the ocean. The mask is part of the museum's permanent "Infinity of Nations" collection at the Heye Center. Master carver Bob Harris, who was a member of the Song Makers Clan and a hereditary chief of the New Vancouver Tribe, carved the mask at a time when the Canadian government outlawed potlatches. Today, Harris is considered to have been one of the greatest carvers among his tribe.

History Notebook
Encourage students to complete the Curating History page for Chapter 1 in their History Notebooks as they read.

Brainstorm a List

Ask students to brainstorm a list of different artifacts they think might be included in a Native American museum. Create and display a master list. Tell students they will learn about several artifacts from collections at the National Museum of the American Indian.

TEACH

Guided Discussion

1. **Describe** What different materials are used in the Odawa moccasins and Tlingit canoe paddles? *(The moccasins are made with silk, beads, and animal hide. The canoe paddles are made with yellow cedar.)* **ASK:** Why might the Odawa and Tlingit have decorated everyday items like moccasins and canoe paddles? *(Answers will vary. Possible response: The Odawa and Tlingit probably took pride in craftsmanship and wanted to express things that were important in their culture.)*

2. **Draw Conclusions** What does the Chief of the Undersea mask reveal about the New Vancouver Tribe? *(Answers will vary. Possible responses: The fact that the mask is made of red cedar indicates that the tribe lived in a forested area. The mask depicts an undersea chief and includes fish scales, which implies that the ocean and fishing played important roles in the life of the tribe. All details on the mask are intentional, and the presence of ceremonial designs indicates that the tribe had organized religious beliefs.)*

Curating History

The National Museum of the American Indian's website is a useful resource for learning more about Native American culture. Access the museum's website and demonstrate how to find the Odawa moccasins, Tlingit canoe paddles, or Chief of the Undersea mask in the collection. Then encourage students to select another object to examine. As a group, ask students to point out details on the objects and ask questions or make speculations about them. Then read the object's caption aloud and discuss that information as it relates to the earlier discussion. Finally, ask groups of students to explore the site on their own and choose another artifact from the collection. Ask groups to present the artifact to the class.

Active Options

On Your Feet: Sort the Artifacts Arrange students in teams of four and ask them to examine the museum's online collection and complete two Concept Clusters like those shown below. In one cluster, students should identify everyday items. In the other, students should identify a different class or genre of artifacts, to be determined by the team. When teams are finished, ask them to share their Concept Clusters with the class.

Inclusion

Narrate the Artifacts This lesson might pose a challenge to the visually impaired. Ask students who are not visually challenged to describe in detail the artifacts featured in the lesson by including their textures, shapes, patterns, intensity of shades, and designs.

Gifted & Talented

Design and Create a Magazine Ad Provide examples of ads from travel magazines for students to examine. Then ask students to design and create an ad inviting people to come to an exhibit of these Native American artifacts at the National Museum of the American Indian. Ask students to include details about the artifacts that might draw potential visitors to the exhibit. Suggest that students illustrate their ads with drawings or other images. Ask students to display and share their completed ads.

See the Chapter Planner for more strategies for differentiation.

CURATING HISTORY

Answers will vary. Possible responses: The Odawa moccasins and the Tlingit canoe paddles were used for everyday activities. The Chief of the Undersea mask was only for ceremonies.

ODAWA MOCCASINS

Answers will vary. Possible responses: The moccasins are skillfully crafted. The silk cuffs are evenly stitched and beaded. The matching diamond and teardrop shapes on each moccasin are intricately beaded. The stitching on the moccasins is so tight it looks like it was done by machine.

1.6 Native American Environments

MAIN IDEA Before European settlement, 500 Native American tribes inhabited North America. Geography helped to shape their diverse cultures.

PHYSICAL AND HUMAN GEOGRAPHY

When you examine how geography affected people and culture, you are taking a **geographic perspective**. That is, you are looking at culture through the lens of geography. You can examine two aspects of geography: physical geography and human geography.

Physical geography refers to the physical characteristics of a region. It includes the surface of the earth, soil, bodies of water, climate, and glaciers and ice sheets. It also includes plant and animal life.

Human geography examines how people and their cultures are affected by physical geography, and how human activities affect

the environment. For example, geography has a great impact on how people make a living. People who live near the sea often make a living by fishing, and in regions with fertile soils, farming is usually an important economic activity.

Use physical geography and human geography to study these Native American tribes before the arrival of Christopher Columbus in the Americas. For each group, you will find an explanation of their physical geography and human geography.

Carved polar bear knife handle, Alaska

Native American Nations, 1491

0   250   500 Miles
0   250   500 Kilometers

Earthenware bowl, New Mexico

ARCTIC AND SUBARCTIC

NORTHWEST COAST

GREAT BASIN AND PLATEAU

GREAT PLAINS

NORTHEAST

SOUTHEAST

SOUTHWEST

PACIFIC OCEAN

Stone point, Eastern Woodlands

PHYSICAL GEOGRAPHY	HUMAN GEOGRAPHY
ARCTIC AND SUBARCTIC	
The Inuit, Aleut, and other tribes of this region lived in one of the harshest environments on Earth—the land that we now call Alaska. It is a land of snow and ice, with little vegetation in the winter.	The people living in the far north creatively adapted to their harsh environment. They hunted for seals and whales and built igloos out of ice to protect themselves from the extreme cold.
NORTHWEST COAST	
The tribes of the Northwest Coast lived in the region that is now the states of Washington and Oregon and the Canadian province of British Columbia. It is a rich environment with lush forests and rivers filled with fish.	The tribes of the Northwest included the Chinook and the Tlingit. They fished and hunted for bears and other large game. The abundance of the region allowed families to accumulate wealth. Families gained honor by giving away part of their wealth in a ceremony called the potlatch.
GREAT BASIN AND PLATEAU	
This region, west of the Great Plains, features soaring mountains and plateaus with long stretches of grassland. The land supported large mammals, including antelope, moose, elk, mountain goat, and bison.	The Utes, Shoshone, and other tribes hunted for game and fished in the rivers for salmon and trout. Some Native Americans even created dances to mimic the movement of the grass in the wind.
SOUTHWEST	
The Southwest, which includes today's Arizona and New Mexico, is a region of deserts with very little rainfall. The climate is harsh, with temperatures soaring to 110 degrees Fahrenheit or more in the summer. But the region also has rivers.	The rivers are critical to this region because of the lack of rainfall. The Pueblo tribes, who lived near the Rio Grande in what is now New Mexico, planted maize (corn) and other crops near the river.
GREAT PLAINS	
The Great Plains stretch from present-day Iowa to Wyoming. The region is flat, with plains and tallgrass prairies. The most important resource was once the bison, or buffalo, which numbered at least 30 million in the 1400s.	The Great Plains had many tribes, including the Lakota, the Blackfoot, and the Mandan. These tribes had one thing in common—they used the bison for food, shelter, and clothing.
NORTHEAST	
The Northeast region spans the present-day states from Virginia to Maine. This land has ample rainfall, many rivers and streams, and a wealth of natural resources, including wild game, fish, and fertile soil.	The Algonquian- and Iroquois-speaking people who lived in this region used the many rivers and streams as highways. They built canoes out of wood and birchbark to use for long-distance trading.
SOUTHEAST	
The Southeast reaches from today's North Carolina to Florida and offers many natural gifts: a mild climate, plentiful rainfall, and fertile soil.	The Cherokee, the Choctaw, and other groups grew maize, beans, squash, and other crops in the fertile soil. Because of the mild climate, the land supported a large population and tribes thrived.

THINK LIKE A GEOGRAPHER

1. **IDENTIFY MAIN IDEAS AND DETAILS** How did different Native American groups adapt to the amount of rainfall they received?

2. **MAKE INFERENCES** What does the potlatch reveal about the attitudes toward wealth among Native Americans of the Northwest?

Objective

Understand the relationship between physical geography and human geography.

Critical Thinking Skills for Lesson 1.6

• Identify Main Ideas and Details
• Monitor Comprehension
• Make Inferences
• Compare and Contrast
• Make Connections
• Interpret Maps

Essential Question for Chapter 1

How were early civilizations in the Americas, Africa, and Europe both similar and different?
Geography affects human activities, and human activities affect geography. Lesson 1.6 discusses the interplay between physical and human geography among Native Americans in different cultural regions in North America before European contact.

Background for the Teacher

The potlatch was primarily a means for maintaining or gaining status. In the traditional potlatch, the host threw elaborate celebrations, often lasting for days, that included massive feasts, dancing, singing, and speeches. Since guests were expected to reciprocate by hosting their own potlatch, a host could punish rivals by setting the bar so high that the rivals might have to give away all of their possessions to meet the obligation, losing status in the process. Potlatches also served as a way for a family who had been dishonored to regain status.

While primarily aimed at prestige, potlatches also helped redistribute resources through feasting and gift giving. The potlatch was alien to European views of property and wealth. Troubled by the excesses of the potlatch, the Canadian government outlawed the ceremonies between 1884 and 1951.

INTRODUCE & ENGAGE

Activate Prior Knowledge

Direct students' attention to the map of North America showing cultural regions. Ask volunteers to share what they already know about the geography in each region and about the cultures of the Native American groups that lived there before 1500. Draw on Lessons 1.1 to 1.4 and ask questions such as, What is the physical geography like in the Southwest? What is one Native American group who lived there before 1500? How did they supply themselves with food? Discuss as a class.

TEACH

STEM

Guided Discussion

1. **Compare and Contrast** Which tribes lived in harsh environments, and how did the environments differ? *(The Inuit, Aleut, and other tribes of the Arctic and Subarctic region and the Pueblo tribes of the Southwest faced harsh conditions. The Arctic and Subarctic region was covered with snow and ice. In winter almost nothing grew. The Pueblo tribes in the Southwest experienced little rainfall and temperatures that could reach 110 degrees Fahrenheit, so the Rio Grande was crucial to their survival.)*

2. **Make Connections** How were the lives of the tribes in the Northwest and the Great Basin and Plateau region similar? *(The tribes all hunted game and fished for food. They celebrated with ceremonies and dances.)*

Geography in History

Interpret Maps Tell students to study the map and the chart. Point out that the map and chart are color coordinated. **ASK:** How was the human geography of the Great Plains shaped by the physical geography of the area? *(Because the Great Plains is such a huge area, there was room for many native tribes. The bison that shared this area provided the meat for food and hides for clothing and shelter, making hunting the bison an important activity for all the tribes.)*

Active Options

On Your Feet: Fishbowl Tell part of the class to sit in a close circle facing inward; the other part of the class sits in a larger circle around them. Tell students on the inside to discuss what they have learned about the physical geography of the regions, including climate and water. Those on the outside should listen for new information and decide what might have been omitted from the discussion. Then groups reverse positions and the new inner circle discusses what they have learned about human geography in the regions. Those on the outside should listen for new information and decide what might have been omitted from the discussion.

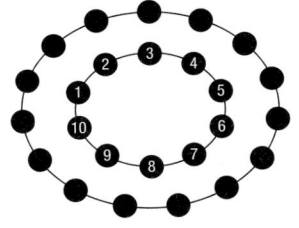

NG Learning Framework: Determine the Effects of Geography

SKILL Collaboration

KNOWLEDGE Our Living Planet

Tell small teams of students to work together to identify ways that geography, such as mountains, rivers, and plains, affected different Native American cultures. Tell students to list positive and negative effects from each cultures' perspective. Ask them to write a short paragraph to summarize their findings. Ask teams to share their paragraphs with the class.

DIFFERENTIATE

Striving Readers

Ready, Set, Recall After reading, ask students to work independently to list everything they recall about the physical and human geography of the regions. Then allow small teams to combine their lists within a given time limit. Finally, ask teams to contribute one item at a time to a class list on the board until all teams run out of items.

English Language Learners   **ELD**

Give a Thumbs Up or Thumbs Down Help students at the **Bridging** level reinforce comprehension. Write a set of true-false statements about the lesson, such as, "Physical geography refers to the physical characteristics of a region." Read the lesson aloud with students following along. Then tell them to close their books and listen as you read the true-false statements. Students should give a thumbs up if a statement is true and a thumbs down if a statement is false.

See the Chapter Planner for more strategies for differentiation.

THINK LIKE A GEOGRAPHER

ANSWERS

1. The Pueblo in the Southwest had little rainfall, so they planted crops near the Rio Grande. The Cherokee, Choctaw, and Southeast people had plentiful rainfall and farmed, growing their crops in the fertile soil. The Algonquian- and Iroquois-speaking people in the Northeast used rivers, supplied by ample rainfall, to practice long-distance trading.

2. Answers will vary. Possible response: Native Americans in the Northwest gave away some of their accumulated wealth through potlatches. Given that the potlatch was a way for families to gain honor, they must have viewed having an excess of wealth as something to be avoided.

The Middle Ages

For hundreds of years, the Roman Empire united much of Europe. So when the western part of the empire fell in A.D. 476, its laws and social structures collapsed, too. With the empire no longer in control, "Now what?" could well have been the question on almost everyone's mind.

MAIN IDEA During the Middle Ages, Western Europe underwent many political, economic, and social changes.

A FEUDAL SOCIETY

Political, economic, and social problems led to the decline of the Western Roman Empire. As the empire weakened, Germanic tribes from Northern Europe invaded Western Europe and overthrew the emperor.

The end of the Western Roman Empire signaled the beginning of a period known as the **Middle Ages**, which lasted from about A.D. 500 to 1450. With no central government after the fall of Rome, Western Europe largely consisted of small kingdoms ruled by Germanic tribes, such as the Franks, Visigoths, and Vikings. Over time, the kingdoms grew and became very powerful.

To help the leaders of these kingdoms hold onto their land and protect their subjects, a political and social system called **feudalism** developed. Feudalism helped ensure the defense and security of kingdoms, which were constantly at war with one another. It achieved this security by maintaining a strict social **hierarchy**, or order.

Kings sat atop this structure. They gave pieces of their land to noblemen, known as lords. A lord, in turn, granted parts of this land to lesser noblemen called **vassals**. Vassals paid taxes on the land and pledged their military service to the lord.

Structure of Feudal Society

A *king* inherited his position, but none could rule without the support of the noblemen.

Church officials and noblemen often exercised more power than the king.

Knights fought to aristocracy

Serfs worked the land. In exchange for protection, a serf provided loyalty, labor, and crops.

The Plague Doctors

When the bubonic plague swept through medieval Europe in the 1300s, medical science was still 500 years away from understanding its cause. At that time, some doctors believed the plague was spread by bad air or odors. In the 1600s, a French physician created the costume, shown here, to protect against such odors and supposedly against the plague. But the problem was not odors. The problem was infected rats and their fleas. Rats spread throughout medieval cities, which lacked sanitation. Fleas living on the rats spread the disease by biting people. The victim then often suffered swelling, vomiting, back pain, delirium, and, finally, death.

Many vassals themselves were soldiers in the army and served as knights, who were warriors on horseback. Peasants called **serfs** were at the bottom of the heap.

The **manor system** emerged as a result of feudalism. The system consisted of peasants bound to a lord's land, or manor. Landowners maintained a tight grip on both their land and their workers, while the peasant workers received a level of military protection they could not provide for themselves. Feudalism and the manor system remained in place throughout the Middle Ages, providing some stability to Western Europe.

WARS, TRADE, AND TOWNS

Still, feudalism was not the only source of stability. The Roman Catholic Church served as the strongest unifying force in medieval Europe. Late in the 11th century, the Church waged the **Crusades**, wars against the spread of **Islam**. That religion's followers, called **Muslims**, had seized control of the Holy Land—the city of Jerusalem and the surrounding area. They'd also begun to attack the Christian Byzantine Empire, once the eastern half of the Roman Empire.

The Crusades continued for two centuries, allowing Crusaders to acquire land in areas previously conquered by Muslims. The land acquisition led to the establishment of trade centers. Though the Crusaders were ultimately unsuccessful—they eventually lost any land they captured—their actions increased trade between Europe and the eastern Mediterranean region.

As trade increased in Europe, businesses and the economy grew. Towns grew, too, as people left their positions on the manors for better jobs.

Outbreaks of a devastating disease called the bubonic plague also created jobs. In the 14th century, the plague killed as many as one-third of all Europeans. Those laborers lucky enough to survive the illness found better work prospects as a result of the decline in population. Less competition led to greater opportunities for those who survived.

The plague, along with the movement to cities and towns, helped bring about the decline of feudalism and the end of the Middle Ages. Europe began to experience cultural changes that would mark the beginning of a new age of creativity.

HISTORICAL THINKING

1. **READING CHECK** How are the manor system and feudalism similar to each other?

2. **EVALUATE** In what way were the Crusaders both successful and unsuccessful?

3. **COMPARE AND CONTRAST** How did feudalism and the Church affect Europe similarly and differently?

PLAN

Objective
Analyze the changes that occurred in Western Europe during the Middle Ages.

Critical Thinking Skills for Lesson 2.1
- Identify Main Ideas and Details
- Monitor Comprehension
- Evaluate
- Compare and Contrast
- Integrate Visuals
- Make Connections
- Draw Conclusions

Essential Question for Chapter 1
How were early civilizations in the Americas, Africa, and Europe both similar and different?
The collapse of the Western Roman Empire ended its central government. Lesson 2.1 discusses how feudalism emerged and factors that affected the growth of trade, businesses, and towns.

Background for the Teacher
The growth of trade, towns, and cities during the Middle Ages had many causes and consequences. As global trade increased and markets and towns grew in size and number, money began to replace barter as the medium of exchange. Banking and new accounting methods emerged to handle the need to exchange money, supply credit to merchants, and maintain accounts. Merchants represented a new social class that did not easily fit into the traditional feudal social structure. Their wealth and their influence in towns and cities led them to demand more privileges and independence, thereby weakening the feudal system and helping set the stage for the Renaissance.

K-W-L Chart

Provide each student with a K-W-L Chart. Tell students to brainstorm what they already know about the Middle Ages, such as details about feudalism, the Crusades, or the plague. Then tell students to write questions that they would like to answer as they study the lesson, such as "What advantages did feudalism provide?" or "What were some of the consequences of the Crusades?" Allow time at the end of the lesson for students to fill in what they have learned.

K What Do I Know?	W What Do I Want To Learn?	L What Did I Learn?

TEACH

Guided Discussion

1. **Integrate Visuals** How was feudal society organized? Use the illustration and text to support your response. *(In a feudal society, there was one king above everyone else. Church officials and noblemen, called lords, were below the king, but they sometimes had equal or greater power. Knights came next. There were more knights than noblemen because their job was to protect the lords. Serfs were at the bottom of the social order, and their great number provided the labor that supported feudal society. The text explains that this strict social order made kingdoms safe and defensible against other kingdoms.)*

2. **Make Connections** What positive effects did the Church, the Crusades, and the plague have on society in medieval Europe? *(The Church served as a unifying force and provided stability; the Crusades increased trade between Europe and the eastern Mediterranean region; the plague created jobs by reducing the number of people competing for work.)*

Draw Conclusions

How did feudalism benefit those at the top levels of the social hierarchy? *(The king counted on the lords to help rule his kingdom and to protect it from enemies. Higher-ranking noblemen benefited from the land given to them by the king, through the taxes the vassals paid on the land the lords granted them and the vassal's military service. Everyone at the top of the hierarchy benefited from the labor the serfs provided.)*

Active Options

On Your Feet: Create a Concept Web Arrange students in groups of four around a section of a bulletin board or a table. Provide each group with a large sheet of paper. Assign each group one of the following three topics: Crusades, Towns and Trade, or the Plague. Instruct group members to take turns contributing a concept or phrase to a Concept Web that has their topic at the center. When time for the activity has elapsed, call on volunteers from each group to share their webs.

NG Learning Framework: Write a Diary Entry

ATTITUDE Curiosity

KNOWLEDGE Our Human Story

Ask students to select one of the classes of feudal people they are still curious about after reading this lesson. Guide students to research the everyday life of this class of people using appropriate print sources and websites. Instruct students to use details from their research to write a diary entry from the perspective of an individual who might have lived during the Middle Ages. Invite students to present their entries to the class.

Inclusion

Monitor Comprehension Assign students into pair groups and tell them to take turns reading the text aloud, paragraph by paragraph. Tell them to stop at the end of each paragraph and use these sentence frames.

• This paragraph is about _____.

• One detail that stood out to me is _____.

• The word _____ means _____.

• I don't think I understand _____.

Encourage students to help each other with any part of the text that they do not understand.

Gifted & Talented

Create a Poster Encourage students to research a specific aspect of the Middle Ages that interests them, such as the knights' code of conduct, manor life, or the plague, using library or online sources. Ask students to create a "Did You Know?" poster listing five of the most interesting facts they discovered in their research. Encourage students to be creative in their designs. Ask students to present their completed posters to the class.

See the Chapter Planner for more strategies for differentiation.

HISTORICAL THINKING

ANSWERS

1. Under both systems, peasants are tied to a lord's land and receive protection in exchange for their work on the land.

2. The Crusaders managed to expand trade successfully between Europe and the eastern Mediterranean region. However, they were unsuccessful at keeping the land they had originally captured.

3. Both feudalism and the Church provided stability in different ways. Feudalism provided security and defense for warring kingdoms through its strict social hierarchy. The Church served as the strongest unifying force in medieval Europe. In addition, the Church helped stimulate trade by launching the Crusades.

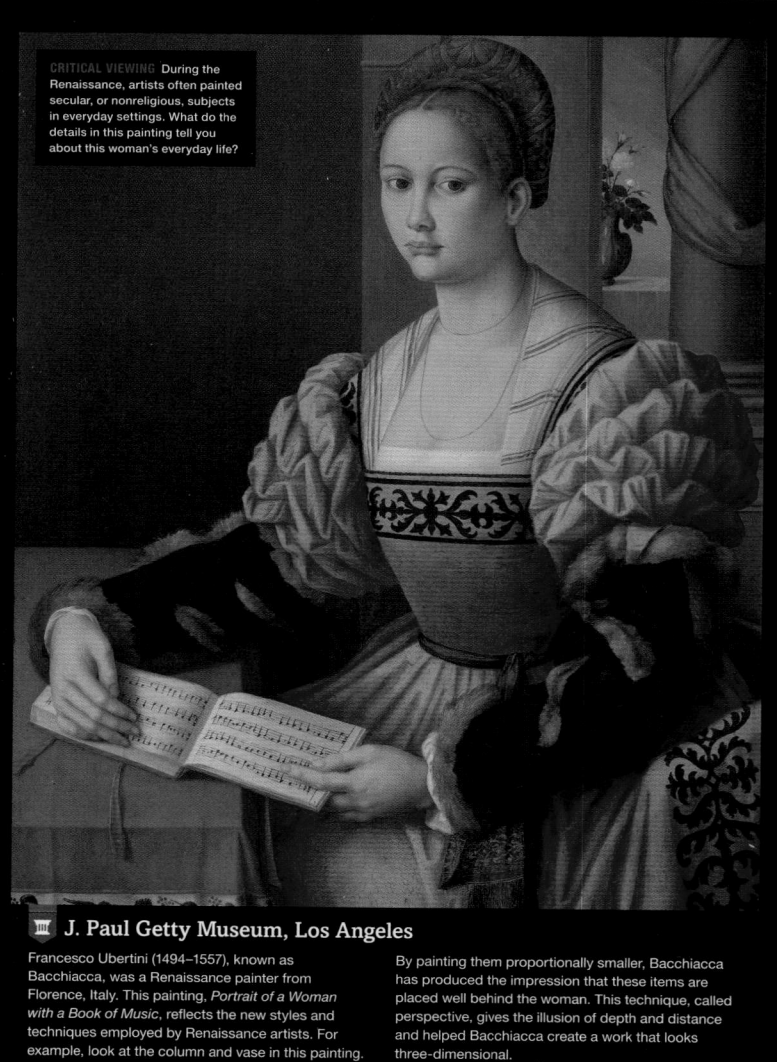

🏛 **J. Paul Getty Museum, Los Angeles**

Francesco Ubertini (1494–1557), known as Bacchiacca, was a Renaissance painter from Florence, Italy. This painting, *Portrait of a Woman with a Book of Music*, reflects the new styles and techniques employed by Renaissance artists. For example, look at the column and vase in this painting.

By painting them proportionally smaller, Bacchiacca has produced the impression that these items are placed well behind the woman. This technique, called perspective, gives the illusion of depth and distance and helped Bacchiacca create a work that looks three-dimensional.

2.2 Renaissance and Reformation

In the 1300s, a revolution began to brew in Europe. But this revolution didn't involve weapons and war. It involved ideas. People focused on the individual and believed every person had unlimited possibilities. These, indeed, were revolutionary ideas.

MAIN IDEA The Renaissance marked a time of curiosity, learning, experimentation, communication, and change.

REBIRTH OF ART AND LEARNING

Historians called the revolutionary movement that began at the end of the Middle Ages the **Renaissance**, which means "rebirth." The Renaissance originated in Italy and spread to other parts of Europe. The movement had its roots in the classical writings of ancient Greece and Rome and the philosophy of **humanism**. Humanists encouraged freedom of thought and the development of new ideas.

The Renaissance also saw the revival of elements of ancient Greek and Roman architecture, such as columns and arches. This revival enabled generations of artists and architects to achieve levels of artistic creation not seen in Europe for a thousand years. Painters such as Raphael and Michelangelo, and architects such as Brunelleschi, created works that still inspire awe in people today. **Leonardo da Vinci** is considered by many to be the ideal Renaissance figure. Leonardo not only painted artistic masterpieces, but he was also an inventor, sculptor, and architect. His studies of anatomy and other sciences proved to be ahead of their time.

The ideas of the Renaissance also had an effect on literature. In the mid-1400s, **Johann Gutenberg's** invention of the **printing press**, which used movable metal type to print pages, allowed for mass distribution of classical and humanist literary works. As the availability of printed materials increased, more people learned to read, and the philosophy of the Renaissance and humanist movement began to spread rapidly across Europe.

DIVISIONS IN THE CHURCH

Around the time of the Renaissance, the Catholic Church began to lose some of its power. Some members charged the Church with corruption and called for reform. This gradual progression toward change within the Church eventually led to the **Reformation**, a split from the Catholic Church that took place in the early 16th century. **Martin Luther**, a German pastor and university professor, led this movement. He believed biblical scripture was more important than the pope's authority. He also believed that Christians achieved God's favor through faith rather than by doing good works. Luther was eventually excommunicated, or expelled, from the Catholic Church for his teachings.

Followers of the Reformation became known as **Protestants**, and the Church split between the Protestants and Catholics. Over time, many different Protestant churches, called denominations, developed, each with its own set of beliefs within the framework of Christianity.

HISTORICAL THINKING

1. **READING CHECK** From which ancient cultures did the Renaissance receive inspiration?

2. **DESCRIBE** Why was the printing press such an important invention during the Renaissance?

3. **DRAW CONCLUSIONS** Why do you think the Catholic Church excommunicated Martin Luther?

Objective
Discover why the Renaissance is considered the rebirth of enthusiasm for art and learning.

Critical Thinking Skills for Lesson 2.2
- Identify Main Ideas and Details
- Monitor Comprehension
- Describe
- Draw Conclusions
- Form and Support Opinions
- Make Connections

Essential Question for Chapter 1
How were early civilizations in the Americas, Africa, and Europe both similar and different?
Freedom of thought was aided by the printing press, and it found expression in art, literature, and the Reformation—a split in the Roman Catholic Church. Lesson 2.2 introduces the Renaissance and Martin Luther's role in the Reformation.

Background for the Teacher
Leonardo da Vinci's paintings and sculptures were informed by his study of anatomy, geometry, and mechanics. As a scientist, he applied the scientific method to his art. He dissected corpses to understand the structures and functions of the human body and drew in exquisite detail, accurately portraying perspective and proportion. Leonardo also conducted various scientific experiments and visualized futuristic inventions. His approach to art and science bridged the gap between unscientific medieval methods and the emergence of humanism and scientific inquiry.

INTRODUCE & ENGAGE

Give It a Twirl

Tell students that, in this lesson, they will learn about the Renaissance and Reformation. Copy the following mnemonic on the board and tell students to use the TWIRL strategy to prepare for the lesson.

Think of a question you would like to ask about the Renaissance or Reformation.
Write your question on a piece of paper.
Interact with a partner by discussing your questions and possible answers.
Report details about your discussion with the class.
Listen politely as other students talk about their discussions.

TEACH

Guided Discussion

1. **Form and Support Opinions** Why do you think many people consider Leonardo da Vinci the ideal Renaissance figure? *(Possible response: Leonardo had a very broad range of interests and accomplishments. In addition to painting, he sculpted, explored anatomy and other sciences, invented, and worked as an architect. Such freedom of thought and development of new ideas are characteristic of the Renaissance.)*

2. **Make Connections** What events paved the way for the Reformation? *(The rebirth of humanism caused people to think freely and not rely on the authority of the Church. After the printing press was invented, free-thinking people, such as Martin Luther, could publish their ideas. One new idea, under the leadership of Luther, was to reform the corrupt Church.)*

⛪ Virtual Museum Visit

The J. Paul Getty Museum at Getty Center in Los Angeles houses a collection of European works, including many Renaissance drawings, paintings, and sculptures. Access the museum's website and find Bacchiacca's *Portrait of a Woman with a Book of Music*. Point out the use of light and dark to create the folds of the woman's dress and the intricate detail in the tablecloth border and the woman's scarf. Discuss the use of perspective. Then ask groups of students to explore the site on their own and choose a work of art from the same period. Ask groups to present their work to the class.

Active Options

On Your Feet: Inside-Outside Circle Arrange students in concentric circles facing each other. Each student in the outside circle asks a question about the Renaissance or Reformation. Then students in the inside circle answer their partners' question. On a signal, students on the inside circle rotate counterclockwise to meet a new partner and begin again. On a different signal, students trade roles so those in the inside circle ask the questions and those in the outside circle answer the questions.

NG Learning Framework: Learn More About Gutenberg's Printing Press

SKILL Collaboration

KNOWLEDGE New Frontiers

Organize students into three groups. Ask each group to research one of these topics:

• how Johann Gutenberg's printing press worked

• Gutenberg's Latin Bible and its impact

• impact of the printing press on society

Once groups have completed their research, instruct students to reassemble and share what they learned.

DIFFERENTIATE

Striving Readers

Use a Detail Web Tell students to summarize information using a Detail Web. Provide the following words for the center circle: *Renaissance* and *Reformation*. Instruct students to complete the web using details from the lesson.

Pre-AP

Interview Martin Luther Allow students to work in teams of two to plan, write, and perform a simulated television interview with Martin Luther. Tell students that the purpose of the interview is to focus on the views of Martin Luther concerning the Roman Catholic Church. Encourage students to conduct their finished interviews for the class.

See the Chapter Planner for more strategies for differentiation.

HISTORICAL THINKING

ANSWERS

1. The Renaissance was inspired by ancient Greece and Rome.

2. The printing press allowed the ideas of the Renaissance to spread quickly, and more people had access to printed texts.

3. Possible response: The Church excommunicated Luther because his beliefs and teachings went against official doctrine and he had begun to attract followers.

CRITICAL VIEWING The woman's elegant dress, with its fur and fine detailing, and her gold necklaces suggest that she is a member of a wealthy family. The room's pillars and the vase of flowers also suggest wealth. Her ivory hands give the impression she does not perform physical work or spend time outdoors. She is holding a book of music, which indicates that she can read music and values it.

2.3 Trade Expands

Just as the Renaissance spurred an expansion in people's thoughts and attitudes, it also inspired a spirit of adventure and curiosity about the world. Sea voyagers set out to explore new lands and, above all, to find new trading opportunities and markets.

MAIN IDEA New sea routes and developments in sailing technology allowed for an expansion of trade between European societies and the East.

EXPANDING TRADE WITH ASIA

In the mid-15th century, the Turks of the Ottoman Empire captured the city of Constantinople. Located on a peninsula between Europe and Asia, Constantinople joined the two continents. Capturing the city gave the Turks complete control of the land trade routes that connected the continents. This control allowed the Turks to charge Europeans high prices for Asian goods. Turkish merchants could then make a **profit**, or earn more money than they spent, on the goods.

To avoid trading with the Turks over land, Europeans explored new sea routes to Asia. At the end of the 15th century, Portuguese navigator **Vasco da Gama** sailed to India via one of these routes. He and his fleet traveled around the Cape of Good Hope at the southern tip of Africa. Portuguese navigator **Bartholomeu Dias** had first discovered this route about a decade earlier. Da Gama was able to return from his trip with Indian spices. This journey helped reestablish direct trade between Europe and the East.

PORTUGAL AND AFRICA

In the early 1400s, **Prince Henry the Navigator** established a school on the Atlantic coast in Sagres, Portugal. The school consisted of mathematicians, mapmakers, astronomers, instrument makers, and other instructors who taught students about sailing. Henry's goal was to train sailors about shipbuilding and **navigation**, or planning and following a route. He wanted to send his students on ocean explorations.

Students learned, among other lessons, how to build a special new ship called a **caravel**. The caravel was a light sailing ship that was both quick and able to sail windward, or into the wind. These characteristics made the ship a particularly good choice for the long voyages Henry had in mind.

Caravels made it possible for explorers to sail farther down the West African coast—and elsewhere. Even Christopher Columbus used two caravels during his historic voyage to the Americas in 1492. In the 1420s, Henry began funding caravel expeditions to Africa. Though Henry himself never joined these expeditions, he instructed his sailors to return with goods from Africa's western coast. During part of the Middle Ages, Portugal was under Islamic rule, and Muslim traders had long told stories about a "land of gold" near the African coast. A series of powerful African empires had inspired these stories. And the stories weren't that far from the truth.

HISTORICAL THINKING

1. **READING CHECK** What was the new sea route that Bartholomeu Dias first discovered and Vasco da Gama later followed to get to India?

2. **ANALYZE CAUSE AND EFFECT** Why did Europeans want to find new sea routes to Asia in the 15th century?

3. **EVALUATE** What might have been some of the advantages and disadvantages of taking a long voyage in a caravel?

CRITICAL VIEWING This sculpture in Lisbon, Portugal, called *Monument to the Discoveries*, celebrates the voyages of Portuguese explorers of the 15th and 16th centuries. Henry the Navigator stands at the top part of the monument, which is shaped like the front of a ship. Behind him are explorers, mapmakers, and others who played an important role in early exploration. Why is the monument's setting a fitting choice?

PLAN

Objective
Learn how shipbuilding technology and desire for trade opened Asia and Africa to Europeans.

Critical Thinking Skills for Lesson 2.3
- Identify Main Ideas and Details
- Monitor Comprehension
- Analyze Cause and Effect
- Evaluate
- Make Inferences
- Make Connections
- Integrate Visuals

Essential Question for Chapter 1
How were early civilizations in the Americas, Africa, and Europe similar and different? New ships and new markets led to trade among Europe, Asia, and Africa in the 1400s. Lesson 2.3 shows how explorers contributed to this expansion.

Background for the Teacher
Caravels were versatile ships. The caravel's width and rounded bottom made it stable in the water and suitable for hauling goods. Its shallow draft, or depth below water, made it safer for sailing close to shore, adding to its stability and making it ideal for sailing along the African coast. Caravels could be rigged with triangular lateen sails, square sails, or a combination of both. Triangular lateen sails—preferred rigging along the African coast—allowed the ships to sail into the wind without capsizing because the sails could be turned to catch the wind on either side of the sail. This design also allowed sailing in lighter winds.

INTRODUCE & ENGAGE

Preview and Predict

Tell students to read the lesson title, the Main Idea statement, and the heads of each section. Tell them to use that information to write sentences that predict what the lesson is about. Allow pairs of students to compare sentences. Then tell students that they will learn about how new sea routes and the development of the caravel helped expand European trade.

TEACH

Guided Discussion

1. **Make Inferences** How did the Ottoman Turks' capture of Constantinople in the mid-15th century affect European trade? *(The capture of Constantinople gave the Turks control of the land route between Europe and Asia, allowing the Turks to charge Europeans high prices for Asian goods. To avoid trading with the Turks over land, Europeans looked for new sea routes to Asia. At the end of the 15th century, Portuguese navigator Vasco da Gama sailed to India and returned with spices, establishing direct trade between Europe and Asia.)*

2. **Make Connections** How did Prince Henry the Navigator contribute to ocean exploration and trade? *(Henry established a school in Sagres, Portugal, that taught shipbuilding and navigation. Students learned to build caravels. These quick, light ships were able to sail into the wind, making them good choices for exploring the West African coast, or in Christopher Columbus's case, voyaging to the Americas. Henry encouraged his sailors to return with trade goods from Africa's western coast.)*

Integrate Visuals

Direct students' attention to the photograph of the *Monument to the Discoveries*. Ask them to read the caption describing the monument and then relate the monument to the text. Then ask the following questions:

- Why do you think the monument's creator placed Henry the Navigator at the top part of the monument? *(Answers will vary. Students might suggest that Henry is at the top of the monument because he and his school at Sagres played such important roles in Portugal's quest for a sea route to Asia.)*
- What type of ship is Henry holding? *(The ship is probably a caravel since that was the ship built at Sagres and used in Portuguese exploration.)*

Active Options

On Your Feet: Question and Answer Ask half the class to write True-False questions based on information in the lesson. Ask the other half to create answer cards, with "True" written on one side and "False" on the other. As each question is read aloud, students in the second group should display the correct answer to the question. When discrepancies occur, review the question and discuss which answer is correct.

NG Learning Framework: Research Caravels

ATTITUDE Curiosity

SKILLS Collaboration, Communication

Tell students to review the text discussion about why caravels were a good choice for exploring the West African coast. Then ask students to work with partners to research the specific sailing technologies, such as lateen sails, that enabled the caravel to sail into the wind and close to the coast. Tell them to write a brief description of the technologies. Ask students to share their reports with the rest of the class.

DIFFERENTIATE

Striving Readers

Use Examples Define and review the following words from this lesson, using context clues or outside dictionaries if necessary: *capturing, established, funding,* and *expeditions.* Provide examples of each one that are recognizable and familiar to students. Then ask students to use each word in a sentence.

English Language Learners **ELD**

Summarize Pair students at the **Emerging** and **Expanding** levels and assign each pair a subsection of Lesson 2.3 to read together. Encourage students to use a Main Idea and Details List such as the one below to make notes about their part of the lesson. Ask each pair to write a brief summary of their subsection.

Main Idea:
Detail:
Detail:
Detail:

See the Chapter Planner for more strategies for differentiation.

HISTORICAL THINKING

ANSWERS

1. The routes that Dias and da Gama followed to arrive in India went around the Cape of Good Hope, the southern tip of Africa.

2. They wanted to avoid trading with the Turks on land routes. Using sea routes let them trade directly with countries such as India.

3. Answers will vary. Possible response: The caravel was light and quick and could sail into the wind. Its maneuverability made it safer to sail. Since the caravel was a new ship, however, there was probably a shortage of sailors with experience sailing it. It was probably small, with less room for crew, supplies, and goods.

CRITICAL VIEWING Possible response: The monument overlooks the water, which is fitting because it pays tribute to the Portuguese explorers and their important sea voyages.

3.1 The Kingdom of Ghana

After Arab traders reached West Africa during the 700s, they talked of a land where even the horses were draped in gold cloth. This was the land of Ghana, and for centuries it was the wealthiest kingdom in West Africa.

MAIN IDEA West Africa's location made it a major trade center, leading to the rise of the kingdom of Ghana and the spread of Islam.

Salt Caravans
This desert caravan is carrying salt blocks through the Danakil Desert in Ethiopia. Caravans similar to this one carried salt across the Sahara from northern Africa to Ghana many centuries ago.

Trans-Saharan Trade Routes, c. 1050–1500

Legend:
- Ghana, c. 1050
- Mali, c. 1300
- Songhai, c. 1500
- Trans-Saharan trade route
- Gold deposit
- Copper deposit
- Salt
- Slaves

GOLD AND SALT IN GHANA

To reach the golden land, the kingdom of Ghana in West Africa, traders had to cross the largest hot desert in the world, the **Sahara**. Covered in dunes, rippling sheets of sand, and rocky formations, the desert extends over an area a little smaller than the United States. South of the desert is a **steppe** region of West Africa called the Sahel. Steppes are flat grasslands with very few trees.

The Sahara could have easily isolated the lands south of it. Extreme heat and a lack of water made travel through the region difficult for humans.

Travelers had to carry enough fresh water to last until the next **oasis**, one of those rare areas in the desert that contain freshwater sources.

People who traveled across the Sahara discovered that camels were well suited to the desert climate and could carry humans and goods long distances through the Sahara. Camels can survive traveling up to 100 miles without water, and they can carry heavy loads. Nomadic traders began to lead camel **caravans**, or groups of people traveling together. In their caravans, they carried goods on **trans-Saharan** trade routes between sub-Saharan Africa and northern Africa, which lay within reach of Europe and Southwest Asia. Market towns started to flourish where trading routes met.

Two kinds of goods dominated trans-Saharan trade: gold and salt. Gold was mined in the forests south of Ghana and was regularly used as a trade item. Salt, however, was not produced naturally in this area. People had to look north to the Sahara, which had an abundance of this valuable and essential nutrient. In fact, buildings in the Saharan trading town of Taghaza were constructed of salt blocks because that was the building material in largest supply.

A POWERFUL KINGDOM

Gold and salt traders met in West Africa, with gold flowing north and salt moving south. Near the midway point, the **kingdom of Ghana** grew and profited from the rising economy as the king collected taxes on the import and export of goods.

By the ninth century, Ghana was rich and powerful and able to conquer nearby lands with its strong army. The kingdom was structured according to a feudal system, with many princes ruling over various parts of the kingdom on behalf of the king.

In addition to goods, traders from North Africa carried their Islamic faith. Islam was the dominant religion of much of southwestern Asia at this time. Rising Muslim empires in North Africa made efforts to **convert**, or change, the people of West Africa to Islam and take over Ghana's trade, which weakened the power of the kingdom's rulers.

These efforts were so successful that in the mid-11th century, a historian named al-Bakri from al-Andalus (now Spain) described Ghana's capital as consisting of two towns. One was home to Muslim traders. The other was the palace of the king. By 1100, Ghana had declined as a result of droughts and unrest, providing an opportunity for a new Muslim empire to take control of the region.

HISTORICAL THINKING

1. **READING CHECK** How did Ghana's location help it become wealthy?

2. **INTERPRET MAPS** Identify two geographic features that the people of West Africa would have to travel through to trade with others.

3. **MAKE INFERENCES** Why did the movement of traders help spread the influence of Islam?

PLAN

Objective
Understand how climate and location influenced the economy and history of Ghana.

Critical Thinking Skills for Lesson 3.1
- Identify Main Ideas and Details
- Monitor Comprehension
- Interpret Maps
- Make Inferences
- Describe
- Draw Conclusions

Essential Question for Chapter 1
How were early civilizations in the Americas, Africa, and Europe both similar and different?
In West Africa, as in Europe and the Americas, trade gave rise to market towns, enriched kingdoms, and helped to spread religions. Lesson 3.1 explores how trade in gold and salt affected the kingdom of Ghana and the spread of Islam.

Background for the Teacher
Trading caravans led by Berber traders started crossing the Sahara around the fifth century. The Berbers were descendants of the original inhabitants of North Africa. When Arabs conquered North Africa, they converted many Berbers to Islam, who then spread the religion to sub-Saharan Africa.

Trading transactions often included the silent barter, in which the two sides never met face-to-face. North African salt traders, for instance, would place their salt in piles at a designated place, signal the beginning of trading with a drumbeat, and then leave. West African gold traders would arrive, inspect the salt, place bags of gold dust next to each pile, and leave. The salt traders would return and, if they approved of the amount of gold, would take it and leave. If not, trading would continue until both sides were satisfied with the exchange.

INTRODUCE & ENGAGE

Preview with the Map

Direct students' attention to the map of the trans-Saharan trade routes and help them locate Ghana, Mali, and Songhai. Tell students to locate the legend and note where on the map different goods are found. Explain that goods are an important factor in an economy's growth. Then ask students to share what they think has to happen for an economy to grow. **ASK:** Based on the map, what goods are most important to the economy of Ghana? (*Gold and salt are found closest to Ghana on the map, so they are probably the most important.*)

TEACH

Guided Discussion

1. **Describe** What role did the camel play in the history of West Africa? (*Answers will vary. Possible response: The Sahara could have isolated West Africa from North Africa, Europe, and Southwest Asia, but camels could carry people and goods many miles through the desert, making trans-Saharan trade possible. This trade connected West Africa to North Africa, and from there, to Europe and Southwest Asia. Market towns developed along the trade routes. In addition, Arab traders brought their Islamic faith with them to West Africa.*)

2. **Draw Conclusions** How did trade in salt and gold benefit the kingdom of Ghana and also contribute to Ghana's decline? (*Trade helped make Ghana rich and powerful because the king collected taxes on the import and export of goods. Other North African empires started to take over Ghana's trade and spread their religion, weakening the power of Ghana's rulers.*)

More Information

Importance of Salt Students may wonder why salt was such an important trade item. Point out that the human body needs salt to survive. People who eat mainly grains must add salt to their diet. Point out the salt symbols along the coast on the map of trans-Saharan trade routes. Explain that West Africans living on or near the coast could get salt from the ocean by evaporating salt water. People could also obtain some salt by consuming milk or meat. But in much of the interior of West Africa, salt was in short supply. Mining large salt slabs in the Sahara and transporting them to the south by camel provided a stable source of salt. Because salt was necessary for human survival, traders could demand high prices and make handsome profits.

Active Options

On Your Feet: Stage a Quiz Show Tell each student to write one question about the kingdom of Ghana. Then ask groups of five students to take turns coming to the front of the class to take part in a quiz. Pose questions in turn to each group. Students should signal their readiness to answer by raising their hands.

NG Learning Framework: Explore Modern Trans-Saharan Trade

| **ATTITUDE** | Responsibility |

| **SKILL** | Observation |

Explain that the photo provides information about the transportation of salt through Ethiopia. Then ask students to research the salt trade in West Africa today and write a short report. Tell them to use information from the photo and caption as well as additional source material, such as encyclopedia articles and websites. Ask students to share their completed reports, focusing on presenting information clearly and efficiently.

DIFFERENTIATE

Striving Readers

Strengthen Vocabulary Ask students to write the word *steppe* in a Word Square and then write its definition and characteristics. Tell students to provide examples and non-examples of it. After students complete the Word Square, ask them to create a Word Square for one of these other vocabulary words: *oasis, caravans,* or *trans-Saharan.*

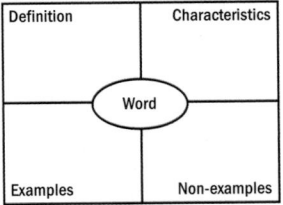

Inclusion

Work in Pairs Pair special needs students with students at a higher proficiency level or with a teacher's aide to examine the map. Help special needs students trace the boundaries of Ghana and the trade routes that led to Walata. Then ask them to identify each resource and point to one example on the map. Make sure they understand that Ghana was the first and smallest of the kingdoms and that salt traveled south along the trade routes and that gold traveled north.

See the Chapter Planner for more strategies for differentiation.

HISTORICAL THINKING

ANSWERS

1. Ghana was located near the meeting point for gold traders and salt traders. Ghana was able to collect taxes on the goods.

2. To trade with others, the people of West Africa might travel through the Sahara to the north or the forests to the south.

3. Answers will vary. Possible response: During this period of time, many traders who passed through West Africa were of the Islam religion, and they practiced their religion wherever they traveled. They also sought to covert others to Islam.

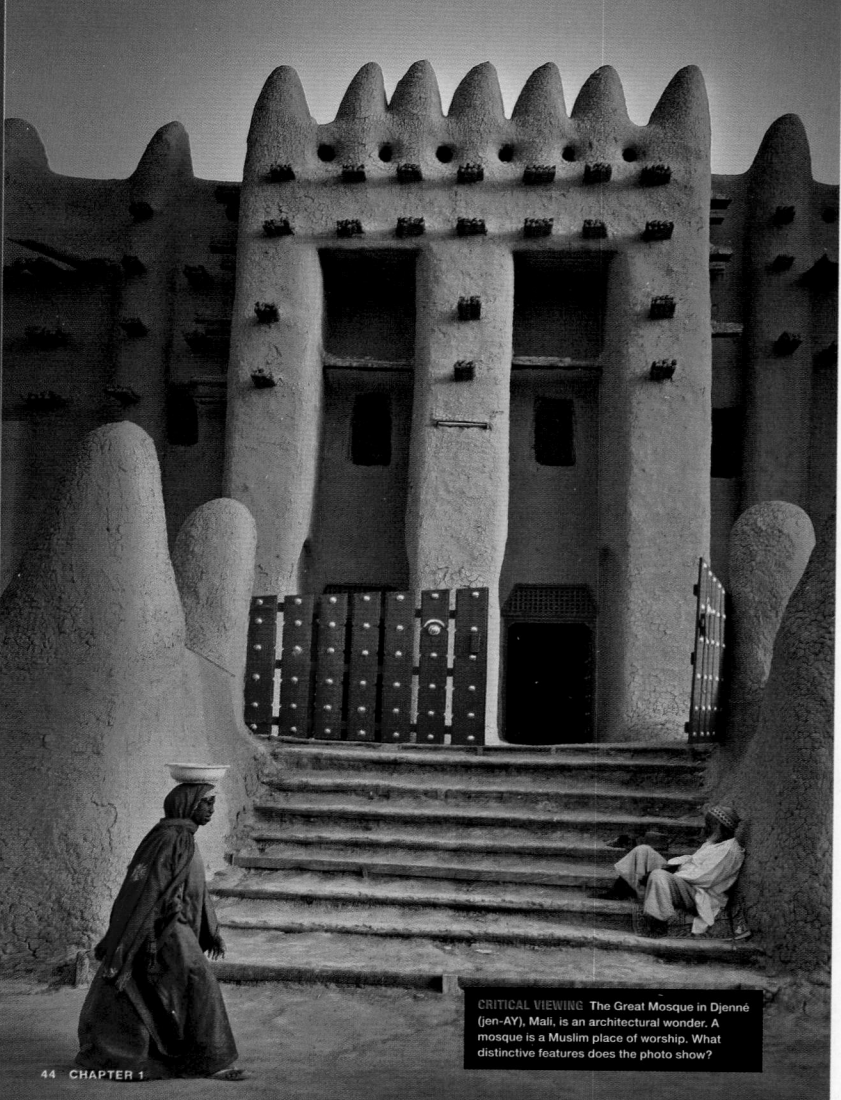

3.2 Mali and Songhai

In the 1300s, new legends spread to Europe about an impossibly wealthy king from West Africa who traveled with hundreds of camels and thousands of servants. This man, Mansa Musa, gave away so much gold that it led to a decline in the precious metal's value in parts of Africa.

MAIN IDEA Wealth from the kingdoms of Mali and Songhai spread along trans-Saharan trade routes to northern Africa and Europe.

MALI TAKES OVER GHANA

After Ghana's decline in the 1200s, the kingdom of **Mali** took control of the gold and salt trades in West Africa. Mali's first king was **Sundiata Keita** (sun-JAHT-ah KAY-tah). Sundiata led military forces to defeat the weakened kingdom of Ghana, uniting the conquered lands into a peaceful, prosperous empire stretching along the Niger River and up into the Sahara.

Though Sundiata ruled well, it was **Mansa Musa** who first introduced Mali to the world. Musa became king in the 1300s. As a Muslim, he decided to make a **pilgrimage**, or religious journey, to the holy city of Mecca in 1324. He took thousands of servants and dozens of camels. The caravan gave gold and other luxurious goods to people along the way. Europeans and Asians, upon hearing accounts of the generous king, became more motivated to trade with the wealthy empire.

Mansa Musa returned from Mecca a year later with new knowledge and ideas. He turned the city of Timbuktu into a center for culture and learning. He also encouraged his people to learn Arabic so they could study the holy book of Islam, the Qur'an.

SONGHAI

The **Songhai** people lived to the east of the Mali Empire. Their capital city, Gao, became such a wealthy, thriving city that the Mali Empire conquered it in 1325 and ruled over it for the next 50 years. When the Songhai finally retook their capital city, they began to build their own empire. In the process, Songhai assumed control of trans-Saharan trade. The Songhai ruler Askia Mohammed then continued to expand the kingdom and strengthen ties with other Muslims. He also reformed government, banking, and education. Later rulers fought each other for control, making the Songhai vulnerable to the ambitions of their envious neighbors. Songhai lost Timbuktu and its capital, Gao, when Morocco captured the two cities in 1591. The invasion by Morocco marked the end of the Songhai Empire.

As Ghana, Mali, and Songhai rose and fell, other West African cultures developed. The Hausa (HOW-suh) and Yoruba (YOR-uh-buh) practiced agriculture and crafts. While the Hausa and Yoruba were allied with each other, they never combined forces to engage in war for other territories. The kingdom of Benin (buh-NEEN) rose to power in the late 1400s, conquered many of its neighbors, and successfully engaged in trade with Europeans.

The Europeans, meanwhile, had set their sights on other lands by the late 1400s. Soon they would be exploring territory in the Americas.

HISTORICAL THINKING

1. **READING CHECK** How did the rise of Mali and Songhai affect trans-Saharan trade?

2. **ANALYZE CAUSE AND EFFECT** How did Mansa Musa's pilgrimage lead to changes in Timbuktu?

3. **COMPARE AND CONTRAST** How were the empires of Mali and Songhai similar?

CRITICAL VIEWING The Great Mosque in Djenné (jen-AY), Mali, is an architectural wonder. A mosque is a Muslim place of worship. What distinctive features does the photo show?

PLAN

Objective
Understand the roles of economics and the spread of religions in the rise of cultures.

Critical Thinking Skills for Lesson 3.2
- Identify Main Ideas and Details
- Monitor Comprehension
- Analyze Cause and Effect
- Compare and Contrast
- Make Inferences
- Make Connections
- Analyze Visuals

Essential Question for Chapter 1
How were early civilizations in the Americas, Africa, and Europe both similar and different?
Like Ghana, Mali and Songhai built their wealth on trade and gold. Lesson 3.2 explores how trade and Islam helped shaped the kingdoms of Mali and Songhai.

Background for the Teacher
At its height, Timbuktu was home to 100,000 people, three large mosques, and the University of Sankore, which had around 25,000 students. The university's main purpose was the study of the Qur'an, although courses also included law, medicine, history, and literature. Students were required to learn Arabic. Scholars flocked to the university to study and teach. As a result, hundreds of thousands of manuscripts were brought to or created in Timbuktu. The manuscripts were devoted to subjects including religion, medicine, astronomy, poetry, law, and mathematics. When Islamic extremists took over parts of Mali in 2012, members of the Mamma Haidara Library in Timbuktu rescued 350,000 manuscripts from Timbuktu-area libraries and transported them to safety.

Review and Predict

Direct students' attention to the map of the trans-Saharan trade routes in Lesson 3.1. Tell students to locate the kingdoms of Mali and Songhai. **ASK:** What can you tell about the size of Mali and Songhai compared to the earlier kingdom of Ghana? *(Mali was larger than Ghana, and Songhai was even larger than Mali.)* Based on details you see on the map, what prediction could you make about the role of trade in the Mali and Songhai empires? *(Answers will vary. Possible response: Resources must have been so plentiful that trade along the trans-Saharan trade routes helped each kingdom to expand its territory.)*

TEACH

Guided Discussion

1. **Make Inferences** What motivated Europeans and Asians to trade with Mali? *(Answers will vary. Possible response: Europeans and Asians heard about Mansa Musa giving away gold and expensive gifts to people. They probably assumed that, with so much wealth to spare, the kingdom would be a good place to sell their goods at high prices.)*

2. **Make Connections** Why do you think the Songhai ruler Askia Mohammed strengthened ties with other Muslims? *(Answers will vary. Possible response: Askia Mohammed strengthened ties with other Muslims because he probably remembered what had happened in the past when Gao, the capital, was conquered by the Mali Empire. With Muslim allies, he'd be better prepared to defend his kingdom.)*

Analyze Visuals

Explore the photograph and caption with students. **ASK:** What do you think the walls are made of? *(Answers will vary. Possible response: The walls appear to be made of dried mud. The material probably comes from nearby because the road is the same color.)* Where do you see wood in the building? *(There are wood beams that jut from the front of the building, and a gate stands at the top of the stairs.)* Tell students that the mud walls need to be repaired by replastering regularly. Djenné holds a celebration each year in which the residents replaster the walls of the mosque. People climb up and sit on the timbers while applying the new mud. The hand application of mud creates the rounded edges.

Active Options

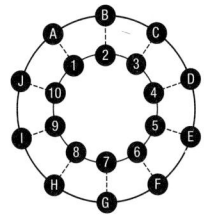

On Your Feet: Fishbowl Arrange students in an inner and outer circle, both facing the center. Use a Fishbowl strategy to have students in the inner circle pose questions and take notes about the emergence of the kingdom of Mali. Then tell students to switch places to pose questions and take notes about Songhai.

NG Learning Framework: Compare Mali and Songhai

ATTITUDE Curiosity

SKILLS Observation, Collaboration

Have students work in teams to collaborate on lists of observations about how Islam and trade impacted Mali and Songhai. Once they have completed their lists, have each team exchange its list with another team. Have each team write two questions about the other team's observations. Reconvene as a class and review the lists of observations and questions posed.

English Language Learners

Identify Main Ideas and Details Ask students at the **Emerging** and **Expanding** levels to complete a Main Idea Cluster using the diagram below. Point out that a main idea is often written in the first sentence of a paragraph and that details give examples or specific information about the main idea.

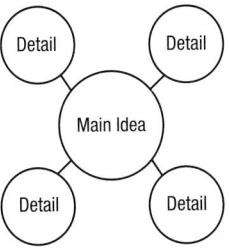

Pre-AP

Research Mansa Musa Ask students to prepare a presentation on Mansa Musa's pilgrimage to Mecca and to include details about the caravan's size, makeup, displays of wealth, and others' reactions to Mansa Musa's wealth.

See the Chapter Planner for more strategies for differentiation.

ANSWERS

1. Possible response: As Mali rose to power, it took control of trans-Saharan trade that Ghana once dominated. Eventually, Songhai became more powerful and took control of trade from Mali.

2. Possible response: Mansa Musa returned from Mecca with new ideas and decided to turn Timbuktu into a cultural center. He promoted the learning of Arabic to enable people to read and study the Qur'an.

3. Possible response: Both Mali and Songhai expanded their kingdoms through conquest, gained wealth by controlling trans-Saharan trade, were Muslim, and had leaders who introduced significant reforms.

CRITICAL VIEWING Answers will vary. Possible response: The mosque's high entry has a zigzag top, resembling a crown, which continues along the roofline, making it look like a castle. The wood and metal on the gate are finely crafted.

DOCUMENT-BASED QUESTION
Impressions of Mali

Travelers have long recorded their observations as they explore new places. Travel journals from the past reveal details about places as they were long ago and also give us insight into how people reacted to different cultures.

This painting is an illustration from an Arabic manuscript from the 1200s and shows a wealthy pilgrim on his hajj, or pilgrimage to Mecca in present-day Saudi Arabia. Moroccan traveler Ibn Battuta (IBH-uhn bah-TOO-tuh) began his travels by going on his hajj in 1325. This was one year after Mansa Musa made his hajj. Stopping in

Cairo, Ibn Battuta heard about Mansa Musa. The two never met, but later Ibn Battuta visited Mali. There he met Mansa Musa's brother Mansa Suleyman and began recording his observations.

CRITICAL VIEWING What mood does the painting convey?

DOCUMENT ONE
Primary Source: Atlas
from the *Catalan Atlas*, c. 1375

Drawn by a European mapmaker, this detail from a medieval map shows West Africa and Mansa Musa, the man wearing a gold crown and holding a ball of gold. The map was made after Mansa Musa's pilgrimage to Mecca, which literally put West Africa on the map.

CONSTRUCTED RESPONSE What does this image suggest about the impression Mansa Musa made on people outside of Mali?

DOCUMENT TWO
Primary Source: Travel Memoir
from *Travels in Asia and Africa 1325–1354*, by Ibn Battuta

Ibn Battuta traveled throughout Africa, Europe, and Asia and wrote about his experiences. His writings help us understand the history and cultures of the places he visited. In this excerpt from his writing, he describes the entrance of the sultan, or ruler, of Mali, Mansa Suleyman.

CONSTRUCTED RESPONSE What impression do you think the sultan made on his audience?

On certain days the sultan holds audiences in the palace yard, where there is a platform under a tree, with three steps. . . . The sultan comes out of a door in a corner of the palace, carrying a bow in his hand and a quiver on his back. . . . His usual dress is a velvety red tunic, made of the European fabrics called "mutanfas." The sultan is preceded by his musicians, who carry gold and silver guimbris [two-stringed guitars], and behind him come three hundred armed slaves. He walks in a leisurely fashion. . . . As he takes his seat the drums, trumpets, and bugles are sounded.

DOCUMENT THREE
Primary Source: Travel Memoir
from *Travels in Asia and Africa 1325–1354*, by Ibn Battuta

As a Muslim, Ibn Battuta was interested to see how people in other regions practiced his religion. In this excerpt, he notes what he witnessed about the observance of Islam in Mali. He admired the commitment of the people there to the religion.

CONSTRUCTED RESPONSE What does this description tell you about the importance of Islam in Mali?

On Fridays, if a man does not go early to the mosque, he cannot find a corner to pray in, on account of the crowd. It is a custom of theirs to send each man his boy [to the mosque] with his prayer-mat; the boy spreads it out for his master in a place befitting him [and remains on it] until he comes to the mosque. . . . Yet another is their zeal for learning the Koran [Qur'an] by heart. They put their children in chains if they show any backwardness in memorizing it, and they are not set free until they have it by heart.

SYNTHESIZE & WRITE

1. **REVIEW** Review what you have learned about travel, trade, and religion in West Africa.

2. **RECALL** Think about your responses to the constructed response questions above. What details in the documents caused you to form these impressions?

3. **CONSTRUCT** Write a topic sentence that answers this question: What impressions did Mali make on those who traveled there?

4. **WRITE** Using evidence from this chapter and the documents, write a paragraph that supports your topic sentence.

PLAN

Objective
Synthesize impressions of the kingdom of Mali from primary source documents.

Critical Thinking Skills for Lesson 3.3
- Synthesize
- Identify Main Ideas and Details
- Analyze Visuals
- Monitor Comprehension
- Evaluate

Essential Question for Chapter 1
How were early civilizations in the Americas, Africa, and Europe both similar and different?
Trade and Islam helped shape Mali's culture. Lesson 3.3 provides a medieval map of West Africa and excerpts from Ibn Battuta's *Travels in Asia and Africa, 1325–1354* to explore the impressions people had of the kingdom of Mali.

Background for the Teacher
Muslims perform the hajj, or pilgrimage to Mecca, once in their lifetimes if they are financially and physically able. The hajj occurs in the last month of the Islamic calendar, beginning on the seventh and ending on the 12th. The hajj is one of the Five Pillars of Islam—the five duties every faithful Muslim should perform: (1) profess the Muslim faith; (2) pray five times a day in the prescribed manner; (3) give alms to the poor; (4) fast during Ramadan; and (5) perform the pilgrimage to Mecca. Mecca, Islam's holiest site, is located in western Saudi Arabia and was the birthplace of the Prophet Muhammad, the founder of Islam.

Prepare for the Document-Based Question

Before students start on the activity, briefly preview the three documents. Remind students that a constructed response requires full explanations in complete sentences. Emphasize that students should use what they have learned about travel, trade, and religion in West Africa in addition to the information in the documents.

Guided Discussion

1. **Analyze Visuals** Examine the map and explain how the mapmaker informs you about the economy of West Africa. Use details from the map in your answer. *(The mapmaker includes a large ship with sails approaching the coast and portrays the trans-Saharan trade routes as roads paved with stones. These details suggest that the economy of West Africa was based on trading with people from outside Africa as well as from within.)*

2. **Monitor Comprehension** What picture does Ibn Battuta paint of Mansa Suleyman and the people of Mali? *(Ibn Battuta portrays Mansa Suleyman as a wealthy and powerful ruler. Details about the people of Mali suggest they are devout Muslims.)*

Evaluate

After students have completed the Synthesize & Write activity, allow time for them to exchange paragraphs and read and comment on the work of their peers. Guidelines for comments should be established prior to this activity so that feedback is constructive and encouraging in nature.

Active Options

On Your Feet: Host a DBQ Roundtable Divide the class into groups of four. Tell groups to move desks together to form a table where they all can sit. Hand each group a sheet of paper with the question, *What is one thing the documents helped you understand about the kingdom of Mali?* The first student in each group should write an answer, read it aloud, and pass the paper clockwise to the next student. The paper should circulate around the table several times. Reconvene as a class and discuss groups' responses.

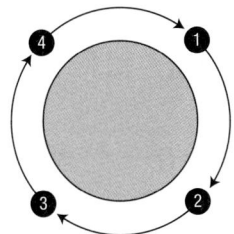

Inclusion

Facilitate Comprehension Pair special needs students with readers who can help them understand the content by minimizing distractions by photocopying or printing for them the documents in Lesson 3.3. Ask special needs students to highlight words that they do not understand and concepts that confuse them. Ask proficient partners to help them look up words and direct them to information in the text to help answer their questions.

Gifted & Talented

Explore Ibn Battuta's Writings Encourage students to further explore Ibn Battuta's impressions of Mali. Ask them to conduct research to find additional descriptions Ibn Battuta made about life in Mali. Once they complete their research, tell students to write a brief report. Ask students to explore how their research agrees with or differs from the documents in Lesson 3.3.

See the Chapter Planner for more strategies for differentiation.

ANSWERS

1. Answers will vary.

2. Answers will vary.

3. Possible response: Travelers to Mali were impressed by the sultan's wealth and power and the people's commitment to Islam.

4. Students' paragraphs should include their topic sentence from the previous question and several details from the documents and chapter to support the sentence.

CONSTRUCTED RESPONSE

Document 1: Possible response: Mansa Musa is sitting on his throne, holding a piece of gold as a trader approaches. He wears a gold crown and holds a gold staff. His portrayal suggests that outsiders viewed him as a ruler of a rich kingdom with whom they should trade.

Document 2: Possible response: Mansa Suleyman's grand entrances, his fine garments, the procession of musicians playing gold and silver guitars, and his hundreds of armed slaves probably made his audience believe that this man was wealthy and powerful.

Document 3: Possible response: Huge crowds at the mosques for prayer suggests that there were many devoted believers. Children memorized the Qur'an, so Islam was very important to the people of Mali beginning at an early age.

CRITICAL VIEWING Possible response: The banners, trumpets, and people's gestures suggest a festive mood. The people seem to be pleased to be on a pilgrimage to Mecca.

1 REVIEW

VOCABULARY

Use each of the following vocabulary terms in a sentence that shows an understanding of the term's meaning and its connection to the information in this chapter.

1. civilization
   Once humans started growing their own food, cities and civilizations could grow.
2. migrate
3. matrilineal
4. slash-and-burn agriculture
5. feudalism
6. navigation
7. trans-Saharan
8. caravan

READING STRATEGY
COMPARE AND CONTRAST

If you haven't already, complete your table to list the characteristics of the three societies discussed in the chapter. List at least four characteristics of each. Then answer the question.

Americas	Europe	Africa
empires		

9. What conflicts might arise among these three societies based on what you've learned about them?

MAIN IDEAS

Answer the following questions. Support your answers with evidence from the chapter.

10. How did the land in Mesoamerica contribute to the rise of civilizations there? **LESSON 1.1**
11. What determined whether a group of people in North America took up farming or continued to live as hunter-gatherers? **LESSON 1.2**
12. What was the significance of the Green Corn festival in the lives of the people of southeastern North America? **LESSON 1.3**
13. Why did the Roman Catholic Church begin the Crusades? **LESSON 2.1**
14. How did the Renaissance influence religious thought and pave the way for the Reformation? **LESSON 2.2**
15. Why did Prince Henry the Navigator establish a school to train sailors? **LESSON 2.3**
16. What caused the eventual decline of the kingdom of Ghana? **LESSON 3.1**
17. How did Mansa Musa increase his trade business on his pilgrimage to Mecca? **LESSON 3.2**
18. Why are the writings of Ibn Battuta considered such an important source for understanding West Africa in the 1300s? **LESSON 3.3**

HISTORICAL THINKING

Answer the following questions. Support your answers with evidence from the chapter.

19. **SUMMARIZE** What purposes did mounds serve in the Adena, Hopewell, and Mississippian cultures?

20. **ANALYZE CAUSE AND EFFECT** Why did trading across continents become important to European merchants?
21. **MAKE INFERENCES** What do you think happened to the kingdom of Songhai as other kingdoms and empires arose in the region?
22. **DRAW CONCLUSIONS** In what way did the Crusades help weaken feudalism?
23. **FORM AND SUPPORT OPINIONS** Which South American, Mesoamerican, or North American civilization do you think was most advanced? Explain and support your answer.

INTERPRET MAPS

Look closely at this map of Vasco da Gama's voyage around Africa to reach India and return to Europe. Then answer the questions that follow.

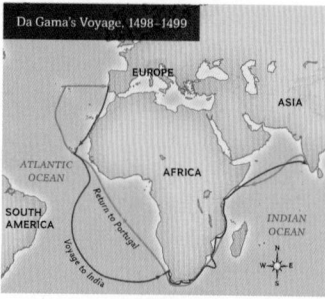
Da Gama's Voyage, 1498–1499

24. As you have read, overland trade routes were used for centuries to link Europe and Asia. Why did Vasco da Gama sail all the way around Africa to reach the same Asian trading centers?
25. Do you think Europeans who followed da Gama traded only with Indian merchants? What information on the map helped you answer the question?

ANALYZE SOURCES

Here is an account of an experience from Vasco da Gama's ship's log. The encounter he describes took place near the southern tip of Africa in 1498. Read the passage and answer the question.

On the following day (November 10) fourteen or fifteen natives came to where our ships lay. The captain-major landed and showed them a variety of merchandise, with the view of finding out whether such things were to be found in their country. This merchandise included cinnamon, cloves, seed-pearls, gold, and many other things, but it was evident that they had no knowledge whatever of such articles, and they were consequently given round bells and tin rings.

26. Why do you think the captain-major wants to know if "such things were to be found in their country"?

CONNECT TO YOUR LIFE

27. **ARGUMENT** Think about the way trading across societies and continents affected the civilizations you have read about in this chapter. Today, nations still trade with one another. Does modern trade have the same cultural impact as it did 600 years ago or more? Write a paragraph stating your opinion, and offer reasons to support your opinion.

TIPS

- Look back on the chapter and list ways in which trading affected the cultures. Then think about how trade affects cultures today. What are the similarities and differences? Make notes and then review them to help you formulate your opinion.
- Include examples of similarities or differences to support your opinion. Use evidence from the text and two or three key terms from the chapter to make your point.
- Conclude your argument by restating your opinion and summarizing your reasoning.

VOCABULARY ANSWERS

1. Once humans started growing their own food, cities and civilizations could grow.
2. The Blackfoot migrated to follow the bison herds they hunted for food.
3. The Iroquois were matrilineal and traced their family lines through their mothers.
4. Eastern Woodlands people practiced slash-and-burn agriculture in order to farm in heavy forests.
5. Serfs were at the bottom of the social hierarchy under feudalism.
6. It took skillful navigation for the Portuguese to explore the West African coast.
7. Ghana grew rich as a market center for trans-Saharan trade.
8. Camel caravans carried salt and gold across the Sahara.

READING STRATEGY ANSWER

Americas	Europe	Africa
empires	kingdoms	kingdoms
cities	cities	cities
trade	trade	trade
Native American religions	Catholic and Protestant	Islam

9. Possible response: The three societies might come into conflict over issues related to trade, religion, and political power. When people from different societies meet for the first time, their beliefs, their ways of life, and their level and types of technology might be very different. If people disagree about religious customs, it may start a conflict over religion. If one group has more advanced technology than another, that group may be tempted to take advantage of the other.

MAIN IDEAS ANSWERS

10. The land in Mesoamerica was fertile. People living there could grow enough crops to feed the larger populations characteristic of civilizations.

11. The environment in which a group of people lived determined if they engaged in agriculture or remained hunter-gatherers. Tribes who lived in an environment rich in game and wild edible plants had plenty of food, so they did not have to provide more through farming. Many groups who lived in an environment with good soil and water resources but sparser game began to farm to have enough food to eat.

12. The Green Corn festival was a religious ceremony that celebrated agriculture. It occurred in the summer as the corn, an important Native American crop, began to ripen.

13. The Roman Catholic Church embarked on the Crusades to stop the spread of Islam and win back control of the Holy Land.

14. By returning to the philosophy of humanism, which encouraged freedom of thought and the development of new ideas, Renaissance thinkers led people to rethink traditions and laws, including the authority and practices of the Church. This questioning resulted in the Reformation.

15. Prince Henry's goal in establishing a school was to teach navigation and to encourage exploration and trade.

16. Ghana declined as a result of droughts and unrest, which provided an opportunity for a new Muslim empire to take control of the region.

17. Mansa Musa gave gold and other luxuries to the people he encountered along his journey. When traders in Europe heard of his generosity, they were more motivated to trade with him.

18. Ibn Battuta traveled throughout Africa, Europe, and Asia in the 1300s, and his writing contains many valuable observations about the time in which he was living and the places he visited.

HISTORICAL THINKING ANSWERS

19. Some mounds served as burial sites; other mounds served as temples. In addition to temples, the Mississippians topped some of their mounds with residences for their chiefs.

20. Possible response: As cities formed and grew in Europe, the merchant class grew, and trade expanded from city to city and from nation to nation. Once a few European merchants began traveling, especially to Asia, and returned with fine goods that sold for a good price, more Europeans started to trade over long distances as well.

21. Possible response: Just as Songhai took over the trans-Saharan trade once dominated by Mali, rising kingdoms eventually gained control of these routes from Songhai.

22. Possible response: The Crusades weakened feudalism by increasing trade. As trade increased, market towns grew. People left the manors for better jobs in towns, and this weakened feudalism.

23. Answers will vary. Students' opinions about the most advanced civilization should be supported by evidence from the text.

INTERPRET MAPS ANSWERS

24. The Turks controlled trade with the East. Vasco da Gama hoped that by finding a sea route to Asian trading centers, Portugal could bypass the Turks' hold on trade with Asia.

25. Possible response: I think Europeans traded with more than just Indian merchants. The map shows that Europeans made stops along the African coast before sailing on to India.

ANALYZE SOURCES ANSWER

26. Possible response: The captain-major wanted to learn whether the people of South Africa were familiar with trade goods such as cinnamon, cloves, seed pearls, and gold to determine whether Europe should be trading with them.

CONNECT TO YOUR LIFE ANSWER

27. Students' paragraphs will vary. Students should identify similarities and differences between how trade affected cultures in the past and how it affects cultures today. Students might suggest that the cultural impacts are the same in some ways but different in others. Trade is different now because goods can be transported much faster and trading partners tend to know more about each other. But trade still requires people from different cultures to interact with one another. This interaction can lead to the spread of cultures, but it can also lead to conflict between cultures.

UNIT 1 RESOURCES

UNIT INTRODUCTION

UNIT TIME LINE

UNIT WRAP-UP

NATIONAL GEOGRAPHIC | **CONNECTION**

National Geographic Magazine Adapted Articles
- "First Americans"
- "Scurvy Struck Columbus's Crew" ONLINE

Unit 1 Inquiry: Establish an Empire

NG Learning Framework Activities
- Create a Map
- Think Like an Archaeologist

Unit 1 Formal Assessment

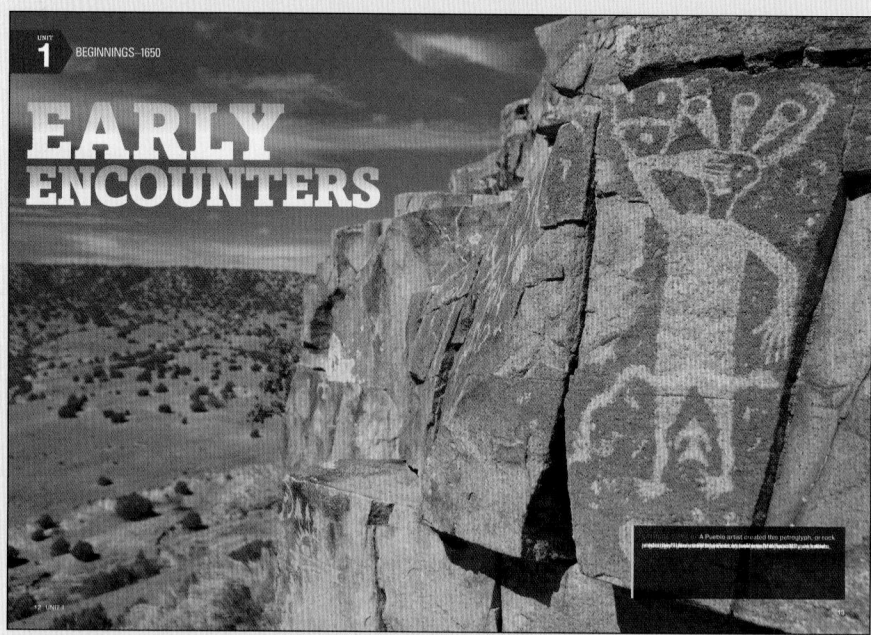

CHAPTER 2 RESOURCES

Available at NGLSync.Cengage.com

TEACHER RESOURCES & ASSESSMENT

Reading and Note-Taking

Vocabulary Practice

Social Studies Skills Lessons
- Reading: Draw Conclusions
- Writing: Write an Explanation

Formal Assessment
- Chapter 2 Pretest
- Chapter 2 Tests A & B
- Section Quizzes

Chapter 2 Answer Key

ExamView®
One-time Download

STUDENT DIGITAL RESOURCES

- **eEdition** (English)
- **eEdition** (Spanish)
- **Handbooks**

- **Online Atlas**
- **American Gallery Online**
- **History Notebook**

- **Active History**
- **Projects for Inquiry-Based Learning**

Chapter 2 Spanish Resources are available at NGLSync.Cengage.com.

The Missions of New Mexico

- Primary Sources
- On Your Feet: Three Corners

| **NG Learning Framework:**
Compare Missions, Past and Present

SECTION 1 RESOURCES
SPAIN CLAIMS AN EMPIRE

LESSON 1.1
The Age of Exploration

- On Your Feet: Inside-Outside Circle

| **NG Learning Framework:**
Identify World Voyages

LESSON 1.2
AMERICAN VOICES
Christopher Columbus

- On Your Feet: Three-Step Interview

| **NG Learning Framework:**
Create a Technology Chart

LESSON 1.3
Conquering the Aztec and Inca

- On Your Feet: Think, Pair, Share

 The Inca Empire

LESSON 1.4
Conquistadors in the North

- On Your Feet: Rotating Discussion

| **NG Learning Framework:**
Map New Encounters

SECTION 2 RESOURCES
EUROPE FIGHTS OVER NORTH AMERICA

LESSON 2.1
Competing Claims

- On Your Feet: Follow the Map
- Active History: Compare European Explorers

LESSON 2.2
Defeat of the Spanish Armada

- On Your Feet: Team Word Webbing

| **NG Learning Framework:**
Write a Biography

LESSON 2.3
French and Dutch Colonies

- On Your Feet: Card Responses

| **NG Learning Framework:**
Analyze Environmental Concepts

SECTION 3 RESOURCES
SPANISH RULE IN THE AMERICAS

LESSON 3.1
Spanish Colonial Rule

- On Your Feet: Think, Pair, Share

| **NG Learning Framework:**
Write a Persuasive Letter

LESSON 3.2
NATIONAL GEOGRAPHIC EXPLORER
PARDIS SABETI
Genetics, Disease, and Native Americans

- On Your Feet: Ready, Set, Recall

| **NG Learning Framework:**
Research the Researchers

LESSON 3.3
The Columbian Exchange

- ▶ Map of a Pizza
- On Your Feet: History Relay

| **NG Learning Framework:**
Explore Introduced Species

SECTION 4 RESOURCES
SLAVERY BEGINS IN THE AMERICAS

LESSON 4.1
A New Kind of Slavery

- On Your Feet: Use a Jigsaw Strategy

| **NG Learning Framework:**
Collect Data on the Middle Passage

LESSON 4.2
The Growth of Slavery

- On Your Feet: Word Chain

| **NG Learning Framework:**
Research the Slave Trade

CHAPTER 2 REVIEW

Strategy ❶
Turn Titles into Questions

Before reading each lesson, display a question based on the lesson title. After reading the lesson, have students work in pairs to answer the question with evidence from the text.

Lesson 1.3: How did the Spanish conquer the Aztec and Inca empires?
Lesson 2.2: What were the causes and effects of the Spanish Armada's defeat?
Lesson 3.1: What was life like under Spanish colonial rule?

Use with Lessons 1.3, 2.2, and 3.1 *Additional option: Have students choose another lesson from Chapter 2 and rewrite its title as a question. Students can trade questions with a partner and work on answering them after reading the chosen lesson.*

Strategy ❷
Ready, Set, Recall

After reading, set a short time limit, and have students write a list of everything they remember about the lesson. Then direct them to work in small teams to compare and combine their lists. Have teams take turns sharing items from their combined lists with the class until they run out of new details. The last team to run out of details to contribute wins.

Use with All Lessons

Strategy ❸
Use Supported Reading

Have students work in pairs to read each lesson aloud. At the end of each lesson, have them pause and use these sentence frames to monitor their comprehension of the text.

- This lesson is mostly about _____.
- Other topics this lesson talked about are _____.
- One question I have about this lesson is _____.
- One of the vocabulary words is _____. It means _____.
- One word I do not recognize is _____.

Use with All Lessons *Pair more proficient readers with less proficient readers.*

Strategy ❶
Modify Vocabulary Lists

Limit the number of Key Vocabulary terms for which students will be responsible. Have students create vocabulary flash cards for the terms from your modified list as they progress through the lessons. Encourage students to add examples, synonyms, or even illustrations to the definitions on their flash cards. Students should be prompted to refer to these cards whenever they encounter the terms in their reading until they feel they have mastered the definitions.

Use with All Lessons

Strategy ❷
Sequence Events

To build understanding of the critical events in a lesson and their relationships to each other in time, have students note them in a Sequence Chain. Remind students that they may add ovals to their Sequence Chains if necessary.

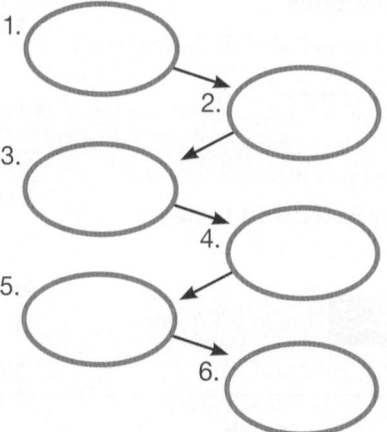

Use with All Lessons

ENGLISH LANGUAGE LEARNERS

Strategy 1
Use a Word in a Sentence

After students have read a lesson, have them locate a word that is unfamiliar to them. Have students work in pairs, with **Emerging** students partnered with **Bridging** students, to write a definition using their own words and use the word correctly in a new sentence.

Use with All Lessons

Strategy 2
Ask Either/Or Questions

To confirm students' understanding of the Key Vocabulary terms, ask questions such as the ones below. Instruct students to say or write the correct response. After students have answered the questions, have them work with partners to check their answers. Challenge students at **All Proficiencies** to write their answers in complete sentences.

1. Does Taino mean a group of people or a place? *(Taino are a group of people.)*
2. Were the conquistadors kings or explorers? *(Conquistadors were explorers.)*
3. Did the Catholic Church persecute or welcome Protestants? *(The Catholic Church persecuted Protestants.)*
4. Were plantations a type of farm or city? *(Plantations were a type of farm.)*

Use with Lessons 1.1, 1.3, 2.1, 3.1, 3.3 *Provide sentence stems for students at the **Emerging** level. Encourage students at the **Bridging** level to develop more complex sentences.*

Strategy 3
Make Word Cards

Help students at **All Proficiencies** make word cards for Key Vocabulary terms from this chapter. Instruct students to write one term on the front of each card. On the back, prompt them to include relevant information about the term, such as definitions, examples, pictures to help them recall meaning, and related words or phrases. Then have students use these cards to write one original sentence using each term.

Some Key Vocabulary terms include:

- mercantilism
- conquistadors
- viceroy
- mission
- Columbian Exchange
- slavery
- triangular trade

Use with Lessons 1.1, 1.3, 3.1, 3.3, and 4.1

GIFTED & TALENTED

Strategy 1
Present a Television Documentary

Have students split into small groups to conduct research about Spanish missions in the Americas. Ask them to choose a specific mission and present a short television-style documentary about it. Tell students to include information on the mission's founders, its history, its present-day uses, and its architecture, using images if available. Remind students to discuss which Native American groups would have been most affected by this mission and its missionaries. Invite groups to present their documentaries to the class.

Use with Lesson 3.1

Strategy 2
Teach a Class

Before beginning the chapter, have students choose one of the lessons and prepare to teach a class on it. Students should prepare questions to ask the class and be prepared to answer classmates' questions as well. Remind students to consider in advance whether they will use any visual or audio materials in their teaching.

Use with All Lessons *Provide students with an appropriate time limit for their teaching presentations. You may wish to have students work in pairs.*

Pre-AP

Strategy 1
Form a Thesis

Have students select one of the lessons from the chapter and develop a thesis around one of its related topics. Remind students that the thesis statement must make a claim they can support with evidence from the lesson, the chapter, or outside sources.

Use with All Lessons *Students may also work in pairs or groups to compare and refine their thesis statements.*

Strategy 2
Create an Annotated Time Line

Have students create and annotate a time line for the Age of Exploration in the Americas. Time lines may include expeditions, the founding of different settlements, and other political or religious events that took place between 1492 and 1650. Remind students that their time lines should include dates or date ranges for all events. Prompt students to illustrate their time lines with images from the text or from outside sources.

Use with Lessons 1.1–2.3

EUROPEAN EXPLORATION OF
THE AMERICAS
1492–1650

ESSENTIAL QUESTION
What impact did European exploration have on the Americas?

READING STRATEGY

DRAW CONCLUSIONS
Drawing conclusions between ideas and events in informational texts is important to building understanding. As you read this chapter, use a chart like this one to note specific details about how European exploration affected the Western Hemisphere.

"Set sail...
at 8 o'clock, and proceeded with a strong breeze till sunset."
—Christopher Columbus

A reproduction of one of Columbus's ships sets sail more than 500 years after that world-changing voyage in 1492. Today, replicas of the *Niña* and the *Pinta* make stops in ports along the East Coast, the Great Lakes, and the Mississippi River as traveling museums for visitors to enjoy.

INTRODUCE THE PHOTOGRAPH

Floating Museums

Have students study the photograph that opens this chapter. Make sure students understand that the ship is a replica, or reproduction, of one of Christopher Columbus's ships. Explain that scholars and shipbuilders working with an organization called the Columbus Foundation constructed replicas of the *Niña* and *Pinta*. The designer of the *Niña* did thorough historical research to design the ship and used traditional techniques to build it. The replica ships serve as a touring museum for visitors to come aboard and explore. **ASK:** What might you expect to learn by touring a ship reproduction? *(Answers will vary. Possible responses: Visitors might learn how quickly the original ships could travel, how the ships handled bad weather, and what it was like to live or work on these ships.)*

For Chapter 2 Spanish Resources, visit the Resources Menu. Chapter 2 Resources are available at NGLSync.Cengage.com.

Share Background

Once introduced, caravels quickly became known as small, lightweight ships that could sail much faster than many ships of their day. Consequently, they were popular choices for long-distance travel and exploration. No plans or drawings of the actual *Niña* or *Pinta* exist. Researchers and engineers built these replicas based on information from Spanish shipwrecks from Columbus's era. They also examined documents such as the *Libro de Armadas*, which contains records of the *Niña*'s size, sail rigging, and cargo. From these studies and documents, researchers concluded that the *Niña* would have been between 65 and 70 feet long and had a tonnage (cargo capacity) of approximately 75 to 100 tons.

INTRODUCE THE ESSENTIAL QUESTION

What impact did European exploration have on the Americas?

Brainstorm Activity: The Ripple Effects of Exploration This activity prompts students to draw on their prior knowledge and make predictions about the possible ways exploration can affect communities, resources, and economies. Divide the class into three groups and have each group sit together. Assign each group two discussion questions as follows:

Group 1:
What are some ways that communities might react to the arrival of strangers? What factors affect how a community chooses to react?

Group 2:
In what ways might each community affect the other's resources? How might the communities decide what to share or exchange with each other?

Group 3:
How might the arrival of new explorers change the economies of a place? How might exploration affect the economies of the explorers' countries?

Have students in each group discuss their assigned questions. Display a three-column chart labeled Communities, Resources, Economies. When students have finished their discussions, call on students from each group to add their ideas to the chart.

INTRODUCE CHAPTER VOCABULARY

Word Maps

As they read the chapter, have students complete Word Maps for Key Vocabulary words. Tell students to make a Word Map for each word. Have them write the word in the center oval, and, as they encounter the word in the chapter, complete the Word Map for that word. Model an example for students on the board, using the graphic organizer below.

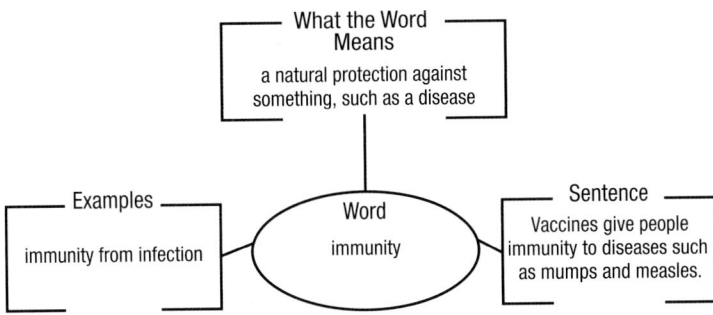

INTRODUCE THE READING STRATEGY

DRAW CONCLUSIONS
Remind students that when they are drawing conclusions about ideas or events, it can be helpful to keep track of all the details related to a particular idea. Looking at the details in one place can make it easier to draw a sound conclusion supported by all of the evidence. Model completing the Draw Conclusions Chart. Point out that the center circle is the event to which all of the other details should be related. Ask for examples of a detail related to European exploration of the Western Hemisphere and fill out a square of the chart as a class. Ask students what this detail tells them about European exploration. Remind students to make use of the chart by adding details to it as they read the chapter.

KEY DATES FOR CHAPTER 2

1494	Treaty of Tordesillas
1521	Hernán Cortés conquers Tenochtitlán
1539	Hernando de Soto lands in present-day Florida
1540	Coronado explores American Southwest
1588	Queen Elizabeth I defeats the Spanish Armada
1608	First French settlement in North America
1626	Dutch purchase the island of Manhattan
1680	Popé's revolt

 AMERICAN STORIES ONLINE For instructional support for the online American Story "The Missions of New Mexico," go to NGLSync.Cengage.com.

For more on resources of the Americas, see *EXPLORE PERUVIAN GOLD*. **STEM**

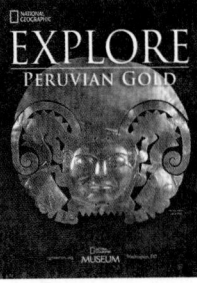

1.1 The Age of Exploration

Imagine setting sail in a direction no one you know has ever gone. Would you be excited or scared? European explorers probably felt both as they set out without smartphones, GPS, or even accurate maps. Now, that's an adventure!

MAIN IDEA The search for a western route to Asia during the late 15th and early 16th centuries opened the Americas to European settlement.

The exact location where Christopher Columbus and his crew landed in October 1492 remains a mystery, but this sandy beach on the island of Samana Cay in the Bahamas might be one possibility. Scientists used Columbus's navigation log with computer modeling to determine his journey.

COLUMBUS SETS SAIL

In the 1440s, Portugal established trade on the West African coast. Seeing the success of the Portuguese, merchants from other countries also tried to participate. However, Pope Nicholas V gave Portugal sole possession of the African and Indian coasts in 1455.

King Ferdinand and **Queen Isabella** of Spain were determined to continue trading despite the pope's decree. They found a strong willed and obsessed navigator to search for a western route to Asia. **Christopher Columbus** gladly accepted the challenge for the Spanish monarchs. In October 1492, Columbus and his fleet of ships arrived in the Bahamas. As he traveled from island to island, he believed—incorrectly, of course—that he was exploring islands south of China. He encountered people called the **Taino** (TIE-noh) and received gold in return for his goods. Leaving a few men behind, Columbus set out for home in January 1493. When he returned a year later, he discovered that the Taino had killed all his crew after his men had abused and badly harmed them. The men's actions were the start of the mistreatment of Native Americans that would last for centuries.

Ferdinand and Isabella petitioned Pope Alexander VI to allow them to colonize the lands Columbus claimed for Spain. Spain's economy was based on **mercantilism**, a system in which countries kept the sole right to trade with their colonies. Under this system, more colonies equaled more wealth—and power.

In 1494, the **Treaty of Tordesillas** established a boundary—called the **Line of Demarcation**—that passed vertically through the Atlantic and present-day Brazil. The boundary gave Portugal a portion of South America to colonize, control of the sea routes around Africa, and control of the Atlantic slave trade. Spain received permission to colonize all of the land west of the line.

Both Portugal and Spain also sent **missionaries**, or people who travel to other places to spread their own religion, to these new lands. The two countries wanted to convert the people who lived there to Christianity.

EXPLORING NEW LANDS

As Europeans continued exploring lands in the Western Hemisphere, they realized that Columbus had not reached Asia. In 1499 and 1501, the Italian captain **Amerigo Vespucci** (uh-MEHR-ih-goh veh-SPOO-chee) made two voyages—one for Spain and one for Portugal. His explorations revealed that South America was a huge landmass, which he later named **Mundus Novus**, meaning "New World" in Latin. Of course, the land was only new to the Europeans; Native Americans had already been living there for centuries. Vespucci's explorations inspired a German cartographer to name the continents *America*, after Vespucci's given name, *Amerigo.*

In 1513, Vasco Núñez Balboa led explorers across the Isthmus of Panama, and they became the first Europeans to see the eastern rim of the Pacific Ocean. Balboa claimed everything he saw for Spain.

Six years later, Ferdinand Magellan departed Spain with five ships to sail around South America and on to Asia. But the Pacific Ocean was much wider than the navigator expected. By the time the ships reached the island of Guam, the sailors were near starvation. After inhabitants killed Magellan, another sailor, Sebastian del Cano, took command of the one remaining ship. He returned to Spain after a three-year voyage, completing the first navigation around the world.

The Controversy Over Columbus Day
Was Christopher Columbus a great explorer or a ruthless invader? The question is at the heart of the controversy over Columbus Day, an annual mid-October holiday that celebrates the explorer's "achievements."

Supporters of the holiday argue that Columbus opened two continents to trade and further settlement, forever changing the world. Opponents say the holiday glorifies a man who nearly destroyed the livelihood of the native peoples of the Americas. They argue instead for celebrating Indigenous Peoples Day to remember the native peoples lost through European colonization. Various city councils have replaced Columbus Day observances with celebrations of Indigenous Peoples Day. The state of South Dakota renamed the holiday Native Americans' Day.

HISTORICAL THINKING

1. **READING CHECK** Why did the Spanish want to find a western route to Asia?

2. **DRAW CONCLUSIONS** In what ways did the Treaty of Tordesillas support Spain's mercantilist economy?

3. **IDENTIFY MAIN IDEAS AND DETAILS** How did further exploration prove that Christopher Columbus had not landed in Asia?

PLAN

Objective

Understand how the search for a western route to Asia led to the European discovery and exploration of the Americas.

Critical Thinking Skills for Lesson 1.1

- Identify Main Ideas and Details
- Monitor Comprehension
- Draw Conclusions
- Make Inferences
- Evaluate
- Form and Support Opinions

Essential Question for Chapter 2

What impact did European exploration have on the Americas? Lesson 1.1 describes how Spanish expeditions led to the European discovery of lands in the Western Hemisphere, the establishment of colonies, and mistreatment of Native Americans.

Background for the Teacher

The marriage of Ferdinand II of Aragon and Isabella I of Castile brought their two kingdoms together as a united Spain. One of their chief objectives was to "modernize" Spain, which meant enforcing Roman Catholicism as the sole religion. This effort resulted in both the Spanish Inquisition, a court dedicated to enforcing Catholicism that largely targeted the Muslim and Jewish populations, and the conquest of the Muslim kingdom of Granada. The battle for control of Granada took almost 10 years and was a tremendous financial drain. When King Ferdinand and Queen Isabella finally triumphed in 1492, the monarchs were able to direct their resources elsewhere—including the support for Christopher Columbus's expeditions.

Financial Literacy

To extend their knowledge and understanding about the concepts in this lesson, refer students to the Financial Literacy handbook.

INTRODUCE & ENGAGE

Locate Destinations

Display a world map and have students identify these locations: Spain, the Bahamas, China, India, and South America. Point out each region on the map as students identify it. Explain that Christopher Columbus hoped to travel from Spain to Asia but instead ended up in the Bahamas. **ASK:** What route must he have been trying to take to India? *(southwest across the Atlantic)* Given that Europeans at the time did not know about North and South America, does his mistake make sense? *(Yes, Columbus had no way of knowing what Asia looked like and thought he had traveled the correct distance in the right direction.)*

TEACH

Guided Discussion

1. **Make Inferences** Based on what you can infer from the text, how did European explorers and rulers view the native people who lived in the Americas? *(Answers will vary. Possible response: Students may infer that Europeans did not consider the native people to have rights to the land, which is demonstrated by the fact that Europeans intended to colonize the lands even though people lived there.)*

2. **Evaluate** Was the Treaty of Tordesillas ultimately more beneficial to Spain or Portugal? Why? *(Possible responses: Some students may say that the treaty was more beneficial to Spain because Portugal largely kept the rights it already had, while Spain discovered many lands west of the Line of Demarcation. Other students might note that Portugal received control of the Atlantic slave trade, which at that time had economic potential.)*

Form and Support Opinions

Review the Columbus Day sidebar with students. **ASK:** Should celebrations of Columbus's "achievements" be stopped altogether? Students should support their responses with evidence from the reading. *(Possible responses: Yes, the celebrations should be halted because Columbus's arrival triggered the mistreatment of Native Americans. No, the celebrations should not be stopped but should include remembering the indigenous people whose land was taken and who were harmed by exploration and colonization.)*

Active Options

On Your Feet: Inside-Outside Circle Arrange students in concentric circles facing each other. Have students in the outside circle ask students in the inside circle a question about the lesson. Then have the outside circle rotate one position to the right, to create new pairs. Repeat for five questions, and then have students switch roles and continue.

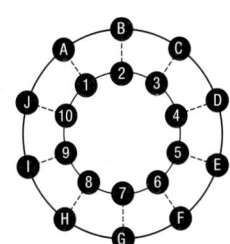

NG Learning Framework: Identify World Voyages

ATTITUDE Curiosity

KNOWLEDGE Our Human Story

Have students conduct online research to learn about other attempts explorers—past or present—have made to circumnavigate the globe. Instruct students to write a brief profile of one successful voyage. They should identify the person or people who made the trip, when they traveled, the modes of transportation used (ship, airplane, multiple modes), and how long the voyage took, as well as any interesting facts about the trip. Encourage students to share their profiles with the class.

DIFFERENTIATE

Striving Readers

Complete Sentence Starters Provide these sentence starters for students to complete after reading. You may also want to have students preview the sentence starters to set a purpose for reading.

- Spain was searching for a western route to _____. *(Asia)*

- Columbus's fleet arrived in the Bahamas in _____. *(October 1492)*

- The Spanish economy was based on a system called _____. *(mercantilism)*

- _____ gave Spain control of the lands claimed by Columbus. *(the Treaty of Tordesillas)*

- _____ explored what is now called South America and named it Mundus Novus. *(Amerigo Vespucci)*

Inclusion

Track Historical Events Pair students who are visually impaired with sighted partners. Have pairs listen to an audio recording of the text. After each paragraph, have pairs stop the recording and discuss the major events described. Students may wish to record the events on a time line or in a chronological list.

See the Chapter Planner for more strategies for differentiation.

HISTORICAL THINKING

ANSWERS

1. Spanish merchants wanted to participate in West African and Asian trade, but their routes were limited since the pope had given Portugal control of the lands to the south of Europe and east toward India.

2. Under Spain's mercantilist economy, it had the sole right to trade with its own colonies. The Treaty of Tordesillas gave Spain the right to colonize lands in the Americas, which would support Spain's economy.

3. Vespucci's explorations revealed South America to be a huge landmass that was not part of Asia. Balboa discovered the Pacific, and the Magellan-del Cano voyage revealed the vastness of the Pacific.

1.2 Christopher Columbus 1451–1506

"By prevailing over all obstacles and distractions, one may unfailingly arrive at his chosen goal or destination." —Christopher Columbus

Of course, since Christopher Columbus's chosen goal was Asia, he didn't actually arrive at his destination. He got distracted by North America, which he confused with India. And Columbus didn't know that a group of Vikings led by Leif Eriksson got to North America more than 500 years before him. Still, in a very real sense, Columbus didn't fail at all. His discoveries and the impact they had were far greater than the route he set out to find.

EXPLORATION OBSESSION

Like many boys born in the coastal city of Genoa, Italy, in the 1400s, young Christopher Columbus sought his fortune on the sea. He first set sail in 1465, when he was just a teenager. About 10 years later, he was on a ship bound for the Mediterranean when the vessel was sunk by pirates. Luckily, Columbus was able to cling to a bit of wreckage from the ship and swim to shore.

With perhaps even greater luck, he ended up in Lisbon, Portugal, where the exploration craze was at its height. There, Columbus studied navigation, cartography (mapmaking), and astronomy, and became obsessed with finding a westward route to Asia. He also read accounts of the riches of the East and decided he would try to bring these precious items back to Europe.

Hero or villain? The debate over Columbus's legacy has raged, particularly over the last several decades. Whether he's seen as the discoverer of the New World or the destroyer of native peoples, the fact is that Columbus's voyages opened up the world. Our global society wouldn't exist without him.

Columbus planned his journey to Asia based on the misinformation that most Europeans of the time accepted as fact—including an underestimation of Earth's circumference. Based on what he thought he knew, Columbus calculated the distance from Portugal to Japan and determined that the seagoing vessels of the day could handle it. Plan in hand, he looked for a sponsor to fund his journey. He finally found his backers in King Ferdinand and Queen Isabella of Spain.

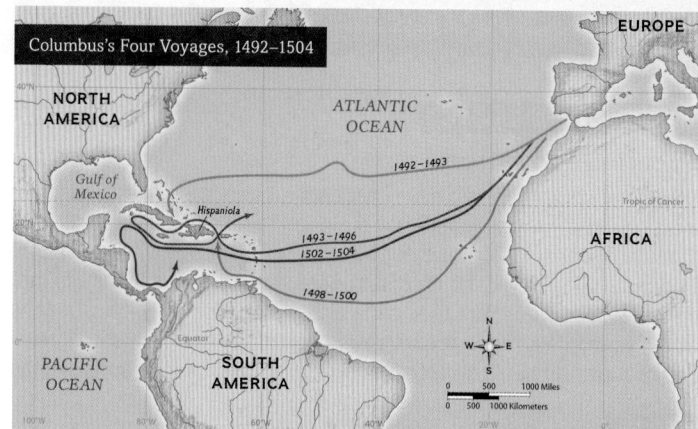

Columbus's Four Voyages, 1492–1504

EUROPE
NORTH AMERICA
ATLANTIC OCEAN
1492–1493
Gulf of Mexico
Hispaniola
1493–1496
1502–1504
AFRICA
Tropic of Cancer
1498–1500
PACIFIC OCEAN
SOUTH AMERICA
0   500   1000 Miles
0   500   1000 Kilometers

Portraits of Columbus

These three portraits of Columbus are very different because no one really knows what he looked like. But his contemporaries described him as a tall man with blond or red hair and beard and blue eyes.

VOYAGES TO THE "NEW WORLD"

On October 8, 1492, as Columbus neared the island he would call San Salvador, he declared "the air soft as that of Seville [a city in Spain] in April, and so fragrant that it was delicious to breathe it." It must have seemed a promising beginning, but his voyages did not turn out the way he hoped.

On the first voyage, he established a settlement on the island of Hispaniola. On the second voyage, he discovered the settlement had been destroyed. He left his two brothers in charge and then returned on his third voyage to find the colonists in revolt. The situation got so bad that a new governor was sent to the island, and Columbus was brought back to Spain in chains. Ferdinand and Isabella eventually pardoned him and even funded his fourth voyage. But he returned from this final trip empty-handed.

Columbus died a few years later, still believing he had found a route to Asia. No matter, though. While he hadn't discovered the riches he dreamed of, he had blazed a trail from Europe to what came to be known as the West Indies. He had opened up a "new world" to exploration and colonization and changed the course of history.

HISTORICAL THINKING

1. **READING CHECK** How did Columbus plan to sail to Asia?

2. **ANALYZE CAUSE AND EFFECT** What happened as a result of Columbus's voyages?

3. **MAKE INFERENCES** What qualities do you think Columbus must have possessed to plan and carry out his voyages?

PLAN

Objective

Learn about Christopher Columbus's path to becoming an explorer and the effects of his expeditions to the Americas.

Critical Thinking Skills for Lesson 1.2

- Identify Main Ideas and Details
- Monitor Comprehension
- Analyze Cause and Effect
- Make Inferences
- Summarize
- Draw Conclusions

Essential Question for Chapter 2

What impact did European exploration have on the Americas? Lesson 1.2 discusses Christopher Columbus's youth, his four voyages to the "New World," and his misconceptions about what he found there.

Background for the Teacher

Columbus made a number of critical errors in planning his journey—although not, as some have thought, the error of assuming the world was flat. He estimated the distance across the Atlantic Ocean based on the length of the route to Asia traveling east. Unfortunately, he chose an incorrect measurement of that distance—one that suggested a far longer route. The mile unit in the 15th century was not an absolute. Columbus may have calculated coastal miles and nautical miles differently. One agreed-upon conclusion is that his calculations fell short of the actual distance and direction to Asia. By mere coincidence, the islands of the Bahamas are located approximately where Columbus expected to find Japan (Cipango).

History Notebook

Encourage students to complete the American Voices page for Chapter 2 in their History Notebooks as they read.

INTRODUCE & ENGAGE

Preview with Visuals

Point out the multiple portraits of Christopher Columbus on this spread, including the large portrait. Ensure that students have read the caption explaining that nobody knows what Columbus actually looked like, apart from a few very general details. **ASK:** How are the portraits similar or different? How does your impression of Columbus change as you view each portrait? *(Answers will vary. Students may point out that the portraits show Columbus in different clothing and hairstyles and possibly at different ages. The large portrait gives the impression of an older, serious man. The center and right portraits show a younger, more stylish, perhaps more adventurous person.)*

TEACH

Guided Discussion

1. **Summarize** How did Christopher Columbus become an explorer? *(Columbus first set sail as a teenager, and after he survived a pirate attack, his career developed in Portugal. Here he studied skills needed for exploration, such as mapmaking, navigation, and astronomy. His confidence and skill, and the support of others, helped him to succeed.)*

2. **Draw Conclusions** Why did Columbus continue expeditions to the New World, despite the difficulties he faced? Have students support their responses with evidence from the text. *(Columbus believed that he had found Asia and that he would eventually bring incredible riches back to Spain.)*

American Voices

   Much of what we know about Christopher Columbus is derived from his journals and the letters he wrote to his patrons. These documents provide vivid descriptions of the people and places Columbus encountered in the Americas. In one letter, Columbus writes, "All these islands are very beautiful, and of quite different shapes; easy to be traversed, and full of the greatest variety of trees reaching to the stars. The convenience of the harbors in this island, and the excellence of the rivers . . . surpass human belief, unless one should see them." He tells of peaceful encounters with "well formed" and "intelligent" inhabitants of these new lands—and mentions that weapons "are entirely unknown to them." Thus, they could be more easily conquered and "converted to our Holy Faith by love than by force."

Active Options

On Your Feet: Three-Step Interview Have students work in pairs and discuss the quotation from Christopher Columbus that opens the lesson. Ask students to consider the following: What does this quotation suggest about Columbus's personality? Prompt students to interview each other using more detailed or wide-ranging questions about the quotation. For example: What values does he consider important? Do you agree with him? Why or why not? How does this quotation reflect values important in the United States today? Once students have completed their interviews, have them share the information they learned from their partners with the class.

NG Learning Framework: Create a Technology Chart

`SKILL` Collaboration

`KNOWLEDGE` New Frontiers

Have students do research to learn more about the technologies that allowed European explorers during the 15th and 16th centuries to go farther and faster than their predecessors. Divide the class into three groups, and assign each group a topic related to technology in the Age of Exploration: ship design, navigation, or mapmaking. When groups have completed their research, have them share their findings. Working with the class, record their responses to create a chart about the technology used in the Age of Exploration.

DIFFERENTIATE

English Language Learners

Ask and Answer Questions Pair students at the **Emerging** level with English-proficient students and have them read the lesson together. After each paragraph, have students pause and ask one another *who, what, where, when,* or *why* questions about the text they have just read. Students may wish to use a 5Ws Chart.

Who?
What?
Where?
When?
Why?

Pre-AP

Research Columbus's Journals Have students conduct online research on the journals Columbus wrote documenting his expeditions. Ask them to report to the class about one of the following:

- the regions Columbus and his crew explored on each expedition
- how long the cross-ocean voyages took and what Columbus and his crew discovered
- Columbus's impressions of the people he encountered

See the Chapter Planner for more strategies for differentiation.

HISTORICAL THINKING

ANSWERS

1. Columbus planned to sail west from Portugal to Japan, based on calculations he made using inaccurate data about the size of Earth.

2. Columbus's voyages opened the "New World" to exploration and colonization.

3. Answers will vary. Possible responses: Columbus had a background in navigation, mapmaking, and astronomy. He possessed confidence in his skills and was courageous and optimistic. He also was determined, disciplined, and able to manage hardships.

1.3 Conquering the Aztec and Inca

The Aztec and Inca were more curious than worried when Spanish soldiers first arrived on horseback. Little did they know that Spanish invaders would enlist allies and topple both empires.

MAIN IDEA A variety of factors helped Spanish soldiers and adventurers conquer the Aztec and Inca empires in the 16th century.

INVADING MEXICO

For several decades, the Spanish had little interference from other Europeans in exploring and colonizing the Americas. **Conquistadors** (kon-KEE-stuh-dohrz), or Spanish soldiers and adventurers, conquered the native tribes of many Caribbean islands, claiming the lands for Spain. They then moved through present-day Mexico and Central America. By 1543, Spanish settlements extended south to Chile, north to present-day Florida, and west to California.

Hernán Cortés was one of the most successful conquistadors. In 1519, he launched an expedition into the vast Aztec Empire in Mexico. As Cortés and his small Spanish force moved toward the Aztec capital of Tenochtitlán (tay-nohch-teet-LAHN), they recruited allies from some Native American tribes that were dissatisfied with

The Museum of Fine Arts, Houston

The Inca were spectacular artisans. This figure, fashioned from silver, copper, shell, and polished stone, dates from between 1200 and 1532. The Spanish melted most such figures to reuse the precious metals.

Aztec rule. They seized the Aztec emperor **Moctezuma** (mahk-tuh-ZOO-muh), who believed the light-skinned, bearded Spaniards signaled the return of the Aztec god Quetzalcoatl (kwet-sul-kuh-WAH-tuhl). Some historians think this is one reason Cortés was able to capture Moctezuma.

Controlling Tenochtitlán proved more difficult. When the Spanish outlawed human sacrifice—an important part of Aztec religion—and demanded more gold, the Aztec rebelled. They forced the Spanish and their allies to retreat, killing many in the process. After Cortés regrouped, he returned in May 1521 with more Spanish troops and allies and laid siege to Tenochtitlán.

The Aztec fought bravely, even though they were already weakened by a deadly outbreak of a disease the Spanish carried, called **smallpox**. In the end, though, the Spanish destroyed the city of Tenochtitlán. Over time, the Spanish colonizers spread their culture throughout Mexico. In fact, the Spanish built Mexico City on the ruins of Tenochtitlán.

CRITICAL VIEWING In the late 1600s, an unknown artist depicted the conquest of Tenochtitlán. Based on details you notice in the painting, what advantages did the Spanish and the Aztec each have as they faced each other in battle?

PIZARRO'S QUEST FOR GOLD

When the Spanish arrived in the Americas, the Inca already controlled a powerful empire stretching along the Andes Mountains in South America. Stories of Inca gold and silver interested the Spanish conquistador **Francisco Pizarro**. So in the 1530s, with around 180 men and a small number of horses, Pizarro set out from Panama to conquer the Inca.

In 1532, the Inca emperor **Atahualpa** invited Pizarro and his men to a meeting in the northern part of present-day Peru. At the meeting, Atahualpa and Pizarro exchanged gifts to show goodwill toward each other. Atahualpa was confident that the presence of his 6,000 warriors would discourage Pizarro from attacking. But the emperor was wrong.

Pizarro's men opened fire on the mostly unarmed Inca and took Atahualpa prisoner. Atahualpa offered Pizarro gold and silver, which Pizarro took. Then he had Atahualpa killed. By 1537, the Spanish had crushed Inca opposition.

Several factors helped the Spanish conquer the Aztec and the Inca. Smallpox and other European diseases killed or weakened many Aztec, Inca, and Native Americans. The Spanish were masterful at forming alliances with Native American groups, especially with tribes opposing the Aztec. Aztec and Inca weapons were no match for the guns and swift horses of the Spanish. Finally, the Spanish used violence and forced labor to control Native American populations and put down revolts.

HISTORICAL THINKING

1. **READING CHECK** What was the goal of the Spanish conquistadors?

2. **ANALYZE CAUSE AND EFFECT** What factors helped the Spanish defeat the Aztec and Inca?

3. **DRAW CONCLUSIONS** What might have led Aztec and Inca leaders to underestimate the Spanish invaders?

PLAN

Objective

Analyze the factors that helped Spanish explorers conquer the Aztec and Inca empires.

Critical Thinking Skills for Lesson 1.3

- Identify Main Ideas and Details
- Monitor Comprehension
- Analyze Cause and Effect
- Draw Conclusions
- Compare and Contrast

Essential Question for Chapter 2

What impact did European exploration have on the Americas? Relatively small numbers of Spanish conquistadors defeated the powerful Aztec and Inca empires, overwhelmingly changing the power structures in many parts of the Americas. Lesson 1.3 explains the various reasons the conquistadors were able to overcome these two mighty empires.

Background for the Teacher

Before conquering the Aztec, explorer Diego Velásquez—along with Hernán Cortés—had conquered Cuba. Both men had powerful positions in the settlement there, and when the opportunity arose to send an expedition to conquer the inhabitants of present-day Mexico, Velásquez put Cortés in charge. Before long, however, Velásquez decided to replace him. Cortés left Cuba before he could do so. When Cortés arrived on the mainland, he cut ties with Velásquez entirely. Concerned that his soldiers might mutiny, Cortés did the unthinkable. He sank his own fleet, making it impossible for his army to turn back.

History Notebook

Encourage students to complete the American Gallery page for Chapter 2 in their History Notebooks as they read.

INTRODUCE & ENGAGE

Brainstorm a List

Have students brainstorm qualities that might help an empire extend its power or protect itself from enemies. If necessary, prompt them to consider such issues as population size, military strength, wealth, negotiating ability, and alliances. Record their responses. **ASK:** Which qualities might help a smaller fighting force overcome a larger force? *(Answers will vary. Students might suggest that superior weaponry or alliances between smaller groups might work to overcome a larger force.)* Explain that in this lesson, students will learn about what happened when the Spanish explorers encountered the Aztec and Inca empires.

TEACH

Guided Discussion

1. **Compare and Contrast** How were the conquests of the Aztec and the Inca similar and different? *(The conquest of the Aztec Empire involved multiple attempts and the cooperation of Native American tribes. The conquest of the Inca involved a single attempt. Both conquests began with capturing the ruler of the empire; both involved a long process of controlling the populations.)*

2. **Draw Conclusions** Which factor do you think had the biggest impact on the Spanish conquest of the Inca and Aztec, and why? *(Answers will vary. Possible response: Europeans' introduction of diseases such as smallpox decimated Inca and Aztec populations and left the empires weak.)*

🏛 Virtual Museum Visit

The collections at the Museum of Fine Arts in Houston include more than 65,000 items, ranging from paintings and sculptures to jewelry, furniture, and even wallpaper. Access the museum's website and find the collection of Inca metalwork. Point out the various figures and ask students to identify their similarities and differences. Then ask student groups to explore the site on their own and select three items to study. Have groups discuss what the different works suggest about Inca life. When groups are finished, have them share their selections with the class.

Active Options

On Your Feet: Think, Pair, Share Give students a few minutes to think about these questions: Based on Moctezuma's beliefs about the Spaniards, how do you think he treated them on their arrival? How might this attitude have contributed to his defeat? Then have students choose partners and talk about the questions for five minutes. Finally, encourage individual students to share their ideas with the class.

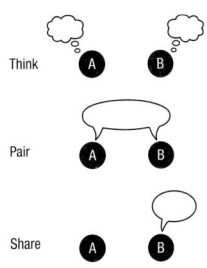

Think   A   B

Pair   A   B

Share   A   B

AMERICAN GALLERY
ONLINE

The Inca Empire Invite students to explore the American Gallery. Have them select one of the items and do additional research to learn more about it. Ask questions that will inspire additional inquiry about the chosen gallery item. Here are some examples: What purpose does the item serve? Where and when was it created, and by whom? Why was it created? What is it made of? Why does it belong in this lesson? What else would you like to know about it?

DIFFERENTIATE

Striving Readers

Preview the Text Help students preview Lesson 1.3. Point out the text features, such as the title, main idea statement, and subheadings. Then have students examine the images and image captions. **ASK:** Based on these features, what do you expect this lesson to be about? *(how the Spanish adventurers and soldiers managed to conquer the Aztec and Inca empires)* **ASK:** Who and what do you think the important people and places in this lesson will be? *(the Aztec and Inca, Mexico, Pizarro)*

Gifted & Talented

Write Journal Entries Invite students to imagine that they are Inca soldiers at the time of Atahualpa's meeting with Pizarro. Instruct them to write two journal entries, one from just before the meeting and one from after the attack. In the entries, have students consider the following:

- How might you have felt upon first meeting European explorers?
- How might you have felt about Atahualpa's invitation to the Spanish?
- How might you have felt in the aftermath of Pizarro's attack?

See the Chapter Planner for more strategies for differentiation.

HISTORICAL THINKING

ANSWERS

1. The goal was to conquer lands in the Americas and claim them for Spain.

2. The factors that helped the Spanish conquer the Aztec and Inca were the introduction of European diseases, the creation of Native American alliances, superior military technology and horses, and ruthless treatment of Native Americans.

3. Answers will vary. Possible response: Both Cortés and Pizarro led small groups of men, while the Aztec and Inca empires had large armies.

CRITICAL VIEWING Answers will vary. Possible response: The Aztec are shown hiding in the water or fighting from small, light boats, which suggests they had the advantage of knowing the area and moving quickly. However, the Spanish are displayed having the advantage of armor, horses, and powerful ships.

1.4 Conquistadors in the North

When conquistadors eager for riches, power, and fame heard news of Cortés's and Pizarro's triumphs, they may have thought to themselves, "How hard could it be?" As it turned out, it was pretty hard.

MAIN IDEA Conquistadors exploring North America in the 1540s were less successful than Cortés and Pizarro.

EXPLORERS REACH FLORIDA

In their search for wealth and new lands, the Spanish did not limit their American explorations to Mesoamerica and South America. Soon they set their sights northward. **Álvar Núñez** (NOO-nyez) **Cabeza de Vaca** was part of an expedition that sailed from Spain in 1527 aiming to claim North America for the king. After he and his fellow voyagers landed on the west coast of present-day Florida, they marched north through insect- and snake-infested swamps. They kidnapped a Native American chief, which triggered an attack from his people. They fled on hastily built rafts, quickly became lost in the Gulf of Mexico, and were captured by Native Americans after a hurricane washed them up on an island near the western shore of the Gulf.

After befriending and living with their captors for several years, de Vaca and three others escaped. They traveled west, passing through southwestern deserts all the way to the Gulf of California. Finally, they encountered other Spaniards near the Pacific coast of Mexico in 1536. De Vaca later commented that on that day the men were "dumbfounded at the sight of me, strangely dressed and in the company of Indians." In his tales, de Vaca mentioned the possibility of riches to the north, which inspired more explorers to try their luck. He returned to Spain the next year and became a governor and judge, standing up for better treatment of Native Americans.

In 1539, **Hernando de Soto**, the governor of Cuba, launched a three-year expedition through the southeast part of North America. His expedition also landed on the west coast of Florida and then trekked northward on foot. The group traveled through the Southeast to the Tennessee River Valley and then turned south toward the Gulf of Mexico, destroying Native American communities, stealing from them, and enslaving or killing people who resisted them. De Soto caught a fever and died in 1542, and the survivors of the expedition returned to Spain.

THE SEARCH FOR GOLDEN CITIES

As the Spanish explored and conquered new lands in the Americas, they set up a system to rule these faraway places. **Viceroys** were colonial leaders who were appointed by the king. Viceroys governed **viceroyalties**, or territories in the Americas "owned" by Spain.

In 1540, the viceroy of one of these territories, **New Spain,** ordered **Francisco Vásquez de Coronado** to lead an expedition of 336 Spaniards and nearly 1,000 Native Americans through the American Southwest. The expedition was to search for the golden cities described in Native American legends.

Conquistador Spur
This sparkling spur is similar to those worn by Spanish explorers on their boots to control their horses. It is an early version of the types of spurs some American cowboys wear today.

Traveling through the Southwest and the Great Plains, Coronado and his men saw and experienced many things not known to the Spanish before. They encountered the Hopi, Native Americans who lived in the Southwest. They also saw giant herds of buffalo, and some of the party stood on the rim of the Grand Canyon. But they found no gold. They returned to Mexico empty-handed.

Two years later, **Juan Rodríguez Cabrillo** (kuh-BREE-yoh) led a voyage of exploration north from Mexico along the California coast in search of a northern water route from the Pacific to the Atlantic Ocean. His expedition may have traveled as far as the Pacific Northwest before turning back south, but he never returned home. He died from injuries received in a battle with Native Americans, and his crew brought his ships back to Mexico.

None of these conquistadors found cities of gold or riches. Despite these failures, Europeans' interest in claiming land in the Americas continued. As you will learn, these interests would lead to international tensions and even war.

Conquistador Routes, 1527–1542

- Álvar Núñez Cabeza de Vaca
- Hernando de Soto
- Francisco Vásquez de Coronado
- Juan Rodríguez Cabrillo

Cities of Gold

De Soto, de Vaca, Coronado, and Cabrillo explored a great deal of southern North America. De Soto hunted the southeastern forests of North America for Cofitachiqui (koh-FEE-tah-CHEE-kee), a rich Native American city. De Vaca and his shipmates searched the Southwest looking for a kingdom called Cíbola (SEE-bow-lah). Coronado also searched for Cíbola in lands farther north on the southern Great Plains. Cabrillo hoped to find wealthy civilizations as he sailed along the California coast. In the end, none of these explorers found what they were looking for because the rumored cities of gold had never existed.

HISTORICAL THINKING

1. **READING CHECK** Why weren't Spanish explorations successful in North America?

2. **ANALYZE CAUSE AND EFFECT** What social impact did conquistadors have on native populations of the American Southwest and Southeast?

3. **INTERPRET MAPS** Look at the routes of the conquistadors on the map. What is one common feature of each of these expeditions?

PLAN

Objective
Describe the routes taken and setbacks faced by conquistadors in North America.

Critical Thinking Skills for Lesson 1.4
- Identify Main Ideas and Details
- Monitor Comprehension
- Analyze Cause and Effect
- Interpret Maps
- Identify
- Draw Conclusions
- Make Inferences

Essential Question for Chapter 2
What impact did European exploration have on the Americas? In the mid-1500s, European nations expanded their explorations of the Americas. Lesson 1.4 traces the routes of some of the Spanish expeditions, which failed to find riches but strengthened Spain's claims in North America.

Background for the Teacher
Coronado's soldiers carried a wide variety of armor and equipment. The conquistadors were soldiers, but they were not an army in the way we often think of armies today. They did not wear uniforms, apart from very basic items, such as helmets. Soldiers wore and carried whatever they could find. Since they paid for their own equipment, many settled for out-of-date equipment. Wealthier soldiers might wear full suits of metal armor, while poorer soldiers wore partial armor, chain mail, or thick leather to protect themselves against enemy weapons. The leaders of the expedition were best equipped. The equipment list from one of Coronado's expeditions mentions that Coronado brought with him four suits of armor—for his horses.

Word Web

Have students use a Word Web to brainstorm the words and phrases that come to mind when they hear the word *conquistador*. Then have students share their associations with the class and discuss. Allow time at the end of the lesson for students to add new associations to their webs.

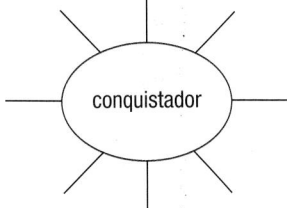

conquistador

Guided Discussion

1. **Identify** What setbacks did Alvar Nuñez Cabeza de Vaca and his crew encounter on his expedition? *(They were attacked after kidnapping a Native American chief. They fled on rafts but got lost in the Gulf of Mexico. Then they encountered a hurricane. After they washed up onshore, Native Americans captured them.)*

2. **Draw Conclusions** What do the Spanish expeditions into North America in the 1500s tell you about Spain's goals for the "New World"? *(Possible response: The searches for "cities of gold" suggest that Spain was mostly interested in quick, tremendous wealth.)*

Make Inferences

Discuss with students the explorers' experiences with Native Americans they encountered on their routes. **ASK:** How did Alvar Nuñez Cabeza de Vaca's experiences as a captive change his opinions about Native Americans? Make sure students support their response with evidence from the text. *(Answers will vary. Possible response: Prior to his capture, de Vaca was willing to help kidnap a Native American chief. After he returned to Spain, de Vaca became a governor and a judge and fought for better treatment of Native Americans. This suggests that his experience may have taught him to be sympathetic to or respect Native Americans.)*

Active Options

On Your Feet: Rotating Discussion Have students form a large circle, facing inward. Ask a question about the lesson and then toss a beanbag to a student, who then must answer the question. After answering the question, the student tosses the beanbag to another student, who may choose to add information to the first answer or ask another question. Continue until all students have either asked or answered a question. If students become stuck on a question, tell them they may toss the beanbag to you, and provide clarification.

NG Learning Framework: Map New Encounters

ATTITUDE Curiosity

KNOWLEDGE Our Human Story

Have students choose one of the exploration routes shown on the map in this lesson and trace it onto a blank map of North America (or trace the lesson map onto their own paper). Encourage students to use lessons in Chapter 1 and other resources to identify the various Native American groups the conquistadors might have encountered during their journeys and label their locations along the explorers' routes. After they have finished, have students compare and contrast their maps with classmates.

English Language Learners

Summarize Lesson 1.4 has eight paragraphs. Have students work in pairs or small groups, with students at the **Emerging** level working with students at the **Expanding** or **Bridging** level. Assign each pair or group one paragraph to read. Then each group should summarize the paragraph in one or two sentences for the class.

Pre-AP

Research a Conquistador Have students choose and research one of the conquistadors from Lesson 1.4. Ask students to create a short presentation covering the chosen conquistador's life, expeditions, patrons or supporters, and death. Students may wish to illustrate their presentations with relevant maps, images, or time lines.

See the Chapter Planner for more strategies for differentiation.

ANSWERS

1. Many conquistadors searched for gold but did not find it. Cabrillo and de Soto died while on expedition. De Vaca was captured and lived with his captors for some time.

2. The conquistadors' expeditions were devastating to many Native American communities. They brought disease, stole things, and enslaved and killed many. De Vaca, however, eventually befriended the Native Americans with whom he lived.

3. Answers will vary. Possible response: All the routes suggest that the conquistadors wandered in search of riches rather than having specific destinations. Each expedition covered a different territory.

2.1 Competing Claims

You're probably used to friendly competitions in your classroom or among friends. For European countries in the 1500s, however, intense competition for land and resources in North America led to some not-so-friendly conflicts.

MAIN IDEA Struggles arose in Europe when other countries challenged the claims Spain and Portugal had made in the Americas.

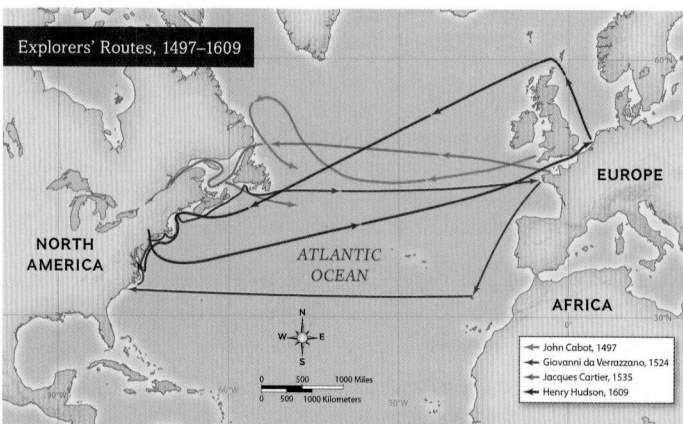

Explorers' Routes, 1497–1609

NORTH AMERICA

ATLANTIC OCEAN

EUROPE

AFRICA

0   500   1000 Miles
0   500   1000 Kilometers

→ John Cabot, 1497
→ Giovanni da Verrazzano, 1524
→ Jacques Cartier, 1535
→ Henry Hudson, 1609

THE NORTHWEST PASSAGE

European kings and queens hoped to find a water route to Asia through the Western Hemisphere. Several monarchs sent explorers to find such a route, or a **Northwest Passage**. In 1497, King Henry VII of England commissioned the Italian navigator **John Cabot**. Cabot left the harbor at Bristol, England, and sailed to Newfoundland, in present-day Canada, where he claimed land for the king. France sent another Italian, **Giovanni da Verrazzano**, to the Americas in January 1524. His ship *La Dauphine* landed near Cape Fear, North Carolina, and continued north along the coast to Newfoundland.

Ten years later, French seafarer **Jacques Cartier** explored the coast of Canada and the St. Lawrence River three different times. His interactions with the Native Americans there led to the name *Canada*. The name is derived from the Huron-Iroquois word *kanata*, meaning "village or settlement."

After voyaging to the Americas twice for England, an explorer named **Henry Hudson** made his final trip in 1609—this time for the Dutch in the Netherlands. Hudson sailed along the Atlantic coast after failing to navigate the Arctic Ocean. Today, a river, a strait, and a bay carry his name.

Just as the conquistadors who searched for golden cities failed, none of these explorers found what they were looking for: a western route to Asia. However, the knowledge gained from these explorations did prove useful. It aided the countries when they later laid claim to land in North America.

TENSIONS GROW

While explorers searched for a Northwest Passage, religious and political unrest grew in Europe. The Spanish were already angry with the French and English for claiming lands in the New World. Tensions increased when France and England challenged Catholicism, the dominant faith in Spain.

As you have read, the Reformation began in 1517 when a German monk named Martin Luther accused the Catholic Church of corruption. At the time, Catholic priests were selling indulgences, which forgave sins in exchange for money. In response, Luther put together a document called the 95 Theses, which pointed out the Church's hypocritical and greedy practices. Luther's teachings divided European Christians, as some common people and rulers alike adopted his Protestant beliefs. Some of Luther's followers formed the branch of Protestantism that now bears his name: Lutheranism. The Catholic Church officially excluded him from Church rituals and membership. In addition, the Catholic Church **persecuted**, or punished, all followers of Protestantism.

One Protestant group, the French Huguenots, looked to the Americas for refuge. They tried settling in Brazil and South Carolina before founding a colony near St. Augustine, Florida, around 1564. This enraged Spain's **King Philip II**, but not only because he was Catholic. The Huguenots had chosen South Carolina with the intention of attacking Spanish ships carrying silver. It was not enough that they were **heretics**, or people who held beliefs different from teachings of the Catholic Church. Philip perceived them as a menace. The king sent General Pedro Menéndez de Avilés to remove the Huguenot colony. After a brief encounter at sea, Menéndez captured the French settlement at Fort Caroline. Most of the men who refused to return to Catholicism were killed.

The Cleveland Museum of Art, Cleveland

Looking at this gold, enamel, and citrine cameo, it may be hard to believe that King Philip II was actually in financial trouble during his reign. When he took the throne in 1556, he assumed the kingdom's debt. The debt only grew as Philip waged war after war and built a lavish palace. Eventually, Philip's spending would be a factor in the fall of the Spanish Empire.

King Philip II of Spain

HISTORICAL THINKING

1. **READING CHECK** What was Spain's response to the claims of other European countries in North America?

2. **INTERPRET MAPS** Based on the sea routes shown on the map, which countries were likely competing over land claims in the Western Hemisphere?

3. **DRAW CONCLUSIONS** How did the Protestant Reformation influence European relations in the Americas?

European Exploration of the Americas **61**

Objective

Analyze why European countries challenged Spanish and Portuguese dominance in the Americas.

Critical Thinking Skills for Lesson 2.1

- Identify Main Ideas and Details
- Monitor Comprehension
- Interpret Maps
- Draw Conclusions
- Make Connections
- Identify

Essential Question for Chapter 2

What impact did European exploration have on the Americas? Europeans exploring North America claimed the lands they found along the way. Lesson 2.1 discusses the social, political, and economic forces in Europe that affected exploration and colonization in the Americas.

Background for the Teacher

Although the explorers of the 16th century failed to find the Northwest Passage, later explorers were more successful. The Northwest Passage, a link between the Atlantic and Pacific oceans, runs through the Arctic Archipelago, a group of islands located in the Arctic Ocean in northern Canada. After hundreds of years of effort and many lost ships and crews, the first person to make it through the Northwest Passage by sea was Norway's Roald Amundsen in 1905. Earlier explorers had managed to complete the journey by traveling over land when the ice became impassable. Today, as rising temperatures make Arctic waters easier to travel, the international community continues to debate how best to use and manage the Northwest Passage and the resources found in the region.

Preview with the Map

Have students examine the map showing the explorers' routes. Encourage them to notice the differences and similarities of the routes taken by the explorers. Prompt students to consider what they already know about exploration in the Americas. Invite them to share their observations about the topics below.

- the destinations of each expedition
- which routes cover the most distance or travel the farthest into North America
- how later routes differ from earlier routes
- what each route suggests about that expedition's possible goals

TEACH

Guided Discussion

1. **Make Connections** Why was finding a Northwest Passage a logical goal for English, Dutch, and French explorers? *(Possible responses: They knew they could profit from a faster route to Asia, and Spanish explorers had shown that southern and western routes were not possible; a Northwest Passage would bypass Spanish-controlled areas of North America.)*

2. **Identify** What two reasons does the text give for Spain's conflict with the French Huguenots? *(Spain viewed them as heretics and a threat to their silver-carrying ships.)*

🏛 Virtual Museum Visit

The Cleveland Museum of Art in Cleveland, Ohio, held its Inaugural Exhibition in 1916 with a small, mostly donated or loaned collection. Today, it is home to almost 45,000 works of art. It is also home to the Ingalls Library, which keeps hundreds of thousands of volumes and slides for researchers and students. Access the museum's website and locate the carved gem portrait of Phillip II in the European Painting and Sculpture collection. Read the description of the cameo and its materials aloud, pointing out that the citrine might have come from "a newly opened source in South America." **ASK:** Why might the artist have chosen this material for a portrait of the king of Spain? *(Possible response: The artist might have wanted to reference the Spanish exploration of the Americas.)* Have students explore the site on their own and choose a work from the same time period to present to the class.

Active Options

On Your Feet: Follow the Map Divide the class into four groups and assign each group one of the exploration routes shown on the map. Explain that one side of the room will represent Europe, and the other will represent the Americas. Indicate which walls will represent north, south, east, and west. Have students study their assigned routes and plot them out using the classroom as a "map." Then have students travel their routes on foot, starting at the appropriate spot on the "European" side. As they walk, they should pay attention to which routes take longest and where they encounter other groups.

Active History: Compare European Explorers Extend the lesson by using either the PDF or Whiteboard version of the activity. These activities take a deeper look at a topic from, or related to, the lesson. Explore the activities as a class, turn them into group assignments, or even assign them individually.

Striving Readers

Expand Main Idea Statements After students have read Lesson 2.1, have them copy the lesson's Main Idea and expand it into a few sentences. If students need additional support, assist by providing sentence frames.

Main Idea: Struggles arose in Europe as more countries challenged the claims Spain and Portugal had made in the Americas.

Two other countries that claimed land were _____ *(France)* and _____. *(England)*

They hoped to find _____. *(a water route from west to east)*

Another source of conflict was _____. *(religion)*

Inclusion

Use Echo Reading Pair students so there is a proficient reader in each pair. Have the proficient reader read the Main Idea statement at the beginning of Lesson 2.1 aloud, and have the other student "echo" the statement in his or her own words.

See the Chapter Planner for more strategies for differentiation.

HISTORICAL THINKING

ANSWERS

1. The Spanish were angry about British and French claims in the New World. Spain continued its own exploration and attempted to halt by force the exploration and settlement of the French Huguenots and others.

2. The Netherlands and France competed, with Hudson overlapping Verrazzano's earlier expedition along the eastern coast of North America.

3. Protestants such as the Huguenots came to the New World to escape religious persecution. However, European conflicts followed them. The French Huguenots battled the Spanish in Florida. This resulted in the surrender of the Protestant Huguenots, and the Spanish killed those who refused to convert to Catholicism.

Defeat of the Spanish Armada

Fans of any sport love a major upset. In much the same way, when England's small but mighty fleet of ships defeated Spain in 1588, the world took notice.

MAIN IDEA Because of England's strong naval fleet, an English victory at sea challenged Spanish dominance in Europe and the Americas.

MONARCHS AND SEA DOGS

Spain had a head start on settling North America, but England started to catch up, largely because of **Queen Elizabeth I**. The Protestant queen ascended to the English throne in 1558. She saw Spain as a threat to England's independence. Her brother-in-law, Philip II of Spain, like many Catholics, wished to see Elizabeth unseated from the throne. He supported Mary, Queen of Scots, Elizabeth's Catholic cousin and the heir to the English throne. But after being implicated in a plot to take Elizabeth's life, Mary was arrested, tried, and beheaded for conspiracy.

Both Philip and Elizabeth had powerful navies. Spain's fleet was made up of large, full-rigged sailing ships called **galleons**, mainly used to transport goods from the Americas. They were heavily armed, but their cannons weren't secured to the deck, which made these large weapons difficult to reload and discharge.

By contrast, English ships were nimble. They carried fewer goods and soldiers, but their mounted artillery was more quickly discharged. English ships were also fast, and their sailors, the **Sea Dogs**, appreciated this quality.

Perhaps the most famous of these sailors was Francis Drake. Drake and other Sea Dogs were **privateers**, or seafarers licensed by a monarch to attack enemy ships. Drake sailed the world stealing treasure from Spanish ports and ships. He and his crew were the first Englishmen to **circumnavigate**, or sail around, the globe.

ENGLISH VICTORY

Under the leadership of Elizabeth I, England challenged Spain's claims to the Western Hemisphere. England supported the Dutch revolt against Philip II. When part of the Netherlands declared its independence from Spain and became the United Provinces in 1585, Elizabeth sent aid there. In doing so, she was essentially declaring war on Spain.

King Philip sent his "invincible" navy to conquer England in May 1588. The **Spanish Armada** was a fleet of about 130 warships. Knowing their vessels were slower and had fewer and smaller cannons than the English, the Spanish captains hoped to take advantage of their own greater numbers. Their plan was to have their men board the enemy ships and defeat the English in hand-to-hand combat.

Stormy weather delayed the armada. This gave English admiral Charles Howard, commander of England's fleet, a chance to join up with Francis Drake's advance force. England's fleet had smaller ships and fewer soldiers, but its superior speed and artillery demolished the Spanish. Many thousands of Spanish men were killed, while England lost several hundred. With only 60 ships remaining, the Spanish returned home in shame.

The defeat of the Spanish Armada was a blow to Spain's position as the dominant world power in both Europe and the New World. Through its victory, England ensured its own continued independence from foreign domination while preserving the Netherlands' United Provinces.

Spain's power weakened further as Sea Dogs continued to harass Spanish vessels and ports. At the same time, Protestant sects in Europe and later in the New World would continue to challenge the supremacy of Spain and the pope on colonization and commerce. Spain found itself on the defensive.

Queen Elizabeth I
In a society where women rarely held any political authority, Elizabeth ruled as a popular, strong, and capable monarch. During the 45 years of her reign, England prospered and became one of the most powerful nations in history. In this portrait, painted around 1588, the English fleet appears behind Elizabeth, likely an acknowledgment of England's increasing naval power.

HISTORICAL THINKING

1. **READING CHECK** What political changes did England's defeat of the Spanish Armada bring to Europe?

2. **COMPARE AND CONTRAST** What were the different advantages and disadvantages of the Spanish and English ships?

3. **DRAW CONCLUSIONS** How did the Spanish captains' strategy to combat the English fleet lead to their own defeat?

CRITICAL VIEWING French artist Philippe-Jacques de Loutherbourg painted *Defeat of the Spanish Armada, 8 August 1588* in 1796. How does the artist use color to show the drama of the battle?

PLAN

Objective

Learn how the defeat of the Spanish upset the balance of power in Europe and the Americas.

Critical Thinking Skills for Lesson 2.2

- Identify Main Ideas and Details
- Monitor Comprehension
- Compare and Contrast
- Draw Conclusions
- Summarize
- Analyze Visuals

Essential Question for Chapter 2

What impact did European exploration have on the Americas? Lesson 2.2 describes how the English defeat of the Spanish Armada and challenges from colonial Protestants weakened Spain's position on commerce and trade.

Background for the Teacher

When Elizabeth I came to power in 1558, England had been embroiled in a conflict over religion for more than 20 years. The new Protestant ruler faced opposition both at home and abroad. This atmosphere of danger was nothing new to the young queen. Her father, Henry VIII, had ordered her mother, Anne Boleyn, beheaded when Elizabeth was only two years old. After Henry's death in 1547, his 10-year-old son, Edward VI, took over the throne. When Edward died in 1553, Mary I, Elizabeth's older half sister, became queen. Mary was a devout Catholic who was married to King Philip II of Spain. When Protestants rebelled against her strict Catholic reign, Mary had Elizabeth imprisoned in the Tower of London for two months. Later, after Mary's death, Elizabeth ascended to the throne.

Describe Surprising Upsets

Begin a class discussion about the concept of an "upset" and how it might be applied to sports, politics, or other competitions. Then have students work in small groups to brainstorm a list of famous (or not-so-famous) upsets they know about. Have each group choose one of the events and share it with the class, describing the expected outcome and the actual outcome and explaining what makes this particular event an "upset."

TEACH

Guided Discussion

1. **Draw Conclusions** Why would a monarch unofficially support privateers like the Sea Dogs? *(Privateers were considered pirates who would steal treasure from others and then share their gains with the monarch. If the monarch did not support them, he or she would not profit from the gains.)*

2. **Summarize** How were the English able to defeat the Spanish Armada? *(Bad weather delayed the Armada's arrival, giving the English extra time to prepare. Meanwhile, Admiral Charles Howard combined his fleet with Sir Francis Drake's ships. When the Armada arrived, the two English forces used their faster, better-armed ships to defeat the Spanish.)*

Analyze Visuals

Direct students' attention to the portrait of Elizabeth I and read the caption with them. **ASK:** What might the artist be trying to express about the queen in this portrait? What is significant about the background of the portrait? *(Answers will vary. Students may point out that the queen is shown in heavy jewelry and gold, signifying wealth and power, or that her expression shows calm determination. Students will likely note that there is a ship in the background of the painting, representing Elizabeth I's dominance at sea.)*

Active Options

On Your Feet: Team Word Webbing Divide students into teams of four, give each team a large piece of paper, and each team member a different colored marker. Assign each team the following questions: What error or errors did the Spanish captains make that contributed to their defeat by the English? What could they have done differently to prevent their defeat? Ask students to write words or phrases that provide a possible solution. Have students add to the part of the paper nearest them. Then signal groups to rotate the paper, and have students add to the nearest part again. When finished, tell students to compare their answers. If time permits, encourage groups to share their ideas with the class to create a class list.

NG Learning Framework: Write a Biography

ATTITUDE Curiosity

KNOWLEDGE Our Human Story

Invite students to learn more about Elizabeth I and about England under her reign. Students should consult library or online resources to research Elizabeth I as a ruler and as a member of a volatile royal family. Tell students to write a short biography of her and to include at least one visual, such as a map or painting. When students have completed their biographies, have them share their work with a partner. Encourage the pairs to compare and contrast what they wrote about this powerful queen.

DIFFERENTIATE

English Language Learners [ELD]

Identify Main Ideas and Details Pair students at the **Bridging** level with students at the **Emerging** or **Expanding** level and assign each pair a subsection of the text to read together. Tell students to make notes about the main idea and supporting details in their subsection. Then have each pair write a one- or two-sentence summary.

Gifted & Talented

Write a Social Media Profile Have groups of students work together to learn more about one of the following figures: Elizabeth I, Philip II, or Sir Francis Drake. Ask each group to create a social media profile for their chosen individual, including a summary section, several posts, and images. Invite students to share their profiles with the class. Then encourage each group to interact with another group that has chosen a different figure. Have them share messages about relevant events that the figures might have exchanged had social media been available in the late 1500s.

See the Chapter Planner for more strategies for differentiation.

HISTORICAL THINKING

ANSWERS

1. Spain's influence decreased after the defeat of the Spanish Armada. The Sea Dogs continued to steal from the Spanish galleons, and Protestant sects challenged Spanish rule.

2. The Spanish galleons were larger but slower. Their long-range cannons were more difficult to load and discharge. The English ships were smaller and more maneuverable. Their mounted artillery could be more quickly discharged and reloaded, but the ships needed to be closer to their targets.

3. The Spanish captains expected to use their greater numbers to board the English ships and defeat the English in close quarters. But the faster English ships defeated the Spanish before they could do so.

CRITICAL VIEWING Possible response: The artist uses vivid reds and orange to reflect the Spanish ships in flames and the intensity of battle. He uses grays to depict the choking smoke, with a gap of blue sky, perhaps signifying hope.

2.3 French and Dutch Colonies

If you visit a coffee shop in Burlington, Vermont, you might see a menu that has both French and English descriptions. Walk around New York City and you'll see Dutch names for streets. Different languages and names are the remnants of European exploration in the 17th century.

MAIN IDEA The French and Dutch claimed North American lands as rich sources of trade and wealth, but they had trouble establishing colonies.

OUTPOSTS IN NEW FRANCE

In 1608, explorer and cartographer **Samuel de Champlain** established a fur-trading base at a point along the St. Lawrence River that became the first permanent French settlement in North America. For two decades, Champlain explored the **watershed** lands, or the area drained by rivers, surrounding his post. As he explored, he strengthened trading ties with the Huron, the Algonquian, and the Montagnai. Champlain also allied with these Native Americans against the Iroquois. Champlain's new trading partners brought him valuable furs, which he then shipped to Europe to be sold. Hearing of Champlain's success, other French traders joined him. This system resulted in an international fur trade so robust the country claimed the region, naming it **New France**.

Population growth in New France was slow. Twenty years after Champlain began his business, the post, which was later named Quebec (kuh-BEK), was home to only about 100 people. By comparison, Jamestown, Virginia, grew from 105 people at its founding in 1607 to 1,240 people in 1622.

In an effort to encourage French people to settle in New France, Champlain's company expanded its charter to include lands from Florida to the Arctic. The company sent Jesuit priests to Native American villages in the hope of learning their languages and converting them to Christianity in accordance with France's Catholic beliefs. However, the French government's refusal to allow Protestants, the most likely immigrants, to settle in the Americas kept the outposts' populations small.

Another factor limiting population growth in New France was its social structure. France was still a feudal society, and settlers brought this system to the Western Hemisphere. Large manors belonged to wealthy settlers. All others worked as tenant farmers. Peasants living in France saw little chance to improve their status in the Americas, where they still could not own and work their own land.

CONFLICT IN NEW NETHERLAND

As you have read, Henry Hudson was searching for a passage to Asia through North America when he discovered the river that would bear his name in what is today New York State. On behalf of the Dutch, Hudson sailed up the river, trading European knives and beads for furs from the Native Americans. The pelts brought a good price in Holland, the Dutch homeland, which is also known as the Netherlands. Traders responded by setting up a post near Albany, New York. In 1614, the Dutch built **Fort Nassau** in that same area. Like the French, the Dutch cooperated with local tribes to establish a thriving fur trade, and the colony of **New Netherland** was established.

The Dutch purchased the island of Manhattan from Native Americans in 1626. They developed the community of New Amsterdam, named for the capital of the Netherlands, but there was a misunderstanding. The Native Americans believed they had sold rights to share the land and could continue using it themselves. The Dutch believed they had purchased exclusive rights to the land. By 1640, the Dutch and the Native Americans were at war over the misunderstanding.

AMERICAN PLACES
Manhattan, New York

Long before skyscrapers towered above its shores, members of the Lenape tribe lived on this island at the mouth of the Hudson River. They called it Mannahatta, "the island of many hills." Compare and contrast the two views of Manhattan shown below. The photo on top is a computer model that suggests what the island might have looked like when Henry Hudson arrived in 1609. The photo at the bottom shows Manhattan 400 years later, in 2009. Manhattan is a borough of New York City, which is the largest city by population in the United States.

The conflict over Manhattan represented a larger issue. Native American tribes, such as the Abenaki and Powhatan, had been living in eastern North America for centuries before Europeans arrived. English settlements in New England and near Chesapeake Bay were agricultural societies, while the French, Dutch, and Swedes focused on trade. Conflicts over land arose between Europeans and Native Americans in these areas. Different European groups sometimes involved Native American trading partners in their arguments over trading opportunities. Some disputes ended in violence. Additionally, many Native Americans succumbed to European diseases, resulting in a decrease in their populations.

HISTORICAL THINKING

1. **READING CHECK** How did explorers influence international trade during the 17th century?

2. **FORM AND SUPPORT OPINIONS** In your opinion, what could the French have done differently to attract settlers and grow the population of New France? Support your opinion with evidence from the text.

3. **INTERPRET VISUALS** What physical features might have made Mannahatta an attractive place for the Dutch to build a community?

PLAN

Objective
Describe the French and Dutch colonies established in North America during the 17th century.

Critical Thinking Skills for Lesson 2.3
- Identify Main Ideas and Details
- Monitor Comprehension
- Form and Support Opinions
- Interpret Visuals
- Compare and Contrast
- Analyze Cause and Effect

Essential Question for Chapter 2
What impact did European exploration have on the Americas? The influence of the French and Dutch colonies in North America can still be seen in languages and place names. Lesson 2.3 discusses the factors that kept these colonies from growing and thriving.

Background for the Teacher
Dutch commerce and trade were strong during the early 17th century. The Dutch East India Company, founded in 1602, sent ships around the globe and established bases in present-day Indonesia. The Dutch West India Company, founded in 1621, did much the same for the colonies in North America. The company had the power to sign treaties and even declare war. It assigned new settlers land to farm (although the company owned the land), sponsored their journeys overseas, and also provided them with supplies.

INTRODUCE & ENGAGE

Establish a Colony

Tell students that the class will work together to plan a new colony. Guide the planning process by having students consider the following questions:

• What is the purpose of the colony? Should it be permanent or temporary?

• What kind of climate and geography would be best for the colony? Why?

• How will the colony be run? Who is in charge? What rights do the colonists have?

As students offer ideas, write them on the board, editing them as they evolve through discussion.

TEACH

Guided Discussion

1. **Compare and Contrast** In what ways were the expeditions of Samuel de Champlain and Henry Hudson similar to other expeditions? In what ways were they different? *(Possible response: Like the Spanish and Portuguese explorers, de Champlain and Hudson were looking for valuable resources and possible wealth; unlike the Spanish explorers, they traded for goods rather than taking them by force, and they formed alliances with Native American groups.)*

2. **Analyze Cause and Effect** What caused the Dutch and Native Americans to be at war in 1640? *(The Dutch bought the island of Manhattan from the Native Americans. The Dutch claimed exclusive rights to the territory, but the Native Americans thought they would be able to share the use of the land. This misunderstanding led to the war.)*

American Places

The island of Manhattan is only one part—the smallest part—of the sprawling city of New York, but it is probably what most people think of when they hear someone mention New York City. More than 1.5 million people live on the island, which is a mere 22.6 square miles, and another 30 million visit each year. How do they all fit on such a small island? They go up! New York has more skyscrapers than any other city. Tourists flock to attractions such as the Statue of Liberty, Central Park, Times Square, the theaters of Broadway, and the Metropolitan Museum of Art. However, Manhattan is also home to dozens of small neighborhoods with strong and vibrant communities.

Active Options

On Your Feet: Card Responses Direct half the class to write six True-False statements based on the lesson. Direct the other half to create answer cards, writing "True" on one side and "False" on the other. Students from the first group should take turns reading their statements. Students from the second group should hold up their cards, showing either "True" or "False" in response to the statements. Have students keep track of their correct responses. Have volunteers modify each "False" statement into a true statement.

NG Learning Framework: Analyze Environmental Concepts

ATTITUDES Curiosity, Responsibility

KNOWLEDGE Our Living Planet

Encourage students to learn more about the fur trade in North America by conducting research using library or online sources. Have students consider the following questions as they research. Then tell students to prepare a short report about the fur trade and have them present it to the class.

• What kinds of animals were most affected by the fur trade?

• How long was the fur trade in North America active?

• How have attitudes about fur trading changed over time?

DIFFERENTIATE

Striving Readers

Use a Concept Cluster Have students work in pairs to summarize the lesson using a Concept Cluster like the one below. Tell students to label the center circle "Eastern North America in the 17th Century." Then have students fill in the smaller circles with details from the lesson.

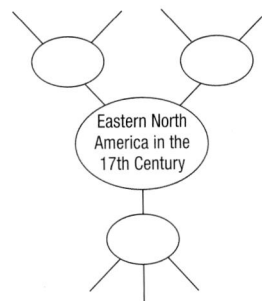

Eastern North America in the 17th Century

Pre-AP

Design a Poster Have students design a poster for the French government that tries to persuade people to move to French settlements in North America during the 17th century. The poster should feature information about the settlements and the kinds of opportunities available there. Students may also wish to include disclaimers, disclosing the potential drawbacks to settlement.

See the Chapter Planner for more strategies for differentiation.

HISTORICAL THINKING

ANSWERS

1. French and Dutch explorers traded with Native Americans for furs, which were considered valuable in Europe. The fur trade led France and the Netherlands to establish colonies.

2. Possible response: The French could have allowed Protestants to settle in the Americas or it could have allowed peasants to own land there.

3. Manhattan's access to water and its forests, which provided lumber and animals for fur trading, might have made it appealing. Also, its location was ideal for the docking of ships importing and exporting goods.

Spanish Colonial Rule

Imagine invaders from far away taking over your town. They would know little about your culture and would likely try to change it. When the Spanish claimed territory in the Americas, they forced a number of social and economic changes, many of which were far from positive.

MAIN IDEA Spanish colonial social and agricultural practices in the Americas had a dramatic effect on Native American cultures.

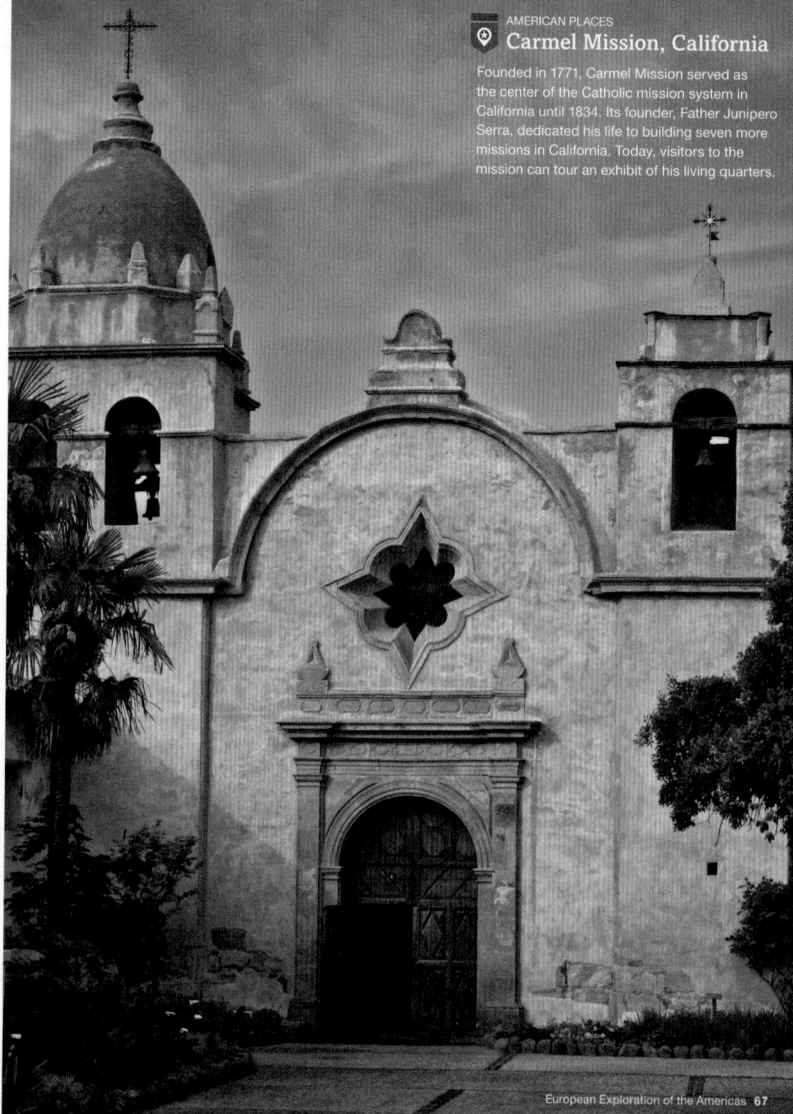

Carmel Mission, California

Founded in 1771, Carmel Mission served as the center of the Catholic mission system in California until 1834. Its founder, Father Junipero Serra, dedicated his life to building seven more missions in California. Today, visitors to the mission can tour an exhibit of his living quarters.

A SOCIAL PYRAMID

As you have read, to control such a huge and distant territory in the Americas, the king of Spain divided it into two viceroyalties. Viceroys governed New Spain and Peru from their capitals, Mexico City and Lima, respectively.

Society in Spanish colonies was hierarchical, or organized like a pyramid. Spanish-born people and their American-born children, called Creoles, were the smallest but most powerful group. **Mestizos** (mes-TEE-zohs), people of mixed Spanish and Native American ancestry, occupied the middle part of society. Native Americans and enslaved Africans were the least powerful but most numerous group.

The Spanish government gave the wealthiest Spanish colonists **haciendas** (hah-see-EHN-dah), or tracts of land to farm. On Caribbean islands, most haciendas were sugarcane **plantations**, or large farms. Sugarcane was an important crop from which colonists made sugar and molasses, which they traded with Europe.

With the hacienda came an **encomienda** (en-coe-mee-AYN-dah), a grant to owners of a certain number of Native American laborers. In return for their labor, the Native Americans received protection from enemies, but never any payment. Native Americans had little power within this social and labor system. Additionally, so many Native Americans died from working in hot and dangerous conditions that the Spanish began to import enslaved Africans to replace them.

IMPACT OF THE CHURCH

The Catholic Church played a major role in Spanish colonization by establishing hundreds of **missions**, or religious settlements, in the Americas. Priests and missionaries wanted to convert Native Americans to Christianity and they also taught skills such as masonry and carpentry.

Some priests brutally punished those who would not adopt Spanish culture. **Bartolomé de Las Casas**, a Spanish priest himself, wrote about the abuses of Native Americans that he'd witnessed. He convinced the Spanish king to pass laws to protect Native Americans from mistreatment, but landowners forced the reversal of those laws.

In 1680, a Pueblo leader named **Popé** led a revolt in present-day New Mexico and drove the Spanish from the area. Popé freed the region of Spanish influence, but Spain restored its control after his death in 1692. By 1700, Spain controlled much of the Americas and remained a powerful presence and a major social influence into the 1800s.

HISTORICAL THINKING

1. **READING CHECK** Who were the mestizos and where did they fit in Spanish colonial society?

2. **COMPARE AND CONTRAST** How did the encomienda and mission systems compare?

3. **ANALYZE CAUSE AND EFFECT** How did the Spanish mission system affect Native American societies?

PLAN

Objective

Learn about Spanish colonies and missions and their impact on Native American populations.

Critical Thinking Skills for Lesson 3.1

• Identify Main Ideas and Details

• Monitor Comprehension

• Compare and Contrast

• Analyze Cause and Effect

• Evaluate

• Draw Conclusions

Essential Question for Chapter 2

What impact did European exploration have on the Americas? Lesson 3.1 discusses how Spain's colonial policies—such as forced labor and the imposed adoption of religion and language—destroyed or permanently altered Native American cultures during the 17th and 18th centuries.

Background for the Teacher

Since direct enslavement of the Native American populations failed in Hispaniola and other colonies, the Spanish sought ways to obtain labor for their mining and agriculture needs. The encomienda system the Spanish instituted in the Americas was adapted from a system used during the Reconquista in Spain and Portugal. Under that system, Muslims who lived in Spanish controlled areas were forced to pay hefty tributes. The system was meant to be an improvement upon outright slavery, but it failed. In effect, the encomienda system in the Americas became an indirect form of slavery for Native Americans.

Activate Prior Knowledge

Provide each student with a K-W-L Chart. Have students brainstorm what they already know about Spanish conquistadors, their first interactions with Native American populations, and their goals in exploration. After reading and discussing the lesson, have students revisit their charts and answer these questions: How were the Spanish colonies organized? What effect did these colonies have on Native Americans?

TEACH

Guided Discussion

1. **Evaluate** What role did ancestry play in the social hierarchy of the Spanish colonies? *(The Spanish colonial hierarchy gave the most power to those born in Spain or with Spanish parents, less power to those with partial Native American ancestry, and the least to full Native Americans or Africans.)*

2. **Draw Conclusions** Why did efforts to protect Native Americans from abuses fail? *(Possible responses: The Spanish settlers who received land grants were to employ the Native Americans who lived on that land without pay, provide protection, and convert them religiously. However, the greed of the Spanish for the profits from their haciendas forced the Native Americans into continual work in harsh conditions and left the Native Americans in a state of destitution, unable to care for their own family needs, with deteriorating health and no independence.)*

American Places

The Carmel Mission, officially called the San Carlos Borromeo de Carmelo Mission, was the core of Catholicism in California until the mid-1800s. Today, it is still an active Catholic parish and services are held daily. The site has five separate museums on the premises, with exhibitions on Spanish colonial and religious art, artifacts and heirlooms from a local family, and documentation of the mission's restoration during the 20th century. The mission also hosts concerts, weddings, and festivals.

Active Options

On Your Feet: Think, Pair, Share Tell students to reread the paragraphs discussing the goals of Spanish colonial missions. Remind them that the missionaries believed they were helping Native Americans by converting them to Christianity. Have pairs of students discuss this concept and form opinions about it. Then ask pairs to share their conclusions with the class.

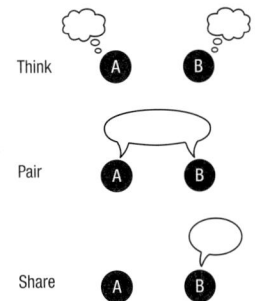

NG Learning Framework: Write a Persuasive Letter

ATTITUDES Responsibility, Empowerment

SKILL Communication

Explain to students that throughout his life, Bartolomé de Las Casas wrote letters and books denouncing the abuse of Native Americans by the Spanish. Encourage them to follow Las Casas's lead and write a persuasive letter of their own. Students should address their letters to a person in power, such as a government official. They should cover an issue they feel strongly about and attempt to convince that person that a change must be made.

English Language Learners ELD

Use Sentence Strips Choose a paragraph from the lesson and make sentence strips out of it. Read the paragraph aloud, having students follow along in their books. Then have students close their books, and give them the sentence strips. Students should put the strips in order. Have students at the **Emerging** and **Expanding** levels work in pairs. Have students at the **Bridging** level work independently. Encourage students to check their sentences by reading them aloud.

Gifted & Talented

Stage a Debate Divide the class into two groups. Tell students to imagine they are Pueblo people living under Spanish colonial rule. Their leader, Popé, wants to organize a revolt against the Spanish colonists. As a community, they are going to debate the idea. Group One will argue for the revolt, while Group Two will argue against it. If time permits, have students conduct additional research on Pueblo culture to help develop their arguments.

See the Chapter Planner for more strategies for differentiation.

HISTORICAL THINKING

ANSWERS

1. The mestizos were people with mixed Spanish and Native American heritage. They occupied the middle class of Spanish colonial society.

2. Both systems attempted to dominate the Native Americans. Both used harsh methods, and each was only partially successful. They differ in that the mission system worked to convert Native Americans to Christianity while the encomienda system kept them under control to supply forced labor to landowners.

3. The mission system provided protection for Native Americans and taught them skills that were useful in colonial society, but it forced them to adapt to Spanish culture at the expense of their own.

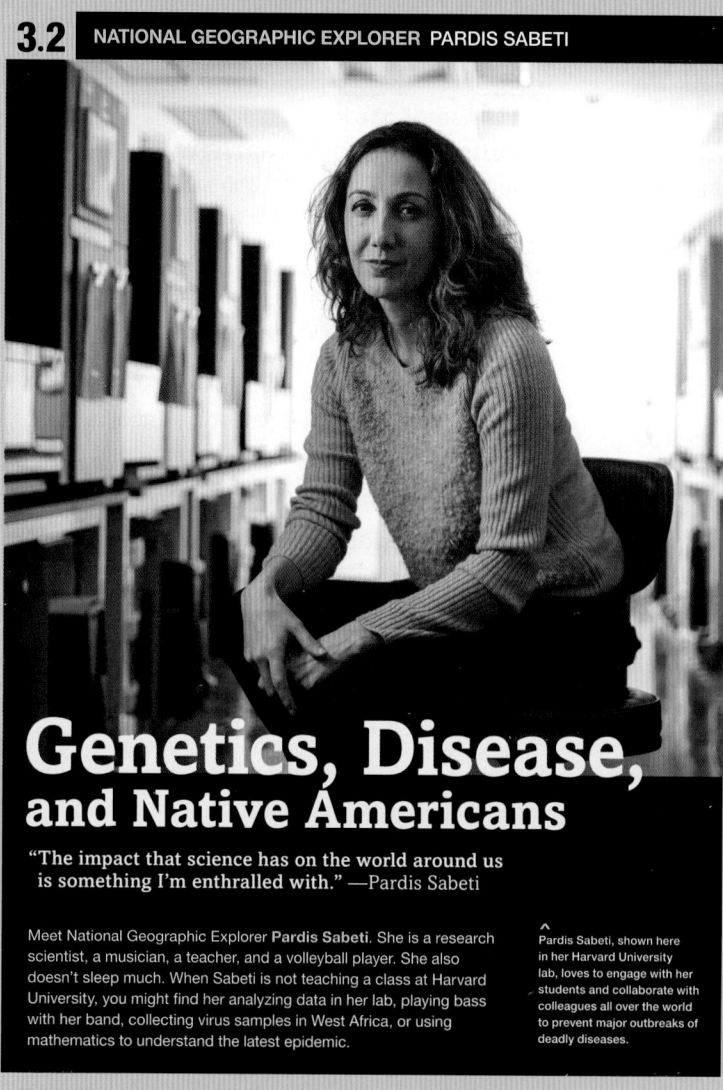

Genetics, Disease, and Native Americans

"The impact that science has on the world around us is something I'm enthralled with." —Pardis Sabeti

Meet National Geographic Explorer **Pardis Sabeti**. She is a research scientist, a musician, a teacher, and a volleyball player. She also doesn't sleep much. When Sabeti is not teaching a class at Harvard University, you might find her analyzing data in her lab, playing bass with her band, collecting virus samples in West Africa, or using mathematics to understand the latest epidemic.

^ Pardis Sabeti, shown here in her Harvard University lab, loves to engage with her students and collaborate with colleagues all over the world to prevent major outbreaks of deadly diseases.

MAIN IDEA Modern scientific research can help explain how diseases from Europe impacted Native Americans in North America.

REFUGEE TO RESEARCH SCIENTIST

When Pardis Sabeti was two years old, she and her family escaped Iran just before its 1979 revolution and settled in Florida. In school, Sabeti learned that she loved math. That's right: math. She followed her interests into medical school, where she fell in love with research and data analysis. That's right: research and data analysis.

While in graduate school, Sabeti developed a pathbreaking algorithm, or a procedure for solving a problem or analyzing data using a computer. She used this algorithm to analyze a specific gene, or the part of a cell that controls growth, appearance, and traits. She knew she'd made a great discovery. She recalls, "I realized I'd found a trait that had to be the result of natural selection—a trait that likely helped the population I was looking at cope with malaria better than others. It was an amazing feeling because at that moment I knew something about how people evolved that nobody else knew."

Today, Sabeti specializes in the study of infectious diseases, or diseases that spread from person to person. She uses mathematical and computer science tools to analyze the different ways diseases change over time and how they influence changes in human biology. Sabeti works in her lab at Harvard University and in countries impacted by diseases such as malaria and Lassa fever.

UNDERSTANDING DISEASE

Sabeti's research has an urgency, and it's risky. Recently, she led a research team during an outbreak of Ebola in Sierra Leone, a country in West Africa. She and her colleagues determined that the Ebola virus actually spread through human-to-human contact, not from contact with bats or other animals. This knowledge helped health professionals stop, or at least slow down, the epidemic and save many lives.

Her research also reveals how infectious diseases have been some of the most important factors in human history. According to Sabeti, more soldiers have died of infections or from exposure to new

Doctors dread seeing the smallpox virus, shown here, in patients. Smallpox is highly contagious and could cause a major human catastrophe if uncontrolled.

climates—and therefore new diseases—than from battle itself. Disease also played an enormous role when Europeans and Native Americans came into contact with each other. Europeans brought diseases to North America, including tuberculosis and smallpox. Europeans likely had inherited immunity, or a genetic protection, against these diseases. But Native Americans had not yet been exposed to them. Smallpox, especially, ravaged Native American populations. This disease also became a weapon of war when European colonizers realized the effect that blankets infected with smallpox could have on native populations.

If you ask Sabeti what she most enjoys about her work, she'd likely respond with more than one answer. She's inspired by colleagues in Africa researching the treatment and prevention of Lassa fever. She thrives on working with her students in classes and in the lab. And she's thrilled to be utilizing her skills in math, research, and data analysis to help develop new treatments for devastating diseases like malaria, a disease that kills more than 1 million people every year.

HISTORICAL THINKING

1. **READING CHECK** What kind of research does Pardis Sabeti do?

2. **SUMMARIZE** In what ways have infectious diseases shaped human history?

3. **MAKE INFERENCES** In what ways might understanding how diseases change over time help doctors prevent future epidemics?

PLAN

Objective

Learn how Pardis Sabeti's work reveals how diseases have affected human history.

Critical Thinking Skills for Lesson 3.2

- Identify Main Ideas and Details
- Monitor Comprehension
- Summarize
- Make Inferences
- Draw Conclusions
- Analyze Cause and Effect

Essential Question for Chapter 2

What impact did European exploration have on the Americas? European explorers brought devastating diseases to the Americas. Lesson 3.2 discusses how scientist Pardis Sabeti studies the impact of genetics and disease in human history.

Background for the Teacher

Pardis Sabeti does more than study diseases. She recently made a discovery that connects Native Americans to their Asian ancestors. During a study of the genomes of 179 people from around the world, Sabeti discovered a gene that increases the number of sweat glands within people who have it. She found that the gene emerged in China 30,000 years ago and traveled to the Americas as Asian populations migrated there. Sabeti believes the mutation has been passed through the generations because it helps regulate body temperature during strenuous activity.

History Notebook

Encourage students to complete the Explorer page for Chapter 2 in their History Notebooks as they read.

INTRODUCE & ENGAGE

Activate Prior Knowledge

Write the term *epidemic* on the board. Ask students to think about where they might have heard this term before and what they understand about its meaning. Students might indicate being familiar with the term from news reports about diseases; they may also have heard it used to describe behaviors (an epidemic of texting while driving). Record students' responses on the board. Then explain that *epidemic* refers to something that spreads quickly and affects large numbers of people. Discuss how this meaning connects to diseases. Tell students that in this lesson, they will be learning about a person who studies epidemics and how her work can also teach us about human history.

TEACH

STEM

Guided Discussion

1. **Draw Conclusions** How could Sabeti's discovery in graduate school help people with malaria? *(Possible response: By using an algorithm she created, Sabeti was able to examine a specific gene and find the trait that showed how a certain population adapted to their environment to better deal with malaria. She could use this research to find ways to prevent malaria or cope with it based on this trait.)*

2. **Analyze Cause and Effect** Why was Sabeti's work able to slow down the Ebola epidemic in West Africa? *(Because Sabeti's work determined that the disease was spread from person to person, the health professionals there were able to change how they handled the disease and prevent more people from being infected.)*

More Information

The Ebola Virus The Ebola virus made global news in 2014 during a widespread outbreak in West Africa. The outbreak was suspected of causing more than 28,000 infections, with more than 15,000 confirmed—and more than 11,000 deaths. Ebola refers to any one of five different viruses, four of which can affect humans. The virus is most commonly spread through contact with an infected person's bodily fluids or contaminated clothing or instruments. People caring for infected patients (such as doctors, nurses, or family members) and people responsible for burying the virus's victims are among those most at risk of infection. Certain animals can also carry the virus, infecting people who eat them or are bitten by them. Careful management of the disease is critical to preventing widespread death from Ebola, which has a mortality rate ranging from 25 percent to 90 percent.

Active Options

On Your Feet: Ready, Set, Recall Have students work in small numbered groups to write down all the details they recall from their reading of Lesson 3.2. Then have groups take turns sharing one fact at a time from their lists with the class. Write all contributions on the board under the group's number. When a group runs out of items, the members must drop out of the game, but they can rejoin if they recall a fact that has not yet been shared. Continue until time is up. The group with the most facts listed is the winner.

NG Learning Framework: Research the Researchers

ATTITUDE Curiosity

KNOWLEDGE New Frontiers

Point out that research science includes a wide variety of topics. Have students work in pairs or small groups to learn more about the different types of research scientists are doing today. They should look for information on where research scientists might work, how much education they need, what fields they work in, and what technologies they use or develop. Have each student create a diagram, such as an idea web, for the type of research scientist he or she finds most interesting, and display the diagrams on the board.

DIFFERENTIATE

Striving Readers

Identify Main Ideas and Details Have students complete a Main Idea and Details List for one of the main ideas in Lesson 3.2. Remind students that a main idea is a statement that tells one of the most important points of a text. Details are facts, descriptions, or explanations that relate to the main idea. If students struggle, work with them to identify some of the text's most important ideas. Once students have identified a main idea from the lesson, have them record three supporting details in their lists.

Pre-AP

Map an Epidemic Have students use the Internet and other resources to research a major epidemic from recent or past history. Then have them create a map or annotated time line of the epidemic, showing where it began, where it spread and when, and the number of people affected. Finally, students should prepare a presentation of their research. Remind them to briefly introduce the disease they have studied: how it spreads, what its symptoms are, and how it is treated or cured. They should conclude with an explanation or prediction of this epidemic's effect on human history.

See the Chapter Planner for more strategies for differentiation.

HISTORICAL THINKING

ANSWERS

1. Sabeti researches infectious diseases, including how they change over time and how they affect human biology and history.

2. Infectious diseases have killed more soldiers than battles have, possibly affecting the outcome of wars. They also led to the destruction of many Native American populations, through accidental and intentional exposure by Europeans.

3. Understanding how diseases changed in the past can help researchers make predictions about how they may change in the future. Then researchers can develop more effective preventions and treatments.

3.3 The Columbian Exchange

One of the best parts about traveling to different places is encountering new and unusual foods, plants, and animals. Beginning in the 1500s, European explorers and colonists encountered and introduced hundreds of new and amazing things.

MAIN IDEA The Columbian Exchange was a significant biological event that changed societies and environments around the world.

TWO WORLDS CONNECT

Millions of years ago, the landmasses of North and South America were connected to Eurasia and Africa. Over time, they drifted far apart and an ocean filled the gap between them. The two hemispheres developed in isolation from each other, resulting in distinct plants and animals evolving in each half of the world. Farmers in the two hemispheres developed and planted different crops and raised different livestock.

The European encounter with the Americas coincided with improved methods of sea travel and the desire to explore and conquer new lands. The combined impact was enormous. Places and people that were once isolated from one another became part of a global exchange network. The contact and trade between these far-flung lands helped some people—and harmed others.

When Europeans crossed the Atlantic in 1492, they carried more than just their ideas—they also brought plants and animals. As they prepared to sail home, they packed new plants and animals they found in the Americas to introduce to the people of Europe. This period of biological mixing between the New World of the Americas and the Old World of Europe, Africa, and Asia is known as the **Columbian Exchange**—named after Christopher Columbus. This momentous swap of biological matter had major economic and social effects in the Americas, both good and bad.

Some of the species the Europeans introduced to the Americas caused significant environmental changes. For example, the Spanish transported livestock, including cattle, horses, sheep, and goats, to the Americas. These animals' roaming and grazing habits altered native landscapes. Europeans also slashed and burned forests to clear lands for farming.

Additionally, Europeans introduced deadly new diseases to the Western Hemisphere. Because they had already encountered diseases such as smallpox, Europeans had developed an **immunity**, or a natural protection, to those diseases. They could even carry the diseases without showing symptoms or appearing sick.

Native Americans had not been exposed to European diseases, so they did not have immunity to them. Epidemics of smallpox, influenza, measles, and other diseases spread quickly after Europeans arrived in the Americas. Between 1519 and 1565, the native population of Central America fell from about 25 million to 2.5 million due to disease alone. Within three centuries of Columbus's landing, about 90 percent of the Native American population had died of disease.

CHANGES FOR THE BETTER

Not all of the consequences of the Columbian Exchange were so negative, however. The great transatlantic swap introduced positive things to both sides. Europeans imported pigs, chickens, and other domesticated animals and brought horses with them, which Native Americans incorporated into their cultures. Europeans also introduced new crops to the Americas. Wheat, barley, rye, rice, and cotton were some of the plants introduced to the Western Hemisphere.

The Columbian Exchange

Other crops included bananas, coffee beans, and sugarcane, all of which grew especially well in Central and South America.

The Western Hemisphere also contributed an important medicine called **quinine** to Europe, Africa, and Asia. Europeans learned about quinine, which comes from the bark of a tree in South America, in the 1600s. For about 300 years, it served as the only effective remedy for malaria, which is carried by mosquitoes. Quinine's use as a treatment for malaria benefited millions of people, but it allowed Europeans to later colonize malaria-ridden areas of the world.

The Columbian Exchange affected the lives of people throughout the world. Some changes were positive, such as improved nutrition because of a greater variety of foods. However, the effect of the Columbian Exchange on native populations in the Americas was disastrous.

More Options, New Troubles

The exchange of crops and animals increased agricultural options and enriched diets on the continents of Europe, North America, Africa, and South America. Some elements of the exchange, such as tobacco and a host of European diseases, were not as positive.

HISTORICAL THINKING

1. **READING CHECK** Why was the Columbian Exchange such an important phenomenon in world history?

2. **INTERPRET MAPS** Based on what you notice on the map, what foods do you enjoy today that originated in the Americas?

3. **DRAW CONCLUSIONS** Which hemisphere benefited most from the Columbian Exchange and why?

70 CHAPTER 2

European Exploration of the Americas 71

PLAN

Objective

Analyze the ecological and cultural impact of the Columbian Exchange.

Critical Thinking Skills for Lesson 3.3

- Identify Main Ideas and Details
- Monitor Comprehension
- Interpret Maps
- Draw Conclusions
- Make Inferences
- Form and Support Opinions
- Categorize

Essential Question for Chapter 2

What impact did European exploration have on the Americas? The exchange of animals, crops, and diseases between Europe, Africa, and the Americas dramatically impacted the cultures of these locations. Lesson 3.3 discusses critical elements and effects of the Columbian Exchange.

Background for the Teacher

Smallpox first spread throughout Europe, Asia, and Africa before spreading to the Americas. While researchers are not exactly sure when smallpox began infecting populations, scholars believe it may go back many thousands of years—as far back as ancient Mesopotamia and the Nile River Valley. Descriptions of diseases with symptoms matching smallpox appear in accounts of terrible plagues from ancient Greece and Rome. Smallpox is thought to have traveled to Europe with soldiers returning from the Crusades. The disease caused fever, aches, vomiting, and a blistering rash that often left permanent, horrible scars. It killed almost a third of its victims. Smallpox is the only infectious disease to be successfully eradicated through vaccination and continual monitoring.

History Notebook

Encourage students to complete the Reid on the Road video series page for Chapter 2 in their History Notebooks after they view the video.

70 CHAPTER 2

Create a Cultural Exchange List

Have students think of and volunteer the foods, music, media, or fashion they enjoy. Write their responses on the board. Ask the class to identify any items that come from another region, country, or culture. Then direct students' attention to the diagram of the Columbian Exchange. **ASK:** How might this diagram look different if we were describing cultural exchange today? *(Possible responses: The arrows would point to many different areas; the items on the arrows might be clothing, music, art, or technology.)*

TEACH   STEM

Guided Discussion

1. **Make Inferences** Based on what you have read, why might European explorers have brought their own crops and livestock with them? *(Answers will vary. Possible responses: They may have been unsure they would find edible food or useful animals in the Americas; they may have hoped to reproduce familiar lifestyles in the new land.)*

2. **Form and Support Opinions** Was the introduction of quinine to the Europeans a more positive or more negative development? Support your opinions using evidence from the lesson. *(Answers will vary. Possible responses: Some students will say quinine was a positive development because it saved countless lives as the only effective malaria treatment for 300 years. Others may say the ability it gave Europeans to "later colonize malaria-ridden parts of the world" may have harmed as many lives as it saved.)*

Categorize

Have students examine the Columbian Exchange items listed in the lesson and on the map. Ask them to use a Three-Column Chart to sort the items into one of three categories: Mostly Helpful, Mostly Harmful, or Both. *(Answers will vary. Possible*

Mostly Helpful	Mostly Harmful	Both

responses: Mostly Helpful—tools and technologies; new fruits, vegetables, and other crops; horses, pigs, and chickens; Mostly Harmful—weapons, diseases; Both—livestock, agriculture/farming, quinine)

Active Options

On Your Feet: History Relay Divide the class into two teams. Allow time for students to think of two questions about the lesson. Have students from each team take turns asking their questions to students on the other team. Students who answer incorrectly must switch to the "asking" team. If a student answers correctly, then the asker must switch teams. Continue until each student has asked a question or time is up. The team with the most students at the end of the game is the winner.

NG Learning Framework: Explore Introduced Species

ATTITUDES Curiosity, Empowerment

KNOWLEDGE Critical Species

Remind students that exchanges of plants, animals, diseases, and other biological elements are continuous. Have them choose a more recent instance of an introduced species in one part of the world and research its features, issues, and contributions. Students should prepare a presentation on their chosen species, explaining how and when it was introduced, the consequences of its introduction, and, in the case of negative impacts, what steps people are taking to remedy the situation. If students need help choosing a topic, here are some suggestions: rabbits in Australia; zebra mussels in the Great Lakes region; kudzu vines in the southeastern United States; beavers in Argentina.

DIFFERENTIATE

Inclusion

Describe Visuals Pair students who are visually impaired with those who are not. Have the latter describe the Columbian Exchange map in detail to their partners. Students may wish to work together to answer the Interpret Maps question in the Historical Thinking section.

English Language Learners

Pose and Answer Questions Have students pose and answer questions about the lesson using the 5Ws. Remind them that *Who* refers to people, *What* refers to events, *When* refers to time, *Where* refers to places, and *Why* refers to reasons. Pair **Emerging** students with **Bridging** students and invite each pair to share their answers with each other. Suggest that students use a 5Ws Chart to organize their thoughts.

See the Chapter Planner for more strategies for differentiation.

HISTORICAL THINKING

ANSWERS

1. Answers will vary. Possible response: The Columbian Exchange introduced people on both sides of the world to new plants, animals, and germs. It improved nutrition and expanded cultures but also resulted in millions of Native American deaths due to the transfer of diseases.

2. Answers will vary. Possible responses: Sweet potatoes, potatoes, corn, peanuts, peppers, beans, and different types of squashes all originated in the Americas.

3. Answers will vary. Many students will argue that the Eastern Hemisphere benefited more because it was much less affected by the spread of new diseases.

4.1 A New Kind of Slavery

Hundreds of newly enslaved people chained together so they can barely move sounds horrifying, because it was. In the 1600s, Europeans seeking wealth in the Americas turned to an ancient and brutal practice: slavery.

MAIN IDEA Demand for labor in Europe and the Americas drove the development of a new kind of slavery, beginning with the capture of people in West Africa.

A NEW FORM OF SLAVERY

Slavery is a social system in which human beings take complete control of others. It has existed throughout human history. In ancient societies around the world, prisoners of war were a main source of slaves. People also bonded themselves into slavery to pay off debts. Such slaves rarely stayed in bondage all their lives. They could usually buy or work for their freedom, and many of them had certain legal rights. Their children almost never became slaves themselves.

However, during European colonization of the Americas, a new kind of slavery developed. Under chattel slavery, people were classified as goods with virtually no human rights. Their bondage—and that of their children—was permanent.

Chattel slavery originated in the mid-1400s when the Portuguese started to trade with West African kingdoms for slaves to work on sugar plantations. Kingdoms such as Dahomey and Ashanti became powerful centers of slave trade commerce, partly by capturing people in raids on inland villages. Raiders marched captives in chains to the coast and locked them in holding pens. The slave traders exchanged goods for the newly enslaved people and shipped them across the Atlantic.

Slave Ship Diagram
The slave trade involved a lot of money and investment on the part of slave traders, merchants, and ship captains. This slave ship diagram shows the precise planning that went into transporting humans across the Atlantic Ocean.

CRITICAL VIEWING The Middle Passage was horrific. These illustrations show a cross-section and a detail of a slave ship. Notice how very little space was allotted for enslaved people during the voyage. What details do you notice in these illustrations?

THE TRIANGULAR TRADE

As you read earlier in this chapter, the Columbian Exchange transformed the Americas and Europe through a massive transfer of plants, animals, and diseases. Another exchange also transformed the Americas, only this one included humans as goods. This exchange formed part of the triangular trade, a three-part system of trade that connected Europe, Africa, and the Americas during the 17th and 18th centuries.

In the first leg of the triangular trade route, traders from Europe brought goods to West Africa to exchange for captured and enslaved Africans. The second and most infamous leg was the Middle Passage. Slave traders forced enslaved Africans onto ships where they were confined in sickening, often fatal conditions. The 5,000-mile voyage took from three weeks to three months. Approximately 10 to 15 percent of the people held captive on slave ships died of disease or despair before reaching the Americas.

Once the ships reached port, the captured Africans were sold again or traded for goods. On the third leg of the voyage, ships loaded with products from the Americas returned to Europe, and the pattern repeated.

The triangular trade lasted until the slave trade was abolished in the early 1800s. Meanwhile, the people who were captured, transported, and sold were unlikely ever to taste freedom again.

HISTORICAL THINKING

1. **READING CHECK** How was chattel slavery different from most forms of slavery practiced in ancient societies?

2. **SUMMARIZE** What was the triangular trade?

3. **INTEGRATE VISUALS** How would you describe the Middle Passage? Use details from the illustrations and the text in your description.

PLAN

Objective
Examine the development of chattel slavery and the triangular trade.

Critical Thinking Skills for Lesson 4.1
- Identify Main Ideas and Details
- Monitor Comprehension
- Integrate Visuals
- Draw Conclusions
- Make Inferences
- Evaluate

Essential Question for Chapter 2
What impact did European exploration have on the Americas? Demands for labor in European colonies led to widespread use of chattel slavery. Lesson 4.1 explains the triangular trade that brought chattel slavery to the Americas and describes the brutal conditions its victims endured.

Background for the Teacher

Though exact numbers are not available, scholars believe that 10 to 12 million people were transported across the Atlantic during the international slave trade. Most of these people were transported during the 18th century. Enslaved men and women resisted their bondage in many different ways. Various forms of rebellion were common, from refusing food to attempting suicide and mutiny. In 1839, enslaved people aboard the ship *Amistad* successfully overthrew the captain and later won their freedom in court. Rebellions were generally most successful when they took place near African shores. Failed rebellions were met with immediate violence, and those resisting were severely punished.

INTRODUCE & ENGAGE

Preview Using Visuals

Point out the slave ship diagram and illustration. Tell students that the diagram depicts an actual slave trading ship. **ASK:** What information about slave ships does the diagram provide? *(Answers will vary. Possible response: The diagram shows the amount of planning that went into filling the ships with as many enslaved people as possible.)* Have them compare and contrast the diagram and the illustration. **ASK:** What details about the Middle Passage does the illustration provide that the diagram does not? *(Answers will vary. Possible response: The illustration shows what the ship looked like, the amount of space enslaved people were given compared with the cargo and how they were positioned.)*

TEACH

Guided Discussion

1. **Draw Conclusions** Why did chattel slavery begin to replace the earlier forms of slavery during the mid-15th century? Support your response with evidence from the text. *(Answers will vary. Possible responses: The text indicates that the chattel system made kingdoms such as Dahomey and Asante very powerful. The bondage of enslaved people and their children was permanent, and therefore it was more profitable—owners did not have to free and replace enslaved people.)*

2. **Make Inferences** What impact did triangular trade have on West Africa? *(Answers will vary. Possible response: Many people were taken from their homes in Africa, thus affecting the population and the social structure of communities.)*

Evaluate

ASK: What other event does the text compare to the triangular trade? *(the Columbian Exchange)* Do you think this is an effective comparison? Explain why or why not. *(Answers will vary. Possible responses: This is an effective comparison because both events were examples of international interactions that dramatically impacted several parts of the world. This is not an effective comparison because the Columbian Exchange had some positive effects, but the enslaving of human beings is only negative.)*

Active Options

On Your Feet: Use a Jigsaw Strategy Group students into three "expert" groups. Each group will use the lesson and outside sources to study one of the following "legs" of the triangular trade: Europe to Africa, the Middle Passage, and the Americas to Europe. After all groups have finished studying their leg of the journey, have students form several groups of three, with each group having one of each type of expert. Have each student in the group take turns sharing his or her subject knowledge while the others take notes and ask questions for clarification.

NG Learning Framework: Collect Data on the Middle Passage `STEM`

`SKILL` Collaboration

`KNOWLEDGE` Our Human Story

Encourage students to work together to gather data on the Middle Passage. Place them in pairs or small groups and have them use the Internet to locate data and statistics about the number of ships that sailed, the number of people who embarked and disembarked from slave ships, and which regions in the Western Hemisphere received the highest number of enslaved people. Tell students to create graphs or charts that summarize their data. Have groups present their findings to the class.

DIFFERENTIATE

English Language Learners

Practice Vocabulary Have students work in pairs to read Lesson 4.1. As they read, they should make lists of unfamiliar words. When they have completed their reading, have them use context clues to determine the meanings of the words. They can then confirm the meanings using a dictionary or glossary. Finally, challenge students to use each word in a new sentence.

Pre-AP

Create a Map Have students use Lesson 4.1 and online resources to create a map showing different triangular trade routes in detail. Students should label the destinations on each continent. Maps should detail the goods and people moved on each leg and how long it took to complete each portion of the trip.

See the Chapter Planner for more strategies for differentiation.

HISTORICAL THINKING

ANSWERS

1. Answers will vary. Possible response: Chattel slavery was permanent, and the enslaved person lost almost all rights. In earlier societies, slaves were often able to work or buy off their freedom, and some people even bonded themselves to slavery to pay debts.

2. The triangular trade was the three-part system that connected Europe, Africa, and the Americas. Traders from Europe brought European goods to Africa and exchanged them for enslaved people. Then slave traders sold these enslaved people in the Americas for payment in products from the Americas, which they brought to Europe.

3. Answers will vary. Possible response: Ships on the Middle Passage were overcrowded, with enslaved people lined up in tightly packed rows. They did not have room to sit up or lie down and were shackled to prevent movement.

CRITICAL VIEWING Answers will vary. Students may notice that people were shackled together with no room to move. The cross-section shows they had no access to windows, and therefore no light or fresh air. The people on the ship are portrayed as cargo.

4.2 The Growth of Slavery

In 2015, author Ta-Nehisi Coates described enslaved Africans as "people turned to fuel for the American machine." The slave labor system that Europeans established in the Americas had an enormous human cost.

MAIN IDEA European access to African slave labor paved the way for the growth of slave labor in the Americas and the expansion of the slave trade.

SLAVERY IN THE AMERICAS

The encomienda and hacienda systems established in Spain's American colonies encouraged the growth of sugar plantations in the West Indies and set the stage for the growth of slavery in North America. These plantations supplied the European market with sugar, and they required a considerable workforce in order to grow and process enough sugarcane to make a profit.

At first, the Spanish forced the islands' Native American populations to work in the sugarcane fields, but ultimately this plan failed. Many Native Americans died of European diseases, while others escaped their bondage.

The inability to force Native Americans into slavery led Spain to turn to Africa as a source of captive labor. At first, the Spanish bought Africans who had been enslaved on the Portuguese plantations. Soon, however, they began buying enslaved Africans directly from West Africa. By the end of the 1500s, 75,000 enslaved Africans were working on Spanish plantations in the Caribbean. The North American slave trade expanded from there.

FAR FROM HOME

Europeans began to buy and ship so many people to the Americas that West African slave hunters had to travel farther into the continent in order to capture and enslave more people to meet the demand. The forced march to the coast was even longer and more brutal, and many people died before they even boarded a ship. Because the slave raiders captured the youngest and most productive members of inland societies, the transatlantic slave trade devastated entire cultures and economies in Africa.

Altogether, the slave trade between Africa and the Americas lasted for about 400 years. From the 16th to the 19th century, traders shipped between 7 and 10 million people to the Western Hemisphere. The removal of so many Africans from their homeland to the Americas is known as the **African diaspora**.

Slavery became an **institution**, or an established and accepted practice, in North America, particularly in the Southern Colonies and then in the new nation, the United States. The international slave trade ended in 1807, and the United States abolished slavery completely in 1865. There is no doubt that slavery as an institution shaped the social, economic, and cultural development of the United States and that it still casts its shadow today.

HISTORICAL THINKING

1. **READING CHECK** How did the slave trade change as demand for African slaves grew?

2. **MAKE INFERENCES** In what ways did the African diaspora change the population of the African continent?

3. **DRAW CONCLUSIONS** How did Portuguese slave trading off the western coast of Africa help contribute to the development of slavery in the Americas?

The Jamaica Train
When sugar refining first began, enslaved workers used four vats of decreasing size called the Jamaica Train. One of the most dangerous jobs on a sugar plantation was boiling the sugarcane water in vats like the ones shown here. When enough liquid had evaporated from one vat, the water was ladled into the next, smaller, vat. The process occurred two more times with more batches following. Enslaved workers had to move quickly so that all the vats were always full.

Indoor Sugar Refining
This painting by William Clark captures work in a large sugar plantation after technology improved the sugar refining process. Moving this process indoors better regulated the heat. Using brick ovens reduced the number of fires needed to boil the sugarcane, but these advances did not make the work much easier for enslaved workers. They still faced scalding, heat exhaustion, and grueling physical labor.

In 1843, Norbert Rillieux invented an evaporating machine. Additional inventions, such as steam power and a process that lowered the boiling point of liquid, continued to improve the sugar refining process.

PLAN

Objective
Discuss how slavery became an institution in the Americas.

Critical Thinking Skills for Lesson 4.2
- Identify Main Ideas and Details
- Monitor Comprehension
- Make Inferences
- Draw Conclusions
- Analyze Cause and Effect

Essential Question for Chapter 2
What impact did European exploration have on the Americas? European plantation owners in American colonies turned to slavery to maximize their profits. Lesson 4.2 explains how Europeans expanded the slave trade and established slavery as an institution in the Americas.

Background for the Teacher

Not all colonists supported the increasingly entrenched practice of slavery. Some considered it deeply immoral. Others thought violent revolts were an inevitable response to the overwhelming mistreatment of enslaved people. In North America, the Quakers became very early opponents of slavery. In Great Britain, abolition movements also gained ground. Writers such as Olaudah Equiano, who had been enslaved, wrote moving accounts of their experiences, and activists worked to expose slavery's most barbaric practices. Their efforts built strong support in the public and Parliament, and in 1807, Great Britain outlawed the international slave trade throughout its colonies. As it happened, the United States had passed a law banning the importation of slaves just three weeks earlier; however, neither law took immediate effect nor did these laws end the practice of slavery.

Preview and Predict

Direct students' attention to the photo and painting. **ASK:** Based on details you notice and information in the captions, what can you predict about what you might learn about the lives of people who worked on sugar plantations? *(Answers will vary. Possible response: From the size of the containers in the photo, the steam in the illustration, and the information in the captions, I infer that the labor required on the plantations was extremely hard, hot, and dangerous.)*

TEACH

Guided Discussion

1. **Analyze Cause and Effect** How did the development of the encomienda and hacienda systems help lead to an increase in the slave trade? *(The encomienda and hacienda systems led to the creation of large plantations, which depended on a huge number of laborers. The cheapest way of obtaining the necessary labor was by buying slaves. As the number of plantations grew, the demand for slaves also grew.)*

2. **Make Inferences** Aside from the chance to make a profit, what other reasons might West African slave traders have had for participating in raids of other villages? *(Answers will vary. Possible response: West African slave traders may have wanted to take over rival villages to reduce competition for resources or to get revenge against enemies.)*

More Information

Sugarcane Before Christopher Columbus sailed to the Americas, sugar was a rare luxury available to rich Europeans only through trade with Asia. The explorer, and those who followed him, planted sugarcane across the Caribbean and parts of South America and what is now the southern United States. As supply increased, prices dropped, and sugar became available for the first time to the middle class and poor. By the mid-17th century, sugar had transformed from a luxury to a mainstay of the European diet. By the 18th century, sugar plantations could be found wherever the climate was right. A seemingly endless supply of laborers was needed to perform the backbreaking work of processing sugarcane, and the planters brought millions of enslaved Africans across the ocean to harvest and mill the sweet crop.

Active Options

On Your Feet: Word Chain Have students form three lines. Hand a piece of paper to the first person in each line with one of these terms: *slave trade, African diaspora, institution.* The first in line adds a word that relates to the original term. Students pass the paper from person to person, each adding a word or phrase they associate with the previously written word. Have a volunteer from each group read the Word Chain, and ask the rest of the class to listen for any words used more than once or any that may not connect correctly.

NG Learning Framework: Research the Slave Trade

ATTITUDE Responsibility

KNOWLEDGE Our Human Story

Have students work in small groups and use other resources to learn more about the practice of slavery in a place other than North America, such as Brazil, during the time of the international slave trade. Students might research and answer such questions as: How were the lives of enslaved people similar or different in this place? What industries used slave labor? When did this place end the practice of slave labor? Ask groups to present their research to the class, using relevant images or maps.

DIFFERENTIATE

Inclusion

Monitor Comprehension Have students work together in small groups to read the lesson, one paragraph at a time. Following each paragraph, students should confirm with their group their understanding of the paragraph's main ideas, important details, and vocabulary. If necessary, provide students with a list of check-in questions to answer following each paragraph.

- What was this paragraph about?
- What details do I remember best?
- What words did I not understand?

Gifted & Talented

Research Slave Market Sites Challenge students to research a West African slave market site. Encourage them to find several sources online, including text, maps, paintings, and illustrations, to gain a better understanding of how the slave trade worked. Students should give an oral report of their findings to the class.

See the Chapter Planner for more strategies for differentiation.

HISTORICAL THINKING

ANSWERS

1. As demand increased, more Africans were captured in slave raids. They were treated more harshly, had longer marches to sea, and endured the horrendous Middle Passage voyage to the Americas.

2. Answers will vary. Possible response: The African diaspora reduced the population of Africa by millions. Africans lived in fear that their villages would be raided and their families ripped apart. The slave trade ruined the culture and economies of these villages.

3. Answers will vary. Possible response: The Spanish colonists in the Americas initially bought enslaved Africans from Portuguese plantations when they could no longer use Native American forced labor. Eventually, they purchased enslaved Africans directly from the same source as the Portuguese and adopted the same practices.

2 REVIEW

VOCABULARY

Use vocabulary words to complete the sentences.

1. In the 1500s, Spain's economy was based on _____.

2. King Philip II considered Protestants to be _____ because they held beliefs different from those of the Catholic Church.

3. Francis Drake and his crew were the first Englishmen to _____ the globe.

4. Francisco Pizarro was a _____ who conquered the Inca in the 1530s.

5. Spain divided the lands it claimed in the Americas into two _____.

6. The Catholic Church _____ followers of Protestantism in the 16th century.

7. _____ were large tracts of land granted to wealthy Spanish colonists.

8. Native Americans did not have _____ against diseases carried by Europeans.

READING STRATEGY
DRAW CONCLUSIONS

If you haven't already, complete your chart to analyze how European exploration affected the Western Hemisphere. List three details, and then answer the question.

9. What were the ways in which Europeans transformed the Western Hemisphere?

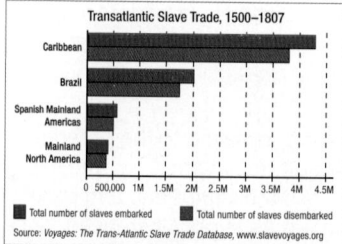

MAIN IDEAS

Answer the following questions. Support your answers with evidence from the chapter.

10. Why were European countries seeking a western route to Asia? **LESSON 1.1**

11. What strategies did the Spanish use to topple the Aztec and the Inca? **LESSON 1.3**

12. What challenges did the conquistadors encounter in North America? **LESSON 1.4**

13. Why did the French Huguenots feel they needed to escape Europe? **LESSON 2.1**

14. Why did King Philip II want Mary, Queen of Scots, to rule England instead of Queen Elizabeth I? **LESSON 2.2**

15. How did the feudal system hinder the growth of New France? **LESSON 2.3**

16. What effect did Spanish rule have on Native American cultures? **LESSON 3.1**

17. What were some of the effects of the Columbian Exchange? **LESSON 3.3**

18. In what ways did the slave trade change cultures and economies in Africa? **LESSON 4.1**

19. Why did the Spanish and Portuguese choose to use slave labor in their New World colonies? **LESSON 4.2**

HISTORICAL THINKING

Answer the following questions. Support your answers with evidence from the chapter.

20. **DRAW CONCLUSIONS** How did competition for land and resources in the Americas lead to conflicts in Europe?

21. **MAKE GENERALIZATIONS** How did the use of slave labor by Europeans in the Americas differ from its use in ancient societies?

22. **MAKE INFERENCES** Why did Bartolomé de Las Casas set himself apart from other Spaniards?

23. **COMPARE AND CONTRAST** What was similar about the colonization of New France and New Netherland? What was different?

24. **FORM AND SUPPORT OPINIONS** What do you think was the most important social or economic effect of the Columbian Exchange? Support your opinion with evidence.

INTERPRET GRAPHS

This bar graph shows numbers of enslaved Africans who got on (embarked) and got off (disembarked) slave ships from West Africa between 1500 and 1807. Study the graph and answer the questions below.

Transatlantic Slave Trade, 1500–1807

Caribbean
Brazil
Spanish Mainland Americas
Mainland North America

0 500,000 1M 1.5M 2M 2.5M 3M 3.5M 4M 4.5M

■ Total number of slaves embarked   ■ Total number of slaves disembarked

Source: Voyages: The Trans-Atlantic Slave Trade Database, www.slavevoyages.org

25. Which region in the Americas imported the most enslaved Africans between 1500 and 1807?

26. What do the two bars for each region show, and what evidence about the Middle Passage do they provide?

ANALYZE SOURCES

In 1524, Giovanni da Verrazzano wrote a letter to King Francis I of France. He described an encounter with Native Americans that he'd witnessed. Read the passage and answer the question.

We sent one of our young sailors swimming ashore to take the people some trinkets, such as little bells, mirrors, and other trifles, and when he came within four fathoms of them, he threw them the goods and tried to turn back, but he was so tossed about by the waves that he was carried up onto the beach half dead. Seeing this, the native people immediately ran up; they took him by the head, the legs, and arms and carried him some distance away. Whereupon the youth, realizing he was being carried away like this, was seized with terror, and began to utter loud cries.

27. Based on the excerpt, do you think the young sailor misread the intentions of the Native Americans? Explain your answer.

CONNECT TO YOUR LIFE

28. **EXPLANATORY** In his letter, Verrazzano describes a crew member's first interaction with a new culture. Connect your knowledge about cultural encounters in the 1500s to a time in your life when you experienced something new for the first time. Write a paragraph connecting the two events.

TIPS

• After you decide on a story of your own to share, use a Venn diagram to organize similarities and differences between your story and Verrazzano's story.

• Use text evidence to compare or contrast the crew member's behavior with actions in your own story.

• After you have finished writing, reread your paragraph to make sure the essay does not slip into informal language, especially when telling your own story.

VOCABULARY ANSWERS

1. mercantilism
2. heretics
3. circumnavigate
4. conquistador
5. viceroyalties
6. persecuted
7. haciendas
8. immunity

READING STRATEGY ANSWER

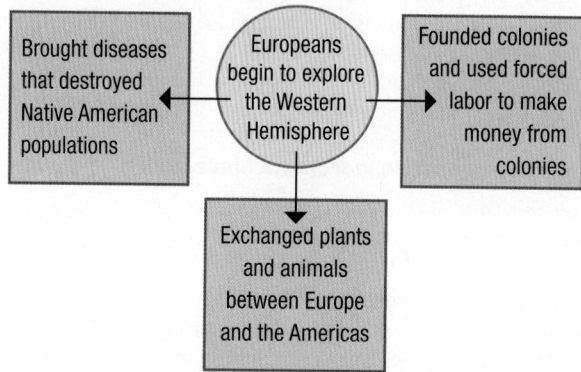

9. By opening the Western Hemisphere to exploration, conquest, and trade, Europeans transformed the hemisphere's populations, agriculture, and economies.

MAIN IDEAS ANSWERS

10. Europeans hoped that a western route to Asia would be faster and easier than the eastern route. The pope had also given control of much of the eastern route to the Portuguese, so other nations had to find new routes.

11. Cortés recruited other Native American tribes who were dissatisfied with Aztec rule. Pizarro ambushed the Inca emperor Atahualpa at a meeting, attacking the mostly unarmed Inca. Both also took advantage of the populations being weakened by smallpox and other illnesses.

12. The conquistadors fought Native Americans, suffered and died from fevers and other illnesses, and failed to find any of the "cities of gold" they sought.

13. The French Huguenots left Europe because Catholics in France were persecuting them for leaving the Church.

14. King Philip II favored Mary, Queen of Scots, over Elizabeth because Mary was Catholic. Elizabeth was a Protestant.

15. The feudal system gave land only to wealthy settlers of New France. French peasants saw no reason to risk the voyage across the Atlantic if they couldn't own their own land.

16. Spanish rule imposed the Spanish language and Christianity on Native Americans under its control, sometimes eliminating native languages and belief systems. It also damaged Native American cultures by greatly reducing the population through disease and removing people for forced labor.

17. Disease spread through Native American tribes, killing up to 90 percent of Native Americans. Firearms, horses, pigs, and many new crops were introduced to the people of North and South America. Europeans enjoyed new crops, such potatoes and corn, and the medicine quinine, which helped cure malaria.

18. The slave trade devastated African communities and cultures by removing so many people from their home cultures and economies.

19. The Portuguese needed more people than they had to work the large plantations they founded in the New World. They first enslaved Native Americans, but disease and abuse killed many. As a result, they looked to Africa to find more slave labor. The Spanish had the same problem with their encomienda system and soon followed Portugal's lead.

HISTORICAL THINKING ANSWERS

20. The possibility of a Northwest Passage, which many nations wanted to find and control, led to tensions between the nations searching for it. Colonists from France, the Huguenots, planned to attack and capture Spanish ships carrying silver, which increased tensions between Catholic and Protestant groups in Europe.

21. The slaves in earlier societies were not chattel; they often had some rights, and sometimes were set free.

22. De Las Casas spoke out against the mistreatment of the Native Americans. Many other Spaniards involved in mission life contributed to the destruction of the Native Americans' communities and lives.

23. Both colonies started as trading posts, and both had settlers that worked with local tribes to start their business in furs. New France had trouble expanding because of limitations set by the French government. New Netherland had trouble expanding because a misunderstanding over the purchase of land (Mannahatta) from the local tribes led to ongoing conflict and war.

24. Answers will vary. Some students may say that disease was the most significant aspect because it so drastically reduced the populations of Native American groups in the Americas and allowed Europeans to take greater control of their lands. Other students may say the exchange of crops and food was the most significant because many of those items continue to affect peoples' diets today.

INTERPRET GRAPHS ANSWERS   STEM

25. The Caribbean imported the most enslaved Africans between 1500 and 1807.

26. The red bar shows how many enslaved Africans embarked, or got on the ships, and left Africa. The blue bar shows how many disembarked, or arrived at their destination, after the Middle Passage. Together they provide evidence that many slaves died during the Middle Passage, since the blue bar is always smaller than the red one.

ANALYZE SOURCES ANSWER

27. Answers will vary. Possible responses: Yes; he had no way of knowing if the people were friendly or not. Verrazzano's expedition was not the first one from Europe, so his sailors may have heard about hostile Native American groups from other sailors. No; he was in distress after being thrown onto the beach, and he needed help. They did not treat him roughly.

CONNECT TO YOUR LIFE ANSWER

28. Students' paragraphs will vary but should clearly describe the student's own experience and accurately identify similarities between that experience and the experience retold by Verrazzano. Possible points of connection between cultural encounters in the 1500s and students' present-day experiences might include moving to a new place, entering a new school, or joining a new group. Students' responses should use formal language and cite evidence directly from the text when making comparisons between their own experience and that of the sailor in Verrazzano's letter.

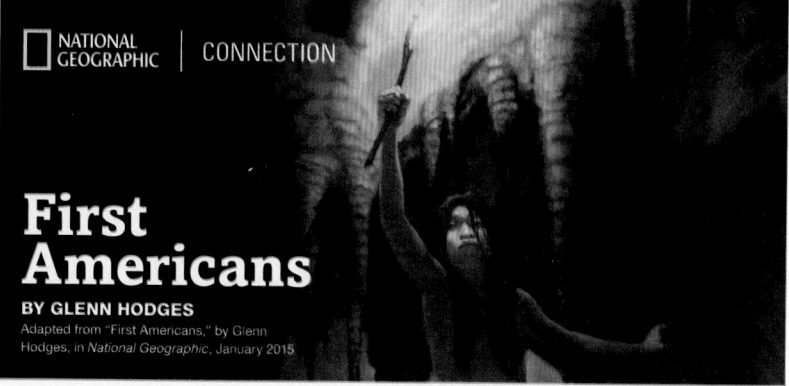

First Americans

BY GLENN HODGES

Adapted from "First Americans," by Glenn Hodges, in *National Geographic*, January 2015

The story begins with an unlucky teenage girl who fell to her death in a cave in Mexico's Yucatán about 12,000 to 13,000 years ago. But her prehistoric bad luck is modern science's good fortune. The skeleton, called Naia (NY-ah), turned out to be one of the oldest ever found in the Americas, and it provides evidence of North America's first inhabitants.

In 2007, a team of Mexican divers led by Alberto Nava made a startling find: an immense submerged cavern they named Hoyo Negro, the "black hole." At the bottom of the abyss, their lights revealed a bed of prehistoric bones, including a nearly complete human skeleton. It was intact enough to provide a foundation for a facial reconstruction. Geneticists were even able to extract a sample of DNA.

Together, these clues may help explain a mystery about the peopling of the Americas. If Native Americans are descendants of Asian trailblazers who migrated into the Americas toward the end of the last Ice Age, why don't they look like their ancient ancestors?

By all appearances, the earliest Americans were a rough bunch. If you look at the skeletal remains of Paleo-Americans, more than half the men have injuries caused by violence. Their wounds do not appear to have been the result of hunting accidents or warfare. Instead, it appears that these men fought violently among themselves. Female skeletons do not reveal the same kinds of injuries. Additionally, female skeletons are much smaller than male skeletons, and they show signs of malnourishment.

Jim Chatters, archaeologist and co-leader of the Hoyo Negro research team that found Naia, theorizes that the earliest Americans were bold pioneers whose behaviors and physical traits changed as they became more settled. This change over time, he explains, is why the earliest Americans' facial features look so different from those of later Native Americans.

According to this hypothesis, men fought for dominance in the group. They also ate better, grew larger, and lived longer than the women did. The men who were able to establish their dominance in the group were the ones who were able to pass on their genes. As a result, their strong traits and features were selected over the softer and more domestic features evident in later, more settled populations.

Chatters's hypothesis is speculative, but his team's findings are not. Naia has the facial features typical of the earliest Americans as well as the genetic signatures common to modern Native Americans. This means that the two groups do not look different because later groups from Asia replaced the earliest populations. Instead, they look different because the first Americans changed after they got here.

For most of the 20th century, anthropologists pointed to spearpoints found near Clovis, New Mexico, and dated to 13,000 years ago as the oldest evidence of ancient hunters. They concluded that the first Americans had followed mammoths and other prey out of Asia, across Beringia, and then south into North America. But in 1997, archaeologists confirmed new evidence of human occupation in Monte Verde, Chile, and the story of the peopling of the Americas was thrown wide open. How did they get there? Given that the Monte Verde people made it all the way to southern Chile more than 14,000 years ago, it would be surprising if they hadn't journeyed by boat.

The story of how and when humans began to inhabit the Americas continues to develop. What is clear is that the Americas hosted diverse communities of people long before the Clovis culture began to spread across North America. We may never know the whole story, but each new discovery gets us closer to a more complete one.

For more from National Geographic, check out "Scurvy Struck Columbus's Crew" online.

UNIT INQUIRY: Establish an Empire

In this unit, you learned about three worlds before 1500 and about the European exploration of the Americas. Based on your reading, what happened when people from Europe, Africa, and the Americas encountered each other on African and American soils? Which societies fared better than others, particularly when Europeans began to establish empires in North, Central, and South America? Why did Europeans establish empires? Which empires were more successful and why?

ASSIGNMENT

Design an empire you think would be successful today. Consider factors such as geography, government, the economy, social structure, and culture. Be prepared to present your plan for an empire to the class.

Gather Evidence As you design your empire, gather evidence from this unit about the factors that made European empires successful and what factors eventually led to their fall. Make a list of both sets of factors. Then develop a plan about how you would use similar or different strategies in your empire. Use a graphic organizer like this one to help organize your thoughts.

Produce Use your notes to produce detailed descriptions of each component of your empire. Write a short paragraph describing your empire's geography, government, economy, social structure, and culture. To support your ideas, make sure to use evidence from the chapters in this unit.

Present Choose a creative way to present your empire to the class. Consider one of these options:

- Write an introduction to a travel guide that describes your empire. Use a narrative style that gives your audience a "tour" of your empire.

- Draw a map of your empire to accompany the descriptions you provide. Include a legend, geographic features, and other details that help give a visual summary of your empire.

- Create a multimedia presentation using photos, drawings, text, and maps to illustrate your empire and its various components.

NATIONAL GEOGRAPHIC | LEARNING FRAMEWORK ACTIVITIES

Create a Map

SKILLS Observation, Collaboration
KNOWLEDGE Our Living Planet

Team up with a partner to create a map of the continents discussed in this unit. Include as many civilizations, landforms, bodies of water, and labels on your map as possible. Draw arrows to represent migration routes, or how groups of people began to move from place to place. You might also consider using arrows to show these civilizations' trade routes and drawing icons to represent products that were traded along those routes. When you have finished your map, compare it to other teams' maps. Offer your own observations, and ask your classmates to make observations about your map.

Think Like an Archaeologist

ATTITUDE Curiosity
KNOWLEDGE Our Human Story

Civilizations leave behind clues about what they were like and how people lived. Archaeologists all over the world follow very strict procedures when they excavate a site to ensure that no information is lost. They also have to make sure that in digging, they don't destroy or ruin artifacts, structures, or art. In groups of four, imagine that you are in charge of a dig site in the location of one of the civilizations covered in this unit. Make a list of items you might find on your site and describe what challenges you think your crew might face on the dig. Then share your imagined dig experience with the class.

NATIONAL GEOGRAPHIC CONNECTION

Guided Discussion for "First Americans"

1. **Identify Main Ideas and Details** What mystery about human occupation of North America are archaeologists trying to solve? *(Archaeologists are using extracted DNA and facial reconstruction on the remains found in a Mexican cave to help explain why Native Americans, the supposed descendants of Asians who migrated across Beringia, have different physical features from their ancient ancestors. Archaeologists point to human occupation in Monte Verde dating from about 14,000 years ago as evidence that the peopling of the Americas may have been accomplished by groups who journeyed by boat, instead of migrating from Asia via Beringia.)*

2. **Evaluate** According to Jim Chatters, the earliest Americans' features differ from those of later populations of Native Americans. What evidence does Chatters's team offer to explain this change over time? *(Chatters's team points out that Naia possesses the facial features of typical earliest Americans as well as genetic signatures of modern Native Americans. This indicates that Asian populations did not replace the earliest Americans but that the earliest Americans changed over time after arriving on the continent.)*

Guided Discussion for "Scurvy Struck Columbus's Crew"

1. **Make Connections** What is scurvy and why was it a problem for sailors? *(Scurvy is a disease caused by a severe vitamin C deficiency. It causes lethargy, anemia, and the re-opening of old wounds. It was a problem for sailors who did not have access to sources of vitamin C while aboard ships for long periods of time.)*

2. **Explain** Why, when surrounded by sources of fruits and vegetables rich in vitamin C, did Columbus's crew still suffer from a deficiency? *(While in La Isabela, the sailors did not venture beyond their stockade to take advantage of the fruits and vegetables growing on the island; Columbus and some of his crew were more interested in finding gold than in feeding themselves; they were under constant attack by the Taino, which discouraged them from foraging; they preferred foods sent from Europe, which were not rich in vitamin C.)*

UNIT INQUIRY PROJECT RUBRIC

Assess

Use the rubric to assess each student's participation and performance.

SCORE	ASSIGNMENT	PRODUCT	PRESENTATION
3 GREAT	• Student thoroughly understands the assignment. • Student engages fully with the project process.	• Descriptions are well thought out. • Descriptions include a number of details about empire components supported by chapter evidence. • Descriptions contain all of the key elements listed in the assignment.	• Presentation is clear, concise, and logical. • Presentation does a good job of creatively presenting an empire to the class. • Presentation engages the audience.
2 GOOD	• Student mostly understands the assignment. • Student engages fairly well with the project process.	• Descriptions are fairly well thought out. • Descriptions include at least two details about empire components supported by chapter evidence. • Descriptions contain most of the key elements listed in the assignment.	• Presentation is fairly clear, concise, and logical. • Presentation does an adequate job of creatively presenting an empire to the class. • Presentation somewhat engages the audience.
1 NEEDS WORK	• Student does not understand the assignment. • Student minimally engages or does not engage with the project process.	• Descriptions are not well thought out. • Descriptions include few or no details about empire components supported by chapter evidence. • Descriptions contain few or none of the key elements listed in the assignment.	• Presentation is not clear, concise, or logical. • Presentation does an inadequate job of presenting the empire to the class. • Presentation does not engage the audience.

NATIONAL GEOGRAPHIC LEARNING FRAMEWORK RUBRIC

Assess

Use the rubric to assess how each student applies the National Geographic Learning Framework.

SCORE	ASSIGNMENT	ASSIGNMENT	FINAL PRODUCTS
3 GREAT	• Map reflects **Observation** and **Collaboration** well. • Map explores **Our Living Planet** well.	• List and description demonstrate **Curiosity** well. • List and description explore **Our Human Story** well.	• Final products are engaging, creative, and well presented.
2 GOOD	• Map reflects **Observation** and **Collaboration**. • Map explores **Our Living Planet**.	• List and description demonstrate **Curiosity**. • List and description explore **Our Human Story**.	• Final products are interesting, logical, and complete.
1 NEEDS WORK	• Map does not reflect **Observation** or **Collaboration**. • Map does not explore **Our Living Planet**.	• List and description do not demonstrate **Curiosity**. • List and description do not explore **Our Human Story**.	• Final products are not creative, complete, or interesting.

Pilgrims Bid Farewell to the *Mayflower*

After their arrival at Plymouth in December 1620, the Pilgrims lived on the *Mayflower* while they constructed houses. Throughout the cold, wet winter, they rowed ashore to work during the day and returned to the ship to sleep. The ship did not have private cabins or beds for each person, and it was cold and damp. Many people died between the Pilgrims' arrival and the departure of the ship.

By March 1621, the Pilgrims had built enough houses for everyone. After people were settled, the *Mayflower* left Plymouth on its return voyage to England on April 5, 1621. The painting *The Departure of the Mayflower* depicts the scene as imagined by artist Newell Wyeth.

The fate of the *Mayflower* remains a mystery. After 1624, there are no records of the ship. Some people in England claim to own a piece of the original *Mayflower*, and there is a barn supposedly constructed of wood from the *Mayflower*, but no historical proof supports these stories. **ASK:** Why do you think people in England might want to claim that they own a piece of the *Mayflower*? *(Answers will vary. Possible response: The voyage of the Pilgrims on the* Mayflower *was a significant event, so a piece of the ship would be a valuable historical artifact.)*

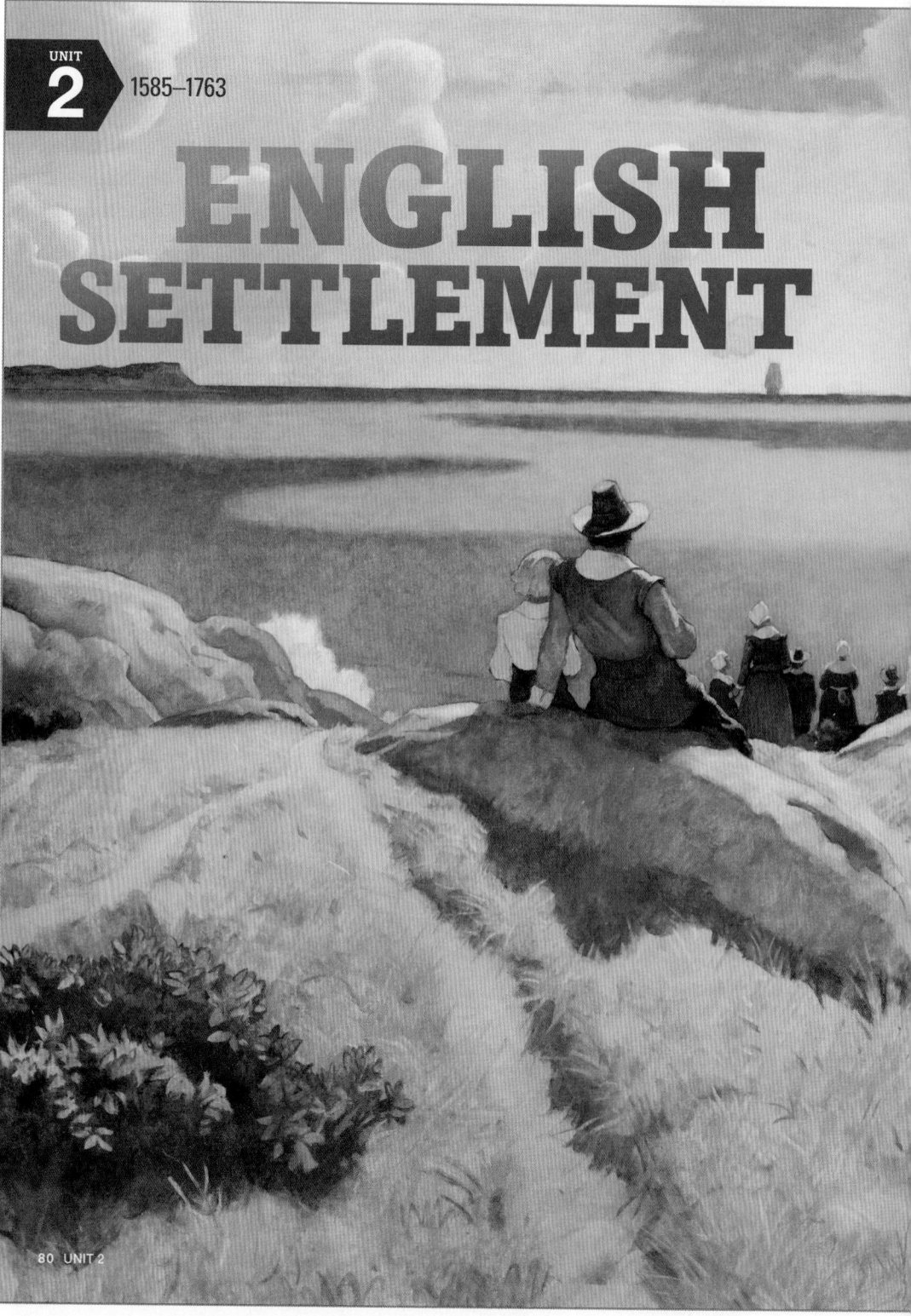

UNIT
2 1585–1763

ENGLISH SETTLEMENT

80 UNIT 2

In this 1941 painting by Newell Wyeth, the Pilgrims watch the *Mayflower* depart on its return voyage to England in April, 1621. What mood does the artist convey by showing the Pilgrims as they watch their ship return to England?

81

Newell Wyeth

Newell Convers Wyeth was one of the foremost artists of the 20th century. In the early 1900s, his pictures of the American West appeared in leading magazines. He also created advertisements for products such as cereal and soft drinks. His illustrations for New York Life Insurance, the Pennsylvania Railroad, and other companies were featured on calendars and posters. Several publishing companies hired Wyeth to illustrate classic stories, including *Treasure Island* and *Robinson Crusoe*. Wyeth also created murals for hotels, banks, and state capitol buildings.

The Departure of the Mayflower is part of a series of murals of Pilgrim life commissioned by the Metropolitan Life Insurance Company. The series depicts major events, such as the coming of the *Mayflower* and preparation for the first Thanksgiving, as well as daily tasks, such as harvesting crops and attending church. Due to Wyeth's sudden death in 1945, his son Andrew Wyeth and his son-in-law John McCoy completed the murals.

CRITICAL VIEWING Answers will vary. Possible response: The artist conveys a peaceful mood with the blue skies and tranquil ocean, but there is also sadness. Based on the distance the *Mayflower* has traveled, the Pilgrims have been watching the ship sail for a long time. This suggests that they are reluctant to lose sight of their physical connection to their homeland. By depicting the Pilgrims from behind—some embracing—and gazing out to sea, the artist reinforces a feeling of wistfulness and longing.

c. 1620 AFRICA:
Kingdom of Dahomey

Dahomey was founded in West Africa after King Agaja conquered the surrounding areas in an effort to improve access to European traders on the coast. The kingdom was established as an absolute monarchy in which the king ruled with unchallenged authority over royalty, commoners, and slaves. The king also maintained a large army, which conquered other territories to expand the boundaries of the kingdom and to capture prisoners who became slaves. Slaves worked on royal plantations, providing food for the army and the royal court, or were traded to Europeans for weapons.

Women played important roles in Dahomey's culture as hunters, palace bodyguards, and warriors. Although it is unclear when or why Dahomey first recruited female soldiers, historical records document their participation in a battle with the Yoruba around 1730. Records indicate that by the mid-1800s, about 6,000 women served in Dahomey's army. They were well trained to fight and die for king and country, and thousands lost their lives in battle. The women warriors of Dahomey were known for their ferocity in battle, and even their enemies praised their courage. **ASK:** Why might Dahomey's king have recruited women for the army? *(Answers will vary. Possible responses: There might not have been enough men to defend the kingdom. Perhaps women had more loyalty to the king. The king may have wanted to provide a show of force to his enemies that required extra soldiers.)*

UNIT 2

ENGLISH SETTLEMENT

COLONIAL AMERICA

1607
English settlers found Jamestown in Virginia. *(sealing wax stamp owned by Jamestown resident)*

1620
Pilgrims sign the Mayflower Compact, establishing a self-governing colony at Plymouth, Massachusetts.

1676
Nathaniel Bacon leads a rebellion against the governor of Virginia and demands war against the Native Americans.

1585
Roanoke, the first English colony, is established. *(engraving showing the English arriving in Virginia in 1585)*

1600

1500

c. 1620 AFRICA
The West African kingdom of Dahomey, which would become rich in part through the Atlantic slave trade, is founded.

1644 ASIA
The Manchus overthrow the Ming and found the Qing dynasty in China. *(lion statue before palace of Ming and Qing emperors)*

THE WORLD

82 UNIT 2

1735
John Peter Zenger is tried for printing articles criticizing the English governor of New York. *(block of movable type used in 1700s America)*

HISTORICAL THINKING: DETERMINE CHRONOLOGY

What two events, nearly 70 years apart, indicate the American and British concern with the power of government?

1763
After the French and Indian War ends, the Proclamation of 1763 is issued.

1692
The Salem witch trials are held in Massachusetts.

1754
The French and Indian War between Great Britain and France is fought on American soil. *(pipe tomahawk, a blend of Native American and European cultures)*

1688 EUROPE
Britain's Glorious Revolution begins and results in greatly increased power for Parliament.

1722 ASIA
Chinese emperor Kangxi dies after reigning for 61 years.

c. 1750 EUROPE
The Industrial Revolution begins in Great Britain. *(spinning jenny, which helped industrialize Britain's textile production)*

1700 **1800**

English Settlement **83**

INTRODUCE TIME LINE EVENT

c. 1750 EUROPE:
Industrial Revolution

In the early 1700s, manufacturing in Great Britain was part of a domestic system in which workers owned the machines, worked at home or in small workshops, and decided their hours. In this cottage system of small, rural manufacturers, industry relied on horses, waterwheels, or windmills as sources of power. Inventions revolutionized production, and the factory system replaced individual cottage industries.

Workers migrated to cities in search of jobs and found employment in large "manufactories" where men, women, and children worked long hours for low pay in places that often were unsafe. Jobs were plentiful, but living conditions were crowded and substandard. **ASK:** What were the advantages and disadvantages of the Industrial Revolution in Great Britain? *(Answers will vary. Possible response: Production increased and cities became industrial centers. The factory system changed where and how people worked. People lived in crowded conditions and worked long hours for low pay in unsafe factories.)*

HISTORICAL THINKING: DETERMINE CHRONOLOGY

Answer: The signing of the Mayflower Compact in 1620 indicated that colonists wanted self-government. Britain's Glorious Revolution in 1688 showed that people wanted to curb the power of the monarch.

UNIT 2 RESOURCES

UNIT INTRODUCTION

UNIT TIME LINE

UNIT WRAP-UP

NATIONAL GEOGRAPHIC | CONNECTION

National Geographic Magazine Adapted Articles
• "Before New York"
• "America, Found and Lost" ONLINE

Unit 2 Inquiry: Envision an Ideal Community

NG Learning Framework Activities
• Prepare a Leadership Memo
• Create a Trade Network

Unit 2 Formal Assessment

CHAPTER 3 RESOURCES

Available at NGLSync.Cengage.com

TEACHER RESOURCES & ASSESSMENT

Reading and Note-Taking

Vocabulary Practice

Document-Based Question Template

Social Studies Skills Lessons
• Reading: Make Inferences
• Writing: Write an Informative Text

Formal Assessment
• Chapter 3 Pretest
• Chapter 3 Tests A & B
• Section Quizzes

Chapter 3 Answer Key

ExamView®
One-time Download

STUDENT DIGITAL RESOURCES

• **eEdition** (English)
• **eEdition** (Spanish)
• **Handbooks**
• **Online Atlas**
• **American Gallery Online**
• **History Notebook**
• **American Voices (Biographies)**
• **Active History**
• **Projects for Inquiry-Based Learning**

Chapter 3 Spanish Resources are available at NGLSync.Cengage.com.

AMERICAN STORIES | The Lost Colony of Roanoke

- Primary Sources
- On Your Feet: Inside-Outside Circle
- **NG Learning Framework:** Investigate Archaeology

SECTION 1 RESOURCES

EARLY COLONIES HAVE MIXED SUCCESS

LESSON 1.1
Colonizing Virginia

- ▶ Plimoth Plantation
- On Your Feet: Think, Pair, Share
- **NG Learning Framework:** Write a Biography

American Voices Biography
John Smith ONLINE

LESSON 1.2
CURATING HISTORY
Voorhees Archaearium Jamestown, Virginia

- On Your Feet: Sort the Artifacts

LESSON 1.3
NATIONAL GEOGRAPHIC EXPLORER
WILLIAM KELSO
Uncovering Where America Began

- On Your Feet: Inside-Outside Circle
- **NG Learning Framework:** Write About Building Jamestown Fort

LESSON 1.4
Conflicts with Native Americans

- On Your Feet: Time Line
- **NG Learning Framework:** Negotiate a Peace Treaty

SECTION 2 RESOURCES

NEW ENGLAND COLONIES

LESSON 2.1
Pilgrims and Puritans

- On Your Feet: Compare and Contrast

AMERICAN GALLERY ONLINE A Portrait of the Pilgrims

American Voices Biographies
Ann Hutchinson ONLINE
John Winthrop

LESSON 2.2
AMERICAN VOICES
Squanto

- On Your Feet: Make Inferences about Character
- **NG Learning Framework:** Investigate the First Thanksgiving

LESSON 2.3
DOCUMENT-BASED QUESTION
Foundations of Democracy

- On Your Feet: Host a DBQ Roundtable

LESSON 2.4
War and Witch Trials

- On Your Feet: Sequence Events
- **NG Learning Framework:** Learn More about King Philip's War

SECTION 3 RESOURCES

MIDDLE AND SOUTHERN COLONIES

LESSON 3.1
The Middle Colonies

- On Your Feet: Tell Me More
- **NG Learning Framework:** Research William Penn

LESSON 3.2
Forming Alliances

- On Your Feet: Team Word Webbing
- **NG Learning Framework:** Explore the Fur Trade

LESSON 3.3
The Southern Colonies

- On Your Feet: Host a Quiz Show
- **NG Learning Framework:** Advertise a Colony

LESSON 3.4
GEOGRAPHY IN HISTORY
Economic Activities in the Thirteen Colonies

- Active History: Compare North American Settlements
- **NG Learning Framework:** Research Natural Resources

LESSON 3.5
Werowocomoco, the Powhatan Capital

- On Your Feet: Compare and Contrast
- **NG Learning Framework:** Investigate Diseases

CHAPTER 3 REVIEW

Strategy ❶
Collect Exit Slips

For a quick, informal assessment tool, direct students to respond in writing to a single question at the end of a lesson. Preview the following questions before reading each lesson. After reading the lesson, pass out strips of paper. Tell students to write their responses to the questions on the paper strips. Collect students' written responses as they exit the class.

1.1 What was the first representative assembly in the American colonies? *(House of Burgesses)*

1.3 What clues led William Kelso to the site of the original fort at Jamestown? *(fragments of pottery, dark-stained dirt, ruins of church tower)*

1.4 What were the terms of the treaty between the colonists and the Powhatan in 1646? *(The Powhatan had to live north of the York River and give the colonists 20 beaver skins each year.)*

Use with Lessons 1.1, 1.3, and 1.4

Strategy ❷
Use Pair-Share Reading

Allow students to work in pairs and divide each lesson into two parts. Have students decide which part each one will handle. Tell both students to read the first part. The student responsible for it verbally summarizes the important information in that part. The second student makes notes and asks a question about the information. Then students switch roles and repeat the procedure with the second part.

Use with All Lessons

Strategy ❸
Modify Main Idea Statements

Ask each student to work with a partner to preview the chapter by reading and copying each lesson's Main Idea statement onto a sheet of paper. Then tell students to look at all maps, photos, and illustrations in the text and add to each lesson's Main Idea. They can write complete sentences or notes on the page.

Use with Lessons 1.1, 1.3, 1.4, 2.1, 2.4, and 3.1–3.4

Strategy ❶
Build Concept Clusters

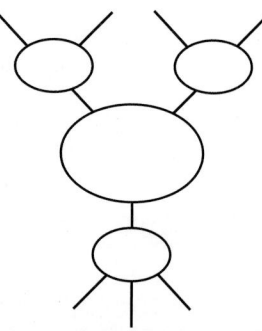

Write *New England Colonies, Middle Colonies,* and *Southern Colonies* on the board. As students read about each group of colonies, have them build a Concept Cluster by adding words, phrases, or pictures to a graphic organizer like the one shown here. Guide students to use their completed graphic organizers to summarize what they have learned about each group of colonies.

Use with Lessons 1.4, 2.1, 2.4, 3.1–3.3 *You may wish to have students of mixed ability levels work in teams to complete the Concept Clusters. Review each Concept Cluster as it is completed and then use all three to compare and contrast the regions.*

Strategy ❷
Provide Terms and Names on Audio

Decide which terms and names from each lesson are important for mastery. Ask volunteers to record the pronunciation and a short sentence defining each word. Encourage students to listen to the recordings as often as necessary.

Use with All Lessons *You might also use the recordings to quiz students on their mastery of the terms and names. Divide students into two teams and play one definition from the recording. Teams take turns trying to identify the term or name. Keep track of which team scores the most points.*

ENGLISH LANGUAGE LEARNERS

Strategy ❶
Prepare for Reading

Help students use the PREP strategy to prepare for reading. Pairs students at the **Emerging** and **Expanding** levels with students at the **Bridging** level and then write the following acrostic on the board:

PREP

Preview title.

Read Main Idea statement.

Examine visuals.

Predict what you will learn.

Tell students to write their prediction and share it with their partner. After reading, ask students to write another sentence that begins "I also learned… ." Instruct students at the **Bridging** level to help their partners with their sentences.

Use with All Lessons

Strategy ❷
Used Paired Reading

Students at the **Emerging** level may benefit by a paired reading with students at the **Bridging** level. Assign partners. Pairs read a passage from the text aloud. Then:

1. Partner 1 reads another passage; Partner 2 retells the passage in his or her own words.
2. Partner 2 reads a different passage; Partner 1 retells it.
3. Pairs repeat the whole exercise, switching roles.

Use with Lessons 1.1–1.2, 1.4, 2.1–2.4, and 3.1–3.3 *For Lesson 1.2, ask Partner 1 to read the description in the text and Partner 2 to describe each artifact in his or her own words. Then ask partners to switch roles.*

Strategy ❸
Create a Word Wall

Work with students at the **Emerging** and **Expanding** levels to select three words from each lesson to display in a grouping on a Word Wall. Choose words students are likely to encounter in other chapters, such as *alliance, doctrine,* and *neutrality.* Keep the words displayed throughout the lessons and discuss each one as it comes up during reading. Suggest that English-proficient students and students at the **Bridging** level contribute by adding phrases or examples to each word to develop understanding.

Use with All Lessons

GIFTED & TALENTED

Strategy ❶
Write a Dialogue

Instruct students to write a dialogue that might have taken place between Nathaniel Bacon and Governor William Berkeley. Encourage students to address the issues of land rights, relationships between colonists and Native Americans, and colonists' voice in government.

Use with Lessons 1.4 *Students might work in pairs to write the dialogue and then present it to the class.*

Strategy ❷
Present a Point of View

Assign students one of the following illustrations in the text: the Salem witch trials or the signing of the treaty with the Lenni Lenape. Encourage students to read the text and to consult other references regarding the events shown in the illustrations. Then ask each student to choose one of the participants depicted in the illustration and to describe the scene from that person's point of view.

Use with Lessons 2.4 and 3.1 *Have students present their descriptions to the class and discuss the reasons for the points of view expressed.*

Pre-AP

Strategy ❶
Interview a Leader

Allow students to work in pairs to research a leader they encounter in this chapter. Tell them to prepare interview questions and answers and then conduct the interview for the class in which one student represents the leader and the other represents the interviewer.

Use with Lessons 1.1, 1.4, 2.1, 2.2, 2.4, 3.1–3.3

Strategy ❷
Write a Profile of a Colonist

Have students review the chapter and identify the diverse groups of individuals who settled the first 13 colonies. Then have students write a profile on an ordinary colonist from one of the groups they identified. Remind students not to write about a famous colonist, but to focus instead on an ordinary person. Encourage students to share their profiles with the class.

Use with All Lessons *You might divide students into groups and assign a region to each group so that the profiles represent a broad range of colonists.*

THE THIRTEEN
COLONIES
1585–1732

ESSENTIAL QUESTION
How did early settlers cope with challenges as they established the first 13 colonies?

AMERICAN STORIES The Lost Colony of Roanoke

SECTION 1 **Early Colonies Have Mixed Success**
KEY VOCABULARY

charter	joint-stock company
indentured servant	traitor

SECTION 2 **New England Colonies**
KEY VOCABULARY

banish	King Philip's War	self-governance
dissenter	levy	separatist
Fundamental Orders of Connecticut	Mayflower Compact	

SECTION 3 **Middle and Southern Colonies**
KEY VOCABULARY

alliance	natural resource	raw material
confederacy	neutrality	royal colony
doctrine	proprietor	tributary
economic activity		

AMERICAN GALLERY
ONLINE A Portrait of the Pilgrims

READING STRATEGY

MAKE INFERENCES
When you make inferences, you use what you already know to figure out the meaning of the text. Use a chart like this one to make inferences about the challenges settlers faced as they established the first 13 colonies.

I READ	I KNOW	AND SO
The settlers lived under difficult conditions.	Many settlers died of diseases.	

84 CHAPTER 3

"As a **city upon a hill,** the eyes of all people are upon us."
—John Winthrop

Founded in 1947, Plimoth Plantation, a living museum in Plymouth, Massachusetts, provides an experience of what life was like for the Pilgrims and the Native Americans after the Pilgrims' arrival in 1620. From details in the photo, what materials can you identify that Pilgrims used to build houses and objects that were once part of daily life?

The Thirteen Colonies 85

INTRODUCE THE PHOTOGRAPH

Plimoth Plantation

Direct students' attention to the photograph. Tell students that in this chapter they will learn about life in the 13 colonies. Explain that Plimoth Plantation in Plymouth, Massachusetts, is a re-creation of the original 17th-century settlement built by the Pilgrims. The colonial village includes homes furnished with reproductions of authentic household items, kitchen gardens, and historic breeds of livestock. Visitors roam the village and encounter staff members dressed in period clothing playing the roles of Plymouth colonists, demonstrating and explaining daily tasks and answering visitors' questions using a 17th-century dialect. **ASK:** What is the value of a living museum like this one? *(Answers will vary. Possible response: It allows people to gain a better understanding of the past.)*

Share Background

The remains of the original Plymouth Colony are buried beneath the present-day city of Plymouth, Massachusetts. The re-created village was constructed through careful research and educated guesswork. It is only about one-third the size of the original settlement, but it sits on a hill, like the village built by the Pilgrims. The name *Plimoth* is based on Governor William Bradford's written history of the colony.

CRITICAL VIEWING Answers will vary. Possible response: Pilgrims used wood to build houses, barrels, fences, and stools. They forged metal for straps on the barrels and used straw for roofs.

For Chapter 3 Spanish Resources, visit the Resources Menu. Chapter 3 Resources are available at NGLSync.Cengage.com.

INTRODUCE THE ESSENTIAL QUESTION

How did early settlers cope with challenges as they established the first 13 colonies?

Four Corners Activity: Challenges This activity encourages students to consider what challenges early settlers faced. Post one of the following topics in each corner of the classroom:

1. Providing food and shelter

2. Establishing relationships with Native Americans

3. Adjusting to a harsh, new environment

4. Establishing rules to govern behavior and resolve conflicts

Ask students to choose a topic and think about how it challenged early settlers. Then have students go to the corner of their chosen topic and discuss their answers. Ask one member of each group to summarize the ideas for the class.

INTRODUCE CHAPTER VOCABULARY

Vocabulary Pyramids

As students read the chapter, instruct them to complete Vocabulary Pyramids for Key Vocabulary words. Tell students to make a pyramid for each word, fill in what they know about each word before reading, and then add to or correct the pyramid after they encounter the word in the chapter. Model an example for students on the board, using the graphic organizer below.

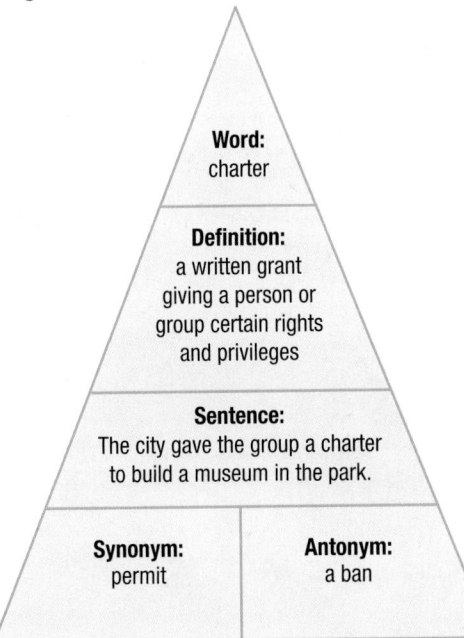

Word:
charter

Definition:
a written grant giving a person or group certain rights and privileges

Sentence:
The city gave the group a charter to build a museum in the park.

Synonym:
permit

Antonym:
a ban

INTRODUCE THE READING STRATEGY

MAKE INFERENCES

Remind students that inferences are not stated in the text. Explain that students must combine prior knowledge with what they read to make an inference. Use a chart like the one below to model making an inference. Read aloud the paragraph in Lesson 1.1 about Jamestown settlers dying from malaria. Then read the information in the first two columns of the chart. **ASK:** Based on what we have read and what we know, what inference can we make about why so many Jamestown settlers died of malaria? *(Answers will vary. Possible response: Jamestown settlers did not have the medical knowledge needed to cure malaria.)* Have students complete the chart with inferences they make as they read the chapter.

I READ	I KNOW	AND SO
The settlers lived under difficult conditions.	Many settlers died of diseases.	

KEY DATES FOR CHAPTER 3

1607	Jamestown founded
1620	Pilgrims create and sign Mayflower Compact
1621	First Thanksgiving
1630	Migration of Puritans
1639	Fundamental Orders of Connecticut
1681	Pennsylvania founded
1692	Salem witch trials
1733	Settlers arrive in Georgia

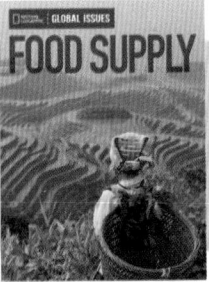

For more on providing people with adequate food, see *GLOBAL ISSUES: FOOD SUPPLY.*

STEM

Objectives

- Learn why England wanted to establish colonies in North America.
- Learn why the Roanoke Island colony did not receive the support it needed.
- Understand how John White's return to England for supplies affected the fate of Roanoke.
- Consider how views regarding the fate of Roanoke have changed over time.
- Study primary sources: artwork and maps of John White, governor of Roanoke.

Critical Thinking Skills for "The Lost Colony of Roanoke"

- Make Connections
- Draw Conclusions
- Analyze Cause and Effect
- Make Inferences
- Compare and Contrast
- Synthesize
- Make Predictions

Background for the Teacher

This American Story introduces students to the settlement of Roanoke, including the reasons for English colonization in North America and speculations about the mysterious disappearance of the colonists. This high-interest story will help students understand the failure of Roanoke, the importance of relations with the Native Americans who lived there before the colonists arrived, how science helps uncover the past, and what historians and archaeologists have discovered about the mystery of the lost colony of Roanoke.

The upcoming chapter, The Thirteen Colonies, covers the founding of the first English colonies in North America, the reasons for the settlements, and issues the colonists faced. This American Story introduces consequences of the interactions between Native Americans and early European colonists.

History Notebook

Encourage students to complete the American Story page for Chapter 3 in their History Notebooks as they read.

Note to the Teacher

Use this American Story as a teaser for content students will encounter in Chapter 3.

AMERICAN STORIES | NATIONAL GEOGRAPHIC

Dasamonquepeuc

Roanoac

CRITICAL VIEWING Which groups are represented in this historical map of Roanoke Island, and how did you identify them?

THE LOST COLONY OF
ROANOKE

Have you ever read about an unsolved mystery
that really haunts you? Something unexplainable has
happened, and you just can't get it out of your mind. The
"Lost Colony" of Roanoke is an unsolved mystery that has
haunted Americans since the late 1500s, when a group of
118 English colonists disappeared from the shore of North
Carolina sometime between 1587 and 1590.

**Watercolor by John White
of the Roanoke Colony**

TRYING TO COLONIZE

In 1584, nearly 100 years
after Christopher Columbus
had landed in North America,
Queen Elizabeth of England
grew tired of watching the
Spanish grow rich off the "New
World." Eager for the wealth and
fame that the colonies might
bring, and for the opportunity
to expand English control, she
granted nobleman Walter Raleigh
permission to set up a colony in North
America. Raleigh sent more than 100 colonists
to Roanoke Island, part of the island chain now
known as the Outer Banks of North Carolina.

The colony lasted less than
a year. The colonists had
no farming or fishing skills
and had to rely on trade
with Native Americans
named the Roanoac to feed
themselves. Foolishly, they
soured relations with the
tribe by treating them with
suspicion and ordering the
killing of a Roanoac chief. When
the explorer Sir Francis Drake
arrived with his fleet in June 1586, the
colonists were sorely in need of food and supplies
and desperate to leave. They gladly accepted
Drake's offer to bring them back to England.

Brainstorm a Need-to-Know List

Divide students into small groups and ask them to
brainstorm a list of things they would need to know
about an unfamiliar island before they moved there
and why. Invite groups to share their lists with the
class. Explain that in the late 1500s, England wanted
to claim and settle new lands in order to gain more
wealth, fame, and power. Tell students they are going
to read an American Story about England's first
attempts to establish a colony on an island off the
coast of present-day North Carolina.

K-W-L Chart

Provide each student with a K-W-L Chart. Ask students
to brainstorm what they might already know about the
lost colony of Roanoke, such as that Native American
inhabitants already lived on the land and why it is called
the "lost colony." Then tell students to write questions
they would like to answer as they study the lesson, such
as: What do historians think happened to the colony?
Allow time at the end of the lesson for students to fill in
what they have learned.

CRITICAL VIEWING Possible response: Native Americans
are represented by figures hunting on the island,
paddling on the water, and grouped in a circle on the
mainland in a tribal village. Shipwrecks may represent
explorers or colonists who came from Europe and
attempted to land their ships at the island but were
unsuccessful.

The Algonquians

In addition to the Croatoan and the Roanoac, the area was home to the Algonquians, a tribe with a population between 10,000 and 15,000 people. The area shared by the tribes was populated with many small towns. Most houses were constructed of poles covered with mats made from rushes. The mats could be raised or lowered depending on the weather. Houses covered with bark, a material that was hard to collect in large quantities, were easier to heat and are thought to be where the royal class, also called *weroances*, lived. While some Native American commoners lived in town, many lived near the fields, forests, and streams where food and water could be readily gathered.

Settling Roanoke Island

Sir Water Raleigh intended for the new colonists to settle along the Chesapeake Bay, quite a bit north of Roanoke Island. He hired Portuguese privateer Simon Fernandes to transport the colonists there, as Fernandes was familiar with the area. However, when Fernandes reached Roanoke Island to check on the 15 men who had remained from the previous year's unsuccessful settlement, he ordered the new settlers off his ship. Rather than taking the colonists to the Chesapeake Bay, he was more interested in resuming his search for Spanish ships to plunder. The new settlers discovered that the men from the first settlement had been killed by native people. With no other options, the new settlers repaired the fort on the island and set about creating a new home.

Rings of Evidence

Archaeologists can sometimes use trees rings to accurately tell the date of a site, building, or artifact. Because environmental conditions cause distinctive patterns in the width of tree rings, similar kinds of trees in the same area show the same pattern of wide and narrow bands. Scientists can therefore work backwards, looking at the rings of progressively older trees for areas where the ring pattern overlaps, establishing one long chronology of tree rings stretching into the past. One sequence of tree rings for bristlecone pine trees in California can be traced back thousands of years. Archaeologists can then use the sequence to tell, for example, in which year a tree was cut and used to build a log cabin. The study of tree-ring dating is called dendrochronology.

AMERICAN STORIES

SOMETIMES, EVIDENCE GROWS ON TREES

Scientists who study tree rings have offered an intriguing clue about the fate of the lost colony. Trees grow a new outer layer of wood each year during the growing season—that's why you can tell the age of a tree by counting its rings. In years with good growing conditions, a wider ring forms. Narrow rings indicate poor years for growth. Long-lived trees, such as the bald cypress trees in some North Carolina rivers, can help researchers determine what growing conditions were like centuries ago.

By studying local trees, scientists have determined that Roanoke Island experienced one of its worst droughts in centuries during the years 1587–1589. Which explanation for the colony's disappearance do you think this evidence supports?

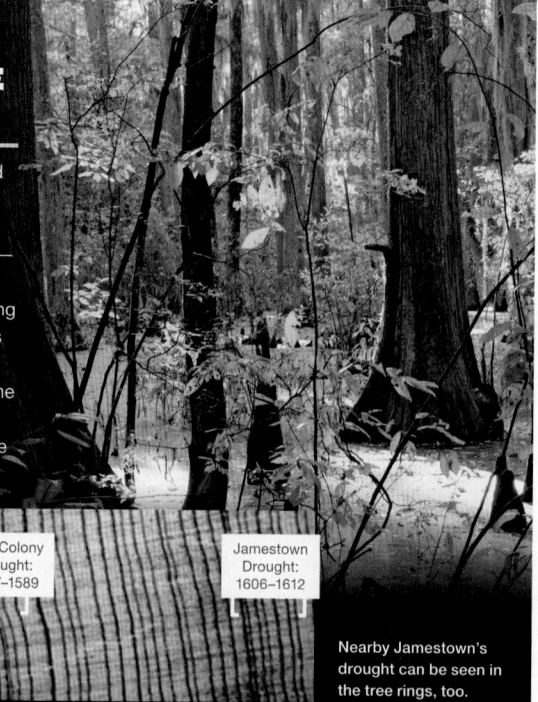

Lost Colony Drought: 1587–1589

Jamestown Drought: 1606–1612

Nearby Jamestown's drought can be seen in the tree rings, too.

FOUND AND LOST

Soon, Raleigh decided to try again, this time with a different type of colony. Unlike the all-male group that made the first attempt, these colonists would be a mixed group of men, women, and some children—families aspiring to be planters in the new colony. The governor would be John White, who had been a member of the earlier, failed expedition and had some knowledge of the local geography and tribes. Among the settlers were White's pregnant daughter Eleanor and her husband Ananias Dare.

The colonists reached Roanoke Island in July 1587. Because of the first colony's experiences, they were wary of the Roanoac, but they began a friendly relationship with a different local tribe, the Croatoan. On August 18, 1587, Virginia Dare was born, the first English baby born in North America.

The settlers soon realized they would need more supplies to get through the coming winter. In August, John White returned to England with the ships that had brought the colonists, intending to ask Raleigh for the much-needed goods. But because of England's war with Spain, White was unable to return to Roanoke for three years.

When John White came ashore on an eerily silent Roanoke Island in August 1590, not a single human—colonist or Native American—was present. White found the word *CROATOAN* carved into a post in the former settlement's gate, and a nearby tree bore the letters *CRO*. According to his journal, White concluded that the settlers were "safe . . . at Croatan, where . . . the Savages of the Island [are] our friends." But he would never learn whether his assumption was correct.

The next day, a strong storm blew up, forcing White's ships away from the Outer Banks. Under an onslaught of continuing bad weather, the small fleet had no choice but to retreat to England. White never succeeded in mounting another expedition to Roanoke or finding the missing colonists.

CRITICAL VIEWING This woodcut shows John White examining the carved word *Croatoan*. What can you infer from the men's expressions and body language?

LOST COLONY FOUND?

Like John White in 1590, researchers today wonder about what happened to the missing colonists. Were the colonists indeed with the Croatoan, just a few miles away from White as he searched the ruined settlement? Did baby Virginia Dare grow up in America? Many plausible explanations exist. The colonists may have moved in with the Croatoan and eventually become part of the tribe. It is also possible they were killed by a hostile native group or by soldiers from a passing Spanish ship.

In recent years, two teams of researchers have found new evidence about the colony's possible fate. In 2012, one group took a closer look at a map of the region drawn by John White. Underneath a paper patch on the map, they found a star-shaped symbol indicating a spot about 50 miles inland from Roanoke. Archaeologists digging at the spot, which they named Site X, uncovered pottery in a style that was also used by the Roanoke colonists.

Meanwhile, researchers digging at Cape Creek on Hatteras Island, where the Croatoan lived, have also discovered a number of objects that may have come from the Roanoke colony.

Many believe the finds at Cape Creek and Site X indicate that the Roanoke colonists left the island to live with different native tribes. Definite proof of the colonists' fate, however, remains tantalizingly out of reach. Charles Ewen, an archaeologist at East Carolina University, sums up the situation. "We still don't know what happened," he reflects, "and we are waiting to be persuaded."

THINK ABOUT IT

How does the story of Roanoke remind you of fictional mystery stories you have read or watched?

The Thirteen Colonies **89**

TEACH

Guided Discussion

1. **Analyze Cause and Effect** What major event contributed to the demise of the colony on Roanoke Island? *(John White returned to England for supplies for the colony, but England was at war with Spain, which prevented his return for three years.)*

2. **Make Inferences** Why are archaeologists unable to answer with certainty what happened to the colonists of Roanoke? Use evidence from the text to support your answer. *(Answers will vary. Possible response: Most of the evidence has been lost or deteriorated. There are clues but not enough factual evidence to have definitive answers.)*

Active Options

On Your Feet: Inside-Outside Circle Use the Inside-Outside Circle strategy to check students' understanding. Direct students in the outer circle to pose questions (e.g., Why did men of the first colony want to return to England?). Direct students in the inner circle to answer them. Then ask students to trade inside/outside roles and relocate to create new partnerships.

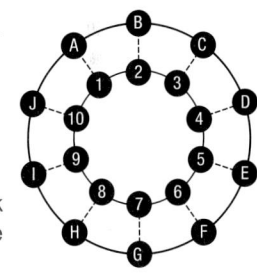

NG Learning Framework: Investigate Archaeology

SKILL Collaboration

KNOWLEDGE Our Human Story

Have groups collaborate to learn how archaeologists work. Tell students to write the following headings on their paper: Choose Site, Plan Dig, Secure Site, Collect Artifacts. Ask groups to assign topics to share the work and research and write a short report. Allow students time to plan, revise, and edit their work. Encourage them to include a graphic or photo and to present the reports.

CRITICAL VIEWING Answers will vary. Possible response: The men's expressions are serious and show uncertainty. John White's hand is extended as though asking, "Is this a clue about where the colonists went?" Two men hold weapons, and they are probably concerned about their own safety.

THINK ABOUT IT

Answers will vary. Possible response: The story of Roanoke is similar to murder mysteries in novels and on TV in which a detective carefully gathers physical evidence in various locations, studies the clues, and comes up with an educated guess as to what happened.

Guided Discussion

1. **Compare and Contrast** Why do you think Manteo remained with the English but Wanchese returned to his people? *(Answers will vary. Possible response: Manteo may have hoped interpreting for and remaining friendly with the English would prevent conflicts between them and his people. During Wanchese's visit in England, he may have realized the English were interested in colonial expansion and not preserving relations with Native Americans, so he decided to spend the rest of his days with his people.)*

2. **Draw Conclusions** How are John White's drawings helpful to historians today? Provide text evidence to support your answer. *(White's drawings are primary sources. The map lets historians know the location where the colonists were first situated. His drawing of Pomeiooc and a chief show the arrangement of a 17th-century Native American town and Native American dress, face paint, and bow.)*

Virtual Museum Visit

The First Colony Foundation (FCF) is an organization dedicated to researching America's beginnings, including the Roanoke Island colonies. At present, the FCF is concerned that the erosion of the Roanoke Island northern coastal areas is impeding efforts of archaeologists and historians to find answers about Roanoke's history. Since artifacts may have been washed into Roanoke Sound, archaeological research in this area is both above ground and underwater. Visitors to the FCF website can explore one of FCF's most important finds—evidence of "Old Fort Raleigh," a small "earthwork" fort.

WRITE ABOUT HISTORY

Compose a Letter Home To help students make connections between the real people involved in this American Story and their own lives, have them imagine they are a member of the colony and write a letter to someone back home in England. The letter might be set at the time of the birth of Virginia Dare or during the years colonists were waiting desperately for supplies. Students might include reasons they moved to North America as well as more personal thoughts students imagine the settlers may have had.

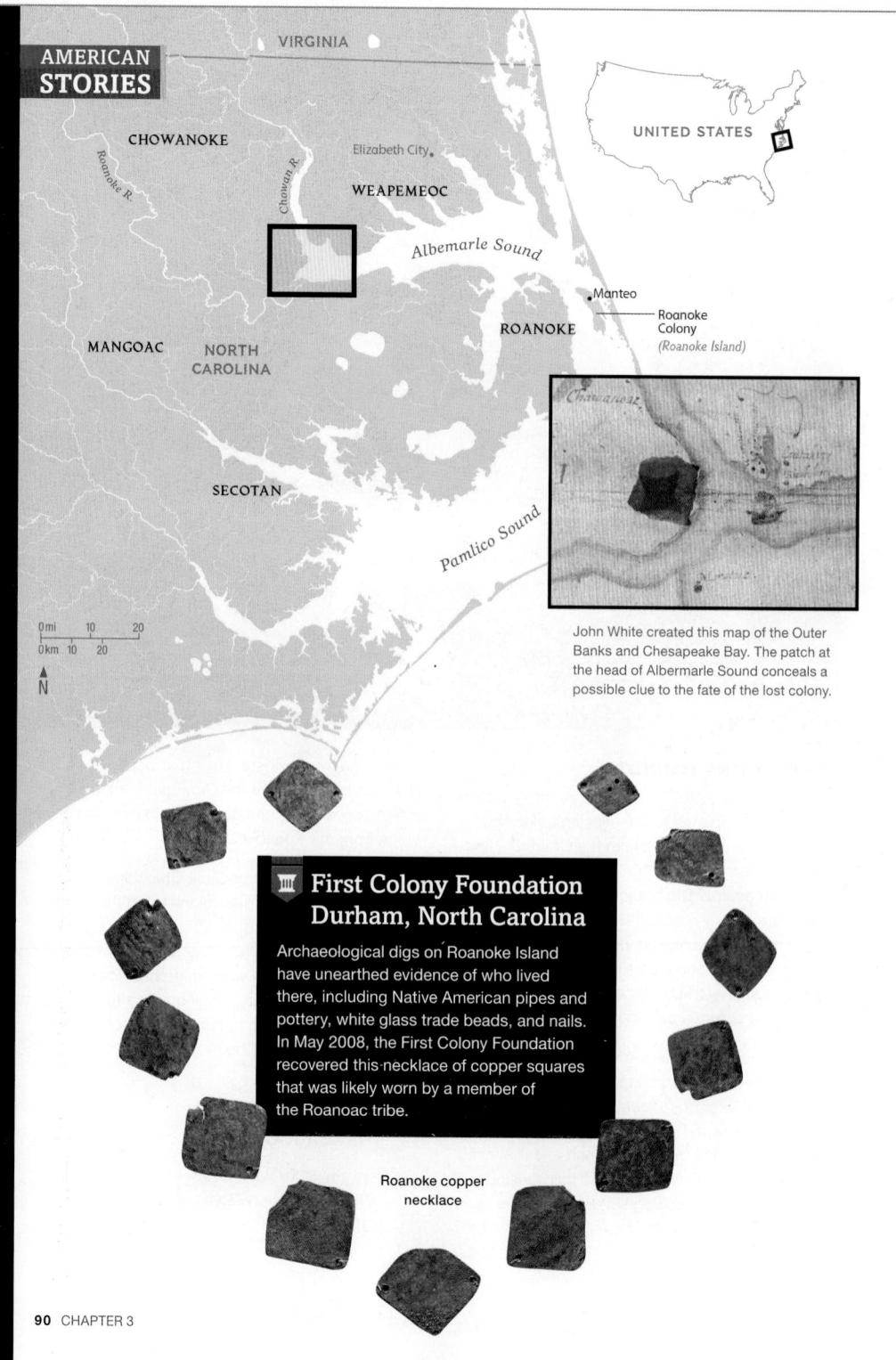

John White created this map of the Outer Banks and Chesapeake Bay. The patch at the head of Albermarle Sound conceals a possible clue to the fate of the lost colony.

First Colony Foundation
Durham, North Carolina

Archaeological digs on Roanoke Island have unearthed evidence of who lived there, including Native American pipes and pottery, white glass trade beads, and nails. In May 2008, the First Colony Foundation recovered this necklace of copper squares that was likely worn by a member of the Roanoac tribe.

Roanoke copper necklace

THE ARTWORK OF JOHN WHITE

John White was an accomplished artist and cartographer. In 1585, he voyaged from England to the Outer Banks. During his year-long stay at Roanoke, he created more than 70 watercolor drawings of indigenous people, plants, and animals to give the English a sense of the environment in the "New World."

John White's watercolor of the Native American town of Pomeiooc

MANTEO AND WANCHESE

Manteo and Wanchese were two of the first Native Americans to have extensive contact with the English. Manteo was a Croatoan chief, and Wanchese was from the Roanoac tribe. Both men encountered a scouting party that Walter Raleigh sent before the first Roanoke colony, and both returned with the group to England.

Wanchese came to dislike the English and felt like a prisoner in England. Manteo, on the other hand, became friendly with the English and remained loyal to them for years. Both Manteo and Wanchese came to Roanoke with the first colony. Wanchese rejoined his people, but Manteo stayed with the English as an interpreter and guide. When the first colony failed, Manteo returned to England with the former settlers. Later, he accompanied White's group of colonists, once again serving as an interpreter and helping to smooth relations with the Croatoans. In August 1587, before White left for England, Manteo was baptized and officially converted to Christianity.

John White's watercolor of a Native American chief

The Thirteen Colonies **91**

DIFFERENTIATE

Striving Readers

Record and Compare Facts After reading each spread, ask students to write at least three facts they can recall. Allow pairs of students to compare and check their facts and then combine their facts into one longer list for the entire American Story. Challenge pairs to assemble the longest list of accurate facts.

Gifted & Talented

Illustrate Roanoke Arrange students in pairs and ask them to illustrate a scene based on what they've learned about the Lost Colony of Roanoke. Ask students to draft their ideas by drawing preliminary sketches. Suggest that students write captions and dialogue bubbles, if appropriate. Invite students to present or display their illustrations.

See the Chapter Planner for more strategies for differentiation.

HISTORICAL THINKING

Ask and have students answer the following questions.

1. **READING CHECK** What clues about the missing colonists did John White find at Roanoke, and why are they important?

2. **SYNTHESIZE** Why is the mystery of Roanoke an important topic to historians?

3. **MAKE PREDICTIONS** Based on the American Story you just read, how do you predict the topics in the story will relate to Chapter 3: The Thirteen Colonies?

ANSWERS

1. John White found *CROATOAN* carved into a post and the letters *CRO* carved into a tree, presumably done by the colonists since Native Americans didn't write in English.

2. Possible response: Historians work from facts based on evidence. Finding new evidence that could explain the disappearance of the colonists would add to our knowledge and possibly change an interpretation of history.

3. Answers will vary.

1.1 Colonizing Virginia

Imagine settling in an entirely new place, far across an ocean from your home. How would you prepare for this adventure? The founders of Jamestown, Virginia, found out the hard way just what it was like.

MAIN IDEA Virginia's first colonists struggled with starvation, wars, and disease before finally finding success in their new home.

FOUNDING JAMESTOWN

In the early 1600s, England began establishing colonies in America. As with Spain and its colonies, England pursued the economic policy of mercantilism, giving it a trade monopoly with its colonies. The colonies provided raw materials to England, where workers made them into goods. Finished goods were then shipped back to the colonies and sold or traded, helping England increase its wealth.

At the same time, merchants and investors developed a new type of business, called a **joint-stock company**. Wealthy individuals invested in a venture, or business project. Their funds paid for the endeavor, and the individuals shared ownership in the venture. This business raised money for

AMERICAN PLACES
The Chesapeake Bay

The Chesapeake Bay is a large inlet that extends through the present-day states of Virginia and Maryland. It is a rich ecosystem, with more than 150 rivers and streams flowing into it. The area around the bay provided rich farmland to colonists who established farms and plantations there.

exploring trade routes and establishing markets in new locations. In late 1606, a joint-stock company called the **Virginia Company** funded the first English settlement at **Jamestown** in the colony of Virginia. King James I had provided a **charter**, or written grant detailing rights and privileges, to the company to settle the colonies. After a difficult winter voyage across the Atlantic Ocean, more than 100 settlers arrived in the **Chesapeake Bay** and established a fort along the James River.

The settlers were ill-equipped to establish a colony. They had little experience with farming, hunting, or fishing and were more interested in searching for gold. Soon they were starving. To make matters worse, Jamestown was located in a low-lying area—perfect for mosquitoes that carried malaria, a disease that killed many settlers.

Colonial officer John Smith established a mutually beneficial trade relationship with the Powhatan, a Native American tribe. The Powhatan grew corn that the settlers could use, and the English had goods that the Powhatan wanted, such as weapons. In 1608, Smith became president of the colony and put the settlers to work planting crops, fishing, and building houses. The state of the colony improved.

Then in September 1609, Smith was injured and returned to England. That same year, the Virginia Company angered Chief Powhatan, who then cut off trade with the settlers. Winter came, and the settlers began to starve again. Any colonist who left the fort risked being attacked. Only 60 colonists survived the winter. In 1614, Chief Powhatan's daughter, Pocahontas, married colonist John Rolfe. The marriage helped usher in peace between the two groups.

SUCCESS AT LAST

In about 1612, Rolfe started to grow a new variety of tobacco in Virginia. He used seeds he had acquired in the West Indies. Rolfe's new tobacco was less bitter than the variety that had been grown in the colony, and by the following year, he began shipping it to England, where it became very popular. Tobacco farmers tried to produce enough to meet rising demand, and tobacco became a driving economic force in the colonies.

In 1619, the Virginia Company tried to persuade English citizens to move to Virginia to build this labor force. Some citizens were freeholders who

Pocahontas
Artists have portrayed Pocahontas in various ways, almost always based on information rather than actually seeing her. The top left painting as Lady Rebecca Rolfe in England (1616) is the only known portrait of her from life. Other artists have imagined her as the Powhatan princess who captivated John Rolfe (top right, painting dated 1945), and shortly after her marriage to Rolfe in 1614 (painting dated c. 1852).

paid their own transportation and received land in exchange. Others were **indentured servants**, who gave up several years of freedom to have their travel fees paid by the company or another person. Indentured servants were bound for a certain length of time to work to pay off their traveling expenses.

Also in 1619, the Virginia Company established an assembly of elected delegates in Virginia, called the **House of Burgesses**. It became the first representative assembly in the American colonies, and it gave the colonists more local control.

HISTORICAL THINKING

1. **READING CHECK** What was the purpose for establishing an English settlement in Virginia?

2. **FORM AND SUPPORT OPINIONS** How important do you think John Smith was to the settlers? Use evidence from the reading to support your opinion.

3. **MAKE INFERENCES** Why did John Rolfe's marriage to Pocahontas bring about peace between the Powhatan and the colonists?

PLAN

Objective
Learn about the development of Jamestown colony.

Critical Thinking Skills for Lesson 1.1
- Identify Main Ideas and Details
- Monitor Comprehension
- Form and Support Opinions
- Make Inferences
- Analyze Cause and Effect
- Make Connections

Essential Question for Chapter 3
How did early settlers cope with challenges as they established the first 13 colonies? Virginia's first settlers were unprepared for the challenges they faced in America. Lesson 1.1 discusses how strong leadership helped colonists survive hardships, forge relationships with Native Americans, and establish a successful economy.

Background for the Teacher
The Virginia Company viewed Jamestown as a business and settlers as company employees. The company instructed the first colonists to search for gold and silver and establish profitable industries and trade. The colonists, many of whom were wealthy adventurers, failed to produce and became aimless. Sir Thomas Dale, who arrived in Jamestown as governor in 1611, quickly established martial law and required reasonable hours of work with harsh punishments for noncompliance. A first offender was tied neck to heels all night. A second offense merited whipping, and punishment for a third offense was death. The harsh laws caused a scandal in England and discouraged settlers from coming to the colony.

History Notebook
Encourage students to complete the Reid on the Road video series page for Chapter 3 in their History Notebooks as they read.

Brainstorm a List

Engage in a short class discussion to brainstorm a list of what settlers would need to survive in an entirely new place. Ask students to speculate about the preparation for this adventure. Use students' answers to create a master list on the whiteboard. Direct students' attention to the photograph of Chesapeake Bay. **ASK:** Based on the list, how do you think settlers would have done in a setting like Chesapeake Bay? Discuss answers and possible obstacles to survival.

TEACH

Guided Discussion

1. **Analyze Cause and Effect** What problems made it difficult for the settlers to survive in the early years of the colony? *(Answers will vary. Possible response: The colonists built their fort along the James River in a low-lying area prone to malaria-carrying mosquitoes. As a result, many colonists died of malaria. In addition, the colonists were not used to farming, hunting, and fishing, so they had to rely on corn from the Powhatan. When Chief Powhatan stopped trading with the settlers, many starved. Conflict between the Powhatan and the settlers also put settlers at risk of attack when they left the fort.)*

2. **Make Connections** What factor contributed to Jamestown's ultimate success? *(John Rolfe started growing a form of tobacco from the West Indies that was not as bitter as the old variety. Demand for the new tobacco was so high in England that the economy became centered on growing tobacco, and the colony prospered.)*

American Places

John Smith's remarkable work of mapping the Chesapeake Bay region helped open Virginia to European exploration, settlement, and trade. Smith traveled some 2,500 miles around the Chesapeake in separate expeditions in 1608, recording observations in a journal and creating a detailed map of the area. The map included the sites of more than 200 Native American villages. Smith's map of Virginia was published in England in 1612, and it remained the primary map of the Chesapeake Bay region for decades.

Active Options

On Your Feet: Think, Pair, Share Ask students what, in their opinion, was most responsible for the success of Jamestown. Tell students to think about their answer, discuss it with a partner, and then share it with the class. Possible answers may include, but are not limited to, an individual's specific contribution, the rich land at the location of the colony, help from the Powhatan, self-government, or the development of a tobacco crop. Make sure students support their answers with information from the text.

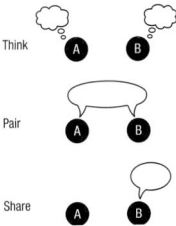

Think

Pair

Share

NG Learning Framework: Write a Biography

SKILL Communication

KNOWLEDGE Our Human Story

Pocahontas has fascinated people from 17th-century artists to 21st-century filmmakers. Tell students to find out more about her life and the impact of her marriage to John Rolfe in 1614. Instruct them to create a biographical sketch of Pocahontas and explain how the visuals in the lesson relate to the events of her life. Students may alternatively create original illustrations. Invite students to share their biographical sketches and illustrations with the class.

Striving Readers

Record and Compare Facts After students read the lesson, ask them to write three important facts they learned about Jamestown. Ask pairs of students to compare and check their facts and then combine their facts into one list. Finally, ask one student from each pair to write the most important fact from their list on the board. As a group, decide if the list includes the most important facts about Jamestown or if something needs to be added or changed.

Gifted & Talented

Create a Multimedia Presentation Instruct students to create a multimedia presentation about the Chesapeake Bay ecosystem during the early 1600s using photos, spoken words, and written text. The presentations should describe geological features, such as rivers and streams, as well as plants and animals that colonists would have used in establishing farms and plantations. Invite students to share their presentations with the class.

See the Chapter Planner for more strategies for differentiation.

HISTORICAL THINKING

ANSWERS

1. England established settlements in Virginia to gain wealth through mercantilism. Settlers provided raw materials to make goods in England that could then be shipped to the colonies for sale or trade.

2. Answers will vary. Possible response: John Smith helped to keep settlers alive and productive. He established trade with the Powhatan to exchange goods for corn and put the settlers to work planting crops, fishing, and building houses.

3. The marriage brought about peace because it bound the two groups together.

1.2 Voorhees Archaearium Jamestown, Virginia

Located near the site of the original Jamestown Settlement, America's first permanent English colony, the Voorhees Archaearium captures the story of Virginia in the 1600s. Artifacts from the arrival of English colonists to Jamestown in 1607 and the earliest cultural encounters and events are housed in this archaeology museum. Visitors can explore the cultures of the Native Americans, Europeans, and Africans who intersected in 17th-century Virginia, and trace Jamestown's beginnings in England. They can even climb aboard replicas of the three ships, moored nearby, that crossed the Atlantic, bringing the earliest colonists from England to Virginia. What can you infer about the lives of the colonists based on the artifacts below?

Brass Thimble
This 16th-century thimble was made in Nuremberg, Germany, and is one of 11 brass thimbles found at the James Fort. Several tailors joined the Jamestown colonists in 1607 and 1608, and their ability to sew and repair cloth was important to the frontier settlement. Other tailoring tools have also been found, including needles, irons, and pins.

Ear Picker
Believe it or not, a Jamestown colonist once used this silver sea creature to scrape teeth, clean dirt from fingernails, and scoop out earwax. Gold and silver grooming tools were often worn like jewelry in Europe during the late 1500s and early 1600s. The first settlers at Jamestown included a surgeon and a barber who could perform basic medical care like removing infected teeth—and excessive earwax.

Tailors sometimes used earwax to make their thread stronger if they had no beeswax!

Lead Toy Horse
A collection of tiny toy horses like this one was found in a trash heap along with food remains, broken pottery, and shattered glassware from the James Fort. Long ago, this horse may have carried a toy rider in its saddle and had wheels so a child could push or pull it around.

Gaming Dice
Excavations have revealed more than 60 gaming dice at the James Fort. Many of the dice are made of animal bone, but some are made of ivory or lead. It's possible that the lead dice may have been made by a soldier who also made lead shot (fired by weapons) at the fort. Like modern dice, the opposing sides of the Jamestown dice add up to seven. Soldiers passed the long hours at the remote fort playing dice games.

Why might the English have felt it was safer to drink wine than water in the early 1600s?

Monogrammed Wine Bottles
Discovered by Jamestown archaeologists, these wide glass bottles were made in England between 1680 and 1700 and found upright on the dirt floor of a rectangular cellar. One of the intact bottles is marked with the initials *FN*, which reveals it once belonged to someone of wealth and status. During the 17th century, high-ranking gentlemen liked to order wine bottles from England stamped with their personal seal.

PLAN

Objective
Identify artifacts relating to the Jamestown Settlement.

Critical Thinking Skills for Lesson 1.2
- Make Connections
- Analyze Visuals
- Make Generalizations
- Draw Conclusions

Essential Question for Chapter 3
How did early settlers cope with challenges as they established the first 13 colonies?
Archaeological excavations at the site of the original Jamestown Settlement have produced a treasure trove of artifacts that provide insights into how the early English colonists lived. Lesson 1.2 shows artifacts from the Voorhees Archaearium collection and examines what they tell us about daily life in colonial Virginia in the 1600s.

Background for the Teacher
The 7,500 square-foot Voorhees Archaearium [ark-ee-AIR-ee-uhm] opened in 2006 as a place to showcase the beginnings of English colonial life in America. More than 4,000 artifacts are on display, including items from the Jamestown Rediscovery project, an ongoing archaeological effort that has located the original James Fort and its principal buildings. Visitors to the museum can view historical objects within sight of the locations where they were originally used. The museum's website includes an interactive time line tracing the history of Jamestown back to the first known steps of an Englishman on the shores of Chesapeake Bay.

History Notebook
Encourage students to complete the Curating History page for Chapter 3 in their History Notebooks as they read.

Preview with Artifacts

Before students read the text, direct their attention to the artifacts. Ask them to speculate about how each object was used. **ASK:** Which objects are similar to objects we use today? *(The toy horse, dice, thimble, and bottle are familiar objects that are used today.)* **ASK:** How do these similarities help us form a connection to the past? *(Answers will vary. Possible response: They show that people who lived long ago were like us in some ways: children had toys, people played games, and they sometimes put their initials on their belongings.)* Allow time for students to discuss which artifact they find most interesting and what they would like to find out about the object.

TEACH

Guided Discussion

1. **Make Generalizations** What details about the toy horse might archaeologists want to study from a historical perspective? *(Answers will vary. Possible response: Archaeologists might want to compare the toy horse and saddle to real horses and saddles from the time period. For example, they might want to determine if Europeans braided their horses' manes and cut their tails short. They might also want to determine the purpose of the saddle design. In addition, archaeologists might try to determine how and where the toy was manufactured.)*

2. **Draw Conclusions** Based on workmanship and materials, what conclusions can you draw about the origins of the dice and ear picker? *(Answers will vary. Possible response: The lead dice might have been made in Jamestown, but the ivory dice likely came from England. The bone dice might have been made in Jamestown or England. The ear picker appears to have been made by a skilled worker and was probably brought from England.)*

🏛 Curating History

The Voorhees Archaearium website is a useful resource for learning more about Jamestown artifacts. Choose an artifact from the lesson to investigate. Access the museum's website and demonstrate how to find the artifact in the collections. For example, locate the dice in the Entertainment Collection. Ask a volunteer to read the information about the dice from the website. Then direct the class to discuss how the information expands their understanding of the artifact. Ask groups of students to find other artifacts from the lesson in the website collections and report their findings to the class.

Active Options

On Your Feet: Sort the Artifacts Direct students to work in teams of four to examine the museum's online collections and complete two Concept Clusters like those shown below. In one cluster, students should identify artifacts related to colonial entertainment. In the other, students should identify a different class or genre of artifacts, to be determined by the team. When teams are finished, ask them to share their Concept Clusters with the class.

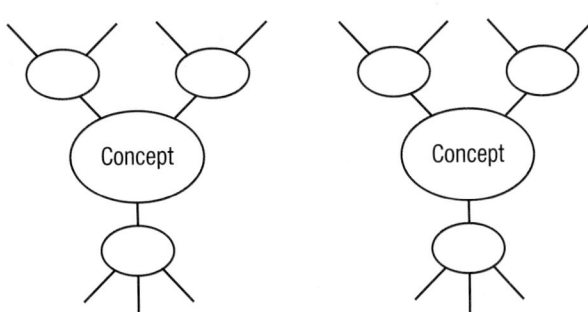

Inclusion

Describe Artifacts Pair students who are visually impaired with sighted partners. Tell pairs to listen to an audio recording of the text. After each description, ask pairs to stop the recording and discuss the artifact described. Sighted students may clarify understandings for their partners based on the photographs.

Pre-AP

STEM

Summarize Processes Direct students to view one or more of the videos on the Voorhees Archaearium website that describe the work of project archaeologists. Then have them summarize processes that archaeologists use to unearth artifacts. Encourage students to present their summaries to the class and be prepared to field questions from the class.

See the Chapter Planner for more strategies for differentiation.

CURATING HISTORY

Answers will vary. Possible response: The colonists provided toys for their children, and they played dice games for entertainment. The thimble shows that there were tailors among the colonists who either repaired or made clothing. The silver ear picker provides evidence of the colonists' methods of personal hygiene, and the monogrammed wine bottles indicate that the colonists brought or made and drank wine.

MONOGRAMMED WINE BOTTLES

Answers will vary. Possible response: The fort at Jamestown was built in a low-lying area, so the water supply may have been unsafe to drink, particularly in times of disease or during hot summer months. As the population grew, water quality may have gotten worse, since there was no sanitation system.

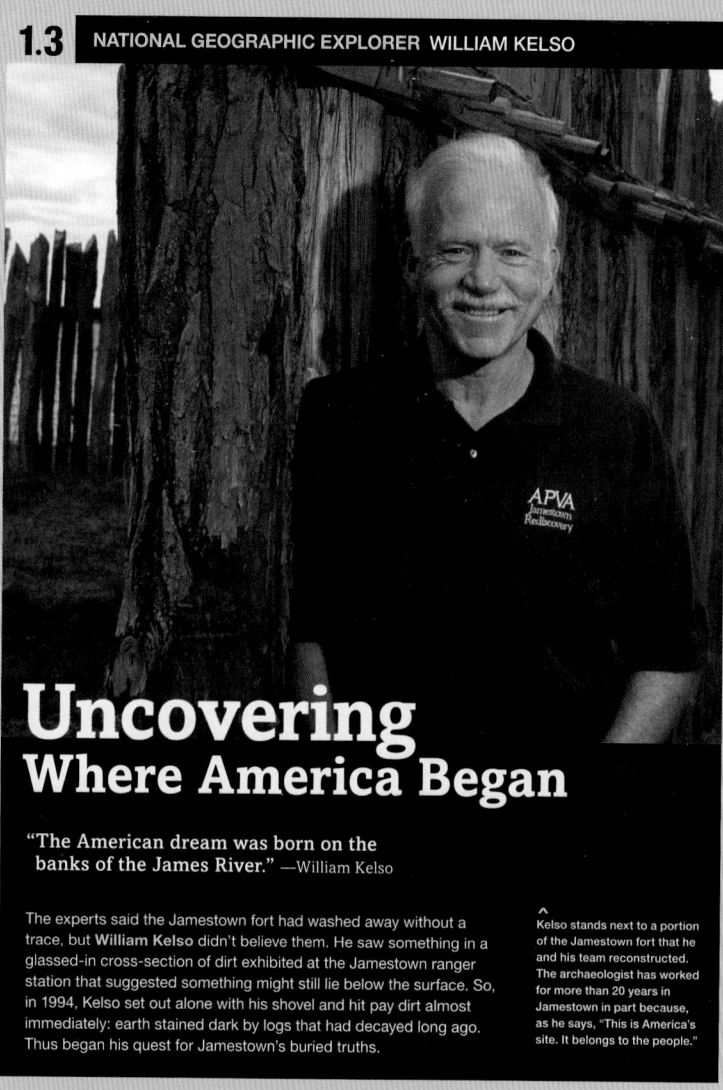

Uncovering
Where America Began

"The American dream was born on the banks of the James River." —William Kelso

The experts said the Jamestown fort had washed away without a trace, but **William Kelso** didn't believe them. He saw something in a glassed-in cross-section of dirt exhibited at the Jamestown ranger station that suggested something might still lie below the surface. So, in 1994, Kelso set out alone with his shovel and hit pay dirt almost immediately: earth stained dark by logs that had decayed long ago. Thus began his quest for Jamestown's buried truths.

^
Kelso stands next to a portion of the Jamestown fort that he and his team reconstructed. The archaeologist has worked for more than 20 years in Jamestown in part because, as he says, "This is America's site. It belongs to the people."

MAIN IDEA Archaeologist William Kelso has uncovered evidence at Jamestown that is changing how people view the settlement.

EARLY DISCOVERIES

National Geographic Explorer William Kelso's search began in 1994. In anticipation of the 400th anniversary of Jamestown's founding, the Association for the Preservation of Virginia Antiquities had announced plans to investigate the island. Kelso volunteered for the job.

About all he had to go on were some historical accounts and documents, including a roughly drawn Spanish map from 1608 showing the triangular Jamestown fort. But he also knew that the only aboveground ruins that had survived in Jamestown were parts of a church tower. Kelso reasoned that the settlers would have built the fort near the church, so he began there. Fragments of early 1600s ceramics and the dark-stained dirt told him that he was on the right track.

THE TRUTH ABOUT JAMESTOWN

In time, Kelso identified evidence of all but one corner of the fort's structure as well as thousands of artifacts. He and his team—at this point, Kelso wasn't working alone anymore—began reconstructing the fort, using the materials and tools available to the Jamestown settlers. During this process, he discovered just how tough the settlers had been. Kelso says, "They were cutting down trees, digging holes, building forts, building buildings, digging ditches." The skeletons that Kelso has excavated also reveal how hard the settlers' lives were. Many died during the starving time of the early years and in the wars with Native Americans. Others couldn't adapt to the new environment. Lifespans were short.

One misconception about Jamestown is that it was a failure, but the settlers got many things right. Historians have often faulted them for establishing their colony in what was basically a

This map shows the triangular Jamestown fort and the houses that stood within it. Chief Powhatan sits at the top right of the map, while ships full of settlers arrive on the island along the James River.

marsh. But they needed to find a place where they could defend themselves against the Spanish. Locating their settlement on an island worked—the Spanish never attacked. Above all, they developed a new form of government. Around 1619, the settlers organized a representative assembly that met at the church. According to Kelso, "That's when liberty got out of the bag, and nobody could stuff it back in."

These findings have told us a lot about the site, and Kelso hopes to uncover more. But now the sea level around Jamestown Island is rising. Soon, important evidence may disappear. And Kelso believes the site is worth preserving. For, as he says, "This is where America began. This is where the English settlers first became American."

HISTORICAL THINKING

1. **READING CHECK** What did Kelso learn about the Jamestown settlers from his excavations?

2. **ANALYZE CAUSE AND EFFECT** Why did the settlers choose Jamestown as the site for their colony?

3. **DRAW CONCLUSIONS** What action on the settlers' part was key to the development of American constitutional democracy?

Objective
Learn what new information William Kelso's work has revealed about Jamestown.

Critical Thinking Skills for Lesson 1.3

- Identify Main Ideas and Details
- Monitor Comprehension
- Analyze Cause and Effect
- Draw Conclusions
- Distinguish Fact from Opinion
- Evaluate
- Analyze Visuals

Essential Question for Chapter 3

How did early settlers cope with challenges as they established the first 13 colonies?
Excavations of Jamestown's fort uncovered new evidence about life in early Jamestown. Lesson 1.3 discusses details from the archaeological site.

Background for the Teacher

As a young man, William Kelso's main interest in life was football. He played for Baldwin Wallace College, where he also studied history. Later, as a high school history teacher and football coach, Kelso spent summers at archaeological digs. His interest in archaeology led to a distinguished career. He has received numerous awards, including being named a Commander of the British Empire. Kelso led Britain's Queen Elizabeth II on a tour of Jamestown during its 400th anniversary celebration in 2007. Kelso's efforts continue to reveal truths—sometimes grim realities—about colonial life. In 2012, his team discovered that Jamestown residents had resorted to cannibalism of corpses to survive the "starving time" in the winter of 1609–1610.

History Notebook

Encourage students to complete the Explorer page for Chapter 3 in their History Notebooks as they read.

INTRODUCE & ENGAGE

Think Like an Explorer

Explain that some questions about what happened in Jamestown can be answered by historical study and research. Ask students to think about the following questions: What is one thing you would like to know about Jamestown? How might you find the answer? Allow time for students to share their questions and ideas about finding answers with the class. Explain that this lesson is about National Geographic Explorer William Kelso's work at the fort at Jamestown.

TEACH   STEM

Guided Discussion

1. **Distinguish Fact from Opinion** What evidence did Kelso find to support his opinion that experts were wrong about Jamestown's fort having "washed away without a trace"? *(A cross-section of dirt Kelso saw at a ranger station caught his attention. When he went to the site and began digging, he found earth that was stained dark by decayed logs. He went on to find evidence of all but one corner of the fort. He also found broken ceramics and thousands of other buried artifacts from the 1600s.)*

2. **Evaluate** How did reconstructing the fort influence Kelso's view of Jamestown's settlers? *(Kelso and his team reconstructed the fort using materials and tools that the settlers would have used. The difficulty of doing this convinced Kelso that the settlers were very tough and had a hard life.)*

Analyze Visuals

Direct students' attention to the early map of the Jamestown fort. **ASK:** What can we learn about Jamestown from the map? Divide students into small groups to discuss their answers. Then have members of each group share their observations with the class. *(Answers will vary. Possible responses: The fort was built in a triangular shape, with the broad side and gate facing the water; All of the settlers' houses were located inside the fort; The fort was located near the Powhatan; Ships could approach the fort by sailing up the James River.)*

Active Options

On Your Feet: Inside-Outside Circle Have students brainstorm a list of questions to ask William Kelso about his work. List questions on the board. Then provide time for students to formulate answers Kelso might give, based on information in the lesson and additional research. Arrange students in concentric circles facing each other. Have each student in the outside circle ask a question from the list, and have the student in the inside circle answer it as Kelso might. Have the outside circle rotate one position to the right and repeat the process. After a few minutes, have students switch roles, with those in the inside circle asking questions and those in the outside circle answering.

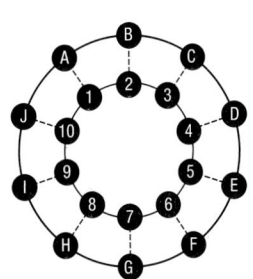

NG Learning Framework: Write About Building Jamestown Fort

SKILL Collaboration

KNOWLEDGE Our Living Planet

Have student teams imagine they are colonists building the Jamestown fort. Ask students to write journal entries about the difficulties and challenges they encounter as they clear the site, gather the building materials, and construct the fort. Suggest that students record their experiences and conversations with the other settlers. Then ask students to read aloud their journal entries and share their recordings with the class.

DIFFERENTIATE

English Language Learners   ELD

Summarize the Main Idea Help students identify the main idea of the lesson by filling out a 5Ws Chart answering the questions: *Who? What? Where? When?* and *Why? (Who: William Kelso; What: the Jamestown fort; Where: Jamestown, Virginia; When: 1994; Why: to find evidence of the fort)* Have students at **All Proficiencies** use the information in their chart to state a sentence that summarizes the main idea of the lesson.

Gifted & Talented   STEM

Create a Model Have students design and construct a whole or partial model of the Jamestown fort to present to the class. They may use craft sticks, cardboard, or other materials. Have students use visuals and information in the lesson as well as additional images on the Jamestown Rediscovery website to guide their work. Ask students to prepare a brief report on one feature of the fort or one aspect of its historical significance that they can illustrate with their model.

See the Chapter Planner for more strategies for differentiation.

HISTORICAL THINKING

ANSWERS

1. When Kelso excavated skeletons, he learned that settlers had hard, short lives. Skeletons indicated that many settlers died during the starving time. Others died in wars with Native Americans or because they could not adjust to the environment.

2. The settlers chose to establish the colony on an island in order to defend themselves in the event the Spanish attacked.

3. The settlers developed a new form of government that included a representative assembly. This was key to the development of an American constitutional democracy.

1.4 Conflicts with Native Americans

When something that belongs to you is taken away, it can be difficult to keep the peace. Native Americans in the 1600s faced this challenge when colonists began to take over their ancestral lands.

MAIN IDEA Wars between Native Americans and Virginian colonists raged on and off for decades as each group laid claim to the land.

WARS WITH THE POWHATAN

For about eight years after John Rolfe and Pocahontas were married, the Jamestown colonists and the Powhatan lived in peace. During that time, the Powhatan helped the colonists plant corn, catch fish, and capture wild fowl. But as thousands of new colonists arrived to work for the Virginia Company, the Powhatan saw their land and culture taken away. In 1622, one Powhatan leader staged a rebellion against the English and their European and Christian customs. Colonists killed him, and the Powhatan responded by launching an attack on the colony, killing hundreds of settlers.

This attack set off a 10-year war. When peace finally came, it lasted for more than a decade. But even during the peaceful years, the colonists' desire for land continued to provoke the Powhatan. As the demand for tobacco as a cash crop increased, colonists, claiming the English king owned the colony and its land, simply grabbed land they deemed to be unoccupied. Although no one lived on the land, the Powhatan hunted, fished, and farmed on it. Two years later, the Powhatan attacked the colony again, triggering yet another war. In 1646, the Powhatan surrendered. Their leader was captured and later killed.

The two groups signed a treaty that required the Powhatan to live on lands north of the York River. They also had to make a yearly payment to the colonists of 20 beaver skins. The Powhatan had lost their power in Jamestown.

BACON'S REBELLION

As years passed, conflicts between Native Americans and colonists increased. In the 1660s, the governor of Virginia, William Berkeley, urged colonists to interact peacefully and maintain trading to avoid a costly war. However, by 1670, tensions surfaced among colonists who owned land and those who did not. Landless freemen resented their lack of property and wanted a stronger voice in Virginia's government.

Chesapeake Bay Colonies, 1650–1700

Areas settled by 1650
Areas settled by 1675
Areas settled by 1700

Many of them had the right to purchase land, but low tobacco prices and high land prices made it difficult for them to find land they could afford to buy. They also claimed that the Powhatan controlled too much land, even though this land had been granted to the Native Americans by the 1646 treaty.

A young councilman and wealthy planter named Nathaniel Bacon, who was actually Berkeley's cousin by marriage, challenged Berkeley's leadership. He argued that the governor held too much power and that the colonists should be more involved with the government. He also wanted to claim more land from the Powhatan. Bacon and a group of landless followers attacked Native Americans in 1676 in an attempted revolution later called **Bacon's Rebellion**.

Berkeley accused Bacon of being a **traitor**, or someone disloyal to his or her own people or cause, because he believed Bacon had challenged the power of the governor and his fellow wealthy planters. Bacon had growing public support, however. Bowing to this pressure, Berkeley agreed to be lenient with Bacon if he turned himself in and went to England to be tried before King Charles II. But the House of Burgesses did not approve of Berkeley's leniency. They forced Bacon to apologize to Berkeley. The power struggle between Bacon and Berkeley continued for several months. Bacon and his army even burned Jamestown to the ground in September 1676.

The rebellion ended a month later when Bacon died unexpectedly. Berkeley ordered Bacon's fellow leaders to be executed. Angered by

CRITICAL VIEWING Bacon's followers included men from all walks of life. In his painting of the burning of Jamestown in 1676, Howard Pyle shows Bacon in the center but not ahead of everyone else. What can you infer from Bacon's placement about the spirit of the rebellion?

these events, King Charles II demanded that Berkeley return to England. Some historians have interpreted Bacon's Rebellion as a fight against the authority of the local government, while others have described it as a power struggle between a powerful governor and a wealthy colonist. However, the Native Americans who were driven from their lands were ultimately the ones who lost the most.

HISTORICAL THINKING

1. **READING CHECK** How did the treaty of 1646 lead to Bacon's Rebellion?

2. **INTERPRET MAPS** How does the map reflect Native American concerns about land?

3. **MAKE INFERENCES** Why did Nathaniel Bacon have public support for his rebellion?

PLAN

Objective

Examine causes and effects of wars between Native Americans and colonists in Virginia.

Critical Thinking Skills for Lesson 1.4

- Identify Main Ideas and Details
- Monitor Comprehension
- Interpret Maps
- Make Inferences
- Analyze Cause and Effect
- Form and Support Opinions

Essential Question for Chapter 3

How did early settlers cope with challenges as they established the first 13 colonies? Conflicts over land led to wars between the colonists and the Powhatan and tension within the colony. Lesson 1.4 examines the conflicts and how the desire for land and a greater voice in local government caused rebellion within the colony.

Background for the Teacher

William Berkeley graduated from Oxford University, studied law, and became a playwright whose work was performed in the royal court. His service in the English Civil Wars earned him a knighthood, and King Charles I appointed Berkeley governor of Virginia in 1641. He went on to serve two terms (1641–1652 and 1660–1677), making him the colony's longest-serving governor.

Nathaniel Bacon was intelligent, arrogant, well connected, and Berkeley's younger cousin by marriage. He likely came to Virginia to escape a lawsuit over his participation in a fraudulent land scheme. Berkeley appointed Bacon to the Governor's council in 1675, soon after his arrival in Virginia. By the following year, the 70-year-old governor and his 29-year-old cousin were locked in a power struggle with severe consequences for Jamestown.

INTRODUCE & ENGAGE

Explore Concepts

Display the Concept Web shown here and ask students why land is important to people. Ask students to brainstorm ideas and attitudes related to the concept of land. Then ask volunteers to share their ideas. Record the answers in the circles on the Concept Web. Tell students that in this lesson they will learn how conflicts over land led to wars and rebellions in 17th-century Virginia.

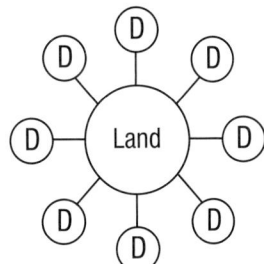

TEACH

Guided Discussion

1. **Analyze Cause and Effect** How did differences in land use cause conflicts between the Powhatan and the Virginia colonists? *(The Powhatan used the land to provide for their needs, but they didn't live on or occupy the land. The colonists claimed individual ownership of the land to raise a cash crop for profit.)*

2. **Form and Support Opinions** Do you agree or disagree with Berkeley's accusation that Bacon was a traitor? Support your opinion with evidence from the text. *(Answers will vary. Possible responses: Yes, because Bacon was disloyal to the governor and ignored laws. No, because Bacon wanted colonists to have more involvement in government.)*

Interpret Maps

Point out that the Chesapeake Bay Colonies map includes settlements in Maryland as well as in Virginia. Ask students to locate Maryland and Virginia on the map. Then ask students to locate the settlements in Virginia that were established between 1607 and 1650. *(Henrico, Williamsburg, and Fort Henry)* Then ask them to locate Virginia settlements established between 1650 and 1700. *(Norfolk, Yorktown, and Hampton)* **ASK:** Based on the map, what conclusion can you draw about the rate of expansion in the Chesapeake Bay colonies? *(Answers will vary. Possible response: The greatest expansion occurred after 1675.)*

Active Options

On Your Feet: Time Line Pair students to complete a time line of events in this lesson. Ask them to include the dates discussed in the text and a key event for each date. Work with students to space their dates appropriately on the time line. Then discuss the sequence of events as well as cause-and-effect relationships.

NG Learning Framework: Negotiate a Peace Treaty

| ATTITUDE | Responsibility |
| KNOWLEDGE | Our Human Story |

Arrange students in two groups, one representing the Virginia colonists and the other the Powhatan. Tell each group to list requirements for a peaceful settlement of land claims. Then ask them to negotiate a treaty that is acceptable to both sides. Remind students to be respectful and to consider multiple perspectives as they negotiate. Ask them to designate a secretary to record accepted terms and a scribe to create and print the final treaty. When the treaty is finalized, display the printed document in the classroom.

DIFFERENTIATE

Striving Readers

Use Examples Define and review the following words from this lesson, using context clues or outside dictionaries, if necessary: *lenient, ultimately, tensions,* and *provoke.* Provide synonyms or examples of each word that are recognizable and familiar to students. Then ask students to use each word in a sentence.

Pre-AP

Prepare a News Broadcast Tell students to prepare a news broadcast about the burning of Jamestown in 1676. Using information in the text as well as other resources, students portraying newscasters should describe the scene and interview the people involved. Other students may play the roles of Bacon, his followers, residents of Jamestown, and Governor Berkeley and answer the interviewers' questions.

See the Chapter Planner for more strategies for differentiation.

HISTORICAL THINKING

ANSWERS

1. The treaty required the Powhatan to live on lands north of the York River, limiting the area that landless freemen could purchase for themselves. Bacon used colonists' frustration to rebel against the colonial government that supported the treaty.

2. The map shows how, as the years passed, colonists settled larger areas of land, pushing Native Americans out.

3. Landless freemen shared Bacon's goals of gaining a stronger voice in government as well as more land from the Powhatan.

CRITICAL VIEWING Answers will vary. Possible response: Although Bacon was a wealthy planter, he represented the views of people who were not wealthy and did not own land. In the painting, his followers walk ahead of or beside Bacon, which suggests that the rebellion embodied a spirit of democracy.

2.1 Pilgrims and Puritans

"Are we there yet?" You've probably asked this question during a long car ride. Imagine sailing across an ocean in a cramped wooden ship. Colonists who braved the long voyage from England to North America may have thought they'd never arrive.

MAIN IDEA The New England colonies became a new home for groups who wished to create societies centered on their religious principles.

THE PILGRIMS FIND A HOME

During the early 1600s, European settlers continued to arrive in the American colonies, despite ongoing conflicts between Native Americans and colonists. At this time in England, religious **dissenters**, or people who disagreed with the beliefs of the Church of England, could be imprisoned or fined. Dissenters yearned for religious freedom so intensely that they left their homes, sailed across the ocean, and settled in the colonies. They became **separatists**, or people who created their own congregations outside of the Church of England.

The **Pilgrims** were one such group. They did not believe in the reforms instituted by the Church of England and saw complete separation as their only spiritual option. In September 1620, a group of Pilgrims boarded the *Mayflower* in England, bound for the northern part of Virginia. The ship strayed off course and landed on Cape Cod. Once they realized they would not land in Virginia, the Pilgrims established and signed the **Mayflower Compact**. This agreement laid out a plan for governing a new colony.

From Cape Cod, the Pilgrims moved to the area around what is now Plymouth, Massachusetts. During their first winter, half of the Pilgrims died from illness or exposure to the cold. The following spring, Native Americans who lived nearby, including Squanto, a member of the Pawtuxet, helped the Pilgrims grow their own food. They identified which crops grew best and when to plant them. They also showed the Pilgrims how to use herring, a local fish, to fertilize the crops. As experienced local planters, Native Americans also shared their knowledge of how to plant corn, beans, and squash together for the best results. The two groups celebrated the Pilgrims' first harvest in a three-day celebration considered the first Thanksgiving.

Eyeglasses with wooden case

🏛 **Pilgrim Hall Museum**
Plymouth, Massachusetts

Even Pilgrims wore spectacles. These eyeglasses, on display at Pilgrim Hall Museum in Plymouth, Massachusetts, were probably made in England sometime in the 17th century. They are made of glass, horn, wood, and leather. The case is carved from pinewood.

A CITY UPON A HILL

Like the Pilgrims, the **Puritans** believed that the Church of England needed additional reform. Unlike the Pilgrims, however, the Puritans wanted to reform the church from within.

Beginning in 1630, the Puritans began their migration from England to Massachusetts Bay. They arrived as part of the Massachusetts Bay Company, believing God wanted them to create a moral community. As Puritan leader John Winthrop said, the colony would be "as a City upon a Hill, the Eyes of all people are upon us."

The Puritans' system of self-governance was called the New England Way. The church was the center of the community, and all citizens were required to attend. Puritans believed that a congregation, bound by a sacred oath, held all authority and could punish members who disagreed with church doctrine. People who tried to leave a congregation could lose their property. The Puritans were dissenters who did not allow dissent within their own communities.

Not all Puritans agreed with the New England Way. In 1636, clergyman Thomas Hooker and a group of Puritans left Massachusetts to found a new colony in Connecticut. Three years later, in a sermon, Hooker provided inspiration for the **Fundamental Orders of Connecticut**. This document established a General Assembly of representatives from many towns. Unlike in Massachusetts, church membership was not a condition for voting.

In 1631, religious dissenter and Pilgrim minister **Roger Williams** arrived in Massachusetts Bay Colony. He attacked laws requiring church attendance and tax support of Puritan churches and was **banished**, or sent away from the colony. In 1636, he bought land from the Narragansett and founded the colony of Rhode Island. He based this new colony on the idea that church and state affairs should be kept separate.

In 1637, Massachusetts Bay Colony leaders banished another dissenter, **Anne Hutchinson**. had angered orthodox Puritans by teaching that people had to respond directly to God, not the church, for their actions. Hutchinson also believed that ministers were unnecessary. She founded a settlement in the colony of Rhode Island.

Built in England in 1956, the *Mayflower II* is a full-scale replica of the vessel that brought the Pilgrims from England to North America in 1620. Upon completion, it sailed from England to New England following the Pilgrims' route. It remains a working sailing ship, moored at Plymouth, Massachusetts.

HISTORICAL THINKING

1. **READING CHECK** What was the Mayflower Compact and why was it important?

2. **MAKE INFERENCES** Why did the Puritans link citizenship to church membership?

3. **MAKE GENERALIZATIONS** Why did some groups leave the Massachusetts Bay Colony to establish new colonies?

PLAN

Objective

Learn about the role religion played in establishing colonies in New England.

Critical Thinking Skills for Lesson 2.1

- Identify Main Ideas and Details
- Monitor Comprehension
- Make Inferences
- Make Generalizations
- Summarize
- Evaluate

Essential Question for Chapter 3

How did early settlers cope with challenges as they established the first 13 colonies? The Pilgrims and Puritans wanted to practice their religion free of interference. Lesson 2.1 explores how they governed themselves in accordance with, and sometimes in opposition to, their beliefs.

Background for the Teacher

The quote, "As a city upon a hill, the eyes of all people are upon us," references the Sermon on the Mount from the New Testament: "You are the light of the world. A city set on a hill cannot be hidden." John Winthrop's Puritan following would have recognized this in his sermon, "A Modell of Christian Charity," and been uplifted by the perception that their Puritan community in New England would be an example of Christian charity to the world. The quote continues to resonate in American politics and appears in speeches given by a number of U.S. presidents, including John F. Kennedy in a speech just days before his inauguration in 1961, Ronald Reagan in his Farewell Address to the Nation in 1989, and Barack Obama in his University of Massachusetts at Boston Commencement Address in 2006.

📄 History Notebook

Encourage students to complete the American Gallery page for Chapter 3 in their History Notebooks as they read.

INTRODUCE & ENGAGE

Take an Imaginary Voyage

Direct students' attention to the photo of the *Mayflower II, a* replica of the original *Mayflower*. Point out that the original *Mayflower* was a cargo ship, not a passenger ship. Explain that the crew's quarters were on the upper decks, while the Pilgrims traveled in lower decks that normally carried cargo. **ASK:** What do you think it was like to travel for more than two months aboard the *Mayflower* in 1620? After students have time to think, encourage them to share their ideas with the class.

TEACH

Guided Discussion

1. **Summarize** What factors accounted for the Pilgrims' survival upon arriving in America? *(The Pilgrims planned how to govern themselves and kept the group together. After the first winter killed half of the group, the Pilgrims made friends with the Pawtuxet, who helped the Pilgrims grow crops.)*

2. **Evaluate** Why were the Mayflower Compact and the Fundamental Orders of Connecticut significant to the development of self-government in the colonies? *(Both documents were created by the colonists and provided rules and plans for governing the colonies. These documents were not imposed by the king of England nor subject to England's laws. In addition, the Fundamental Orders established a General Assembly that included representatives from towns and did not limit voting to church members.)*

Virtual Museum Visit

Pilgrim Hall Museum opened in 1824 to preserve the history of Plymouth, Massachusetts, and tell the story of the Pilgrims of Plymouth Colony. The museum's collections include possessions of the Pilgrim settlers, such as a bible owned by William Bradford, Plymouth's long-time governor; the sword of Myles Standish, the colony's military leader; a sampler embroidered by Standish's daughter; and the cradle of Peregrine White, the first Pilgrim baby born in New England. Access Pilgrim Hall Museum's website and allow students to explore the online exhibits. Provide time for students to discuss how the information added to their understanding of the Pilgrims.

Active Options

On Your Feet: Compare and Contrast Divide the class into two teams and assign Pilgrims to one and Puritans to the other. Members of each team should write as many facts about their group as they can. Ask teams to compare and contrast Pilgrims and Puritans by recording differences in the outside circles and similarities in the overlapping section of a Venn diagram. Use the completed diagram as the basis for a discussion about the lesson.

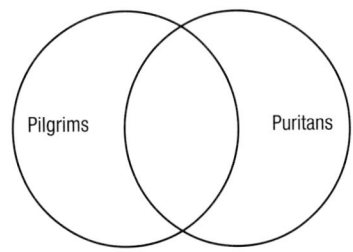

Pilgrims   Puritans

AMERICAN GALLERY **ONLINE** **A Portrait of the Pilgrims** Invite students to explore the American Gallery. Tell them to select one of the items and do additional research to learn more about it. Ask questions that will inspire additional inquiry about the chosen gallery item, such as: What or who is this? When was this painted or created? By whom? What is it made of? Why does it belong in this chapter? What else would you like to know about it?

DIFFERENTIATE

Inclusion

Pose and Answer Questions Pair strong readers with students who have reading or perception issues. Instruct the pairs to work together to read each paragraph in the lesson. After each paragraph, allow the student with reading issues to ask questions for clarification. The strong reader should pose one simple recall question for each paragraph. The student with reading issues should answer the question or ask for further clarification of the text.

English Language Learners `ELD`

Analyze Word Parts Pair proficient students with students at the **Emerging** level and pair students at the **Expanding** level with each other. Ask students at the **Bridging** level to work independently. Write the nouns *dissenters* and *separatists* on the board. Point out that the base words *dissent* and *separate* are verbs and the suffixes *-ers* and *-ists* mean "people who." Ask pairs to complete the chart. Suggest that students add other words from the lesson that follow the same pattern, such as *settlers* or *representatives*.

Noun	Verb	Meaning of Noun	Sentence
dissenters			
separatists			

See the Chapter Planner for more strategies for differentiation.

HISTORICAL THINKING

ANSWERS

1. The Mayflower Compact outlined how the Pilgrims would govern themselves when they realized they wouldn't be living in Virginia under its laws. It was important because it was a new plan of governance.

2. The Puritans linked citizenship to church membership to maintain control over all people in the community. The congregation was bound to the church by a solemn oath that gave it authority to punish members who went against church doctrine.

3. Answers will vary. Possible response: The laws in Massachusetts Bay were strict and rigid. Those who left the colony had different ideas about how things should be run. They wanted to separate church and state affairs.

Squanto

c. 1580–1622

"[Squanto] was a special instrument sent of God for [the Pilgrims'] good beyond their expectation."

—from the journal of William Bradford, governor of Plymouth Colony

The Pilgrims certainly couldn't have expected that a fluent English-speaking Native American would happen on the scene and choose to act as their interpreter and guide. So Squanto, also known as Tisquantum, must have seemed like a gift indeed. He taught the Pilgrims how to grow maize and where to catch fish, and generally showed them the ropes so they could survive in Plymouth. Squanto even died in the Pilgrims' service. What we don't know for sure is exactly what came before.

EARLY LIFE

Part folk hero, part myth, much of what we know—or think we know—about Squanto comes from often conflicting eyewitness accounts. According to some sources, he was kidnapped from his Massachusetts home in 1605 by Englishman George Weymouth and taken to England. While there, he was apparently treated well and taught English—the idea being that he would serve as an interpreter for those settling the colonies. John Smith, one of the founders of Jamestown Colony, is said to have returned him to America for that purpose around 1615.

Remarkably, Squanto was kidnapped a second time, an event on which most authorities agree. One of Smith's men,

Wooden sculpture of Squanto

🏛 **Pilgrim Hall Museum**
Plymouth, Massachusetts

The nation's oldest continuously operating public museum, Pilgrim Hall, tells the founding story of America: the Pilgrims' arrival, struggles, and first Thanksgiving in Plymouth. This 19th-century sculpture of Squanto forms part of the museum's collection. It shows what one artist thinks the Native American guide might have looked like.

Thomas Hunt, took Squanto and several other Native Americans to Spain where the Englishman hoped to sell them into slavery. Fortunately, Squanto managed to get away. Some say Spanish priests rescued him. Most accounts, though, have him escaping to England and befriending merchants in London. This period, then, may have been when Squanto learned English. In 1619, he sailed with the merchants to New England to help them establish trade with the Native Americans.

LIFE AMONG THE PILGRIMS

Squanto returned to his homeland only to find that most of his people—the Pawtuxet—had been wiped out by disease. For a time, he lived with the Wampanoag (WAHMP-uh-noh-ag). Then, in early 1621, a Native American named Samoset brought Squanto to Plymouth Colony. Samoset had been the first Native American to greet the Pilgrims. But, with his limited understanding of English, he couldn't really speak to them. Squanto, he knew, had a far better command of the language.

Guide—and Troublemaker?

Squanto was known for his role as the Pilgrims' guide. But stories have also circulated about trouble he caused. For example, fearful of losing his position of power, Squanto tried to pit the Pilgrims against the Native Americans. He spread rumors that Massasoit was joining forces with other tribes in a plan to attack the Pilgrims.

When Squanto's plot was uncovered, Massasoit demanded that Squanto be turned over for punishment. Certain that the Wampanoag chief would execute Squanto, William Bradford refused. With more colonial ships arriving in the area, Bradford knew that he and the new settlers would need Squanto more than ever.

Before long, Squanto became an indispensable member of the colony. He taught the settlers how to plant local crops and served as their ambassador on trading expeditions. He even helped negotiate a peace treaty between the Pilgrims and the Wampanoag chief, Massasoit. In the fall of 1621, the Wampanoag, the Pilgrims, and Squanto celebrated the peace and Plymouth's successful harvest with the first Thanksgiving.

Squanto's time in Plymouth turned out to be brief. While guiding William Bradford on an expedition around Cape Cod, the Native American contracted a fever and died. According to some sources, Squanto said to Bradford on his deathbed, "Pray for me, Governor, that I might go to the Englishmen's God in heaven." Apparently, the Pilgrims had had a powerful influence on Squanto. He could have no idea that his own influence and aid had helped secure the survival of the colonists.

HISTORICAL THINKING

1. **READING CHECK** How did Squanto help the Pilgrims in Plymouth?

2. **FORM AND SUPPORT OPINIONS** Do you think the treaty with the Wampanoag could have been created without Squanto? Why or why not?

3. **DRAW CONCLUSIONS** Based on his dying words, what did Squanto learn from the Pilgrims?

Objective

Learn about Squanto's early life and his contributions to the lives of the Pilgrims.

Critical Thinking Skills for Lesson 2.2

- Identify Main Ideas and Details
- Monitor Comprehension
- Form and Support Opinions
- Draw Conclusions
- Make Connections

Essential Question for Chapter 3

How did early settlers cope with challenges as they established the first 13 colonies? Squanto, an English-speaking Pawtuxet, helped the Pilgrims survive the challenges they faced establishing Plymouth Colony. Lesson 2.2 examines the myths and facts surrounding the events in Squanto's life.

Background for the Teacher

Unlike the Powhatan living near Jamestown, the Wampanoag were already badly weakened by European diseases and subject to attacks by the Massachusetts and Narragansett. Having a peaceful relationship with the Pilgrims provided the Wampanoag with some degree of security and a possible ally in case of attack.

The treaty that Squanto brokered had six main points of agreement: (1) neither side would injure members of the other side; (2) if anyone was hurt, the offender would be turned over to the aggrieved side for punishment; (3) any tools taken from either side would be returned; (4) each side would assist the other in case of war; (5) the Wampanoag would encourage their allies to join the peace; and (6) both sides would disarm during meetings.

📄 **History Notebook**

Encourage students to complete the American Voices page for Chapter 3 in their History Notebooks as they read.

INTRODUCE & ENGAGE

K-W-L Chart

Provide students with a K-W-L Chart like the one below. Instruct students to brainstorm and list what they already know about Squanto, such as the fact that he was a Pawtuxet who helped the Pilgrims plant and grow crops. Then ask them to write questions that they would like to have answered as they study the lesson. Allow time at the end of the lesson for students to fill in what they have learned.

K What Do I Know?	W What Do I Want To Learn?	L What Did I Learn?

TEACH

Guided Discussion

1. **Make Connections** How did Squanto's early life prepare him for his role as the Pilgrims' interpreter and guide? *(Answers will vary. Possible response: Because Squanto was kidnapped and taken to Europe, he learned to speak English fluently. That experience prepared him to be an interpreter for the Pilgrims. Squanto had been raised in the area where the Pilgrims settled, which prepared him to be their guide.)*

2. **Form and Support Opinions** Which of Squanto's contributions do you think was most important to the Pilgrims' survival? Support your answer with text evidence. *(Possible responses: Teaching the Pilgrims how to plant crops ensured a food supply that helped them survive the winters. Serving as a trade ambassador provided the Pilgrims with a way to get needed supplies. Negotiating a peace treaty ensured the Pilgrims' safety for a time and provided a model for dealing with other Native Americans.)*

🔖 American Voices

An incident reported in Bradford's *Of Plymouth Plantation* illustrates Squanto's importance to the Pilgrims. Bradford feared that Corbitant, a lesser chief among the Wampanoag, was planning to break the peace treaty with the Pilgrims. He sent Squanto and a companion to Corbitant's village, where they were seized. When word reached Bradford that Squanto might be dead, the governor sent a rescue party with instructions to save Squanto if alive, or to avenge his death by killing Corbitant. The rescuers found Squanto alive and well, but three members of Corbitant's tribe were injured during the raid. The Pilgrims returned to Plymouth with Squanto and the injured members of the tribe, whose wounds were tended. The Pilgrims' actions helped to ensure peace and won the respect of Corbitant and the other chiefs who had opposed the treaty.

Active Options

On Your Feet: Make Inferences about Character Instruct students to work in pairs to conduct Three-Step Interviews. Have one student interview the other asking the question, What do you think Squanto's actions show about his character? Then have students reverse roles. Provide time for students to share the results of their interviews.

NG Learning Framework: Investigate the First Thanksgiving

ATTITUDE Curiosity

KNOWLEDGE Our Human Story

Ask students to frame a question about the first Thanksgiving to address their curiosity about the event. Tell them to use the Pilgrim Hall Museum website and other sources to investigate and answer their questions. Ask students to share their findings and discuss whether the information supported or contradicted their previously held ideas.

DIFFERENTIATE

English Language Learners

Give a Thumbs Up or Thumbs Down Prepare a set of true-false statements about the lesson, such as "Squanto was born and raised in England." Direct students at **All Proficiencies** to reread the lesson. Then tell them to listen, with books closed, as you read the true-false statements. To check students' comprehension, instruct them to give a thumbs up for true statements or a thumbs down for false ones. Ask students to verify or change their responses by finding information in the lesson.

Gifted & Talented

Write a Documentary Script Ask students to work in pairs to write a short scene from Squanto's life based on information in the lesson and additional research. Have students write in script form and include a cast, a description of the setting, and dialogue. The action might center on an event from Squanto's early life, his life among the Pilgrims, peace negotiations, or his travels to Europe. Invite students to share and discuss their scripts.

See the Chapter Planner for more strategies for differentiation.

HISTORICAL THINKING

ANSWERS

1. Squanto served as an interpreter, guide, and trading ambassador and taught the Pilgrims how to plant local crops.

2. Answers will vary. Possible responses: Squanto was indispensable because he was fluent in both English and the Wampanoag language. Samoset, with his limited English, might have brokered a treaty because maintaining peace was crucial to the Wampanoag.

3. Squanto's words on his deathbed indicate his learned belief in Puritan Christianity and his hope that the Englishmen's god would welcome him.

2.3 Foundations of Democracy

Democracy is founded on a number of principles, one of which is equality. Throughout history, legal documents have outlined rights and created rules for governing communities fairly. Some of these writings inspired the authors of the Declaration of Independence and the Constitution.

In colonial New England, the Puritans established a style of governing that revolved around town hall meetings. These meetings were some of the first experiments in American democracy. Certain requirements limited who could vote in the meetings, however. In most cases, only male, property-owning church members had a vote. Today, all citizens can participate fully in town hall meetings, regardless of gender, race, or wealth.

CRITICAL VIEWING Old Town Hall, located in Canterbury, New Hampshire, was built in 1736. It continues to function as a meeting and polling place. Below, a Canterbury citizen leaves Old Town Hall after voting in a primary during the 2012 election. What details from the photo indicate that the citizens of Canterbury value their town hall?

DOCUMENT ONE
Primary Source: Legal Document from the Magna Carta, 1215

The Magna Carta, or "Great Charter," served as a peace treaty between King John of England and his barons, who rebelled against the heavy taxes the king **levied** on them, or required that they pay. The original document contained 63 clauses detailing laws that everyone was expected to follow. Principles in the Magna Carta were later embodied in the 1689 English Bill of Rights, such as the right to a trial by jury and protection from excessive fines and cruel punishment.

CONSTRUCTED RESPONSE Why is it significant that the Magna Carta includes the phrase "lawful judgment of his equals"?

> No free man shall be seized or imprisoned, or stripped of his rights or possessions, or outlawed or exiled, or deprived of his standing in any other way, nor will we proceed with force against him, or send others to do so, except by the lawful judgment of his equals or by the law of the land.

DOCUMENT TWO
Primary Source: Legal Document from the Mayflower Compact, 1620

Just prior to settling Plymouth, Massachusetts, the settlers-to-be signed the Mayflower Compact on board their ship. The agreement established **self-governance**, or control of the colony based on the democratic principle of common consent.

CONSTRUCTED RESPONSE What reasons do the Mayflower Compact signers give for working together as a "civil body politic"?

> Having undertaken . . . a voyage to plant the first colony in the northern parts of Virginia, do . . . solemnly and mutually in the presence of God and one another, covenant [promise], and combine ourselves together into a civil body politic, for our better ordering and preservation, and furtherance of the ends aforesaid; and . . . to enact, constitute, and frame such just and equal laws . . . as shall be thought most meet and convenient for the general good of the colony.

DOCUMENT THREE
Primary Source: Legal Document from the Fundamental Orders of Connecticut, 1639

The founders of Connecticut drafted a plan of government called the Fundamental Orders of Connecticut. The document created an assembly of elected representatives from each town in the colony. The ideas captured in this document were later reflected in the U.S. Constitution.

CONSTRUCTED RESPONSE Why do you think it was important to the colony founders that the representatives lived in the towns they represented?

> It is Ordered . . . and decreed, that there shall be yearly two General Assemblies or Courts. The first shall be called the Court of Election, wherein shall be yearly chosen from time to time, so many Magistrates and other public Officers as shall be found requisite [necessary] . . . which choice shall be made by all that are admitted freemen and have taken the Oath of Fidelity [loyalty], and do cohabit within this Jurisdiction . . . of the Town wherein they live.

SYNTHESIZE & WRITE

1. **REVIEW** Review what you have learned about the Magna Carta, the Mayflower Compact, and the Fundamental Orders of Connecticut.

2. **RECALL** On your own paper, write the main ideas about government expressed in the Magna Carta, the Mayflower Compact, and the Fundamental Orders of Connecticut.

3. **CONSTRUCT** Construct a topic sentence that answers this question: How is the Magna Carta, written in 1215, similar to the Mayflower Compact and the Fundamental Orders of Connecticut?

4. **WRITE** Using evidence from this chapter and the documents, write a paragraph that supports your topic sentence in Step 3.

PLAN

Objective
Synthesize information about the foundations of democracy from primary source documents.

Critical Thinking Skills for Lesson 2.3
- Synthesize
- Identify Main Ideas and Details
- Monitor Comprehension
- Evaluate

Essential Question for Chapter 3
How did early settlers cope with challenges as they established the first 13 colonies? One of the challenges settlers faced was how to create rules to govern their colonies. Lesson 2.3 discusses how the Magna Carta, Mayflower Compact, and Fundamental Orders of Connecticut provided foundations for democratic government.

Background for the Teacher
Several versions of the Magna Carta were created in the 13th century. Of the four surviving copies from 1215, only one bears the seal of King John, and all four are housed in England. One has been kept in Salisbury in the Salisbury Cathedral for nearly 800 years, and two copies have been kept in the British Library in London since 1753. The remaining copy is kept in Lincolnshire in the Lincoln Cathedral, but it has traveled to the United States several times, where it has been displayed in Massachusetts and Washington, D.C. During World War II, it was stored in Fort Knox, Kentucky, along with the Declaration of Independence and the Bill of Rights.

Prepare for the Document-Based Question

Before students start on the activity, briefly preview the three documents. Remind students that a constructed response requires full explanations in complete sentences. Emphasize that students should use what they have learned about the Mayflower Compact and the Fundamental Orders of Connecticut in addition to the information in the documents.

TEACH

Guided Discussion

1. **Identify Main Ideas and Details** What prompted the writing of the Magna Carta? *(English barons rebelled against the heavy taxes King John levied on them. The Magna Carta served as a peace treaty detailing laws that everyone was expected to follow.)*

2. **Monitor Comprehension** How do the Mayflower Compact and the Fundamental Orders of Connecticut show that colonists valued the principle of equality? *(Answers will vary. Possible response: The Mayflower Compact mentions just and equal laws and the need for people to work together for the common good. The Fundamental Orders of Connecticut calls for elected officials to represent the people.)*

Evaluate

After students have completed the Synthesize & Write activity, allow time for them to exchange paragraphs and read and comment on the work of their peers. Guidelines for comments should be established prior to this activity so that feedback is constructive and encouraging in nature.

Active Options

On Your Feet: Host a DBQ Roundtable Divide the class into groups of four. Tell groups to move their desks together to form a table where they all can sit. Hand each group a sheet of paper with the question, Why was equality an important principle of government in the colonies? The first student in each group should write an answer, read it aloud, and pass the paper clockwise to the next student. The paper should circulate around the table several times. Reconvene as a class and discuss the group's responses.

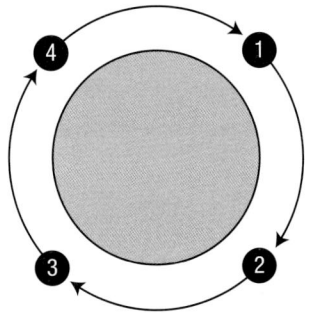

DIFFERENTIATE

Striving Readers

Summarize Main Ideas Arrange students in pairs to read information about each document presented in the lesson. Instruct them to pause after reading about a document and ask each other *Who? What? Where? When?* and *Why?* questions. Students may use a 5Ws chart to organize their questions and answers. Then ask them to use their responses to summarize the main ideas about each document.

Pre-AP

Research Art Instruct students to use Internet or other resources to research artistic depictions of the signing of the Mayflower Compact. Encourage students to analyze similarities and differences among the works. Then ask them to create a visual presentation to share their findings with the class.

See the Chapter Planner for more strategies for differentiation.

SYNTHESIZE & WRITE

ANSWERS

1. Answers will vary, but should list details from and about each document.

2. Answers will vary, but there should be one concise main idea for each document.

3. Possible response: Even though 400 years separates the Magna Carta from the Mayflower Compact and the Fundamental Orders of Connecticut, all three discuss democratic ideas that influenced the establishment of the U.S. government.

4. Students' paragraphs should include their topic sentence from Step 3 and provide several details from the documents to support the sentence.

CONSTRUCTED RESPONSE

Document 1: Possible response: Up to this point, the king could probably do whatever he wanted. A judgment by equals ensured fairer treatment of citizens.

Document 2: Possible response: The signers believe that working together will contribute to a more peaceful way of life and aid in their survival.

Document 3: Possible response: They would better understand the needs of the town's citizens because they would know firsthand what was happening there.

CRITICAL VIEWING Answers will vary. Possible response: The building is well preserved and maintained, having clean windows and what looks like fresh paint. The date *1736* is displayed above the door, telling visitors and reminding citizens how long the building has been standing.

2.4 War and Witch Trials

The continued takeover of Native American lands by colonists caused conflicts in the 1670s. Conflicts also arose among colonists, and in one New England town, accusations of witchcraft and wickedness flew.

MAIN IDEA In the late 1600s, wars with Native Americans raged in the New England colonies and witch trials nearly tore the town of Salem apart.

KING PHILIP'S WAR

In 1671, because of increasing tensions with Native Americans, the Plymouth government forced the Wampanoag to surrender their guns. Four years later, a chain of events led to a bloody war.

A Native American named John Sassamon was a convert to Christianity and an interpreter for English colonists. Soon after he warned of an impending attack by a Wampanoag leader named **Metacom**, he was found dead. With little or no evidence, authorities tried and hanged three Wampanoag for his murder.

In response, Metacom and his troops attacked 52 towns throughout New England, destroying 12 of them completely. By the next summer, Metacom's troops were suffering from disease, hunger, and a shortage of weapons, so the campaign came to an end.

English settlers had given Metacom the nickname "King Philip"—no one remembers why—and these attacks became known as **King Philip's War**. Around 600 colonists and thousands of Native Americans died in the war, including Metacom.

ACCUSATIONS IN SALEM

In February 1692, authorities in the village of Salem, Massachusetts, accused three women of witchcraft. Presumably, the charges stemmed from the strange behavior of some village girls. But it didn't take long for people to believe that witches existed and were living in Salem.

Authorities began to arrest people accused by fellow villagers. Nearly 200 women and men were accused and brought to trial for witchcraft.

"Evidence" consisted largely of accusations and little more. Twenty of the accused were put to death, most by hanging.

Historians think the issue underlying the trials may have been women's ownership of property. In Puritan society, women were rarely allowed to own property. When a man died, his son or sons usually inherited his property. If he had no male children, his wife or daughter could inherit.

Many Salem residents accused of witchcraft were women who had inherited property. Their status as property owners went against the societal norm and threatened to challenge traditional gender roles. The threat posed by women as property owners may have driven many witchcraft accusations.

Governor William Phips and Increase Mather, an influential minister, initially supported the trials but then realized things had gone too far. By May 1693, Phips had pardoned all of those still imprisoned. Additionally, courts dismissed charges and returned not-guilty verdicts in the remaining cases. The strange episode of the Salem witch trials was over.

HISTORICAL THINKING

1. **READING CHECK** Why did Metacom attack New England towns?

2. **ANALYZE CAUSE AND EFFECT** What effect did King Philip's War have on Native Americans in the region?

3. **MAKE INFERENCES** Why were landowning women targets of witchcraft accusations?

The Wonders of the Invisible World.
OBSERVATIONS
As well Historical as Theological, upon the NATURE, the NUMBER, and the OPERATIONS of the
DEVILS.
Accompany'd with,
I. Some Accounts of the Grievous Molestations, by DÆ-MONS and WITCHCRAFTS, which have lately annoy'd the Countrey; and the Trials of some eminent Malefactors Executed upon occasion thereof: with several Remarkable Curiosities therein occurring.
II. Some Councils, Directing a due Improvement of the terrible things, lately done, by the Unusual & Amazing Range of EVIL SPIRITS, in Our Neighbourhood: & the methods to prevent the Wrongs which those Evil Angels may intend against all sorts of people among us; especially in Accusations of the Innocent.
III. Some Conjectures upon the great EVENTS, likely to befall, the WORLD in General, and NEW-ENGLAND in Particular; as also upon the Advances of the TIME, when we shall see BETTER DAYES.
IV. A short Narrative of a late Outrage committed by a knot of WITCHES in Swedeland, very much Resembling, and so far Explaining, That under which our parts of America have laboured!
V. THE DEVIL DISCOVERED: In a Brief Discourse upon those TEMPTATIONS, which are the more Ordinary Devices of the Wicked One.
By Cotton Mather.
Boston, Printed by Benj. Harris for Sam. Phillips. 1693.

CRITICAL VIEWING The fiery New England preacher named Cotton Mather wrote a book on the Salem witch trials. At left is a page from his book. In the 1890s, 200 years after the Salem witch trials, illustrator Joseph E. Baker reimagined the events reported to have taken place in Salem. What are the different ways witches are portrayed in Mather's writing and these drawings?

PLAN

Objective

Learn how war and witch trials challenged New England colonists in the late 1600s.

Critical Thinking Skills for Lesson 2.4

- Identify Main Ideas and Details
- Monitor Comprehension
- Analyze Cause and Effect
- Make Inferences
- Make Generalizations
- Analyze Visuals

Essential Question for Chapter 3

How did early settlers cope with challenges as they established the first 13 colonies? Conflicts between Native Americans and New England colonists intensified in the 1670s, while accusations of witchcraft caused conflicts among colonists. Lesson 2.4 discusses the impact of these events.

Background for the Teacher

By the late 1600s, belief in witchcraft had long been a part of traditional European culture. In England, witchcraft had been a capital offense since the early 16th century. Colonial governments in America followed suit in condemning those who gave "entertainment to Satan." During the 17th century, Puritan governments in New England accused more individuals of witchcraft than did other English colonies.

The witchcraft accusations in Salem in the 1690s at first resembled those in other places and times. But in Salem, accusations fell on prosperous church members, a minister, a wealthy shipowner, and several town officials, as well as women who stood to inherit property. In Salem, accusations were less about witchcraft, and more about power.

INTRODUCE & ENGAGE

Activate Prior Knowledge

Read the introduction to the lesson to the class. Ask students to define the word *accusation* and then consider situations in which individuals have been accused of wrongdoing. Discuss the reasons for unsupported accusations and the harm that they can do. Ask students to think about why someone would accuse someone of something that was provably untrue or only suspected. Then tell students that they will read about legal trials in which unsupported accusations resulted in the accused being put to death.

TEACH

Guided Discussion

1. **Make Inferences** Which actions of Plymouth's leaders in the late 1600s indicated a lack of trust in Native Americans? *(Forcing the Wampanoag to surrender their guns and hanging three Wampanoag without evidence of guilt indicated Plymouth's leaders did not trust the Native Americans to keep the peace.)*

2. **Make Generalizations** What evidence is there that women had less power than men in Puritan society? *(In most cases, women could not own property. When a man died, his property went to his sons. Wives and daughters could only inherit property in the absence of male heirs.)*

Analyze Visuals

Direct students' attention to the top illustration, which shows a method of punishment called a pillory. Explain that a pillory consisted of a platform with a wood framework topped by an upright horizontal board. The board was hinged or divided in half with openings for a person's neck and wrists. When the offender's head and hands were in place, the two parts of the board were fastened together. A pillory often stood in the main square of a town. **ASK:** Why do you think a pillory was used as a punishment for witchcraft and other offenses? *(Answers will vary. Possible response: It made the offender an object of public ridicule. The offender was held in an awkward, uncomfortable position with no defense against insults or physical abuse.)*

Active Options

On Your Feet: Sequence Events As a class, review the chain of events that led to King Philip's War. Call on volunteers to record students' responses on the board. Then direct students to work in small groups to complete a Sequence Chain by placing the events in order. Tell groups to share their work with the class. **ASK:** What does this sequence of events demonstrate about cause and effect? *(The effect of one event can be the cause of another.)*

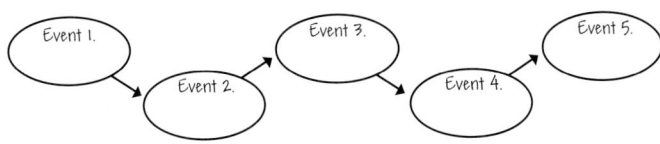

NG Learning Framework: Learn More about King Philip's War

SKILL Problem-Solving

KNOWLEDGE Our Human Story

Divide students into two groups. Instruct one group to research King Philip's War from the Native Americans' point of view and the other group to research the conflict from the colonists' point of view. Guide students to use appropriate Internet sources in addition to the text and print sources available in the classroom or library. Ask each group to present its perspective of the conflict. Then discuss how learning about both sides of a conflict enhances understanding of historical events.

DIFFERENTIATE

Inclusion

Use Supported Reading Pair special-needs students with students at a higher proficiency level to read the lesson aloud together. Assign one paragraph to each pair. At the end of their paragraph, students should complete the following sentence frames.

This paragraph is about _____ .

One fact I learned is _____ .

I had trouble understanding _____ .

I figured out the meaning by _____ .

Encourage students to help each other with parts of the text that they do not understand.

Gifted & Talented

Research the Salem Witch Trials Ask students to go on a fact-finding mission to learn more about the Salem witch trials. Students should explore the following questions in their research: Who were the so-called witches? Why were they accused of witchcraft? What happened at the trials? What might explain this episode of colonial history? Invite students to present their findings.

See the Chapter Planner for more strategies for differentiation.

HISTORICAL THINKING

ANSWERS

1. Without evidence, the colonists hanged three Wampanoag for the murder of John Sassamon, a Native American who had warned the colonists of an impending attack by Metacom. Metacom retaliated.

2. Native Americans troops suffered from disease, hunger, and a lack of weapons, so the campaign failed. Thousands of Native Americans, including Metacom, died.

3. The women's status as property owners gave them power. This power challenged traditional gender roles and social norms.

CRITICAL VIEWING Possible response: The top drawing depicts witches as frightened, restrained criminals at the mercy of a jeering crowd. The bottom drawing features a woman throwing books at officials or making the books fly. Expressions on onlookers' faces suggest that they might be afraid.

3.1 The Middle Colonies

Have you ever traveled to a new place and discovered a culture different from that of your hometown? A colonist traveling south from New England to the Middle Colonies would meet people from European countries who were forging a unique colonial identity.

MAIN IDEA The Middle Colonies included a diverse mix of cultures and religions as people from different countries began to settle in the region.

NEW NETHERLAND TO NEW YORK

Situated in the mid-Atlantic region of North America, the **Middle Colonies** included New York, New Jersey, Pennsylvania, and Delaware. Settlers from countries such as England, France, the Netherlands, Germany, Sweden, and Portugal came to the colonies for different reasons. Some were fleeing religious wars in their home countries. Others were conducting trade.

The first Dutch settlers arrived about 1614 and began trading with Native Americans. In 1624, Cornelius Jacobsen May, working on behalf of the Dutch West India Company, founded New Netherland to provide a base for trade in the Hudson River region. The first settlers of New Netherland worked for the company.

For about 15 years, colonists maintained good relations with Native Americans. However, disputes over land ownership grew. In particular, Native Americans objected to the Dutch settling on lands without a clear agreement that they could do so. Eventually, wars broke out.

In 1664, King Charles II of England gave his brother James, the duke of York, permission to force the Dutch out. The overwhelming English presence in the area made doing so easy and ensured the English complete control of eastern North America. James took over the colony and renamed it New York, and the English made peace with Native Americans living there.

Middle Colonies, 1704

New England Colonies
Middle Colonies
Southern Colonies

PENN'S WOODS

After assuming control of New York, James granted land between the Delaware and lower Hudson rivers to Lord John Berkeley and Sir George Carteret, who named the area New Jersey. New Jersey eventually split into West Jersey and East Jersey.

In 1681, Charles II granted a charter for a colony to an Englishman named **William Penn**. Penn wanted to establish a safe home for his fellow **Quakers**—members of the Religious Society of Friends, a Christian movement devoted to peaceful principles. Quakers emphasized education and equality and rejected formal worship and ministry. Because they were perceived by others as

CRITICAL VIEWING In 1682, William Penn met with leaders of the Lenni Lenape under an elm tree at a spot on the Delaware River in present-day Philadelphia. There they signed a treaty together promising cooperation. In this relief from the U.S. Capitol Rotunda, Penn is in the center, gesturing toward the activity around the chest. What details in this relief reveal the reactions of the participants in this treaty signing?

anti-authority and even dangerous, thousands of Quakers were persecuted in England and even in the American colonies. Penn named his colony Sylvania, which means "woods." Charles II renamed it Pennsylvania, after Penn's father.

Penn set out to create a colony based on the Quaker **doctrine**—a principle or policy accepted by a group—that all are equal in the eyes of God. By applying this doctrine, he made Pennsylvania into an extremely diverse society, partly by encouraging religious minorities to settle there. Quaker doctrine also emphasized tolerance for others. In Pennsylvania, all colonists, no matter their religion, could worship in their own way.

Penn encouraged diversity in other ways, too. He kept peace with Native Americans, such as the Lenni Lenape. He purchased land from them, which he then sold to a variety of buyers—people from other colonies, different countries in Europe, and the West Indies. The Swedes, Finns, and Dutch who already inhabited the area became English subjects under Penn.

European settlers who lived in the "Lower Counties" in the southern part of the colony did not like living under Penn's government and at times clashed with Pennsylvania's authority. Penn tried unsuccessfully to unite the English and the Europeans, but in 1704, after two decades of difficulties, he allowed Delaware to form its own assembly. Elsewhere, and following Penn's death, conflicts between Native Americans and colonists continued.

HISTORICAL THINKING

1. **READING CHECK** What factors contributed to the diversity of the Middle Colonies?

2. **ANALYZE CAUSE AND EFFECT** What caused William Penn to allow Delaware to form its own assembly?

3. **INTERPRET MAPS** Locate Delaware on the map. Why does it make sense that Penn might have difficulty uniting people who settled there with the settlers who lived in the rest of Pennsylvania?

PLAN

Objective

Understand how diversity influenced events in the Middle Colonies.

Critical Thinking Skills for Lesson 3.1

- Identify Main Ideas and Details
- Monitor Comprehension
- Analyze Cause and Effect
- Interpret Maps
- Make Inferences
- Compare and Contrast

Essential Question for Chapter 3

How did early settlers cope with challenges as they established the first 13 colonies? The Middle Colonies' population included Europeans from various countries, people from other English, Dutch, and West Indies colonies, and Native Americans. Lesson 3.1 explores the reasons for this diversity and the challenges it brought.

Background for the Teacher

William Penn spent a great deal of time planning his Pennsylvania colony. He established an assembly with two houses, both elected by adult males who owned property. During the early decades, when servants received 50 acres at the end of their term of service, nearly every man in Pennsylvania could vote. However, Penn did not extend that right to women.

Penn intended to make a fortune from Pennsylvania. But, in this respect, his colony was a deep disappointment to him. Land sales reaped smaller profits than he had hoped, the costs of administering the colony soared, and he went into debt. Although the province became prosperous and quite successful as a tolerant, diverse society, Penn reckoned it a failure.

INTRODUCE & ENGAGE

Compare Visions of Equality

Introduce this lesson by explaining that William Penn hoped to establish his colony of Pennsylvania on the principle that all people are equal. Ask students to consider what a colonial society based on equality might look like. Record their responses on the board and then ask the class to compare this list to what they see and experience in society today. Revisit the list at the end of the lesson and compare students' suggestions with society in colonial Pennsylvania.

TEACH

Guided Discussion

1. **Make Inferences** How does the history of New Netherland illustrate the importance of establishing good relations with Native Americans? *(Answers will vary. Possible response: The Dutch were able to prosper through trade with Native Americans as long as the colonists maintained good relations. However, land disputes led to war when the colonists began settling on land without first getting an agreement from Native Americans. Disputes over land ownership eventually led to war. This warfare may have contributed to the English being able to oust the Dutch.)*

2. **Compare and Contrast** How did William Penn's purpose for establishing a colony differ from Cornelius Jacobsen May's? *(Penn wanted to establish a place where Quakers and others could enjoy religious freedom, equality, and tolerance and live peacefully with Native American neighbors. May wanted to provide a base for trade with Native Americans.)*

Interpret Maps

Direct students' attention to the key on the map of the Middle Colonies. **ASK:** What is indicated by the area marked with yellow and green stripes? *(The area was populated by colonists from both the New England Colonies and the Middle Colonies.)* **ASK:** What might you infer about the interactions among colonists in this area? *(Answers will vary. Possible response: There may have been conflicts among the colonists over the land.)* Tell students that armed conflicts between colonists were common in the disputed area and that the dispute was finally resolved in 1777 when Vermont was established.

Active Options

On Your Feet: Tell Me More Divide students into two teams and assign *New Netherland* to one team and *Pennsylvania* to the other. Members of each team should write as many facts about their topic as they can. Then bring the class together and tell the first team to stand up. The other team calls out, "Tell me more about New Netherland!" The team recites a fact. The other team again calls, "Tell me more!" until the group runs out of facts. Then the teams reverse roles and the second team presents facts about Pennsylvania. Keep track of which team shares the most facts.

NG Learning Framework: Research William Penn

ATTITUDE Responsibility

KNOWLEDGE Our Human Story

Tell students that William Penn is one of only a few people whom Congress has made an honorary citizen of the United States. Ask student pairs to research Penn and make observations about how his personal values shaped the founding and history of colonial Pennsylvania. Tell students to use Internet and print sources to conduct their research. Reconvene the class and invite pairs to share their observations and research. Then discuss their varying perspectives in assessing whether Penn deserved honorary U.S. citizenship.

DIFFERENTIATE

Striving Readers

Preview the Lesson Help students preview the lesson by pointing out text features, such as the lesson title, Main Idea statement, and headings. **ASK:** Based on the headings, what do you expect this lesson to be about? Tell students to study the relief and Critical Viewing caption. As students begin reading, help them confirm their understanding of each paragraph before moving on to the next one.

English Language Learners

Pose and Answer Questions Pose a question about the text, such as: How did Penn make his colony a diverse society? Help students at the **Bridging** level restate the question to frame the answer, such as: Penn made his colony a diverse society by encouraging people of different religions to settle there. Pair students at the **Bridging** level with proficient students and ask them to take turns framing and answering questions using the model provided.

See the Chapter Planner for more strategies for differentiation.

HISTORICAL THINKING

ANSWERS

1. People from England, France, the Netherlands, Germany, Sweden, Finland, Portugal, and other countries came to the Middle Colonies. These people brought their own religious beliefs and cultures, contributing to the diversity of the colony.

2. European settlers living in the Lower Counties disliked Penn's government and its authority. Penn tried for two decades to unite the Europeans and the English but was unsuccessful. To end the conflict, Penn allowed Delaware to form its own assembly.

3. Delaware was separated geographically from the rest of Pennsylvania.

CRITICAL VIEWING Answers will vary. Possible response: The Lenni Lenape and Quakers on Penn's right appear friendly. All look pleased and interested in the treaty. At Penn's left, a Lenni Lenape chief, or a man of status, carries a bow and arrows but wears a calm expression. Penn's inviting gesture suggests equality.

3.2 Forming Alliances

Have you ever heard the phrase "strength in numbers"? In the 1600s, as Native Americans and Europeans battled with each other in the Middle Colonies, they discovered that it's sometimes better to be part of a larger group than to stand alone.

MAIN IDEA The Iroquois Confederacy consisted of five tribes that worked together to defeat other Native American tribes and the French.

Wampum Accessory
Wampum are white and purple beads made from the shells of a certain clam and sea snail. Native Americans made woven items from strings of wampum. The decorations recorded information and sometimes confirmed authority of the wearer.

CLASHES AMONG CULTURES

As white colonists continued moving into New England and the Middle Colonies, two groups of Native Americans began to feel increasingly threatened by their presence.

One group that banded together was the Algonquian (al-GON-kwee-uhn). It consisted of the tribes who lived along the Atlantic coast and spoke similar languages. The Pequot tribe resided in New England. The Lenape inhabited the region that became the Middle Colonies. The Algonquian were hunters and gatherers. While they also fished and planted crops, they moved each season to follow the supply of food and lived in temporary camps while away from their villages.

Historically, the Algonquian were the enemies of another united group of tribes, the Iroquois (IHR-uh-kwoy). The Iroquois lived in what is currently central New York State. The French gave these Native Americans the name *Iroquois*, but they called themselves the Haudenosaunee (hah-duh-NAH-suh-nee), or "People of the Longhouse," for the style of home that they built and lived in with their families.

Native American Nations, 1650

OJIBWA
OJIBWA
MENOMINEE
HO-CHUNK
OTTAWA
POTAWATOMI
SAUK
FOX
KICKAPOO
MIAMI
ILLINOIS
NEUTRAL
ERIE
SHAWNEE
ALGONQUIN
MICMAC
PENOBSCOT
ABENAKI
HURON
IROQUOIS
SENECA CAYUGA ONONDAGA ONEIDA MOHAWK
MOHICAN
MASSACHUSET
WAMPANOAG
NARRAGANSET
PEQUOT, MOHEGAN
SUSQUEHANNOCK
DELAWARE
POWHATAN
TUSCARORA
ATLANTIC OCEAN

0   100   200 Miles
0   100   200 Kilometers

Present-day boundary

The arrival of colonists from Europe added another source of tension to the region. Yet another wave of settlers was now occupying disputed tribal territories, disrupting hunting grounds, communities, and sacred sites.

UNITED WE STAND

Even before Europeans began colonizing and claiming land in North America, conflicts among groups of Native Americans led some of them to form **alliances**, or agreements, with one another. One of the most important alliances was the **Iroquois Confederacy**. A **confederacy** is an agreement among several groups to protect and support one another in battle or other endeavors. In about 1600, the Iroquois Confederacy joined together five tribes: the Mohawk, Onondaga, Oneida, Cayuga, and Seneca, ending the fighting that had once raged among them. The addition of the Tuscarora about 120 years later would change the confederacy's name to the Six Nations.

By banding together, Native Americans hoped to protect their lands and culture and prevent further strife, but they also formed alliances with the French and British. These alliances shifted over time. Sometimes Native Americans even pitted the French, British, and colonists from other countries against one another.

The Iroquois—the Mohawk, in particular—often traded furs with Dutch and British settlers in exchange for firearms. In this way, the trading partners came to rely on each other, and they supported each other in battle. Likewise, the Lenape and the Huron, both enemies of the Iroquois, allied with the French.

Battles between the French and Iroquois over control of the fur trade continued. Due to high demand for their fur, beavers became scarce in the East by the mid-1600s. As a result, the Iroquois Confederacy moved west to gain greater access to beavers in the region, warring with competing tribes along the way. The Iroquois also attacked New France in the North, hoping to end French fur trading in the Ohio Valley and beyond.

In 1689, the Iroquois attacked the settlement of Lachine, near Montreal, in present-day Canada. The attack was in response to a raid two years earlier in which the French had destroyed Iroquois corn. The Iroquois killed about 250 settlers and burned the settlement. More back-and-forth retaliation followed until both sides grew weary of conflict. The weakened Iroquois made peace and, in 1701, signed a treaty of **neutrality**, in which they agreed not to take sides in future wars. But the conflict over land and furs was to grow even more.

HISTORICAL THINKING

1. **READING CHECK** How did forming alliances help the members of the Iroquois Confederacy?

2. **MAKE INFERENCES** In what ways did the demand for beaver fur affect alliances among Native Americans and Europeans?

3. **INTERPRET MAPS** How does the map help you understand why some Native Americans living near the Great Lakes might have been easy targets for the Iroquois Confederacy?

PLAN

Objective
Discover how forming alliances helped Native American tribes defeat their enemies.

Critical Thinking Skills for Lesson 3.2
- Identify Main Ideas and Details
- Monitor Comprehension
- Make Inferences
- Interpret Maps
- Draw Conclusions
- Analyze Cause and Effect
- Make Connections

Essential Question for Chapter 3
How did early settlers cope with challenges as they established the first 13 colonies? Native American groups had conflicts among themselves and with colonists. Lesson 3.2 describes how forming alliances affected these conflicts.

Background for the Teacher
The Iroquois initially established their confederacy as a way to maintain peace and cooperation among the different Iroquois nations. But the confederacy also gave the Iroquois strength and security when negotiating with other tribes or with colonists and when conducting warfare against enemies. This became increasingly important with the advent of colonial trade and settlement. The Iroquois Confederacy was more effective than most other Native American alliances, in part because its complex political structure was well defined and ritualized. While villages retained local control, the sachems, or peace chiefs, from the different nations came together to resolve conflicts and set policies.

INTRODUCE & ENGAGE

Strength in Numbers

Display a single pencil and a group of pencils banded together. **ASK:** Why would the group of pencils be harder to break than the single pencil? *(The group is stronger.)* Tell students to brainstorm other examples that support the phrase "strength in numbers." Tell them this lesson describes how some groups of Native Americans and colonists employed the strategy of strength in numbers in the 1600s.

TEACH

Guided Discussion

1. **Draw Conclusions** How might the arrival of European colonists and fur traders have increased tensions between the Algonquian and Iroquois? *(Answers will vary. Possible response: The Algonquian and Iroquois lived in close proximity and clashed over tribal territory and hunting grounds. Fur traders and settlers further encroached on disputed land and made the Iroquois and Algonquian competitors for furs, particularly after the Iroquois moved westward in search of a more plentiful supply of beavers.)* Using the map, point out the Algonquin tribe north of the Great Lakes. Explain that the Algonquin are a specific tribe that lived in the Ottawa River Valley of Quebec and Ontario. Explain that the Algonquian discussed in the text is the vast language group of Native American tribes who lived along the Atlantic coast.

2. **Analyze Cause and Effect** What chain of events led the Iroquois to eventually sign a treaty of neutrality in 1701? *(The Iroquois fought the French to gain control of the fur trade in the Ohio Valley. They warred with competing tribes and attacked towns in New France. In 1689, they attacked and burnt the settlement of Lachine, near Montreal, killing about 250 settlers. The French retaliated, and fighting continued. Finally, the Iroquois signed a treaty of neutrality in 1701, promising not to take sides in future wars.)*

Make Connections

Point out that the British as well as the French wanted the Iroquois to remain neutral in future wars. **ASK:** What geographic and economic factors might have led the French and British to want the confederacy to remain neutral in future wars? *(Possible response: Fur trading was important to the French, British, and the Iroquois, whose villages were located near waterways important to the trade. The Iroquois's participation in warfare would disrupt the fur trade and decrease profits.)*

Active Options

On Your Feet: Team Word Webbing Divide students into teams of four and give each team a large sheet of paper and each student a different colored marker. Tell students to write *confederacy* in the center of the paper. Have each student add a related word or phrase on the part of the web nearest him or her. On a signal, they rotate the paper and add to the nearest part again. Repeat the process with *alliance* and *neutrality*. After all Word Webs have been completed, ask teams to share and discuss their work.

NG Learning Framework: Explore the Fur Trade   **STEM**

SKILL Collaboration

KNOWLEDGE Critical Species

Have teams of students work together to research the trade in beaver furs in colonial North America. Tell groups to consider two questions in their research:

• How did the beaver fur trade benefit European colonists and Native Americans?

• What impact did this fur trade have on the environment?

Encourage students to collaborate on their research and on creating a visual presentation of the information they gather. Have teams present their findings to the class and then conduct a class discussion about their findings.

English Language Learners

Make Vocabulary Cards Have students at **All Proficiencies** make and use flash cards to learn and practice unfamiliar words they encounter in this lesson. On one side of each card, they should write the target word. On the other, they should write related words they are familiar with, draw or glue images that will help them recall the meaning of the target word, or write out other mnemonic devices. Encourage students to use their flash cards for review.

Gifted & Talented

Research and Compare Alliances Tell students to research a present-day alliance and compare it to an alliance they read about in the lesson. Then ask students to present their findings to the class.

See the Chapter Planner for more strategies for differentiation.

HISTORICAL THINKING

ANSWERS

1. By banding together rather than fighting one another, the Iroquois had more strength and could better withstand enemies or wage wars.

2. The Iroquois traded furs with the Dutch and British, while the Lenape and Huron tended to trade with the French. Because these trading relationships were important to both Native American and colonial economies, trade partners also made political alliances.

3. The Great Lakes are near the lands claimed by the Iroquois Confederacy, so it would have been easy for the members of the confederacy to attack Native Americans who lived there.

3.3 The Southern Colonies

Have you ever made a plan that didn't work out as you expected? Leaders developed detailed plans for the Southern Colonies. But as more colonists arrived, some of the plans worked better than others.

MAIN IDEA The Southern Colonies provided economic opportunities and social challenges for the colonists who settled in them.

COLONIAL EXPANSION AND COMMERCE

As you have read, in 1607 Jamestown became the first colonial settlement. In 1699, Williamsburg became the new capital of the Virginia colony. Over time, Europeans established settlements in many parts of the South. Maryland, Virginia, North Carolina, South Carolina, and Georgia together formed the **Southern Colonies.**

In 1632, King Charles I of England granted a charter to George Calvert, who held the title Lord Baltimore, to establish a new colony called Maryland, made up of the northern part of Virginia. Most of its settlers were small landowners and renters. Upon Calvert's untimely death, his son became Lord Baltimore and Maryland's **proprietor**—the person responsible for the colony. Maryland's location on the Chesapeake Bay provided easy access to trade, and the region's rich, fertile soil was ideal for growing tobacco. Wealthy plantation owners and merchants built docks on **tributaries**, or small rivers that flow into larger bodies of water, of the Chesapeake Bay. There, they could more easily load ships with tobacco for export and receive ships from around the world loaded with goods.

By 1670, Carolina had become a colony. By 1691, it had split into two colonies: North Carolina, already settled by small planters from Virginia, and South Carolina. Many of South Carolina's settlers came from Barbados in the West Indies. They established large plantations where they grew tobacco, rice, cotton, sugarcane, and other crops. They purchased enslaved Africans to work these plantations. By 1729, both Carolinas had become **royal colonies**, or colonies with a governor and council appointed by the king.

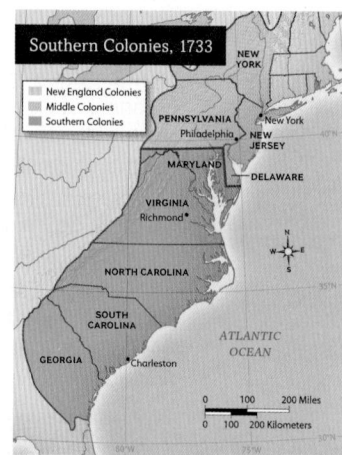

Southern Colonies, 1733

New England Colonies
Middle Colonies
Southern Colonies

GEORGIA: A GRAND EXPERIMENT FAILS

Most of Britain's American colonies were founded for profit or religious freedom. But Georgia, the last mainland British colony in North America, began with a different idea. **James Oglethorpe** and Viscount John Percival envisioned a colony in which debtors and the very poor could make a new start.

King George II wasn't interested in helping the poor, but he understood that Georgia could be a military buffer between Spanish Florida and South Carolina. He granted the charter, placing control of the colony in the hands of trustees who could neither receive financial gain from Georgia nor own

land within it. As governor, Oglethorpe required that all colonists follow three rules based on his own beliefs: no slaves, no liquor, and limited land ownership for each settler. His lofty vision did not last long.

Settlers began arriving in 1733. Many of them found the colony's strict policies unreasonable, so Georgia's population grew slowly. Its role as military buffer between the Spanish and British colonies soon became a source of conflict. The Spanish, suspecting the British of smuggling slaves and goods into Spanish provinces, began searching British ships. Then, in 1740, Oglethorpe attacked Florida, in an attempt to drive the Spanish out. The Spanish, in turn, invaded Georgia in 1742. After a number of other conflicts, both sides gave up, and calm was restored to the buffer zone.

The trustees recognized that Georgia would not thrive under Oglethorpe's strict rules. By 1750, laws allowed liquor and slavery, and there were no limits on land ownership. In 1752, control of Georgia returned to Great Britain. The grand experiment had failed.

CRITICAL VIEWING Tobacco was one of the major crops in the Southern Colonies. Today, the work of planting, harvesting, and preparing tobacco for market is much the same as it was during the colonial period. In the top photo, a man in Tennessee harvests the whole tobacco plant by chopping it at its base. In the bottom photo, bundles of tobacco hang to cure, or dry and preserve. Based on details you notice in both photos, what kinds of challenges do you think tobacco farmers encounter?

HISTORICAL THINKING

1. **READING CHECK** In what ways was Georgia different from the other Southern Colonies?

2. **MAKE INFERENCES** Why might James Oglethorpe have insisted on limiting the amount of land a settler could have?

3. **INTERPRET MAPS** Find the city of Charleston on the map. What advantages do you think this city enjoyed due to its geographic location?

PLAN

Objective

Discover why colonists moved to and settled in the Southern Colonies.

Critical Thinking Skills for Lesson 3.3

• Identify Main Ideas and Details
• Monitor Comprehension
• Make Inferences
• Interpret Maps
• Draw Conclusions
• Form and Support Opinions

Essential Question for Chapter 3

How did early settlers cope with challenges as they established the first 13 colonies? The location and resources of the Southern Colonies provided new opportunities and new challenges for settlers. Lesson 3.3 discusses the expansion of colonies and commerce in the Southern Colonies and Georgia's role in the conflict with the Spanish.

Background for the Teacher

Tobacco was a successful crop in the Southern Colonies, but it proved labor intensive to plant, harvest, and cure. Tobacco seeds were planted in beds in the winter and tended until the seedlings were ready to transplant to the fields in the spring, when the plants were placed in knee-high hills of soil. Tasks, such as weeding, pruning, and removing worms and other pests, required manual labor during the intense summer heat. The tobacco was harvested in late summer after it had reached a height of between six to nine feet. Once the tobacco was cured, turning from greenish-yellow to tan, it was sorted by hand and packed in barrels to be shipped to England.

Activate Prior Knowledge

Provide each student with a K-W-L Chart like the one shown below. Ask students to recall what they know about why Virginia was founded, who settled there, and how colonists lived. Tell students to record their answers in the first column of the chart. Then ask them to write questions they would like to have answered as they learn about the Southern Colonies. Allow time at the end of the lesson for students to fill in what they have learned.

K What Do I Know?	W What Do I Want To Learn?	L What Did I Learn?

TEACH

Guided Discussion

1. **Draw Conclusions** Why were many of South Carolina's settlers slave owners? *(Answers will vary. Possible response: Many settlers were from Barbados in the West Indies, and they created large plantations of crops such as tobacco, rice, cotton, and sugarcane. The plantations required many workers, so the owners bought slaves to work the fields.)*

2. **Form and Support Opinions** Was James Oglethorpe's grand experiment doomed to failure from the outset? Support your opinion with evidence from the text. *(Answers will vary. Possible responses: No, new opportunities provided an incentive for debtors and poor people to settle in the colony, so Oglethorpe's plan seemed promising. Yes, Oglethorpe's strict rules, which banned slavery and liquor and limited land ownership, discouraged settlers, so the plan was doomed to failure from the beginning.)*

Interpret Maps

Tell students to locate Maryland on the map of the Southern Colonies. **ASK:** Why would Maryland's location be good for tobacco farmers? *(Answers will vary. Possible response: Tobacco was an export crop, so farmers needed to get their cured tobacco to seaports for shipping to England. Maryland's location on the Chesapeake Bay and its many tributary rivers made transporting tobacco easy for farmers.)*

Active Options

On Your Feet: Host a Quiz Show Ask each student to write one question about the Southern Colonies. Then bring teams of five students to the front of the class to take part in a quiz show. Ask for student volunteers to alternate as quiz show hosts. Instruct hosts to pose student questions. Keep track of questions that stumped players and, as a class, answer those questions.

NG Learning Framework: Advertise a Colony

SKILL Collaboration

KNOWLEDGE Our Human Story

Ask students to imagine they are in charge of an ad campaign to attract settlers to one of the Southern Colonies. Instruct them to collaborate on choosing a colony and creating a poster that advertises the advantages of living there. Emphasize that the goal of the poster should be to persuade settlers to move that colony, so students should use persuasive language and visual media to that end. Invite groups to share their posters with the class.

Striving Readers

Strengthen Vocabulary Ask pairs to write the word *proprietor* in a Word Square and collaborate to write its definition and characteristics, examples, and non-examples. Repeat with *tributaries* and *royal colonies*. After completing the Word Squares, ask students to use each Key Vocabulary word in a sentence to confirm understanding.

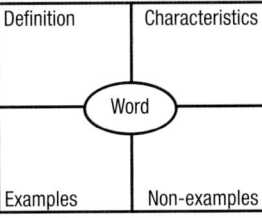

Definition	Characteristics
	Word
Examples	Non-examples

Inclusion

Describe Photographs Pair students who are visually impaired with sighted partners. Ask sighted students to describe the photographs and read the caption aloud to their partners. Allow students with visual impairments to ask for clarification of the description and text. Then ask partners to discuss the Critical Viewing question.

See the Chapter Planner for more strategies for differentiation.

HISTORICAL THINKING

ANSWERS

1. Georgia was run by a board of trustees who could not own land or receive money from land sales. Other colonies generated profit for their proprietors. In Georgia, unlike other Southern Colonies, slavery was forbidden, and settlers had limited land ownership.

2. Possible response: Limiting the amount of land each person could buy helped maintain equality among colonists.

3. Answers will vary. Possible response: Charleston's location on the coast made it easily accessible to the Southern Colonies and attractive to merchants engaged in commerce. It was a valuable port where goods could be imported and exported.

CRITICAL VIEWING Possible response: The photos suggest that tobacco farming requires manual labor, so farmers have to pay a large labor force to cut, bundle, and hang the tobacco. The plants are open to the air to dry, so farmers have to deal with insects and wet weather.

3.4 Economic Activities in the Thirteen Colonies

MAIN IDEA Colonists used the abundant resources around them to develop thriving economies in three colonial regions.

SHAPING THE COLONIAL ECONOMY

When European settlers came to North America, they took advantage of the region's **natural resources**. Natural resources are divided into two categories: living and nonliving. The earth provides living resources, such as plants, trees, and animals, that help feed, shelter, and clothe humans. The earth also provides nonliving resources, such as minerals, water, and soil. Both living and nonliving natural resources provide **raw materials**, or substances used to make products.

People use natural resources to engage in **economic activities**, or the production, distribution, and consumption of goods and services. When you go to the store to buy groceries, you are engaging in an economic activity.

How are natural resources, raw materials, and economic activities related? Consider this example. Colonists in New England chopped down trees in the region's thick forests for timber, or wood used for building. Timber became one of New England's most important raw materials. Shipbuilding became one of its most important economic activities.

The natural resources and raw materials available in different regions shaped how the colonies developed. Some natural resources, raw materials, and economic activities were unique to one region, but others were common among all three.

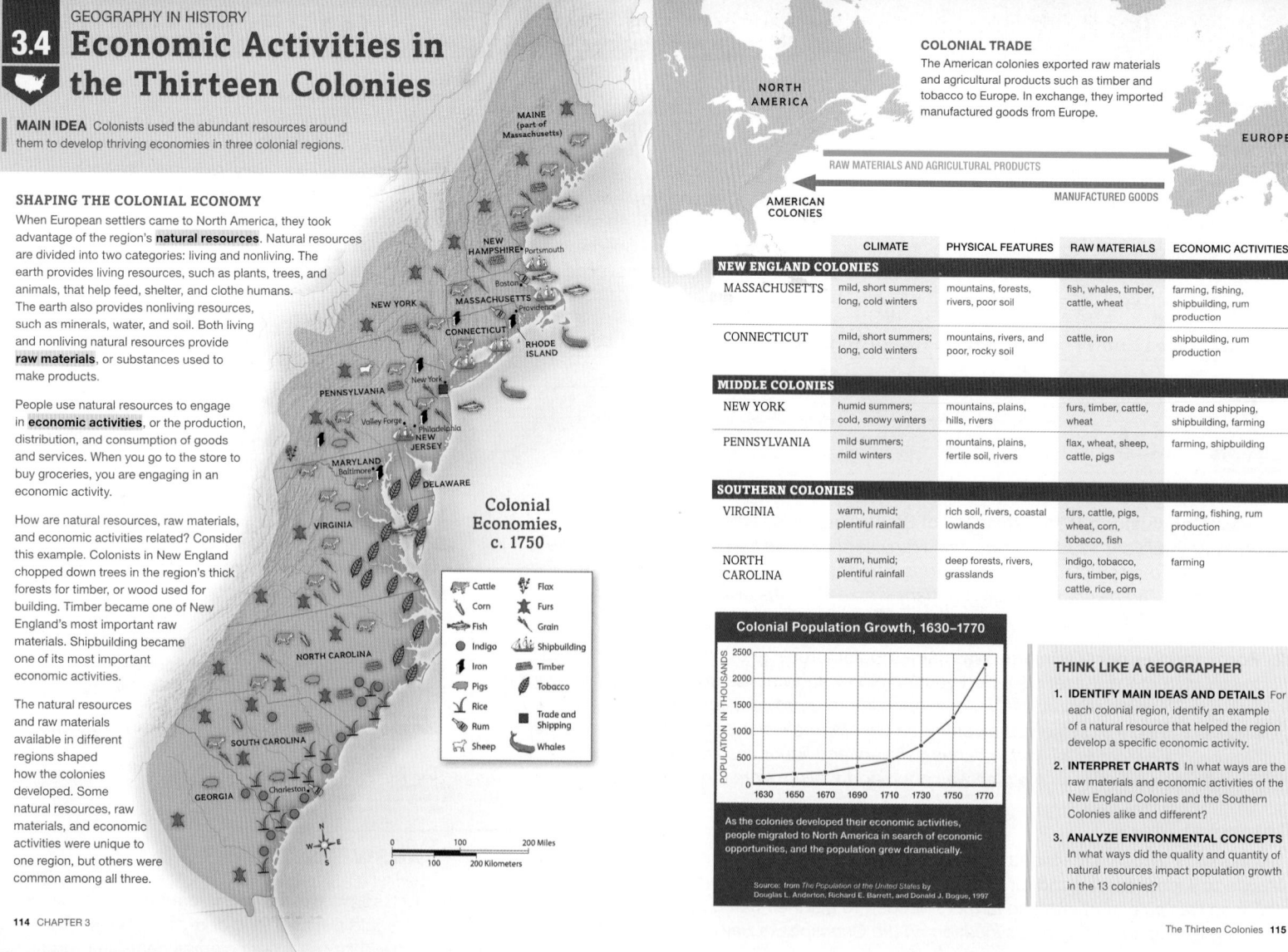

Colonial Economies, c. 1750

Legend:
- Cattle
- Corn
- Fish
- Indigo
- Iron
- Pigs
- Rice
- Rum
- Sheep
- Flax
- Furs
- Grain
- Shipbuilding
- Timber
- Tobacco
- Trade and Shipping
- Whales

COLONIAL TRADE
The American colonies exported raw materials and agricultural products such as timber and tobacco to Europe. In exchange, they imported manufactured goods from Europe.

NORTH AMERICA — AMERICAN COLONIES — EUROPE

RAW MATERIALS AND AGRICULTURAL PRODUCTS →
← MANUFACTURED GOODS

	CLIMATE	PHYSICAL FEATURES	RAW MATERIALS	ECONOMIC ACTIVITIES
NEW ENGLAND COLONIES				
MASSACHUSETTS	mild, short summers; long, cold winters	mountains, forests, rivers, poor soil	fish, whales, timber, cattle, wheat	farming, fishing, shipbuilding, rum production
CONNECTICUT	mild, short summers; long, cold winters	mountains, rivers, and poor, rocky soil	cattle, iron	shipbuilding, rum production
MIDDLE COLONIES				
NEW YORK	humid summers; cold, snowy winters	mountains, plains, hills, rivers	furs, timber, cattle, wheat	trade and shipping, shipbuilding, farming
PENNSYLVANIA	mild summers; mild winters	mountains, plains, fertile soil, rivers	flax, wheat, sheep, cattle, pigs	farming, shipbuilding
SOUTHERN COLONIES				
VIRGINIA	warm, humid; plentiful rainfall	rich soil, rivers, coastal lowlands	furs, cattle, pigs, wheat, corn, tobacco, fish	farming, fishing, rum production
NORTH CAROLINA	warm, humid; plentiful rainfall	deep forests, rivers, grasslands	indigo, tobacco, furs, timber, pigs, cattle, rice, corn	farming

Colonial Population Growth, 1630–1770

(graph: POPULATION IN THOUSANDS vs years 1630, 1650, 1670, 1690, 1710, 1730, 1750, 1770; values from 0 to 2500)

As the colonies developed their economic activities, people migrated to North America in search of economic opportunities, and the population grew dramatically.

Source: from *The Population of the United States* by Douglas L. Anderton, Richard E. Barrett, and Donald J. Bogue, 1997

THINK LIKE A GEOGRAPHER

1. **IDENTIFY MAIN IDEAS AND DETAILS** For each colonial region, identify an example of a natural resource that helped the region develop a specific economic activity.

2. **INTERPRET CHARTS** In what ways are the raw materials and economic activities of the New England Colonies and the Southern Colonies alike and different?

3. **ANALYZE ENVIRONMENTAL CONCEPTS** In what ways did the quality and quantity of natural resources impact population growth in the 13 colonies?

PLAN

Objective

Explore the connection between resources and economic activities in the colonies.

Critical Thinking Skills for Lesson 3.4

- Identify Main Ideas and Details
- Monitor Comprehension
- Interpret Charts
- Analyze Environmental Concepts
- Make Generalizations
- Interpret Maps

Essential Question for Chapter 3

How did early settlers cope with challenges as they established the first 13 colonies? The availability of natural resources was key to meeting economic challenges in the colonies. Lesson 3.4 describes how colonists used plentiful raw materials to develop successful economies.

Background for the Teacher

Shipbuilding in the New England colonies soon gave rise to shipbuilding playing a key role in the Atlantic economy. The fishing industry in New England spurred the growth of maritime trade and encouraged local shipbuilding. Oak forests provided raw materials, and with the building of ships, associated trades arose, such as sail, rope, and candle making. Shipbuilding in the Chesapeake Bay area produced the tobacco boat, which could transport five to ten 1000-pound barrels of tobacco. The quality of timber was important, and Georgia's live oak—dense and resistant to rot—was a desired shipbuilding material. The shipbuilding industry along the Atlantic coast helped the 13 colonies begin to attain financial independence from Britain.

Financial Literacy

To extend their knowledge and understanding about the concepts in this lesson, refer students to the Financial Literacy handbook.

Preview and Predict

Have students preview the Colonial Economies map. **ASK:** What generalizations can you make about the colonial economy based on the map? *(Answers will vary. Possible responses: Farming and agriculture were important in all of the colonies, as was the timber industry. Fur trapping was important in western regions, and shipbuilding, fishing, and whaling were important industries along the northeastern coast.)*

Guided Discussion

1. **Make Generalizations** Based on the three visuals and what you read in the text, state why shipbuilding was vital to the economy of the colonies. Point to evidence in the lesson to support your statements. *(Possible response: The map shows the colonies covered a vast area along the coast with an abundance of raw materials. The geography and economics chart details the colonies' use of raw materials for both manufacturing and exporting. The population growth graph indicates a growing population. Therefore, ships played a vital role because they were necessary to move goods for trade with Europe and to distribute raw materials, manufactured goods, and consumable goods within the colonies to support a growing population.)*

2. **Analyze Environmental Concepts** According to the map, which crops in the Southern Colonies grew mainly in the coastal lowlands, and what does that tell you about the plants? *(Answers will vary. Possible response: Indigo, rice, and tobacco grew mainly in the coastal lowlands, which indicates that they could grow in hot, wet conditions.)*

Geography in History

Interpret Maps Have students identify the symbol for Trade and Shipping in the map key and locate the city it marks on the map. **ASK:** Why was New York a center for trade and shipping? *(Answers will vary. Possible response: It is located on the coast and on a major river. Its location made it accessible to and from other colonies as well as to and from Europe.)* Ask students to identify other cities on the map that were likely centers for trade and shipping. *(Boston, Philadelphia, Baltimore, Charleston, Providence, and Portsmouth)*

Active Options

Active History: Compare North American Settlements Extend the lesson by using either the PDF or Whiteboard version of the activity. These activities take a deeper look at a topic from, or related to, the lesson. Explore the activities as a class, turn them into group assignments, or even assign them individually.

NG Learning Framework: Research Natural Resources

ATTITUDE Curiosity

KNOWLEDGE Our Living Planet

Tell students to work in pairs to research one of the natural resources on the map that interests them. Students can use online or library resources for their research. Tell students to identify their chosen natural resource, how it was used in the colonial period, and if it is still used. Some students may want to trace the history of their resource from the colonial period to the present day. Tell students to organize the information on posters or in multimedia presentations and encourage them to share their findings with the class.

Inclusion

Provide Terms and Names on Audio Decide which of the terms and names are important for mastery and have a volunteer record the pronunciations and a short sentence defining each word. Encourage students to listen to the recording as often as necessary.

English Language Learners   ELD

Complete Sentence Frames Use sentence frames such as those below to help students at the **Emerging** level demonstrate their understanding of the Colonial Economies map and the geography and economics chart. You may wish to allow students to choose the correct word to fill in the blanks from a list on the board.

- A natural resource in the colony of _____ is _____.
- The climate in the colony of _____ is _____.
- A physical feature in the colony of _____ is _____.
- An economic activity in the colony of _____ is _____.

See the Chapter Planner for more strategies for differentiation.

ANSWERS

1. Answers will vary. Possible response: New England's forests and iron deposits helped develop a shipbuilding industry. The fertile soil of the Middle Colonies helped develop wheat farming. The rich soil and grasslands of the Southern Colonies helped farmers grow crops and raise livestock.

2. Answers will vary. Possible response: People of both the New England and Southern Colonies trapped animals for fur, harvested timber, farmed, raised cattle, and produced rum. Rich soil in the Southern Colonies gave way to plantations and crops for export. In New England, shipbuilding grew out of the importance of ocean fishing and whaling.

3. Because of the abundance and high quality of natural resources available to the colonists, the population increased by more than 2,000,000 people.

3.5 Werowocomoco, the Powhatan Capital

In 1607, Europe had long-established capital cities such as London, Paris, and Madrid. When the Jamestown colonists first met the Native American chief they called Powhatan, they visited him in an equally sophisticated capital.

MAIN IDEA In the 1600s, Werowocomoco was the capital of the Powhatan tribes. Today researchers are exploring its site to learn about the tribes and their interactions with English colonists.

SEAT OF POWER FOR A CHIEFDOM

It was in Werowocomoco (wayr-wuh-KAH-muh-koh) that John Smith first met Powhatan's daughter Pocahontas, who eventually married colonist John Rolfe. Smith would later tell a dramatic tale of being rescued by Pocahontas from certain execution at the hands of Chief Powhatan's warriors. Historians suspect the true story of the meeting was a little less exciting, but it nevertheless was a key moment in the relationship between the colonists and the Powhatan people.

The village of Werowocomoco must have presented a real contrast to the Jamestown Colony in 1607. While Jamestown had been built on swampy ground, Werowocomoco was built on bluffs above the Pamunkey River, which the Europeans later renamed the York River, in present-day Virginia.

The village had many geographical advantages. River bluffs and nearby creeks served as natural defenses against attackers. Nearby waterways were a source of drinking water and fish. The surrounding

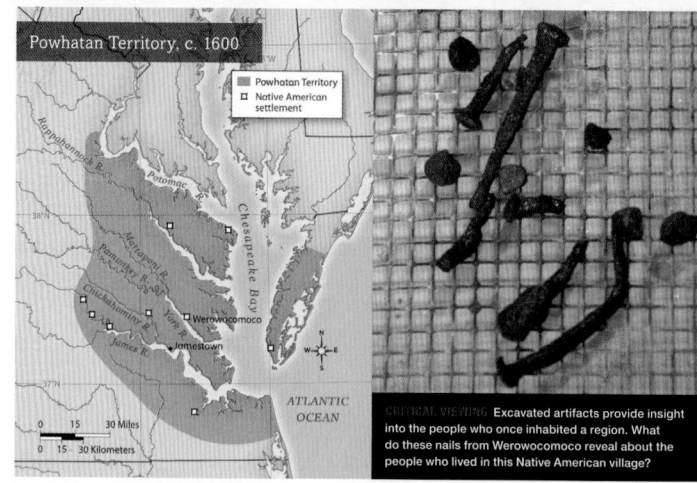

Powhatan Territory, c. 1600

CRITICAL VIEWING Excavated artifacts provide insight into the people who once inhabited a region. What do these nails from Werowocomoco reveal about the people who lived in this Native American village?

land was suitable for farming, and nearby forests provided wood for building and fires.

Archaeological evidence suggests that Virginia Indians had lived on the Werowocomoco site since around 8000 B.C. By the early 1600s, the village was the seat of power for Chief Powhatan. He ruled over a group of more than 30 Algonquian-speaking tribes spread out over more than 8,000 square miles around Chesapeake Bay.

EXPLORING WEROWOCOMOCO TODAY

Today, Werowocomoco's wealth lies in the knowledge it reveals about Powhatan society. In 1609, Chief Powhatan abandoned the village, and in time the location of Werowocomoco was forgotten. Then in 2003, researchers announced they had used evidence from historical maps and documents to pinpoint the village's location. Since then, archaeologists have been actively excavating the site.

Finding Werowocomoco has allowed researchers to learn not only about how Powhatan society evolved but also about the meeting of the English and Native American cultures that took place between 1607 and 1609. Archaeologists found a number of English artifacts that closely

resembled lists of trade goods John Smith kept in his Jamestown journals. These included several copper-alloy items such as a pot, fragments of a spoon, and small beads. In order to enhance his importance among local tribes, Chief Powhatan had tried to maintain an exclusive trade in objects such as these with the English.

Within a few years, the English and the Powhatan would be at war. Werowocomoco preserves evidence that for brief but significant moments before the conflict, the two sides engaged in mutual bonds of trade and cultural exchange.

Archaeologists and members of Virginia's Native American tribes spend long hours carefully excavating the Werowocomoco dig site adjacent to the York River.

HISTORICAL THINKING

1. **READING CHECK** What types of items did the Powhatan and the Jamestown settlers trade with each other?

2. **MAKE CONNECTIONS** Think about what you learned about Jamestown in this chapter. In what ways did geography affect the relationship between Jamestown and Werowocomoco?

3. **MAKE GENERALIZATIONS** What purposes do exploring and preserving sites like Werowocomoco serve?

Objective

Learn about contact between colonists and the Powhatan from archaeological discoveries.

Critical Thinking Skills for Lesson 3.5

- Identify Main Ideas and Details
- Monitor Comprehension
- Make Connections
- Make Generalizations
- Integrate Visuals
- Draw Conclusions
- Interpret Maps

Essential Question for Chapter 3

How did early settlers cope with challenges as they established the first 13 colonies?
Jamestown settlers encountered sophisticated Native-American societies in Virginia. Lesson 3.5 discusses archaeological discoveries that suggest early cultural exchanges were peaceful.

Background for the Teacher

The discovery of one of the most significant sites in American colonial history was the result of a woman walking her dog. In 1996, Lynn Ripley was exploring her recently purchased farm along the York River and noticed pieces of broken pottery sticking up from the ground. She began collecting the ceramic pieces, arrowheads, pipe stems, and other items she found on her walks. In 2001, the Ripleys mentioned Lynn's collection to two local archaeologists who contacted Randolph Turner at the Virginia Department of Historic Resources. Turner had spent 30 years trying to locate the Powhatan capital based on John Smith's writings and an old Spanish map. After doing some preliminary surveys of the Ripleys' property, Turner concluded, "This is Werowocomoco!"

Frame Questions

Invite students to imagine they are members of a team of archaeologists who have discovered ruins or a site from a past culture. Ask them to frame questions they would want to answer by excavating the site. List the questions on the board. At the end of the lesson, allow students to revisit the questions to find out which questions have been answered.

TEACH

Guided Discussion

1. **Integrate Visuals** Based on information in the text and map, why might Powhatan have chosen Werowocomoco as his seat of power? *(Answers will vary. Possible response: The map shows that Werowocomoco was centrally located. The location was easily defensible because it was built on bluffs above the Pamunkey River with direct navigation to the Chesapeake Bay. From this advantageous location, Powhatan traded with and controlled more than 30 Algonquian-speaking tribes under his leadership.)*

2. **Draw Conclusions** How has new information about Werowocomoco changed or confirmed interpretations of history? *(New information indicates that the Powhatan were not the first to settle Werowocomoco. Virginia Indians first occupied the site around 8000 B.C. Archaeological evidence also confirms European historical records, such as information about trade goods in John Smith's journals and the location of Werowocomoco on historical maps.)*

Interpret Maps

Have students study the map of Powhatan Territory. **ASK:** Based on what you see on the map, where did the Powhatan live in 1600? *(The Powhatan lived on the Atlantic coast and in and along Chesapeake Bay.)* What do you notice about the locations of settlements? *(Many of them are on rivers or along inlets.)* Why might access to locations on or near bodies of water be important? *(Access to locations on or near water would be important for trade, for fresh water, and fishing.)*

Active Options

On Your Feet: Compare and Contrast Divide students into two teams to compare and contrast Jamestown and Werowocomoco. As a class, have students determine bases of comparison, such as location, resources, advantages, leaders, and size. Then assign Jamestown to one team and Werowocomoco to the other. Based on information in the text and other sources, have team members fill in a Venn diagram. Remind students to list differences in the outer parts of the circles and similarities in the overlapping part. Discuss the diagrams as a class.

NG Learning Framework: Investigate Diseases   STEM

ATTITUDE Curiosity

KNOWLEDGE Our Living Planet

Encourage students to form teams and consult online or library sources to research the similarities and differences between the locations and physical features of Jamestown and Werowocomoco. Students should identify why such features were or were not conducive to the spread of diseases such as dysentery, malaria, and cholera. Have students compare and contrast their findings with other teams and then present them to the class.

Striving Readers

Record and Compare Facts After reading the lesson, ask students to write three important facts they learned about Werowocomoco. Allow pairs of students to compare and check their facts. Ask a volunteer from each pair to write the most important fact from their list on the board. Then combine students' facts into one list.

Gifted & Talented

Create a Multimedia Display Direct students to research the archaeological evidence uncovered at Werowocomoco to discover how science supports historical inquiry. Have students create a multimedia display illustrating artifacts archaeologists have found. Then have them play the role of archaeologists and answer students' questions about the historical significance of each artifact.

See the Chapter Planner for more strategies for differentiation.

HISTORICAL THINKING

ANSWERS

1. Trade goods included such items as copper pots, spoons, and beads.

2. Although both settlements were located on rivers off Chesapeake Bay, Werowocomoco was built above the water on bluffs. Jamestown's location on low, swampy land made it necessary for settlers to seek help from the Powhatan to survive.

3. Exploring sites provides information about the changes in Native American societies over time, such as how they maintained control over their territories and interacted with European settlers. Preserving these sites allows future researchers to build on accumulated knowledge.

3 REVIEW

VOCABULARY

Use vocabulary words to complete the sentences.

1. _____ had to work for a set number of years to pay off their passages to the colonies.

2. Governor Berkeley accused Nathaniel Bacon of being a _____ .

3. The Virginia Company was known as a _____ because its shareholders also owned stock in the company.

4. When Lord Baltimore died, his son became the _____ of the Maryland colony.

5. The company had received a _____ from King James I to establish a colony in Virginia.

6. Governed by the crown through an appointed governor and council, Carolina was a _____ .

7. In the early 1600s, a _____ who disagreed with the beliefs of the Church could be punished.

READING STRATEGY
MAKE INFERENCES

If you haven't already, complete your chart of inferences about the challenges of establishing the first 13 colonies. List at least four inferences. Then answer the question.

8. What kind of physical dangers did settlers face in the colonies?

I READ	I KNOW	AND SO
The settlers lived under difficult conditions.	Many settlers died of diseases.	

MAIN IDEAS

9. How did John Smith help keep the settlers from starving at Jamestown? **LESSON 1.1**

10. What caused the conflict between colonists at Jamestown and the Powhatan? **LESSON 1.4**

11. Why did Nathaniel Bacon stage a rebellion? **LESSON 1.4**

12. How were the Pilgrims' and Puritans' involvement with the Church of England different? **LESSON 2.1**

13. What was the reason for massive arrests in Salem in 1692? **LESSON 2.4**

14. How did England benefit from taking control of New Netherland? **LESSON 3.1**

15. How did William Penn's Quaker beliefs help influence the diverse makeup of Pennsylvania? **LESSON 3.1**

16. Why did the Iroquois attack New France? **LESSON 3.2**

17. How did Maryland's access to the Chesapeake Bay benefit the colony? **LESSON 3.3**

HISTORICAL THINKING

Answer the following questions. Support your answers with evidence from the chapter.

18. **EVALUATE** In what ways was control of land central to struggles between Native Americans and European colonists?

19. **SYNTHESIZE** Why did the American colonies represent a safe haven for religious groups willing to move to a new place in the 17th and 18th centuries?

20. **COMPARE AND CONTRAST** How were the settlers in the New England colonies different from and similar to settlers in the Middle Colonies?

21. **FORM AND SUPPORT OPINIONS** Why do you think some Puritans in Salem might have felt threatened by women owning property? Use information from the chapter to support your opinion.

22. **DISTINGUISH FACT AND OPINION** Was the idea that Georgia could help debtors and the very poor overcome their difficulties a fact or an opinion? Explain why you think so.

INTERPRET MAPS

Look closely at the map of the Pilgrims' intended route and where they actually sailed. Then answer the questions that follow.

23. What was the Pilgrims' planned destination?

24. Between what latitudes did the Pilgrims go off their planned course, and where did they land?

Pilgrims' Route, 1620

ANALYZE SOURCES

Transcriptions of court records from the 1692 Salem witch trials include testimony from the accused. In the following transcription, Reverend Increase Mather relays information about his conversation with prisoner Mary Bridges. Read the passage and answer the question.

> Goodwife Bridges said that she had confessed against herself things which were all utterly false; and that she was brought to her confession by being told that she certainly was a witch, and so made to believe it,—though she had no other grounds so to believe.

25. What does Mather's statement reveal about the likely cause of many people's confessions?

CONNECT TO YOUR LIFE

26. **INFORMATIVE** Think about how and why people left their homelands to settle in the 13 colonies. Then think of a present-day group of people who have moved to a new place. Write a paragraph that connects the two groups.

TIPS

- Before you start writing, organize your ideas in a two-column chart. On the left, list your two groups. On the right, list the reasons why each group decided to move.

- Include textual evidence and one or two vocabulary terms from the chapter.

- Conclude the paragraph with your observations about the reasons why colonists came to America and why the group you selected decided to move to a new place.

VOCABULARY ANSWERS

1. indentured servants

2. traitor

3. joint-stock company

4. proprietor

5. charter

6. royal colony

7. dissenter

READING STRATEGY ANSWER

I READ	I KNOW	AND SO
The settlers lived under difficult conditions.	Many settlers died of diseases.	

8. Answers will vary. Possible response: Settlers faced physical dangers from diseases, the harsh climate, starvation, and attack. Diseases, such as malaria, and harsh winters caused the death of many colonists. Inexperience in farming and hunting in the new environment sometimes led to starvation. Clashes with Native Americans led to death or injury.

MAIN IDEAS ANSWERS

9. Smith traded with the Powhatan for corn, and he later had the settlers plant crops.

10. The colonists continued to claim more land, and the Powhatan resented the takeover of their lands and feared for their culture.

11. Nathaniel Bacon staged a rebellion because the governor held too much power and Bacon thought colonists should be more involved with the government. He also wanted to claim more Powhatan land.

12. Pilgrims were separatists who completely split from the Church of England to form their own congregation. Puritans wanted to reform the church from within rather than completely separate from it.

13. Villagers accused three women of witchcraft. Once people believed that witches were living in the village, more accusations arose. The accused were arrested and faced trial.

14. By taking over New Netherland, the English gained complete control of eastern North America.

15. Because Penn believed that all were equal in the eyes of God, he allowed many different groups of people to live and worship in Pennsylvania.

16. The Iroquois wanted to end French fur trading in and near the Ohio Valley. Also, the French were allies of the Lenape and the Huron, and these groups were enemies of the Iroquois.

17. The region's resources included soil that was good for raising tobacco, and the bay allowed the colony easy access to trade.

HISTORICAL THINKING ANSWERS

18. Native Americans and colonists frequently fought over land because the colonists wanted to own land and often obtained it by pushing Native Americans out of their territories. This happened in places such as Jamestown, where the Powhatan and colonists fought, and in New England, where Algonquians and colonists battled.

19. Both the Pilgrims and the Puritans viewed the colonies as places where they could practice their religion freely and not suffer from the prejudice they experienced in their native England. William Penn saw Pennsylvania as a haven for his fellow Quakers, a place where they could live according to their Quaker ideals.

20. The settlers in the New England colonies were mainly Pilgrims and Puritans from England. The settlers in the Middle Colonies came from multiple countries, so they brought varied cultures with them. Settlers in the Middle Colonies had a wider variety of religious backgrounds, too. Many settlers in both New England and the Middle Colonies came to the colonies seeking the freedom to worship as they pleased.

21. Answers will vary, but should include the fact that Puritan women rarely owned property because property passed from fathers to sons. Some Puritans may have felt threatened by women owning property because it upset what they considered to be the natural order of things.

22. The idea was an opinion. Answers will vary but should include that the James Oglethorpe-Viscount John Percival plan for Georgia did not last long. Many found the colony's strict policies unreasonable.

INTERPRET MAPS ANSWERS

23. The Pilgrims intended to land in Virginia.

24. They went off course between 40° and 42° N latitude. They landed in Plymouth.

ANALYZE SOURCES ANSWER

25. Many people probably confessed just because others convinced them that they were witches.

CONNECT TO YOUR LIFE ANSWER

26. Students' paragraphs will vary, but students should make a connection between the people who settled the 13 colonies and a present-day group of immigrants. Students' paragraphs should include textual evidence, Key Vocabulary terms, and a conclusion that offers observations about why both groups decided to move to a new place.

UNIT 2 RESOURCES

UNIT INTRODUCTION

UNIT TIME LINE

UNIT WRAP-UP

NATIONAL GEOGRAPHIC | CONNECTION

National Geographic Magazine Adapted Articles
- "Before New York"
- "America, Found and Lost" ONLINE

Unit 2 Inquiry: Envision an Ideal Community

NG Learning Framework Activities
- Prepare a Leadership Memo
- Create a Trade Network

Unit 2 Formal Assessment

UNIT 2   1585–1763

ENGLISH SETTLEMENT

CRITICAL VIEWING. In this 1941 painting by Newell Wyeth, the Pilgrims watch the Mayflower depart on its return voyage to England in April, 1621. What mood does the artist convey by showing the Pilgrims as they watch their ship return to England?

CHAPTER 4 RESOURCES

Available at NGLSync.Cengage.com

TEACHER RESOURCES & ASSESSMENT

Reading and Note-Taking

Vocabulary Practice

Document-Based Question Template

Social Studies Skills Lessons
- Reading: Identify Main Ideas and Details
- Writing: Write a Narrative

Formal Assessment
- Chapter 4 Pretest
- Chapter 4 Tests A & B
- Section Quizzes

Chapter 4 Answer Key

ExamView®
One-time Download

STUDENT DIGITAL RESOURCES

- **eEdition** (English)
- **eEdition** (Spanish)
- **Handbooks**
- **Online Atlas**
- **American Gallery Online**
- **History Notebook**
- **American Voices (Biographies)**
- **Active History**
- **Projects for Inquiry-Based Learning**

Chapter 4 Spanish Resources are available at NGLSync.Cengage.com.

Colliding Cultures: The Fur Trade

- Primary Sources
- On Your Feet: Identifying Issues

NG Learning Framework:
Make a Historical Connection

SECTION 1 RESOURCES
NEW ENGLAND: COMMERCE AND RELIGION

LESSON 1.1
Harvesting Land and Sea

- On Your Feet: Four Corners

NG Learning Framework:
Investigate Whale Products

LESSON 1.2
Colonial Trade

- On Your Feet: Fishbowl

NG Learning Framework:
Debate the Navigation Acts

LESSON 1.3
Society and Religion

- On Your Feet: History Roundtable

NG Learning Framework:
Research African Americans in Colonial New England

LESSON 1.4
Education and Literacy

- On Your Feet: One-on-One Interviews

NG Learning Framework:
Investigate Colonial Apprenticeships

LESSON 1.5
NATIONAL GEOGRAPHIC EXPLORER DONALD SLATER
Graveyards, Buildings, and American Identity

- On Your Feet: Numbered Heads

AMERICAN GALLERY ONLINE Colonial Graveyards

SECTION 2 RESOURCES
THE SOUTHERN COLONIES

LESSON 2.1
Slavery Expands

- On Your Feet: Jigsaw

NG Learning Framework:
Learn More About Colonial Rice Production

LESSON 2.2
From Plantations to the Backcountry

- On Your Feet: Question and Answer

NG Learning Framework:
Analyze Labor Systems

LESSON 2.3
Life Under Slavery

- On Your Feet: Team Word Webs

NG Learning Framework:
Research the Stono Rebellion

LESSON 2.4
DOCUMENT-BASED QUESTION
Slave Narratives

- On Your Feet: Use a Jigsaw Strategy
- Active History: Analyze Primary Sources

SECTION 3 RESOURCES
THE MIDDLE COLONIES

LESSON 3.1
Agricultural Production

- On Your Feet: Create a Quiz

NG Learning Framework:
Diagram Grain's Path from Field to Table

LESSON 3.2
A Diverse Society

- On Your Feet: Inside-Outside Circle

NG Learning Framework:
Explore Colonial Cities

LESSON 3.3
Cultures of the Middle Colonies

- On Your Feet: Tell Me More

NG Learning Framework:
Discuss Quaker Opposition to Slavery

SECTION 4 RESOURCES
ROOTS OF AMERICAN DEMOCRACY

LESSON 4.1
Colonial Men and Women

- On Your Feet: Turn and Talk on Topic

NG Learning Framework:
Research Women's Work Roles in Colonial America

LESSON 4.2
Great Awakening and Enlightenment

- On Your Feet: Conduct Talk-Show Interviews

NG Learning Framework:
Trace Influences on the Enlightenment

LESSON 4.3
Rights in England and the Colonies

- On Your Feet: Identify Issues

NG Learning Framework:
Research the Magna Carta and English Bill of Rights

LESSON 4.4
John Peter Zenger and Free Speech

- On Your Feet: Defend a Viewpoint

NG Learning Framework:
Create a Zenger Trial Time Line

SECTION 5 RESOURCES
THE FRENCH AND INDIAN WAR

LESSON 5.1
War Begins

- On Your Feet: Numbered Heads

NG Learning Framework:
Explore the Fort Necessity Campaign

American Voices Biography
Sieur de la Salle ONLINE

LESSON 5.2
Quebec and the British Victory

- On Your Feet: Build a Living Time Line

NG Learning Framework:
Convince General Braddock

LESSON 5.3
Impact of the War

- On Your Feet: Think, Pair, Share

NG Learning Framework:
Analyze Treaties

CHAPTER 4 REVIEW

Strategy ❶
Use a TASKS Approach

Help students get information from visuals by using the following TASKS strategy:

T Look for a **Title** that may give the main idea.
A **Ask** yourself what the visual is trying to show.
S Determine how **Symbols** are used.
K Look for a **Key** or legend.
S **Summarize** what you learned.

Use with All Lessons

Strategy ❷
Make Predictions About Content

Before students read the lessons listed below, have them examine the headings and visuals in each one and write their predictions on what the lesson will be about. After students read the lessons, have them check to see whether their predictions were accurate.

Use with Lessons 1.3, 2.1, 3.1, 3.3, 4.1–4.4, and 5.1–5.3 *You might want to pair students whose predictions were inaccurate with students who correctly predicted the content of the lessons and have them compare the conclusions they drew from viewing the headings and visuals in each one.*

Strategy ❸
Read and Recall

Invite students to work in groups of two to four. First have each student read the same lesson independently. After reading, students should meet without the book and share ideas they recall. One student should take notes. As a group, students should look at the lesson and decide what should be added or changed in the notes.

Use with All Lessons *For an extension of this strategy, have different groups compare their notes.*

Strategy ❶
Preview Content Using a Map

Use the following suggestions to preview content using a map:

- Point to the map key and discuss how it explains the map's content. Tell students that the different colors on the map represent different things.
- Remind students that they can identify continents and bodies of water by their labels on the map.
- Call out specific map features, such as rivers, mountain ranges, oceans, battles, cities, colonies, and countries, and ask students to point to them.

Use with Lessons 1.2, 5.1, and 5.3 *Invite volunteers to help visually impaired students by describing the visuals in detail.*

Strategy ❷
Sequence Events

Provide students with a list of events from Section 5 in random order and a Sequence Chain like the one shown. Have students fill in the chain, putting the events in chronological order.

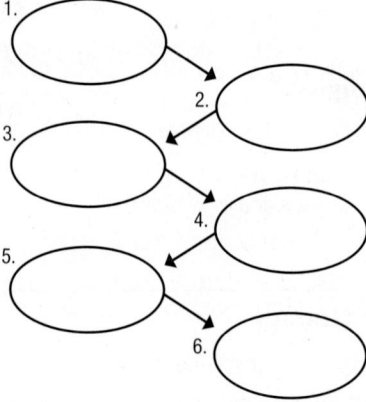

Use with Lessons 5.1–5.3

ENGLISH LANGUAGE LEARNERS

Strategy ❶
Use Paired Reading

Pair **Expanding** and **Bridging** students to read passages from the text aloud.

1. Partner 1 reads a passage; partner 2 retells the passage in his or her own words.
2. Partner 2 reads a different passage; partner 1 retells it.
3. Pairs repeat the whole exercise, switching roles.

Use with All Lessons

Strategy ❷
Teach and Learn

Pair **Emerging** students with English-proficient students. Have English-proficient students model using words that appear in various forms throughout Section 2. Tell pairs to compose a sentence for each word and then share their sentences with the class. Suggest the following words:

- plants, planter, plantation
- slaves, enslaved, slaveholders, slaveowners
- farms, farmworkers, farmland
- rebels, rebelled, rebellion

Use with Lessons 2.1–2.4

Strategy ❸
Use a Vocabulary Word Map

Ask students to use a graphic organizer like the one shown to make Word Maps for the Key Vocabulary words *diversity* in Lesson 3.2 and *tolerance* and *conformity* in Lesson 3.3. For the word *diversity*, for example, suggest that students consider the root word *diverse* and use a dictionary if necessary. Have students at the **Emerging** and **Expanding** levels work in pairs. Have students at the **Bridging** level work independently.

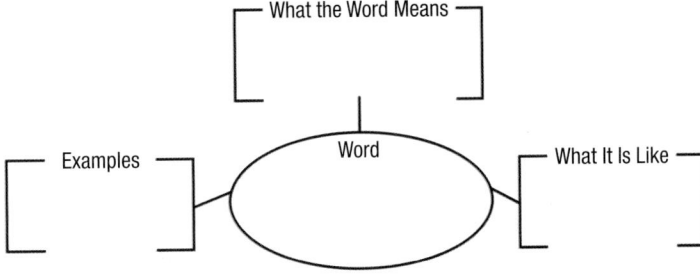

Use with Lessons 3.2–3.3

GIFTED & TALENTED

Strategy ❶
Annotate a Time Line

Have students annotate a time line of events that took place during the colonial period between 1651 and 1763. Students should use the information in the chapter as well as Internet research. Tell students to include details such as dates, locations, and important events and people. Students might also include images with their time lines. Have students share their time lines with the class.

Use with Lessons 1.2–1.4, 2.1, 2.3, 3.2–3.3, 4.2, 4.4, and 5.1–5.3

Strategy ❷
Explain the Significance

Allow students to choose one term below to investigate and ask them to design a presentation that explains the significance of the term to the development of the colonies.

- religious freedom
- triangular trade
- slavery
- literacy
- gristmill
- Native Americans
- Enlightenment
- trading post

Use with Lessons 1.2–1.4, 2.1, 2.4, 3.1–3.2, 4.2, and 5.1

Pre-AP

Strategy ❶
Create a Podcast

Before beginning the chapter, allow students to choose one of the lessons listed below and use the information to prepare an episode of a history podcast. Tell students that their podcast should take a point of view on the content so that it is both informative and entertaining. Suggest that they think about any sound effects they might want to include. Then have students either present their episode to the class or record it on a phone or other device.

Use with Lessons 1.1, 2.1, 3.1, 4.1, 4.4, and 5.2

Strategy ❷
Extend Knowledge

Students may work individually or in pairs to research and examine the long-term effects of the European settlement of North America. As an alternative, assign teams and have each team choose one of the following aspects on which to focus: trade, technology, or government. Suggest that students develop a graphic organizer to display the results of their investigation.

Use with Lessons 1.1–1.3, 2.1, 3.1–3.2, 4.1–4.3

4

COLONIAL DEVELOPMENT
1651–1763

ESSENTIAL QUESTION
How did a developing American identity unite the colonies?

AMERICAN STORIES ONLINE
Colliding Cultures: The Fur Trade

AMERICAN GALLERY ONLINE
Colonial Graveyards

READING STRATEGY

IDENTIFY MAIN IDEAS AND DETAILS
To identify a main idea and details, state the most important idea and find facts that support it. Use a diagram like this one to find a main idea and details about the development of the colonies as you read the chapter.

Colonial Development

Main Idea:
Detail:
Detail:
Detail:

"The ground is very fruitful,
and produceth plentiful crops with great speed."
—Nathaniel Shrigley, author and British Army officer

CRITICAL VIEWING The Piedmont in Virginia and North Carolina, shown here, is a land of rolling hills and rich farmland. How does the photo illustrate the description in the quotation above?

Colonial Development 121

INTRODUCE THE PHOTOGRAPH

The Piedmont

Have students study the photograph of the Piedmont. Explain that the region lies between the coastal plain along the Atlantic Ocean and the Appalachian Mountains. Tell students that European settlers began farming there in the early 1700s, but Native Americans had long lived among the rolling hills and dense forests. **ASK:** What can you tell about today's farms from the photo? *(Answers will vary. Possible response: Farms appear to be relatively small, and the pastures and fields are spread out over the land. Trees cover areas that are not cleared for crops or pastures.)*

Share Background

When European settlers first arrived in the Piedmont, they had to clear dense forests to farm. The best farmland was in the valleys and near the waterfalls that separated the coastal plain and the Piedmont. The soil was heavily clayed but fertile. Today, farms still dot the landscape, with fields and pastures intertwining with forests. The climate helps make it a good place to farm. There are at least 180 frost-free days throughout the year, and more than 20 inches of rainfall during the growing season.

CRITICAL VIEWING Answers will vary. Possible response: The photo shows an area of the Piedmont today that looks fertile and includes farms with fields of crops and pastures.

For Chapter 4 Spanish Resources, visit the Resources Menu. Chapter 4 Resources are available at NGLSync.Cengage.com.

How did a developing American identity unite the colonies?

Roundtable Activity: Uniting Through Identity This activity prompts students to think about what it means to have a common identity and how having a common identity can unite groups of people.

Divide the class into groups of four or five students and assign each group a number. Hand the odd-numbered groups a sheet of paper with this question at the top: *What does it mean to have a common identity?* Hand the even-numbered groups a sheet of paper with this question at the top: *How could having a common identity unite people?* The first student in each group should write an answer and then pass the paper clockwise to the next student, who may add a new answer.

After reading the chapter, revisit these same questions as a class to see how students' understandings of unity through identity may have changed based on what they learned in the chapter.

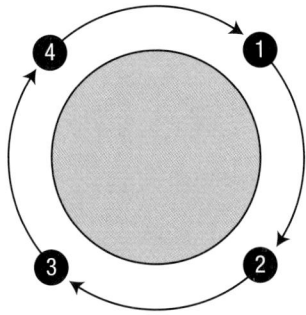

Word Maps

As they read the chapter, have students complete Word Maps for Key Vocabulary words. Tell students to make a Word Map for each word. Have them write the word in the center oval and, as they encounter the word in the chapter, complete the Word Map for that word. Model an example for students on the board, using the graphic organizer below.

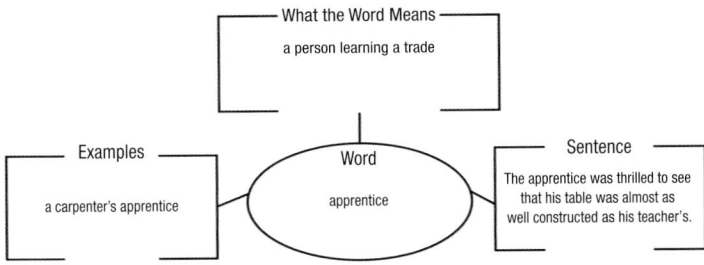

IDENTIFY MAIN IDEAS AND DETAILS

Remind students that they will better understand the text if they identify a main idea and determine which facts support that idea as they read. Use Lesson 2.1 to model how to use the Main Idea and Details List diagram. Ask students to suggest a relevant detail in the first paragraph to support the main idea that the use of enslaved African labor increased over time in the Southern Colonies. *(Answers will vary. Possible response: Plantation owners depended on enslaved West Africans to grow rice.)* Instruct students to add additional details when they study the lesson. Encourage them to use a Main Idea and Details List in each lesson to determine main ideas and record relevant details.

Colonial Development

Main Idea: Enslaved African labor increased over time in the Southern Colonies.
Detail: Plantation owners depended on enslaved West Africans to grow rice.
Detail:
Detail:

1651	Navigation Acts
1689	English Bill of Rights
1735	John Peter Zenger libel trial
1739	Stono Rebellion
1754	French and Indian War begins
1755	Battle of Monongahela
1759	British capture Quebec
1760	British capture Montreal
1763	Treaty of Paris
1763	Pontiac's Rebellion

AMERICAN STORIES ONLINE For instructional support for the online American Story "Colliding Cultures: The Fur Trade," go to NGLSync.Cengage.com.

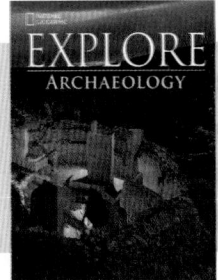

For more on how archaeologists work, see *EXPLORE ARCHAEOLOGY*.

STEM

Sperm whales, like the one shown here, have huge heads and a full set of teeth along the inside of their long jaws. Colonial whalers frequently hunted this type of whale, venturing far out to sea to search for them. The oil of these whales burned more brightly than other whale oils and made finer candles, which became important export items.

1.1 Harvesting Land and Sea

In 17th-century New England, you basically had two choices: toil day and night as a farmer, or toil day and night as a sailor. Neither option left much time for anything else.

MAIN IDEA New England's colonial economy was based on agriculture, commerce, and small-scale manufacturing.

FARMING HILLY, ROCKY LAND

Most New England colonists were farmers. Their farms were small and were frequently located on hilly and forested land with rocky soil. The long, cold winters made for a short growing season.

Farmers relied on their large families to clear the fields, plant and harvest the crops, and care for the farm animals. This all added up to something called **subsistence farming**. This means the farmers produced about enough food to provide for their family with only a little, if any, left over to sell or trade. In other words, they were barely scraping by. Without much in savings or extra food, a poor year of farming could ruin a family.

Because farming was so tough, the size and quality of a family's farmland mattered. Colonists were at the mercy of their town's powerful Puritan founders, who led the church and the town. The founders decided the location and amount of land a family received. One man might be given 50 acres with grazing fields attached, another only 3 acres with grazing fields a mile away. It wasn't fair, and these differences in land ownership created distinct social classes within the town.

Harpoon
Whalers used harpoons to stun and capture their prey. Sailors launched whaleboats from the ship, surrounded the whale, and threw their weapons. Once the whale was fully pierced by harpoons, which were attached to ropes, the sailors towed the huge animal back to the ship.

FISHING, WHALING, AND TRADE

The Atlantic Ocean provided greater economic opportunities than agriculture. Colonial fishers could engage in international trade, selling their catch to London merchants in exchange for goods such as shoes, textiles, and metal products. Whaling provided the colonists with many commercial products, including whale oils and waxes, meat, fat, bones, and leather. Colonists sold and exported the whale meat and blubber, or fat. People used the blubber to light oil lamps, make candles, and soften leather.

Fishing and whaling led to the growth of a shipbuilding industry. New England's plentiful forests supplied the shipyards with timber—and employment. Building a single ship could employ 200 workers. Shipbuilders also kept sawmills, rope makers, and iron foundries busy. By the end of the 1700s, New England built one-third of all British ships and almost all of its own merchants' and fishers' ships. This economic activity made New England a natural center of colonial trade.

HISTORICAL THINKING

1. **READING CHECK** What four economic activities were important in New England?

2. **DRAW CONCLUSIONS** What conclusion can you draw about the relationship between a family's farm and its social class?

3. **ANALYZE CAUSE AND EFFECT** In what ways were the goods provided by the Atlantic Ocean essential to the livelihood, economy, and culture of the New England colonists?

Objective
Learn about characteristics of the colonial New England economy.

Critical Thinking Skills for Lesson 1.1
- Identify Main Ideas and Details
- Monitor Comprehension
- Draw Conclusions
- Analyze Environmental Concepts

Essential Question for Chapter 4
How did a developing American identity unite the colonies? Unequal land distribution by Puritan leaders drove many colonists to fishing and the manufacture of ships. Lesson 1.1 looks at New England's economy and how ocean and timber resources helped the region develop a new identity as the center of colonial trade.

Background for the Teacher
The early colonists in New England practiced drift whaling—harvesting beached whales. This was a practice used successfully by Native Americans prior to the colonists' arrival. Although drift whales were considered community property, the profit from their oil and other raw materials was large enough that communities established laws governing how the whales would be divided. The colonial government demanded its fair share of each whale, payable in oil, which the government then sold to England.

Around 1650, New England colonists began shore whaling as well. Shore whaling made whaling a private business rather than a communal enterprise. The men who pursued whales offshore formed companies that retained the profits from the captured whales.

INTRODUCE & ENGAGE

Understand Risk Taking

Point out the photographs of the sperm whale and harpoon and read the captions aloud. Tell students that sperm whales can grow to around 60 feet long and weigh some 60 tons. Ask students to imagine going after such a large creature in a small rowing boat with only harpoons and lances as weapons. **ASK:** Why do you think colonial whalers were willing to risk their lives to hunt sperm whales? *(Answers will vary. Possible response: The sperm whales' oil was a valuable commercial product. Whalers made a lot money from sperm whale oil, making the profit worth the risk.)*

TEACH

Guided Discussion

1. **Analyze Environmental Concepts** What evidence is there that the Atlantic Ocean provided greater economic opportunities than farmland in New England? *(Answers will vary. Possible response: New England's rocky soil and short growing season meant that farmers practiced subsistence farming. They had little left over to sell or trade after feeding their families. In contrast, the Atlantic Ocean was bountiful. It provided fish that could be sold to London markets and whales that supplied blubber for oil, as well as meat, bone, leather, and wax for sale and export.)*

2. **Identify Main Ideas and Details** What products and goods were part of the import-export trade between New England and England? *(New England exported such items as cod, whale meat, whale oil, and ships to England and imported manufactured goods, such as metal products, textiles, and shoes.)*

More Information

Sperm Whale Oil The oil that colonial whalers harvested from sperm whales is a fluid called spermaceti. It's different from other types of whale oil, which are harvested from the animal's blubber, bones, and meat. By contrast, spermaceti is actually a fluid found in large quantities in the sperm whale's head. Its function remains a mystery to scientists, but some theorize that clues can be found in how the substance changes. Spermaceti hardens from liquid to wax when it gets cold. Some scientists believe this helps the sperm whale regulate its buoyancy so it can dive down into the depths in search of food and then swim back to the surface efficiently.

Active Options

On Your Feet: Four Corners Label the four corners of the classroom *Subsistence Farming, Fishing, Whaling,* and *Shipbuilding.* Allow students time to write down what they know about all four sectors of the New England economy. Then have students move to a corner of their choice and discuss the economic sector they chose by asking and answering questions. Finally, have at least one student from each corner share a summary of the corner discussion.

NG Learning Framework: Investigate Whale Products STEM

ATTITUDE Curiosity

KNOWLEDGE Critical Species

Encourage students to learn more about the many products made from whales. Have students conduct research using library and online sources to gather information about how producers used spermaceti, baleen, and ambergris. Instruct students to investigate the sources of these raw materials, the products that were made from them, and the places where the products were traded. Ask students to write a summary of their findings to share with the class.

DIFFERENTIATE

Striving Readers

Record and Compare Facts After they have read the lesson, ask students to write down at least three facts they can recall. Then have them work in pairs to compare the facts they wrote down and check them for accuracy. Tell each pair to combine their lists into one longer list, and challenge them to become the pair with the longest list of accurate facts.

Gifted & Talented

Write a Persuasive Blog Entry Encourage students to research the debate about whaling today. What arguments do whalers make to justify their activities, and how do conservationists respond? Tell students to research the role whales play in the marine ecosystem and the efforts being made to protect them. Then instruct them to write a blog entry in which they choose a side in the debate and convince readers to support it.

See the Chapter Planner for more strategies for differentiation.

HISTORICAL THINKING

ANSWERS

1. The important economic activities included farming, fishing, whaling, and shipbuilding.

2. The Atlantic Ocean provided food, trade goods, industries, and life on the sea for many New England colonists.

3. Answers will vary. Possible response: Ship manufacturing provided employment for builders and those who supplied shipbuilding materials, such as wood, iron, and rope. In addition, the ships were sold to merchants and fishers in the colonies and to customers overseas, thereby generating profits for colonial shipbuilders.

1.2 Colonial Trade

It was good to be a trader in New England. The region's shipyards turned out many ships that carried goods along the North American coast and across the Atlantic. If colonial trade were a race, the merchants of New England were winning.

MAIN IDEA New England merchants expanded the colonial economy through Atlantic trade.

TRADE IN THE ATLANTIC

As its fishing and whaling industries continued to thrive, New England found itself at the center of America's trade. New England merchants traded with other colonies. They also engaged in direct trade with Europe. Soon the New England merchants became the chief traders along the coast from Newfoundland to Georgia.

The merchants also conducted business through the triangular trade. As you have learned, the triangular trade routes crossed the Atlantic and connected North America, Europe, and Africa. New England merchants sent goods such as rum and cotton to Europe. The merchants received imported goods including wine, fruit, and salt from islands off the coast of North Africa. Molasses, rum, sugar, and dyes came from the Caribbean. Food and drink weren't the only goods New England merchants traded. As you know, the merchants also acquired enslaved people from Africa in exchange for rum and other goods.

The growth of trade across the Atlantic created great demand for sailors and other workers. Shipbuilders and sailmakers crafted vessels.

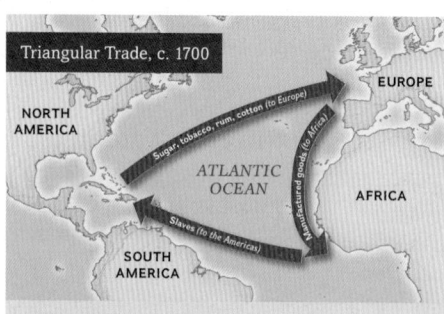

Triangular Trade, c. 1700

NORTH AMERICA

EUROPE

ATLANTIC OCEAN

AFRICA

SOUTH AMERICA

Sugar, tobacco, rum, cotton (to Europe)

Manufactured goods (to Africa)

Slaves (to the Americas)

Colonial Trade Routes and Goods

The colonial economy depended on ships trading goods between North America, Europe, and Africa. So did the economies of most European countries. France, England, the Netherlands, Portugal, and Spain were willing to fight for a share of the wealth the trade routes generated. Many ships on the triangular trade routes sailed only between North America and Africa or Europe and Africa. Some ships bound for New England also stopped in Brazil or the Caribbean, where some of the enslaved Africans onboard were sold.

Suppliers stocked ships with **provisions**, which consisted of the food, water, and other supplies needed for the voyages. Dockworkers loaded and unloaded goods that laborers transported in carts. As a result of the thriving trade, port cities sprang up in New York, Philadelphia, and Charleston after 1750. Colonial trade was no longer dominated entirely by the merchants of Boston and other port cities in Massachusetts and Rhode Island.

Blackbeard the Pirate

Smuggling was not the only illegal activity on the high seas. Pirates prowled the Atlantic looking for ships and cargo to steal. One such pirate was called Blackbeard.

According to some, the English pirate's real name was Edward Teach. He tried to make his appearance frightening by putting pieces of burning rope under his hat, as shown in the illustration. For two years, he and his pirates terrorized merchant ships in the Atlantic and the Caribbean. In 1718, Blackbeard met his end at the hands of Lieutenant Robert Maynard of the Royal Navy. Maynard chopped off the pirate's head and threw his body overboard.

ENGLAND'S CUT OF THE PROFITS

When New England began to earn huge profits from trade, the English decided to begin taking their cut. To ensure their share of the profits, the English passed a series of laws called the **Navigation Acts** in 1651. The acts required that goods brought to England or its colonies in Asia, Africa, or America be carried on English ships or ships made in the colonies. Furthermore, the acts identified a list of colonial products that could only be sold to England or its colonies. These products included tobacco, sugar, cotton, and dyes.

The acts also made sure that England controlled—and taxed—all trade to and from the colonies. So, for instance, all European goods bound for the colonies had to go to England first. There, English dockworkers would unload, inspect, and reload the goods back onto English or colonial-made ships. These ships then carried the goods to colonial ports where the English charged additional taxes on the imports. Worst of all for the colonists, the English taxed all colonial goods that were not going to be shipped to England.

Not surprisingly, the colonists resented the additional charges to products going in both directions. Some colonists turned to trading goods illegally, or **smuggling**. The colonists proved hard to control as they resisted attempts to enforce the acts.

While New England colonists protested their treatment at the hands of the English government, many in their own society had far more cause for complaint. But enslaved African Americans and some Protestant groups were powerless to change their situation.

HISTORICAL THINKING

1. **READING CHECK** What different types of trade did New England merchants carry out?

2. **ANALYZE CAUSE AND EFFECT** Why did Parliament pass the Navigation Acts?

3. **INTERPRET MAPS** How do the items sent from North America differ from those exported from Europe?

PLAN

Objective

Understand Atlantic trading patterns and their effects on the colonial economy.

Critical Thinking Skills for Lesson 1.2

- Identify Main Ideas and Details
- Monitor Comprehension
- Analyze Cause and Effect
- Interpret Maps
- Form and Support Opinions
- Integrate Visuals

Essential Question for Chapter 4

How did a developing American identity unite the colonies? Atlantic trade helped shape the colonies' economy and character. Lesson 1.2 examines the structure of colonial trade and the effects of the Navigation Acts.

Background for the Teacher

Colonial trade operated within the English mercantilist system, which consisted of regulations on trade and manufacturing. For mercantilism to work to England's benefit, the colonies had to produce raw materials and agricultural staples for England and serve as a market for its manufactured goods. The Navigation Acts established the mercantilist system and helped to forge a common identity in the American colonies. All along the eastern seaboard after 1740, families indulged in what has been called a "consumer revolution," purchasing cloth, clothing, carpets, paper, gloves, mirrors, clocks, silverware, china tea sets, pottery, and books. Under the Navigation Acts, they could only import these items from England.

Financial Literacy

To extend their knowledge and understanding about the concepts in this lesson, refer students to the Financial Literacy handbook.

Activate Prior Knowledge

Provide students with a K-W-L Chart like the one below. Have students think about what they have already learned about colonial trade in general and about the triangular trade. Then ask them to write questions that they would like to have answered as they study the lesson. Allow time at the end of the lesson for students to fill in what they have learned.

K What Do I Know?	W What Do I Want To Learn?	L What Did I Learn?

TEACH

Guided Discussion

1. **Analyze Cause and Effect** What effect did the growth of Atlantic trade have on employment in the colonies, and why? *(Atlantic trade increased the demand for workers in port cities. Workers were needed to build the ships and make the sails. Workers were also needed to stock the ships with provisions and to move cargo.)*

2. **Form and Support Opinions** Do you think the Navigation Acts worked as planned for England? Support your opinion with text evidence. *(Answers will vary. Possible response: England lost a portion of the potential tax revenue because the acts led to smuggling and were hard to enforce, so the acts only partially worked as intended.)*

Integrate Visuals

Tell students to examine the Triangular Trade map and reread the text on Atlantic trade. **ASK:** Based on the text, what details could you add to the map? *(In addition to sugar, tobacco, rum, and cotton, North American merchants sent molasses and dye from the Caribbean. They received manufactured goods from Europe and wine, fruit, and salt from the islands off the coast of Africa.)* Encourage students to research other goods associated with the triangular trade routes to further expand the map.

Active Options

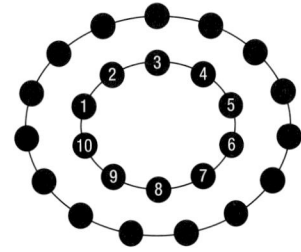

On Your Feet: Fishbowl Have one half of the class sit in a close circle, facing inward. The other half of the class should sit in a larger circle around them. Post the following statement: *The triangular trade affected the movement of slaves and goods.* Students in the inner circle should discuss the statement for five minutes while those in the outer circle listen to the discussion and evaluate the points made. Then have the groups reverse roles and continue the discussion.

NG Learning Framework: Debate the Navigation Acts

SKILL Problem-Solving

KNOWLEDGE Our Human Story

Invite students to engage in a class debate about the Navigation Acts. One half of the class should represent colonial merchants, shipbuilders, and consumers. The other half should represent the English government, English merchants, and English manufacturers. Have each group research the advantages and disadvantages of the Navigation Acts for the members of their group. Then have the two groups select members to participate in a panel debate on whether the Navigation Acts should be repealed, revised, or continued.

Striving Readers

Preview Text Encourage students to preview the lesson. Ask them to read the title, the Main Idea, and the subheadings. Tell them to examine the map and the illustration as well. Then have them list information about trade in colonial New England that they expect to find in the text. After they read the lesson, students should discuss with a partner what they learned and whether it matched their expectations.

English Language Learners

Use Sentence Strips Choose a paragraph from the lesson and make sentence strips out of it. Read the paragraph aloud, and tell students at **All Proficiencies** to follow along in their books. Then ask students to close their books, and give them the sentence strips. Students should put the strips in order and read the sentences aloud.

See the Chapter Planner for more strategies for differentiation.

HISTORICAL THINKING

ANSWERS

1. New England merchants formed partnerships among themselves and with English merchants to conduct trade along the North American coast and across the Atlantic. They were involved in food, drink, and textile trade as well as the slave trade.

2. Parliament passed the Navigation Acts to shut out foreign competition and to force American colonists to do business only with England. Also, English merchants could make extra profit when they added charges to re-export goods.

3. The goods shipped from North America consist of rum and raw materials, such as sugar, tobacco, and cotton. Europe ships manufactured goods.

1.3 Society and Religion

In New England, some African Americans performed tasks that were not available in other colonies—small consolation for their far-from-equal treatment.

MAIN IDEA New England was different from other colonial regions in terms of its use of enslaved labor and its religious views.

ENSLAVED LABOR IN NEW ENGLAND

Enslaved African Americans accounted for only 2 to 3 percent of New England's population. But this wasn't really due to colonial opposition to enslavement. Some of the wealthiest New England merchants made their money in the slave trade. The low percentage was due to geography and economics. New England farms were generally small. Most colonial farmers had no need for large numbers of enslaved workers, and they couldn't afford them, anyway.

The enslaved African Americans who came to New England worked as household servants, farmhands, artisans, and laborers. In the Southern Colonies, slaveholders generally wanted to purchase enslaved people who could work in the fields immediately, but slaveholders in New England were often more willing to purchase young people who could be trained for specific household or business duties.

Enslaved people generally lived in their masters' houses and worked by their sides. They practiced carpentry, printing, baking, and making cloth, shoes, and clothing, among other trades. In seaport towns, enslaved African Americans sometimes worked alongside free African Americans in the shipyards and on the docks as fishers, whalers, and shipbuilders.

Some African Americans were born free, but most free African Americans spent part of their lives in enslavement. Some achieved freedom by fulfilling the terms of a work contract. Some escaped. Others were freed by their master for faithful service or as part of their master's will. Although both enslaved and free African Americans in New England enjoyed some legal rights, they were not treated equally. For example, a 1703 Massachusetts law stated that African Americans could not be outdoors after 9:00 P.M. unless they were on business for their masters.

THE DECLINE OF PURITANISM

Some religious groups were treated unfairly, although not to the extent suffered by African Americans. The Puritans saw other Protestant groups, such as the Quakers and Baptists, as a threat to the harmony of their society. Therefore, Puritan leaders allowed only the male members of the Puritan church to vote and hold most public offices. Puritans clashed with other Protestant sects that disagreed with their teachings. They punished citizens who did not share their beliefs and even hanged several Quaker missionaries. They also objected to a newly emerging merchant class and its focus on commercial values and worried that the younger generation was only concerned with making money.

Beginning in 1650, membership in the Puritan church had begun to decline, especially among men. Quakers who had been deported from Massachusetts kept coming back. King Charles II of England sent a letter forbidding the execution of Quakers. Quaker communities and Baptist congregations began to flourish throughout New England.

The crown gave the Puritans two options: they could either obey the terms of the colonial charter of Massachusetts Bay or they could have the charter revoked. And the charter guaranteed **religious freedom**, or the right to practice the religion of one's choosing, for all.

But the Puritan leaders believed themselves to be the highest authority in Massachusetts and did not feel that they answered to the king. Charles II disagreed. In 1684, the king canceled the colonial charter of Massachusetts Bay. Charles died in 1685, but that didn't do the Puritans any good. Charles's successor, James II, tried to strengthen English control even more. He combined Massachusetts with other northern colonies to form the **Dominion of New England**.

Eventually, the Dominion included Massachusetts Bay, Plymouth, New Hampshire, Maine, Rhode Island, Connecticut, New York, and New Jersey. Both the decision to create the Dominion and to appoint its new governor were extremely unpopular with the colonists. They felt stripped of the rights and freedoms they had enjoyed under their own colonial charters.

In 1691, Massachusetts received a new charter to replace the one King Charles had canceled. It guaranteed religious freedom for all Protestants, further undermining Puritan influence. It also opened up the right to vote to any man owning property, regardless of his religion. The number of property owners was much greater than the number of churchgoers. As a result, the charter led to a large increase in the number of voters in New England.

As Puritanism declined, education in New England was on the rise. Acquiring knowledge was becoming a new priority in the colony.

🏛 **New Britain Museum of American Art**
New Britain, Connecticut

In *Gentleman with Attendant*, painted between 1785–88, artist Ralph Earl characterizes the enslaved African Americans of New England as serving their masters more directly. This is in contrast to slavery in the Southern Colonies, where enslaved people worked in fields far from the owners, under the supervision of hired bosses.

HISTORICAL THINKING

1. **READING CHECK** Why was the percentage of enslaved African Americans low in New England?

2. **IDENTIFY MAIN IDEAS AND DETAILS** What types of tasks did most enslaved and free African Americans in New England perform?

3. **ANALYZE CAUSE AND EFFECT** What impact did the 1691 Massachusetts charter have on Puritanism?

PLAN

Objective

Understand the characteristics of slavery and the impact of Puritanism in New England.

Critical Thinking Skills for Lesson 1.3

- Identify Main Ideas and Details
- Monitor Comprehension
- Analyze Cause and Effect
- Make Inferences

Essential Question for Chapter 4

How did a developing American identity unite the colonies? New England's Puritan roots separated it culturally from the other colonial regions. That began to change as Puritanism declined toward the end of the 1600s. Lesson 1.3 examines the factors that led to this decline and some of the changes it brought.

Background for the Teacher

For Massachusetts Puritans, the Dominion of New England was a disaster. King James's governor, Sir Edmund Andros, made sweeping changes that undercut the Puritan notion of a covenanted community. He levied taxes without the approval of a representative assembly, restricted the power of town meetings, and mandated religious toleration. Andros also enforced the Navigation Acts, favored his own cronies over the Puritan elite in distributing patronage, required landowners to obtain new land titles from the crown, and took control of common lands. A number of colonists who rebelled by refusing to pay taxes were jailed and fined. Finally, on April 18, 1689, the people of Boston joined with militias from neighboring towns. Numbering more than a thousand, the insurgents deposed the dominion government.

INTRODUCE & ENGAGE

Preview Using Lesson Features

Have students preview the lesson's Main Idea, headings, and painting. **ASK:** Based on these text features, what questions do you expect to have answered in the lesson? *(Answers will vary. Possible response: What kinds of work did enslaved African Americans perform in colonial New England? What caused Puritanism to decline in New England?)* List students' questions on the board. Later, after they have read and discussed the lesson, write answers they may have found. For questions not answered in the lesson, ask students to research the answers using library or online sources.

TEACH

Guided Discussion

1. **Make Inferences** How were the lives of enslaved African Americans in New England different from the lives of enslaved people in the Southern Colonies? *(Possible response: Slaves in New England generally lived in the masters' homes, were often skilled in trades, and had contact with colonial society. Slaves in the South were used primarily as field workers and isolated on plantations away from their owners and society.)*

2. **Analyze Cause and Effect** What actions by Massachusetts Puritans contributed to Charles II canceling the colony's charter? *(Possible response: Charles II warned that he would revoke Massachusetts' charter if the Puritans did not guarantee religious freedom. The Puritans, however, believed that the Quakers and Baptists threatened societal harmony. As a result, the Puritans allowed only church members to vote and punished citizens who did not share their beliefs.)*

🏛 Virtual Museum Visit

Explain that *Gentleman with Attendant* is an unsigned painting, but experts at the New Britain Museum of American Art believe, based on its style, that the artist is Ralph Earl. The museum dates the painting to the late 1780s, while Earl was confined to debtors' prison. Help students locate and read the description of the painting on the museum's website. **ASK:** According to the website, how does the artist depict the social status of the two subjects in the painting? *(The man looks confidently at the viewer, while the boy stares faithfully at the man. The boy's mouth is open and shows his teeth, while the man's mouth is closed. Showing teeth was not appropriate in 18th-century society, and this stark contrast in expression underscores the subjects' difference in status.)*

Active Options

On Your Feet: History Roundtable Divide the class into groups of four or five. Hand each group a sheet of paper containing the following question: How did events in Massachusetts show that the colonists were becoming a more democratic society? The first student in each group should write an answer, read it aloud, and pass the paper clockwise to the next student. Have students circulate the paper until they run out of answers or time is up.

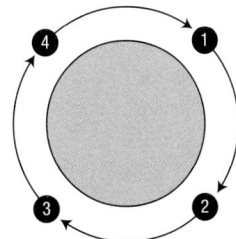

NG Learning Framework: Research African Americans in Colonial New England

SKILL Collaboration

KNOWLEDGE Our Human Story

Assign small groups of students to work together to develop a presentation about free and enslaved African Americans in colonial New England. Encourage them to divide tasks among themselves, researching changes in the size of the two populations over time, laws that governed the rights of the two groups, and how living arrangements affected enslaved people's families and social lives. Students should include images and create charts and diagrams. Have each group share their presentation with the class.

DIFFERENTIATE

Striving Readers

Summarize Read the lesson aloud while students follow along in their books. At the end of each paragraph, ask students to summarize in one sentence what you read. Allow them time to write the summary on their own paper.

English Language Learners

Thumbs Up or Thumbs Down Help students at the **Bridging** level reinforce comprehension. Write a set of True-False statements about the lesson, such as the following: *The original Massachusetts charter guaranteed religious freedom.* Then have students close their books and listen as you read the True-False statements. Students should give a thumbs up if a statement is true and a thumbs down if a statement is false.

See the Chapter Planner for more strategies for differentiation.

HISTORICAL THINKING

ANSWERS

1. Most New England farmers had no need for large numbers of enslaved workers because their farms were generally small.

2. Most enslaved African Americans worked as household servants, farmhands, artisans, and laborers. Many free African Americans worked in the shipyards and on the docks as fishers, whalers, and builders.

3. Answers will vary. Possible response: The charter required Puritans to tolerate other religions. It guaranteed freedom for all Protestants and based voting rights on property ownership rather than church membership.

1.4 Education and Literacy

Why do you read? Probably for fun or to learn new things. Colonial children mostly learned to read so they could understand the Bible.

MAIN IDEA Education and literacy were important to New England colonists and had a major impact on the region's economic and social development.

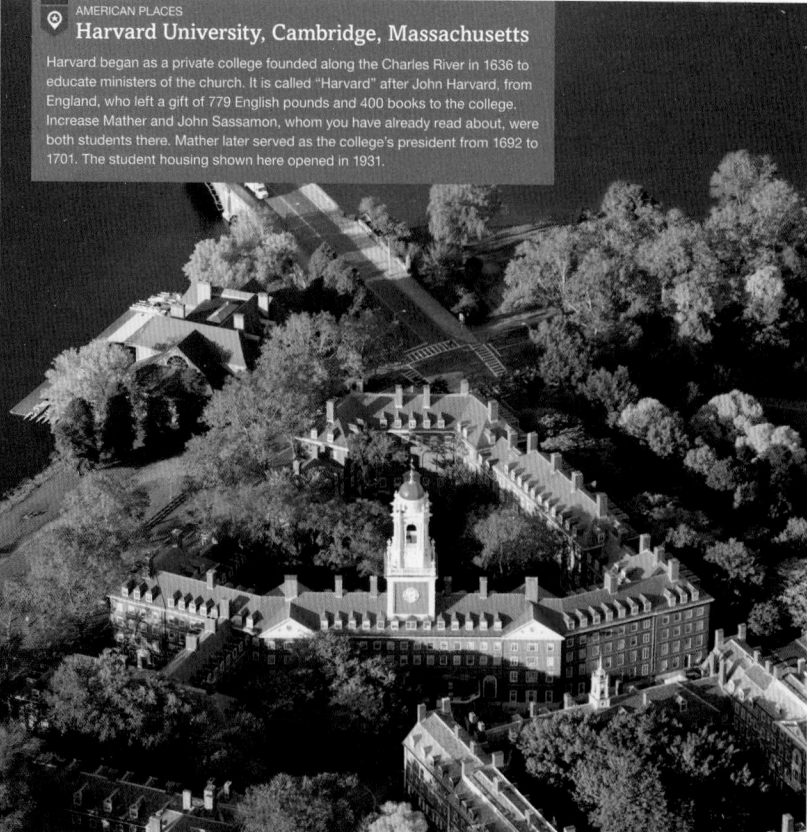

AMERICAN PLACES
Harvard University, Cambridge, Massachusetts
Harvard began as a private college founded along the Charles River in 1636 to educate ministers of the church. It is called "Harvard" after John Harvard, from England, who left a gift of 779 English pounds and 400 books to the college. Increase Mather and John Sassamon, whom you have already read about, were both students there. Mather later served as the college's president from 1692 to 1701. The student housing shown here opened in 1931.

A NEW ENGLAND EDUCATION
New Englanders believed people needed to be able to read so they could learn about God. They set up schools that focused on the Bible, religious study, and texts that taught moral behavior. In the 1640s, the Massachusetts legislature established **common schools**, the colonial name for elementary schools, and secondary schools called Latin grammar schools. Connecticut and other colonies followed with similar legislation. Eventually, more people in New England were able to read than in any other colony.

Early education also involved teaching children skills that would help them thrive in their community. For many colonial boys, this meant becoming an **apprentice**. An apprentice lived with a master craftsman for a set number of years in order to learn a trade, such as butchering, baking, or carpentry. Girls, on the other hand, often stayed with their mothers to learn cooking, sewing, and other skills necessary to manage a household.

Communities established colleges for older students. The Puritans founded Harvard College in Massachusetts in 1636 and Yale College in Connecticut in 1701. Harvard and Yale joined William and Mary College in Virginia to make up the only three colleges in the colonies. All three have grown into modern universities that offer a wide range of subjects and the chance to earn many different degrees. Most of the graduates of colonial colleges became members of the clergy. None, however, were women. Colonial colleges only admitted men.

NEWSPAPERS AND BOOKS
The rising rate of literacy throughout the colonies created a big demand for newspapers and books. Starting in 1704, newspapers popped up in Boston, Philadelphia, New York, and Charleston. These early newspapers focused on European events and politics. They helped colonists feel less separated from faraway Europe and more connected to England.

The general reading tastes of colonial people ranged across many subjects, but readers especially enjoyed topics unique to the American experience. In New England, books about being captured by Native Americans attracted interest. One of the most popular of these was by **Mary Rowlandson**. In her account, she describes being taken prisoner with her three children during King Philip's War. The Native Americans who had captured her then released her for 20 pounds' ransom. After her husband, a Puritan minister, died, Rowlandson moved to Boston and wrote the story for which she is famous.

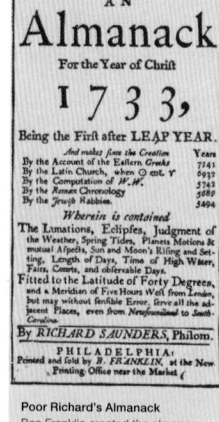

Poor Richard's Almanack
Ben Franklin created the almanac under the name Richard Saunders, but he credited himself as the volume's printer.

Another favorite genre, the almanac, stuffed many types of useful information together in one volume. *Poor Richard's Almanac*, published by **Benjamin Franklin**, proved a best seller. It mixed calendars, information about the weather and planting, medical advice, and witty proverbs, such as "Fish and visitors stink after three days." Also around this time, writers began to compose the first histories of their lives in the colonies. Meanwhile, to the south, life was very different—particularly for African slaves.

HISTORICAL THINKING

1. **READING CHECK** What types of schools did colonial New Englanders establish?

2. **DRAW CONCLUSIONS** What role did religion play in the importance of education in New England?

3. **MAKE GENERALIZATIONS** Why would a newspaper's emphasis on European events and politics be helpful to colonial merchants?

PLAN

Objective
Learn how education and literacy influenced New England society.

Critical Thinking Skills for Lesson 1.4
- Identify Main Ideas and Details
- Monitor Comprehension
- Draw Conclusions
- Make Generalizations
- Make Inferences

Essential Question for Chapter 4
How did a developing American identity unite the colonies? Colonial New England's emphasis on literacy may have had religious roots, but it also prompted widespread reading of newspapers and popular literature. Lesson 1.4 explores how New Englanders became educated and developed a taste for topics about the American experience.

Background for the Teacher
Governments in colonial New England considered a person's ability to understand the Bible and civil laws so important that they enacted education laws. For example, a 1642 Massachusetts education law fined adults who failed to teach their children and apprentices to read. The law even allowed magistrates to remove children from the home and place them with people who would teach them to read.

A more comprehensive 1647 Massachusetts law shifted the responsibility for education from the family to the town. It required towns with more than 50 families to hire someone to teach reading and writing. Towns with more than 100 families were required to open a Latin grammar school to prepare boys for college. Consequently, about 70 percent of men and 45 percent of women in New England could read by 1700.

Discuss Civic Responsibility

Ask students to consider some of the responsibilities of good citizens, such as following laws, voting, and working for the good of the community and larger society. Make a list on the board, then discuss how being able to read and being knowledgeable about issues and events help people carry out these responsibilities more effectively. Tell students that in Lesson 1.4 they will learn about the importance colonial leaders in New England placed on being able to read in order to understand the Bible and the government's laws.

TEACH

Guided Discussion

1. **Draw Conclusions** If New England society valued formal education, why did colonial education also include apprenticeships? *(Answers will vary. Possible response: Colonial leaders believed citizens should be able to read, write, and have basic academic skills. However, most colonial jobs did not require formal education. Many jobs, such as carpentry, butchering, and baking, required hands-on skills that were best taught through apprenticeships.)*

2. **Make Inferences** How did newspapers and books help colonists forge a common identity? *(Answers will vary. Possible response: By focusing on European events and politics, newspapers made colonists feel less isolated from English society. Books may have also helped build a common colonial identity by highlighting the uniqueness of colonists' American experiences.)*

⬡ American Places

Colonial male students entered Harvard around the age many other boys would be starting apprenticeships with tradesmen. Students were assigned a rank in the college based on their academic skills and the social status of their families. While many of Harvard's students studied for the clergy, the school also offered courses in literature, science, and the arts. The goal was to train students to be the leaders of colonial society. Student life was very formal and strict. All but freshmen wore academic gowns, and undergraduates were expected to take off their caps when passing the house of the college president and salute him when meeting him in the street.

Active Options

On Your Feet: One-on-One Interviews Group students into pairs. Tell each pair to write three questions about the general reading tastes of colonial people. Ask students to conduct interviews with each other as if on a talk show and then take questions from the class. Students' answers should demonstrate an understanding of the importance of reading in colonial New England, as well as colonists' reading abilities and interests.

NG Learning Framework: Investigate Colonial Apprenticeships

ATTITUDE Curiosity

KNOWLEDGE Our Human Story

Direct students to work in pairs to learn more about apprenticeships in colonial New England. Tell partners to choose a specific trade that interests them and use library and online sources to research such facts as the age at which children were apprenticed, how apprenticeships were arranged, the length of apprenticeships, and what the experience was like. Ask partners to present their findings to the class.

English Language Learners ELD

Ask and Answer Questions Pair students at the **Emerging** level with English-proficient students and have them read the lesson together. After each paragraph, have partners pause and ask one another *who, what, where, when,* or *why* questions about the text they have just read. Students may wish to use a 5Ws Chart.

Who?
What?
Where?
When?
Why?

Pre-AP

Write a Review Help students locate a copy of Mary Rowlandson's *Narrative of the Captivity and Restoration of Mrs. Mary Rowlandson* online. Tell students to select a chapter and use it as the basis for a book review for a colonial newspaper. Encourage students to analyze the book from the perspective of a colonial reader rather than a modern reviewer looking back in history. Ask students to post their reviews for others to read.

See the Chapter Planner for more strategies for differentiation.

HISTORICAL THINKING

ANSWERS

1. Colonial New Englanders established common schools and Latin grammar schools. They also established Harvard College in 1636 and Yale College in 1701.

2. Answers will vary. Possible response: New Englanders thought that people needed to be able to read so they could understand the Bible and learn about God. Most graduates from New England colleges joined the clergy.

3. Answers will vary. Possible response: Colonial merchants depended on Atlantic trade. Political decisions and events in Europe, such as war, affected trade.

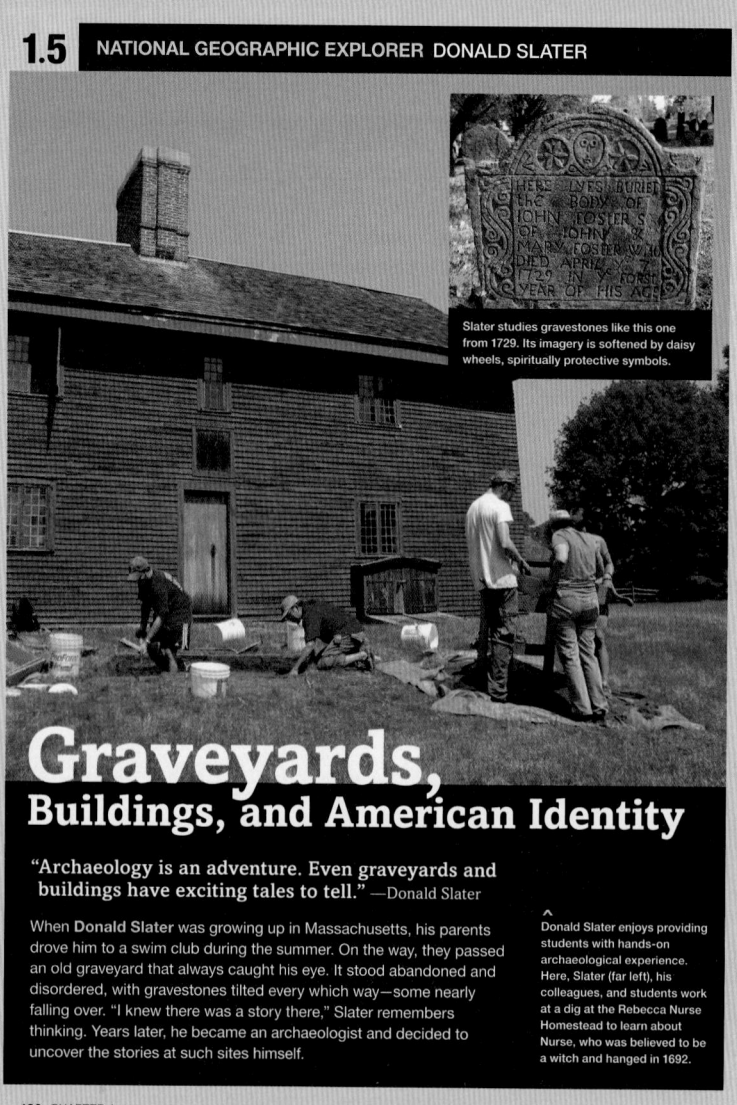

Slater studies gravestones like this one from 1729. Its imagery is softened by daisy wheels, spiritually protective symbols.

Graveyards,
Buildings, and American Identity

"Archaeology is an adventure. Even graveyards and buildings have exciting tales to tell." —Donald Slater

When **Donald Slater** was growing up in Massachusetts, his parents drove him to a swim club during the summer. On the way, they passed an old graveyard that always caught his eye. It stood abandoned and disordered, with gravestones tilted every which way—some nearly falling over. "I knew there was a story there," Slater remembers thinking. Years later, he became an archaeologist and decided to uncover the stories at such sites himself.

^
Donald Slater enjoys providing students with hands-on archaeological experience. Here, Slater (far left), his colleagues, and students work at a dig at the Rebecca Nurse Homestead to learn about Nurse, who was believed to be a witch and hanged in 1692.

MAIN IDEA Archaeologist Donald Slater investigates colonial New England graveyards and architecture to learn about American culture.

THE GRAVE WHISPERER

National Geographic Explorer Donald Slater studies graveyards from the 1600s and 1700s. Luckily for him, he lives in New England where there are lots of graveyards from these periods. One of his favorites is the Old Burying Ground, established in 1634 in Ipswich, Massachusetts. It contains the region's oldest documented gravestones, including those of the wife and child of John Winthrop, Jr., the town's chief founder.

As Slater examines a graveyard, he pays particular attention to the iconography of the gravestones— the stone's carved design. Although the details are hotly debated among scholars, Slater believes that changes in the designs point to evolving religious ideas in the New England Colonies. A death's head, showing a stylized skull with wings or crossed bones, appeared on most early gravestones. As the 18th century progressed, however, death's heads were replaced by winged cherub, or angel, heads.

Slater believes a religious movement that began in the 1720s caused the graveyard iconography to soften. The movement—called the Great Awakening—which you'll learn more about later in this chapter, emphasized the idea that people could ascend to heaven by demonstrating their faith in God. Earlier Puritan beliefs held that people's place after death—heaven or hell—was predestined, or determined, by God at birth.

Around the same time, the epitaphs, or inscriptions, carved on the gravestones also became more hopeful. Instead of focusing on mortality, later epitaphs celebrate the deceased's reward in heaven for a life well lived. Some provide a brief narrative of the person's life. According to Slater, one such epitaph reveals that the man buried was born a slave but died free.

OUR AMERICAN IDENTITY

Like gravestones, colonial architectural styles also evolved over time. Some of these changes reflect cultural change—and the increasing American identity of the colonies. In the early 1600s, builders

Slater reads a gravestone at the South Parish Burial Ground in Andover, Massachusetts. Established in 1709, the cemetery is Andover's oldest museum.

in New England based their structures on English architecture. But instead of brick, the colonists most often used wood and other rustic building materials, which resulted in a uniquely American style. Builders adapted structures to conditions in the colony. For example, they constructed summer kitchens at the rear of a house to avoid heating up the entire home, applying construction techniques they used in England.

Much of New England is a treasure trove of colonial sites and artifacts. But what if you don't live there? Slater suggests you visit your local historical society to learn about early American sites in your community, including those of Native Americans, or ask your neighborhood librarian for information. All these sources can help you discover your American identity. And Slater believes this is important. For, as he says, "There is no better way to preserve our cultural heritage than to educate today's youth on the subject, because it is they who will be making tomorrow's decisions that will determine whether sites are protected or destroyed."

HISTORICAL THINKING

1. **READING CHECK** What does Slater study when he investigates colonial graveyards?

2. **ANALYZE CAUSE AND EFFECT** According to Slater, why might a cherub head have replaced the death's head on later graves?

3. **MAKE INFERENCES** What do you think the architectural developments by the early 1700s suggest about New England colonists?

PLAN

Objective

Learn how studying New England gravestones can provide insight into colonial culture.

Critical Thinking Skills for Lesson 1.5

- Identify Main Ideas and Details
- Monitor Comprehension
- Analyze Cause and Effect
- Make Inferences
- Draw Conclusions
- Make Connections

Essential Question for Chapter 4

How did a developing American identity unite the colonies? Many of the New England colonists were united by a common religion and culture. Lesson 1.5 examines how Donald Slater studies graveyards and architecture to better understand that shared identity.

Background for the Teacher

Donald Slater is not alone in his view that design changes in gravestone iconography point to evolving religious ideas in colonial New England. In the 1960s, James Deetz and Edwin Dethlefsen, two archaeologists responsible for one of the foundational studies of New England gravestones, noted a shift from death's heads to cherubs. They argued that this shift occurred as Puritanism declined and the Puritans' harsh religious views concerning death gave way to the more uplifting views of immortality embodied in the Great Awakening. Some experts call this interpretation into question, however, arguing that cherubs never completely replaced death's heads in the 1700s.

History Notebook

Encourage students to complete the Explorer and American Gallery pages for Chapter 4 in their History Notebooks as they read.

Gravestone Iconography

Write the word *iconography* on the board, and underline *icon*. **ASK:** What is an icon? *(An icon is a symbol.)* Then ask students to brainstorm a list of religious or spiritual symbols. Discuss how the symbols on the list are associated with different cultures or religions. End by telling students that Lesson 1.5 explores the use and significance of iconography on colonial-era gravestones.

TEACH

Guided Discussion

1. **Draw Conclusions** What does the fact that scholars hotly debate the significance of gravestone iconography tell you about how archaeological theories are developed? *(Answers will vary. Possible response: Since different archaeologists interpret evidence differently, it probably takes a long time for a theory to be accepted.)*

2. **Make Connections** How might learning about early American sites in your community help you make decisions about preserving America's cultural heritage sites in the future? *(Answers will vary. Possible response: Learning about local sites helps you appreciate how places and cultures change over time. By appreciating your own cultural heritage, you might see the importance of protecting cultural heritage sites.)*

More Information

Preserving Colonial History The Rebecca Nurse Homestead is located in Danvers, Massachusetts, the site of Salem Village. Rebecca and Francis Nurse leased the property in 1678 and developed the land into a productive farm. Generations of the Nurse family continued to live in the house until 1784. The property was restored in the early 1900s and turned over to the Society for the Preservation of New England Antiquities. Today, the property is owned and operated by a living history organization. It is believed that Rebecca's family may have secretly buried her body on the property after she was hanged for witchcraft.

Active Options

On Your Feet: Numbered Heads Organize students into groups of four and assign each group member a number from one to four. Tell them to think about and discuss a response to this question: How was the colonial identity and culture reflected in the architecture and art of New England? Then call a number and have the student from each group with that number report for the group.

1 2
Think Time
4 3

1 2
Talk Time
4 3

Share 2's Time

AMERICAN GALLERY
ONLINE
Colonial Graveyards Invite students to explore the American Gallery. Have them select one of the photos and do additional research to learn more about it. Ask questions that will inspire additional inquiry about the chosen photo, such as: What is this? Where and when was this created? By whom? Why was it created? What is it made of? Why does it belong in this chapter? What else would you like to know about it?

Inclusion

Narrate a Colonial Graveyard The American Gallery images might pose a challenge to the visually impaired. Ask students who are not visually challenged to narrate the gravestones to a visually impaired partner by describing the iconography and messages. Encourage visually impaired students to ask questions, and remind their partners to give detailed answers.

Gifted & Talented

Compare Architecture Ask students to conduct online research to find examples of colonial structures in New England from the 1600s and 1700s. Encourage students to download photos and organize them into a presentation that illustrates and demonstrates the similarities and differences of the architecture of the two centuries.

See the Chapter Planner for more strategies for differentiation.

HISTORICAL THINKING

ANSWERS

1. Slater analyzes the iconography and epitaphs on colonial gravestones in order to understand evolving religious ideas in the 1600s and 1700s.

2. Slater believes that a religious movement that began in 1720 replaced the idea that a person's place after death was determined at birth with the view that people could get to heaven by demonstrating faith in God.

3. Answers will vary. Possible response: Colonial builders constructed buildings adapted to colonial conditions rather than simply using local materials to construct English designs. This might indicate that colonists were thinking of themselves as more American than English and were developing a uniquely American design.

2.1 Slavery Expands

A person journeying from New England to the Southern Colonies would be amazed by its large plantations—quite a contrast to New England's small farms. And the warm climate would probably make the traveler shed his or her jacket. What a difference geography makes!

MAIN IDEA The Southern Colonies developed a system of plantation agriculture that relied on increasing numbers of enslaved Africans.

PLANTATION CROPS

The geography of New England was very different from that of the Southern Colonies. The fertile land and milder climate of the Southern Colonies—Maryland, Virginia, the Carolinas, and Georgia—made it possible to grow **cash crops**, crops grown for sale rather than for use by the farmers themselves. The main cash crops were tobacco, rice, and **indigo**, a plant whose leaves provide a source of blue dye for cloth. Tobacco thrived in the hot and humid growing season of Virginia and coastal Maryland. Rice was well suited to the swampy lowlands and tidal areas of coastal rivers in the Carolinas. However, the colonists had no experience in rice cultivation. They depended on enslaved Africans, who had been taken from rice-growing regions in West Africa, to farm the rice and ensure successful yields.

Plantations sprang up along the rivers so planters could use the water for their rice fields. Ships sailed up tributaries from the Chesapeake Bay and docked at the plantations. Because of the ease of transporting goods directly from their farms, southern colonists had little need for port cities.

One exception was the busy seaport of **Charles Town** (now called Charleston). As Carolina planters developed cash crops, Charles Town grew as a port. Many plantation owners lived there part of the year to escape the isolation of their plantations. Although Charles Town became the fourth-largest colonial city, after Boston, Philadelphia, and New York, it never grew larger because English and New England shippers controlled its trade. Without

a strong merchant community, the city failed to attract large numbers of new workers.

NEW SLAVE TRADING

Planters in the Southern Colonies originally hired white indentured servants to work for several years in exchange for a plot of land. But in 1698, England gave all English merchants permission to participate in slave trading. As a result, planters who lived in the **Chesapeake**, the settled land around the Chesapeake Bay, turned to enslaved Africans to farm their land. In 1660, only 900 Africans resided in the Chesapeake, some of whom had arrived as servants and lived free. By 1720, one-fifth of the population of that area were Africans. By 1770, that number ranged from one-third to one-half. African populations in Virginia and the Carolinas also increased dramatically during this period. By 1750, African Americans accounted for over 40 percent of Virginia's total population and more than half of South Carolina's. More than 90 percent of the total African-American population was enslaved.

HISTORICAL THINKING

1. **READING CHECK** Why were tobacco and rice good cash crops for Virginia, Maryland, and the Carolinas?

2. **ANALYZE VISUALS** After which step in the rice process are the grains of rice collected?

3. **IDENTIFY MAIN IDEAS AND DETAILS** What factors led to the expansion of slave labor in the Southern Colonies?

RICE PRODUCTION

Rice production required many steps and many people to grow enough grain to make a profit. Below are some of the steps of this labor-intensive process.

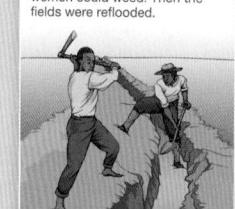

1 Flooding
Farmworkers built flood gates and dug ditches. They planted, then opened the floodgates to fill the rice fields with water. After the seeds sprouted, the fields were drained so the women could weed. Then the fields were reflooded.

2 Harvesting
Workers harvested, or reaped, the ripened rice plants with a cutting tool called a scythe (SIGHTH).

3 Threshing
On colonial plantations, threshing meant beating the plants with a stick called a flail until the grains fell from the plants.

4 Winnowing
Winnowing was the process of tossing the rice grains in a basket to separate them from their tissue-like outer coating, or chaff.

5 Pounding
The winnowed rice was poured into a hollowed-out log and pounded with a staff called a mortar. This removed the tough outer husk from the grain.

In 1915, when these photographs were taken, slavery had been abolished, but workers still used tools similar to ones that had been used more than 200 years ago.

Colonial Development 133

PLAN

Objective

Trace slavery's development in the Southern Colonies and its role in plantation agriculture.

Critical Thinking Skills for Lesson 2.1

- Identify Main Ideas and Details
- Monitor Comprehension
- Analyze Visuals
- Analyze Cause and Effect
- Make Inferences

Essential Question for Chapter 4

How did a developing American identity unite the colonies? The Southern Colonies developed an economy based on plantation agriculture and enslaved labor. Lesson 2.1 explores the characteristics of plantation agriculture and the origins of its reliance on slavery.

Background for the Teacher

Chesapeake settlers learned early that Native Americans, who escaped enslavement and died in catastrophic numbers, would not fill their labor needs. White indentured servants from Europe filled the gap until about 1675, when their numbers began to decline. The decline was due in part to the founding of new colonies where land was plentiful, giving emancipated servants a wider range of options. In choosing slavery as an alternative labor source, colonists followed the example of the Portuguese, Spanish, Dutch, and the English in the West Indies. They considered humans superior to animals, Christians superior to "heathens," and Europeans superior to the people of sub-Saharan Africa. These beliefs helped Europeans justify chattel slavery.

Activate Prior Knowledge

Provide students with a K-W-L Chart. Have them think about what they know about the slave trade and slavery in the Americas. Then ask them to write questions they would like to have answered as they study this lesson about the expansion of slavery in the Southern Colonies. Allow time at the end of the lesson for students to complete their charts with what they have learned.

TEACH

Guided Discussion

1. **Analyze Cause and Effect** What factors affected the growth of port cities in the Carolinas? *(Answers will vary. Possible response: Since plantations were located along rivers, planters transported their goods by water. Shippers from New England and England controlled Charles Town, the major seaport. This control meant that the seaport did not develop a strong merchant class or attract a large number of workers.)*

2. **Make Inferences** What economic inferences can you make based on the rise in the African-American population in the Southern Colonies in the 1700s? *(Answers will vary. Possible response: The rise in the African-American population suggests that the demand for enslaved workers increased as more planters used slave labor and as the size and number of plantations increased. The rise also suggests that the number of merchants participating in the slave trade might have increased.)*

Analyze Visuals

Direct students' attention to the Rice Production feature. Allow time for students to study the illustrations and photos and reread the captions. **ASK:** Based on the visuals and text, why was rice production such a labor-intensive task? *(Answers will vary. Possible response: Rice production involved many physically difficult steps. Workers had to dig ditches, build floodgates, and harvest the individual plants by hand. The rice grains had to be separated from the plant, then the chaff had to be separated from the grain, and the grain's husk had to be removed by tossing the rice in a basket and pounding it in a hollowed-out log.)*

Active Options

On Your Feet: Jigsaw Divide students into three "expert" groups and assign each group one of the following topics: plantation crops, Charles Town, and slave trading. Groups should study their assigned topic in depth. Then have students reorganize so that each new group has at least one member from each expert group. Have students in each new group share what they learned about their topic.

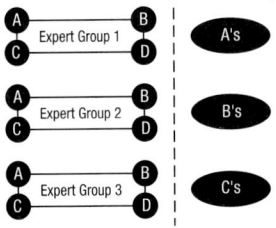

NG Learning Framework: Learn More About Colonial Rice Production

SKILL Collaboration

KNOWLEDGE Our Human Story

Have students work in small groups to research the roles enslaved Africans played in the development and success of rice production in the Carolinas. Assign each group one of the following topics:

• the knowledge the West Africans possessed from growing rice in their homelands;

• the challenges of clearing and preparing the Carolina swampland for planting;

• the labor-intensive aspects of tending and harvesting the rice.

Instruct students to use their pooled research to create a multimedia presentation on colonial rice production in the Carolinas.

English Language Learners ELD

Identify Main Idea and Details Pair students at the **Emerging** level with those at the **Bridging** level and pair students at the **Expanding** level together. Give each pair a piece of construction paper or a flip chart with the main idea of the lesson written on it: *The Southern Colonies developed a system of plantation agriculture that relied on increasing numbers of enslaved Africans.* Ask each pair to list as many details from the lesson as they can to support the main idea. They should write their details on the flip chart or construction paper. Then have the pairs compare their lists.

Pre-AP

Research Charles Town Have students investigate Charles Town's role in the African slave trade in the 1700s. Instruct students to ask questions such as the following: How did the number of Africans arriving annually in Charles Town change over time? What were the homelands of the arriving Africans? What role did Sullivan Island play in the slave trade? Instruct students to conduct research to answer their questions. Encourage students to share their findings with the class.

See the Chapter Planner for more strategies for differentiation.

ANSWERS

1. Tobacco thrived in Virginia and coastal Maryland's hot, humid growing season. Rice was well suited to the semitropical, swampy lowlands and tidal areas of coastal rivers in the Carolinas.

2. The rice grains were collected after step three, the threshing.

3. Answers will vary. Possible response: The need for workers with rice-growing experience and the ruling that all English merchants could participate in the slave trade led to the expansion of slave labor.

2.2 From Plantations to the Backcountry

There's a saying that "the rich get richer," and it seemed to be true on the large plantations. More land and slaves meant more cash crops—and more money.

MAIN IDEA Life in the coastal areas of the Southern Colonies differed greatly from life further inland, and revolved extensively around slavery.

WEALTH AND CLASS

Over time, wealthy planters in Maryland, Virginia, and the Carolinas bought more and more land and slaves. The expanding plantations produced increasing amounts of tobacco, rice, and indigo. The owners reaped the profits.

Not all farmers became wealthy, but the owners of the largest plantations became so wealthy and powerful that distinct classes formed among southern farmers. With their luxurious homes and leisurely lifestyle, rich landowners lived like nobles in Europe.

An army of slaves made this way of life possible. The work the slaves performed depended on where they lived. In South Carolina, each enslaved person received certain jobs to complete each day—a field to hoe, a fence to build. In the Chesapeake, most enslaved people worked on the plantation for a specific number of hours or until the **overseer**, or supervisor, told them to stop. As a result, many slaves worked long into the night.

While some plantation owners treated enslaved people fairly well, others did not. But the terrible workload took its toll on all the laborers. As work increased and the hours grew even longer, death rates among enslaved people surged dramatically.

THE BACKCOUNTRY

A different kind of culture arose as some settlers in the Southern Colonies sought their fortune in the backcountry. The **backcountry** stretched along the Appalachian Mountains from Pennsylvania south through the Shenandoah Valley to the Carolinas. This region included the rich soil, rolling hills, and deep forests of the **Piedmont**, a relatively flat area between the mountains and the coastal plain.

In the early 1700s, European settlers such as the Scots-Irish, immigrants from the northern part of Ireland, came to the colonies. They began settling in the backcountry and establishing farms outside the first English settlements, carving their farmland out of the forests.

Backcountry farmers learned to be self-sufficient. They used one of the most plentiful natural resources of this region—timber—to build simple log cabins. They hunted and raised enough crops and livestock to feed their families. Women in the backcountry worked in the home, the fields, and the wild. Many of them carried guns. Also, unlike many people in the Southern Colonies, most of the immigrants living in the backcountry didn't rely on slaves.

HISTORICAL THINKING

1. **READING CHECK** What was the social structure like in the Chesapeake in the 1700s?

2. **COMPARE AND CONTRAST** How did work patterns differ for slaves in South Carolina and the Chesapeake?

3. **ANALYZE CAUSE AND EFFECT** How did the environment of the backcountry affect how the people settling there made a living?

Shenandoah Valley
In the 1700s, Scots-Irish settlers who had come to Pennsylvania began moving into the Shenandoah Valley in present-day West Virginia and Virginia. The rich soil of the valley made it a dream for farming, and at the time, the Scots-Irish had little competition from other Europeans. They did, however, compete for the land with Native Americans who had long called the region home.

Colonial Development 135

PLAN

Objective
Describe differences between coastal and backcountry regions of the Southern Colonies.

Critical Thinking Skills for Lesson 2.2
- Identify Main Ideas and Details
- Monitor Comprehension
- Compare and Contrast
- Analyze Cause and Effect
- Synthesize

Essential Question for Chapter 4
How did a developing American identity unite the colonies? Two very different farming cultures emerged in the Southern Colonies. Lesson 2.2 explores the differences between plantation agriculture along the coast and backcountry farming in the Piedmont.

Background for the Teacher
Chesapeake society was made up of many classes of people based on wealth. Enslaved people, who owned no property and had little hope for freedom, occupied the bottom rungs of the Chesapeake social structure. Above them were the 40 to 50 percent of white families who rented land and owned some livestock and household goods but rarely held servants or slaves. These white families were often in debt to the local merchant-planter for goods such as ammunition, fabric, shoes, and tools. Small landholders, with incomes that allowed them to live more comfortably, in nicer (though still quite small) homes, occupied the next step up in the Chesapeake social structure. The upper five percent of Chesapeake society included the gentry, or people who owned many slaves and held large acreages. The gentry served as trade intermediaries for smaller planters, who often owed them substantial debts.

Compare Regions

Have students recall the information they have already learned about the geography of the coastal areas of the Southern Colonies. **ASK:** How would you characterize the physical geography of the coastal regions? *(swampy, low-lying tidal areas, many navigable rivers)* Then have students look at the photo of the Shenandoah Valley. **ASK:** How does the physical geography shown in this photo of the Shenandoah Valley contrast with what you know about the coastal region's physical geography? *(Answers will vary. Possible response: It is very different. The photo shows a hilly terrain bordered by mountains. The land is forested with patches of dry grasslands.)* Tell students that they will learn about the differences between the two regions in this lesson.

TEACH
Guided Discussion

1. **Synthesize** How did the reliance on enslaved labor help the owners of the largest plantations maintain their wealth and leisurely lifestyles? *(Answers will vary. Possible response: The owners became wealthy because they had more land on which to plant cash crops. However, the planting required more labor. Owners of large plantations solved their labor needs by using enslaved labor instead of wage labor. Enslaved labor was cheaper than wage labor, and since the enslaved workers could be sold, they were considered to be part of the slaveholder's wealth.)*

2. **Compare and Contrast** In what ways were farmers in the backcountry similar to farmers in colonial New England? *(Answers will vary. Possible response: Farmers in both regions carved farms out of hilly, forested land. Because the farms were generally small in both regions and relied primarily on the labor of the families, most farmers raised only enough crops and livestock to feed their families.)*

More Information

Settling the Backcountry Hunger for cheap land was not the only reason for settling the backcountry. Colonial governments in coastal regions wanted the land settled as a buffer against attacks by Native Americans and encroachment by the French. They also wanted to lessen the threat of runaway slaves creating communities in the Appalachian Mountains. But settling the backcountry was no easy task. The rapids and waterfalls made getting there by river impractical. Instead, settlers traveled along Native American trails, such as the Great Trading Path and what came to be called the Great Wagon Road.

Active Options

On Your Feet: Question and Answer Have half the class write True-False statements based on the information in the Wealth and Class section of the lesson and the other half write True-False statements based on the information in The Backcountry section. Have each group create answer cards with "True" written on one side and "False" on the other. Then have groups take turns reading aloud their questions while the other group displays the correct answers. Review and discuss the information when discrepancies occur.

NG Learning Framework: Analyze Labor Systems

ATTITUDE Curiosity

KNOWLEDGE Our Human Story

As students learned in Lesson 2.2, plantation owners in South Carolina organized the work of their slaves differently than plantation owners in the Chesapeake. Have students research the two labor systems—referred to as the task system and gang system—to learn more about how they operated. Encourage students to also find information on why the two regions used different systems. Then invite students to share their findings through a guided class discussion of the two systems.

DIFFERENTIATE
Striving Readers

Set a Purpose for Reading Before reading, have students use the subheadings in the lesson to create purpose-setting questions:

- How did wealth affect class in the coastal regions?

- What was life like for settlers in the backcountry?

After reading, have student pairs answer the questions. Then ask for student volunteers to share their answers.

Gifted & Talented

Investigate Backcountry Living Have students work in pairs to conduct research on life in the backcountry. Direct them to focus on one of the following topics:

- how the settlers competed with the Native Americans for land;

- how the settlers cleared and planted their land;

- how work was divided among family members;

- how the settlers built and used market towns.

Ask students to give a short presentation of their findings to the class. Encourage students to be prepared to answer questions their classmates might have about their presentation.

See the Chapter Planner for more strategies for differentiation.

HISTORICAL THINKING

ANSWERS

1. At the top were the wealthy and powerful planters who owned large amounts of land and many slaves. Below them were the owners of smaller plantations and the farmers who never became wealthy. At the bottom were the vast numbers of enslaved people who worked the plantations.

2. In South Carolina, each slave received a certain amount of work to perform each day. In the Chesapeake, most slaves on plantations labored for a specific number of hours or until they were told to stop.

3. Answers will vary. Possible response: The backcountry's fertile soil attracted farmers. However, because it took a lot of work to clear the forest, farms were small.

2.3 Life Under Slavery

After days of hard work, enslaved Africans gathered together—sometimes secretly—on Sundays. They cooked African foods and played music based on African rhythms. As much as they could, they hung on to pieces of their past.

MAIN IDEA Plantation slaves kept their African culture and traditions alive, even though their living and working conditions were often very difficult.

LIVING CONDITIONS

As you've read, most plantation slaves—both men and women—spent long hours planting, weeding, and harvesting tobacco, rice, and indigo. Overseers sometimes used whips and other harsh instruments and measures to force workers to work harder or more productively. Some owners also recruited slaves, called drivers, to push their fellow workers to pick up the pace.

Work in the slaveowner's household was sometimes less brutal. Both men and women cooked and did gardening chores. Women often took care of the children as well. Some

men became **artisans**, or skilled workers who crafted things by hand. Some women served as nurses and weavers.

Marriage between slaves was illegal in the colonies. An enslaved couple had to obtain their master's permission to live together as husband and wife. Slave marriages were torn apart when

Slave Housing
Only nine of the 27 slave houses that once stood at Boone Hall Plantation near Charleston, South Carolina, still remain. The houses together make up what is called a "slave street." The nine houses, five of which appear in this photograph, were home to the servants at the plantation house. Each house was divided into two rooms and had either a dirt or a wooden floor. Dirt floors were common in the houses provided for slaves.

one of the pair was sold to a different slaveowner. In those cases, slaves often walked long distances at night to visit and hold the family together.

Slaves often built their own houses, which were typically one-room cabins. Many planters provided only basic foods for their enslaved workers, such as corn and a little pork. Enslaved people often planted gardens with vegetables like yams and squash to enhance their diet. They also raised hogs and chickens and hunted and fished for extra food.

People from different parts of West Africa often found themselves thrown together on large plantations. To speak to each other, they blended African languages with English. By this means, such African words as *yam* and *tote* were introduced into the English language.

Africans influenced colonial culture, as well as that of early national America, in many other ways. Their music, with its rhythmic beat, had a huge impact on jazz and blues. They made clay pottery, baskets, and musical instruments with African designs. They also popularized new foods, including okra, melons, and bananas. In Boston, a slave taught his owner the practice of vaccination, which he had learned in Africa. As a result of the slave's help, the city's people were protected from a smallpox outbreak.

ACTS OF REBELLION

Enslaved people did what they could to cope with their situation, but many actively rebelled against their treatment. They resisted the slave owner's power by staging slowdowns, faking illness, and secretly destroying crops and tools. Others ran away. Some enslaved people became violent, killing the slave owners or setting fire to fields and homes.

In 1739, a group of more than 50 enslaved people revolted near the Stono River in South Carolina. Their leader was a literate slave named Jemmy (also known as Cato) whose master had taught him to read and write. When armed planters defeated the rebels in battle, some of the slaves headed to St. Augustine, Florida, where the Spanish government had promised them freedom. But the South Carolina militia pursued them, putting to death everyone suspected of being involved. Although similar rebellions had already taken place in the Middle Colonies, the **Stono Rebellion** sent fear throughout the American colonies.

The South Carolina legislature enacted a harsh slave code in 1740 in an effort to prevent future revolts. The new code made all enslaved people and their children permanent slaves. In addition, the code prohibited enslaved people from learning to read and write. In spite of these new laws, some slaves did learn to read and write. And they used this knowledge to tell their stories and let the world know what was happening to them.

Banjo
Africans on plantations played instruments made of a gourd cut in half with a goatskin stretched over it, a stick, and three strings. The banjo shown here was made in Baltimore, Maryland, in 1845. In this banjo, the gourd has been replaced with a circular wooden frame and the stick with a flat piece of wood. In other modern versions, the frame is sometimes made of metal.

HISTORICAL THINKING

1. **READING CHECK** What measures did owners use to force slaves to work harder?

2. **IDENTIFY MAIN IDEAS AND DETAILS** What are some of the ways in which enslaved people asserted their humanity and kept their traditions alive?

3. **ANALYZE CAUSE AND EFFECT** What were the long-term negative consequences of the Stono Rebellion on enslaved people?

PLAN

Objective
Learn how enslaved Africans retained their culture and traditions.

Critical Thinking Skills for Lesson 2.3
- Identify Main Ideas and Details
- Monitor Comprehension
- Analyze Cause and Effect
- Identify Problems and Solutions
- Draw Conclusions
- Analyze Visuals

Essential Question for Chapter 4
How did a developing American identity unite the colonies? Lesson 2.3 explores how enslaved Africans developed a culture that retained and adapted elements of their African heritage.

Background for the Teacher
Enslaved Africans and African Americans kept their cultures alive through language, music, dance, and religion. Some newly arrived Africans knew European languages from former contacts in Africa or the West Indies. In order to communicate with other slaves and with Europeans, most adopted Creole speech, which evolved from English and various African languages. Enslaved Africans retained traditional concepts of the hereafter, where the deceased reunited with ancestors, and combined these beliefs with European ideas about heaven. Mourners buried the dead facing Africa, with traditional rituals, music, and dance. Enslaved Africans also passed down African medical practices, which combined physical and psychological treatments, including magic.

Categorize Topics

On the board, write these three categories: *plantation life*, *slave culture*, and *rebellion*. Then ask students to think about topics they would like to know more about for each category. Next to or under each category, write down student topics. After reading the lesson, revisit the topics to see if students still have questions.

TEACH

Guided Discussion

1. **Identify Problems and Solutions** How did plantation slaves improve their living conditions and protest their working conditions? *(Answers will vary. Possible response: Slaves often built their own houses, and many planted gardens, raised animals, and hunted and fished to provide better food for themselves. They also developed ways to retain their cultures, such as with music. To protest their working conditions, they staged acts of rebellion, such as slowdowns, faking illnesses, and destroying crops and tools.)*

2. **Draw Conclusions** What factors in the Stono Rebellion might have contributed to South Carolina's decision to outlaw teaching slaves to read and write? Support your answer with evidence from the text. *(Answers will vary. Possible response: The South Carolina legislature may have believed that literate slaves would make future rebellions easier to plan and execute because written information would be easier to circulate among plantations and hide from overseers and plantation owners.)*

Analyze Visuals

Explore the photograph of the slave houses and its caption with students. **ASK:** What do you notice about the construction of the houses? *(Answers will vary. Possible response: They look soundly built of brick and have tile roofs. They each have a fireplace and a window with a wooden shutter. The caption indicates they have two rooms and either wood or dirt floors.)* **ASK:** Who lived in these houses? *(These particular houses were homes of enslaved people who worked in the plantation house.)* Conduct a class discussion about why house servants might have been provided better housing than field hands.

Active Options

On Your Feet: Team Word Webs Divide the class into two teams. Give each team a sheet of paper, one with the phrase "Living Conditions" in the center and the other with the phrase "Acts of Rebellion" in the center. Give students a few minutes to create a team Word Web about their phrase, listing what they know from the lesson. Then have one team share their web with the other team.

NG Learning Framework: Research the Stono Rebellion

ATTITUDE Empowerment

KNOWLEDGE Our Human Story

Tell students to conduct online research to learn more about the Stono Rebellion. Instruct students to consider the following questions in their research:

• How did the slaves and the colonists perceive the rebellion?

• What factors might have contributed to the timing of the revolt?

• How did events unfold over the course of the rebellion?

• What were the short- and long-term consequences of the revolt?

Have students use their findings to create a short report on the rebellion. Encourage students to share their report with the class.

Striving Readers

Use Supported Reading Have students work in pairs. Assign each pair one paragraph to read aloud together. At the end of each paragraph, have them use the following sentence frames to tell what they do and do not understand:

• This paragraph is about _____.

• One fact that stood out to me is _____.

• _____ is a word I had trouble understanding, so I figured it out by _____.

Be sure students understand the content before moving on to the next paragraph.

Pre-AP

Write a News Story To help students appreciate how enslaved Africans retained their culture in the 1700s, ask them to research today's Gullah and Geechee communities. To direct their research, have students pose questions such as:

• Who are the Gullah and Geechee?

• Where are their communities located?

• What West African ethnic traditions can be seen in Gullah/Geechee culture?

Challenge students to write news stories highlighting what they have discovered about the Gullah and Geechee. Have students share their news stories with the class.

See the Chapter Planner for more strategies for differentiation.

HISTORICAL THINKING

ANSWERS

1. Overseers sometimes used whips and other punishments to force slaves to work harder or more productively.

2. Answers will vary. Possible response: Slaves grew African crops, produced traditional arts and crafts, and played African music. They asserted their humanity with activities from growing a garden to faking an illness or running away.

3. Answers will vary. Possible response: The rebellion led the South Carolina legislature to pass a harsh slave code in 1740. It prohibited slaves from learning to read and write and made slavery permanent for all slaves and their offspring.

2.4 Slave Narratives

After gaining their freedom, some former slaves wrote about their experiences and the cruelty they'd endured. They wanted to open up people's eyes to the true nature of slavery.

Olaudah Equiano (oh-LOW-duh ehk-wee-AHN-oh) was born in Benin, an empire in Africa that you have learned about previously. Equiano was sold into slavery at the age of 11. About 10 years later, he bought his freedom from his last owner, a Quaker from Philadelphia. He made his way to England, where he lectured on the evils of slavery.

In 1789, in London, Equiano published his autobiography, an excerpt from which appears on the next page. He had the image shown here created for the book. Copies sold quickly, and the popularity of *The Interesting Narrative of the Life of Olaudah Equiano* contributed to a law being passed in England in 1807 that made slavery illegal in England and its colonies. By then, as you will learn, America was no longer a British colony.

CRITICAL VIEWING Why do you think Equiano wanted to have his portrait show him holding a book?

Engraving of Olaudah Equiano from his book, *The Interesting Narrative of the Life of Olaudah Equiano*

DOCUMENT ONE

Primary Source: Autobiography
from *The Interesting Narrative of the Life of Olaudah Equiano*, 1789

In this excerpt from his autobiography, Equiano describes the brutal conditions aboard the slave ship during the passage from Africa to the Americas—the notorious Middle Passage.

CONSTRUCTED RESPONSE What details help you understand the horror the slaves endured in the Middle Passage?

I was soon put down under the decks, and there I received such a salutation [greeting] in my nostrils as I had never experienced in my life: so that, with the loathsomeness of the stench [smell], and crying together, I became so sick and low that I was not able to eat, nor had I the least desire to taste any thing.

. . . Many a time we were near suffocation from the want [lack] of fresh air, which we were often without for whole days together. This, and the stench of the necessary tubs, carried off [killed] many.

DOCUMENT TWO

Primary Source: Autobiography
from *A Narrative of the Most Remarkable Particulars in the Life of James Albert Ukawsaw Gronniosaw, An African Prince, as Related by Himself*, 1772

James Albert Ukawsaw Gronniosaw was sold into slavery at age 15. Upset with his family, Gronniosaw had believed the promise of a slave merchant and voluntarily left his home in Africa. He realized his mistake too late.

CONSTRUCTED RESPONSE How does the merchant make the idea of going with him sound like a fascinating adventure rather than the entry into a nightmare?

About this time there came a merchant from the Gold Coast. . . . He told me that if I would go with him I should see houses with wings to them walk upon the water, and should also see the white folks; and that he had many sons of my age, which should be my companions; and he added to all this that he would bring me safe back again soon. I was highly pleased with the account of this strange place, and was very desirous of going.

DOCUMENT THREE

Primary Source: Autobiography
from *A Narrative of the Life and Adventures of Venture, a Native of Africa: But Resident Above Sixty Years in the United States of America*, 1798

Venture Smith was born in West Africa, captured as a young child by an enemy army, and then sold as a slave in Rhode Island. He published his autobiography in 1798. The excerpt details how he obtained freedom for his family.

CONSTRUCTED RESPONSE What can you infer about the personal qualities that enabled Venture Smith to accomplish all that he describes?

Being thirty-six years old, I left Col. Smith once for all . . . [having] paid an enormous sum for my freedom. . . . When I had [raised enough money to purchase] my two sons, I had then left more than one hundred pounds. . . . The rest of my money I laid out in land, in addition to a farm which I owned before, and a dwelling house thereon . . . [In] my forty-fourth year, I purchased my wife Meg . . . Being about forty-six years old, I bought my oldest child Hannah . . . I had already redeemed from slavery, myself, my wife and three children.

SYNTHESIZE & WRITE

1. **REVIEW** Review what you have learned about the slave trade and slavery in colonial America.

2. **RECALL** On your own paper, write the main ideas expressed in each document.

3. **CONSTRUCT** Construct a topic sentence that answers this question: How did formerly enslaved persons endure and overcome slavery?

4. **WRITE** Using evidence from this chapter and the documents, write an informative paragraph that supports your topic sentence in Step 3.

PLAN

Objective

Synthesize information about the slave experience from primary source documents.

Critical Thinking Skills for Lesson 2.4

- Synthesize
- Identify Main Ideas and Details
- Monitor Comprehension
- Evaluate

Essential Question for Chapter 4

How did a developing American identity unite the colonies? Enslaved Africans shared the awful experience of being captured and forced to endure the horrors of the Middle Passage and bondage. Lesson 2.4 provides insight into these experiences through excerpts from three slave narratives.

Background for the Teacher

Enslavement and transit across the Atlantic Ocean was dehumanizing and perilous. About half of those sold into slavery died while still in Africa awaiting transport or during the Atlantic passage. As European sea captains made successive trips, African traders had to travel farther to find enough people to enslave. Some captives marched 500 miles or more in lines of shackled prisoners called coffles. On the coast, they were confined for long periods without adequate food and drink. European slave traders branded the newly enslaved people and loaded them into ships for the voyage across the Atlantic. Weather permitting, the captives spent their days on deck—the men in chains, the women and children unrestrained. At night, and around the clock in bad weather, slaves were forced into small spaces in the hold of the ship.

Prepare for the Document-Based Question

Before students start on the activity, briefly preview the three documents. Remind students that a constructed response requires full explanations in complete sentences. Emphasize that students should use what they have learned about the slave trade, Middle Passage, and slavery in addition to the information in the documents.

TEACH

Guided Discussion

1. **Identify Main Ideas and Details** How did Equiano and Gronniosaw feel when they were first sold into slavery? *(Answers will vary. Possible response: Equiano was upset by the conditions on the ship and was so sick and low that he couldn't eat. Gronniosaw was excited and wanted to go with the merchant because he believed his lies.)*

2. **Monitor Comprehension** What relevant information does Venture Smith provide in his account that helps you know he was dedicated to the goal of reuniting his family? *(Answers will vary. Possible response: He gives the ages at which he bought his own and his family members' freedom, which indicates that his goal was so important to him that he stuck with it for 10 years.)*

Evaluate

After students have completed the Synthesize & Write activity, allow time for them to exchange paragraphs and read and comment on the work of their peers. Guidelines for comments should be established prior to this activity so feedback is constructive and encouraging.

Active Options

On Your Feet: Use a Jigsaw Strategy Organize students into three "expert" groups and have students from each group analyze one of the documents and summarize the main ideas in their own words. Then have the members of each group count off using the letters A, B, C, and so on. Regroup

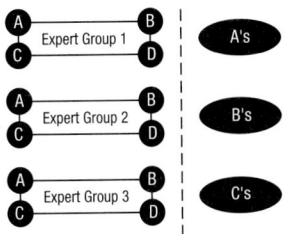

students into three new groups so each new group has at least one member from each expert group. Have students in the new groups take turns sharing the simplified summaries they came up with in their expert groups.

Active History: Analyze Primary Sources Extend the lesson by using either the PDF or Whiteboard version of the activity. These activities take a deeper look at a topic from, or related to, the lesson. Explore the activities as a class, turn them into group assignments, or even assign them individually.

DIFFERENTIATE

Striving Readers

Use Reciprocal Teaching Have partners take turns reading each excerpt aloud. At the end of the excerpt, the reading student should ask the listening student questions about the excerpt. Students may ask their partners to state the main idea and details or summarize the excerpt in their own words. Then have students work together to answer the Constructed Response questions.

Gifted & Talented

Analyze Slave Narratives Tell students to read additional excerpts from these three autobiographies. Encourage them to distinguish between the facts and opinions in the excerpts. Suggest that students also note parts of the excerpts that evoke historical empathy. Have students write a brief summary of each excerpt, highlighting any new insights into the authors' experiences with slavery, the slave trade, or the Middle Passage.

See the Chapter Planner for more strategies for differentiation.

SYNTHESIZE & WRITE

ANSWERS

1. Answers will vary but should include details from each document.

2. Answers will vary, but there should be one concise main idea for each document.

3. Answers will vary. Possible response: Some formerly enslaved people asserted their humanity by sharing their life stories to alert others to the horrors of slavery.

4. Students' paragraphs should include their topic sentence from Step 3 and provide several details from the documents.

CONSTRUCTED RESPONSE

Document 1: Possible response: Equiano describes the sounds of people crying out, the crowded conditions where people are packed so closely they can barely breathe, and the smell, which is so bad that he becomes ill and cannot eat.

Document 2: Possible response: The merchant depicts the slave ships as magical houses with wings that can walk on water. He makes the "white folks" sound like people who Gronniosaw would like to meet, rather than slaveholders.

Document 3: Possible response: Smith was likely a determined, focused, loving, and hardworking man, because he worked for 10 years to save money to reunite his family.

CRITICAL VIEWING Answers will vary. Possible response: Equiano wants readers to understand that he is literate and intelligent, and thus his narrative is reliable.

3.1 Agricultural Production

The basics of farming haven't changed. Farmers today need fertile soil and a good climate to grow abundant crops, just like their counterparts in the colonies. Good climates in the Middle Colonies attracted immigrant farmers from Britain and other parts of Europe.

MAIN IDEA The fertile land of the Middle Colonies allowed farmers to raise cash crops and livestock for sale and export, resulting in a booming economy.

FARMLAND AND FREEDOM

Just like the settlers of New England and the Southern Colonies, immigrants who came to the Middle Colonies of New York, New Jersey, Pennsylvania, and Delaware found ways to support themselves in their new environment. There were navigable rivers and harbors, and rich farmland rolled across the region. The area's weather was warmer than New England's but avoided the sticky heat farther south. Settlers soon discovered that grains such as wheat, corn, rye, and barley thrived in the climate. As a result, the region earned the nickname "breadbasket of the colonies."

Immigrants from all over Europe heard about the **arable**, or fertile, land and decided to move to the Middle Colonies. Attracted by cheap land, limited government control, and religious tolerance, more than 100,000 Germans immigrated to the area between 1683 and 1783.

The majority of Germans headed for the backcountry of Pennsylvania. They brought with them new farming techniques, such as providing shelter for their animals in the winter. Some farmers used indentured servants and enslaved people to tend their fields. As the settlers grew wealthier, they sold more of their harvest as cash crops and raised livestock for sale and export.

The residents of the breadbasket enjoyed more prosperous lives than farmers in New England. Unfortunately, there was a cost—though not directly to the settlers. Their growing farms continued to edge out the Native Americans who lived on the land.

GRIST FOR THE MILL

Many Middle Colony farmers grew grains, and wheat was the most popular grain in colonial America. The plant made a finer flour than corn, which in turn produced softer bread. Colonists enjoyed wheat bread with their meals, but making the flour required grinding. Grinding the grain by hand took a long time and resulted in flour that was rough in texture. Farmers found they could save time and energy by taking their wheat to a **gristmill**, a building that housed machinery for grinding grain.

Since human and animal labor was in short supply in the Middle Colonies, many colonists built their gristmills near a river and harnessed the power of water to operate the gristmill. At that time, water mills were the latest technology. The water spun a wheel outside that turned grinding stones within the gristmill.

Workers called millers ran the gristmills and generally took a portion of the flour they ground as payment. They also took other goods in exchange. Some millers opened stores to sell the surplus flour, grain, or other goods. These stores became the centers of communities. Neighbors would gather there to exchange goods and catch up on news. As demand grew, some millers bought larger mills or moved their mill to a spot on the river with a faster current.

But not all of the immigrants who came to the Middle Colonies became farmers or millers. Some settled in the cities hoping to find greater opportunities in the fast-growing coastal towns.

How a Gristmill Works

With the exception of a few metal parts and the stone grinding blocks, most colonial gristmills were made of wood. Some had foundations of stone. A channel called a millrace was dug from a stream or river to direct fast-running water to the waterwheel. Water falling from the millrace turned the wheel. The moving waterwheel then turned gears inside the building, which rotated the top grinding block. This block could be raised and lowered to vary its closeness to the bottom block, depending upon the size of the grain being ground between the stones. As the top block turned, it pressed and rolled the grains, cracking away the hard outer layers and grinding all the parts into soft flour.

grain

sluicegate

hopper

top stone (rotates)

millrace

bedstone (stays still)

flour

waterwheel

HISTORICAL THINKING

1. **READING CHECK** Why were farmers in the Middle Colonies able to raise cash crops and livestock for sale and export?

2. **IDENTIFY MAIN IDEAS AND DETAILS** Why were the Middle Colonies called the "breadbasket of the colonies"?

3. **ANALYZE VISUALS** Use the diagram to explain how the flour got into the sacks.

PLAN

Objective
Discover why and how the Middle Colonies were able to create a thriving economy.

Critical Thinking Skills for Lesson 3.1
- Identify Main Ideas and Details
- Monitor Comprehension
- Analyze Visuals
- Compare and Contrast
- Draw Conclusions

Essential Question for Chapter 4
How did a developing American identity unite the colonies? The fertile soil of the Middle Colonies attracted farmers from all over Europe. Lesson 3.1 explores how these settlers created a booming agricultural economy.

Background for the Teacher

Two main types of vertical waterwheels were used in colonial gristmills: overshot and undershot. The illustration shows an overshot wheel. In an overshot mill, the water that turned the wheel ran over the top of the wheel. This was the most efficient wheel, since it used anywhere from 50 to 70 percent of the water's energy. It also had the potential to generate the most horsepower. In an undershot mill, the water ran under the wheel. It was less efficient, using only about 15 to 30 percent of the water's energy. The millwright had to decide which size and type of wheel would be best for the mill's location, what types of paddles or buckets to use on the wheel, and where to place the millraces. Millwrights also often had to design dams and millponds to hold water during dry periods.

INTRODUCE & ENGAGE

Preview Using Visuals

Direct students' attention to the illustration. Ask them to read the text describing the gristmill's operation. **ASK:** What was the purpose of the gristmill? *(It ground grain into flour.)* What does the inclusion of the diagram in this lesson tell you about farming in the Middle Colonies? *(Students might indicate that farmers in the Middle Colonies must have grown grain crops.)* Tell students that in this lesson they will learn about the use of gristmills in agricultural production in the Middle Colonies.

TEACH

Guided Discussion

1. **Compare and Contrast** How did the Middle Colonies differ from New England and the Southern Colonies in terms of geography and agriculture-based economic activity? *(Answers will vary. Possible response: The climate of the Middle Colonies was warmer than New England but not as hot and sticky as the Southern Colonies. Unlike New England's rocky soil, the Middle Colonies' soil was fertile and farmland was plentiful. Farmers could meet their own needs and have surplus grain to sell or export. Unlike the Southern Colonies, which relied on slave labor to raise cash crops, only some Middle Colonies used enslaved people or indentured servants to work the fields.)*

2. **Draw Conclusions** How might millers and gristmills in the Middle Colonies have been important to westward expansion? *(Answers will vary. Students may point out that flour was easier to transport than whole grain. If farmers who settled farther west had access to a local gristmill, they could grind their surplus grain and bring the flour to markets along the coast. Also, stores opened by millers to sell their surplus flour, grain, or other goods supported the development and growth of western communities.)*

More Information

Colonists and Technology Much of the colonial economy was based on furs, fish, forests, and farms. European colonists brought technology with them that helped them establish a fur trade and fishing and logging industries. Shipbuilders brought knowledge about how to build and sail ships. Farmers brought hand tools, domesticated animals, new crops, and waterwheel technology. Colonial water-powered technology originated in the Old World, and water-powered mills, such as the gristmill and later textile mills, would eventually transform a colonial economy into an international, industrialized economy.

Active Options

On Your Feet: Create a Quiz Organize students into two teams and have each team write five True-False statements about agricultural production in the Middle Colonies. Then have each team respond to the statements created by the other team. Review student answers as a class and have teams keep track of their correct answers.

NG Learning Framework: Diagram Grain's Path from Field to Table `STEM`

`ATTITUDE` Curiosity

`KNOWLEDGE` New Frontiers

Have students use the information in the lesson and additional research to trace the path that grain might have taken to get from a farm in the Middle Colonies into a loaf of bread on a table in Britain. Tell students to use their research to make a list of the steps the grain had to go through and then use their list to create a diagram tracing the path. Hang the diagrams on a wall and have students discuss the differences between them.

DIFFERENTIATE

Striving Readers

Summarize Have students work in pairs, and assign each student a paragraph to read aloud. The partner should summarize what he or she hears in one or two spoken sentences. Encourage students to ask each other questions as they come across complex information.

English Language Learners `ELD`

PREP Before Reading Instruct students to use the PREP strategy to prepare for reading. Write this acrostic on the board.

PREP **P**review title.

Read the Main Idea statement.

Examine visuals.

Predict what you will learn.

Tell students to write their prediction and share it with a partner. Provide students at the **Emerging** level with the following sentence stem: *I think this lesson is about _____.* Ask students at the **Bridging** level to give reasons for their prediction. After reading, ask students at **All Proficiencies** to write another sentence that begins: *I also learned _____.*

See the Chapter Planner for more strategies for differentiation.

HISTORICAL THINKING

ANSWERS

1. The region had fertile soil and a climate in which grains such as wheat, corn, rye, and barley thrived. Also, the settlers brought farming techniques from Europe that helped them tend their crops and livestock.

2. It was called the "breadbasket of the colonies" because grains used to make bread, such as wheat, corn, rye, and barley, thrived in the region.

3. Answers will vary. Possible response: Grain was poured into the hopper, where it flowed to the grinding blocks. Water flowed down the millrace to turn the waterwheel. The waterwheel then turned gears inside the building, which rotated the top stone to grind the grain into flour. The flour fell through a chute into the flour bags.

3.2 A Diverse Society

What would you look for if you were searching for a new homeland? You might look for a place that was prosperous and productive and tolerant of differences. For many immigrants, the Middle Colonies seemed like such a place.

MAIN IDEA In addition to being economically successful, the Middle Colonies were culturally diverse.

GROWTH OF CITIES

A stream of settlers, hungry for new opportunities, moved to cities along the Atlantic coast, especially the ports of New York City and Philadelphia. As the colonies produced more and more goods, trade from these ports also grew, and people could find a variety of work in the cities.

Founded in 1681, Philadelphia was the fastest-growing city in the colonies. It started out as a village on the Delaware River and grew to more than 2,000 people in 1700. By 1760, the population had rocketed to roughly 23,000 people, outstripping New York and Boston. The city thrived on crops and trade. Philadelphia's merchants forged relationships with farmers who needed to sell their wheat, livestock, and lumber and with dealers who wanted to market these **commodities**, or goods, in the West Indies and elsewhere.

Philadelphia was an attractive city. Pennsylvania's founder, William Penn, drew up plans for Philadelphia while establishing his own colony. He conceived the city as a large "green country town," with wide streets in a grid pattern, public parks, ample lots, and brick houses.

One of Philadelphia's most famous brick buildings is Independence Hall, which was called the Pennsylvania State House when it was first established in 1753.

Meanwhile, New York City was also expanding. The English acquired the city in 1664 as part of their takeover of the Dutch colony New Netherland. The brick houses with low-sloping tile roofs that lined the city's cobblestoned streets looked exactly like those in Dutch towns. As the city expanded, the English made their mark by building houses of brick and wood in their own style.

After the English took over the city, New York merchants maintained ties with the Netherlands and its colony, the Dutch West Indies. They continued to ship grain, flour, dried fish, timber, and other goods to Amsterdam. Because of these ties, New York City's population more than doubled between 1720 and 1760.

American Products
Cities in the colonies wouldn't have grown without the work of artisans like Cornelius Kierstede of New York. He made this silver teapot around 1720. He shaped the spout into the form of a bird and engraved the purchaser's initials into the side.

AMERICAN PLACES
Philadelphia Rowhouses
The houses of Society Hill date to around 1690. Rowhouses like these helped support the growing number of people living near the busy docks where goods were traded.

VARIETY OF IMMIGRANTS

When the English took possession of New Netherland, it was already home to the Dutch, Swedes, Finns, Norwegians, French Protestants, Jews, and other settlers. This **diversity**, or wide variety of people, was partly due to the Dutch, who had opened immigration to many different groups. It made the population of the Middle Colonies unique among the regions of America.

After the English takeover, most new immigrants came from England and Germany. German artisans created the Pennsylvania long rifle for hunting. They also designed the **Conestoga wagon**, which was capable of carrying up to four tons of cargo. Other German artisans were ironworkers and makers of glass, furniture, and kitchenware.

The farmland and cities drew immigrants to the Middle Colonies. But immigrants also came to enjoy something that was much less concrete but, perhaps, even more important: religious freedom.

HISTORICAL THINKING

1. **READING CHECK** What ideas or events caused the populations of Philadelphia and New York City to change over time?

2. **COMPARE AND CONTRAST** What caused the population of the Middle Colonies to differ from that of New England and the Southern Colonies?

3. **IDENTIFY MAIN IDEAS AND DETAILS** How did German immigrants contribute to the success of the Middle Colonies?

PLAN

Objective

Understand why the Middle Colonies were economically successful and culturally diverse.

Critical Thinking Skills for Lesson 3.2

- Identify Main Ideas and Details
- Monitor Comprehension
- Compare and Contrast
- Synthesize
- Make Connections

Essential Question for Chapter 4

How did a developing American identity unite the colonies? The Middle Colonies were home to a culturally diverse population that came together in the pursuit of economic opportunities and religious freedom. Lesson 3.2 explores the diverse societies that developed in the Middle Colonies.

Background for the Teacher

The Conestoga wagon takes its name from the area where it was developed—the Conestoga Creek region in Pennsylvania. German immigrants designed the wagon to carry goods to market over rough roads. Its floor was curved to keep cargo from sliding around while going over bumps or hills. Its large, broad wheels smoothed the ride, and its hooped canvas cover kept the freight dry during bad weather. Four or five stout horses could pull a Conestoga wagon, but six horses were often used to haul heavy loads. In addition to employing drivers, the wagons also created jobs for blacksmiths, wheelwrights, and wagon builders, who took great pride in their creations.

Word Map

Tell students to discuss the meaning of the word *diversity*. Begin by adding the word to the center of a Word Map. Complete the Word Map during classroom discussion. Discuss the word's root and use a dictionary, if necessary. Revisit this activity at the end of the lesson to complete the Word Map with any missing details.

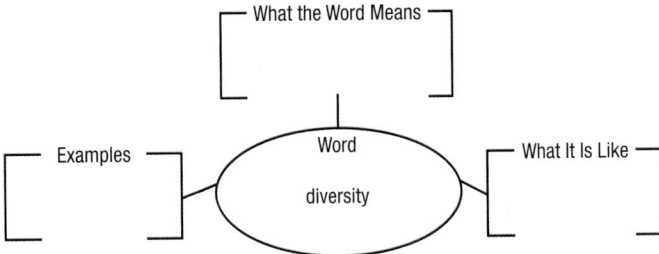

TEACH

Guided Discussion

1. **Synthesize** How did merchants forge ties that helped Philadelphia and New York City thrive? *(Philadelphia merchants connected frontier farmers selling wheat, livestock, and lumber with markets overseas. New York City merchants maintained ties with the Netherlands and the Dutch West Indies even after the English acquired the city. As a result, they were able to find additional markets for goods produced in the colony. In both cases, the cities thrived because of these economic ties.)*

2. **Make Connections** How do you think cultural diversity affects the attitudes of the residents of a particular location? Why do you think so? *(Answers will vary. Possible response: People who live in areas of greater diversity are exposed to a wide variety of cultures and many different points of view. They are therefore more likely to be open-minded about the differences between people.)*

American Places

In 1682, William Penn awarded land to the Free Society of Traders, a company that promoted business in Pennsylvania. Residents soon began referring to the land as "the Society's Hill." By 1776, the area was home to an ethnically and economically diverse population. Wealthy members of the community built mansions and grand rowhouses. Smaller structures housed servants and workers. In 1958, the neighborhood was officially named Society Hill to commemorate its history, and today it is listed on the Philadelphia Register of Historic Places and the National Register of Historic Places.

Active Options

On Your Feet: Inside-Outside Circle Arrange students in concentric circles facing each other. Tell students in the outside circle to ask students in the inside circle a question about the lesson. After students answer, have the outside circle rotate one position to the right to create new pairings. After five questions, have students switch roles and continue.

NG Learning Framework: Explore Colonial Cities

SKILL Collaboration

KNOWLEDGE Our Human Story

Invite students to work in pairs or small groups to research colonial Philadelphia and New York City. Assign each group a topic, such as Penn's grid system for Philadelphia, housing and architectural styles, employment opportunities, or major commodities. Encourage students to use their research to create a brochure or multimedia presentation for the class. Tell students to be prepared to answer questions their classmates might have about their findings.

Inclusion

Clarify Text Pair visually impaired students with sighted partners. As they listen to an audio recording of the text, have the visually impaired students indicate if there are words or passages they do not understand. Their partners can clarify meanings by repeating passages, emphasizing context clues, and paraphrasing.

Pre-AP STEM

Create a Graph Tell students to use historical census data from the U.S. Census Bureau website to create a graph comparing population growth in Philadelphia, New York City, and Boston from 1730 to 1790. Encourage students to share their graphs with the class and discuss the population growth.

See the Chapter Planner for more strategies for differentiation.

HISTORICAL THINKING

ANSWERS

1. Philadelphia and New York City grew rapidly because they were port cities with a growing trade in cash crops and other commodities. As such, they attracted many settlers hoping to take advantage of the wide variety of opportunities.

2. Answers will vary. Possible response: The open immigration policies of the Dutch in New York City and religious tolerance in Pennsylvania caused the population in the Middle Colonies to be much more diverse than other regions.

3. Answers will vary. Possible response: German immigrants helped make the Middle Colonies successful through the technical and artistic skills and knowledge they brought from Europe. For example, German immigrants created the Pennsylvania long rifle and the Conestoga wagon, brought their ironworking skills to the colonies, and produced furniture, kitchenware, and glassware.

3.3 Cultures of the Middle Colonies

You probably know this from your own experience with your classmates: Things just go better if you try to get along. For the most part, that's what people in the Middle Colonies discovered, too.

MAIN IDEA While the Middle Colonies made an honest attempt to tolerate different religions, tensions still existed between different races.

Quaker Meeting, by an unidentified British artist, c. 1700–1825

RELIGIOUS TOLERANCE

With people from all walks of life pouring into the Middle Colonies, neighbors needed to show religious **tolerance**, or acceptance of others, in order to establish community. This open-mindedness was part of the legacy of the Dutch. In the Netherlands, Jews practiced their religion freely and became citizens. The Dutch also welcomed many Protestant groups not recognized by the church, including Puritans, Quakers, and Lutherans. In fact, the Pilgrims who settled at Plymouth, Massachusetts, had originally gone to live in the city of Leiden in the Netherlands because of the religious tolerance they found there. The Dutch carried their practice of tolerance across the sea to New Netherland, where it continued after the English took over.

Less than 100 miles away, William Penn founded Pennsylvania as a free colony—not just for Quakers, but for other religions as well. He promised equal rights and opportunities. As a result, the colony attracted many different Protestant faiths, including the Amish. This group emphasized personal faith and a simple life. They also valued humility and submission.

Quakers believed all people were equal in the eyes of God. They saw religion as a personal matter, and they did not demand **conformity**, or obedience, to a strict set of beliefs. Quakers were also the first group in America to ban slaveholding.

TENSIONS BETWEEN RACES

But most people in the Middle Colonies didn't share the Quakers' view. When the English acquired New Netherland in 1664, an estimated 20 percent of the population was African. The Dutch West India Company provided "half freedom" to older enslaved Africans. This meant that the company released the older slaves, but not their children, from slavery. Other slaves worked for wages to buy their freedom. As a result, by 1664, one-fifth of all Africans were free. But tolerance for diversity did not extend to these Africans and African Americans, whether they were free or slaves.

Most African Americans in the Middle Colonies lived in New York City. By 1711, about 40 percent of white households there had at least one slave. Many enslaved people were skilled workers and lived and worked next to free and indentured whites.

Enslaved African Americans whose owners had run out of tasks for them often sought work on their own, looking for paid work throughout New York. However, the sight of so many African Americans on the streets of New York made white people fearful. A law was put into effect requiring that all hiring of slaves be done at one place, the slave market. This put still more restrictions on the lives of the African Americans, and in turn, white people began to worry about a slave rebellion.

These fears became reality on the night of April 6, 1712, when about 20 enslaved people set fire to a building, attacking the white men who came to put it out. Nine white people were killed, and terror spread up and down the Atlantic coast.

As in the case of later slave revolts and conspiracies, the revenge taken on the African-American community far outweighed any violence the rebels had committed. In the wake of the New York revolt, 13 enslaved African Americans were hanged, 3 were burned at the stake, 1 was tortured, and another starved to death in chains.

Some white colonists, however, questioned the morality of slavery. Wasn't it a violation of the Bible's golden rule, which says to act toward others as you want others to act toward you? A person who enslaves another certainly would not like to be enslaved in return. Other whites opposed slavery simply because they feared slave rebellions. Despite these considerations, slavery became a part of early American culture and would remain so for more than 150 years.

🏛 Museum of Fine Arts, Boston

Like many Protestant groups, Quakers did not have a paid clergy. Instead, they believed every individual should decide how to worship. People sat silently at Quaker meetings, thinking and praying, until they felt that God moved them to speak. They wore plain clothes and spoke plainly, even to nobility. This painting by an unknown artist from the late 1700s or early 1800s captures the feeling of a Quaker meeting.

HISTORICAL THINKING

1. **READING CHECK** How did the Dutch colonists show tolerance for religious diversity in New Netherland?

2. **MAKE INFERENCES** Why do you think Quakers accepted other religions and races?

3. **EVALUATE** The text claims that "the revenge taken on the African-American community far outweighed any violence the rebels had committed." What evidence supports this?

Objective

Learn about religious tolerance and racial tension in the Middle Colonies.

Critical Thinking Skills for Lesson 3.3

- Identify Main Ideas and Details
- Monitor Comprehension
- Make Inferences
- Evaluate
- Make Connections
- Form and Support Opinions

Essential Question for Chapter 4

How did a developing American identity unite the colonies? The Middle Colonies were ethnically, religiously, and racially diverse. Lesson 3.3 explores the extent and limits of religious and racial tolerance in the region.

Background for the Teacher

In establishing Pennsylvania, William Penn hoped to provide a haven for Quakers. Quakers had faced persecution in England because they would not pay tithes for church support or attend Anglican services. Penn conceived of his colony as a "holy experiment," a place where Quakers could exercise their beliefs without interference. The Swedes, Dutch, and Finns already living in the region integrated with the new Quaker arrivals, though not without friction. These "old residents" became naturalized as English subjects, but they continued to worship in their own congregations. The old residents were concentrated in the southern part of the colony, and in 1704, after two decades of conflict, the three southern counties formed their own separate Delaware assembly.

INTRODUCE & ENGAGE

Explore Concepts

Display the Concept Web shown here. Discuss the concept of tolerance with the class. Have students think about the benefits and challenges of practicing tolerance in a diverse community. Then call on volunteers to share their thoughts. Record the responses in the circles of the Concept Web. Tell students that in this lesson they will learn about religious and racial tolerance in the Middle Colonies.

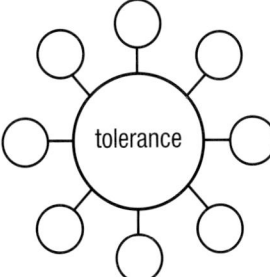

tolerance

TEACH

Guided Discussion

1. **Make Connections** Why was it important for people in the Middle Colonies to practice religious tolerance? *(Answers will vary. Possible response: People from many different religions lived in the Middle Colonies, including Quakers, Amish, and other Protestant faiths, as well as Jews. With this much diversity, tolerance was necessary to prevent conflict and establish a successful community.)*

2. **Form and Support Opinions** How might the New York slave market law and the South Carolina slave code you learned about in Lesson 2.3 have had similar effects on free African Americans in both regions? *(Answers will vary. Possible response: Both laws placed restrictions on African Americans. The New York law restricted their movement and made it more difficult to find employment. The South Carolina slave code restricted enslaved people from learning to read and write and made slavery permanent.)*

Virtual Museum Visit

Boston's Museum of Fine Arts has nearly 500,000 works of art in its collections. *Quaker Meeting* is part of its European collection. Access the museum's website and search for *Quaker Meeting.* Point out the top bench in the painting. Note that the top bench was reserved for the elders, those members with a gift for ministry. **ASK:** What can you tell about who could be an elder from the painting? *(Both men and women could be elders.)* Point out the hat hanging on the wall. Note that colonial Quakers took off their hats when they felt they were in the presence of God. **ASK:** What can you infer about the man who is standing? *(He might feel he is in the presence of God.)* Have students use the close-up details of the painting to make other inferences about colonial Quaker meetings.

Active Options

On Your Feet: Tell Me More Have students form four groups. Assign each group one of the following topics: Dutch legacy, Quakers' views, enslaved and free African Americans, or slave rebellions. Each group should write down as many facts about its topic as it can. Have the class reconvene and have each group stand up, one at a time. The class calls out "Tell me more about [the topic]." The group recites one fact. The class continues to request a fact until the group runs out of facts to share. Then the next group presents its facts.

NG Learning Framework: Discuss Quaker Opposition to Slavery

ATTITUDE Curiosity

KNOWLEDGE Our Human Story

Assign students to small groups. Ask members of each group to research the role of Quakers in the early abolitionist movement in colonial America. Have students write short sentences describing what they learned. Use the sentences as the basis of a class discussion on religious efforts to overturn slavery.

DIFFERENTIATE

Striving Readers

Make Lists Have students work in pairs. Post the title "What I Learned About Tolerance in the Middle Colonies." Ask each pair to copy the title and then work together to list facts they learned from the lesson. Encourage students to share their lists with the class.

Gifted & Talented

Prepare an Interview Invite pairs of students to use online sources to read, discuss, and analyze information about the slave rebellion that occurred in New York City on April 6, 1712. Then ask them to imagine they could interview a witness to the event or its aftermath. Tell students to come up with 10 questions to ask about the rebellion or its aftermath. Pairs should then take turns sharing several of their questions and answers with the class.

See the Chapter Planner for more strategies for differentiation.

HISTORICAL THINKING

ANSWERS

1. The Dutch in New Netherland carried over tolerant practices from the Netherlands: Jews were able to practice their religion freely and become citizens, and many Protestant dissenters were welcomed.

2. Answers will vary. Possible response: Quakers believed that all people were equal in the eyes of God and that religion was a personal matter. Religious and racial tolerance supported their ideals of equality and individuality.

3. Answers will vary. Possible response: Only 9 white people were killed during the revolt, but 13 slaves were hanged, 3 burned at the stake, 1 tortured, and another starved to death in chains.

Colonial Men and Women

As a girl, can you imagine rights reserved only for boys? As a boy, can you imagine being denied rights because of your family's lack of wealth? That's the way it was in the colonies.

| MAIN IDEA Rights and wealth were not evenly distributed across religions, social classes, races, and genders in colonial American society.

RIGHTS AND WEALTH

Between 1720 and 1763, the diverse American population experienced changes in many aspects of their lives. In science, doctors made strides in understanding how diseases spread. People reexamined traditions and laws. The changes spread throughout the colonies.

However, other ideas were resistant to change. Voting was restricted to white men—and to a select group. Only landowning men could vote. But there were exceptions. Men who were Catholic or Jewish were denied the vote based on religion. Servants, slaves, and men without property were also barred. Men with a small amount of land or personal property had to pay to vote.

Although land was plentiful and industry booming, wealth in the colonies was not evenly distributed. This was especially visible in the cities. Fabulously wealthy merchants built mansions and bought coaches with income from trade with other nations or colonies. Less fortunate city dwellers worked for low wages or lacked employment altogether. For instance, seamen and artisans who relied on trade could be out of a job if the demand for goods decreased. In addition, the **burgeoning**, or quickly growing, towns lacked sanitation, putting many people at risk from the spread of disease.

ROLE OF WOMEN

Life was tough for both colonial men and women, but the women had even fewer choices. In rural areas, white wives cooked, cleaned, sewed, reared children, and helped with farm tasks. Many also made candles, soap, and other items to sell or exchange for goods. Most African-American

women were enslaved. They worked in the fields, cooked, cleaned, and tended to the slaveholder's family. Only the wives of plantation owners led an easy life. They supervised the household slaves and servants and oversaw meal preparation.

In cities, women cared for their children and the household. Wealthier wives employed servants, and some depended on slaves. Some worked alongside their husbands in shops and businesses. Other women served as **midwives**, helping deliver babies. Poor women often made money by mending, washing, and ironing clothes or providing domestic services. Few women worked outside the home.

Women had few legal rights throughout most of the colonial period. They could not vote. They lost the right to manage their property and earn a living once they married. Many women relied on the church for their social life. Soon, all colonists would be asked to pay more attention to their spiritual lives as well.

HISTORICAL THINKING

1. **READING CHECK** What requirements did a person have to meet to be eligible to vote in colonial America?

2. **IDENTIFY MAIN IDEAS AND DETAILS** What details support the idea that wealth was not evenly distributed in colonial American cities?

3. **ANALYZE VISUALS** Which household task may have posed the biggest problem for colonial women? Use the information in the visual to explain your answer.

BOX IRON

Easy-care fabrics did not exist in colonial times, so ironing was an essential part of laundry, which was hard work at every stage. The box iron had a hatch in the back where the woman inserted a hot metal piece called a slug. One slug sat on the fire until the one in the iron cooled. Then the woman switched them.

The first **electric iron** was introduced in 1882.

handle
hatch lever
hatch door
hatch
slug
box
soleplate
slug heated in the fire
slug placed in box

ALL IN A DAY'S WORK

In the days before electricity and grocery stores, colonial women—and, later, the women of early national America—labored to maintain their homes and families. There was cream to churn into butter, and there were fires to stoke and clothes to iron, along with all the other aspects of making sure the family was fed and warm.

BUTTER CHURN

For a colonial woman, making butter began with milking a cow. The milk sat in a container until the cream rose to the top. Then the woman skimmed off the cream and put it into a butter churn. She moved the dasher up and down and in circles, churning the cream. After what could be minutes or hours, butter formed, along with buttermilk. The final step was to strain the butter to separate the two.

The first U.S. **butter factory** opened in 1856.

dasher
splasher top
cream
plunger disc

BED WARMER

Heat from the fireplace of a colonial home did not spread from room to room. If the house couldn't be heated, however, the beds could. A colonial woman filled the pan of a bed warmer with glowing coals and took it from room to room. She moved the pan around under the covers to distribute the heat evenly. Then she went along to the next bed.

The first **electric blanket** was introduced in 1912.

holes to vent
hot coals, rocks, or brick

PLAN

Objective

Learn how race, gender, and religion affected the colonists' rights and ability to gain wealth.

Critical Thinking Skills for Lesson 4.1

- Identify Main Ideas and Details
- Monitor Comprehension
- Analyze Visuals
- Compare and Contrast

Essential Question for Chapter 4

How did a developing American identity unite the colonies? A colonist's rights and opportunity for wealth were largely determined by his or her religion, race, gender, and social class. Lesson 4.1 examines the uneven distribution of rights and property in colonial society.

Background for the Teacher

Colonial leaders believed voting was both a right and an important civic obligation. But many leaders also believed it was a right that was best limited to white men who had a vested interest in society. That vested interest came from the ownership of a significant amount of land or personal property or from the payment of taxes. The reasoning behind this view was that if a person owned property and paid taxes, he had enough resources to be an independent thinker and would be genuinely interested in the success of the community. Wage earners and the landless, on the other hand, were beholden to other people, such as employers and wealthy landlords, and thus might be swayed by their influence.

Discuss Voting Rights

Generate a discussion about voting rights. **ASK:** How should a society decide who can vote? Tell students to write answers to this question, answering in as many ways as they can. When they have finished writing, encourage volunteers to share their ideas, and write those ideas on the board. Explain that this lesson will examine how the colonies decided who could—and could not—vote.

TEACH

Guided Discussion

1. **Identify Main Ideas and Details** What details support the idea that some segments of society had few legal rights? *(Male servants and slaves, men without property, Catholic and Jewish men, and women could not vote. Married women could not manage their own property or earn a living.)*

2. **Compare and Contrast** How were the roles of white women in rural areas and cities similar and different? *(Possible responses: Women always took care of the home and children. In rural areas, women also helped with farm tasks, and many made items, such as soap, to sell or exchange. In cities, some women made money by mending, doing laundry, or providing other domestic services. Wives may have worked in their husbands' shops or businesses.)*

Make Connections

Direct students' attention to the items pictured in the All in a Day's Work feature. Tell them to read the captions to understand the steps and time involved in the use of each item. **ASK:** How does the information contained in the feature help you understand how daily life in colonial America was different from daily life in the United States today? *(Answers will vary but should reflect the fact that much more time needed to be spent on domestic chores in colonial times.)* Conduct a class discussion about how having to spend more time on simple chores would alter students' lives.

Active Options

On Your Feet: Turn and Talk on Topic Arrange students into three to five groups. Give each group this topic sentence: Women in colonial American society had fewer rights, freedoms, and options than men. Tell students to build a paragraph on that topic by having each student in the group contribute one sentence. Allow each group to present its paragraph to the class by having each student read her or his statement.

NG Learning Framework: Research Women's Work Roles in Colonial America

SKILL Communication

KNOWLEDGE Our Human Story

Invite students to learn more about the kinds of work women in colonial America performed. Instruct small groups of students to conduct research to prepare a short oral presentation about the role colonial women filled in health care as doctors, nurses, midwives, and apothecaries who grew plants and made medicines. Encourage students to include at least one visual when they share their presentation with the class.

Inclusion

Narrate the Feature The All in a Day's Work feature might pose a challenge to the visually impaired. Ask students who are not visually challenged to narrate the photos and technical drawings by describing them in detail and discussing how colonial women used each item.

Pre-AP

Research the Spread of Scientific Ideas Tell students to investigate the smallpox epidemic that hit Boston in 1721. In their research, suggest that students read about the method and effectiveness of the inoculations. Invite students to share their findings with the class in a short oral report.

See the Chapter Planner for more strategies for differentiation.

ANSWERS

1. To be eligible to vote, a person had to be a white adult male landowner. Adult white men who owned only a little land or personal property had to pay a tax to vote.

2. Answers will vary. Possible response: Some merchants, wealthy from colonial and international trade, built mansions, owned coaches, and hired servants. Many city dwellers were unemployed or worked for low wages.

3. Answers will vary. Possible response: Churning butter was probably the most complicated task because of the number of steps and time necessary. It required milking cows, setting the milk, skimming off cream, and then churning and straining to separate the butter.

Great Awakening and Enlightenment

Have you ever listened to someone who made you think about a familiar topic in a new way? Something like that happened to colonists in the early 1700s and reawakened their dedication to religion.

MAIN IDEA The Enlightenment, emphasizing reason, and the Great Awakening, a religious renewal, helped shape colonial thought.

Church of England minister George Whitefield appealed to many races and classes with his promise of a more equal, or egalitarian, relationship between believers and their God. Here, artist John Collet portrays a meeting during one of Whitefield's seven visits to the colonies. The painting dates to the mid-1700s.

THE GREAT AWAKENING

You probably remember that many of the first colonists came to America to seek religious freedom. But once they'd achieved it, they began to focus on the material concerns of everyday life. People concentrated on their work and their homes. As a result, by the early 1700s, people's passion for religion had begun to die down. Some even stopped going to church regularly.

Many Protestant ministers feared that colonists were losing sight of the importance of God. In an effort to inspire people to recommit to their spiritual beliefs, these ministers gave stirring—and sometimes frightening—sermons during a series of religious revivals known as the **Great Awakening**.

One of the most effective of these ministers was **Jonathan Edwards** of Massachusetts. In 1734, he began preaching sermons on **salvation**, or the deliverance from sin. In his most famous sermon, "Sinners in the Hands of an Angry God," Edwards compared his listeners to spiders. God, he said, held them by a string over the fires of hell. If they failed to seek salvation, he warned, God would simply let go of the string.

Another minister, **George Whitefield**, came from Britain to preach salvation to the colonists. With his theatrical gestures and thundering words, he appealed to people's emotions and brought them to tears. Some even fainted.

The revivals of the Great Awakening changed how people viewed religion and morality. People began to believe they did not need church officials to

A Ray of Hope

Jonathan Edwards delivered "Sinners in the Hands of an Angry God" in 1741 to a congregation in Connecticut. Unlike George Whitefield, Edwards spoke in a quiet voice and used few gestures, but his message caused near-hysteria in his listeners. In this excerpt from the sermon, after threatening his audience with damnation, Edwards offers them a chance to be saved. How do you think Edwards's listeners responded to his words of hope?

PRIMARY SOURCE

And now you have an extraordinary opportunity, a day wherein Christ has thrown the door of mercy wide open, and stands in the door calling and crying with a loud voice to poor sinners. How awful is it to be left behind at such a day! To see so many rejoicing and singing for joy of heart, while you have cause to mourn for sorrow of heart. How can you rest one moment in such a condition? Therefore let every one that is out of Christ [that has not accepted Christ], now awake and fly from the wrath [fury] to come.

—from "Sinners in the Hands of an Angry God," by Jonathan Edwards, 1741

connect with God. Even more dangerously, they began to challenge authority and think themselves equal to those in power.

THE ENLIGHTENMENT

The Great Awakening was not the only movement that helped pave the way for revolutionary fervor. The intellectual movement known as the **Enlightenment** spread from Great Britain to the colonies in the 1700s. Enlightenment thinkers believed that the "light" of human reason would shatter the "darkness" of ignorance, superstition, and unfair authority. In part, they were influenced by the **Scientific Revolution**, which began in Europe around the mid-1550s and used logical thinking to answer scientific questions. The Enlightenment encouraged people to use logic and ask questions instead of just accepting what religious and political figures told them.

The ideas of **John Locke**, a 17th-century English philosopher, greatly influenced Enlightenment thought. Locke asserted that humans were born free and equal with **natural rights**, or rights such as life or liberty that a person is born with. He

also claimed that a leader could rule only with the consent of the people. If a ruler failed to protect the people's rights, Locke believed they had the right to overthrow him.

These ideas would prove hugely influential in the colonies. American Enlightenment leaders included Benjamin Franklin, who devoted his life to public service and science. In time, Franklin and many other American founders would start to demand their own rights and freedoms.

HISTORICAL THINKING

1. **READING CHECK** What was the Great Awakening?

2. **IDENTIFY MAIN IDEAS AND DETAILS** What were some of John Locke's beliefs?

3. **DRAW CONCLUSIONS** What did the Enlightenment and the Great Awakening contribute to colonial views about equality and government?

Colonial Development **149**

PLAN

Objective
Understand how the Great Awakening and the Enlightenment affected colonial society.

Critical Thinking Skills for Lesson 4.2
- Identify Main Ideas and Details
- Monitor Comprehension
- Draw Conclusions
- Make Inferences
- Analyze Visuals

Essential Question for Chapter 4
How did a developing American identity unite the colonies? The Great Awakening and the Enlightenment helped shape colonial views on religion, authority, and individual rights. Lesson 4.2 examines these two movements and their impact on colonial thinking.

Background for the Teacher
The Enlightenment arose out of earlier shifts in thinking that focused on reason, observation, and the importance of the individual. The most direct influence was the Scientific Revolution, which applied reason and observation to scientific inquiry, thereby challenging traditional religious-based views of nature. Enlightenment thinkers applied the same tools to the study of government and society. The Enlightenment also owed much to the humanism of the Renaissance and the focus on individual freedom and equality of the Reformation. Like the Scientific Revolution and the Renaissance, the Enlightenment also borrowed from classical Greek philosophers who emphasized logic and reason and from Roman philosophers who developed the idea of natural laws.

Complete a Concept Cluster

Tell students to draw a Concept Cluster such as the one shown. Assign the term *Great Awakening* to half the class and *Enlightenment* to the other half. Then ask students to identify associations that come to mind when they think of their assigned term. After students have individually written their associations, discuss their thoughts as a class. You might want to have them revisit and revise their Concept Clusters after they have read the lesson.

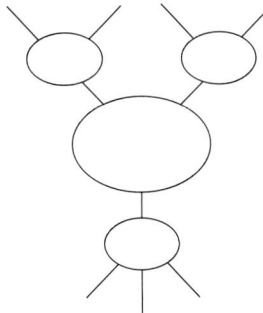

TEACH

Guided Discussion

1. **Draw Conclusions** Ask students to reread the excerpt from Jonathan Edwards's "Sinners in the Hands of an Angry God" sermon. What about the message might have led people to believe they did not need church officials to connect with God? *(Answers will vary. Possible response: Edwards reassures the congregation that all they need to do is accept Christ without church officials intervening on their behalf.)*

2. **Make Inferences** Why is the idea of natural rights associated with an egalitarian society? *(Answers will vary. Possible response: Natural rights mean that all people are born with the same rights, such as life and liberty, and should be free and equal in society, regardless of gender, race, or wealth.)*

Analyze Visuals

Direct students' attention to John Collet's painting of George Whitefield preaching. **ASK:** How does the crowd listening to Whitefield preach differ from the Quaker congregation in the painting in Lesson 3.3? *(Possible response: Whitefield is preaching outside to a crowd of men, women, and children who appear to be actively participating, sitting and standing together without regard to social rank or gender. The Quaker congregation is separated by gender and sits quietly in personal reflection.)*

Active Options

On Your Feet: Conduct Talk-Show Interviews Have teams of three students conduct talk show interviews on either the Great Awakening or the Enlightenment. Student 1, the interviewer, develops a question to ask Student 2, the show's guest and an expert on the movement. Student 2 answers, citing information from Lesson 4.2. Student 3, a member of the studio audience, asks a spin-off question that the whole class can answer. Have participants ask and answer several questions to ensure a solid review of the topic.

NG Learning Framework: Trace Influences on the Enlightenment

SKILL Collaboration

KNOWLEDGE Our Human Story

Invite students to work in small groups to trace the influences of classical Greek and Roman philosophers, Christianity, the Renaissance, the Reformation, and the Scientific Revolution on Enlightenment ideas. Ask students to share research tasks to assure that everyone participates. On a large sheet of chart paper or a whiteboard, have groups pool their findings to create a Concept Cluster displaying the influences.

DIFFERENTIATE

English Language Learners

Make Word Cards Help students of **All Proficiencies** make word cards for the proper nouns in Lesson 4.2. On each card, students should write the proper noun on one side. On the other side, they can list words or phrases related to the proper noun. Tell students to write a brief sentence on each card, using the proper noun in its appropriate context. You may wish to provide sentence stems for **Emerging** students.

Pre-AP

Research Charles-Louis Montesquieu Have students research Enlightenment thinker Charles-Louis Montesquieu to determine his views on government, the separation of governmental powers, the ways laws should be formed, and the nature of liberty. Instruct students to write a summary paragraph about each view. Encourage students to share and discuss their summaries.

See the Chapter Planner for more strategies for differentiation.

PRIMARY SOURCE

Answers will vary. Edwards' listeners might have been so relieved to hear a message of hope that they ran toward him, exclaimed their thanks aloud, or fell to their knees and praised God to be spared from God's wrath.

HISTORICAL THINKING

ANSWERS

1. The Great Awakening was a series of religious revivals that began in the 1730s. Ministers from various faiths used them to call for a return to church participation and a recommitment to spiritual beliefs.

2. Answers will vary. Possible response: John Locke argued that all humans were born with natural rights, such as life and liberty, that governments could rule only with consent of the people, and that people had a right to overthrow unjust rulers.

3. Answers will vary. Possible response: The Great Awakening invited people to connect with God without church officials and to think of themselves as equals with those in power or socially higher. Enlightenment thinkers emphasized reason and freedom over superstition and ignorance and encouraged people to challenge unjust authority to protect their natural rights.

4.3 Rights in England and the Colonies

The colonists considered themselves English and felt they were entitled to the same rights that the citizens of England enjoyed. And for a while, the English government let them think that.

MAIN IDEA Political changes in England that balanced the power between Parliament and the king helped set the American colonies on the path to democracy.

ENGLISH PARLIAMENT

Of course, the English themselves hadn't always enjoyed many rights. As you have learned, the Magna Carta, or Great Charter, began to change all that. The Magna Carta put protections in place to keep the English people from losing their freedom or property unless the law of the land ruled against them.

This important document helped give rise to **Parliament**, the legislative body of England, and later, Great Britain. Parliament consisted of two houses: the House of Lords, made up of nobles and high church officials, and the House of Commons, whose members were elected by male landowners.

Parliament's power grew in the late 1600s after clashing with King James II, who was a Catholic. Fearing James would make England a Catholic country under authoritarian rule, parliamentary leaders exiled him to France. They then invited his Protestant daughter, Mary, and her husband, William, to take the throne.

The Magna Carta and the Colonies
This stained glass in the Mansion House in London, England, home to the city's Lord Mayor, depicts the signing of the Magna Carta. The document established that the king was not above the law. Henry III, John's successor, reissued slightly revised Magna Cartas in 1216, 1217, and 1225. The 1225 version became English law in 1297. Hundreds of years later, the English colonists believed that they, too, possessed the rights guaranteed in the Magna Carta. During the American Revolution, colonists drew on principles in the Magna Carta for their Declaration of Independence and rebellion against the tyranny of King George III.

CRITICAL VIEWING James II was often in conflict with the Parliament in England and with the colonies. He revoked colonial charters from New Jersey to Maine and established the Dominion of New England. What details in this painting convey the king's high status?

At the same time, Parliament permanently limited the English monarch's power. It established Parliament's control of taxation, and its right to pass laws, and it also secured the independence of the courts. Parliament's consent was necessary for raising an army in peacetime and in the case of any foreign invasions. The bloodless overthrow of James II and the transferring of power to Parliament was called the Glorious Revolution. Parliament created the **English Bill of Rights of 1689** (more formally known as "An Act Declaring the Rights and Liberties of the Subject and Settling the Succession of the Crown") to officially protect the rights of English citizens and Parliament.

Many believed the balancing of powers would prevent a single individual or social group from becoming too dominant. Power shared by the king, the nobles, and the common people was thought to be the way to avoid more destructive forms of government that could threaten the liberty of some portion of the population.

COLONIAL ASSEMBLIES

The American colonies modeled their governments after Parliament by forming elected assemblies similar to the House of Commons. The colonial assemblies consisted of representatives elected by property owners. The assemblies could collect money through taxes and decide how to spend it.

Unlike the English legislature, however, elected officials in the assemblies lived in the area they represented. The colonists believed that representatives who lived among the people who elected them would better understand local interests and needs.

As colonists came to enjoy making decisions and managing some of their own affairs, they began to resent English authority. The colonists had no representatives in Parliament and sometimes felt they were treated unfairly—especially when Parliament passed laws the colonists didn't like.

For the most part, though, the English government was busy fighting foreign wars and dealing with disagreements within the country itself. So the government adopted a policy of **salutary neglect** toward the colonies. Under this policy, the English government did not strictly enforce its colonial policies. As a result, the colonies grew happily accustomed to living in relative isolation from British authority and largely governing themselves. They were generally content with British rule. But that state of affairs was about to change.

HISTORICAL THINKING

1. **READING CHECK** How did Parliament influence the growth of representative government in the colonies?

2. **SUMMARIZE** How did the Magna Carta pave the way for the English Bill of Rights?

3. **IDENTIFY MAIN IDEAS AND DETAILS** What rights did Parliament establish in the English Bill of Rights?

Objective

Discuss how English parliamentary traditions affected colonial views on government.

Critical Thinking Skills for Lesson 4.3

• Identify Main Ideas and Details
• Monitor Comprehension
• Summarize
• Analyze Cause and Effect
• Evaluate
• Ask and Answer Questions

Essential Question for Chapter 4

How did a developing American identity unite the colonies? Slowly pulling away from Parliament's grasp, colonies established assemblies to govern locally. Lesson 4.3 examines the history of English Parliament and the growth of a representative government in the colonies.

Background for the Teacher

The English Bill of Rights would have a major influence on drafting the Declaration of Independence and the Bill of Rights. In addition to establishing Parliament's rights and limiting the power of the monarchy, the English Bill of Rights outlined rights for citizens. For example, the document guaranteed the right to free elections and freedom of speech and debate in Parliament. It guaranteed Protestants the right to bear arms, a right they had been denied under the Catholic James II. It also guaranteed citizens the right to petition the monarch without fear of prosecution, limited the use of excessive bail and fines, set guidelines for juries, and prohibited levying fines and forfeitures before conviction. Some of these guarantees were first laid out in the Magna Carta.

INTRODUCE & ENGAGE

Activate Prior Knowledge

Invite students to share what they have already learned about the Magna Carta. Use their responses to complete a 5Ws Chart. Students might remember that the Magna Carta was a peace treaty signed in 1215 between rebelling barons and King John of England. The barons rebelled because of the heavy taxes the king had levied on them. The document included 63 laws that everyone was expected to follow and guaranteed the right to a fair trial. Tell students that they will learn more about the Magna Carta as they read about the history of English rights and law.

TEACH

Guided Discussion

1. **Analyze Cause and Effect** What events and concerns led Parliament to permanently limit the English monarch's power? *(Parliament fought with the Catholic James II during his authoritarian rule. Its leaders eventually exiled him and brought his Protestant daughter, Mary, and her husband, William, to the monarchy. To prevent another despotic monarchy, Parliament limited the monarch's power and took over key responsibilities of government, such as taxation and passing laws.)*

2. **Evaluate** How did the English government's policy of salutary neglect benefit the representative government in the American colonies? *(Salutary neglect meant that the English government did not strictly enforce its policies in the colonies, making it easier for the colonial assemblies to set policies about taxing and spending. Thus, a representative government was established.)*

Ask and Answer Questions

Direct students' attention to the photo of the Mansion House stained glass and its caption about the Magna Carta. **ASK:** Which version of the Magna Carta became English law, and when? *(The 1225 version became law in 1297.)* Why was such an old document of interest to the English colonists? *(They believed they possessed the rights outlined in the Magna Carta.)*

Active Options

On Your Feet: Identify Issues Divide students into four groups and have them move to different corners of the classroom. Ask each group to address the following question: How did political changes in England contribute to the beginnings of a democracy in the American colonies? Encourage students to consider the question individually and then discuss their responses as a group. Suggest that one person in the group act as the recorder. Then invite recorders to take turns stating their group's conclusions.

NG Learning Framework: Research the Magna Carta and English Bill of Rights

ATTITUDE Responsibility

KNOWLEDGE Our Human Story

Have students locate online copies of the 1225 version of the Magna Carta and the English Bill of Rights of 1689. Instruct them to work in pairs to develop a list of the rights contained in the documents that would be relevant to establishing a representative government in the 1700s. Point out that some points in the documents will be specific to the time and events that led to their creation and may not be relevant. Have student pairs come together to defend their choices and compile a master list of rights to share with the class.

DIFFERENTIATE

Striving Readers

Summarize Information Assign each paragraph in the English Parliament section to an individual student. Have each student read his or her paragraph independently and write a one- or two-sentence summary of the paragraph. Provide dictionaries and pronunciation help as necessary. Have students combine their paragraph summaries into a single summary for the section.

English Language Learners

Pose and Answer Questions Tell students at the **Emerging** level to work in pairs to read the lesson. Instruct them to pause after each paragraph and ask one another *who, what, when, where,* or *why* questions about what they have just read. Suggest students use a 5Ws Chart to help them organize the information.

See the Chapter Planner for more strategies for differentiation.

HISTORICAL THINKING

ANSWERS

1. The colonists modeled Parliament by forming elected colonial assemblies that were similar to the House of Commons.

2. The Magna Carta protected people from having their property and freedom taken away without due process of the law. By the time the English Bill of Rights was written, these rights were well established.

3. The English Bill of Rights gave Parliament the right to create taxes and pass laws, and it protected citizens' rights. It made the courts independent and prevented the monarch from raising an army and invading countries without Parliament's permission.

CRITICAL VIEWING Answers will vary. Possible response: James II is wearing a styled wig and a polished suit of armor and helmet, intricately decorated with gold and red trim. His scarf and shirt appear to be made of expensive materials, such as silk, velvet, and lace.

John Peter Zenger and Free Speech

Today, we expect talk show hosts to joke about politicians and criticize our government. We take for granted that people in the media are free to say what they want. That was not always the case in the colonies.

MAIN IDEA The trial of John Peter Zenger helped pave the way for freedom of the press.

LIBEL OR FREE SPEECH?

Under Great Britain's policy of salutary neglect, the colonists became used to determining what they could and couldn't do. In 1733 by British law, it was illegal to criticize the government in print. But **John Peter Zenger**, the publisher of the *New-York Weekly Journal*, did it anyway. In his newspaper, he printed a series of articles about the British colonial governor of New York, William Cosby. A few years before, Cosby had removed a judge who had ruled against him and then tried to rig, or tamper with the outcome of, an election.

Another person, a lawyer named James Alexander, wrote the articles, but his name didn't appear in the paper. Unable to determine the author, Cosby went after Zenger. Police arrested Zenger for **libel**, the publishing of lies, in November 1734. He remained in jail until his trial in August 1735.

Governor Cosby expected the trial to be an open and shut case. Any criticism of the government, true or not, was considered libel. The paper had definitely criticized the governor—there was no question about that—so as far as Cosby was concerned, the jury had to find Zenger guilty.

Andrew Hamilton, John Peter Zenger's lawyer, reasoned convincingly on Zenger's behalf. In this illustration from 1877, Hamilton makes his case before the judge.

High Court Upholds Students' Peaceful Protest

Free Speech Rights

Today, the U.S. Constitution protects almost all forms of free speech. In 1965 in Des Moines, Iowa, North High School suspended Mary Beth Tinker and her brother, John (shown here), for wearing armbands to mourn American soldiers who had been killed in the Vietnam War. They appealed, and the U.S. Supreme Court ruled that the right to free speech extends to students in school. The students were allowed to wear their armbands.

ZENGER CLEARED

Although he was confident of the outcome, Cosby didn't want to take any chances. He packed the jury with his own supporters. However, Zenger's wife Anna found out and revealed Cosby's misdeed in the *New-York Weekly Journal*, which she had continued to publish while her husband was in jail. The judge replaced Cosby's jury with a jury of colonists, but Zenger's problems continued. The judge dismissed Zenger's lawyers when they challenged the judge's authority. Meanwhile, Zenger's friends brought Andrew Hamilton, a famous Philadelphia lawyer, to take over the case.

Hamilton took a novel approach. He admitted that Zenger had printed articles criticizing Cosby. Hamilton argued, however, that the jury should consider the fact that the criticisms were true. Should Zenger be jailed for doing his job correctly as a newspaper publisher by printing the truth? Hamilton went on to argue that freedom of the press was especially important in the colonies because it acted as a check against the abuses of colonial governors. In his closing, Hamilton urged the jury to grant "that, to which Nature and the Laws of our Country have given us a Right, . . . both of exposing and opposing arbitrary Power . . . by speaking and writing Truth."

After a short time, the jury returned to the court with a verdict of not guilty, and Zenger was released. The victory paved the way to gaining freedom of the press. It also unified the colonists in their pursuit of their rights. But the colonists still considered themselves British citizens. Soon, they'd unite and join forces with Britain in war.

HISTORICAL THINKING

1. **READING CHECK** Why was John Peter Zenger charged with libel?

2. **IDENTIFY MAIN IDEAS AND DETAILS** Why did William Cosby assume that John Peter Zenger would be found guilty?

3. **SYNTHESIZE** How was the outcome of *Tinker* v. *Des Moines* similar to the outcome of Zenger's trial?

PLAN

Objective

Discuss the issues of free speech involved in the trial of John Peter Zenger.

Critical Thinking Skills for Lesson 4.4

- Identify Main Ideas and Details
- Monitor Comprehension
- Synthesize
- Summarize
- Draw Conclusions

Essential Question for Chapter 4

How did a developing American identity unite the colonies? Like British citizens, the colonists could not criticize government officials without facing charges of libel. Lesson 4.4 examines the outcome of the libel trial of John Peter Zenger.

Background for the Teacher

James Alexander was more than just a writer for the *New-York Weekly Journal*—he was the mastermind behind it. Alexander was part of a political organization that stood in opposition to Governor William Cosby. The organization needed a platform from which to attack Cosby. Since the only other paper in town, the *New York Gazette*, was being heavily censored by one of Cosby's cronies, Alexander approached John Peter Zenger with the proposal to launch the *New-York Weekly Journal*. Alexander also appeared to have intentionally advocated for free speech and a free press. He used the paper to reprint *Cato's Letters*, a series of essays by two British journalists who argued that free speech was an essential safeguard to liberty and that truth was a defense for libel. It is this defense that Andrew Hamilton used to defend Zenger.

INTRODUCE & ENGAGE

Define Terms

Write the terms *free speech* and *libel* on the board. Ask for volunteers to offer definitions of each, and write the definitions on the board. Once the terms are defined, ask the class to brainstorm a list of reasons why free speech is important in a democracy and a list of any limits they think a society should place on free speech. Ask students to discuss their lists. Tell them that issues of free speech were at the heart of John Peter Zenger's libel trial.

TEACH

Guided Discussion

1. **Summarize** How did Andrew Hamilton convince the jury that John Peter Zenger was not guilty? *(Answers will vary. Possible response: Hamilton admitted that Zenger printed the negative articles about Cosby. However, he argued that Zenger should not be found guilty because what he printed was true. Hamilton claimed it was the responsibility of the press to use the truth to expose and oppose abuses of power.)*

2. **Draw Conclusions** Why do you think the victory in the Zenger trial helped pave the way to increasing freedom of the press? *(Answers will vary. Possible response: The jury supported Zenger's right to print the truth. This may have made government officials less likely to want to bring libel cases to court, since juries might be reluctant to find defendants guilty if they were speaking the truth.)*

More Information

Mary Beth Tinker As an adult, Mary Beth Tinker has remained an outspoken proponent of First Amendment rights. In 2013, she and attorney Mike Hiestand started the Tinker Tour, which visits schools, college campuses, and other venues around the country to teach about freedom of speech, freedom of the press, and other First Amendment issues relevant to student rights. In recognition of Tinker's work in support of student rights, the Marshall-Brennan Project at American University's Washington College of Law named its annual youth advocacy award after her in 2000. Then in 2006, the ACLU National Board of Directors' Youth Affairs Committee renamed its annual youth affairs award the Mary Beth Tinker Youth Involvement Award.

Active Options

On Your Feet: Defend a Viewpoint On one wall of the classroom, post a sign that says "All forms of free speech should be protected." On the opposite wall, post a sign that says "No offensive forms of free speech should be protected." Tell students to find the position on an imaginary line between the two signs that best represents their opinion. Have students explain their viewpoint.

NG Learning Framework: Create a Zenger Trial Time Line

SKILL Collaboration

KNOWLEDGE Our Human Story

Tell small groups of students to use the text and additional research to create a time line of events surrounding the Zenger trial. Have groups include William Cosby's unethical actions, the establishment of the newspaper, James Alexander's articles, Cosby's actions against the paper, Zenger's arrest, the various phases of the trial, and any relevant events that happened after the trial. Ask students to include a basic description of each event. Encourage groups to assign tasks so all students can contribute. Invite groups to share their time lines with the class.

DIFFERENTIATE

English Language Learners ELD

Clarify Meanings The term *free speech* is used to refer to more than just spoken words, so it may cause confusion. Working with students at **All Proficiencies**, break down the term into its two parts. Help students clarify what is meant by *free* (not restricted by the government). Then explore the meaning of the word *speech* in this context (either spoken or written words or symbols or actions that communicate a message). Provide examples of symbolic speech for students, such as wearing a black armband or engaging in sit-ins or other protests.

Gifted & Talented

Analyze Freedom of Speech Instruct students to use library or online sources to locate a summary of the U.S. Supreme Court case *Tinker v. Des Moines Independent Community School District*. Have them research the case and summarize the majority and dissenting opinions. Then have them use the information to prepare a short oral presentation on the case. Encourage students to take questions and comments from the class.

See the Chapter Planner for more strategies for differentiation.

HISTORICAL THINKING

ANSWERS

1. Zenger's paper, the *New-York Weekly Journal*, printed articles criticizing William Cosby, the governor of New York.

2. Answers will vary. Possible response: At the time, it was illegal to criticize the government in print, even if the criticisms were true. Zenger's paper had printed articles that criticized the governor, so by definition, he was guilty of libel.

3. Answers will vary. Possible response: In both trials, the side that was arguing for free speech came out victorious.

Battles in New France, 1754–1760

NEW FRANCE

Louisbourg, 1758

St. Lawrence River

Fort Beausejour, 1755
ACADIA

NOVA SCOTIA

Halifax

Québec, 1759

MAINE
(part of Massachusetts)

Montréal
(Surrendered, 1760)

Lake
Champlain

Fort Ticonderoga, 1758, 1759

NEW
HAMPSHIRE

Fort Frontenac, 1758

Fort William Henry, 1757

Lake Ontario

Boston

Fort Oswego, 1756

MASS.

NEW YORK

Fort Niagara, 1759

Lake Huron

CONN.

RHODE ISLAND

Hudson R.

New York

ATLANTIC
OCEAN

Lake Erie

PENNSYLVANIA

Allegheny R.

NEW
JERSEY

Philadelphia

Monongahela, 1755

Fort Necessity, 1754

Fort Duquesne

Susquehanna R.

MARYLAND

DELAWARE

OHIO VALLEY

VIRGINIA

Ohio R.

James R.

Roanoke R.

NORTH CAROLINA

SOUTH
CAROLINA

British territory
French territory
Disputed territory
British victory
French victory

0   100   200 Miles
0   100   200 Kilometers

154

5.1 War Begins

Finders keepers. That's what the French might have said when they claimed prime real estate in the Ohio Valley for themselves. But the British and the American colonists begged to differ.

MAIN IDEA Competition for land and furs involved France and Great Britain in many years of war in North America, starting with the French and Indian War.

SEEDS OF CONFLICT

When French fur traders first came to North America in the 1600s, they set up a few forts and **trading posts** in the St. Lawrence Valley. As you may recall, the French traded with the Huron and Algonquian there for almost 100 years. But after French trappers killed many of the animals in the area and fur supplies dwindled, they resettled in the Ohio Valley. This land was also claimed by Great Britain. So in the 1740s, the British joined forces with the Iroquois and pushed the French traders out of the valley.

The fertile land of the Ohio Valley appealed to colonial settlers. In 1749, they were eager to buy land shares from the Ohio Company of Virginia, which promoted the westward settlement of colonists from Virginia. But the French hadn't given up their claim to the land. They built a number of forts there, including Fort LeBoeuf (luh-BUHF) in northwest Pennsylvania. Then in 1752, the French destroyed Pickawillany, a colonial trading post. In an effort to settle the dispute over the Ohio Valley peacefully, the British governor of Virginia sent a young colonial army leader named **George Washington** to Fort LeBoeuf to ask the French to leave. Not surprisingly, they refused.

COLONIAL INVOLVEMENT

In 1754, the British decided to take more forceful measures and sent the newly promoted Colonel Washington and a small number of troops to capture Fort Duquesne (doo-KAYN) in present-day Pittsburgh. When he arrived, Washington quickly realized he was outnumbered. Scrambling to defend his troops, he built a wooden barrier, or

stockade, which he fittingly named Fort Necessity. But the situation was hopeless. French and Native American troops surrounded the fort and attacked, causing heavy losses for Washington's troops. Defeated, Washington surrendered and abandoned the fort.

Many consider this battle the beginning of the **French and Indian War**. For Britain and France, this war would become part of a larger one, called the Seven Years' War, that officially began in 1756. It pitted these two great powers in a struggle over land in Europe.

The colonists, meanwhile, were concerned with land in North America. Seven colonies sent delegates to a congress in Albany, New York, to discuss uniting the colonies to fight the French for that land. The delegates adopted Benjamin Franklin's **Albany Plan of Union**, which proposed granting a central government the power to tax, pass laws, and oversee military defense for the colonies. When the delegates returned home with the proposal, none of the colonies approved it. But the colonists were united in their determination to fight for land they considered theirs. And they soon persuaded the British to help them.

HISTORICAL THINKING

1. **READING CHECK** How did the fur trade cause conflict between the French and the British?

2. **INTERPRET MAPS** Around what bodies of water were many of the battles fought?

3. **IDENTIFY MAIN IDEAS AND DETAILS** What was the purpose of the Albany Plan of Union?

Colonial Development **155**

PLAN

Objective

Learn how conflict over land and fur trading set the stage for the French and Indian War.

Critical Thinking Skills for Lesson 5.1

• Identify Main Ideas and Details

• Monitor Comprehension

• Interpret Maps

• Make Connections

• Determine Chronology

Essential Question for Chapter 4

How did a developing American identity unite the colonies? The desire for cheap and fertile land made the Ohio Valley attractive to colonists. Lesson 5.1 examines how conflict over land and trade launched the French and Indian War.

Background for the Teacher

The French attack on Pickawillany was an important event in the buildup to the French and Indian War. The trading post had been built by an Irish immigrant named George Croghan. Croghan spoke several Native American languages and was instrumental in negotiating treaties with the Miami and other Native American groups that opened the Ohio Valley to British trade. Because Croghan's traders had access to quality British trade goods at reasonable prices at a time when the British were blocking French goods, they were able to weaken Native American loyalties to the French. This is what led the French to attack Pickawillany in 1752. Charles-Michel Mouet de Langlade, a French soldier of Ottawa and French heritage, led a Native American raiding party against Pickawillany, destroying the trading post and much of the village.

Preview Using the Map

Point out the Ohio Valley on the map in Lesson 5.1. Then assess what students remember about New France, French fur trading, and French alliances with Native Americans. **ASK:** Why would France care if British settlers and traders moved into the Ohio Valley? *(Answers will vary. Possible response: According to the map, the Ohio Valley was part of French territory. British settlers moving there might cause territorial disputes or infringe upon the trade that France had established with the Native Americans.)* Tell students that they will learn in this lesson how France reacted.

TEACH

Guided Discussion

1. **Make Connections** What events led the British governor of Virginia to send George Washington to Fort LeBoeuf? *(The French refused to give up their claim to the Ohio Valley and built a series of forts in the area. After they attacked the Pickawillany trading post, the Virginia governor sent George Washington to ask the French to leave in an effort to find a peaceful end to the conflict.)*

2. **Determine Chronology** How is the 1754 battle at Fort Necessity connected to the Seven Years' War? *(Answers will vary. Possible response: Many consider the battle at Fort Necessity to be the first battle in the French and Indian War, which eventually became part of the Seven Years' War when Britain declared war on France over land in Europe in 1756.)*

Build Time Lines

Have students work in small groups to use information from the map to create a time line of the battles in New France between 1754 and 1760. Instruct students to indicate the victors in each battle by using red for British victories and blue for French victories. **ASK:** Based on your time line, what is one generalization you can make about the progress of the war? *(Answers will vary. Possible response: The French had many victories early in the war, but the tide turned in favor of the British in later years.)* Have groups share their generalizations with the class.

Active Options

On Your Feet: Numbered Heads Organize students into groups of four and assign each group member a number from one to four. Tell students to think about and discuss a response to this question: Why do you think the colonies failed to approve the Albany Plan of Union? Then call a number and have the student from each group with that number report the group's answer to the class.

NG Learning Framework: Explore the Fort Necessity Campaign

ATTITUDE Curiosity

KNOWLEDGE Our Human Story

Ask students to use the school or local library to learn more about George Washington's 1754 Fort Necessity campaign. Get them started by having them research answers to these questions: What was on the site of Fort Duquesne before the French built the fort? What happened at Jumonville Glen? Why did Washington build Fort Necessity? What events led to Washington's surrender? Have students share their findings with the class.

DIFFERENTIATE

Striving Readers

Preview Text Help students preview the lesson. Point out the text features, such as the lesson title, Main Idea, headings, and map. **ASK:** Based on the text features, what do you expect this lesson to be about? As students begin reading, help them confirm their understanding of each paragraph before moving on to the next one.

Pre-AP

Prepare an Interview Invite students to prepare a mock interview with Benjamin Franklin about the Albany Plan of Union. Direct students to use the Internet to learn more about the Albany Plan of Union and the Albany Congress by answering the following questions: Why did the colonies call the Albany Congress? Why did members of the Congress favor the proposed Albany Plan of Union? What were the details of the plan? Have pairs of students use their research to write interview questions and responses and then conduct their interviews for the class.

See the Chapter Planner for more strategies for differentiation.

HISTORICAL THINKING

ANSWERS

1. To expand their fur trade, the French moved onto lands the British considered to be their territory. Britain joined forces with the Iroquois and sent troops to try to take the land back.

2. Many of the battles were fought around Lake Ontario and Lake Champlain and along the St. Lawrence, Hudson, and Allegheny rivers.

3. Benjamin Franklin hoped to unify the colonies to defend against the French. He wanted to create an overarching colonial government that had the power to tax, pass laws, and supervise military defense.

5.2 Quebec and the British Victory

The stakes were high in the French and Indian War. Ultimately, the outcome of the war would determine which countries controlled North America.

MAIN IDEA The British and French fought for control of North America in the French and Indian War, with extensive losses on both sides.

CRITICAL VIEWING At the moment captured here in the Battle of the Monongahela, Washington is still on his horse and in command as the wounded General Braddock falls before him. Junius Brutus Stearns painted *Washington as a Captain in the French and Indian War* around 1851. In a time before photography, how did this painting effectively convey information about the battle?

EARLY BRITISH LOSSES

In response to the colonists' request for help, the British jumped into the fight. In 1755, they sent British general Edward Braddock and two regiments to North America to destroy French forts. George Washington accompanied Braddock as he marched with his more than 2,000 soldiers through the Virginia backcountry on a mission to capture Fort Duquesne. Braddock was confident that his highly trained soldiers would quickly defeat the enemy.

He was wrong. The British soldiers were totally unprepared for fighting on the frontier. Their wagons were too big for the paths, and they offended many of the Native American scouts they'd recruited to lead the way, causing most of them to abandon the soldiers. The army's slow progress gave the French plenty of notice of their clumsy arrival.

As a result, the French and Native American troops were lying in wait for them. In the **Battle of the Monongahela**, fought just east of present-day Pittsburgh, they hid behind trees and ambushed Braddock's army as it marched by. Used to fighting on battlegrounds where both sides formed neat rows,

the British soldiers were caught completely off guard. Washington suggested they break ranks and fight from behind trees like the French, but Braddock refused. Within a few hours, nearly two-thirds of the British forces lay dead or wounded. Braddock himself soon died of his wounds. Washington, his uniform ripped by bullets, helped lead the retreat.

Losses continued to plague the British in the early years of the war. In New York, the French seized Fort William Henry, Fort Oswego, and 2,000 British soldiers at Lake George. The British defeats emboldened Native American tribes allied with the French to attack British settlements in the backcountry, where they killed and captured hundreds of settlers. Things looked bleak for the British and colonial forces.

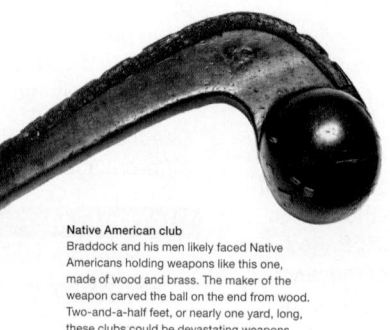

Native American club
Braddock and his men likely faced Native Americans holding weapons like this one, made of wood and brass. The maker of the weapon carved the ball on the end from wood. Two-and-a-half feet, or nearly one yard, long, these clubs could be devastating weapons.

FRENCH DEFEATS

The tide turned after British statesman **Sir William Pitt** poured money and men into the war. In July 1758, the British captured Louisbourg in Nova Scotia (NOH-vuh SKOH-shuh). Alarmed, the French pulled their troops from the Ohio Valley so they could protect Quebec and Montreal. The retreat allowed the British to take control of the west. Cut off from French supplies and weakened by smallpox, Native Americans ended their war in the backcountry.

Even with extra troops, the French could not save Quebec. The British captured the city in 1759 during the **Battle of Quebec**. Encouraged by these victories, the Iroquois joined forces with Britain. In 1760, the British captured Montreal, ending French control of Canada.

The defeat of the French in Canada marked the end of the war with France in North America. A treaty would be signed, but the war had a lasting impact on everyone who had taken part in it. For

one thing, thousands of colonists had joined the British army. They found that, at best, the British soldiers and officers looked down on them, and at worst, the British dealt out severe punishments to soldiers for small offenses. Colonial soldiers didn't feel they'd been treated like allies. The war would also cause great suffering to Native Americans. Soon settlers would invade even more of their homeland.

HISTORICAL THINKING

1. **READING CHECK** How did Braddock's defeat at Fort Duquesne show that the British were not ready to fight a frontier war?

2. **IDENTIFY MAIN IDEAS AND DETAILS** What turned the tide of the French and Indian War?

3. **DETERMINE CHRONOLOGY** What happened after Braddock and Washington marched to capture Fort Duquesne?

PLAN

Objective
Understand the events that led to the British victory in the French and Indian War.

Critical Thinking Skills for Lesson 5.2
- Identify Main Ideas and Details
- Monitor Comprehension
- Determine Chronology
- Analyze Cause and Effect
- Draw Conclusions
- Analyze Visuals

Essential Question for Chapter 4
How did a developing American identity unite the colonies? The French and Indian War helped unite the American colonists and weaken their loyalties to Britain. Lesson 5.2 examines the significant battles in the French and Indian War.

Background for the Teacher
George Washington was not the only American colonist who played a pivotal role in the Battle of the Monongahela. The expedition westward might not have even taken place if Benjamin Franklin had not solved a serious logistical problem. He secured the wagons and teamsters the army needed to carry supplies. The trek through the Virginia backcountry was difficult for Edward Braddock and his men. They had to cut a 12-foot-wide military road through mountainous and heavily forested land as they traveled toward Fort Duquesne. Although the battle ended in a British defeat, Braddock's road proved vital to future British military efforts. It allowed the army to shift its focus from the Atlantic coast and the St. Lawrence River to the interior, which made it possible to defeat the French. Once Fort Duquesne fell to the British, the road also opened the Ohio Valley to a flood of traders, hunters, and settlers.

INTRODUCE & ENGAGE

Make Word Connections

Write the words *recruit, ally,* and *coalition* on the board and ask students to offer definitions and synonyms for these words. Engage in a short class discussion about how these words relate to each other. Explain that in this lesson students will learn about how and why the French had much better luck than the British in recruiting a coalition of Native American allies in the early years of the war.

TEACH

Guided Discussion

1. **Analyze Cause and Effect** What factors contributed to the British defeat in the Battle of the Monongahela? *(Answers will vary. Possible responses: Braddock was overconfident in the skill of his British soldiers. The British offended the Native American scouts, causing most to abandon the British troops. The troops' slow movement along the frontier paths made them easy targets for ambush. Once ambushed, Braddock refused to follow Washington's advice to break ranks and fight from behind trees.)*

2. **Draw Conclusions** Why do you think the Iroquois waited so long to join forces with the British? *(Answers will vary. Possible response: They wanted to see if the British had a good chance of winning the war before joining them. Being allies of the British would have caused problems for them if the French won the war.)*

Analyze Visuals

Explore the painting and caption for this lesson with students. Make sure they understand that the men in brown are the colonial militiamen. **ASK:** How does the artist portray British troops? *(Answers will vary. Possible response: The artist has the British soldiers standing passively in rows in the background as the militiamen fight under Washington's leadership. The only British soldiers in the foreground are the wounded Braddock, the soldier supporting him, and another wounded soldier under the tree. British soldiers seem ineffectual compared to the militiamen.)*

Active Options

On Your Feet: Build a Living Time Line Invite student teams to create a living time line of events from the French and Indian War. Provide teams with sheets of paper with the following events written on them, shuffled out of order: General Braddock arrives in North America; Battle of the Monongahela; French seize Fort William Henry and Fort Oswego; French capture 2,000 British soldiers; British capture Louisbourg; British capture Quebec; British capture Montreal. Tell teams to arrange themselves in the order in which the events occurred. Then, as a class, determine if students' living time line is accurate.

NG Learning Framework: Convince General Braddock

> SKILL Communication

> KNOWLEDGE Our Human Story

Encourage students to investigate Benjamin Franklin's and George Washington's roles in helping General Braddock plan and execute his attack on Fort Duquesne. Instruct students to write a persuasive essay from the point of view of either Franklin or Washington. Essays from Franklin's point of view should inform General Braddock of the supplies he will need to take on the march and warn him of the challenges he will face on the way. Essays from Washington's point of view should attempt to convince Braddock to abandon traditional fighting techniques and take on the techniques of the enemy. Have students present their essays to the class in character.

DIFFERENTIATE

Inclusion

Narrate the Painting Pair students who are visually impaired with students who are not. Ask the latter to describe in detail the painting *Washington as a Captain in the French and Indian War* and discuss the artist's techniques and focus. Then invite student pairs to work together to answer the Critical Viewing question.

English Language Learners

Pose and Answer Questions Invite **Expanding** and **Bridging** students to pose and answer questions that begin with the 5Ws. Remind them that *Who* refers to people, *What* to events, *Where* to places, *When* to dates or time, and *Why* to reasons. Encourage students to share their questions and answers.

See the Chapter Planner for more strategies for differentiation.

HISTORICAL THINKING

ANSWERS

1. French troops and their Native American allies ambushed the British from behind trees. The British soldiers, used to fighting in neat rows, were exposed to the enemy. Braddock refused to let his soldiers break rank and fight from behind trees.

2. Answers will vary. Possible response: Sir William Pitt contributed money and troops. British troops attacked targets in Nova Scotia, causing the French to pull their troops out of the Ohio Valley. Native Americans ended their war in the backcountry, enabling the British to take control of the west.

3. Braddock's army was ambushed by the French and their Native American allies. Nearly two-thirds of the British forces were wounded or killed. After Braddock was mortally wounded, Washington had to help lead the retreat.

CRITICAL VIEWING Answers will vary. Possible response: The painting conveyed the wilderness terrain where the battle took place, details about the troops and their equipment and uniforms, and the moment when General Braddock fell.

5.3 Impact of the War

The colonists celebrated Britain's victory in the French and Indian War. New York City even raised a statue of King George III. Would the colonists' love of the king endure? We'll see.

MAIN IDEA Victory in the French and Indian War expanded British territory but led to conflict with Native Americans in the Ohio Valley.

THE TREATY OF PARIS

In 1763, diplomats from Britain and France met in Paris to negotiate a **treaty**, or peace agreement. The resulting **Treaty of Paris** officially ended the French and Indian War.

According to its terms, France lost all of its territory—and thus all of its power—in North America. As Britain's ally, Spain acquired New Orleans and the Louisiana Territory west of the Mississippi. The British gained Canada from France and Florida from Spain in exchange for Cuba and the Philippines. Britain now controlled all of the land in North America east of the Mississippi River.

The colonists also reaped some rewards from the treaty. They received the right to fish in the North Atlantic off the coast of Canada. The colonists also assumed they were now free to settle the Ohio Valley.

PONTIAC'S REBELLION

Not everyone in North America was happy when the French and Indian War ended. The war had been a disaster for Native Americans. While the French had presented them with gifts each year, the British ended this custom and then raised prices on trade goods. Worse yet, the British government limited what—and how

much—Native Americans could trade. Additionally, white settlers streamed into the Ohio Valley after the war, in clear violation of existing treaties.

The British trade policies and land-grabbing drove large numbers of Delaware, Shawnee, Iroquois, and other Native Americans to take up arms.

Treaty of Paris, 1763

Map legend:
- British territory
- French territory
- Spanish territory
- Russian territory

PRIMARY SOURCE

When I go to see the English commander and say to him that some of our comrades are dead, instead of bewailing their death, as our French brothers do, he laughs at me and at you. If I ask for anything for our sick, he refuses with the reply that he has no use for us. From all this you can well see that they are seeking our ruin. Therefore, my brothers, we must all swear their destruction and wait no longer.

—Chief Pontiac in a speech to a council of Native Americans near Detroit, May 1763

Ottawa leader **Pontiac** urged Native Americans in the region to band together and rise up against the British. Many listened.

Pontiac had fought alongside the French in the French and Indian War. In 1763, he led Native Americans in launching what came to be called **Pontiac's Rebellion**. His forces defeated 13 British outposts. However, the British successfully defended their most important forts, including Fort Pitt, sometimes by ruthless means.

When Pontiac launched his rebellion, he needed help to replenish ammunition supplies and strengthen the Native Americans' ranks throughout the Great Lakes region and western Pennsylvania. He counted on the French to come to his aid. But they never did. Then, when British commanders met with Native American leaders at Fort Pitt, they are said to have given them smallpox-infested blankets and handkerchiefs as gifts, hoping to spread disease among many of the tribes.

Fighting continued for two more years. Sick of war, the king issued a proclamation that colonists could not settle west of a line drawn along the crest of the Appalachian Mountains from Maine to Georgia. This angered colonists, who wondered what they had been fighting for. They also resented the continued presence of British troops in their homeland. The soldiers and their somewhat coarse behavior served as a daily reminder of the mother colony. In time, colonists began to regard British authority more critically.

HISTORICAL THINKING

1. **READING CHECK** How did the Treaty of Paris affect power in North America?

2. **INTERPRET MAPS** Which countries gained the most territory after 1763?

3. **SYNTHESIZE** How did the outcome of the war impact Native Americans?

Colonial Development **159**

Objective

Analyze the effects of the war on colonial territory and conflict with Native Americans.

Critical Thinking Skills for Lesson 5.3

- Identify Main Ideas and Details
- Monitor Comprehension
- Interpret Maps
- Synthesize
- Evaluate
- Make Connections
- Analyze Language Use

Essential Question for Chapter 4

How did a developing American identity unite the colonies? Lesson 5.3 examines some of the consequences of the British victory in the French and Indian War.

Background for the Teacher

One of the outcomes of the French and Indian War was a shift in the way Native Americans in the Ohio Valley and farther west saw themselves. After growing accustomed to fighting alongside one another, many Native Americans began to think in terms of common interests rather than purely tribal interests. Native American religious leaders were often the first to call for unity among tribes. One such leader was Neolin, a Delaware, who argued that Native Americans had betrayed their way of life by allowing white settlers onto Indian land and by relying on European goods. Neolin pushed for Native Americans to abandon white ways and force British settlers out. Pontiac heard Neolin's message and called on others to join him in fighting the British. Most Native Americans in the Ohio Valley heeded the call.

INTRODUCE & ENGAGE

Brainstorm a List

Ask students to brainstorm a list of reasons why the outcome of the French and Indian War may have been more beneficial for British colonists than for Native Americans. Record their reasons on chart paper or on the board. Discuss them as a class, and encourage students to copy the list and revisit it after reading and discussing the lesson.

TEACH

Guided Discussion

1. **Evaluate** How did the benefits of the French and Indian War fall short of the colonists' expectations? *(Answers will vary. Possible response: The colonists' belief that the Treaty of Paris would open the Ohio Valley to settlement was not correct. The British government angered the colonists when it issued a proclamation in 1763 that prohibited colonists from settling west of a line drawn along the crest of the Appalachian Mountains from Maine to Georgia.)*

2. **Make Connections** What evidence would support the text claim that the British sometimes used ruthless means to defend their most important forts? *(Answers will vary. Possible response: The British are suspected of giving smallpox-infected blankets and handkerchiefs as gifts to Native American leaders when they met with British commanders at Fort Pitt. The infected articles would spread smallpox among the tribes and kill them.)*

Analyze Language Use

What words and images does Pontiac use in his speech to persuade others to join his rebellion? *(Answers will vary. Possible response: Pontiac refers to the French and the Native American council members as "brothers" to show the British as a common enemy. He uses "bewailing" to call forth an image of grieving for death that the British don't share with his "brothers." He uses the phrase "seeking our ruin" and drives home the point that the British want to destroy Native American culture and not just win a war or territory.)*

Active Options

On Your Feet: Think, Pair, Share Give students a few minutes to think about this question: What are some of the most effective ways to encourage people to join a cause? Then have students choose partners and talk about the question for five minutes. Finally, allow individual students to share their ideas with the class.

NG Learning Framework: Analyze Treaties
ATTITUDES Empowerment, Responsibility
SKILLS Communication, Collaboration

Invite student teams to consider the elements of fair and successful treaties. Have teams conduct further research on the Treaty of Paris using library and online sources, and then encourage them to research another treaty that ended a war. Students should identify similarities and differences between the Treaty of Paris and the additional treaty they research and be able to situate both in their historical contexts. After teams have completed their research, have them make presentations to the class.

DIFFERENTIATE

Striving Readers

Expand Main Idea Statements After students have read Lesson 5.3, have them copy the lesson's Main Idea and expand it into a few sentences. If students need additional support, assist by providing sentence frames.

Main Idea: Victory in the French and Indian War expanded British territory but led to conflict with Native Americans in the Ohio Valley.

Territory gained by Britain included _____ (Canada) from France and _____ (Florida) from Spain.

The British ended the French custom of _____ (presenting gifts) to Native Americans.

Gifted & Talented

Create a Map Have students create an annotated map showing the major events in Pontiac's Rebellion. Instruct students to include and annotate the British forts taken by Native Americans, the British forts not taken, battle sites, and colonial towns. Also have students indicate the homelands of the various Native American tribes in the Ohio Valley and Great Lakes region. Encourage students to present their maps to the class.

See the Chapter Planner for more strategies for differentiation.

HISTORICAL THINKING

ANSWERS

1. France lost all of its territory in North America. The British obtained Canada and Florida, thereby gaining control of all land east of the Mississippi River. Spain acquired New Orleans and territory west of the Mississippi River.

2. Britain and Spain gained the most territory after 1763.

3. Answers will vary. Possible response: The British victory in the French and Indian War was bad for Native Americans. The British ended the French custom of giving gifts each year and limited what and how much Native Americans could trade. In addition, settlers ignored treaties and began moving into the Ohio Valley.

4 REVIEW

VOCABULARY

Use each of the following vocabulary words in a sentence that shows an understanding of the term's meaning.

1. subsistence farming

   If a family practices subsistence farming, they usually harvest just enough food to survive and sometimes will have a little left over to sell.

2. provisions
3. religious freedom
4. apprentice
5. cash crop
6. backcountry
7. gristmill
8. diversity
9. libel
10. trading post

READING STRATEGY
IDENTIFY MAIN IDEAS AND DETAILS

If you haven't done so already, complete your chart to identify details about the development of the colonies. Then answer the question.

Colonial Development

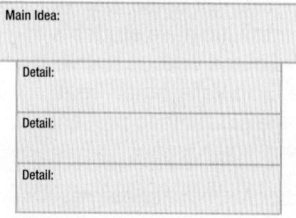

Main Idea:

Detail:

Detail:

Detail:

11. Why did the use of enslaved African labor grow over time in the Southern Colonies?

MAIN IDEAS

Answer the following questions. Support your answers with evidence from the chapter.

12. Why was fishing important to the economy of New England? **LESSON 1.1**

13. How did triangular trade contribute to the expansion of slavery? **LESSON 1.2**

14. Why did Charles Town remain smaller than the largest northern cities? **LESSON 2.1**

15. What was the Stono Rebellion? **LESSON 2.3**

16. How did gristmills affect the economy of the Middle Colonies? **LESSON 3.1**

17. What were indicators of racial tension in New York City in the early 1700s? **LESSON 3.3**

18. In what ways did women add to the colonial economy? **LESSON 4.1**

19. How did ministers like Jonathan Edwards and George Whitefield contribute to the Great Awakening? **LESSON 4.2**

20. What led to the creation of the Albany Plan of Union? **LESSON 5.1**

21. Why did Pontiac rebel? **LESSON 5.3**

HISTORICAL THINKING

Answer the following questions. Support your answers with evidence from the chapter.

22. **MAKE INFERENCES** How did the Navigation Acts lead to an increase in smuggling?

23. **ANALYZE CAUSE AND EFFECT** How did the beliefs of the Puritans lead to the growth of education in the colonies?

24. **COMPARE AND CONTRAST** How was society in the backcountry different from society in the Chesapeake and South Carolina?

25. **SYNTHESIZE** How did the Great Awakening and the Enlightenment contribute to revolutionary thought?

26. **FORM AND SUPPORT OPINIONS** Were the Native Americans better off dealing with French fur traders or the British settlers? Support your opinion with evidence from the chapter.

27. **DRAW CONCLUSIONS** How did the British victory in the French and Indian War change the distribution of power in North America?

INTERPRET MAPS

Look closely at the map of the African-American population in the British colonies around 1760. Then answer the questions that follow.

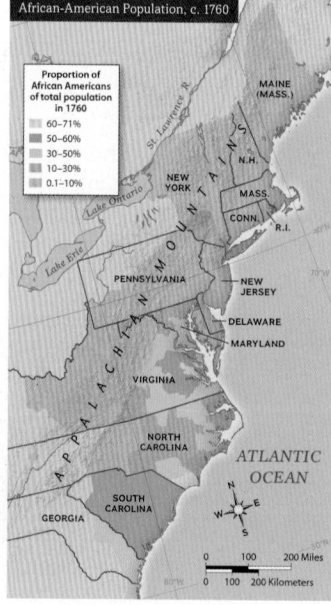

African-American Population, c. 1760

Proportion of African Americans of total population in 1760

- 60–71%
- 50–60%
- 30–50%
- 10–30%
- 0.1–10%

28. Which two areas had the highest proportion of African Americans in their population?

29. How did the African-American population in South Carolina differ from that in Virginia?

ANALYZE SOURCES

In 1704, French and Native American forces attacked Deerfield, Massachusetts, killing 50 people and taking 112 captives. Stephen Williams, an 11-year-old captive, kept a journal while a prisoner. Here he describes the attack. Read the excerpt and answer the question.

> The French and Indians came and surprised our fort and took it. And after they had broken into our house and took us prisoners, they barbarously murdered a brother and sister of mine as they did several of our neighbors. They rifled our house and then marched away with us that were captives, and set our house and barn afire as they did the greatest part of the town.

30. How does this source help to develop an understanding of the attack?

CONNECT TO YOUR LIFE

31. **NARRATIVE** Think about the tasks and adjustments of someone who moves and starts at a new school. What work is involved in physically moving? What does a person do to get to know new neighbors, teachers, and friends? Write a paragraph in which you make connections between this experience and that of the colonists.

TIPS

- List the challenges that the colonists faced coming to British America. Then make a list of the challenges involved in moving.
- Use two or three vocabulary terms from the chapter in your narrative.
- Conclude the narrative with a comment that ties the colonists' experiences to that of a modern student's move.

VOCABULARY ANSWERS

1. If families practice subsistence farming, they usually harvest just enough food to survive and sometimes will have a little left over to sell.

2. New England merchants made money supplying provisions for trading ships.

3. Many immigrants came to New England and the Middle Colonies in search of religious freedom.

4. A boy could learn a job by being an apprentice in a bakery.

5. The owners of large plantations became wealthy by growing tobacco and other cash crops.

6. Many Scots-Irish moved to the backcountry in search of cheap land to farm.

7. Pennsylvania farmers relied on their local gristmill to turn wheat into flour.

8. The diversity of the Middle Colonies made toleration of other religions important.

9. John Peter Zenger was charged with libel for publishing articles critical of the governor of New York.

10. Native Americans and European traders met at trading posts to exchange goods, such as furs and ammunition.

READING STRATEGY ANSWER

Colonial Development

Main Idea: Enslaved African labor increased over time in the Southern Colonies.

Detail: Plantation owners depended on enslaved West Africans to grow rice.

Detail: In 1698, England granted permission to all English merchants to join in the slave trade.

Detail: Over the next 50 years, the number of enslaved Africans in the Chesapeake grew enormously.

11. After England opened the slave trade to all English merchants in 1698, planters in the Chesapeake turned to enslaved labor to work on plantations. An expanded slave trade meant there was an ample supply of enslaved workers to meet the need as the number and size of plantations increased over time.

MAIN IDEAS ANSWERS

12. Fishing allowed the colonies to engage in international trade. New England fishers sold their catch to English merchants in exchange for English goods. In addition, fishing contributed to the growth of the shipbuilding industry.

13. New England merchants shipped rum and other goods to Africa in exchange for enslaved Africans.

14. English and New England shippers controlled Charles Town's trade. As a result, it never built a strong merchant community and thus was unable to attract large numbers of workers.

15. The Stono Rebellion was a 1739 slave revolt in South Carolina. It involved more than 50 enslaved people led by a literate slave named Jemmy, or Cato. Armed planters defeated the rebels, and everyone suspected of being a rebel was put to death.

16. Gristmills enabled farmers to grind their wheat into flour, making it easier to ship. In addition, millers often opened stores where goods could be exchanged.

17. New York City passed a law saying that enslaved Africans could seek extra work only at the slave market. Then on April 6, 1712, about 20 slaves set fire to a building and attacked the white men who came to put out the fire, killing nine. In response, 17 slaves were killed and one was tortured.

18. Rural white women performed farm tasks and made goods to sell or trade. Enslaved African-American women worked in the fields or the households of their masters. Some women in cities acted as midwives or worked alongside their husbands in stores. Poor women in cities often provided domestic services.

19. Edwards and Whitefield preached sermons about salvation that appealed to people's emotions, and their listeners came to believe that they did not need church officials to have a connection with God.

20. Disputes over land between the colonists and the French led to the Albany Plan of Union.

21. After the French and Indian War, Pontiac felt that the British were not trading fairly with the Native Americans and too many white colonists were settling in the Ohio Valley.

HISTORICAL THINKING ANSWERS

22. Answers will vary. Possible response: Some colonists turned to smuggling to circumnavigate the restrictions and avoid the taxes of the strict Navigation Acts.

23. Puritans believed that people needed to be able to read the Bible and other moral texts. This led the Massachusetts legislature to pass laws establishing common schools and Latin grammar schools. The Puritans also needed schools to educate their ministers. This led to the establishment of universities, such as Harvard.

24. Society in the Chesapeake and South Carolina was hierarchical and based on slave labor and cash crops. Society in the backcountry was primarily non-slaveholding and centered on small farms that enabled settlers to grow their own food.

25. Answers will vary. Possible response: The Great Awakening's focus on equality in religion caused colonists to apply the same thinking to society. The Enlightenment paved the way for revolutionary change by emphasizing the use of reason to question previously accepted beliefs and traditions.

26. Answers will vary. Possible response: Native Americans were better off dealing with French fur traders because the French provided trade goods in exchange for furs and provided annual gifts. The British treated the Native Americans poorly and felt that victory in the French and Indian War entitled them to Native American land.

27. France lost all of its territory, and thus all of its power, in North America. The British gained Canada from the French and Florida from Spain. The British now controlled all land east of Mississippi River. Spain acquired New Orleans and French territory west of the Mississippi River.

INTERPRET MAPS ANSWERS

28. Coastal areas in Virginia and North Carolina had the highest proportion of African Americans.

29. The African-American population was fairly evenly distributed in South Carolina, but in Virginia, the population varied by region.

ANALYZE SOURCES ANSWER

30. Answers will vary. Possible response: The source provides an eyewitness account of the attack from the perspective of one of the captives. This primary source appears to be a credible one because Williams provides specific details of the attack. The reader learns that it was a surprise attack and can conclude from the details that the French and Indian forces were victorious, since they killed and captured townspeople and burned much of the town.

CONNECT TO YOUR LIFE ANSWER

31. Answers will vary but should include information from the chapter about the challenges colonists faced coming to British America.

NATIONAL GEOGRAPHIC | CONNECTION

Before New York

BY PETER MILLER

Adapted from "Before New York," by Peter Miller, in *National Geographic*, September 2009

Of all the visitors to New York City in recent years, one of the most surprising was a beaver named José. No one knows exactly where he came from. He just showed up one wintry morning in 2007 on a riverbank in the Bronx Zoo, where he built a lodge.

During the early 17th century, when the city was the Dutch village of New Amsterdam, beavers were widely hunted for their pelts, which were fashionable in Europe. The fur trade grew into such a profitable business that a pair of beavers earned a place on the city's official seal, where they remain today.

Because of the high demand for their pelts, the real animals vanished. According to Eric Sanderson, an ecologist at the Wildlife Conservation Society (WCS) headquartered at the Bronx Zoo, "There hasn't been a beaver in New York City in more than 200 years." That's why he was skeptical when a colleague told him he'd seen evidence of a beaver during a walk along the river. But it was true. Sanderson and his colleague found José's lodge, and a couple of weeks later, they ran into José himself.

The beaver's return to the Big Apple was hailed as a victory by those who have spent more than three decades restoring the health of the Bronx River, once a dumping ground for abandoned cars and trash. José was named in honor of José E. Serrano, the congressman from the Bronx who'd secured more than $15 million in federal funds to support the river cleanup.

For almost a decade, Sanderson has led a project at WCS to imagine and digitally recreate what the island of Manhattan might have looked like before the city took root. The Mannahatta Project, as it's called (after the Lenape name for "island of many hills"), is an effort to turn back the clock to 1609, just before Henry Hudson and his crew sailed into New York Harbor and spotted the island.

Long before its hills were bulldozed and its wetlands paved over, Manhattan was a wilderness of chestnut, oak, and hickory trees. It was full of salt marshes and grasslands with turkey, elk, and black bear—and "as pleasant a land as one can tread upon," Hudson reported. Sandy beaches ran along stretches of both coasts on the narrow, 13-mile-long island where the Lenape feasted on clams and oysters. More than 66 miles of streams flowed through Manhattan.

"You might find it difficult to imagine today, but 400 years ago there was a red maple swamp right here in Times Square," Sanderson mentioned while waiting to cross Seventh Avenue. "Just over there was a beaver pond," he said, as a bus rumbled by.

"The landscape in Manhattan is so transformed, it makes you wonder what was here before," Sanderson remarked. As a landscape ecologist, his goal is to figure out how wild places work. So he and his colleagues built a landscape from the bottom up. They began by listing the various ecosystems they could safely assume existed on the island, such as old-growth forests, wetlands, or plains. In all, they identified 55 different ecological communities. Then they filled in the wildlife, discovering a dense network of relationships among species, habitats, and ecosystems. In the end, they identified 1,300 species and at least 8,000 relationships linking them to one another and their habitats.

Sanderson hopes his project will stimulate a new curiosity about what existed on Manhattan before Hudson arrived. "I'd like every New Yorker to know that they live in a place that had this fabulous ecology," he said. "New York isn't just a place of fabulous art, music, culture, and communications. It's also a place of amazing natural potential—even if you have to look a little harder here."

For more from National Geographic, check out "America, Found and Lost" online.

UNIT INQUIRY: Envision an Ideal Community

In this unit, you learned about the visions different groups had about what newly founded communities should be. Some groups built communities based on shared religious beliefs. Other groups focused on profiting from the rich natural resources the new continent offered. Based on your understanding of the text, what factors are involved in envisioning a new community? How might some groups' visions conflict with others?

ASSIGNMENT

Envision an ideal community. All new colonies began with people who imagined a new way of living or a new world. Consider factors such as what the "goal" of your community is, what sort of rules would govern your community, and how the community would thrive. Be prepared to present your community to the class.

Gather Evidence As you envision your community, gather evidence from this unit about the various factors that founders of new communities had to consider. Make a list of categories and subcategories that you consider the most important. Review the unit to gather evidence that supports your vision. Use a graphic organizer like this one to help organize your thoughts.

Produce Use your notes to produce a detailed vision of your new community. Write a short paragraph on each component, using evidence from this unit to support your ideas.

Present Choose a creative way to present your ideal community to the class. Consider one of these options:

- Create a commercial to persuade people to move to your new community. Include details that describe where it is, who would prosper there, what the "goal" of the community would be, and what people who move there might expect.

- Organize teams and hold a classroom discussion on establishing a new community. Explore questions such as who would hold power, who might be included (or excluded), and how the community would support its residents.

- Design a flag or symbol for your new community. Describe how the elements you include on your flag represent your community and why these factors would be important to people who might choose to settle there.

NATIONAL GEOGRAPHIC | LEARNING FRAMEWORK ACTIVITIES

Prepare a Leadership Memo

ATTITUDE Responsibility

SKILLS Observation, Problem-Solving

Effective leaders possess solid diplomatic, communication, and problem-solving skills. Choose a leader that you read about in this unit and, using evidence from the reading, prepare a memo from that leader's point of view. In your memo, outline what you as that leader accomplished—or wish you had—by approaching problems in your community or colony with diplomacy. Offer examples of specific events or problems that your leader participated in or encountered. Then present your leadership memo to the class.

Create a Trade Network

SKILL Collaboration

KNOWLEDGE Our Human Story

Work with a team of classmates to create a trade network. Decide what products or resources you would trade with other groups and what products or resources you would like to acquire. Collaborate with your classmates on setting prices and quantities for products and resources to be traded. Then determine how your network will exchange goods. Illustrate your trade network on a classroom whiteboard. When all groups have added their networks to the board, discuss the ways in which the networks are similar to and different from each other.

NATIONAL GEOGRAPHIC CONNECTION

Guided Discussion for "Before New York"

1. **Compare and Contrast** In what ways is present-day Manhattan similar to and different from the island Henry Hudson encountered in 1609? *(Answers will vary. Possible response: Today, Manhattan is located in the same place geographically, but instead of being covered with salt marshes and dense forest, much of the city is covered in pavement and skyscrapers.)*

2. **Describe** What are the goals of the Mannahatta Project? *(The goals of the Mannahatta Project are to stimulate a new curiosity about what Manhattan was like before European settlement and to help New Yorkers and others realize the hidden natural features that still exist there.)*

Guided Discussion for "America, Found and Lost"

1. **Make Connections** Why does the author of the article refer to tobacco, honeybees, and domestic animals as "weapons"? *(Answers will vary. Possible response: Tobacco, honeybees, and domestic animals are referred to as "weapons" because their introduction to the North American continent resulted in massive transformation of the ecosystem, which, in many ways, led to the demise of many Native American communities.)*

2. **Explain** In what ways did various diseases impact Jamestown colonists and Native Americans? *(Jamestown colonists were impacted by the diseases of typhoid, dysentery, and salt poisoning, all caused by tainted water. Native Americans were impacted by malaria and other diseases brought over by the English colonists.)*

UNIT INQUIRY PROJECT RUBRIC

Assess

Use the rubric to assess each student's participation and performance.

SCORE	ASSIGNMENT	PRODUCT	PRESENTATION
3 GREAT	• Student thoroughly understands the assignment. • Student participates fully in the project process. • Student works well with team members.	• Ideal community is well thought out. • Ideal community includes evidence that supports its vision. • Ideal community contains all of the key elements listed in the assignment.	• Presentation is clear, concise, and logical. • Presentation does a good job of creatively representing an ideal community. • Presentation engages the audience.
2 GOOD	• Student mostly understands the assignment. • Student participates fairly well in the project process. • Student works fairly well with team members.	• Ideal community is fairly well thought out. • Ideal community includes evidence that supports its vision. • Ideal community contains most of the key elements listed in the assignment.	• Presentation is fairly clear, concise, and logical. • Presentation does an adequate job of creatively representing an ideal community. • Presentation somewhat engages the audience.
1 NEEDS WORK	• Student does not understand the assignment. • Student minimally participates or does not participate in the project process. • Student does not work well with team members.	• Ideal community is not well thought out. • Ideal community does not include evidence that supports its vision. • Ideal community contains few or none of the key elements listed in the assignment.	• Presentation is not clear, concise, or logical. • Presentation does an inadequate job of representing an ideal community. • Presentation does not engage the audience.

NATIONAL GEOGRAPHIC LEARNING FRAMEWORK RUBRIC

Assess

Use the rubric to assess how each student applies the National Geographic Learning Framework.

SCORE	ASSIGNMENT	ASSIGNMENT	FINAL PRODUCTS
3 GREAT	• Memo reflects **Responsibility** well. • Memo demonstrates **Observation** and **Problem-Solving** well.	• Trade network demonstrates **Collaboration** well. • Trade network explores **Our Human Story** well.	• Final products are engaging, creative, and well presented.
2 GOOD	• Memo reflects **Responsibility**. • Memo demonstrates **Observation** and **Problem-Solving**.	• Trade network demonstrates **Collaboration**. • Trade network explores **Our Human Story**.	• Final products are interesting, logical, and complete.
1 NEEDS WORK	• Memo does not reflect **Responsibility**. • Memo does not demonstrate **Observation** and **Problem-Solving**.	• Trade network does not demonstrate **Collaboration**. • Trade network does not explore **Our Human Story**.	• Final products are not creative, complete, or interesting.

Washington Crossing the Delaware

After suffering a series of defeats over several months, General George Washington decided to stage a surprise attack on Hessian troops in Trenton, New Jersey, over Christmas 1776. Washington ferried across the Delaware River at night and reached New Jersey on the morning of December 26 with about 2,400 soldiers. Another 3,000 soldiers were supposed to join Washington and his men at the meeting point on the Jersey shore but, because of the darkness and icy conditions, failed to arrive. The Americans struck without them. At 8 a.m., they surrounded the Hessians and overpowered them.

Have students study the painting and identify General Washington at the front of the boat. Point out some of the historical inaccuracies of the painting. For one thing, the boat is much smaller than the one he would have actually sailed on. For another, while Washington sailed during the night, the painting is filled with light. But stress that the painting is not meant to depict the actual event. The artist wanted to celebrate the American Revolution and the fight for independence and democracy.

ASK: What do you notice about the people in Washington's boat? *(Possible responses: They represent a cross section of the colonies. The rower at the front is a pioneer from the backcountry. The rower in the red shirt may be a woman.)* Have students point out and discuss other interesting figures in the boat. Ask them why the artist might have chosen to present such a cross section of America.

History Notebook

Encourage students to complete the Reid on the Road video series page for Unit 3 in their History Notebooks after they watch the video.

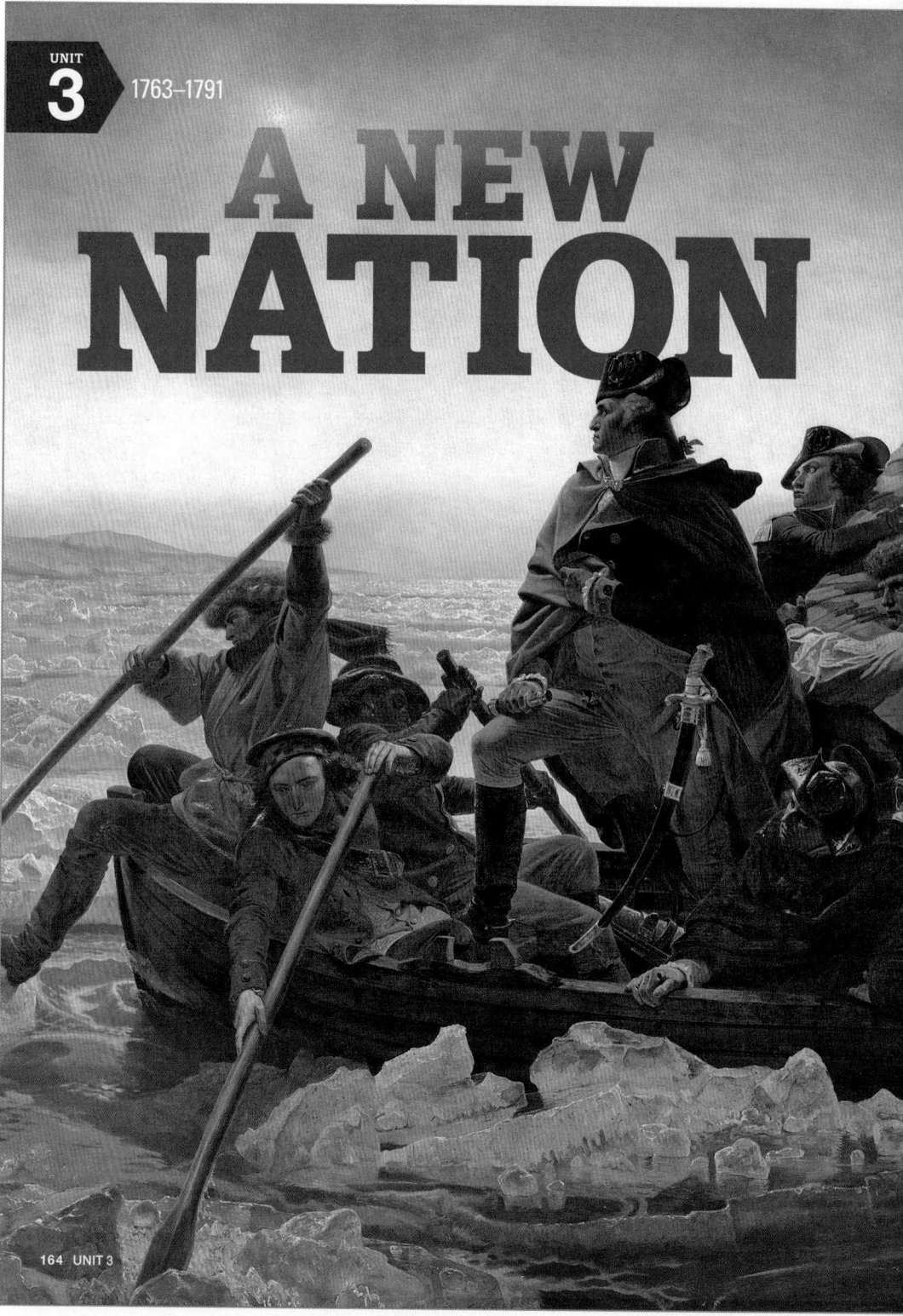

UNIT **3** 1763–1791

A NEW NATION

164 UNIT 3

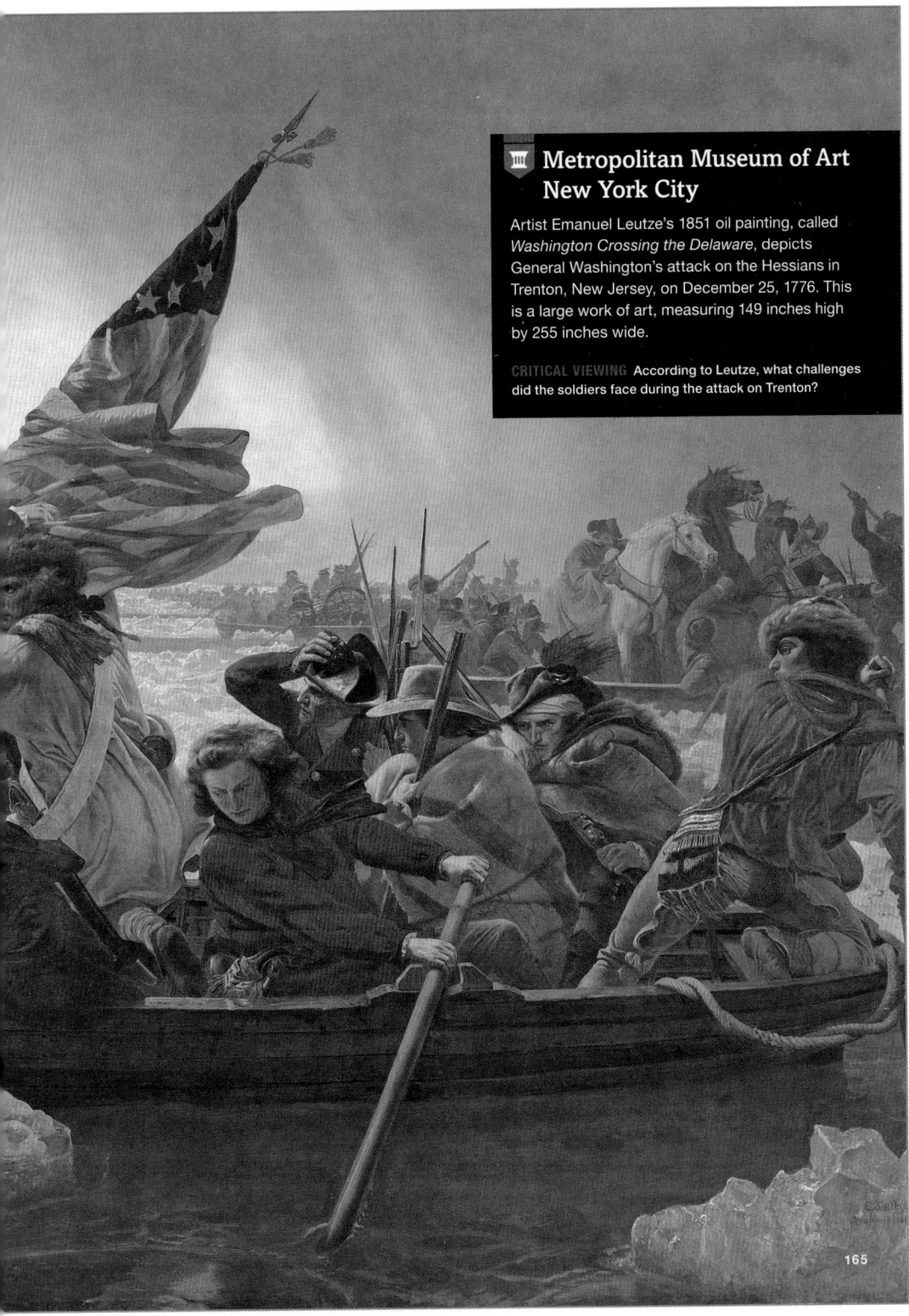

Metropolitan Museum of Art New York City

Artist Emanuel Leutze's 1851 oil painting, called *Washington Crossing the Delaware*, depicts General Washington's attack on the Hessians in Trenton, New Jersey, on December 25, 1776. This is a large work of art, measuring 149 inches high by 255 inches wide.

CRITICAL VIEWING According to Leutze, what challenges did the soldiers face during the attack on Trenton?

165

Virtual Museum Visit

The Metropolitan Museum of Art in New York City is the largest art museum in the United States. The collection spans 5,000 years and includes more than 2 million works of art from all over the world. The museum's website includes #metkids, which allows users to explore some of the works, learn fun facts, and view videos made by kids.

CRITICAL VIEWING Answers will vary. Possible response: The soldiers had to battle the ice in the river and strong winds as they rowed to Trenton. During the attack, the ragtag army would have been tired from their journey and not well equipped for the fight.

1770 OCEANIA:
Great Britain Claims Australia

Seventeen years after James Cook explored Australia's coast, British ships sailed for Australia. From 1788 to 1868, the British government sent convicts to overseas colonies in order to decrease overcrowding in British prisons. When the American colonies established independence in 1776, the government needed a new place to send convicts. British colonization began in Australia as a way for the government to transport its convicts to prisons overseas.

Most transported convicts were young, healthy, and unmarried. Only 20 percent were women. Those who were married sometimes brought their families with them. The majority of convicts came from the working classes in England and Ireland. The government used convicts' skills and relied on their labor to build the colonies. Convicts built roads, bridges, buildings, and farms as they served their sentences.

Though these settlers were British prisoners, they had certain freedoms. For example, many were allowed to live in their own homes and run their own businesses. At the end of their prison terms, freed convicts often remained in the colonies. Their contributions helped the Australian colonies to grow. **ASK:** Why do you think many freed convicts chose to remain in Australia? *(Answers will vary. Possible response: They had set down roots and built a life there.)*

UNIT 3

A NEW NATION

THE UNITED STATES

1776
The Declaration of Independence, which announces the formation of the United States of America and its independence from Britain, is adopted on July 4. *(the original Declaration of Independence)*

1775
After a shot is fired in Lexington, Massachusetts, the American Revolution begins.

1773
Colonists board three ships in Boston Harbor and throw 342 boxes of tea overboard to protest the Tea Act. The protest comes to be known as the Boston Tea Party.

1765
The Stamp Act is imposed, requiring American colonists to pay a tax on nearly every piece of paper they use. *(colonial teapot protesting the Stamp Act)*

1770

1760

THE WORLD

1765 ASIA
China invades Burma and begins a war with that country.

1763 AMERICAS
France is defeated in the French and Indian War and surrenders most of its North American colonies to Britain and Spain.

1770 OCEANIA
British captain James Cook explores the east coast of Australia and claims the region for Great Britain. *(replica of James Cook's ship, the Endeavour)*

HISTORICAL THINKING: DETERMINE CHRONOLOGY

What world events occurred at the same time as events leading to the formation of the United States?

1789
George Washington becomes the first president of the United States. *(Statue on the steps of New York's Federal Hall celebrates the site of Washington's inauguration.)*

1787–1788
Delegates at the Constitutional Convention draft, sign, and ratify the U.S. Constitution, which becomes the supreme law of the land.

1791
The Bill of Rights, guaranteeing individual rights, is added to the U.S. Constitution.

1790

1783
The United States defeats Britain, and the American Revolution ends when representatives from both sides sign the Treaty of Paris.

1791 AMERICAS
In the French colony of Saint-Domingue on the Caribbean island of Hispaniola, slaves rebel against French authority.

1800

1780

1779 AFRICA
Luanda, a city on Africa's Atlantic coast, becomes the leading port in the African slave trade.

1789 EUROPE
Inspired by Enlightenment thinkers, the French people attack the Bastille, a prison in Paris, and start a revolution. *(Storming of the Bastille by Jean-Pierre Houël)*

1789 EUROPE:
The French Revolution

In 1789, France exploded into revolution. Most historians point to the inequality among France's prerevolutionary social classes, or estates, as a main cause. The First Estate was the Catholic clergy, who had significant powers and privileges. The Second Estate was the nobility, who lived in privileged isolation at the king's court in Versailles. The nobles enjoyed lavish lifestyles and, like the members of the First Estate, were only lightly taxed.

The Third Estate was the common people, the vast majority of France. The Third Estate had its own hierarchy. At the top was the bourgeoisie, or middle class, made up of relatively prosperous and educated professionals and merchants. Beneath the bourgeoisie were the peasants, who made up the majority of the population. Hard work, hunger, and poverty were the norm for most peasants.

The Third Estate paid the largest share of the nation's taxes but had no say in government. It was largely members from this class who stormed the Bastille and triggered the revolution. **ASK:** What do you think members of the Third Estate wanted to accomplish by starting a revolution? *(Answers will vary. Possible response: They probably wanted a fair tax system and to be represented in government.)*

HISTORICAL THINKING: DETERMINE CHRONOLOGY

Answer: The French and Indian War, China's invasion of Burma, and the exploration of Australia occurred around the same time.

UNIT 3 A NEW NATION

UNIT 3 RESOURCES

UNIT INTRODUCTION
▶ Crossing the Delaware

UNIT TIME LINE

UNIT WRAP-UP

NATIONAL GEOGRAPHIC | CONNECTION

National Geographic **Magazine Adapted Articles**
- "Patriots in Petticoats"
- "Two Revolutions" `ONLINE`

Unit 3 Inquiry: Prepare an Argument

NG Learning Framework Activities
- Research a Colonial American
- Build a Time Line

Unit 3 Formal Assessment

CHAPTER 5 RESOURCES

Available at NGLSync.Cengage.com

TEACHER RESOURCES & ASSESSMENT

Reading and Note-Taking

Vocabulary Practice

Document-Based Question Template

Social Studies Skills Lessons
- Reading: Analyze Cause and Effect
- Writing: Write a Narrative

Formal Assessment
- Chapter 5 Pretest
- Chapter 5 Tests A & B
- Section Quizzes

Chapter 5 Answer Key

ExamView®
One-time Download

"These are the times **that try men's souls.**"
—Thomas Paine

STUDENT DIGITAL RESOURCES

- **eEdition** (English)
- **eEdition** (Spanish)
- **Handbooks**

- **Online Atlas**
- **American Gallery Online**
- **History Notebook**

- **American Voices (Biographies)**
- **Active History**
- **Projects for Inquiry-Based Learning**

Chapter 5 Spanish Resources are available at NGLSync.Cengage.com.

AMERICAN STORIES | Our American Identity

- Primary Sources
- On Your Feet: Question and Answer

AMERICAN GALLERY ONLINE Colonial Boston

SECTION 1 RESOURCES
BRITISH CONTROL

LESSON 1.1
Limits on Freedom

- On Your Feet: Turn and Talk on Topic

NG Learning Framework:
Write a Story

LESSON 1.2
Taxation without Representation

- On Your Feet: Rotating Discussion

NG Learning Framework:
Settle a Dispute

LESSON 1.3
The Stamp Act

- On Your Feet: Word Chain

NG Learning Framework:
Write a Biography

LESSON 1.4
AMERICAN VOICES
Benjamin Franklin

- On Your Feet: Three-Step Interview

NG Learning Framework:
Research an Invention

SECTION 2 RESOURCES
REBELLION IN THE COLONIES

LESSON 2.1
Colonial Protests Grow

- On Your Feet: Take a Stand

NG Learning Framework:
Connect Historical Events

LESSON 2.2
The Boston Massacre

- On Your Feet: Question and Answer

AMERICAN GALLERY ONLINE Colonial Boston

LESSON 2.3
The Boston Tea Party

- On Your Feet: Question and Answer

NG Learning Framework:
Organize a Peaceful Protest

LESSON 2.4
CURATING HISTORY
Museum of the American Revolution, Philadelphia

- On Your Feet: Sort the Artifacts

SECTION 3 RESOURCES
LEXINGTON AND CONCORD

LESSON 3.1
Preparing to Fight

- On Your Feet: Fishbowl

NG Learning Framework:
Explore the Meaning of Liberty

LESSON 3.2
The Midnight Ride of Paul Revere

▶ Myths of 1776

- On Your Feet: Inside-Outside Circle

NG Learning Framework:
Research the Five Riders

LESSON 3.3
Shot Heard Round the World

- On Your Feet: Three Corners

NG Learning Framework:
Create a Storyboard

LESSON 3.4
AMERICAN PLACES
North Bridge Concord, Massachusetts

- On Your Feet: Numbered Heads

NG Learning Framework:
Identify a Community Landmark

SECTION 4 RESOURCES
DECLARING INDEPENDENCE

LESSON 4.1
Colonial Army Forms

- On Your Feet: Chart Relay

NG Learning Framework:
Research the Continental Army

LESSON 4.2
GEOLOGY IN HISTORY
How Geology Shapes the Battlefield

- On Your Feet: Turn and Talk on Topic

NG Learning Framework:
Devise a Strategic Defense

LESSON 4.3
Breaking with Britain

- On Your Feet: Create a Concept Web

NG Learning Framework:
Form an Opinion

LESSON 4.4
Drafting the Declaration

- Active History: Analyze Primary Sources

NG Learning Framework:
Hold a Colonial Town Hall Meeting

American Voices Biographies
John and Abigail Adams ONLINE

LESSON 4.5
DOCUMENT-BASED QUESTION
Declarations of Freedom

- On Your Feet: Use a Jigsaw Strategy

CHAPTER 5 REVIEW

Strategy ❶
Turn Titles into Questions

To help students set a purpose for reading, have them read the title of each lesson in a section and then turn that title into a question they believe will be answered in the lesson. Students can record their questions and write their own answers, or they can ask each other their questions.

Use with All Lessons *For example, in Lesson 1.1, the question could be: What limits were placed on the colonists' freedoms?*

Strategy ❷
Complete a Cause-and-Effect Chart

Have students complete a graphic organizer like the one below to show what led to the Boston Tea Party.

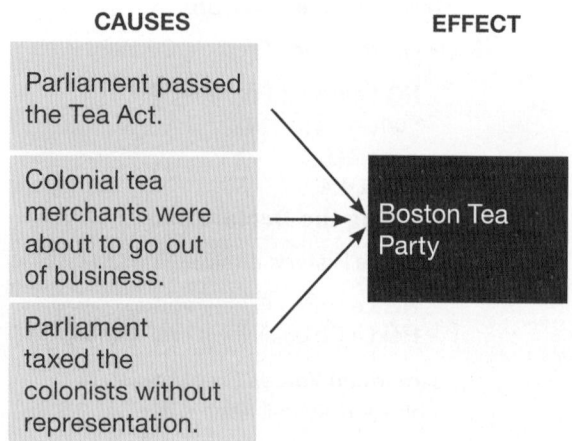

CAUSES — Parliament passed the Tea Act. / Colonial tea merchants were about to go out of business. / Parliament taxed the colonists without representation. **EFFECT** — Boston Tea Party

Use with Lesson 2.3

Strategy ❸
Play the "I Am . . ." Game

To reinforce the meanings of Key Vocabulary and important names, places, and events, assign every student one term or name that appears in the chapter and have them write a one-sentence clue beginning with "I am." Have students take turns reading clues and calling on other students to guess answers.

Use with All Lessons

Strategy ❶
Provide Terms and Names on Audio

Decide which of the terms and names are important for mastery and have a volunteer record the pronunciations and a short sentence defining each word. Encourage students to listen to the recording as often as necessary.

Use with All Lessons *You might also use the recording to quiz students on their mastery of the terms. Play one definition at a time from the recording and ask students to identify the term or name described.*

Strategy ❷
Describe Lesson Visuals

Pair visually challenged students with students who are not visually challenged. Ask the latter to help their partners "see" the visuals in the chapter by describing the images and answering any questions the visually impaired students might have.

Use with All Lessons *For example, for the anti–Stamp Act visual in Lesson 1.3, students might describe the skull and crossbones on the image and read aloud the visual's text and caption.*

ENGLISH LANGUAGE LEARNERS

Strategy ❶
Create a Word Web

To activate prior knowledge and build vocabulary, work with students at the **Expanding** level to create a Word Web for the word *tyranny* before beginning Section 1 and the term *unalienable right* before beginning Section 4.

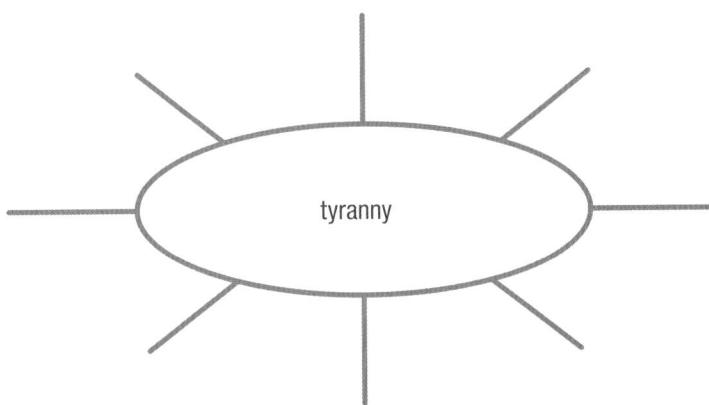

tyranny

Use with Lessons 1.2 and 4.3 *For the web for* tyranny, *encourage students to think of words they associate with dictators from the past or present whom they might know about.*

Strategy ❷
Pair Partners for Dictation

After students read each lesson in the chapter, have them write a sentence summarizing its main idea. Have students get together in pairs and dictate their sentences to each other. Then have them work together to check the sentences for accuracy and spelling.

Use with All Lessons *You may wish to place students in pairs, such as students at the **Emerging** level with those at the **Bridging** level, and have more advanced students assist less advanced students in checking the accuracy and spelling of their sentences.*

Strategy ❸
Use Visuals to Predict Content

Before reading, ask students at the **Emerging** level to read the lesson title and look at any visuals. Then ask them to write a sentence for each visual that predicts how it is related to the lesson title. Repeat the exercise after reading and ask volunteers to read their sentences.

Use with All Lessons

GIFTED & TALENTED

Strategy ❶
Teach a Class

Before beginning the chapter, allow students to choose one of the lessons listed below and prepare to teach the content to the class. Give them a set amount of time in which to present their lesson. Suggest that students think about any visuals or activities they want to use when they teach.

Use with Lessons 2.1–2.3, 3.2–3.3, and 4.2

Strategy ❷
Interview a Historical Figure

Allow students to work in teams of two to plan, write, and perform a simulated television interview with Benjamin Franklin or with Benedict Arnold. Tell students that the purpose of the interview is to focus on the achievements, actions, and goals of the historical figure.

Use with Lessons 1.4 and 4.1 *Invite students to do research to learn more about the historical figure they have chosen. Encourage them to elicit in-depth answers by asking the historical figures why and how they did the things they did.*

Pre-AP

Strategy ❶
Write a Feature Article

Have students use the Internet to research the battles of Lexington and Concord. Ask students to write a detailed feature article describing what they have learned. Articles should focus on the time frame of events, the movement of both British and American troops, and specific individuals who were involved. Encourage students to include photos, illustrations, or charts in their articles.

Use with Lesson 3.3

Strategy ❷
Build a Time Line

Ask students to build an online time line of the major events and ideas leading to the American Revolution. Tell them to include basic descriptions of events as well as a written analysis of each event's significance. When students have completed their time lines, they can post them to a class blog or website or on an Internet document sharing site.

Use with Lessons 2.2, 3.3, and 4.1

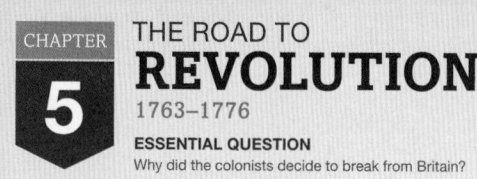

THE ROAD TO
REVOLUTION
1763–1776

ESSENTIAL QUESTION
Why did the colonists decide to break from Britain?

AMERICAN STORIES **Our American Identity**

SECTION 1 **British Control**
KEY VOCABULARY

boycott	militia	repeal	Stamp Act
Currency Act	Proclamation of 1763	revenue	Sugar Act
duty	Quartering Act	Sons of Liberty	tyranny
grievance			

SECTION 2 **Rebellion in the Colonies**
KEY VOCABULARY

Boston Massacre	committee of correspondence	Townshend Acts
Boston Tea Party	Tea Act	writ of assistance

SECTION 3 **Lexington and Concord**
KEY VOCABULARY

First Continental Congress	Loyalist	Patriot
Intolerable Acts	minutemen	

SECTION 4 **Declaring Independence**
KEY VOCABULARY

artillery	earthwork	Second Continental Congress
Continental Army	geology	terrain
Declaration of Independence	Hessian	unalienable right
drumlin		

AMERICAN GALLERY
ONLINE **Colonial Boston**

READING STRATEGY

ANALYZE CAUSE AND EFFECT
When you analyze cause and effect, you note the consequences of an event, an action, or a condition. As you read the chapter, use a graphic organizer like this one to identify the causes of the colonies' separation from Britain.

Causes   Effect

The colonies declare independence from Britain.

CRITICAL VIEWING In this photo by National Geographic photographer Kenneth Garrett, reenactors stage a battle in Leesburg, Virginia. What details in the photo convey what fighting on the front lines of this battle might have been like?

"These are the times
that try men's souls."
—Thomas Paine

INTRODUCE THE PHOTOGRAPH

Battle Reenactment

Tell students to study the photograph of the battle that opens this chapter. Make sure students understand that this is a reenactment of a battle that took place in Leesburg, Virginia. Explain that historical reenactment is a popular hobby for many people. In order to stage an authentic scene, reenactors wear clothing from the period, much of which can be quite elaborate. They also assume the language and accents of their subjects and try never to "break character"—or slip back into their present-day identities. Tell students that in this chapter they will learn about the factors and events that led the American colonies to stage a revolution against one of the most powerful empires in history.

NATIONAL GEOGRAPHIC PHOTOGRAPHER
Kenneth Garrett

Ken Garrett grew up in Virginia and still lives there. He has worked on more than 50 stories for *National Geographic* magazine, and he has published several of his own books. He specializes in photographing the artifacts and sites of past civilizations, from ancient Egypt to Mesoamerica. He also has a special fondness for historical sites in the United States. He knows the power places have in shaping national identities. Places also help tell good stories, and he shares those stories with his camera.

CRITICAL VIEWING Answers will vary. Possible response: Details about what fighting might have been like on the front lines at the battle at Leesburg, Virginia, include fire from the cannons and how close soldiers are to the fire and to each other. Smoke and glare from the fire would have made it hard to see well to reload and aim the rifles. There must have been a lot of noise and confusion.

For Chapter 5 Spanish Resources, visit the Resources Menu. Chapter 5 Resources are available at NGLSync.Cengage.com.

INTRODUCE THE ESSENTIAL QUESTION

Why did the colonists decide to break from Britain?

Roundtable Activity: Elements of a Revolution This activity introduces students to different elements of the American Revolution: economics, sacrifices, strategies, and political thinkers and ideas. Divide the class into four groups and have each group sit at a table. Assign the following questions to the groups:

Group 1: What economic factors might cause a colony to revolt from its governing country?

Group 2: What kinds of sacrifices were revolutionaries willing to make to win independence?

Group 3: How might differing strategies about achieving independence complicate efforts or affect the outcome of a revolution?

Group 4: What effects do political thinkers and ideas have on revolutions?

Ask students at each table to take turns answering the question. When they have finished their discussion, ask a representative from each table to summarize that group's answers.

INTRODUCE CHAPTER VOCABULARY

Vocabulary Pyramids

As they read the chapter, encourage students to complete Vocabulary Pyramids for Key Vocabulary words. Tell students to make a pyramid for each word, fill in what they know about each word before reading, and then add to or correct the pyramid after they encounter the word in the chapter. Model an example for students on the board, using the graphic organizer below.

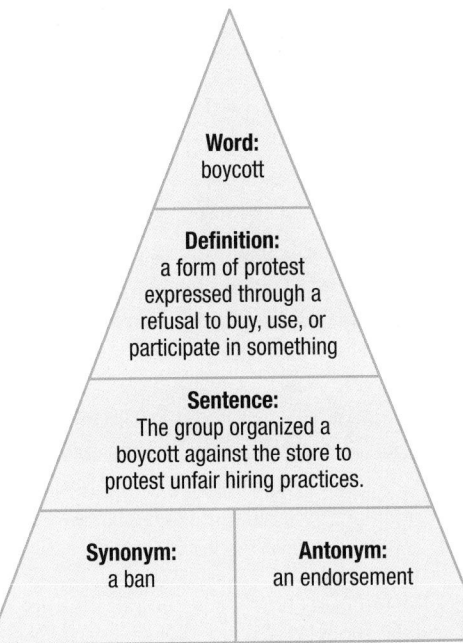

Word:
boycott

Definition:
a form of protest expressed through a refusal to buy, use, or participate in something

Sentence:
The group organized a boycott against the store to protest unfair hiring practices.

Synonym:
a ban

Antonym:
an endorsement

INTRODUCE THE READING STRATEGY

ANALYZE CAUSE AND EFFECT
Remind students that when analyzing cause and effect, it is useful to keep track of the consequences of specific events, actions, or conditions. Sometimes, multiple causes lead to a singular effect, as in the many causes that spurred the colonists to break from Britain. Other times, one cause might lead to several effects, as in the many consequences that stemmed from British colonization. Model completing the Cause-and-Effect Chart. Point out the two sections of the chart, one labeled "Causes" and the other labeled "Effect." Ask for suggestions for one example of cause and effect and fill in the chart for that entry as a class. Remind students to make use of the chart as they read the chapter.

Causes   Effect

The colonies declare independence from Britain.

KEY DATES FOR CHAPTER 5

1754	French and Indian War begins
1764	Sugar Act
1765	Stamp Act
1770	Boston Massacre
1773	Boston Tea Party
1774	First Continental Congress meets
1775	Battle of Lexington and Concord
1776	Thomas Paine publishes *Common Sense*
1776	Declaration of Independence

For more on protecting human rights, see *GLOBAL ISSUES: HUMAN RIGHTS.*

Objectives

- **Learn about the history of the American flag.**
- **Analyze flags and other symbols of a nation and their significance throughout history and today.**
- **Consider your American identity and any symbols you identify with.**
- **Study primary sources: "The Star-Spangled Banner" and the Pledge of Allegiance.**

Critical Thinking Skills for "Our American Identity"

- Make Connections
- Draw Conclusions
- Compare and Contrast
- Evaluate
- Make Inferences
- Analyze Visuals
- Synthesize
- Make Predictions

Background for the Teacher

This American Story introduces students to the concept of identity, specifically American identity, through primary source material, engaging photographs, and a compelling narrative about an important symbol—the American flag—from its origin to the present day. Use this high-interest story to hook students before they read the chapter and inspire them to consider what being an American means to them.

This chapter, The Road to Revolution, discusses the period in history when the colonies were struggling under British rule and colonists were trying to determine their identity, both as individuals and as a nation separate from Great Britain. This American Story will serve as a thought-provoking and relatable entry point into one of the major themes discussed in chapter content: American identity.

History Notebook

Encourage students to complete the American Story page for Chapter 5 in their History Notebooks as they read.

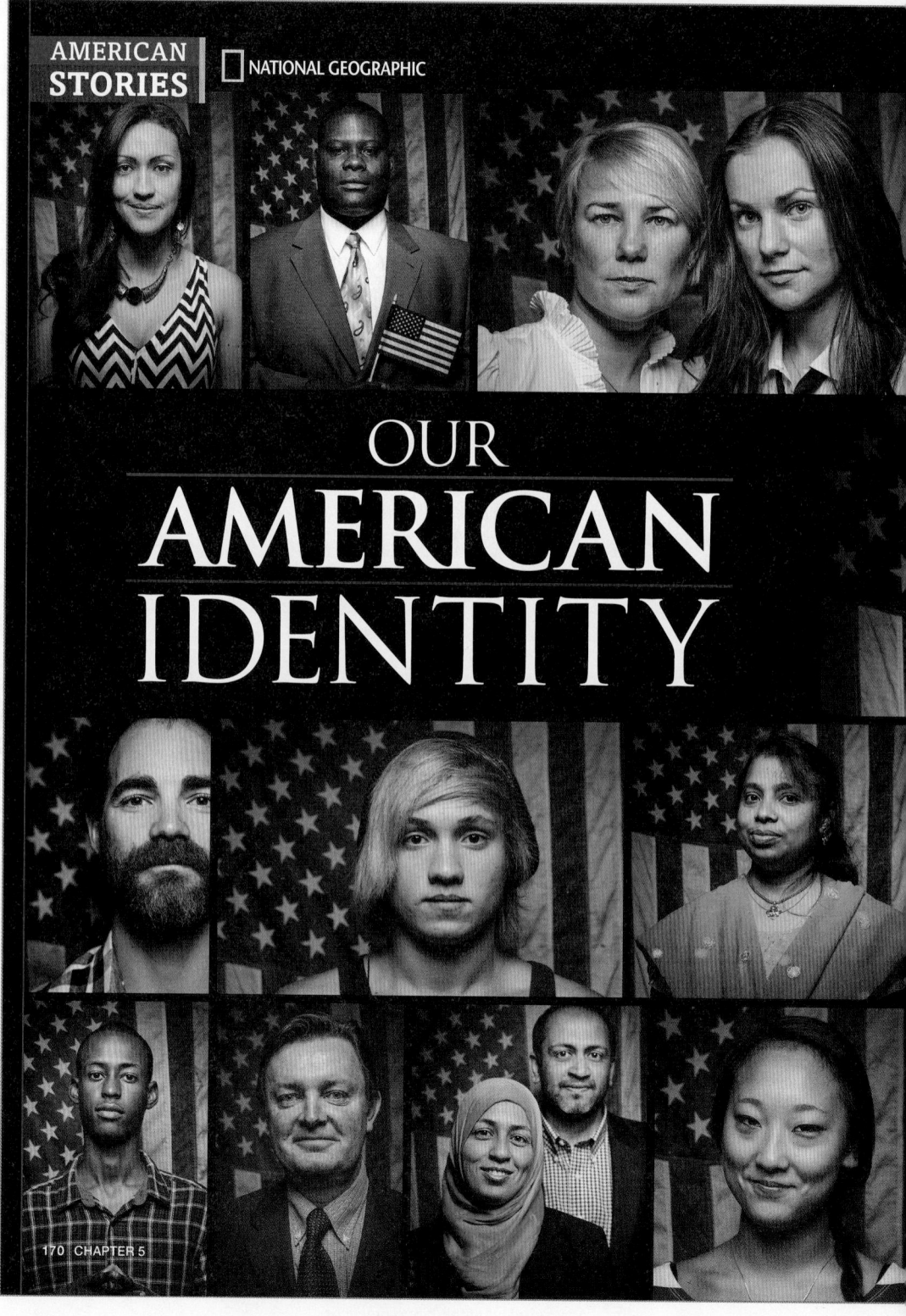

AMERICAN STORIES | NATIONAL GEOGRAPHIC

OUR AMERICAN IDENTITY

170 CHAPTER 5

Their faces may be different, but these individuals all identified as Americans and first-time voters in the 2012 presidential election. Here they are shown posing in front of the American flag after casting their ballots in Bridgeport, Connecticut.

The American flag is one of the most recognizable national symbols. For many of us, seeing it at just the right moment or in just the right setting sends shivers down our spines, raises goosebumps on our arms, or brings tears to our eyes.

Why does a simple piece of cloth have the power to provoke such a physical reaction in so many people? The answer may be simple: identity. For many, being an American is part of our identity, and the flag may be a symbol of that part of us. It reminds us that being part of a country influences who we are as individuals.

The Stars and Stripes solemnly drapes the caskets of fallen heroes returning from battle, sheltering them with the gratitude of their country as they are laid to rest. The flag waves proudly at sporting events, representative of the strength and perseverance the United States was built upon and the country's passion for sports and competition. Clothing that bears the flag is often worn to make a statement—to identify the wearer. It says: I'm a firefighter. I'm a soldier. I'm a Girl Scout. I'm an astronaut. I'm a veteran. I'm an athlete. I'm a relief worker. I live in the United States. I represent the United States. I support the United States.

Where did this important icon come from, and what does its story tell us about the establishment of national identity?

Survey and Write

Conduct an informal survey among students to establish how many students are American citizens, hold dual citizenship, or are citizens of another country. If needed, prompt a short discussion of what it means to be a citizen of a country (not just the United States) and then what it means to be "American." Then write the following prompt on the board or whiteboard: *What is American identity?* Ask students to spend two minutes writing words or sentences that correspond to the writing prompt. Invite volunteers to share what they have written. Then tell students they are going to read an American Story about American identity and how it varies for every American.

Selfies

Tell each student to take a selfie in front of a patriotic background or flag, similar to the mosaic of images that opens this American Story. Post the selfies in the classroom and allow each student to caption his or her photo with a sentence that describes what it means to be an American.

K-W-L Chart

Provide each student with a blank four-column K-W-L Chart. In the first column, ask students to list the following topics: American Identity, The Pledge of Allegiance, Fort McHenry, "The Star-Spangled Banner." Next, ask students to complete the second and third columns with what they already know about the topic and questions they would like to have answered as they read the American Story. Finally, as students read the American Story, allow time for them to fill in what they learned about each topic in the remaining column.

Fort McHenry

Built between 1799 and 1802, Fort McHenry was constructed in the shape of a five-pointed star. Each point was visible from the points on either side of it and provided a great view of the land surrounding the fort. The solid brick fort included four barracks where soldiers lived, a guardhouse, and a powder magazine, where flammable gunpowder was carefully stored. The fort itself underwent major improvements in the 1830s and can still be toured today, as it is now a National Monument and Historic Shrine. In the summer months, the Fort McHenry Guard performs drill, musket, and artillery demonstrations for the visitors who come to see "The Birthplace of the American National Anthem."

Patriotic Music

For many people, the music of their country inspires great feelings of patriotism. "The Star-Spangled Banner" has many verses, but none are as widely known as the first verse. Introduce students to the second verse below, discuss it, and analyze its meaning. Then consider playing other types of patriotic American music for the class to listen to, discuss, and analyze.

"THE STAR-SPANGLED BANNER"
(second verse)
by Francis Scott Key

On the shore, dimly seen through the mists of the deep,
Where the foe's haughty host in dread silence reposes,
What is that which the breeze, o'er the towering steep,
As it fitfully blows, half conceals, half discloses?
Now it catches the gleam of the morning's first beam,
In full glory reflected now shines on the stream:
'Tis the star-spangled banner! O long may it wave
O'er the land of the free and the home of the brave!

More Patriotic Songs

"My Country 'Tis of Thee"
"Yankee Doodle Dandy"
"America the Beautiful"
"Battle Hymn of the Republic"
"The Stars and Stripes Forever"
"God Bless America"
"This Land Is Your Land"

AMERICAN STORIES

On July 4, 1776, representatives of the 13 American colonies approved the Declaration of Independence, formally announcing their break with Britain. Soon after the Declaration was drafted, the Continental Congress passed an act establishing an official flag for the new nation: "Resolved, that the flag of the United States be thirteen stripes, alternate red and white; that the union be thirteen stars, white in a blue field, representing a new constellation." This description doesn't fit the look of the flag as we know it today, but it describes the first of many versions of the flag—the earliest official national symbol and the emblem of independence from Great Britain.

Fast forward to September 13, 1814. The War of 1812 rages on, with British and American troops battling fiercely at Fort McHenry in Baltimore, Maryland. At this point in history, the American flag featured 15 stars and 15 stripes. Fort McHenry served both as the military stronghold that stood between the harbor and the city and as the United States' last hope to prevent a major British military victory. As British rockets and bombs flew from ships, letting loose a deadly deluge of shrapnel and fire over the fort, American gunners responded with their own fire, pushing the British back. The fighting continued all night as a young Washington lawyer named Francis Scott Key watched from a boat in the harbor. While the fiery battle carried on, Key wondered which country would emerge victorious and whose flag he would see flying above the fort in the morning.

It was the American Stars and Stripes—a huge flag measuring 30 feet by 42 feet, made out of red, white, and blue wool by a Baltimore seamstress. The sight of the flag flying proudly over Fort McHenry that morning was so moving it inspired Key to draft the original version of the poem that would become our national anthem: "The Star-Spangled Banner."

CRITICAL VIEWING Think about a time you attended an event or game that began with "The Star-Spangled Banner," and consider this photograph of the stadium. What might a person from another country infer about American identity from these traditions?

THE STAR-SPANGLED BANNER

O say can you see, by the dawn's early light,
What so proudly we hail'd at the twilight's last gleaming,
Whose broad stripes and bright stars through the perilous fight
O'er the ramparts we watch'd were so gallantly streaming?
And the rocket's red glare, the bombs bursting in air,
Gave proof through the night that our flag was still there,
O say does that star-spangled banner yet wave
O'er the land of the free and the home of the brave?

Inspired by the sight of the American flag after a U.S. victory over the British during the War of 1812, Francis Scott Key wrote the 1814 lyrics that were set, ironically, to the tune of a popular British song and became "The Star-Spangled Banner." This song is still the go-to musical expression of patriotism in the United States.

After the United States entered World War I, patriotic music was often played at professional baseball games. In game one of the 1918 World Series, the Cubs and Red Sox players faced the American flag while the band played "The Star-Spangled Banner" with the crowd singing along. This sparked the tradition of playing the song at U.S. sporting events, even though it wouldn't be declared the national anthem by Congress until 1931.

This three-cent stamp honoring Francis Scott Key was issued August 9, 1948. It features Key's portrait and home, the American flags of 1814 and 1948, and Fort McHenry.

Guided Discussion

1. **Compare and Contrast** Provide students with two different audio recordings of "The Star-Spangled Banner," which are widely available online. Consider using a nontraditional version, such as a recording of Jimi Hendrix performing it live or a pop singer performing it at the Super Bowl, as well as a more traditional version. Play the recordings for students and use a T-Chart to record their observations. **ASK:** What mood or emotions does each one evoke? What instruments are used? Which one do you like best?

2. **Evaluate** Tell students to examine the second verse of "The Star-Spangled Banner" (available here and on the Fort McHenry page of the National Park Service website). If possible, project the lyrics on a whiteboard or provide students with a photocopy of the lyrics. Work as a class to discuss the second verse of the song and "translate" it into modern language. Discuss the meaning, symbolism, and historical context of each verse.

CRITICAL VIEWING Answers will vary. Possible response: Someone from another country might infer that sporting events are a major part of American culture, and therefore many of them open with a deeply American song.

The Pledge of Allegiance

Explore the photograph of the naturalization ceremony with students. Explain that once a prospective American citizen has an approved application and has passed a citizenship interview, that person recites an oath that makes him or her a fully naturalized U.S. citizen. This usually takes place at an oath ceremony, like the one shown in the photograph. Oath ceremonies can be held in a courtroom, a federal or state building, a historic landmark, or even a large stadium. **ASK:** Why do you think a swearing-in ceremony is part of becoming a U.S. citizen? *(It gives new citizens the opportunity to profess their allegiance to their new country. It is a special way to make the citizenship feel important and official.)* What symbols are part of a naturalization ceremony? *(Symbols of the naturalization ceremony include the oath itself, the American flag, and sometimes a historic American building.)*

Discuss other types of oaths students may be familiar with. Examples may include being sworn in to testify in a court of law or pledges recited as part of a scouting organization or other group. Discuss the significance of publicly pledging an oath versus doing it privately.

If your classroom discussion includes the topic of the separation of church and state in regard to the Pledge of Allegiance, accept all viewpoints and responses, and acknowledge that it is also appropriate for students to refrain from commenting on this complicated issue.

THINK ABOUT IT

Answers will vary. Possible response: Students may suggest animals, trees, shapes, and any other symbol.

For the next 100 years, American military families cared for and proudly displayed the famous Fort McHenry flag. During the Civil War, they hid the flag to keep it safe. Until 1880, small pieces of the flag were even cut and given to war veterans and others—something considered disrespectful and unpatriotic by today's standards. The flag finally landed safely in the Smithsonian National Museum in 1912, 98 years after it flew over Fort McHenry. It remains part of the Smithsonian collection today.

The look of the American flag has evolved along with the nation. Stars and stripes have been added and relocated as the country has expanded, endured the horrors of civil and global wars, and acquired new territories. But the impact and symbolic value of the flag has remained steadfast to many Americans. Many of us view the American flag as a symbol of our identity as U.S. citizens, but it's not the only symbol of national identity, nor does a person have to attach to *any* symbol in order to establish his or her identity. Maybe your identity as an American is revealed in a different way. Or maybe a different symbol of national identity has more meaning to you. A person. A logo. A slogan. A poem. When it comes to what defines your unique identity, you have many rich and wonderful choices.

THINK ABOUT IT

What type of symbol represents your identity as an American? Why?

THE PLEDGE OF ALLEGIANCE

I pledge allegiance to the flag of the United States of America, and to the republic for which it stands, one nation under God, indivisible, with liberty and justice for all.

If you go to school in the United States, you've probably recited the Pledge of Allegiance many times. Written in 1892 by Francis Bellamy, a Baptist minister from New York, the pledge was intended as a salute to the American flag, to be read in unison by schoolchildren. Over time, its words have been changed and debated—especially the phrase "under God," which some people feel violates the constitutional separation of church and state. What do you think?

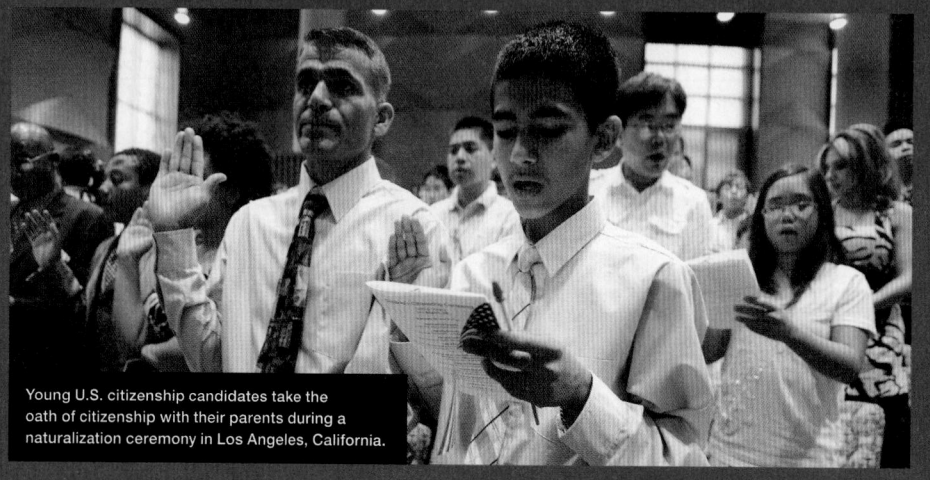

Young U.S. citizenship candidates take the oath of citizenship with their parents during a naturalization ceremony in Los Angeles, California.

A SYMBOL OF A NATION

You'd expect to see the American flag on American soil, but the Stars and Stripes can be seen in many interesting and meaningful places across the world—and out of this world!

Why might people visiting faraway destinations want others to know about their nation's flag? Maybe it's the item they feel identifies them most clearly as Americans. Think about what symbol of national identity you might use when visiting another country.

1 Marchers carry American and Cuban flags at a 2015 rally focused on human rights abuses by the Castro regime. The United States restored diplomatic ties with Cuba in late 2014 after 53 years of distrust.

2 The famous sculpture at the Marine Corps Memorial in Arlington, Virginia, depicts U.S. Marines raising the flag on the island of Iwo Jima, Japan, after a major victory during World War II. The sculpture is based on a photo of the actual flag-raising captured by photographer Joe Rosenthal in February 1945.

3 This customized version of the flag was used at a peaceful protest at the Washington Monument in 1969.

4 Astronaut Buzz Aldrin posed for this 1969 photograph beside the American flag he and Neil Armstrong planted on the moon.

The Road to Revolution **175**

Active Options

On Your Feet: Question and Answer Ask half the class to write True-False questions based on factual information found in this American Story. Ask the other half to create answer cards with "True" written on one side and "False" on the other. As each question is read aloud, students in the second group should stand and display the correct answer to the question. When discrepancies occur, review the question and discuss which answer is correct.

AMERICAN GALLERY
ONLINE **Colonial Boston** Invite students to explore the American Gallery. Have them select one of the images and do additional research to learn more about it. Ask questions that will inspire additional inquiry about the chosen gallery image, such as: What is this? Where and when was this created? By whom? Why was it created? What is it made of? Why does it belong in this chapter? What else would you like to know about it?

History Notebook
Encourage students to complete the American Gallery page for Chapter 5 in their History Notebooks as they read.

Guided Discussion

1. **Make Inferences** What are some of the benefits of keeping an American artifact like the Fort McHenry flag in a museum? *(The flag can be kept in a temperature-controlled setting and in low light. Professionals can monitor it for damage and repair it if needed. The public can see the flag and learn more about it. The flag is safe from theft or vandalism.)*

2. **Analyze Visuals** Why would the gantry shown in the fourth photograph on the opposite page be a necessary tool in restoring the flag? *(The flag is large, so it would be impossible to reach the middle of it without walking or crawling on the flag itself.)*

🏛 Virtual Museum Visit

The National Museum of American History in Washington, D.C., contains more than 3 million national artifacts, from Abraham Lincoln's top hat to the gowns of the American first ladies. The exhibits revolve around major themes in American history and culture, from the American Revolution to today. Visitors view collections of artifacts that explore transportation, military conflicts, presidencies, and pop culture. The museum's website is a great resource for students—encourage them to take a virtual visit, or do so as a class.

WRITE ABOUT HISTORY

Connect to Your American Identity This American Story tells the story of a major American symbol, the flag, and describes how symbols like this can be part of someone's national identity. To help students make connections between the American Story and their own lives, have them write a short essay on the topic of what the phrase "American identity" means to them. Remind them of the activity they did before reading the American Story, when they considered what the concept of American identity was without connecting it to their own lives and experiences. Pair students to edit each others' essays and make suggestions for revision. Provide guidance about the writing process as necessary.

CRITICAL VIEWING Answers will vary. Possible response: The glass enclosure allows visitors to see the flag without damaging it but also protects the flag from light, dust, and temperature changes. The viewing area gives people space to sit or stand and experience the flag comfortably but safely.

AMERICAN STORIES 🏛 National Museum of American History
Washington, D.C.

PRESERVING THE STAR-SPANGLED BANNER

The enormous flag raised over Baltimore's Fort McHenry to announce the American victory over the British during the War of 1812 has seen better days. Time, use, and questionable storage have rendered it dirty and fragile, and the flag itself—this important relic of American history—is now at risk of falling apart.

Beginning in 1998, great efforts have been made to preserve this 1814 flag, the inspiration for Francis Scott Key's composition of "The Star-Spangled Banner." The flag has been safely housed in the National Museum of American History since the early 1900s. It is now stored with attention to preservation, at a 10-degree angle in a low-oxygen, low-light chamber. Experts routinely examine the flag's delicate fibers with microscopes, looking for signs of decay or damage.

As you read about the events leading up to the American Revolution in this chapter, consider why having a flag to represent an emerging American identity would have been important to the colonists.

CRITICAL VIEWING What details from these photographs reveal how this museum balances preserving the flag with displaying it for public view?

176 CHAPTER 5

1. For more than 30 years, the Star-Spangled Banner hung in the central Flag Hall at the museum. But in 1998, the flag entered a 10-year-long restoration process.

2. To repair the flag, the conservation team had to first remove its soiled linen backing. This meant clipping about 1.7 million stitches that had held the backing in place since 1914 and using tweezers to lift each one away.

3. The team used dry sponges to gently remove dirt from the side of the flag that had been covered by the linen. The dirt itself was analyzed to learn more about the flag's history.

4. Much of the restoration of the flag was done in a special lab that allowed museum visitors to watch the process through a glass wall. A movable bridge called a gantry allowed conservation team members to hang above the flag as they restored it.

The Road to Revolution 177

English Language Learners ELD

Pose and Answer Questions Arrange students at the **Emerging** and **Expanding** levels in mixed pairs and ask them to reread the American Story together. Instruct them to pause after each paragraph and ask one another *who, what, when, where,* or *why* questions about what they have just read. Suggest students use a 5Ws Chart to help organize their questions and answers. Ask students at the **Expanding** level to assist students at the **Emerging** level as needed.

Pre-AP

Investigate Different Versions of the Flag Direct students do to online research individually or in small groups to learn more about how the look of the American flag evolved over time, including the symbolism and arrangement of the stars and stripes. Ask them to create a time line or other visual or a report to document what they have discovered.

See the Chapter Planner for more strategies for differentiation.

HISTORICAL THINKING

Ask and have students answer the following questions.

1. **READING CHECK** What was the original purpose of the Pledge of Allegiance?

2. **SYNTHESIZE** Why might different Americans identify more strongly with different symbols of the United States?

3. **MAKE PREDICTIONS** Based on the American Story you have just read, how do you predict the topics in the story will relate to Chapter 5: The Road to Revolution?

ANSWERS

1. The Pledge of Allegiance was originally intended as a salute to the American flag, to be read in unison by schoolchildren.

2. The flag might evoke strong feelings of patriotism or allegiance in some Americans. Other Americans might identify more with another symbol, such as a bald eagle or an American bison. Still others may not identify with a physical symbol.

3. Answers will vary.

1.1 Limits on Freedom

As far as the British were concerned, 1763 was a great year. They had won the French and Indian War—a major victory. Business in the colonies was booming, which put money into the British economy. What could possibly go wrong?

MAIN IDEA After the French and Indian War, the British government enacted laws that restricted some of the colonies' freedoms.

PROBLEMS ARISE

At the end of the French and Indian War, the British colonists in North America had plenty of reasons to be optimistic about their future as British subjects. The colonies' **militias**, or groups of local men who organized to protect their town or colony, had proven themselves to be able fighters alongside British soldiers. After decades of economic growth, the colonies were prosperous. Still, some of the colonists felt a growing dissatisfaction.

The British colonies were the only European settlements in North America where ordinary people could vote for their local legislatures. This freedom to govern, however, was limited by **King George III** and the British Parliament. King George believed the role of a colony was to support the mother country. He was determined to maintain control of Britain's North American colonies.

Concerned about the high cost of the French and Indian War, the king was eager to limit contact between the Native Americans and the colonists in order to keep the peace. As you have read, the king issued a law

CRITICAL VIEWING This hand-colored engraving (right) shows British soldiers housed in an American home during the 1770s. What do the details in this image help you infer about the colonists' reactions to the Quartering Act?

requiring colonists to stay east of a line drawn on a map along the crest of the Appalachian Mountains. This law was called the **Proclamation of 1763**.

Settlers in the western areas objected to the proclamation. They felt the king was restricting their freedom to expand colonial territories westward. In fact, people continued to settle west of the line decreed by the proclamation. The British government, weighed down by debt from the French and Indian War, could not afford to send soldiers to enforce the law.

SOLDIERS IN THE COLONIES

Soon, colonists along the eastern coast also found themselves frustrated by laws they found oppressive. After the war, many British soldiers were moved into port cities such as New York and Boston to help enforce laws. In 1765, the British Parliament passed the **Quartering Act**. The Quartering Act required colonists to provide

The Proclamation of 1763

This historical map shows the land assigned to the colonists and Native Americans by the Proclamation of 1763. The colonists resented the proclamation, and many continued to push west of the Appalachians into land long inhabited by Native Americans. This migration weakened an agreement called the Covenant Chain. A covenant is an agreement or promise between two parties.

The Covenant Chain was a complicated system of alliances established between the nations of the Iroquois League and the northernmost colonies. The chain originated around 1677 and lasted for a century. It helped European settlers and some Native American groups maintain mostly peaceful relationships, but that friendship was tested as new settlers began to claim Native American lands.

Territories and Colonies, 1763

CRITICAL VIEWING Consider the label on the map that refers to Native Americans and what you know about the Covenant Chain. To what extent do you think this covenant was fulfilled?

housing for British soldiers. If a city did not have barracks to house the soldiers, the men were housed in local inns, homes, and stables, or vacant houses or barns.

While the Quartering Act did not allow the British troops to kick people out of their homes, local governments and residents still resented being forced to house the soldiers. The New York colonial assembly refused to enforce the Quartering Act. In all the colonies, the presence of British troops provoked tension and hostility between soldiers and the civilians who had begun to identify less with the British and more as Americans.

HISTORICAL THINKING

1. **READING CHECK** What were the goals of the Proclamation of 1763 and the Quartering Act?

2. **COMPARE AND CONTRAST** In what ways were the complaints of eastern and western colonists similar and different?

3. **DETERMINE WORD MEANING** What does *prosperous* mean in the sentence, "After decades of economic growth, the colonists were prosperous"?

---

178 CHAPTER 5

PLAN

Objective
Analyze how laws passed by British Parliament provoked frustration among the colonists.

Critical Thinking Skills for Lesson 1.1
- Identify Main Ideas and Details
- Monitor Comprehension
- Compare and Contrast
- Determine Word Meaning
- Make Inferences
- Form and Support Opinions
- Interpret Maps

Essential Question for Chapter 5
Why did the colonists decide to break from Britain? The colonists objected to the Proclamation of 1763 and the Quartering Act passed by the British Parliament. Lesson 1.1 discusses the colonists' frustration with those laws.

Background for the Teacher

The Proclamation of 1763 was an attempt by the British to organize British territories and provide Native Americans with lands free of colonial settlement. The act prohibited settlement on Native American land west of the Appalachian Mountains and required settlers already established there to leave. The provisions of the Proclamation of 1763 were in response to an attempt by several united tribes to expel all settlers from their ancestral homes. Carefully orchestrated attacks led by the Ottawa chief Pontiac, known collectively as Pontiac's War (1763–1764), succeeded in capturing eight of 12 fortified British forts. Eventually, British soldiers were able to subdue the attacks, and a peace treaty was concluded in July 1766.

Consider Reactions to Imposed Laws

Remind students that at the end of the French and Indian War, the British government passed a law that forbade colonists from settling west of a specific line running through the Appalachian Mountains from Maine to Georgia. Explain that students will be reading about the colonists' reactions to this and other laws imposed by the British government. **ASK:** How would you feel and what might you do if freedoms that you enjoy, such as moving to a different city, were taken away? If you were a member of the government imposing the laws, how might you prepare for the reactions of the people? Write students' responses to the questions on the board, including the likely reactions of the people and likely preparations by the government. After reading the lesson, revisit students' responses and ask if they would add or change their responses.

TEACH

Guided Discussion

1. **Make Inferences** What message was the New York general assembly sending to the British Parliament when it refused to endorse the Quartering Act? *(The New York general assembly was telling the British that it would defy unfair laws imposed upon the colonists.)*

2. **Form and Support Opinions** Were the colonists' responses to the Quartering Act justified? Support your opinion with evidence from the text. *(Possible response: They were justified because quartering soldiers caused both a financial and personal burden on the colonists.)*

Interpret Maps

Direct students' attention to the map. Read the information about the Proclamation of 1763. Have students find the label on the map that identifies land reserved for Native Americans. **ASK:** How did the Proclamation of 1763 change the established borders of the colonies? *(It created a new border across all of the colonies that significantly reduced the amount of land available for settlement.)*

Active Options

On Your Feet: Turn and Talk on Topic Have students form three groups. Give each group this topic sentence: The British Parliament caused increased resentment in the colonists by imposing several restrictions on them. Tell students to build a paragraph on that topic by having each student contribute one sentence. Suggest that students first discuss why British actions were unreasonable from the colonists' perspective. Allow each group to present its paragraph to the class by having the groups form lines and having each student read his or her sentence in the correct order.

NG Learning Framework: Write a Story

SKILL Problem-Solving

KNOWLEDGE Our Human Story

Encourage students to learn more about the Quartering Act. Tell them to use library or Internet sources to research how colonists might have responded to this act. Then have them imagine themselves as colonists living under the act and write a first-person fictional story about the impact of the law. Each story should explain the problems the Quartering Act imposed on the character's family and how the family addressed each problem.

DIFFERENTIATE

Striving Readers

Understand Main Ideas Have students work in pairs to complete a Cause-and-Effect Web for the Quartering Act and for the Proclamation of 1763. Students should write the names of the two acts in the circle and then add three effects of each act.

Pre-AP

Analyze Impacts Divide students into two groups and provide chart paper to each. Assign the Proclamation of 1763 to one group and the Quartering Act to the other. Ask students to brainstorm the financial and social impacts of their assigned law and then list them on chart paper. Post the charts and ask students to compare them, circling impacts that are similar or common to both. Then have students write a concluding statement about the collective impact of these two laws on the colonists.

See the Chapter Planner for more strategies for differentiation.

HISTORICAL THINKING

ANSWERS

1. The Proclamation of 1763 was supposed to keep peace by limiting colonists to lands east of the crest of the Appalachian Mountains. The Quartering Act required colonists to house British soldiers.

2. Both were frustrated with oppressive laws. Eastern colonists did not like the Quartering Act, but they housed soldiers because the law was usually enforced. Western colonists ignored the Proclamation of 1763 because the British government could not afford to send soldiers to enforce it.

3. The word *prosperous* means the colonists were doing well financially.

CRITICAL VIEWING Answers will vary. Possible response: The colonists' expressions show fear and anger. Some are cringing and cowering. One is pointing and making a fist. The colonists are portrayed as angered by and also afraid of the British soldiers.

CRITICAL VIEWING Answers will vary. Possible response: The Covenant Chain helped people moving west establish peaceful relations with Native Americans. It was mostly unfulfilled because colonists kept moving farther west, encroaching on Native American lands.

Taxation Without Representation

If you borrow money from a friend to buy an amazing pair of sneakers, eventually you'll have to pay off your debt. But how can you do that if you don't have any money? The answer seems obvious—earn some money. But it wasn't that simple for King George and Parliament.

MAIN IDEA British attempts to impose taxes and exert greater control over the colonies caused growing anger and resentment among colonists.

WAR DEBT

The French and Indian War had been an expensive undertaking for the British government. Maintaining and supplying an army in distant colonies had left King George with a hefty debt. In addition, Britain was still keeping 10,000 soldiers in North America to protect the colonies. The British government needed **revenue**, or income, to pay off its debts and expenses.

King George appointed a new prime minister, George Grenville, who agreed that the colonies should be strictly controlled by Britain. Grenville concluded that the colonies should pay for the war debt and the continuing maintenance of the troops in North America. After all, he reasoned, the colonies had benefited the most from the French and Indian War. To raise the money, Grenville sought ways to tax the colonies directly, rather than allowing colonial assemblies to pass taxes. What followed was a series of acts that would have big consequences.

King George III
King George III (1738–1820) ruled Britain for 59 years. "Born and educated in this country," he said, "I glory in the name of Britain." But the war with America was hard on George. He became seriously ill around 1788 and continued to decline until 1811, when his son, George IV, became the acting king and eventually took the throne. A 2005 study of a hair sample from George III suggested that the king may have become ill and died from arsenic poisoning.

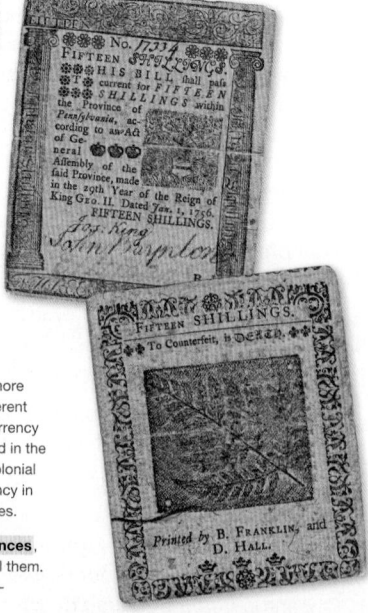

Colonial Currency
Colonial currency came in different shapes, and its designs were very detailed, as the five-pound note (left) issued in New York in 1759 shows. The Pennsylvania 15-shilling note below was produced by Benjamin Franklin and issued on January 1, 1756. It featured multiple anti-counterfeiting processes invented by Franklin, including the blue thread that ran through the note.

ACTS OF PARLIAMENT

The **Sugar Act** of 1764 was among the first of the new taxes. This law was designed to raise revenue as well as to reinforce British control over the colonies. The Sugar Act actually lowered the **duty**, or tax, on the imported molasses used to produce rum in the colonies. The goal of the Sugar Act was to encourage merchants to pay the lower duty instead of smuggling molasses into the colonies to avoid paying the tax, as they had been doing before. This would then increase revenue to the British government.

The **Currency Act**, also passed in 1764, aimed to more tightly control the colonial economy. Previously, different colonies had issued their own paper money. The Currency Act declared that only British currency could be used in the colonies. As colonists discarded the now-useless colonial paper money, the resulting shortage of British currency in the colonies created a number of economic difficulties.

Not surprisingly, the colonists voiced several **grievances**, or objections, to Britain's attempts to tax and control them. They had come to resent the policy of mercantilism—trade designed to bring wealth primarily to the mother country—which was now strengthened by the Sugar Act and Currency Act. The colonists were further frustrated when a new prime minister tightened the Navigation Acts, which controlled colonial trade and shipping, to benefit Britain.

Some accused the British of **tyranny**, or unjust rule by an absolute ruler. They used the slogan "no taxation without representation." Colonists argued that Parliament did not have the right to impose direct taxes on them because they did not have representatives in Parliament who could vote on taxes.

HISTORICAL THINKING

1. **READING CHECK** In what ways did the British government try to raise revenue and control the colonies at the same time?

2. **MAKE INFERENCES** How did the Sugar Act and Currency Act reinforce Britain's policy of mercantilism?

3. **ANALYZE CAUSE AND EFFECT** What impact did these acts likely have on the ways colonists did business?

Objective

Identify the financial and political impacts of the Sugar Act and the Currency Act.

Critical Thinking Skills for Lesson 1.2

• Identify Main Ideas and Details

• Monitor Comprehension

• Make Inferences

• Analyze Cause and Effect

• Evaluate

• Make Predictions

• Analyze Visuals

Essential Question for Chapter 5

Why did the colonists decide to break from Britain? Many colonists objected to new taxes passed by Parliament. Lesson 1.2 discusses how the Sugar Act, the Currency Act, and Britain's tightening grip on colonial trade deepened colonial resentment of British rule over the colonies.

Background for the Teacher

The Molasses Act was among the Navigation Acts passed by the British Parliament in the 17th and 18th centuries. The intent of the Navigation Acts was to control trade by restricting the types of goods that could be bought and sold across the empire. Passed in 1733, the Molasses Act attempted to monopolize the colonial sugar market by forcing buyers to purchase sugar from the British West Indies rather than France and other nations.

The colonists needed sugar to create molasses, a key ingredient in the production of rum, and an important industry in colonial New England. The Molasses Act threatened to raise the price of molasses, thus making rum distilling less profitable.

Financial Literacy

To extend their knowledge and understanding about the concepts in this lesson, refer students to the Financial Literacy handbook.

Hands on the Money

Photocopy the images of colonial currency and make five or six sets of the copies. Divide students into five or six groups and give each group a set of the copies and a $1 bill. Point out the currency images and read the information in the caption. Explain that each colony had its own unique currency because there was no single, unifying economic system. Encourage students to examine the copies of the colonial currency, compare them with the $1 bill, and describe the similarities and differences. Then ask students to discuss the key elements that both currencies include.

TEACH

Guided Discussion

1. **Evaluate** Why did the French and Indian War lead to increased taxation on the colonists? *(Britain was looking for a way to cover its war debt and to pay to keep soldiers in the colonies to enforce its laws.)*

2. **Make Predictions** How might the British Parliament react to grievances expressed by the colonists? *(Possible response: The British Parliament might become more insistent that the colonists respect and obey the laws it passes.)*

Analyze Visuals

Direct students' attention to the portrait of George III and read the information to the students. Focus on the details in the portrait, including the horse, the sky, and the clouds. **ASK:** How is King George gesturing? *(He is pointing toward the ocean.)* What does it look like the horse is about to do? *(The horse looks like it's about to spring forward, as if charging into battle.)* What might the artist be conveying by the use of dark clouds with a small break in the clouds? *(The artist could be suggesting that difficult times are ahead, but soon the storm will be over.)*

Active Options

On Your Feet: Rotating Discussion Divide students into four teams and assign each team a corner of the room. Ask each team to prepare several questions about how the Sugar Act and Currency Act impacted colonists. Start the discussion by tossing a beanbag or other soft object to Team 1 and asking a question. After the members of Team 1 answer the question, they toss the beanbag to another team while asking one of their prepared questions. Continue until all teams have exhausted their questions.

NG Learning Framework: Settle a Dispute

ATTITUDE Empowerment

SKILLS Problem-Solving, Collaboration

Have two students act out a conversation about the Sugar Act between a colonial merchant arguing against the Sugar Act and a British member of Parliament arguing for it. Have the class make a list of the points made by each individual. Divide the class into small groups. Tell each group to consider the points made by the merchant and the member of Parliament. Then have groups identify one point on which both individuals can agree. Tell groups to share their ideas. As a class, discuss the importance of understanding another person's position and looking for common ideas when engaging in a dispute.

Inclusion

Work in Pairs Allow students with disabilities to work with other students who can read the lesson aloud to them. Encourage the partner without disabilities to describe the visual as well. Have students work together to determine their answers to the Historical Thinking questions. Give students the option of recording their answers rather than writing them out.

English Language Learners

Word Cards Have students at the **Expanding** level make vocabulary cards using the words *revenue, tyranny, grievances, duty,* and *currency.* Tell students to write the word on one side of the card and illustrate the term on the opposite side. Ask students to write the vocabulary word in their first language under the illustration. Students then pair with another student, present each illustration, and ask their partner to determine which vocabulary word is illustrated and explain what the word means. Each pair continues until all cards are shared.

See the Chapter Planner for more strategies for differentiation.

HISTORICAL THINKING

ANSWERS

1. The British government imposed taxes such as the Sugar Act and the Currency Act to pay its debts and to maintain troops in North America.

2. The Sugar Act and Currency Act both brought wealth only to Britain through trade in British colonies.

3. The Sugar Act caused merchants to buy molasses within the colony instead of smuggling it in from other colonies to get it cheaper. The Currency Act caused a shortage in British currency, creating economic difficulties. Both of these acts made colonists work harder while reducing the amount of money they made.

1.3 The Stamp Act

In 1765, the easiest way to become unpopular with your neighbors
was to be appointed by the king to collect his latest tax.

MAIN IDEA An attempt to impose a new type of tax sparked open protests and violent action, which forced the British government to repeal the tax.

A NEW KIND OF TAX

Passed by Parliament in 1765, the **Stamp Act** provoked an even greater storm of protest. Unlike previous laws, the Stamp Act did nothing to further Britain's mercantilist aims. Instead, it was designed purely to raise revenue to pay for the soldiers stationed in the colonies.

The Stamp Act required that all printed materials have a special government stamp. Items subject to the law included newspapers, playing cards, court documents, and sales receipts for land. So, for example, a person selling or buying a piece of land would also pay a British official to stamp the sales document. Colonists could only pay officials for the stamp with gold or silver coins—both of which were rare in the colonies. British courts enforced the Stamp Act by taking away any land or property involved in sales conducted without the stamps.

To the colonists, the Stamp Act was a shocking example of taxation without representation. Philadelphia merchant John Reynell said, "The point in dispute is a very important one, if the Americans are to be taxed by a Parliament where they are not nor can be Represented, they are no longer Englishmen but Slaves."

PROTESTING BRITISH GOODS

Colonial reactions to the Stamp Act were increasingly angry. **Patrick Henry** was a young politician and newly elected to Virginia's House of Burgesses. He persuaded the assembly to pass a series of resolutions that defended the colonists' right to tax themselves rather than to be taxed by Parliament. The resolutions declared that "the General Assembly of this colony . . . have the sole right . . . to lay taxes and impositions upon its inhabitants." When newspapers spread word of

Stamp Act Resistance
The hated Stamp Act was scheduled to take effect on November 1, 1765. Philadelphia newspaper printer William Bradford designed the October 31 "tombstone edition" of the *Pennsylvania Journal* with this skull and crossbones "stamp" to represent the death of the newspaper due to the Stamp Act. Bradford then ignored the act and continued publishing his paper.

Virginia's action, other colonies responded. Rhode Island instructed officials to ignore the stamp tax. Several other colonies passed resolutions similar to Virginia's resolution.

Colonists in cities such as Boston and Philadelphia soon realized they had more in common with each other than with Britain, and they began to organize. In Boston, a group rioted against the Stamp Act.

🏛 Museum of Fine Arts, Boston

Paul Revere was a father, husband, silversmith, and member of the Sons of Liberty. He left his mark on America by crafting many treasures relating to the American Revolution. Some of Revere's finest work is housed in Boston's Museum of Fine Arts.

The Sons of Liberty Bowl featured the engraved names of 92 members of the Massachusetts House of Representatives. In 1767, they refused to retract a letter sent throughout the colonies protesting the Townshend Acts, which taxed paper, tea, glass, and other goods imported from Britain. This act of peaceful protest by the "Glorious Ninety-Two" was a major step leading to the American Revolution.

In the same year that Paul Revere crafted the Sons of Liberty Bowl, artist John Singleton Copley (KOP-lee) honored the silversmith by painting his portrait. Copley's decision to represent Revere as an artisan at work embodies the concept of Americans as builders and crafters throughout history.

Sons of Liberty Bowl Commissioned by the Sons of Liberty and made by Paul Revere, this silver bowl joins the Declaration of Independence and the Constitution as the nation's three most precious historical treasures.

Paul Revere In 1768, Copley painted Paul Revere engraving a teapot. It is his only finished portrait of an artisan at work.

They damaged the home of Andrew Oliver, the official in charge of stamping documents, and destroyed the governor's house. Oliver promptly resigned. Protestors in other colonies also acted to prevent the distribution of stamps. By the end of 1765, the stamp distributors in all the colonies except Georgia had resigned.

Some of the men who led the angry crowds called themselves the **Sons of Liberty**. They were mostly merchants, shopkeepers, and craftsmen. The Sons of Liberty also organized a **boycott**, a form of protest that involves refusing to purchase goods or services. Merchants in New York City, Boston, and Philadelphia agreed to stop importing goods from Britain.

In 1766, the protestors succeeded. Parliament **repealed**, or canceled, the Stamp Act. The colonists had taken their first major step toward independence from Britain and creating a new American identity.

HISTORICAL THINKING

1. **READING CHECK** How did the Stamp Act raise revenue for the British government?

2. **MAKE INFERENCES** Why did the Stamp Act provoke such a strong response?

3. **ANALYZE CAUSE AND EFFECT** What events led up to the repeal of the Stamp Act?

PLAN

Objective
Learn how the colonists reacted to a new type of tax imposed by the British government.

Critical Thinking Skills for Lesson 1.3
- Identify Main Ideas and Details
- Monitor Comprehension
- Make Inferences
- Analyze Cause and Effect
- Evaluate

Essential Question for Chapter 5
Why did the colonists decide to break from Britain? As it was well within its power, Parliament passed the Stamp Act without consulting the colonists. Lesson 1.3 discusses the colonists' increasing anger and frustration with the British government's authority and their first major step toward independence.

Background for the Teacher
Paul Revere began his career as a silversmith at an early age and took charge of his family's shop at the age of 19, when his father died. Over the next 20 years, he proved himself one of the best precious-metal artists in colonial America, producing beautiful bowls, pots, knives, and forks. In addition to silversmithing, Revere dabbled in dentistry—or for what passed as such in the 1700s. Above all, he took an active role in colonial events and affairs. Revere fought in the French and Indian War. Once colonists began challenging British authority, he joined groups that pressed for independence, including the Sons of Liberty. Often, Revere combined his interests and talents, as demonstrated by the Sons of Liberty Bowl presented in this lesson.

INTRODUCE & ENGAGE

Preview Using Visuals

Point out the drawing of the stamp in the lesson. Explain that this image was used to represent many colonists' feelings about the Stamp Act. Discuss the skull and crossbones drawing. **ASK:** What does this image symbolize? *(death)* Then read aloud the text that borders the drawing on three sides. Tell students that the creator of the stamp, William Bradford, used the skull and crossbones to symbolize the death of the newspaper. **ASK:** Based on the image, what do you think Bradford and other colonists thought of the Stamp Act? *(They hated it and violently opposed its passage.)*

TEACH

Guided Discussion

1. **Make Inferences** Why do you think colonists who were engaged in selling or buying land had to pay for the stamp with gold or silver coins? *(These coins were rare. If colonists couldn't manage to come up with the coins, the British could take their land or property.)*

2. **Evaluate** What new American identity began to take shape as a result of protesting the Stamp Act? *(Answers will vary. Possible response: A new American identity as a united people, determined to resist outside authority and to abide laws that their own representatives passed began to take shape. Colonists were moving away from the traditions of Parliament and toward creating their own political identity.)*

Virtual Museum Visit

Boston's Museum of Fine Arts, or MFA, is one of the largest museums in the United States, with nearly 500,000 works of art on display. The collection represents artists from all over the world, from ancient civilizations to today. The MFA's Arts of the Americas collection is particularly renowned. Access the museum's website and find the Sons of Liberty Bowl in this collection. Point out the engraved words *Magna Charta* (usually spelled *Magna Carta*) and *Bill of Rights* and ask students why these documents are identified on the bowl. Read aloud the caption, which describes other engravings that appear on the work. Then ask groups of students to explore the site on their own and choose a work of art from the same period. Have groups present the work to the class.

Active Options

On Your Feet: Word Chain Have students form three lines. Hand a piece of paper to the first person in each line with one of these words or terms from the text: *Stamp Act, Sons of Liberty, boycott.* The first student in line adds a word to the list that relates to the original word or term. Students pass the paper from person to person, each one adding a word or phrase they associate with the previously written word. Have a volunteer from each group read off the Word Chain, and ask the rest of the class to listen for words that are used more than once or that may not connect correctly.

NG Learning Framework: Write a Biography

`ATTITUDE` Curiosity

`KNOWLEDGE` Our Human Story

Have students learn more about Paul Revere. Instruct them to write a short biography or profile about Revere using information from the chapter and additional print and digital source materials. Encourage students to explore the myths surrounding Revere and compare those with the historical facts they note as they research Revere. Remind students to quote and paraphrase the conclusions of others, avoiding plagiarism and following a standard format for citation.

DIFFERENTIATE

Striving Readers

Understand Main Ideas Check students' understanding of the main ideas in Lesson 1.3 by asking them to correctly complete either/or statements such as the following:

- Most of the colonists [loved or hated] the Stamp Act.
- The Stamp Act was passed by [the British Parliament or the general assembly of Virginia].
- The Sons of Liberty encouraged colonists to [buy or refuse to buy] English goods.
- In reaction to protests, Britain [canceled or passed] the Stamp Act.

English Language Learners

Identify Facts Arrange students in mixed proficiency groups and guide them to conduct a Round Robin activity to review what they have learned in the lesson. Ask groups to generate facts for about three to five minutes, with all students contributing. You might ask students at the **Expanding** and **Bridging** levels to assist students at the **Emerging** level. Finally, invite one student from each group to share his or her group's responses. Write all the facts on the board.

See the Chapter Planner for more strategies for differentiation.

HISTORICAL THINKING

ANSWERS

1. The Stamp Act required that colonists pay for all printed materials to receive a special British government stamp.

2. The Stamp Act provoked a strong response because the colonists had not been consulted about its passage. It was another instance of "taxation without representation."

3. Resolutions to ignore the Stamp Act, riots against it, and boycotts of British goods led to the act's repeal.

Benjamin Franklin 1706–1790

"To succeed, jump as quickly at opportunities as you do at conclusions."—Benjamin Franklin

Benjamin Franklin seized just about every opportunity that came his way. When he was 17, he ran away from his home in Boston to seek a fresh start in a new city. He eventually ended up in Philadelphia. There, the multitalented Franklin worked as a printer, an inventor, and a scientist. His experiments on the nature of electricity, conducted with his famous kite, brought him international fame. But it is as a statesman that he is best known—and honored.

A REPRESENTATIVE IN ENGLAND

When the Stamp Act was passed in 1765, Franklin was in England, serving as a colonial representative. He'd been in the country off and on since 1757 and, by all accounts, enjoyed his stay there. Franklin liked to dine in fine restaurants and go to the theater—comforts that the more rustic colonies lacked. He opposed the Stamp Act but didn't think it could be stopped. Franklin had even ordered British stamps to be used in his Philadelphia printing firm.

The colonists' response to the passage of the act took him completely by surprise. Franklin learned that mobs of Americans were joining together to prevent the act's enforcement. He also discovered that his acceptance of the despised Stamp Act

The National Portrait Gallery Washington, D.C.

French artist Joseph Siffred Duplessis painted two very similar portraits of Benjamin Franklin, but only this one hangs in the National Portrait Gallery. For the most part, only the color and style of Franklin's coat differ in the two paintings. In both, as one person noted, the subject's "large forehead suggests strength of mind" and his expression conveys "the smile of an unshakeable serenity."

Our American Identity

You may have seen the "Join, or Die" cartoon before, but did you know that Franklin was the artist? The pieces of the snake are meant to roughly represent the 13 colonies. "N.E." stands for the New England colonies of New Hampshire, Massachusetts, Rhode Island, and Connecticut.

Franklin's cartoon found its most popular meaning later, when the colonists' futures were at risk. For many, the choice to support the colonies in North America involved abandoning their identity as Europeans and, instead, identifying themselves as Americans at a time when no one knew what that might mean. The stakes were high, but the eloquent words of people like Franklin carried the day.

CRITICAL VIEWING: Franklin's famous political cartoon is shown today tattooed on someone's calf. Based on what you know about the cartoon and its message, what might you infer about this person, regardless of what you think of tattoos?

had begun to tarnish his reputation. Stirred to action, Franklin spoke eloquently to Parliament, condemning the act and explaining the colonists' position. His speech was instrumental in the act's repeal. The experience made Franklin feel what he called his "Americanness" as never before. He also began to question his loyalty to Britain and its treatment of the colonies.

A SUPPORTER OF INDEPENDENCE

Over the next few years, Franklin tried to smooth over the differences between Britain and the colonies and help each side understand the other. To achieve that goal, he worked closely with Thomas Hutchinson, the governor of Massachusetts. Hutchinson was supposed to defend the rights of the colonists, but he really acted on behalf of King George. Secretly, he was working to limit the colonists' rights. When Franklin uncovered letters that detailed Hutchinson's intentions, he sent them to America. The letters fueled the colonists' anger with British rule.

The letters' release also led the British government to condemn Franklin, who shortly thereafter returned to America. His experiences in England had convinced him that the colonies should break away from Britain. At the outset of the French and Indian War in 1754, Franklin had created a political cartoon called "Join, or Die" to urge the colonies to unite and fight with Great Britain against the French. Now the cartoon came to symbolize colonial unity against the British.

As colonial protests mounted against Britain and the king, Franklin became a strong voice for independence and democracy. He would help draft the Declaration of Independence and was among the first to sign it, saying as he did so, "We must indeed all hang together, or most assuredly we shall all hang separately."

HISTORICAL THINKING

1. **READING CHECK** What official role did Franklin have while he lived in England?

2. **ANALYZE CAUSE AND EFFECT** What realization led to Franklin's dissatisfaction with British rule?

3. **MAKE INFERENCES** Franklin said he was feeling his "Americanness" as never before. How might Franklin have described the American identity at that time in history?

PLAN

Objective

Learn about Benjamin Franklin's experience as a colonial representative in England.

Critical Thinking Skills for Lesson 1.4

- Identify Main Ideas and Details
- Monitor Comprehension
- Analyze Cause and Effect
- Make Inferences
- Summarize
- Draw Conclusions

Essential Question for Chapter 5

Why did the colonists decide to break from Britain? Benjamin Franklin was instrumental in getting the Stamp Act repealed. Lesson 1.4 discusses how the experience made Franklin feel his "Americanness" and begin to think that the colonies should break away from Britain.

Background for the Teacher

Benjamin Franklin is known for his invention of the lightning rod and the experiments he conducted with it, but another of his inventions may surprise people: swim fins. An enthusiastic swimmer, Franklin came up with the idea for the fins at the age of 11. But instead of going on the feet, Franklin's fins fit on the hands. Describing them, he wrote, "I made two oval pallets, each about ten inches long, and six broad, with a hole for the thumb, in order to retain it fast in the palm of my hand." The fins helped push him through the water faster, but, as Franklin pointed out, they wore out his wrists. For his promotion of swimming—and, no doubt, for his swim fins—Franklin was inducted into the International Swimming Hall of Fame in 1968.

History Notebook

Encourage students to complete the American Voices page for Chapter 5 in their History Notebooks as they read.

Ask Questions

As a class, come up with a list of questions about Benjamin Franklin and his accomplishments. Write students' questions on the board. After reading the lesson, review the questions and ask volunteers to write answers on the board. If necessary, provide students time to research answers to particular questions they could not answer.

TEACH

Guided Discussion

1. **Summarize** How did Franklin initially view the Stamp Act? *(He opposed it, but because Parliament was acting within its power, he didn't think it could be stopped.)*

2. **Draw Conclusions** What did Franklin mean when he said, "We must all hang together, or assuredly we shall all hang separately"? *(He meant that the colonists should all unite against Britain in a revolution or individual rebellious colonists would be hanged by the British for treason.)*

American Voices

Benjamin Franklin is the prototype American voice. An American Renaissance man, he has been called "the harmonious human multitude." As one of the Framers, he helped draft the Declaration of Independence and the U.S. Constitution. He even wrote an anti-slavery tract in 1789. Franklin's civic contributions include forming the first fire brigade in Philadelphia, founding the first lending library in the colonies, and launching the American Philosophical Society. In his spare time, he was a scientist, mathematician, mapmaker, and inventor. When Franklin died at the age of 84, about 20,000 people came to his funeral.

Active Options

On Your Feet: Three-Step Interview Have students work in pairs to discuss the third question in Historical Thinking. Ask students what they think Benjamin Franklin meant when he said that he was feeling his "Americanness" as never before. As pairs conduct their interviews, tell them to use more detailed questions about the quotation. For example: What do you think it meant to be an American in colonial times? What might have been the American identity then? What does it mean to be an American today? Remind students to listen closely as their partner answers so they can report what they hear to the rest of the class.

NG Learning Framework: Research an Invention   STEM

ATTITUDE Curiosity

KNOWLEDGE New Frontiers

Remind students that Benjamin Franklin was an inventor as well as a statesman. Ask students to work in small groups to briefly research one of Franklin's inventions and then come up with a way to improve it. Students should provide a printed image or sketch of Franklin's original invention as well as a drawing of their improved version. Ask students to label and describe the specific change, indicating the specific improvement.

DIFFERENTIATE

Inclusion

Clarify Text Have visually impaired students work with sighted partners. As they listen to an audio recording of the text, have the visually impaired students indicate if there are words or passages they do not understand. Their partners can clarify meanings by repeating passages, emphasizing context clues, and paraphrasing.

Pre-AP

Create a Top 10 List Have groups of students research to learn more about Benjamin Franklin. Then have them create a list of 10 interesting facts about him. Tell groups to list the facts beginning with number 10, the least important, and ending with number 1, the most important. Then have the groups take turns reading the lists to the class.

See the Chapter Planner for more strategies for differentiation.

HISTORICAL THINKING

ANSWERS

1. He served as a colonial representative in England.

2. He realized that Thomas Hutchinson, who was supposed to be defending the colonists' rights, was in fact working to limit their rights.

3. Answers will vary. Possible response: He may have described American identity as being loyal to America and willing to speak up—and even fight—for democratic rights and independence.

CRITICAL VIEWING Answers will vary. Possible response: The person might feel a sense of patriotism or may find meaning in the notion of uniting together for a common cause.

2.1 Colonial Protests Grow

You're a young Boston colonist in 1768. "Sorry, son. There's no tea today," your mother says at breakfast. "We're boycotting British imports again." How would you feel about doing without your favorite food or drink to make a point?

MAIN IDEA Britain's attempt to raise revenue and control the colonies through the Townshend Acts led to protests and violence.

THE TOWNSHEND ACTS

Colonists celebrated the Stamp Act's repeal. However, the British government insisted that it had not lost any authority over the colonies. But with the Stamp Act repealed, Britain had to figure out other ways of gaining revenue.

In 1767, Parliament passed the **Townshend Acts**, named after Charles Townshend, a British royal treasurer. The acts placed duties on tea, glass, paper, lead, and paint—all goods that the colonies were required to purchase only from Britain. The revenue from the Townshend Acts would be used by the British to pay the salaries of colonial governors and judges. Previously, these officials had been paid by the colonial assemblies. By paying officials directly, the British government would establish greater control over the day-to-day running of the colonies.

The Townshend Acts also required colonial courts to provide **writs of assistance**, or search warrants, so officials could search houses and businesses for smuggled goods. Writs of assistance had existed for several years, and colonists had protested them. To the colonists, the writs allowed the British to search without cause and to justify random searches, and the Townshend Acts only expanded their use.

THE COLONISTS REACT

Colonists once again protested and accused the British government of tyranny. The protestors were strongly influenced by the 17th century British philosopher **John Locke**, who wrote that a leader could rule only with the consent of the people.

Daughters of Liberty

In the 1770s, colonial women contributed significantly to the anti-British movement. They even spun yarn to reduce colonial dependence on British textiles, prompting Samuel Adams to declare, "With the ladies on our side, we can make every Tory tremble."

This image of a colonial woman holding a flintlock musket appeared on a broadside, a single-sided newspaper, around 1779. A symbol of strength and patriotism, she wears a man's hat, holds her weapon and powder horn, and is pictured in front of a British fort.

He stated that government exists to uphold natural rights, or rights such as life or liberty that a person is born with. Any government that failed in this task should be overthrown. The colonists strongly identified with Locke's way of thinking.

Samuel Adams was a follower of Locke's philosophy, a member of the Massachusetts Assembly, and a leader of the Sons of Liberty. In 1768, Adams cowrote a letter with lawyer James Otis to the other colonial assemblies. The letter objected to the new duties and proposed a boycott of British goods. The British governor of Massachusetts threatened to dismiss the assembly if it did not take back the letter. Defiantly, the assembly refused, and it was disbanded.

Samuel Adams and the Sons of Liberty vigorously continued to support actions against the Townshend Acts. Colonists in Boston signed an agreement to boycott British imports, and merchants in New York soon followed. Women also used their purchasing power to protest the Townshend Acts. A group called **Daughters of Liberty** boycotted imported tea and clothing. To replace imported cloth, they wove their own fabric, known as homespun, from American yarn and wool.

The Great Awakening of the 1730s and 1740s also helped push the colonists toward rebellion and independence. During that revival movement, believers challenged the authority of their church leaders. They learned to use their own judgment in matters of religion. The habit of thinking independently spread throughout the colonies. By the 1770s, the ideas of the Great Awakening had helped create a revolutionary fervor among the colonists, which led them to challenge Britain's authority.

Tar and Feathers

Sometimes angry protestors used tar and feathers to punish people who supported British taxes. Victims would be dragged to a public place. Then they would be coated with hot, sticky tar and covered in feathers, as shown in this 1774 political cartoon. Tarring and feathering was often portrayed in a humorous way, but it was in fact horribly painful.

HISTORICAL THINKING

1. **READING CHECK** How were the Townshend Acts intended to accomplish Britain's goals in the colonies?

2. **ANALYZE CAUSE AND EFFECT** In what ways did Locke's philosophy influence the colonists in their protest against British actions?

3. **MAKE PREDICTIONS** What might result from the boycotts against the Townshend Acts?

PLAN

Objective

Analyze how the Townshend Acts impacted colonial life.

Critical Thinking Skills for Lesson 2.1

- Identify Main Ideas and Details
- Monitor Comprehension
- Analyze Cause and Effect
- Make Predictions
- Make Connections

Essential Question for Chapter 5

Why did the colonists decide to break from Britain? The 17th-century writer John Locke, who wrote that government can only rule with the consent of the people, influenced Samuel Adams and others. Lesson 2.1 describes the Townshend Acts and how colonists reacted to increased British authority.

Background for the Teacher

One of the leaders of the Great Awakening in New England was Jonathan Edwards, an academic and pastor in Northampton, Massachusetts. Edwards preached against the doctrine that God chooses certain individuals for salvation while rejecting others. In his famous sermon, "Sinners in the Hands of an Angry God," Edwards argued:

God has laid himself under no obligation by any promise to keep any natural man out of hell one moment. God certainly has made no promises either of eternal life, or of any deliverance or preservation from eternal death.

Jonathan Edwards and John Locke influenced the development of morality in the colonies. The Great Awakening contributed to dissent from established churches, division within religious denominations, and a greater tolerance of religious diversity. This changing attitude toward religion contributed to the idea of religious freedom among the colonists.

Analyze a Political Cartoon

Point out the "Tar and Feathers" political cartoon and read the caption. Explain that in a political cartoon the artist might use gross exaggeration to get across a point. Inform students that this cartoon was published in a British newspaper and depicts a tax collector being tarred and feathered by colonists. Ask students to write a list of the details in the cartoon and then discuss the political message the cartoon conveys. **ASK:** What is the artist's message and what makes you think so? *(Possible responses: This cartoon offers a criticism of the colonists' extreme actions towards the British. The colonists are shown with evil grins and enjoying themselves while torturing their victim. In the background, men are shown dumping tea from a ship, showing the extent to which colonists are breaking laws.)*

TEACH

Guided Discussion

1. **Analyze Cause and Effect** What was the reaction of many colonists to the Townshend Acts? Why? *(Colonists reacted with petitions and boycotts. They resented both paying duties on British goods and the restrictions on their daily lives.)*

2. **Make Connections** Describe the relationship between the moral and political ideas of the Great Awakening and the development of revolutionary fervor. *(Answers will vary. Possible response: The ideas of the Great Awakening encouraged independent thought, so when colonists felt oppressed, they challenged Britain's authority.)*

More Information

The English Bill of Rights Explain that the English Bill of Rights passed by Parliament in 1689 ensured certain rights of British citizens. Like the Declaration of Independence, the English Bill of Rights was influenced by the political thinking of John Locke. In particular, it guarantees freedom of speech and the right to petition the government. North American colonists were British citizens, and many believed the English Bill of Rights still applied to them. The history of inherited rights was not a new concept. In 1215, King John signed the Magna Carta, granting certain liberties to "free men" and their heirs. The English Bill of Rights reasserted rights that had been curtailed under King James II. The Framers of the Declaration of Independence would find precedent in both of these documents. **ASK:** Why did many colonists feel the rights guaranteed to British citizens were being denied to them? *(Possible responses: The colonists were denied representation in British Parliament and were taxed without representation. British authorities were disbanding colonial assemblies that proposed boycotts, further denying colonists representation in government.)*

Active Options

On Your Feet: Take a Stand Point out the Daughters of Liberty image. Read and discuss the information above it. Set up four different colonial shops in the classroom, such as dresses and hats, furniture, paint and glass, tea and biscuits. Assign a merchant to each shop. Divide the class into four groups. Assign each group to visit one shop and act as Sons and Daughters of Liberty. At the shop, they should reject British goods and then determine if the goods are necessary and how they could replicate them through home and local trade craftsmanship. Have groups share their ideas in a group discussion.

NG Learning Framework: Connect Historical Events

SKILL Collaboration

KNOWLEDGE Our Human Story

Divide the class into small groups. Display a Cause-and-Effect Web and have groups replicate it on chart paper. Students should review the lesson and add details to the web to show the effects of the Townshend Acts. Suggest that artistic students add images to provide visual representations of the information. Have students share their charts and display them in the room. Use the details in the charts to discuss and connect the effects of the Townshend Acts with why colonists became angry and protested British rule.

DIFFERENTIATE

Striving Readers

Preview and Review the Text Have students preview the lesson. Have them read the title, the Main Idea, subheadings, visuals, and questions. Then have them write questions they have about colonial resistance to British authority that they expect to be answered in the text. After students read the lesson, have them work in groups to discuss what they learned and find answers to their questions.

Pre-AP

Research the Sons of Liberty Have students write three questions about the Sons of Liberty. Questions should seek a deeper understanding of *who* they were, *how* they acted, and *why* they were motivated to act. Then have students conduct online research, assessing the credibility of each source, to answer their questions. Have students summarize their findings in a brief report and conclude with a one-paragraph analysis of the impact of the Sons of Liberty.

See the Chapter Planner for more strategies for differentiation.

HISTORICAL THINKING

ANSWERS

1. The British would use the revenue from the Townshend Acts to pay the salaries of colonial governors and judges. This would allow the British government greater control over the day-to-day running of the colonies.

2. Locke felt that a leader could rule only with the consent of the people. Samuel Adams followed Locke's philosophy and organized a boycott of British goods. The Sons of Liberty and the Daughters of Liberty acted against the Townshend Acts. Locke's philosophies inspired the colonists to think independently and oppose British authority.

3. Answers will vary. Possible response: The boycotts might cause British authorities to impose even more strict laws to try to control the colonists.

2.2 The Boston Massacre

If you place a flame too close to a powder keg full of explosive gunpowder, it will blow up spectacularly. In 1770, Boston was like a powder keg, and a hot flame was quickly approaching.

MAIN IDEA Tensions between the British troops and the colonists in Boston reached a breaking point when some soldiers fired on an angry crowd of citizens.

TENSIONS RISE

In response to growing protests and increasing unrest among colonists, British authorities brought additional troops to Boston. Some of the soldiers camped out on Boston Common, an open area that was intended for all Bostonians to use.

This arrangement made for a tense situation. Frequent fights broke out between soldiers and civilians. To annoy the British soldiers, children followed them in the streets, taunting them and calling them names such as "redcoats" and "lobsterbacks" because of the bright red uniforms they wore.

In addition, the British soldiers were poorly paid. To make extra money, they took jobs as workers during their off-duty hours. This took jobs away from some Bostonians, who were angry at losing work to soldiers they already despised.

On March 5, 1770, a boy began yelling insults at a British soldier standing guard at a government building. The soldier hit the boy with his gun. A rowdy crowd gathered around the commotion, and Captain Thomas Preston led a group of seven additional soldiers out to diffuse the situation. The crowd grew larger, throwing snowballs, ice, and sticks at the soldiers. Then someone hit a soldier with a club, knocking his gun out of his hands.

TENSIONS EXPLODE

Suddenly Preston's men were firing at the crowd. Five townspeople were killed and six were injured. This event soon became known as the **Boston Massacre**. To the colonists, the killings would come to symbolize all that they hated about British rule.

The first man shot and killed was **Crispus Attucks**, an African American and former slave who worked as a sailor and rope maker in Boston. Attucks is considered to be the first person to die in the quest for American independence.

After the shooting, the soldiers were arrested and put on trial for murder. At the trial, they were represented by lawyer **John Adams**, a cousin of Samuel Adams. This surprised some people because John Adams was a well-known Patriot, or supporter of colonial self-rule, in addition to being a respected lawyer. But he was also a firm believer in the right to a fair trial for everyone, no matter how unpopular they were.

Adams claimed that the soldiers had fired in self-defense. He made his case so eloquently that Captain Preston and all but two of the soldiers were found not guilty. Many people, including John Adams, thought this trial would be the end of his legal career. Yet in the end, Bostonians came to respect Adams for making the unpopular but ethical choice. He went on to have a distinguished career in politics, including serving as the first vice president and second president of the United States.

HISTORICAL THINKING

1. **READING CHECK** What events led up to the Boston Massacre?

2. **MAKE INFERENCES** What was the general feeling in Boston in 1770?

3. **ANALYZE VISUALS** What similarities and differences can you identify in the two depictions of the Boston Massacre at right?

The Bloody Massacre

American Patriot Paul Revere wasn't the first person to use a tragic incident to sway people's opinions, but he did it particularly effectively in the engraved print on the left. Titled *The Bloody Massacre in King Street*, the print shows a line of British soldiers firing into an unarmed crowd when, in fact, violence erupted on both sides. If you look closely at the white building on the right—the Customs House—you can also see that Revere changed its name to "Butcher's Hall." You may also notice that Crispus Attucks isn't represented in the print.

In fact, Attucks wouldn't be portrayed as a person of color until artist William L. Champney depicted him at the event in his 1855 drawing *Boston Massacre*. The antislavery movement was at its height, so the artist placed Attucks squarely in the center of the action. He also shows the colonists taking a more active role in the fight—probably a more accurate depiction of the incident.

PLAN

Objective

Understand how tensions between British soldiers and townspeople led to the Boston Massacre.

Critical Thinking Skills for Lesson 2.2

- Identify Main Ideas and Details
- Monitor Comprehension
- Make Inferences
- Analyze Visuals
- Make Connections

Essential Question for Chapter 5

Why did the colonists decide to break from Britain? Relations between British soldiers and many Boston townspeople continued to deteriorate in 1770. Lesson 2.2 discusses the tension and events that led to the Boston Massacre, as well as the consequences of this important turning point in British and colonial relations.

Background for the Teacher

Prior to the Boston Massacre, conflict in Massachusetts was not confined to tensions between colonists and British soldiers. The Sons of Liberty also focused their attention on colonists whom they believed were sympathetic to the British. Early in 1770, the Sons of Liberty began posting signs on businesses that ignored the boycott of British goods. Tensions between boycott-defying merchants and the Sons of Liberty escalated when on February 22, 1770, a crowd attacked Ebenezer Richardson's home with stones as he attempted to take down a Sons of Liberty sign on a neighbor's business. In the anger and confusion, Richardson fired his gun, hitting 11-year-old Christopher Seider, who died later that night. On March 5, 1770, the situation finally exploded with the events surrounding the Boston Massacre.

History Notebook

Encourage students to complete the American Gallery page for Chapter 5 in their History Notebooks as they read.

INTRODUCE & ENGAGE

Preview Vocabulary

Read the word *massacre*. **ASK:** What do you think the word *massacre* means? *(Answers will vary. Possible response: A massacre is when a lot of people are killed.)* Write responses on the board. As students read the lesson, encourage them to compare their definitions with the way the word is used in the text. Revisit the student list at the end of the lesson. **ASK:** Why do you think some Bostonians used the term *massacre* to define the event that happened on March 5, 1770? *(Answers will vary. Possible response: They used the term* massacre *to show that they believed that the British deliberately shot at the colonists.)*

TEACH

Guided Discussion

1. **Make Connections** What details support the idea that a new American identity was emerging in Boston? *(Possible response: With new taxes, more British troops, and off-duty troops taking their jobs, Bostonians realized that their interests were different from those of the British and adopted an "us against them" viewpoint. The crowd of colonists saw in the soldier everything they hated about being under British rule and turned into an angry mob. Colonists united against a common enemy and helped to create a new American identity.)*

2. **Identify Main Ideas and Details** How did the right to a fair trial apply to the British soldiers involved in the Boston Massacre? *(Possible response: John Adams, who represented them, pointed out that they had this right the same as everyone.)*

Analyze Visuals

Direct students' attention to the first print of the Boston Massacre. **ASK:** What is shown in this print by Paul Revere, and what do you think was his intended purpose? Tell students to base their opinions only on details in the print. Ask students to share their ideas. *(Possible response: It shows a one-sided assault by British soldiers. Revere wanted to influence public opinion against British authority.)* Then direct students' attention to the second print. **ASK:** Do you have to revise your opinions to accurately describe the event as portrayed here? Ask students to suggest reasons why, almost 100 years later, William Champney depicted the event differently. *(Possible response: In 1855, the nation was starting to splinter over the issue of slavery, so the artist may have wanted to emphasize the African-American role in the Revolution to argue for the end of slavery and full citizenship for African Americans.)*

Active Options

On Your Feet: Question and Answer Tell half the class to write True-False questions based on the information about the Boston Massacre. Ask the other half to create answer cards with "True" written on one side and "False" on the other. Then ask the students who wrote questions to read them aloud. Students in the second group should respond by holding up either "True" or "False." When discrepancies occur, review the question and the text and discuss which answer is correct.

AMERICAN GALLERY ONLINE **Colonial Boston** Invite students to explore the American Gallery. Have them select one of the images and do additional research to learn more about it. Ask questions that will inspire additional inquiry about the chosen gallery image, such as: What is this? Where is this? Who might have created it? Why was it created? What is it made of? Why does it belong in this chapter? What else would you like to know about it?

DIFFERENTIATE

Inclusion

Identify a Sequence Pair special needs students with helper students and ask them to reread the lesson together. Draw a Sequence Chart for students to copy. Ask students to identify two events in sequence that led to the Boston Massacre. For the last box, ask students to write an original sentence explaining what happened during the Boston Massacre.

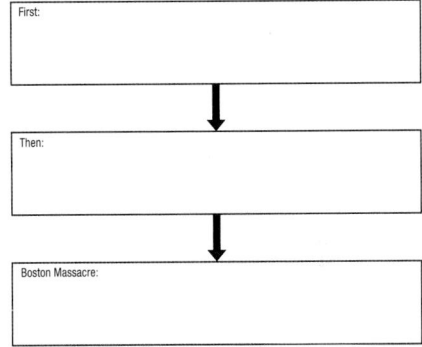

Gifted & Talented

Explore Art as Propaganda Ask students to consider how Paul Revere used the events of the Boston Massacre as propaganda against the British. Then ask students to find an example of art as propaganda from another time in history and to prepare a short visual presentation to exhibit and explain their findings.

See the Chapter Planner for more strategies for differentiation.

HISTORICAL THINKING

ANSWERS

1. Unhoused British soldiers camped out on Boston Common, an area designated for Bostonians. The low-paid soldiers took on off-duty work, taking Bostonians' jobs and creating tense relations. When a boy yelled insults at a soldier standing guard, the soldier hit him. The resentful crowd turned violent, and the soldiers fired at them.

2. The general feeling in Boston in 1770 was tension and anger.

3. Answers will vary. Possible responses: Similarities include the same setting and position of soldiers. Differences include Champney's inclusion of Crispus Attucks, the aggressive stance of the colonists, and a fallen British soldier.

2.3 The Boston Tea Party

Sit-ins, marches, posters, and chants are the tools of peaceful protest. They help people express displeasure or opposition without violence. The colonists were angry with the British, but sometimes they found ways to make their feelings known without lifting a weapon.

MAIN IDEA When Parliament imposed new laws to regulate tea, colonists responded by throwing a cargo of British tea into Boston Harbor.

NEW LAW, OLD TAX

At about the same time as the Boston Massacre, the British government decided to repeal most of the Townshend Acts. The taxes on all the items listed in the act were lifted, except for the tax on tea. There were fewer protests, and for two years, the relationship between Britain and the colonies was generally calm.

But in 1772, Patriots in Rhode Island burned a British ship that had been searching local boats for smugglers. When news of the attack reached England, Parliament once again began passing laws to gain greater control over the colonies. In Massachusetts, Samuel Adams responded by forming a **committee of correspondence**. This group made a list of British offenses against the colonies' rights and published it in Massachusetts. Other colonies joined in the movement by forming their own committees.

The committees soon had a new complaint. In 1773, Parliament passed the **Tea Act**, allowing the British East India Company to sell tea directly in the colonies. This lowered the price of tea, but it also took money away from colonial tea merchants. The prime minister also refused to repeal the Townshend Acts' tax on tea.

Despite the fact that cheaper tea would now be available, the new law fanned the flames of colonial resentment toward Britain. Colonial tea merchants were close to going out of business, and Parliament was still taxing the colonists without representation.

TEA OVERBOARD!

At first, the colonists protested by making it difficult for the British East India Company to deliver shipments of tea. Workers in major cities refused to unload shipments of tea from ships in port. In New York and Philadelphia, the ships' captains were told to return to England.

On the night of December 16, 1773, members of the Sons of Liberty disguised themselves as Native Americans and boarded three ships loaded with tea in Boston Harbor. Without harming the ships' other cargo, they dumped the tea into the icy water while thousands of people on shore watched the events of the **Boston Tea Party** unfold.

The Boston Tea Party was not the only act of colonial defiance that involved tea. On October 14, 1774, in Annapolis, Maryland, a ship with a cargo of tea was set on fire. King George was furious. Soon Parliament would enact new laws to punish the colonists for their actions, and the stage would be set for further conflicts.

HISTORICAL THINKING

1. **READING CHECK** In what ways did the colonists protest the Tea Act?

2. **FORM AND SUPPORT OPINIONS** Was the Boston Tea Party an effective form of protest? Support your opinion with evidence from the text.

3. **MAKE GENERALIZATIONS** How did the Tea Act reflect the attitude of the British government toward the colonies?

Objective

Learn about the events of the Boston Tea Party and the legacy of protest.

Critical Thinking Skills for Lesson 2.3

- Identify Main Ideas and Details
- Monitor Comprehension
- Form and Support Opinions
- Make Generalizations
- Evaluate
- Make Connections

Essential Question for Chapter 5

Why did the colonists decide to break from Britain? When conflicts between governments and citizens reach a breaking point, sometimes disagreements turn into full-scale protests. Lesson 2.3 describes the reasons for and outcomes of the Boston Tea Party.

Background for the Teacher

Before the early 1600s, tea was basically unknown in Europe. However, once introduced, it became a popular beverage, along with coffee and chocolate. Drinking tea involved elaborate rituals, and it soon became part of the daily routine in England.

Colonists brought tea rituals with them when they moved to America. So when Britain imposed various taxes on tea, the colonists responded by boycotting British tea, smuggling in their own, and switching to coffee or Liberty Tea, an herbal tea colonial women made using indigenous plants. The Boston Tea Party was the ultimate protest of British regulations the colonists perceived as unfair. It was also a symbolic rejection of the mother country's ritual beverage. After the Revolution, Americans continued to drink tea. Coffee did not take over as the main hot beverage until the 19th century.

K-W-L Chart

Provide each student with a K-W-L Chart. Have students brainstorm what they already know about the Boston Tea Party, such as listing different sides involved in the conflict and the grievances the colonists had against the British. Then tell students to write questions that they would like to answer as they study the lesson, such as: Why did the colonists throw tea overboard? or Why did this event occur in Boston? Allow time at the end of the lesson for students to fill in what they have learned.

K What Do I Know?	W What Do I Want To Learn?	L What Did I Learn?

TEACH

Guided Discussion

1. **Evaluate** Remind students of the idea of American identity that they read about and discussed in the American Story. **ASK:** What role did committees of correspondence play in helping to establish an American identity throughout the colonies? *(Committees of correspondence published lists of British offenses against the colonies, establishing the idea that colonists were developing an identity that was no longer British.)*

2. **Make Connections** Why was tea a strategic target for colonists' rebellion against the British government? *(Tea was popular among the British, and therefore colonists, and colonial merchants sold a lot of tea. Tea was also taxed, so refusing to buy tea, destroying tea by throwing it into Boston Harbor, or setting shipments of it on fire would be a symbolic protest against taxation without representation.)*

A Global Perspective

Explore the photograph and caption for this lesson with students. **ASK:** What connections do you see between the 2015 protest in France and the 1773 protest in Boston? *(Both were peaceful; both were protests about governmental decisions.)* What symbols did the protestors in both events rely upon? *(The Sons of Liberty targeted tea, a British-imported product and a cultural beverage. The French protestors used pairs of shoes to represent people who would have been at the protest had it not been canceled.)* Conduct a class discussion about other forms of peaceful protest and ask students what they think inspires protests, both peaceful and not peaceful.

Active Options

On Your Feet: Question and Answer Have half the class write True-False questions based on information in Lesson 2.3. Ask the other half to create answer cards with "True" written on one side and "False" on the other. As each question is read aloud, students in the second group should stand and display the correct answer to the question. When discrepancies occur, review the question and discuss which answer is correct.

NG Learning Framework: Organize a Peaceful Protest

ATTITUDE Empowerment

SKILL Collaboration

Divide students into small groups and instruct them to organize a peaceful protest about an issue for which they have strong feelings. Encourage students to consider issues on the school, community, national, and international levels. Each group should make a plan that includes a description of the issue, the location of the protest, and the targeted audience. Once all groups have devised their plans, have leaders present their groups' peaceful protest plans to the class.

DIFFERENTIATE

Striving Readers

Complete Sentence Starters Provide these sentence starters for students to complete after reading. You may also have students preview the starters to set a purpose for reading.

- In 1772, Samuel Adams formed the _____. *(committees of correspondence)*
- The British government refused to repeal the _____. *(Townshend Acts)*
- Colonial merchants were angry about taxation without _____. *(representation)*
- The Boston Tea Party took place on December 16, _____. *(1773)*
- The Boston Tea Party is an example of colonial _____. *(defiance)*

English Language Learners

Pose and Answer Questions Have students at the **Emerging** level work in pairs to read Lesson 2.3. Instruct them to pause after each paragraph and ask one another *who, what, when, where,* or *why* questions about what they have just read. Suggest students use a 5Ws Chart.

See the Chapter Planner for more strategies for differentiation.

HISTORICAL THINKING

ANSWERS

1. Colonists made deliveries of tea difficult, refused to offload tea shipments in port, and forced ships' captains to turn back from ports.

2. Answers will vary. Possible responses: The Boston Tea Party was an effective form of protest because it got the attention of King George and fueled other protests. No, it wasn't an effective form of protest because it caused the British Parliament to enact more laws to punish the colonists.

3. The Tea Act sent the message that the colonies were at the mercy of British merchants and the British East India Company.

A GLOBAL PERSPECTIVE Answers will vary. Possible response: Both protests were meant to be dramatic displays to capture the attention of people or groups making decisions protestors disagreed with. Unlike the Boston Tea Party, the 2015 protest was peaceful and silent and no property was destroyed.

2.4 Museum of the American Revolution, Philadelphia

The Museum of the American Revolution is located in the heart of historic Philadelphia. Visitors find themselves across the street from Carpenter's Hall, the first meeting place of the Continental Congress, and a short walk to the home of founding father Benjamin Franklin. The museum's rich collection of artifacts includes many personal belongings of George Washington, early American weapons, artwork, documents, and thousands of other items that date to the American Revolution. These items help tell the earliest stories of American independence from Britain. How would each of the artifacts shown have been used during the war?

Engraved Powder Horn

Virginia rifleman William Waller used this ornate powder horn as he fought British and Hessian soldiers during a battle at Fort Washington on November 16, 1776. Waller was captured.

Made of cow, ox, or buffalo horn, this elaborate version bears popular slogans from the American Revolution, including "Liberty or Death," and "Kill or be Kill(e)d." Powder horns were vital pieces of equipment for soldiers during the American Revolution. Riflemen used them to carry and protect the gunpowder they needed to fire their rifles.

> Riflemen often engraved their horns with names, dates, and artwork to personalize them.

American War Drum

This drum dates to 1740, well before the American Revolution had begun. It is believed to be the second-oldest dated American drum that exists. The drum is inscribed with the name of its maker, Robert Crosman, from Taunton, Massachusetts.

Considered a piece of standard equipment for New Englanders, drums and small, shrill flutes called fifes served as signal instruments for the infantry. They provided musical "commands" to soldiers in the battlefield and around camp. Fife and drum music also distracted soldiers from the drudgery of long marches.

> What role did fife and drum music play in the American Revolution?

> "The need for wider, **deeper understanding of the Revolution,** and respect for those who championed the cause at the time, has never been greater than now."
>
> —David McCullough
> Pulitzer Prize-winning author

> The stamp or brand on this musket is unique. It reads "U. States," which was a label required by the Congress to show that this gun was American-made, not European.

> The design on the musket's flintlock was modeled after the Continental three-dollar bill.

American Military Musket

Made around 1775, this musket is pretty rare. By 1777, weapons imported from France and other countries had replaced American-made firearms from the early days of the American Revolution. This particular musket features a flintlock mechanism. The flintlock creates a spark that lights the gunpowder stored in the barrel of the gun. What challenges might the use of this weapon have posed to soldiers?

PLAN

Objective

Identify artifacts relating to the soldiers of the American Revolution.

Critical Thinking Skills for Lesson 2.4

- Make Connections
- Analyze Visuals
- Describe
- Draw Conclusions

Essential Question for Chapter 5

Why did the colonists decide to break from Britain? Soldiers in the Colonial Army needed weapons to survive on the battlefield, but they also needed to keep their spirits up. Lesson 2.4 shows several of the tools of war during the American Revolution from the collection of the Museum of the American Revolution and explains their significance.

Background for the Teacher

The Museum of the American Revolution's collection was started more than 100 years ago when a history-minded minister in Valley Forge, Pennsylvania, raised the money needed to purchase the original tent that George Washington used as his command center during the American Revolution. This very tent is a showpiece of the museum's collection today. In fact, the tent purchase marked the beginning of an ever-growing rich and diverse collection, including British, French, and American weapons used in battle, numerous pieces of fine art, personal and military-issued gear for soldiers, uniforms, currency, and priceless documents.

History Notebook

Encourage students to complete the Curating History page for Chapter 5 in their History Notebooks as they read.

Brainstorm a List

Ask students to form small groups and brainstorm a list of equipment and items soldiers in the Continental Army or British Army would have been likely to carry as they traveled on foot over rough terrain and lived outdoors in many types of weather. Reconvene as a class and ask each group to share their list. Use the group lists to create a master list on the whiteboard. Discuss the best way to transport the gear and the challenges this would pose. Then tell students they will learn about some of the equipment that was vital to the survival of Continental soldiers.

TEACH

Guided Discussion

1. **Describe** How did soldiers use powder horns during the American Revolution? *(Powder horns were containers of gunpowder made, as the name suggests, out of the horn of an animal, such as a cow, ox, or buffalo. Soldiers used them to keep their gunpowder dry because wet gunpowder would not fire.)* **ASK:** Why might soldiers have personalized their powder horns? *(Personalizing would help them identify their gear. It would also allow soldiers to express their own personality, heritage, or beliefs.)*

2. **Draw Conclusions** Choose one of the artifacts. What does it reveal about the life of a Continental soldier? *(Answers will vary. Possible responses: The drum reveals that music and culture were important parts of warfare. Soldiers liked hearing the beat of a drum or the sound of a fife, as music probably reminded them of happier times or home, and also kept them in line as they marched into battle. The musket reveals one of the ways that soldiers battled during the American Revolution and serves as an example of the level of technology they had to work with. The powder horn makes me realize it must have been hard to fire frequently or successfully if you had to dump gunpowder into your musket each time. But the powder horn also reveals that soldiers took pride in their belongings.)*

Curating History

The Museum of the American Revolution's website is a useful resource for learning more about this time period. Access the museum's website and demonstrate how to find the drum, powder horn, or musket in its collection. Then encourage students to select another object to examine. As a group, have students point out details on the objects and ask questions or make speculations about them. Then read each object's caption aloud and discuss that information as it relates to the earlier discussion. Finally, ask groups of students to explore the site on their own and choose another artifact from the collection. Have groups present the artifact to the class.

Active Options

On Your Feet: Sort the Artifacts Have students work in teams of four to examine the museum's online collection and complete two Concept Clusters like those shown below. In one cluster, students should identify various weapons of war that the soldiers on both sides of the war used. In the other, students should identify a different class or genre of artifacts, to be determined by the team. When teams are finished, have them share their Concept Clusters with the class.

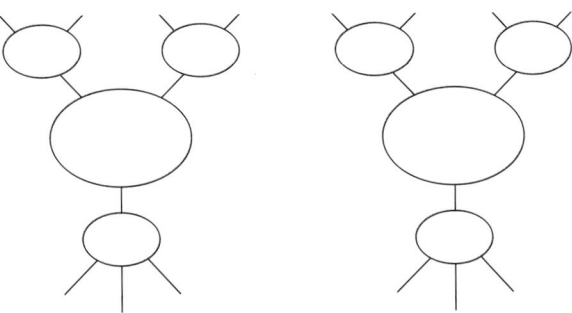

Inclusion

Identify New Words Pair special needs students with students at a higher proficiency level. Have them reread the lesson. Then have students identify three words from the lesson that were unfamiliar to them before they read the lesson. Have them use the Two-Column Chart below to record each word and its meaning.

Word	Meaning

Pre-AP

Research Revolutionary Weapons Challenge students to research the weapons soldiers used during the American Revolution. Students should give an oral report about their findings to the rest of the class.

See the Chapter Planner for more strategies for differentiation.

CURATING HISTORY

Answers will vary. Possible response: Soldiers would have used the powder horn to fill their muskets with gunpowder. They would have used the drum for entertainment and to keep marching in unison. They would have used the musket to fire at their enemies during battle.

AMERICAN WAR DRUM

Answers will vary. Possible response: During battle, drums and fifes were used to signal battle commands to the infantry. Music played on the instruments during marches, and maybe in the evenings, helped to distract soldiers by taking their minds off the harshness of war.

AMERICAN MILITARY MUSKET

Answers will vary. Possible response: The musket looks heavy and harder to fire than modern rifles. The information about the powder horn makes me think this musket was probably hard to use in bad weather.

3.1 Preparing to Fight

King George had reached his limit. He believed the colonies were out of control and had to be reined in. Maybe the king didn't understand that the colonists had reached their limits, too. Could there be a war on the horizon?

MAIN IDEA Britain enacted a series of laws to punish Boston and force the colonies into obedience, but the colonies united to resist the laws.

INTOLERABLE LAWS

Parliament decided to punish the Bostonians. It passed a series of laws called the Coercive Acts. In the colonies, these laws quickly became known as the **Intolerable Acts**.

The Intolerable Acts prevented Massachusetts from governing itself. The Massachusetts Assembly would no longer be made up of representatives elected by the people of the colony. Instead, it was to be replaced by a ruling council of officials appointed by the king. The Quartering Act was strengthened. Now, if no barracks were available, troops could take over private homes. In addition, the port of Boston would be closed until the residents could pay for the tea they had destroyed.

The British government expected the new laws to isolate Boston and convince the other colonies to be obedient. Instead, towns near Boston sent much-needed supplies to the city and took in Bostonians looking for work. Other colonies called for a meeting to decide on a united response to the Intolerable Acts. According to the Virginia House of Burgesses, "an attack made on one of our sister colonies . . . is an attack made on all British America."

Patrick Henry
Patrick Henry was known for crafting speeches on the spot with no notes. In one of his most famous speeches, given on March 23, 1775, Henry ended with the now-famous phrase, "Give me liberty or give me death!"

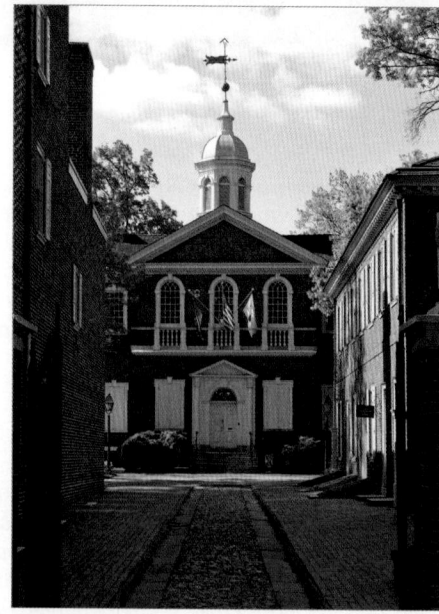

AMERICAN PLACES
Carpenters' Hall Philadelphia

Books were hard to find in the 1700s, so in 1731, Benjamin Franklin established the Library Company of Philadelphia, America's first lending library. For the first time, the public had access to a collection of books that could be borrowed and shared. In September 1773, the library moved to Carpenters' Hall (left).

Members of both Continental Congresses used the library, making it the first unofficial Library of Congress. Officers of the British Army were also permitted to borrow books, provided that they returned them in good condition.

SEEDS OF WAR

The meeting of the colonies—called the **First Continental Congress**—took place in Philadelphia on September 5, 1774. Every colony except Georgia sent delegates. The 56 representatives included Patrick Henry, Samuel and John Adams, and George Washington. The main purpose of the First Continental Congress was to discuss ways to have the Intolerable Acts repealed.

The delegates wanted to assert the rights of the 13 British colonies in North America. One of the resolutions they passed stated that the Intolerable Acts were "gross infractions of those rights to which we are justly entitled by the laws of nature, the British constitution, and the charter of this province." However, the First Continental Congress was not ready to declare independence. In the end, the delegates simply voted to end all trade with Britain and Ireland—still a significant step.

Several delegates believed it was also time to start training for a possible fight with Britain. One of the other resolutions stated that everyone qualified to fight should learn "the art of war as soon as possible." Some delegates may have believed that if there was any fighting, it would be over quickly. But others, like Patrick Henry, expected all-out war.

HISTORICAL THINKING

1. **READING CHECK** How did the colonies react to the Intolerable Acts?

2. **MAKE INFERENCES** What might learning "the art of war" have meant to colonists?

3. **ANALYZE CAUSE AND EFFECT** What were the Intolerable Acts, and how did they backfire on the British government?

Objective

Analyze the consequences of the Coercive Acts.

Critical Thinking Skills for Lesson 3.1

- Identify Main Ideas and Details
- Monitor Comprehension
- Make Inferences
- Analyze Cause and Effect
- Identify
- Draw Conclusions

Essential Question for Chapter 5

Why did the colonists decide to break from Britain? Parliament used the Coercive Acts to punish Boston and convince other colonies to obey British laws. Lesson 3.1 describes why the Coercive Acts became known as the Intolerable Acts and how they led to greater colonial unity.

Background for the Teacher

The adoption of the Declaration and Resolves of the First Continental Congress in 1774 was not a call to break from Great Britain through war. It was an affirmation that colonists were "free and natural-born subjects" with the right to be protected by laws that govern all British citizens. In an echo of Enlightenment thinkers such as John Locke, the document insisted that colonists had "immutable" rights including "life, liberty and property," which could not be infringed upon. The document also argued that colonists were "entitled to a free and exclusive power of legislation," which Britain was violating by repressing the Massachusetts Assembly.

The Declaration dismissed the ability of Parliament to maintain a standing army in the colonies "in times of peace," a blatant rebuke of the Quartering Act. The failure of Parliament to adequately address these grievances was one of the primary causes of the American Revolution.

INTRODUCE & ENGAGE

Preview Using Visuals

Point out the painting of Patrick Henry addressing his fellow Virginians. Read the caption. Draw attention to the faces of those listening. Tell students to make individual lists of the emotions they might notice. Then ask them to share their answers. **ASK:** What different responses to Patrick Henry's speech does the artist convey? *(The responses include shock, anger, and anxiety.)* Why do you think the artist conveyed all of these emotions? *(The artist wanted to show the difficult decision faced by the colonists.)*

TEACH

Guided Discussion

1. **Identify** What were the results of the First Continental Congress? *(The Congress resulted in greater unity among the colonies, the passage of resolutions and trade restrictions, and the possibility of war.)*

2. **Draw Conclusions** What was the significance of the statement from the Virginia House of Burgesses that "an attack made on one of our sister colonies . . . is an attack made on all British America"? *(The statement meant the colonies were beginning to view themselves as politically united.)*

◉ American Places

Located on Chestnut Street in Philadelphia, Carpenters' Hall was built in 1770 and was the meeting place for the First Continental Congress. Delegates were pleased with the building and divided their work between the large first-story room for the Congress and the second-story rooms for committee work. Although the building was not used for the Second Continental Congress, it remained important throughout early American history. During the American Revolution it was used as a hospital, and weapons were stored in the basement. In 1791, it was home to the first Bank of the United States. Today, Carpenters' Hall is part of the Independence National Historical Park. Inside, visitors can see the delegates' chairs and original banner carried during the 1788 constitutional parade.

Active Options

On Your Feet: Fishbowl One half of the class sits in a small circle, facing inward. The other half of the class sits in a larger circle around them. Post the question: What concerns did the delegates debate when meeting as the First Continental Congress? Students in the inner circle should discuss the question while those in the outer circle listen to the discussion and evaluate the points made. Then the groups reverse roles and continue the discussion.

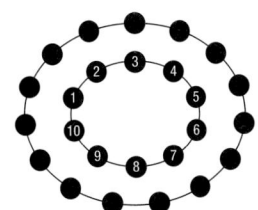

NG Learning Framework: Explore the Meaning of Liberty

ATTITUDE Responsibility

SKILL Collaboration

Draw a Detail Web on the board and write the word *Liberty* In the center. Tell students that the delegates to the First Continental Congress met to define their ideas of liberty and to act on them. Point out that the document they sent to King George III and the British Parliament articulated those strong beliefs and that the idea of liberty is central to our democracy. **ASK:** What does liberty mean to you? How do you and other people express the belief in liberty today? What are some ways the government can protect or deny one's liberty? Encourage students to be open to the ideas of others. Complete the Detail Web as students share their ideas.

DIFFERENTIATE

Striving Readers

Summarize With students working in pairs, assign each student a paragraph to read aloud while a partner listens and takes notes. Tell students that after the first student reads, the partner will summarize the paragraph in one or two spoken sentences. Encourage students to ask each other questions as they come across complex information.

Gifted & Talented

Write a Blog Choose some examples of political blogs and tell students to read them to see how writers present facts and opinions. Invite students to imagine they have traveled back in time and are delegates to the First Continental Congress. Then ask students to write a blog about their imagined experience. Remind them to include facts about the First Continental Congress as well as their opinions about the events, people, and outcomes of the meeting.

See the Chapter Planner for more strategies for differentiation.

HISTORICAL THINKING

ANSWERS

1. The colonies joined together to support Boston by sending supplies and calling for a meeting to decide how they all could stand against Britain.

2. Learning "the art of war" for those qualified to fight meant learning how to shoot and perform as a soldier in preparation for a possible conflict with Britain.

3. Known to the British as the Coercive Acts, the Intolerable Acts were intended to punish Bostonians. The Intolerable Acts prevented self-government, strengthened the Quartering Act, and closed the port of Boston until residents paid for the tea they had destroyed. The Intolerable Acts backfired on the British government by unifying the colonies to work together and form the First Continental Congress.

3.2 The Midnight Ride of Paul Revere

If you wanted to spread important news, you'd probably text it or put it out on social media for everyone to see. In 1775, spreading information wasn't that simple. "Social media" meant a man on a horse racing from town to town.

MAIN IDEA The British wanted to take control of military supplies in the colonies, but Paul Revere and others warned colonists of the coming attack.

STORED ARMS

After the First Continental Congress, militia units across the colonies began to step up their training and stockpile supplies. Remember, militias were not professional soldiers; they were groups of local men who organized to protect their town or colony. Companies of handpicked, specially trained militia members called **minutemen** were also assembled. The minutemen were known for their ability to be ready to fight with practically no warning—in a "minute."

Revere's Lantern
This iron and glass piece of American history was identified as one of the two lanterns used to signal that the British were coming by sea. It's an important artifact. Without it, the minutemen might not have been prepared for the arrival of the British troops, and Paul Revere's late-night ride might have been in vain.

General Thomas Gage, the British governor of Massachusetts, was ordered by the British government to take forceful action against the militias. In April 1775, he learned that the Massachusetts militia was storing military supplies in the town of Concord. He decided to take the supplies and also to arrest Samuel Adams and **John Hancock**. Both men were staying in Lexington, on the road from Boston to Concord. Like Adams, Hancock was a leading figure in the protests against British laws and a member of the First Continental Congress.

ONE IF BY LAND, TWO IF BY SEA

Gage's plans were leaked, however. Paul Revere, a silversmith who had taken part in the Boston Tea Party, formed a plan to warn the Massachusetts militias. He arranged to signal the Sons of Liberty in Charlestown when the British soldiers left for Concord. He would use lanterns in the Old North Church steeple, which was visible from Charlestown. If the British troops left Boston by land, there would be one lantern in the steeple. If they left by water, there would be two lanterns.

On the night of April 18, 1775, Revere learned that British soldiers were preparing to cross the bay. He had a friend hang two lanterns in the steeple, and he rowed to Charlestown in a small boat. There, the Sons of Liberty had a horse waiting for him, and he set off on his famous ride, stopping at houses and villages to warn the local militias that the British troops were coming.

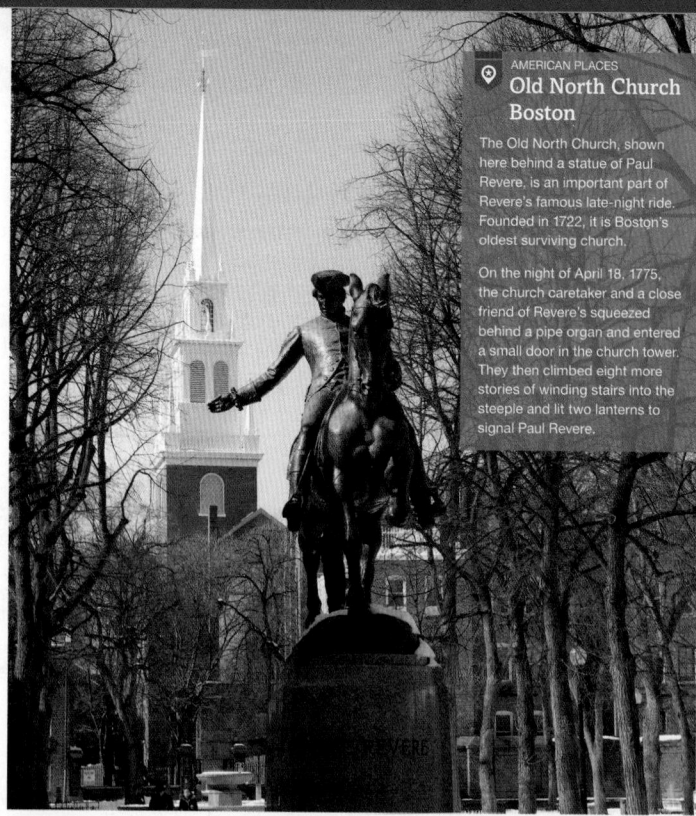

AMERICAN PLACES
Old North Church
Boston

The Old North Church, shown here behind a statue of Paul Revere, is an important part of Revere's famous late-night ride. Founded in 1722, it is Boston's oldest surviving church.

On the night of April 18, 1775, the church caretaker and a close friend of Revere's squeezed behind a pipe organ and entered a small door in the church tower. They then climbed eight more stories of winding stairs into the steeple and lit two lanterns to signal Paul Revere.

Paul Revere was not the only rider that night. When he stopped in Lexington to tell Adams and Hancock that the troops were on their way, he was joined by William Dawes. A third rider, Dr. Samuel Prescott, caught up with Revere and Dawes farther down the road.

Soon, a patrol of British soldiers stopped the riders. Dawes and Prescott escaped, but Revere was held and questioned by the soldiers. Prescott was able to complete the ride and alert the militia in Concord. When the British troops arrived, the minutemen were ready.

HISTORICAL THINKING

1. **READING CHECK** How did Paul Revere and others alert the Massachusetts militia about the approaching British soldiers?

2. **INTERPRET VISUALS** How do the photo and caption above help you understand the events described in the text?

3. **FORM AND SUPPORT OPINIONS** Is Paul Revere an important figure in American history? Why or why not?

PLAN

Objective
Explore the reasons and details behind Paul Revere's legendary midnight ride.

Critical Thinking Skills for Lesson 3.2
• Identify Main Ideas and Details
• Monitor Comprehension
• Interpret Visuals
• Form and Support Opinions
• Make Predictions
• Identify Problems and Solutions

Essential Question for Chapter 5
Why did the colonists decide to break from Britain? By 1775, colonists were already dissatisfied with the British government. Lesson 3.2 describes how the colonial government in Massachusetts tried to take control of military supplies and how the militias and individuals worked together to foil the British plan.

Background for the Teacher
Militias and minutemen played integral roles in the American Revolution, but militias did not originate in the 1770s. In fact, militias existed in the colonies as early as the 1630s, and minutemen participated in the French and Indian War in the 1750s. By the time the American Revolution began, militias and minutemen were well regarded as groups that helped defend the colonies from Native American attacks, rioting, and various forms of social unrest. These military units were not centrally organized or commanded, so when colonists realized a full-scale army was necessary to fight the British, these units disbanded and a colonial army formed.

History Notebook
Encourage students to complete the Reid on the Road video series page for Chapter 5 in their History Notebooks after they view the video.

INTRODUCE & ENGAGE

Team Up: Community Response

Have students form small groups to discuss what would happen if they needed to communicate information about an emergency in their community. Help guide the discussions by encouraging groups to think about the following:

• What forms of communication individuals might use to communicate information

• What community leaders might do to help get the word out

• Why it is important to reach all members of a community in an emergency

TEACH

Guided Discussion

1. **Make Predictions** What might have been the course of events had Paul Revere not been able to signal that the British were coming? (*If the British had caught the colonists by surprise, they may have succeeded in suppressing the colonists' rebellion.*)

2. **Identify Problems and Solutions** What problem did the militias solve for the colonists on the verge of revolution? (*The colonists had no defense against the British government until they used organized militias to protect their towns and colonies.*)

American Places

The Old North Church in Boston, Massachusetts, is still standing. More than half a million people visit this important American Revolution site every year. Visitors can tour the church, learn about the families who "owned" its pews over the years, tour the bell-ringing chamber, and descend into the crypt underneath the church. Tourists can also check out Captain Jackson's Historic Chocolate Shop, named after Captain Newark Jackson, and learn about 18th-century chocolate making. Old North Church's congregation continues to hold services every Sunday.

Active Options

On Your Feet: Inside-Outside Circle Arrange students in concentric circles facing each other. Have each student in the outside circle ask a question about the minutemen or Paul Revere's ride. Then have each student in the inside circle answer his or her partner's question. On a signal, have students on the inside circle rotate counterclockwise to meet new partners and begin again. On a different signal, have students trade roles so that those in the inside circle ask questions and those in the outside circle answer questions.

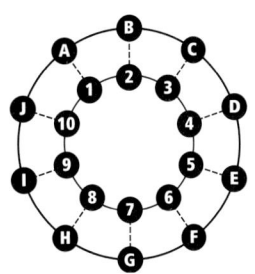

NG Learning Framework: Research the Five Riders

ATTITUDE Curiosity

KNOWLEDGE Our Human Story

As students learn in Lesson 3.2, Paul Revere was not the only rider who alerted colonists about an impending attack by the British. Have students conduct online research to learn who the five riders were. Instruct them to write profiles on two of the five riders. Students should identify names, interesting points about the riders, and where and when they rode. When students have finished researching and writing their profiles, allow time for them to present to the class.

DIFFERENTIATE

Inclusion

Monitor Comprehension Have students work in small groups, reading aloud the text paragraph by paragraph. At the end of each paragraph, have them stop and use these sentence frames:

• This paragraph is about _____.

• One detail that stood out to me is _____.

• The word _____ means _____.

• I don't think I understand _____.

Encourage students to help each other with any part of the text that they do not understand.

Gifted & Talented

Map Revere's Ride Encourage students to research Paul Revere's route using library or online sources. Then have students create an illustrated and annotated map of his route, including notable locations along the way, such as the Old North Church. Tell students to annotate their maps with more information about Paul Revere, the Sons of Liberty, local militias, and other riders. Encourage students to be creative in their map designs and color schemes. When students have completed their maps, have them present them to the class.

See the Chapter Planner for more strategies for differentiation.

HISTORICAL THINKING

ANSWERS

1. Paul Revere and other riders alerted the militia about the coming of the British by using lanterns in the Old North Church steeple as signals. They also rode from house to house and village to village to warn colonists.

2. The Old North Church steeple is very tall, and it is hard to imagine how someone was able to signal Revere with lanterns from that spot. Understanding that the church caretaker was a friend of Revere's helps the story make sense, because someone with insider knowledge would have had to hang the lanterns for Revere's plan to work.

3. Revere helped communicate important information about a critical event, but he wasn't the only one who did so. His importance is probably more symbolic than literal, and in that way he is a significant historical figure.

3.3 Shot Heard Round the World

In 1837, American poet Ralph Waldo Emerson referred to a bullet fired in Lexington, Massachusetts, as "the shot heard round the world" in his poem "Concord Hymn." Nobody knows who fired that shot, but it started a revolution that changed the world.

MAIN IDEA The American Revolution began when Massachusetts militia fought the British forces in the towns of Lexington and Concord.

THE REVOLUTION BEGINS

As the British Army marched toward Concord, they heard church bells and saw lights in windows. The colonists were awake and aware. Soon after sunrise on April 19, the troops reached Lexington. There, they met about 70 armed militiamen, nearly half of the town's adult males. But the Lexington militia was inexperienced and faced a much larger British force.

The scene was chaos as both the British commander and the militia leader called orders to their troops. The British officer, Major John Pitcairn, wanted to disarm the Americans, not engage in battle. But as the British advanced, a shot rang out. Then there were several more. Pitcairn tried to stop his troops, but the shooting continued for 20 minutes, leaving eight Lexington men dead and 10 wounded. Only one British soldier was wounded and none were killed.

The British reached Concord at about eight o'clock in the morning. Using previously hidden military supplies, the Americans inflicted more casualties than the British did this time. The British soldiers attempted an orderly retreat back to Boston. But hundreds of militiamen fired at them from behind trees, walls, rocks, and buildings and forced many British soldiers to panic. The British countered by sending advance parties to set fire to homes and kill residents along the way back to Boston.

The fighting at **Lexington and Concord** is considered the first battle of the American Revolution. By the end of the day, British losses totaled 73 dead and 200 wounded or missing. The Americans counted 49 killed and at least 39 wounded or missing.

CHOOSING SIDES

As tensions between Britain and the colonies turned into open violence, colonists took sides in the conflict. Those who called themselves **Patriots** supported the right of the colonies to rule themselves. At first, not all Patriots wanted to separate from Britain. Over time, however, those on the Patriot side became convinced that independence was necessary.

The **Loyalists**, colonists who supported Britain, increasingly found themselves an uncomfortable minority. As time went on, it became dangerous to sympathize with the British cause. Some Loyalists were beaten or saw their homes burned by fellow colonists. In 1775, a Loyalist who spoke openly about his opinions was ordered to leave Maryland by the Maryland Provincial Convention.

HISTORICAL THINKING

1. **READING CHECK** What were the results of the fighting at Lexington and Concord?

2. **ANALYZE CAUSE AND EFFECT** Why did the battles of Lexington and Concord increase tensions between Patriots and Loyalists?

3. **IDENTIFY MAIN IDEAS AND DETAILS** What details support the idea that the Patriots won the battles?

LOYALISTS CALLED THE **PATRIOTS**

Whig! Rebel! Yankee!

PATRIOTS CALLED THE **LOYALISTS**

King's Man! Royalist! Tory!

COLONIAL ARMY **SOLDIER**

BRITISH ARMY **SOLDIER**

FAMOUS **PATRIOTS**
George Washington
Thomas Jefferson
James Madison
Patrick Henry
John Adams
Alexander Hamilton
Benjamin Franklin

FAMOUS **LOYALISTS**
John Howe
Mary Dowd
Myles Cooper
William Franklin
Thomas Hutchinson

DAILY COLONIAL ARMY RATIONS
1 1/2 lb. Bread or Flour
4 oz. Whiskey
1 lb. Beef or 3/4 lb. Pork

DAILY BRITISH ARMY RATIONS
1 1/2 lb. Bread or Flour
8 oz. Rum
1/4 pint Canned Peas and 1 oz. Rice
1 oz. Butter
1 lb. Beef or 1/2 lb. Pork

COLONISTS VS BRITISH

ALLIES
France Spain
United Netherlands

ALLIES
Many Native American Tribes
Hessian Troops

2.5 Million American Colonists

BATTLES WERE FOUGHT ACROSS THE **GLOBE**

Europe
North America
Caribbean

11 Million People in Great Britain

20% Supported Britain

2.5 Million Colonists in America

SOURCE: Civil War Trust Online

The Road to Revolution **199**

Objective
Describe the beginnings of the American Revolution and the divisions that defined the colonies following Lexington and Concord.

Critical Thinking Skills for Lesson 3.3
- Identify Main Ideas and Details
- Monitor Comprehension
- Analyze Cause and Effect
- Determine Chronology
- Make Connections
- Analyze Visuals

Essential Question for Chapter 5
Why did the colonists decide to break from Britain? The military conflict at Lexington and Concord is considered the first battle of the American Revolution. Lesson 3.3 explains the events surrounding the conflict and the divisions between Patriots and Loyalists in the colonies.

Background for the Teacher
About one-third of British colonists identified themselves as Loyalists, most of whom served the British crown as officials, were members of the Anglican Church, or had an economic interest in the colonies remaining loyal to Britain. Motivated by the British promise of freedom and hope for a better life, thousands of enslaved African Americans supported the British government.

As colonies declared independence from Britain, Loyalists were often treated harshly. Strict laws prevented Loyalists from holding office or from voting and heavily taxed or confiscated their property. Because of this treatment, approximately 100,000 Loyalists fled their homes, many eventually ending up in Canada, where the British government provided asylum and offered some compensation for claims of lost property. Many African-American Loyalists feared they would be enslaved. The British, however, allowed thousands of African-American Loyalists to leave America for Nova Scotia, Jamaica, and Britain.

Explore Idioms

Read the lesson title. Lead a discussion about the significance of the phrase "heard round the world." **ASK:** What does "round the world" suggest? *(Answers will vary. Possible response: It suggests something that had far-reaching effects, and not just for Britain. It also suggests that countries around the globe were aware of the conflict in the British colonies in North America.)* **ASK:** What recent or current events have been "heard round the world"? *(Answers will vary. Students should make connections between events and their global impact.)*

TEACH

Guided Discussion

1. **Determine Chronology** How did one event lead to another at Lexington and Concord on April 19, 1775? *(First, the British marched toward Concord. When troops reached Lexington, a group of 70 inexperienced militiamen were waiting. Leaders from both sides yelled orders to their men, and in the confusion a shot was fired. The first shot led to more shots, and then fighting continued for 20 minutes, leaving eight Lexington men dead. When the British reached Concord later that morning, Americans were armed with weapons they had hidden. The militiamen fired from behind trees and buildings, forcing the British to retreat over the course of the day.)*

2. **Make Connections** What method of fighting by the Massachusetts militiamen caused the British to have significantly greater casualties than the colonists? *(The militiamen fought from behind trees, walls, rocks, and buildings rather than in formed lines facing the British soldiers.)*

Analyze Visuals

Direct students' attention to the infographic. **ASK:** What advantages did the colonists have at the beginning of the war? *(The colonists had help from foreign allies as well as support from 80 percent of the people.)* What advantages did the British have? *(The British had a larger population of potential soldiers, more plentiful rations, and support from many Native Americans.)* At the outset of the fighting, who do you think should have been "favored" to win this war? *(Answers will vary. Student responses should include information from the infographic and text for support.)*

Active Options

On Your Feet: Three Corners Post these signs in three corners of the classroom: Patriots for Independence, Patriots Against Independence, Loyalists. Organize students into groups around each sign and have them discuss that group's likely opinion about "the shot heard round the world." Then have students from each group travel to explain its viewpoint to each of the other two groups.

NG Learning Framework: Create a Storyboard

SKILL Communication

KNOWLEDGE Our Human Story

Instruct groups of students to work together to create a storyboard about the events of April 19, 1775. Their storyboards should tell more about the human story of the day's events than about the actual battles. Explain that students should focus on how the townspeople, militiamen, and British soldiers reacted as the day unfolded. Tell students to imagine how they might have thought and felt and what they might have said. Encourage students to include captions and dialogue in their storyboards.

DIFFERENTIATE

English Language Learners

Explore the 5Ws Explain to students that reporters use the questions *Who? What? Where? When?* and *Why?* to guide their reporting and that students can use the same questions to understand the information in the lesson. Pair students at the **Emerging** level with English-proficient students and tell them to work in pairs to answer the five questions about the events of April 19, 1775, at Lexington and Concord. Suggest that English-proficient students help students at the **Emerging** level understand the meaning of each 5W word before the pair answers each question.

Pre-AP

Engage in a Debate Tell students to select and research one of the Patriots or Loyalists named on the infographic. After students take notes and gather information, ask them to assume the role of their chosen historical figure and participate in a debate concerning whether the colonies should remain loyal to Britain.

See the Chapter Planner for more strategies for differentiation.

HISTORICAL THINKING

ANSWERS

1. After Lexington and Concord, colonists began to choose sides. Some were still loyal to Britain, and others supported the right of the colonies to rule themselves.

2. As fighting began, people had to choose sides. The Loyalists found themselves in the minority and were treated harshly for sympathizing with the British.

3. British losses totaled 73 dead and 200 wounded or missing. Massachusetts counted 49 killed and 43 wounded or missing.

3.4 North Bridge
Concord, Massachusetts

North Bridge is more than just a quaint path over the Concord River in Massachusetts. Located in **Minute Man National Historical Park**, it's a solemn place—American hallowed ground. It is also the site where some of the first shots of the American Revolution were fired on April 19, 1775. The original "battle bridge" that existed when the war broke out has long since been replaced, but the symbolism of this historical landscape remains. Based on what you see here, how might the geography of this place have impacted colonial and British soldiers?

CRITICAL VIEWING The 1875 bronze Minute Man statue (right background) was made from melted Civil War cannons for the 100th anniversary of the battle in this location. It symbolizes the colonial farmers who replaced their plows with muskets to defend their land and liberty. What does this tell you about how the colonial soldiers differed from British soldiers?

The Road to Revolution 201

PLAN

Objective

Discover the historical importance of North Bridge, the now-peaceful site where the American Revolution began.

Critical Thinking Skills for Lesson 3.4

- Analyze Visuals
- Make Connections
- Compare and Contrast
- Identify

Essential Question for Chapter 5

Why did the colonists decide to break from Britain? Conflict between the British and the American colonists had been building up for more than a decade. Lesson 3.4 introduces students to the place where the American Revolution began.

Background for the Teacher

The symbolic importance of North Bridge cannot be overstated. Colonists firing on British soldiers was considered an act of treason, or a crime of betrayal against one's country. The British considered colonists as British subjects. Rebelling colonists had decided to shed their British identities in favor of new American ones. While no one is quite sure which side fired first, the fact remains that a colonial militia engaged the king's troops in armed, open combat. For the Patriots, there was no turning back.

History Notebook

Encourage students to complete the American Places page for Chapter 5 in their History Notebooks as they read.

INTRODUCE & ENGAGE

Categorize Descriptions

As a class, take a few minutes to study the photograph of North Bridge in Lesson 3.4. Have students volunteer words that describe what they see in the photo as you write them on the board. Then have students categorize the words they volunteer. For example, one category might be "Nature" and another one "Structure." Encourage students to think of words that relate to the photo that may evoke a particular emotion or time period.

TEACH

Guided Discussion

1. **Compare and Contrast** How is North Bridge similar to and different from bridges you have crossed or visited? *(Answers will vary. Responses may include that students are more familiar with bridges made of steel or bridges that are much bigger.)*

2. **Identify** Why would the Minute Man statue have been created from melted Civil War cannons? *(Answers will vary. Possible response: Melting down cannons just used in a civil war to create a statue of a minuteman, a hero of the American Revolution, may have been a way that Americans wanted to symbolically recall and celebrate American unity.)*

American Places

Patriot's Day celebrations are held every April at Minute Man National Historical Park. People dress in costumes ranging from colonial militia and British soldiers to ordinary colonists. Participants reenact the fighting along Battle Road Trail and other battles that took place on the site. Historical interpreters tell stories from the point of view of colonists who shaped the events of April 19, 1775.

Active Options

On Your Feet: Numbered Heads Organize students into groups of four. Tell students to think about and discuss a response to this question: Does it matter which side fired the first shot? Then call a number and have the student from each group with that number report for the group.

NG Learning Framework: Identify a Community Landmark

ATTITUDE Curiosity

KNOWLEDGE Our Human Story

Remind students that history and historical landmarks are all around us, if we look hard enough. Divide the class into teams. Have each team work together to identify and research an important landmark or historical site in the community. It could be a human-made feature, such as a building, or it could be an important physical feature, such as a strategic river. Have each team prepare a multimedia presentation about the landmark. Allow time in class for teams to present the landmarks they have discovered and learned about.

DIFFERENTIATE

Striving Readers

Summarize Have students work together in pairs or small groups to read and summarize the text, caption, and information they gather from the photograph of North Bridge. Tell students to use a Summary Chart like the one shown below to organize their notes. Suggest students provide three notes per category. After they have completed taking notes, have students create a summary statement about Lesson 3.4.

Text	Caption	Photograph
1.	1.	1.
2.	2.	2.
3.	3.	3.
SUMMARY STATEMENT		

Pre-AP

Write Journal Entries Invite students to imagine they were present at North Bridge on April 19, 1775. Tell them to create a historical character based on what they have read in this and previous lessons. Then have them write journal entries from their character's point of view. Have them consider the following questions:

• What kinds of difficulties have you encountered leading up to this day?

• How do you feel when you see so many troops ready to fight?

• Do you want revolution, or do you want to stay under British control?

Encourage students to present their journal entries to the class. Consider pairing opposing sides or like-minded individuals together for a readers' theater experience.

See the Chapter Planner for more strategies for differentiation.

AMERICAN PLACES

Answers will vary. Students might mention that soldiers would have had to figure out how to cross rivers or take control of bridges during battles.

CRITICAL VIEWING Answers will vary. Possible response: The symbolism of a statue created from melted-down cannons drives home the point that colonial soldiers had to fend for and outfit themselves, while the British soldiers were supplied by one of the largest armies—and empires—in the world.

4.1 Colonial Army Forms

You nervously count and recount your bullets as you and your fellow militiamen stand at the top of the hill. Below, a line of red-coated British soldiers marches toward you, pausing only to fire in unison. This is it. This is war.

MAIN IDEA Colonial leaders remained reluctant to fully declare independence, but battles between the British and colonial militias continued to break out.

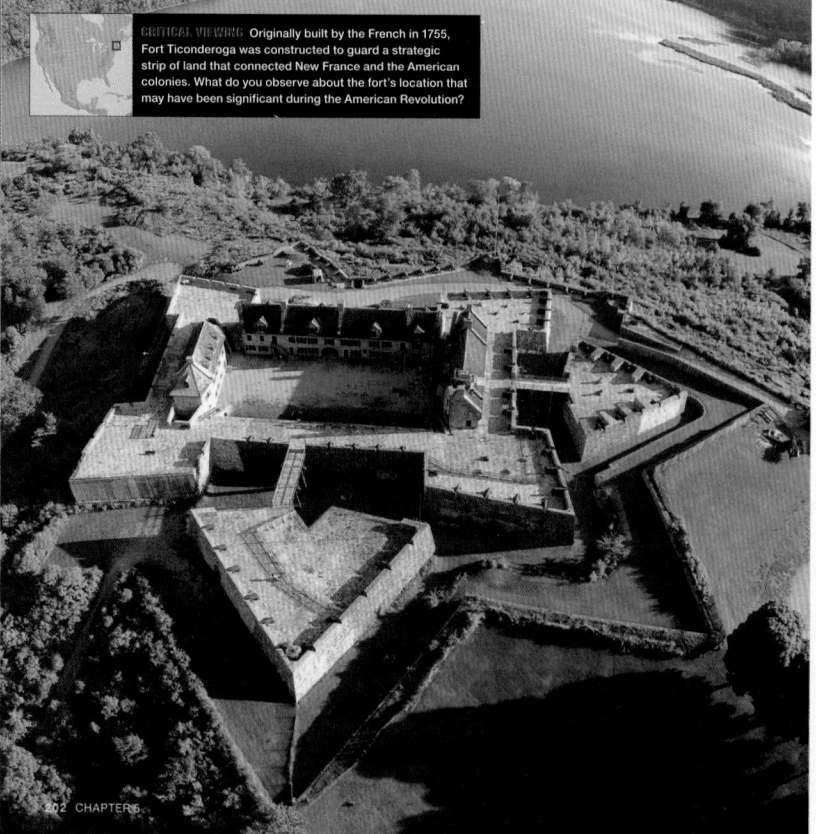

CRITICAL VIEWING Originally built by the French in 1755, Fort Ticonderoga was constructed to guard a strategic strip of land that connected New France and the American colonies. What do you observe about the fort's location that may have been significant during the American Revolution?

VICTORY AT FORT TICONDEROGA

The next battle in the growing conflict took place on May 10, 1775. At dawn that morning, **Ethan Allen**, a Patriot and colonial leader from Vermont, and **Benedict Arnold**, from Connecticut, led a troop of militia in an attack on Fort Ticonderoga in northeastern New York. In a classic example of "timing is everything," the militia known as the Green Mountain Boys surprised the sleeping British soldiers and captured the fort without firing a shot.

The victory at Fort Ticonderoga gave the colonial forces an important advantage. The Green Mountain Boys captured the fort's **artillery**, or large guns that could fire a long distance. In all, they claimed 59 cannons and 19 other pieces of heavy artillery for the colonies. It was an epic gain.

On the same day that Ethan Allen took Fort Ticonderoga, the **Second Continental Congress** met in Philadelphia. Many of the delegates had also been part of the First Continental Congress. New delegates included Thomas Jefferson of Virginia and Benjamin Franklin of Pennsylvania.

The Congress recognized the need to prepare for war and wanted to make sure the army would be under its control. So it appointed **George Washington** as the commander in chief of the colonial forces, which would now be called the **Continental Army**. Despite this warlike decision, however, many of the delegates were still opposed to declaring independence.

BATTLE OF BUNKER HILL

Before Washington could even take command of the troops, another battle broke out. The militia around Boston learned that the British were planning to seize the hills overlooking the city. On June 16, a troop of militiamen occupied Bunker Hill and Breed's Hill to prevent the British from taking the high ground.

The next morning, the British troops attacked. The militia fighters were greatly outnumbered. They were also short of ammunition, so they had to make every shot count. Colonel William Prescott, their commander, is said to have told his men, "Don't fire until you can see the whites of their eyes."

An American Traitor
Benedict Arnold was an early hero in the American Revolution who went on to become one of the most infamous traitors in American history. After helping capture Fort Ticonderoga in 1775, Arnold continued his support of the American war efforts but felt his work went unrecognized. In 1779, he secretly negotiated with the British to turn over an American post in exchange for a commanding position in the British army and a cash reward. Arnold's plot was discovered by the Americans, but he escaped to British territory.

The militia did have one key advantage: the British troops had to charge uphill to reach them. The redcoats tried storming Breed's Hill three times. The first two attempts failed, resulting in a huge loss of lives. On the third try, the Patriots were overrun by the redcoats. Britain won the battle, but at an enormous cost. Today, the encounter is known as the Battle of Bunker Hill, even though most of the fighting took place on Breed's Hill.

HISTORICAL THINKING

1. **READING CHECK** What happened at the battles of Fort Ticonderoga and Bunker Hill?

2. **ANALYZE CAUSE AND EFFECT** Why did the Second Continental Congress decide to prepare for war?

3. **FORM AND SUPPORT OPINIONS** Do you think peace between Britain and the colonies could have been possible in 1775? Why or why not?

PLAN

Objective
Explain the significance of the battles at Fort Ticonderoga and Bunker Hill.

Critical Thinking Skills for Lesson 4.1
- Identify Main Ideas and Details
- Monitor Comprehension
- Analyze Cause and Effect
- Form and Support Opinions
- Draw Conclusions
- Make Predictions
- Evaluate

Essential Question for Chapter 5
Why did the colonists decide to break from Britain? Lesson 4.1 describes the significance of the capture of Fort Ticonderoga and the Battle of Bunker Hill, as well as the steps taken by the Second Continental Congress to prepare for war with Britain.

Background for the Teacher

The Second Continental Congress placed its faith in George Washington to lead the Continental Army. As a veteran of the French and Indian War, where he fought with and learned from the British, Washington was perhaps the colonies' most experienced military leader.

Washington's task of raising and training an army was a formidable one, as colonists lacked the training and discipline of British soldiers. In fact, when taking command on July 3, 1775, he described the Continental Army as "a mixed multitude of people under very little discipline, order or government." To rectify this, Washington worked to instill discipline in his soldiers through the use of harsh punishments such as lashings and frequent court-martials. However, despite Washington's best efforts, many men resisted his methods, as they felt their responsibilities were first to their families and farms.

INTRODUCE & ENGAGE

Activate Prior Knowledge

Point out the portrait of Benedict Arnold and read the caption. Ask students if they've ever heard anyone called a "Benedict Arnold." **ASK:** What do you think calling someone a "Benedict Arnold" means? *(Answers will vary. Possible response: It means that someone double-crossed another person for personal gain or to be on the winning side of a conflict.)* After students share their ideas, explain that Arnold's actions are considered to have been so despicable that in American culture his name is synonymous with the word *traitor*.

TEACH

Guided Discussion

1. **Draw Conclusions** What conclusions can you draw about the strengths and weaknesses of colonial forces in 1775? *(Colonial forces had a strong determination and were fighting on terrain they understood. However, they were a newly formed army lacking in resources needed for battle.)*

2. **Make Predictions** Given the events of 1775, why might someone predict a quick end to the conflict between the colonies and Britain? *(Answers will vary but should note the British forces' victory at the Battle of Bunker Hill, Parliament's resolve to control the rebellion, or the Second Continental Congress's reluctance to declare independence.)*

Evaluate

Ask students to think about the strategic importance of Breed's Hill. **ASK:** Why do you think the British made a third assault up Breed's Hill after suffering such a huge loss of life in the first two attempts? *(Securing the high ground provided military advantage for the British. In addition, they didn't want to allow the colonists another victory.)*

Active Options

On Your Feet: Chart Relay Tape large pieces of paper to the wall. Put students in teams of four. Provide each team with a marker. Tell them to make four columns on their paper and label them as follows: Victory at Fort Ticonderoga, Battle of Bunker Hill, Formation of Continental Army, and Second Continental Congress. Allow teams time to discuss the topics. Inform students that each team must provide four facts for each topic. Tell team members to arrange themselves in order from one to four. On your signal, team members who are number one write their first fact on the chart. When finished, they hand the marker to the second team member, and so on. The first team to complete their chart wins.

Victory at Fort Ticonderoga	Battle of Bunker Hill	Formation of Continental Army	Second Continental Congress

NG Learning Framework: Research the Continental Army

ATTITUDE Curiosity

SKILL Collaboration

Tell groups of four students to review Lesson 4.1. Instruct them to collaborate in writing two questions about the Continental Army they would like to answer. Then have the groups split into pairs and have each pair pursue an answer to one of the questions through research at the library or online. When finished, ask students to report their findings to the other members of the group.

DIFFERENTIATE

Striving Readers

Complete Sentence Starters Provide these sentence starters for students to complete after reading. You may also ask students to preview the sentence starters to set a purpose for reading.

- On May 10, 1775, colonial forces under the leadership of Ethan Allen and Benedict Arnold were able to capture _____. *(Fort Ticonderoga)*
- The Second Continental Congress formed the Continental Army and appointed _____ to lead it. *(George Washington)*
- The costly Battle of Bunker Hill was won by _____. *(the British)*

Gifted & Talented

Create a Presentation Ask students to conduct research about the Battle of Bunker Hill. Tell them to create a short multimedia presentation focusing on the battle's chronology and its significance for the colonists and the British. The presentation may include visuals such as maps, primary sources, and photographs.

See the Chapter Planner for more strategies for differentiation.

HISTORICAL THINKING

ANSWERS

1. Colonial forces gained an important advantage with the capture of Fort Ticonderoga by capturing the fort's artillery. While the British won the Battle of Bunker Hill, they suffered great losses.

2. Because of the escalating conflict and tension between colonists and Britain, the Second Continental Congress knew that war was increasingly likely.

3. Answers will vary. Possible responses: No; there were different opinions concerning who should hold power in the colonies, and colonial and British blood had already been shed. Yes; many Loyalists opposed the war, and colonists faced a daunting prospect in formally fighting the British military.

CRITICAL VIEWING The fort is strategically placed on high ground and on the water. An impending enemy attack by water or land easily could be seen, providing a defensive advantage. Also, its location along a waterway may have been important in controlling the flow of supplies to the colonies from Canada.

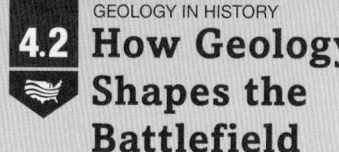

4.2 How Geology Shapes the Battlefield

MAIN IDEA Geologic forces shape the landscape, impacting the outcome of many battles.

By Andrés Ruzo, **National Geographic Explorer**

TAKE THE HIGH GROUND

Taking advantage of a battlefield can mean the difference between victory and defeat, and there is a geologic story behind every great battle. An area's **geology**—the local geologic features such as rocks, landforms, and the processes that created and shaped them—can define a battlefield. Over millions, even billions of years, colliding tectonic plates and volcanic activity give rise to great landforms like mountain ranges. Erosion from weathering, moving glaciers, and other destructive forces break down these landforms. The eroded material is transported and re-deposited, customizing each region with its distinctive **terrain**, the physical features of the land.

Throughout history, successful commanders were the ones who understood how to use the local terrain to their advantage. The names of American Revolution battle sites like Brooklyn Heights (New York), Bunker Hill (Massachusetts), and Kings Mountain (South Carolina) are clues to the importance of battlefield geology. Hills, cliffs, bluffs, and other elevated landforms played a key role in the war. Elevation gave soldiers a strategic military advantage. Think about running uphill with a heavy rifle straight into enemy gunfire. Now consider the benefits of firing down on your enemies from a well-fortified position as they advance up difficult terrain. It's no wonder military commanders try to "take the high ground."

BUNKER HILL

Study the map of Bunker Hill. This landscape tells a geologic story. Over 20,000 years ago, a massive melting glacier slowly began to reveal the

Breed's or Bunker?
On June 16, 1775, more than 1,000 colonists set out to fortify Bunker Hill, but they passed it in the dark and fortified Breed's Hill instead.

Battle of Bunker Hill, 1775

Mystic River

Bunker Hill

Mill Pond

Warren's Redoubt

Breed's Hill

Tricky Terrain
Seemingly open stretches of land were obstacle courses for the British. Tall grasses hid rocks and holes. Fences and stone walls also slowed them down.

Falcon

Glasgow

CHARLESTOWN

British troops
Patriot troops
British advance
Patriot advance
British ship

Lively

Taking the High Ground
The colonists didn't have many cannons, and they weren't very good at firing the ones they did have. But they did have a strong position on high ground, just across the water from Boston. This forced the British to attack before they were fully ready to do so.

BOSTON

landscape that would one day become Boston. Geologically, Bunker Hill and Breed's Hill are called **drumlins**, smooth-sloped hills made of glacial sediments. In 1775, the Americans took the high ground and fortified these drumlins by building 6-foot **earthworks**, human-made land modifications, out of the silty glacial soils. This put the Americans in an ideal defensive position overlooking the battlefields.

But taking the high ground doesn't always ensure victory. At Bunker Hill, the Americans held their ground until they ran out of ammunition. As you

have read, the British won the battle, but at a terrible cost. Over 1,000 British soldiers were killed or wounded, compared to over 400 Americans. This showed that the Patriots could hold their own against a better-trained, better-equipped, and far larger British force. Clearly local terrain played a role in how the battle unfolded.

War commanders probably don't think much about the geologic story that shaped their battlefields, but that doesn't mean the geology isn't significant.

THINK LIKE A GEOLOGIST

1. **IDENTIFY MAIN IDEAS AND DETAILS** If you were a commander defending your city, where would you set up troops? Why?

2. **DESCRIBE** What advantages or disadvantages would your local terrain present in battle?

3. **INTERPRET MAPS** Aside from hills, which geologic features do you think affected the battle?

PLAN

Objective

Explain how American forces attacked and defended from high ground during key battles, gaining advantage over the British.

Critical Thinking Skills for Lesson 4.2

• Identify Main Ideas and Details
• Monitor Comprehension
• Describe
• Interpret Maps
• Summarize
• Make Inferences

Essential Question for Chapter 5

Why did the colonists decide to break from Britain? Geologic processes and terrain played a big role in battles during the American Revolution. Lesson 4.2 discusses how geology and knowledge of the terrain helped the Americans win important battles and attain their goal of breaking from Britain.

Background for the Teacher

A year after the Battle of Bunker Hill, the landscape would play an important role in General Washington's strategy for the Battle of Long Island. Knowing the British would attempt to take control of New York City, Washington split his nearly 20,000 troops, placing them on the high ground of Brooklyn Heights, the Heights of Guan, and near Gowanus Bay. This, he believed, would force the British to move slowly through heavily wooded terrain, giving the advantage to the Americans.

British general William Howe had other plans, however. He had grown cautious since Bunker Hill, and he had a secret weapon—his subordinate Henry Clinton had spent time hunting in the area as a boy. Clinton proposed the British use a little-known pass through the heights, called Jamaica Pass, to flank the Americans. Howe led 10,000 soldiers through the unguarded pass and attacked the Americans from the rear, winning the battle and forcing Washington to retreat from Long Island.

Hands-On Geology

Tell students that in this lesson they will learn how geologic processes have shaped landscapes. One such process involves tectonic plates, whose movement can cause earthquakes, move glaciers, form mountain ranges, and carve out basins. Use two blocks of wood to demonstrate how the plates move against one another. Begin by explaining that geologists have identified 12 large plates on Earth's surface that are constantly moving and coming into contact with one another. Ask students to suppose that each block of wood you are handling represents a plate. Demonstrate the four kinds of movements:

- one plate diving under another (subduction)
- two plates pulling apart from each other (divergence)
- two plates colliding, slowly pushing up the parts that collide (convergence)
- two plates sliding past each other (transform)

TEACH   STEM

Guided Discussion

1. **Summarize** What strategies did commanders in the American Revolution use to control a battlefield? *(They used local resources to build defensive fortresses and secured useful viewpoints on high ground so they could see the enemy coming.)*

2. **Make Inferences** What disadvantages did the British forces face by fighting on American soil? *(They were unfamiliar with the terrain and so didn't always know where they could conceal themselves. Also, when they attacked the American forces, they often were forced to charge uphill, making them easy targets.)*

Geology in History

Interpret Maps Have students study the map showing the British and American troops at the Battle of Bunker Hill on Charlestown Peninsula. Explain that the map shows the topography of the area, with contour lines indicating elevation. Point out Breed's Hill at the lower elevation. Ask students to identify the British and American troops and trace their movements on the map. Point out Warren's Redoubt, where the American soldiers had built fortifications. Point out, too, the fortifications built along the west side of the peninsula. **ASK:** How did the British troops advance on the Americans? *(They advanced straight up Breed's Hill.)* What did they find at the top of the hill? *(They encountered American troops ready to fire on them.)* What advantages did the American troops have in the attack? *(They could see the British advancing.)* Why did the Americans build fortifications along the west side of the peninsula? *(They wanted to prevent a flank attack.)*

Active Options

On Your Feet: Turn and Talk on Topic Have students form three lines. Give each group this topic sentence: Generals of the American Revolution used the local terrain to help them win the Battle of Bunker Hill. Tell students to build a paragraph on that topic by each one adding one sentence. Allow each group to present its paragraph to the class by having each student read his or her statement.

NG Learning Framework: Devise a Strategic Defense

ATTITUDE Curiosity

KNOWLEDGE Problem-Solving

Have students get together in groups. Ask them to imagine they are army leaders during the American Revolution and they must plan a strategy for defending a terrain that consists of a series of rolling hills overlooking flat meadowland. Have each group come up with a plan for defending the area and defeating the British soldiers who are about to advance on it. Once the groups have devised a plan, tell them to share it with the class.

English Language Learners

Outline and Take Notes To help students at **All Proficiencies** develop their comprehension skills, ask them to work in pairs to write an outline of this lesson. Pair students at the **Emerging** level with a student at either the **Expanding** or **Bridging** level. The following format can help them start writing their outlines.

Outline

I. *Battlefield Terrain* _____

   A. _____

   B. _____

II. *Advantages of Elevation* _____

   A. _____

   B. _____

III. *Knowledge of Terrain* _____

   A. _____

   B. _____

Gifted & Talented

Infographic of Mountain Formation Have students research and produce an infographic showing how the Appalachian Mountains were formed. The infographic should show the mountains, the plates beneath the mountains, and arrows showing the movement of the plates.

See the Chapter Planner for more strategies for differentiation.

THINK LIKE A GEOLOGIST

ANSWERS

1. Answers will vary. Possible response: Students might say they would set up troops on elevated terrain so they would see the enemy advancing.

2. Answers will vary. Possible response: Students may say the local geography is relatively flat, the disadvantage being that there is no high ground, or that knowing the area is an advantage because they could take routes the enemy soldiers don't know and sneak up and surround them.

3. Answers will vary. Possible response: Soldiers in the valleys would have been more exposed and easier to attack. Soldiers may have hidden behind the trees or tried to escape to the rivers and ponds.

4.3 Breaking with Britain

Congress has always had a difficult job, making decisions that will impact a large number of people. In 1775, the Second Continental Congress faced a hard choice: pursue peace or prepare for war.

MAIN IDEA The Second Continental Congress made one last attempt to make peace with Britain, but fighting continued and public opinion moved toward declaring independence.

PEACE REJECTED

During the summer of 1775, the Continental Congress made moves toward both peace and war. In an attempt to restore peace with Britain, delegates sent the king a petition. They asked him to resolve the conflict between the colonies and Parliament. Instead, he proclaimed that the colonies were in "an open and avowed rebellion."

At the same time, Congress sent an army north to invade Canada and take on the British forces there. This proved to be a poor decision. The Canada campaign was long, bloody, and unsuccessful. British troops successfully pushed the colonial army back into New York.

In December 1775, Parliament decided to punish the colonies by cutting off all trade. Then in January 1776, King George signed a treaty with Germany that allowed him to hire more than 20,000 German soldiers and send them to the colonies. These soldiers for hire were known as **Hessians**, and they had a reputation as fierce fighters. For many Americans, these actions proved that the British government intended to crush the colonies both militarily and economically, at any cost.

Hessian miter cap

🏛 National Museum of American History Washington, D.C.

This hat, called a miter cap, was worn by a Hessian infantry soldier from the Fusilier Regiment, which served under the British Army during the American Revolution. The cap has a cloth body covered with a brass cap plate and is stamped with a Hessian lion.

TIME TO PART

Meanwhile, the colonial army was meeting with greater success in Boston. George Washington had arrived there during the summer of 1775, determined to drive the British from the city. The following winter, he sent troops to drag the heavy guns from Fort Ticonderoga and install them on high ground overlooking Boston. In the spring of 1776, under the threat of the looming artillery, the British withdrew from the city. They sailed north to Canada in preparation for an eventual invasion of New York City. More than a thousand Loyalists left with the British because they feared they would not be safe from angry Patriots if they stayed in Boston.

Alarmed by the colonists' show of force in Boston, the British government sent a massive force to put down the revolt. Nearly 400 ships set sail from England carrying 32,000 troops, including at least 12,000 Hessians. The soldiers would join the British troops already gathering in Canada for an attack on New York City. The warships would attack seaports and disrupt colonial shipping.

Printing *Common Sense*

Colonial printers working on printing presses similar to the one shown here created publications one page at a time. They carefully folded paper onto set and inked letters and then used a lever to press the images and words onto the page.

Thousands of copies of *Common Sense* were printed, sold, and read aloud in meeting rooms and inns throughout the colonies. Because it was originally anonymous, many initially attributed *Common Sense* to Ben Franklin. As you have read, before he was a scientist and revolutionary, Ben Franklin was a printer and publisher in Philadelphia. He even owned his own printing press, so it is not a surprise that some would think he published *Common Sense*.

Printing Press

Ink Ball
The printer uses the ink ball to apply an oil-based ink onto the type.

Press
The printer rolls the type box under the press and uses the handle to imprint letters onto the paper.

Paper Holder
The printer inserts paper in the holder and folds it onto the inked type.

Type Box
The printer arranges the letters in the type box.

In January 1776, **Thomas Paine** published a pamphlet called *Common Sense* to argue the case for independence. In the pamphlet, Paine made several practical arguments for independence. He claimed that France and Spain would only aid the colonies if they broke with Britain. He also pointed out that European countries would continue to purchase American exports if the colonies declared independence. "'Tis time to part," he urged his readers. As the eventful year unfolded, more and more Americans agreed with him.

HISTORICAL THINKING

1. **READING CHECK** Which events in 1775 and 1776 led the colonies toward independence?

2. **ANALYZE CAUSE AND EFFECT** Why did the British government respond with overwhelming force to events in North America, and what was the colonial response?

3. **IDENTIFY MAIN IDEAS AND DETAILS** What was Thomas Paine's principal argument in favor of independence?

PLAN

Objective

Analyze how the colonies attempted to achieve peace while anticipating war.

Critical Thinking Skills for Lesson 4.3

- Identify Main Ideas and Details
- Monitor Comprehension
- Analyze Cause and Effect
- Determine Chronology
- Evaluate

Essential Question for Chapter 5

Why did the colonists decide to break from Britain? With the king rejecting a petition by Congress to reconcile differences, colonists moved closer to formally declaring their independence. Lesson 4.3 explains the influence of Thomas Paine and the final events that drove Congress toward severing ties with Britain.

Background for the Teacher

As George Washington assumed command of the Continental Army on July 3, 1775, he was concerned about the lack of gunpowder and cannons needed to force the British from their stronghold in Boston. With its valuable stash of weaponry, Fort Ticonderoga (captured earlier that year) seemed to solve this problem. But there was a catch—it was located 300 miles from Boston.

Washington sent Henry Knox to transport artillery from New York to Massachusetts. Knox and his men built sleds to move 59 artillery pieces weighing approximately 120,000 pounds. Oxen hauled the cannons on the sleds during an arduous 56-day journey. Members of the expedition struggled through harsh winter conditions. When Knox reached his destination, the cannons were soon positioned at Dorchester Heights, overlooking Boston. Recognizing their peril, British troops and Loyalists abandoned Boston on March 17, 1776.

INTRODUCE & ENGAGE

Printing Then and Now

Direct students' attention to the illustration of the printing press. Ask them to identify and read the descriptions of the different parts. Tell students that before the printing press was invented in the 15th century, information was spread verbally or by copying texts by hand. Explain that the printing press allowed news to quickly reach a wider audience, much like the Internet does today. Show students photos of a typewriter, a computer (with monitor and keyboard), and a cell phone. Ask students to compare the items in the photos with the drawing of the printing press and comment on the similar features of each. Encourage students to tell how each was a major change in information technology.

TEACH

Guided Discussion

1. **Determine Chronology** How did the timing of the publishing of Thomas Paine's *Common Sense* help move the colonies toward a break with Britain? *(It came shortly after Parliament decided to cut off all trade with the colonies and at the time King George signed a treaty with Germany allowing him to hire Hessians.)*

2. **Evaluate** Why did King George's statement that the colonies were in "an open and avowed rebellion" help push the colonies toward a full break with Britain? *(The word* rebellion *implied that reconciliation between the colonies and Britain was no longer possible. The colonists had reached a point from which they could not turn back.)*

Virtual Museum Visit

The National Museum of American History's online exhibitions and the Smithsonian's History Explorer provide many interactive teacher resources. Access the museum's website and search for "Hessian miter cap" in the search field. Examine the cap in detail and read the information provided. Ask students why they think the lion is positioned upright holding a sword. Then arrange students in small groups and ask them to explore the site on their own and choose an artifact from the same period to examine. Encourage groups to present a printed image of the artifact to the class and tell its significance.

Active Options

On Your Feet: Create a Concept Web Position students in groups of four around a section of a bulletin board or a table. Provide each group with a large sheet of paper. Tell groups to draw a Concept Web with the topic *Break with Britain* in the center. Encourage group members to take turns writing a concept or phrase on the web to contribute to the topic. When time for the activity has elapsed, call on volunteers from each group to share their webs.

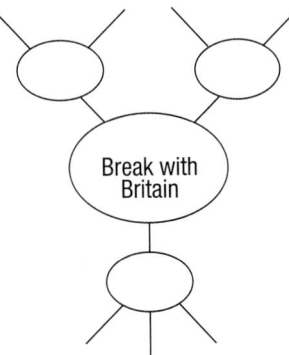

Break with Britain

NG Learning Framework: Form an Opinion

ATTITUDE Empowerment

SKILL Problem-Solving

Invite students to imagine they were one of the delegates at the Continental Congress. Place them in small groups and tell them to discuss: What is your response to the actions of King George, including his rejection of the petition, the cutting off of trade, and the hiring of Hessians? Should the colonies break free from Britain? Is war inevitable? Instruct groups to come to a consensus concerning their ideas and share them with the class.

DIFFERENTIATE

English Language Learners   ELD

Teach Compound Words Remind students that two words can be put together to make a new word. Write the following words and tell students to copy them.

seaports   warships

Ask students to circle the two words within each word. Then help them define each of the two smaller words and the resulting compound word. Tell students to locate the words in the lesson and read the sentences aloud. To verify students' understanding, ask them to paraphrase each sentence without using the compound word. Pair students at the **Emerging** level with students at the **Expanding** level. Students at the **Bridging** level can work independently.

Pre-AP

Create a Pamphlet Ask students to read portions of Thomas Paine's *Common Sense* online. Then tell them to examine other examples of pamphlets from the period. Ask students to use what they learned to design a pamphlet expressing their reasons for either maintaining ties with Britain or declaring independence. Students may illustrate their pamphlets with drawings modeled after those from the period.

See the Chapter Planner for more strategies for differentiation.

HISTORICAL THINKING

ANSWERS

1. The king rejected the Continental Congress's petition to resolve the conflict, the king hired Hessian soldiers to fight against the rebellion, and Parliament punished the colonies by cutting off trade.

2. The British government wished to quickly put down the rebellion. As a result, the colonies fought back and were pushed closer toward declaring independence.

3. Paine argued that European countries would continue to buy American exports if the colonies declared independence.

4.4 Drafting the Declaration

Every Fourth of July, the air fills with the sound of marching bands and the night sky with fireworks—all to celebrate a piece of paper? It's not just any piece of paper. It's the document that launched a new country and gave a name and an identity to the United States of America.

MAIN IDEA In 1776, the Continental Congress formally declared the independence of the United States of America from Great Britain.

MOVING TOWARD INDEPENDENCE

By the spring of 1776, the Continental Congress was making decisions for the colonies as a whole, serving in effect as the colonial government. In this role, the Congress declared that American ports would accept ships from any country—except, however, for Great Britain. The Congress also encouraged the colonies to establish their own independent governments.

Then, on June 7, Richard Henry Lee of Virginia placed a shocking resolution before the delegates. It stated that "these United Colonies are, and of right ought to be, free and independent States."

Not all the delegates were in favor of Lee's resolution to separate completely from Britain. Still, the Congress appointed a committee to draft an official statement to declare independence. **Thomas Jefferson** of Virginia, a brilliant scholar and persuasive writer, would be the principal author.

John Adams and Benjamin Franklin were also on the committee to create the document. Franklin had lived in England for several years, serving as a representative from several colonies to the British government. Adams suggested that Jefferson should write the first draft. Franklin gave Jefferson advice and helped revise the document.

On July 2, 1776, the Continental Congress voted to approve independence from Britain. Two days later, the Congress adopted Jefferson's document, the **Declaration of Independence**.

Thomas Jefferson
In addition to drafting the Declaration of Independence, Jefferson served his country for more than 50 years as a historian, public official, president, and founder of the University of Virginia. His famous words captured the voice and identity of a new America like no one else's could.

SELF-EVIDENT TRUTHS

Many of the ideas expressed in the Declaration of Independence can be traced to John Locke. The first part states, "We hold these truths to be self-evident, that all men are created equal, that they are endowed by their Creator with certain unalienable Rights, that among these are Life, Liberty, and the Pursuit of Happiness." An **unalienable right** is one that cannot be taken away.

National Archives Washington, D.C.

Visitors to Washington, D.C., can stop by the Rotunda of the National Archives Building to see the original Declaration of Independence, safely encased in bulletproof glass and under the watchful eye of armed guards. You can read the Declaration in its entirety in the Citizenship Handbook.

Yet the unalienable rights of two large groups were not discussed in the Declaration. In his first draft, Jefferson had listed slavery as one of the king's offenses. After an intense debate, this section was removed. The Declaration was silent on the rights of women, too, even though John Adams's wife, Abigail, had pleaded with him in a letter to "remember the ladies and be more generous and favorable to them than your ancestors."

The second part of the Declaration listed the offenses of the king against the colonies. These included refusing to approve laws passed by the colonial assemblies, placing a standing army in the colonies, and imposing taxes without colonial consent. For these reasons and more, the Continental Congress declared the 13 colonies "free and independent states," the United States of America.

HISTORICAL THINKING

1. **READING CHECK** What are the principal parts of the Declaration of Independence?

2. **ANALYZE LANGUAGE USE** What is an "unalienable right," and how did the inclusion of these words in the Declaration point to a new philosophy of governing?

3. **MAKE CONNECTIONS** What laws did Jefferson refer to when he listed the complaints against the British king?

Objective

Analyze the purpose and content of the Declaration of Independence.

Critical Thinking Skills for Lesson 4.4

- Identify Main Ideas and Details
- Monitor Comprehension
- Analyze Language Use
- Make Connections
- Make Inferences
- Draw Conclusions

Essential Question for Chapter 5

Why did the colonists decide to break from Britain? The Declaration of Independence officially asserted the colonies' separation from Great Britain. Lesson 4.4 describes how the Continental Congress adopted the Declaration and explains the essential elements.

Background for the Teacher

The principles of the Magna Carta, specifically regarding the rights of people, were also embodied in the English Bill of Rights and the Declaration of Independence. King John had imposed taxes on English barons who had not served in his war against Philip II of Spain. In the original Magna Carta (the "Articles of the Barons"), the barons changed the wording from "any baron" to "any freeman," introducing the idea that the rights granted extended to all British people.

The English Bill of Rights asserted that King James II's offenses were "contrary to the known laws and statutes and freedom of this realm." The Framers of the Declaration of Independence asserted the "unalienable rights" of people and justified the "Right of the People to . . . institute new Government." Guaranteeing rights and freedoms is a unifying principle in all three documents.

Write a Declaration

Draw attention to the portrait of Thomas Jefferson. Point out that Jefferson is the author of the Declaration of Independence. Explain that a declaration is a firm statement and that with the Declaration of Independence, the colonies declared their independence from British rule due to the many violations of natural rights they believed they had suffered. Remind students of the concept of the natural rights of freedom, equality, and liberty that they have encountered in the chapter. Have a short class discussion about injustices in today's world that inhibit the natural rights of freedom, equality, or liberty. Then tell students to write a declaration stating an injustice and what rights are being violated. Ask volunteers to share their ideas.

TEACH

Guided Discussion

1. **Make Inferences** Why were the delegates shocked by Richard Henry Lee's resolution? *(Breaking with Britain would mean certain war and the hard task of forming a new government. This was probably beyond what some delegates were willing to consider.)*

2. **Draw Conclusions** Why do you think the portion of the Declaration of Independence mentioning slavery was removed? *(Answers will vary. Possible response: Slavery was present throughout the colonies—especially the South—and if the Declaration of Independence formally denounced slavery, some Southern Colonies might not support the break from Britain.)*

🏛 Virtual Museum Visit

The National Archives was established by Congress in 1934 to preserve important government documents. In 1935, records from various places were moved to the new National Archives building in Washington, D.C. Three of the most important documents in the history of the United States—the Declaration of Independence, the United States Constitution, and the Bill of Rights—are displayed within the building. Access and display the museum's website and find the page on the Rotunda for the Charters of Freedom. Ask students to comment on the design of the room. Then ask small groups of students to access the page on the Declaration of Independence. Tell groups to view the original copy of the declaration and read through the articles in the section Learn More about the Declaration. Then ask the groups to share one important fact about the document with the class. Make a list as they share facts. Afterward, instruct them to categorize the facts.

Active Options

Active History: Analyze Primary Sources Extend the lesson by using either the PDF or Whiteboard version of the activity. These activities take a deeper look at a topic from, or related to, the lesson. Explore the activities as a class, turn them into group assignments, or even assign them individually.

NG Learning Framework: Hold a Colonial Town Hall Meeting

ATTITUDE Empowerment

SKILLS Collaboration, Communication

Help students deepen their understanding of the Framers' arguments by holding a colonial town hall meeting in which students defend Thomas Jefferson's argument that "all men are created equal" and "endowed by their Creator with certain unalienable rights." Tell students to adopt the mindset of colonists who have just heard about the Declaration of Independence and are in agreement with the break from Great Britain. In preparation for the meeting, encourage students to recall what colonists have experienced in the years leading up to the Declaration and to clearly define and understand the terms *equal* and *unalienable*. Tell students to use the definitions in their statements defending Jefferson's argument. Encourage students to reach a consensus on Jefferson's exact meaning.

Striving Readers

Summarize Arrange students in pairs or small groups and tell them to summarize Lesson 4.4 by creating a Word Web with "Declaration of Independence" in the center oval. Ask them to complete their webs with relevant information about the document's content and purpose.

Gifted & Talented

Compare Drafts of the Preamble Tell groups of students to research and compare the first and final drafts of the preamble to the Declaration of Independence. Using a chart like the one below, instruct students to list specific differences in the language between the two drafts. After they complete the comparison, ask students to write a paragraph explaining how the Declaration's meaning changed and how the changes unified the colonies as a new nation in opposition to Great Britain.

Declaration of Independence

First Draft	Final Draft

See the Chapter Planner for more strategies for differentiation.

HISTORICAL THINKING

ANSWERS

1. The first part states unalienable rights of people: life, liberty, and the pursuit of happiness. The second part lists offenses of King George against the colonies, including placing a standing army in the colonies and imposing taxes without the consent of colonial assemblies.

2. Answers will vary. Possible response: An unalienable right is one that cannot be taken away. The words point to a governing philosophy that frees the people from the tyranny of an absolute ruler.

3. In his complaints, Jefferson is referring to the Quartering Act, the Sugar Act, the Stamp Act, and the Intolerable Acts.

4.5 Declarations of Freedom

Beginning in the late-1600s, political thinkers put forth new ideas about natural rights and human equality in books, articles, essays, and pamphlets. These writings set the stage for a revolution that created a nation and transformed the world.

This painting by John Trumbull, titled *Declaration of Independence,* depicts the moment on June 28, 1776, when the first draft of the document was presented to the Second Continental Congress in the Pennsylvania State House. In the painting, Thomas Jefferson, thought to be the main author of the document, places the document in front of John Hancock, who was the president of the Congress, surrounded by members of the committee who helped create the draft.

CRITICAL VIEWING What do you notice about the people who are gathered for the presentation of the first draft of the Declaration of Independence?

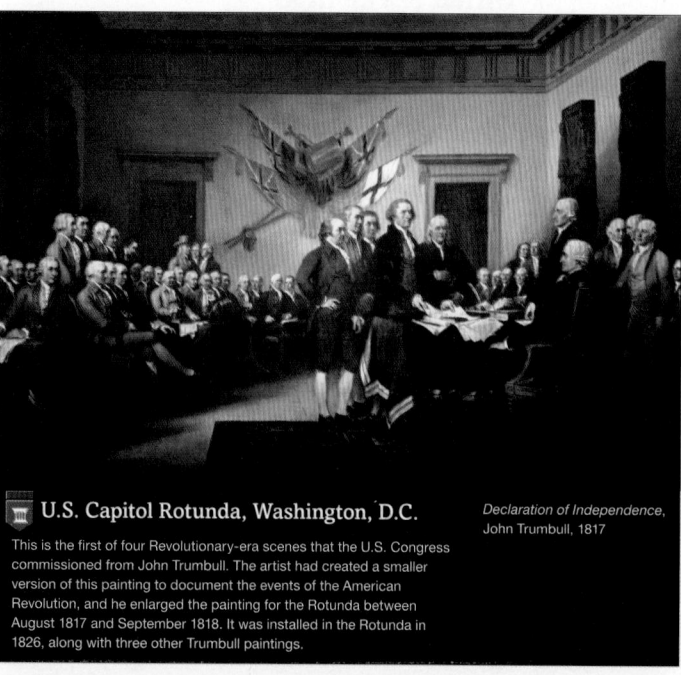

U.S. Capitol Rotunda, Washington, D.C.

This is the first of four Revolutionary-era scenes that the U.S. Congress commissioned from John Trumbull. The artist had created a smaller version of this painting to document the events of the American Revolution, and he enlarged the painting for the Rotunda between August 1817 and September 1818. It was installed in the Rotunda in 1826, along with three other Trumbull paintings.

Declaration of Independence,
John Trumbull, 1817

DOCUMENT ONE

Primary Source: Legal Document
from the Declaration of Independence, 1776

The Declaration of Independence begins with a clear statement of its writers' beliefs. The goal of the Declaration was to unify the colonies as one new nation in opposition to Great Britain.

CONSTRUCTED RESPONSE In what ways is this vision of governing different from how the British monarchy governed?

> We hold these truths to be self-evident, that all men are created equal, that they are endowed by their Creator with certain unalienable Rights, that among these are Life, Liberty and the pursuit of Happiness. That to secure these rights, Governments are instituted among Men, deriving their just powers from the consent of the governed, That whenever any Form of Government becomes destructive of these ends, it is the Right of the People to alter or to abolish it, and to institute new Government.

DOCUMENT TWO

Primary Source: Legal Document
from the Declaration of Independence, 1776

The second part of the Declaration contains a long list of offenses by the king against the colonies. In total, Jefferson included 27 grievances that referred to the Quartering Act, the Intolerable Acts, and several other British attempts to impose their will on the colonies.

CONSTRUCTED RESPONSE Why do you think the writers included such a complete list of grievances against the king?

> To prove this, let Facts be submitted to a candid world.
>
> He has refused his Assent to Laws, the most wholesome and necessary for the public good.
>
> He has dissolved Representative Houses repeatedly, for opposing with manly firmness his invasions on the rights of the people.
>
> He has kept among us, in times of peace, Standing Armies without the Consent of our legislatures.

DOCUMENT THREE

Primary Source: Essay
from *Two Treatises on Government,* by John Locke, 1689

Nearly a century before the American Revolution, John Locke outlined his theories of government in two treatises, or essays. In the second treatise, he explained his thoughts on liberty and the consent of people to be governed. Thomas Jefferson drew heavily on Locke's political theories when creating the Declaration.

CONSTRUCTED RESPONSE In what ways did Locke's ideas directly influence the actions of the colonies and the writing of the Declaration of Independence?

> Men being . . . by nature, all free, equal, and independent, no one can be put out of this estate, and subjected to the political power of another, without his own consent. The only way . . . any one divests himself of his natural liberty, and puts on the bonds of civil society, is by agreeing with other men to join and unite into a community, for their comfortable, safe and peaceable living one amongst another.

Read the full Declaration of Independence in the Citizenship Handbook.

SYNTHESIZE & WRITE

1. **REVIEW** Review what you have learned about the events leading up to the Declaration of Independence.

2. **RECALL** On your own paper, write the main ideas about government expressed in the Declaration of Independence and Locke's *Second Treatise on Government.*

3. **CONSTRUCT** Construct a topic sentence that answers this question: How did beliefs about the nature of government and human freedom lead to the colonies' break with Britain?

4. **WRITE** Using evidence from this chapter and the documents, write an informative paragraph that supports your topic sentence in Step 3.

Objective
Synthesize information about the nature of government from primary source documents.

Critical Thinking Skills for Lesson 4.5
- Synthesize
- Identify Main Ideas and Details
- Monitor Comprehension
- Evaluate

Essential Question for Chapter 5
Why did the colonists decide to break from Britain? The Declaration of Independence presented the principles on which the United States was founded. Lesson 4.5 provides excerpts from the Declaration and a treatise on government by John Locke that explain the theories behind America's break from Britain.

Background for the Teacher
The U.S. Capitol Rotunda contains eight iconic paintings illustrating important events in early American history. John Trumbull's *Declaration of Independence* was the first to be hung in the Rotunda. Today, there are four scenes of early exploration and four scenes of the revolutionary period—those last four are all by Trumbull. Placed together, Trumbull's four paintings provide a narrative of the development of America's republican form of government.

The narrative begins with *The Declaration of Independence,* which depicts the principles of government being agreed on. It continues with two paintings depicting key battles of the American Revolution: *Surrender of Burgoyne at Saratoga* and *Surrender of Lord Cornwallis at Yorktown.* The narrative ends with *General George Washington Resigning His Commission,* in which Washington peacefully gives up his position and defers to the collective authority of the new United States.

INTRODUCE & ENGAGE

Prepare for the Document-Based Question

Before students start on the activity, briefly preview the three documents. Remind students that a constructed response requires full explanations in complete sentences. Emphasize that students should use what they have learned about the Declaration of Independence and the colonists' struggle for liberty in addition to the information in the documents.

TEACH

Guided Discussion

1. **Identify Main Ideas and Details** According to the Declaration of Independence, how do governments get their power? *(Governments get their power from their citizens, who agree to give them power as long as they don't abuse it.)*

2. **Monitor Comprehension** In John Locke's opinion, what is the only way people put on the bonds of civil society? *(People put on the bonds of civil society by agreeing to unite in a community and live peaceably together.)*

Evaluate

After students have completed the Synthesize & Write activity, allow time for them to exchange paragraphs and read and comment on the work of their peers. Establish guidelines for comments prior to this activity so that feedback is constructive and encouraging in nature.

Active Options

On Your Feet: Use a Jigsaw Strategy Organize students into three "expert" groups and have students from each group analyze one of the documents and summarize the main ideas of it in their own words. Then have the members of each group count off using the letters A, B, and C. Regroup students into three new groups so that each new group has at least one member from each expert group. Have students in the new groups take turns sharing the simplified summaries they came up with in their expert groups.

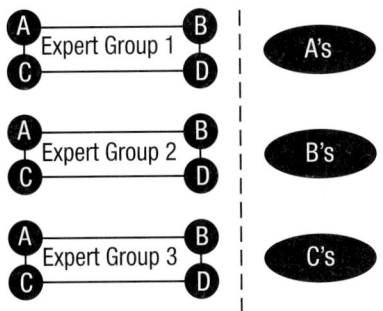

DIFFERENTIATE

Striving Readers

Summarize Read each document aloud to students. Have one small group of students work together to reread each document and summarize it for the larger group. After each document is summarized, read the constructed response question with the larger group and make sure all students understand it. Then have volunteers suggest responses.

Gifted & Talented

Create Social-Networking Profiles Ask groups of students to research to learn more about the Enlightenment and Enlightenment thinkers, including John Locke, Voltaire, Montesquieu, and Mary Wollstonecraft. Then have each group select a thinker and create a social-networking profile on him or her, providing a brief summary and "photos." Have the groups share their profiles with the rest of the class. Then invite students to "friend" the Enlightenment thinkers and send them messages about their lives and ideas.

See the Chapter Planner for more strategies for differentiation.

SYNTHESIZE & WRITE

ANSWERS

1. Answers will vary.

2. Answers will vary.

3. Answers will vary. Possible response: Beliefs about democracy and human equality led to the colonies' break with Britain.

4. Answers will vary. Students' paragraphs should include their topic sentence from Step 3 and provide several details from the documents to support the sentence.

CONSTRUCTED RESPONSE

Document 1: Possible response: The Declaration of Independence envisions a government formed by the people, not by a monarch.

Document 2: Possible response: The writers wanted to show that they had valid reasons for declaring independence.

Document 3: Possible response: Locke's ideas about equality, political power, and peaceful community life directly influenced the actions of the colonies and the writing of the Declaration of Independence.

CRITICAL VIEWING Answers will vary. Possible response: They appear dignified and formal. The seated men are paying close attention to the presentation of the Declaration of Independence.

5 REVIEW

VOCABULARY

Use each of the following vocabulary words in a sentence that shows an understanding of the term's meaning.

1. revenue
   Because the British government needed money after the French and Indian War, it imposed taxes to raise revenue.

2. unalienable right

3. militia

4. tyranny

5. boycott

6. committee of correspondence

7. repeal

8. artillery

READING STRATEGY
ANALYZE CAUSE AND EFFECT

If you haven't already, complete your chart to analyze the causes that led up to the colonies' break with Britain. List at least four key causes. Then answer the question.

Causes → Effect

The colonies declare independence from Britain.

9. What changes in the way Britain treated the American colonies caused the colonies to revolt?

MAIN IDEAS

Answer the following questions. Support your answers with evidence from the chapter.

10. What changes did the British government make in the colonies after the French and Indian War? **LESSON 1.1**

11. Why did the colonists protest the Sugar Act and Currency Act as forms of "taxation without representation"? **LESSON 1.2**

12. How did the colonists bring about the repeal of the Stamp Act? **LESSON 1.3**

13. Why did the colonists consider the Townshend Acts to be oppressive? **LESSON 2.1**

14. Why did the Tea Act result in such violent opposition? **LESSON 2.3**

15. In what ways did the Intolerable Acts build on earlier British laws? **LESSON 3.1**

16. What was the result of the battles at Lexington and Concord for the British and the colonists? **LESSON 3.3**

17. How did the Second Continental Congress pursue both peace and war? **LESSON 4.1**

18. What were the main goals of the two parts of the Declaration of Independence? **LESSON 4.4**

HISTORICAL THINKING

Answer the following questions. Support your answers with evidence from the chapter.

19. **SYNTHESIZE** How did the events of the French and Indian War help lead to the American Revolution?

20. **MAKE INFERENCES** Why did the Patriots find the ideas of John Locke appealing?

21. **ANALYZE CAUSE AND EFFECT** How did the passage of the Townshend Acts lead to the Boston Tea Party?

22. **EVALUATE** Were boycotts an effective form of protest against British taxes and laws? Explain.

23. **FORM AND SUPPORT OPINIONS** Which of the British laws and taxes placed the greatest burden on the colonies? Support your opinion with evidence from the chapter.

INTERPRET MAPS

Look closely at the map of eastern North America in 1763. Then answer the questions that follow.

Territories and Colonies, 1763

— Proclamation Line of 1763
▢ Thirteen colonies
FOX Native American settlements
▢ Other British territory
▢ Spanish territory

24. What groups were impacted the most by the Proclamation of 1763?

25. How did the geography of the Proclamation Line make it hard for the British to enforce it?

26. Compare this historical map to a present-day map of the eastern part of the United States. What similarities do you observe? What differences? How might those similarities and differences be explained?

ANALYZE SOURCES

In *Common Sense*, published in January 1776, Thomas Paine included a variety of arguments in favor of independence. In addition to the reasons you have already read, he stated the one below. Read the passage and answer the question.

> As to government matters, it is not in the power of Britain to do this continent justice: The business of it will soon be too weighty, and intricate, to be managed with any tolerable degree of convenience, by a power, so distant from us, and so very ignorant of us; for if they cannot conquer us, they cannot govern us.

27. What argument does Paine make about the British government in this passage?

CONNECT TO YOUR LIFE

28. **NARRATIVE** Think about the events that led up to the Declaration of Independence and why the colonists felt they had to separate from Great Britain. Make a connection between that time in history and a recent protest that you have read about, heard about, or seen. Write a paragraph connecting the two events.

TIPS

- Make a time line of the principal events leading up to the colonists' action or decision. Then make a time line showing what led up to the present-day protest you have chosen.

- Use textual evidence and two or three vocabulary terms from the chapter in your narrative.

- Conclude the narrative with a comment that ties the colonists' actions to those of people today.

VOCABULARY ANSWERS

1. Because the British government needed money after the French and Indian War, it imposed taxes to raise revenue.

2. Unalienable rights cannot be taken from any individual.

3. Before they established an official army, the colonies organized militias made up of local men.

4. When people are ruled by an absolute monarch and are forced to obey, they are living under tyranny.

5. Today, people still boycott certain goods, refusing to buy them until an injustice is corrected.

6. Before the American Revolution, committees of correspondence collected information about British actions and spread the word throughout the colonies.

7. When the Stamp Act was repealed, colonists no longer had to pay for stamps to be placed on all written materials.

8. Artillery was used to launch heavy attacks on cities such as Boston.

READING STRATEGY ANSWER

Causes

- Currency Act and Sugar Act try to raise revenue
- Quartering Act forces colonists to house British soldiers
- Stamp Act imposes a new kind of tax
- Intolerable Acts seek to punish colonies
- British troops and militia fight at Lexington and Concord

→

Effect

The colonies declare independence from Britain.

9. In an effort to raise money and exert greater control over the colonies, Britain imposed increasingly oppressive laws and harsh punishments. Eventually, the anger on both sides led to bloodshed.

212 CHAPTER 5

MAIN IDEAS ANSWERS

10. The British government enacted a proclamation limiting the ability of the colonies to spread westward. Through the Quartering Act, it also required colonies to house the British soldiers who were stationed in North America.

11. Both acts involved direct British control of the colonies. The Sugar Act was a tax imposed directly by the British government rather than by the colonial assemblies. The colonists objected because they had no representatives in the British Parliament to vote for or against the new laws.

12. The colonists brought about the repeal of the Stamp Act in a variety of ways: Several colonial assemblies resolved that only they had the right to impose taxes, some colonists rioted and intimidated tax collectors, and the Sons of Liberty organized a boycott of British goods.

13. The Townshend Acts taxed goods that the colonies were allowed to buy only from Britain. They also brought the colonial government under closer British control by paying governors and judges directly and by forcing colonial courts to cooperate in enabling British troops to search homes and businesses for smugglers.

14. Even though it lowered the price of tea, the Tea Act put colonial tea merchants out of business by allowing the British East India Company to bypass them. The Townshend Acts' tax on tea was still in force, and colonists argued that it was an example of taxation without representation.

15. The Intolerable Acts intensified British attempts to control the colonies by strengthening the Quartering Act and by dissolving the Massachusetts assembly, thus establishing direct British control over the colony.

16. The colonists inflicted more casualties and forced the British to retreat to Boston. The British soldiers, however, did much damage by burning buildings on their way back to the city.

17. The Second Continental Congress appealed directly to the king to end the conflict. At the same time, it sent an army to attack British forces in Canada, and George Washington retook Boston from the British.

18. The first part of the declaration explains the rights of citizens. The second part lists the colonies' reasons for declaring independence from the king.

HISTORICAL THINKING ANSWERS

19. The British government spent a lot of money and sent large numbers of troops to fight the French and Indian War. As a result, it needed new sources of revenue, so it taxed the colonies. Taxes antagonized the colonists and pushed them toward revolt. The quartering of British troops in the colonies after the French and Indian War also caused ill will among the colonists.

20. Locke stated that people have a right to govern themselves. This idea was in opposition to the monarchy of Britain that was trying to impose its control over the colonies. Locke's ideas aligned with the colonists' desire to be free from oppressive British rule.

21. First, the British imposed the Townshend Acts taxing goods colonists bought from Britain. Then the colonists protested and boycotted British goods. As a result, the British repealed all the Townshend taxes except the tax on tea. Two years later, the British enacted a new tea law and refused to repeal the tea tax. The Boston Tea Party took place soon after that.

22. Britain enacted the taxes and laws in order to gain more revenue from the colonies. Boycotts greatly reduced the amount of goods that British businesses could sell in the colonies, thus defeating the purpose of the laws and reducing Britain's revenues.

23. Answers will vary. Students should clearly state their opinion regarding which of the laws and taxes placed the greatest burden on the colonies and support that opinion with evidence from the chapter.

INTERPRET MAPS ANSWERS

24. Native Americans west of the Appalachians benefited the most from the proclamation.

25. The line was very long, and its entire length followed a chain of mountains. The British would have had great difficulty posting enough soldiers to prevent settlers from crossing unseen in the rough terrain.

26. Similarities: physical features such as shape of the continent and location of mountains, rivers, and lakes noted on each map are the same. Differences: names of places are different; instead of names of Native American nations, the present-day map of the United States shows names of states and current political borders.

ANALYZE SOURCES ANSWER

27. Paine argues that Britain cannot govern the colonies because North America is too far away and because the British government does not understand the colonies well enough. The argument is based on common sense because it offers practical reasons why British control of the colonies cannot work for long.

CONNECT TO YOUR LIFE ANSWER

28. Answers will vary. Students should incorporate a time line of the main events of the protest they are describing, use textual evidence and at least three Key Vocabulary words, and conclude with a connection between colonists' protests and the protest they have described.

UNIT 3 RESOURCES

UNIT INTRODUCTION
▶ Crossing the Delaware

UNIT TIME LINE

UNIT WRAP-UP

NATIONAL GEOGRAPHIC | CONNECTION

National Geographic Magazine Adapted Articles
• "Patriots in Petticoats"
• "Two Revolutions" ONLINE

Unit 3 Inquiry: Prepare an Argument

NG Learning Framework Activities
• Research a Colonial American
• Build a Time Line

Unit 3 Formal Assessment

UNIT 3 1763–1791

A NEW NATION

Metropolitan Museum of Art New York City

Artist Emanuel Leutze's 1851 oil painting, called *Washington Crossing the Delaware*, depicts General Washington's attack on the Hessians in Trenton, New Jersey, on December 25, 1776. This is a large work of art, measuring 149 inches high by 255 inches wide.

CRITICAL VIEWING According to Leutze, what challenges did the soldiers face during the attack on Trenton?

CHAPTER 6 RESOURCES

Available at NGLSync.Cengage.com

TEACHER RESOURCES & ASSESSMENT

Reading and Note-Taking

Vocabulary Practice

Social Studies Skills Lessons
• Reading: Form and Support Opinions
• Writing: Write an Explanation

Formal Assessment
• Chapter 6 Pretest
• Chapter 6 Tests A & B
• Section Quizzes

Chapter 6 Answer Key

ExamView®
   One-time Download

CHAPTER 6 THE AMERICAN **REVOLUTION** 1775–1783

ESSENTIAL QUESTION
What factors helped America win the war?

AMERICAN STORIES **Bitter Winter at Valley Forge**

SECTION 1 **Early War Years**
KEY VOCABULARY
Articles of Confederation | mercenary
counterattack | reinforcements
defensive war | republic
fortification

SECTION 2 **The War Expands**
KEY VOCABULARY
bayonet | financier
blockade | espionage | skirmish

SECTION 3 **The Path to Victory**
KEY VOCABULARY
expertise | provisions
guerrilla | republicanism
pacifist | Treaty of Paris of 1783

AMERICAN GALLERY ONLINE **Colonial Vernacular Architecture**

READING STRATEGY

FORM AND SUPPORT OPINIONS
You often form opinions while reading. As you read the chapter, decide what factor was most important in achieving an American victory in the Revolution. Use a graphic like this one to write your opinion and record your reasons for supporting it.

"It is a common observation here that **our cause is the cause of all mankind.**"
—Benjamin Franklin

STUDENT DIGITAL RESOURCES

• **eEdition** (English)	• **Online Atlas**	• **American Voices (Biographies)**
• **eEdition** (Spanish)	• **American Gallery Online**	• **Active History**
• **Handbooks**	• **History Notebook**	• **Projects for Inquiry-Based Learning**

Chapter 6 Spanish Resources are available at NGLSync.Cengage.com.

AMERICAN STORIES | Bitter Winter at Valley Forge

- Primary Sources
- On Your Feet: Team Word Webbing

SECTION 1 RESOURCES
EARLY WAR YEARS

LESSON 1.1
War in the Middle States

▶ Battle of Long Island

- Active History: Analyze Different Points of View

NG Learning Framework:
Analyze Concepts in 1776 Virginia State Constitution

LESSON 1.2
The Struggle for New York

- On Your Feet: Inside-Outside Circle

NG Learning Framework:
Write a Biography

LESSON 1.3
Battles of Saratoga

- On Your Feet: Numbered Heads

NG Learning Framework:
Explore an American Revolution Battlefield

SECTION 2 RESOURCES
THE WAR EXPANDS

LESSON 2.1
Seeking Help from Europe

- On Your Feet: Create a Concept Cluster

NG Learning Framework:
Negotiate an Alliance

LESSON 2.2
Hardship and Challenges

- On Your Feet: Rotating Discussion

NG Learning Framework:
Diary from a War Zone

LESSON 2.3
Women's Roles in the Revolution

- On Your Feet: Jigsaw

NG Learning Framework:
Write an Exclusive Interview

American Voices Biography
Women of the Continental Army ONLINE

LESSON 2.4
War at Sea

- On Your Feet: History Relay

NG Learning Framework:
Learn More About Naval Battles

SECTION 3 RESOURCES
THE PATH TO VICTORY

LESSON 3.1
War in the Southern Colonies

- On Your Feet: Turn and Talk on Topic

NG Learning Framework:
Analyze Battle Tactics

LESSON 3.2
The Tide Turns

- On Your Feet: Think, Pair, Share

NG Learning Framework:
Take a Stand

LESSON 3.3
The War Ends

- On Your Feet: Word Chain

NG Learning Framework:
Explore the Art of the Revolution

LESSON 3.4
GEOGRAPHY IN HISTORY
An Ally in the American Victory

- On Your Feet: Four Corners

NG Learning Framework:
Explore a River

LESSON 3.5
Legacy of the War

- On Your Feet: Three-Step Interview

AMERICAN **GALLERY** ONLINE | Colonial Vernacular Architecture

CHAPTER 6 REVIEW

Strategy ❶
Sequence Events

To build understanding of the critical events in a section and their relationships to each other in time, have students note them in a Sequence Chain like the one shown.

Use with Lessons 1.1–1.3, 2.2, 2.4, 3.1–3.2

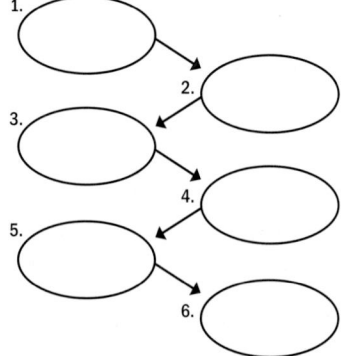

Strategy ❷
K-W-L Chart

Provide each student with a K-W-L Chart. Have students brainstorm what they already know about the American Revolution, such as its causes, participants, important battles, and goals. Have students add these ideas to the chart. Then have students write in the second column of the chart three questions they have about the American Revolution, such as "Did the Americans have any other allies?" or "How did the war affect ordinary citizens living in the colonies?" Remind students to complete their charts as they read the chapter.

Use with all Lessons

Strategy ❸
Write a Tweet

As students read the lesson, direct them to pause after each paragraph and write a tweet, or 140-character message, summarizing the paragraph's main idea in their own words. Have students read their tweets aloud to the class, small group, or partner one at a time, with the first student reading his or her tweet about the first paragraph, the second student reading a tweet about the second paragraph, and so forth.

Use with All Lessons *If students need additional support, have them work in pairs to compose or revise their tweets.*

Strategy ❶
Modify Main Idea Statements

To help students anticipate and organize content, provide modified Main Idea statements before reading. Several examples are provided below.

1.2 The British made mistakes that kept them from taking over the Hudson River Valley.

1.3 Saratoga was an important victory for the Americans.

2.1 Help from other nations made it more possible for the Americans to win the war.

2.3 Women could not join the army, but they helped the war effort in other ways.

3.1 The Patriots had to learn to fight differently in the Southern Colonies.

3.4 Features of the land have played an important role in many events in history.

Use with All Lessons

Strategy ❷
Provide a Summary Chart

Provide a summary of important events, people, and outcomes for students to use as they preview Lessons 1.1–1.3. Explain that they will be learning about important battles of the American Revolution, as well as the challenges faced by each side.

Battles	People	Outcomes
Battle of Trenton (1776)	• Washington (American) • Howe (British)	• Americans won.
Battle of Germantown (1777)	• Washington (American) • Howe (British)	• British won.
Battles of Saratoga (1777)	• Burgoyne (British) • Gates (American) • Arnold (American)	• Americans won.

Use with Lessons 1.1–1.3

ENGLISH LANGUAGE LEARNERS

Strategy 1
Word Wall

Work with students to choose three words from each section to display on a Word Wall. Encourage students of **All Proficiencies** to choose words they may encounter in other chapters, such as *reinforcements*, *republic*, or *expertise*. Keep the words displayed as the class works through the lessons. Discuss each word as it appears in the reading, asking volunteers to add definitions, related words, and examples to the Word Wall to reinforce comprehension.

Use with All Lessons

Strategy 2
Use Pronunciation Keys

Preteach the meaning and pronunciation of Key Vocabulary terms for students at **All Proficiences**. After you have given a brief example of the word, pronounce it slowly and carefully several times, with students repeating it after you. Then have students create a pronunciation key for each word on a notebook page or note cards. At the end of each lesson, have students write sentences about the lesson using each word, and read them aloud. Provide sentence stems for students at the **Emerging** level. Encourage students at the **Bridging** level to develop more complex sentences for each word.

Use with All Lessons

Strategy 3
Either/Or Questions

Monitor students' comprehension of the lesson by asking them to answer either/or questions. After students have answered the questions, have students at the **Emerging** level pair with students at the **Bridging** level to check their answers.

- Were Franklin and Adams successful or unsuccessful on their mission to France? *(successful)*
- Were the French and Spanish enemies or allies? *(allies)*
- Did blockades help or hurt the Americans during the war? *(hurt)*
- Was Congress able or not able to pay for the war with taxes? *(not able)*

Use with Lesson 2.1

GIFTED & TALENTED

Strategy 1
Write an Essay

Encourage students to write an essay in which they explain the impact of the American Revolution on each of the following groups: Native Americans, African Americans, and women. Essays should compare and contrast each group's participation in the war effort with the benefits each group received (or did not receive) after the American victory. Students may use outside sources in addition to evidence from the text to explain their ideas.

Use with All Lessons

Strategy 2
Read Historical Biographies

Have students use the school or local library to locate a historical biography on an individual they encountered in this chapter. Tell students to read their chosen biography independently and then develop a profile for the person they read about. Encourage students to share their profiles with the class.

Use with Lessons 1.2, 1.3, 2.3–2.4, 3.2–3.3

Pre-AP

Strategy 1
Annotate a Time Line

Tell students to annotate a time line of critical events in the American Revolution, extending from 1776 to 1783. For each event, they should include the date and at least two details. For at least three events, they should include a relevant image, map, or diagram. Encourage students to conduct additional research to support the information provided in the chapter or to find relevant images. Students may create their time lines digitally and display them online or post paper time lines in the classroom.

Use with All Lessons

Strategy 2
Extend Knowledge

Invite students to conduct research to find out more about a topic or event introduced in Chapter 6. For example, students might choose to research Revolution-era military technology, women's roles in the Revolution, or frontier battles involving different Native American groups. Have students present their findings in an oral report to the class or in a digital report posted on a class blog.

Use with All Lessons

CHAPTER

6

THE AMERICAN
REVOLUTION
1775–1783

ESSENTIAL QUESTION
What factors helped America win the war?

AMERICAN STORIES Bitter Winter at Valley Forge

SECTION 1 **Early War Years**
KEY VOCABULARY

Articles of Confederation	mercenary
counterattack	reinforcements
defensive war	republic
fortification	

SECTION 2 **The War Expands**
KEY VOCABULARY

bayonet	desert	financier
blockade	espionage	skirmish

SECTION 3 **The Path to Victory**
KEY VOCABULARY

expertise	provisions
guerrilla	republicanism
pacifist	Treaty of Paris of 1783

AMERICAN GALLERY
ONLINE **Colonial Vernacular Architecture**

READING STRATEGY

FORM AND SUPPORT OPINIONS
You often form opinions while reading. As you read the chapter, decide what factor was most important in achieving an American victory in the Revolution. Use a graphic like this one to write your opinion and record your reasons for supporting it.

Opinion:

Supporting statement:
Supporting statement:
Supporting statement:
Supporting statement:

CRITICAL VIEWING Historical reenactors try to represent clothing and weapons as authentically as possible. Here, a reenactor prepares his musket for firing. What details of the musket reveal what it might be like to carry this weapon into battle?

"It is a common observation here that **our cause is the cause of all mankind.**"

—Benjamin Franklin

214 CHAPTER 6

The American Revolution 215

INTRODUCE THE PHOTOGRAPH

American Revolution Uniforms

Have students study the uniform in the photograph and note the colors and details. Tell students that the Continental Army did not adopt this uniform until 1779, when Congress passed a resolution authorizing General Washington to establish a standard uniform. In the early years of the war, soldiers wore uniforms in a variety of colors and types of cloth. Those without uniforms often wore hunting shirts and long breeches. Washington chose dark blue for the official jacket and different colored facings for regions and regiments. Point out that the red facing in the photograph was used for Pennsylvania, Delaware, Maryland, and Virginia.
ASK: Why might Congress have wanted Continental soldiers to wear standard uniforms? *(Answers will vary. Possible response: Having a standard uniform strengthened the impression that the Continental Army was well trained and professional.)*

For Chapter 6 Spanish Resources, visit the Resources Menu. Chapter 6 Resources are available at NGLSync.Cengage.com.

Share Background

In addition to muskets like the one shown in the photograph, soldiers in the Continental Army also made use of rifles, axes, swords, bayonets, and pistols. A rifle is a long gun like a musket, but with grooves, or "rifling," in the barrel that make it more accurate and usable over longer distances than a musket, ideal for snipers or guerrilla fighters. However, rifles of the Revolution were slower to load than muskets and could not be fitted with bayonets, which made them much less useful during up-close, hand-to-hand fighting. Since hand-to-hand fighting was a large part of most critical battles in the American Revolution, handheld weapons such as swords, axes, and bayonets were some of a soldier's most important equipment.

CRITICAL VIEWING Answers will vary. Students may point out that the firing mechanism looks as though it may be complicated and the musket itself looks long and heavy. These details reveal that the weapon may have been heavy and clumsy to carry or use in a battle.

214 CHAPTER 6

INTRODUCE THE ESSENTIAL QUESTION

What factors helped America win the war?

Four Corners Activity: The War Effort This activity introduces students to several of the factors that can affect the outcomes of a conflict. Label the four corners of the classroom with these categories: Strategy, Leadership, Support from Allies, and Chance. Divide the class into four groups and assign each group to one of the corners of the room. Tell each group to discuss the question and prepare a response to present to the class.

- **Corner 1: Strategy**

What role does strategy play during a war?

- **Corner 2: Leadership**

How important is leadership during a war?

- **Corner 3: Support from Allies**

What impact can support from allies have during a war?

- **Corner 4: Chance**

In what ways can chance affect outcomes during a war?

As groups discuss their questions, encourage them to consider what they already know about the causes and people involved in the American Revolution. When all four groups have finished discussing and answering the question, reassemble as a class and engage in a short discussion about their responses.

INTRODUCE CHAPTER VOCABULARY

Word Webs

Have students complete Word Webs for selected Key Vocabulary words as they read the chapter. Ask them to write each word in the center of an oval. Have them look through the chapter to find examples, characteristics, and descriptive words that may be associated with the vocabulary word. At the end of the chapter, ask student what they learned about each word. Model an example for students on the board, using the graphic organizer below.

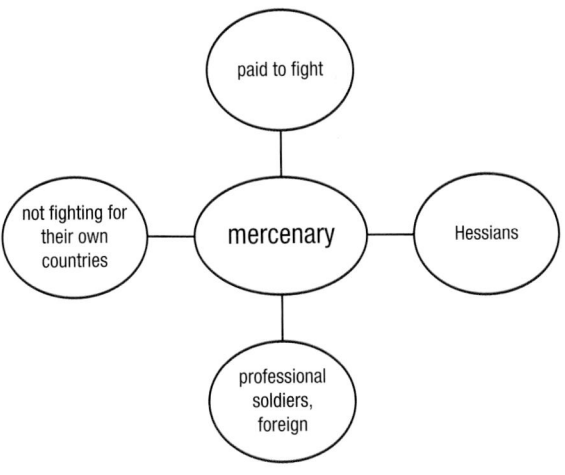

INTRODUCE THE READING STRATEGY

FORM AND SUPPORT OPINIONS
Remind students that keeping track of the evidence that supports a particular view will help them evaluate which opinion has the most or best supporting evidence. Model completing the Form and Support Opinions diagram. Based on what they have read in earlier chapters, ask students to suggest an initial opinion about what factor might be most important in the American victory. Fill in the top row of the diagram. Then have students continue to suggest supporting statements for that opinion.

> Opinion: I think that gaining supporters and allies will be the most important factor.

> Supporting statement: The British Army was very large and powerful.

> Supporting statement: Not all people living in the colonies supported the Revolution.

> Supporting statement: It would be hard to find enough soldiers and weapons among the colonists.

KEY DATES FOR CHAPTER 6

1776	Battle of Trenton
1777	Congress adopts Articles of Confederation
1777	Washington and troops winter at Valley Forge
1778	France signs Treaty of Alliance with United States
1779	John Paul Jones captures the British ship *Serapis*
1780	Battle of Kings Mountain turns the tide for the Americans
1781	Cornwallis surrenders at Battle of Yorktown
1783	Treaty of Paris

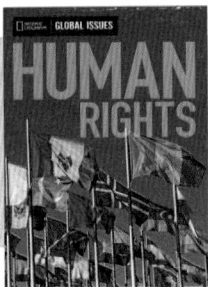

For more on the fight for human rights around the world, see *GLOBAL ISSUES: HUMAN RIGHTS.*

Objectives

- Learn about the events at the Valley Forge encampment during the winter of 1777–1778.
- Describe the actions of Congress regarding the Continental Army.
- Evaluate Washington's plan for rebuilding his army.
- Learn about the turning points reached with improved methods for obtaining supplies and new training.
- Study primary sources: letter of Rebecca Franks and memoir of soldier Joseph Plumb Martin.

Critical Thinking Skills for "Bitter Winter at Valley Forge"

- Make Connections
- Draw Conclusions
- Identify Problems and Solutions
- Evaluate
- Compare and Contrast
- Analyze Visuals
- Synthesize
- Make Predictions

Background for the Teacher

This American Story introduces students to the encampment at Valley Forge during the winter of 1777–1778. This high-interest story will help students understand what life was like for the soldiers of the Continental Army and how the harsh weather and lack of resources affected the camp. Students will also learn how physical geography and location served as an advantage and understand the turning points that helped Washington and his soldiers emerge as a confident and trained army.

The upcoming chapter, The American Revolution, covers the early years of the war, key battles and turning points during the war, how the war grew, and how the Americans triumphed over the British. This American Story introduces the coming challenges and triumphs experienced by the Continental Army during the American Revolution.

History Notebook

Encourage students to complete the American Story page for Chapter 6 in their History Notebooks as they read.

Note to the Teacher

Introduce this American Story after the class has engaged with the content in Section 2.

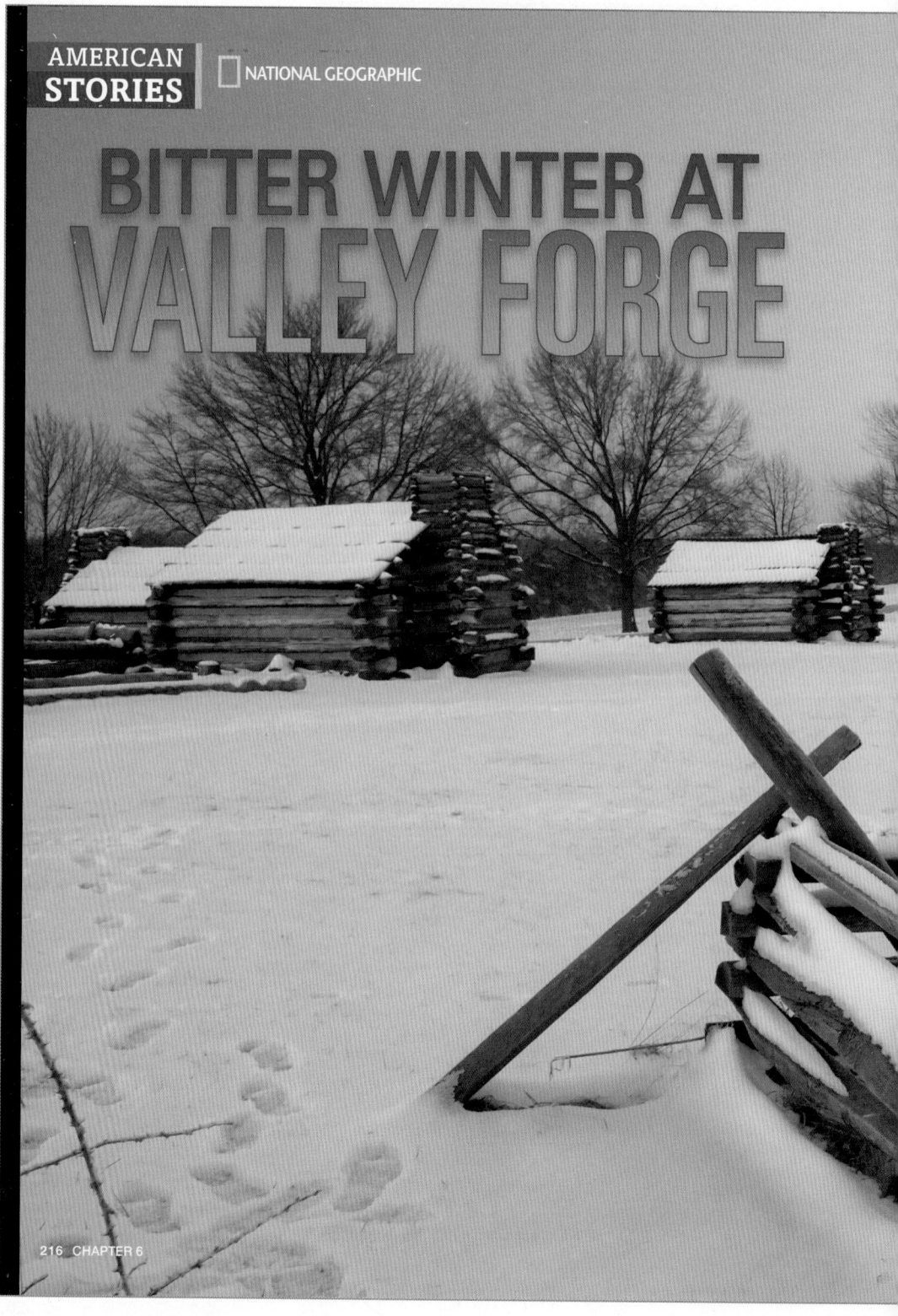

AMERICAN STORIES

NATIONAL GEOGRAPHIC

BITTER WINTER AT VALLEY FORGE

216 CHAPTER 6

Valley Forge is now a National Historical Park in Pennsylvania. These re-created soldier cabins in the park give visitors a sense of what the living conditions were like for the Continental Army in the winter of 1777–78.

The American Revolution 217

Brainstorm Resources

Ask students to brainstorm the resources they would need to go camping. If needed, prompt a short discussion by asking if any students have gone camping and what items they brought for the trip. As a class, create a list of supplies, including food and clothing. Tell students that during the American Revolution, soldiers had to create camps to rest and regroup. Guide students to discuss the resources needed to maintain a camp with 11,000 soldiers during cold winter months. Then tell students they are going to read an American Story about the encampment at Valley Forge and what life was like for the soldiers there.

Discuss and Write

Share a list of movies from popular culture in which a main character or group overcomes great obstacles, such as *The Karate Kid, Remember the Titans, A League of Their Own, 42,* and any of the *Star Wars* films. Ask students if they are familiar with any of these movies and ask them to share other examples. Discuss with students what the character(s) did to defy the odds. Write the following prompt on the board or whiteboard: What do you do when the odds are against you? Ask students to spend two minutes writing their response to the question. Invite volunteers to share what they have written. Then tell students they are going to read an American Story about the obstacles faced by the Continental Army and how the soldiers overcame the odds to become a strong, well-trained army.

Preview with Visuals

Review the photograph with students and read the caption. Have students describe the weather shown in the image. **ASK:** How do you think the weather affected living conditions at Valley Forge? *(Answers will vary. Possible response: The snow and cold weather probably made it difficult to stay warm. Some soldiers might have gotten sick from the cold.)* Tell students that Valley Forge is where the Continental Army went to rest before the next battle. Then discuss with students the advantages and disadvantages of staying at Valley Forge.

Lack of Supplies

As Washington encamped at Valley Forge, the lack of much-needed supplies was apparent. Washington's soldiers began the work of building wooden huts for shelter. Since they did not have enough blankets for everyone, soldiers also searched for straw to keep themselves warm. Once at the camp, Washington was told there were only 25 barrels of flour and a small amount of salt pork to feed some 11,000 soldiers and the approximately 500 women and children who joined them. One-third of Washington's soldiers had no shoes, and many of them did not have an appropriate coat.

Native Americans at Valley Forge

Although the exact number is unknown, it is estimated that several hundred Oneida, Tuscarora, Mohican, and Native Americans from other tribes enlisted in the Continental Army, many serving as scouts. Approximately 50 Native Americans were among the soldiers at Valley Forge. On May 20, 1778, a group of Native Americans leading an American reconnaissance mission prevented British forces from capturing the Marquis de Lafayette. They did so by ambushing British soldiers and providing delay tactics as the 2,200 soldiers, including Lafayette, made their way back to Valley Forge.

Martha Washington

Many women, including officers' wives, joined their husbands at Valley Forge. While George Washington believed women should not be there, he realized their importance in the care and survival of the army. Martha Washington came to Valley Forge at the beginning of February and stayed until June. She provided much-needed support for the troops. She wrote to governors' wives for financial support and supplies and often made rounds at the camp, visiting soldiers. She gave as much food to them as she could contribute, sewed socks and other clothing, and asked local women for their help. She also cared for soldiers who were sick or dying. Her care and support endeared her to the soldiers, who, with respect, addressed her as "Lady Washington."

AMERICAN STORIES

COLD, HUNGRY, AND SICK

Think of the images you have seen of U.S. Army units marching on parade. The soldiers are strong, healthy, and clothed in matching uniforms. They move with assurance and discipline, each soldier knowing his or her place in the formation. It's a sight that inspires confidence in the armed forces.

In the winter of 1777, the sight of George Washington's troops straggling into Valley Forge would have inspired anything but confidence. Instead, some viewers felt pity and shock. The army had been defeated twice by the British, and now the soldiers were going into winter quarters to rest and regroup. The city of Philadelphia, 20 miles away, was in British hands.

The soldiers were in desperate need of relief. They were exhausted, underfed, diseased, and freezing. Albigence Waldo, an army doctor, described their plight in his journal: "There comes a Soldier, his bare feet are seen thro' his worn out Shoes." Joseph Plumb Martin, an army private, later recalled his fellow soldiers walking barefoot "till they might be tracked by their blood upon the rough frozen ground." At one point during the long winter, 7,000 soldiers were too sick to be on duty.

NO RELIEF IN SIGHT

George Washington was well aware of his men's suffering. In a letter to Congress, he wrote, "I am now convinced, beyond a doubt that unless some great and capital change suddenly takes place . . . this Army must inevitably be reduced to one or other of these three things. Starve, dissolve, or disperse in order to obtain subsistence [food] in the best manner they can."

Congress, however, did not send Washington the relief he needed in the form of either supplies or money. Instead, some members pressured him to send his starving army against the British troops in Philadelphia. Some, including John Adams, had lost confidence in General Washington and wanted to replace him. Another Patriot, Alexander Hamilton, demonstrated his faith in Washington by joining the general's staff in 1777, a position he would hold until 1781.

Of even greater concern was the trust of Washington's officers and men. In all, 1,000 soldiers deserted during that harsh winter, and several hundred officers resigned. Most, however, remained loyal to their general and their cause. Joseph Plumb Martin wrote, "We had engaged in the defense of our injured country and were . . . determined to persevere."

Boots weren't exactly weatherproof in the 1700s. Valley Forge soldiers lucky enough to have footwear wore boots like these. Others simply wrapped their feet in rags, which provided little protection from the hard ground and cold snow.

Valley Forge

After British forces took control of Philadelphia, George Washington and his troops fled 20 miles northwest to take refuge at Valley Forge. This location was close enough to put pressure on the British but far enough away to make an enemy attack unlikely.

Schuylkill River

Varnum's Brigade
Star Redoubt
Huntington's Brigade
McIntosh's Brigade
Huntington's Quarters
Washington's Headquarters
General Varnum's Quarters
Adjutant General's Quarters
Ft. Huntington
Conway Huts
Redan
SITE OF 2004 EXPERIMENT
Conway's Brigade
GRAND PARADE
Ft. Greene
Redan
Maxwell's Brigade
Muhlenberg's Brigade
Weedon's Brigade
Patterson's Brigade
Learned's Brigade
Glover's Brigade
Redan
Ft. Muhlenberg
Gulph Road
Knox's Artillery Brigade
OUTER LINE OF DEFENSE
Mount Misery
Valley Creek
Mount Joy
INNER LINE OF DEFENSE
Ft. Washington
Scott's Brigade
1st Pa. Brigade
2nd Pa. Brigade
Poor's Brigade
Covered bridge
Woodford's Brigade
OUTER LINE OF DEFENSE
Lord Stirling's Quarters
Maxwell's Quarters
Knox's Quarters
Lafayette's Quarters

Army engineers laid out the camp wisely in a triangle shape. Each side of the triangle measured seven miles. On two sides, the ridgeline and two high hills provided the camp's main defenses. The Schuylkill River, a natural barrier to enemies, made up the third side of the triangle.

■ Brigade
□ Fort/Redoubt
■ Hut/Cabin

N
0 mi   0.25   0.5
0 m   250   500

TOLERABLY COMFORTABLE

In 2004, a team of park rangers and volunteers used "experimental archaeology" to discover how well cabins like those the soldiers built and lived in at Valley Forge sheltered the soldiers during the winter of 1777. First, the team reviewed historical documents and soldiers' personal accounts for details about their living experiences. Then the team spent six days and five nights living in a re-created cabin at Valley Forge, capturing temperature, humidity, and weather data. While conditions weren't cozy, the study led the team to conclude the soldiers' cabins were well-built and relatively comfortable.

SOURCE: National Park Service

The cabin door was usually located on the south end of the cabin to let in sunlight for added warmth.

Bunks closest to the hearth were the warmest. Higher-ranking officers, sick soldiers, and those who did hard manual labor may have earned warmer bunks.

CABIN FLOOR PLAN

Soldiers built the cabins using logs harvested from the surrounding woods and a mix of mud and straw as mortar.

log walls
14 Feet
door
dirt floor
hearth
lower bunk
middle bunk
upper bunk
16 Feet

8–12 soldiers shared about 200 square feet of living space.

The hearth kept the soldiers warm and dried the dirt floor and log walls.

The team measured temperatures inside the re-created cabin up to 50° F warmer than outdoor conditions during the day, and up to 35° F warmer at night. They concluded that the well-designed structures likely made the soldiers feel like it was **"April inside while it was January outside."**

Guided Discussion

1. **Identify Problems and Solutions** In what condition was the Continental Army when it first arrived at Valley Forge? *(The army came to the camp defeated, so morale was low. Soldiers were tired and starving. Many soldiers were too sick to do any work. They were freezing, and some did not have shoes and walked barefoot in the snow.)*

2. **Evaluate** Why did some soldiers choose to desert the army while other soldiers remained? *(The living conditions were harsh and supplies were limited. Soldiers were tired, sick, cold, and hungry. After Congress denied aid, some soldiers probably doubted Washington's leadership and saw no chance of relief. The soldiers who stayed despite these hardships must have been deeply devoted to the cause and felt loyalty to Washington.)*

Active Options

On Your Feet: Team Word Webbing Draw attention to the cabin floor plan shown on the map. Invite students to read the descriptions and identify the various features of the cabin. Divide students into teams of four and provide each team with a large piece of paper. Assign each group the following question: What are the positive and negative features of the cabin? Tell students to write down cabin features and identify them as positive or negative. Have each student add to the part of the paper nearest him or her. Then signal groups to rotate the paper, and have students add to the nearest part again. When finished, tell students to compare their answers. If time permits, encourage groups to share their ideas with the class to create a class list.

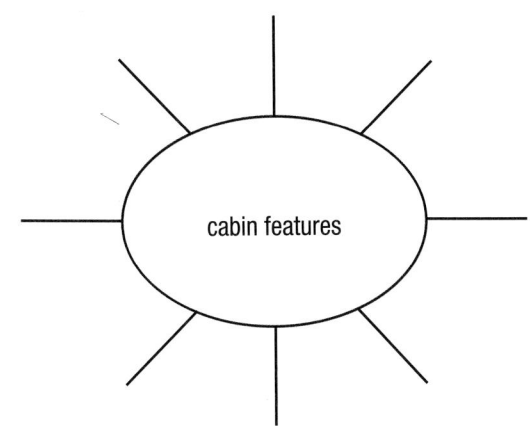

cabin features

Guided Discussion

1. **Compare and Contrast** Review the primary sources. How did life in Philadelphia compare with life for the Continental soldiers at Valley Forge? *(Life in Philadelphia was filled with social events and plenty of food and entertainment, but life at Valley Forge was extremely difficult, with soldiers starving, freezing, and just trying to survive the bitter winter.)*

2. **Analyze Visuals** How effective do you think the ice creepers would be for crossing snow and ice? *(Answers will vary. Possible response: The ice creepers might work well in soft snow but would be ineffective on hard ice. They look like they would fall off shoes easily and would not help soldiers who lacked shoes.)*

The Battle of Monmouth

On June 28, 1778, Washington moved 11,000 soldiers to meet the British at the Battle of Monmouth. Intense fighting continued throughout the day in 100-degree heat. By day's end, many British and American troops had been killed or wounded. Washington saw British campfires burning in the distance and believed the British were resting for the evening. His troops rested overnight as well, preparing to resume the battle the next morning. At sunrise, Washington realized that the British had escaped and marched to New York. With the British retreat, the Americans claimed victory. But did they really win the Battle of Monmouth? Some historians believe the battle had no clear winner. Whether the Americans won or not, the Battle of Monmouth once again showed Washington's courage and leadership in the face of seemingly impossible odds.

WRITE ABOUT HISTORY

Connect to the Winter at Valley Forge This American Story tells of the soldiers' hardship at Valley Forge and their stamina and determination. To help students make connections between the American Story and what it takes to overcome obstacles, ask them to choose a real person who persevered and succeeded in conquering what seemed like an insurmountable challenge. Students should write a blog entry from the person's point of view, describing how he or she faced the obstacle and including the character traits and solutions needed to triumph in the end.

THINK ABOUT IT

Answers will vary. Possible response: Students might say that they would feel betrayed and abandoned by Congress. Isolated from battle, Congress does not understand the hard work, sacrifice, and challenges faced by soldiers fighting for liberty.

AMERICAN STORIES

GATHERING STRENGTH AND TRAINING

The painful irony was that the Continental Army was starving in a land of plenty. The area around Valley Forge was fertile farmland. However, the Americans were competing with the British for the region's resources, and the British were very effective at buying—or taking—what they wanted.

Once the soldiers were fed, they would also need training to fight the well-equipped, professional British Army. The soldiers came from state militias that were each organized differently. They did not know how to work together as an effective force.

Fortunately, Washington had two men at Valley Forge who could address these problems. He put General Nathanael Greene in charge of supplies. Greene organized groups of soldiers to go foraging, or seeking food, in the countryside. Greene found ways to help the army get food and horses, and he set up a system of supply sites and roads for moving the goods. By springtime, the troops were properly fed and supplied.

At Ben Franklin's suggestion, Friedrich von Steuben (FREE-drihk von STOO-buhn), formerly an officer in the Prussian Army, came to Valley Forge to train Washington's troops. Von Steuben was an expert in the military tactics used by modern armies. A colorful figure, he barked out commands in German, drilling the soldiers for hours each day. Private Martin recalled, "I was kept constantly, when off other duty, engaged in learning the Baron de Steuben's new Prussian exercise." The Americans emerged from von Steuben's special brand of boot camp ready to fight like professionals.

The Continental Army marched out of Valley Forge on June 19, 1778. The tattered, starving, desperate group had been transformed into a confident, disciplined army. A week later, Washington's soldiers fought the British Army at the Battle of Monmouth. There was no turning back on the path to independence.

THINK ABOUT IT

How would you feel if you were a soldier in the Continental Army and you felt you lacked the support of Congress?

Soldiers strapped these iron and leather ice creepers to their ragged shoes or boots to cross the ice and snow.

LIFE GOES ON

While the soldiers starved, struggled, and battled illness at Valley Forge, life went on as usual in Philadelphia. This is evident in these two wildly different personal accounts of the same time period. Read and compare these primary sources.

PRIMARY SOURCE

You can have no idea of the life of continued amusement I live in. I can scarce have a moment to myself. I have stole this while everybody is retired to dress for dinner . . . and most elegantly am I dressed for a ball this evening at Smith's where we have one every Thursday.

—from a letter by Rebecca Franks, 1778

PRIMARY SOURCE

I lay two nights and one day, and had not a morsel of any thing to eat all the time, save half of a small pumpkin, which I cooked by placing it upon a rock, the skin side uppermost, and making a fire upon it; by the time it was heat through I devoured it with as keen an appetite as I should a pie made of it at some other time.

—from *Memoir of a Revolutionary Soldier,* by Joseph Plumb Martin, 1830

Despite the grim living conditions—or perhaps because of them—the men at Valley Forge found ways to have fun when they were not drilling or scouting for food. Sometimes, soldiers would play "base," a very early form of baseball. George Washington himself once joined a group of men playing cricket, a British sport that also involves a type of bat and ball. Some officers put on plays in a stone building on the Valley Forge site. The men were not allowed to play cards or gamble, but many ignored this rule to pass the time with a friendly card game or two. After all, the winter nights at Valley Forge were long, dull, and uncomfortable.

These French paper playing cards somehow made their way into the hands of bored Continental soldiers trying to pass the time at Valley Forge.

Soldiers also played games of dice by shaking ivory dice in this leather cup and rolling them out.

The American Revolution **221**

English Language Learners `ELD`

Outline and Take Notes To help students develop comprehension skills, ask **Emerging** students to partner with **Bridging** or English-proficient students and write an outline of the story using the headings "Tired, Hungry, and Freezing," "No Relief in Sight," and "Gathering Strength and Training."

Gifted & Talented

Build a Model Have students locate an illustration of a cabin at Valley Forge. Tell them to use the illustration and additional research to build a 3-D model of the cabin. They can use 3-D software for a digital rendering or modeling clay or other materials to reconstruct a cabin. Remind students to build the cabin to scale. Students could include bunks and other items inside the cabin.

See the Chapter Planner for more strategies for differentiation.

HISTORICAL THINKING

Ask and have students answer the following questions.

1. **READING CHECK** Why did Washington encamp the Continental Army at Valley Forge?

2. **SYNTHESIZE** What helped Washington's soldiers survive the winter at Valley Forge and become a more disciplined army?

3. **MAKE PREDICTIONS** Based on what you just read, how do you think the Continental Army might perform in battles to come?

ANSWERS

1. Washington needed a safe place to wait out the winter and watch the British army while resting, supplying, and training his troops.

2. Soldiers lived in cabins and received supplies of meat and clothing, learned to gather food, and were trained by Friedrich von Steuben.

3. Possible response: A healthy, well-trained Continental Army should fight well because soldiers feel stronger and more confident.

1.1 War in the Middle States

Have you ever been surprised when a team that seems to have no chance at all actually wins the big game? The Continental Army was that kind of team.

MAIN IDEA Despite its disadvantages, the Continental Army managed to win important battles early on in the American Revolution.

CREATING AN ARMY

In 1775, Great Britain had one of the most powerful armies in the world. Its soldiers were well-trained, experienced professionals, and about 42,000 of them came to fight in the colonies. Great Britain was prepared to meet the troops' needs for arms and other supplies. As you have read, the British also hired Hessian soldiers to join them in the colonies—about 30,000 men. These **mercenaries**, or soldiers who are paid to fight for a country other than their own, further swelled the number of British forces.

On September 9, 1776, the Continental Congress voted to rename the colonies the "United States of America," but the new nation did not have a strong central government. Congress did not have the power to provide funding for arms, other supplies, or soldiers' pay.

This situation didn't change until the next year, when the Continental Congress drafted and adopted the **Articles of Confederation** in 1777. Under the Articles of Confederation, the 13 states mostly governed themselves as small **republics**. A republic is a form of government in which the people elect representatives to speak for them and enact laws based on the people's needs. James Madison helped organize the state government of Virginia. The Articles granted Congress the authority to call on states to help fund the war.

Compared with the British Army, the young Continental Army was ill prepared and disorganized. The Patriots had other problems as well. George Washington faced a huge challenge in turning a collection of local militias into a disciplined, united fighting force. He also had trouble recruiting more troops. Few eligible men had formal military training, and many were

unwilling to leave their farms or jobs. Also, not everyone was eager for independence. Families and communities found themselves split between Loyalists and Patriots.

Both free and enslaved African Americans were in a unique situation when it came to deciding where their loyalties lay. The British promised freedom to many enslaved people if they promised to fight on the British side. Other African Americans, both free and unfree, were motivated to try to secure freedom for all and served in the war with the Patriots.

In 1776, only around 20,000 men had joined the Continental Army, but despite this and its numerous other problems, the Continental Army did have some advantages over the British. Most importantly, its soldiers were fighting a **defensive war**, or a war to protect one's own land, on familiar ground, while the British Army was far from home. And Americans were fighting for their homes and way of life.

EARLY VICTORIES AND DEFEATS

Even though the Revolution started in New England, it quickly spread to the Middle States of New York, New Jersey, Pennsylvania, and Delaware. In July 1776, British troops landed on New York's Staten Island and pushed American troops back to Manhattan Island and then New Jersey. The Continental Army soon had to escape across the Delaware River into Pennsylvania.

But the Continental Army had a change of luck by the end of the year. When they crossed the icy Delaware River on Christmas Day, Washington and his troops surprised and defeated the Hessian defenders in Trenton, New Jersey. The Hessian commander had received orders to build defenses

around Trenton, but he had ignored them. On the night before the battle, he got a message informing him that the Continental Army was on its way. He ignored this as well, and the result was a major defeat for the British. After this American victory, called the **Battle of Trenton**, British general **William Howe** withdrew most of his army back to New York. In the words of one British officer, the Americans had "become a formidable [fearsome] enemy." This victory resulted in a wave of support and enthusiasm for the American cause, which encouraged recruitment—and greater victories.

Each December, the Old Barracks Museum in Trenton, New Jersey, hosts a reenactment of the battle that showed the determination of American troops as they marched in blinding snow. The leaflet shown here provides an account of the battle—which lasted only 35 minutes—and the American victory. It took the news 11 days to reach Salem, Massachusetts, and appear in print on January 6.

HISTORICAL THINKING

1. **READING CHECK** What advantages and disadvantages did the Continental Army have at the start of the American Revolution?

2. **FORM AND SUPPORT OPINIONS** How do you think questions over national identity might have affected military recruitment? Explain why.

3. **ANALYZE CAUSE AND EFFECT** How did the Articles of Confederation impact the American Revolution?

Objective

Analyze how the Continental Army won critical early battles in the American Revolution.

Critical Thinking Skills for Lesson 1.1

- Identify Main Ideas and Details
- Monitor Comprehension
- Form and Support Opinions
- Analyze Cause and Effect
- Draw Conclusions

Essential Question for Chapter 6

What factors helped America win the war? In Lesson 1.1, students will read about how certain advantages helped the Continental Army win early battles and gain support from the American public.

Background for the Teacher

African-American and white colonists were not the only people whose loyalties varied before and during the Revolution. Many Native Americans believed that an American victory would endanger their own lands. Under British rule, the Proclamation of 1763 prohibited colonists from moving west of the Appalachians. Concerned that under American rule the proclamation might no longer apply, many Native American groups sided with the British. Some groups, such as the Iroquois, remained neutral, at least initially. Still others, such as the Catawba in South Carolina, worked with the Patriots throughout the war.

History Notebook

Encourage students to complete the Reid on the Road video series page for Chapter 6 in their History Notebooks after they view the video.

INTRODUCE & ENGAGE

Preview with Visuals

Direct students' attention to the photo of the Battle of Trenton reenactment. **ASK:** What does this photo suggest about American Revolution soldiers and their uniforms? *(Answers will vary. Possible response: The uniforms do not seem warm enough for cold weather. Soldiers do not all have the same uniforms.)* Tell students that in this lesson they will learn about the Battle of Trenton and early victories and defeats of the Continental Army.

Guided Discussion

1. **Draw Conclusions** Why might the Continental Congress have chosen to avoid forming a strong central government, even when having one could have meant more funding for the Continental Army? *(The Congress may have wanted to avoid re-creating the same tyranny colonists had experienced under British rule.)*

2. **Analyze Cause and Effect** In what ways did the American victory at Trenton change attitudes about the Continental Army on both sides of the conflict? *(The victory caused more Americans to support and to join the army and forced British military leaders to evaluate the threat of the Continental Army as more serious.)*

More Information

Mercenaries The term *Hessian* is derived from Hesse-Cassel, a state in the Holy Roman Empire in present-day Germany. In the 1700s, the state earned revenue by exporting well-trained and disciplined soldiers as mercenaries throughout Europe. The Hessians were well paid in comparison to what they would have earned as laborers or farm workers in their homeland. They were accustomed to supplementing their incomes with plunder (property stolen from civilians). In the colonies, this added to the hostility Americans already felt toward them. Even so, when the American Revolution ended, about 3,000 Hessians stayed in America and made it their new home.

Active Options

Active History: Analyze Different Points of View Extend the lesson by using either the PDF or Whiteboard version of the activity. These activities take a deeper look at a topic from, or related to, the lesson. Explore the activities as a class, turn them into group assignments, or even assign them individually.

NG Learning Framework: Analyze Concepts in 1776 Virginia State Constitution

SKILLS Collaboration, Communication

KNOWLEDGE Our Human Story

Organize students into small groups and help them locate online the Virginia Declaration of Rights and Constitution (June 12 and June 29, 1776), Sections I and XIII. Tell students to analyze the language and explain how specific American political institutions or ideas have developed from it (in particular, how the federal government governs the military today). Then have each group present their ideas to the class.

DIFFERENTIATE

English Language Learners `ELD`

Complete Sentence Frames Provide sentence frames like the ones below and have students at the **Emerging** and **Expanding** levels work in pairs to complete them. The first two sample frames cover the section titled Creating an Army, and the last two cover the section Early Victories and Defeats. Students may choose to split up the frames by section or to work together on each one.

- The British hired Hessian _____, or soldiers who are paid to fight for another country. *(mercenaries)*
- The Continental Army had the advantage of fighting a _____ war. *(defensive)*
- Washington defeated the Hessians in a surprise attack on _____. *(Trenton)*
- The victory at Trenton caused more people to _____ the Continental Army. *(support)*

Gifted & Talented

Create a Recruitment Poster Tell students to imagine they are in charge of recruitment for the Continental Army. Washington has just won the Battle of Trenton, but enlistment is still far too low. Have them design posters meant to persuade farmers, workers, and other eligible people to enlist in the fight against the British. Encourage students to do Internet research for examples of real recruitment posters from various eras. Remind them to incorporate details from the lesson into their posters.

See the Chapter Planner for more strategies for differentiation.

HISTORICAL THINKING

ANSWERS

1. The Continental Army's disadvantages were lack of men, training, and funding; not being supported by an established government; and divided loyalties among the people. Its biggest advantages were that it was fighting a defensive war and fighting on familiar land.

2. Answers will vary. Possible response: Without a unified nation, people do not know exactly what they are fighting for. A lot fewer people would want to fight when the cause is uncertain.

3. They gave Congress the power to ask states to contribute to the war effort.

1.2 The Struggle for New York

One of the worst things you can do is underestimate an opponent. The Americans looked like a ragtag bunch, but they had advantages the more disciplined British failed to see, and this oversight cost them.

MAIN IDEA Due to poor planning, the British expectation that they would dominate the Hudson River Valley proved to be incorrect.

HUDSON RIVER VALLEY

Even though Washington's troops were victorious in New Jersey, the British still controlled New York City. From there, they planned to capture the Hudson River Valley. They hoped to divide New England from the rest of the states and bring a swift conclusion to the colonial rebellion.

General Howe, a lieutenant general of British forces in North America, planned to seize the Hudson River Valley using three armies. In 1777, he sent a regiment under the command of British general **John Burgoyne** from Boston to Canada. Burgoyne's troops were to move by boat down Lake Champlain. Howe's own troops would move north to meet them. Another force, led by British lieutenant colonel Barry St. Leger, would move east from western New York along the Mohawk River to link up with the other two armies in Albany, New York.

On their way south from Lake Champlain, Burgoyne's troops took Fort Ticonderoga, but they quickly ran into problems. Burgoyne had overloaded his troops with baggage, including cartloads of his own clothing. American forces chopped down trees and rolled boulders into the path of the British troops, making a march of 23 miles take 24 days. Then, near Saratoga, New York, the Americans surrounded Burgoyne's troops. When Burgoyne called

Revolutionary Battles in New York, 1777

Map legend:
- American forces
- British forces
- American victory
- British victory
- Fort

for **reinforcements**, or more soldiers and supplies, from New York, he found that Howe had changed his plans. Instead of joining Burgoyne's troops, Howe had decided to head for Philadelphia. His route there was roundabout. He sailed around Delaware and up Chesapeake Bay to Pennsylvania. Washington tried and failed to block Howe's advance through Pennsylvania. The British

A Mohawk Loyalist

Joseph Brant was born by the Ohio River and educated at an Indian charity school in Connecticut. His sister married a British Army officer, whom Brant followed into battle during the French and Indian War. His loyalties remained with the British throughout the American Revolution, and he skillfully led Iroquois Loyalist troops in battle throughout the Mohawk Valley. After the war, he worked for peace on the frontier. For his service, the British awarded him land in Canada, where he and his followers eventually settled.

A gorget was worn by officers to protect their throats during battle. King George gave this gorget to Brant as a gift.

occupied and successfully defended Philadelphia and nearby Germantown against another attack by Washington's troops in October 1777.

ALONG THE MOHAWK RIVER

Meanwhile, St. Leger continued to push toward Albany. After crossing Lake Ontario, he led his army along the Mohawk River. And he was not alone. Iroquois warriors from the region supported St. Leger's troops.

The Six Nations of the Iroquois had formed their alliance around 1720. They signed a treaty with Britain in 1768 to establish a boundary between Native American and European lands. Then, in 1775, as the American Revolution approached, the Six Nations agreed to remain neutral. However, after war broke out, both the Americans and the British pressured the nations in the alliance to choose sides. Eventually the Six Nations decided to split their loyalties. The Mohawk sided with the British.

Mohawk chief **Joseph Brant** commanded his troops as they fought alongside St. Leger in the Mohawk River Valley. But they encountered American resistance at Fort Stanwix in 1777. When they heard that officer Benedict Arnold was approaching from the east with more American troops—and Native American allies—St. Leger and his Iroquois allies retreated. Their flight and Howe's change of plans meant that no one would be coming to help Burgoyne once he got to Albany.

HISTORICAL THINKING

1. **READING CHECK** What errors did Burgoyne make as he headed to the Hudson River Valley?

2. **INTERPRET MAPS** Along what river did most of the American victories occur in 1777?

3. **FORM AND SUPPORT OPINIONS** Do you think Burgoyne and Howe were ready for battle in America? Why or why not?

PLAN

Objective
Analyze how errors prevented the British from taking control of the Hudson River Valley.

Critical Thinking Skills for Lesson 1.2
- Identify Main Ideas and Details
- Monitor Comprehension
- Interpret Maps
- Form and Support Opinions
- Describe
- Make Predictions

Essential Question for Chapter 6
What factors helped America win the war?
Although the British managed to hold Philadelphia, their attempt to control the Hudson River Valley was foiled. Lesson 1.2 details how British missteps allowed American fighters to gain the upper hand.

Background for the Teacher
During the battle at Germantown, Pennsylvania, the American forces were hampered by a dense fog. In addition, Washington's plan called for several simultaneous attacks, which led to one group of American soldiers accidentally firing upon another. Though the Continental Army lost the battle at Germantown, its efforts were not entirely wasted. Washington's 11,000 troops failed to defeat the British forces, and he lost almost twice as many men as his opponent. However, Washington's bold, elaborate battle strategy impressed the French. It helped convince them of his military capability at a time when they were still debating whether to lend support to the American cause.

INTRODUCE & ENGAGE

Analyze Military Strategy

Direct students' attention to the map in this lesson and ask them to locate the Hudson River. **ASK:** Where is New York City in relation to the Hudson River? *(New York city is at the terminus of the river.)* Why might the control of the Hudson River be a smart military strategy? *(Controlling rivers allows an army to control what moves on the river, from other troops to supplies. Controlling the Hudson River would allow the British to maintain control of New York City.)* Remind students that the area around the Hudson River is called the Hudson River Valley. Then tell them that in this lesson, they will learn about battles for control of the Hudson River Valley and the Mohawk River.

TEACH

Guided Discussion

1. **Describe** How did General Howe plan to take control of the Hudson River Valley, and what went wrong when he tried to put the plan into action? *(Howe planned to use three armies: his own, Burgoyne's, and St. Leger's. Burgoyne's troops would come south from Canada and meet up with Howe's troops, which would be traveling north. Then these armies would move to Albany, where St. Leger's forces would meet them from the east. Burgoyne's excess baggage and American sabotage of the roads slowed his army's travel. St. Leger faced stronger American opposition than the plan anticipated. Howe did not implement his own part of the plan.)*

2. **Make Predictions** Based on what you have read in the lesson, what do you predict will happen when Burgoyne's troops reach Albany? *(Answers will vary. Possible response: He will not have enough help fighting Washington's armies, and he will lose the battle.)*

Interpret Maps

Direct students' attention to the map of battles in New York. Review the map legend and remind students that the arrows represent British and American movements. **ASK:** Which side had more victories in this period of the war? *(neither)* **ASK:** Based on this map, what conclusions could you draw about the two armies and the war overall during the years 1776 and 1777? *(Answers will vary. Possible responses: The armies seem to be evenly matched; it seems like either side could potentially win or lose the war.)*

Active Options

On Your Feet: Inside-Outside Circle Have each student write one question about information in Lesson 1.2. Then arrange students in two concentric circles, with the outer ring of students facing inward and the inner ring of students facing out. Have students on the outer ring ask their inner-ring partners their questions. After all inner-ring students have had some time to answer the questions, signal the inner-ring students to rotate one place and read their questions to the outer ring. Repeat as time permits.

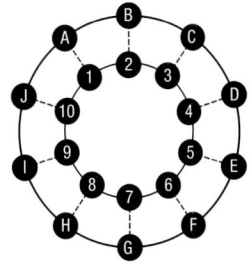

NG Learning Framework: Write a Biography

ATTITUDE Curiosity

KNOWLEDGE Our Human Story

Have students learn more about Joseph Brant or another Native American who played a major role in the American Revolution. Instruct them to write and submit a short biography or profile about their chosen subject, using information from the chapter and additional source material. Encourage students to share their biographies with the class.

DIFFERENTIATE

Striving Readers

Understand Main Ideas Check students' understanding of the main ideas in Lesson 1.2 by asking them to correctly complete either/or statements such as the following by choosing the correct answer of the two in brackets:

- General Howe [planned or did not plan] to have his three armies meet in Philadelphia.
- Washington [succeeded or failed] at taking control of Philadelphia in 1777.
- The Mohawk people chose to support [the Americans or the British].

Inclusion

Complete a 5Ws Chart Guide students to complete a 5Ws Chart like the one below to aid in their comprehension of the text. As they read the lesson, encourage them to pause after each paragraph and identify any information they should add to their charts.

What?
Who?
Where?
When?
Why?

See the Chapter Planner for more strategies for differentiation.

HISTORICAL THINKING

ANSWERS

1. He had his troops carry too much baggage, which slowed them down when the Americans sabotaged their path.

2. Most of the American victories in 1777 occurred along or near the Mohawk River.

3. Answers will vary. Possible response: Burgoyne was not ready because he brought too much unnecessary equipment and could not navigate the territory well. Howe did not follow his own plan or predict that Burgoyne might need reinforcements.

1.3 Battles of Saratoga

Sometimes things just don't go as planned. Unexpected events can derail even the best strategy—events like being hopelessly outnumbered, for example.

MAIN IDEA American planning and coordination, along with British miscalculation, led to Patriot victories at Saratoga and a turning point in the American Revolution.

AMERICAN PLACES
Saratoga Battlefield, New York

In order to hold off British forces, American troops under General Horatio Gates built two fortified walls along Bemis Heights, overlooking the Hudson River and the road beside it. They lined up 22 cannons along the walls, which helped them successfully defend their line. Today, the battlefield where these important American victories were won is open to all as part of the Saratoga National Historical Park.

A TURNING POINT

As you have read, General Burgoyne found himself in a tricky situation as he moved south—without backup—toward Albany after his victory at Fort Ticonderoga. He expected to be joined by British troops moving north from New York, but that support never came.

Here's what happened: In September 1777, 12,000 members of the Continental Army under General Horatio Gates surrounded Burgoyne and his 5,800 men at Saratoga, New York. The Americans were well prepared for this clash. Gates and Polish military engineer Tadeusz Kościuszko (tah-DAY-oosh kos-CHOOS-ko) had overseen a plan to build up American **fortifications**, or structures built to protect a place from attack.

They had brought in reinforcements from other states as well, including the Light Horse Volunteers commanded by Colonel John Langdon. One of Langdon's men was Wentworth Cheswell, an African-American government official from Massachusetts. Though the British Army had been more welcoming of African-American volunteers, soldiers such as Cheswell had started to support the Patriot cause in larger numbers.

On September 19, 1777, the British and Continental armies clashed at what would later be known as the First Battle of Saratoga, also called the Battle of Freeman's Farm. Burgoyne failed to cross Gates's lines. The British struck at the Americans again on October 7, but General Benedict Arnold staged a strong American **counterattack**, or attack in response, in what would be known as the Second Battle of Saratoga. At this point, 20,000 American troops surrounded Burgoyne's men. Burgoyne had requested that General Howe send reinforcements, but, as you may recall, Howe and his troops were on their way to Philadelphia. Greatly outnumbered, Burgoyne surrendered at Saratoga on October 17.

An African-American Hero of the Revolution

Wentworth Cheswell is most often remembered today as one of the early African-American heroes of the American Revolution. As the town messenger of Newmarket, New Hampshire, Cheswell once had to ride all night to warn his community of an impending British invasion. He also served in the Continental Army with John Langdon's Light Horse Volunteers.

But this was just one facet of a man whose career in politics lasted nearly 50 years. His ancestry was part European, part African American. Formally educated in Byfield, Massachusetts, the 22-year-old Cheswell was elected in 1768 to his first political office—town constable of Newmarket. Over the course of his impressive career, he held other prominent posts, including justice of the peace for Rockingham County, New Hampshire.

Wentworth Cheswell

A NEW ALLY

The **Battles of Saratoga** proved to be an important turning point in the American Revolution. As with the Battle of Trenton, the victories boosted Americans' morale and gave them hope that they could defeat a larger, well-established army.

Success at Saratoga also earned the Americans a valuable asset: an alliance with France. France was already supporting the United States with economic and military assistance, and these victories convinced the French government that the Americans could win the war. No longer feeling outmatched, the Americans now had military help from a wealthy nation, and they had experienced significant victories themselves.

HISTORICAL THINKING

1. **READING CHECK** Why were the battles of Saratoga important for the Continental Army?

2. **ANALYZE CAUSE AND EFFECT** How did an error in strategy affect the outcome of the Battles of Saratoga?

3. **IDENTIFY PROBLEMS AND SOLUTIONS** What problems did the Continental Army face at Saratoga, and what steps did it take to solve them?

Objective

Explain how victories at Trenton and Saratoga were a turning point for the Continental Army.

Critical Thinking Skills for Lesson 1.3

- Identify Main Ideas and Details
- Monitor Comprehension
- Analyze Cause and Effect
- Identify Problems and Solutions
- Form and Support Opinions
- Make Inferences

Essential Question for Chapter 6

What factors helped America win the war?

The Continental Army's victories at Trenton and Saratoga helped turn the tide of the war. Lesson 1.3 analyzes how the Americans won the critical battles, including shrewd American planning and British miscalculation.

Background for the Teacher

American Revolution hero Tadeusz Kościuszko (ta-DE-oosh kahs-CHOO-sko) (1746–1817) might not have been in the colonies at all were it not for some bad luck in love. As a tutor in Poland, Kościuszko had attempted to marry his employer's daughter, which enraged his employer, a general. After fleeing the general, Kościuszko went to America, where his military training helped him rise quickly through the ranks of the Continental Army. Throughout the war he planned critical fortifications, which earned him American citizenship. Later he returned to Poland and led a rebellion against Russian occupation that failed after he was taken prisoner. After his release, Kościuszko returned briefly to the United States, where he was received warmly by the people and began a long friendship with Thomas Jefferson.

INTRODUCE & ENGAGE

Design a Fortification

Tell students that in Lesson 1.3, they will be learning about the role of fortifications in two battles. **ASK:** What is a fortification's purpose? *(to protect troops, other people, and supplies from attack)* What are some things forts have in common? *(strong walls; guarded entries; watchtowers)* Have the class work together to design a fortification to protect a colonial location they have read about, such as Boston. Ask volunteers to sketch out the design on the board. Return to the class design after reading the lesson to give students a chance to add or change elements of the design.

TEACH

Guided Discussion

1. **Form and Support Opinions** Which factor was more important in the American victories at Saratoga: American planning or British error? Support your opinion with evidence from this lesson and Lesson 1.2. *(Answers will vary. Some students may identify American planning, which allowed strong fortifications and an increased number of soldiers, as the main factor forcing Burgoyne to surrender. Others may say that without British error, Burgoyne would have had more troops and may have won.)*

2. **Make Inferences** Based on what you have read in this lesson and Lesson 1.1, why might free and enslaved African Americans have become more motivated to support the Patriots' cause? *(Answers will vary. Possible response: As the Continental Army fought more successfully against the British, African Americans may have thought that they had a better chance at securing freedom for all if they supported the Patriots' cause.)*

American Places

The battlefield at Saratoga has been preserved as a National Historical Park. In addition to the battlefield, the park includes the home of Continental Army general Philip Schuyler, the woods into which Burgoyne and his men retreated, and a 155-foot-tall monument to the American soldiers who fought at Saratoga. Visitors can schedule guided tours or explore the park on their own with audio guides or smartphone apps. Virtual tours of the park are also available on the National Park Service's website.

Active Options

On Your Feet: Numbered Heads Have students form groups of four and give each student a number: one, two, three, or four. Present the following questions to all groups: What might France have hoped to gain from supporting the Americans? Why might the French have wanted evidence that the Americans could win the war before providing support? Allow time for groups to arrive at a consensus. Then call out a number and have the student in each group with that number report the group's answers.

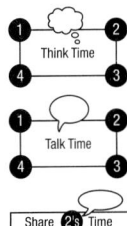
Think Time
Talk Time
Share 2's Time

NG Learning Framework: Explore an American Revolution Battlefield

`ATTITUDE` Responsibility

`KNOWLEDGE` Our Living Planet

Explain to students that many battlefields have been preserved as landmarks. Have students choose a battlefield and research how it is used and preserved today. Questions to consider include:

• Where is the battlefield located?

• What evidence remains of the former battle (or battles)?

• How might war have changed the landscape?

• What are the reasons for preserving this battlefield?

Have students assemble a brief presentation on their chosen battlefield, using images and maps where possible to support and emphasize their points.

DIFFERENTIATE

Striving Readers

Set a Purpose for Reading Before reading, have students use the title, headings, the Main Idea statement, and proper nouns to create purpose-setting questions for Lesson 1.3.

• Who won the Battles of Saratoga?

• Why was Saratoga a turning point in the war?

• Who was General John Burgoyne?

• Who was General Horatio Gates?

• What roles did African Americans play in the Battles of Saratoga?

• Who became the Americans' new ally?

Pre-AP

Write a Letter Have students reread the section on Wentworth Cheswell in Lesson 1.3. Instruct them to use this information, as well as outside sources if time permits, to write a letter from Cheswell to a family member or friend following the Battles of Saratoga. The letter should include information about Cheswell's location, his role in the battles, and his thoughts about serving in the Continental Army as an African American. You may wish to provide students with examples of letters written during the American Revolution or direct students to conduct an online search to help them find their own models.

See the Chapter Planner for more strategies for differentiation.

HISTORICAL THINKING

ANSWERS

1. The victories at Saratoga were a turning point in the army's morale and led to France offering more military support.

2. General Howe's decision to take his troops to Philadelphia rather than reinforce Burgoyne at Saratoga contributed to Burgoyne's surrender.

3. Answers will vary. Possible response: The Continental Army faced a British force that was fresh off a victory at Fort Ticonderoga, so American leaders knew they had to be prepared. They built up fortifications before Burgoyne and his men got to Saratoga and assembled reinforcements so they outnumbered the British force.

2.1 Seeking Help from Europe

It's hard to face a tough challenge alone. This is especially true in times of war. During the Revolution, America looked for help from other countries.

MAIN IDEA Assistance from European powers and from heroes of various backgrounds helped Americans overcome some of their disadvantages in the American Revolution.

POWERFUL FRIENDS

The alliance between France and the United States did not happen immediately. Taking advantage of the Continental Army's momentum, the Continental Congress sent Benjamin Franklin and John Adams to Europe. Congress hoped to persuade France to become an official ally of the United States. The French considered Britain to be their main enemy and wanted to avenge their loss in the French and Indian War. These considerations helped Franklin and Adams convince France to sign the Treaty of Alliance in February 1778 and provide the United States with financial assistance.

France and Spain were allies, and they both had lost significant lands in North America at the end of the French and Indian War. In addition to money and supplies, France provided the Americans with troops. Both nations helped the Americans by drawing Britain's military and naval attention in different directions. The French navy engaged the British in the West Indies, pulling resources away from the North American mainland. Spanish military leader Bernardo de Gálvez forced the British to send troops to the Mississippi Valley to defend forts formerly held by the Spanish. Then Gálvez helped defeat the British in Florida and claimed that territory for Spain.

HEROES FROM HOME AND ABROAD

France and Spain also played pivotal roles in affecting the course of the war. You've learned that Tadeusz Kościuszko from Poland helped win the Battles of Saratoga. You've also read about the contributions of Prussia's **Baron Friedrich von Steuben** at Valley Forge. From von Steuben, the inexperienced American soldiers rapidly

learned skills such as marching, making quick decisions in combat, and using weapons, including the **bayonet** (BAY-uh-net), a sharp blade attached to a musket.

The **Marquis de Lafayette** (mar-KEE duh lah-fy-EHT), a French nobleman, had already offered his assistance to the American war effort and had become a general in the Continental Army. He took a break from the fighting and returned to France to help Franklin and Adams get funding and support from the king. With that goal accomplished, Lafayette came back to America and took part in many battles, including the one that would end the war.

Although the Continental Army did not actively welcome African Americans, those who sympathized with the Patriot cause found ways to help. An enslaved man named **James Armistead** was allowed by his owner to spy for Lafayette. Gaining the trust of British officers, Armistead gathered information that helped the Americans win key battles.

Even with France and Spain helping to pay for some of the costs of the war, the United States faced major economic challenges during the conflict. Before the war, Britain and the West Indies had been markets for American goods and sources of goods for the American markets. Now British ships **blockaded** American ports by refusing to let vessels enter or leave these harbors. Towns and farms were destroyed as battles raged near or around them. And war is expensive. American troops had to be fed, and they needed uniforms, dependable weapons, and a steady supply of ammunition. Battle wounds and

Boston Athenaeum, Boston

In this 1853 painting by Andre Jolly, Benjamin Franklin is shown as the center of attention among French royalty at the home of Princess Elizabeth. Diane de Polignac, placing a laurel wreath on Franklin's head, ran the household. Elizabeth stands behind her brother, King Louis XVI, who is seated at the right. To his right is his wife, Marie-Antoinette, the queen.

outbreaks of disease led to an increasing need for medical supplies. And, of course, the soldiers expected to be paid.

Unfortunately, Congress did not have the power to collect taxes to help fund the war. Instead, Congress decided to make up for the shortfall by printing more money, even though it had no real wealth to back it up. In 1782, John Adams obtained a loan from Dutch bankers but also looked to American citizens for additional help.

Many Americans contributed what they could to the cause. For example, American Jewish **financier** Haym Salomon lent funds to help pay the costs of the revolution. A financier raises and provides funds for a business or undertaking. Salomon's generous gesture was never repaid, however, and he died in 1785 without a penny to his name. Financial problems were not the only challenges Americans faced, however. The war was still far from over.

HISTORICAL THINKING

1. **READING CHECK** How did France and Spain help the Americans?

2. **MAKE INFERENCES** Why did other nations offer to help the Americans?

3. **DRAW CONCLUSIONS** How did Britain wage war against the Americans off the battlefield?

PLAN

Objective

Describe how allies aided the Continental Army during the Revolution.

Critical Thinking Skills for Lesson 2.1

- Identify Main Ideas and Details
- Monitor Comprehension
- Make Inferences
- Draw Conclusions
- Form and Support Opinions
- Analyze Visuals

Essential Question for Chapter 6

What factors helped America win the war?
In order to defeat the powerful British Army in the American Revolution, the Continental Army needed training, guidance, and money. Lesson 2.1 illustrates how a variety of allies provided help that affected the course of the war.

Background for the Teacher

When Marie-Joseph-Paul-Yves-Roch-Gilbert du Motier (otherwise known as Marquis de Lafayette) arrived in America to offer his aid to George Washington, he was neither a seasoned military leader nor an experienced diplomat. Rather, he was a wealthy, orphaned courtier to Louis XVI—and only 19 years old. The young soldier quickly proved himself a capable fighter. As a commander, Lafayette used his personal resources to improve conditions for soldiers, which helped stem the tide of deserters. Washington regarded the young soldier as a son. In 1824 when he returned to the United States after the war, Lafayette found himself universally admired and honored for his contributions to the Revolution.

INTRODUCE & ENGAGE

Preview Terms

Introduce the concept of an *alliance*. If necessary, have students use a dictionary to define the word, and then ask students to offer comparisons and examples (from history, literature, or pop culture) in a classroom discussion. At the end of the lesson, revisit the discussion to include alliances made during the American Revolution.

TEACH

Guided Discussion

1. **Form and Support Opinions** Who would have benefited more from their alliance, the Americans or the French, and why? (*Answers will vary. Some students may say that the Americans benefited more from receiving immediate money and help in battle. Others may say that the French might have benefited more in the long run from weakening their enemy, Britain, and having the Americans on their side in the future.*)

2. **Analyze Visuals** What details in the painting by Andre Jolly might be symbolic of the relationship between the French and the Americans? (*Answers will vary. Possible response: The elaborate gowns, coats, and hairstyles of the French royalty, compared with Franklin's plain coat and loose hair, might be symbols of the contrast between the French nobles' wealth and the Americans' need. The woman placing a wreath on Franklin's head might symbolize the French granting their support to the Americans.*)

Virtual Museum Visit

The motto of the Boston Athenaeum in Massachusetts is appropriate for one of the nation's oldest libraries: "Sweet are the fruits of letters." Founded in 1807, the library began hosting art exhibits in 1827. Today, in addition to housing more than 500,000 texts, the Athenaeum is home to approximately 600 permanent works of art and several permanent exhibitions. A growing selection of paintings and sculptures appears on the museum's website, along with detailed background information and scholarly essays on the works and their artists. Encourage students to conduct a virtual visit, or do so as a class.

Active Options

On Your Feet: Create a Concept Cluster Have students form teams of three or four around a table with a large piece of paper or by a section of the board. Instruct students to sketch a Concept Cluster, like the one shown here, with "Support from Allies" in the center. Group members should take turns contributing events or details to the cluster. Prompt students to consider all types of support described in the lesson: military, economic, and strategic.

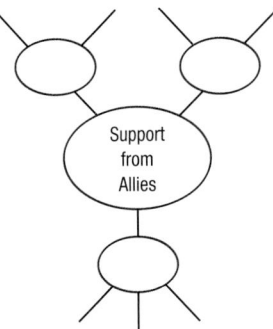

NG Learning Framework: Negotiate an Alliance

ATTITUDE Empowerment

SKILLS Collaboration, Problem-Solving

Tell students to form four groups, representing the Americans, the French, the Spanish, and private individuals (such as James Armistead and Haym Salomon). Have the group representing the Americans use what they learned in Lesson 2.1 and prior lessons to present a case for supporting the Revolution. The groups representing France, Spain, and private individuals should ask questions of the Americans and debate the pros and cons of offering support. When all of their questions have been answered, tell the French, Spanish, and private individual groups to draft their alliance agreements with the Americans.

DIFFERENTIATE

English Language Learners

Practice Vocabulary Have students choose one of the following Key Vocabulary terms from Lesson 2.1: *bayonet*, *blockaded*, or *financier*. Pair students at the **Emerging** level with English-proficient students. Instruct students to present their chosen term to their partner, defining the term in their own words and using examples or sketches to further explain its meaning. Students can use a Word Square like the one below to organize their presentations.

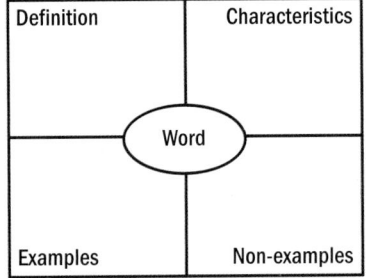

Gifted & Talented

Present a News Report Challenge students to use the information in Lesson 2.1 to create a modern-day newscast reporting on foreign and domestic efforts to support the Continental Army. Encourage students to use the Internet and other resources to locate or create relevant visual aids, such as paintings of people or places in the lesson. Students may work individually or in groups. Invite them to present their newscasts live in class or in video format.

See the Chapter Planner for more strategies for differentiation.

HISTORICAL THINKING

ANSWERS

1. They provided financial assistance, soldiers, and supplies. Their armies and navies also fought against Britain in different locations, which kept the British engaged on multiple fronts.

2. France and other nations were impressed with the Americans after victories such as the ones at Saratoga. France and Spain also wanted revenge on Britain for their losses in the French and Indian War.

3. The British blockaded American ports, cutting off Americans from essential trade. This led to economic hardship.

2.2 Hardship and Challenges

Even the most satisfying success can be short-lived, especially in wartime. You're up one day and down the next. Challenging as it may be, you just have to hang in there.

MAIN IDEA The Continental Army faced hardship and challenges at Valley Forge and on the frontier.

VALLEY FORGE

As you have read, the victory at Saratoga boosted American morale, but there was much more work to be done. The focus of the war shifted to Pennsylvania, where General Howe now occupied Philadelphia. You probably remember that the Continental Army set up camp at **Valley Forge**, northwest of the city, in the dead of the winter of 1777. George Washington set up camp alongside his men high atop a series of hills. Washington vowed to "share in the hardship" and "partake of [take part in] every inconvenience" his soldiers experienced. While Washington certainly suffered, he lived with his aides in a stone house at Valley Forge. His men lived in the small wooden huts they'd built themselves and used straw they gathered for bedding.

Meanwhile, General **Henry Clinton** had become the new commander of British forces in North America. In contrast to the Americans, Clinton and his men settled into quarters in Philadelphia, where they lived in relative comfort. Loyalist families gave them places to stay, and Clinton and his officers enjoyed parties and good food.

As you've read, the soldiers in the Continental Army suffered greatly from the cold and a lack of food, and some chose to **desert**, or run away from the army. But despite the horrible conditions, most soldiers chose to stay. Loyal to General Washington and determined to keep up the fight, they spent the winter training under von Steuben.

As winter wore on, others arrived to help the American cause. Lafayette came to command a division at Valley Forge. In addition to sharing his men's hardships, the Frenchman provided uniforms and muskets to those who needed them.

Spring's arrival brought not only better weather but also great news. Word of the alliance between America and France reached the camp. To celebrate, Washington had his men line up and shoot their guns in the air. They were poised and ready to do battle at Monmouth.

WAR ON THE FRONTIER

Pennsylvania wasn't the only place where war raged. From New York to Georgia, **skirmishes**, or small, short battles, took place along the rural western boundary of the frontier. Small divisions of the British Army guarded forts in this region, supported by Native American volunteers. Remember that at the outset of the American Revolution, many Native Americans supported the British. They feared that if the Americans won, they would take over more Native American land.

British general Henry Hamilton and his Native American allies planned to invade the frontier. But American frontiersman George Rogers Clark heard of these plans and led a small force in a surprise attack on one of the British bases, Fort Vincennes (vihn-SEHNZ). Hamilton surrendered, and the joint British–Native American offensive was halted.

Despite Clark's victory at Vincennes, American settlers found themselves constantly battling Iroquois forces. The fighting caused homelessness and food shortages in many communities.

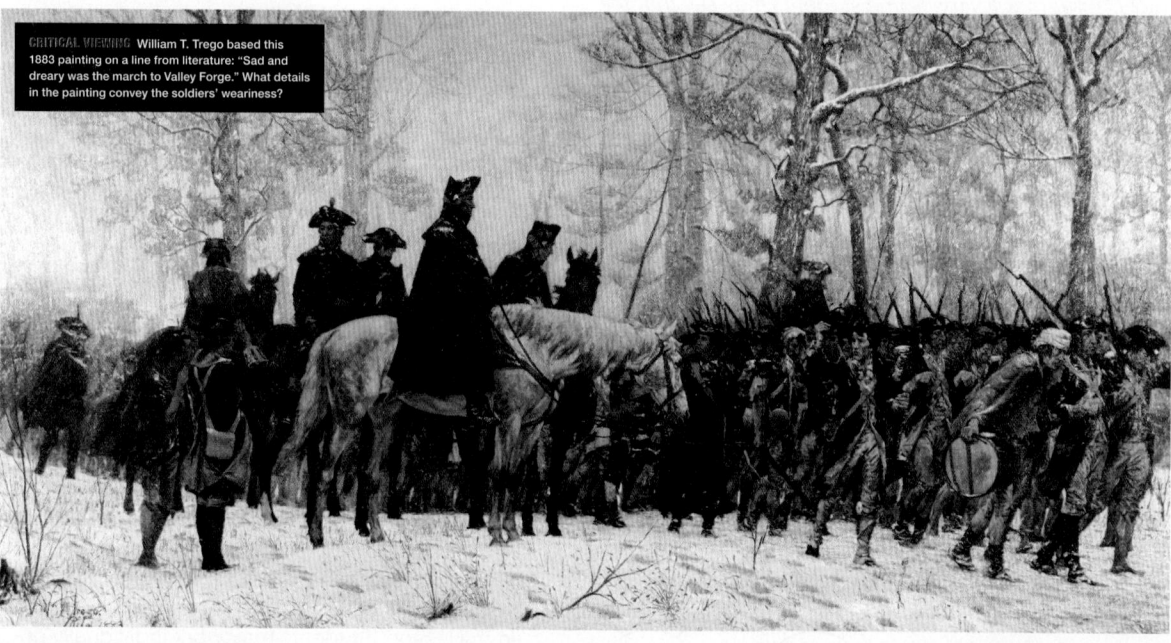

CRITICAL VIEWING William T. Trego based this 1883 painting on a line from literature: "Sad and dreary was the march to Valley Forge." What details in the painting convey the soldiers' weariness?

HISTORICAL THINKING

1. **READING CHECK** What did George Washington's men have to do when they first arrived at Valley Forge?

2. **COMPARE AND CONTRAST** How did the experiences of the British and Continental armies in the winter of 1777–78 differ?

3. **IDENTIFY MAIN IDEAS AND DETAILS** How and why did Native Americans participate in the American Revolution?

PLAN

Objective

Describe the Continental Army's challenges at Valley Forge and on the western frontier.

Critical Thinking Skills for Lesson 2.2

- Identify Main Ideas and Details
- Monitor Comprehension
- Compare and Contrast
- Make Inferences
- Make Predictions
- Form and Support Opinions

Essential Question for Chapter 6

What factors helped America win the war?
Lesson 2.2 explores how the Continental Army persisted in spite of difficult hardships, keeping the Revolution alive until aid from France arrived. The lesson also details how battles with Native Americans brought the war to the frontier.

Background for the Teacher

George Rogers Clark achieved victory at Fort Vincennes not only by surprising the British and Native American forces holding the fort but also through the use of psychological intimidation. Clark's small force arrived at Vincennes exhausted, cold, and hungry; they had had no provisions for several days during their march. Clark doubted his weary men could defeat the occupying soldiers, so instead of storming the fort, he bluffed. Before reaching Vincennes, Clark sent exaggerated warnings of a massive, imminent attack to the townspeople around the fort and threatening letters to the British general, Henry Hamilton. Upon arrival, Clark had his soldiers surround the fort and fire their guns often so that it would sound as though he had more troops than he did.

Identify Coping Traits

Tell students that in this lesson, they will be exploring one of the most challenging periods faced by the Continental Army during the American Revolution. **ASK:** What kinds of things help people cope with hardship? Have students write a list of four or five thoughts, actions, traits, or motivations that might help someone get through hard times. Then have the class share and discuss their lists. After the lesson, have students revisit their lists and circle any items that apply to Washington's soldiers at Valley Forge.

TEACH

Guided Discussion

1. **Make Inferences** Why would it have been important for Continental Army leaders like Washington and Lafayette to share in the hardship experienced by their soldiers? *(Answers will vary. Possible response: The American Revolution was being fought in the name of freedom and equality. If the soldiers believed that some people were suffering more than others, they may have decided to leave or rebel against the inequality.)*

2. **Make Predictions** Based on what you have read in this lesson and what you already know, do you think the conflicts between American settlers and the Iroquois will improve after the war? Explain your prediction. *(Answers will vary. Possible response: The conflicts will not improve because the American settlers will continue to live on and invade Native American lands.)*

Form and Support Opinions

Have students review the section of Lesson 2.2 that describes the conditions for soldiers during the winter at Valley Forge. You might also wish to review the American Story feature that opens this chapter. **ASK:** Do you think that Washington kept his vow to live the way his soldiers lived? *(Answers will vary. Some students may say that by living in sturdier housing with aides, Washington did not really share his men's hardships. Other students may say that Washington mostly kept his vow, since he suffered along with them in other ways and did not opt to live in luxury like the British soldiers.)*

Active Options

On Your Feet: Rotating Discussion Assign students to one of four corners in the room. Then instruct each team to think of several questions about the winter at Valley Forge or the skirmishes on the frontier. Start a discussion by tossing a beanbag to one team and asking them a question about the lesson, such as "Why did Washington's troops choose to camp at Valley Forge?" *(It was near Philadelphia and General Howe's occupying British forces.)* When one team answers the question, they will toss the beanbag to another team and ask their own question. Continue until all groups have asked and answered a question.

NG Learning Framework: Diary from a War Zone

ATTITUDE Responsibility

KNOWLEDGE Our Human Story

Remind students that soldiers were not the only people affected by the chaos of the American Revolution. Families of soldiers often followed the troops, and civilians living in occupied cities faced hardships of their own. Have students use library or online sources to research the experiences of civilians during the war.

Then encourage students to use their research to write one or two diary entries from the perspective of a person living near a major battlefield, a citizen of an occupied city (such as Philadelphia), or a family member following a soldier. Students may present their diary entries to the class or post them on a class blog.

Striving Readers

Pose and Answer Questions Have students work in pairs to read the text aloud. At the end of the lesson, have each partner ask the other *who*, *what*, *where*, *when*, and *why* questions about the content they read. If students struggle to answer the questions, they can ask their partners for a clue, such as which paragraph or section contains the answer. Remind students to reread slowly and carefully as they locate the answers.

Inclusion

Monitor Comprehension Have students work in pairs or small groups to read the lesson aloud. At the end of each paragraph, instruct them to complete the following sentence frames:

• This paragraph is about _____.

• One detail I remember from this paragraph is _____.

• This detail is important because _____.

• One word I did not understand was _____.

• I think this word might mean _____.

See the Chapter Planner for more strategies for differentiation.

HISTORICAL THINKING

ANSWERS

1. When they first arrived at Valley Forge, Washington's men had to set up camp for the winter months, building wooden shelters and finding straw for bedding.

2. Thanks to Loyalist supporters, most of the British lived in relative comfort in Philadelphia, enjoying "parties and good food." Most Continental soldiers spent the winter cold and starving at Valley Forge.

3. Many Native Americans fought on the side of the British, helping them guard forts and attacking settlements on the frontier. They feared that if the Americans won, they would take even more land.

CRITICAL VIEWING Answers will vary. Students may note that details suggesting weariness include the muted colors, the postures of the soldiers walking, and the glum faces of the men on horseback.

2.3 Women's Roles in the Revolution

If colonial women could time travel to the present day, many would probably be surprised to see American women working alongside men in most settings. But some would feel right at home.

MAIN IDEA Even though they could not officially serve in the army, women played many key roles in the American Revolution.

BEFORE THE REVOLUTION

Colonial women had long stood with men against the British. For instance, do you remember that before the American Revolution, the Daughters of Liberty helped organize a boycott of British goods? **Mercy Otis Warren** was an outspoken supporter of these boycotts. She became active in colonial politics through one of the committees of correspondence and went on to become a notable historian of the Revolutionary era.

John Adams's wife, **Abigail Adams**, also played a vital role from the earliest days of the Revolution. Along with Mercy Otis Warren and the governor's wife, Hannah Winthrop, Adams was appointed by the Massachusetts Colony General Court to question and report on local women suspected of being Loyalists. Both Adams and Warren were sharp thinkers and skilled writers who freely voiced their ideas about liberty, independence, women's rights, and a new government.

DURING THE REVOLUTION

As often happens in wartime, women took over many duties at home traditionally performed by men. Women ran farms, shops, and businesses. They also supported soldiers who passed through their communities, giving them housing and food. Some women took more direct action. They traveled with the troops, working as nurses, cooking men's meals, and washing their clothes.

You may be surprised to learn that some women excelled at espionage, or spying. This was due in great part to the fact that men tended to

underestimate them. Many of these spies worked as maids or cooks for British officers and so had access to valuable information. Some women even took part in combat, disguising themselves as men or at times simply stepping into battle. They risked not only the dangers of combat but also jail if it were discovered that they were women.

In 1777, **Sybil Ludington** rode more than 40 miles in a single night to warn forces commanded by her father of a British attack in Connecticut. The British planned to destroy American supplies there. She also warned the people along the way.

When women did not have a defined role in the war, they were resourceful in finding ways to help—some of which could be very risky. Abigail Adams's appeal to her husband still did not bring equal rights to American women. But colonial women had shown their ability to participate in the building of a new nation.

HISTORICAL THINKING

1. **READING CHECK** How did women contribute to the success of the American Revolution?

2. **FORM AND SUPPORT OPINIONS** Which woman named in this lesson do you think contributed most to the American Revolution? Use evidence from the text to explain and support your opinion.

3. **DRAW CONCLUSIONS** In what way do Abigail Adams's comments to her husband reflect ideas in the Declaration of Independence?

Remember the Ladies

The four women featured on this page—Abigail Adams, Anna Smith Strong, Mary Ludwig Hays McCauly, and Phillis Wheatley—provide examples of women who were every bit as involved and took the same or greater risks in the American Revolution as the men.

Abigail Adams wrote the following to her husband, John Adams, affirming that women were as much a force behind the war as men and deserved to be heard.

"In the new Code of Laws which I suppose it will be necessary for you to make I desire you would **Remember the Ladies** . . . we are determined to foment a Rebellion, and will not hold ourselves bound by any Laws in which we have no voice, or Representation."

—Abigail Adams in a letter to John Adams, March 31, 1776

Portrait of Abigail Adams by Benjamin Blyth, c. 1766

Molly Pitcher at the Cannon's Mouth postcard, 1909

Mary Ludwig Hays McCauly carried water to cool off the soldiers and the hot cannon her husband was firing during battles. This earned her the nickname Molly Pitcher. She also worked with her husband to fire the cannon. Other women served in combat during the war. One of them was Margaret Corbin, who is buried and honored with a monument at the United States Military Academy at West Point, New York. The woman in the postcard above represents not just Molly Pitcher but all the brave women who faced combat during the Revolution.

Phillis Wheatley proved the pen could also be a mighty weapon. She was born in Africa, enslaved as a young girl, and sold to a family of Boston Quakers who provided her with a good education. She became a poet who called for freedom for all, praised George Washington, and supported the American Revolution. She was the first African-American poet to have her work published.

Anna Smith Strong was a member of a spy ring on the coast of New York. She used a code based on how she hung out her laundry to let other members of the ring know when a messenger with information was arriving. A black petticoat on her clothesline meant the messenger was coming. The number of handkerchiefs scattered on the line indicated the cove in which he would land.

PLAN

Objective

Discuss the status and contributions of women during the American Revolution.

Critical Thinking Skills for Lesson 2.3

- Identify Main Ideas and Details
- Monitor Comprehension
- Form and Support Opinions
- Draw Conclusions
- Make Inferences
- Evaluate
- Analyze Primary Sources

Essential Question for Chapter 6

What factors helped America win the war?
The American Revolution was not won by battle victories alone. Lesson 2.3 analyzes the roles of women during the war, as well as efforts by women like Abigail Adams to secure political rights.

Background for the Teacher

Women on both sides of the American Revolution acted as spies. Ann Bates, recruited by the British Army for her knowledge of weapons, worked her way into Washington's headquarters. Her reports affected the outcome of the battle at Newport in 1778. Other women spying for the Loyalists were less successful; one spy's incorrect information may have helped bring about the British defeat at Yorktown. On the opposing side, Martha Bratton of North Carolina proudly admitted to sabotaging American ammunition before the British could seize it. Later, she arranged a surprise attack on the British soldiers sleeping in her neighbor's house. The level of secrecy surrounding female spies means that even today we do not know the true identities of many of these women.

Hands Up, Hands Down

Read off the names of each of the women discussed in this chapter. As you read each name, have students raise their hands if they have heard of the person or leave them down if they have not. For each woman, ask students who raise their hands if they can provide any details about her. **ASK:** Are you surprised by how many or how few of these names you recognize? *(Answers will vary depending upon students' prior knowledge.)* Tell students they will be learning about the contributions of women during the American Revolution.

TEACH

Guided Discussion

1. **Make Inferences** Based on what you have read about Adams and Warren, why might women have been eager to support the colonists over the British? *(Answers will vary. Possible response: Many women would have agreed with the ideals of liberty and equality that fueled the Revolution and would hope that if the Americans won, those ideals would also apply to them.)*

2. **Evaluate** In what ways did women during the American Revolution take advantage of their status in society? *(Possible response: Women spies took advantage of their less important status to gather information without looking like a threat. Women like Abigail Adams used their position as wives of leaders to influence policies.)*

Analyze Primary Sources

Have students review the excerpt from Abigail Adams's letter to John Adams. Then have students review the following lines of the Declaration of Independence:

– That to secure these rights, Governments are instituted among Men, deriving their just powers from the consent of the governed, – That whenever any Form of Government becomes destructive of these ends, it is the Right of the People to alter or to abolish it.

Instruct students to pay attention to the statements' tone, content, and purpose. **ASK:** In what ways do both documents express classical liberal principles, such as ideas about freedom and limited government? *(Possible response: Both documents express the importance of having a say in the government and suggest rebellion against a government that does not meet this need.)* **ASK:** In what ways are these documents different? *(Possible response: Adams's letter uses less formal language; she cushions her ideas in phrases such as "I suppose" and "I desire you would." The Declaration, as a legal document, uses less forceful, more formal language: "alter or to abolish" instead of "foment a rebellion.")*

Active Options

On Your Feet: Jigsaw Organize students into three groups, and assign each group one category of women's participation in the American Revolution: writers and organizers; spies; workers on the home front and the battlefield. Have each group study their assigned category and become "experts" on it. Which women performed each role? What were the contributions of each role? What were the risks? Invite students to reorganize into groups of three, with each group containing one "expert" on each category. Have each member present his or her expert knowledge to the group.

NG Learning Framework: Write an Exclusive Interview

ATTITUDE Curiosity

SKILL Communication

Tell students to imagine they have been hired to write profiles and interviews for a magazine feature called "Women of the Revolution." Have each student select and research a woman who contributed to the war effort and use the information to write a profile or interview in which they ask the individual about her experiences. Encourage students to include relevant images, if available. Have students submit their work to a class blog or display them on a bulletin board.

DIFFERENTIATE

Striving Readers

Who's Who Assign pairs of students to make flash cards or review cards for each of the women mentioned in Lesson 2.3. Have students determine what each woman was known for and include key facts and details on one side of the card. Prompt students to choose a visual symbol that represents each woman's contributions to the American Revolution and include this symbol on the other side of the card. Encourage partners to use their cards with each other or trade cards with another pair and use the other pair's cards to review the lesson.

Pre-AP

Compare Across Time: Women at War Have students research American women's participation in war efforts from the Revolution through the present day. Students should then write a brief essay or prepare a short presentation explaining how women's wartime roles have and have not changed over time. Remind students to include relevant images where available.

See the Chapter Planner for more strategies for differentiation.

HISTORICAL THINKING

ANSWERS

1. They kept shops, farms, and businesses running at home. They supported troops through cooking, cleaning, and nursing. Some women participated in battle. Others served as spies. They also wrote and spoke about independence and equal rights.

2. Answers will vary, but they should be supported with evidence from the text. For example, some students may identify Sybil Ludington and other spies because they affected the outcomes of battles. Others may identify Abigail Adams because she influenced leaders like John Adams.

3. Adams asks her husband to ensure that women are given equal rights and a voice in the new government, as the Declaration of Independence sought from the British.

2.4 War at Sea

When you're used to walking on land, it can be hard to adjust to the tossing and swaying of a boat. Some people refer to this as "getting your sea legs." Sailors in the Continental Navy were about to get theirs.

MAIN IDEA The Continental Navy needed teamwork, determination, and strategy as it faced almost impossible odds against Britain's Royal Navy.

ATTACKS ON MERCHANT SHIPS

On land, Americans had the advantage of fighting on familiar terrain, or landforms and other physical features. And even though the British sent great numbers of troops to fight in North America, they were spread out across vast distances, so the Continental Army often faced smaller numbers of British troops at a time. In this way, it was able to hold its own.

The war at sea was a different story. Through the efforts of John Adams, the Continental Congress had established the Continental Navy in 1775, but the navy never had many ships. In contrast, Britain's Royal Navy was the largest and most powerful in the world, capable of causing great damage to the Americans' forces and economy. Even as the American Revolution began, British naval vessels had blockaded American harbors. Now they were attacking both American naval and merchant ships. The tiny Continental Navy could not hope to match its enemy's strength and resources.

Quickly building up and supporting a naval fleet was much more difficult than recruiting troops for land conflict. However, Benjamin Franklin's visit to France paid off. The French and Spanish navies helped swell the ranks of the Continental Navy.

Americans also turned to privateers—privately owned ships authorized to participate in warfare—to help protect their own shipping industry and damage Britain's. The Continental Congress granted privateers official permission to attack any British naval and merchant ships they encountered. During the war, as many as 2,000 vessels were put into use for privateering.

Privateer crews included a number of African-American sailors, both enslaved and free. Slave catchers rarely tried to capture runaway slaves who had stowed away on a ship. And the pay onboard was good, even though all privateer sailors worked in dangerous conditions. In fact, they were often captured and taken as prisoners of war.

Teenage African-American crewmember **James Forten** was taken aboard a British ship when it captured his vessel, the *Royal Louis*. The British captain assigned Forten to care for his young son, and the two became fast friends. As a result, the

Calling All Able Sailors
This handbill advertised for experienced sailors to sail with the *Washington*, a vessel that went on to capture several enemy ships.

The Ordeal of John Paul Jones
Illustrator Anton Otto Fischer captures the drama on the *Bonhomme Richard* as John Paul Jones (background, right) and his crew fight to keep sailors on the British ship *Serapis* from boarding their ship. About 150 people were killed on each side in this battle.

captain's son asked his father to grant Forten his freedom instead of turning him over to a prison ship. The captain offered Forten a chance to return to Britain with them, but Forten refused. He believed in the principles of the American Revolution, especially the natural rights of freedom and the opportunity for democracy.

JOHN PAUL JONES

What the Continental Navy lacked in ships it made up for in determination, strategy, and sheer heroism. One American captain, **John Paul Jones**, had all three of these strengths. In September 1779, Jones was in command of a ship called the *Bonhomme Richard* when he encountered the British ship *Serapis*. The *Serapis* was escorting British merchant ships carrying military supplies. Jones attacked the *Serapis*, and the battle was on.

Disaster struck for the American ship when its main gun battery exploded. Soon after, the *Bonhomme Richard* caught fire and was damaged beyond repair. Legend has it that with both ships fighting side by side, the British called on Jones to surrender. But he yelled back, "I have not yet begun to fight!" The battle raged on, and soon it fell to the British to surrender. Jones boarded and took control of the *Serapis*. In a war with few victories for the Continental Navy, Jones's success boosted American morale as the conflict moved into its final stage.

HISTORICAL THINKING

1. **READING CHECK** How was the Continental Navy able to hold its own against Britain's Royal Navy?

2. **ANALYZE CAUSE AND EFFECT** How were France and Spain affected by the war at sea?

3. **MAKE INFERENCES** What do you think James Forten hoped to gain by fighting to uphold the American principles of freedom?

PLAN

Objective
Explain the strategies and alliances that helped the Continental Navy win critical naval battles.

Critical Thinking Skills for Lesson 2.4
- Identify Main Ideas and Details
- Monitor Comprehension
- Analyze Cause and Effect
- Make Inferences
- Draw Conclusions
- Make Connections
- Analyze Visuals

Essential Question for Chapter 6
What factors helped America win the war?
Lesson 2.4 demonstrates how allies, privateers, and smart leadership helped the Continental Navy hold its own against Britain's powerful Royal Navy.

Background for the Teacher
As students may have inferred from the name, the *Bonhomme Richard* was a gift from France. Unfortunately, although John Paul Jones went on to fame and honor, the *Bonhomme Richard* did not. The ship sank shortly after its famous battle with the *Serapis*. Since then, two other ships in the U.S. Navy have been named after the *Bonhomme Richard* in honor of Jones's great victory. The first, launched in 1944, saw service in three wars: WWII, the Korean War, and the Vietnam War. The second was christened in 1997. Since 2005, the U.S. Navy and many other research organizations have led several expeditions to locate the original *Bonhomme Richard*, using manned and unmanned vehicles, sonar, and divers. So far, however, these efforts have been unsuccessful.

Consider Challenges and Advantages

Remind students that the American Revolution took place not only on land but also at sea. **ASK:** What challenges would sea battles pose that land battles would not? *(Answers will vary. Possible responses: Ships can sink, endangering all of the sailors. It might be impossible to call for help. Reinforcements and supplies would take longer to arrive.)* **ASK:** What are some advantages of fighting at sea? *(Possible responses: You might have only one or two targets rather than a large, spread-out fighting force. Ships could move faster than soldiers on the ground.)* Tell students that in this lesson they will be learning about some of the challenges the new Continental Navy faced in its battles against the British.

TEACH

Guided Discussion

1. **Draw Conclusions** Based on what you have read in this lesson, what two things were the British trying to accomplish with their naval actions against the Americans? *(The British Royal Navy wanted to defeat the Continental Navy and its allies while also weakening the Americans' economy by denying them access to trade and supplies.)*

2. **Make Connections** The text describes the actions of James Forten as upholding the principles of the American Revolution. In what ways did John Paul Jones do the same? *(Answers will vary. Some students might point to his determination in the battle with the* Serapis.*)*

Analyze Visuals

Have students examine the illustration of the *Bonhomme Richard* during its battle with the *Serapis*. **ASK:** What details stand out most to you in this illustration? *(Answers will vary. Possible response: The ships are very close, and the sailors on the* Bonhomme Richard *seem to be fighting using their own fallen sails.)* Then have students determine which figure represents John Paul Jones. **ASK:** What do you notice about the artist's depiction of Jones? *(Answers will vary. Possible response: He shows Jones standing above the chaos and the crowd, wearing full dress uniform, and making a dramatic, commanding gesture; it seems to show him as a distinctive, heroic figure.)*

Active Options

On Your Feet: History Relay Give students time to formulate at least one question about the material in Lesson 2.4. Then have them form two lines, taking their questions with them. Invite students to take turns posing their questions to the other team. If the other team answers correctly, the asker must switch sides. If the other team answers incorrectly, the answerer must switch sides. Have students continue until time is up, or all students have asked a question. The team with the most students at the end of the game wins.

NG Learning Framework: Learn More About Naval Battles

SKILL Collaboration

KNOWLEDGE Our Human Story

Tell students to work in teams to learn more about the naval battles during the American Revolution. Students should use library or online sources to conduct their research. Encourage students to consider the following questions as they research:

• What sizes and types of ships fought these battles?

• What kinds of weaponry did the ships use? Did sailors also carry weapons?

• How did battles begin, and how were they fought? What signaled a victory?

Have students use relevant, verifiable information to prepare a short presentation for the class on one or more elements of naval battles of the American Revolution.

Inclusion

Visual Partners Pair visually impaired students with sighted students to interpret the illustration and poster that accompany this lesson. Make sure the pairs explain the events and individuals shown in the illustration of the *Bonhomme Richard*. Remind partners to discuss the important details given by the recruitment poster: the name of the ship and captain *(the* Washington, *captained by John Dyson),* the job for which it is advertising *(crew on a privateer),* and what it promises to sailors *(they will "make their fortunes in a few months").*

Gifted & Talented

Write a Documentary Script Remind students of the philosophy of civic republicanism, which calls on people to put the common good ahead of their own self-interest. Have students use the information in Lesson 2.4 and additional research online to write a script for a five-minute documentary about how people such as the privateers, James Forten, and John Paul Jones exemplified civic republicanism by putting the goals of the American Revolution ahead of their own safety and gain. Have students present their scripts to the class, casting classmates as historical figures or expert "talking heads."

See the Chapter Planner for more strategies for differentiation.

HISTORICAL THINKING

ANSWERS

1. The Continental Navy had the support of the French and Spanish navies, and they enlisted privateers into the naval effort. American naval leaders such as John Paul Jones also made up for the lack of ships with determination and strategy.

2. Because of Ben Franklin's visit to Europe, France and Spain sent ships to help the small Continental Navy fight the war at sea.

3. Forten may have hoped that if the colonies won their freedom from Britain, all Americans, even the enslaved, would also be granted their freedom.

3.1 War in the Southern Colonies

When you're losing a game, sometimes it helps to change your strategy. That's what the British decided to do. But would moving the war south help or hurt them?

MAIN IDEA At first, southern battles went badly for the Continental Army, but the Patriots soon found ways to torment the British.

EARLY LOSSES

The British deployed a new strategy in the Southern Colonies in 1778. They counted on Loyalist and African-American support in Georgia, the Carolinas, and Virginia. They used the islands of the British West Indies to gather and transport supplies and recruits for the British and their allies.

But French-held territory in the Caribbean provided aid to the Continental Army's southern campaign. The French Colonial Army recruited many soldiers for the American cause from its islands, such as Saint-Domingue (san dom-ANG), or present-day Haiti. Their numbers included enslaved men willing to fight against the British.

Enslaved African Americans in the Southern Colonies were also recruited to fight for the British. General Henry Clinton offered freedom to enslaved men who joined the British Army. As a result, African-American support for the British grew in the Southern Colonies.

In 1778, Clinton sent thousands of troops to Georgia. There they captured Savannah and Augusta, followed by Charleston, South Carolina. In an effort to combat the British onslaught, in July 1780, American general Horatio Gates arrived to build a new southern army. But Gates failed to prepare these troops properly for battle. **Lord Cornwallis**, the British commander, had learned of Gates's movements and attacked the Americans at Camden, South Carolina. The British scored an overwhelming victory that spelled disaster for the Continental Army and disgrace for Gates.

THE SWAMP FOX

While the Continental Army suffered major losses in the South, nontraditional military units strengthened the American cause. **Guerrilla** units, or independent military groups that used methods such as sneak attacks, thrived in the rural wetlands of the American Southeast. South Carolina officer **Francis Marion** and his small group of guerrillas harassed British troops through the swamps of Georgia and the Carolinas. Because he was so clever and good at dodging the British, Marion soon earned the nickname "the Swamp Fox."

Marion had once been a regular soldier fighting for the Patriots. But General Gates dismissed him before the disastrous Battle of Camden to focus on defending other territories. Marion soon discovered his genius for guerrilla warfare—conducting surprise attacks on the British, gathering intelligence about the enemy, and winning the loyalty of local people. Despite the many early American defeats in the Southern Colonies, guerilla leaders such as Marion caused enough trouble for the British to keep the United States competitive—and, eventually, on the path to victory.

HISTORICAL THINKING

1. **READING CHECK** What early wins did the British score in the Southern Colonies?

2. **IDENTIFY MAIN IDEAS AND DETAILS** What role did France play in the war in the Southern Colonies?

3. **DRAW CONCLUSIONS** What characteristics of a fox did Francis Marion demonstrate as a guerrilla leader?

CRITICAL VIEWING In 1780, Francis Marion lured a British force 26 miles into the heart of a South Carolina swamp. Will Anderson illustrated this episode in a mural he painted in 2001. Why do you think the British (on horseback) might have had a difficult time fighting on the Swamp Fox's terms?

PLAN

Objective
Explain how the Continental Army defended against the British in the Southern Colonies.

Critical Thinking Skills for Lesson 3.1
- Identify Main Ideas and Details
- Monitor Comprehension
- Draw Conclusions
- Compare and Contrast
- Analyze Cause and Effect

Essential Question for Chapter 6
What factors helped America win the war?
Lesson 3.1 examines how nontraditional guerrilla fighters and support from French Caribbean territories helped the Continental Army endure despite military losses in the Southern Colonies.

Background for the Teacher
In the early years of the war, many African Americans who supported the Patriots found themselves turned away from the Continental Army, even as it struggled to recruit soldiers. Beginning in 1777, the Continental Army and state militias began to permit free African-American men, and later still, enslaved men, to join. Ultimately, approximately 5,000 African Americans served in some capacity. The majority of them came from northern states and served in integrated forces. Following the war, several New England states began passing laws to end the practice of slavery; however, slavery in the South became more entrenched than ever, and free African Americans in all regions faced substantial discrimination.

INTRODUCE & ENGAGE

Activate Prior Knowledge

Write the vocabulary word *guerrilla* on the board. **ASK:** What things or ideas do you associate with this word? *(Answers will vary. Possible responses: war, fighting, secrecy, sneak attacks, unofficial fighters)* Then draw students' attention to the mural shown in Lesson 3.1. **ASK:** What elements of this image fit your understanding of the term *guerrilla*? *(the soldiers hiding behind trees, the soldier in clothing that blends in with the surroundings)* Explain that students will encounter this word often when reading about warfare and other conflicts.

TEACH

Guided Discussion

1. **Compare and Contrast** How did African Americans' reasons for joining the French Colonial Army compare with their reasons for joining the British Army? *(African Americans in the French territories were willing to join up because the French opposed the British; enslaved African Americans in the Southern Colonies joined up with the British because they were promised their freedom.)*

2. **Analyze Cause and Effect** How did Francis Marion become a guerrilla fighter in the American Revolution? *(He had fought as a regular soldier under General Gates, but Gates sent him away to lead a small group of fighters against the British.)*

Draw Conclusions

Ask students to identify the problems faced by American military leaders such as General Gates. *(Answers will vary. Possible responses: difficulty recruiting enough soldiers, poor training of soldiers, better equipped and trained British enemy)* Display students' responses on the board. Then have students review the section describing Francis Marion, the "Swamp Fox." **ASK:** Why was Marion able to avoid the problems the Continental Army faced in the Southern Colonies? *(Answers will vary. Possible responses: He had been a member of the Continental Army, so he knew firsthand why things were not working. He did not have to worry about running a "traditional" army.)* **ASK:** Why was the success of guerrilla groups like Marion's an effective contribution to the American war effort? *(Answers will vary. Possible response: The guerrillas distracted and caused trouble for the British while keeping local people loyal to the American cause even when the Continental Army was struggling.)*

Active Options

On Your Feet: Turn and Talk on Topic Have students form three lines, and give each line the same topic sentence: *The British strategy in the Southern Colonies depended on the support of Loyalists and African Americans in the area.* Direct each student in the line to add one sentence to this topic sentence, forming a paragraph. Then have each group share its paragraph with the class.

NG Learning Framework: Analyze Battle Tactics

ATTITUDE Curiosity

KNOWLEDGE Our Human Story

To extend knowledge about battle tactics, encourage students to conduct research using online or library sources about battle tactics used during the American Revolution. Questions to consider while they research might include: How were soldiers supposed to behave in battle? How did armies use the environment to their advantage? How are Revolutionary military battle tactics similar to and different from modern ones? Tell students to use the information they gather to prepare a short class presentation. Alternatively, students could provide written analyses that could be posted in the classroom or on a class blog.

DIFFERENTIATE

English Language Learners

Clarify Word Meaning Ensure that students understand the meaning of the word *guerrilla* as it is used in Lesson 3.1. Explain that *guerrilla* comes from the Spanish word *guerra*, meaning "war," and prompt students to explain what this suggests about the meaning of *guerrilla*. Remind students that when they encounter an unfamiliar word, they can use context, root words, or a dictionary to determine the meaning. Then have students use *guerrilla* in a sentence. You may want to provide sentence stems for students at the **Emerging** level.

Pre-AP

Write an Editorial Present students with the following question: In wartime, are guerrilla tactics just or unjust? Have students write an editorial from the perspective of an American or British soldier during the American Revolution. Students should take a position on this question and support their argument using evidence from the lesson. Encourage students to conduct research using online or library sources to strengthen their arguments. Invite students to share their editorials with the class.

See the Chapter Planner for more strategies for differentiation.

HISTORICAL THINKING

ANSWERS

1. The British achieved early wins in Augusta, Savannah, Charleston, and Camden.

2. France recruited soldiers from its Caribbean colonies to help the Americans fight the British.

3. Answers will vary. Possible response: As a guerrilla leader, Francis Marion demonstrated cleverness, skill at hiding from his enemy, and an ability to use his environment to his advantage, all characteristics associated with foxes.

CRITICAL VIEWING Answers will vary. Possible responses: The horses would have a difficult time navigating swamp terrain. The British, arranged in a large, orderly group, make a big, visible target for Marion's fighters. Also, they might not have been expecting the American fighters to hide or camouflage themselves.

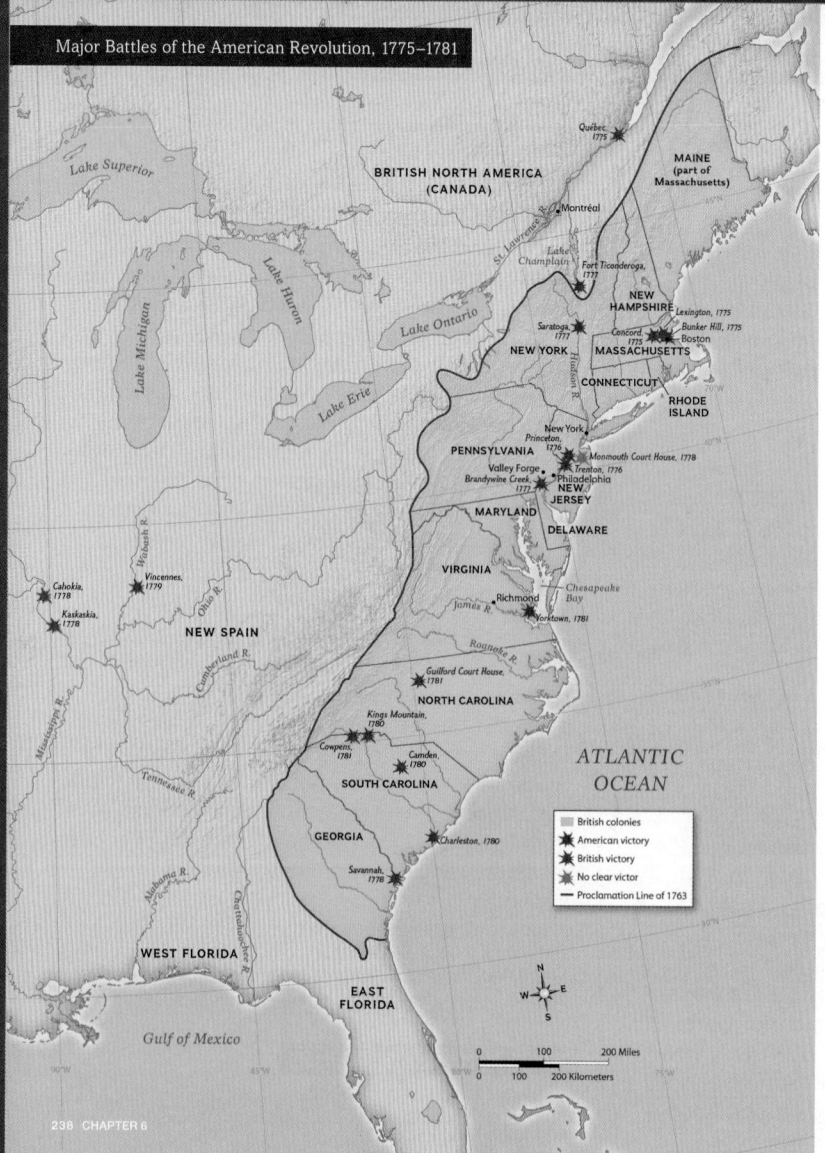

BRITISH NORTH AMERICA
(CANADA)

MAINE
(part of
Massachusetts)

Québec,
1775

Montréal

Lake Superior

Lake Huron

Lake Michigan

Lake Erie

Lake Ontario

Lake Champlain

St. Lawrence R.

Fort Ticonderoga,
1777

NEW
HAMPSHIRE

Lexington, 1775
Concord, 1775
Bunker Hill, 1775
Boston

Saratoga,
1777

MASSACHUSETTS

NEW YORK

CONNECTICUT

RHODE
ISLAND

New York,
1776

Princeton,
1776

PENNSYLVANIA

Monmouth Court House, 1778

Valley Forge
Brandywine Creek,
1777

Trenton, 1776
Philadelphia

NEW
JERSEY

MARYLAND

DELAWARE

VIRGINIA

Chesapeake
Bay

Richmond

Yorktown, 1781

James R.

Cahokia,
1778

Vincennes,
1779

Ohio R.

Kaskaskia,
1778

NEW SPAIN

Cumberland R.

Tennessee R.

Roanoke R.

Guilford Court House,
1781

NORTH CAROLINA

Kings Mountain,
1780

Cowpens,
1781

Camden,
1780

SOUTH CAROLINA

ATLANTIC
OCEAN

GEORGIA

Charleston, 1780

Savannah,
1778

Alabama R.

Chattahoochee R.

WEST FLORIDA

EAST
FLORIDA

Gulf of Mexico

British colonies
★ American victory
★ British victory
★ No clear victor
— Proclamation Line of 1763

0   100   200 Miles
0   100   200 Kilometers

N W E S

238 CHAPTER 6

3.2 The Tide Turns

Sometimes a new leader brings new energy and ideas to a situation and makes all the difference. That's just what happened when a new commander was brought in to lead the southern troops.

MAIN IDEA A change in leadership and a victory in the Carolinas helped change the course of the war in the Southern Colonies.

A NEW GENERAL

The tide of the war in the Southern Colonies began to turn in 1780. That's when General **Nathanael Greene** replaced Horatio Gates as commander of the Continental Army's southern troops. As a Quaker, Greene should have been a **pacifist**, or a person who stood against war and violence. So when Greene expressed his desire to organize troops against the British, the Quakers expelled him. After serving with Washington and leading troops in New York, New Jersey, and Pennsylvania, Greene was sent to the Southern Colonies to try to change the direction of the war for the Americans.

Greene's strategy involved increasing the Continental Army's mobility and agility. Spread out over the Southern Colonies, the large British Army had trouble moving quickly and changing plans. Greene used smaller forces to draw British troops away from strategic locations. He also benefited from a growing southern dislike of the British, whose troops and supporters had destroyed local houses and farms, executed prisoners of war, and made false promises of protection. Greene impressed southern colonists, including Loyalists, by protecting their property and enforcing order. Growing numbers in the Southern Colonies joined Greene's army or guerrilla forces.

PATRIOTS AND LOYALISTS CLASH

While the Americans changed their strategy, the British did not. British strategy in the Southern Colonies depended heavily on Loyalist support. The British relied on pitting American Loyalists and Patriots against each other, with little British troop involvement. That strategy failed at the **Battle of Kings Mountain**.

In the fall of 1780, Lord Cornwallis headed north from South Carolina, believing the time had come for British forces to conquer all the Southern Colonies. His troops met with heavy resistance. At Kings Mountain, near the border between the Carolinas, 2,000 Patriots, fighting independently from the Continental Army, clashed with an enemy force made up almost entirely of other Americans. These frontier Patriots dealt a resounding defeat to 1,100 Loyalist soldiers fighting under Major Patrick Ferguson, the only British Army member at the battle. Patriot fighters put to death some Loyalists who surrendered, perhaps as revenge for recent British executions of American prisoners.

The Battle of Kings Mountain was the first of many victories for the Patriots in the Southern Colonies. Loyalists sustained big losses at Cowpens in South Carolina, and Cornwallis and his troops suffered casualties at Guildford Court House in North Carolina. As a result, Cornwallis headed back toward Virginia. Because of the importance of the Battle of Kings Mountain, Thomas Jefferson called it "the turn of the tide of success."

HISTORICAL THINKING

1. **READING CHECK** How did Nathanael Greene's leadership affect the war in the Southern Colonies?

2. **INTERPRET MAPS** Why might frontiersmen have fought the Battle of Kings Mountain?

3. **SUMMARIZE** Why did Cornwallis's plan to control the Southern Colonies by enlisting the aid of Loyalists fail?

Objective

Analyze how a change in leadership and strategy turned the tide for the Americans.

Critical Thinking Skills for Lesson 3.2

- Identify Main Ideas and Details
- Monitor Comprehension
- Interpret Maps
- Summarize
- Compare and Contrast
- Make Connections
- Identify Problems and Solutions

Essential Question for Chapter 6

What factors helped America win the war?
Lesson 3.2 discusses how a change in leadership and strategy helped the Americans win important battles and gain momentum toward overall victory.

Background for the Teacher

Although the battle at Guilford Courthouse drove Lord Cornwallis back toward Virginia, the battle actually ended in victory for the British. Greene retreated first, but the British had lost over a quarter of their soldiers in the battle, while the Americans had relatively few casualties. Moreover, in their haste to fight Greene, the British had abandoned many of their supplies, and after the battle they were forced to withdraw as well. Cornwallis would later report that the Americans "fought like demons."

INTRODUCE & ENGAGE

Preview with Maps

Point out the map and its key in this lesson. Ensure that students understand how the map indicates battles and victories. Draw students' attention to the battles' dates. Tell them to locate the battles discussed in Lesson 3.1: Savannah, Charleston, and Camden. **ASK:** Based on this map, in which direction did the British troops move? *(They moved north and west.)* **ASK:** What do you notice about the southern battles that followed Camden? *(The Americans have two victories in battles following Camden, contrasting with none before.)* Have students combine the map and the lesson title to make a prediction about the lesson.

TEACH

Guided Discussion

1. **Compare and Contrast** How did British and American treatment of colonists in the Southern Colonies differ? *(The British destroyed the colonists' farms and executed prisoners. Under Greene, the Americans protected the colonists' property and enforced order, even for Loyalists.)*

2. **Make Connections** Recall that before the American Revolution began, colonists had resented the behavior of British troops stationed in the colonies after the French and Indian War. In what ways was the situation in the Southern Colonies during the American Revolution similar? *(In the Southern Colonies, the British Army destroyed property, executed prisoners, and broke promises. In both cases, the actions of British troops made formerly loyal people unhappy enough to support the other side.)*

More Information

Quakers and the American Revolution The Society of Friends, also known as the Quakers, is a religious group founded in England in the 17th century. From its earliest days, the Society has opposed fighting and warfare. In the years leading up to the American Revolution, the Quakers, like other colonists, protested British taxation and boycotted British goods. As Britain and and its American colonies grew closer to war, though, the Quakers hoped for reconciliation with Britain. While the official Quaker stance was neutrality, in reality, some sided with the Patriots and others with the Loyalists. Some, like Nathanael Greene, took up arms against Britain and were no longer welcome in the group. In Pennsylvania, several hundred Quakers were disowned for this reason.

Active Options

On Your Feet: Think, Pair, Share Have students use the Think, Pair, Share strategy to consider the major turning points in the war. Ask them to form pairs and discuss in detail why battles such as Saratoga and Kings Mountain were turning points. Students should identify how these battles differed from others and what their outcomes were. Then have one student from each pair present his or her conclusions to the class.

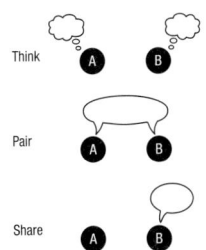

Think   A   B

Pair   A   B

Share   A   B

NG Learning Framework: Take a Stand

ATTITUDE Empowerment

SKILL Communication

Point out that individual Americans looked at the American Revolution from a variety of different perspectives. Divide the class into pairs and have each pair choose one of these debates: pacifism versus support for war or Patriot versus Loyalist. Instruct the partners to take opposing sides, and have each partner write a persuasive speech defending his or her stance. Encourage partners to share their speeches with the class.

DIFFERENTIATE

Striving Readers

Summarize As students read Lesson 3.2, have them pause at the end of each paragraph to write a brief summary of it. Students could also work in pairs or groups, summarizing paragraphs together or dividing the paragraphs among group members. Summaries should identify the main idea and one or two important supporting details. Work with students, or have students work in pairs, to check their summaries and revise if necessary.

Inclusion

Describe Maps Pair visually challenged students with students who are not. Invite the latter to ask and answer questions that will confirm and strengthen their partner's understanding of how the dates and locations of American victories on the battle map show an overall shift in the course of the war. Work with pairs to answer questions about the map.

See the Chapter Planner for more strategies for differentiation.

HISTORICAL THINKING

ANSWERS

1. Greene used a strategy that depended on smaller groups of American soldiers being able to move quickly in order to force British troops away from important locations. This led to Americans starting to win battles in the South.

2. Kings Mountain, on the border between North and South Carolina, near the colonies' western frontier, may have been difficult for the official Continental Army to reach. Frontiersmen would have lived nearby and been familiar with the territory.

3. Answers will vary. Possible response: Cornwallis's strategy failed because the Loyalist forces were mostly unable to defeat the Patriots in critical battles. Loyalists were outnumbered in the Battle of Kings Mountain and took heavy losses at Cowpens. Also, many Loyalists in the Southern Colonies withdrew their support due to the harsh actions of British troops.

3.3 The War Ends

How often does winning against impossible odds happen in real life?

When that first shot was fired in Lexington, no one could have predicted that 13 small colonies would defeat one of the world's greatest armies.

MAIN IDEA The British defeat at the Battle of Yorktown brought an end to the American Revolution.

A PIVOTAL YEAR

As you've read, British hopes for victory in the South began to fade after their defeat at Kings Mountain. In 1781, American general Nathanael Greene moved south to regain South Carolina and Georgia, where the British still had 8,000 men spread thinly throughout the large region. Greene's 1,500 Continental soldiers and the guerilla units helping them were able to defeat small groups one by one. Americans were able to take back most of the area. Meanwhile, in Virginia, Lord Cornwallis replaced

Benedict Arnold as commander of the British forces in the area. In Yorktown, with an army of almost 8,000 men, Cornwallis camped on a peninsula facing the York River. His aim was to protect the harbor for the use of the British fleet. Cornwallis requested more troops from New York, but the British were slow in sending them.

U.S. Capitol Rotunda, Washington, D.C.

John Trumbull's painting *Surrender of Lord Cornwallis* depicts the British surrender in Yorktown. In the painting, American troops (on the right) and French troops (on the left) are all on horseback. Cornwallis's soldiers appear in the center of the painting. Why do you think the British soldiers are all on foot?

Setting up camp on the peninsula would prove to be a fatal mistake for Lord Cornwallis and his soldiers.

THE WORLD TURNED UPSIDE DOWN

American and French troops surrounded Cornwallis's camp by land and by sea. French naval officer admiral Comte de Grasse (duh-GRAHS) commanded a French fleet on the York River. He approached the British camp from the water. Meanwhile, a combined army of French soldiers, commanded by Comte de Rochambeau (ROH-sham-BOH), and Americans, led by General George Washington, marched south from New York, approaching the camp by land. In a show of military **expertise**, or skill, these three commanders led their 17,000 troops against Cornwallis, trapping him on the peninsula. Cornwallis had no choice but to surrender.

Charles O'Hara, second in command to Cornwallis, tried to surrender his general's sword to Rochambeau, but the French leader steered him to Washington instead. The British military band played a song called "The World Turned Upside Down," a fitting comment on the victory. The **Battle of Yorktown** was the last major battle of the war. In 1782, more than six years after the first shots were fired, the British Parliament officially voted to end the war.

The impact of this victory was staggering. Once only the dream of a group of visionaries seeking freedom from unreasonable laws and taxes, the young country had come through the fire of war to take its place as a full-fledged nation. In the decades and centuries that followed, the United States of America—established with the promise of equality for all—would rise to become one of the most powerful and influential nations on Earth. In time, people in many countries around the world would draw inspiration from America's example and fight for their own freedom and independence.

Remembering the Victors

This stamp commemorates the 150th anniversary of the victory at Yorktown. We all know George Washington, who is shown in the middle, but what about the other two leaders who helped the Americans win at Yorktown?

Comte de Rochambeau (on the left), was born in Vendôme, France. Commissioned into the French army at age 17, he was a veteran of 14 military sieges in Europe. King Louis XVI sent him to lead the French force in America in 1780.

Comte de Grasse (on the right), was born in Le Bar, France, and started working on ships when he was only about 12 years old. At 18, he joined the French navy. DeGrasse was fighting the British in the West Indies when General Washington asked for his help in Virginia against Cornwallis. The rest is history.

HISTORICAL THINKING

1. **READING CHECK** What factors led to the American victory at Yorktown?

2. **DRAW CONCLUSIONS** What statement was Rochambeau making when he made O'Hara surrender the British general's sword to Washington?

3. **ANALYZE CAUSE AND EFFECT** What happened as a result of the American victory in both the long- and short-term?

PLAN

Objective

Analyze the American victory in the Battle of Yorktown and its effects on the war.

Critical Thinking Skills for Lesson 3.3

- Identify Main Ideas and Details
- Monitor Comprehension
- Draw Conclusions
- Analyze Cause and Effect
- Make Connections

Essential Question for Chapter 6

What factors helped America win the war? To protect the harbor at Yorktown, British commander Lord Cornwallis camped his army on a peninsula there. Lesson 3.3 analyzes how this decision allowed American and French forces to surround him completely, forcing his surrender and, shortly afterward, the end of the war.

Background for the Teacher

It might seem as though losing a multiyear war and 13 of your nation's colonies would be enough to ruin any career. Lord Cornwallis, however, went on to achieve significant success after his defeat at Yorktown. As the governor-general of India, he worked to bring an end to widespread corruption among British officials, a process he would repeat some five years later as viceroy of Ireland. Although not all of his reforms in India proved successful, the British government honored him with the title of marquess for his work there. In 1805, he returned to India as governor-general again but died before he could resume his work.

INTRODUCE & ENGAGE

Discuss Rituals of Victory and Surrender

Ask students to describe any celebrations or ceremonies they may have seen or participated in that marked a victory or a surrender. For example, students may have attended a sports awards banquet or seen a parade honoring a winning team; they may be familiar with political concession speeches. **ASK:** How might the victors celebrate when a war ends? How might the losers formalize their surrender? Then tell students they will learn about how people marked victory and surrender after the American Revolution.

TEACH

Guided Discussion

1. **Make Connections** View the image of the stamp celebrating the 150th anniversary of the Battle of Yorktown. Given what you have read about the French military's role in this battle, why might it be important that the three portraits are the same size? *(Having all three portraits the same size suggests that the French contributions to the battle were just as important to victory as George Washington's, and the French deserve credit.)*

2. **Draw Conclusions** Why do you think the British chose to play the song they did during O'Hara's surrender to Washington? *(The British had one of the most powerful armies in the world, and for them to be defeated by a small, new nation was as surprising as the world turning upside down.)*

🏛 Virtual Museum Visit

Visitors to the U.S. Capitol Building in Washington, D.C., are sure to notice the Capitol Rotunda with its enormous dome towering above the building's center. The Rotunda, which is often used for ceremonies and other important events, also houses works of art honoring important people, places, and events in American history. In addition to Trumbull's *Surrender of Lord Cornwallis*, artwork on permanent display in the Rotunda includes three other iconic Trumbull paintings and an elaborate frieze—a horizontal band of paintings that decorates a wall—depicting important periods in American history. Have students access the Architect of the Capitol website, where they can view the Rotunda paintings as well as art displayed throughout the Capitol. Have students select a work of art and present it to the class, explaining how it is connected to U.S. history.

Active Options

On Your Feet: Word Chain Arrange students in three lines. Hand a piece of paper to the first person in each line with one of these names or terms: *Lord Cornwallis, Yorktown, expertise*. The first student in line adds a word that relates to the original word or term. Students pass the paper down the line, each adding a word or phrase they associate with the previously written word. Have a volunteer from each group read the Word Chain, and ask the class to listen for any words that were used in more than one. Discuss the associations between words as well as any words that do not seem to connect correctly. Use the discussion to monitor students' comprehension of Lesson 3.3.

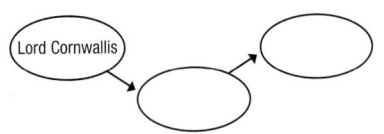

NG Learning Framework: Explore the Art of the Revolution

SKILLS Collaboration, Observation

KNOWLEDGE Our Human Story

Have students work in small teams to identify and research other works of art that portray events of the American Revolution. Each team should prepare a short presentation on one work. Presentations should identify the artist, the event portrayed, and why the event was significant. Students should also work to identify similar elements—themes, colors, styles—between their chosen image and the painting of Cornwallis's surrender.

DIFFERENTIATE

English Language Learners [ELD]

Interpret Multiple Meaning Words Point out to students at **All Proficiencies** the word *staggering* in the lesson's concluding paragraph. Explain that the word has two different, though related, meanings: When used as an intransitive verb, *staggering* means "to move in an unsteady way." When used as an adjective, it means "very shocking or overwhelming." **ASK:** Which meaning do you think the word *staggering* has in the lesson? *(very shocking or overwhelming)* Have students explain why this definition applies.

Gifted & Talented

Make a Short Film Have students work together to make a short film about the Battle of Yorktown, researching to find additional information as necessary. They could choose to create a documentary, incorporating maps and historical drawings or paintings. Alternatively, they could create a narrative script with dialogue, act it out, and film it. Have students show their finished film to the class.

See the Chapter Planner for more strategies for differentiation.

HISTORICAL THINKING

ANSWERS

1. Cornwallis and his troops camped on a peninsula, a mistake that allowed American and French forces to surround them. The British were slow in sending additional troops. The French and American forces amassed a large army and fleet of ships that trapped Cornwallis and his troops.

2. Answers will vary. Possible response: Rochambeau was showing respect for Washington and making it clear that the victory belonged to the American people, not the French.

3. In the short term, the colonies gained their independence. In the long term, the nation rose to become one of the most powerful countries in the world.

VIRTUAL MUSEUM VISIT

Answers will vary. Some students may suggest that the British are on foot to symbolize their defeat. Others may suggest that it is a safety precaution—they cannot launch a surprise attack if they are on foot and unarmed.

3.4 An Ally in the American Victory

MAIN IDEA The physical and human characteristics, as well as the "site" and "situation," of locations have helped shape events in history.

In 1776, no one in the world believed the American colonists could defeat the mighty British Army. Yet throughout history, geography has affected how events have unfolded, and this was certainly the case during the American Revolution. The Continental Army had several types of geographic advantages: terrain, population distribution, distance, and climate. For example, the Continental Army spent the winter of 1777–78 at Valley Forge in Pennsylvania. The climate there was cold—and the cold shaped events. As you know, the soldiers suffered greatly from a lack of sufficient clothing and shelter. Yet the bad weather prevented the British from attacking them.

Study these examples of the geographic advantages that favored the Continental Army. Consider the information provided about each site—the physical characteristics of the example given. Then consider the situation or the location of each site in relation to other places.

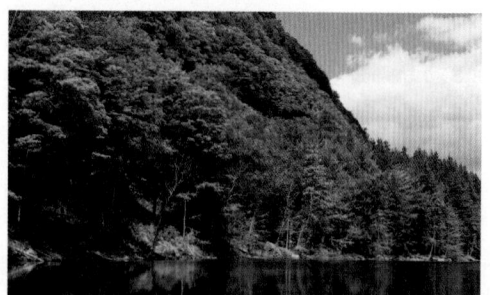

The Catskill Mountains in New York State are covered with thick forests that provided cover for the Continental Army and challenges for the British as they approached.

European Claims in North America, 1776

unexplored

BRITISH CLAIM

SPANISH CLAIM

AMERICAN COLONIES

West Florida

East Florida

TERRAIN

SITE The terrain of upstate New York is mountainous and heavily forested, with many rivers and streams.

SITUATION The Americans were familiar with the terrain, which gave them an enormous advantage. For example, in 1777, British troops marched from Canada toward New York to attack the Continental Army. Americans cut down trees and wrecked bridges, slowing down British troops. This gave the Americans time to gather more than 11,000 troops at Saratoga, where they defeated the British.

The Original Thirteen Colonies, 1776

40,000 people
population of Philadelphia in 1776

1,580 miles
from northern border of Maine to southern border of Georgia

POPULATION DISTRIBUTION

SITE The area of the colonies was large, but the population was relatively small—about 2.5 million people. Cities were also small, as most people lived on farms, so the population was widely scattered.

SITUATION The population was so widely distributed that the British couldn't simply attack one or two cities to defeat the Americans. In addition, the Continental Army could hide from British troops in unpopulated territory.

COLONIAL POPULATION, 1776

Philadelphia, PA	40,000
New York, NY	25,000
Boston, MA	15,000
Charleston, SC	12,000
Newport, RI	11,000

Source: *The Economist*

97 miles
from New York City to Philadelphia

370 miles
from New York City to Fort Pitt

3,460 miles
from London, England, to New York City

763 miles
from New York City to Charleston

DISTANCE

SITE The colonies stretched more than 1,500 miles from north to south and more than 350 miles from east to west.

SITUATION The 13 colonies were located more than 3,000 miles from Great Britain. The distance created enormous problems for the British. They had to transport soldiers, supplies, and munitions by sailing ships. When the troops reached North America, they took weeks to march from one field of combat to another.

CLIMATE

SITE The British were not used to the cold winters of the northern states. The heat and humidity of the southern states were unfamiliar to the British, too.

SITUATION The Americans used their knowledge of the climate during the war. In the winter of 1775, Washington wanted artillery transported from New York to Boston. Colonel Henry Knox used 42 sleds pulled by oxen to transport the artillery over snow and ice. The Americans used the weapons to drive the British out of Boston.

THINK LIKE A GEOGRAPHER

1. **IDENTIFY MAIN IDEAS AND DETAILS** Why did distance pose problems for British troops during the American Revolution?

2. **ANALYZE CAUSE AND EFFECT** How did the Americans use geography to gain an advantage over the British?

3. **FORM AND SUPPORT OPINIONS** Of the four geographic factors, which one do you think had the greatest impact on the war? Explain your reasons.

PLAN

Objective
Explore geographic advantages on which the Americans capitalized during the Revolution.

Critical Thinking Skills for Lesson 3.4
- Identify Main Ideas and Details
- Monitor Comprehension
- Analyze Cause and Effect
- Form and Support Opinions
- Draw Conclusions
- Make Inferences
- Interpret Maps

Essential Question for Chapter 6
What factors helped America win the war? In the American Revolution, a new, much smaller army defeated a major imperial power. Lesson 3.4 explores four advantages the Americans had over the British because they were fighting on home turf.

Background for the Teacher
Rivers are especially strategic during wartime, and it was no different in the American Revolution. General Washington knew that the Hudson River—the lifeline of the Hudson River Valley and central to interregional commerce—had to remain under American control at all costs. The Hudson River was a major travel route, linking New York Harbor to Canada, with many ferry-crossing sites and connecting roads. The British wished to capture control of the Hudson in order to divide the New England Colonies from the Middle Colonies and to cut off the transportation of food and supplies within the colonies. Today, West Point, the United States Military Academy, overlooks the Hudson River from the Hudson Highlands, once the site of some of the most important military strategy of the American Revolution.

Activate Prior Knowledge

Direct students' attention to the two maps in the lesson. Remind them that different European countries had made territorial claims in North America. Students should also remember that the line demarcating the Proclamation of 1763 granted Britain the land east of the line. British and American colonists were prohibited from settling west of that line, though many did anyway. Tell students that in this lesson they will learn how American colonists used the geographic advantages of the land set aside by the Proclamation against the British during the Revolution.

TEACH   STEM

Guided Discussion

1. **Draw Conclusions** What advantages and disadvantages might cities situated on the coastline have experienced during the Revolution? *(Advantages: able to send and receive supplies and troops via ship; soldiers in the cities could see the British approaching. Disadvantages: The British could capture ports and paralyze cities; coastline locations allowed British ships armed with powerful guns to fire on cities.)*

2. **Make Inferences** Based on what you can infer from the map and text, where would you want to be stationed if you were a British soldier sent to fight in the American colonies? *(Answers will vary. Some students may mention that if they lived in London or another British city, they would want to be stationed in a colonial American city because that would be familiar. Others may say they would like to be stationed somewhere with a similar climate to their home in England.)*

Geography in History

Interpret Maps Have students compare the map of the 13 colonies with a present-day map of the United States. **ASK:** What are the ways in which the area of the colonies compares and contrasts with the area of the United States today? *(Responses should include size, shape, and addition of other physical features, such as deserts, rivers, mountains, and coastlines.)* How do the locations of colonial cities compare with the locations of present-day cities? *(Many colonial cities were located near rivers or the coast; today, cities can be located in those places but also in the middle of deserts because of modern transportation systems.)*

Active Options

On Your Feet: Four Corners Divide students into four groups and assign each group a corner of the room. Have students make cards that say "Terrain," "Population Distribution," "Distance," and "Climate." Tell members of each group to develop a list of the ways in which each geographic theme provided an advantage for the Americans over the British. Then have groups present their lists to the class. Ask students to vote on the advantage they think was the most significant and then rank the results on the board, from most to least significant. Encourage students to debate the results based on their understanding of the text and map.

NG Learning Framework: Explore a River

SKILL Observation

KNOWLEDGE Our Living Planet

Encourage students to identify and research a river located in one of the original 13 colonies. Students should explore important facts about the river's route, how the river has been used for economic or military purposes, the health of the river today, and any folklore, poetry, or music associated with the river. Tell students to prepare a multimedia presentation on the river. Some students may wish to work in pairs or groups. When the presentations are completed, have a River Day in class to allow students and groups to present their findings.

Inclusion

Mark Up Maps Help students identify cities and features discussed in the lesson. Provide sentence frames for students to complete based on the map of the colonies.

- The city of Boston is in _____. *(Massachusetts)*
- Virginia is located _____ of Maryland. *(south)*
- The southernmost colony is _____. *(Georgia)*
- The light blue lines on the map represent _____. *(rivers)*

Pre-AP

Research a Colony Have students extend their knowledge about one of the 13 colonies that fought in the Revolution. Students should approach their colony from the geographic standpoint to learn more about their colony's terrain, population distribution, important locations, and climate. Students should also include particular battles that were fought in their colony and determine if geography affected the outcomes of those battles.

See the Chapter Planner for more strategies for differentiation.

THINK LIKE A GEOGRAPHER

ANSWERS

1. Distance was a problem because Britain was more than 3,000 miles from the colonies. Sending soldiers and supplies took a long time. Once British troops arrived, they had to march from one battle to another, which was taxing.

2. The Americans knew their own terrain and outsmarted the British, who were unfamiliar with the colonies. Americans were used to the various climates where they lived, and populations were widely scattered and not concentrated in cities.

3. Answers will vary but should demonstrate an understanding of the text.

Legacy of the War

With the war finally over, the young country assessed its costs and looked toward the future. The citizens of the United States had some hard decisions to make. What direction would the new country take?

MAIN IDEA Once a formal treaty was negotiated and signed, the United States began to forge its new identity as an independent nation.

NEGOTIATING THE PEACE

The American Revolution was over. It would soon inspire other nations, including France and the French colony of Haiti, to revolt and demand democracy. But war always comes at a high price. Thousands of soldiers—both American and British—lost their lives in combat, and even more died of disease. Now it was time to heal and begin building the nation. First, though, the United States and Great Britain had to make peace. The two countries did so in the **Treaty of Paris of 1783**.

Benjamin Franklin, John Jay, and John Adams negotiated skillfully for the United States. The treaty they produced included two extremely important **provisions**, or legal conditions, that aided the country. The British agreed both to recognize the independence of the United States of America and to approve the new American boundaries. The new country was bounded on the west by the Mississippi River, on the north by Canada, and on the south by Florida. The United States would have plenty of growing room.

Florida, from which Britain had created **East Florida** and **West Florida**, went back to Spain in a separate agreement. The British also made a separate agreement with France over parts of the West Indies and Canada.

A NEW IDENTITY

Not all Americans were happy with the outcome of the war. Many Loyalists and Native Americans, furious that their British allies had signed away their lands, moved to Canada. Some former slaves freed by the British also made their way to Canada, but others were returned to slavery. The majority of Americans, though, stayed right where they were

and began rebuilding. Britain's economic control and taxation had spurred the Revolution. Freedom of trade took firm hold, laying the groundwork for growing commerce and industry.

Liberty and equality were central to the new national identity as well. In 1781, an enslaved woman named Mum Betts sued and won her freedom in court. Taking the name **Elizabeth Freeman**, she inspired Massachusetts to become the first state to abolish slavery. In Delaware, **Richard Allen** bought his freedom and later founded one of the first independent black churches in Philadelphia.

The most difficult task facing the United States was establishing a plan for government. Citizens favored **republicanism**, a system with no king or queen, where the people choose representatives to make their laws. They also stressed civic republicanism, or responsibility for the common good. Americans hoped to blend civic republicanism and ideals of classical liberal principles, including private property and individual and religious freedoms, to create their new government.

HISTORICAL THINKING

1. **READING CHECK** How did the Treaty of Paris of 1783 secure the future of the United States?

2. **DESCRIBE** How did the U.S. government plan reflect the ideals of civic republicanism, classical liberal principles, and English parliamentary traditions?

3. **FORM AND SUPPORT OPINIONS** Do you think African Americans were better off after the revolution? Explain why or why not.

CRITICAL VIEWING As David Hartley of Great Britain and John Adams, Benjamin Franklin, and John Jay of the United States signed the Treaty of Paris, shown here, each man added his wax seal—the red patch to the left of each name. The seal was made by dripping melted wax onto a surface and pressing a personalized metal stamp into the wax before it cooled. In the 18th century, a wax seal confirmed the identity of the signer of a document. Why might a personalized seal have been required on a document like this one?

PLAN

Objective

Discuss the war's legacy and the ways in which the United States forged a national identity.

Critical Thinking Skills for Lesson 3.5

• Identify Main Ideas and Details
• Monitor Comprehension
• Describe
• Form and Support Opinions
• Identify
• Explain

Essential Question for Chapter 6

What factors helped America win the war?
Lesson 3.5 discusses the role that the principles of freedom and representation in government would play as Americans transitioned from a group of rebellious colonies to a new, united nation.

Background for the Teacher

The Treaty of Paris of 1783 was just one part of a series of treaties called the Peace of Paris, in which Britain made separate agreements with the United States, France, Spain, and the Netherlands. The United States government viewed the treaty as a victory, but many other groups were less satisfied with its provisions. Native Americans who had fought on the British side were not pleased to be under American control or to have their lands signed away. They felt betrayed by the British, who they believed had not worked hard enough to protect Native Americans' rights and lands in the negotiations. The Spanish would continue to fight with the United States over unclear boundaries between American and Spanish territories. Finally, the provisions meant to protect former Loyalists and to return their lands caused disputes as well.

History Notebook

Encourage students to complete the American Gallery page for Chapter 6 in their History Notebooks as they read.

INTRODUCE & ENGAGE

Make a List

As a class, briefly review the causes of the American Revolution and the principles and goals of those who fought in it. Then, tell students to imagine they have been given the task of negotiating the peace with Britain. **ASK:** What are the most important things you would want this treaty to guarantee? Ask students to write a list of four or five things they would request in their peace treaties, and have them explain in writing why each of these is important. Ask volunteers to share their lists with the class.

TEACH

Guided Discussion

1. **Identify** Where were the official boundaries of the new United States, as outlined in the treaty with Britain? *(Canada was the northern boundary, the Mississippi River was the western boundary, and Florida was the southern boundary.)*

2. **Explain** Why was forming a post-Revolution government a difficult task for the new nation? *(Answers will vary. Possible response: The new government would have to balance authority with freedom and protect individual rights while having just a few people representing many.)*

More Information

Republicanism Rooted in ancient Greek and Roman thought and Renaissance ideas, republicanism is a political philosophy that places the authority to govern in the hands of the people. A key concept is civic virtue—the responsibility of citizens to participate in society and government through such activities as voting, paying taxes, and working for the common good. **ASK:** Why might balancing republicanism and individual rights and freedoms be a challenge? *(Answers will vary. Possible response: Working for the common good involves putting aside your own self-interest in favor of doing what is good for the community or country. This means that individuals might have to endure limits on their personal rights and freedoms in order to secure benefits or protections for others.)*

Active Options

On Your Feet: Three-Step Interview Have students work in pairs to interview each other about the national identity that emerged in the United States following the American Revolution. Ask students to consider how they would describe this new identity. As pairs conduct their interviews, have them ask more specific questions, such as: What parts of the nation's identity seemed to be the most important during this time? Did the nation struggle with any part of its new identity? What elements of America's new identity seem directly related to the causes of the war? After both students have had the chance to interview, have them report what they have learned from their partners to the class.

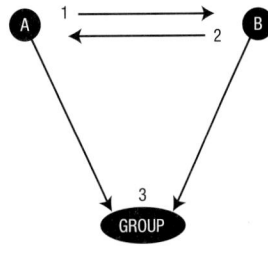

AMERICAN GALLERY
ONLINE
Colonial Vernacular Architecture Invite students to explore the American Gallery. Have them select one of the images and do additional research to learn more about it. Ask questions that will inspire further inquiry about the image, such as: What is this? Where is it located, and when was it created? What is it made of? What else would you like to know about it?

DIFFERENTIATE

Striving Readers

Use a Main Idea Cluster Tell students to work in pairs to complete a Main Idea Cluster covering Lesson 3.5. Assign each student in the pair one section of the lesson. Students should work together to identify the lesson's main idea and write it in the center. Then, each student will contribute at least two supporting details from his or her section.

Gifted & Talented

Research State Constitutions Encourage students to research how the state constitutions created during the American Revolution laid the foundation for a U.S. government based on republicanism and the protection of freedom. Tell students to use library or online sources to learn how the states handled such concepts as popular sovereignty, the structure of the legislature, limits on government power, voting rights, and the protection of individuals' rights and freedoms. Ask students to use their research to create a short presentation for the class.

See the Chapter Planner for more strategies for differentiation.

HISTORICAL THINKING

ANSWERS

1. The treaty required Britain to recognize the independence of the United States, and it set generous boundaries for the new nation that would eventually allow it to expand.

2. Citizens pushed for a government that blended the ideal of individual freedom with a system in which the people choose representatives to make laws.

3. Answers will vary. Many students will say African Americans were not better off, since most remained enslaved. Some may say African Americans were better off, since the new nation's ideals valued freedom and some states began to end slavery.

CRITICAL VIEWING Answers will vary. Possible response: It would be essential to be able to prove that all signatures were real because a forged signature might mean that the people with the authority to make the treaty had not actually approved it. In that case, the treaty might not be valid, and its agreements might not be honored.

6 REVIEW

VOCABULARY

Match the following vocabulary terms with their definitions.

1. mercenary
2. blockade
3. skirmish
4. desert
5. pacifist
6. provision
7. republicanism
8. espionage

a. legal condition or requirement
b. the act of spying to gather information
c. to leave military service illegally
d. a soldier who is paid to fight for a country other than his or her own
e. a small, short battle
f. a form of government in which the people elect representatives
g. to use ships or other means to keep ships and commerce from entering a port
h. a person who stands against war and violence

READING STRATEGY
FORM AND SUPPORT OPINIONS

If you haven't already, complete your chart listing your opinion and supporting statements regarding the factor that most helped secure an American victory in the Revolution. Then answer the following question.

9. What factor was key to the U.S. victory in the American Revolution? Include your supporting statements in your answer.

Opinion:
Supporting statement:
Supporting statement:
Supporting statement:
Supporting statement:

MAIN IDEAS

Answer the following questions. Support your answers with evidence from the chapter.

10. What disadvantages did the Americans face at the beginning of the war? **LESSON 1.1**

11. How did the alliances and treaties made by Native Americans affect their relationships with both the Patriots and the British? **LESSON 1.2**

12. How did other nations come to the aid of the Americans? **LESSON 2.1**

13. Compare the experiences of the American and British armies in the winter of 1777–78. **LESSON 2.2**

14. Why did Abigail Adams ask her husband to "Remember the Ladies"? **LESSON 2.3**

15. What strategy did the Americans use to face the powerful British Navy? **LESSON 2.4**

16. How did Nathanael Greene and Francis Marion help change the course of the war in the Southern Colonies? **LESSON 3.2**

17. How did the Americans earn a victory at Yorktown? **LESSON 3.3**

18. How did American calls for independence inspire other nations, such as France and the French colony of Haiti? **LESSON 3.5**

HISTORICAL THINKING

Answer the following questions. Support your answers with evidence from the chapter.

19. **ANALYZE CAUSE AND EFFECT** Besides the death toll, what was a negative effect of the war?

20. **SYNTHESIZE** How did American women and men work together in the war?

21. **DRAW CONCLUSIONS** What groups of people did not benefit from the Revolution?

22. **FORM AND SUPPORT OPINIONS** What British mistake led most directly to their defeat?

INTERPRET MAPS

Look closely at the map of the Battle of Yorktown. Then answer the questions that follow.

Battle of Yorktown, 1781

23. According to the map, what happened in the Battle of the Capes?

24. How does the map illustrate cooperation between the Americans and the French?

ANALYZE SOURCES

Timothy Pickering, Jr., was an officer in the Continental Army. In 1778, when he read that his father, a Loyalist, was dying, Pickering wrote him a letter. Read the excerpt from the letter and answer the question.

> When I look back on past time, I regret our difference of sentiment in great as well as (sometimes) in little politics; as it was a deduction [subtraction] from the happiness otherwise to have been enjoyed. Yet you had always too much regard to freedom in thinking & the rights of conscience, to lay upon me any injunctions [commands] which could interfere with my own opinion of what was [my] duty. Often have I thanked my Maker for the greatest blessing of my life—your example & instructions in all the duties I owe to God, and my neighbor. They have not been lost upon me.
>
> —Letter from Timothy Pickering, Jr., to Timothy Pickering, Sr., February 23, 1778

25. What emotions does Pickering express toward his father?

CONNECT TO YOUR LIFE

26. **EXPOSITORY** Think about the different people you read about in the chapter. How did individuals, both Americans and others, show heroism in the American Revolution? Write a paragraph about two individuals mentioned in the chapter, explaining why they should be considered heroes.

TIPS

- Review the chapter and choose two individuals whom you consider heroes. Write a topic sentence about their heroism during the American Revolution.

- Support your choices with evidence from the chapter.

- Conclude your paragraph with a summary of the individuals' heroism.

VOCABULARY ANSWERS

1. d. a soldier who is paid to fight for a country other than his or her own

2. g. to use ships or other means to keep ships and commerce from entering a port

3. e. a small, short battle

4. c. to leave military service illegally

5. h. a person who stands against war and violence

6. a. legal condition or requirement

7. f. a form of government in which people elect the representatives

8. b. the act of spying to gather information

READING STRATEGY ANSWER

Opinion: Foreign allies were the key to the U.S. victory in the American Revolution.
Supporting statement: France provided financial assistance that kept the Americans afloat.
Supporting statement: France and Spain provided military and naval support that stretched Britain's resources.
Supporting statement: Individuals from France and Prussia provided crucial training that helped the Americans fight the British more effectively.

9. Possible response: Foreign allies were the key factor in the American victory in the American Revolution because they provided military, naval, and financial support without which the Americans could never have defeated the much more powerful British Army and Navy.

MAIN IDEAS ANSWERS

10. Disadvantages that Americans faced included: a lack of an established government; divided loyalties among the American public; few trained military members; and not enough money for weapons, supplies, and soldiers' pay.

11. As war approached, the Six Nations of the Iroquois decided to remain neutral. But after fighting broke out, the nations split their loyalties, with some, such as the Mohawk, siding with the British, and others fighting on the side of the Americans.

12. France and Spain contributed money, supplies, and men. They also fought against the British in locations such as the West Indies, which kept the British engaged on multiple fronts.

13. General Howe's British troops spent the winter in Philadelphia in comfortable surroundings; they were warm and well fed. Americans at Valley Forge camped in rough shelters and nearly froze or starved to death. During this miserable time, however, they received valuable military training under Friedrich von Steuben.

14. Abigail Adams asked her husband to "Remember the Ladies" because she believed women had made just as much of a contribution to the war effort as men and that they deserved to have a voice and representation in the new government.

15. Americans used privateers to supplement their small navy. Privateers helped protect American shipping and disrupted British naval and commercial activities. Aid from the French and Spanish navies also helped the Americans compete against the British by providing more ships and sailors.

16. Greene put together an effective strategy built on mobility. Marion led guerrilla fighters, who were able to attack British forces stealthily. Both of these elements helped the Americans win some critical victories and drive back the British forces.

17. At Yorktown, the British forces were camped on a peninsula, a piece of land that was easily surrounded. Additionally, they did not receive reinforcements from New York in time. Combined American and French forces were able to surround the British camp by land and sea, forcing the British to surrender.

18. The Americans' victory in the American Revolution inspired the people of France and the French colony of Haiti to revolt against their own governments and demand democracy.

HISTORICAL THINKING ANSWERS

19. Answers will vary. Possible response: Aside from the death toll, one negative effect of the war was the continuation of slavery in many of the former colonies. Another negative effect would be damaged relationships with many Native American groups.

20. Answers will vary. Possible response: On the home front, women took over many tasks and positions when men left to fight. Women often followed the soldiers to provide support, such as cooking and laundry. Women took advantage of men's lack of suspicion to serve effectively as spies for both sides. They also sometimes fought in battle disguised as men—or not disguised, as in the case of "Molly Pitcher." Finally, women writers worked to persuade people to support the war and to make the case for women's rights in the new nation.

21. Answers will vary. Possible response: Overall, women did not benefit much from the Revolution. They did not gain any new liberties, other than independence from Britain. Most African Americans did not benefit. The practice of slavery continued, though the cause of abolition did gain support in the North. Native Americans found that their land had been signed away in the Treaty of Paris. France and Spain did not gain the lands in North America that they had expected.

22. Answers will vary but should indicate specific mistakes made by the British. Students may cite the British military's tendency to underestimate the Continental forces in battles such as Trenton, their disorganization in their attempts to control the Hudson Valley, the behavior of troops in the Southern Colonies that cost them Loyalist supporters, or the poor choice of location at Yorktown and the British delay in sending reinforcements.

INTERPRET MAPS ANSWERS

23. At the Battle of the Capes, an American and allied naval force led by De Grasse met with British naval forces led by Graves and Hood. The Americans and allies won and drove the British forces back north.

24. Signs of American and French cooperation on the map include Lafayette's move toward Yorktown and the note about Washington and Rochambeau leading troops together toward Yorktown at the same time. The map also shows that De Grasse, a French ally, won at the Battle of the Capes.

ANALYZE SOURCES ANSWER

25. Pickering expresses sadness and regret over his differences with his father. He also expresses admiration and respect for how his father allowed him the freedom to form his own opinions and make his own choices about fighting, even though it seems his father would have disagreed with his decision.

CONNECT TO YOUR LIFE ANSWER

26. Answers will vary, but students should pick two of the individuals discussed in the chapter, list their specific contributions to the war effort (supported by evidence from the text), and end with a summary of why they think those contributions were heroic.

UNIT 3 RESOURCES

UNIT INTRODUCTION
▶ Crossing the Delaware

UNIT TIME LINE

UNIT WRAP-UP

NATIONAL GEOGRAPHIC | **CONNECTION**

National Geographic Magazine Adapted Articles
• "Patriots in Petticoats"
• "Two Revolutions" ONLINE

Unit 3 Inquiry: Prepare an Argument

NG Learning Framework Activities
• Research a Colonial American
• Build a Time Line

Unit 3 Formal Assessment

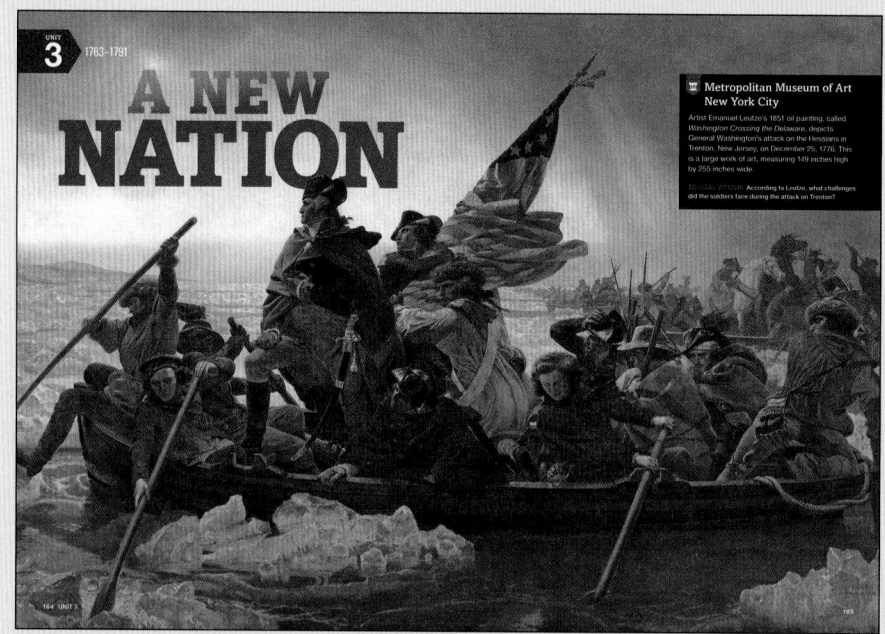

CHAPTER 7 RESOURCES

Available at NGLSync.Cengage.com

TEACHER RESOURCES & ASSESSMENT

Reading and Note-Taking

Vocabulary Practice

Document-Based Question Template

Social Studies Skills Lessons
• Reading: Determine Chronology
• Writing: Write an Explanation

Formal Assessment
• Chapter 7 Pretest
• Chapter 7 Tests A & B
• Section Quizzes

Chapter 7 Answer Key

ExamView®
One-time Download

STUDENT DIGITAL RESOURCES

• **eEdition** (English)
• **eEdition** (Spanish)
• **Handbooks**

• **Online Atlas**
• **American Gallery Online**
• **History Notebook**

• **American Voices (Biographies)**
• **Active History**
• **Projects for Inquiry-Based Learning**

Chapter 7 Spanish Resources are available at NGLSync.Cengage.com.

- Primary Sources
- On Your Feet: Inside-Outside Circle

NG Learning Framework:
Research Convention Delegates

SECTION 1 RESOURCES
THE CONFEDERATION ERA

LESSON 1.1
State and National Governments

- On Your Feet: Three-Step Interview

NG Learning Framework:
Explore State Constitutions

LESSON 1.2
Ordinances of 1785 and 1787

- On Your Feet: Word Chain

NG Learning Framework:
Investigate Education

LESSON 1.3
Controversies About the Articles

- On Your Feet: Debate

NG Learning Framework:
Research American Rebellions
in 1786 to 1787

SECTION 2 RESOURCES
DRAFTING THE CONSTITUTION

LESSON 2.1
The Constitutional Convention

AMERICAN GALLERY ONLINE Historic Philadelphia

NG Learning Framework:
Profile a Framer

American Voices Biography
James Madison ONLINE

LESSON 2.2
The Big Question: How to Divide Power

- Active History: Categorize Government Responsibilities

NG Learning Framework:
Explore Women's Rights

LESSON 2.3
Slavery and Trade

- On Your Feet: Three Corners

NG Learning Framework:
Create a Trade Simulation

SECTION 3 RESOURCES
RATIFICATION AND THE BILL OF RIGHTS

LESSON 3.1
Federalists and Antifederalists

- On Your Feet: Turn and Talk on a Topic

NG Learning Framework:
Hold a 21st Century Bill of Rights
Panel Discussion

LESSON 3.2
DOCUMENT-BASED QUESTION
Constitutional Debates

- On Your Feet: Jigsaw

LESSON 3.3
The Bill of Rights

- On Your Feet: Rotating Discussion

NG Learning Framework:
Understand the Bill of Rights

CHAPTER 7 REVIEW

STRIVING READERS

Strategy ❶
Turn Titles into Questions

To help students set a purpose for reading, have them read the title of each lesson in a section and then turn that title into a question they believe will be answered in the lesson. Students can record their questions and write their own answers, or they can ask each other their questions.

Use with All Lessons *For example, in Lesson 1.1, the question could be, "How did state and national governments work together?*

Strategy ❷
Play Vocabulary Tic-Tac-Toe

Write nine Key Vocabulary words on a tic-tac-toe grid on the board. Position the words on the grid so that an X or O can be written below each word. Player A chooses a word. If the player correctly pronounces, defines, and uses the word in a sentence, he or she can put an X or O in that box in the grid. Play alternates until one person has a row of Xs or Os.

Use with All Lessons *This game can also be played using teams. Divide the class into two teams, Team A and Team B, and alternate play until one team has a row of Xs or Os.*

Strategy ❸
Make a Top Five Facts List

After reading a lesson, have students write in their own words five important facts they learned from the lesson. Tell students to consider the 5Ws–*who, what, where, when,* and *why*–as they decide on their top five facts. Have students meet with a partner to compare lists and consolidate the two lists into one final list. Call on students to offer facts from their lists.

Use with All Lessons

INCLUSION

Strategy ❶
Modify Vocabulary Lists

Using your standards as a guide, limit the number of Key Vocabulary words that students will be required to master. As they read, have students create a vocabulary card for each word in the modified list. Students may create a picture to illustrate each word or write definitions, synonyms, or examples. Encourage students to refer to their vocabulary cards often as they read.

Use with All Lessons

Strategy ❷
Analyze Primary Sources

In order to facilitate comprehension, have students work in pairs to analyze the primary source excerpts in Lesson 3.2. Provide the graphic organizer below for students to complete. Students should identify the author and title of each document, each document's main idea, and one idea in each document that students would like to know more about.

Use with Lesson 3.2.

Author and Title	Main Idea	Want to Know More

ENGLISH LANGUAGE LEARNERS

Strategy ❶
Provide Sentence Frames

Have students of *All Proficiencies* read the lessons and complete the sentences below.

1.1 a. State constitutions gave leaders the idea for a _____ constitution for the nation. *(new)*

b. Americans liked the Articles of Confederation because states had _____. *(more power)*

1.2 a. The Wilderness Road helped people reach the _____ that included present-day Ohio, Indiana, Illinois, Michigan, Wisconsin, and part of Minnesota. *(western lands)*

b. The Ordinance of 1785 divided the Northwest Territory into _____. *(townships)*

1.3 a. _____ is being able to buy something and pay it back over time. *(credit)*

b. Massachusetts passed the _____ after Shays's Rebellion. *(Riot Act)*

Use with Lessons 1.1–1.3. *For Sections 2 and 3, have students at the **Emerging** and **Expanding** levels work in pairs to write their own sentence frames for each lesson. Pairs can then trade sentence frames with another pair and complete them together. Students at the **Bridging** level can work independently and exchange frames with a partner.*

Strategy ❷
Pair Partners for Dictation

After students read each lesson in the chapter, have them write a sentence summarizing its main idea. Pair students at the **Emerging** and **Expanding** levels with students at the **Bridging** level and have them dictate their sentences to each other. Then have them work together to check the sentences for accuracy and spelling.

Use with All Lessons

Strategy ❸
Preteach Key Terms

To build background, preteach the following Key Vocabulary words for students at the **Emerging** level before beginning Lesson 3.1 and Lesson 3.3.

1. federalist
2. antifederalist
3. amendment
4. Bill of Rights
5. statute

Use with Lessons 3.1 and 3.3

GIFTED & TALENTED

Strategy ❶
Write a Historical Dialogue

Tell students to review Lesson 2.2. Have them use facts from the lesson to write a dialogue between Edmund Randolph, William Paterson, and Roger Sherman. If students want more information about these historical figures, they can conduct online research or reference other source materials to learn more about these men and their plans for dividing governmental power. Encourage students to present their dialogues to the class using props, such as hats, to play the parts of the different historical figures.

Use with Lesson 2.2

Strategy ❷
Interview a Framer

Allow students to work in pairs to plan and write a question and answer news article interview with a Framer of the Constitution. Tell students to focus on the debates during the Constitutional Convention, and the arguments that he supported. Invite students to use online sources to learn more about the chosen Framer. Encourage students to ask in-depth questions about Framer why and how he debated the way he did. Have students share the interview with the class.

Use with Lessons 2.1, 2.3, and 3.1

Pre-AP

Strategy ❶
Form a Thesis

Have students develop a thesis statement for a specific topic related to one of the lessons in the chapter. Be sure the statement makes a claim that is supportable with evidence either from the chapter or through further research. Ask students to present their thesis statements to the class.

Use with All Lessons

Strategy ❷
Persuade Colleagues

Several delegates and leaders spoke passionately about their views on ratification of the Constitution. Have students choose a leader from the Constitutional Convention and research their chosen leader's position as a federalist or antifederalist. Encourage students to consult the writings and speeches of their selected leader to understand their perspective in the context of their lives. After they have gathered information, instruct them to write a persuasive speech from that person's perspective. Encourage students to practice and then deliver their speech to the class.

Use with Lessons 3.1 and 3.2

FROM CONFEDERATION TO
CONSTITUTION
1776–1791

ESSENTIAL QUESTION
How did ideas about the role of state and national government evolve?

READING STRATEGY

DETERMINE CHRONOLOGY
When you analyze chronology, you determine how ideas and events unfold over time. As you read the chapter, use an organizer like this one to record how ideas about state and national government developed in the United States.

For Chapter 7 Spanish Resources, visit the Resources Menu. Chapter 7 Resources are available at NGLSync.Cengage.com.

> "The people are the only legitimate fountain of **power.**"
> —James Madison

CRITICAL VIEWING The National Mall in Washington, D.C., is a park that extends about two miles from the Capitol Building to the Lincoln Memorial, with the Washington Monument in between. Americans gather there to celebrate and to express various aspects of our democracy as embodied in the Constitution. How does the crowd gathered for President Barack Obama's first inauguration represent our unity as a nation?

249

INTRODUCE THE PHOTOGRAPH
The National Mall

Have students study the photograph of the National Mall in Washington, D.C. Tell students that this photograph captures the moment when President Barack Obama was delivering the inaugural address for his first term as president. Explain that in this chapter they will learn about how the people who founded the United States created a new government structure for the nation, determined power divisions, and established roles of government, which included how citizens vote for a new president. **ASK:** What do you think of when you see people gathered for this kind of event? (*Answers will vary.*)

Share Background

When architect Pierre L'Enfant designed the city plan for the new national capital in 1791, his vision included a wide and open tree-lined boulevard with intersecting streets that would connect to important buildings and monuments in the city. L'Enfant's boulevard became the National Mall. Over the years, the Mall was neglected and overgrown with trees, and at one point even had a railroad station on it. Around 1900, plans were made to revitalize the Mall to reinstate its original design. Now the Mall has open space and is used as a public gathering area. The Mall includes the Capitol Building, the Lincoln Memorial, and the Washington Monument, in addition to several public museums.

CRITICAL VIEWING Answers will vary. Possible response: The crowd represents our nation's unity because the people are there to witness and celebrate the swearing-in ceremony of the president of the United States.

INTRODUCE THE ESSENTIAL QUESTION

How did ideas about the role of state and national government evolve?

Fishbowl Activity: The Power of Ideas This activity helps students explore how ideas have the power to change governments and societies. Encourage students to use prior knowledge about how and why the American colonies broke away from Great Britain. Suggest that they also draw on what they know about present-day political changes or revolutions in governments that they might read about in the news.

Have students form an inner circle and an outer circle, both facing the center. Tell the inner circle to discuss the following question while the outer circle listens and takes notes: What ideas prompted American colonists to protest British rule and ultimately fight for independence?

Then have students switch places and tell the "new" inner circle to discuss the following question while the outer circle listens and takes notes: How did the ideas of the American Revolution become the foundation for a new nation?

Reconvene as a class and discuss the common themes each circle touched upon in their discussions. Tell students that in this chapter, they will learn about how the new nation grappled with setting up state and national governments after the Revolution.

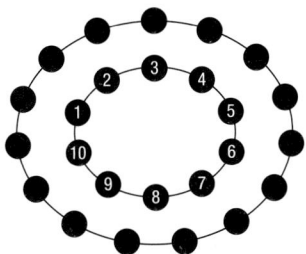

INTRODUCE CHAPTER VOCABULARY

Definition Chart

As they read the chapter, have students complete a Definition Chart for Key Vocabulary words. Have students list the Key Vocabulary words in the far left column of their charts. Then, as they encounter the words in the chapter, tell them to write the Key Vocabulary word's definition in the center column and what the word means using their own words in the far right column. Model an example for students on the board, using the graphic organizer below.

Word	Definition	In My Own Words
constitution	a plan for government	

INTRODUCE THE READING STRATEGY

Determine Chronology

Remind students that when determining chronology, it is useful to keep track of key events and when they occurred. This strategy will also help students better understand how events are related to each other in time. Explain that in this chapter, students will learn how the roles of state and national government evolved over time. Model completing the Sequence Chain. Since Chapter 7 begins with the Articles of Confederation, complete that entry for oval #1. Remind students to make use of the Sequence Chain as they read the chapter.

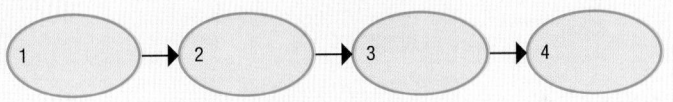

KEY DATES FOR CHAPTER 7

1781	Thirteen states ratify the Articles of Confederation
1784	First ordinance for western lands passes
1785	Ordinance of 1785 organizes western lands
1786	Shays's Rebellion
1787	Northwest Ordinance of 1787
1787	Constitutional Convention meetings start in May
1787	Framers sign the Constitution in September
1788	*The Federalist* is published
1791	Congress adds the Bill of Rights to the Constitution

For instructional support for the online American Story "Philadelphia, Summer of 1787," go to NGLSync.Cengage.com.

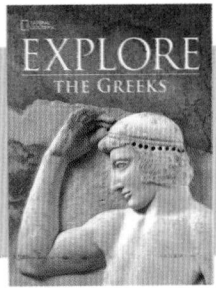

To learn about the ancient roots of American government, see *EXPLORE THE GREEKS.*

1.1 State and National Governments

The last thing revolutionaries who have broken free from oppressive rulers want is the same way of governing. American revolutionaries wanted a new style of government—and one with limited power.

MAIN IDEA The Articles of Confederation limited the power of the new national government, while state governments retained much of their independence.

CREATING ORDER

Part of the legacy of the American struggle for independence included the establishment of a government based on republicanism, or the idea that government's power comes from its citizens and their representatives. Even as the war raged, each state moved forward and set up its own government.

Elected representatives from each state met and drafted a **constitution**, or a plan for government. Many state constitutions included lists of rights to which every citizen was entitled, such as the freedom to practice any religion. Once the constitutions were drafted and revised, the state representatives **ratified**, or approved, them.

Many states decided to organize their governments with governors and two-house legislatures elected by the people. Organizing legislatures into two parts, instead of one, ensured that lawmakers would have to share power and limited the power of governors. Some states, such as Pennsylvania, opted for no governor at all.

State constitutions were a new concept at the time. Most western European countries did not grant such power to elected legislatures. The

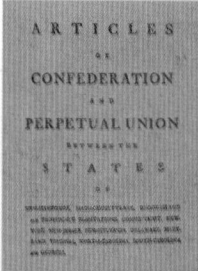

The Articles of Confederation went through six drafts between 1775 and 1777 before Congress finally approved it and then submitted it to the 13 states for ratification.

process of writing and ratifying state constitutions served as a model for the new national government to introduce future political institutions and ideas. One of the new ideas that emerged was a constitution that would govern all American states.

A NATIONAL PLAN

After the states ratified their constitutions, they decided to band together to defeat the British. Representatives from many of the states started meeting regularly to draft a plan for unification called the Articles of Confederation.

The Articles of Confederation gave Congress the ability to make decisions about the military. They also outlined a national plan of **sovereign**, or self-governing, states. The **federal**, or national, government would have little power of its own, nor would it include a president or a federal court system. It would simply serve as an administrator to help unify the states. This limited federal government reflected the ideals first put forth in the Declaration of Independence, which stated that a government should derive its powers "from the consent of the governed."

The Articles of Confederation assigned foreign affairs and relations with Native Americans, the ability to declare war and peace, and the postal service to Congress. The national government could produce money but not levy taxes. If it needed money, it had to ask the states for funds. Congress needed to approve any legislation that would affect the country.

Americans liked these ideas because they addressed liberties denied to them under British rule. They also laid the foundation for **constitutionalism**, an approach to government that strictly defines and limits its powers. In March 1781, all 13 states finally ratified the Articles of Confederation, which would serve as the first constitution of the United States for eight years.

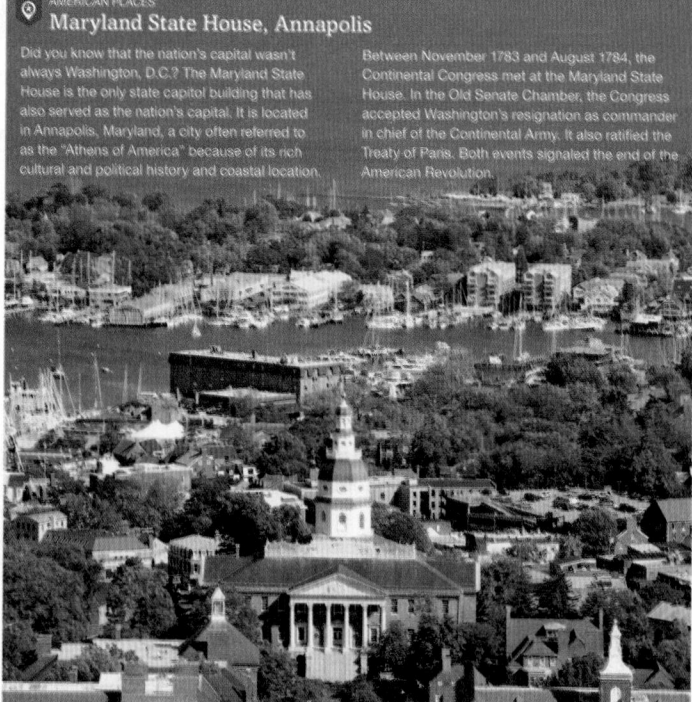

AMERICAN PLACES
Maryland State House, Annapolis

Did you know that the nation's capital wasn't always Washington, D.C.? The Maryland State House is the only state capitol building that has also served as the nation's capital. It is located in Annapolis, Maryland, a city often referred to as the "Athens of America" because of its rich cultural and political history and coastal location.

Between November 1783 and August 1784, the Continental Congress met at the Maryland State House. In the Old Senate Chamber, the Congress accepted Washington's resignation as commander in chief of the Continental Army. It also ratified the Treaty of Paris. Both events signaled the end of the American Revolution.

HISTORICAL THINKING

1. **READING CHECK** What responsibilities did the national government have under the Articles of Confederation?

2. **ANALYZE CAUSE AND EFFECT** How did the development of state constitutions influence the national plan for government?

3. **IDENTIFY MAIN IDEAS AND DETAILS** How were the ideals put forth in the Declaration of Independence reflected in the new American government?

PLAN

Objective

Learn how the nation devised a new system of government after the American Revolution.

Critical Thinking Skills for Lesson 1.1

- Identify Main Ideas and Details
- Monitor Comprehension
- Analyze Cause and Effect
- Make Inferences
- Draw Conclusions

Essential Question for Chapter 7

How did ideas about the role of state and national government evolve? Americans wanted a new form of government in which representatives elected by the people had to share power. Lesson 1.1 discusses the states' efforts at drafting and upholding state constitutions that led to a national plan of unification under the Articles of Confederation.

Background for the Teacher

It might surprise you to find out that the Articles of Confederation and the Declaration of Independence were both being written at the same time: during June of 1776. One of the documents, the Declaration, stated the basis for forming a new nation. The other, the Articles, put in place practical means to do so.

Why it might be surprising is that we tend to think of things linearly: there was the Declaration, then there were the Articles of Confederation, but actually they were both going on at once. The Declaration of Independence was approved by state delegates during a July 4, 1776, meeting of the Second Continental Congress.

INTRODUCE & ENGAGE

Make a List

Conduct a class discussion and ask volunteers to share what they know about state and national governments today. For example, students might mention that the leader of the United States government is the president, the leader of a state government is the governor, and that both levels of government have groups of people that make laws. Record their responses on the board. **ASK:** What do you think are the most important responsibilities of state and national governments? *(Possible response: The most important responsibilities of both governments are making laws, enforcing laws, and deciding what laws mean.)*

TEACH

Guided Discussion

1. **Make Inferences** What conflicts could arise from states having different constitutions? *(Possible response: The states may differ on which citizens' rights their constitutions would protect.)*

2. **Draw Conclusions** Why do you think the Articles of Confederation gave Congress the ability to make military decisions but not the ability to levy taxes? *(The Representatives who drafted the Articles may have recognized that the national government should control the military to create a strong, unified front against enemies, but that citizens were still angry over taxes that had been imposed by Britain and would not want to be taxed by the national government.)*

American Places

The wooden dome on the Maryland State House was added by colonial architect Joseph Clark, who completed it in 1794. The dome is topped with two distinct structures: a lightning rod and a mostly decorative acorn. The lightning rod provides protection from lightning, based on Benjamin Franklin's idea that an iron rod grounds lightning strikes by directing the electrical energy through the conductive metal and down to the ground where the energy can be discharged. The rod runs through the middle of the acorn, which stabilizes the rod. While the rod is the original wrought iron, the acorn had to be replaced in 1996 because of water damage. A new acorn was created using 31 separate pieces of wood from cypress trees and covered with copper, made by craftspeople from across Maryland. These parts were then put together to make the replacement acorn.

Active Options

On Your Feet: Three-Step Interview Have students work in pairs to discuss the Articles of Confederation. Have one student play the role of an interviewer by asking the other student this question: *Do you think the Articles of Confederation struck a good balance between the states and the national government? Why or why not?* Have the interviewer ask follow-up questions based on the answers provided. Then ask students to reverse roles. Finally, allow students to share their ideas from the interview with the class.

NG Learning Framework: Explore State Constitutions

ATTITUDE Responsibility

SKILL Collaboration

Instruct students to explore state constitutions between 1777 and 1781 to learn how American political ideals and institutions were developed. Tell students to use library resources or to search online to find the state constitutions as well as resources such as The Founders' Constitution, maintained by the University of Chicago Press. Have students analyze the principles and concepts behind the political ideals that provided the basis for the state constitutions and to write a summary of their findings. Encourage students to share their summaries with the class.

DIFFERENTIATE

Striving Readers

Understanding Main Ideas Check students' understanding of the main ideas in Lesson 1.1 by asking them to complete either/or statements such as the following:

- Most of the states wrote their own [constitutions or Articles of Confederation].

- The sovereign states under the Articles of Confederation [elected representatives themselves or were ruled by a president].

- In 1781 all 13 states [approved or disapproved] the Articles of Confederation.

English Language Learners

Set Up a Word Wall Work with students at the **Emerging** and **Expanding** levels to select three words from each lesson to display in a grouping on a Word Wall. It might be useful to choose words that students are likely to encounter in other chapters, such as *federal* or *sovereign*. Keep the words displayed throughout the lessons and discuss each one as it comes up during reading. Encourage volunteers to add words, phrases, and examples to each word to develop understanding.

See the Chapter Planner for more strategies for differentiation.

HISTORICAL THINKING

ANSWERS

1. Under the Articles of Confederation, the national government handled foreign and Native American relations, had the power to declare war and peace, governed the postal service, and produced money.

2. The national plan for government used ideas and followed the processes the states used when they wrote and ratified their constitutions.

3. The Declaration of Independence stated that a government should get its powers "from the consent of the governed." In the new government, citizens elected representatives, and the national government could not act without representatives' approval.

Ordinances of 1785 and 1787

When large groups of people get together but have few rules to follow, things can get wild fast. As settlers moved into territory northwest of the Ohio River, the new United States struggled to maintain law and order beyond its official boundaries.

MAIN IDEA The ordinances of 1785 and 1787 allowed the federal government to better regulate westward expansion and distribute land to new settlers.

GO WEST!

You have read that the Treaty of Paris of 1783 granted the United States most of the territory from the Atlantic Ocean to the Mississippi River. This land extended north to the St. Lawrence River and the Great Lakes and south to the Spanish colony of Florida. Under the Articles of Confederation, the national government controlled all this territory.

Fertile soil attracted white settlers to the land beyond the Appalachian (a-puh-LATCH-uhn) Mountains. Settlers had begun arriving there in 1775, when frontier adventurers such as

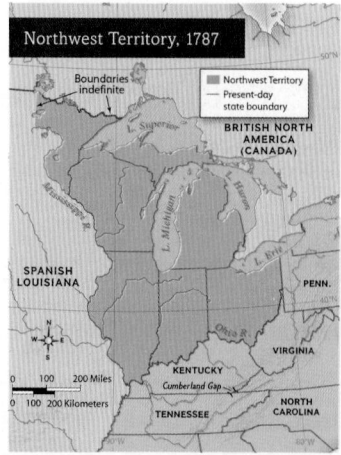

Northwest Territory, 1787

Daniel Boone and some companions created a route through the Appalachian Mountains from Virginia to Kentucky. The new route, called the **Wilderness Road**, enabled large numbers of people to move west. The "western lands," as they were called, included present-day Ohio, Indiana, Illinois, Michigan, Wisconsin, and part of Minnesota.

THE NORTHWEST TERRITORY

Territorial expansion and its consequences created a new set of problems for the federal government. Congress recognized the need to provide safety and order within the new settlements, and it also wanted to establish a strong governmental presence in the western lands. Operating under the Articles of Confederation, Congress passed a series of **ordinances**, or laws, for settling the western lands. These ordinances established an orderly system for transferring federally owned land into private holdings, townships, and states. The first ordinance, passed in 1784, divided the territory into a small number of self-governing districts that could later become states.

The second ordinance was the **Ordinance of 1785**. It called for surveying and organizing districts into townships. The townships would be further divided into lots that the government would sell at a minimum of $1 per acre. Each township also had to set aside land for a school.

Finally, the **Northwest Ordinance of 1787** renamed the land the **Northwest Territory**. The ordinance provided for ownership of land by individuals and for the creation of new states out of this territory. Because it applied a portion of funds

AMERICAN PLACES
Cumberland Gap, Appalachian Mountains

Many Americans who moved west to settle in the Northwest Territory traveled through the Cumberland Gap. It was the only place where settlers could reasonably cross the Appalachian Mountains from Virginia into Kentucky. As the map to the left shows, the Cumberland Gap is located where the states of Virginia, Kentucky, and Tennessee meet.

from the sale of lands toward building schools, it established the first system of public education and reinforced the Founders' belief that the success of a republican government relies on an educated people. The ordinance prohibited slavery in the Northwest Territory. It guaranteed the rights of the people who settled there and stated that "the utmost good faith shall always be observed" toward Native Americans. The ordinances of 1785 and 1787 created a plan for westward expansion. They also caused some unforeseen problems for the new nation. One of these problems would be growing conflict with Native Americans in the Northwest Territory.

HISTORICAL THINKING

1. **READING CHECK** What problems did territorial expansion create for the new nation?

2. **DETERMINE CHRONOLOGY** How did the Articles of Confederation and each of the land ordinances build on one another to pave the way for settlement?

3. **INTERPRET MAPS** Based on what you see on the map, what major waterways were newly available to settlers in the Northwest Territory?

Consider Westward Expansion

Ask students why Americans in the new nation might have wanted to move to and settle on western lands. Have students think about the question for a few minutes and record their ideas on a piece of paper. Then lead a class discussion and encourage volunteers to share their ideas with the class. After discussing the ideas, tell students that in this lesson they will learn more about westward expansion and the laws that governed how settlers moved into new territory.

TEACH

Guided Discussion

1. **Identify** What factors influenced large numbers of people to move west? *(People heard there was fertile soil west of the Appalachian Mountains, and a new route through the mountains, called the Wilderness Road, made it easier for people to travel west.)*

2. **Make Connections** Read the following quote from Thomas Jefferson aloud: "If a nation expects to be ignorant and free, in a state of civilization, it expects what never was and never will be." Discuss the meaning of Jefferson's words. **ASK:** How are Jefferson's ideals reflected in the provisions placed in the Northwest Ordinance of 1787? *(The Northwest Ordinance set aside funds to build schools and prohibited slavery. The Founders, including Thomas Jefferson, believed that an educated population is necessary for the success of a republican government.)*

American Places

The Cumberland Gap is part of the Cumberland Mountain Range, which is in the southern third of the Appalachian Mountain Range. The Appalachians are long, running from Georgia and Alabama in the south, to New Brunswick, Canada, in the north. The Appalachians were a natural barrier for early settlers who were traveling west. The gap that runs through the Cumberland Mountains is a low valley that has been shaped by weathering and erosion over the years. Scientists also believe that the impact of a meteor or possibly the collapse of an underground sinkhole may have created this landform. The result is a natural gap that Native Americans and animals used long before white settlements moved to the Northwest Territory. Historians speculate that 300,000 people traveled the Cumberland Gap between 1775 and 1810. Today, a national park and a roadway tunnel mark the historic path.

Active Options

On Your Feet: Word Chain Have students create a Word Chain about how the ordinances of 1785 and 1787 privatized national resources and transferred federally owned lands into private holdings, townships, and states. Tell students to form five lines. Hand a piece of paper to the first person in each line with one of these words from the text: *ordinances; federally owned lands; private holdings; townships; states.* The first student in line adds a word to the list that relates to the original word or term. Students pass the paper from person to person, each one adding a word or phrase they associate with the previously written word. Have a volunteer from each group read the Word Chain and ask the rest of the class to listen for any words that may not connect correctly. Conclude the activity by reviewing how the ordinances transferred lands.

NG Learning Framework: Investigate Education

ATTITUDE Curiosity

KNOWLEDGE Our Human Story

Encourage students to investigate more about education in the Northwest Territory. Direct them to briefly research church schools, dame schools, and home schooling of the period. Ask students to then choose one form of education to research further. Have students demonstrate their research by writing a period editorial or giving a period speech, using information from the lesson and new source material.

Striving Readers

Determine Chronology Check students' understanding of chronological order in Lesson 1.2 by asking them to place the ordinances in order by numbering them 1, 2, 3:

____(3)____ This ordinance renamed the "western lands" the Northwest Territory.

____(1)____ An ordinance was passed dividing the western lands where people were settling into smaller, self-governing sections that could later become states.

____(2)____ This ordinance organized land sections into townships.

Pre-AP

Research Native American Tribes Tell students to research the Native American tribes that lived in and around the Cumberland Gap. Instruct students to list the tribes and note facts that describe each culture and its connection to the geography of the Cumberland Gap. Ask students to pick a tribe to research further. Then ask students to synthesize what they learned and share their findings with the rest of the class.

See the Chapter Planner for more strategies for differentiation.

HISTORICAL THINKING

ANSWERS

1. Territorial expansion caused conflicts with Native Americans in the Northwest Territory.

2. First, the Articles of Confederation granted the national government land west of the Appalachians to the Mississippi River. Then, in 1784, a land ordinance divided the land into districts and set rules for attaining statehood. The Land Ordinance of 1785 divided districts into townships and required each township have a school. Finally, the Northwest Ordinance of 1787 renamed the region the Northwest Territory and established rights for settlers.

3. Most of the boundaries of the Northwest Territory follow the shores of the Great Lakes or the Ohio and Mississippi rivers.

1.3 Controversies About the Articles

Have you ever thought of a brilliant solution to a problem that only led to more problems? In the 1780s, the Articles of Confederation were exactly that: a solution that led to more problems.

MAIN IDEA The Articles of Confederation limited the federal government's effectiveness and led to economic problems and challenges to its authority.

THE PRICE OF WAR

The Articles of Confederation provided a governing structure during the Revolution but quickly proved inadequate for the needs of the new nation. The Articles created 13 sovereign states instead of one unified nation. So when the national government faced growing economic problems, it did not have an effective system in place to solve them.

One economic problem was the amount of debt that remained after the Revolution. By 1790, the U.S. government owed around $50 million to American merchants and farmers and also to the French government. The shortfall in funds also meant soldiers could not be paid, which led to angry protests.

Because of the limitations of the Articles, Congress could not impose taxes or regulate trade. Individual states refused to contribute enough money to help the national government pay these debts. Rewriting the Articles so that Congress could levy taxes was nearly impossible because the representatives of all 13 states had to approve such a measure. Few, if any, states were likely to offer their support, so the debts went unpaid.

Before the war, many Americans relied on receiving **credit**, or the privilege of purchasing something and paying the cost back over time. British companies wanted to encourage the colonists to buy their goods, and giving credit made that possible. As British subjects, farmers could repay their debts with goods, such as livestock and crops. After the war, British manufacturers demanded that all debts be repaid with money instead of goods. At the same time, state governments started to impose heavy taxes upon their citizens. Few farmers had cash on hand, and many Americans, especially farmers, faced financial ruin. When farmers failed to repay their debts, they often faced prosecution and the loss of their farms.

In some states, those who owed money demanded new laws that would allow them to settle their debts and pay taxes with goods. Citizens also wanted fewer requirements for voting so that they would have better representation in state governments. When governments did not respond, citizens challenged their authority and legitimacy by rebelling.

SHAYS'S REBELLION

In the fall of 1786, Daniel Shays, a veteran of the American Revolution, led rifle-carrying farmers into various Massachusetts courthouses and demanded the end of debt hearings. The Massachusetts government frantically asked Congress for help to put down the armed rebellion. In turn, Congress requested that the states help by sending money and soldiers, but the states refused. Its inability to respond to the domestic crisis of citizen rebellion revealed how ineffective Congress was under the Articles of Confederation.

Citizens became angrier when the state of Massachusetts passed the Riot Act, which prohibited armed groups from gathering in public. To prove its point, the state government sent armed troops, who defeated Shays's men easily. Shays and his supporters risked losing their voting rights and even imprisonment. However, Shays's Rebellion inspired other people to stand up to the government. One effect of the uprising was that in the following year's election, voter participation increased dramatically. Citizens wanted input into how problems such as debt repayment could be resolved.

CRITICAL VIEWING A protestor attacks an official during Shays's Rebellion in an attempt to disrupt court proceedings in Springfield, Massachusetts. Protests over the repayment of debts occurred in many states but reached a higher level of intensity in Massachusetts. Confrontations between farmers and government officials also occurred in the Massachusetts towns of Northampton, Concord, and Worcester. What details in the illustration convey the drama of Shays's Rebellion?

Tricorn hat

🏛 Memorial Hall Museum Deerfield, Massachusetts

Tricorn hats like this one, dated 1775, were popular in Europe and America in the 1700s. Notice how the tricorn hat appears in the illustration on the opposite page, flying off the head of the man attacking the official. Other men in the scene are wearing tricorn hats as well.

HISTORICAL THINKING

1. **READING CHECK** How did the Articles of Confederation limit the effectiveness of the federal government?

2. **DETERMINE CHRONOLOGY** In what ways did the economics of the American Revolution lead to Shays's Rebellion?

3. **ANALYZE CAUSE AND EFFECT** What effect did Shays's Rebellion have on the election of 1787?

PLAN

Objective
Understand the effects of an ineffective national government under the Articles of Confederation.

Critical Thinking Skills for Lesson 1.3
- Identify Main Ideas and Details
- Monitor Comprehension
- Determine Chronology
- Analyze Cause and Effect
- Compare and Contrast
- Ask and Answer Questions

Essential Question for Chapter 7
How did the ideas about the role of state and national government evolve? The Articles of Confederation provided a governing structure, but it was inadequate for unifying 13 sovereign states. Lesson 1.3 describes the effects of the Articles of Confederation and the challenges that resulted.

Background for the Teacher
The colonial economy used trading commodities such as livestock or crops, coins from Spain and Britain, credit, and bartering. In 1775, the Continental Congress began issuing fiat money, or paper currency, made by the government but not backed by a commodity. This fiat money was called "Continentals," and its value was determined by the people who used it. They viewed the actual value as low. Since the Continental was not backed by something of value, it was subject to inflation or deflation. People would often use the phrase "not worth a continental" for worthless goods.

Financial Literacy
To extend their knowledge and understanding about the concepts in this lesson, refer students to the Financial Literacy handbook.

Examine Historical Protests

Direct students' attention to the illustration of Shays's Rebellion. Ask them to recall similar images from earlier chapters such as the illustration "Tar and Feathers" in Chapter 5, Lesson 2.1. Guide a discussion that reviews the violent and nonviolent protests in Chapter 5, reminding students about the Boston Tea Party and the boycotts following the Townshend Acts. Conduct a short class discussion on different forms of protest.

TEACH

Guided Discussion

1. **Compare and Contrast** How did Americans make purchases before the war, and how did that change after the war? *(Credit was used before and after the war as a way for Americans to pay for purchases. Before the war, however, debts could be repaid with goods, such as crops. After the war, companies demanded money instead of goods to repay debt, which many farmers could not pay due to low cash flow and higher taxes.)*

2. **Ask and Answer Questions** What questions and answers might a reporter and Daniel Shays exchange about debt hearings? *(Possible responses: A reporter may ask why Shays thought he had a right to not pay his debts, or why he thought it was acceptable to storm a courthouse with a rifle. Shays may respond that debts to him for his military service went unpaid and because of this, he didn't have any money to pay his debts. He might say that he was accustomed to standing up for his rights by using force.)*

🏛 Virtual Museum Visit

The Memorial Hall Museum in Deerfield, Massachusetts, opened in 1880 with a collection of artifacts assembled by antiquarian George Sheldon. Housed in a former school building, the Memorial Hall Museum is one of the oldest museums in the United States. It holds 19 rooms of art, including paintings, Native American artifacts, textiles, and other items of historical significance. In addition, the building next to the museum is the Pocumtuck Valley Memorial Association (PVMA) Library, which holds a number of primary sources from colonial America, such as diaries, account ledgers, and town records.

Active Options

On Your Feet: Debate Divide the class into two groups. One group will represent the perspective of Congress and the other group will represent the perspective of state representatives. The debate should focus on the topic of Congress wanting to revise the Articles of Confederation so it could impose federal taxes in order to pay for war debts. Instruct groups to review their notes from the text, organize their arguments, and generate counterarguments to prepare for the debate. Then give both groups the opportunity to debate, changing the speaker for each group at regular intervals so all students can share their ideas. Encourage the class to vote on which side won the debate.

NG Learning Framework: Research American Rebellions in 1786 to 1787

ATTITUDE Empowerment

SKILL Communication

Have students conduct online research to learn about the rebellions that followed Shays's Rebellion. Instruct students to write a report on one rebellion that interests them. Students should include in their reports where the rebellion took place, why it happened, and who participated in it. Ask students why the rebellion they chose interested them. Allow time for students to present their reports to the class.

DIFFERENTIATE

Striving Readers

Preview Text Help students preview the lesson by pointing out the text features, such as the lesson title, Main Idea, and subheadings. **ASK:** Based on the subheadings, what do you expect this lesson to be about? Direct students to study the drawing and its accompanying Critical Viewing caption. Ask students to make notes about specific details in the illustration to help them with their Critical Viewing answer. Help students confirm their understanding of each paragraph before moving on to the next one.

Inclusion

Summarize Information Use a Fishbowl activity to review the lesson. Place students of mixed ability levels in each circle. Call on more advanced students to take turns summarizing the lesson content. When the first group of students has concluded its summary, switch positions and have inclusion students review the lesson content.

See the Chapter Planner for more strategies for differentiation.

HISTORICAL THINKING

ANSWERS

1. The Articles created sovereign states instead of a central government, making it difficult for Congress to tax, regulate trade, or raise money to pay off war debts.

2. After the war, businesses expected farmers to pay their debts with currency only. Farmers could not pay cash and went deeply into debt. Farmers demanded that state governments change laws affecting debt and voting. When governments offered no help, Daniel Shays led a group of farmers in a revolt against the Massachusetts government.

3. Shays's Rebellion encouraged more people to vote in the election of 1787 than had voted before.

CRITICAL VIEWING Possible response: One onlooker appears to be waving his hat and cheering on the attacker. The attacker appears to be choking the official. No one is stopping the attack or helping the official.

The Constitutional Convention

Would you like to travel for weeks by horse-drawn wagon along bumpy dirt roads in bad weather to help decide your country's fate? That's what 55 government representatives did to attend a meeting in the spring of 1787.

MAIN IDEA American leaders met at the Constitutional Convention to debate and decide how to reform the national government.

CRITICAL VIEWING This mural is one of two large-scale scenes painted by Barry Faulkner in 1936. It hangs in the Rotunda for the Charters of Freedom in the National Archives. What do you think the artist meant to convey by the setting he created for James Madison's presentation of the U.S. Constitution to George Washington?

Legend 1 James Madison   3 George Washington   5 Gouverneur Morris
        2 George Mason   4 Benjamin Franklin   6 Alexander Hamilton

DELEGATES GATHER

By 1787, it was clear the Articles of Confederation were not very effective. The United States was growing geographically and economically, and the Articles were not able to address complications from that growth. Robert Morris of Pennsylvania and **Alexander Hamilton** of New York pointed to Shays's Rebellion and other crises as evidence in support of their message. Morris and Hamilton believed the country needed a stronger government in order to deal with its problems.

Leaders called for a meeting to discuss reform. The meeting, held in Philadelphia on May 25, 1787, was called the **Constitutional Convention**.

Every state sent **delegates**, or representatives, except Rhode Island. The tiny state did not trust the concept of a powerful federal government, which it feared would be the outcome of the Constitutional Convention. Rhode Island's decision not to send delegates irritated many, including the normally even-tempered George Washington.

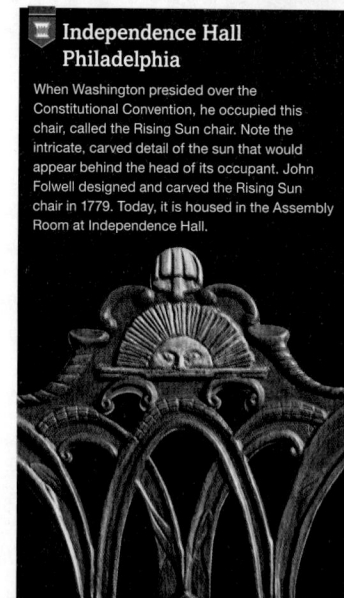

Independence Hall Philadelphia

When Washington presided over the Constitutional Convention, he occupied this chair, called the Rising Sun chair. Note the intricate, carved detail of the sun that would appear behind the head of its occupant. John Folwell designed and carved the Rising Sun chair in 1779. Today, it is housed in the Assembly Room at Independence Hall.

Those who gathered at the Convention to create the Constitution became known as the **Framers**. The Framers were wealthy, influential, and well educated. Many of the Framers had also been leaders during the Revolution, including Pennsylvania delegate Benjamin Franklin. The Framers elected George Washington from Virginia to lead the Convention.

Of the Framers at the Convention, James Madison, from Virginia, was the best prepared to craft a constitution for the new nation. His research and knowledge proved the most influential in shaping the ideas the delegates debated and ultimately included in the final document. Because of his active role, Madison is often called the "Father of the Constitution."

Some notable American leaders did not attend. Thomas Jefferson and John Adams were serving as ministers to France and Great Britain. Patrick Henry refused to attend because he fiercely opposed a strong central government.

GOALS AND CHALLENGES

The delegates debated for four months. Because of their experience, the Framers aimed to create a government that was neither too strong, like the British monarchy, nor too weak, as under the Articles of Confederation. The delegates wanted national, state, and local governments to share governing power, an idea called **federalism**. They also felt **dual sovereignty**, or giving state governments certain powers that the national government could not overrule, was important.

Delegates at the Convention agreed upon other main principles. One was republicanism. In a republican government, citizens elect officials to represent them, and these officials must act and govern according to the law. Another principle that guided the delegates was that elections and legislative votes would be decided by majority rule. Majority rule requires that the candidates or legislation receive at least one more than one-half of all votes, even when there are more than two choices. Majority rule means that support for a successful candidate or law must be strong.

Convention delegates supported the idea of federalism but debated how to divide state-federal power. They disagreed about how much power state and national governments should have and about how much authority they should grant the three branches of the federal government.

HISTORICAL THINKING

1. **READING CHECK** In what ways did James Madison contribute to the Constitutional Convention?

2. **DESCRIBE** What were the main issues of debate among delegates at the Constitutional Convention?

3. **FORM AND SUPPORT OPINIONS** Which principle under debate at the Convention do you think was most important to the new nation? Support your opinion with evidence from the text.

Objective

Understand why representatives reformed the national government.

Critical Thinking Skills for Lesson 2.1

- Identify Main Ideas and Details
- Monitor Comprehension
- Describe
- Form and Support Opinions
- Compare and Contrast
- Make Connections

Essential Question for Chapter 7

How did ideas about the role of state and national government evolve? Fifty-five delegates discussed how to reform the national government. Lesson 2.1 discusses the Constitutional Convention, at which delegates debated the roles of the federal and state governments.

Background for the Teacher

At the start of the Constitutional Convention, the Framers agreed upon rules and adopted them without debate. James Madison logged these rules in a journal. Among the rules were "That nothing spoken in the House be printed, or otherwise published, or communicated, without leave."

A cloud of secrecy surrounded the Constitutional Convention. While secrecy may contradict the idea of democratic ideals and philosophies that were the basis of the Constitutional Convention documents, the Framers had extensive experience with meetings to create new governments. As a result, they wanted to debate their ideas, make compromises, and establish the infrastructure for a new government without debate from the general public during the convention.

History Notebook

Encourage students to complete the American Gallery page for Chapter 7 in their History Notebooks as they read.

INTRODUCE & ENGAGE

Preview Using Visuals

Draw students' attention to the mural and details in it, such as the way the men are posed, their style of dress, and the use of walking sticks. **ASK:** Based on the details you see, what can you infer about the men in the mural and what they are doing? *(Possible response: The men are dressed formally and posed in a stately manner. They look older, wealthy, and probably educated, too. Perhaps they are merchants and gentlemen rather than farmers. Some are carrying documents.)* Explain that the mural depicts some of the leaders who attended the Constitutional Convention in Philadelphia in 1787.

TEACH

Guided Discussion

1. **Compare and Contrast** How did Patrick Henry's views about government differ from those of Alexander Hamilton and Robert Morris? *(Both Hamilton and Morris wanted a stronger federal government to handle the growing problems, and Patrick Henry was strongly against giving more power to a central government.)*

2. **Make Connections** How did the ideas of federalism and dual sovereignty discussed at the Constitutional Convention reflect ideals of the Declaration of Independence? *(Federalism reflected ideals in the Declaration of Independence because federalism prevented one authority from taking too much power, which was a main objection. Dual sovereignty related to the Declaration of Independence because it helped to maintain that some states' rights could not be overruled by a national government. Both ideas relate to the Declaration of Independence because they are meant to prevent the tyranny the colonists experienced under British rule.)*

Virtual Museum Visit

Draw students' attention to the image of the Rising Sun chair, which resides in Independence Hall, within Philadelphia's historic district. The chair is of the Chippendale style, inspired by designs by British cabinet maker, Thomas Chippendale. Philadelphia cabinet maker, John Folwell, used this popular 18th-century style when crafting the Rising Sun chair. The mahogany high-back chair has seen much wear and tear over time, and it was recently restored. As part of the restoration, the chair was reupholstered with stressed leather to make it look as if it has been used for hundreds of years.

Active Options

AMERICAN GALLERY ONLINE
Historic Philadelphia Invite students to explore the American Gallery. Have them select one of the images and do additional research to learn more about it. Ask questions that will inspire additional inquiry about the chosen image, such as: What is this? Where and when was it created? By whom? Why was it created? What is it made of? Why does it belong in this chapter? What else would you like to know about it?

NG Learning Framework: Profile a Framer

SKILL Communication

KNOWLEDGE Our Human Story

Encourage students to learn more about the men who attended the Constitutional Convention. Tell partners to choose one Framer to study in-depth and to find at least three primary sources produced by the Framer. Instruct students to work together to write a magazine article that profiles the Framer. Ask students to include information about his background, education, wealth, and the values that the Framer brought to the Convention. Students should also provide a brief explanation of how the Framer's background influenced the positions he took at the Constitutional Convention. When students have finished, allow time for them to share their articles with the rest of the class.

DIFFERENTIATE

Striving Readers

Review Concepts Draw attention to two concepts from Lesson 2.1: *republicanism* and *majority rule*. Have students prepare a T-Chart. Point out where the two terms are explained in Lesson 2.1. Then have students fill in their T-Chart, listing the terms *republicanism* and *majority rule and* recording important information about each in the correct column.

Inclusion

Reinforce Main Ideas Pair special needs students with students who are at a higher proficiency level. Have the pair reread the lesson, and then have them identify the main idea, along with supporting details, for each paragraph. They can use a diagram like the one below to record the main idea and details.

See the Chapter Planner for more strategies for differentiation.

HISTORICAL THINKING

ANSWERS

1. James Madison had the most active role in shaping the ideas of the Constitution and drafting it. For this reason, he is called the "Father of the Constitution."

2. The main debates consisted of how to divide power between the people and the government, the state and federal governments, and the three branches of the federal government.

3. Answers will vary, but responses should include one of the principles listed in the lesson, and evidentiary support should be given for all opinions.

CRITICAL VIEWING Possible response: The setting suggests a government building because of the columns and stairs. While it's unlikely that this event actually happened on the steps of a building, the artist probably wanted to emphasize that this was a historic moment.

The Big Question: How to Divide Power

Imagine listening in on the debates at the Constitutional Convention. Delegates from more populous states want more representatives than smaller states. Other delegates want the same number of representatives for all states. How do they resolve this issue? They compromise.

MAIN IDEA Delegates at the Constitutional Convention decided how to divide power in the government and how to elect the president.

THE GREAT COMPROMISE

As you have read, the Constitutional Convention embraced the idea that the federal government should rely on three branches of government based on the principles of **separation of powers** and **checks and balances**. Each branch would have unique powers. None would have more power than any other, and each branch would be a check on the other two. The **legislative branch** would create and pass legislation, or make laws. The **executive branch** would lead the nation and enforce laws, and the **judicial branch** would interpret laws.

Most delegates agreed on a judicial branch headed by a **Supreme Court** and that one leader, a president, should head the executive branch. But they could not agree on how the legislative branch should work. Delegates Edmund Randolph and William Paterson proposed two different plans, the **Virginia Plan** and the **New Jersey Plan**, shown at right. Smaller states, such as Delaware, Maryland, and New Jersey, were uncomfortable with the Virginia Plan. Larger states didn't like the New Jersey Plan. Delegates voted for the Virginia Plan as the draft framework for the Constitution, but many remained dissatisfied.

Roger Sherman of Connecticut combined the best ideas from both plans to craft the **Great Compromise**. He proposed a legislative branch with two houses. Delegates voted in favor of Sherman's plan and established the legislative branch that exists today.

PRESIDENTIAL ELECTIONS

The delegates agreed on the executive role of the president of the United States, but not on how to select this leader. Some argued for a direct election—the candidate with the majority of votes would win. Others wanted Congress or the state legislatures to choose, fearing that the people might elect someone unqualified for the job.

The Convention delegates landed on another compromise: the **electoral college**. States would be granted a specific number of electors equal to their numbers of senators and representatives in Congress. States would then choose their electors, who would cast their votes for president based on their voters' preferences. Though voting rights would eventually expand over time, after the Revolution, voting was limited to white males.

HISTORICAL THINKING

1. **READING CHECK** What compromises did the Convention delegates reach when planning for the legislative and executive branches?

2. **DETERMINE CHRONOLOGY** What two proposals preceded the Great Compromise?

3. **FORM AND SUPPORT OPINIONS** Of the Virginia Plan and the New Jersey Plan, which do you think best reflected the spirit of the new nation? Support your opinion with evidence from the text.

TOTAL POPULATION OF THE UNITED STATES, 1790: **3,929,214**

Population of Virginia **19%, 747,610**

Population of New Jersey **4.7%, 184,139**

= one representative from Virginia

= one representative from New Jersey

Edmund Randolph's **Virginia Plan**
TWO HOUSES

UPPER HOUSE
LOWER HOUSE

The number of representatives from each state is **proportionate to the state's population.**

This plan made delegates from small states nervous.

William Paterson's **New Jersey Plan**
ONE HOUSE

Each state has an equal number of representatives, regardless of population.

Delegates from larger states didn't like this plan.

ROGER SHERMAN'S
GREAT COMPROMISE

HOUSE OF REPRESENTATIVES

The number of representatives from each state is **proportionate to the state's population.**

SENATE

Each state has an equal number of representatives, **regardless of population.**

Source: United States Census Bureau

SEPARATION OF POWERS

THREE BRANCHES OF GOVERNMENT

LEGISLATIVE BRANCH	EXECUTIVE BRANCH	JUDICIAL BRANCH
MAKES LAWS	ENFORCES LAWS	INTERPRETS LAWS

Objective

Evaluate the compromises delegates made when dividing the power in the government.

Critical Thinking Skills for Lesson 2.2

- Identify Main Ideas and Details
- Monitor Comprehension
- Determine Chronology
- Form and Support Opinions
- Identify Problems and Solutions
- Describe
- Analyze Visuals

Essential Question for Chapter 7

How did ideas about the role of state and national government evolve? Delegates created a federal government structure. Lesson 2.2 discusses the agreements on a presidential election process and the Great Compromise.

Background for the Teacher

Roger Sherman was the only person to sign all four founding documents of government: the Continental Association, the Declaration of Independence, the Articles of Confederation, and the Constitution. Before his political life began, though, Sherman held several other jobs. Sherman grew up in a farm family. His father taught him the trade of a cordwainer, making shoes, belts, and other things from leather. Soon, he educated himself in mathematics. His abilities with numbers landed him a career surveying land in Connecticut.

While living in New Milford, Connecticut, Sherman opened a mercantile store that sold household goods, furniture, and other items. Sherman also published almanacs, studied law, and served in public posts.

INTRODUCE & ENGAGE

Activate Prior Knowledge

Write the words *represent* and *representative* on the board. Ask for volunteers to offer definitions of the words. Then ask students to offer examples of each word. Engage in a short class discussion about what students might know about who represents their communities in state government, and who represents their state in the federal government. Tell students that in this lesson they will learn about how the current system of federal representation was established.

TEACH

Guided Discussion

1. **Identify Problems and Solutions** What problem did the Great Compromise solve? *(The main problem was that delegates could not agree on the number of representatives each state should have. The Great Compromise endorsed a legislative branch with two houses, one with representation based on state population and one with an equal number of representatives for each state.)*

2. **Describe** Why did the delegates at the Constitutional Convention establish the electoral college for electing a president? *(The delegates were concerned that the people might elect an unqualified candidate for the job in a direct election.)*

Analyze Visuals

Direct students' attention to the infographic of the Great Compromise. Make sure students understand that the pie chart shows the size of the population of the United States in 1790, while the slices show each state's proportion of that population. **ASK:** What states were the most populous? *(Virginia, South Carolina, and Pennsylvania)* Point out that the pie slices that are the smallest, Delaware and Rhode Island, had the fewest people living in them. **ASK:** Based on the chart, why do you think the delegates were divided on their support of the Virginia or New Jersey plans? *(The states with more people living in them wanted representation based on population so they would have more power; states with fewer people wanted an equal number of representatives so they wouldn't be at a disadvantage.)*

Active Options

Active History: Categorize Government Responsibilities Extend the lesson by using either the PDF or Whiteboard version of the activity. These activities take a deeper look at a topic from, or related to, the lesson. Explore the activities as a class, turn them into group assignments, or even assign them individually.

NG Learning Framework: Explore Women's Rights

ATTITUDE Empowerment

KNOWLEDGE Our Human Story

Have students work in small groups to analyze the rights that women had during the early national period. Ask them to include women's representation and voting rights, their right to own property, and any other rights students want to know about. The groups can conduct online research to learn more details about the status of women. Tell groups to write a summary of their findings. Then have the groups present their summaries. Encourage students to include at least one visual for the presentation.

DIFFERENTIATE

English Language Learners

PREP Before Reading Have students of **All Proficiencies** use the PREP strategy to prepare for reading.

Preview title.
Read Main Idea Statement.
Examine Visuals.
Predict what you will learn.

Have students write their prediction and share it with a partner. Tell students at the **Expanding** level to give their reasons for their prediction. After reading, ask students to write another sentence that begins with "I also learned. . ."

Pre-AP

Write a News Article Encourage students to research and write a news article reporting on the debates at the Constitutional Convention. Instruct them to research the Convention to ensure that their article includes facts about what decisions were made, which new structures created, and any other rules or principles developed. Ask students to write an attention-getting headline for their article and to share it with the class.

See the Chapter Planner for more strategies for differentiation.

HISTORICAL THINKING

ANSWERS

1. The delegates combined their ideas and reached the Great Compromise, which set up two houses for the legislature, with different kinds of representation in each, establishing a new pattern for running a government. Another compromise was for an electoral college, which let state electors choose the president based on the vote of the people of each state.

2. The Virginia Plan and the New Jersey Plan preceded the Great Compromise.

3. Possible responses: The Virginia Plan reflected the spirit of the new nation because it proposed representation in proportion to the population size of each state. The New Jersey Plan reflected the spirit of equality in the new nation because it called for an equal number of representatives from each state no matter the size of the population.

2.3 Slavery and Trade

When people in power make decisions, the consequences are often immediate and long-lasting. That was the case during the Constitutional Convention when the Framers made decisions about slavery and trade.

MAIN IDEA Before the delegates approved the final draft of the Constitution, they had to compromise about slavery and settle issues about commerce.

SLAVERY AND REPRESENTATION

Even though the word *slavery* does not appear in the original body of the Constitution, slavery was a major topic at the Constitutional Convention. In fact, the delegates negotiated several compromises that firmly preserved the institution of slavery.

All delegates, whether from the North or the South, were especially concerned with how the practice of slavery affected state representation in Congress. Southern states depended more on enslaved labor than northern states. As a result, southern delegates wanted enslaved people to be counted as members of a state's population. Doing so would increase the number of delegates representing southern states in the House of Representatives. It would also increase the region's electoral votes. Northerners argued that enslaved people should not be counted because they were legally defined as property.

As part of the Great Compromise, the Convention delegates decided that five enslaved Americans would count as three free persons and approved inserting what is called the Three-Fifths Compromise into Article 1 of the Constitution. The Three-Fifths Compromise increased the power of white voters in the South at the expense of enslaved African Americans, who were each counted as less than a full person.

Article 1 also included a slave importation clause stating that Congress could not ban the importation of slaves for 20 years and that the tax on importing an enslaved person could not exceed $10 per person. Southern delegates also supported

Enslaved Population, 1790

Region	Total Population	Enslaved Population	Percentage of Population
New England	1,009,522	3,886	0.38%
Middle Atlantic	1,017,726	45,371	4.46%
South	1,866,387	645,023	34.56%
TOTAL	3,893,635	694,280	17.83%

Source: United States Census Bureau

the addition of the fugitive slave clause into Article 4 of the Constitution. This clause barred people who had escaped slavery in the South from living as free people in northern states.

Some delegates, especially those from northern states, wondered if the nation's ideals of freedom, liberty, and democracy could coexist alongside slavery. Benjamin Franklin wanted to abolish slavery from Pennsylvania altogether, but other representatives from northern free states approved the provisions. Most did not oppose slavery.

FREE AND OPEN TRADE

The southern representatives' other concern was the government's taxation of exports. The South's strong agricultural economy depended on the export of goods to other countries. Southerners believed that requiring foreign buyers to pay taxes on exported goods would hurt this trade. A weakened agricultural trade, in turn, would hurt the southern economy. The delegates agreed.

The Constitution placed few limits on the nation's commerce. One exception was the commerce clause, which gave Congress the power "to

regulate commerce with foreign nations, and among the several states, and with the Indian tribes." Under the commerce clause, Native American tribes were considered sovereign governments and were not subject to the same regulations as states. The coinage clause required all states to use common coinage, or the same kind of money. Finally, according to the full-faith and credit clause, all states were required to respect the public acts, records, and judicial proceedings of all other states. Together, these three clauses gave Congress the authority to oversee interstate commerce and keep trade free and open among states. Delegates decided the country's economy would work under a common market, which meant that no tax could be charged on trade between states.

At last, the delegates had settled the most important issues for the new nation. Gouverneur Morris, a delegate from New York, perfected the wording of the proposed Constitution and organized it into seven articles, or main sections. On September 15, 1787, the delegates approved the final draft. They signed it two days later. As he observed the signing of the Constitution, Benjamin Franklin commented that the sun on George Washington's chair at the Convention must be a rising sun. The United States was at the beginning, and not the end, of its time.

Thirty-nine of the 55 Convention delegates, or more than two-thirds, signed the document. Some delegates who approved of the final draft did not sign it because they were not in attendance. After it was signed, the Constitution was sent to the states for ratification and became the subject of yet more debate.

HISTORICAL THINKING

1. **READING CHECK** How did the Constitution reflect specific concerns of southern states?

2. **ANALYZE DATA** Why did southern delegates want to insert clauses about slavery into the Constitution? Use evidence from the population chart and the text to support your answer.

3. **MAKE GENERALIZATIONS** What advantages did the states experience under the common market?

Washington and Slavery
George Washington speaks with an overseer at his Mount Vernon farm in this 1851 painting by Junius Brutus Stearns. Twenty-five of the 55 delegates to the Convention owned slaves. Only Washington would grant some of his slaves freedom. His will specified that 123 of the 317 slaves at Mount Vernon be freed upon the death of his wife. Instead, Martha Washington freed them in 1800, before she died.

PLAN

Objective
Understand why compromises were made on slavery and trade during the Convention.

Critical Thinking Skills for Lesson 2.3
• Identify Main Ideas and Details
• Monitor Comprehension
• Analyze Data
• Make Generalizations
• Make Inferences

Essential Question for Chapter 7
How did ideas about the role of state and national government evolve? Before signing the Constitution, delegates debated slavery and trade. Lesson 2.3 discusses how the delegates compromised to address these issues.

Background for the Teacher
George Washington first acquired slaves when he was 11 years old through his father's will. He owned slaves for the rest of his life, freeing some of them in his own will. In a letter Washington sent in September 1786, he wrote, "I never mean … to possess another slave by purchase; it being among my first wishes to see some plan adopted by … which slavery in this Country may be abolished." However, he did not share his ambivalence toward slavery publicly, nor did he set his slaves free during his lifetime.

Washington was not able to free all of the slaves at Mount Vernon in his will. When Martha Washington's first husband, Daniel Parke Custis, died, by law, Martha received one third of the slaves Custis owned. These slaves were called "dower slaves." By Virginia law, the Washingtons could not will freedom to the dower slaves. After the Washingtons' deaths, the dower slaves went back to the Custis estate and were divided among the Custis descendants.

Preview and Predict

Direct students' attention to the painting of George Washington on his farm with an overseer and enslaved people working in a field. Note that, like Washington, the majority of the Framers at the Constitutional Convention owned slaves. **ASK:** How could the nation's ideals of freedom, liberty, and democracy be adopted alongside slavery? Have students think about this question and write down a prediction on a piece of paper regarding how the Framers handled the contradiction in ideals. Tell students they will learn about how the Framers addressed slavery when they finalized the Constitution. Have students revisit their predictions after completing the lesson to see if they were correct.

TEACH

Guided Discussion

1. **Make Inferences** Why do you think the original body of the Constitution did not have the word *slavery* in it? *(Possible responses: The delegates may have realized that the institution of slavery contradicted the ideals of freedom, liberty, and democracy, as declared in the Constitution. Gouverneur Morris, who perfected the wording of the documents, may have thought using the word could make them look bad.)*

2. **Make Predictions** What do you think were the long-term costs of slavery, both to people of African descent and to the nation? *(African Americans suffered physical, emotional, and psychological trauma because of the institution of slavery. That kind of suffering continued through efforts to gain freedom, liberty, and a part in the democracy the nation is based on. The nation suffers when its people do.)*

Analyze Data

STEM

Draw students' attention to the Enslaved Population, 1790 chart. Tell students that in some counties in the South, the slave populations represented nearly half of the county populations. **ASK:** In which region did the lowest proportion of enslaved people live? *(New England)* **ASK:** According to the chart, which region would receive the least benefit from compromising? *(New England included the smallest number of enslaved people in the United States, so it would not benefit as much from the slavery clauses.)*

Active Options

On Your Feet: Three Corners Organize students into three groups. Then have students search online for the document that was written at the Constitutional Convention. Assign one of the following excerpts from the Constitution for each group to analyze and discuss: Article 1, Section 2; Article 1, Section 10; and Article 4, Section 2. Ask students to analyze the compromises the Framers adopted to produce this single document and how it preserved the institution of slavery. After the groups have discussed the topic, have one student from each group present their conclusions to the class.

NG Learning Framework: Create a Trade Simulation

ATTITUDE Empowerment

SKILL Communication

Divide students into groups and tell them each group represents a state with its own trade rules and currency. Distribute classroom supplies among the groups so that each group has only one product. For example, one group has all the pencils; another has all the paper; another has all the laptops. Provide all groups with different forms of currency. Have each group come up with a plan for trading with the other groups. Once the groups have devised their plans, have them use their plans to trade materials with each other. Allow time after the trading for groups to share what they noticed about the advantages or disadvantages of not having an agreed-upon set of trade rules or currency. Review the commerce clause and its constituent parts, including the full-faith and credit clause, and then point out how conflicts that arose among the groups could have been avoided.

DIFFERENTIATE

Striving Readers

Pose and Answer Questions Have students work in pairs to read the lesson. Instruct them to pause after each paragraph and ask one another a *what, who, where, when,* or *why* question about what they have just read. Suggest students use a 5Ws Chart to help organize their questions and answers.

What?
Who?
Where?
When?
Why?

Gifted & Talented

Create a Presentation Tell students to conduct research to evaluate how the country benefited from the Ordinances of 1785 and 1787 combined with the commerce clause and the common market standards. After students have completed their research, have them create a brief presentation that demonstrates through text and visuals what connection they've made between these ideas. Encourage students to share their presentations with the class.

See the Chapter Planner for more strategies for differentiation.

HISTORICAL THINKING

ANSWERS

1. The southern states had concerns about their populations of enslaved people. The Three-Fifths Compromise addressed concerns about representation in Congress, and the fugitive slave clause prohibited free states from granting freedom to escaped slaves. Additionally, the South pressed for and received a prohibition on export taxes.

2. About 35 percent of the South's population consisted of enslaved people. Southern states would be granted fewer representatives (and therefor have less power) if enslaved people were not counted as part of the population.

3. Possible response: Eliminating taxes and using common coinage made trade between the states easier, more profitable, and helped the states work together.

3.1 Federalists and Antifederalists

Sometimes a fight between two people can spread until everyone takes a side. After the Constitutional Convention, citizens in the new nation faced this situation as two separate groups argued that their ideal vision was the right one.

MAIN IDEA Americans with opposite views about a strong central government engaged in intense debates over the ratification of the Constitution.

DIFFERENT POINTS OF VIEW

September 17, 1787, was a big day for the new United States. It was the day its Framers signed the Constitution. However, after it was signed, much more work was yet to come. Every state legislature had to ratify this new document. Given the spirited debates at the Constitutional Convention itself, it is not surprising that legislators and citizens quickly split into two factions. Those who supported the Constitution as it was written were known as **federalists**. Those who opposed all or parts of the Constitution were called **antifederalists**.

As you have read, federalism is a principle of governing in which a strong national government shares powers with the states. Federalists tended to live in big coastal cities and work in commerce. They hoped for more international trade and wanted to establish a strong and stable federal government. Some federalists were also frontier settlers, and they believed a strong central government could help defend them against attacks by Native Americans.

Antifederalists believed the Constitution did not provide strong enough barriers against the potential abuse of power by the federal government. They favored giving more power to state governments and believed only a government closest to the people could properly protect their liberties. Antifederalists tended to be from more rural areas, and they perceived the federal government as distant and separate from their interests. Antifederalists Patrick Henry and **George Mason**, a delegate from Virginia, gave impassioned speeches criticizing the Constitution.

Many newspapers supported the federalist cause. In New York, James Madison, Alexander Hamilton, and **John Jay**, who had been working behind the scenes in helping to craft the new government, published a series of essays in newspapers that argued in favor of the Constitution. In the spring of 1788, they published a book of the 85 essays called *The Federalist*. Despite these convincing essays, some key states, such as North Carolina, Virginia, and New York, resisted ratification at first.

RATIFYING THE CONSTITUTION

Each state held a convention to debate and vote on the Constitution. Delaware was the first to ratify, followed by Pennsylvania, New Jersey, Georgia, Connecticut, and Massachusetts. Except for Pennsylvania, all these states had small populations. Delegates to conventions in these states understood the advantages of joining a union in which their representation was equal to that of larger states. In Pennsylvania, federalists led by James Wilson moved quickly to secure ratification before antifederalists in the rural west could organize.

Many state constitutions already included a bill of rights, and the federalists argued that for this reason, another bill of rights was unnecessary. But in Virginia, antifederalists George Mason and Patrick Henry argued that adding a bill of rights to the Constitution was necessary to protect individuals and states and to prevent abuse of power by the federal government. Political writer Mercy Otis Warren also advocated for a bill of rights. In 1788, horrified by the violence she witnessed during Shays's Rebellion, she argued that the revolutionaries did not fight against Britain only to meet with more tyranny.

CRITICAL VIEWING In 1939, Congress commissioned artist Howard Chandler Christy to paint *Signing of the Constitution* in honor of the 150-year anniversary of the Constitution. It is an enormous work, 20 by 30 feet in size, and it hangs in the House wing of the U.S. Capitol. In this painting, Christy depicts the events of September 17, 1787. George Washington stands in front of his Rising Sun chair during the signing, which was held at Independence Hall. The 81-year-old Ben Franklin listens to something Alexander Hamilton is telling him, and Richard Spaight signs the document. How does this painting convey the importance of the event it depicts?

By July 1788, all but two states—North Carolina and Rhode Island—had voted for ratification. Rhode Island, again a holdout, refused to ratify the Constitution until a list of changes was included. The vote for ratification was so close that James Madison finally proposed to Congress that a set of 12 official **amendments**, or changes, be added to the Constitution to provide greater constitutional protection for individual liberties. The states ratified 10 of these amendments, and Congress added them to the Constitution. These amendments, which place specific restrictions on governmental power, became known as the **Bill of Rights**. Together, the Constitution and the Bill of Rights have provided the foundation for the U.S. government for more than 200 years.

HISTORICAL THINKING

1. **READING CHECK** What were the main arguments between the federalists and the antifederalists?

2. **COMPARE AND CONTRAST** What are some general characteristics of the people who identified as federalists and those who identified as antifederalists?

3. **DESCRIBE** Why did Congress add the Bill of Rights to the Constitution?

PLAN

Objective
Describe the opposing political philosophies of the leaders who debated ratification.

Critical Thinking Skills for Lesson 3.1
- Identify Main Ideas and Details
- Monitor Comprehension
- Compare and Contrast
- Describe
- Identify
- Form and Support Opinions

Essential Question for Chapter 7
How did ideas about the role of state and national government evolve? Two groups debated the Constitution, resulting in the addition of the amendments that became known as the Bill of Rights. Lesson 3.1 discusses the opposing philosophies of the federalists and antifederalists.

Background for the Teacher
An official copy of the Constitution needed to be written before it could be sent to the states for ratification. Jacob Shallus, an assistant clerk for the legislature of Pennsylvania, handwrote the 4,543 words of the Constitution on four large pieces of vellum parchment. This was done after the Constitutional Convention closed late on Saturday, September 15, 1787.

Copying other documents into one entirely new and official document would be a labor-intensive task for anyone, but Shallus was not even a delegate at the Convention. He completed the arduous task by Monday, September 17, 1787. Shallus's handwritten copy, done in inked calligraphy, resides in the Rotunda of the National Archives Museum in Washington, D.C.

Compare and Contrast Political Parties

Before reading this lesson, take time as a class to compare and contrast the present-day Democratic and Republican political parties. Draw a Venn Diagram on the board and record students' responses. Write details about the Democratic party in the left circle and about the Republican party in the right circle. In the area of overlap, include details about how the parties are alike. Explain that these differing ideas about government are similar to the debate between federalists and antifederalists, groups that emerged during constitutional debates.

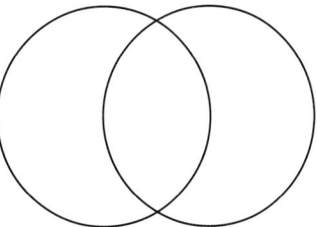

TEACH

Guided Discussion

1. **Describe** What are some ways the American idea of constitutionalism preserves individual rights? *(The idea of constitutionalism, which limits the powers of the government, is found in the Constitution and Bill of Rights, which protect against the abuse of power and set limits on the amount of power that can be given to a government.)*

2. **Identify** Who were the most vocal federalists and antifederalists during the ratification process? How did they express their opinions? *(James Madison, Alexander Hamilton, and John Jay were staunch federalists. They published their views in newspapers and a book of essays called* The Federalist. *Strong antifederalists included Patrick Henry, George Mason, and Mercy Otis Warren. They spoke out vocally against the Constitution and in favor of guaranteeing more individual and states' rights within it.)*

Form and Support Opinions

Instruct students to closely examine the text to understand more about the debate between the federalists and antifederalists. Then ask students to share their opinion about whether they believe the Constitution would have been ratified without including a Bill of Rights. Tell students to support their answers with evidence from the reading. *(Answers will vary, but should include evidence that supports the opinion.)*

Active Options

On Your Feet: Turn and Talk on a Topic Divide the class into four groups and have each group form a line. Give each group this topic sentence: Federalists and antifederalists expressed their differences on national government and the Constitution. Starting with the first person in line, have each student take a turn providing a supporting statement to the next person in line building a paragraph on the topic. Allow each group to present its paragraph to the class by having each student share his or her statement.

NG Learning Framework: Hold a 21st Century Bill of Rights Panel Discussion

ATTITUDE Curiosity

SKILL Collaboration

Encourage students to explore the current implications of the adoption of the Bill of Rights. Assign students to teams of two and tell them to research one amendment in the Bill of Rights as it applies to Americans in the 21st century. Teams should explore what rights the amendment protects, why the amendment is a point of contention (if it is), and what American society today might look like without that particular amendment. Students can use online or library sources for research. Ideally, teams will locate a news story that demonstrates the ways in which their amendment is still relevant, more than 200 years after it was added to the Constitution. Allow time for a Bill of Rights panel discussion in class, and encourage teams to prepare an oral presentation about their amendment.

DIFFERENTIATE

Striving Readers

Summarize Have students read Lesson 3.1 in pairs and write a sentence that restates the main idea of each paragraph as they read. Then have students review those sentences and write a four- or five-sentence paragraph that summarizes the whole lesson. Remind students that they should use their own words in their summary and include only the most important ideas and details.

Inclusion

Define Key Vocabulary Pair students with learning disabilities with students who are proficient readers. Direct partners to work together as they go through the lesson, filling in a Word Map for each Key Vocabulary word. Then ask students to use each word in a sentence and have their partner verify that it is used correctly.

See the Chapter Planner for more strategies for differentiation.

HISTORICAL THINKING

ANSWERS

1. Federalists supported the Constitution, favored a strong federal government, and believed that a central government was necessary to protect them from attacks. Antifederalists did not believe the Constitution as written protected citizens from the abuses of power Americans experienced as British subjects and wanted more power to reside with state and local governments.

2. Federalists mostly lived in big cities, worked in commerce, and wanted more trade with other countries. Antifederalists tended to be from more rural areas and viewed the federal government as disconnected from their interests.

3. In order to reach an agreement, James Madison proposed changes to the Constitution that eventually became ratified as the Bill of Rights.

CRITICAL VIEWING Answers will vary. Possible response: The men are in deep discussion; and have serious facial expressions; George Washington, one of the nation's foremost leaders, presides over the group on a raised platform.

3.2 Constitutional Debates

Legislators and ordinary citizens had a lot to say both for and against ratifying the proposed Constitution. As people on both sides of the debate published their arguments, it became clear that some kind of compromise was necessary for this plan of government to survive.

Federalists and antifederalists circulated their opinions to appeal to and persuade their audiences. As you have read, Alexander Hamilton, John Jay, and James Madison published *The Federalist* in support of ratification of the Constitution as written. Writer

George Mason argued against the Constitution without certain guarantees. Writing under the pen name of "A Columbian Patriot," Mercy Otis Warren presented a strong antifederalist argument, which antifederalist newspapers used to challenge federalist ideas.

CRITICAL VIEWING John Singleton Copley painted this 1763 portrait of Mercy Otis Warren. Warren grew up in a wealthy and politically active family. Though she did not receive a formal education, she became a poet, a playwright, and a historian. Her social position allowed her a unique view of the events of the American Revolution. What details in her portrait convey her social status?

DOCUMENT ONE

Primary Source: Essay
from "Federalist No. 1," by Alexander Hamilton, 1788

Originally appearing as an anonymous series of 85 newspaper essays in favor of the Constitution, the authors' work was bound into the book *The Federalist* in 1788. These essays are considered among the most important examples of political philosophy in American history. This excerpt, from the first essay, was written by Hamilton.

CONSTRUCTED RESPONSE What was the author's opinion about a strong government versus the opinions of those who advocated for more rights for the people?

History will teach us that [dangerous ambition] has been found a much more certain road to the introduction of despotism [government with an absolute ruler] than the [firmness and efficiency of government], and that of those men who have overturned the liberties of republics, the greatest number have begun their career by paying . . . court to the people; commencing demagogues [absolute rulers], and ending tyrants.

DOCUMENT TWO

Primary Source: Essay
from "Objections to the Constitution of Government Formed by the Convention," by George Mason, 1787

During the Constitutional Convention in 1787, George Mason wrote an essay about why he refused to sign the Constitution. In his essay, which was published in the *Virginia Journal*, Mason predicted what would become of the union if individual rights weren't made clear. His ideas reflected principles in the Declaration of Independence.

CONSTRUCTED RESPONSE How does Mason's essay about government differ from ideas expressed in *The Federalist*?

This government will set out a moderate aristocracy [a class system based on birth or wealth]: it is at present impossible to foresee whether it will, in its operation, produce a monarchy, or a corrupt, tyrannical aristocracy; it will most probably vibrate some years between the two, and then terminate in the one or the other.

DOCUMENT THREE

Primary Source: Essay
from "Observations on the New Constitution," by Mercy Otis Warren, 1788

As a woman in the new United States, Mercy Otis Warren could not vote or take part in any conventions or lawmaking. That did not stop her from voicing a strong antifederalist viewpoint in the hopes of swaying those who had the power to ratify or reject the Constitution.

CONSTRUCTED RESPONSE What concerns about the Constitution did Warren express?

[The] Constitution, which, by the undefined meaning of some parts, and the ambiguities of expression in others, is dangerously adapted to the purposes of . . . tyranny. There is no security in the proffered [presented] system, either for the rights of conscience, or liberty of the press. There are no well-defined limits of the Judiciary Powers. The Executive and Legislative are so dangerously blended as to give just cause of alarm.

SYNTHESIZE & WRITE

1. **REVIEW** Review what you have learned about the arguments for and against the ratification of the Constitution.

2. **RECALL** On your own paper, write details about the arguments in favor of and opposed to the ratification of the Constitution, as revealed by the three excerpts.

3. **CONSTRUCT** Construct a topic sentence that answers this question: What were the main philosophies that supported the arguments for and against the ratification of the Constitution?

4. **WRITE** Using evidence from this chapter and the documents, write an informative paragraph that supports your topic sentence in Step 3.

PLAN

Objective
Synthesize information about the debates surrounding the ratification of the Constitution from primary source documents.

Critical Thinking Skills for Lesson 3.2
- Synthesize
- Identify
- Compare and Contrast
- Evaluate

Essential Question for Chapter 7
How did the ideas about the role of state and national government evolve? Citizens of the new nation published federalist and antifederalist views about the powers of state and national governments as outlined in the Constitution. Lesson 3.2 provides excerpts from three primary sources that illustrate the debates over the ratification of the Constitution.

Background for the Teacher
Mercy Otis Warren had a long and prolific writing career. She published her early work, mainly plays, anonymously, but her later work was published under her name. Warren came from a wealthy family and pushed her father to allow her to be tutored alongside her brother.

She published poems and satirical political pieces in the *Boston Gazette*. Her play, *The Adulateur*, which poked fun at Massachusetts Governor Thomas Hutchinson, was published by the *Massachusetts Spy* in 1772. Whether satirical or not, her work was characterized by a theme of revolutionary spirit, strength, and republican ideals.

INTRODUCE & ENGAGE

Prepare for the Document-Based Question

Before students start on the activity, briefly preview the three documents. Remind students that a constructed response requires full explanations in complete sentences. Emphasize that students should use what they have learned about the constitutional debates and the positions of the federalists and antifederalists in addition to the documents.

TEACH

Guided Discussion

1. **Identify** According to Alexander Hamilton in *The Federalist*, what human trait is most likely to lead to absolute or tyrannical leadership? *(Hamilton states that "dangerous ambition has been found a much more certain road to the introduction of despotism.")*

2. **Compare and Contrast** George Mason and Mercy Otis Warren were both antifederalists. How were their arguments similar? How were they different? *(Both argue that the Constitution could set up a system that would lead to tyranny. Mason believes tyranny will stem from the aristocracy. Warren mentions specific rights that are lacking in the Constitution, such as term limits on the judicial branch—omissions that could lead to tyranny.)*

Evaluate

After students have completed the Synthesize & Write activity, allow time for them to exchange paragraphs and read and comment on the work of their peers. Establish guidelines for comments prior to this activity so that feedback is constructive and encouraging in nature.

More Information

John Singleton Copley John Singleton Copley was an American painter born in 1738. He was widely commissioned by middle-class patrons in New England to paint their portraits. His painting style depicted his subjects in their daily lives and with everyday objects. Copley's painting style captured his subjects while conveying a feeling of realism that was not common in paintings by American artists, as it was a European technique–one that was in demand by Copley's patrons. **ASK:** Why might Copley's American patrons be interested in being portrayed in their everyday life by an artist who used European techniques? *(Possible response: Patrons may have wanted a portrait portraying them in European style to give the impression that they had a lot of wealth.)*

Active Options

On Your Feet: Jigsaw Organize students into three "expert" groups and have students from each group analyze one of the documents and summarize the key points of the arguments in their own words. Then have students in each group count off using letters A, B, and C. Regroup students into three new groups so that each new group has at least one person from each expert group. Have students in the new groups take turns sharing the main points of the arguments they came up with in their expert groups.

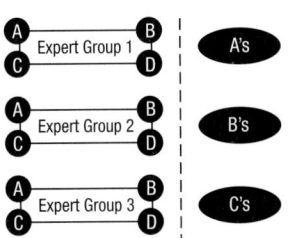

DIFFERENTIATE

English Language Learners

Identify Main Ideas and Details Tell students at the **Emerging** level to work in pairs to read Lesson 3.2. Instruct them to pause after each paragraph and state the main idea of the paragraph. Encourage pairs to work together to fill in a Main Idea and Details List for each paragraph, including the three primary source documents. Finally, invite one student from each pair to share their responses.

Gifted & Talented

Host a Talk Show Invite students to host a talk show featuring Alexander Hamilton, George Mason, and Mercy Otis Warren. Tell students to conduct research to determine the appropriate questions for each guest. Then have students decide who will represent each guest and who will be the host. Encourage the group to present their talk show to the class, and tell the host to field questions for the guests from the class.

See the Chapter Planner for more strategies for differentiation.

SYNTHESIZE & WRITE

ANSWERS

1. Answers will vary.

2. Answers will vary.

3. Possible response: Federalists believed in a strong national government while antifederalists believed in a smaller central government, with a focus on individual liberties.

4. Students' paragraphs should include their topic sentence from Step 3. Students should include a quotation or detail from the excerpt of *The Federalist* to support federalist ideas. Students should include one to two details from both "Objections to the Constitution of Government Formed by the Convention" and "Observations on the New Constitution" to support the antifederalists' points.

CONSTRUCTED RESPONSE

Document 1: Possible response: The author, Hamilton, felt that a strong government was essential to secure liberty, while those who advocated for more rights for the states thought a strong federal government would lead to tyrannical rule.

Document 2: Possible response: Mason differs from the writers of *The Federalist* in that he believed the federal government described in the Constitution would likely turn into a monarchy or tyrannical aristocracy.

Document 3: Possible response: Warren believed the Constitution was ambiguous and could lead to an oppressive government unless there were provisions for freedom of the press, limits on judiciary powers, and separation of the executive and legislative branches.

CRITICAL VIEWING Possible response: Warren wears an ornately decorated gown with expensive material, which indicates that she has wealth and social status.

The Bill of Rights

Americans enjoy many rights every day, from freely expressing opinions in public and in the press to protesting government actions. These and other fundamental rights are part of our identity as a nation, and we have the Framers of the Constitution to thank for them.

MAIN IDEA The Framers included a Bill of Rights in the Constitution to protect the fundamental rights and individual liberties of all citizens.

AMENDING THE CONSTITUTION

In 1787, the United States Constitution represented a bold new way of governing based on the consent of the governed. It also established a government that has survived for more than 200 years. Its survival has resulted from the control of power and interests through a system of checks and balances. Through Article 5, the Constitution provided a process by which it could adapt to the needs of a changing society. This process made possible a series of amendments protecting individual liberties from governmental abuses.

In order to amend, or change, the Constitution, Congress or two-thirds of the state legislatures must propose an amendment. Then three-fourths of the state legislatures must approve it. If they do, the amendment is ratified. This vigorous process helps protect citizens from unreasonable amendments.

Congress added the first 10 amendments, known as the Bill of Rights, to the Constitution in 1791. The amendments were intended to protect the freedoms of life, liberty, and the pursuit of happiness—all ideals that were put forth in the Declaration of Independence.

INDIVIDUAL FREEDOMS

The First Amendment protects fundamental individual freedoms: freedom of religion, freedom of speech and the press, and freedom of peaceful assembly and petitioning. In 1786,

THE BILL OF RIGHTS

FIRST AMENDMENT	Freedoms of speech, religion, the press, and the right to peacefully assemble and to petition the government
SECOND AMENDMENT	The right to form a well-regulated militia and to keep and bear arms
THIRD AMENDMENT	Protection from being forced to quarter soldiers
FOURTH AMENDMENT	Protection against searches and seizures without a warrant based on reasonable grounds
FIFTH AMENDMENT	The right of an arrested individual to know what he or she is accused of; protection against being tried for the same crime twice; protection against unjustified deprivation of life, liberty, or property; the right to refuse to testify against oneself
SIXTH AMENDMENT	The right to a fair and speedy trial by jury; the right to a lawyer
SEVENTH AMENDMENT	The right to a jury trial in certain civil cases
EIGHTH AMENDMENT	Protection against excessive bail and cruel or unusual punishment
NINTH AMENDMENT	Protection against others taking away rights not mentioned in the Bill of Rights
TENTH AMENDMENT	The right of states and citizens to retain powers not given to the federal government

See the Citizenship Handbook for the full text of the United States Constitution.

CRITICAL VIEWING On August 28, 1963, 250,000 participants at the March on Washington for Jobs and Freedom gathered in front of the Lincoln Memorial in Washington, D.C., where they heard speeches on issues of racial equality and economic justice. The event concluded with Dr. Martin Luther King, Jr., delivering his "I Have a Dream" speech. What does this photo convey about the participants' confidence in enjoying the protection of the First Amendment?

Thomas Jefferson wrote a **statute**, or a law written by a legislative body, for the state of Virginia that served as a forerunner to the First Amendment. In the Statute for Religious Freedom, Jefferson strongly advocated for religious liberty and the separation of church and state. Some delegates objected to including this idea in the Constitution, believing that the Constitution should reflect the nation's Christian foundation. Other delegates, such as James Madison, contended that safeguarding people's "natural right" to worship freely, or not worship at all, was more important. Because of the First Amendment, Americans have the right to practice any religion or no religion without fear of discrimination or persecution.

Freedom of the press, another First Amendment right, was a new concept in the 1780s, when governments routinely blocked the publication of stories they disliked. Governments also forced newspapers to print articles that suited their own purposes. The First Amendment made both acts illegal, and today the American press can report and publish freely. The First through Eighth Amendments focus on individual rights. The Ninth Amendment protects any personal freedoms not specified in the Bill of Rights. The Tenth Amendment allows citizens and states to keep any powers not mentioned in the Constitution.

Throughout our nation's history, we, the people, have added additional amendments to the Constitution to expand and clarify our rights. These amendments have been vital to the development of an American identity. They have established many of the essential freedoms Americans enjoy today.

HISTORICAL THINKING

1. **READING CHECK** Why was protecting the rights and freedoms listed in the Bill of Rights important to citizens of the new nation?

2. **MAKE GENERALIZATIONS** In what ways are natural rights protected in the Bill of Rights?

3. **EXPLAIN** What requirements are involved for proposed and ratified amendments, and why is this process in place?

PLAN

Objective
Understand how the Constitution was amended to protect the rights and liberties of citizens.

Critical Thinking Skills for Lesson 3.3
- Identify Main Ideas and Details
- Monitor Comprehension
- Make Generalizations
- Explain
- Make Inferences
- Form and Support Opinions

Essential Question for Chapter 7
How did the ideas about the role of state and national government evolve? Individual state laws influenced the amendments included in the Bill of Rights. Lesson 3.3 describes how the Constitution can be amended and covers the liberties that the Bill of Rights protects.

Background for the Teacher

Freedom of religion was so important to Thomas Jefferson that he noted authoring the Virginia Statute for Religious Freedom as one of his greatest accomplishments. This statute heavily influenced the First Amendment to the U.S. Constitution. Among the reasons he believed religious freedom was so important was because the British government imposed taxes on the people to fund the Church of England.

While some of the colonists chose to worship at the Church of England, many others came to the colonies because they were seeking religious freedom. Taxes were a point of contention, and the government had to assess whether it was fair to use taxes to support churches. There were many religious groups that occupied the colonies including: Quakers, Catholics, Baptists, Jews, and Presbyterians, among others, and the Framers needed to give careful thought to the role of religion in the government.

INTRODUCE & ENGAGE

Rank the Rights

Point out the chart showing the Bill of Rights. Explain to students that before the Constitution was ratified, engaged citizens insisted that these rights be guaranteed for all Americans. Ask students to create a list of rights that they would like to see at their school. List their proposed rights on the board. Have each student rank these rights in a list of their own, based on what they believe is most important. Encourage students to share their lists. **ASK:** How do you think life would be different if your school implemented your Bill of Rights? (*Answers will vary.*)

TEACH

Guided Discussion

1. **Make Inferences** How do you think Article 5 supports a changing American identity throughout time? (*Article 5 allows for the Constitution to be amended, so as American identity, culture, and technology evolve, distinct from the time of the Framers, then the Constitution can be amended to support those changes.*)

2. **Form and Support Opinions** What rights do you think are covered by the Ninth Amendment? (*Possible responses should include evidence that supports the opinion.*)

Build Time Lines

Organize students into groups of four or five. Tell students they will be constructing their own time lines about how specific rights included in the Bill of Rights have played out over time. Invite each group to choose one protected right from the amendments, such as the right to assemble peacefully. (Or teachers can assign each group a specific right to research.) Have the groups research examples of key historical events of when citizens executed that right. Encourage students to consider how these liberties have come to be defined in practice over time, noting each event on their time lines. Once groups have completed their time lines, have them summarize their conclusions for the class.

Active Options

On Your Feet: Rotating Discussion Assign teams of students to each of the four corners in the room. Have each team think of several questions about the Bill of Rights. Start the discussion by tossing a bean bag or other soft object to Team A and asking a question. When Team A answers, have them toss the bean bag to another team while asking one of their prepared questions. Continue until all questions have been answered.

NG Learning Framework: Understand the Bill of Rights

ATTITUDE Empowerment

KNOWLEDGE Our Human Story

Divide students into small groups. Tell groups to review the reasons the Framers added the Bill of Rights to the Constitution, including the impact of the colonial experience, to understand why these freedoms were important to citizens. Students should take into account the underlying reasons, from broad emphasis on religious and political freedom, to more specific protections, such as the prohibition against quartering of troops. Have each group choose one amendment to present to the class. Encourage presenters to assume the role of one of the Framers and state the reasons for including that amendment in the Bill of Rights.

DIFFERENTIATE

English Language Learners

Make Key Vocabulary Cards Have students of **All Proficiencies** make and use flashcards to learn and practice unfamiliar vocabulary words from this lesson. On one side of the card, they write the key term. On the other side, they write the definition and description and draw a picture that helps them recall the meaning. Encourage students to use the flashcards for review.

Gifted & Talented

Teach a Class Invite students to teach a class on the First Amendment. Tell them to research and prepare a short multimedia presentation about the purpose and meaning of the First Amendment. Students might focus on the relationship between Jefferson's Statute for Religious Freedom and the First Amendment. Once students have presented, encourage them to ask their classmates what the First Amendment means to them and to field questions from the class.

See the Chapter Planner for more strategies for differentiation.

HISTORICAL THINKING

ANSWERS

1. The rights and freedoms listed in the Bill of Rights were important because they were intended to protect the freedoms of life, liberty, and the pursuit of happiness, religious and political freedom, and protection from being forced to quarter soldiers—all ideas that were put forth in the Declaration of Independence.

2. Fundamental rights are protected in the Bill of Rights by ensuring freedom of speech and freedom of religion under the First Amendment. The Third and Fourth Amendments protect property.

3. The requirements to ratify amendments include the following: Congress or two-thirds of the state legislatures must propose the amendment; three-fourths of the state legislatures must approve the proposal. This process is difficult so that one small faction cannot push through an amendment that most people would disapprove of.

CRITICAL VIEWING Possible response: People are holding hands and singing together. They seem at ease with the demonstration because peaceful assembly is a First Amendment right.

7 REVIEW

VOCABULARY

Write a sentence for each group of words that explains the relationship between them.

1. federalist / antifederalist
2. commerce clause / common market
3. legislative branch / executive branch / judicial branch
4. Bill of Rights / amendment
5. separation of powers / checks and balances
6. constitution / constitutionalism
7. statute / ordinance
8. sovereign / dual sovereignty
9. delegates / Framers

READING STRATEGY
DETERMINE CHRONOLOGY

If you haven't done so already, complete your sequence chain to show how the roles of state and federal governments evolved in the early United States. Then answer the question.

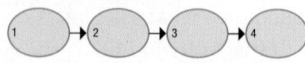

10. From 1776 to 1791, how did the role of the federal government develop in the United States?

MAIN IDEAS

Answer the following questions. Support your answers with evidence from the chapter.

11. In what ways did the Articles of Confederation limit the effectiveness of the national government? **LESSON 1.1**
12. What did the ordinances of 1785 and 1787 regulate? **LESSON 1.2**

13. What were Daniel Shays and his followers protesting? **LESSON 1.3**
14. What was the purpose of the Constitutional Convention of 1787? **LESSON 2.1**
15. What three principles did delegates at the Constitutional Convention want to include? **LESSON 2.1**
16. Why did the Framers insist on separation of powers in the Constitution? **LESSON 2.2**
17. How did the Great Compromise help both large and small states? **LESSON 2.2**
18. What was the Three-Fifths Compromise and who did it benefit? **LESSON 2.3**
19. How did James Madison, Alexander Hamilton, and John Jay present the arguments of the federalists? **LESSON 3.1**
20. Why was the Bill of Rights added to the Constitution? **LESSON 3.3**

HISTORICAL THINKING

Answer the following questions. Support your answers with evidence from the chapter.

21. **ANALYZE CAUSE AND EFFECT** What factors prompted leaders to work to replace the Articles of Confederation with a new constitution?
22. **IDENTIFY PROBLEMS AND SOLUTIONS** What problem did the establishment of the electoral college solve?
23. **SYNTHESIZE** How does the Bill of Rights represent the ideals that Americans fought for in the American Revolution?
24. **FORM AND SUPPORT OPINIONS** Do you think the Constitution reflects a fair balance between federalist and antifederalist arguments? Support your opinion with evidence from the chapter.

25. **EVALUATE** How did the Framers reconcile the ideals of freedom, liberty, and democracy with slavery?
26. **EXPLAIN** Why did James Wilson want a quick ratification of the Constitution?

ANALYZE VISUALS

This statue, called *Guardianship*, stands in front of the National Archives building in Washington, D.C., where the foundational documents of the United States are housed. The inscription at the base of the statue reads, "Eternal vigilance is the price of liberty." Study the statue and its inscription. Then answer the questions below.

27. Why might the inscription on this statue refer to "eternal vigilance," or keeping a careful watch over something, as the "price of liberty"?
28. *Guardianship* means taking care of something. In what ways were the Framers guardians of the new nation?

ANALYZE SOURCES

In 1788, as part of "Federalist No. 38," James Madison wrote the following opinion about the process of forming a government through history. Read the passage and answer the question.

> It is a matter both of wonder and regret, that those who raise so many objections against the new Constitution should never call to mind the defects of that which is to be exchanged for it. It is not necessary that the former should be perfect; it is sufficient that the latter is more imperfect.

29. What is Madison saying to those who disagree with the new Constitution?
30. To what is Madison referring when he mentions "the defects of that which is to be exchanged for it"?

CONNECT TO YOUR LIFE

31. **NARRATIVE** Review the rights granted by the First Amendment. Think about a time when one of the rights played a role in your own life or that of someone you know. Write a paragraph connecting that right to your life as an American today.

TIPS

- Read through the text of the First Amendment. List the specific freedoms mentioned. Then choose a freedom that has had an impact on your life.
- Use textual evidence from the amendment in your paragraph. Cite the specific language used to describe the freedom, and then explain the impact that freedom has had on your life.
- Conclude the paragraph with a comment about what you think is most important about the First Amendment.

VOCABULARY ANSWERS

1. Federalists wanted a strong national government, while antifederalists wanted states to have more power.

2. The commerce clause allowed Congress to regulate commerce among states and allowed states to work under a common market without changing currency or paying extra taxes.

3. The legislative branch, or Congress, is in charge of making laws; the executive branch, which includes the president, is in charge of enforcing the laws; and the judicial branch is in charge of evaluating and interpreting the laws.

4. The Bill of Rights, consisting of 10 amendments that were ratified by the states, was added to the Constitution.

5. Separation of powers ensures that each branch of the federal government has unique and equal power; checks and balances allow each branch to be a check on the other two.

6. Constitutionalism is an approach to government that limits its powers, while the Constitution is a plan for the government.

7. An ordinance is a law similar to a statute, which is a law written by a legislative body.

8. A sovereign state is self-governing while dual sovereignty gave individual states power that could not be overruled by the national government.

9. The delegates that represented each state at the Constitutional Convention as representatives have become known as the Framers of the Constitution.

READING STRATEGY ANSWER

10. Under the Articles of Confederation, the national government was ineffective and had little power other than declaring war and peace. Under this government, the states had no obligation to provide funds for national resources, including the military. Congress didn't have the funds to pay for wars, and states declined requests from Congress to pay war debts, so many soldiers were not paid for their service. At the convention, the delegates had to compromise on several issues, including the Great Compromise, which established a legislative branch with two houses. As the new Constitution was being ratified, 10 amendments, known as the Bill of Rights, were added to protect individual and states' rights.

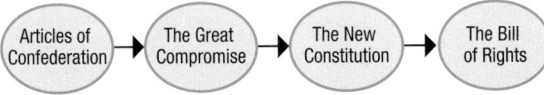

Articles of Confederation → The Great Compromise → The New Constitution → The Bill of Rights

MAIN IDEAS ANSWERS

11. Under the Articles of Confederation, the national government could not tax its citizens. It had to rely on the states for money.

12. The ordinances regulated how the sections of land in the Northwest Territory would be distributed, sold, and governed.

13. They were protesting debt hearings that resulted from the changes to how citizens could pay debts.

14. The purpose of the Constitutional Convention was to discuss how to reform the national government.

15. Answers will vary, but should include three of the following ideas: republicanism, federalism, dual sovereignty, separation of powers, checks and balances, majority rule, and constitutionalism.

16. They insisted on a separation of powers so that each branch of government could provide a check on the others to prevent any one branch from having too much power.

17. The Great Compromise helped larger states by giving them more delegates in the House, because it made the number of representatives proportionate to each state's population. It helped smaller states by allowing each state regardless of size, the same number of representatives in the Senate.

18. The Three-Fifths Compromise benefited southern states, which had the largest population of enslaved people, because it counted five slaves to equal three free people. This increased their number of representatives in the house.

19. They wrote a series of essays which were published in newspapers. The essays were later published in a book called *The Federalist.*

20. The Bill of Rights was added in order to uphold ideals set forth in the Declaration of Independence, which includes the rights to life, liberty, and the pursuit of happiness.

HISTORICAL THINKING ANSWERS

21. Under the Articles of Confederation, the central government's inability to enforce laws, levy taxes, and regulate trade led to debt for the country and many citizens. Shays's Rebellion and other events highlighted the national government's weakness in controlling uprisings. These factors caused leaders to replace the Articles of Confederation, and the effects included implementing the new Constitution.

22. The electoral college was designed as part of the checks and balances system, in the event that the people voted to elect an unqualified candidate.

23. The Bill of Rights represents ideals as it ensures certain rights of the American people that were violated under British rule, such as freedom of speech, religion, peaceful assembly, the right to petition the government, and protection from being forced to house soldiers.

24. Answers will vary, but students should mention the arguments of the federalists and antifederalists and note how the views of each are addressed in the Constitution.

25. The purpose of the Constitution was to embed the ideals of freedom, liberty, and democracy into the governing document for the nation; however, slavery went against all three of these ideals. The Framers reconciled the differences among the ideals when each side compromised on the divisive issues. The Framers added the Three-Fifths Compromise, the slave importation clause, and the fugitive slave clause to the Constitution to placate the southern states. Most of the representatives from the northern states did not intensely oppose slavery, so they made concessions to reconcile the competing ideals of freedom, liberty, and democracy and the institution of slavery.

26. James Wilson wanted to ratify the Constitution before the antifederalists in western lands could organize opposition to its ratification.

ANALYZE VISUALS ANSWERS

27. Possible response: It means that in order to protect out liberty, we must keep a careful watch on it or it may be taken away.

28. The Framers were guardians of the new nation because they wrote a Constitution that protected the citizens' rights and guarded their freedoms.

ANALYZE SOURCES ANSWERS

29. Madison is surprised by those who disagree with the new Constitution because even though it isn't perfect, it is significantly better than anything that came before it.

30. Madison means problems or deficiencies with the previous government and the Articles of Confederation.

CONNECT TO YOUR LIFE ANSWER

31. Students should identify one of the rights granted in the First Amendment (freedom of speech, freedom of the press, freedom of religion, the right to assembly, or the right to petition). Their narrative should explain how that right played a role in a specific event in their own lives.

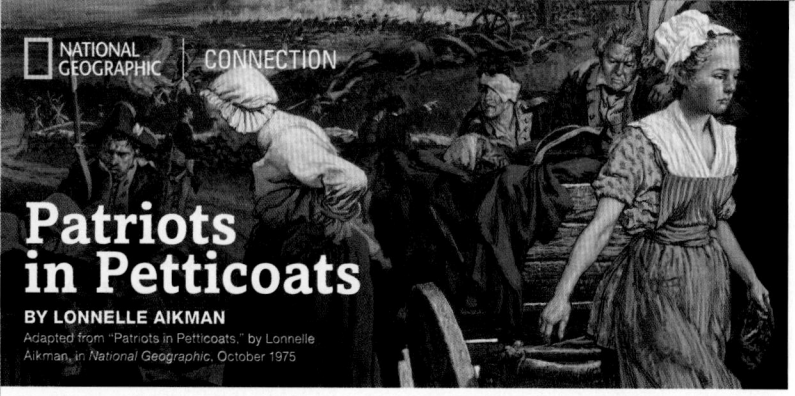

NATIONAL GEOGRAPHIC | CONNECTION

Patriots in Petticoats

BY LONNELLE AIKMAN

Adapted from "Patriots in Petticoats," by Lonnelle Aikman, in *National Geographic*, October 1975

Schooled in an untamed land of hardships, the women of colonial America were conditioned to independence. They grew their own food, sewed their own clothing, and made their own medicines. All this, while rearing children and running their families.

Given their willingness to endure, women in colonial America were more than ready to give up imported luxuries rather than submit to British taxation. Better, they said, to wear plain homespun dresses than to wear European imports. As for British tea, there were plenty of native substitutes—such as sage and currant—which they brewed and served as Liberty Tea. As the war began and spread, women of all classes, from frontier wives to managers of great plantations, participated fully in the conflict. Throughout the colonies, women replaced soldier-husbands in fields and shops and often spied on the enemy.

Abigail Adams, one of the first American women patriots, promoted activities from sewing uniforms to making bullets. She fed and sheltered soldiers and welcomed temporary refugees from neighboring towns. She also provided military and political intelligence to her husband by reporting on enemy troops and ships, as well as on Tories, inflation, and other American problems. John Adams appreciated Abigail's specific and accurate information, saying that she supplied him "with dearer and fuller Intelligence, than I can get from a whole Committee of Gentlemen."

Martha Washington traveled with General Washington throughout the war, which may astonish those who think of her as a sheltered elite. She was with him in New York City, Morristown, Valley Forge, and Middlebrook, and she helped him through two mutinies by his starving troops. Even after the guns were silent, Martha was with George while both waited impatiently for news of the final peace treaty in 1783.

If following the army was hard on the general's wife, it was more challenging for the ordinary women who trudged with the troops. Armies reluctantly allowed women to work alongside their husbands and other men of the corps, to carry water, to swab cannons, and to ease the wounded on the battlefield.

Some women fought side-by-side with men, including Margaret Cochran Corbin. When her husband John joined an artillery corps, Margaret went along. "Molly," as her comrades called her, helped the gunner's team swab out the bore and ram down the ammunition. When John was shot and killed, Margaret jumped into his battle station. Then she, too, went down, her shoulder torn by grapeshot. She never regained the use of her arm. Recognizing her courage under fire, Congress made her the first woman to receive a pension from the United States.

An equally brave woman posed as a man in order to fight. When Deborah Sampson was a child, poverty forced her widowed mother to give her up for indentured service. She emerged a strong woman, quite able to take on men's work. When the Revolution began, she made herself a man's suit, walked to a recruiting post in another town, and enlisted as Robert Shurtleff. She was wounded twice but managed to keep her secret until she went to Philadelphia as a general's orderly. There she came down with a "malignant fever" and was sent to a hospital, where a startled doctor discovered that she was a woman.

Martha Washington, Deborah Sampson, and Abigail Adams were women of strength who continue to capture the spotlight of history. Behind them stand all those others, the nameless Founding Mothers, without whom independence would have been impossible.

For more from National Geographic, check out "Two Revolutions" online.

UNIT INQUIRY: Prepare an Argument

In this unit, you learned about the factors that led to the American Revolution, the war itself, and the creation of the Constitution. Use what you learned from the text and do further research if necessary to determine why all colonists didn't support separating from Great Britain.

ASSIGNMENT

Prepare an argument for or against independence from Great Britain from the perspective of a Patriot and a Loyalist, respectively. Your arguments should offer examples of the benefits and drawbacks or risks involved in becoming independent from Great Britain. Be prepared to present both sides to your class.

Gather Evidence As you consider both sides of the argument, use what you learned in this unit to think of the reasons an American colonist would have either supported or opposed the separation from Great Britain. Make a list of these reasons, and try to incorporate them into your argument. Use a table like this one to help organize your evidence.

Patriot Reasons	Loyalist Reasons

Produce Use your notes to craft a solid argument for both sides of the issue—thinking like a Loyalist and like a Patriot. You may wish to write the arguments in paragraph form or bullet points on index cards and label them either "Patriot" or "Loyalist."

Present Choose a creative way to present both sides of this debate to the class. Consider one of these options:

- Use two different props, such as different hats, to transform yourself into a Patriot and a Loyalist. Wearing the Patriot hat, give a short speech expressing why it makes sense for the colonies to separate from Great Britain. Then put on the Loyalist hat and give a short speech expressing the other side of the debate. Alternate between Patriot and Loyalist hats to change your persona and add to each side of the argument.

- Organize your classmates into teams (Patriots and Loyalists). Familiarize each team with one side of the argument, and have a classroom debate about the benefits or dangers of separating from Great Britain.

NATIONAL GEOGRAPHIC | LEARNING FRAMEWORK ACTIVITIES

Research a Colonial American

ATTITUDE Curiosity

KNOWLEDGE Our Human Story

Choose one of the historical figures from this unit that you are still curious about, and do online research to learn more about him or her. Develop a biography for this individual in a traditional written format, or do something more visual, such as a poster or digital presentation. You could even give a costumed speech to your class as that individual. Be sure your biography—in whatever form it takes—includes common information such as birth and death dates, where the person lived, and the work he or she did. Also consider including information about how this person influenced colonial America, how the American Revolution or the Constitution might have been different without him or her, and the legacy this person left behind.

Build a Time Line

SKILLS Collaboration, Communication

KNOWLEDGE Our Human Story

Work with a partner or small group to capture the "story" of the formation of the United States in the form of a time line. First discuss how your time line will work. For example, decide if it will flow left to right or top to bottom, how it will be divided into intervals, and when the time line will start and end. Then refer to the chapters in this unit to determine which significant events will be included on your time line. Once you have gathered the information you need, work together to craft the physical time line. Consider the following questions: Will you use a symbol or color to represent types of events, such as battles? Will you use each side of the time line to represent different events or eras? What will make your time line clear and easy to read?

NATIONAL GEOGRAPHIC CONNECTION

Guided Discussion for "Patriots in Petticoats"

1. **Identify** In what ways did colonial women support and participate in the American Revolution? *(Colonial women participated in and supported boycotts of British goods; they spied on the British; they fought in battles, sometimes disguised as men; they helped soldiers on the battlefield; they sewed uniforms and made bullets; they sheltered and fed soldiers.)*

2. **Ask and Answer Questions** Imagine that you had the chance to interview one of the women mentioned in the article. What questions would you ask her, and how do you think she might respond? *(Answers will vary, but should demonstrate an understanding of the text and provide thoughtful questions and answers for the articles' subjects.)*

Guided Discussion for "Two Revolutions"

1. **Compare and Contrast** How were the American and French revolutions similar and different in terms of their origins and outcomes? *(Both were revolutions against monarchies; both were intended to usher in liberty and democracy. They differed in that the French Revolution resulted in the deaths of the king and queen, unlike the American Revolution in which the king was not killed; also, the French Revolution produced figures such as Robespierre, who encouraged the deaths of the French monarchs.)*

2. **Summarize** In what ways did the French support the Americans in their revolution against British rule? *(Individuals such as Lafayette volunteered to fight with the Americans; the French government sent soldiers, warships, money, and war supplies to help the Americans.)*

Assess

Use the rubric to assess each student's participation and performance.

SCORE	ASSIGNMENT	PRODUCT	PRESENTATION
3 GREAT	• Student thoroughly understands the assignment. • Student participates fully in the project process. • Student works well with team members.	• Argument is well thought out. • Argument offers a number of examples of the benefits and drawbacks of independence from Britain. • Argument contains all of the key elements listed in the assignment.	• Presentation is clear, concise, and logical. • Presentation does a good job of creatively representing both sides. • Presentation engages the audience.
2 GOOD	• Student mostly understands the assignment. • Student participates fairly well in the project process. • Student works fairly well with team members.	• Argument is fairly well thought out. • Argument offers at least two examples of the benefits and drawbacks of independence from Britain. • Argument contains most of the key elements listed in the assignment.	• Presentation is fairly clear, concise, and logical. • Presentation does an adequate job of creatively representing both sides. • Presentation somewhat engages the audience.
1 NEEDS WORK	• Student does not understand the assignment. • Student minimally participates or does not participate in the project process. • Student does not work well with team members.	• Argument is not well thought out. • Argument does not offer examples of the benefits and drawbacks of independence from Britain. • Argument contains few or none of the key elements listed in the assignment.	• Presentation is not clear, concise, or logical. • Presentation does an inadequate job representing both sides. • Presentation does not engage the audience.

Assess

Use the rubric to assess how each student applies the National Geographic Learning Framework.

SCORE	ASSIGNMENT	ASSIGNMENT	FINAL PRODUCTS
3 GREAT	• Biography reflects **Curiosity** well. • Biography explores **Our Human Story** well.	• Time line demonstrates **Collaboration** and **Communication** well. • Time line explores **Our Human Story** well.	• Final products are engaging, creative, and well presented.
2 GOOD	• Biography reflects **Curiosity**. • Biography explores **Our Human Story**.	• Time line demonstrates **Collaboration** and **Communication**. • Time line explores **Our Human Story**.	• Final products are interesting, logical, and complete.
1 NEEDS WORK	• Biography does not reflect **Curiosity**. • Biography does not explore **Our Human Story**.	• Time line does not demonstrate **Collaboration** and **Communication** • Time line does not explore **Our Human Story**.	• Final products are not creative, complete, or interesting.

The University of Virginia

Thomas Jefferson called architecture the "hobby of my old age." He drew much of his architectural inspiration from the classical designs of the Greeks and Romans, as well as from the architecture he had observed during his time in France. As a result, many of his designs fall into the category of neoclassical. In the early years of the American republic, he gave advice on the design of many government buildings and the layout of the new capitol building in Washington, D.C.

By 1819, Jefferson had begun designing what he called an "academical village," in which students and professors would live and work closely together. He wanted to create a school in which the design itself would help to foster three academic priorities: discussion, collaboration, and enlightenment. The result was a U-shaped plan of neoclassical buildings set around a central lawn, headed by the graceful Rotunda, as shown in this photograph. Student and faculty housing was interspersed around the lawn, encouraging scholars and teachers alike to work across disciplines and ages—the university, by Jefferson's instructions, had no set curriculum requirements.

Have students examine the photograph, which shows that many of Jefferson's original buildings and details have been preserved. Tell students that the buildings along the right side of the photograph are still used for student and faculty housing, as they were in Jefferson's day. **ASK:** What elements of the photograph seem to reflect Jefferson's ideals, and why? *(Answers will vary. Possible responses: The fact that Jefferson designed the buildings in the style of Roman temples suggests a desire to preserve the ideals of ancient architecture in a purposeful way. Jefferson was proud of founding the University of Virginia, as noted on his grave marker, and he created a beautiful and stately place of learning as evidence of his respect for education.)*

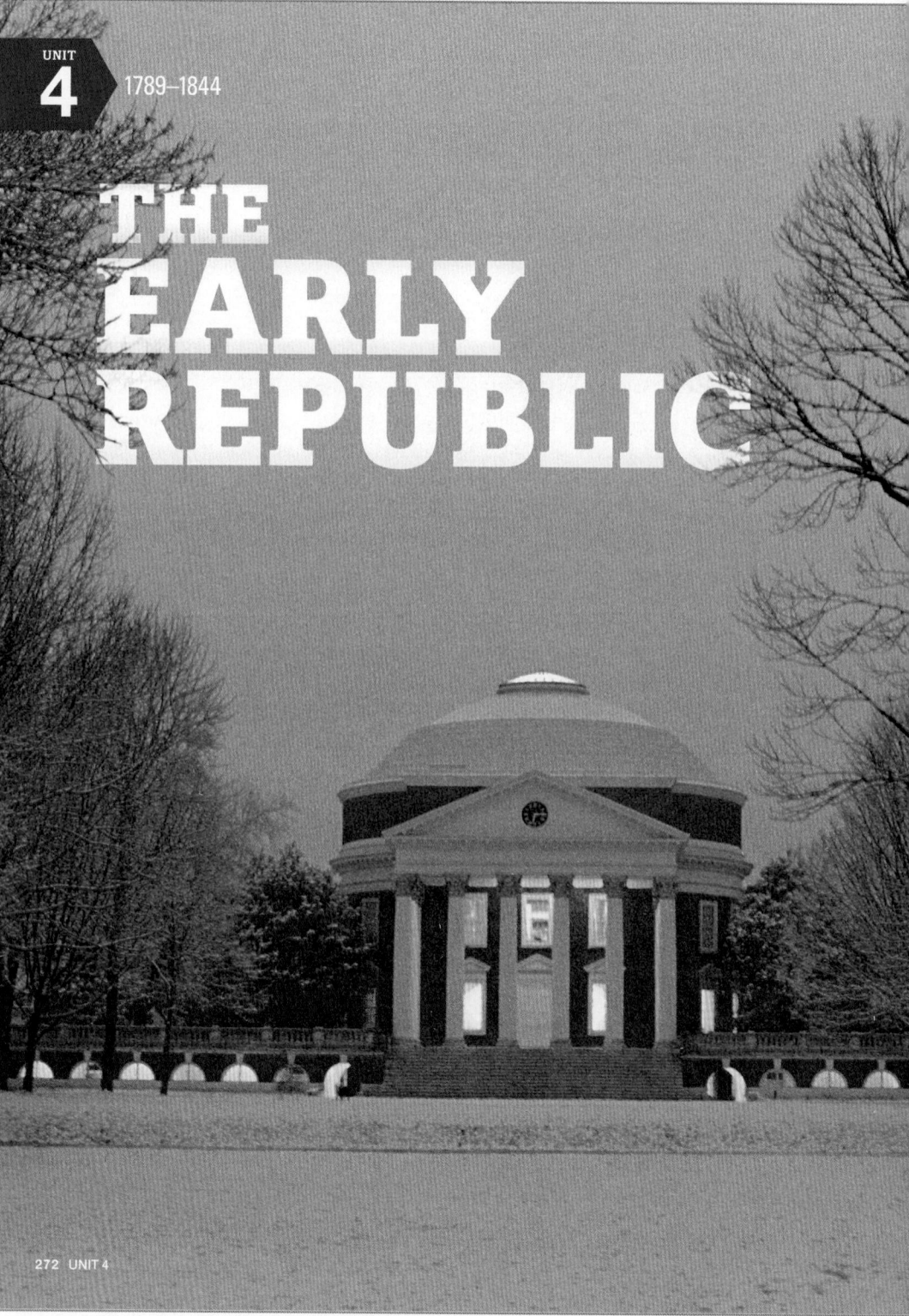

UNIT **4** 1789–1844

THE EARLY REPUBLIC

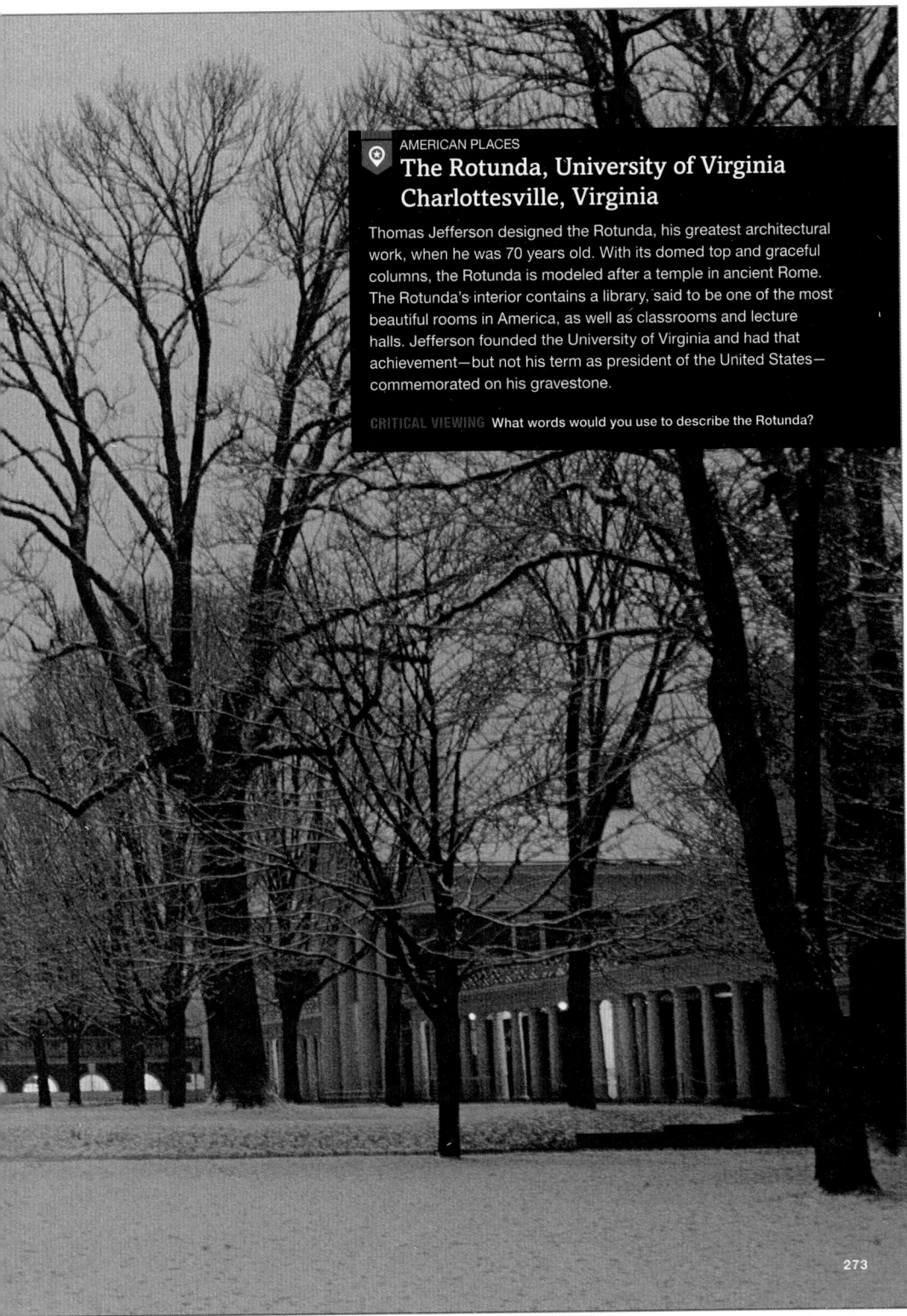

AMERICAN PLACES

The Rotunda, University of Virginia
Charlottesville, Virginia

Thomas Jefferson designed the Rotunda, his greatest architectural work, when he was 70 years old. With its domed top and graceful columns, the Rotunda is modeled after a temple in ancient Rome. The Rotunda's interior contains a library, said to be one of the most beautiful rooms in America, as well as classrooms and lecture halls. Jefferson founded the University of Virginia and had that achievement—but not his term as president of the United States—commemorated on his gravestone.

CRITICAL VIEWING What words would you use to describe the Rotunda?

American Places

The Rotunda and its surrounding buildings at the University of Virginia are now known as the Jeffersonian Precinct, which has been declared a UNESCO World Heritage Site. They are all still in use as some of the university's key buildings. In 1895, the Rotunda itself was nearly destroyed by a fire and later almost completely rebuilt; however, the restoration effort aimed at keeping Jefferson's inspiration and vision intact. Visitors to the university can arrange for tours of the Rotunda and its rooms; groups and individuals can also reserve many of the rooms for private or public functions.

CRITICAL VIEWING Answers will vary. Possible responses: *symmetrical*, *graceful*, *noble*, *elite*, *Roman*, *fancy*, *official*. Some students may note the similarity to other famous government buildings.

1799 EUROPE:
Napoleon Bonaparte Comes to Power

The French Revolution of 1789 involved the revolt of the common people, or Third Estate, against the wealthy nobility and clergy. The revolt led to the overthrow of the monarchy. In its place arose a government called the National Convention, and later, the Directory. All along, revolutionary and counterrevolutionary factions fought within the government.

Napoleon took control of France in a coup d'état. He believed only a military dictatorship could prevent a return to monarchy. Thanks to the revolution, Napoleon was well respected in France. Following the coup, Napoleon became first consul of the new government, called the Consulate. Its constitution gave him enormous power, which he used to institute a series of judicial, educational, military, and administrative reforms. These changes transformed France and secured many of the rights and protections for which the revolutionaries had fought.

In 1804, Napoleon declared France an empire, with hereditary succession, and he declared himself emperor. In this role, his main ambition was to expand French control throughout Europe. He launched a series of wars of conquest now known as the Napoleonic Wars, which would have serious consequences for the newly independent United States. **ASK:** Do you think Napoleon's rule was mostly a gain or a loss for the ideals of the French Revolution? *(Answers will vary. Possible responses: Napoleon's rule was mostly a gain because he helped reform the government in ways the revolutionaries had wanted. Napoleon's rule was mostly a loss because France ended up as a dictatorship rather than a democratic republic.)*

UNIT
4

THE EARLY
REPUBLIC

THE UNITED STATES

1797
John Adams, a Federalist, becomes president, while Thomas Jefferson, a Democratic-Republican, becomes vice president.

1789
George Washington takes office as president and sets up his government.

1803
Thomas Jefferson sends Meriwether Lewis and William Clark on an expedition to explore the western territory included in the Louisiana Purchase. *(coin featuring Sacagawea, Lewis and Clark's Native American interpeter)*

1780

1800

1789 EUROPE
France explodes into revolution against the royal ruling class.

1799 EUROPE
Napoleon Bonaparte seizes control of the French government. *(statue of Napoleon on horseback)*

THE WORLD

1812
The War of 1812 erupts between Britain and the United States over British violations of American rights at sea. *(American infantry drum used during the War of 1812)*

HISTORICAL THINKING: DETERMINE CHRONOLOGY

Which strong leaders came to power within ten years of each other?

1844
Samuel Morse's invention of the telegraph allows messages to be sent between Washington, D.C., and Baltimore, Maryland. *(early telegraph developed by Samuel Morse)*

1813
As the textile industry expands during the Industrial Revolution, the first Lowell mill is built in Massachusetts.

1831
Nat Turner leads an armed rebellion in an effort to free the slaves.

1820

1840

1833 EUROPE
Britain abolishes slavery in the British Empire.

1836 AFRICA
The Boers, farmers of Dutch, French, and German descent, undertake their "Great Trek" through southern Africa.

1821 AMERICAS
Venezuela gains independence from Spain.

1839–1842 ASIA
The first Opium War is fought between China and Britain after the Chinese government tries to stop the trade of opium in its country. *(Chinese junk boat similar to those used by China during the Opium War)*

The Early Republic 275

INTRODUCE TIME LINE EVENT

1821 AMERICAS:
Venezuela Gains Independence from Spain

Venezuela's struggle for independence from Spain began in 1797 when a group of Creoles (social elites of the colonial system) unsuccessfully declared Venezuela an independent republic. When Napoleon Bonaparte invaded Spain in 1808, the Venezuelans took advantage of Spain's divided attention. The revolutionaries declared independence again in 1811, and in 1813, named Simón Bolívar as leader. Bolívar defeated the Spanish in 1821, aided by mercenaries from abroad.

Bolívar became president but soon left to fight for the liberation of Peru. With Bolívar gone, General José Antonio Páez established himself as military dictator. Páez created some stability and prosperity, but he also gave the central government supreme power, restricted voting rights, and supported enslaved labor. An opposing Liberal Party formed, and in 1846, a new president sent Páez into exile. For nearly 100 years afterward, Venezuelan politics were marked by civil war, military dictatorships, and turmoil. **ASK:** How were the American Revolution and the Venezuelan War of Independence similar and different? *(Answers will vary. Possible response: In both, foreign mercenaries helped rebelling forces win, and the leader of the revolution became president. In the United States, the Constitution balanced state and federal powers, but in Venezuela, the first president established the central government as the supreme power, and years of military dictatorships followed.)*

HISTORICAL THINKING: DETERMINE CHRONOLOGY

Answer: George Washington and Napoleon Bonaparte came into power within 10 years of each other.

UNIT 4 THE EARLY REPUBLIC

UNIT INTRODUCTION

UNIT TIME LINE

UNIT WRAP-UP

NATIONAL GEOGRAPHIC | CONNECTION

National Geographic Magazine Adapted Articles
- "Searching for Sacagawea"
- "Lost Missouri" ONLINE

Unit 4 Inquiry: Define Good Citizenship

NG Learning Framework Activities
- Propose a New Invention
- Write a Campaign Speech

Unit 4 Formal Assessment

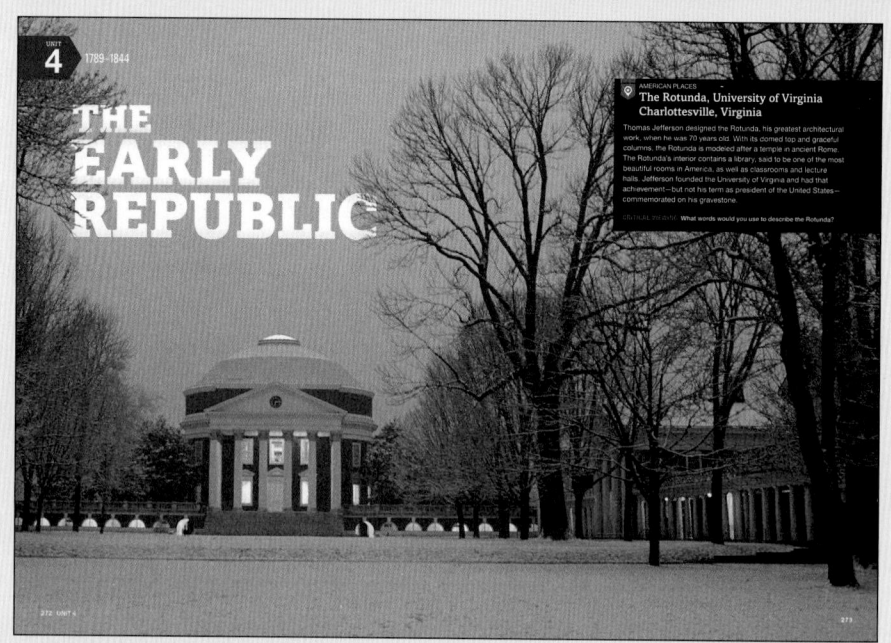

CHAPTER 8 RESOURCES

Available at NGLSync.Cengage.com

TEACHER RESOURCES & ASSESSMENT

Reading and Note-Taking

Vocabulary Practice

Document-Based Question Template

Social Studies Skills Lessons
- Reading: Identify Problems and Solutions
- Writing: Write an Explanation

Formal Assessment
- Chapter 8 Pretest
- Chapter 8 Tests A & B
- Section Quizzes

Chapter 8 Answer Key

ExamView®
One-time Download

STUDENT DIGITAL RESOURCES

- **eEdition** (English)
- **eEdition** (Spanish)
- **Handbooks**

- **Online Atlas**
- **American Gallery Online**
- **History Notebook**

- **American Voices (Biographies)**
- **Active History**
- **Projects for Inquiry-Based Learning**

Chapter 8 Spanish Resources are available at NGLSync.Cengage.com.

AMERICAN STORIES ONLINE | **George Washington's Mount Vernon**

- Primary Sources
- On Your Feet: Hold a Roundtable Discussion

NG Learning Framework:
Research Slavery at Mount Vernon

SECTION 1 RESOURCES
WASHINGTON'S PRESIDENCY

LESSON 1.1
Setting Up the Government

- On Your Feet: Inside-Outside Circle

NG Learning Framework:
Campaign for George Washington

American Voices Biography
George Washington ONLINE

LESSON 1.2
Cabinet and Courts

AMERICAN **GALLERY** ONLINE   Federal Washington

NG Learning Framework:
Investigate Change

LESSON 1.3
Hamilton's Economic Plan

- On Your Feet: Think, Pair, Share
- Active History: Create a Personal Budget

LESSON 1.4
AMERICAN PLACES
Broadway, New York City

- On Your Feet: Perform a Skit

NG Learning Framework:
Write a Historical Song

SECTION 2 RESOURCES
POLITICS IN THE 1790s

LESSON 2.1
Political Parties Form

- On Your Feet: Question and Answer

NG Learning Framework:
Promote a Political Party

LESSON 2.2
Competition for Territory and the French Revolution

- On Your Feet: Turn and Talk

NG Learning Framework:
Describe a Conflict

LESSON 2.3
DOCUMENT-BASED QUESTION
Washington's Farewell Address

- On Your Feet: Host a DBQ Roundtable

LESSON 2.4
The Parties in Conflict

- On Your Feet: Think, Pair, Share

NG Learning Framework:
Understand the Free Press

CHAPTER 8 REVIEW

Strategy 1
Focus on Main Ideas

Tell students to locate the Main Idea statement at the beginning of each lesson. Explain that these statements summarize the important ideas of the lesson and will be useful for helping them pay attention to what matters most in the text.

Use with All Lessons *Throughout the chapter, help students get in the habit of using the Main Idea statements to set a purpose for reading.*

Strategy 2
Clarify Multiple Meaning Words

To help Striving Readers' text comprehension, point out prominent words in this chapter that have other, more familiar meanings. List these words and definitions on the board:

address: the exact place on a street where a building is located/a speech

cabinet: a piece of furniture for storing things/a council that gives advice

Have students identify which meaning fits the context.

Use with Lesson 1.1 *Throughout the chapter, call out and clarify other multiple meaning words.*

Strategy 3
Turn Headings into Outlines

To help Striving Readers organize lesson content, explain that headings can provide an outline of the lesson. Model for students how to use the lesson title and subheadings to create an outline structure. Encourage students to add to their outlines as they read.

Use with All Lessons

Strategy 1
Describe Lesson Visuals

Pair visually challenged students with students who are not visually challenged. Ask the latter to help their partners understand the visuals in the chapter by describing the images and answering any questions the visually impaired students might have.

Use with Lessons 2.1, 2.2, and 2.4 *Students who are not visually challenged can help visually challenged students derive meaning from and gain impressions of the campaign buttons, the painting* Washington Reviewing the Western Army at Fort Cumberland, Maryland, *and the photograph of the North Korean soldiers.*

Strategy 2
Use Supported Reading

Guide small groups of students to read the chapter aloud lesson by lesson. At the end of each lesson, ask them to stop and use these frames to tell what they comprehended from the text:

This lesson is about _____.

One detail that stood out to me is _____.

The vocabulary word _____

   means _____.

I don't think I understand _____.

Guide students with portions of text they do not understand. Be sure all students understand a lesson before moving on to the next one.

Use with All Lessons

ENGLISH LANGUAGE LEARNERS

Strategy ❶
PREP Before Reading

Encourage students at **All Proficiencies** to use the PREP strategy to prepare for reading. Write this acrostic on the board:

PREP   **P**review the title.
        Read Main Idea statement.
        Examine visuals.
        Predict what you will learn.

Use with All Lessons *Encourage students at the **Emerging** level to ask questions if they have trouble writing a prediction. Students at the **Bridging** level might want to help **Emerging** and **Expanding** level students write their predictions.*

Strategy ❷
Review Transitional Words

To help students put events in chronological order and summarize what they read, display these transitional words on the board: *first, next, then, also,* and *finally.* Have students at the **Emerging** and **Expanding** levels work together to write a series of simple sentences that tell what happens in each lesson. Encourage them to use transitional words to tell about the time-order of events. Have students at the **Bridging** level construct a paragraph that summarizes the material. Encourage them to use transitional words and to vary their sentence structure.

Use with All Lessons

Strategy ❸
Look for Cognates

Suggest that as students read they look for words that are similar in spelling and meaning to words in their home language. For example, the word *president* has a cognate in Spanish—*presidente.* For each word they identify, have students of **All Proficiencies** make a vocabulary card. On one side, have them write the English word and definition. On the other side, have them write the word and its definition in their home language. Encourage them to think about and note any differences they notice in the meaning of the two words.

Use with All Lessons *You may wish to pair students at the **Emerging** level with students at the **Bridging** level.*

GIFTED & TALENTED

Strategy ❶
Compare Historical Biographies

Work with the school librarian to find biographical information about the major participants in the early United States government, such as George Washington, John Adams, Thomas Jefferson, and Alexander Hamilton. Have students read about these historical figures and compare them. Then have them design a way to present a comparison of the biographies to the class.

Use with All Lessons

Strategy ❷
Write a Dramatic Skit

Invite students to create a short skit about an event or issue from the first two presidential administrations, such as the debate over the National Bank, the formation of political parties, the Whiskey Rebellion, the XYZ Affair, or the Alien and Sedition Acts. Allow time for students to perform their skits for the class.

Use with All Lessons *Invite students to do more research about the topic of their choice. Remind them that conflict— with others or with oneself—is the basis of drama.*

Pre-AP

Strategy ❶
Interview Thomas Jefferson

Encourage students to prepare a mock interview with Thomas Jefferson about events during the Washington and Adams administrations. Direct students to use the Internet to find out more about Jefferson's opinions on such matters as the National Bank, political parties, the Whiskey Rebellion, and the Alien and Sedition Acts. Then instruct pairs of students to develop a list of questions to ask Thomas Jefferson about the direction of the government under Washington and Adams. Ask pairs of students to act out their interviews before the class.

Use with Lessons 1.3, 2.1–2.2, and 2.4

Strategy ❷
Analyze Party Systems

Instruct students to research political-party systems in different countries. Suggest they study the differences between one-party systems, two-party systems, and multi-party systems and then write a short essay comparing and contrasting them. Suggest they identify some specific countries where these different systems currently exist and consider advantages and disadvantages of each.

Use with Lesson 2.1

GROWING PAINS
IN THE NEW REPUBLIC
1789–1800

ESSENTIAL QUESTION
What challenges did Americans in the new republic confront?

READING STRATEGY

IDENTIFY PROBLEMS AND SOLUTIONS
By identifying problems and solutions, you can better understand why decision-makers took the courses of action they did. As you read the chapter, use a graphic organizer like this one to identify and analyze each problem the new nation faced and how it was solved.

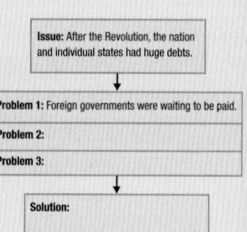

Issue: After the Revolution, the nation and individual states had huge debts.

↓

Problem 1: Foreign governments were waiting to be paid.
Problem 2:
Problem 3:

↓

Solution:

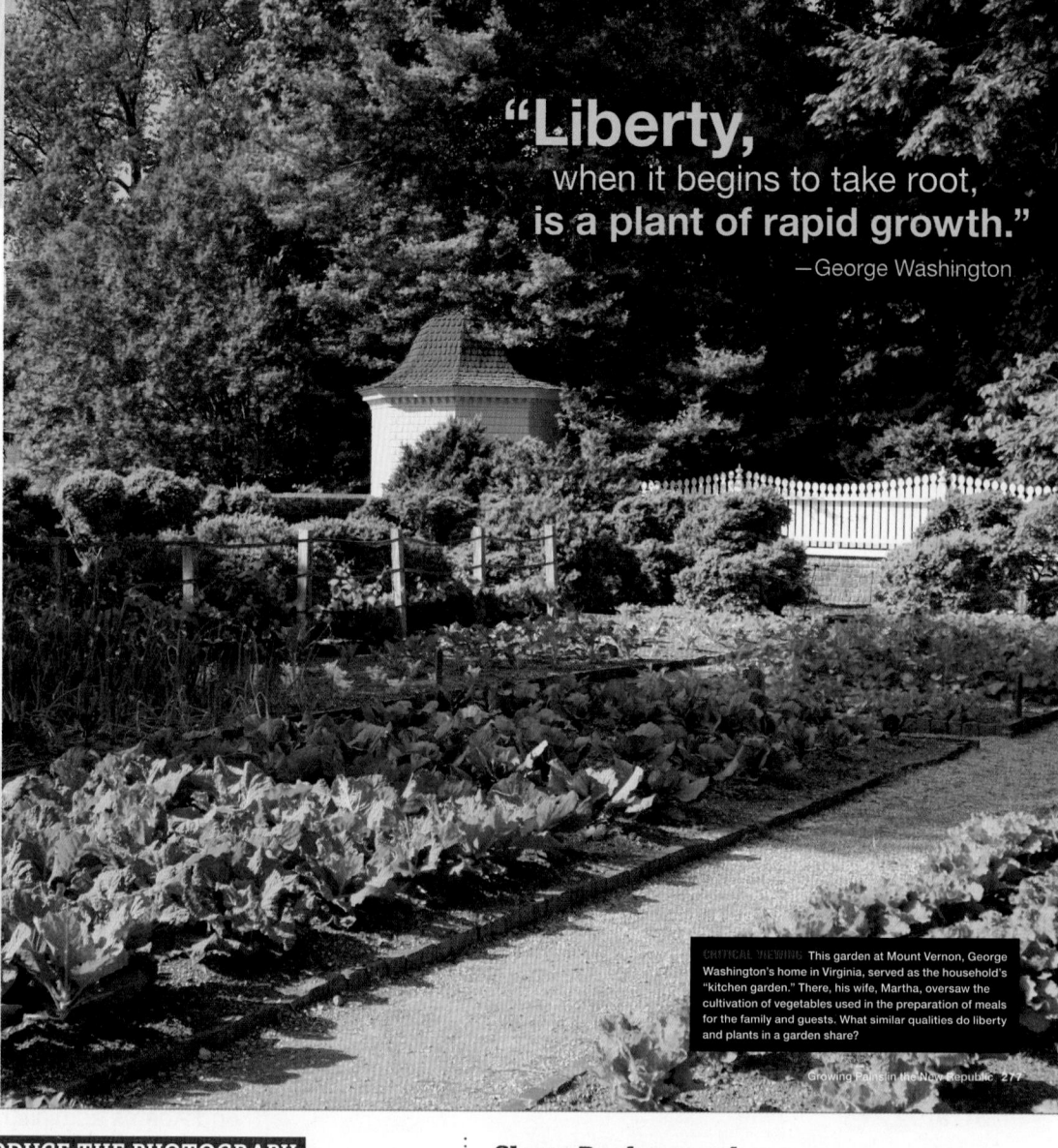

"Liberty,
when it begins to take root, is a plant of rapid growth."

—George Washington

CRITICAL VIEWING This garden at Mount Vernon, George Washington's home in Virginia, served as the household's "kitchen garden." There, his wife, Martha, oversaw the cultivation of vegetables used in the preparation of meals for the family and guests. What similar qualities do liberty and plants in a garden share?

Growing Pains in the New Republic 277

INTRODUCE THE PHOTOGRAPH

Kitchen Garden

Focus students' attention on the photograph of the garden at Mount Vernon. Note the variety of plants being grown. Explain to students that many homes had "kitchen gardens" to provide fruits, vegetables, and herbs for home consumption in early America. **ASK:** Why do you think this was the case? *(If you had a little land, you could grow your own food instead of buying it in a market. Transportation was difficult for getting produce to markets and for getting to a market to buy vegetables.)* Point out to students that having a garden helps one to be independent and self-sufficient. Explain that students will learn about the early leaders of the United States and how they set up the government of the new nation to promote self-sufficiency and independence from other nations.

Share Background

Today, fresh fruits and vegetables are important parts of the American diet. But in the early republic, Americans did not focus on these staples. Most colonial-era Americans lived on farms able to grow an abundance of plants, but the typical American dinner plate contained mostly meat and grain. This diet may have been carried over from England, where fruits and vegetables were scarce. On large plantations such as Mount Vernon, however, exotic vegetables such as artichokes were often served during fancy dinners, as they were seen as a symbol of refinement and good taste.

CRITICAL VIEWING Students might suggest that both liberty and garden plants are living, resilient, light-seeking, and always growing.

For Chapter 8 Spanish Resources, visit the Resources Menu. Chapter 8 Resources are available at NGLSync.Cengage.com.

INTRODUCE THE ESSENTIAL QUESTION

What challenges did Americans in the new republic confront?

Brainstorming Activity: Challenges of a New Republic Explain to students that, under the leadership of George Washington, the United States faced many challenges in its journey to become a new, independent country. Lead students to brainstorm some difficult questions that might have arisen during the early years of the United States. Record student responses on the board. Point out that many of these questions could be answered by historical study or research. If students need help getting started, encourage them to think about these categories and sample questions:

Political Questions How should leaders be chosen? How can citizens make their voices heard?

Economic Questions How will the economy function? Should the government regulate trade?

Foreign Policy Questions How should we interact with other nations? What do we do in case of foreign aggression?

Constitutional Questions How will the government work? What powers should the government have?

INTRODUCE CHAPTER VOCABULARY

Word Maps

As they read the chapter, direct students to complete Word Maps for Key Vocabulary words. Tell students to make a Word Map for each word. Instruct them to write the word in the center oval and, as they encounter the word in the chapter, complete the Word Map for that word. Model an example for students on the board, using the graphic organizer below.

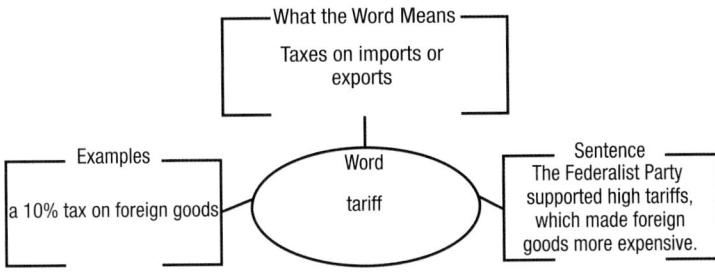

What the Word Means — Taxes on imports or exports

Examples — a 10% tax on foreign goods

Word — tariff

Sentence — The Federalist Party supported high tariffs, which made foreign goods more expensive.

INTRODUCE THE READING STRATEGY

IDENTIFY PROBLEMS AND SOLUTIONS

Remind students that sometimes one solution might resolve several problems. Other times, multiple solutions might be proposed to solve a problem or group of problems, as students will read about in this chapter. Model completing the Problem-and-Solution Chart. Point out the three sections of the chart: Issue, Problems, and Solution. Ask for suggestions for one example of an issue, the problems that arise from it, and the solution to the problems. Fill in the chart for that entry as a class. Remind students to make use of the chart as they read the chapter.

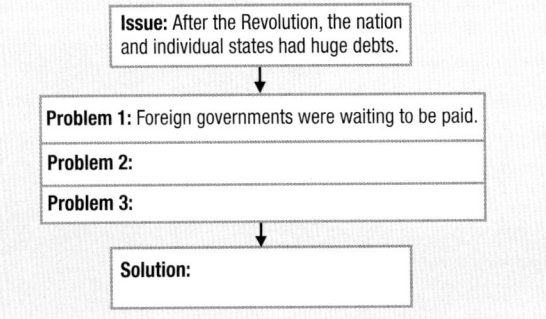

Issue: After the Revolution, the nation and individual states had huge debts.

Problem 1: Foreign governments were waiting to be paid.

Problem 2:

Problem 3:

Solution:

KEY DATES FOR CHAPTER 8

1789	George Washington becomes president
1789	The first Cabinet is created
1789	Federal Judiciary Act is passed
1791	National Bank is created
1794	Whiskey Rebellion is suppressed
1795	Treaty of Greenville
1797	John Adams becomes president
1797	XYZ Affair
1798	Alien and Sedition Acts become law

AMERICAN STORIES ONLINE For instructional support for the online American Story "George Washington's Mount Vernon," go to NGLSync.Cengage.com.

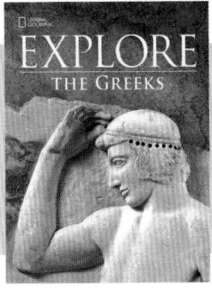

EXPLORE THE GREEKS

For more on theories of government, see *EXPLORE THE GREEKS.*

1.1 Setting Up the Government

Would you want to be president of the United States? You might be surprised to hear that George Washington did *not* want the job. He knew that being the first president of the new country wouldn't be easy. But his countrymen wanted Washington.

MAIN IDEA The Constitution established some guidelines, but for the first president, starting up the new government was a complex and difficult undertaking.

THE FIRST PRESIDENT

George Washington was the obvious choice to be the nation's first president—he was a dignified man of strong character. Better yet, he was a natural leader, which he had proved during the American Revolution. Success in the new republic was not at all assured, but Washington accepted the challenge. Even though he didn't want the job, Washington guided the new government through its early years.

As the newly written Constitution directed, the electoral college determined who would be president in this first election—not the people. Every one of the 69 electors voted for Washington. The reluctant candidate won hands down. John Adams, who was runner-up, became the vice president.

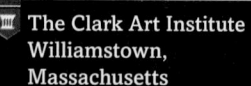

The Clark Art Institute Williamstown, Massachusetts

Gilbert Stuart painted 104 portraits of George Washington, including the one shown here, which was painted some time between 1796 and 1803. John Jay, whom you may remember as an author of *The Federalist* papers, introduced Washington to the painter. Stuart began creating his likenesses of the president in 1795. Washington became extremely impatient sitting for his portrait, however. Even though Stuart was known as an entertaining conversationalist, Washington remained mostly silent during their sessions.

On April 23, 1789, thousands of cheering citizens in New York City, the country's temporary capital, welcomed Washington. He took the oath of office a week later and began his difficult task. Washington had to invent the role of president as he went along. "My station is new; and . . . [I] walk on untrodden ground," he wrote in a letter. Everything he did would set a **precedent**, or establish an example, for all future presidents.

Washington particularly wanted to make it clear that he was *president* of the United States, not its *king*. He dressed plainly for his **inauguration**, the ceremony that marked the beginning of his presidency, in an American-made brown suit. And he refused to be called "His Excellency" or "Your Highness," as John Adams had suggested. After much debate, Washington decided that "Mr. President" would do just fine.

AN OCEAN OF DIFFICULTIES

Once in office, Washington got to work—and there was a lot to do. As he himself described it, the nation faced "an ocean of difficulties." The new government had to deal with problems within the country as well as conflicts in the Northwest Territory and wars across the Atlantic.

To tackle all these situations, both the president and Congress had certain responsibilities and powers, as spelled out in the Constitution. Essentially, Congress would make the laws, and the president would ensure they were carried out.

But not everything was covered in the Constitution. Here, too, Washington set precedents. For example, he took control of treaty negotiations, bypassing Congress, and established a policy of neutrality in foreign conflicts—insisting it was within the president's power to do so.

Fortunately, the framers of the Constitution did foresee the need for departments to assist the president. Congress had the power to create the departments, and the president decided who would head them. Together, the heads of the departments are called a **Cabinet**.

Washington picked men from a variety of geographical areas and with a mix of political views for his Cabinet. He strongly advocated political moderation and tried to keep himself, as president, above the bickering that went on between political factions. That way, he believed, he could do what was best for the country. Washington appointed a group of highly talented men to his Cabinet—and hoped they'd put aside their political differences, too.

The First Inaugural Address

Washington wasn't required to give a speech at his inauguration, but he decided to do so. Every president since has done the same. To mark the occasion, people attending the ceremony could purchase copper buttons, like the ones below, as souvenirs.

As he gave this First Inaugural Address, Washington was nervous. His hands and voice trembled, but his words were powerful: "The preservation of the sacred fire of liberty, and the destiny of the Republican model of government, are justly considered as deeply . . . staked on the experiment entrusted to the hands of the American people." In other words, the future of the country depended on the success of this new government.

Washington inaugural souvenirs

HISTORICAL THINKING

1. **READING CHECK** Why did George Washington write that he was walking "on untrodden ground"?

2. **IDENTIFY PROBLEMS AND SOLUTIONS** How did Washington deal with treaty negotiations, since no process was spelled out in the Constitution?

3. **MAKE CONNECTIONS** How did Washington's presidency help establish an American identity?

PLAN

Objective

Analyze the challenges that come with setting up a new government.

Critical Thinking Skills for Lesson 1.1

- Identify Main Ideas and Details
- Monitor Comprehension
- Identify Problems and Solutions
- Make Connections
- Make Inferences
- Form and Support Opinions

Essential Question for Chapter 8

What challenges did Americans in the new republic confront? George Washington was elected the first president of the United States in spite of his reservations. Lesson 1.1 discusses the challenges he faced in forming a new government and the precedents he set for future presidents.

Background for the Teacher

When George Washington was elected the first president of the United States, his wife, the former Martha Dandridge Custis, became the first First Lady. Just as her husband recognized the need to invent the role of president, Washington realized that she had to invent a role for herself. Being the first First Lady meant that her actions would establish protocol for the wives of all future presidents. While living in the capital, Martha managed the household, dressed formally, received visitors, and met with important members of society. She set up a weekly reception at the president's house on Friday evenings to which all were welcome. Opening the house to citizens was viewed as a sign that the new government would be responsive to the needs of ordinary citizens, unlike the British government had been.

Debate a Question

Write this question on the board and ask students to debate: What powers should the federal government have? If necessary, prompt students with ideas such as engaging in war and negotiating treaties, acquiring land, and making laws. Ask students to decide whether the president, Congress, or the states should make the final decision about these matters. Then inform students that many of these questions were unanswered in the early days of the United States, and solutions evolved over time.

Guided Discussion

1. **Make Inferences** Why was George Washington so careful to avoid acting like a king? *(As an opponent of the British monarchy, Washington wanted to show that American republicanism was unique and different.)*

2. **Form and Support Opinions** Why do you think Washington wanted a diverse Cabinet? Support your response with evidence from the text. *(Answers will vary. Possible response: In Washington's inaugural address, he expressed how deeply he felt about "the destiny of the Republican model of government." By appointing a diverse Cabinet, he hoped that the interests and political views of the American people would be heard.)*

Virtual Museum Visit

The Clark Art Institute in Williamstown, Massachusetts, originated as a place for Sterling and Francine Clark to display their private artwork. It has become home to a world-renowned collection of American and European art and a forum for shaping art history. Access the museum's website and locate the portrait of George Washington by Gilbert Stuart in the American collection. Read the description of the portrait aloud, pointing out that it is one of many portraits of Washington by Stuart. **ASK:** Why might the artist have painted a number of portraits of George Washington? *(Possible response: The artist might have thought that a founder of the new republic was a man likely to hold interest for many people.)* Encourage students to explore the site, choose a different portrait from the American collection, and discuss how it is similar to or different from the Washington portrait.

Active Options

On Your Feet: Inside-Outside Circle Arrange students in concentric circles facing each other. Ask students in the outside circle to pose questions about the challenges faced by the new government; for example: What precedent did Washington set by establishing policy about foreign conflicts? Guide students in the inner circle to answer. Then tell students to trade inside/outside roles and rotate to create new partnerships.

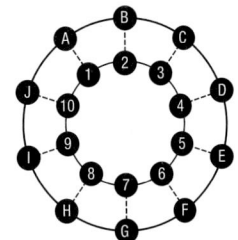

NG Learning Framework: Campaign for George Washington

SKILL Problem-Solving

KNOWLEDGE Our Human Story

Ask students to write a short speech supporting Washington for president using evidence from online primary sources. Guide students to conduct their research to locate two or more primary sources about George Washington's life and military career that include evidence explaining why Americans wanted him to be the United States' first president. Remind students of what constitutes a primary source. Encourage students to check Library of Congress online collections for primary sources.

Striving Readers

Understand Main Ideas Monitor students' understanding of the main ideas by asking them to correctly complete statements such as these:

- The [electoral college] determined that Washington would be the first president.
- Washington had to invent the role of [president] because there was no [precedent] for how he should behave in his new role.
- The [Constitution] defines the responsibilities of the president and Congress.

English Language Learners

Make Word Cards To clarify the similar-sounding words *precedent* and *president,* help students make word cards on which they list phrases about or write definitions for the words, such as these:

- *precedent*: an example someone sets that helps people know what to do in the future
- *president*: the leader of the United States

Encourage students at the **Emerging** and **Expanding** levels to work in pairs. Ask students at the **Bridging** level to work independently.

See the Chapter Planner for more strategies for differentiation.

ANSWERS

1. He meant that he was doing a job no one had done before. The presidency was established by the Constitution, but as the nation's first president, Washington would set precedents about how to use presidential powers.

2. Washington decided to bypass Congress and control treaty negotiations himself. He decided the United States should be neutral in foreign conflicts.

3. Washington set a tone with his presidency that influenced American identity. He built the role of president based on virtues important to him and his growing country. He was dignified, of strong character, and respectful of diverse opinions.

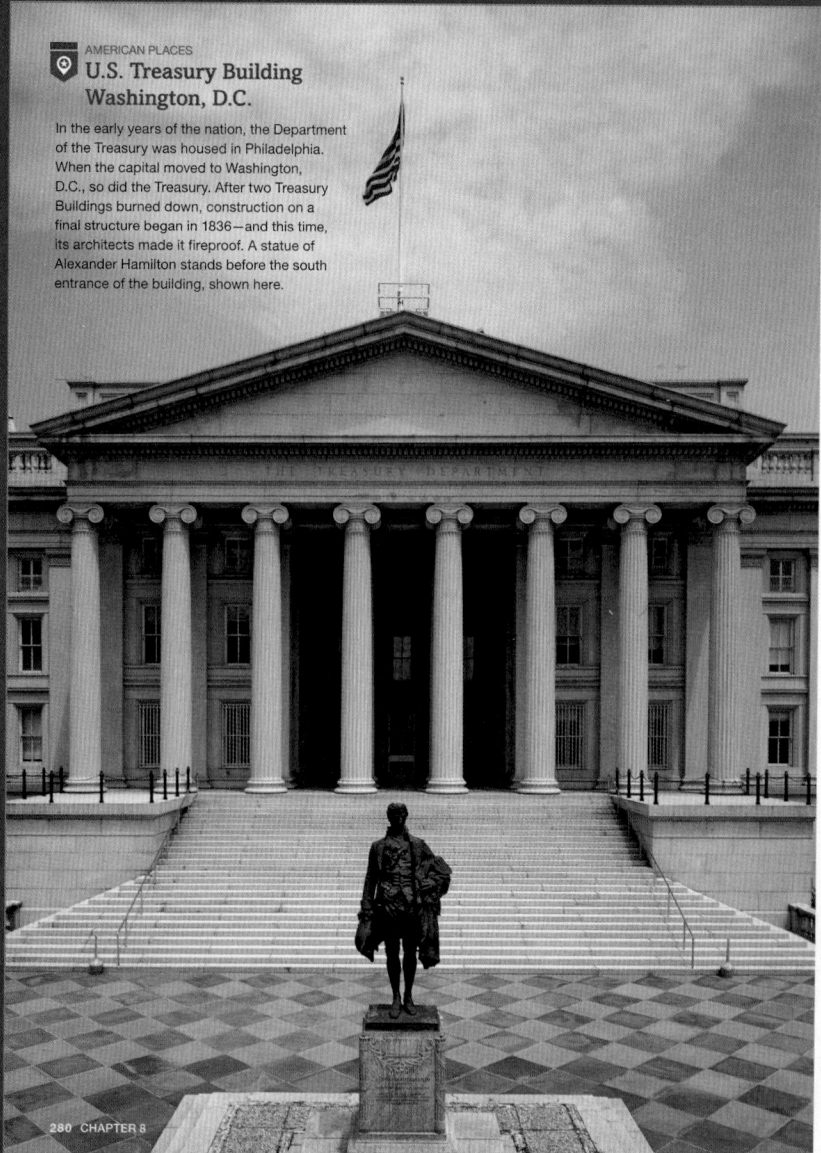

U.S. Treasury Building
Washington, D.C.

In the early years of the nation, the Department of the Treasury was housed in Philadelphia. When the capital moved to Washington, D.C., so did the Treasury. After two Treasury Buildings burned down, construction on a final structure began in 1836—and this time, its architects made it fireproof. A statue of Alexander Hamilton stands before the south entrance of the building, shown here.

1.2 Cabinet and Courts

Imagine trying to play a game of soccer or basketball without any teammates. It wouldn't work. George Washington didn't guide the new country alone, either. He gathered an A-list of team members to help him.

MAIN IDEA The first order of business for George Washington and Congress was to assemble a presidential Cabinet and create a court system.

ASSEMBLING A TEAM

In the summer of 1789, Congress created the Departments of State, Treasury, and War as part of the executive branch. Washington appointed the department heads, called secretaries, and they formed his Cabinet.

To oversee relations with other countries, Washington chose Thomas Jefferson as Secretary of State. As Secretary of War, former general Henry Knox would see to the country's defense. And to manage the government's money, Washington selected Alexander Hamilton as Secretary of the Treasury. Congress also created the office of the **attorney general**, whose primary role was to represent the United States before the Supreme Court. He would be a member of Washington's Cabinet, but unlike the others, he would not head an executive department. Edmund Randolph served as the first attorney general.

The president called his Cabinet secretaries together for regular meetings. However, you might be surprised to learn that Vice President John Adams was *not* invited to these meetings. The vice president soon realized the limitations of his position. "My country," he wrote, "has in its wisdom contrived [designed] for me the most insignificant office that ever the invention of man contrived or his imagination conceived."

THE HIGHEST COURT IN THE LAND

In addition to building the Cabinet, Washington and Congress created a court system. The Constitution established a Supreme Court as the nation's highest court. But it left the question of how many justices would sit on the Court to

Congress and didn't specify what its powers would be. So, in 1789, Congress passed the Federal Judiciary Act. It called for the Supreme Court to have six justices—one **Chief Justice** and five associate justices. Today, eight associate justices sit on the court. The Chief Justice presides over the judicial branch of the U.S. government as well as over the Supreme Court itself. John Jay became the country's first Chief Justice.

The act created the world's first dual-court system, with responsibilities split between state and federal courts. Federal courts handled interstate and international cases, disputes regarding the U.S. Constitution, and civil and criminal cases relating to federal laws. State courts dealt with cases involving state laws and civil disputes within states. The act also created lower, or less powerful, federal courts.

The federal government established executive departments and a working system of courts, but more challenges lay in store. For one thing, there was the small matter of a very large war debt to be paid.

HISTORICAL THINKING

1. **READING CHECK** What departments made up Washington's Cabinet?

2. **DRAW CONCLUSIONS** What do the Cabinet departments suggest about what was important to the new government?

3. **MAKE INFERENCES** Why do you think the Federal Judiciary Act created both state and federal courts?

PLAN

Objective

Explain the purpose and organization of the United States' first Cabinet and court system.

Critical Thinking Skills for Lesson 1.2

- Identify Main Ideas and Details
- Monitor Comprehension
- Draw Conclusions
- Make Inferences
- Evaluate

Essential Question for Chapter 8

What challenges did Americans in the new republic confront? Washington and the first Congress had to organize the new government. Lesson 1.2 describes how they established a presidential Cabinet and a dual-court system that split responsibilities between state and federal courts.

Background for the Teacher

Often-overlooked Founding Father John Jay was active across all branches of government at every level and played an influential role in making the U.S. Constitution possible. President George Washington thought so much of Jay that he offered him any position within his new Cabinet, and Jay chose to be the Chief Justice of the United States. As the nation's first Chief Justice, Jay established rules and procedures for the Supreme Court and helped define the role of the Court. In 1794, Jay took a break from the Court to work as a diplomat, negotiating an important treaty with Great Britain. While away, he was elected governor of New York, a position he held for six years. In 1800, he ran for president and received one electoral vote.

History Notebook

Encourage students to complete the American Gallery page for Chapter 8 in their History Notebooks as they read.

Start a Country

Prompt students to think about how difficult it would be to start a new country. **ASK:** As a leader, what problems would you need to solve? *(Answers will vary. Possible response: facing attacks from enemies, deciding who is in charge of what, giving fair access to resources, creating laws)* How could others help you solve these problems? *(Possible response: They could gather information, help with planning, or provide expertise.)* Ask students to suppose they are in charge of a new country. Have students brainstorm a list of the types of experts they would hire to help them lead successfully. As they make suggestions, ask them to explain how each would be useful.

TEACH

Guided Discussion

1. **Evaluate** Which of Washington's four original Cabinet positions do you think was most crucial to ensuring the country's success? *(Answers will vary. Possible response: I think the role of Secretary of the Treasury was most crucial to the success of the country, given the importance of financial planning and management.)*

2. **Make Inferences** Why do you think the Framers did not lay out the details of the Supreme Court and the court system in the Constitution? *(Answers will vary. Possible response: The Framers wanted the structure of the government to reflect a balance of power different from a monarchy. They wrote the Constitution as a guide, leaving room for leaders to govern within the context of a different historical period.)*

American Places
The U.S. Treasury Building is the oldest departmental building in Washington, D.C. It was built over a period of 33 years, and when completed in 1869, the enormous structure was one of the largest office buildings in the entire world. Its Greek Revival style, reflected in its large granite columns, is typical of many buildings in our nation's capital.

Active Options

AMERICAN GALLERY ONLINE **Federal Washington** Invite students to explore the American Gallery. Have them select one of the images and do additional research to learn more about it. Ask questions that will inspire additional inquiry about the chosen gallery image, such as: What is this? Where and when was this created? By whom? Why was it created? What is it made of? Why does it belong in this chapter? What else would you like to know about it?

NG Learning Framework: Investigate Change
SKILL Collaboration
KNOWLEDGE Our Human Story

Encourage students to learn more about John Adams's role as the first vice president. Instruct them to write a short description, using information from the chapter and additional source material, of his feelings concerning his role in the Washington Administration. Then direct small groups of students to research the role of the modern vice president and work together to identify three ways the duties of the job have changed over time.

DIFFERENTIATE

Striving Readers

Understand Main Ideas Direct students to make a T-Chart, labeling the first column Who? and the second column Did What? Have students use the chart to record the name of each secretary, the attorney general, the vice president, and the first Chief Justice and list phrases that tell about the duties of each.

Who?	Did What?

Gifted & Talented

Research a Problem Direct students to research a historical figure from the lesson, identifying one problem that person had to solve and that person's solution. Have students share their findings with the class.

See the Chapter Planner for more strategies for differentiation.

HISTORICAL THINKING

ANSWERS

1. The Department of State, the Department of Treasury, and the Department of War each had a leader called a secretary. These secretaries, together with the attorney general, made up the president's Cabinet.

2. The department names suggest that defense, relations with other countries, management of the government's money, and legal representation were important to the new government.

3. The Federal Judiciary Act was created to balance power between federal and local government. State courts ruled on their own laws and disputes between their citizens. The federal courts handled disputes between states, international disputes, and questions about the U.S. Constitution.

1.3 Hamilton's Economic Plan

Can you spare a cool $54 million? The American Revolution was a success, but that's how much the Patriots had to borrow to pull it off. Now it was time to pay back the debt. The question was how?

MAIN IDEA The United States had to develop an economic strategy for the new nation, but conflicting political points of view made planning difficult.

THE PRICE OF WAR

In addition to America's whopping **national debt**, individual states collectively owed another $25 million. Foreign governments and Americans who had helped finance the war were waiting to be repaid. Secretary of the Treasury Alexander Hamilton wanted the U.S. government to demonstrate it could be trusted to take care of its financial responsibilities. Doing so would improve America's credit and encourage new business.

An ardent federalist, Hamilton suggested that the federal government assume, or take over, the war debts of each state. This strategy would give the government more power to run the country's financial affairs. Under Hamilton's plan, sales of federal lands in the West would finance the repayment of European loans. More money would come from increased **tariffs**, or taxes on imports and exports. Tariffs would also encourage Americans to buy American goods, which would help protect industries from foreign competition.

Hamilton suggested the government pay off the rest of its debts by levying, or charging, certain taxes and by issuing new bonds, or investments promising interest on money

loaned. Investors would buy these bonds because the interest would produce big profits over the long run. Finally, to stabilize the nation's finances, Hamilton proposed a common currency and a National Bank. This bank would collect taxes, hold government funds, and promote business and industry by issuing loans. Hamilton envisioned the United States as a strong industrial nation.

The engraving of Alexander Hamilton, shown here, appears on the ten-dollar bill. Very narrow lines are used to create the engravings on U.S. money, making them so detailed that it is virtually impossible to copy exactly, or counterfeit, paper money.

Silver Dollar

During the American Revolution, individual states and the Continental Congress printed their own paper money. Those notes lost value very quickly and were worth almost nothing by the end of the war. Later, when the Constitution gave Congress the sole power to issue national currency, Alexander Hamilton recommended the nation adopt a silver dollar coin. He also suggested using fractional coins to represent smaller parts of a dollar. The Coinage Act of 1792 established the United States Mint—a facility for manufacturing coins—and regulated the coinage of the United States.

The act established the dollar, half-dollar, quarter-dollar, "disme," "half-disme," cent, and half-cent as the denominations of coins. The word *disme* became what we know as "dime." A "half-disme" is now a nickel.

The first dollar coin, called the "Flowing Hair Dollar," from 1794, showed Liberty as a woman on one side (top) and an eagle surrounded by a wreath on the other (bottom). In 1790, you could have used this coin to buy a bag or two of groceries. Ten of the coins could buy you a cow.

CRITICS WEIGH IN

Thomas Jefferson, on the other hand, envisioned an agricultural nation. He and other antifederalists opposed the strong central government and National Bank that Hamilton envisioned. A National Bank, they feared, would favor the interests of business over agriculture—specifically, the interests of the industrial North over those of the agricultural South. And southern states had even more reasons to oppose Hamilton's plan. Most had already paid their war debts. Hamilton ultimately won the South's favor by promising to relocate the nation's capital to Virginia, in an area that would eventually become Washington, D.C., the current capital of the United States.

Jefferson also opposed a National Bank because he believed it would give the federal government unlimited powers and go against the Constitution. But since the Constitution didn't expressly forbid the creation of a National Bank, Hamilton claimed the federal government had every right to establish one. Congress agreed. In 1791, it passed a bill creating a National Bank for a term of 20 years, and President Washington, who also supported Hamilton's views, signed it into law. In December of 1791, the Bank of the United States opened its doors in Philadelphia. Branches soon were established in major cities such as Boston, New York, Charleston, and Baltimore.

Both Jefferson and Hamilton were dedicated to the success of the new administration and the country. However, each man often advised Washington to ignore the counsel of the other. This made them personal adversaries, or opponents. In a letter to Washington written in 1792, Jefferson claimed that Hamilton's allies in Congress were a "corrupt squadron [military unit]," whose "ultimate object . . . is to prepare the way for a change, from the present republican form of government, to that of a monarchy, of which the English constitution is the model." The very nasty and public feud that developed between Jefferson and Hamilton greatly distressed Washington.

HISTORICAL THINKING

1. **READING CHECK** Why did Hamilton think it was crucial for the United States to repay its debts to European nations right away?

2. **COMPARE AND CONTRAST** Describe Jefferson's and Hamilton's different visions for the new nation.

3. **IDENTIFY PROBLEMS AND SOLUTIONS** How did Hamilton propose to pay off the national debt?

PLAN

Objective

Analyze the economic ideas of Alexander Hamilton and Thomas Jefferson.

Critical Thinking Skills for Lesson 1.3

- Identify Main Ideas and Details
- Monitor Comprehension
- Compare and Contrast
- Identify Problems and Solutions
- Make Inferences
- Draw Conclusions

Essential Question for Chapter 8

What challenges did Americans in the new republic confront? The new republic had huge debts from the American Revolution. Lesson 1.3 discusses Alexander Hamilton's economic plan and Thomas Jefferson's opposition to that plan.

Background for the Teacher

The Department of the Treasury was one of the three original Cabinet positions established during Washington's presidency, but the roots for a Department of Treasury began much earlier. Before the American Revolution, money was needed to buy ammunition and supplies for colonial soldiers. But the Continental Congress did not have the power to levy and collect taxes, and foreign investors only agreed to support the United States after a formal declaration of independence. In June 1775, the Continental Congress resolved to issue 2 million dollars in paper money, in the form of bills of credit, to fund the American Revolution. It promised repayment in coin after the war. Hamilton viewed repaying this debt as vital to the United States' reputation, both at home and abroad.

Financial Literacy

To extend their knowledge and understanding about the concepts in this lesson, refer students to the Financial Literacy handbook.

INTRODUCE & ENGAGE

Preview Using Visuals

Point out the silver dollar image in the lesson. Explain that this image depicts the first dollar coin of the new nation. Discuss the woman and eagle images. **ASK:** What do you think these images represent? *(They represent liberty.)* **ASK:** How are the images on this coin like the images on today's U.S. coins? How are they different? *(Answers will vary. Possible response: Coins still carry the word* liberty *and some show eagles. Today's coins have portraits of real people, such as Washington.)*

TEACH

Guided Discussion

1. **Make Inferences** How did Hamilton's economic plan illustrate his Federalist beliefs? *(Hamilton's plan illustrated the Federalists' belief in a strong central government. His plan gave the federal government great power to run the nation's financial affairs, allowing for the use of taxation and the establishment of a National Bank.)*

2. **Draw Conclusions** What did Jefferson mean when he said that Hamilton and his followers were a "corrupt squadron [military unit]," whose "ultimate object . . . is to prepare the way for a change, from the present republican form of government, to that of a monarchy, of which the English constitution is the model"? *(Jefferson believed that the Federalists were too closely aligned with British thinking and they would strengthen the central government in a way that resembled a monarchy rather than a republic.)*

Compare and Contrast

Comparison of Thomas Jefferson and Alexander Hamilton can offer students insight into the administration of George Washington and demonstrate that the success of the new republic was not at all assured. Guide students to use shadow outlines of Hamilton's and Jefferson's profiles to create "historical heads," helping students distinguish between the radically different views of the two men regarding the role of government in the new nation. Students should contrast the perspectives of Hamilton and Jefferson on issues such as these: the funding and assumption of Revolutionary debt, the use of taxes, the establishment of a National Bank, the strength of the federal government compared to state and local governments, and the vision of an industrial or agricultural nation. Students can write the views of each man inside the appropriate outline or beneath the profile. Explain that Jefferson's and Hamilton's strongly opposing views represent a fundamental tension in American politics.

Active Options

On Your Feet: Think, Pair, Share Have students work in pairs to discuss how they would choose between the different advice of key advisors as Washington did with Hamilton and Jefferson. First, instruct students to imagine they are Washington, and invite them to think of questions they'd ask both Jefferson and Hamilton about their economic plans. Next, tell students to discuss their questions with a partner. Finally, encourage students to share their questions with the class.

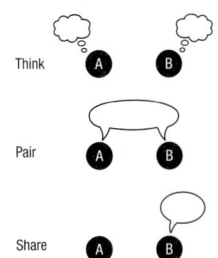

Active History: Create a Personal Budget Extend the lesson by using either the PDF or Whiteboard version of the activity. These activities take a deeper look at a topic from, or related to, the lesson. Explore the activities as a class, turn them into group assignments, or even assign them individually.

DIFFERENTIATE

Striving Readers

Discover Motivation Help students to briefly research online the backgrounds of Thomas Jefferson and Alexander Hamilton for clues that help explain the motivation for their political beliefs. For example, what explains why Jefferson favored agriculture over industry? Why did Hamilton feel a strong nation required industry? Guide students to find a few facts that help them understand these historical figures. Then invite them to share their facts and ideas with the class.

Pre-AP

Write a Comparison Guide students' close reading of primary source excerpts to help them learn more about the clash of political opponents and personal adversaries Thomas Jefferson and Alexander Hamilton. Ask students to analyze Hamilton's notes for a speech at the Federal Convention of June 1787 and Jefferson's letter to Washington of May 1792. Instruct them to write a short comparison of the men's central claims, using information from the primary source excerpts. Then have students present their comparisons to the class.

See the Chapter Planner for more strategies for differentiation.

HISTORICAL THINKING

ANSWERS

1. Hamilton believed that other countries would help the United States financially only if the United States proved it could be trusted to honor its debts.

2. Jefferson, a southern farmer, pictured a nation built on agriculture and did not want a strong federal government. Hamilton, on the other hand, pictured the United States as an industrialized nation with a strong central government.

3. Hamilton believed he could pay off the national debt by selling off western land and by raising money through tariffs and taxes.

AMERICAN PLACES

1.4 Broadway, New York City

New York's theater district revolves around a street you've probably heard of—Broadway. Some 40 theaters make up this famous district, including the Majestic, the Gershwin, and the Richard Rodgers Theatre, where *Hamilton: An American Musical* (shown below) made its Broadway debut in 2015. Since the early 1900s, small theaters have nestled between large ones under the glow of colorful signs advertising the latest productions. Countless actors have launched their careers in Broadway shows like *Cats*, *The Phantom of the Opera*, *Mamma Mia!*, and *The Lion King*, because if you've made it to Broadway, you've made it big. How is theater a part of American culture?

"My name is Alexander Hamilton
And there's a million things I haven't done
But just you wait
Just you wait."

—lyrics from the song "Alexander Hamilton"
by Lin-Manuel Miranda

CRITICAL VIEWING Tony Award-winning *Hamilton* is likely the most unique Broadway production in decades. The hip-hop musical tells the story of Founding Father Alexander Hamilton, who authored several of the Federalist Papers. Actor Lin-Manuel Miranda (center) played Hamilton on Broadway to sold-out crowds and critical acclaim. Based on the photo, how do you think *Hamilton* connects a modern audience to American history?

284 CHAPTER 8

Growing Pains in the New Republic 285

PLAN

Objective

Learn how art can be used to interpret history.

Critical Thinking Skills for Lesson 1.4

- Analyze Visuals
- Make Connections
- Form and Support Opinions
- Make Inferences

Essential Question for Chapter 8

What challenges did Americans in the new republic confront? Alexander Hamilton was a key figure in shaping the economic trajectory of the country. Lesson 1.4 introduces students to a musical based on Hamilton's life that depicts challenges Hamilton faced in his personal life as well as in his role as a Founding Father.

Background for the Teacher

New York City–born *Hamilton* creator Lin-Manuel Miranda grew up in a musically inclined family, taking piano lessons, listening to Broadway musicals, and developing a love for hip-hop. While studying at Wesleyan College, Miranda developed his first musical, *In the Heights*, which went on to win four Tony Awards. He got the idea for *Hamilton: An American Musical* while reading a biography on vacation. Miranda saw the Founding Father's story— his immigrant upbringing, scandalous life, penchant for debate, and tragic death—as a hip-hop story. Even though the historical figures were exclusively white, the production uses a cast filled with diverse actors—Miranda is of Puerto Rican descent— connecting Hamilton's story to the lives of modern day immigrants and minorities.

History Notebook

Encourage students to complete the American Places page for Chapter 8 in their History Notebooks as they read.

Preview Using Visuals

As a class, take a few minutes to study the photograph from *Hamilton: An American Musical*. Encourage volunteers to share their experiences with musicals or plays they have seen in person or on a recorded medium. Inform students that *Hamilton: An American Musical* is a popular Broadway show based on events that took place during the time period covered in this chapter. **ASK:** How does the image from the text compare with your ideas of what early U.S. citizens looked like? *(The people are dressed in historical attire, but the diversity of the cast is surprising because it does not match most textbook descriptions of the period.)*

TEACH

Guided Discussion

1. **Form and Support Opinions** Why do you think theater remains a popular form of entertainment? *(Answers will vary. Possible response: Many theatrical productions are based on universal and popular stories, and live actors can make audiences feel they are seeing the events as they unfold.)*

2. **Make Inferences** Lin-Manuel Miranda chose to tell the story of Alexander Hamilton in a modern style with a diverse cast. Which aspects of Hamilton's story, described in Lesson 1.3, could happen today? Which issues are rooted in a specific time and place? *(Answers will vary. Possible response: High-level officials can still have very different visions for the nation; people still argue about the balance of power between the states and the federal government; today, the United States is an industrial nation and the federal bank has long been established.)*

⬤ American Places

While theaters are found across the United States, Broadway is the most famous area for live theater in the country. This theater district covers several blocks in Manhattan, New York City, including Times Square. Performing a show in one of these 40 theaters exposes it to a huge and potentially lucrative audience. In 2016, Broadway shows together sold more than 13 million tickets at a combined cost of more than 1 billion dollars. Typically, musicals are the most successful and longest-running Broadway shows. Every year, a group of theater professionals honors the year's best Broadway shows by presenting Tony Awards in such categories as Best Play, Best Musical, and Best Original Score. In 2016, *Hamilton: An American Musical* won 11 Tony Awards.

Active Options

On Your Feet: Perform a Skit Place students into small groups. Direct them to review the conflicts between Hamilton and Jefferson as described in this chapter. Then have them work together to write a skit that uses modern language and references to dramatize the conflict. Ask the groups to perform their skits for the class.

NG Learning Framework: Write a Historical Song

| SKILL | Communication |

| KNOWLEDGE | Our Human Story |

Explain that *Hamilton: An American Musical* uses hip-hop music to tell the story of Hamilton's life. Then allow pairs of students to choose another historical figure from the time period. Have them discuss their chosen figure and write a short hip-hop song that conveys the important events in the person's life. Point out that they can review information presented in Chapter 8 or they can research briefly to find additional information.

DIFFERENTIATE

Striving Readers

Summarize Have students work in pairs to read and summarize the text, the caption, and information they gather from the photograph of *Hamilton: An American Musical*. Tell students to use a Summary Chart like the one shown below to organize their notes. Suggest students provide three notes per category. After they have completed taking notes, guide students to create a summary statement about Lesson 1.4.

Lesson Title and Text	Critical Viewing Caption	Photograph
1.	1.	1.
2.	2.	2.
3.	3.	3.
Summary Statement		

Gifted & Talented

Analyze a Scene Assign students to view different examples of historical films, plays, or musicals, such as *John Adams*, *Pocahontas*, or *1776*. Ask students to choose one scene and present it to the class. As part of the presentation, students should analyze the historical accuracy of the scene. After the presentations, discuss as a class the strengths and weaknesses of dramatizing historical events.

See the Chapter Planner for more strategies for differentiation.

AMERICAN PLACES

Answers will vary. Students might mention the popularity of school plays and community theater in addition to small- and large-scale professional theater productions. They may also mention historical plays that some communities mount during heritage celebrations.

CRITICAL VIEWING Possible response: The musical features a multiethnic cast, flashy costumes, choreography, modern music, and an interesting set to make the story feel more contemporary.

2.1 Political Parties Form

You've probably seen the ads. "Vote for me! Don't vote for" — whomever. The candidates are usually from different political parties. You can thank (or blame) Hamilton and Jefferson for laying the groundwork for such parties.

MAIN IDEA Leaders formed political parties to promote their ideas, forming the basis of the modern American political system.

TAKING SIDES

During the 1790s, many congressional representatives sided with either Hamilton, who fought for a strong central government, or Jefferson, who feared the power such a government could wield. Eventually, the two sides formed two political parties—the **Federalist Party** and the **Democratic-Republican Party**. The Federalists backed Hamilton. The Democratic-Republicans sided more with Jefferson.

The Constitution made no provision for political parties, but it did not prohibit them. Still, the idea of divided political parties shocked the older leaders of the Revolutionary era. Washington warned against their "baneful [harmful] effects." If they were to play any role at all, he said, they needed to be kept in check. But the process was now in motion. Political parties had established themselves as a powerful force, and sides had been taken.

FACING OFF

On one side stood the Federalist Party, whose **power base**, or area of biggest influence, was in New England and the Middle Atlantic states. John Adams, Washington's vice president, joined the Federalists. They favored commercial development, a National Bank, the development of infrastructure to build canals, roads, and schools through land grants, and high tariffs to spur manufacturing. They also believed in a **loose interpretation** of the Constitution—one that gave broad powers to Congress and the president. Federalists were more likely than their opponents to be critical of slavery and so gained the allegiance of free African Americans in both the North and the South. Because their power base

lay in the Northeast, many Federalists didn't back the idea of western expansion and sometimes supported the rights of Native Americans.

On the other side was the Democratic-Republican Party, whose power base was in the South and the West. The party included many former antifederalists. Like Jefferson, the Democratic-Republicans believed in a **strict interpretation** of the Constitution—one that strictly followed the document and honored the rights of states over federal power. They opposed too much federal support for manufacturing and commerce. With its southern backing, the party rejected efforts to abolish slavery. Because it favored westward expansion and had little sympathy for the rights of Native Americans, the party also had the support of westerners on the frontier. The fundamental tension created by the development of a two-party system continues to influence American politics today.

In addition to these internal divisions within the government, the United States had to confront more fundamental challenges to its authority and legitimacy. Trouble was brewing in the Northwest Territory and abroad.

HISTORICAL THINKING

1. **READING CHECK** What regions of the United States supported each party, and why?

2. **IDENTIFY PROBLEMS AND SOLUTIONS** What problems might either a loose or strict interpretation of the Constitution create or solve?

3. **EVALUATE** What are the advantages and disadvantages of political parties?

Two-Party System

Although the parties have changed and shifted over the years, the United States still has two major political parties: the Democrats and the Republicans. A two-party system is relatively unique in the world. Some countries have only one party, while others have many. The symbols of each U.S. party are shown below: a donkey for the Democrats and an elephant for the Republicans. Neither modern party aligns closely with the political ideas of the Federalists or the Democratic-Republicans. However, like the parties in the 1790s, the parties today have regional characteristics. The Republicans tend to be stronger in the South and the West, and the Democrats stronger on the coasts, the Northeast, and the upper Midwest.

The campaign buttons shown are from the second half of the 20th century. Remember, though, that supporters purchased buttons honoring George Washington at his inauguration. In the 1840 election, people wore campaign buttons sewn on clothing. Pins were added around 1860, along with the first photograph to appear on a campaign button—a picture of Abraham Lincoln.

PLAN

Objective

Understand how conflicts between Thomas Jefferson and Alexander Hamilton led to the two-party system in the United States.

Critical Thinking Skills for Lesson 2.1

- Identify Main Ideas and Details
- Monitor Comprehension
- Identify Problems and Solutions
- Evaluate
- Form and Support Opinions

Essential Question for Chapter 8

What challenges did Americans in the new republic confront? Hamilton's and Jefferson's differing ideas gave rise to opposing political parties. Lesson 2.1 discusses Federalist and Democratic-Republican views on slavery, westward expansion, the Constitution, and states' rights.

Background for the Teacher

Historically, the two major U.S. political parties have represented a diverse set of beliefs. While most U.S. senators and representatives are elected as Democrats or Republicans, each party's membership has historically included a wide range of differing ideas and opinions. A Democrat, therefore, might vote with other Democrats on some issues but with Republicans on other issues. This has allowed for more liberal Republicans and Democrats to form alliances against more conservative Democrats and Republicans, and vice versa. However, in recent times, opinions within the political parties have become more polarized, which has made compromise and alliances more difficult. Because of this polarization, today, Democrats rarely support ideas proposed by Republicans, and Republicans usually oppose solutions recommended by Democrats.

Create a Party Platform
Invite students to share what they know about the modern Democratic and Republican parties. Then tell students that the class is going to create a new political party. On the board, pose the following questions: What will the party be called? What should its symbol be? What principles will the party stand for? Have students brainstorm a list of ideas based on these questions. Then inform students that in this lesson, they will discover how the party system began in the early days of the republic.

TEACH
Guided Discussion
1. **Identify Problems and Solutions** George Washington believed that political parties were harmful and should be kept in check. Why do you think Washington felt this way? How do you think parties could be "checked"? *(Possible response: Washington worried that parties would bring disunity to the new country. To prevent this, Congress could be split evenly between the parties, or parties could be given equal time to make their case before the public regarding policy issues.)*

2. **Form and Support Opinions** In a 1797 letter to a friend, Thomas Jefferson wrote: "You and I have formerly seen warm debates and high political passions. But gentlemen of different politics would then speak to each other and separate the business of the Senate from that of society. It is not so now." Do you agree with Jefferson that it is dangerous if people cannot separate politics from social interactions? Explain your answer. *(Possible response: Jefferson is right; if people cannot get past political differences, it makes compromise difficult, which is harmful to the country.)*

More Information
Political Philosophies Explain to students that the fundamental tension between and among political parties in the United States has roots in the very early years of the new nation. Comparing the philosophies of Jefferson and Hamilton can help students understand the development of a two-party system. Washington understood the differences between Jefferson and Hamilton, but he was also concerned that too much conflict might derail the new republic. **ASK:** What are some of the ways in which different philosophies can both help and hinder a new nation? *(Differing political philosophies can help refine and strengthen a nation's identity; however, too much conflict can sometimes lead to disruption or revolt, which is what worried Washington.)*

Active Options
On Your Feet: Question and Answer Instruct half the class to write True-False statements based on information in Lesson 2.1. Direct the other half to create response cards with "True" written on one side and "False" on the other. As each statement is read aloud, students in the second group should stand and respond to the statement by displaying either the "True" or "False" card. When discrepancies occur, review the statements and discuss which response is correct.

NG Learning Framework: Promote a Political Party
SKILL Communication
KNOWLEDGE Our Human Story

Direct small groups of students to further research the platforms of the Federalist Party or the Democratic-Republican Party. Then have them create a sales pitch to promote their chosen party. Instruct them to identify a particular audience for their promotion, such as farmers, laborers, the wealthy, or the poor. Then guide them to choose an appropriate medium, such as a speech, a letter to the editor, a poster, or a multimedia presentation. Finally, have groups create and present their promotion. After the presentation, have the class vote on whether the promotion was effective at persuading the intended audience to support the party.

DIFFERENTIATE
Inclusion
Make a Graphic Organizer Pair students with disabilities with proficient readers. Have pairs create a T-Chart, labeling the left column Federalists and the right column Democratic-Republicans. Ask proficient readers to read aloud from the lesson and help their partners complete the T-Chart, together identifying and organizing the ideas of the two parties.

Pre-AP
Trace the History of U.S. Political Parties Encourage students to research how the various major political parties in the United States have changed over time. Suggest they make an annotated time line showing the rise and fall of different parties and noting any fundamental changes of philosophy. On their time lines, they should identify important people and events that helped bring about the birth, change, or demise of a party.

See the Chapter Planner for more strategies for differentiation.

HISTORICAL THINKING
ANSWERS
1. New England and the Middle Atlantic states, where industry and commerce thrived, favored the Federalists. The South was more agricultural, so southern voters generally preferred the more agriculturally oriented Democratic-Republicans.

2. A loose interpretation of the Constitution could offer flexibility but could lead to laws that changed with each administration. A strict interpretation of the Constitution could create stability but could prevent the nation from changing laws to respond to changing situations.

3. Advantages may include: Political parties support certain ideas, so voters get clues about a candidate by identifying his or her party; having clearly defined parties might help people discuss and debate issues. Disadvantages may include: People might vote for a candidate based solely on party affiliation, not competence; parties can serve to divide the nation.

Competition for Territory and the French Revolution

George Washington had dealt with many challenging situations, but as president, he probably got more than he bargained for. As political conflict grew among U.S. citizens, conflicts over western lands heated to the boiling point.

MAIN IDEA As the young republic pushed west, conflicts both at home and abroad caused a host of challenges for the United States.

CONFLICTS IN THE WEST

The problem area was the Northwest Territory, located north of the Ohio River, between the western boundary of Pennsylvania and the Mississippi River. As you may remember, the Treaty of Paris of 1783 had established new boundaries for the United States and tried to settle claims on this land. But in the 1790s, the land seemed to be up for grabs once again. Spain, Britain, the United States, and Native American groups all claimed parts of the vast expanse for their own.

The United States mostly fought with Native Americans over rights to this land. Americans wanted to settle the land, not only for its rich soil but also for its minerals, such as copper, iron, and silver. Native Americans had lived in this region for thousands of years and attacked settlers who moved onto the land. In response, Washington sent in two military expeditions, but the Miami of Ohio, led by

Chief Little Turtle, defeated them both. Then, in 1794, federal troops defeated the Miami at the Battle of Fallen Timbers. The British, who had usually helped the Miami, refused to protect them this time. They were tired of war. Without British support, the Miami and other Native Americans in the region signed the **Treaty of Greenville**, which **ceded**, or gave up, their lands in present-day Ohio and Indiana to the United States.

🏛 Metropolitan Museum of Art, New York

Washington Reviewing the Western Army at Fort Cumberland, Maryland depicts Washington arriving to review the militia during the Whiskey Rebellion. The president's mere presence was enough to put an end to the protestors' armed attacks. The episode demonstrated how much people respected Washington and the central government. Artist Frederick Kemmelmeyer created the painting sometime after 1795—shortly after the rebellion took place.

Meanwhile, another conflict brewed in western Pennsylvania. Farmers had been protesting a whiskey tax, claiming it was unfair. Secretary of the Treasury Alexander Hamilton had proposed the tax, which was passed by Congress in 1791 to raise money to pay down the national debt. The angry farmers who made, consumed, sold, and traded whiskey, tarred and feathered tax collectors and threatened armed attacks in what is known as the **Whiskey Rebellion**. President Washington sent nearly 13,000 soldiers into the region to demonstrate the power of the federal government. The rebels soon stood down.

THE FRENCH REVOLUTION

Across the Atlantic, the people in France were involved in a rebellion of their own. They sought to put an end to upper-class privilege and demanded equality for the lower classes. Many in the United States, and particularly the Democratic-Republicans, supported the **French Revolution**. But then in 1793, **radicals**, or people who support complete social or political change, executed the French king, Louis XVI. France then declared war on Spain, Britain, and other neighboring nations. In this international conflict, the Federalists sided with Britain, thereby increasing the division between the two American parties. So even though France had supported the American Revolution, Washington declared in 1793 that the United States would remain neutral, not taking sides with anyone.

But Britain made neutrality difficult. Its Royal Navy captured American citizens and forced them to work on British ships. They also blocked trade in the British West Indies and seized American ships. To make peace, Washington sent Chief Justice John Jay to England to work out a deal. Jay's Treaty required the British to pay for the American ships they had damaged, but it failed to reopen trade in the West Indies.

Meanwhile, **Thomas Pinckney**, an American statesman, traveled to Spain and negotiated Pinckney's Treaty in 1796 to maintain friendly relations between the United States and Spain. The treaty opened the Mississippi River to free navigation, allowed Americans to use the Spanish port of New Orleans, and settled a conflict regarding the Spanish colony of West Florida.

Guillotine
One of the most striking images of the French Revolution is the guillotine (GEE-yuh-teen), the machine used to execute thousands, including Louis XVI. The guillotine had a blade that plunged down grooves in two upright posts to slice through the victim's neck, beheading him or her in one stroke.

HISTORICAL THINKING

1. **READING CHECK** Why did farmers in western Pennsylvania stage the Whiskey Rebellion?

2. **IDENTIFY PROBLEMS AND SOLUTIONS** Describe the conflicts between American settlers and Native Americans in the Northwest Territory and how they were resolved.

3. **MAKE INFERENCES** Why do you think the United States wanted to remain neutral during the French Revolution?

PLAN

Objective

Understand how the United States government dealt with foreign and domestic skirmishes.

Critical Thinking Skills for Lesson 2.2

- Identify Main Ideas and Details
- Monitor Comprehension
- Identify Problems and Solutions
- Make Inferences
- Analyze Cause and Effect
- Compare and Contrast

Essential Question for Chapter 8

What challenges did Americans in the new republic confront? The new republic faced hostilities in the Northwest Territories, Pennsylvania, and Europe. Lesson 2.2 examines how the U.S. government used military and diplomatic means to address problems with Native Americans, farmers, and foreign governments.

Background for the Teacher

The Whiskey Rebellion gave the federal government a chance to assert its authority. Proposed by Alexander Hamilton and passed by Congress in 1791, a tax on whiskey and other spirits was created to help chip away at the national debt. To many small farmers, this tax presented a big problem because whiskey—an alcoholic beverage made with grain—played a central role in the economy and social lives of many out west. As a result, many farmers refused to pay the tax and destroyed the distilling equipment of those who did pay. However, by sending troops, including nearby state militias, to quash the rebellion, President George Washington proved that the federal government could impose and enforce this kind of tax and punish those who failed to comply.

Resolve a Conflict

Lead students in brainstorming some tools a government might use to resolve a conflict with another nation or with a contentious domestic group. Record their responses on the board. For example, students might suggest military force, diplomacy, economic sanctions, and other ideas. Then discuss the following questions:

• Under what circumstances might a government decide to go to war?

• How and why might a government avoid going to war?

Tell students they will learn about how George Washington's administration dealt with conflicts at home and abroad.

TEACH

Guided Discussion

1. **Analyze Cause and Effect** Questions concerning the land in the Northwest Territory dated back to the country's founding. Why do you think these issues arose again in the 1790s? *(As the population of the United States grew, people needed more land opened up for farming, thus pushing them west into land occupied by Native Americans. In addition, minerals were discovered on the land, and people wanted to exploit them.)*

2. **Compare and Contrast** In what ways were the American Revolution and the French Revolution alike? In what ways were they different? *(Alike: Both involved people rising up against authority. In both, people fought for ideals, such as freedom and equality. Different: In the French Revolution, people fought against class inequality; in the American Revolution, people fought for independence from a foreign power.)*

🏛 Virtual Museum Visit

Some online features at the Metropolitan Museum of Art's website offer personal perspectives on art and art themes from artists, curators, and other museum personnel. Access the museum's website and go to Online Features. Under Connections, you may wish to access the brief video "War and Conflict" as a class. Then ask groups of students to explore the section on their own, viewing videos about art on topics that interest them. Have groups share what they have found with the class.

Active Options

On Your Feet: Turn and Talk Ask students to form three to five groups. Give each group this topic sentence: During George Washington's presidency, the United States met and responded to several conflicts at home and abroad. Tell students to build a paragraph on that topic by having each student in the group contribute one sentence. The sentences should provide evidence to support the topic sentence. Allow each group to present its paragraph to the class by having each student read her or his statement.

NG Learning Framework: Describe a Conflict

ATTITUDE Curiosity

KNOWLEDGE Our Human Story

Have students select one of the conflicts they are still curious about after reading this lesson. Instruct them to write a short description of this conflict using information from the lesson and additional source material. The description should analyze the claims of each side of the conflict and include an evaluation of which side had the stronger argument.

DIFFERENTIATE

Inclusion

Complete a 5Ws Chart Guide students in completing a 5Ws Chart to help them understand the major events (such as the Treaty of Greenville and the French Revolution) discussed in the lesson. Review vocabulary words that students might have difficulty comprehending, such as *ceded* and *radicals*.

Who?
What?
Where?
When?
Why?

English Language Learners

Identify Main Ideas and Details Lesson 2.2 has two subsections. Pair students at the **Emerging** and **Expanding** levels and assign each pair a subsection of the text to read together. Have students use a graphic organizer to make notes about the main idea and supporting details in their part of the lesson. Students at the **Bridging** level can work individually. Then ask students to write a one- or two-sentence summary.

See the Chapter Planner for more strategies for differentiation.

HISTORICAL THINKING

ANSWERS

1. Farmers in western Pennsylvania objected to a whiskey tax they felt was unfair.

2. When settlers moved onto the lands on which Native Americans had lived for thousands of years, the Native Americans fought them. Defeated by federal troops, Native American groups signed the Treaty of Greenville, giving up their lands.

3. Possible response: Taking sides could cause divisions among the American public; the United States probably wanted to maintain diplomatic and commercial ties to different European countries and did not want to get pulled into a costly foreign war.

2.3 Washington's Farewell Address

At the end of his first presidential term, George Washington wrote a goodbye letter to the American people. Then he ended up running for a second term. The letter—Washington's Farewell Address—was finally published in 1796, and it is an important American document.

When his eighth year as president was drawing to a close, Washington shared the letter with John Jay and Alexander Hamilton. The three men spent four months revising the letter, ensuring that Washington's ideas were crystal clear. Washington handwrote a clean copy of the finished letter—32 pages long—and addressed it to "Friends & Fellow-Citizens." It was published in the Philadelphia newspaper, *American Daily Advertiser*,

on September 19, 1796. It was then printed in other newspapers throughout the country. Following his service as president of the United States, Washington moved back to Mount Vernon (shown in the photo), his home and plantation in Virginia. Washington grew up at Mount Vernon and had always dreamed of returning to his home life there. He lived at Mount Vernon until his death in 1799 and is buried there.

Mount Vernon, George Washington's home

DOCUMENT ONE

Primary Source: Historical document from Washington's Farewell Address, 1796

In this excerpt from his address, Washington tells Americans that they form one united nation. United, he tells them, they are stronger and more secure than they could ever be as separate individuals.

CONSTRUCTED RESPONSE Why does Washington urge people to be proud to be called Americans?

The unity of government . . . is a main pillar in the edifice [structure] of your real independence, . . . of your tranquility at home, your peace abroad; of your safety; of your prosperity; of that very liberty which you so highly prize. The name of American, which belongs to you in your national capacity, must always exalt the just pride of patriotism.

DOCUMENT TWO

Primary Source: Historical document from Washington's Farewell Address, 1796

Washington felt that political parties could pit one group of people against another, posing a threat to national unity. Here, he discusses the dangers of rival political parties.

CONSTRUCTED RESPONSE According to Washington, how might rival political parties affect a community?

In contemplating the causes which may disturb our Union, it occurs as matter of serious concern that any ground should have been furnished for characterizing parties by geographical discriminations [differences], . . . whence [by which] designing men may endeavor to excite a belief that there is a real difference of local interests and views.

DOCUMENT THREE

Primary Source: Historical document from Washington's Farewell Address, 1796

In 1796, France was at war with many other European countries, including Britain. As you've read, some Americans supported the French cause, while others supported Britain. In this excerpt, Washington warns against forming permanent alliances and argues for neutrality in all overseas affairs. He believes such alliances would open the country to foreign influence and unnecessary wars.

CONSTRUCTED RESPONSE What did Washington's speech suggest about the policy the United States should follow with other nations?

Nothing is more essential than that permanent, inveterate antipathies [harsh opposition] against particular nations, and passionate attachments for others, should be excluded and that, in place of them, just and amicable [friendly] feelings towards all should be cultivated. Excessive partiality for one foreign nation and excessive dislike of another cause those whom they actuate [fire up] to see danger only on one side, and serve to veil [cover up] . . . the influence on the other. The great rule of conduct for us in regard to foreign nations is in extending our commercial relations, to have with them as little political connection as possible.

SYNTHESIZE & WRITE

1. **REVIEW** Review what you have learned about Washington's Farewell Address.

2. **RECALL** On your own paper, write the main idea that Washington expressed in each excerpt from his farewell address.

3. **CONSTRUCT** Construct a topic sentence that answers this question: What factors did Washington fear could disrupt the unity and peace of the United States?

4. **WRITE** Using evidence from this chapter and the documents, write an informative paragraph that supports your topic sentence in Step 3.

Objective

Understand the main arguments made in George Washington's Farewell Address.

Critical Thinking Skills for Lesson 2.3

- Synthesize
- Identify Main Ideas and Details
- Monitor Comprehension
- Evaluate

Essential Question for Chapter 8

What challenges did Americans in the new republic confront? As Washington ended his tenure as the first U.S. president, the new nation faced many foreign and domestic challenges. Lesson 2.3 provides excerpts of Washington's parting advice about how to pursue national unity and good relationships with other nations.

Background for the Teacher

In addition to his duties as a military general and president, George Washington remained a gentleman farmer, yearning for life back home at Mount Vernon. He had inherited Mount Vernon in 1761 and made many improvements over the years, including adding a distillery and gristmill. He first cultivated tobacco, then wheat. Washington designed several gardens at Mount Vernon—ornamental gardens, a "kitchen garden" that provided vegetables for consumption on the estate, and even a greenhouse for rare and exotic plants. Washington watched over orchards of apple, peach, pear, and cherry trees. He continued to supervise farm activities until his death. George and Martha Washington are buried at Mount Vernon.

INTRODUCE & ENGAGE

Prepare for the Document-Based Question

Before students start on the activity, briefly preview the three documents. Remind students that a constructed response requires full explanations in complete sentences. Emphasize that students should use what they have learned about conflicts between political parties and other American groups, as well as policies regarding foreign relations, in addition to the information in the documents.

TEACH

Guided Discussion

1. **Identify Main Ideas and Details** What does Washington suggest is important for ensuring tranquility, peace, safety, and prosperity? *(He suggests that a united government is crucial.)*

2. **Monitor Comprehension** Why does Washington suggest it's unwise to strongly favor one nation over another? *(Possible response: If you prefer one nation to another, you are likely to overlook signs of danger from the preferred nation and suspect trouble only from the less favored nation.)*

Evaluate

After students have completed the Synthesize & Write activity, allow time for them to exchange paragraphs and read and comment on the work of their peers. Establish guidelines for comments prior to this activity so that feedback is constructive and encouraging in nature.

Active Options

On Your Feet: Host a DBQ Roundtable Arrange the classroom for a DBQ Roundtable and divide the class into small groups. Read this statement aloud from another section of Washington's Farewell Address: "Of all the dispositions and habits which lead to political prosperity, Religion and Morality are indispensable supports" and this one, written by John Adams: "Our Constitution was made only for a moral and religious people." Give each group this discussion starter: Consider how these ideas expressed by Washington and Adams support a loose interpretation of the Constitution. If necessary, suggest to students that they consider issues such as slavery and treatment of Native Americans. Direct students to list their ideas. Then reconvene as a class and discuss groups' responses.

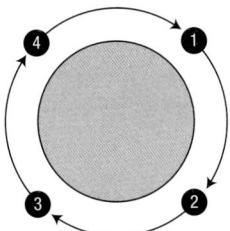

DIFFERENTIATE

Striving Readers

Understand Synonyms Point out that several formal words used in Washington's Farewell Address have more common synonyms. Write these synonym groups on the board: *tranquility: peacefulness, calmness; partiality: favoritism; prosperity: success, wealth, or well-being; just: fair.* Then ask students to use each of the more formal words in a sentence.

Inclusion

Work in Pairs Allow students with disabilities to work with other students who can read the lesson aloud to them. Encourage the partner without disabilities to read slowly and distinctly, especially when reading the longer words and more formal language of the excerpts. Ask pairs to work together to answer the Constructed Response and Synthesize & Write questions. If possible, give students the option of recording their answers rather than writing them out.

See the Chapter Planner for more strategies for differentiation.

SYNTHESIZE & WRITE

ANSWERS

1. Answers will vary.

2. Answers will vary.

3. Possible response: Washington feared that the unity of the United States could be disrupted by entanglements with foreign governments, divisiveness between political parties, and lack of national identity and unity.

4. Students' paragraphs should include their topic sentence from Step 3 and provide several details from the documents to support the sentence.

CONSTRUCTED RESPONSE

Document 1: Possible response: Washington wants people in the United States to have a sense of belonging and pride in their nation above their sense of identity and loyalty to their individual communities, states, or regions.

Document 2: Possible response: Washington suggests that political parties can encourage a focus on the differences between people and communities and thus cause divisiveness.

Document 3: Possible response: Washington's speech suggests that the United States should follow a policy of neutrality, engaging in trade without taking sides in political matters.

2.4 The Parties in Conflict

Politicians making negative remarks about each other. Citizens deeply divided over the candidates. A modern-day election? Nope. This happened in 1796, when political parties first competed in an election.

MAIN IDEA Political clashes tested U.S. relationships abroad and the constitutionality of laws passed at home.

ADAMS VS. JEFFERSON

The Federalists and Democratic-Republicans waged a bitter campaign in 1796. John Adams ran on the Federalist side, and Thomas Jefferson represented the Democratic-Republicans. After attacks on both sides, Adams won with 71 electoral votes. He was the first president to govern from Washington, D.C. Jefferson came in second with 68 electoral votes and became vice president. It was not a happy arrangement.

Problems abroad claimed their attention. France began seizing American ships in an effort to prevent U.S. trade with Britain. In response, Adams sent three **envoys**, or ambassadors, to France to settle the problem. The envoys met with French agents known to the American public simply as X, Y, and Z. When the French agents made unreasonable demands and even insisted on being paid a bribe to begin negotiations, the shocked envoys turned them down and returned home.

The **XYZ Affair**, as the negotiations came to be called, further soured American relations with France. It also hurt the reputation of the Democratic-Republicans, who had supported the French Revolution. When Adams made reports of the affair public, most Americans felt their honor had been attacked, and war fever swept the country. Congress expanded the army, established the navy, and authorized naval vessels to attack French ships that threatened American merchant ships. Congress stopped all trade with France and ended the U.S. alliance with the country.

THE ALIEN AND SEDITION ACTS

Americans cheered Adams's response to the French threat. Riding on a wave of popularity, the Federalists passed the **Alien and Sedition Acts**. The Alien Act allowed the president to expel, for any reason, new immigrants, or aliens, living in the United States—most of whom were Democratic-Republicans. The Sedition Act targeted U.S. citizens, including journalists, who criticized the government. **Sedition** is the act of provoking rebellion.

Democratic-Republicans were quick to respond. For example, in the Kentucky Resolutions, Jefferson condemned the excess of the Alien and Sedition Acts, claiming they violated citizens' freedom of speech and freedom of the press. Adams's opponents fought the acts using a theory called **states' rights**, which declares that individual states have rights the federal government cannot violate. By 1802, the acts had expired, but they had undermined Adams's popularity. In the presidential election of 1800, Jefferson defeated him. The election marked the first peaceful transfer of power from one party to another.

HISTORICAL THINKING

1. **READING CHECK** How did Jefferson become Adams's vice president in 1796?

2. **ANALYZE CAUSE AND EFFECT** Why did the XYZ Affair increase Adams's popularity?

3. **SYNTHESIZE** How did the Sedition Acts contradict the rights guaranteed under the First Amendment?

A GLOBAL PERSPECTIVE When Congress passed the Sedition Act in 1798, the legislation threatened citizens' freedom of speech and press. Fortunately, Americans can protest against laws they deem unfair and work to overturn them. This is not the case today in North Korea, where any criticism of the government and its leaders results in imprisonment—or worse. The government uses a strong military to enforce its rigid laws. In the 2007 photo shown here, North Korean soldiers take part in a celebration of the 75th anniversary of the founding of the Korean People's Army. What impression do you think the soldiers conveyed to the people of North Korea and the world?

PLAN

Objective

Analyze how John Adams's administration handled diplomatic problems overseas and worked to silence critics in the United States.

Critical Thinking Skills for Lesson 2.4

- Identify Main Ideas and Details
- Monitor Comprehension
- Analyze Cause and Effect
- Synthesize
- Evaluate
- Describe

Essential Question for Chapter 8

What challenges did Americans in the new republic confront? The United States faced diplomatic problems at home and abroad. Lesson 2.4 explores the political and the public reaction to the XYZ Affair and how the Adams Administration used the Alien and Sedition Acts to silence critics.

Background for the Teacher

The Alien and Sedition Acts were passed by the Federalist majority in Congress in 1789 and were intended to thwart some very specific groups of people for political reasons. For example, the Naturalization Act targeted Irish immigrants, who tended to vote Democratic-Republican, by lengthening the time it took to become an American citizen. The Sedition Act made it unlawful for a person to speak, write, print, or publish statements criticizing the government, Congress, or the president. Those who defied the law risked fines or imprisonment. Under the Sedition Act, the secretary of state launched court cases against several Democratic-Republican–leaning newspapers, intentionally interfering with their ability to weigh in on the 1800 election.

INTRODUCE & ENGAGE

Plan a Succession

Ask students to identify some traits that make a good leader. Write their responses on the board. Then ask them to think about which of George Washington's traits would be helpful for a president to have and which new traits might be valuable in the president succeeding Washington. Guide them in a discussion about what they think voters should look for in a candidate to succeed Washington as president. Tell them they will be learning about the man who took office after Washington.

TEACH

Guided Discussion

1. **Evaluate** How much power should the federal government have and what should it do? Should the federal government be able to override states' rights? Should the states be able to override federal laws? *(Possible response: The federal government shouldn't be able to take away rights granted in the Bill of Rights. States should be able to make their own laws as long as they are constitutional. However, states should not have the ability to override federal laws.)*

2. **Describe** Review with students what they have learned over the last several lessons, particularly the ways in which the government evolved in the early years of the new nation. **ASK:** How did the government change during the early years of the republic? *(Possible response: During the early years, the power of the federal government expanded, becoming far stronger than it was under the Articles of Confederation. This is illustrated by examples such as the creation of a National Bank and the passage of the Alien and Sedition Acts.)*

A Global Perspective

Explore the photograph and caption for this lesson with students. **ASK:** What do you notice about the formation in this picture? *(It looks extremely precise, with not one soldier out of position.)* What do you think would happen if a soldier decided not to participate in this display? *(The soldier might be imprisoned or killed.)* Why do you think many oppressive governments have strong and organized militaries? *(Possible response: The militaries can be used to enforce laws and intimidate citizens.)*

Active Options

On Your Feet: Think, Pair, Share Direct individual students to think about these questions: For what reasons might some people support the Alien and Sedition Acts? For what reasons might other people oppose them? Have students pair up and share their answers. Then have one student from each pair share that pair's answers with the class.

NG Learning Framework: Understand the Free Press

ATTITUDE Responsibility

SKILL Collaboration

To help students identify the functions and responsibilities of a free press, ask them to work in pairs. One partner should research countries in which the press has a high degree of freedom, such as Finland, Costa Rica, and New Zealand, while the other partner should research countries without a free press, such as China, Cuba, and Libya. When they have finished their individual research, they should work together to analyze their findings and answer these questions: How does a free press function in society? What happens when the government controls the press? Can journalists and/or citizens abuse a free press? If so, how? In countries in which the press is limited, are there ways to get around these controls? Invite pairs to share their analysis with the class.

DIFFERENTIATE

English Language Learners

Summarize Lesson 2.4 has five paragraphs. Place students of **All Proficiencies** in pairs or groups, and assign each pair or group one paragraph to read together. Then groups should summarize their paragraph in one or two sentences for the class.

Pre-AP

Create a TV News Report Invite interested students to research the Alien and Sedition Acts. They should answer questions such as the following:

- When and under whose authority were the acts imposed?
- Which specific groups were the intended target of the acts? How and why did the acts target them?
- How did the public react?
- What constitutional questions were raised by the acts?
- How did the acts come to an end?

Students can present their information to the class in the form of a TV news magazine report, either as a news story or as a commentary.

See the Chapter Planner for more strategies for differentiation.

HISTORICAL THINKING

ANSWERS

1. Adams won the highest number of electoral votes, and Jefferson won the second highest number of electoral votes.

2. The French seized American ships, and the French envoys expected bribes from American diplomats to resolve the matter. The American people liked that Adams strengthened the military and stopped trade with France instead of giving in.

3. In seeking to suppress criticism of the government, the Sedition Acts put limits on free speech and freedom of the press, both guaranteed in the First Amendment.

A GLOBAL PERSPECTIVE Possible response: The soldiers are likely to be seen as very intimidating, which makes dissent and opposition rare.

8 REVIEW

VOCABULARY

Complete each of the sentences below with one of the vocabulary words or terms from this chapter.

1. The department heads in Washington's _____ did not always agree.

2. Placing a _____ on imported goods helped make American goods more competitive.

3. U.S. journalists who criticized the government could be accused of _____ .

4. Federalists preferred a _____ of the Constitution rather than a rigid one.

5. Antifederalists tended to favor _____ rather than a strong central government.

6. The first presidential _____ took place in New York City.

READING STRATEGY
IDENTIFY PROBLEMS AND SOLUTIONS

Complete your chart to identify the problems the new nation faced. List at least three key problems. Then answer the question below.

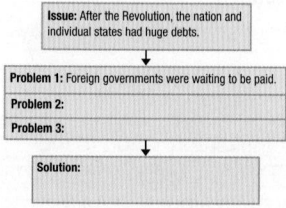

Issue: After the Revolution, the nation and individual states had huge debts.

Problem 1: Foreign governments were waiting to be paid.

Problem 2:

Problem 3:

Solution:

7. How did Alexander Hamilton solve the problem of the nation's debt?

MAIN IDEAS

Answer the following questions. Support your answers with evidence from the chapter.

8. Why was George Washington the obvious choice to be the first president? **LESSON 1.1**

9. What three departments did Congress first create to be part of the executive branch? **LESSON 1.2**

10. What did the Federal Judiciary Act call for? **LESSON 1.2**

11. How did Hamilton's economic plan reflect his federalist philosophy? **LESSON 1.3**

12. Why did the South tend to support the Democratic-Republican Party? **LESSON 2.1**

13. Why did Washington warn against divided political parties? **LESSON 2.1**

14. Why did Native Americans in the Northwest Territory sign the Treaty of Greenville? **LESSON 2.2**

15. Why did Congress stop all U.S. trade with France? **LESSON 2.4**

16. What freedoms did the Sedition Act target? **LESSON 2.4**

HISTORICAL THINKING

Answer the following questions. Support your answers with evidence from the chapter.

17. **SYNTHESIZE** How did the choice of George Washington as the country's first president help to shape American identity?

18. **EVALUATE** Why would Washington want to avoid any suggestion that the office of president of the United States was similar to that of a king?

19. **MAKE CONNECTIONS** Identify a controversial issue mentioned in this chapter that is still causing disagreement today.

20. **DRAW CONCLUSIONS** Why did George Washington think it was important to leave some parting words to the American people in his farewell address?

21. **MAKE INFERENCES** Why might Adams have wanted to pass the Alien Act?

22. **IDENTIFY PROBLEMS AND SOLUTIONS** What new problem did the XYZ Affair cause, and what measures did Congress put in place to solve it?

INTERPRET MAPS

Study this map, which shows the results of the 1796 presidential election between John Adams and Thomas Jefferson. Note that the numbers represent the number of electoral college votes for each state. Remember that the electoral college consists of electors representing each state who vote to elect a president and vice president. The boxed numbers represent the number of electors in that state who voted differently from the others in the state. Then answer the questions that follow.

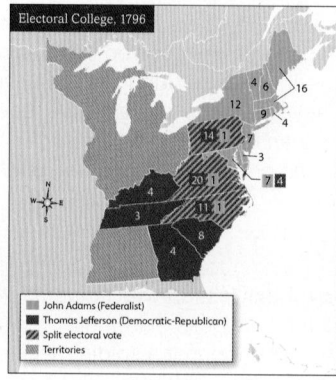

Electoral College, 1796

- John Adams (Federalist)
- Thomas Jefferson (Democratic-Republican)
- Split electoral vote
- Territories

23. Which state had the most electoral votes?

24. What generalization can you make regarding the geographic distribution of results?

ANALYZE SOURCES

In this excerpt from a letter written on February 28, 1796, by Thomas Jefferson to John Adams, Jefferson explains why he thinks Americans are especially suited to a democratic form of government. Read the passage and answer the question.

> Never was a finer canvas presented to work on than our countrymen. All of them engaged in agriculture or the pursuits of honest industry, independent in their circumstances, enlightened as to their rights, and firm in their habits of order and obedience to the laws. This I hope will be the age of experiments in government, and that their basis will be founded on principles of honesty, not of mere force.

25. How does Jefferson characterize the American people?

CONNECT TO YOUR LIFE

26. **EXPLANATORY** Think about the election of 1796, the first to involve political parties. Make a connection between that presidential election and a recent one. Write a paragraph explaining how the two elections are similar and different.

TIPS

- Take notes on the two elections. You may wish to use a Venn diagram or other graphic organizer to help organize your ideas.

- State your main idea clearly and support it with relevant facts, details, and examples.

- Use at least two vocabulary terms from the chapter.

- Provide a concluding statement about how the elections are similar and different.

VOCABULARY ANSWERS

1. Cabinet

2. tariff

3. sedition

4. loose interpretation

5. states' rights

6. inauguration

READING STRATEGY ANSWER

Issue: After the Revolution, the nation and individual states had huge debts.

↓

Problem 1: Foreign governments were waiting to be paid.

Problem 2: The United States needed to improve its credit and encourage new business.

Problem 3: The federal goverment had to prove itself trustworthy.

↓

Solution: Raise money by selling land, levying taxes and tariffs, and issuing bonds.

7. Alexander Hamilton urged the federal government to assume the debts owed by each state, then paid the debt by raising money through land sales, taxes, tariffs, and bonds.

MAIN IDEAS ANSWERS

8. After the American Revolution, Washington was probably the most popular man in the United States. His leadership during the war, his dignity and character, and his support for a republican government made him the obvious choice.

9. Congress created the departments of State, Treasury, and War.

10. The Federal Judiciary Act called for a dual-court system with authority split between state and federal courts and established the structure of the Supreme Court.

11. As a Federalist, Hamilton favored a strong central government. Therefore, his economic plan included having the federal government assume the debts of states. This would consolidate all debts at the national level and give the federal government increased power, a central Federalist idea.

12. The South tended to support the Democratic-Republicans because of that party's support of agriculture, slavery, and westward expansion.

13. Washington believed political parties would harm national unity by pitting people against one another.

14. The Native Americans signed the Treaty of Greenville because they were tired of war and did not think they could defeat federal troops without the help of the British.

15. Congress stopped all trade with France because France began seizing American ships and, to make matters worse, French agents (in the XYZ Affair) expected to be paid a bribe to get the matter resolved.

16. The Sedition Act targeted freedom of speech and freedom of the press.

HISTORICAL THINKING ANSWERS

17. Washington was the ultimate American role model. He set a precedent in how he created the role of president. He served out of a sense of love for his country and not out of personal ambition. He didn't behave like a monarch; for example, he wore a plain suit to his inauguration. He put together a Cabinet of advisors with differing political points of view and favored neutrality with foreign states. All this helped cement the American identity as one that is grounded in moderation, peace, and greater equality among citizens.

18. Washington wanted to separate American democracy from previous forms of government. Making the president distinct from a king was a way to distance the U.S. form of government from that of a monarchy.

19. Answers will vary. Possible response: People still debate about states' rights vs. federal authority and whether a strict or loose interpretation of the Constitution is best.

20. At the end of his second term, Washington was tired and discouraged by the many problems facing the nation and by the political bickering. He wanted to help shape the country's future after finishing his final term as president, so he offered advice to Americans by publishing his thoughts in the newspaper, where many people would read them.

21. The Alien Act allowed the federal government to deport new immigrants, many of whom voted Democratic-Republican. Removing these voters strengthened Federalist control of the government.

22. The XYZ Affair soured American relations with France and hurt the reputation of the Democratic-Republicans. Congress expanded the army, established the navy, and authorized navy vessels to attack French ships that threatened American merchant ships. Congress stopped all trade with France and ended an alliance with the country.

INTERPRET MAPS ANSWERS

23. Virginia

24. The North supported Federalists, the South supported the Democratic-Republicans, and the Middle Atlantic states were the most likely to split votes.

ANALYZE SOURCES ANSWER

25. Jefferson is proud of the American people and believes they have the strong character required for this "experiment in government," describing them as honest, independent, enlightened, orderly, and lawful.

CONNECT TO YOUR LIFE ANSWER

26. Students' paragraphs will vary, but students should use textual evidence and at least two vocabulary terms and conclude with an explanation of how the two elections were similar and different.

UNIT 4 THE EARLY REPUBLIC

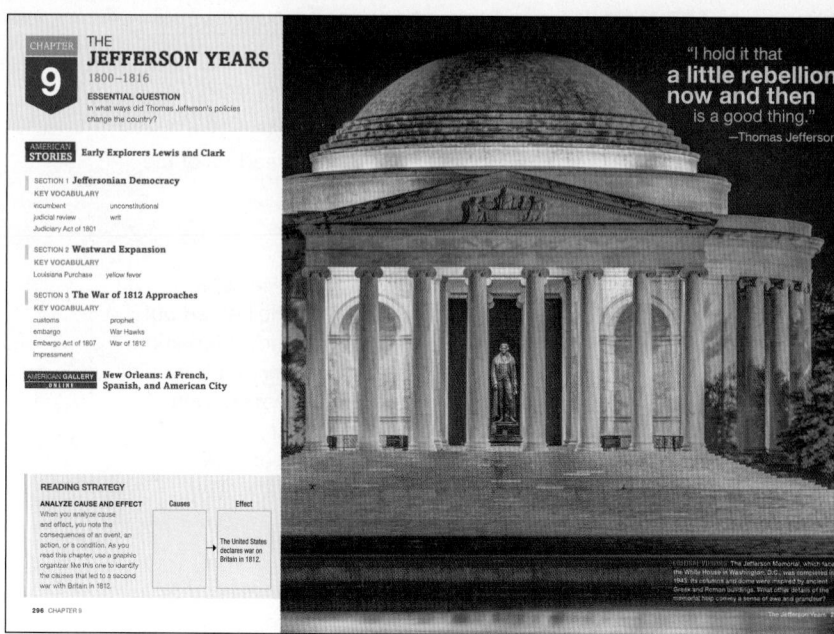

Chapter 9 Spanish Resources are available at NGLSync.Cengage.com.

AMERICAN STORIES | Early Explorers Lewis and Clark

- Primary Sources
- On Your Feet: Create a Quiz

NG Learning Framework:
Use a Compass

American Voices Biography
Sacagawea ONLINE

SECTION 1 RESOURCES
JEFFERSONIAN DEMOCRACY

LESSON 1.1
Jefferson's Vision for America
- ▶ Monticello
- On Your Feet: Question and Answer

NG Learning Framework:
Analyze Jefferson's 1801
Inaugural Address

LESSON 1.2
AMERICAN VOICES
Thomas Jefferson
- On Your Feet: Fishbowl

NG Learning Framework:
Learn More About Jefferson's Writing

LESSON 1.3
The Supreme Court
- On Your Feet: Create a Concept Cluster

NG Learning Framework:
Learn More About *Marbury* v. *Madison*

SECTION 2 RESOURCES
WESTWARD EXPANSION

LESSON 2.1
The Louisiana Purchase
- On Your Feet: Three-Step Interview

 New Orleans: A French, Spanish, and American City

LESSON 2.2
GEOGRAPHY IN HISTORY
The Discoveries of Lewis and Clark
- Active History: Research Native Cultures

NG Learning Framework:
Conduct a Cost-Benefit Analysis

LESSON 2.3
NATIONAL GEOGRAPHIC DIGITAL NOMAD
ROBERT REID
Sharing the World
- On Your Feet: Conduct Talk Show Interviews

NG Learning Framework:
Develop a Travel Itinerary

SECTION 3 RESOURCES
THE WAR OF 1812 APPROACHES

LESSON 3.1
Neutrality or War?
- On Your Feet: Debate

NG Learning Framework:
Analyze Political Cartoons

LESSON 3.2
Native Americans Unite
- On Your Feet: Create a Quiz

NG Learning Framework:
Examine Treaties

LESSON 3.3
The War of 1812
- On Your Feet: Tell Me More

NG Learning Framework:
Create a Social Media Profile

CHAPTER 9 REVIEW

Strategy ❶
Record and Compare Facts

After reading a lesson, ask students to write two important facts they learned. Allow pairs of students to compare and check their facts and then combine their facts into one longer list. Ask a volunteer from each pair to read the most important fact from the list.

Use with All Lessons

Strategy ❷

Use a TASKS Approach

Help students get information from visuals by using the following TASKS strategy:

T Look for a **title** that may give the main idea.
A **Ask** yourself what the visual is trying to show.
S Determine how **symbols** are used.
K Look for a **key** or legend.
S **Summarize** what you learned.

Use with All Lessons

Strategy ❸

Play Vocabulary Tic-Tac-Toe

Write nine Key Vocabulary words on a tic-tac-toe grid on the board. Position the words on the grid so that an X or O can be written below each word. Have Player A choose a word. If the player correctly pronounces, defines, and uses the word in a sentence, he or she can put an X or O in the box in that square. Play alternates until one person has a row of Xs or Os.

Use with All Lessons *This game can also be played using teams. Divide the class into two teams, Team A and Team B, and alternate play until one team has a row of Xs or Os.*

Strategy ❶
Build Time Lines

Provide students a copy of a time line such as the one below. Have students select key events and dates from the chapter to add to their time lines as they read.

- In Lessons 2.1 and 2.2, point out the map key and discuss that it contains dates and information that help explain the content on the map. Instruct students to use the map key to find at least one event to add to their time lines.
- After students have read each lesson, have them skim for dates and events to add to their time lines.
- Remind students to review photo captions for details that they can add to their time lines.

Use with Lessons 1.1, 1.2, 2.1–2.2, and 3.1–3.3 *For example, in Lesson 2.1, students might add 1803: the Senate ratifies Louisiana Purchase treaty. Explain that some dates may carry multiple events.*

Strategy ❷
Set a Purpose for Reading

Direct students to read and find at least three examples of how Thomas Jefferson contradicted himself. After reading, have students record their examples in a list. Allow partners to compare their lists to see if they arrived at the same conclusion.

Use with Lesson 1.2

ENGLISH LANGUAGE LEARNERS

Strategy ❶
Use Paired Reading

To help students with comprehension, pair **Expanding** and **Bridging** students to read passages from the text aloud:

1. Partner 1 reads a passage; Partner 2 retells the passage in his or her own words.
2. Partner 2 reads a different passage; Partner 1 retells it.
3. Pairs repeat the whole exercise, switching roles.

Use with All Lessons

Strategy ❷
Pair Partners for Dictation

Pair **Emerging** and **Bridging** students. After reading a lesson, direct each student to write one sentence about a main idea from the reading. Then have student pairs take turns dictating their sentences to each other. Allow them to work together to check the spelling and accuracy of sentences.

Use with All Lessons

Strategy ❸
Make Word Cards

Help students of **All Proficiencies** make word cards for Key Vocabulary terms from this chapter. Instruct students to write one term on the front of each card. On the back, prompt them to include relevant information about the term, such as definitions, examples, pictures to help them recall meaning, and related words or phrases. Then have students write one original sentence for each term.

Some Key Vocabulary words to include:

- incumbent
- writ
- judicial review
- yellow fever
- Louisiana Purchase
- prophet
- War Hawks
- War of 1812

Use with Lessons 1.1, 1.3, 2.1, and 3.2–3.3
For Lesson 3.2 have students also create a word card for the word profit *to help them understand the difference between* profit *and* prophet.

GIFTED & TALENTED

Strategy ❶
Analyze Impact

Explain to students that Native American leader Tecumseh spoke out against the destruction of traditional cultural practices as a result of influence from the United States. Ask students to choose a Native American tribe, such as the Shawnee, and write a report analyzing how the tribe was changed through contact with Europeans.

Use with Lesson 3.2

Strategy ❷
Produce a Political Video

Have students imagine they are political analysts during the election of 1800. Tell students to research, write, and record a short "talking head" video about the tie between Thomas Jefferson and Aaron Burr. Encourage students to talk about how the problem arose, what information can be verified and what is speculation, what information is relevant to the election, and what people like Alexander Hamilton are doing to try to sway events. Allow time for students to share their videos with the class.

Use with Lesson 1.1

Pre-AP

Strategy ❶
Annotate a Multimedia Time Line

Have students create an annotated, multimedia time line of events leading up to the War of 1812. Instruct students to use the information in the chapter as well as online resources. Tell students to include details such as dates, locations, important events, and people. Encourage students to include illustrations or photos, audio, or other multimedia features in their time lines. Invite students to share their time lines with the class.

Use with Lessons 3.1–3.3

Strategy ❷
Tweet About the War

Ask students to imagine that they are living in either Washington, D.C., or New Orleans during the War of 1812. Have them write a series of tweets about the British burning the Capitol and the White House or about the battle in New Orleans. Encourage students to do additional research online to provide details for their tweets. Have students post their tweets in the classroom for others to read.

Use with Lesson 3.3

THE JEFFERSON YEARS
1800–1816

ESSENTIAL QUESTION
In what ways did Thomas Jefferson's policies change the country?

AMERICAN STORIES Early Explorers Lewis and Clark

SECTION 1 **Jeffersonian Democracy**

KEY VOCABULARY

incumbent	unconstitutional
judicial review	writ
Judiciary Act of 1801	

SECTION 2 **Westward Expansion**

KEY VOCABULARY

Louisiana Purchase	yellow fever

SECTION 3 **The War of 1812 Approaches**

KEY VOCABULARY

customs	prophet
embargo	War Hawks
Embargo Act of 1807	War of 1812
impressment	

AMERICAN GALLERY
ONLINE New Orleans: A French, Spanish, and American City

READING STRATEGY

ANALYZE CAUSE AND EFFECT
When you analyze cause and effect, you note the consequences of an event, an action, or a condition. As you read this chapter, use a graphic organizer like this one to identify the causes that led to a second war with Britain in 1812.

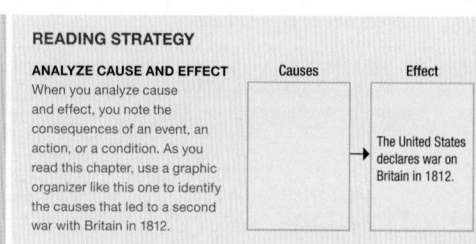

Causes → Effect

The United States declares war on Britain in 1812.

"I hold it that **a little rebellion now and then** is a good thing."
—Thomas Jefferson

CRITICAL VIEWING The Jefferson Memorial, which faces the White House in Washington, D.C., was completed in 1943. Its columns and dome were inspired by ancient Greek and Roman buildings. What other details of the memorial help convey a sense of awe and grandeur?

The Jefferson Years 297

INTRODUCE THE PHOTOGRAPH

The Jefferson Memorial

Direct students' attention to the photograph of the Jefferson Memorial and ask a student to read the caption aloud. **ASK:** What features do you see that remind you of Greek and Roman architecture? (Answers will vary. Possible responses: the dome, the style of the columns, the trim, the sculpture over the entrance, the arches) Explain to students that the design of the memorial was controversial. Point out that John Russell Pope, the memorial's architect, chose the classical design to mirror Thomas Jefferson's own taste in architecture, as Jefferson was an architect who designed several buildings. The design pays homage to Monticello and the Rotunda at the University of Virginia, both of which Jefferson designed. Tell students that they will learn more about Thomas Jefferson's political and personal accomplishments in this chapter.

For Chapter 9 Spanish Resources, visit the Resources Menu. Chapter 9 Resources are available at NGLSync.Cengage.com.

Share Background

Congress commissioned the Jefferson Memorial, and construction began in 1938. The architects chose to use materials that were symbolic of the natural resources of the United States, including the territories that were added during Jefferson's time in office. For example, the outer stone work of the memorial is marble from Vermont. Stonework on the inside of the memorial includes granite from Minnesota and marble from Missouri. Parts of Minnesota and all of Missouri were acquired in the Louisiana Purchase. President Franklin D. Roosevelt laid the cornerstone for the memorial in a ceremony on November 15, 1939. The memorial was dedicated on the 200th anniversary of Jefferson's birth—April 13, 1943.

CRITICAL VIEWING Possible response: The size of the memorial and the detail in the stonework and sculpture are impressive. Additionally, the dramatic lighting draws attention to details inside the memorial and makes the centerpiece, Jefferson's dark bronze statue, stand out against the night sky.

INTRODUCE THE ESSENTIAL QUESTION

In what ways did Thomas Jefferson's policies change the country?

Brainstorming Activity: Setting Presidential Policies Ask students to think about and predict how a president in the early 1800s might change a country through his or her policies. Prompt students to identify broad categories of issues about which President Jefferson might want to set policies. Then guide students to make a list of specific issues within each category. For example:

- **Government:** small versus large federal government, federal role versus states' role, taxes

- **Environment:** exploration, expansion, land use

- **Foreign Relations:** free trade versus restricted trade, war versus peace or neutrality

- **Native Americans:** land disputes, treaties versus armed conflict

Then ask students to discuss how a president's policies on these matters could change a country. After reading the chapter, revisit students' lists and encourage them to refine their categories and issues based on what they learned.

INTRODUCE CHAPTER VOCABULARY

Vocabulary Pyramids

Encourage students to complete Vocabulary Pyramids for Key Vocabulary words as they read the chapter. Tell students to make a pyramid for each word, fill in what they know about each word before reading, and then add to or correct the pyramid after they encounter the word in the chapter. Model an example for students on the board, using the graphic organizer below.

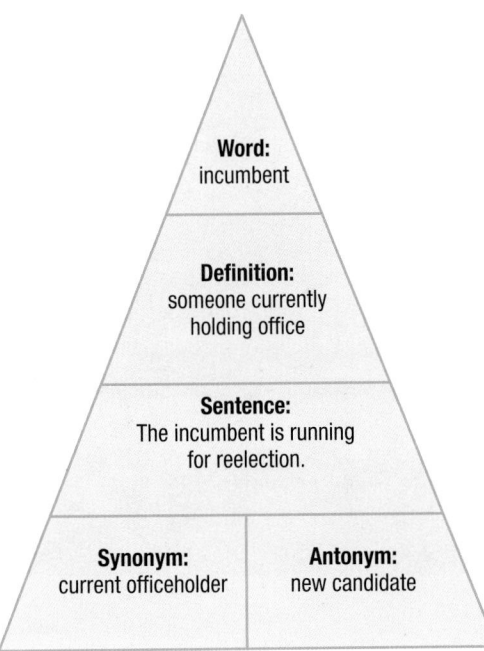

Word:
incumbent

Definition:
someone currently holding office

Sentence:
The incumbent is running for reelection.

Synonym:
current officeholder

Antonym:
new candidate

INTRODUCE THE READING STRATEGY

ANALYZE CAUSE AND EFFECT

Remind students that cause and effect involves figuring out why things happen. A cause is an action or condition that makes something else happen. An effect is what happens as a result of the cause. An effect often has several causes. Point out the two sections of the chart, one labeled "Causes" and the other labeled "Effect." Model completing the chart by reading the first paragraph under "A Nation at Odds" in Lesson 3.3 and adding the phrase *War Hawks push for war* in the "Causes" box. Remind students to add to the chart as they read the chapter.

Causes	Effect
American sailors are impressed into the British navy.	The United States declares war on Britain in 1812.
Britain responds to Non-Importation Act with aggression.	
Americans suspect an alliance between Britain and Native Americans.	
War Hawks push for war.	

KEY DATES FOR CHAPTER 9

1801	Thomas Jefferson becomes third president
1801	Judiciary Act of 1801
1803	Louisiana Purchase
1804	Thomas Jefferson reelected president
1804	Lewis and Clark travel up Missouri River
1807	Embargo Act of 1807
1808	James Madison wins presidential election
1811	Battle of Tippecanoe
1812	War of 1812 begins
1814	Treaty of Ghent

For more on the impact of territorial expansion on species' habitats, see *HABITAT PRESERVATION*.

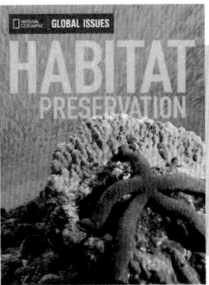

GLOBAL ISSUES

HABITAT PRESERVATION

Objectives

- Analyze the challenges and the successes of the Lewis and Clark expedition.
- Describe the purpose of the expedition and the discoveries made along the way.
- Understand the relationship between Native Americans and explorers.
- Study primary sources: Lewis and Clark's journals.

Critical Thinking Skills for "Early Explorers Lewis and Clark"

- Make Connections
- Draw Conclusions
- Form and Support Opinions
- Determine Chronology
- Make Inferences
- Analyze Data
- Integrate Visuals
- Analyze Environmental Concepts
- Synthesize
- Make Predictions

Background for the Teacher

This American Story introduces students to Lewis and Clark's 1804 expedition to explore the uncharted West. Through a detailed narrative, artifacts, a time line, and several primary source documents, students will understand the planning and preparations made for the journey, the importance of relations with the Native Americans in the West, the physical landscape as seen through Lewis and Clark's observations, and how the explorers recorded and communicated their discoveries.

Use the compelling story of Lewis and Clark to engage students and introduce them to Chapter 9, The Jefferson Years, in which they will learn about the influence of President Thomas Jefferson and the impact of the Louisiana Purchase on the nation's westward expansion. This American Story will help students understand why the Lewis and Clark expedition became a dramatic turning point in America's history.

History Notebook

Encourage students to complete the American Story page for Chapter 9 in their History Notebooks as they read.

Note to the Teacher

Use this American Story as a teaser for content students will encounter in Chapter 9.

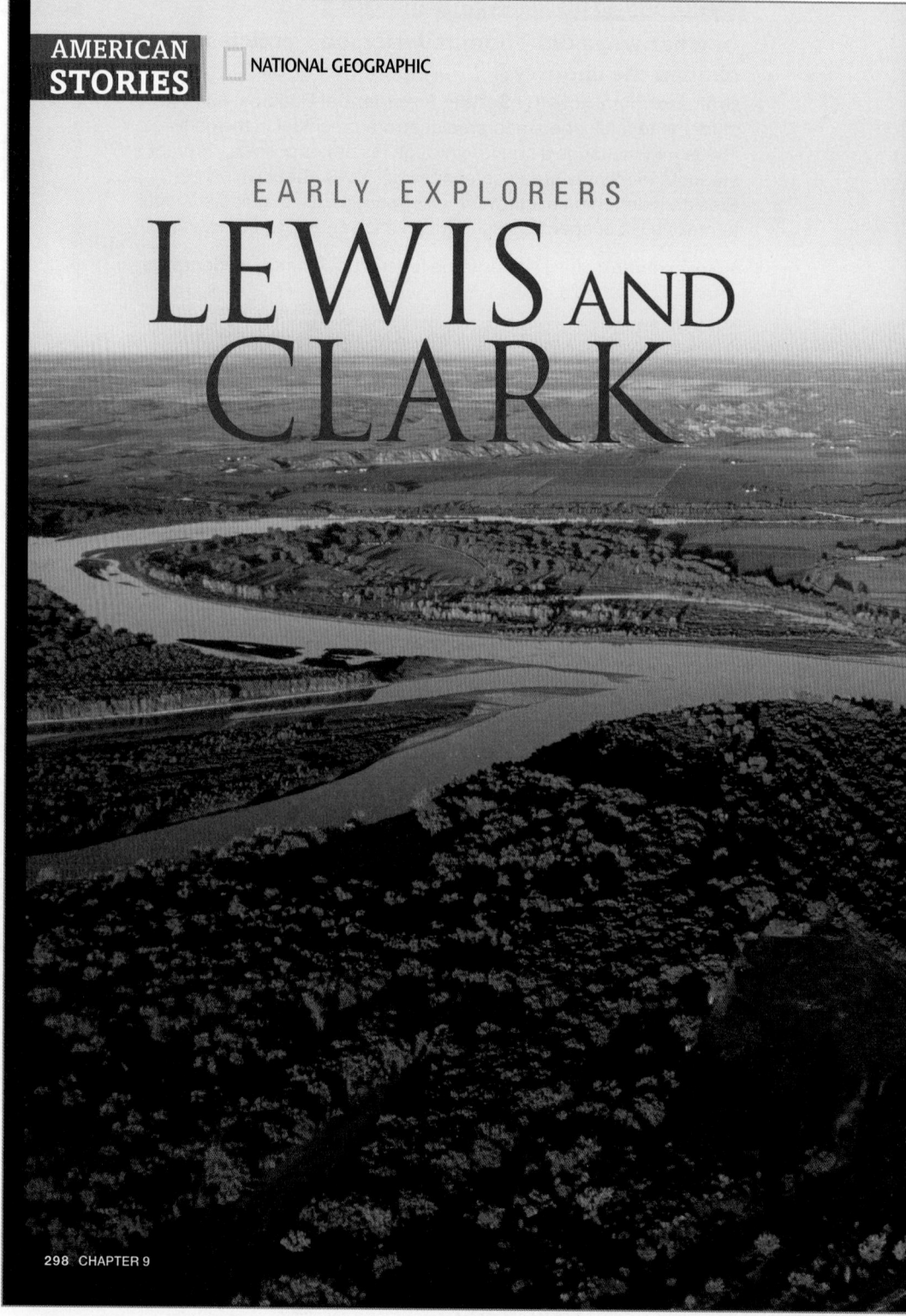

AMERICAN STORIES

NATIONAL GEOGRAPHIC

EARLY EXPLORERS

LEWIS AND CLARK

298 CHAPTER 9

Captain
Meriwether Lewis

Second Lieutenant
William Clark

In 1803, Thomas Jefferson

sent Meriwether Lewis and William Clark to find a water route to the Pacific and explore the uncharted West. Jefferson believed woolly mammoths, erupting volcanoes, and a mountain of pure salt awaited them. What they found was no less mind-boggling: some 300 species unknown to science, nearly 50 Indian tribes, and the Rocky Mountains.

Lewis was Jefferson's private secretary, an army officer, and an enthusiastic amateur scientist. Clark was a friend of Lewis and also an army officer. On May 14, 1804, the two men set off from a camp near St. Louis, Missouri, accompanied by a group of about 40 men that they dubbed the Corps (KOR) of Discovery. Most of the explorers were soldiers, and one was Clark's African-American slave—a man named York. Packed into three boats along with their supplies, the men headed upstream on the Missouri River toward the regions that now have familiar names such as Kansas, North Dakota, and Idaho. In 1804, this area was called the Louisiana Territory. As far as Jefferson was concerned, it was the great unknown.

National Geographic photographer Sam Abell captured this image of the merging of the Yellowstone River (left) with the Missouri River (right) at one of the locations visited by Lewis and Clark during their expedition.

The Jefferson Years **299**

Preview Using Visuals

As a class, study the photograph. Have students volunteer words that describe what they see in the photo and write those on the board. Encourage students to imagine that they are standing in this place as Lewis and Clark did and to think about what sounds they would hear, what they would see that might surprise them, and what smells there would be that would be new to them. Ask volunteers to come up with a sentence describing the landscape and share it with the class.

Activate Prior Knowledge

Direct students' attention to a map of the present-day United States. Ask a volunteer to point out Missouri and Kansas, another to point out North Dakota and Montana, and another to identify the Pacific coast at the border of Washington and Oregon. Explain that Lewis and Clark started their expedition in Missouri and the states students identified are some of the ones that Lewis and Clark traveled through on their expedition. **ASK:** Where is Missouri in relation to the Pacific coast? *(It is located hundreds of miles east of the coast.)* Discuss with students whether they think this was the most logical route to take and why the explorers may have chosen that route.

NATIONAL GEOGRAPHIC PHOTOGRAPHER
Sam Abell

Growing up in Ohio, Sam Abell first learned about photography from his father, a teacher. Now living in Virginia, Abell is a photographer, teacher, and writer. He has worked with the National Geographic Society since 1970, producing more than 20 stories on wilderness subjects and on the everyday lives of people and places across the globe. His photographic journeys have taken him to Australia, Cuba, the Galapagos, Italy, and the Mississippi River. Abell worked with author Stephen Ambrose on the book *Lewis & Clark: Voyage of Discovery.* Throughout his career, Sam Abell has captured moments in time through his camera lens and shared them for the world to enjoy.

Preparing for the Expedition

In January 1803, President Jefferson sent a letter to Congress requesting $2,500 for an expedition westward to the Pacific Ocean. Although the French had claimed a large chunk of land west of the Mississippi River, Congress approved the funds on February 28, 1803. Plans for the expedition quickly moved forward with the July 1803 announcement of the Louisiana Purchase, which involved the acquisition from France of a vast territory west of the Mississippi River. Before the Louisiana Purchase, the expedition would have had to cross land claimed by a foreign government. Because of the Louisiana Purchase, Lewis and Clark could freely explore the great unknown lands to the west.

The Mandan

The Mandan lived along the banks of the Upper Missouri River in permanent lodges that housed up to 60 people. The more prominent families lived in the center of the village near a sacred cedar post. The Mandan grew a variety of crops including corn, beans, squash, and tobacco. The Mandan village served as a trade center for the region at which other Native American tribes, including the Cheyenne, Cree, Crow, and Sioux, as well as Europeans, gathered in the fall to trade goods. Items such as musical instruments, horses, and meat products were traded for Mandan corn.

18th-Century Technology STEM

The spyglass is a type of telescope that uses different types of lenses within a tube. These lenses refocus the light that is reflected from an object so the eye perceives the object as larger. The spyglass used by Meriwether Lewis was a continuous-draw design. Earlier spyglasses were designed as a single-draw tube made up of segments that needed to be screwed together, with the eyecup attached to the final segment.

The continuous-draw tube appeared around 1800, with smaller tubes containing the lenses fitted inside the larger tube when the eyeglass was collapsed. This design improvement allowed the tubes to slide smoothly into each other, making them more portable than earlier spyglasses. The continuous-draw design was also sturdier, as a single-draw design came apart easily.

AMERICAN STORIES

TO FORT MANDAN AND BEYOND

One of Jefferson's goals for the expedition was to establish friendly relationships with the Indian tribes living in the West. Lewis and Clark had mixed success with this effort. Some tribes welcomed the explorers' gifts and offers of alliance, while others were either uninterested or hostile. The Mandan, living in present-day North Dakota, were among the more welcoming groups. The Corps arrived at the villages of the Mandan and Hidatsa in October 1804. After being warmly received, Lewis and Clark decided to build their winter quarters nearby.

While building their camp, the explorers met Sacagawea (SAK-uh-juh-WE-uh), who would become an important member of the Corps of Discovery. She was a young woman of the Shoshone tribe, which lived just east of the Rocky Mountains. She had been kidnapped from her people as a small child and was now married to a French-Canadian trader named Toussaint Charbonneau. Knowing they would meet the Shoshone later in their travels, Lewis and Clark hired Sacagawea and Charbonneau as interpreters.

In April 1805, the Corps of Discovery broke camp and resumed its journey west. At the same time, they sent a boat back to Thomas Jefferson in Washington, D.C., loaded with 108 botanical specimens, 68 mineral specimens, and a map of the United States drawn by William Clark.

QUITE A SHOPPING LIST

Knowing they would be gone for a long time, Lewis and Clark stocked up on gear for the trip. Below are just a few items from the Corps of Discovery's supply list. Lewis spent $2,324 on supplies for the years-long expedition. That's the equivalent of around $40,000 in 2016 dollars.

Camping Equipment:
- 150 yards of cloth for making tents and sheets
- 25 hatchets
- 10.5 pounds of fishing hooks
- 12 pounds of soap
- 193 pounds of "portable soup"

Medicine:
- 50 dozen of "Rush's Thunderclapper" pills
- syringes
- tourniquets
- 3,500 doses of sweat inducer

Gifts for Native American Tribes:
- 12 dozen pocket mirrors
- 4,600 sewing needles
- 8 brass kettles
- 20 pounds of beads
- 288 brass thimbles

Meriwether Lewis also brought his spyglass on the expedition.

TIME LINE OF EVENTS

May 14, 1804 The Corps of Discovery leaves its camp near St. Louis and begins the journey west.

Early September 1804 The Corps enters the Great Plains. Lewis and Clark begin sighting unfamiliar animal species.

October 24, 1804 The Corps arrives at the villages of the Mandan and Hidatsa tribes near present-day Bismarck, North Dakota.

November 11, 1804 Lewis and Clark hire Sacagawea and Toussaint Charbonneau as interpreters for the rest of the journey.

1804

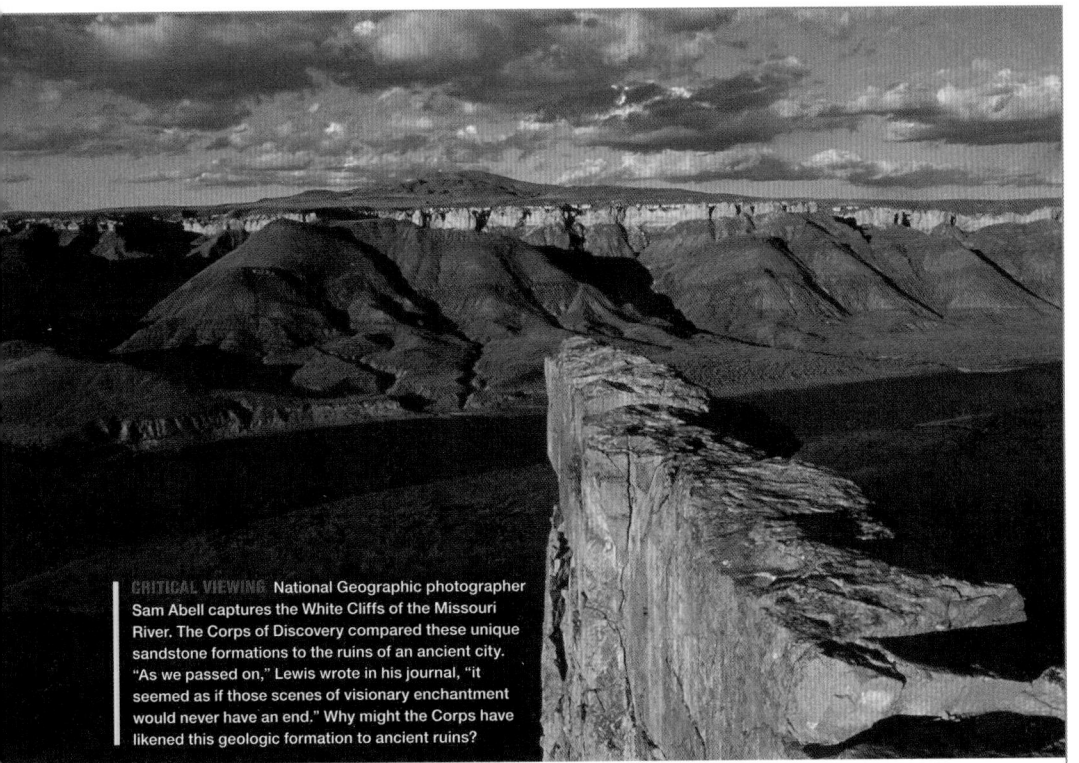

CRITICAL VIEWING National Geographic photographer Sam Abell captures the White Cliffs of the Missouri River. The Corps of Discovery compared these unique sandstone formations to the ruins of an ancient city. "As we passed on," Lewis wrote in his journal, "it seemed as if those scenes of visionary enchantment would never have an end." Why might the Corps have likened this geologic formation to ancient ruins?

TEACH

Guided Discussion

1. **Form and Support Opinions** Which item on the shopping list do you think was most critical for survival? Support your opinion with evidence from the text. *(Answers will vary.)*

2. **Determine Chronology** What events occurred while the Corps was camped at the Mandan village? *(They met Sacagawea and her husband, whom they hired as interpreters for the rest of the trip, and they built Fort Mandan near the village.)*

Make Inferences

Read the last paragraph of the spread aloud. Have students speculate on what it must have been like when Sacagawea realized she was back in the village of her birth. **ASK:** Why do you think Sacagawea continued on with the Corps rather than stay in her village? *(Answers will vary. Possible responses: She may have been committed to the success of the mission; she may have wanted to stay with her husband; she knew that her knowledge of the region was valuable to the Corps of Discovery.)*

CRITICAL VIEWING Answers will vary. Possible response: The landscape looks like the remnants of ancient buildings built high into the landscape that are slowly turning into broken rock and sand.

FROM THE ROCKIES TO THE PACIFIC

Throughout the summer, the Corps made progress toward the Rocky Mountains, nervously watching as the imposing, snow-capped peaks grew taller and taller as they approached. When they reached the region we now call northern Montana, Lewis scouted ahead of the expedition, and came across "the grandest sight I ever beheld"—the Great Falls of the Missouri, along with four additional waterfalls immediately upriver. The expedition had no choice but to portage, or carry their canoes over land, for 18.5 miles in order to get around the falls. Extreme summer heat, dangerous storms, prickly pear cacti, and brush made the portage more challenging and time-consuming than anticipated, and the journey took nearly a month.

In August, the Corps reached a Shoshone village just east of the mountains. Here, they hoped to buy horses to help them cross the mountains. The next thing that happened could be described as one of history's most stunning coincidences. The Shoshone villagers recognized Sacagawea. To everyone's shock and delight, she learned that the chief of this group was her long-lost brother.

December 24, 1804 The Corps finishes building Fort Mandan near the Indian villages.

April 7, 1805 The Corps leaves Fort Mandan to resume its westward travel.

May 16, 1805 One of the expedition's boats almost flips over. Sacagawea saves many journals and important papers from going overboard.

August 17, 1805 The Corps reaches the Shoshone camp on the eastern edge of the Rockies. There, Sacagawea realizes the chief is her long-lost brother.

1805

Analyze Data

STEM

Have students review the data on the infographic. **ASK:** Which set of data do you find the most surprising? *(Answers will vary.)* Which is most important when considering the purpose of the Lewis and Clark expedition? *(Answers will vary. Possible response: discovering a large number of new plants and animals)* Using a map application on their smartphones or tablets, or an online distance graph, have students find a location 8,000 miles from the school's location to find a point of reference and distance comparison with the Lewis and Clark expedition. Then, with the distance comparison in mind, discuss with students whether they believe Lewis and Clark would have enthusiastically agreed to the expedition if they had known beforehand how far it would take them, how many new discoveries they would make, and how many different Native American tribes they would encounter.

BUILD BACKGROUND

Sacagawea

Sacagawea proved to be a vital member of the expedition team not only for her help as an interpreter but also as a guide through the uncharted landscape. On the return trip, her memory of Shoshone trails from childhood helped guide the Corps through the mountains to the Yellowstone River (now Bozeman Pass, Montana). Although Sacagawea received no pay for her work on the expedition, her husband, Charbonneau, was given between $400 and $500 (accounts vary on this point) and 320 acres of land for his scouting services.

When the Corps returned to the Hidatsa-Mandan villages, Sacagawea, Charbonneau, and their child Jean Baptiste remained behind as Lewis and Clark made their way back east. Sacagawea gave birth to a daughter, Lisette, six years later. There are a number of accounts of Sacagawea's life following the birth of Lisette. One account states that she died in 1812 at age of 25 from a persistent illness while living at Fort Manuel in present-day South Dakota. This account also states that Clark adopted both of Sacagawea's children after her death. Other accounts tell of Sacagawea's return to the Shoshones and death on April 9, 1884, on Wyoming's Wind River Reservation.

AMERICAN STORIES

THE CORPS OF DISCOVERY BY THE NUMBERS

PREVIOUSLY UNKNOWN PLANTS DESCRIBED
178

PREVIOUSLY UNKNOWN ANIMALS DESCRIBED
122

INDIAN TRIBES ENCOUNTERED
48

CORPS MEMBER CASUALTIES
ONE BY NATURAL CAUSES, PROBABLY APPENDICITIS

THE JOURNEY SPANNED OVER **8,000 MILES** AND WENT ON FOR . . . **863 DAYS.**

JOYFUL ARRIVAL

At the end of August, the expedition set out to cross the Rockies with the 29 horses they had purchased. The crossing was brutal. At one point, the men lost the trail in the midst of a blinding snowstorm. By the time they stumbled out of the mountains, the men and Sacagawea were exhausted, almost frozen, and near starvation. Happily for the Corps, the Nez Perce Indians, who lived on the west side of the Rockies, were welcoming and willing to share their food.

Soon, the explorers were on the last leg of their westward journey, making their way down the swift-flowing Columbia River toward the Pacific Ocean. On November 7, Clark wrote in his journal, "Ocian in view! O! The joy!" In fact, the Corps had just reached the place where the Columbia widened before meeting the Pacific. The men were still 20 miles from the coast. Three weeks later, after battling fierce storms, the expedition finally reached the shore of the Pacific.

With winter approaching, the Corps built a settlement they named Fort Clatsop, after the Indians living nearby. Lewis and Clark hoped to avoid recrossing the Rockies on the return trip east. American and British trading ships often stopped near the mouth of the Columbia, and the plan was to take passage on one of these ships. However, the expedition never spotted a single ship during a long, dreary winter that had only 12 days without rain.

TIME LINE OF EVENTS *CONTINUED*

September 11, 1805 The Corps begins climbing up into the Bitterroots, a range of the Rocky Mountains.

September 23, 1805 The expedition completes the mountain crossing and meets the Nez Perce Indians.

October 16, 1805 They reach the Columbia River.

November 24, 1805 The Corps reaches the Pacific Ocean and decides to build Fort Clatsop on the south side of the Columbia.

1806

HOMEWARD BOUND

When spring finally arrived, the expedition was more than ready to leave Fort Clatsop. The trip back to St. Louis was difficult and filled with dangers. The Corps failed in its first attempt to cross the Rockies and had to try a second time. Before leaving the mountains, the expedition split into two to explore more territory, and both groups had hostile encounters with Native American groups. The two halves of the party had a dramatic reunion when a member of Clark's group fired at what he believed was an elk, only to discover that he had shot Lewis in the leg. Luckily, the error did not result in an injury that was life-threatening.

On September 23, the Corps of Discovery came ashore in St. Louis, nearly two and a half years after their departure. The entire city turned out to celebrate the return of the heroes who had been given up for dead. Unlike many earlier explorers, Lewis and Clark did not set off in search of gold or other monetary rewards. Instead, they were returning with a far richer treasure—knowledge about the people, places, plants, and animals in the lands far west of the Mississippi.

THINK ABOUT IT

Use the time line to help you describe the most significant challenges and successes of the Lewis and Clark expedition.

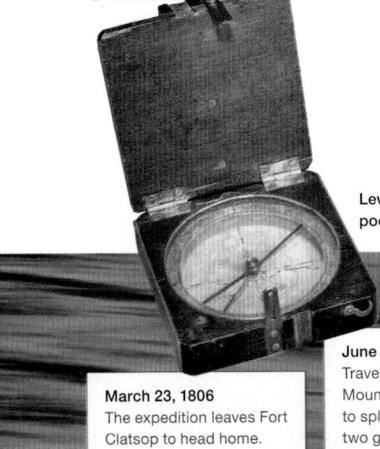

Lewis's silver
pocket compass

SACAGAWEA

Kidnapped at the age of 12 by the Hidatsa, Sacagawea, a Shoshone, was taken from the Rocky Mountains to the Hidatsa-Mandan villages in North Dakota. That's where she met the Corps of Discovery in November 1804. Sacagawea's knowledge of languages and the land proved to be very valuable to the Corps as it moved west, passing through the territories of many Native American tribes, some of which had never seen white men before. When tribes saw Sacagawea and her baby traveling with the Corps, they knew the Corps was a friendly group disinterested in war. This statue of Sacagawea stands in a park in Portland, Oregon.

March 23, 1806
The expedition leaves Fort Clatsop to head home.

June 30, 1806 They pause at Traveler's Rest in the Bitterroot Mountains. Lewis and Clark decide to split up and divide the Corps into two groups to cover more ground.

August 12, 1806
The Corps reunites. From here, the swift-flowing Missouri River allows for rapid travel eastward.

September 23, 1806
The Corps of Discovery arrives at St. Louis and receives a hero's welcome.

1807

The Jefferson Years 303

Active Options

On Your Feet: Create a Quiz Tell each student to write one question about the Lewis and Clark expedition. Collect the questions. Then have groups of five students take turns coming to the front of the class to take part in a quiz. Pose a few of the questions to each group. Students should confer about the answer and then signal their readiness to respond by raising their hands.

NG Learning Framework: Use a Compass STEM

ATTITUDE Curiosity

KNOWLEDGE Our Human Story

For this activity, have students use a physical compass or compass application on their smartphones or other devices. Tell students to work in pairs to map out a route from one location in the classroom to another, figuring out an estimate for the number of steps and direction of travel to complete the route. Then have students test their route. Once pairs have completed a route, have them trade routes with another pair. Each pair should then follow the path given to them using their compasses. Discuss with students what it might have been like for early explorers like Lewis and Clark to move mainly by following a compass to provide their direction of travel.

THINK ABOUT IT

Answers will vary. Possible response: Their greatest challenge was crossing the mountains, and their greatest success was that they actually completed the expedition.

Guided Discussion

1. **Draw Conclusions** How do you think Lewis and Clark were able to create maps of such detail without the advantage of modern technology? *(Answers will vary. Possible response: The Corps of Discovery took the time needed to make notes on compass markings and take measurements of lengths and curves of rivers, as well as note elevations as they moved up and down the mountains.)*

2. **Integrate Visuals** What do you notice about the artifacts and the field journal entries that were made by Lewis and Clark? *(Possible response: They entries are very thorough. They and the artifacts provide a detailed history of geography and the plant and animal life.)*

Analyze Environmental Concepts

How would the increase in settlements made possible by Lewis and Clark's expedition impact the environment? *(New and increased settlement would impact the environment because humans would hunt and fish, change the landscape to build roads, homes, and businesses, and they could potentially decimate certain populations of animals, such as the American bison.)*

WRITE ABOUT HISTORY

Write a Field Journal Entry This American Story tells of the adventures and discoveries of the Lewis and Clark expedition. Much of what is known about their expedition was recorded in their field journals. Tell students to think about the route they take to get to school, a park, or another place to which they frequently travel. Instruct students to write a journal entry about one part of that path. Tell them to include a detailed drawing of an object, plant, or animal that they observed along the way. Also tell them to add information about what they see and hear. Their entry should have enough detail that someone reading it will be able to visualize what they experienced.

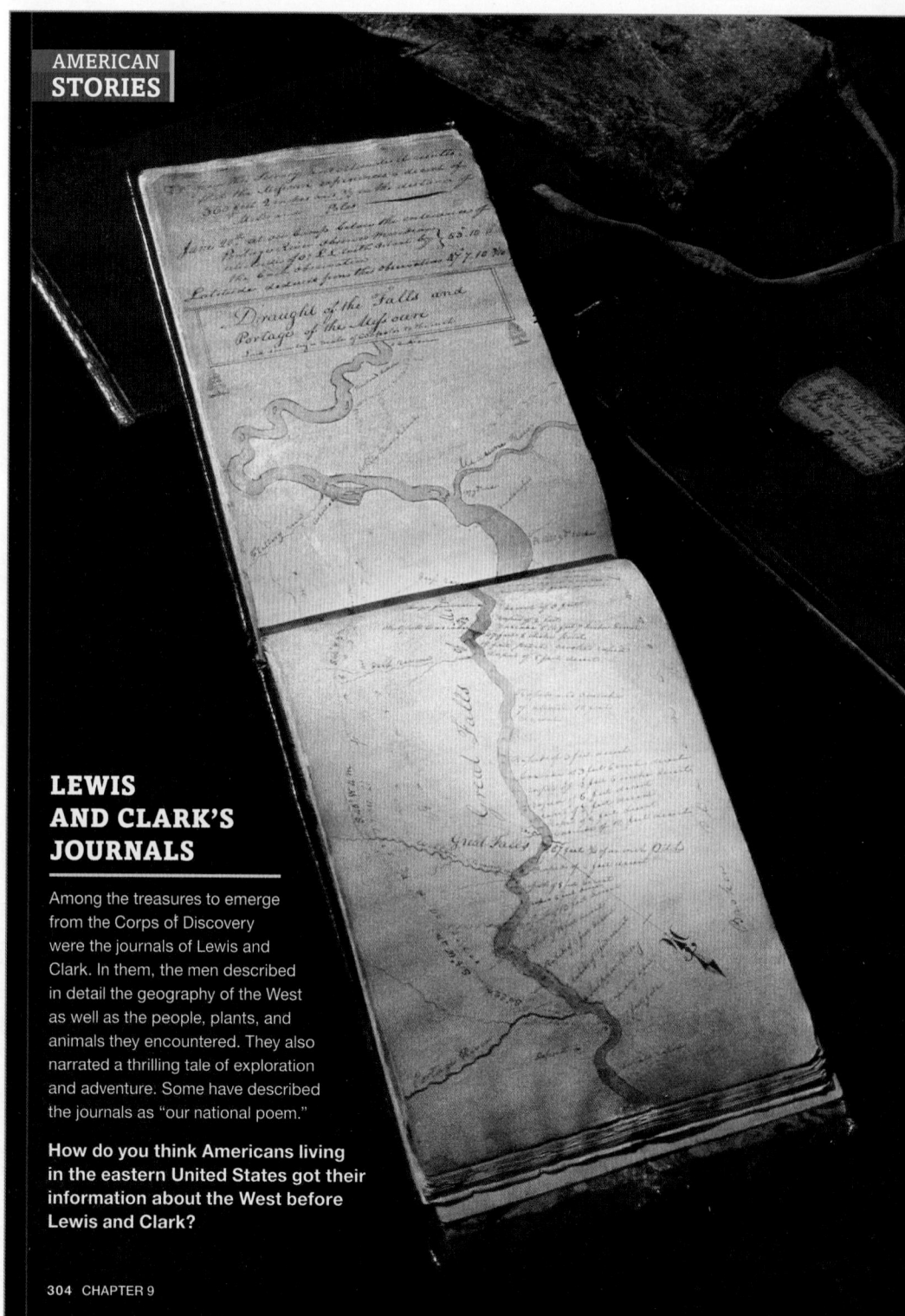

AMERICAN STORIES

LEWIS AND CLARK'S JOURNALS

Among the treasures to emerge from the Corps of Discovery were the journals of Lewis and Clark. In them, the men described in detail the geography of the West as well as the people, plants, and animals they encountered. They also narrated a thrilling tale of exploration and adventure. Some have described the journals as "our national poem."

How do you think Americans living in the eastern United States got their information about the West before Lewis and Clark?

304 CHAPTER 9

The Indian woman recognizes the country and assures us that this is the river on which her relations [the Shoshone] live, and that the three forks are at no great distance. This piece of information has cheered the spirits of the party who now begin to console themselves with the anticipation of shortly seeing the head of the Missouri yet unknown to the civilized world.

—from the *Journals of the Lewis and Clark Expedition*, entry by Meriwether Lewis, 1803–1806

While it's uncertain exactly how Lewis and Clark assembled their field journals, it's likely that the men first made quick notes in portable notebooks they carried with them, including simple maps and sketches. When they returned to camp, they probably combined their notes and rewrote them into the more clear and detailed pages you see here.

The Jefferson Years **305**

DIFFERENTIATE

Striving Readers

Summarize Have students work in pairs and assign each student a paragraph to read aloud. The listening partner should summarize what he or she hears in one or two spoken sentences. Have the pair record their spoken sentences on paper to complete a written summary of the whole lesson.

Gifted & Talented

Map the Expedition Invite students to research Lewis and Clark's route. Then have students create an illustrated and annotated map of their route, including notable locations and Native American tribes they met along the way. Tell students to annotate their maps with more information about Lewis and Clark, the Corps of Discovery, Sacagawea, and others on the expedition. When students have completed their maps, have them present them to the class.

See the Chapter Planner for more strategies for differentiation.

HISTORICAL THINKING

Ask and have students answer the following questions.

1. **READING CHECK** How did Lewis and Clark prepare for their expedition?

2. **IDENTIFY MAIN IDEAS AND DETAILS** What motivated the Corps of Discovery to continue on their mission to reach the Pacific Ocean?

3. **MAKE PREDICTIONS** What do you think will result from the discoveries about the natural resources west of the Mississippi River?

ANSWERS

1. They organized a group of about 40 explorers and former soldiers and gathered sufficient supplies, including tents, medicines, and gifts, and packed the supplies and crew into boats.

2. Possible responses: The explorers were given a mission by the president of the United States. They needed to explore the new lands and hoped to find a waterway for trade and new resources. They were supported by Sacagawea's dedication and knowledge.

3. Possible response: There will be more settlers and adventure seekers migrating west.

1.1 Jefferson's Vision for America

John Adams and Thomas Jefferson didn't actually come to blows during the election of 1800, but they probably came close. They certainly exchanged insults. But when the dust settled, Jefferson was the winner.

MAIN IDEA After the election of Thomas Jefferson, the nation steered a course to a more limited and less expensive government.

BREAKING THE TIE

The election of 1800 was filled with tension and political divisions, and the fact that the frontrunners were the **incumbent**, or current, president and vice president added to it. President Adams, the Federalist, had spent the past four years building a strong government. Vice President Thomas Jefferson, the Democratic-Republican, believed Adams had favored businessmen from the North. To persuade the nation to elect him, Jefferson promised a limited government and lower taxes.

Jefferson favored Aaron Burr as his candidate for vice president. But remember that, at that time, potential running mates ran on their own. So for Burr to become Jefferson's vice president, Jefferson needed to receive the most votes, and Burr needed to come in second.

As it turned out, Jefferson and Burr received an equal number of votes for president. The tie had to be broken by the Federalist-dominated House of Representatives.

Replicas of Burr-Hamilton dueling pistols

🏛 New York Historical Society, New York

In the early 1800s, men engaged in pistol fights called duels to defend their honor. Although dueling was illegal in most states, it was an accepted practice.

On the morning of July 11, 1804, Vice President Aaron Burr and Alexander Hamilton dueled in a field in Weehawken, New Jersey. Burr had challenged Hamilton to the duel; Hamilton had provided the pistols. The men's rivalry had been building for a decade. In 1791, Burr defeated Hamilton's father-in-law in an election. In 1800, Burr publicly shamed Hamilton by publishing a private essay Hamilton had written criticizing his fellow Federalist, President John Adams. The final straw for Burr was when he read a newspaper article that quoted some of Hamilton's negative opinions of him.

Before that fateful morning, Hamilton had written in letters that he had no intention of killing Burr. The aim of Hamilton's first shot is disputed. Some say he pointed his pistol up in the air; others say he fired at Burr and missed. But Burr didn't miss. He shot Hamilton in the stomach, and Hamilton died the next day. Not only did the showdown end Hamilton's life, it also ended the vice president's political career. Burr was charged with Hamilton's death but received no punishment for the crime.

The World's Best Hope

Jefferson tried to unite Americans in his 1801 Inaugural Address and soothe their fears about what had happened in France during the French Revolution. In that country, radical elements in a republican government had seized control and terrorized the French people. In this excerpt from his address, Jefferson explains why he doesn't believe such a thing could happen in the United States. Why does Jefferson believe the United States has the strongest government on earth?

> **PRIMARY SOURCE**
>
> *I know, indeed, that some honest men fear that a republican government can not be strong, that this Government is not strong enough, but would the honest patriot . . . abandon a government which has so far kept us free and firm on the theoretic and visionary [imaginary] fear that this Government, the world's best hope, may . . . want [lack] energy to preserve itself? I trust not. I believe this, on the contrary, the strongest Government on earth. I believe it the only one where every man . . . would meet invasions of the public order [would defend the country] as his own personal concern.*
>
> —from Thomas Jefferson's First Inaugural Address, March 4, 1801

The House spent six days casting votes 36 separate times. At first, most Federalists supported Burr, but Burr's bitter enemy Alexander Hamilton rallied support for Jefferson. On February 17, 1801, the House cast the final votes. Jefferson became the nation's third president, and Burr became his vice president.

SOOTHING FEARS

Jefferson's inauguration took place the following month, the first to be held in the new capital city of Washington, D.C. The new president was aware of the division in the country following the election. Many Federalists feared what they considered Jefferson's radical views. They saw what had happened during the French Revolution, when extreme revolutionaries took control and executed thousands of people. In his inaugural address, Jefferson tried to soothe their fears by saying, "We are all Republicans; we are all Federalists."

Jefferson's call for unity set the tone for his years in office. He clearly laid out his plan for governing to the people—and followed it. He lowered taxes and reduced the size of the federal judiciary. In addition, Jefferson continued to support the power of the states and championed low government spending. But he did not dismantle all Federalist institutions. He left the military and Hamilton's National Bank mostly intact.

A popular president, Jefferson easily won re-election in 1804. In his second term, Jefferson continued to combine Democratic-Republican beliefs with wise politics, shrinking the federal government, military, and national debt. Further, Jefferson's personal humility, or humbleness, went hand-in-hand with his philosophy of small government. Instead of hosting showy and expensive events, he insisted on meeting personally with members of Congress and foreign leaders for dinner and conversation. A seat at that table would have been a sought-after invitation for most. These dinners showcased not only Jefferson's taste for fine food but also his many talents.

HISTORICAL THINKING

1. **READING CHECK** What was Thomas Jefferson's political philosophy, and how was it reflected in his policies as president?

2. **MAKE INFERENCES** Based on what you have learned about the ideological differences between Jefferson and Hamilton, what can you infer about Hamilton's support of Jefferson in the 1800 election?

3. **DISTINGUISH FACT AND OPINION** What facts and opinions does Jefferson use to reduce the country's fears and unite Americans?

PLAN

Objective
Understand Thomas Jefferson's vision for America and how he implemented it.

Critical Thinking Skills for Lesson 1.1
- Identify Main Ideas and Details
- Monitor Comprehension
- Make Inferences
- Distinguish Fact and Opinion
- Analyze Cause and Effect
- Draw Conclusions

Essential Question for Chapter 9
In what ways did Thomas Jefferson's policies change the country? Unlike John Adams who advocated for a strong central government, Thomas Jefferson supported a limited central government. Lesson 1.1 discusses some of the actions Jefferson took to achieve his goal.

Background for the Teacher
The American public disliked the French because of the XYZ Affair and French takeover of U.S. merchant ships. This attitude helped the anti-French Federalists sweep the 1798 congressional elections. Federalists hoped to continue their success in the 1800 election by painting the pro-French Democratic-Republicans as un-American. But President Adams tried to end hostilities before the election. While this action prevented war, it hurt Adams as Federalists opposed his decision. Democratic-Republican leader Thomas Jefferson benefited because of this split.

📓 History Notebook
Encourage students to complete the Reid on the Road video series page for Chapter 9 in their History Notebooks after they view the video.

INTRODUCE & ENGAGE

Activate Prior Knowledge

Provide each student with a K-W-L Chart. Lead students in a discussion to brainstorm what they already know about how the Federalists and Democratic-Republicans differed in their views on the role of the federal government. Then ask them to write questions that they would like to have answered as they study this lesson about Democratic-Republican Thomas Jefferson's presidency. Allow time at the end of the lesson for students to complete their charts with what they have learned.

K What Do I Know?	W What Do I Want To Learn?	L What Did I Learn?

TEACH

Guided Discussion

1. **Analyze Cause and Effect** What factors caused tension during the election of 1800? *(Possible response: First, the election pitted two incumbents—President John Adams and Vice President Thomas Jefferson—against each other as the candidates for opposing political parties. Second, Jefferson wanted Aaron Burr as his running mate, but the two tied in votes, causing the election to be thrown into the Federalist-controlled House of Representatives, which took 36 ballots and more than six days to decide the outcome in favor of Jefferson as president.)*

2. **Draw Conclusions** What do you think Thomas Jefferson meant when he said, "We are all Republicans; we are all Federalists"? *(Answers will vary. Possible response: Jefferson was saying that the two political parties might differ on specific ideas and courses of action, but all Americans were united in their support of republican principles and the federal system that divided power between the central government and the states.)*

🏛 Virtual Museum Visit

The New York Historical Society, founded in 1804, is New York City's oldest museum. Access the museum's website and demonstrate how to find the pistols in its "Alexander Hamilton: The Man Who Made Modern America" online exhibit. As a class, listen to the audio about the pistols and discuss the duel. Then encourage small groups of students to examine other parts of the online exhibit such as events in the time line, documents in the Hamilton Log, Hamilton's letter in support of Thomas Jefferson's election as president in the Document Viewer, or entries in the Gallery of Peers. Have groups present the information they find to the class.

Active Options

On Your Feet: Question and Answer Have half the class write True-False questions based on information in Lesson 1.1. Ask the other half to create answer cards, with "True" written on one side and "False" on the other. As each question is read aloud, students in the second group should stand and display the correct answer to the question. When discrepancies occur, review the question and discuss which answer is correct.

NG Learning Framework: Analyze Jefferson's 1801 Inaugural Address

SKILL Collaboration

KNOWLEDGE Our Human Story

Instruct students to work in groups to analyze the full text of Thomas Jefferson's 1801 Inaugural Address. Encourage students to use what they know about events and policies during the first two presidential administrations and conduct additional research as needed to understand references in the address. You may wish to assign groups specific paragraphs to analyze or assign them specific questions, such as, *How do specific lines in the address reflect Jefferson's political philosophy? What fears is Jefferson trying to calm? To which historical events do specific lines refer? Why is the address significant in terms of policy?* Have groups share their analyses with the class.

DIFFERENTIATE

Striving Readers

Monitor Comprehension Tell students to work in pairs, reading the text aloud paragraph by paragraph. At the end of each paragraph, have them stop and use these sentence frames:

- This paragraph is about _____.
- One detail that stood out to me is _____.
- The word _____ means _____.
- I don't think I understand _____.

Pre-AP

Research Dueling Direct students to conduct research on the practice of dueling in early America to understand why Alexander Hamilton engaged in a duel with Aaron Burr even though it was illegal. Ask students to explore the following questions: *Why did men challenge one another to duels? How did the rituals surrounding dueling generally prevent opponents from engaging in an actual duel? Why did these rituals fail to prevent the duel between Hamilton and Burr? What effect did the duel have on Burr and his political career?* Have students summarize and share their findings with the class.

See the Chapter Planner for more strategies for differentiation.

HISTORICAL THINKING

ANSWERS

1. Jefferson believed in limited government and lower taxes. As president, he lowered taxes and government spending and reduced the size of the federal judiciary.

2. Possible response: Alexander Hamilton did not agree with the politics of either Democratic-Republican candidate, but he and Aaron Burr were bitter enemies.

3. Answers will vary. Possible response: In his inaugural address, Jefferson stated the opinion that all Americans were Republicans and Federalists, and thus more alike than different. He offered the fact that the U.S. government had kept people "free and firm" so far.

PRIMARY SOURCE

Jefferson believes that the United States has the strongest government on earth because the United States is a government of the people, and therefore, every man will defend it out of a personal concern.

1.2 Thomas Jefferson 1743–1826

"I like the dreams of the future better than the history of the past." —Thomas Jefferson

A gifted writer, architect, scientist—you name it—Thomas Jefferson had the chops to carry out his dreams. He proposed a plan that laid the basis of our school system, restocked the Library of Congress with his own books, and penned America's creed. At a dinner at the White House in 1962, President John F. Kennedy remarked to a group of dignitaries that they represented the greatest talent ever assembled there, "with the possible exception of when Thomas Jefferson dined alone."

MONTICELLO

Because Jefferson was born into one of Virginia's foremost families, he received an education that allowed his natural abilities to flourish. As a young man, he studied law and, in time, developed a successful practice. While trying and winning most of the cases that came his way, the young lawyer met Martha Wayles Skelton, who would become his wife. A few years before they married, Jefferson began to design and build Monticello, which would be their home—aside from his years in the White House—for the rest of their lives.

Jefferson built Monticello on land in Charlottesville, Virginia, that he inherited from his father. The home became his architectural masterpiece, which he constantly reimagined and reworked over more than 40 years. The exterior of the house, with its columns and dome, was inspired by ancient Greek and Roman temples. The interior, with its 40-plus

New York Historical Society New York City

American artist Rembrandt Peale painted this portrait in 1805 after Jefferson won reelection in a landslide victory. Jefferson posed for the portrait in the White House, wearing a cape with a fur-lined collar, perhaps to lend an air of informality to the painting.

Monticello, Charlottesville, Virginia

When Jefferson rebuilt the front of Monticello, he had the eight-sided dome, shown here, constructed. A radical design feature at the time, the dome was the first in America to be installed on top of a private residence.

rooms, held some of Jefferson's own inventions, including a "turning-machine" for holding and rotating the clothes in his closet.

The extensive gardens at Monticello also contained his inventions and improvements, such as a sundial and a plow that could easily lift and turn the soil cut by the machine. Jefferson was a dedicated gardener. He cultivated seeds he'd obtained from Europe and Mexico and even some from Lewis and Clark's westward expedition. Jefferson's gardens were a botanic laboratory where he used the scientific method to determine which seeds and plants grew best in its soil and climate.

MAN OF CONTRADICTIONS

Unfortunately, Jefferson's building projects at Monticello and his lavish lifestyle—he loved to entertain—caused him to fall deeply in debt. This may seem odd for a man who once said, "Never spend your money before you have it," but then, Jefferson was full of contradictions. In the Declaration of Independence, he wrote that "all men are created equal," yet he owned more than 100 slaves. And while George Washington granted freedom to many of his slaves in his will, Jefferson only freed a handful of his. He staunchly supported states' rights, but as president, greatly expanded the power of the national government. In many ways, he embodied the social and political contradictions of America itself.

Jefferson died at Monticello on July 4, 1826—50 years to the day after the signing of the Declaration of Independence. By a strange coincidence, his old friend and rival, John Adams, died on the same day. The pair had often locked horns politically but had always maintained a strong mutual respect. When Adams died, his last words were, "Thomas Jefferson survives." He didn't know that his friend had passed away just a few hours before.

HISTORICAL THINKING

1. **READING CHECK** What were some of Jefferson's talents and accomplishments?

2. **EVALUATE** Why do you think it might have been difficult for Jefferson to live up to his principles?

3. **MAKE INFERENCES** Why do you think Adams might have been thinking of Jefferson in his last moments?

PLAN

Objective

Learn about Thomas Jefferson's life and accomplishments outside of politics.

Critical Thinking Skills for Lesson 1.2

- Identify Main Ideas and Details
- Monitor Comprehension
- Evaluate
- Make Inferences
- Make Connections
- Draw Conclusions

Essential Question for Chapter 9

In what ways did Thomas Jefferson's policies change the country? Thomas Jefferson's ideas and actions helped guide the United States through the early decades of nationhood. Lesson 1.2 explores Jefferson's life and contributions outside of politics.

Background for the Teacher

It's not surprising that Jefferson died in debt. He entertained frequently, and on some nights as many as 50 overnight guests filled Monticello. Jefferson's heavy debt helps explain why he failed to free his slaves, even in his will—they were bound to his creditors as collateral. After Jefferson died, his daughter sold off most of Monticello's slaves, furnishings, farm animals, and equipment to pay down the debt. However, the family was forced to sell Monticello. Eventually, Uriah P. Levy, a naval officer who admired Jefferson, purchased and restored the property, and by 1837 Levy was providing guided tours. After Levy died in 1862, Monticello returned to a state of disarray. In 1923, the Thomas Jefferson Foundation purchased Monticello and opened it to the public in 1924.

History Notebook

Encourage students to complete the American Voices page for Chapter 9 in their History Notebooks as they read.

INTRODUCE & ENGAGE
Preview Using Visuals

Call students' attention to the painting of Jefferson and the photograph of Monticello in the lesson. Ask volunteers to read the captions. Lead a discussion to share students' thoughts on both images. Write their responses on the board. Then note that Jefferson is often characterized as a man of contradictions. **ASK:** Do the portrait and the house lend any evidence to that claim? *(The caption states that Jefferson wanted to appear informal by wearing plain clothing, but his elaborate and formal-style mansion counters this idea.)*

TEACH
Guided Discussion

1. **Make Connections** How did Jefferson's life at Monticello reflect both upper-class southern society and respect for science and reason that grew out of the Enlightenment? *(Answers will vary. Possible response: Like other plantation owners in the South, Jefferson relied on large fields of agricultural goods for his livelihood. He used enslaved labor to work the fields and staff his household to maintain the daily lifestyle that was typical for white southern society before the Civil War. He also entertained lavishly in the southern style. The Greek and Roman-inspired design of Monticello, his scientific pursuits and inventions, and the scientific methods he used in planting and tending his gardens reflect Jefferson's Enlightenment influences.)*

2. **Draw Conclusions** What do you think the text means when it says that Jefferson "embodied the social and political contradictions of America itself?" *(The Declaration of Independence and the Bill of Rights championed equality and individual rights. Yet slavery persisted, and enslaved African Americans were viewed as property. Jefferson promoted individual rights and equality while he continued to hold people in bondage.)*

American Voices

Thomas Jefferson was a great American voice who hated to speak in public. John Adams noted that Jefferson spoke few words during the meetings of the Continental Congress. His fear of public speaking did not lessen as he aged. During both of his inaugural addresses, his voice was so soft that few in the crowd could hear him. He was so self-conscious of his tendency to mumble that as president he never delivered his annual message to Congress in person. However, on paper, Jefferson was a prolific and eloquent wordsmith, writing for many hours each day.

Active Options

On Your Feet: Fishbowl Instruct one half of the class to sit in a close circle, facing inward. Direct the other half of the class to sit in a larger circle around them. Then read the last sentence in the first paragraph of the lesson aloud. **ASK:** Why is President Kennedy's observation a fitting tribute to Jefferson? Students in the inner circle should discuss the question for 10 minutes while those in the outer circle listen to the discussion and evaluate the points made. Then have the groups reverse roles and continue the discussion.

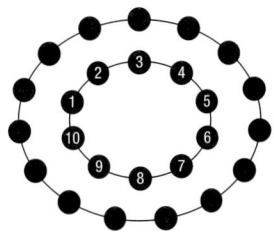

NG Learning Framework: Learn More About Jefferson's Writing
ATTITUDE Curiosity
SKILL Collaboration

Thomas Jefferson was a gifted writer who is quoted frequently. However, many of the quotations attributed to him are spurious, or wrong. Prompt groups of students to choose three quotations that are credited to Jefferson and assess the source. Then ask students to investigate the quotations to verify if they are from Thomas Jefferson. Encourage groups to share their chosen quotations and the results of their investigation with the class.

DIFFERENTIATE
Inclusion

Describe Lesson Visuals Pair visually impaired students with sighted partners. Ask the latter to describe the portrait of Jefferson and the photo of Monticello and answer questions the visually impaired student might have.

Gifted & Talented

Create a Multimedia Presentation Instruct students to use the Thomas Jefferson Foundation's Monticello Explorer interactive website to create a multimedia presentation of life at Monticello during Jefferson's lifetime. Encourage students to focus on an aspect of the plantation or plantation life that interests them, such as the architecture of the house, the layout of the plantation, the gardens and grounds, or domestic life. Invite students to share their completed presentations with the class.

See the Chapter Planner for more strategies for differentiation.

HISTORICAL THINKING
ANSWERS

1. Possible response: Jefferson's talents and accomplishments included being a gifted writer, scientist, architect, lawyer, inventor, and gardener.

2. Possible response: Although Jefferson held lofty ideals—such as equality, states' rights, and not spending money one didn't have—his lifestyle and political realities sometimes caused him to act against those ideals. For example, as a plantation owner, he relied on enslaved labor.

3. Answers will vary. Possible response: Adams might have been thinking of Thomas Jefferson because it was the Fourth of July, 50 years after the signing of the Declaration of Independence. They were two of the few remaining leaders from that era and had a mutual respect for one another, even though they had been rivals.

1.3 The Supreme Court

After winning the presidency, Thomas Jefferson might have thought that he and his opponents would be able to put aside their differences and work together. He didn't know John Adams would take one more parting shot.

MAIN IDEA The introduction of judicial review brought greater power to the Supreme Court and greater balance among the three branches of government.

MARSHALL'S COURT

John Adams and the Federalists lost the presidential and congressional elections in 1800, but they made the most of their remaining time in office. Just before the Democratic-Republicans took over, Congress passed the **Judiciary Act of 1801**. The act reduced the number of justices on the Supreme Court from six to five, which would deny Jefferson the chance to appoint a new justice when the next justice died or resigned. This power is important because the position of a Supreme Court justice is a lifetime appointment. The act also allowed Adams to appoint many new, Federalist lower-court judges before he stepped down. Adams worked late into the night of his last day signing commissions for these judges, who became known as "midnight judges."

Adams also chose a new Chief Justice of the United States, **John Marshall**—a Federalist. One of Marshall's earliest and most important cases was *Marbury* v. *Madison*. The case pitted one of Adams's midnight judges, William Marbury, against Jefferson's secretary of state, James Madison.

MARBURY V. MADISON

The case arose because Adams had signed Marbury's commission but left office before it was delivered. Adams believed that his signature alone made the commission valid. Jefferson disagreed and ordered Madison to block the commission. Marbury sued, saying that the Judiciary Act of 1789 required the Supreme Court to force Madison to give him his commission.

It seemed like a straightforward case. The Court had to decide three questions. First, was Marbury entitled to have the commission delivered to him? The Court said yes. Second, was it within the law

to have the courts issue a **writ**, or legal document, commanding Madison to deliver the commission? Again, the Court agreed. Third, was it legal for the Supreme Court to issue this writ? Here, the Court surprised everyone. Marshall answered with a resounding "No!" and decided against Marbury.

Even though the Judiciary Act of 1789 stated that the Supreme Court could issue such writs, Marshall argued that the U.S. Constitution did not give such power to the Court. The Court declared that part of the act to be **unconstitutional**, or against the Constitution. No law had ever been declared unconstitutional before. With his ruling, Marshall established **judicial review**, the power to invalidate any law the Court deems unconstitutional. *Marbury* v. *Madison* established the judiciary's role in the protection of the freedoms and individual rights detailed in the Bill of Rights. The case also strengthened the balance among the three branches of government, promoting the principle of checks and balances. Jefferson, however, would soon test the limits of the power of the branches and the Constitution.

HISTORICAL THINKING

1. **READING CHECK** How was Marbury appointed as a judge?

2. **ANALYZE CAUSE AND EFFECT** What unintended consequence did John Adams's plan to appoint midnight judges bring about?

3. **EVALUATE** What was surprising about Marshall's decision that the Supreme Court did not have the power to issue Marbury's writ?

AMERICAN PLACES
⊙ The Supreme Court, Washington, D.C.

Surprisingly, the Supreme Court was not provided with its own building until 1935. Until that time, members of the Court met in several places, including the Capitol Building. Finally, Chief Justice William Howard Taft—who had also served as president—persuaded Congress to construct a permanent home for the Court. When work got underway, the architect built it in the style of an ancient Roman temple, similar to the style of nearby congressional buildings. The result was as Taft wished: "a building of dignity and importance suitable for use as the home of the Supreme Court of the United States."

Review the Judiciary Act of 1789

Write *Judiciary Act of 1789* on the board. Ask students what they remember about the act from Chapter 8, Lesson 1.2. List their responses on the board. Students might recall that the act established the number of Supreme Court justices, defined their powers, and created a dual-court system that split responsibilities between state and federal courts. Tell students that they will read how the Supreme Court reacted to provisions of the act.

TEACH

Guided Discussion

1. **Draw Conclusions** Why might the Judiciary Act of 1801 have been seen as an attempt by the Federalists to keep their influence alive even though they lost the presidency and Congress? *(Possible response: Federalist presidents had appointed the current Supreme Court justices. By reducing the number of Supreme Court judges from six to five, the act lessened the chance that Jefferson would have an opportunity to appoint a Democratic-Republican to the Supreme Court. In addition, packing the lower courts with Federalist judges reinforced Federalist influence across the nation.)*

2. **Summarize** How did the decision in *Marbury* v. *Madison* strengthen the balance among the three branches of government and promote the principle of checks and balances? *(Possible response:* Marbury v. Madison *strengthened the balance of power and promoted the principle of checks and balances by declaring that the Supreme Court had the right to review laws passed by Congress and void laws that were unconstitutional. Thus it provided a "check" upon the legislative and executive branches and expanded the power of the judicial branch.)*

American Places

When the federal government was headquartered in New York City, the Supreme Court met in the Merchants Exchange Building. After the federal government relocated to Philadelphia, the Court moved to Independence Hall and then City Hall. When the federal government moved the capital to Washington, D.C., the Supreme Court wandered from place to place across the city. Later, in 1932, Congress authorized $9,740,000 for the construction of a permanent Supreme Court Building. Much of the building is constructed from marble quarried in Vermont, Georgia, and Alabama, and the wood is American white oak. The architects wanted the scale and the design of the building to reflect the judiciary's coequal power with the other two branches of government.

Active Options

On Your Feet: Create a Concept Cluster Have students form groups of four around a section of a bulletin board or a table. Provide each group with a large sheet of paper. Have group members take turns contributing a concept or phrase to a Concept Cluster with the phrase *Marbury* v. *Madison* at the center. When time for the activity has elapsed, call on volunteers from each group to share their clusters. Use the clusters to explore the case's short-term and long-term significance.

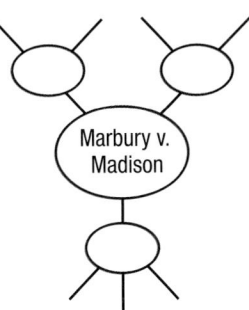

Marbury v. Madison

NG Learning Framework: Learn More About *Marbury* v. *Madison*

ATTITUDE Curiosity

KNOWLEDGE Our Human Story

Have students work in groups to research the arguments Chief Justice John Marshall used in *Marbury* v. *Madison* to declare part of the Judiciary Act of 1789 unconstitutional. Instruct students to investigate Article 3 of the Constitution because Marshall used to it justify his position. Then have groups use their research to write a short Supreme Court opinion in modern language that mirrors Marshall's reasoning. Have groups share their opinions with the class.

English Language Learners ELD

Create Webs for Key Words Write the Key Vocabulary word *unconstitutional* on the board and draw a circle around it. Allow students to volunteer words that are related to something being unconstitutional. Draw spokes from the circle and write the words suggested at the ends of the spokes. Have students at the **Emerging** and **Expanding** levels work with students at the **Bridging** level to write or say sentences that use words added to the web.

Pre-AP

Research Judicial Review Chief Justice John Marshall established the Supreme Court's right to exercise judicial review, but he was not the first to advocate the principle. Alexander Hamilton and James Madison posed arguments in favor of judicial review in the *Federalist Papers*. Have students research Hamilton's and Madison's arguments and share with the class why the two men thought judicial review was an important safeguard. To expand the activity, encourage students to research and present other examples of judicial review in U.S. history.

See the Chapter Planner for more strategies for differentiation.

HISTORICAL THINKING

ANSWERS

1. After the Federalists lost the election in 1800, Congress passed the Judiciary Act of 1801, enabling President John Adams to appoint new Federalist judges before he left office. He appointed Marbury and others.

2. Possible response: Adams hoped to pack the courts with Federalists in order to counter Jefferson's presidential power. However, his strategy resulted in the Supreme Court establishing judicial review, giving the Court authority to invalidate a law it deems unconstitutional.

3. Possible response: People were surprised because they did not expect Marshall to rule unconstitutional the part of the Judiciary Act of 1789 that gave the Supreme Court the right to issue writs. It was the first time that the Supreme Court had declared a law unconstitutional.

2.1 The Louisiana Purchase

We all know our nation spans the continent from "sea to shining sea," but in the early 1800s, the western border of the United States was the Mississippi River. Thomas Jefferson took steps to change that.

MAIN IDEA Thomas Jefferson negotiated a deal with France to purchase the Louisiana Territory and doubled the size of the United States.

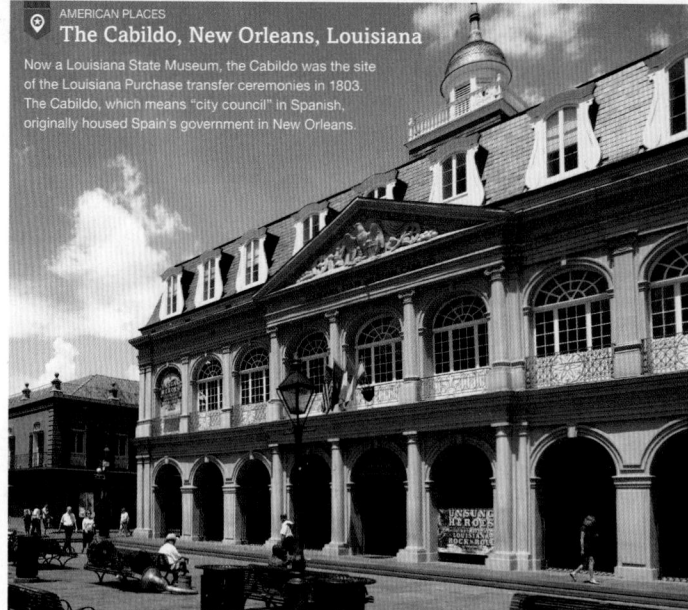

AMERICAN PLACES
The Cabildo, New Orleans, Louisiana

Now a Louisiana State Museum, the Cabildo was the site of the Louisiana Purchase transfer ceremonies in 1803. The Cabildo, which means "city council" in Spanish, originally housed Spain's government in New Orleans.

PORT OF NEW ORLEANS

While the Supreme Court dealt with the midnight judges, Jefferson set his sights on expansion. The population in the region between the Appalachian Mountains and the Mississippi River had grown steadily. Now farmers were settling the area and shipping their crops down the tributaries of the Mississippi to New Orleans. From there, ships carried cargo to ports all over the world. Jefferson wanted to acquire New Orleans. Only France stood in his way.

In 1799, **Napoleon Bonaparte** overthrew the revolutionary government in France and took power. In 1800, he signed a secret treaty requiring Spain to return Louisiana to France. The Spanish government had decided that, with only 50,000 settlers in all of Louisiana, the area was too expensive to maintain and produced too little profit. But Jefferson feared that once France owned Louisiana, it would interfere with American shipping in New Orleans. Fortunately for Jefferson, France now felt as burdened with Louisiana as Spain had and was very willing to sell the territory to another nation. Soon, peaceful negotiations began between Napoleon and the United States.

NAPOLEON'S OFFER

Jefferson began by sending James Monroe to France in 1803 to help negotiate the purchase of territory at the mouth of the Mississippi, including New Orleans. However, negotiations began to stall on the French side. Napoleon was having trouble in another part of the Americas—the Caribbean colony of Saint-Domingue, now known as Haiti, on the island of Hispaniola. In 1791, **Toussaint L'Ouverture** (TOO-sahnt LOH-ver-toor) had led a successful revolution to free slaves in the French colony. L'Ouverture governed the island until 1802, when Napoleon decided he wanted the colony back. But his actions resulted in an all-out war.

Napoleon had had enough of the Americas. His forces had been reduced by yellow fever, an often-fatal disease carried by mosquitoes in tropical climates, and he surrendered to Haitian independence. Without Saint-Domingue, Napoleon felt that Louisiana had little value. As a result, the French leader decided to give up all his territory in continental North America. Instead of selling only New Orleans to the United States, Napoleon suggested selling the entire Louisiana Territory—all 828,000 square miles of it—for $15 million. In October 1803, the U.S. Senate ratified the treaty that established the Louisiana Purchase. France officially transferred the land to the United States, doubling the size of the nation.

Jefferson had some misgivings about the deal. He debated the constitutionality of the purchase, saying, "The General Government has no powers but such as the Constitution gives it. . . . It has not given it power of holding foreign territory, and still less of incorporating it into the Union. An amendment of the Constitution seems necessary for this." But Jefferson ended up putting his concerns aside. The land, he believed, would provide space for generations of American farmers and allow people in the region to trade freely on the Mississippi. Soon after the treaty with France was finalized, Jefferson funded an expedition to take a good look at the land and natural resources the country had bought. He could hardly wait to hear what the explorers learned about the plants, animals, and people in the region.

Louisiana Purchase, 1803

Map legend:
- Original United States by Treaty of 1783
- Louisiana Purchase, 1803
- British territory
- French territory
- Spanish territory

HISTORICAL THINKING

1. **READING CHECK** Why did Jefferson want to purchase Louisiana from France?

2. **ANALYZE CAUSE AND EFFECT** What happened as a result of war in Saint-Domingue?

3. **INTERPRET MAPS** What major river did the United States acquire the rights to in the Louisiana Purchase?

PLAN

Objective

Analyze Thomas Jefferson's decision to expand the United States with the Louisiana Purchase.

Critical Thinking Skills for Lesson 2.1

- Identify Main Ideas and Details
- Monitor Comprehension
- Analyze Cause and Effect
- Interpret Maps
- Evaluate

Essential Question for Chapter 9

In what ways did Thomas Jefferson's policies change the country? Jefferson supported westward expansion as a way to provide more land for farmers. Lesson 2.1 describes how Jefferson doubled the size of the United States through the Louisiana Purchase.

Background for the Teacher

In 1795, while New Orleans was under Spanish rule, the United States and Spain signed Pinckney's Treaty, also called the Treaty of San Lorenzo. The treaty guaranteed the United States free navigation on the Mississippi River and the right to bring goods to New Orleans for temporary warehousing and duty-free shipment from the port. The situation changed, however, when Spain returned control of Louisiana back to France, and in 1802, Spanish officials in Louisiana blocked Americans from depositing goods and shipping out of New Orleans. As some factions began calling for war, Jefferson stepped up negotiations with France by sending James Monroe to Paris to represent the United States. He gave Monroe the authority to pay up to $10 million for New Orleans and Florida in order to protect shipping.

History Notebook

Encourage students to complete the American Gallery page for Chapter 9 in their History Notebooks as they read.

Preview with the Map
Direct students' attention to the Louisiana Purchase map. As a class, note the locations of the original United States and its territories, the Mississippi River, New Spain, and finally, the Louisiana Purchase. **ASK:** Why might Thomas Jefferson have thought that the Louisiana Purchase would be positive for the United States? *(Answers will vary. Students may suggest that the added territory would make the country larger and more powerful; others might suggest that acquiring the Louisiana Territory would limit the influence and reach of Spain.)*

TEACH
Guided Discussion
1. **Analyze Cause and Effect** Why did Spain agree to return Louisiana to France, and why did the decision worry Jefferson? *(Spain agreed to return Louisiana to France because it was not populated enough or profitable enough to warrant the expense of maintaining it. The decision worried Jefferson because he feared France would interfere with the United States shipping goods out of New Orleans.)*

2. **Evaluate** What considerations did Jefferson take into account when deciding to move forward with the Louisiana Purchase? *(Possible response: Jefferson worried that the deal with France might be unconstitutional since the Constitution did not explicitly state how to acquire territory from other nations. However, he also envisioned America as a nation based on farming, and the Louisiana Purchase provided new land for generations of farmers. Jefferson decided to put aside his constitutional concerns in favor of his agricultural vision.)*

⌾ American Places
The Cabildo is located on Jackson Square in New Orleans in the heart of the French Quarter. The building sits on the site of the original Spanish government building that was destroyed by a series of fires in the late 1700s. Architect Don Gilberto Guillemard designed the current building along with the neighboring Cathedral of St. Louis and the Presbytere, which had also been destroyed by fire. The Louisiana State Museum acquired the Cabildo in 1908, and it was declared a National Historic Landmark in 1960. Today, the building stands as one of the few remnants from Spain's control of the Louisiana Territory.

Active Options
On Your Feet: Three-Step Interview Have students work in pairs. One student should interview the other using this question: *How did international events help Thomas Jefferson expand U.S. territory?* Then students should reverse roles. Finally, each student should share the results of his or her interview with the class.

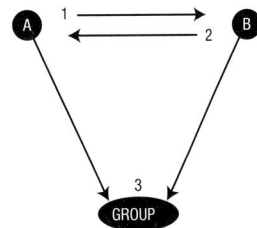

AMERICAN GALLERY
ONLINE
New Orleans: A French, Spanish, and American City Invite students to explore the American Gallery. Have them select one of the images and do additional research to learn more about it. Ask questions that will inspire additional inquiry about the chosen gallery image, such as: What does it show? How does it reflect the history of New Orleans? How does it reflect the cultural diversity of New Orleans? How does it reflect the people of New Orleans? What else would you like to know about the subject or subjects in the image?

Striving Readers
Use Reciprocal Teaching Have students read Lesson 2.1 in pairs. Instruct students to take turns reading each paragraph aloud. At the end of the paragraph, have the reading student ask the listening student a question or two about what he or she has just heard.

Inclusion
Provide Terms and Names on Audio Decide which of the terms and names are important for mastery and have a volunteer record the pronunciations and a short sentence defining each word. Encourage students to listen to the recording as often as necessary. You might also use the recordings to quiz students on their mastery of the terms. Play one definition at a time from the recording and ask students to identify the term or name described.

See the Chapter Planner for more strategies for differentiation.

ANSWERS
1. Economic factors motivated Jefferson to purchase Louisiana from France. The United States needed access to the Mississippi River and the port at New Orleans in order to ship crops and cargo to world markets. The purchase also allowed the United States to acquire vast fertile farmlands and other resources.

2. The war in Saint-Domingue went badly for the French forces, forcing Napoleon to surrender to Haitian independence. In the wake of the defeat, Napoleon decided Louisiana had little value. Thus he offered to sell all of his continental territory to the United States.

3. Mississippi River

2.2 The Discoveries of Lewis and Clark

MAIN IDEA Lewis and Clark's expedition cleared up some of the geographic unknowns of the new, expansive lands that President Jefferson bought from France.

A SCIENTIFIC EXPEDITION

As you have read, Meriwether Lewis and William Clark's Corps of Discovery traveled almost 8,000 miles from St. Louis, Missouri, to the Pacific Ocean, then back to St. Louis. Few accurate maps of the West existed at that time, and there were many geographic unknowns about the region. Lewis and Clark's recorded observations changed Americans' understanding of the physical landscapes of the West.

Their journey also resulted in the discovery of plants and animals never seen before by European-Americans. Lewis and Clark recorded more than 120 new animal species, including mule deer and coyote. They described 178 new species of plants, like the big leaf maple, the Oregon crabapple, and the ponderosa pine.

Follow the journey of Lewis and Clark on the map below. Then read about three geographic unknowns in the West and the new geographic knowledge the explorers gained through their travels and observations.

Lewis and Clark's Expedition Route, 1804–1806

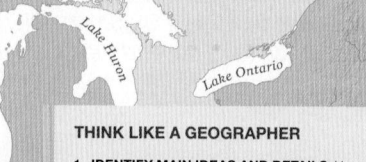

GEOGRAPHIC UNKNOWN	GEOGRAPHIC KNOWLEDGE

THE MISSOURI RIVER AND THE MARIAS RIVER

In June 1805, Lewis and Clark were sailing up the Missouri River in present-day Montana when they came to another river. One river flowed from the north, and the other flowed from the south. Which one was the main stem of the Missouri River? Which one should they continue to follow?

Most members of Lewis and Clark's expedition wanted to follow the river that flowed from the north. Lewis and Clark were not so sure. They split up, with Clark scouting the river to the south and Lewis scouting the river to the north. They returned from their quick explorations and agreed—the south branch was the Missouri River and the one they should continue to follow upstream. Lewis named the river to the north the Marias River, after his cousin Maria.

THE NORTHWEST PASSAGE

Jefferson had hoped Lewis and Clark would find a Northwest Passage, a water route that would connect the Missouri River to the Pacific Ocean and the riches of Asia. The country that found such a route first would control it. When the explorers arrived at the origin of the Missouri River in August 1805, they expected to have a short portage to the Columbia River, which would carry them to the Pacific.

Lewis reached Lemhi Pass, a two-mile span bridging the gap between the ranges of the Rockies near the border of present-day Montana and Idaho. There, Lewis discovered "immence ranges of high mountains still to the West of us with their tops partially covered with snow." There would not be a short portage to the Columbia River. Instead, the expedition had to cross the rugged Bitterroot Mountains, which took them until October. The hopes for a Northwest Passage had died.

BISON

When Lewis and Clark embarked on their expedition, they knew about bison. However, they had no idea how large the herds were or how vital these animals were to the Native Americans of the Great Plains. They also didn't know where the bison roamed.

As Lewis and Clark traveled west, they found enormous herds of bison and, like the Native Americans, they came to depend on the bison for the animals' nutritious meat. The explorers found no bison west of the Rocky Mountains, but when they took different routes east through the Rockies, the bison reappeared.

THINK LIKE A GEOGRAPHER

1. **IDENTIFY MAIN IDEAS AND DETAILS** How did Lewis and Clark determine that the Northwest Passage did not exist?

2. **ANALYZE ENVIRONMENTAL CONCEPTS** How might settlement in the lands obtained through the Louisiana Purchase affect the biological diversity of the plants and animals Lewis and Clark discovered?

3. **DRAW CONCLUSIONS** How did Lewis and Clark's perceptions of the West change as a result of their expedition?

PLAN

Objective

Describe the geographic information Lewis and Clark discovered about the western territory.

Critical Thinking Skills for Lesson 2.2

- Identify Main Ideas and Details
- Monitor Comprehension
- Analyze Environmental Concepts
- Draw Conclusions
- Make Inferences
- Make Connections
- Interpret Maps

Essential Question for Chapter 9

In what ways did Thomas Jefferson's policies change the country? Jefferson's decision to send Lewis and Clark's expedition across the Louisiana Territory to the Pacific Ocean resulted in insight into the geography of the region. Lesson 2.2 explores what the expedition discovered during the journey.

Background for the Teacher

Jefferson chose Meriwether Lewis to lead the Corps of Discovery because he wanted "a person who to courage, prudence, habits & health adapted to the woods, & some familiarity with the Indian character, joins a perfect knowledge of botany, natural history, mineralogy & astronomy." To prepare for his task, Lewis had some of the leading scientists of the day tutor him in mapmaking and surveying, mathematics, botany, zoology, fossils, anatomy, and medicine. Lewis also purchased Seaman, a Newfoundland dog, and designed a 55-foot keelboat to carry men and supplies. Lewis sent this keelboat back to St. Louis from Fort Mandan filled with journals, maps, Native American artifacts such as a painted Mandan buffalo robe, mineral samples, and plant and animal specimens that included a live prairie dog.

Review the Route

Direct students' attention to the map in Lesson 2.2. Remind them that they learned about Lewis and Clark's expedition in the chapter's American Stories feature. Point to St. Louis and have students describe the significance of the location based on their prior knowledge. Continue with other places along the route that students have already learned about, such as Fort Mandan, the Rocky Mountains, Shoshone Village, and Fort Clatsop. Note that the names of the tribes of Native Americans, such as the Osage, are shown on the map in the areas they occupied. Tell students that in this lesson, they will learn about the geographic knowledge the explorers gained as they traveled the route.

TEACH **STEM**

Guided Discussion

1. **Analyze Environmental Concepts** What does the fact that Lewis and Clark found many new species of plants and animals tell you about the environment of the western lands? *(Possible response: The new species indicate environments different from those in the east.)*

2. **Make Connections** How did taking separate return routes back through the Rockies help Lewis and Clark understand the roaming range of bison? *(On the way westward, Lewis and Clark observed bison along their Missouri River route. After they entered the Rockies, the bison disappeared and were not found west of the Rockies. On the return trip, the men took different routes. Both men observed bison once they were east of the mountains. This showed that bison roamed across large swaths of the Great Plains and did not live in mountain habitats.)*

Geography in History

Interpret Maps Have students study the map of Lewis and Clark's expedition route. **ASK**: How did the physical geography of the route change as the expedition moved westward? *(The first part of the journey was across the Great Plains, so the land was relatively flat and grassy. As the group got closer to the Rocky Mountains, the elevation increased and the topography changed from flat, to hilly, then to steep mountains.)* What does the red dotted line along the Rocky Mountains represent? *(Continental Divide)*

Active Options

Active History: Research Native Cultures Extend the lesson by using either the PDF or Whiteboard version of the activity. These activities take a deeper look at a topic from, or related to, the lesson. Explore the activities as a class, turn them into group assignments, or even assign them individually.

NG Learning Framework: Conduct a Cost-Benefit Analysis

SKILL Collaboration

KNOWLEDGE Our Living Planet

Point out that the Lewis and Clark expedition discovered valuable natural resources, such as fertile soil, navigable rivers, mineral deposits, and new plants and animals. Organize students into groups and have them create a list of advantages these natural resources might offer the young republic. Then have students come back together as a class and use their lists to discuss how a demand for natural resources might have influenced Thomas Jefferson's decision to spend money on the Louisiana Purchase and the expedition even though he was concerned about reducing the national debt.

Inclusion

Describe Physical Geography Have visually impaired students work with sighted partners to learn the details of Lewis and Clark's Expedition Route map. Have the sighted partner describe where the route begins and each territory or significant land feature it passes through to reach the Pacific Ocean. Allow the visually impaired students to ask questions as needed.

Pre-AP

Create an Exhibit Have students research some of the new species of plants and animals Lewis and Clark found on their expedition. Then have them use the information to create a virtual exhibit of species of their choosing. Students should create a theme and title for their exhibit, provide drawings or photos of the species, and write descriptive labels.

See the Chapter Planner for more strategies for differentiation.

THINK LIKE A GEOGRAPHER

ANSWERS

1. When Lewis and Clark reached the origin of the Missouri River, they expected the Columbia River to be close by. At Lehmi Pass, Lewis realized that the Bitterroot Mountains were in the way and the Missouri and Columbia rivers were not close enough to make any sort of connection. Thus the Northwest Passage did not exist.

2. Settlement in the lands might harm the plants and animals, causing them to adapt to new conditions, decrease in number, or even die away.

3. Possible response: Lewis and Clark had believed that there might be a Northwest Passage but found that it did not exist. While they probably expected to encounter new kinds of plants and animals, they may have been surprised at the large number of new species they did find.

Sharing the World

"Try to say yes when you travel. You'll open yourself up to so many new experiences." —Robert Reid

You might say **Robert Reid** has a pretty great job. As National Geographic's Digital Nomad, he investigates the whys and hows of how we experience the world, sharing his adventures with a global audience via social media, blog posts, and the occasional informal travel video.

Reid has traveled from coast to coast in the United States and extensively abroad, from Vietnam to England to Australia. He's been to Canadian Mountie boot camp, counted mustaches in Siberia, and poked around Atlantic City, New Jersey. He's even parachuted from a World War II-era plane in the middle of Russia. He gets around. Reid uses his own hobbies and interests to build trip itineraries, research articles, and provide a framework for the video storytelling he is famous for. (Look him up!)

^
The East African country of Kenya is only one of the amazing destinations Robert Reid has visited during his career as a travel writer.

MAIN IDEA Digital Nomad Robert Reid explains how travel enriches our lives.

ROAD TRIPPING

In spite of his extensive international travel experience, Reid admits if he could only visit one country for the rest of his life, it would be the United States. "It's so diverse," he explains, highlighting some of his favorite American places. "I love the Great Plains. Mountains are great, but they get in the way of a good view." He's also fond of New York City because of its cultural icons and famous places. Oregon, Reid's home state, is another favorite location. "Oregon is the most underrated state in the country. It has everything. Coastlines. Waterfalls. You name it. It's also where Lewis and Clark ended their great American road trip."

Reid identifies with Lewis and Clark in many ways. "I think the ultimate road trip of all time belongs to those guys," he says. "Their journey was just so American. Americans take road trips to understand their country, and that's what Lewis and Clark were doing." Reid points out the ability of the explorers to travel 8,000 miles—and survive—more than 200 years ago is downright incredible, but explainable. "They didn't overpack. We know that, because they left us lists of exactly what they brought. They knew how important it was to rely on the knowledge of the locals, so they used native guides who knew the language, the terrain, and the culture. And nearly everyone survived the expedition. That's incredible!"

TIPS FROM A TRAVELER

Most importantly to Reid as a travel writer, Lewis and Clark documented their journey. Extensively. So what suggestions does this travel guru have to offer the average tourist today? First, take photographs—lots of them—because they'll help you remember your trip. Secondly, write about who and what you encounter on your journey. Visit a place from different angles and talk to locals who can offer unique perspectives. For example, says Reid, "Go to Wyoming and find a geologist who

When he travels, Robert Reid gets to know the locals—in this case, a Rosie the Riveter reenactor he met in Ronks, Pennsylvania.

is walking every square inch of the state to make maps. That person knows the land better than anyone and knows how to better appreciate things most people miss."

Everywhere he visits, Reid talks to people who live there and tries to see the place from their perspective, not from that of an outsider. "When you travel, do and see the things the locals like to do and see—and make sure you do that with the locals," he advises. Sound advice from someone who knows how to travel.

Check out the Reid on the Road videos online in this history program.

HISTORICAL THINKING

1. **FORM AND SUPPORT OPINIONS** Reid believes it's vital to interact with local residents when you travel. Why does he recommend this? Do you agree? Use evidence in the text to support your answer.

2. **COMPARE AND CONTRAST** What does Robert Reid have in common with Lewis and Clark? How are they different?

PLAN

Objective
Learn about Robert Reid's experiences as a National Geographic Digital Nomad.

Critical Thinking Skills for Lesson 2.3
- Identify Main Ideas and Details
- Monitor Comprehension
- Form and Support Opinions
- Compare and Contrast
- Make Connections
- Summarize

Essential Question for Chapter 9
In what ways did Thomas Jefferson's policies change the country? Jefferson's decision to send Lewis and Clark to explore the western lands acquired in the Louisiana Purchase provided a wealth of information that helped later travelers. Lesson 2.3 discusses the travels of Lewis and Clark and of contemporary traveler Robert Reid.

Background for the Teacher
Robert Reid likes the challenge and fun of presenting his travels in a video format. He approaches the task in much the same way he writes an article—by conducting research, collecting statistics and quotes, and developing a point of view. Reid notes that the Internet has changed travel writing. When he wrote print guidebooks, it often took a year before information about new hotels or restaurants reached the public. Now information can be shared quickly through websites and social media. Regardless of how travel writers share information, they remain, in Reid's view, a valuable resource because of the way they travel. Unlike travelers who post online reviews of the places they visit, travel writers seek out at a wide variety of businesses and places of interest, thereby offering a broader overview.

History Notebook
Encourage students to complete the Digital Nomad page for Chapter 9 in their History Notebooks as they read.

INTRODUCE & ENGAGE

Plan a Road Trip

Ask students to suggest places they would like to visit if they could travel anywhere. Then, as a class, compile a list of things students would want to know in order to get the most out of their travels. **ASK:** How could you find this information? *(Answers will vary. Possible responses: travel guides, online sites, talking to people who have been there)* Tell students that in this lesson they will learn how Robert Reid approaches traveling to new places in order to get the most out of his trips.

TEACH

Guided Discussion

1. **Make Connections** Why is technology important to Robert Reid's mission as a National Geographic Digital Nomad? *(Part of Reid's mission is to share his adventures with a global audience. His use of photographs and videos helps him document the physical and cultural features of the places he visits, and his use of social media and blog posts helps him share his experiences and perspectives with people around the globe.)*

2. **Summarize** How does Reid characterize the Lewis and Clark expedition, and why does he describe it that way? *(Reid characterizes the Lewis and Clark expedition as "the ultimate road trip" because Lewis and Clark, like Americans on road trips today, set out to understand their country. Reid thinks the journey was incredible because almost everyone survived the 8,000-mile expedition. He attributes this to the fact that they didn't overpack and relied on locals for information and help.)*

More Information

Travel Advice Robert Reid has valuable advice for travelers, including not passing up travel opportunities—something he has done more than once himself. In 1989, for instance, he passed up a chance to make a quick side trip to the Berlin Wall, little knowing that it would be torn down two months later. On another occasion, a Hungarian film crew invited him to camp with them at a Siberian gulag. He politely declined, suggesting that he might do it another time—as if another time was likely to present itself. Reid suggests the best way to avoid travel regrets is to listen to your future self when making travel decisions today.

Active Options

On Your Feet: Conduct Talk Show Interviews Assign students to teams of three and tell them to prepare questions to conduct talk show interviews on how to be a successful traveler. Student 1, the interviewer, develops a question to ask the show's "guest." Student 2, an "expert" on traveling, answers the question, citing information from the lesson. Student 3, a member of the studio audience, asks a spin-off question for the whole class to answer. Have participants ask and answer several questions to ensure a solid review of the topic.

NG Learning Framework: Develop a Travel Itinerary

ATTITUDE Curiosity

SKILL Communication

Invite students to work in groups to develop present-day trip itineraries based on following part of Lewis and Clark's route to the Pacific and back. Students should list departure and destination points for their segment of the trail, points of interest and historical facts, and photo or video opportunities. Encourage students to conduct online research to build their itineraries. Have students share their completed itineraries with the class.

DIFFERENTIATE

English Language Learners

Ask the Five Ws Remind students that reporters use *who, what, where, when,* and *why* questions to guide their reporting. Explain to students that they can use the same questions to understand nonfiction text. Pair students at the **Emerging** and **Expanding** levels of proficiency and have them ask and answer five questions about Robert Reid's travels and his advice on being a successful traveler.

Gifted & Talented

Create a Travel Video Have students select a location in their neighborhood or community to present in an informal travel video. In planning their video, tell students to talk to local people, conduct research, and think about why the place is worthy of being included on someone's travel itinerary. Have students share their videos with the class.

See the Chapter Planner for more strategies for differentiation.

HISTORICAL THINKING

ANSWERS

1. Answers will vary. Reid suggests that travelers should interact with locals because locals offer a unique perspective on a place. Students may agree because, as Reid notes, someone like a Wyoming geologist who has walked all across the state would notice things most travelers would miss. In addition, locals can share information about where they like to go and what they like to do.

2. Like Lewis and Clark, Reid records what he sees and relies on the knowledge of locals. How he records what he sees differs, though. Lewis and Clark kept written journals. Reid makes use of modern technology like photographs and videos.

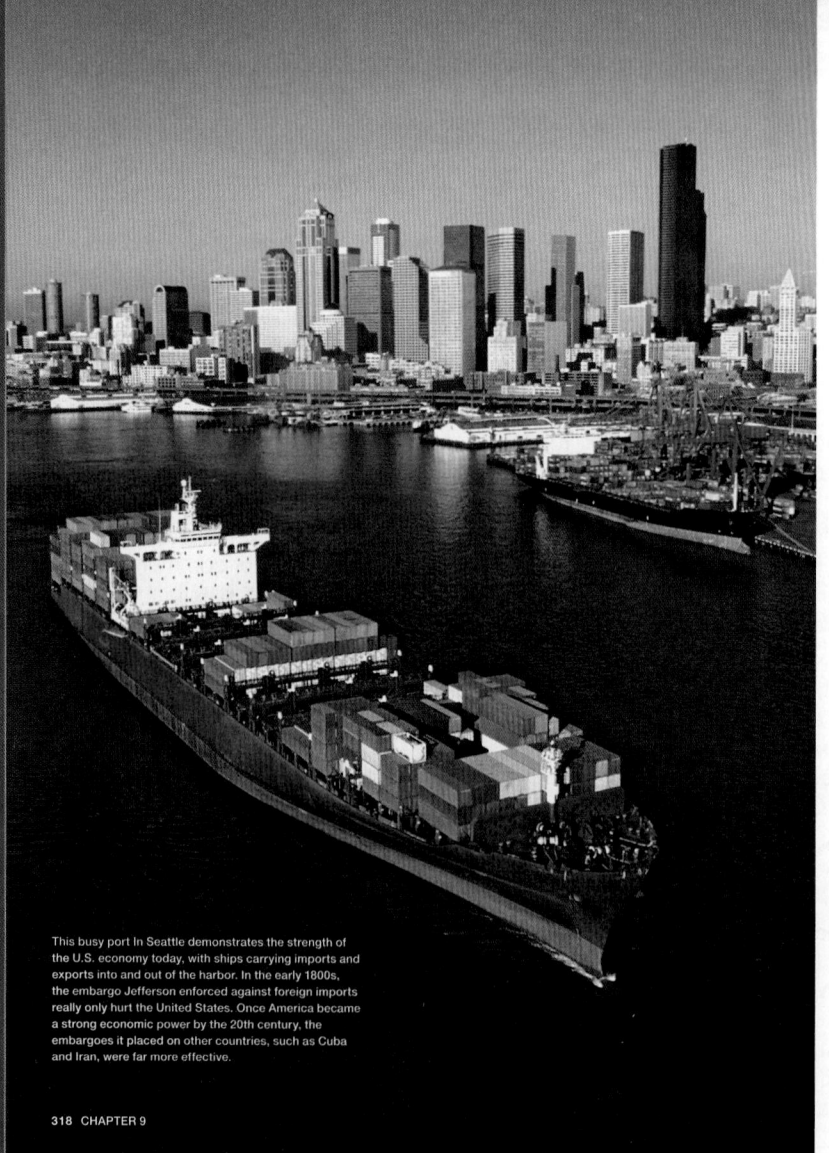

This busy port In Seattle demonstrates the strength of the U.S. economy today, with ships carrying imports and exports into and out of the harbor. In the early 1800s, the embargo Jefferson enforced against foreign imports really only hurt the United States. Once America became a strong economic power by the 20th century, the embargoes it placed on other countries, such as Cuba and Iran, were far more effective.

3.1 Neutrality or War?

When people get into a fight, do you join in or walk away? Thomas Jefferson probably wanted to focus on Lewis and Clark's discoveries in the Louisiana Territory. Unfortunately, the war brewing abroad kept demanding his attention.

MAIN IDEA Jefferson's plan to remain neutral during a war between Britain and France backfired.

JEFFERSON'S FOREIGN POLICY

In his 1801 Inaugural Address, Jefferson had explained his foreign policy. The United States, he said, was "separated by nature and a wide ocean from the exterminating havoc [deadly chaos] of one quarter of the globe." The last part referred to Europe. Among his "essential principles of government" were "peace, commerce, and honest friendship with all nations, entangling alliances with none." In other words, he wished the United States to remain neutral. Easier said than done.

After Napoleon gave up on expansion in North America, he turned to Europe and began a war with Britain in 1803. At first, American merchants profited from U.S. neutrality and sold provisions and weapons to both countries. Yet soon the British and French navies tried to block American ships from supplying their enemy. In addition, Britain authorized its navy to capture American ships and force the sailors to serve the British Navy—an act called **impressment**.

CUTTING OFF TRADE

Although many Americans called for war, the United States remained neutral. But trade with Britain and France became more difficult after Napoleon threatened to seize any ship that engaged in trade with Britain. In response, Jefferson urged Congress to pass the Non-Importation Act, which banned British imports. He also closed U.S. ports and waters to British ships. The British answered by continuing impressment, firing on U.S. coastal towns, and entering the Chesapeake Bay.

In response, Congress passed the **Embargo Act of 1807**. An **embargo** is a law that restricts commerce with one or more nations. The act was supposed to stop all foreign imports from arriving in American harbors, but smugglers still got through. Congress allowed the president to use militia against these illegal traders.

While these steps stopped the smuggling, the embargo had disastrous effects on the U.S. economy. The Treasury's chief source of income—**customs**, or taxes placed on imported and exported goods—dwindled. The embargo particularly affected New England farmers, whose crops were no longer being exported abroad, and New England merchants, who depended on European trade for much of their business. After New Englanders demanded an end to the embargo, Congress passed laws in 1809 that reopened trade with all nations except Britain and France.

Despite the impact of the embargo, Jefferson remained popular. His endorsement of fellow Democratic-Republican James Madison in the 1808 presidential election resulted in a landslide victory against the Federalists. The election proved that Americans still supported the policies of Jefferson's Democratic-Republicans. As it turned out, these policies would soon be tested at home.

HISTORICAL THINKING

1. **READING CHECK** What was Jefferson's foreign policy?

2. **ANALYZE CAUSE AND EFFECT** How did the Embargo Act of 1807 affect Americans?

3. **SUMMARIZE** What foreign actions tested Jefferson's policy of neutrality?

PLAN

Objective

Describe Thomas Jefferson's foreign policy decisions and their consequences.

Critical Thinking Skills for Lesson 3.1

• Identify Main Ideas and Details
• Monitor Comprehension
• Analyze Cause and Effect
• Summarize
• Draw Conclusions

Essential Question for Chapter 9

In what ways did Thomas Jefferson's policies change the country? Jefferson's decision to cut off foreign trade in an effort to stay neutral in the war between Britain and France hurt the U.S. economy. Lesson 3.1 explores the causes and effects of the Non-Importation Act and the Embargo Act of 1807.

Background for the Teacher

Jefferson and Madison believed that the Embargo Act of 1807 would be detrimental to the warring parties, particularly Britain. In reality, the neutrality caused a financial problem for the United States. The war initially boosted American exports from $66.5 million to $102.2 million between 1803 and 1807. However, following the passage of the embargo, exports dropped by 80 percent. Farm foreclosures increased and agricultural prices declined. Smuggling helped offset some of the losses; however, smuggling was not beneficial to most citizens, and New Englanders demanded an end to the embargo. On March 1, 1809, Congress replaced the embargo with the Non-Intercourse Act, which reopened trade with all countries except Britain and France. Congress passed the law just days before Jefferson's term ended, resulting in Jefferson leaving office without solving the nation's international and financial troubles.

Discuss Neutrality

Write the following lines from Thomas Jefferson's first inaugural address on the board: "It is proper you should understand what I deem the essential principles of our government...— peace, commerce, and honest friendship with all nations, entangling alliances with none..." Ask students to speculate on what Jefferson meant. If necessary, lead them to understand that Jefferson is talking about the United States remaining neutral in foreign wars. Have students suggest why Jefferson might take this stance. Tell students that they will learn about the effects of Jefferson's views on neutrality in this lesson.

TEACH

Guided Discussion

1. **Analyze Cause and Effect** What were the causes and consequences of the Non-Importation Act? *(Congress passed the Non-Importation Act, which banned the import of British goods, in response to Napoleon's threats to seize any ship that engaged in trade with Britain. Britain retaliated by continuing to impress American sailors, firing on coastal towns, and entering the Chesapeake Bay even though Jefferson had closed U.S. ports to British ships.)*

2. **Draw Conclusions** Why do you think Congress responded to calls for the embargo's end in the way it did? *(Answers will vary. Possible response: By reopening trade with all nations except Britain and France, Congress enabled farmers, merchants, and the Treasury to make money through trade. By excluding Britain and France, the United States could maintain neutrality.)*

More Information

Impressment of American Sailors Many British sailors deserted the British navy during the war with France and joined the American merchant marines. To combat the problem, Britain employed "press gangs" to board American ships and retrieve deserters. The gangs often took anyone who looked British. As a result, only about 10 percent of the sailors impressed from American ships were actually British. Most were Americans who simply could not prove their citizenship.

Active Options

On Your Feet: Debate Divide the class into two groups and have one side discuss and write reasons why they might support the Embargo of 1807, while the other side develops and writes claims to argue against it. Have students from each group take turns debating the topic. Make sure each side responds to the claims of the other. See if either group can persuade opposing students to change sides. At the end, reward the side with the most remaining students as the winner of the debate.

NG Learning Framework: Analyze Political Cartoons

SKILL Communication

KNOWLEDGE Our Human Story

Have students work in groups to locate and analyze political cartoons—such as *The Embargo (Ograbme) 1807*—from the early 1800s that express the effects of impressment or the Embargo Act. Have groups share their cartoons with the class and explain the meanings behind the cartoons.

Striving Readers

Use Context Clues Model how to use textual definitions and context clues to understand Key Vocabulary words in this lesson: *impressment, embargo,* and *customs.* Then guide students in using context to understand other unfamiliar academic vocabulary words such as *alliances, commerce,* and *importation.*

English Language Learners

Build Vocabulary Help students at the **Emerging** and **Expanding** levels understand words used in Lesson 3.1 that may be unfamiliar to them. Begin with the Key Vocabulary words for this lesson: *impressment, embargo,* and *customs.* Provide students with index cards or paper. Have students write each word and its definition based on context clues in the text. Then have them compare their definitions with definitions in the Glossary. Once students have established solid definitions, have them write sentences using the Key Vocabulary. Tell students to follow these steps for other unfamiliar words in Lesson 3.1, using a dictionary to check their definitions.

See the Chapter Planner for more strategies for differentiation.

HISTORICAL THINKING

ANSWERS

1. Jefferson's foreign policy was based on the United States remaining neutral and not forming alliances.

2. The Embargo Act stopped most of the trade between America and other nations, resulting in an economic slump. New England was hit especially hard because farmers could not ship their crops and merchants were cut off from the European trade that accounted for much of their business. In addition, the Treasury's income dropped because of the lost customs.

3. The war between Britain and France tested Jefferson's policy of neutrality because both sides interfered with U.S. merchants who tried to provide supplies to the other side. Additionally, the British practiced impressment, and France threatened to seize ships trading with the British.

3.2 Native Americans Unite

Thomas Jefferson kept the United States out of war. But in the years shortly after he left office, the threat of war continued to grow. Conflict was in the air, and not only in Europe.

MAIN IDEA Native Americans across North America united to fight against the American government and its increasing expansion into their traditional lands.

TECUMSEH'S IDEA

While the United States was trying to maintain neutrality in the war in Europe, trouble was developing at home. American expansion into the Northwest Territory had increased conflict with Native American nations. Shawnee chief **Tecumseh** (tuh-KUM-suh), in particular, began to speak out against the destruction of native cultures and economies. He also criticized Native American leaders who sold their land to the United States.

To present a united front against the United States, Tecumseh visited Native American tribes, including the Miami, the Delaware, and the Potawatomi, and spoke to them about forming a confederation, or alliance. In 1809, while Tecumseh traveled the country, the U.S. government negotiated the Treaty of Fort Wayne with several other tribes. According to the terms of the treaty, the Native American leaders who signed the agreement sold 2.9 million acres of their land to the government for a fraction of a penny per acre. This type of "deal" was just what Tecumseh had been trying to prevent. The treaty was the last straw and inspired many more Native American groups to join Tecumseh's cause.

A Gift from the British

This ceremonial tomahawk and pipe was a gift to Tecumseh from British colonel Henry Proctor. The two men fought together on the frontier and in Canada, but they fell out over Proctor's reluctance to attack American troops in Ohio. Proctor hoped to win back Tecumseh's respect and friendship by offering him this weapon, which was most likely made in France.

Pipe tomahawk, c. 1810–1812

THE BATTLE OF TIPPECANOE

Meanwhile around 1808, Tecumseh had established **Prophetstown** on the Tippecanoe (tih-pee-kuh-NOO) River in the Indiana Territory. Prophetstown was a community devoted to Native American unity and opposition to U.S. expansion. Tecumseh's brother, Tenskwatawa (tens-qwah-TAH-wah), lived there, and people called him "the Prophet." A **prophet** is someone who is believed to deliver messages that come from God or some other divine source. Tecumseh's brother had become a religious leader in Prophetstown, and many of its inhabitants looked to him to foretell the future. The Prophet promoted a return to traditional ways of life and insisted that Native Americans reject all aspects of European culture.

In 1811, the governor of the Indiana Territory, William Henry Harrison, led about 1,000 men to attack the community and put an end to Tecumseh's confederacy. Tecumseh was away, trying to recruit Native Americans in the South to his cause. Acting against his brother's orders, the Prophet led an attack of his own on Harrison's camp early one morning but was soon forced to retreat. The next day, Harrison's forces found Prophetstown deserted and burned it to the ground. The skirmish came to be known as the **Battle of Tippecanoe**.

The battle infuriated many Americans. Rumors swirled that British forces in Canada had encouraged Tecumseh's confederacy and attacks by Native Americans. Some Americans who favored war, called **War Hawks**, even believed that the British had already formed an alliance with Native Americans against the United States. Many leaders felt, too, that the new nation had to demonstrate its viability, or skill, on the international stage. The War Hawks' anger boiled over in the Capitol, resulting in a call to arms. The shadow of war was falling on the country.

Tecumseh's Eloquence

Tecumseh traveled throughout the United States and Canada, persuading other tribes to join his confederacy. In one speech, he told the Osage that they "belong to one family" and were all "children of the Great Spirit." His goal of confederation, he explained, was "to assist each other to bear our burdens." Tecumseh insisted, "We walk in the same path. . . . We must be united; we must smoke the same pipe; we must fight each others' battles."

HISTORICAL THINKING

1. **READING CHECK** What was Tecumseh's plan, and how did he hope to accomplish it?

2. **ANALYZE CAUSE AND EFFECT** What main factors led Tecumseh to formulate his plan?

3. **EVALUATE** In what ways was Tecumseh's plan a good one, and in what ways was it likely to fail?

320 CHAPTER 9

The Jefferson Years **321**

PLAN

Objective
Understand the impact of territorial expansion on Native Americans.

Critical Thinking Skills for Lesson 3.2
• Identify Main Ideas and Details
• Monitor Comprehension
• Analyze Cause and Effect
• Evaluate
• Make Connections

Essential Question for Chapter 9
In what ways did Thomas Jefferson's policies change the country? American expansion westward led to increased tension with Native Americans, particularly in the Northwest Territory. Lesson 3.2 examines Shawnee chief Tecumseh's attempt to unite Native Americans against American expansion.

Background for the Teacher
Under George Washington and John Adams, the federal government approved 12 treaties with Native Americans between 1789 and 1798. These treaties usually involved incorporating forcibly ceded Native American land into the United States. The Treaty of Greenville is one example. It was signed in 1795, reaffirming the ceding of Northwest Indian lands covering nearly two-thirds of present-day Ohio. The practice continued under the administrations of Thomas Jefferson and James Madison. Jefferson instituted a series of treaties aimed at transforming Native Americans into settled farmers, establishing trade, and acquiring Native American land. The loss of land led to growing discontent among Native Americans.

INTRODUCE & ENGAGE
Take a Stand
Ask students to consider what they would do if their land and way of life were being threatened by a conquering people. For example, would they adapt to the new culture? Would they join together and fight? What might a leader say to sway their opinion? Lead a class discussion and ask volunteers to share their ideas with the class. Tell students that Lesson 3.2 explores Shawnee chief Tecumseh's efforts to persuade Native Americans to band together to fight U.S. expansion.

TEACH
Guided Discussion
1. **Make Connections** How did the Treaty of Fort Wayne affect Tecumseh's recruitment? *(Possible response: As part of the terms of the Treaty of Fort Wayne, Native American leaders gave up 2.9 million acres of land to the U.S. government for less than a penny per acre. Tecumseh realized native cultures were being destroyed by leaders selling land, so he fueled anger over the treaty and inspired Native American groups to join his confederacy.)*

2. **Sequence Events** Describe the events that led to the Battle of Tippecanoe. *(Prophetstown was a community of the Native American opposition, located on the Tippecanoe River, founded by Tecumseh and his brother, Tenskwatawa. While Tecumseh was away, and aware that William Henry Harrison was planning an attack on the town, Tenskwatawa led an attack against Harrison, but had to retreat. The next day, Harrison attacked the town, burning it to the ground, but Tenskwatawa and the others had already abandoned it. The skirmish became known as the Battle of Tippecanoe.)*

Evaluate
As a class, evaluate the unintended consequences of the Battle of Tippecanoe. **ASK:** How did the Battle of Tippecanoe help propel the United States toward war with Britain? *(The battle infuriated many Americans because they believed that the British had encouraged Native American attacks and Tecumseh's confederacy. The War Hawks went a step further and argued that the British had formed an alliance with Native Americans against the United States.)*

Active Options
On Your Feet: Create a Quiz Have students work in groups to create a fill-in-the-blank quiz about the causes and consequences of Native American resistance to westward expansion. Encourage students to use the text to confirm their answers. Then have each group ask another group their questions. Have students keep track of the number of correct answers for their group scores.

NG Learning Framework: Examine Treaties
ATTITUDE Responsibility
SKILL Collaboration

Divide students into four teams to investigate and examine the major treaties the United States signed with Native American nations during the administrations of Washington, Adams, Jefferson, and Madison. Assign each team one administration. Have students examine the treaties and then outline the terms of the treaties and their varying outcomes. Ask groups to share their outlines with the whole class. After all the administrations have been discussed, have students analyze similarities and differences in the consequences of these treaties.

DIFFERENTIATE
Striving Readers
Use Reciprocal Teaching Have students read Lesson 3.2 in pairs. Instruct students to take turns reading each paragraph aloud. At the end of the paragraph, the reading student should ask the listening student a question or two about what they have just heard. For example, students may ask their partners to summarize the paragraph in their own words.

Gifted & Talented
Analyze a Speech Assign students different speeches—or portions of speeches—given by Tecumseh. Have them read the speech as a group and then write a short paragraph analyzing its meaning. Tell them to research any unfamiliar words or references. Then have groups read an excerpt of the speech to the class. After the reading, have the group share their analysis of the speech.

See the Chapter Planner for more strategies for differentiation.

HISTORICAL THINKING
ANSWERS
1. Tecumseh planned to unite Native American tribes against the Americans by visiting and negotiating with the tribes in the United States and Canada. He believed a confederacy of tribes could stop the takeover of Native American land.

2. Tecumseh's plan was a reaction to the expansion of U.S. settlements into the Northwest Territory. He wanted to prevent Native American leaders from selling or ceding more land to the United States.

3. Answers will vary. Possible response: Tecumseh's plan was good because a strong confederacy of tribes might have resisted settlers and soldiers from encroaching onto Native American lands. On the other hand, the plan was destined to fail because Native American tribes were so geographically distant that an effective organization of forces against the U.S. military would have been impossible.

3.3 The War of 1812

Americans value their independence. That's what the American Revolution had been about, after all. Turns out, many Americans would be willing to fight for it a second time.

MAIN IDEA The War of 1812 unified the people of the United States and set the stage for expansion and economic prosperity.

A NATION AT ODDS

In June 1812, the War Hawks got their way. Congress declared war against Britain—again. However, despite the widespread belief that the British and Native Americans were working together, Americans had mixed feelings about the **War of 1812**. As you know, the war with Britain was especially unpopular with New England farmers and merchants for economic reasons.

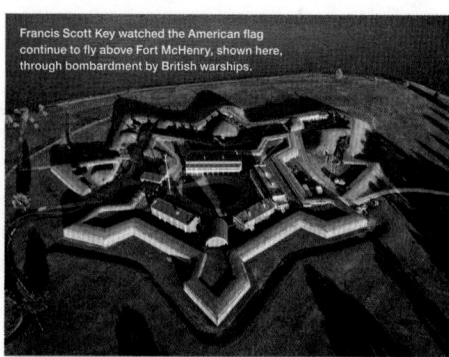

Francis Scott Key watched the American flag continue to fly above Fort McHenry, shown here, through bombardment by British warships.

Politicians also wondered how President James Madison planned to pay for the war. The National Bank's charter had expired, leaving only the less stable state banks to provide war loans. Also, you may remember that the United States had ended trade with Britain and France while those two countries were at war. The government had lost a great deal of income from tariffs as a result.

THROUGH THE PERILOUS FIGHT

At first, busy fighting Napoleon, Britain all but ignored the war with the United States. However, Britain had to act when American forces attacked its fort near Detroit, Michigan. The British repelled the attack and even forced the U.S. militia to surrender Detroit. Things were beginning badly for the Americans.

In September 1813, American troops won their first victory when **Oliver Hazard Perry** and his fleet of ships defeated British troops on Lake Erie.

Soon after, William Henry Harrison's forces retook Detroit and defeated British forces at the Battle of the Thames (tehmz). Shawnee chief Tecumseh died on that battlefield fighting for the British.

By the summer of 1814, Britain's war against Napoleon in Europe was drawing to a close, so the country sent more troops to North America. British forces captured Washington, D.C., and burned down the Capitol and White House. Less than a month later, the British also attacked **Fort McHenry** and Baltimore, Maryland, but failed to take the city. The American flag flying amid the battle's flaming rockets and bombs inspired **Francis Scott Key** to memorialize the scene in his poem "The Star-Spangled Banner." The poem was later set to music and became the national anthem of the United States. (You can read more about Key's famous lyrics and our flag earlier in this text in the American Story, "Our American Identity.")

By the end of 1814, neither Britain nor the United States saw much hope for victory. Delegates from both countries met in Ghent, a city in present-day Belgium, where they signed the Treaty of Ghent and formally ended the war. News of the treaty did not come soon enough to stop one last British naval and ground attack on New Orleans, however. **Andrew Jackson**, a military leader from Tennessee, and his troops countered the attack and killed, captured, or wounded more than 2,000 British soldiers. Jackson lost only 13 soldiers.

The terms of the treaty restored things to the way they were before the war. All territory captured during the war was returned to its original owner, and all prisoners of war were freed.

Although the treaty did not declare a winner, many Americans felt they'd scored a diplomatic victory. The war confirmed U.S. sovereignty and boosted Americans' self-confidence and patriotism. It also encouraged yet more expansion and a new economic prosperity.

🏛 The White House
Washington, D.C.

This painting by Tom Freeman, called *Burning of the White House, 1814*, shows the structure in flames after British soldiers torched it during the War of 1812. Before their arrival, Madison's wife, Dolley, had a full-length portrait of George Washington removed and taken from the building for safekeeping.

CRITICAL VIEWING What emotions is the painting probably meant to inspire?

HISTORICAL THINKING

1. **READING CHECK** Why were Americans divided over fighting the War of 1812?

2. **ANALYZE CAUSE AND EFFECT** What happened because news of the Treaty of Ghent didn't arrive immediately?

3. **FORM AND SUPPORT OPINIONS** Do you think Americans were justified in their belief that they had won the war? Explain why or why not.

PLAN

Objective
Understand the political and economic causes and consequences of the War of 1812.

Critical Thinking Skills for Lesson 3.3
- Identify Main Ideas and Details
- Monitor Comprehension
- Analyze Cause and Effect
- Form and Support Opinions
- Summarize
- Draw Conclusions

Essential Question for Chapter 9
In what ways did Thomas Jefferson's policies change the country? Westward expansion and the impact of Jefferson's embargo on Britain pitted the War Hawks against many New Englanders over support for the War of 1812. Lesson 3.3 examines the war and its consequences.

Background for the Teacher

The War Hawks were mainly Democratic-Republicans in Congress from the South and West regions of the United States. They believed the war could aid western expansion and increase the possibility of gaining possession of Spanish Florida and even Canada. The Federalists opposed the war, and these disgruntled delegates met in 1814 at the Hartford Convention. They discussed the war and the possibility of New England's secession from the Union. Calmer heads quieted talk of secession, but the delegates brought proposals to Congress calling for an end to the war and for constitutional amendments to limit Democratic-Republican power. However, these proposals fell on deaf ears when news of the Treaty of Ghent arrived from Europe. In the end, an outpouring of postwar patriotism eroded the stature of the Federalist Party.

Preview Using Visuals

Direct students' attention to the photo of Fort Henry and the painting of the White House burning. Call on volunteers to predict what they will learn in the lesson based on what they see in the images. At the end of the lesson, have students review their predictions to see how accurate they were.

TEACH

Guided Discussion

1. **Summarize** Why did U.S. politicians worry about paying for the war with Britain? *(Politicians worried about paying for the war because the National Bank's charter had expired. This meant that the government had to rely on the less stable state banks to finance the war. In addition, the government's financial reserves were low because the trade embargoes had reduced the amount of money the government brought in through tariffs.)*

2. **Draw Conclusions** Based on what you know about the war, why do you think both sides decided to seek peace? *(Answers will vary. Possible response: Both sides had victories and losses in battles, but there were no decisive victories that suggested one side would pull ahead and win the war. Since the attack on New Orleans had not yet happened, peace seemed a good option.)*

Virtual Museum Visit

Tom Freeman painted *The British Burning the White House, 1814* at the request of the White House Historical Association in 2004. The association wanted a panoramic view of the event, since there was no visual record of the burning. In preparation for creating the painting, Freeman read accounts of the night, met with historians, and studied British uniforms and the way fire moves. Freeman later supplied additional pencil and watercolor sketches of the event for historian William Seale's book *The Night They Burned the White House: The Story of Tom Freeman's Painting.* Today, several of Freeman's paintings and prints hang in the White House.

Active Options

On Your Feet: Tell Me More Have students form two teams and assign each team one of the following topics: *American actions during the war* or *British actions during the war.* Instruct each group to write down as many facts about their topic as they can. Have the class reconvene and have each group stand up, one at a time. The sitting group calls out, "Tell me more about [American actions or British actions]!" The standing group recites one fact. The sitting group again calls, "Tell me more!" until the standing group runs out of facts to share. Then the groups switch places.

NG Learning Framework: Create a Social Media Profile

ATTITUDE Curiosity

KNOWLEDGE Our Human Story

Invite students to select an individual from this chapter and create a social media profile for him or her. Students can supplement information from the text with online or library research. Encourage students to include visuals with their profiles, such as photos or illustrations. Profiles should include information such as likes, dislikes, friends, political affiliation, and a short "About Me" section that situates their person in historical context. Have students share their profiles with the class.

Inclusion

Narrate Lesson Visuals This lesson might pose a challenge to the visually impaired. Have students who are not visually challenged help their classmates understand the photo of Fort Henry and the Freeman painting by describing them in detail and answering questions posed.

Gifted & Talented

Write Journal Entries Have students conduct research to learn more about an event in the War of 1812, such as Oliver Hazard Perry's Lake Erie victory, the British attack on Fort Henry, the British burning of the Capitol and White House, or Andrew Jackson's victory at New Orleans. Then ask students to write a series of journal entries from the perspective of someone viewing or participating in the event. Tell students to include information from their research in their journal entries. Ask for volunteers to read some entries aloud.

See the Chapter Planner for more strategies for differentiation.

HISTORICAL THINKING

ANSWERS

1. The War Hawks favored the war, in part because they thought the British and Native Americans were working together to resist westward expansion. New England farmers and merchants, on the other hand, worried that the war would hurt them economically.

2. Because of the time it took for news of the Treaty of Ghent to reach the United States, British and American troops engaged in battle in New Orleans after peace had already been negotiated.

3. Answers will vary. Possible response: No, neither side won. The terms of the treaty merely restored things to the way they were before the war. Neither side gained land, and all prisoners of war were released. A diplomatic victory is not the same thing as winning the war.

CRITICAL VIEWING Answers will vary. Possible response: The painting may be meant to stir emotions of shock and horror at the idea of the British burning down the White House.

9 REVIEW

VOCABULARY

Use each of the following vocabulary words in a sentence that shows an understanding of the term's meaning.

1. judicial review
   After judicial review, the Supreme Court decided that the new law was invalid.

2. Louisiana Purchase

3. incumbent

4. unconstitutional

5. impressment

6. customs

7. embargo

READING STRATEGY
ANALYZE CAUSE AND EFFECT

If you haven't already done so, complete your chart to analyze causes that led President Madison to declare war on Britain in 1812. List at least four causes. Then answer the question.

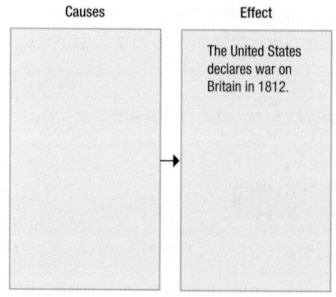

Causes	Effect
	The United States declares war on Britain in 1812.

8. How did Britain's war with France influence the outbreak of the War of 1812?

MAIN IDEAS

Answer the following questions. Support your answers with evidence from the chapter.

9. How was the 1800 election decided? **LESSON 1.1**

10. What were the effects of the Judiciary Act of 1801? **LESSON 1.3**

11. Why did William Marbury think *Marbury* v. *Madison* was a good case? **LESSON 1.3**

12. In what way did the Louisiana Purchase contradict Jefferson's philosophy of government? **LESSON 2.1**

13. What were some difficulties the United States encountered while remaining neutral during the war between Britain and France? **LESSON 3.1**

14. What geographic factor made Tecumseh's plan for union difficult? **LESSON 3.2**

15. What role did the War Hawks play in the War of 1812? **LESSON 3.2**

16. How would you summarize Britain's military situation during the War of 1812? **LESSON 3.3Z**

17. How was the Treaty of Ghent different from traditional treaties? **LESSON 3.3**

HISTORICAL THINKING

Answer the following questions. Support your answers with evidence from the chapter.

18. **COMPARE AND CONTRAST** How were Jefferson's beliefs similar to and different from those of the Federalists?

19. **ANALYZE CAUSE AND EFFECT** What was the most important lasting effect of the Judiciary Act of 1801?

20. **FORM AND SUPPORT OPINIONS** Do you think the Louisiana Purchase was constitutional? Explain why or why not.

21. **EVALUATE** What were the purpose, challenges, and economic incentives of the Lewis and Clark expedition?

22. **SYNTHESIZE** Why did the War of 1812 increase American patriotism?

23. **IDENTIFY** What experiences contributed to Napolean's loss of interest in the Americas?

INTERPRET MAPS

Look closely at the map below. Then answer the questions that follow.

Western Exploration, 1803–1807

24. Based on the boundaries of the Louisiana Territory, which European nations might have come into conflict with the United States over territorial boundaries?

25. What two explorations does the map show, and which of these went into territory owned by another nation?

ANALYZE SOURCES

In an 1811 letter to Secretary of War William Eustis, William Henry Harrison, governor of the Indiana Territory, described Tecumseh's work in building a confederation to keep U.S. settlers and soldiers off Native American lands. Read the excerpt and answer the questions.

> The implicit [absolute] obedience and respect which the followers of Tecumseh pay to him, is really astonishing, and . . . bespeaks him [suggests that he is] one of those uncommon geniuses which spring up occasionally to produce revolutions. . . . If it were not for the vicinity of the United States, he would, perhaps, be the founder of an empire that would rival in glory that of Mexico or Peru. . . . I hope, however, . . . that that part of the fabric [unity among the tribes] which he considered complete, will be demolished, and even its foundations rooted up.

26. According to Harrison, how do other Native Americans regard Tecumseh?

27. What seems to be Harrison's opinion of Tecumseh?

CONNECT TO YOUR LIFE

28. **NARRATIVE** Choose an important U.S. figure from 1800 to 1816, such as Thomas Jefferson or John Marshall. Make a connection between that historical figure and a well-known person today. Write a paragraph in which you imagine what would happen if the two met.

TIPS

- List the historical figure's qualities and accomplishments. Then make a similar list for the present-day person you have chosen.

- Use textual evidence and vocabulary words from the chapter in your narrative.

- Include dialogue to convey the figures' personalities and philosophies.

- Conclude with a description of the connection that ties the two figures together.

VOCABULARY ANSWERS

1. After judicial review, the Supreme Court decided that the new law was invalid.

2. The Louisiana Purchase doubled the size of the land area of the United States.

3. As the incumbent, Jefferson endorsed James Madison to follow him as president.

4. The Supreme Court has the power to declare a law or an executive action unconstitutional.

5. The impressment of American sailors into the British Navy was one cause of the War of 1812.

6. The Embargo Act of 1807 prevented the government from collecting customs on imports and exports.

7. The embargo against trading with France and Britain caused economic problems for New England merchants.

READING STRATEGY ANSWER

Causes	Effect
American sailors are impressed into the British navy.	
Britain responds to Non-Importation Act with aggression.	The United States declares war on Britain in 1812.
Americans suspect an alliance between Britain and Native Americans.	
War Hawks push for war.	

8. Britain's war with France brought naval blockades and dangerous passage for U.S. trading ships, as well as extensive impressment of American sailors into the British Navy, all factors leading to the War of 1812.

MAIN IDEAS ANSWERS

9. The 1800 election initially resulted in a tie between Thomas Jefferson and Aaron Burr. The House of Representatives voted 36 times over the course of six days and finally gave Thomas Jefferson a majority vote.

10. The Judiciary Act of 1801 reduced the number of justices on the Supreme Court, which would prevent Jefferson from filling a seat when one became vacant. It also allowed President Adams, a Federalist, to appoint lower court judges just before he left office. This resulted in fewer Democratic-Republicans in the judicial system when Jefferson became president.

11. Marbury believed his case was valid because President Adams signed his commission before he left office.

12. Jefferson believed that the federal government only had the powers given by the Constitution, which does not mention the power to obtain new lands. Jefferson decided to go ahead with the deal because he believed the Louisiana Purchase would strengthen the nation.

13. Maintaining neutrality was difficult for the United States because the British and French each blocked American ships from supplying the other country with supplies. Britain took American ships and impressed sailors. Even as Jefferson closed U.S. ports to British ships, the British fired on coastal towns and entered the Chesapeake Bay.

14. Tecumseh was trying to unite Native Americans over a wide geographic area stretching from Canada through the Northwest Territory to the south of the United States. This meant that he had to do a great deal of traveling in his efforts to persuade tribes to join his confederacy.

15. The War Hawks were members of Congress who, because they believed the British were encouraging Native American uprisings, supported war. Their anger put added pressure on President Madison when he was deciding what action to take.

16. Britain was fighting two wars: one with France and one with the United States. Britain focused only on France at first. Once the battle with France started going well, Britain shipped troops to North America to fight the United States.

17. The Treaty of Ghent was different because it did not declare a winner of the war. Its purpose was to hold Britain and the United States to the agreement that their relationship would go back to how it was before the war.

HISTORICAL THINKING ANSWERS

18. Answers will vary. Possible response: Jefferson and the Federalists believed in a strong federal government and keeping states' rights, but Jefferson promised to limit federal government to gain votes. While Federalists were aligned with businessmen in the North, Jefferson championed farmers. Jefferson believed in paying down the national debt, but Federalists believed having a national debt was not a problem.

19. Answers will vary. Possible response: The most important lasting effect of the Judiciary Act of 1801 was that it led to the Supreme Court case of *Marbury* v. *Madison*. As a result of this case, Chief Justice Marshall's Court established the Supreme Court's right to judicial review—the power to determine whether a law was constitutional—thereby strengthening the balance of power and promoting checks and balances.

20. Answers will vary. Possible response: Although Jefferson worried that the Louisiana Purchase might be unconstitutional because the Constitution did not explicitly state that the federal government could acquire foreign land, the purchase was probably constitutional. The president has the power to initiate treaties that are then ratified by Congress. Congress ratified the Louisiana Purchase, so it was constitutional.

21. Answers will vary. Possible response: The Lewis and Clark expedition was charged with the challenging task of exploring and mapping a new territory, searching for the Northwest Passage, establishing friendly relations with the Native American groups they met, and collecting samples of the land's plant, animal, and mineral resources. Westward expansion, natural resources, and trade with Native Americans were all economic incentives. In addition, by exploring the West, Lewis and Clark strengthened future U.S. claims to the region.

22. Answers will vary. Possible response: Although the United States did not gain land by the terms of the treaty, Americans believed they had achieved a diplomatic victory by standing up to Britain and confirming U.S. sovereignty. This boosted patriotism.

23. After Napoleon suffered losses in Saint-Domingue, he felt that Louisiana was not valuable enough to keep.

INTERPRET MAPS ANSWERS

24. Britain and Spain

25. The map shows Lewis and Clark's expedition of 1804 to 1806 and Pike's exploration of 1806 to 1807. Pike's journey went into the Spanish lands of New Spain.

ANALYZE SOURCES ANSWERS

26. Harrison indicates that Tecumseh's followers show him absolute obedience and respect.

27. Harrison shows great admiration for Tecumseh's abilities and leadership, yet he hopes that the Native American chief's work will be "demolished" and "rooted up."

CONNECT TO YOUR LIFE ANSWER

28. Paragraphs will vary, but students should use textual evidence, chapter vocabulary, dialogue, and a conclusion in their narrative.

UNIT 4 RESOURCES

UNIT INTRODUCTION

UNIT TIME LINE

UNIT WRAP-UP

NATIONAL GEOGRAPHIC | CONNECTION

National Geographic Magazine Adapted Articles
- "Searching for Sacagawea"
- "Lost Missouri" ONLINE

Unit 4 Inquiry: Define Good Citizenship

NG Learning Framework Activities
- Propose a New Invention
- Write a Campaign Speech

Unit 4 Formal Assessment

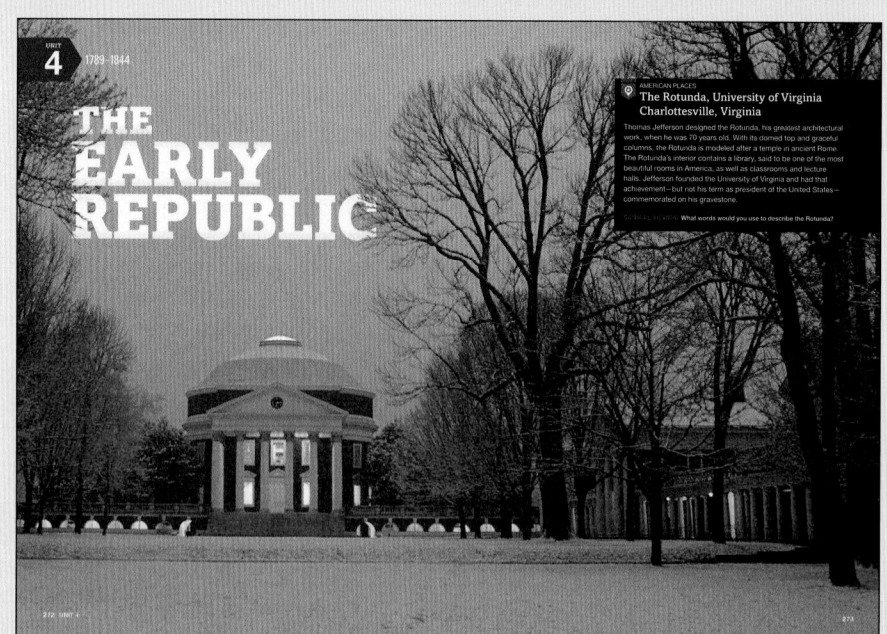

CHAPTER 10 RESOURCES

Available at NGLSync.Cengage.com

TEACHER RESOURCES & ASSESSMENT

Reading and Note-Taking

Vocabulary Practice

Document-Based Question Template

Social Studies Skills Lessons
- Reading: Draw Conclusions
- Writing: Write a Narrative

Formal Assessment
- Chapter 10 Pretest
- Chapter 10 Tests A & B
- Section Quizzes

Chapter 10 Answer Key

ExamView®
One-time Download

STUDENT DIGITAL RESOURCES

- **eEdition** (English)
- **eEdition** (Spanish)
- **Handbooks**

- **Online Atlas**
- **American Gallery Online**
- **History Notebook**

- **American Voices (Biographies)**
- **Active History**
- **Projects for Inquiry-Based Learning**

Chapter 10 Spanish Resources are available at NGLSync.Cengage.com.

The Mighty Mississippi

- Primary Sources
- On Your Feet: Create a Concept Web

‖ **NG Learning Framework:**
Make a Transportation Time Line

SECTION 1 RESOURCES

AMERICA'S FIRST INDUSTRIAL REVOLUTION

LESSON 1.1
From Farm to Factory

- On Your Feet: Four Corners

‖ **NG Learning Framework:**
Design Strike Posters

American Voices Biographies
Francis Cabot Lowell ONLINE
Lucy Larcom

LESSON 1.2
Innovations and Inventions

- Active History: Evaluate Industrial Revolution Inventions

‖ **NG Learning Framework:**
Annotate a Technology Time Line

American Voices Biographies
Samuel Morse
Mary Dixon Kies ONLINE

LESSON 1.3
GEOGRAPHY IN HISTORY
Roads, Railroads, and Canals

 The American Railroads

‖ **NG Learning Framework:**
Plan a Journey

LESSON 1.4
AMERICAN PLACES
The Mississippi River

- On Your Feet: Turn and Talk

‖ **NG Learning Framework:**
Create a Presentation About Mark Twain

SECTION 2 RESOURCES

PLANTATIONS AND SLAVERY SPREAD

LESSON 2.1
CURATING HISTORY
The Henry Ford Museum Dearborn, Michigan

- On Your Feet: Sort the Artifacts

LESSON 2.2
Growth of the Cotton Industry

- On Your Feet: Word Chain

‖ **NG Learning Framework:**
Learn More About Slave Dwellings

LESSON 2.3
Slavery and Resistance

- On Your Feet: Question and Answer

‖ **NG Learning Framework:**
Compare African-American Experiences

SECTION 3 RESOURCES

NATIONALISM AND SECTIONALISM

LESSON 3.1
A Young Nation Expands

- ▶ State Shapes
- On Your Feet: Use a Jigsaw Strategy

‖ **NG Learning Framework:**
Evaluate Supreme Court Decisions

American Voices Biography
James Monroe ONLINE

LESSON 3.2
Increasing Regional Tensions

- On Your Feet: Inside-Outside Circle

‖ **NG Learning Framework:**
Negotiate a Compromise

LESSON 3.3
DOCUMENT-BASED QUESTION
The Monroe Doctrine

- On Your Feet: Think, Pair, Share

LESSON 3.4
Women in the Early Republic

- On Your Feet: Three-Step Interview

‖ **NG Learning Framework:**
Study Family Life in the New Republic

CHAPTER 10 REVIEW

Strategy 1
Create a 3-2-1 Summary

After they read a lesson, direct students to complete a 3-2-1 summary by writing three important ideas under the number three, two Key Vocabulary terms and their definitions under the number two, and one main idea question to ask another student under the number one.

Use with Lessons 1.1, 1.2, 2.3–3.2

Strategy 2
Use a Word Sort Activity

Display the following Key Vocabulary terms and direct students to sort them into categories or groupings. Have students then explain, orally or in writing, how the words in each group are connected.

American System	spirituals	tariff
strike	abolition	passive resistance
subsidy	interchangeable parts	Missouri Compromise
cotton gin	Industrial Revolution	interstate slave trade

Use with All Lessons *Encourage students to identify some terms that may belong in more than one category and explain their reasoning.*

Strategy 3
Turn Titles into Questions

To help students set a purpose for reading, have them read the titles of selected lessons in each section and turn them into questions they think might be answered in the lesson. Students can record their questions and write their own answers as they complete the lessons, or partners can ask each other their questions.

Use with All Lessons *For example, the title of Lesson 1.1, "From Farm to Factory," might be reworded as "Why did the American economy shift from farms to factories?"*

Strategy 1
Monitor Comprehension

Have students choose one Key Vocabulary word, one name, and one date for each lesson. Guide students to write each item on a sticky note and put the note on the page next to where the item appears in context. Suggest students add a definition, context clues, or other information to the sticky note to help them understand and remember each item.

Use with All Lessons *Encourage students to retain each lesson's sticky notes and use them to track each item as they continue through the rest of the chapter.*

Strategy 2
Pose and Answer Questions

Pair students who have reading or perception issues with more proficient readers. Have pairs work together to read each paragraph of the lesson. After each paragraph, allow the student with reading difficulties to ask questions for clarification. Have the more proficient readers pose one recall question per paragraph for their partners to answer.

Use with All Lessons

Strategy ❶
Ask Yes/No Questions

To reinforce vocabulary comprehension, have students at the **Expanding** level answer yes/no questions about Key Vocabulary after reading lessons.

- Was the **textile** industry the first in America to begin using factories? *(yes)*
- Was using **interchangeable parts** a way of making items more difficult to build? *(no)*
- Were **spirituals** a form of violent protest against slavery? *(no)*
- Did **republican motherhood** refer to people who belonged to a specific political party? *(no)*

Use with Lessons 1.2, 2.3, 3.1, and 3.4 *To ensure comprehension, you might ask students at the **Bridging** level to pair with students at the **Emerging** level and help them review their answers.*

Strategy ❷
Create Word Webs

To expand vocabulary and preview lesson content, have students at **All Proficiencies** create a Word Web for the word *innovation* before beginning Section 1, the word *expansion* before beginning Section 2, and the word *nationalism* before beginning Section 3.

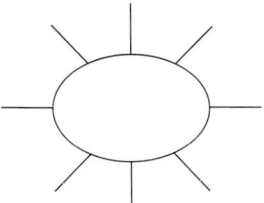

Use with Lessons 1.1, 2.1, and 3.1 *Encourage students to make Word Webs for Key Vocabulary words as they read the lessons.*

Strategy ❸
Illustrate Key Vocabulary

Encourage students at the **Emerging** level to draw pictures or other visual cues that will help them recall the meanings of Key Vocabulary terms, such as *strike, textile, passive resistance,* or *monopoly*. Students can include these illustrations on flash cards and review them often as they read the chapter. Encourage students at the **Expanding** and **Bridging** levels to make flash cards with a Key Vocabulary word on one side and the definition on the other side.

Use with All Lessons

Strategy ❶
Write Journal Entries

Have students write a series of short journal entries from the perspective of one of the following individuals: a worker in the Lowell textile mills, an enslaved African American, a free African American in the South, a young woman about to attend Catherine Beecher's Hartford Female Seminary, or a plantation owner. Encourage students to research their chosen narrator and to include the narrator's reflections on daily life and opinions about national events.

Use with Lessons 1.1, 2.2–2.3, and 3.4

Strategy ❷
Teach a Class

Before beginning the chapter, have students choose one of the lessons listed below and prepare to teach its contents to the class. Provide a set amount of time for students to present the essential information from their lessons. Encourage them to research and prepare any visual or audio media and any class or group activities they may want to use as they teach.

Use with Lessons 1.1–1.3, 2.2–2.3, 3.1–3.2, and 3.4

Strategy ❶
Consider Both Sides

Have students write a short essay about the Industrial Revolution and its effects on American society in the early 1800s. Instruct students to present both positive and negative effects of the shift to a factory system, the development of widespread transportation networks, and the rise of new technologies. Tell students to conclude with their opinion on whether the Industrial Revolution was more harmful or more beneficial. Have students exchange and compare essays with a partner to determine which is more convincing.

Use with Lessons 1.1–3.2 *Suggest that students first make a list of the pros and cons of the Industrial Revolution in the United States and refer to it as they write.*

Strategy ❷
Write a Summary

Remind students of the Essential Question: How did new industries and inventions transform the United States economically, socially, and geographically? Tell students to review the chapter and identify industries and inventions that caused changes. Then have students write a summary using the examples they identify to answer the Essential Question.

Use with All Lessons *Encourage students to use a Three-Column Chart to organize their ideas.*

EXPANSION AND GROWTH
1800–1844

ESSENTIAL QUESTION
How did new industries and inventions transform the United States economically, socially, and geographically?

READING STRATEGY

DRAW CONCLUSIONS
When you draw conclusions, you support them with evidence from the text. As you read the chapter, use a graphic organizer like this one to draw conclusions about the expansion and growth of the United States during the 1800s.

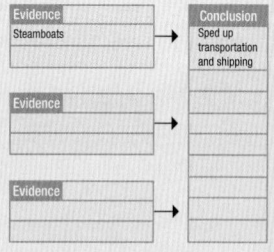

Evidence: Steamboats → Conclusion: Sped up transportation and shipping

Evidence →

Evidence →

> **"Railroad iron is a magician's wand,** in its power to evoke the sleeping energies of land and water."
> —Ralph Waldo Emerson

The railroad is one of the iconic symbols of U.S. expansion. During the early 19th century, Americans built railroads, canals, and roads that made traveling and trading with distant places easier and more efficient. The growing transportation network unified the country physically and culturally.

327

INTRODUCE THE PHOTOGRAPH
The American Railroad

Have students study the photograph and quotation that open this chapter. Tell students that Ralph Waldo Emerson was a famous American writer, thinker, and poet. Born in 1803, Emerson would have witnessed the birth of many technologies, including the railroad. **ASK:** Why might Emerson have described the railroad as a "magician's wand"? *(Possible responses: It had the ability to change the entire landscape; it could do things people previously thought were impossible.)* **ASK:** In what ways does this photograph reflect a similar attitude toward the railroad? *(Answers will vary. Possible response: The train appears to be traveling through an almost magical landscape—a sort of fairy-tale version of autumn.)*

Share Background

The locomotive shown in this photograph is steam powered, as were all of the earliest locomotives. In these engines, coal or wood was used to heat large amounts of water to create steam, which powered the machine. The engine then vented the steam, earning this train the name "steam engine." Trains carried the fuel and water that powered them in a tank or in a container called a tender.

American steam engines were powerful and relatively easy to maintain. They could run over cheap rails, travel around tight turns, and provide access to cities and agricultural regions that were not located near convenient waterways or ports, connecting vast stretches of the United States. Eventually, diesel and electric locomotives replaced their steam-powered ancestors.

For Chapter 10 Spanish Resources, visit the Resources Menu. Chapter 10 Resources are available at NGLSync.Cengage.com.

INTRODUCE THE ESSENTIAL QUESTION

How did new industries and inventions transform the United States economically, socially, and geographically?

Brainstorm Activity: Innovation and Expansion Have students brainstorm effects that a single invention might have on a society, using an example of a recent technology, such as the Internet.

As a class, use a Cause-and-Effect Chain like the one shown to map out the effects this invention had on economies, societies, and the way we use or think about geography.

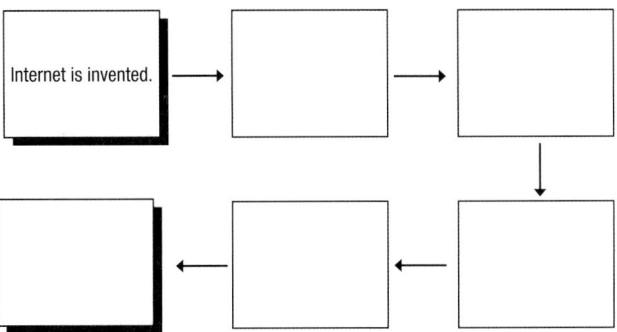

Encourage students to complete their Cause-and-Effect Chains as they encounter other inventions in this chapter. Explain that in this chapter, students will explore how new technologies caused rapid changes to the newly founded United States.

INTRODUCE CHAPTER VOCABULARY

Definition Charts

As students read the chapter, have them complete a Definition Chart for Key Vocabulary words. Have students list the Key Vocabulary words in the far left column of their chart. Then, as they encounter the words in the chapter, tell students to write each Key Vocabulary word's definition in the center column and explain the word's meaning in their own words in the far right column. Model an example for students using the graphic organizer below.

Word	Definition	In My Own Words
monopoly	control over all of a specific good or service in an area	when a company doesn't compete with other companies because it has cornered a market

INTRODUCE THE READING STRATEGY

DRAW CONCLUSIONS

Remind students that when they draw conclusions they combine evidence to make a statement. Model completing the Draw Conclusions Diagram. Point out that the diagram shows how multiple pieces of evidence should support a conclusion. Guide students to use the image and quotation that open the chapter as sources of evidence. Work as a class to complete the diagram and draw a conclusion about expansion and growth in the United States.

KEY DATES FOR CHAPTER 10

1793	Eli Whitney invents cotton gin
1807	Congress bans international slave trade
1811	National Road built
1817	Construction of Erie Canal begins
1819	*McCulloch* v. *Maryland*
1820	Missouri Compromise
1823	Monroe establishes Monroe Doctrine
1824	*Gibbons* v. *Ogden*
1826	Baltimore & Ohio Railroad founded
1831	Nat Turner's rebellion

 For instructional support for the online
American Story "The Mighty Mississippi,"
go to NGLSync.Cengage.com.

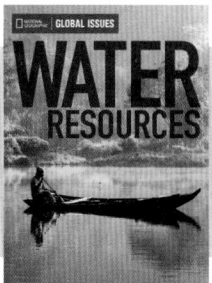

For more on water resources and development, see *GLOBAL ISSUES: WATER RESOURCES.*

STEM

1.1 From Farm to Factory

On a farm or in a factory—where would you rather work? In the first half of the 1800s, new inventions sparked the growth of factories. Many people left farm life behind, and this shift changed American culture in many ways.

MAIN IDEA Industrialization in the early 19th century transformed the ways in which Americans lived and worked.

CHANGES IN THE ECONOMY

In the early 1800s, different regions of the United States became more interdependent and connected. One factor that made this possible was the **market revolution**, or the transition from a pre-industrial economy to a market-oriented, capitalist economy. In part, this economic transition was prompted by the **Industrial Revolution**, or the widespread production by machinery, that had been underway in Europe since the mid-1700s.

The beginning of the Industrial Revolution in the United States is often dated to 1793, when **Samuel Slater** opened his first cloth factory in Rhode Island. Industrialization in the Northeast transformed social structures and had important consequences for the nation's economy and international position.

Newly introduced machines produced goods more rapidly and efficiently than people could make by hand, one at a time. A **factory system**, or a method of production in which large crews of people perform work in one location, developed. Mechanized production in factories and mills replaced skilled craftspeople. Factory managers recruited men and women from rural areas, many of whom embraced the idea of factory work.

New locations and types of work profoundly affected how people lived and worked. They also transformed the family economy. Furthermore, instead of working together on farms or in shops, men and women began to work in separate spheres. This shift was especially true for the emerging middle class.

THE MILL GIRLS

The United States entered the Industrial Revolution through the **textile** industry, which produced cloth and clothing from cotton and other raw materials. Initially, individual workers wove thread into large pieces of cloth on hand-operated looms. In 1785, an Englishman named Edmund Cartwright introduced the first power loom. Power looms required multiple workers, but by 1813, improvements had eliminated the general need for all but one person. This single-operator model became the basis for a faster, more efficient power loom developed by **Francis Cabot Lowell** at his textile mill in Massachusetts.

A mill town named in Lowell's honor was founded in 1823. Mill owners hired young girls and women because they would work for less pay than men. These female textile workers, some as young as 10 years old, were called the "Lowell girls." The Lowell girls lived in boarding houses and worked in the mills instead of attending school. Their letters home revealed that many enjoyed the independence factory work provided. These young women also published a monthly magazine of poetry and fiction, called the *Lowell Offering*.

Eventually, the Lowell workers' low wages and long hours in dangerous conditions soon became intolerable, so the young women banded together to protest. In the 1830s, the Lowell workers organized several **strikes**, or work stoppages, to protest cuts in wages. Their activism led to the formation of the Lowell Female Labor Reform Association, the first organization of working women in the United States.

A 19th-Century Textile Mill

Textile mills in the 19th century relied on water to power the different machines needed to transform raw materials into textiles. Machines inside the mill performed a variety of tasks, including preparing the cotton and fibers for spinning, spinning fibers into threads, and weaving threads into cloth.

Power Looms Noisy and fast-moving power looms weave yarn into cloth.

Spinning Powerful spinning machines combine thread from 10 to 15 different bobbins into strong yarn.

Carding and Drawing Fine metal teeth in carding machines brush the fibers so they face the same direction. The resulting loosely formed rope is then fed into a drawing frame to combine the fibers into a single strand.

Water Wheel Moving water turns a geared wheel that drives a series of belts and gears to power the machines inside the mill.

Raw Materials Bales of cotton arrive at the mill via horse-drawn wagon.

HISTORICAL THINKING

1. **READING CHECK** How did work change in the early 19th century?

2. **INTERPRET VISUALS** Based on the illustration and captions, describe how raw materials were transformed into cloth at textile mills.

3. **DETERMINE CHRONOLOGY** In what ways did the establishment of mill towns in the northeastern United States rely on earlier economic and technological developments?

PLAN

Objective

Analyze how the Industrial Revolution affected industries and workers in the United States.

Critical Thinking Skills for Lesson 1.1

- Identify Main Ideas and Details
- Monitor Comprehension
- Interpret Visuals
- Determine Chronology
- Make Predictions
- Summarize

Essential Question for Chapter 10

How did new industries and inventions transform the United States economically, socially, and geographically? The market revolution shifted American workers from rural areas to urban ones. Lesson 1.1 examines the example of the Massachusetts mill town Lowell.

Background for the Teacher

A magazine called the *Lowell Offering* began its run in 1840. Founded by a pastor, the Reverend Abel Charles Thomas, the magazine originally aimed to showcase inspirational works on topics such as science and nature alongside humorous sketches and religious messages. In 1842, Harriet Farley—herself a Lowell textile mill employee—took over as editor, and the magazine was written and produced almost exclusively by women. Farley continued to publish religious and literary texts but expanded the magazine's mission to include "diminishing prejudice against factory operatives" and addressing class bias. As labor unrest grew in Lowell, however, Farley attempted to keep the *Offering* neutral, and the decision proved unpopular with her readers. In 1845, amid harsh criticism, the *Offering* folded.

INTRODUCE & ENGAGE

Preview Concepts

Ask students to identify the factors they would consider important when looking for a job or a career, such as work conditions or future opportunities. Then preview the concepts of the Industrial Revolution and the factory system by having students consider the question that opens the lesson. **ASK:** Would you rather work on a farm or in a factory? *(Answers will vary.)* As a class, discuss the factors that students find appealing or off-putting about each kind of work: location, tasks, pay, stability, and social opportunities.

Guided Discussion

1. **Make Predictions** Under the factory system, men and women began to "work in separate spheres," especially in the middle class. What long-term effects might this change have? *(Possible response: A division between men's work and women's work might lead to greater inequality; women might begin fighting for better opportunities.)*

2. **Summarize** What advantages and disadvantages did the Lowell mill jobs offer their workers? *(The mill jobs offered the advantages of independence and social opportunities. The disadvantages included long hours, dangerous conditions, and a lack of education because the young girls in the mills worked instead of attending school.)*

More Information

Historical Fiction Many novels have been set in the mill towns of the Industrial Revolution. While the characters are fictional, they offer insight into questions about why people went to work in mills and what their day-to-day lives were like there. Read aloud or distribute excerpts from narratives about the Industrial Revolution, such as Katherine Paterson's historical novel *Lyddie*, that describe the working lives of people—especially women—in textile mills and other factories. Guide students to discuss how the rise of factories might have changed the meaning of "work" in the first half of the 19th century and why people in that time period might have chosen this new kind of work.

Active Options

On Your Feet: Four Corners Label the four corners of the room as follows: Farm Workers, Factory Owners, Factory Workers, and Consumers. Organize students into four groups, and assign each group to a corner. Tell groups to use information from this lesson to summarize the effects of the Industrial Revolution and the market revolution on the people they represent. Then have them share their ideas with the class.

NG Learning Framework: Design Strike Posters

ATTITUDE Empowerment

KNOWLEDGE Our Human Story

Invite students to use print or online resources to learn more about the daily lives of mill workers and the early labor disputes that led to strikes in the Lowell mills. For example, they could look up works published by mill workers in the *Lowell Offering*. Encourage students to consider the following questions as though they were mill workers themselves: What issues are most important? What demands should we make? Then have students work in groups to create signs the strikers could carry during their protests. Signs may include slogans, demands, complaints, or suggested solutions. Ask students to present their signs to the class, explaining the meaning behind each one.

DIFFERENTIATE

Striving Readers

Write Paragraph Summaries Lesson 1.1 has seven paragraphs under the subheadings Changes in the Economy and The Mill Girls. Have students work with a partner to write short summaries of each paragraph. Instruct partners to work together to craft one or two sentences that summarize the lesson as a whole.

English Language Learners

Use Sentence Frames Have students at the **Emerging** and **Expanding** levels work with a partner to complete these sentence frames as they read.

- The _____ involved an increase in production by machines. *(Industrial Revolution)*

- In a _____ system, large crews perform work in one place. *(factory)*

- The first U.S. industry to rely on factory work was the _____ industry. *(textile)*

- Mills often hired _____ in order to pay lower wages. *(women or girls)*

- Lowell workers organized a _____ to protest their low wages. *(strike)*

See the Chapter Planner for more strategies for differentiation.

HISTORICAL THINKING

ANSWERS

1. In the 19th century, machines produced goods more quickly and efficiently, replacing skilled craftspeople. People moved from farms to cities as jobs were concentrated in factories.

2. The cotton was first run through a carding machine that prepared it for spinning. Next, a spinning machine wove the threads into strong yarn, and power looms wove the yarn into fabric.

3. Answers will vary. Possible response: Francis Cabot Lowell introduced the power loom in his Massachusetts mill. This faster, more efficient loom was based on Edmund Cartwright's 1785 weaving machine that had replaced the hand-operated loom.

1.2 Innovations and Inventions

In your lifetime, new ideas and technology have transformed communication in dramatic ways. During the early 1800s, new technologies started speeding up transportation and communication.

MAIN IDEA New inventions made American workers more productive, created new industries, and contributed to the nation's economic growth.

NEW MANUFACTURING METHODS

As industries began to flourish in the United States, innovative thinkers were making manufacturing more efficient and profitable. Eli Whitney, John Deere, Robert Fulton, and Samuel Morse were just a few of the many Americans who introduced new technologies in the early 19th century.

Eli Whitney, one of the most influential of these inventors, was born in 1765 in Massachusetts. From an early age, he showed a natural talent for mechanics and was able to skillfully improve useful items. In 1797, war between the United States and France seemed likely, and the nation's military needed more weapons. Whitney came up with an ambitious plan to supply the federal government

with 10,000 rifles in just two years' time. The challenge was this: Every weapon already in use was unique. Any repair required making a new custom part for that specific gun. So Whitney made his rifles using **interchangeable parts**. Each of his guns had the exact same parts.

Whitney completed the government's order in eight years, but his method of using interchangeable parts set the machine age in motion. The use of interchangeable parts soon spread to the production of nearly all goods. Having all parts ready to use meant that goods could be produced quickly and at a lower cost. This efficiency helped shape the identity of the United States as a nation of problem-solving, ingenuity, and progress.

CRITICAL VIEWING Today's combine harvesters definitely look different from Deere's original plow. These machines accomplish all the harvesting tasks: they thresh, separate, clean, and collect the grain. What effect do you think these machines have on farm life and food production?

🏛 John Deere Historic Site, Grand Detour, Illinois

As Americans moved west, they developed new technologies to tackle the challenges they faced. Blacksmith John Deere found the soil of the American prairie to be harder to work with than eastern soil. Farmers typically used cast-iron plows to turn up soil before planting seeds, but their regular plows weren't enough. The dirt just clumped and stuck to the plow.

To solve this problem, Deere developed a plow made of hard, polished steel. The shape and material of his plow kept the soil from clumping, and he began selling his successful invention in 1838. Deere solved an agricultural problem by examining the design and function of a common tool, and paved the way for more improvements in farming technology. Today, Deere & Company manufactures plows and combines, which perform all the tasks associated with crop harvesting in one step.

John Deere's steel plow

STEAMBOATS AND TELEGRAPHS

New technologies also changed shipping, communication, and agriculture. Robert Fulton's **steamboats**, or boats outfitted with steam boiler engines to power their paddle wheels, revolutionized river travel and made shipping quicker. By 1811, Fulton had designed a steamboat powerful and sturdy enough for the strong currents of the Mississippi River. Soon, an upstream journey on the Mississippi and Ohio rivers from New Orleans to Louisville, Kentucky was shortened from several months to just 14 days. But even the swiftest ship could not carry a message across miles in a matter of minutes.

Samuel F. B. Morse's **telegraph** sent messages over electrical wires using a series of long and short pulses known as Morse code. An operator in one location tapped out a message on a device called a key. The message moved through wires to a machine that printed it out as dots and dashes punched onto a strip of paper. Another operator then transcribed the code into words. The first telegraph message was transmitted on May 24, 1844. Soon, telegraph wires stretched throughout the nation, and operators could interpret the code in real time. Widespread use of the telegraph for personal, business, and government communication continued for more than 100 years.

Innovations changed life on the farm as well. Cyrus Hall McCormick's horse-drawn mechanical **reaper** quickly cut, or reaped, stalks of wheat from the field and gathered them up for processing. Farmers who used this new machine no longer had to harvest wheat by hand. The reaper helped increase wheat production throughout the Great Plains. It changed not only American farming but also many of the world's farming methods. McCormick's reaper was so successful that he opened a factory in Chicago to produce his machines, advancing both rural farming technology and urban manufacturing techniques.

HISTORICAL THINKING

1. **READING CHECK** What was significant about manufacturing with interchangeable parts?

2. **DRAW CONCLUSIONS** How did McCormick's mechanical reaper contribute to agricultural and urban growth?

3. **MAKE CONNECTIONS** McCormick's reaper connected both rural and urban innovation. How might another invention described in the text connect the country and the city?

PLAN

Objective

Understand the effects of new technologies in the 19th century on people and industries.

Critical Thinking Skills for Lesson 1.2

- Identify Main Ideas and Details
- Monitor Comprehension
- Draw Conclusions
- Make Connections
- Evaluate
- Make Generalizations

Essential Question for Chapter 10

How did new industries and inventions transform the United States economically, socially, and geographically? Technologies developed in the 19th century changed American industries. In Lesson 1.2, students will learn how four critical innovations transformed agriculture, communication, and transportation.

Background for the Teacher

Like the power loom and other important inventions of the 19th century, the electric telegraph was born out of earlier technologies. Even the term *telegraph* predates Morse's 1844 system: It originated in the 1700s to describe a French communication system and was used to describe many systems that sent coded messages at a distance. Some early telegraph systems included semaphore towers with rotating arms that spelled out messages letter by letter and towers with moving shutters that opened and closed in patterns. Towers placed at regular intervals sent messages along the chain from origin to destination.

Imagine Innovations

Have students brainstorm some technologies that they use or see every day. **ASK:** Which of these technologies improve on something that existed before? (*Possible responses: smartphones, tablets, hybrid or electric cars*) Prompt students to discuss what makes each of these technologies an improvement. For example, the smartphone is a portable combination of telephone and computer. **ASK:** What do you think the next big innovation might be? (*Answers will vary.*) Explain that in this lesson, students will learn about four innovations that had an enormous impact on the American economy in the 19th century.

TEACH

Guided Discussion

1. **Evaluate** Did Eli Whitney's interchangeable parts solve the problem they were meant to solve? (*Whitney's innovation did not solve the specific problem of building 10,000 weapons in two years. However, it did solve the much larger problem of how to produce a wide range of goods quickly, cheaply, and on a large scale.*)

2. **Make Generalizations** What was the overall effect of new technologies in the 19th century? (*The overall effect was to make existing activities and industries, such as communication, travel, manufacturing, and farming, faster and more efficient.*) In what ways did new technologies shape human activities? (*Possible response: The improved plow led people to move west and transform prairie into farmland.*) In what ways did they result in human modifications to the landscape? (*Mass production of the reaper and other factory-made products led to increased urbanization.*)

More Information

John Deere Historic Site The John Deere Historic Site in Grand Detour, Illinois, is located where Deere first invented his steel plow. Deere moved to Grand Detour from his native Vermont in 1837, setting up shop as a blacksmith. Before long, he was experimenting with new kinds of plows. Ten years later, he moved his operations to the more conveniently located town of Moline, Illinois, on the Mississippi River. Visitors can view the original Deere smithy, found by archaeologists in 1963, and the home Deere shared with his wife, children, and many apprentices. These places offer a glimpse into the challenging lives of midwestern farmers and pioneers during the 19th century.

Active Options

Active History: Evaluate Industrial Revolution Inventions Extend the lesson by using either the PDF or Whiteboard version of the activity. These activities take a deeper look at a topic from, or related to, the lesson. Explore the activities as a class, turn them into group assignments, or even assign them individually.

NG Learning Framework: Annotate a Technology Time Line

ATTITUDE Curiosity
KNOWLEDGE New Frontiers

Have students work in small groups to select one of the inventions discussed in this lesson and find more information to create an annotated time line for it. Time lines should include important events or developments leading to the creation of the invention, the period of its most widespread use, and the point at which it either evolved or became obsolete. Students may also want to include important historical events in which their chosen invention played a large part. Encourage students to look for relevant images or videos to illustrate their time lines. Have students present their completed time lines to the class or display them on classroom walls.

DIFFERENTIATE

Inclusion

Work in Pairs Consider pairing students with disabilities with more proficient readers. Have the proficient reader read the lesson text aloud. After each paragraph, the listening student should briefly summarize the information or ask questions if needed to clarify the material.

Pre-AP

Interview an Inventor Have students work with a partner to prepare an interview with one of the inventors mentioned in the lesson. Partners research their chosen inventor and use the information to craft a television-news-style interview, with one student asking questions and the other answering in the persona of the inventor. Students posing as inventors should answer questions in ways that are supported by evidence from the lesson or student research. Invite students to record their interviews or conduct them in front of the class.

See the Chapter Planner for more strategies for differentiation.

HISTORICAL THINKING

ANSWERS

1. Interchangeable parts made the manufacturing process more efficient because pieces did not need to be custom-made for each finished item.

2. The mechanical reaper contributed to agricultural growth by allowing farmers to harvest a larger amount of wheat more quickly. It contributed to urban growth because McCormick opened a Chicago factory to build reapers, which brought more jobs and workers to that city.

3. Answers will vary. Students might mention that the telegraph connected both urban and rural communities or that interchangeable parts were used in farm machines and guns and soon spread to nearly all goods used in the country and in cities.

CRITICAL VIEWING Because these machines do so many different tasks, they can probably get through the same amount of work with fewer workers and expand the number of acres that could be farmed.

1.3 Roads, Railroads, and Canals

MAIN IDEA Between 1800 and 1850, the United States built the most advanced transportation network in the world.

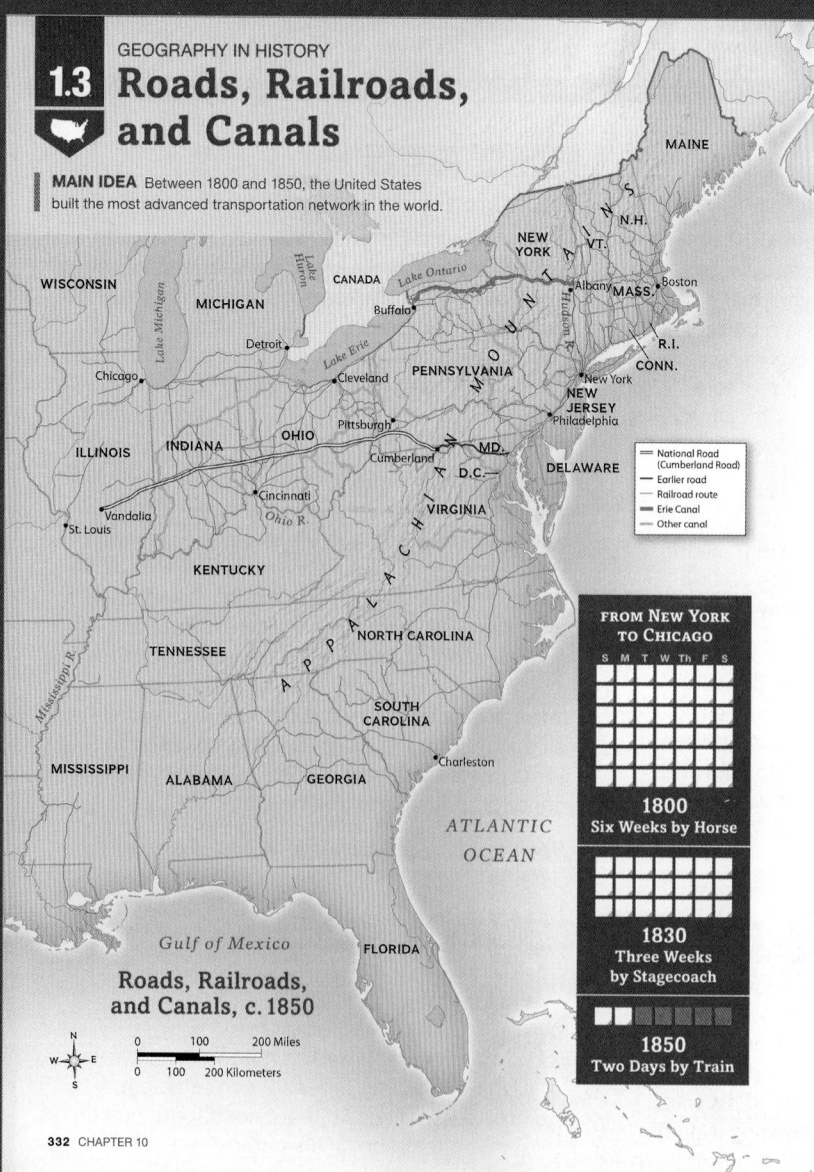

Roads, Railroads, and Canals, c. 1850

FROM NEW YORK TO CHICAGO

1800
Six Weeks by Horse

1830
Three Weeks by Stagecoach

1850
Two Days by Train

Map legend:
- National Road (Cumberland Road)
- Earlier road
- Railroad route
- Erie Canal
- Other canal

OVERCOMING OBSTACLES

In the early 1800s, Americans moving west and south soon realized they needed more efficient ways to move people and goods across the country. But they faced several geographic challenges. One of these was distance. Today, you can fly from New York City to Miami, Florida, in a few hours. However, in 1800, that trip took three uncomfortable weeks by horse-drawn stagecoach. Travelers called stagecoaches "shake guts" because they shook so much as they rumbled over roads filled with holes and tree stumps.

The Appalachian Mountains represented another geographic challenge. This mountain range stretches north to south for more than 1,500 miles from Canada to Alabama and is up to 300 miles wide. Often steep and densely wooded, the Appalachians formed a physical barrier between the interior regions of the United States and thriving eastern ports such as New York City, Boston, Charleston, and Philadelphia. Americans innovated new solutions and overcame geographic challenges to build an enormous transportation network that produced major economic benefits.

TRANSPORTATION INNOVATION	ECONOMIC BENEFITS
THE NATIONAL ROAD	
During the early years of the United States, the roads were terrible. But in 1811, the federal government built the National Road, also known as the Cumberland Road. The road stretched west from Cumberland, Maryland, to Vandalia, Illinois. A good stretch of it had pavement, making for a much smoother ride. The states charged travelers tolls for their carriages and wagons—and even for their cattle!	The National Road moved mail, goods, and settlers between the East and the growing states of the Northwest Territory, including Ohio, Indiana, and Illinois. The federal government, states, and private companies soon built more roads connecting the East, the South, and the West. Trade expanded between the nation's interior and its bustling port cities, from Boston south to Charleston.
THE B&O RAILROAD	
During the 1820s, merchants in Baltimore, Maryland, struggled to compete with the merchants of New York City, who had the benefit of the Erie Canal to move goods. In 1826, a group of enterprising businessmen founded the Baltimore & Ohio (B&O) Railroad. They needed a steam-operated railroad to connect Baltimore to the growing cities of the interior, such as Cincinnati, Ohio, and St. Louis, Missouri. A steam locomotive called the Tom Thumb ran on the earliest line and proved that steam-powered cars could handle the steep, winding route.	The B&O proved an enormous success. Trains transported coal from the mines of western Virginia and Pennsylvania to the factories and furnaces of the East. The success of the B&O encouraged companies to build other railroads linking states and territories of the East, South, and West. By the 1850s, railroads were carrying all kinds of products. They transported Chesapeake Bay oysters, Florida oranges, and Georgia peaches to the restaurants of New York City. By 1860, the United States had 30,500 miles of track, about as much as the rest of the world.
THE ERIE CANAL	
Americans built a system of constructed waterways called canals that allowed boats and ships to travel inland to move goods. The largest of them, the Erie Canal, connected the Hudson River to the Great Lakes. It cut through 363 miles of land in upstate New York and linked New York City to growing cities such as Buffalo, Cleveland, Detroit, and Chicago.	Building the Erie Canal took eight years. But after it was completed, farmers in Ohio, Illinois, Indiana, and other states in the Midwest could ship their grain much more cheaply and quickly to the East. Before the canal, farmers had to pay $100 per wagon to ship their grain. By using the canal, their cost was only $10 per shipment. Instead of 20 days, the journey took just eight.

THINK LIKE A GEOGRAPHER

1. **IDENTIFY MAIN IDEAS AND DETAILS** What were some geographic challenges the young United States faced?

2. **INTERPRET MAPS** Study the map. How did the road, railroad, and canal systems work together as one transportation network?

PLAN

Objective
Analyze and compare advances in U.S. transportation between 1800 and 1850.

Critical Thinking Skills for Lesson 1.3
- Identify Main Ideas and Details
- Monitor Comprehension
- Interpret Maps
- Draw Conclusions
- Form and Support Opinions

Essential Question for Chapter 10
How did new industries and inventions transform the United States economically, socially, and geographically? As the United States expanded, people needed faster and more reliable transportation. Lesson 1.3 outlines how the development of roads, railroads, and canals helped the American economy keep up with the growing nation.

Background for the Teacher
Early railroads were faster than traveling by horseback or stagecoach, but they were not necessarily more comfortable. The first rail cars on lines such as the B&O were patterned on road coaches and often built by the same companies. The early rail cars, set on four wheels, offered a swaying, "galloping" ride. Some featured rooftop seats to relieve overcrowding—exposing riders to the dangers of smoke, weather, and low bridges. Worst of all, the four-wheelers were incredibly dangerous. They were prone to derailment and heated by stoves that would ignite the wooden coaches in an accident. As rail travel grew more popular and longer trips became the norm, rail car designers began to develop safer and more comfortable coaches.

History Notebook
Encourage students to complete the American Gallery page for Chapter 10 in their History Notebooks as they read.

INTRODUCE & ENGAGE

Compare Transportation

As a class, complete a Three-Column Chart with the pros and cons of different forms of transportation. Then prompt students to consider what they have already read about expansion in the early 19th century. **ASK:** What kinds of problems would Americans have faced in moving people and goods? *(a need to travel longer distances; obstacles such as mountains and forests; difficulty moving heavy goods)* Explain that in this lesson, students will learn how American transportation in the 1800s evolved to meet these challenges.

Roads	Railroads	Canals and Waterways
Pros: Cons:	Pros: Cons:	Pros: Cons:

TEACH

Guided Discussion

1. **Draw Conclusions** Based on the map and the text, what cities might have benefited most from the advances in transportation? Why? *(Possible response: Cities such as Cleveland, Detroit, and Buffalo may have benefited most because they were directly accessible by railroad, road, and canal.)*

2. **Form and Support Opinions** Which transportation innovation do you think had the greatest economic impact on the United States in the early 1800s? Support your opinion with evidence from the text, map, and graph. *(Answers will vary but should be supported with clear textual evidence.)*

Geography in History

Interpret Maps Direct students' attention to the map. **ASK:** Which form of transportation seems to cover the most area on this map? *(railroads)* Why do you think that is? *(Students may point to the text, which suggests that railroads' early success made people more likely to build more of them.)* **ASK:** How does the infrastructure—roads, railroads, and canals—vary between the Northeast, South, and West? *(Students should recognize that there are more roads, including the National Road, in the North and that very little infrastructure extends to the West.)*

Active Options

 The American Railroads Invite students to explore the American Gallery. Have them select one of the images and do additional research to learn more about it. Ask questions that will inspire additional inquiry about the chosen gallery image, such as: What is this? Where and when was it created? Who created it? Why does it belong in this chapter? What else would you like to know about it?

NG Learning Framework: Plan a Journey

ATTITUDE Responsibility

SKILLS Problem-Solving, Collaboration

Organize students into small groups and assign each group a set of two to four different cities. Have groups use the map to plan possible routes that someone in the early 1800s might have used to travel from one city to the next. Then ask students to use the chart showing modes of travel to estimate the amount of time each journey would take by horse, stagecoach, and train. Have groups collaborate to create a timetable for each mode of travel. Display the completed timetables in the classroom.

DIFFERENTIATE

Striving Readers

Identify Facts Assign students to pairs and tell them to work together to review the lesson by identifying and listing facts. Finally, invite one student from each pair to share the pair's responses. Write all the facts on the board.

Gifted & Talented

Write a Travel Blog Have students write a travel-blog entry in the voice of a person from the mid-1800s traveling across the United States. Explain that students' blog entries should describe the experience of traveling in one or more forms of transportation discussed in this lesson. Have students research to learn more about these forms of transportation and about the cities through which a 19th-century traveler would pass. Tell students their entry should explain where the traveler is going, why, and what he or she sees and experiences while passing through different regions of the country.

See the Chapter Planner for more strategies for differentiation.

THINK LIKE A GEOGRAPHER

ANSWERS

1. Some geographic challenges included large distances and mountain ranges—specifically the Appalachian Mountains—that were steep and covered by forests in many places.

2. Answers will vary. Possible response: Roads, railroads, and canals intersected at many points, so people or goods could change modes of transportation and direction to reach their destinations. Carts might carry raw materials to a canal where boats would carry them to a railroad that might carry the raw materials to a factory in the East. Manufactured goods could be loaded and moved to the West. A wagon could carry the manufactured goods, such as machinery, to a farm or store.

1.4 The Mississippi River

CRITICAL VIEWING Steamboats have been chugging down the Mississippi River since the early 1800s, transforming how people and goods moved across the United States. Examine the front of the first steamboat (left) and the rear of the second steamboat (right). What can you infer about how these boats move through the water?

The mighty Mississippi is the largest river in North America and one of the largest in the world. It lies entirely within the United States and flows south from Minnesota, collecting water from the Ohio and Missouri rivers and spilling from Louisiana into the Gulf of Mexico. As one of the world's busiest commercial waterways, the river is the lifeblood of a highly industrialized country. It snakes through some of the nation's most fertile farmland and moves most of our agricultural exports. The unique role the Mississippi has played in American history and literature has woven it deeply into the fabric of the country's folklore. As American author Mark Twain once said, "The Mississippi River will always have its own way; no engineering skill can persuade it to do otherwise." How might a geologic feature like a river serve as a "character" in a book?

334 CHAPTER 10

Expansion and Growth 335

Objective

Discover the historical and cultural importance of the Mississippi River.

Critical Thinking Skills for Lesson 1.4

- Analyze Visuals
- Make Connections
- Analyze Cause and Effect
- Make Inferences

Essential Question for Chapter 10

How did new industries and inventions transform the United States economically, socially, and geographically? Innovations in transportation made the Mississippi River a critical part of American agriculture, trade, and travel. In Lesson 1.4, students learn about the impact the river has had on the American imagination.

Background for the Teacher

Inventors had been experimenting with steamboats since the late 1700s. By 1811, steamboats were operating on the lower Mississippi River, traveling all the way to New Orleans. The basic design of the boats changed over time to navigate the shallow waters of the Mississippi so that the boats did not ride so low in the water. These boats carried loads of sugar and cotton. They also carried passengers in luxurious surroundings that mimicked fancy hotels. Some featured orchestras on board. The heyday of steamboats declined in the latter part of the 1800s as railroads proved a more efficient mode of transportation.

History Notebook

Encourage students to complete the American Places page for Chapter 10 in their History Notebooks as they read.

INTRODUCE & ENGAGE

Preview with the Photograph

Have students examine the photograph of the Mississippi River. Ask students to explain their initial impressions of the river in a few words, based on what they see. Record their impressions on the board in an Idea Web. After students have completed the lesson, return as a class to the Idea Web and update it to include any new ideas students have.

TEACH

Guided Discussion

1. **Analyze Cause and Effect** The Mississippi River and its tributaries affected the growth and development of many states, communities, and regions in the early United States. What kinds of conflict might result from people's dependence on the river? (*Students may suggest possible conflicts over access to the river, use of its water, crowding and pollution, and competing business interests.*)

2. **Make Inferences** Based on the lesson text and the photograph, why might steamboat travel still occur on the Mississippi River, despite the existence of more modern boats? (*Possible response: The text suggests that the Mississippi River plays an important role in American history and literature; people might enjoy reliving that history or those books. People might see it as a romantic or picturesque way of traveling.*)

📍 American Places

Depending upon when and how it is measured, the Mississippi River runs for at least 2,340 miles through the continental United States. It is both an impressive force of nature and a marvel of human engineering, with dams and levees holding back its floodwaters and shaping its course. The Mississippi serves many diverse purposes—and creatures. The river and its surroundings are home to about a quarter of all North American fish species and at least 200 species of mammals, amphibians, and reptiles. At least 50 cities use the Mississippi River as a water source. Share this information with students and use it as a springboard for a discussion of how water rights might be fairly apportioned for different communities and uses.

Active Options

On Your Feet: Turn and Talk Have students form small groups. Give each group this topic sentence: *A river could serve as a character in a book.* Tell groups to build a paragraph on that topic by having each member contribute one sentence. Suggest that students first discuss how an actual river might play an important role in a story by flooding, providing a fishing place, or offering a transportation avenue. Suggest they consider how a river might seem to take on human qualities, moods, or motivations. Allow each group to present its paragraph to the class.

NG Learning Framework: Create a Presentation About Mark Twain

ATTITUDE Curiosity

KNOWLEDGE Our Human Story

Instruct students to use outside source material to prepare a short presentation on Mark Twain's life and work. For example, students might read excerpts from Twain's *Life on the Mississippi*. Presentations should include details about Twain's experiences on and connections to the Mississippi River and how he drew on his experiences as he created literary works that reflect daily life on the river. Encourage students to use a variety of media in their presentations. Invite students to share their presentations with the class or record them on video and post them to a class blog.

DIFFERENTIATE

English Language Learners ELD

Identify Visual Features Pair students at the **Emerging** level with students at the **Bridging** level or with English-proficient students. Ask pairs to identify the features mentioned in the Critical Viewing question (the front and rear of the boats, the wheel on the right-hand steamboat). Then have them work together to answer the Critical Viewing question.

Pre-AP

Explore Artistic Depictions Have students use the Internet and other resources to research depictions of the Mississippi River in painting, literature, music, theater, or film. Tell students to select three depictions and prepare a report or presentation explaining the artist or artists behind the works, the role the river plays in them, and the eras in which they were created. Encourage students to make connections or highlight contrasts among the depictions they select and research.

See the Chapter Planner for more strategies for differentiation.

AMERICAN PLACES

Answers will vary. Students might mention that because the river plays such a large role in the economies and communities around it, the river can affect events as much or more than any human character. Students may also note that the river has characteristics that change from day to day, much like a human character, and it may seem to be acting intentionally.

CRITICAL VIEWING The image suggests that large, rear-mounted wheels with paddles attached to them rotate, pushing water past the boats and moving the boats forward. The smokestacks on the front of one of the boats suggest that the wheels are powered by steam.

2.1 The Henry Ford Museum Dearborn, Michigan

One of the world's wealthiest and most influential innovators, Henry Ford grew up on a farm and never lost his ties to rural life. He became a collector of objects from ordinary people and examples of industrial progress and opened a museum in 1929 to share them with the public. The Henry Ford Museum's mission is to provide unique educational experiences based on authentic objects, stories, and lives that represent America's ingenuity, resourcefulness, and innovation. Its impressive collection of American artifacts includes many items related to the cotton industry. How do the artifacts below reflect the cotton production process?

Spinning Wheel
Spinning fibers into yarn that was then woven into cloth was an important task in many households in the 1600s and 1700s. Young or unmarried women often became experts at this tedious and physically tiring task. This large spinning wheel would have required its spinner to alternate between spinning fibers into yarn and winding the yarn onto the spindle.

Fluffy raw wool or cotton fibers were spun into fine yarn used to make clothing.

One bale of cotton can make 1,217 men's T-shirts or 313,600 $100 bills.

Cotton Blossom
Cotton grows on shrubs in 17 states across the southern half of the country. Cotton plants first produce blossoms, which change from white to pink and fall off after a few days. In their place grow small green pods called bolls. Cotton seeds and their attached hairs develop within the bolls, which swell and grow. When the boll is ripe, it bursts into the white, fluffy balls shown here. The seed hair has turned into the fibers used to make cloth and thread.

"Ford's perspective on history was informed by a strong belief in **the power of learning by doing.**"
—Marc Greuther, Chief Curator, The Henry Ford Museum

Once the cotton gin made cotton easier to process, cotton became the primary crop in the American South.

Cotton Gin
Invented by Eli Whitney in 1793, the cotton gin machine revolutionized the process of cleaning seeds out of cotton. Whitney was visiting a friend in the South when he heard about how farmers struggled to efficiently process their cotton crops. He quickly solved their problem with a device that pulled the cotton through a set of wire teeth mounted on a spinning cylinder. The cotton fibers could fit through narrow slots in the machine, but the seeds couldn't.

Why would advertising thread have been so common during the 1800s?

Cotton Thread Trade Cards
Without cotton, there is no thread, and without thread, there is no clothing! The cotton industry remained strong throughout American history, as demonstrated by these trade cards for "spool cotton" or thread, which date to the late 1800s. Advertisers appealed to customers with colorful ads promoting consumer goods such as thread.

PLAN

Objective
Identify artifacts related to cotton production in the 1800s.

Critical Thinking Skills for Lesson 2.1
• Make Connections
• Analyze Visuals
• Describe
• Draw Conclusions

Essential Question for Chapter 10
How did new industries and inventions transform the United States economically, socially, and geographically? The growth of the textile industry transformed some northeastern states into manufacturing centers and transformed some southern states into cotton producers. In Lesson 2.1, students will explore several objects and their connections to the cotton industry.

Background for the Teacher

In the 1920s, Henry Ford began to turn his personal collection of objects into an official museum. The Henry Ford Museum in Dearborn, Michigan, is a vast complex that includes a 12-acre indoor museum and an operational Ford truck plant. It also includes Greenfield Village, an 80-acre open-air museum consisting of painstakingly preserved and restored buildings from throughout U.S. history. Ford began this project with his own childhood home, which he rescued from demolition in 1919 and worked to restore. By 1928, he had plans to build an entire village, complete with schools, homes, and fully functioning manufacturing buildings. Today, the village boasts 83 buildings, including a re-creation of Thomas Edison's Menlo Park laboratory.

History Notebook
Encourage students to complete the Curating History page for Chapter 10 in their History Notebooks as they read.

Compare Advertisements

Ask students to name common products in ads. *(Possible responses: cleaning supplies, kitchen gadgets, personal care products)* Then ask students to describe techniques advertisers use. *(Possible response: Advertisers compare their products with a competitor's or suggest their product will make you look or feel better.)* Point out the larger trade card. **ASK:** What conclusions can you draw from this ad? *(Answers will vary. Possible response: Thread was a common household item. The ad shows rival spools tipping over, suggesting that those brands of thread might jam machines.)*

TEACH

Guided Discussion

1. **Describe** How did the cotton gin make cotton processing more efficient? *(The machine pulled the cotton through narrow slots that caught the seeds, quickly separating the unnecessary seeds from the useful fiber. Instead of pulling out seeds slowly by hand, a person only needed to turn the crank.)*

2. **Draw Conclusions** Based on the information in the images and captions, which machine was used first during the production process: the cotton gin or the spinning wheel? Explain why. *(The cotton gin would have been used first to clean the cotton fibers that would later be spun into yarn on the spinning wheel.)*

🏛 Curating History

The Henry Ford Museum's full collections consist of more than 250,000 objects and artifacts and millions of documents and images. Many of these are now accessible through the museum's digital collections. Using the museum's digital collection website, demonstrate how to locate the cotton gin shown in Lesson 2.1. Then have students select another object from the category "cotton industry." As a class, read the object's caption and discuss how it relates to the other objects in the lesson. Finally, have students explore the website and choose items to create their own collections of four or five artifacts. Have students present their collections to the class, explaining the significance of each item and connecting it to what they have read about the Industrial Revolution.

Active Options

On Your Feet: Sort the Artifacts Have students work in teams of four to examine the Henry Ford Museum's digital collections that are related to the Industrial Revolution. Then have them complete two Concept Clusters like those shown below. In one cluster, students should identify tools, machines, and other objects related to the production of cotton. In the second cluster, students should identify a different class or genre of artifacts, to be selected by the team. When teams are finished, have them share their Concept Clusters with the class.

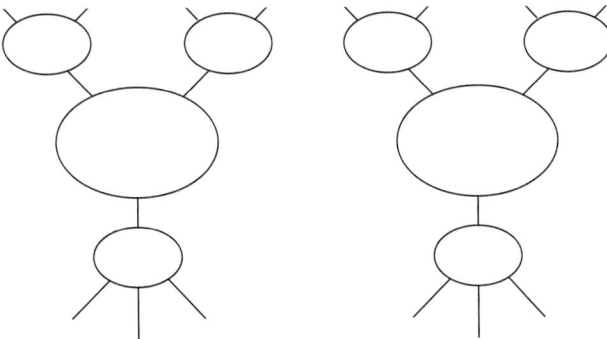

Striving Readers

Complete Sentence Starters Monitor students' comprehension by having them complete the following sentence starters.

- Cotton grows in 17 states across _____. *(the southern half of the country)*

- The cotton gin revolutionized _____. *(the process of cleaning seeds out of cotton)*

- Cotton fibers were made into yarn using _____. *(a spinning wheel)*

- Cotton yarn and thread were then used to make _____. *(cloth; clothing)*

Inclusion

Describe Lesson Visuals Students with visual impairments may have difficulty understanding the images of artifacts in this lesson. Pair these students with others who are not visually challenged. Ask the latter to describe the parts of the different machines and help their partners understand how each one works to process cotton at different stages. Ask them also to help their partners understand the images and messages on the cotton thread trade cards.

See the Chapter Planner for more strategies for differentiation.

CURATING HISTORY

Possible response: The artifacts represent cotton production at each stage of the process: the raw material (cotton plant), the cleaning of seeds from cotton fibers (cotton gin), the creation of yarn or thread (spinning wheel), and the sale of thread (advertising cards).

COTTON THREAD TRADE CARDS

Possible response: Thread advertisements may have been common during the 1800s because many people made their own clothing and other items. As a result, people would have needed to purchase thread on a regular basis.

2.2 Growth of the Cotton Industry

Today, economies all over the world are connected to each other in visible and sometimes not-so-visible ways. The same was true for two seemingly very different parts of the United States—the South and the North—in the 19th century.

MAIN IDEA A new invention enabled southern plantation owners to grow more crops and increase profits.

THE COTTON BOOM

The South differed from the North in several ways. For example, the South relied more on an agrarian economy, while the North was rapidly becoming a major industrial center. But one invention brought the two regions closer together.

In 1793, Eli Whitney visited a southern plantation and observed that the system used to remove seeds from picked cotton was slow and labor intensive. To solve this problem, he designed the **cotton gin**, which, as you have read, is a machine fitted with teeth to grab the seeds and separate them from cotton tufts. The cotton gin increased the productivity of enslaved laborers,

and cotton became the main cash crop on many southern farms that had previously grown tobacco. Most southern farmers embraced cotton because years of tobacco cultivation had depleted the soil of the nutrients needed for growing healthy tobacco plants.

Because of more efficient cotton production in the early 19th century, cotton quickly became a central part of the U.S. economy. Both the South and the North relied on this crop. Slave labor produced the cotton and raw materials that enabled northern manufacturers, financiers, and other business interests to thrive. This, in turn, spurred a new consumer culture in individual families connected to the slave-based economy.

CRITICAL VIEWING *Plantation Economy*, by William Aiken Walker, c. 1881, depicts enslaved people working in a southern cotton field. What does the painting convey about the process of cotton production?

The Slave Dwelling Project
In 2010, Joseph McGill began a series of overnight stays in houses once occupied by slaves. His experiences resulted in the Slave Dwelling Project. Its mission is to preserve the places where enslaved people lived. By 2016, he had visited slave dwellings in 17 states. McGill invites others to visit and sleep in these dwellings. The dwelling featured here is located at Magnolia Plantation in South Carolina.

SLAVERY EXPANDS

Even with the advent of the cotton gin, growing and picking cotton was labor intensive, and the production of cotton relied on the labor system created to support it: slavery. The "peculiar institution" of slavery shaped the South's political, social, economic, and cultural development.

Southern plantation owners who wanted to maximize their profits from cotton production tried to do so by acquiring more land. As you have read, in the early 19th century, the federal government intentionally seized Native American lands. So when some southern landowners and farmers did the same in order to expand their farmlands, they did so with the blessing of the federal government. This land grab forced tribes to leave the Southeast and move to relocation areas in the West. Many Native Americans were permanently displaced from their homes.

Southern plantation owners also tried to maximize profits by increasing their enslaved workforces. In January 1807, Congress passed a new law that would "prohibit the importation of slaves into any port or place within the jurisdiction of the United States … from any foreign kingdom, place, or

country." However, the slave importation clause that had been inserted into the Constitution 20 years prior prevented this new law from taking effect until January 1808. Once enacted, the ban caused the **interstate slave trade**, or the slave trade *within* the United States, to increase. Slave owners urged enslaved women to have more children. They then sold some slaves at slave auctions to make a profit and bought others to staff their plantations with specially skilled enslaved workers. Slave auctions separated families. Enslaved communities responded to forced separations by broadening kinship bonds, which meant considering non-blood-related fellow slaves as family members.

HISTORICAL THINKING

1. **READING CHECK** What impact did the cotton gin have on cotton production?

2. **DRAW CONCLUSIONS** How did the interstate slave trade affect enslaved communities?

3. **EVALUATE** In what ways did the institution of slavery shape the economic development of both the South and the North?

PLAN

Objective

Trace the effects of the expanding cotton industry on the North and South.

Critical Thinking Skills for Lesson 2.2

- Identify Main Ideas and Details
- Monitor Comprehension
- Draw Conclusions
- Evaluate
- Make Inferences
- Analyze Cause and Effect

Essential Question for Chapter 10

How did new industries and inventions transform the United States economically, socially, and geographically? The invention of the cotton gin led to the growth of the cotton industry. Lesson 2.2 analyzes the changes that followed, including the expansion of slavery.

Background for the Teacher

Eli Whitney expected his cotton gin to make him rich. He patented his invention, which gave him exclusive rights to the technology for 14 years and, presumably, to the profits. Unfortunately, planters pirated his technology and learned to make their own versions of the cotton gin. Within a few years, Whitney and his business partner, Phineas Miller, were out of business. After years of failed lawsuits, Whitney and Miller ended up earning only about $90,000 in license fees. Whitney wasn't completely out of luck, though; a few years later, his invention of a musket made from interchangeable parts put him on the path to fortune.

Consider Consequences

As a class, discuss what might happen when large industries, such as the auto industry, experience a sudden change. Work with students to map out on the board a chain of events that might follow when a new technology makes a business more efficient. Guide students to consider such issues as profitability, workers, consumer prices, and so on. Explain that in this lesson, students will explore some of the consequences—intended and unintended—of new developments in the cotton industry during the early 1800s.

TEACH

Guided Discussion

1. **Make Inferences** How did developments in cotton production lead to a consumer culture in both the North and the South? *(The growth of the cotton industry led to more profits in the South, for plantation owners, and in the North, for manufacturers and workers. With more money to spend, people could afford more consumer goods.)*

2. **Analyze Cause and Effect** In what way did the ban on the importation of slaves have the opposite effect from the one Congress intended? *(The ban on importing slaves from abroad was meant to limit slavery and the slave trade. However, slave owners and traders got around this by increasing the domestic, or interstate, trade in enslaved people.)*

Draw Conclusions

Display a map of the United States showing states and boundaries as they were in the early 1800s. As a class, identify the rough boundaries between the North and the South. **ASK:** Based on what you have read, which states do you think produced cotton during the 1800s? *(Students should identify southern states, such as Georgia, North Carolina, South Carolina, Mississippi, Tennessee, Virginia, Louisiana, Alabama, and Florida.)* Can you think of geographic reasons that helped the South become an agricultural region while the North did not? *(The South's warmer climate made it better suited to farming.)* Start a class discussion on the possible effects of a country having two regions with very different economies.

Active Options

On Your Feet: Word Chain Have students form three lines. Hand a piece of paper to the first person in each line with one of these words or terms from the text: *cotton gin*, *landowners*, and *interstate slave trade*. The first student in line adds a word to the list that relates to the original word or term. Students pass the paper from person to person, each adding a word or phrase they associate with the previously written word. Have a volunteer from each group read the Word Chain aloud. Ask the rest of the class to listen for words that are used in more than one chain or that may not connect correctly.

NG Learning Framework: Learn More About Slave Dwellings

ATTITUDE Responsibility

KNOWLEDGE Our Human Story

Divide the class into small groups and invite the groups to learn more about Joseph McGill's Slave Dwelling Project. Suggest students use additional Internet or library resources to research the towns, plantations, and other locations McGill and his groups have visited. Have students use the Slave Dwelling Project as a springboard to explore differences in the lives of free and enslaved African Americans, plantation owners, and other white southerners. Encourage students to use the information they find—particularly photographs, paintings, or first-person accounts—to describe the lives of people living and working in these places. Ask each group to prepare a short summary of one of McGill's overnight stays and share it with the class.

English Language Learners

Make Vocabulary Cards Have students at **All Proficiencies** make flash cards with unfamiliar words and terms they encounter in the lesson. One side should have the word or term and its pronunciation, and the other side should have the definition, drawings, words, or hints that help students memorize and understand the meaning. Encourage the use of the flash cards for review.

Pre-AP

Explore the Modern Cotton Industry Provide students with these questions to guide a research project on the modern cotton industry: Where is most cotton grown? Why? What modern products and industries depend on cotton? What are labor conditions like? How does the industry use new technologies? Have students prepare a short oral report on their findings to present to the class. Encourage students to explain one or two ways in which the industry has or has not changed over time.

See the Chapter Planner for more strategies for differentiation.

HISTORICAL THINKING

ANSWERS

1. The cotton gin removed seeds quickly and efficiently, making cotton production more profitable. Plantation owners seized Native American lands to grow more cotton and acquired more enslaved workers to pick it, thereby expanding slavery.

2. The interstate slave trade separated families with the buying and selling of family members for profit. As a result, strong "kinship bonds" developed among enslaved people who were not blood relatives.

3. In the South, cheap enslaved labor made plantations profitable. Wealthy landowners acquired more land and more enslaved labor and produced more cotton. The North used cotton and other raw materials from the South in its manufacturing centers.

CRITICAL VIEWING Answers will vary. Students may say the painting shows that labor was done entirely by enslaved people and largely by hand. Some students may feel that the painting shows a peaceful scene that romanticizes the idea of the plantation and its enslaved laborers.

2.3 Slavery and Resistance

When one group of people oppresses another, the oppressed group eventually revolts. During the 19th century, enslaved communities and individuals alike rose up.

MAIN IDEA People trapped in the institution of slavery created a culture of survival, resistance, and, ultimately, rebellion.

THE SOCIETAL IMPACT OF SLAVERY

The institution of slavery affected all parts of southern society: wealthy or poor, slave or free, white or black. Plantation owners greatly advanced their wealth through slavery. Even though the majority of southern white farmers workers did not own slaves, they supported the practice of slavery. In the **antebellum**, or prewar, South, the poorest whites held higher status than any African Americans.

During the early 19th century, more than 100,000 free African Americans lived in the South, and they most certainly did not support slavery. Though they were free, they could not vote, own property, or receive an education. Legally, their status was constantly in question. Traveling was dangerous because they ran the risk of being accused of being runaway slaves and losing their freedom. In order to prove their free status, free African Americans had to go to court for Certificates of Freedom. Even then, some were kidnapped and sold into slavery.

The greatest impact of slavery, of course, was on enslaved people themselves. Slaves were considered chattel, or property, of their owners and were denied rights, freedom, and sometimes even their lives. Slave owners held a particularly ominous form of power over slaves with the constant possibility of family separation. Just the threat of sale allowed slave owners to exercise enormous control over their slaves. Enslaved parents routinely saw their children sold away from them. Spouses and siblings were separated, and they knew that future contact would be nearly impossible.

Shackles

Tax badge

🏛 Chicago History Museum, Chicago

The system of slavery relied on preventing escapes. Slave owners placed shackles like these on enslaved people's wrists or ankles. The cuffs were held closed by a screw. In Charleston, South Carolina, enslaved workers who were hired out by their owners had to wear tax badges engraved with tax registration numbers and job categories.

SURVIVAL AND RESISTANCE

Despite the horrific conditions under which they lived, enslaved people resisted the circumstances they faced every day. Many slave owners imposed their own religious beliefs on slaves because they suggested that a belief in Christianity would make slavery an acceptable situation. But enslaved people interpreted scripture for themselves, in ways that encouraged a quest for freedom. They also composed songs called **spirituals** based on scripture and biblical figures such as Moses, who led the Israelites out of slavery in Egypt.

In addition to their own religious practices, enslaved people developed a distinct African-American culture. They retained and adapted traditional customs including music, food, and dancing, as well as varied family structures. They created rich communities bound together by common experiences and shared traditions. In this way, enslaved people asserted their humanity, which could not be taken away by slave owners.

Passive resistance, or the nonviolent refusal to obey authority and laws, was another way enslaved people resisted slavery. Forms of passive resistance included breaking tools, working slowly, pretending to be ill, and learning to read.

Sometimes, though, resistance meant armed rebellion. Inspired by a slave uprising in Haiti, in 1800, a slave named **Gabriel Prosser**, who bore the last name of his cruel owner, Thomas Prosser, planned a revolt in Virginia. In 1822, a freed slave named **Denmark Vesey** used scripture to inspire others to take over arsenals and burn down buildings in Charleston, South Carolina. Most revolts, including these, were put down quickly before whites were killed, and they resulted in the deaths of the enslaved people who had planned the rebellions.

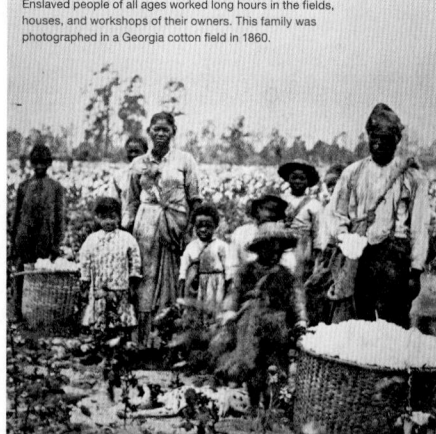

Enslaved people of all ages worked long hours in the fields, houses, and workshops of their owners. This family was photographed in a Georgia cotton field in 1860.

But in 1831, **Nat Turner** led a small group of fellow slaves in a violent rebellion in which more than 50 people were killed in one night. Turner and his men were captured and hanged. Southerners reacted to Turner's rebellion—as they had to others—with violence. Some took matters into their own hands and murdered hundreds of innocent slaves.

Like Gabriel Prosser and Denmark Vesey, Turner was a literate man who led an open, violent revolt against slave-owning whites. Southern authorities reacted to Turner's revolt forcefully and by instituting severe restrictions, including a ban on teaching slaves to read and write.

HISTORICAL THINKING

1. **READING CHECK** In what ways did enslaved people resist slavery?

2. **DRAW CONCLUSIONS** Why did free African Americans need Certificates of Freedom?

3. **MAKE CONNECTIONS** Why was literacy for slaves a threat to slave owners?

PLAN

Objective

Learn how enslaved people resisted the institution and the experience of slavery.

Critical Thinking Skills for Lesson 2.3

- Identify Main Ideas and Details
- Monitor Comprehension
- Draw Conclusions
- Make Connections
- Compare and Contrast
- Evaluate

Essential Question for Chapter 10

How did new industries and inventions transform the United States economically, socially, and geographically? The growth of the cotton industry led to slavery becoming entrenched in the South. In Lesson 2.3, students will read about ways in which enslaved African Americans coped with and resisted oppression.

Background for the Teacher

Denmark Vesey was born into slavery but purchased his freedom in 1800 with $600 he won in a street lottery. A self-educated man, Vesey read antislavery material and had closely followed the controversy about whether to admit Missouri as a slave state. As a free man, Vesey was dissatisfied with his limited rights. In 1822, he organized a plan to seize Charlestown, South Carolina, possibly with as many as 9,000 people. He believed that the defiant slaves would kill their owners, and he and his rebels would all sail to Haiti, where slavery was illegal. Had he succeeded, it would have been the largest slave revolt in U.S. history. However, authorities learned of the plot and suppressed it. Many African Americans, including Vesey, were hanged; others were exiled.

Define Resistance

Have students discuss the meaning of the term *resistance*. Begin by adding the word to the center of a Word Map. **ASK:** What does the word *resistance* mean to you? *(Answers will vary. Possible responses: fighting, refusing)* Work with students to list examples of resistance from history, current news, or students' experiences. **ASK:** What are some concepts or events that you associate with the word *resistance*? *(Answers will vary. Possible responses: protests, sabotage, resistance fighters)* Add to the map as discussion continues. Revisit the map after the lesson to add new meanings or associations.

TEACH

Guided Discussion

1. **Compare and Contrast** Compare the political and economic opportunities of free African Americans with those of southern whites. Did freedom from slavery necessarily mean equality? Why or why not? *(Compared with southern whites, even the poorest ones, free African Americans had very few rights and did not experience equality. They could not vote, own property, or get an education. They were also in constant danger of being kidnapped and taken into slavery despite their free status.)*

2. **Evaluate** In what ways did enslaved people use Christianity and African-American culture as forms of resistance? *(Possible response: Both helped strengthen African-American communities in the face of constant family separation and dehumanization.)*

🏛 Virtual Museum Visit

The Chicago History Museum is an institution that has risen from the ashes—literally. Originally known as the Chicago Historical Society, it lost its original building and most of the original collections to the Great Chicago Fire of 1871. The society rebuilt and continued to grow its collections of artifacts, documents, art, and photographs. These collections now span Chicago's vibrant literary, artistic, political, cultural, and commercial history. In 2006, the Chicago Historical Society became the Chicago History Museum. Encourage students to visit the museum's website, where they can view many of the museum's 22 million artifacts, including the shackles shown in this lesson.

Active Options

On Your Feet: Question and Answer Tell half the class to write True-False statements about the impacts of slavery and the resistance efforts used by enslaved and free African Americans. Ask the other half to create response cards with "True" written on one side and "False" on the other. Then ask the students who wrote statements to read them aloud. Students in the second group should respond by holding up either "True" or "False." When discrepancies occur, review the statement and text and discuss which response is correct.

NG Learning Framework: Compare African-American Experiences

ATTITUDE Curiosity

KNOWLEDGE Our Human Story

Have students work in small groups to research the experiences of free African Americans in the North and free African Americans in the South. Tell students to consider questions such as: How did African-American experiences of freedom in the North differ from those in the South? How were they similar? How did the opportunities of free African Americans in the North differ from those in the South? Have groups use their research to prepare a short oral report to present to the class.

DIFFERENTIATE

Striving Readers

Use Exit Slips Preview the following questions before reading the lesson:

- What rights did free African Americans lack in the antebellum South?
- What roles did religion and culture play in the lives of enslaved African Americans?
- What is passive resistance?
- What happened to people who planned violent uprisings against slavery?

After students have read the lesson, direct them to return to the questions and provide brief written responses to each on strips of paper and hand in the strips as they exit the class.

Gifted & Talented

Create a Multimedia Presentation Have students use the Internet and other resources to research and create a multimedia presentation on African-American spirituals. Students might analyze the role spirituals played during the antebellum period, after the abolition of slavery, or in the civil rights movements of the 1960s. Encourage students to incorporate recordings or videos of spirituals into their presentations.

See the Chapter Planner for more strategies for differentiation.

HISTORICAL THINKING

ANSWERS

1. Enslaved people resisted slavery by teaching religious beliefs promoting freedom, forming communities with their own cultures, passively refusing to obey authority, and planning armed rebellions.

2. Free African Americans had to prove they were not runaway slaves to protect themselves from being arrested. Many were kidnapped and sold into slavery anyway.

3. Slave owners feared educated enslaved people might not accept their owners' authority. For example, enslaved people might begin to read antislavery literature—or write it themselves—and be more encouraged to rebel.

3.1 A Young Nation Expands

Being part of a strong family or a successful organization makes members proud to belong to that group. The same kind of pride developed in the early 1800s among Americans witnessing the massive changes in transportation and commerce in the United States.

MAIN IDEA Americans developed a strong national identity during the administrations of presidents James Madison and James Monroe.

TRANSPORTATION AND COMMERCE

The market revolution changed how people worked, traveled, and did business. Eventually, it also encouraged a new philosophy of **nationalism**. Nationalism is the concept of loyalty and devotion to one's nation.

Congressmen **Henry Clay** and **John C. Calhoun** argued for tariffs, or taxes on imported goods, to promote American manufacturing and stimulate commerce. In 1816, Calhoun was instrumental in establishing the Second Bank of the United States. Clay and Calhoun also supported government **subsidies**, or government funds for improvements or support of commerce. Land subsidies, or land granted to private companies by the federal government, became an important part of building roads and railroads. Clay, Calhoun, and others engaged in heated debates with other legislators who favored a more limited federal government role in financing a national infrastructure. Ultimately, tariffs on import goods, the establishment of the National Bank, and government subsidies became known as the **American System**.

Under the American System, improvements in road systems, trains, and waterways united the country geographically and culturally. In 1817, construction began on the **Erie Canal**, which stretched from Buffalo near Lake Erie in western New York to Albany. The Hudson River connected Albany to New York City. When the canal was completed eight years later, farmers could ship their crops within the state and to international destinations through the port at New York City. The canal also encouraged the development of more industrial sites because improved transportation made it easier to move goods to markets.

The **Illinois and Michigan Canal**, completed in 1848, connected Lake Michigan to the Illinois and Mississippi rivers near the city of Chicago. After the construction of these canals, crops and manufactured goods could be shipped all the way from New York City to New Orleans on a water route. The canals also made it easier for people to move their families and belongings west.

NEW BOUNDARIES, NEW DECISIONS

At the same time, the nation was growing in size. General Andrew Jackson became a hero with his successful military campaigns in the War of 1812, including victory in the Battle of New Orleans. His reputation grew when he subdued Native Americans in the Southeast and wrested Florida from Spanish control. Under the terms of the Transcontinental Treaty of 1819, the United States formally received Florida from Spain and gave Spain sovereignty over Texas.

The years that followed the War of 1812 were fairly peaceful and smooth. Territorial conflicts with other nations were temporarily settled, and the economy was growing. The administration of **James Monroe**, who was elected president of the United States in 1816, is remembered as the **Era of Good Feelings**. When Monroe ran for re-election in 1820, the Federalist Party didn't even offer a candidate to oppose him. By 1820, the Federalist Party was no longer a national force.

The Erie Canal, Then and Now
Cranes powered by horses lifted buckets of rock from the canal bed, swung them around, and dumped the rocks at the top of the canal bank. George Catlin's 1825 lithograph, *Process of Excavation, Lockport*, illustrates the ingenuity of this process. The original canal had 83 locks. The photograph at right is a present-day aerial view of the Erie Canal and two of the 35 modern locks positioned on the canal.

During this period, important Supreme Court rulings strengthened the federal government's power. In 1819, the Court affirmed the constitutionality of the Second Bank of the United States in the *McCulloch* v. *Maryland* decision. According to the Necessary and Proper Clause in the Constitution, Congress has **implied powers**, or powers not explicitly stated in the Constitution. In short, because a National Bank had previously been established, Congress could establish the Second Bank of the United States. Additionally, the state of Maryland did not have the power to tax that national bank.

In 1824, the case of *Gibbons* v. *Ogden* expanded federal control over interstate commerce, or business affairs between states. Aaron Ogden, who owned steamboats that traveled on the Hudson River, sued Thomas Gibbons for running steamboat operations in the same waters. Gibbons argued that Congress alone had the power to regulate interstate commerce, and that New York had been wrong to grant Ogden the sole right to running his steamboats in the waterway in the first place. The Court ruled in favor of Gibbons to prevent the formation of a **monopoly**, or complete control of an industry by one company. More importantly, the decision solidified the federal government's power to regulate interstate commerce by eliminating the individual states' sole control over it.

HISTORICAL THINKING

1. **READING CHECK** Why did nationalism grow stronger during the administrations of Madison and Monroe?

2. **DRAW CONCLUSIONS** What parts of the American System are still in effect today?

3. **SUMMARIZE** Why is Monroe's presidency remembered as the Era of Good Feelings?

Objective
Analyze how the federal government promoted economic growth and national identity.

Critical Thinking Skills for Lesson 3.1
- Identify Main Ideas and Details
- Monitor Comprehension
- Draw Conclusions
- Summarize
- Make Inferences
- Analyze Cause and Effect

Essential Question for Chapter 10
How did new industries and inventions transform the United States economically, socially, and geographically? New growth and new ideas brought the nation together. Lesson 3.1 discusses how the federal government helped to develop a capitalist economic system.

Background for the Teacher
In the early 1800s, a number of Supreme Court decisions supported capitalistic ventures and upheld the sanctity of contracts. The *Gibbons* v. *Ogden* decision supported the growth of new competing businesses by preventing monopolies. The *McCulloch* v. *Maryland* decision solidified the federal government's sole control over interstate commerce. In *Dartmouth College* v. *Woodward*, the Court ruled that private contracts and charters were protected under the U.S. Constitution.

Financial Literacy
To extend their knowledge and understanding about the concepts in this lesson, refer students to the Financial Literacy handbook.

History Notebook
Encourage students to complete the Reid on the Road video series page for Chapter 10 in their History Notebooks after they view the video.

INTRODUCE & ENGAGE

Preview Using Visuals

Have students view the illustration and read the caption. **ASK:** What do you notice about this illustration? *(Answers will vary. Students may point out the large scale of the project, the horse-powered cranes, or the enormous rock piles.)* Have students list elements needed for such a project, such as workers, raw materials, and machinery. Explain that this lesson discusses ways the early United States supported massive projects like this one.

TEACH

Guided Discussion

1. **Make Inferences** How might improvements in roads, railways, and canals unite the country culturally? *(Answers will vary. Possible response: With better, faster transportation, people could move and travel to different regions more easily, bringing their cultural ideas with them.)*

2. **Analyze Cause and Effect** Why would the idea of implied powers result in a strengthening of the federal government? *(Answers will vary. Possible response: With implied powers, the government might go beyond the specific powers given to it in the Constitution and take on extra powers to do work it considered necessary.)*

More Information

Folk Music and Canal Culture Explain that traveling along the Erie Canal and other waterways on a boat pulled by mules was slow going. Canal boat workers and passengers sometimes whiled away the hours making up folk songs about life on the canals. As with many folk songs, the tunes or lyrics changed over time and as people carried the song from one canal system to another. The most well-known canal song today is "Low Bridge, Everybody Down" (sometimes called "Fifteen Miles on the Erie Canal"), which was not written until the early 20th century. **ASK:** What tone or mood would you expect a canal song to convey? What kinds of details would you expect to hear? *(Answers will vary.)*

Active Options

On Your Feet: Use a Jigsaw Strategy Organize students into four groups. Assign each group one of the following topics: the American System, canals, new territories and borders, or Supreme Court decisions. Have groups use the lesson text to become "experts" on their topics. Then reshuffle students into four different groups so that each new group contains at least one expert on each of the topics. Each group will pool the members' knowledge of the four topics, with students reporting on their area of expertise. Groups should then use what they have learned to complete a short written summary of the lesson.

NG Learning Framework: Evaluate Supreme Court Decisions

ATTITUDE Responsibility

SKILL Collaboration

Review the Supreme Court decisions *Gibbons* v. *Ogden* and *McCulloch* v. *Maryland*. Encourage interested students to research the *Dartmouth College* v. *Woodward* decision. Have students work in pairs to evaluate and discuss these decisions and their impact on U.S. history. Ask students to consider the following questions: Which decision would have had the most drastic effect in the short term? Why? Which decision might have had the greatest effect on the nation in the long term? Combine pairs of students into groups of four and ask them to compare and contrast their answers to these questions. Groups should then present their conclusions to the class.

DIFFERENTIATE

English Language Learners   ELD

Use Key Vocabulary in a Sentence Pair students at the **Emerging** level with English-proficient students. Model, or have proficient students model, using a term from the lesson in a sentence. Then have pairs compose a sentence for each of the following Key Vocabulary words: *subsidy, nationalism, monopoly.* Invite pairs to share their sentences and discuss other possible ways of using these words.

Gifted & Talented

Prepare a Speech Remind students that after the Louisiana Purchase, the U.S. government had to manage and develop a nation that had doubled in size. Have students use chapter text and other resources to research the economic and political conditions during the early national period. Direct them to focus on two issues: national and state debts and the debate over federal versus state control of resources. Tell students to prepare a short speech, citing supporting evidence, explaining whether the United States was ready for the Louisiana Purchase.

See the Chapter Planner for more strategies for differentiation.

HISTORICAL THINKING

ANSWERS

1. Answers will vary. Possible responses: The growth of commerce and transportation brought together people from different regions. Economic success, the addition of new territories, and victory in the War of 1812 increased national pride.

2. The United States still has a national banking system, and the government still subsidizes transportation projects. Although free trade has expanded in modern times, the federal government still sets tariffs on international trade.

3. Monroe's presidency was marked by few international conflicts, a lack of political conflict, and major economic achievements.

3.2 Increasing Regional Tensions

When people find it impossible to agree, they may need to work out a compromise to resolve the issue. In the early 1800s, Americans wanted to maintain a balance of power between free states and slave states, so they came up with a compromise.

MAIN IDEA As the United States expanded its territory and its power, it negotiated how each new state would deal with the issue of slavery.

Missouri Compromise, 1820

THE MISSOURI COMPROMISE

Nationalism grew during the years of Madison's and Monroe's presidencies, and so did **sectionalism**. Sectionalism is the identification with and loyalty to a particular part of the country, such as the North or the South. The rise of sectionalism was driven by two main factors: the different economies of these regions and the practice of slavery. For the most part, the North was an industrial region, with mills and wage laborers, while the South was an agricultural region, producing cotton through slave labor.

The federal government wanted to admit the Missouri Territory as the 23rd state. The trick was

how to do so without upsetting the balance of 11 slave states and 11 free states. Americans worried that admitting Missouri would create an imbalance in power between slave and free states. In 1819, the Senate proposed the **Missouri Compromise**. In it, the people of the state of Missouri could own slaves. Missouri would be admitted to the Union at the same time as Maine, a free state, which maintained the balance between the number of slave states and free states. The compromise prohibited slavery in all the lands acquired in the Louisiana Purchase north of the 36° 30' N latitude line. These lands were considered **unorganized territory**, or lands governed by the federal government but not belonging to any state. As

a result of the compromise, any states formed from this unorganized territory would be free states. Even so, the compromise stated that enslaved people who escaped to free states could be captured and returned to their owners.

THE MONROE DOCTRINE

In December 1823, President Monroe delivered a speech in which he introduced a new approach to foreign policy. In it he stated, "The American continents, by the free and independent conditions which they have assumed and maintained, are henceforth not to be considered as subjects for future colonization by any European power." Monroe also promised that the United States would not fight in any European wars. In simple terms, the president said, "You stay out of our hemisphere, and we'll stay out of yours." His ideas became known as the **Monroe Doctrine**. Monroe warned European nations against interfering in the Western Hemisphere. Doing so would be considered an act of aggression that would result in military action from the United States. Monroe's declaration was bold because the United States had no actual authority over Central America or South America.

Part of the inspiration for the Monroe Doctrine stemmed from colonies in Central and South America rebelling against European rule. Monroe was concerned about European countries having so much presence and authority in Central and South America. He feared that European countries might try to re-assert their colonial power. He also had concerns over Russia's presence in what is now Alaska. Russia had issued a statement in 1821 that non-Russians could not enter its territory. Monroe did not want Russia to try to expand its North American territory.

Though Russia and Spain denounced the Monroe Doctrine, they tolerated it. Wars among European countries had wearied them, and they had little desire to expand their involvement in the Americas.

The Monroe Doctrine Desk
While serving as a minister to France under President George Washington, James Monroe purchased this mahogany desk in Paris. When he moved into the White House in 1817, he brought this desk with him and likely wrote the Monroe Doctrine while sitting at it. About 100 years after his presidency, Monroe's great-great-grandson discovered letters from Washington, Madison, Franklin, and Jefferson to Monroe, hidden in the desk's secret compartment.

HISTORICAL THINKING

1. **READING CHECK** What was Monroe's concern about Central and South America?

2. **IDENTIFY PROBLEMS AND SOLUTIONS** How did the Missouri Compromise attempt to solve a problem and cause a potential problem at the same time?

3. **INTERPRET MAPS** Based on details you notice on the map, what territories were open to slavery and what territories were closed to slavery?

Objective
Analyze regional tensions between slave and free states caused by expanding U.S. borders.

Critical Thinking Skills for Lesson 3.2
- Identify Main Ideas and Details
- Monitor Comprehension
- Identify Problems and Solutions
- Interpret Maps
- Draw Conclusions
- Form and Support Opinions
- Make Connections

Essential Question for Chapter 10
How did new industries and inventions transform the United States economically, socially, and geographically? The economies of the North and South led to regional differences. Lesson 3.2 discusses the reasons for and impact of the Missouri Compromise, created to settle disputes over slavery.

Background for the Teacher
Not long after Henry Clay, "the Great Compromiser," used his impressive negotiation skills to bring about the Missouri Compromise, he found he had to do it all over again. After the agreement was made to admit Missouri as a slave state, Missouri's constitutional convention attempted to add a provision that would allow the state to exclude free African Americans and people of mixed race. The provision caused an outcry in Congress and led to the Second Missouri Compromise. Under this compromise, Missouri could keep its exclusionary clause but never use it against U.S. citizens. Only after this second compromise was Missouri admitted to the Union.

INTRODUCE & ENGAGE

Preview with the Map

Direct students' attention to the Missouri Compromise map. **ASK:** What does the color-coding on this map suggest to you? *(Possible response: Much of the nation is clearly split into two regions that show northern and southern states, but the western part of the nation seems less clearly divided.)* Tell students that they will use the map to understand how the Missouri Compromise affected the balance between slave states and free states.

TEACH

Guided Discussion

1. **Draw Conclusions** Given the structure of the U.S. Congress, why might it have been so important for the planners of the Missouri Compromise to maintain a balance between free and slave states? *(Each new state would have representatives in the House and the Senate. If the number of free and slave states remained even, neither the North nor the South would have more power in Congress.)*

2. **Form and Support Opinions** Was the Monroe Doctrine truly necessary? Support your opinion with evidence from the text. *(Possible responses: The Monroe Doctrine was necessary because it outlined how the United States would respond, or not respond, to international conflicts. The Monroe Doctrine was not necessary because nations such as Russia and Spain were not interested in expanding their lands in the Americas.)*

Make Connections

As a class, review some of the geographic, economic, and political differences between the North and South, as discussed in Lesson 3.2 and earlier lessons. **ASK:** Why would both sides see westward expansion as a benefit? *(Answers will vary. Possible response: With more territory, the South could expand its farmlands, giving the North more raw materials for manufacturing.)* How were each region's ideals and aspirations for the nation similar and different? *(Possible responses: The North hoped for an industrial, urban economy, while the South wanted an agriculturally dominated economy. The North also did not want slavery to expand, while the South did.)* Prompt students to outline why these differing ideals made westward expansion more complicated.

Active Options

On Your Feet: Inside-Outside Circle Arrange students in concentric circles facing each other. Have each student in the outside circle ask a question about the Missouri Compromise or the Monroe Doctrine. Then have the student's partner in the inside circle answer the question. On a signal, have students on the inside circle rotate counterclockwise to meet new partners and begin again. On a different signal, have students trade roles so that those in the inside circle ask questions and those in the outside circle answer.

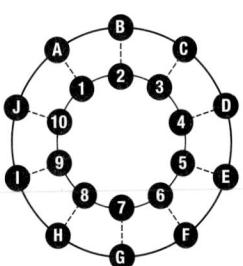

NG Learning Framework: Negotiate a Compromise

ATTITUDE Empowerment

SKILL Problem-Solving

Guide students to brainstorm some issues in their school or community about which people have strong opinions and differing ideas. Have small groups of students choose one of the issues and work to come up with a solution that is a compromise. Encourage them to be creative with their solutions, but instruct them that their alternatives must not include violent conflict.

DIFFERENTIATE

Striving Readers

Create 5Ws Charts Help students understand the two different situations discussed in the lesson by having them work in pairs to complete a 5Ws Chart for each section. Remind students to use information from the headings, map, captions, and the lesson text when completing their charts. Pairs may divide the lesson into one section per partner or work on both as a team.

Pre-AP

Hold a Press Conference Have students hold a press conference announcing the results of the Missouri Compromise to the public. Provide video of a present-day press conference for reference. Tell students to act as public officials who will make the announcement and then answer questions. Encourage students to prepare detailed notes on all parts of the agreement. Direct the rest of the class to draft a set of questions about the compromise based on information from the text. After the students acting as public officials make their announcement, have them answer questions posed by the rest of the class.

See the Chapter Planner for more strategies for differentiation.

HISTORICAL THINKING

ANSWERS

1. Monroe was concerned that Central and South American rebellions would result in attempts by European powers to reassert dominance over former colonies. He wanted European nations to stop interfering in the affairs of the Americas.

2. The Missouri Compromise attempted to balance power between the slave and free states. It created the possibility of future imbalance by declaring the unorganized territory to be free but allowing for escaped enslaved people to be returned into slavery.

3. Area north of the Missouri Compromise line was closed to slavery, while territory south of the line (the Arkansas Territory) was open to slavery. Florida Territory was open to slavery even before the compromise.

3.3 The Monroe Doctrine

In the early 19th century, the United States began to position itself as a world power. One part of that new role for the young country, according to President James Monroe, was protecting countries in Central and South America from future interference from European monarchies. The Monroe Doctrine, as his 1823 statement came to be known, would shape U.S. foreign policy for more than a century.

On December 2, 1823, President Monroe delivered his seventh annual message to Congress, or what we know today as a State of the Union address. Monroe touched on many topics, but most significantly, he introduced a new policy toward Europe and the Western Hemisphere.

CRITICAL VIEWING In this 1912 painting by Clyde DeLand, titled *Birth of the Monroe Doctrine*, President Monroe is outlining his new policy to his cabinet in preparation for his address. Notice the map and the globe. What do you think their significance is?

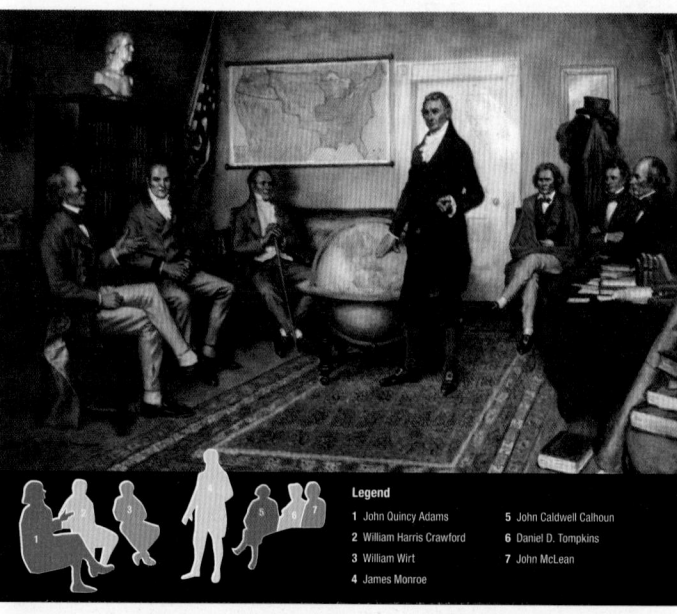

Legend

1 John Quincy Adams
2 William Harris Crawford
3 William Wirt
4 James Monroe
5 John Caldwell Calhoun
6 Daniel D. Tompkins
7 John McLean

DOCUMENT ONE

Primary Source: Speech
from War Message to Congress,
by James Madison, June 1, 1812

The U.S. Navy was young compared to Great Britain's. While navigating Atlantic waters, American sailors had to deal with frequent interference from Great Britain. President Madison delivered this speech as a warning that further activity would initiate an open conflict.

CONSTRUCTED RESPONSE How does Madison's summary of British actions make a case for retaliation?

British cruisers have been in the practice also of violating the rights and the peace of our coasts. They hover over and harass our entering and departing commerce. When called on, nevertheless, by the United States to punish the greater offenses committed by her [Britain's] own vessels, her government has bestowed on their commanders additional marks of honor and confidence.

DOCUMENT TWO

Primary Source: Speech
from Seventh Annual Message to Congress,
by James Monroe, December 2, 1823

In this speech, President Monroe declared that from that point on, European monarchies were not allowed to interfere in Central and South America. At the same time, he promised that the United States would stay out of European affairs.

CONSTRUCTED RESPONSE How does Monroe's speech communicate a strategy for both peacetime and military action, if provoked?

In the wars of the European powers in matters relating to themselves we have never taken any part, nor does it comport with our policy to do so. It is only when our rights are invaded or seriously menaced that we resent injuries or make preparation for our defense. With the movements in this hemisphere we are of necessity more immediately connected, and by causes which must be obvious to all enlightened and impartial [unbiased] observers.

DOCUMENT THREE

Primary Source: Essay
from "The Monroe Doctrine and Spanish America,"
by Juan Bautista Alberdi, c. 1850

Juan Bautista Alberdi, a political thinker from Argentina, expressed concern that Monroe's new policy would threaten the political and economic independence of the countries it promised to protect.

CONSTRUCTED RESPONSE How does Alberdi's opinion of the Monroe Doctrine differ from Monroe's description of his new policy?

The doctrine attributed to Monroe is a contradiction, the daughter of egoism [self-centeredness]. Even though the United States owes everything to Europe, it wants to isolate America from Europe, from any influence that does not emanate [originate] from the United States, which will make the United States the only custom house [official port] for the civilization of transatlantic origin.

SYNTHESIZE & WRITE

1. **REVIEW** Review what you have learned about the position of the United States as a rising world power in the early 1800s.

2. **RECALL** On your own paper, write down the main ideas expressed in the excerpts from Madison's and Monroe's speeches and Alberdi's essay.

3. **CONSTRUCT** Construct a topic sentence that supports or opposes this statement: In the early 1800s, the United States established itself as a world power through a policy of protection and European nonintervention in the Americas.

4. **WRITE** Write a paragraph that presents an argument for or against the statement in Step 3 using evidence from the documents.

PLAN

Objective

Synthesize information about the Monroe Doctrine from primary source documents.

Critical Thinking Skills for Lesson 3.3

- Synthesize
- Draw Conclusions
- Distinguish Fact and Opinion
- Evaluate

Essential Question for Chapter 10

How did new industries and inventions transform the United States economically, socially, and geographically? By 1823, the United States was expanding geographically and economically. Lesson 3.3 provides excerpts from primary sources that show how the Monroe Doctrine became a blueprint for U.S. foreign policy.

Background for the Teacher

When Juan Bautista Alberdi wrote his argument against the Monroe Doctrine, he had the benefit of hindsight. By the 1850s, the Monroe Doctrine had been in effect for some time. Alberdi, who was born in 1810 and a child when Monroe gave his famous speech, had become a prominent political and social thinker. His work inspired those who wrote Argentina's constitution, but he did not limit himself to matters of government. One prominent Argentine academic noted that "many generations will pass, before the South Americans are able to speak of railroads, ports, canals, commerce, industry, population, immigration, education and teaching, wealth and national taxation, American politics, and peace and international justice without . . . a thought of Alberdi."

INTRODUCE & ENGAGE

Prepare for the Document-Based Question

Before students start on the activity, briefly preview the three documents. Remind students that a constructed response requires full explanations in complete sentences. Emphasize that students should use what they have learned about the Monroe Doctrine and about growth and expansion in the United States during the early 1800s in addition to the information in the documents.

TEACH

Guided Discussion

1. **Draw Conclusions** Based on the excerpts from Madison's and Monroe's speeches, how did American leaders think other nations viewed the United States? *(Possible response: From Madison's description of the British government honoring commanders and Monroe's mention of rights being "invaded or seriously menaced," a reader could conclude that American leaders did not feel respected or recognized by other nations.)*

2. **Distinguish Fact and Opinion** What parts of Monroe's and Alberdi's statements reflect their personal opinions about the United States? *(Possible response: Monroe expresses the opinion that the U.S. connection with the Western Hemisphere is "obvious to all enlightened and impartial observers." Alberdi expresses the opinion that the United States is suffering from "egoism" and "owes everything to Europe.")*

Evaluate

After students have completed the Synthesize & Write activity, allow time for them to exchange paragraphs and read and comment on the work of their peers. Establish guidelines for comments prior to this activity so that feedback is constructive and encouraging in nature.

Active Options

On Your Feet: Think, Pair, Share Have students review each excerpt and consider the following questions: In the early 1800s, did the United States consider itself a world power? Did other nations agree? Then have them discuss and compare their answers with a partner. Tell pairs to write out their final answers to the questions, supporting them with evidence from the documents. Invite one member from each pair to share their answers with the class.

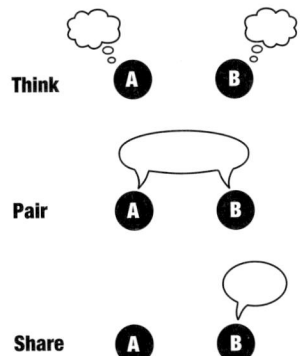

DIFFERENTIATE

English Language Learners

Rewrite in Your Own Words Pair students at the **Emerging** and **Expanding** levels with English-proficient partners. Have pairs work together to rewrite the following lines in their own words.

* "They hover over and harass our entering and departing commerce."
* "In the wars of the European powers in matters relating to themselves we have never taken any part."

Students at the **Bridging** level may work independently. Prompt all students to use dictionaries and other reference works as necessary.

Gifted & Talented

Host a Talk Show Have volunteers assume the roles of James Madison, James Monroe, and Juan Bautista Alberdi. Have another student act as the host of a talk show. Tell students to research their assigned figures to learn about their lives, careers, and philosophies. Instruct hosts to use the chapter text and other resources to write discussion questions for each of the figures, asking them to explain their opinions on early 19th-century events. Have students record their talk shows or conduct them in class.

See the Chapter Planner for more strategies for differentiation.

SYNTHESIZE & WRITE

ANSWERS

1. Answers will vary.

2. Answers will vary.

3. Answers will vary. Possible response: By issuing the Monroe Doctrine, the United States showed the nations of Europe that it was prepared to interact with them as an equal, and it expected to be treated as such.

4. Answers will vary. Students' paragraphs should include their topic sentence from Step 3 and provide evidence from the documents for support.

CONSTRUCTED RESPONSE

Document 1: Possible response: Madison points out that the British government supports the attacks on U.S. vessels. This helps make his case for retaliation as a way to stop the harassment.

Document 2: Possible response: Monroe's statement of U.S. foreign policy was intended to maintain peace while declaring that European intervention in the Americas would create a cause for military action against the intervening country. It's basically saying "we will stay out of your hemisphere, but we expect you to stay out of ours."

Document 3: Possible response: Alberdi sees the declaration of U.S. policy as a strategy for the United States to put itself in charge of the Western Hemisphere. Monroe describes it as a way to keep the Americas free from European interventions and invasions.

CRITICAL VIEWING Students may see them as symbols of the United States taking its place in the world or as showing Monroe's focus on the Western Hemisphere and not the world as a whole.

3.4 Women in the Early Republic

To people living in the 21st century, the saying "a woman's place is in the home" is not only dated, it's inaccurate. However, in the early years of the republic, home was considered the ideal sphere for a woman's power and influence.

MAIN IDEA Increased access to education and the rise of women's organizations expanded women's roles in the early republic.

Catharine Beecher
In a family portrait taken around 1860, Catharine Beecher is seated second from the left. Beecher championed free public education for all and a rigorous education for women. However, her support of women's education did not extend to other rights for women. She opposed granting women the right to vote. She believed that women should limit their efforts to home and school and that a woman's greatest roles were those of wife and mother. Even so, she never married or had children, and she supported herself throughout her life as an educator, writer, and lecturer.

REPUBLICAN MOTHERHOOD

In the years after the Revolution, a strong nationalist spirit took hold as the young United States began to grow and prosper. Citizens embraced their new, republican government. As you have read, in the context of the early republic, the word *republican* did not refer to a political party, but to the new form of representative rule. Citizens also embraced the ideal of civic republicanism, or promoting the common good in order to protect liberty. According to the ideal of republicanism, good government and virtuous citizens worked toward the public good instead of private interests.

What did that mean for women in the early republic? Many had fully participated in the American Revolution, just as their husbands and sons had done. But after the war, women returned to their roles as wives and mothers. No matter their race or class, women were not allowed to vote or even, in many cases, to own their

own property or hold public office. However, they participated in the republic by teaching republican ideals to their children—especially to their sons, who would grow up to be voters, property owners, and maybe even public officials or statesmen. Historians refer to this set of societal expectations for mothers as **republican motherhood**.

Mother as Teacher
The early 19th-century woman had a lot to live up to. Literature, art, and social expectations defined roles for women in narrow ways. Paintings such as this one cast women in a nearly angelic light and featured them as doting mothers.

THE IMPORTANCE OF EDUCATION

In the early 1800s, the ideal woman was pure, religiously devout, and a good housekeeper and mother. She also willingly deferred to all her husband's wishes. Such a role did not require women to be well educated, and few learned more than language arts and basic arithmetic—subjects that aided them in running an efficient home. But without adequate education, how could mothers be expected to teach their children, especially their sons, the basics of civic life and service in a republic?

This question had been brewing since the American Revolution, when Abigail Adams argued that in order to support male education, women should be educated as well: "If we mean to have heroes, statesmen, and philosophers, we should have learned [educated] women."

A few years later, **Judith Sargent Murray,** an American essayist and playwright in the early republic, was known for commenting on public issues, especially women's rights. She wrote that women were not intellectually inferior to men, as some believed. She argued that daughters could not reach their full potential if they were simply trained to be wives, housekeepers, and mothers. In order to teach their children republican values, mothers needed to learn science and higher math, which were traditionally taught only to men.

In 1822, **Catharine Beecher** founded the Hartford Female Seminary, a school for women in Connecticut. Students learned algebra, Latin, logic, and philosophy, among other subjects. The curriculum emphasized physical education and training in home economics. Many women who attended became teachers themselves.

As more girls and women received formal educations, women began to establish organizations that focused on helping others. Many of the organizations had a specific focus, such as helping orphans, people with physical handicaps, or war widows. Members soon began to see the positive effects of their work. Women's organizations grew and expanded, and their leaders became important agents for social change. Some of these women's organizations also laid the groundwork for budding political and social movements, such as securing the vote for women and the **abolition** of, or putting an end to, slavery.

HISTORICAL THINKING

1. **READING CHECK** How does the concept of republican motherhood align with the ideals women were expected to live up to in the early republic?

2. **DRAW CONCLUSIONS** What conclusions can you draw about the work that 19th-century women's organizations did?

3. **MAKE CONNECTIONS** How might a more comprehensive education and the expectation of rearing good citizens lead women to seek broader civic roles for themselves?

PLAN

Objective

Explore how ideals about womanhood and motherhood shaped women's lives in the new republic.

Critical Thinking Skills for Lesson 3.4

- Identify Main Ideas and Details
- Monitor Comprehension
- Draw Conclusions
- Make Connections
- Summarize
- Make Inferences

Essential Question for Chapter 10

How did new industries and inventions transform the United States economically, socially, and geographically? Civic duty was an important facet of the new republic. Lesson 3.4 examines how understandings of civic duty shaped the roles and expectations for women.

Background for the Teacher

Judith Sargent Murray expressed ideas that were radical for her time, and in many ways she lived those ideas. As the child of wealthy parents, she received a better education than many women, but she could see that her brother was getting an even better one. In the 1780s, Murray began publishing essays under the pseudonym "Constantia." Later, she would adopt the male pseudonym "Mr. Gleaner" in the hopes of attracting a larger audience of men. In essays such as "On the Equality of the Sexes" (1790), Murray argued forcefully for equal education of girls and boys. She was also the first American playwright—man or woman—to have her plays performed at the Boston Theatre, although the plays were unsuccessful. In 1802, Murray and her cousin opened an academy for girls near Boston in the hopes of providing girls with the education Murray knew they deserved.

Activate Prior Knowledge

Ask students to recall what they have learned previously about women's roles in U.S. society. **ASK:** What kinds of roles did women play in the American Revolution? *(Women ran the homes and businesses of men who went to fight; they followed and cared for soldiers in the field; some fought in battles.)* As a class, discuss how women might have thought of themselves and their responsibilities following the war. Explain to students that in this lesson, they will examine how women's roles changed as the new nation grew and developed.

TEACH

Guided Discussion

1. **Summarize** In what ways did women's roles and opportunities change after the American Revolution? *(During the Revolution, women participated in the war effort almost equally with men; after the Revolution, they were expected to stay home as wives and mothers. They did not gain voting or property rights, so they lacked political and economic power.)*

2. **Make Inferences** Why might women's organizations working for the right to vote have been likely to get involved with the abolition movement? *(Possible responses: As women's organizations fought against the injustice they faced, they might have become more aware of other injustices, such as slavery. They might have thought that the two movements could work in concert to achieve equality for everyone.)*

More Information

The Cult of Domesticity Explain that the value system known as the Cult of Domesticity or True Womanhood, prominent among the 19th-century white middle and upper classes, defined femininity by four key virtues: piety, purity, domesticity, and submissiveness. These virtues formed a yardstick against which women could be judged. According to this ideal, women were expected to seek and find happiness within the confines of a well-run home. Few married women in the middle and upper classes worked outside the home. **ASK:** Why do you think this ideal applied to middle- and upper-class white women, but not working-class women, women of color, or enslaved women? *(Possible response: The other women did not have the luxury of choosing not to work.)*

Active Options

On Your Feet: Three-Step Interview Direct students to choose a partner. Have one partner interview the other using the following questions: What reasons did women in the early republic give for needing better education? What were the results of this increased education? Based on this, how do you think women felt about their roles in the republic? Students then reverse roles. Finally, have students share the results of their interviews with the class.

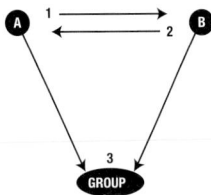

NG Learning Framework: Study Family Life in the New Republic

| ATTITUDE | Curiosity |
| KNOWLEDGE | Our Human Story |

Have students work on their own or in pairs to research how some of the pressures and opportunities women faced in the early years of the United States affected family life. Direct each student or pair to choose one of the following regions: the Northeast, the frontier, or the South. Tell students to use chapter text and outside resources to prepare an oral presentation on family life during the first half of the 1800s in the region they chose. Encourage students to include relevant visuals and primary sources in their presentations.

Striving Readers

Set a Purpose for Reading Before students begin the reading, have them use the title and subheadings in Lesson 3.4 to create purpose-setting questions such as the following: What were women's roles and experiences in the new republic? What did "republican motherhood" involve? Why was education important to the new republic? After students read the lesson, have them work in pairs to answer the questions. If they struggle to answer, prompt them to review that section of text. Ask for volunteers to share their responses with the class.

Inclusion

Clarify Text and Visuals Have visually challenged students work with sighted partners. As they listen to an audio recording of the text, have the visually challenged students indicate words or passages they do not understand. Ask sighted partners to clarify meaning by repeating passages, identifying context clues, and paraphrasing. Encourage sighted partners to describe shading, textures, body language, and the expressions of the subjects in the visuals to help aid understanding.

See the Chapter Planner for more strategies for differentiation.

HISTORICAL THINKING

ANSWERS

1. The ideal woman was supposed to be a good wife and mother who deferred to her husband in all things. Women were expected to teach their children, especially sons, to be good citizens of the republic.

2. Answers will vary. Possible response: Women did charitable work, such as caring for orphans and war widows. This suggests that women were encouraged to provide care for others as an extension of their roles as wives and mothers.

3. Answers will vary. Possible response: With more education, women might understand their own capabilities and develop their own ideas. Since part of women's civic duty was teaching their sons to be involved in the republic, women might think of ways that they could help the republic as well.

10 REVIEW

VOCABULARY

Use vocabulary words to complete the sentences.

1. Eli Whitney's invention of the _____ made the production of cotton more efficient.

2. *Gibbons* v. *Ogden* declared that a single company could not have a _____ on an industry.

3. _____ made manufacturing more structured and uniform, producing pieces that could fit in any component of its kind.

4. Young girls were recruited to work in mills in the _____ industry.

5. The _____ brought crews of people to one main site where work was done with machinery.

6. Congress used _____ in establishing the Second Bank of the United States.

7. _____ grew as the United States acquired more land, improved its financial system, and encouraged patriotic ideals.

8. The division between the North and the South was an example of _____.

READING STRATEGY
DRAW CONCLUSIONS

If you haven't already, complete your chart with evidence from the text to support conclusions. List at least three key conclusions. Then answer the question.

9. What is one conclusion you can draw about the growth and changes in the United States between 1800 and 1844, and what evidence helped you to draw that conclusion?

MAIN IDEAS

Answer the following questions. Support your answers with evidence from the chapter.

10. What type of work did the factory system replace? **LESSON 1.1**

11. How did Eli Whitney plan to deliver the most rifles ever produced by one factory? **LESSON 1.2**

12. Why did plantation owners want to use enslaved labor? **LESSON 2.2**

13. How did religion play a role in motivating the leaders of slave rebellions? **LESSON 2.3**

14. How did a strong economy benefit the spread of nationalism during the Era of Good Feelings? **LESSON 3.1**

15. What conditions gave rise to sectionalism in the United States? **LESSON 3.2**

16. What did President Monroe hope to achieve through his message to European powers in the Monroe Doctrine? **LESSON 3.3**

17. How did education help to change women's roles in society? **LESSON 3.4**

HISTORICAL THINKING

Answer the following questions. Support your answers with evidence from the chapter.

18. **MAKE GENERALIZATIONS** How did technological advancements change agriculture in the early 19th century?

19. **SEQUENCE EVENTS** What were the major events of the Industrial Revolution in the United States? Create a time line to illustrate your answer.

20. **DESCRIBE** What were enslaved people's daily lives like in the antebellum South?

21. **EVALUATE** How did the country become more connected in the first half of the 19th century?

22. **FORM AND SUPPORT OPINIONS** Which territorial expansions were of the most value to the United States? Support your opinion with evidence from the chapter.

INTERPRET MAPS

Cotton spindles are part of cotton spinning machinery. Larger mills had more spindles. Study the map and then answer the questions below.

Cotton Mills, 1840

- Under 5,000 spindles
- 5,000 to 24,999
- 25,000 to 99,999
- 100,000 to 249,999
- 250,000 to 500,000

23. Which northern and southern states had the largest mills?

24. According to the map, where might ships carrying raw cotton be headed?

ANALYZE SOURCES

After visiting a plantation in Georgia in 1793, Eli Whitney designed a new machine to remove seeds from cotton. He wrote a letter to his father about his invention. Read the excerpt and then answer the question below.

> I tried some experiments. In about ten Days I made a little model, for which I was offered . . . a Hundred Guineas [about $450]. I concluded [decided] to . . . turn my attention to perfecting the Machine. I made one . . . which required the labor of one man to turn it and with which one man will clean ten times as much cotton as he can in any other way before known and also cleanse it much better than in the usual mode. This machine may be turned by water or with a horse, with the greatest ease, and one man and a horse will do more than fifty men with the old machine. It makes the labor fifty times less.

25. What benefits did Whitney point to when describing his new invention?

CONNECT TO YOUR LIFE

26. **NARRATIVE** Review the inventions and innovations in this chapter and consider how they changed people's lives. Then think of a new technology that has affected your life. Write a paragraph connecting your experience with the experience of someone in the early to mid-1800s whose life was similarly affected.

TIPS

- Make a list of important engineering or technological advances in the early to mid-1800s.

- Use two or three vocabulary terms from the chapter in your narrative.

- Reflect on new machines, products, or building projects during your lifetime.

- Conclude by stating how you think new technology changes people's lives.

VOCABULARY ANSWERS

1. cotton gin
2. monopoly
3. interchangeable parts
4. textile
5. factory system
6. implied power
7. nationalism
8. sectionalism

READING STRATEGY ANSWER

Evidence	Conclusion
Railroads and canals made cross-country travel faster and easier.	Changes in the United States during this time made the nation more connected than before.
Textile factories in the North needed the cotton from the South as raw material.	
New technologies made communication across distances easier.	

9. Answers will vary. Possible response: Between 1800 and 1844, new technologies made American economic and geographic expansion possible. Evidence to support this includes the canal and railroad systems, which helped agriculture expand in the nation's new territories, and the cotton gin, which made the textile industry more efficient and profitable.

CHAPTER 10 **EXPANSION AND GROWTH**

MAIN IDEAS ANSWERS

10. The factory system replaced people doing work at home. Manufactured textiles and goods replaced handmade items.

11. Whitney planned to produce this massive number of rifles by making them with interchangeable parts. With this method, each rifle would use the exact same parts, making assembly simpler and faster.

12. Plantation owners wanted to use enslaved labor because an unpaid workforce they controlled would allow them to maximize their profits.

13. Christianity, although initially forced upon enslaved people, became a source of hope and helped to strengthen African-American communities. African Americans took biblical stories and teachings about leading people out of suffering as inspirations for their own rebellions.

14. The strong economy made it possible to pursue projects that improved life for Americans. Nationalism spread easily while the citizens of the country were secure and successful.

15. Sectionalism grew as states developed identities based on the economies of and products produced in their regions. The two main sections of the country were the North and the South. The North was a mainly industrial region employing paid labor, while the South was mainly agricultural and used enslaved labor. These regions, often divided by conflicting economic and political goals, began to compete for power in Congress and control of new territories.

16. Monroe hoped to keep European powers from expanding their hold on territories in the Western Hemisphere, thereby securing the U.S. position as the dominant power. He also hoped to keep the United States out of costly and complicated European wars.

17. Women began using their educations to organize groups that addressed social and political problems, such as slavery and poverty. They also began to work as writers and educators.

HISTORICAL THINKING ANSWERS

18. Several inventions during the early 1800s, such as the steel plow, mechanical reaper, and the cotton gin, allowed farmers to produce and harvest more crops with less effort. Meanwhile, transportation innovations such as railroads and canals allowed them to ship goods farther and more cheaply. Overall, technological innovation made agriculture more efficient and profitable.

19. Answers will vary. Students might mention the factory system; invention of the cotton gin; use of interchangeable parts; and the development of steamboats, the telegraph, and the railroad system. Students' time lines should accurately represent information from the text that is included in their responses.

20. Enslaved peoples' lives in the antebellum South were full of suffering. Enslaved people knew they could be sold away from their families at any time and would likely never see their loved ones again. Women were forced to have children who would also become enslaved. The efficiency of the cotton gin meant they worked larger plots of land and processed more cotton. However, they also formed extended kinship networks and developed religious communities.

21. In the first half of the 19th century, the nation became more connected physically, through the development of railroads, canals, and roads. It also became more connected economically, with the manufacturing economy of the North relying upon the raw materials from the agricultural South.

22. Answers will vary. Students should defend their choice of territory with evidence from the chapter.

INTERPRET MAPS ANSWERS

23. Massachusetts in the North and Georgia in the South had the largest mills.

24. The map suggests that ships carrying raw cotton would be likely to head for states in the Northeast.

ANALYZE SOURCES ANSWER

25. Advantages Whitney mentions in his letter include how much more cotton it cleans than a person performing the task by hand, how it cleans the cotton better than a person could, and how it can be run by water or horsepower, allowing one machine to do the work of 50 laborers.

CONNECT TO YOUR LIFE ANSWER

26. Students' narratives will vary but should draw a connection between their experiences with a modern invention and an important technological advance from the 1800s. Paragraphs should use two or three Key Vocabulary terms and conclude with a general statement about how new technology changes peoples' lives.

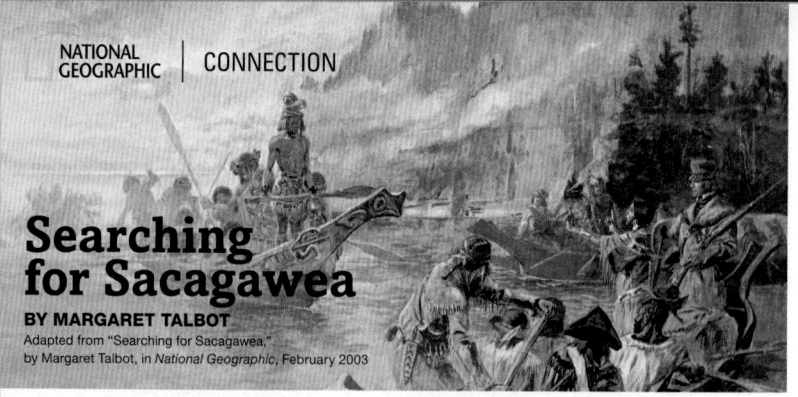

Searching for Sacagawea

BY MARGARET TALBOT

Adapted from "Searching for Sacagawea,"
by Margaret Talbot, in *National Geographic*, February 2003

The glimpses we are allowed of Sacagawea in Lewis and Clark's expedition journals tell us more about her than about almost any other Native American woman of her time. But the very sketchiness of our knowledge has permitted novelists, feminists, and Native American tribes to project what they wish upon Sacagawea. Many see her as a metaphor more than a human being. But who was Sacagawea, really?

From the age of about 13, Sacagawea had lived with the Hidatsa near the confluence of the Missouri and Knife rivers. Lewis and Clark first met Sacagawea when she was about 17 and pregnant with her first child. In November 1804, the Corps of Discovery, as the expedition was known, had arrived among the Mandan and Hidatsa on the upper Missouri River, in what is now North Dakota.

One warm afternoon in 2002, I spent some time there trying to reimagine Sacagawea's world. With me was Amy Mossett, a Mandan-Hidatsa from New Town, North Dakota, and an expert on Sacagawea. On a bluff above the Knife River, Mossett and I look out over shallow, bowl-shaped indentations in the ground where her ancestors' earth lodges once stood. "This is where I feel closest to Sacagawea," says Mossett.

The Corps of Discovery set out from its winter quarters on April 7, 1805. Less than two months after giving birth, Sacagawea gathered up her infant son and embarked with her husband, a French-Canadian fur trader, on a roughly 5,000-mile, 16-month journey. Contrary to her romanticized image, Sacagawea was not the expedition's "girl-guide." Most of the territory they passed through was as unfamiliar to her as it was to Lewis and Clark.

One of Sacagawea's greatest contributions was her mere presence, which seems to have disarmed potentially hostile tribes along the way. The journals record one of those fortunate coincidences.

Sacagawea, who spoke Hidatsa and Shoshone but neither English nor French, was to translate a Shoshone chief's words into Hidatsa for her husband, who was to translate into French for a member of the corps, who would translate into English for the captains. They were just about to begin this unwieldy relay when Sacagawea suddenly recognized the Shoshone chief. He was, of all people, her long-lost brother.

After the 21 months in which Sacagawea's story intersects with that of the expedition, she disappears almost entirely from our view. The best evidence we have suggests that she died in her mid-20s shortly after giving birth to a daughter. For many years, most white Americans wrote about Sacagawea as the archetypal "good Indian"—one who, like Pocahontas, had aided white men. But in recent decades, and especially for Native Americans, Sacagawea has become a different sort of symbol. She is a reminder of the extent to which the Lewis and Clark story is also a Native American story.

Disputes remain about where and when Sacagawea died and even how to spell and pronounce her name. For the 400 or so remaining Lemhi Shoshone who live on a reservation in Idaho, the connection to Sacagawea is one thread on which to hang their hopes for federal tribal recognition and a return of ancestral lands. The Wind River Shoshone in Wyoming insist "Sacajawea" (their spelling) died on their reservation, though most historians dispute this. But the Shoshone's cultural claim on Sacagawea anchors them in the Lewis and Clark story.

Some historians wonder why Sacagawea didn't stay behind with the Shoshone and her brother. Perhaps she had come to feel more like a Hidatsa than a Shoshone. Or perhaps she had been seized with curiosity about what came next and where the journey would take her.

For more from National Geographic, check out "Lost Missouri" online.

UNIT INQUIRY: Define Good Citizenship

In this unit, you learned about the political, economic, and geographic growth of the United States in the years of the early republic. Based on your understanding of the text, in what ways was good citizenship central to the success of the early republic? What role did citizenship play in how Americans defined themselves and others? Which groups of Americans were excluded from full citizenship, and why?

ASSIGNMENT

Create your own definition for good citizenship. Your definition should include several elements, including a statement of what constitutes good citizenship, why citizenship mattered in the early republic, and why citizenship still matters today. Be prepared to present your definition of citizenship to the class and explain your reasoning.

Gather Evidence As you develop your definition of good citizenship, gather evidence from this unit about the different ways in which concepts of citizenship shaped communities and a young nation. Think about the active roles citizens played in the early republic. Also consider the rights and responsibilities American citizens had—or did not have—and why. Use a graphic organizer like this one to help organize your thoughts.

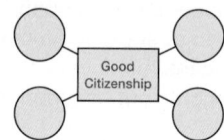

Good Citizenship

Produce Use your notes to produce descriptions of the elements that make up your definition of good citizenship. Write a short paragraph on each element using evidence from this unit to support your ideas.

Present Choose a creative way to present your definition of good citizenship to the class. Consider one of these options:

- Interview citizens in your community about what they think good citizenship entails. Ask them what they do to be good citizens and what rights and responsibilities are the most important to them. Present your interviews to the class.

- Create a good citizenship award. Work with a small team to design the award. Identify a person in your school who you think deserves this honor. Hold an award ceremony and appoint a class member to describe the ways in which your award recipient exemplifies good citizenship.

- Design a collaborative wall mural that illustrates the rights and responsibilities of good citizenship using words and drawings.

NATIONAL GEOGRAPHIC | LEARNING FRAMEWORK ACTIVITIES

Propose a New Invention

ATTITUDES Responsibility, Empowerment

SKILL Problem-Solving

Part of being a good citizen is taking care of the people and environment around you. The men and women who innovated new technologies in the early republic were all trying to solve some sort of problem or make a process more efficient. Using evidence from the reading, develop a proposal for a new invention. Define the problem that you are solving and how your invention would benefit your community or even the world. Consider including illustrations of your invention. Present your proposal to the class as if you were presenting to a panel of financial backers.

Write a Campaign Speech

SKILLS Collaboration, Communication

KNOWLEDGE Our Human Story

Political campaigns have been a part of American democracy since it began. Effective campaigns and their candidates have to deliver a clear message to potential voters if they want to win elections. Work with a small team of classmates to write a campaign speech about an important issue during the early republic. Use evidence from the reading to define your issue, craft your message, and select the candidate who would best deliver the speech. Present your team's speech and be prepared to listen to other teams' speeches.

Guided Discussion for "Searching for Sacagawea"

1. **Summarize** What were Sacagawea's roles on the Corps of Discovery's expedition? *(Sacagawea provided a disarming presence with tribes the Corps encountered. She also served as a translator.)*

2. **Make Inferences** In what ways is Sacagawea a symbol for Native Americans? *(Sacagawea is a reminder of the extent to which the Lewis and Clark story is also a Native American story. Various tribes claim her as their own, either as a point of pride or as a means to asserting ancestral and tribal rights.)*

Guided Discussion for "Lost Missouri"

1. **Describe** What was Jim Harlan's goal? *(Harlan wanted to create historically accurate maps of Lewis and Clark's outward and return trips across Missouri.)*

2. **Make Connections** What experiences and skills did Harlan rely upon to complete his project? *(As a boy, he developed a fascination for local history. Later, he joined the army. He then pursued a master's degree in geography.)*

UNIT INQUIRY PROJECT RUBRIC

Assess

Use the rubric to assess each student's participation and performance.

SCORE	ASSIGNMENT	PRODUCT	PRESENTATION
3 GREAT	• Student thoroughly understands the assignment. • Student participates fully in the project process.	• Definition of citizenship is well thought out. • Definition contains all of the key elements listed in the assignment. • Definition supports ideas with evidence from the unit.	• Presentation is clear and creative. • Presentation does a good job of portraying a definition of good citizenship. • Presentation engages the audience.
2 GOOD	• Student mostly understands the assignment. • Student participates fairly well in the project process.	• Definition of citizenship is fairly well thought out. • Definition contains most of the key elements listed in the assignment. • Definition supports most ideas with evidence from the unit.	• Presentation is fairly clear and creative. • Presentation does an adequate job of portraying a definition of good citizenship. • Presentation somewhat engages the audience.
1 NEEDS WORK	• Student does not understand the assignment. • Student minimally participates or does not participate in the project process.	• Definition of citizenship is not well thought out. • Definition contains few or none of the key elements listed in the assignment. • Definition supports few or no ideas with evidence from the unit.	• Presentation is not clear or creative. • Presentation does an inadequate job of portraying a definition of good citizenship. • Presentation does not engage the audience.

NATIONAL GEOGRAPHIC LEARNING FRAMEWORK RUBRIC

Assess

Use the rubric to assess how each student applies the National Geographic Learning Framework.

SCORE	ASSIGNMENT	ASSIGNMENT	FINAL PRODUCTS
3 GREAT	• Proposal reflects **Responsibility** and **Empowerment** well. • Proposal demonstrates **Problem-Solving** well.	• Speech demonstrates **Collaboration** and **Communication** well. • Speech explores **Our Human Story** well.	• Final products are engaging, creative, and well presented.
2 GOOD	• Proposal reflects **Responsibility** and **Empowerment**. • Proposal demonstrates **Problem-Solving**.	• Speech demonstrates **Collaboration** and **Communication**. • Speech explores **Our Human Story**.	• Final products are interesting, logical, and complete.
1 NEEDS WORK	• Proposal does not reflect **Responsibility** or **Empowerment**. • Proposal does not demonstrate **Problem-Solving**.	• Speech does not demonstrate **Collaboration** and **Communication**. • Speech does not explore **Our Human Story**.	• Final products are not creative, complete, or interesting.

Objectives

- **Discuss the concept of a "hometown" and how a hometown can change over time.**
- **Analyze a township map.**
- **Learn how to construct a personal American story using historical events.**

Critical Thinking Skills for "Why Study U.S. History?"

- Make Inferences
- Make Connections
- Draw Conclusions
- Determine Chronology

Background for the Teacher

On these pages, Fred Hiebert, National Geographic's Archaeologist-in-Residence, invites students to investigate their own hometown and what it reveals about U.S. history. Use Hiebert's own community's story to prompt a discussion about street names and buildings in students' own neighborhoods.

Make Inferences Using Visuals

Direct students' attention to the map of Haverford Township and the callouts provided. **ASK:** What inferences can you make about the township in 1875? *(Answers will vary. Possible responses: There were several mills along the eastern border; many families owned large chunks of land; a new railroad was being proposed.)*

WHY STUDY U.S. HISTORY?

To tell your American story

You've been reading about the founding of the country and the establishment of the American republic. Think about the individuals and families who established their homes in the United States. What does the idea of a "hometown" mean to you? And what can you learn when you investigate your own hometown?

Fred Hiebert
▶ Watch the Why Study U.S. History? video

This map of Haverford Township, published in 1875, reveals the kind of ground-level details those who lived there would have recognized—homes and farms belonging to prominent citizens, numerous creeks and ponds created for early mills, and the proposed Philadelphia–Chester County rail line.

354

If you look around my hometown (suburban Philadelphia), it's an area of houses and parks. But there are all sorts of clues to our history—strange names that don't seem to make sense. Like an old building called Nitre Hall on Karakung Drive, or a nearby street on a hillside called Lakeview Avenue (though there is no lake in sight).

So here's what I learned by going to my local library and historical society: This area west of Philadelphia has great agricultural land, watered by streams and creeks, and was acquired from Governor William Penn in 1680 for agricultural development. The largest stream in our part of Delaware County is Cobb's Creek, but the original name given by the Lenape Native Americans was *Karakung* (the place of wild geese). This name is still preserved as a road name.

Electric trolleys similar to this one were introduced in Haverford around the turn of the century. The electric railway transformed settled farmland into a thriving suburb accessible by a growing middle class.

By the early 1800s, the creeks were dammed, and the water flow was used to power mills of all sorts. A gunpowder mill operated from 1810 to 1840, using nitre (saltpeter), charcoal, and sulfur (all brought in), mixed here using the power of the waterwheels. Nitre Hall is actually the original house where the powder master (who mixed the dangerous powder together) lived. At that time, Nitre Hall Powder Mill was the second-largest black powder mill in the United States.

By 1840, the mills were converted to use water power to spin cotton and wool. During the Civil War, cloth for Union soldiers' uniforms was produced here. Following the Civil War and the increased dependence on steam power, the water mills disappeared. The last mill was a sawmill that closed in the mid-20th century.

It was pretty quiet here until—boom!—at the beginning of the 20th century, with the development of electric railways. In 1907, a tramline was built to the region from Philadelphia, and the area opened to provide housing for workers employed in Philadelphia. To increase visitors and make the suburbs more attractive, a large amusement park was built nearby with an artificial lake for boating. Lakeview Avenue was built near Nitre Hall. After three years of bad weather, however, the amusement park was an economic bust and the lake dried up.

Today, Nitre Hall is a local museum located on Karakung Drive, and the name Lakeview Avenue is all that's left of the lake. But together they tell the story of my neighborhood's place in the history of the United States.

What's your American story?

You can begin to recognize the connections between the events of our past and your life today. Look around your neighborhood and find an interesting street name or building name—you can discover your hometown's place in U.S. history, too.

 Use your History Notebook to comment on what you've read. And check out the "Documenting My America" project online to start telling your own American story.

355

Guided Discussion

1. **Make Connections** How do historical events explain street and place names like Karakung Drive, Nitre Hall, and Lakeview Avenue? *(Karakung Drive reflects the fact that the land was once occupied by the Lenape; Nitre Hall reflects the existence of a gunpowder mill in the early 1800s; Lakeview Avenue references the artificial lake built in the early 1900s to make the suburbs more attractive.)*

2. **Determine Chronology** What historical events tell the story of how Haverford Township changed from a farming community to a suburb over time? *(Possible response: The land was acquired for agricultural development from William Penn in 1680; in the early 1800s, the creeks were dammed to develop different kinds of power mills, including a gunpowder mill and later textile mills; the mills disappeared after the Civil War with the shift to steam power; a building boom began in 1907, when an electric tramline connected the region to Philadelphia, turning the town into a suburb of the city.)*

Active Option

NG Learning Framework: Create Time Lines

ATTITUDE Curiosity

SKILL Collaboration

Ask groups of students to do online research about their hometown and then use their findings to create a time line. Encourage them to include important historical events and the people who influenced the town at various points in time. Suggest that they also include photographs and illustrations if possible. Then have groups share and compare their time lines.

DIFFERENTIATE

Striving Readers

Summarize Have students work in pairs, and assign each student a paragraph to read aloud. The partner should summarize what he or she hears in one or two spoken sentences.

Pre-AP

Suburban Trolleys The Philadelphia & West Chester Traction Company operated the electric trolleys that transformed Haverford into a suburb of Philadelphia. Ask students to research the company and then give an oral presentation of their findings. Presentations should describe the company's history and influence and should include a few visuals if possible.

INTRODUCE THE PAINTING

Depiction from *The Last of the Mohicans*

Thomas Cole created several paintings based on the work of novelist James Fenimore Cooper. This one depicts a scene from *The Last of the Mohicans,* in which a Huron man named Magua has petitioned the Delaware for the return of several people whom he had previously taken prisoner. One of the prisoners, Cora (kneeling, with her arms raised up), pleads with Tamenund, an elder and former chief of the Delaware people, to release her sister Alice from captivity.

ASK: What do you notice first about the people in this painting? *(Possible response: The people are shown very small and off to one side, as if they're not important. It's difficult to determine what they are doing or who they are.)* Have students discuss the effect that the size of the people relative to the rest of the painting has on their impressions of the painting overall. **ASK:** Why might an artist choose to depict a dramatic scene in this way? *(Answers will vary. Students may say that this painting emphasizes the vast scale and power of nature and suggests that humans are relatively unimportant or powerless.)* Point out that emphasizing the power and scale of nature was a feature of many of Cole's paintings.

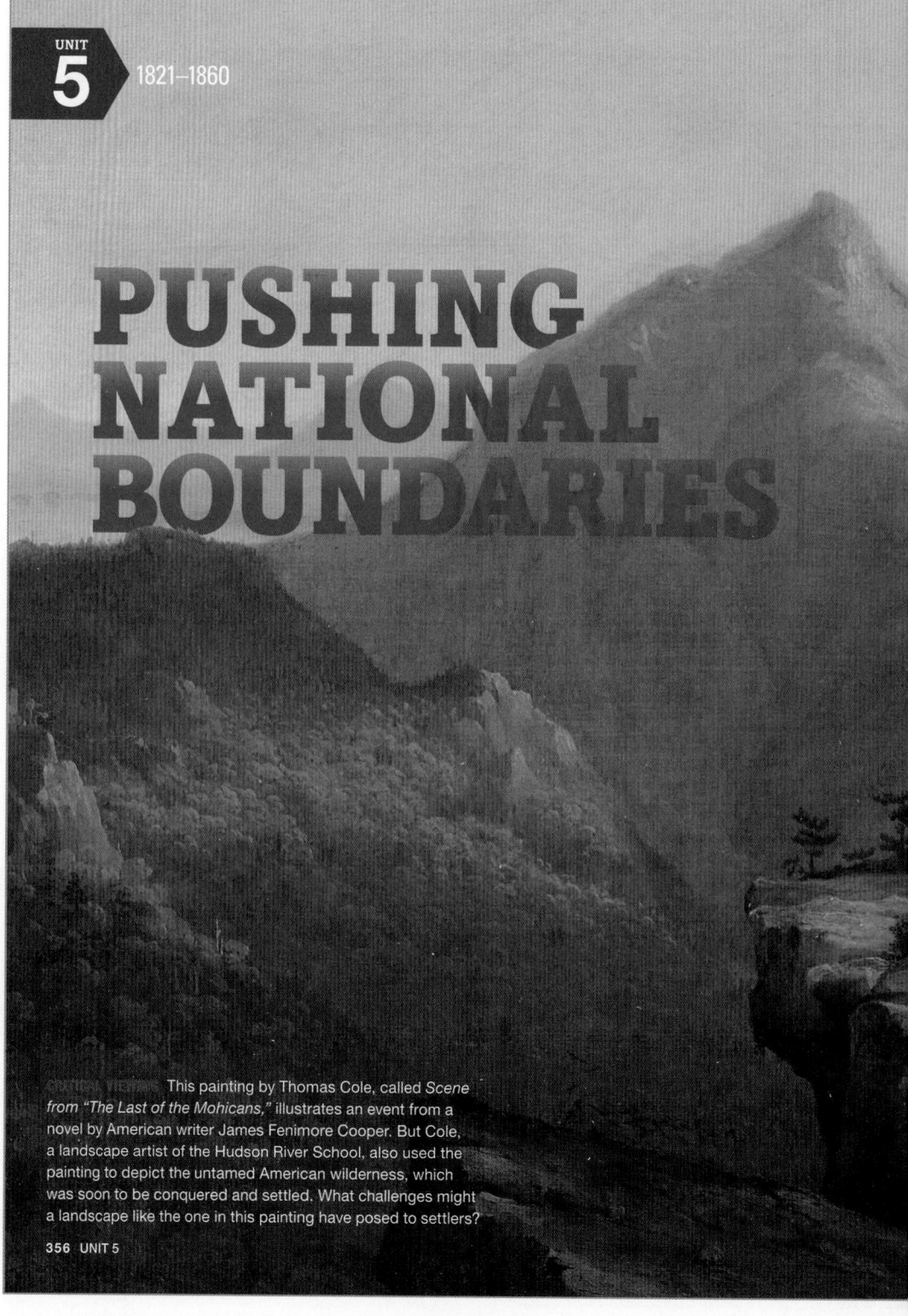

UNIT
5 1821–1860

PUSHING NATIONAL BOUNDARIES

CRITICAL VIEWING This painting by Thomas Cole, called *Scene from "The Last of the Mohicans,"* illustrates an event from a novel by American writer James Fenimore Cooper. But Cole, a landscape artist of the Hudson River School, also used the painting to depict the untamed American wilderness, which was soon to be conquered and settled. What challenges might a landscape like the one in this painting have posed to settlers?

356 UNIT 5

357

The Hudson River School

The Hudson River School was the name given to a group of landscape painters of the mid-19th century who were based in New York City. The movement took shape around the works of Thomas Cole, which brought a new sensibility to the American landscape—one that recognized nature's power and ability to inspire fear. Cole had been born in England but trained as a painter in Philadelphia after his family emigrated.

After settling in the Hudson River Valley in 1826, Cole began to document his surroundings. His work quickly caught the attention of New York City's art community, and soon prominent artists became Cole's followers. Although Cole achieved significant success as a painter with his imaginative and sometimes symbolic landscapes, later followers of the Hudson River School shifted to less dramatic subjects and depictions.

CRITICAL VIEWING Answers will vary. Students may point out that the landscape is characterized by mountains, cliffs, and dense forests, through which travel would be difficult or dangerous given the terrain and the possibility of unfriendly encounters.

1838 AFRICA:
The Zulu and Boers Clash

The term *Boer* refers to Dutch settlers and their descendants in South Africa. In 1806, Britain took over the Dutch settlement of Cape Colony on the Cape of Good Hope, and some Boers began to leave the main colony. Throughout the 1830s, these *Voortrekkers*, or pioneers, left the colony to establish new settlements in inland South Africa. Originally, it was thought that the *Voortrekkers* left because they disapproved of Britain's policy on freeing slaves—a theory largely established by the British. Now, however, some argue that they mostly left in search of economic opportunity.

As they made their way inland, the *Voortrekkers* began to enter lands controlled by the Zulu under King Dingane. Clashes between the groups came to a head in 1838, when well-armed Boer forces provoked the Zulu to attack them. The battle, which was a devastating loss for the Zulu, later came to be known as the Battle of Blood River. It led to the end of Dingane's reign as well as the end of Zulu conflict with the Boers.

Boer settlement in South Africa's interior continued to be marked with conflict throughout the 19th century. In particular, the Boers clashed with the British over mining resources such as gold. In 1899, war broke out between the two sides. The Boers, who had previously been granted independence, were defeated and brought into the British Empire. **ASK:** How and why might historians have revised their views on the *Voortrekkers* over time? *(Answers will vary. Possible response: Historians question previous theories about their motivations for leaving the main colony because the British, who spread the original theory, were likely biased against the Boers after the war.)*

UNIT 5

PUSHING NATIONAL BOUNDARIES

1828
Andrew Jackson, a southerner, is elected president. *(Jackson presidential campaign poster)*

HUZZA FOR Gen. Jackson! DOWN WITH THE YANKEES!

1836
Texans declare independence from Mexico. *(illustration of the Battle of the Alamo, a fort in San Antonio, Texas, where Texans fought Mexican troops)*

1838–1839
The journey of about 17,000 Cherokee forced to leave their homeland becomes known as the Trail of Tears.

1837
A panic over the state of the economy results in a severe depression.

1840

THE UNITED STATES

1830

1820

1821 AMERICAS
Mexico gains its independence from Spain.

1838 AFRICA
Zulus clash with Boers in what is known today as South Africa. *(Zulu shield and weapons)*

1839 AMERICAS
Antonio López de Santa Anna regains control of Mexico and rules as a dictator.

THE WORLD

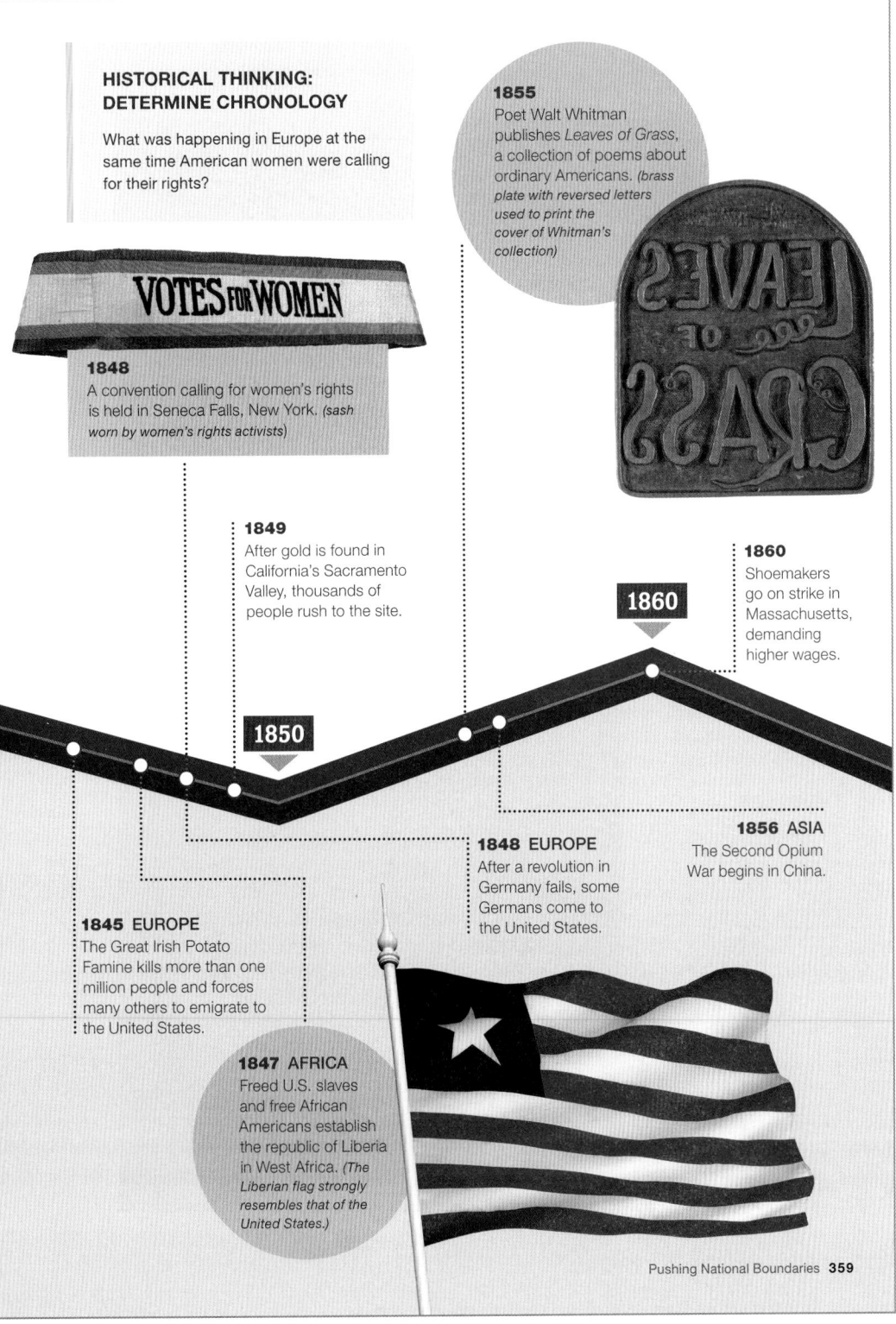

HISTORICAL THINKING: DETERMINE CHRONOLOGY

What was happening in Europe at the same time American women were calling for their rights?

1848
A convention calling for women's rights is held in Seneca Falls, New York. *(sash worn by women's rights activists)*

1849
After gold is found in California's Sacramento Valley, thousands of people rush to the site.

1855
Poet Walt Whitman publishes *Leaves of Grass*, a collection of poems about ordinary Americans. *(brass plate with reversed letters used to print the cover of Whitman's collection)*

1860
Shoemakers go on strike in Massachusetts, demanding higher wages.

1848 EUROPE
After a revolution in Germany fails, some Germans come to the United States.

1856 ASIA
The Second Opium War begins in China.

1845 EUROPE
The Great Irish Potato Famine kills more than one million people and forces many others to emigrate to the United States.

1847 AFRICA
Freed U.S. slaves and free African Americans establish the republic of Liberia in West Africa. *(The Liberian flag strongly resembles that of the United States.)*

Pushing National Boundaries **359**

INTRODUCE TIME LINE EVENT

1856 ASIA:
The Second Opium War

Despite its name, the Second Opium War was not fought directly over opium. It was, instead, the continuation of an earlier conflict between the Chinese government and European powers over the opium trade. In the First Opium War (1839), China had attempted to halt the flow of opium into its borders, angering the British government and merchants who stood to profit. The war ended with British victory, however, and China was forced to give Britain and other Western nations significant trading rights and access. Britain also gained control over Hong Kong.

Tensions did not resolve following the First Opium War, as Britain felt that the Qing government was not honoring its treaties. Britain also sought greater trading access than the treaties had allowed. Finally, in 1856, British troops began attacking Chinese ships and bombing port cities such as Canton and Tianjin. With help from the French, the British won this Second Opium War as well. China was forced to sign treaties giving even more rights and access to Britain and several other Western nations; those rights eventually included the legalization of the opium trade in China. Despite the defeat, China continued to fight and negotiate for two more years. **ASK:** Why do you think Britain would have wanted China to grant similar new rights to other Western nations following the Opium Wars? *(Answers will vary. Possible response: to prevent conflict among European powers over Britain's greater access to Chinese trade rights)*

HISTORICAL THINKING: DETERMINE CHRONOLOGY

In 1848, at the same time as women began calling for their rights in the United States, a failed revolution in Germany caused some Germans to leave for the United States.

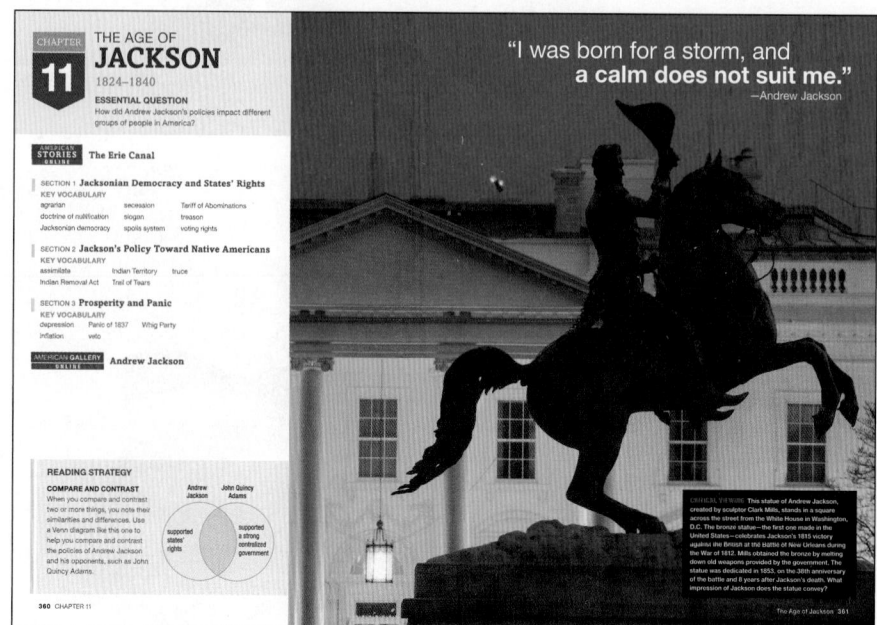

Chapter 11 Spanish Resources are available at NGLSync.Cengage.com.

AMERICAN STORIES ONLINE | The Erie Canal

- Primary Sources
- On Your Feet: Question and Answer

NG Learning Framework:
Research Geographic Obstacles

SECTION 1 RESOURCES

JACKSONIAN DEMOCRACY AND STATES' RIGHTS

LESSON 1.1
Expanding Democracy

- On Your Feet: Team Word Webbing

NG Learning Framework:
Create a Storyboard

LESSON 1.2
President of the People?

- On Your Feet: Debate

 AMERICAN GALLERY ONLINE Andrew Jackson

LESSON 1.3
Debating States' Rights

- On Your Feet: Present Both Sides

NG Learning Framework:
Analyze the Doctrine of Nullification

SECTION 2 RESOURCES

JACKSON'S POLICY TOWARD NATIVE AMERICANS

LESSON 2.1
Expanding into Native American Lands

- On Your Feet: Numbered Heads

NG Learning Framework:
Form an Opinion

American Voices Biography
Sequoyah ONLINE

LESSON 2.2
Native American Resistance

- On Your Feet: Create a Living Time Line

NG Learning Framework:
Write a News Article

LESSON 2.3
The Trail of Tears

- Active History: Analyze a Different Perspective

NG Learning Framework:
Compare Relocation Routes

American Voices Biography
John Ross ONLINE

SECTION 3 RESOURCES

PROSPERITY AND PANIC

LESSON 3.1
Economic Crises

- On Your Feet: State and Respond

NG Learning Framework:
Create a Line Graph

LESSON 3.2
A New Party System

- On Your Feet: Turn and Talk on Topic

NG Learning Framework:
Write a Campaign Speech

CHAPTER 11 REVIEW

Strategy ①
Create Idea Webs

Have students summarize the chapter by creating three Idea Webs. They should write *Andrew Jackson* in the center of first Idea Web, *Native Americans* in the second Idea Web, and *Bank Crisis* in the third Idea Web. Ask them to complete each web with relevant information as they read the lessons.

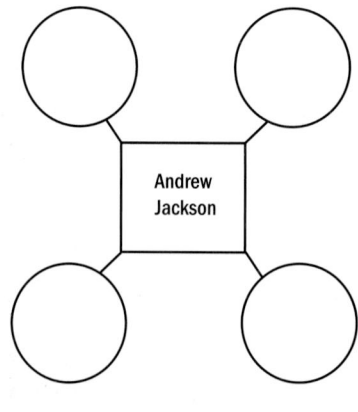

Andrew Jackson

Use with All Lessons *For example, for Andrew Jackson students could add* states' rights, spoils system, common man, *or* bank charter.

Strategy ②
Review Main Ideas

Check students' understanding by asking them to complete either/or statements such as the following:

- The 1823 Supreme Court decision in *Johnson* v. *M'Intosh* [helped or harmed] the Cherokee. *(helped)*
- In 1838, the federal government sent soldiers to [assist or remove] Native Americans in what became known as the Trail of Tears. *(remove)*
- As a result of the Trail of Tears, the Cherokee people and their culture [thrived or suffered]. *(suffered)*

Use with Lesson 2.3

Strategy ③
Clarify Information

Students may have trouble understanding that Lesson 3.1 describes the 1830s economic crisis. To help students clarify and organize their reading, have them take notes for the text under each subheading using a 5Ws Chart.

Use with Lesson 3.1

Strategy ①
Preview Using Maps

To help students comprehend lesson text, preview the Removal of the Native Americans map from Lesson 2.3. Tell students to place a finger on the yellow patch marked *CHEROKEE* on the right (eastern) part of the map, then trace the yellow line until it ends at the yellow patch on the left (western) part of the map. Explain that the line shows the movement of the Cherokee people during the Trail of Tears. Have them explore the routes of other Native American groups. Point out that, in each case, the Native Americans were moved from east to west.

Use with Lesson 2.3

Strategy ②
Describe Lesson Visuals

Pair visually challenged students with students who are not visually challenged. Ask the latter to describe the visuals and answer any questions the visually impaired students might have.

Use with All Lessons *For example, for the Trail of Tears sculpture in Lesson 2.3, students might describe the body positions of the woman and child and read aloud the visual's caption.*

ENGLISH LANGUAGE LEARNERS

Strategy 1
Sound Out Words

Before reading, preview with students at **All Proficiencies** long or unusually spelled Key Vocabulary terms that students may have difficulty sounding out, such as: *agrarian*, *abominations*, *nullification*, *secession*, *assimilate*, *Whig*, and *vetoed*. Say the words slowly, breaking them into syllables. Suggest students write word cards for each word, writing definitions and pronunciation hints for themselves.

Use with Lessons 1.3, 2.1, 3.1, and 3.2

Strategy 2
Use a Term in a Sentence

Pair English language learners with English-proficient students. Have the proficient students model using Key Vocabulary words in sentences. Then have each pair compose a sentence for each word. Invite pairs to share their sentences and discuss different ways to use each word. Suggest the following words:

- voting rights
- slogan
- treason
- truce
- depression

Use with All Lessons *You may wish to place students in pairs, such as students at the **Emerging** level with those at the **Bridging** level, and have English-proficient students assist less proficient students in checking the accuracy and spelling of their sentences.*

Strategy 3
Use Sentence Strips

Choose a paragraph from the lesson and make sentence strips from it. Read the paragraph aloud while students follow along in their books. Have students close their books and give them the set of sentence strips. Students should put the strips in order and then read the paragraph aloud.

Use with All Lessons *Before reading, ask students at the **Emerging** level to read sentence strips aloud. Then ask them to point out meaningful words in the sentence. Repeat the exercise with another paragraph.*

GIFTED & TALENTED

Strategy 1
Present a Skit

Invite students to research the Webster-Hayne debate. Have them use what they learn to write a short skit about the historic meeting. Encourage students to consider writing two different endings: one that reflects the historical events and one that imagines a different outcome. Encourage students to present their skits to the class and to perform both endings.

Use with Lesson 1.3

Strategy 2
Research Sequoya's Syllabary

Have students research Sequoya's Syllabary. Instruct them to find out how the syllabary worked, what the characters looked like, and how it was used. Then have them sound out their own names or other words and write the words using characters from the Syllabary. Allow students to present what they have learned to the class, and display their written words around the room.

Use with Lesson 2.1

Pre-AP

Strategy 1
Investigate Native American Artifacts

Challenge students to research Native American artifacts that date back to the early or mid-1800s. Students should investigate what the artifacts were made from and how they were used. Some may wish to investigate items from the Trail of Tears forced migration. Encourage students to present their artifacts to the rest of the class.

Use with Lessons 2.1–2.3

Strategy 2
Compare Historical and Current Events

Tell students that the protection of individual civil rights remains important to Americans today, as described in the Threatened by Oil feature in Lesson 2.2. Have students think about recent instances in which people believed their civil rights had been violated. Have students choose one of these instances and research the arguments on both sides of the issue. Invite students to present the issue to the class, explaining the reasoning on both sides.

Use with Lesson 2.2 *You might also wish to have students compare the outcome of the 1824 election and Jackson's reaction to it, as described in Lesson 1.1, with recent U.S. presidential elections.*

THE AGE OF
JACKSON
1824–1840

ESSENTIAL QUESTION
How did Andrew Jackson's policies impact different groups of people in America?

AMERICAN STORIES ONLINE The Erie Canal

SECTION 1 Jacksonian Democracy and States' Rights
KEY VOCABULARY

agrarian	secession	Tariff of Abominations
doctrine of nullification	slogan	treason
Jacksonian democracy	spoils system	voting rights

SECTION 2 Jackson's Policy Toward Native Americans
KEY VOCABULARY

assimilate	Indian Territory	truce
Indian Removal Act	Trail of Tears	

SECTION 3 Prosperity and Panic
KEY VOCABULARY

depression	Panic of 1837	Whig Party
inflation	veto	

AMERICAN GALLERY ONLINE Andrew Jackson

READING STRATEGY

COMPARE AND CONTRAST
When you compare and contrast two or more things, you note their similarities and differences. Use a Venn diagram like this one to help you compare and contrast the policies of Andrew Jackson and his opponents, such as John Quincy Adams.

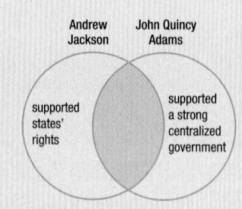

Andrew Jackson — supported states' rights

John Quincy Adams — supported a strong centralized government

"I was born for a storm, and a calm does not suit me."
—Andrew Jackson

CRITICAL VIEWING This statue of Andrew Jackson, created by sculptor Clark Mills, stands in a square across the street from the White House in Washington, D.C. The bronze statue—the first one made in the United States—celebrates Jackson's 1815 victory against the British at the Battle of New Orleans during the War of 1812. Mills obtained the bronze by melting down old weapons provided by the government. The statue was dedicated in 1853, on the 38th anniversary of the battle and 8 years after Jackson's death. What impression of Jackson does the statue convey?

INTRODUCE THE PHOTOGRAPH

Jackson's Equestrian Statue

Direct students' attention to the photograph of the equestrian statue of Andrew Jackson. Discuss the location of the statue and the proximity of the statue to the White House, which is in the background of this photo. Read the caption of the photo aloud. Note that the quote is also by Andrew Jackson. **ASK:** How do you think the quote applies to the photo? *(Answers will vary. Possible response: Jackson sounds fearless in the quote and looks fearless in the photo.)* **ASK:** Why do you think Jackson's statue was installed near the White House? *(Answers will vary. Possible response: because Jackson lived in the White House when he was president)* Tell students that in Chapter 11 they will learn about the influence Andrew Jackson had on national politics and on the nation's economy. The chapter also explains how Jackson's policies dramatically affected Native Americans and forever changed their way of life.

For Chapter 11 Spanish Resources, visit the Resources Menu. Chapter 11 Resources are available at NGLSync.Cengage.com.

Share Background

Clark Mills began his sculpting career after inventing a new way to cast busts of human faces to create living masks. This new way of casting masks eventually evolved into casting statues. His bronze sculpture of Jackson was the first equestrian statue cast in bronze in the United States. Mills's success with the Jackson statue resulted in more federal commissions for statues, including one of George Washington installed at Washington Circle in Washington, D.C., in 1860 and "Statue of Freedom," a sculpture designed by artist Thomas Crawford. "Statue of Freedom" was first cast in five sections and finally installed in the Capitol in 1863.

CRITICAL VIEWING Answers will vary. Possible response: The statue conveys a sense of strength and leadership and a willingness to charge into danger. Jackson appears to be someone who is looking for an adventure.

How did Andrew Jackson's policies impact different groups of people in America?

Four Corners Activity: Compromise Label each corner of the room with one of the following: Democracy, Economy, States' Rights, Native Americans. Divide the class into four groups and have each group move to a corner to discuss these questions.

Group 1: Democracy: How is voting related to the idea of democracy? Who should be allowed to vote?

Group 2: Economy: What is the foundation for a strong economy?

Group 3: States' Rights: Should states have the right to change a law made by federal lawmakers?

Group 4: Native Americans: In 1824, Native Americans were members of their own sovereign nations and were not considered U.S. citizens. What might be the advantages and disadvantages for Native Americans under this system?

Ask students in each group to discuss their question and come to an agreement on a response. Have each group read their question and answer to the class. Record student answers and revisit them at the end of the chapter.

Word Web

Have students complete a Word Web for Key Vocabulary words as they read the chapter. Ask them to write each word in the center of an oval. Have them look through the chapter to find examples, characteristics, and descriptive words that may be associated with the vocabulary word. At the end of the chapter, ask students what they learned about each word. Model an example for students on the board, using the graphic organizer below.

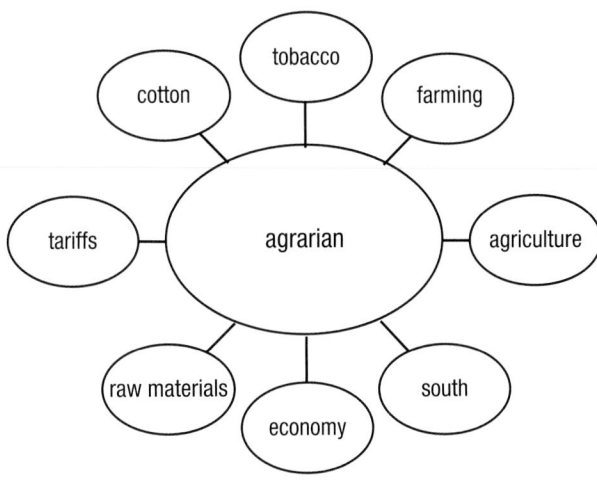

COMPARE AND CONTRAST
Remind students that Venn Diagrams are used to show what is alike and what is different about two individuals or events. Details that show how the two things are different are placed in the outside circles—in this case, details that tell only about Jackson or only about Adams. Details that show how Jackson and Adams are alike are placed in the overlapping area. Have students copy the Venn Diagram. Tell them that they should add at least two main policy differences to the diagram as they read through the chapter to compare and contrast the policies of President Andrew Jackson with those of President John Quincy Adams.

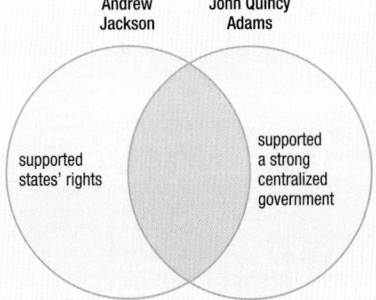

1824	John Quincy Adams elected president
1828	Andrew Jackson elected president
1828	Tariff of 1828
1830	Indian Removal Act
1833	Congress reduces tariffs
1834	Whig Party founded
1837	Panic of 1837
1837	Federal forces capture Osceola
1838	Trail of Tears

AMERICAN STORIES ONLINE For instructional support for the online American Story "The Erie Canal," go to NGLSync.Cengage.com.

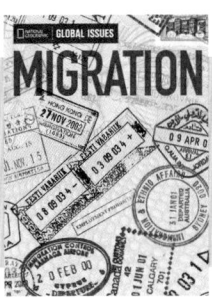

For more about the movement of people from one place to another, see *GLOBAL ISSUES: MIGRATION.*

1.1 Expanding Democracy

You back the candidate who's got your back. It's human nature. He or she supports your causes and promises to fix all the things you think are broken. Of course, these promises aren't always kept.

MAIN IDEA Regional differences fueled a battle over the presidency in the 1820s between John Quincy Adams and Andrew Jackson.

THE TIGHT ELECTION OF 1824

The presidential election of 1824 pitted **John Quincy Adams**, the current secretary of state and son of John Adams, against Andrew Jackson, who, as you may remember, fought in the War of 1812. The two candidates embodied the regional differences that divided the country. Adams represented the businessmen of the East. He wanted to build canals and roads to improve the nation's transportation system, and he promoted science and education. Jackson, representing the farmers of the West, supported states' rights. Adams and Jackson were the main candidates in 1824, but other candidates ran as well, including William Crawford, the secretary of the treasury, and Henry Clay, the speaker of the House of Representatives.

Andrew Jackson received the most popular votes in the election by a large margin. He also won the most electoral votes. However, he failed to win more than half of the total electoral votes, which then, as now, is required for victory. As a result, according to the 12th Amendment to the Constitution, the responsibility of choosing a winner among the top three candidates—Jackson, Adams, and Crawford—fell to the House of Representatives. By one vote, the House chose Adams to lead the country.

Adams took office in March 1825 and appointed Henry Clay as the secretary of state shortly thereafter. The appointment outraged Jackson. He believed that Adams and Clay had made a deal in which Clay persuaded other members of the House to vote for Adams in exchange for the prestigious, or highly respected, cabinet position. Jackson called the deal a "corrupt bargain" and

claimed the men stole the election from him. As president, Adams didn't gather much backing for his proposed canals and roads, in part because Jackson's supporters in Congress blocked them.

READY FOR A REMATCH

Meanwhile, Jackson had his eyes on the 1828 presidential election. Both Adams and Jackson were Democratic-Republicans, but the party had become deeply split. According to Jackson, on one side stood Adams and the rich easterners whose interests Adams favored. Jackson himself claimed to champion hardworking people whom he called the "common man." Eventually, two new parties arose. Adams and his followers formed the **National Republicans**. Jackson and his camp were known as **Democrats**.

During the 1828 campaign, both parties used speeches, parades, **slogans**, or sayings, and songs to build excitement for their candidate—an approach that changed the way politicians ran for office. Supporters on both sides also took part in mudslinging, or using insults to attack an opponent. In spite of all the name-calling, Jackson easily beat Adams in the election.

Voting rights, or laws that dictate which Americans have the right to vote, had been extended so more people could vote. You may recall that previously, only white men who owned property and paid taxes could vote. By contrast, in 1828, most white men in many states could vote whether they owned property or not. As a result, about 782,000 more "common men" participated in the 1828 election than in the previous one. Most Americans viewed Jackson's win as a victory over the privileged. **Jacksonian democracy** was the

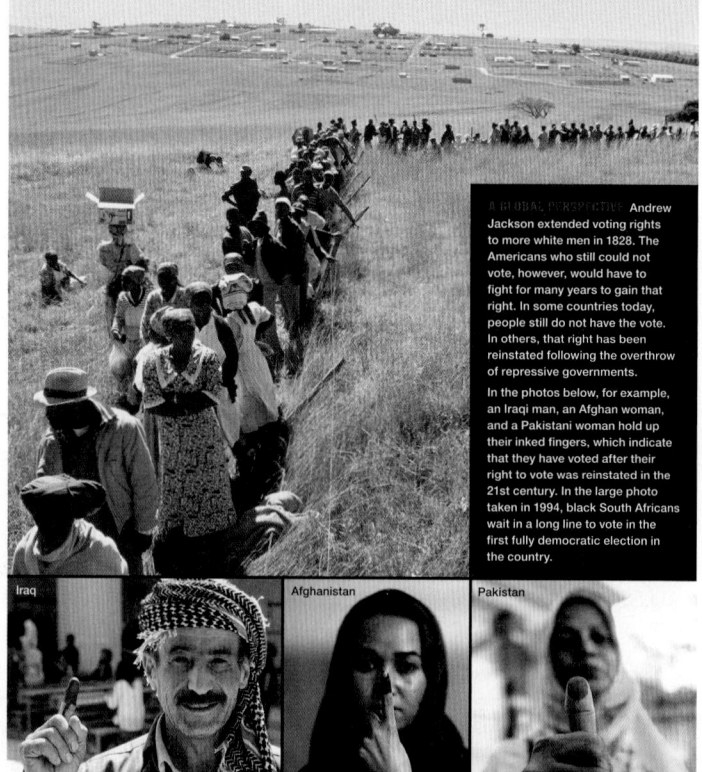

Iraq

Afghanistan

Pakistan

A GLOBAL PERSPECTIVE Andrew Jackson extended voting rights to more white men in 1828. The Americans who still could not vote, however, would have to fight for many years to gain that right. In some countries today, people still do not have the vote. In others, that right has been reinstated following the overthrow of repressive governments.

In the photos below, for example, an Iraqi man, an Afghan woman, and a Pakistani woman hold up their inked fingers, which indicate that they have voted after their right to vote was reinstated in the 21st century. In the large photo taken in 1994, black South Africans wait in a long line to vote in the first fully democratic election in the country.

political movement that celebrated the common man—farmers, craftsmen, laborers, and middle-class businessmen—and defended the will of the people. But women, African Americans, and Native Americans still could not vote or hold office. Nevertheless, Jackson's election in 1828 reflected the steady expansion of white male suffrage, symbolized the shift of political power to the West, and opened a new era of political democracy in the United States. President Jackson was a symbol of his age. People now believed they were represented by one of their own in the White House.

HISTORICAL THINKING

1. **READING CHECK** How was the presidential election of 1824 decided?

2. **COMPARE AND CONTRAST** How was Jacksonian democracy different from what had existed before?

3. **DRAW CONCLUSIONS** Why was Jacksonian democracy such an important development?

PLAN

Objective
Learn how political party differences influenced the 1828 election.

Critical Thinking Skills for Lesson 1.1
• Identify Main Ideas and Details
• Monitor Comprehension
• Compare and Contrast
• Draw Conclusions

Essential Question for Chapter 11
How did Andrew Jackson's policies impact different groups of people in America? The 1828 election saw the expansion of voting rights for some, but not all citizens. Lesson 1.1 discusses the growth of two political parties and the impact of that political division on the 1828 election.

Background for the Teacher
The 1824 presidential election was not the only election to be decided by the House of Representatives. The election of 1800 saw a more heated battle for president unfold in the House. The candidates were Thomas Jefferson and Aaron Burr. Burr was actually Jefferson's running mate, but under the voting rules of the day, each received 73 electoral votes. When it came time for the House to break the tie, no victor emerged. Representatives from each of the 16 states voted more than 30 times but neither candidate gained the nine votes needed to declare a majority. After weeks of deadlock, Delaware's James Bayard shifted his support away from Burr, giving the presidency to Jefferson. In both the 1800 and 1824 elections, the involvement of the House raised concerns that the strength of political parties and closed-door political deals were what truly elected the president, not the will of the people.

INTRODUCE & ENGAGE

Discuss Political Campaigns

Prompt students to consider local or national political campaigns they are familiar with. Guide them to discuss things they've noticed about candidates and their campaigns, such as the tone and content of advertisements, whether the candidates debate each other, and how they get their messages across. Encourage students to identify character traits or defining issues for a candidate they would support. **ASK:** Do you think voters in one region might tend to vote for different candidates than voters in another region? Why or why not? *(Possible response: Yes; people in the same region are likely to face similar problems, so they would tend to vote for the candidate who addresses those problems.)*

TEACH

Guided Discussion

1. **Compare and Contrast** In what ways did the differences between John Quincy Adams and Andrew Jackson reflect the different regions and people who supported them? *(Adams stood for the businessmen of the East and supported improvements in the transportation system, science, and education. Jackson supported those in the West, specifically the farmers, and he advocated for states' rights.)*

2. **Draw Conclusions** While voting rights were expanded for the 1828 election, not all people in the South shared the views of democratic politics of the Jacksonian era that were popular among his supporters. What might be some of the limitations of Jacksonian democracy for those in the South? *(Possible response: Unlike many white men, African-American men were not allowed to vote and almost certainly did not feel their views were represented by Jackson. Much of the population in the South was made up of enslaved men.)*

A Global Perspective

Explore the photographs and caption for this lesson with students. **ASK:** What do you think it means to individuals denied the opportunity to vote to finally have that opportunity? *(Answers will vary. Possible response: It would mean a lot because they would finally have a voice in how their country was run.)* How do you view the importance of voting in the United States in local, state, and federal elections? *(Answers will vary. Possible response: Voting is the obligation of every American citizen who has the right to vote.)*

Active Options

On Your Feet: Team Word Webbing Organize students into teams of four and have them record what they know about voting and the electoral process on a piece of paper. Encourage students to build on their teammates' entries as they rotate the paper from one member to the next. Then call on volunteers from each group to make statements about how the president of the United States is elected based on their webs.

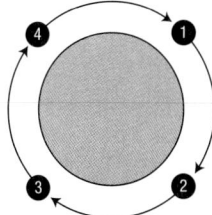

NG Learning Framework: Create a Storyboard

SKILLS Collaboration, Communication

KNOWLEDGE Our Human Story

Encourage students to work together to create a storyboard about events leading to the 1828 election of Andrew Jackson, including events surrounding the 1824 election of John Quincy Adams. Students should begin by illustrating the story of the 1824 election, the election results, the subsequent actions of the House of Representatives, the expansion of voting rights, and the division of political parties leading to the 1828 election. When the storyboards are completed, invite groups to share them with the class.

DIFFERENTIATE

English Language Learners ELD

Create Word Charts Help students at the **Emerging** level understand specific word meanings. Display the chart below and write the following four words above it: *elect, party, candidate, representative.* Tell students to copy the chart and complete the four parts of the chart for each word.

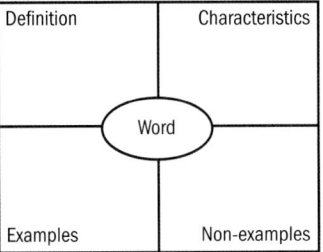

Definition	Characteristics
	Word
Examples	Non-examples

Pre-AP

Create Campaign Posters Remind students of the types of campaigning that preceded the 1828 presidential election. Have students create campaign posters for John Quincy Adams and for Andrew Jackson. The posters should reflect the division of political parties and pitch their candidate to both the candidates' base of support as well as undecided voters. Once students are finished, have them share their completed posters with the class.

See the Chapter Planner for more strategies for differentiation.

HISTORICAL THINKING

ANSWERS

1. A vote by the House of Representatives decided who became president.

2. Most of the white male population could vote in 1828, whether they held property or not, so many more people voted and did not support the privileged class.

3. Possible response: Jacksonian democracy championed the "common man," such as farmers and laborers. It was an important development because it was seen as an effort to support and defend the will of the people and as a movement away from the will of the eastern elite.

President of the People?

When you're considered an outsider and achieve something big, people expect great things of you. That was the position Andrew Jackson was in when he won the presidency, and now all eyes were on him.

MAIN IDEA Andrew Jackson rose from humble beginnings to become a U.S. president who symbolized a new brand of democracy.

FROM HARDSHIP TO HERO

Andrew Jackson was the first president who didn't come from a wealthy Virginia or Massachusetts family. In fact, he was born into poverty in 1767 and grew up in North Carolina. His father died before his birth, leaving his mother to raise him and his brothers.

During the American Revolution, young Jackson served as a messenger for the Continental Army. British soldiers discovered what he was doing and took him prisoner. While Jackson was being held, a British soldier ordered the boy to clean his boots. Jackson refused, and the soldier slashed him with his sword. Jackson also contracted smallpox and survived, but his mother and brothers weren't as lucky. He was an orphan by the age of 14.

Despite his hard childhood, Jackson achieved great success. He moved to the Tennessee frontier and became a lawyer in 1787. He practiced law in the small but growing town of Nashville and met his future wife, Rachel Donelson Robards, while boarding with her family. Later, he made a successful run for Congress. In 1804, Jackson purchased a

🏛 The Cabildo – Louisiana State Museum, New Orleans

In 1815, wearing this uniform coat, Jackson led the American victory at the Battle of New Orleans, which ended the War of 1812. Jackson is also wearing the coat in the 1817 portrait by Ralph E.W. Earl, shown on the opposite page. What details in the coat might indicate that the person wearing it is a general?

425-acre farm, later known as the Hermitage, where he built a plantation and used enslaved people to labor in his fields.

When the War of 1812 broke out between the United States and Great Britain, Jackson served as a general in command of soldiers from Tennessee. After crushing the British at the Battle of New Orleans, Jackson became a national hero.

A CLEAN SWEEP

Jackson's success was crowned by his election as president of the United States in 1828. About 30,000 people witnessed his inauguration in March 1829. But he endured the ceremony with a heavy heart. During the campaign, some of the mudslinging had been directed at his wife's reputation. When she died of a heart attack three months before her husband's inauguration, Jackson believed the personal attacks had caused her death.

Once he took office, however, Jackson assumed the presidency with enthusiasm and began carrying out the government reforms he'd promised to make during his campaign. First, Jackson replaced many of Adams's government officials with his own supporters. These appointees included newspaper editors who had been loyal to Jackson during the presidential campaign.

Critics claimed that what he'd done was corrupt. They believed Jackson was using the appointments to assume greater control of the federal government. But Jackson defended his actions by pointing out that completely removing officials from time to time prevents any one party from maintaining a stranglehold on government. The practice of rewarding political backers with government jobs became known as the **spoils system**, and it continues today. The term comes from the saying, "to the victors belong the spoils [goods or benefits] of the enemy." In this case, the "spoils" were the political positions Jackson had given to his supporters.

Controversy over appointments was just one of the problems Jackson faced early in his presidency. Soon he would find himself in a battle over taxes and states' rights that threatened to tear apart the Union.

Portrait of General Andrew Jackson, 1817

Mathew Brady photo of Jackson, 1845

HISTORICAL THINKING

1. **READING CHECK** What challenges did Andrew Jackson face growing up?

2. **COMPARE AND CONTRAST** How did Jackson differ from all preceding presidents?

3. **FORM AND SUPPORT OPINIONS** Do you think Jackson was right to initiate the use of the spoils system to appoint government officials? Support your opinion.

Objective

Learn about the reforms Andrew Jackson made early in his presidency.

Critical Thinking Skills for Lesson 1.2

• Identify Main Ideas and Details

• Monitor Comprehension

• Compare and Contrast

• Form and Support Opinions

• Make Inferences

• Analyze Cause and Effect

Essential Question for Chapter 11

How did Andrew Jackson's policies impact different groups of people in America? After the election of 1828, Jackson rewarded his supporters with political appointments. Lesson 1.2 discusses Jackson's life before the 1828 election and the controversies that arose after he became president.

Background for the Teacher

The Hermitage played an important role in Jackson's life. He originally purchased the small, 425-acre farm in 1804. Not long after he moved in, he quit his job as a superior court judge to focus on the farm and his other businesses. Over the years, he added land and brought slaves to the Hermitage. The house underwent major remodeling in 1831 after Jackson became president and again in 1834 after it was heavily damaged by fire. At its height, the farm became a 1,000-acre plantation worked by approximately 150 slaves. Its main cash crop was cotton, which was labor-intensive and required many hands. In 1856, 11 years after Andrew Jackson's death, Andrew Jackson, Jr., sold the Hermitage to the state of Tennessee and the Jackson family became tenants on the farm.

📓 History Notebook

Encourage students to complete the American Gallery page for Chapter 11 in their History Notebooks as they read.

Identify Historical Heroes

Ask students to identify people in history who are considered heroes for the common people, such as Abraham Lincoln. Write the names of the heroes on the board. Then work together to brainstorm characteristics that heroes possess. Add these characteristics on the board. Tell students in this lesson they will learn about President Andrew Jackson. At the end of the lesson, refer students back to the list of heroes from history and discuss Jackson's legacy and whether they think Jackson was a hero for the common people.

TEACH

Guided Discussion

1. **Make Inferences** Which event in Jackson's life helped him the most in becoming president of the United States? *(Answers will vary. Possible response: Jackson's victory at the Battle of New Orleans made him a national hero, which probably helped him win the election.)*

2. **Analyze Cause and Effect** How did Jackson's initial government reforms lead to the spoils system? *(Jackson replaced many government officials with his own supporters. Critics thought this action was corrupt and that Jackson was appointing his political followers to key positions in order to gain more control of the government.)*

🏛 Virtual Museum Visit

The Cabildo is located on Jackson Square in New Orleans. Inside is a wealth of artifacts highlighting American history, such as Andrew Jackson's military coat from the Battle of New Orleans. The museum's collection showcases the diverse groups of people who have contributed to Louisiana's history. On the museum's website, a virtual tour of the third floor offers a glimpse of the museum's collection.

Active Options

On Your Feet: Debate Divide the class into two groups. Have one side represent the pros of the spoils system and the other side represent the cons. To organize their arguments, have the pro group discuss the reasons why the spoils system benefits the workings of government and the policy decisions of the president, and have the con group find reasons for the opposite. Each group should also generate some suggestions to address the concerns of the other group. Then give the groups turns debating the topic by presenting their arguments and suggestions. See if either group can persuade opposing students to change sides. After the debate, have the class vote to determine the winner of the debate.

AMERICAN GALLERY
ONLINE

Andrew Jackson Invite students to explore the American Gallery. Have them select one of the items and do additional research to learn more about it. Ask questions that will inspire additional inquiry about the chosen gallery item, such as: What is the item? Where and when was it created? Why was it created? What is it made of? Why does it belong in this chapter? What else would you like to know about it?

Striving Readers

Sequence Events Have students work in pairs to determine the sequence of events in Andrew Jackson's life. Tell students to illustrate four big events in the order in which they happened and write a caption for each event.

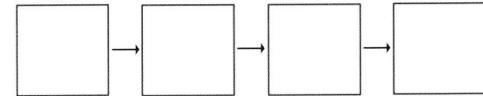
Events in the Life of Andrew Jackson

Gifted & Talented

Teach a Class Encourage students to prepare to teach this lesson to the class. Provide a set amount of time for students to present their lessons. Encourage them to research and prepare any visual or audio media, as well as any class or group activities, they may want to use as they teach.

See the Chapter Planner for more strategies for differentiation.

HISTORICAL THINKING

ANSWERS

1. Jackson grew up in poverty and was taken prisoner by the British during the American Revolution. Also, at age 14, his whole family contracted a serious illness that he survived but that claimed his mother and brothers.

2. Unlike previous presidents, who all came from wealthy families in Virginia or Massachusetts, Jackson was born into poverty and grew up in North Carolina.

3. Answers will vary. Possible response: I don't think he was right to give his supporters jobs because they may not have been qualified for high-level, public service jobs. For example, some of the people he appointed were newspaper editors, without public service or government experience.

THE CABILDO

The epaulets on the shoulders and the stripes on the sleeves might indicate that the coat belonged to a general.

When you get together with friends for a movie, you probably disagree sometimes about which one to see. Will it be sci-fi, a romantic comedy, or a thriller? But the real question is: Do you compromise or split up and see different films?

MAIN IDEA Conflicts over tariffs caused tensions—and triggered threats—in different parts of the country.

In this painting by George P.A. Healy, *Webster's Reply to Hayne*, Daniel Webster stands and delivers his speech in the Senate. Hayne sits to Webster's right with his hands held in front of him.

TROUBLE OVER TAXES

In the early years of Andrew Jackson's presidency, regions of the country were having trouble compromising. In particular, the Northeast and the South disagreed over tariffs, which are taxes a foreign country charges on its imported goods. The Northeast welcomed tariffs. Many northeasterners worked in manufacturing. Tariffs made foreign goods more expensive than those produced in the Northeast, and so increased sales of local goods. But people in the South didn't like tariffs. The South had an **agrarian**, or agricultural, economy. Southerners were mostly farmers who had to buy manufactured goods from other countries. Tariffs increased the cost of these goods.

So southerners were angry when Congress passed a bill in the last months of John Quincy Adams's presidency that greatly increased tariffs. The bill raised the price of foreign products sold in the United States. It also contained a clause that raised taxes on U.S. raw materials sold abroad. The clause hurt the South because it depended on the overseas sale of such raw materials as cotton and tobacco. Taxes made these items more expensive and, as a result, less attractive to foreign buyers.

The Tariff of 1828, as the bill was called, was a win-win for the federal government and the Northeast. Tariffs were the government's main source of revenue, or income. The fees caused foreign countries to charge more for their goods and helped protect northeastern industries. As you may recall, Adams represented the interests of the Northeast. In fact, the Adams-packed Congress passed the bill to appeal to northeastern voters.

Not surprisingly, southerners were outraged. They called the bill the **Tariff of Abominations**. An abomination is something that stirs feelings of disgust or hatred, which is exactly how southerners felt. But the bill backfired on Adams. The South helped vote him out of office partly in reaction to the tariff hike.

STATE VERSUS FEDERAL POWER

Political leaders in South Carolina hated the bill so much, they began to talk about the state's withdrawal from the Union. To prevent the country from breaking apart, South Carolina senator John C. Calhoun applied the **doctrine of nullification**, also called the states' rights doctrine. According to this doctrine, a state could nullify, or reject, a federal law it considered unconstitutional. By promoting the idea that a state could override a federal law, the doctrine opened up the debate over states' rights versus the authority of the federal government.

The issue placed Jackson in a tough position. He supported states' rights, and he had picked Calhoun to be his vice president. But he disagreed with Calhoun's notion that states should be able to prevent the federal government from acting on behalf of the nation as a whole.

Soon, other politicians joined in. Most famously, two senators took part in the **Webster-Hayne debate** in 1830. **Daniel Webster** from Massachusetts argued against nullification, claiming that it threatened the Union and freedom.

In a passionate plea, he called for "Liberty and Union, now and forever, one and inseparable!" Robert Y. Hayne from South Carolina made the case for nullification. He claimed that a state had the right to nullify a federal law, and he criticized those who, as he said, "are constantly stealing power from the States and adding strength to the Federal Government."

To ease the situation, Jackson and Congress agreed to reduce the tariff in 1832, but South Carolina's representatives still thought it was too high. They rejected the tariff in 1828 and 1832. The state's representatives even threatened **secession**, or withdrawal from the country, if the federal government tried to force it to pay the tariffs. Jackson responded by warning the representatives that he would consider secession an act of **treason**, or disloyalty to one's country. And Congress authorized Jackson to use force to collect tariffs.

The crisis finally ended in 1833 when Congress passed yet another bill that gradually reduced tariffs. However, tensions between the North and the South did not go away. On the contrary, tensions would continue to escalate throughout the first half of the 1800s.

But, meanwhile, another crisis was brewing. Americans' demand for more land in the West was driving Native American populations from their homes. Jackson answered with a new set of policies toward Native Americans.

HISTORICAL THINKING

1. **READING CHECK** How did the doctrine of nullification help assert states' rights?

2. **ANALYZE CAUSE AND EFFECT** How did the Tariff of 1828 affect the agrarian economy in the South?

3. **FORM AND SUPPORT OPINIONS** Do you think states should have the right to nullify a federal law? Explain your answer.

PLAN

Objective
Understand how tariffs led to tension between the North and South.

Critical Thinking Skills for Lesson 1.3
- Identify Main Ideas and Details
- Monitor Comprehension
- Analyze Cause and Effect
- Form and Support Opinions
- Summarize
- Compare and Contrast
- Make Generalizations

Essential Question for Chapter 11
How did Andrew Jackson's policies impact different groups of people in America? The Tariff of 1828 resulted in disagreements between the North and the South. Lesson 1.3 discusses the tension between the two regions over the legislative power of the federal government and states' rights.

Background for the Teacher
The Webster-Hayne debate was not an organized debate but an impromptu series of speeches given on the Senate floor. When Connecticut Senator Samuel A. Foote proposed limits on how western land could be sold, Senator Hayne claimed the limits would lead to high prices and corruption and would undermine states' independence. Senator Webster argued against Hayne's view of states' rights. Webster felt that it was slavery, not the land sale proposal, that was the real root of the South's problems. Three months later, it became apparent that the federal versus states' rights rift went to the top of the government. President Jackson gave a toast at a dinner, saying, "Our Federal Union. It must be preserved." Vice President Calhoun responded with a toast of his own, "The Union—next to our liberty, the most dear."

INTRODUCE & ENGAGE

Take a Stand

Engage in a short class discussion about who determines laws in the United States today: state governments or the federal government. Point out that laws regarding some issues, such as immigration, are decided at the federal level, while others, such as medical malpractice, are decided at the state level. Ask students to identify areas where they believe laws should be developed at the federal level and areas where they believe laws should be developed at the state level. Then tell students that they will read about the issue of states' rights and the debate that almost divided the nation.

TEACH

Guided Discussion

1. **Summarize** How did the issue of tariffs divide the country? *(The Northeast wanted tariffs because they raised the price of imported goods so that people were more inclined to buy local goods. For the South, tariffs increased the price of the imported goods they needed for farming. The bill also raised taxes on American materials sold overseas. The South sold raw materials such as cotton and tobacco to other countries and tariffs made these materials more expensive in foreign markets.)*

2. **Compare and Contrast** What was the mood in Congress before and after Congress passed a bill in 1833 that gradually reduced tariffs? *(Before the bill passed, tensions were so high that South Carolina threatened to secede from the country. The bill ended the secession crisis, but tensions between northern and southern states remained.)*

Make Generalizations

Do you think southern objections to the Tariff of 1828 were more about a general concern for states' rights or specifically a concern about how the tariff would affect the sale of cotton and tobacco abroad? *(Answers will vary. Possible response: I think it was a greater concern for the rights of states to pass laws governing their state, and in particular laws governing their economy.)* How would a tariff on cotton hurt its sale to Europe? *(It would increase the cost of U.S. cotton, perhaps making it more expensive to buy than cotton from other countries.)*

Active Options

On Your Feet: Present Both Sides Divide students into two groups, one representing the state governments and the other representing the federal government. Give the state group this topic sentence: State governments should have the power to reject a federal law. Give the federal group this topic sentence: The federal government acts in the interests of the nation as a whole. Tell groups to discuss their ideas and to create a paragraph by having each student contribute one sentence to support the topic. Allow each group to organize their ideas and present its paragraph to the class by having the groups form lines and having each student read his or her sentence in the correct order.

NG Learning Framework: Analyze the Doctrine of Nullification

ATTITUDE Curiosity

SKILL Observation

Tell students to work in groups to research the doctrine of nullification and learn why the doctrine violated the Constitution. Students should find out why senators from southern states believed the doctrine was essential to the South's cotton-producing economy. Tell students to record their findings. Once students have finished researching and recording their notes, have the groups present their findings to the class.

DIFFERENTIATE

Striving Readers

Use Exit Slips Give each student an exit slip with the following question: *Why were states' rights important to the southern states?* Tell students to read the lesson, write their answer on the slip, and give their answer to a classmate who will add a sentence to support or reject the answer. Have students hand in their slips when they leave class.

Inclusion

Team Up Assign students to teams of two to work through the Historical Thinking questions together. One student should read the question first. Then the team should discuss a response, and the other student can write down the answer. When teams are finished, have them trade answers with another team to check for accuracy.

See the Chapter Planner for more strategies for differentiation.

HISTORICAL THINKING

ANSWERS

1. It declared that a state could reject a federal law within that state's borders.

2. The tariff raised taxes on imported goods, which the South relied on. The tariff also raised taxes on American raw materials being exported overseas, which hurt southerners exporting cotton and tobacco.

3. Answers will vary. Possible answer: If states could nullify a federal law, then the union of states would be at risk. There would be no reason to have a federal government, and especially no reason for Congress, since federal laws would be passed but could not be enforced.

Expanding into Native American Lands

Native Americans had lived in North America for centuries, enduring natural disasters, wars, and disease. Soon they would be forced to try to survive Andrew Jackson's Native American policies.

MAIN IDEA Native Americans lost land to white settlers as Andrew Jackson and the U.S. government forced their westward relocation.

TREATIES AND BATTLES

Andrew Jackson had a long history with Native Americans. After the War of 1812, he battled the Creek in Georgia and negotiated a treaty with them on behalf of the federal government. According to the terms of the treaty, the Creek gave up 22 million acres of land (an area larger than the state of South Carolina) to the government, which then sold pieces of the land to settlers.

More battles and treaties followed with the Creek, Cherokee, Choctaw, and Chickasaw, who held large areas of land throughout the South. Little by little, many of these groups were forced onto lands less suited to farming, as white settlers moved into what had once been Native American territory.

When Jackson became president, he offered Native Americans in the South two choices: either assimilate, or adopt, European ways of life and accept the authority of the states in which they lived, or move west of the Mississippi River. More than any other southeastern tribe, the Cherokee assimilated, taking up many aspects of white culture and customs. They dressed in western-style clothing and built plantations and ranches similar to those of white settlers.

One Cherokee named Sequoya (sih-KWOY-uh) developed a writing system and began publishing a newspaper. As a result, literacy quickly spread among the Cherokee. They even wrote a constitution, using the U.S. Constitution as a model, and established the Cherokee Nation. Despite these efforts, the Cherokee were under constant pressure to leave the region. The pressure came to a head in 1828, when Americans discovered gold on Cherokee lands in Georgia. Now both settlers and miners were eager to grab the land. That's when southern states passed laws allowing them to take over Native American lands.

THE INDIAN REMOVAL ACT

Jackson supported these laws and, in 1830, approved another law that took Native American relocation a step further. The law was the Indian Removal Act, which ended the U.S. government's earlier policy of respecting the rights of Native Americans to remain on land they'd lived on for generations. Under this policy, they were forced to move to an area of land that included present-day Oklahoma and parts of Kansas and Nebraska. The area came to be known as Indian Territory.

The act required the government to peacefully negotiate treaties with Native Americans and not force them off their land. But the U.S. government and Jackson often ignored this requirement. Jackson considered Native Americans conquered subjects of the United States. As such, he believed the government could decide where they would live.

Not all Americans supported the removal act. Many opposed it because of their dislike of Jackson. Others protested the cruelty of sending Native Americans into an unknown wilderness. Religious groups, such as the Quakers, opposed the act on moral grounds, claiming it wasn't just or right. Many Native Americans gave in and left their homes. But not all would go without a fight.

National Museum of the American Indian, Washington, D.C.

While the Cherokee assimilated European styles, they also held onto their own culture, as the traditional artifacts shown here demonstrate. The man's coat is made from the hide of deer, which the Cherokee hunted. Like all Cherokee baskets, the one shown here was woven by a woman and was used to store all sorts of household goods. The Cherokee would have filled the wooden water drum with a quantity of water to get a deep, echoing sound.

Man's coat, c. 1820

Basket of woven and dyed rivercane, c. 1900

Water drum and drumstick, c. 1890

HISTORICAL THINKING

1. **READING CHECK** What was Jackson's attitude toward Native Americans?

2. **MAKE INFERENCES** What do you think the Cherokee hoped to gain by establishing their own constitution?

3. **COMPARE AND CONTRAST** How were the stated policies toward Native Americans different from what actually occurred?

Objective

Analyze how westward expansion into Native American lands affected Native Americans.

Critical Thinking Skills for Lesson 2.1

- Identify Main Ideas and Details
- Monitor Comprehension
- Make Inferences
- Compare and Contrast
- Describe
- Analyze Cause and Effect

Essential Question for Chapter 11

How did Andrew Jackson's policies impact different groups of people in America? The Indian Removal Act forced Native Americans from their ancestral lands. Lesson 2.1 describes Native Americans' experience as white settlers moved into their territory, pushing them westward.

Background for the Teacher

Sequoya's writing system, or syllabary, at first used one graphic symbol for each word. When that became too cumbersome, Sequoya devised a new system where a unique character stood for each syllable. Eventually, Sequoya devised a total of 86 symbols. The writing system was used to produce the Cherokee nation's official newspaper. The first issue of the *Cherokee Phoenix* was published on February 21, 1828. When the Cherokee were displaced and moved west of the Mississippi River, they took their writing system with them, using it to produce official documents and newspapers. Over time, use of Sequoya's syllabary declined, although it was used for the next 100 years in descriptions of Cherokee medicine, in private letters, and in translations of the Bible.

INTRODUCE & ENGAGE

Predict the Outcome

Read the title of the lesson aloud. Explain that in this lesson students will learn about what happened when white settlers moved westward into Native American lands. Ask students to predict what they think will happen as white settlers move west. Write their predictions on the board. Then at the end of the lesson, review the predictions and compare them with the actual outcomes.

TEACH

Guided Discussion

1. **Describe** How did the writing system developed by Sequoya benefit the Cherokee culture? *(It increased literacy, expanded the ability of the Cherokee to communicate and share ideas, and provided the means to write a constitution that established the Cherokee Nation.)*

2. **Analyze Cause and Effect** What prompted southern states to pass laws allowing miners and settlers to take over Native American lands? *(Gold was discovered on Cherokee lands in Georgia in 1828.)*

🏛 Virtual Museum Visit

Today the Cherokee Nation is the largest tribal nation in the United States and one of the largest employers in northeastern Oklahoma. In June 2016, the Cherokee Nation donated $500,000 to the National Museum of the American Indian to support a special 10-year exhibit called *Americans* as well an educational initiative titled *Native Knowledge 360°*. The *Americans* exhibit will present imagery of Native American history spanning six centuries. Importantly, the exhibit will examine the consequences of the 1830 Indian Removal Act. *Native Knowledge 360°* will introduce students in grades 4 through 12 to historically accurate informational materials on Native American history.

Active Options

On Your Feet: Numbered Heads Organize students into groups of four. Tell students to think about and discuss a response to this question: In what ways did Andrew Jackson's presidency usher in a particularly difficult time for Native Americans? Then call a number and have the student from each group with that number report for the group.

NG Learning Framework: Form an Opinion

ATTITUDES Responsibility, Empowerment

SKILL Problem-Solving

Assign students to small groups. Ask them to imagine they are leaders of a Native American tribe during the westward expansion and that Andrew Jackson has given them the choice to either assimilate European ways or move west of the Mississippi. Ask students which choice they think their tribe should make. Have each group come to an agreed-upon decision and plan for action using information from the text or from additional research to support their decision. Encourage groups to share their decisions with the class, explaining how they reached their decisions.

DIFFERENTIATE

Inclusion

Analyze Visuals Pair special needs students with students at a higher proficiency level. Have them reread the lesson and caption. Then have students describe the three items shown on the page. Have them use the three-column chart below to record each item, how it was used, and if this item would still be useful today.

Item	Purpose	Currently Used

Gifted & Talented

Explore Effects on Native Cultures Allow students to choose one Native American tribe affected by the Indian Removal Act. Suggest that they use online sources to learn about the history of the tribe and how its members were affected by the Indian Removal Act. Suggest that they also learn about the tribe's culture, including traditions, dress, food, and art, and how the culture changed after relocation. Students can present their findings in visual form, such as a time line, a map, an original work of art, or a multimedia presentation.

See the Chapter Planner for more strategies for differentiation.

HISTORICAL THINKING

ANSWERS

1. Jackson considered Native Americans to be conquered subjects of the United States. As such, he expected them to either move west to make way for European settlers or assimilate into the culture of the European settlers.

2. They hoped to be seen as a separate nation with laws and sovereignty over their lands.

3. The United States government ignored the part of the Indian Removal Act that required peaceful treaty negotiations and instead forced Native Americans to relocate to areas of present-day Oklahoma, Kansas, and Nebraska.

2.2 Native American Resistance

Sometimes you have to fight for your rights, even when it seems like a losing battle. But the fight is that much harder when the other side doesn't play fair.

MAIN IDEA Some Native Americans took up arms to resist their forced relocation by the U.S. government.

A TRAP IS SET

The **Seminole** were among the Native Americans who refused to leave their homes. They lived near the Everglades, a large wetlands region in southern Florida. After the Seminole rejected a removal treaty, President Jackson and the federal government declared war on them in 1835. But it didn't turn out to be an easy fight.

Seminole villages lay deep within the dangerous swampland of the Everglades, providing plenty of places where the Native Americans could hide and giving them a clear geographic advantage. When American soldiers came on the attack, Seminole leader **Osceola** (ahs-ee-OH-luh) and his warriors took them by surprise. They ambushed the soldiers, killing them with their tomahawks and

Threatened by Oil
Some Native Americans continue to protest their treatment today. In this photo, a Native American member of the Cowboy and Indian Alliance joined other Native Americans and non-native protestors in front of the Capitol in Washington, D.C., in April 2014. The thousands who gathered objected to the building of an oil pipeline through their land in the Great Plains region, saying it threatened water and other natural resources.

Black Hawk
Black Hawk visited Washington, D.C., in 1837 to witness the sale of the last of Sauk land to the United States. During that visit, artist Charles Bird King painted Black Hawk's portrait. Homer Henderson painted this copy in the late 1800s from a print of the original. In the painting, the Native American leader wears a medallion, depicting an unknown man, which he probably received as a treaty gift from U.S. officials.

muskets. The Seminole also burned the homes and crops of American settlers, hoping to drive them from the region.

At the end of 1837, the government arranged to meet with Osceola at a so-called peace conference. The two sides had declared a **truce**, an agreement to stop fighting, while their leaders met to talk. But the meeting was actually a trap. As soon as Osceola arrived, American soldiers took him prisoner. He died three months later in captivity.

Fighting continued off and on for five more years before the Seminole finally surrendered. Some of the Seminole migrated to Indian Territory, but they never entirely left the Everglades. Their descendants continue to live there today.

THE BLACK HAWK WAR

Native Americans in other parts of the country also resisted removal. At first, tribes north of the Ohio River in Illinois, including the Shawnee, Ottawa, Potawatomi, Sauk, and Fox, signed a treaty agreeing to relocate west of the Mississippi River. Once they had moved, however, the Sauk and Fox struggled to grow enough food for their people. They faced starvation. Then, in 1832, they rebelled. A Sauk leader named **Black Hawk** led his people and the Fox back to their lands in Illinois, where they meant to stay.

The U.S. military and Illinois militia had other ideas. To intimidate the Sauk and Fox, troops built large forts in the area. They also recruited members of other Native American tribes to fight Black Hawk and his followers. A young man named **Abraham Lincoln** served as a captain during this campaign. The Black Hawk War dragged on for a few months, but the Sauk and Fox were eventually overpowered. The war was brief but bloody, particularly for the Sauk and Fox. As many as 600 Native Americans died in the fighting, while only about 70 American soldiers perished.

In August 1832, Black Hawk surrendered, and the military imprisoned him for a time in a Virginia fort. He told his captors that he was not sorry for what he'd done. He was defending his land and his people from what he called "cheating men." When the American people read Black Hawk's words, many sympathized with him. Still, the Black Hawk War did not put an end to the government's efforts to drive Native Americans from their lands. Many more would be forced to leave—and at great cost.

HISTORICAL THINKING

1. **READING CHECK** How did Native Americans fight back against attempts to remove them?

2. **COMPARE AND CONTRAST** How were the reactions of Osceola and Black Hawk similar when they were forced to move westward?

3. **MAKE INFERENCES** Who were the "cheating men" Black Hawk referred to, and why did he characterize them in that way?

Objective
Learn how Native Americans reacted to forced relocation by the United States government.

Critical Thinking Skills for Lesson 2.2
• Identify Main Ideas and Details
• Monitor Comprehension
• Compare and Contrast
• Make Inferences
• Form and Support Opinions
• Evaluate
• Analyze Visuals

Essential Question for Chapter 11
How did Andrew Jackson's policies impact different groups of people in America? Native American tribes in southern Florida and the Great Lakes region resisted relocation efforts by the U.S. government. Lesson 2.2 discusses each side's role in the conflict.

Background for the Teacher
The 1835–1842 war between the Seminole and the U.S. government was the second of three Seminole wars. The first occurred from 1817 to 1818, when U.S. troops led by General Andrew Jackson crossed into Spanish-held Florida to capture enslaved African Americans who had escaped and were living amongst the Seminole. U.S. soldiers burned Seminole villages and captured Pensacola and St. Marks from the Spanish. The Third Seminole War took place between 1855 and 1858. The U.S. military was sent to track down the small population of Seminole that remained in Florida. By the end of the third war, only about 200 Seminole had survived the relocation efforts, many of them by hiding deep in the Everglades.

Connect to Today

Have students read the caption "Threatened by Oil" aloud. Discuss the significance of protests. **ASK:** Why do individuals or groups protest? *(Answers will vary. Possible responses: to bring attention to something they feel isn't right; to inform the greater public)* **ASK:** What is an example of a recent protest you feel was successful in informing others of an unfair situation? *(Answers will vary. Students may reflect on a local, state, or national protest event.)*

TEACH

Guided Discussion

1. **Form and Support Opinions** Was the military justified in using deception to capture Native American leaders as a way to end conflict? Support your opinion with evidence from the text. *(Answers will vary. Possible response: No. Using deception showed a lack of respect for Native American leaders and for their plight in trying to save their people from being forced from their native lands and a lack of integrity in deceiving an adversary who agreed to meet on peaceful terms to discuss a compromise.)*

2. **Evaluate** How did the Sauk and Fox tribes react to the relocation? *(They initially agreed to relocate but then found that they could not grow enough food for their people, so they defied the treaty and moved back to their original lands.)*

Analyze Visuals

Compare the clothing and hairstyle worn by the Native American protesting in front of the U.S. Capitol Building with the cultural attire worn by Black Hawk as depicted in the painting by Homer Henderson. **ASK:** How does their cultural attire make a statement about their Native American heritage? *(The cultural attire establishes an identity and cohesiveness among members of a tribe.)*

Active Options

On Your Feet: Create a Living Time Line Tell students to work in pairs to create a time line showing the events and dates associated with the relocation of the Seminole and the Sauk. Have pairs write each of the dates from their time line on an index card. Then mix up the cards and distribute them among students. Ask students to use the dates on their index cards to arrange themselves in a line in correct chronological order, keeping in mind that dates will have more than one student representing the date. Then have each student, or a representative from a group for that date, in turn explain the significance of the date he or she is holding.

NG Learning Framework: Write a News Article

ATTITUDE Curiosity

KNOWLEDGE Our Human Story

Encourage students to learn more about Abraham Lincoln's military involvement in the Black Hawk War. Have students work in pairs to frame a list of questions they have about the war and the role that Lincoln played in that war. Then have pairs use library resources or conduct online research to find answers to their questions and write a short news article reporting on Lincoln's role in the Black Hawk War. Encourage pairs to share their articles with the class.

DIFFERENTIATE

English Language Learners `ELD`

Identify Facts Arrange students in mixed-proficiency groups and guide them to conduct a Round Robin activity to review what they have learned in the lesson. Ask groups to spend three to five minutes generating facts, with all students contributing and taking notes. You might ask students at the **Expanding** and **Bridging** levels to assist students at the **Emerging** level. Finally, invite one student from each group to share his or her group's responses. Write all the facts on the board.

Pre-AP

Analyze Black Hawk's Farewell Speech Have students access, read, and, if available, listen to a dramatic reading of Black Hawk's 1832 Farewell Speech, which is available online. Ask students to analyze the speech and explain Black Hawk's interpretation of the way white men treated him and his fellow Indians. Invite students to summarize Black Hawk's Farewell Speech for the class and draw parallels to Chief Osceola's experience.

See the Chapter Planner for more strategies for differentiation.

HISTORICAL THINKING

ANSWERS

1. The Seminole refused to leave their homes and fought back when the federal government declared war on them. They tried to drive out white settlers by burning their homes and crops. The Sauk and the Fox warred with the federal government in an attempt to reclaim their lands.

2. Both Osceola and Black Hawk fought against leaving their lands. Osceola fought the soldiers and tried to drive settlers off the land. Black Hawk battled against the U.S. Army and state militias to take back tribal lands.

3. Answers will vary. Possible response: The cheating men were U.S. government officials. Black Hawk felt that deception had been used against the Sauk and other Native American tribes in order to take their native lands away from them.

2.3 The Trail of Tears

When people believe a policy is unfair or unconstitutional, they can take it to the highest court in the land. You would think that everyone would have to abide by a Supreme Court ruling, right?

MAIN IDEA In defiance of a ruling from the Supreme Court, Andrew Jackson forced the Cherokee to relocate to Indian Territory.

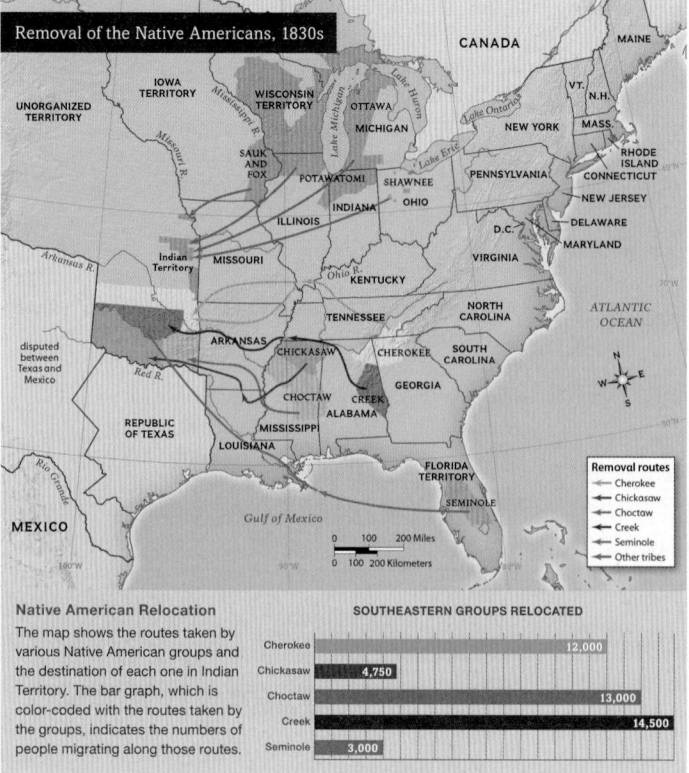

Removal of the Native Americans, 1830s

Removal routes
- → Cherokee
- → Chickasaw
- → Choctaw
- → Creek
- → Seminole
- → Other tribes

0 100 200 Miles
0 100 200 Kilometers

Native American Relocation
The map shows the routes taken by various Native American groups and the destination of each one in Indian Territory. The bar graph, which is color-coded with the routes taken by the groups, indicates the numbers of people migrating along those routes.

SOUTHEASTERN GROUPS RELOCATED

Group	Number
Cherokee	12,000
Chickasaw	4,750
Choctaw	13,000
Creek	14,500
Seminole	3,000

ONE LAST STAND

In an 1823 decision, *Johnson* v. *M'Intosh*, the Supreme Court had offered some protection for Native American lands. So, in 1832, the Cherokee turned to the Supreme Court to seek legal means to stay on their land. The Court ruled in their favor, determining that the Indian Removal Act was unconstitutional and that it violated previous treaties with the Cherokee. But the state of Georgia and President Andrew Jackson opposed the Supreme Court's decision. They wanted the Cherokee to go.

A small group of Cherokee signed the treaty, deciding that doing so was their only hope. They soon left for Indian Territory. But most of the Cherokee—about 17,000 people—opposed the treaty and remained on their land. **John Ross**, the principal chief of the Cherokee, led the resistance and tried to negotiate a better treaty. However, Jackson wasn't willing to enter into negotiations. In 1838, he sent General **Winfield Scott** and 7,000 federal troops into Cherokee lands in Georgia and Alabama. The soldiers forced people from their homes and placed them in camps. White settlers then looted and destroyed the Cherokee villages, leaving the Native Americans with only the few possessions they had taken to the camps.

A GRUELING MARCH

After the Cherokee had been confined in the camps for months, American soldiers forced them on a march to Indian Territory. The terrible journey lasted about four months, during the fall and winter of 1838 and 1839. The Cherokee weren't given adequate food, shelter, or clothing as they struggled in the rain and snow. Some soldiers even stole the few supplies that had been provided for the Native Americans.

Trail of Tears Sculpture
This sculpture from the Trail of Tears exhibit at the Cherokee Heritage Center in Tahlequah, Oklahoma, represents a Cherokee couple on the forced march. The exhibit includes a gallery that focuses on how the Cherokee started over after their relocation.

As a result, about 4,000 people died from cold, illness, and starvation on the march. One survivor remembered, "Children cry and many men cry, and all look sad like when friends die, but they say nothing." A witness to the forced migration reported that even old women "were traveling with heavy burdens attached to the back—on the sometimes frozen ground, and sometimes muddy streets, with no covering for the feet." Because of the suffering the Cherokee endured, the journey became known as the **Trail of Tears**.

To add to their burden, the soldiers made the Cherokee pay settlers for passing through their farms and boatmen for transporting them across rivers. By the time the Cherokee reached Indian Territory, they had little money left. They faced other challenges as well. Native Americans already living in the territory resented the newcomers. Not long after the Cherokee resettled, the Osage fought them over land. In addition, many Cherokee sought revenge against those of their tribe who had signed the treaty agreeing to move.

The Cherokee felt they had given up a part of their identity when they left their homeland. They had lost a spiritual connection to their ancestors, and they believed they had been betrayed by the U.S. government. Jackson's policies carried undertones of racial and political superiority and had a devastating impact on Native Americans.

HISTORICAL THINKING

1. **READING CHECK** What happened when some of the Cherokee resisted moving west?

2. **DESCRIBE** What challenges endured by Native Americans on the forced march to Indian Territory caused the journey to be known as the Trail of Tears?

3. **INTERPRET MAPS** Which southeastern Native American tribe traveled the farthest?

PLAN

Objective
Analyze the effects of President Jackson's defiance of the Supreme Court's ruling.

Critical Thinking Skills for Lesson 2.3
- Identify Main Ideas and Details
- Monitor Comprehension
- Describe
- Interpret Maps
- Make Inferences
- Identify
- Interpret Graphs

Essential Question for Chapter 11
How did Andrew Jackson's policies impact different groups of people in America? The forced migration of the Cherokee caused conflict within the tribe and with other Native American tribes. Lesson 2.3 discusses the Cherokee relocation route known as the Trail of Tears.

Background for the Teacher
Before the federal government started to remove the Cherokee from their homelands in 1838, a group of about 100 Cherokee, commonly known as the Treaty Party signed the Treaty of New Echota in 1835. This treaty was the basis for the federal government to justify removing the Cherokee from their ancestral lands. The Treaty Party included Major Ridge, who was a Cherokee leader, though he was not authorized to represent the whole tribe.

The terms of the treaty included surrendering ancestral lands east of the Mississippi. The compensation for their homelands included money, livestock, tools, and land in Indian Territory, among other benefits. However, the Cherokee Nation Council had passed a law prohibiting anyone from agreeing to relinquish tribal lands, decreeing death as the punishment for anyone breaking this law. After the treaty was signed, several Treaty Party members, including Major Ridge and his son, were killed by other Cherokees for violating the law.

K-W-L Chart

Provide each student with a K-W-L Chart. Have students brainstorm what they already know about the forced relocation of Native Americans. Then direct students' attention to the map. After reviewing the map, tell students to write questions inspired by the map, such as: Why were Native Americans moved so far from their native lands? How did the removal of Native Americans from their native lands affect the people and their tribal cultures? Allow time at the end of the lesson for students to fill in what they have learned.

K What Do I Know?	W What Do I Want To Learn?	L What Did I Learn?

TEACH

Guided Discussion

1. **Make Inferences** What was the impact on the Cherokee as they saw their villages destroyed? *(Answers will vary. Possible response: They probably felt great sadness and a sense of betrayal, anger, and fear about would happen to them next.)*

2. **Identify** What problems did the Cherokee face once they reached Indian Territory? *(Most of them had little money left to settle down with, and other tribes who settled there first fought with them over land.)*

Interpret Graphs

STEM

How many people were forcibly removed in the 1830s? *(47,250)* On average, how many people per tribe were removed from their homelands? *(9,450)* How did you arrive at your answers? *(Adding the numbers of all five groups together yields the total number; dividing the total number by the number of tribes yields the average.)*

Active Options

Active History: Analyze a Different Perspective Extend the lesson by using either the PDF or Whiteboard version of the activity. These activities take a deeper look at a topic from, or related to, the lesson. Explore the activities as a class, turn them into group assignments, or even assign them individually.

NG Learning Framework: Compare Relocation Routes

ATTITUDE Curiosity

KNOWLEDGE Our Human Story

Tell students to study the map showing the removal of Native Americans in the 1830s from lands east of the Mississippi River. Ask them to review the route each group of Native Americans was forced to take. Then have them use information from the lesson and additional source material to write sentences comparing and contrasting the relocation routes. Suggest that they include challenges each group faced based on their route. As a class, discuss what students discovered from their comparisons.

DIFFERENTIATE

Striving Readers

Pose and Answer Questions Have students work in pairs to read the lesson. Instruct them to pause after each paragraph and ask one another *what, who, where, when,* or *why* questions about what they have just read. Suggest students use a 5Ws Chart to help organize their questions and answers.

Gifted & Talented

Create a Podcast Tell students to research the relocation of Native Americans in the 1800s by investigating the searing accounts of removal and the Cherokees' Trail of Tears. Students should use their research to create a podcast discussing the relocation efforts and their effects on Native Americans' way of life. Invite students to share their podcasts with the class, lead a discussion on the credibility of the source, and draw conclusions about the accounts.

See the Chapter Planner for more strategies for differentiation.

HISTORICAL THINKING

ANSWERS

1. Seven thousand federal troops marched into Cherokee territory and forced people from their homes.

2. The Native Americans suffered during the four-month migration. They didn't have adequate clothing, food, or shelter. Many died of starvation, exposure, and illness.

3. The Seminole had the longest route to the Indian Territory. Their homelands were the farthest east.

3.1 Economic Crises

In the 1830s, people were moving west. New railroads and canals carried people and goods from state to state. These were good times for the country. Most people thought they'd never end.

MAIN IDEA Andrew Jackson helped destroy the Second Bank of the United States, which had a severe impact on the economy.

Land Sales, 1836–1854
The graph shows the impact of the Panic of 1837 on land sales after the government required people to buy land with only gold and silver.

Source: United States Census Bureau

THE BANK WAR

Andrew Jackson's domestic policies devastated the lives of Native Americans, but for many white Americans, life was good. The U.S. economy prospered during Jackson's presidency. Much of this prosperity was due to the country's powerful National Bank, the Second Bank of the United States, which played a big role in regulating the economy. Founded in 1816 after the first National Bank, the Second Bank was a huge federal bank

that held power over smaller banks. It controlled the nation's money supply and, by doing so, kept down **inflation**. Inflation is a decrease in the value of money that causes an increase in the price of goods and services. The Second Bank also provided loans to many people who wanted to buy property or launch businesses.

Jackson hated the Second Bank. For one thing, he didn't trust paper currency or any form of money other than gold or silver. For another, Jackson claimed that the bank, led by its president

Bank Notes
The $5,000 bank note (top) is a copy of one that Nicholas Biddle might have issued to customers taking out a loan. As you can see, the Second Bank used the name "Bank of the United States" on its paper currency.

The 6-cent note (below) is actually a political cartoon commenting on the extent to which money had lost its value after 1837. The bank that supposedly issued the note is the "Humbug Glory Bank"—*humbug* means "false or deceiving." And the images at the top of the note may symbolize Andrew Jackson. The donkey represents the Democratic Party to which Jackson belonged, and the hickory leaf may be a reference to his nickname: "Old Hickory."

Nicholas Biddle, held a monopoly over all other banks. He thought its policies favored the wealthy over working people. Jackson may also have disliked the bank because it often made loans to members of Congress, possibly giving Biddle influence over the legislators.

The bank became a central issue during the 1832 election. The bank's charter was due to expire in 1836. Jackson's opponent in the 1832 election, National Republican Henry Clay, sponsored a bill to renew the bank's charter early. The bill passed in Congress, but Jackson **vetoed**, or rejected it— and beat Clay in the election.

When Jackson won the presidency in 1832, he believed his victory proved that the people supported his position on the bank. So in the four years that remained of its charter, Jackson waged an all-out war to destroy the bank. He had his treasury secretary withdraw government funds and deposit them in state banks. Jackson's opponents called these state banks his "pet banks." Biddle retaliated by withholding bank loans from customers, but his actions only turned more people against the bank. In time, Jackson got his way, and the Second Bank went out of business.

THE PANIC OF 1837

After the Second Bank closed, people flocked to Jackson's pet banks. These banks made it easier to take out loans. But this easy money led to inflation. During the last years of Jackson's presidency, he required that people use gold or silver to buy land rather than paper money as a way to fight the inflation.

Because the economy still seemed to be in good shape, Jackson's vice president, **Martin Van Buren**, easily won the presidential election in 1836. But within a few weeks of his inauguration, it became clear that the state banks were in trouble. Fear about the condition of the economy spread throughout the country. This widespread fear, or panic, became known as the **Panic of 1837**.

Panicked people ran to the banks to exchange their money for gold and silver, but the banks quickly ran out of the precious metals. When many of the banks closed, businesses collapsed and people lost their jobs and land. Soon, the country sank into a deep economic **depression**, or a period of slow economic activity. States no longer had enough money to finish public projects for developing infrastructure, such as building canals and roads. It wasn't the first depression the nation faced, and it wouldn't be the last. The country's economic problems did not improve during Van Buren's presidency, and he did little to try to resolve them. Van Buren's inaction made him unpopular with the people and set the stage for a change in government and politics.

HISTORICAL THINKING

1. **READING CHECK** Why did Jackson veto the bill to renew the National Bank's charter?

2. **ANALYZE CAUSE AND EFFECT** How did the Panic of 1837 affect the country economically and politically?

3. **INTERPRET GRAPHS** How would you describe land sales between 1836 and 1842?

PLAN

Objective

Analyze how the country's economy went from growing prosperity to economic depression.

Critical Thinking Skills for Lesson 3.1

- Identify Main Ideas and Details
- Monitor Comprehension
- Analyze Cause and Effect
- Interpret Graphs
- Form and Support Opinions
- Compare and Contrast
- Analyze Visuals

Essential Question for Chapter 11

How did Andrew Jackson's policies impact different groups of people in America?
Jackson's dislike of the National Bank resulted in economic problems for Americans. Lesson 3.1 describes Jackson's efforts to close the bank and the ensuing economic consequences.

Background for the Teacher

Why would Henry Clay sponsor a bill to renew the Second Bank's charter in 1832 when the original charter wouldn't expire until 1836? The answer lies in a political strategy that backfired on Clay. Under Biddle's watch, the Second Bank had stabilized the national economy. Clay feared that if Jackson was reelected, he would let the bank's charter expire in 1836 and close the bank. Clay reasoned that given the bank's success, Jackson would never veto a bill to renew its charter in an election year. Biddle advised against the move, fearing the bank would become embroiled in campaign politics. Biddle was correct. Jacksonians viewed the recharter bill as a political attack on Jackson. They wagered that after a veto, and with Jackson as president, Congress would avoid addressing the National Bank's charter again until 1836.

Financial Literacy

To extend their knowledge and understanding about the concepts in this lesson, refer students to the Financial Literacy handbook.

Preview Using Visuals

Draw students' attention to the copy of a real bank note and the cartoon bank note. Have a volunteer read the caption aloud. Discuss the differences in the bank notes and have students identify details of each note. **ASK:** What do the illustrations in the real bank note represent about the United States? *(federal government, honesty, prosperity)*. **ASK:** What is the cartoonist's message and what makes you think so? *(The cartoonist is making a statement about how the federal government is managing the economy. The note shows little value, the name of the bank indicates it's not a good bank, and the illustrations make fun of Jackson.)*

TEACH

Guided Discussion

1. **Form and Support Opinions** Do you agree with Jackson's view of the Second Bank and his reasons for shutting it down? Have students support their opinions with evidence from the text. *(Possible response: I disagree with Jackson because the federal bank kept down inflation and provided loans to individuals and businesses.)*

2. **Compare and Contrast** How was the nation's economy managed before and after the closing of the Second Bank? *(Before the Second Bank closed, loans were secured through it, and it controlled the nation's money supply. After the closing, state banks issued easy loans, driving up inflation. Gold and silver were required to buy land rather than paper money as a way to fight inflation. Eventually, many state banks closed, resulting in great financial difficulties for Americans.)*

Analyze Visuals

Invite students to use the lesson as a starting point to research political cartoons created about Jackson's presidency. Tell them to focus on cartoons about the Second Bank published in newspapers. Have them save or print out three cartoons they find to be the most interesting and creative and write a report analyzing the opinions expressed by the political cartoons. Then have volunteers share their reports with the class, relating what the cartoons add to what they learned in the lesson.

Active Options

On Your Feet: State and Respond Have half the class write 10 statements based on the lesson. Tell students to focus on decisions made by Jackson regarding the Second Bank and the economic consequences of those decisions. Have the other half create response cards, writing "Positive Consequences" on one side and "Negative Consequences" on the other side. Then have students from the first group read their statements. Students from the second group should hold up their cards, showing either "Positive Consequences" or "Negative Consequences" as their response to the statement. For any statement with an obvious discrepancy between students who feel the consequences were positive or negative, discuss the statement and reasoning for their responses.

NG Learning Framework: Create a Line Graph

SKILLS Observation, Problem-Solving

STEM

KNOWLEDGE Our Human Story

Have students learn more about economic depressions in the United States from 1776 through 1836. Tell students to create a line graph that shows the inflation rates during that time. As a class, discuss the trends shown by the inflation rate graph and how it relates to economic depressions. Discuss whether Jackson's opinion about the worth of paper currency (also known as fiat money) versus gold and silver was a valid argument in the context of the economic patterns indicated on the graph.

English Language Learners

Use a Term in a Sentence To demonstrate their understanding of the terms *inflation*, *veto*, and *depression*, have students write two sentences using each word appropriately and draw a picture to go with each word. If needed, show students illustrations or charts to help them visualize the economic terms *inflation* and *depression*. Have students at the **Emerging** and **Expanding** levels work in pairs. Have students at the **Bridging** level work independently.

Pre-AP

Write Blog Posts Tell students that Alexis de Tocqueville was a French writer who visited the United States in the 1830s. Have them research de Tocqueville and find a summary of his book *Democracy in America*. Then ask them to imagine they are taking a trip across the United States today and to write blog posts comparing de Tocqueville's description of national character in the 1830s with the people they would expect to meet on their trip today. Have the rest of the class make comments on the blog posts.

See the Chapter Planner for more strategies for differentiation.

ANSWERS

1. Jackson hated the National Bank and thought the bank violated states' rights because it controlled private state banks.

2. The Panic of 1837 resulted in inflation and a rush to exchange paper money for gold and silver. This rush caused banks and businesses to close, which resulted in a loss of jobs and land and an economic depression. Initially, the panic seemed to have little political impact, but later, President Van Buren's inaction made him unpopular with the people.

3. Sales of land dropped significantly from 1836 to 1842. There was a small rebound in 1839, but by 1842 land sales had dropped to a few million acres.

A New Party System

When something isn't working, you probably want to change it—out with the old, in with the new. It often works that way in politics, too.

MAIN IDEA A new political party formed to oppose Jackson, and its candidate won the 1840 presidential election.

A CHANGE OF PARTIES

The old way of doing things definitely wasn't working in the United States in the late 1830s. While the economy slumped, the depression dragged on. Most of the factories in the East had let their workers go and closed down. Many of the unemployed in the cities went hungry and lived on the streets.

President Martin Van Buren didn't believe that government should interfere with the economy. But Jackson's old opponent, Senator Henry Clay, disagreed. He and Senator Daniel Webster claimed the government should step in and help fix the economic situation. Clay wanted the government to impose tariffs that would raise the price of imports and encourage Americans to buy domestically produced goods. He believed the federal government should fund infrastructure development by building a network of roads, canals, and railroads. Clay also

called for the establishment of a new national bank. His economic program was called the American System.

In 1834, senators Clay and Webster had formed a new political party, which they called the **Whig Party** after a British political group that had criticized the monarchy. Clay, Webster, and other opponents of Andrew Jackson chose the name because they believed Jackson had exceeded his powers as president. In fact, they often referred to him as "King Andrew." Unlike the Democrats, who supported an agrarian society, the Whigs promoted business and the expansion of industry.

Harrison Campaign Flag
Throughout the 1840 presidential campaign, the Whigs made much of William Henry Harrison's war experience 28 years earlier at the Battle of Tippecanoe, where he won a victory over the Shawnee. The party created this banner, combining a picture of Harrison with the American flag and a label underscoring his heroism at Tippecanoe.

THE HERO OF
TIPPECANOE

THE ELECTION OF 1840

As the 1840 presidential election approached, the Whigs believed they had a good chance of winning it. Many Americans blamed the country's economic woes on Van Buren and seemed ready for a change. The Whigs nominated William Henry Harrison of Ohio as their candidate for president and **John Tyler** of Virginia as his running mate.

Harrison was a national figure because he had led U.S. Army troops against the Shawnee at the Battle of Tippecanoe in 1811. He'd also been a hero during the War of 1812. Making the most of Harrison's war experience, the Whigs came up with the catchy slogan "Tippecanoe and Tyler too."

Because Harrison lived on a farm, he also gained the reputation as a "common man" of the frontier. As a matter of fact, he came from a wealthy family. But that didn't stop the Whigs from including pictures of a rustic log cabin in banners and Harrison's campaign pamphlets. They also held parades, sang songs, and had their candidate go out on the campaign trail himself. Harrison was the first presidential candidate to do so.

Harrison narrowly defeated Van Buren in the 1840 election, but just 32 days after taking office, he died. He had delivered a long inaugural address—the longest on record—without wearing a hat or overcoat on a cold March day and came down with pneumonia.

Tyler took Harrison's place after his death but received little support from his party. Tyler's views were actually more in line with those of the Democrats. The Whigs had chosen him to attract southern voters. In time, they expelled him from the party and took to calling him "His Accidency." In spite of their differences, Tyler worked well with the mostly Whig Congress. During his single term in office, Tyler focused on strengthening the country by expanding and opening up the West.

DID YOU KNOW?

There is something unique and unusual about each of the presidents you have read about in this lesson.

Martin Van Buren
Eighth president
- First president to be born a U.S. citizen rather than a British subject
- Nicknamed "Old Kinderhook" for his hometown, Kinderhook, New York. The expression "OK" (or okay) came into use during his presidency.

William Henry Harrison
Ninth president
- President for only 32 days
- First president to die in office
- Attended medical school to become a doctor, but he could not afford the tuition after his father died. He dropped out and joined the military.

John Tyler
Became tenth president when William Henry Harrison died in office
- Only former U.S. president to side with the Confederacy in the Civil War
- Father of 14 children who lived into adulthood

HISTORICAL THINKING

1. **READING CHECK** Why were the Whigs in a good position to win the 1840 election?

2. **COMPARE AND CONTRAST** How did the agrarians' and the industrialists' views on the economy differ?

3. **MAKE INFERENCES** Why did the Whigs use pictures of a log cabin in Harrison's campaign?

Objective

Understand how the Whig Party formed before the election of 1840.

Critical Thinking Skills for Lesson 3.2

- Identify Main Ideas and Details
- Monitor Comprehension
- Compare and Contrast
- Make Inferences
- Identify
- Make Connections
- Distinguish Fact and Opinion

Essential Question for Chapter 11

How did Andrew Jackson's policies impact different groups of people in America?
Jackson's economic policies resulted in high unemployment in the East. Lesson 3.2 discusses the rise of the Whig Party and changes in federal economic policies.

Background for the Teacher

Henry Clay once said, he'd "rather be right than be president," yet he tried quite hard to be elected to the highest office in the land. True to what he said, in the end, his stance against slavery and his support of the American System proved to be right, as those are the policies that the citizens of the country supported.

Between 1824 and 1848, Clay made five unsuccessful attempts to be president. In 1824, he ran as a Democratic-Republican. In 1832, Clay was unanimously nominated by the National Republicans but lost the election to Jackson. In 1840, he attempted to be the Whigs' candidate for president but lost that bid to William Henry Harrison. Nominated by the Whig Party in 1844, Clay lost the national election to James K. Polk. In 1848, he lost the Whig nomination for a presidential run to Zachary Taylor, who won the election. Though he was never elected president, Clay proved to be a major influence in national politics.

INTRODUCE & ENGAGE

Activate Prior Knowledge

Discuss what students know about political parties in the United States today. **ASK:** What are the current political parties? *(The Democratic Party and the Republican Party are the two major parties. Other parties include the Libertarian Party and the Green Party.)* Explain that these were not always our political parties and that in this lesson students will learn about how a new party system was formed.

TEACH

Guided Discussion

1. **Identify** What did Daniel Webster and Henry Clay believe the role of the federal government should be? *(Webster and Clay believed the federal government should manage the nation's economy and build its roads, canals, and railroads.)*

2. **Make Connections** Why was it important for the Whig Party to portray William Harrison as a military hero in his bid for the presidency? *(Possible response: The Whigs were seen as the party that catered to the interests of the wealthy and business and industry. To get Harrison elected, he needed to be portrayed as a man people could relate to and also as someone who served the country.)*

Distinguish Fact and Opinion

Discuss Harrison's political campaign with students. Explain that sometimes with campaigns it is difficult to distinguish fact from opinion. **ASK:** Based on details in the text, which descriptions of the candidates were based on facts, and which were based on opinion? *(Possible response: Fact: Harrison attended medical school at one point; Opinion: Harrison was a "common man." Fact: Van Buren was the first president to be born a U.S. citizen; Opinion: Van Buren was responsible for the country's economic woes.)*

Active Options

On Your Feet: Turn and Talk on Topic Divide the class into four groups and provide each group with the same topic sentence: The old way of doing things definitely wasn't working in the United States in the late 1830s. Tell groups to discuss examples of what wasn't working. Then instruct students to create a paragraph on that topic by having each student contribute one sentence to support why the old way was not working. Allow each group to organize their ideas and present its paragraph to the class by having the groups form lines and having each student read his or her sentence in the correct order.

NG Learning Framework: Write a Campaign Speech

ATTITUDES Responsibility, Empowerment

KNOWLEDGE Our Human Story

Arrange students in small groups. Prompt the groups to choose a candidate for the 1840 election: William Henry Harrison or Martin Van Buren. Instruct students to review information presented in the lesson and to conduct additional research about their candidate. Have them work together to craft a campaign speech for that candidate, based on what they learned about the candidate's personality, his political beliefs, and events leading up to the election. Each group should then nominate one person to deliver the speech to the class.

DIFFERENTIATE

Striving Readers

Connect Details to a Main Idea Remind students that a main idea is a statement that summarizes the key idea of an article, speech, or paragraph. Details are facts, dates, events, and descriptions that support a main idea. Ask students to write one main idea and two details about the creation of the Whig Party. Have students share their ideas when they have finished. An example using William Harrison is shown below.

Main Idea: William Henry Harrison was elected president in 1840.
Detail: Member of the Whig Party
Detail: War hero
Detail: Died in office
Detail:
Detail:

Gifted & Talented

Interview a Historical Figure Have students work in pairs to plan, write, and perform a television interview with either Henry Clay, Martin Van Buren, William Henry Harrison, or John Tyler. Students can focus on before or after the election of 1840. Invite students to research their selected historical figure and focus on his actions, goals, and achievements. Encourage pairs to conduct their interviews in front of the class.

See the Chapter Planner for more strategies for differentiation.

HISTORICAL THINKING

ANSWERS

1. In the 1830s, the economy was failing. People blamed Jackson and Van Buren and wanted a different political party in charge.

2. The industrialists who formed the Whig party focused mainly on building factories, canals, and roads, while the agrarians focused on the negative effects of tariffs on the price of imports and exports.

3. The Whigs wanted to give the appearance that William Harrison was a "common man" who could relate to the people.

11 REVIEW

VOCABULARY

Use each of the following vocabulary words in a sentence that shows an understanding of the term's meaning.

1. agrarian

   The economy of the South was mostly agrarian, or based on farming.

2. voting rights

3. depression

4. inflation

5. spoils system

6. doctrine of nullification

7. assimilate

8. truce

READING STRATEGY
COMPARE AND CONTRAST

If you haven't done so already, complete your diagram to compare and contrast the policies of Andrew Jackson and John Quincy Adams. List at least two policies to compare and contrast. Then answer the question.

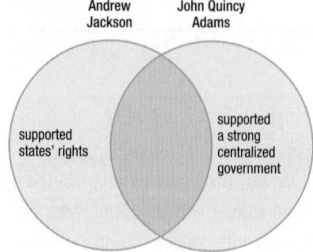

Andrew Jackson | John Quincy Adams

supported states' rights

supported a strong centralized government

9. What were some of the main policy differences between Jackson and Adams?

MAIN IDEAS

Answer the following questions. Support your answers with evidence from the chapter.

10. Why did Andrew Jackson think he had been robbed of the presidential election in 1824? **LESSON 1.1**

11. How does the spoils system work? **LESSON 1.2**

12. Why did Daniel Webster believe nullification would threaten the Union and freedom? **LESSON 1.3**

13. What two options did President Jackson offer Native Americans in the South? **LESSON 2.1**

14. What policy did the Indian Removal Act set in place? **LESSON 2.1**

15. How did the U.S. government trick Osceola? **LESSON 2.2**

16. What did John Ross hope to achieve by resisting the move west? **LESSON 2.3**

17. How did Andrew Jackson bring about the end of the Second Bank of the United States? **LESSON 3.1**

18. How did his opponents react to Andrew Jackson's transfer of funds out of the Second Bank? **LESSON 3.1**

19. What economic factors formed part of Henry Clay's American System? **LESSON 3.2**

HISTORICAL THINKING

Answer the following questions. Support your answers with evidence from the chapter.

20. **SYNTHESIZE** How did Andrew Jackson change the country?

21. **ANALYZE CAUSE AND EFFECT** How did Andrew Jackson's use of the spoils system lead to charges of corruption against him?

22. **COMPARE AND CONTRAST** In what ways were the rebellions of Black Hawk and the Cherokee similar and different?

23. **MAKE CONNECTIONS** John C. Calhoun applied the states' rights doctrine to prevent the country from breaking apart. When was states' rights first invoked, and what was it used to fight?

24. **DISTINGUISH FACT AND OPINION** Both Andrew Jackson and William Henry Harrison were said to represent the "common man." Did this label represent a fact or an opinion?

25. **FORM AND SUPPORT OPINIONS** Considering the legacy of Jackson's policies, do you think he lived up to his reputation as a hero for common people? Explain your answer.

INTERPRET MAPS

Study the map of the electoral college results for Andrew Jackson and John Quincy Adams in the 1828 presidential election. Then answer the questions that follow.

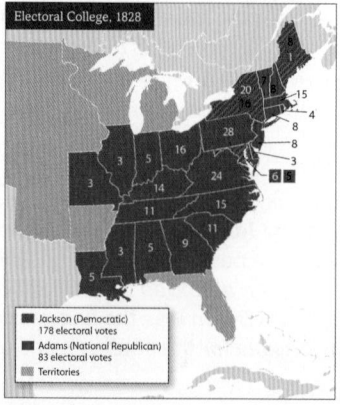

Electoral College, 1828

■ Jackson (Democratic)
178 electoral votes
■ Adams (National Republican)
83 electoral votes
☐ Territories

26. Based on the map, what can you conclude about Jackson's victory?

27. Where did Adams gain votes and why?

ANALYZE SOURCES

In 1835, some Cherokee representatives signed, and Congress ratified, the Treaty of New Echota, in which the Cherokee sold all their lands east of the Mississippi River to the United States. The next year, Cherokee leader John Ross wrote a letter to Congress in response.

Neither myself nor any other member of the regular delegation to Washington, can . . . ever recognize that paper as a Treaty, by assenting to its terms, or the mode of its execution. They are entirely inconsistent with the views of the Cherokee people. Three times have the Cherokee people formally and openly rejected conditions substantially [largely] the same as these. The Cherokee people, in two protests . . . spoke for themselves against the Treaty, even previous to its rejection by those whom they had selected to speak for them.

28. What does this excerpt tell you about Ross's opinion of the Treaty of New Echota?

CONNECT TO YOUR LIFE

29. **EXPLANATORY** This chapter describes many disputes among different groups of people. Think about disagreements you have had with others in your own life. How were they resolved? Make a connection between what you have learned about problem solving and how this information can be applied to resolve a dispute. Then write a paragraph in which you help two opposing groups overcome their dispute.

TIPS

• Fill in a problem-and-solution chart, listing the problem between the groups at the top, the steps for fixing the problem in the middle, and the plan's conclusion at the bottom.

• Include evidence and one or two vocabulary terms from the chapter.

• Conclude with a comment tying your suggested resolution of the argument to your own life.

VOCABULARY ANSWERS

1. The economy of the South was mostly agrarian, or based on farming.

2. By the 1820s, voting rights had expanded to include more white males.

3. Jackson's closing of the Second Bank of the United States led to a depression, which is a period of slow economic activity.

4. Inflation decreases the value of money.

5. Andrew Jackson's spoils system rewarded his supporters with government jobs.

6. The doctrine of nullification declared that states could reject a law passed by Congress.

7. Andrew Jackson encouraged Native Americans to assimilate to European American culture.

8. American soldiers misled Osceola when they called a truce and then took him hostage.

READING STRATEGY ANSWER

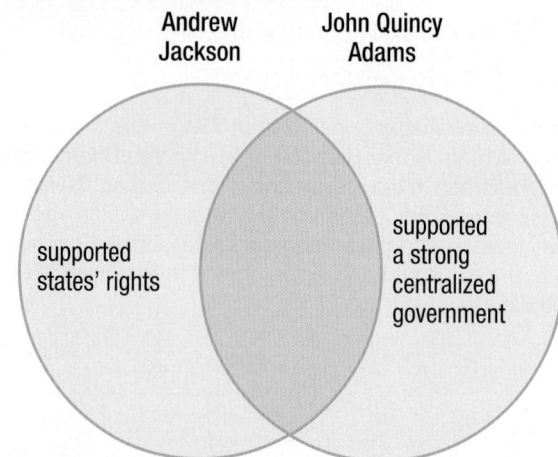

Andrew Jackson | John Quincy Adams

supported states' rights

supported a strong centralized government

9. Adams believed in a strong federal government and supported tariffs. Jackson supported states' rights, believed tariffs hurt the southern economy, and worked to end the National Bank.

MAIN IDEAS ANSWERS

10. After the House of Representatives awarded the election to Adams, President Adams gave Clay the job of secretary of state. Jackson believed that Adams and Clay had made a "corrupt bargain" in which Clay persuaded the House members to vote for Adams in exchange for the cabinet position.

11. The spoils system works by permitting each new president to reward political backers with government jobs.

12. Webster believed that nullification had the potential of tearing apart the Union as states determined which federal laws they could reject, weakening the ties that bound the states together.

13. Jackson told Native Americans they could choose to either assimilate European ways of life and accept the authority of the states in which they lived or be forced to move west of the Mississippi River.

14. Under this policy, Native Americans were forced to leave their lands in the South and relocate to an area west of the Mississippi known as Indian Territory.

15. The government set up a meeting with Osceola for what was supposed to be a "peace conference" but then captured and imprisoned him.

16. Ross wanted to negotiate a treaty that would be more beneficial for the Cherokee.

17. Jackson removed all government funds from the Second Bank of the United States and deposited the money in various state banks.

18. Jackson's opponents called the state banks where Jackson deposited federal funds "pet banks," and Biddle used his power to withhold bank loans from customers.

19. Henry Clay's American System called for establishing a new National Bank and advocated for the building of roads, canals, and railroads by the federal government.

HISTORICAL THINKING ANSWERS

20. Jackson's transfer of funds from the Second Bank of the United States to state banks caused a financial panic that took place just after Van Buren became president. The country sank into a major economic depression during Van Buren's presidency. Van Buren was unable to fix the problem and lost his second bid for president. Jackson also changed the country for Native Americans, who were removed from their homelands and moved west.

21. Jackson's opponents saw the spoils system as corrupt because, when Jackson took office as president, he replaced previous officials with his own supporters. In effect, Jackson was rewarding his supporters—some of whom were newspaper editors—with government jobs.

22. Native Americans in both regions were forced out of their tribal lands against their will and onto lands in the West. Black Hawk tried to lead his people back to their homelands and keep them united as a tribe. A small group of Cherokee made a deal against the wishes of the rest of the tribe, which caused fighting and violence within the tribe after they were forced off their land.

23. Calhoun first applied the states rights' doctrine in South Carolina to fight against the Tariff of 1828. The southern states believed the Tariff of 1828 hurt their cotton and tobacco economies and believed states could reject a federal law that was viewed as harmful to the state.

24. Possible response: It was an opinion, because neither man was "common" by the time he was elected president. This opinion was more justifiable for Andrew Jackson, however, because he actually grew up in poverty and tended to take the side of working people. William Henry Harrison was a wealthy man. The idea to present him to voters as a "common man" was mostly made up by the Whigs as a campaign claim.

25. Possible response: While he believed his policies supported hard-working common people, his economic policies ultimately hurt the people because banks failed and many lost their land, jobs, and businesses.

INTERPRET MAPS ANSWERS

26. Possible response: Jackson did better in New York than he did in most of the other northeastern states. Van Buren's influence probably helped him secure more votes there.

27. Adams gained votes in the East, because he represented businessmen and their interests, such as improving the nation's transportation infrastructure.

ANALYZE SOURCES ANSWER

28. This excerpt indicates that Ross does not believe the treaty is in the Cherokees' best interest. He notes that the Cherokee have repeatedly rejected treaties that were basically the same as the one being offered and states that he and his people cannot agree to it.

CONNECT TO YOUR LIFE ANSWER

29. Answers will vary, but students should include a personal experience and use text evidence to discuss what they learned about problem solving.

UNIT 5 RESOURCES

UNIT INTRODUCTION

UNIT TIME LINE

UNIT WRAP-UP

NATIONAL GEOGRAPHIC | CONNECTION

**National Geographic Magazine
Adapted Articles**
- "The Way West"
- "People of the Horse" ONLINE

Unit 5 Inquiry: Organize a Reform Campaign

NG Learning Framework Activities
- Research a Mining Boomtown
- Encounter Nature

Unit 5 Formal Assessment

CHAPTER 12 RESOURCES

Available at NGLSync.Cengage.com

TEACHER RESOURCES & ASSESSMENT

Reading and Note-Taking

Vocabulary Practice

Document-Based Question Template

Social Studies Skills Lessons
- Reading: Identify Main Ideas and Details
- Writing: Write an Argument

Formal Assessment
- Chapter 12 Pretest
- Chapter 12 Tests A & B
- Section Quizzes

Chapter 12 Answer Key

ExamView®
  One-time Download

STUDENT DIGITAL RESOURCES

- **eEdition** (English)
- **eEdition** (Spanish)
- **Handbooks**
- **Online Atlas**
- **American Gallery Online**
- **History Notebook**
- **American Voices (Biographies)**
- **Active History**
- **Projects for Inquiry-Based Learning**

Chapter 12 Spanish Resources are available at NGLSync.Cengage.com.

AMERICAN STORIES The Golden City

- Primary Sources
- On Your Feet: Gold Rush Roundtable

NG Learning Framework:
Establish Points of View

SECTION 1 RESOURCES
TRAILS WEST

LESSON 1.1
The Pull of the West

- On Your Feet: Create a Concept Cluster

NG Learning Framework:
Learn More About Trailblazers

LESSON 1.2
DOCUMENT-BASED QUESTION
Manifest Destiny

- On Your Feet: Host a DBQ Roundtable

LESSON 1.3
Trails to the West

- On Your Feet: Four Corners

 The Westward Trails

LESSON 1.4
Pioneers and Native Americans

- Active History: Illustrate the Rain Shadow Effect

NG Learning Framework:
Depict Frontier Life

SECTION 2 RESOURCES
THE TEXAS REVOLUTION

LESSON 2.1
The Tejanos

- On Your Feet: Jigsaw

NG Learning Framework:
Learn About Stephen F. Austin

LESSON 2.2
Settlement and Rebellion

- On Your Feet: Cause-and-Effect Chain

NG Learning Framework:
Research the Alamo's Heroes

American Voices Biographies
David Crockett ONLINE
James Bowie

LESSON 2.3
Independence and Annexation

- On Your Feet: Think, Pair, Share

NG Learning Framework:
Create a Campaign Poster

LESSON 2.4
AMERICAN VOICES
Samuel "Sam" Houston
Antonio López de Santa Anna

- On Your Feet: Analyze Character Traits

NG Learning Framework:
Conduct an Interview

LESSON 2.5
CURATING HISTORY
San Jacinto Museum of History
La Porte, Texas

- On Your Feet: Sort the Artifacts

SECTION 3 RESOURCES
THE WAR WITH MEXICO

LESSON 3.1
Tensions with Mexico

- On Your Feet: Create a Cause-and-Effect Map

NG Learning Framework:
Take a Stand

LESSON 3.2
The United States at War

- On Your Feet: Ready, Set, Recall

NG Learning Framework:
Compare Artistic Depictions

LESSON 3.3
Consequences of the War

- On Your Feet: Annotate a Time Line

NG Learning Framework:
Explore Mexican Culture in the Southwest

SECTION 4 RESOURCES
THE CALIFORNIA GOLD RUSH

LESSON 4.1
The Spanish and Mexicans in California

- On Your Feet: Team Word Webbing

NG Learning Framework:
Find Out More about the Mission System

LESSON 4.2
The Gold Rush

- The Gold Rush
- On Your Feet: Fishbowl

NG Learning Framework:
Evaluate Primary Sources

LESSON 4.3
The Mining Frontier

- On Your Feet: Three-Step Interview

NG Learning Framework:
Perform Skits

CHAPTER 12 REVIEW

Strategy ❶
Play "Who Am I?"

Choose from the names below and distribute a list to students. Have them make game cards with the name on the front and a clue to the person's identity on the back. For example, for Sam Houston, students might write "defeated Santa Anna." Use the cards to play a whole-group, small-group, or partner review game.

Jedediah Smith	James K. Polk
Jim Beckwourth	Zachary Taylor
Brigham Young	John C. Frémont
Stephen F. Austin	Winfield Scott
Antonio López de Santa Anna	Sam Houston
Junípero Serra	John Sutter

Use with Lessons 1.1, 1.3, 2.1–2.4, 3.1–3.2, and 4.1

Strategy ❷
Use Reciprocal Teaching

Tell partners to take turns reading each paragraph of the lesson aloud. At the end of the paragraph, the reading student should ask the listening student questions about the paragraph. Students may ask their partners to state the main idea, identify important details that support the main idea, or summarize the paragraph in their own words. Then have students work together to answer the Historical Thinking questions.

Use with All Lessons

Strategy ❸
Modify Vocabulary Lists

Limit the number of vocabulary words, terms, and names students will be required to master. Have students write each word from your modified list on a colored sticky note and put it on the page next to where it appears in context.

Use with All Lessons *Encourage students to create and keep a list of unfamiliar words they encounter and to add definitions and contexts as they read.*

Strategy ❶
Summarize Information

Use a Fishbowl activity to review the lesson. Place students of mixed ability levels in each circle. Call on more advanced students to take turns summarizing the lesson content. When the first group of students has concluded its summary, switch positions and have inclusion students review the lesson content.

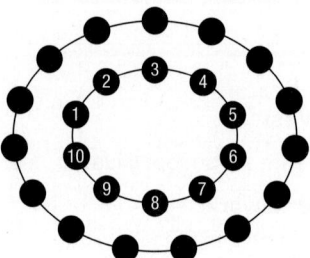

Use with All Lessons *Encourage students to write an outline and refer to it as they review the lesson content.*

Strategy ❷
Build a Time Line

Select key events from Lesson 1.3. Then have students use the events to create a time line on the board. Guide students to add to the time line as they read other lessons.

1821 Mexico
wins independence
from Spain

Use with Lesson 1.3 *For example, key events from Lesson 1.3 might include the opening of the Santa Fe Trail in 1822 and settlement of the Oregon Territory boundary in 1846.*

ENGLISH LANGUAGE LEARNERS

Strategy ❶
Pair Partners for Dictation

After reading a lesson, direct students to write in their own words a sentence telling an important idea from the reading. Pair students and let them take turns dictating their sentences to each other. Then allow them to work together to check spelling and accuracy.

Use with All Lessons *You may wish to pair students at the* **Emerging** *level with those at the* **Bridging** *level.*

Strategy ❷
Use Pronunciation Keys

Preteach the pronunciation of vocabulary words. Give a brief definition and pronounce each word slowly and clearly. Encourage students at **All Proficiencies** to repeat each word after you and then create a pronunciation key to help them remember how to say it.

Use with All Lessons

Strategy ❸
Build Vocabulary

Help students at **All Proficiencies** learn unfamiliar words by introducing synonyms they may know. Write these word pairs from the American Story on the board:

> brutally/awfully
>
> penalties/fines

Tell students to try replacing the first word of each pair with the second word when they find the first word in a sentence. Then encourage them to use a thesaurus when they come to other difficult words to look among the synonyms and find one that makes sense in context.

Use with All Lessons *Look for opportunities in all lessons to use synonyms and a thesaurus to aid comprehension. For example, in Lesson 4.1, students may benefit by using a thesaurus to understand* priority *(first concern) and* controversy *(disagreement).*

GIFTED & TALENTED

Strategy ❶
Create a Travel Brochure

Ask students to work in pairs or teams to create a travel brochure to help visitors explore one of the historical sites discussed in Chapter 12. Instruct students to research the place of their choice to find out what visitors might see or do there, including activities surrounding historical places or events. Allow students to create their brochure in the medium of their choice and to share their work with the class.

Use with Lessons 2.2, 3.2, and 4.1–4.3

Strategy ❷
Interview a Pioneer Woman

Allow students to work in pairs to plan, write, and perform a radio or podcast interview with a pioneer woman. Invite students to choose a historical figure or create a fictional character based on information from the text. Tell students the purpose of the interview is to focus on how the role of women changed during the first half of the 19th century.

Use with Lessons 1.2, 2.2, and 4.3 *Encourage students to include questions that prompt the pioneer woman or character to give her opinion about how her life changed.*

Pre-AP

Strategy ❶
Form a Thesis

Ask students to develop a thesis statement for a specific topic related to one of the lessons in the chapter. Instruct them to be sure their statement makes a claim that is supportable with evidence either from the chapter or through further research. Allow students to work in pairs to compare their statements and determine which makes the stronger or more supportable claim.

Use with Lessons 1.2–1.4

Strategy ❷
Write an Essay

Instruct students to write an essay explaining the significance of manifest destiny. Tell them to explain the idea of manifest destiny, summarize how the idea arose, and describe its short- and long-term consequences.

Use with All Lessons *Encourage students to include visuals with their essays, such as maps, fine art, and photos of artifacts.*

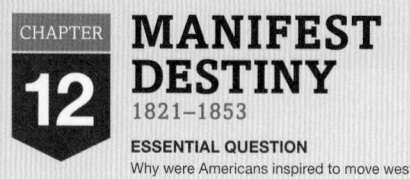

CHAPTER 12
MANIFEST DESTINY
1821–1853

ESSENTIAL QUESTION
Why were Americans inspired to move west?

AMERICAN STORIES The Golden City

SECTION 1 **Trails West**
KEY VOCABULARY

annex	individualism	pioneer
Continental Divide	manifest destiny	rendezvous
exodus	mountain men	wagon train

SECTION 2 **The Texas Revolution**
KEY VOCABULARY

margin   presidio   siege

SECTION 3 **The War with Mexico**
KEY VOCABULARY

contiguous	Gadsden Purchase	parallel
diplomat	insurrection	proviso

SECTION 4 **The California Gold Rush**
KEY VOCABULARY

boomtown	forty-niner	rancho
Californio	prospector	

AMERICAN GALLERY
ONLINE   The Westward Trails

READING STRATEGY

IDENTIFY MAIN IDEAS AND DETAILS
When you identify main ideas and details, you determine the most important idea in the text. Finding key details in the text helps you determine the main ideas they support. As you read the chapter, use an organizer like this one to record main ideas and details about the westward movement of Americans.

Main Idea:

Detail:

Detail:

Detail:

"We are the nation of **human progress.**"

—John L. O'Sullivan

CRITICAL VIEWING A stream winds through a valley in the Rocky Mountains of Colorado, presenting a wide-open vista for people looking for a new home. How does this photo convey the invitation many felt to move west in search of new lives and opportunities?

For Chapter 12 Spanish Resources, visit the Resources Menu. Chapter 12 Resources are available at NGLSync.Cengage.com.

INTRODUCE THE PHOTOGRAPH

Rocky Mountain Valley

Direct students' attention to the photograph that opens this chapter. **ASK:** Which parts of this landscape might have attracted pioneers? Which parts might have caused them worry? *(Possible response: The green valley, trees, and water source probably seemed appealing to pioneers; the mountains represented a major challenge and obstacle in their path.)* Point out that western trails took pioneers through varied landscapes, but most routes faced the same challenge—crossing the Rocky Mountains. Those who followed the mountain route of the Santa Fe Trail may have encountered autumn scenery like that shown in the photograph. Just beyond the peaceful valleys in Colorado, however, lay the treacherous Raton Pass. Like other routes through the mountains, this path was steep and narrow, and it took a toll on people, wagons, and draft animals.

Share Background

The son of a diplomat, John Louis O'Sullivan (1813–1895) was educated in Europe before he came to New York City to attend college. He worked as a lawyer and served in the New York State assembly. O'Sullivan became the founder and editor of the *Democratic Review*, a prestigious monthly journal that featured literature from some of the best-known authors of the time, including Nathaniel Hawthorne, Edgar Allan Poe, Henry David Thoreau, and Walt Whitman. The journal also presented political commentary, including O'Sullivan's 1839 essay "The Great Nation of Futurity," in which the quotation on this page appears.

CRITICAL VIEWING Possible response: The image shows open land with plentiful woods and water, and the mountains may have mineral resources. It shows land that is not crowded like cities on the East coast. This space might look inviting to those who sought adventure or an opportunity to live on the land.

INTRODUCE THE ESSENTIAL QUESTION

Why were Americans inspired to move west?

Think, Pair, Share: Discussing Moving Experiences Help students establish a personal connection to the essential question by asking them to think about a time when they or someone they know moved to a different location. Give students a few minutes to jot down some notes in response to these questions:

• Who moved? Was it you and your family? A relative? A friend?

• Where did you or the people move? Was it near or far away?

• Was the move sudden, or had it been planned?

• What were the reasons for the move?

• Were those moving happy about it? Why or why not?

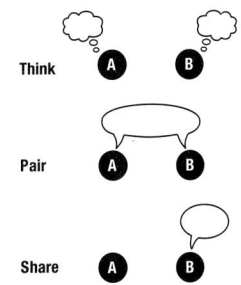

Group students into pairs to compare their responses. Challenge them also to think about additional responses. Then call on pairs to share their ideas on these topics:

• What circumstances inspire people to move?

• How do you determine whether a move has been beneficial?

As students read the chapter, encourage them to look for information that addresses these topics.

INTRODUCE CHAPTER VOCABULARY

Word Maps

As students read the chapter, have them complete Word Maps for Key Vocabulary words. Tell students to make a Word Map for each word. Have them write the word in the center oval, and, as they encounter the word in the chapter, complete the Word Map for that word. Model an example for students on the board, using the graphic organizer below.

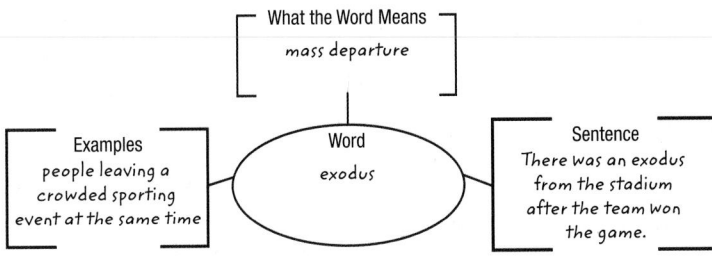

INTRODUCE THE READING STRATEGY

IDENTIFY MAIN IDEAS AND DETAILS

Remind students that identifying a main idea and determining which facts support that idea helps them understand the text. The main idea is the key point the author wants readers to understand. Authors often state the main idea near the beginning or end of a paragraph or section of text, but sometimes they imply the main idea rather than state it outright. If a main idea is not stated, students need to evaluate details to determine the main thing the author wants them to know about a topic. Model completing the Main Idea and Details Chart.

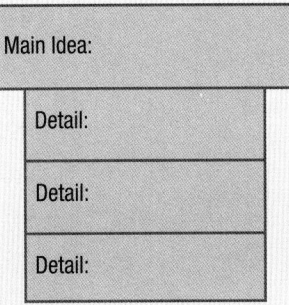

KEY DATES FOR CHAPTER 12

1821	Mexico gains independence from Spain
1836	Texas becomes the Lone Star Republic
1845	Texas becomes a state
1846	Bear Flag Revolt
1847	Mexican-American War ends
1849	Gold rush begins
1850	California becomes a state
1853	Gadsden Purchase

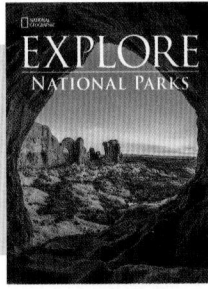

For more on exploration in the West, see *EXPLORE NATIONAL PARKS.*

Objectives

- Learn about the California gold rush.
- Describe the lives of miners, immigrants, and Native Americans during the gold rush.
- Explain how the gold rush affected the economy and the growth of large cities in California.
- Study primary sources: "Ho! For California!," a mining song, and an excerpt from Luzena Stanley Wilson's 1881 memoir.

Critical Thinking Skills for "The Golden City"

- Make Connections
- Draw Conclusions
- Analyze Environmental Concepts
- Interpret Maps
- Analyze Data
- Distinguish Fact and Opinion
- Integrate Visuals
- Evaluate
- Determine Chronology

Background for the Teacher

In this American Story, students get a feel for the gold rush era and its importance in U.S. history by tracing the early days of San Francisco, a town that rose to prominence as miners and businesspeople moved and settled there. Historical and contemporary photographs, as well as a first-person account from a woman who ran a successful hotel during the gold rush, help tell the tale of miners, immigrants, Native Americans, and others whose lives were changed because of the lure of gold.

This chapter, Manifest Destiny, discusses the many causes and effects of westward expansion—which groups pushed westward, how and why they traveled, and how the United States fought for and won vast new tracts of land. This American Story will help students envision what life was like during a particularly colorful episode in settling the West.

History Notebook

Encourage students to complete the American Story page for Chapter 12 in their History Notebooks as they read.

Note to the Teacher

Introduce this American Story after the class has engaged with the content in Section 4.

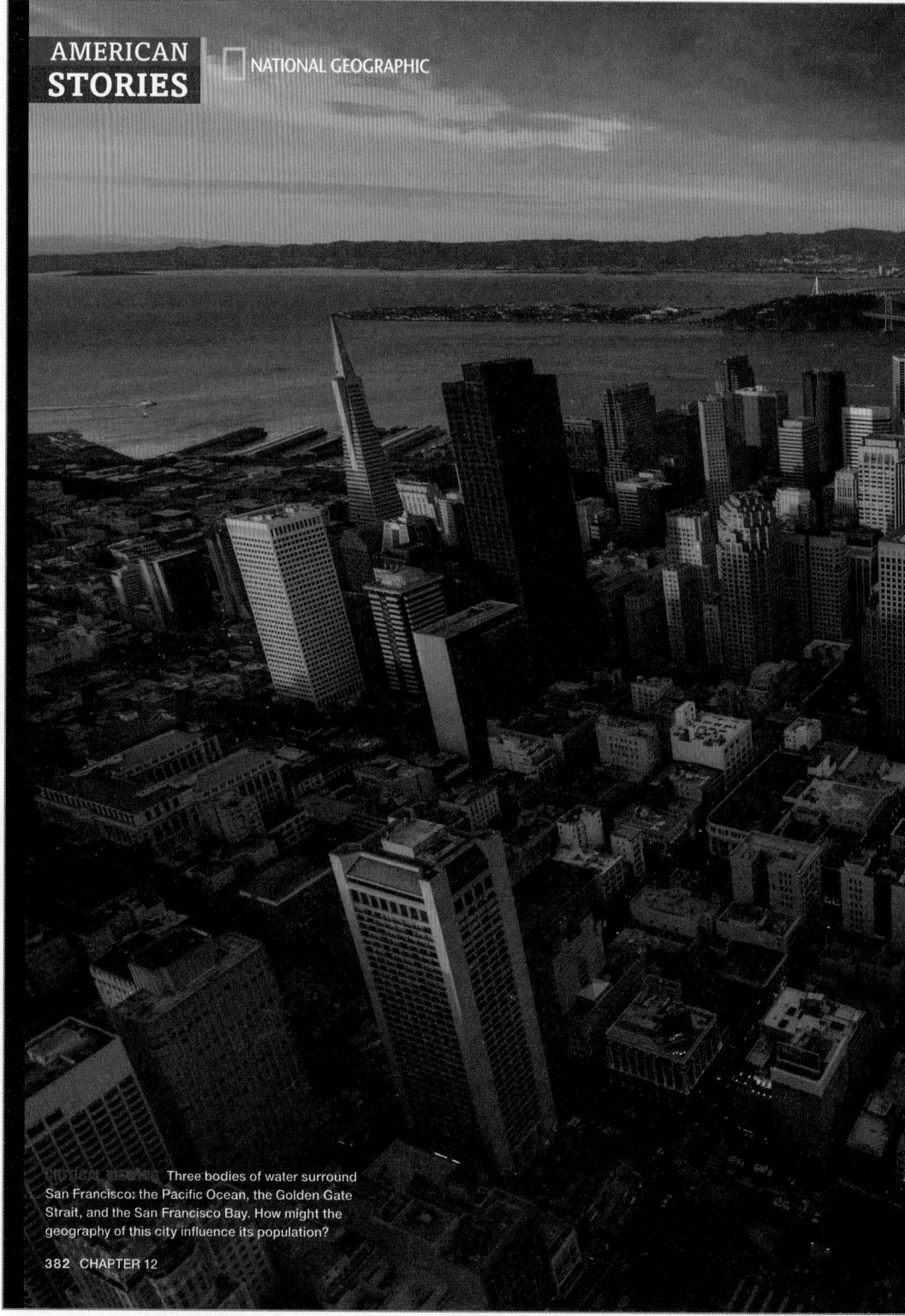

AMERICAN STORIES

NATIONAL GEOGRAPHIC

Three bodies of water surround San Francisco: the Pacific Ocean, the Golden Gate Strait, and the San Francisco Bay. How might the geography of this city influence its population?

382 CHAPTER 12

THE GOLDEN CITY

San Francisco is a vibrant, modern city known for its unique coastal skyline, diverse neighborhoods, sweeping bridges, and notorious fog. It's the Golden City in the Golden State— a city "built on gold" during the 1848 California gold rush.

Manifest Destiny 383

INTRODUCE & ENGAGE

Preview Using Visuals

Examine the photograph of the San Francisco skyline with the class. Have students identify the different types of buildings that make up the city skyline, pointing out buildings they find particularly interesting. Discuss what seems to be the age of the buildings and the type of architecture seen in the photo. Have students read the text below the title and separate words into two groups: words that name things (nouns) and words that describe (adjectives). **ASK:** Which words describe downtown San Francisco? *(Possible response: modern, coastal, diverse)* **ASK:** What things are found in San Francisco? *(bridges, neighborhoods, fog, skyline)*

Ask Questions

Discuss with students why they think San Francisco is called the Golden City. Then ask students to consider some categories of information that will help them learn more about San Francisco's role in the country's growth as Americans moved west: *People, Industry, Human Relations, Inventions.* Write the four categories as headings in a chart. Have students brainstorm three questions for each category. Add those questions to the chart. At the end of the chapter, have students return to their questions and answer them as a group.

CRITICAL VIEWING Answers will vary. Possible response: The water provides easy access by boat to the city, allowing people from faraway places to settle in San Francisco.

Gold Fever

Gold seekers moving west had to choose between traveling across land and taking a water route. By land, many forty-niners traveled from Independence or St. Joseph, Missouri, along the Oregon Trail, branching off to follow the Humboldt River and then crossing the Forty-Mile Desert before scaling the Sierra Nevada. About 25,000 forty-niners took a sea route. They packed boats for the 13,000-mile voyage around Cape Horn—a dangerous trip that could take up to eight months. Others attempted to cross through Panama. While the sea route was shorter, the people who traveled that way often fell victim to the ills of the tropical climate. Whether by land or by sea, forty-niners confronted many perils in their effort to strike it rich in California.

Music of the Forty-Niners

"Ho! For California!" often was sung as forty-niners set off to seek their fortune in gold in California. The song speaks of a water route to California and also of the belief in the abundance of gold and the ease of finding it.

"Ho! For California!"
(selected verses)
by Jesse Hutchinson, Jr., 1849

*We've formed our band, and we're all well manned
To journey afar to the promised land
Where the golden ore is rich in store
On the banks of the Sacramento shore*

*As off we roam through the dark sea foam
We'll ne'er forget kind friends at home
But memory kind shall bring to mind
The love of those we left behind*

*As the gold is thar most any whar
And they dig it out with an iron bar
And where 'tis thick, with a spade or pick
They can take out lumps as big as a brick*

*As we explore the distant shore
We'll fill our pockets with the shining ore
And how 'twill sound as the wind goes 'round
Of our picking up gold by the dozen pound*

AMERICAN STORIES

This nugget sparked the gold rush after workers found it near Sutter's Mill in 1848.

It all started on January 24, 1848. James Marshall set out to inspect the progress his workers had made on a sawmill they were building for John Sutter on the American River near Coloma, California. Overnight, Marshall had left a trickle of water flowing through the mill to wash away some loose dirt and gravel. To his great surprise, some bright flakes of gold were left behind that morning. Shocked, Marshall showed the gold to his crew, swearing them to secrecy. He needed some time to process what had just happened before he took action. He also figured he'd better finish building Sutter's Mill.

But an exciting secret like that is impossible to keep. The word spread quickly, and over the next few years, hundreds of thousands of people streamed into California hoping to get rich. By 1856, around $465 million worth of gold had been mined in California.

A MINER'S LIFE

The Americans who moved from the East to California in 1849 in search of gold were nicknamed the "forty-niners." Most of them came with the plan to work hard for a short time, find enough gold to get rich, and return home wealthy.

In reality, mining was then, and still is, brutally hard work and very dangerous. During the gold rush, supplies were extremely expensive because the items were in such high demand. One miner reported that pork cost $1.25, beans $1, sugar $.75, and coffee $.50. That sounds pretty reasonable until you realize that a dollar in 1850 was worth about $30 today. Most miners only found enough gold to cover their expenses.

The dangerous and difficult nature of the work caught many new miners by surprise. One of them, William Swain, described his life in a letter to his brother back in New York: "George, I tell you this mining among the mountains is a dog's life."

CHALLENGES FOR IMMIGRANTS

William Swain was joined in his quest for gold by thousands of immigrants from Mexico, Chile, Peru, Germany, France, Turkey, China, and other countries. In China, people dreaming of California riches sometimes called the United States "the gold mountain." By 1848, the first Chinese miners began arriving in San Francisco, leaving behind China's high taxes and farming challenges. The arrival of so many different groups to California shaped the diversity of this exciting new place.

As the number of immigrants grew and as the U.S. economy weakened, the attitude of Americans toward the immigrants became increasingly resentful and discriminatory. In 1850, California's government placed a $20 tax on each immigrant miner—a tax American miners did not have to pay.

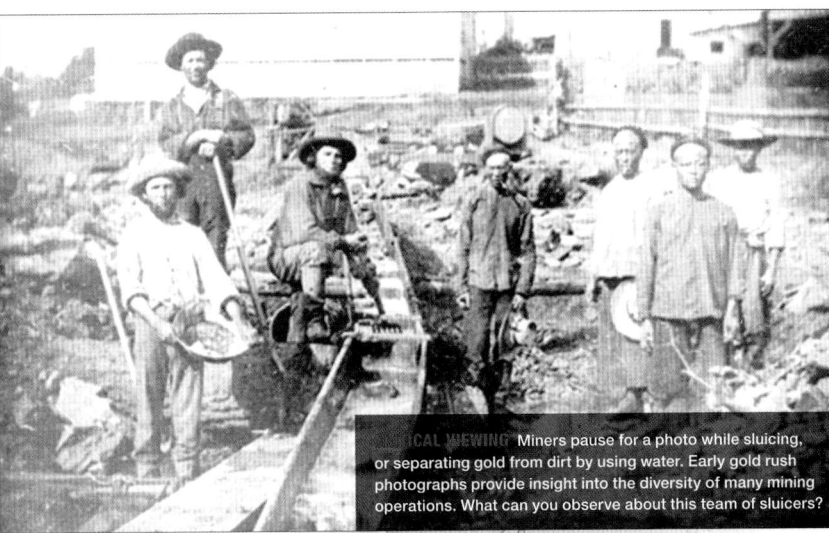

CRITICAL VIEWING Miners pause for a photo while sluicing, or separating gold from dirt by using water. Early gold rush photographs provide insight into the diversity of many mining operations. What can you observe about this team of sluicers?

The Chinese endured other tough penalties. In 1852, the government imposed another tax on Chinese miners. When California governor John Bigler suggested the wave of Chinese immigrants should be stopped, a Chinese man responded in the *Daily Alta California*: "The effect of your late message has been thus far to prejudice the public mind against my people, to enable those who wait [for] the opportunity to hunt them down, and rob them of the rewards of their toil."

Many of the Chinese men who came to California were literate and eager for new possibilities, but the state's increasingly hostile social climate made mining unwise—and unsafe—for them to continue. Forced out of mining, they found other work, building railroads and operating laundries and stores. Despite ongoing discrimination, thousands of Chinese immigrants stayed in California, seeking refuge in the San Francisco neighborhood known as Chinatown, and contributing greatly to the state's economy and culture.

Gold Rush Mine Locations

· Historic gold mine location

Marysville
Sacramento
San Francisco · · Oakland
· San Jose
· Stockton
Lake Tahoe
UTAH TERRITORY
CALIFORNIA
Sacramento R.
San Joaquin R.
Tulare Lake
· San Luis Obispo
· Santa Barbara
· Los Angeles
NEW MEXICO TERRITORY
Colorado R.
PACIFIC OCEAN
· San Diego

385

TEACH

Guided Discussion

1. **Analyze Environmental Concepts** In what ways did extracting gold from the earth impact mountains and rivers in California during the gold rush? (*Answers will vary. Possible response: Because miners and mining companies had to set up structures for mining and sluicing, the natural landscape would have been altered. Rivers might have been impacted by pollution from the mining or humans.*)

2. **Interpret Maps** Have students study the locations of gold mines on the map. **ASK:** What physical features are found near the gold mines? (*rivers*) **ASK:** What do you notice about the location of gold mines in California? (*Mines were scattered across California, but many were clustered near cities, such as Sacramento, and along the rivers.*)

CRITICAL VIEWING Answers will vary. Possible response: The team shows the diversity of people who came to California to mine for gold. The tools and the harsh landscape suggest mining was hard work for this team.

Guided Discussion

1. **Make Connections** What factors contributed to San Francisco becoming a major city in California? *(Possible response: San Francisco is situated on a bay, making it an ideal arrival city for immigrants who needed housing, goods, and jobs. The gold rush brought hopeful miners who had similar needs, which helped build San Francisco's economy.)*

2. **Analyze Data** Tell students to study the infographic. **ASK:** How many people became residents of San Francisco between 1848 and 1855? *(55,000 – 812 = 54,188)* **ASK:** If 750,000 pounds of gold were mined during the gold rush, and the value of that gold was $456 million, how much was one pound of gold worth? *($456,000,000 ÷ 750,000 = $608)*

More Information

California Property Law Explain that in 1850 women made up only about 3 percent of those who immigrated to California to find their fortune in gold. By 1860, when the gold rush had ended, women made up about 19 percent of the non-native population. Not only women from east of the Mississippi, but also women from other countries, including France, Peru, and China, made the arduous journey to California. An 1849 provision in the California constitution allowed married women the right to own property, a right they did not have in other states. **ASK:** How might the right to own property separate from their husbands have helped women during the years of the gold rush? *(Possible response: The right made it possible for women to own businesses and be independently successful.)*

American Places

The oldest and second-largest Chinatown in North America, San Francisco's Chinatown is home to about 15,000 Chinese. Densely populated, Chinatown serves as a center of commerce and culture for the thousands of Chinese living in and around San Francisco. It is a protected historic district and a major tourist attraction, with approximately 2 million visitors a year. One popular event is the Chinese New Year Parade held in late February.

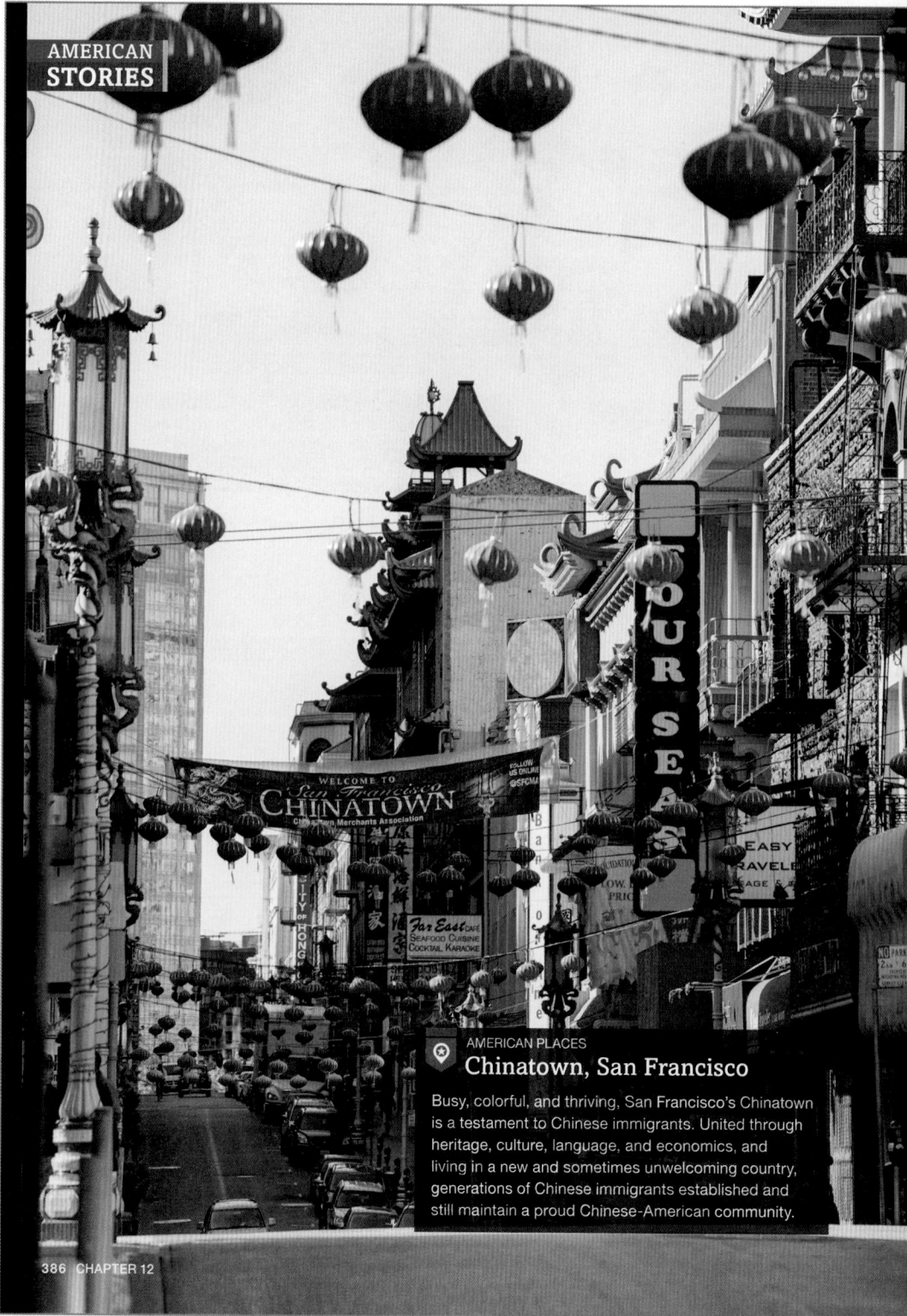

AMERICAN STORIES

AMERICAN PLACES
Chinatown, San Francisco

Busy, colorful, and thriving, San Francisco's Chinatown is a testament to Chinese immigrants. United through heritage, culture, language, and economics, and living in a new and sometimes unwelcoming country, generations of Chinese immigrants established and still maintain a proud Chinese-American community.

386 CHAPTER 12

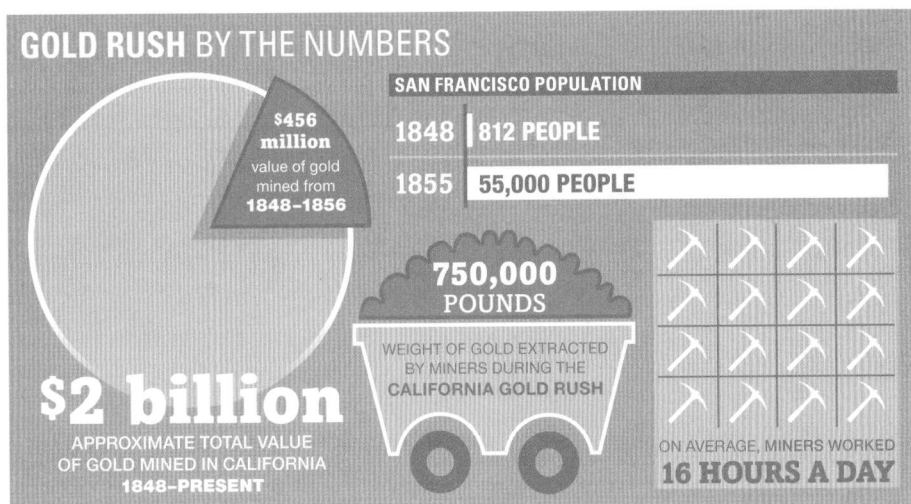

GOLD RUSH BY THE NUMBERS

$456 million
value of gold mined from
1848–1856

$2 billion
APPROXIMATE TOTAL VALUE
OF GOLD MINED IN CALIFORNIA
1848–PRESENT

SAN FRANCISCO POPULATION

1848 | 812 PEOPLE
1855 | 55,000 PEOPLE

750,000 POUNDS
WEIGHT OF GOLD EXTRACTED
BY MINERS DURING THE
CALIFORNIA GOLD RUSH

ON AVERAGE, MINERS WORKED
16 HOURS A DAY

NATIVE AMERICAN STRUGGLES

While many immigrants faced prejudice and opposition, the harshest treatment was reserved for the people who had been living in California all along. White miners used Native Americans for cheap labor and made them targets of violence. William Swain was upset by abuse against Native Americans that he witnessed, writing, "Such incidents have fallen under my notice that would make humanity weep and men disown their race." Historians estimate that around 150,000 Native Americans were living in California in 1848, but by 1870, fewer than 30,000 remained. Among the causes for the decline were starvation, violence, and diseases introduced by the miners.

A CITY ARISES

As the Native American population declined, populations of forty-niners and immigrants in northern California cities increased. In March of 1848, the *California Star* newspaper listed the city of San Francisco's population of non–Native Americans as 575 men, 177 women, 60 children— a total of 812 people. Within two years, the city's population had skyrocketed to more than 20,000.

San Francisco's natural wealth lay in its geography, a sheltered port on the Pacific Ocean. Immigrants and forty-niners arriving by ship passed through San Francisco, and many decided to stay. Clever businesspeople established shops, hotels, restaurants, and banks to accommodate the

miners' needs, forming the base for what would evolve into a thriving local economy.

The money and people flooding into California also sped up the time it took for it to be granted statehood. In 1848, the federal government purchased the land that included California from Mexico as part of the treaty that ended the Mexican-American War. Just two short years later, California was admitted as the 31st state in the Union.

By the end of the 1850s, the gold rush had ended, but it had lasting effects. Like San Francisco, many cities that got their start during the gold rush still exist. And entrepreneurs who set up shop to sell goods to the miners established brands that are still familiar. In 1852, the bankers Henry Wells and William Fargo opened an office in San Francisco. Wells Fargo Bank remains one of America's top banking institutions. In the same year, Domingo Ghirardelli opened a sweet shop in San Francisco, launching the famous brand of chocolate many people enjoy today.

The California gold rush only lasted a few years, but it helped form a state and change a nation. California would play an increasingly significant role in the national economy.

THINK ABOUT IT

How did the California gold rush affect the economy and population of the United States?

Active Options

On Your Feet: Gold Rush Roundtable Have students hold a roundtable discussion to collect details about the California gold rush. Arrange students in groups of four. Each student writes a different detail about the gold rush. Afterward, have groups share their collected details.

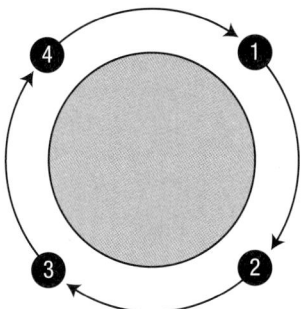

NG Learning Framework: Establish Points of View

SKILLS Communication, Collaboration

KNOWLEDGE Our Human Story

Divide the class into groups of four. Assign each group one of the following categories: white miners, women migrants, Chinese men, Native Americans. Have students find information about their category in this American Story. Then have each group create a one-minute dialogue that identifies who they are and quickly summarizes both positive and negative aspects of the California gold rush from their point of view.

THINK ABOUT IT

Possible response: The California gold rush brought many people to the United States and resulted in a booming national economy.

Guided Discussion

1. **Distinguish Fact and Opinion** What does Luzena Stanley Wilson actually mean when she says, "I was a queen"? *(Possible response: She is referring not specifically to herself but to how all women were viewed and treated. Because there were so few women, their skills were revered and they were treated like royalty.)* Tell students to compare what Wilson says in her memoir with facts in the historical note about her. **ASK:** Do you think most women of the gold rush would feel like queens? Why or why not? *(Answers will vary. Possible response: Yes, because men missed their wives or girlfriends and treated the few women they saw with great respect. No, because they had to work very hard and most were probably not as successful as Wilson was. It sounds as if Wilson herself worked very hard to succeed—not exactly a life of royal ease.)*

2. **Integrate Visuals** Instruct students to study the photo of Bodie, California, and recall what they have read about the gold rush. **ASK:** Why do you think Bodie became a ghost town instead of continuing to grow once the gold rush ended? *(Possible response: The photograph suggests that Bodie was a bleak and isolated place, with nothing to offer aside from mining. Once the gold ran out, miners left in search of better opportunities, and the businesses that had supported mining folded.)*

Link Discrimination from the Past and Present This American Story describes the struggles of miners as they sought to find fortune during the California gold rush. It also discusses the discrimination and hardship suffered by immigrants and Native Americans. To help students make connections between the American Story and their own lives, have them write a short essay about discrimination today. Remind them of the struggles of the Chinese during the gold rush and of their ability to maintain their cultural traditions and language. In their essays, have students emphasize how individuals overcome discrimination while maintaining cultural cohesiveness. Pair students to edit each other's essays and make suggestions for revisions. Provide guidance about the writing process as necessary.

AMERICAN STORIES

Luzena Stanley Wilson

EVERY WOMAN A QUEEN

Luzena Stanley Wilson was one of the few women to travel to California during the gold rush. She, her husband, and their two young sons left their cabin in Missouri to head west in the spring of 1849. It wasn't long before Wilson got her first inkling that she could make money in California. A man offered to buy a biscuit from her, saying he would pay "$10 for bread made by a woman."

The Wilsons settled in Sacramento and opened a hotel where Luzena did the cooking. Again she found that many miners would pay a premium for a meal made by an experienced female cook. The Wilsons went on to own several successful hotels in different California cities. After Luzena's husband left the family in 1872, she moved to San Francisco and made a living buying and selling real estate. She died in that city in 1902, at the age of 83.

PRIMARY SOURCE

I was a queen. Any woman who had a womanly heart, who spoke a kindly, sympathetic word to the lonely, homesick men, was a queen, and lacked no honor which a subject could bestow. Women were scarce in those days. I lived six months in Sacramento and saw only two.

—from *Luzena Stanley Wilson '49er, Her Memoirs as Taken Down by Her Daughter in 1881,* by Correnah Wilson Wright, 1937

BODIE, CALIFORNIA: GHOST TOWN

Shortly after the initial gold rush, Bodie, California, became a thriving mining town and home to nearly 10,000 people. Now it's a ghost town, an abandoned place that has fallen into ruin after a natural disaster, war, or economic depression. An 1875 mine cave-in led to the discovery of gold in Bodie, which went from a town of a few dozen people to a bustling boomtown. Today it sits in a state of arrested decay, visited by tourists, tumbleweeds, and maybe an occasional ghost.

LONG TOM

Many independent miners used a device called a long tom to separate gold from the California dirt. The largest part of the long tom was a shallow wooden trough about 15 feet long. This had to be placed near a water source, because a steady stream of water needed to flow through it.

A miner would put gold-bearing dirt at the top of the trough. The water washed the dirt through a screen that removed larger rocks. Next, the water flowed into a shallow box with wooden riffles sticking up from the bottom. The gold flakes caught on the riffles while the water and the rest of the dirt flowed out of the box. Shoveling dirt into a long tom all day was back-breaking work.

WATER IN

DIRT AND GRAVEL IN
Miners pour pay dirt into the top of the long tom. Water washes over the dirt.

CRITICAL VIEWING Museum volunteers, or docents, demonstrate the art of using a long tom in the American River in Coloma, California. Based on details you notice in the photo, how did long tom operators use forces of gravity and motion to separate gold from dirt?

GOLD SEPARATES
Flowing water helps separate gold from rocks and dirt particles.

SCREEN

RIFFLE BOX

RIFFLES CATCH GOLD
Heavy gold flakes get caught in the riffles. Light dirt and sand wash away.

HOW THE **LONG TOM** WORKS

WATER OUT

SETTLING POND

Manifest Destiny 389

Striving Readers

Make a Top Five Facts List Tell students to reread the information about how the gold rush contributed to the growth of San Francisco and to the national economy. Then have students write in their own words five facts they have learned. Have students meet with a partner to compare lists and consolidate the facts into one final list.

Gifted & Talented

Market the Gold Rush Have students research travel brochures to analyze the use of hyperbole. Then divide students into teams. Have each team design a brochure as a way to market travel to California to mine for gold. The brochures should be colorful, showcase both the adventures of land and water travel to California, and use hyperbole in an attempt to attract prospective miners. Have teams share their brochures with the rest of class. Discuss the effectiveness of students' brochures and whether they would be successful at persuading people to join the California gold rush.

See the Chapter Planner for more strategies for differentiation.

HISTORICAL THINKING

Ask and have students answer the following questions.

1. **READING CHECK** How did the gold rush shape the population of California?

2. **EVALUATE** Why were the Chinese treated harshly by white miners?

3. **DETERMINE CHRONOLOGY** How long did the gold rush last?

ANSWERS

1. Thousands of people from all over the world came to seek their fortune. Most failed to find gold, but many stayed, creating a population of many cultures.

2. Chinese miners faced discrimination from white miners who felt threatened by the competition in a failing economy.

3. The gold rush lasted about 10 years.

CRITICAL VIEWING The water flowed from the higher part of the long tom to the lower part. The force of the water moved the dirt from one point to another. Gravity caused dirt and rocks to fall through the screen as the water flowed from the high point to the low point.

1.1 The Pull of the West

If you had trouble finding work and heard about opportunities in a completely different part of the country, you just might pack up and move. That's exactly what settlers from the eastern half of the United States did in the 19th century. They packed up and moved west.

MAIN IDEA A tough economy and the promise of a rich and exciting future led Americans to look for opportunities in the West.

As they moved west, Americans built new settlements. In this 1868 painting, *Across the Continent* by Frances Palmer, Native Americans on horseback watch from afar as excited settlers greet an incoming train.

OPENING THE WEST

The boundaries of the nation shifted dramatically in the early 19th century, and the westward migration of easterners profoundly changed American culture. The West inspired ideals of **individualism**, or a self-reliant independence, and rugged frontier life that dramatically influenced our national self-image and sense of the American past.

In the early 19th century, Americans began to explore, move to, and live in the West. In 1806, Zebulon Pike led an expedition to discover the headwaters of the Arkansas River and was one of the first white men to explore the wilderness of Colorado. Many of these adventurous individuals were fur trappers and explorers, called **mountain men**. They spent most of their time in the wilderness trapping small animals for furs. Every summer from about 1825 to 1840, trappers met with fur traders at temporary markets called **rendezvous** (RAHN-deh-voo) to sell and buy goods and supplies. Trade opportunities like this were one of the economic incentives that drew people to the West.

Several mountain men became legendary. Kit Carson, a successful fur trapper in California, would later use his skills to guide U.S. Army officers in a war with Mexico. Another legend was **Jedediah Smith**. Smith had read of Lewis and Clark's expeditions and decided to explore the West for himself. He would eventually explore more of the unknown territory of the West than any other single person. In 1826, Smith crossed the Mojave (moh-HAH-vee) Desert into southern California. The next year, he hiked through California's high

A Seasoned Mountain Man
Jim Beckwourth's adventures took him from the Everglades of Florida to northern Mexico, southern Canada, and the Pacific coast. While exploring the West, he lived with a Crow tribe for several years. He was also a prospector and a U.S. Army scout, and he learned to overcome many challenges of the frontier.

mountains, the Sierra Nevada, and became the first white American to travel overland from the East to California and back. Another mountain man who explored the Sierra Nevada was **Jim Beckwourth**. He had been born into slavery but was set free when he was 25. In 1850, he discovered a mountain pass through the Sierra Nevada for settlers to follow as they traveled to northern California. Today, that pass is still called Beckwourth Pass.

The mountain men's explorations opened lands that had previously seemed inaccessible. After the Panic of 1837, many Americans faced economic difficulties. Newly explored lands in the West started to look attractive to unhappy easterners, new immigrants, independent women, and others who were seeking a new start.

MANIFEST DESTINY

In 1845, magazine editor John O'Sullivan wrote an editorial urging the United States to **annex**, or add, Texas as a state. He also wrote that Americans had a "**manifest destiny**" to overspread and possess the whole of the continent." The word *manifest* means "obvious," and *destiny* refers to the unavoidable events of the future. The phrase, and the purpose underlying manifest destiny, reflected several cultural assumptions, including the certainty that the United States would—indeed, should—one day stretch from the Atlantic Ocean to the Pacific Ocean. Those who embraced this concept were driven by more than just the promise of new opportunities. O'Sullivan's editorial described a belief that God intended for white Protestant Americans to take over the continent. Such an idea blatantly ignored the fact that there were already people living on these lands.

For several decades, the federal government pursued the territorial acquisition of western lands. The Oregon Territory promised timber, furs, and rich fisheries. California offered fertile farmland and abundant mineral resources, and both California and Oregon provided ports on the Pacific Ocean for seaboard merchants to ship and receive goods. Texas held deposits of minerals and metals, such as silver. The desire for riches and the belief in manifest destiny inspired settlers and politicians to move westward.

HISTORICAL THINKING

1. **READING CHECK** How did the concept of manifest destiny encourage Americans to move west?

2. **IDENTIFY MAIN IDEAS AND DETAILS** What natural resources served as economic incentives for people moving west?

3. **EVALUATE** Why might lands in the West have seemed inaccessible to many Americans?

PLAN

Objective

Learn how the lure of adventure and possibility changed the economic landscape of the West.

Critical Thinking Skills for Lesson 1.1

• Identify Main Ideas and Details
• Monitor Comprehension
• Evaluate
• Analyze Cause and Effect
• Make Predictions
• Analyze Visuals

Essential Question for Chapter 12

Why were Americans inspired to move west?
With the expansion of national boundaries in the early 19th century, adventurers began to explore unknown territories. Lesson 1.1 discusses what drew settlers from the East and how the westward movement both reflected and created a new national self-image.

Background for the Teacher

While the mountain men were exploring the West on foot, the government-sponsored United States Exploring Expedition, sometimes called U.S. Ex Ex, was exploring part of the West by water. The expedition's assignment to study the entire Pacific Ocean placed special emphasis on Antarctica and, in order to gather data that would bolster the government's claim to the region, the northern parts of the West Coast.

The U.S. Ex Ex helped establish Oregon as a goal of American manifest destiny. The team compiled charts showing 800 miles of the Oregon coast, 100 miles of the Columbia River, and the overland route from Oregon to San Francisco. After his return, Charles Wilkes, captain of the expedition, urged Congress to annex the Oregon Territory. Wilkes also published an influential narrative of the expedition that, along with later narratives, enticed aspiring settlers with descriptions of the forests, furs, and fisheries of Oregon.

Consider Motivations

Encourage students to recall people they know who have moved to another part of the United States or to another country. Questions to prompt class discussion include the following: Why did they move? What might motivate you to move to a different region or country? Where would you go and why? Call on volunteers to share their responses with the class. Ask students to consider as they read how the motivations of people today are similar to and different from the motivations of Americans who moved to the West in the 19th century.

TEACH
Guided Discussion

1. **Analyze Cause and Effect** How do you think the rendezvous and the concept of the frontier provided an incentive for people to move west? *(Answers will vary. Possible responses: The markets may have convinced people they could make money on the frontier. The rugged lifestyle of the trappers at the rendezvous may have appealed to some adventurers.)*

2. **Make Predictions** What was the likely outcome of American settlers moving onto land that was already inhabited by others? *(Answers will vary. Possible response: Conflicts or wars between groups of people would likely take place.)*

Analyze Visuals

Direct students' attention to the painting *Across the Continent*. **ASK:** How does the painting reflect the purpose, challenges and economic incentives of westward expansion in the 19th century? *(Answers will vary. Possible response: The abundant natural resources around the town suggest that people could earn a living off the land. The covered wagons leaving the town suggest even further opportunities. The men using axes and shovels show that living in the West was hard work. The people's excitement about the arrival of the train suggests that loneliness was another challenge. The presence of Native Americans is a reminder that the settlers were taking over Native American lands.)*

Active Options

On Your Feet: Create a Concept Cluster Form groups of four students around a section of bulletin board or a table. Provide each group with a large sheet of paper. Have group members take turns contributing a word, name, or phrase to a Concept Cluster focused on the word *individualism*. Encourage students to name and include characteristics of people from the lesson who exhibited individualism, such as Zebulon Pike, Jedediah Smith, and James Pierson Beckwourth. Provide time at the end of the activity for groups to share their Concept Clusters.

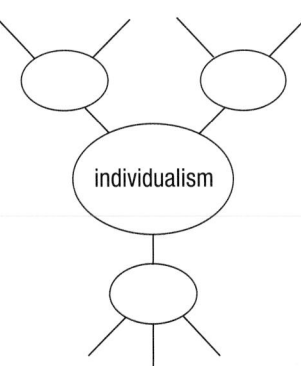

NG Learning Framework: Learn More About Trailblazers

ATTITUDE Curiosity

KNOWLEDGE Our Human Story

Organize students into three groups. Assign each group one of the following trailblazers: Zebulon Pike, Jedediah Smith, or Jim Beckwourth. Encourage groups to use library or online sources to learn more about their assigned trailblazer. Once groups have completed their research, tell them to organize the information into a biographical sketch. Groups should also create a map showing their trailblazer's explorations. Have groups share their work and discuss the impact these people had on the settlement of the West.

Striving Readers

Summarize Ask students to read Lesson 1.1 in pairs. Tell them to write a sentence that restates the main idea of each paragraph as they read. Then instruct students to review their sentences and write a paragraph consisting of four or five sentences that summarizes the whole lesson. Remind students to use their own words in their summary and to include only the most important ideas and details. Call on volunteers to share their summaries with the class.

Gifted & Talented

Write an Editorial Ask students to write a newspaper editorial in which they put themselves in the place of the editor of a newspaper in a 19th-century western town and urge Americans to look for opportunities in the West. Remind students that their editorial should support the basic ideas of manifest destiny and include compelling arguments for people to move to California or Oregon. Students may publish their editorials in a class newspaper.

See the Chapter Planner for more strategies for differentiation.

HISTORICAL THINKING

ANSWERS

1. The concept of manifest destiny encouraged the belief that it was God's will that white Protestant Americans occupy the entire continent from the Atlantic Ocean to the Pacific Ocean.

2. The Northwest had valuable resources, such as forests and fisheries. California had mineral resources and fertile farmland. Texas had minerals and metals. The West also had a large amount of land available for settlement.

3. Getting to lands in the West required a long and difficult journey crossing deserts and high mountain ranges, a seemingly impossible task to many Americans.

1.2 Manifest Destiny

John O'Sullivan might have thought he was onto something when he coined the phrase "manifest destiny." However, he could not have predicted the impact that Americans' movement west would have on the nation's identity.

For the 19th-century Americans already considering moving westward, the idea of manifest destiny—that they had not only the right but also the responsibility to help expand the nation—was quite appealing. Settlers by the hundreds began crossing the Mississippi River and heading west.

John Gast's 1872 painting *American Progress* depicts the "spirit of America" as a goddess-like woman bathed in light and floating westward. She is leading **pioneers**, or people moving to a new and unfamiliar land, as they

leave their settled lives and communities behind. The spirit carries a schoolbook, and she strings telegraph wire as she moves across the open land. Notice Gast's use of light and dark in this painting and how Native Americans and wildlife seem to react to the people headed their way.

CRITICAL VIEWING What do you notice about the direction the painting's subjects are facing? How does that reflect the concept of manifest destiny?

🏛 **Autry Museum of the American West, Los Angeles**

Gast painted *American Progress* just a few years after the end of the Civil War. In some ways, the painting's themes of modernization and new frontiers reflect a cultural desire to begin anew.

DOCUMENT ONE

Primary Source: Essay
from "The Great Nation of Futurity,"
by John L. O'Sullivan, 1839

The concept of manifest destiny originated in John L. O'Sullivan's essay about what he perceived as the great future for the United States.

CONSTRUCTED RESPONSE On what authorities does O'Sullivan rest his ideas about the "onward march" of the United States?

The expansive future is our arena. We are entering on its untrodden space, with the truths of God in our minds, beneficent objects in our hearts, and with a clear conscience unsullied by the past. We are the nation of human progress, and who will, what can, set limits to our onward march? Providence is with us, and no earthly power can. We point to the everlasting truth on the first page of our national declaration. In its magnificent domain of space and time, the nation of many nations is destined to manifest to mankind the excellence of divine principles.

DOCUMENT TWO

Primary Source: Artifact
Wheel from a covered wagon, wood and iron, c. 1830

The wheels on the covered wagons that carried the pioneers, like the wagon depicted in *American Progress* at left, were about four feet across. An iron band encircled the outside of the wheel, and iron strengthened the opening for the axle.

CONSTRUCTED RESPONSE What characteristics of the wheel can you see that make it suited to carrying a one-ton load more than 1,000 miles?

DOCUMENT THREE

Primary Source: Diary
from "The Letters and Journals of Narcissa Whitman,"
by Narcissa Whitman, 1836

Some of the first white settlers in the West were missionaries. Narcissa Whitman and her husband Marcus traveled to Oregon Country, hoping to spread Christianity among the Native Americans. Her diaries and letters home capture the experience of traveling the Oregon Trail and living in the Northwest. This excerpt is from July 27, 1836.

CONSTRUCTED RESPONSE How does Whitman describe the hardships of travel to the West?

We are still in a dangerous country; but our company is large enough for safety. Our cattle endure the journey remarkably well. They supply us with sufficient milk for our tea and coffee, which is indeed a luxury. Do not think I regret coming. No, far from it; I would not go back for a world. I am contented and happy, notwithstanding I sometimes get very hungry and weary. Have six week's steady journey before us. Feel sometimes as if it were a long time to be traveling. Long for rest, but must not murmur. Feel to pity the poor Indian women, who are continually traveling in this manner during their lives, and know no other comfort.

SYNTHESIZE & WRITE

1. **REVIEW** Review what you have learned about the cultural, geographic, and political context in which the idea of manifest destiny emerged.

2. **RECALL** On your own paper, write the main ideas about manifest destiny inspired by Gast's painting, the writings of O'Sullivan and Whitman, and the wagon wheel.

3. **CONSTRUCT** Construct a topic sentence that answers this question: In what ways did Americans incorporate the idea of manifest destiny into their decisions about moving west?

4. **WRITE** Using evidence from this chapter and the documents and artifact, write an informative paragraph that supports your topic sentence in Step 3.

PLAN

Objective

Synthesize information about westward expansion from primary sources and an artifact.

Critical Thinking Skills for Lesson 1.2

- Synthesize
- Make Inferences
- Compare and Contrast
- Evaluate

Essential Question for Chapter 12

Why were Americans inspired to move west?

Nineteenth-century Americans interpreted manifest destiny in different ways. Lesson 1.2 examines how primary sources depict the challenges and incentives associated with westward expansion.

Background for the Teacher

John Gast's painting, just 11½ by 15¾ inches in size, was commissioned by publisher George Crofutt, who reproduced the painting in his popular western travel guides. It portrays the concept of 19th-century Americans' national identity, the passage of time, and the advance of technology. From left to right, the population of the frontier changes from Native Americans to miners to farmers and settlers. Transportation technology advances from horseback and travois, a sled-like transport for goods made of two connected poles, to covered wagons and stagecoaches to railroads and steamships. Progress and enlightenment spreads from east to west as the spirit of America brings light to the darkness of the unexplored frontier.

INTRODUCE & ENGAGE

Prepare for the Document-Based Question

Before students start on the activity, briefly preview the documents and artifact. Remind students that a constructed response requires full explanations in complete sentences. Emphasize that students should use what they have learned about manifest destiny and Americans' westward movement in addition to the information in the documents and details about the artifact.

TEACH

Guided Discussion

1. **Make Inferences** Why do you think John Gast included a schoolbook and telegraph wire in his painting? *(Answers will vary. Possible response: The schoolbook suggests that education is a form of progress settlers were bringing to the West. The telegraph wire shows the importance of communication as a means of connecting the nation.)*

2. **Compare and Contrast** What are some similarities and differences between the writings of John L. O'Sullivan and Narcissa Whitman? *(Answers will vary. Possible response: Both were written at about the same time. O'Sullivan's essay defends the concept of manifest destiny. Whitman's diary details the experience of moving west.)*

Evaluate

After students have completed the Synthesize & Write activity, allow time for them to exchange paragraphs and read and comment on the work of their peers. Guidelines for comments should be established prior to this activity so that feedback is constructive and encouraging in nature.

Active Options

On Your Feet: Host a DBQ Roundtable Divide the class into groups of four. Have groups move desks together to form a table where they all can sit. Hand each group a sheet of paper with these questions: What were some reasons Americans accepted the idea of manifest destiny? How did these reasons affect the nation's identity? Have one student in each group write a response, read it aloud, and pass the paper clockwise to the next student. Have each group circulate the paper around the table several times before discussing their responses. Reconvene as a class and have groups share their responses.

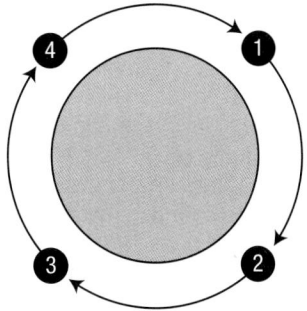

DIFFERENTIATE

Inclusion

Work in Pairs Allow students with visual disabilities to work with partners who can read the lesson aloud to them. Encourage the partner without disabilities to describe the painting and the artifact as well. Instruct students to work together to determine their answers to the Critical Viewing and Synthesize & Write questions. You may also want to give students the option of recording their paragraphs rather than writing them out.

Pre-AP

Identify Points of View Assign pairs Gast's painting, O'Sullivan's writing, or Whitman's writing. Ask students to identify the artist's or writer's point of view on manifest destiny and to determine the context in which the painting or writing originated. Have pairs develop written or infographic summaries to share with the class.

See the Chapter Planner for more strategies for differentiation.

SYNTHESIZE & WRITE

ANSWERS

1. Answers will vary.

2. Answers will vary.

3. Possible response: In the 1840s, many white settlers decided to move west because they believed that God had a plan for the United States to extend to the Pacific Ocean.

4. Students' paragraphs should include their topic sentence from Step 3 and several details from the documents and about the artifact to support the sentence.

CONSTRUCTED RESPONSE

Document 1: Possible response: O'Sullivan uses God and the foundations of democracy to support his ideas. He states, "Providence is with us," suggesting that no power on Earth can interfere. He also refers to the Declaration of Independence as support for the nation's destiny to span the continent.

Document 2: Possible response: The wooden parts of the wheel look sturdy enough to hold heavy loads. The iron that covers the rim and reinforces the opening for the axle would prevent wooden parts from being easily damaged while rolling over rough ground and rocks for hundreds of miles.

Document 3: Possible response: Despite sometimes suffering hunger and fatigue, Whitman says she is content and does not regret making the journey. Although she longs for rest, she reminds herself not to complain because she feels that her life is easier than the lives of "Indian women" who had to travel constantly.

CRITICAL VIEWING Answers will vary. Possible response: The subjects in the painting are facing west, which supports the idea that westward expansion to the sea was purposeful and inevitable.

1.3 Trails to the West

Think of times when you've had several choices in front of you. In the mid-19th century, westward-bound Americans had to decide which road—or, more accurately, which trail—they would take.

MAIN IDEA Between 1841 and 1866, as many as a half million Americans followed trails to new lives in the West.

TRAVELING BY TRAIL

The story of one of the most important trails to the West begins in 1821, the year that Mexico won its independence from Spain. Under Spanish rule, trade with the United States had been heavily restricted. Mexico was eager to support individual land ownership and trade with the United States. Settlements at Santa Fe and Taos in the New Mexico territory, then part of Mexico, were ideally located for Mexican trade with the westernmost territories.

In 1822, a trader named William Becknell opened a new route that covered a distance of more than 900 miles from Independence, Missouri, to Santa Fe. Soon other traders began using this route, which became known as the **Santa Fe Trail**. They hauled their goods in caravans of covered wagons, similar to Conestoga wagons. Near the trail's western end, traders used a branch of the trail called the Cimarron Cutoff so they could avoid crossing the rugged Sangre de Cristo (SAHN-gray day KREE-stoh) Mountains.

From Santa Fe, traders traveled to the Pacific coast along the **Old Spanish Trail**, through territory controlled by Mexico. They brought Mexican woolen goods across the trail to trade for horses

Trails to the West, 1840s

in California. Extending across high mountains and the scorching Mojave Desert, it was the most dangerous and difficult of the trails.

In the midst of building a new nation, Mexico struggled to govern its settlements along the American border, where traders and settlers from both countries lived. Cultural clashes over such issues as slavery—which had been outlawed in Mexico—were common.

The Santa Fe Trail represented only one of several important routes to the West. Independence was also the starting point for two other important

trails. The **Oregon Trail** led to the Oregon Country in the Northwest. This region included the present-day states of Oregon, Washington, and Idaho as well as parts of Montana and the Canadian province of British Columbia.

In 1846, the United States and Great Britain signed a treaty setting the boundary between their territories in the Oregon Country. The treaty settled disputed land claims between the two nations, and the resulting stability encouraged even more American settlers to move to the **Oregon Territory**, the American portion of what had been Oregon Country. Between 1840 and 1860, from 300,000 to 400,000 Americans traveled the Oregon Trail. By 1860, about 52,000 people had settled in the new state of Oregon. Many settled in the fertile valley of the Willamette River located at the end of the trail.

THE MORMON TRAIL

Some trails were forged by people seeking new economic opportunities. But others were inspired by the religious faiths of the travelers. One of those was the **Mormon Trail**. In 1830, Joseph Smith founded the Mormon religion, the Church of Jesus Christ of Latter-day Saints, in New York. Smith and his followers moved west, establishing a community in Nauvoo, Illinois. There, because of the economic and political power they had achieved, they suffered harassment from their non-Mormon neighbors. When a mob killed Smith, the Mormons' new leader, **Brigham Young**, decided to move even farther west so that he and his fellow Mormons could practice their religion freely.

In 1846, Young led an **exodus**, or mass departure, of Mormons. They traveled westward until they reached the Missouri River near present-day Omaha, Nebraska. After wintering there, they continued west, sometimes following the Oregon Trail. When they neared the **Continental Divide**,

🏛 The National Museum of American History, Washington, D.C.

This sunstone carved from limestone is one of 30 that adorned the grand temple of the Church of Jesus Christ of Latter-day Saints, completed in 1846 in Nauvoo, Illinois, by architect William Weeks. Images of the sun, moon, and stars are important to Mormon symbolism and may pertain to the Old Testament story of Joseph. Joseph Smith said that a sun with a face like this had come to him in a vision.

the high point in the Rocky Mountains that divides the watersheds of the Atlantic and Pacific oceans, they headed southward into territory still owned by Mexico. After an arduous trek over the Rockies, they reached the Great Salt Lake. There, in present-day Utah, Young declared that they had reached their destination, and they established the community of Salt Lake City.

HISTORICAL THINKING

1. **READING CHECK** Where did the Santa Fe, Oregon, and Mormon trails begin and end?

2. **ANALYZE CAUSE AND EFFECT** Why did the Mormons move west from Illinois?

3. **INTERPRET MAPS** What major physical features did all or most of the trails shown on the map share?

PLAN

Objective

Describe the challenges Americans faced as they traveled overland to the West.

Critical Thinking Skills for Lesson 1.3

- Identify Main Ideas and Details
- Monitor Comprehension
- Analyze Cause and Effect
- Interpret Maps
- Make Connections

Essential Question for Chapter 12

Why were Americans inspired to move west?
Reaching destinations in California and Oregon presented many challenges, such as crossing mountains and deserts. Lesson 1.3 describes routes to the West and explores reasons why settlers seeking new opportunities chose to follow these trails.

Background for the Teacher

Mormon leaders had been planning a westward migration before Joseph Smith's death. However, continuing persecution forced the first group of about 3,000 people to flee in February 1846. Leaders had planned to get to Utah by the end of the year. The first stage of the journey, traveling 265 miles from Nauvoo to Omaha, Nebraska, took more than four months. Many families forgot to pack important provisions, and few had the skills to survive on the trail. Although they arrived in June, the group established "winter quarters" in Omaha until the following spring. More than 400 members died that winter. In April 1847, the first wagon train left Omaha to travel nearly 1,000 miles to Salt Lake City. The Mormons reached the Great Salt Lake in July, and during the next two decades almost 70,000 Mormons followed.

📓 History Notebook

Encourage students to complete the American Gallery page for Chapter 12 in their History Notebooks as they read.

INTRODUCE & ENGAGE

Design a Word Wall

Ask students to brainstorm a list of words they associate with the western frontier. Tell them the words may be about people, places, animals, modes of transportation, objects, or concepts. Provide index cards or slips of paper on which students may write their words. If students encounter one of their words in the lesson, have them display the word on a wall or bulletin board in the classroom as a means of review and as a way to verify accurate understanding of the western frontier.

TEACH

Guided Discussion

1. **Analyze Cause and Effect** What were the effects of the 1846 treaty between the United States and Great Britain? *(Answers will vary. Possible response: The treaty settled a boundary dispute and created the Oregon Territory as part of the United States. Americans could then settle the Willamette Valley, which attracted a large enough population to form the state of Oregon.)*

2. **Make Connections** How was the Mormon migration to Oregon in the 1800s similar to the Puritan migration to the colonies in the 1600s? *(Both groups sought religious freedom and opportunities for a better life. Both groups traveled a great distance, facing challenges, hardship, and loss of life, in their efforts to reach their destinations and establish settlements.)*

Interpret Maps

Why was the location of Santa Fe an advantage and a disadvantage for Mexico and the United States? *(Santa Fe was located on the Rio Grande, where it became a trading center for newly independent Mexicans and Americans headed to California. The settlement was also on the border between Texas and Mexico, so it likely became a site for cultural and territorial clashes.)*

Active Options

On Your Feet: Four Corners Label each of the four corners of the room with one of the following words: Challenges, Destinations, Incentives, Purposes. Tell students to consider how each of these ideas influenced the westward movement of Americans in the mid-19th century. Then ask them to go to the corner labeled with the idea they think was the most important influence. Allow members of each group to discuss their reasons. Call on volunteers from the groups to explain the influence of their idea to the class.

The Westward Trails Invite students to explore the American Gallery. Have them select one of the images and do additional research to learn more about it. Ask questions that will inspire additional inquiry about the chosen gallery image, such as: Why does this image belong in this chapter? How does it aid your understanding of manifest destiny? What else would you like to know about the image?

DIFFERENTIATE

English Language Learners   ELD

Use Sentence Stems Before reading, provide students at the **Emerging** level with the sentence stems listed below. Add a word bank if needed. Have students complete the stems as they read. After reading, have students compare completed sentences with a partner.

1. Much of the land in the West was part of _____, which had won independence from Spain. *(New Mexico territory)*

2. A trade route from Independence, Missouri, to Santa Fe became known as the _____. *(Santa Fe Trail)*

3. The _____ was the most dangerous route to the West because it crossed high mountains and the Mojave Desert. *(Old Spanish Trail)*

4. A treaty between the United States and _____ settled the boundary between their territories in the Oregon Country. *(Britain)*

5. Brigham Young led the _____ from Illinois to the Great Salt Lake to seek religious freedom. *(Mormons)*

Gifted & Talented

Write a Diary Have students choose a trail described in the lesson and imagine they were following it in the mid-1800s. Have them write diary entries describing their experiences. Ask students to conduct research using maps and documents to make their diary entries realistic. Provide opportunities for them to share their diaries.

See the Chapter Planner for more strategies for differentiation.

HISTORICAL THINKING

ANSWERS

1. The Santa Fe and Oregon Trails began at Independence, Missouri. The Santa Fe Trail ended at the city of Santa Fe. The Oregon Trail ended in the Willamette Valley. The Mormon Trail started in Nauvoo, Illinois, and ended at the Great Salt Lake.

2. The Mormons left Illinois because non-Mormons were persecuting them and killed their leader. They traveled west to find a safe place to practice their religion.

3. Answers will vary. Possible response: Most of the trails followed rivers for part of their routes and crossed mountains on their way to western lands.

1.4 Pioneers and Native Americans

Most people don't enjoy doing chores, even with the help of modern conveniences. Imagine how hard it was for families traveling along the Oregon Trail in the 1840s to prepare meals or wash clothes while also coping with illness and injuries in unfamiliar territory.

MAIN IDEA Pioneers who moved west endured hardships, and their encounters with Native Americans had profound effects on both cultures.

Like other mid-19th century painters, Albert Bierstadt depicted the splendor and beauty of the American landscape. He painted this work, *Oregon Trail*, around 1850. What details in this painting convey the challenges and adventures of life on the frontier?

A DIFFICULT JOURNEY

Pioneers heading west usually traveled in groups of covered wagons called **wagon trains**. No matter the destination, the journey was grueling and took several months. Wagon trains crossed rivers and mountains as well as arid lands where water and vegetation were scarce. The long days demanded difficult chores and wearying travel.

Pioneers dealt with severe weather, including sandstorms, snowstorms, and floods. They also fought diseases such as cholera and typhoid. Because of the long distances between outposts, or settlements, running out of food, water, and supplies was a constant worry.

Pioneer women performed tasks such as cooking and cleaning. They also worked alongside men—tending to livestock, gathering supplies, and repairing tools and wagons. Everyone pitched in, no matter who they were or what job needed to be done.

Life on the frontier wagon trains changed conventional gender roles. Excerpts from men's and women's diaries and letters capture both the hope and excitement of seeing new lands, the day-to-day tasks they had to do, and the great losses and hardships endured on the trail. The journal entries below, of a man and a girl, describe very different pioneer experiences.

PRIMARY SOURCES

Today we met a large company, homeward bound. Some of our company purchased two milk cows from them. They say we never can get through, because there is no grass ahead, and the cholera is getting worse. Their wagons are crowded with sick men. Now our hearts began to fail us again and when we reflect that we have hardly made an introduction to our journey, the task becomes harder and we almost get weary of life.

—from "Journal of John Wood," by John Wood, 1852

One pleasant evening some Indian boys wanted to display their skill with bow and arrow. When we gave them a biscuit they would set it up, step off some distance and pierce it with an arrow. Father got a pan of biscuits and he would measure off a distance, set up one and tell them to shoot at it. The one who struck it first got it for his own. They had considerable sport over the biscuits.

—from *One Woman's West*, by Martha Gay Masterson, 1892

CULTURAL ENCOUNTERS

Westward trails passed through lands inhabited by various Native American tribes. On the Great Plains, pioneers encountered the **Lakota**, and in the Oregon Territory they met the **Nez Perce**. Traders who traveled the Santa Fe Trail to the New Mexico territory interacted with southwestern tribes such as the **Zuni**.

The Lakota, Nez Perce, and Zuni had distinctive customs. Traditionally, the Lakota lived in tepees and hunted bison. The Nez Perce tended to settle along streams that provided a steady supply of food. Up to 30 families could live in one of their roomy lodges. The Zuni lived in adobe houses or dwellings built into cliffs.

Encountering Native Americans was a new experience for pioneers and for the people hearing about such encounters back home. In addition, works of fiction about westward journeys often exaggerated accounts of Native American attacks on pioneers. In reality, attacks were rare. Of the nearly 400,000 people who traveled the Oregon Trail in the mid-19th century, about 400 were killed in attacks by Native Americans. Most encounters were friendly, and Native Americans and settlers engaged in trade and sometimes helped each other.

Even so, as new settlers intruded on Native American land, conflicts did arise. In one instance, a cow wandered away from one of the pioneers traveling on the Oregon Trail, and was killed by a Native American. U.S. Army soldiers intervened by talking to the Native American chief. At first everyone behaved reasonably, but misunderstandings and a nervous soldier shooting his gun led to a battle near Fort Laramie, a U.S. military post in present-day Wyoming. By the time it ended, the Native American chief and 29 American soldiers had been killed in what is referred to as the Grattan Massacre of 1854.

HISTORICAL THINKING

1. **READING CHECK** In general, what were interactions between pioneers and Native Americans like?

2. **IDENTIFY MAIN IDEAS AND DETAILS** What kinds of challenges did pioneers heading west in wagon trains face?

3. **EVALUATE** What do we learn about family life on the frontier from the letters and diaries of travelers moving west?

PLAN

Objective

Describe how the lives of pioneers and Native Americans changed as a result of people moving west.

Critical Thinking Skills for Lesson 1.4

- Identify Main Ideas and Details
- Monitor Comprehension
- Evaluate
- Make Generalizations
- Make Inferences

Essential Question for Chapter 12

Why were Americans inspired to move west?
Life on the trail was more difficult than most pioneers expected. Lesson 1.4 discusses the realities of the journey west as well as pioneer encounters with Native Americans.

Background for the Teacher

The 2,170-mile trek along the Oregon Trail from Missouri to the Willamette Valley took four to six months. The timing of the journey was essential to its success. Leaving Independence in April or May increased the chances of crossing the western mountain passes before snowfall. The trail was littered with treasured belongings families were forced to abandon to lighten the wagonload. Loved ones who died of starvation, disease, or accidents were left behind in unmarked trailside graves. In spite of the challenges, thousands of pioneers reached their destination. Traces of their journey can be seen today in well-preserved wagon wheel ruts along the Oregon National Historic Trail.

INTRODUCE & ENGAGE

Imagine a Long Journey

Invite students to discuss problems people might encounter today if they were going on a long trip through unfamiliar territory. *(Possible responses: A car might break down. An airplane flight might be delayed or canceled. Travelers might get lost. Their baggage might be lost. They might not like the place when they get there.)* As they study this lesson, tell students to compare and contrast these present-day travel problems with the problems pioneers faced on their journey to the West.

TEACH

Guided Discussion

1. **Make Generalizations** Based on the primary sources, what generalizations can you make about the experience of traveling west on a wagon train? *(Answers will vary. Possible response: Adults were concerned about the number of sick people, the difficulty of the journey, and the threat of diseases, such as cholera. The girl's journal entry suggests that adults spent some time distracting children, such as by playing with the Indian boys, to make the journey less harsh.)*

2. **Make Inferences** What do the descriptions of the Lakota, Nez Perce, and Zuni indicate about Native Americans of the West? *(Answers will vary. Possible response: Native Americans were a peaceful, diverse group with distinctive customs and ways of life. The West was not just open land waiting for settlers. It was populated by many groups of people who had been there for a long time.)*

Active Options

Active History: Illustrate the Rain Shadow Effect Extend the lesson by using either the PDF or Whiteboard version of the activity. These activities take a deeper look at a topic from, or related to, the lesson. Explore the activities as a class, turn them into group assignments, or even assign them individually.

NG Learning Framework: Depict Frontier Life

| ATTITUDE | Empowerment |
| SKILL | Collaboration |

Invite students to assume the roles of people on the frontier. Divide students into groups of four or five and direct each group to create a tableau, or a motionless scene, depicting one of the aspects of frontier life discussed in Lesson 1.4. As each group presents its tableau, ask other members of the class to write a sentence describing the scene. At the end of the activity, encourage students to share their sentences and discuss how, together, their tableaux capture the adventure and challenges of frontier life.

DIFFERENTIATE

Striving Readers

Record and Compare Facts After they read the lesson, ask students to write three important facts they learned about the pioneers' westward journey. Allow pairs of students to compare and check their facts and then combine their facts into one list. Call on volunteers to come to the board and write the most important fact from their list.

Pre-AP

Examine Historical Accounts Ask students to examine additional accounts of the incident described in the last paragraph of the lesson, which is known as the Grattan Massacre. Ask them to examine the eyewitness account by James Bordeau, newspaper articles from 1854, and secondary accounts from reliable sources. Remind students to distinguish verifiable from unverifiable information. Hold a class discussion in which students present their findings.

See the Chapter Planner for more strategies for differentiation.

HISTORICAL THINKING

ANSWERS

1. Despite some conflicts, most travelers and Native Americans interacted peacefully and traded with each other.

2. They had to cross rivers, arid lands, and mountains. The weather could be punishing. They sometimes ran out of food or other supplies. Disease was common.

3. Answers will vary. Possible response: Reading what people wrote about their own experiences allows historians to understand pioneers' day-to-day activities and concerns. The diaries in this lesson indicate that men worried about protecting and feeding their families, and that life on the trail wasn't always harsh.

CRITICAL VIEWING Answers will vary. Possible response: The scene is at night, and travelers have stopped by a river. Traveling through new and scenic country must have been an adventure. People are doing laundry in the river, and one man is carrying wood to keep a fire going. Challenging chores like these must have been constant, but in the evening the travelers might have had time to relax around the fire.

2.1 The Tejanos

When Mexico took control of the territory that later became Texas, the Mexican government was concerned about how few people lived there. The solution? Offer free land and hope people would move there.

MAIN IDEA After achieving independence from Spain, Mexico encouraged American settlement in the territory of Texas.

SPANISH TERRITORY

In the early 1800s, some westward-bound Americans ended up in Spanish territory. What we know today as the state of Texas used to be the Spanish territory called **Tejas** (TAY-hahs). In 1598, Spanish conquistador Juan de Oñate (oh-NYAH-tay) and his soldiers reached the Rio Grande. De Oñate claimed all the land around the river for Spain, leading to 200 years of Spanish rule.

Tejas lay north of the Nueces (noo-AY-suhs) River and extended into present-day Louisiana. Spain established missions throughout the area, starting with San Francisco de los Tejas. Catholic priests and missionaries moved to these missions in order to convert the Coahuiltecan (koh-uh-WEEL-tek-un) and the Caddo (KAH-doh) people. **Presidios**, or military settlements, surrounded most missions. Other Spanish settlers built farms close to the presidios.

Tejas shared a border with the United States. As a result, Spain worried about the influence its northern neighbor might have on the territory. Settlers of Spanish or Mexican descent, called **Tejanos** (tay-HAH-nohs), were forbidden to trade with other countries. Even so, many Americans entered the territory illegally to do business with Tejanos. Spanish authorities pursued and arrested Americans who did so. Meanwhile, many Native Americans attacked Spanish settlements because they were resentful that Spain limited their chances to trade with the United States and suspicious of the actions of Spanish missionaries. Spain tried to maintain peace with Native Americans in Tejas because it wanted to remain in control of the region. But the Spanish were unable to bring about stability there.

Mexico, c. 1821

A bronze statue of a Tejano sitting astride his horse is part of the striking Tejano Monument, located on the grounds of the Texas state capitol in Austin. The monument honors the contributions of Tejanos and their roles in shaping Tejas—and eventually Texas.

LAND GRANTS AND SETTLERS

After an 11-year war, Mexico won its independence from Spain. As a result, in 1821, the Tejanos found themselves part of Mexico and no longer under Spanish rule. The new nation of Mexico included the lands that make up present-day Texas, New Mexico, Arizona, California, Nevada, and Utah, as well as parts of Colorado and Wyoming.

Few people lived in Tejas, and the Mexican government feared conflicts between Tejano settlements and Native Americans. Hoping that a larger population of settlers would stabilize the territory, Mexico encouraged American immigration and settlement and, unlike Spain, welcomed trade with Americans.

The Mexican government also gave land grants to American farmers and merchants. One American merchant received permission to form a colony even before Mexican independence. In 1820, Moses Austin persuaded the Spanish governor to allow him to bring a few hundred families to settle in Tejas. He died a year later, before he could carry out his plan, but his son, **Stephen F. Austin**, inherited the land grant. Austin moved 300 American families into southeastern Tejas, establishing the territory's first legal American settlement. A rush of other American immigrants soon followed.

HISTORICAL THINKING

1. **READING CHECK** What influence did Mexican independence have on Americans' presence in Tejas?

2. **IDENTIFY MAIN IDEAS AND DETAILS** What did Mexico hope to accomplish through the land grants?

3. **INTERPRET MAPS** Based on details you notice on the map, describe the borders and territory of Mexico in 1821.

PLAN

Objective

Describe the settlement of the Texas territory in the early 1800s.

Critical Thinking Skills for Lesson 2.1

- Identify Main Ideas and Details
- Monitor Comprehension
- Interpret Maps
- Synthesize
- Make Inferences
- Analyze Visuals

Essential Question for Chapter 12

Why were Americans inspired to move west?
Before Mexico gained independence, Spain controlled lands southwest of the United States. Lesson 2.1 examines how Mexican control over those lands affected American settlement of the West.

Background for the Teacher

The Tejano Monument, unveiled in 2012, consists of a large granite pedestal with 10 life-size bronze statues that represent the development of Tejano settlement. In chronological order, the statues depict a Spanish explorer, a mounted Tejano vaquero, a family of rancheros including a father and mother with an infant, and a young boy and girl tending a goat and a sheep. All details of the statues are authentic representations of the time periods they depict. The vaquero's clothing and equipment, as well as his mustang and the two longhorn cattle he leads, accurately represent 19th-century Tejano ranching. Five bronze plaques along the front of the monument summarize major historical contributions of Tejanos from 16th-century Spanish exploration to 20th-century Mexican-American culture.

INTRODUCE & ENGAGE

Frame Questions

Direct students' attention to the map and ask them to interpret the information in the legend. Instruct students to develop questions that they have about the map and its content. Have volunteers share their questions with the class. List questions on the board and guide students to frame them in a way that can be answered through historical study and research. At the end of the lesson, revisit the questions to see which ones have been answered and which require additional research.

TEACH

Guided Discussion

1. **Synthesize** What factors motivated Spain's policies in Tejas? *(Answers will vary. Possible response: Religion motivated Spain to build missions to convert Native Americans. Economic concerns motivated Spain to build presidios and to forbid trade with Americans in order to keep control of the territory.)*

2. **Make Inferences** Why do you think American families wanted to move to Austin's colony in Tejas? *(Answers will vary. Possible response: Austin's colony provided a legal opportunity to own land and do business in Tejas.)*

Analyze Visuals

Direct students' attention to the photograph of the Tejano statue. **ASK:** What aspects of Tejano culture did the artist capture in the details of the statue? *(Answers will vary. Possible response: The Tejano is shown wearing a finely embroidered vest, suggesting pride and wealth. The inclusion of the horse shows that ranching was important to the culture.)* Ask a volunteer to read the caption aloud. **ASK:** What is the significance of having a Tejano monument on the grounds of the Texas state capitol? *(Answers will vary. Possible response: The monument honors the history and diversity of the state's population.)*

Active Options

On Your Feet: Jigsaw Divide students into four "expert" groups. Assign each group one of the following topics: the locations of Mexican settlements in areas that are now part of the United States, the land-grant system, the cultural traditions of Mexican settlers, or the ranching economy Mexican settlers established. After groups have studied their topic in depth, regroup students so that each new group has at least one member from each expert group. Then ask experts to share the results of their study.

NG Learning Framework: Learn About Stephen F. Austin

ATTITUDE Responsibility

SKILL Collaboration

Allow students to work in pairs or small groups to find out more about Stephen F. Austin. Ask them to compile notes about Austin's background, his role in establishing an American colony in Tejas, and the difficulties he faced in carrying out his father's plan. Ask groups to share their notes. Then discuss reasons why Austin is called the "Father of Texas."

DIFFERENTIATE

Inclusion

Use Supported Reading In small groups, guide students with learning or cognitive disabilities to read the lesson aloud. At the end of the lesson, have them use these frames to self-evaluate what they understood from the text.

- This lesson is about _____.
- One detail that stood out to me is _____.
- The vocabulary word _____ means _____.
- One thing I would like to understand more clearly is _____.

Review portions of the text students do not understand. Make sure all students understand this lesson before moving on to the next lesson.

English Language Learners   ELD

Use Sentence Strips Choose a paragraph from the lesson and make sets of sentence strips with the text. For students at the **Emerging** level, read the paragraph aloud, having students follow along in their books. Instruct students to close their books. Distribute sets of sentence strips and ask students to put the strips in order and read the paragraph aloud. Ask questions to monitor comprehension.

See the Chapter Planner for more strategies for differentiation.

HISTORICAL THINKING

ANSWERS

1. Unlike Spain, Mexico encouraged American trade and settlement in Tejas.

2. The land was sparsely populated, so the Mexican government used land grants to increase the population to in turn reduce incidents of conflict between Tejanos and Native Americans.

3. In 1821, the territory of Mexico extended from the Gulf of Mexico to the Pacific Ocean. The northern boundary extended east from the Pacific coast along 42° N latitude to 105° W longitude, south to the Arkansas River, east to 100° W longitude, south to the Red River, east along the Red River, and then south to the Gulf of Mexico.

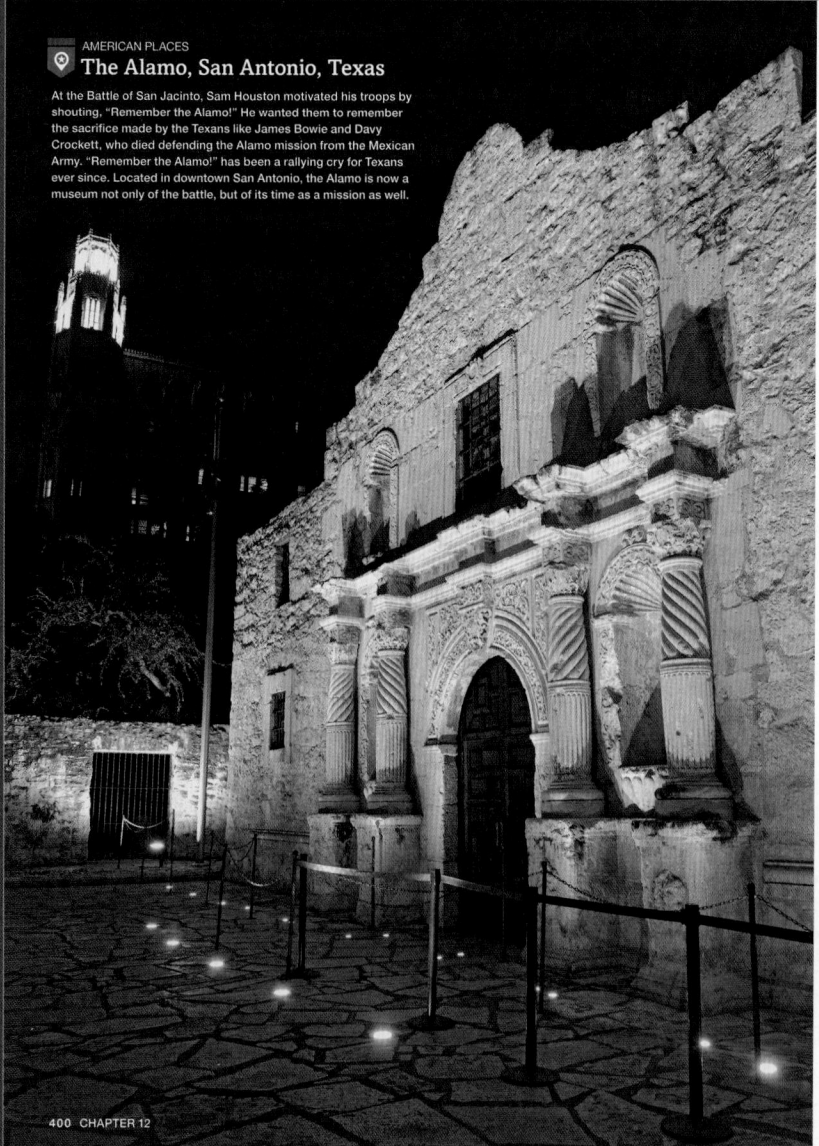

The Alamo, San Antonio, Texas

At the Battle of San Jacinto, Sam Houston motivated his troops by shouting, "Remember the Alamo!" He wanted them to remember the sacrifice made by the Texans like James Bowie and Davy Crockett, who died defending the Alamo mission from the Mexican Army. "Remember the Alamo!" has been a rallying cry for Texans ever since. Located in downtown San Antonio, the Alamo is now a museum not only of the battle, but of its time as a mission as well.

2.2 Settlement and Rebellion

Inviting new friends to your home for a party can sometimes lead to unexpected surprises. Mexico thought that inviting Americans to move to Texas would boost the population. It didn't anticipate what would happen next.

MAIN IDEA Cultural differences and disagreements with the Mexican government led Texans to declare independence from Mexico.

GROWING NUMBER OF SETTLERS

With the opportunity to own a great deal of land in exchange for a small fee, thousands of Americans arrived in Tejas—or Texas, as they called the territory—to take advantage of Mexico's settlement policies. Here, women were able to inherit land grants, and many owned and ran huge, profitable ranches. Women worked alongside men in the day-to-day operations of raising and selling livestock.

Texas quickly became a mix of cultures. Most American settlers were English-speaking Protestants, and the vast majority of Mexicans were Spanish-speaking Catholics. American settlers continued the practice of slavery in Texas, even though Mexico had outlawed slavery in 1829.

Though it had invited American settlement, the Mexican government grew concerned as the population of Texas became more American and less Mexican. By 1830, about 21,000 Americans lived there, including about 1,000 enslaved African Americans. On April 6, 1830, Mexico banned all further American settlement in Texas. Many European countries had already outlawed slavery, and the Mexican government hoped that a stronger European presence would encourage an end to the practice of slavery in the territory.

Texans—Americans and Tejanos alike—who disliked these changes called for more representation within the Mexican government. Revolts in 1832 and 1833 sent the message: Texans wanted Texas statehood within Mexico. General **Antonio López de Santa Anna**, who had recently become the president of Mexico, rejected this demand. Texans rebelled and the Texas War for Independence began.

TEXAS WAR FOR INDEPENDENCE

The war started in October 1835 with the Battle of Gonzales, a victory for Texas. More battles followed, and Santa Anna soon led an army from Mexico City to put down the rebellion. He reached San Antonio by mid-February 1836, where he encountered roughly 180 Texans guarding the **Alamo,** a mission building. For 13 days, 1,800 Mexican soldiers held the Alamo and its defenders under **siege**, which meant no one could leave or enter the building to bring food, supplies, or reinforcements. On March 2, Texans declared themselves a separate nation, the Republic of Texas. On March 6, the Mexican Army breached the Alamo's walls and killed almost everyone inside, including frontiersmen James Bowie, designer of the Bowie knife, and Davy Crockett, a U.S. congressman.

In response, on April 21, **Sam Houston**, the Texan Army's commander, attacked the Mexican Army near the San Jacinto River. He won the **Battle of San Jacinto** (sahn hah-SEEN-toh) and captured Santa Anna. Santa Anna agreed to withdraw and surrender. Texas had achieved independence.

HISTORICAL THINKING

1. **READING CHECK** Why did Texans want independence from Mexico?

2. **ANALYZE CAUSE AND EFFECT** How did the Texans' defeat at the Alamo affect the final outcome of the Texas War for Independence?

3. **DESCRIBE** What opportunities did Tejas offer women who settled and lived there?

PLAN

Objective
Identify causes and effects of the Texas War for Independence.

Critical Thinking Skills for Lesson 2.2
- Identify Main Ideas and Details
- Monitor Comprehension
- Analyze Cause and Effect
- Describe
- Form and Support Opinions
- Compare and Contrast

Essential Question for Chapter 12
Why were Americans inspired to move west?
The Mexican government invited American settlers to Tejas. Lesson 2.2 examines the changes brought about by this policy.

Background for the Teacher
The rebels who occupied the Alamo in early 1836 included Americans Davy Crockett, William Barret Travis, and James Bowie. Most of the defenders were Americans or European immigrants and Tejanos who had joined the rebellion. Travis assumed command after Bowie became ill. In a letter addressed to the "people of Texas and all Americans in the world," Travis requested help and pledged to "never surrender or retreat." Help did not arrive. Nearly every Alamo defender was killed during a 90-minute battle on March 6. The few who survived were executed at General Antonio López de Santa Anna's order, but several women and children were spared. In the Battle of San Jacinto a few weeks later, a force of 900 Texans and the Tejano cavalry defeated Santa Anna in an 18-minute battle that changed Texas history.

INTRODUCE & ENGAGE

Brainstorm a Rallying Cry

Ask students to brainstorm a list of rallying cries. As they shout out examples, write the words or phrases on the board. **ASK:** What is the purpose of a rallying cry? *(Answers will vary. Possible response: It encourages people to unite in support of a group or a cause.)* Tell students that in this lesson they will learn why "Remember the Alamo!" became a rallying cry for Texans.

TEACH

Guided Discussion

1. **Form and Support Opinions** Do you think American and Tejano settlers in Texas were more united by their concerns about actions of the Mexican government or more separated by their different cultural traditions and attitudes toward slavery? *(Answers will vary. Students' opinions may include that differences in religion and language separated American and Tejano settlers and that some Americans supported slavery, while Tejanos opposed it, or that Americans and Tejanos were united in the demand for independence from Mexico.)*

2. **Compare and Contrast** What were the advantages and disadvantages for both sides in the Battle of the Alamo? *(The Mexican Army was much larger than the Texan forces, but it took a 13-day siege to defeat the defenders. The Texans were determined to win independence, but they had no reinforcements and the siege caused them to run low on food and supplies.)*

American Places

The Alamo is a National Historic Landmark visited by more than 2 million people each year. Although much of the original compound is gone, the mission church, part of the barracks, and some of the cannons remain. Visitors can view what the Alamo looked like in 1836 from various vantage points. Many educational events throughout the year, including monthly living-history interpretations and annual ceremonies observing the battle anniversary, enhance the experience of visiting the Alamo.

Active Options

On Your Feet: Cause-and-Effect Chain Conduct this exercise as a whole-class activity or divide the class into small teams. On the board or on a large sheet of paper, create a Cause-and-Effect Chain like the one shown here. In the first box, write: Mexico offers land grants in Tejas. At each step, call on a student from the class or ask a team to send a member to write one major effect of the cause preceding it. Continue to have students write and explain causes and effects until they exhaust information from the lesson.

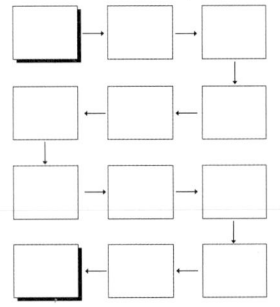

NG Learning Framework: Research the Alamo's Heroes

ATTITUDE Curiosity

KNOWLEDGE Our Human Story

Have students explore the life of one of the defenders of the Alamo. Students may choose well-known leaders, such as William Barret Travis, Susannah Dickinson, James Bowie, Davy Crockett, or Gregorio Esparza, or a less famous defender who died in the battle. Ask students to conduct research and then write a paragraph about the person they chose. Then ask students to share their paragraphs with the class. After the presentations, use these questions to prompt a class discussion: What did these individuals have in common? Why were they willing to give their lives for Texas independence?

DIFFERENTIATE

Striving Readers

Pose and Answer Questions Allow students to read the lesson in pairs. Instruct them to pause after each paragraph and ask each other a *who, what, when, where,* or *why* question to check their comprehension. Suggest students use a 5Ws Chart to help them organize their questions and answers.

Gifted & Talented

Give On-the-Scene News Reports Instruct students to research the Battle of the Alamo. Then have them assume the role of news reporters and write on-the-scene reports of the events from February 23 to March 6, 1836. Remind students that their role is to describe the events without bias. Then ask volunteers to perform their news reports for the class.

See the Chapter Planner for more strategies for differentiation.

HISTORICAL THINKING

ANSWERS

1. Texans felt that they were not being represented in the Mexican government. They were angered by laws that outlawed slavery and banned further American settlement of Texas.

2. Sam Houston's rallying cry "Remember the Alamo!" helped motivate the rebels to fight at San Jacinto, reminding them of those who lost their lives at the Alamo. They went on to capture Santa Anna, ultimately winning the revolution.

3. Mexico's policies in Tejas allowed women to inherit land grants. This made it possible for women to own and run profitable ranches and raise livestock for sale.

2.3 Independence and Annexation

A "political football" is an issue that political opponents fight over. In 1836, the issue of annexing Texas became a political football in the United States, and it would be kicked back and forth for nearly a decade.

MAIN IDEA The annexation of the Republic of Texas as the 28th state caused tension between northern and southern states.

THE LONE STAR REPUBLIC

After the Texas War for Independence, Texas became an independent nation, the Republic of Texas. Texans elected Sam Houston as their first president. The flag of Texas, with a single star, earned the nation the nickname of **Lone Star Republic**. As proud as they were of their victory, Texans knew they were vulnerable to further attacks from Mexico. They also lacked an established economy. Most Texans favored annexation by the United States.

The United States initially rejected this plan, however. In 1836 and 1837, President Andrew Jackson and his successor Martin Van Buren turned down Texas lawmakers' proposals. For

one thing, they argued, annexing Texas would hurt American relations with Mexico and perhaps even lead to war. They also knew the American people were divided on the question, primarily because of the issue of slavery.

Before independence, Texas clashed with Mexico over slavery, which was prohibited by Mexican law. The ongoing use of enslaved labor in the Republic of Texas also became a concern for northern states in the United States. Admitting Texas as a state would upset the balance between states that had outlawed slavery and states where slavery was still practiced. Presidents Jackson and Van Buren argued that annexation was not in the best interest of the country.

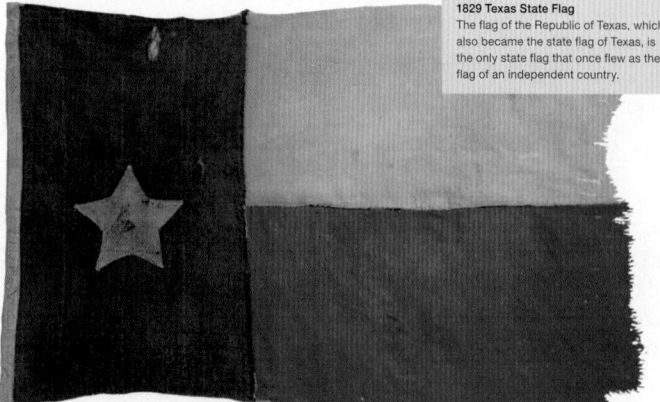

1829 Texas State Flag
The flag of the Republic of Texas, which also became the state flag of Texas, is the only state flag that once flew as the flag of an independent country.

A GLOBAL PERSPECTIVE In recent decades, some Texans have supported a movement for Texas to leave the United States and become an independent republic again. Proponents of this effort believe that the state gives too much power and money to the federal government. Some have compared these views with those advocated by "Brexit," the British movement that voted to leave the European Union (EU) in June 2016. The Texan movement earned a similar nickname, "Texit," a combination of the words *Texas* and *exit*. In this photo, campaigners for and against Brexit pass out flyers in London. What historical precedent might supporters of Texit cite as evidence that Texas should leave the United States?

ANNEXATION OF TEXAS

Texas remained independent for almost 10 years. Then, in 1844, annexation gained a supporter in the White House—**James K. Polk**. Polk had been the Speaker of the House and the governor of Tennessee, but he was not a superstar politician. When the Democrats nominated him for president in 1844, he was an unknown candidate who had little chance of winning. But despite running as an unknown against Henry Clay, the prominent Whig candidate, Polk won the presidency, barely, with 49.5 percent of the popular vote and an electoral college **margin**, or amount by which something is won or lost, of 170–105.

As president, Polk managed to turn his political ambitions into policy. He supported the ideas of manifest destiny and favored the annexation of

Texas. He also believed that the United States should take complete control of the Oregon Territory, up to the latitude of 54° 40'. One of Polk's campaign slogans was "Fifty-four forty or fight!" Polk brought an enthusiasm to his presidency for expanding the country. Under his leadership, Texas became the 28th state.

HISTORICAL THINKING

1. **READING CHECK** What were the arguments against the annexation of Texas as a state?

2. **IDENTIFY MAIN IDEAS AND DETAILS** How was Polk's argument for annexation informed by the concept of manifest destiny?

3. **EVALUATE** What made James K. Polk an attractive but unlikely candidate for president?

Objective

Examine conflicting viewpoints as Texas progressed toward statehood.

Critical Thinking Skills for Lesson 2.3

- Identify Main Ideas and Details
- Monitor Comprehension
- Evaluate
- Draw Conclusions
- Make Inferences

Essential Question for Chapter 12

Why were Americans inspired to move west?
Texas became an independent republic, but many Texans favored annexation by the United States. Lesson 2.3 discusses arguments for and against statehood for Texas.

Background for the Teacher

Mexico's policies had restricted slavery in Texas but had not ended it. In 1836, there were about 5,000 slaves in Texas, approximately 13 percent of the population. Most of these slaves had immigrated to Texas with their owners from slave states in the United States. The Constitution of the Republic of Texas protected slaveholders and allowed slaves to be imported to Texas from the United States but not from Africa. By 1850, the number of enslaved people had increased to more than 58,000, which was then 27 percent of the population. Most slaves worked on cotton plantations in the eastern part of Texas, but the economic potential of cotton and the fertile land in other parts of the state ensured the growth of slavery.

INTRODUCE & ENGAGE

Consider Independence

Ask students to think about the challenges they might face when they become independent from their parents. Record responses on the board. *(Answers will vary. Possible responses: finding a place to live, getting a job, learning how to manage money)* Tell students that in this lesson they will learn about the challenges the Republic of Texas faced once it became independent of its former "parent" nation, Mexico.

TEACH

Guided Discussion

1. **Draw Conclusions** What benefits did Texans hope to gain from annexation by the United States? *(Answers will vary. Possible response: Being part of the United States would provide opportunities for economic development. The United States had an army that could defend Texas against Mexican attacks.)*

2. **Make Inferences** Which groups of voters likely supported James K. Polk in the 1844 election? *(Texans, because Polk supported annexation; pro-slavery southerners, because Polk did not oppose adding a slave state to the Union; proponents of manifest destiny, because Polk favored westward expansion of the country)*

A Global Perspective

Direct students' attention to the photograph and caption. **ASK:** What can you conclude about the Brexit campaign based on the photo? *(Answers will vary. Possible response: Opinions were divided. The campaign involved people of different age groups. Both sides promoted their ideas peacefully.)* **ASK:** What connection do you see between Brexit and Texit? *(Answers will vary. Possible responses: Both movements involve a small but powerful political unit withdrawing from a larger political unit in order to gain more control over its own affairs. Both movements are controversial.)*

Active Options

On Your Feet: Think, Pair, Share Invite students to use the Think, Pair, Share strategy to develop arguments for and against the U.S. annexation of Texas. Ask pairs to decide what they believe was in the best interest of both Texas and the United States. Then have pairs share their arguments with the class.

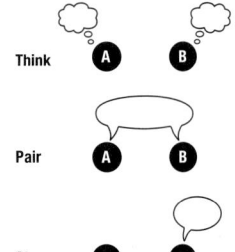

Think   A   B

Pair   A   B

Share   A   B

NG Learning Framework: Create a Campaign Poster

SKILL Communication

KNOWLEDGE Our Human Story

Invite students to imagine they are in charge of the election campaign for James K. Polk. Direct them to work in groups to collaborate on a poster that might persuade citizens to vote for Polk. Remind students to conduct research and combine information from other sources with information from the text to highlight Polk's qualifications and his plans for the nation. Encourage groups to display their posters for the whole class.

DIFFERENTIATE

English Language Learners   ELD

Use Sentence Stems Before reading, provide students at the **Expanding** level with the following sentence stems. Have them complete the stems with information they encounter as they read.

- Texas became an independent country called the _____. *(Republic of Texas)*
- Most people in the Republic of Texas wanted to join _____. *(the United States)*
- At first, the United States _____ the plan to annex Texas because of concerns about slavery and relations with Mexico. *(rejected)*
- James K. Polk believed in _____, so he wanted to annex new lands. *(manifest destiny)*

Pre-AP

Analyze Effects Remind students that in Lesson 2.2 they learned that Tejanos played an important role in winning the Texas War for Independence. Have students conduct research to determine what effects Texan independence had on Tejanos. Instruct students to research immediate, short-term, and long-term effects. Hold a panel discussion with the whole class to have students describe their findings.

See the Chapter Planner for more strategies for differentiation.

HISTORICAL THINKING

ANSWERS

1. Many American leaders feared that annexation would lead to war with Mexico and that annexing Texas would upset the balance between slave states and free states.

2. Polk was a proponent of manifest destiny and enthusiastically supported U.S. territorial expansion. Annexation of Texas would expand the territory of the country.

3. Possible response: Polk had political experience as governor of Tennessee and Speaker of the House, but he was a relatively unknown candidate running against Henry Clay, a popular politician.

A GLOBAL PERSPECTIVE Possible response: When Texas seceded from Mexico in 1836, it established a precedent of becoming independent in response to deep disagreements with government policies.

Samuel "Sam" Houston
1793–1863

Antonio López de Santa Anna
1794–1876

"Santa Anna, living, can be of incalculable [great] benefit to Texas."—Sam Houston

CRITICAL VIEWING During the Battle of San Jacinto, Houston was shot in the leg but continued to fight. In this painting by William Huddle, called *Surrender of Santa Anna*, Houston lies on a mat with his leg bandaged, while Santa Anna stands before him. Why do you think Houston's men surround Santa Anna?

Houston became known as the "George Washington of Texas." The city of Houston was named after him.

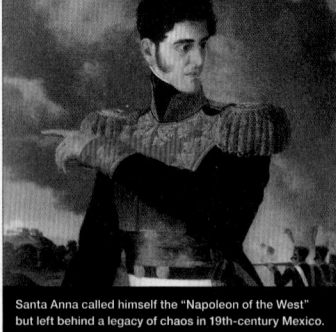

Santa Anna called himself the "Napoleon of the West" but left behind a legacy of chaos in 19th-century Mexico.

Not everyone agreed with Sam Houston about the value of Antonio López de Santa Anna's life. When the Texans won the Battle of San Jacinto, many of Houston's soldiers called for the Mexican leader's execution. After all, Santa Anna hadn't shown any mercy to the Texans at the Alamo. But Houston wanted independence for Texas—not revenge.

CONTRASTING PERSONALITIES

Houston and Santa Anna fought on opposite sides during the Texas War for Independence, but they had a number of things in common. Both pursued careers in the military and in politics. And, in the 1800s, both men were legends and dominant figures in the lands they loved—Houston in Texas and Santa Anna in Mexico.

But that's where the resemblance ended. Houston consistently demonstrated his loyalty and duty to the United States. He fought heroically in the War of 1812 under Andrew Jackson, whom Houston considered his mentor. It was Jackson

who encouraged Houston to enter politics. While living in Tennessee, Houston was first elected to Congress and later became governor of the state.

Santa Anna, on the other hand, often placed self-interest above duty, switching sides based on what was in it for him. He entered the Spanish army at 16 and fought with Spain when the war for Mexican independence broke out. (Mexico was a Spanish colony at that time.) But in 1821, Santa Anna shifted his loyalty and led the Mexican rebels to independence. As a reward, he was appointed governor of the Mexican state of Veracruz.

In 1833, the Mexican people elected Santa Anna president, but he soon lost interest in the office and left the real governing to his vice president. However, when the vice president began reforming the church, state, and army, Santa Anna was furious because the reforms threatened his interests. In response, he used military force to remove his vice president.

CLASHING ARMIES

Resuming authority, Santa Anna introduced a less democratic form of government in Mexico and in Texas. The Texans became dissatisfied with their lack of freedom and, in 1835, began a revolution. They called on Houston, who had relocated to Texas, to lead the rebel force.

From the outset, the Texans were outnumbered. They suffered terrible defeats at the Alamo and in the Texas town of Goliad, where about 350 rebels were taken prisoner and executed. The Texans finally seized their chance in 1836 when Santa Anna and a small number of his soldiers arrived at San Jacinto. Houston organized a surprise attack and quickly overpowered the Mexican Army.

For a time after his embarrassing defeat, Santa Anna fell from favor in Mexico. He returned to power eventually, but as you'll see, American troops would once again bring about his downfall.

As for Houston, he became the first president of the Republic of Texas and served as senator after Texas achieved statehood. He'd just been elected its governor when a number of southern states voted to separate from the United States. When Houston refused to allow Texas to join the southern states, he was removed from office.

HISTORICAL THINKING

1. **READING CHECK** In which two areas did both Houston and Santa Anna pursue careers?

2. **COMPARE AND CONTRAST** How did Houston's treatment of the enemy in the Texas War for Independence differ from the way in which Santa Anna treated his prisoners?

3. **EVALUATE** In what way did Santa Anna's character and judgment affect Texas and Mexico?

PLAN

Objective

Learn about the similarities and differences between opposing leaders in the Texas War for Independence.

Critical Thinking Skills for Lesson 2.4

- Identify Main Ideas and Details
- Monitor Comprehension
- Compare and Contrast
- Evaluate
- Synthesize
- Make Inferences

Essential Question for Chapter 12

Why were Americans inspired to move west?
Texas independence provided new opportunities for settlers in the West. Lesson 2.4 discusses two prominent leaders who played very different roles in the fight for Texas independence.

Background for the Teacher

As a teen, Sam Houston spent time living with Cherokee people in Tennessee, which gave him an understanding of the Native Americans' language and culture. He distinguished himself in Tennessee politics, though he resigned as governor before the end of his first term. Eventually, he made his way to Texas, where he became one of its greatest heroes.

Antonio López de Santa Anna served as president of Mexico for 11 nonconsecutive terms during the particularly tumultuous period from 1833 to 1855, when the presidency changed hands 36 times. He also managed to turn a military wound into a political advantage. He attained hero status when part of his leg was amputated as a result of battle, and he had the limb buried with full military honors.

History Notebook

Encourage students to complete the American Voices page for Chapter 12 in their History Notebooks as they read.

INTRODUCE & ENGAGE

Preview Using Visuals

Direct students' attention to the painting *Surrender of Santa Anna*. **ASK:** What can people infer about history from paintings of historical events? *(Possible response: Paintings show what key places and people looked like or may have looked like. They can help viewers imagine what it was like to live through the events.)* **ASK:** Why do you think artists often depict battlefield scenes? *(Possible response: Wars affect people's lives. The outcome of a war may have long-term effects on a country.)* Tell students that they will learn more about the leaders of the opposing sides in the battle that is the subject of the painting.

TEACH

Guided Discussion

1. **Synthesize** How does the term *dominant figure* apply to both Houston and Santa Anna? *(Possible response: Each man was well known for his military service and fought in his country's wars. Each also served in his country's government and was a well-known political leader.)*

2. **Make Inferences** Why was the outcome of the Battle of San Jacinto considered "an embarrassing defeat" for Santa Anna? *(Possible response: Santa Anna had defeated the Texans in previous battles. His troops greatly outnumbered the Texans. He lost the Battle of San Jacinto because he was unprepared for a surprise attack.)*

American Voices

Call on a volunteer to read the captions under the paintings of Houston and Santa Anna. Remind students that George Washington led the Continental Army to victory in the American Revolution, and then he became the first president of the new nation. Tell them that Napoleon was a French military leader who conquered much of Europe, and then he crowned himself emperor. Divide the class into two groups and have one group research character traits and achievements of Washington and the other group do the same with Napoleon. Then ask each group to explain the comparison between Houston and Washington or between Santa Anna and Napoleon.

Active Options

On Your Feet: Analyze Character Traits Divide the class into two groups and assign Houston to one group and Santa Anna to the other. Have groups work in separate areas of the classroom to complete a graphic organizer like the one shown. Instruct members of each group to use information from the text as well as from other sources to list actions of their subject and identify character traits demonstrated by each action. Then have members of each group take turns portraying the actions they have listed and allow members of the opposite group to identify the character traits the actions demonstrate. Use the activity as the basis for a class discussion in which students compare and contrast the two men.

Person	Actions	Character

NG Learning Framework: Conduct an Interview

ATTITUDE Empowerment

KNOWLEDGE Our Human Story

Have students imagine they are going to interview Houston and Santa Anna. Allow them to work in small groups to write questions that will demonstrate how the interviewees are alike or different. Encourage each group to choose two members to play the roles of Houston and Santa Anna and answer the questions as those historical figures would. The remaining members will be reporters who ask the questions. Each group should present its interview for the class.

DIFFERENTIATE

Inclusion

Explore Visuals Provide questions to help students describe *Surrender of Santa Anna*. **ASK:** Why is one man lying down? Which person is probably a doctor, and how can you tell? What details show that many of the people around the man are soldiers? How can you tell that not everyone fought on the same side in the battle? Encourage students to point to details that they don't understand and to elicit help from other students to frame questions about the details.

English Language Learners

Ask Yes/No Questions After reading, ask students at the **Emerging** level the questions below and have students say or write *yes* or *no* in response. Then allow students to work with a partner who is a fluent English speaker to correct any sentence with *no* as an answer. *(1 and 4)*

1. Houston and Santa Anna fought on the same side during the Texas War for Independence.

2. Houston fought in the War of 1812.

3. Santa Anna fought with Spain in the war for Mexican independence.

4. Houston became president of the United States.

See the Chapter Planner for more strategies for differentiation.

HISTORICAL THINKING

ANSWERS

1. Houston and Santa Anna both served in the military and in political offices.

2. Santa Anna executed the prisoners at the Alamo and at Goliad. Houston spared Santa Anna's life after defeating him.

3. Possible responses: Santa Anna was a chameleon who switched careers and policies frequently based on his own self-interest. He was a ruthless military leader who executed survivors after battles.

CRITICAL VIEWING Possible responses: Houston was injured, so his men were protecting him. Santa Anna was a dangerous man and might try to escape. Many of Houston's soldiers wanted to execute Santa Anna.

2.5 San Jacinto Museum of History La Porte, Texas

A museum with a unique location, the San Jacinto is housed in the base of the San Jacinto Monument. It was established as a steward of history to honor those who fought in the Texas War for Independence from Mexico and showcase the history of Texas and the Spanish Southwest. Visitors can view art and artifacts from the Spanish conquest, Spanish colonial life, the Mexican Revolution, the colonization of Mexican Texas, early Texas statehood, and the Civil War. What can you infer about the relationship between Mexico and Texas by examining the artifacts below?

Mexican Badge
This heavy brass badge, likely worn by a soldier in the Mexican Army, features the Mexican military insignia, an eagle perched on a cactus plant. The streamer beneath the eagle's talons reads: "LIBERTAD MEXICANA" (Mexican freedom).

Soldiers sharpened the curve on the top of the blade, called a clip point, to inflict a more serious wound as the knife was pulled out.

Texas Army Bowie Knife
Alamo hero and knife-fighter Jim Bowie knew what he wanted in a knife. He worked with blacksmiths to create knives like this one that had curved blades and cross-guards to protect hands. It was a handy weapon, useful for hunting, digging, or cutting down trees, as well as in hand-to-hand combat.

Santa Anna's Knee Buckle
In the late 1700s, many men wore knee buckles to secure their short pants, or breeches, at the knee. This buckle has 22 square diamonds, a handsome design, and an impressive history. Santa Anna gave this buckle to Sam Houston after Houston defeated him in the Battle of San Jacinto. Historians agree Santa Anna was a strong leader with a dynamic personality, but he also lacked principles and loved military glory, which often led Mexico down the wrong path.

Notice this pistol's unusual octagon-shaped barrel.

Texas Army Percussion Pistol
This wood and brass pistol belonged to Euclid M. Cox, who used it during the 1838 Battle Creek Massacre. A group of 25 Texan surveyors, who were studying the land for its settlement potential, encountered 300 members of the Kickapoo tribe. After failing to heed a warning to leave, the Texans were ambushed. Only seven survived.

Do you think this sword belt would have been a practical accessory? Why or why not?

Texas Army Military Sword Belt
A sword belt like this one, made of gold braid and maroon leather, was an important part of a soldier's uniform. This one belonged to Thomas Jefferson Chambers of the Texas Army. The belt's decorative round buckle is trimmed with leaves and berries and has a silver, five-pointed star set in the center. The two chains attached to the belt end in hooks that Chambers would have fastened to his sword's scabbard, or sheath.

Manifest Destiny 407

PLAN

Objective
Identify artifacts relating to those who fought in the Texas War for Independence.

Critical Thinking Skills for Lesson 2.5
• Make Connections
• Analyze Visuals
• Draw Conclusions
• Make Inferences

Essential Question for Chapter 12
Why were Americans inspired to move west?
The Texan victory at San Jacinto created an independent Texas. Lesson 2.5 examines some of the weapons used in the battle that helped open Texas to settlement and paved the way for settlement of other western territories.

Background for the Teacher
The San Jacinto Monument is a 570-foot stone column. Built of Texas Cordova shellstone, it includes the imprints of 100-million-year-old fossils. Crowned with a 34-foot rendition of a nine-pointed star symbolizing the Republic of Texas, the monument towers over a reflecting pool. An observation floor high in the monument allows visitors to view the battleground site from a height of nearly 500 feet. The San Jacinto Museum of History in the monument's base chronicles more than 400 years of Texas history. The monument and museum are part of the San Jacinto Battleground State Historic Site, where an annual reenactment of the Battle of San Jacinto dramatizes the birth of the Republic of Texas.

History Notebook
Encourage students to complete the Curating History page for Chapter 12 in their History Notebooks as they read.

INTRODUCE & ENGAGE

Evaluate Sources

Ask students to brainstorm different sources of information they might use to learn about 19th-century Texas history. Students might suggest textbooks, historical documents, maps, paintings or other artwork, letters, diaries, historical fiction, or other sources of information. Ask students to choose which source they think is the most credible and to give a reason to support their choice. Tell students that in this lesson they will study artifacts from the Texas War for Independence. At the end of the lesson, discuss whether students think the artifacts are a credible source of information.

TEACH

Guided Discussion

1. **Draw Conclusions** Why do you think James Bowie had to work with blacksmiths to create a special knife? *(Answers will vary. Possible response: The knife design that he wanted was not available. A custom design for this knife meant it could be used for hunting or clearing land as well as for combat.)*

2. **Make Inferences** What do the knee buckle artifact and its history reveal about Antonio López de Santa Anna? *(Answers will vary. Possible response: The diamond buckle indicates that Santa Anna was wealthy. The fact that Santa Anna gave the buckle to Sam Houston shows that he may have respected his opponent or perhaps that he was grateful that Houston spared his life.)*

Curating History

The San Jacinto Museum of History website provides a searchable database of artifacts. Access the website and demonstrate how to find one of the artifacts featured in the lesson. Then encourage students to choose another artifact from the collection and discuss what they can learn from it. Ask groups of students to explore the museum's website to determine what other sources of information it offers. As a class, discuss why the available sources of information are credible and what students could learn from them.

Active Options

On Your Feet: Sort the Artifacts Have students work in teams of four to examine the museum's online collection and complete two Concept Clusters like those shown below. In one cluster, students should identify various weapons that the soldiers on both sides of the war used. In the other, students should identify a different class or genre of artifacts to be determined by the team. When teams are finished, have them share their Concept Clusters with the class.

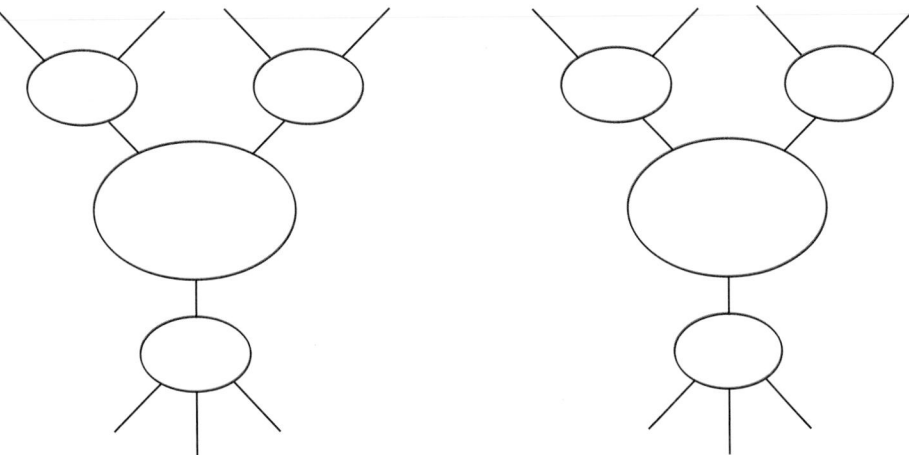

DIFFERENTIATE

Striving Readers

Summarize Have students work in pairs to read the caption that accompanies each artifact in Lesson 2.5. Instruct pairs to make a list of words they do not understand. Then discuss and define the words with students. Finally, ask the pairs to go back and summarize each caption in their own words. Call on volunteers to share their captions with the group.

Inclusion

Pose and Answer Questions Pair students who have visual disabilities with a partner who does not. Have the student without disabilities read the captions and describe the artifacts in the lesson. Encourage students to ask any necessary clarification questions. Then have each partner pose one simple recall question to the other for each artifact and caption.

See the Chapter Planner for more strategies for differentiation.

CURATING HISTORY

Answers will vary. Possible response: The artifacts show that soldiers on both sides were proud defenders of their causes. The Bowie knife and the sword belt bear the lone star symbol of Texas. The Mexican badge features the symbol and motto of the Mexican Army. The weapons show the bravery of soldiers on both sides who fought hand to hand in battle. The artifacts indicate similarities between the people of Mexico and Texas even though they fought against each other.

TEXAS ARMY MILITARY SWORD BELT

Answers will vary. Possible response: This sword belt looks more decorative than useful. However, it was a useful part of the soldier's uniform because it attached to the sword's scabbard.

Tensions with Mexico

When you heat water in a teakettle, pressure builds until the water reaches the boiling point. In the 1840s, tensions between the United States and Mexico reached their boiling point: war.

MAIN IDEA The annexation of Texas upset the balance of slave and free states and led to the Mexican-American War.

POLK'S MISSION

James K. Polk was a firm believer in the concept of manifest destiny. When he became president in 1844, he focused on territorial expansion, including the annexation of Texas and the acquisition of California and Oregon. Southerners favored Polk because of his plans to annex Texas. Since slavery had long been practiced there, Texas would join the Union as a slave state. This infuriated northerners because it meant that slave states would outnumber free states. The threat of an unequal number of slave and free states had already reared its head in 1820, with Missouri's request to become a state. The political firestorm that ensued led to a solution in the Missouri Compromise. That solution proved to be temporary, as Congress voted to annex Texas as a new slave state in 1845.

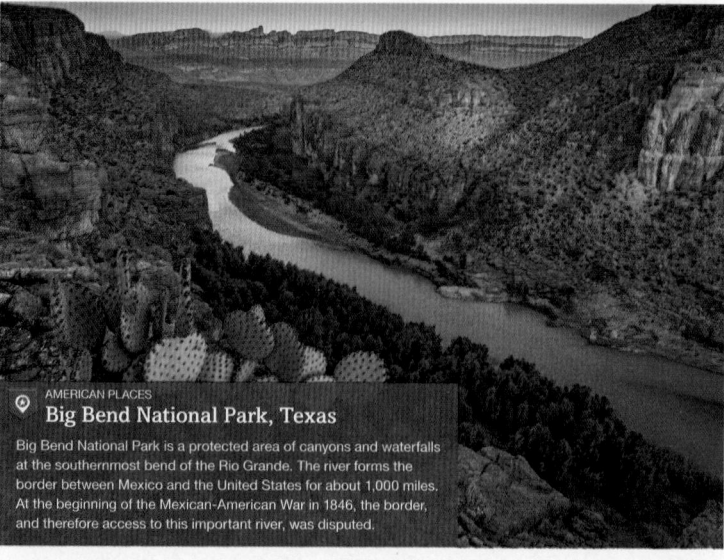

AMERICAN PLACES
Big Bend National Park, Texas

Big Bend National Park is a protected area of canyons and waterfalls at the southernmost bend of the Rio Grande. The river forms the border between Mexico and the United States for about 1,000 miles. At the beginning of the Mexican-American War in 1846, the border, and therefore access to this important river, was disputed.

CROSSING THE NUECES RIVER

Relations between the United States and Mexico had been tense since the creation of the Republic of Texas. Mexican president Antonio López de Santa Anna had signed the Treaties of Velasco, giving Texas its independence, but the Mexican government never formally acknowledged the treaties as legal. Santa Anna had signed the treaties while he was a prisoner of the Texan Army, they argued, and therefore Texas was still a part of Mexico. Given this history, it's not surprising that Texas's annexation further worsened relations between the United States and Mexico.

At the time, Texas extended only as far south as the Nueces River. President Polk insisted that Texas's southern border should be the Rio Grande, much farther south than the Nueces. In July 1845, Polk sent American troops, led by General **Zachary Taylor**, to secure the area between the Rio Grande and the Nueces River. Polk also sent John Slidell, a **diplomat**, or person sent to represent a country, to Mexico City with an offer. Texas would extend to the Rio Grande, and the United States would buy California for $25 million. The Mexican government refused to negotiate.

Hearing about the snub, Polk told Taylor to advance on the Rio Grande. A skirmish between American and Mexican troops near the river gave Polk the excuse he needed to call for war. In an address to Congress, he declared that Mexico "has invaded our territory and shed American blood upon American soil." Even the Whigs, who had wanted to avoid conflict with Mexico, gave in. The **Mexican-American War** started on May 13, 1846.

Although Congress voted overwhelmingly in favor of the war, many Americans opposed Polk's tactics. Notable New Englanders, including John Quincy Adams and James Russell Lowell, claimed the war was a scheme to expand slavery. Henry David Thoreau even landed in jail when he refused to pay taxes to support the war. Abraham Lincoln, then a young congressman from Illinois, agreed with the New Englanders. He demanded an answer from Polk about "the particular spot of soil on which the blood of our citizens was so shed." Despite the protests, the United States remained at war with Mexico for more than a year.

MAJOR GENERAL ZACHARY TAYLOR

🏛 **Dallas Historical Society**
Dallas, Texas

Zachary Taylor is memorialized as the king of diamonds on this 19th-century playing card. He is wearing a bicorn hat and elaborate epaulettes, or shoulder ornaments—both of which were typical of American and European military officers beginning in the 1790s.

HISTORICAL THINKING

1. **READING CHECK** What did President Polk want from Mexico, and how did the president of Mexico respond?

2. **IDENTIFY MAIN IDEAS AND DETAILS** What were the causes of the Mexican-American War?

3. **EVALUATE** How did President Polk use emotion to persuade Congress to vote for war with Mexico?

PLAN

Objective

Explain how Texas statehood led to war between the United States and Mexico.

Critical Thinking Skills for Lesson 3.1

- Identify Main Ideas and Details
- Monitor Comprehension
- Evaluate
- Draw Conclusions
- Synthesize

Essential Question for Chapter 12

Why were Americans inspired to move west?
To fulfill the idea of manifest destiny, Americans needed the territories Mexico controlled in the West. Lesson 3.1 explains how the annexation of Texas affected relations between the United States and Mexico.

Background for the Teacher

The events leading up to the Mexican-American War involved mistakes on both sides. Diplomatic relations between Mexico and the United States had ended when the United States annexed Texas. President Polk wanted to force Mexico into negotiating with the United States, but his strong stand indicated a lack of respect for the Mexican government. President José Herrera refused to meet with John Slidell for fear of being overthrown by opponents in Mexico. Polk was already preparing a war message to Congress when he learned of the hostilities along the Texas boundary. This may have been an excuse rather than a cause for war, and Polk used it to his advantage. He was willing to risk war because he did not expect the Mexicans to put up much of a fight. In a twist of fate, Antonio López de Santa Anna convinced Polk to help him return from his exile in Cuba to Mexico, where he would negotiate peace. When Santa Anna reached Mexico, however, he became commander of the Mexican forces.

INTRODUCE & ENGAGE

Preview Using Text Features

Direct students' attention to the playing card and read the information below it. Ask students to use details from the card (such as Zachary Taylor's military attire), information from the lesson title and introduction, and their prior knowledge of James K. Polk, Texas, and Mexico to predict what they will learn in this lesson.

TEACH

Guided Discussion

1. **Draw Conclusions** How did President Polk's belief in manifest destiny cause a division among people in the United States? *(Possible response: Polk's plan to expand U.S. territory included annexing Texas, which would be a slave state. Southerners supported the plan, but northerners strongly opposed it.)*

2. **Synthesize** What was the basis of opposition to Polk's tactics? *(Answers will vary. Possible response: Some people questioned Polk's motives for going to war. Others questioned whether Mexico had actually invaded American territory.)*

American Places

Big Bend National Park is in a remote area 300 miles southeast of El Paso, Texas, the nearest major city. The park's dominant feature is the Rio Grande. The river rises as a snow-fed stream in the San Juan Mountains of Colorado before cutting through New Mexico and winding its way between Texas and the Mexican states of Chihuahua, Coahuila, Nuevo León, and Tamaulipas to the Gulf of Mexico. For thousands of years, the Rio Grande has influenced the lives of people in the region. Use a map to trace the river from its source to its mouth. Have students identify the land between the Rio Grande and the Nueces River that was at the root of the boundary dispute between the United States and Mexico. Ask students to research the Rio Grande and find one important fact to share with the class.

Active Options

On Your Feet: Create a Cause-and-Effect Map On the board, create a large Cause-and-Effect Map like the one shown. In each Original Cause box, write a cause from the lesson or from the list below:

- Santa Anna signs treaties while prisoner of the Texan Army.
- John Slidell presents an offer to Mexico.
- Mexican and American troops skirmish near the Rio Grande.

Divide the class into two teams. Have Team One members discuss an Original Cause and send a member to the board to complete its First Effect box. Have Team Two add a second effect. Continue this process, alternating teams. Then allow each team to challenge and correct the answers supplied by the other team. Continue challenges and corrections until both teams agree that the entire map is correct.

NG Learning Framework: Take a Stand

ATTITUDE Curiosity

KNOWLEDGE Our Human Story

Instruct students to review the reasons for and against the Mexican-American War. Then ask them to work with a partner to choose one reason and create a pro-war or antiwar poster that promotes their chosen position. Display the completed posters around the classroom and have students discuss which posters are most effective and why.

DIFFERENTIATE

English Language Learners ELD

Give a Thumbs Up or Thumbs Down Prepare a set of true-false statements about the lesson, such as "Texas joined the Union as a free state." Read the lesson aloud as students follow along in their books. Then have them close the books and listen as you read the true-false statements. Tell students to give a thumbs up if a statement is true and a thumbs down if a statement is false. Pair students at the **Emerging** level with students at the **Expanding** or **Bridging** level. Repeat the false statements and ask partners to work together to correct them.

Pre-AP

Analyze a Speech Assign students to work in pairs to analyze Polk's message to Congress asking for a declaration of war on Mexico. Tell them to choose an excerpt that shows how Polk justified going to war. Then have students hold a panel discussion in which they provide their analyses to the class.

See the Chapter Planner for more strategies for differentiation.

HISTORICAL THINKING

ANSWERS

1. President Polk wanted the border of Texas to extend to the Rio Grande, so he wanted to extend Texas and buy California from Mexico. The Mexican president refused to negotiate with the diplomat that Polk sent.

2. Disagreement over borders led to the Mexican-American War. When the United States annexed Texas, President Polk wanted the boundary set farther south, at the Rio Grande. A skirmish between Mexican troops and the U.S. troops sent to secure the area was the immediate cause for the United States to declare war.

3. Even though Polk had ordered American troops into the area, he said that Mexican soldiers had shed "American blood upon American soil," appealing to people's emotions and sense of outrage.

3.2 The United States at War

California's state flag features an unusual combination of items: a grizzly bear, a lone red star, and the words "California Republic." The history of this unique flag stems from an event that took place in the 1840s.

MAIN IDEA The United States took control of New Mexico and California after forcing Mexico to surrender at the end of the Mexican-American War.

TERRITORIAL SETTLEMENTS

Despite some Americans' opposition to the Mexican-American War, the United States had the upper hand from the start. On August 18, 1846, General **Stephen Kearny** and his troops marched into Santa Fe, the capital of the New Mexico Territory. They had expected to face strong opposition from Mexican troops and militia, but they found the city unguarded. For unknown reasons, Santa Fe's Mexican governor, Manuel Armijo (ahr-MEE-hoh), had decided not to fight. The United States claimed the New Mexico Territory without a single soldier firing a weapon.

Meanwhile, dramatic events unfolded in California. On June 14, 1846, American settlers took over the town of Sonoma and declared their independence from Mexico. They declared that their land was now the Republic of California. Because of their flag—which featured a grizzly bear—their insurrection, or rebellion, would become

known as the **Bear Flag Revolt**. American explorer and survey expedition leader **John C. Frémont** headed to Sonoma, where he gave his support to the settlers.

The Republic of California, with Frémont as its elected leader, had a very short life, however. The insurrection had been carried out by a group of settlers who were not connected with, or acting under orders from, the U.S. government. Within days, American forces took control of the area and claimed California for the United States. In August 1846, the U.S. Army also captured the city of Los Angeles, and by November, the conquest was complete.

By 1847, the United States controlled all of California and New Mexico. American military leaders then turned toward Mexico itself. The Mexican Army was busy in the California and New Mexico territories, leaving strategic Mexican cities vulnerable to attack.

State of California Flag
The present-day state flag of California is much like the one used by the California battalion that supported the U.S. Army in taking control of California. It includes the same elements as the Bear Flag of that battalion. The grizzly bear symbolizes strength, the star stands for independence, and the red color represents courage.

INVADING MEXICO

Zachary Taylor, the leader of the troops that had crossed the Nueces River to spark the war, had enjoyed some success near the Rio Grande. Taylor now entered Mexico, pursuing retreating Mexican troops. He fought Santa Anna at Buena Vista in 1847. Though the battle seemed to be an even fight, Santa Anna withdrew his troops, and Taylor now controlled northern Mexico.

Because Taylor was reluctant to mount a large-scale invasion of Mexico, Polk changed the American strategy. He ordered General **Winfield Scott** to take his troops to Mexico by sea. Scott and his men landed at Veracruz, which they captured after a three-week siege. They then fought their way toward the capital, Mexico City.

After another fierce battle on the outskirts of the city, American troops entered the capital. In September 1847, Scott gained control of Mexico City and raised the flag of the United States.

Mexico had surrendered and the war was over, but politicians were divided about what to do with the conquered territory. Some wanted the United States to claim all of the territory conquered in the war, while others wanted to claim only the disputed territories. Some politicians argued that the United States should claim no territory at all. Any treaty between the United States and Mexico would have to settle this debate.

HISTORICAL THINKING

1. **READING CHECK** What was the Bear Flag Revolt?

2. **EXPLAIN** How did the battles over New Mexico and California territories give the U.S. Army an advantage?

3. **DRAW CONCLUSIONS** Why did some politicians argue that the United States should not claim any territory in Mexico?

Objective

Chronicle events leading up to the United States victory in the Mexican-American War.

Critical Thinking Skills for Lesson 3.2

- Identify Main Ideas and Details
- Monitor Comprehension
- Explain
- Draw Conclusions
- Make Inferences

Essential Question for Chapter 12

Why were Americans inspired to move west?
The United States defeated Mexico in 1847. Lesson 3.2 discusses events leading up to Mexico's surrender and the questions the outcome raised.

Background for the Teacher

Christopher (Kit) Carson, a legendary hero, was a mountain man and trapper who traveled throughout the West using his knowledge of the terrain and his experiences with Native Americans to become a well-known guide. John Frémont hired Carson to accompany him on expeditions through the Rocky Mountains and Great Basin and to Oregon and California. Carson fought in the Bear Flag Revolt. Frémont sent him to Washington with messages for President Polk, but on the way, Carson met up with General Stephen Kearny, who enlisted him to guide U.S. troops from New Mexico to California. Carson fought with Kearny's forces in the Battle of San Pasqual.

After the Mexican-American War, Carson settled in New Mexico, where he became a rancher and federal Indian agent before serving as the leader of the New Mexico volunteers in the Civil War. Following the Civil War, Carson led several military actions against Native American tribes in New Mexico and Texas.

Activate Prior Knowledge

Ask students to recall what they learned in Lessons 2.2 and 2.3 about how Texas became an independent republic. Create a 5Ws Chart on the board and call on volunteers to fill in the first column with words or phrases to answer *what, who, when, where,* and *why* questions about the Lone Star Republic. Tell students that in this lesson they will learn how California also briefly became an independent republic. At the end of the lesson, ask students to complete another 5Ws Chart with information about the California Republic.

TEACH

Guided Discussion

1. **Draw Conclusions** Why did the U.S. Army take over California, which had already declared independence from Mexico? *(Possible response: The Bear Flag Revolt was not a government-approved rebellion. The United States wanted control of the territory.)*

2. **Make Inferences** Why do you think President Polk ordered Winfield Scott to take his troops to Mexico by sea rather than by land? *(Answers will vary. Possible response: The overland distance from Veracruz to Mexico City was much shorter than from northern Mexico. Scott's troops could gain control of the capital before Zachary Taylor's troops could get there.)*

More Information

The Bear Flag The history of the Bear Flag began with its creation in 1846 and ended with its adoption as California's state flag 65 years later. The original flag included the same details as today's flag. However, the crudely drawn grizzly was criticized for looking more like a pig than a bear. The historic Bear Flag was destroyed in the 1906 San Francisco earthquake, but the design had been documented in the letters and drawings of the teenage son of a navy commander at Sonoma. California adopted the Bear Flag as its state flag in 1911. Standardization of the design and statutes for its display became effective in 1953. Encourage students to find out when and how the state flag may be displayed.

Active Options

On Your Feet: Ready, Set, Recall After the class has read the lesson, instruct small groups of students to list everything they recall. Then have groups, in round-robin order, send a member to the board to write one item from the group's list to compile a class list. When group members run out of items, the group must drop out of the game. However, if any members think of a new item, the group can get back in the game.

NG Learning Framework: Compare Artistic Depictions

ATTITUDE Curiosity

KNOWLEDGE Our Human Story

Ask students to suggest a word to describe Christian Mayr's painting of General Scott's entrance into Mexico City. *(Possible responses: celebration, triumph, orderly, happy)* Have students find Carl Nebel's painting of the same event online and compare the two paintings. **ASK:** How is Nebel's portrayal of the event different from Mayr's? *(Answers will vary. Possible response: The scene is not a celebration. People are not welcoming the Americans.)* **ASK:** How is Nebel's historical point of view different from Mayr's? *(Answers will vary. Possible response: Nebel seems sympathetic to the defeated Mexicans, whereas Mayr seems to focus on the victorious Americans.)* Encourage students to think about how an artist's point of view affects our understanding of history. Allow students to discuss their ideas with a partner and then call on volunteers to share their responses with the class.

DIFFERENTIATE

Striving Readers

Preview and Predict Before students read the lesson, direct them to preview the title, the Main Idea statement, and the headings. Guide students to use that information to help them write a sentence that predicts what the lesson will be about. Allow pairs of students to compare sentences.

Gifted & Talented

Analyze Nicknames Tell students one of the American generals in this lesson was nicknamed "Old Rough and Ready" and another was called "Old Fuss and Feathers." Ask them to guess who merited each nickname and why. Then tell students to research the correct answers and to write a paragraph explaining the characteristics that earned each general his nickname. Have students share their paragraphs with the class.

See the Chapter Planner for more strategies for differentiation.

HISTORICAL THINKING

ANSWERS

1. The Bear Flag Revolt was a rebellion of American settlers in California who declared themselves independent from Mexico and established the Republic of California.

2. The U.S. Army won both the battles over New Mexico and California, giving the United States control over both territories. While the Mexican Army was still defending New Mexico and California, the U.S. Army was in a position to invade Mexico.

3. Answers will vary. Possible response: Many people had objected to war with Mexico and believed that claiming Mexican territory would further damage relations between the countries. Since settlers in California had already established a republic, they could choose to seek annexation as Texas had.

CRITICAL VIEWING Answers will vary. Possible response: The artist shows well-dressed Mexicans waving and cheering as Scott's troops enter Mexico City. The Mexicans appear to be welcoming the U.S. Army.

3.3 Consequences of the War

Restless Americans dreaming of new opportunities set westward expansion in motion. Then the United States seized vast new western territories in a war with Mexico. Some Americans' dream of manifest destiny seemed to be coming true.

MAIN IDEA After a series of treaties, land purchases, and international agreements, the United States stretched from the Atlantic to the Pacific.

OCEAN TO OCEAN

With the fall of Mexico City, the United States had won the Mexican-American War. The war officially ended in February 1848, when the United States and Mexico signed the **Treaty of Guadalupe Hidalgo**. The treaty set the Rio Grande as the border between Texas and Mexico and, in exchange for $15 million, Mexico gave up its northernmost territories. These territories included present-day California, Nevada, and Utah, as well as parts of Arizona, New Mexico, Colorado, and Wyoming. Upon the signing of the treaty, tens of thousands of people who had previously considered themselves Mexicans became Americans overnight.

The United States now stretched from the Atlantic Ocean to the Pacific Ocean. But the victory over Mexico aggravated an already looming problem.

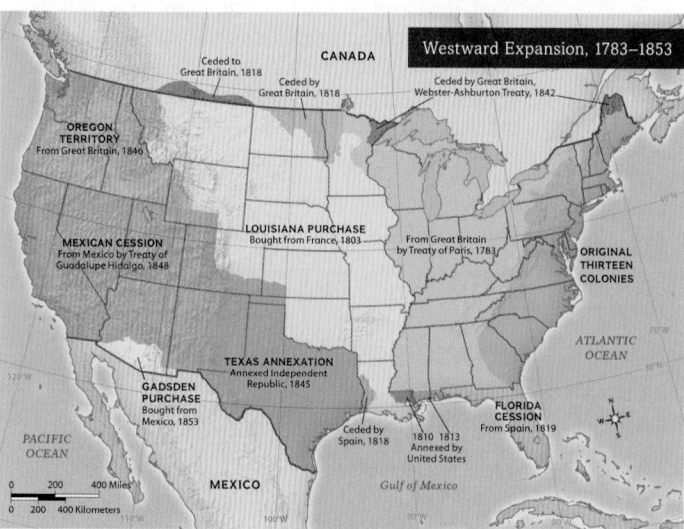

Westward Expansion, 1783–1853

The addition of so much land only worsened conflicts over slavery. The new territories were not part of the Missouri Compromise. What would happen when they gained enough population to become states? Would these states be free states or slave states?

While the Mexican-American War was still in progress, Representative David Wilmot of Pennsylvania introduced a plan called the **Wilmot Proviso**. A **proviso** is a condition attached to a legal document or legislation. The Wilmot Proviso was originally attached to a bill meant to pay for a portion of the Mexican-American War. It called for slavery to be barred from any territory gained from the Mexican-American War. President Polk and other pro-slavery southerners opposed this plan and offered an alternate proposal: to extend the Missouri Compromise line westward. Slavery would be allowed in territories south of the line and prohibited in territories north of it. The Wilmot Proviso passed several times in the House of Representatives but not in the Senate. Without passage of this proviso into law, the subject of slavery in new states remained a major concern.

NEW BORDERS, NORTH AND SOUTH

At the same time the United States was adding land in the West, it began to clash with Great Britain over land in the Northwest: the Oregon Territory. Fortunately, diplomacy, not war, ended this conflict. Lawmakers from the United States and Britain agreed to a compromise, setting the northern border of the United States at the 49th **parallel**, or line of latitude, located 49° N of the equator.

Another puzzle piece of American territory fell into place in 1853, when Mexico sold the United States a sliver of land located along the southern edges of present-day Arizona and New Mexico. This $10 million deal, called the **Gadsden Purchase**, granted the United States land it needed to complete a southern transcontinental railroad. It also completed the borders of the **contiguous**, or connected, United States.

The Mexican-American War led to a monumental increase in the size of the United States and an important addition to American culture and identity. For generations, Mexican Americans have contributed to and shaped the United States, and their culture has particularly deep roots in the region that once belonged to Spain and Mexico. Place names throughout the Southwest reflect their Hispanic heritage, and Mexican cultural traditions shape life and identity in many southwestern communities. Spanish and Mexican people and their descendants also played a large role in California's story as it moved toward statehood.

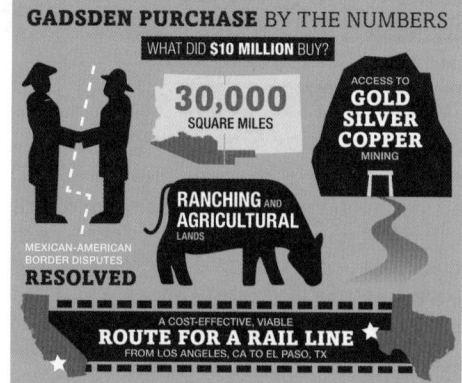

GADSDEN PURCHASE BY THE NUMBERS
WHAT DID **$10 MILLION** BUY?
30,000 SQUARE MILES
ACCESS TO GOLD SILVER COPPER MINING
MEXICAN-AMERICAN BORDER DISPUTES **RESOLVED**
RANCHING AND AGRICULTURAL LANDS
A COST-EFFECTIVE, VIABLE **ROUTE FOR A RAIL LINE** FROM LOS ANGELES, CA TO EL PASO, TX

HISTORICAL THINKING

1. **READING CHECK** What events finalized the borders of the western United States?

2. **IDENTIFY MAIN IDEAS AND DETAILS** Why did each acquisition of new territory renew conflicts over slavery?

3. **INTERPRET MAPS** Locate present-day state borders on the map. How many states or parts of states were added to U.S. territory between 1803 and 1853?

PLAN

Objective

Discover how the United States acquired lands that fulfilled the idea of manifest destiny.

Critical Thinking Skills for Lesson 3.3

- Identify Main Ideas and Details
- Monitor Comprehension
- Interpret Maps
- Summarize
- Integrate Visuals

Essential Question for Chapter 12

Why were Americans inspired to move west?
Through treaties and land purchases, the United States completed its westward expansion. Lesson 3.3 discusses some of the consequences of acquiring new territories in the West.

Background for the Teacher

As a consequence of the Mexican-American War, both the United States and Mexico experienced several long-lasting effects. On the negative side, nearly 6,000 American soldiers were killed or wounded, and more than twice that many died from diseases. For Mexico, losses included not only thousands of military casualties but also extensive damage to cities and roads. Mexico also suffered a loss of national honor, and the war worsened the country's political instability.

On the positive side, the Mexican-American War was a proving ground for U.S. military forces. It was the nation's first war fought on foreign soil, and it involved complex military operations. It shaped the military careers of Robert E. Lee, Ulysses Grant, Jefferson Davis, George Meade, and others who would distinguish themselves during the Civil War.

Consider the Importance of Land

Ask students to identify reasons why land is valuable. List responses on the board. Reasons may include the following: Land may have natural resources, such as fertile soil, minerals, or trees. The land may be a good location for an office building or mall or a good investment for future sale. Tell students that they will find out in this lesson why the federal government was willing to pay millions of dollars for lands in the West in the 19th century.

TEACH

Guided Discussion

1. **Summarize** How were the Wilmot Proviso and President Polk's proposal to extend the Missouri Compromise line alike and different? *(Both plans would limit slavery in the West. The Wilmot Proviso would ban slavery in any territory acquired in the Mexican-American War. Polk's plan would allow slavery south of the Missouri Compromise line.)*

2. **Integrate Visuals** Why was the United States willing to pay almost as much for the Gadsden Purchase as for all the rest of Mexico's territories? Use details from the text and the infographic to answer. *(Possible response: Without the Gadsden Purchase, the United States could not complete a railroad connecting California and Texas. The area included valuable land for ranching and farming and valuable minerals to be mined.)*

More Information

An Ongoing Influence Explain that many Mexican Americans have influenced the history and culture of the United States. Cesar Chavez (1927–1993) used nonviolent means to promote the rights of Mexican-American farm workers and showed the inequalities that they workers suffered. Sandra Cisneros (b. 1954) is an award-winning author whose writing describes the Chicana experience. Ask students to research a prominent Mexican American, such as one of the following, and present a biographical sketch that includes the contribution he or she has made to the development of California and the United States.

Rudolfo Anaya	Alberto Gonzalez	Salma Hayek
Nancy Lopez	Ellen Ochoa	Mario J. Molina

Active Options

On Your Feet: Annotate a Time Line Label five large sheets of paper with these dates: 1803, 1845, 1846, 1848, and 1853. Divide the class into five groups and assign each one date. Have the groups use information from the lesson to list key events of their assigned year and at least one consequence. When groups have finished, draw a time line, hang the segments in chronological order, and have groups share their events and consequences.

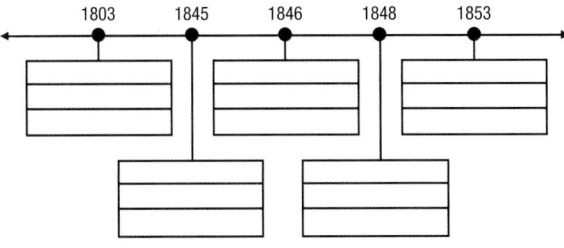

NG Learning Framework: Explore Mexican Culture in the Southwest

ATTITUDE Curiosity

KNOWLEDGE Our Human Story

Have students investigate the influence of Mexican culture in the southwestern United States. Ask groups to choose and research a place, style of architecture, type of food, celebration, or custom. Have groups create posters or displays to share their findings.

DIFFERENTIATE

Inclusion

Describe Details in Maps Pair students who have visual impairments with students who do not. Ask students without impairments to describe the details of the map for their partners. Encourage students with visual impairments to ask questions for clarification. Then have partners work together to gain an understanding of the relative size of lands that were added to the United States in the 19th century.

Pre-AP

Analyze the Treaty of Guadalupe Hidalgo Instruct students to work in pairs to study the Treaty of Guadalupe Hidalgo, especially Articles VIII and IX. Have each pair create a blog post listing the rights and protections given to Mexicans living in the lands acquired by the United States. Then ask pairs to write a few comments on the post from the viewpoints of a Mexican and of an American affected by the treaty. Ask pairs to share and comment on each other's blogs.

See the Chapter Planner for more strategies for differentiation.

HISTORICAL THINKING

ANSWERS

1. The Treaty of Guadalupe Hidalgo gave the United States a large piece of Mexican territory. The Gadsden Purchase transferred a final piece of the Southwest to the United States. A compromise with Great Britain set the northern border of the United States at the 49th parallel.

2. As new territories were acquired, the question of slavery had to be decided again to maintain the balance between free states and slave states.

3. All or parts of the following 26 states were added between 1803 and 1853: Maine, Florida, Alabama, Mississippi, Minnesota, Iowa, Missouri, Arkansas, Louisiana, North Dakota, South Dakota, Nebraska, Kansas, Oklahoma, Texas, Montana, Wyoming, Colorado, New Mexico, Idaho, Nevada, Utah, Arizona, Washington, Oregon, and California.

The Spanish and Mexicans in California

Maps tell us about geography, but they also tell us about history. Just look at a map of California, and you'll see names such as Los Angeles, Palo Alto, and Sierra Nevada—evidence of a past rooted in Spanish culture.

MAIN IDEA Long before the United States acquired California, Spanish and Mexican settlers were founding missions and settlements there.

This statue of Junípero Serra, sculpted by Arthur Putnam in 1918, is located in the cemetery garden at Mission San Francisco. Serra founded Mission San Francisco, also known as Mission Dolores, in 1776.

SPANISH MISSIONS IN CALIFORNIA

As you have read, Spanish conquistadors first explored and claimed the area that is now California in the 16th century. The Spanish were slow to settle in California. The colonial government considered California too far north from its base in Mexico for the region to be a priority. In the 1700s, however, British and Russian fur traders expanded westward into the region to take advantage of the land's natural resources. As a defensive measure, Spain sent an expedition to establish communities in southern California in 1769.

One member of the expedition was **Father Junípero Serra** (hoo-NEE-peh-roh SEH-rah), a Catholic priest from Spain. Serra founded the first mission in California at San Diego. His relationship to the Native Americans he sought to convert to Christianity is still the subject of controversy. Some historians see him as a courageous and generous man who worked hard to improve Native American lives. Others point to his participation in the mistreatment and enslavement of Native Americans.

Over time, the Spanish established 21 missions in California. The names of these missions echo the cities that eventually grew up around them, such as San Francisco, Santa Clara, and San Luis Obispo.

The mission system itself was complicated. Mission residents established farms on the nearby lands and tried to convert Native Americans to Christianity. Spanish treatment of Native Americans was often cruel. Many settlers exploited and enslaved Native Americans they encountered near their farms. They pushed thousands of Native Americans off their land and forced hundreds of others to live and work at the missions.

MEXICAN RULE OF CALIFORNIA

When Mexico gained independence from Spain in 1821, California was one of the new nation's northernmost territories. Because of its enormous size and its great distance from Mexico City, California was difficult for Mexico to rule. As in Texas, the local Mexican government was often ineffective and corrupt.

In 1824, Mexico passed an act that granted land to settlers in the form of large estates. These land grants became new estates, called **ranchos**, which consisted of sprawling tracts of land covering thousands of acres. The ranchos formed the basis of the economy of the Mexican settlements in the region. The rancheros, or owners, raised huge herds of cattle and traded hides and the processed fat of the cattle for manufactured goods along the Pacific coast.

The economy expanded as American traders, trappers, farmers, and businesspeople moved into the territory in the decades after Mexican independence. Some received land grants for ranchos or other parcels of land.

One of these new settlers was a Swiss immigrant named **John Sutter**, who received several land grants from the Mexican government to start a colony. In 1843, he built what became known as Sutter's Fort, a huge, high-walled adobe structure at the future site of Sacramento. Sutter kept herds of cattle like other California rancheros, but he also helped diversify the region's economy and agriculture by raising grapes and wheat.

By 1848, Americans who had moved to California accounted for more than half of its non-Native American population. They faced a government they felt did not represent them, and as a result, the Americans entertained the idea of independence from Mexico.

They got their wish with the signing of the Treaty of Guadalupe Hidalgo in 1848. The United States acquired California just in time for an amazing discovery at a sawmill that John Sutter was building in the foothills of the Sierra Nevada.

HISTORICAL THINKING

1. **READING CHECK** Why did the Spanish establish communities in California?

2. **COMPARE AND CONTRAST** How were the histories of Texas and California alike under the rule of Spain and Mexico?

3. **IDENTIFY MAIN IDEAS AND DETAILS** How did the California economy change as American settlers received land grants?

PLAN

Objective

Describe how Spanish and Mexican missions and ranchos influenced the history and culture of California.

Critical Thinking Skills for Lesson 4.1

- Identify Main Ideas and Details
- Monitor Comprehension
- Compare and Contrast
- Evaluate
- Make Inferences

Essential Question for Chapter 12

Why were Americans inspired to move west?
Mexican land grants in California created an economy based on cattle ranching and drew Americans to the area. Lesson 4.1 discusses how American settlers diversified the region's economy and paved the way for independence from Mexico.

Background for the Teacher

At the height of their power, California missions served not only as churches but also as towns with their own schools, farms, and prisons. Missions often existed near a *presidio*, or military fort, and a *pueblo*, or farming community. In the 1830s, the missions were secularized, and the government gave most of their lands, in the form of ranchos, to private individuals. After the decline of the missions, ranchos became the dominant feature of California's fertile lands. Most land grants were awarded to wealthy families that became an elite group known as *Californios*. Rancho workers were mostly Native Americans who had learned Spanish while living and working at missions. Under the terms of the Treaty of Guadalupe Hidalgo and other legislation, the United States guaranteed the property rights of Mexican citizens in California, but lengthy and costly legal processes often resulted in the loss of these lands.

INTRODUCE & ENGAGE

Preview with Maps

Display a present-day map of California. Set a time limit and challenge students to locate as many cities as they can that begin with *San* or *Santa*. Discuss the results of their search. Point out that many cities in California are named for saints, which reflects the Spanish and Mexican heritage of the state. Tell students that many of these cities grew up around Spanish missions started in the 1700s. Explain that in this lesson students will learn how the mission system influenced life in California.

TEACH

Guided Discussion

1. **Evaluate** Why is the legacy of the California missions considered controversial? *(Possible response: The missions were established to spread Christianity, which some might see as positive and others as negative. Mission residents settled the land and created farming communities, which can be seen as a good thing, but mission residents also mistreated Native Americans and forced many off their lands.)*

2. **Make Inferences** How did the activities and attitudes of settlers in California reflect the idea of manifest destiny? *(Possible response: Manifest destiny was the idea that Americans had a special purpose to settle the whole continent, so settlers felt they had the right to take over land and resources in California. Settlers also wanted independence from Mexico so that California would belong to the United States.)*

More Information

Mission San Francisco de Asís Founded in 1776, San Francisco de Asís was the sixth Spanish mission in California. The small chapel, built in 1791, survived the great earthquake and fire of 1906. The chapel was restored in the 1990s, and its three original bells are still in use. The mission gardens were also restored and planted with trees, shrubs, and flowers that were native to the area when the mission was founded. The cemetery holds the remains of many Ohlone and Miwok people who built the mission and became its first residents, as well as several noteworthy non-native pioneers, including the first Mexican governor of California.

Active Options

On Your Feet: Team Word Webbing Organize students into teams of four and give each team a large sheet of paper with the word *rancho* in the center. Give each student a different colored marker. Instruct students to write what they know about ranchos. At your signal, have students rotate the paper clockwise. Encourage students to build on their teammates' entries. After each student has written on all four sides of the paper, call on volunteers from each team to make statements about ranchos based on their web.

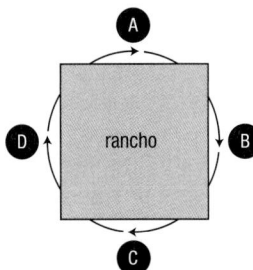

NG Learning Framework: Find Out More about the Mission System

SKILL Collaboration

KNOWLEDGE Our Human Story

Encourage students to work together in small groups to find maps, time lines, and other documents online about the California missions. Suggested topics include the art, architecture, and layout of a mission; daily life for adults and children; and types of work done at a mission. Students may choose to investigate the history of a particular mission or research the development of missions from south to north. Encourage groups to share their findings in some creative way, such as drawing maps or diagrams of a mission, making a video presentation, performing a play, or writing a first-person account from the viewpoint of a resident or missionary.

DIFFERENTIATE

Striving Readers

Expand the Main Idea Statement After they read the lesson, direct students to copy the Main Idea statement and write additional sentences to create a paragraph that expands on the statement and summarizes the lesson.

English Language Learners

Summarize Lesson 4.1 has two sections. Pair students at the **Emerging** and **Expanding** levels with students at the **Bridging** level, and assign each pair a section of the text to read together. Encourage students to use a Main Idea and Details list such as the one below to make notes. Answer any questions after pairs have finished. Then have each pair share and discuss their notes with a pair who were assigned the other section of the chapter.

Main Idea:
Detail:
Detail:
Detail:

See the Chapter Planner for more strategies for differentiation.

HISTORICAL THINKING

ANSWERS

1. The Spanish wanted a stronger presence in California to defend against the expansion of British and Russian fur traders.

2. Texas and California were settled by Spain at about the same time, and both became home to Catholic missions. When Mexico gained independence in 1821, it took ownership of both territories. Americans moved into both territories and worked for independence from Mexico.

3. The Mexican economy was based on ranching. Americans who received land grants helped diversify the economy by raising grapes and wheat. American settlers also included trappers, traders, farmers, and businesspeople.

4.2 The Gold Rush

A fever of sorts broke out in the late 1840s. Victims from all around the world quit their jobs, left their families, and set off on long, dangerous journeys. The "illness" they suffered from? Gold fever.

MAIN IDEA The discovery of gold in California in 1848 led to a boom in population and wealth.

EUREKA!

By the late 1840s, Sutter's Fort had become a thriving farm community. Various new projects were underway, including the construction of a sawmill upstream on the American River. You might recall from the American Story in this chapter that this was where workers spotted a few flecks of gold on January 24, 1848. Sutter swore the workers to secrecy, but the word soon got out. The next few years would be chaos for Sutter. His men immediately stopped working, abandoned the colony, and went hunting for gold instead.

At first, **prospectors**, or people in search of valuable resources in the earth, found a wealth of gold deposits that were easy to access. They struck gold by digging into hills or mountainsides, or by panning in rivers or streams. Panning involves using a shallow pan to scoop up gravel from the bed of a stream, dipping the pan in the stream to collect some water, and swishing the water around to wash away dirt, clay, and silt. Heavier materials, including particles of gold, remain in the pan.

When prospectors struck gold, they yelled "Eureka!" *Eureka* is an ancient Greek word that means "I have found it." During the California gold rush, shouts of "Eureka!" expressed the thrill and excitement accompanying the discovery of riches. The word was so closely associated with the gold rush that it would become the California state motto.

News of the gold discovery spread to the East Coast and then around the world. Thousands of people bitten by the "gold bug" began heading west to strike it rich.

CRITICAL VIEWING In 1858, George W. Northrup posed as a prospector for a photo to send home to his family in Minnesota. He is holding a pickaxe, a hoe, a pan, and two pistols. Note that he also has a bag labeled "gold" on his lap. What image do you think Northrup was trying to convey by posing in this way?

PATENT RIVETED CLOTHING
The Best in USE FOR
FARMERS, Mechanics AND MINERS
LEVI STRAUSS & CO. SAN FRANCISCO, CAL.

Levi Strauss's Blue Jeans
One merchant who became rich during the gold rush was **Levi Strauss**. A German immigrant, he arrived in San Francisco in 1850. His goal was to manufacture tents and wagon covers for miners. But after noticing a demand for durable work pants, he began producing trousers made from the tent canvas he had purchased.

People loved the pants. Strauss sold enough to open a factory and started to produce the pants using a denim cloth known as *gênes* in French. Levi Strauss invented blue jeans and founded a company and a unique American brand.

THE FORTY-NINERS

By the following year, around 80,000 new gold-seekers had moved to California. They earned the nickname **forty-niners** because they arrived in 1849. The forty-niners came from all over the United States and the world. Consequently, the mining towns that sprang up to house and feed the forty-niners included diverse mixes of nationalities and cultures. Because slavery was not commonly practiced in California, many free African Americans decided to try their luck in the gold fields. Thousands of immigrants also arrived from China.

Most of the fortune-seekers were single men who hoped to find riches quickly and move on. Others headed to California with plans to settle there permanently. Whether they struck gold or not, many ended up staying. The boom in population created opportunities for all kinds of settlers. With a bit of creativity and business knowledge, people could make a fortune providing goods and services to the miners and other new residents of California.

However, the gold rush did not have a positive impact on everyone. Many people who had long lived in California found their livelihoods destroyed. **Californios**, or residents of Spanish or Mexican descent, had thrived on California's abundant farmland and prosperous ranchos. Newcomers to the area did not respect Californios' customs or legal rights, and in some cases they seized Californios' property. In addition, thousands of Native Americans died at the hands of gold miners or from the diseases that they and other settlers brought into the region.

California's population increased quite rapidly because of the gold rush. Before 1848, about 1,000 non-native people lived there. By the end of 1849, that number reached nearly 100,000. Even though most of the easily found gold deposits had been depleted by then, more fortune-seekers arrived each day. With that fast-growing population came a need for the laws and government that statehood could provide.

HISTORICAL THINKING

1. **READING CHECK** How did the California gold rush start?

2. **ANALYZE CAUSE AND EFFECT** In what ways did the discovery of gold and the migration of the forty-niners affect Californios and others who had long lived in California?

3. **SUMMARIZE** How did the population of California change, and why?

PLAN

Objective
Explain why the population of California increased dramatically in the late 1840s.

Critical Thinking Skills for Lesson 4.2
- Identify Main Ideas and Details
- Monitor Comprehension
- Analyze Cause and Effect
- Summarize
- Make Inferences
- Evaluate
- Analyze Visuals

Essential Question for Chapter 12
Why were Americans inspired to move west?
Thousands of gold-seekers flocked to California in the late 1840s. Lesson 4.2 explains the causes and effects of the gold rush.

Background for the Teacher

In spite of California's fertile farmlands, many forty-niners faced starvation. The food supply could not keep up with the rapid influx of settlers, and the growing demand allowed merchants to charge outrageous prices for their goods. Chicken eggs sold for a dollar or more apiece, a price equivalent to nearly $29 per egg today. Some entrepreneurs found a new source of eggs for the protein-hungry newcomers. They sailed to the Farallon Islands off the coast of San Francisco to gather murre eggs, which they sold to restaurants and grocery stores. Murres are penguin-like birds that lay their large eggs on steep cliffs. Egging, as the work was called, was dangerous, but the enterprise touched off a competitive, and often violent, egg rush in California.

History Notebook
Encourage students to complete the Reid on the Road video series page for Chapter 12 in their History Notebooks after they view the video.

INTRODUCE & ENGAGE

Solve a Riddle

Pose this riddle for students: When is a fever not a symptom of an illness? If students have difficulty guessing, ask them to consult a dictionary to find alternative meanings of *fever*. Then encourage them to brainstorm examples of the kind of fever that describes excitement or enthusiasm over something. *(Possible responses: spring fever, baseball fever, fever for a sports team or famous person)* Tell students that in this lesson they will learn how an event in California in the 1840s caused people to develop gold fever.

TEACH

Guided Discussion

1. **Make Inferences** Based on the description of prospectors' work, what characteristics would a prospector need to be successful? *(Possible response: A prospector would need to be strong because mining was hard physical labor. A prospector would need patience and determination because panning for gold was a tedious process.)* **ASK:** How might those traits help people contribute to the economy of western communities? *(These would all be helpful traits for living and working in a rugged frontier environment.)*

2. **Evaluate** How did the values of the forty-niners conflict with those of the Californios? *(Possible response: The Californios had received their ranchos through land grants and had established a prosperous and settled way of life. But the forty-niners wanted to get rich quickly. They sometimes seized Californios' property while seeking a fortune.)*

Analyze Visuals

Direct students' attention to the Levi Strauss advertisement. **ASK:** What makes this ad appealing to potential customers? *(Possible response: It is colorful, and the banner clearly indicates what Strauss is selling. It shows a prosperous farmer who has a nice house and fenced property. The clothing appears comfortable and well made. The text states the clothing is best for mechanics and miners as well as farmers.)* Call on a volunteer to read the caption aloud. **ASK:** How does Strauss's story reflect new sources of immigration and the contributions of immigrants to the economy of California? *(Possible response: People from all over the world moved to California to seek their fortune. Strauss was a German immigrant who became successful by opening a factory to meet the needs of the growing population. He contributed to the economy by employing other people in his factory.)*

Active Options

On Your Feet: Fishbowl Arrange students so that half of the class sits in a close circle facing inward. The other half of the class sits in a larger circle around them. Pose the question: What were the positive and negative impacts of the gold rush on California? Direct students in the inner circle to discuss the question for 10 minutes while those in the outer circle listen to the discussion and evaluate the points made. Then ask the groups to reverse roles and continue the discussion.

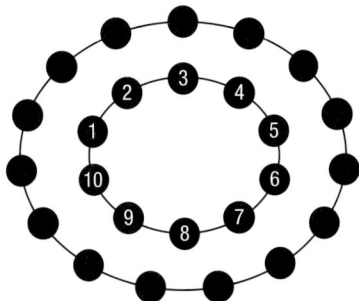

NG Learning Framework: Evaluate Primary Sources

ATTITUDE Curiosity

KNOWLEDGE Our Human Story

Instruct students to work individually or in small groups to conduct online research for primary sources about the California gold rush. Encourage them to examine newspaper articles, songs or poems written in the 1840s, or journals and diaries of the forty-niners. Have each student or group share one source with the class and explain how it adds to the class's understanding of the gold rush. Ask students to assess the credibility of the sources they examined and draw conclusions based on their research.

DIFFERENTIATE

English Language Learners ELD

Match Words and Definitions To preteach Key Vocabulary for students at the **Emerging** level, scramble the order of definitions and have students match each word to its definition. Then allow students at the **Emerging** level to partner with students at the **Expanding** level to write a sentence using each word.

1. prospectors	a. people who went to California during the gold rush
2. forty-niners	b. Spanish or Mexican farmers and ranchers in California
3. Californios	c. people who search for valuable resources in the earth

Gifted & Talented

Create a Business Plan Instruct students to create a business plan for striking it rich in California in the 1840s. Encourage them to consider different aspects of the economy based on what they learned in the lesson. When students have finished, have them pitch their idea to the class, presenting print or oral advertisements for their product or service.

See the Chapter Planner for more strategies for differentiation.

HISTORICAL THINKING

ANSWERS

1. Workers discovered gold while constructing a sawmill for John Sutter.

2. The population increased quickly as gold-seekers came to California. Newcomers often disregarded the rights of residents. Californios lost property, and Native Americans died from abuse or diseases.

3. Many prospectors were single men who planned to make a fortune and leave. Free African Americans came to California because slavery was uncommon there. Some new immigrants planned to start farms or businesses. Many people emigrated from China.

CRITICAL VIEWING Possible response: With the bag of gold, Northrup was probably trying to impress friends and family. The tools and pistols show prospecting as a difficult, dangerous job.

4.3 The Mining Frontier

It's 1849 and you've journeyed to California to hunt for gold. You dreamed of adventure and riches, but the living and working conditions are miserable. Worst of all, you haven't found a speck of gold!

MAIN IDEA A population boom and growing lawlessness caused by the gold rush led to the demand for California statehood.

LIFE IN A MINING CAMP

When 100,000 people crowd into the same region within a short period of time, there are bound to be problems. Few of the single men who rushed west to search for gold were interested in building stable communities. A region that had been mostly rural was suddenly covered with **boomtowns**, or mining camps that grew into crowded towns overnight. These boomtowns had neither strong leadership nor government of any kind. Law enforcement could not keep up with the boomtowns of the gold rush. Thieves and swindlers often got richer than gold miners. Bored miners living far from home spent their free time gambling and fighting with each other.

As you have read, many westward moving pioneers arrived in wagon trains on overland trails. But others decided to travel by ship. Starting on the East Coast, they sailed southward around Cape Horn at the southernmost tip of South America, and then back north to California. Overland trips took from four to six months, and the Cape Horn route took about six months.

Immigrants arrived from many countries, including Chile, Mexico, and China. San Francisco's location made it particularly accessible for people crossing the Pacific Ocean. Immigrants from China were the most numerous. Many settled in California permanently, even though they had not planned on doing so initially.

As a result, these newly established communities included people who spoke different languages, had different customs, and practiced different religions. Sometimes, cultural differences led to misunderstandings or even violence. Among white Americans, prejudices against Native Americans, African Americans, and Chinese immigrants often boiled over into fights. When gold discoveries slowed down, competition for the dwindling gold became more intense. Tensions increased, and so did crime.

Women who moved to boomtowns were far outnumbered by men and faced many challenges. In addition to the hard labor typical of living in a frontier region, they also handled domestic duties for their households. To make extra money, some even took on housekeeping tasks for single men living around them. Many women discovered a liberating independence in California because they could make a good living there. In this frontier region, few laws existed to prohibit women from owning property or businesses. Women opened profitable boarding houses, taverns, and other businesses that catered to the populations of the mining camps. Others tried their luck at mining, and a few even struck gold.

STATEHOOD FOR CALIFORNIA

Many American territories waited years before achieving statehood, but not California. With its population booming and lawlessness plaguing its mining camps, California needed a strong government right away. Since it now easily met the population requirements, many people felt that it was time for California to become a state.

In 1849, territory leaders met at a convention in Monterey to draft a constitution and to make a plan to petition the federal government for statehood. California's first constitution prohibited

San Francisco, 1848

San Francisco, 1860

The California gold rush transformed the small mission of San Francisco into a thriving, vibrant city. Between 1848 and 1849, its population rose from 1,000 to 25,000. By 1860, the city had more than 50,000 people. The top illustration shows the city before the gold rush. The bottom lithograph, by the French illustrator Auguste-Victor Deroy, captures the city as he saw it in 1860. How do these two illustrations show how the landscape of San Francisco changed as more people arrived?

slavery. However, it did not grant civil rights to all of the state's nonwhite or female populations. Like the nation's other states at this time, California's constitution granted only white men the highest level of legal rights and protections.

In September 1850, less than two years after Sutter's workers glimpsed those first specks of gold in a Sierra mountain stream, California became the 31st state. Not surprisingly, its admission as a free state heightened the crisis over slavery that was already threatening to tear the country apart.

HISTORICAL THINKING

1. **READING CHECK** How did the gold rush lead to California's application for statehood?

2. **IDENTIFY MAIN IDEAS AND DETAILS** What opportunities were women able to pursue during the gold rush, and why?

3. **EVALUATE** Did the leaders at the 1849 California constitutional convention support ideas of freedom and equality? Support your response with evidence from the text.

PLAN

Objective
Explain how and why California became a state.

Critical Thinking Skills for Lesson 4.3
- Identify Main Ideas and Details
- Monitor Comprehension
- Evaluate
- Analyze Environmental Concepts
- Make Generalizations

Essential Question for Chapter 12
Why were Americans inspired to move west?
The gold rush led to a population boom in California. Lesson 4.3 explains how this sudden increase in population sped up the process of California's admission to the Union.

Background for the Teacher
After the gold ran out, some boomtowns in California turned into ghost towns, including one called Bodie on the eastern edge of the Sierra Nevada range. The town was founded after Waterman S. Body discovered gold in the area in 1859. Townspeople named the town after Body but changed the spelling of his name. Bodie became a thriving town but gained a wild reputation as a result of the many killings, robberies, and street fights that took place there. By 1879, Bodie boasted a population of about 10,000. Not long after, though, the town began to decline. In the early 1880s, many of the mines played out, and fire later destroyed the business district. Today, Bodie and its remaining buildings are preserved for visitors, and the site has been designated as a California State Historic Park.

INTRODUCE & ENGAGE

What's in a Name?

Write the following place names on the board: Old Dry Diggins, Angels Camp, Fiddletown, Sawyers Bar, and French Gulch. Ask students to describe the images each name brings to mind. **ASK:** What do you think these places have in common? *(They were California mining towns during the gold rush.)* Tell students that in this lesson they will learn what life was like in boomtowns such as these.

TEACH

Guided Discussion

1. **Analyze Environmental Concepts** Based on details you notice in the two paintings, in what ways do you think the sudden population growth of San Francisco might have changed the physical characteristics of its location? *(The bay was once unpopulated and pristine. When people moved to the area, they quickly built homes and businesses, carved out streets on the land, and built docks on the water.)*

2. **Make Generalizations** What did the frontier represent to immigrants? *(Possible response: It represented a new beginning and greater opportunities.)* What did the frontier mean to the nation as a whole? *(Possible response: It represented freedom, rugged individualism, and opportunity.)*

More Information

A Bilingual Constitution According to Article XI of California's 1849 constitution, all the state's laws had to be published in Spanish as well as English. The constitution, therefore, also needed to be translated into Spanish. That task fell to William E.P. Hartnell, a delegate fluent in Spanish. Hartnell also translated the other laws created at California's 1849 Constitutional Convention. **ASK:** Why do you think the delegates wanted to make laws available in both English and Spanish? *(Possible response: Because of its history as part of Mexico, California was home to many people whose primary language was Spanish. Having documents available in Spanish as well as English helped them better understand their rights and responsibilities as citizens of the new state.)*

Active Options

On Your Feet: Three-Step Interview Tell students many historians consider the California gold rush a turning point in U.S. history. Ask students who agree with the statement to stand on one side of the room and those who disagree to stand on the other side. Instruct students to pair with someone who has the opposite viewpoint. Have partners interview each other and compare answers and reasons. Finally, ask pairs to summarize their ideas for the class.

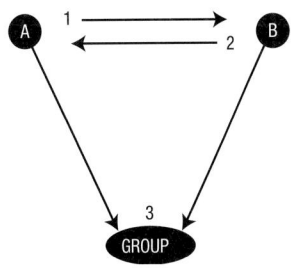

NG Learning Framework: Perform Skits

SKILL Communication

ATTITUDE Responsibility

Assign students to work in pairs or small groups to create and perform skits about life in a California boomtown. Encourage them to portray the diverse population, including women, prospectors, immigrants, and lawmen. Instruct them to use information from the text and other sources to help them accurately depict daily life on the frontier. At the end of the performances, hold a class discussion about the advantages and disadvantages of living in California in the late 1840s.

DIFFERENTIATE

Inclusion

Work in Pairs Pair students with visual disabilities with students who can describe the visuals and caption to them. Encourage students with disabilities to ask questions to clarify their understanding of the visuals. Instruct students without disabilities to pose a question about the caption to check their partner's comprehension.

Pre-AP

Interpret Maps and Documents Tell students to investigate land or sea routes that helped open the West to settlement. Some students could research the routes that ships sailed from New York to San Francisco and examine maps, diaries, and other primary source documents about the voyages. Others could trace wagon train routes to San Francisco and locate letters, memoirs, or other documents that describe the trips. Encourage students to present their findings to the class or share them via a class blog.

See the Chapter Planner for more strategies for differentiation.

HISTORICAL THINKING

ANSWERS

1. Because of the gold rush, California's population quickly surpassed the population requirement for statehood. Also, lawlessness in the mining camps led to demands for stronger government.

2. Women in California were able to own property or start businesses. Some ran successful boarding houses or taverns, suddenly in demand as the population exploded. Others succeeded as prospectors because traditional gender roles had changed on the frontier.

3. Possible response: No, they did not really support the ideas of freedom and equality. The constitution they drafted prohibited slavery, but it granted full civil rights only to white men. African Americans, women, and immigrants were poorly represented by these leaders.

ANALYZE ENVIRONMENTAL CONCEPTS Possible response: The illustration of San Francisco in 1848 shows a sparsely populated landscape with few structures. The illustration of San Francisco in 1860 shows many structures, such as homes, churches, docks, walls, and streets.

12 REVIEW

VOCABULARY

Use each of the following vocabulary words in a sentence that shows an understanding of the term's meaning.

1. exodus
   The hurricane warning prompted an exodus of thousands of people from their coastal communities.

2. presidio
3. prospector
4. annex
5. proviso
6. rancho
7. insurrection
8. siege

READING STRATEGY
IDENTIFY MAIN IDEAS AND DETAILS

If you haven't done so already, complete your chart to identify details about Americans' westward movement. Then answer the question.

Main Idea:
Detail:
Detail:
Detail:

9. What factors drove Americans west between 1821 and 1853?

MAIN IDEAS

Answer the following questions. Support your answers with evidence from the chapter.

10. How did the concept of manifest destiny contribute to American expansion? **LESSON 1.1**

11. What groups traveled on the Santa Fe, Oregon, and Mormon Trails? **LESSON 1.3**

12. Why did the Mexican government encourage American settlement in Texas? **LESSON 2.1**

13. Describe the events and outcome of the Battle of the Alamo. **LESSON 2.2**

14. What was James K. Polk's stance on the concept of manifest destiny? **LESSON 2.3**

15. What was the significance of American troops crossing the Nueces River in 1845? **LESSON 3.1**

16. Who participated in the Bear Flag Revolt, and why? **LESSON 3.2**

17. What were the consequences of the Mexican-American War? **LESSON 3.3**

18. Who were the forty-niners? **LESSON 4.2**

19. What did California's first constitution say about slavery? **LESSON 4.3**

HISTORICAL THINKING

Answer the following questions. Support your answers with evidence from the chapter.

20. **IDENTIFY PROBLEMS AND SOLUTIONS** Why did the expansion of the United States create new problems regarding slavery?

21. **MAKE GENERALIZATIONS** How did the ideals of individualism and rugged frontier life shape American identity during the 1800s?

22. **DRAW CONCLUSIONS** Why did the Mexican government regret encouraging American settlement in Texas?

23. **DESCRIBE** In what ways had the borders of the United States changed by the 1850s?

24. **EVALUATE** How did the gold rush provide new opportunities for women, immigrants, and free African Americans?

INTERPRET MAPS

Look closely at the map of the Mexican-American War. Then answer the questions that follow.

25. What was the final battle of the war, and when did it take place?

26. Based on the map, what type of war were the Mexicans fighting? Explain the reasons for your response.

27. Using the map scale, about what was the greatest distance from the United States that any battle was fought?

28. Which military expedition followed the Gila River? Why might it have done so?

Mexican-American War, 1846–1848

ANALYZE SOURCES

William Gilpin was an explorer, an author, and the first governor of the Colorado Territory. He wrote reports for the government, including "The Untransacted Destiny of the American People" for a U.S. Senate committee in 1846. Read the following excerpt from his report.

29. How were Gilpin's claims similar to President Polk's goals for the United States?

30. What does Gilpin mean when he says that the destiny of Americans is to "subdue the continent?"

> Two centuries have rolled over our race upon this continent. From nothing we have become 20,000,000. From nothing we are grown to be . . . the first among nations existing or in history. So much is our destiny—so far, up to this time—transacted, accomplished, certain, and not to be disputed. The untransacted [unfinished] destiny of the American people is to subdue the continent—to rush over this vast field to the Pacific Ocean.

CONNECT TO YOUR LIFE

31. **ARGUMENT** Think about the way the West represented a new frontier for Americans in the 1800s. Also think about the motivations of pioneers who moved west. Then consider what kinds of frontiers inspire the same kind of exploration today. Identify one present-day frontier that you would like to explore and write a paragraph that presents an argument for exploring the new frontier. In your argument, take into account new technologies and skills that you might need to explore the frontier.

TIPS

- Look back at the chapter and list ways in which expansion affected the United States during the 1800s. Then think about how present-day frontiers inspire exploration today. Make notes and then review them to help you craft your argument.

- Support your argument with examples of similarities and differences. Use evidence from the text and two or three key terms from the chapter to make your claims.

- Conclude your paragraph by restating your argument and summarizing your reasoning.

VOCABULARY ANSWERS

1. The hurricane warning prompted an exodus of thousands of people from their coastal communities.

2. In Tejas, missions were located near presidios for protection.

3. Many prospectors left their homes and moved to California in the hopes of finding gold.

4. The city government wanted to annex the neighboring township to extend its tax base.

5. One proviso in the new town charter states that street parking in the city center is prohibited during rush hours.

6. People who received a title to a rancho usually raised cattle or farmed the fertile land.

7. Settlers staged an insurrection because they wanted independence from Mexico.

8. The defenders of the Alamo were strong and courageous to withstand the siege.

READING STRATEGY ANSWER

Main Idea:	From the 1820s through the 1850s, the United States expanded westward.
Detail:	Settlers and traders traveled westward on trails by covered wagon.
Detail:	American settlers in Texas won independence from Mexico.
Detail:	The Treaty of Guadalupe Hidalgo and the Gadsden Purchase transferred California, the New Mexico territory, Texas north of the Rio Grande, and other southwestern territories to the United States.
Detail:	A treaty with Britain set the northern border of the Oregon Territory.
Detail:	The California gold rush and resulting population boom helped to bring about California's statehood.

9. Answers will vary. Possible response: Manifest destiny, the acquisition of lands in the West from Mexico and Great Britain, and the California gold rush were some factors that drove Americans west.

MAIN IDEAS ANSWERS

10. The concept of manifest destiny justified some Americans' belief that the United States had a right and a responsibility to expand as far west as the Pacific Ocean.

11. Traders traveled on the Santa Fe Trail; settlers traveled on the Oregon Trail; Mormons escaping persecution traveled on the Mormon Trail.

12. Texas was sparsely populated, and it was difficult to govern because it was far from Mexico City. The Mexican government hoped American settlers would stabilize the region against Native American attacks.

13. During the Texas War for Independence, about 180 Texans held off a siege against the Alamo by the Mexican Army. After 13 days, Mexicans breached the walls and killed almost everyone inside. The incident led Sam Houston's forces to attack the Mexican Army at San Jacinto and win independence from Mexico.

14. Polk believed in manifest destiny, and he pushed for the United States to annex Texas and to take control of the Oregon Territory to latitude 54° 40′.

15. When Texas was annexed by the United States, its southern border with Mexico was the Nueces River, but Polk thought the border should be the Rio Grande. Polk ordered troops across the Nueces in order to force a battle. This gave him an excuse to call for war with Mexico.

16. American settlers in Sonoma, California, who no longer wanted to be under Mexican rule, declared their independence and established the Republic of California.

17. As a result of the Mexican-American War, the United States gained present-day California, Nevada, and Utah and parts of Arizona, New Mexico, Colorado, and Wyoming. The boundary between Mexico and the state of Texas was set at the Rio Grande. The United States had achieved its manifest destiny, but the addition of new territories worsened the conflict over slavery.

18. Forty-niners were people who arrived in California, starting in 1849, to seek gold.

19. California's first constitution prohibited slavery.

HISTORICAL THINKING ANSWERS

20. The acquisition of new territories by the United States led to proposals to create new states. An equal number of slave states and free states meant that neither side had a majority in the U.S. Senate, but each request for statehood created a crisis because it threatened to tip the balance in favor of one side or the other. The Wilmot Proviso called for the line established by the Missouri Compromise to be extended westward. Slavery would be prohibited in states north of the line and allowed in states south of the line. The Wilmot Proviso did not pass, however, and tensions over the slavery issue continued to build.

21. Answers will vary. Possible response: Americans moved west because of the desire for land or the opportunity to become rich by finding gold. Many people recognized an opportunity to become financially successful by establishing businesses to provide goods and services in the West.

22. The culture of American settlers in Texas differed from that of Tejanos. Some settlers were slave owners, and most were not Catholic. American settlers also brought their ideas of freedom, which inspired both Americans and Tejanos to rebel against what they believed were unfair edicts from the Mexican government. Eventually, Texas won independence from Mexico.

23. By the 1850s, the United States extended west to the Pacific Ocean, north to the 49th parallel, and south to the Rio Grande.

24. Laws in California did not prohibit women from owning property or businesses, so many became successful business owners. Some also became prospectors. Since slavery was not widespread in California, free African Americans moved there to look for gold. Immigrants from China arrived to seek their fortune. The gold rush also provided opportunities to make a fortune providing goods and services to miners and other settlers.

INTERPRET MAPS ANSWERS

25. The final battle was the United States victory in Mexico City on September 13–14, 1847.

26. Mexicans were fighting a defensive war because most battles took place in Mexico.

27. The greatest distance from the U.S. border was about 600 miles.

28. Kearny's 1846 military expedition followed the Gila River. The Gila River offered a direct route to San Diego and provided a source of water and a means of transportation.

ANALYZE SOURCES ANSWERS

29. Gilpin's claims reflect Polk's goals to extend the United States to the Pacific Ocean.

30. After declaring that the United States has already accomplished greatness, Gilpin states that it is the country's destiny to take control of the continent and to expand all the way to the Pacific Ocean. Polk's actions as president were motivated by his belief in this same destiny.

CONNECT TO YOUR LIFE ANSWER

31. Answers will vary. Students may suggest that the boldest frontier today is space or an area that is sparsely inhabited, such as Antarctica. In their responses, students should incorporate textual evidence and a few Key Vocabulary words as they compare and contrast their chosen frontier with the West of the 1800s. They should discuss what people might be seeking in exploring this new frontier, along with the benefits and challenges of exploration.

UNIT 5 RESOURCES

UNIT INTRODUCTION

UNIT TIME LINE

UNIT WRAP-UP

NATIONAL GEOGRAPHIC | **CONNECTION**

National Geographic Magazine Adapted Articles
- "The Way West"
- "People of the Horse" ONLINE

Unit 5 Inquiry: Organize a Reform Campaign

NG Learning Framework Activities
- Research a Mining Boomtown
- Encounter Nature

Unit 5 Formal Assessment

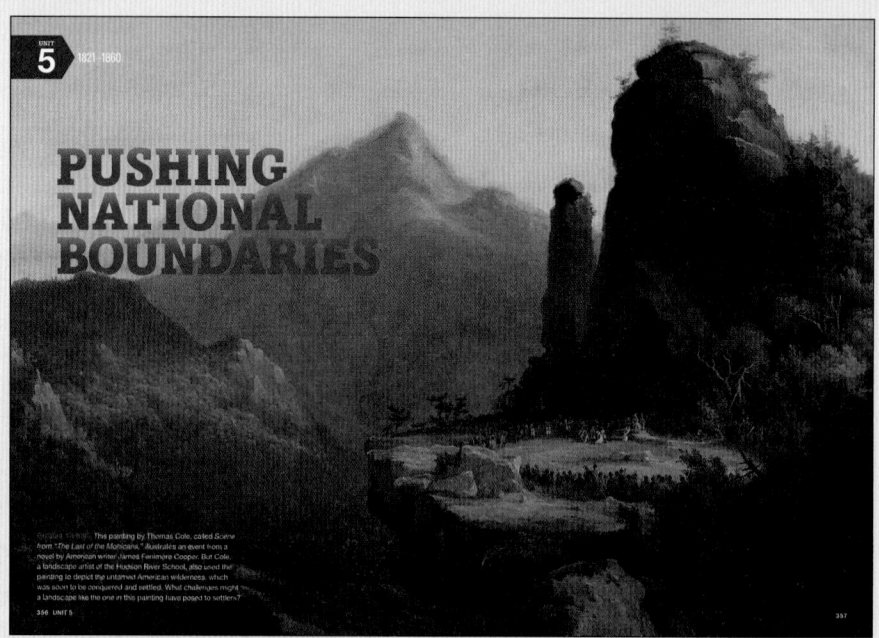

CHAPTER 13 RESOURCES

Available at NGLSync.Cengage.com

TEACHER RESOURCES & ASSESSMENT

Reading and Note-Taking

Vocabulary Practice

Document-Based Question Template

Social Studies Skills Lessons
- Reading: Synthesize
- Writing: Write an Explanation

Formal Assessment
- Chapter 13 Pretest
- Chapter 13 Tests A & B
- Section Quizzes

Chapter 13 Answer Key

ExamView®
One-time Download

STUDENT DIGITAL RESOURCES

- **eEdition** (English)
- **eEdition** (Spanish)
- **Handbooks**

- **Online Atlas**
- **American Gallery Online**
- **History Notebook**

- **American Voices (Biographies)**
- **Active History**
- **Projects for Inquiry-Based Learning**

Chapter 13 Spanish Resources are available at NGLSync.Cengage.com.

AMERICAN STORIES | The Underground Railroad

- Primary Sources
- On Your Feet: Four Corners

| **NG Learning Framework:** Investigate U.S. Currency

SECTION 1 RESOURCES

THE IMMIGRANT EXPERIENCE

LESSON 1.1
The Lure of America

- On Your Feet: Card Responses

| **NG Learning Framework:** Annotate a Map of Immigration

LESSON 1.2
From Different Countries

- On Your Feet: Word Chain

| **NG Learning Framework:** Compare Famines as Push Factors

LESSON 1.3
AMERICAN PLACES
Central Park New York City

- On Your Feet: Descriptive Words

| **NG Learning Framework:** Investigate Olmsted's Spaces

LESSON 1.4
Opposition to Immigration

- On Your Feet: Three-Step Interview

| **NG Learning Framework:** Analyze Political Cartoons

American Voices Biography
Know-Nothing Party ONLINE

SECTION 2 RESOURCES

REFORMING AMERICAN SOCIETY

LESSON 2.1
The Second Great Awakening

- On Your Feet: Tell Me More

| **NG Learning Framework:** Research Temperance Activism

LESSON 2.2
Educating and Advocating

- On Your Feet: Numbered Heads

| **NG Learning Framework:** Create a Time Line

LESSON 2.3
Fighting for Better Pay

- On Your Feet: Fishbowl

| **NG Learning Framework:** Interpret Child Labor Laws

LESSON 2.4
Creative Expression

- On Your Feet: Team Word Webbing

| **NG Learning Framework:** Create a Documentary

SECTION 3 RESOURCES

ABOLITION AND WOMEN'S RIGHTS

LESSON 3.1
The Abolition Movement

- On Your Feet: Create a Quiz

| **NG Learning Framework:** Publish an Antislavery Pamphlet

American Voices Biography
Sojourner Truth ONLINE

LESSON 3.2
DOCUMENT-BASED QUESTION
Voices Against Slavery

- On Your Feet: Use a Jigsaw Strategy

LESSON 3.3
Women's Rights and Seneca Falls

- Active History: Analyze Primary Sources

 AMERICAN GALLERY ONLINE Women's Rights

American Voices Biographies
Susan B. Anthony
Elizabeth Cady Stanton ONLINE

CHAPTER 13 REVIEW

Strategy ❶
Set a Purpose for Reading
Before reading each lesson in Section 1, display the associated question below. Instruct students to answer the questions as they read. At the end of a lesson, ask students to exchange their answers with a partner and discuss.

1.1 What are push-pull factors?

1.2 Where did new immigrants to the United States in the 1800s come from? Why?

1.4 What groups opposed immingation? Why?

Use with Lessons 1.1, 1.2, and 1.4

Strategy ❷
Make a Concept Cluster
As students read lessons in Sections 2 and 3, have them complete a Concept Cluster. Instruct students to write the word *reform* in the center circle. Then prompt them to fill the outer circles with the types of reform movements that emerged during the early 1800s. Finally, tell students to add specific details about each reform movement to their Concept Cluster.

Use with Lessons 2.1–2.3, 3.1, and 3.3

Strategy ❸
Analyze Main Ideas
Direct students to read the Main Idea statements aloud for each lesson. Explain that these statements identify and summarize the key idea for each lesson. As students read the lessons, encourage them to make notes about details they find in the text that connect to the Main Idea statements. Tell them this process will help them identify and remember the most important information.

Use with All Lessons

Strategy ❶
Modify Vocabulary Lists
Limit the number of Key Vocabulary terms you will ask students to master. Direct students to create flash cards for the remaining words using illustrations, definitions, and synonyms (or context clues from the lesson text). Remind students to refer to these cards when they encounter the terms in their texts.

Use with All Lessons

Strategy ❷
Build a Time Line
Tell students that one way to track many events is to build time lines. Write key events on index cards and read the events aloud. Tell students to put the events in chronological order, add dates and verify them using the text, and then record the events in order on their time lines.

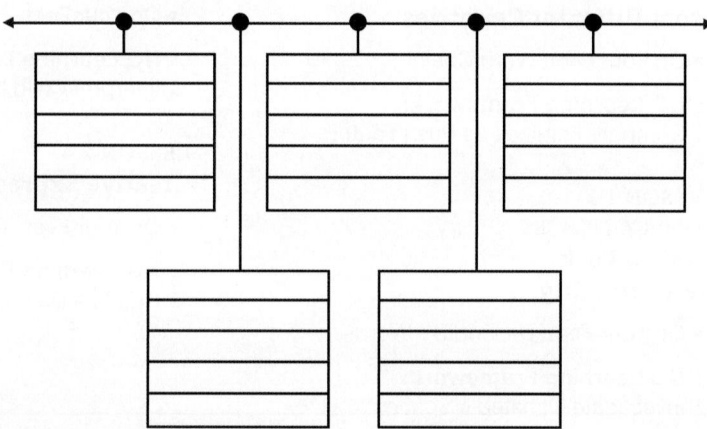

Use with Lessons 2.2–2.3, 3.1, and 3.3 *For example, in Lesson 2.2, students might record the following: 1821—Troy Female Seminary founded; 1833—First asylum opened at Massachusetts General Hospital; 1834—Canterbury School attacked and closed; 1837—Mount Holyoke Female Seminary founded, Horace Mann begins common school movement; 1841—Dorothea Dix joins the cause to provide asylums for the mentally ill.*

ENGLISH LANGUAGE LEARNERS ELD

Strategy 1
Design a Word Wall

Direct students at **All Proficiencies** to choose three or four Key Vocabulary words from each section to group together on a Word Wall. Keep the Word Wall on display as students work through the chapter and encourage students to add definitions and examples as they encounter each Key Vocabulary word.

Use with All Lessons

Strategy 2
Create Word Squares

Tell pairs to create Word Squares for at least three Key Vocabulary words from the chapter. Encourage them to choose terms they have had difficulty understanding. Then have pairs trade their Word Squares with another group.

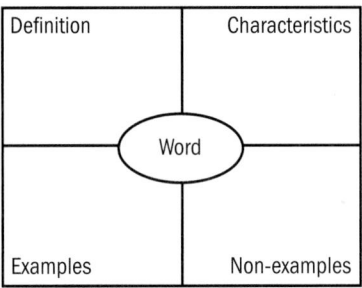

Use with All Lessons *You may wish to place students in pairs, such as students at the **Emerging** level with those at the **Bridging** level.*

Strategy 3
Illustrate Key Vocabulary

Direct students at the **Emerging** level to choose three Key Vocabulary words from Section 1 and illustrate them using drawings and symbols. Then ask students to use their illustrations as a prompt to write new sentences using each word.

Use with All Lessons *Alternatively, invite students at the **Expanding** and **Bridging** levels to pair with students at the **Emerging** level and use computer software to create Key Vocabulary cards. Suggest students use definitions from approved online dictionaries and illustrate cards with clip art or computer-generated original drawings.*

GIFTED & TALENTED

Strategy 1
Present a Museum Exhibit

Direct students to use the chapter text and online resources to design and prepare a museum exhibit about early 19th-century immigration. Encourage students to use letters, newspaper articles, illustrations, and other primary source documents. Direct students to display their exhibits in the classroom and give a brief presentation of their work.

Use with All Lessons

Strategy 2
Create a Profile

Tell students to create a social media profile for one of the following people and interact as they would on social media: Charles Grandison Finney, Dorothea Dix, David Walker, Harriet Tubman, Sarah Bagley, Sojourner Truth, Prudence Crandall, Ralph Waldo Emerson, William Lloyd Garrison, Horace Mann, Walt Whitman, Frederick Douglass, Susan B. Anthony. Have students include a profile, visual representations, likes, dislikes, and details that illustrate the person's life and beliefs. Ask students to act as the individual and present their profile. Invite others to act as their chosen person and "friend" the presenter, asking questions and commenting on shared interests and goals.

Use with Lessons 2.1–2.4 and 3.1–3.3

Pre-AP

Strategy 1
Write a Feature Article

Instruct students to research a reform movement and write a feature article. Tell them to focus on causes, individuals' positions or goals, and reactions of opponents to the attempted reform. Encourage the use of visual elements and quotations from primary sources.

Use with Lessons 2.1–2.3, 3.1, and 3.3 *You may wish to provide examples of feature articles as a guide.*

Strategy 2
Perform a Dramatic Reading

Ask students to choose and read a poem or section of text aloud by a writer or poet mentioned in the chapter and explain how the selection illustrates an important event, idea, or belief from the 19th century. Remind students to use tone, volume, and cadence to express and emphasize meaning.

Use with Lesson 2.4 *For example, a selection from Thoreau's* Walden *could be used to illustrate the idea of self-reliance as found in the philosophy of transcendentalism.*

THE CHANGING AMERICAN
IDENTITY
1830–1860

ESSENTIAL QUESTION
How did immigration and reform influence American identity?

AMERICAN STORIES The Underground Railroad

SECTION 1 **The Immigrant Experience**
KEY VOCABULARY

assimilate	famine	prejudice
blight	immigrate	push-pull factor
domestic service	Know-Nothing party	steerage
emigrate	nativist	

SECTION 2 **Reforming American Society**
KEY VOCABULARY

asylum	revival meeting
common school movement	Second Great Awakening
craft union	temperance movement
evangelize	transcendentalism
labor union	

SECTION 3 **Abolition and Women's Rights**
KEY VOCABULARY

abolitionist	suffrage
emancipation	Underground Railroad
Seneca Falls Convention	

AMERICAN GALLERY
ONLINE Women's Rights

READING STRATEGY

SYNTHESIZE
When you synthesize, you combine related ideas into a single idea, a synthesis. As you read the chapter, use a chart like this one to synthesize ideas about the ways American identity changed between 1830 and 1860.

"I went to the woods because I wished to **live deliberately.**"

—Henry David Thoreau

The calm waters of Walden Pond, a lake located in Concord, Massachusetts, reflect the light of sunset. For two years in the 1840s, Henry David Thoreau lived in a cabin at Walden Pond. He wanted to live simply, in nature. His book *Walden*, published in 1854, is based on his years at Walden Pond.

The Changing American Identity 423

INTRODUCE THE PHOTOGRAPH

Walden Pond

Originally part of the lands owned by Ralph Waldo Emerson's family, today Walden Pond is part of a 335-acre state reservation. Various organizations are committed to preserving the area much as it was in Thoreau's day. Visitors to the park can swim, hike, ski, or explore Thoreau's replica cabin. Have students examine the photograph and read the accompanying quotation. **ASK:** What do you think it means to "live deliberately"? *(Answers will vary. Students might say that one lives deliberately by making purposeful decisions based on specific ideas and then creating a life around those ideas.)*

Share Background

As a young man, Henry David Thoreau became friends with Ralph Waldo Emerson and joined a group of thinkers and writers called the transcendentalists. This group valued self-reliance and believed that living in nature would help humans escape the influence of institutions. The transcendentalists also valued the concept of reform, an idea embraced by many Americans in the 19th century. Thoreau made the decision to "live deliberately" after a period of professional hardship and personal grief. Though his time living at Walden Pond is possibly the best-known period of his life, it lasted only two years. In September 1847, Thoreau moved into the Emerson household, while Emerson was in Europe, and never returned to his cabin at Walden Pond.

For Chapter 13 Spanish Resources, visit the Resources Menu. Chapter 13 Resources are available at NGLSync.Cengage.com.

How did immigration and reform influence American identity?

Numbered Heads: What Is Identity? Engage in a short class discussion about the elements that make up a national identity, such as values, symbols, institutions, and culture.

Organize students into groups of four and assign each group member a number. Tell students to think about and then discuss a response to the following question: How would you describe the American identity?

When students have completed their discussions, call out a number from one to four. Each student with that number will then report on his or her group's conclusions.

Explain that in this chapter, students will be examining how several events and movements helped to form and change the American identity throughout the 19th century.

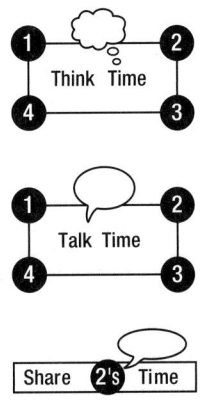

INTRODUCE CHAPTER VOCABULARY

Word Webs

Have students complete a Word Web for Key Vocabulary words as they read the chapter. Ask them to write each word in the center of an oval. Have them look through the chapter to find examples, characteristics, and descriptive words that are associated with the vocabulary word. At the end of the chapter, ask students what they learned about each word. Model an example for students on the board, using the graphic organizer below.

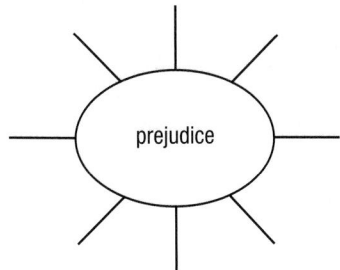

INTRODUCE THE READING STRATEGY

SYNTHESIZE

Remind students to keep track of ideas as they read to help them see connections among concepts in a new way and synthesize them into new conclusions. Model completing the Synthesis Diagram below. Read the ideas in the outer bubbles aloud and discuss how the ideas are related. Then provide students with an example of a synthesis of those ideas: *In the 19th century, some women worked to end slavery and fought for their own rights.* Challenge students to develop other syntheses from the information.

KEY DATES FOR CHAPTER 13

1790s	Second Great Awakening begins
1823	James Fenimore Cooper publishes *The Pioneers*
1831	Prudence Crandall opens Canterbury School
1831	William Lloyd Garrison publishes *The Liberator*
1837	Horace Mann helps establish common school system
1840	Famine begins in Ireland
1848	Seneca Falls Convention
1851	Sojourner Truth delivers "Ain't I a Woman?" speech
1874	Massachusetts passes the 10-hour workday

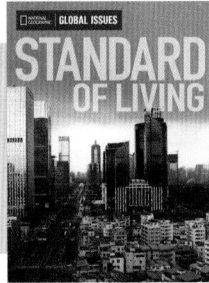

For more on the factors that influence people's economic well-being, see *GLOBAL ISSUES: STANDARD OF LIVING.*

PLAN

Objectives

- **Learn about Harriet Tubman and her role in the Underground Railroad.**
- **Explore the purpose and history of the Underground Railroad.**
- **Understand the ways in which people resisted slavery.**
- **Analyze primary sources related to the Underground Railroad.**

Critical Thinking Skills for "The Underground Railroad"

- Make Connections
- Draw Conclusions
- Analyze Language Use
- Analyze Visuals
- Describe
- Make Inferences

Background for the Teacher

This American Story introduces students to the Underground Railroad and perhaps its most famous conductor, Harriet Tubman. Through an analysis of primary source material, fine art, and photographs, students will be immersed in the life of Harriet Tubman and the history of the Underground Railroad. Use this American Story to provide depth, context, and deeper understanding of the resistance to slavery and one way people escaped it.

This chapter, The Changing American Identity, analyzes the economic, political, and social changes that took place in early America due to such factors as immigration, religion, and the birth of reform movements. This American Story will serve as an entry point into two divisive issues of the era—slavery and the abolition movement—and how they contributed to bringing about the nation's Civil War.

History Notebook

Encourage students to complete the American Story page for Chapter 13 in their History Notebooks as they read.

Note to the Teacher

Introduce this American Story after the class has engaged with the content in Section 3.1.

AMERICAN STORIES | NATIONAL GEOGRAPHIC

"I think slavery is the next thing to hell."
—Harriet Tubman

CRITICAL VIEWING African-American artist Jacob Lawrence captured the spirit of the Underground Railroad in his moody, nighttime painting called *Forward Together*. Harriet Tubman is believed to be the figure wearing the red cloak on the right. How many other people can you find in the painting?

THE UNDERGROUND RAILROAD

The Changing American Identity **425**

INTRODUCE & ENGAGE

Discuss Ways to Support Change

Ask students what they would do about an unjust law. Have them think about what they would do to change that law. Would they:

• Work through politics to change the law?

• Actively break the law?

• Peacefully protest the law?

Encourage students to explain why they would take their chosen action and if they think it would be successful at ending the unjust policy. After the discussion, tell students they are going to read an American Story about Harriet Tubman and how she worked with the Underground Railroad to help many enslaved African Americans escape to freedom.

K-W-L Chart

Provide each student with a blank four-column K-W-L Chart. In the first column, have students list the following topics: Slavery, Underground Railroad, Harriet Tubman. Next have students complete the second and third columns with what they already know about each topic and questions they would like to have answered as they read the American Story. Finally, as students read, allow time for them to complete the K-W-L Chart with what they learned about each topic.

Create a Secret Code

Ask students if they've used a secret code to share information with a friend. Tell students to imagine they will be creating symbols to convey secret information to help runaway slaves escape into freedom. As a class, brainstorm what information would be most useful in helping people. Then have students create a pattern or symbol that could be used to pass along that information. Have volunteers share their symbols with the class and explain their meanings. Tell students they will be reading about code words that operators of the Underground Railroad used to share information and about quilt patterns that may have conveyed information to help enslaved people find safe paths to freedom.

CRITICAL VIEWING Answers will vary. Possible response: There are 13 or 14 other people in the painting. It's difficult to tell exactly because the figures are hidden in the shapes of the trees. The artist may have been making the point that escaped slaves had to remain well hidden to make it to freedom.

Life On the Run

To flee the South and head north, escapees relied on the unchanging position of the North Star, the knowledge that moss grows on the north face of trees, and maps provided by abolitionists and previous travelers. Safe houses provided occasional meals, baths, and lodging, but freedom seekers often traveled under the darkness of night, foraging plants and hunting meat in the forest. The knowledge of plants as medicine also proved to be particularly useful during the long journey. Wild echinacea protected the immune system, and mint aided digestion.

Slavery and Freedom in Maryland

Harriet Tubman grew up in Maryland, where the line between freedom and slavery was often complicated. Her father Ben was freed at age 45, but, with limited employment and living options, he continued working for his former owners. His wife and children remained slaves. Harriet grew up surrounded by a large extended family, some of whom were free, others enslaved. This was not unusual in Maryland. By 1810, the state was home to the largest free black population in the country, and it was common for both free and enslaved African Americans to form communities and meet to worship and socialize. Harriet met her husband John in this way. Even though John was free, his and Harriet's children would have been slaves, as the mother determined a child's status.

The Fugitive Slave Act

In 1850 the United States government passed the Fugitive Slave Act, which made it a federal offense to assist or hide escaped enslaved persons and called for heavy fines and jail time for violators. Prior to the act, enslaved persons who reached a northern free state were essentially safe. After passage of the act, many slaveholders pursued escaped enslaved people into northern states to return them to the South. This law was bitterly opposed in parts of the North, such as in Boston, where the recapture and arrest of Anthony Burns resulted in riots and protests. Escapees traveling the Underground Railroad had to make it all the way to Canada before they could experience true freedom.

CRITICAL VIEWING Answers will vary. Possible response: Photographs were probably rarely taken, so people dressed in their best clothing and were carefully posed. Tubman's expression is serious, so people must not have smiled when being photographed. It was probably easier not to smile in order to hold a pose for the long exposures required in early photography.

AMERICAN STORIES

"When I found I had crossed that line, I looked at my hands to see if I was the same person. There was such a glory over everything; the sun came like gold through trees, and over the fields, and I felt like I was in Heaven."

—Harriet Tubman

CRITICAL VIEWING Based on details in this photograph, what would you infer about photographic practices in the late 1800s?

If you didn't know better,

you might think the Underground Railroad was similar to a city subway. In reality, this amazing railroad never had a single mile of track. In the years before the Civil War, the Underground Railroad was a path to freedom for enslaved African Americans, and its most famous conductor was Harriet Tubman.

Tubman was born into slavery with a different name—Araminta Ross—around 1822 in Dorchester County, Maryland. Minty, as she was called, was first put to work at five years old. By the time she was seven years old, she was cleaning her master's house and taking care of the family's baby. Throughout her childhood and youth, Minty was forced to do difficult jobs, both indoors and out in the fields. She was poorly fed and often beaten by her masters. However, hard work and cruel punishments never crushed Minty's independent nature.

In 1844, Minty married John Tubman, a free black man living in Maryland. Despite her marriage to a free man, she remained enslaved. That meant she could be sold to another owner far from her husband, possibly in the South where conditions for slaves were even worse.

In 1849, Minty learned that she might be sold, so she resolved to flee to Pennsylvania, the free state north of Maryland. As part of her escape, she changed her name to Harriet Tubman. Harriet was her mother's name; Tubman, of course, was her husband's. John Tubman chose to stay in Dorchester County, so Harriet was left to make the risky journey to freedom on her own.

One of the people who helped Tubman escape was a Quaker woman. As you have read, Quakers believed that all people, regardless of skin color, were created equal and that slavery was wrong. This unnamed woman sheltered Tubman for a night and helped her enter the Underground Railroad.

A DIFFERENT KIND OF RAILROAD

The Underground Railroad had no trains, nor was it a single path to freedom. Instead, it was a network of ways that enslaved people could escape to the northern states or Canada. An Underground Railroad "station" was a home or other building in which escaped slaves could take shelter and hide. "Conductors" risked their lives to guide groups of fugitive slaves on the perilous trek from the South and help them navigate the railroad's hidden network.

Because the Underground Railroad operated in deep secrecy, nobody knows exactly how many enslaved people it brought to freedom. One estimate is that around 100,000 people made their way to freedom and safety via the Underground Railroad between 1810 and 1860. Although there were some white supporters of the Underground Railroad, such as the Quakers, free African Americans in the North played the most active role in operating the Underground Railroad. And one of them was Harriet Tubman.

SINGING TO FREEDOM

Escaping slaves needed a secret way to communicate with each other and their conductors. Often they passed messages through songs with a religious theme, called spirituals. Singing while they worked was a tradition among enslaved people, so owners did not suspect an escape was underway when they heard them singing. Harriet Tubman told her biographer that she used the spirituals "Go Down Moses" and "Bound for the Promised Land" to signal to groups of fugitives when they should take cover and when it was safe to come out. "Wade in the Water" was another spiritual used by conductors to communicate with their groups. It was an instruction to jump into a river or stream to shake off possible pursuers.

PRIMARY SOURCE

Wade in the Water. God's gonna trouble the water.
Who are those children all dressed in Red?
God's gonna trouble the water.
Must be the ones that Moses led.
God's gonna trouble the water.

Who are those children all dressed in White?
God's gonna trouble the water.
Must be the ones of the Israelites.
God's gonna trouble the water.

Who are those children all dressed in Blue?
God's gonna trouble the water.
Must be the ones that made it through.
God's gonna trouble the water.

Chorus: *Wade in the Water, wade in the water children.*

THE CODE OF THE RAILROAD

The Underground Railroad used code words to conceal its operations from slave catchers. Several of the code words had their origins in the Bible. Moses—Harriet Tubman's code name—was especially appropriate, because she had a deep faith.

GOSPEL TRAIN the Underground Railroad	**HEAVEN** Canada, freedom
STATION home or other building where slaves could take shelter and hide	**BUNDLES OF WOOD** a group of fugitives that was expected at a station
STATION MASTER person who owned a station and told fugitives how to get to the next station	**STOCKHOLDER** person who donated money, food, or clothing to help the escaping slaves
AGENT person who planned the courses of escapes and contacted the helpers	**LOAD OF POTATOES** fugitives hidden under fruits or vegetables in a farm wagon
MOSES Harriet Tubman (in the Bible, prophet who helped the Israelites escape slavery in Egypt)	**RIVER JORDAN** the Ohio River (a river in Southwest Asia, mentioned in the Bible)

427

TEACH

Guided Discussion

1. **Analyze Language Use** Have students read the quote from Harriet Tubman. Instruct them to think about the meaning of Tubman's words and what they can infer about her reaction to her situation. **ASK:** How does Harriet Tubman's choice of words convey her reaction to reaching freedom? *(She is overwhelmed with happiness as illustrated by her use of the words* glory, gold, *and* heaven.*)*

2. **Draw Conclusions** Why was "Wade in the Water" an appropriate song used by escaping slaves and conductors to communicate with each other? *(Enslaved people traditionally sang spirituals while working, so it would not be unusual for owners to hear this song being sung. "Wade in the Water" was particularly appropriate because it instructed slaves to hide in the water until it was safe to pass.)*

Make Connections

Engage in a class discussion about the role of religion in the Underground Railroad and the abolition movement. Many of the conductors were Quakers, and some of the code words were biblical in origin. Tell students to read and then discuss the codes used on the Underground Railroad. **ASK:** Why were the code words *bundles of wood* and *stockholder* appropriate? *(Answers will vary. Possible response: Comparing the escaped slaves to wood, a valuable raw material in the South, suggests that those who helped, or stockholders, were investing in something of value by helping people reach freedom.)*

Active Options

On Your Feet: Four Corners Assign students to one of four corners in the room, labeled Getting Directions, Identifying Safe Houses, Getting Supplies, and Avoiding Capture. Instruct each group to brainstorm methods by which they could communicate this information to escaping slaves on the Underground Railroad and then to choose the two methods they like best. Once groups have made their choices, ask them to explain the choices to the class.

NG Learning Framework: Investigate U.S. Currency

ATTITUDE Curiosity

KNOWLEDGE Our Human Story

After reading and discussing the feature Harriet On the $20, have groups of students use online sources to investigate the process by which subjects are selected for representation on U.S. currency. Tell students to use government websites (.gov) to locate information about the guidelines for selecting subjects and designs. Ask groups to prepare a brief report on the process and then make their own unanimous selection of a candidate for inclusion on U.S. currency. Invite a representative from each group to present and give reasons for their selection to the class.

WRITE ABOUT HISTORY

Compare to Present Day To help students make connections between the American Story and their own life, have them write a short essay about a person they consider to be a present-day Harriet Tubman. For this essay, ask students to choose a person—one they know in person, someone famous, or even a fictional character—and explain how this person is similar to Harriet Tubman. Students might include comparisons of Tubman's traits, such as courage and determination, with the person they select.

CRITICAL VIEWING Harriet Tubman cared deeply about the lives of her fellow African Americans. She dedicated her life to helping those often forgotten by society. Even after the end of slavery, she continued working to help African Americans, from raising money for schools to caring for the elderly.

THINK ABOUT IT

Answers will vary. Possible response: "Underground Railroad" is a good name because it was concealed from the eyes of the law but also ran across established routes. Today, a similar network might use airplanes and be called "Above-the-Radar Airlines."

AMERICAN STORIES

"I was the conductor of the Underground Railroad for eight years, and I can say what most conductors can't say — I never ran my train off the track and I never lost a passenger."

—Harriet Tubman

CRITICAL VIEWING After the Civil War, Harriet Tubman returned to the home she had purchased in Auburn, New York, and began the next phase of her work: caring for elderly African Americans. This photo from c. 1885 shows Tubman (far left) with friends, family members, and some of the aged people she cared for in Auburn. Based on this image and information you have read about Tubman, what conclusions can you draw about the nature of her work and the tasks that motivated and interested her?

CONDUCTOR AND HERO

Once she successfully made her own escape, Tubman decided her family and other slaves should also be free. For her, the best way to do that was to become a conductor herself.

Being a conductor required courage, intelligence, and nerves of steel. Slave catchers were always on the lookout for fugitives. Hired by slave owners to capture escaped slaves, the slave catchers, or bounty hunters as they were sometimes called, were not afraid to use force.

Quick thinking and tough, Tubman was up to the task. According to her own recollections, Tubman made around 19 trips back into Maryland and rescued up to 300 slaves, including her own parents. She gave directions to at least 70 more slaves so they could make their own escapes. Harriet Tubman was one of the most important faces of the Underground Railroad.

When the Civil War broke out, Tubman found other ways to help African Americans and support the Union Army. She worked as a nurse, aiding sick and wounded Union soldiers and escaped slaves. She also acted as spy, passing unnoticed in southern territory disguised as a slave. In 1863, she helped lead Union soldiers and African-American scouts in a raid on the Combahee River in South Carolina. The raid freed over 750 slaves.

After the Civil War, Tubman moved to Auburn, New York, but she did not retire from her mission to help others. She raised money to support schools for freed slaves in the South, participated in antislavery meetings, and campaigned for women's right to vote. She also established a home for elderly and disabled African Americans.

On March 10, 1913, Harriet Tubman died of pneumonia. She was buried in Fort Hill Cemetery in Auburn, New York, with full military honors.

THINK ABOUT IT

Do you think "Underground Railroad" is an appropriate name for the network to aid fugitive slaves? Why or why not? What might such a network be named today?

QUILTED CODES?

Some historians theorize quilts similar to these may have been used to communicate with enslaved people waiting to escape, or with those on the path to freedom. For example, a pattern like the Wagon Wheel could have been hung by seamstresses on plantations. A pattern like the Log Cabin could have been a welcome sight for weary travelers.

The patterns on this quilt may have been used as "maps" for escapees.

 The **WAGON WHEEL** design may have told escapees to pack for traveling. It also could have meant escapees would be hiding in a wagon with a secret compartment.

 Similar to the Wagon Wheel, the **TUMBLING BLOCKS** pattern might have announced a conductor was in the area, so it was time to pack for the journey.

 The **BOW TIE** design could have meant escapees should wear disguises when they journeyed on the Underground Railroad.

 The **BEAR PAW** pattern advised passengers to take a hidden path made by bear tracks, which would lead to water and food.

Like the Bow Tie pattern, the **BRITCHES**, or pants, pattern may have told escapees to dress like free people.

 The **CROSSROADS** block represented the city of Cleveland, Ohio, one of the main corridors of the Underground Railroad.

 The simple design of the **LOG CABIN** may have indicated that a home was a safe house, or a place where escapees could rest.

  The floral pattern of the **ROSE WREATH** might have been an announcement that someone had died along the journey to freedom.

HARRIET TUBMAN ON THE $20 BILL?

In 2016, Treasury Secretary Jacob Lew announced his plan to replace President Andrew Jackson with Harriet Tubman on the $20 bill in 2020. However, a new administration entered the White House in 2017. Its leaders suggested they might block the plan or place Tubman on a $2 bill.

The Changing American Identity **429**

Inclusion

Describe Lesson Visuals Pair visually challenged students with students who are not visually challenged. Ask the latter to help their partners experience the visuals by describing them and answering any questions the visually impaired student might have.

Gifted & Talented

Write Song Lyrics Explain that Harriet Tubman and other slaves not only used code as a way to communicate, but they also used songs to provide secret directions. Tell students to research and read about coded songs used during the operation of the Underground Railroad. Then have students create their own coded song lyrics that provide some sort of direction. Encourage students to present their lyrics to the class and see if the class can figure out the secret instructions.

See the Chapter Planner for more strategies for differentiation.

HISTORICAL THINKING

Ask and have students answer the following questions.

1. **READING CHECK** What was the purpose of the Underground Railroad?

2. **DESCRIBE** What hardships did Harriet Tubman face while enslaved?

3. **MAKE INFERENCES** Why did the Underground Railroad operate in secrecy?

ANSWERS

1. The Underground Railroad was a network of safe passages that enslaved people used to escape from the South and reach freedom in free states and Canada.

2. She was subjected to insufficient food, hard work, and severe punishment. She could have been sold and forced to move away from family and friends at any time.

3. Participants in the Underground Railroad were breaking the law and had to operate secretly to avoid being caught.

The Lure of America

Imagine sleeping in a small bed in a cramped room on a ship bound for New York City. The sea is rough. You try to ignore how sick you feel. Instead, you think about the new life you will make in America.

MAIN IDEA In the mid-1800s, millions of people from around the world left their homelands and moved to the United States.

PUSH AND PULL

When groups of people decide to move to a new country, they consider two types of reasons for the move. Some reasons push, or encourage people to **emigrate**, or leave their home countries. Other reasons pull, or encourage people to **immigrate**, or move to another country. Together, these reasons are known as **push-pull factors**.

Throughout history, crop failures, overpopulation, religious persecution, and wars have pushed people from their homelands. Immigrants usually chose to move to countries with plenty of land to farm, a better economy, and freedoms that appealed to them. For example, the Pilgrims' disagreements with the Church of England pushed them to leave England. Available land, the chance to earn a living, and the opportunity to practice their religion freely pulled them to North America. In every century that has followed, the promise of a better life has pulled immigrants to the United States from around the world.

Between 1840 and 1870, more than 7.5 million immigrants came to the United States. That's more people than the total U.S. population in 1810. Wars in Europe acted as a push factor on the people there. At the same time, the United States continued to exert pull factors on people experiencing hardship across the oceans.

LOOKING FOR OPPORTUNITIES

As you have read, in 1848, word spread in newspapers around the world that miners had discovered gold in California. Many Chinese men emigrated from China, in hopes of finding work in the American West.

Chinese men weren't the only people to immigrate to the United States or its territories to build new lives. Immigrants from northern Europe—including Britain, Ireland, Germany, and Scandinavia—also traveled across the ocean alone or with their families. Their journeys were often difficult. Many immigrants could only afford to travel in **steerage**, a small, confined space between the main decks of the ship. Steerage class was an inexpensive way to travel. However, it was crowded and dark, with almost no comforts. Steerage passengers had to bring mattresses, cooking pots, and even their own food for the voyage. Travelers in steerage class also dealt with rats, lice, and fleas during the journey. Seasickness and other illnesses made the area smelly, unpleasant, and unsanitary. Disease could spread rapidly, which was a problem because any illness put immigrants at risk for rejection when they reached the United States.

As new industries expanded in the northeastern United States, immigrants became an important source of labor. They arrived ready to take whatever work they could find in order to survive. The many job opportunities and the established immigrant population of large American cities encouraged many newcomers to stay in the city of their arrival. In fact, New York City had a large immigration center, called Castle Garden, which accepted new immigrants into the country. Immigrants joined with others from their home countries, and they established neighborhoods where people shared similar customs and traditions and spoke the same language. These neighborhoods grew and became vibrant parts of American culture.

The United States welcomed immigrants throughout the 19th and 20th centuries. Some immigrants decided to uproot their families because they hoped for new opportunities. Others wanted to escape a bleak future, or simply to feed their families.

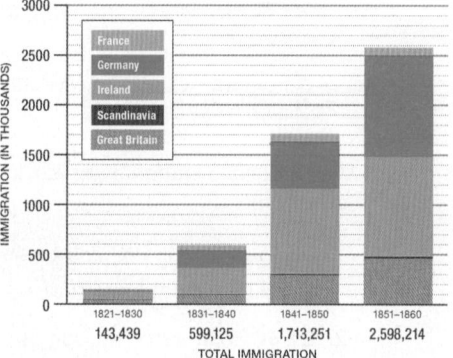

European Immigration to the United States, 1821–1860

IMMIGRATION (IN THOUSANDS)

Legend:
- France
- Germany
- Ireland
- Scandinavia
- Great Britain

	1821–1830	1831–1840	1841–1850	1851–1860
TOTAL IMMIGRATION	143,439	599,125	1,713,251	2,598,214

Source: Department of Homeland Security

CRITICAL VIEWING An Irish man in Dublin, Ireland, scours a poster advertising voyages to New York City in this lithograph by T.H. Maguire titled *Outward Bound*, c. 1840–1860. What details do you notice that indicate why he might be interested in leaving Ireland?

HISTORICAL THINKING

1. **READING CHECK** Name two push-pull factors that drove mass immigration in the mid-1800s.

2. **ANALYZE GRAPHS** According to the graph, when did the largest number of Irish immigrants move to the United States?

3. **SYNTHESIZE** How do push factors and pull factors work together?

PLAN

Objective

Analyze factors that drew immigrants to the United States during the mid-1800s.

Critical Thinking Skills for Lesson 1.1

- Identify Main Ideas and Details
- Monitor Comprehension
- Analyze Graphs
- Synthesize
- Make Predictions
- Make Inferences
- Draw Conclusions

Essential Question for Chapter 13

How did immigration and reform influence American identity? In the mid-1800s, more than 7.5 million people immigrated to the United States. Lesson 1.1 explores push and pull factors and the experiences of people whose journeys took them across oceans to the United States.

Background for the Teacher

While many people recognize the name Ellis Island and know about its role in American immigration history, fewer are familiar with Castle Garden. For more than 30 years, Castle Garden was the United States' official immigrant-processing center. Located at the southern tip of Manhattan Island, the building originally served as a fortification during the War of 1812. After the war, the city of New York took over the building and turned it into a public resort that included a restaurant and theater. In 1855, the building was reborn as the point of entry for new immigrants. From then until its closure in 1890, Castle Garden processed two-thirds of the immigrants coming to the United States—more than 8 million people. Today, it houses the ticket offices for another immigration landmark—the Statue of Liberty.

Consider Motivations

Introduce this lesson by asking students to consider why people move from one country to another. **ASK:** Why might people want to emigrate from the country of their birth? *(Possible responses: war; political unrest; lack of rights, jobs, or education)* Then have students consider some of the positive elements that draw immigrants to places like the United States. **ASK:** Can you think of a nation you would be willing to move to? *(Answers will vary.)* Ask student volunteers to share their responses and explain their reasoning. Tell students that in this lesson, they will learn about some of the factors that pushed people out of their countries and pulled them to the United States during the 1800s.

Guided Discussion

1. **Make Predictions** What changes did European and Asian immigration bring to the United States? *(Possible response: Immigrants introduced new languages, religions, and foods into the United States.)*

2. **Make Inferences** Why might U.S. immigration authorities reject immigrants who were ill? *(Possible response: The United States may have wanted to prevent the spread of contagious illnesses to its population. It may also have wanted to prioritize healthy people who could work and care for themselves.)*

Draw Conclusions

This lesson describes the kinds of communities and neighborhoods immigrants built after arriving in the United States. As a class, list some of the practical benefits of living in such a community. *(Possible response: Living around people who speak your language might help you navigate the city and find housing, jobs, and childcare.)* **ASK:** What emotional or cultural benefits might these neighborhoods provide for new immigrants? *(Communities like these might help with homesickness, keep cultural and religious practices alive, and make dealing with the challenges of immigration less stressful.)*

Active Options

On Your Feet: Card Responses Divide the class into two teams. Tell the first team to write a list of all of the push and pull factors mentioned in the lesson and then write one factor on each card. Each team member should hold one card. Tell the second team to make two cards, one reading "Push Factor" and the other reading "Pull Factor." Direct the first team to take turns holding up a card. The second team should respond with all members holding up the card that correctly identifies the factor as "Push" or "Pull." Keep track of correct answers and discuss incorrect responses as a class.

NG Learning Framework: Annotate a Map of Immigration

SKILLS Observation, Collaboration

KNOWLEDGE Our Human Story

Arrange students in small groups and provide them with blank world maps. Encourage students to use the text and chart as well as additional research to annotate the map to show European immigration to the United States between 1821 and 1860. Tell students to create a legend for their map that identifies different European countries by color. Then suggest that students work together to decide how to show which groups immigrated, when they immigrated, and where they landed. Invite groups to display their maps in the classroom.

Striving Readers

Identify Facts Have pairs conduct a Round Robin activity to review what they have learned in the lesson. Ask students to generate facts for 3–5 minutes. Finally, invite one student from each pair to share their responses. Write all the facts on the board.

Gifted & Talented

Analyze Statistics Tell students to conduct a short research project comparing immigration in the present-day United States to immigration in the mid-1800s. Tell students to use the text and several additional sources to find facts and statistics, focusing on factors such as country of origin, push-pull factors, gender, work experience, and education. Have students prepare a short presentation, including visual elements such as maps, graphs, or charts, to display their findings.

See the Chapter Planner for more strategies for differentiation.

ANSWERS

1. Push factors included wars in Europe and economic hardship. Pull factors included discovery of gold in California and growing industry in the northeastern United States.

2. The largest number of Irish immigrants arrived between 1851 and 1860.

3. Push factors give people reasons to leave their home countries. Pull factors draw those people to a new destination. The two work together because, without an appealing place to go, people might not be willing to leave their homes.

CRITICAL VIEWING Answers will vary. Possible response: The details such as the sack carrying his belongings, his tattered clothes, and the single coin in his hand, indicate that the man has been experiencing economic hardship in Ireland for a while.

1.2 From Different Countries

You can probably think of a time when you were assigned a tough or boring task you didn't want to do. For some immigrants, only the hardest, lowest-paid work was available when they arrived in their new country.

MAIN IDEA Many immigrants came to the United States to escape food shortages and political conflicts in their home countries.

ESCAPING DISEASE AND POVERTY

Between the 1830s and 1860s, Irish immigrants represented the largest number of newcomers to the United States. Most were poor farmers who had no opportunities to improve their lives in their homeland. For centuries, Britain had claimed sovereignty over Ireland, and many of the Irish were dissatisfied with the oppression of British rule. To make matters worse, the country was experiencing widespread starvation due to the Great Irish Famine. A **famine** is an extreme shortage of food. From 1845 to 1852, a plant disease called **blight** killed the country's entire potato crop. The famine was made worse by the system of farming imposed by the British, because British landlords took what little food the Irish were able to farm. Approximately 1 million people died before the famine was over. For these reasons, or push factors, Irish immigrants came to the United States in record numbers.

Opportunities for jobs and new beginnings were pull factors for many Irish immigrants. American business owners recruited Irish immigrants because they would work for lower wages than many American workers. While skilled workers such as carpenters or bakers could earn adequate wages, most Irish men were unskilled. They found jobs building railroads, digging canals, and loading cargo onto ships. The work was difficult, dangerous, and paid the lowest wages. For Irish women, unskilled labor meant **domestic service**, or housework in another person's home. Maids and kitchen servants received about a dollar a day in 1870, which was better pay than most factories offered. Plus, domestic service often included food and housing.

British immigrants didn't flee from famine, but they did hope to escape from the rigid British class system. Just as in Irish society, few opportunities existed for British farmers to avoid living in poverty. From their perspective, owning inexpensive and fertile American land was a chance at a whole new, and likely better, life.

When they arrived in the United States, most British and Irish immigrants wanted to **assimilate**, or become part of, their new country. But they also held on to their culture and traditions. In the neighborhoods where they lived close to each other, they formed groups and clubs and attended community dances, meals, and church services together. Preserving and maintaining many of their customs and traditions offered a relief from the strain of assimilation.

MOVING TO THE MIDWEST

Poverty and hunger were not the only push factors. Civil unrest, or open conflict within a society, also encouraged people to leave. For example, in the middle of the 19th century, areas in Germany experienced a series of revolutions. As a result, many Germans fled to the United States.

German immigrants differed in some ways from other groups of immigrants. One difference was that Germans held diverse religious beliefs. Most German immigrants were Protestant, many others were Catholic or Jewish. Also, unlike those who came to escape poverty and famine, many German immigrants were not poor and did not have to travel in steerage. They could afford to continue traveling after they arrived in the country, oftentimes choosing to settle in the farmland between the present-day states of Nebraska and Minnesota. So many of them settled in this region, in fact, that the area became known as the "German Belt."

Especially after the 1860s, immigrants from Sweden, Norway, and Denmark joined the Germans in the upper Midwest. The population of Sweden was growing, farmland was scarce, and the same potato blight that hit Ireland struck Sweden around 1868. Some Swedes and other Scandinavian immigrants sought land in the United States. Others came for the growing number of well-paid factory jobs in midwestern cities such as Chicago and Minneapolis. Immigration increased the population and enriched the culture of the United States, but not all Americans welcomed the newcomers.

Immigrants brought their possessions in large trunks. This handmade wooden trunk with rope handles belonged to a Swedish immigrant.

CRITICAL VIEWING In 1850, British artist Frederick Goodall painted *An Irish Eviction*. He drew upon his experience of traveling in Ireland during the famine. Landlords eager to rid their lands of destitute laborers and farmers evicted hundreds of thousands of families. What details in Goodall's painting capture the despair of evicted tenants during the famine?

HISTORICAL THINKING

1. **READING CHECK** What factors prompted people to emigrate from their home countries?

2. **SYNTHESIZE** What pull factor drew so many different groups to the United States between 1830 and 1860?

3. **MAKE GENERALIZATIONS** What kinds of choices could wealthier immigrants make once they arrived in the United States?

PLAN

Objective

Examine why many Europeans emigrated from their home countries in the 19th century.

Critical Thinking Skills for Lesson 1.2

- Identify Main Ideas and Details
- Monitor Comprehension
- Synthesize
- Make Generalizations
- Identify Problems and Solutions
- Make Predictions
- Analyze Visuals

Essential Question for Chapter 13

How did immigration and reform influence American identity? Many immigrants were escaping disease, poverty, and civil unrest. Lesson 1.2 discusses European and Scandinavian immigrants and the roles they took on in America.

Background for the Teacher

The fungus that caused the Great Irish Famine actually traveled from the United States to Ireland. The potato blight that destroyed years' worth of potato harvests was a strain of a pathogen called *Phytophthora infestans*, a water mold that most likely traveled to Europe in potatoes carried aboard ships from North America. The pathogen covered the leaves of potato plants with black splotches and turned the potatoes into an inedible mush.

Ireland was particularly vulnerable because Irish farmers grew only a few varieties of potato—varieties that were highly affected by the blight. In 2013, scientists took DNA samples from potato leaves preserved from the years of blight and were able to identify the exact strain that led to widespread starvation. Understanding how crop diseases evolve has helped scientists and farmers develop more disease-resistant crops.

Imagine a Cargo Trunk

Point out the photo of the trunk and read the caption aloud. **ASK:** Why do you think the Swedish family painted tulips on the trunk? *(Answers will vary. Students may suggest that tulips are associated with Sweden and other Scandinavian countries.)* Have students imagine that they are moving to a new country and have a similar trunk in which they would pack their belongings. **ASK:** What designs and decorations would you paint on or apply to your family trunk that would tell about your family? *(Answers will vary. Students may mention including the family name, initials, significant dates, photos, or depictions of events associated with their family history.)*

Guided Discussion

1. **Identify Problems and Solutions** If the British had wanted to prevent mass emigration from Ireland and Britain, how might they have done so? *(Possible response: By changing their landlord policies in Ireland, the British might have eased the famine and made it possible for people to stay. If they had made the class system less rigid, poor farmers and workers might have felt they could build better lives at home.)*

2. **Make Predictions** Based on the last sentence of the lesson, predict some of the reasons Americans might have had for not welcoming newcomers. *(Possible response: Americans may have disliked the extra competition for jobs, crowding caused by increased population, or the unfamiliar religious or cultural practices of immigrants.)*

More Information

Domestic Service The high demand for Irish domestic servants enabled many servant girls to choose their employer and negotiate terms. Financially, they did well, earning about 50 percent more than female Irish sales clerks and 25 percent more than female textile workers. Not having household expenses, they were able to send money to their relatives in Ireland.

Active Options

On Your Feet: Word Chain Arrange students in three lines. Hand a piece of paper to the first person in each line with one of these Key Vocabulary words from the text: *famine, assimilate, steerage.* The first student in line adds a word to the list that relates to the original term. Students pass the paper from person to person, each one adding a word or phrase they associate with the previously written word. Have a volunteer from each group read off the Word Chain and ask the rest of the class to listen for words that were used in more than one or any that may not connect correctly.

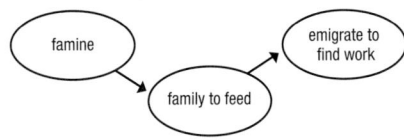

NG Learning Framework: Compare Famines as Push Factors

Curiosity, Responsibility

Collaboration

Arrange students in small groups and have them research famine as a push factor. Tell students to briefly research present-day famines and choose one to compare to the Irish famine. Instruct students to locate relevant data and statistics about changes in the two populations and where people immigrated. Ask students to present statistical information in charts or graphs and display them in a presentation to the class. After students' presentations, hold a discussion about famine as a push factor in different countries.

Inclusion

Monitor Comprehension Tell student pairs to read the lesson paragraph by paragraph. At the end of each paragraph, have students pause and complete the following sentences:

• This paragraph is about _____.

• One detail that stood out to me is _____.

• One thing I did not understand was _____.

• One unfamiliar word I want to look up is _____.

English Language Learners ELD

Use Sentence Stems Before reading, give students at the **Expanding** level the following sentence stems to complete as they read:

• Many immigrants came from Ireland because of a _____. *(famine)*

• In the United States, Irish immigrants often worked for low _____. *(wages)*

• Some people came from Germany because of civil _____. *(unrest)*

• Unlike other groups of immigrants, many German immigrants were not _____. *(poor)*

• Many German immigrants settled on farms in the _____. *(Midwest)*

See the Chapter Planner for more strategies for differentiation.

ANSWERS

1. Push factors such as civil unrest, famine, poverty, and lack of opportunities prompted people to emigrate from their countries.

2. Economic opportunities in industrial jobs and farming pulled many different groups to the United States in the mid-1800s.

3. Wealthier immigrants could afford to travel inland when they arrived, so they could choose a place to live based on their preferences, specific opportunities they may have had, and their ability to purchase land.

CRITICAL VIEWING Answers will vary. Possible response: The children look frightened, the woman is crying, and the man looks angry and grim. All these details suggest despair.

1.3 Central Park
New York City

On July 21, 1853, the New York State Legislature set aside more than 750 acres of land in the middle of Manhattan Island to establish America's first major landscaped park. Sensibly called "the Central Park," it was designed by architects and social reformers who believed that great parks would benefit public health and contribute to a "civil society." Central Park sparked the urban park movement, one of the most significant developments in 19th-century America. After several decades of disrepair and neglect, the park was restored during the late 1900s and early 2000s, and it has never been more beautiful, safe, and clean. It proudly represents the American ideals of great public spaces, health and wellness, and the preservation of nature within an urban setting. Which different physical features do you observe in the photo of Central Park?

CRITICAL VIEWING New Yorkers and visitors alike seek out Central Park, a natural refuge in "the city that never sleeps." The park's ponds, meadows, grassy hills, and rocky paths are a welcome break from the loud streets and towering buildings of the city. What does this photograph reveal about the types of activities people can do in Central Park?

434 CHAPTER 13

The Changing American Identity 435

PLAN

Objective
Learn about the history of New York City's Central Park in the heart of Manhattan.

Critical Thinking Skills for Lesson 1.3
- Analyze Visuals
- Make Connections
- Make Inferences
- Describe

Essential Question for Chapter 13
How did immigration and reform influence American identity? A growing population during the 1800s led to crowded, noisy conditions in many American cities. In some cities, social reformers and urban planners sought to create public green spaces for people who lived in cramped tenements or towering apartments. Lesson 1.3 introduces students to Central Park, a public space that has become an American icon.

Background for the Teacher
Central Park was the brainchild of poet William Cullen Bryant and landscape architect Andrew Jackson Downing. The city held a competition for the best park design, and the winning design came from British architect Calvert Vaux and an American named Frederick Law Olmsted. Olmsted had studied some engineering and written a book on English landscaping, but he was a journalist and not a working architect. His work with Vaux proved so successful, however, that from that point on he devoted his career to landscape architecture. Olmsted went on to design many of the United States' most famous public parks and spaces, including Belle Isle Park in Detroit, the grounds of the U.S. Capitol Building in Washington, D.C., and Chicago's Jackson Park, originally the home of the World's Columbian Exposition in 1893.

History Notebook
Encourage students to complete the American Places page for Chapter 13 in their History Notebooks as they read.

INTRODUCE & ENGAGE

Preview Using Visuals

Direct students' attention to the photograph of Central Park. **ASK:** What do you notice first about this photograph? *(Answers will vary.)* How would you describe the areas that surround the park? *(Answers may vary. Possible responses: extremely crowded, almost entirely made up of buildings)* Have students discuss why a park like the one shown might be very important to the people who live in the city around it. Then present students with a map showing Manhattan and have them locate Central Park. **ASK:** Why might people want, or not want, a large public space in this location? *(Possible responses: The central location would be easy for people to find. Some people might think the land would be more valuable as space for housing or businesses.)*

TEACH

Guided Discussion

1. **Make Inferences** Why might social reformers have expected public parks to contribute to a "civil society"? *(Possible responses: Public parks might help to reduce the stress of urban life, making people happier and more productive. Public parks might bring together people of different ages, races, and economic levels in a peaceful way.)*

2. **Describe** What type of environment does Central Park offer in the middle of New York City? *(Possible responses: The park is a relief from the loud and crowded city. The park offers a natural environment in the midst of buildings, busy streets, and concrete sidewalks.)*

American Places

New York City's Central Park is about half a mile wide and approximately 2.5 miles long, running from 110th Street on its north side to 59th Street on its south side. Within those boundaries, visitors will find a park designed to provide interesting views and activities wherever they go. In addition to the baseball diamonds visible in the photograph, the park is home to a theater, a zoo, and seasonal attractions such as an ice-skating rink.

Active Options

On Your Feet: Descriptive Words Distribute two sticky notes to each student. Then have students closely examine the photograph. Direct students to write one word or a short phrase describing Central Park on each sticky note. Tell students to place their notes on the board or a wall. As a class, discuss the posted descriptions and sort them into general categories such as appearance, size, or use.

NG Learning Framework: Investigate Olmsted's Spaces

ATTITUDE Curiosity

KNOWLEDGE Our Human Story

Invite students to choose one of Frederick Law Olmsted's spaces and prepare a short presentation discussing its history, present-day uses, and design. Encourage students to research Olmsted's work using library or online sources. Review using search terms effectively and assessing the credibility and accuracy of each source. Remind students that when they quote or paraphrase information or conclusions from a source, they should provide a citation for that source. Provide a standard format for citation and ask students to document their sources. Encourage students to incorporate maps, photographs, sketches, and other visual elements into their presentations.

DIFFERENTIATE

Striving Readers

Use a Detail Web Have students use a Detail Web like the one below to summarize information on New York City's Central Park. Direct students to exchange and discuss their web with a partner and add details they missed.

Pre-AP

Debate an Issue Engage students in a short discussion about the pros and cons of large public spaces like Central Park. Then organize students into pairs. Tell them to imagine they are on a mid-1800s city planning committee considering a proposal for the construction of a large, centrally located, public park. Half of the pairs will argue in support of the park's construction and half will argue against it. Allow students time to improve their arguments by researching 19th-century cities. Ask each pair to write their argument, including organized evidence and a concluding statement that supports their claim, and share it with the class.

See the Chapter Planner for more strategies for differentiation.

AMERICAN PLACES

Answers will vary. Students may note physical features such as trees, rocks, ponds, pathways, and lawns.

CRITICAL VIEWING Answers will vary. Students may point out that the paths look as though they are marked for biking and walking (and some even for driving); people may be able to sail or fish on the ponds; baseball diamonds suggest that people can play ball there.

1.4 Opposition to Immigration

Some people feel afraid when they face something new or unfamiliar. Their fear may make them lash out toward others. In the mid-1800s, some Americans reacted negatively to the arrival of new immigrants.

MAIN IDEA Some native-born Americans tried to restrict immigrants' rights because they feared change and worried about the financial impact of immigration.

FEAR AND JUDGMENT

The numbers of immigrants coming to the United States alarmed some native-born Americans, or Americans who were born in the United States. They feared that the influence of new languages, different religious practices, and new cultural traditions might change the culture of the United States. Their fears inspired many **prejudices**, or broad judgments about groups of people that are not based on reason or fact.

Because many immigrants accepted jobs for very little pay, some native-born Americans believed their own wages would be reduced as a result. Newspaper articles reporting the failed rebellions in Germany gave some Americans the impression that immigrants would try to inspire revolution in the United States. They also worried that local governments would increase taxes and strain public services in order to care for so many poor immigrants. As one American writer put it, "They increase our taxes, eat our bread, and encumber [clog] our streets."

Some elected officials proposed passing **nativist** laws, or laws that favored native-born Americans over immigrants, often focusing on religion. Most native-born Americans were Protestant. Some Protestants formed prejudices against Catholic immigrants entering the country—especially the Irish. Protestants feared that Catholics held an allegiance to a foreign power because the leader of their church, the Pope, reigned over the Catholic Church from Italy. At times, violence erupted between Protestants and Catholics. Anti-Catholic mobs burned a convent, or a dwelling for nuns, near Boston in 1834. Prejudice against Catholics also influenced immigration laws.

EXCLUDING IMMIGRANTS

During the 1840s, nativists organized groups to oppose immigration. One of these groups called itself the American Party. Its leaders told new members to say "I know nothing" if anyone asked what the party did, so people began calling the American Party the **Know-Nothing party**. The party proposed laws that prevented immigrants, especially Irish Catholics, from voting and holding public office. They also wanted to require immigrants to live in the country for 21 years before they could become citizens.

Membership in the party continued to grow. In 1855, 43 members of Congress belonged to the Know-Nothing party. But Congress refused to pass most of the party's proposed legislation, and party members' involvement in violence and corruption in various states made the party increasingly unpopular. By 1860, differing views on slavery broke up the party, but that was not the end of nativist ideas in the United States.

HISTORICAL THINKING

1. **READING CHECK** What issues increased American prejudice toward immigrants in the mid-1800s?

2. **ANALYZE VISUALS** In which different ways do these two political cartoons portray immigrants, native-born Americans, and the political process?

3. **EVALUATE** What role did religion play in nativist prejudices?

These two cartoons from the 1850s reflect nativist attitudes toward immigrants. The first cartoon, published in a Know-Nothing newspaper, portrays an Irish and a German immigrant running away from a voting site with the ballot box, which they have stolen in the midst of a brawl. They are "clothed" in barrels that held whiskey and beer.

The second cartoon, from *Harper's Weekly*, shows a voter being pulled in two directions. On the left, a nativist politician attempts to persuade the voter. On the right, an Irish politician tries to do the same. What different characterizations of immigrant voters are shown in these cartoons?

PLAN

Objective

Examine the causes and consequences of the rise of nativism in the United States.

Critical Thinking Skills for Lesson 1.4

- Identify Main Ideas and Details
- Monitor Comprehension
- Analyze Visuals
- Evaluate
- Categorize
- Draw Conclusions
- Form and Support Opinions

Essential Question for Chapter 13

How did immigration and reform influence American identity? The influx of immigrants to the United States brought new languages and cultures. Lesson 1.4 explores the nativist attitude toward immigrants during the mid-1800s and its impact on the nation's laws and political parties.

Background for the Teacher

Fear of the potential political impact of new immigrants was not unique to the mid-1800s. In 1798, John Adams signed The Naturalization Act, which extended the residency requirement for new citizens to fourteen years, making it more difficult for Democratic-Republicans to attract immigrant votes. Similarly, nativist groups in the mid-1800s feared new Irish and German voters would become an influential bloc. Because the Constitution left decisions on voting rights to the states, requirements for suffrage varied widely. As a result, immigrants often obtained the right to vote (especially in state and local elections) very quickly. In some states, they could even vote as long as they merely intended to become citizens. Suffrage only applied to white males; women and African Americans could not vote.

INTRODUCE & ENGAGE

Preview Terms

Write *nativist* on the board. Ask students to raise their hands if they have heard the term before. **ASK:** What does it often mean when a word ends in *-ist*? *(Possible response: a person who does or believes in something)* What might *nativist* mean? *(Answers will vary. Students may infer that the word has something to do with supporting or believing in natives.)* What does it mean to be a native? *(Answers will vary. Students may identify natives as people born in a place or as the original inhabitants of a place.)* Tell students that in this lesson, they will be examining why nativists started a political movement in the 1800s.

TEACH

Guided Discussion

1. **Categorize** Sort each of the nativists' objections to immigration into one of the following categories: political, economic, or cultural. Some objections may fall into more than one category. *(Answers will vary. Possible response: political: objections to Catholics' allegiance to the Pope, fears that German immigrants would start revolutions; economic: fears of increased taxes and lower wages; cultural: dislike of unfamiliar religious practices, fears of Catholic allegiance to the Pope)*

2. **Draw Conclusions** What does the request that members respond "I know nothing" when asked about their activities suggest about the American Party? *(Possible response: It suggests that the American Party was paranoid about people outside of it or felt that people would object to its activities.)*

Form and Support Opinions

ASK: Was the Know-Nothing party an effective political movement? Explain why or why not, using evidence from the text to support your opinion. *(Possible responses: The party was not effective because Congress would not pass most of its laws, and its members gave it a reputation for corruption and violence. The party was effective because it brought nativist views to the public and had 43 members in Congress.)*

Active Options

On Your Feet: Three-Step Interview Assign students to pair groups. One student interviews the other on the following question: How did nativist groups plan to solve what they saw as problems with immigration? Then direct students to reverse roles. Finally, ask each student to share the results of the interview with the class.

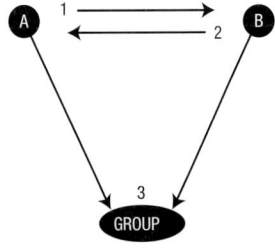

NG Learning Framework: Analyze Political Cartoons

ATTITUDE Curiosity

SKILL Collaboration

Encourage students to learn more about attitudes surrounding immigration in the 19th century by analyzing political cartoons. Students can research using library or online sources. The Library of Congress website is a particularly good resource. Tell students to choose two or three cartoons to research, identifying the artist, the year, and the immigration issue each cartoon represents. Invite students to present their chosen cartoons and analysis of the artists' viewpoints to the class.

DIFFERENTIATE

Inclusion

Describe Details Pair students who are visually impaired with students who are not. Ask the latter students to describe the details in each of the political cartoons that accompany this lesson before working together to answer the Critical Viewing question.

English Language Learners

Identify Context Clues To encourage students to use context clues for comprehension, pair students at the **Emerging** level with English-proficient students. Instruct pairs to read the lesson aloud with students at the **Emerging** level signaling when they encounter words or sentences that are confusing. Prompt English-proficient students to point out context clues to help their partners understand the meanings of unfamiliar words. Students may also work together to restate challenging sentences in their own words.

See the Chapter Planner for more strategies for differentiation.

HISTORICAL THINKING

ANSWERS

1. The large numbers of immigrants, the issue of low wages, and differences in religion all contributed to American prejudice toward immigrants during the mid-1800s.

2. The political cartoons portray immigrants as heavy drinkers (in the top cartoon) and corrupt (in both cartoons). The bottom cartoon portrays native-born Americans as respectable and well-dressed, trying to persuade a voter without bribery. Both portray the political process as full of conflict and corruption.

3. Most nativists, who were Protestant, feared the Pope would have too much influence over Catholic immigrants.

CRITICAL VIEWING The top cartoon characterizes immigrant voters as heavy drinkers and brawlers who will steal votes. The bottom cartoon characterizes them as being of a lower class than nativists and possibly willing to accept or offer a bribe.

2.1 The Second Great Awakening

Being part of a large gathering can be exciting and inspiring. In the mid-1800s, some religious events were so popular that they drew huge crowds, much like a music festival or sporting event does today.

MAIN IDEA In the early 19th century, new ideas about religion inspired people to reform problems in society.

A RETURN TO THE CHURCH

As you've read, the Enlightenment was a period in American history when political philosophers applied reason and logic to religion and society. New concepts about equality and government sparked the American Revolution. At the same time, scientific knowledge was expanding. The rush of new ideas caused many people to become skeptical of the power churches seemed to hold. Influenced by the Enlightenment, some people established new religions, such as Unitarianism, that combined the practical ideas of the Enlightenment with the teachings of the Bible.

In the 1790s, some Christians reexamined their religious practices. Many began to believe they should have a direct and emotional relationship with God. This movement is called the **Second Great Awakening**. To revive, or reawaken, religious enthusiasm, many Methodists and Baptists, among other denominations, organized **revival meetings**, or informal religious events held outdoors or in tents. Revivals became very popular because they drew people out of church buildings and into nature. Some preachers drew thousands of spectators. Audience members cried, shook, or rolled on the ground as preachers delivered sermons. Often, preachers **evangelized**, or spread the Christian gospel by delivering dramatic sermons and sharing personal experiences.

Many new believers joined Methodist and Baptist congregations as a result of the revivals. At these events, people felt a sense of freedom in worshiping with their friends and neighbors outside the formal organization of the church.

REFORMING SOCIAL PROBLEMS

One of the most prominent figures of the Second Great Awakening was a former lawyer and religious skeptic, or person who questions something others believe to be true, named **Charles Grandison Finney**. Finney became a fervent, or eager, Christian and preacher after his law studies led him to read and examine the Bible. He used his experience in arguing court cases to persuade others to adopt his beliefs.

Finney was as passionate about social reform as he was about his faith. He believed a just society had the responsibility to improve the lives of all its members. He delivered lively sermons calling for the end of slavery, the improvement of education for all citizens, and women's rights. Many other revivalist preachers shared Finney's views. As a result, religious groups actively promoted social reform causes.

The **temperance movement** was one part of this social reform effort. The word *temperance* means "moderation" or "self-restraint." This movement's proponents crusaded against the overuse of alcohol, which had become an integral part of daily life. On balance, 19th-century Americans consumed a lot of alcohol. In 1830, the average American drank seven gallons of alcohol per year—three times the average amount consumed today. Farmers earned extra money by making whiskey with leftover crops, local economies relied on alcohol sales, and drinking during working hours was commonplace. However, both public drunkenness and alcoholism had become significant social problems.

CRITICAL VIEWING In 1839, J. Maze Burbank captured the fervor of a revival in his painting *Religious Camp Meeting*. Revival meetings were also known as "camp meetings." Most were located on the frontier where churches had yet to be built. How does this painting convey what people who attended this revival meeting might have experienced?

Temperance reformers approached the issue from different angles. Some wanted to curb the use of alcohol because they feared drunkenness was a threat to social order and economic prosperity. Others, motivated by the fervor of the Second Great Awakening, saw drinking as a sin. Some reformers wanted to protect women and children from neglect and mistreatment resulting from their husbands' and fathers' abuse of alcohol. Finally, medical professionals wanted Americans to limit their alcohol use for health reasons.

The reformers also looked beyond alcohol-related issues. They called attention to poor living conditions in overcrowded cities and advocated for working children's rights in factories and mills. Many, including California pioneer Annie Bidwell, also promoted free public education and voting rights for women.

HISTORICAL THINKING

1. **READING CHECK** What was the Second Great Awakening?

2. **DESCRIBE** How did Charles Grandison Finney play a significant role in society?

3. **COMPARE AND CONTRAST** What were the different ways in which reformers approached alcohol consumption in the 19th century?

PLAN

Objective

Analyze the connection between 19th-century religious and social reform movements.

Critical Thinking Skills for Lesson 2.1

- Identify Main Ideas and Details
- Monitor Comprehension
- Describe
- Compare and Contrast
- Make Connections
- Make Generalizations

Essential Question for Chapter 13

How did immigration and reform influence American identity? Reform movements of the 19th century led to shifts in American attitudes and behavior. Lesson 2.1 explores origins of reforms and their ties to the Second Great Awakening.

Background for the Teacher

Although Charles Grandison Finney was a popular preacher, he drew fire from some mainstream denominations. He was criticized for such matters as the emotionalism of his meetings and for his "New Measures," which included holding meetings over several days instead of just on Sundays, allowing women to pray in meetings that men also attended, using music to set the mood at the meetings, and urging converts to register their decisions publicly. Among Finney's admirers, however, were abolitionists who invited him to teach at Oberlin College in Ohio. Finney eventually became the school's president, and it was in that position that he advocated most strongly for social reforms.

INTRODUCE & ENGAGE

Make a List

Ensure that students understand the meaning of the term "reform movement." **ASK:** What reform movements can you think of, whether from history or today? *(Answers will vary. Possible responses: environmental movement, minimum wage movement, Tea Party movement, Occupy movement)* List students' examples on the board. **ASK:** Do these movements have anything in common? *(Answers will vary. Students may suggest that all movements aim to change conditions or solve a problem.)* Tell students that in this lesson, they will explore how reforms aimed to improve social problems.

TEACH

Guided Discussion

1. **Make Connections** In what ways did the religious practices of the Second Great Awakening reflect Enlightenment ideals? *(New religious groups and practices emphasized individual experience and each person's power to have a relationship with God instead of the traditional church power structure.)*

2. **Make Generalizations** What values were supported by reformers who emerged from the Second Great Awakening? Support your statement with text evidence. *(Reformers such as Charles Grandison Finney supported abolition, women's rights, temperance, and education. This suggests that reformers who came out of the Second Great Awakening valued equality, health, and the protection and care of children.)*

More Information

Key Vocabulary Etymology The word *evangelize* (and its noun form, *evangelism*) comes from a Greek verb that means "to announce good news." Evangelists of the Second Great Awakening saw themselves as announcers of the good news that people could have a personal relationship with God. As explained in this lesson, the Second Great Awakening helped promote social reform as well. **ASK:** What relationship might there be between having an awakening of faith and becoming involved in reform causes? *(Answers will vary. Possible response: An awakened faith might lead a person to care more about other people and to want to help people who are suffering.)*

Active Options

On Your Feet: Tell Me More Organize students into four teams. Assign each team one of the following topics: the Second Great Awakening, revival meetings, Charles Grandison Finney, or the temperance movement. Ask team members to list as many facts about their topic as possible. Then have each team stand up in turn. Direct the rest of the class to call out "Tell me more about [topic]!" Standing team members then share one fact each about their topic. Rotate to the next team and repeat until all teams have shared several facts.

NG Learning Framework: Research Temperance Activism

| ATTITUDE | Curiosity |
| SKILL | Communication |

Tell students to draw on several sources to research the history of temperance activism in a particular state. To allow for multiple avenues of exploration, direct students to work in groups to generate a question they can research in order to create a short presentation on a chosen aspect of temperance activism. Students might answer such questions as the following: Who were the key activists? Where did the movement start and why? What actions did activists engaged in? What factors affected the success or failure of the movement? Invite students to present their findings to the class.

DIFFERENTIATE

Striving Readers

Understand Main Ideas Check understanding of the main ideas in the lesson by asking students to complete either/or statements.

- The Enlightenment [challenged or supported] the power held by many churches.
- Revival meetings were [formal or informal] religious gatherings.
- Charles Grandison Finney preached [for or against] abolition and women's rights.
- The word *temperance* refers to [limiting or increasing] one's use of alcohol.
- Many temperance activists [considered or did not consider] alcohol abuse a moral issue.

Gifted & Talented

Write an Editorial Tell students to imagine they live in the 19th century in a state that is considering legislation to ban alcohol. Have them write a short editorial, either supporting or opposing the ban, from the viewpoint of one of the following: a doctor, farmer, factory owner, or restaurant owner. Remind students to support their arguments with evidence from the text and additional research they might do. Challenge students who oppose the ban to propose alternative solutions to one or more of the problems outlined by the temperance movement.

See the Chapter Planner for more strategies for differentiation.

HISTORICAL THINKING

ANSWERS

1. It was a religious movement that drew on Enlightenment thinking. It included new religions, such as Unitarianism, and a shift in Christian practices toward a more direct relationship with God.

2. Charles Grandison Finney spoke out about social reform and inspired other preachers to do the same.

3. Reformers in the 19th century approached alcohol consumption as a medical problem, a cause of poverty and abuse, and a sin.

CRITICAL VIEWING Answers will vary. Students may note the portrayal of a range of experiences, such as people holding their hands in the air as if worshiping, lying down covering their eyes as if overcome by emotion, and turned away from or ignoring the preacher as if disinterested.

2.2 Educating and Advocating

When you see a situation that seems unjust, you want to do something about it. Likewise, positive changes in society have often started with one brave person raising his or her voice.

MAIN IDEA Reform movements in the 1830s and 1840s led to improvements in the treatment of mental illness, the prison system, and public education.

EDUCATION FOR ALL

If you were female, African American, or an immigrant, it was hard to get a good education in the United States during the early 19th century. To address the lack of education for girls and women, a number of women established schools for them, including Emma Willard, who founded the Troy Female Seminary in 1821, and Mary Lyon, who founded Mount Holyoke Female Seminary in 1837. Schools and colleges for girls and women were a step forward, but women's literacy rates were still half those of men. Further, most young people who attended school, whether male or female, came from wealthy families. Many lower-income, working-class, and immigrant children could not afford formal education. They chose work over school to help support their families.

African-American children faced other obstacles in education as well. Laws barred enslaved African Americans from studying at all, and free African Americans could only attend certain schools. **Prudence Crandall**, an educator from Connecticut, took a bold step to address racism in education. When she opened the Canterbury School for young African-American girls in 1831, her small Connecticut town became the center of controversy. Crandall was arrested several times for unlicensed instruction, the school's water well was poisoned, and townspeople threw eggs and stones at her students. Crandall's school closed in 1834 after a violent mob broke windows and ransacked the classrooms. Clearly, racism against African Americans was not confined to the South.

Individuals and groups worked to correct these injustices and to reform the education system as a whole. The clear solution was to offer every American child a public education. Religious and women's groups campaigned for a public investment in education, or free public schools that would be funded by the collection of property taxes and managed by the local government. This education reform was known as the **common school movement**.

In 1837, **Horace Mann** put the ideas of the common school movement into action. Mann wanted the public education system to be rooted in good citizenship and moral education that would prepare students for society and the workforce. His crusade helped establish a public education system in Massachusetts for students of all social classes, genders, races, ethnicities, and faiths. Soon, other states followed. The Northeast took the lead in establishing free public schools, but the South lagged behind the rest of the nation for several decades.

REFORMING INSTITUTIONS

In the early 1800s, people knew little about what caused mental illnesses or how to treat them. A mental illness is a long-term disorder, such as depression or addiction, that alters one's personality or way of thinking. Those who suffered from such ailments were often feared and misunderstood. Many mentally ill patients ended up living in prisons or poorhouses.

A shocking visit to a prison inspired **Louis Dwight**, a minister from Massachusetts, to help the mentally ill. While visiting inmates, Dwight recognized the need to remove people with mental illnesses from prisons and place them in hospitals called **asylums**. Because of Dwight's efforts, Massachusetts General Hospital opened the state's first asylum at Worchester in 1833.

Dorothea Dix, a teacher from Maine, joined Dwight's cause in 1841 after witnessing mentally ill women shivering in an unheated jail cell. The authorities tried to convince her that, because they were mentally ill, the women could not feel the cold. After that visit, Dix toured hundreds of prisons, jails, and poorhouses. She persuaded state legislators to develop tax-supported systems of care. Her influence helped open more asylums.

At the same time, Dwight, Dix, and others called for improvements in the treatment of prisoners. They believed it was better to rehabilitate inmates, or restore them to health, instead of putting them in solitary confinement, where they were locked up with no human contact. Reformers cited tragedies from the past to make their case.

For instance, in 1821, wardens of Auburn Prison in New York had placed 80 prisoners into solitary confinement for long periods of time. Some prisoners were confined for their entire sentence, which caused many to become mentally ill. In the weeks following their release, many prisoners committed suicide. Soon after, Auburn Prison eliminated solitary confinement for prisoners. The Auburn Prison's change in policies supported the reformers' insistence that solitary confinement damaged prisoners. Reformers went on to fight for prison libraries and literacy classes, programs that can still be found in prisons today.

CRITICAL VIEWING Primers were small books used in schools to teach beginning reading and arithmetic. This primer was printed on cloth and sewn together by a Boston printer around 1860. What do you notice about the illustrations used in this primer?

Q is for Quarters, guarded with care.

R is Retreat, may you never be there.

S is a Sailor, who respected will be.

T is a Traitor, that was hung on a tree.

HISTORICAL THINKING

1. **READING CHECK** How did the common school movement address inequalities in education?

2. **MAKE CONNECTIONS** What connections do you see between the school system Horace Mann helped establish and today's schools?

3. **DRAW CONCLUSIONS** How did American reformers help mentally ill and imprisoned people in the 19th century?

PLAN

Objective

Explore reforms aimed at children, women, African Americans, and the institutionalized.

Critical Thinking Skills for Lesson 2.2

• Identify Main Ideas and Details
• Monitor Comprehension
• Make Connections
• Draw Conclusions
• Describe
• Make Inferences

Essential Question for Chapter 13

How did immigration and reform influence American identity? Reform movements of the 1800s introduced many of our present-day American values. Lesson 2.2 describes how reform movements emphasized education, equality, and humane treatment for all.

Background for the Teacher

The antebellum South lagged behind the North in education and other reforms because of regional differences that became more defined during the 1800s. As the North industrialized, its cities grew, drawing in poor workers from rural areas and immigrant workers from abroad. Concerns about the concentration of poverty, lack of education, poor and crowded housing conditions, and alcohol abuse inspired many of the 19th century's reform movements. The South, which had not industrialized, did not share these urban concerns. Southerners continued to educate children privately or in church schools. Additionally, the strong connection between many reform movements and the abolition movement led some in the South to reject them. As a result, the South did not benefit from advances made in the North.

INTRODUCE & ENGAGE

Education Quickwrite

Give students a few minutes to write a response to this question: How should an education benefit me? Invite volunteers to share their responses. **ASK:** How can education help you in the workplace? *(Possible response: It can give me the skills or information I need to do a certain job.)* How else can education help you? *(Possible response: It can teach me how to think critically and how to work with others.)* Tell students that in this lesson, they will learn how educational reforms benefited Americans.

TEACH

Guided Discussion

1. **Describe** What obstacles did African Americans face when attempting to get an education? *(Enslaved African Americans were forbidden to get an education at all, while free African Americans could only attend certain schools. Educators who opened schools for African-American children faced controversy, terrorism, and violence.)*

2. **Draw Conclusions** Why did reformers like Horace Mann think public education was the clear solution to education inequality in the United States? *(Possible response: A public school system could admit any student, regardless of race, religion, or economic status. It would be free, so poor students could attend.)*

Make Inferences

Tell students to recall what they have learned about the population, politics, and economy of the South. **ASK:** What distinguished the South from the rest of the nation that might have caused the region to lag behind in public education? *(Answers will vary. Possible responses: The region may not have felt the need for literacy and public education since its economy was based primarily on agriculture rather than industry. Because of its importance to the economy of the South, maintaining a labor force of enslaved African Americans was probably a more pressing issue than public education in the early and mid-1800s.)*

Active Options

On Your Feet: Numbered Heads Organize students into groups of four and assign each student a number. Tell students to think about and discuss as a group the following question: What ideas from the reform movements discussed in this lesson are still common in the United States today? Then call out a number and have the student with that number from each group share the group's answer with the class.

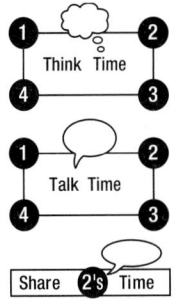

NG Learning Framework: Create a Time Line

ATTITUDE	Responsibility

SKILL	Communication

The work of reformers such as Dorothea Dix and Lewis Dwight was part of a long, ongoing effort to protect the rights and opportunities of people with disabilities. Encourage students to use library and online sources to create a time line of critical movements, laws, and events (such as the passage of the Americans with Disabilities Act) related to disability rights in the United States. Time lines should include short annotations explaining the basic details and significance of each event. Invite students to present their time lines to the class.

DIFFERENTIATE

English Language Learners

Use Word Maps Pair students at the **Emerging** and **Expanding** levels with students at the **Bridging** level. Tell students to build a Word Map for three words they struggle with. Have groups trade Word Maps and review.

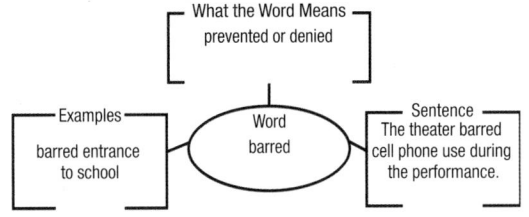

Pre-AP

Write an Argument Direct students to research how young people lived in the 1830s and analyze how public education likely affected their lives. Students should use their research to write an argument for or against present-day public education as a public investment. Tell students to include evidence from their research to support their claim. Have students share their arguments with the class to generate discussion of education as a public investment.

See the Chapter Planner for more strategies for differentiation.

HISTORICAL THINKING

ANSWERS

1. The common school movement favored admitting students who had previously been denied an education, including African Americans, women, and immigrants.

2. Like Horace Mann's common schools, public schools today admit all students regardless of gender, race, ethnicity, or class, and charge no tuition. Property taxes still pay for schools, and local governments still manage them.

3. Reformers called for asylums for mentally ill patients and the rehabilitation of imprisoned people. They fought for prison reforms such as banning solitary confinement and providing literacy classes and libraries.

CRITICAL VIEWING Answers will vary. Students may notice that the letters on the page are all styled like American flags or that all of the rhymes and illustrations instill patriotic values.

2.3 Fighting for Better Pay

The phrase "strength in numbers" applies to many situations. During the 1830s and 1840s, American workers in many different industries realized that groups were stronger than individuals.

MAIN IDEA During the mid-1800s, American workers banded together and demanded better, safer labor conditions.

Leather Shoes
These leather baby shoes were produced by a Massachusetts shoe factory during the mid-19th century.

LONG DAYS, HARD WORK

By the early 19th century, factory work had become widespread. Working conditions in most factories, however, were far from ideal.

Most factory workers toiled 10 to 14 hours per day, 6 days a week, no matter if they were elderly or 10 years old. They operated large and dangerous machines without safety gear. Many machine operators were maimed or killed on the job. If workers were injured during their shifts, they received no payment or paid time off to recover, and they often lost their jobs.

At the same time, the costs of living, such as rent and groceries, continually rose. Workers wanted better wages. They also wanted their employers to be held responsible for accidents on the job. Individually, workers knew they had little power to change their working conditions. In the 1820s, workers began to organize **labor unions**, or groups that advocate for workers rights and protections. Together, unionized workers had a much more powerful voice in demanding better pay and safer work environments.

A mill worker poses for a photograph around 1850. Many children worked in the textile mills, including this young girl. Her job may have been to straighten strands of cotton as they moved into the loom.

Craftsmen such as carpenters and shoemakers also formed organizations called **craft unions**. Craft unions differed from labor unions because most craftsmen did not work in factories, and they had learned a specialized skill. However, their objectives were the same: better wages and working conditions.

Labor and craft unions made progress in improving workplace conditions. But then in 1836, an economic depression hit the nation. Within a year, many factory workers and craftsmen were unemployed. Those fortunate enough to have jobs saw their wages cut by almost half. Displaced and underpaid workers were willing to take on whatever work they could find, and factory and shop owners knew it. As the economy struggled, the power of labor and craft unions decreased.

A WIN FOR WORKERS

When the economy improved in the early 1840s, unions reorganized. **Sarah Bagley**, a millworker in Lowell, Massachusetts, led the way for women's labor unions. She and her female coworkers worked up to 14 hours a day for lower wages than their male counterparts. In 1844, they joined together and established the **Lowell Female Labor Reform Association (LFLRA)**.

Bagley gave speeches denouncing her employer for not acknowledging the issues the mill workers faced daily. After she stopped working at the mill, she published stories about her experiences. Some politicians disliked her honesty and her critical view of mill owners. But her efforts improved the lives of women in the workforce.

Under the leadership of Bagley, the LFLRA appealed to the Massachusetts legislature to enact laws for shorter workdays. The legislature refused to confront mill owners, who agreed to shorten the workday to 13 hours only after public opinion pressured them into doing so in 1847. The LFLRA continued to advocate for shorter workdays. In 1853, mill owners cut the workday to 11 hours.

The actions of the LFLRA inspired other unions in the Northeast. In 1860, a shoe manufacturer in Massachusetts refused the shoemaker unions' request for wage increases. The shoemakers fought back by organizing a strike, or work stoppage. The workers walked out of the factory in protest. Their bold action encouraged similar strikes across New England. Ultimately, 20,000 shoemakers in 25 towns participated. As a result, most of the employers met the unions' demands. The successful strike emboldened the unions, which grew in strength and numbers and soon began to organize on a national level. Even so, Massachusetts did not pass a 10-hour workday law until 1874.

HISTORICAL THINKING

1. **READING CHECK** Why did factory workers and craftsmen form unions?

2. **SYNTHESIZE** Describe how and why the power of labor unions diminished in the 1830s.

3. **MAKE GENERALIZATIONS** What was work life like for 19th-century laborers?

PLAN

Objective
Learn about the rise of organized labor during the 1800s.

Critical Thinking Skills for Lesson 2.3
- Identify Main Ideas and Details
- Monitor Comprehension
- Synthesize
- Make Generalizations
- Draw Conclusions
- Evaluate
- Make Connections

Essential Question for Chapter 13
How did immigration and reform influence American identity? Reform movements pushed to improve many facets of society. Lesson 2.3 explores the influence of labor unions on working conditions and wages during the 1800s.

Background for the Teacher
Only sparse information about Sarah George Bagley survives outside of her brief time as a prominent figure in the early labor movements in New England. However, she did have a few ventures after her split with the Lowell Female Labor Reform Association. In 1846, she took a position as superintendent of the Lowell telegraph office, making her one of the first female telegraph operators in the nation. She left the job in 1848 and returned, for unknown reasons, to work in the mills before traveling throughout New England lecturing on health care, women's rights, and working conditions. After her marriage in 1850, Bagley and her husband moved to Albany, New York, and operated a health care clinic for women and children. They manufactured herbal medicines in the 1860s and eventually moved to Brooklyn Heights, New York. Bagley died around 1883, but the exact date is uncertain.

INTRODUCE & ENGAGE

Define a Good Job

ASK: What elements make up a job? *(Answers will vary. Most students should note that a job requires doing something for payment.)* **ASK:** What makes a job good or bad? *(Answers will vary. Possible responses: A good job pays well, offers interesting work, and has safe working conditions. A bad job does not pay enough for how difficult the work is or how unpleasant the conditions are.)* Guide students in a discussion about what workers can do when their working conditions aren't safe or their wages aren't fair. Explain that this lesson is about early efforts by workers to address these two issues.

TEACH

Guided Discussion

1. **Draw Conclusions** Why might manufacturing workers have felt they had little individual power? *(Possible response: Factory workers probably feared they would lose their jobs if they complained about their pay or working conditions. An individual worker had no power to change the situation other than to quit or be fired.)*

2. **Evaluate** Which labor union tactics were most effective in getting workers' demands met? *(Possible response: Based on the text, the strikes in Massachusetts were more effective than other tactics because, in addition to persuading employers to meet strikers' demands, the strikes inspired other unions to strike for similar benefits.)*

Make Connections

Point out the photograph of the millworker and read the caption. **ASK:** What can you infer about widespread attitudes toward children during the 1830s and 1840s? *(Answers will vary. Possible response: People saw children as having similar responsibilities as adults.)* Ask students to recall what they read about the educational reform efforts of Horace Mann. **ASK:** Why might the movement toward mandatory free public schooling have been so important? *(Possible response: In addition to creating a better-educated population, it also removed children from dangerous factory jobs and long work hours.)* **ASK:** Who might have objected to public schooling for all children and why? *(Possible responses: Parents who needed children's income and factory owners who wanted the cheapest possible labor would have wanted to keep children in the workforce.)*

Active Options

On Your Feet: Fishbowl Arrange students in two groups. Direct Group 1 to sit in a close circle and discuss the conditions that led to the formation of labor and craft unions during the 1800s. Tell Group 2 to form a circle around Group 1 and take notes to summarize the discussion. Then have groups switch positions and repeat the activity.

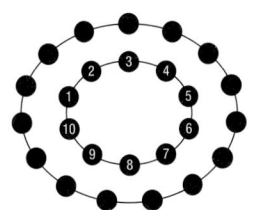

NG Learning Framework: Interpret Child Labor Laws

ATTITUDE Responsibility

SKILL Problem-Solving

Tell students that one result of the reform era was a changing attitude toward child workers. Direct students to government websites to research current child labor laws in their state. Point out that the state may have separate laws for different types of work, such as work on farms or in family businesses. Assign students to write a short report to answer the following questions: Are you currently allowed to work in your state? What jobs could you get? Whose permission would you need?

DIFFERENTIATE

Striving Readers

Complete a Cause-and-Effect Map Reinforce students' understanding of the relationships between events by having them work in pairs to complete the Cause-and-Effect Map below.

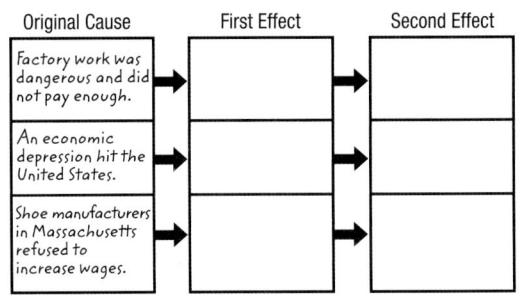

Inclusion

Review Concepts Model creating summaries of key concepts from the subsection Long Days, Hard Work:

- Factory workers worked long hours, had low wages, and were often injured by machinery.

- Workers formed labor unions and craft unions to try to fix the problems with their jobs.

- Unions had less power during a bad economy and more power during a good economy.

Have pairs create summaries of each paragraph in the subsection A Win for Workers.

See the Chapter Planner for more strategies for differentiation.

HISTORICAL THINKING

ANSWERS

1. Individual factory workers and craftsmen had little power to change their working conditions, long hours, and low pay, so they organized to act as one body.

2. The power of labor unions diminished in the 1830s when an economic depression made jobs hard to find and people were willing to work for lower wages rather than be jobless. This meant that employers now had more power than the unions.

3. Laborers were often underpaid and worked in hard, dangerous jobs. They were not respected or cared for by their employers and had very little individual power.

2.4 Creative Expression

In every civilization, writers and artists ask important questions and help shape and define culture and identity. In the 19th century, American literature and art exploded with creativity.

MAIN IDEA Nineteenth-century American writers and artists helped define what it means to be an American.

AMERICAN AUTHORS ON THE RISE

As reformers advocated for solutions to social problems, writers in the 19th century set out to shape the American identity. Some used the events of American history as their setting. Others reflected social and intellectual movements.

Washington Irving's 1820 story "Rip Van Winkle" was a comment on the dramatic change the American Revolution had brought about. **Henry Wadsworth Longfellow's** poem "Paul Revere's Ride" created an American legend by fictionalizing and bringing to life one of the most exciting events of the Revolution. **James Fenimore Cooper** wrote the first American novel in 1823. *The Pioneers* described life for ordinary Americans on the New York frontier in the late 1700s, before the nation began its westward expansion.

Some 19th-century authors wrote about conflict and individualism. **Nathaniel Hawthorne** wrote during the mid-1800s, but his novel, *The Scarlet Letter*, focused on love and guilt among the Puritans of Massachusetts in the 1640s. **Herman Melville's** *Moby Dick* told the story of Captain Ahab pursuing the great white whale. The novel was Melville's allegory for Americans' reckless westward expansion and obsession with wealth.

One especially rich source of inspiration for some 19th-century writers was **transcendentalism**, an intellectual and social movement of the mid-1800s led by **Ralph Waldo Emerson**. The movement's goal was to transcend, or rise above, the expectations society placed on people. Transcendentalists thought that people should be self-reliant and connected to the natural world. Emerson's book *Nature* reflected these values.

Walt Whitman first published *Leaves of Grass* in 1855. One of the best-known poems in the collection is "Song of Myself," Whitman's celebration of individualism.

PRIMARY SOURCE

I CELEBRATE myself, and sing myself,
And what I assume you shall assume,
For every atom belonging to me as good
    belongs to you.
. . .
I too am not a bit tamed, I too am
    untranslatable,
I sound my barbaric yawp over the roofs of
    the world.

—from "Song of Myself," by Walt Whitman, 1855

One of Emerson's students, **Henry David Thoreau**, lived alone in a simple cabin by Walden Pond for 26 months to write his memoir, *Walden*. **Louisa May Alcott**, the daughter of Bronson Alcott, a transcendentalist, grew up in the company of Emerson and Thoreau. Alcott wrote about family relationships and growing up as a female in the 19th century—the focus of her most successful work, *Little Women*.

Walt Whitman and **Emily Dickinson** forged new paths in poetry by breaking traditional rules. Poetry of the period was flowery and romantic, but Whitman and Dickinson wrote honestly and directly. In his most important work, *Leaves of Grass*, Whitman used free verse, or poetry that doesn't rhyme or depend upon a strict meter. Emily Dickinson also wrote poems that ignored established rules about rhyme and rhythm. She shared them with so few people that even her family members were not aware of all her poems until after her death.

Transcendentalists supported women's rights, abolition, and other social reforms. Organized religion, restrictive laws and social institutions, and industrialization inhibited individuals from fully expressing themselves. Certain authors gave a voice to those who were sometimes overlooked. Whitman, for example, wrote openly about love as well as same-sex relationships. His work also celebrated laborers, immigrants, and people who were all part of the growing diversity of the nation.

PAINTING AMERICAN BEAUTY

Nineteenth-century visual artists also shaped American identity through landscape paintings that celebrated the diverse beauty of the United States. **Thomas Cole** was one of the early leaders of an art movement known as the **Hudson River School**. In the 1820s, Cole hiked in New York's Catskill Mountains and painted magnificent scenes of the Hudson River Valley. Hudson River School painters became known for their landscapes, which often highlighted people's relationship with nature.

Asher B. Durand and **Frederic Edwin Church**, friends of Cole, were two artists to emerge from the Hudson River School. Cole inspired Durand to switch from painting portraits to painting landscapes. Church painted natural phenomena such as waterfalls, volcanoes, icebergs, and rainbows. A German immigrant and artist named **Albert Bierstadt** painted panoramic scenes of the Rocky Mountains, the Grand Canyon, and the Yosemite Valley using Hudson River School styles.

🏛 Crystal Bridges Museum of American Art, Bentonville, Arkansas

In 1848, Asher B. Durand completed *Kindred Spirits*, which he painted as a tribute to the friendship of painter Thomas Cole and poet William Cullen Bryant. The two artists are overlooking Fawns Leap and the Kaaterskill Falls—two sites in the Catskill Mountains of New York that cannot actually be viewed at the same time. Throughout their artistic lives, all three men—Durand, Cole, and Bryant—used the beauty of nature as their inspiration.

CRITICAL VIEWING Why might Durand have created a scene that brought two separate sites together?

HISTORICAL THINKING

1. **READING CHECK** What historical events influenced American literature and art in the 19th century?

2. **DESCRIBE** In what ways did common themes in artistic expression reveal the ideals and aspirations of the new nation?

3. **SYNTHESIZE** How did writers, visual artists, and transcendental thinkers shape American identity in the 19th century?

PLAN

Objective

Discuss how 19th-century American art and literature reflected ideals of the new nation.

Critical Thinking Skills for Lesson 2.4

- Identify Main Ideas and Details
- Monitor Comprehension
- Describe
- Synthesize
- Analyze Language Use
- Draw Conclusions

Essential Question for Chapter 13

How did immigration and reform influence American identity? The early 19th century saw the emergence of new American ideals and aspirations. Lesson 2.4 explores writers and artists who shaped, reflected, and challenged the still-forming American identity.

Background for the Teacher

Born in 1819, Walt Whitman spent the early part of his life as a teacher and a journalist, writing poetry in his spare time. He self-published the first of nine versions of *Leaves of Grass* in 1855, bringing his new poetic style to a mostly unenthused public. In his poems, he called on Americans to embrace liberty, nature, and the connections among people. Ralph Waldo Emerson admired the work, but many of Whitman's contemporaries criticized it, particularly for its frank depictions of sex and nature and its rejection of poetic rules. Whitman's later poetry, collected in *Drum-Taps* and *Sequel to Drum-Taps*, reflected various emotions surrounding the Civil War, from patriotism, horror, and—upon the assassination of Abraham Lincoln—deep grief.

INTRODUCE & ENGAGE

Preview Using Visuals

Ask students to suggest words and phrases to describe the mood of the painting in this lesson. *(Answers will vary. Possible responses: peaceful, hopeful, inspiring)* **ASK:** Based on the painting, how do you think American artists viewed the American landscape? *(Possible response: They admired and idealized it.)* Then read the caption aloud. **ASK:** What can you infer about the American art world in the 19th century from this information? *(Answers will vary. Possible response: Writers and painters had close relationships and shared similar views on nature.)*

TEACH

Guided Discussion

1. **Analyze Language Use** How does the word *untranslatable* help you understand Walt Whitman's view of individualism? *(Possible response: The word "untranslatable" suggests that there is something in each person that is unique and cannot be understood by others, and that is what makes a person valuable as an individual.)*

2. **Draw Conclusions** How did ideas and events combine to produce the American art and literature of the 19th century? *(Possible response: Ideas about liberty, the individual, and nature combined to form artistic movements that glorified America as a place of incredible natural beauty and great freedom. This new sense of liberty was generated by America's separation from Europe and expansion into new territories.)*

🏛 Virtual Museum Visit

The Crystal Bridges Museum of American Art in Bentonville, Arkansas, houses American works of art. Founded in 2005, the museum's mission is "to welcome all to celebrate the American spirit in a setting that unites the power of art with the beauty of nature." Expansive windows and glass-enclosed bridges allow viewing of the museum's natural setting alongside its art. Access the museum's website and locate works by painters mentioned in the lesson. Ask students to point out similarities and differences in the artists' styles and subjects. Tell groups to explore the site on their own and choose a work from a different artist. Invite groups to present the work to the class, explaining why it fits in with the works they have already viewed.

Active Options

On Your Feet: Team Word Webbing Organize students into groups of three or four to discuss the themes, people, and important works of American art and literature in the 19th century. Arrange teams around a large sheet of paper and give each team member a different color marker or pencil. Encourage students to add their ideas to the part of the page closest to them. On your signal, tell students to rotate the page and add new ideas to the area in front of them. When the page has rotated back to its original position, tell groups to summarize their ideas and share their webs with the class.

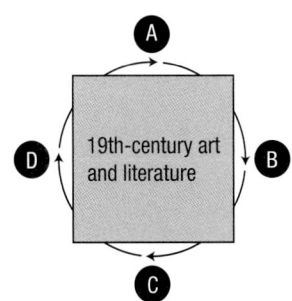

NG Learning Framework: Create a Documentary

SKILL Collaboration

KNOWLEDGE Our Human Story

Arrange students into small groups. Tell students to choose one writer or artist discussed in the lesson and use additional resources to research his or her life and work. Instruct students to assign and share tasks to prepare a brief documentary that includes excerpts from the person's most famous works and information about his or her important life events and achievements. Students may choose to present their documentary in person to the class or record and play a video of it.

DIFFERENTIATE

English Language Learners   ELD

Describe a Visual Ask students at the **Expanding** and **Bridging** levels to assist students at the **Emerging** level in brainstorming words that describe the painting. Tell students to use the words to write one or two complete sentences about the painting and then discuss their sentences with their partners as they check for spelling, grammar, and clarity.

Gifted & Talented

Experience Early American Music Explain that students will use library and online sources to research 19th-century American music. Direct students to identify the era's most popular or important composers and locate recordings of their work. Ask students to choose one recording and prepare a short presentation in which they play all or part of the recording for the class and explain how it reflects an aspect of the 19th-century American identity.

See the Chapter Planner for more strategies for differentiation.

HISTORICAL THINKING

ANSWERS

1. The American Revolution and westward expansion helped to shape American art and literature in the 19th century.

2. The individual rising above social expectations, the pursuit of wealth or greatness, and the breaking of tradition reflected the national ideals of independence and self-reliance and the national aspiration toward growth.

3. Writers, visual artists, and transcendental thinkers of the 19th century created narratives and images portraying a self-reliant American in touch with nature and not bound to tradition or established rules.

CRITICAL VIEWING Answers will vary. Students may suggest that Durand combined two impressive natural sites to create visual drama and reinforce the theme of kindred spirits, with the sites representing his two friends' work and ideas.

3.1 The Abolition Movement

Reformers in the 19th century didn't have cell phones or social media to spread the word. Instead, they wrote letters and newspaper articles, gave speeches, and even sent secret messages to communicate their ideas.

MAIN IDEA Brave individuals spoke out about the injustices of slavery in an attempt to end the institution in the United States.

William Lloyd Garrison published the weekly newspaper *The Liberator* for 35 years, beginning in 1831. The masthead, or title area, depicts enslaved people before and after liberation.

SPEAKING OUT AGAINST SLAVERY

Many reformers who spoke out about social issues were also **abolitionists**, or people who wanted to end slavery. However, some Americans did not agree with abolitionists. Southerners and northerners alike considered abolitionists and their ideas too radical—as well as dangerous, un-Christian, and even unpatriotic.

In 1831, an abolitionist named **William Lloyd Garrison** published the first issue of his newspaper, *The Liberator*. His paper called for the immediate **emancipation**, or freedom, for all enslaved people. **Wendell Phillips**, a wealthy attorney, soon allied with Garrison. He wrote for *The Liberator* and contributed financially to the movement.

In 1839, former President John Quincy Adams argued that the ideals of the Declaration of Independence applied to all people. He called for a constitutional amendment to make every child born in the United States after July 4, 1842, free. He also proposed that no new state could enter the Union if it allowed slavery, but neither idea became law.

The Iron Collar
One of the most horrifying tools slave owners subjected enslaved people to was the iron collar. They used this device to punish slaves, especially for attempts to escape. The prongs made it impossible to lie down to rest or sleep. They also caught on bushes and underbrush, making it hard to run. Abolitionists pointed to this kind of cruelty in demanding an end to slavery.

Two sisters, **Sarah Grimké** and **Angelina Grimké**, witnessed the cruelty of slavery firsthand while growing up on their parents' plantation in South Carolina. When the sisters took up the abolitionist cause, as some southerners did, their family disowned them. These determined women joined the Quakers and traveled the country giving speeches in support of abolition. In 1863, Angelina Grimké married fellow abolitionist **Theodore Weld**, a trainer and recruiter for the American Anti-Slavery Society.

STANDING UP FOR FREEDOM

Both free and enslaved African Americans actively challenged the existence of slavery. **David Walker** was a free African-American man who wrote for *Freedom's Journal*, an abolitionist newspaper. As the owner of a secondhand clothing store in Boston in the 1820s, Walker printed antislavery pamphlets and sewed them into the pockets of clothing he sold to sailors. Walker hoped the pamphlets would reach people in many ports, especially those in the South. One of his pamphlets, entitled *An Appeal to the Coloured Citizens of the World*, became one of the most radical antislavery documents of the movement, and southern states reacted by prohibiting the circulation of abolitionist literature.

Another African-American abolitionist was **Charles Remond**, who was born to a wealthy, free African-American family in Salem, Massachusetts. He worked as an agent of the Massachusetts Anti-Slavery Society, and he traveled and spoke with Garrison, Phillips, and others.

Robert Purvis was the son of a wealthy cotton broker and a free African-American woman. When he was nine years old, his family moved from South Carolina to Philadelphia. As an adult, Purvis became very active in abolition and in the **Underground Railroad**. In fact, he and his wife, **Harriet Forten**, housed escapees in their home, also known as the Purvis "safe house."

At the beginning of the chapter, you read about the courageous work of **Harriet Tubman**. Other African-American women played significant roles in the abolitionist movement as well. **Harriet Jacobs**, born into slavery, escaped to New York in 1842. She published *Incidents in the Life of a Slave Girl* in 1861, considered one of the most extensive slave narratives written by a woman.

Sojourner Truth was also a powerful abolitionist voice. Like Tubman and Jacobs, Truth was born into slavery. When she told a white neighbor that her owner broke his promise to release her, the neighbor paid the owner $20 for her and then set her free. She changed her enslaved name, Isabella, to Sojourner Truth. She captivated people with her simple, clear message: that all people deserved the same rights as white men.

HISTORICAL THINKING

1. **READING CHECK** How did abolitionists work to end slavery?

2. **DRAW CONCLUSIONS** Why did most Americans consider abolitionists' ideas radical?

3. **ANALYZE VISUALS** What details do you notice in the photo, and how might those—and the photo itself—have impacted people who saw it in the mid-1800s?

PLAN

Objective
Describe the contributions of important leaders to the abolition movement.

Critical Thinking Skills for Lesson 3.1
- Identify Main Ideas and Details
- Monitor Comprehension
- Draw Conclusions
- Analyze Visuals
- Make Inferences
- Compare and Contrast

Essential Question for Chapter 13
How did immigration and reform influence American identity? The reform movements of the 19th century sought to solve social problems. Lesson 3.1 describes how influential abolitionists worked to end slavery.

Background for the Teacher

Long before the South began the secession movement that triggered the Civil War, abolitionist William Lloyd Garrison called for secession of the North. An abolitionist since age 25, Garrison originally supported the colonization movement, a plan under which African Americans would be freed but sent to settle in Africa. After spending more time with African-American abolitionists, however, Garrison decided to reject colonization. In his years running *The Liberator*, Garrison's opinions became increasingly radical, culminating in his call for abolitionists to reject all institutions—such as churches and political parties—which had long tolerated slavery and for northern states to secede from the slave-holding South. In 1865, shortly after the issuance of the Emancipation Proclamation, Garrison published his last issue of *The Liberator*, stating that "my vocation as an abolitionist is ended."

Preview Using Visuals

Direct students' attention to the masthead of *The Liberator* and read the caption aloud. **ASK:** What does the verb *liberate* mean? *(to free)* What is the difference between the left and right side of the illustration? *(The left side depicts people in slavery and the right shows them living in freedom.)* Tell students that in this lesson they will learn how abolitionists worked to end slavery.

TEACH

Guided Discussion

1. **Make Inferences** Why did abolitionists focus their efforts on pamphlets and newspapers such as *The Liberator*? *(Newspapers and pamphlets were a way of spreading information and ideas to large numbers of people. Pamphlets could also be distributed in secret, as with David Walker's pamphlets.)*

2. **Compare and Contrast** In what ways were free African-American abolitionists from the North and the South different? *(Some free African Americans from the North who worked as abolitionists were born into freedom and never directly experienced slavery. On the other hand, many of the free African-American abolitionists from the South had once been enslaved.)*

More Information

Reaction to the Abolition Movement Groups against abolition destroyed antislavery pamphlets and newsletters sent through the mail and threatened those who helped to distribute them with capture or injury. Prominent abolitionists, such as William Lloyd Garrison, and publishers, such as Elijah P. Lovejoy, were physically attacked. Some, such as Lovejoy, were murdered. **ASK:** Why might anti-abolition violence focus on printed works and their writers or publishers? *(Possible response: Anti-abolitionists may have wanted to stop abolitionist ideas from spreading, especially into the hands of enslaved people.)* Have students discuss other possible reasons for violent opposition.

Active Options

On Your Feet: Create a Quiz Organize students into two teams. Tell each team to write one True-False question about each individual mentioned in the lesson (12 questions total). Then have each team answer the other team's questions. Review the answers to the quizzes as a class, having students keep track of correct responses. The team with the most correct answers wins.

NG Learning Framework: Publish an Antislavery Pamphlet

ATTITUDES Responsibility, Empowerment

SKILLS Collaboration, Communication

Direct students to library and online resources to find examples of antislavery publications, such as *The Liberator*. Tell small groups to produce their own antislavery pamphlet based on their research. Encourage students to include illustrations and other text features for visual emphasis or effect. Tell students to print and distribute their pamphlets to the class. Use students' pamphlets to generate a discussion about techniques and language used in antislavery publications.

Striving Readers

Write Paragraph Summaries Assign pairs to write short summaries of each paragraph in the lesson. When students have completed their summaries, have them write a sentence that summarizes the lesson as a whole.

Pre-AP

Hold a Panel Discussion Ask groups of students to extend their reading about the abolition movement in the United States with additional resources. Then direct them to host a panel discussion to answer the following questions:

• What strategies did the abolition movement use to share and support its positions?

• What strategies were most effective in winning supporters or changing laws?

• What were the major abolitionist groups and how were they similar and different?

Arrange seating so that students can hold the panel discussion in front of the class. Invite all students to participate in a Q-and-A session following the discussion.

See the Chapter Planner for more strategies for differentiation.

HISTORICAL THINKING

ANSWERS

1. Abolitionists gave speeches against slavery, published articles and newspapers, wrote and distributed pamphlets, and operated the Underground Railroad.

2. Most Americans felt the liberation of enslaved people was contrary to the Christian religion, dangerous to society, and unpatriotic.

3. Answers will vary. Students may note the cumbersome collar around the man's neck, his gray, thinning hair, and the expression on his face. These details might have helped people in the 1800s realize how cruelly slaves were treated, including the elderly.

3.2 Voices Against Slavery

Abolitionists relied on shocking testimonials and appeals to good conscience in their fight to end slavery. They dared to write and publish newspaper articles to condemn the injustices of slavery. Others marshalled their strength to stand on a stage and share the indignities they had witnessed or personally endured.

In the first issue of the *The Liberator*, William Lloyd Garrison called slavery "America's all-conquering sin." He wrote, "I do not wish to think, or to speak, or write, with moderation. . . . I will not equivocate . . . I will not excuse . . . I will not retreat a single inch . . . AND I WILL BE HEARD!" Garrison also helped to found the American Anti-Slavery Society, members of which appear at a convention in New York in this 1850 photo. He would ally with women and men, African American and white, and wealthy and poor in his decades-long fight against slavery.

CRITICAL VIEWING What do you notice about the individuals gathered for a photo at this convention?

DOCUMENT ONE

Primary Source: Speech
from "Address to the Slaves of the United States," by William Lloyd Garrison, 1843

When William Lloyd Garrison published this speech in *The Liberator*, slavery had long been the basis for the southern economy. Garrison's passion for the abolitionist cause is evident in the way he addresses enslaved people directly.

CONSTRUCTED RESPONSE How does Garrison describe enslaved people, and what specific actions does he encourage them to take?

> We advise you to seize every opportunity to escape from your masters, and, fixing your eyes on the North Star, travel on until you reach a land of liberty. You are not the property of your masters. God never made one human being to be owned by another. Your right to be free, at any moment, is undeniable; and it is your duty, whenever you can, peaceably to escape from the plantations on which you are confined, and assert your manhood.

DOCUMENT TWO

Primary Source: Speech
from "On the Injustice of Slavery," by Sojourner Truth, 1856

Sojourner Truth dictated her life story to Olive Gilbert for her book *Narrative of Sojourner Truth, a Northern Slave*, published in 1850. In the following address to the Friends of Human Progress, Truth shares her grief over the loss of her children. Her story provided clear evidence of the ongoing mistreatment of vast numbers of people who were unable to care for their children or even keep them from being sold.

CONSTRUCTED RESPONSE How does Truth's account reflect the lack of basic freedom enslaved people endured?

> I want to know what has become of the love I ought to have for my children? I did have love for them, but what has become of it? I cannot tell you. I have had two husbands, but I never possessed one of my own. I have had five children and never could take one of them up and say, "My child" or "My children," unless it was when no one could see me.

DOCUMENT THREE

Primary Source: Speech
from "What the Black Man Wants," by Frederick Douglass, 1865

Frederick Douglass, sitting next to the table in the photo on the left, was an escaped slave who taught himself to read and write. Douglass became one of the most powerful and outspoken opponents of slavery, and proponents, or supporters, of women's rights. He delivered this speech to the Massachusetts Anti-Slavery Society in 1865.

CONSTRUCTED RESPONSE Why does Douglass reject the pity and sympathy of other abolitionists?

> I understand the anti-slavery societies of this country to be based on two principles—first, the freedom of the blacks of this country; and, second, the elevation of them. Let me not be misunderstood here. I am not asking for sympathy at the hands of abolitionists, sympathy at the hands of any. What I ask . . . is not benevolence, not pity, not sympathy, but simply justice.

SYNTHESIZE & WRITE

1. **REVIEW** Review what you have learned about 19th-century abolitionists, their ideas and motivations, and their movement.

2. **RECALL** On your own paper, write the main ideas expressed by Garrison, Truth, and Douglass.

3. **CONSTRUCT** Construct a topic sentence that answers this question: In what ways did abolitionists appeal to their fellow citizens' morality in order to gather support to abolish slavery?

4. **WRITE** Using evidence from this chapter and the documents, write an informative paragraph that supports your topic sentence in Step 3.

PLAN

Objective

Synthesize information about 19th-century abolitionists from primary source documents.

Critical Thinking Skills for Lesson 3.2

- Synthesize
- Compare and Contrast
- Make Inferences
- Evaluate

Essential Question for Chapter 13

How did immigration and reform influence American identity? Abolitionists fought to end slavery, an institution many considered immoral. Lesson 3.2 provides excerpts from speeches that provide perspectives about slavery and the abolition movement.

Background for the Teacher

The photograph featured in this lesson shows a crowd of both men and women, but women were not always allowed to attend antislavery events. Women's participation in the abolitionist movement was at times a source of debate and division. William Lloyd Garrison's inclusion of women in the American Anti-Slavery Society split the organization. In 1840, an antislavery convention held in London denied floor seats to female delegates whose number included Elizabeth Cady Stanton and Lucretia Mott. Their experience inspired them to begin planning their own convention for women's rights.

INTRODUCE & ENGAGE

Prepare for the Document-Based Question

Before students start on the activity, briefly preview the three documents. Remind students that a constructed response requires full explanations in complete sentences. Emphasize that students should use what they have learned about the institution of slavery in the United States and the abolition movement in addition to the information in the documents.

TEACH

Guided Discussion

1. **Compare and Contrast** How does Sojourner Truth's perspective in her speech differ from that of Frederick Douglass and William Lloyd Garrison? *(Sojourner Truth focuses her speech on the direct effects of slavery on the enslaved person. Douglass and Garrison speak about the injustice of slavery from a general perspective.)*

2. **Make Inferences** Douglass gave his speech to the Massachusetts Anti-Slavery Society. Based on this excerpt, what kinds of people may have made up his audience? *(Possible response: His statement that he does not want pity or sympathy from his audience suggests that it may have been made up of white people who had never witnessed slavery or African Americans who had never been enslaved.)*

Evaluate

After students have completed the Synthesize & Write activity, allow time for them to exchange paragraphs and read and comment on the work of their peers. Establish guidelines for comments prior to this activity so that feedback is constructive and encouraging in nature.

Active Options

On Your Feet: Use a Jigsaw Strategy Organize students into three "expert" groups and have students from each group analyze one of the documents and summarize its main ideas in their own words. Then have the members of each group count off using the letters A, B, and C. Regroup students into three new groups so that each new group has at least one member from each expert group. Have students in the new groups take turns sharing the simplified summaries they came up with in their expert groups.

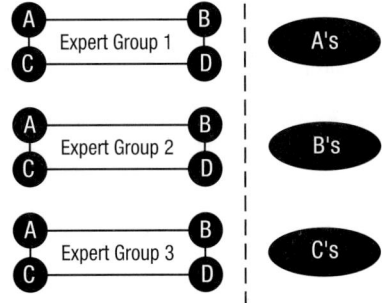

DIFFERENTIATE

Striving Readers

Provide Sentence Frames Have students complete the following sentence frames to help them understand the arguments made by each of the speakers:

Document 1: Enslaved people should attempt to _____ their _____ whenever possible. *(escape; masters)*

Document 2: Being enslaved meant that Sojourner Truth was not free to truly _____ her husbands or _____. *(acknowledge; children)*

Document 3: Frederick Douglass did not want _____ from abolitionists; instead, he wanted _____. *(sympathy; justice)*

Inclusion

Highlight and Summarize Provide students with a copy of the three excerpts printed on a separate piece of paper to minimize distractions. Model for them the strategy of highlighting the most important phrases and sentences in the texts. Then have them write brief summaries of each excerpt in their own words.

See the Chapter Planner for more strategies for differentiation.

SYNTHESIZE & WRITE

ANSWERS

1. Answers will vary.

2. Answers will vary.

3. Answers will vary. Possible response: Abolitionists appealed to their fellow citizens' morality by arguing that enslaved people were human beings and human beings should not be mistreated.

4. Answers will vary. Students' paragraphs should include their topic sentence from Step 3 and provide several details from the documents to support the sentence.

CONSTRUCTED RESPONSE

Document 1: Possible response: Garrison describes enslaved people as human beings with the right to be free. He encourages them to escape from their masters whenever they have the opportunity and travel north to freedom.

Document 2: Possible response: Truth's account reflects the basic lack of freedom for enslaved people to openly have families and love them.

Document 3: Possible response: Douglass rejects pity and sympathy because those emotions are not important compared to actually achieving justice by making enslaved people free.

CRITICAL VIEWING The individuals at the convention include different races and genders, which suggests the diverse coalition of people who opposed slavery.

3.3 Women's Rights and Seneca Falls

Like activists in modern civil rights movements, 19th-century activists in the women's rights movement felt an urgent sense of purpose. And when it came to establishing basic rights for women, failure was impossible.

MAIN IDEA In 1848, supporters of women's rights laid the groundwork for a movement that would change the lives of American women.

LEADERS FOR WOMEN'S RIGHTS

Throughout the early 1800s, women played active roles in social reform and abolition movements. Yet women continued to occupy a secondary place to men in society. When women earned wages outside of the home, their pay was much lower than the wages men received for doing the same job. Married women could not own or purchase property or enter into contracts. Single women had all the property rights a man had but were taxed on that property by a government in which they had no voice. Furthermore, because educational and career opportunities were so limited for women, marriage was often the only possible path to a financially stable life for most women.

The fight for women's rights had its roots in the abolition movement. Female abolitionists gained public speaking and organization experience, and some began to ask why women were not granted the same rights as men. **Elizabeth Cady Stanton** and **Lucretia Mott** were early leaders in the women's rights movement, and both were abolitionists.

Elizabeth Cady came from a wealthy family and received an excellent education at Troy Female Seminary. She married abolitionist Henry Brewster Stanton, became an abolitionist herself, and met many other abolitionists, including Lucretia Mott. Mott was a Quaker from Massachusetts who housed escapees traveling on the Underground Railroad.

In 1848, Mott and Stanton organized the **Seneca Falls Convention** in central New York. There, they issued a "Declaration of Sentiments and Resolutions." The Declaration of Sentiments

Susan B. Anthony shows a document to Elizabeth Cady Stanton, seated, in 1900. In 1902, Anthony wrote to Stanton: "It is fifty-one years since we first met, and we have been busy through every one of them, stirring up the world to recognize the rights of women."

framed the injustices faced by women in familiar language. As you know, the Declaration of Independence introduced the idea that all men are created equal. The Declaration of Sentiments inserted "and women" into that fundamental idea to reinforce the assertion that "all men and women are created equal." In this spirit, Stanton went a

AMERICAN PLACES
Women's Rights National Historical Park Seneca Falls, New York

The Women's Rights National Historical Park honors women who produced the Declaration of Sentiments. The statues featured here are the centerpiece of the park's visitors' center lobby. Notice Frederick Douglass standing with the women. Like many women's rights activists, he supported both abolition and women's rights.

step further and included women's **suffrage**, or the right to vote, in the Declaration of Sentiments. She knew opponents of women's suffrage would claim the demand was outrageous, and that it might hinder the acceptance of other ideas about women's rights. But because Stanton believed the right to vote was essential, she and Mott listed it as the first grievance in the Declaration of Sentiments.

CONTINUING THE WORK

In 1851, Sojourner Truth, who had attended Seneca Falls, delivered a powerful speech at the Women's Rights Convention in Ohio. She asked, "Ain't I a woman?" and drew attention to race in the fight for women's rights. Truth was a passionate supporter of equality for men and women of all races. That same year, Elizabeth Cady Stanton met **Susan B. Anthony**. Coming from a Quaker family, Anthony supported both temperance and abolition. The two women began

a friendship and a political partnership that lasted more than 50 years. They traveled together, delivered speeches to lawmakers, planned campaigns, and published *The Revolution*, a newspaper devoted to women's rights.

During the 1850s and 1860s, issues regarding women's rights became less pressing because of the impending Civil War. However, after the war was over, women's rights activists picked up the cause again. In 1869, Anthony and Stanton founded the **National Woman Suffrage Association**, the first national women's rights organization. Anthony believed that the best way to bring attention to women's suffrage was to violate the law—by voting. When she tried to vote in the 1872 election, she was arrested and fined. Anthony never paid the fine and never went to jail.

The campaign for women's rights began in the early 1800s and continued through the rest of the 19th century and into the 20th. Some leaders worked until the day they died. Mott, Stanton, Truth, Anthony, and many other women's rights activists dedicated their lives to securing political and social equality for women.

HISTORICAL THINKING

1. **READING CHECK** What was the Seneca Falls Convention, and why was it significant?

2. **MAKE CONNECTIONS** In what ways were the movements for abolition and women's rights intertwined?

3. **SYNTHESIZE** How did women's rights activists link women's rights to the Founding Fathers' positions on equality and natural rights?

PLAN

Objective
Trace the development and goals of the 19th-century women's rights movement.

Critical Thinking Skills for Lesson 3.3

- Identify Main Ideas and Details
- Monitor Comprehension
- Make Connections
- Synthesize
- Draw Conclusions
- Describe

Essential Question for Chapter 13

How did immigration and reform influence American identity? Reform movements in the 19th century fought to give rights and opportunities to those denied them. Lesson 3.3 traces the development of the women's rights movement.

Background for the Teacher

Most early women's rights activists advocated for women's suffrage. But other issues were important as well, including naming and dressing conventions. In 1855, a college-educated women's rights and abolition lecturer named Lucy Stone chose to keep her maiden name after marriage, prompting others (who came to be known as Lucy Stoners) to follow her lead. Around the same time in Seneca Falls, Amelia Bloomer discussed a new kind of clothing in her newspaper, *The Lily*, and accidentally gave her name to the new trend of women wearing pants.

History Notebook

Encourage students to complete the American Gallery page for Chapter 13 in their History Notebooks as they read.

INTRODUCE & ENGAGE

Create a Word Web

Display a Word Web with the phrase *women's rights* in the center. **ASK:** What ideas, events, and people do you associate with this phrase? *(Answers will vary.)* Add students' contributions to the diagram or direct students to complete their own diagrams. Tell students that in this lesson, they will learn more about how the American movement for women's rights began. After students have completed the lesson, allow time for them to add any new terms or people they have learned about.

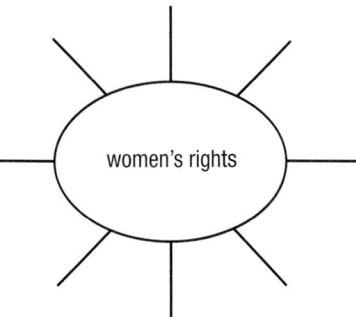

women's rights

TEACH

Guided Discussion

1. **Draw Conclusions** Tell students to consider ways in which 19th-century reform movements were connected. **ASK:** Why do periods of reform arise at certain historical moments? *(Possible response: Many women's rights reformers were abolitionists, and many education reformers had dedicated themselves to improving education for women and African Americans. Peoples' conditions in society are connected, and in trying to solve one problem, reformers begin to see other problems around them.)*

2. **Describe** Describe how the text is organized in presenting information about the development of the women's rights movement. Use text evidence to explain your answer. *(The text is organized sequentially, first showing that during the abolition movement, women spoke out for the rights of African Americans and then asserted the necessity of equal rights for women. Presenting information sequentially shows how the movement developed and grew from the early 1800s to the moment when Susan B. Anthony tried to vote in 1872.)*

🏛 American Places

At the Women's Rights National Historical Park in Seneca Falls, New York, visitors can see the home of activist Elizabeth Cady Stanton, view films and exhibits at the Visitor Center, and tour the Wesleyan Chapel, where the Seneca Falls convention was held. On the National Park Service's website, students can view and download photos, read documents, such as the Declaration of Sentiments and Resolutions, and take virtual tours of various locations.

Active Options

Active History: Analyze Primary Sources Extend the lesson by using either the PDF or Whiteboard version of the activity. These activities take a deeper look at a topic from, or related to, the lesson. Explore the activities as a class, turn them into group assignments, or even assign them individually.

AMERICAN GALLERY
ONLINE

Women's Rights Invite students to explore the American Gallery. Have them select one of the images and do additional research to learn more about it. Ask questions that inspire additional inquiry about the chosen gallery image, such as: Which people or events does this image show? When was it created, and by whom? For what purpose? Why does it belong in this section? What else would you like to know about it?

DIFFERENTIATE

English Language Learners

Create a Meaning Map Students may be confused by the word *suffrage* because of its similarity to *suffering*. Pair students at the **Emerging** level with more proficient students and have them complete a Meaning Map for *suffrage*. Tell students to use *suffrage* in a sentence and then trade sentences with another pair to check for accuracy and spelling.

Gifted & Talented

Compare and Contrast Declarations Have students locate the full text of the Declaration of Sentiments and Resolutions and a copy of the Declaration of Independence. Tell students to compare and contrast the texts. Then ask students to write a short essay describing the ways in which the Declaration of Sentiments viewed the concept of freedom similarly to and differently from the Declaration of Independence. Tell students to conclude their essays with a paragraph that answers the question: What did freedom mean and how did it change over time?

See the Chapter Planner for more strategies for differentiation.

HISTORICAL THINKING

ANSWERS

1. The Seneca Falls Convention was a gathering at which Lucretia Mott and Elizabeth Cady Stanton presented the Declaration of Sentiments and Resolutions. It began a larger discussion of injustices faced by women and introduced the fight for women's suffrage.

2. The movements for abolition and women's rights shared many activists and both fought for basic rights for groups that did not have them.

3. Women's rights activists used the language of the Declaration of Independence, adapting it to refer specifically to women.

13 REVIEW

VOCABULARY

Use each of the following vocabulary terms in a sentence that shows an understanding of the term's meaning.

1. nativist
   Members of Congress passed nativist laws to limit the rights of immigrants.

2. blight

3. steerage

4. evangelize

5. labor union

6. revival meeting

7. temperance movement

8. suffrage

9. emancipation

READING STRATEGY
SYNTHESIZE

If you haven't already done so, complete the graphic organizer for this chapter. List at least three ideas and their synthesis. Then answer the question.

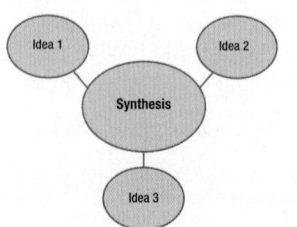

10. In what ways did the American identity change between 1830 and 1860?

MAIN IDEAS

Answer the following questions. Support your answers with evidence from the chapter.

11. Why did many immigrants choose to stay in the city of their arrival? **LESSON 1.1**

12. How did political problems in Europe affect immigration to the United States in the early 1800s? **LESSON 1.2**

13. How did the Know-Nothing party try to limit the freedoms of immigrants to the United States? **LESSON 1.4**

14. What role did religion have in changing the American identity? **LESSON 2.1**

15. What work did Dorothea Dix and Louis Dwight do? **LESSON 2.2**

16. What did the members of the Lowell Female Labor Reform Association seek to change? **LESSON 2.3**

17. From what sources did mid-19th century writers and artists draw their inspiration? **LESSON 2.4**

18. In what ways did abolitionists use print sources to build a case for the abolition of slavery? **LESSON 3.1**

19. Why was Susan B. Anthony arrested in 1872? **LESSON 3.3**

HISTORICAL THINKING

Answer the following questions. Support your answers with evidence from the chapter.

20. **SUMMARIZE** What were the goals of the 19th-century reform movements?

21. **IDENTIFY PROBLEMS AND SOLUTIONS** What problem did Horace Mann seek to solve?

22. **EVALUATE** How did Americans' understanding of the concept of freedom change during the 19th century?

23. **MAKE GENERALIZATIONS** Why did Elizabeth Cady Stanton and Lucretia Mott organize a convention at Seneca Falls?

24. **FORM AND SUPPORT OPINIONS** Which reform effort improved society the most during the 19th century? Support your opinion with evidence from the chapter.

INTERPRET MAPS

The map shows Underground Railroad routes from southern slave states to northern free states. The width of a path on the map corresponds to the number of people following it. Look closely at the map and then answer the questions that follow.

Underground Railroad Routes, 1830–1860

25. What routes indicate that the Underground Railroad was an international network?

26. In what ways did Underground Railroad routes rely on major rivers? Support your answer with details from the map.

ANALYZE SOURCES

Margaret Fuller's *Woman in the Nineteenth Century*, published in 1845, is a transcendentalist argument for women participating fully in society. Fuller points out that women constitute half of humanity. She goes on to argue that women's development contributes to the growth of men, too. Fuller makes the case that men are better off when women are able to lead fulfilling lives.

> Not a few believe, and men themselves have expressed the opinion that . . . the idea of Man, however imperfectly brought out, has been far more so [expressed] than that of Woman . . . that she, the other half of the same thought, the other chamber of the heart of life, needs now take her turn in the full pulsation, and that improvement in the daughters will best aid in the reformation of the sons of this age.

27. Why do you think Fuller describes women as "the other half of the same thought?"

CONNECT TO YOUR LIFE

28. **EXPLANATORY** Think about a 19th-century reform movement and a cause you support today. What common threads can you trace between then and now? Write a paragraph in which you describe how the cause you support can trace its roots to reform movements of the past.

TIPS

- Consider the mix of reforms happening at this time, and list the facts and details that best align with the cause you support.

- Explain your reasons for supporting your cause, and connect them with the reasons of early reformers.

- Use two or three vocabulary terms from the chapter in your paragraph.

VOCABULARY ANSWERS

1. Members of Congress passed nativist laws to limit the rights of immigrants.

2. In Ireland, blight caused by a fungus killed the potato crop.

3. Many poor immigrants traveled to the United States in steerage, cramped and exposed to rats and lice between the main decks.

4. The preacher began to evangelize by shouting scripture, pointing at the congregation, and recounting his conversion to Christianity.

5. The workers in the textile mills in Massachusetts formed a labor union to improve working conditions.

6. Some revival meetings had thousands of attendees who came to listen to Christian preachers.

7. Many women worked within the temperance movement in an attempt to reduce people's consumption of alcohol.

8. Women and African Americans were denied suffrage, or the right to vote.

9. William Lloyd Garrison argued for emancipation of the enslaved, which would have given them immediate freedom.

READING STRATEGY ANSWER

10. Between 1830 and 1860, reformers worked to make America more inclusive by fighting for equal rights and educational opportunities for African Americans, women, and the poor.

MAIN IDEAS ANSWERS

11. Large immigrant communities were often already established in arrival cities, and there were more job opportunities in urban, industrial areas than in small towns. Also, immigrants may not have had enough money to move further into the country.

12. Revolutions and civil unrest, as in Germany, made some people refugees. Political conditions and famine in Ireland drove many Irish immigrants to the United States.

13. The Know-Nothing party proposed laws barring the foreign-born from voting or holding public office and advocated a 21-year residency requirement before granting citizenship.

14. The Second Great Awakening inspired Americans to think differently about life and their responsibilities to others. Religious beliefs fueled reform movements such as abolition and temperance.

15. Dix and Dwight were concerned with the treatment and placement of mentally ill people within the prison system. They worked to create new institutions and helped the medical profession treat the mentally ill as patients instead of as criminals.

16. Members of the LFLRA wanted to shorten the workday.

17. Some authors and artists drew inspiration from American history, as Longfellow did with his poem about Paul Revere's famous ride during the American Revolution. Other authors and artists, such as Thoreau and Durand, wrote about and painted nature.

18. John Quincy Adams insisted that the Declaration of Independence was the basis for equality for all people. William Lloyd Garrison wrote and printed articles to argue for abolition, and David Walker sewed antislavery pamphlets into clothes he sold to sailors to circulate abolitionist ideas as widely as possible.

19. Susan B. Anthony was arrested for attempting to vote in the 1872 election.

HISTORICAL THINKING ANSWERS

20. Reformers in the 19th century worked to improve education, achieve greater rights for women, emancipate enslaved African Americans, bargain for better wages and working conditions, reduce alcohol abuse, and improve conditions in prisons and asylums.

21. Through free public schools, Horace Mann wanted to solve the problem of unequal access to education due to race, economic status, religion, ethnicity, and gender.

22. Americans argued that freedom should apply to a more diverse set of people, including women and African Americans. In addition, an education and a livable wage were recognized as necessary for a people to be free.

23. Lucretia Mott and Elizabeth Cady Stanton organized the Seneca Falls convention in order to issue their "Declaration of Sentiments and Resolutions" and begin a national discussion on the injustices faced by women.

24. Answers will vary. Possible response: The movement to reform education improved society the most during the early 19th century because it succeeded in establishing free public schools. Other reform movements struggled, and sometimes failed, to achieve many of their goals during the first half of the 1800s.

INTERPRET MAPS ANSWERS

25. The escape routes that run from the South into Canada and from Georgia and Florida to the Caribbean show that the Underground Railroad was an international network.

26. The map shows heavy traffic along the Mississippi and Ohio rivers, so people escaping from slavery relied on these rivers to get to free states.

ANALYZE SOURCES ANSWER

27. Answers will vary. Possible response: Fuller asserts that women make up half of the population and should receive the same consideration as the other half. If the "thought"—or an idea such as a freedom or a right—applies to men, then women, as "the other half" should be granted the same freedom or right.

CONNECT TO YOUR LIFE ANSWER

28. Answers will vary. Student responses should connect a 19th-century reform movement with a cause the student supports. Responses should include reasons for the connection supported by facts and details and at least two vocabulary terms.

The Way West

BY JOHN G. MITCHELL

Adapted from "The Way West," by John G. Mitchell, in *National Geographic*, September 2000

The naysayers said it couldn't be done. No one had ever rounded up a party of tenderfoot pioneers, pointed their noses toward sundown, and, without benefit of compass or reliable map, dared them to bet their boots, wagons, and lives against the fearsome 2,000 miles between them and California. But at the far edge of Missouri, where the United States of America had come to a full stop, moving west was on people's minds. They *had* to try it. So in the spring of 1841, a handful of brave souls started out. No matter that they'd have to abandon their wagons on the arid plains and slaughter their livestock to survive in the mountains. All those who stayed the course—34 of them—got to California. It had never been done that way. But they did it.

In 1848, the year Mexico ceded California to the United States and gold was discovered at Sutter's Mill, California could claim a population of 14,000 Anglos and Hispanics. By the end of 1849, emigration by land and sea had pushed the population past 100,000. This number was sufficient for folks to start demanding that the territory be admitted to the Union, which it was on September 9, 1850. In the span of just one generation, even after most of the gold lodes had played out, nearly a quarter million emigrants came into the promised land the old-fashioned way, on foot and by wagon on the California Trail.

By some accounts, the few surviving ruts of that trail reflect one of the greatest human migrations in recorded history. Between the migration's peak years, 1849 to 1852, travelers described the scene as having the appearance of an army on the move. The journey started at the Missouri River, where feeder trails that originated from Independence, Westport Landing, St. Joseph, Council Bluffs, and other frontier towns converged near Fort Kearny on the River Platte. From the Platte's north fork, the trail picked up the Sweetwater River, crossed the Great Divide at South Pass, then dodged one mountain range after another on its way to Fort Hall, a fur post on the Snake River.

A bit beyond Fort Hall, the main trail split and the right fork—the homestretch of the Oregon Trail—continued down the Snake toward Oregon. The left fork turned southwest toward California. In the 1850s, some Oregonians liked to claim that at another place where the trails diverged, a pile of gold-bearing quartz showed the path to California, while a signpost with a written legend guided the traveler toward Oregon. Those who couldn't read, the slur alleged, went to California.

By one estimate, 20,000 people died on the California Trail between 1841 and 1859—an average of 10 graves for every mile. Most died from accidents, disease, contaminated water, inadequate food, or exhaustion from the constant toil. Contrary to what dime novelists would have had the world believe, trouble with Native Americans figured little with the mortality rate on the overland trails. Until 1849, fewer than 50 westward migrant deaths were attributed to Native American attack, and many of those occurred along the pathways to Oregon. However, as the numbers of overlanders increased, so did the fatal encounters. By 1860, pioneer casualties probably totaled close to 400. Even more Native Americans were killed by pioneers.

In the longer view of the great migration, gold was only one of many incentives that lured the wagonfolk west. More lasting was the human hunger for fertile land. But why would a family pack up and set out on a four-month journey when cheap and arable land was still available in the frontier states of the Mississippi Valley?

Perhaps there were as many motives as there were travelers to act on them. A politician might have attributed it all to manifest destiny and the course of empire. But that could not begin to explain the American people's westering tilt, and only the Pacific Ocean would prove big enough to stop it.

For more from *National Geographic*, check out "People of the Horse" online.

UNIT INQUIRY: Organize a Reform Campaign

In this unit, you learned about the ways in which the United States changed in the first part of the 19th century. New national boundaries enlarged the country, and immigrants from around the world enriched the population. Based on your understanding of the text, in what ways did these and other new developments lead to injustices or intensify social problems? What issues did reformers focus on?

ASSIGNMENT

Organize a reform campaign. Identify an injustice or social problem that you learned about in this unit. Then organize a reform campaign. Your plan should include specific actions the campaign could take and communication strategies to broadcast your campaign. Be prepared to present your campaign to the class and explain how it would address the issue you select.

Gather Evidence As you organize your reform campaign, gather evidence from this unit about the different challenges that Americans faced during this time period. Think about the ways in which some developments benefited one group over another. Also consider what principles motivated people to organize reform movements. Use a graphic organizer like this one to help organize your thoughts.

Produce Use your notes to produce descriptions of the specific actions your reform campaign will take and the different audiences it will try to reach. Write a short paragraph on each action and audience using evidence from this unit to support your ideas.

Present Choose a creative way to present your reform campaign to the class. Consider one of these options:

- Create slogans for your campaign that identify the injustice or social problem you are addressing. Carefully consider the campaign message you want to be the most prominent and memorable. Write your slogans on posters, banners, cards, or other forms of visual signage.

- Host a debate that engages different sides of the injustice or social problem your campaign aims to reform. Prepare research memos and talking points for both sides.

- Present your campaign in the character of a reformer from this unit. Research your reformer and consider dressing up as that person.

REFORM CAMPAIGN	
ACTIONS	COMMUNICATION

NATIONAL GEOGRAPHIC | LEARNING FRAMEWORK ACTIVITIES

Research a Mining Boomtown

ATTITUDES Empowerment, Curiosity
KNOWLEDGE Our Human Story

The mining boomtowns of the West were exciting places. In some ways, their remote locations and lack of formal structure allowed different groups a measure of freedom they did not enjoy in 19th-century society. Research the history of a western mining boomtown of your choice. Create a time line that includes major events during the heyday of the town, profiles of important figures and the different groups of people who sought opportunities there, and documents and artwork about the town. Present your research to the class.

Encounter Nature

SKILLS Observation, Collaboration
KNOWLEDGE Our Living Planet

Nineteenth-century artists celebrated the beauty and wonder of the American landscape through visual arts and creative writing. Select a nature site near you to explore. It could be a local park, a beach, a nature trail, or some other site. Explore the nature site you select with a group of classmates. While you are there, take notes on what you observe, including plant life, animals, and birds and the physical features of the site. Gather your notes and present your observations about your site to the class.

NATIONAL GEOGRAPHIC CONNECTION

Guided Discussion for "The Way West"

1. **Describe** What life-threatening dangers existed for travelers on the California Trail? *(Dangers included accidents, disease, contaminated water, inadequate food, and exhaustion.)*

2. **Form and Support Opinions** Why do you think Americans moved west in the 19th century? *(Answers will vary but should be supported by textual evidence. Possible response: Some Americans moved west to get rich during the gold rush. Others wanted to embark on new adventures and new opportunities.)*

Guided Discussion for "People of the Horse"

1. **Identify Main Ideas and Details** What impact did the arrival of the horse in 1500 have on Native American cultures? *(Horses allowed people to hunt more efficiently and helped transport supplies from camp to camp. They became highly valued and ushered in social classes of people who owned horses and people who did not.)*

2. **Summarize** In what ways are horses an integral part of Native American culture? *(Horses are a source of pride for individuals and families that care for them and train them, and they are a link to ancestors and heritage.)*

Assess

Use the rubric to assess each student's participation and performance.

SCORE	ASSIGNMENT	PRODUCT	PRESENTATION
3 GREAT	• Student thoroughly understands the assignment. • Student participates fully in the project process.	• Campaign is well thought out. • Campaign identifies a cause, offers multiple actions, and identifies multiple audiences. • Campaign contains all of the key elements listed in the assignment.	• Presentation is engaging and creative. • Presentation does a good job of addressing different sides of the injustice or social issue. • Presenter addresses the audience in character as a reformer from unit.
2 GOOD	• Student mostly understands the assignment. • Student participates fairly well in the project process.	• Campaign is fairly well thought out. • Campaign identifies a cause, offers at least one action, and identifies at least one audience. • Campaign contains most of the key elements listed in the assignment.	• Presentation is fairly engaging and creative. • Presentation does an adequate job of addressing different sides of the injustice or social issue. • Presenter addresses the audience in character as a reformer from unit but is not fully understood.
1 NEEDS WORK	• Student does not understand the assignment. • Student minimally participates or does not participate in the project process.	• Campaign is not well thought out. • Campaign does not identify a cause or offer actions and does not identify an audience. • Campaign contains few or none of the key elements listed in the assignment.	• Presentation is not creative or engaging. • Presentation does an inadequate job addressing different sides of the injustice or social issue. • Presenter does not address the audience in character as a reformer from the unit.

Assess

Use the rubric to assess how each student applies the National Geographic Learning Framework.

SCORE	ASSIGNMENT	ASSIGNMENT	FINAL PRODUCTS
3 GREAT	• Research and time line reflect **Empowerment** and **Curiosity** well. • Research and time line explore **Our Human Story** well.	• Nature site presentation demonstrates **Observation** and **Collaboration** well. • Nature site presentation explores **Our Living Planet** well.	• Final products are engaging, creative, and well presented.
2 GOOD	• Research and time line reflect **Empowerment** and **Curiosity**. • Research and time line explore **Our Human Story**.	• Nature site presentation demonstrates **Observation** and **Collaboration**. • Nature site presentation explores **Our Living Planet**.	• Final products are interesting, logical, and complete.
1 NEEDS WORK	• Research and time line do not reflect **Empowerment** or **Curiosity**. • Research and time line do not explore **Our Human Story**.	• Nature site presentation does not demonstrate **Observation** and **Collaboration**. • Nature site presentation does not explore **Our Living Planet**.	• Final products are not creative, complete, or interesting.

Civil War Battle Reenactment

Historical reenactment communities vary widely in what they do and how accurate they attempt to be, but they all share the common goal of exploring the past through direct experience. Explain that these groups and their performances grow and change over time as interpretations and portrayals of history change. For example, the Civil War and American Revolution reenactment communities now include many African Americans, and women's roles in the communities have changed as people have learned more about women's participation in past wars.

Reenactments of major battles, such as Gettysburg, are tremendously popular. On weekends from April through October, "living historians" set up camp at Gettysburg National Park and produce demonstrations and reenactments of Civil War camp life and military technology. Important anniversaries of major battles might see enormous reenactment productions. One Gettysburg anniversary event involved more than 20,000 performers. Reenactment groups will often use the funds raised by such events for the preservation of battlefields and other historical sites.

Direct students' attention to the photograph. Point out that although photography did exist during the Civil War, it was a very new technology. **ASK:** Do you think a photograph like this, taken of a reenactment, can provide information about the Civil War experience that photographs taken during the war could not? Explain your answer. *(Possible response: Yes; photography during the Civil War required light and a motionless subject, so a photographer couldn't have captured the action in this scene of a battle at night. In addition, the historically accurate reenactors provide details on which the photographer can focus to make a point or give viewers a specific historical perspective.)*

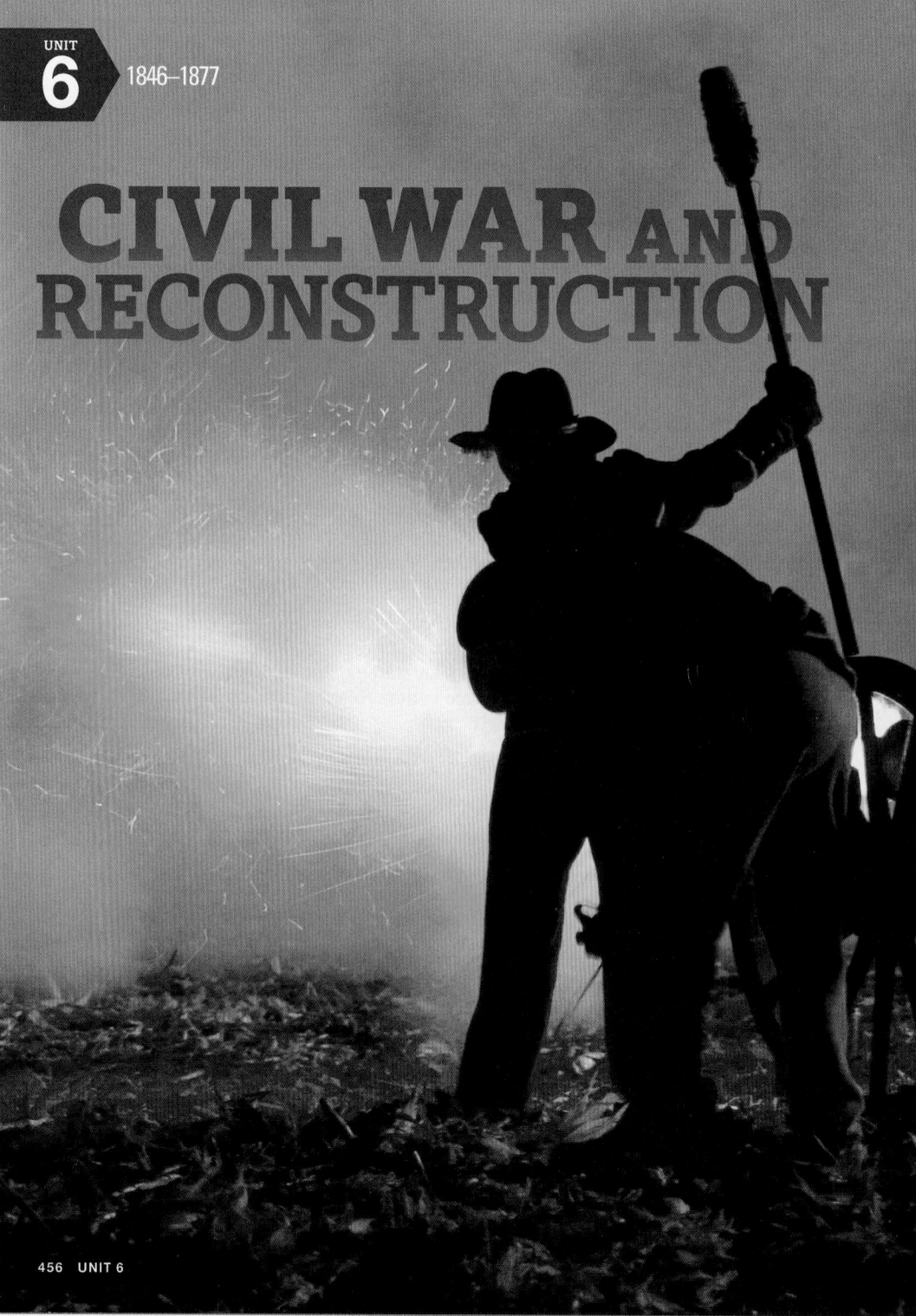

UNIT
6 1846–1877

CIVIL WAR AND RECONSTRUCTION

CRITICAL VIEWING Modern-day Civil War reenactors fire a cannon in this photograph of a battle scene. Fighting during the Civil War was fierce and bloody, often resulting in staggering numbers of casualties among both northern and southern soldiers. Improved technologies, including more high-powered cannons, contributed to the high death toll. What details in the photo help convey what fighting in a Civil War battle must have been like?

457

Birth of the Army Signal Corps

In addition to breakthroughs in artillery and weapons technology, the Civil War also saw the birth of the Army Signal Corps, the part of the U.S. Army that manages all of the major communications systems on which the army relies. The Corps was the brainchild of Major Albert J. Myer, who had previously worked as a telegraph operator and developed language "codes" to help people with hearing and speech impairments communicate. Even before the Civil War, Myer had begun working on a signal system called "wigwag," a flag-based code similar in some ways to semaphore, a signal system using poles or the arms to indicate letters of the alphabet. Myer presented the idea of a dedicated signal office to an initially skeptical military in 1860, and the Corps became an official Union Army branch in 1863.

At the start of the war, Myer proposed that the Signal Corps not only rely on his system of signaling with flags and torches, which was less effective in bad weather, but also on telegraph technology. He devised a system of "flying telegraph lines"—telegraph systems carried from place to place on wagons and assembled in the field—that brought communications to areas regular civilian and military telegraph systems did not cover. The combination of flag signals and telegraph lines allowed for faster, more reliable communication across distances than was possible before the war.

The Confederate Army had a Signal Corps of its own, with similar flag codes and ciphers (coded writing), although the Union had less difficulty breaking Confederate ciphers than the other way around. Unfortunately, little is known about the Confederate Signal Corps because most of its records have been lost or destroyed.

CRITICAL VIEWING Answers will vary. Possible response: The uneven ground would have made positioning and aiming the cannon difficult. Engaging in battle at night, soldiers would have been firing into the darkness, dealing with glare from the cannon's blast and low visibility created by the cannon smoke. Protective helmets and gear weren't yet invented, so operating a cannon must have been particularly hazardous.

1857 ASIA:
Sepoy Rebellion in India

In the mid-1800s, British efforts to control and influence India through the British East India Company were meeting with increasing unrest. Many Indians felt their rights were ignored or threatened by British reforms to the legal and property systems. Hindus and Muslims alike resented the intrusion of Christian missionaries. Western education styles and technologies were perceived as attacks on tradition.

Amid this atmosphere of distrust and anger, sepoys began to protest the introduction of a new type of weapon, the Enfield rifle. They objected to the rifle because they believed that its cartridges, which they had to bite before loading, had been lubricated with pork and beef fat—forbidden for both Muslims and Hindus to eat. When the protesting soldiers were punished with jail time, violence broke out. The rebellion spread to three provinces and was marked by brutal massacres, to which the British responded by executing hundreds of sepoys after they had reasserted control.

The failed rebellion led to a number of changes in British India. The British government stripped the British East India Company of its powers and took more direct control. Under this new system, the British were to give Indians a greater voice in governing and avoid any interference with either Hindu or Muslim religious practices. However, the British also decreased the percentage of Indians in the military to prevent future rebellion. The social and cultural relationships between Indians and British citizens living in India had been permanently damaged. **ASK:** In what ways were the conflicts in British India similar to conflicts in the United States in the mid-1800s? *(Answers will vary. Possible response: In both nations, groups who were oppressed on the basis of race began to protest, sometimes violently, the way they were being treated.)*

UNIT 6 CIVIL WAR AND **RECONSTRUCTION**

THE UNITED STATES

1860 Abraham Lincoln is elected president. Soon after, South Carolina secedes from the Union. *(hat worn by Lincoln when he was assassinated in 1865)*

1852 Harriet Beecher Stowe's novel, *Uncle Tom's Cabin*, is published and stirs the debate over slavery. *(cover from 1897 edition of the book)*

1850 Congress passes the Compromise of 1850, which seeks to maintain a balance between slave and free states.

1861 The Civil War begins after the South attacks Fort Sumter, a garrison under federal control.

1846 Because he lives in a free state, Dred Scott sues for his freedom from slavery after his owner dies.

1840   **1850**   **1860**

1848 EUROPE Nationalism incites unrest and revolution across Europe.

1861 EUROPE The serfs in Russia are freed.

THE WORLD

1857 ASIA Indian soldiers, called *sepoys*, revolt against British rule in India. *(illustration of sepoys)*

458 UNIT 6

HISTORICAL THINKING: DETERMINE CHRONOLOGY

How long after Russia freed its serfs did the United States grant African-American men the right to vote?

1870
The 15th Amendment grants voting rights to African-American men. (*1884 glass ballot jar set in a slotted wooden box*)

1865
On April 9, the Civil War ends when southern general Robert E. Lee surrenders to northern general Ulysses S. Grant. On April 15, Lincoln is assassinated. (*Lee signed a letter of surrender at this table.*)

1867
The Reconstruction Acts of 1867 are passed, requiring southern states to satisfy several conditions before they can reenter the Union.

1863
The Union wins the Battle of Gettysburg, but both sides suffer thousands of casualties.

1877
Newly inaugurated president Rutherford B. Hayes puts an end to Reconstruction.

1870

1876 AFRICA
The European scramble for African territory begins.

1880

1864 AMERICAS
Napoleon III crowns Archduke Maximilian emperor of Mexico.

1867 ASIA
The Tokugawa shogunate is overthrown, and Meiji rule brings a period of modernization in Japan. (*Japanese print of a steam engine in a Tokyo station*)

Civil War and Reconstruction **459**

INTRODUCE TIME LINE EVENT

1867 ASIA:
The End of the Tokugawa Shogunate

The Tokugawa shogunate had controlled Japan since 1603. Under its leaders, the nation had gradually closed itself off from the influences of foreign governments, merchants, and religions. The shogunate solidified Japan's rigid class system, forbidding virtually all social mobility. At the same time, however, the government also promoted significant economic development in both rural and urban areas, creating a thriving merchant class. The result was widespread economic expansion and political stability known as the Edo period.

While many social classes saw positive changes during this period, others, such as the peasant and warrior classes, were locked out of economic benefits. Economic dissatisfaction, combined with increasing pressure to engage again with foreign governments, set the stage for a group of men from the warrior class, known as *samurai*, to stage a coup and overthrow the shogun.

Under the Meiji rule, Japan ended its feudal system and implemented economic and social reforms, including universal education. Many reforms were significantly influenced by nations in the West. However, the new government was not uniformly popular, and uprisings and revolts continued well into the 1880s. By the end of the Meiji era, Japan's modernizing technology, government, culture, and economic system had made the formerly isolated nation into a world power. **ASK:** How did Japan's feudal system contribute to the end of the Tokugawa shogunate? (*Possible response: By forbidding people to move between classes, the feudal system denied some classes economic benefits and left people with no means to change their situations except through revolt.*)

HISTORICAL THINKING: DETERMINE CHRONOLOGY

Answer: The United States granted African-American men the right to vote nine years after Russia freed its serfs.

UNIT 6 RESOURCES

UNIT INTRODUCTION

UNIT TIME LINE

UNIT WRAP-UP

NATIONAL GEOGRAPHIC | CONNECTION

National Geographic Magazine Adapted Articles
- "Lincoln's Funeral Train"
- "Civil War Battlefields" ONLINE

Unit 6 Inquiry: Develop a Conflict Resolution Strategy

NG Learning Framework Activities
- Create an Illustrated Time Line
- Compose a Letter Home

Unit 6 Formal Assessment

CHAPTER 14 RESOURCES

Available at NGLSync.Cengage.com

TEACHER RESOURCES & ASSESSMENT

Reading and Note-Taking

Vocabulary Practice

Document-Based Question Template

Social Studies Skills Lessons
- Reading: Identify Main Ideas and Details
- Writing: Write an Informative Text

Formal Assessment
- Chapter 14 Pretest
- Chapter 14 Tests A & B
- Section Quizzes

Chapter 14 Answer Key

ExamView®
One-time Download

STUDENT DIGITAL RESOURCES

- **eEdition** (English)
- **eEdition** (Spanish)
- **Handbooks**
- **Online Atlas**
- **American Gallery Online**
- **History Notebook**
- **American Voices (Biographies)**
- **Active History**
- **Projects for Inquiry-Based Learning**

Chapter 14 Spanish Resources are available at NGLSync.Cengage.com.

The Pony Express

- Primary Sources
- On Your Feet: I See, I Read, And So

NG Learning Framework:
Find Historical Relationships

SECTION 1 RESOURCES

GROWING TENSIONS BETWEEN NORTH AND SOUTH

LESSON 1.1
Controversy Over Territories

- On Your Feet: Create a Quiz

NG Learning Framework:
Analyze Henry Clay's Strategy

LESSON 1.2
Slavery and Racism

- On Your Feet: Rotating Discussion

NG Learning Framework:
Learn About the Underground Railroad

SECTION 2 RESOURCES

SLAVERY DOMINATES POLITICS

LESSON 2.1
A Country in Crisis

- On Your Feet: Numbered Heads

NG Learning Framework:
Learn More About "Bleeding Kansas"

LESSON 2.2
The Dred Scott Decision

- On Your Feet: Team Word Webbing

NG Learning Framework:
Evaluate a Historical Figure

LESSON 2.3
DOCUMENT-BASED QUESTION
Lincoln and Douglas

- Active History: Debate an Issue
- On Your Feet: Think, Pair, Share

SECTION 3 RESOURCES

LINCOLN'S ELECTION AND SOUTHERN SECESSION

LESSON 3.1
The Election of 1860

- On Your Feet: Fishbowl

NG Learning Framework:
Write a Campaign Song

American Voices Biography
Abraham Lincoln ONLINE

LESSON 3.2
Southern States Secede

- On Your Feet: Sequence Chain

AMERICAN **GALLERY**
ONLINE Abraham Lincoln

American Voices Biography
Jefferson Davis ONLINE

LESSON 3.3
Efforts at Compromise

- On Your Feet: Jigsaw Experts

NG Learning Framework:
Compare Primary Sources

CHAPTER 14 REVIEW

Strategy ❶
Summarize a Lesson

Read the lesson aloud while students follow along in the text. At the end of each paragraph, ask students to write a sentence on their own paper to summarize what they read. Invite volunteers to write their summary sentences on the board as paragraphs in the order they appear in the lesson. Point out to students that taken together, the summary sentences represent a summary of the whole lesson.

Use with All Lessons

Strategy ❷
Chart the Parties

Have students use a chart to keep track of the views and actions of the Democratic and Republican parties in the 1850s and early 1860s. Examples are shown below.

Fact	D	R
Lost antislavery members to the Free-Soil Party	X	
Party of Stephen A. Douglas, who proposed the Kansas-Nebraska Act	X	
Party founded in 1854 to fight the expansion of slavery		X
Gave the "House Divided" speech		X

Use with Lessons 1.1, 2.1–2.3, and 3.1–3.3

Strategy ❸
Make a Top Five Facts List

Tell students to reread the lesson and to review any visuals that it contains. Then ask students to write down five facts that they remember from the text. Have students meet with a partner to compare lists and consolidate the two lists into one final list. Encourage student pairs to state facts from their lists.

Use with All Lessons

Strategy ❶
Preview and Predict

Pair visually impaired students with students who are not visually challenged. Instruct them to read the lesson title and subheadings together. Tell sighted students to describe lesson visuals in detail to help their partners understand them. Then have partners work together to tell what they think the lesson will be about. After reading, ask pairs to review the activity to see whether their predictions were confirmed.

Use with Lessons 1.2, 2.1, and 3.1–3.3

Strategy ❷
Use Supported Reading

In small groups, have students read the chapter aloud lesson by lesson. Instruct them to stop at the end of each lesson and use these sentence frames to monitor their comprehension of the text:

- This lesson is mostly about _____.
- Other topics in this lesson _____.
- One question I have about the lesson is _____.
- One of the vocabulary words is _____. It means _____.
- One word I do not recognize is _____.

Use with All Lessons

ENGLISH LANGUAGE LEARNERS ELD

Strategy 1
Use Vocabulary Word Maps

Pair students at the **Emerging** level with those at the **Bridging** level. Have them use a graphic organizer like the Word Map below for any of the Key Vocabulary words. As students work, they can discuss the words and clear up any misunderstandings. You may want students to compare their responses with responses from other students.

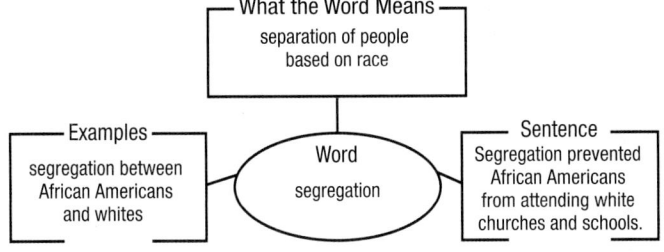

Use with Lessons 1.1–1.2, 2.1, and 3.2–3.3

Strategy 2
Review Suffixes

To build vocabulary, work with students at **All Proficiencies** to study the adjective-forming suffix -ial. Write the following words on the board: presidential, controversial, social, industrial, and racial. Underline the suffix -ial in each word. Explain that this word ending usually turns a noun into an adjective. Then show how the noun president becomes the adjective presidential. Ask students what presidential means. (relating to or connected with a president) Explain that "relating to or connected with" expresses the meaning of -ial in other words, too. Have students define each word and use it in a sentence.

Use with Lessons 1.1–1.2 and 2.2–2.3 Provide sentence stems for students at the **Emerging** level. Encourage students at the **Bridging** level to develop more complex sentences for each word.

Strategy 3
Chart Events

To build comprehension of the issues and events leading up to the Civil War, have students at **All Proficiencies** chart these developments: the Compromise of 1850, the Kansas-Nebraska Act, the Dred Scott case, the Lincoln-Douglas debates, and John Brown's raid on Harpers Ferry. Guide students to understand that the issue of slavery was central to each event but that political leaders struggled to avoid war.

Use with Lessons 1.1 and 2.1–2.3 You may want to pair students at the **Emerging** and **Expanding** levels with students at the **Bridging** level.

GIFTED & TALENTED

Strategy 1
Write News Reports

Assign students the role of journalists reporting on an influential governmental decision made between 1850 and 1861. Point out that news reports begin with the most important information and usually answer most or all of the questions Who?, What?, Where?, When?, Why?, and How?, by the end. Invite students to post their articles on a class blog or publish them on a class, grade, or school website.

Use with Lessons 1.1, 2.1–2.2, and 3.3

Strategy 2
Create a Gallery Walk

To help them learn more about ways in which the debate over slavery was expressed in public, instruct students to locate online resources such as photographs and illustrations relating to slavery, reproductions of newspaper headlines, or portraits and quotations from key individuals. Ask students to work together to group their findings, either by medium or by theme, and to set up stations around the classroom. Then conduct a Gallery Walk, inviting students to stop at each station.

Use with Lessons 1.1–2.3

Pre-AP

Strategy 1
Build an Annotated Time Line

Direct students to use online resources to find out more about Abraham Lincoln's life prior to the election of 1860. Students can create an annotated time line including dates, events, and an explanatory sentence about each event. They will then write a brief paragraph about the significance of these events in shaping the future president. Encourage them to display both their time lines and their paragraphs.

Use with Lessons 2.3–3.3

Strategy 2
Host a Podcast

Invite students to engage in a podcast discussion about the best way to resolve the slavery issue facing the United States in the 1850s and 1860s. Focus the discussion on this question: What is better, compromise on or abolition of slavery? Ask students to assume the roles of a podcast host, an abolitionist, and a politician who supports compromise. Encourage students playing each role to prepare by drafting questions and researching their assigned positions. Students can record their podcast and upload it to a class or school website or another approved host site.

Use with Lessons 2.3 and 3.1–3.3

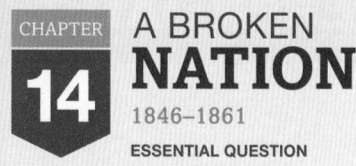

CHAPTER 14

A BROKEN NATION

1846–1861

ESSENTIAL QUESTION
How did slavery divide the country?

AMERICAN STORIES ONLINE The Pony Express

SECTION 1 Growing Tensions Between North and South

KEY VOCABULARY
federal marshal   racism   segregation

SECTION 2 Slavery Dominates Politics

KEY VOCABULARY
Dred Scott decision   popular sovereignty   Republican Party

SECTION 3 Lincoln's Election and Southern Secession

KEY VOCABULARY
Confederacy   garrison   Unionist
Crittenden Plan   secede

AMERICAN GALLERY ONLINE Abraham Lincoln

READING STRATEGY

IDENTIFY MAIN IDEAS AND DETAILS
When you identify a text's main idea and details, you state the most important idea about a topic and determine which facts support that idea. As you read the chapter, use a graphic organizer like this one to identify main ideas and details relating to the issue of slavery.

Main Idea: Tensions grew between slave states and free states.

Detail   Detail

CRITICAL VIEWING This monumental statue of a seated Abraham Lincoln is situated within the Lincoln Memorial in Washington, D.C. The memorial was completed in 1922, and the statue, designed by sculptor Daniel Chester French, took four years to carve. At 19 feet tall and 19 feet wide, the imposing statue creates a sense of awe and power. What characteristics does Lincoln's face convey?

"A house **divided against itself** cannot stand."
—Abraham Lincoln

A Broken Nation **461**

460 CHAPTER 14

INTRODUCE THE PHOTOGRAPH

The Lincoln Memorial

Direct students' attention to the photograph of the statue of Abraham Lincoln, the centerpiece of the Lincoln Memorial. Read the caption. **ASK:** Why do you think Americans wanted to create this statue and monument? *(Possible response: People felt that Lincoln's accomplishments as president were worthy of being remembered for a long time to come.)* Explain that the following words are inscribed in the wall behind the statue: "In this temple, as in the hearts of the people for whom he saved the Union, the memory of Abraham Lincoln is enshrined forever." Tell students that in this chapter they will learn more about Abraham Lincoln and the challenges he faced as president.

Share Background

Construction of the Lincoln Memorial began in 1914, but Congress had started making plans for it in 1867. Sculptor Daniel Chester French studied photographs of and writings about Lincoln and created several models before producing the final statue. His work—and the work of architect Henry Bacon, who designed the memorial itself—has been a major inspiration of the civil rights movement. African-American singer Marian Anderson sang at the Lincoln Memorial in 1939 after she had been denied a booking at another venue because of her race. In 1963, Martin Luther King, Jr., delivered his "I Have a Dream" speech from the memorial's front steps.

CRITICAL VIEWING Answers will vary. Possible response: Lincoln's face conveys a calm determination. His thoughtful gaze looks ahead as if he is imagining a time when war will end and the Union will be restored.

For Chapter 14 Spanish Resources, visit the Resources Menu. Chapter 14 Resources are available at NGLSync.Cengage.com.

INTRODUCE THE ESSENTIAL QUESTION

How did slavery divide the country?

Three Corners Activity: Analyze the Effects of Slavery Label three corners of the room with one of the following: Social, Economic, Political. Divide the class into three groups and direct each group to a corner to discuss these questions:

Group 1: Social: What were the social effects of slavery? What social effects might the abolition of slavery bring about?

Group 2: Economic: What were the economic effects of slavery? What economic effects might the abolition of slavery bring about?

Group 3: Political: What were the political effects of slavery? What political effects might the abolition of slavery bring about?

Ask students in each group to discuss their questions and come to an agreement on the responses. Have each group read their questions and answers to the class. Record student answers and revisit them at the end of the chapter.

INTRODUCE CHAPTER VOCABULARY

Definition Charts

As they read the chapter, have students complete Definition Charts for Key Vocabulary words. Instruct students to list the Key Vocabulary words in the far left column of their charts. Then, as they encounter the words in the chapter, tell them to write each word's definition in the center column and paraphrase the definition in the far right column. Model an example for students on the board, using the graphic organizer below.

Word	Definition	In My Own Words
popular sovereignty	the idea that the people of an area decide for themselves how they will be governed	the people who live in a place can make their own rules

INTRODUCE THE READING STRATEGY

IDENTIFY MAIN IDEAS AND DETAILS

Explain that when students use a Main Idea Chart they should record details that specifically support the main idea, not every tiny detail that may appear in a passage. Point out that the chart has two detail boxes but that more could be added. Note that sometimes a key word in the main idea statement can help students find supporting details. Model completing the Main Idea Chart. Ask students to suggest details that support the main idea: Tensions grew between slave states and free states. Remind students to make use of the graphic organizer as they read the chapter.

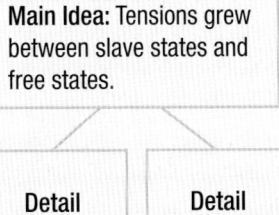

Main Idea: Tensions grew between slave states and free states.

Detail   Detail

KEY DATES FOR CHAPTER 14

1850	Fugitive Slave Act
1854	Kansas-Nebraska Act
1856	Beginning of "Bleeding Kansas"
1857	*Dred Scott* decision
1859	John Brown's forces attack Harpers Ferry
1860	Abraham Lincoln is elected president
1860	South Carolina secedes from the Union
1861	Crittenden Plan is proposed
1861	The Confederate States of America is founded
1861	Confederate forces fire on Fort Sumter

AMERICAN STORIES ONLINE For instructional support for the online American Story "The Pony Express," go to NGLSync.Cengage.com.

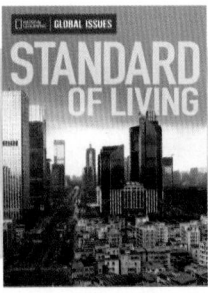

For more on the impact of war on society, see *GLOBAL ISSUES: STANDARD OF LIVING.*

1.1 Controversy Over Territories

Sometimes friends disagree, and sometimes these disagreements can get out of hand. The United States had gained new territory, but the North and the South couldn't agree on how to use it.

MAIN IDEA Disputes over slavery in new territories and states led to growing tensions between the North and the South.

THE COMPROMISE OF 1850

As the middle of the 19th century approached, slavery had become too divisive, or a cause of conflict, for political leaders to ignore any longer. One of the major issues they debated was whether slaveholding should be allowed in new territories and any new states carved from them.

The Missouri Compromise had temporarily settled the issue in 1820. However, the nation once again split over the debate about the expansion of slavery into newly created western territories and states, especially after the Mexican-American War and the discovery of gold in California. In the run-up to the presidential election of 1848, people hotly argued over the future of the new western territories. Disappointed in the position taken by their parties' presidential candidates, antislavery Whigs and a few antislavery Democrats joined together to create the **Free-Soil Party,** which was dedicated to keeping slavery out of the new territories and states.

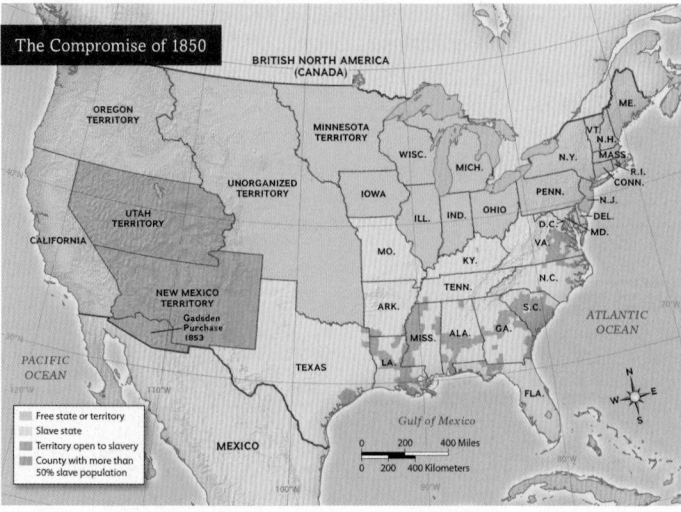

The Compromise of 1850

Free state or territory
Slave state
Territory open to slavery
County with more than 50% slave population

In 1849, a national crisis erupted when California applied for statehood as a free state. For most of the period after the Missouri Compromise, the United States had been evenly split between free states and slave states. Statehood for California would upset this balance and give free states a majority in the U.S. Senate. They already enjoyed a majority in the U.S. House of Representatives. Fearing loss of political power and the possibility that slavery might be outlawed, the slave states threatened to withdraw from the Union.

Remember Henry Clay, the main force behind the Missouri Compromise? In January 1850, he presented a plan for a new compromise. It called for California to be admitted as a free state and for the issue of slavery to be left open in the other territories won from Mexico. Clay and two other famous legislators, John C. Calhoun and Daniel Webster, led a passionate debate over the plan, which lasted for eight months.

Finally, in September, the **Compromise of 1850** became law, preventing the Union from splitting apart. Statehood for California that same year would also give rise to the **Pony Express** in 1860. This mail service, delivered by horseback riders, established communication between the East and the West and so helped keep California connected to the rest of the country.

THE FUGITIVE SLAVE ACT

One of the most controversial parts of the Compromise of 1850 was the **Fugitive Slave Act**. The act strengthened an earlier Fugitive Slave Act passed by Congress in 1793 by enforcing greater penalties on runaways and those who aided them. Under this harsh new act, **federal marshals**, or law enforcers who worked for the U.S. government, could force ordinary citizens to help them capture runaway slaves. In addition, anyone who helped a slave escape faced penalties, as did any marshal who failed to enforce the law. Further, the law denied accused fugitives the right to a trial by jury.

The law provoked bitter anger in the northern states. Many people defied it, and some states passed new laws that protected runaway slaves. Armed groups confronted slave catchers and freed slaves from jails. Nevertheless, slavery continued to expand in the South.

Webster-Calhoun Debate

After Henry Clay proposed his plan, John Calhoun's speech was read in the Senate. Calhoun was too ill to stand and deliver it himself. Three days later, Daniel Webster responded to Calhoun, speaking for more than three hours. In the following excerpts from their speeches, Calhoun speaks for the South, while Webster pleads for saving the Union.

PRIMARY SOURCES

The equilibrium [balance] between [the North and the South] . . . has been destroyed. One section has the exclusive power of controlling the government, which leaves the other without any adequate means of protecting itself against its encroachment and oppression.

—John C. Calhoun, 1850

I wish to speak today, not as a Massachusetts man, nor as a Northern man, but as an American. It is not to be denied that we . . . are surrounded by very considerable dangers to our institutions of government. I speak today for the preservation of the Union. Hear me for my cause.

—Daniel Webster, 1850

HISTORICAL THINKING

1. **READING CHECK** Why did California's application for statehood upset some people?

2. **COMPARE AND CONTRAST** What conflicting views on state and federal authority are revealed in Webster's and Calhoun's speeches?

3. **INTERPRET MAPS** According to the Compromise of 1850, in which territories would settlers be allowed to decide whether slavery would be legal or illegal?

PLAN

Objective

Learn how the North and the South clashed over slavery in new territories and states.

Critical Thinking Skills for Lesson 1.1

- Identify Main Ideas and Details
- Monitor Comprehension
- Compare and Contrast
- Interpret Maps
- Identify Problems and Solutions
- Analyze Language Use
- Make Inferences

Essential Question for Chapter 14

How did slavery divide the country? As the United States expanded westward, questions about the expansion of slavery intensified. Lesson 1.1 examines events leading to the Compromise of 1850 and the effect of the new law, especially its inclusion of the Fugitive Slave Act.

Background for the Teacher

The Whig candidate for president in 1848 was Zachary Taylor, who had been a general in the Mexican-American War. The fact that he was a slaveholder caused the antislavery Conscience Whigs to withdraw their support. The Democrats chose Lewis Cass of Michigan. Cass advocated letting settlers of new territories make their own decisions about slavery—a view that infuriated proslavery Democrats. In addition, Cass was unpopular with Democrats who had wanted Martin Van Buren as their candidate. Many of these Van Buren Democrats joined the Conscience Whigs and the abolitionist Liberty Party in forming the Free-Soil Party, with Van Buren as the candidate. On Election Day, Taylor won the electoral vote, but he and Cass each won 15 states, reflecting the increasingly divisive spirit in the country.

Discuss Compromise

Present this scenario: Six classmates are working on a project. Three want to dress in historical costumes and speak as historical characters; the other three want to present information in a news program format. Eventually they compromise and present information as historical characters being interviewed on a news program. **ASK:** Did either side "win"? Explain. *(Both sides won something. Each side had some of its idea used, but neither side got everything it wanted.)* Explain that a compromise is a way of settling differences so that each side gets part of what it wanted. Tell students they will learn how the Compromise of 1850 worked to settle differences over slavery.

TEACH

Guided Discussion

1. **Identify Problems and Solutions** What problem was the Compromise of 1850 meant to solve, and what was the solution? *(The Compromise of 1850 was meant to solve the problem of whether slavery would be allowed in the territories won in the Mexican-American War. The solution was to make California a free state but to allow settlers in the other territories to decide the matter for themselves.)*

2. **Analyze Language Use** Reread the quotations from John Calhoun and Daniel Webster. What do words like *encroachment* and *oppression* and words like *American* and *preservation* suggest about the two men's points of view? *(Possible response: Calhoun's words suggest that he sees the antislavery forces as enemies, and Webster's words suggest that he views safeguarding the Union as the most important thing.)*

Make Inferences

Direct students' attention to the map. Have students use the legend to distinguish free states from slave states. **ASK:** Suppose that California had been a slave state (yellow) instead of a free state (green). How might that have changed the thinking in Congress? *(Possible response: The Compromise of 1850 might have offered a slave state, rather than a free state, as part of the compromise, while the issue of slavery would still remain open in the new territories.)*

Active Options

On Your Feet: Create a Quiz Organize students into two teams and have each team write five or six True-False statements about the Compromise of 1850. Then direct each team to respond to the statements the other team created. Review the student responses as a class and ask teams to keep track of their number of correct responses.

NG Learning Framework: Analyze Henry Clay's Strategy

ATTITUDE Responsibility

SKILL Problem-Solving

Invite students to revisit the information on Henry Clay in Lesson 1.1 and to imagine themselves in his place. Tell them to consider the following questions:

• What did Clay want to achieve with the Compromise of 1850?

• Why do you think states eventually agreed on the compromise?

• What were the positive aspects of Henry Clay's strategy?

• How would you have tried to settle the dispute?

Instruct students to write a short speech from the point of view of Henry Clay describing his reaction to the Compromise of 1850 becoming law. Ask students to present their speeches to the class.

Inclusion

Use Supported Reading Assign pairs of students paragraphs to read aloud together. At the end of each paragraph, have them use the following sentence frames to identify what they do and do not understand:

• This paragraph is about _____.

• One fact that stood out to me was _____.

• I had trouble understanding _____, so I figured it out by _____.

Be sure all students understand the content before moving on to the next paragraph.

Pre-AP

Extend Knowledge Have students gather information about the Fugitive Slave Act from multiple print and digital sources and write a paragraph or two describing their findings. Encourage them to use primary and secondary sources and to quote or paraphrase them as appropriate. Remind students to cite their sources. Invite volunteers to share their findings with the class.

See the Chapter Planner for more strategies for differentiation.

HISTORICAL THINKING

ANSWERS

1. Some people feared that if California were admitted to the Union as a free state, free states and their antislavery representatives would have a majority in the Senate. The power of the slave states would then be weakened, and slavery could be outlawed.

2. Calhoun suggests states should have influence over the workings of the federal government. Webster suggests the Union is more important than individual states.

3. Settlers in the Utah Territory and New Mexico Territory could make the choice regarding slavery.

1.2 Slavery and Racism

Enslaved people in the South thought running away from their plantations would change their lives for the better. But would freedom in the North live up to its promise?

MAIN IDEA Racism and slavery were defining forces in the lives of African Americans in both the South and the North.

AFRICAN AMERICANS IN THE SOUTH

While some Americans began to harbor misgivings over slavery, the slave trade continued to thrive in the South. Enslaved people from Africa were no longer imported. But since the children of enslaved people in the United States also became slaves, the slave population grew steadily in the South. By 1860, there were nearly four million enslaved African Americans in the region.

Racism, or the belief that one race is superior to others, was the foundation upon which slavery was built. Many slave owners justified slavery by claiming that African Americans were better off under the care of plantation owners than they would be by caring for themselves. But, as you know, many slaves endured lives of unspeakable cruelty. Laws such as the Fugitive Slave Acts made sure their lives could never improve by sharply curbing their freedom and economic opportunities.

Racist attitudes also affected the lives of the more than 250,000 free African Americans in the South. Local laws prevented them from traveling or assembling in large groups. Free African Americans were also discouraged from organizing churches, schools, and fraternal orders, or social organizations, like the Masons.

Slavery was central to the economy and culture of the agrarian South. Concerned about the health of the South's economy, southern leaders not only fought for slavery but they also battled against tariffs. They argued that high tariffs favored the industrial North and hurt the South by forcing plantation owners to pay higher prices for manufactured goods.

Some wealthy plantation owners even tried to convince the U.S. government to acquire Cuba from Spain as a slave state. Their proposal was presented in the 1854 Ostend Manifesto and included the provision that the island be taken by force if necessary. The manifesto fell through, but it became a rallying cry for northern abolitionists, who saw the move as an attempt to extend slavery.

AFRICAN AMERICANS IN THE NORTH

Though some enslaved people dreamed of escaping to the North, those who succeeded found themselves facing many of the challenges they thought they had left behind. Many northerners held the same racist beliefs that were common among southerners. They did not want to live near, work with, or have their children go to school with African Americans. They cared little about ending slavery and looked upon free African Americans with scorn. Even as they worked to try to end the institution of slavery, some abolitionists held racist attitudes toward African Americans.

Discrimination took several forms. Some states passed laws restricting the rights of African Americans to vote, own property, and move about freely. **Segregation**, or the separation of people based on race, was common in northern cities, and African Americans often were forbidden from entering white churches, schools, and many other buildings. They were often blocked from employment for skilled jobs. Free African Americans even feared for their lives. Daily threats included attacks by white mobs and the possibility of being captured and sent back to a life of slavery.

The Impact of Slavery
The damage done to people by slavery is evident in these two photos. The man above, photographed in 1863, is scarred from being whipped, and fear is evident in the faces of the children at the right.

A writer named **Harriet Beecher Stowe** channeled her anger over slavery into a novel called *Uncle Tom's Cabin*. This 1852 painting called *An American Slave Market*, by an artist known only as Taylor, depicts a scene in the novel in which a slave trader purchases a child.

Published in 1852, *Uncle Tom's Cabin* sold 300,000 copies in that year alone and was also turned into popular plays. It dramatically changed the national debate over slavery and racism.

HISTORICAL THINKING

1. **READING CHECK** What was the relationship between racism and slavery?

2. **IDENTIFY MAIN IDEAS AND DETAILS** What forms of discrimination did African Americans face in the North?

3. **COMPARE AND CONTRAST** How were the situations of free African Americans in the North and the South similar?

Objective

Understand how racist attitudes affected African Americans in the North and the South.

Critical Thinking Skills for Lesson 1.2

- Identify Main Ideas and Details
- Monitor Comprehension
- Compare and Contrast
- Make Connections
- Make Generalizations

Essential Question for Chapter 14

How did slavery divide the country? Settlement of the slavery issue seemed impossible. Lesson 1.2 explores the meaning of racism and some of the ways in which racism was manifested in both the South and the North.

Background for the Teacher

The idea of slavery is so abhorrent to people today that it is difficult to understand how it could have ever been an accepted practice. In addition to presenting economic reasons, advocates of slavery pointed to history, noting that many ancient nations practiced slavery. They sometimes used the Bible to defend their position, explaining that slaves appear in the Bible and suggesting that Africans were a "cursed" people. Proslavery arguments also centered on "scientific racism"—that is, the idea that Africans were "naturally" inferior to Europeans. In fact, a very popular book titled *Vestiges of the Natural History of Creation*, published in 1844 by Robert Chambers, proposed that each race was at a different point in the development of humanity and that some races were more advanced than others.

INTRODUCE & ENGAGE

Preview Using Visuals

Point out the historical photographs in the lesson. Invite students to comment about details in the images and the emotional responses that the images evoke. **ASK:** Why do you think photographs like these were taken and published? *(Possible response: The photographs provide stark evidence about the realities of life under slavery. They also could be used by abolitionists to stir up public feeling against slavery.)*

TEACH

Guided Discussion

1. **Make Connections** What was the relationship between plantation owners' opposition to tariffs and their determination to keep slavery in place? *(Possible response: Because tariffs caused plantation owners to pay high prices for manufactured goods, plantation owners could say that they needed to create as much profit as possible to afford those goods—and that they needed slaves to make that profit possible.)*

2. **Make Generalizations** Were the northern states truly free for African Americans living there? Why or why not? *(Answers will vary. Possible response: No; African Americans could not feel completely free in the North. Laws in some states kept them from owning property, voting, or even moving around freely, and they were often discriminated against and sometimes threatened by white people.)*

More Information

Uncle Tom's Cabin Harriet Beecher Stowe based the plot and characters in *Uncle Tom's Cabin* on slave narratives she had read and stories told to her by former slaves who worked for her in Cincinnati. The heroes of her novel are Uncle Tom, a slave whose trust in God helps him suffer abuse from a cruel master, and Eliza, a slave who bravely escapes to freedom with her baby by crossing the partially frozen Ohio River. **ASK:** The scene of Eliza's escape gripped readers of the novel and audiences watching dramatized versions of the story. Why do you think the scene would be powerful? *(People probably responded to the danger of the escape and a mother's desire to protect her baby.)*

Active Options

On Your Feet: Rotating Discussion Help students understand the antebellum South by comparing the lives of plantation owners, other white southerners, free African Americans, and enslaved African Americans. Prompt them to consider how the Fugitive Slave Acts of 1793 and 1850 and other discriminatory laws benefited or harmed each group. Divide students into four teams and assign each team a corner of the room. Ask each team to prepare several questions about one of the four groups listed above, including whether and how the laws affected the group's freedoms. Start the discussion by tossing a beanbag or other soft object to Team 1 and asking a question. After the members of Team 1 answer the question, they toss the beanbag to another team while asking one of their prepared questions. Continue until all teams have exhausted their questions.

NG Learning Framework: Learn About the Underground Railroad

ATTITUDE Empowerment

KNOWLEDGE Our Human Story

Encourage pairs or small groups of students to use library or online resources to gather information about the Underground Railroad—the network of people who, in various ways, helped escaping slaves reach freedom. Have students present their findings to the class, incorporating maps and profiles of some of the "conductors" of the Underground Railroad, such as Harriet Tubman and Thomas Garrett, if possible.

DIFFERENTIATE

Striving Readers

Create Word Squares Ask students to write the word *racism* in the center oval of a Word Square and to write the definition and characteristics in the appropriate boxes. Guide them to identify examples and non-examples. Then instruct them to create a Word Square for *segregation*.

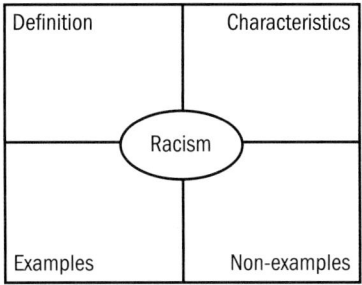

Definition	Characteristics
	Racism
Examples	Non-examples

English Language Learners ELD

Summarize Allow students at the **Bridging** level to work in pairs to summarize the lesson by completing the following sentences using words and phrases from the text.

- By 1860, almost 4 million _____ African Americans lived in the South. *(enslaved)*

- Some southern plantation owners wanted the United States to take the country of _____ from Spain and make it a slave state. *(Cuba)*

- Preventing African Americans from owning property and attending white schools were examples of _____. *(discrimination)*

See the Chapter Planner for more strategies for differentiation.

HISTORICAL THINKING

ANSWERS

1. Many slave owners held the racist view that African Americans were inferior and that it was good for African Americans to be under their "care," as they saw it.

2. In some places, they could not vote, own property, or move about freely. In many cities, African Americans could not enter white schools and churches. They were blocked from skilled jobs and could be attacked by mobs or illegally sold into slavery.

3. In both the South and the North, African Americans were often viewed as inferior and became victims of discrimination.

2.1 A Country in Crisis

In 1820 and again in 1850, compromises had held the United States together. But how many times can you compromise before someone finally cries, "enough already"?

MAIN IDEA The Kansas-Nebraska Act deepened the conflict over slavery and led to the eruption of violence in these territories.

THE KANSAS-NEBRASKA ACT

The discovery of gold in California in 1848 had increased interest in building a railroad to the Pacific coast. **Stephen A. Douglas**, a senator from Illinois, lobbied for the railroad to run through his state. Douglas, who was a great supporter of national expansion, proposed a route stretching from the Illinois city of Chicago west to San Francisco, California.

However, there were problems with this route. Before a railroad could cross the territory west of Minnesota, Iowa, and Missouri, the territory would have to be organized into new states. But the Missouri Compromise had banned slavery in this area. The prospect of new free states infuriated, or enraged, southerners and once again threatened the country's unity.

Douglas introduced a bill that dealt with these issues. It called for the territory to be split into two smaller territories called Kansas and Nebraska, which could then become states. It also called for the repeal of the Missouri Compromise, which would end the long-standing ban on slavery in the North.

The bill, however, did not dictate whether slavery would actually be permitted in the new states. It left that decision to the people. This approach is called **popular sovereignty** (SAHV-run-tee) and allows residents to decide an issue by voting. Douglas had developed this idea, but many northerners, especially in New England, disagreed with it. Despite the strong opposition to popular sovereignty, Douglas managed to push the bill through Congress. It was signed into law in May 1854 as the **Kansas-Nebraska Act**.

Three Compromise Acts, 1820–1854

- Free states
- Slave states
- Territories closed to slavery
- Territories open to slavery
- Non-U.S. areas

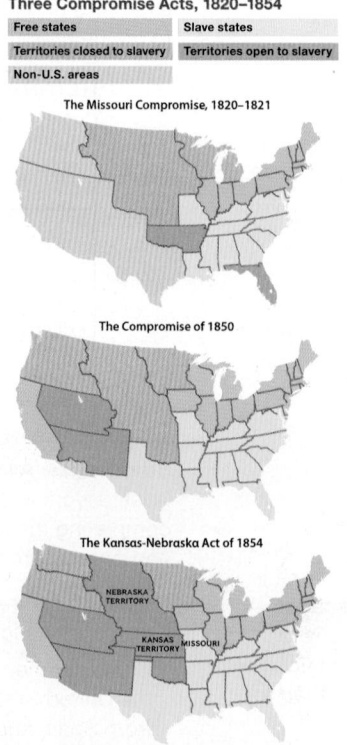

The Missouri Compromise, 1820–1821

The Compromise of 1850

The Kansas-Nebraska Act of 1854

"BLEEDING KANSAS"

Douglas predicted that the Kansas-Nebraska Act would "impart peace to the country [and] stability to the Union." Instead, Kansas became a battleground in the slavery conflict. Antislavery "Free-Soilers," or members of the Free-Soil Party in the North, organized like-minded groups of people to settle in the new territory and vote against slavery there. Free-Soilers hoped that by populating Kansas with people who felt as they did, they could ensure that the territory would become a free state.

But southerners were just as determined to make Kansas a slave state. When elections were held, thousands of slavery supporters from Missouri crossed the border to vote illegally. These "border ruffians," as they were called, were actually not needed because many southerners and slavery supporters already lived in Kansas. Proslavery forces gained control of the legislature in 1855 and passed a series of harsh laws against those who opposed slavery. Antislavery settlers then created their own government within the state and worked through the summer and fall of 1855 to write their own constitution. Over the winter, the Free-Soilers elected a legislature and governor. Groups sympathetic to their cause in the Northeast sent them rifles, while southerners sent a 300-man expedition to support the proslavery settlers.

The situation soon turned violent. In May 1856, a large group of slavery supporters raided the town of Lawrence, Kansas, a free-soil stronghold. They burned down a hotel, destroyed a newspaper office, and threw printing presses into the river. In revenge, a militant, or extremist, abolitionist named **John Brown** led four of his sons and several other men to a proslavery settlement at Pottawatomie (pot-uh-WAH-tuh-mee) Creek. There, they pulled five men out of their houses and brutally murdered them. Federal troops pursued Brown, but he managed to escape. Brown fled north where he was protected by other abolitionists. Because of the violence in Lawrence, Pottawatomie Creek, and other places, Americans

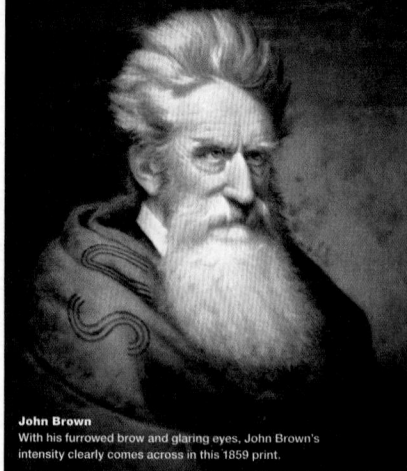

John Brown
With his furrowed brow and glaring eyes, John Brown's intensity clearly comes across in this 1859 print.

began calling the territory "Bleeding Kansas." Eventually, order was restored in Kansas, but the political struggle over slavery continued.

The violence even reached Washington, D.C. Preston Brooks, a representative from South Carolina, had been angered by an antislavery speech given by Massachusetts senator Charles Sumner. When Brooks entered the Senate chamber, he severely beat Sumner with a cane. Soon, the split in the country over slavery would involve the Supreme Court.

HISTORICAL THINKING

1. **READING CHECK** What approach did the Kansas-Nebraska Act take toward the issue of slavery in the Kansas and Nebraska territories?

2. **ANALYZE CAUSE AND EFFECT** What violent incident occurred as a result of a senator's speech opposing slavery?

3. **INTERPRET MAPS** How did U.S. territories represented in the Compromise of 1850 map change after the Kansas-Nebraska Act was passed?

PLAN

Objective
Understand the reasons for and results of the Kansas-Nebraska Act.

Critical Thinking Skills for Lesson 2.1
- Identify Main Ideas and Details
- Monitor Comprehension
- Analyze Cause and Effect
- Interpret Maps
- Evaluate
- Make Connections

Essential Question for Chapter 14
How did slavery divide the country? Plans to build a transcontinental railroad caused further disputes about slavery. Lesson 2.1 discusses how the Kansas-Nebraska Act, meant to settle those disputes, actually increased tensions.

Background for the Teacher
When Stephen A. Douglas introduced the bill that later became the Kansas-Nebraska Act, it met with widespread criticism that reflected Americans' sharply divided views of slavery. In the Senate, six Free-Soilers (including Salmon P. Chase and Charles Sumner) called the bill a plot by a "Slave Power" and predicted that its passage would turn Nebraska into a "dreary region of despotism, inhabited by masters and slaves." Outside of Congress, newspapers in the North condemned the bill, and ministers preached against it. Although opposition was strong, it was not strong enough to keep the bill from passing in the House by a vote of 113 to 100 and in the Senate by a vote of 35 to 13.

Analyze Consequences

Point out that sometimes the solution to a problem can have unintended consequences and may end up creating one or more new problems. Direct students' attention to the first sentence in the lesson. **ASK:** What advantage would a railroad have over other ways of getting to California? *(It would be much faster than other forms of transportation.)* **ASK:** What kinds of problems can you foresee arising from the plan to build a railroad to the Pacific coast? *(Answers will vary. Possible responses: It would cost a lot of money. It might bring on conflict with Native American groups. It would have to cross a difficult landscape.)* Explain that in this lesson students will learn how the plan to build the railroad sparked more conflicts over the issue of slavery.

TEACH

Guided Discussion

1. **Evaluate** Did the Kansas-Nebraska Act guarantee that the North and South would continue to clash over the issue of slavery, or was there hope that tensions would pass once the law went into effect? *(Answers will vary. Possible response: Douglas hoped for an end to the conflict. By this time, however, opinions about slavery were so strongly held that neither side was likely to support the law.)*

2. **Make Connections** In what way did the actions of antislavery settlers in Kansas echo what the American colonists had done about 80 years earlier? *(In both cases, people who did not agree with the established government broke away and created their own government.)*

Interpret Maps

Direct students' attention to the maps and the legend. Invite comments about the meaning of the changing colors on the maps. **ASK:** How did the status of the land that became California change between the Missouri Compromise and the Compromise of 1850? *(In that 30-year period, it went from not even being part of the United States to being a state. Its green color means it became a free state.)* Invite students to ask and answer other questions about the maps.

Active Options

On Your Feet: Numbered Heads Count students off in groups of four. Have the groups discuss how the Kansas-Nebraska Act made the national division over slavery worse instead of better. Then choose a number and ask the student with that number from each group to summarize the group's discussion for the class.

NG Learning Framework: Learn More About "Bleeding Kansas"

ATTITUDE Empowerment

KNOWLEDGE Our Human Story

Invite students to learn more about "Bleeding Kansas." Tell them to think of a question they would like answered about the conflicts. Then have them use library or online resources to research the answer. Instruct students to use their research to generate and answer related questions, such as: How might things have been done differently to prevent or stop the violence? Ask volunteers to read their questions and answers aloud, then lead a class discussion about their views.

DIFFERENTIATE

Inclusion

Work in Pairs Pair special needs students with students at a higher proficiency level or with a teacher's aide. Have students trace the boundaries of each type of area (signified by color) on each map, especially the "closed to slavery" and "open to slavery" territories. Make sure that students understand the importance of the changes brought about by the Kansas-Nebraska Act.

Gifted & Talented

Present a Documentary Invite students to prepare and present a short documentary in which they explore the tactics adopted by proslavery and antislavery forces to advance their causes and whether those tactics were justified. Encourage students to review what they have learned about border ruffians, John Brown, and Free-Soilers and to conduct additional research about the situation in Kansas. Follow the presentation with a discussion about the tensions that led to "Bleeding Kansas."

See the Chapter Planner for more strategies for differentiation.

HISTORICAL THINKING

ANSWERS

1. The act let the people of Kansas and Nebraska decide whether or not to allow slavery in their territories.

2. The senator, Charles Sumner, was attacked by Representative Preston Brooks, who beat Sumner with a cane.

3. The main change was that before the act took effect, the land that became the Kansas Territory and Nebraska Territory was closed to slavery; afterward, the territories were open to slavery.

The Dred Scott Decision

When things are going badly, we like to think that, at least, they can't get any worse. Until, of course, they do.

MAIN IDEA The Dred Scott case and John Brown's attack on Harpers Ferry further divided the North and the South over the issue of slavery.

THE REPUBLICAN PARTY

The Kansas-Nebraska Act caused the political differences in the United States to erupt. The repeal of the Missouri Compromise and the opening of new territories to slavery angered many northerners and deepened North-South divisions in the Whig and Democratic parties. Many northerners began to feel that none of the existing political parties reflected their growing concerns over slavery.

In reaction, antislavery leaders founded a new party in 1854 dedicated to fighting the expansion of slavery. The **Republican Party**, as it was named, found a following among former Whigs, Free-Soilers, Democrats, and Know-Nothings.

When the 1856 presidential election approached, the Republicans picked John C. Frémont, who was well-known for his explorations of the West, as their candidate. The Democrats chose **James Buchanan** to represent their party. Buchanan secured the presidency, but Frémont made a strong showing, winning 11 northern states. From the outset, the Republicans proved they were a force to be reckoned with.

DRED SCOTT AND JOHN BROWN

In March of 1857, two days after Buchanan took office, the U.S. Supreme Court issued a decision in *Dred Scott* v. *Sandford*, which had begun in 1846. The case involved a slave named

Dred Scott was about 60 years old when this photo was taken during his Supreme Court case. His former master's sons purchased and freed Scott after the decision, but he died nine months later.

Dred Scott. He had sued for his freedom on the grounds that his master had taken him to live in the free state of Illinois and in the Wisconsin Territory, where slavery was also prohibited.

The Court ruled that Scott should remain a slave, and the **Dred Scott decision** sent shockwaves through the nation. In his explanation of the ruling, Chief Justice **Roger Taney** asserted that "members of the negro African race" were not actually citizens of the United States. Therefore, Scott did not have the right to bring a lawsuit to a federal court. Taney further declared that since slaves were the personal property of slaveholders, Congress had never had the authority to restrict slavery in the territories. This rendered the Missouri Compromise of 1820 unconstitutional. The strongly proslavery decision sparked outrage in the North and raised fears that southerners might try to extend slavery to the whole country. The chasm between North and South grew even wider.

Two years later, yet another dramatic event in the struggle over slavery took center stage. John Brown, the abolitionist responsible for the Pottawatomie Creek massacre in Kansas, led an attack on the town of **Harpers Ferry**, in the part of Virginia that later became West Virginia. He and his armed band of 21 men captured a federal arsenal and a rifle-manufacturing plant and took dozens of hostages. Brown hoped to trigger a

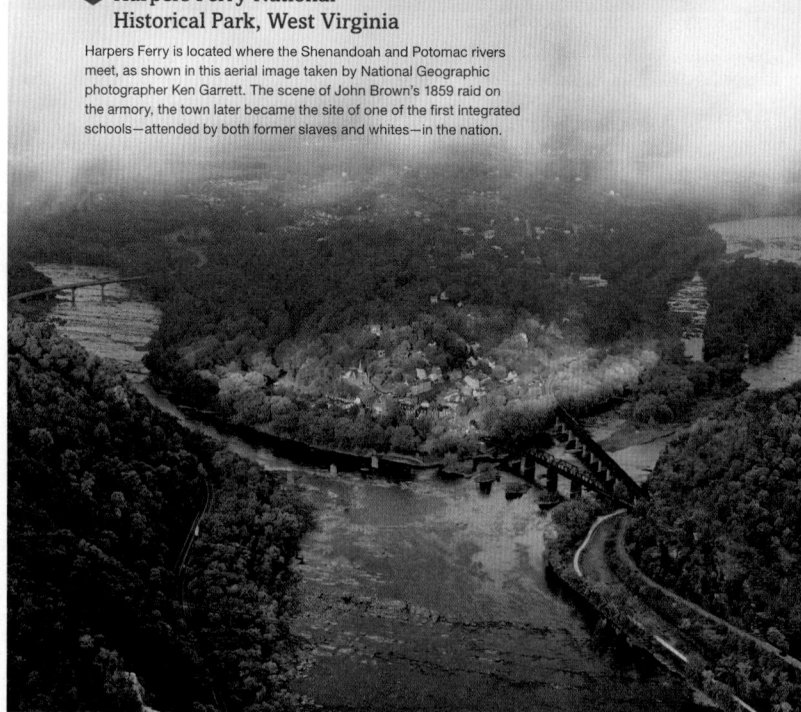

Harpers Ferry National Historical Park, West Virginia

Harpers Ferry is located where the Shenandoah and Potomac rivers meet, as shown in this aerial image taken by National Geographic photographer Ken Garrett. The scene of John Brown's 1859 raid on the armory, the town later became the site of one of the first integrated schools—attended by both former slaves and whites—in the nation.

slave revolt and create an "army of emancipation" that would free slaves across the South. He was wounded and captured, however, and ten of his men were killed. After a short trial, he was hanged just six weeks after the attack. To the dismay of southerners, many northerners refused to condemn Brown. Instead, they viewed him as a hero and a martyr, or a person willing to die for his or her beliefs, to the cause of abolition. The raid at Harpers Ferry increased southerners' fear of slave rebellions and further heightened the tension between the North and the South. As a result, slavery was about to bring the country to the breaking point.

HISTORICAL THINKING

1. **READING CHECK** Why did Dred Scott believe he should be freed from slavery?

2. **IDENTIFY MAIN IDEAS AND DETAILS** What political ideas led to the formation of the Republican Party?

3. **DISTINGUISH FACT FROM OPINION** Is Roger Taney's assertion that "members of the negro African race" were not actually citizens of the United States a fact or opinion? Explain your answer.

PLAN

Objective
Learn how the *Dred Scott* decision and the Harpers Ferry attack inflamed views on slavery.

Critical Thinking Skills for Lesson 2.2
- Identify Main Ideas and Details
- Monitor Comprehension
- Distinguish Fact from Opinion
- Identify
- Summarize

Essential Question for Chapter 14
How did slavery divide the country? In 1857, the Supreme Court's controversial decision in the *Dred Scott* case intensified the already strong division between antislavery and proslavery Americans. Lesson 2.2 examines the details of that decision and its violent repercussions.

Background for the Teacher
Although Dred Scott had spent much time in the free states of Illinois and Wisconsin, he did not sue for his freedom while there. Instead, he began the lawsuit while living in St. Louis, Missouri. When the *Dred Scott* case came before the Supreme Court, the Court consisted of five southern Democrats, two northern Democrats, one northern Republican, and one northern Whig. There was, therefore, a strong proslavery sentiment on the Court; in fact, many of the justices came from families that owned slaves. Democrats on the Court wanted to hand down a ruling that would definitively settle the issue of slavery in new states and territories, and the vote went 7 to 2 against Scott.

Activate Prior Knowledge

Invite students to share what they know about the groups from which the Republican Party was formed. Ask these questions and write students' responses on the board:

• What belief united the Free-Soilers? *(keeping slavery out of new territories and states)*

• Whom did the Whigs support more: businesspeople or planters? *(businesspeople)*

• Was the Democratic Party in favor of slavery or opposed to it? *(in favor of it)*

Discuss how these facts suggest that the Republican Party would be more in tune with the interests of the North.

TEACH
Guided Discussion

1. **Identify** What reason did the Supreme Court give for deciding against Dred Scott? *(As stated by Chief Justice Roger Taney, Scott was not a citizen of the United States but merely the property of his master.)*

2. **Summarize** What happened at the town of Harpers Ferry, Virginia, in 1859? *(John Brown led an armed attack on the town in hopes of starting a slave revolt. His band took hostages and captured a federal arsenal and a rifle-manufacturing plant. Ten of Brown's men were killed, he and the rest were captured, and Brown was hanged.)*

🛡 American Places

Harpers Ferry National Historical Park covers 3,670 acres, offering opportunities for visitors to hike more than 20 miles of trails and explore Civil War battlefields. One of the park's most visited sites is Lower Town, whose buildings appear in the center of the lesson's photograph. Lower Town is home to several museums, including the John Brown Museum. In conjunction with the Harpers Ferry Historical Association, Lower Town offers a look at 19th-century life through workshops that focus on skills such as blacksmithing, sewing, and tinsmithing. It also presents a variety of living history events each year.

Active Options

On Your Feet: Team Word Webbing Organize students into teams of four and have them record what they know about the *Dred Scott* decision on a piece of paper. Encourage students to build on their teammates' entries as they rotate the paper from one member to the next. Then call on volunteers to use their team's web to make statements about that historic Supreme Court ruling.

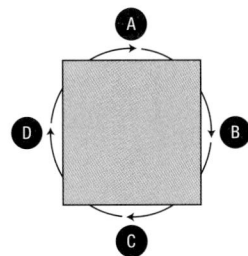

NG Learning Framework: Evaluate a Historical Figure

ATTITUDE Responsibility

SKILL Observation

Explain that some Americans have revered John Brown, celebrating him in artwork and song as a heroic martyr, but others view him as a radical and a terrorist. Encourage students to learn more about John Brown. Instruct them to reflect on their findings and to then write a short evaluation of Brown, supporting their views with information from the chapter and additional source material. Remind them to consider whether sources they find contain facts, opinions, or both.

Striving Readers

Use Reciprocal Teaching Pair striving readers with more proficient readers, and have these pairs read the lesson together. Instruct students to take turns reading each paragraph aloud. At the end of the paragraph, the reading student should ask the listening student a question or two about what the listener has just heard. For example, students may ask their partners to summarize the paragraph in their own words.

Pre-AP

Explore Human Drama Instruct students to look beyond the facts of the *Dred Scott* decision to find background information about Scott and his wife, their lives, and the events leading up to the legal conflicts. Then invite students to dramatize the events in a short play or a rap that emphasizes the personal perspective of the main characters.

See the Chapter Planner for more strategies for differentiation.

ANSWERS

1. Scott believed that he had the right to freedom because he had lived for extended periods in a free state and a free territory.

2. The passage of the Kansas-Nebraska Act convinced many northerners that none of the existing political parties shared their concerns over the spread of slavery.

3. Taney's assertion is an opinion. The opposite viewpoint could be supported with evidence as well.

2.3 Lincoln and Douglas

Republican Abraham Lincoln and Democrat Stephen Douglas opposed each other in two political races. In 1858, they fought for the U.S. Senate seat in Illinois, which Douglas won. In 1860, they ran against each other for president, with Lincoln the victor. Although both men disliked slavery, they had different views on the issue.

Lincoln and Douglas engaged in a series of debates during their race for the Illinois Senate seat. Their fourth debate was held on September 18, 1858, in Charleston, Illinois. There, Douglas attacked Lincoln by saying that his opponent favored racial equality, an unpopular position at the time, even in the North. The painting below shows Lincoln speaking to the crowd gathered for the outdoor event. Douglas sits to Lincoln's right, waiting his turn to speak.

CRITICAL VIEWING How does the artist portray the debate?

Abraham Lincoln and Stephen A. Douglas Debating at Charleston by Robert Marshall Root, 1918

DOCUMENT ONE

Primary Source: Speech
from Abraham Lincoln's speech at the Republican Convention in Springfield, Illinois, on June 16, 1858

This speech is known as the "House Divided" speech. Lincoln used a Bible metaphor, comparing the nation to a house, to express his view of the impact that conflicting laws about slavery were having on the country as a whole.

CONSTRUCTED RESPONSE What does Lincoln think will happen to the Union if the division continues?

"A house divided against itself cannot stand." I believe this government cannot endure, permanently, half slave and half free. I do not expect the Union to be dissolved; I do not expect the house to fall; but I do expect it will cease to be divided. It will become all one thing, or all the other.

DOCUMENT TWO

Primary Source: Speech
from Stephen Douglas's speech at the Lincoln-Douglas debate in Freeport, Illinois, on August 27, 1858

In a debate held in Freeport, Illinois, Douglas addressed a question that Lincoln had put to him: Could the people of a territory keep slavery out? Douglas believed they could and, in this excerpt, he explains how.

CONSTRUCTED RESPONSE Describe how Douglas uses cause and effect to explain how people can keep slavery out of a territory.

The people have the lawful means to introduce it [slavery] or exclude it as they please, for the reason that slavery cannot exist a day or an hour anywhere, unless it is supported by local police regulations. Those police regulations can only be established by the local legislature, and if the people are opposed to slavery they will elect representatives to that body who will by unfriendly legislation effectually prevent the introduction of it into their midst.

DOCUMENT THREE

Primary Source: Political Cartoon
from *Harper's Weekly*, 1860

This political cartoon suggests that the issue of slavery is tearing the United States apart. Seen here are the four candidates in the 1860 presidential election. From left to right are Abraham Lincoln, Stephen Douglas, John C. Breckinridge, and John Bell.

CONSTRUCTED RESPONSE What details in the cartoon suggest that slavery is tearing the United States apart?

SYNTHESIZE & WRITE

1. **REVIEW** Review what you have learned about Abraham Lincoln and Stephen Douglas and their debates.

2. **RECALL** On your own paper, write the main idea expressed in each document.

3. **CONSTRUCT** Construct a topic sentence that answers this question: What differing positions did Lincoln and Douglas take on the issue of slavery?

4. **WRITE** Using evidence from this chapter and the documents, write an informative paragraph that supports your topic sentence in Step 3.

PLAN

Objective
Synthesize information about Lincoln and Douglas from primary source documents.

Critical Thinking Skills for Lesson 2.3
- Synthesize
- Make Generalizations
- Describe
- Evaluate

Essential Question for Chapter 14
How did slavery divide the country? Stephen A. Douglas and Abraham Lincoln held differing views regarding slavery. Lesson 2.3 provides excerpts from key speeches by these politicians and a political cartoon that expresses one view of the division caused by their differences.

Background for the Teacher

Douglas was not a staunch supporter of slavery, but he did believe in popular sovereignty, which made slavery possible in some new territories. He also felt strongly that slavery should be dealt with as a political issue rather than as a moral issue. In contrast, Lincoln presented slavery as morally indefensible in the 1858 debates, a set of seven debates to which Douglas agreed only reluctantly. The election was close, and Lincoln lost the Senate seat to Douglas. However, the campaign gave him exposure that would benefit him when he took on Douglas for the presidency two years later.

INTRODUCE & ENGAGE

Prepare for the Document-Based Question

Before students start on the activity, briefly preview the three documents. Remind students that a constructed response requires full explanations in complete sentences. Emphasize that students should use what they have learned about the national debate over slavery in addition to the information in the documents.

TEACH

Guided Discussion

1. **Make Generalizations** According to the Douglas excerpt, what restriction is placed upon police as enforcers of the law? *(The police can act only within the laws that are established by the local legislature.)*

2. **Describe** According to the political cartoon, which part of the United States was of special interest to each of the candidates in 1860? *(The part of the map that each candidate is trying to claim indicates that Bell was interested in the North, with its free states, and that Breckinridge was interested in the South, with its slave states. Lincoln and Douglas were interested in the new territories, where slavery was an especially intense issue.)*

Evaluate

After students have completed the Synthesize & Write activity, allow time for them to exchange paragraphs and read and comment on the work of their peers. Establish guidelines for comments prior to this activity so that feedback is constructive and encouraging in nature.

Active Options

Active History: Debate an Issue Extend the lesson by using either the PDF or Whiteboard version of the activity. These activities take a deeper look at a topic from, or related to, the lesson. Explore the activities as a class, turn them into group assignments, or even assign them individually.

On Your Feet: Think, Pair, Share Give students a few minutes to think about this question: What other issues could result in a "house divided" and threaten the Union through differing state or regional values? Then have students choose partners and talk about the question for five minutes. Finally, allow individual students to share their ideas with the class.

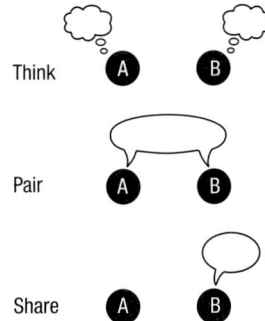

Think A B

Pair A B

Share A B

DIFFERENTIATE

Inclusion

Synthesize Help students minimize distractions by creating a document that includes the two excerpts alone. Give a copy to each student along with a highlighter. Tell students to highlight important words that appear in the excerpts. Then have them write a summary sentence for each excerpt using several of the words.

English Language Learners

Clarify Multiple Meaning Words Make sure students understand that some words have more than one meaning. To determine which meaning is meant in a particular sentence, students may be able to find context clues, but sometimes referring to a dictionary is more efficient. Have students at the **Expanding** and **Bridging** levels assist students at the **Emerging** level in determining the correct meaning of these words from the two speech excerpts: *stand, dissolved, introduce,* and *body.*

See the Chapter Planner for more strategies for differentiation.

SYNTHESIZE & WRITE

ANSWERS

1. Answers will vary.

2. Answers will vary.

3. Answers will vary. Possible response: Douglas believed in popular sovereignty, but Lincoln felt that slavery should be allowed either everywhere or nowhere.

4. Answers will vary. Students' paragraphs should include their topic sentence from Step 3 and provide several details from the documents and Chapter 14 to support the sentence.

CONSTRUCTED RESPONSE

Document 1: Possible response: Lincoln states his belief that if the division continues, the Union will fail.

Document 2: Possible response: Douglas says that if the people of a territory elect lawmakers who are opposed to slavery, the effect will be that these lawmakers can pass legislation to prevent its introduction.

Document 3: Possible response: The cartoon depicts four presidential candidates with differing views regarding slavery. They are tearing apart a map, which symbolizes the divisive nature of the slavery question in the United States.

CRITICAL VIEWING Answers will vary. Possible response: The artist portrays the debate as a formal event held outside for the public to view. Lincoln is shown in a heroic stance while all the other men are seated, perhaps giving greater weight to what he is saying.

3.1 The Election of 1860

Say you belong to a club and two groups within it often disagree. Should they try to work things out? Or should one group break away and form a new club? Maybe it depends on whether they're into politics.

MAIN IDEA The growing divide between the North and the South had a strong impact on the 1860 presidential election.

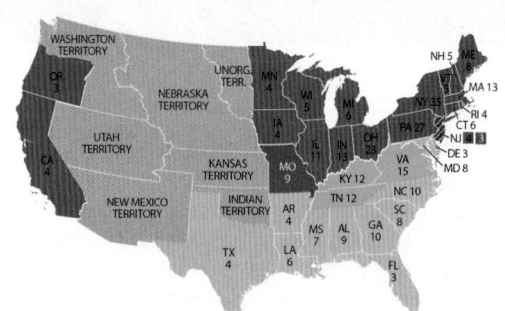

1860 Presidential Election

Lincoln, Republican
Electoral Vote: 180 votes, 59.4%
Popular Vote: 1,866,452 votes, 39.8%

Douglas, Northern Democrat
Electoral Vote: 12 votes, 3.9%
Popular Vote: 1,380,202 votes, 29.5%

Breckinridge, Southern Democrat
Electoral Vote: 72 votes, 23.8%
Popular Vote: 847,953 votes, 18.1%

Bell, Constitutional Unionist
Electoral Vote: 39 votes, 12.9%
Popular Vote: 590,901 votes, 12.6%

POLITICAL PARTIES BREAK APART

"Bleeding Kansas," the Dred Scott decision, John Brown's raid at Harpers Ferry: each of these developments had left the United States more divided over slavery. The Democratic Party found it harder to hold itself together as tensions grew between its powerful southern faction, or group, and its smaller northern faction. When the two factions could not agree on a candidate for the 1860 presidential election, the party split in two. Northern Democrats nominated Stephen Douglas of Illinois, and southern Democrats nominated **John Breckinridge** of Kentucky.

Around this same time, a group of former Whigs and Know-Nothings founded the conservative **Constitutional Union Party**. It appealed to people who believed that preserving the Union and protecting the

Constitution outweighed concerns about slavery. For the election, **Unionists**, as members of the Constitutional Union Party were called, sought a compromise candidate who could appeal to both northerners and southerners. They chose John Bell, a highly regarded former U.S. senator from Tennessee.

Lincoln Campaign Banner

Lincoln's running mate in the 1860 election was Hannibal Hamlin, a senator from Maine. In this cotton flag, Lincoln's first name is spelled "Abram," possibly to enable his name to appear larger. "Abram" is also the original spelling of the biblical Abraham. The portrait of Lincoln may have been printed sideways so the flag could be hung vertically.

THE NOMINATION OF LINCOLN

In May 1860, Republicans gathered in Chicago, Illinois, for their national convention. Party strategists identified four states that would be key to winning the upcoming election: Illinois, Indiana, New Jersey, and Pennsylvania. The first three bordered southern states and were more moderate in their views about slavery than states farther north. The party decided to place its presidential hopes on a moderate from Illinois: Abraham Lincoln.

Born in a one-room log cabin, Lincoln grew up on frontier farms in Kentucky and Indiana. His mother died when he was just nine. Because the family was poor, they moved from place to place, struggling to survive. Young Lincoln developed a love of reading but had to work, so he received very little formal schooling. When Lincoln was 21, he moved with his family to Illinois. There, he taught himself law, built a thriving legal practice, and launched a successful political career. He served four terms in the Illinois state assembly and one term in the U.S. House of Representatives. He failed twice in bids for the U.S. Senate, but that didn't stop him from running for president in 1860.

In the presidential campaign, Lincoln did not try to win over southern voters, and Breckinridge spent little effort on the North. Southerners refused to consider Lincoln because they believed he was too antislavery, while northerners rejected

Breckinridge's proslavery views. Bell focused his attention on like-minded Unionists in the states between the North and the South. Douglas, however, campaigned in both the North and the South, defending the Union and warning against voting along sectional lines. Because Bell and Douglas didn't propose enacting laws one way or the other on slavery, they were considered the moderate candidates.

When voters cast their ballots on election day, Lincoln won almost 40 percent of the popular vote, and he captured the electoral votes in every northern state except New Jersey, which he split with Douglas. Not surprisingly, he didn't win any electoral votes in the South. For the most part, voters cast their ballots along regional lines. The election proved they were tired of compromising. And for many southerners, the election also drew a line in the sand that they were not afraid to cross.

HISTORICAL THINKING

1. **READING CHECK** Why were there two Democratic candidates in the 1860 election?

2. **MAKE INFERENCES** Why might Abraham Lincoln's background have appealed to voters?

3. **INTERPRET MAPS** Why did winning just the northern states guarantee that Lincoln would secure the majority of electoral votes?

PLAN

Objective

Describe the divisive issues in the presidential election of 1860 and the election's outcome.

Critical Thinking Skills for Lesson 3.1

- Identify Main Ideas and Details
- Monitor Comprehension
- Make Inferences
- Interpret Maps
- Form and Support Opinions
- Analyze Cause and Effect
- Categorize

Essential Question for Chapter 14

How did slavery divide the country? As the 1860 election approached, Americans continued to be divided in their views on slavery. Lesson 3.1 discusses how this division shaped political parties and how the election's outcome offered little hope for reconciliation.

Background for the Teacher

Campaign slogans have long been a way of summarizing a party's stance, and the slogans used in 1860 were no exception. The Constitutional Union Party backed John Bell with slogans supporting national unity, such as "The Union as it is, and the Constitution as it is." John Breckinridge, the candidate of the southern Democrats, was proslavery, but he also wanted to see the Union kept whole—a view signaled in the slogan "Our Rights, the Constitution and the Union." Republicans drew on Abraham Lincoln's folksy persona with slogans such as "Honest Old Abe—the People's Choice" and "The Rail-Splitter of 1830/The President of U.S. 1861." They also tried to focus on issues other than slavery with the slogan "Vote Yourself a Farm," a promise of free land for settlers in the west. Stephen A. Douglas, representing northern Democrats, took direct aim at Lincoln with "No Rail-Splitter Can Split This Union."

INTRODUCE & ENGAGE

Convention Quickwrite

Have students take a few minutes to write something that they have read, seen, or heard about political conventions in a presidential election year. Then ask volunteers to share what they wrote. Explain that the Democratic Convention in 1860 was among the most turbulent in American history.

TEACH

Guided Discussion

1. **Form and Support Opinions** The Constitutional Union Party ignored the issue of slavery. Do you think that was a wise decision? Why or why not? Support your opinion with evidence from the text. *(Answers will vary. Some students may feel that it was unwise not to take a stand on such an important issue; others may suggest that party leaders believed that their ticket would get more votes if the issue of slavery were not part of the platform.)*

2. **Analyze Cause and Effect** Reread the last two paragraphs of the lesson. Does the text present information sequentially, comparatively, or causally? What makes you say so? *(The information is presented causally; it tells why voters voted as they did.)*

Categorize

Draw a Three-Column Chart on the board and label columns with these categories: Party, Position on Slavery, and Target Voters. As a class, identify each party, the party's position on slavery, and the segment of the voting population to which the party directed its efforts. Students should recognize that northern Democrats were relatively quiet regarding slavery and appealed to northerners; southern Democrats were proslavery and appealed to southerners; Republicans were against slavery in new territories and appealed to northerners; and Unionists took no position on slavery in hopes of appealing to both northerners and southerners.

Party	Position on Slavery	Target Voters
Northern Democrat		
Southern Democrat		
Republican		
Constitutional Union		

Active Options

On Your Feet: Fishbowl One half of the class sits in a small circle facing inward. The other half of the class sits in a larger circle around them. Post the question: How did the issues of slavery and preservation of the Union influence the selection of candidates and the outcome of the 1860 presidential election? Students in the inner circle should discuss the question while those in the outer circle listen to the discussion and evaluate the points made. Then the groups reverse roles and continue the discussion.

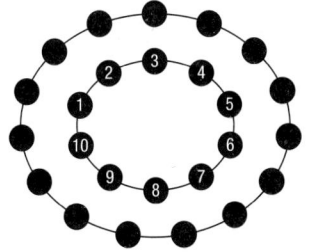

NG Learning Framework: Write a Campaign Song

ATTITUDE Curiosity

SKILLS Collaboration, Communication

Invite students to work in groups to learn more about Abraham Lincoln as a folk hero. After they complete their investigation using library and online sources, tell students to use their findings to write lyrics for a campaign song for Lincoln. Students may put new words to a familiar melody or may write an original melody. Alternatively, have students locate and present a recording of "Lincoln and Liberty Too," the actual campaign anthem.

DIFFERENTIATE

Inclusion

Describe Lesson Visuals Pair visually impaired students with students who are not visually challenged. Ask the latter to describe the elements of Lincoln's campaign banner (for example, the wording, including the name Abram Lincoln; the image of Lincoln without a beard; the ring of stars and the four corner stars, totaling 33 to represent the 33 states in the Union in 1860). Guide sighted partners to answer questions the visually impaired students might have.

English Language Learners

Study Idioms Students of **All Proficiencies** may come across idioms that are confusing to them. Explain that idioms are expressions whose meaning is different from the literal meaning of the words. Explain that in the idiom *cast their ballots*, the word *ballot* comes from the Italian word *ballotta*, which means "little ball," and that long ago, people often voted by tossing (casting) a small colored ball into a container to show their choice. *Draw a line in the sand* refers to setting a boundary against someone; anyone defying that boundary (by crossing the line) increases the likelihood of conflict. Help students secure their understanding of these expressions by acting them out.

See the Chapter Planner for more strategies for differentiation.

HISTORICAL THINKING

ANSWERS

1. Northern Democrats and southern Democrats could not agree on a candidate, so the party split in two.

2. Answers will vary. Possible response: Voters might have felt that because Lincoln grew up poor, he could better relate to the common people. They might also have found him appealing as a "self-made man."

3. The number of electors per state is based in part on the state's population. This guaranteed Lincoln a majority of electoral votes because the northern states were significantly more populous than the southern states.

3.2 Southern States Secede

A crack in a mirror often starts out small, hardly visible. But over time, rough handling causes the crack to deepen and run the length of the glass. Pretty soon, the smallest added pressure will make it snap and break in two.

MAIN IDEA The election of Abraham Lincoln as president in 1860 led southern states to secede from the Union.

THE SOUTH DEBATES INDEPENDENCE

The South had reached its breaking point. Abraham Lincoln's victory in the 1860 election shocked and angered most southerners. They were suddenly faced with a northern president who had not won a single southern state. In fact, his name had not even appeared on the ballot in most of them. After all, Lincoln represented a party founded by people who wanted to keep slavery out of new territories and states.

Although Lincoln had not called for the abolition of slavery many proslavery southerners felt certain this was his goal. You've already read one excerpt from Lincoln's "House Divided" speech, delivered in 1858. In that speech he also said, "Either the opponents of slavery will arrest the further spread of it, . . . or its advocates [supporters] will push it forward, till it shall become alike lawful in all the States." In the South, many assumed this meant that Lincoln wished to abolish slavery throughout the United States.

On the day after the election, South Carolina's legislature gathered to debate the possibility of **seceding**, or formally withdrawing from the Union and becoming independent. Secession was not a new idea. Slave states had threatened to leave the Union on numerous occasions. In fact, South Carolina had come very close to doing so during the nullification crisis of the 1830s.

Supporters of secession justified it in terms of states' rights. The right that southern leaders most wanted to protect was their perceived right to own slaves. They argued that under the Constitution, the states retained certain rights,

1860 campaign buttons feature Lincoln (left) and his running mate, Hamlin (right).

including the right to secede. Just as each state had once decided to join the Union, each state could decide to withdraw from it.

VOTES FOR SECESSION

On December 20, 1860, South Carolina became the first state in the nation to secede from the Union. The state's secession came in response to the presidential election of Abraham Lincoln the month before, even though he was not to take office until March 1861. South Carolina decided that Lincoln's presidential win as a Republican—a party that supported the Free-Soil platform, not the end of slavery in territories where it already existed—signaled that it could not continue as part of the United States.

South Carolina was joined by 10 other states in the coming months. In March 1861, the **Confederate States of America**, or the **Confederacy**, united and quickly formed a temporary government in Montgomery, Alabama, and adopted a new constitution. It was much like the U.S. Constitution, but it protected slavery and states' rights.

Jefferson Davis, a Mississippi senator who had spoken out against secession just weeks earlier, was chosen to be the temporary president of the Confederacy. In his inaugural address, Davis placed the blame for the secessions on the Union,

Abraham Lincoln
This 1860 photo by Alexander Hesler reveals Lincoln's lined face and rugged features.

arguing that protecting slavery had been the "well-known intent" of the Founders. Meanwhile, the issue of secession was proving to be divisive in the more northern part of the South. Many people opposed secession, calling it treason. They believed secession would be disastrous for the South. Others thought it would be best to wait before making a decision. For the time being, Virginia, Tennessee, North Carolina, and Arkansas remained in the Union. They still held out hope that the differences between the North and the South could be resolved.

HISTORICAL THINKING

1. **READING CHECK** Why did Lincoln's election drive southern states to secede from the Union?

2. **MAKE INFERENCES** Why do you think the Confederacy adopted a constitution that was very similar to the U.S. Constitution?

3. **DRAW CONCLUSIONS** What fundamental challenge to the Constitution did secession and the doctrine of nullification pose?

Objective

Learn how the 1860 election led directly to the founding of the Confederate States of America.

Critical Thinking Skills for Lesson 3.2

- Identify Main Ideas and Details
- Monitor Comprehension
- Make Inferences
- Draw Conclusions
- Ask and Answer Questions
- Form and Support Opinions

Essential Question for Chapter 14

How did slavery divide the country? Proslavery states could not abide the idea that Abraham Lincoln would be the next president. Lesson 3.2 examines how the philosophical division over slavery resulted in a formal division through secession and the founding of the Confederacy.

Background for the Teacher

When Lincoln was elected, Democrats controlled the Senate and the Supreme Court. However, many southern leaders feared that when he became president, Lincoln would give Republicans federal positions throughout the South and that these officials might undermine slavery from within. The South Carolina legislature, meeting the day after Lincoln's election, called for an election to be held two months later, in January, to select delegates who would then decide the course the state should follow. Legislators hoped that in the meantime support for secession would grow throughout the South. Support indeed grew—so quickly, in fact, that South Carolina decided to secede before the planned-for election could take place.

History Notebook

Encourage students to complete the American Gallery page for Chapter 14 in their History Notebooks as they read.

INTRODUCE & ENGAGE

Activate Prior Knowledge

Review the Tenth Amendment to the Constitution with the class by reading its text aloud. Remind students that according to the Tenth Amendment, any powers that are not specifically given to the federal government belong to the states and to American citizens. **ASK:** How might the concept of states' rights figure into the debate over slavery? *(Many Americans might have believed that states, not the federal government, had the right to decide whether to allow slavery.)* Explain that the concept of states' rights was applied in a new way after the election of Abraham Lincoln.

TEACH

Guided Discussion

1. **Ask and Answer Questions** If you had been part of the South Carolina legislature discussing the possibility of seceding, what questions would you have raised in the discussion? *(Answers will vary. Possible response: How quickly can we get other states to join us? How might the North retaliate?)*

2. **Form and Support Opinions** Do you agree or disagree with Jefferson Davis that the Union was to blame for the secessions? Why or why not? Support your opinion with evidence from the text. *(Possible responses: Yes; antislavery factions in the Union intended to end slavery, which would hurt the economy of the South. No; the South was to blame for placing more importance on keeping slaves than on preserving the Union.)*

More Information

Buchanan's Reaction When South Carolina seceded, James Buchanan was still president. He made no attempt to respond to that secession nor to the others that followed while he was still in office, leaving that task to Lincoln. Buchanan declared that the secession was illegal, but he also declared that taking government action to stop it would be illegal. He blamed the secession on the "intemperate interference of the northern people with the question of slavery" and stated that the Union could be saved if the slave states were allowed "to manage their domestic institutions in their own way." Buchanan apparently was relieved that he didn't have to resolve the crisis, for he is said to have told Lincoln, "If you are as happy in entering the White House as I shall feel on returning to Wheatland [his home in Pennsylvania], you are a happy man."

Active Options

On Your Feet: Sequence Chain Have groups of students trace the events described in the lesson by summarizing them in a Sequence Chain. When groups have completed their work, guide students from the groups to stand up and form a physical chain, with volunteers reading one event after the other as they form the successive links.

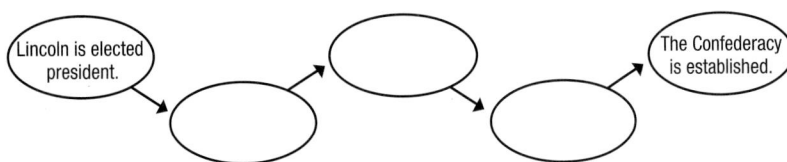

AMERICAN **GALLERY**
ONLINE

Abraham Lincoln Invite students to explore the American Gallery. Have them select one of the photos and do additional research to learn more about it. Ask questions that will inspire additional inquiry about the chosen photo, such as: Why do you think this photograph is important? How does it help to create an "image" for Abraham Lincoln?

DIFFERENTIATE

Striving Readers

Identify Main Ideas and Details Remind students that a main idea is a statement that summarizes the key idea of an article, speech, paragraph, or other written or spoken work. Details are facts, dates, events, and descriptions that support a main idea. Ask students to use their own words to write one main idea and three details about the secession of southern states. Encourage students to share their completed work and reach a consensus about the most important main ideas and details.

Main Idea:
Detail:
Detail:
Detail:

Pre-AP

Research the Secessionist States Have students do research to learn more about each of the states that seceded. Then invite them to present their findings to the class. Instruct students to find out not just when the states seceded but also what statements their leaders made when they did so. Guide the class to look for common themes in the material presented.

See the Chapter Planner for more strategies for differentiation.

HISTORICAL THINKING

ANSWERS

1. Southerners were motivated to secede because Lincoln was a northerner who had not won any southern states, his party had been founded upon antislavery principles, and he had proclaimed that the country could not remain divided between free states and slave states.

2. Leaders of the Confederacy wanted to protect the right to slavery and states' rights, but they still believed in the basic principles of the U.S. Constitution.

3. If a state could decide that a federal policy or decision was unconstitutional and did not apply to the state, then the federal government didn't really have the power to make laws for the entire country.

3.3 Efforts at Compromise

Who among your friends is the peacemaker? There's usually one who brings those in conflict together and tries to find common ground and iron out differences. Sometimes these efforts pay off. Sometimes they don't.

MAIN IDEA Leaders in the North and the South tried to resolve the secession crisis, but their attempts to reach a compromise failed.

Lincoln with His Cabinet and Generals
In this engraving from 1866, Lincoln meets with his Cabinet and military leaders to discuss their response to the South's secession. Lincoln did not want war with the South, but he wanted to be prepared for it if it couldn't be avoided.

THE CRITTENDEN PLAN

After South Carolina seceded from the Union, John J. Crittenden, a senator from Kentucky, tried to step in as peacemaker. In 1861, he offered a proposal that came to be known as the **Crittenden Plan**. Under the terms of this compromise plan, the federal government would have no power to abolish slavery in the states where it already existed. Further, the Missouri Compromise line would be reestablished and extended all the way to the Pacific Ocean. Slavery would be prohibited in territories north of the line, but in territories south of it, local residents would decide whether to allow slavery.

The proposal found many supporters in both the North and the South, and President James Buchanan pushed for its speedy approval in Congress. President-elect Abraham Lincoln and many Republicans, however, strongly objected to extending slavery in any new territories. After much debate, the Crittenden Plan was defeated in Congress, and the secession crisis continued.

A Perpetual Union

At the beginning of his inaugural address, Lincoln stated that he was going to get directly to the point and talk about the matter of greatest concern to the country at that moment: the threat of southern secession. He assured the South that he did not support freeing its slaves. But he also emphasized that there was no constitutional basis for withdrawing from the Union.

LINCOLN BECOMES PRESIDENT

As his inauguration approached, Lincoln put together his government. For his Cabinet, he purposely chose men who represented competing factions within the Republican Party. Some of them could barely stand one another.

Surprisingly, four of the top positions went to men who had competed with Lincoln for the Republican nomination. He would later defend these appointments by saying, "We needed the strongest men of the party in the Cabinet. These were the very strongest men. Then I had no right to deprive the country of their services." Some have called the men he assembled "a team of rivals."

Lincoln took office on March 4, 1861, as the 16th president of the United States. In his inaugural address, Lincoln spoke sternly and directly about the crisis facing the country. He said his first task was to reunite the nation. Secession was illegal, he declared; no state could simply decide on its own to leave the Union. The Union was therefore

PRIMARY SOURCE

I hold that, in contemplation of universal law and of the Constitution, the Union of these States is perpetual [everlasting]. Perpetuity [This permanence] is implied, if not expressed, in the fundamental law of all national governments. It is safe to assert that no government proper ever had a provision in its organic law [system of laws] for its own termination [end]. . . . The Union will endure forever.

—from Abraham Lincoln's First Inaugural Address, March 4, 1861

still intact, and he vowed to use his powers as president to protect places and property belonging to the federal government. He assured the South, however, that he did not intend to interfere with slavery where it already existed, and there would be no invasion or use of force by the government. "We are not enemies, but friends," Lincoln said. "Though passion may have strained, it must not break our bonds of affection."

Lincoln's words had little effect. The day after his address, a message arrived in Washington from **Fort Sumter**, which lay at the entrance to the harbor in Charleston, South Carolina. The fort was under threat from Confederate forces, and its **garrison**, or defense force, of about 85 federal soldiers would soon run out of food. After South Carolina seceded, the U.S. government

took control of the fort. But in January 1861, local militias prevented a ship from bringing supplies and additional troops to Fort Sumter. President Lincoln wanted to avoid conflict with the South, but a civil war looked more and more likely.

HISTORICAL THINKING

1. **READING CHECK** What compromise did the Crittenden Plan propose?

2. **IDENTIFY MAIN IDEAS AND DETAILS** Who did Lincoln choose to be in his Cabinet, and why did he appoint these individuals?

3. **DRAW CONCLUSIONS** Why did Confederate forces threaten Fort Sumter?

PLAN

Objective

Discuss how reconciliation failed, bringing the North and the South to the brink of war.

Critical Thinking Skills for Lesson 3.3

- Identify Main Ideas and Details
- Monitor Comprehension
- Draw Conclusions
- Identify
- Distinguish Fact and Opinion
- Identify Problems and Solutions

Essential Question for Chapter 14

How did slavery divide the country? Despite worsening tensions between leaders of the North and South, there was still hope for compromise as James Buchanan's administration drew to a close. Lesson 3.3 examines that attempt, its failure, and the threat of war as Abraham Lincoln's administration began.

Background for the Teacher

Between Lincoln's election and his inauguration, politicians in both the North and the South worked to avoid secession. In addition to the Crittenden Plan, there was talk about creating a constitutional amendment to make slavery permanent, about purchasing Cuba and making it a place where slavery was allowed, and about going to war as a way of unifying the country. For as long as he could, Lincoln tried to minimize the move toward secession, saying, "Let it alone, and it will go down of itself." However, the movement grew, and Lincoln had to become more concerned about death threats. Some took a view of "let it go" instead of "let it alone"; Frederick Douglass, for example, declared, "If the Union can only be maintained by new concessions to the slaveholders, then ... let the Union perish."

INTRODUCE & ENGAGE

Preview Using Visuals

Direct students' attention to the engraving. **ASK:** What details suggest that this meeting will consider military issues? *(Of the 10 men depicted, 7 are dressed in military uniforms. One of those military men seems to be leading the discussion and is pointing to a map, an act that suggests military strategy.)* You may wish to mention that the man pointing to the map is General Winfield Scott, a hero of the Mexican-American War and a Whig presidential candidate in 1852. Although he was commanding general of the U.S. Army when the Civil War began, he retired in early 1862 due to advanced age and ill health.

TEACH

Guided Discussion

1. **Identify** According to the excerpt from Lincoln's inaugural address, what is true of the laws that shape every nation's government? *(Those laws never spell out a procedure for ending the government.)*

2. **Distinguish Fact and Opinion** Reread Lincoln's description of the people he appointed to his Cabinet. Is he expressing a fact or an opinion? How can you tell? *(He is expressing an opinion. Someone could argue that other men were stronger Republicans than the men he chose and that other men would be of better service to the country in that time of crisis.)*

Identify Problems and Solutions

Review the information about the threat to Fort Sumter. **ASK:** Why do you think the Confederacy created this particular problem? *(Answers will vary. Possible response: Fort Sumter was located in the first state to secede. Confederate leaders did not want to see a Union-run fort in operation on Confederate land.)* Point out that the lesson closes with Lincoln's pondering whether to resupply Fort Sumter. **ASK:** If you were Lincoln, what would you do? *(Answers will vary, but students should note that an attempt to resupply the fort would almost certainly lead to open conflict.)* Note that in Chapter 15, Lesson 1.1, students will learn of Lincoln's decision and its aftermath.

Active Options

On Your Feet: Jigsaw Experts Gather students into three "expert" groups and give each group one of the following topics: the Crittenden Plan, Lincoln's inauguration and Cabinet, or the threat to Fort Sumter. Ask each group to do additional research on its topic. Then have students form new groups so that every group has at least one "expert" for each topic. Ask student experts to report on their topic to the rest of the group, and invite students to take notes as they listen to use as a review for the lesson.

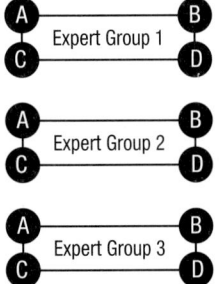

NG Learning Framework: Compare Primary Sources

SKILL Communication

KNOWLEDGE Our Human Story

Divide students into three groups and assign one of the following to each group: the excerpt from the "House Divided" speech in Lesson 2.3, the third and fourth paragraphs of Lincoln's first inaugural address, or the second paragraph of the Declaration of Independence. Have each group write a summary of the assigned text. Then ask volunteers to read the primary text and their group's summary. Initiate a class discussion about how Lincoln's speeches relate to the Declaration of Independence.

DIFFERENTIATE

English Language Learners

Monitor Comprehension Monitor students' comprehension by asking them to answer either/or questions such as the following:

- Was the goal of the Crittenden Plan to abolish slavery or to keep the peace between North and South? *(keep the peace)*
- Were Lincoln's Cabinet members more likely to agree or disagree with one another? *(disagree)*
- Did troops at Fort Sumter face a food shortage or face a rebellion among the soldiers stationed there? *(a food shortage)*

Ask students at the **Expanding** and **Bridging** levels to assist students at the **Emerging** level.

Gifted & Talented

Analyze the Compromises Ask students to review the constitutional compromises that forestalled the division of the Union in the first half of the 19th century, including the Missouri Compromise, the Compromise of 1850, the Kansas-Nebraska Act, and the Crittenden Plan. Instruct students to use library and online sources to create a visual presentation that analyzes how political leaders sought to avoid war at all costs and how, despite their efforts, the series of compromises ultimately paved the way for the Civil War. Invite students to share their presentations with the class.

See the Chapter Planner for more strategies for differentiation.

HISTORICAL THINKING

ANSWERS

1. The Crittenden Plan called for the Missouri Compromise line to be revived and extended to the Pacific Ocean.

2. Lincoln filled four Cabinet positions with men who had opposed him for the Republican nomination. Even though they had been his rivals, Lincoln appreciated their strengths and abilities and felt they were the best people for the jobs.

3. The threat demonstrated the Confederacy's sovereignty, its rejection of Lincoln, and its willingness to engage in open conflict in order to preserve its way of life.

14 REVIEW

VOCABULARY

Use each of the following terms in a sentence that shows an understanding of the term's meaning.

1. secede
   Southern states secede, *breaking away from the United States.*

2. federal marshal

3. racism

4. segregation

5. popular sovereignty

6. Dred Scott decision

7. garrison

8. Confederacy

READING STRATEGY
IDENTIFY MAIN IDEAS AND DETAILS

If you haven't done so already, complete your chart to identify the main ideas and details relating to the issue of slavery. List at least four main ideas and their supporting details. Then answer the question.

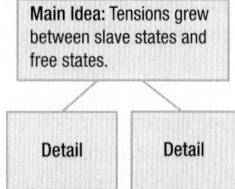

Main Idea: Tensions grew between slave states and free states.

Detail   Detail

9. What impact did Lincoln's "House Divided" speech have on the South and slavery?

MAIN IDEAS

Answer the following questions. Support your answers with evidence from the chapter.

10. How did the Compromise of 1850 help save the Union? **LESSON 1.1**

11. How did segregation affect free African Americans living in northern states? **LESSON 1.2**

12. Why did the Kansas Territory become known as "Bleeding Kansas"? **LESSON 2.1**

13. How did the Supreme Court decision in the Dred Scott case widen the divide between the North and the South? **LESSON 2.2**

14. Why did Jefferson Davis blame the Union for the secession? **LESSON 3.2**

15. Why did the election of Abraham Lincoln cause southern states to secede from the Union? **LESSON 3.2**

16. Under the terms of the Crittenden Plan, how would the issue of slavery be handled south of the Missouri Compromise line? **LESSON 3.3**

HISTORICAL THINKING

17. **SYNTHESIZE** Why didn't the compromises made in the first half of the 19th century last?

18. **DRAW CONCLUSIONS** How did John Brown's raid at Harpers Ferry increase tensions between the North and the South?

19. **MAKE CONNECTIONS** How did slavery as a political, economic, and social institution divide the country and lead to civil war?

20. **IDENTIFY MAIN IDEAS AND DETAILS** Why did the Supreme Court rule that Dred Scott should remain a slave?

21. **FORM AND SUPPORT OPINIONS** Based on the slavery-related developments of the 1850s, was it inevitable that southern states would eventually decide to separate from the Union? Support your opinion with evidence from the chapter.

22. **MAKE INFERENCES** What do you think might have been the strengths and weaknesses of having a "team of rivals" in Lincoln's Cabinet?

INTERPRET MAPS

The map below shows the percentage of enslaved people throughout the United States in 1860. The darkest green shading indicates areas in which more than 50 percent of the residents were enslaved. The lightest green shading indicates areas with no slaves. Look closely at the map and then answer the questions.

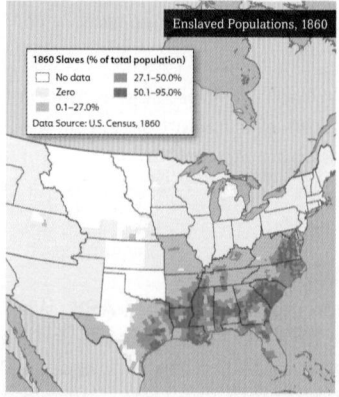

Enslaved Populations, 1860

1860 Slaves (% of total population)
- No data
- Zero
- 0.1–27.0%
- 27.1–50.0%
- 50.1–95.0%

Data Source: U.S. Census, 1860

23. What does this map reveal about the general geographic distribution of slavery across the South?

24. In which sections of the country were there zero populations of enslaved people?

ANALYZE SOURCES

In Harriet Beecher Stowe's novel *Uncle Tom's Cabin,* Eliza is an enslaved woman whose child has been sold to another plantation owner. Rather than see her son turned over to a new slaveholder, Eliza flees with her son in the early spring across the Ohio River to the free state of Ohio. The river is still partly frozen, and she crosses it by jumping from one block of ice to another. Read the following excerpt from the novel and then answer the question.

> Eliza made her desperate retreat across the river just in the dusk of twilight. The gray mist of evening, rising slowly from the river, enveloped her as she disappeared up the bank, and the swollen current and floundering [shifting] masses of ice presented a hopeless barrier between her and her pursuer.

25. What details in the excerpt help build suspense?

CONNECT TO YOUR LIFE

26. **INFORMATIVE** Think about what you have learned about slavery and how deeply it divided the United States. What issues divide the country today? Choose one issue and write a paragraph summarizing it and discussing its impact on the country.

TIPS

- Introduce the topic with a clear main idea statement.

- Develop the topic with relevant facts and concrete details. Be sure to present both sides of the issue.

- Compare the impact of the issue you have chosen to the impact of slavery.

- Provide a concluding statement that follows from and supports the information that you have presented.

VOCABULARY ANSWERS

1. Southern states seceded, breaking away from the United States.

2. Federal marshals caught the escaped criminal and returned him to prison.

3. Racism allowed many people to justify the institution of slavery.

4. Laws that supported segregation kept African Americans from receiving fair and equal treatment in the United States.

5. Under the principle of popular sovereignty, some regions could choose for themselves whether or not to allow slavery.

6. In issuing the *Dred Scott* decision, the Supreme Court ruled that slaves were property and that African Americans were not citizens.

7. Every soldier in the garrison checked his weapons and prepared for battle.

8. The southern states that seceded formed the Confederacy to stand against the federal government.

READING STRATEGY ANSWER

Main Idea: Tensions grew between slave states and free states.

The *Dred Scott* decision (1857) declared that slaves were property, not citizens, and created further division.

Lincoln's election outraged the South and triggered the founding of the Confederate States of America.

9. Answers will vary. Possible response: Lincoln's speech made little, if any, difference. The proslavery South was determined to keep its way of life, even if doing so meant seceding from the Union.

MAIN IDEAS ANSWERS

10. Slave states had threatened to split from the Union if California was admitted as a free state. The Compromise of 1850 appeased these states by declaring that other new territories would be open to slavery.

11. African Americans were not allowed to enter some public buildings, such as churches and schools, and they often were not allowed to take skilled jobs.

12. The term "Bleeding Kansas" originated with the violence that erupted between proslavery and antislavery factions after the passage of the Kansas-Nebraska Act.

13. The fact that the decision supported slavery and slave owners angered northerners and made them worry that slavery could be extended to the whole country.

14. Davis argued that the Founders had supported slavery and therefore the North had no right to oppose it.

15. Southern leaders worried that Lincoln would take steps to end slavery, which was central to the South's economy.

16. Inhabitants of territories south of the line could make their own decisions about slavery.

HISTORICAL THINKING ANSWERS

17. The territories addressed by the compromises could be carved into new states, and the addition of each new state threatened to upset the balance between free states and slave states.

18. Many northerners thought of John Brown as a hero, but most southerners condemned him.

19. Answers will vary. Possible response: Slavery caused political divisions regarding new territories and states, economic divisions because only the South relied on it to provide labor, and social divisions because North and South disagreed about its morality.

20. The Court decided that because Scott was an African-American slave, he was not a citizen and therefore had no right to file a lawsuit in federal court.

21. Answers will vary, but in supporting their opinions, students should discuss such developments as the Compromise of 1850, the Kansas-Nebraska Act, "Bleeding Kansas," the *Dred Scott* decision, John Brown's raid on Harpers Ferry, and the election of Abraham Lincoln.

22. Answers will vary. Possible response: The main strength would be that having a variety of viewpoints might lead to better decision-making. The main weakness would be that rivalries might cause arguments and personal conflicts.

INTERPRET MAPS ANSWERS

23. The map shows that slavery was prevalent throughout the South, although most southern states had regions with relatively small percentages of enslaved people.

24. There were zero populations of enslaved people in the Northeast, the Midwest, and most of the far western territories.

ANALYZE SOURCES ANSWER

25. Suspense is built through the details that suggest the dangers of the setting: the mist and growing darkness, the swollen river, and the moving masses of floating ice. Word choices such as *desperate retreat* and *hopeless barrier* increase the tension of the narrative.

CONNECT TO YOUR LIFE ANSWER

26. Paragraphs will vary but should demonstrate students' understanding of the divisiveness caused by slavery in the past, the divisiveness caused by the chosen issue today, and the similarities and differences between the two.

UNIT 6 RESOURCES

UNIT INTRODUCTION

UNIT TIME LINE

UNIT WRAP-UP

NATIONAL GEOGRAPHIC | CONNECTION

National Geographic Magazine Adapted Articles
- "Lincoln's Funeral Train"
- "Civil War Battlefields" ONLINE

Unit 6 Inquiry: Develop a Conflict Resolution Strategy

NG Learning Framework Activities
- Create an Illustrated Time Line
- Compose a Letter Home

Unit 6 Formal Assessment

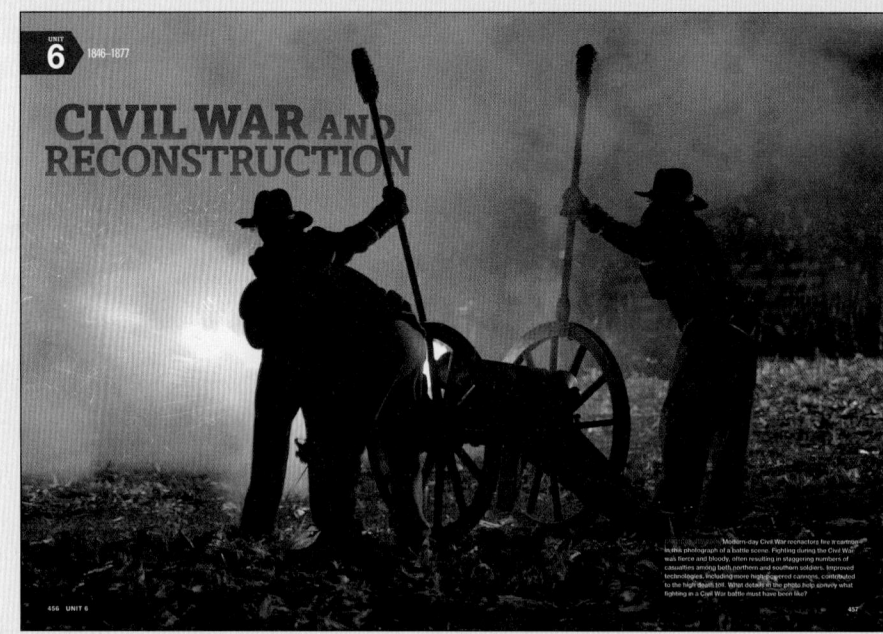

CHAPTER 15 RESOURCES

Available at NGLSync.Cengage.com

TEACHER RESOURCES & ASSESSMENT

Reading and Note-Taking

Vocabulary Practice

Social Studies Skills Lessons
- Reading: Summarize
- Writing: Write an Argument

Formal Assessment
- Chapter 15 Pretest
- Chapter 15 Tests A & B
- Section Quizzes

Chapter 15 Answer Key

ExamView®
  One-time Download

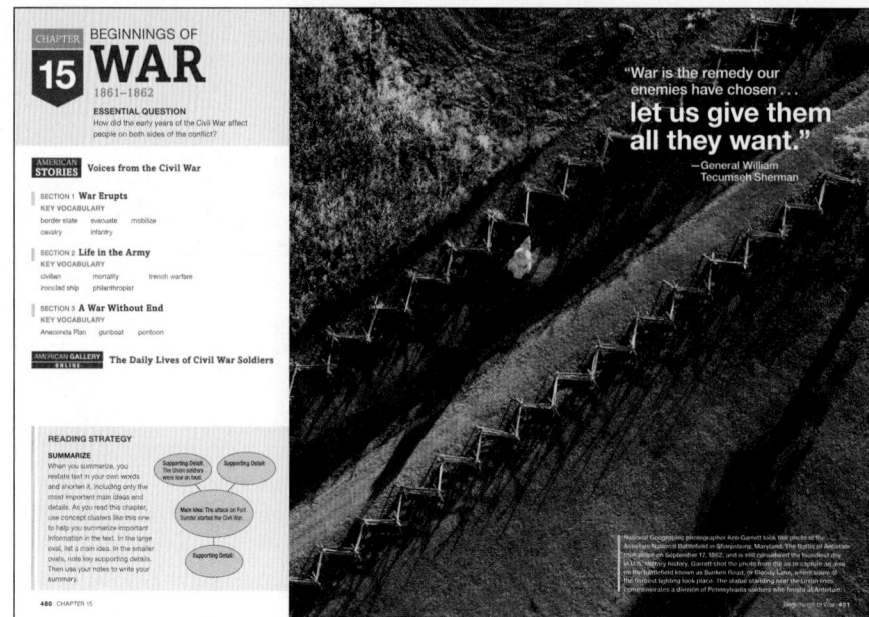

STUDENT DIGITAL RESOURCES

- **eEdition** (English)
- **eEdition** (Spanish)
- **Handbooks**
- **Online Atlas**
- **American Gallery Online**
- **History Notebook**
- **Active History**
- **Projects for Inquiry-Based Learning**

Chapter 15 Spanish Resources are available at NGLSync.Cengage.com.

CHAPTER PLANNER **479B**

AMERICAN STORIES | Voices from the Civil War

- Primary Sources
- On Your Feet: Create a Concept Web

NG Learning Framework:
Recruit Supporters

SECTION 1 RESOURCES
WAR ERUPTS

LESSON 1.1
Shots at Fort Sumter

- On Your Feet: Create a Quiz

NG Learning Framework:
Advise the President

LESSON 1.2
An Early Confederate Victory

- On Your Feet: Form a Human Sequence Chain

NG Learning Framework:
Write a Résumé

LESSON 1.3
CURATING HISTORY
Confederate Memorial Hall New Orleans, Louisiana

- On Your Feet: Sort the Artifacts

SECTION 2 RESOURCES
LIFE IN THE ARMY

LESSON 2.1
Hardship and Weapons

- ▶ Civil War Medicine
- On Your Feet: Complete a Cause-and-Effect Web

AMERICAN **GALLERY** **ONLINE** The Daily Lives of Civil War Soldiers

LESSON 2.2
Women and the War

- On Your Feet: Hold a Roundtable Discussion

NG Learning Framework:
Research the Red Cross

LESSON 2.3
NATIONAL GEOGRAPHIC PHOTOGRAPHER
KEN GARRETT
Through the Lens— Civil War Photography

- On Your Feet: Evaluate Ways of Learning

NG Learning Framework:
Interview a Photographer

SECTION 3 RESOURCES
A WAR WITHOUT END

LESSON 3.1
Different Strategies

- On Your Feet: Form a Human Venn Diagram
- Active History: Compare Resources

LESSON 3.2
GEOGRAPHY IN HISTORY
Differences Between North and South

- On Your Feet: Become an Expert

NG Learning Framework:
Create Charts and Graphs

LESSON 3.3
War in the West and East

- On Your Feet: Think and Discuss

NG Learning Framework:
Evaluate Civil War Navies

LESSON 3.4
Bloody 1862

- On Your Feet: Hold a Class Discussion

NG Learning Framework:
Commemorate a Battle

CHAPTER 15 REVIEW

Strategy ❶
Organize Information

To help students organize information about the various Civil War battles, guide them to create a facts card about each major battle as they read. Instruct them to include the name and date of the battle, list the important military leaders, tell who won, and record any other information that makes the battle stand out. For example, they should note that the attack on Fort Sumter began the Civil War.

Use with Lesson 1.1–1.2 and 3.3–3.4

Strategy ❷
Make a Tree Diagram

Help students focus on the important ideas in a lesson by making a Tree Diagram like the one below. As students read each lesson, instruct them to record three important ideas on their diagram. After students have read the lesson and completed their diagrams, ask them to use the ideas to summarize the lesson in one or two sentences.

```
           ┌─ 1. _____
Lesson 1 ──┤  2. _____
           └─ 3. _____
```

Use with All Lessons *Student summaries may be written or oral. Call on volunteers to share their summaries with the class.*

Strategy ❸
Create a 3-2-1 Summary

After students read a lesson, direct them to create a 3-2-1 summary by writing three important details, two Key Vocabulary words with definitions, and one main idea. Have students use their summaries to help them write three questions (one each about details, Key Vocabulary, and the main idea) to ask another student. Encourage students to share their summaries with a partner and answer each other's questions.

Use with All Lessons

Strategy ❶
Partner for Critical Viewing

Pair students who have visual impairments with students who are not visually impaired to answer Critical Viewing questions. Have the partner without visual impairments describe the photographs and answer any questions. Both partners then use information from the visual, the lesson text, and their prior knowledge to answer the Critical Viewing question.

Use with Lessons 2.1–2.2 and 3.3 *You might also wish to pair students with and without visual impairments to preview maps and photographs in other lessons.*

Strategy ❷
Play Vocabulary Tic-Tac-Toe

Write nine Key Vocabulary words on the board in a tic-tac-toe grid. Organize students into two teams, Team X and Team O. Allow a player from Team X to choose a word. If the player can correctly pronounce the word, define it, and use it in a sentence, he or she can mark the square with an X. Alternate play until one team has marked a horizontal, vertical, or diagonal row of words.

Use with All Lessons *This game can also be played with pairs of students.*

ENGLISH LANGUAGE LEARNERS

Strategy ❶
Predict Word Meanings

Before they read a lesson that has two or more Key Vocabulary terms, use a matching task like the example below to help students predict word meanings. Have them write each word next to the definition they predict is correct. After they finish reading, have students revisit their predictions and correct any mistakes.

mobilize	cavalry	infantry

1. _____ soldiers who walk

2. _____ get soldiers ready for war

3. _____ soldiers who ride horses

Use with Lessons 1.1–1.2 and 2.1–2.2 *Pair students at the **Emerging** level with students at the **Expanding** or **Bridging** levels to predict and verify meanings.*

Strategy ❷
Create Labels for Visuals

Have students at the **Emerging** level preview a lesson by looking at the visuals. Help them identify and label important features in each picture. Then have them work with a partner at the **Expanding** or **Bridging** level to create labels for the visuals. Each label should be a word that will support understanding of the lesson.

Use with Lessons 1.1–1.2, 2.1–2.2, 3.1, and 3.3
Students might use sticky notes for labels.

Strategy ❸
Rewrite Captions

Challenge students at the **Emerging** and **Expanding** levels to rewrite one-sentence captions for the visuals in Lesson 1.3 in their own words. Ask students at the **Bridging** level to write captions of a few sentences or a short paragraph to accompany the visuals in the lesson. Suggest they vary the sentence structure of their captions.

Use with Lesson 1.3 *This strategy may be used with other lessons. You might pair students at the **Emerging** level with different proficiency levels to help them read the captions.*

GIFTED & TALENTED

Strategy ❶
Present a Monologue

Ask students to portray a historical figure and present a monologue from that person's point of view. For example, Dorothea Dix or Clara Barton might discuss women's participation in the war effort or the experience of tending to the wounded on the battlefield. George McClellan might justify his cautious decisions.

Use with Lessons 1.1, 2.2, 3.1, and 3.3–3.4 *Student pairs could present a dialogue between two historical figures.*

Strategy ❷
Plan an Itinerary

Prompt students to research one of the historical sites from the chapter, such as the Fort Sumter National Monument, and plan an itinerary for visiting it. The itinerary should include the location of the site, the hours of operation, and things to see and do there. Encourage groups to create a multimedia presentation to share with the class.

Use with Lessons 1.1–1.2 and 3.3–3.4

Pre-AP

Strategy ❶
Recommend a Book

Invite students to read a biography or a historical fiction book related to the chapter. Establish criteria for evaluating the book, such as readability, interest, and historical accuracy. Based on the criteria, ask students to rate the book and write a review to share with the class.

Use with All Lessons

Strategy ❷
Research Confederate Troops

Tell students to choose one Confederate state and use library or online sources to research how men were assembled in that state and mustered into the Confederate Army. Ask students to include how men were notified to report for duty, where troops were assembled, and how troops were discharged at the end of the war. Invite students to present their findings in a panel discussion. Prompt the rest of the class to comment and ask questions.

Use with Lessons 1.1–1.2

ESSENTIAL QUESTION
How did the early years of the Civil War affect people on both sides of the conflict?

AMERICAN
STORIES **Voices from the Civil War**

SECTION 1 **War Erupts**
KEY VOCABULARY

border state   evacuate   mobilize
cavalry   infantry

SECTION 2 **Life in the Army**
KEY VOCABULARY

civilian   mortality   trench warfare
ironclad ship   philanthropist

SECTION 3 **A War Without End**
KEY VOCABULARY

Anaconda Plan   gunboat   pontoon

AMERICAN **GALLERY**
ONLINE   **The Daily Lives of Civil War Soldiers**

READING STRATEGY

SUMMARIZE
When you summarize, you restate text in your own words and shorten it, including only the most important main ideas and details. As you read this chapter, use concept clusters like this one to help you summarize important information in the text. In the large oval, list a main idea. In the smaller ovals, note key supporting details. Then use your notes to write your summary.

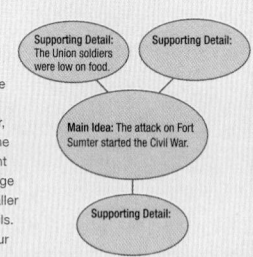

Supporting Detail: The Union soldiers were low on food.

Supporting Detail:

Main Idea: The attack on Fort Sumter started the Civil War.

Supporting Detail:

"War is the remedy our enemies have chosen . . .
let us give them all they want."
—General William Tecumseh Sherman

National Geographic photographer Ken Garrett took this photo of the Antietam National Battlefield in Sharpsburg, Maryland. The Battle of Antietam took place on September 17, 1862, and is still considered the bloodiest day in U.S. military history. Garrett shot the photo from the air to capture an area on the battlefield known as Sunken Road, or Bloody Lane, where some of the fiercest fighting took place. The statue standing near the Union lines commemorates a division of Pennsylvania soldiers who fought at Antietam.

INTRODUCE THE PHOTOGRAPH
Antietam National Battlefield

Direct students' attention to the photograph. Explain that before the Battle of Antietam, a dirt path worn into the ground by farmers was known as Sunken Road. On September 17, 1862, Confederate troops waited behind fence rails they had piled along the high ground beside the road. As Union troops moved into range, the Confederates opened fire. After three hours of intense combat, more than 5,000 soldiers were dead or wounded. Neither side had won a decisive victory, but since then Sunken Road has been called Bloody Lane.

Visitors to Antietam National Battlefield can see the restored zig-zag fences that mark the site of the original fences. **ASK:** Why do you think the photographer chose to present an aerial view of the battlefield? *(Possible response: It provides the viewer with an idea of the size and physical characteristics of the area.)*

NATIONAL GEOGRAPHIC PHOTOGRAPHER
Kenneth Garrett

Ken Garrett's interest in history and his training in photojournalism have led to an interesting career. Garrett's photographs of artifacts from different ancient cultures have appeared in *National Geographic* as well as in books and exhibits throughout the world. For a book called *Journey Through Hallowed Ground*, Garrett photographed sites that have special significance to American history. Part of the Hallowed Ground territory includes Civil War battlefields in Virginia. Garrett believes it is important to preserve the history and heritage of the area. His photographs are one way of doing that.

For Chapter 15 Spanish Resources, visit the Resource Menu. Chapter 15 resources are available at NGLSync.Cengage.com.

INTRODUCE THE ESSENTIAL QUESTION

How did the early years of the Civil War affect people on both sides of the conflict?

Discuss the Effects of War Organize students into two groups, with one half sitting in a close circle facing inward and the other half sitting in a larger circle around them. Pose the question: How does war both unite and divide people? Have students in the inside circle discuss the topic, while those in the outside circle listen and evaluate the discussion. Then reverse roles. Ask students to write a paragraph predicting how the uniting and divisive effects of war might apply to the North and the South during the early years of the Civil War. Call on volunteers to share their predictions.

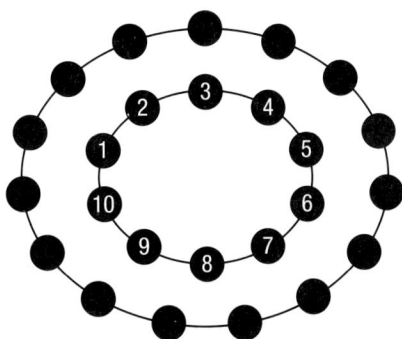

INTRODUCE CHAPTER VOCABULARY

Vocabulary Pyramids

As students read the chapter, encourage them to complete Vocabulary Pyramids for Key Vocabulary words. Tell students to make a pyramid for each word. Have them write the word at the top of the pyramid. As they encounter the word in the chapter, instruct them to complete the information for that word. Model an example for students on the board using the graphic organizer below.

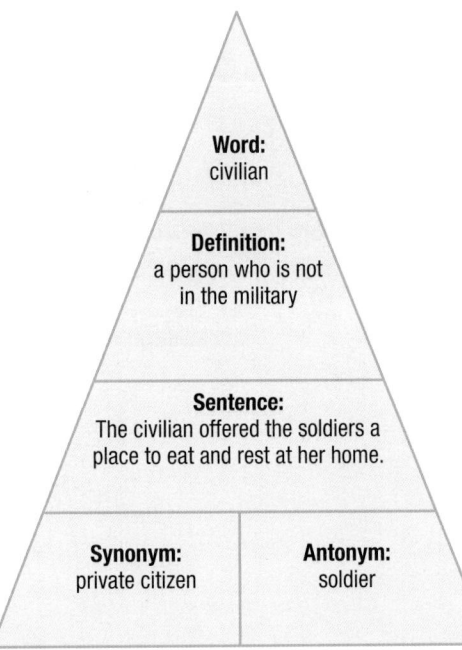

INTRODUCE THE READING STRATEGY

SUMMARIZE

Remind students that when they summarize text, they restate the main ideas and the major, or most important, details in their own words. Encourage students to use a Concept Cluster to keep track of the main ideas and details they might include in a summary of a lesson. After students have read Lesson 1.1, help them complete the Concept Cluster below as a model. Then have them write a summary of the lesson based on their notes. Suggest that students create a Concept Cluster for the remaining lessons of the chapter.

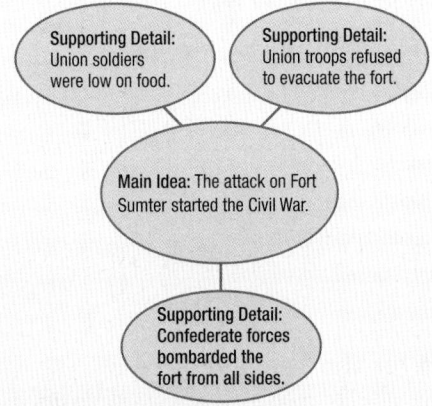

KEY DATES FOR CHAPTER 15

April 1861	Confederates fire on Fort Sumter
April 1861	Volunteer nurses march on Washington, D.C.
July 1861	First Battle of Bull Run
March 1862	First skirmish between ironclad ships
April 1862	Battle of Shiloh
June 1862	Seven Days' Battles begin
September 1862	Battle of Antietam
December 1862	Battle of Fredericksburg
June 1863	West Virginia becomes part of the Union

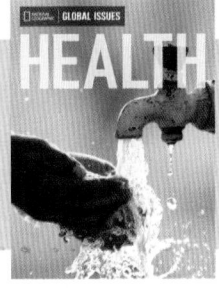

For more on the effects of war on people's health, see *GLOBAL ISSUES: HEALTH.*

Objectives

- **Learn how soldiers and civilians experienced the Civil War through firsthand accounts.**
- **Consider different points of view concerning national identity.**
- **Describe the living conditions for Civil War soldiers and civilians.**
- **Compare the homecoming experiences of Union and Confederate soldiers.**
- **Study primary sources: memoirs, journals, and photographs from the Civil War.**

Critical Thinking Skills for "Voices from the Civil War"

- Make Connections
- Draw Conclusions
- Analyze Language Use
- Identify Problems and Solutions
- Make Generalizations
- Make Inferences

Background for the Teacher

With this American Story, students can delve into the history of the Civil War using primary source documents and photos. Through the actual words of Civil War soldiers, students learn about the real challenges and deep sadness experienced by soldiers both on and off the battlefield. Use this American Story to deepen students' understanding of the harsh reality of Civil War experiences that affected soldiers on a personal level.

This American Story provides a backdrop to the chapter, Beginnings of War, starting with Fort Sumter and moving through the expansion of the Civil War in the West and the East. The chapter discusses not only early battle successes but also the toll the war took on soldiers and the instrumental role women played in hospitals serving wounded and dying soldiers.

History Notebook

Encourage students to complete the American Story page for Chapter 15 in their History Notebooks as they read.

Note to the Teacher

Use this American Story as a teaser for content students will encounter in Chapter 15.

AMERICAN STORIES | NATIONAL GEOGRAPHIC

VOICES FROM THE CIVIL WAR

PRIMARY SOURCES

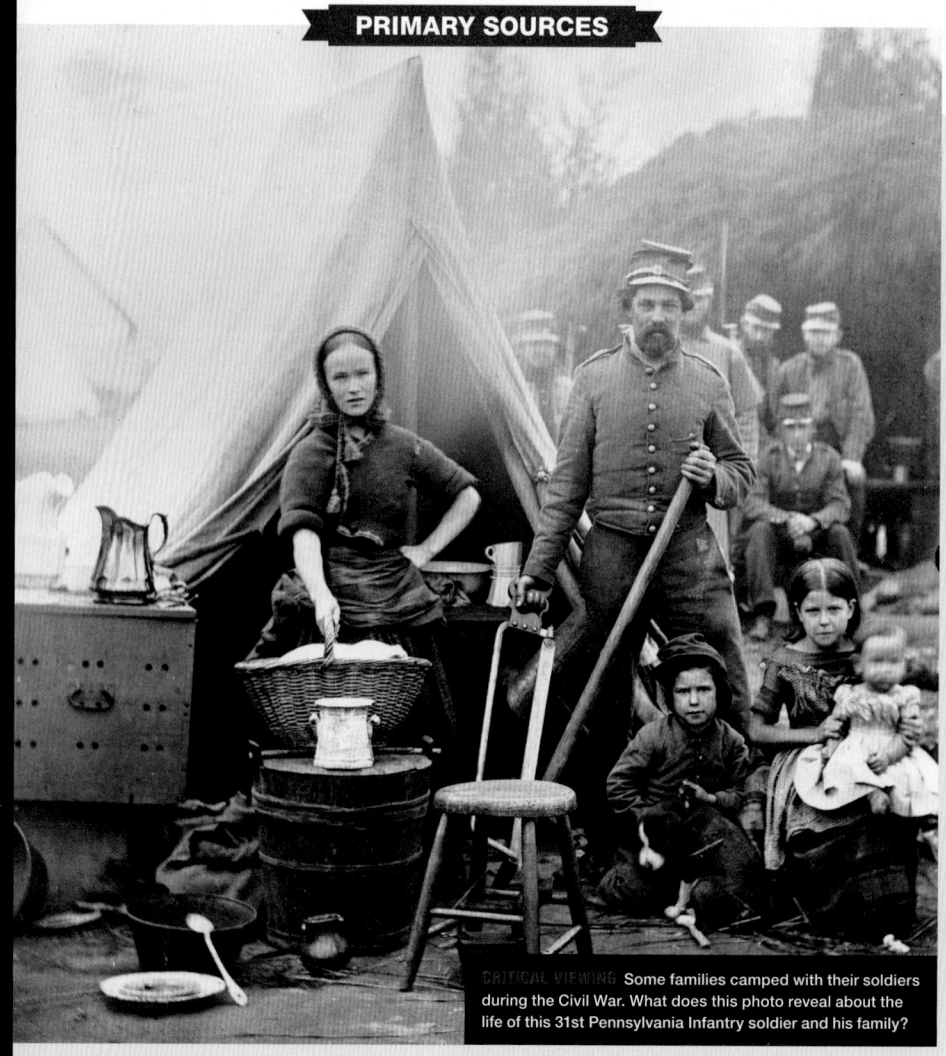

CRITICAL VIEWING Some families camped with their soldiers during the Civil War. What does this photo reveal about the life of this 31st Pennsylvania Infantry soldier and his family?

482 CHAPTER 15

In the 1860s, an event transformed the lives of all Americans. The Civil War between the northern and southern states would leave no person untouched. In the 1800s, people had limited options for describing their experiences. They used letters and journals, charcoal and paints, and photographs as their voices and means of expression. After the war, they wrote memoirs and recollections to preserve their stories and process their experiences.

You're about to read about the daily lives and hardships of the soldiers, the suffering of civilians in a battle zone, the agony of a family divided, and other struggles of a people divided by war. Through these primary sources, you will gain a firsthand understanding of what it was like to live through the Civil War, one American voice at a time.

JOHN D. BILLINGS

First, [the hardtack biscuits] may have been so hard that they could not be bitten; it then required a very strong blow of the fist to break them.

The second condition was when they were mouldy [moldy] or wet.

The third condition was when from storage they had become infested with maggots and weevils. These weevils were, in my experience, more abundant than the maggots. They were a little slim, brown bug an eighth of an inch in length, having the ability to completely riddle [poke holes in] the hardtack.

But hardtack was not so bad an article of food, even when traversed by insects. Eaten in the dark, no one could tell the difference between it and hardtack that was untenanted. It was no uncommon occurrence for a man to find the surface of his pot of coffee swimming with weevils, after breaking up hardtack in it . . . but they were easily skimmed off and left no distinctive flavour behind.

—from *Hardtack and Coffee*, by John D. Billings, 1888

HARDTACK

In the humorous excerpt from his postwar memoir (left), Union Army soldier John D. Billings describes the challenges of hardtack biscuits, one of the most common camp foods. Hardtack (shown here) is a hard cracker made of flour and water. It was a problematic food, but as you can see, some soldiers actually developed a fondness for it.

Soldiers from both the North and the South learned to live with minimal comfort when they were on the march or in camp. At night, they crowded into small tents, sometimes packed together so tightly, if one soldier wanted to roll over, he had to get his tent mates to roll over, too.

The food tasted awful and was sometimes inedible. When soldiers received "fresh" meat, it had often already gone bad. Preserved meat was so filled with salt that it had to be soaked in water for hours before a soldier even attempted to eat it. In southern camps, these poor rations were likely to run out, especially in the war's later years when many farms in the South had been destroyed.

Identify Primary Sources

Write the title of this American Story on the board. **ASK:** What is meant by "Voices" in this title? *(Possible response: "Voices" refers to those who actually experienced the Civil War.)* **ASK:** What type of primary sources would historians use to understand voices from the Civil War? *(photos, diaries, letters)* Point out that artifacts such as tools and weapons also help historians understand the experiences of soldiers. Explain that in this American Story, students will read firsthand accounts of life during the Civil War.

Compare with Today

Discuss with students why people today might share their experiences on social media. **ASK:** Do you think social media is a good way to share personal stories? Why or why not? *(Possible response: It's the best way to share a story because information can get out to a large group of people immediately.)* Explain that during the Civil War, soldiers and their families shared experiences through letters, journals, and memoirs. **ASK:** How do primary sources such as personal letters from the past and posts on social media today help us interpret moments in history? *(They provide a first-person account of events as they were unfolding or soon after.)*

Describe Civil War Food

Share the recipe for hardtack with students. Explain that hardtack continues to be used today as survival food for individuals who need to keep food for a long time without having it spoil. Invite students to speculate on the taste of hardtack. **ASK:** What food is commonly sold today that might be similar to hardtack? *(Students might suggest that saltine crackers might be similar.)*

Hardtack Recipe
(makes nine hardtack crackers)
3 cups white flour
2 teaspoons salt
1 cup water

Mix flour and salt in a bowl. Add water to make the dough. Roll dough until about ½-inch thick. Cut into nine squares. Use a nail to poke holes in the dough. Bake in a 350°F oven for about 30 minutes.

CRITICAL VIEWING Answers will vary. Possible response: Life must have been difficult because the family was living in a tent and does not look happy.

Soldiers' Uniforms

Southern soldiers wore uniforms made of a durable wool-cotton denim material. Soldiers wore shirts and undergarments made of cotton and shoes that did not hold up well on the battlefield. Union soldiers wore uniforms made in northern mills from wool fabric, which was superior to the fabric used for Confederate uniforms. Union soldiers also wore forage caps with leather visors, and Confederate soldiers wore caps called "kepis."

Siege of Port Hudson, Louisiana

As part of the Vicksburg campaign, the Battle of Port Hudson lasted 48 days and remains one of the longest battles in American history. During that time, some 7,500 Confederate soldiers sought safety behind earthen fortifications against a powerful force of 40,000 Union soldiers. At stake was control of the Mississippi River. Twice Union forces attempted to overrun the Confederates but lost almost 4,000 troops, including 600 African-American soldiers from the First and Third Louisiana Native Guards. It wasn't until the Confederates at Port Hudson learned of the fall of Vicksburg that they finally surrendered.

A 12-Mile Circle

As the siege of Vicksburg raged on, the Union army fortified a 12-mile ring encircling the embattled city. The people who huddled in what the Union troops called "Prairie Dog Village" endured 47 days of shell fire during the Battle of Vicksburg. Vicksburg residents built a network of caves as temporary homes—even moving parlor and bedroom furniture into them. Cooking took place outside of the caves. Though the citizens of Vicksburg suffered great hardship, dehydration, starvation, and the hazards of battle, most survived the siege.

AMERICAN STORIES

A SOLDIER'S GEAR

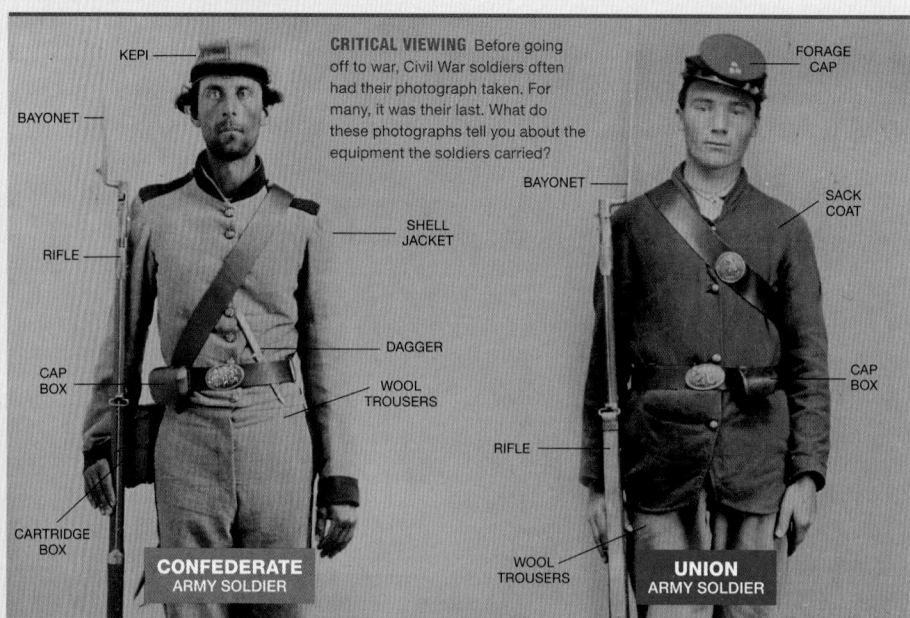

CRITICAL VIEWING Before going off to war, Civil War soldiers often had their photograph taken. For many, it was their last. What do these photographs tell you about the equipment the soldiers carried?

CONFEDERATE ARMY SOLDIER

KEPI · BAYONET · RIFLE · CAP BOX · CARTRIDGE BOX · SHELL JACKET · DAGGER · WOOL TROUSERS

UNION ARMY SOLDIER

FORAGE CAP · BAYONET · SACK COAT · CAP BOX · RIFLE · WOOL TROUSERS

GEORGE ALLEN

A woolen blanket and a piece of shelter tent twisted together, and thrown over our shoulders; haversack [knapsack] loaded with a dozen hard tack and a small piece of "salt horse," little bag of coffee and sugar, . . . all sorts of hats or caps; little to eat, but plenty of ammunition.

—from *Forty-Six Months with the Fourth R.I. Volunteers*, by Corp. George H. Allen, 1887

A SOLDIER'S GEAR

When a Union soldier like George Allen from Rhode Island joined the army, he was, of course, equipped with a rifle. He also received other gear, like a knapsack, a wool blanket, a cartridge box on a shoulder strap, a canteen, a bag for carrying food, and eating utensils. All together, he might find himself carrying 40 to 50 pounds of weapons and gear. But as time went on, most soldiers threw away the items they found to be unnecessary to make marching and moving easier. Corporal Allen's description of the simplicity of his gear after a year of fighting gives a sense of how practicality outweighed comfort.

coffee beans · coffee can · tin cup · food sack · cloth for patching · sewing kit

THE CIVILIANS OF VICKSBURG

As the fighting raged through the border states and the South, civilians often found themselves on the front lines of the war. The people of Vicksburg, Mississippi, experienced life in a battle zone between 1861 and 1863.

Vicksburg sits on a high bluff overlooking the Mississippi River. At the start of the war, the Confederacy controlled Vicksburg, and therefore it controlled the river traffic that passed by the city. The Union Army made multiple attempts to take Vicksburg, and eventually put the city under siege, blocking the paths into town so that no food or ammunition could be brought in. Day and night, Union soldiers rained shells down onto Vicksburg from the opposite side of the Mississippi River. Abandoning their ruined houses, residents dug caves into the hillside beneath the town. As the weeks dragged on, food ran short. People were forced to eat mules, horses, dogs, and rats.

The siege ended on July 4, 1863, when the military commander of the Vicksburg troops surrendered. A chaplain for the southern troops commented, "We surrendered to famine, not to [the northern army]." One woman kept a diary of the civilians' daily life during the siege of Vicksburg. She described the cave she was living in as "suffocating" and like "a living tomb." Read more from her diary in the excerpt below.

April 28, 1863—I never understood before the full force of those questions—what shall we eat? what shall we drink? and wherewithal shall we be clothed?

May 28—The regular siege has continued. We are utterly cut off from the world, surrounded by a circle of fire. The fiery shower of shells goes on day and night. People do nothing but eat what they can get, sleep when they can, and dodge shells. There are three intervals when the shelling stops, either for the guns to cool or for the gunners' meals, I suppose— about eight in the morning, the same in the evening, and at noon. In that time we have to both prepare and eat ours. Clothing cannot be washed or anything else done. I think all the dogs and cats must be killed or starved; we don't see any more pitiful animals prowling around.

—from "A Woman's Diary of the Siege of Vicksburg," published in *The Century Illustrated Monthly Magazine,* 1885

CRITICAL VIEWING The Shirley family, who owned the house shown in this 1863 photograph, were forced to live in a manmade cave, like the ones dug into the ground in the photo, to avoid the cannon fire flying past their home. What does this photo reveal about the impact of the Civil War on the civilian population of cities like Vicksburg?

Guided Discussion

1. **Analyze Language Use** Which group of words in the excerpt written by George H. Allen conveys his sense of dismay? *("…all sorts of hats or caps; little to eat, but plenty of ammunition.")* What do you think Allen is saying about his situation? *(Possible response: He is saying that leaders care more about the soldiers' readiness to fight than they care about whether the soldiers have enough food to eat.)*

2. **Identify Problems and Solutions** Tell students to imagine they are civilians in 1863 living in a cave at Vicksburg with the war raging around and above them. **ASK:** What would be the most difficult problem in this situation? *(Answers will vary. Possible response: The most difficult problem would be staying warm and having enough food to eat because it would be very dangerous to leave the cave.)* How do you think the civilians living in the caves solved the problem you identified? *(Possible response: They most likely ate whatever they could, including rats and mice living in the caves.)*

CRITICAL VIEWING Answers will vary. Possible response: The photographs show that most of the soldiers' equipment was fighting related: rifle, cap box, cartridge box, bayonet.

CRITICAL VIEWING Answers will vary. The civilian population was terrorized by war, and people could not live in their own homes. They had to find safety in underground shelters.

Active Options

On Your Feet: Create a Concept Web Form groups of four around a section of a bulletin board or a table. Provide each group with a large sheet of paper. Have students create a Concept Web on their paper and write *Civil War soldier* in the center. Group members should take turns contributing a concept or phrase to the web. When time for the activity has elapsed, call on volunteers from each group to share their webs.

NG Learning Framework: Recruit Supporters

ATTITUDE Empowerment

SKILL Communication

Point out that actual words, photos, and personal experiences of troops could be powerful tools for recruiting soldiers to fight on either side of the Civil War—or for recruiting citizens to join an anti-war campaign. Guide students to consider how the photos and accounts in "Voices from the Civil War" might be used to spur people to action. Then have them work in groups to use elements such as these to create a recruitment poster for the Union, the Confederacy, or an anti-war group. They can locate historical photos to incorporate or draw their own, based on those shown in the lesson. Display the finished posters.

WRITE ABOUT HISTORY

Share a Personal Point of View This American Story provides a first-person view into the lives of Civil War soldiers and civilians. To help students make connections between the American Story and their own lives, have them write a personal account about their experience as a family member or friend of someone serving or who has served in the military. Students who do not have a personal connection can use library or online sources to locate personal accounts of individuals who have served in the military.

CRITICAL VIEWING Possible response: Soldiers had to rebuild their lives as they returned to their homes. They may have also had to deal with battlefield memories or injuries that left them unable to work.

THINK ABOUT IT

Possible response: Primary sources are very useful because they tell the story from the perspective of a person who experienced the event.

FAMILIES DIVIDED

They may not look much alike, but David Keener Shriver (left) and Mark Shriver (right) were family members—cousins, in fact—fighting on opposite sides of the Civil War.

David joined up to fight with Company 1 of the Union Army's 190th Regiment of Pennsylvania Volunteers. His cousin Mark was a member of the Confederate Army's 1st Virginia Cavalry. Because the young soldiers' parents were siblings, it's likely loyalty to opposing armies was a source of division and tension in the family.

D.P. CONYNGHAM

I had a Sergeant Driscoll, a brave man, and one of the best shots in the Brigade. When charging at Malvern Hill, a company was posted in a clump of trees, who kept up a fierce fire on us, and actually charged out on our advance. Their officer seemed to be a daring, reckless boy, and I said to Driscoll, "if that officer is not taken down, many of us will fall before we pass that clump."

"Leave that to me," said Driscoll; so he raised his rifle, and the moment the officer exposed himself again bang went Driscoll, over went the officer, his company at once breaking away.

As we passed the place I said, "Driscoll, see if that officer is dead—he was a brave fellow."

I stood looking on. Driscoll turned [the young soldier] over on his back. He opened his eyes for a moment, and faintly murmured "Father," and closed them forever.

I will forever recollect the frantic grief of Driscoll; it was harrowing to witness. [The young soldier] was his son, who had gone South before the war.

—from *The Irish Brigade and Its Campaigns,* by Union Army Capt. D.P. Conyngham, 1867

TRAGIC ENCOUNTERS

Most Americans sided with their home state in the Civil War, but some found it harder to choose a side. Political or personal beliefs, loyalty to the federal government, and pressure from loved ones often made for conflicted soldiers and broken family bonds.

The most heartbreaking tales of the Civil War may be those of families first divided, then reunited as enemies in battle. The personal account of Captain D.P. Conyngham of the Union Army (left) describes a tragic scene he witnessed during the battle at Malvern Hill, Virginia, on July 1, 1862.

CRITICAL VIEWING During the Grand Review in May 1865, the great armies of Grant and Sherman received a hero's welcome in Washington, D.C. What challenges do you think Union soldiers faced after the cheers subsided and they returned to their lives?

LEANDER STILLWELL

I now had only two miles to go, and was soon at the dear old boyhood home. My folks were expecting me, so they were not taken by surprise. There was no "scene" when we met, . . . but we all had a feeling of profound contentment and satisfaction which was too deep to be expressed by mere words.

When I returned home I found that the farm work my father was then engaged in was cutting up and shocking corn. So, the morning after my arrival, September 29th, I doffed my uniform of first lieutenant, put on some of father's old clothes, armed myself with a corn knife, and proceeded to wage war on the standing corn. The feeling I had while engaged in this work was "sort of queer." It almost seemed, sometimes, as if I had been away only a day or two, and had just taken up the farm work where I had left off.

—from *The Story of a Common Soldier of Army Life in the Civil War* by Leander Stillwell, 1920

GOING HOME

For some soldiers, the return home after the Civil War was warm, yet surprisingly undramatic. In his personal account (left), Union soldier Leander Stillwell describes his return home to Illinois.

When the war ended in 1865, thousands of soldiers were mustered out (dismissed from service). But first, for many Union soldiers, there was the Grand Review in Washington, D.C. Over the course of two days in May, thousands of Union troops paraded through the streets of the capital to the applause of large crowds. Then, with the cheers still ringing in their ears, the men returned to their homes.

On the Confederate side, it was harder for soldiers to return home. The war had left southern cities and farms in ruins, and the recovery process would be long and difficult.

Personal accounts shed new light on history.

When you read the words of someone who lived through an event like the Civil War, you draw conclusions that are probably different from those you'd draw from a secondary source like a textbook.

Primary sources like those included in this American Story provide varied perspectives and points of view. They capture the voices of the Civil War and help tell the story of this country-changing event in American history.

THINK ABOUT IT

How useful and credible are primary sources like those included in this American Story in helping you understand soldiers' and civilians' lives during the Civil War?

Beginnings of War **487**

Striving Readers

Summarize Have students work together in pairs or small groups to read and summarize the text, excerpts, and photos they encounter. Tell students to create a Three-Column Chart to organize their notes. They should use the following column categories: *Text, Excerpt, Photo*. Suggest students provide three notes per category. Tell students to use their notes to create a summary statement about the American Story.

Pre-AP

Analyze Sources Ask students to compare and contrast a minimum of two secondary source articles written about the citizens of Vicksburg with a minimum of three primary sources written by individuals who lived in caves during the 47-day Battle of Vicksburg. Encourage students to write an analysis of what they learned from their research and then present their findings to the class.

See the Chapter Planner for more strategies for differentiation.

HISTORICAL THINKING

Ask and have students answer the following questions.

1. **READING CHECK** What hardships did both Union and Confederate soldiers experience in camp?

2. **MAKE GENERALIZATIONS** From the viewpoints expressed in the primary sources in this American Story, what statement can be made that is true about all of the documents?

3. **MAKE INFERENCES** Do you think family divisions caused by the Civil War were easily repaired once the war ended? Why or why not?

ANSWERS

1. Soldiers had to share small tents. They had limited food rations, and the food tasted awful and had often already gone bad.

2. Possible response: All the documents describe great struggles and hardships faced by those who experienced the Civil War.

3. Possible response: Most likely the divisions caused by the Civil War remained after the war ended because it would be difficult for individuals to forgive the death and destruction caused by the Civil War.

1.1 Shots at Fort Sumter

Imagine a hot, dry landscape where rain hasn't fallen for months. It would take only a spark to send the whole area up in flames. The spark that ignited the Civil War was the attack on Fort Sumter.

MAIN IDEA Once the northern states declared war and most southern states had seceded, the country waited to see whether the states in between would remain in the Union.

THE SPARK THAT CAUSED THE FIRE

As you have read, President Abraham Lincoln declared that secession was illegal under the Constitution. Southerners, on the other hand, claimed secession as a states' right guaranteed by the document. They decided to secede because they perceived Lincoln's election as a threat to the lawful institution of slavery.

After they split from the Union, the newly formed Confederate states declared that everything owned by the U.S. government within their boundaries now belonged to the Confederacy. Fort Sumter in Charleston, South Carolina, was among the possessions they claimed.

Union major **Robert Anderson**, who was in charge of the fort, had watched the people of Charleston get swept up in secession fever, and he was worried. More than 5,000 Confederate soldiers surrounded Anderson and his men, and the Union soldiers were so low on provisions that they faced starvation. Lincoln sent a message to the southern leaders stating that he was going to send food, but not weapons, to the soldiers at Fort Sumter.

On April 11, 1861, before the Union's provisions arrived, Confederate leaders demanded that the Union troops **evacuate**, or leave, the fort. Otherwise, Confederate forces would take the stronghold by force. Lincoln and Anderson refused to agree to this demand, and the next day, Confederate forces began bombarding the fort from all sides. The shelling lasted for 34 hours. On April 14, with no more food or ammunition, Anderson surrendered.

War was unpopular among northerners, but the attack stirred the Union to action. Lincoln declared South Carolina to be in rebellion and called to form a militia. The Civil War had begun. Its purpose then was not to end slavery but to reunite the nation.

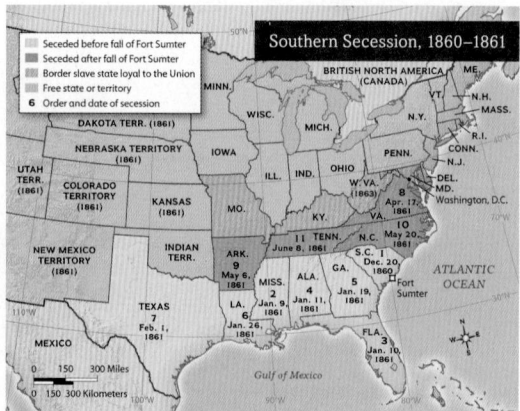

Southern Secession, 1860–1861

- Seceded before fall of Fort Sumter
- Seceded after fall of Fort Sumter
- Border slave state loyal to the Union
- Free state or territory
- **6** Order and date of secession

THE GEOGRAPHY OF WAR

Within two days of Lincoln's call to arms, Virginia seceded. The Confederacy established its capital at Richmond, Virginia. Soon after, Arkansas, Tennessee, and North Carolina left the Union. However, four states bordering both the Union and the Confederacy—Maryland, Delaware, Missouri, and Kentucky—remained undecided. These states, called the **border states**, lay in the middle ground between the warring North and South and so were very important geographically.

Maryland, for example, bordered Washington, D.C., on three sides. If the state joined the Confederacy, the Union's capital would be completely surrounded by Confederate states. In an effort to keep Maryland in the Union, Lincoln threatened to jail any Confederate soldier who entered the state.

Missouri was also vital to the Union cause. With its large population, Missouri could supply the Union with many soldiers. The state also produced a great deal of food and protected the western side of the Union. In addition, its biggest city, St. Louis, was an important commercial and transportation center.

In Kentucky, both Confederate recruiters and pro-Union leaders tried to sway the state's citizens. But when Confederate forces invaded Kentucky in September 1861, the state asked the federal government for help. Lincoln sent troops to the state, the invaders were driven out, and Kentucky stayed in the Union.

The president gained more ground when 50 counties in northwest Virginia decided to form a new state. The people in those counties no longer wanted to be a part of pro-slavery Virginia and so, in 1863, West Virginia became part of the Union. Overall, Lincoln succeeded in keeping the border states in the Union. He would need all the forces he could gather to prepare for war and fight the long, tough battles ahead.

HISTORICAL THINKING

1. **READING CHECK** What happened after the Confederates attacked Fort Sumter?

2. **SUMMARIZE** Why was it important for the Union to keep the border states out of the Confederacy?

3. **IDENTIFY PROBLEMS AND SOLUTIONS** How did Lincoln deal with Confederate attempts to seize the border states?

PLAN

Objective
Describe the role of the attack on Fort Sumter and the importance of border states in the Civil War.

Critical Thinking Skills for Lesson 1.1
- Identify Main Ideas and Details
- Monitor Comprehension
- Summarize
- Identify Problems and Solutions
- Make Inferences
- Draw Conclusions

Essential Question for Chapter 15
How did the early years of the Civil War affect people on both sides of the conflict? Within weeks after President Lincoln's inauguration, the Civil War erupted. Lesson 1.1 describes the event that marked the beginning of the war.

Background for the Teacher
President Lincoln's call to arms and his threat to detain Confederates in Maryland were wartime measures taken without the approval of Congress. In a message to Congress on July 4, 1861, Lincoln explained his actions and asked for congressional authorization for war. The president reminded Congress that in his inaugural address he had told the seceding southerners, "You can have no conflict without being yourselves the aggressors." Since Confederate forces had initiated the attack on Fort Sumter, President Lincoln believed that the U.S. government had no choice but to resist.

Lincoln further defended his decision to suspend the writ of *habeas corpus* (the constitutional right of prisoners to contest unlawful detention) in the case of those accused of aiding the Confederacy. The president asked Congress to provide the soldiers and money to carry out a war that he believed would be "short and decisive."

INTRODUCE & ENGAGE

Activate Prior Knowledge

Ask students to consider this question: Why was there a Civil War? Complete a K-W-L Chart with student responses that show what they already know about reasons for the Civil War. If necessary, guide the discussion by asking about compromises that postponed the separation of the Union in the first half of the 19th century. Then elicit and record in the K-W-L Chart questions that students would like to answer as they study the lesson. At the end of the lesson, provide time for a discussion to fill in the last column of the K-W-L Chart with what they have learned.

TEACH

Guided Discussion

1. **Make Inferences** Both Lincoln and those in favor of secession pointed to the Constitution to support their views. Why were their interpretations of the Constitution so different? *(Lincoln and southerners had opposite views on what was in their own and the nation's best interest; each side wanted to prove that the Constitution supported their position.)*

2. **Draw Conclusions** Based on information in the map and text, how did West Virginia's statehood benefit the Union? *(West Virginia remained loyal to the Union and could provide people and resources. It also became another border state between the North and South, linking the existing border states of Kentucky and Maryland.)*

American Places

Charleston, South Carolina, was one of the most important ports along the southeast coast of the United States. Three forts had been built to defend the harbor: Castle Pinckney, Fort Moultrie, and Fort Sumter. When South Carolina seceded, Charleston Harbor belonged to the Confederacy, but the forts were still in control of Union troops. In December 1860, Union major Robert Anderson moved his men to Fort Sumter from Fort Moultrie. Anderson believed Fort Sumter, with thick walls and a more strategic position, would be easier to defend than Fort Moultrie, where guns provided protection from attacks by sea but not from land. However, although Fort Sumter could withstand attacks in the 1820s when it had been built, it proved vulnerable to the Confederate bombardment of 1861. Today, visitors to the Fort Sumter National Monument can still see evidence of the battle.

Active Options

On Your Feet: Create a Quiz Organize students into two teams and have the teams move to opposite sides of the room. Instruct each team to write 10 true-false statements or multiple-choice questions about the Southern Secession map in this lesson. Have teams alternate reading a statement or asking a question to which the other team will respond. Keep track of the number of correct answers for each team.

NG Learning Framework: Advise the President

SKILL Communication

KNOWLEDGE Our Human Story

Tell students to imagine that it is early in 1861, shortly before the battle at Fort Sumter. Arrange students in small groups and assign each group one of the following leaders: Secretary of State William Seward, General Winfield Scott, Secretary of the Navy Gideon Welles, Major Robert Anderson, or President Jefferson Davis. Instruct groups to research what action their assigned leader believed Abraham Lincoln should take regarding the fort, the reasons the leader supported that plan, and the results the leader expected. Have groups use their findings to write a letter to Abraham Lincoln, advising Lincoln what action to take on Fort Sumter and why. Then have a volunteer from each group read its letter aloud to the class. Discuss similarities and differences in opinion among Lincoln's advisors.

DIFFERENTIATE

Striving Readers

Use Reciprocal Reading Have partners take turns reading aloud each paragraph of the lesson and the captions on the map and photograph. After reading each paragraph or caption, the reader should ask the listener questions about it. Students may ask their partners to state the main idea, identify important details that support the main idea, or summarize the material in their own words. When partners have finished reading the lesson, have them work together to answer the Historical Thinking questions.

Gifted & Talented

Make a Documentary Ask students to pose questions about the Battle of Fort Sumter that can be answered through research. Then have them consult print and online resources to find answers. Have them create a documentary about the battle, using the medium of their choice, to share with the class.

See the Chapter Planner for more strategies for differentiation.

HISTORICAL THINKING

ANSWERS

1. After the attack on Fort Sumter, the Union troops surrendered, but the Confederacy's act of aggression led President Lincoln to call for troops to put down the rebellion.

2. The border states provided a buffer between the North and the South. Maryland prevented the nation's capital from being surrounded by Confederate states. The border states also had populations and resources that were valuable to the Union.

3. Lincoln sent troops to the border states to drive out Confederate invaders.

1.2 An Early Confederate Victory

Sometimes you jump into something before you're really ready. Without enough time to make a plan or devise a strategy, you could find that you just have to "wing it." In a way, that's what happened to the Union and Confederate armies.

MAIN IDEA Confederate forces gained an early victory by winning the Battle of Bull Run.

The first official Confederate flag is shown at the left. Often called the "Stars and Bars," it sometimes caused confusion on the battlefield because it looked so much like the U.S. flag. The flag below was first flown by a Virginia regiment. Soon other regiments began using it, but the Confederacy never officially adopted the flag.

Robert E. Lee

Born into a celebrated Virginia family, Robert E. Lee wanted to make a name for himself. He enrolled in the U.S. Military Academy at West Point in New York and was one of only six soldiers in his class who graduated with a clean record of behavior. After graduating, Lee met and married a descendant of Martha Washington, George Washington's wife. During the Mexican-American War, Lee impressed his commanding officer, General Winfield Scott, with his keen military mind. He became an officer in the Confederate Army after turning down Lincoln's offer to command the Union Army. His loyalty to his home state outweighed the president's request.

PREPARING FOR WAR

War had begun, but neither the Union nor the Confederacy was actually prepared for it. In April 1861, the Union forces included only 16,000 professional soldiers, while the Confederacy had fewer than 2,000. Both sides quickly took steps to **mobilize**, or organize and prepare troops for active service.

The North and the South enlisted troops at the local and state levels. A local leader would encourage men to join and serve under his command, or a group of men would get together and elect their commander. Many military units also formed along ethnic lines. Some northern regiments consisted only of European immigrants who communicated in their native language. Germans were the largest European immigrant group fighting for the Union. European immigrants also fought for the South, and a Texas regiment consisting of Mexicans called the Tejas soon joined the Confederate cause as well. Mobilization helped swell the ranks on both sides, but neither army was at full strength.

THE BATTLE OF BULL RUN

The armies were put to the test in July 1861. Hoping to bring a swift end to the war, Lincoln decided to send Union forces to seize Richmond. To carry out his plan, Lincoln first ordered General Irvin McDowell to attack the Confederate forces in Manassas, Virginia, a town less than 100 miles from Richmond. McDowell and his troops were in Washington, D.C., only 40 miles east of Manassas. But McDowell didn't believe his 35,000 volunteers were ready for battle, so he and his troops left

Washington, D.C., more than a week later than planned. When the Confederate general stationed in Manassas, P.G.T. Beauregard, learned of the delay, he sent for help. Soon 11,000 more Confederate soldiers arrived to strengthen his forces.

The battle began on July 21, when Union forces crossed a small creek called Bull Run to attack the Confederates. As the Confederate soldiers charged, they unleashed a high-pitched battle cry that could be heard for miles. The earsplitting cry came to be known as the "rebel yell." Many Union soldiers wrote in letters and diaries about the terror the scream inspired.

During the battle, Confederate general Thomas Jackson and his forces filled a gap in the line of Confederate soldiers. He held the line so bravely that another general told his men to take heart from the sight of Jackson, "standing like a stone wall!" Jackson would be known by the nickname **Stonewall Jackson** for the rest of his life. Meanwhile, **J.E.B. Stuart**, the leader of the Virginia Confederate **cavalry**, or soldiers on horseback, watched Union movements on a hill overlooking the battlefield. At a critical point in the battle, Stuart's cavalry charged and scattered the

Union **infantry**, or foot soldiers. The charge forced the Union troops to retreat to Washington, D.C.

The Confederacy won the battle, but both sides suffered heavy casualties: about 3,000 soldiers for the North and more than 1,700 for the South. Another battle at Bull Run would take place more than a year later. Once again, the Confederates, under General **Robert E. Lee**, would win but with staggering casualties: nearly 15,000 for the Union and 9,000 for the Confederacy. These extremely high casualty rates continued to make the war unpopular in the North. Lincoln knew it would be a long and grueling war.

HISTORICAL THINKING

1. **READING CHECK** How did the North and the South prepare for the war?

2. **ANALYZE CAUSE AND EFFECT** How did the first Battle of Bull Run affect the course of the early part of the war?

3. **DRAW CONCLUSIONS** How did this battle reflect the beginnings of a broad pattern of leadership in the North and the South?

Objective

Describe how the Battle of Bull Run affected the course of the Civil War.

Critical Thinking Skills for Lesson 1.2

- Identify Main Ideas and Details
- Monitor Comprehension
- Analyze Cause and Effect
- Draw Conclusions
- Make Predictions
- Form and Support Opinions

Essential Question for Chapter 15

How did the early years of the Civil War affect people on both sides of the conflict? In 1861, neither the North nor the South was prepared for war. Lesson 1.2 explains how the early Confederate victory at Bull Run influenced the course of the Civil War.

Background for the Teacher

Some witnesses to the Battle of Bull Run learned the hard way that war is no picnic. When the Battle of Bull Run began on Sunday, July 21, 1861, interested spectators from Washington, including some members of Congress, went to witness the event. Many packed a picnic lunch since the battle site was about 25 miles, or a seven-hour carriage ride, from their homes. Some brought opera glasses to get a better view of combat from a safe distance away. The picnic atmosphere changed when Union generals called for retreat, and soldiers ran for their lives in the direction of the spectators. Most of the onlookers joined in the retreat and returned to Washington unharmed. Some senators tried to convince the soldiers to go back and fight. One member of Congress was captured by Confederates and imprisoned in Richmond.

Brainstorm Descriptive Terms

Write the term *game plan* on the board. **ASK:** What does it mean to have a game plan? *(Possible response: having a strategy for success)* Have students brainstorm other terms with similar meanings. *(Possible responses:* blueprint, design, big idea, road map*)* Then ask students to brainstorm terms that describe doing something without a plan. *(Possible responses:* wing it, ad-lib, improvise, play it by ear*)* Tell students that they will find out which terms best describe how the Union and Confederate armies operated.

TEACH

Guided Discussion

1. **Make Predictions** Based on the numbers of the Union and Confederate forces at the beginning of the war, what prediction would most observers have made about the outcome? *(Based on the size of the forces, the Union seemed likely to quickly defeat the Confederacy.)* How did the Battle of Bull Run change that prediction? *(The outcome of Bull Run made a quick win for the Union appear less likely.)*

2. **Form and Support Opinions** What was the greatest advantage for the Confederacy in the Battle of Bull Run? Why do you think so? *(Possible responses: an opportunity for more soldiers to arrive; the rebel yell; strong military leaders; the use of cavalry)*

More Information

Battle Names The battle discussed in this lesson is known by two different names. To northerners, it was the Battle of Bull Run because the Union usually named battles after nearby geographic features, often bodies of water. To southerners, it was the Battle of Manassas because the Confederacy usually named battles after nearby towns or railroad stations. Challenge students to complete the table below with Union and Confederate names for Civil War battles. *(Pittsburg Landing/Shiloh; Antietam/Sharpsburg; Pea Ridge/Elkhorn Tavern; Stones River/Murfreesboro)*

Union name for battle	Confederate name for battle
Pittsburg Landing	
	Sharpsburg
Pea Ridge	
	Murfreesboro

Active Options

On Your Feet: Form a Human Sequence Chain Organize students into small groups and provide each group with six large sheets of paper. Have group members work together to choose six events from the lesson that form a sequence from the preparation for the Battle of Bull Run to its end result. Instruct students to write one event on each sheet of paper. At your signal, have members of each group stand and, holding up the six papers, arrange themselves in order to present their events in the proper sequence. Allow groups to analyze each other's work and make suggestions for changes.

NG Learning Framework: Write a Résumé

ATTITUDE Empowerment

SKILL Collaboration

Make sure students understand that the purpose of a résumé is to show that a person has the qualifications and experience for a job. You might want to provide an example of a résumé for students to use as a model. Then have students work in small groups to write a résumé for Robert E. Lee indicating why he was suited to command Confederate troops. Encourage students to use information from other sources in addition to the text to make sure their résumé is accurate. Allow groups to present their résumés to the class.

English Language Learners

Illustrate Vocabulary Have students at the **Emerging** level draw pictures to represent the Key Vocabulary words *cavalry* and *infantry*. Then have them write a caption for each picture to explain the meaning of the word. You may have students at the **Bridging** or **Expanding** levels help formulate the captions.

Pre-AP

Portray Soldiers' Viewpoints Assign all or parts of James McPherson's *What They Fought For, 1861–1865*. After students have completed the reading, have them work together to present a dramatization in which they portray the viewpoints of different soldiers in the Civil War. Encourage them to include excerpts from the book in their presentations. Then ask the whole class to reflect on and discuss the different viewpoints dramatized in the presentations.

See the Chapter Planner for more strategies for differentiation.

HISTORICAL THINKING

ANSWERS

1. Both sides enlisted and trained troops. Although many men joined the armies, neither the North nor the South had enough soldiers.

2. The victory at Bull Run made the Confederates feel they could win the war, while heavy casualties caused a loss of support for the war among northerners.

3. Lincoln had planned to seize Manassas and Richmond in order to bring about a quick end to the war. However, his general did not carry out the plan. Meanwhile, Confederate military leaders showed they could make and carry out successful battle plans.

1.3 Confederate Memorial Hall New Orleans, Louisiana

Confederate Memorial Hall opened its doors in New Orleans on January 8, 1891. The oldest museum in Louisiana, it celebrates southern heritage and history with a focus on Civil War artifacts from the Confederate Army. In fact, the museum houses one of the largest collections of

Confederate memorabilia in the United States, including uniforms and boots, weapons, personal items, and photographs. What challenges and advantages might a museum face in choosing to showcase items from one side of a war rather than from both sides?

Binoculars and Case

These 1863 binoculars and leather case belonged to a Confederate soldier. Cavalry generals—generals who commanded soldiers on horseback—and officers carried binoculars as part of their gear. Confederate soldiers also commonly carried a canteen, blanket roll (similar to a sleeping bag), ammunition and a weapon, and very simple food.

How might binoculars like these have helped officers on the battlefield?

New Yorker William Ketchum designed and patented this Civil War hand grenade.

Ketchum Hand Grenade

Unexploded hand grenades make an interesting addition to any wartime museum exhibit—especially early ones from the Civil War. Confederate and Union soldiers tossed these three- and five-pound hand grenades like darts into enemy territory during battles. The weapons have been recovered from famous battle sites such as Vicksburg and Petersburg.

Tintype Portrait

A photographer captured this 1861 tintype portrait of Sergeant Joseph Corneille, a member of the 22nd Louisiana Infantry, in his full dress uniform. Tintypes were invented in the 1850s and involved the transfer of a photograph to a thin sheet of iron coated with enamel. These portraits were prized possessions. They were also expensive. People bought elaborate frames like the one shown here, so they could put their portraits on display. They also carried them in cases or envelopes so the tintypes would be protected.

Many Civil War soldiers in full uniform had a tintype created before they headed off to battle. Why do you think the soldiers wanted to have these portraits created?

Confederate Battle Flag

Many Confederate regiments designed and adopted their own personalized battle flags during the Civil War. The red and white Van Dorn battle flag shown below was used by the regiments under the command of Confederate general Earl Van Dorn in Louisiana, Missouri, Mississippi, and Arkansas between 1862 and 1863. The 13 white stars represent the 13 Confederate States of America.

PLAN

Objective
Identify artifacts from the Confederate Army.

Critical Thinking Skills for Lesson 1.3
• Make Connections

• Analyze Visuals

• Draw Conclusions

• Make Inferences

Essential Question for Chapter 15
How did the early years of the Civil War affect people on both sides of the conflict? During the Civil War, 80 percent of the eligible free men in the South were recruited for military service. Lesson 1.3 reveals the experiences of Confederate soldiers through artifacts from their daily lives.

Background for the Teacher
Confederate Memorial Hall was a gift to the Louisiana Historical Association from philanthropist Frank Howard. Until it was built, the artifacts were housed in the Howard Library next door, a building also funded by Howard. Both buildings were designed by the nationally prominent architect Henry Hobson Richardson, who lived nearby in the city. His style, Richardsonian Romanesque, was popular in the late 1800s. On the day the museum opened, the New Orleans *Daily Picayune* praised the building itself and referred to the displays as a "wonderland," stating, "There is not another building in this city like it in interior finish and contents." Confederate Memorial Hall remains a popular tourist attraction in New Orleans.

History Notebook
Encourage students to complete the Curating History page for Chapter 15 in their History Notebooks as they read.

Plan an Exhibition

Tell students to imagine that the school district is choosing items for an exhibition showcasing the daily life of students in the 21st century. Ask them what items should go in the exhibition. List the items on the board and discuss how helpful and credible each item would be for future generations who want to understand the day-to-day lives of today's students. Tell students that in this lesson they will examine items used by Confederate soldiers in the Civil War in order to gain insight into the daily lives of those soldiers.

TEACH

Guided Discussion

1. **Draw Conclusions** What conclusions can you draw about Civil War combat based on the Ketchum hand grenade? *(Answers will vary. Possible response: Technology was not very advanced. Opposing forces must have been close to each other because the grenades were too heavy to throw long distances.)*

2. **Make Inferences** Why do you think Confederate regiments used personalized battle flags? *(Answers will vary. Possible responses: Personalized flags showed soldiers' pride in their regiment or respect for their commanding officer. Flags may also have been a way for soldiers to identify their unit on the battlefield.)*

Curating History

A Confederate soldier's uniform typically consisted of a kepi hat, cotton jacket and pants, and brogans, or heavy leather shoes that reached the ankle. Some Confederate soldiers, however, had no shoes at all. Uniform colors varied from blue or gray to a tan or butternut shade. Officers generally wore knee-length coats instead of jackets. As the war dragged on, uniforms were in short supply, and shoes were especially hard to replace. Due to lack of resources and industry in the South, many Confederate soldiers lacked adequate clothing.

Access the Confederate Memorial Hall website and encourage students to explore the museum's collection of uniforms, weapons, and personal items. Then hold a class discussion about these primary source materials and what conclusions can be drawn from them.

Active Options

On Your Feet: Sort the Artifacts Have students work in teams of four to examine the museum's online collection and complete two Concept Clusters like those shown below. In one cluster, students should identify various personal items, such as the binoculars and case. In the other, students should identify a different class or genre of artifacts to be determined by the team. When teams are finished, have them share their Concept Clusters with the class.

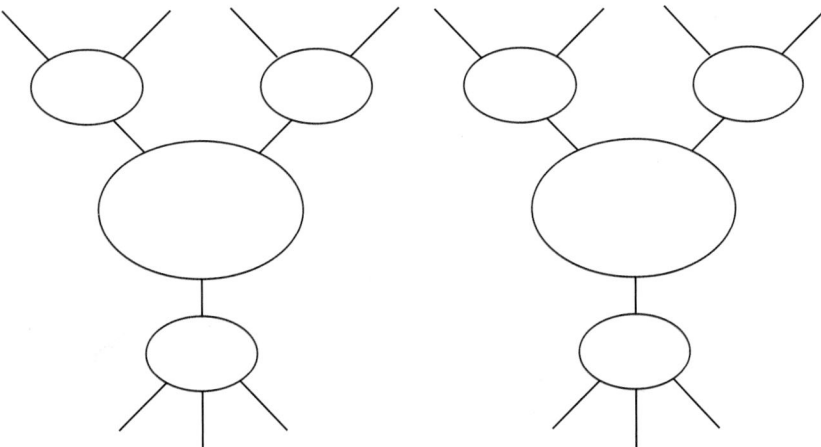

Striving Readers

Summarize Captions Allow students to work in pairs to read the captions together. Explain that after reading the captions, one partner will choose a photograph and tell about it in his or her own words, including information from the caption, and the other partner can add additional details. Partners will take turns choosing photographs and describing them.

Inclusion

Describe the Artifacts Pair students who have visual impairments with students who do not. Ask students without visual disabilities to read the captions and describe the artifacts in detail for their partners. Encourage students to ask questions as needed for clarification. Then have the partners work together to answer the questions in the lesson.

See the Chapter Planner for more strategies for differentiation.

CURATING HISTORY

Answers will vary. Possible response: The country was reunited by the time the museum opened, so some people may have felt both sides of the conflict should be represented. Others may have wanted to preserve the heritage of the South. Since the museum is located in the South, artifacts from the Confederacy may have been easier to collect.

BINOCULARS AND CASE

Answers will vary. Possible response: Binoculars allowed officers, especially those on horseback, to see opposing troop movements from a distance. The officers could position their soldiers accordingly.

TINTYPE PORTRAIT

Answers will vary. Possible response: The soldiers were proud to serve the Confederacy and wanted to preserve a picture of themselves in uniform. They may have wanted to provide their families with a permanent remembrance in case they did not survive.

2.1 Hardship and Weapons

Siblings fight over all kinds of things: household chores, toys, television programs. During the Civil War, however, some siblings argued over a much larger issue: whether to support the Union or the Confederacy.

MAIN IDEA Soldiers in the Civil War faced difficulties at home and in the field, including dealing with technological advances on the front lines.

A SOLDIER'S LIFE

The Civil War divided not only a nation but also families. Siblings, parents, and even spouses sometimes found themselves on different sides of the debate. It was not uncommon to hear of two brothers serving in opposing armies. No one was spared from these divisions, not even Abraham Lincoln. His brother-in-law, Ben Hardin Helm, was a Confederate general.

Whichever side the soldiers served on, life was difficult and dangerous. For every 30 days in the field, the average soldier engaged in battle one day and drilled, trained, and marched the remaining 29. Army leaders had difficulty keeping track of their units' needs, so supplies didn't always arrive when required. The soldiers were often cold and hungry as a result. Disease killed more men than fighting did.

And now army leaders had more soldiers under their command. After Bull Run, both the Confederate and Union leaders realized they needed larger armies. Farmers under the age of 30 made up about half of the men on both sides. Some older men joined the ranks as well, and boys as young as 12 served as

Wooden Legs, Iron Arms
Approximately 70,000 soldiers lost limbs during the battles of the Civil War. The government offered veterans money to buy prosthetic, or artificial, arms, feet, and legs, like this one, to replace their missing limbs. Many options made of wood, iron, and leather were soon available. Few, however, were comfortable or functional. Most soldiers chose to use crutches and hooks instead.

drummers and buglers. About a quarter of the Union volunteers were young immigrants, mainly from Germany, Ireland, Canada, and England. Another group of people, African-American men, could have been drafted into fighting, but it would be several years before either army began to recruit them or even allow them to enlist.

A NEW KIND OF WAR

The Civil War battlefield was far more dangerous than it had been in previous American wars. Advances in technology made fighting more efficient and deadlier than ever. In earlier wars, soldiers carried muskets, which were not very accurate. The inside of a musket's barrel was polished smooth, causing the bullet's flight to be unpredictable. And a man fighting on the battlefield with a musket had to stand within 80 yards of his enemy in order to hit him. All that changed in the 1850s when a new kind of rifle replaced the musket. The grooves carved inside the barrel made the bullet spin as it hurtled toward its target. The spinning made the bullet fly in a straighter line and gave it a greater range—more than 1,000 yards.

CRITICAL VIEWING As this 1862 photograph of the Union Army reveals, Civil War soldiers used heavy guns and fought from trenches. What might have been some of the disadvantages of fighting and living in trenches such as these?

Some Union soldiers had another technological advantage in their hands: the repeating rifle. Instead of having to reload a gun after each shot, a soldier armed with a repeating rifle could fire several times before having to replenish his ammunition. These technological advances would continue to be improved and affect how future wars were fought.

With improvements to both rifles and larger cannons, soldiers increasingly resorted to **trench warfare** during the Civil War. Opposing armies dug lines of trenches, or ditches, roughly parallel to each other. The trenches gave soldiers both a vantage point from which to fire and a place to shelter from incoming rounds of ammunition. Advances in naval technology also brought changes to warfare at sea. Before, ordinary wooden ships were vulnerable to cannon and rifle fire. New **ironclad ships**, or ships plated with thick metal, could withstand this heavy artillery.

Unfortunately, the technology of medical treatment had not transformed as fast as the technology of war. Effective treatments for infections, such as antibiotics, had not yet been invented. **Mortality**,

or the death rate, from wounds and disease was high. And the hundreds of thousands of sick and wounded required medical attention, which in turn created a shortage of people to care for them. Hard-working male doctors and nurses set up hospitals in makeshift buildings and did their best to treat the soldiers, but they struggled to keep up with the flood of patients. The acute need for more caregivers was soon answered, however. Large numbers of women volunteered to provide much-needed care as nurses and administrators.

HISTORICAL THINKING

1. **READING CHECK** What sort of struggles did Civil War soldiers face before they arrived on the battlefield?

2. **DETERMINE WORD MEANING** What context clues help you understand what *replenish* means?

3. **MAKE INFERENCES** What impact do you think technological advances had on the soldiers' mortality rate?

Objective

Describe how divided family loyalties and improved weapons affected Civil War soldiers.

Critical Thinking Skills for Lesson 2.1

- Identify Main Ideas and Details
- Monitor Comprehension
- Determine Word Meaning
- Make Inferences
- Analyze Cause and Effect

Essential Question for Chapter 15

How did the early years of the Civil War affect people on both sides of the conflict? The Civil War divided American families and introduced new technologies that made warfare more dangerous than ever before. Lesson 2.1 discusses the experiences of soldiers on and off the battlefield.

Background for the Teacher

Drummers and buglers played important roles in the Union and Confederate armies. These musicians were generally young boys who had enlisted with or without their parents' permission, sometimes by lying about their age. At camp, buglers played reveille to wake up the soldiers in the morning and taps to signal the end of the day. There were also specific bugle calls for assembly, sick call, and other daily routines. In battle, more than 40 bugle calls were used to communicate commands. These sounds could be heard much more clearly than an officer's voice. Drummers had similar responsibilities. Drumbeats regulated drills and signaled orders on the battlefield.

History Notebook

Encourage students to complete the American Gallery page for Chapter 15 in their History Notebooks as they read and the Reid on the Road video series page after they view the video.

Imagine Battlefield News

As a class, discuss the kinds of news Civil War families might hope to learn in a letter from the battlefield. *(Possible responses: that their loved one is safe and healthy, what camp life is like, stories of battles, or insights into the war's progress)* Then ask students to discuss the kind of report a soldier would like to receive in a letter from home. *(Possible responses: that his family is well, that his town is safe from the war, that a sweetheart is waiting for him, family news, or political news that might not make it to the battlefield)* Tell students that in this lesson they will learn about life in camp and on the battlefield.

TEACH

Guided Discussion

1. **Analyze Cause and Effect** How do you think the early part of the Civil War affected farming in both the North and the South? *(Possible responses: Farm families suffered hardships because many farmers had to serve in the army. Crop production may have been smaller due to lack of workers or destruction of fields by troops.)*

2. **Make Inferences** Why do you think medical technology did not advance as fast as military technology did during the Civil War? *(Possible responses: Government resources were focused on the war instead of on medical research. Advances in war technologies were new, and the medical profession had yet to encounter the types of injuries those technologies could cause.)*

More Information

Minié Balls Rifle-muskets were the most popular weapon used by infantry in both the North and the South. Loading and firing a muzzle-loaded rifle-musket required a nine-step process in which a musket ball had to be forced into the barrel of the gun. A technological advance called the minié ball improved the use of rifles for combat. The minié ball was a bullet named for its inventor, French army officer Claude-Étienne Minié. The bullet's size and conical shape made it easier and faster to load than a musket ball. The minié bullet also offered more accurate shots and inflicted more damage. **ASK:** In addition to the use of trenches, how might new, more accurate weapons have had an effect on future warfare? *(Possible response: It might have pushed armies to adopt stealthier tactics, such as sniper fire and camouflage uniforms, or to develop protective gear and vehicles such as tanks.)*

Active Options

On Your Feet: Complete a Cause-and-Effect Web Display a large version of a Cause-and-Effect Web. In the center circle, write *Civil War*. Invite students to write a word or phrase in one of the Effect boxes. They can list effects in any order. If a student cannot think of an effect, allow classmates to help. After everyone has had a turn, ask the class to organize the effects in some logical way. For example, they might categorize positive and negative effects or determine who was affected in each case.

AMERICAN GALLERY ONLINE **The Daily Lives of Civil War Soldiers** Invite students to explore the American Gallery. Have them select one of the images and do additional research to learn more about it. Ask questions that will inspire additional inquiry about the chosen gallery image, such as: What is this? Where and how was it used? By whom? Why does it belong in this chapter? What else would you like to learn about it?

English Language Learners

Use Sentence Frames Provide students with a set of sentence frames that summarize the lesson. Leave one blank per sentence for students at the **Expanding** level and more than one blank for students at the **Bridging** level. Depending on your students' proficiency, you might wish to provide a word bank or list of answers for students to use to complete the sentences. After they complete the sentence frames individually, allow students to work in pairs to compare answers and read the sentences.

Gifted & Talented

Investigate Effects of Warfare Prompt students to research how technologies developed during the Civil War affected subsequent warfare. Examples include the use of trenches, advances in weapons and naval technology, and organization of military structure. Have students develop a slide show or other media presentation to share the results of their research with the class. Encourage classmates to ask questions about the presentations.

See the Chapter Planner for more strategies for differentiation.

HISTORICAL THINKING

ANSWERS

1. Many soldiers were cold and hungry because provisions could not always be delivered, some suffered from disease, and some faced family strife over which side of the conflict they chose.

2. The phrases *instead of having to reload* and *repeating rifle could fire several times* signal that *replenish* means "to refill or add more."

3. Technological advances in weapons likely increased the mortality rate because soldiers could fire faster, farther, and more accurately. Ironclad ships likely reduced the mortality rate because the ships could withstand heavy artillery attacks.

CRITICAL VIEWING Trenches became wet, muddy, and uncomfortable when it rained. Grenades could be thrown in, and soldiers wouldn't be able to escape. Soldiers could not see over the top, so they might have been shot when they came out.

2.2 Women and the War

Think of a time when you stepped up and took on a role you'd never shouldered before. You might have felt uncomfortable about assuming the role, but—like women during the Civil War—you probably felt that you had to do it.

MAIN IDEA Women took an active role in the Civil War, both on the battlefield and at home.

CRITICAL VIEWING A nurse feeds a wounded Union soldier in a hospital in Pennsylvania in 1861. How would you describe the conditions in the hospital?

WOMEN ON THE BATTLEFIELD

Just as they had in the American Revolution, women during the Civil War took on roles that brought them closer to the field of battle. Many women, in particular, became nurses. Before the war, society considered it inappropriate for women to care for injured and ill men. The Civil War quickly changed all that. Soon, most nurses were women, and at least one woman, **Mary Edwards Walker**, became a doctor.

In the North, Dorothea Dix and a **philanthropist** named **Clara Barton** led the nursing effort. A philanthropist is someone who actively promotes human welfare. Already known for her work on behalf of the mentally ill, Dix led volunteer nurses in a march on Washington in April 1861, demanding that women be allowed to help the Union forces. As a result, the Secretary of War gave Dix the responsibility of recruiting female nurses. Dix insisted that her volunteers be no younger than 30 years old. More than 2,000 women volunteered. For her part, Barton collected and delivered medical supplies, clothing, and food for Union soldiers throughout the war. She aided many wounded Union soldiers and the Confederate prisoners they captured.

In the South, a young woman named **Sally Tompkins** led the effort to provide nursing care through her private hospital in Richmond, which she supported with her own personal fortune. The hospital treated more than 1,300 soldiers during the four years it was open, and it returned more men to the battlefield than any other hospital. In

addition, more than 600 nuns from 12 different Catholic religious communities also served as nurses during the war and attended to both Union and Confederate soldiers.

The founder of the American Red Cross, Clara Barton was 29 years old when this photo was taken (1850). A former teacher, Barton was working as a clerk at the U.S. Patent Office in Washington, D.C., when the Civil War began. Determined to support the war effort, she set out to help the soldiers, some of whom were once her students. Soon, Barton was following the Union Army to the battlefields, where she tended to the wounded and dying.

WOMEN AT HOME

While some women helped on the battlefield, many more did their part at home. When war came, women all over the country took over the roles of their husbands, brothers, and sons in order to keep family farms and businesses running. On small farms, women and children took charge of raising animals and planting, tending, harvesting, and selling crops. On southern plantations, women directed the overseers and enslaved people. In the cities, women took jobs in factories and offices, replacing the men who had left to fight. Many women also volunteered to raise food and money, make clothing, and provide medical supplies for the troops and their communities.

Even for those women who stayed at home, the war sometimes came uncomfortably close. **Civilians**, or people not in the military, who lived near the battlefields had to deal with the sounds and dangers of battle. They could only

watch as enemy combatants marched through their towns and raided their homes for supplies. To add to the stress, a family's only means of communicating with husbands and sons at war was through letters. Since troops were constantly on the move, delivering mail to them was difficult. If a soldier was killed or missing in action, the bad news arrived by letter. And since soldiers carried no official identification, many families were not informed at all. If a loved one's letters stopped coming, his family had to assume that he was not coming home.

HISTORICAL THINKING

1. **READING CHECK** How did Dorothea Dix open up the occupation of nursing to women?

2. **SUMMARIZE** What new roles did women play during the Civil War?

3. **ANALYZE CAUSE AND EFFECT** How did the war impact women, combatants, and civilians in different ways?

Objective

Explain how women's roles changed during the Civil War.

Critical Thinking Skills for Lesson 2.2

• Identify Main Ideas and Details

• Monitor Comprehension

• Summarize

• Analyze Cause and Effect

• Draw Conclusions

• Make Connections

Essential Question for Chapter 15

How did the early years of the Civil War affect people on both sides of the conflict? The Civil War affected every part of American society. Lesson 2.2 explores how the war impacted women.

Background for the Teacher

Mary Edwards Walker was an eccentric who was often criticized for wearing men's trousers under her dress, but she was also a skilled surgeon at a time when female doctors were rare. When the Civil War began, Walker offered her services as a doctor, but she was refused. Eventually, Walker became an assistant surgeon in the Union Army. She was captured by Confederates and imprisoned for several months.

Shortly after the war, Walker was awarded the Medal of Honor for her service. In 1917, however, Congress revoked medals (including Walker's) that had been given to anyone who had not served in combat. Walker nevertheless continued to wear her medal until she died in 1919. Sixty years later, Congress reinstated Walker's award, making her the only woman to have won the Medal of Honor.

INTRODUCE & ENGAGE

Identify Gender Roles

List the following jobs on the board: doctor, soldier, business owner, farmer, nurse, factory worker, fundraiser, office worker. Point to each job and ask students to vote, by raising their hands, whether these jobs are performed mostly by men, by women, or equally by both genders in the United States today. Ask students to defend their opinions if there are disagreements. Then tell them they will learn how some gender roles changed as a result of the Civil War.

TEACH

Guided Discussion

1. **Draw Conclusions** What did Clara Barton's actions reveal about her attitude toward the war? *(Answers will vary. Possible responses: Barton collected supplies for Union soldiers and followed the Union army in battle, which suggests that she supported the Union cause. Barton helped both Union soldiers and Confederate prisoners of war, which suggests that she was more interested in helping people than in taking sides.)*

2. **Make Connections** Metal identification tags like soldiers wear today first began to appear during the Civil War. What problem did the tags help address? *(Possible response: Lack of official identification in the Civil War meant that families often were not notified if their loved one was killed in battle. The use of metal ID tags helped provide a means of identifying soldiers who had been hurt or killed.)*

More Information

Albert Cashier During the Civil War, hundreds of women disguised themselves as men in order to fight as soldiers in the Union and the Confederate armies. Jennie Hodgers was one of them. In 1862, Hodgers joined the 95th Illinois Infantry as Albert Cashier. She fought in more than 40 battles, including the Siege of Vicksburg. After the war, Hodgers continued to live as a man in order to collect a military pension. Her secret was not discovered until 1910 when she was hit by a car and treated for a broken leg. **ASK:** Why do you think women wanted to participate in combat? *(Answers will vary. Possible responses: They felt strongly about the war and wanted to support their side. They thought taking part in the fighting was a more significant contribution than the ways in which women were allowed to participate.)*

Active Options

On Your Feet: Hold a Roundtable Discussion Arrange students in groups of four. Ask them to discuss the following question: What was the most important change women experienced during the Civil War? Instruct roundtable groups to discuss the answers among themselves and come to a consensus about the most important change women experienced. Have groups share their ideas with the class.

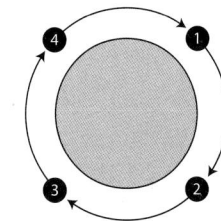

NG Learning Framework: Research the Red Cross

SKILL Communication

KNOWLEDGE Our Human Story

Assign students to small groups. Ask each group to choose some aspect of the American Red Cross, such as its beginnings, the services it provides, or its present-day status. Instruct them to gather and summarize relevant information from multiple primary and secondary sources, including both print and digital references, using search terms effectively. Remind students to assess the credibility and accuracy of the sources they use and to cite sources appropriately when quoting or paraphrasing. Allow time for students to share the results of their research with the class.

DIFFERENTIATE

Inclusion

Complete an Idea Web To help students with learning disabilities keep track of details, draw an Idea Web on the board. In the center box, write "Women's Roles." Then instruct students to complete the outer circles with examples of different roles women played during the Civil War. Use the completed Idea Web to review the lesson.

Pre-AP

Profile a Woman of the Civil War Ask students to research Clara Barton, Dorothea Dix, Mary Edward Walker, Jennie Hodgers/Albert Cashier, Sally Tompkins, or another Civil War woman of their choosing. Then prompt them to write a profile about the woman they chose, including biographical information as well as any insight into the motivations that propelled the woman to take on the role she did during the Civil War. Encourage students to read their profile to the class, or post them on a class blog or website.

See the Chapter Planner for more strategies for differentiation.

HISTORICAL THINKING

ANSWERS

1. Dorothea Dix led volunteers in a march on Washington to demand that women be allowed to tend Union soldiers.

2. Women took on tasks such as managing farms and plantations, planting and harvesting crops, caring for livestock, working in offices and factories, and caring for the sick and wounded as nurses.

3. Women took on new roles on the battlefield and at home, performing many jobs previously done by men. Combatants were separated from their families, and many were killed or suffered injuries and illnesses. Civilians were exposed to the dangers of war, and many civilians lost loved ones.

CRITICAL VIEWING Answers will vary. Possible response: The hospital room looks crowded and unsanitary by today's standards. The blankets look like they may have come from someone's home. Medical supplies seem inadequate. The nurse is mixing something in a cup, perhaps food or medicine.

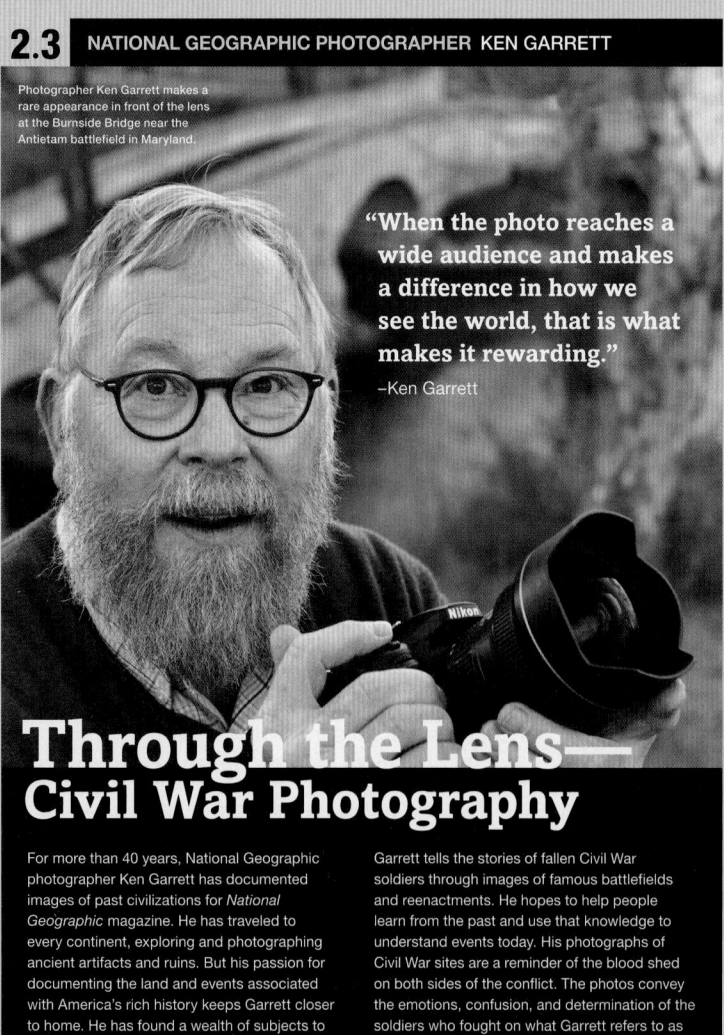

Photographer Ken Garrett makes a rare appearance in front of the lens at the Burnside Bridge near the Antietam battlefield in Maryland.

"When the photo reaches a wide audience and makes a difference in how we see the world, that is what makes it rewarding."

–Ken Garrett

Through the Lens— Civil War Photography

For more than 40 years, National Geographic photographer Ken Garrett has documented images of past civilizations for *National Geographic* magazine. He has traveled to every continent, exploring and photographing ancient artifacts and ruins. But his passion for documenting the land and events associated with America's rich history keeps Garrett closer to home. He has found a wealth of subjects to photograph on the Civil War.

Garrett tells the stories of fallen Civil War soldiers through images of famous battlefields and reenactments. He hopes to help people learn from the past and use that knowledge to understand events today. His photographs of Civil War sites are a reminder of the blood shed on both sides of the conflict. The photos convey the emotions, confusion, and determination of the soldiers who fought on what Garrett refers to as "hallowed ground."

Lincoln Cemetery in Gettysburg, Pennsylvania, is the burial site of about 30 members of the U.S. Colored Troops. During the Civil War, African-American veterans were prohibited from being buried in the Soldiers' National Cemetery. In this photo taken by Garrett, reenactors pay tribute to African-American Civil War veterans during a Remembrance Day parade.

SIZING UP A SITE

When Garrett photographs a Civil War site, he likes to scout the area with a guide who can help him understand the events of the historic battle. The guide's insights help Garrett determine how to use his camera to capture the decisions made during the battle. He uses photography to show why one place was important to defend or what made another a superior place in which to hide, prepare, and attack.

Battery-powered lighting equipment helps Garrett capture the right photograph in the right light or season. "You should try to photograph a site during the season when the action took place," he adds. For example, by photographing Brandy Station, Virginia, during the summer, Garrett was able to provide insight into the heat and humidity both armies endured at this site of the largest cavalry battle in U.S. history.

Gettysburg is Garrett's favorite Civil War battlefield to photograph. "It is a very emotional place, where you really get an understanding of the horror of war. The thought that those boys walked out into that open field to be killed, sometimes by their own brothers, is a shocking realization." Gettysburg is also a popular site for reenactments. These re-creations put contemporary people in the shoes of people from 150 years earlier, bringing history to life and giving us valuable perspective on historic events.

A selection of Garrett's Gettysburg photographs as well as others from his Civil War collection are included in the following photo essay on the Civil War.

HISTORICAL THINKING

MAKE CONNECTIONS Why are Ken Garrett's Civil War photographs relevant today?

PLAN

Objective

Explain how Ken Garrett uses photography to document the Civil War.

Critical Thinking Skills for Lesson 2.3

- Identify Main Ideas and Details
- Monitor Comprehension
- Make Connections
- Summarize
- Evaluate

Essential Question for Chapter 15

How did the early years of the Civil War affect people on both sides of the conflict?

Photographs of Civil War sites can help people learn about history. Lesson 2.3 discusses how Ken Garrett uses photography to give modern viewers insight into battles and soldiers of the Civil War.

Background for the Teacher

The Journey Through Hallowed Ground is a National Heritage area extending from Gettysburg, Pennsylvania, through Maryland and West Virginia to Thomas Jefferson's home at Monticello in Charlottesville, Virginia. It includes the nation's largest concentration of Civil War sites. The Journey Through Hallowed Ground partnership hired photographer Ken Garrett to capture the area's natural beauty and historical significance. Garrett's photos were exhibited at Dulles International Airport in Washington, D.C., and they appear in a book titled *Journey Through Hallowed Ground: Birthplace of the American Ideal.* Commenting on the title, Garrett said, "We think these places are so important that they have a spiritual meaning."

History Notebook

Encourage students to complete the Explorer page for Chapter 15 in their History Notebooks as they read.

Think Like a Photographer

Ask students to think of a photograph that they especially like, taken by themselves or someone else. **ASK:** What makes a good photograph? *(Possible responses: subject, light, clarity, or angle from which it was taken)* **ASK:** If you wanted to take a photograph that conveyed a certain mood or attitude, how would you go about it? *(Answers will vary. Students might suggest techniques such as using shadow and light, emphasizing facial expressions, or creating black-and-white images.)* Tell students in this lesson they will learn about techniques National Geographic photographer Ken Garrett uses to capture images that help people understand the past.

Guided Discussion

1. **Summarize** What techniques does Garrett use when photographing historic sites? *(Possible responses: He uses a guide who is familiar with the site to help him understand what took place there and what it was like. He photographs under conditions that are similar to those at the time the event took place.)*

2. **Evaluate** What is the value of reenacting Civil War battles? *(Answers will vary. Possible responses: Battle reenactments help people understand what soldiers wore and what weapons they used. People can gain insights into battle strategies. Participants and viewers may see a battle in more human terms, rather than as a set of statistics.)*

More Information

Remembrance Day The annual Remembrance Day parade and reenactment ceremonies take place on or around November 19, the anniversary of President Lincoln's dedication of the cemetery for white soldiers in 1863. In 1867, a group of African-American citizens known as the Sons of Goodwill bought land nearby to bury African-American soldiers who had died in the war. Direct students' attention to the photograph of Remembrance Day reenactors and the quote that appears beside the photo of Garrett. **ASK:** How might this photo make a difference in how people see the role of African-American soldiers in the Civil War? *(Possible responses: Garrett's photo focuses on African-American reenactors, and the low angle gives them an air of heroism. The photo may help people appreciate the contributions of the black soldiers who were originally denied the respect given to white soldiers.)*

Active Options

On Your Feet: Evaluate Ways of Learning Have students work in pairs to discuss different ways of learning about history, such as reading textbooks and historical fiction, watching plays, and examining photographs and other visuals. Ask students to interview each other about how and why the different formats offer historical insight. For example: Which is your favorite way to learn about history? What information does each format provide? When might photographs be helpful? Remind students to listen closely as their partner answers so they can report what they hear to the rest of the class.

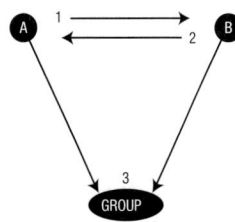

NG Learning Framework: Interview a Photographer

ATTITUDE Curiosity

SKILL Collaboration

Invite student teams to prepare questions for an interview with Ken Garrett. Encourage teams to develop a list of questions about Garrett's work, especially his photographs of Civil War sites and his reasons for wanting to document history through photography. Have teams share their lists of questions. As a class, prepare a master list of interview questions for Garrett.

Striving Readers

Make a List Post the following heading on the board: Three Things I Know about Ken Garrett and His Work. After students read the lesson, have them work in pairs to write three sentences to go with the heading. Call on volunteers to share their sentences with the class.

Gifted & Talented

Write a Narrative Allow students to work individually or in pairs to write a narrative or a poem that tells a story about the photograph of Remembrance Day reenactors. Encourage them to choose some appropriate music to accompany their words. Then ask students to share their work with the class.

See the Chapter Planner for more strategies for differentiation.

ANSWER

Answers will vary. Possible responses: Garrett's photographs help people today understand the sites where battles took place. Photographs of reenactments provide viewers with an emotional connection to the past by sharing the experiences of those who fought in battles.

Objective

- **Analyze how photographs can convey information about the past.**

Critical Thinking Skills for "A Civil War Photo Essay"

- Make Connections
- Analyze Visuals
- Make Inferences
- Describe
- Form and Support Opinions

Background for the Teacher

Photographs allow us to communicate and express ideas using images. A single photograph—such as the image of three firefighters raising an American flag amid the ruins of the World Trade Center on 9/11—can become an unforgettable symbol of an event. A photo essay builds on that idea by presenting a series of images that tell a story. These photos from Ken Garrett's Civil War collection include historical artifacts, memorials, and reenactments at the sites of actual battles. The photos reinforce and extend the knowledge students have gained through reading.

To help students gain the most benefit from the photo essay, give them time to study each photograph and direct their attention to details. Encourage students to pose questions that can be answered through historical research. Use the Guided Discussion questions to provoke analysis and enhance comprehension.

History Notebook

Encourage students to complete the Photo Essay page for Chapter 15 in their History Notebooks.

THINK ABOUT IT

Possible responses: The photo essay has a setting, characters, and action. Each photo shows a particular perspective on the war.

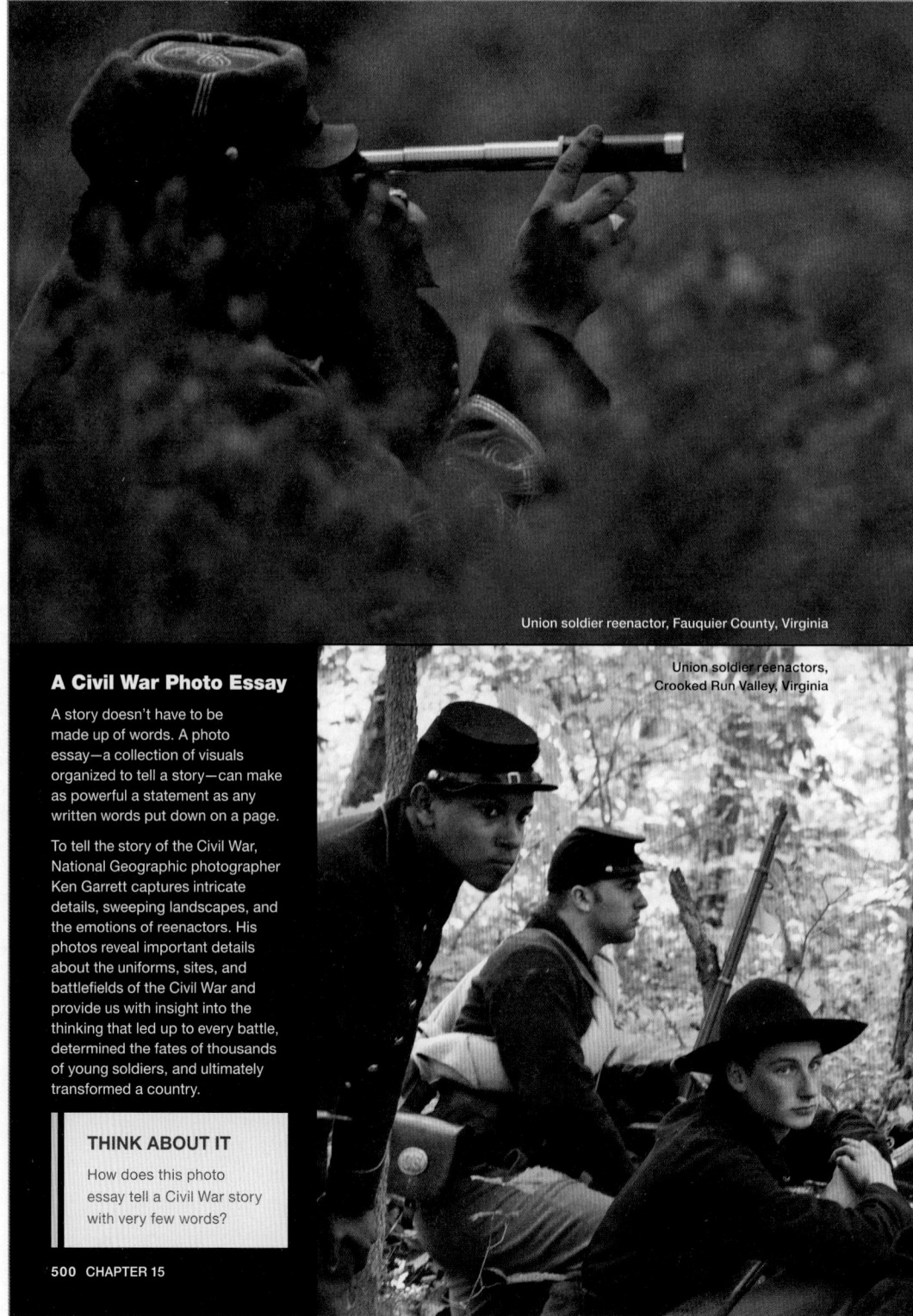

Union soldier reenactor, Fauquier County, Virginia

Union soldier reenactors, Crooked Run Valley, Virginia

A Civil War Photo Essay

A story doesn't have to be made up of words. A photo essay—a collection of visuals organized to tell a story—can make as powerful a statement as any written words put down on a page.

To tell the story of the Civil War, National Geographic photographer Ken Garrett captures intricate details, sweeping landscapes, and the emotions of reenactors. His photos reveal important details about the uniforms, sites, and battlefields of the Civil War and provide us with insight into the thinking that led up to every battle, determined the fates of thousands of young soldiers, and ultimately transformed a country.

THINK ABOUT IT

How does this photo essay tell a Civil War story with very few words?

500 CHAPTER 15

Battle of Bull Run reenactment, Manassas, Virginia

Lincoln Cemetery, burial site for Gettysburg's African-American soldiers

Beginnings of War **501**

Interpret a Saying

On the board, write the saying "A picture is worth a thousand words." Ask students to explain what the saying means and whether they agree with it. Have them brainstorm some things they might learn from photographs that they could not learn from words alone. Then introduce the term *photo essay* and have students predict how a photo essay might be similar to or different from a written essay.

Bull Run Reenactment

Bull Run was the site of two major Civil War battles, the first on July 21, 1861, and the second on August 28–30, 1862. The photo depicts a reenactment of the first of those battles. People watching this present-day reenactment already know how the battle turned out— unlike Union leaders and the citizens of Washington who came out to watch the battle over a picnic lunch, only to be shocked by the Union's defeat.

Lincoln Cemetery

Lincoln Cemetery consists of about four acres of land on the west side of Gettysburg, Pennsylvania. Many African-American residents of the town are buried there, including 30 Civil War veterans. The site is also known as Goodwill Cemetery after the group who bought the land for the burial of those who "without the benefit of citizenship . . . fought for freedom."

Guided Discussion

1. **Analyze Visuals** Direct students' attention to the photos of reenactors on the first page of the photo essay. Call on volunteers to describe what they notice. Have students identify clues that suggest the man in the top photo is an officer. *(age, uniform, telescope)* **ASK:** From what you see in the photos, what do you think are some qualifications for being a reenactor? *(Possible responses: Reenactors must be able to accurately portray people and events of the past. They have to wear clothing and use equipment that may be uncomfortable.)*

2. **Make Inferences** Discuss what students find notable about the photo of the reenactment of the Battle of Bull Run. *(It seems like a real battle, with military formations and weaponry in use.)* Discuss what is happening in the bottom photo. *(It appears to be a parade, with spectators in modern dress.)* **ASK:** Based on these photos, what inferences can you make about these Civil War sites? *(Possible response: The sites are still of interest to Americans today because many people participate in the reenactments or visit the sites and the events held there.)*

Pickett's Charge Reenactment

The Confederate attack known as Pickett's Charge took place on July 3, 1863, during the Battle of Gettysburg. For two days, Confederate General Robert E. Lee had launched unsuccessful advances against General George Meade's Union forces. Lee decided to attack the center of the Union line. Under heavy fire, the Confederate infantry advanced across an open field and over a stone fence. Of the nearly 15,000 Confederate troops who took part in the battle, General George Pickett led a unit of about 6,000. Of Pickett's men, more than half were killed, wounded, or captured.

Confederate Cannon

Most Civil War cannons were muzzle loaders that required several steps to fire: An iron projectile and a cloth bag filled with gunpowder were rammed into the barrel; a metal pick poked through a hole near the back of the gun pierced the bag; a friction primer was inserted into the hole and attached to a rope; when the rope was pulled, the charge ignited and fired the projectile.

Grant at Vicksburg

This statue commemorates a key Union victory in the Civil War. On July 4, 1863, after a 47-day siege by Grant's forces, the Confederate fort at Vicksburg surrendered. The victory gave the Union control of the Mississippi River and propelled Grant's rise to the command of all Union forces.

Soldiers' National Cemetery

Best known as the site of Lincoln's Gettysburg Address, the Soldiers' National Cemetery is the burial place of more than 3,000 Union soldiers who died in the Battle of Gettysburg in July 1863. Beginning that October, a committee began recovering the bodies from battlefield graves and providing proper burial in the soldiers' cemetery. Hundreds of markers indicate the graves of unknown soldiers. In 1872, the remains of Confederate soldiers buried in battlefield graves were recovered and shipped to cemeteries in the South.

Military Earthworks

Both Union and Confederate forces used military earthworks as a defensive tactic. Confederates had dug a 10-mile trench line around Petersburg, a vital Confederate supply center, in 1862; by 1864, the system of earthworks extended nearly 40 miles. Advancing Union forces constructed their own trenches, sometimes less than 400 yards from the Confederate line. For several months, opposing forces carried on combat there. Those who survived mud, insects, and diseases in the trenches risked death from enemy fire simply by raising their heads above the protection of the earthworks.

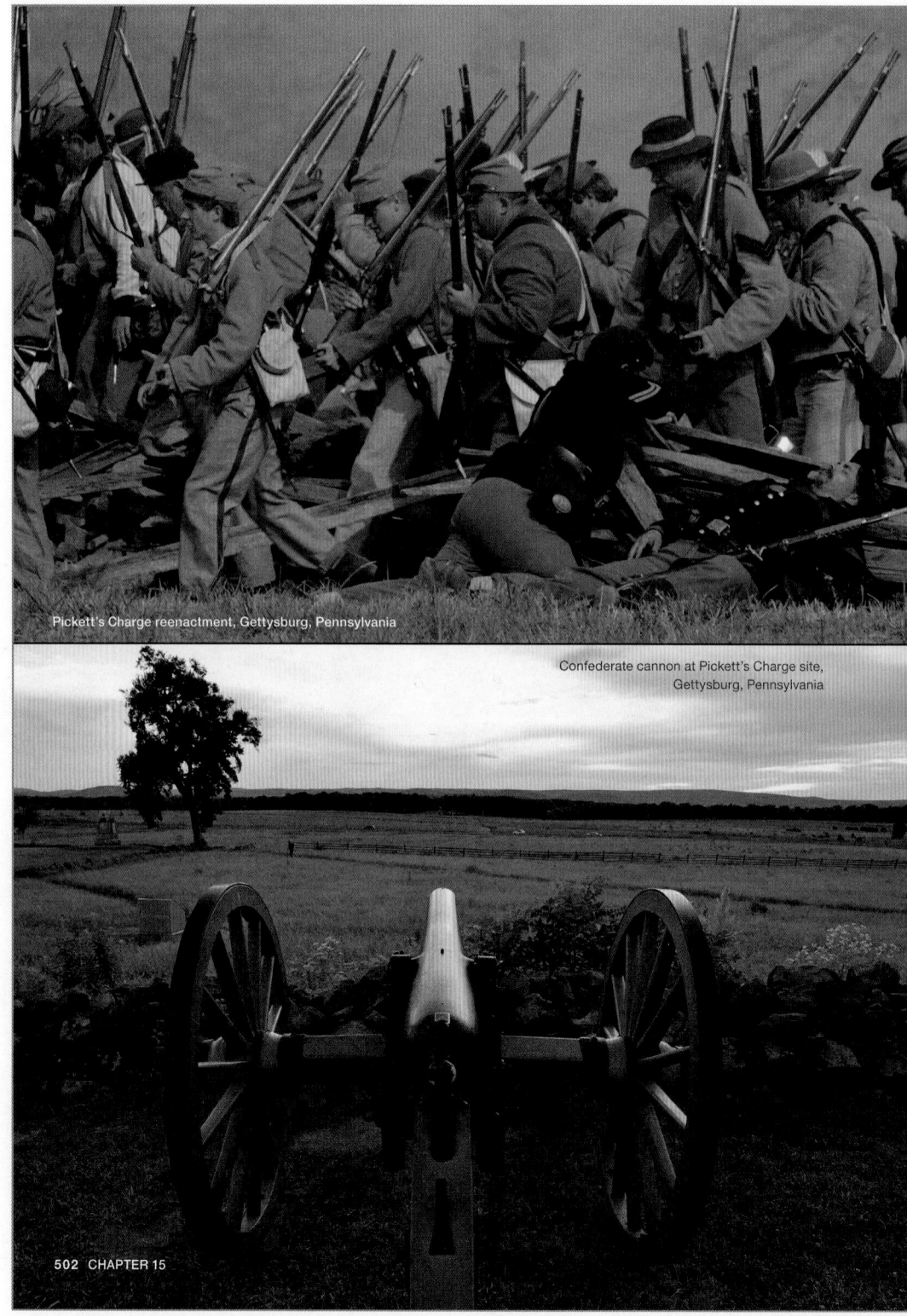

Pickett's Charge reenactment, Gettysburg, Pennsylvania

Confederate cannon at Pickett's Charge site, Gettysburg, Pennsylvania

502 CHAPTER 15

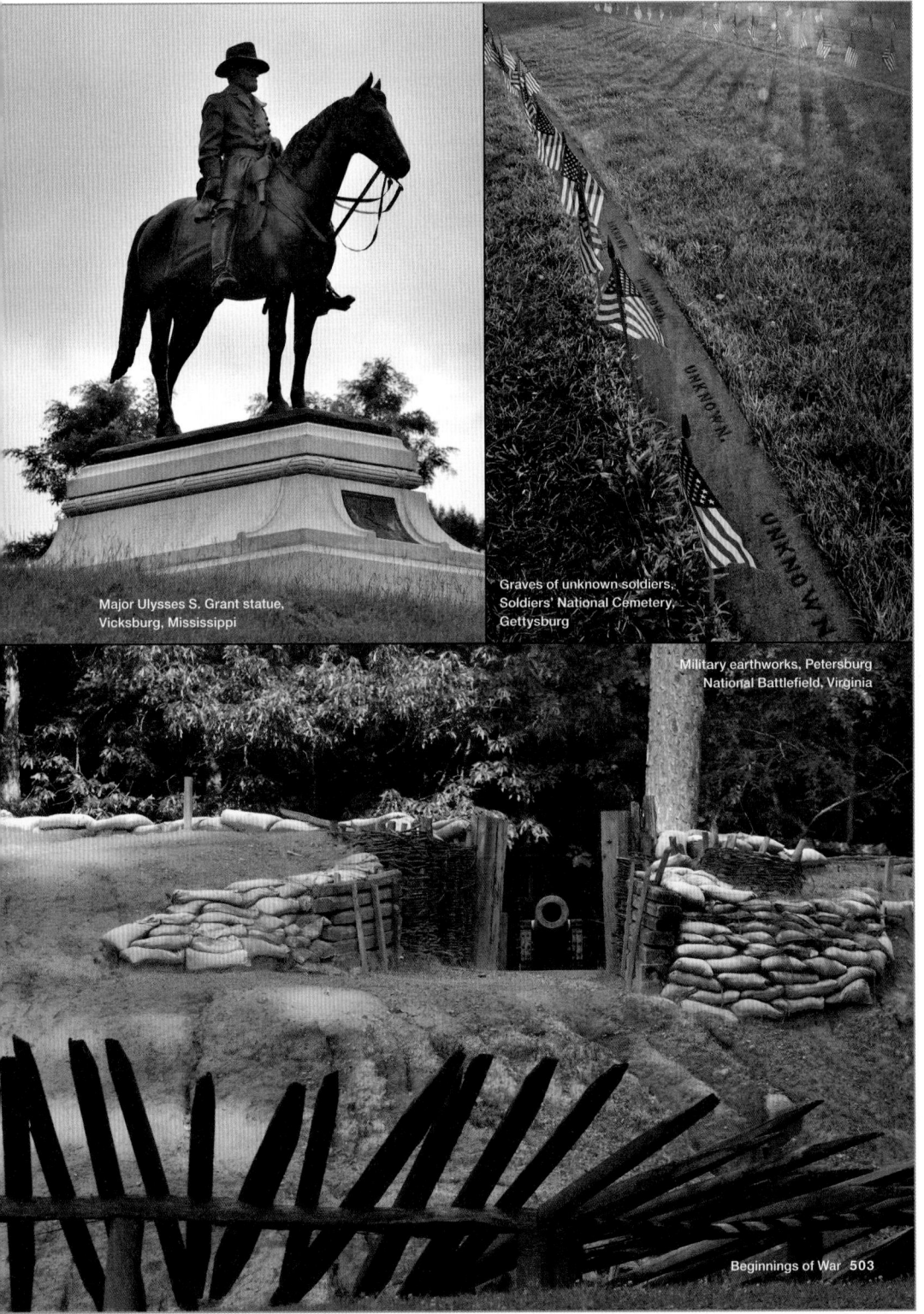

Major Ulysses S. Grant statue, Vicksburg, Mississippi

Graves of unknown soldiers, Soldiers' National Cemetery, Gettysburg

Military earthworks, Petersburg National Battlefield, Virginia

Beginnings of War 503

Guided Discussion

1. **Describe** As a class, review the purpose or purposes of a photo essay. (*A photo essay tells a story with visual images, helping the viewer understand where and when an event took place; it allows the viewer to share the experiences of people who lived long ago; it may cause an emotional response.*) **ASK:** What emotions do these photos evoke, or bring to mind? (*Answers will vary. Possible responses: Pickett's Charge: confusion, anxiety; Confederate cannon: sadness; Grant statue: respect; National Cemetery: sorrow; Earthworks: curiosity*)

2. **Form and Support Opinions** Which photograph in the photo essay do you think could be a symbol for the Civil War? Support your opinion with details from the photographs in this photo essay. (*Answers will vary, but students should use details from the photographs and statements about the Civil War to express reasons for their choices.*)

DIFFERENTIATE

English Language Learners `ELD`

Match Words and Pictures Provide a list of words or terms for students at the **Emerging** level to match with the images in the photo essay. Examples include *cemetery, telescope, cannon, battle, soldiers, parade,* and *monument*. Then ask students at the **Expanding** level to use each word in a sentence to describe the photograph. Encourage students at the **Bridging** level to combine the sentences to create a paragraph about the photo essay.

Gifted & Talented

Create a Photo Essay Challenge students to work with a partner or a small group to create their own photo essay about a local history topic. Establish guidelines, such as being respectful of property and getting permission before photographing people or their property. Encourage students to choose five or six of their photos to showcase in a photo essay to share with the class.

See the Chapter Planner for more strategies for differentiation.

Everyone has strengths and weaknesses. You may be good at math and sports but not so great at science and card games. The trick is figuring out how to use what you've got to the best advantage.

MAIN IDEA Both the Union and the Confederacy had advantages and disadvantages, and each came up with strategies for winning the war.

STRENGTHS AND WEAKNESSES

During the Civil War, both the North and the South had strengths and weaknesses. The North had a much larger population than the South. And Union states were home to large cities, which were centers of business and industry. More than 100,000 factories were located in Union states— about five times the industrial capacity of the agrarian South.

The Union also boasted a stronger military infrastructure. It had a navy and many more ships than the South. West Point, the best military academy in the country to train leaders in the midst of war, was in the North. Many northern officers had trained there. However, the South also had talented graduates of West Point leading its soldiers. You may remember that Robert E. Lee graduated from the military academy, and so did Jefferson Davis, the Confederate president.

With its smaller numbers, the South fought the war largely on the defensive. Simply trying to defend itself seemed to be the best way to win the war, at least initially. As a result, most of the fighting took place in Confederate states. But this gave the Confederate forces a geographic advantage. They were fighting in areas they knew well, while the Union Army found itself on unfamiliar ground.

The South also used more offensive tactics to wear down the North. Confederate leaders encouraged private ship owners to intercept and capture northern merchant ships and their cargo in the Atlantic. And some southern generals planned to concentrate their forces and exert pressure on the northern capital of Washington, D.C., which bordered southern states.

MAKING A GAME PLAN

One of the renowned generals who led the Union, Winfield Scott, a hero of the Mexican-American War and the War of 1812, also had a plan. When the Civil War began, Scott was the commander-in-chief of the U.S. Army. In early 1861, he formulated a strategy he hoped would put an end to the war. His plan called for blocking Confederate ports along the Atlantic and Gulf coasts with Union warships. The North hoped to cripple the Confederate war effort and economy by preventing the delivery of weapons and halting cotton exports. Scott also proposed sending troops to gain control of the Mississippi River and capture major cities and river ports, creating divisions in the South.

Scott's massive blockade was risky. No blockade of this size had ever been tried before. There were more than 3,000 miles of coastline to block with fewer than 40 ships! Scott's idea was nicknamed the **Anaconda Plan** after a type of snake that strangles its prey. Within a week after the loss of Fort Sumter, Lincoln ordered the blockade to be carried out, and it was somewhat successful. However, many northern leaders ridiculed the plan. They wanted to take action and fight.

To counter the plan, the South tried to create a cotton shortage on the European market. The Confederacy hoped the shortage would force Great Britain and France, two major cotton consumers, to join the Confederate cause and help break up the Union blockade. The attempt backfired when both countries bought cotton from Egypt and India instead. Meanwhile, the Confederate Army engaged in terrible battles on the ground that would claim many lives and, eventually, give the South greater hope.

SCOTT'S GREAT SNAKE

The **Anaconda Plan** was meant to strangle the South by cutting off all trade among southern states and allowing the Union to take control of the Mississippi River. Scott believed his plan would put an early end to the war and limit the number of casualties.

Scott proposed sending a large naval force down the **Mississippi River** that would capture forts and towns along its banks.

Union ships patrolled the coastal border to prevent deliveries of weapons and supplies to southern states.

corn   oranges   cattle   sheep   coal
cotton   tobacco   hay   apples
peaches   horses   banking   sugar cane

Scott's plan was never fully implemented, but a naval blockade was maintained throughout the war. The blockade succeeded in cutting off the South's resources and probably did shorten the war. But not even Scott knew how the war would develop. He guessed it would go on for two years, not four.

HISTORICAL THINKING

1. **READING CHECK** What was General Scott's strategy for winning the war?

2. **COMPARE AND CONTRAST** What geographic advantages did the South have over the North?

3. **ANALYZE VISUALS** What resources did the Anaconda Plan attempt to prevent from being traded in the South?

Objective
Explain how strengths and weaknesses of both sides influenced strategies during the Civil War.

Critical Thinking Skills for Lesson 3.1
• Identify Main Ideas and Details
• Monitor Comprehension
• Compare and Contrast
• Analyze Visuals
• Evaluate
• Synthesize
• Draw Conclusions

Essential Question for Chapter 15
How did the early years of the Civil War affect people on both sides of the conflict? Both the North and the South had strengths and weaknesses. Lesson 3.1 explains how military leaders on both sides built on their strengths and took advantage of their opponent's weaknesses.

Background for the Teacher
At the outset of the war, the South seemed to have the advantage in both political and military leadership. Jefferson Davis had served in both houses of Congress and had held the position of secretary of war under Franklin Pierce. Davis was a graduate of West Point with a distinguished record of service in the Mexican-American War. Abraham Lincoln, on the other hand, had served one term in the House of Representatives, and his military experience consisted of service in the Black Hawk War, during which he did not fight in any battles. Davis served as his own secretary of war, whereas Lincoln struggled to find competent advisors.

At the start of the war, Confederate generals also outshone Union generals in training and experience. Early in the war, Lincoln had to replace his aging general in chief, Winfield Scott, with the indecisive George McClellan. Even among regular troops, more Confederate soldiers had military experience and the ability to live off the land.

Name a Campaign

Challenge students to suggest appropriate names for various kinds of campaigns, such as campaigns to elect student council representatives, to cut down on wasted food in the cafeteria, to raise funds for a class field trip, or to donate toys for charity. Encourage them to think of action names that describe the purpose or strategy of the campaign, or names that compare the campaign to an animal, weather pattern, or object. List responses on the board. Point out that military campaigns often have names that describe a strategy. Tell students in this lesson they will learn about a Civil War campaign called the Anaconda Plan. Invite them to speculate about the kind of strategy the name implies.

TEACH

Guided Discussion

1. **Evaluate** What were the advantages and disadvantages of having the military leaders of both sides trained at the same academy? *(Answers will vary. Possible response: Both sides would have excellent leaders, but the leaders would probably be trained in the same strategies and tactics so they could anticipate what their opponent might do.)*

2. **Synthesize** Why were Great Britain and France important to the Confederate economy? *(They provided a market for cotton, the South's most important export.)*

Draw Conclusions

Direct students' attention to the map and the accompanying text. **ASK:** Was the Anaconda Plan an offensive or a defensive strategy? Explain your answer. *(Possible responses: The blockade was a defensive strategy because it did not involve a Union attack on the Confederacy. Capturing cities and ports on the Mississippi River was an offensive strategy because it involved sending troops into enemy territory.)*

Active Options

On Your Feet: Form a Human Venn

Diagram Divide the class into three groups, and assign each group one of the following categories: Union, Confederacy, or Both. Instruct students in each group to work together to make a list of strengths and weaknesses for their assigned category. Have them write each strength and weakness on a separate sheet of paper. Suggest they consider these topics: population, leadership,

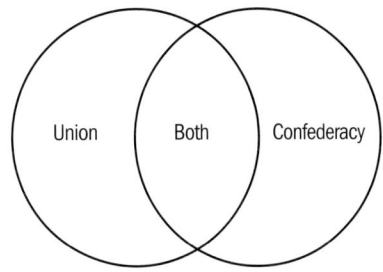

geography, and motivation, as well as any others they brainstorm. Then use rope, tape, or chalk on the floor to create a large Venn Diagram, like the one shown, with areas designated for Union, Confederacy, and Both. Have students stand in the correct area of the circle to compare and contrast first the strengths and then the weaknesses of the sides. For example, a student holding a sheet with the strength *well-trained leaders* might stand in the Both area where the circles overlap, while a student holding *industrial strength* would stand in the Union circle. As an alternative, create the Venn Dagram on the board and have volunteers write the strengths or weaknesses in the appropriate places.

Active History: Compare Resources Extend the lesson by using either the PDF or Whiteboard version of the activity. These activities take a deeper look at a topic from, or related to, the lesson. Explore the activities as a class, turn them into group assignments, or even assign them individually.

English Language Learners

Answer Questions Ask questions to monitor comprehension of the lesson, adapting answer requirements according to students' proficiency levels. For students at the **Emerging** level, ask questions that require an either/or answer. **ASK:** Did the North have a larger or a smaller population than the South? *(larger)* Show students at the **Expanding** level how to restate questions in their answers. **ASK:** Where did most of the fighting take place? *(Most of the fighting took place in the South.)* Help students at the **Bridging** level use transitional words or phrases *(but, however, because, as a result)* to express comparisons or causes and effects. **ASK:** Why did Scott blockade the South? *(Scott blockaded the South because he wanted to cut off trade.)*

Pre-AP

Compare Governments Assign one or more students to represent Abraham Lincoln and the Union and one or more students to represent Jefferson Davis and the Confederacy. Instruct each side to research the advantages and disadvantages its government had when preparing for the war. Then have students portray Abraham Lincoln or Jefferson Davis and explain to the class the strategies they used to benefit from the advantages and minimize the disadvantages of their government. After the presentations, have the class discuss which side had a stronger government and why.

See the Chapter Planner for more strategies for differentiation.

HISTORICAL THINKING

ANSWERS

1. Scott planned to gain control of the Mississippi River and major river ports and cities to divide the Confederacy. He also intended to blockade the Atlantic and Gulf coasts to cut off Confederate trade with Europe and cripple the South's economy.

2. Southern forces were fighting a defensive war on familiar land. They could use geography to their advantage because northern troops did not know the territory.

3. The Anaconda Plan was created to prevent the South from exporting cotton and importing weapons.

Differences Between North and South

MAIN IDEA At the start of the Civil War, the Union and the Confederacy each had important geographic advantages.

GEOGRAPHIC ADVANTAGES

Geography is critically important in any war. Mountains and rivers can serve as natural defenses, helping an army to defend itself from invaders. Hills can provide a visual advantage for soldiers who are watching for enemy troops. Trees felled in a forest can slow down an army as it tries to pass through.

In the Civil War, the Union and the Confederacy had other types of geographic advantages. You've learned that the Union had a greater population spread across a wide geographic area, which helped boost the size of its army. It also had many industrial centers. As you know, too, the Confederacy had the advantage of fighting the war on familiar terrain. And the South grew abundant cotton, which could be sold to help cover Confederate war expenses.

Read the following text and examine the maps to see how four important geographical factors—population, railroads, industry, and agriculture—critically affected the Civil War.

POPULATION

In 1860, the North had a population of about 18.5 million people, of which about 3.8 million free men were of military age. In contrast, the South had about 5.5 million free persons and 3.5 million enslaved people. Only 1.1 million free men were of military age, and 80 percent of these went to war. This percentage reflects the South's dedication to the cause for independence, since Jefferson Davis and the Confederacy relied on the voluntary cooperation of state governments for troops.

Additionally, 19 of the largest cities in the United States were part of the Union. Because the South was an agricultural society with few industrial cities to attract large populations, the Confederacy had only two, New Orleans and Charleston.

RAIL TRANSPORTATION

As you can see on the large map, the Union had more than twice as many miles of railroad lines as the Confederacy. In the South, most railroads went from Mississippi, Alabama, and Georgia to Charleston, carrying cotton for exporting.

The Civil War was one of the first wars in which railroads played a critical role. The Union and the Confederacy both used railroads to ship equipment, weapons, and troops. Sometimes, officers even sent spies on trains to learn about the opponent's troop movements. However, the Confederacy began the war at a disadvantage. Their railroads were in bad shape, and repairs often had to wait. Many railroad workers had quit to fight the war.

INDUSTRY

Manufacturing, especially of iron and steel, was critically important to both the Union and the Confederacy during the Civil War. The large map shows the location of factories in the North and the South. As you've learned, the majority of the factories were in the North, but the Confederacy did have some in Virginia and other states. The largest Confederate iron works was in Richmond, Virginia. Confederate officers fought to protect their factories because they were so important to the South.

Because the Union did more manufacturing, it was able to produce more of the rifles, cannons, railroad tracks, locomotives, and other materials its army needed for war. That was a definite advantage.

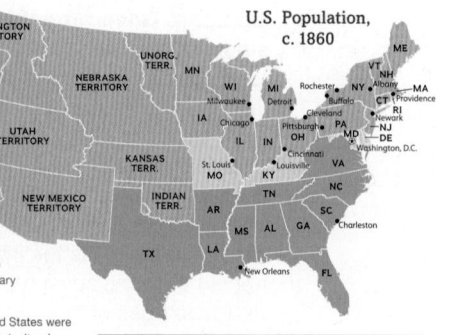

U.S. Population, c. 1860

Legend: Union state or territory | Border state not seceding | Confederate state | • City with population over 40,000

Industry and Agriculture in the North and the South, 1850

Legend:
- Textiles
- Other manufacturing
- Cotton
- Railroads

ATLANTIC OCEAN

Gulf of Mexico

AGRICULTURE

As the map above shows, cotton was king in the South. The region devoted the majority of its economic and technological energy to this cash crop. As a result, the South supplied most of the world's cotton, producing 77 percent of the cotton used by Great Britain, the largest maker of textiles in the world.

Cotton was critical to the Confederacy's ability to raise the huge amounts of money needed to fight a war. In addition to Great Britain, the South exported cotton to France and other European countries and used the profits to buy weapons and equipment and to fund the Confederate government. Even textile mills in the North bought cotton from the South. The Confederacy also borrowed against the promise of future cotton crops to pay for its war efforts.

THINK LIKE A GEOGRAPHER

1. **IDENTIFY MAIN IDEAS AND DETAILS** What geographic advantages did the Confederacy have, and why were they important?

2. **ANALYZE CAUSE AND EFFECT** How did the Union's superiority in rail transportation contribute to its victory in the war?

3. **FORM AND SUPPORT OPINIONS** In your opinion, what was the most important geographic factor in the outcome of the war?

PLAN

Objective

Explain how geographic factors influenced the outcome of the Civil War.

Critical Thinking Skills for Lesson 3.2

- Identify Main Ideas and Details
- Monitor Comprehension
- Analyze Cause and Effect
- Form and Support Opinions
- Compare and Contrast
- Interpret Maps

Essential Question for Chapter 15

How did the early years of the Civil War affect people on both sides of the conflict?
Geographic differences provided advantages to both the Union and the Confederacy. Lesson 3.2 explains how differences in population, rail transportation, industry, and agriculture affected the war.

Background for the Teacher

In addition to having more railroad lines than the Confederacy, the Union had the resources and expertise to use rail transportation effectively. Herman Haupt, a Union brigadier general and railroad engineer, supervised railroad line repair and bridge construction. He also upgraded telegraph communications along the railroads. In spite of challenges such as weather, lack of proper tools, and inexperienced workers, Haupt organized an efficient support system for the war effort. In some areas, an officer in the field could telegraph a request for needed supplies and have those supplies arrive by railroad within a day. On the return trip, railroad cars carried wounded soldiers to hospitals. The Union's effective use of railroads for military purposes was key to its victory in the Civil War.

INTRODUCE & ENGAGE

Choose a State

Ask students to choose a state—their own or a different one—and brainstorm a list of its geographic advantages. Examples may include such factors as the state's location, its physical features, its economy, or its cities. Allow time for volunteers to "sell" their chosen state by telling about its advantages. Then tell students they will learn how geographic advantages of the Union and the Confederacy influenced the Civil War and its outcome.

TEACH   STEM

Guided Discussion

1. **Analyze Cause and Effect** The South had a relatively small number of young men to draw on from which to pull fighting forces. What consequences did this situation have for the South and for the Confederate Army? *(Possible response: A greater percentage of men had to join the Confederate Army, and Confederate soldiers were outnumbered by Union soldiers. With most of the male population in the South fighting the war, the burden of farming and other tasks became the responsibility of women.)*

2. **Compare and Contrast** How did the North and the South differ in the ways in which they obtained weapons and equipment for their troops? *(Possible response: The North had the industrial means to produce war materials, while the South exported cotton to get money to buy weapons and other war materials.)*

Geography in History

Interpret Maps Instruct students to compare the U.S. Population map with the Industry and Agriculture map. **ASK:** Based on both maps, what geographic advantages did the Confederacy's major cities have? *(Possible responses: Both New Orleans and Charleston are located along a coast, so they had access to overseas trade. New Orleans is located at the mouth of the Mississippi River, so river trade also passed through it. Both were also served by railroads, which allowed troops and goods to move through them. Both cities are located far from the Union, so they could be defended from attack.)* Ask students to explain how they combined information from both maps to answer the question. Then challenge them to think of another question that requires a similar process.

Active Options

On Your Feet: Become an Expert Organize students into four "expert" groups and have each group move to a different location in the classroom to study one of the categories of geographic advantages presented in the lesson. Instruct group members to use information from the text as well as from other sources to become informed about their topic. Then regroup students so that each new group has at least one member from each of the original "expert" groups. Have members of the new groups take turns sharing what they learned about their topic.

NG Learning Framework: Create Charts and Graphs

ATTITUDE Responsibility

SKILLS Collaboration, Communication

Remind students that data can be presented in different ways. For example, the text presents data in words and numbers, and the maps present data visually. Challenge students to present the data from Lesson 3.2 in charts or graphs. Allow them to work in pairs or small groups to create an appropriate means of representing the data. Display the completed charts and graphs. Then discuss as a class which ways of presenting data are most helpful and why.

DIFFERENTIATE

Inclusion

Preview Maps Before reading the lesson, pair students who have learning disabilities with other students who can help them preview the maps. Provide a list or ask students without disabilities to create a list of specific questions to aid understanding of the colors, symbols, and labels on the maps. Encourage students with disabilities to use their fingers as needed to trace boundaries of the Union and Confederacy on the population map and to trace coastlines and rivers on the industry and agriculture map.

English Language Learners   ELD

Summarize Information Pair students at the **Expanding** and **Bridging** levels and assign one of the following topics to each pair: population, rail transportation, industry, or agriculture. Instruct pairs to write a sentence summarizing important information from the lesson about their topic. Review the sentences as a group. Then have the writers assist students at the **Emerging** level to read the summary sentences aloud.

See the Chapter Planner for more strategies for differentiation.

THINK LIKE A GEOGRAPHER

ANSWERS

1. The Confederacy fought on land that was familiar to soldiers, so they could use physical geographic features, such as rivers and mountains, to their advantage. The Confederacy's abundant cotton crop could be sold to fund the war effort.

2. The Union used railroads to transport its troops, which was much faster than having armies travel on foot. Railroads also moved weapons and equipment throughout the North, which gave the Union an advantage.

3. Answers will vary. Possible responses: Population gave the North an advantage in the number of soldiers available. Railroads provided the North with an efficient way to move troops and equipment. Industry allowed the North to produce materials needed for the war. Agriculture was the South's main method of funding the war.

3.3 War in the West and East

You may have heard the phrase "divide and conquer" from a parent or coach. Union military leaders used the same strategy to try to defeat the South.

MAIN IDEA The Union attacked strategic areas in the western and eastern parts of the Confederacy in the early years of the Civil War.

THE BATTLE OF SHILOH

In 1862, Union and Confederate forces clashed in important battles in the western part of the Confederacy. The region had some of the Confederacy's most important assets, including New Orleans, its largest city, and many major ports along the Mississippi River. The North set its sights on capturing the region.

To that end, two Union generals, **Ulysses S. Grant** and **William T. Sherman**, sailed troops on a fleet of 19 riverboats up the Tennessee River. Seven of the vessels were gunboats, small, fast ships carrying mounted guns. The fleet successfully captured two key forts in Tennessee, Fort Henry and Fort Donelson, forcing the Confederate Army to retreat. On February 25, the Union Army continued its march across Tennessee with the goal of reaching Corinth, Mississippi—a major rail center—where 20,000 more Union soldiers awaited them. If Grant captured the railroads at Corinth, the Union would control most of the western part of the Confederacy.

However, General Albert Sidney Johnston, the Confederate commander in the region, learned of Grant's plan and ambushed the Union general's forces near a church in Shiloh, Tennessee, on April 6. The larger Confederate forces drove Grant's troops back. By the next day, however, more Union forces had arrived, and Grant led a counterattack. The Confederates conceded defeat and withdrew to Corinth.

The two-day **Battle of Shiloh** was the bloodiest battle in the war to that point. The South lost more than 10,000 men, including General Johnston. Even though it won the battle, the Union Army actually lost more men: about 13,000 soldiers. Because of the high casualty count, some people called for Grant's removal, but Lincoln refused. He is said to have remarked, "I can't spare this man [Grant]; he fights!"

Ulysses S. Grant
After graduating from West Point, Ulysses S. Grant served with General Winfield Scott during the Mexican-American War, as had his Confederate opponent, Robert E. Lee. After the Civil War, Grant became president of the United States in 1868, when he was only 46 years old. His presidency was plagued by scandal, although Grant himself was an honest man.

CRITICAL VIEWING This illustration shows the *Monitor* (in the front) firing its guns at the *Virginia* (in the back) at Hampton Roads Harbor, Virginia. The *Virginia* began its life as a standard steam-powered vessel built in the North, when it was called the *Merrimack*. The Confederates salvaged the *Merrimack* from a navy yard in Norfolk and refitted it as an ironclad. How did the successful use of ironclad ships probably affect future warfare?

THE SEVEN DAYS' BATTLES

Meanwhile, the Union had undertaken another campaign in the eastern part of the Confederacy with the goal of capturing the Confederate capital of Richmond, Virginia. On March 9, 1862, the Confederate ironclad ship, the C.S.S. *Virginia*—also known as the *Merrimack*—faced off against the Union ironclad, the U.S.S. *Monitor*. It marked the first skirmish between ironclad warships. The battle took place in the harbor of Hampton Roads, Virginia, and ended in a standoff.

Lincoln urged General George B. McClellan to continue the advance toward Richmond. McClellan had replaced Winfield Scott as the leader of the Union Army and was a brilliant general. But McClellan's tendency to overestimate the enemy's strength and postpone troop movement often frustrated Lincoln. McClellan eventually set sail with about 120,000 troops to the coast of the Virginia Peninsula. The Union forces battled their way to within a few miles of Richmond. But, fearing that he might be outnumbered, McClellan pulled his men back.

On June 1, rebel forces led by the new commander of the Confederate Army, Robert E. Lee, took advantage of McClellan's caution and moved to protect Richmond. From June 25 to July 1, Lee and his forces went on the attack and fought an offensive war, called the **Seven Days' Battles**. Lee forced McClellan to retreat back down the Virginia Peninsula, but even as they were being pursued, the Union forces still managed to inflict heavy casualties on the Confederates.

Nonetheless, the victory of the Seven Days' Battles boosted southern morale, saved the Confederate capital, and made Lee a hero. But as Lee's star was rising, McClellan's was falling. McClellan's failures made Lincoln's opinion of him sink even lower.

HISTORICAL THINKING

1. **READING CHECK** What did the Union Army hope to accomplish in the western part of the Confederacy in 1862?

2. **SUMMARIZE** Describe the Union advance toward Richmond.

3. **ANALYZE CAUSE AND EFFECT** How did the Seven Days' Battles affect the combatants and the leaders of the war?

PLAN

Objective

Describe the Union's purpose for targeting eastern and western parts of the Confederacy.

Critical Thinking Skills for Lesson 3.3

• Identify Main Ideas and Details
• Monitor Comprehension
• Summarize
• Analyze Cause and Effect
• Synthesize
• Compare and Contrast
• Form and Support Opinions

Essential Question for Chapter 15

How did the early years of the Civil War affect people on both sides of the conflict? The Union developed strategies for conquering both the eastern and western regions of the Confederacy. Lesson 3.3 describes the outcomes, casualties, and effect on morale of major campaigns.

Background for the Teacher

Ironclad warships were not the only advance in naval warfare made during the Civil War. By 1861, both the Union and the Confederacy worked to develop a practical submarine. The *H.L. Hunley*, named for its southern inventor, arrived in Charleston by train in August 1863, with hopes that it could break the Union blockade. On its first attempt, the crew submerged the vessel before all hatches were closed, sinking the ship and drowning five crew members. The recovered ship set out on a diving exercise in October 1863, this time with the inventor himself on board, but the submarine sank again, killing all on board. In February 1864, the twice-recovered ship succeeded in its mission. It rammed the Union warship *U.S.S. Housatonic* and planted a charge that exploded, sinking the ship and killing five Union sailors. The *Hunley*, however, was also lost during this mission, bring to more than 20 the total number of Confederate crew members killed on the submarine over its lifetime.

INTRODUCE & ENGAGE

Make a Decision

Pose several questions for students to consider, such as *Should I watch a movie with a friend or study for tomorrow's test? Should I buy that item I want now or wait until it goes on sale? Should I help my grandparents or accept an invitation to a party?* Display a Decision Matrix and call on volunteers to complete it with information that would help them make a decision. Tell students they will learn about the choices, pros and cons, and decisions that had a major impact on the Civil War.

Choice	
Pros	Cons
Decision	

TEACH

Guided Discussion

1. **Synthesize** During the Civil War, in what ways were rivers in western regions important to the Union? *(Possible responses: In order to control the western region, the Union planned to capture Confederate ports and cities along the Mississippi River. The Union used gunboats on the Tennessee River to capture Confederate forts.)*

2. **Compare and Contrast** How were the Union and Confederate strategies in the Seven Days' Battles similar to and different from their strategies in the first Battle of Bull Run that you read about in Lesson 1.2? *(Possible response: Similarities: Both battles halted a Union attempt to conquer Richmond, Virginia. Union delays allowed Confederates to move troops before both battles. Differences: The Confederacy fought a defensive battle at Bull Run, but Lee's forces fought an offensive war in the Seven Days' Battles.)*

Form and Support Opinions

Do you think Lincoln should have replaced McClellan after the Seven Days' Battles? Support your opinion with evidence from the text. *(Answers will vary. Possible responses: No, because McClellan was a brilliant leader, and no general can win every battle. Yes, because Lincoln had to command him to take action against the Confederates several times. McClellan not only failed to capture Richmond, but Confederate troops chased him out of Virginia.)*

Active Options

On Your Feet: Think and Discuss Organize students into groups of four in separate areas of the classroom. Assign each student in a group a number (one, two, three, or four). **ASK:** Which battles were more important to the outcome of the Civil War—those fought in the East or those fought in the West? Why? Instruct students to think about and then discuss a response. Allow time for discussion within groups, then call a number and have the student from each group with that number explain the group's response to the question.

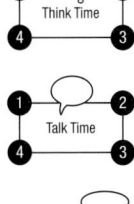

NG Learning Framework: Evaluate Civil War Navies

ATTITUDE Curiosity

SKILL Collaboration

Invite students to explore this question: Was naval warfare critical to either side during the Civil War? Divide students into teams of three or four. Challenge each team to use print and online resources to find five facts about the Union and Confederate navies. Poll teams about their findings and combine their facts into a list on the board. Then have students collaborate in their original teams to write a paragraph that answers the question about the importance of naval warfare during the Civil War, using the facts to support their position.

DIFFERENTIATE

Striving Readers

Complete a Cause-and-Effect Chart Remind students to look for cause-and-effect relationships as they read. Allow students to work in pairs to complete this chart. Then have them look for other causes and effects in the lesson to add to the chart.

Cause	Effect
Important Confederate resources were in the western region.	

Pre-AP

Compare Military Leaders Ask each student to choose a Civil War general. Tell them to use library and online sources to research their general and prepare a presentation that includes the following: a brief biographical sketch; a summary of the general's participation in the war, including battles and outcomes; one or more quotes that express his views; a summary statement of how the general's military leadership affected the war. Allow students to use the medium of their choice to share their presentations with the class.

See the Chapter Planner for more strategies for differentiation.

HISTORICAL THINKING

ANSWERS

1. The Union wanted to capture the region that included New Orleans and other river ports as well as railroad centers. Doing so would cripple the Confederacy's war effort.

2. McClellan landed troops along the Virginia coast and battled to within a few miles of Richmond before pulling back.

3. Confederate combatants suffered heavy casualties, but their victory gave them confidence. The battles made Lee a hero, while McClellan lost favor.

CRITICAL VIEWING Answers will vary. Possible response: The ability of ironclad ships to withstand attack probably inspired future navies to build warships with iron sides.

Civil War Battles Map

Bull Run (Manassas)
July 21, 1861 Aug. 28–30, 1862

Chancellorsville
May 1–4, 1863

Fredericksburg
Dec. 11–15, 1862

Spotsylvania Court House
May 8–21, 1864

VIRGINIA

James R. Richmond

Seven Days
June 25–July 1, 1862

Appomattox
Court House
(Lee surrenders
to Grant Apr. 9, 1865)

Siege of
Petersburg
June 20, 1864–
Apr. 2, 1865

Hampton Roads
Mar. 8–9, 1862
(Monitor vs.
Merrimack)

MD.
Washington, D.C.
DEL.

0 25 50 Miles
0 25 50 Kilometers

NEW YORK

PENNSYLVANIA

Gettysburg
July 1–3, 1863

NEW
JERSEY

Antietam
Sept. 17, 1862

MD.

DELAWARE

ILLINOIS   INDIANA

OHIO

Washington, D.C.

WEST
VIRGINIA
(1863)

Louisville

VIRGINIA Richmond

MISSOURI

Missouri R.
Ohio R.

KENTUCKY

Appomattox Court House
(Lee surrenders to Grant
Apr. 9, 1865)

Richmond

Fort Henry
Feb. 4, 1862

Fort Donelson
Feb. 6, 1862

Tennessee R.

NORTH CAROLINA

ARKANSAS

Shiloh
Apr. 6–7,
1862

TENNESSEE

Chattanooga
Nov. 23–25, 1863

Chickamauga
Sept. 19–20, 1863

Wilmington

Kennesaw Mountain
June 27, 1864

Atlanta (occupied
Sept. 2, 1864)

Columbia

SOUTH
CAROLINA

MISSISSIPPI

ALABAMA

GEORGIA

Charleston

MISSISSIPPI

Jackson

Vicksburg
May 19–July 4, 1863

Natchez

Montgomery

Fort Sumter
Apr. 12–14, 1861

Savannah
(occupied Dec. 21, 1864)

ATLANTIC
OCEAN

N E
W
S

LOUISIANA

Mobile

New Orleans
(captured Apr. 25,
1862)

Mobile Bay
Aug. 2–23, 1864

Olustee
Feb. 20, 1864

Sanderson

Gulf of Mexico

FLORIDA

0 100 200 Miles
0 100 200 Kilometers

☐ Union state
☐ Confederate state
☐ Border state
✦ Union victory
✦ Confederate victory

3.4 Bloody 1862

When a friend lets you down, you likely give him or her one more chance. But at a certain point, you get fed up. As Lincoln realized, you can give someone "just one more chance" only so many times.

MAIN IDEA The bloody battles of Antietam and Fredericksburg exacted a high cost from both Union and Confederate forces.

THE BLOODIEST DAY

You've read about the first Battle of Bull Run in 1861. A second battle took place there in 1862. After driving General George McClellan and his troops back to Washington, D.C., General Robert E. Lee marched his men northward to battle again at Bull Run outside Manassas, Virginia. On the third day of fighting, the Confederates forced the Union soldiers to retreat. Afterward, Lee went on the offensive and marched his troops north into Maryland. He wanted to move the war into the Union states.

President Lincoln called McClellan back into action and ordered him to defend the Union capital. On his way to meet Lee, McClellan got lucky. By chance, a Union soldier found a packet of cigars in a field, dropped by a careless Confederate officer. Wrapped around the cigars were Lee's detailed plans for the assault on Maryland. McClellan learned that Lee's forces were in two groups several miles apart. If McClellan moved quickly, he could destroy Lee's army before the groups joined up. But McClellan acted too late. The Confederate Army met Union soldiers on the battlefield at Antietam (an-TEE-tuhm) Creek near Sharpsburg, Maryland, on September 17.

The casualties for both sides at the **Battle of Antietam** numbered at least 23,000 men. The day of the battle would later be called "America's Bloodiest Day." The Union considered it a victory because Lee's forces left Maryland. But Lincoln was frustrated with McClellan's errors. He said, "If General McClellan does not want to use the army, I would like to borrow it for a time." The president named Ambrose Burnside as the new commander.

THE BATTLE OF FREDERICKSBURG

For his first campaign, General Burnside decided to lead his troops back toward Richmond to try to capture the Confederate capital. To reach Richmond, Burnside marched to Falmouth, near Fredericksburg, Virginia, where he planned to cross the Rappahannock River. The Union troops arrived at Falmouth in December 1862, but Lee's army had got there first and destroyed all the bridges. Burnside ordered army engineers to build floating bridges using **pontoons**, or hollow metal cylinders, but Confederate soldiers shot at the Union engineers while they worked.

Meanwhile, Lee and the rest of his troops dug into the hills above Fredericksburg and readied their artillery. When Burnside finally crossed the Rappahannock River, his forces fought for three days in an unsuccessful effort to take the hills. The Battle of Fredericksburg ended when Burnside retreated across the river.

After so many defeats, northern civilians were becoming restless. They did not like the turn the war had taken, and neither did Lincoln.

HISTORICAL THINKING

1. **READING CHECK** How did McClellan discover Lee's plans at the Battle of Antietam?

2. **SUMMARIZE** How did these two battles reflect broader strategic patterns in the war?

3. **INTERPRET MAPS** Where were most of the Civil War battles fought, in the North or in the South? Explain why.

PLAN

Objective
Describe how the battles of Antietam and Fredericksburg affected the course of the war.

Critical Thinking Skills for Lesson 3.4
- Identify Main Ideas and Details
- Monitor Comprehension
- Summarize
- Interpret Maps
- Draw Conclusions
- Compare and Contrast

Essential Question for Chapter 15
How did the early years of the Civil War affect people on both sides of the conflict? Some of the war's bloodiest battles took place in 1862. Lesson 3.4 discusses how these battles affected civilians as well as soldiers.

Background for the Teacher
During the Civil War, more than 10,000 conflicts took place throughout the country in 26 states as far west as New Mexico and as far north as Minnesota. They ranged from minor clashes with little impact on the war to major battles with significant historical importance. The Civil War Sites Advisory Commission identified 384 principal battles, of which 123 were fought in Virginia. Today, the National Park service maintains as parks, monuments, and historical sites the locations of many Civil War battles, including Antietam and Fredericksburg.

INTRODUCE & ENGAGE

See the Big Picture

Ask students to roll a sheet of paper lengthwise and use it like a telescope. Call on volunteers to look through the tube and describe what they can see. Then instruct students to loosen the roll a bit to make it bigger and notice how it expands their view. Remind students that when fighting erupted at Fort Sumter in April 1861, no one knew how the war would develop nor how it would end. **ASK:** What are some ways that a limited view of events might affect attitudes toward the war? *(Answers will vary. Possible response: People might be sure the war will be won quickly and that their side is bound to win.)* Tell students that by 1862, people had begun to see the bigger picture. Ask students to predict how attitudes toward the war might change as a result.

TEACH

Guided Discussion

1. **Draw Conclusions** In what sense could Antietam be considered a Union defeat as well as a victory? *(Possible response: Antietam could be considered a victory because the Union succeeded in defending the capital from the Confederate assault and Lee's forces retreated after the battle. It could be considered a defeat because a large number of soldiers were killed. Had McClellan acted quickly, the battle may not have even happened.)*

2. **Compare and Contrast** How were McClellan and Burnside alike and different? *(Answers will vary. Possible response: Both generals failed to act quickly, thereby giving their opponents an advantage. McClellan succeeded in turning back Lee's forces at Antietam, but Burnside retreated from Lee at Fredericksburg.)*

More Information

Civil War Photographers Explain that Mathew Brady, a well-known portrait photographer of the mid-1800s, set out to document the Civil War. Using his own money, Brady hired photographers who followed troops into battle. Two of those photographers—Alexander Gardner and James F. Gibson—captured images of Antietam. Their pictures of dead soldiers on the battlefield were displayed in Brady's New York studio, a sight that disturbed many viewers. These photos were the first to show the horror of an actual battlefield. **ASK:** Do you think Brady should have displayed photos of the dead soldiers? Why or why not? *(Possible responses: Yes; people should know the truth about the horrors of war. No; the photos must have upset people, including the families of soldiers.)*

Active Options

On Your Feet: Hold a Class Discussion Create four signs with the following labels: Military War, Political War, Economic War, and Cultural War. Tape one sign to each corner of the room. Then pose this question: How did both sides in the Civil War wage war militarily, politically, economically, and culturally? Allow students to choose one of the posted topics, or assign a topic to each student. Instruct students to research their topic and then move to the designated corner to discuss it. Finally, ask volunteers to summarize their group's discussion for the class.

NG Learning Framework: Commemorate a Battle

ATTITUDE Responsibility

KNOWLEDGE Communication

Invite students to choose a battle from the Civil War Battles map and research the important details in order to create an exhibition commemorating the battle. Have students write a brief summary describing the battle and honoring those who participated. Encourage students to enhance their summary with a map, photos, a time line, or other images to create an appropriate display to post in the classroom so that the class can acknowledge the event on its anniversary.

DIFFERENTIATE

Inclusion

Determine Main Ideas and Details Allow students with reading or learning disabilities to work in pairs or pair them with students who do not have disabilities to compete a Main Ideas and Details Chart. Guide pairs to restate the lesson's Main Idea and write it in the Main Idea box. Then have them identify and write supporting details.

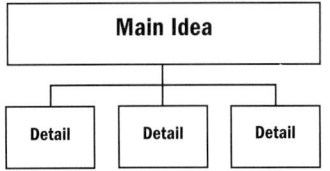

Gifted & Talented

Write a Ballad Direct students to review the events discussed in this lesson, including the errors made by both sides: the misplaced plans for Lee's assault and the failure to act by both McClellan and Burnside. Then prompt them to compose a folk ballad based on some or all of the events. Point out that folk ballads often embellish or exaggerate facts.

See the Chapter Planner for more strategies for differentiation.

HISTORICAL THINKING

ANSWERS

1. A Union soldier discovered Lee's plans wrapped around a packet of cigars that had been dropped by a Confederate soldier.

2. The battles of Antietam and Fredericksburg showed the need for more decisive action on the part of Union military leaders. These battles also indicated that General Lee was capable of using both offensive and defensive strategies to defeat the Union.

3. Most battles were fought in the South. The original purpose of the war was to restore the Union, so Union troops invaded the South to gain control of the seceded states. That resulted in the South fighting a mainly defensive war.

15 REVIEW

VOCABULARY

Use each of the following vocabulary words in a sentence that shows an understanding of the term's meaning.

1. cavalry

   The <u>cavalry</u> rode in on their horses to defend their fellow Union soldiers.

2. trench warfare

3. evacuate

4. gunboat

5. ironclad ship

6. mobilize

7. mortality

8. philanthropist

9. civilian

READING STRATEGY
SUMMARIZE

If you haven't done so already, complete your concept cluster of important information discussed in this chapter. Create at least four content clusters and summarize the information in each one. Then answer the question.

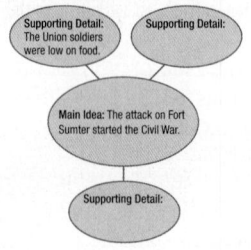

Supporting Detail: The Union soldiers were low on food.

Supporting Detail:

Main Idea: The attack on Fort Sumter started the Civil War.

Supporting Detail:

10. What was life like for a typical soldier in the Union or Confederate army?

MAIN IDEAS

Answer the following questions. Support your answers with evidence from the chapter.

11. How did the call for soldiers affect the states on the border between the North and the South? **LESSON 1.1**

12. Why did the first battle of the Civil War take place near Manassas, Virginia? **LESSON 1.2**

13. What new technological advances in weapons were introduced during the Civil War? **LESSON 2.1**

14. Who made up about half of the men who enlisted in the war on both sides? **LESSON 2.1**

15. What did Sally Tompkins contribute to the war effort? **LESSON 2.2**

16. Why did most of the fighting in the Civil War take place in the Confederate states? **LESSON 3.1**

17. Why did General Grant want to capture the railroads at Corinth, Mississippi? **LESSON 3.3**

18. What did Lee's troops do before Union troops arrived at Falmouth? **LESSON 3.4**

HISTORICAL THINKING

Answer the following questions. Support your answers with evidence from the chapter.

19. **MAKE INFERENCES** Why do you think Lincoln sent a message to southern leaders, stating that he would be sending only food, and not ammunition, to Fort Sumter?

20. **DRAW CONCLUSIONS** How did the attack on Fort Sumter make it clear that war was the necessary step to take toward reunification?

21. **COMPARE AND CONTRAST** What advantages did an ironclad ship have over a wooden ship?

22. **MAKE GENERALIZATIONS** Why was General McClellan unwilling to act quickly when leading the Union Army?

INTERPRET VISUALS

Look closely at the photograph of Union soldiers taken during the Civil War, and then answer the questions that follow.

24. What do the men in the photo appear to be doing?

25. What does the photo reveal about the lives of soldiers during the Civil War?

ANALYZE SOURCES

Clara Barton not only gathered supplies and clothing for the Union Army, but she also provided nursing care to wounded Union soldiers on many battlefields, including the Battle of Antietam. In this excerpt from one of her journals, Barton describes the danger she put herself in to help a soldier at Antietam. Read the excerpt and answer the question that follows.

> A man lying upon the ground asked for drink—I stooped to give it, and having raised him with my right hand, was holding the cup to his lips with my left, when I felt a sudden twitch of the loose sleeve of my dress—the poor fellow sprang from my hands and fell back quivering in the agonies of death—a ball [bullet] had passed between my body—and the right arm which supported him—cutting through the sleeve, and passing through his chest from shoulder to shoulder.

26. What happened as Barton was giving the soldier a drink?

23. **SEQUENCE EVENTS** What were the major early battles of the Civil War? Create a time line of the battles in which you indicate their significance.

CONNECT TO YOUR LIFE

27. **ARGUMENT** The Civil War was a terrible conflict, resulting in great loss of life. But, as you'll learn in the next chapter, the war had positive aspects as well, including helping to put an end to slavery. Think about conflicts in your life. Should they have been avoided, or did some good come out of them? Write a paragraph in which you make an argument for or against conflict.

TIPS

- Make a list of the positive and negative outcomes of conflicts you've experienced.

- Determine whether the positives outweighed the negatives, or vice versa.

- State your position on conflict in a topic sentence and support it with evidence from your own experience.

- Conclude your paragraph with a sentence summarizing your position.

VOCABULARY ANSWERS

1. The cavalry rode in on horses to defend Union soldiers.

2. The use of trench warfare allowed soldiers to be sheltered in ditches while firing at the enemy.

3. To avoid being caught in a battle, people evacuated to nearby towns, leaving their belongings behind.

4. Soldiers on the small, fast gunboat sailed up the river, firing its mounted rifles.

5. An ironclad ship had large pieces of metal attached to its sides to protect it from gunfire.

6. Lincoln's call to arms was a signal to mobilize troops for war.

7. The highest mortality rates occurred at the Battle of Antietam, at which thousands of soldiers lost their lives.

8. Clara Barton was a philanthropist who gave her time to the medical care of wounded soldiers.

9. Civilian volunteers aided soldiers on both sides of the war.

READING STRATEGY ANSWER

10. Soldiers spent most of their time training for battle and marching. They often lacked adequate food and supplies. More soldiers died from disease than from battle.

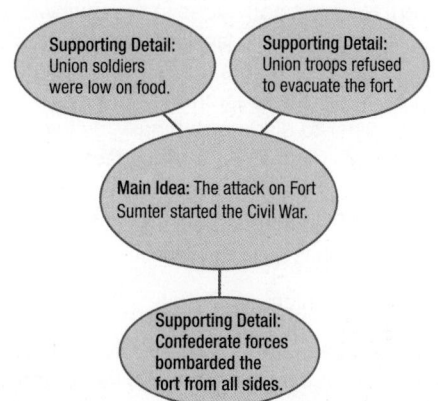

Supporting Detail: Union soldiers were low on food.

Supporting Detail: Union troops refused to evacuate the fort.

Main Idea: The attack on Fort Sumter started the Civil War.

Supporting Detail: Confederate forces bombarded the fort from all sides.

MAIN IDEAS ANSWERS

11. The call for a militia forced the border states to choose which side they would fight on.

12. The Battle of Bull Run took place near Manassas because President Lincoln ordered General McDowell to attack the Confederate soldiers there in a bid to seize Richmond.

13. Rifles were more accurate than muskets and had a longer range. Repeating rifles could be fired several times without reloading. Ironclad ships could withstand heavy gunfire.

14. About half the enlisted men on both sides were farmers under the age of 30.

15. Sally Tompkins saw the first wounded soldiers come back from the battlefields and decided to help them by providing medical care. She started a private hospital using her own money.

16. The South had a smaller army than the North, so Confederates fought a mostly defensive war on their own land.

17. Capturing the railroads at Corinth would give the Union control of most of the western part of the Confederacy.

18. General Lee's troops destroyed the bridges the Union forces needed to cross the Rappahannock River.

HISTORICAL THINKING ANSWERS

19. Answers will vary. Possible responses: Lincoln wanted to avoid war. His message indicated that he was not preparing the soldiers at Fort Sumter to fight the Confederates.

20. Answers will vary. Possible response: The attack on Fort Sumter was an act of war against the Union, which required a military response.

21. Unlike a wooden ship, an ironclad ship would not be damaged by cannonballs or rifle fire.

22. Answers will vary. Possible responses: McClellan was a cautious man. He wanted to make sure his men were ready for battle. He overestimated the enemy's strength. He knew that any bad decision he made would cost lives.

23. The time line should include the following battles: Fort Sumter (April 1861) marked the beginning of the Civil War; Bull Run (July 1861) showed that the Confederates would not be easily defeated and the war would last longer than expected; Shiloh (April 1862) was the bloodiest battle up to that point; the Seven Days' Battles (June 1862) saved the Confederate capital and made Lee a hero; Antietam (Sept. 1862) had the highest number of casualties on both sides and caused Lincoln to replace McClellan; Fredericksburg (Dec.1862) caused the Union to retreat and made northerners question the war effort.

INTERPRET VISUALS ANSWERS

24. The men at the table appear to be writing letters or journals. The man in front appears to be mending his clothes.

25. Answers will vary. Possible responses: The photo shows that when soldiers were not fighting battles they spent time taking care of tasks or communicating with their families.

ANALYZE SOURCES ANSWER

26. While Barton was supporting a wounded man with her arm to give him a drink, a bullet passed between them, cutting through her sleeve and killing the man.

CONNECT TO YOUR LIFE ANSWER

27. Answers will vary, but students should relate a personal dispute they have experienced to the rising tensions of the Civil War. Their response should state a position, weigh positives and negatives, and support an argument for or against conflict.

UNIT 6 CIVIL WAR AND RECONSTRUCTION

UNIT 6 RESOURCES

UNIT INTRODUCTION

UNIT TIME LINE

UNIT WRAP-UP

NATIONAL GEOGRAPHIC | CONNECTION

National Geographic Magazine Adapted Articles
- "Lincoln's Funeral Train"
- "Civil War Battlefields" ONLINE

Unit 6 Inquiry: Develop a Conflict Resolution Strategy

NG Learning Framework Activities
- Create an Illustrated Time Line
- Compose a Letter Home

Unit 6 Formal Assessment

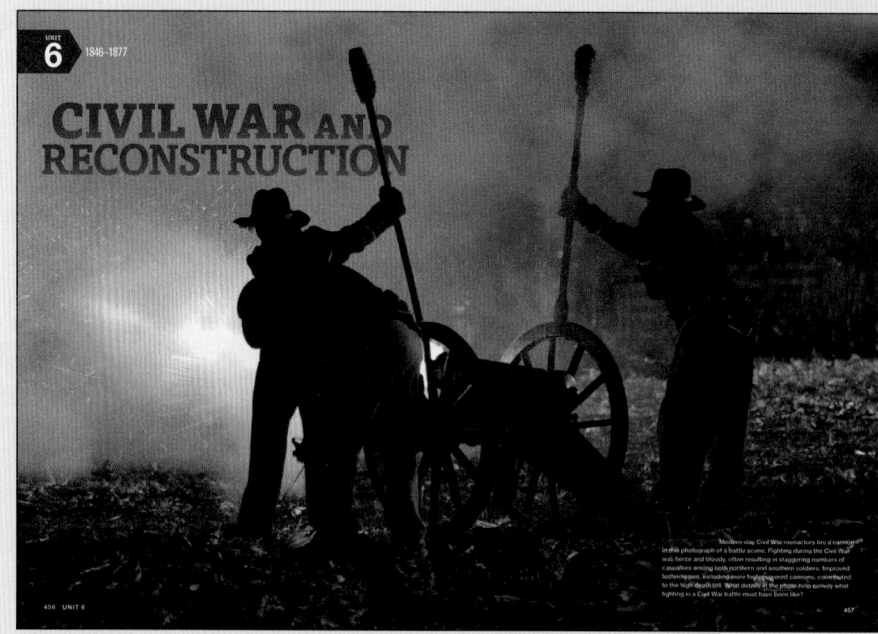

CHAPTER 16 RESOURCES

Available at NGLSync.Cengage.com

TEACHER RESOURCES & ASSESSMENT

Reading and Note-Taking

Vocabulary Practice

Document-Based Question Template

Social Studies Skills Lessons
- Reading: Analyze Language Use
- Writing: Write a Narrative

Formal Assessment
- Chapter 16 Pretest
- Chapter 16 Tests A & B
- Section Quizzes

Chapter 16 Answer Key

ExamView®
One-time Download

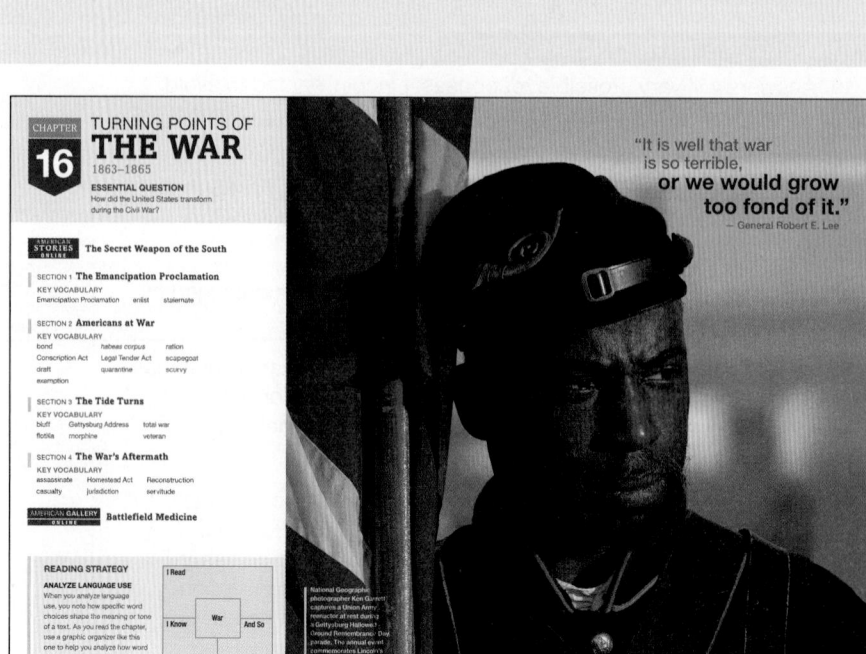

STUDENT DIGITAL RESOURCES

- **eEdition** (English)
- **eEdition** (Spanish)
- **Handbooks**
- **Online Atlas**
- **American Gallery Online**
- **History Notebook**
- **American Voices (Biographies)**
- **Active History**
- **Projects for Inquiry-Based Learning**

Chapter 16 Spanish Resources are available at NGLSync.Cengage.com.

AMERICAN
STORIES
ONLINE **The Secret Weapon of the South**

- Primary Sources

- On Your Feet: Ready, Set, Recall

NG Learning Framework:
Think Like a Marine Archaeologist

SECTION 1 RESOURCES

THE EMANCIPATION PROCLAMATION

LESSON 1.1
Lincoln Issues the Emancipation Proclamation

- On Your Feet: Inside-Outside Circle

NG Learning Framework:
Analyze a Speech

American Voices Biography
Martin Luther King, Jr. ONLINE

LESSON 1.2
AMERICAN VOICES
Frederick Douglass

- On Your Feet: Card Responses

NG Learning Framework:
Write a Persuasive Speech

LESSON 1.3
African-American Soldiers

- On Your Feet: Turn and Talk on Topic

NG Learning Framework:
Research African Americans
During the War

SECTION 2 RESOURCES

AMERICANS AT WAR

LESSON 2.1
Conflicts over the Draft

- On Your Feet: Stage a Quiz Show

NG Learning Framework:
Debate Draft Exemptions

LESSON 2.2
Paying for War

- On Your Feet: Three Corners

NG Learning Framework:
Explore Confederate Impressment

LESSON 2.3
Wartime Prison Camps

- On Your Feet: Fishbowl

NG Learning Framework:
Investigate Diseases

SECTION 3 RESOURCES

THE TIDE TURNS

LESSON 3.1
Battles of Vicksburg and Gettysburg

- ▶ Gettysburg Reenactors

- Active History: Solve a Puzzle

NG Learning Framework:
Write a Biography of a General

LESSON 3.2
Sherman's March and Grant's Victory

- On Your Feet: Team Word Webbing

NG Learning Framework:
Investigate Consequences of Total War
on Civilians

American Voices Biographies
Robert E. Lee
Ulysses S. Grant ONLINE

LESSON 3.3
DOCUMENT-BASED QUESTION
Lincoln's Vision

- On Your Feet: Host a DBQ Roundtable

LESSON 3.4
Appomattox

AMERICAN **GALLERY**
ONLINE Battlefield Medicine

NG Learning Framework:
Investigate Medical Technology

LESSON 3.5
AMERICAN PLACES
**Ball's Bluff National Cemetery
Leesburg, Virginia**

- On Your Feet: Rotating Discussion

NG Learning Framework:
Research National Cemeteries

SECTION 4 RESOURCES

THE WAR'S AFTERMATH

LESSON 4.1
Landmark Amendments and Terrible Loss

- On Your Feet: Word Chain

NG Learning Framework:
Compare Opinions

LESSON 4.2
The Legacy of the War

- On Your Feet: Hold a Panel Discussion

NG Learning Framework:
Determine Economic Data

CHAPTER 16 REVIEW

Strategy ❶
Use Supported Reading

In small groups, have students read the chapter aloud lesson by lesson. At the end of each lesson, have them stop and use these frames to tell what they comprehended from the text:

- This lesson is about _____.

- One detail or fact that stood out to me is _____.

- The vocabulary word _____ means _____.

- I don't think I understand _____.

Use with All Lessons

Strategy ❷
Use a TASKS Approach

Help students get information from visuals by using the following TASKS strategy:

T Look for a **title** that may give the main idea.
A **Ask** yourself what the visual is trying to show.
S Determine how **symbols** are used.
K Look for a **key** or legend.
S **Summarize** what you learned.

Use with Lessons 3.2 and 4.2

Strategy ❸
Use Paired Reading

Pair students and assign each pair two passages in the lesson. Tell them that they will each take one passage, read it, take notes, become an expert on it, and share their expertise with their partner. After students have had time to prepare their passages, have them report on their reading to each other. Tell each listener to write two clarifying questions.

Use with All Lessons

Strategy ❶
Provide Terms and Names on Audio

Decide which of the terms and names are important for mastery and ask a volunteer to record the pronunciations and a short sentence defining each word. Encourage students to listen to the recording as often as necessary.

Use with All Lessons *You might also use the recordings to quiz students on their mastery of the terms. Play one definition at a time from the recording and ask students to identify the term or name described.*

Strategy ❷
Build a Time Line

Select key events from Lessons 1.1 and 1.3. Then have students use the events to start a time line on the board. Tell students to add to the time line as they read the chapter.

1863
Jan. 1
Emancipation
Proclamation
goes into effect

Use with Lessons 1.1, 1.3, 2.1–2.2, 3.1–3.2, 3.4, and 4.1–4.2 *For example, key events from Lesson 1.3 might include 1863 / July 18 / 54th Massachusetts storms Fort Wagner.*

ENGLISH LANGUAGE LEARNERS ELD

Strategy ❶
Modify Vocabulary Lists

Limit the number of vocabulary words, terms, and names students at the **Emerging** level will be required to master. Have students write each word from your modified list on a colored sticky note and put it on the page next to where it appears in context.

Use with Lessons 2.1, 2.3, and 4.1

Strategy ❷
Use Visuals to Predict Content

Direct students at the **Emerging** and **Expanding** levels to read the lesson title and look at the visuals. Then ask them to write a sentence predicting how the visual is related to the lesson. After reading, you may wish to have students verify their predictions and reword sentences if necessary.

Use with All Lessons

Strategy ❸
Build a Concept Cluster

Write the Key Vocabulary word *total war* on the board and ask students for words, phrases, or pictures that come to mind. Have volunteers write the words and draw simple pictures around *total war* to build a Concept Cluster. Call on students to create sentences about the words and pictures. Then tell students each to ask a question they would like to have answered about the Key Vocabulary word.

Use with Lesson 3.2 *You may wish to pair students at the **Emerging** level with students at the **Expanding** and **Bridging** levels and have more advanced students assist less advanced students.*

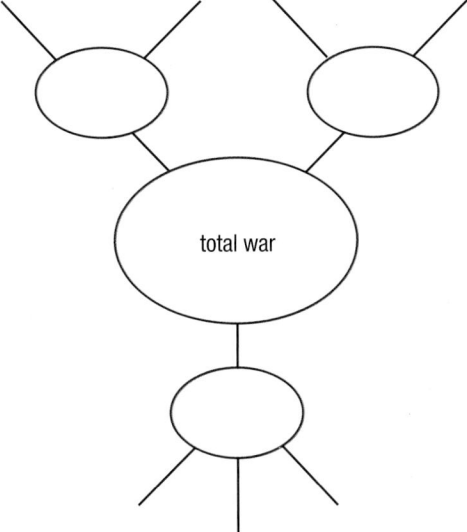

GIFTED & TALENTED

Strategy ❶
Teach a Class

Before beginning the chapter, allow students to choose one of the lessons listed below and prepare to teach the content to the class. Give them a set amount of time in which to present their lesson. Suggest that students think about any visuals or activities they want to use when they teach.

Use with Lessons 1.3, 2.1, 2.3, 3.1–3.2, and 3.4

Strategy ❷
Write a Historical Dialogue

Tell students to use the facts they have learned to write a dialogue that might have taken place between generals Grant and Sherman as Sherman planned and executed his total war in the South. Encourage students to convey Grant's and Sherman's views on warfare through the dialogue. Students may want to supplement their dialogues with additional research. Remind them to use academic sources in their research.

Use with Lesson 3.2

Pre-AP

Strategy ❶
Form a Thesis

Have students develop a thesis statement about an immediate consequence of the Civil War. Tell students to make sure the statement makes a claim that is supportable with evidence either from the chapter or through further research. Then have pairs compare their statements and determine which makes the strongest or most supportable claim.

Use with All Lessons

Strategy ❷
Analyze Effects

Tell students to work individually or in pairs to research and examine the long-term effects of the Civil War. As an alternative, assign teams and have each team choose one of the following aspects on which to focus:

• social changes

• economic changes

• political changes

Suggest that students develop a graphic organizer to display the results of their investigation.

Use with Lesson 4.2

CHAPTER 16

TURNING POINTS OF THE WAR
1863–1865

ESSENTIAL QUESTION
How did the United States transform during the Civil War?

READING STRATEGY

ANALYZE LANGUAGE USE
When you analyze language use, you note how specific word choices shape the meaning or tone of a text. As you read the chapter, use a graphic organizer like this one to help you analyze how word choices help convey the realities of war.

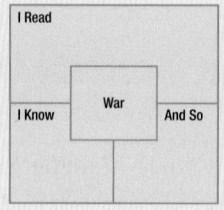

I Read

I Know   War   And So

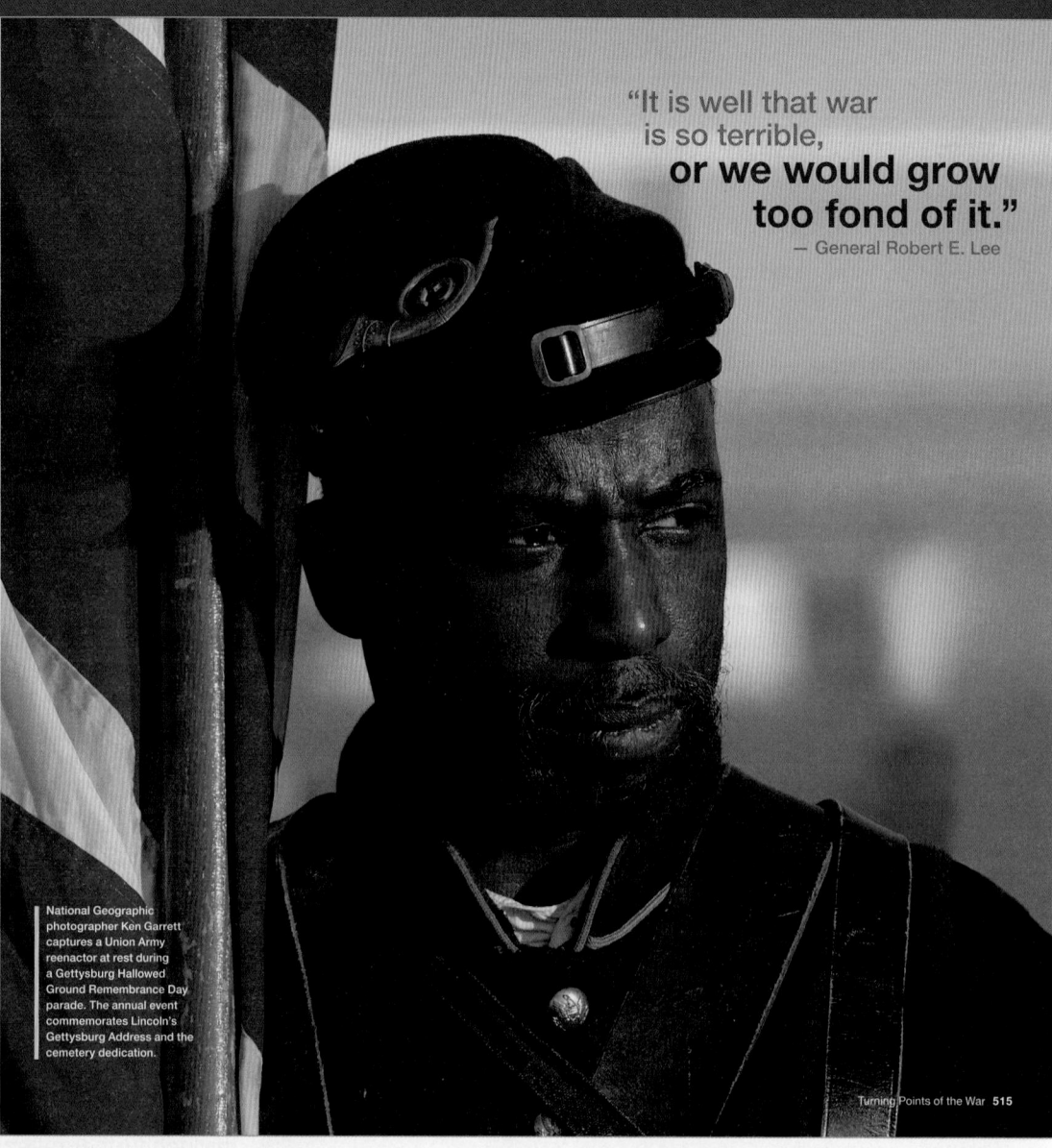

"It is well that war is so terrible, **or we would grow too fond of it.**"
— General Robert E. Lee

National Geographic photographer Ken Garrett captures a Union Army reenactor at rest during a Gettysburg Hallowed Ground Remembrance Day parade. The annual event commemorates Lincoln's Gettysburg Address and the cemetery dedication.

INTRODUCE THE PHOTOGRAPH
African-American Soldiers

Point out that while no African-American units fought with the Union Army at Gettysburg, nearly 200,000 African-American soldiers and sailors served on the Union side during the Civil War. The custom of the time meant that African Americans were not buried in the national cemetery at Gettysburg. About 30 members of the U.S. Colored Troops are buried in nearby Lincoln Cemetery along with early members of Gettysburg's African-American community. Tell students that in this chapter they will learn about the turning points in the Civil War and how President Lincoln opened military service to African Americans and shifted the focus of the war from saving the Union to ending slavery.

NATIONAL GEOGRAPHIC PHOTOGRAPHER
Kenneth Garrett

National Geographic photographer Kenneth Garrett carries on a proud family tradition. His father, Wilbur "Bill" Garrett, was a longtime National Geographic photographer and served as the editor of *National Geographic* magazine in the 1980s. Garrett remembers that dinner conversation when he was growing up often centered on photography, spurred on by the professional photographers who were frequent guests. His father believed that photographers should be photojournalists and visual storytellers. Garrett agrees, although he admits that he grew into that view. As a child, he saw photography as a way to explore. As an adult, he has achieved both.

For Chapter 16 Spanish Resources, visit the Resources Menu. Chapter 16 Resources are available at NGLSync.Cengage.com.

How did the United States transform during the Civil War?

Four Corners Activity: Transformations This activity introduces students to the idea that the Civil War transformed the United States in significant ways by asking them to think about the different ways a civil war might change a nation. Designate a section of the room to each area of transition below and tell students to move to the area that interests them most. Once students are organized in their groups, have them discuss the question provided. Then call on volunteers from each group to summarize the group's thoughts for the class.

Social How might a civil war change social relationships and aspects of culture?

Economic How might a civil war cause economic changes, either good or bad?

Political How might a civil war cause political changes, both during and after the fighting?

Geographic How might a civil war change the physical and human geography of a region?

Word Maps

Have students work together to create Word Maps for Key Vocabulary words. Pairs make a map for each word, writing what they know about the word before reading and then adding to the map during reading. Model an example for students on the board, using the graphic organizer below.

What the Word Means
situation in which neither side has a path to victory

Examples
a war in which neither side is winning

Word
stalemate

Sentence
Our game resulted in a stalemate when neither of us could capture the other's king.

ANALYZE LANGUAGE USE
Remind students to note how specific word choices shape the meaning or tone of a text. Point out the topic in the center square and use the chart to model analyzing Lincoln's words from the Gettysburg Address. Write the following quote under I Read: "Now we are engaged in a great civil war, testing whether that nation or any nation so conceived and so dedicated can long endure." Point out the words *testing* and *endure* and ask students to suggest connotations, such as difficulty or hardship. Add connotations under I Know. Work with the class to write a conclusion about what Lincoln's use of language conveys about the realities of war. Add the conclusion to the And So box. Remind students to make use of the chart as they read the chapter.

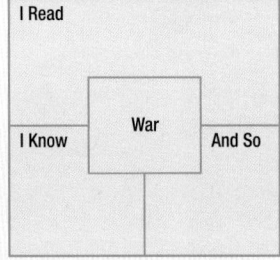

I Read

I Know | War | And So

January 1863	Emancipation Proclamation
July 1863	Battle of Gettysburg
July 1863	New York draft riots erupt
July 1863	54th Massachusetts storms Fort Wagner
November 1863	Gettysburg Address
September 1864	Sherman captures Atlanta
November 1864	Lincoln elected to second term
April 1865	Lee surrenders at Appomattox Court House
April 1865	Lincoln is assassinated

AMERICAN STORIES ONLINE For instructional support for the online American Story "The Secret Weapon of the South," go to NGLSync.Cengage.com.

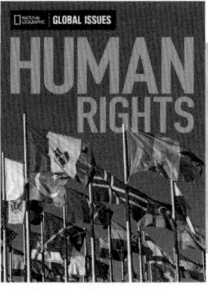

For more on protecting human rights, see *GLOBAL ISSUES: HUMAN RIGHTS.*

1.1 Lincoln Issues the Emancipation Proclamation

In a game of tug-of-war, if both sides pull with equal force, neither wins. In the summer of 1862, the Union and Confederate armies were both tugging equally, and President Lincoln had to find a way to end the standoff.

MAIN IDEA In 1863, Abraham Lincoln issued the Emancipation Proclamation, which freed slaves in states under Confederate control.

GIVING PURPOSE TO THE WAR

Before September 17, 1862, the name "Antietam" referred only to a creek near Sharpsburg, Maryland. But by sunset that day, Antietam would become the name of one of the bloodiest battles ever fought on American soil. Despite battle after battle, the war had reached a **stalemate**, with neither side holding a clear path to a final victory. And still, the body count rose.

CRITICAL VIEWING President Lincoln meets with General McClellan in the general's headquarters after the Battle of Antietam. What do you notice about the flags in the photo?

In both the North and the South, the loss of so many lives led many to question why Americans were fighting against one another. In the midst of all this suffering, President Lincoln sought to define a greater moral purpose for the war. He realized the Union could not defeat the Confederacy without first destroying slavery.

From the beginning of the war, President Lincoln had faced pressure from abolitionists to end slavery. Although personally opposed to the

institution, Lincoln was initially reluctant to abolish it outright. Instead, he envisioned a gradual end to slavery, with slaveholders being paid for the loss of their property. Northern Democrats, whose support he needed, opposed abolition. Many of them were sympathetic to the South and to the cause of slavery, even as they remained loyal to the Union. They warned Lincoln against the social, economic, and political fallout of bringing an end to slavery, whether slowly or abruptly.

From a military standpoint, however, the institution of slavery gave the Confederacy an advantage over the Union. Slave labor kept the southern agrarian economy running, which meant more white southern men could join the Confederate Army. Although some members of Lincoln's party urged him to allow African-American men to fight on the side of the Union, the president remained hesitant to offend the border states by doing so. By the summer of 1862, Union troops had secured the slave-owning states of Missouri and Kentucky.

FOREVER FREE

The North had been fighting to preserve the Union, but a clearer moral purpose was emerging from the bloodshed. Five days after the Union victory at Antietam, Lincoln shifted the focus of the war. He issued a decree that emancipated, or freed, all Confederate slaves. Lincoln had purposely waited to submit a draft of the **Emancipation Proclamation** to his cabinet because he knew the timing had to be right for such a dramatic move. The five-page document declared that all slaves in

> **PRIMARY SOURCE**
>
> *That on the first day of January, in the year of our Lord one thousand eight hundred and sixty-three, all persons held as slaves within any State or designated part of a State, the people whereof shall then be in rebellion against the United States, shall be then, thenceforward, and forever free.*
>
> —from the Emancipation Proclamation, issued by Abraham Lincoln, January 1, 1863

rebel states were "thenceforward, and forever free." It committed the government and armed forces of the United States to liberate enslaved people in rebel states. The final draft of the proclamation allowed the Union to accept freed slaves into its fighting forces. On January 1, 1863, Lincoln formally issued the Emancipation Proclamation.

At the time Lincoln wrote the proclamation, approximately 4 million enslaved people lived in the United States. However, the proclamation did not apply to slaves in the Union's slave-holding border states of Maryland, Missouri, Kentucky, Delaware, or West Virginia. Lincoln feared that emancipating slaves in all Union-controlled territories might cause border states to join the Confederacy. The Union couldn't afford that loss.

As you have read, the Declaration of Independence states that "all men are created equal." However, according to the Constitution, enslaved African Americans were not equal citizens with equal rights. By issuing the Emancipation Proclamation, Lincoln began the long process of addressing the vast discrepancies between the words of the Declaration of Independence and the realities experienced by African Americans, both enslaved and free.

Slaveholders in Confederate states did not consider themselves bound by U.S. law, and they refused to acknowledge the proclamation. In order to become free, enslaved people still had to escape to Union-controlled territory. About 500,000 African Americans emancipated themselves by escaping. Some young men who did so fled to Union camps and, after 1863, even joined the Union Army. However, many enslaved people in the South knew nothing about the Emancipation Proclamation until the war was over.

HISTORICAL THINKING

1. **READING CHECK** What were the goals of the Emancipation Proclamation?

2. **MAKE INFERENCES** To what extent did the Emancipation Proclamation extend the principles of the Declaration of Independence?

3. **ANALYZE CAUSE AND EFFECT** What factors affected President Lincoln's decision to issue the Emancipation Proclamation?

PLAN

Objective

Understand why Abraham Lincoln issued the Emancipation Proclamation.

Critical Thinking Skills for Lesson 1.1

- Identify Main Ideas and Details
- Monitor Comprehension
- Make Inferences
- Analyze Cause and Effect
- Summarize
- Analyze Language Use

Essential Question for Chapter 16

How did the United States transform during the Civil War? The Emancipation Proclamation shifted the focus of the war toward freeing enslaved people, who could then also fight as soldiers in the Union Army. Lesson 1.1 discusses how the Emancipation Proclamation changed the course of the Civil War.

Background for the Teacher

Lincoln first informed his Cabinet of his intention to issue the Emancipation Proclamation on July 22, 1862. Secretary of State Seward argued that Lincoln should wait until after a Union victory so that the proclamation would not look like the act of a desperate administration. Lincoln heeded the advice, waiting until after the Union victory at Antietam to issue a preliminary Emancipation Proclamation on September 22. The preliminary proclamation served as a warning to Confederate states. When no states in the Confederacy responded, Lincoln signed the final proclamation on January 1, 1863. The differences between the two documents reflected Lincoln's changing views over time.

Discuss the Value of Purpose

Remind students that Thomas Jefferson used the Declaration of Independence to outline colonial grievances against Great Britain and to justify declaring independence. Discuss the value of Jefferson's purpose with the class. Ask students how having a clear purpose might have helped generate colonial support for the American Revolution. Tell students that they will learn about how Abraham Lincoln used the Emancipation Proclamation to define a greater moral purpose for the Civil War in an effort to defeat the Confederacy.

TEACH

Guided Discussion

1. **Summarize** How did Lincoln's positions on slavery and African Americans in the military change between the beginning of the war and the release of the final Emancipation Proclamation? *(At the beginning of the war, Lincoln favored a gradual end to slavery that included paying slaveholders for the loss of their slaves and allowing African-American men to serve in the military. Faced with a stalemate in the war, Lincoln decided that ending slavery was a military necessity and the moral thing to do.)*

2. **Analyze Cause and Effect** Why did the Emancipation Proclamation have only a limited impact on slavery? *(Answers will vary. Possible response: Because Confederate slaveholders refused to acknowledge the Emancipation Proclamation, many enslaved people in Confederate states did not learn about emancipation until after the war. In addition, the proclamation did not apply to border states or to Confederate states that were not yet under Union control.)*

Analyze Language Use

Allow time for students to reread the excerpt from the Emancipation Proclamation. **ASK:** What point do you think Lincoln was trying to make when he stated that all slaves in rebel states "shall be then, thenceforward, and forever free"? *(Answers will vary. Possible response: Lincoln was making the point that the freedom granted to African Americans would not be taken away at a later date.)*

Active Options

On Your Feet: Inside-Outside Circle Arrange students in concentric circles facing each other. Tell students in the outside circle to pose questions about the goals and outcomes of the Emancipation Proclamation, such as: Why did the Emancipation Proclamation not free all slaves? Tell students in the inner circle to answer their partner's question. On a signal, students trade roles so that those in the inside circle ask questions and those in the outside circle answer the questions.

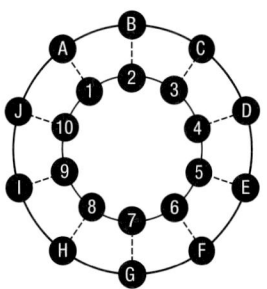

NG Learning Framework: Analyze a Speech

SKILL Collaboration

KNOWLEDGE Our Human Story

Have students explore the link between the Declaration of Independence and the Emancipation Proclamation by analyzing Martin Luther King, Jr.'s address delivered on September 12, 1962, to commemorate the centennial of the Emancipation Proclamation. Instruct students to work in small groups to locate the speech online and summarize King's major points in support of his claim that the Emancipation Proclamation was the offspring of the Declaration of Independence. Then ask students to use the summaries as the basis of a class discussion.

Striving Readers

Use Context Clues Define and review some of the words used in this lesson, using context clues or outside dictionaries if necessary: *stalemate, moral, institution, emancipation, proclamation,* and *thenceforward.* Provide examples that are recognizable and familiar to students. Then ask students to use each word in a sentence.

Pre-AP

Write a Report Direct students to gather relevant information from several library or online sources to write a report on the military benefits that the Emancipation Proclamation provided for the Union, including its effect on the Confederacy's efforts to obtain foreign support. Encourage students to use search terms effectively, assess the credibility and accuracy of their sources, include properly formatted citations, and paraphrase their data and conclusions to avoid plagiarism. Have students share their reports with the class.

See the Chapter Planner for more strategies for differentiation.

HISTORICAL THINKING

ANSWERS

1. It aimed to free enslaved people in the rebel states and provide a moral purpose for the war by shifting the focus to ending slavery.

2. Possible response: When the Declaration of Independence stated "all men are created equal," it did not mean enslaved African Americans, who were not considered citizens. The Emancipation Proclamation began the process of extending to African Americans the rights promised in the Declaration of Independence.

3. Enslaved labor gave the Confederacy a military advantage, so ending slavery could provide African-American troops and give an advantage to the North. However, Lincoln didn't want to anger the border states. The Emancipation Proclamation was a solution because it only focused on states in rebellion against the Union.

CRITICAL VIEWING Answers will vary. Possible response: The U.S. flag is carefully draped over a table, while the Confederate flag is lying on the ground.

AMERICAN VOICES
Frederick Douglass 1818–1895

"The white man's happiness cannot be purchased
by the black man's misery."—Frederick Douglass

Frederick Douglass was deeply familiar with the miseries suffered by black men and women living in slavery. Born to an enslaved mother in 1818, he spent the early years of his childhood living on a plantation in Maryland. There, he endured cold and hunger, and he witnessed other slaves being whipped.

BALTIMORE AND BEYOND

When he was around eight years old, Douglass was sent to live in Baltimore with a shipbuilder named Hugh Auld. Auld's wife Sophia taught the young boy the alphabet. Auld quickly put a stop to the lessons because it was illegal to teach a slave to read. However, the child's passion for learning had been ignited, and he taught himself to read and write.

In 1832, Douglass was sent to work on a plantation, where he was regularly beaten and given little to eat. In his own words, he was "broken in body, soul, and spirit" as "the dark night of slavery closed in upon me." Eventually, he returned to Baltimore to work in the shipyards, where he made his escape in 1838 by fleeing to New York City. After his escape, he changed his name to reduce the risk of being found by slave catchers. Before, he had been called Frederick Augustus Washington Bailey. From this point on, he would call himself Frederick Douglass.

🏛 Art Institute of Chicago

This photograph by Samuel J. Miller shows Frederick Douglass in formal dress, staring forcefully at the viewer. Douglass, the most photographed American of the 19th century, insisted on posing this way. He wanted to reteach people how to see African Americans by replacing the stereotype of the oppressed slave with the portrait of a dignified, proud fellow citizen.

FIGHTER FOR FREEDOM

Douglass settled in New Bedford, Massachusetts, where he worked as a laborer and furthered his education by reading widely. In 1841, he made his first speech describing his life in slavery and calling for an end to the brutal practice. It was the beginning of a lifelong career in public speaking.

Douglass's speeches were so eloquent that some people suspected him of simply pretending to be a former slave. They reasoned that a man born in slavery could never have learned to speak with such brilliance. In many ways, Douglass remade how his fellow citizens viewed African Americans.

To tell his full story, Douglass wrote *Narrative of the Life of Frederick Douglass, an American Slave* in 1845. Publishing the autobiography was a special act of courage because it revealed details about his life that might enable slave catchers to find him. He traveled to Great Britain, where he promoted his book and gave lectures. There, he could speak out without fear of being captured. Over the course of his two-year tour, he gained many new friends and supporters, who helped him purchase his freedom.

Back in the United States, Douglass founded an abolitionist newspaper, wrote two more influential books, and continued to speak out. In 1852, he delivered one of his most famous speeches, "The Meaning of July Fourth for the Negro." In it, he asked why enslaved people should celebrate the country's freedom when they did not benefit from it themselves. "We need the storm, the whirlwind, the earthquake," he thundered. "[The] conscience of the nation must be roused."

When the Civil War broke out, Douglass helped recruit African-American soldiers, and he met with President Abraham Lincoln several times. After the war he held various government posts, including U.S. Marshall for the District of Columbia. He continued promoting civil rights for all Americans until his death in 1895.

CRITICAL VIEWING This painting, *Three Great Abolitionists: A. Lincoln, F. Douglass, J. Brown,* was created by William H. Johnson around 1945. Frederick Douglass stands in the middle, clasping hands with Abraham Lincoln on his left and John Brown on his right. Johnson depicted the three using a "primitive" style of painting, characterized by the work's bright colors and two-dimensional figures. Just behind John Brown, African Americans raise their hands in celebration of the abolitionists. What aspects of Civil War–era African-American life are depicted in the background of the painting?

HISTORICAL THINKING

1. **READING CHECK** Why was Douglass in danger of being enslaved again, even after he became well known?

2. **ANALYZE CAUSE AND EFFECT** How did a few lessons from Sophia Auld change the course of Douglass's life?

3. **DRAW CONCLUSIONS** Why do you think Douglass took the Fourth of July as a theme for a speech on slavery?

PLAN

Objective

Learn about Frederick Douglass's life and his views on abolishing slavery.

Critical Thinking Skills for Lesson 1.2

• Identify Main Ideas and Details
• Monitor Comprehension
• Analyze Cause and Effect
• Draw Conclusions
• Form and Support Opinions

Essential Question for Chapter 16

How did the United States transform during the Civil War? Abolitionist Frederick Douglass called for an end to slavery before and during the Civil War. Through his speeches, Douglass changed the way some people viewed African Americans. Lesson 1.2 describes the life of Frederick Douglass and his efforts to end slavery.

Background for the Teacher

According to Frederick Douglass, being sent to Baltimore in his youth changed his life and set the stage for his later successes. In Baltimore, Douglass learned about the work of abolitionists, and he met his future wife, Anna Murray, there when he was sent back to the city as an adult. His work continued when he moved to New Bedford, Massachusetts, where he attended abolition meetings and began reading *The Liberator,* the weekly abolitionist journal published by William Lloyd Garrison. After settling in Rochester, New York, Douglass published his own abolitionist newspaper, the *North Star,* from 1847 to 1860. During the Civil War, Douglass advised President Lincoln to include African Americans in the military and to make ending slavery the war's focus.

📝 History Notebook

Encourage students to complete the American Voices page for Chapter 16 in their History Notebooks as they read.

Preview Using Visuals

Point out the painting by William H. Johnson. Read the caption under the painting. Draw attention to how the three abolitionists are posed and the images in the background. Tell students to make individual lists of the emotions and actions they notice. Then ask them to share their lists. **ASK:** What do you think the artist conveys in the painting? *(Answers will vary. Possible response: The artist shows that Douglass, Brown, and Lincoln worked together to end slavery. The shaking of hands shows that they were in agreement in their beliefs.)* Explain to students that they will learn more about Frederick Douglass's life and his work to end slavery.

TEACH

Guided Discussion

1. **Draw Conclusions** How did Frederick Douglass turn his experiences on the plantation and in Baltimore into a powerful weapon against slavery? *(Answers will vary. Possible response: He told of his own experiences of life as a slave. Using speeches and his writings, Douglass was able to convincingly argue for the end of slavery.)*

2. **Form and Support Opinions** How much power does one person have in changing people's views of groups of others? *(Answers will vary. Possible responses: One person can offer strong evidence and change people's views, as Douglass did in changing some people's views about African Americans. If people have extremely strong views, even the strongest evidence may not be able to change them.)*

American Voices

Frederick Douglass cared about how he presented himself to the public through his speaking and writing and how he appeared in photographs. He believed that maintaining a strong and serious public image helped him participate in society on equal footing with whites. He was particularly fond of photographs because he believed that they did not lie, even if the photographer was a racist. Photographs allowed him to show an image tailored to the meaning he wanted to project. He refrained from smiling in photographs because he thought smiling played into racist stereotypes of a happy slave.

Active Options

On Your Feet: Card Responses Instruct half the class to write 15 True-False or Yes-No questions based on the lesson. The other half creates answer cards, writing "True" or "Yes" on one side of the cards and "False" or "No" on the other side. Students from the question group take turns asking their questions. Tell students from the answer group to hold up cards showing the correct answer. Have students keep track of their correct answers.

NG Learning Framework: Write a Persuasive Speech

ATTITUDE Empowerment

SKILL Communication

Frederick Douglass used the power of speech to share his experience and views of slavery. Instruct them to write a persuasive speech about an issue that is important to them. Encourage students to consider issues on the school, community, national, and international levels. Tell students to share their own view about the issue as well as facts that support their view. Remind students to use quotations and visuals in the speech to help persuade others to act on the issue. Call on volunteers to present their speeches to the class.

English Language Learners ELD

Identify Facts Place students in mixed proficiency pairs and guide them in a round-robin activity to review facts about Frederick Douglass. Ask pairs to generate facts for about three to five minutes. Have students at the **Expanding** and **Bridging** levels assist students at the **Emerging** level. Invite one student from each pair to share their responses. Display all facts.

Gifted & Talented

Host a Talk Show Arrange students in pairs and direct them to locate an online transcript of Frederick Douglass's "The Meaning of July Fourth for the Negro" speech. Tell students to assume the roles of a talk show host and Frederick Douglass and to plan, write, and perform an interview focusing on Douglass's views expressed in his speech. Invite pairs to present their talk show to the class.

See the Chapter Planner for more strategies for differentiation.

HISTORICAL THINKING

ANSWERS

1. Douglass was a runaway slave. If slave catchers had identified him by the information he included in his autobiography or speeches, he could have been taken back into slavery.

2. The alphabet lessons awakened Douglass's passion for learning. He taught himself to read and write and, as an adult, furthered his education by reading extensively.

3. Answers will vary. Possible response: The Fourth of July is a day to celebrate independence, so using it as a theme when speaking about the evils of slavery points out the contradiction between the ideals expressed in the Declaration of Independence and the experiences of enslaved African Americans.

CRITICAL VIEWING The painting shows African Americans performing slave labor such as picking cotton and plowing with a mule. While it shows some African Americans lifting up their hands in what looks like worship, it also depicts the harsh reality of a lynching.

African-American Soldiers

Sometimes in war, people put goals ahead of prejudices. During the Civil War, the U.S. military accepted African-American soldiers into its ranks. Defeating the South had become more important than excluding fellow Americans from military service.

MAIN IDEA In 1863, African Americans began to join U.S. military units and proved to be valuable soldiers for the Union.

AFRICAN AMERICANS JOIN THE FIGHT

When the Civil War first began, many free African-American men rushed to **enlist** in, or join, the Union Army, but they were turned away. A 1792 law barred African Americans from joining the U.S. military. At first, members of Lincoln's administration resisted changing this prohibition. But the Emancipation Proclamation reversed the law with its provision that African-American men "will be received into the armed service of the United States," a critical development that affected the war's outcome.

By the end of the Civil War, African-American soldiers in the U.S. Army totaled nearly 180,000, or about 10 percent of total Union enlistments. Additionally, 19,000 African Americans served in the U.S. Navy. African-American troops faced the same danger and fought with as much commitment as white soldiers, but they were not treated equally.

The army assigned African-American soldiers to segregated units commanded by white officers. African-American soldiers received lower wages than most white soldiers until June 1864, when Congress granted equal pay to African-American military units.

Like all 19th-century American women, African-American women were barred from enlisting in the army. Still, some African-American women, including Harriet Tubman, served as nurses, spies, and scouts. As you have read, Tubman led people to freedom on the Underground

Railroad. Tubman also worked as a nurse and scouted behind Confederate lines for the Union's 2nd South Carolina Volunteers. In 1863, she helped free 727 slaves at one time during the Combahee River Raid. That raid was the single largest liberation of slaves in American history.

THE 54TH MASSACHUSETTS REGIMENT

In February 1863, the governor of Massachusetts issued the first formal call for African-American soldiers to join the U.S. Army. He selected the **54th Massachusetts** infantry regiment under the command of Colonel **Robert Gould Shaw**, a white officer. In just two weeks, more than 1,000 African Americans enlisted. Charles and Lewis Douglass, two sons of Frederick Douglass, were among them.

On July 18, 1863, the 54th Massachusetts prepared to storm **Fort Wagner**, which guarded the Port of Charleston, South Carolina. At dusk, Shaw gathered 600 of his men on a narrow strip of sand just outside Fort Wagner's walls. He told them, "I want you to prove yourselves. The eyes of thousands will look on what you do tonight."

As night fell, Shaw led his men over the walls of the fort. They were met by 1,700 Confederate soldiers waiting inside the fort. The brutal hand-to-hand combat that followed took its toll: 281 of the 600 charging soldiers were killed, wounded, or captured. Shaw himself was shot in the chest and died instantly. The 54th lost the battle at Fort Wagner, but its valor, or courage, was beyond

🏛 **Smithsonian National Gallery of Art, Washington, D.C.**

In 1897, Augustus Saint-Gaudens unveiled his 14-year project of honoring the members of the 54th Massachusetts in a bronze relief called the Robert Gould Shaw Memorial. The sculpture depicts the regiment marching down Beacon Street in Boston, on its way to fight Confederate troops in South Carolina. The following year in Paris, Saint-Gaudens exhibited a second version of the memorial made of plaster and covered with bronze metallic paint. Today, the bronze-painted sculpture shown above is housed at the Smithsonian National Gallery of Art in Washington, D.C. The original sculpture is located at the Boston African American National Historic Site on Beacon Street, across the street from the Massachusetts State House. An inscription on the Boston memorial reads, "Together they gave to the nation and the world undying proof that Americans of African descent possess the pride, courage, and devotion of the patriot soldier."

question. For his bravery in the fight, **William H. Carney** became the first African American to receive the Congressional Medal of Honor.

For the next two years, the 54th Massachusetts took part in a number of sieges in South Carolina, Georgia, and Florida. The service and bravery of its members helped to win acceptance for other African-American regiments and solidified their importance in the war effort. Despite increased African-American enlistment, the need for more soldiers in both the North and the South grew.

HISTORICAL THINKING

1. **READING CHECK** Why did the Union wait until after the Emancipation Proclamation to enlist African Americans in the army?

2. **DRAW CONCLUSIONS** Why did the 54th Massachusetts gain great respect in the Union Army despite losing its first battle?

3. **ANALYZE LANGUAGE USE** What made the words Colonel Shaw used with his troops before the battle at Fort Wagner particularly effective?

PLAN

Objective

Understand how African-American soldiers helped the Union war effort.

Critical Thinking Skills for Lesson 1.3

- Identify Main Ideas and Details
- Monitor Comprehension
- Draw Conclusions
- Analyze Language Use
- Make Connections
- Evaluate

Essential Question for Chapter 16

How did the United States transform during the Civil War? The Emancipation Proclamation lifted the 1792 ban on African Americans serving in the U.S. military, and as a result Union forces gained an advantage in the war. Lesson 1.3 describes the role of African-American soldiers in the war effort.

Background for the Teacher

As the first African-American regiment in the North, the 54th Massachusetts faced public scrutiny and doubt. Some whites argued that African Americans lacked the ability to fight effectively. Massachusetts governor John A. Andrews, an abolitionist, believed that African-American soldiers could lead successfully, but he yielded to pressure and appointed commissioned white officers to head the regiment. Few African-American officers received commissions, and most had to work their way up the enlisted ranks. The discrepancy in pay between African-American and white soldiers was significant. The War Department authorized $10 a month for African-American soldiers and deducted $3 for clothing. White soldiers earned $13 with no clothing deductions. Soldiers in the 54th Massachusetts protested this discrepancy by refusing their pay. They eventually received back pay after Congress remedied the imbalance.

Discuss a Quote

Explore the following words of Frederick Douglass with the class: "Once let the black man get upon his person the brass letter, U.S., let him get an eagle on his button, and a musket on his shoulder and bullets in his pocket, there is no power on earth that can deny that he has earned the right to citizenship." Consider displaying the excerpt on the board or providing students with handouts. Discuss with students what Douglass meant. Write students' ideas on the board. After reading the lesson, revisit the students' ideas and ask if they would add or change their responses.

TEACH

Guided Discussion

1. **Make Connections** What information in the text supports the idea that African-American soldiers were not always treated equally? *(The military assigned African-American soldiers to segregated units under the command of white officers. In addition, African-American soldiers were initially paid less than white soldiers.)*

2. **Evaluate** How did Harriet Tubman's actions benefit the Union war effort? *(Tubman served as a nurse, giving aid to Union soldiers, and scouted behind enemy lines, providing information to the Union Army. She helped free 727 slaves during the Combahee River Raid, depriving the Confederacy of workers.)*

🏛 Virtual Museum Visit

The Smithsonian National Gallery of Art was created through the generosity and efforts of financier Andrew W. Mellon, an avid art collector. Mellon got the idea for a world-class national art museum while serving as secretary of state from 1921 to 1932. He proposed his idea to President Franklin D. Roosevelt in 1936, offering to pay for construction of a building and to donate $25 million in art. Congress approved the plan in 1937, and the National Gallery of Art opened in 1941. Access the museum's website and find the archived pages from the "Tell It with Pride: The 54th Massachusetts Regiment and Augustus Saint-Gaudens' Shaw Memorial" exhibit. Ask a volunteer to read the accompanying information about the sculpture aloud. Then ask groups of students to explore other artifacts and photographs in the exhibit on their own and choose one to present to the class.

Active Options

On Your Feet: Turn and Talk on Topic Have students form four lines. Give each group this topic sentence: African-American soldiers were valuable to the Union cause. Tell them to write a paragraph by having each student in the line add a sentence that supports the topic. Direct groups to present their paragraph to the class by having each student in line read his or her sentence in the correct order.

NG Learning Framework: Research African Americans During the War

ATTITUDE Curiosity

KNOWLEDGE Our Human Story

Have students work in small collaborative teams to research the contributions and challenges faced by African-American soldiers or African-American women volunteers in the Civil War. Tell students to select the group that is of most interest to the team and collect first-person accounts, statistics, photographs, and anecdotes. Then ask teams to present their findings to the class in a multimedia format.

DIFFERENTIATE

Inclusion

Describe Details Pair students who are visually impaired with students who are not. Ask the latter to read the caption aloud and describe in detail the bronze-painted memorial to Shaw and the 54th Massachusetts. Tell visually impaired students to ask clarifying questions as necessary.

Pre-AP   STEM

Design a Website Have students work in small groups to design a website about the battle for Fort Wagner. Tell them to begin by designing a home page and then supplying a site map of supporting pages. The website should include information about the strategic importance of Fort Wagner, the physical setting, the regiments and military leaders who participated, accounts of the battle, acts of bravery, and the outcome. Encourage students to share their designs with the class.

See the Chapter Planner for more strategies for differentiation.

HISTORICAL THINKING

ANSWERS

1. Until the Emancipation Proclamation was made law, African Americans were barred from enlisting in the U.S. military.

2. The African-American soldiers of the 54th Massachusetts showed great valor in battle even though they were greatly outnumbered and nearly half of them were killed, wounded, or captured.

3. Answers will vary. Possible response: Shaw's words showed his pride and faith in his troops and reminded the men that this battle was an opportunity for them to prove that African-American troops would be an asset in the Union Army.

2.1 Conflicts over the Draft

Imagine being told you have to fight in a war you may not even support. Then consider that your wealthy neighbor is told the same thing but can pay someone else to take his place. During the Civil War, many men realized they were getting a bad deal.

MAIN IDEA In reaction to forced military service during the Civil War, people in both the North and the South staged riots.

MILITARY SERVICE IN THE SOUTH

Waging a civil war required a steady supply of men volunteering to fight as soldiers. At first, men from both the North and the South rushed to sign up. However, as battles wore on, numbers of enthusiastic volunteers began to dwindle. The South was first to acknowledge this problem.

When war first broke out, 100,000 southern men volunteered to fight for the Confederacy. But as their yearlong enlistments were ending, many soldiers returned home to their families and farms. In 1862, the Confederate government, worried that its armies would be short of men as the Union was stepping up its attacks, instituted a **draft**, or a mandatory term of military service. The Confederacy required three years of service for all white men between the ages of 18 and 35.

The draft didn't apply to every man equally, however. Wealthy southerners could pay other men to serve in their places. They could also choose to pay a fee of $500—an amount out of reach for most men. Individuals who owned 20 slaves or more were excused from the draft and their voluntary enlistments altogether.

Military **exemptions**, or releases from the obligation to serve, widened the growing divide between rich and poor in the South. A non-slaveholding man named Jasper Collins remarked that exemptions made the Civil War a "rich man's war, and a poor man's fight." Some soldiers deserted, or left, their units. Desertion remained a major problem for the Confederacy throughout the war.

The gap between rich and poor spread beyond military service. Convinced that greedy merchants were hoarding flour and supplies, women rioted in Richmond, the Confederate capital. They smashed storefronts and stole bread and everything else they could grab, from bacon to boots. One young girl explained, "We are starving . . . each of us will take a loaf of bread. That is little enough for the government to give us after it has taken all our men."

DRAFTING SOLDIERS IN THE NORTH

The North also faced the need for new soldiers. Death, disease, and desertion continually reduced the size of the army, so the Union instituted its own draft in the form of a law called the **Conscription Act** in March 1863. Men between 20 and 45 years of age were liable to be drafted into the military, but, as in the South, they could pay to avoid service for $300—a fee only wealthy families could afford. These exemptions ignited draft riots in cities throughout the Northeast.

On July 13, the attempt to enforce the draft in New York City set off the most destructive civil disturbance in the city's history. Rioters torched government buildings. Police struggled for three days to control the riot. Eventually, Union troops had to rush from the battlefields in Pennsylvania to New York City to aid the police. Union soldiers fired into groups of fellow citizens who were rioting. About 300 people, more than half of them police officers and soldiers, were injured, and more than 100 people died, most of them rioters.

Some whites in New York blamed African Americans for the unrest surrounding the draft riots. In fact, African Americans became **scapegoats**, or individuals or groups blamed for the mistakes or faults of others. Some people claimed that African Americans were responsible for the war and that they were taking jobs away from white workers. Angry white rioters killed many African Americans and destroyed their homes. Such violence prompted many African Americans to flee New York City during the draft riots. They feared for their lives.

In an effort to control riots and curb criticism of the war, the Lincoln administration suspended the writ of **habeas corpus**, or the right of an arrested person to be brought before a judge before going to jail. More than 14,000 people were jailed after being accused of disloyalty to the Union. As a result of the riots, some New York men with families who had no other means of financial support received exemptions from the draft.

HISTORICAL THINKING

1. **READING CHECK** Why did both the North and the South enact military drafts?

2. **ANALYZE LANGUAGE USE** How did Jasper Collins describe the Civil War, and why?

3. **COMPARE AND CONTRAST** In what ways were the Confederate and Union drafts similar, and in what ways were they different?

CRITICAL VIEWING In this photo still from the 2016 film *Free State of Jones*, Newton Knight, center, and his fellow soldiers fight off Confederate troops trying to put down their rebellion. What do you notice about the men in the photo?

Open Rebellion in Mississippi

Newton Knight of Mississippi enlisted in the Confederate Army in July 1861. Angered by the law exempting white men who owned 20 or more slaves, Knight deserted his battalion in October 1862. Back home, he witnessed his fellow southerners suffer abuses at the hands of Confederate soldiers, and he decided to form an opposition group. Other deserting soldiers and escaped slaves joined him, and by late 1863, they had organized into the Jones County Scouts.

The Jones County Scouts eventually numbered more than 1,000. To symbolize their open rebellion, Knight and his men raised the American flag over the Jones County courthouse. They evaded capture by disappearing into the swamps, with local civilians supplying them with weapons, food, and information. Though Confederate officers eventually subdued the rebellion, the Jones County Scouts fought against the Confederacy until it fell.

PLAN

Objective
Analyze the effects of the military draft during the Civil War.

Critical Thinking Skills for Lesson 2.1
- Identify Main Ideas and Details
- Monitor Comprehension
- Analyze Language Use
- Compare and Contrast
- Analyze Cause and Effect
- Form and Support Opinions
- Evaluate

Essential Question for Chapter 16
How did the United States transform during the Civil War? Mandatory terms of service and draft exemptions widened the gap between rich and poor in the South and led to riots in the North. Lesson 2.1 examines tensions created by the draft.

Background for the Teacher

Many among New York City's working class opposed the Emancipation Proclamation and the draft. Democratic Party newspapers and politicians, including New York governor Horatio Seymour, fueled this opposition by railing against the draft and warning the city's Irish and German immigrants that the Emancipation Proclamation would result in waves of African Americans coming to New York City to take their jobs.

Opposition was particularly high among Irish immigrants, who often competed with African Americans for jobs. Like other laborers, the Irish had been hit hard by the economic downturn in the first year of the war and by rising prices as the war progressed. They were also discouraged and alarmed by mounting casualties among Irish units in the Union Army. Word that 23,000 Union soldiers had been killed, injured, or were missing at Gettysburg only heightened resistance to the draft.

INTRODUCE & ENGAGE

Consider Draft Options

Pose this situation to students: There is a war, and every able-bodied man and woman between 20 and 35 must serve in the military. However, people able to pay a fee equal to half the average worker's annual income can avoid service. Have students consider the advantages and disadvantages of this arrangement. After a few minutes, make a list of students' ideas. Revisit the list after reading the lesson and compare students' ideas with conflicts they read about.

TEACH

Guided Discussion

1. **Analyze Cause and Effect** What effect did the draft riots have on African Americans in New York City? *(Many whites accused African Americans of being the cause of the draft riots and killed African Americans or destroyed their homes or businesses. Fearing for their lives, many African Americans fled the city.)*

2. **Form and Support Opinions** Was the Lincoln administration justified in suspending *habeas corpus*? Support your opinion with evidence from the text. *(Answers will vary. Possible responses: Suspending* habeas corpus *was justified because the riots needed to be controlled. This action was not justified because depriving citizens of the right to see a judge and hear charges against them may have been unconstitutional.)*

Evaluate

Draw students' attention to the photograph and the information below it. **ASK:** What role did the Jones County Scouts play in the Civil War? *(The Jones County Scouts were an opposition group in Jones County, Mississippi. They were angry over draft laws that exempted white men who owned at least 20 slaves, so they fought against the South until the end of the war.)*

Active Options

On Your Feet: Stage a Quiz Show Instruct students to write one question about the draft laws or the conflicts over the laws in the North and South. Collect the questions. Then have groups of five students take turns coming to the front of the class to take part in a quiz. Pose a few of the questions to each group and allow students to confer about the answer. Tell them to signal their readiness to respond by raising their hands.

NG Learning Framework: Debate Draft Exemptions

`ATTITUDE` Responsibility

`SKILL` Communication

Direct students to work in groups to conduct additional research on the draft in the North and the South. Tell them to stage a debate about whether the military exemptions both sides built into their draft laws were warranted based on wartime conditions. One side will argue the affirmative and the other side the negative. Tell students to write their arguments to prepare for the debate and to support their claims with evidence from their research. Allow groups to pick the members who will debate and the members who will serve as debate judges.

DIFFERENTIATE

English Language Learners

Create Word Squares Pair students at the **Expanding** and **Bridging** levels. Display Key Vocabulary words *draft, exemption, habeas corpus, Conscription Act,* and *scapegoat.* Display the chart below. Ask pairs to copy and complete the chart for each word on the list.

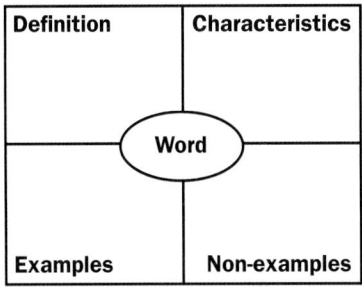

Definition	Characteristics
	Word
Examples	Non-examples

Gifted & Talented

Write a Newspaper Article Direct students to use the text and online research to learn more about the New York City draft riots. Tell students to use their research to write a newspaper article about the causes and consequences of the rioting. Encourage students to include quotes from eyewitnesses and statistics. Invite students to share their articles with the class.

See the Chapter Planner for more strategies for differentiation.

HISTORICAL THINKING

ANSWERS

1. Soldiers were deserting both the Union and Confederate armies, so military drafts solved the problem of supplying troops.

2. Answers will vary. Possible response: Jasper Collins described the Civil War as a "rich man's war, and a poor man's fight." He meant that rich men made the decisions, but poor men did the actual fighting.

3. They both allowed rich men to pay money to avoid service. They differed in age requirements, and southerners with 20 or more slaves were exempt.

CRITICAL VIEWING Possible response: The photo shows a mix of white and African-American men dressed in a variety of clothing, reinforcing the idea that they are a diverse group of rebels rather than a formal army.

Paying for War

Raising money to fight a war is difficult. In 1861, the federal government implemented several financial strategies to support the war effort. The Confederate government struggled with hard economic realities as it tried to do the same.

MAIN IDEA During the Civil War, both the North and the South had to devise new methods of funding their war efforts.

FINANCIAL STRATEGIES

War is incredibly expensive. Even though the Union and the Confederacy were both rich by any international standard, neither had ever supported a large army. Thousands of soldiers needed food, shelter, transportation, uniforms, weapons, ammunition, medical care, and a host of other supplies. As the costs increased, leaders on both sides discovered they had only a few choices: loans, new taxes, and the creation of paper money.

In the North, the federal government issued $2 billion worth of treasury **bonds**. Bonds are certificates offered for sale to the public with the promise that the government will pay the money back at a later date, usually with interest. In August 1861, Congress passed the first federal income tax in U.S. history. This law required citizens who earned more than $600 per year to pay a portion of their income to the government to fund the war.

In 1862, Congress passed the **Legal Tender Act**, an act that replaced currencies of individual banks with one national currency. Because the back of the money was colored green, the national notes were soon called "greenbacks." The Union issued $450 million in greenbacks during the war.

The sudden increase in money in the North had unexpected negative consequences. Greedy manufacturers took advantage of federal funds and urgent demand to produce poorly made and even defective goods. Uniforms sometimes fell apart in the first rain or had no buttons. Some shoemakers produced boots with soles made of cardboard. Not surprisingly, these boots didn't last on long

marches. Some suppliers mixed sawdust in with the gunpowder that filled artillery shells. Dishonest businessmen profited from supplying Union troops with spoiled meat. A new word was invented to describe defective war material: *shoddy*.

PRINTING MONEY, SEIZING CROPS

As you have read, the North had a distinct industrial advantage over the agrarian South. It also had the support of the federal government. The South's lack of an industrial base and a strong government made it difficult for the Confederacy to raise funds to pay for war. It tried to borrow money from Britain and France, and it raised taxes to meet expenses. The Confederacy also printed money, but unlike in the North, this strategy resulted in severe inflation: prices for goods increased and the purchasing value of money decreased. The Confederate government also issued war bonds, but most southerners were too poor to buy them. Those wealthy enough to afford bonds soon discovered that inflation was rising faster than the rate of interest on their bonds.

In 1863, the Confederacy passed a law requiring all farmers to give 10 percent of all the crops they raised to the government for use in the war effort. In addition, Confederate citizens were subjected to impressment, a practice that allowed military officers to take anything they thought might be useful to the war effort, including slaves.

Thousands of African Americans were forced to leave their families to perform forced labor for the Confederate military. Many of them rebelled and escaped to the Union lines where they offered their

A GLOBAL PERSPECTIVE No matter when or where they are fought, civil wars have devastating consequences for ordinary people. Financial resources of nations are diverted away from supporting citizens in order to pay for war. Young men, and sometimes boys, are forced into military service. Day-to-day lives are disrupted, people are displaced from their homes and countries, and economies are damaged. These characteristics all apply to the civil war that took place after the African country of South Sudan achieved independence in 2011.

During that civil war, government spending on weapons took priority over other responsibilities, thousands of people were killed, and more than 1 million people fled the country. The military limited the movements of those who remained, which meant farmers could not plant crops, trade harvests, or tend livestock. The result was massive starvation and famine by 2016. How might the experience of South Sudanese like the young man shown below be similar to what families in the United States experienced during the Civil War?

Lynsey Addario is a National Geographic conflict photographer who documents the human impact of war, drought, and violence. She photographed Lat Padang, a young soldier, while he was recovering from injuries sustained during South Sudan's civil war.

labor to the Union. Southern farms and plantations no longer had the labor necessary to grow food and cash crops.

Meanwhile, many southerners watched helplessly as armies stripped their farms of food and livestock. Some farmers grew cotton because it stored well and they thought it would fetch a high price after the war. As a result, the Confederacy devoted land and labor to growing cotton instead of growing food for its hungry citizens.

HISTORICAL THINKING

1. **READING CHECK** What methods did the North and the South use to raise money for the war?

2. **DESCRIBE** In what ways were civilians in the North and the South affected by the war?

3. **COMPARE AND CONTRAST** In terms of its economy and government, what advantages did the North have over the South?

PLAN

Objective

Learn about the financial strategies the North and South used to pay for the war.

Critical Thinking Skills for Lesson 2.2

- Identify Main Ideas and Details
- Monitor Comprehension
- Describe
- Compare and Contrast
- Draw Conclusions
- Analyze Cause and Effect

Essential Question for Chapter 16

How did the United States transform during the Civil War? Financial strategies and laws put in place on both sides of the war left a lasting impact. Lesson 2.2 describes the different ways the North and South financed the war as well as the consequences of their strategies.

Background for the Teacher

When faced with the need to raise money for the war, Congress favored an income tax over taxing personal property. The first income tax measure was passed (but never implemented) in the summer of 1861. It applied a 3 percent tax on yearly incomes of more than $800. The Internal Revenue Act of 1862 replaced this tax with a tiered system that applied a 3 percent tax on incomes between $600 and $10,000 and a 5 percent tax on incomes of more than $10,000. Rates were increased two more times during the war. The tax was considered relatively progressive because few laborers made more than $600 and thus paid no taxes. The income tax, along with other government-imposed taxes, provided about 21 percent of the funds for the war. Having served its purpose, the income tax was repealed in 1872.

Financial Literacy

To extend their knowledge and understanding about the concepts in this lesson, refer students to the Financial Literacy handbook.

Count the Expenses of War

As a class, discuss the following question: Why are wars so expensive? To encourage discussion, have students identify what is needed during a war, from supplies to shelter. Explain that the cost of war isn't limited to the needs of troops and ask students to identify other costs that might be incurred during a war. Invite students to share their responses. Tell students that in this lesson they will learn about how the North and the South raised money to fight the Civil War.

TEACH

Guided Discussion

1. **Draw Conclusions** Why would some manufacturers and businessmen produce and sell shoddy materials? *(By using cheap materials to make products, they kept their costs low and were able to make a profit. It may also be that good materials were scarce during wartime, so manufacturers could not provide well-made products.)*

2. **Analyze Cause and Effect** Why did some farmers in the South grow cotton during the Civil War, and how might that have affected people after the war? *(Some farmers grew and stored cotton for sale after the war, hoping prices would increase. This meant less land was available for growing food for citizens and soldiers when the war ended.)*

A Global Perspective

Explore the photograph and caption for this lesson with students. **ASK:** What connections do you see between government actions in South Sudan during its civil war and government actions in the North and South during the Civil War in the United States? *(Possible response: The governments in both civil wars spent money on the war that might have been used to help citizens. They also took actions that restricted the freedoms and rights of citizens.)* Why do you think National Geographic photographer Lynsey Addario chooses to document conflict? *(Possible response: Addario might believe it is important to document the impact of war and violence so that people think about the human consequences of conflict.)*

Active Options

On Your Feet: Three Corners Post signs in three corners of the classroom: Bonds, Taxes, and Printing Money. Organize students into groups around each sign and ask them to discuss the effectiveness of their strategy to raise money in the North and the South. To compare the strategies, have students from the bonds group travel to explain their strategy's effectiveness to each of the other two groups. Then repeat the process with the other two groups.

NG Learning Framework: Explore Confederate Impressment

ATTITUDE Curiosity

KNOWLEDGE Our Human Story

Draw a Detail Web on the board and write the word *impressment* in the center. Organize students into groups and have them research the South's use of impressment during the Civil War and its effects on the home front. Instruct students to take notes on the forms of impressment, the effectiveness of the strategy, the impact on civilians, and reactions to the strategy. Complete the web as groups share their findings with the class.

DIFFERENTIATE

Striving Readers

Summarize Have pairs summarize the lesson by creating two Word Webs with *North* and *South* in the center ovals. Ask students to complete each web with information about how both the North and the South financed the war.

Inclusion

Check Understanding Tell students to write the letters *A, B,* and *C* on three separate index cards. Then check students' understanding by asking questions with answer choices *A, B,* and *C.* Tell students to hold up the card with the letter that corresponds to the correct answer. Help students find the answers in the lesson for any questions that cause them difficulty.

See the Chapter Planner for more strategies for differentiation.

HISTORICAL THINKING

ANSWERS

1. The North issued bonds, passed a federal income tax, and established a national currency. The South tried to borrow money from France and Britain, raised taxes, printed money, and issued bonds.

2. Northerners paid higher taxes and dealt with shoddy goods from greedy manufacturers. Southerners had higher taxes and inflation and surrendered a portion of their crops and property. Thousands of African Americans were forced to provide labor for the Confederates.

3. The North had an industrial base and a strong federal government. The agrarian South had difficulties raising funds.

A GLOBAL PERSPECTIVE The South Sudanese, like Americans during the Civil War, faced forced military service and the loss of young men, disrupted lives, displacement, war-damaged economies, and restricted rights. The South Sudanese faced starvation because the war interfered with planting and harvesting, and the South also faced food shortages during the war.

2.3 Wartime Prison Camps

In war, there are always unintended consequences. During the Civil War, neither side was prepared to provide shelter and food for thousands of war prisoners. For those unfortunate enough to be captured, imprisonment could be worse than death.

MAIN IDEA Thousands of soldiers on both sides of the conflict died from exposure and disease in Civil War prison camps.

On July 6, 1864, the first 400 Confederate prisoners arrived at the barracks of Camp Rathbun, soon to become the prison camp at Elmira, New York. The barracks could accommodate 6,000 soldiers, but housed more than 10,000 prisoners between 1864 and 1865. Based on details you notice in this photo of the Elmira prison camp, how would you describe the camp and the conditions for prisoners?

PRISONERS IN THE NORTH

In the early years of the Civil War, the Union and the Confederacy exchanged prisoners of war rather than maintaining prisons. Cooperation soon broke down between the two sides, however, and captured soldiers were confined in military prison camps on both sides.

Camp Douglas in Illinois received its first prisoners—approximately 5,500—in February 1862. It would house more than 26,000 Confederate prisoners by the end of the war. Many prisoners were already sick or wounded when they arrived at the camp, and many died while there due to lack of medical care. Poor sanitation, harsh weather conditions, and reduced **rations**, or supplied food, weakened the remaining prisoners. These circumstances left the prisoners susceptible to infectious diseases such as pneumonia and smallpox. Still others died from **scurvy**, a disease linked to malnutrition and a diet lacking in fruits and vegetables. The total death toll has been estimated to be as many as 6,129 men, the greatest mortality statistic of any Union prison.

Alton was another Illinois prison camp. Originally the first state penitentiary built in Illinois, it closed in 1860, but then reopened in 1862 to relieve overcrowding in other Union prisons. Soon Alton became overcrowded as well. When smallpox swept through the camp in 1862 and 1863, authorities built a hospital on an island in the Mississippi River to **quarantine** infected prisoners, or keep them away from those who had not yet contracted the disease.

Elmira prison camp in New York operated from July 6, 1864, until July 11, 1865. Even though it was set up for 6,000 men, more than 10,000 arrived. Because of overflow, some prisoners camped along the nearby Chemung River.

CAMPS IN THE SOUTH

The largest and most notorious Confederate military prison camp was **Andersonville**, located in Georgia. A creek that flowed through the 16-acre compound provided water for the prisoners, but it quickly became polluted with human waste, making it a perfect breeding ground for contagious diseases. The camp, built for 10,000 men, soon held 33,000 prisoners.

Situated on a 54-acre island in the James River near Richmond, Virginia, Belle Isle prison camp operated from 1862 to 1865, housing more than 30,000 men. In 1864, Surgeon De Witt Peters described the horrific conditions experienced by Union prisoners at Belle Isle.

PRIMARY SOURCE

Laboring under such diseases as chronic diarrhea, . . . scurvy, frost bites, general debility, caused by starvation, neglect, and exposure. Many of [the prisoners] had partially lost their reason. They were filthy in the extreme, covered in vermin. . . . nearly all were extremely emaciated [very thin]; so much so that they had to be cared for even like infants.

—from testimony to the U.S. Sanitary Commission, by De Witt Peters, 1864

Approximately 13,000 of the 45,000 Union prisoners eventually held at Andersonville died because of exposure, starvation, and brutality. Northerners were enraged when they heard about the conditions at the military prison. After the war, Andersonville's commander, Captain **Henry Wirz**, was executed for war crimes.

Overall, between 12 and 16 percent of southern and northern prisoners died in military prison camps during the war. The deplorable prison camp conditions, both in the North and in the South, led to prison reform efforts after the war to build safer, more sanitary, and more humane prisons in the United States.

HISTORICAL THINKING

1. **READING CHECK** What were the general conditions of most Civil War prison camps? Provide evidence to support your answer.

2. **ANALYZE LANGUAGE USE** What words did De Witt Peters use to describe Belle Isle prison camp, and why might he have chosen those words?

3. **ANALYZE CAUSE AND EFFECT** What effect did wartime deaths at prison camps have on the U.S. prison system after the war?

PLAN

Objective

Explain the conditions at prison war camps and their impact on soldiers.

Critical Thinking Skills for Lesson 2.3

• Identify Main Ideas and Details

• Monitor Comprehension

• Analyze Language Use

• Analyze Cause and Effect

• Make Connections

• Summarize

• Analyze Visuals

Essential Question for Chapter 16

How did the United States transform during the Civil War? Horrific conditions in prison camps led to thousands of deaths on both sides of the war and later led to prison reform. Lesson 2.3 examines conditions at several wartime prison camps in the North and South.

Background for the Teacher

Historians estimate that about 56,000 soldiers died in Confederate and Union prison camps during the war. The Union camp at Elmira lost about 25 percent of its prisoners, and approximately 29 percent of the prisoners at Andersonville in Georgia died. The makeshift nature of some camps made matters worse. The South's Belle Isle, built on an island in the James River, lacked permanent shelters. The camp's approximately 300 tents, meant to house 10 men each, were far from adequate to shelter a population that soared to more than double the camp's intended capacity. Most prisoners were forced to build their own shelters out of whatever they could find.

INTRODUCE & ENGAGE

Preview and Predict

Read the lesson title and introduction aloud. **ASK:** Why might imprisonment be worse than death? *(Possible response: It means that being captured and suffering in prison is a terrible fate. One might rather die than be imprisoned.)* Tell students to think about this phrase and then predict what they will learn about the conditions in the Civil War prison camps. Write students' predictions on the board. At the end of the lesson, review the list to see which predictions were correct.

TEACH

Guided Discussion

1. **Make Connections** Why might crowded conditions and an inadequate diet contribute to death by disease? *(Possible response: Overcrowding would lead to unsanitary conditions, which would help spread disease. A poor diet would make people more susceptible to disease, and they would not have the strength to fight off illness.)*

2. **Summarize** Why was Captain Henry Wirz executed? *(Wirz was executed for war crimes committed under his command.)*

Analyze Visuals

Direct students' attention to the photograph of the Elmira prison camp and read the caption aloud. Ask students to describe the details in the photo. Point out the number of tents, the size and shape of the tents, and the hills in the background. **ASK:** Why might tents cause problems for prisoners in a setting like Elmira? *(Possible response: The surrounding hills would likely funnel rainwater into the camp during storms, and the tents would provide little protection. The tents would also offer little defense from cold and snow during the winter.)*

Active Options

On Your Feet: Fishbowl Direct one half of the class to sit in a circle facing inward and the other half to sit in a larger circle around them. Tell students on the inside to discuss conditions in wartime prison camps and contrast them with what they know about conditions in modern prisons. Students in the outer circle listen to the discussion and take notes on the information they hear. Then have the groups reverse positions and repeat the same activity.

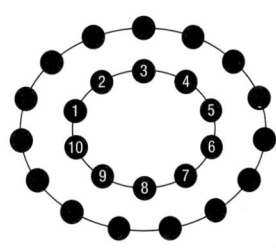

NG Learning Framework: Investigate Diseases

STEM

ATTITUDE Curiosity

KNOWLEDGE Our Human Story

Ask students to research the science behind the diseases and epidemics that caused so many deaths in Civil War prison camps. Organize students into groups and assign each group one of the following conditions: dysentery, scurvy, pneumonia, or smallpox. Have students explore the conditions that cause the diseases as well as the mechanism for transmission. Suggest that students present their findings in the form of a poster or multimedia presentation.

DIFFERENTIATE

English Language Learners ELD

Use Meaning Maps Pair students at the **Emerging** level with students at the **Expanding** or **Bridging** levels. Have them use a Meaning Map for three words they are struggling with in the lesson. Direct pairs to trade Meaning Maps and review.

Gifted & Talented

Research Prison Camps Tell students to conduct a short research project to answer questions about prison camps used during other wars in history. Ask students to generate an initial research question based on information in the lesson. To provide multiple avenues of exploration, encourage students to draw on several sources to generate additional related, focused questions until they develop a specific question to research. Have students research their questions and share their findings with the class.

See the Chapter Planner for more strategies for differentiation.

HISTORICAL THINKING

ANSWERS

1. Prison camps on both sides were crowded and unsanitary with little medical care. Low rations led to malnutrition and scurvy, and polluted water sources spread infectious diseases.

2. De Witt Peters described the prisoners at Belle Isle as "filthy in the extreme, covered with vermin" and having to be "cared for like infants." He might have chosen these words to create vivid images in his testimony and provoke a strong response from the commission.

3. The extremely high number of wartime deaths at camps led to reforms that made prisons safer and more humane.

CRITICAL VIEWING Answers will vary. Possible response: Living conditions were clearly cramped, but the photo, taken from a distance and revealing few details, shows the tents, buildings, and standing prisoners to be deceptively neat and orderly.

3.1 Battles of Vicksburg and Gettysburg

Sometimes you can recall the exact moment when things suddenly change and get either much better or much worse. For Civil War generals, two battles in particular dramatically shifted the war's direction.

MAIN IDEA The battles of Vicksburg and Gettysburg were the key turning points in the Union's eventual victory in the Civil War.

SPLITTING THE CONFEDERACY

In the first months of 1863, the war was not going well for Union generals. In January, after a disastrous defeat at Fredericksburg, Lincoln replaced General **Ambrose Burnside** with General **Joseph Hooker** as commander of the Army of the Potomac. Then in May, Lee's army defeated Hooker's forces near **Chancellorsville**, Virginia. Hooker resigned after the loss and was replaced by General **George Meade**. Lee lost his own most capable commander when Stonewall Jackson was accidentally shot by one of his own soldiers. However, Lee's victory at Chancellorsville is widely considered his greatest of the entire war.

The battle that ensued further south, in Vicksburg, Mississippi, began to change the course of the war for the Union. By 1863, Vicksburg had been a Confederate stronghold for more than a year. Its position allowed the Confederacy to control a wide part of the region from **bluffs**, or cliffs, 200 feet above the Mississippi River. Capturing the city and silencing Confederate guns became a strategic necessity for the Union.

During the early spring of 1863, Union forces commanded by General Grant tried to find a way to take the city from their vantage point on the western bank of the river. But Confederate troops commanded by General **John C. Pemberton** turned them back. Then in early May, Admiral **David Porter**, under Grant's orders, ran a **flotilla**, or small fleet, of gunboats and barges past

Confederate forces at Vicksburg under cover of night. Porter used these vessels to ferry Grant's troops across the river south of the city.

From there, Grant's troops marched northeastward before doubling back toward Vicksburg and cutting the city off from the east. In only three weeks, Grant's men marched 180 miles, won 5 battles, and captured 6,000 prisoners. Vicksburg was now surrounded and under siege. Food ran out and the residents began to starve. Pemberton surrendered on July 4, 1863. The Union victory at the **Battle of Vicksburg** gave the Union control of the Mississippi Valley and split the Confederacy in half. It also convinced President Lincoln of Grant's outstanding military ability.

THE TIDE TURNS AT GETTYSBURG

Despite his victory at Chancellorsville, Lee realized that the North's manpower advantage might be wearing down Confederate troops and that a victory on the attack would boost Confederate morale. He decided that his most effective move was to invade the North again. In late June 1863, Lee's troops advanced into Pennsylvania, where they met Meade's troops at the **Battle of Gettysburg**. At first, Lee succeeded in sending the Union troops into retreat. Then, on July 1, reinforcements arrived for both sides, bringing troop numbers to approximately 90,000 for the Union and about 75,000 for the Confederates. Union forces stopped retreating and stationed themselves on **Cemetery Hill**, where the high vantage point gave them a defensive edge.

CRITICAL VIEWING Photography played a new and important role in the Civil War. This iconic photo, captured by Timothy O'Sullivan in July 1863, shows about 20 of the more than 3,100 fallen Union soldiers after the Battle of Gettysburg. What effect do you think this photo might have had on Americans who saw it in 1863?

On Friday, July 3, hoping to outflank Union forces on Cemetery Hill, Lee ordered Major General **George Pickett** and about 15,000 of his men to attack the Union troops on a plain just below the hill. Lee's strategy proved disastrous. The Union repelled Pickett's charge, killing or wounding more than half of Pickett's troops. The next day, Lee retreated, eventually crossing the Potomac River to Virginia. This retreat marked a turning point in the war. It put the Confederacy on the defensive and the Union in a favorable position for victory.

On November 19, 1863, President Lincoln delivered the **Gettysburg Address** at the battle site to commemorate the loss of so many men and to dedicate a military cemetery there. Throughout his speech, Lincoln referred to the Declaration of Independence directly and to its ideas. His address reinforced the Declaration's principles of equality and freedom for which the war was fought and for which so many died, and were still dying.

HISTORICAL THINKING

1. **READING CHECK** How did the battles of Vicksburg and Gettysburg affect the Civil War?

2. **IDENTIFY PROBLEMS AND SOLUTIONS** What challenges did Grant and his troops face, and how were they eventually able to capture the city of Vicksburg?

3. **EVALUATE** How did the Union's position on Cemetery Hill contribute to its victory at Gettysburg?

PLAN

Objective

Learn why the battles of Vicksburg and Gettysburg were key turning points in the war.

Critical Thinking Skills for Lesson 3.1

- Identify Main Ideas and Details
- Monitor Comprehension
- Identify Problems and Solutions
- Evaluate
- Summarize

Essential Question for Chapter 16

How did the United States transform during the Civil War? Following victories at Vicksburg and Gettysburg, President Lincoln used the Gettysburg Address to reaffirm principles of freedom and equality expressed in the Declaration of Independence. Lesson 3.1 discusses the battles of Vicksburg and Gettysburg and their significance.

Background for the Teacher

Pennsylvania had purchased 17 acres for the Gettysburg cemetery and hired a specialist to lay out burial plots so that no state would be offended by the amount of space devoted to its fallen men. Since October 27, burial crews had been moving the bodies of Union dead, initially buried where they died by comrades or townspeople or buried side by side on farms. Only about a third of the reburials had taken place when Lincoln arrived, and caskets remained stacked at the station. When he spoke at the dedication of the cemetery, Lincoln saw it as a chance to impart a sense of purpose to the Union cause. In his speech, Lincoln attempted to shift the purpose of the war from union for union's sake to union for freedom's sake, calling for a "new birth of freedom," and speaking of equality as the fundamental purpose of the war.

History Notebook

Encourage students to complete the Reid on the Road video series page for Chapter 16 in their History Notebooks after they view the video.

Think About Geography

Explain that the Confederate stronghold of Vicksburg sat on a bluff 200 feet above the Mississippi River, while the small town of Gettysburg was located in the hilly farmland of south central Pennsylvania, a landscape dotted with open fields, orchards, woods, granite boulders, and ridges. Tell students to think about the geographic features of these two different terrains and discuss advantages and obstacles presented by each. Ask students to keep their discussion ideas in mind as they read about the battles of Vicksburg and Gettysburg.

TEACH

Guided Discussion

1. **Summarize** What changes in military leadership occurred in the first months of 1863, and why? *(Lincoln replaced General Ambrose Burnside with General Joseph Hooker after the Union defeat at Fredericksburg. Hooker resigned after the Union loss at Chancellorsville and was replaced by General George Meade. The Confederacy lost General Stonewall Jackson after he was accidentally shot by one of his own soldiers.)*

2. **Identify Problems and Solutions** Why did General Lee decide to invade the North in 1863? *(Lee worried that the North's superior number of troops was wearing down his men, so he decided to engage in battle and win while on the attack to encourage them.)*

More Information

Mathew Brady The Civil War was the first American war to be documented by photography. Mathew Brady, who was already one of the most respected photographers in the country, organized teams of photographers to follow the Union troops, recording the daily lives of the soldiers as well as the horrors of the battlefields. Timothy O'Sullivan apprenticed with Mathew Brady but left his service after a dispute over crediting photographs. He then teamed up with Alexander Gardner, another former Brady apprentice. Gardner included the O'Sullivan photograph used in this lesson in his *Photographic Sketch Book of the War,* published in 1866. He titled the photograph *A Harvest of Death.* **ASK:** Why do you think Gardner chose this title? *(Possible response: Many deaths resulted from the battle, and, similar to a harvest, the bodies are lying on the ground waiting to be removed. Gardner used* harvest *ironically, suggesting that years of war resulted in bodies rather than the fruits of labor.)*

Active Options

Active History: Solve a Puzzle Extend the lesson by using either the PDF or Whiteboard version of the activity. These activities take a deeper look at a topic from, or related to, the lesson. Explore the activities as a class, turn them into group assignments, or even assign them individually.

NG Learning Framework: Write a Biography of a General

ATTITUDE Curiosity

KNOWLEDGE Our Human Story

Invite students to learn more about one of the generals discussed in the lesson. Instruct them to write a short biography or profile about the general using information from the chapter and additional source material. Encourage students to find out more about the general's role in the Civil War, other battles in which he may have fought, and his viewpoints on the war. Suggest that students use quotes and visuals in their biographies. Have students share their completed biographies with the class.

DIFFERENTIATE

Striving Readers

Describe Key Words and Phrases Have students read the lesson in pairs. As they read, instruct them to record notes about each name or phrase below. Then ask them to reread and add notes as their understanding increases.

What	When	What Happened
Vicksburg		
Gettysburg		
Gettysburg Address		

Pre-AP

Compare Documents Encourage students to compare Abraham Lincoln's Gettysburg Address with the Declaration of Independence to determine similar themes. Ask students to use their comparisons to write a brief essay about what Lincoln's references to the Declaration of Independence indicate about his view of the ultimate purpose of the Civil War. Invite students to share their essays with the class.

See the Chapter Planner for more strategies for differentiation.

HISTORICAL THINKING

ANSWERS

1. The battles signaled a turning point in the war that favored the Union. Vicksburg gave the Union control of the Mississippi River and split the Confederacy in half. Gettysburg put the Confederacy on the defensive.

2. Under Grant's orders, Admiral David Porter ferried Union troops across the Mississippi River south of the city during the night. Grant's troops then doubled back toward Vicksburg and cut it off from the east.

3. The Union forces had the high ground on Cemetery Hill and defended their position, driving back Confederate forces.

CRITICAL VIEWING Answers will vary. Possible response: The photograph probably shocked Americans who saw it and brought home the reality of bodies strewn on a battlefield and the high death toll.

3.2 Sherman's March and Grant's Victory

Can you think of someone you know who, when challenged by what looks like impossible odds, simply refuses to give up? Historians attribute this kind of persistence to General Grant, especially in the last year of the Civil War.

MAIN IDEA Grant and his generals brought the full power of the Union Army down on the South in their campaign to capture the Confederate capital.

AMERICAN PLACES
Savannah Historic District
Savannah, Georgia

The Savannah Historic District is a National Historic Landmark. James Oglethorpe founded the city in 1733 when Georgia was a British colony. Savannah's distinctive 18th- and 19th-century architecture is reflected in its numerous historic homes, gardens, and monuments. General Sherman used the Greene-Meldrim House, shown here, as a base of operations between 1864 and 1865. The house was built in 1853 in the Gothic Revival architectural style.

MARCHING THROUGH GEORGIA

In March 1864, President Lincoln named Ulysses S. Grant, the victor of Vicksburg, as commanding general of the Union Army. Grant immediately put a plan in place to wear down the Confederacy with a series of widespread and relentless attacks. Following a Union victory at Chattanooga, Tennessee, in 1864, Grant sent General William T. Sherman to deliver destruction to the heart of the Confederacy—Atlanta, Georgia, which Sherman captured in September 1864. This was an important feat because Atlanta was a railroad hub and the industrial center of the Confederacy.

The city was also a symbol of Confederate pride and strength. Its fall made even the most loyal southerners doubt that they could win the war. "Since Atlanta," South Carolinian Mary Chesnut wrote in her diary, "I have felt as if . . . we are going to be wiped off the earth."

From Atlanta, Sherman marched 62,000 Union troops through Georgia to Savannah, located on the Atlantic shore. His goal was to destroy southern property, crops, and other supplies. Early in 1865, Sherman and his men left Savannah, burning their way northward to Columbia, South Carolina. From there, they marched into North Carolina, battling Confederate troops before destroying the Fayetteville arsenal. In Bentonville, the Confederacy challenged Sherman for three days, but his troops gained the upper hand.

A **total war** is one in which all rules and laws of war are ignored and all resources are poured into defeating the enemy no matter what the cost. Sherman waged total war against the Confederacy, and his strategy was brutal and destructive. But it did what it was meant to do. It was a blow to southern morale and fighting

capacity. It led to a feeling in the North that the Union was winning the war and so helped with President Lincoln's reelection in November 1864.

Sherman and his troops spared the city of Savannah instead of burning it as they did Atlanta. Why? There are a number of theories, some more plausible than others. One is that Sherman found Savannah too beautiful to burn. Another is that he was lenient because city leaders surrendered before he could enter the city, agreeing they would not put up a fight if he spared life and property. Perhaps the strongest theory is that Savannah had a large port that could prove very useful to the Union.

GRANT FACES LEE

General Grant was pleased with Sherman's success in the South, and he became even more determined to capture Richmond, Virginia, the Confederate capital. The first large battle of Grant's campaign was the **Battle of the Wilderness**, fought in a heavily wooded area west of Fredericksburg and north of Richmond. The armies engaged in battle for two days with heavy casualties, especially on the Union side. Grant refused to retreat. Instead, he moved his army farther south. Lee followed him. On May 8, 1864, Grant attacked Lee's troops near **Spotsylvania**, beginning a battle that raged for 12 days. The Union's Army of the Potomac lost 18,000 men at the Battle of Spotsylvania; the Confederates lost

12,000. In less than three weeks, Grant had lost 33,000 men. On May 31, Lee and Grant collided again at **Cold Harbor**, where Grant's forces were defeated with heavy losses. The Union lost about 13,000 troops; the Confederates lost only 2,500 or fewer.

In 1865, Grant's forces broke through the last line of Richmond's defenses, and the city fell on April 3. Confederate troops and government officials fled Richmond, setting fire to parts of the city as they left to prevent Union troops from using it for shelter and supplies. The Union took control of what was left of the city. The Confederate capital was captured. President Lincoln traveled to Richmond a few days later to see the evidence of this significant Union victory for himself.

HISTORICAL THINKING

1. **READING CHECK** What was Grant's strategy in the South?

2. **ANALYZE LANGUAGE USE** Mary Chesnut used a figurative expression to describe how she felt about the fall of Atlanta. How did she articulate how she felt about the war? Use evidence from the text to support your answer.

3. **MAKE PREDICTIONS** What effect could you predict the Union capture of Richmond would have on the Civil War's outcome?

Sherman's March, 1864–1865

[Map showing Sherman's March through the southeastern United States with labels: VIRGINIA, TENNESSEE, NORTH CAROLINA, SOUTH CAROLINA, ALABAMA, GEORGIA, FLORIDA, Chattanooga, Dalton, Atlanta Sept. 2, 1864, Columbia Feb. 17, 1865, Charleston, Savannah Dec. 21, 1864, Fayetteville, Bentonville March 19, 1865, Sherman enters Raleigh, Apr. 13, 1865, Wilmington, ATLANTIC OCEAN, Gulf of Mexico. Scale: 0 50 100 Miles / 0 50 100 Kilometers. Legend: Union state, Confederate state, Union victory, Union advance, Confederate advance, Confederate retreat]

PLAN

Objective

Analyze the strategies generals Grant and Sherman used to achieve victory in the South.

Critical Thinking Skills for Lesson 3.2

- Identify Main Ideas and Details
- Monitor Comprehension
- Analyze Language Use
- Make Predictions
- Interpret Maps
- Draw Conclusions

Essential Question for Chapter 16

How did the United States transform during the Civil War? The Union Army swept through the South, eventually taking the Confederate capital of Richmond. Lesson 3.2 describes the relentless line of attack by the Union to capture the capital and the consequences.

Background for the Teacher

General William T. Sherman set out across Georgia on his march from Atlanta to Savannah a week after Lincoln's 1864 reelection. His goal was twofold—to conquer Confederate territory and to send a clear message. "If we can march a well-appointed army right through [Confederate] territory," Sherman explained, "it is a demonstration to the world, foreign and domestic, that we have a power which Davis cannot resist."

In the wake of Sherman's path to Savannah during the fall of 1864, large numbers of Union and Confederate deserters, fugitive slaves, and outlaws took advantage of the situation, causing widespread destruction and panic. When Sherman's forces finally reached the city on December 21, the victorious general sent Lincoln a buoyant telegraph: "I beg to present to you, as a Christmas gift, the city of Savannah."

Preview Using Maps
Direct students' attention to the map of Sherman's march. Point out Atlanta and Savannah. **ASK:** What actions did the two armies take before Sherman began his march from Atlanta to Savannah? *(Both armies advanced from Chattanooga, Tennessee, to Atlanta. Confederate forces retreated from Atlanta as Sherman advanced south.)* Tell students that they will read about Sherman's march and Grant's victories.

TEACH
Guided Discussion
1. **Interpret Maps** According to the map of Sherman's march, what did the Confederate forces do after Sherman took Savannah? *(The Confederate forces retreated to Charleston, South Carolina. From there, they continued their retreat northward through North Carolina, passing through Fayetteville and Bentonville until they reached Raleigh.)*

2. **Draw Conclusions** What conclusions can you draw about Grant's effectiveness as a general? *(Answers will vary. Possible response: Grant was effective because he would not retreat, even in defeat. His campaigns were successful because he was willing to sacrifice tens of thousands of lives to achieve victory.)*

American Places
In addition to its Georgian, Greek Revival, and Gothic architecture, the Savannah Historic District is noted for its grid pattern of public squares. Founder James Oglethorpe originally laid out 24 public squares, and all but two remain. The Green-Meldrim House is located on the west side of Madison Square. The elaborate and spacious house was built in the 1850s by Charles Green, a British immigrant who made his fortune in cotton and shipping. As the Union Army advanced on the city, Green offered his home to General Sherman as a headquarters in hopes of saving it and his cotton from destruction. Sherman accepted, and it was in the Green-Meldrim House that Sherman composed his telegram presenting Savannah to Lincoln.

Active Options
On Your Feet: Team Word Webbing Organize students into teams of four and instruct them to record on a piece of paper what they know about Grant facing off against Lee in the South. Encourage students to build on their teammates' entries as they rotate the paper from one member to the next. Then call on volunteers from each team to read statements about the face-off from their team's web.

NG Learning Framework: Investigate Consequences of Total War on Civilians
ATTITUDE Responsibility
KNOWLEDGE Our Human Story

Tell students that Sherman's march was a success for the Union, but it had dire consequences for many civilians in the South. Ask students to conduct online research, making sure to use credible primary and secondary sources, to learn about the effects of Sherman's campaign on the people in his path. Then have students use their findings to describe the consequences civilians experienced during and after Sherman's march.

DIFFERENTIATE
Inclusion
Mark Up Maps Provide a printout of the map of Sherman's march. Direct students to circle the names of Confederate cities and states in which battles occurred. Work with students to ensure they understand the items listed on the legend and how to locate each on the map. Provide sentence frames for students to complete based on the map.

• Sherman started his advance in _____.
• Cities where Sherman's forces won battles were _____.
• The Confederates retreated from _____.
• Sherman reached Savannah on _____.

Gifted & Talented
Create a Social-Networking Profile Have students use credible online resources to research Ulysses S. Grant's military strategies and operational views once he became commander of the Union Army. Encourage students to find quotes by Grant and secondary sources that express his views. Instruct students to use their research to create a social-networking profile for the general. Invite them to share their profiles with the class.

See the Chapter Planner for more strategies for differentiation.

HISTORICAL THINKING
ANSWERS
1. Grant planned to wear down the South with constant attacks, using all his resources to capture Richmond, the Confederate capital.

2. Mary Chesnut expressed her feelings of devastation by stating, "We are going to be wiped off the earth." By writing her feelings in her diary, Chesnut preserved her thoughts about the destruction she witnessed.

3. The Union's capture of Richmond, the Confederate capital, would likely lead to a Union victory in the Civil War.

3.3 Lincoln's Vision

Politicians and public officials use speeches to express their views on public policy. During his political career, Abraham Lincoln delivered a number of speeches, several of which became some of the most formative speeches in U.S. history.

For nearly 100 years, historians believed that no photos existed of Lincoln delivering the Gettysburg Address. But in 1952, National Archives employee Josephine Cobb was examining a crowd shot taken by photographer Mathew Brady at Gettysburg on November 19, 1863. She had the photo enlarged and examined where she thought Lincoln might have been standing in that crowd. And right there, in the middle of the crowd, she identified the out-of-focus—but unmistakable image—of Abraham Lincoln delivering the Gettysburg Address. You can see this rare photo below.

Lincoln was not known as a speaker gifted with a captivating voice or dramatic delivery. Rather, the force

of his speeches came from the words themselves. For example, the Gettysburg Address is just 272 words long, and it took only around three minutes for Lincoln to deliver it. But in this succinct address, Lincoln reminded Americans of the foundation on which the United States was built and on which it still rested. Quite intentionally, he framed his words around the principles of liberty and equality as set forth in the Declaration of Independence.

CRITICAL VIEWING Locate Abraham Lincoln in the photograph below. What do you notice about Lincoln's position in the crowd and how it differs from the ways in which the president is protected in public today?

DOCUMENT ONE

Primary Source: Speech
The Gettysburg Address, by Abraham Lincoln, November 19, 1863

As president, Lincoln used the opportunity of a battle site dedication to appeal to his fellow citizens to take up "unfinished work" of those who had died. He begins by situating his words in time by using the phrase "fourscore and seven" as a way of expressing the number 87. The word *score* means 20, so *fourscore* equals 80. By referring to 87 years ago, Lincoln asks his listeners to remember the American Revolution and the nation's founding principles of liberty and equality.

CONSTRUCTED RESPONSES

What did Lincoln mean by "testing whether that nation or any nation so conceived and so dedicated can long endure"?

What action did Lincoln propose as the best way to honor those who had died at Gettysburg?

Fourscore and seven years ago our fathers brought forth on this continent a new nation, conceived in liberty and dedicated to the proposition that all men are created equal.

Now we are engaged in a great civil war, testing whether that nation or any nation so conceived and so dedicated can long endure. We are met on a great battlefield of that war. We have come to dedicate a portion of that field as a final resting-place for those who here gave their lives that that nation might live. It is altogether fitting and proper that we should do this.

But in a larger sense, we cannot dedicate, we cannot consecrate, we cannot hallow this ground. The brave men, living and dead who struggled here have consecrated it far above our poor power to add or detract. The world will little note nor long remember what we say here, but it can never forget what they did here.

It is for us the living rather to be dedicated here to the unfinished work which they who fought here have thus far so nobly advanced. It is rather for us to be here dedicated to the great task remaining before us—that from these honored dead we take increased devotion to that cause for which they gave the last full measure of devotion—that we here highly resolve that these dead shall not have died in vain, that this nation under God shall have a new birth of freedom, and that government of the people, by the people, for the people shall not perish from the earth.

DOCUMENT TWO

Primary Source: Speech
from Second Inaugural Address, by Abraham Lincoln, March 4, 1865

When Lincoln delivered this speech in March 1865, the North was close to victory. Lincoln did not speak of happiness, nor did he gloat about the South's impending defeat. Instead, he spoke about his sadness over the loss of life during the war. Just over a month later, the president who had saved the Union would be assassinated.

CONSTRUCTED RESPONSE What was Lincoln referring to when he called on Americans "to bind up the nation's wounds"?

With malice toward none, with charity for all, with firmness in the right as God gives us to see the right, let us strive on to finish the work we are in, to bind up the nation's wounds, to care for him who shall have borne the battle and for his widow and his orphan, to do all which may achieve and cherish a just and lasting peace among ourselves and with all nations.

SYNTHESIZE & WRITE

1. **REVIEW** Review what you have learned about the events leading up to Lincoln's address at Gettysburg and his Second Inaugural Address.

2. **RECALL** On your own paper, write the main themes that emerge from the Gettysburg Address and this excerpt from Lincoln's Second Inaugural Address.

3. **CONSTRUCT** Construct a topic sentence that answers this question: What was President Lincoln's vision for the United States after the Civil War, and how did he try to persuade Americans to support that vision?

4. **WRITE** Using evidence from this chapter and the documents, write a persuasive paragraph that supports your topic sentence in Step 3.

PLAN

Objective

Synthesize information about Lincoln's vision for the nation from primary source documents.

Critical Thinking Skills for Lesson 3.3

- Synthesize
- Identify
- Analyze Language Use
- Evaluate

Essential Question for Chapter 16

How did the United States transform during the Civil War? The United States broke apart during the Civil War. As the war came to a close, the challenge was how to put the country back together. Lesson 3.3 looks at President Lincoln's vision for the nation as expressed in the Gettysburg Address and his Second Inaugural Address.

Background for the Teacher

Abraham Lincoln was not the only speaker at the Gettysburg Cemetery dedication on November 19, 1863. The first speaker was Edward Everett, a famed orator who spoke for two hours. Afterward, in a letter congratulating Lincoln on his speech, Everett expressed the hope that he had done in two hours what Lincoln had managed to do in three minutes—sum up the central idea of the day.

Lincoln made at least five handwritten copies of the Gettysburg Address, and the phrasing in each is slightly different. He gave the first two copies to his personal secretaries, John Nicolay and John Hay, and the copies are now housed at the Library of Congress. The president produced the other three copies for charitable events to raise money for Union causes. The last of the charitable copies— often called the Bliss copy because it was made for Alexander Bliss—is on display at the White House.

Prepare for the Document-Based Question

Before students start on the activity, briefly preview the two documents. Remind students that a constructed response requires full explanations in complete sentences. Emphasize that students should use what they have learned about the Civil War and Lincoln's view about it in addition to the information in the documents.

TEACH

Guided Discussion

1. **Identify** According to Lincoln in his Gettysburg Address, what will be the outcome for the nation if the Union continues the work of the fallen soldiers? *(The nation will have a rebirth of freedom and the democratic government will survive.)*

2. **Analyze Language Use** In his Second Inaugural Address, what does Lincoln mean when he says, "with firmness in the right as God gives us to see the right"? *(Answers will vary. Possible response: Lincoln is suggesting that the war is just and that he believes it is part of God's plan, but only God knows if that is true.)*

Evaluate

After students have completed the Synthesize & Write activity, allow time for them to exchange paragraphs and read and comment on the work of their peers. Establish guidelines for comments prior to this activity so that feedback is constructive and encouraging in nature.

Active Options

On Your Feet: Host a DBQ Roundtable Divide the class into groups of four. Arrange desks to form a table where all group members can sit. Hand each group a sheet of paper with the following question: What specific language in the two speeches indicates how Lincoln hopes to mend the nation? The first student in each group should write an answer, read it aloud, and pass the paper clockwise to the next student. The paper should circulate around the table several times. Reconvene as a class and discuss groups' responses.

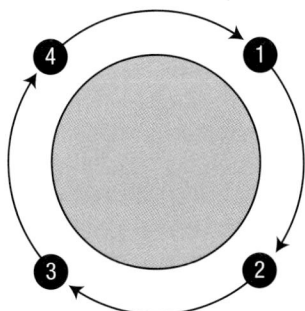

DIFFERENTIATE

Striving Readers

Provide Sentence Frames Provide students with these sentence frames to help them understand Lincoln's main points.

- **Document 1** The war is testing whether a nation founded on _____ *(liberty)* and _____ *(equality)* can endure.

- **Document 2** Lincoln wants people to _____ *(mend)* the nation's wounds by _____ *(helping each other)* and not having _____ *(bad feelings)* toward anyone.

Pre-AP

Chart the Progression of Lincoln's Views Tell students to use Lincoln's First Inaugural Address, Emancipation Proclamation, Gettysburg Address, and Second Inaugural Address to chart the changing meaning of the war over the course of Lincoln's presidency. Instruct students to read each document and create a succinct summary of Lincoln's points of view. Then ask students to use the summaries to create a flowchart showing the evolution in Lincoln's thoughts. Encourage students to use their charts to hold a class discussion on the following question: How and why did the Civil War become a war to end slavery?

See the Chapter Planner for more strategies for differentiation.

SYNTHESIZE & WRITE

ANSWERS

1. Answers will vary.

2. Answers will vary.

3. Answers will vary. Possible response: Lincoln envisioned a fair and lasting peace for the United States if people were willing to reunite without seeking retribution for the Civil War.

4. Answers will vary. Students' paragraphs should include their topic sentence from Step 3 and provide several details from the chapter and the documents to support the sentence.

CONSTRUCTED RESPONSE

Document 1: Possible response: Part 1: Lincoln meant that the war was testing the idea that a democracy is based on liberty and equality. Part 2: Lincoln suggested that the best way to honor the dead was for the living to carry on and win the war and reunite the nation.

Document 2: Possible response: Lincoln didn't want people to seek retribution for the causes or losses of the war. Instead, they were to work together to heal and reunite the country. He was suggesting an attitude of compassion rather than hostility.

CRITICAL VIEWING Lincoln is seated with the crowd surrounding and turned toward him. Present-day presidents would not give a speech from the middle of a crowd, where a Secret Service detail couldn't provide protection.

3.4 Appomattox

Forgiving a sibling or a friend after a fight is hard to do. Generals Grant and Lee had a difficult task in front of them when they met to end the war. Grant wondered: Was it better to forgive former enemies, or punish them further?

MAIN IDEA The Civil War ended with the surrender of the Confederacy at a simple ceremony in Virginia.

SURRENDER AT LAST

By the beginning of 1865, war had nearly completely devastated the South. Sherman continued to march through the Carolinas, burning homes, barns, and crops. Knowing the end was near, Confederate president Jefferson Davis sent his vice president, **Alexander Stephens**, to meet with Lincoln on February 3, 1865. His goal was to negotiate peace and bring the war to an end. Not interested in negotiating, Lincoln demanded that the Confederacy surrender completely. Stephens refused, and the war continued.

Meanwhile, General Lee finally had to abandon his defense of Richmond after the Confederate government fled and Union troops marched in to take over the city. But Lee still had hopes of turning the situation around. He tried to move his forces south in order to join other Confederate forces in North Carolina. Lee's army never reached that goal. Union cavalry surrounded Lee and his troops near the Virginia town of **Appomattox Court House**, halting his progress. Following a brief battle, Lee agreed to surrender.

On April 9, 1865, Lee met Grant in the front room of Wilmer McLean's home in Appomattox Court House. Grant arrived in his muddy field uniform, while Lee wore his full dress uniform. Lee accepted Grant's terms of surrender. All Confederate officers and soldiers were pardoned. They could keep their private property, including their horses, which they would need for spring planting. Confederate officers were also allowed to keep their side arms. Grant made sure that Lee's men, many of whom were starving, would receive Union rations. Grant told his officers: "The war is over. The Rebels are our countrymen again."

The Confederacy had fought with courage and endured almost unimaginable hardships. But courage was not enough to defeat the resources and manpower of the far more powerful industrial North. The Union prevailed.

COSTS OF THE WAR

In dollars and cents, the Union spent more than $3 billion on the war; the Confederacy spent about $1 billion. But these amounts of money for military expenditures barely compared to the massive loss of life. Roughly 620,000 men had died: 360,000 Union soldiers and 260,000 Confederate soldiers, the most American lives lost in any conflict to date.

Two out of every three deaths occurred not from battle, but from disease. The most common diseases in army camps were typhoid fever, smallpox, measles, diarrhea, pneumonia, malaria, and tuberculosis. Army surgeons relieved the pain of sick and wounded soldiers by prescribing millions of doses of a highly addictive medication called **morphine**. Morphine worked well to ease wounded soldiers' pain, but many Civil War **veterans**, or people who had served in the military, became addicted to it.

The war had direct economic consequences for American families. The loss of fathers or sons often meant the loss of family breadwinners. Countless wounded veterans were unable to work, and families fell into poverty. Many homes, farms, and businesses, particularly in the South, had been destroyed. Lives, careers, and communities had to be rebuilt.

Even after financial costs were recovered, the emotional toll of such intense loss persisted for generations. The war itself became the subject or backdrop for art and literature. In 1862, Louisa May Alcott served as a nurse in Washington, D.C., during the war. She was sent home when she contracted a serious disease called typhoid from the unsanitary conditions in the hospital. In 1863, Alcott published *Hospital Sketches*, a collection of stories crafted from her letters home about her hospital experiences. Thirty-two years later Stephen Crane published *The Red Badge of Courage*, a novel based on the life of Private Henry Fleming. Crane was not yet born when the war broke out, but his novel captured the horrific details of battlefield experiences nonetheless. That Crane's novel still resonated with American readers three decades after the war ended speaks to the profound effect the Civil War had on the country.

CRITICAL VIEWING To commemorate the centennial anniversary of the end of the Civil War, the National Geographic Society commissioned Tom Lovell to paint *Surrender at Appomattox*. Lee, dressed in gray, signs the surrender terms while Grant and his officers look on. Their meeting was somber, but friendly. Upon signing, Lee is reported to have said, "This will have a very happy effect on my army." Based on details you notice in the painting, how did Grant treat Lee during the signing?

HISTORICAL THINKING

1. **READING CHECK** What were the terms of surrender that Grant delivered to Lee?

2. **ANALYZE LANGUAGE USE** What do you think Grant was saying about what it means to be an American when he stated, "The war is over. The Rebels are our countrymen again"?

3. **FORM AND SUPPORT OPINIONS** Explain whether you think the financial losses or personal losses of the war were greater, and support your opinion with information from the text.

PLAN

Objective
Learn how the Civil War ended and describe the war's human and financial costs.

Critical Thinking Skills for Lesson 3.4
- Identify Main Ideas and Details
- Monitor Comprehension
- Analyze Language Use
- Form and Support Opinions
- Analyze Cause and Effect
- Make Connections
- Analyze Visuals

Essential Question for Chapter 16
How did the United States transform during the Civil War? The Civil War exacted a heavy financial, physical, and emotional toll on Americans, and for some it lasted for decades. Lesson 3.4 describes Lee's surrender at Appomattox and the lasting effects of the war on the United States.

Background for the Teacher
The Civil War did not immediately end with Lee's surrender at Appomattox. Lee only surrendered the Army of Northern Virginia, and only the troops at Appomattox were immediately pardoned. The War Department then extended the terms of surrender to the troops in the Army of Northern Virginia who were still in the field, hoping they would voluntarily surrender. Those who failed to surrender would not be pardoned and would be treated as prisoners of war if captured. General Joseph E. Johnston continued fighting in North Carolina until April 26, when he surrendered his Army of Tennessee and other forces under his command to General Sherman. The remaining Confederate generals east of the Mississippi surrendered their commands in May, and the last of the Confederate forces west of the Mississippi River surrendered in June.

History Notebook
Encourage students to complete the American Gallery page for Chapter 16 in their History Notebooks as they read.

INTRODUCE & ENGAGE

Preview Using Visuals

Direct students' attention to the painting of Lee's surrender at Appomattox. Have a volunteer read the caption. **ASK:** What do you think Lee meant when he said, "This will have a very happy effect on my army"? *(Answers will vary. Possible response: Lee knew that his troops were tired of fighting and that victory was no longer a possibility. He was suggesting that his troops would be happy to have the war over and to go home.)* Tell students they will read about the conditions of Lee's surrender.

TEACH

Guided Discussion

1. **Analyze Cause and Effect** What were the main causes of death among Union and Confederate soldiers? *(Diseases, not battle, accounted for two-thirds of all deaths, including typhoid fever, smallpox, and measles.)*

2. **Make Connections** What literary evidence shows that the Civil War has had a lasting impact on Americans? *(During the war, Louisa May Alcott published* Hospital Sketches, *a collection of stories based on her experiences as a Civil War nurse in Washington, D.C. Decades later, Stephen Crane published the novel* The Red Badge of Courage, *which recounts the battlefield experiences of a young Union soldier.)*

Analyze Visuals

Direct students' attention to the painting by Tom Lovell. **ASK:** What do you notice about the uniforms worn by Lee and the Confederate officer versus those worn by Grant and the other Union officers? *(The Confederates are dressed in clean, pressed uniforms, while the Union officers, including Grant, are in dirty, rumpled battlefield uniforms.)* **ASK:** What conclusion can you draw from this difference? *(Answers will vary. Possible response: Having been captured by the Union Army, Lee would not have been leading troops immediately prior to signing and had time to make himself presentable. In surrender, Lee may have wanted, or been allowed, to present himself in a dignified manner.)*

Active Options

 Battlefield Medicine Invite students to explore the American Gallery. Have them select one of the images and do additional research to learn more about it. Ask questions that will inspire additional inquiry about the chosen gallery image, such as: What details do you see? What purpose do the objects in the photo serve? What is the physical setting? What is happening? How would the photo be different if it were taken today?

NG Learning Framework: Investigate Medical Technology

ATTITUDE Curiosity

KNOWLEDGE New Frontiers

Tell students to research the science and technology behind battlefield medicine during the Civil War and to consider how the challenges of treating the wounded and sick helped advance medicine into the modern age. Then direct students to write a report about a medical technology that developed from the treatment of Civil War soldiers. Instruct students to gather relevant information from multiple print and online primary and secondary sources, using search terms effectively. Remind students to assess the credibility and accuracy of each source, to quote or paraphrase the data and conclusions of others without plagiarizing, and to follow a standard format for citation. Invite students to share their reports.

DIFFERENTIATE

Inclusion

Describe Details Pair students who are visually impaired with students who are not. Ask the latter to describe the details in Lovell's painting of Lee's surrender at Appomattox. Then have pairs work together to answer the Critical Viewing question.

English Language Learners

Use Sentence Strips Choose a paragraph from the lesson and make sentence strips out of it. Read the paragraph aloud, having students at the **Emerging** level follow along in their books. Have students close their books and give them the set of sentence strips. Instruct students to put the strips in order and then read the paragraph aloud.

See the Chapter Planner for more strategies for differentiation.

HISTORICAL THINKING

ANSWERS

1. All Confederate officers and soldiers were pardoned. They could keep their private property and their horses. Officers could keep their small weapons, and Lee's starving soldiers were provided with food.

2. Possible response: Grant was saying that Confederates were once again American citizens and should be treated with fairness and equality.

3. Possible responses: The greatest losses were financial because, in addition to the billions of dollars spent executing the war, many homes, businesses, and farms were destroyed, with families losing their primary breadwinners. The greatest losses were personal. While financial losses could be recovered, the loss of life, effects of soldiers' injuries, and sense of personal loss lasted for generations.

CRITICAL VIEWING Possible response: Grant and his men have removed their hats and are watching Lee quietly, and the artist conveys the gravity of the moment through their serious, not gloating, expressions. Lee, seated at a table larger and finer than Grant's, has an aide or officer at his side, in keeping with a general's status.

3.5 Ball's Bluff National Cemetery Leesburg, Virginia

The need to lay soldiers to rest respectfully after battle led to the creation of national cemeteries during the Civil War. These sites honor the bravery and sacrifice of the men and women who have served their country throughout its history.

In 1861, a Union raiding party crossed the Potomac River at Ball's Bluff in Leesburg, Virginia. They tangled with a Confederate patrol, and a skirmish began, moving down the steep slope of the bluff and into the river. Many soldiers drowned, dragged under the water by the weight of their heavy gear. Using their geographic advantage, Confederate troops shot down at Union soldiers from the top of the bluff, causing even more fatalities. To the horror of President Lincoln, the bodies of many Union soldiers washed up on the shores of the Potomac in Washington, D.C., after the battle. The embarrassing and devastating defeat prompted Congress to form a committee to investigate Union losses, the treatment of wounded soldiers, illegal trade with Confederate states, and military contracts.

More than 50 of the Union soldiers who fell at Ball's Bluff were buried near the battle site, at what would become a national cemetery. In what ways does a cemetery like Ball's Bluff serve as a shrine to the fallen?

CRITICAL VIEWING The Ball's Bluff National Cemetery is one of the nation's smallest military cemeteries. Established in 1865 as the burial place for Union soldiers killed at Ball's Bluff, only the name of one soldier is known: James Allen, a Union soldier and member of Company H, 15th Massachusetts Infantry. What does the unique perspective of this photo by National Geographic photographer Ken Garrett reveal about the cemetery?

PLAN

Objective
Discover the historical importance of Ball's Bluff National Cemetery, one of the nation's smallest national cemeteries.

Critical Thinking Skills for Lesson 3.5
- Analyze Visuals
- Make Connections
- Compare and Contrast
- Analyze Cause and Effect

Essential Question for Chapter 16
How did the United States transform during the Civil War? The high death toll in Civil War battles led to the creation of national cemeteries. Lesson 3.5 discusses the history behind the national cemetery at Ball's Bluff.

NATIONAL GEOGRAPHIC PHOTOGRAPHER
Kenneth Garrett

National Geographic photographer Kenneth Garrett raises awareness of a lesser-known Civil War memorial with his photo of the Ball's Bluff National Cemetery. The remains of 54 soldiers are buried in 25 graves in a semicircle around a center flagpole in the half-acre cemetery. Two monuments outside the walls of the cemetery commemorate Clinton Hatcher, a fallen Confederate soldier, and Union colonel Edward D. Baker, a senator from Oregon and a close personal friend of President Lincoln. Hatcher and Baker are both buried elsewhere. Baker led the Union charge at Ball's Bluff. His death triggered the hasty retreat that resulted in 900 fallen and injured Union soldiers. In addition, 700 Union troops were captured in the battle.

History Notebook
Encourage students to complete the American Places page for Chapter 16 in their History Notebooks as they read.

INTRODUCE & ENGAGE

Activate Prior Knowledge

Explain that the photograph shows one of many national cemeteries in the United States. Ask volunteers to share what they already know about national cemeteries, such as Arlington. Ask questions, such as: What is the purpose of a national cemetery? Why might a nation want to honor the dead in this way? Discuss the significance of a national cemetery with the class.

TEACH

Guided Discussion

1. **Compare and Contrast** Display a photo of Arlington National Cemetery. **ASK:** How is Ball's Bluff National Cemetery similar to and different from other national cemeteries you might have seen in photos or on the news, such as Arlington? *(Answers will vary. Possible response: Ball's Bluff is similar in that it has headstones arranged in an orderly fashion, but the headstones differ in layout and size, and they are enclosed by a wall on all four sides. Only 25 headstones form the partial circle, so the more than 50 soldiers buried there must share graves. Also unlike Arlington, it is small and isolated and includes only Union soldiers.)*

2. **Analyze Cause and Effect** How might the geography of the region have made the Union advance ill advised? *(Answers will vary. Possible response: The Confederates, with their superior position on the bluff, could easily see and fire on Union soldiers advancing from below. The slope made advancing difficult for Union forces, and the river hindered escape.)*

🛡 American Places

In 1861, the western bank of the Potomac River marked not only the boundary between Maryland and Virginia but also the boundary between the Union and the Confederacy. On the Maryland side of the river, the land consisted of a wide, fertile floodplain devoted to agriculture. The Virginia side was marked by a narrow floodplain walled off by a high, rugged escarpment that rose to the Ball's Bluff plateau, which was heavily wooded. The plateau was cut off by deep ravines on the north and south, greatly complicating the Union soldiers' retreat in the battle of Ball's Bluff. The soldiers descended the steep bluff in hopes of reaching Harrison's Island in the middle of the Potomac, which the Union Army held. The land on which Ball's Bluff National Cemetery and the battlefield are located looks much as it did in 1861. Both the cemetery and battlefield have been designated National Historic Landmarks by the National Park Service.

Active Options

On Your Feet: Rotating Discussion Have students form a large circle, facing inward. Ask a question about the lesson and then toss a beanbag to a student, who must answer the question. After answering, the student asks a question of his or her own and tosses the beanbag to another student. Remind students to support their responses with information from the text.

NG Learning Framework: Research National Cemeteries

ATTITUDE Curiosity

KNOWLEDGE Our Human Story

National cemeteries began during the Civil War to handle the high number of casualties and to respect and honor fallen soldiers. Divide the class into teams. Have each team select and research one of the Civil War–era national cemeteries and prepare a multimedia presentation about it. Allow time in class for teams to make their presentations.

DIFFERENTIATE

Striving Readers

Pose and Answer Questions Arrange students in pairs and tell them to read the lesson. Instruct partners to take turns asking each other a *what, who, where, when,* or *why* question about what they have just read. Suggest that students use a 5Ws Chart to help organize their questions and answers.

Gifted & Talented

Write an E-Zine Article Have students research the battle at Ball's Bluff. Tell them to write an e-zine article about the battle's geographical obstacles and challenges, each side's military tactics, and the outcome. Instruct students to pay special attention to events surrounding Edward D. Baker and his forces and to include graphics, such as diagrams and illustrations, to enhance their articles. Invite students to publish their articles on the class blog or home page.

See the Chapter Planner for more strategies for differentiation.

AMERICAN PLACES

Possible response: Students might mention that Ball's Bluff National Cemetery serves as a shrine by providing a quiet place where the fallen are respectfully buried.

CRITICAL VIEWING Answers will vary. Possible response: Garrett's perspective reveals the small size and square shape, the semicircle layout of the headstones, the thickness of the surrounding wall, and the single entrance and exit to the cemetery. Some of these details could have been lost if Garrett had positioned himself at the gate rather than diagonally. The perspective also reveals sky through the trees at the right, emphasizing the height of the bluff.

Landmark Amendments and Terrible Loss

The end of slavery was a great moral victory for the nation. But it became a source of rage for some—rage that triggered violence and terrible loss.

MAIN IDEA Abraham Lincoln planned to rebuild the South and restore the Union, but others would have to follow through for him.

SLAVERY IS ABOLISHED

In January 1865, three months before Lee would surrender, Congress passed the **13th Amendment**, which prohibited slavery in the United States. As with all amendments, it was sent to the states for ratification. By December 1865, three-quarters of the states had approved it, and the 13th Amendment was added to the Constitution.

Slavery was over. Georgia, a former Confederate state, provided the final vote needed for ratification. The amendment states, "Neither slavery nor involuntary **servitude** [being enslaved] . . . shall exist within the United States, or any place subject to their **jurisdiction** [the authority to enforce laws within a given area]." The 13th Amendment abolished slavery, but African Americans were not guaranteed full equality under the law until 1868, with the ratification of the **14th Amendment**. African-American men received voting rights when the **15th Amendment** was ratified in 1870.

Outlawing the practice of slavery was a giant step toward equality and justice. However, discrimination and racism did not magically disappear with the passage of the 13th, 14th, and 15th Amendments. African Americans were frequent victims of violence at the hands of whites. With few options for employment, many southern African Americans went back to work on plantations, where they earned poverty-level wages. Further, African Americans could not depend on a legal system that still favored whites.

LINCOLN'S ASSASSINATION

After the Civil War ended, Lincoln's primary goal was, once again, reuniting the nation. He recognized that integrating newly freed African Americans into society and rebuilding the physical and social structures of the South would be a delicate operation. He planned to implement measures to remedy the injustices of slavery, bring the former Confederate states back into the Union, and rebuild the South.

These plans became known as **Reconstruction**. Lincoln knew he would have to act with careful diplomacy in order to carry out these measures without inflaming already volatile racial and sectional tensions. However, he realized some issues would cause an uproar, no matter the diplomacy used in proposing them. For example, on April 11, 1865, he suggested that some African-American men should have the right to vote. As you have read, that right would not be guaranteed for another five years.

Just three days later on April 14, 1865, **John Wilkes Booth**, an actor and Confederate sympathizer, fatally shot Lincoln at Ford's Theatre in Washington, D.C., as the president watched a play. Audience members rushed the president from Ford's Theatre to the Petersen House, a boarding house across the street. Lincoln never regained consciousness, and he died the next morning. For the first time in U.S. history, a sitting president had been **assassinated**, or murdered for political reasons.

On April 21, Lincoln's funeral train began a somber journey to Springfield, Illinois, where he had lived before becoming president. Thousands of Americans lined the train's route to mourn. Lincoln was buried on May 4, 1865.

Vice President **Andrew Johnson** succeeded Lincoln as president. Johnson favored Lincoln's Reconstruction policies, but he lacked Lincoln's leadership skills. Also, Republican congressmen distrusted him because he was a former Democrat and former slaveholder.

Johnson could not stop Congress from enacting harsh penalties on the southern states. In particular, the **Radical Republicans** believed the former Confederacy should be punished for secession and war. Their treatment of the South caused long-standing resentment and discontent among many southerners.

Lincoln's steady leadership had brought an end to the Civil War. Following his death, the nation struggled to regain a true sense of unity as it rebuilt without the leader who had saved it. The far-reaching consequences of his loss were yet to be realized. The morning he died, Lincoln's Secretary of War, Edwin M. Stanton, is reported to have said either, "Now he belongs to the ages" or "Now he belongs to the angels." For Americans in 1865, both statements rang true.

🏛 Chicago History Museum

After Lincoln was shot, he was taken to a small bedroom in the Petersen House and laid in this bed, diagonally, because he was so tall. Today, you can see Lincoln's death bed at the Chicago History Museum. *The Last Hours of Abraham Lincoln,* painted by Alonzo Chappel in 1868, hangs above the bed. It dramatizes Lincoln's last hours, features Mary Todd Lincoln weeping on his chest, and includes many of the people who visited Lincoln before he died.

HISTORICAL THINKING

1. **READING CHECK** How did Lincoln plan to reunite and heal the nation after the Civil War?

2. **ANALYZE LANGUAGE USE** What do you think is meant by the phrase "or any place subject to their jurisdiction" in the 13th Amendment?

3. **EVALUATE** In what ways did Lincoln's assassination affect Reconstruction and attitudes in the South?

PLAN

Objective

Describe amendments ending slavery, Lincoln's plan for unity, and Lincoln's assassination.

Critical Thinking Skills for Lesson 4.1

- Identify Main Ideas and Details
- Monitor Comprehension
- Analyze Language Use
- Evaluate
- Draw Conclusions
- Make Inferences

Essential Question for Chapter 16

How did the United States transform during the Civil War? Passage of the 13th, 14th, and 15th amendments redefined the federal government's role in protecting civil rights. Lesson 4.1 discusses these amendments and the changes brought about by President Lincoln's assassination.

Background for the Teacher

The Emancipation Proclamation had only ended slavery in Confederate regions that rebelled against the United States. Border states and other areas not in rebellion were not affected. The only way to guarantee the end of slavery throughout the nation was through a constitutional amendment. Leaving it up to individual states to ban slavery on their own through their state constitutions—even as a condition for being readmitted to the Union— was no guarantee. States could go back at a later date and change their constitutions. The 13th Amendment took control out of the hands of the state governments and placed it in the hands of the federal government. This was a significant shift. By forbidding slavery, the federal government was for the first time using the Constitution to control the behavior of individuals rather than to control the actions of government.

K-W-L Chart

Provide each student with a K-W-L Chart. Have students think about what they already know about slavery and the Civil War. Then tell them to write questions that they would like to answer as they study the lesson, such as: Why was the Emancipation Proclamation not enough to end slavery in the United States? or What were people's reactions to the end of slavery? Allow time at the end of the lesson for students to write what they have learned.

K What Do I Know?	W What Do I Want To Learn?	L What Did I Learn?

TEACH

Guided Discussion

1. **Draw Conclusions** Why were the 13th, 14th, and 15th amendments important to the goals of Reconstruction? *(Reconstruction aimed to readmit the Confederate states to the Union and rebuild the South. This meant that the South had to permanently abandon slavery and integrate African Americans into society. The 13th Amendment ensured the end of slavery, the 14th Amendment guaranteed formerly enslaved people full equality under the law, and the 15th Amendment gave African-American men the right to vote.)*

2. **Make Inferences** What events might have triggered John Wilkes Booth to assassinate President Lincoln when he did? *(Answers will vary. Possible response: Booth was a Confederate sympathizer, and the assassination may have been in response to Lincoln's recent suggestion that some African-American men should have the right to vote.)*

Virtual Museum Visit

Between April 9, 2016, and February 20, 2017, the Chicago History Museum held an exhibition titled "Lincoln's Undying Words," which explored Abraham Lincoln's changing views on slavery through five of his most famous speeches: the "House Divided" speech, First Inaugural Address, Gettysburg Address, Second Inaugural Address, and the speech on Reconstruction. Encourage students to visit the museum's online collection, where they can view photos of the bed on which Lincoln died, the table on which General Lee signed his surrender at Appomattox, devastated southern cities, and Lincoln's funeral train. Have students share descriptions of what they find with the class.

Active Options

On Your Feet: Word Chain Arrange students in three lines. Hand a piece of paper to the first person in each line with one of these terms from the lesson: *13th Amendment, 14th Amendment, 15th Amendment.* Instruct the first student to add a word to the list that relates to the term based on information from the lesson. Tell students to pass the paper from person to person in the line, each one adding a word associated with the previously written word. Ask a volunteer from each group to read off the word chain. Ask the rest of the class to listen for any words that were used in more than one chain or any that may not connect correctly with the original word.

NG Learning Framework: Compare Opinions

SKILLS Collaboration, Communication

KNOWLEDGE Our Human Story

Direct students to work in groups to use lesson information and online research to compile a list of Lincoln's views and the views of the Radical Republicans on Reconstruction. Then have groups use their lists to create a Venn diagram showing how the two sets of views were similar and different. Tell students to refer to their Venn diagrams as they hold a class discussion on approaches to Reconstruction.

DIFFERENTIATE

English Language Learners ELD

Complete Sentence Starters Before reading, provide students at the **Emerging** and **Expanding** levels with the sentence starters listed below. Call on volunteers to read the sentences aloud and explain any unclear vocabulary. After reading, ask students to complete the sentences in writing and compare them with a partner's.

- Congress passed the 15th Amendment to _____.
- Reconstruction was the plan to _____.
- John Wilkes Booth was responsible for _____.
- Andrew Johnson lacked Abraham Lincoln's _____.
- The Radical Republicans wanted to _____.

Pre-AP

Extend Knowledge Point out that John Wilkes Booth's original plan was to kidnap Lincoln with the help of a group of co-conspirators, but over time the plan changed. Have students conduct online research about the evolving plan, including reasons for the change. Ask students to present their findings to the class.

See the Chapter Planner for more strategies for differentiation.

HISTORICAL THINKING

ANSWERS

1. Lincoln planned to integrate African Americans into society and rebuild broken structures in the South without provoking already unstable social and racial tensions.

2. The phrase "any place subject to their jurisdiction" means any place where the federal government has the authority to enforce its laws.

3. Lincoln's death left Andrew Johnson, whom the Radical Republicans didn't trust, to oversee Reconstruction. Johnson did not have Lincoln's leadership skills, and by not stopping the Radical Republicans from trying to punish the South, he caused long-standing resentment among southerners.

4.2 The Legacy of the War

The Civil War was one of the most formative events in American history. Four years of battle and loss resulted in both positive and negative consequences.

MAIN IDEA The Civil War left a legacy of unresolved economic and political issues that would have long-lasting effects on the United States.

REBUILDING THE NATION

Conditions in the North and the South after the Civil War contrasted dramatically. The devastated South struggled to recover from the financial and physical destruction it suffered during the war. Its economy had been based on growing and exporting crops for cash. Invading armies had burned down farms and destroyed crops and fields, and, at least initially, few resources existed to rebuild them. The North's naval blockade of southern exports resulted in plantation owners' financial ruin. The biggest economic blow, however, was the abolition of slavery and the resulting loss of "free" labor. Southern plantation owners would have to find other ways to profit from agriculture as the South rebuilt.

Although the North had suffered some destruction and hundreds of thousands of **casualties**, or dead or injured men, it emerged from the war more prosperous than ever. The war effort had led to a rapid growth of the North's industrial economy. Manufacturing had expanded because of the need to build products necessary to fight the war, from guns to railroad cars to uniforms and shoes. Many northern business owners grew rich on wartime profits and the industrial boom that followed. Even northern agriculture prospered during and after the war, as the Union's farms began using more farm machinery to grow and harvest crops with fewer farmers in the fields. In fewer than 50 years after the Civil War, the expansion of primarily northern manufacturing, mining, and transportation made the United States the world's leading industrial nation.

LAND GRANTS AND HOMESTEADS

The Civil War achieved two significant goals: the preservation of the Union and the abolition of slavery. The United States banned slavery later than some other countries. Great Britain had outlawed slavery throughout its empire, including the British West Indies, with the 1833 **Slavery Abolition Act**. In the Western Hemisphere, many South American countries had already abolished slavery as well, though Brazil didn't outlaw the institution until 1888.

Another result of the war was the greatly expanded power and size of the federal government. The balance of power shifted from individual states and regions to Washington, D.C. The federal government was quick to use its power, and one of its goals was to encourage the settlement and development of the West. The government had already begun to put some of its planned programs in motion even before the end of the Civil War.

The **Morrill Act**, signed into law by President Lincoln on July 2, 1862, provided each state with 30,000 acres of federal land grants for each member of its congressional delegation. The land was then sold to the states, and the proceeds were used to fund public colleges that focused on agriculture and the mechanical arts. These land grants funded 69 colleges, including Cornell University, the Massachusetts Institute of Technology, and the University of Wisconsin at Madison.

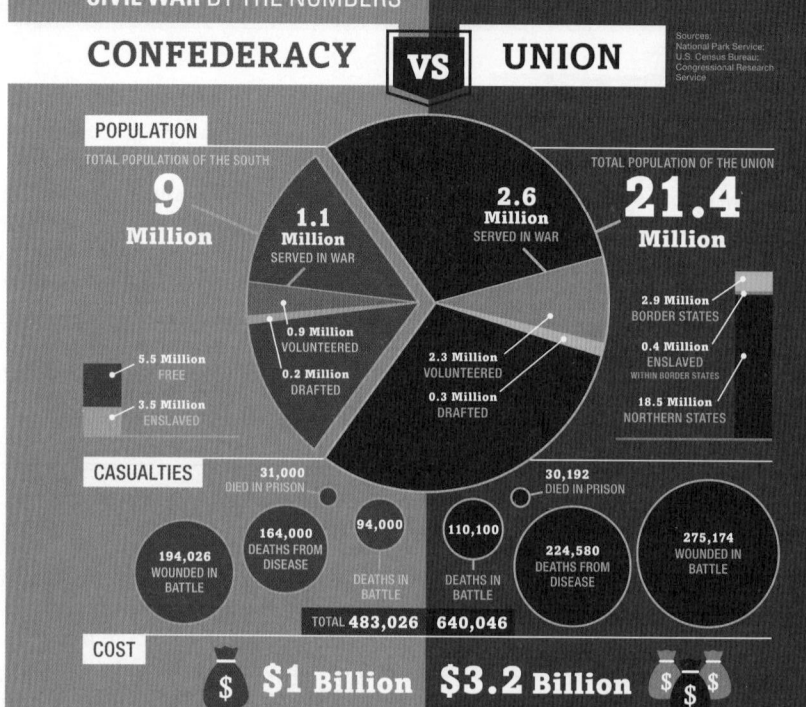

CIVIL WAR BY THE NUMBERS

CONFEDERACY VS UNION

Sources: National Park Service; U.S. Census Bureau; Congressional Research Service

POPULATION

TOTAL POPULATION OF THE SOUTH
9 Million

- 1.1 Million SERVED IN WAR
- 0.9 Million VOLUNTEERED
- 0.2 Million DRAFTED
- 5.5 Million FREE
- 3.5 Million ENSLAVED

TOTAL POPULATION OF THE UNION
21.4 Million

- 2.6 Million SERVED IN WAR
- 2.3 Million VOLUNTEERED
- 0.3 Million DRAFTED
- 2.9 Million BORDER STATES
- 0.4 Million ENSLAVED WITHIN BORDER STATES
- 18.5 Million NORTHERN STATES

CASUALTIES

- 31,000 DIED IN PRISON
- 194,026 WOUNDED IN BATTLE
- 164,000 DEATHS FROM DISEASE
- 94,000 DEATHS IN BATTLE
- 110,100 DEATHS IN BATTLE
- 30,192 DIED IN PRISON
- 224,580 DEATHS FROM DISEASE
- 275,174 WOUNDED IN BATTLE

TOTAL **483,026**   **640,046**

COST

$ **$1 Billion**   **$3.2 Billion** $ $

The **Homestead Act**, signed into law on May 20, 1862, set in motion a program of public land grants to small farmers. It provided that any adult citizen who headed a family could qualify for a grant of 160 acres of public land by paying a small registration fee and living on the land continuously for five years.

The main task of the country's political leaders, however, was, in Lincoln's words, "to bind up the nation's wounds." Many years would pass before the nation would recover politically, economically, and socially. This struggle would be especially difficult for the South.

HISTORICAL THINKING

1. **READING CHECK** What were the major economic and political impacts of the Civil War on American life?

2. **COMPARE AND CONTRAST** How did the aftermath of the Civil War affect the southern agricultural economy and northern industrial economy differently?

3. **ANALYZE CAUSE AND EFFECT** What effect did the land grants have on education and farming?

PLAN

Objective
Learn about the human, economic, and political consequences of the Civil War.

Critical Thinking Skills for Lesson 4.2
- Identify Main Ideas and Details
- Monitor Comprehension
- Compare and Contrast
- Analyze Cause and Effect
- Analyze Visuals

Essential Question for Chapter 16
How did the United States transform during the Civil War? The Civil War ended slavery, physically and financially devastated the South, led to a booming economy in the North, and greatly expanded the size and power of the federal government. Lesson 4.2 discusses how these changes influenced the nation's recovery.

Background for the Teacher
After the Civil War, economic recovery was slow in the South: Cities were in ashes, railroads were destroyed, and farm prices fell dramatically. In Georgia, for example, as late as 1870 the state recorded 1 million fewer pigs, 200,000 fewer cattle, and 3 million fewer acres under cultivation than in 1860. Just as damaging in the long run, lines of credit were severed. Before emancipation, planters used their slaves as collateral for loans. Now, with the absence of collateral, few people outside the South were willing to lend money to planters or other investors, making it difficult to revive the economy. The war also brought a steep price in social disorder in both the South and the North because of the high death toll.

Ask Questions

As a class, come up with a list of questions about the Civil War and its consequences, such as: How did families get by in the South when so many breadwinners were killed? What happened to deserters on both sides after the war? Write students' questions on the board. After reading the lesson, review the questions and ask volunteers to write answers on the board. If necessary, provide students time to research answers to particular questions they could not answer.

TEACH

Guided Discussion

1. **Compare and Contrast** How did the United States compare with other countries in ending slavery? *(The United States ended slavery later than many other countries, including Great Britain, which outlawed slavery in 1833. The United States did abolish slavery ahead of Brazil, which didn't outlaw the practice until 1888.)*

2. **Analyze Cause and Effect** How did the Civil War affect the roles of state and federal governments? *(The federal government expanded its authority and quickly used its power to enact new laws, which shifted the balance of power from individual states to the federal government.)*

Analyze Visuals

Direct students' attention to the infographic. **ASK:** Based on the numbers, what advantages did the Union have over the Confederacy in waging war? *(The Union had the advantage of a larger population, which meant it could raise a larger army and more money for war efforts.)*

Active Options

On Your Feet: Hold a Panel Discussion Build on the first two Historical Thinking questions by asking volunteers to stage a panel discussion in front of the rest of the class about the impact of the Civil War on the North and the South. Students can choose to discuss any impact they learned about in the lesson.

NG Learning Framework: Determine Economic Data STEM

SKILL Communication

KNOWLEDGE Our Human Story

Arrange students in groups to research and create infographics on the economic consequences of the Civil War for the North and the South. To complete their infographics, tell groups to research economic indicators for the North and South in 1860 and 1870. Possible indicators might include such things as number of livestock, acreage under cultivation, amount of crops, number of manufactured goods, exports, miles of railroads, and number of factories. Instruct students to translate the data into an infographic and encourage them to be creative in their designs. Invite groups to share and discuss their data.

Inclusion

Describe Charts Pair visually challenged students with students who are not visually challenged. Ask the latter to describe the Civil War By the Numbers infographic by reading data and answering any questions the visually impaired partner might have.

Gifted & Talented

Calculate Percentages Tell students to compare the relative impact of the war on the Confederacy and the Union by converting the numerical data in the Civil War By the Numbers infographic to percentages. Instruct students to organize their comparison by generating a set of questions based on the data, such as: Which side had the greatest percentage of casualties caused by battle deaths? Invite students to share their comparisons with the class.

See the Chapter Planner for more strategies for differentiation.

HISTORICAL THINKING

ANSWERS

1. The Civil War caused the northern industrial economy to boom and devastated the southern economy through destruction of land, disruption of trade, and the end of slavery. Politically, the Civil War expanded the power and size of the federal government.

2. The southern economy was agricultural, and when slavery ended, plantation owners lost cheap labor. The destruction of farmland destroyed crops, and even if there were crops to sell, trade was blocked. The northern industrial economy boomed because it was able to produce and sell many goods during and after the war and because of the need for farm machinery.

3. The sale of federal land grants authorized by the Morrill Act positively impacted education and farming by funding public colleges that focused on farming and mechanical arts. Land grants associated with the Homestead Act benefited small farmers by providing public land to heads of household at a minimal cost.

VOCABULARY

Use each of the following vocabulary words in a sentence that shows an understanding of the term's meaning.

1. stalemate
   Since they could not agree on a single point, their argument ended in a stalemate.

2. exemption

3. quarantine

4. conscription

5. scapegoat

6. bluff

7. Homestead Act

8. servitude

READING STRATEGY
ANALYZE LANGUAGE USE

If you haven't done so already, complete your graphic organizer to analyze how word choices throughout the text help convey the realities of war. Then answer the question.

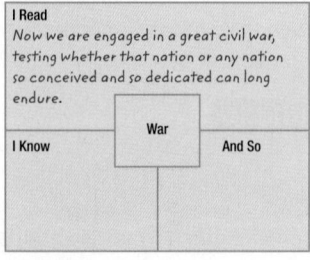

I Read
Now we are engaged in a great civil war, testing whether that nation or any nation so conceived and so dedicated can long endure.

I Know   War   And So

9. How do the words used by President Lincoln in the Gettysburg Address help you understand the impact of the Civil War on the United States?

MAIN IDEAS

Answer the following questions. Support your answers with evidence from the chapter.

10. What major change in the war led to Lincoln's decision to issue the Emancipation Proclamation? **LESSON 1.1**

11. What challenges did the members of the 54th Massachusetts face as new members of the U.S. Army? **LESSON 1.3**

12. What provision of the 1863 Conscription Act was most responsible for sparking draft riots throughout the Northeast? **LESSON 2.1**

13. What measures did the North and the South take to pay for the war? **LESSON 2.2**

14. What problems did prison camps in the North and the South share? **LESSON 2.3**

15. Why are the Union victories at Vicksburg and Gettysburg considered turning points in the war? **LESSON 3.1**

16. What was the main military goal of Sherman's march through Georgia? **LESSON 3.2**

17. What were the main provisions of Grant's terms of surrender? **LESSON 3.4**

18. In what ways did Lincoln's assassination affect the treatment of the South during Reconstruction? **LESSON 4.1**

19. How did the federal government support its goal of expansion into western states after the war? **LESSON 4.2**

HISTORICAL THINKING

Answer the following questions. Support your answers with evidence from the chapter.

20. **MAKE CONNECTIONS** In what ways did having a strong central government help Lincoln wage war against the Confederacy?

21. **MAKE INFERENCES** How did the battles fought during Sherman's march through the South reflect broader struggles during the war?

22. **EVALUATE** How and why did the war become a war to end slavery?

23. **DRAW CONCLUSIONS** What is the main reason Lincoln chose Grant to lead the Union armies after the Battle of Vicksburg?

24. **SYNTHESIZE** How did the Civil War change the United States?

25. **FORM AND SUPPORT OPINIONS** What was the most important factor in the Union victory over the Confederacy? Support your opinion with evidence from the text.

26. **SEQUENCE EVENTS** What amendments followed the Civil War, and what meaning did they have? Create an annotated time line to illustrate your answer.

ANALYZE SOURCES

In his 1863 political cartoon, Thomas Nast imagines what impact emancipation would have on African Americans. Look closely at the cartoon and then answer the following questions.

27. How is slavery depicted in this cartoon?

28. How is emancipation depicted in this cartoon?

29. Why does Nast include Lincoln in this cartoon?

30. How might Americans in the North and the South have viewed this cartoon differently? Explain.

CONNECT TO YOUR LIFE

31. **NARRATIVE** Think about the events that became turning points in the Civil War. Connect your knowledge about this time in history to your own life. Have there been any turning points in your life? Do you expect there to be any turning points in your life in the future? Write a paragraph in which you compare turning points on a national scale like those in the Civil War to more personal turning points like those you've experienced or expect to experience in your life.

TIPS

- Make a time line of principal turning points in the Civil War. Then make a time line of possible turning points in your own life.

- Use two or three vocabulary terms from the chapter in your narrative.

- Conclude the narrative with a comment that ties Civil War turning points to your own life.

VOCABULARY ANSWERS

1. Since they could not agree on a single point, their argument ended in a stalemate.

2. Exemptions enabled some men to legally avoid the Civil War draft.

3. Authorities decided to quarantine troops to keep diseases from spreading.

4. Both sides in the Civil War passed conscription laws that drafted men to fight.

5. African Americans became scapegoats even though they were not responsible for starting the war.

6. Vicksburg's position on bluffs above the Mississippi River made the city difficult to capture.

7. The Homestead Act encouraged the growth of farms in western lands.

8. The 13th Amendment abolished slavery in the United States.

READING STRATEGY ANSWER

I Read
But in a larger sense, we cannot dedicate, we cannot consecrate, we cannot hallow this ground.

I Know   War   And So

9. Lincoln chose words that cast the Civil War as a moral fight to save a nation based on liberty and equality. Words such as *dedicate*, *consecrate*, and *hallow* suggest that the war created deep wounds in people with hard-held beliefs on both sides and that the wounds have been difficult to heal.

MAIN IDEAS ANSWERS

10. The Union victory at Antietam, ending a string of Union defeats, persuaded Lincoln to issue the Emancipation Proclamation.

11. The men of the 54th Massachusetts faced the challenge of proving that they could fight as bravely and effectively as white soldiers.

12. The exemption provision, which allowed men to escape the draft by paying $300, was most responsible for sparking draft riots.

13. Both the North and the South issued bonds, raised taxes, and printed money. The South also tried to borrow foreign money and used impressment.

14. Prison camps were crowded and lacked adequate sanitation, food, and shelter, so they became sources of disease.

15. Vicksburg gave the Union control of the Mississippi River, splitting the Confederacy in half. Gettysburg put the Confederacy on the defensive.

16. Sherman's goal was to wear down the spirit and morale of the Confederacy by destroying southern property, crops, and supplies, as well as the industrial city of Atlanta.

17. All officers and soldiers were pardoned and could keep their horses and other private property. Officers were allowed to keep their sidearms, and the starving troops received Union rations.

18. Lincoln's assassination allowed Radical Republicans in Congress to impose much harsher restrictions on the defeated South than Lincoln had wanted.

19. The federal government supported western expansion by offering land grants through the Morrill Act and the Homestead Act.

HISTORICAL THINKING ANSWERS

20. Having a strong central government helped Lincoln organize the draft, coordinate the manufacture and distribution of supplies, and raise money through taxes, bonds, and printing money.

21. The brutality of Sherman's tactics underscored the struggle inherent in a civil war. In fighting to save the Union, the North destroyed property and devastated the lives of people who would be U.S. citizens again if the North won.

22. Lincoln's position on ending slavery evolved. At first he was reluctant to end slavery outright, fearing the reaction of the border states and Democrats. Then he realized that ending slavery was a military strategy that would deprive the South of manpower. Finally, Lincoln came to see the end of slavery as a moral goal tied to the American principles of liberty and equality.

23. After Vicksburg, Lincoln felt that Grant had proved that he had the military talent and determination to lead the Union armies.

24. The war left the South struggling to rebuild financially, physically, and emotionally. It left the North with a stronger industrial base, improved agriculture, and a booming economy. The federal government expanded and gained more power over the states than before the war.

25. Answers will vary. Students should clearly state their opinion regarding the most important factors and support that opinion with evidence from the chapter.

26. The 13th Amendment (1865), which abolished slavery, the 14th Amendment (1868), which guaranteed equality under the law, and the 15th Amendment (1870), which gave African-American men the vote, followed the Civil War. Students' time lines should illustrate the events in chronological order.

ANALYZE SOURCES ANSWERS

27. The cartoon shows the horrible conditions of chattel slavery: men and women being sold, beaten, and abused.

28. Emancipation is shown as giving African Americans the freedom to live with their families, have their own homes, and freely gather on the street.

29. Nast presents Lincoln as the person responsible for emancipation.

30. Americans in the North might have been gratified by the cartoon because it depicts emancipation as a justifiable reason for fighting the war. Americans in the South, however, might have been angered by the depiction of free African Americans because the end of slavery contributed to their economic and social problems.

CONNECT TO YOUR LIFE ANSWER

31. Answers will vary. Students should include a time line of turning points in the Civil War and a time line of turning points in their own lives and then use textual evidence and two or three Key Vocabulary words to compare turning points. Students should conclude by connecting Civil War turning points to their own lives.

UNIT 6 RESOURCES

UNIT INTRODUCTION

UNIT TIME LINE

UNIT WRAP-UP

NATIONAL GEOGRAPHIC | **CONNECTION**

National Geographic Magazine Adapted Articles
- "Lincoln's Funeral Train"
- "Civil War Battlefields" ONLINE

Unit 6 Inquiry: Develop a Conflict Resolution Strategy

NG Learning Framework Activities
- Create an Illustrated Time Line
- Compose a Letter Home

Unit 6 Formal Assessment

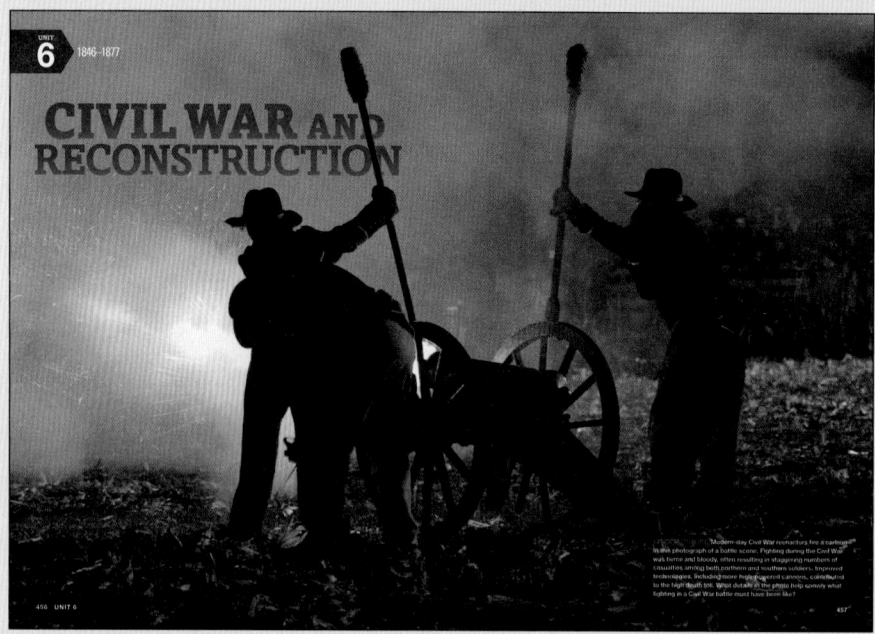

CHAPTER 17 RESOURCES

Available at NGLSync.Cengage.com

TEACHER RESOURCES & ASSESSMENT

Reading and Note-Taking

Vocabulary Practice

Social Studies Skills Lessons
- Reading: Draw Conclusions
- Writing: Write an Expository Paragraph

Formal Assessment
- Chapter 17 Pretest
- Chapter 17 Tests A & B
- Section Quizzes

Chapter 17 Answer Key

ExamView®
One-time Download

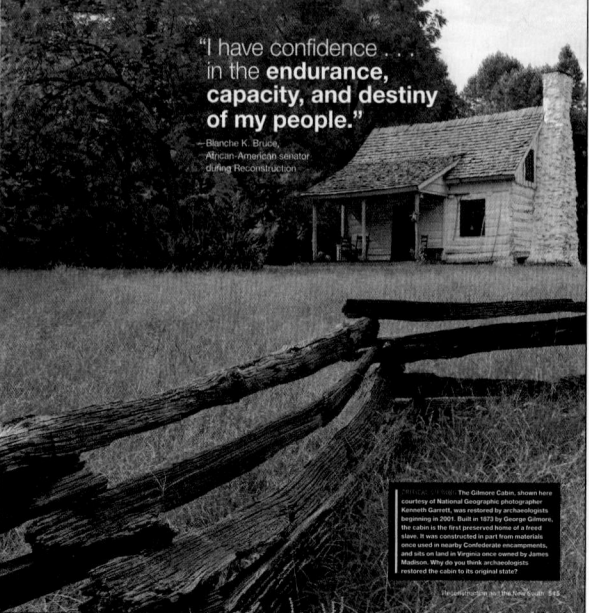

STUDENT DIGITAL RESOURCES

- **eEdition** (English)
- **eEdition** (Spanish)
- **Handbooks**
- **Online Atlas**
- **American Gallery Online**
- **History Notebook**
- **Active History**
- **Projects for Inquiry-Based Learning**

Chapter 17 Spanish Resources are available at NGLSync.Cengage.com.

AMERICAN STORIES | Freedom Readers

- Primary Sources
- On Your Feet: Fishbowl

NG Learning Framework:
Research Female Literacy

SECTION 1 RESOURCES
REBUILDING THE UNION

LESSON 1.1
Reconstruction Under Andrew Johnson

- On Your Feet: Three Corners

NG Learning Framework:
Learn About the Presidential Pardon

LESSON 1.2
Radical Reconstruction

- On Your Feet: Living Time Line

NG Learning Framework:
Debate the Two Reconstructions

SECTION 2 RESOURCES
RECONSTRUCTION CHANGES DAILY LIFE

LESSON 2.1
Free African Americans Gain a Voice

- On Your Feet: Card Response

NG Learning Framework:
Write a Biography

LESSON 2.2
Education and Land

 AMERICAN GALLERY ONLINE   The Freed Slaves of the Civil War

NG Learning Framework:
Discover an HBCU

LESSON 2.3
Resistance in the South

- On Your Feet: Build a Paragraph

NG Learning Framework:
Explore Social Justice Organizations

SECTION 3 RESOURCES
THE END OF RECONSTRUCTION

LESSON 3.1
Grant's Presidency

- Active History: Amend the Constitution

NG Learning Framework:
Create a Campaign Item

LESSON 3.2
The Election of 1876

- On Your Feet: Three-Step Interview

NG Learning Framework:
Research Voter Suppression

CHAPTER 17 REVIEW

Strategy ❶
Use Context Clues

Define and review some of the Key Vocabulary words used in this chapter using context clues or dictionaries if necessary. Consider starting with the following Key Vocabulary: *social justice, sharecropping, poll tax, defected.* Then ask students to use each one in a sentence.

Use with Lessons 2.1–2.2 and 3.1–3.2

Strategy ❷
Annotate a Time Line

Have students use the lessons as references to complete and annotate a time line that shows major events during Reconstruction. Students should use the dates 1865 and 1877 as their beginning and end dates. Tell students they may add more boxes to the line if needed.

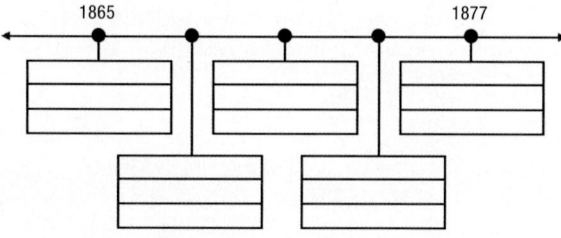

Use with All Lessons

Strategy ❸
Play Vocabulary Tic-Tac-Toe

Choose nine Key Vocabulary words and place them on a tic-tac-toe grid on the board. Position the words on the grid so that an X or O can be written below each word. Player A chooses a word. If the player correctly pronounces, defines, and uses the word in a sentence, he or she can put an X or O in that square. Play alternates until one person has a row of Xs or Os.

Use with All Lessons *This game can also be played using teams.*

Strategy ❶
Use Supported Reading

In small groups, have students read the chapter aloud, lesson by lesson. At the end of each lesson, have them stop and use these frames to tell what they understood from their reading:

• This lesson is about _____.

• One detail I remember is _____.

• Two terms I did not understand were _____ and _____.

• One question I have is _____.

Use with All Lessons *Guide students through portions of text they do not understand. Be sure all students understand a lesson before moving on to the next one.*

Strategy ❷
Ask Yes/No Questions

Ask students the questions below and have them say or write *yes* or *no* in response. Then reread the questions and ask students to correct the information in any sentence that has *no* as an answer.

Were the black codes laws that protected African Americans' rights? *(no)*

Did literacy increase among African Americans during Reconstruction? *(yes)*

Under sharecropping, did African Americans own their own land? *(no)*

Use with Lessons 1.2 and 2.2

ENGLISH LANGUAGE LEARNERS

Strategy 1
Present a Word

Pair students at the **Emerging** level with English-proficient students and pair students at the **Expanding** level with students at the **Bridging** level. Have each partner choose a Key Vocabulary word from the lesson and present it to the other partner, using a variety of tools such as illustrations, gestures, example sentences, and definitions. After each partner presents a word, the other partner writes a complete sentence using it correctly.

Use with All Lessons

Strategy 2
Apply Key Vocabulary

Pair English language learners with English-proficient students. Ask the proficient students to model using Key Vocabulary words in sentences. Then prompt each pair to compose a sentence for each word. Invite pairs to share their sentences and discuss different ways to use each word. Suggest the following words:

- impeachment
- social justice
- wage economy
- poll taxes
- corruption

Use with Lessons 1.2, 2.1–2.2, and 3.1–3.2 *You may wish to place students in pairs, such as students at the* **Emerging** *level with those at the* **Bridging** *level, and have English-proficient students assist less proficient students in checking the accuracy and spelling of their sentences.*

Strategy 3
Pair Partners for Dictation

After students of **All Proficiencies** read each lesson in the chapter, have them write a sentence summarizing its main idea. Have students get together in pairs and dictate their sentences to each other. Then have them work together to check the sentences for accuracy and spelling.

Use with All Lessons *You may wish to pair students at the* **Emerging** *level with students at the* **Expanding** *or* **Bridging** *levels for dictation.*

GIFTED & TALENTED

Strategy 1
Create a Multimedia Presentation

Invite students to choose a topic related to Reconstruction or African-American civil rights in the late 1800s and create a multimedia presentation. Tell students to conduct outside research and incorporate media such as photographs, political cartoons, and maps. The presentation should be structured around asking and answering a historical question.

Use with All Lessons *For example, students might explore the question, Why was the 15th Amendment ineffective at protecting African-American voting rights?*

Strategy 2
Conduct an Interview

Direct students to choose an individual from the chapter and write an interview that could appear in a magazine. Students should use information from the text and outside resources to compile information about the person's life and career. Direct students to include a brief biographical description followed by an interview with two or three questions answered in the voice of the chosen individual.

Use with Lessons 1.1–1.2, 2.1–2.2, and 3.1–3.2

Pre-AP

Strategy 1
Write a Feature Article

Ask students to select a topic from the chapter that relates to the social or political consequences of Reconstruction. Have them use library or online resources to research their topic and write a feature article. Encourage students to include statistics, photos, and first-person accounts in their article, if appropriate. Have students share their articles with the class.

Use with Lessons 1.1–2.3

Strategy 2
Use the PERSIA Approach

Have students use the chapter text and library or online resources to write an essay exploring the short- and long-term effects of Reconstruction on the United States. Display the following on the board and direct students to focus on one or more categories as they structure their essays:

Political
Economic
Religious
Social
Intellectual
Artistic

Use with All Lessons

ESSENTIAL QUESTION
In what ways did Reconstruction both succeed and fail?

READING STRATEGY

DRAW CONCLUSIONS
When you draw conclusions, you make a judgment based on what you have read. You analyze the facts, make inferences, and use your own experiences to form your judgment. As you read the chapter, use a diagram like this one to draw conclusions about the impact of Reconstruction on American society.

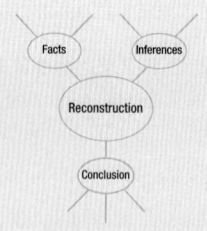

Facts   Inferences

Reconstruction

Conclusion

"I have confidence . . . in the **endurance, capacity, and destiny of my people.**"

—Blanche K. Bruce,
African-American senator
during Reconstruction

CRITICAL VIEWING The Gilmore Cabin, shown here courtesy of National Geographic photographer Kenneth Garrett, was restored by archaeologists beginning in 2001. Built in 1873 by George Gilmore, the cabin is the first preserved home of a freed slave. It was constructed in part from materials once used in nearby Confederate encampments, and sits on land in Virginia once owned by James Madison. Why do you think archaeologists restored the cabin to its original state?

INTRODUCE THE PHOTOGRAPH
Historical Cabin Restoration

Direct students' attention to the photograph of the cabin and the caption that accompanies it. Ensure that students understand the cabin is a restoration of an original home, meaning archaeologists have used historical records, artifacts found on the property, and information from the owners' descendants to present the building as it would have looked in the 1870s. Encourage students to share their impressions of the building. **ASK:** Why might restorations like this one be an important tool for studying the lives of former slaves after the Civil War? *(Answers will vary. Possible response: Restorations show the kinds of economic conditions people dealt with after the war and how they lived.)*

NATIONAL GEOGRAPHIC PHOTOGRAPHER
Kenneth Garrett

Photographer Ken Garrett uses his art as a tool to preserve historic places. He notes, "We need to make sure we don't lose it before it's too late." One such place is the Gilmore Cabin. The cabin's builders and original occupants were the Gilmore family—George Gilmore, his wife Polly, and their three children. The family was, relatively speaking, a success story. George started out by renting the land and eventually bought it outright. He owned it until his death, upon which he passed it on to his family. Since 2005, the cabin has been open to visitors and school groups. Inside the cabin, visitors can explore the details of everyday life for some African Americans on their path from slavery to citizenry.

CRITICAL VIEWING Possible responses: Archaeologists may have restored the cabin to honor the memory of people who were freed from slavery or to show people what life was like for some formerly enslaved people after the Civil War.

For Chapter 17 Spanish Resources, visit the Resources Menu. Chapter 17 Resources are available at NGLSync.Cengage.com.

INTRODUCE THE ESSENTIAL QUESTION

In what ways did Reconstruction both succeed and fail?

Roundtable Activity: Make Predictions This activity introduces students to key questions about Reconstruction. Have students form four groups. Direct each group to address one of the topics listed below and make predictions to answer the questions that follow.

A. Economic: How will the South adjust to the loss of enslaved labor? What place will free African Americans have in the new economy?

B. Legal: How will the rights of newly freed African Americans compare to those of other citizens? How will they gain and protect their rights?

C. Social: How will white southerners and northerners react to including newly freed African Americans in society? How will free African Americans change their communities to meet their new needs?

D. Political: What roles will African-American voters and leaders play in the political system? How might political parties help or hinder Reconstruction?

Assign one student in each group to take notes and another student to present the group's predictions to the class. Students may then revisit their predictions when they have completed the chapter.

INTRODUCE CHAPTER VOCABULARY

Vocabulary Pyramids

As students read the chapter, have them complete Vocabulary Pyramids for Key Vocabulary words. Tell students to make a pyramid for each word, add what they know about each word before reading, and then add to or correct the pyramid after they encounter the word in the chapter. Model an example for students on the board, using the graphic organizer below.

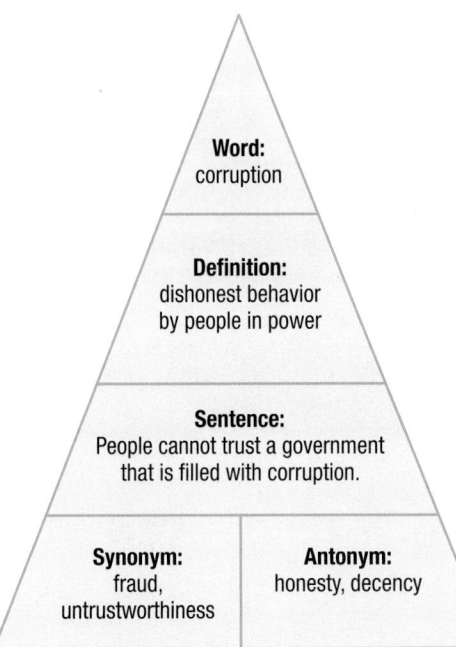

Word: corruption

Definition: dishonest behavior by people in power

Sentence: People cannot trust a government that is filled with corruption.

Synonym: fraud, untrustworthiness

Antonym: honesty, decency

INTRODUCE THE READING STRATEGY

DRAW CONCLUSIONS

Remind students that when they draw conclusions, they combine facts and inferences to make a statement. Explain that graphic organizers can help them keep track of facts and inferences. Model completing the Concept Cluster. Point out that the center circle is labeled "Reconstruction." Add one fact related to Reconstruction to a "Fact" branch, such as "Reconstruction was the period immediately after the Civil War." Help students make and record inferences about Reconstruction. Model combining facts and inferences to draw a conclusion. Remind students to complete their Concept Clusters as they read the chapter.

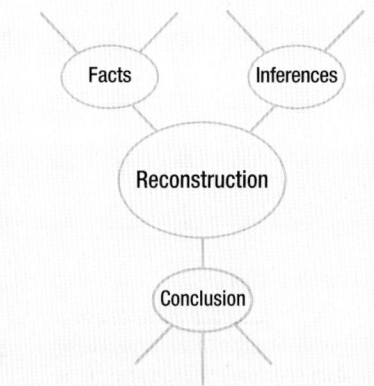

Facts

Inferences

Reconstruction

Conclusion

KEY DATES FOR CHAPTER 17

1865	Civil War ends
1866	Civil Rights Act of 1866
1867	Reconstruction Acts of 1867
1868	Impeachment trial of President Andrew Johnson
1868	Ulysses S. Grant wins presidential election
1870	15th Amendment becomes part of Constitution
1870–1871	Congress passes Enforcement Acts
1873	Panic of 1873 causes economic depression
1876	*U.S.* v. *Cruikshank*; *U.S.* v. *Reese*
1877	Compromise of 1877 ends Reconstruction

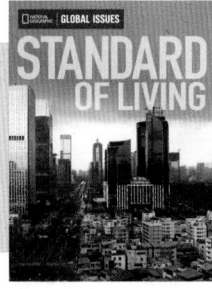

For more on factors that shape a population's well-being, see *GLOBAL ISSUES: STANDARD OF LIVING.*

Objectives

- **Learn how enslaved people used the power of literacy to escape slavery.**
- **Compare viewpoints about African-American literacy in the North and in the South.**
- **Discuss the concept of universal literacy.**
- **Understand how literacy and education changed after the Civil War.**

Critical Thinking Skills for "Freedom Readers"

- Make Connections
- Draw Conclusions
- Make Inferences
- Summarize
- Analyze Visuals
- Categorize
- Identify
- Synthesize

Background for the Teacher

This American Story encourages students to explore the history of literacy and African Americans during and after slavery. Use this high-interest narrative to underscore the chapter's coverage of changes in the lives of African Americans following the end of the Civil War and to remind students of the restrictions under which most African Americans lived, both before and after the war.

This chapter, Reconstruction and the New South, includes information about improved educational opportunities for African Americans after the Civil War. This American Story will provide a context, helping students understand what literacy meant to African Americans and how people worked—sometimes in secret, sometimes risking punishment—to make that ability a reality.

History Notebook

Encourage students to complete the American Story page for Chapter 17 in their History Notebooks as they read.

Note to the Teacher

Use this American Story as a teaser for content students will encounter in Chapter 17.

AMERICAN STORIES

NATIONAL GEOGRAPHIC

CRITICAL VIEWING This mid-1800s photograph of enslaved women and children outside their southern cabin is unique in a significant way: it shows a young woman reading aloud to the group. How might the ability to read and write have affected the life of a slave before and after the Civil War?

546 CHAPTER 17

FREEDOM READERS

BY FRAN DOWNEY

Vice President and Publisher,
National Geographic *Explorer* Magazine

African rebellion leaders Nat Turner, Gabriel Prosser,
Touissant L'Ouverture, and Denmark Vesey shared
one important power: literacy. Enslaved people
realized the value of reading, and many risked
everything—including their lives—to learn.
They were America's freedom readers.

When slavery first began in the colonies, slave owners often encouraged their slaves to read. In fact, literacy became a way for slave owners to assert control over them. Slave owners wanted to convert enslaved Africans to Christianity in order to "civilize" them, and believed that all Christians needed to be able to read the Bible. Helping his or her slaves learn to read was a critical part of a slave owner's "civilization" plan. Some slave owners also used scripture to justify the concept of slavery, believing the Bible implied it was acceptable to enslave people.

Many enslaved people had a very different goal in mind as they learned to read and write. They saw it as a way to resist bondage. Like breaking tools, working slowly, and pretending to be ill, learning to read and write was a passive way for the enslaved to revolt against the enslaver. Literate African Americans could learn about the larger world. They could read newspapers, plan escapes and rebellions, and send messages. A few, whose voices you have heard throughout this book, even wrote slave narratives, which exposed the evils of slavery. Instead of a lock that kept them shackled, enslaved people saw literacy as a way to unlock the chains of slavery.

Over time, slave owners began to fear the potential power of literate free and enslaved African Americans. States like North Carolina passed laws that severely punished African-American students and those who helped them. These laws forced African Americans to get inventive. Some slaves tricked their owners into teaching them. Others watched and listened as white children were taught to read, and practiced in secret.

Reconstruction and the New South **547**

Make a List of Advantages

Discuss the power of literacy with students. Explain that even a basic ability to read and write enables people to do things that are challenging for people who haven't learned these skills. Have students brainstorm a list of tasks for which literacy is a clear advantage by completing this sentence:

Because I can read and write, I can _____.

Provide this sentence as an example: Because I can read and write, I can fill out a job application. Encourage students to think about reading tasks that do not involve today's technology, such as reading text on a TV or computer screen or using social media. As you review the completed list, tell students they will read an American Story about the value of literacy for enslaved people before and after the Civil War.

Preview Using Visuals

Direct students' attention to the photograph and invite them to describe the scene. Write their responses on the board. Then ask for a volunteer to read the Critical Viewing caption and question. Take some initial responses now, but tell students that they will be able to answer the question in more detail after they read.

CRITICAL VIEWING Possible response: Before the Civil War, being able to read and write might have made it easier for a slave to figure out and communicate an escape plan. After the war, that skill might have made it easier for a former slave to find a job.

The Stono Rebellion

The slaves who set out from a spot near the Stono River outside of Charleston (known then as Charlestown) were responding to an offer from the government of Spanish-owned Florida: slaves who came to Florida from an English colony would be free and would receive land. Some historians think that the rebellion was purposely staged on a Sunday, when slave owners were likely to be in church and without weapons. Indeed, the rebellion took place just a few weeks before a law requiring white men to carry a gun at all times was to go into effect in South Carolina.

The African Methodist Episcopal Church

The African Methodist Episcopal (AME) Church is an example of what the power of literacy can achieve. The AME got its start from the Free African Society (FAS), a charitable organization. Richard Allen, a founder of the FAS, also ministered as a preacher for the black members of Philadelphia's St. George's Methodist Episcopal Church. The break from that church, in 1794, resulted from rising discrimination from the church's white members, including segregated seating and a refusal to allow black members to pray on their knees. Allen won two court cases that established the independence of his new church. Black worshipers in other such churches began forming their own AME congregations leading to the movement's official designation as a denomination. The AME is still active today with congregations around the world.

David Walker

After the reward was offered for David Walker's capture, his friends urged him to leave Boston and go to Canada. Walker refused to flee, saying "Somebody must die in this cause. I may be doomed to the stake and the fire, or to the scaffold tree, but it is not in me to falter if I can promote the work of emancipation." Devout in his Christian faith, Walker pronounced abolition a "glorious and heavenly cause." In June of 1830, Walker published yet a third edition of his *Appeal*. He was dead two months later. Some suspected that Walker was poisoned, but no evidence supports this allegation. Research into his life revealed that his daughter had died of tuberculosis a week earlier, suggesting this as the likely cause of Walker's death. In 1866, Walker's only son, Edwin G. Walker, became the first black man elected to the Massachusetts state legislature.

Nat Turner's Rebellion in 1831, as represented by this illustration, panicked the South and prompted legislation that prevented the education, movement, and assembly of enslaved people.

EARLY LAWS AND LITERACY

Southern lawmakers began to outlaw African-American literacy as early as 1740. This date is no coincidence. A year earlier, 20 slaves in South Carolina tried to escape to Florida. This unsuccessful uprising, known as the Stono Rebellion, resulted in the deaths of 60 people. Believing that those who planned the rebellion had used reading and writing to communicate, lawmakers outlawed teaching slaves to write. This law did not impose a penalty on enslaved African Americans, who were considered property. Rather, it punished free people who taught slaves with a fine of 100 pounds.

In the New England Colonies, where slavery was less common, literacy rates among enslaved African Americans were higher. In the 1770s, literate slaves read that many colonists wanted to break from Britain. Believing these revolutionary leaders would be sympathetic to their cause, literate slaves in Massachusetts wrote to the legislature to request their freedom. Enslaved African Americans in Connecticut did the same about five years later. While neither legislature granted the slaves' request, one by one, northern states slowly began to end slavery in the 1780s.

After the American Revolution, African Americans continued to occupy the same social, economic, and political positions in the Northeast. But they began to create institutions to advance their rights and develop communities without racial discrimination. For example, Richard Allen, Absalom Jones, and others founded the African Methodist Episcopal Church in 1816. Additionally, some northern states passed laws to educate their newly emancipated fellow citizens. The state of New York did not abolish slavery until 1827. As a result, the New York African Free School, founded in 1787, became a haven for free African-American students and enslaved people whose owners allowed them to attend.

UNIVERSAL LITERACY?

One of the premises of the new republican government was that the nation's very existence depended on universal literacy—literacy for all. Even Thomas Jefferson, a slave owner himself, argued, "If a nation expects to be ignorant and free, in a state of civilization, it expects what never was and never will be."

Reinforcing the importance of education in the new nation, George Washington declared in his will that the enslaved children he owned who did not have parents should be taught a vocation, or trade, and educated. However, Washington's desire to teach enslaved children to read and write was not shared by most slave owners. In 1800, southern lawmakers passed a new law that restricted all "mental instruction" of both free and enslaved people of African descent, including teaching or simply talking about reading, writing, or mathematics.

The law also prohibited free and enslaved African Americans from gathering between sunset and sunrise. This restriction made it more difficult for African Americans to set up informal schools and gave authorities the right to barge in on anyone who they suspected of holding these "unlawful" meetings. This law punished both free and enslaved lawbreakers with a whipping, stating law officers, or justices of the peace, could "inflict corporal punishment on the offender or offenders . . . not exceeding twenty lashes."

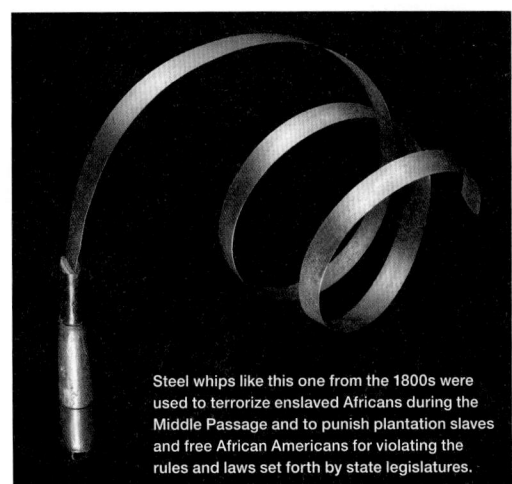

Steel whips like this one from the 1800s were used to terrorize enslaved Africans during the Middle Passage and to punish plantation slaves and free African Americans for violating the rules and laws set forth by state legislatures.

FEARING THE LITERATE

Slave owners' worst fears about literate African Americans were realized in 1829, when David Walker, a free African-American abolitionist, published his *Appeal to the Colored Citizens of the World.* He wanted African Americans, especially slaves, to read his *Appeal,* in which he urged them to resist oppression violently, if necessary. He also argued for racial equality.

Born in North Carolina, Walker was considered free because his mother was free, but he had seen the impact of slavery. Walker became a radical voice against slavery. When authorities in the South discovered the first copies of the *Appeal,* they worried slaves had already been preparing a violent attack. African Americans in Charleston and New Orleans were promptly arrested for distributing Walker's *Appeal,* and a reward was offered for Walker: $10,000 alive, $1,000 dead.

TEACH

Guided Discussion

1. **Make Inferences** Point out to students that the 1740 law against literacy followed the failure of the Stono Rebellion. **ASK:** Why do you think the law was aimed at people who taught slaves to read instead of the slaves themselves? *(Possible response: Lawmakers probably believed that punishing the teachers would discourage them from teaching slaves who were not yet literate.)*

2. **Summarize** Prompt students to restate Thomas Jefferson's quotation in their own words. **ASK:** How does Jefferson's quote apply to literacy education for African Americans? *(Possible response: A nation isn't truly civilized and free if its people are denied a basic education. The quotation suggests that ignorance and freedom are mutually exclusive.)*

Active Options

On Your Feet: Fishbowl Direct half the class to sit in a close circle, facing inward. Tell the other half of the class to sit in a larger circle around them. Instruct students in the inside circle to discuss what they know about efforts in the young republic to improve the lives of free and enslaved African Americans through institutions, education, and laws. Then call on volunteers in the outside circle to summarize what they heard. Tell students to switch places and ask those now on the inside circle to discuss what they know about efforts to restrict the freedom of free and enslaved African Americans through laws. The outside circle should listen and then summarize what they heard.

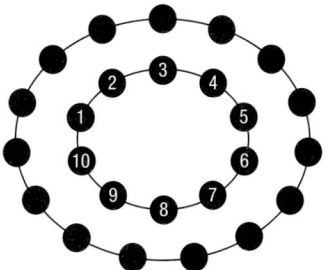

NG Learning Framework: Research Female Literacy

SKILL Communication

KNOWLEDGE Our Human Story

Point out that low levels of literacy among young girls and women is a problem in some areas of the world today. Have students work in groups to research where this is a problem, how big the problem is from a statistical point of view, why low levels are a problem from a social perspective, and what efforts are being made to remedy the problem. Encourage groups share their findings with the class.

Guided Discussion

1. **Analyze Visuals** Direct students' attention to the painting and read the caption. **ASK:** What details do you notice in the painting and what does it convey about education? *(Possible response: The children look serious, and some are gathered around one book while one is standing alone. It's dark in the cabin, implying that learning had to be done in secret. Education was prohibited, so the small number of children may be because of the risk involved in teaching them.)* Then direct students' attention to the photograph. **ASK:** What does the photograph convey about education? *(Possible response: There are many children at the school, each has a book, and they are engrossed in their reading, suggesting how much they value learning. Since they are free and not enslaved, they are able to get a basic education legally.)*

2. **Categorize** Which of the three African Americans in the Runaway Reading feature used the ability to read as a key to escape and which used the ability after escaping? *(Possible response: John Sella Martin used his ability to read while still a slave, presumably to help plan his escape. Mattie Jackson and Willis used it after their escape: Mattie to help her tell and sell her story and Willis to forge papers that would help him avoid being returned to slavery.)*

WRITE ABOUT HISTORY

Blog About Education This American Story provides an overview of the challenges that African Americans faced in securing an education and their use of literacy as a powerful tool in their lives. To help students make connections between the American Story and their own lives, have them write a reflective essay on what they feel are the qualities of a good education and how they hope their education will serve them in the future. Invite students to read their essays to the class or to post them in a blog format on a school or other approved website.

THINK ABOUT IT

Answers will vary. Possible response: Because of the freedom that the Civil War ensured, African Americans gained access to education, opening the door to jobs and mobility within society.

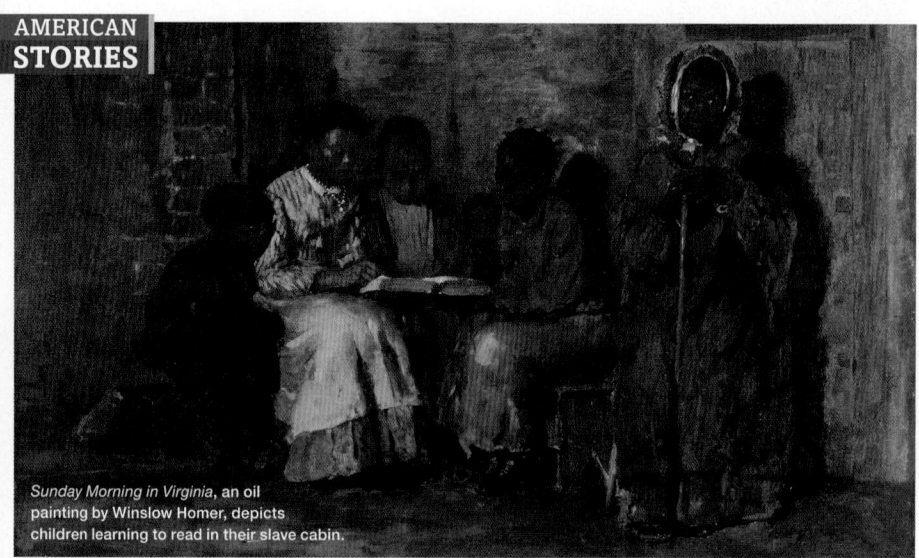

AMERICAN **STORIES**

Sunday Morning in Virginia, an oil painting by Winslow Homer, depicts children learning to read in their slave cabin.

LITERACY LAWS CONTINUE

By 1830, southern authorities had taken further steps to curb literacy among African Americans. They prohibited free African Americans, especially those from the North, from meeting with the enslaved, in an attempt to prevent slaves from gaining access to information.

Some northerners also grew concerned about educating free African Americans. You have read about the boarding school Prudence Crandall opened in Connecticut in 1832 for African-American girls. In 1833, the state passed a law requiring all African-American students be residents of the state. Authorities quickly arrested Crandall for violating this law. African Americans from Connecticut were still allowed to attend school, but those from out of state could not. Lawmakers feared migrating students would increase the state's African-American population, resulting in the "injury of the people." This way of thinking contributed to the characterization of free and educated African Americans as a separate and dangerous community.

AFTER THE CIVIL WAR

The Civil War was a watershed event that marked an important shift in American history and the end of slavery. Emancipation brought about many social changes, including the transformation of the

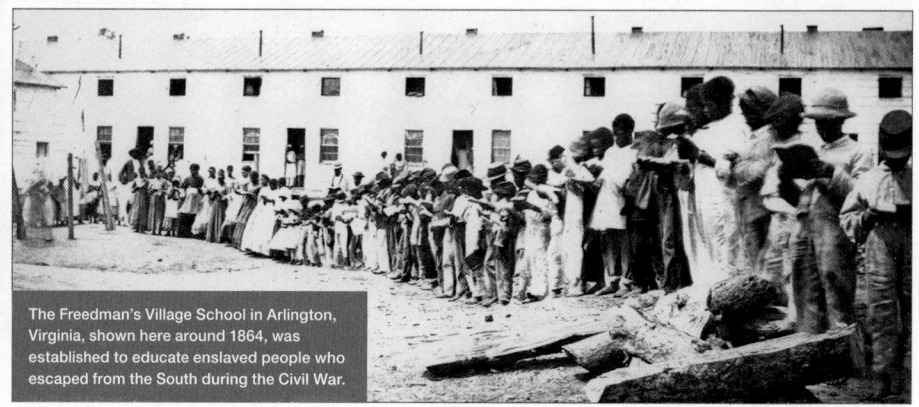

The Freedman's Village School in Arlington, Virginia, shown here around 1864, was established to educate enslaved people who escaped from the South during the Civil War.

RUNAWAY READING

As antiliteracy laws were passed and enforced, enslaved African Americans continued to disregard them. They learned to read and write, and then used these skills to escape slavery. Let's look at some of their remarkable stories.

WILLIS

As valuable as reading was to slaves, writing was equally useful. An enslaved man called Willis used writing to escape slavery. What we know about him comes from a newspaper ad in which he is described as being 30 years old, stooped and downcast, and walking with a limp. On November 25, 1862, Willis ran away from his owner, W.H. Medlin, in South Carolina and headed north. Medlin placed the ad so people would look for Willis, but Willis had a special skill that helped him. To avoid capture, he wrote and signed a note that declared him free. He used his literacy skills to gain his freedom.

MATTIE JACKSON

Slavery crippled bodies and separated families, but it didn't stop people's quest for freedom. When Mattie Jackson was five years old, she and her mother tried to escape from Missouri to Chicago, but they were caught and sold back into slavery. Mattie decided to learn to read and demonstrated her literacy and resistance to slavery openly at times to her owner. When she finally managed to escape to Indiana, Mattie dictated, or spoke the story of her life so someone could record it, and sold the story. She used the money to pay for her education.

Martin's photograph is part of a collection called Portraits of American Abolitionists, which features people who represent a wide range of viewpoints in the slavery debate.

JOHN SELLA MARTIN

Runaway slave and abolitionist John Sella Martin (shown above) learned to read by listening. Working in a hotel in Georgia, he secretly listened to white co-workers as they played games and spelled words. By memorizing the sounds and spellings, Martin learned to spell even before he saw the shapes of the letters in the alphabet. He then applied this knowledge by trying to decode signs on the stores he walked by.

Other enslaved people saw Martin spelling words and assumed he could read. One day, three illiterate men gave him a newspaper and dared him to read it to them. Martin thought he might have to pretend he could read it. Instead he found he could read the headline and much of the article, which was about an abolitionist. Amazed and proud, Martin then knew there were abolitionists fighting slavery. And, perhaps even more important, he knew he could read.

Enslaved friends brought Martin newspapers and books they had stolen from their masters so he could practice reading, risking punishment for helping him. For Martin and other slaves, learning to read was one step on the road to freedom.

education system and a significant increase in the literacy rate among African Americans.

During the postwar Reconstruction era, the number of schools for African Americans rose substantially. Newly emancipated African Americans, or freedmen, recognized the value of literacy and education and set out to establish new schools and colleges. In 1865, Congress established an organization called the Freedmen's Bureau to provide support to the newly freed. The bureau aided the spread of African-American

schools in the South, renting buildings for schools, providing books for teachers, and offering protection for students and teachers threatened by the opponents of black literacy. In the face of segregation, violence, and opposition, African Americans would continue to be challenged by the pursuit of equal education for many years.

THINK ABOUT IT

Why might access to public education have been one of the most important outcomes of the Civil War for African Americans?

Inclusion

Use Supported Reading Pair special needs students with a proficient reader. Have the proficient reader read the narrative aloud. Then have the other student use these frames to tell what they understood from the text:

• This American Story is about _____.
• Two details that stood out to me are _____ and _____.
• The person named _____ is important to this narrative because _____.

Pre-AP

Discuss a Primary Source In *My Bondage and My Freedom*, Frederick Douglass offers his account of his quest as a young slave to learn how to read. Tell students to locate the account *My Bondage and My Freedom* online and to identify the chapters that describe how and when Douglass learned to read. After students have read the account, invite them to hold a panel discussion to summarize and share their insights about Douglass's account.

See the Chapter Planner for more strategies for differentiation.

HISTORICAL THINKING

Ask and have students answer the following questions.

1. **READING CHECK** Why did white Americans disagree about teaching African Americans to read?
2. **IDENTIFY** How did enslaved people benefit from the ability to read and write?
3. **SYNTHESIZE** Why is the topic in this American Story important to all Americans?

ANSWERS

1. Some white Americans believed in universal literacy, but others feared it would lead slaves to revolt or push free African Americans to move into white communities to attend school.
2. They used the ability to read and write as a way to rebel against slavery, learn about current events, plan escapes, send messages, write about slavery, and write to lawmakers asking for their freedom.
3. The fight for the freedom to get an education reflects a national belief in education for all.

1.1 Reconstruction Under Andrew Johnson

Imagine you've been fighting with your friend. You both said and did terrible things, but you know it's time to forgive. How do you become friends again? That was the dilemma President Andrew Johnson faced after the Civil War.

MAIN IDEA President Johnson and Congress clashed over different goals for Reconstruction.

AMERICAN PLACES
Arlington National Cemetery
Arlington, Virginia

Arlington National Cemetery was established in 1864 on land that had belonged to Robert E. Lee. Thousands of Union soldiers, including free African Americans, had already been buried there. Lee's home, which rises in the photo's background, now serves as a museum.

LEADING THE WAY

1865 was a rough year. The war had torn the nation in two, and the war's end did not repair this division. Lincoln was dead, and citizens mourned the loss of his thoughtful guidance and strong leadership. The new president, Andrew Johnson, faced the monumental challenge of rebuilding the United States politically, socially, and economically. Many decisions had to be made. How should the Confederate states be readmitted to the Union? Should Confederate leaders be punished? What role should free African Americans play in the country?

Johnson had been an unusual choice as Lincoln's vice president. He was a southerner from Tennessee who had served in Congress as a Democrat. But he was definitely pro-Union, a stance fueled by his dislike for wealthy southern planters. When Tennessee seceded, he remained in the U.S. Senate. Lincoln later appointed Johnson as military governor of Tennessee. During the Civil War, military governors worked to re-establish the governments of southern states conquered by the Union Army.

When the 1864 election rolled around, the Republicans chose Johnson to run as Lincoln's vice president based on his loyalty to the Union. But Johnson didn't support equal rights for African Americans. Like most southern whites, he was deeply prejudiced, which offended many Republicans.

Among the first decisions Johnson made as president was to oversee Reconstruction himself, an approach called **Presidential Reconstruction**. Johnson's plan required Confederate states to ratify the 13th Amendment—which, as you may recall, abolished slavery—and create new governments with new constitutions before they could rejoin the Union.

Although he had repeatedly stated, "Treason is a crime, and crime must be punished," Johnson quickly pardoned, or legally forgave, most Confederates who took an oath of loyalty to the Union. The pardons restored their civil rights and protected their property from being seized. Only wealthy planters and high-ranking Confederate leaders had to apply individually for presidential pardons. Many in Congress felt Johnson's plans were too lenient, or forgiving. Congress wanted Confederates to pay for their actions.

THE FREEDMEN'S BUREAU

Johnson's perceived leniency toward the former rebels was not the only problem Republicans had with his plan. They were equally alarmed that Presidential Reconstruction did not provide a way for African-American men to vote, a right African Americans deeply desired. African Americans also wanted the right to own property. Without the protection of full citizenship and property rights, African Americans worried that white southerners would take away their newly won freedoms and economic opportunities.

Republicans shared their concerns. In 1865, Congress created the Bureau of Refugees, Freedmen, and Abandoned Lands—more popularly known as the **Freedmen's Bureau**—to help the formerly enslaved, as well as impoverished white southerners. Congress appointed General Oliver Otis Howard to run the bureau. Army officers acting as bureau agents provided medicine, food, and clothing to newly freed African Americans and others displaced by the war. The officers also tried to settle former slaves on southern land that had been abandoned or seized during the war. Agents drew up labor contracts between landowners and African-American workers and created courts to settle conflicts between African Americans and whites.

Howard also saw education as a way to improve living conditions and economic opportunities for African Americans. The Freedmen's Bureau worked with northern aid groups to establish schools for the newly freed. By 1869, approximately 3,000 schools serving more than 150,000 students reported to the bureau. Yet in spite of this progress, neither President Johnson nor most whites were ready to grant full rights to African Americans. As a result, the Republicans in Congress decided to take control of Reconstruction.

HISTORICAL THINKING

1. **READING CHECK** What were the original aims of Reconstruction?

2. **MAKE INFERENCES** Why might Johnson have chosen to be lenient toward many Confederates?

3. **SUMMARIZE** How did the Freedmen's Bureau affect newly freed African Americans?

Reconstruction and the New South **553**

PLAN

Objective

Describe the postwar roles of Presidential Reconstruction and the Freedmen's Bureau.

Critical Thinking Skills for Lesson 1.1

- Identify Main Ideas and Details
- Monitor Comprehension
- Make Inferences
- Summarize
- Make Connections
- Form and Support Opinions

Essential Question for Chapter 17

In what ways did Reconstruction both succeed and fail? Andrew Johnson sought to restore the Union but did not prioritize the rights of newly freed African Americans. Lesson 1.1 explores Johnson's Reconstruction policies and the efforts of the Freedmen's Bureau to help the formerly enslaved.

Background for the Teacher

While the Freedmen's Bureau made some progress, particularly in the realm of education, it could not ultimately achieve its lofty goals. The Bureau largely failed to grant freed African Americans land, leaving many dependent on white landowners to support them and their families. This system, known as sharecropping, trapped many in a brutal cycle of poverty. The Freedmen's court system was somewhat more effective, providing African Americans with legal recourse in states where they were subject to harsher sentences or limited access to courts. However, the court system did not operate for very long, and without its protection, African Americans found themselves routinely mistreated.

INTRODUCE & ENGAGE

Activate Prior Knowledge

Ask a student volunteer to read the lesson introduction aloud. Have students recall what they know about the end of the Civil War. Discuss whether the metaphor of the two sides as friends who have had a fight seems accurate. **ASK:** What do you think would be most important to the North following the war? *(Possible response: to ensure the end of slavery, the return of Southern states into the Union, and the possible punishment of Confederate leaders)* **ASK:** What do you think would be most important to the South? *(Possible response: to restore the South's economy and rebuild damaged cities)* Explain that in this lesson, they will learn about the early efforts to rebuild the war-torn nation.

TEACH

Guided Discussion

1. **Make Connections** How did Johnson's priorities in Presidential Reconstruction reflect his personal beliefs? *(Johnson's dislike of wealthy planters made him pro-Union. During Reconstruction, he was harsher on wealthy planters and Confederate leaders than on other southerners. His prejudice against African Americans was reflected in his failure to emphasize their rights.)*

2. **Form and Support Opinions** Do you think the efforts of the Freedmen's Bureau were necessary? Support your opinion with evidence from the text. *(Possible response: The Bureau was necessary to protect formerly enslaved African Americans because they didn't have voting and property rights, they were likely unprepared for life as free citizens, and they faced racism and prejudice.)*

🛡 American Places

Arlington National Cemetery (ANC) today serves as a museum, a memorial, and an operating cemetery. Its gravesites and memorials honor fallen soldiers from every U.S. war, as well as two presidents, astronauts killed in space shuttle disasters, and other prominent civilians, such as Senator Robert Kennedy. Visitors to the cemetery can schedule formal tours or use a mobile app to find the locations of individual graves or memorials. Have students visit the Monuments and Memorials page of the ANC website and explore the various memorials. Then ask them to choose one or two they would be interested in visiting. Prompt volunteers to share which memorials they chose and why.

Active Options

On Your Feet: Three Corners Create three signs: Social Reconstruction, Political Reconstruction, Economic Reconstruction. Place each sign in a corner of the room. Tell students that after the Civil War, the country had pressing problems to solve. Assign each student to one of the three groups. Ask them to discuss the pressing problems in their category. Then instruct each group to send a member to each of the other groups to exchange information. When they have finished, have students return to their original groups and compile the new information with their own. Ask students to tell which problems they think would be the most difficult to solve.

NG Learning Framework: Learn About the Presidential Pardon

ATTITUDE Curiosity

SKILL Collaboration

President Johnson's decision to pardon many Confederates was highly controversial. Have students work in pairs to use online sources to research the history of the presidential pardon: how it works, how various presidents have used it, and whether anyone can change or stop a pardon once issued. Direct them to choose one instance of a famous presidential pardon and prepare a brief summary of the event for the class.

DIFFERENTIATE

Striving Readers

Set a Purpose for Reading Before reading, have students examine the lesson title and subheadings to create purpose-setting questions such as the following:

• What was Andrew Johnson's role in Reconstruction?

• How did Johnson "lead the way" toward Reconstruction?

• What was the Freedmen's Bureau and what did it do?

After students have completed the reading, set aside time for them to revisit and respond to these questions with details from the text.

Pre-AP

Design a Web Page Have students use the text and outside resources to further research the Freedmen's Bureau. Ask them to use what they have learned to create a design for a Freedmen's Bureau web page (either digitally or on paper). Page designs might include relevant images, links to important services or projects, and profiles of people who worked for or were helped by the Bureau. You may wish to show students examples of web pages for present-day nonprofit organizations or state governments as examples of similar content. Have students present their designs to the class.

See the Chapter Planner for more strategies for differentiation.

HISTORICAL THINKING

ANSWERS

1. Reconstruction aimed to readmit Confederate states to the Union and have them ratify the 13th Amendment.

2. Answers will vary. Possible response: Johnson may have been lenient with the Confederates because he was from Tennessee, a Confederate state.

3. The Freedmen's Bureau provided medicine, food, and clothing to newly freed African Americans. It also established schools, set up courts to settle conflicts between African Americans and whites, and created labor contracts.

1.2 Radical Reconstruction

In a debate, you're pitted against a team that wants to make its case as badly as you do. In 1866, the president and Congress both wanted to win control of the South. The struggle deteriorated into name-calling and power grabs.

MAIN IDEA Unhappy with Johnson's Reconstruction plans, the Republican Congress took the responsibility away from him.

JOHNSON VERSUS CONGRESS

Made bold by the lenient terms of Presidential Reconstruction, some southern states refused to ratify the 13th Amendment. They even refused to admit that secession had been illegal. Southern states also passed **black codes**—laws for controlling African Americans and limiting their rights. The codes granted African Americans a few rights, such as the right to marry and pursue a lawsuit in court, but most of the codes dealt with what African Americans could not do. For example, they could not own land, work in certain industries, or serve on a jury.

Congress was furious over the black codes and the leniency of Johnson's Reconstruction plans. As a result, Republicans proposed the **Civil Rights Act of 1866**. The bill granted full equality and citizenship to "every race and color." Johnson vetoed the bill, but Republicans in Congress overrode the veto, and the bill became law. To solidify these rights, Radical Republicans also proposed the 14th Amendment. As you've read, this amendment guarantees citizenship and equal protection under the law to all American-born people. On President Johnson's urging, many southern states refused to ratify the new amendment. It took two years for two-thirds of the states to ratify it.

THE RECONSTRUCTION ACTS OF 1867

Shocked northerners watched as delegates at southern state conventions refused to accept the 14th Amendment. When Republicans won control of Congress in the 1866 elections, they decided it was time to take Reconstruction out of the president's hands. They put themselves in charge of the process by passing the **Reconstruction Acts of 1867**. Their plan of action came to be called **Radical Reconstruction**.

CRITICAL VIEWING Carl Schurz moved from Wisconsin to Missouri, where he was elected U.S. senator in 1868. In this political cartoon from 1872, he is shown as a carpetbagger. What details in the cartoon suggest what southerners thought of Schurz and other carpetbaggers?

The Reconstruction Acts placed all of the former Confederate states except Tennessee, which had already officially been readmitted to the Union, into five districts under military rule. Once military leaders decided that order had been established, the states could draw up new constitutions. Each constitution had to accept the 14th Amendment. Then the majority of a state's citizens and the U.S. Congress had to approve the new constitution. Republican delegates were given the task of writing the new state constitutions. Many of the delegates were southern white Republicans who had opposed secession. Those in the South who hated Radical Reconstruction called the southern white Republicans "scalawags," or dishonorable people.

Northern white Republicans also made up a sizeable number of the delegates. Many southerners believed the northern white

Republicans had come to the South to get rich and called them "carpetbaggers," implying they had thrown everything they owned into a cheap suitcase, or carpetbag, and headed south. In reality, most of the Republicans from the North were Union veterans, preachers, teachers, or social workers. Free African Americans made up the rest of the delegates. Most were ministers or teachers.

To prevent Johnson from interfering with Radical Reconstruction, Congress passed the Tenure of Office Act, which prevented the president from removing government officials without Senate approval. The act clearly violated and ignored a Constitutional provision that granted the president the right to hire and fire Cabinet members. Johnson defied the act in August 1867, when he replaced his Secretary of War, Edwin M. Stanton, with Civil War hero Ulysses S. Grant. Stanton had been the only member of Johnson's Cabinet to support Radical Reconstruction. Congress responded by beginning the **impeachment** process, officially charging Johnson with "high crimes and misdemeanors," or extreme misconduct, while in office. They hoped to remove him from the presidency, and this was the first step. But the Senate tried Johnson and acquitted him, or found him not guilty, by one vote.

HISTORICAL THINKING

1. **READING CHECK** What had to be done before a state could be readmitted to the Union?

2. **DRAW CONCLUSIONS** Why did many in Congress want to remove Johnson from the presidency?

3. **INTERPRET MAPS** Which southern state was the last to be readmitted to the Union?

Military Districts and Readmission, 1866–1870

Military District No. 1
Military District No. 2
Military District No. 3
Military District No. 4
Military District No. 5
1870 Date of readmission to the Union

VA. Jan. 26, 1870
N.C. July 24, 1866
TENN. July 24, 1866
S.C. Jun. 25, 1868
GA. July 15, 1870
ALA. July 14, 1868
FLA. Jun. 25, 1868
MISS. Feb. 23, 1870
ARK. Jun. 22, 1868
LA. Jun. 25, 1868
TEXAS Mar. 30, 1870

0   150   300 Miles
0   150 300 Kilometers

Gulf of Mexico

PLAN

Objective

Analyze the goals and methods of the Republicans' Radical Reconstruction plan.

Critical Thinking Skills for Lesson 1.2

- Identify Main Ideas and Details
- Monitor Comprehension
- Draw Conclusions
- Interpret Maps
- Determine Chronology
- Evaluate

Essential Question for Chapter 17

In what ways did Reconstruction both succeed and fail? Under Johnson's Reconstruction plan, some states failed to ratify the 13th Amendment. Lesson 1.2 explores the efforts of Republicans in Congress to take control of Reconstruction away from President Johnson.

Background for the Teacher

Carl Schurz, the senator portrayed in the cartoon, was born in Prussia but fled to the United States after escaping from prison for his role in the failed German revolution of 1848. Upon reaching America, he became an active abolitionist, joined the Union Army at the outset of the Civil War, and commanded troops at the Battle of Gettysburg. Following the war, he continued to argue for the full rights of African Americans, clashing with Presidents Johnson and Grant along the way. He served only one term in the Senate but later worked as the Secretary of the Interior under Rutherford Hayes. Carl Schurz Park in New York City is named for Schurz and is the site of Gracie Mansion, the official residence of the mayor.

Preview Terms

Point out the title of this lesson. **ASK:** What does the word *radical* mean to you? *(Answers will vary. Students might suggest the words* extreme, upheaval, change, *or* reform.) Explain that *radical* can have both positive (newness and transformation) and negative (extreme or dangerous) connotations. **ASK:** Based on what you know about Reconstruction under President Johnson, what do you think a Radical Reconstruction will be like? *(Possible response: A Radical Reconstruction might involve a change in southern governments, harsh punishments for Confederate leaders, or protection of rights for African Americans.)* When students have finished reading, have them revisit their predictions.

TEACH

Guided Discussion

1. **Determine Chronology** How did the Republican strategy towards Reconstruction change over time? *(Republicans in Congress initially attempted to address Presidential Reconstruction by passing laws, such as the Civil Rights Act of 1866, which protected the rights of African Americans. Eventually, Republicans had to take over Reconstruction entirely, and when Johnson continued to oppose them, they impeached him.)*

2. **Evaluate** Based on the information in the lesson and on the map, was the decision to make states ratify the 13th and 14th amendments before rejoining the Union an effective way of ratifying those amendments? Explain. *(Possible response: It was an effective plan. As illustrated by their actions under Presidential Reconstruction, the states would not have ratified the amendments without harsher enforcement by Congress. However, as seen by the map, under military rule, all the states had accepted the new amendments by 1870.)*

More Information

Abolition in Early State Constitutions Well before the Civil War, northern states had revised their constitutions or otherwise passed laws to ban slavery. The first state to do so was Vermont, which included these elements in its constitution as early as 1777. The Massachusetts constitution declared all men "free and equal," and in 1783, the courts decided this provision made slavery essentially illegal in the state. Other states, such as Pennsylvania, Connecticut, and Rhode Island, passed laws calling for a gradual end to slavery in the state in the 1780s. New York and New Jersey followed later, also passing laws for gradual abolition. **ASK:** Why might many states have called for gradual abolition rather than immediate abolition? *(Possible response: They may have feared economic or social disruption if they immediately freed all enslaved people in a state.)*

Active Options

On Your Feet: Living Time Line Have students work in pairs. Assign each pair an event from the lesson or from the map (for example, Tennessee is readmitted to the Union). Direct pairs to find their assigned event in the lesson to determine when it took place. Then ask all students to form a living time line by positioning themselves in order according to the year of their event. Remind students that some years will contain multiple events. When students have formed the time line, have them state their events in chronological order.

NG Learning Framework: Debate the Two Reconstructions

ATTITUDE Empowerment

SKILLS Collaboration, Communication

Organize the class into two groups and direct them to hold a debate about which Reconstruction plan was more effective at working toward the goal of healing and restoring the Union. Using the information in this section, have one team argue in favor of Johnson's Reconstruction and the other in favor of Radical Reconstruction. When both sides have argued their cases, have a whole-class discussion on how either plan could have been improved.

English Language Learners `ELD`

Use Sentence Stems Before beginning the lesson, provide students at the **Expanding** level with the sentence stems below. After reading, have students complete the stems in writing and compare completed sentences with a partner.

- Southern states restricted the rights of African Americans through _____. *(black codes)*
- The two amendments states had to ratify before rejoining the Union were _____. *(the 13th and 14th)*
- Under Radical Reconstruction, southern states were controlled by the _____. *(military)*
- When President Johnson continued to work against Reconstruction, Congress began the process of _____. *(impeachment)*

Inclusion

Describe a Map Have students with visual impairments partner with students who are not visually challenged. Ask the latter to describe in detail the map of states readmitted to the Union. Then direct students to work together to answer the Interpret Maps question in the Historical Thinking section.

See the Chapter Planner for more strategies for differentiation.

HISTORICAL THINKING

ANSWERS

1. Under Radical Reconstruction, states had to revise their constitutions to include the 14th Amendment and have the constitution approved by a majority of its citizens and the U.S. Congress.

2. Congress wanted to remove Johnson because he worked against their Reconstruction goals by removing officials who supported Radical Reconstruction and vetoing Republican legislation such as the Civil Rights Act of 1866.

3. Georgia was the last state to be readmitted to the Union, in July 1870.

CRITICAL VIEWING Answers will vary. Details such as Schurz's grasping fist and scowling face suggest that southerners viewed him and other carpetbaggers as greedy people.

2.1 Free African Americans Gain a Voice

Think of a time when you've stepped up to be a leader or you've done something hard and unfamiliar. You probably felt both nervous and proud. That may well have been how many African Americans felt as they took part in the political process for the first time.

MAIN IDEA During Radical Reconstruction, African Americans participated in government, established churches of their own, and tried to reestablish kinship structures.

TAKING PUBLIC OFFICE

After Congress passed the Reconstruction Acts, African Americans attained political freedom and wanted to exercise their new political power. As a result, many African-American citizens from the North, newly organized as Republicans, moved to the South hoping to fill appointed or elected government positions. African Americans from the South, some of whom had been free before the war, also sought leadership roles. These men became the backbone of the Republican Party in southern districts with large African-American populations.

African Americans everywhere wanted the ability to make their own choices. Many wanted to be involved in their states' readmission into the Union. Throughout the South, local African-American leaders, ministers, and Republicans encouraged newly freed men to register and vote. Their efforts helped Republican delegates dominate state constitutional conventions in every state except Georgia. African Americans also participated as delegates in all state conventions. Across the South, in fact, African Americans accounted for some 265 delegates out of a total of slightly more than 1,000. Between 1865 and 1877, African Americans influenced the direction of southern politics and elected 22 members of Congress. Republican-dominated legislatures established the first publicly financed education systems in the South, provided debt relief to the poor, and expanded women's rights.

About 600 African Americans also participated directly in the new state legislatures. Although no African Americans were elected governor, several served as lieutenant governors, secretaries of state, judges, or treasurers. **Pinckney Pinchback**, the lieutenant governor of Louisiana, became the acting governor when the state charged his boss with corruption.

African Americans became leaders at the national level when **Hiram Rhodes Revels** and **Blanche K. Bruce** served in the U.S. Senate. Revels, who was born a free man, served in Mississippi's state senate. He went on to fill a U.S. Senate seat left vacant when Mississippi seceded from the Union. He was the first African American to serve in the U.S. Senate. Bruce, who had been born into slavery, also represented Mississippi. He was the second African American to serve in the U.S. Senate and the first to be elected to a full term. In addition, 14 African Americans served in the U.S. House of Representatives during the Reconstruction era.

CHURCH AND FAMILY

Hiram Revels was already familiar in the African-American community in Mississippi through his work as a minister in the African Methodist Episcopal Church. Churches had long been at the center of African-American life. Because ministers were often the most educated members of the community, they became natural leaders—not only in religious matters but also in politics.

Following the Civil War, African Americans quickly established their own churches. The new churches were often Baptist because that denomination allowed each congregation to start a church independently and organize the services the way it wanted. By 1890, about 1.3 million African Americans were members of Baptist churches, mostly in the South. Churches were central to the African-American quest for social justice, or fair distribution of opportunities and privileges, including racial equality and rights. In addition to providing a place of worship, African-American churches often served as gathering places for social and political events and housed schools.

Like churches, family life had always been important to African Americans. But as you know, slavery had often split up families when members were sold to different owners. During Reconstruction, many African Americans tried to locate and reunite with their families. They were helped in this effort by the Freedmen's Bureau. In some cases, the bureau succeeded, particularly when the separated members of a family had gone to nearby plantations. Unfortunately, in other cases, family members had been sent far away. Some African Americans traveled hundreds of miles searching for their loved ones—often in vain.

First African Americans in U.S. Congress
The seven men in this print from 1872 are the first African Americans to serve in the U.S. Congress. Together, the seven represented five southern states. From left to right, the men are Senator Hiram Rhodes Revels of Mississippi (who filled the Senate seat that Jefferson Davis had held), Congressman Benjamin S. Turner of Alabama, Congressman Robert C. De Large of South Carolina, Congressman Josiah T. Walls of Florida, Congressman Jefferson F. Long of Georgia, Congressman Joseph Rainey of South Carolina, and Congressman Robert B. Elliot of South Carolina.

HISTORICAL THINKING

1. **READING CHECK** How did African-American political participation help strengthen the Republican Party in the South?

2. **MAKE INFERENCES** Why do you think it was important for African Americans to establish their own churches?

3. **DRAW CONCLUSIONS** Why were African Americans strongly motivated to influence and become leaders in government?

PLAN

Objective

Describe the impact of Reconstruction on African-American political participation, religion, and family life.

Critical Thinking Skills for Lesson 2.1

- Identify Main Ideas and Details
- Monitor Comprehension
- Make Inferences
- Draw Conclusions
- Make Generalizations
- Describe

Essential Question for Chapter 17

In what ways did Reconstruction both succeed and fail? The Reconstruction Acts allowed African Americans to experience greater freedom within the South. Lesson 2.1 discusses ways African Americans worked to build political, religious, and family structures during Reconstruction.

Background for the Teacher

African Americans often established Baptist churches because the denomination allowed them to organize independently. The Baptist church in the South grew rapidly during the First Great Awakening of the 1700s, at which time many enslaved people were brought into the church. With the end of slavery, African-American participation in Baptist churches increased even further, and by 1900 it had more African-American members than any other denomination. The relationship between African Americans and the Baptist denomination remains strong to the present. Surveys conducted in 2007 showed that African Americans were more likely than many other groups to belong to a church, and approximately 40 percent were Baptist.

Hands Up, Hands Down

List the names of some former or current African American members of Congress, such as Maxine Waters, Tim Scott, Kamala Harris, and John Lewis. Instruct students to raise their hands when they recognize a name and tell what they know about the person. Inform students that prior to Reconstruction, no African Americans had served in Congress. Then have students examine the print of the first African Americans in Congress and read the caption. Finally, tell students that in this lesson they will learn about some African Americans who worked to build political power during Reconstruction. **ASK:** Can you predict what effect it had on U.S. politics for African Americans to become involved in the process? *(Answers will vary.)*

TEACH

Guided Discussion

1. **Make Generalizations** What were the goals of the Republican Party in the South during this era? *(The Republican Party during this era sought to expand the rights for citizens, such as women, African Americans, the poor, and children.)*

2. **Describe** How did Reconstruction affect African-American families? *(Under slavery, African-American families were often separated. During Reconstruction, African Americans could look for relatives and maintain kinship ties.)*

More Information

Frederick Douglass's Speech When African Americans gained their freedom, they did not automatically gain the right to vote. Share with students the following passage from Frederick Douglass's 1865 speech, "What the Black Man Wants."

> I believe that when the tall heads of this Rebellion shall have been swept down, as they will be swept down, when the Davises and Toombses and Stephenses, and others who are leading this Rebellion shall have been blotted out, there will be this rank undergrowth of treason [. . .] growing up there, and interfering with, and thwarting the quiet operation of the Federal Government in those states. You will see those traitors, handing down, from sire to son, the same malignant spirit which they have manifested and which they are now exhibiting, with malicious hearts, broad blades, and bloody hands in the field, against our sons and brothers.

Help students interpret Douglass's rhetoric in the excerpt. **ASK:** What does Douglass think will happen in the South after the war? *(People in the South will fight the federal government and continue oppressing African Americans.)* **ASK:** How might political power have protected African Americans against this hostility? *(If African Americans had power in local governments, they would not need to rely on the federal government.)*

Active Options

On Your Feet: Card Response Divide the class in half and then have one half write ten true-false statements about the impact of Reconstruction on African Americans. Have the other half create response cards, writing "True" on one side and "False" on the other side. Students from the first group take turns reading their statement. Students from the second group hold up their response cards, showing either "True" or "False."

NG Learning Framework: Write a Biography

ATTITUDE Curiosity

KNOWLEDGE Our Human Story

Invite students to use online and print resources to research and write a short biography of one of the African-American political leaders mentioned in this lesson, focusing on his life during Reconstruction and time working within the government. Students may then present their biographies to the class or post them online in a class blog. Have the class discuss similarities and differences among the experiences of the leaders.

DIFFERENTIATE

Striving Readers

Read and Recall Allow students to work in pairs. First, have each student read the lesson independently. Then have students meet without the text and share ideas they recall. One person should take notes. Then have pairs look at the lesson together and decide what should be added or changed in the notes.

Gifted & Talented

Give a Campaign Speech Have students choose one of the individuals mentioned in the lesson—including those identified in the print—and use the text and outside resources to gain an understanding of his political positions. Tell students to prepare a short campaign speech in the persona of the individual, naming the office for which the person was running, the policies he supported, and what he hoped to achieve in office. Encourage students to find campaign slogans used or to invent one based on his positions. Have students present their speeches to the class.

See the Chapter Planner for more strategies for differentiation.

HISTORICAL THINKING

ANSWERS

1. African Americans participated in state conventions, registered and voted as Republicans, and ran for office as Republicans. Some African Americans from the North moved to the South to participate in politics.

2. Possible response: Establishing their own churches allowed African Americans to build communities for education, politics, and social justice, as well as religion.

3. African Americans were motivated to influence and become political leaders to protect and expand their rights after the end of slavery.

2.2 Education and Land

Like most Americans, you probably consider the education you receive as your right, rather than a privilege. But to African Americans during Reconstruction, school was an important sign of their new freedom.

MAIN IDEA The Freedmen's Bureau made education available to African Americans in the South, but other aspects of their lives changed very little.

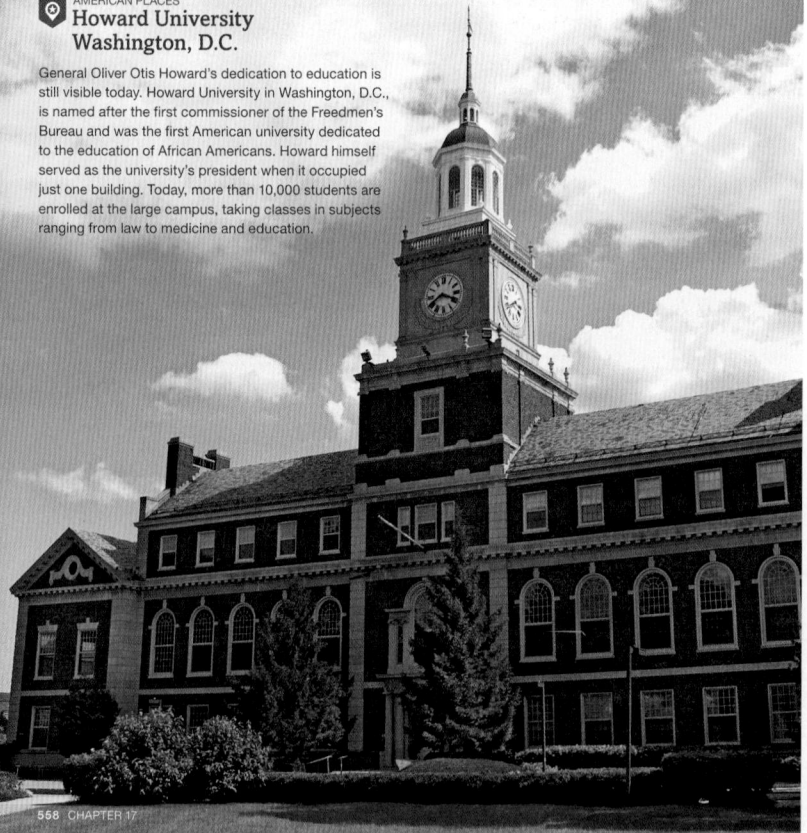

AMERICAN PLACES
Howard University
Washington, D.C.

General Oliver Otis Howard's dedication to education is still visible today. Howard University in Washington, D.C., is named after the first commissioner of the Freedmen's Bureau and was the first American university dedicated to the education of African Americans. Howard himself served as the university's president when it occupied just one building. Today, more than 10,000 students are enrolled at the large campus, taking classes in subjects ranging from law to medicine and education.

AN OPPORTUNITY TO LEARN

African Americans appreciated the value of education. Slavery had denied many of them the opportunity to learn, so they saw education as a path to empowerment. **Literacy**, or the ability to read and write, and a solid working knowledge of mathematics gave African Americans the tools they needed to understand labor contracts. Education helped them advance in a **wage economy**, or an economy in which people are paid for their work. With a good education, they could fully participate in the political process and understand their civil rights.

The Freedmen's Bureau helped provide educational opportunities. The bureau and aid groups worked with individual communities to fund, build, and staff hundreds of Freedmen's Schools for African-American children and adults. These schools were often built on land owned by African Americans or housed in their churches. The schools were free, but since most African-American families counted on the labor or income their older children could provide, parents sacrificed a lot to send their children to school.

A shortage of teachers and space meant that schools often had to rotate students in three-hour groups. Typically, teachers worked all day teaching children and then held classes for adults at night. In some schools, however, young people worked and learned alongside adults in the classroom. In return, teachers experienced the satisfaction of teaching enthusiastic and motivated students. By the time the Freedmen's Bureau closed, about 150,000 students had attended classes.

BACK TO WORKING THE LAND

A good education was important to African Americans in the South because it offered their only chance for advancement. For the most part, uneducated African Americans worked the land of white landowners, but they faced discrimination in a southern economy on the edge of collapse. As a result, many former slaves wanted to obtain their own land to farm. Some freed African Americans had this wish fulfilled—at least for a short time.

In January 1865, General William T. Sherman issued Special Field Order No. 15, which set aside the Sea Islands for newly freed African Americans. The Sea Islands were located south of Charleston, South Carolina, and encompassed an area of approximately 400,000 acres. Each family would receive 40 acres to farm and a mule. News of the offer spread quickly, and about 40,000 African Americans rushed to settle on the land. But by the fall of 1865, President Andrew Johnson had overturned Sherman's order. The land was returned to the southern planters who had owned it before the Civil War.

With no land of their own, many African Americans went back to working for white landowners. At first, landowners insisted that the newly freed African Americans work in gangs, as they had under slavery. Over time, however, an agricultural system called **sharecropping** developed. In sharecropping, a farmer raised crops for a landowner in return for part of the money made from selling the crops. Some poor white families, devastated by the war, also took up sharecropping. But they did not face the discrimination that African Americans endured.

Sharecropping often left African-American families in debt to landowners. The sharecroppers needed supplies, such as tools and seeds, to work the land. Landowners would sell or rent the supplies to the sharecroppers on credit and at a high rate of interest. By the time the crops were harvested, sharecroppers had usually run up a large bill and, as a result, would receive very little of the profits from selling the crops. Sharecropping tied African Americans to a landowner's land and resulted in **black peonage**, a sort of economic slavery.

Unable to earn a living as sharecroppers or find other work, many African Americans began moving north or west. Some also fled to escape the terror generated by groups of white southerners.

HISTORICAL THINKING

1. **READING CHECK** How did the Freedmen's Bureau help educate former slaves?

2. **ANALYZE CAUSE AND EFFECT** What factors led to the development of sharecropping in the South?

3. **DRAW CONCLUSIONS** In what way did sharecropping replace slavery?

PLAN

Objective
Discuss the efforts of groups to empower and educate freed African Americans.

Critical Thinking Skills for Lesson 2.2
- Identify Main Ideas and Details
- Monitor Comprehension
- Analyze Cause and Effect
- Draw Conclusions
- Make Inferences
- Form and Support Opinions

Essential Question for Chapter 17
In what ways did Reconstruction both succeed and fail? Despite the efforts of aid groups during Reconstruction, freed African Americans faced obstacles. Lesson 2.2 explores the establishment of schools and the sharecropping system.

Background for the Teacher
After his time as head of the Freedmen's Bureau, Oliver Otis Howard returned to military service under President Ulysses S. Grant. Grant sent him to negotiate peace with the Apache, and later, to move Chief Joseph's Nez Percé group out of their homelands—whether through negotiation or force. During the Civil War, Howard's convictions led him to work on behalf of formerly enslaved people. Later, as a representative of the military in the West, Otis found himself sympathetic to the plight of the Native Americans. Some complained Howard gave too many concessions to the Apache, and while he was obligated by military orders to move the Nez Percé to a reservation, he later argued for the decision to be reversed.

History Notebook
Encourage students to complete the American Gallery page for Chapter 17 in their History Notebooks as they read.

Brainstorm with Visuals

Have students view the photograph. Explain that Howard University was founded shortly after the Civil War to educate African Americans. **ASK:** What impression of Howard University do you get from this photograph? *(Students may say that it seems important, official looking, grand, or inspirational.)* Remind students that most enslaved people were forbidden to attend school or even learn to read. **ASK:** How do you think formerly enslaved people might feel about attending a school like Howard? *(Possible responses: empowered, respected, inspired, ambitious)* Tell students that in this lesson, they will learn about how African Americans' lives changed during Reconstruction.

TEACH

Guided Discussion

1. **Make Inferences** Why would the Freedmen's Bureau establish schools on African-American–owned land or in African-American churches? *(The Freedmen's Bureau may have been unable to afford land, or it might have been difficult to find people willing to sell land. African Americans may have felt safer attending classes in familiar areas.)*

2. **Form and Support Opinions** What was the main reason for Reconstruction's failures? Support your opinion with evidence from the text. *(Answers will vary. Possible response: The main reason for Reconstruction's failures was racial prejudice. People in power, such as Andrew Johnson, were reluctant to give African Americans the land and help they needed to become truly equal. This resulted in systems like sharecropping and in African-American schools operating with little staff or space.)*

🔾 American Places

Howard University is one of over 100 Historically Black Colleges and Universities (HBCUs) in the United States. In order to be classified as an HBCU, a school must have been founded before 1964 for the purpose of educating black students—although the school can admit students of all races and ethnicities. Today, Howard University consists of 13 schools and colleges and is home to a hospital, a television station, and commercial and student radio stations. Prominent alumni include Nobel Prize-winning author Toni Morrison and the first African-American justice of the Supreme Court, Thurgood Marshall.

Active Options

AMERICAN GALLERY ONLINE **The Freed Slaves of the Civil War** Invite students to explore the American Gallery. Have them select one of the images and do additional research to learn more about it. Ask questions that will inspire further inquiry about the chosen gallery images, such as: What or whom is shown in this image? Who took the picture, and why? What might the photographer want people to think about this subject? Why does it belong in this chapter? What else would you like to know about it?

NG Learning Framework: Discover an HBCU

ATTITUDE Curiosity

KNOWLEDGE Our Human Story

Invite students to use online sources to identify the Historically Black Colleges or Universities located in the United States. Direct students to choose one of the schools they find and do research to determine its location, the history of its founding, and what its enrollment and areas of focus are today. Tell students they might include details about the mascot, school colors, famous alumni, and other interesting details about the campus and student life. Have students prepare a short presentation on their chosen school and deliver it to the class.

DIFFERENTIATE

Inclusion

Use Echo Reading Pair students with special needs with proficient readers. Have the latter read the Main Idea statement aloud. Then have the student with special needs read back the same statement. Have pairs repeat this process for the first paragraph of the lesson and each of the subheadings.

Pre-AP

Write a Persuasive Essay Tell students to imagine they are General Sherman and have just heard that President Johnson plans to overturn Special Field Order No. 15. Then direct them to write a persuasive essay to convince the president that the order must be preserved. Students should use evidence from the lesson as well as from outside sources to support their arguments. Have students present their essays to the class or share them on a class blog.

See the Chapter Planner for more strategies for differentiation.

HISTORICAL THINKING

ANSWERS

1. The Freedmen's Bureau helped to educate formerly enslaved people by working with communities to build, staff, and run schools attended by children and adults.

2. A lack of farmland for African Americans, a need for farm labor in the post-war southern economy, and an absence of other opportunities for former slaves led to the development of sharecropping.

3. Sharecropping, like slavery, forced African Americans to do physical farm labor for white landowners. While they were technically working for a wage, African-American sharecroppers were often heavily in debt and could not get ahead financially.

2.3 Resistance in the South

Terror is a powerful weapon. When combined with racism, its damage can last for generations. A reign of terror in the South set back African-American political gains and broke the Republican Party's hold in the region.

MAIN IDEA Afraid of losing political and economic power, some white southerners used terror tactics against African Americans and Republicans.

THE KU KLUX KLAN

Radical Reconstruction angered many white southerners and created a resistance movement based on racism and discrimination. Few white southerners accepted African Americans as their equals. Sometimes whites turned to violence in an attempt to keep African Americans from voting and exercising other rights. In 1866, white mobs attacked unarmed African-American men, women, and children and rioted in Memphis, Tennessee, and New Orleans, Louisiana. The mobs killed or injured many African Americans. In Memphis, the rioters, who included police officers, committed **arson** by purposefully burning homes, churches, and schools in African-American communities.

That same year, a group of young men in Tennessee founded the **Ku Klux Klan**. Originally intended as a social club, the group's purpose changed dramatically in 1867 when African Americans gained voting rights in the state under the Reconstruction Acts and began holding public office. Thereafter, the Ku Klux Klan, under the leadership of former Confederate officer Nathan Bedford Forrest, dedicated itself to maintaining the social and political power of white people.

To achieve its goals, members of the Klan terrorized and killed African Americans. They also attacked white people who associated with Republicans or supported African-American rights. To conceal their identities and maximize the terror, Klan members rode out at night dressed in hooded costumes. They whipped, tar-and-feathered, and even **lynched**, or hanged, their victims. They also committed arson. The Klan became the face of violent discrimination, carrying out punishments against people whom they felt had overstepped racial boundaries. Boosted by popular sentiment and federal acceptance, the Klan's popularity quickly spread across the South and even beyond.

CRITICAL VIEWING In 1874, this political cartoon by Thomas Nast appeared in *Harper's Weekly*. Why do you think the cartoonist included the words "worse than slavery" over the heads of the African-American family?

The Klan Through the Years
The Ku Klux Klan members in this photo traveled from New Jersey to take part in a Klan parade held in Washington, D.C., in 1926. The legal action brought against the Klan in 1871 drove its members into hiding, but it did not destroy the organization. Further actions by the government never succeeded in dissolving the group either. The Klan resurfaced in the 1920s, fueled by the arrival of immigrants whom they accused of taking jobs away from "real" Americans.

The Klan began to grab newspaper headlines once again as the civil rights movement gathered momentum in the 1950s and 1960s. After three civil rights volunteers were killed in Mississippi in 1964, FBI agents discovered the murderers were Klan members and police officers. Seven men were arrested for the murders. The Klan still exists today, although it is widely despised and wields very little political power. As of April 2014, official Klan groups were registered in 41 states with a total of as many as 8,000 members.

A POWER SHIFT

In response, the Republican-dominated Congress passed the Enforcement Acts in 1870 and 1871. The acts made it a crime to use violence or threats to interfere with a citizen's right to vote, hold office, or serve on a jury. The acts authorized the federal government to supervise congressional elections and gave the president the power to enforce the acts. The intent of the acts was to stop Klan activities and protect African-American rights.

Armed with the Enforcement Acts, the federal government took legal action against the Klan in 1871. In state after state, the government charged Klan leaders with crimes. The Klan became less visible, but their scare tactics had already damaged the Republican Party by preventing African Americans from voting. As a result, the Democratic Party began to gain back control in the South, and the number of African-American officeholders fell dramatically.

Meanwhile, many white voters in the North also thought the Radical Republicans had gone too far in promoting African-American rights. Even though the country would elect a Republican president in 1868, Reconstruction was starting to lose steam.

Members of the Ku Klux Klan often wore metal membership badges like these. The 1921 Klan badge on the right is shaped like the hood Klan members wore to scare and intimidate their victims.

HISTORICAL THINKING

1. **READING CHECK** What tactics did the Ku Klux Klan use to terrorize African Americans and white Republicans?

2. **MAKE INFERENCES** Why do you think the Klan's activities were allowed to continue in the South until 1870?

3. **SUMMARIZE** How did Klan activities change the balance of political power in the South?

Objective
Trace the development of southern resistance to Reconstruction through the rise of the KKK.

Critical Thinking Skills for Lesson 2.3
- Identify Main Ideas and Details
- Monitor Comprehension
- Make Inferences
- Summarize
- Make Connections
- Evaluate
- Analyze Visuals

Essential Question for Chapter 17
In what ways did Reconstruction both succeed and fail? African Americans' economic and political gains led to violent backlash from white southerners. Lesson 2.3 discusses how terrorism and intimidation drove southern African Americans out of the political process.

Background for the Teacher
In viewing the political cartoon, students may note that it shows a handshake between two men, one labeled "KKK," and the other labeled "White League." Unlike the Ku Klux Klan, the White League does not have a presence in the United States today. However, in the 1870s, this paramilitary group and others like it were the cause of substantial violence in the South. Leaders of the White League were often prominent locals who generally did not hide their identities. Their tactics ranged from political intimidation through election disruption to outright assassination and violence. In 1873, well-armed White Leaguers in Colfax Parish, Louisiana, attacked a state militia and killed about 100 African Americans. This attack, known sometimes as the Colfax Massacre or the Battle of Colfax, set a pattern for later violence.

Preview, Review, and Predict

Have students read the lesson title, the introductory paragraph in blue text, and the Main Idea statement. **ASK:** Why were white southerners afraid of losing political power? *(Under Reconstruction, African Americans and white Republicans who supported them had begun to build political power in southern local and state governments.)* Next, tell students to write a sentence predicting what this lesson will be about. When they have finished reading, ask students to revisit their predictions and evaluate whether the predictions were accurate.

TEACH

Guided Discussion

1. **Make Connections** In what way were attacks on African-American schools and churches a reaction to Reconstruction policies? *(Under Reconstruction, African-American schools spread throughout the south, and churches became centers of African-American political activity. Attacking these African-American institutions was an attack on African-American gains made through Reconstruction policies.)*

2. **Evaluate** Were the Enforcement Acts an effective tool against the Klan and other groups like it? Why or why not? *(Possible responses: The Enforcement Acts were an effective tool because they helped the government arrest leaders of groups, such as the Klan, and made the Klan less visible. They were not an effective tool because the damage had already been done, and Klan members simply went underground.)*

Analyze Visuals

Direct students' attention to the photograph. **ASK:** What can you infer from the men's uncovered faces? *(Answers will vary. Possible response: The men are not ashamed to be identified as part of the Klan.)* As a class, discuss what the uncovered faces suggest about the Klan's acceptance in society. Then have students examine the membership badges shown below the photograph. **ASK:** For what reasons might someone wear these badges? *(Possible responses: to intimidate any African Americans they encountered; to signal their opinions to others who might share them; to threaten people who might disagree)*

Active Options

On Your Feet: Build a Paragraph Instruct students to stand in four lines. Present the class with a topic sentence: White southerners used terror and violence to hinder African Americans' progress under Reconstruction. Then direct each line of students to build a paragraph based on the topic sentence, adding sentences one student at a time. Have the groups record their paragraphs (in audio or writing) and share them with the class.

NG Learning Framework: Explore Social Justice Organizations

ATTITUDES Empowerment, Responsibility

SKILL Collaboration

Remind students that the Ku Klux Klan and other groups like it still exist in society, but so do groups dedicated to promoting social justice. Organize students into small groups and direct them to use online sources to research social justice organizations such as the Southern Poverty Law Center and the Anti-Defamation League. Have students choose an organization and identify its main goals and actions. Then ask them to brainstorm a list of ways they could contribute to the work these groups do. Post student lists on a class bulletin board or wall.

Striving Readers

Understand Main Ideas Check students' understanding of the lesson's main ideas by asking students to correctly complete either/or statements such as the following:

- Many white southerners [supported or opposed] Radical Reconstruction.

- Members of the Ku Klux Klan [encouraged or rejected] violence against African Americans.

- The Klan's actions were [popular or unpopular] with many white southerners.

- Congress [canceled or passed] the Enforcement Acts to protect African Americans against the Klan.

- Because of Klan threats, the number of African Americans in government [rose or fell].

English Language Learners

Use Word Parts Help students at the **Bridging** level expand their vocabularies by examining word parts. Write *enforcement* on the board and underline the suffix *-ment*. Explain that the suffix *-ment* changes the verb *enforce* into a noun that means the act of enforcing something. Have students write a sentence telling why the name "Enforcement Acts" is an accurate one for the laws described in the lesson.

See the Chapter Planner for more strategies for differentiation.

HISTORICAL THINKING

ANSWERS

1. The Ku Klux Klan rode out in costumes, burning houses, schools, and churches. They assaulted and even murdered African Americans and white sympathizers.

2. Possible response: Many people in the South agreed with the Klan's activities, even if they didn't participate, because they were prejudiced against African Americans.

3. By preventing African Americans from voting, the Klan weakened the Republican Party and helped the Democratic Party regain power, dramatically reducing the number of African-American officeholders.

CRITICAL VIEWING Possible response: "Worse than slavery" suggests that life for African Americans in the South was more dangerous and oppressive under the threat of groups like the KKK than it had been under slavery.

Grant's Presidency

Think about how much has been at stake in recent presidential elections. The election of 1868 was similar, especially for Republicans and African Americans. A Democratic victory could deliver the end of Reconstruction.

MAIN IDEA After their party's victory in the 1868 presidential election, Republicans helped pass the 15th Amendment.

THE ELECTION OF GENERAL GRANT

In the 1868 presidential race, the Republicans nominated Ulysses S. Grant, the great Union hero of the Civil War. Although Grant had no experience in government, Republicans believed their candidate would be able to please members of both parties. When Grant accepted the nomination, he said, "Let us have peace." That phrase became a theme for the campaign. Republicans were aware that white voters had become less willing to help African Americans. As a result, the party did not promise to expand Reconstruction or to further promote the rights of African Americans.

The Democrats nominated **Horatio Seymour**, the former governor of New York, as their candidate. Seymour was part of a group of Democrats called the **Copperheads**. As you probably know, a copperhead is a poisonous snake. During the Civil War, this group, who called themselves "Peace Democrats," opposed emancipation and the draft. Republicans called the group "Copperheads" because they believed its members were Confederate sympathizers.

Seymour and the Copperheads relied on fear and racism to attract voters. Seymour criticized the Republicans for their aggressive handling of Reconstruction. He felt the government placed too much importance on African-American rights. His ideals appealed to many midwestern farmers who felt the Republicans did not understand their way of

1868 Campaign Buttons
Grant's running mate was Schuyler (SKY-ler) Colfax, a prominent Radical Republican. The candidates' campaign buttons feature ferrotypes, or photos printed on tin.

life. He also appealed to urban whites who believed free African Americans would move to the North and take their jobs.

Despite Seymour's rhetoric, or use of persuasive language, Grant led the Republicans to victory in the 1868 election. About 500,000 African Americans voted for Grant, helping him receive 53 percent of the ballots. In his inaugural speech, Grant declared, "I shall on all subjects have a policy to recommend, but none to enforce against the will of the people." He promised, unlike Andrew Johnson, to carry out the laws that Congress passed.

THE 15TH AMENDMENT

After the 1868 election, Republicans pushed for the adoption of the **15th Amendment** to the Constitution. Under the amendment's terms, the federal and state governments could not restrict the right to vote because of race, color, or

CRITICAL VIEWING Called *The 15th Amendment*, this 1870 print illustrates a parade celebrating the amendment's passage. The large image is surrounded by portraits of those who helped pass the amendment, including Abraham Lincoln, and scenes depicting African-American life. What do some of the scenes illustrate?

previous condition of servitude—in other words, slavery. The amendment would complete the political reforms sought by Reconstruction. Congress approved the amendment in February 1869 despite Democratic opposition, and it became part of the Constitution in 1870.

The intent of the amendment was to limit the southern states' ability to prevent African Americans from participating in the political process. But the new law did little for African Americans outside the former Confederacy. It also did not restrict or change any of the laws that states had placed on the rights of males to vote, such as charging **poll taxes**. A poll tax is a fee charged when people register to vote. Meanwhile, the Amnesty Act of 1872 removed voting restrictions on most of those who had belonged to the Confederacy.

The adoption of the 13th, 14th, and 15th amendments fundamentally changed the nation by establishing citizenship rights and full equality for anyone born in the United States. However, over the next couple of decades, courts and political interests would undermine the intent of the amendments.

Still, rights and equality were not on the minds of most people in the 1870s. They wanted their elected leaders to pay more attention to problems closer to home, including a severe economic depression. As an Illinois newspaper observed, "the negro is now a voter and a citizen. Let him hereafter take his chances in the battle of life."

HISTORICAL THINKING

1. **READING CHECK** What was the theme of Grant's presidential campaign?

2. **COMPARE AND CONTRAST** What differing views characterized the Republican and Democratic presidential candidates in the election of 1868?

3. **DRAW CONCLUSIONS** Why would a poll tax prevent African Americans from voting?

PLAN

Objective

Analyze the effects of Grant's election and the 15th Amendment on Reconstruction.

Critical Thinking Skills for Lesson 3.1

- Identify Main Ideas and Details
- Monitor Comprehension
- Compare and Contrast
- Draw Conclusions
- Make Inferences
- Identify Problems and Solutions
- Form and Support Opinions

Essential Question for Chapter 17

In what ways did Reconstruction both succeed and fail? Amid resistance in the South and economic strife, Radical Reconstruction began to lose support. Lesson 3.1 explores how the election of Ulysses S. Grant reflected a change in the Republican Party's approach to Reconstruction.

Background for the Teacher

Horatio Seymour's opposition to the Republican Party predated the Civil War. In the 1850s, as governor of New York, he argued for compromise over war. Once the war started, Seymour opposed Lincoln on issues such as emancipation and the draft. By contrast, Seymour's running mate, Francis Blair, Jr., had supported gradual emancipation followed by deportation. Blair campaigned for Lincoln, served in Congress as a Republican, and was at least partly responsible for keeping Missouri in the Union. Nonetheless, by 1868, Blair had changed parties and was willing to run on a campaign whose supporters sometimes wore badges stating, "This is a White Man's Country; Let White Men Rule."

Connect to Today

Ask students to consider what they know about or associate with present-day presidential elections. **ASK:** In what ways are presidents sometimes different during a campaign than they are in office? *(Answers will vary. Students may point out that they do not always focus on the same issues or that they change their positions on some issues.)* Discuss some reasons why presidential candidates might compromise on issues, either before or after an election. *(Possible responses: in order to win more votes; in order to please voters after the election; because circumstances have changed)* Explain that in this lesson, students will be reading about an election in which Republicans modified their positions on Reconstruction.

TEACH
Guided Discussion

1. **Make Inferences** How might Grant and the Republicans' campaign for peace have meant different things to different people? *(Answers will vary. Possible response: Northern whites and African Americans might have viewed it as a promise to end the violent backlash in the South, while Southern whites might have viewed it as a promise to end the military occupation and Reconstruction.)*

2. **Identify Problems and Solutions** What were the weaknesses of the 15th Amendment? *(Answers may vary. Possible response: The 15th Amendment did not eliminate laws intended to obstruct African-American voting, such as poll taxes.)*

Form and Support Opinions

Direct students to review the descriptions of Grant's campaign and his presidency. **ASK:** Based on what you have read, do you think Grant changed his position on Reconstruction either during the campaign or during his presidency? *(Answers will vary. Possible responses: Yes, because he helped to pass the 15th Amendment without promising to expand Reconstruction. No, because the 15th Amendment only made official the existing goals of Reconstruction.)* **ASK:** Do you think Grant was right to take a more moderate stance on Reconstruction during his campaign? Explain why or why not. *(Answers will vary, but students should support them with evidence from the chapter.)*

Active Options

Active History: Amend the Constitution Extend the lesson by using either the PDF or Whiteboard version of the activity. These activities take a deeper look at a topic from, or related to, the lesson. Explore the activities as a class, turn them into group assignments, or even assign them individually.

NG Learning Framework: Create a Campaign Item

SKILLS Collaboration, Observation

KNOWLEDGE Our Human Story

Organize students into pairs and tell them to use library and online sources to research examples of political posters, buttons, and leaflets from the late 1800s. Tell students to look for the kinds of imagery, design, and content the campaign materials have in common. Have students use their research to help them design a campaign item for Ulysses S. Grant and Schuyler Colfax. Direct them to use information from the lesson to determine content that might influence a voter in the 1868 presidential race. When students have finished, display their work in the classroom.

DIFFERENTIATE
Striving Readers

Create Main Idea Diagrams Give pairs of students a Main Idea Diagram. Have them write the Main Idea statement in the top box. As they read, they should record important supporting details from the text in the smaller boxes of the diagram. Encourage students to draw additional detail boxes or create a second Main Idea Diagram if necessary.

Pre-AP

Research the 15th Amendment Direct students to research the arguments made for and against the 15th Amendment during the late 1860s and early 1870s and then to write a short paper outlining the major arguments on both sides of the issue. Encourage students to draw on primary sources, both print and digital, such as statements made in Congress or newspaper editorials from the late 1860s and early 1870s, as well as secondary sources. Provide students with guidelines for using search terms effectively and assessing the credibility and accuracy of sources. Emphasize that students are use a standard format for citation when quoting or paraphrasing information to avoid plagiarism. Then hold a panel discussion with the whole class to have students present the findings of their research.

See the Chapter Planner for more strategies for differentiation.

HISTORICAL THINKING

ANSWERS

1. The theme of Grant's presidential campaign was "Let us have peace."

2. Grant supported Reconstruction but did not promise expansions or promote new rights for African Americans. Seymour opposed Reconstruction and promoted economic fear.

3. Economic depression, discrimination, and sharecropping meant that many African Americans lacked economic opportunities and would be unable to afford a poll tax.

CRITICAL VIEWING Answers will vary. Possible responses: Scenes depict African Americans leading troops, working on farms, reading, giving speeches, voting, getting married, and teaching in a school. All of these scenes portray African Americans in everyday activities that had been denied them during slavery.

3.2 The Election of 1876

With our 24/7 online news feed, it can be hard to focus on one important problem when other issues arise. But this also happened in the 1870s, when scandals and economic woes distracted Americans from Reconstruction.

MAIN IDEA As scandals and a depression arose, a compromise reached over a contested election brought Reconstruction to an end.

SCANDAL AND PANIC

Ulysses S. Grant had been an effective general, but he proved to be a poor administrator. He often relied on Congress to make the types of decisions he should have made as the country's leader. He also was unable to keep his party from splintering into different factions, or groups, each promoting a different political viewpoint. The **Liberal Republicans** were among these factions. They believed the government had become too large and too powerful. They favored free trade and an end to Reconstruction. In American politics of the 1870s, the word *liberal* referred to someone who embraced these ideas.

Leading up to the election of 1872, the Liberal Republicans **defected**, or broke away, from the Republican Party and formed an alliance with Democrats. They nominated Horace Greeley, a newspaper editor from New York City, as the Democratic presidential candidate. Greeley's main goal was to end Reconstruction, but that was not enough to appeal to voters. Grant easily won re-election.

But accounts of dishonest behavior plagued Grant's second term. These scandals involved **bribery**, or offers of money or privileges in exchange for political favors. Financial wrongdoing among legislators and Cabinet members surfaced. For instance, Congress investigated Secretary of War William Belknap for **corruption**, another word for dishonesty. Congress accused Belknap of accepting cash gifts from army suppliers, which led to his resignation.

This painting by Howard Pyle called *The Rush from the New York Stock Exchange on September 18, 1873* conveys the fear and confusion sparked by the Panic of 1873.

To make matters worse, economic disaster struck in 1873 when bank and railroad failures triggered an economic crisis called the **Panic of 1873**. Many people lost their money when banks closed and lost their jobs when businesses collapsed. As unemployment rose, the country slid into a depression that lasted six years.

END OF RECONSTRUCTION

As the depression wore on, economic concerns overshadowed the nation's interest in Reconstruction. In 1876, two court cases dealt a further blow to the cause of African Americans' civil rights. The U.S. Supreme Court ruled in *U.S.* v. *Cruikshank* that the civil rights amendments only allowed the federal government to prevent states from abusing African Americans' civil rights. The job of punishing individuals fell to the states. In *U.S.* v. *Reese*, the Court ruled that the 15th Amendment only made it illegal to deny a person the right to vote based on race. States could use other criteria, such as **literacy tests**, or tests of one's ability to read and write, to exclude voters.

By the 1876 presidential election, Democrats had regained control of several southern states and the U.S. House of Representatives. Democrats nominated Samuel J. Tilden as their candidate. The Republican nominee was **Rutherford B. Hayes**. The race was extremely close, with election results in several states disputed. Congress created an electoral commission to decide the election, but while it met, Democrats and Republicans got together to negotiate a deal. In what came to be called the **Compromise of 1877**, Democrats agreed to award the victory to Hayes if Republicans agreed to end Reconstruction and pull federal troops out of the South. The deal was struck.

In the end, Reconstruction fell short of its goals. It had raised and then dashed hopes that African Americans would achieve equality. To some degree, African Americans made advances. But to help African Americans overcome the effects of hundreds of years of slavery and racism entirely would have required a great expansion of federal power. Still, although the promise of the 13th, 14th, and 15th amendments remained unfulfilled during Reconstruction, these amendments became the legal basis for the civil rights movement of the 1960s.

HISTORICAL THINKING

1. **READING CHECK** What views did Liberal Republicans promote?

2. **ANALYZE CAUSE AND EFFECT** What impact did the 1872 Amnesty Act, the 1876 election, and the withdrawal of federal troops from the South have on civil rights for African Americans?

3. **INTERPRET MAPS** How many contested electoral votes did Tilden need to win the election?

The Election of 1876

Hayes (Republican)		
Uncontested Electoral: 165 votes		
Electoral Vote: 185 votes, 50.1%		
Popular Vote: 4,034,311 votes, 48.5%		

Tilden (Democrat)		
Uncontested Electoral: 184 votes		
Electoral Vote: 184 votes, 49.9%		
Popular Vote: 4,288,546 votes, 51.5%		

Territories, No Returns

Contested Electoral Votes

Twenty electoral votes from Florida, Louisiana, Oregon, and South Carolina were contested, or disputed, following charges of voter fraud. The controversial election was finally settled by the Compromise of 1877. All 20 votes went to Hayes, giving him the win by one electoral vote.

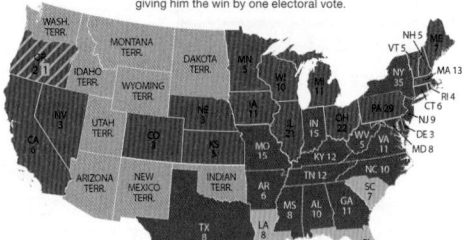

Objective

Analyze social, political, and economic factors that led to the end of Reconstruction.

Critical Thinking Skills for Lesson 3.2

- Identify Main Ideas and Details
- Monitor Comprehension
- Analyze Cause and Effect
- Interpret Maps
- Summarize
- Draw Conclusions

Essential Question for Chapter 17

In what ways did Reconstruction both succeed and fail? Reconstruction had promised African Americans equality but failed to ensure it in practice. Lesson 3.2 discusses the election of 1876, factors that led to its outcome, and how it brought about the end of Reconstruction.

Background for the Teacher

In 1876, the Republican Party nominated Rutherford B. Hayes as its presidential candidate, partly as an antidote to Grant. Hayes's military and political careers had been impeccably ethical in contrast to the scandal-ridden Grant administration. In 1864, Hayes had easily won a congressional election without even campaigning—he had felt it would be immoral to campaign instead of serving in the Union Army. As governor of Ohio, he continued to serve as a strong moral voice and built widespread popularity. By the time he ran for president in 1876, he had the backing of many famous American Republicans. Despite his determination to serve with integrity, however, he was not successful in building Republican support in the South.

Preview Using Visuals

Direct students' attention to the painting, *The Rush from the New York Stock Exchange on September 18, 1873*. **ASK:** What do you notice about the people in the painting? *(Possible responses: The people are all men wearing suits and hats, so they are probably businessmen. Their expressions show numb disbelief, and some appear to be struggling in the crowd or hurrying in a panic.)* **ASK:** Based on the caption, what do you think has happened at the stock exchange? *(It has likely crashed.)* Discuss how societies might react to large economic disruptions.

TEACH

Guided Discussion

1. **Summarize** How did Grant's presidency weaken the Republican Party and the efforts of Reconstruction? *(Grant's inability to keep his party unified, along with scandal and corruption in his administration, gave more influence to Liberal Republicans, who did not support the expansion of Reconstruction.)*

2. **Analyze Cause and Effect** What was the effect of various Supreme Court decisions on Reconstruction and the 15th Amendment? *(The Supreme Court undermined Reconstruction's goals through a series of decisions that limited the protections of the 15th Amendment and the ability of the federal government to enforce them.)*

Draw Conclusions

Prompt students to identify the major events leading up to the end of Reconstruction. **ASK:** What does the Compromise of 1877 suggest about American attitudes toward African Americans' rights and about Reconstruction efforts? *(The Republicans' willingness to trade Reconstruction for the White House suggests that they had lost enthusiasm for it. Reconstruction and African Americans' rights were less of a priority than other issues, such as the economy.)* Finally, have students examine the map. **ASK:** Based on this map, what can you conclude about the regional divisions that helped to cause the Civil War? *(The regional divisions between the North and the South were not eliminated by the Civil War and Reconstruction.)*

Active Options

On Your Feet: Three-Step Interview Assign students partners or have them select their own. Ask one student to interview the other about the following questions: What factors led to the end of Reconstruction? Was Reconstruction ultimately a success or failure? Then have students switch roles. Remind them to support their answers with evidence from the text. Ask partners to summarize for the class what they learned in the interview.

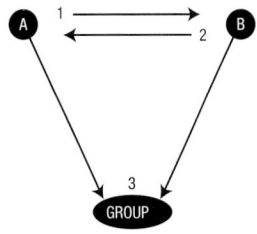

NG Learning Framework: Research Voter Suppression

ATTITUDE Responsibility

KNOWLEDGE Our Human Story

Instruct students to use print and digital resources to learn more about voter suppression in both the Reconstruction South and in present-day elections. Ask students also to research methods used to fight voter suppression. Coach students in using search terms effectively and in locating credible sources by assessing their biases and accuracy. Remind students to follow a standard format for citation of sources when quoting or paraphrasing information and conclusions of others to avoid plagiarizing. Allow time for students to share and discuss their findings.

English Language Learners

Use Terms in a Sentence To strengthen their understanding of the Key Vocabulary words *defect*, *bribery*, and *corruption*, have students write one sentence using each word correctly. Ask students at the **Expanding** and **Bridging** levels to work in pairs with students at the **Emerging** level. When pairs have completed their sentences, have them trade sentences with another pair and compare their work.

Gifted & Talented

Research Civil Rights Movements Have students use outside resources to conduct a research project exploring the connection between the Reconstruction-era amendments and the 1960s civil rights movement. Prompt students to develop specific research questions, such as: How did the civil rights activists of the 1960s use Reconstruction-era amendments as a legal basis for change? What had changed by the 1960s that spurred the civil rights movement? Have students use their research to write a short paper. Then hold a panel discussion in which students present their papers and the entire class comments and asks questions.

See the Chapter Planner for more strategies for differentiation.

HISTORICAL THINKING

ANSWERS

1. Liberal Republicans promoted smaller federal government, free trade, and an end to Reconstruction.

2. The 1872 Amnesty Act restored the voting rights of ex-Confederates, meaning that forces opposed to African Americans' civil rights had greater voting power. This, combined with the end of Reconstruction and the withdrawal of federal troops from the South, hindered the advances made in civil rights for African Americans.

3. Tilden needed one contested electoral vote to win the election.

VOCABULARY

Use each of the following vocabulary words in a sentence that shows an understanding of the term's meaning.

1. black codes
   Southern states used black codes to restrict the rights of African Americans.

2. corruption

3. Freedmen's Bureau

4. impeachment

5. Radical Reconstruction

6. sharecropping

7. 15th Amendment

8. Panic of 1873

READING STRATEGY
DRAW CONCLUSIONS

If you haven't done so already, complete your diagram to draw conclusions about the impact of Reconstruction on American society. Then answer the question.

9. How did Reconstruction redefine what it meant to be an American?

MAIN IDEAS

Answer the following questions. Support your answers with evidence from the chapter.

10. Why was President Johnson at odds with many Republicans? LESSON 1.1

11. What did Presidential Reconstruction fail to do for African Americans? LESSON 1.1

12. What legislation did Congress propose to counteract Johnson's Reconstruction plans? LESSON 1.2

13. Why did African Americans often establish Baptist churches? LESSON 2.1

14. Why was education a symbol of their new freedom to African Americans in the South? LESSON 2.2

15. What was the goal of the Ku Klux Klan? LESSON 2.3

16. How did the 15th Amendment fail African Americans? LESSON 3.1

17. What was the Compromise of 1877? LESSON 3.2

HISTORICAL THINKING

Answer the following questions. Support your answers with evidence from the chapter.

18. DRAW CONCLUSIONS What did the outcome of Johnson's impeachment trial indicate about the power of Radical Republicans in the Senate?

19. EVALUATE What did the election of Blanche K. Bruce to the U.S. Senate probably mean to African Americans?

20. ANALYZE CAUSE AND EFFECT What impact did Reconstruction have on the political and social structures of the North and the South?

21. MAKE INFERENCES Why do you think some states charged poll taxes and made voters take literacy tests?

22. MAKE CONNECTIONS How were the 13th, 14th, and 15th amendments connected to Reconstruction?

INTERPRET PHOTOGRAPHS

The lives and work of sharecroppers remained largely unchanged for decades after the end of the Civil War. Look closely at the photograph of a sharecropper in Mississippi taken in the 1930s. Then answer the questions that follow.

23. How would you describe the work the woman is doing?

24. In what way is this work similar to that performed by enslaved persons?

ANALYZE SOURCES

In his second inaugural address delivered on March 4, 1873, Ulysses S. Grant discussed the problems African Americans still faced in the South. Read the following excerpt from the speech and answer the question.

> The effects of the late civil strife have been to free the slave and make him a citizen. Yet he is not possessed of the civil rights which citizenship should carry with it. This is wrong, and should be corrected. To this correction I stand committed, so far as Executive influence can avail [be of service or help].
>
> Social equality is not a subject to be legislated upon, nor shall I ask that anything be done to advance the social status of [an African American], except to give him a fair chance to develop what there is good in him, give him access to the schools, and when he travels let him feel assured that his conduct will regulate the treatment and fare [prices charged, food, material] he will receive.

25. Based on the excerpt, what is Grant's position on African-American civil rights?

CONNECT TO YOUR LIFE

26. EXPOSITORY Review the reasons many African Americans saw the opportunity for education as a way to improve their lives. Think about an activity you enjoy doing, for instance, reading comic books or playing basketball. Write a paragraph explaining how your education helps you better enjoy that activity.

TIPS

• Pick an activity you enjoy doing. Use an idea web to brainstorm what school subjects are involved in doing that activity.

• Conclude your paragraph with a comment about how your education has enabled you to enjoy the activity.

• Have you addressed the topic? Revise or rewrite your paragraph, as needed.

VOCABULARY ANSWERS

1. Southern states used black codes to restrict the rights of African Americans.

2. William Belknap, the Secretary of State during Grant's administration, resigned due to charges of corruption.

3. The Freedmen's Bureau provided assistance to formerly enslaved people.

4. Through impeachment, Andrew Johnson was charged with extreme misconduct, but he was acquitted by one vote.

5. Radical Reconstruction emphasized African-American civil rights.

6. Without their own land to farm, many African Americans turned to sharecropping.

7. The 15th Amendment was passed to guarantee African Americans the right to vote.

8. The Panic of 1873 led to an economic depression.

READING STRATEGY ANSWER

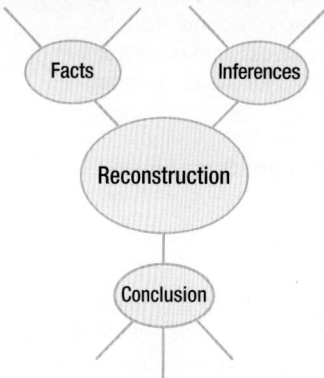

Possible Facts: the 14th and 15th amendments, the Freedmen's Bureau, the KKK, and violence against African Americans

Possible Inferences: social and political power and the influence of white southerners

Possible Conclusion: Reconstruction led to gains for African Americans, but they still faced many obstacles.

9. Possible response: Through the passage of the 13th, 14th, and 15th amendments, Reconstruction redefined what it meant to be "American" by including people of all races.

MAIN IDEAS ANSWERS

10. President Johnson was at odds with Republicans because he was a southern Democrat who took a lenient approach towards Reconstruction.

11. Presidential Reconstruction failed to provide a way for African Americans to vote, protect their property, and become full citizens.

12. Congress proposed the Civil Rights Act of 1866, which gave full equality to African Americans, in an effort to counteract Johnson's Reconstruction plans.

13. African Americans often established Baptist churches because the Baptists allowed each congregation to start a church independently and organize it the way they wanted.

14. Before the Civil War, it was illegal for enslaved people to attend school. After Reconstruction, African Americans understood that learning to read, write, and do math would help them get better jobs. They also knew that reading and writing were key to participating fully in the political process and to exercising their civil rights.

15. The goal of the Ku Klux Klan was to maintain the supremacy of white people by terrorizing African Americans and white sympathizers.

16. The 15th Amendment failed African Americans because it did not outlaw many of the state laws—such as poll taxes—that made it difficult for African Americans to exercise voting rights.

17. The Compromise of 1877 gave the presidency to Rutherford B. Hayes, a Republican, in exchange for the end of Reconstruction and the removal of federal troops from the South.

HISTORICAL THINKING ANSWERS

18. The outcome of Johnson's impeachment trial, which found him not guilty by only one vote, suggested that while the Radical Republicans did not have overwhelming power in the Senate, they had quite a lot of support.

19. The election of Blanche K. Bruce was significant because, while he was the second African American to serve in the Senate, he was the first to have been born into slavery. To African Americans, this would have meant that all African Americans, even formerly enslaved people, could serve in high office.

20. Politically, Reconstruction cemented the identities of the political parties. The Republicans became associated with the rights of African Americans and with strong Reconstruction policies. The party was strongest in the North. The Democrats, on the other hand, became the party of white Southerners and opposed Reconstruction. Socially, although slavery was abolished and amendments seemed to guarantee rights, most African Americans remained on the outside of American society due to prejudice and discrimination.

21. States charged poll taxes and used literacy tests because they could not explicitly prevent people from voting based on race. To get around this, states made sure that poor people and uneducated people could not vote. This disenfranchised many formerly enslaved African Americans, who had been denied education and had limited economic opportunities.

22. After the Civil War, the Radical Republicans worried that the South would fall back into a social, political, and economic system similar to slavery. The 13th, 14th, and 15th amendments were passed to prevent this by ensuring that African Americans' rights were federally protected by the Constitution.

INTERPRET PHOTOGRAPHS ANSWERS

23. Answers may vary. Possible response: The woman seems to be doing difficult, physical, outdoor agricultural labor.

24. Many enslaved persons did an identical kind of outdoor agricultural labor.

ANALYZE SOURCES ANSWER

25. Grant believes that African Americans have not achieved the civil rights that citizens should possess. He believes that is wrong and should be corrected. However, he seems to suggest that he is not in favor of more legislation to protect African-American rights and does not think that laws can make them socially equal. Instead, he asks white Americans to give African Americans access to education and treat them fairly.

CONNECT TO YOUR LIFE ANSWER

26. Paragraphs will vary but should include an activity that the student enjoys and an explanation of how the student's education improves his or her enjoyment of the activity.

National Geographic | Connection

Lincoln's Funeral Train

by Adam Goodheart

Adapted from "How Abraham Lincoln's Funeral Train Made History," by Adam Goodheart, news.nationalgeographic.com, April 18, 2015

On the drizzly morning of April 19, 1865, when the train carrying the murdered president's coffin pulled out of Washington's central depot, it embarked on a journey that resonated deeply with many chapters of his life. As a 27-year-old novice state legislator in the 1830s, he was already advocating the construction of new train lines. He later served as an attorney for the Illinois Central and other companies.

In 1861, when Lincoln journeyed to Washington for his first inauguration, he traveled farther to reach the White House than any previous president-elect. As he made his way through midwestern and northern states, he reassured Americans that the nation would be saved. The trip itself was a powerful statement. It was a reminder of the 30,000 miles of steel that already bound the nation together, of the industrial economy that was vaulting the North ahead of the South, and of plans to build a transcontinental line joining Atlantic to Pacific.

Four years later, the funeral trip that carried Lincoln home for burial in Springfield, Illinois, was designed to recall the earlier journey. On the second day of travel, as it crossed the border between Maryland and Pennsylvania, the train rode over tracks that just a few years earlier had been used by slaves escaping to freedom. During the Civil War, trains laden with wounded soldiers often passed here as well, trundling their human burden from Virginia battlefields to the Union military hospitals in Pennsylvania.

On the 1865 trip, just two cars made the entire journey. One carried high-ranking military personnel and members of the Lincoln family. The other was the funeral car itself, named the United States. It had been completed in February 1865 as a lavish presidential office on wheels, a 19th-century version of Air Force One. It boasted gilded wood, etched glass, and wheels designed to accommodate tracks of varying gauges. For the funeral trip, it was draped inside and out in heavy black cloth fringed with silver.

The train's passage through towns and villages, usually in darkness, was an unparalleled event. "As we sped over the rails at night, the scene was the most pathetic ever witnessed," wrote one member of the entourage. "At every crossroads, the glare of innumerable torches illuminated the whole population from [old] age to infancy kneeling on the ground, and their clergymen leading in prayers and hymns."

Especially in the rural Midwest, ordinary Americans felt a connection with Lincoln that went beyond the tragedy of his assassination. Like him, they had suffered the agonies and triumphs of four years of war, and this emotional journey was bound up with memories of the railroad, too. It was at the local depots—the same ones where the funeral train now passed—that, long before, many had caught their last glimpses of sons and brothers who would never return. It was here that civilians brought the bandages, clothing, food, and flags that they contributed to the war effort. It was here that the first news of defeats and losses on distant battlefields arrived, carried by the telegraph lines that ran along the tracks.

For the 150th anniversary of the funeral journey, some people resurrected memories of when Lincoln's funeral car carried history through the midwestern heartland. It stopped in Springfield for a reenactment of the Lincoln funeral, two days shy of the actual anniversary.

A coffin—empty, of course—was unloaded onto a horse-drawn hearse and driven to the old Illinois State House for an all-night vigil. The next day, it was taken to Oak Ridge Cemetery. As in 1865, the last few miles of the homeward journey were powered by horses, not steam engines. But the ghostly presence of the railroad, like that of the murdered president himself, hovered somewhere close at hand.

> For more from National Geographic, check out "Civil War Battlefields" online.

UNIT INQUIRY: Develop a Conflict Resolution Strategy

In this unit, you learned about the issues that fueled the Civil War and about the challenges that the United States faced after the war ended. Based on your understanding of the text, what unresolved conflicts eventually drove Americans to war? How did these conflicts get resolved? How did the Civil War and Reconstruction shape the American identity?

ASSIGNMENT

Develop a strategy that you think would have been successful in resolving one of the conflicts that Americans wrestled with before, during, and after the Civil War. Since you have knowledge about how events unfolded, your strategy should take into consideration the factors that led to conflict. Be prepared to present your strategy to the class and explain your reasoning.

Gather Evidence As you plan your strategy, gather evidence from this unit about the different ways in which conflicts and the way Americans did or didn't resolve them shaped the American identity. Also think about what Americans hoped to achieve through war and how the war affected ordinary citizens. Make a list of the causes and consequences of the war and address the most significant ones in your strategy. Use a graphic organizer like this one to help organize your thoughts.

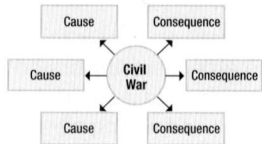

Produce Use your notes to produce descriptions of the causes and consequences of the Civil War. Write a short paragraph on each, using evidence from this unit to support your ideas.

Review Your Paragraphs Is the writing appropriate for your audience? Do you meet the purpose of the assignment? Revise or edit as needed.

Present Choose a creative and engaging way to present your conflict negotiation strategy to the class. Consider one of these options:

- Play the role of a diplomat and explain why a peaceful solution or compromise is preferable to a full-scale civil war.

- Write a dialogue between two people, one from the North and one from the South, that describes their perspectives on the causes and consequences of the Civil War.

- Create a multimedia presentation using paintings, photographs, and excerpts of documents to illustrate what caused the war, the realities of the war, and the consequences of the war.

NATIONAL GEOGRAPHIC | LEARNING FRAMEWORK ACTIVITIES

Create an Illustrated Time Line

SKILL Observation
KNOWLEDGE Our Human Story

Keeping track of events and their details can be a challenge, but understanding how events flow and relate to each other is how we make sense of them. Create an illustrated time line of the events surrounding the Civil War. You can organize events and details horizontally or vertically and illustrate the events you find most compelling. Include important dates and people. When you have completed your time line, share your work with the class.

Compose a Letter Home

ATTITUDE Empowerment
SKILLS Collaboration, Communication

In any war, letters from the front reveal the hard realities facing people on the front lines. Imagine that you are a soldier, medic, or reporter during the Civil War. Write a letter home that describes your experiences. Include specific details about time and place and observations about the people around you. Consider working with a partner who, as the recipient of your letter home, writes a letter back. When you have completed your letter or letters, present them to the class.

NATIONAL GEOGRAPHIC CONNECTION

Guided Discussion for "Lincoln's Funeral Train"

1. **Describe** How does Adam Goodheart describe the journey of Lincoln's funeral train? *(Answers will vary. Possible response: Lincoln's funeral train departed from Washington, D.C., and consisted of two cars—one for family and one draped in black cloth for Lincoln's coffin. The train moved through the same states that had just experienced war, and mourners gathered to pay respects to Lincoln as the train passed through communities on its way to Springfield, Illinois.)*

2. **Make Connections** Why were Americans in the rural Midwest particularly attached to Lincoln, according to the author? *(Answers will vary. Possible response: Like Lincoln, who was from the region, Americans in the Midwest had endured four years of Civil War, and their lives during and surrounding the years of the war were intimately connected with the railroad.)*

Guided Discussion for "Civil War Battlefields"

1. **Identify Main Ideas and Details** Why are Civil War battlefields in danger of being lost to development? *(Answers will vary. Possible response: Though the federal government began to preserve Civil War battlefields in the 1890s, Congress did not appropriate enough funds, so many battlefields are not protected from development.)*

2. **Summarize** According to Goodheart, what is the purpose of recognizing and preserving Civil War battlefields? *(Answers will vary. Possible response: The battlefields of the Civil War are important not only because of the losses and heroism of that war but also because these sites help us connect with a part of American history that would vanish without our attention.)*

UNIT INQUIRY PROJECT RUBRIC

Assess

Use the rubric to assess each student's participation and performance.

SCORE	ASSIGNMENT	PRODUCT	PRESENTATION
3 GREAT	• Student thoroughly understands the assignment. • Student participates fully in the project process.	• Strategy is well thought out. • Descriptions of causes and consequences of Civil War include substantial text evidence. • Strategy contains all of the key elements listed in the assignment.	• Presentation is clear, concise, and logical. • Presentation does a good job of creatively offering a negotiation strategy. • Presentation engages the audience.
2 GOOD	• Student mostly understands the assignment. • Student participates fairly well in the project process.	• Strategy is fairly well thought out. • Descriptions of causes and consequences of Civil War include some text evidence. • Strategy contains most of the key elements listed in the assignment.	• Presentation is fairly clear, concise, and logical. • Presentation does an adequate job of creatively offering a negotiation strategy. • Presentation somewhat engages the audience.
1 NEEDS WORK	• Student does not understand the assignment. • Student minimally participates or does not participate in the project process.	• Strategy is not well thought out. • Descriptions of causes and consequences of Civil War include little or no text evidence. • Strategy contains few or none of the key elements listed in the assignment.	• Presentation is not clear or engaging. • Presentation does an inadequate job of creatively offering a negotiation strategy. • Presentation does not engage the audience.

NATIONAL GEOGRAPHIC LEARNING FRAMEWORK RUBRIC

Assess

Use the rubric to assess how each student applies the National Geographic Learning Framework.

SCORE	ASSIGNMENT	ASSIGNMENT	FINAL PRODUCTS
3 GREAT	• Illustrated time line reflects **Observation** well. • Illustrated time line explores **Our Human Story** well.	• Letter demonstrates **Empowerment** well. • Letter demonstrates **Collaboration** and **Communication** well.	• Final products are engaging, creative, and well presented.
2 GOOD	• Illustrated time line reflects **Observation**. • Illustrated time line explores **Our Human Story**.	• Letter demonstrates **Empowerment**. • Letter demonstrates **Collaboration** and **Communication**.	• Final products are interesting, logical, and complete.
1 NEEDS WORK	• Illustrated time line does not reflect **Observation**. • Illustrated time line does not explore **Our Human Story**.	• Letter does not demonstrate **Empowerment**. • Letter does not demonstrate **Collaboration** and **Communication**.	• Final products are not creative, complete, or interesting.

Lower Manhattan, c. 1915

The development of New York City as we know it today—a massive urban center with multiple boroughs—began with the island of Manhattan. Lower Manhattan is home to the city's Financial District as well as neighborhoods such as the Lower East Side, Little Italy, and the Bowery. In 1915, Manhattan was already a center of finance, manufacturing, and trade, boasting 25,000 factories and the headquarters of many of the nation's largest companies. Its biggest industry was clothing, made possible by a large labor force that included many southern and eastern European immigrants who settled on the Lower East Side.

The Lower East Side in the early 1900s was one of the most crowded neighborhoods in the world. It had undergone many transformations by this time, from a German neighborhood known as "Kleindeutschland" (Little Germany) to an area with a rising Italian population (Little Italy) and finally to a predominantly Jewish neighborhood. The demographics of Lower Manhattan's neighborhoods continue to change as waves of immigration bring more new residents to the United States. In the early years of the 21st century, a majority of immigrants living in the area were from China or the Dominican Republic.

Have students examine the photograph and identify the many elements of urban life it documents. **ASK:** What kind of neighborhood does this one seem to be, commerical or residential? *(Possible response: It appears to be a commercial neighborhood because there are storefronts at street level and a lot of activity on the street. The presence of horse-drawn carts, streetcars, and automobiles suggests that goods and people are coming and going.)* **ASK:** Does it appear wealthy or poor and why? *(Possible response: The neighborhood appears wealthy. People on the street are well dressed, and the buildings look clean and well maintained.)*

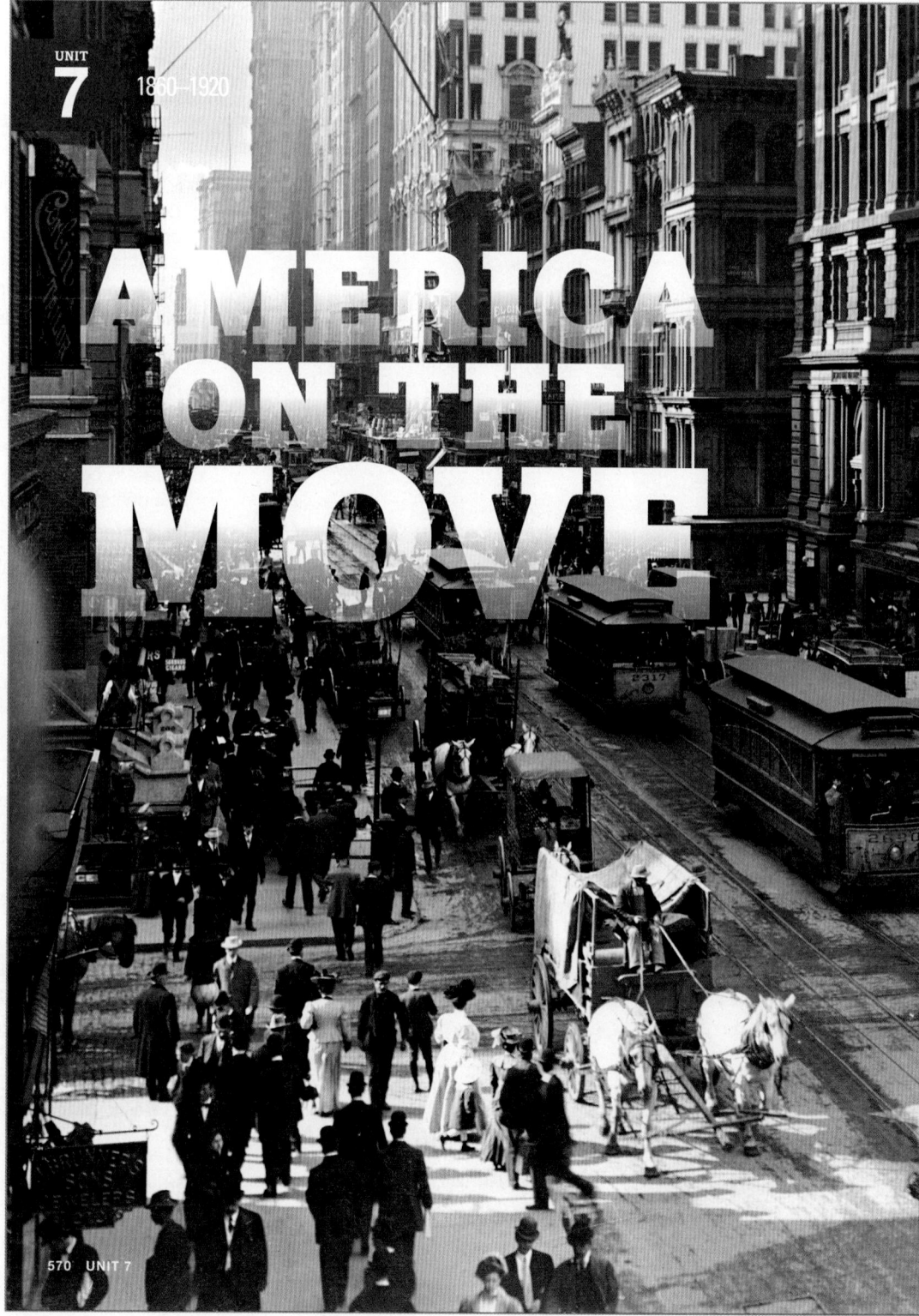

UNIT
7
1850–1920

AMERICA ON THE MOVE

570 UNIT 7

CRITICAL VIEWING People, cars, and horse-drawn carriages fill New York City's Lower Manhattan neighborhood in this photo taken around 1915. During the early 1900s, millions of mostly European immigrants flocked to American cities. What do you think life might have been like for the immigrants who lived or worked in Lower Manhattan?

New York's Subway System

In addition to the streetcar, the photograph shows a structure labeled "Subway Entrance" in the lower right of the frame. The New York subway began operation in 1904, running a single line from Lower Manhattan to 145th Street on the island's north end. A pamphlet from the subway's official opening heralded a future of "pleasure excursions through long, broad, airy passages" punctuated by stations decorated with glazed tiles, glass roofs, and marble. The original system ran local and express trains every 3 to 10 minutes.

The system, run by the Interborough Rapid Transit Company, quickly expanded. By 1915, lines likely ran to Brooklyn, Queens, and the Bronx, as well as within Manhattan. Other companies followed suit, establishing their own subway and bus lines. The city did not control the subways and elevated trains until 1940.

With reliable subways, elevated trains, and bridges providing access to workplaces in Manhattan, immigrants began to spread out, leaving their densely populated neighborhoods in Lower Manhattan for more space in the outer boroughs.

CRITICAL VIEWING Answers will vary. Possible response: Life for immigrants in Lower Manhattan might have been difficult, noisy, crowded, dirty, and busy. Judging by the number of people and shops, some immigrants may have been working hard and making a good living.

1896 EUROPE:
First Modern Olympic Games

The original Olympic Games of ancient Greece were one of several religious festivals marked by physical competition. The list of events grew over time to include foot races, chariot races, wrestling, boxing, and even street fighting. The Roman Empire and its leaders did not approve of the games, however, and banned them around A.D. 400.

In 1890, French educator Baron Pierre de Coubertin, began working with English doctor William Brookes to develop a plan for an international sporting competition. Greece had been holding successful national "Olympiads" for about 30 years, and Coubertin argued that athletics could be "the free trade of the future" and a tool for establishing peaceful relations between nations. The idea was not tremendously popular. Nonetheless, Coubertin managed to arrange for the first modern Olympics to take place in 1896.

The 1896 Athens Olympics included 43 events—summer events only, as the Winter Olympics were not officially established until 1924—and did not permit women to compete. In the early years of the Olympics, most nations did not have national teams. Instead, amateur athletes from various organizations competed for honor, for glory, and sometimes for their lives. In the original 1,200-meter swim competition, swimmers were simply left 1,200 meters out at sea and had to make it safely to shore. The winner admitted that he cared less about finishing first than he did about surviving the swim.
ASK: Why might Coubertin have thought the Olympics would be a good way to establish peace among nations? *(Answers will vary. Possible responses: If nations could gain pride from peaceful competition, they might not feel the need to compete violently. If people were exposed to individuals from other nations in a peaceful setting, they might not want to start conflicts with those nations.)*

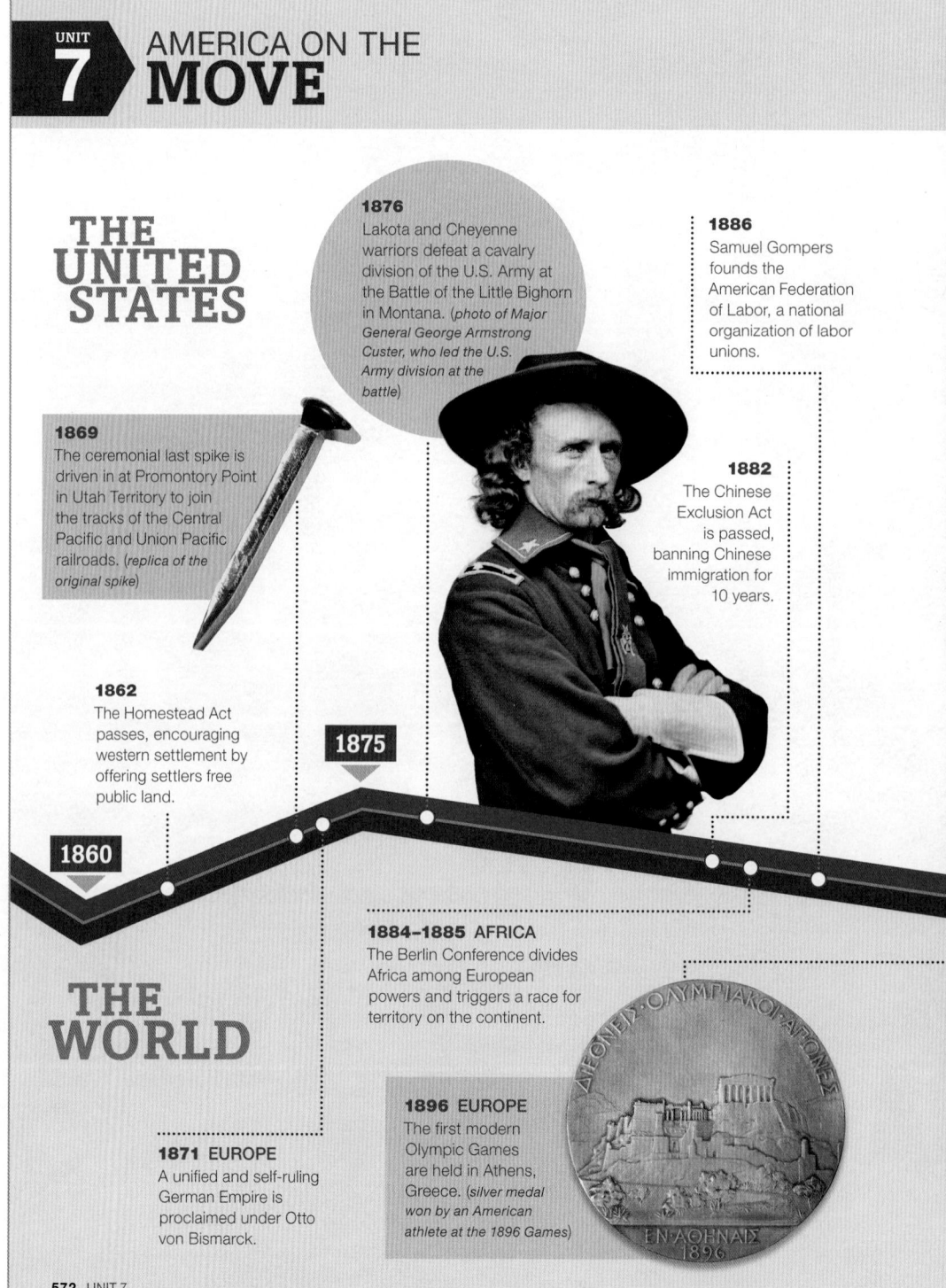

UNIT 7 AMERICA ON THE **MOVE**

THE UNITED STATES

1876
Lakota and Cheyenne warriors defeat a cavalry division of the U.S. Army at the Battle of the Little Bighorn in Montana. (*photo of Major General George Armstrong Custer, who led the U.S. Army division at the battle*)

1886
Samuel Gompers founds the American Federation of Labor, a national organization of labor unions.

1869
The ceremonial last spike is driven in at Promontory Point in Utah Territory to join the tracks of the Central Pacific and Union Pacific railroads. (*replica of the original spike*)

1882
The Chinese Exclusion Act is passed, banning Chinese immigration for 10 years.

1862
The Homestead Act passes, encouraging western settlement by offering settlers free public land.

1875

1860

1884–1885 AFRICA
The Berlin Conference divides Africa among European powers and triggers a race for territory on the continent.

THE WORLD

1896 EUROPE
The first modern Olympic Games are held in Athens, Greece. (*silver medal won by an American athlete at the 1896 Games*)

1871 EUROPE
A unified and self-ruling German Empire is proclaimed under Otto von Bismarck.

1892
Ellis Island opens and becomes the country's busiest immigration station. (*teddy bear belonging to an immigrant child who came through Ellis Island*)

HISTORICAL THINKING: DETERMINE CHRONOLOGY

What similar events occurred in the Americas and Asia in the late 1800s and early 1900s?

A WOMAN LIVING HERE HAS REGISTERED TO VOTE THEREBY ASSUMING RESPONSIBILITY OF CITIZENSHIP

1898
The Spanish-American War erupts after U.S. intervention in Cuba's war of independence against Spain.

1896
In *Plessy* v. *Ferguson*, the Supreme Court rules that facilities for African Americans can be "separate but equal."

1914
The United States finishes construction of the Panama Canal, which connects the Atlantic Ocean with the Pacific Ocean.

1919
The passage of the 19th Amendment grants women the right to vote. (*Women displayed signs like this one to show that they had exercised their right to vote.*)

1890
The U.S. Army kills nearly 200 Native Americans at Wounded Knee in South Dakota.

1905

1920

1890

1910 AMERICAS
The Mexican Revolution is fought to overthrow dictator Porfirio Díaz.

1912 ASIA
Two thousand years of imperial rule in China come to an end when revolutionary forces overthrow the Qing dynasty.

1914 EUROPE
Archduke Franz Ferdinand is assassinated, sparking the start of World War I. (*1914 illustration of the assassination*)

1917 EUROPE
The Russian Revolution begins. (*This Soviet poster of a man breaking his chains celebrates the revolution.*)

America on the Move **573**

INTRODUCE TIME LINE EVENT

1917 EUROPE:
The Russian Revolution

The Russian Revolution of 1917 was actually made up of two revolutionary movements. The first began in March and ended the rule of Tsar Nicholas and the Romanov dynasty, which had controlled Russia since 1613. The seeds had been sown 12 years earlier, when a series of protests, riots, and general strikes across the Russian Empire, referred to as the Russian Revolution of 1905, forced the tsar to create a representative government (the Duma) and a functional constitution.

In the years that followed, however, Tsar Nicholas largely failed to honor the spirit of these changes. The resulting widespread distrust of the tsar, combined with the economic and military devastation caused by World War I, prompted civilian and military riots that forced him off the throne. He and his immediate family were executed in 1918.

The provisional government that took the tsar's place proved ineffective—it could neither maintain control of the military nor fully address the chaos that had spread through the empire. In the meantime, groups such as the Socialist Revolutionaries, the Mensheviks, and especially the Bolsheviks were gaining in popularity. In November, the second phase of the Russian Revolution of 1917 began when the Bolsheviks took over the government through a coup. **ASK:** What were the chief causes of the first phase of the Russian Revolution of 1917? (*Possible response: distrust of the tsar and the effects of World War I on Russia's military and economy*)

HISTORICAL THINKING: DETERMINE CHRONOLOGY

Answer: In the late 1800s and early 1900s, nations in Asia and the Americas experienced political upheavals and political revolutions. Cuba began a war for independence from Spain, and in Mexico and China, revolutions overthrew a dictator and a dynasty, respectively.

UNIT 7 RESOURCES

UNIT INTRODUCTION

UNIT TIME LINE

UNIT WRAP-UP

NATIONAL GEOGRAPHIC | CONNECTION

National Geographic Magazine Adapted Articles

• "This Land is Your Land"
• "The Native American Photography of Edward Sheriff Curtis" ONLINE

Unit 7 Inquiry: Innovate a New Solution

NG Learning Framework Activities

• Research American Species
• Write a Journal Entry

Unit 7 Formal Assessment

CHAPTER 18 RESOURCES

Available at NGLSync.Cengage.com

TEACHER RESOURCES & ASSESSMENT

Reading and Note-Taking

Vocabulary Practice

Social Studies Skills Lessons

• Reading: Categorize
• Writing: Write an Argument

Formal Assessment

• Chapter 18 Pretest
• Chapter 18 Tests A & B
• Section Quizzes

Chapter 18 Answer Key

ExamView®
One-time Download

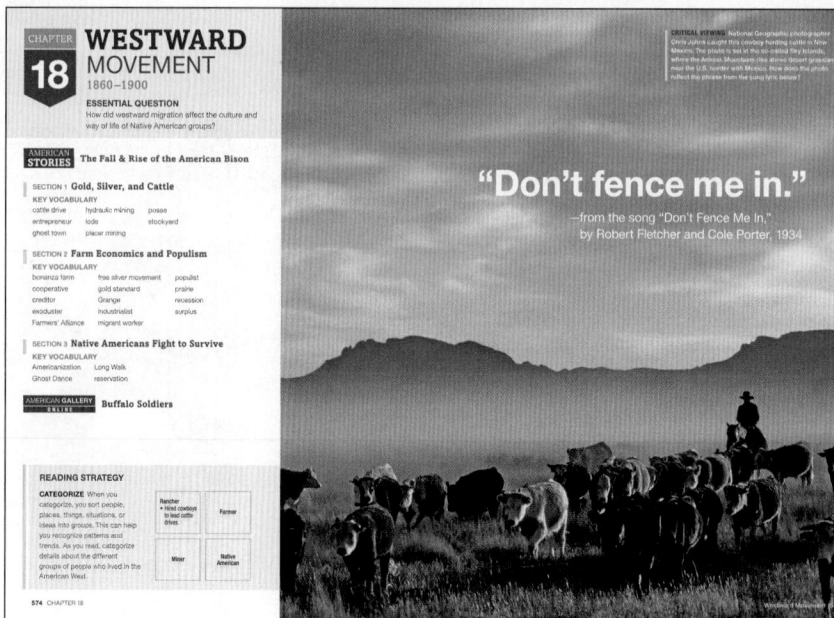

STUDENT DIGITAL RESOURCES

• **eEdition** (English)
• **eEdition** (Spanish)
• **Handbooks**

• **Online Atlas**
• **American Gallery Online**
• **History Notebook**

• **American Voices (Biographies)**
• **Active History**
• **Projects for Inquiry-Based Learning**

Chapter 18 Spanish Resources are available at NGLSync.Cengage.com.

AMERICAN STORIES | The Fall & Rise of the American Bison

- Primary Sources
- On Your Feet: Write a Verse

NG Learning Framework:
Collect Data

SECTION 1 RESOURCES
GOLD, SILVER, AND CATTLE

LESSON 1.1
Mining Boomtowns

- On Your Feet: Fishbowl

NG Learning Framework:
Create an Infographic

LESSON 1.2
Cattle and the Long Drive

- On Your Feet: Concept Cluster

NG Learning Framework:
Write Diary Entries

SECTION 2 RESOURCES
FARM ECONOMICS AND POPULISM

LESSON 2.1
Farming in the West

- On Your Feet: Turn and Talk on Topic

NG Learning Framework:
Make a Homesteading Plan

LESSON 2.2
Women and Children on the Prairie

- On Your Feet: Tell Me More

NG Learning Framework:
Compare Responsibilities

LESSON 2.3
Farmers and Populism

- On Your Feet: Card Responses

NG Learning Framework:
Create a Political Advertisement

SECTION 3 RESOURCES
NATIVE AMERICANS FIGHT TO SURVIVE

LESSON 3.1
Native Americans of the Plains

- Active History: Solve a Puzzle

AMERICAN GALLERY ONLINE Buffalo Soldiers

American Voices Biographies
Sitting Bull
George Armstrong Custer **ONLINE**

LESSON 3.2
NATIONAL GEOGRAPHIC PHOTOGRAPHER JOEL SARTORE
Conservation of the American Bison

- On Your Feet: Think, Pair, Share

NG Learning Framework:
Explore Wildlife Photography

LESSON 3.3
Native Americans of the Northwest and Southwest

- On Your Feet: Three-Step Interview

NG Learning Framework:
Create a Podcast

LESSON 3.4
Wounded Knee

- On Your Feet: Sequence Chain

NG Learning Framework:
Research Boarding Schools

CHAPTER 18 REVIEW

NATIVE AMERICAN CONFEDERACIES & NATIONS

- On Your Feet: Talking Stick Debate

NG Learning Framework:
Write a Blog Post

Strategy ❶
Connect Titles to Main Ideas

Before reading, remind students that lesson titles hold clues to the main ideas in the lessons. After reading, display the following sentence starters. Ask students to complete the sentences to express main ideas. Encourage pairs of students to compare sentences.

1.1 Mining boomtowns grew because _____.

1.2 Customers in the East appreciated the cattle boom and the long drive because _____.

2.1 Many homesteaders started farming in the West because _____.

2.3 Many farmers supported populism because _____.

3.1 Native Americans of the Great Plains faced the problem of _____.

3.4 Wounded Knee is the place where _____.

Use with Lessons 1.1–1.2, 2.1, 2.3, 3.1, and 3.4 *Each lesson is represented by one sentence starter above.*

Strategy ❷
Pose and Answer Questions

Have students read each lesson in pairs. Instruct them to pause after each paragraph and ask each other *who, what, where, when,* or *why* questions about what they have just read. Encourage them to use a 5 Ws Chart.

Use with All Lessons

Strategy ❸
Use a Sorting Activity

Write these terms on the board. Ask students to sort them into four groups of four related terms and then write a paragraph that shows how the terms are related.

gold standard	Farmers' Alliance
placer mining	bonanza farms
hydraulic mining	free silver movement
Populist Party	migrant workers
exodusters	creditors
recession	lodes
cooperatives	prairie
entrepreneurs	Grange

Use with Lessons 1.1, 2.1, and 2.3

Strategy ❶
Modify Vocabulary Lists

Using your standards as a guide, limit the number of Key Vocabulary words and other content-specific terms that students will be required to master. As they read, have students create a vocabulary card for each word in the modified list. Allow students to create a picture to illustrate each word or write definitions, synonyms, or examples. Encourage students to refer to their vocabulary cards often as they read.

Use with Lessons 1.1, 2.1, 2.3, 3.1, and 3.4 *You may want to focus on the content-specific terms that may be the most unfamiliar to students, such as* lodes, placer mining, hydraulic mining, exodusters, bonanza farms, recession, Grange, populist, reservations, Americanization, *and* Dawes General Allotment Act.

Strategy ❷
Use Echo Reading

Point out that the Main Idea statements all relate in some way to land use in the West. Section 1 focuses on using the land for mining and raising cattle; Section 2 focuses on using the land for farming; and Section 3 focuses on using the land after clashing with and supplanting the Native Americans who were living there. Pair each inclusion student with a proficient reader. Ask the proficient reader to read the Main Idea statement at the beginning of a lesson aloud. The less proficient partner will "echo" by reading the same statement.

Use with All Lessons

ENGLISH LANGUAGE LEARNERS

Strategy ❶
Compose Captions

Pair students at the **Emerging** and **Expanding** levels with English-proficient students. Have students work together to write original captions for the photographs in the chapter. You may want pairs to compare their captions with the captions written by other pairs.

Use with Lessons 1.1, 2.1–2.2, and 3.1–3.4 *For Lesson 3.4, make sure that students caption both photographs. You also may wish to expand this activity to include the artwork in Lessons 1.2 and 2.3.*

Strategy ❷
Create Word Squares

Give students at **All Proficiencies** the following list of Key Vocabulary words and display a Word Square diagram. Ask students to copy and complete the four parts of the diagram for each word on the list.

cooperative   migrant worker   recession   creditor
populist   surplus   industrialist prairie

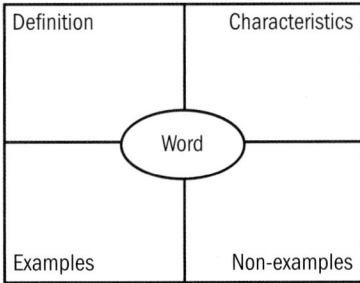

Use with Lessons 2.1 and 2.3

Strategy ❸
Summarize Text

Each lesson presents information in two subsections. Organize students into pairs and assign each pair one subsection to read together. Then each pair should summarize the assigned subsection, collaborating so that students at **All Proficiencies** can contribute. English-proficient students and students at the **Bridging** level can be particularly helpful in making the summaries clear. Encourage students to compare their summaries and discuss discrepancies.

Use with All Lessons

GIFTED & TALENTED

Strategy ❶
Write a Dialogue

Tell students to write and perform a dialogue that might have taken place among settlers in the Great Plains. For example, students may choose to imagine a conversation between a homesteader and the resident of a prairie town, between two children in a one-room schoolhouse, or between two farmers at a Grange meeting. Encourage students to include details about life on the plains and the concerns of the people who lived there in the second half of the 19th century.

Use with Lessons 2.1–2.3 *Follow up by inviting the class to share insights about the issues brought up in the dialogue.*

Strategy ❷
Plan a Historical Tour

Have students work individually or in pairs to identify a heritage site for a Native American group discussed in the lesson. Tell students to plan an informational tour of the site, including its location and geography and information from the chapter about the tribes. Encourage students to present their findings in a tour brochure that includes an annotated map.

Use with Lessons 3.1 and 3.3–3.4

Pre-AP

Strategy ❶
Design an Infographic STEM

Instruct students to review the chapter and to conduct additional research about roles that railroads played in American life between 1860 and 1900. Ask students to create an infographic that uses data and other visual information to show both the advantages and disadvantages of the growing railroad system. Invite students to compare infographics and generate a master list of advantages and disadvantages.

Use with Lessons 1.2, 2.1, 2.3, and 3.1

Strategy ❷
Produce a Commercial

Have students write and perform a commercial urging easterners to move to the West. Direct students to choose a target audience—for example, miners, homesteaders, businesspeople, or cowboys—and craft an appropriate appeal. Encourage students to use photos and fictional testimonials to enhance the appeal. Students may present a video recording of the commercial or perform it live.

Use with Lessons 1.1, 1.2, and 2.1 *Follow up by inviting the class to evaluate the historical accuracy and sales pitch of each appeal.*

ESSENTIAL QUESTION
How did westward migration affect the culture and way of life of Native American groups?

READING STRATEGY

CATEGORIZE When you categorize, you sort people, places, things, situations, or ideas into groups. This can help you recognize patterns and trends. As you read, categorize details about the different groups of people who lived in the American West.

Rancher • Hired cowboys to lead cattle drives.	Farmer
Miner	Native American

CRITICAL VIEWING National Geographic photographer Chris Johns caught this cowboy herding cattle in New Mexico. The photo is set in the so-called Sky Islands, where the Animas Mountains rise above desert grasslands, near the U.S. border with Mexico. How does the photo reflect the phrase from the song lyric below?

"Don't fence me in."
—from the song "Don't Fence Me In,"
by Robert Fletcher and Cole Porter, 1934

INTRODUCE THE PHOTOGRAPH
"Don't Fence Me In"

As a class, take a moment to study the photograph. Explain that the Sky Island region has a mix of landforms and a diverse population of plants and animals. The photograph is set in the area that includes the Chihuahuan Desert, North America's largest desert. Read the caption. **ASK:** According to the caption, the cowboy is herding cattle. What does that mean? *(Possible response: He is guarding the cattle as they graze and perhaps is moving them to another grazing area.)* Tell students that in this chapter they will learn more about cowboys, other settlers of the West, and the Native Americans with whom they interacted.

NATIONAL GEOGRAPHIC PHOTOGRAPHER
Chris Johns

Born in Oregon, Chris Johns has traveled the world as a photographer for *National Geographic*, a job he began in 1985. He became editor in chief of the magazine in 2005 and chief content officer for the magazine and many other National Geographic publications in 2014. He is currently executive director of the National Geographic Society Centers of Excellence. Johns says of photography, "There has to be lyricism—memorable pictures that don't just show you what it's like to be there, but what it *feels* like to be there, or to be that animal or that person, or in that landscape."

CRITICAL VIEWING Answers will vary. Possible response: "Don't fence me in" indicates a desire to be free and unlimited. The photo suggests an open landscape that offers the freedom to travel and live without boundaries.

For Chapter 18 Spanish Resources, visit the Resources Menu. Chapter 18 Resources are available at NGLSync.Cengage.com.

INTRODUCE THE ESSENTIAL QUESTION

How did western migration affect the culture and way of life of Native American groups?

Brainstorm Migration Issues Invite students to begin thinking about the consequences of western migration by brainstorming ideas in response to the following questions:

1. What are some of the reasons that drive large groups of people to migrate to a new place?

2. What kinds of conflicts might develop between newcomers and people who already live there?

3. In what ways might cultures change when newcomers arrive in a community?

4. Should the government have a role in mediating disputes, and if so, what role?

Write each question on chart paper and add students' ideas. Revisit the questions at the end of each lesson and ask students to suggest additional answers based on what they learned.

INTRODUCE CHAPTER VOCABULARY

Word Webs

Encourage students to complete a Word Web for Key Vocabulary words as they read the chapter. Ask them to write each word in the center of an oval and then look through the chapter to find examples, characteristics, and descriptive words that they may associate with the vocabulary word. At the end of the chapter, ask students what they learned about each word. Model an example for students on the board, using the graphic organizer below.

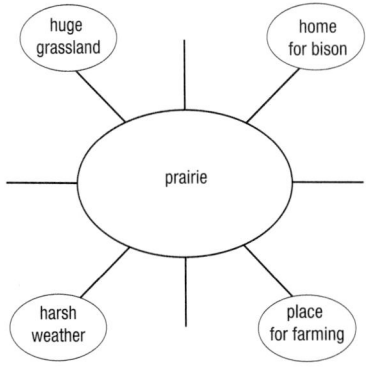

INTRODUCE THE READING STRATEGY

CATEGORIZE

Ask students to read the headings in the Four-Square Diagram. Explain that the key to categorizing is having a clear understanding of what the headings mean. In this case, the headings direct students to look for and record important, specific details about four kinds of westerners. Point out that the diagram shows one detail under Rancher but that more could be added. Model completing the diagram by reading the first paragraph of Homesteaders and Exodusters in Lesson 2.1 and noting this detail under Farmer: *Many moved to the West because of the Homestead Act.* Remind students to complete their Four-Square Diagrams as they read the chapter.

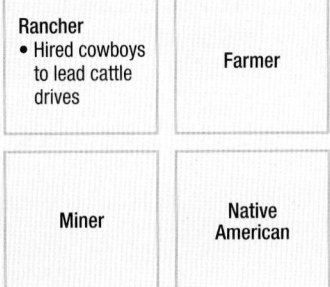

KEY DATES FOR CHAPTER 18

1864	Sand Creek Massacre
1867	The Grange is founded
1875	Battle of the Little Bighorn
1877	Chief Joseph and the Nez Perce surrender
1879	Largest group of exodusters arrives in Kansas
1887	Dawes General Allotment Act
1890	Wounded Knee Massacre
1892	Populist Party forms

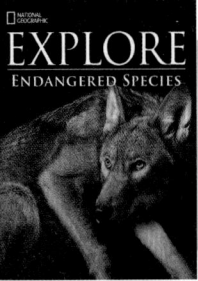

For more on the impact of habitat loss and hunting, see *EXPLORE ENDANGERED SPECIES.*

 STEM

Objectives

- Learn about the American bison and its role as an American symbol.
- Identify the reasons for the decline of the American bison.
- Learn about the efforts to reestablish the American bison in the United States.
- Understand the importance of the American bison in Native American society.
- Study a primary source: "Home on the Range."

Critical Thinking Skills for "The Fall & Rise of the American Bison"

- Make Connections
- Draw Conclusions
- Interpret Graphs
- Analyze Visuals
- Analyze Environmental Concepts
- Compare and Contrast
- Make Inferences

Background for the Teacher

This American Story introduces students to the vital role of the American bison in North American history. Through the study of a compelling narrative—coupled with an analysis of graphs, paintings, photographs, and even song lyrics—students will understand the importance of the bison to Native American tribes, the reasons for its population collapse, and the steps taken to reestablish this mighty creature.

The upcoming chapter, Western Movement, explores the reasons for and the impact of large numbers of American settlers pouring into the western states and territories. While the text examines the social, economic, and political impacts of this migration, this American Story provides an understanding of the ecological and environmental costs of this period.

▌ NATIONAL GEOGRAPHIC PHOTOGRAPHER
Joel Sartore

Joel Sartore is the founder of Photo Ark, a project focused on documenting every species held in captivity. Sartore has visited 40 countries and photographed more than 6,000 species, including the rare Florida panther and Indian rhinoceros. Examples of these stunning images can be found on the National Geographic website.

History Notebook

Encourage students to complete the American Story page for Chapter 18 in their History Notebooks as they read.

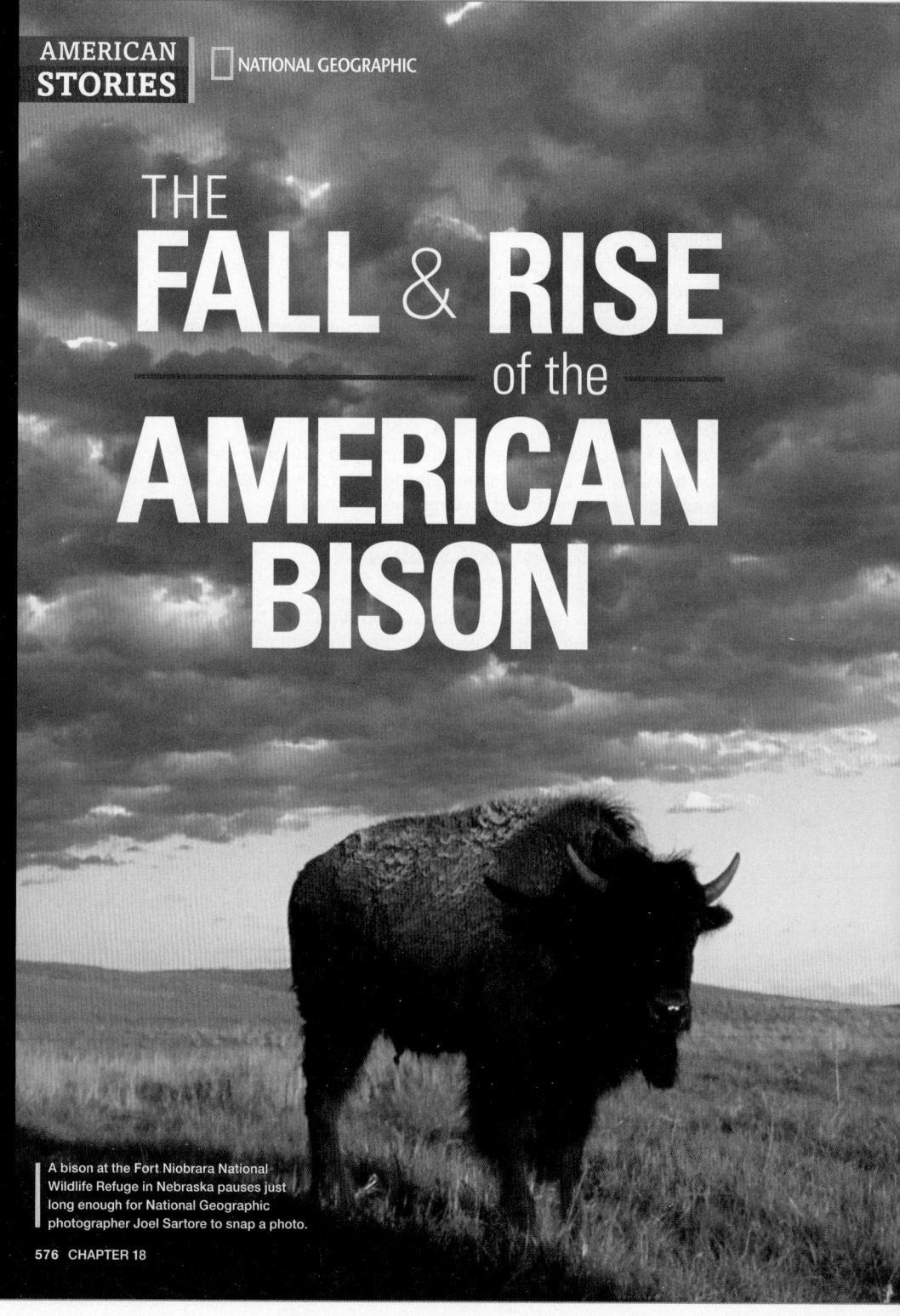

AMERICAN STORIES   NATIONAL GEOGRAPHIC

THE
FALL & RISE
of the
AMERICAN
BISON

A bison at the Fort Niobrara National Wildlife Refuge in Nebraska pauses just long enough for National Geographic photographer Joel Sartore to snap a photo.

576 CHAPTER 18

Everyone knows that the national animal of the United States is the bald eagle. But in 2016, President Barack Obama signed the National Bison Legacy Act, designating the American bison as the official national mammal.

Even if you've never seen one in person, you probably know what an American bison looks like. Commonly referred to as a buffalo, the American bison is portrayed on coins, company and sports team logos, and even the Wyoming state flag. What is the attraction to this unique North American mammal?

For one thing, the American bison is enormous. It can weigh more than 2,000 pounds and measure, at its shoulder, nearly 7 feet tall. It is also incredibly fast and strong. Because of its power, strength, and resilience, the American bison has become a national symbol for many Americans. It stands for both our past and our future, for damage done and the hope that arises when people unite to repair it.

Before 1500, tens of millions of bison roamed the North American plains. When horses and guns arrived on the continent, bison numbers declined drastically. By 1900, this iconic American mammal had become nearly extinct. How did this happen? To understand the decline and rise of the American bison, you have to go back to the beginning, thousands of years ago.

Westward Movement **577**

Preview Using Visuals

Point out the photograph of the bison. **ASK:** What words would you use to describe the image? *(vast, wild, large sky, solitary)* Inform students that the animal seen in the photograph is the American bison, which played an important part in American history. Then have students read the caption. **ASK:** What does the word *refuge* mean? *(a safe place)* Explain to students that there once were tens of millions of bison living across North America, but today's wild populations are confined to a few refuges. Then tell students they are going to read an American Story about how the American bison population collapsed and is slowly being rebuilt.

Chart Symbols of Identity

Create a T-Chart with the heading Symbol for one column and Meaning for the other column. Add to the Symbol column the names of several important American landmarks, such as the Statue of Liberty and the Lincoln Memorial. **ASK:** What do these landmarks tell us about the American identity? *(Americans believe in a country that accepts people of different cultures and races.)* Then have students brainstorm natural landforms, plants, or animals—such as the Grand Canyon or bald eagle—that are important symbols of American identity. Record their responses in the Symbol column. Discuss with students what each symbol conveys about the United States, noting their ideas in the Meaning column. After the chart is completed, have students vote on which symbol they feel best represents the American identity.

Explore Conservation

Write the word *conservation* in the center circle of a Concept Cluster. Ask students what they think of when they hear the word *conservation*. Discuss with students the things they have conserved or have been asked to conserve in their lives. As a class, identify different categories of things, such as resources, plants, or food, that people often conserve. Write the categories in the circles of the Concept Cluster. Then have students brainstorm examples of conservation for each category, and record the responses in circles branching out from the center circle. After brainstorming, guide students to discuss why it's important to conserve and who leads conservation efforts.

What's In a Name?

In the United States, the terms *buffalo* and *bison* are often used interchangeably, but these animals are not of the same species. The American bison is found exclusively in North America, while two types of buffalo make their homes in parts of Asia and Africa. Bison and buffalo are both members of the Bovidae family, and each has a distinct look. The American bison has a much larger head, a noticeable hump, and smaller, cowlike horns as opposed to the huge, sweeping horns of the buffalo. The naming confusion arose from early European explorers who called the bison *bufello* due to their resemblance to their Asian and African counterparts. Because of this mistake, even today, the bison is often referred to by the incorrect name.

Many Uses of Bison

Many Native American tribes on the Great Plains made great use of the American bison—almost no part of the animal was wasted. A typical bison weighed 2,000 pounds and supplied 800 pounds of meat, which is about twice as much as a cow. The meat was cut into thin strips and dried in the sun, which enabled it to be easily transported and stored for months or even years. Native Americans used the nonedible parts of the animal as well: bones were turned into tools, hides were used for blankets or shelter materials, fat was converted to soap, the teeth were fashioned into necklaces, the bladder worked as a bag, and the thick skin at the top of the head became a useful bowl.

Bison Today

While American bison populations have rebounded since the late 1800s, their modern numbers are minuscule compared with their historical peaks. As of now, there are approximately 500,000 bison living in North America, but only a small fraction of these are wild. These wild herds are found in Canada, Mexico, and the United States and are managed by the government or environmental groups. However, wild bison no longer migrate because the required vast amount of open land no longer exists. In addition, a lack of genetic diversity due to their small numbers makes them susceptible to disease. Today, the majority of bison are privately owned and found on ranches where, similar to cattle, they are fenced in and raised for their meat.

CRITICAL VIEWING On horseback, Native Americans could more easily keep up with the bison, making a hunt more efficient.

AMERICAN STORIES

Bison Population in **Millions**
1500–1884

325

1500   1750   1884

Sources: National Geographic,
U.S. Fish and Wildlife Service

FROM MILLIONS TO A FEW HUNDRED

For thousands of years, bison hunting was central to many Native American cultures, especially those living on the Great Plains. They relied on bison herds for survival, especially on the animals' meat for food and skins for shelter coverings. When Europeans arrived in the early 1500s, about 50 million bison ranged across most of the present-day United States. Spanish conquistadors brought horses with them, introducing a new species to the continent. Native Americans adopted the horse, specifically for hunting. Instead of following herds on foot, hunters pursued them on horseback, making the hunt more efficient. By 1750, bison numbers had fallen to 30 million.

When settlers arrived in the West, bison numbers declined rapidly for several reasons. Consumers in the East loved items made of bison skin or fur. Railroads wanted to eliminate the grazing herds that blocked trains for hours or even days. Ranchers wanted to use the land for grazing their cattle. Some army officers believed killing bison would starve out Native American groups in conflict with the U.S. government. In the 1860s and 1870s, hunters hired by the railroads and ranchers killed thousands of bison a day.

White hunters were not the sole threat. A severe drought in the mid-1880s and 1890s, diseases introduced by the settlers' cattle, and Native American hunters also contributed to the reduction in herd numbers. Whatever the precise causes, the result was devastating. By 1884, only 325 wild bison remained in the United States.

CRITICAL VIEWING Nineteenth-century artist George Catlin featured Native Americans in his paintings of the American West. In *The Buffalo Hunt,* painted in 1844, Catlin captures a bison hunt. Based on details you notice in the painting, what advantages would bison hunters on horseback have?

THE COMEBACK

At the height of the bison hunting and slaughter, many people expressed shock and worry. One observer in 1884 described it as "the ruthless, selfish destruction of what should have been protected as State property." Even so, the government voted down proposed measures to protect the bison.

In 1899, William Hornaday, the first director of the Bronx Zoo in New York City, took action. He acquired several bison and started a herd at the zoo. In 1905, Hornaday established the American Bison Society. President Theodore Roosevelt and several other influential men were members. In 1907, the Society persuaded Congress to set aside land in Oklahoma for bison from the Bronx Zoo herd to roam safely and freely. In the decades that followed, additional preserves were established. Soon, bison numbers climbed from the hundreds into the thousands.

BUFFALO BILL CODY

By the late 1800s, the sympathy of the American people had swung in favor of the bison, thanks in part to Buffalo Bill Cody. In the 1860s, the Kansas & Pacific Railroad had hired Cody to hunt bison to feed the railroad's workers. By his own report, he killed more than 4,000 bison in 18 months.

Cody popularized the bison, which eventually aided their preservation. In 1883, he launched a traveling show called Buffalo Bill's Wild West, featuring staged bison hunts using real animals. Other acts included skilled riders, sharpshooters, and Native Americans reenacting famous battles. People who saw the show emerged with an image of the American West as a place of thrills and adventure. Americans soon embraced the idea of the Wild West as part of the nation's identity. Front and center in this vision was the American bison.

More than 100 years after this bison left the Bronx Zoo for a new home in Oklahoma, the American Bison Society, in partnership with the Wildlife Conservation Society and many other conservation groups, continues to work toward the ecological restoration of the bison.

Guided Discussion

1. **Interpret Graphs** Direct students' attention to the graph showing bison population. Have students identify the title of the graph and think about the information being conveyed. **ASK:** What change does the graph show? *(The graph shows the decline of the bison population over a period of more than 300 years.)* **ASK:** What caused the decline? *(The decline was caused by the introduction of horses, hunting by Americans, drought, and disease.)*

2. **Analyze Visuals** Prompt students to examine the photograph of the caged bison and read the accompanying caption. **ASK:** How does the photograph of the bison contrast with the iconic image of bison in American history? *(The iconic image of bison is of large herds roaming freely across the Great Plains. This image shows the opposite—a single bison, caged, with no space to move.)*

Analyze Environmental Concepts

Guide students to consider how the management of the U.S. bison population changed over time. **ASK:** Who worked to manage the bison population in the 1860s and 1870s, and how did they do so? *(Ranchers and railroad workers tried to manage the population by killing off vast numbers to make way for grazing land and railroad efficiency.)* **ASK:** Who worked to manage the bison population in the early 1900s, and how did they do so? *(Conservationists including William Hornaday, President Theodore Roosevelt, and the American Bison Society sought to increase the bison population by setting aside land for them to roam freely and safely.)*

Active Options

On Your Feet: Write a Verse As a class, read the lyrics from "Home on the Range." Arrange students in groups of four. Ask each group to write an additional verse to the song by having each student add one line of lyrics. Allow each group to present the new verse by singing or speaking the lyrics.

NG Learning Framework: Collect Data **STEM**

ATTITUDE Responsibility

KNOWLEDGE Critical Species

After students read Bison of Yellowstone, explain that Yellowstone is home to numerous species of birds and fish and 61 different species of mammals, many of which have been threatened due to contact with humans. Divide the class into groups and have each group select a species, such as the grizzly bear, gray wolf, or bald eagle, found in Yellowstone. Instruct groups to research the species' population over a specific time period and record the data in a graph. Groups should also research how contact with humans has impacted that species and the steps taken—if any—to help the population recover. When finished, invite groups to present their findings to the class.

WRITE ABOUT HISTORY

Human Impact on the Environment To help students make connections between the American Story and their own life, invite them to write an opinion piece about how actions in their community and their own actions have impacted the natural environment. For this op-ed, students should choose two specific actions and explain how they impact the natural environment positively, negatively, or in both ways. Remind students to support their opinions with evidence. Students might discuss topics such as water conservation, recycling, or public transportation.

THINK ABOUT IT

What probably started as thinning the herds of bison resulted in nearly wiping out the entire species. Recognizing the bison's importance in the Native American culture and its growth as an American icon and symbol of the Wild West, the federal government began to manage and preserve the bison population in Yellowstone.

Bison Population in **Thousands**, 1884–2016

600

IN CAPTIVITY

300

325

WILD

0

1884   1919   2016

Sources: National Geographic, U.S. Fish and Wildlife Service

PROTECTING AN AMERICAN ICON

Today, Native American groups are heading up one of the major efforts to save bison in the wild. The Intertribal Bison Cooperative has 51 member tribes and has successfully established herds on reservation lands. Other organizations, including the National Park Service and the Nature Conservancy, are reintroducing bison in preserves throughout their original range. The American Prairie Reserve in Montana focuses on increasing bison numbers, specifically on bison roaming freely on 1 million acres.

Thanks to the decades-long efforts of many concerned individuals and groups, American bison numbers have grown steadily. Estimates of the current population vary, but according to the National Geographic Society, the number on ranches in the United States stands at around 500,000. Who knows how bison numbers—protected and wild—might grow as citizens, scientists, and agencies work together to protect them? What's certain is that this symbolic and unique American species has a real hope for survival.

THINK ABOUT IT

What factors have changed over time that make both Native American and non-Native American groups want to restore the bison?

HOME, HOME ON THE RANGE

Perhaps you've heard the song "Home on the Range" on TV, in movies, or hummed by an older relative. To many, the song symbolizes the American West. The opening line inspires images of wide-open spaces and peacefully grazing bison herds. Brewster Higley wrote the song, originally as a poem, in the early 1870s. By 1934, "Home on the Range" was one of the most popular songs on the radio. In 1947, Kansas adopted it as its state song.

Home on the Range

Oh, give me a home where the buffalo roam,
Where the deer and the antelope play,
Where seldom is heard a discouraging word
And the skies are not cloudy all day.

Chorus

Home, home on the range,
Where the deer and the antelope play;
Where seldom is heard a discouraging word
And the skies are not cloudy all day.

Why do you think this song became so popular?

THE BISON OF YELLOWSTONE

Yellowstone National Park is the only place in the United States, outside of Alaska, where free-ranging bison have lived continuously for thousands of years. Established in 1872, the park sheltered some of the very few American bison to survive the slaughter of the 1800s.

In the early 1900s, the U.S. Army administered Yellowstone and protected the bison living there from illegal hunting. Today, the National Park Service runs the park and manages its bison herd, which numbers around 5,000.

Managing a free-ranging herd is a complex and delicate project. Ranchers and others who live or work near the park worry about the massive, sometimes dangerous animals wandering onto their land. Some bison carry a disease that can make cattle ill as well. The National Park Service works with government and tribal agencies that manage land around Yellowstone to balance the interests of both humans and bison.

What are the benefits and problems of having bison and people living near each other?

A frost-covered bison rests in Yellowstone National Park. The bison's thick fur offers impressive protection against winter. Its coat retains the animal's body heat incredibly well—even snow that falls on its back doesn't melt, keeping the animal dry.

Westward Movement **581**

1.1 Mining Boomtowns

Some opportunities sound too good to pass up, and everyone wants to be a part of them. In the 19th century, when people heard claims of gold and silver in the West, thousands traveled to find out if the claims were true.

MAIN IDEA The discovery of valuable metals in the American West caused a population explosion as people rushed to work in the mines or start businesses to support the miners.

MINING IN THE WEST

The Civil War delayed the dream of manifest destiny for many Americans, but once the war ended, people began to hit the westward trails again in record numbers, seeking new opportunities. The hot, arid climate of the West made farming a challenge, but the quest for land brought many farmers to the Great Plains. Opportunities in mining and cattle ranching also drew people west.

After the gold rush era ended in California in the late 1850s, it didn't take long for miners and merchants to move beyond California to seek mineral wealth. Prospectors began scouring the West for gold, silver, and other valuable metals and discovered gold and silver in Colorado, Nevada, and South Dakota. They also unearthed copper in Arizona and New Mexico. In 1859 in the mountains of Nevada, one of the largest deposits, or **lodes**,

of silver and gold in the West was found. The discovery of rich mineral lodes continued over the next few decades.

The mines provided resources essential to the nation's industrial development. Some miners set up operations near land that Native Americans had lived and hunted on for centuries. Eventually, the U.S. government forced the tribes off those lands, devastating tribal ways of life.

Early on, individual miners who panned for surface gold in riverbeds used a process called **placer mining**. This method works because gold is highly dense and sinks in water faster than other materials. As surface gold was depleted, individual miners went to work for mining companies that began to practice **hydraulic mining**. Workers shot pressurized water onto rocky mountainsides to remove topsoil and gravel, which they then processed with toxic chemicals, such as mercury, to draw out the precious metals. The mercury and mining waste was dumped into streams and rivers, affecting the usefulness of the water sources used by farmers, wildlife, and communities.

For years, farmers fought against mining companies to prevent this environmental damage. In 1884, hydraulic mining was outlawed in the West, but it continued to be used on a small scale. Still, the abandoned mines left ugly scars on the landscape, some of which remain to this day.

MINING CAMPS AND BOOMTOWNS

Populations in mining areas expanded quickly. Initially miners set up camps. Most camps quickly turned into bustling boomtowns, as **entrepreneurs**, such as merchants and business people, arrived to offer goods and services to the miners. People of all ethnicities came to the boomtowns to improve their lives. A few enslaved African-American women, who gained their freedom in the West, became successful business women and landowners.

Boomtowns throughout the West were similar in nature. No matter the state or territory, the pattern of quick growth was much the same. It was difficult to maintain order with a rapidly growing population, so boomtowns were often lawless places. Instead of a regular police force, residents formed **posses**, or groups selected by a sheriff to hunt down criminals.

Similar to the gold rush of 1848, after the mineral deposits were depleted, many boomtowns quickly faded into **ghost towns**, or abandoned towns that have fallen into ruin. Western states today list hundreds of ghost towns. In contrast, cities such as San Francisco and Sacramento, where businesses other than mining had taken hold, continued to flourish and grow.

Like Bodie, California, which you've already read about, Castle, Montana, shown here, sprang up after a mine opened nearby. Years later, Castle became a ghost town. At its peak around 1890, the town had 1,500 residents. By 1920, it had been completely abandoned.

HISTORICAL THINKING

1. **READING CHECK** How did the discovery of valuable mineral resources change the character of western North America?

2. **ANALYZE ENVIRONMENTAL CONCEPTS** What problem did hydraulic mining solve, and what problems did it cause for humans and the land?

3. **CATEGORIZE** List words from the text that describe life in a boomtown, then sort the words into two categories: *positive* and *negative*. What is one pattern or trend you see as you analyze the categories?

PLAN

Objective
Learn how the influx of miners to the West affected the land and the lives of native people.

Critical Thinking Skills for Lesson 1.1
- Identify Main Ideas and Details
- Monitor Comprehension
- Analyze Environmental Concepts
- Categorize

Essential Question for Chapter 18
How did westward migration affect the culture and way of life of Native American groups? The discovery of precious metals in the West was a major moment in American history. Lesson 1.1 explains how the lure of wealth changed the West, focusing on what miners searched for, how mining was conducted, and the settlements miners created and left behind.

Background for the Teacher
The Comstock Lode, discovered in the 1850s in western Nevada, was named for Henry Comstock, who took over the claim from the two miners who discovered the silver deposit. Getting precious metals out of the Comstock Lode made panning for gold in riverbeds look easy. The Comstock Lode was worked through a set of underground mines, where the miners faced sweltering heat and cave-ins, especially in the mines' early years. As they did in California, miners in Nevada used toxic chemicals and mercury (as much as seven tons of mercury in all) to separate out the precious metals, contaminating surrounding land and water in the process. In addition, lumber companies cut down about 60 miles of trees in the eastern Sierra Nevada to provide lumber for the mines and the boomtowns that sprang up around the mines. The deforestation led to floods in the area.

Discuss Population Growth

Explain that a growing population can affect an area in many ways. Point out that the "rush" for gold and other metals caused a great growth of population in the largely undeveloped West. **ASK:** How do you think the region had to change to support this population growth? Write students' responses on the board, drawing special attention to responses relating to the challenge of supplying the newcomers' basic needs and to competition among these new arrivals or between newcomers and people already living there.

TEACH   `STEM`

Guided Discussion

1. **Analyze Environmental Concepts** How did mining practices impact the environment beyond the immediate area surrounding mining operations? *(Possible response: As mining contaminants were dumped into waterways, water carried the poisonous materials downstream to pollute a broader area.)*

2. **Analyze Environmental Concepts** How might hydraulic mining practices have affected the resources and agricultural products people consumed? *(Possible response: Mercury and other toxic substances poisoned waterways, leaving less water for human or agricultural use. Water quality would have directly affected whether livestock or crops could survive or be healthful to consume.)*

More Information

Biddy Mason and Mary Ellen Pleasant Two African-American women to make their mark upon the West were Biddy Mason and Mary Ellen Pleasant. Biddy Mason gained her freedom in 1856 after her owner's family moved to California, a free state. Living in Los Angeles, Mason saved her earnings as a nurse and midwife, and in 1866, she bought two lots, becoming one of the nation's first African-American women to own land. She also was well known for giving to those in need in her community. Mary Ellen Pleasant was born into slavery, but in 1849 she came to San Francisco from Boston as a free woman with an inheritance from her first husband. With that money, plus what she made as a cook and the owner of a boardinghouse, Pleasant helped freed slaves find jobs and provided low-interest loans to African Americans.

Active Options

On Your Feet: Fishbowl Arrange one half of the class sitting in a close circle facing inward. The other half of the class sits in a larger circle around them. Present this question: How did the West change because of the search for mineral wealth? Students in the inner circle should discuss the question for five minutes while those in the outer circle listen to the discussion and evaluate the points made. Then direct the groups to reverse roles and continue the discussion.

NG Learning Framework: Create an Infographic

`SKILL` Collaboration

`KNOWLEDGE` Our Living Planet

Tell groups of students to review the information about hydraulic mining. Then instruct them to create an infographic that explains why hydraulic mining came to be used in the West, how the technology worked, and how it affected the environment. Invite groups to share their infographics and comment upon how the use of hydraulic mining changed America.

English Language Learners   `ELD`

Explore New Terms Students at the **Emerging** level may be unfamiliar with the term *boom*, as in *boomtown*. Explain that a boom refers to something that grows very quickly. In the lesson, *boomtown* refers to a town that grew very quickly because of the arrival of miners and people who served their needs. Tell students to look up the meaning of other kinds of booms, such as manufacturing boom and baby boom. Then invite students to use *boom* in original oral or written sentences.

Pre-AP   `STEM`

Connect Past and Present Challenge students to conduct research across multiple print and digital sources and then write a report on a modern effort to reclaim land or water poisoned by hydraulic mining or to protect Americans today from its toxic residue. As students do their research, remind them to use search terms effectively and to evaluate the credibility and accuracy of each source. Remind students not to plagiarize but to document any data that they quote or paraphrase and to follow a standard format for citation.

See the Chapter Planner for more strategies for differentiation.

ANSWERS

1. The miners' rush to obtain mineral wealth (and the rush of entrepreneurs seeking to make their fortunes off the miners) increased the population of the West, dispossessed many Native Americans, and created environmental damage.

2. Hydraulic mining solved the problem of getting valuable minerals from the earth after the minerals from the surface had been taken. The debris created by the practice and toxic chemicals used to process the topsoil and gravel were dumped into waterways, polluting them.

3. Positive language includes *bustling*, *entrepreneurs*, *strike it rich*, and *successful*. Negative language includes *lawless places*, *posses*, *hunt down criminals*, and *ghost towns*. An analysis of the categories suggests that the lure of the boomtowns was short lived and that towns were dangerous.

1.2 Cattle and the Long Drive

Moving to a new place and experiencing a change of scenery can be thrilling. After the Civil War, many people were eager to reach the West and the Great Plains. The territory was wide open, and there was plenty of work for those who could endure long, hard days.

MAIN IDEA The cattle industry relied upon a wide range of people doing vastly different kinds of work in different parts of the country.

CRITICAL VIEWING *The New Fence*, a 1946 painting by Thomas Hart Benton, shows two ranchers unrolling coils of barbed wire to make a fence. What does the windswept effect of the painting convey about life on the open range?

THE CATTLE BOOM

Mining was only one of the industries pulling Americans west. Cattle ranching was another. Americans' taste for beef, as well as the ability of railroads to transport cattle quickly across the country to market, made ranching very profitable.

Across the Great Plains, from Texas to Montana, ranchers began raising herds of cattle that grazed across the open range. Ranchers depended on cowboys, who led **cattle drives** to move the herds across the plains to cow towns, railroad communities where cattle were loaded on trains to be taken to market. The earliest cow towns were in Kansas: Abilene, Wichita, and Dodge City. As the railroads pushed west, cow towns developed in Nebraska, Wyoming, and Montana.

The cattle were transported by train to **stockyards** at meat processing facilities. A stockyard is an enormous outdoor area where animals are penned until they can be slaughtered. Because it was a railroad hub and closer to the plains than eastern cities, Chicago, Illinois, boasted the nation's largest stockyards. The most successful meat processing companies of the day made innovations in butchering and processing, and were centered in Chicago. After 1878, advances in boxcar cooling and refrigeration allowed beef products to be processed and packaged at the meat company and then delivered to all corners of the United States.

THE LORE OF THE COWBOY

In folklore of the American West, cowboys were rugged, fearless, and self-sufficient heroes of the open range. In reality, cowboys' lives were difficult and dangerous. They worked 14-hour days, slept outside in all weather, spent hours riding and roping, and earned very modest pay. The average cowboy was young—only 24 years old—and just as likely to be a Mexican American, African American, or Native American as a European American. Cowboys worked together in teams to herd and manage the cattle.

Many of the tools western cowboys used originated with the Mexican *vaqueros*, or cattle

Fencing In the Open Range

Joseph Glidden received a patent for barbed wire in 1874. His invention forever changed the frontier and cattle grazing. Ranchers enclosed their land with barbed wire fences and kept their branded cattle within this boundary. Barbed wire fencing led to land disputes among ranchers. It also led to a decline in the need for cowboys. Prior to its use, many cowboys were needed to round up cattle from the open range. Then they had to separate and sort the animals by their brands, or identifying markings, to determine which cattle belonged to which ranch. With herds confined by barbed wire, ranchers no longer needed cowboys to perform this service.

drivers. Mexican ranchers had a long-established tradition of working with cattle. Thus, many of the words associated with cattle ranching developed from Spanish. For example, cowboys wore leather leg coverings called *chaps* (from *chaparreras*) to protect against scrapes from sagebrush or thorny cacti that covered the landscape. They used a looped cord, which was made of braided strips of cowhide, called a *lariat* (from *la reata*) to rope a wayward cow or horse.

About 25 percent of cowboys were African Americans who migrated to the West after the Civil War. The war brought about poor economic conditions in the South and pushed African Americans to build new lives in a new land. They often performed the hardest and most dangerous work, such as taming wild horses, but only rarely became ranchers themselves. One exception was Daniel W. Wallace, who, as a cowboy, became known as "80 John" for the brand—the number "80"—he placed on his cattle. Wallace accepted cattle as payment for his work. He acquired 1,280 acres of land in Texas and became a successful rancher.

Cowboys still herd and manage cattle in the western United States today, but by the end of the 1880s, the era of the great cattle drives had ended. Much of the once-open range had been enclosed by barbed wire, and the railroads had expanded so much that long cattle drives were no longer necessary. The rails had come to the ranchers. Even so, the powerful image of the western cowboy continues to be part of the American identity.

HISTORICAL THINKING

1. **READING CHECK** Why was the West well suited for the cattle industry?

2. **ANALYZE CAUSE AND EFFECT** How did the expansion of the railroad impact cattle ranching and the work of cowboys?

3. **DISTINGUISH FACT AND OPINION** The American cowboy is an idealized figure today. What ideas about cowboys are merely opinions, and what facts does the text provide about cowboys' lives?

PLAN

Objective
Explore the cause of the cattle boom and the technologies and people that made it possible.

Critical Thinking Skills for Lesson 1.2
- Identify Main Ideas and Details
- Monitor Comprehension
- Analyze Cause and Effect
- Distinguish Fact and Opinion
- Describe
- Evaluate
- Make Connections

Essential Question for Chapter 18
How did westward migration affect the culture and way of life of Native American groups? Cattle ranching attracted Native Americans, Mexican Americans, and African Americans. Lesson 1.2 describes the work and workers of the cattle boom.

Background for the Teacher
Before the Civil War, most Americans thought of cattle primarily as producers of dairy products. Pork was a more popular meat because it was relatively inexpensive and was easily preserved. Salt pork was a staple of the rations that soldiers in the Civil War received. After the war, however, beef started to gain in popularity, in part because of the shortage of cattle in the North. Investors could not resist the profit to be made from selling beef in eastern cities and shipping some of it to Europe. As a result, hired workers drove beef cattle to rail lines in Kansas and Nebraska where the animals could be loaded for transport. Overstocked ranges eventually led to less profit, but the cattle boom had a major effect on American culture.

Activate Prior Knowledge

Write the word *cowboy* on the board. Ask students what they may know or may have heard about cowboys; note their responses. The responses may be a mix of fact and fiction, but take advantage of that to point out that the cowboy has become a major figure in American folklore and brings a specific image to the minds of Americans even today. Explain that in this lesson students will learn about the work that cowboys actually did and why they played an important role in the development of the West.

TEACH

Guided Discussion

1. **Describe** What was the purpose of a cattle drive? *(In a cattle drive, cowboys herded the animals from their grazing lands on the range to towns where the cattle were loaded onto trains that would take them to market.)*

2. **Evaluate** What problems did barbed wire solve, and what new problems did it create? *(Barbed wire kept cattle from wandering, and it kept one owner's cattle from getting mixed up with another owner's cattle. However, barbed wire greatly reduced the need for cowboys, and it led to conflicts among ranchers regarding land use.)*

Make Connections

Discuss with students the connection between the Civil War and the cattle boom. In particular, review the situation in the South after the war—Radical Reconstruction. As the lesson points out, the cattle boom encouraged African Americans to move to the West as cowboys. **ASK:** Why do you think that southern African Americans would be attracted to this work? *(Possible response: It offered them better opportunities than sharecropping, and it took them farther away from the organized discrimination going on against African Americans in the South.)* Point out that the challenges of life in the Reconstruction South also motivated some white southerners to move to the West.

Active Options

On Your Feet: Concept Cluster Have students form groups of four or five around a section of a bulletin board or a table. Provide each group with a large sheet of paper. Have group members take turns contributing a concept or phrase to a Concept Cluster with the term *Cattle Boom* at the center. When time for the activity has elapsed, call on volunteers from each group to share their group's cluster. Invite students to make comparisons.

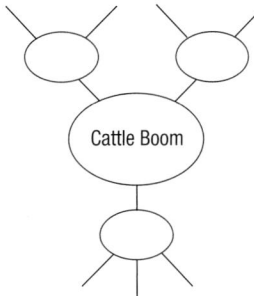

NG Learning Framework: Write Diary Entries

ATTITUDES Curiosity, Empowerment

KNOWLEDGE Our Human Story

Instruct students to research the life as a cowboy on the open range. Then ask them to write a set of diary entries based on their research. Invite students to share the entries, perhaps working with classmates who have completed the same activity to present the material in a reader's theater format.

DIFFERENTIATE

Striving Readers

Use Reciprocal Teaching Have partners take turns reading each paragraph of the lesson aloud. At the end of the paragraph, the reading student should ask the listening student questions about the paragraph. Students may ask their partners to state the main idea of the paragraph, identify important details that support the main idea, or summarize the paragraph in their own words. Then have students work together to answer the Historical Thinking questions.

English Language Learners

Explore Cognates Point out the Spanish origins of *chaps* and *lariat*; add that *vaquero* is based on *vaca*, the Spanish word for *cow*. Encourage students at **All Proficiencies** to look for cognates that can help them understand the meaning of words they read. For example, students may be familiar with these Spanish cognates: *refrigeration/refrigeración; exception/excepción; facility/facilidad; community/comunidad.*

See the Chapter Planner for more strategies for differentiation.

HISTORICAL THINKING

ANSWERS

1. The open areas of grazing land in the West provided a vast supply of food for herds of cattle.

2. As railroads expanded across the West, the need for long cattle drives ended because ranchers could get their cattle to market from railroad stations that were far closer than before.

3. Cowboys did in fact conduct roundups and cattle drives. They also worked long hours and faced dangerous conditions, although they did not make much money. Descriptions such as "rugged, fearless, and self-sufficient heroes of the open range" are opinions.

CRITICAL VIEWING Answers will vary. Possible response: People who worked on the open range had to become accustomed to living in harsh weather conditions.

Farming in the West

Getting something for free sounds really great. How could people turn down 160 acres of land if they didn't have to pay for it? In truth, homesteaders quickly found out that their free land was more expensive than it seemed.

MAIN IDEA Many homesteaders rushed west to claim the free land in the West offered by the U.S. government.

HOMESTEADERS AND EXODUSTERS

As you have read, in 1862 the U.S. government's Homestead Act encouraged westward migration by offering 160 acres of land to every free American citizen or to those intending to become citizens. The offer was open to unmarried, widowed, or divorced women, as well as African Americans, eventually. If they claimed the land and lived there for five years, it became theirs.

By 1868, a steady stream of African Americans began to move to Kansas and farther west to claim land. Kansas had a strong pull factor. It had entered the Union as a free state, and the story of John Brown and his efforts to keep Kansas free were legendary. By 1879, a full-scale exodus, or mass migration, was underway, driven by racism in the South and encouraged by some northern legislators. The thousands of African Americans who headed to Kansas and a new life became known as the **exodusters**. Between 1870 and 1880, Kansas added about 27,000 African-American citizens who established farms, settled in cities, and founded communities such as the Nicodemus Town Company in 1877.

Although the Homestead Act offered a diverse group of people the opportunity to own land, the cost of livestock, seeds, and farm equipment often discouraged newcomers with no previous farming or ranching experience. Families who already had established farms elsewhere were more likely to claim the free land. Only 80 million acres of the 500 million dispersed by the General Land Office between 1862 and 1904 went to homesteaders. Between 1851 and 1871, approximately 130 million acres were given to railroads.

If a new farmer had the money to purchase cattle, the grasslands of the **prairie**, a vast area of flat land covered with tall plants, offered immediate grazing. Unlike in the East with its abundant rain, cultivating crops in the western United States and Great Plains proved challenging. Wheat grew well in this region, but the arid climate made irrigation both necessary and difficult. Farmers wanted to settle near rivers, but not everyone could. Farms farther away from water resources needed a way to transport water across other people's land, which required cooperation among the farmers. Homesteaders often fought over water rights. Discouraged, many farmers turned to ranching instead of growing crops until federal legislation led to irrigation projects at the beginning of the 20th century.

BONANZA!

You have also read that even before the Civil War, agricultural technology began to transform American farming with innovations such as the reaper, the thresher, and the plow. These machines allowed farmers to work larger areas of land with fewer people. In 1873 when the Northern Pacific Railroad needed money to cover its debts, it sold enormous tracts of land—some up to 100,000 acres—to investors who created **bonanza farms**. The name reflects the fact that the owners, who often did not live on the land, believed they would soon find a bonanza—a stroke of extreme good fortune. These farms made the American West and Great Plains major wheat-producing regions.

Bonanza farms specialized in one crop and used a farm manager and crews of **migrant workers**, or laborers who moved from one farm

to another as needed, to cultivate the land. For example, in California's Central Valley, Chinese, Japanese, Hindu, Turkish, Filipino, and Mexican migrant workers toiled on bonanza farms. The workers slept in bunkhouses and ate in dining halls built by the farm managers.

The success of bonanza farms was subject to wheat prices. When the farms produced a **surplus**, or excess, of wheat, the price of the grain dropped. Harvesting required thousands of migrant workers, but with lower wheat prices, there was little or no profit after paying the workers. Farming on a much smaller scale, homesteaders worked their own land. They were less affected by price changes, outlasting the bonanza farms for a time, but the homesteaders faced problems of their own.

Sod Houses
One big problem homesteaders faced on the prairie was that there were almost no trees—certainly not enough to provide wood to build a house or cabin. Families needed shelter in this treeless environment. Fortunately, there was plenty of grass that sent deep roots into the topsoil to form sod. Settlers used thick chunks of sod to build houses. Sod homes were practical: their thick walls kept out the cold in the winter and the heat in the summer. One type of sod home, called a dugout (shown above), was built by digging right into the side of a ridge. Dugouts were the fastest way to create a shelter, as not all sides of the home needed to be constructed using sod bricks.

HISTORICAL THINKING

1. **READING CHECK** What groups of people could take advantage of the Homestead Act?

2. **IDENTIFY PROBLEMS AND SOLUTIONS** How did homesteaders change the land to solve the problems they faced?

3. **ANALYZE ENVIRONMENTAL CONCEPTS** What effect did the sale of land by the Northern Pacific Railroad have on how the land was used?

PLAN

Objective
Analyze the rapid migration of homesteaders to the West and the rise of bonanza farms.

Critical Thinking Skills for Lesson 2.1
- Identify Main Ideas and Details
- Monitor Comprehension
- Identify Problems and Solutions
- Analyze Environmental Concepts
- Analyze Cause and Effect

Essential Question for Chapter 18
How did westward migration affect the culture and way of life of Native American groups? After the Civil War, thousands of Americans found the West an attractive place to make a new start. Lesson 2.1 describes the migration of homesteaders and some of the challenges they faced in farming the land.

Background for the Teacher
One of the greatest promoters of migration to Kansas was Benjamin "Pap" Singleton, a former slave who advertised throughout the South the idea of settlements for African Americans in Kansas. Singleton became known as the "Father of the Exodus." He promoted migration heavily at a convention in 1875, and he helped hundreds of African Americans relocate to Kansas between 1877 and 1879. He also helped found the Nicodemus Town Company. The town of Nicodemus prospered for a time and even began to exercise some clout in Kansas politics. Though smaller than it once was, Nicodemus continues today. In 1996, it was designated a National Historic Site.

Preview Using Visuals

Direct students' attention to the photograph of the family in front of their sod house. Explain the term *sod house* and invite comments about details in the photograph that strike students as unusual, such as the window set into a dirt wall and the horse-drawn wagon on the "roof" of the house. Discuss whether students think the sod house would be a comfortable place to live. **ASK:** Why do you think people moved to the West if it meant living like this? *(Possible responses: They were willing to endure the hardship because they thought they could make a better life for themselves in the West. They may not have realized that they would be living so differently from what they were used to.)*

TEACH
Guided Discussion

1. **Analyze Cause and Effect** Why were many African Americans especially attracted to Kansas? *(African Americans remembered "Bleeding Kansas" and how John Brown, a hero to many, had fought to ensure that Kansas would be a free state.)*

2. **Analyze Environmental Concepts** How did the Homestead Act influence the environment and the biological diversity of the Great Plains? *(By granting legal ownership to free land, the Homestead Act opened up vast areas to human settlement for farmers and ranchers, who brought large herds of cattle and planted wheat on what had previously been prairie land. They also worked to bring water farther from waterways to irrigate dry land.)*

More Information

Dry Farming Water was definitely a problem for farmers in the West, parts of which received no more than 20 inches of rain per year. There were few rivers to tap for irrigation, and few ranchers could afford the equipment required for drilling wells that could reach the water lying deep underground. For most farmers, the answer was dry farming, which used what little water the ground held after the rain. One method used by dry farmers was to till the soil to a depth of three or four inches instead of cutting deeper with a plow. Dry farmers often rotated their crops, giving fields the chance to accumulate moisture during a year of "rest." Dry farming enabled many farmers to succeed; however, over time the practice broke down the soil and the root system of existing grasses, leading to the Dust Bowl of the 1930s.

Active Options

On Your Feet: Turn and Talk on Topic Group students in three lines. Give each line the same topic sentence: After the Civil War, farming changed the West. Tell them to build on that topic by having each student in the line add one sentence. Groups can present their results to the class, with each student reading his or her sentence.

NG Learning Framework: Make a Homesteading Plan

ATTITUDE Empowerment

SKILL Problem-Solving

Tell students to review the text and photograph in the lesson. Ask them to consider what challenges a homesteader would face upon arriving in and starting to farm on the prairie. Examples might include building a home, securing livestock, and buying and planting seed. Allow a few minutes for brainstorming or quickwriting. Then work with students to compile their responses into a plan that a homesteader might use to settle into life as a farmer on the prairie.

DIFFERENTIATE
Inclusion

Analyze Visuals Provide concrete questions to help students describe the photograph of the family and their sod house. **ASK:** Who are the people in the photo? Why is there grass on the walls of their house? What items do you see that might be found at the home of a family today? What work do the horses do? What does their position in the photo tell you about the house? Encourage students to identify details they don't understand, and help them frame questions about these details.

Pre-AP

Research and Role-Play Have students do research to learn how rivers influenced western settlement patterns and how water management in eastern cities, where the supply of water was adequate, compared with water management on the western prairie, where water often was scarce. Suggest that students consider irrigation practices, the use of dams, and water rights and allocation. Ask students to prepare and present interviews in which they role-play an eastern city-dweller and a western farmer, sharing information and insights about the role of water in their daily lives and activities and in their communities. Allow time for the class to ask questions of the presenters.

See the Chapter Planner for more strategies for differentiation.

HISTORICAL THINKING

ANSWERS

1. Free American citizens, including women and people who were planning to become citizens, were able to take advantage of the Homestead Act. Later, African Americans could participate, too.

2. Few trees meant no lumber for homes, so homesteaders cut bricks of sod to build their dwellings. The land was hard to till, and there was little rain, so homesteaders grew wheat, which thrived in a prairie environment. Watering crops often required irrigation systems or other ways of transporting water from a distance.

3. Investors bought thousands of acres to form large farms called bonanza farms. Bonanza farms specialized in one crop and employed a system of farm managers and migrant work crews.

2.2 Women and Children on the Prairie

Do you sew your own clothes? Bake your own bread? On the prairie, everything was made by hand. Daily tasks required demanding, time-consuming labor that was divided between men, women, and children.

MAIN IDEA On the prairie, a new American identity formed around community, religion, and hard work performed by all family members.

CHALLENGES FOR WOMEN

In 1870, the majority of Americans lived in small towns or on farms. Just as farm work on the American prairie was demanding, the responsibilities of rural housekeeping were extensive, and they were handled primarily by women. Women hauled water and kept a fire constantly burning in a stove. Just those two tasks took at least an hour each day. Women sewed by hand the clothing their family wore,

washed the laundry in a tub, and used a heavy iron to press the clothes. In addition, the women had to watch and raise their children and keep a safe and clean home.

Prairie women fed the livestock, gathered chicken eggs, and tended the garden, which provided most of the family's food. They canned, or preserved, the ripened fruits and vegetables for use in the winter.

⬛ Iowa Quilt Museum
Winterset, Iowa

Made by machine and by hand in an unknown pattern, this quilt is from c. 1850–1900. Several U.S. museums, like this one in Iowa, are devoted to preserving the art and history of quilts. American quilts are their own art form, sewn from blocks of fabric. A quilt usually has a name related to its pattern, which can be an illustration or a geometric form, such as the quilt shown here.

Made like a sandwich, quilts usually have a decorated top, a back, and a warm filler in between. Quilts were needed to keep a family warm, but they were also a source of enjoyment. Women on the prairie helped each other at social "bees," where they did handwork together, such as quilting and sewing.

Prairie farms were miles apart, so a woman could go days without contact with anyone except her husband and children. During good weather, everyone looked forward to going to church on Sunday. It was a chance to see others and catch up on the community news. But during the winter, deep snow and dangerous winds kept most people confined to their homes, which contributed to a profound sense of isolation. Author Willa Cather describes the long prairie winters in her book *My Ántonia*: "Winter lies too long in country towns; hangs on until it is stale and shabby, old and sullen."

If a woman's husband died, she was often left alone on the land. Fortunately, she usually had the skills needed to manage the farm. Due to their contributions on the farm and in the home, prairie women gained great respect. It is no surprise that women in the West were the first to win the right to vote when the Wyoming Territory established women's suffrage in 1869.

THE LIVES OF PRAIRIE CHILDREN

In the first half of the 19th century, school was not mandatory in the United States, but most parents wanted their children to get at least a basic education. Many prairie communities built one-room schoolhouses in central locations. To attend, most children walked several miles each way. Early schools had dirt floors and were heated by a coal- or wood-fired stove. Children brought their lunches from home and used the same dipper to drink water from a community bucket. An outhouse stood behind the building; there was no indoor plumbing for bathrooms.

In a one-room schoolhouse, one teacher taught all of the grades. Some teachers managed classes as large as 48 students ranging in age from 6 to 18 years old. Students learned at their own pace. Among the common textbooks found in schools of that time were the **McGuffey Readers**, which were developed by William McGuffey in 1836. Children learned by reading stories that promoted

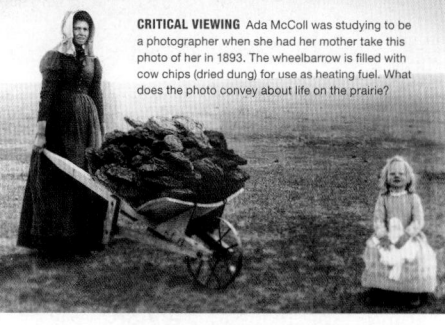

CRITICAL VIEWING Ada McColl was studying to be a photographer when she had her mother take this photo of her in 1893. The wheelbarrow is filled with cow chips (dried dung) for use as heating fuel. What does the photo convey about life on the prairie?

good character, a strong work ethic, and honesty. The books condemned lying, stealing, cheating, laziness, and alcohol use.

Even though education was important for prairie children, their work on the homestead was considered more valuable than schoolwork. Starting at about age four, children had many chores to do and little free time to play. Because families made or grew most of what they ate, children were expected to help milk cows, churn butter, and care for a vegetable garden to help their families survive.

When they finished their chores, the children played games, including many you might recognize, such as jump rope, hopscotch, checkers, and marbles. Prairie children also enjoyed getting together with friends at church socials, the Fourth of July celebration, and other gatherings.

HISTORICAL THINKING

1. **READING CHECK** In what ways did women and children play important roles on the American prairie?

2. **CATEGORIZE** How might you categorize details about the women who lived on the prairie? Explain your reasoning.

3. **COMPARE AND CONTRAST** How were the lives of children living on the prairie during the 19th century similar to and different from the lives of children today? Provide relevant details from the text.

⬛ PLAN

Objective
Describe home and community life of families who farmed the prairie in the late 1800s.

Critical Thinking Skills for Lesson 2.2

- Identify Main Ideas and Details
- Monitor Comprehension
- Categorize
- Compare and Contrast
- Describe
- Make Inferences

Essential Question for Chapter 18
How did westward migration affect the culture and way of life of Native American groups? Prairie living presented challenges to many homesteaders. Lesson 2.2 discusses ways in which homesteading families worked together to meet their daily needs, educate their children, and keep in touch with their community.

Background for the Teacher

Although members of married couples did not have identical daily tasks, they generally realized that it took a partnership for them to succeed. One wife from the Kansas prairie stated, "I already had ideas of my own about the husband being the head of the family. I had taken the precaution to sound him on 'obey' in the marriage pact and found he did not approve of the term. Approval or no approval, that word 'obey' would have to be left out. I had served my time of tutelage to my parents as all children are supposed to. I was a woman now and capable of being the other half of the head of the family. His word and my word would have equal strength."

INTRODUCE & ENGAGE

Activate Prior Knowledge

Some students may be familiar with the *Little House* series of novels, which author Laura Ingalls Wilder based on her childhood in Wisconsin, Kansas, Minnesota, and South Dakota in the 1870s and 1880s. Invite volunteers to recall details about life in the West in those stories. If students have not read the series, ask them to imagine what life was like, based on what they read in Lesson 2.1. *(Answers will vary. Student responses may include living in a sod house, tending a garden, struggling with water shortages, and dealing with blizzards.)* Explain that this lesson will focus on the daily lives of women and children in prairie families.

TEACH

Guided Discussion

1. **Describe** What was family life like for homesteaders on the western prairie? *(Possible response: Life was often very challenging. Family members had to work hard to provide for themselves, and most of what they had they made or prepared for themselves. They spent much of their time isolated from other families.)*

2. **Make Inferences** How might the fact that work on the homestead was considered more valuable than schoolwork have affected attendance at school? *(When children were needed to help at the homestead, during planting and harvesting times, they were most likely kept out of school to work.)*

🏛 Virtual Museum Visit

The Iowa Quilt Museum opened in May 2016 in a renovated store in the town square of Winterset, Iowa. To display and protect a variety of new and heirloom quilts, the museum has several movable walls, equipment that keeps the humidity low, and special LED lighting. Read the caption aloud and ask students whether they know anyone who makes quilts. Invite comments about the pictured quilt, as well, which was part of the museum's inaugural exhibit, "Three Centuries of Red + White Quilts." Explain that red and white quilts are a specific type of quilt that became popular in the 1800s, when cloth colored with a nonfading dye called Turkey red (originally made in Turkey) came to American markets. Finally, ask groups of students to explore the museum's site on their own and present a favorite quilt to the class.

Active Options

On Your Feet: Tell Me More Arrange students in two teams. Assign each team one of the following topics: lives of prairie women or lives of prairie children. Team members should write down as many facts about their topic as possible. When the class reconvenes, have one team stand up. Members of the other team call out, "Tell me more about [the topic]!" A spokesperson for the standing team recites one fact. The other team continues to call, "Tell me more!" until the standing team runs out of facts to share. Then the teams switch roles. Keep track of which team shares more facts.

NG Learning Framework: Compare Responsibilities

ATTITUDE Responsibility

KNOWLEDGE Our Human Story

Gather students into small groups. Instruct them to review the responsibilities of women and children in a homesteading family as presented in the lesson and to record relevant facts in a T-Chart. Have each group write and present a paragraph to assess how each family member's responsibilities contributed to the homestead's success.

DIFFERENTIATE

English Language Learners

Use a Main Idea Cluster Pair students at the **Emerging** and **Expanding** levels with students at the **Bridging** level. Direct pairs to use a Main Idea Cluster to check their understanding. Tell students to take turns reading parts of the lesson. For each part they will record the main idea and four details. Instruct pairs to trade and compare clusters.

Gifted & Talented

Explore Primary Sources Explain that much of what we know about everyday life on the prairie comes from journals kept by homesteading women or letters that they wrote to friends and relatives in the East. Ask students to research print and reputable online sources to find an interesting first-person account in one such primary source, something that can be read aloud in two or three minutes. As students search, encourage them to look for essential information, not incidental details. Invite students to share their selections with the class. Discuss how the information presented reinforces or supplements the information in the lesson.

See the Chapter Planner for more strategies for differentiation.

HISTORICAL THINKING

ANSWERS

1. Women and children did chores, worked farms, and tended gardens and livestock. Widows managed farms and maintained their families. Children learned to farm and went to school for formal education.

2. Prairie women might be categorized by their daily chores, their leisure activities, and their family responsibilities. The text provides details about these parts of a prairie woman's life.

3. Children from both eras have school, chores, and time spent with friends. Chores were harder and more vital to the family in the 19th century, and 19th-century schooling often took a back seat to duties at home. The distances between homes on the prairie meant that children were sometimes isolated from their friends.

CRITICAL VIEWING Answers will vary. Possible response: Homesteaders had to work hard to live on the prairie, including collecting materials such as cow chips for fuel.

It's challenging—and risky—to start a small business, and most of them aren't instantly profitable. In the mid to late 1800s, new farmers struggled to earn a profit, and some lost their farms.

MAIN IDEA Farmers organized to promote political ideas they hoped would change the economy to be more favorable to agriculture.

FARMERS' ECONOMIC PROBLEMS

Farming is a difficult business. Seeds and equipment cost money, and it is especially hard for a new farmer to purchase them without any crops to sell. In the 1800s, many new farmers borrowed money to get started. When crop prices fell during an economic downturn, or **recession**, in the early 1870s, farmers in the South, Midwest, and West faced economic distress. Farmers who failed to pay their debts often lost their land to

their **creditors**, or the people from whom they had borrowed money. After the Civil War, Oliver Kelley, a clerk for the United States Bureau of Agriculture, toured the South to gather information about how best to help farmers during Reconstruction. He observed the struggles most farmers faced. In 1867, he started the **Grange**, an organization that brought farm families together, addressed farmers' economic issues, and encouraged advancements in agriculture.

CRITICAL VIEWING Louis Kurz created this lithograph around 1875. Among those depicted are President Grant, people in finance and transportation, a doctor, and a storekeeper. How does the image represent the dependence of the economy on the American farmer?

I FEED YOU ALL!

As membership in the Grange grew, the organization began to promote farmer-owned **cooperatives**, or groups of farmers who pooled their money to buy the products and services they needed. By buying so many items or services at one time, a cooperative could negotiate better prices for machinery, seeds, and crop storage. This saved members money. The Grange also promoted the regulation of railroad and warehouse rates and operations in several states to control the shipping and storage of harvested crops.

THE POPULIST PARTY

When midwestern blizzards killed entire herds of livestock in the winter of 1887, many farmers and ranchers faced financial ruin. They needed help, and they wanted an alternative to the Republican and Democratic parties, which they believed had failed to support their interests. The **Farmers' Alliance**, an organization similar to the Grange but more political, emerged. The Farmers' Alliance started in the southern cotton belt and spread quickly into the Midwest and West.

The Farmers' Alliance pushed for a third political party, and in 1892, it helped form the **Populist Party**. A **populist** claims to represent the concerns of ordinary people. The Populist Party aimed to give farmers the equivalent political status of business people and **industrialists**, the people who own and run industries. It called on the government to reclaim the land held by railroads and wanted to put more currency, or paper money, into circulation. Doing so would mean farmers would get higher prices for their harvests, making it easier for them to pay their debts. Farmers began thinking of ways in which this could be accomplished.

You have read previously about the relationship between currency and gold and silver. In the 1890s, and continuing into the 1930s, American currency was held to the **gold standard**, a policy requiring that the government could only print an amount of money equal to the total value of its gold reserves. The only way to distribute more money was to obtain more gold. With a limited number of dollars, each dollar's value increased. The overall value of the currency shrank as the value of each dollar rose. As a result, prices of goods were low, and farmers worked harder to maintain the same level of income.

The Populist Party supported the **free silver movement**: Anyone holding silver could have it minted into U.S. silver dollar coins for a small fee, and these coins would be placed into circulation. Silver from American mines was plentiful, so introducing free silver would increase the money supply and inflate prices, as the farmers desired.

Currency was the main issue of the 1896 election. Republican nominee **William McKinley** supported the gold standard, while Democrat **William Jennings Bryan** was pro-silver. Bryan ran as the Democratic Party's presidential candidate in 1896. When the Populist Party chose to support Bryan, its members joined the Democratic Party. The Populist Party came to an end. McKinley won, and the gold standard remained in place until 1933.

The End of the Frontier

The 1890 U.S. census showed that with the arrival of farmers, ranchers, and miners to the West, there was no longer a "frontier," or a line beyond which population was so sparse that the land was considered to be uninhabited. In 1893, historian Frederick Jackson Turner used this fact to declare the American frontier "closed," meaning that there were no longer any wild and unsettled places in the West—only towns, cities, railroads, and lots of people. He wrote that the frontier had contributed to Americans' sense of optimism and rugged independence. It formed an American identity of ingenuity and self-reliance. Although Turner influenced many historians, his accounts left out the stories of women, African Americans, Latinos, Asians, and Native Americans.

HISTORICAL THINKING

1. **READING CHECK** Why did the Grange promote regulation of railroad and warehouse rates and operations?

2. **CATEGORIZE** What categories would you use to sort the interests of different groups of people you read about in this lesson?

3. **MAKE CONNECTIONS** Why did many farmers join the Democratic Party before the 1896 presidential election?

PLAN

Objective
Identify how farmers increased their economic and political power after the Civil War.

Critical Thinking Skills for Lesson 2.3
• Identify Main Ideas and Details
• Monitor Comprehension
• Categorize
• Make Connections
• Compare and Contrast
• Make Inferences

Essential Question for Chapter 18
How did westward migration affect the culture and way of life of Native American groups? As agriculture developed across the West, concerns about the welfare of the American farmer displaced concerns about Native Americans. Lesson 2.3 outlines ways in which farmers promoted their welfare by organizing and seeking political power.

Background for the Teacher
Before working for the Department of Agriculture, Oliver Kelley, chief founder of the Grange, had been an innovative Minnesota farmer who published articles about scientific agriculture. Kelley became convinced that a national organization would benefit farmers. Grange meetings educated farm families and allowed them to socialize. As farmers met and talked, they realized that they shared concerns about high mortgages and the cost of storing and transporting their crops. Their influence led to a series of state-level "Granger laws," which attempted to regulate storage and transportation rates and which led to several court cases that were decided in favor of the states. In the 1880s, some of those decisions were overturned, but in 1887 the Interstate Commerce Act was enacted to provide regulation on a national level.

Financial Literacy
To extend their knowledge and understanding about the concepts in this lesson, refer students to the Financial Literacy handbook.

INTRODUCE & ENGAGE

Draw an Analogy

The effects of the gold standard and free silver on prices may seem counterintuitive to students. Use a more tangible example to prepare them, for the lesson discussion. **ASK:** Which is more plentiful, diamonds or ordinary rocks? *(ordinary rocks)* What do you think would happen to the price of goods if everyone could use rocks to pay for things? *(Prices would go up because people could afford to pay whatever the seller demanded.)* What do you think would happen to prices if people could only use diamonds? *(Prices would go down because people wouldn't have as many diamonds.)* Tell students that in this lesson they will learn about the effects of the gold standard and free silver on prices and politics.

TEACH

Guided Discussion

1. **Identify Main Ideas and Details** The word *Grangerism* refers to the values and work of the Grange. What impact did Grangerism have on farmers and on some of the businesses that worked with farmers? *(Possible response: Through Grangerism, farmers became better organized and cooperated to achieve common goals that would improve their standard of living. Some of the businesses that worked with farmers eventually found themselves regulated by laws that members of the Grange had helped to enact.)*

2. **Compare and Contrast** How were the Grange and the Farmers' Alliance similar and different? *(Both were organizations of farmers, and both had some political influence. The Farmers' Alliance, however, took its political interests to the point of helping to form the Populist Party.)*

Make Inferences

ASK: What personal qualities do you think most Americans imagined when they thought about the people who settled the frontier? *(Answers will vary. Possible responses: an independent spirit; self-reliance; personal pride)* **ASK:** How do you think Frederick Jackson Turner's pronouncement that the frontier was closed might have affected the ways that Americans thought about themselves? *(Answers will vary. Possible response: Americans might have felt disappointed, less confident, and interested in establishing new goals that would promote personal pride.)*

Active Options

On Your Feet: Card Responses Direct half the class to write 10 True-False statements based on the lesson. Tell the other half to create response cards, writing "True" on one side and "False" on the other side. Collectively, the students from the first group should stand before the class and take turns reading their statements. Students from the second group hold up their cards, showing either "True" or "False." Both groups can provide details to support each response. Tell students to keep track of their correct responses.

NG Learning Framework: Create a Political Advertisement

ATTITUDE Curiosity

SKILL Communication

Tell students to review the information about the currency issue in the 1896 election. Ask them to research the arguments for retaining the gold standard and for free silver and then create and present a political advertisement for one of the viewpoints. The advertisement may be a poster, a television commercial, an editorial, or another format that you authorize, but encourage both viewpoints. After the presentation, invite questions and comments from the class.

DIFFERENTIATE

Striving Readers

Use Context Clues Model how to use textual definitions and context to understand the following Key Vocabulary words: *recession*, *creditor*, *cooperative*, *populist*, and *industrialist*. Then guide students in using the text to understand other Key Vocabulary terms, such as *Grange*, *Farmers' Alliance*, *gold standard*, and *free silver movement*. Students can use a chart like the one below to record their ideas.

Key Vocabulary	Context Clues

Inclusion

Describe Details in Artwork Pair students who are visually impaired with students who are not. Ask the latter to describe the Louis Kurz lithograph in detail for their partners, focusing especially on the details in the center scene. Then have pairs work together to answer the Critical Viewing question.

See the Chapter Planner for more strategies for differentiation.

HISTORICAL THINKING

ANSWERS

1. Farmers wanted restrictions on railroads to reduce their own expenses, which included shipping and storage of crops. The Grange promoted regulations that would reduce farmers' financial burdens.

2. Economic concerns drove the interests of farmers, creditors, and members of the Grange; populists and members of the Grange also had political interests.

3. The populists supported "free silver," which meant that anyone holding silver could have it minted into U.S. coins for a small fee. William Jennings Bryan, the Democratic nominee, was pro-silver, so the populists chose to support Bryan by joining the Democratic Party.

CRITICAL VIEWING Answers will vary. Possible response: The illustrator makes the farmer larger than the other occupations shown to indicate his importance—his occupation feeds the population of the country.

3.1 Native Americans of the Plains

Are you a peacemaker or a problem solver? Do you look for solutions that benefit people on both sides of an issue? In the 1860s, white settlers and the U.S. government stopped trying to solve problems and resorted to using force instead.

MAIN IDEA As more people moved onto the plains, Native Americans were forced to fight for their land and their culture.

CHANGING LIVES ON THE PLAINS

You may recall that in the 1830s, Andrew Jackson's Indian removal policies forced the Cherokee and other eastern tribes across the Mississippi River into Indian Territory on the southern plains. By the mid-1800s, Native Americans were once again being forced off their lands. Settlers laid claim to the land for farming and ranching, miners staked claims to areas with rich mineral resources, and railroad companies laid tracks across the entire country. In treaty after treaty with the U.S. government, land was allocated to tribes that were promised annual payments from the government, but one by one, those treaties were broken. Soon, Native Americans were clashing with settlers and the U.S. Army, attempting to defend their lands and their ways of life.

Although many settlers wanted the Native Americans completely removed from the Great Plains, President Grant authorized the U.S. government to set aside specific areas of land, called **reservations**. On the reservations, tribes could live apart from the settlers and, as some settlers believed, learn the "benefits" and values of white society. They were encouraged to farm the land rather than hunt, in exchange for a small government income. The U.S. Army stood by to stop any resistance and to keep the tribes within the reservation boundaries.

THE NATIVE AMERICAN WARS

As settlers claimed land on the Great Plains, they also systematically hunted and killed off the vast bison herds on which Native Americans depended. In some instances, frustrated Native Americans attacked settlers.

The U.S. Army responded by building more forts and sending more troops. These troops included several African-American regiments, who built forts, mapped large areas of wilderness, strung telegraph lines, and protected railroad crews and settlers from Native American attacks on the Great Plains and in the Southwest. The Native Americans gave them the name "Buffalo Soldiers," possibly because of the soldiers' perseverance. In this way, the soldiers may have resembled the buffalo to the Native Americans.

Orlando Scott Goff photographed this Buffalo Soldier at Ft. Custer, Montana, sometime around 1885. The soldier stands in front of a painted background, one of several Goff carried with him in his wagon.

Still, the violence continued. In November 1864, Chief Black Kettle, his band of Cheyenne, and a group of Arapaho encamped near Sand Creek in what is now Colorado. Black Kettle flew both a white flag of peace and an American flag over the camp to show that his people did not seek war. At daybreak on November 29, the men went hunting, leaving the women, children, and elderly behind. Colonel John Chivington ignored the flags and led a volunteer militia into the camp. His troops slaughtered 200 unarmed Native Americans and mutilated the bodies. In response to this atrocity, now known as the **Sand Creek Massacre**, the Cheyenne, Lakota, and Arapaho attacked defenseless settlers.

One of the most well-known battles in the series of Native American wars took place in the **Black Hills** in present-day South Dakota. The Black Hills were part of the Lakota reservation in the 1870s when a government survey found gold there. To the Lakota, the region was, and still is today, sacred.

In 1875, the United States ordered the Lakota off the land, but a year later, **Colonel George A. Custer** and the 7th Calvary found Lakota and Cheyenne hunters camping there, along the Little Bighorn River. Although approximately 2,500 Native American warriors were in an advantageous position and Custer had only 210 men, the colonel ordered an attack. The warriors killed Custer and nearly all of his men in the **Battle of the Little Bighorn**. The victory was short-lived, however. More U.S. troops arrived the next day and forced the Lakota from the Black Hills. Although Native Americans won some battles, they ultimately lost the war.

HISTORICAL THINKING

1. **READING CHECK** What factors led Native Americans of the Great Plains to go to war against the U.S. Army?

2. **COMPARE AND CONTRAST** The Sand Creek Massacre and the Battle of Little Bighorn had different outcomes. How were they similar?

3. **INTERPRET MAPS** What does the map illustrate about the land set aside for Native American reservations?

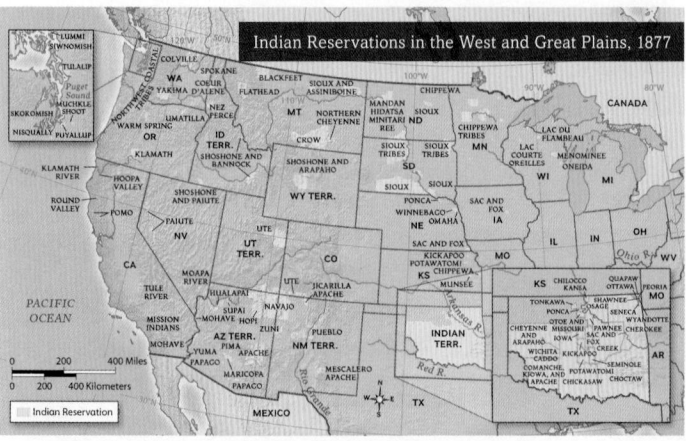

Indian Reservations in the West and Great Plains, 1877

Westward Movement **593**

PLAN

Objective
Analyze causes and effects of relocating Great Plains Native Americans onto reservations.

Critical Thinking Skills for Lesson 3.1
- Identify Main Ideas and Details
- Monitor Comprehension
- Analyze Environmental Concepts
- Interpret Maps
- Evaluate

Essential Question for Chapter 18
How did westward migration affect the culture and way of life of Native American groups? The flood of homesteaders and the expansion of railroads brought Native Americans' dominance of the Great Plains to an end. Lesson 3.1 describes the rise of the reservation system and the start of the Native American wars.

Background for the Teacher
In their first years of operation, the Buffalo Soldiers were under the command of white officers, and some white officers refused assignments to the African-American regiments. In addition, Buffalo Soldiers were not stationed east of the Mississippi due to concerns about racial tensions. The duties of the Buffalo Soldiers included building roads, guarding the U.S. mail, fighting fires, and apprehending poachers and thieves. The name Buffalo Soldiers may indeed have been a Native American reference to the soldiers' toughness, but it also could possibly have referred to the soldiers' curly hair or to the buffalo-skin coats that they might have worn in cold weather. The Buffalo Soldiers themselves were proud of the nickname, and one regiment included a buffalo in its coat of arms.

History Notebook
Encourage students to complete the American Gallery page for Chapter 18 in their History Notebooks as they read.

Use a K-W-L Chart

Provide each student with a K-W-L Chart. Have students use their prior knowledge to brainstorm ideas about conflicts between the federal government and Native Americans in the mid- to late 1800s. Ask students to write questions that they would like to have answered as they study the lesson. Allow time at the end of the lesson for students to complete their charts with what they have learned.

K What Do I Know?	W What Do I Want To Learn?	L What Did I Learn?

TEACH

Guided Discussion

1. **Analyze Environmental Concepts** How did the creation of the reservation system influence land use? *(Possible response: Native Americans were encouraged to switch from hunting to farming. Natural habitats for some animals were probably destroyed as the land was taken over for use in growing crops that were not native to the area.)*

2. **Evaluate** Was the federal government's way of dealing with the situations at Sand Creek and at the Little Bighorn River effective? Explain your answer. *(Answers will vary. Possible response: The attack at Sand Creek was ineffective because it caused the Cheyenne, Lakota, and Arapaho to attack defenseless settlers in response. The attack at the Little Bighorn River was also ineffective because most of the government troops were killed. In addition, the government's response to both situations made conciliation and compromise between the two sides nearly impossible.)*

More Information

General Custer's Defeat News of General Custer's defeat created shock and anger, for Custer was known to have performed bravely in the Civil War. Many Americans mourned the death of someone whom they considered a hero. President Grant, however, stated, "I regard Custer's Massacre as a sacrifice of troops, brought on by Custer himself, that was wholly unnecessary—wholly unnecessary." Indeed, the popular view of Custer has varied over the years. He has been viewed as an egotistical racist, and most people today have a dim view of him. However, some have argued that he was a capable leader who made a miscalculation—for in this battle, the Native Americans, who usually scattered when government troops attacked, fought back. **ASK:** Do you think people would have a different opinion of Custer today if he had won the Battle of the Little Bighorn? Why or why not? *(Answers will vary. Some students might suggest that he would be considered a hero for winning against long odds, while others might suggest that, win or lose, he was still an egotistical racist who did not follow a good plan.)*

Active Options

Active History: Solve a Puzzle Extend the lesson by using either the PDF or Whiteboard version of the activity. These activities take a deeper look at a topic from, or related to, the lesson. Explore the activities as a class, turn them into group assignments, or even assign them individually.

AMERICAN GALLERY
ONLINE
Buffalo Soldiers Invite students to explore the American Gallery. Have them select one of the images and do additional research to learn more about it. Ask questions that will inspire additional inquiry about the chosen gallery image, such as: Why does this image belong in this chapter? How does it aid your understanding of westward movement? What else would you like to know about the subject of the photograph?

English Language Learners

Read in Pairs Pair English language learners at the **Emerging** or **Expanding** level with proficient English speakers and have them read the lesson together. Instruct the proficient speakers to pause whenever they encounter a word or sentence construction that is confusing to their partners. Suggest that the proficient speakers point out context clues to help their partners understand the meanings of unfamiliar terms. Encourage English language learners to restate sentences in their own words.

Pre-AP

Report on a Presidential Plan When Ulysses S. Grant became president, he gave a high priority to Native American concerns. Instruct students to research and present an oral report about Grant's attempts to reform the Indian Bureau and his "Peace Policy" regarding Native Americans. Have students include insights about why Grant thought that he was doing the right thing and about why his plans did not result in the degree of change that he probably wanted.

See the Chapter Planner for more strategies for differentiation.

HISTORICAL THINKING

ANSWERS

1. Settlers, miners, and the railroads pushed Native Americans off their lands. The federal government had broken treaty after treaty and was forcing the tribes onto reservations, prompting their rebellion.

2. In both the Sand Creek Massacre and the Battle of Little Bighorn, members of the U.S. Army made an unprovoked attacked against Native Americans.

3. Possible response: Native American reservations comprised a small fraction of lands that Native Americans had once inhabited. Groups from disparate parts of the country were crowded together in new and unfamiliar lands (especially in so-called Indian Territory).

"The bison is an animal of myth and lore and the backbone of Native American cultures. It is truly an American species." —Joel Sartore

In the back of his truck, Joel Sartore keeps a safe distance from a herd of one of his favorite subjects: the American bison.

Conservation
of the American Bison

In his more than 25 years as a photographer, National Geographic Fellow and photographer Joel Sartore has encountered quite a few unusual situations. He's been chased by hungry animals, infected with flesh-eating parasites, and pinned underneath a truck by an American bison. Why does he do what he does? His mission is to introduce us to the amazing diversity of Earth's animal, bird, and insect life and to make us aware of their shrinking habitats.

A native of Lincoln, Nebraska, Sartore has been on location all over the world. The uniquely American animals he's photographed include bald eagles, gray wolves, grizzly bears, and the American bison. He is especially fond of the bison, which he argues is "the most iconic animal in the United States. The bison is more historically significant than the bald eagle because of human dependence on it."

Sartore is not only a champion of the American bison, but of the hundreds of other species facing habitat loss and threats of extinction. To save species, we have to save their habitats, which for bison means conserving the prairies. For Sartore, everything is connected. "When we save species," he says, "we save ourselves."

On one photo shoot, this bison pinned Sartore underneath a feed truck, so he took his photo, naturally. Most of the time, bison keep their distance from humans. But "they can go from 0 to 40 mph in three hops and zoom into your face like a cannonball." Sartore insists novices like most of us "must never cross a field with bison in it, because you could be killed. Stay in your truck, and use a powerful lens."

PHOTOGRAPHING BISON

Sartore admires bison for their self-sufficiency and their resilience. He remarks, "Bison are brutishly strong and hardier than cattle. They can handle any weather and they're very tough. Bison also herd together well, which helps herds do better. But even when they are confined to and raised on modern ranches for commercial consumption, bison remain wild animals." It is a wildness that he loves.

Sartore prefers photographing bison out in the open, not hidden in grasses, and "in the last 15 minutes of sunlight, so there is a nice glow, no harsh shadows." To capture how massive they are, Sartore photographs them from below. For Sartore, the goal is to be able to see the bison's eyes. And any day he gets to do that, he says, is a good day.

HISTORICAL THINKING

SUMMARIZE Why is Sartore drawn to the bison, and why does he believe it is an American symbol?

Objective

Learn how Joel Sartore uses photography to educate people about endangered animals.

Critical Thinking Skills for Lesson 3.2

- Identify Main Ideas and Details
- Monitor Comprehension
- Summarize
- Distinguish Fact and Opinion
- Make Inferences
- Make Connections

Essential Question for Chapter 18

How did westward migration affect the culture and way of life of Native American groups? As white Americans increasingly populated the Great Plains, they decimated the region's bison. Lesson 3.2 describes how National Geographic photographer Joel Sartore photographs bison to show why bison should be admired and protected.

NATIONAL GEOGRAPHIC PHOTOGRAPHER
Joel Sartore

In 2005, Joel Sartore started the Photo Ark with one goal: to photograph at least one of as many animal, bird, and insect species as he could. The photographs are meant to interest people in the animals shown and, as a result, encourage them to become involved in conservation efforts. Sartore's interest is not limited to large animals, such as bison. He notes: "A mouse is every bit as important as a tiger, and a minnow is as intricate as an elephant. All are of equal size and importance in the Photo Ark." Learn more about the Photo Ark on National Geographic's website.

History Notebook

Encourage students to complete the Explorer page for Chapter 18 in their History Notebooks as they read.

Activate Prior Knowledge

Write the term *endangered animals* on the board. Ask students to define the term. *(animal species that are in danger of becoming extinct)* Then invite volunteers to name examples of animals that they think are endangered. *(Possible responses: gorillas, tigers, whales)* Explain that many organizations and individuals work to protect endangered animals and that an important part of their work is to make people aware of the issue and to get them involved in helping. Tell students that in this lesson they will see how a National Geographic photographer has made it his mission to use his skill with a camera to do just that.

TEACH   STEM

Guided Discussion

1. **Distinguish Fact and Opinion** Is Joel Sartore's comment that the bison is "the most iconic animal in the United States" a fact or an opinion? How can you tell? Use the photographs in the article to help you explain your answer. *(It is an opinion. Even though Sartore gives a reason for his view, other people might choose a different animal and give a reason for their choice.)*

2. **Make Inferences** Sartore says that he tries to get photos in which he can see the bison's eyes. Why do you think that being able to see an animal's eyes might help promote the cause of animal conservation? *(Answers will vary. Possible response: Being able to look an animal in the eye, even in a photo, creates a connection between the viewer and the animal. Knowing that the animal belongs to an endangered species might help encourage the viewer to become involved in protecting that species.)*

Make Connections

Reread Joel Sartore's description of the bison's toughness and ability to adapt. Have students think about what they have learned regarding life on the Great Plains. Tell them that at one time, millions of bison lived on the Great Plains. **ASK:** Why did bison have to be tough and adaptable to thrive there? *(Possible response: Weather on the Great Plains could be very harsh, especially in winter, and water sometimes was scarce. Bison had to adapt to these conditions if the species was going to survive.)*

Active Options

On Your Feet: Think, Pair, Share Give students a few minutes to think about the question: How can photographs help bring about change? Then ask students to choose partners and talk about the question for five minutes, drawing upon what they learned by reading about Joel Sartore as well as their own ideas. Finally, allow individual students to share their thoughts with the class.

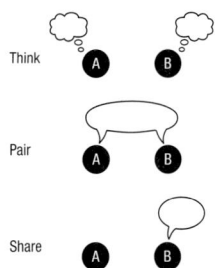

Think A B

Pair A B

Share A B

NG Learning Framework: Explore Wildlife Photography

ATTITUDE Curiosity

KNOWLEDGE Critical Species

Have students learn more about life as a wildlife photographer. Instruct them to write a brief essay in which they explain how one particular wildlife photographer prepares for a photo shoot and what seems to be his or her goal in this career. You may wish to have participants in this activity compare their essays, looking for common characteristics among the photographers.

Striving Readers

Make Lists Post this heading: Three Things I Know About Joel Sartore and His Work. After students read the lesson, ask them to copy the posted heading and add three sentences about the topic. Invite volunteers to share their sentences with the class.

Gifted & Talented

Illustrate a Quotation Direct students' attention to this comment from Joel Sartore: "When we save species, we save ourselves." Challenge students to interpret that comment artistically. For example, they may create a drawing or painting that incorporates the comment, they may use it as the caption for an original photograph that suggests a connection between people and endangered animals, or they may compose a song that includes the comment in its lyrics. Have students collaborate on creating a format for presenting their creations.

See the Chapter Planner for more strategies for differentiation.

ANSWER

Answers will vary. Possible response: Sartore admires the bison's wildness, resilience, and self-sufficiency. He may consider these characteristics to be true of the American spirit as well.

3.3 Native Americans of the Northwest and Southwest

It's bad enough when you're forced to live in one small place if you're used to traveling freely. It's devastating when you're forced to march hundreds of miles from your home to a place that lacks the resources you need to survive.

MAIN IDEA The U.S. government continued to push Native Americans off their ancestral lands and onto reservations throughout the West.

CONFLICT IN THE ROCKIES AND THE NORTHWEST

Native Americans in the Rocky Mountains and northwest regions of the United States faced the same pressures and problems as those on the Great Plains. For example, the Crow lived in the Yellowstone River Valley and northern plains of Montana and Wyoming. During U.S. Army campaigns against other tribes, the Crow actually fought alongside the United States because the Crow leader believed the U.S. government would treat them well after it won. His plan backfired; the Crow were treated just like other tribes and forced to move to a reservation.

In 1855, representatives from several tribes, including the Blackfoot, the Flathead, the Pend d'Oreille (pahn dor-AY), the Nez Perce, and the Cree, met with U.S. government officials. The tribes agreed to use common hunting grounds and stay within set boundaries on the northern plains of Montana. The Blackfoot believed their homeland was safe under this treaty. But by 1862, prospectors had found gold on their lands. Mining camps sprung up across the area, and, as with the Lakota, the U.S. government forced the Blackfoot to leave.

The Nez Perce, led by **Chief Joseph**, refused to move onto a reservation. In 1877, Chief Joseph led his band of about 700 people toward Canada to live free lives outside the reservation system. However, the U.S. Army apprehended them just before they crossed the border and sent them

far south to Indian Territory. There, many died from disease. The surviving members of the group were eventually sent to reservations in the Pacific Northwest. Today, many Nez Perce live in eastern Washington.

CONFLICT IN THE SOUTHWEST

Similar events took place in the Southwest. In 1864, the U.S. government forced thousands of Navajo to walk 300 grueling miles from their homelands in Arizona to the Bosque Redondo (BOH-skeh reh-DOHN-doh) reservation in New Mexico. Hundreds died along the route, which became known as the **Long Walk**. Bosque Redondo was a desolate place with a poor water supply and terrible farming conditions. Nearly one-third of those who lived through the walk starved or died from disease at Bosque Redondo. The Navajo suffered there for four years before the army realized how badly this relocation had failed. The survivors were allowed to return to their traditional lands, where tribe members still live today.

Cochise (koh-CHEES) was an Apache (uh-PA-chee) chief. At first, his people got along so well with settlers that tribe members helped build the Apache Pass stagecoach station in Arizona. The relationship soured in 1861 when Cochise was wrongly accused of kidnapping a rancher's son. He escaped arrest and fled into Arizona's Dragoon Mountains with about 200 of his people. They evaded capture for nearly a decade, and survived by raiding ranches and settlements from their mountain stronghold. Eventually, the government,

eager to end the hostilities, offered to make their homeland a huge reservation. Cochise agreed, and his people settled there.

Another Apache leader, **Geronimo**, was from New Mexico. The U.S. Army confined his people to a reservation in Arizona in the 1870s, but Geronimo refused to stay there. He left the reservation with a small group and raided settlements across the Southwest for two years. In September 1886, the army captured Geronimo, 16 men, 12 women, and 6 children and sent them and 300 others to prison. Released in 1887, Geronimo spent the rest of his life in present-day Oklahoma.

HISTORICAL THINKING

1. **READING CHECK** Why did Native Americans resist moving to reservations?

2. **CATEGORIZE** What categories can you use to describe the situations and actions of the Native Americans discussed in this lesson?

3. **DRAW CONCLUSIONS** What does Chief Joseph's surrender speech reveal about his character?

PLAN

Objective

Analyze the federal government's attempts to relocate western Native Americans.

Critical Thinking Skills for Lesson 3.3

- Identify Main Ideas and Details
- Monitor Comprehension
- Categorize
- Draw Conclusions
- Analyze Cause and Effect
- Compare and Contrast
- Analyze Language Use

Essential Question for Chapter 18

How did westward migration affect the culture and way of life of Native American groups? The federal government wanted Native American lands beyond the Great Plains. Lesson 3.3 outlines how the government's efforts led to conflict in parts of the Northwest and Southwest.

Background for the Teacher

Raiding was a way of life for the Apache. But Geronimo's motivations for raiding changed after Mexican soldiers attacked his camp in the 1850s, killing his mother, wife, and young children while he was away. Raiding then became an act of revenge, and Geronimo rose to power among his band of Apache by showing skill and courage in defeating the soldiers who had killed his family and by attacking Mexican and American settlements. Apache attacks escalated throughout the 1860s, resulting in the U.S. government sending in General George Crook and his troops to settle the Apache on reservations. Crook made clear that he would hunt down any Apache who continued to raid. Unlike some Apache leaders, Geronimo did not heed the warning.

Discuss Fairness

As a class, have a brief discussion about these two topics:

• the meaning of *fairness*

• what happens when people believe in a promise or agreement but are disappointed

Then explain that in this lesson students will learn how Native Americans' hopes for fair treatment by the federal government were not realized.

TEACH

Guided Discussion

1. **Analyze Cause and Effect** Why did the Crow join federal troops in fighting other Native Americans, and what was the result? *(The Crow leader thought that by doing so, the federal government would treat his people favorably. However, the Crow were resettled onto a reservation, just the same.)*

2. **Compare and Contrast** How were Cochise's and Geronimo's relationships to the federal government similar and how were they different? *(Both Apache leaders fought against federal forces by attacking white settlements. Cochise and his people were granted a reservation on their homeland; Geronimo did not stay on the reservation given to his people; he was captured and sent to prison with many of his people.)*

Analyze Language Use

Reread the excerpt from Chief Joseph's speech. Discuss with students how his language, though simple, conveys deep feeling. **ASK:** Which words express Chief Joseph's decision to surrender? *("I will fight no more forever.")* **ASK:** Who are the "chiefs" he mentions? *(They probably are the officers of the federal troops who have tracked down Chief Joseph and his people.)* **ASK:** Which words describe his own feelings? *(the words* tired *and* sad)

Active Options

On Your Feet: Three-Step Interview Arrange students in pairs and tell them to conduct Three-Step Interviews about the Native American leaders Chief Joseph, Cochise, and Geronimo. One student should interview the other using this question: How did [the leader's name] react to life on a reservation? Then students should reverse roles. Finally, each pair should share the results of the interview with the class.

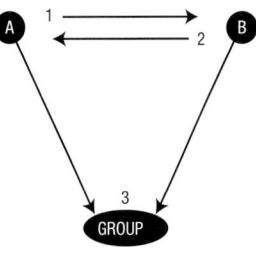

NG Learning Framework: Create a Podcast

SKILLS Collaboration, Communication

KNOWLEDGE Our Human Story

Invite students to work together to learn more about the Long Walk. Instruct them to focus on four areas of research: the relocation itself, the conditions at the Bosque Redondo, the decision to return the Navajo to their homeland, and the meaning of the incident to the Navajo today. Then tell students that they will use their research to create a podcast. Various students can read short essays about the areas studied. Ask students to choose a host and write an introduction and segues for him or her to use. When students have recorded the podcast, invite them to upload it to a class or school website or another approved host site.

DIFFERENTIATE

English Language Learners ELD

Use Sentence Strips Choose a paragraph from the lesson and make sentence strips out of it. Read the paragraph aloud as students at **All Proficiencies** follow along in their books. Tell students to close their books and then give them the set of sentence strips. Students should put the strips in order and read the paragraph aloud.

Gifted & Talented

Present a Dramatic Reading Ask students to reread the excerpt from Chief Joseph's speech and think about his tone. Does he sound angry, noble in defeat, or broken and disillusioned? Invite volunteers to present the excerpt as a dramatic reading, using different tones. Follow each reading with a brief discussion about how using a different tone colors the meaning of the printed words.

See the Chapter Planner for more strategies for differentiation.

HISTORICAL THINKING

ANSWERS

1. The reservations were rarely on or near traditional Native American lands, and Native Americans did not want to be forced to live within designated boundaries.

2. Possible response: Reactions could be categorized as immediate acceptance (the Blackfoot); refusal, leading to forced removal (the Nez Perce and Navajo); and violent rebellion (the Apache leaders Cochise and Geronimo).

3. Answers will vary. Possible response: Chief Joseph's surrender speech shows that he is compassionate. He is more concerned about the lives and well-being of his people than about victory at all costs. From the vow he makes at the end, he seems to be an honorable man.

3.4 Wounded Knee

Does anyone benefit when a group is pressured to assimilate to a different culture? In the late 1800s, the U.S. government forced Native American youths to adopt the language, culture, and norms of American society.

MAIN IDEA Once the U.S. Army defeated Native Americans in the West, the government increased its efforts to force Native Americans to assimilate to American culture.

MASSACRE AT WOUNDED KNEE

By the late 1880s, most Native American tribes had moved to reservations, but they still offered resistance. Some Native Americans, including the Lakota, practiced the **Ghost Dance**, a religion that included rituals believed to make white settlers disappear. This new faith spread quickly throughout reservations in the West, giving hope to disheartened tribes that the land would be restored to Native Americans.

Every six weeks, tribes held a five-day ceremony that included meditation, prayer, chanting, and a nightly Ghost Dance. Dancers wore white shirts decorated with symbols, and they believed these "ghost shirts" could stop bullets.

The government feared the ghost dancers were planning a rebellion. The U.S. Army arrested their leaders, including Lakota Chief **Sitting Bull**, who was killed as he was taken into custody. A ghost dancer himself, Sitting Bull had long resisted government policies. Famous for defeating the U.S. Army at the Battle of the Little Big Horn, his death was a blow to his people, but even that did not stop their dancing.

On December 29, 1890, the army confronted a large group of Lakota ghost dancers at Wounded Knee Creek on the Pine Ridge Reservation in South Dakota and demanded the Lakota hand over their weapons. During the tense interaction, an unknown person fired a shot. U.S. troops opened fire immediately, killing between 200 and 300 Lakota. The **Wounded Knee Massacre** did not end the Ghost Dance, but from then on, the ceremony was performed in secret. Wounded Knee marked the last major violent confrontation between Native Americans and the U.S. Army in the 19th century. As a result, many historians believe the capture of Geronimo and the Wounded Knee Massacre marked the end of the Native American wars.

MORE UNSUCCESSFUL POLICIES

When the wars ended, **Americanization** efforts began. The aim was to teach Native Americans the skills to assimilate into white, "civilized" society. In 1887, Congress passed the **Dawes General Allotment Act**, which divided reservations into parcels, or specific sections, of land for each Native American family. Land was allotted to the male as the head of the family, disregarding the status of females in tribal society. Recipients could not sell or lease their parcels for 25 years. The idea was that Native Americans would establish farms and adopt the "American" way of life. Those who did so could become U.S. citizens. The Dawes Act was intended to help Native Americans, but Congress refused to pass it until it was modified to allow the public sale of any unclaimed land. Few Native Americans participated.

The **Bureau of Indian Affairs**, established in the 1850s, was supposed to manage the reservations to benefit the tribes. However, the Bureau was corrupt, and the administration of the Dawes Act was mismanaged. White settlers quickly purchased the reservation land as "unclaimed," leaving Native Americans with the least desirable parcels. Additionally, Native Americans whose heritage did not include large-scale farming were accustomed to moving with the seasons and hunting. Their attempts to farm unsuitable land led to deteriorating community life on reservations and miserable poverty.

Another method of Americanization urged Native American children to reject their languages and customs. When this plan did not work, reformers decided that children couldn't assimilate if they were living with their own families. They sent Native American children to distant boarding schools where they were forced to speak English and forbidden to observe their own cultural practices.

The Carlisle Indian Industrial School

The children shown in these two photos were among those captured in 1886 with Geronimo in Arizona. From Arizona, they were taken by train to Florida, and two months later, sent to the Carlisle Indian Industrial School of Pennsylvania. They arrived there on November 4, 1886, when the top photo was taken.

Richard Henry Pratt, former commander of a Buffalo Soldier unit, opened the school in 1879. He wanted the Native American students to speak only English and learn jobs he felt would help them fit into society. He thought the students would assimilate into white culture if they no longer practiced their traditional ideas and customs. Boys learned construction and farming; girls learned to clean, cook, and sew. All students learned geography, English, and arithmetic. Discipline was strict and enforced by physical punishment.

The children were desperately homesick, but after returning home, they found themselves lost in their own cultures and unable to use the skills they had learned at school. The school was a failure. Just 12 percent of the students graduated. Many ran away, and others died of disease or despair. The Carlisle School closed in 1918, but Native American children continued to be sent forcibly to boarding schools until the passage of the Indian Child Welfare Act in 1978.

HISTORICAL THINKING

1. **READING CHECK** What was the aim of U.S. government policies toward Native Americans in the late 1800s?

2. **DRAW CONCLUSIONS** Why do you think the U.S. Army arrested Sitting Bull and other leaders of the Ghost Dance religion?

3. **COMPARE AND CONTRAST** What effects did living at the Carlisle Indian Industrial School have on Native American children? Compare the photographs and use text evidence.

PLAN

Objective
Learn about the Native American wars and efforts to "Americanize" Native Americans.

Critical Thinking Skills for Lesson 3.4
- Identify Main Ideas and Details
- Monitor Comprehension
- Draw Conclusions
- Compare and Contrast
- Make Generalizations
- Evaluate

Essential Question for Chapter 18
How did westward migration affect the culture and way of life of Native American groups? By the late 1880s, federal troops had relocated most western Native Americans. Lesson 3.4 discusses the end of this phase of the government's dealings with Native Americans and the start of efforts meant to assimilate them into white society.

Background for the Teacher
The Dawes Act did great damage to Native Americans. Those who had pushed for its adoption, however, claimed to have good intentions. Alice Fletcher, an anthropologist who had lived among the Omaha and who managed the allotment of some Native American lands, stated that under the Dawes Act, "The Indian may now become a free man; free from the thralldom of the tribe; freed from the domination of the reservation system; free to enter into the body of our citizens. This bill may therefore be considered as the Magna Carta of the Indians of our country." There were advocates for Native Americans who opposed the law, believing that it would make the lives of Native Americans worse, not better. They were outnumbered, but, in time, they were proved right.

Preview Using Visuals

Direct students' attention to the paired photographs of Native American children, and invite comments before students have read the caption. In particular, guide them to point out differences in the clothing and hairstyles from one photo to the other. Explain that in this lesson students will learn why many Native American children in the late 1800s went through the same kinds of changes as the children in the photographs did.

TEACH

Guided Discussion

1. **Identify Main Ideas and Details** Why is it said that the Native American wars ended with the Wounded Knee Massacre? *(The defeat of the Lakota at Wounded Knee was the last major clash between a Native American group and federal government forces.)*

2. **Make Generalizations** What was the purpose of sending Native American children to boarding schools? *(It was hoped that Native American children who were sent away from their parents would learn English and assimilate into white society more quickly than they might if they stayed with their families.)*

Evaluate

Remind students that the goal of Americanization was to "civilize" Native Americans and that *civilize* is a term that should be understood with a critical eye. Then share this definition of *civilized* as famously stated by Senator Henry Dawes, who sponsored the bill that became the Dawes Act: "to wear civilized clothes…cultivate the ground, live in houses, ride in Studebaker wagons, send children to school, drink whiskey [and] own property." **ASK:** Why do you think Dawes chose these standards? Do you think that his standards were reasonable? Explain. *(Answers will vary. Possible response: Dawes probably was thinking of standards that to him indicated success in white society. They were not reasonable standards when applied to cultures with different ways of living and different values.)*

Active Options

On Your Feet: Sequence Chain Have students work with partners or in small groups to complete a Sequence Chain that summarizes the main points of the lesson. You may wish to provide a "starting event" statement, such as: The federal government became concerned about ghost dancers. When students have finished their work, ask them to compare chains and come to a consensus about the key events stemming from federal policies toward Native Americans of the West in the late 1800s as presented in the lesson.

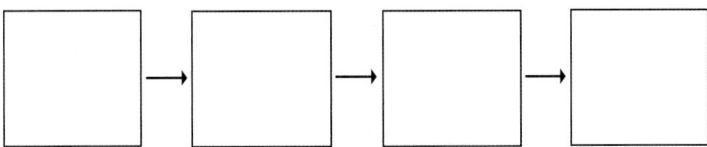

NG Learning Framework: Research Boarding Schools

ATTITUDE Curiosity

KNOWLEDGE Our Human Story

Encourage students to develop a question they would like to answer about life in Native American boarding schools of the late 1800s. Then have them research the topic, looking for personal stories about Native American children's lives at school and their experiences upon returning home. Prompt them to expand their research by asking additional, focused questions and remind them to document their sources. Invite students to share their findings in a reader's theater format.

Inclusion

Describe Details in Photos Pair students who are visually impaired with students who are not. Ask the latter to describe the details in the photos of Native American children so their partners can understand the photos. Consider incorporating the resulting discussion into the Introduce & Engage activity.

Pre-AP

Write an Editorial Encourage students to expand upon the lesson's coverage of the Bureau of Indian Affairs (BIA) by doing some research into the work of the BIA today and finding some present-day opinions of the BIA's work. Instruct students to write an editorial that either commends the BIA or recommends some change in its practices. You might create a display of "pro" and "con" editorials illustrated with photos that students find in support of their viewpoints.

See the Chapter Planner for more strategies for differentiation.

HISTORICAL THINKING

ANSWERS

1. The aim was to lead Native Americans to assimilate into an American (white) way of life.

2. The Ghost Dance was spreading rapidly, and the government feared that it would develop into a full-fledged rebellion. Arresting the leaders demoralized the dancers and kept the leaders from directing any actions that might threaten federal authorities.

3. Answers will vary. Possible response: The photos show a stark difference in clothing and grooming, but there is a definite similarity concerning the children: They all look unhappy. In addition, the schools did not really prepare them for life in white society but alienated them from their own cultures.

18 REVIEW

VOCABULARY

Use each of the following vocabulary words in a sentence that shows an understanding of the term's meaning.

1. cattle drive
   Cowboys moved herds of cattle to cow towns during cattle drives.

2. placer mining

3. stockyard

4. free silver movement

5. gold standard

6. Americanization

7. cooperative

8. reservation

9. Ghost Dance

READING STRATEGY
CATEGORIZE

If you haven't done so already, complete your graphic organizer by categorizing details about each group of people struggling for land in the American West. Then answer the question.

Rancher
• Hired cowboys to lead cattle drives.

Farmer

Miner

Native American

10. Why did conflicts over land take place in the West in the last decades of the 1800s?

MAIN IDEAS

Answer the following questions. Support your answers with evidence from the chapter.

11. Why did boomtowns develop so quickly in the West? **LESSON 1.1**

12. Who played roles in the growing cattle industry in the United States? **LESSON 1.2**

13. What factors led the exodusters to migrate west? **LESSON 2.1**

14. What was the school experience like for children on the prairie? **LESSON 2.2**

15. How did the Grange help bring about populism? **LESSON 2.3**

16. Why did the U.S. government establish the reservation system? **LESSON 3.1**

17. What did the Crow do in the hopes that it would benefit them? **LESSON 3.3**

18. Why did reformers remove Native American children from their families living on the reservations? **LESSON 3.4**

HISTORICAL THINKING

Answer the following questions. Support your answers with evidence from the chapter.

19. **IDENTIFY PROBLEMS AND SOLUTIONS** Describe a technology that offered both solutions and problems in the West and Great Plains. Consider modes of transportation, tools and methods for farming and mining, and weapons in your response.

20. **CATEGORIZE** List and categorize the different reasons for western expansion in this period.

21. **DRAW CONCLUSIONS** Do you think it was wise to homestead on the Great Plains? Why or why not?

22. **MAKE GENERALIZATIONS** Why did the Populist Party appeal to many farmers?

23. **DETERMINE CHRONOLOGY** Choose a Native American tribe mentioned in the text. Describe the sequence of events that led to the tribe's relocation to a reservation.

24. **DISTINGUISH FACT AND OPINION** The U.S. government believed "Americanizing" Native Americans was essential for their welfare. What factors distinguish this idea as a fact or as an opinion? Use evidence from the text to support your response.

INTERPRET MAPS

Look closely at the map showing cities next to rivers flowing through the Great Plains in 1890. Then answer the questions that follow.

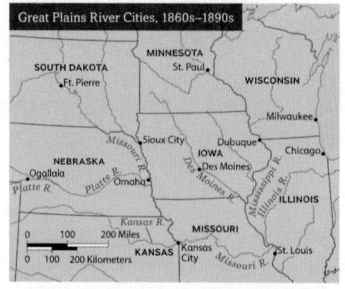

Great Plains River Cities, 1860s–1890s

25. From which cities and rivers could wheat farmers of South Dakota and Minnesota ship their grain south?

26. What is the most direct river route for shipping Kansas produce northward toward Chicago?

27. How many miles did passengers departing from St. Louis have to travel on a riverboat to get to Kansas City?

ANALYZE SOURCES

The Walker family homesteaded in Oklahoma in the late 1800s. As a married woman, Cudia Walker Ealum remembered her life in a sod house on the plains. Read the passage from an interview with Mrs. Ealum closely, and answer the question.

> We had a sod house [dugout], with dirt floor and dirt walls. . . . This was a hole about 12' x 16' and about 6' deep, dirt floors and walls. The top was made of heavy cottonwood logs laid across with grass, with dirt thrown on top. This made a nice snug house, but the bark on the logs was a good housing place for the centipedes. Often when lying awake we would see one crawl out and drop down on the bed, then how we would scramble to get out of bed.

28. What positive and negative memories does Cudia have about living in a sod house?

CONNECT TO YOUR LIFE

29. **ARGUMENT** Consider the inevitable clashes that occur among groups of people trying to claim the same land for themselves. Choose two groups of people who clashed over land in the American West, and ask yourself which group had the better claim to the land. Write a paragraph in which you describe the groups and the conflict, state your stance on it, and support your position with evidence from the text.

TIPS

• Before you write, list facts supporting both sides of the conflict. Decide which side you support and why.

• Note the evidence that best supports your position, and choose the two strongest reasons to include in your paragraph.

• State your argument clearly at the beginning of your paragraph.

• Have you addressed the topic? Revise or rewrite your paragraph, as needed.

VOCABULARY ANSWERS

1. Cowboys moved herds of cattle to cow towns during cattle drives.

2. Many miners searched for gold by using placer mining, panning for gold in riverbeds.

3. The stockyard held the cattle meant for slaughter.

4. Supporters of the free silver movement wanted to be able to have silver coined and put into circulation.

5. The gold standard prohibited the face value of printed money from exceeding the value of federal gold reserves.

6. Americanization was an attempt to incorporate Native Americans into white society.

7. Farmers organized into cooperatives so they could share in the costs of products and services that they needed.

8. The federal government set aside reservations where Native American groups would live apart from white settlers.

9. Participants in the Ghost Dance believed that their religious ceremonies would make the white settlers disappear.

READING STRATEGY ANSWER

Rancher
• Hired cowboys to lead cattle drives

Farmer
• Dug up the prairie to plant crops, primarily growing wheat

Miner
• Searched for mineral wealth across the West

Native American
• Forced to relocate to reservations and adopt new ways

10. Conflicts arose because Native Americans resisted being removed from their homelands by miners, farmers, and ranchers who wanted to use Native American land.

MAIN IDEAS ANSWERS

11. When prospectors found a rich lode of ore, miners and entrepreneurs rushed in to make their fortunes. Their mining camps grew rapidly, turning into boomtowns.

12. Those with money became investors in the cattle industry. Ranchers and cowboys did the daily work of taking care of the cattle and driving them to market. Those who worked at the stockyards and who transported cattle and meat by rail also played a part.

13. The exodusters moved west to escape discrimination and poverty in the South. They hoped to establish farms, towns, and careers for themselves in a new location.

14. On the prairie, children of mixed ages were educated together in a one-room schoolhouse—all by one teacher.

15. The Grange organized farmers for social and economic reasons. Eventually, it took political steps and influenced legislation that benefited the farmers. Other organizations, such as the Farmers' Alliance, also arose. Organized farmers came to use their collective strength to support populism—a political movement that claimed to embrace the concerns of the common man—and subsequently built the Populist Party.

16. The federal government hoped to confine Native Americans to discrete areas where they could be contained and controlled. Attempts to "Americanize" them could be made in these settings, but control and containment were the top priority.

17. The Crow fought alongside federal troops against other tribes in hopes that the government would reward them for their loyalty. These actions yielded little or no benefits.

18. Reformers believed that cutting off Native American children from their people, including their families, would promote the children's assimilation into mainstream American society. Thus, the children were taught English and forbidden to speak their own languages or practice their own customs.

HISTORICAL THINKING ANSWERS

19. Answers will vary. Possible responses: The railroad solved the problem of how to get cattle to market quickly but diminished the role of the cowboy. Guns helped hunters but decimated the buffalo population. Barbed wire fencing created boundaries between ranchers but started many disputes over land.

20. Reasons for expansion include the following: to support various mining endeavors; to claim land for settlement and farming; to use the open range for the growing beef industry; and to construct a growing railroad system.

21. Answers will vary. Some students may say homesteading was not wise because of the hardships, such as isolation, catastrophic weather, wildfires, or tough soil for agriculture. Others may say it was wise because it provided escape from the industrial cities, independence for farmers, or adventure.

22. Farmers were common people, not industrialists or rich businesspeople who could easily influence politicians to make laws favorable to business and industry. They thought the Populist Party would support and advance farmers' concerns and treat farmers with respect as the political force they believed themselves to be.

23. Answers will vary. Possible response: The Apache initially coexisted with white settlers, but the relationship became strained. Fleeing capture, the Apache leader, Cochise, retreated to the mountains with about 200 of his people, where they stayed for 10 years. Their successful raiding convinced federal authorities to offer to make the Apache homeland their reservation. Cochise agreed and the Apache settled there.

24. Possible response: The idea that Americanization was essential is based on an opinion, not a fact. Native Americans had their own cultures and their own ways of life that were different from those of white American society. They did not agree that embracing this different way of life was good for them or even possible for them to achieve. That is why many could not become farmers quickly enough to succeed and why children were not able to assimilate, even when they were pulled away from the influence of their families.

INTERPRET MAPS ANSWERS

25. South Dakota farmers could ship wheat south from Fort Pierre on the Missouri River. Minnesota farmers could ship wheat south from St. Paul on the Mississippi River.

26. Kansas produce could travel from Kansas City to St. Louis on the Missouri River and then travel toward Chicago along the Illinois River.

27. The passengers traveled a little more than 300 miles.

ANALYZE SOURCES ANSWER

28. Possible response: Cudia remembers the sod house as being small but "nice" and "snug." These are positive memories. However, the bark on the roof logs was a home for centipedes, which would drop onto family members as they tried to sleep. This sounds rather negative, since Cudia remembers scrambling out of bed to get away from the centipedes.

CONNECT TO YOUR LIFE ANSWER

29. Paragraphs will vary but should pinpoint two specific groups and show an understanding of their conflicts. Students should state their positions clearly and support them with evidence from the text.

Objective

- **Learn about the cultures of several Native American groups before and after westward expansion.**
- **Identify reasons that some Native American peoples formed leagues, nations, or confederacies.**
- **Analyze the Iroquois Confederacy's Great Law of Peace and its likely influence upon American government.**
- **Explore the portrayal of Native Americans in movies and on television.**

Critical Thinking Skills for "Native American Confederacies & Nations"

- Make Connections
- Draw Conclusions
- Identify Main Ideas and Details
- Interpret Maps
- Compare and Contrast
- Form and Support Opinions
- Synthesize
- Make Inferences
- Identify

Background for the Teacher

This feature explains how various Native American groups banded together to enhance their political and military strength. Use this narrative and its sidebar features to help students explore ways in which Native Americans not only invalidated the claim that they were an "uncivilized" people but also made a rich contribution to the government of the United States.

NATIONAL GEOGRAPHIC PHOTOGRAPHER
Dan Westergren

The opening photograph is the work of Dan Westergren, who has served as the photo editor of *National Geographic Traveler* magazine as well as shooting on his own and teaching workshops for other photographers. His photograph in this feature reflects the American West, but his craft has taken Westergren to all seven continents.

History Notebook

Encourage students to complete the pages for Native American Confederacies & Nations in their History Notebooks as they read.

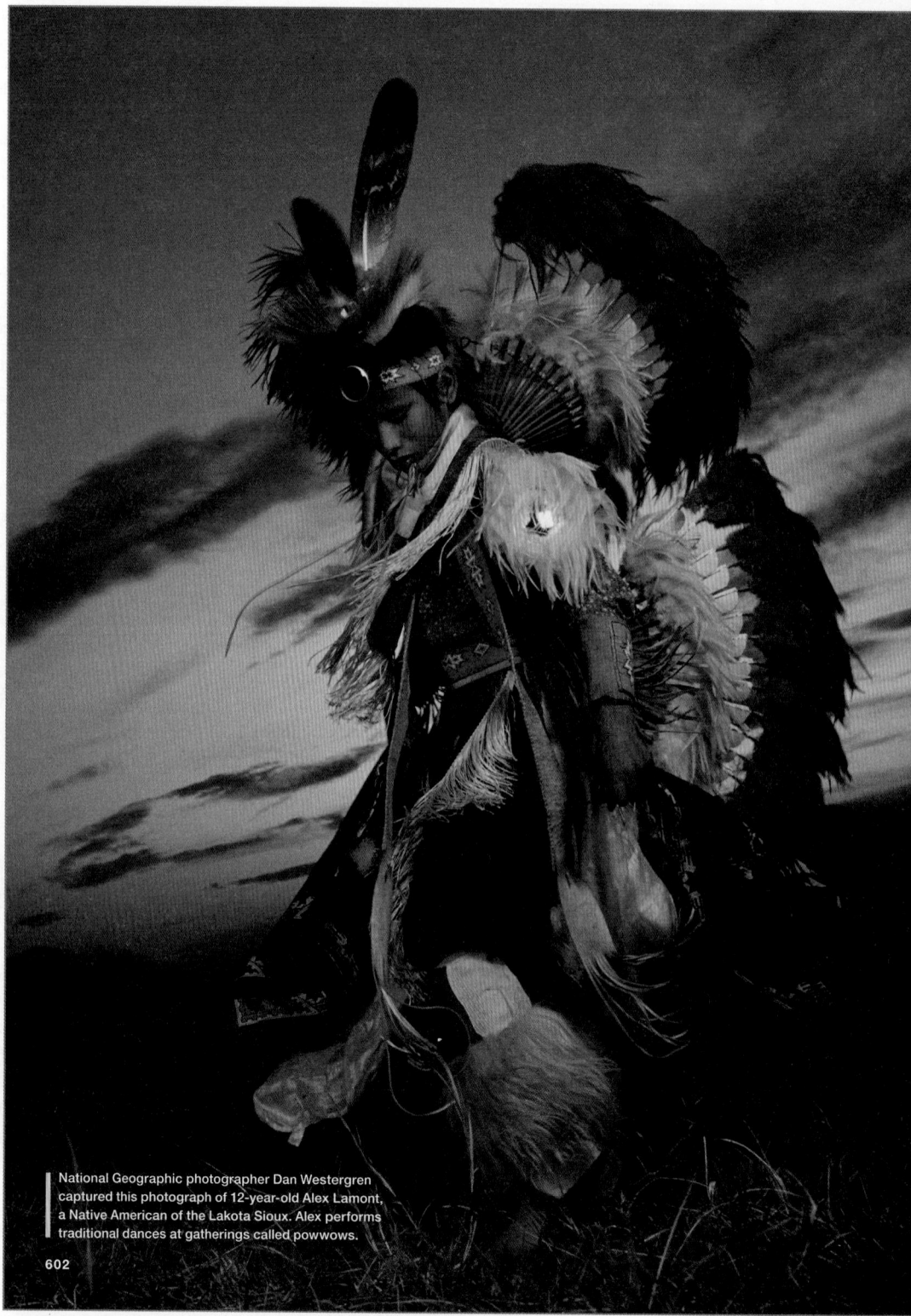

National Geographic photographer Dan Westergren captured this photograph of 12-year-old Alex Lamont, a Native American of the Lakota Sioux. Alex performs traditional dances at gatherings called powwows.

602

NATIVE AMERICAN
CONFEDERACIES
& NATIONS

BY DR. TERENCE CLARK

Director, Shíshálh Archaeological Research Project, University of Saskatchewan, Canada

You've read about how the Founding Fathers worked tirelessly to unite the colonies and create a form of government different from the hierarchies in Europe. But long before the United States was formed, many Native American tribes had determined they were stronger if they banded together. They already had democratic and inclusive governments in place. Some had even established voting rights for all, as well as basic law-making and amendment processes.

We don't know exactly how much the framers of the U.S. Constitution borrowed ideas from early Native American nations and confederacies. We do know that Thomas Jefferson, James Madison, James Monroe, and Benjamin Franklin were familiar with the governmental structure of Native American nations such as the League of the Iroquois. The framers even visited this group to learn from its strength and organization and observe its practices. Franklin in particular was so impressed by the organization of Native American governments, he felt it should be studied—and possibly imitated—by the colonies. And it was.

The Native American confederacy has persevered throughout history, through conflict, land loss, and relocation. Today, there are more than 550 of these federally recognized nations in the United States, including over 200 in Alaska alone. The nations are self-governing, which ensures they can retain and preserve their distinct cultural identities. As you read about two of the largest and most influential North American confederacies, the confederacies of the West and the Iroquois Confederacy, consider how these great nations formed and their impact on Americans and the U.S. government.

603

Preview Using Visuals

Direct students' attention to the photograph that opens this feature. Have them read the caption and describe what strikes them about Alex Lamont, such as his costume, his activity, and the scene in which he appears. Invite students to suggest several questions they would like to ask the young dancer. Write their questions on the board. You may wish to return to this activity after students have read the feature to see whether they can answer any of the questions.

Discuss a Key Term

Point out the title of this feature, and then ask students to place the word *confederacy* at the center of a Word Map. Instruct students to use a dictionary, if necessary, to define the word. After students finish reading this feature, tell them to revisit their Word Maps to add examples and descriptions.

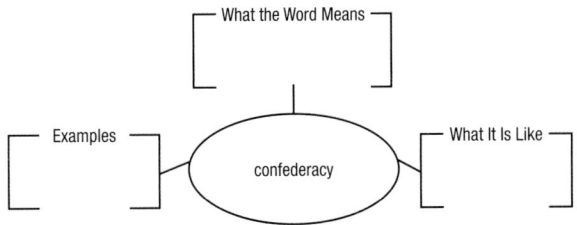

Why Join a Group?

Ask students to spend two minutes making a list of groups that they are members of or that they might like to join sometime in the future. Invite volunteers to share what they have written. Ask them what advantages they see in belonging to a group. *(Possible responses: friendship, unity, common interest or activity, sense of purpose or belonging, greater strength or effectiveness)* Explain that in this feature students will learn about Native American tribes that joined together in confederacies and the advantages they found in doing so.

Tribal Names

The names by which we know many Native American groups today are actually the ones given to them by their enemies. For example, *Sioux* comes from an Ojibwa word meaning "little snakes"; however, the Sioux called themselves *Dakota, Lakota*, or *Nakota* (depending on the dialect), meaning "friends" or "allies." Similarly, *Iroquois* comes from the Algonquian word for "real adders," but, as students will learn in this feature, the Iroquois called themselves *Haudenosaunee*, meaning "people of the long house." The name of the Blackfoot people is a rare case in which the English name is simply a translation of the native name, *Siksika*.

The Sioux Nation

The Sioux were expert hunters. By the time they first encountered Europeans, they were a huge nation, consisting of seven tribes. As Europeans filtered beyond the Mississippi, the Sioux coexisted with the French during the 17th century and with the British in the 18th century. However, the expansion of white settlers into the West in the 19th century brought disease, overhunting of bison, and escalating conflicts over land and ways of life. In the end, the great Sioux Confederacy was defeated.

Wind Cave National Park

Theodore Roosevelt established Wind Cave National Park in 1903, but native peoples' familiarity with the cave and the lands around it goes back thousands of years. In fact, tipi rings appear near the park's elevator building, and the Lakota had many stories describing the "hole that breathes cool air" near the Buffalo Gap. Now we know that the cave "breathes" because of differences in atmospheric pressure between the air outside the cave and the air within its vast reaches. Scientists have used the differences in pressure to calculate the size of the cave, and they have concluded that only about ten percent of this enormous cave has been explored.

LIFE BEFORE CONFEDERACIES

As you have read, the Great Plains are the geographic heart of North America, stretching from the eastern slopes of the Rocky Mountains to the shores of the Mississippi River, from Texas well into Canada. Although they vary geographically, the Great Plains are primarily made up of open grasslands, wooded river valleys, and upland areas. This "sea of grass" has served as a habitat for huge numbers of bison, deer, pronghorn antelope, and other animals—resources relied upon by many Native American groups.

The Native American groups of the northern and western Great Plains, including the Blackfoot, Cheyenne, and Comanche, relied upon hunting large game, fishing, and gathering plants. Groups of the eastern Great Plains, such as the Hidatsa, Mandan, and Arikara, settled in villages and grew maize, beans, and squash, much like their Eastern Woodland neighbors.

Until the 1800s, the Native Americans of the Great Plains lived in small groups and made several short migrations each year. Camps were small but well connected. Trade and social gatherings brought people together into bigger groups to renew social ties and find marriage partners.

CONFEDERACIES OF THE WEST

As American settlers began moving into the Great Plains in the early and mid-1800s, independent Native American groups felt the need to create alliances to protect themselves from the settlers and from potentially hostile Native American neighbors. As you know, westward expansion drew miners, trappers, and traders to the region in search of their own fortunes, and the expansion of the railroad changed the trickle of newcomers to a torrent. As a result, Native American alliances grew and the great confederacies of the West were born.

Two of the most powerful western confederacies were the Sioux (SOO) Confederacy and the Blackfoot Confederacy. These were political and military powerhouses whose territories included large areas of the region. With neighboring communities competing for land and resources and threatening the culture and way of life of local peoples, confederacies gave Native Americans of the Great Plains strength and unity.

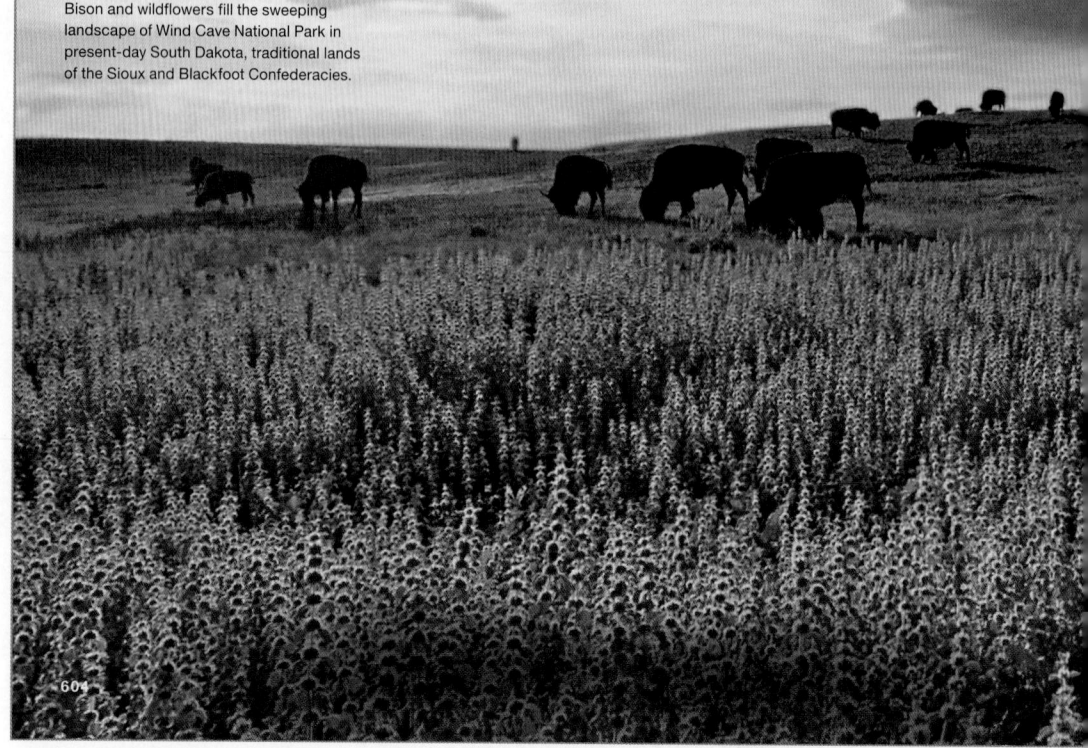

Bison and wildflowers fill the sweeping landscape of Wind Cave National Park in present-day South Dakota, traditional lands of the Sioux and Blackfoot Confederacies.

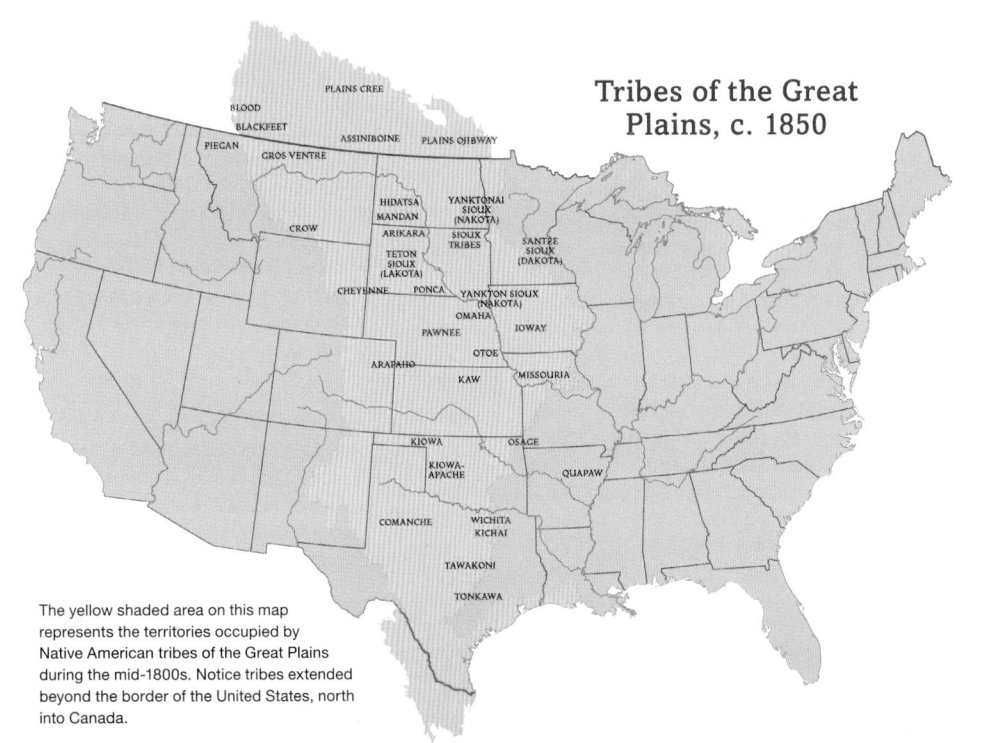

Tribes of the Great Plains, c. 1850

The yellow shaded area on this map represents the territories occupied by Native American tribes of the Great Plains during the mid-1800s. Notice tribes extended beyond the border of the United States, north into Canada.

Guided Discussion

1. **Identify Main Ideas and Details** How did Native Americans' knowledge of the Great Plains and the many plants and animals living there affect their lifestyle? *(Possible responses: Native Americans utilized their knowledge to live off the bounty of the land; some tribes were seminomadic hunters, fishers, and gatherers, while others lived in permanent villages where they raised crops, including maize, beans, and squash.)*

2. **Interpret Maps** Have students form small groups and list details of this map that they think are important. **ASK:** According to the map, where were the Sioux concentrated in the mid-1800s? *(Possible response: The Sioux lived in the northern Great Plains—North and South Dakota, Minnesota, Iowa, and Nebraska.)* **ASK:** What might the fact that the dark yellow area extends beyond the borders of the United States suggest about the Great Plains? *(Possible response: The conditions that made the Great Plains of the United States a good place to live extended into part of southern Canada as well.)*

Crazy Horse Memorial

The Crazy Horse Memorial Foundation is the driving force behind this colossal sculpture to celebrate the traditions and heritage of Native Americans. It honors Crazy Horse, who fought for his people's right to stay on their lands and preserve their way of life. Sculptor Korczak Ziolkowski designed the memorial at the request of Oglala Lakota chief Henry Standing Bear. The design features the Sioux leader atop his horse, carved into a granite mountain in the Black Hills. To accomplish Ziolkowski's design on this memorial which is still under construction, workers use large blasts to remove great chunks of granite, followed by smaller blasts to shape the working area. Finally, they remove rock by hand as they get closer to shaping the surface of the statue. Although Ziolkowski died in 1982, his work continues through several of his children and grandchildren, who carry on the mission.

Native Americans and Hollywood

While most Native Americans in 1950s and 1960s Hollywood films were portrayed by white actors, a few Native American actors did find careers in movies or on TV. For example, Jay Silverheels (the stage name of Harold J. Smith, a Mohawk from Canada) had a long career in Hollywood. Perhaps best known for playing Tonto on the long-running television series, *The Lone Ranger*, Silverheels, like most Native American actors, found work mainly in westerns in roles that often perpetuated stereotypes. Present-day Native Americans have more opportunities to write and produce films. **ASK:** How do you think increased opportunities for Native American writers and producers influences the depiction of Native Americans in film and on television? *(Possible response: Native American writers and producers are probably more interested in telling stories about Native Americans' lives, creating bigger, more interesting roles about well-drawn characters instead of stereotypical "savage" roles with few lines.)*

THE SIOUX AND THE BLACKFOOT

The Great Sioux Nation is a confederacy of groups that speak different dialects, or forms, of the Siouan language: Dakota, Nakota, and Lakota. You have probably seen the Sioux—especially the Lakota Sioux—in famous photographs, paintings, and movies as the proud and famous warriors on horseback from the northern Great Plains. Arguably the most iconic of all Native American groups, Lakota Sioux leaders include Crazy Horse, Sitting Bull, and Red Cloud. Lakota history contains some of the most recognizable Native American conflicts of all time, including the Battle of the Little Bighorn and the Wounded Knee Massacre. The people of the Great Sioux Nation have faced the challenges of relocation to reservations, assimilation, and poverty, and yet the nation has endured and remains strong in North and South Dakota to this day.

The Blackfoot Confederacy was once one of the largest Native American groups in the northern Great Plains. Its territory ran from the North Saskatchewan River in present-day Canada to the Yellowstone River, and from central Saskatchewan to the Rocky Mountains. By the 1750s, the Blackfoot were hunting on horses they got from other tribes with guns they got from British traders. Hunting, raiding, and trading helped the nation gain power and establish a thriving economy. However, a smallpox epidemic in 1837 significantly weakened the population.

In 1855, the U.S. government began the process of removing the confederacy from its native lands and dispersing groups onto reservations in the United States and Canada. Although the Blackfoot Confederacy was broken apart during the removal process, numerous Native American groups that were once part of the nation survived, and continue to thrive in the Great Plains and Canada.

This enormous mountain sculpture in the Black Hills—the Crazy Horse Memorial—has been in progress since 1948. When complete, this tribute to the Lakota Chief Crazy Horse will dwarf Mount Rushmore.

"INDIANS" IN HOLLYWOOD

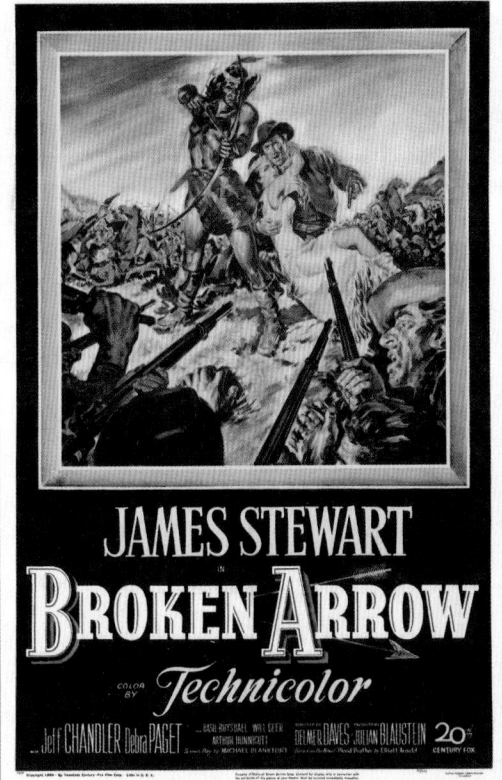

In the 1950s and 1960s, Westerns—fictional television series about the American West in the late 1800s—were on nearly every channel. Movie screens were filled with the same stories of scheming outlaws pursued by handsome lawmen, and noble cowboys protecting cattle from thieves and "civilized" white people from "uncivilized" Indians.

Some Native Americans played a legitimate role in Westerns that required skilled horse riders, but most Westerns represented Native American people as less than human. They were given few spoken lines, and were often shown being shot down or killed. Similarly, women in Westerns were often shown in need of rescue. Yet in reality, many women of the West were fiercely independent, taking on non-traditional roles and responsibilities. And contrary to their portrayal in movies, Native American women had great influence over their tribes and were sometimes warriors.

The 1950 Technicolor Western *Broken Arrow* featured several non-Native American actors playing the roles of Native American chiefs and being paid far more than Native-American actors.

DAVID BALD EAGLE

David Bald Eagle lived an extraordinary life. By the time of his 2016 death at the age of 97, he had been a Lakota tribal chief, a war hero, a champion dancer, a rodeo cowboy, a touring musician, an actor, a professional baseball player, and a race car driver. There was nothing he hadn't tried.

But most importantly, Bald Eagle was an advocate for Native people, a tribal leader, and an elder of the United Native Nations. His grandfathers entertained him with war stories to give him something to remember them by, making him a key connection between the past and present, the traditional and modern cultures.

Active Options

On Your Feet: Talking Stick Debate Prompt students to imagine themselves living in the Great Plains in the mid-1800s. Divide them into two groups on opposite sides of the room: members of the Great Sioux Confederacy on one side and settlers who have moved west to live and work there on the other. Instruct students to list as many facts or reasons as they can for their group's claim to the land and to their way of life. When they have finished, line them up facing each other. Provide a talking stick. Explain that only the person with the stick can talk and that after one side speaks, the speaker must give the stick to someone on the other side. Speakers should use their group's list but should speak directly to the people on the other side, giving the rationale for a claim to the land and a certain way of life. When students finish, have them evaluate the strengths of the claims and arguments.

NG Learning Framework: Write a Blog Post

| ATTITUDES | Curiosity, Empowerment |
| KNOWLEDGE | Our Human Story |

Tell students to research and write a blog post about a Native American who is prominent in the arts. Students may want to learn more about David Bald Eagle's musical talents or the fact that he was accomplished in both native and ballroom dance. Alternatively, students may research other Native Americans, such as the writer, performer, and filmmaker Sherman Alexie or the ballet dancer Maria Tallchief. Students may read their completed posts to each other or share them on an approved website.

Guided Discussion

1. **Compare and Contrast** What are some of the similarities between the government of the Iroquois Confederacy and the government of the United States? *(Possible responses: There are representatives from each tribe/state; they address issues of concern using discussion and debate; the leader is accountable to the people; the people may remove a leader if necessary.)*

2. **Form and Support Opinions** Do you think the U.S. Constitution was modeled on the Iroquois Great Law of Peace? State and support your opinion. *(Possible responses: Yes; the two have many similarities, and some of the Founders admired the Iroquois government. No; many governments have similar characteristics, and some aspects of the Iroquois system, such as equality for women, were not part of the early federal government.)*

Synthesize

Based on what you know about the treatment of Native Americans in the 1800s, do John Marshall's words reflect historical reality? Explain. *(Possible response: Marshall's views about the nationhood and rights of Native Americans seem admirable. Two years earlier, however, President Jackson had signed the Indian Removal Act, ignoring Marshall and the Supreme Court's decision regarding Indian nations and forcing many Native Americans from their homelands. Ultimately, few Native Americans retained "their original natural rights, as the undisputed possessors of the soil.")*

NATIONAL GEOGRAPHIC PHOTOGRAPHER
William Albert Allard

William Albert Allard was born in Minnesota, the son of an immigrant parent. His long professional relationship with National Geographic began with an internship in 1964. Allard specializes in often-overlooked people— from the Amish to blues singers to Native Americans— and photographs them exclusively in color, believing that color and composition are inseparable. Says Allard, "I think the best pictures are often on the edges of any situation," an idea reflected in the photo of the dancers.

WRITE ABOUT HISTORY
Write About Uniting for Change

This feature describes how some Native American tribes came together for greater strength and unity. To help students make connections to their own lives, have them write a short nonfiction narrative about a group that banded together for a specific purpose, such as to change a law, fight a disease, or raise funds. Instruct students to draw on their own experience or find an example from current events. (In case of the latter, remind them to document their sources.) Invite students to read their narratives to the class or to post them in a blog format on an approved website.

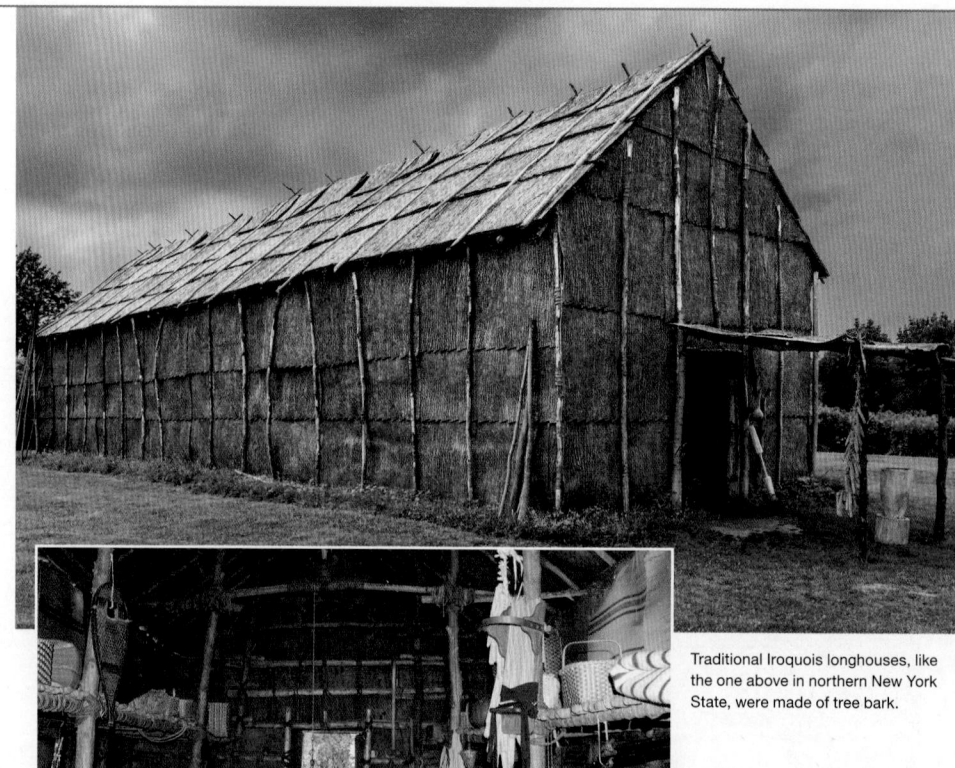

Traditional Iroquois longhouses, like the one above in northern New York State, were made of tree bark.

The interior of this reconstructed 17th-century Seneca longhouse (left) represents how the people of the Iroquois Confederacy would have sheltered and lived.

THE IROQUOIS CONFEDERACY

Another example of a strong Native American nation is the Iroquois Confederacy, which you may remember reading about earlier in this book. This nation formed between 1570 and 1600. At first, this union of five tribes lived in present-day upstate New York and included the Mohawk, Oneida, Onondaga, Seneca, and Cayuga. The tribes were at one time enemies, but a Mohawk chief and an Onondaga speechmaker persuaded them they would be stronger if they united into a single confederacy, or nation. The tribes found security in this bond, forming what is known as the Great Law of Peace, which continues through today and is arguably the longest-lasting treaty in North America. In 1722, a sixth tribe, the Tuscarora, joined the League, and its territory expanded.

You might recall that together, the tribes in the Iroquois Confederacy became known as Haudenosaunee (hoe-dee-no-SHOW-nee)— People of the Longhouse—because of the types of dwellings they lived in. Their government revolved around a Council of Fifty, made up of representatives from the five tribes. This Council gathered to address issues and solve problems involving multiple tribes. All laws had to be passed unanimously, meaning a single person on the Council could block the law. That meant every man or woman—and there were women on the Council—had the same amount of power, regardless of how many members of his or her tribe sat on the Council. How does the structure of the Council of Fifty compare to the structure of today's U.S. government?

608

COMMON GROUND

The Iroquois Confederacy lasted through the 1780s, and at its height, reached from present-day Maine to North Carolina and from the Atlantic Ocean to the Mississippi River. It is possible many of our current U.S. government practices were influenced by those of the League. They include the use of discussion and debate before passing laws, removing leaders who were deemed ineffective, and making leaders accountable to the people. The Iroquois League also distinguished between its military and its civilians, as the United States does today.

It's not difficult to form connections between the tribes that united to form Native American confederacies and the colonies that came together to form the United States. Even the states that came together to form the Union and the Confederacy can be compared in a significant way to the formation of Native American nations: they saw strength in unity. Clearly the influence of Native American nations is evident in the government and social structure of the present-day United States.

> *Indian Nations have always been considered as distinct, independent political communities, retaining their original natural rights, as the undisputed possessors of the soil. The very term "nation" so generally applied to them, means "a people distinct from others."*
>
> —Chief Justice John Marshall, 1832

National Geographic photographer William Albert Allard captured this quiet moment as dancers check their makeup at a powwow on the Rocky Boy Indian Reservation in Montana.

Confederacies and Nations 609

Inclusion

Clarify Text Have visually impaired students work with sighted partners and listen to an audio recording of the text. Instruct the visually impaired students to indicate words or passages they do not understand. Their partners can clarify meanings by repeating passages, emphasizing context clues, and paraphrasing.

Gifted & Talented

Create a Multimedia Presentation Explain that many Native American groups did not have written language; instead, they relied on oral traditions to keep their history and culture alive. Tell students to research how the Great Law of Peace, with all of its precise rules and procedures, survived intact over generations. Direct students to prepare and give a multimedia presentation on the topic, including information about the wampum belt of the Iroquois Great Law of Peace.

See the Chapter Planner for more strategies for differentiation.

HISTORICAL THINKING

Ask and have students answer the following questions.

1. **READING CHECK** What three confederacies were formed by Native American peoples, and what did they achieve?

2. **MAKE INFERENCES** What can you infer about the impact of past portrayals of Native Americans on television and in movies?

3. **IDENTIFY** What is one difference in the way the Iroquois Great Law of Peace and the U.S. Constitution make laws?

ANSWERS

1. Tribes banded together to form the Iroquois, Blackfoot, and Sioux confederacies in order to have greater strength and unity as settlers encroached upon their territory.

2. Possible response: Many film and television portrayals of Native Americans helped develop and perpetuate the stereotype of savage, dangerous, and uncivilized Indians.

3. The Iroquois required a unanimous decision from their Council, but no branch of the federal government requires a unanimous decision in order to pass a law.

UNIT 7 RESOURCES

UNIT INTRODUCTION

UNIT TIME LINE

UNIT WRAP-UP

NATIONAL GEOGRAPHIC | CONNECTION

National Geographic Magazine Adapted Articles
- "This Land is Your Land"
- "The Native American Photography of Edward Sheriff Curtis" ONLINE

Unit 7 Inquiry: Innovate a New Solution

NG Learning Framework Activities
- Research American Species
- Write a Journal Entry

Unit 7 Formal Assessment

CHAPTER 19 RESOURCES

Available at NGLSync.Cengage.com

TEACHER RESOURCES & ASSESSMENT

Reading and Note-Taking

Vocabulary Practice

Document-Based Question Template

Social Studies Skills Lessons
- Reading: Identify Main Ideas and Details
- Writing: Write an Informative Text

Formal Assessment
- Chapter 19 Pretest
- Chapter 19 Tests A & B
- Section Quizzes

Chapter 19 Answer Key

ExamView®
One-time Download

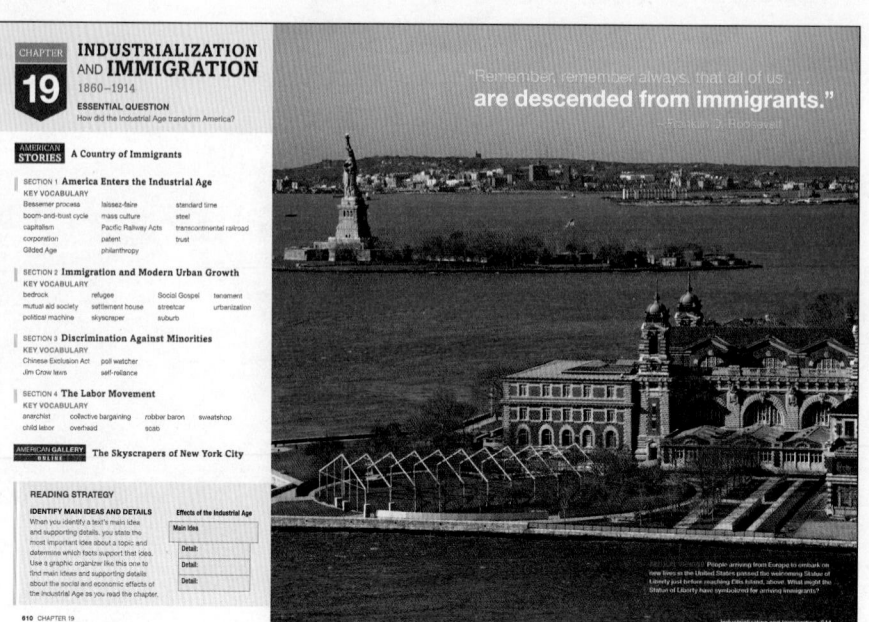

STUDENT DIGITAL RESOURCES

- **eEdition** (English)
- **eEdition** (Spanish)
- **Handbooks**

- **Online Atlas**
- **American Gallery Online**
- **History Notebook**

- **American Voices (Biographies)**
- **Active History**
- **Projects for Inquiry-Based Learning**

Chapter 19 Spanish Resources are available at NGLSync.Cengage.com.

CHAPTER 19 PLANNER

AMERICAN STORIES | A Country of Immigrants

▶ Angel Island

• Primary Sources

• On Your Feet: Numbered Heads

NG Learning Framework:
Create an Immigration Mural

SECTION 1 RESOURCES

AMERICA ENTERS THE INDUSTRIAL AGE

LESSON 1.1
Industrial Revolution Gathers Steam

▶ River as Highway

• On Your Feet: Inside-Outside Circle

NG Learning Framework:
Investigate Consequences of a Railroad System

American Voices Biography
Cornelius Vanderbilt ONLINE

LESSON 1.2
AMERICAN PLACES
The Scenic Railways of the United States

• On Your Feet: I See, I Read, And So

NG Learning Framework:
Research Narrow-Gauge Track

LESSON 1.3
The Age of Invention

• On Your Feet: Rotating Discussion

NG Learning Framework:
Create a Virtual Museum Exhibit

LESSON 1.4
Growth of Big Business

• On Your Feet: Question and Answer

NG Learning Framework:
Research Philanthropy

LESSON 1.5
Mass Culture During the Gilded Age

• On Your Feet: Hold a Panel Discussion

NG Learning Framework:
Identify Exposition Technologies

SECTION 2 RESOURCES

IMMIGRATION AND MODERN URBAN GROWTH

LESSON 2.1
The New Immigrants

• Active History: Map Countries of Origin

NG Learning Framework:
Explore Asian-American Contributions

LESSON 2.2
CURATING HISTORY
Tenement Museum New York City

• On Your Feet: Sort the Artifacts

LESSON 2.3
Cities Grow Rapidly

• On Your Feet: Fishbowl

NG Learning Framework:
Profile the Women of Hull House

LESSON 2.4
GEOLOGY IN HISTORY
How Geology Defines Your Skyline

• On Your Feet: Card Responses

AMERICAN GALLERY ONLINE The Skyscrapers of New York City

LESSON 2.5
DOCUMENT-BASED QUESTION
Urban Poverty

• On Your Feet: Use a Jigsaw Strategy

SECTION 3 RESOURCES

DISCRIMINATION AGAINST MINORITIES

LESSON 3.1
Racism and Segregation

• On Your Feet: Turn and Talk on Topic

NG Learning Framework:
Write a News Article

LESSON 3.2
"Separate but Equal"

• On Your Feet: Three-Step Interview

NG Learning Framework:
Create a Biographical Infographic

LESSON 3.3
Fighting Against Segregation

• On Your Feet: Chart Relay

NG Learning Framework:
Create a Social Media Page

American Voices Biographies
Booker T. Washington ONLINE
W.E.B. DuBois

SECTION 4 RESOURCES

THE LABOR MOVEMENT

LESSON 4.1
The Lives of Workers

• On Your Feet: Travel Around the World

NG Learning Framework:
Create a Photo Exhibit

LESSON 4.2
Rise of Labor Unions

• On Your Feet: Conduct Talk Show Interviews

NG Learning Framework:
Explore Perspectives

LESSON 4.3
Labor Conflicts

• On Your Feet: Labor Conflicts Roundtable

NG Learning Framework:
Investigate a Youth-Organized Strike

American Voices Biography
Cesar Chavez ONLINE

CHAPTER 19 REVIEW

STRIVING READERS

Strategy ❶
Modify Main Idea Statements

Provide these modifications of the Main Idea statements at the beginning of the following lessons:

1.1 Railroads connected the East and West coasts in the late 1860s.
1.3 New technologies helped to develop the Industrial Age.
1.4 Industries expanded in the late 1800s and early 1900s.
1.5 Mass culture emerged in the late 1800s.
2.1 Millions of new immigrants arrived around 1900.
2.3 Cities changed with the arrival of new methods of transportation and construction.
3.1 African Americans and other people of color experienced prejudice.
3.2 In 1896, the Supreme Court upheld segregation laws.
4.1 Many workers faced long days, low wages, and danger.
4.2 Labor unions staged strikes for better working conditions.
4.3 Labor conflicts turned violent in the late 1800s.

Use with Lessons 1.1, 1.3–1.5, 2.1, 2.3, 3.1–3.2, and 4.1–4.3

Strategy ❷
Ask Questions

Have students form groups of four and come up with a list of three questions about industrial growth and inventions. After the lesson, review the questions and have students from each group answer the questions they listed or give them the opportunity to research answers if their particular question was not addressed in the text. Have each group share its questions and answers with the class.

Use with Lessons 1.1–1.3 *This activity can be used with all lessons by changing the topic.*

Strategy ❸
Read and Recall

Tell students to read the lesson independently. After reading, pair students and instruct them to discuss the lesson and share ideas they recall while one person takes notes. Both students then review the lesson together and decide what should be added or changed in the notes.

Use with All Lessons *For an extension of this strategy, encourage student pairs to compare their notes.*

INCLUSION

Strategy ❶
Complete Cloze Sentences

Provide copies of cloze statements for students to complete during or after reading.

3.1 The Chinese Exclusion Act _____ Chinese _____ for a 10-year period. *(prohibited; immigration)*
3.1 Jim Crow laws were designed to _____ the rights of _____ in the South. *(restrict; African Americans)*
3.2 In *Plessy* v. *Ferguson*, the court upheld the practice of _____, allowing governments, businesses, and institutions to enact and enforce _____ policies. *(segregation; "separate but equal")*
3.3 _____ and _____ were two activists who founded the NAACP to combat race-based _____. *(W.E.B. Du Bois; Ida B. Wells; discrimination)*

Use with Lessons 3.1–3.3

Strategy ❷
Use a Word Splash

Present the words on the board in a random arrangement and ask students to choose three pairs of words that are related to each other. Have students use this sentence starter to write how each pair of words is related.

_____ and _____ are related because . . . .

suburbs
streetcars
urbanization
political machines
settlement house
Tammany Hall
Hull House
Ellen Gates Starr
Social Gospel
Jane Addams

Use with Lesson 2.3

ENGLISH LANGUAGE LEARNERS

Strategy ❶
Set Up a Word Wall

Work with students at the **Emerging** and **Expanding** levels to identify three words from each section to display in a grouping on a Word Wall. Choose words that students are likely to encounter in other chapters or contexts, such as *capitalism* or *corporation*. Keep the words displayed throughout the lessons and discuss each one as it comes up during reading. Encourage volunteers to add words, phrases, and examples to each word to develop understanding.

Use with All Lessons

Strategy ❷
PREP Before Reading

Have students at **All Proficiencies** use the PREP strategy to prepare for reading. Write this acrostic on the board:

PREP **P**review title.

Read the Main Idea statement.

Examine visuals.

Predict what you will learn.

Tell students to write their prediction and share it with a partner. After reading, ask students to write a sentence that begins with "I also learned . . ."

Use with Lessons 1.1, 1.3–1.5, 2.1, 2.3, 3.1–3.3, and 4.1–4.3

Strategy ❸
Preview Vocabulary with Visuals

Ask students to look at the visuals and try to figure out clues that help them understand Key Vocabulary words. In Lesson 1.1, have them work out the meaning of *standard time*; in Lesson 2.3, the meaning of *settlement house*; in Lesson 3.1, the meaning of *Jim Crow laws*; and in Lesson 4.2, the meaning of *robber baron*.

Use with Lessons 1.1, 2.3, 3.1, and 4.2 *You may wish to pair students at the **Emerging** level with students at the **Expanding** or **Bridging** levels and have more advanced students assist less advanced students in identifying the connection between visuals and Key Vocabulary words.*

GIFTED & TALENTED

Strategy ❶
Teach a Class

Before beginning the chapter, allow students to choose one of the lessons listed below and prepare to teach the content to the class. Give them a set amount of time in which to present their lesson. Suggest that students think about visuals or activities they might use when they teach.

Use with Lessons 1.1, 1.3–1.5, 2.1, 2.3, 3.1–3.3, and 4.1–4.3

Strategy ❷
Create a Fan Zine

Using any individual mentioned in the text, suggest that students create and share a comic or zine to celebrate and teach about the person. Tell students to use both visuals and text, quotations from or about the individual, and examples illustrating his or her ideas.

Use with Lessons 1.3, 1.4, 2.3, 3.3, and 4.2–4.3

Pre-AP

Strategy ❶
Explain Significance

Ask students to choose one term below and investigate its significance as it relates to immigration. Instruct them to design a presentation that includes a visual, such as a chart or map, that demonstrates the relationship. Invite students to present their findings and visual to the class.

- political machines
- refugees
- mutual aid
- settlement house

Use with Lessons 2.1 and 2.3

Strategy ❷
Extend Knowledge

Encourage students to use library media centers and online resources to investigate child labor during the late 1800s and early 1900s. Suggest that students focus on why factory work offered fewer benefits for children than the older system of apprenticeships and on working conditions in textile mills, canneries, coal mines, and agriculture. Ask students to present their findings in an oral report to the class.

Use with Lesson 4.1

INDUSTRIALIZATION AND IMMIGRATION

1860–1914

ESSENTIAL QUESTION
How did the Industrial Age transform America?

AMERICAN STORIES A Country of Immigrants

SECTION 1 **America Enters the Industrial Age**

KEY VOCABULARY

Bessemer process	laissez-faire	standard time
boom-and-bust cycle	mass culture	steel
capitalism	Pacific Railway Acts	transcontinental railroad
corporation	patent	trust
Gilded Age	philanthropy	

SECTION 2 **Immigration and Modern Urban Growth**

KEY VOCABULARY

bedrock	refugee	Social Gospel	tenement
mutual aid society	settlement house	streetcar	urbanization
political machine	skyscraper	suburb	

SECTION 3 **Discrimination Against Minorities**

KEY VOCABULARY

Chinese Exclusion Act	poll watcher
Jim Crow laws	self-reliance

SECTION 4 **The Labor Movement**

KEY VOCABULARY

anarchist	collective bargaining	robber baron	sweatshop
child labor	overhead	scab	

AMERICAN GALLERY ONLINE The Skyscrapers of New York City

READING STRATEGY

IDENTIFY MAIN IDEAS AND DETAILS
When you identify a text's main idea and supporting details, you state the most important idea about a topic and determine which facts support that idea. Use a graphic organizer like this one to find main ideas and supporting details about the social and economic effects of the Industrial Age as you read the chapter.

Effects of the Industrial Age

Main Idea
Detail:
Detail:
Detail:

"Remember, remember always, that all of us . . .
are descended from immigrants."
—Franklin D. Roosevelt

People arriving from Europe to embark on new lives in the United States passed the welcoming Statue of Liberty just before reaching Ellis Island, above. What might the Statue of Liberty have symbolized for arriving immigrants?

INTRODUCE THE PHOTOGRAPH

Ellis Island

Tell students to examine the photograph that opens this chapter. Students will recognize the Statue of Liberty but may not recognize the island in the foreground. Explain that this is the Main Building of the Ellis Island complex, through which millions of immigrants passed for immigration processing before entering the United States. Tell students to read the Roosevelt quotation and then invite volunteers to name their immigrant ancestors.
ASK: Why do you think Roosevelt emphasized remembering our immigrant heritage? *(Possible response: He wanted us to realize that even with so much diversity, Americans are united by having ancestors who came to this country in search of a better life.)* Tell students that in this chapter, they will learn more about the immigrants of the late 1800s and early 1900s and the rapidly changing America that became their new home.

For Chapter 19 Spanish Resources, visit the Resources Menu. Chapter 19 Resources are available at NGLSync.Cengage.com.

SHARE BACKGROUND

The Main Building in the photograph is not the original processing center. The original pine building, along with other structures on the island, burned to the ground on June 15, 1897. The federal government ordered the immigration station to be rebuilt using fireproof material. The brick-and-limestone building shown here opened on December 17, 1900. On its first day in operation, 2,251 immigrants passed through its doors to be processed in the two-story Registry Room, which was built to accommodate 5,000 immigrants a day. The New York architectural firm of Boring and Tilton designed the building in the Beaux-Arts classical style.

CRITICAL VIEWING Answers will vary. Possible response: The Statue of Liberty might have symbolized immigrants' hopes for a new life in a land where they would be free to pursue their dreams.

How did the Industrial Age transform America?

Roundtable Activity: Traits of an Age This activity introduces students to different characteristics of American life in the late 1800s and early 1900s: industrialization, immigration, and urbanization. Divide the class into three groups and have each group sit at a table. Assign the following questions to the groups:

Group 1: How might advances in technology change the kinds of work that people do for a living?

Group 2: Why might people feel the need to move to a new country?

Group 3: What problems might political leaders face when cities have a rapid growth in population?

Ask students at each table to take turns answering the question. When they have finished their discussion, ask a representative from each table to summarize that group's answers.

Definition Charts

As students read the chapter, have them complete a Definition Chart for Key Vocabulary words. Instruct students to list each Key Vocabulary word in the first column of the chart. Then, as they encounter that word in the chapter, tell them to write its definition in the second column and then use the third column to restate that meaning in their own words. Model an example on the board using the graphic organizer below.

WORD	DEFINITION	IN MY OWN WORDS
overhead	the cost of doing business	what a business spends to produce an item or service, including the price of materials and employee wages

IDENTIFY MAIN IDEAS AND DETAILS

Remind students that they can confirm their understanding of the main idea of a text by identifying details from the text that support the idea. Model the strategy by reading the third and fourth paragraphs aloud in the subsection Arriving in a New Land in Lesson 2.1 and then identifying its main idea and supporting details.

> **Main Idea: Immigrants took a variety of jobs in the United States.**
>
> **Detail:** New York City: construction, shipping, garment industry
>
> **Detail:** Midwest: steel mills, coal mines
>
> **Detail:** West: agriculture, logging, mining, railroads, restaurants

1869	Transcontinental railroad completed
1870	Standard Oil Company founded
1879	Thomas Edison's first practical light bulb
1882	Chinese Exclusion Act
1886	American Federation of Labor formed
1892	Ellis Island opens
1893	World's Columbian Exposition
1896	*Plessy* v. *Ferguson*
1903	Wright brothers' first successful airplane flight
1909	NAACP founded

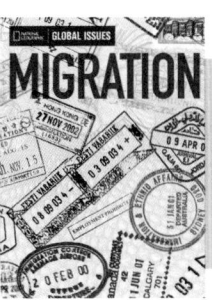

For more on the reasons for and results of migration, see *GLOBAL ISSUES: MIGRATION.*

Objectives

- **Understand the experiences of immigrants in the late 19th and early 20th centuries.**
- **Contrast the experiences of immigrants who entered the United States through Angel Island with those of immigrants who entered through Ellis Island.**
- **Describe how changing patterns of immigration are reflected in urban neighborhoods today.**
- **Study primary sources: an excerpt from *The Bread Givers*, a poem by Emma Lazarus, photographs, and official documents.**

Critical Thinking Skills for "A Country of Immigrants"

- Make Connections
- Draw Conclusions
- Make Inferences
- Analyze Language Use
- Identify
- Make Generalizations
- Analyze Cause and Effect
- Identify Problems and Solutions

Background for the Teacher

This American Story introduces students to the experiences of people who came to the United States in the late 1800s. Use this narrative to spark students' interest before they read Chapter 19 and to remind students that the United States is a nation of immigrants.

This chapter, Industrialization and Immigration, discusses a period of great growth and change in the history of the United States. This American Story will open the door to a key component—immigration—and will underscore the fact that the United States is a nation distinguished by its diversity.

History Notebook

Encourage students to complete the American Story page for Chapter 19 in their History Notebooks as they read and the Reid on the Road video series page after they view the video.

CRITICAL VIEWING Possible response: The man and woman are dressed nicely, so they may be well off. They are carrying few items, which suggests that their belongings are in trunks. The boy doesn't look as well dressed, so he may have been hired to carry the large sack on his shoulder.

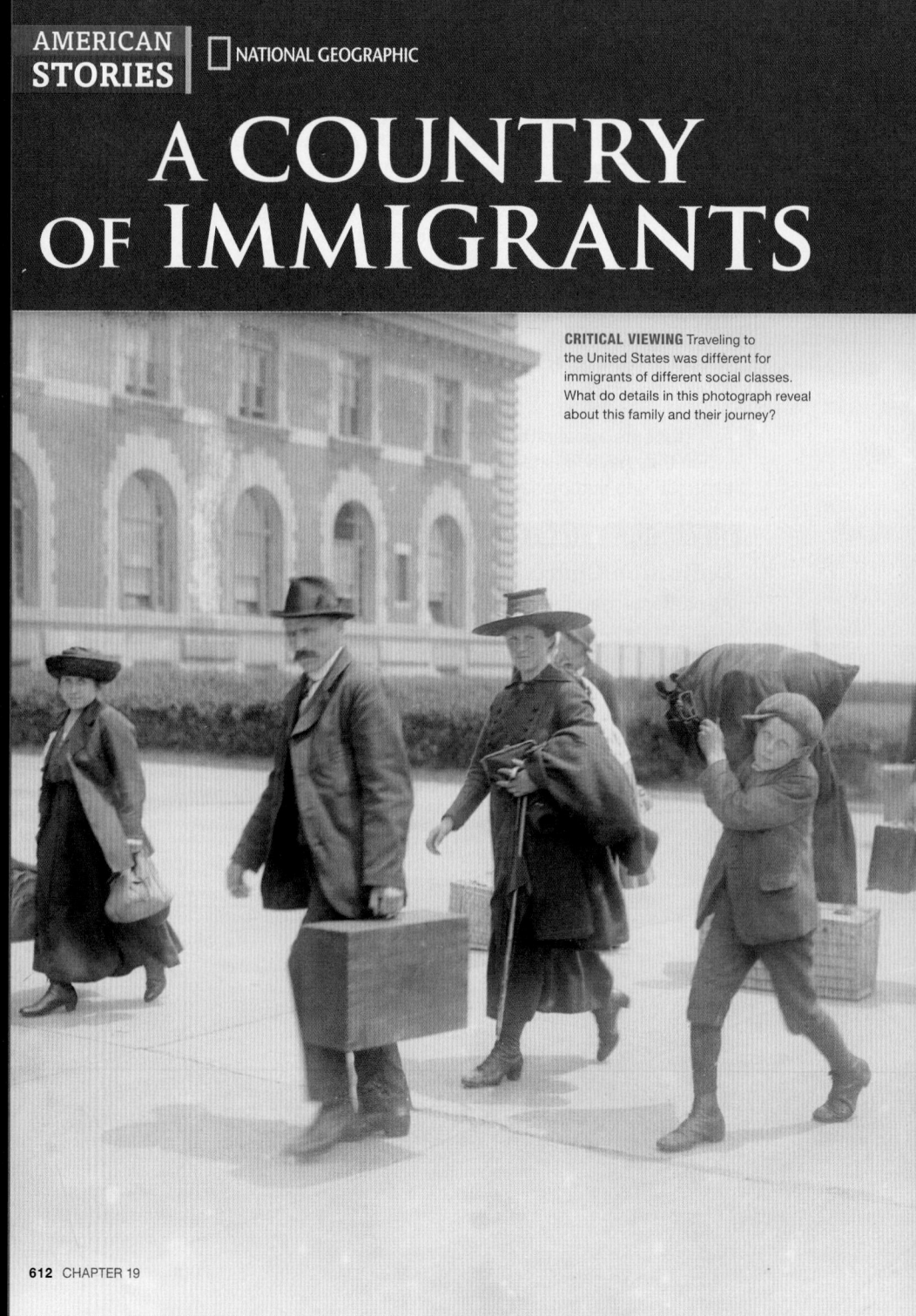

AMERICAN STORIES | NATIONAL GEOGRAPHIC

A COUNTRY OF IMMIGRANTS

CRITICAL VIEWING Traveling to the United States was different for immigrants of different social classes. What do details in this photograph reveal about this family and their journey?

612 CHAPTER 19

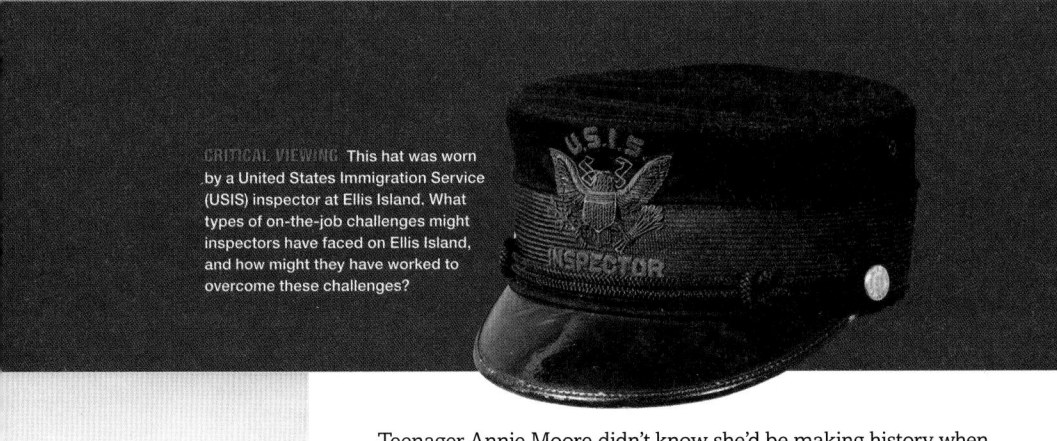

CRITICAL VIEWING This hat was worn by a United States Immigration Service (USIS) inspector at Ellis Island. What types of on-the-job challenges might inspectors have faced on Ellis Island, and how might they have worked to overcome these challenges?

Teenager Annie Moore didn't know she'd be making history when she climbed aboard a boat in Ireland in 1891. On New Year's Day of 1892, she became the first immigrant to step ashore on Ellis Island in New York Harbor. There, a brand-new reception center had been built to receive the immigrants from Europe. Photographers were on hand to capture the moment the first immigrant landed at Ellis Island, making Annie special—but at the same time, she was just one of millions.

CROSSING THE ATLANTIC

Annie Moore was among the immigrants who came to the United States between 1870 and 1920. People seeking new lives arrived from all over the world. Millions of immigrants, many of whom were Jews fleeing persecution, landed on the East Coast from southern and eastern Europe. Others landed on the West Coast from different parts of Asia.

Those who could afford it traveled in comfortable first- or second-class cabins aboard the ships. Most, like Annie, made the journey in steerage—an open space below decks shared by all the poorer passengers. One immigrant described the conditions in steerage: "There must have been two to three hundred people in that huge, cavernous area. [There] was no such things as washing or bathing. The stench, the vermin, it was rat infested." It was a difficult journey, to say the least.

> ### PRIMARY SOURCE
>
> *I'm smart enough to look out for myself. It's a new life now. In America, women don't need men to boss them. Thank God, I'm living in America! I'm going to make my own life. I'm going to live my own life. Nobody can stop me. I'm not from the old country. I'm an American!*
>
> —from *Bread Givers,* by Anzia Yezierska, 1925

Industrialization and Immigration **613**

Preview Using Visuals

Call students' attention to the photograph of the Registry Room on the second spread of this American Story. Then ask a volunteer to read the caption. Ask students to suggest the pros and cons of processing large numbers of immigrants in this setting. Encourage students to consider the issues from the perspectives of inspectors and immigrants. Tell students that they are going to read an American Story about how immigrants from several parts of the world entered the United States generations ago and enriched American life.

Brainstorm Reasons

Ask students to brainstorm answers to this question: For what reasons would you leave your homeland and begin life in a new country? Urge students to think about both push factors, such as religious persecution, and pull factors, such as the chance to give one's family a better quality of life. Write students' responses on the board. If time permits, work with students to identify the top three or four reasons. Then tell students that as they read this American Story, they will see how some—and perhaps all—of these reasons motivated a wide variety of immigrants to come to the United States.

Analyze Primary Sources

Call on a volunteer to read aloud the quotation from Anzia Yezierska. Discuss how Yezierska contrasts her new life in the United States with that in her homeland. **ASK:** What details in Anzia Yezierska's comment suggest a reason for her immigration? Explain. *(Possible response: "In America, women don't need men to boss them" and "Nobody can stop me" suggest that in her homeland, Yezierska felt that other people tried to control her.)* What suggests that she is confident about her new life in the United States? *(Possible responses: She sounds confident when she states, "I'm smart enough to look out for myself" and "I'm going to make my own life.")*

CRITICAL VIEWING Possible response: Inspectors would have needed to speak different languages or have used interpreters to communicate with immigrants who didn't speak English. They might have encountered nervous or sick immigrants, which would have required a compassionate attitude.

The Registry Room

Upon entering Ellis Island, immigrants ascended a set of stairs to the Registry Room, an imposing structure with arching windows and a ceiling that soared to 60 feet. The room was often loud and confusing, with thousands of people filing through in one day. It was restored in 1924 and is now open to visitors as part of The Statue of Liberty National Monument.

The Health Inspection

An immigrant's health inspection began almost as soon as he or she walked upon dry land. As immigrants climbed the stairs to the Registry Room, inspectors assessed whether they had difficulty carrying their bags or appeared short of breath. If so, immigrants were immediately inspected for disease. Those who made it up the stairs were quickly examined by a doctor who checked for conditions such as cholera, ringworm, and mental disability, sometimes suspected when an immigrant had trouble following directions. What most immigrants feared the most, however, was suspicion of trachoma, a contagious eye infection that often blinded its victims and was treated through painful surgery and the use of corrosive chemicals.

From Copper to Green

The Statue of Liberty was the collaborative creation of two Frenchmen, sculptor Frédéric-Auguste Bartholdi and engineer Gustave Eiffel, of Eiffel Tower fame. The base on which the statue stands was designed by Richard Morris Hunt, an American architect. Originally, the statue was the color of copper, the material that covers its surface. However, slowly, due to oxidation, the color changed to its familiar green. Because of the lack of color photography from the era, historians are not sure of the exact rate of greening, but by 1920 the original copper color was gone.

AMERICAN STORIES

ISLE OF TEARS, ISLE OF JOY

In 1907 alone, Ellis Island processed more than 1 million people. By the time the center closed in 1954, more than 12 million immigrants had passed through its halls. By one estimate, more than a third of present-day Americans have at least one ancestor who arrived at Ellis Island.

For many, Ellis Island was an overwhelming place. Few immigrants spoke English, but all had to go through an admission process. They were required to pass a health inspection and answer questions about their countries of origin and their finances.

They also had to reveal if they had relatives already in the United States. Many immigrants worried they would be denied admission to the country.

Some called Ellis Island the "Isle of Tears," but in reality, immigration officials made efforts to treat arriving immigrants decently. They were given meals, and the ill were cared for in an on-site hospital. In all, only about two percent of immigrants were refused entry into the country.

Memories of the Ellis Island experience vary wildly. One woman who arrived as a girl recounted, "[The] first meal we got—fish and milk, big pitchers

CRITICAL VIEWING New arrivals to Ellis Island lined up for health inspections and processing by Immigration Service officers in the Registry Room. On some days, more than 5,000 immigrants passed through this great hall. What do details from this 1900 photograph reveal about how immigrants might have felt while waiting in line in the Registry Room?

LADY LIBERTY

For many immigrants entering Ellis Island, their first glimpse of the United States was the Statue of Liberty towering over New York Harbor. Completed in 1886, the statue was a gift from the French. Officially named "Liberty Enlightening the World," it stands an impressive 305 feet tall on Liberty Island, near Ellis Island. Every year, thousands of visitors climb up inside the hollow statue to enjoy the view through windows placed in its spiky crown.

Since its earliest days, the Statue of Liberty has served as a symbol of welcome to immigrants. In 1883, Emma Lazarus wrote a poem called "The New Colossus" to help raise funds to erect the statue. The poem's most famous lines depict Lady Liberty speaking to the countries of Europe, saying:

Give me your tired, your poor,
Your huddled masses yearning to breathe free,
The wretched refuse of your teeming shore.
Send these, the homeless, tempest-tost to me,
I lift my lamp beside the golden door!

The poem was placed on a plaque at the base of the statue in 1903.

Why do you think Lazarus used a golden door as the image of a gateway to the United States?

of milk and white bread. And I said, 'My God, we're going to have a good time here. We're going to have plenty to eat.'" But another immigrant recalled, "The people had such terrible sad faces. [There's] more tears in Ellis Island to ten people than, say, to a hundred people elsewhere."

An immigrant who arrived in 1921 summed up the experience in practical terms, "You had to wait in line to get the food. You had to get in line to get a blanket. And they weren't unkind, but . . . they had so many people to take care of."

Guided Discussion

1. **Make Inferences** Why do you think some immigrants called Ellis Island the "Isle of Tears"? *(Answers will vary. Possible response: Any immigrant who was refused entry would be devastated, resulting in tears. Immigrants might also have felt sadness at leaving their homeland or have fears about how they would get by in America.)*

2. **Analyze Language Use** How might the official name of the Statue of Liberty, "Liberty Enlightening the World," refer to more than the torch that the statue holds? *(Possible response: By welcoming immigrants to the chance for a new and better life, America—symbolized by Lady Liberty—might be offering spiritual light by demonstrating compassion and a welcoming spirit to the world.)*

CRITICAL VIEWING Possible response: The immigrants were packed closely together on hard benches. Many of them were probably nervous, hot, and tired as they awaited inspection and processing.

Angel Island

Direct students' attention to the photograph of Angel Island. Explain that to reach the immigration station, Chinese immigrants undertook a three-week voyage across the Pacific Ocean. Many could barely even afford steerage accommodations and borrowed money for their ticket from relatives. Since Chinese laborers were being excluded by 1910, the immigrants sometimes borrowed money to buy forged identity papers as well. **ASK:** Why were these immigrants willing to go into debt? *(Answers will vary. Possible responses: They were desperate for a new life in the United States. They believed that they would make enough money to repay their debts.)*

Tell students to compare the photo of Angel Island to the photos of Ellis Island. **ASK:** What do the photos suggest about the welcome that Chinese immigrants received when they arrived? *(Possible response: Chinese immigrants would not be made to feel very welcome. The photos of Ellis Island suggest efficiency and some grandeur, but the photo of Angel Island suggests a grim barracks with basic accommodations.)* Ask for volunteers to read the poems in the photograph and the text. **ASK:** What idea do these poems have in common? *(Possible response: Both poems express a person's unhappiness and frustration at being detained on Angel Island rather than going to the mainland.)*

Asian-American History

Students may want to explore the history of Asian Americans in more depth. Historians Erika Lee and Ronald Takaki have both published works on Asian Americans. Among Lee's books are *The Making of Asian America: A History; At America's Gates: Chinese Immigration during the Exclusion Era, 1882-1943*, and *Angel Island: Immigrant Gateway to America*, which she coauthored with Judy Yung. The late Ronald Takaki, the grandson of a Japanese immigrant, taught and wrote about multiculturalism and race relations in the United States. Among his works are *Strangers from a Different Shore: A History of Asian Americans* and *Democracy and Race: Asian Americans and World War II*. Students might also enjoy reading the novels of Amy Tan, the daughter of Chinese immigrants. Her books, such as *The Joy Luck Club* and *The Bonesetter's Daughter*, focus on the lives of Chinese Americans.

AMERICAN STORIES

Angel Island was more like a detention center than a welcome center. It was designed to control waves of Chinese coming into the country after the passage of the Chinese Exclusion Act of 1882. From 1910 to 1940, Angel Island processed Asian immigrants from China, Japan, Russia, and South Asia.

ANGEL ISLAND

While Ellis Island received European immigrants on the East Coast, a second reception center was built on the West Coast on Angel Island, just offshore from San Francisco. It was at Angel Island that many Hindu, Sikh, Chinese, Japanese, and Korean immigrants landed after journeying across the Pacific Ocean from Asia. While Angel Island is often compared to Ellis Island, the California center was built to exclude most Asian immigrants, not to welcome them.

At Angel Island, immigrants waited for days or weeks to find out whether they would be allowed to enter the United States. By contrast, the average time for processing at Ellis Island was less than a day. Some wrote poems on the walls, like the one shown on the right, to express their despair. One reads, "It's been seven weeks since my imprisonment / On this island—and I still do not know when I can land."

Angel Island closed in 1940. Precise numbers are not available, but it is estimated that officials there refused between 11 and 30 percent of immigrants.

These Chinese characters, which make up part of a poem, were carved into a wall in the Angel Island detention barracks. More than 200 poems written in Chinese have been transcribed from the walls of the immigration center. Hundreds more may have been buried by layers of paint.

Many of the poems at Angel Island express Chinese immigrants' frustration over their poor living conditions. Some even reveal their desire to seek revenge for their unfair treatment. This poet writes, "the American continent is the most difficult of difficulties."

PAPER SONS AND DAUGHTERS

Although the United States tried to keep out some Asian immigrants through Angel Island, they could not keep out Chinese immigrants who were already citizens because their fathers were U.S. citizens. According to immigration laws, Chinese immigrants who could prove their father's U.S. citizenship could not be denied entry into the United States. Immigration inspectors often suspected Chinese immigrants of avoiding Chinese exclusion laws by entering the country as "paper sons and daughters," a term used to describe immigrants who falsely claimed to be related to a U.S. citizen to gain citizenship for themselves.

Immigration inspectors subjected Chinese citizens to a much longer, more grueling admission process than those from Europe, Japan, or Korea. They spent hours interviewing Chinese immigrants with questions like these (right), designed to confirm their identities and call attention to paper sons and daughters. If an immigrant or his or her witnesses fumbled during the questioning process, the immigrant faced potential deportation back to China. Some of the questions were so abstract that even true children and wives occasionally failed the interrogation process.

> What are the birth and death dates of your grandparents? Where are they buried?
>
> Who lives in the third house in the fourth row of houses in your village?
>
> How often did your father [or husband] write and how much money did he send home?
>
> How many guests were at your wedding? What jewelry did your husband give you as wedding presents?
>
> —from "Angel Island Immigration Station," by Judy Yung and Erika Lee, September 2015

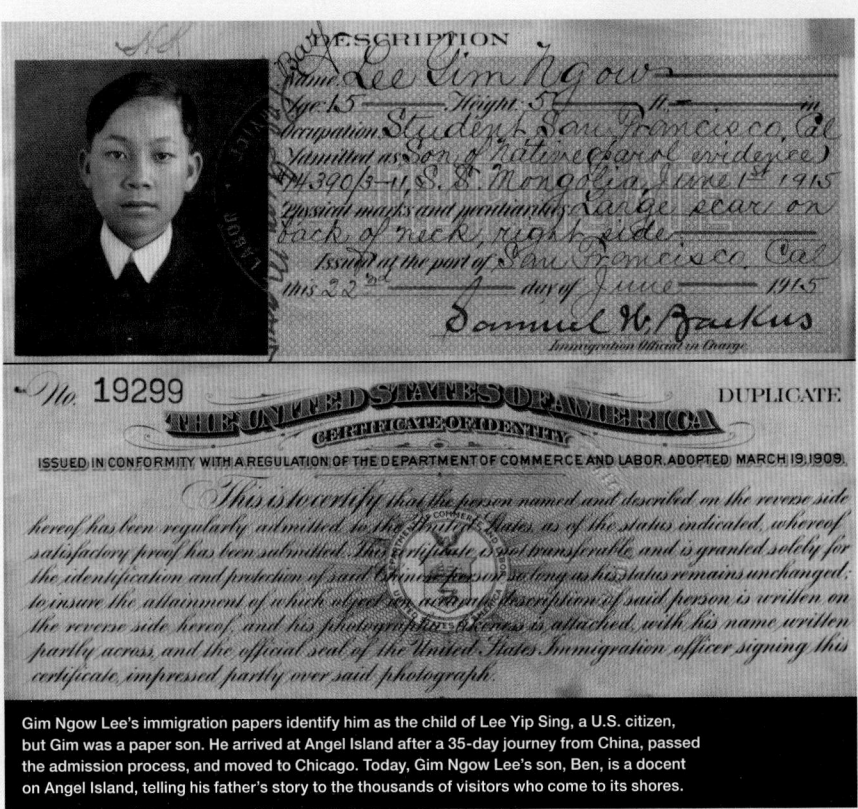

Gim Ngow Lee's immigration papers identify him as the child of Lee Yip Sing, a U.S. citizen, but Gim was a paper son. He arrived at Angel Island after a 35-day journey from China, passed the admission process, and moved to Chicago. Today, Gim Ngow Lee's son, Ben, is a docent on Angel Island, telling his father's story to the thousands of visitors who come to its shores.

Active Options

On Your Feet: Numbered Heads Organize students into groups of four and ask students to number off. Tell students to think about and discuss a response to this question: In what ways did Angel Island differ from Ellis Island? Encourage students to approach the question from a variety of angles, such as differences in setting, purpose, practices, and immigrant experiences. Then call a number and have the student from each group with that number report for the group.

NG Learning Framework: Create an Immigration Mural

ATTITUDES Curiosity, Empowerment

SKILLS Collaboration, Communication

Invite groups of students to create immigration murals. Tell them to discuss the topic and decide on a theme or idea to express. Direct students to print and online sources for visuals to include, such as historical photographs or artistic interpretations. Ask students to organize visuals in a meaningful way. For example, they might arrange them chronologically or in a way that contrasts immigrants' old and new lives. Suggest to students that they might also include relevant quotations by immigrants, historians, or artists in their murals. Prompt students to display their finished murals and ask them to comment on the work they did to bring the project to completion. Encourage comments from the class about parts of each mural that students find especially meaningful.

Guided Discussion

1. **Identify** In what sense does Annie Moore's story illustrate "the diverse and changing face of immigration"? *(Possible response: Annie Moore came from Ireland, in western Europe. The fact that her descendants include "Dominicans, Chinese, Jews, and Italians" shows that immigrants from other parts of the world have populated New York.)*

2. **Make Generalizations** Think about the history of the Pilsen neighborhood in Chicago. From what you read about the Bohemian influences and, later, the Mexican influences in that neighborhood, what impact does immigration have on the characteristics of neighborhoods and even whole cities? *(Answers will vary. Possible response: Immigrants give neighborhoods characteristics that reflect the culture of their homeland, such as distinctive architecture, languages, and art.)*

WRITE ABOUT HISTORY

Compose a Letter Home This American Story tells the story of people who left their homeland to start a new life in an unfamiliar country. To help students make connections between this American Story and their own lives, ask them to imagine themselves as an immigrant coming through Ellis Island or Angel Island. Tell them to write, in character, a letter to someone back home, describing the process of entering the United States and their hopes for a new life. Students may want to do additional research to get a deeper understanding of the topic. Invite students to share their letters with the class.

THINK ABOUT IT

Students may suggest that not all immigrants were welcomed with open arms. European immigrants entered the country more easily than Asian immigrants, suggesting prejudice toward non-Christians with a non-European appearance.

CRITICAL VIEWING Possible response: All the men in the photograph are wearing turbans and have beards, so a tradition about men covering their heads and keeping beards is likely a part of the culture.

AMERICAN STORIES

ANNIE'S TALE

So what happened to Annie Moore after she stepped out of the headlines and into her new life in America? For nearly a century, it seemed she had disappeared without a trace, but in 1986, an elderly woman claimed Annie Moore was her mother. She said Annie had moved to the West, married, and opened the first hotel in Clovis, New Mexico.

It was a great story. The only problem was that the real Annie Moore had relatives who told a different tale. In 2006, Annie's true story came out. She had never been west or even traveled beyond New York City. Instead, she had lived the rest of her life in New York's Irish neighborhood, where she married and raised a large family. When a researcher gathered the real Annie's descendants, they were a diverse group including Dominicans, Chinese, Jews, and Italians. Annie's actual story may be less exciting than the colorful tales of her travels to the West, but it reflects the diverse and changing face of immigration.

Sculptor Jeanne Rynhart created two bronze sculptures of Annie Moore. One stands in Ireland, where Annie began her immigration journey. The other (shown here) is located at Ellis Island, where she landed.

THINK ABOUT IT

In what ways do Ellis Island and Angel Island reflect complex American attitudes toward immigration?

CRITICAL VIEWING Built in 1915 in Stockton, California, this Sikh temple, which Sikhs call a "Gurdwara" (gur-DWAR-ah) was the first permanent Indian religious building in the United States. What does this photograph reveal about the Sikh culture and traditions?

SIKH IMMIGRANTS

Sikhs (SEEKS or SIKZ) are followers of a religion called Sikhism, which was established in India around 1500. About 7,000 Hindu, Muslim, and Sikh immigrants came from India to the United States and Canada between 1899 and 1920. Angel Island records show that hundreds were processed in California.

Many Sikh immigrants had been skilled farmers in India. They sought agricultural jobs in California, and contributed to the state's development of farming. Many became migrant workers in the Sacramento Valley, eventually establishing permanent homes there. Inaccurately known as "Hindu crews," many faced discrimination and judgment in part because they dressed differently from other workers.

Other Sikhs found jobs in the railroad and lumber industries, oftentimes earning a lower wage than white workers doing the same tasks.

A NEIGHBORHOOD OF IMMIGRANTS

Many European immigrants settled in big industrial cities in the North, such as New York, Chicago, Detroit, and Philadelphia. They moved into neighborhoods with others from the same country or who had the same religion. There, they spoke their own languages and maintained their cultures. For example, in New York City, Jewish immigrants settled in the Tenth Ward, and Italians settled along Mott Street and Prince Street.

In the 1870s, a wave of Czech-speaking immigrants from Bohemia, an area of eastern Europe, was drawn to Chicago by the promise of jobs in lumber mills, garment factories, and railroad yards. Additionally, after Chicago's Great Fire in 1871, the city experienced an economic boom. More immigrants moved to Chicago to work to rebuild the city. The Bohemians settled into a neighborhood on the west side of the city. When one man opened a restaurant named after the Bohemian city of Plzen, the name stuck. Soon the whole neighborhood became known as Pilsen.

Like other immigrant groups, the Bohemians of Pilsen imprinted their culture on the neighborhood. They built buildings that reflected the architectural style of their homeland. They established stores, homes, and churches, creating a vibrant community within the larger city of Chicago.

Also like other groups, the Bohemians eventually left the neighborhood. The children and grandchildren of the original immigrants learned to speak English, and gradually moved away. In their place came immigrants from Mexico and other Spanish-speaking countries. Today, Pilsen is still notable for its Bohemian architecture, but now some buildings are decorated with bright, Mexican-themed murals. The language in the streets is Spanish, not Czech. The faces have changed, but Pilsen remains a lively, vital community within the city of Chicago. And so the immigrant story continues.

This 2006 mural is called *The Community*. It was commissioned by the Chicago Artist Coalition (CAC) in collaboration with Chicago's Pilsen community to celebrate the diversity of this neighborhood.

Industrialization and Immigration 619

English Language Learners ELD

Use Word Squares Pair students at the **Emerging** or **Expanding** level with those at the **Bridging** level or with English-proficient students. Have partners use a Word Square to explore unfamiliar terms, such as *reception center, persecution, process, wretched, deportation,* and *abstract*. Encourage students to discuss the terms to clarify meaning.

Gifted & Talented

Host a Talk Show Tell students to use print and online resources to locate personal narratives of immigrants who entered the United States through Ellis Island or Angel Island. Help students choose a few narratives to tell in a talk show format. Direct groups to plan an introduction for each immigrant and to craft questions that all of the immigrants could answer. When students have finished researching and writing questions, ask for volunteers to play the part of the host or one of the immigrants. Students could record the talk show and play the video in class or present it live.

See the Chapter Planner for more strategies for differentiation.

HISTORICAL THINKING

Ask and have students answer the following questions.

1. **READING CHECK** What was the purpose of immigration reception centers?

2. **ANALYZE CAUSE AND EFFECT** Why was processing at Ellis Island an overwhelming experience for many immigrants?

3. **IDENTIFY PROBLEMS AND SOLUTIONS** How did the federal government attempt to solve the problem of Chinese immigrants entering the country illegally?

ANSWERS

At reception centers, inspectors evaluated immigrants' health and ability to work before allowing them into the country.

Upon arrival, immigrants waited for hours in the crowded Registry Room. They may not have slept or eaten, but they had to be examined and questioned.

The government used a long, detailed interview in which immigrants had to prove their father or husband was a U.S. citizen.

1.1 Industrial Revolution Gathers Steam

Imagine traveling to California by train in the 1860s. At one point after lunch, all the windows go dark—you are in a tunnel. When the train emerges, the beautiful peaks of the Sierra Nevada surround you.

MAIN IDEA In the late 1860s, railroads expanded across the Great Plains and the western mountain ranges to connect the East and West coasts.

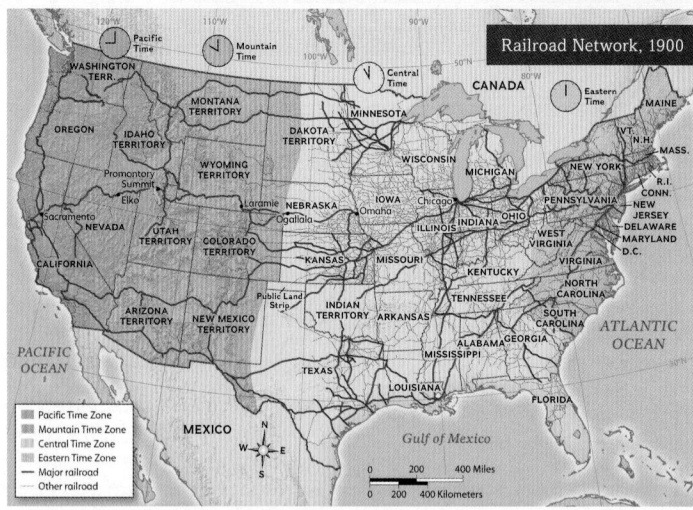

Railroad Network, 1900

RACING TO UTAH

Prior to the 1860s, the journey by land from the Midwest to the Pacific was difficult. To get to California, most settlers spent months traveling by wagon or stagecoach. To address the lack of efficient transportation west, the federal government passed the **Pacific Railway Acts** in 1862 and 1864, which put two companies in charge of building a **transcontinental railroad**, or a railroad that ran across the continent. The acts provided funds for the construction of rail lines by issuing government bonds and land grants. The **Central Pacific Company** would start building from Sacramento, California, and the **Union Pacific Company** from Omaha, Nebraska. They were to meet in the middle, and the federal government would pay for every mile of track the companies laid. The race was on.

The Central Pacific Company started off slowly. Equipment took several months to travel from the East Coast, where it was manufactured, to the West Coast because there were no reliable overland shipping routes through North America. Instead, ships had to carry the equipment all the way around the southern tip of South America and up its western coast in order to reach California.

The Central Pacific also had to figure out how to build a level track through the Sierra Nevada. Its solution was to blast tunnels through the rugged granite peaks. The railroad company had a hard time finding enough people for the difficult, dangerous job, but it eventually hired about 10,000 Chinese immigrants willing to take on the challenge. Even though the Nebraska prairie was smoother terrain than California's mountains, the Union Pacific faced difficulties, too. With few trees on the prairie, workers scrounged for adequate supplies of wood for constructing the ties that held the rails. Workers also faced the threat of attack by Native Americans, who saw the railroad as another invasion of their land.

Railroad laborers worked 12 to 16 hours a day, 7 days a week. They built bridges, blasted tunnels, and laid tracks through bitter winters and scorching summers. On May 10, 1869, the two lines met at Promontory, Utah. **Leland Stanford**, the president of the Central Pacific, hammered one last golden spike into the tracks to celebrate the achievement.

CHANGING TIMES

After the first transcontinental rail line opened, more railroad companies laid their own tracks. **Cornelius Vanderbilt**, who had dominated the steamship and ferry industries in the 1850s, turned his attention to railroads. He helped expand regional networks between Chicago and New York and make railroad transportation more efficient. By 1890, the United States boasted 185,000 miles of railroad track—more than in all of Europe. By 1895, four more railroads, the Northern Pacific, Southern Pacific, Great Northern, and Atlantic and Pacific, crisscrossed the country. People and goods could move across and around the nation in a relatively short time. Train passengers could travel from New York to California in one week instead of four to six months by stagecoach. Speedy rail transportation also opened up a national market. For instance, cattle ranchers in Nebraska could now transport their livestock to Chicago markets, and Chicago meatpackers could ship products to nationwide markets well before the meat spoiled.

The railroads did not benefit everyone, though. Train tracks cut through Native American land and hunting grounds. Small towns popped up quickly along the tracks. As a result, the government took more Native American land to satisfy the increasing desire for property. The natural environment suffered. Hunters came by train to kill buffalo for sport, even though Native Americans depended upon the animals for survival. The blasting of mountains and chopping down of trees required to lay the tracks changed the landscape forever.

The transcontinental railroad brought one unexpected change. Before trains, many towns ran on their own "local time" based on the sun's position in the sky. Railroad lines operated according to the local time of the town in which they originated. When passengers tried to make train connections, though, the differing times caused confusion. So in 1883, the railroads began operating according to four newly established time zones. The general public later adopted the time zones and standardized the time in each region. This concept is called **standard time**.

The transcontinental railroad had a huge impact on the country. But it was not the only major change the United States experienced in the late 1800s. Other important innovations soon followed.

HISTORICAL THINKING

1. **READING CHECK** Why was a transcontinental railroad important to the United States?

2. **ANALYZE ENVIRONMENTAL CONCEPTS** How did the railroads change the landscape, and what impact did they have on Native Americans?

3. **INTERPRET MAPS** What is the time change when traveling from Omaha to Laramie?

PLAN

Objective
Learn how the transcontinental railroad changed the United States.

Critical Thinking Skills for Lesson 1.1

- Identify Main Ideas and Details
- Monitor Comprehension
- Analyze Environmental Concepts
- Interpret Maps
- Summarize

Essential Question for Chapter 19
How did the Industrial Age transform America?
The transcontinental railroad dramatically cut travel time between the East and West coasts, making the movement of people and goods more efficient. Lesson 1.1 discusses the impact of this achievement on westward expansion and Native Americans.

Background for the Teacher

Leland Stanford was one of the driving forces behind the Central Pacific Railroad. Stanford was a former Wisconsin lawyer who moved to California in the early 1850s and became a successful merchant selling supplies to miners. Stanford became president of the Central Pacific Railroad Company in 1861. Then as governor of California from 1862 to 1863, Stanford secured state subsidies and land grants to help build the eastbound section of the transcontinental railroad. He also participated in building other railroads, including the Southern Pacific Railroad, which connected southern California to Arizona and, by connecting with other railroads, provided a route to the port of New Orleans.

History Notebook
Encourage students to complete the Reid on the Road video series page for Chapter 19 in their History Notebooks after they view the video.

Brainstorm Lists

Remind students that in the late 1800s, westward expansion changed both the geography and demography of the country. Farmers, ranchers, and miners pushed Native Americans from homelands in the Great Plains, West, and Southwest, and western cities, such as San Francisco and Sacramento, grew and prospered. Work with students to brainstorm a list of benefits of connecting the continent with a railroad system and a list of challenges that the endeavor would involve. Encourage students to check off items and add to their lists as they read.

TEACH

Guided Discussion

1. **Identify Main Ideas and Details** How did the federal government encourage the westward expansion of the railroad system? *(The federal government provided bonds and land grants and paid railroad companies for every mile of track they laid.)*

2. **Summarize** How did standard time develop? *(The position of the sun relative to specific locations determined local time prior to the establishment of time zones. With the completion of the transcontinental railroad, standard time, in the form of four time zones, was established in order to standardize train schedules.)*

Interpret Maps

What evidence on the map supports the idea that railroads were important to cattle ranching in the West? *(Possible response: Major railroads are shown crisscrossing Kansas and connecting its cow towns to the stockyards and meat processing plants in Chicago.)*

Active Options

On Your Feet: Inside-Outside Circle Arrange students in two concentric circles, facing each other. Each student in the outside circle asks a question about the transcontinental railroad. Then each student in the inside circle answers his or her partner's question. On a signal, students on the inside circle rotate counterclockwise to meet a new partner and begin again. Direct students to trade roles so that those on the inside ask the questions and those on the outside answer them.

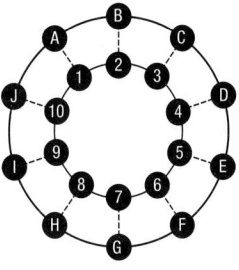

NG Learning Framework: Investigate Consequences of a Railroad System

ATTITUDE Responsibility

KNOWLEDGE Our Living Planet

Instruct students to use the text and print or online research to investigate the demographic and geographic consequences of the growing railroad system for the West and Southwest. Organize students into groups and assign one of the following topics to each group:

• railroad towns

• policy toward Native Americans

• Chinese immigration

• environment

Have groups create a list of facts associated with their topic, sort them into negative and positive consequences, and report their findings to the class.

DIFFERENTIATE

Inclusion

Narrate the Map Pair visually challenged students with students who are not visually challenged. Ask the latter to narrate the map by describing the general characteristics of the routes, explaining the time zones, and answering any questions that may arise.

Pre-AP

Write a Biography Have students review the information about Cornelius Vanderbilt in the lesson. Then instruct them to work in pairs to conduct online research to find out additional information about Vanderbilt including his involvement with the Union Navy during the Civil War. Have students share their biographies with the class.

See the Chapter Planner for more strategies for differentiation.

HISTORICAL THINKING

ANSWERS

1. The railroad cut the travel time from New York to California from four to six months to one week, faster shipping opened national markets, more people moved west, and new towns developed along the tracks.

2. Construction of the railroad required blasting through mountains to make tunnels and cutting down trees to make way for tracks and to make railroad ties. The railroad cut through Native American lands and brought in sport hunters who reduced the number of buffalo, an animal vital to the culture of Native Americans.

3. Traveling west to Laramie results in a gain of one hour.

1.2 The Scenic Railways of the United States

CRITICAL VIEWING Based on what you have read and what you can tell from this image, what would tracklayers' biggest challenges have been when constructing railways like the Georgetown Loop Railroad in the Colorado Rockies?

As the nation continued to expand westward, the railways connected far-flung regions of the country. By the 1860s, tracks had extended westward into the gold- and silver-rich lands of Colorado. There, tracklayers met the towering peaks of the Rocky Mountains—not exactly easy ground for railway construction. But the Denver & Rio Grande Western Railroad Company met the challenge with the slogan "Through the Rockies, not around them." By 1881, the company's railroad had reached the town of Durango, Colorado, near the New Mexico border. A year later, it expanded to the mining town of Silverton, Colorado. There, trains began transporting precious metals down from the mountains. They also carried adventurous passengers who enjoyed both the gorgeous views from the train and the ability to visit parts of the country they would otherwise never have seen.

In recent decades, railway preservationists in Colorado have led a tourism effort beginning with the restoration of the "Painted Train," a gold and black sightseeing train on the Durango & Silverton Narrow Gauge line. A glass-topped car called the "Silver Vista" was also introduced to provide tourists with amazing views of the western scenery. Today, people still take this famous train route through the scenic San Juan range of the Rockies, as well as many other scenic railways throughout the United States.

PLAN

Objective
Discover how trains supported economic opportunities and tourism.

Critical Thinking Skills for Lesson 1.2
• Analyze Visuals

• Make Connections

• Make Inferences

• Compare and Contrast

Essential Question for Chapter 19
How did the Industrial Age transform America?
Railroads serviced the mining industry in the mountains of the West and Southwest and spurred tourism. Lesson 1.2 explores the connection between mining and scenic railways in the United States.

Background for the Teacher
William Jackson Palmer, founder of the Denver & Rio Grande Western Railroad Company, originally planned to extend his railroad to Mexico City to support mining operations there. Competition with the Santa Fe Railway foiled that plan. Palmer focused instead on a railway system through mountainous areas of Colorado, New Mexico, and Utah. To accomplish the difficult task of building in a rough terrain, Palmer used narrow three-foot tracks, rather than the standard wide gauge. The narrow gauge was cheaper and faster to build, and it could handle the sharp turns and steep slopes through the mountains. Palmer promoted his railroad as the "Scenic Line of the World," taking passengers on a breathtaking journey past the steep cliffs, powerful waterfalls, and icy Gunnison River of the Black Canyon in western Colorado.

History Notebook
Encourage students to complete the American Places page for Chapter 19 in their History Notebooks as they read.

Preview Using Visuals

Direct students' attention to the photo of the Georgetown Loop Railroad train. **ASK:** Why is this photo a good example of a scenic railway? *(Answers will vary. Possible response: The train is traveling through a beautiful mountain landscape. People are seated in open observation cars so they can enjoy the view.)* Ask students to share experiences they have had on scenic railways or passenger trains, including sights they enjoyed.

TEACH
Guided Discussion

1. **Make Inferences** Why was routing the Denver & Rio Grande Railroad around the Rockies not an option for the railroad company? *(Possible response: The railroad company made its money in part by transporting precious metals down from the mountains, so the tracks needed to run through the Rockies. The location of the tracks also benefited the tourist side of the business.)*

2. **Compare and Contrast** What difference is there between the function of the scenic railways in the past and their function today? *(Answers will vary. Possible response: In the late 1800s, the railways served a dual purpose by carrying freight to and from mining towns and by enabling tourists to enjoy the Rocky Mountains. Today, the scenic railways are used solely as tourist attractions.)*

American Places

The Georgetown Loop Railroad train featured in the photo is traveling through the Georgetown Loop Historic Mining & Railroad Park located west of Denver, Colorado. The narrow-gauge railroad was originally completed in 1884 to connect the mining towns of Georgetown and Silver Plume. Although the towns were only about two miles apart, more than four miles of track was needed to accommodate the mountainous terrain between them. From the 1880s to the early 1900s, Georgetown and the Georgetown Loop were popular tourist destinations. The Colorado Historical Society began restoration of the railroad in 1973, and it is once again a tourist attraction as part of the Georgetown-Silver Plume National Historic Landmark District.

Active Options

On Your Feet: I See, I Read, And So On a large sheet of chart paper or a whiteboard, create a chart like the one below. As a class, reexamine the photograph of the train. Have volunteers describe something they observe in the photo and something they have read to draw conclusions about laying tracks or riding trains in the Rockies. Record their observations on the chart.

I See	I Read	And So

NG Learning Framework: Research Narrow-Gauge Track

ATTITUDE Curiosity

SKILL Problem-Solving

Instruct students to work in groups to research the characteristics of narrow-gauge track and how it relates to the geography of where it was used. Ask students to write a conclusion about the economic and engineering advantages of using narrow-gauge track and to share it with the class. Encourage students to use a visual, such as a diagram or photograph, to illustrate their conclusions.

Striving Readers

Write About It Tell students to imagine that they are tourists traveling on a scenic railway through the Rockies in the late 1800s. Have them write a diary entry describing this experience. Encourage them to mention geographic details that they would see and the look and feel of the train and tracks. As volunteers share their paragraphs with the class, tell students to notice common elements in the descriptions.

Gifted & Talented

Create an Advertisement Invite students to research one of the scenic railways that exist today in the West or Southwest, such as the Durango & Silverton Narrow Gauge Railroad or the Georgetown Loop Railroad. Instruct students to use their research to create a poster, brochure, or video advertising the railway. Encourage students to use descriptive language and geographic details to attract prospective tourists. Work with students to create a format for sharing their creations with the class.

See the Chapter Planner for more strategies for differentiation.

CRITICAL VIEWING Answers will vary. Possible response: In order to keep routes as short as possible, tracklayers had to go through, not around, mountains. Doing so required laying tracks along the sides of mountains, through tunnels, and over ravines and canyons.

We use electric lights and telephones every day, so it is easy to take both inventions for granted. Thanks to the clever ideas of inventors of the late 1800s, we enjoy bright lights and speedy communication.

MAIN IDEA In the late 1800s, innovations in industries and technologies played important roles in the continued development of the Industrial Age.

NEW INDUSTRIES, NEW INVENTIONS

Railroads were the nation's first big business, but they weren't the only one. Other major industries emerged in the late 1800s that would change the ways Americans lived and worked.

Building railroads requires **steel**, a hard metal made from a mixture of iron and carbon. Railroad companies needed a lot of steel to make railroad tracks, locomotives, and train cars. And they needed it fast. Unfortunately, making steel was expensive and time-consuming. How could steel factories meet the demand? The answer came in the 1870s when improvements were made to a new technique, the **Bessemer process**. The process involved blowing air into molten iron to remove impurities. The result was a stronger metal that took only a half hour to produce. The Bessemer process made mass production of steel possible.

Another revolutionary development in the 1870s was made possible when **Thomas Alva Edison** invented the first reliable electric lights for home use. Within just five years of their debut, electric light bulbs lit 500 homes in New York City. When word about Edison's invention spread, many more people wanted electric lights installed in their homes. But that caused a problem. The lights relied on an electric current that lost power when it traveled from its source to people's homes. A former colleague of Edison's, Nikola Tesla, developed a system for delivering electric power using an alternating current. Alternating current, or AC, electric power could travel longer distances than the direct current, or DC, power Edison and his team had developed. Tesla sold his patent to industrialist George Westinghouse, who quickly embraced and marketed Tesla's new and improved method.

Reliable lights were not Edison's only electric invention. As a young man, Edison invented the electrographic vote recorder. The recorder allowed legislators in Congress to cast their votes electronically instead of voting by voice. Edison also invented the electric pen, which created a stencil as the person wrote. The writer could then use the stencil and ink to make copies of a document.

For his inventions, Edison received 1,093 U.S. **patents**, or exclusive rights granted to inventors. As an entrepreneur, he marketed his inventions to the public and started various manufacturing companies to make and sell devices based on his ideas.

RAPID COMMUNICATION

Other inventions also led to the development of new businesses and an expanding economy. The sewing machine, the refrigerated freight car, and inexpensive paper made from wood pulp were just a few of the inventions that grew into big businesses such as sewing machine manufacturers and paper goods companies. The rise of these businesses would make offices and factories common workplaces.

Edison's Filament Lamp
In 1879, Edison came up with a design for a light bulb that wouldn't burn out instantly. A longer-lasting bulb made lamps like this one more practical for daily use in American homes.

In 1868, **Christopher Sholes** invented the typewriter, a printing machine similar to a computer keyboard. The typewriter allowed people to produce written communication quickly. The need for easily readable notes and the ability to make copies became more important as other industries rapidly developed and expanded.

Eight years after the typewriter appeared, **Alexander Graham Bell** spoke the first words transmitted over a telephone to his assistant: "Mr. Watson—come here—I want to see you." Bell demonstrated his new invention that same year at the Centennial Exposition in Philadelphia. He then joined two investors, Gardiner C. Hubbard and Thomas Sanders, to form the Bell Telephone Company, which expanded rapidly because of Americans' high demand for telephones. Bell's invention has evolved into the cell phones and smartphones we use today. Alexander Graham Bell would become the first president of the National Geographic Society in 1898.

The First Flight
On December 17, 1903, after years of collecting data and building and testing their invention, the Wright brothers attempted the first powered airplane flight near Kitty Hawk, North Carolina. While Orville piloted, Wilbur ran alongside the plane to keep it steady. The first flight lasted just 12 seconds, but by the end of the day, another flight lasted almost a minute. Winter weather didn't allow more flights until the spring, but the Wright brothers knew they had built something that would change the world.

HISTORICAL THINKING

1. **READING CHECK** How did electric power transform American society?

2. **MAKE INFERENCES** In what ways do you think both telephones and typewriters helped make office work faster and more efficient?

3. **ANALYZE CAUSE AND EFFECT** What effect did the Bessemer process have on the steel industry?

PLAN

Objective
Analyze how inventions improved the quality of life and work for Americans in the late 1800s.

Critical Thinking Skills for Lesson 1.3
- Identify Main Ideas and Details
- Monitor Comprehension
- Make Inferences
- Analyze Cause and Effect
- Compare and Contrast

Essential Question for Chapter 19
How did the Industrial Age transform America?
Inventions such as electric lights and the telephone changed the way that many Americans lived and worked. Lesson 1.3 presents some of the major inventors and inventions of the late 1800s.

Background for the Teacher
Thomas Edison waged a very public battle against George Westinghouse for control of the electric power market. Their "War of Currents" centered on the use of direct current (DC), which Edison used in his devices and generators, and alternating current (AC), which Westinghouse used. Heavily invested in DC and convinced that AC was dangerous, Edison launched lawsuits, publicity stunts, and newspaper attacks against Westinghouse. He even tried to persuade the state of New York to use AC to execute criminals and referred to the process as "Westinghouse-style."

In the end, Westinghouse's AC current was deemed more practical since AC generators could deliver power over longer distances and thus service more customers. Confirmation of that choice came when Westinghouse won the contract to provide electric lights for the 1893 World's Columbian Exposition held in Chicago.

Create a "Top Ten" Tech List

Have students make a "Top Ten" list of their favorite technological inventions. Ask them to consider how each invention meets their needs and how their lives might be different without it. Invite volunteers to name inventions from their lists and discuss their reasons. Tell students that Lesson 1.3 discusses some inventions that transformed people's lives in the late 1800s.

TEACH

Guided Discussion

1. **Compare and Contrast** Why can both Thomas Edison and Alexander Graham Bell be considered entrepreneurs as well as inventors? *(Possible response: Edison patented his inventions, marketed them to the public, and started various manufacturing companies to make and sell his devices. Similarly, Bell formed the Bell Telephone Company to provide telephone service to customers.)*

2. **Make Inferences** Why might inexpensive paper and refrigerated freight cars have been important inventions in the late 1800s? *(Answers will vary. Possible response: As the number of businesses and factories expanded, the need for copies of important documents increased. Cheap paper would keep costs down. With farming, ranching, and meat processing moving westward, having refrigerated freight cars to move meat and vegetables to distant markets would be important.)*

More Information

Alexander Graham Bell With an almost completely deaf mother and a father and grandfather who taught elocution, Alexander Graham Bell grew up in a family that shaped his interest in communication. His father focused specifically on teaching the deaf. As a young man, Bell also taught and helped deaf students learn to speak. In his spare time, he worked on various inventions, including developing a harmonic telegraph that could send multiple sounds over a wire at the same time. Bell's work on the harmonic telegraph convinced him that human speech could be transmitted over a wire, leading to his invention of the telephone.

Active Options

On Your Feet: Rotating Discussion Assign each student to one of four corners in the room, creating four teams. Instruct members of each team to create a list of questions about the inventors and inventions discussed in the lesson. Start the discussion by tossing a bean bag or other soft object to Team A and asking a question. When Team A answers the question, have one of its members toss the bean bag to another team while asking one of Team A's prepared questions. Continue until teams have exhausted their questions or as time allows.

NG Learning Framework: Create a Virtual Museum Exhibit

SKILLS Collaboration, Communication

KNOWLEDGE New Frontiers

Arrange students in groups and explain that they will construct a virtual museum exhibit on inventions and inventors of the late 1800s. Assign groups individual inventors, such as Edison, Westinghouse, Sholes, Bell, or the Wright brothers, or specific inventions, such as electric lights, electric generator, sewing machine, inexpensive paper, refrigerated freight car, typewriter, or telephone. Instruct groups to provide information about the individual inventors, describe the inventions, and explain the significance of the new technologies on people and the nation's economy. Encourage groups to include photos or drawings that enhance their presentation. Allow time for groups to share their entries.

English Language Learners

Use a Main Idea Cluster Guide students to use a Main Idea Cluster to aid comprehension. Pair students at the **Emerging** level with English-proficient students and tell them to take turns reading the lesson one paragraph at a time, pausing periodically to check their understanding. Suggest that students locate the main idea and supporting details and complete the cluster together. Encourage student pairs to include at least four details per cluster.

Pre-AP

Research the Bessemer Process Point out that many people contributed over time to the development of the Bessemer process. Organize students into three groups and assign each group one of the following topics to research.

• people who helped to develop the process

• the science and technology behind the process

• impact of the process on the lives of Americans

Instruct groups to pool their research to develop a multimedia presentation explaining the three topics. Have students share their presentations with the class.

See the Chapter Planner for more strategies for differentiation.

HISTORICAL THINKING

ANSWERS

1. Thomas Edison's electric lights and George Westinghouse's electric generator brought reliable electric lighting and power into homes and businesses.

2. Possible response: Using telephones, workers could call other offices, suppliers, or customers instead of going in person or writing letters. Typewriters made it possible to write communications quickly in an easily readable format.

3. The Bessemer process produced strong steel in a short time, enabling factories to mass-produce it.

1.4 Growth of Big Business

In some ways, success breeds more success. For shrewd businessmen in the late 1800s, successful companies relied upon and increased the industrial expansion of the United States.

MAIN IDEA American industries grew in size and complexity in the late 19th and early 20th centuries, and a few of their leaders became wealthy.

STEEL AND OIL

As the nation expanded, industries that enabled that expansion grew as well. In order to operate, industries such as railroads and steel mills needed access to large sums of money. Owners asked other wealthy businessmen to invest money in their companies in exchange for a share of future earnings. As a result, groups of people, rather than an individual or a family, owned the business. A business in which a group of people owns shares in a large company and that acts as one entity is called a **corporation**.

One of the industrial giants of the late 19th century was **Andrew Carnegie**, who bought his first steel plant in 1875. His expanding business eventually became the Carnegie Steel Company. Carnegie cut the cost of producing steel by more than half, which forced many of his competitors out of business. In the 1890s, Carnegie Steel shifted to the open-hearth method of steel production, in which workers added scrap metal to the molten iron ore. The new process surpassed the Bessemer process in efficiency. Steel production doubled between 1890 and 1900 because of the new technique. As production increased, the price of steel dropped even lower. In 1901, Carnegie became the richest man in the world when he sold his company, which became U.S. Steel Corporation.

Opened in 1909, the Manhattan Bridge spans the East River between Manhattan and Brooklyn, New York. It stands just upriver from the iconic Brooklyn Bridge, which opened 26 years earlier.

Andrew Carnegie (left) and John D. Rockefeller (right) both believed in the importance and value of higher education. Carnegie founded what would eventually be named Carnegie Mellon University in Pittsburgh, and Rockefeller helped establish the University of Chicago.

Oil was another high-growth industry in the late 1800s. Before electricity was in every home, Americans depended on oil for heat and light. Industries needed oil to keep machinery running smoothly. Transporting oil was big business for railroads and steamship companies. In 1870, **John D. Rockefeller** founded the Standard Oil Company in Ohio. By the end of the decade, Rockefeller controlled about 90 percent of the country's oil-refining capacity and had assumed control of most of his competitors. In fact, he nearly achieved a monopoly on the industry.

In 1882, Standard Oil became a **trust**, or a group of corporations managed, but not directly owned, by a board, or a group of people. This distinction allowed Standard Oil to bypass state laws and keep its business methods private. As a trust, Rockefeller's business could own stock in other oil companies and operate in multiple states.

POWER AND WEALTH

Corporations, trusts, and other businesses thrived in the United States because of **capitalism**. Capitalism is an economic system in which private individuals or groups, as opposed to the government, own and profit from factories and farms. In the late 1800s, federal and state governments rarely interfered with how businesses made money. This economic policy called **laissez-faire** (leh-say FAIR) capitalism, allowed businesses to operate without much regulation. The phrase *laissez-faire* generally means "leave alone" in French. Leaving businesses alone might have been good for owners, but the lack of regulations and government oversight put workers at a disadvantage.

At the same time that companies and industries were growing larger and more powerful, the economy experienced several recessions, or periods of economic decline, and prolonged financial disruption. Intense **boom-and-bust cycles**, or periods of economic growth followed by sudden economic downturns, characterized the last decades of the 19th century. Boom-and-bust cycles had dramatic consequences on industries and individuals alike.

Though John D. Rockefeller and Andrew Carnegie were shrewd in business, they also believed in the Gospel of Wealth, or the idea that the very wealthy had a responsibility to share their wealth and help others. Both engaged in **philanthropy**, or the financial support of worthy causes.

During his lifetime, Rockefeller donated more than $500 million to various educational institutions, scientific and medical research, medical facilities, and international relief. Likewise, Carnegie established several philanthropic organizations and donated millions of dollars to education, scientific research, and international peace efforts. Carnegie also founded and funded more than 2,500 public libraries throughout the United States. By the end of his life, Carnegie had given away 90 percent of his wealth.

HISTORICAL THINKING

1. **READING CHECK** When and why did Andrew Carnegie and John Rockefeller become so powerful?

2. **DESCRIBE** How did the expansion of the nation depend on and encourage the growth of the steel and oil industries?

3. **IDENTIFY MAIN IDEAS AND DETAILS** What is laissez-faire capitalism, and why did it help industries grow in the late 19th century?

PLAN

Objective

Discuss how industrial leaders and laissez-faire policies shaped business in the late 1800s.

Critical Thinking Skills for Lesson 1.4

- Identify Main Ideas and Details
- Monitor Comprehension
- Describe
- Analyze Cause and Effect
- Summarize

Essential Question for Chapter 19

How did the Industrial Age transform America?
Corporations and new production methods spurred the growth of big business in the late 1800s. Lesson 1.4 explores the people and practices behind this growth.

Background for the Teacher

One of the main reasons Andrew Carnegie was able to undercut his competition in price and outperform them in profit and production was his willingness to innovate. Carnegie was an early practitioner of vertical integration, owning ore mines, steel mills, coal mines, and ships in order to control all aspects of steel production and delivery. He was the first in the United States to adopt the Bessemer process and innovated by controlling all of the steps in the process of making steel. He acquired mines to ensure that he had raw materials, boats to move ore on rivers, railroads to carry it to his mills, and a sales force to market his many products.

Financial Literacy

To extend their knowledge and understanding about the concepts in this lesson, refer students to the Financial Literacy handbook.

Preview Concepts

Write the word *laissez-faire* on the board. Tell students that it is a French term meaning "leave alone" and that under a laissez-faire economic system, businesses are allowed to operate with little government interference. **ASK:** Why might business leaders like the freedom to make their own rules? *(Answers will vary. Possible response: With such freedom, business leaders would be better able to respond to competition, control costs, react to market demands, and make more money.)* Tell students that in the late 1800s, some business leaders became wealthy and powerful by making their own rules.

TEACH

Guided Discussion

1. **Analyze Cause and Effect** What evidence is there that laissez-faire capitalism resulted in less competition in the oil industry? *(Possible response: Rockefeller controlled about 90 percent of the country's oil-refining capacity. He also controlled most of his competitors through trusts that enabled Standard Oil to own stock in other oil companies.)*

2. **Summarize** Why and how did Carnegie and Rockefeller use the wealth they accumulated to impact society in a positive way? *(Possible response: Both men believed in the Gospel of Wealth, which held that the very wealthy had a responsibility to use their wealth for the good of others. Toward this end, they donated money to education, scientific and medical research, and other causes. Carnegie eventually gave away 90 percent of his wealth, and Rockefeller donated more than $500 million.)*

More Information

J. Pierpont Morgan Industrial expansion and commerce in the later 1800s required large sums of money, so bankers became powerful players in the U.S. economy. Perhaps no banker was more powerful than J. Pierpont Morgan. Morgan's bank financed businesses and also lent money to the federal government during economic busts, such as the depression that followed the panic of 1893 and the stock market panic of 1907. In addition, Morgan reorganized the railroad industry and consolidated many businesses, including merging the Federal Steel Company with Carnegie Steel to form U.S. Steel. General Electric and the International Harvester Company are two other major companies he helped create through mergers.

Active Options

On Your Feet: Question and Answer Tell half the class to write True-False questions based on the lesson's information about big business in the late 1800s. Ask the other half to create answer cards, with "True" written on one side and "False" on the other. Ask the question-writing students to read their questions aloud. Instruct students in the second group to display the correct answer to each question. When discrepancies occur, review the question and discuss which answer is correct.

NG Learning Framework: Research Philanthropy

ATTITUDE Curiosity

SKILLS Collaboration, Communication

Arrange students in groups to learn more about the philanthropic efforts of Andrew Carnegie and John D. Rockefeller. Instruct groups to select a specific area of philanthropic interest, such as Carnegie's focus on public libraries or Rockefeller's interest in international relief, to research. Then have groups use their research to create and share a poster or multimedia presentation honoring the philanthropic efforts of these two giants of industry.

DIFFERENTIATE

Striving Readers

Summarize Place students in pairs and tell them to take turns reading the lesson aloud, one paragraph at a time. Encourage students to ask each other questions as they come across complex information. Then ask them to summarize the lesson by creating two Word Webs with *Carnegie* and *Rockefeller* in the center ovals. Ask students to complete each web with relevant information from the lesson.

Pre-AP

Research Business Strategies Tell students to research the roles of Andrew Carnegie, John D. Rockefeller, and investment banker J.P. Morgan in shaping laissez-faire capitalism in the late 1800s. Instruct students to focus on Carnegie's tactics, Rockefeller's trusts, and Morgan's mergers. Ask students to write short profiles of each person and share them with the class, perhaps in an interview format.

See the Chapter Planner for more strategies for differentiation.

HISTORICAL THINKING

ANSWERS

1. Carnegie's and Rockefeller's rise to power began in 1870, when Carnegie founded the Carnegie Steel Company and Rockefeller founded the Standard Oil Company. Carnegie pushed many of his competitors out of business, and Rockefeller took control of his competitors.

2. As the nation expanded, there was an increasing need for steel for railroads, bridges, and buildings, along with oil to provide light and heat and to run machinery. Business grew along with increased demand.

3. Laissez-faire capitalism is an economic system in which private individuals or groups operate their businesses with few government regulations. This policy allowed businesses in the late 1800s to make money and grow in practically any way they wished without interference from the government.

1.5 Mass Culture During the Gilded Age

Nowadays when people get bored, they can play games, read, or watch movies on their phones or computers. Turn-of-the-century Americans enjoyed reading, games, and shows, too—just not on electronic devices.

MAIN IDEA Americans enjoyed a variety of entertainments in the late 1800s, all of which helped to shape the American identity.

ALL THAT GLITTERS IS NOT GOLD

Big business in the United States expanded rapidly between 1870 and 1900, and those who profited from it became extremely rich. Some people believed these newly rich people were generous and moral in the public eye, but shrewd and greedy in private. Rockefeller donated millions of dollars to build schools and hospitals, but he earned that money by dominating his industry and avoiding business laws. Some people saw his philanthropy as a way to distract people from his immoral business tactics. Still, many people hoped to become similarly rich.

In 1873, authors **Mark Twain** and Charles Dudley Warner published *The Gilded Age*, a novel about the greed they believed was corrupting the country. "What is the chief end of man?—to get rich. In what way?—dishonestly if we can; honestly if we must," they lamented. Twain and Warner wrote about the underlying greed that was tarnishing the identity of the United States. They described the age as gilded because things that are gilded are covered in a thin layer of gold to make them appear more brilliant or luxurious. The name caught on, and the last three decades of the 19th century became known as the **Gilded Age.**

CULTURE AND ENTERTAINMENT

Twain and Warner's novel had the power to name a time period because of the development of **mass culture,** a culture that grows out of widespread access to media, music, art, and forms of entertainment. Americans were able to take advantage of this emerging mass culture

because they were more literate. More American children were attending elementary school, and the number of students enrolled in high school rose every year from 1889 to 1900. Growing industry played a role, too. As production processes became more efficient and less expensive, books, magazines, and newspapers became more widely available and affordable. Even those who could not afford to buy books or magazines could visit one of the Carnegie-funded libraries and borrow books.

Urbanization also contributed to the development of mass culture. Working-class youth especially enjoyed the opportunities cities provided. Young men and women living in cities experienced a new independence, both socially and financially. The social convention of dating emerged. Young people met in public spaces such as movie houses, amusement parks, and dance halls. Young men, who on balance earned more than young women, paid their dates' way.

Souvenirs from the World's Columbian Exposition included decorative spoons and dishes, coin purses, and engraved matchboxes like this one featuring the Ferris wheel.

Attending sporting events was another form of entertainment during the Gilded Age, and baseball was the most popular game of all. Cities responded to baseball's popularity by building large stadiums, including Fenway Park in Boston in 1912 and Ebbets Field in Brooklyn in 1913.

In 1893, the city of Chicago hosted the World's Columbian Exposition, to celebrate the 400-year anniversary of Columbus's arrival in the New World. Taking place within the context of rapid industrialization and an unpredictable economy—and only 28 years after the Civil War—this world's fair showcased the "progress of civilization," groundbreaking inventions, and the strength of American industry. One of the highlights for visitors was taking a ride on the world's first Ferris wheel. Purposely built taller than Paris's Eiffel Tower, the Ferris wheel rose 264 feet in the air and offered

a spectacular view of the many buildings of the exposition and the city itself.

Electricity was presented to Americans for the first time at the Chicago World's Fair. Thousands gathered to watch President Grover Cleveland light the fairgrounds with a press of a button.

CRITICAL VIEWING The World's Columbian Exposition of 1893, sometimes called the Chicago World's Fair, occupied 630 acres of the city. More than 27 million people from all over the world visited the exposition between May and October. International fairs like this one were wildly popular with visitors. They were fascinating cultural events as well as opportunities for host cities to establish a national presence. How are the city of Chicago and the World's Fair portrayed through details in this poster?

HISTORICAL THINKING

1. **READING CHECK** What was the Gilded Age?

2. **MAKE CONNECTIONS** How did rising literacy and more efficient production processes lead to the development of mass culture?

3. **IDENTIFY MAIN IDEAS AND DETAILS** What forms of entertainment did Americans enjoy during the Gilded Age?

PLAN

Objective

Learn how mass culture helped shape the American identity during the Gilded Age.

Critical Thinking Skills for Lesson 1.5

- Identify Main Ideas and Details
- Monitor Comprehension
- Make Connections
- Make Inferences

Essential Question for Chapter 19

How did the Industrial Age transform America?
Industrialization, urbanization, and increased literacy gave rise to a mass culture during the Gilded Age. Lesson 1.5 explores elements of this transformation.

Background for the Teacher

The World's Columbian Exposition had a mission beyond merely celebrating the strength of American industry. It was seen as a way to build a spirit of unity and optimism in American society. Chicago was a microcosm of the times. It was an economic and transportation center born of westward expansion, the railroad, and industrialization. It was a city that had experienced rapid population growth largely through a diverse array of immigrants and a place wracked by poverty that created a wide gap between the elites and the working class. Chicago won out over New York City as the site for the fair, and Chicago's leaders hoped that a successful fair would change many people's negative opinions of their city.

Discuss Mass Culture

As a class, discuss the definition of *mass culture*. **ASK:** What kinds of things influence our mass culture today? *(Answers will vary. Possible responses: television, movies, social media, print media, sports, music, fashions, advertising)* Tell students that this lesson explores mass culture during the last three decades of the 19th century.

TEACH

Guided Discussion

1. **Make Connections** How does the view that some people held of Rockefeller's philanthropy relate to the idea that "all that glitters is not gold"? *(Answers will vary. Possible response: The people who were critical of Rockefeller's philanthropy believed that his seeming generosity was meant to distract people from his suspicious business practices. That is similar in effect to covering a plaster figurine in gold paint to give the appearance of value even though the figurine is cheap plaster.)*

2. **Make Inferences** How might urbanization also have contributed to rising literacy rates? *(Answers will vary. Possible response: The availability of schools in cities and the increased need to be able to read and write to gain employment and navigate the city might have spurred school attendance.)*

More Information

World's Columbian Exposition The layout of the World's Columbian Exposition was designed to reinforce the message of a bright future built through commerce, industry, art, science, and technology. The main exhibit buildings—nicknamed the "White City" for their white plaster facades—were designed in a classical style and surrounded by a park-like setting. The grandeur of these buildings was juxtaposed with the bustling Midway, where exhibits from many countries were housed amid concession stands and amusements such as the Ferris wheel.

Active Options

On Your Feet: Hold a Panel Discussion Ask volunteers to stage a panel discussion about similarities and differences between mass culture during the Gilded Age and mass culture today. Suggest that panel members meet briefly to organize their topics. Then provide this overarching question to guide the discussion: How have technological advances influenced mass culture?

NG Learning Framework: Identify Exposition Technologies STEM

ATTITUDE Curiosity

KNOWLEDGE New Frontiers

Direct groups to research the main exhibits at the World's Columbian Exposition. Assign each group one of the following main exhibit buildings to research: Agriculture, Electricity, Machinery, Manufactures and Liberal Arts, Mines and Mining, and Transportation. Instruct students to find out what was considered modern or state of the art in 1893 based on the exhibits in each building. Ask groups to collaborate on a format for sharing their findings with the class.

DIFFERENTIATE

Inclusion

Use Supported Reading Assign pairs one paragraph to read aloud together. At the end of each paragraph, have them use the following sentence frames to tell what they do and do not understand:

- This paragraph is about _____.
- One detail that stood out to me is _____.
- (If applicable) The vocabulary word _____ means _____.
- One thing I would like to understand more clearly is _____.

Tell students to make sure they understand the content before moving on to the next paragraph.

Gifted & Talented

Write a Journal Entry Tell students to imagine that they are young adults in the 1890s who have recently moved to a city. Invite them to write a journal entry describing their impressions of the mass culture they have encountered in the city. Encourage students to research mass culture during the Gilded Age using library or online sources to support their journal entries. Ask students to share their journal entries in a reader's theater format.

See the Chapter Planner for more strategies for differentiation.

HISTORICAL THINKING

ANSWERS

1. The Gilded Age refers to the last three decades of the 19th century, named such for the excesses of wealth that obscured underlying greed and corruption.

2. More efficient production methods lowered the cost of mass-producing newspapers, books, and magazines, making them widely available and affordable for the increasing number of people who could read.

3. Popular forms of entertainment included sporting events such as baseball, movies, dancing, and amusement parks.

CRITICAL VIEWING Possible response: The poster depicts Chicago and the World's Columbian Exposition as beautiful places having ornate buildings, fountains, and wide avenues. The impression is one of cultural refinement and prosperity.

2.1 The New Immigrants

Moving to a different country to start a new life can be exciting, but it can be scary, too. For the millions of immigrants who came to the United States beginning in the late 19th century, it was both.

MAIN IDEA At the turn of the 19th century, millions of people from Europe and Asia moved to the United States.

ARRIVING IN A NEW LAND

Between 1870 and 1900, approximately 12 million people moved to the United States in search of new lives and better opportunities. Most came from countries in southern and eastern Europe and Asia, and from Mexico. In 1892, **Ellis Island** opened in New York, replacing Castle Garden as the main East Coast entry point to the United States. In 1907 alone, approximately 1.25 million immigrants entered through Ellis Island—more people than in any previous year.

The sheer number of people entering the United States strained the housing capacities of some cities. Quickly constructed apartment buildings called **tenements** were built to house immigrants and new city residents.

Southern and eastern European immigrants who came through Ellis Island were mainly Italian, Polish, Hungarian, Russian, and Czech. Many settled in New York City and worked in construction, building bridges and subway systems. Others worked in the shipping industry on the docks, or in the garment industry making clothes. Immigrants to midwestern cities such as Pittsburgh and Cleveland found work in steel mills. Coal mining in Pennsylvania and West Virginia drew many southern and eastern European immigrants.

Mining also drew immigrants to the West. People from Asia arrived on the West Coast, and they settled in California, Washington, and Oregon. Many Asian immigrants worked in agriculture and the logging, mining, railroad, and restaurant industries. People from China, Japan, Korea, India, and the Philippines arrived at different times and for different reasons. Some wanted to embrace new opportunities in the United States. Others wanted to escape poverty or break from oppressive social systems. Still others were **refugees**, or people who flee to another country to escape danger or persecution. Beginning in 1910, immigrants to the West Coast passed through **Angel Island**, located in the bay off the coast of San Francisco, California. Also in 1910, Mexican immigrants began to move to Texas, Arizona, and California where many worked in mining and agriculture.

BECOMING AMERICAN

Native-born Americans expected newly arrived immigrants to assimilate into American culture. Reformers in the late 19th century placed Native Americans in boarding schools and tried to force them to adopt new cultures and traditions. Similarly, some reformers believed that immigrants should "become American" by learning English and adopting American traditions.

Many immigrants wanted to Americanize. They learned English, adopted American holidays and culture, and prepared to become citizens. Others preferred to maintain ties with their home countries. Still others managed to incorporate facets of both worlds into their new American lives.

Immigrant children who entered public schools Americanized faster than their parents. At school, they socialized with native-born schoolmates and adopted American social customs. Most immigrants did not speak English, but children were placed in English-only classrooms. Some adjusted and learned the new language quickly, but others struggled with the language barrier.

CRITICAL VIEWING August Francis Sherman was the chief registry clerk at Ellis Island in the early 1900s. He photographed incoming immigrants, and in 1907, *National Geographic* magazine published some of them. In 2016, artist Jordan Lloyd colorized many of these photos digitally, including the six that appear below with the person's country of origin. Specialists reproduced historically accurate colors in order to bring to life the traditional clothing worn by immigrants who came through Ellis Island. What details do you notice in each of the photos that you might have missed if the photo were not colorized?

Ukraine | India | Italy

Guadeloupe Islands | Russian Empire | Algeria

Whether immigrants settled in the East, Midwest, or West, they established communities, religious organizations, and **mutual aid societies**, or groups that helped other immigrants. At the same time they became American, they introduced their own cultures and traditions to the United States. Today, the legacy of millions of immigrants who ventured to a new country is evident in many cities and communities across the nation, from street signs and restaurants to places of worship.

HISTORICAL THINKING

1. **READING CHECK** What industries did immigrants work in once they arrived in the United States?

2. **IDENTIFY MAIN IDEAS AND DETAILS** In the years between 1870 and 1910, who immigrated to the United States, and why?

3. **DRAW CONCLUSIONS** What impact did Americanization efforts have on immigrants?

PLAN

Objective
Describe experiences of immigrants to the United States in the late 1800s and early 1900s.

Critical Thinking Skills for Lesson 2.1
- Identify Main Ideas and Details
- Monitor Comprehension
- Draw Conclusions
- Analyze Cause and Effect
- Make Connections
- Analyze Visuals

Essential Question for Chapter 19
How did the Industrial Age transform America?
Industrialization created new factory jobs, drawing many immigrants to the United States. Lesson 2.1 discusses push and pull factors for immigrants in the late 19th and early 20th centuries and immigrants' experiences as new Americans.

Background for the Teacher
Immigrant education was an important issue in large cities in the late 1800s. In New York and Chicago, for instance, nearly four out of five school-age children had immigrant parents, and not all immigrant parents favored educating their children. For some, it was an economic choice between having their children work to help support the family or sending them to school. For others, it was a cultural issue, as parents who had farmed in Europe were unused to sending their children to school and often were uneducated themselves. Schools, for their part, often went beyond teaching the standard curriculum and added instruction for immigrant children on citizenship, dress, hygiene, diet, patriotism, and English language skills.

Thumbs Up, Thumbs Down

Ask students to volunteer reasons that might cause them to move from one country to another. List their reasons on the board. Then read the list aloud and have students give each reason a thumbs-up or a thumbs-down, depending on whether they would immigrate for that reason. Tell them that in Lesson 2.1, they will learn about the millions of immigrants who left their homelands and moved to the United States in the late 1800s and early 1900s.

Guided Discussion

1. **Analyze Cause and Effect** Why did immigrant children tend to Americanize faster than their parents? *(Answers will vary. Possible response: Children tended to enter public schools where instruction was in English. Exposure to English all day long would have sped their assimilation.)*

2. **Make Connections** In what ways is the influence of immigrants seen today? *(Answers will vary. Possible response: The influence can be seen in such things as street signs, restaurants, places of worship, and other aspects of American life, especially in cities.)*

Analyze Visuals

Ask students to take a few moments to study the photos of the six immigrants. **ASK:** What do you find striking about the photos? Do you notice similarities or contrasting features? Explain using details from the photos. *(Answers will vary. Possible responses: All of the immigrants are posed in a dignified manner, sitting straight with their clothing neatly arranged. Each has a solemn expression that suggests the seriousness of the occasion. The photographer used different poses and photographed the man from India and the woman from Guadeloupe Islands in profile, possibly to highlight their features.)*

Active Options

Active History: Map Countries of Origin Extend the lesson by using either the PDF or Whiteboard version of the activity. These activities take a deeper look at a topic from, or related to, the lesson. Explore the activities as a class, turn them into group assignments, or even assign them individually.

NG Learning Framework: Explore Asian-American Contributions

ATTITUDES Curiosity, Empowerment

KNOWLEDGE Our Human Story

Ask students to research an Asian American who immigrated to the United States between the end of the 19th and beginning of the 20th centuries and who has made a contribution to American society. You may wish to provide these names or let students find a biographical subject on their own: Sessue Hayakawa, I.M. Pei, Chien-Shiung Wu, Dalip Sing Saund. Instruct students to write a biographical profile about their subject, including a picture of the person and, when possible, a quotation. Tell students to include why the person immigrated to the United States and what experiences he or she had. Encourage students to post their biographies on a "biography wall" in the classroom.

Striving Readers

Use Examples Define and review some of the words used in this lesson, using context clues or dictionaries if necessary: *persecution, oppressive, assimilate, socialized,* and *ventured.* For each word, provide an example that students will find familiar. Then ask students to use each word in a sentence.

English Language Learners

Pose and Answer Questions Pair students at the **Emerging** level with students at the **Expanding** or **Bridging** levels and have students read the lesson together. Tell them to pause after each paragraph and ask each other *who, what, where, when,* or *why* questions about what they have just read. Suggest that students use a 5Ws Chart to help organize their questions and answers.

See the Chapter Planner for more strategies for differentiation.

ANSWERS

1. In general, immigrants who settled in New York City worked in construction, shipping, and garment industries. Immigrants in the Midwest worked in steel mills and mining. Immigrants in the West worked in agriculture, logging, mining, railroad, and restaurant industries. Mexican immigrants in the Southwest often worked in mining and agriculture.

2. Immigrants came from southern and eastern Europe, Asia, and Mexico. They emigrated for various reasons: to escape persecution, poverty, or oppressive social systems or to take advantage of new opportunities in the United States.

3. Many immigrants learned English, adopted American holidays and culture, and prepared to become citizens. Others incorporated facets of their homelands into their new lives.

CRITICAL VIEWING Possible response: Without color it would be difficult to appreciate the richness and depth of details in the beaded necklaces and piecework vest and shirt of the Ukrainian and Russian clothing, the ornately embroidered design on the Indian hat, and intricate folding of the fabric in the hat from the Guadeloupe Islands and turban from Algeria.

2.2 Tenement Museum New York City

The Lower East Side Tenement Museum in Manhattan depicts life in the gritty housing available to the working poor in the late 1800s and early 1900s. The museum itself is housed inside a five-story brick tenement built in 1863 for the working class immigrants entering New York. Tenements were often overcrowded and unsanitary. This particular building had 20 apartments that housed anywhere from 77 to 111 people at any given time. The museum features apartments restored to show visitors how German, Irish, Italian, and eastern European immigrant families may have lived. What do the images below tell you about the lives of immigrants?

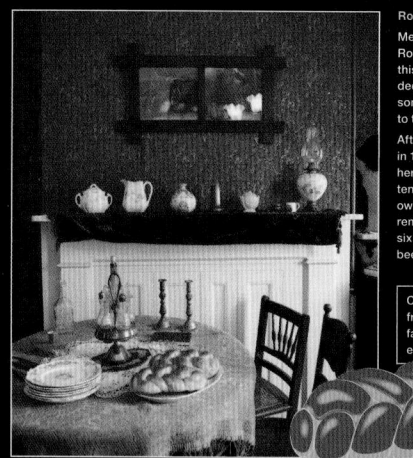

Rogarshevsky Family Parlor

Members of the large Lithuanian Rogarshevsky family moved in and out of this tenement on Orchard Street for three decades. They were part of a group of some 250,000 Lithuanians who immigrated to the United States during the early 1900s.

After the death of her husband, Abraham, in 1918, Fannie Rogarshevsky supported her family by working as a janitor for the tenement. She was known for keeping her own apartment immaculately clean. Fannie remained in this apartment until 1941, six years after the building had officially been closed.

> Challah is a type of bread made from braided dough. Jewish families like the Rogarshevskys eat challah on religious holidays.

Levine Family Parlor

The Levine family emigrated from what is now Poland in 1890. Hundreds of thousands of Poles had moved into the United States seeking better employment opportunities and safety from political unrest. The Levines set up a dress shop in their parlor and sewed garments for a larger company. After paying their employees, the Levines were left to survive on 16 dollars a week.

> Why do you think this sewing machine was placed next to the only window?

Confino Family Kitchen

The Confino family originally lived in the city of Kastoria in present-day Greece. In 1910, when they learned their teenage son Joseph could be drafted into the army, they chose to move to the United States. Ten Confinos lived in this small apartment for three years until they moved to East Harlem with other members of their Jewish community.

> Rachel Confino and her daughters scrubbed their dirty laundry in a large sink using a wooden washboard.

Baldizzi Family Kitchen

Italians Adolpho and Rosaria Baldizzi raised their two children in this apartment. They had emigrated from Palermo, Sicily, in 1923 along with other southern Italians who came to America seeking jobs. Although they entered the country illegally, they later became citizens.

Rosaria spent a lot of time in this kitchen, caring for her family. With the radio blaring in the background, she cooked, cleaned, and joked with Adolpho and the kids. A popular figure in the neighborhood, Rosaria returned to the Lower East Side to socialize and shop even after the family was evicted from this tenement when the building closed in 1935.

> Rosaria Baldizzi worked in a garment factory and likely used her sewing skills at home, too. Which items in this photograph might Rosaria have made herself?

632 CHAPTER 19

Industrialization and Immigration 633

PLAN

Objective
Identify artifacts relating to life in a New York City tenement in the late 1800s and early 1900s.

Critical Thinking Skills for Lesson 2.2
- Make Connections
- Analyze Visuals
- Describe
- Make Inferences

Essential Question for Chapter 19
How did the Industrial Age transform America?
Millions of European immigrants entered the United States through New York City in the late 1800s and early 1900s, and many of them stayed and lived in tenements there. Lesson 2.2 explores four tenement apartments that have been preserved as a New York City museum.

Background for the Teacher
Ruth Abram and Anita Jacobson founded the Tenement Museum to honor America's immigrants. The museum is housed in a former tenement at 97 Orchard Street, part of Manhattan's Lower East Side. This tenement, in which some 7,000 immigrants had lived, was closed in 1935. The founders conducted extensive research in order to accurately portray immigrant life in the restored apartments. The first restored apartment, home to the Gumpertz family in 1878, was opened to the public in 1992. In addition to the apartment tours, the museum offers guided walking tours of the surrounding neighborhood to help visitors understand the immigrant experience.

History Notebook
Encourage students to complete the Curating History page for Chapter 19 in their History Notebooks as they read.

INTRODUCE & ENGAGE

Explore Life Histories Through Objects

Remind students that examining objects is one way that historians understand the past. Direct students' attention to the photo of the Levine family parlor. **ASK:** What can you infer about the family's life from the objects in the photo? *(Answers will vary. Possible responses: The calendar suggests that the Levines were living in New York City in 1897, and, based on the sewing machine, someone in the household made garments. The apartment probably didn't have electricity because the sewing machine is operated by a pedal and the lamp uses oil for fuel.)* Tell students that they will explore the lives of four immigrant families through studying artifacts.

TEACH

Guided Discussion

1. **Describe** How did the Confino family do its laundry? *(The large bucket under the sink suggests the family had to carry water to the sink where they used a washboard to scrub the items. Then they hung the washed items to dry on a line over the sink.)*

2. **Make Inferences** Compare the photographs of the Rogarshevsky family parlor and the Baldizzi family kitchen. What can you infer about the economic circumstances of the two families? *(Answers will vary. Possible response: The Rogarshevskys seem to have been better off economically than the Baldizzis. The Rogarshevsky's parlor appears to be in better condition and the furnishings are a better quality than those in the Baldizzi family kitchen. Maybe the Rogarshevsky family could afford better things because it was larger and had more breadwinners.)*

🏛 Curating History

The Tenement Museum's website is a useful resource for learning more about the immigrant experience. Access the website and guide students to the virtual tours of the Levine, Confino, Rogarshevsky, and Baldizzi apartments. As a class, look at the Levine front room, read the caption, and listen to the audio to learn about the family. Encourage students to explore other rooms in the apartment and to point out details, ask questions, or make speculations about what they hear and see. Then ask groups of students to explore one of the other three apartments on their own and present their observations to the class.

Active Options

On Your Feet: Sort the Artifacts Arrange students in teams of four or five to examine the museum's online virtual tour of one of the apartments featured in this lesson. Instruct teams to use the details they see to complete two Concept Clusters. In one cluster, have students identify kitchen items. In the other, have them identify a different class or genre of artifacts to be determined by the team. When teams are finished, they can share their Concept Clusters with the class and note details that most of the teams identified.

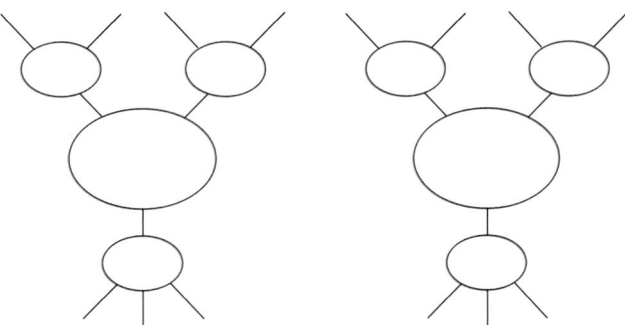

DIFFERENTIATE

Inclusion

Describe Details in Photos Pair students who are visually impaired with students who are not. Ask the latter to describe the details in each photo and answer any questions their partner might have. Then have the pairs of students work together to answer the questions in the text.

Gifted & Talented

Synthesize Sources Have students locate an excerpt from Anzia Yezierska's 1925 novel *Bread Givers*, which focuses on a Jewish immigrant family. Then have them use the Tenement Museum website to select information about immigrant life on the Lower East Side of New York during the same time period. Instruct students to analyze the relationship between how the novel and the website portray the same topic. Have students share their syntheses with the class.

See the Chapter Planner for more strategies for differentiation.

CURATING HISTORY

Answers will vary. Possible response: Immigrants lived in cramped quarters. Rooms often had to serve double duty, such as turning the parlor into a workspace or doing laundry in the kitchen.

LEVINE FAMILY PARLOR

The window would have provided natural light for the person using the sewing machine. When opened, the window would have provided ventilation as well.

BALDIZZI FAMILY KITCHEN

Rosaria might have made the towels, apron, ironing board cover, and quilt on the floor.

2.3 Cities Grow Rapidly

What do you think of when you hear the word *city*? Crowds of people? Traffic jams? In the late 19th and early 20th centuries, American cities were just starting to grow into the bustling places we know today.

> **MAIN IDEA** New methods of transportation and construction transformed American cities, and reformers addressed the challenges of urban poverty.

URBAN LIFE: PROS AND CONS

In the late 19th and early 20th centuries, the rapid and widespread growth of industries such as railroads and steel mills led to the growth of American cities. Economic, industrial, and population patterns shifted from rural areas to cities, a process known as **urbanization**. Rural migrants, including African Americans from the South, and immigrants moved to cities in search of new opportunities.

Beginning in the 1880s, **streetcars** became the main form of transportation in American cities. Streetcars could carry many passengers at once, and they ran on rails, like trains. Some ran directly on rails embedded in the streets. Others were elevated above street level or moved underground as subways. Many cities developed streetcar systems, including Boston, San Francisco, Chicago, and New York.

The shift from walking or riding in a horse-drawn carriage to other forms of transportation allowed **suburbs**, areas on the edges of cities made up mostly of residences, to develop. Suburbs developed along rail lines extending far past the growing city centers. Wealthy people moved away from the crowded cities to the nearby countryside where they could build more spacious homes. Railroad terminals in both cities and suburbs made transportation between them quick, easy, and convenient.

Cities were exciting places in which to live and work, but they were also filled with a range of problems. Corruption in big city governments was an accepted practice and **political machines**,

or agreed-upon, exclusive power structures, were in charge. City officials bribed politicians, contractors, and voters, and these arrangements powered the machines. In cities such as Chicago and New York, political machines were efficient, if corrupt, ways by which mayors and political bosses managed their cities.

In New York City, William Magear Tweed, or "Boss Tweed," led a Democratic Party committee called **Tammany Hall.** Tweed secured city contracts for his supporters and associates to build New York's skyscrapers. In other words, if a person voted for one of Tweed's candidates, he would be more likely to get a well-paid job. Newspapers charged Tweed with corruption. Though the charges against Tweed eventually brought his political power to an end in 1873, political machines continued to operate.

Despite its corruption, Tammany Hall helped New York City's poor as well as immigrant populations. The contracts that Tweed awarded helped build roads and install sewers and gas lines. Impoverished parts of the city were overcrowded and had inadequate sanitation, and their residents were grateful for improvements.

CITIES AND REFORMERS

Help for people in need came from a variety of sources. Protestant ministers who had witnessed the suffering that accompanied poverty preached the gospel to promote social reforms as part of the **Social Gospel** movement. They advocated ending child labor, restricting work on Sundays, and providing disability insurance for workers injured on the job.

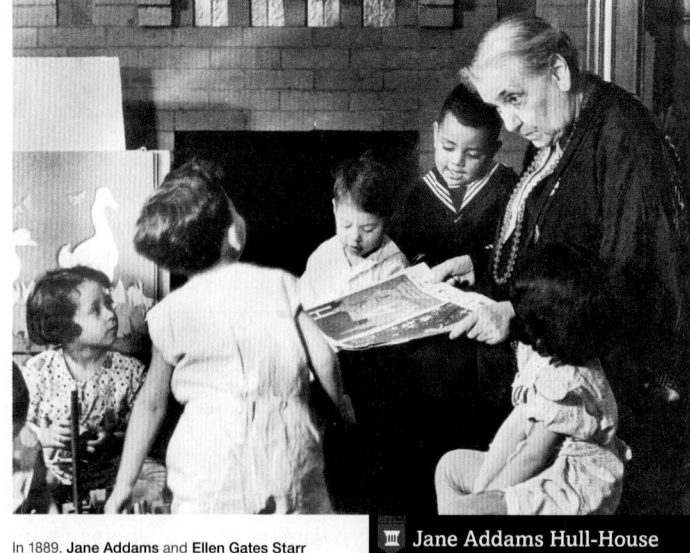

In 1889, **Jane Addams** and **Ellen Gates Starr** opened **Hull House** in a working-class Chicago neighborhood. It provided daycare, an art gallery, and libraries, among other services. Hull House was a **settlement house**, or a place that provided assistance to poor and immigrant residents. In its second year of operation, Hull House helped more than 2,000 people per week, including immigrants from Italy, Ireland, Germany, Russia, Poland, Bohemia, China, Sweden, and Norway. Because education was important to Addams and the other founders, Hull House offered arithmetic, sewing, job-hunting, drawing, and exercise classes. It also provided citizenship classes and language lessons in English, Italian, Latin, French, and German.

Addams, Starr, and others at Hull House also promoted laws that protected children and established social welfare programs. They persuaded Illinois leaders to pass child labor laws and to make public education mandatory for all children. Additionally, these committed reformers inspired the creation of the juvenile court system, so children did not have to be tried as adults.

🏛 Jane Addams Hull-House Museum, Chicago

One of the first programs Jane Addams set up at Hull House was a nursery school, where she often read to and taught young children. The care of children was important to her vision of a diverse, democratic community. To support that view, Hull House also established a kindergarten and an early version of a formal playground, where instructors engaged children in games.

HISTORICAL THINKING

1. **READING CHECK** What structural changes did cities undergo in the late 1800s?

2. **MAKE GENERALIZATIONS** How did Tammany Hall demonstrate the pros and cons of political machines?

3. **IDENTIFY MAIN IDEAS AND DETAILS** What were some of the ways in which different groups tried to address urban poverty?

PLAN

Objective

Learn about the characteristics of cities and city life in the late 1800s and early 1900s.

Critical Thinking Skills for Lesson 2.3

- Identify Main Ideas and Details
- Monitor Comprehension
- Make Generalizations
- Analyze Cause and Effect
- Draw Conclusions

Essential Question for Chapter 19

How did the Industrial Age transform America?
Industrialization prompted a population shift from rural to urban areas, which led to the rapid growth of American cities. Lesson 2.3 focuses on city life in the late 19th and early 20th centuries.

Background for the Teacher

Jane Addams was inspired to build a settlement house in Chicago after visiting Toynbee Hall, a settlement house in London. She and Ellen Gates Starr began Hull House in an abandoned home (originally built by Charles G. Hull) at 800 South Halsted Street, on Chicago's Near West Side. With the addition of 12 new buildings, Hull House grew to cover half a city block. Several prominent social reformers lived and worked at Hull House, including Alice Hamilton, Sophonisba Breckinridge, Julia Lathrop, and Florence Kelley. These women studied the surrounding neighborhood to document conditions and determine the services needed. Their research prompted the creation of programs to address poor sanitation, unsafe working conditions, and other social problems.

INTRODUCE & ENGAGE

Create a Word Web

Create a Word Web like the one shown with the word *cities* in the center. Ask students to suggest words they associate with present-day big cities. Point out any suggestions that could also have described cities like New York and Chicago in the late 1800s and early 1900s. Tell students that this lesson will show how industrialization led to changes in cities and city life.

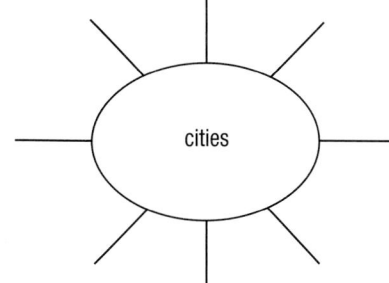

TEACH

Guided Discussion

1. **Analyze Cause and Effect** Why did industrial growth lead to the expansion of cities in the late 19th and early 20th centuries? *(Possible response: Growth in industries led to a shift in population from rural to urban because many people moved to cities to find employment in the expanding job market. Railroads and streetcars made it practical for people to live farther away from the city centers, leading to the growth of suburbs.)*

2. **Draw Conclusions** How did the work of Addams and Starr benefit people beyond the neighborhood that Hull House served? *(Possible response: They pushed for the establishment of social welfare programs that benefited all children, such as child labor laws, mandatory public education, and the creation of the first U.S. juvenile court.)*

Virtual Museum Visit

The Jane Addams Hull-House Museum, housed in the original Hull House and the former Residents' Dining Hall, honors the memory of Jane Addams and those who worked at Hull House. The museum's collection consists of more than 5,500 artifacts, including woven textiles and pottery produced at Hull House and oral histories from former residents and neighbors. Access the museum's website and locate the Urban Experience in Chicago online archive under Educational Materials, which includes photographs and primary sources. Have students work in groups to explore the exhibit and photographs. Ask each group to choose one artifact or photograph and report to the class on its significance to Hull House or to life in a big city at the turn of the century.

Active Options

On Your Feet: Fishbowl Position one half of the class in a close circle facing inward and the other half in a larger circle around them. Instruct students on the inside to discuss what they have learned about Hull House, including what actions Addams and Starr took to help the poor and immigrants. Instruct students on the outside to listen for new information and decide what might have been omitted from the discussion. Then tell groups to swap positions with the new inner circle discussing the same topic.

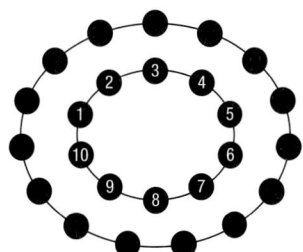

NG Learning Framework: Profile the Women of Hull House

ATTITUDE Curiosity

KNOWLEDGE Our Human Story

Invite students to learn more about the women who founded and worked at Hull House. Tell them to select one of the following women and use library and online sources to research her education, career, and work at Hull House and other institutions: Jane Addams, Ellen Gates Starr, Florence Kelley, Alice Hamilton, Julia Lathrop, Sophonisba Breckinridge, or Grace and Edith Abbott. Encourage students to prepare a biographical profile in the form of a poster and to include photos and other visuals. Allow time for students to present their profiles in class.

DIFFERENTIATE

English Language Learners ELD

Build Vocabulary Remind students at **All Proficiencies** that analyzing word parts can help them understand word meaning. Write *urbanization* and *suburb* on the board. Help students break the words into parts to determine their meaning. Write and discuss the following:

urbanization (noun)
urban = related to a city
-ization = act or process of making
urban + *-ization* = process of becoming a city

suburb (noun)
sub- = near
urbs = city
sub- + *urb* = near city

Pre-AP

Discuss Consequences of Growth Tell groups to use the online *Encyclopedia of Chicago* to locate Blanchard's maps of Chicago in 1862, 1871, 1888, and 1921, and to examine them in chronological order, focusing on changes in the city's physical features and growth over time, including the growth of suburbs. Ask groups to discuss urban and industrial growth and how they likely affected quantities of natural resources the city needed. Encourage students to comment on the location of observed natural resources and their distance from the areas that needed them. Have groups share the maps and their conclusions with the class.

See the Chapter Planner for more strategies for differentiation.

HISTORICAL THINKING

ANSWERS

1. Beginning in the 1880s, cities developed streetcar systems and suburbs began to develop.

2. Tammany Hall was corrupt and bought votes by providing jobs and awarding city contracts to supporters. At the same time, the political machine helped poor and immigrant populations by building roads, sewers, and gas lines in undeveloped areas and by helping people get jobs, assimilate, and become American citizens.

3. Protestant ministers promoted social reforms, such as ending child labor, as part of the Social Gospel movement. Jane Addams and Ellen Gates Starr opened Hull House to provide assistance to immigrants and the poor.

2.4 How Geology Defines Your Skyline

MAIN IDEA Skyscrapers transformed cities, and an understanding of geology made these buildings possible.

By Andrés Ruzo, **National Geographic Explorer**

When you think of **skyscrapers**, Chicago's Willis Tower or New York's Empire State Building probably come to mind. But the first modern skyscraper rose only 10 stories high—and it changed the way cities grew. This historic high-rise was the Home Insurance Building, built in Chicago in 1885. It towered over the wooden buildings of its day. It also looked vastly different. That's because it was supported by a steel frame.

In older buildings, the walls bore the weight of the structure. In this early skyscraper, the frame bore the weight of the walls. It was a revolutionary idea. And with its elevators and modern plumbing system, the Home Insurance Building set the standard for future skyscrapers.

It turned out the secret to building skyscrapers lay not in looking up, but in looking down. Way down. By the early 1900s, engineers had discovered that a skyscraper could be stabilized by anchoring its foundation deep into **bedrock**, the solid rock underlying loose soil. Builders set concrete pillars into the bedrock to support a skyscraper's steel frame and prevent the building from collapsing.

The skyscraper reached its height—literally—in 1931, when the Empire State Building rose 102 stories in the air. One of the reasons the building stands where it does is because the bedrock beneath it lies relatively close to the surface. This made it easier to lay the foundation. Although other factors may have been involved, including population distribution and the location of economic centers, most of New York's tallest buildings stand where the bedrock is shallow.

But sometimes a location's geology isn't so cooperative. In Chicago, a city that sits atop mostly swampy, shifting soil, the bedrock can be as much as 85 feet underground. In the late 1800s, engineers tried to float large buildings on a layer of clay, but this resulted in sinking, uneven floors.

Skyscrapers have come a long way since the Home Insurance Building, climbing from 10 stories to more than 100. We've soared into the sky thanks to improved technology and building methods and a solid understanding of what lies beneath our feet.

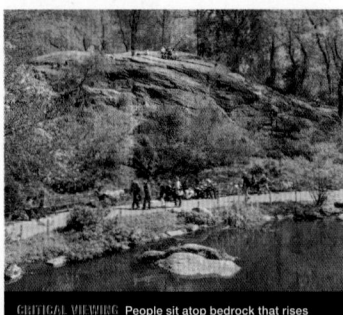

CRITICAL VIEWING People sit atop bedrock that rises high above the ground in New York City's Central Park. Do you think the area around the park is or is not suitable for skyscrapers? Why?

THINK LIKE A GEOLOGIST

1. **IDENTIFY MAIN IDEAS AND DETAILS** How does an area's geology have an impact on urban development?

2. **DRAW CONCLUSIONS** What geologic conclusions can you draw about an area of a city where there are no skyscrapers?

The Empire State Building's antenna spire sketches an exclamation point on New York's skyline. It was the tallest building in the world for 42 years. The diagram shows the concrete pillars anchored in bedrock to support the building's frame.

Labels in diagram: Basement, Column, Pillar cap, Soft soil, Pillar, Clay, Anchor bulb, Bedrock, Pillar, Anchor bulb, Bedrock

---

PLAN

Objective
Understand how bedrock provided stability for the building of skyscrapers.

Critical Thinking Skills for Lesson 2.4
- Identify Main Ideas and Details
- Monitor Comprehension
- Draw Conclusions
- Summarize
- Identify Problems and Solutions
- Analyze Visuals

Essential Question for Chapter 19

How did the Industrial Age transform America?
The use of a steel frame enabled engineers and architects to design and build skyscrapers, forever changing the skyline of American cities. Lesson 2.4 explains the importance of bedrock in making skyscrapers possible.

Background for the Teacher
Outcroppings of schist like the one in Central Park illustrate how close to the surface bedrock is in some areas in Manhattan. Around Times Square, for instance, the bedrock is only about 18 feet below the surface. In Greenwich Village, however, you would have to dig about 260 feet to reach bedrock. Not surprisingly, skyscrapers are common around Times Square and other places in Midtown and Lower Manhattan but are rare in Greenwich Village.

History Notebook
Encourage students to complete the American Gallery page for Chapter 19 in their History Notebooks as they read.

Think Like an Engineer

Have students consider how houses are constructed. **ASK:** How are houses typically anchored in the ground? *(Possible response: The wood frame is attached to a cement slab, cement block, or shallow concrete footings and pilings.)* Then have students speculate on reasons why this method would not work well for a skyscraper. *(Possible response: Skyscrapers are so tall and heavy that they might tip or settle unevenly.)* Tell students that they will learn how design and materials made skyscrapers possible in New York City.

TEACH   STEM

Guided Discussion

1. **Summarize** How did the skyscrapers differ from older buildings? *(Possible response: The skyscrapers were not only taller than older buildings but structurally different. In older buildings, the walls supported the structure; but in skyscrapers, the steel structure supported the building. In addition, skyscrapers had elevators and modern plumbing systems.)*

2. **Identify Problems and Solutions** What problem did engineers face in building skyscrapers in Chicago, and how did they try to solve it? *(Engineers needed to find a way to deal with Chicago's swampy, shifting soil and deep bedrock. They tried floating large buildings on a layer of clay, but the floors sank and became uneven.)*

Geology in History

Analyze Visuals Direct students' attention to the diagram of the Empire State Building's foundation. Point out the labels and have students identify the bedrock, clay, and soft soil. **ASK:** How is the basement attached to the pillars? *(Short columns attach the basement to the pillar caps that sit on top of the pillars.)* How are the pillars attached to the bedrock? *(by anchor bulbs)* Why do you think this system was effective? *(Answers will vary. Possible response: The pillars run the full width of the basement and are attached to the bedrock, providing not only a strong anchor but also additional support for the building.)*

Active Options

On Your Feet: Card Responses Tell half the class to write 10 True-False or Yes-No questions based on the lesson. Tell the other half to create answer cards, writing "True" or "Yes" on one side of the cards and "False" or "No" on the other side. Instruct students from the question group to take turns asking their questions. Tell students from the answer group to hold up their cards, showing the correct answer. Have students keep track of their correct answers and help clarify students' understanding when answers are incorrect.

AMERICAN **GALLERY**
ONLINE

The Skyscrapers of New York City Invite students to explore the American Gallery. Have them select one of the images and do additional research to learn more about it. Ask questions that will inspire additional inquiry about the chosen gallery image, such as: How tall is the building? Where is it located? Who designed it? When was it built? What was it used for? What else would you like to know about it?

Striving Readers

Preview Text Help students preview the lesson. Tell them to read the title, the Main Idea, photo and diagram captions, and questions. Then ask students to make notes about the kinds of information that they expect to find in the text. Have students read the lesson and then discuss with a partner what they learned. Encourage them to revise and add to their preview notes.

Gifted & Talented

Create a Multimedia Presentation Ask small groups of students to conduct research to find photographs of and statistics about early skyscrapers in Chicago and New York City. Tell students to use their findings to create and present a multimedia presentation on early skyscrapers.

See the Chapter Planner for more strategies for differentiation.

THINK LIKE A GEOLOGIST

ANSWERS

1. The location of bedrock is one way that an area's geology impacts urban development. The tallest buildings will be located where bedrock is close to the surface.

2. Answers will vary. Possible response: Where there are no skyscrapers, the bedrock may be so deep or uneven that anchoring a skyscraper there is not practical or economical.

CRITICAL VIEWING Possible responses: Yes; the outcropping indicates that there is bedrock close to the surface, making it a suitable area for anchoring skyscrapers. No; the area may have bedrock close to the surface, but it is uneven and may not be suitable.

2.5 Urban Poverty

How do you get people to pay attention to an uncomfortable problem? In the late 19th and early 20th centuries, photographers, social reformers, and novelists used their talents to highlight the terrible conditions the poor endured in American cities.

Jacob Riis was a Danish immigrant who arrived in the United States at age 21. Often poor and homeless, he bounced from job to job until he landed work as a police reporter in New York City. He taught himself photography and began to capture in words and photos what he saw around him. In 1890, Riis published *How the Other Half Lives*, a pioneering work of photojournalism about the urban poor in late-19th

century New York City. An immediate success, the book included vital statistics as well as Riis's photographs.

CRITICAL VIEWING Riis photographed these children huddled together for warmth in a window well on New York's Lower East Side. What impact do you think this Jacob Riis photo might have had on people who saw it in *How the Other Half Lives*?

DOCUMENT ONE

Primary Source: Nonfiction Book
from *How the Other Half Lives*, by Jacob Riis, 1890

The tenements of New York City were unhealthy places to live. They were also the focus of many reformers who wanted to improve living conditions for their residents. In this excerpt, Riis describes conditions in the city's tenements.

CONSTRUCTED RESPONSE Why do you think tenements might have been a cause of "despair" for public health officials?

To-day three-fourths of its people live in the tenements, and the nineteenth century drift of the population to the cities is sending ever-increasing multitudes to crowd them. The fifteen thousand tenant houses that were the despair of the sanitarian [public health official] in the past generation have swelled into thirty-seven thousand. We know now that there is no way out; that the "system" that was the evil offspring of public neglect and private greed has come to stay.

DOCUMENT TWO

Primary Source: Novel
from *The Jungle*, by Upton Sinclair, 1906

In his novel *The Jungle*, Upton Sinclair explores the terrible working conditions of Chicago's stockyards and the labor abuses of immigrant workers. In this excerpt, Sinclair describes the dismal conditions of the city, as seen by immigrants who have arrived to work in the stockyards.

CONSTRUCTED RESPONSE How did Chicago appear to new immigrant workers in Sinclair's novel?

Down every side street they could see . . . ugly and dirty little wooden buildings. Here and there would be a bridge crossing a filthy creek, with hard-baked mud shores and dingy sheds and docks along it . . . here and there would be a great factory, a dingy building with . . . immense volumes of smoke pouring from the chimneys, darkening the air above and making filthy the earth beneath. But after each of these interruptions, the desolate procession would begin again—the procession of dreary little buildings.

DOCUMENT THREE

Primary Source: Autobiography
from *Twenty Years at Hull-House*, by Jane Addams, 1910

Jane Addams wrote *Twenty Years at Hull-House* about her work and experiences at Hull House, the settlement house she founded in Chicago. In it, she details many of the challenges poor immigrants faced in Chicago.

CONSTRUCTED RESPONSE What point do you think Addams is trying to make about the circumstances poor immigrants face?

This piteous dependence of the poor . . . was made clear to us in an early experience with a peasant woman straight from the fields of Germany, whom we met during our first six months at Hull-House. Her four years in America had been spent in patiently carrying water up and down two flights of stairs, and in washing the heavy flannel suits of iron foundry workers. For this her pay had averaged thirty-five cents a day.

SYNTHESIZE & WRITE

1. **REVIEW** Review what you have learned about these depictions of urban poverty by Riis, Sinclair, and Addams.

2. **RECALL** On your own paper, write down what the three passages and photograph tell you about urban poverty in the late 19th and early 20th centuries.

3. **CONSTRUCT** Construct a topic sentence that answers this question: What challenges did the urban poor encounter during the late 19th and early 20th centuries?

4. **WRITE** Write a paragraph that supports the statement in Step 3 by using evidence from the passages and photograph.

PLAN

Objective
Synthesize information about urban poverty from primary source documents.

Critical Thinking Skills for Lesson 2.5
- Synthesize
- Identify Main Ideas and Details
- Draw Conclusions
- Evaluate

Essential Question for Chapter 19
How did the Industrial Age transform America?
Industrialization created wealth for some people, but many urban dwellers lived in poverty. Lesson 2.5 explores writings that highlight the grim consequences of urban poverty.

Background for the Teacher
Jacob Riis understood using the power of photography to persuade an audience, and he embraced the new technology of flash photography to enhance his work. He believed that people would respond with compassion or concern if they saw how the poor lived. He included his photographs in his books and lectures he gave to middle-class audiences across the country. The flash lamp enabled him to capture scenes in dark, windowless rooms of tenements and in back alleys where the desperately poor and homeless spent their nights.

Riis's photographs of the terrible conditions in police lodging houses caught the attention of Theodore Roosevelt, New York City's police commissioner, and led him to close the lodgings. Riis developed a friendship with Roosevelt that lasted through Roosevelt's governorship of New York and into his presidency. As a strong advocate of redesigning tenements and adding parks and playgrounds for children, Riis was able to inspire many housing reforms.

Prepare for the Document-Based Question

Before students start on the activity, briefly preview the three documents. Remind students that a constructed response requires full explanations in complete sentences. Emphasize that students should use what they have learned about the urban poor in the late 1800s and early 1900s in addition to the information in the documents.

Guided Discussion

1. **Identify Main Ideas and Details** What is Riis's main argument about tenements? *(Possible response: Riis's main point is that tenements, with their overcrowded and unsanitary conditions, are growing in number and are unlikely to change.)*

2. **Draw Conclusions** According to Jane Addams's autobiography, did the German woman's life improve after immigrating to the United States? *(Possible response: It seems that her life may have not improved significantly. She probably did backbreaking work in the fields, and she continued to perform difficult labor in Chicago.)*

Evaluate

After students have completed the Synthesize & Write activity, allow time for them to exchange paragraphs and read and comment on the work of their peers. Establish guidelines for comments prior to this activity so that feedback is constructive and encouraging in nature.

Active Options

On Your Feet: Use a Jigsaw Strategy Organize students into three "expert" groups. Have students from each group analyze one of the documents and summarize its main ideas in their own words. Then have the members of each group count off using the letters A, B, and C. Regroup students into three new groups so that each new group has at least one member from each expert group. Have students in the new groups take turns sharing the simplified summaries they came up with in their expert groups.

Inclusion

Work in Pairs Pair visually impaired students with students who can read the documents aloud to them. Ask the visually impaired students to tell what they learned about each document. You may also want to give students the option of recording their responses.

Pre-AP

Present an Oral Report Ask students to prepare and present oral reports on one of the three books featured in the lesson. Have students choose one or more excerpts to highlight and present to the class. Instruct students to focus on excerpts that illustrate the causes or consequences of urban poverty and that indicate the author's point of view. Encourage students to include multimedia elements in their reports to enhance interest and understanding.

See the Chapter Planner for more strategies for differentiation.

ANSWERS

1. Answers will vary.

2. Answers will vary.

3. Answers will vary. Possible response: The poor had to face crowded and unhealthy living conditions, depressing work environments, and hard work that paid little.

4. Answers will vary. Students' paragraphs should include their topic sentence from Step 3 and provide several details from the documents and photograph to support that statement.

CONSTRUCTED RESPONSE

Document 1: Possible response: The spread of disease would have been a cause of great concern for public health officials. Getting the landlords of the 37,000 crowded and unsanitary tenements to clean up the buildings was probably an impossible task.

Document 2: Possible response: To the immigrant workers, Chicago looked dirty, ugly, and depressing.

Document 3: Possible response: Addams is trying to make the point that even when the poor work very hard, they still struggle to get by because their pay is so low.

CRITICAL VIEWING Answers will vary. Possible response: The children in the photograph look miserable and cold. People who saw the photo were probably moved by the fact that young children were suffering.

Racism and Segregation

Imagine what it might be like to be denied the right to do something that most others are allowed to do. What if you had been denied based on your birthplace or the color of your skin?

MAIN IDEA African Americans and other people of color encountered different forms of prejudice across the United States.

PREJUDICE AND EXCLUSION

The challenges of industrialization, urbanization, and immigration resulted in serious problems, including poverty and discrimination, or the unfair treatment of people based on their age, race, gender, or religious affiliation. Discrimination was not limited to cities or to certain parts of the country. It affected many people in many different ways.

In California, many native-born Americans blamed Chinese immigrants for high rates of unemployment during the economic downturns of the 1870s. As a result, the federal government passed the **Chinese Exclusion Act** in 1882. The act prohibited Chinese immigration for a 10-year period. Only people who could prove they were not coming to find work

HINDUS DRIVEN OUT.

Citizens at Marysville, Cal., Attack Them—British Consul Informed.

MARYSVILLE, Cal., Jan. 27.—Twenty citizens of Live Oak Saturday night attacked two houses occupied by seventy Hindus who had been discharged from the Southern Pacific Company and ordered the Hindus to leave town.

The Hindus were driven to the edge of the town and told to travel. One went to Yuba City and swore to complaints charging the members of the mob with stealing $1,950. They also took the case to the British Consul at San Francisco.

Hostility toward immigrants was often direct and violent, as demonstrated in this *New York Times* article from 1908. The term *Hindu* was often used in reference to any immigrant from India, whether Hindu, Sikh, or Muslim.

could enter the country. Since proving this intention was difficult, very few Chinese immigrants entered the country after 1882.

Native-born Americans also discriminated against other Asian immigrants. On September 4, 1907, a mob of 500 white men in Bellingham, Washington, forced lumber mill workers from India—mostly Sikhs and Hindus—to leave town. Similar assaults against Indian immigrants occurred in Oregon and California.

Prejudice against Asian immigrants became law with the passage of the Immigration Act of 1917. This law banned broadly defined categories of people from entering the country, including "criminals and convicts," "political radicals," and "vagrants." It also introduced literacy tests for incoming immigrants and barred immigration from all Asian and Pacific Island countries, except for Japan and the Philippines.

Mexicans and Americans of Mexican descent also faced social and political barriers. The need for agricultural laborers brought thousands of Mexican immigrants to the West and Southwest. Though welcomed as workers, many became targets of violence.

LEGALIZED DISCRIMINATION

The economy of the South still lagged behind that of other states in the late 1800s. Generally more rural, the South hadn't industrialized as quickly either. Although African Americans gained civil rights after the Civil War, southern politicians quickly stripped these rights away through black codes and laws.

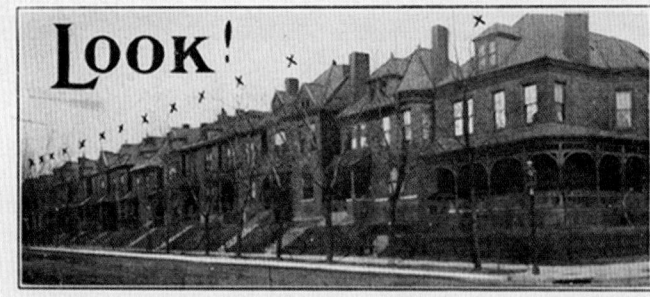

LOOK At These Homes NOW!

An entire block ruined by negro invasion. Every house marked "X" now occupied by negroes. ACTUAL PHOTOGRAPH OF 4300 WEST BELLE PLACE.

SAVE YOUR HOME! VOTE FOR SEGREGATION!

In 1915, a group of white residents in St. Louis, Missouri, distributed this postcard supporting a "reform" ordinance. The legislation, which passed in 1916, prevented people of one race from buying homes in neighborhoods occupied by more than 75 percent of another race. St. Louis became the first northern city to impose racial segregation in housing, and other cities soon followed.

Some of these laws were called **Jim Crow laws**. "Jim Crow" was a derogatory name some whites used toward African-American men. Jim Crow laws varied from state to state. Many states prohibited African Americans and whites from marrying each other, as well as from using the same restrooms, telephone booths, libraries, hospitals, barbers, parks, classrooms, and even cemeteries. Whites used the legalized segregation enforced by Jim Crow laws to establish and maintain economic, social, and political power.

For decades, the Ku Klux Klan had threatened and terrorized African Americans throughout the South. In the 1890s, the Klan increased its activities, partly in response to a populist movement to unite African Americans and poor whites against large landowners, mill owners, and the conservative rulers of the South. Klan members burned large crosses in front of people's homes and lynched African Americans, usually without fear of arrest or conviction.

During the late 19th and early 20th centuries, many southern African Americans moved to northern cities such as New York, Chicago, and St. Louis. Discrimination, poverty, and segregation were the push factors that prompted many to move north. Job opportunities and the chance to start new lives were powerful pull factors.

However, leaving the South did not mean African Americans left discrimination and segregation behind. Northern, white real estate agents and landlords gave preference to whites and enforced racial divisions by refusing to sell or rent to African Americans in primarily white neighborhoods. The North, too, was a racially divided society.

HISTORICAL THINKING

1. **READING CHECK** How did state and federal governments discriminate against different groups of people during the late 19th century?

2. **IDENTIFY MAIN IDEAS AND DETAILS** How did Jim Crow laws protect the social, economic, and political power of whites?

3. **SYNTHESIZE** What push-pull factors contributed to African-American migration to northern cities?

PLAN

Objective

Learn about discrimination aimed at African Americans and Asian immigrants.

Critical Thinking Skills for Lesson 3.1

- Identify Main Ideas and Details
- Monitor Comprehension
- Synthesize
- Analyze Cause and Effect
- Compare and Contrast
- Draw Conclusions

Essential Question for Chapter 19

How did the Industrial Age transform America?
The challenges of industrialization coupled with urbanization, immigration, and economic problems resulted in increased discrimination in the United States. Lesson 3.1 discusses some forms discrimination took.

Background for the Teacher

The mob that forced the immigrants to leave Bellingham, Washington, on September 4, 1907, was organized by the Japanese and Korean Exclusion League, an anti-immigration labor organization that later changed its name to the Asiatic Exclusion League. Tensions had been mounting over the summer after a large influx of South Asian workers came to the area. The union had warned lumber mill owners to stop hiring South Asian workers by Labor Day and had staged a massive parade through Bellingham as a show of force. The workers, however, reported to work as usual after Labor Day. On the day of the riot, whites rampaged through town, breaking windows and rounding up South Asian workers from their boarding houses and the mills. Then the mob hauled the workers to the town jail in the basement of City Hall and held them overnight. The next day, most of the immigrants left town by train, fearful for their safety.

INTRODUCE & ENGAGE

K-W-L Chart

Provide each student with a K-W-L Chart. Tell students to brainstorm what they already know about black codes and the Ku Klux Klan in the South following the Civil War. Then ask students to write questions that they would like to answer as they study the lesson, such as: How were black codes and Jim Crow laws similar? Why did Klan activity increase? Allow time at the end of the lesson for students to fill in what they have learned and to compare notes with one another.

K What Do I Know?	W What Do I Want To Learn?	L What Did I Learn?

TEACH

Guided Discussion

1. **Analyze Cause and Effect** What factors contributed to the increase of Ku Klux Klan activities in the South in the late 1890s? *(Possible response: The Klan's increased activities were, in part, a reaction to seeing African Americans and poor whites unite in a populist movement against large landowners, mill owners, and the conservative rulers of the South.)*

2. **Compare and Contrast** How did the segregation that African-American migrants faced in the North compare to their experiences in the South? *(Possible response: African Americans faced segregation in both locations. Although segregation was not legally enforced in the North, neighborhoods remained racially divided, and real estate agents and landlords often gave preference to whites or refused to sell or rent to African Americans.)*

Draw Conclusions

Ask students to examine and express their reactions to the newspaper clipping and the postcard. **ASK:** Based on these two primary source documents, what can you conclude about one pattern of discrimination? *(Answers will vary. Possible response: Whites banded together to challenge immigrants and African Americans who settled in their neighborhoods.)* How did the Asian immigrants react to the attacks? *(They reported the incident to the police and to the British Consul.)* As a class, discuss the importance of taking action to fight discrimination.

Active Options

On Your Feet: Turn and Talk on Topic Form students into three lines. Give each line this topic sentence: *African Americans and other people of color encountered various forms of prejudice across the United States.* Instruct students to build a paragraph on that topic by asking each student in the line to add a detail that supports the topic sentence. Encourage each line to present its paragraph to the class by having each student read his or her statement aloud.

NG Learning Framework: Write a News Article

ATTITUDE Responsibility

KNOWLEDGE Our Human Story

Instruct students to use the text's discussion of the attack on South Asian immigrants in Bellingham as a starting point for investigating incidents of discrimination against Asian immigrants in California and the Pacific Northwest in the late 1800s and early 1900s. Ask students to select a specific incident and write a short news article describing the event. Invite students to share their articles with the class.

DIFFERENTIATE

English Language Learners

Identify Facts Arrange students at **All Proficiencies** in pairs. You might pair students at the **Expanding** and **Bridging** levels with students at the **Emerging** level. Guide pairs to conduct a Round Robin activity to review the lesson. Ask students to generate facts for three to five minutes and then invite one student from each pair to share their facts. Write correct facts on the board and review the finished list.

Gifted & Talented

Research Legal Discrimination Tell students to conduct a short research project to answer questions about how states and the federal government used laws to discriminate against African Americans and other people of color in the late 1800s. Instruct students to generate an initial research question based on information in the lesson. Encourage them to draw on a variety of sources to generate additional related, focused questions that allow them multiple avenues of exploration. After students research their questions, ask them to share their findings with the class.

See the Chapter Planner for more strategies for differentiation.

HISTORICAL THINKING

ANSWERS

1. The Chinese Exclusion Act kept Chinese immigrants out of the country; the Immigration Act of 1917 subjected all Asian and Pacific Island immigrants to a literacy test; workers with a Mexican heritage sometimes became victims of violence; and Jim Crow and other laws in the South were used to segregate and control African Americans.

2. Jim Crow laws legalized the segregation of African Americans.

3. The segregation and exclusion of African Americans in the South acted as a push factor, while the jobs created by industrialization acted as a pull factor for migration to northern cities.

3.2 "Separate but Equal"

One person's brave actions can change the course of history. When a man sat down in a train car in 1891, the cultural and legal reaction that followed would shape Americans' lives for more than a half century.

MAIN IDEA A Supreme Court ruling in 1896 led to even greater segregation throughout the United States.

A FATEFUL RIDE

Local Jim Crow laws had national consequences. In 1890, Louisiana passed the Separate Car Act. This act mandated "equal but separate accommodations" for white and African-American train passengers. The state government required that railroad companies have the same accommodations for whites and African Americans, but the two groups were not allowed to sit in the same rail cars.

A group of African-American activists in New Orleans formed the Citizens Committee to test the constitutionality of the new law. The Citizens Committee argued the act could not be applied consistently because it did not define what the terms used to describe the two races meant.

In 1891, the committee sent **Homer Plessy** to buy a train ticket in Louisiana. Plessy was one-eighth African American, which means one of his eight great-grandparents was of African descent, so he sat in the car reserved for whites. A train conductor told him to move out of the white car, but he refused. The police arrested him and he stood trial. The court upheld the state law but allowed that Plessy could take his case to a higher court.

Lawyers argued Plessy's case against the railroad company before the Supreme Court in 1896. The court ruled in **Plessy v. Ferguson** that the Separate Car Act did not violate the 14th Amendment, which guarantees "equal protection of the laws" to all citizens.

The Court reasoned that the accommodations on the train were the same for whites and African Americans, even if they were separate. Plessy lost the case, and the Supreme Court upheld the practice of segregation. The ruling allowed governments, businesses, and institutions to enact and enforce "separate but equal" policies for decades to follow.

SEPARATE, *NOT* EQUAL

Jim Crow laws required that African Americans and whites attend different schools as well. White communities received funding for their schools from local and state governments. Many African-American communities, however, had to build schools themselves without public funding.

Without proper funding, African-American schools could not maintain their facilities properly, nor could they improve students' education. Teachers

> In response to the *Plessy* v. *Ferguson* decision, the *Richmond Planet*, an African-American newspaper founded in 1882 by 13 previously enslaved men, published this editorial.
>
> **PRIMARY SOURCE**
>
> *We can be discriminated against, we can be robbed of our political rights, we can be persecuted and murdered and yet we cannot secure a legal redress [remedy] in the courts of the United States. Truly [have] evil days come upon us. But a reckoning day will come and all classes of citizens, sooner or later [will] realize that a government which will not protect cannot demand for itself protection.*
>
> —from "Another Decision," *Richmond Planet*, May 23, 1896

A Northern Critique of Jim Crow
In February 1913, the New York humor magazine *Puck* ran this cartoon. It represents the inequality that automatically results from requiring separate accommodations. In order for African Americans and whites to fly apart, the African-American passengers are crowded onto a platform held up by a balloon and towed by the plane. Though this cartoon was lampooning the idea of "separate but equal," the consequences of Jim Crow laws were far from humorous.

in African-American schools frequently used second-hand supplies and outdated textbooks handed down from white schools.

The invention and acceptance of segregation provided many southern whites with justification for denying African Americans the right to vote. For example, some communities forced eligible citizens to pay a fee called a poll tax before they could register to vote. In some places, even owning a certain amount of property was also considered a requirement for voting.

African-American voters were also required to take literacy tests. **Poll watchers**, or people appointed to guard against voting irregularities, were allowed to deny voting to any person they deemed illiterate, even if the test proved otherwise. In some states, white people who could not read or write were exempted from literacy tests if their fathers or grandfathers had voted.

Both poll taxes and literacy tests purposefully prevented people from voting, and they were specifically directed against African Americans.

Though voting requirements technically applied to all voters, they were mainly used to keep African-American men from voting.

In the late 19th and early 20th centuries, court rulings and state laws undermined the 14th and 15th amendments. This effectively kept many African-American males in the South from voting. African Americans responded by organizing and fighting back against injustices in the South and the rest of the nation.

HISTORICAL THINKING

1. **READING CHECK** How did *Plessy* v. *Ferguson* result in the expansion of segregation laws?

2. **IDENTIFY MAIN IDEAS AND DETAILS** In what ways did poll taxes and literacy tests keep poor people from voting?

3. **DESCRIBE** Why was the "separate but equal" policy never really equal for African Americans?

PLAN

Objective

Understand the effects of the Supreme Court's ruling in the case of *Plessy* v. *Ferguson*.

Critical Thinking Skills for Lesson 3.2

- Identify Main Ideas and Details
- Monitor Comprehension
- Describe
- Evaluate
- Explain
- Analyze Primary Sources

Essential Question for Chapter 19

How did the Industrial Age transform America?
Many African Americans saw their rights restricted during the Industrial Age as southern states passed Jim Crow laws and the Supreme Court supported the principle of "separate but equal." Lesson 3.2 describes these violations of civil rights.

Background for the Teacher

The ruling in *Plessy* v. *Ferguson* was not the first time that the Supreme Court undermined the Civil War amendments. In 1883, the Court declared the Civil Rights Act of 1875 unconstitutional because it made discrimination by individuals a crime. The Court argued that the 14th Amendment did not apply to actions by private individuals and that victims of discrimination by private individuals had to seek relief in state courts, which in the South favored Jim Crow laws. When *Plessy* v. *Ferguson* came before the Court, the majority argued that the 14th Amendment guaranteed political and legal equality but was never meant to abolish distinctions of race or ensure social equality. Judge John Harlan dissented, arguing that the ruling would damage African Americans' civil rights and would encourage states to defeat the intent of the Civil War amendments through state laws.

INTRODUCE & ENGAGE

Preview Using Visuals

Direct students' attention to the cartoon. Read the caption aloud and point out the statement that inequality "automatically results from requiring separate accommodations." **ASK:** Why do you think this might be the case? *(Answers will vary. Possible response: It's an issue of power. Having separate accommodations implies that the two groups are different in some measurable way. The group that establishes the system defines that measure.)* How does the cartoon illustrate this idea? *(Possible response: The plane has power, so it can go wherever it wants. The platform has no power of its own and depends on the towrope to stay afloat. It is an obviously inferior form of transportation.)*

TEACH

Guided Discussion

1. **Evaluate** Why was Homer Plessy a good candidate for testing the constitutionality of the Separate Car Act? *(Possible response: The Separate Car Act failed to define the terms used to describe white and African American. Plessy was one-eighth African American, which meant that determining his race was not clear cut.)*

2. **Explain** Why were literacy tests unfair? Support your response with evidence from the text. *(Possible response: They were unfair because they were applied unequally. Poll watchers sometimes deemed African Americans illiterate even when they passed the literacy test, and whites were allowed to vote in some states without having to take a literacy test if their fathers or grandfathers had voted.)*

Analyze Primary Sources

Review the *Plessy* v. *Ferguson* ruling. Then have students read the primary source editorial from the *Richmond Planet*. **ASK:** Based on your understanding of the Court's ruling, what point do you think the editorial is making? *(Answers will vary. Possible responses: The ruling has undermined the protections guaranteed by the 14th Amendment. Citizens may someday react against the government for failing to protect African Americans.)*

Active Options

On Your Feet: Three-Step Interview Organize students into pairs. Have one student interview the other using this question: *How did* Plessy v. Ferguson *weaken the gains made by African Americans during Reconstruction?* Then have students reverse roles. Finally, invite each student to share the results of his or her interview with a small group or the entire class.

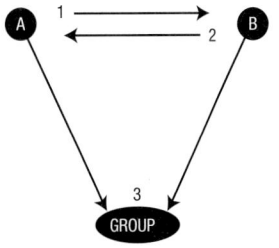

NG Learning Framework: Create a Biographical Infographic

ATTITUDE Responsibility

KNOWLEDGE Our Human Story

Arrange students in groups and ask them to learn more about Homer Plessy. Tell them to gather information about Plessy and the influence of his activism, using information from the chapter and material from reliable print and online sources. Tell groups to use their information to create an infographic to represent their findings. Display the infographics in class and ask students to suggest comparisons and make other constructive comments.

DIFFERENTIATE

Striving Readers

Set a Purpose for Reading Instruct students to identify at least three details about *Plessy* v. *Ferguson* and at least three details about Jim Crow laws in the South. After reading, have students record the details on note cards. Encourage partners to compare cards and discuss the details they chose.

Pre-AP

Research *Brown* v. *Board of Education* Tell students to research and report on *Brown* v. *Board of Education*. Ask them to include in their reports how the verdict reversed *Plessy* v. *Ferguson*. Invite students to present their reports to the class.

See the Chapter Planner for more strategies for differentiation.

HISTORICAL THINKING

ANSWERS

1. By declaring the Separate Car Act constitutional, the Supreme Court validated the concept of segregation, allowing governments, businesses, and institutions to expand and enforce "separate but equal" policies in several areas of society.

2. Poor people might not have had the money to pay the poll tax, disqualifying them from voting. Similarly, they might have had little formal education, making it difficult to pass the literacy test.

3. Answers will vary. Possible response: Separate facilities are inherently unequal because people are forced to be apart. In the case of schools, the government funded white schools, but African Americans often had to build and fund their own schools. Without proper funding, it was difficult to maintain quality.

Fighting Against Segregation

Leaders faced with complicated problems often come up with different solutions. African-American leaders agreed that they should fight discrimination, but they didn't agree on how to go about it.

| **MAIN IDEA** Prominent African-American leaders fought against segregation in American society using different strategies.

EMPOWERING THROUGH EDUCATION

As the effects of the *Plessy v. Ferguson* ruling rippled across the country, African-American leaders began to take action. The educator **Booker T. Washington** became the most influential African-American leader between 1890 and 1915. In 1881, he founded the **Tuskegee Institute** in Alabama to train African Americans to become teachers. Later, the school expanded its focus to include vocational education. Students could learn skilled trades, such as farming techniques and shoemaking, in addition to acquiring teaching techniques. Washington believed the work-related skills of a vocational education would help African-American students become economically independent.

Washington's strategy was to empower African Americans with practical skills and education, or **self-reliance**. By developing self-reliance, he argued, African Americans could "prove" their worthiness and value as functioning members of society. Washington's ideas attracted white philanthropists and helped him raise money for the institute. Andrew Carnegie was among the school's financial supporters. Even though Washington advocated self-reliance, he also funded and supported court challenges to segregation.

Despite Washington's success at drawing support from both whites and African Americans, a number of African-American leaders disagreed

with his approach. **W.E.B. Du Bois** (doo BOYS) was a sociologist, activist, and reformer who refused to accommodate the discriminations of society. He claimed that by trying to prove equality, Washington accepted discrimination and thus allowed it to continue. Du Bois believed that protest, not accommodation, would be the way fundamental change would take place.

PROTESTING RACISM

In 1909, Du Bois and **Ida B. Wells**, another activist, founded the **National Association for the Advancement of Colored People (NAACP)** to combat race-based discrimination. Like Du Bois, Wells believed protest was necessary for achieving justice. Du Bois and Wells led the NAACP in its fight against segregation and discrimination against African Americans.

Long before co-founding the NAACP, Wells taught school in Memphis, Tennessee. She then turned her attention to journalism, working as an editor for an African-American newspaper called the *Free Speech and Headlight*. Wells wrote editorials exposing discrimination against African Americans and eventually became a full-time journalist. After a group of white men lynched three of her friends, Wells began to write extensively about the horrors and violence of lynching. She even traveled to England to raise awareness about lynching in the United States. Many whites in the South became angry with her for speaking out.

When white protestors destroyed her newspaper office, Wells decided to move to Chicago. She married and began working for the *Chicago Conservator,* an African-American newspaper. Wells also wrote pamphlets on lynching and formed anti-lynching societies.

Together with social reformer Jane Addams, Wells worked to keep Chicago schools from becoming segregated. When a Chicago newspaper began campaigning in 1903 for segregating the integrated Chicago schools, Wells asked Addams to meet with the newspaper's editors. Addams did so, and the editors ceased printing more articles. Wells's writing about lynching and other racial injustices brought much-needed attention to the topic. The struggle for justice and equality in society would continue as workers in the late 19th century began to assert their rights.

W.E.B. Du Bois   Ida B. Wells

The Springfield Riots and the NAACP

In 1908, racial tensions turned violent in Springfield, Illinois. When an African-American prisoner accused of a crime against a white woman was transferred out of Springfield by police officers, white residents of the town lashed out. Thousands of white protestors burned houses, shot people, and lynched two men. At least seven people were killed. After the Springfield riots, 60 civil rights activists, including Du Bois and Wells, met in New York City to discuss how to prevent riots and mob violence. Together, those meeting in New York signed a mission statement that marked the beginning of the NAACP.

HISTORICAL THINKING

1. **READING CHECK** How did Booker T. Washington differ from W.E.B. Du Bois and Ida B. Wells on confronting discrimination?

2. **FORM AND SUPPORT OPINIONS** What are the pros and cons of self-reliance and protest as strategies to achieve equality?

3. **SUMMARIZE** What prompted Ida B. Wells to become a civil rights activist? Use details from the text to support your response.

CRITICAL VIEWING The accomplished scientist and inventor George Washington Carver (center) was a teacher at the Tuskegee Institute. What lab work might the class be doing?

PLAN

Objective

Learn about the strategies African-American leaders used to fight segregation.

Critical Thinking Skills for Lesson 3.3

- Identify Main Ideas and Details
- Monitor Comprehension
- Form and Support Opinions
- Summarize
- Identify Problems and Solutions
- Analyze Cause and Effect
- Make Inferences

Essential Question for Chapter 19

How did the Industrial Age transform America?
African-American reformers worked to address the effects of *Plessy* v. *Ferguson* and Jim Crow laws in the late 1800s and 1900s. Lesson 3.2 explains some of the strategies used.

Background for the Teacher

William Edward Burghardt Du Bois grew up in Great Barrington, Massachusetts. After graduating as his high school's valedictorian, Du Bois earned two bachelor of arts degrees, the first from Fisk University and the second from Harvard University. He then received a master of arts and doctorate in history from Harvard. After receiving his doctorate, he briefly taught sociology at the University of Pennsylvania, where he conducted urban research that he published as *The Philadelphia Negro: A Social Study in 1899*.

Before helping form the NAACP, Du Bois served as general secretary of the Niagara Movement, a protest group formed by African-American professionals and scholars. As part of his duties, he edited two of the movement's publications, the *Moon* and the *Horizon*. During his time with the NAACP, he served as editor of *The Crisis*, the association's monthly magazine. In addition to his academic writing and his journalism, Du Bois also wrote poems, plays, and novels.

Preview Terms

Introduce the concept of self-reliance by asking students what it means to rely on someone. Then discuss what the word *self-reliance* means. Have students speculate on how being self-reliant might have helped African Americans in the South in the late 1800s. Tell students that in Lesson 3.3 they will learn about some of the ways African-American leaders responded to segregation, including by teaching self-reliance.

TEACH

Guided Discussion

1. **Identify Problems and Solutions** What problem was Booker T. Washington trying to solve, and how did he go about solving it? *(Possible response: Washington was trying to solve the problem of a lack of economic independence among African Americans. He tried to solve that problem by training students at the Tuskegee Institute to be teachers and by providing vocational training in farming techniques and skilled trades.)*

2. **Analyze Cause and Effect** How did the NAACP come into existence? *(Possible response: The Springfield riots motivated 60 civil rights activists to meet in New York City to discuss preventing race riots and violence. Participants in the conference drafted and signed a mission statement creating the NAACP.)*

More Information

The Civil Rights Movement Explain that the Civil Rights Movement has a long history in the United States and that leaders within the movement have approached the quest for racial equality in different ways. Just as Booker T. Washington and W.E.B. Du Bois differed in how best to achieve racial equality, civil rights advocates in the 1950s and 1960s differed in tactics and objectives. Point out that Martin Luther King, Jr., who emerged as a civil rights leader in the mid-1950s, advocated nonviolent social protest. By the mid-1960s, more militant groups associated with Black Power and Malcolm X's black nationalism emerged. These groups rejected King's approach as too accommodating. Ask students to research the different ways groups have tried to achieve equality and then debate the pros and cons of approaching social change from more than one perspective.

Active Options

On Your Feet: Chart Relay Tape large pieces of paper to the wall in different locations of the classroom. Arrange students in teams of three. Provide each team with a bold marker and one of the sheets of paper. Instruct teams to label three columns on their paper: Washington, Du Bois, and Wells. Allow teams time to assemble three facts they learned about each person. Make each team member responsible for one fact. Then, on your signal, tell teams to write their facts on the charts. The first team to finish wins. Take time for teams to compare their answers to ensure accuracy.

NG Learning Framework: Create a Social Media Page

SKILL Communication

KNOWLEDGE Our Human Story

Direct students to work in groups to research the founding of the NAACP with the purpose of creating a social media page. Explain that their page should reenact the announcement of the formation of the organization as if such technology had been available in 1909. Instruct groups to include the organization's mission statement, provide short biographies of key founding members, and discuss projects or initiatives the organization expects to launch. Encourage students to include photographs where appropriate.

English Language Learners

Use Sentence Strips Choose a paragraph from the lesson and make sentence strips out of it. Read the paragraph aloud, having students at the **Emerging** level follow along in their books. Then have students close their books. Give students the set of sentence strips and instruct students to put the strips in order and read the paragraph aloud.

Gifted & Talented

Write News Tweets Direct students to research the riot that occurred in Springfield, Illinois, in 1908. Tell them to imagine that they are in Springfield during the riot and to write a series of tweets to a friend explaining what is happening. Ask volunteers to share their tweets with the class.

See the Chapter Planner for more strategies for differentiation.

HISTORICAL THINKING

ANSWERS

1. Washington thought that African Americans had to prove themselves to whites, so he focused on hard work and personal development rather than social reform. Activists Du Bois and Wells thought protest was necessary and accepting discrimination only allowed it to continue.

2. Answers will vary. Possible response: Self-reliance provides training that helps individuals advance economically, but it doesn't address issues of discrimination. Protest calls attention to discrimination, but it doesn't help individuals acquire skills to achieve economic independence.

3. After three of her friends were lynched, Wells started to focus much of her writing and speaking on lynching.

CRITICAL VIEWING "Soil Analyses" is written on the chalkboard, and Carver is watching a student pour a liquid over a filter containing some substance. The students are probably analyzing the properties of different kinds of soil.

4.1 The Lives of Workers

What are you doing after school today? Hanging out with friends? Relaxing?

Many children in the late 1800s and early 1900s didn't have these options.

They worked long hours in hard, dangerous jobs for little pay.

MAIN IDEA Work places at the turn of the century often involved dangerous conditions, long days, and low wages, with few labor laws to protect workers.

Child miners pause for a lunch break at the Woodward Coal Mine in Kingston, Pennsylvania, in 1900. Until 1916, mine operators hired boys as young as 8 years old to work 12-hour days, 6 days a week. These workers, called "breaker boys," broke chunks of coal into pieces and separated the coal from rocks, slate, and other debris. They sat on wooden benches and processed the coal with their bare hands. Injuries were common and sometimes deadly, and the breaker boys, like adult miners, had few protections.

WORKING CONDITIONS

Industrial progress brought prosperity to some, but for others, this progress was more problematic. As industrialization expanded in the late 19th century, companies looked for ways to increase profits—much like companies do today. In this regard, they benefited from laissez-faire business practices that allowed them to run their businesses with few restrictions. One way to increase profits was to lower **overhead**, or the cost of doing business. New machines replaced the work of individuals, and factory work became more common. Factory managers wanted the work done as quickly and cheaply as possible.

In the late 1800s and into the 1900s, it was not uncommon for workers in some factories to put in 10- to 12-hour days. Working conditions were often dangerous, and the rates of job-related injuries and deaths were very high. In addition to enduring long days and difficult conditions, workers also received low wages from employers. Because of the low wages, unsafe conditions, and long work hours, people started calling these factories **sweatshops**. Sweatshops were particularly common in the garment, shoe, and soap manufacturing industries.

Some industries had especially dangerous conditions. Coal mining, for example, was one of the most dangerous jobs of the late 19th century. Coal miners used dynamite to blast through underground rock, so they were constantly at risk of having mine tunnels collapse on them. Lethal gases such as methane collected in the tunnels. Such gases killed workers in seconds. When fires broke out, miners were trapped deep inside with no way out. After breathing in coal dust, miners often developed painful, debilitating, and deadly lung diseases.

Like coal miners, railroad workers performed life-threatening work, including setting off dangerous explosions as they blasted through rock to build tunnels. Operating the trains could also prove deadly. The brakemen, who were responsible for stopping trains, had to run on top of the train applying the brakes by hand on each car. Sometimes workers fell between the cars and were killed underneath the trains as they attempted this task.

WOMEN AND CHILDREN

In the late 19th century, native-born women typically entered the workforce as teachers and office workers. Immigrant women more often found work in manufacturing, such as in textile mills or shoe factories.

Working conditions for women were often even worse than they were for men. Not only did women have to work long hours in unhealthy surroundings, but they were paid much less than men. Even when performing the same work, whether as a teacher or factory worker, a woman was paid only about 60 percent of a man's wages.

Child labor continued to be a common practice during the late 19th and early 20th centuries, and few laws existed to protect children. As a result, companies were allowed to hire children to perform dangerous work in textile mills and glass factories. They even worked in the hazardous coal mines. Children often worked just as many hours as adults did. Employers preferred hiring them because they could get away with paying them even lower wages. Families living in poverty needed the wages earned by their children. Many children could not attend school because they were working in factories.

Labor practices and working conditions were far from ideal. As you have read, reformers responded by advocating and providing opportunities for people who were poor and vulnerable. Reformers helped many people get their basic needs met and somewhat improved their quality of life. But the efforts of reformers were not enough. Workers across industries had reached a breaking point and began to demand better conditions and pay.

HISTORICAL THINKING

1. **READING CHECK** What were working conditions like for factory workers in the late 19th and early 20th centuries?

2. **IDENTIFY MAIN IDEAS AND DETAILS** What industries were particularly dangerous, and why did workers enter them anyway?

3. **MAKE GENERALIZATIONS** Why were employers able to pay women and children less?

PLAN

Objective
Discuss working conditions for many Americans in the late 1800s and early 1900s.

Critical Thinking Skills for Lesson 4.1
- Identify Main Ideas and Details
- Monitor Comprehension
- Make Generalizations
- Analyze Cause and Effect
- Analyze Language Use
- Describe

Essential Question for Chapter 19
How did the Industrial Age transform America?
Industrial progress fueled a growing middle class but led to problems for American workers. Lesson 4.1 describes conditions that many working-class men, women, and children faced.

Background for the Teacher
Textile mills, glass factories, and coal mines were not the only industries that hired children. Between 1890 and 1910, the number of children age 14 or younger who worked in industrial jobs grew from 1.5 million to 2 million. Many children worked alongside their parents. In canneries, for instance, children as young as six or seven began work at three in the morning. In seafood canneries, children might shuck oysters or process shrimp for 10 hours a day. In vegetable and fruit canneries, the workdays could stretch to 18 hours. Children might haul heavy crates of fruits and vegetables, shuck corn, or cut the ends off green beans. Injuries in all of these jobs were common, especially near the end of the long workday when the children were physically and mentally exhausted.

Create a Concept Cluster

Display a Concept Cluster like the one shown. Write the term *working class* in the center. Ask students what ideas they associate with the working class and add their responses. Explain that in this lesson, students will learn about conditions in the workplace for most members of the working class during the Industrial Age.

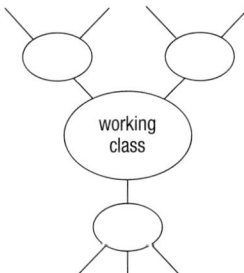

working class

TEACH

Guided Discussion

1. **Analyze Cause and Effect** Why were businesses able to operate with a low overhead? *(The lack of legal restrictions on businesses made it possible for business owners to keep overhead low.)* What were the results of that practice? *(The result was greater profit for businesses but also unpleasant and even dangerous conditions for employees.)*

2. **Analyze Language Use** Why is the term *sweatshops* a fitting way to describe many factories during the Industrial Age? *(Possible response: Working conditions, particularly in the manufacturing industries, were often dangerous, and men, women, and children worked long hours for little pay.)*

Describe

Tell students to reflect on the discussion of coal mines in the lesson and photo caption. **ASK:** What conditions made mines particularly dangerous workplaces? *(Breaker boys often cut their hands when they separated the coal from sharp shale and rocks, and they had to deal with dangerous conveyor belts and coal dust. Workers in the mines faced the risk of tunnel collapses, fire, coal dust, and deadly gases.)*

Active Options

On Your Feet: Travel Around the World Position two students in one corner of the room and one student in each of the other three corners. Ask the two students in the first corner a question about the lesson. Whoever correctly answers the question first becomes the "traveler" and moves to another corner to stand with a new partner while the first partner sits down. Repeat the process for as long as time permits. A traveler who correctly answers one question in each corner has "traveled around the world."

NG Learning Framework: Create a Photo Exhibit

ATTITUDE Responsibility

SKILL Communication

Have students work in groups to locate and select photos that show child labor in coal mines and factories in the late 1800s and early 1900s. Instruct the groups to write research-based captions to accompany the photos. Then have groups organize their photos and captions into a single electronic or print gallery exhibit for the classroom.

Inclusion

Describe a Historical Photo Pair students who are visually impaired with students who are not. Ask the latter to describe the photograph of the breaker boys in detail, read the caption aloud, and answer questions their partners might have.

Pre-AP

Research Social Darwinism Direct students to use both print and digital sources to research the role of Social Darwinism in justifying child labor and the working conditions in the late 1800s. Tell students to use search terms effectively, assess the credibility and accuracy of their sources, and quote or paraphrase without plagiarizing by following the provided format for citations. Instruct students to use their research to create a presentation for the class that explains the following points:

• the basic principles of Social Darwinism

• how Social Darwinists viewed laissez-faire capitalism

• why Social Darwinists opposed legislation to restrict child labor or improve the lives of workers

Encourage the class to ask questions.

See the Chapter Planner for more strategies for differentiation.

HISTORICAL THINKING

ANSWERS

1. Workers often had to work up to 12 hours per day under dangerous conditions and for very little money. Women were paid about 60 percent of what men were paid, even if they were doing the same job. Children made even less money but often worked as hard as adults.

2. Coal mining and railroad work were particularly dangerous, but people took the jobs anyway because they needed to support their families.

3. Answers will vary. Possible response: There were few laws to protect workers' rights, and women and children had little power or social standing.

Rise of Labor Unions

Generally speaking, a group of people can be pushed around and taken for granted only so long before they fight back. When workers in the late 1800s had finally had enough of unfair demands from employers, they did just that.

MAIN IDEA American workers formed labor unions and staged strikes across the country as they advocated for better working conditions and fair wages.

ORIGINS OF LABOR UNIONS

By the late 1800s, long workdays, low wages, and dangerous work conditions began to take their toll. Ultimately, workers decided they needed more protection from employer abuses. Forming labor unions offered a way to achieve this.

In a labor union, people doing similar jobs unite as a group to demand improved working conditions. This is called **collective bargaining**. When an employer is unwilling to bargain for better wages or conditions, the union may call for a strike, refusing to work until its demands are met. The purpose of a strike is to persuade employers to grant the changes employees seek.

As you have read, workers had established craft and labor unions beginning in the 1840s. In the 1860s, unions formed in industries controlled by some of the worst violators of workers' rights, including coal mining, shoemaking, and cigar-making. These unions were often city- or even factory-specific, and they were not always able to assert power and protect workers. With the increase in size and scope of industry in the late 19th century, workers began to strategize on a national level.

Knights of Labor Seal
A seal is a tool that stamps a design to guarantee an official statement or agreement on a document's authenticity. The inscription on this Knights of Labor seal reads, "That is the most perfect government in which an injury to one is the concern of all." The word *Prytaneum* at the center refers to the central hearth or fire in a village in ancient Greece.

In July 1877, railroad workers throughout the country participated in the **Great Railroad Strike**. When the Baltimore and Ohio (B&O) Railroad announced a 10 percent wage cut, the second cut that year, irate workers in Martinsburg, West Virginia, walked off the job. The strike then spread to other cities. When B&O managers tried to break the strike, or put an end to it by bringing in other workers to replace the strikers, rioting broke out in many cities, including Baltimore, Pittsburgh, and Chicago. Eventually, federal troops arrived to curb the violence. In the end, about 100,000 workers had participated in the strike, and about 100 people had been killed in the resulting riots.

THE KNIGHTS OF LABOR

One of the first significant national labor unions in the United States was the **Knights of Labor**, founded in 1869 as a union of Philadelphia tailors. **Terence V. Powderly** became the union's leader in 1879. Under his leadership the union became a national organization of many different types of workers, including farmers, shop owners, and laborers.

The union welcomed both skilled and unskilled workers. It also welcomed women and African

CRITICAL VIEWING Industrial leaders rest on their bags of money, enjoying the comforts of their large bank accounts in this 1893 political cartoon. The workers below bear the load of supporting industrial America while knee-deep in rough waters. Based on details you notice in the cartoon, how do the industrial leaders' bags of money compare to the wages earned by their employees?

Americans, a forward-thinking move for a 19th-century union. The Knights of Labor supported ideas considered radical by many: the abolition of child labor, reasonable working hours, and equal pay for men and women doing the same work.

After the Great Railroad Strike, membership in the Knights of Labor started to grow. Then in 1885, the Knights of Labor went on strike against the ruthless railroad owner **Jay Gould**. Gould had earned a reputation as a **robber baron**, or an industrial leader known for cutthroat tactics against workers and competitors. Within just one year of that first strike against Gould, the union added 500,000 members. Total membership peaked at 700,000 members in 1886.

That same year, in response to the firing of a union member in Texas, the Knights of Labor went on a second, much longer strike against Gould's

railroad. This strike was known as the **Great Southwest Strike**, and it took place in several states and lasted for many months. Eventually, Gould called in the police to break it up.

The Great Southwest Strike was just one of thousands of strikes to take place in 1886. In fact, that year workers staged about 1,600 strikes as tensions between labor and management grew across industries.

HISTORICAL THINKING

1. **READING CHECK** Why did workers use collective bargaining as a strategy?

2. **EXPLAIN** What was Terence Powderly's goal in forming the Knights of Labor?

3. **MAKE INFERENCES** Why do you think membership in the Knights of Labor increased after 1877?

PLAN

Objective
Understand the rise of unions and factors that prompted railroad strikes in the late 1800s.

Critical Thinking Skills for Lesson 4.2
- Identify Main Ideas and Details
- Monitor Comprehension
- Explain
- Make Inferences
- Analyze Cause and Effect
- Form and Support Opinions
- Analyze Language Use

Essential Question for Chapter 19
How did the Industrial Age transform America?
Labor unions grew in size during the late 1800s as workers banded together to demand better pay and working conditions. Lesson 4.2 discusses the rise of unions and early railroad strikes.

Background for the Teacher
Railroads were the first business to confront labor issues nationally due to the number of workers they employed. Many railroad employees—for example, engineers, firemen, and brakemen—were hard to replace during a strike because of their specialized skills. Railroad workers often joined unions based on those skills, such as the Brotherhood of Locomotive Firemen and the Brotherhood of Locomotive Engineers. These unions did not plan the Great Railroad Strike of 1877. Rather, the strike was a spontaneous reaction to poor pay and dangerous working conditions, exacerbated by the depression that followed the Panic of 1873. The strike caused a few railroads to consider providing employee benefits. For the most part, however, management's reaction was not to help workers but to plan stronger ways to keep employees under control.

Preview Using Visuals

Direct students' attention to the political cartoon. Ask students to come up with a word or phrase that describes what they see. Write their responses on the board. **ASK:** What point do you think the cartoonist is trying to make? *(Answers will vary. Possible response: The artist is trying to make the point that industrial leaders are getting rich due to the back-breaking labor of the suffering workers whom they are underpaying.)* Tell students that they will read about the efforts of labor unions to improve conditions for workers.

TEACH
Guided Discussion

1. **Analyze Cause and Effect** Why were the labor unions that formed between the 1840s and 1860s often unable to protect workers? *(These unions were small, often covering workers in a specific city or factory, so they didn't always have the clout to protect workers.)*

2. **Form and Support Opinions** Do you think Jay Gould deserved his reputation as a robber baron? Support your opinion with evidence from the text. *(Answers will vary. Possible response: Yes, Gould deserved that reputation. He used ruthless tactics against his competitors and even against his own workers. For example, he called in police to break up the Great Southwest Strike.)*

Analyze Language Use

Point out the photograph of the Knights of Labor seal and read the caption aloud. **ASK:** What do you think is meant by the motto inscribed on the seal? *(Possible response: The motto means that the government has the responsibility to protect everyone.)* Why might this be a good motto for a labor union? *(Possible response: Labor unions, like governments, should look out for the welfare of their members. It also may suggest that the union is prepared to stand up to a government that fails to protect workers.)*

Active Options

On Your Feet: Conduct Talk Show Interviews Form students into teams of four and explain that students will conduct talk show interviews about the railroad strikes. Student 1, the interviewer, develops a question to ask the show's "guests." Student 2, a representative from railroad management, and Student 3, a representative from a labor union, answer the question, citing information from the lesson. Student 4, a member of the studio audience, asks a follow-up question that the whole class can answer. Have participants ask and answer several questions to ensure a solid review of the topic.

NG Learning Framework: Explore Perspectives

SKILL Communication

KNOWLEDGE Our Human Story

Ask students to conduct research in reputable print and online sources to learn more about Terence V. Powderly and Jay Gould. Tell students they will use the information to write an editorial about Gould from Powderly's point of view or about Powderly from Gould's point of view. Invite students to share their editorials with the class, perhaps in a series of point/counterpoint readings.

DIFFERENTIATE
Striving Readers

Use Context Clues Use *collective bargaining* and *robber baron* to model how to use textual definitions and other context clues to understand Key Vocabulary. Guide students in using the text to understand such words as *violators*, *forward-thinking*, and *radical*. Encourage students to use a chart, such as the one shown, to record definitions and to refer to a print or online dictionary if they need clarification of a specific term.

Term	Definition from Context

Gifted & Talented

Draw Political Cartoons Have students use information in the lesson to create political cartoons addressing the railroad strikes against Jay Gould and Gould's reactions to those strikes. Have students share their political cartoons with the class and discuss the intended points of view.

See the Chapter Planner for more strategies for differentiation.

HISTORICAL THINKING

ANSWERS

1. Workers used this strategy because it gave them more bargaining power than they had as individuals.

2. Terence Powderly wanted to eliminate child labor and convince employers to provide equal pay and reasonable hours to their workers, including African Americans and women.

3. Possible response: The Great Railroad Strike of 1877 focused attention on low wages and poor working conditions, and workers probably began to see that unions could have some effect on improving those things.

CRITICAL VIEWING The industrial leaders' enormous bags of money illustrate the point that industrial leaders are millionaires while their workers make from $6 to $11 per week.

4.3 Labor Conflicts

When you arrive, a man is giving a speech about Congress ignoring the workingmen. Someone shouts "Police!" and you see a line of men walking toward the crowd. Then an explosion rattles the buildings around you, pistol shots fire, and everyone begins to run.

MAIN IDEA A series of violent strikes took place during the late 1800s as workers intensified their demands for better wages and working conditions.

THE HAYMARKET RIOT

As the Great Southwest Strike raged in the spring of 1886, another strike was brewing. In May of that year, workers protested at the McCormick Harvesting Machine Company in Chicago. The demonstration was part of a nationwide effort to establish an eight-hour workday.

On May 3, police officers killed one protestor and injured several others. In response, labor leaders called for a protest meeting the following day in Haymarket Square. Though the meeting on May 4 was initially peaceful, someone in the crowd threw a bomb, and police began shooting. Several police officers and members of the crowd were killed in the explosion and rioting that followed. Dozens more were injured. Afterward, police arrested eight people, claiming they were **anarchists**, or people who advocate lawlessness and the absence of all government. Four of the accused anarchists were hanged for the crime of throwing the bomb, and one was sentenced to 15 years in prison. Their guilt was never adequately proven, however, and the remaining defendants were eventually pardoned. The event became known as the **Haymarket Riot**.

CRITICAL VIEWING Evidence presented at the trial against the accused included these lead pipe bombs. Officers who had been on duty during the Haymarket Riot carried this banner in a parade honoring police veterans of the riot. What is the relationship of these two artifacts?

Many blamed the Knights of Labor for the events in Chicago, though there was no direct connection. As a result, membership in the Knights of Labor rapidly declined. Instead, workers who wanted to unionize joined the newly formed **American Federation of Labor**, which **Samuel L. Gompers** had formed that same year. Many considered that organization to be less radical than the Knights of Labor. Like the Knights of Labor, however, Gompers's organization supported demands for an eight-hour workday.

HOMESTEAD AND PULLMAN

Despite the violence that had overshadowed the Haymarket Riot and the Great Railroad Strike, labor unions grew in membership and strength in the late 1800s. But conflicts continued to flare up between labor and employers.

In 1892, workers at the Carnegie Steel Company in Homestead, Pennsylvania, went on strike. The manager had cut the workers' wages and refused to negotiate with them. He fired all 3,800 union workers and hired 300 private security guards to take over the plant. During the **Homestead Strike** that followed, clashes between the two groups led to the deaths of at least seven workers and three guards. The workers took control of the mill, but the company called in the National Guard to remove them. Then the company hired **scabs**, or people willing to cross union lines to work during a strike, to take the place of union workers.

Just two years later, in 1894, the **Pullman Strike** took place near Chicago. The head of the Pullman Palace Car Company, a railway car manufacturer, had refused to meet with workers to discuss wage cuts and long workdays. Instead, the owner fired them. The workers called a strike and walked off the job. **Eugene V. Debs**, the leader of the American Railway Union, coordinated a boycott of Pullman cars on rail lines. This meant rail workers

Pullman Strike
The Pullman Strike began as a "wildcat strike," meaning the workers at the factory walked out without the formal decision of a union. On July 3, 1894, federal troops arrived in Chicago to prevent interference with the operation of trains. In this photo, troops stand in formation outside the Pullman Arcade building, which housed shops and businesses serving the Pullman company town. Ultimately, as many as 250,000 railroad workers in 27 states went on strike or disrupted train traffic.

refused to handle or service any Pullman cars. The boycott successfully brought midwestern rail traffic to a halt.

To get the trains moving again, President Grover Cleveland sent federal troops to Illinois. Violence erupted, and National Guard members shot and killed strikers. After the strike ended, Debs was arrested. The coming years would see more upheaval as reformers continued pressing for improvements in the lives of workers, immigrants, women, and children.

HISTORICAL THINKING

1. **READING CHECK** Why did labor unions strike in the late 1800s?
2. **IDENTIFY MAIN IDEAS AND DETAILS** How did the federal government respond to labor strikes in the 1890s?
3. **DETERMINE CHRONOLOGY** What events led to the rise of the American Federation of Labor?

PLAN

Objective
Discuss growth of labor unrest and response from employers and the federal government.

Critical Thinking Skills for Lesson 4.3
- Identify Main Ideas and Details
- Monitor Comprehension
- Determine Chronology
- Make Inferences
- Evaluate

Essential Question for Chapter 19
How did the Industrial Age transform America?
Labor conflicts increased and became more violent as workers demanded better working conditions. Lesson 4.3 examines the causes and results of the Haymarket Riot and the Homestead and Pullman strikes.

Background for the Teacher
Workers at the Pullman plant, in Pullman, Illinois, lived in a company town. George Pullman had founded the town in 1880 when he built a new factory on the site. Unskilled workers lived in apartments, skilled workers lived in row houses, and managers lived in modest Victorian single homes. Workers paid rent, which was taken directly out of their paychecks, and they shopped in the Pullman Arcade building.

When Pullman lowered the workers' pay in response to an economic downturn in 1893, he did not lower rents or prices in the stores. With less money to spend but no change in their living expenses, many families came close to starving. Following the strike, the court ordered Pullman to sell off all the town's property that was not directly tied to the plant. The city of Chicago then incorporated the town.

Discuss Outcomes

Have students recount what they have read so far about labor strikes and the reactions of management and the government in the late 1800s. Then have the class consider how these past interactions might affect actions by workers and management. **ASK:** What effect might these past events have on how labor and management deal with one another? *(Answers will vary. Possible response: Both sides would likely be mistrustful of each other. As tensions mount, the potential for violence on the part of strikers and the use of force on the part of management might increase.)* Tell students that they will read about further labor conflicts in this lesson.

TEACH

Guided Discussion

1. **Determine Chronology** What steps did the manager at the Carnegie Steel Company take to deal with protesting workers? *(Rather than negotiate, the manager fired all 3,800 union workers, hired 300 security guards to take over the plant, and hired nonunion workers to replace the strikers.)*

2. **Make Inferences** Why do you think Eugene V. Debs was arrested when the Pullman Strike ended? *(Possible response: Debs had coordinated the boycott that led to the call for federal troops, so Debs was likely held responsible for the deaths of the strikers who were shot.)*

Evaluate

Read the Pullman Strike caption aloud. Tell students to examine the photo to determine the position of the federal troops and the townspeople. **ASK:** Why might placing federal troops at that location be an effective way to intimidate participants in the Pullman strike? *(Pullman was a company town, and the federal troops are positioned to keep the residents away from the Pullman Arcade building where they shop and do business.)*

Active Options

On Your Feet: Labor Conflicts Roundtable Guide students to hold a roundtable discussion to compile details about the labor conflicts discussed in the lesson. Arrange students around tables or in circles in groups of four and instruct them to use information from the lesson to offer a detail about the Haymarket Riot, Homestead Strike, or Pullman Strike. Encourage students to take notes as others offer information. When groups have finished sharing information, invite them to present a summary to the class.

NG Learning Framework: Investigate a Youth-Organized Strike

ATTITUDE Responsibility

SKILL Collaboration

Arrange students in small groups and tell them to investigate the newsboys' strike of 1899. Tell students to find out where, why, and against whom the newsboys organized the strike, how long it lasted, and whether the newsboys' demands were met. Encourage students to briefly explain how the strike impacted child labor on a national level. Invite student groups to present their findings to the class.

English Language Learners

Use Sentence Frames Provide students at the **Expanding** level with these sentence frames in random order. Tell students to complete the sentences and number them in the sequence in which they happened in the Haymarket Riot.

1. Workers at the McCormick Harvesting Machine Company protested because they wanted _____. *(an eight-hour workday)*

2. On May 3, the police _____ and _____. *(killed one protestor; injured several others)*

3. The riot began on May 4, after a _____ went off and police began _____. *(bomb; shooting)*

4. The police arrested eight people who they thought were _____. *(anarchists)*

5. Many people blamed the _____ for the riot and the deaths. *(Knights of Labor)*

Pre-AP

Create an Annotated Time Line Tell students to use print and online sources to research and build an annotated time line of the Homestead or Pullman strike. Instruct them to include dates, descriptions of significant events, and visuals to chronicle how the strike unfolded. Ask students to share their time lines. Invite comparisons and comments from the class.

See the Chapter Planner for more strategies for differentiation.

HISTORICAL THINKING

ANSWERS

1. Labor unions staged strikes to push for eight-hour workdays and fair wages.

2. In the Homestead Strike, federal troops removed strikers from the steel mill. President Cleveland sent the National Guard to Chicago to put down the Pullman Strike by rail workers.

3. Membership in the Knights of Labor declined after it was blamed for the Haymarket Riot. The recently formed American Federation of Labor attracted workers who were still interested in the strength a union provided.

CRITICAL VIEWING The use of the pipe bombs was the cause that led to the parade in which officers carried the banner.

19 REVIEW

VOCABULARY

For each pair of vocabulary words or terms, write one sentence that explains the connection between the two words or terms.

1. capitalism; laissez-faire

   Those who promote laissez-faire economics believe less government intervention in the economy is good for capitalism.

2. standard time; transcontinental railroad

3. overhead; sweatshop

4. Chinese Exclusion Act; Jim Crow laws

5. philanthropy; Social Gospel

6. Bessemer process; steel

7. mass culture; urbanization

8. Gilded Age; robber baron

9. Homestead Strike; scab

READING STRATEGY
IDENTIFY MAIN IDEAS AND DETAILS

If you haven't already, complete your Main Ideas and Details graphic organizer about the social and economic effects of the Industrial Age. Include at least three details. Then answer the question.

Social and Economic Effects of the Industrial Age

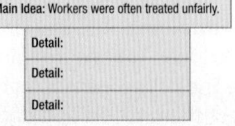

Main Idea: Workers were often treated unfairly.

Detail:

Detail:

Detail:

10. What were the main social problems of the Industrial Age?

MAIN IDEAS

Answer the following questions. Support your answers with evidence from the chapter.

11. How did construction of the first transcontinental railroad affect Native Americans? **LESSON 1.1**

12. What improvements did Andrew Carnegie make to the steel industry? **LESSON 1.4**

13. What did new immigrants experience after arriving in the United States? **LESSON 2.1**

14. What was the goal of the Social Gospel movement? **LESSON 2.3**

15. In what ways did the Ku Klux Klan intimidate African Americans? **LESSON 3.1**

16. What does the phrase "separate but equal" mean? **LESSON 3.2**

17. Why did Booker T. Washington promote self-reliance? **LESSON 3.3**

18. What effect did child labor have on children's education? **LESSON 4.1**

19. What purpose did strikes serve in workers' demands for change? **LESSON 4.2**

20. What event led to the Haymarket Riot in Chicago? **LESSON 4.3**

HISTORICAL THINKING

Answer the following questions. Support your answers with evidence from the chapter.

21. **DESCRIBE** Why were employers able to take advantage of immigrant workers, female workers, and child workers?

22. **SYNTHESIZE** What contributions did Ida B. Wells, Jane Addams, and Ellen Gates Starr make to social welfare programs?

23. **EVALUATE** How did new inventions and industries affect people both positively and negatively during the Industrial Age? Use examples from the chapter.

24. **FORM AND SUPPORT OPINIONS** Which reform movement during the late 19th and early 20th centuries had the biggest impact on people's lives? Use evidence from the chapter to support your answer.

25. **ANALYZE CAUSE AND EFFECT** What changes in transportation in the late 19th and early 20th centuries led to the development of suburbs?

26. **MAKE INFERENCES** Why did groups of American citizens support the Chinese Exclusion Act and other discriminatory practices against Asian Americans?

INTERPRET GRAPHS

Look closely at this graph showing population growth in the United States from 1880 to 1910. Then answer the questions that follow.

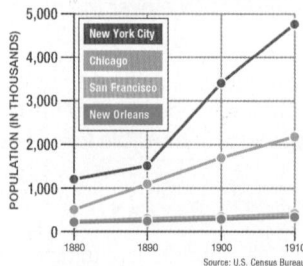

City Populations, 1880–1910

Legend: New York City, Chicago, San Francisco, New Orleans

POPULATION (IN THOUSANDS): 5,000 / 4,000 / 3,000 / 2,000 / 1,000 / 0

Years: 1880, 1890, 1900, 1910

Source: U.S. Census Bureau

27. Which city had the most growth from 1880 to 1890?

28. In which city did the population grow the least during this 30-year time period?

ANALYZE SOURCES

On May 11, 1869, *The New York Times* published news of the transcontinental railroad's completion. The day before, workers had driven the last spike into the railroad, finally linking the coasts. Read the passage and answer the question.

> It was apparent everywhere throughout the City yesterday that an event of more than usual importance was taking place, and that there was an evident disposition among the people to be jubilant. Flags were displayed on the City Hall, on all the newspaper offices, and on the prominent hotels. Every countenance [face] seemed to bear a look of supreme satisfaction, and all were apparently awaiting with anticipations of delight the receipt of most welcome news . . . the last rail of the road connecting our opposite ocean-bound shores was laid; the last spike (a gold one, by the bye) was driven; and thereupon there was booming of cannon . . . and general rejoicing.

29. How did Americans react to the completion of the transcontinental railroad?

CONNECT TO YOUR LIFE

30. **INFORMATIVE** This chapter describes many different people who have had to fight for their own rights or those of others. Choose one of the people discussed in the chapter. Then write a paragraph in which you explain which traits you find admirable about the person. Tell how you try to mirror these same traits in your own life through actions you take.

TIPS

- Fill in a word web, listing the person's name in the middle and the person's admirable traits on the surrounding lines.

- Include in your informative paragraph textual evidence that supports your ideas about the person, along with two or three vocabulary terms from the chapter.

- Conclude the paragraph with a comment that explains how you try to mirror the same traits in your own life.

VOCABULARY ANSWERS

1. Those who promote laissez-faire economics believe less government intervention in the economy is good for capitalism.

2. Passengers who used the transcontinental railroad to cross the United States appreciated the introduction of standard time because it made railroad schedules easier to use.

3. To improve profits, some business owners kept the overhead low, even when such cost-cutting measures resulted in sweatshops where people worked long hours in unsafe conditions for little pay.

4. The Chinese Exclusion Act, which strictly limited immigration from China, and Jim Crow laws, which limited rights of African Americans in the South, were both forms of legalized racism.

5. Some people tried to help the less fortunate through reforms encouraged by the Social Gospel movement and through acts of philanthropy, or generous financial support.

6. The production of steel, a mixture of iron and carbon, was improved through the Bessemer process, in which blowing air into molten iron removed impurities and strengthened the metal.

7. Urbanization, or the movement of people from rural areas into cities, resulted in broader access to media, music, art, and other forms of entertainment, leading to the development of a mass culture.

8. Jay Gould was a robber baron whose harsh, unethical tactics led to the corruption that underlay the Gilded Age.

9. In 1892, the Carnegie Steel Company hired scabs to replace union workers who refused to work during the Homestead Strike.

READING STRATEGY ANSWER

Social and Economic Effects of the Industrial Age

> **Main Idea: Workers were often treated unfairly.**
>
> > **Detail:** Rather than spend money to make workplaces safe, many business owners had employees work in dangerous conditions.
> >
> > **Detail:** Children worked as hard as adults but for less pay.
> >
> > **Detail:** Striking workers seeking fair wages were replaced with scabs, sometimes resulting in violent clashes.

10. Responses will vary but may include poverty, discrimination against immigrants, women, children, and people of color, and the growing gap between the social classes.

MAIN IDEAS ANSWERS

11. The railroad's tracks cut through Native American land and hunting grounds. The towns that sprang up along the tracks took more land from Native Americans. In addition, the sport hunters who arrived by train diminished the number of bison on whom some Native Americans depended for survival.

12. Carnegie improved the steel industry by making steel more cheaply and efficiently.

13. After passing through an immigration center, new immigrants experienced the challenge of deciding how quickly and thoroughly they and their children would assimilate into the mainstream American culture.

14. The goal of the Social Gospel movement was to promote social reform—for example, ending child labor and getting disability insurance for workers—as a way of expressing one's faith.

15. The Ku Klux Klan increased activities meant to terrorize African Americans in the South. The organization's tactics included burning crosses in front of people's homes and murder.

16. Under the principle of "separate but equal," it was considered legal to keep African Americans from sharing certain facilities (rail cars and schools, for example) with whites as long as the separate facilities that African Americans used were equal in quality to the facilities that whites used—a requirement that often was overlooked.

17. Washington promoted self-reliance because he believed that doing so would enable African Americans to "prove" their value as a worthy part of American society.

18. When child labor was a common practice, children were unable to get an education because they worked instead of attending school.

19. Strikes were a way in which workers tried to force employers to provide better wages and working conditions. By refusing to work, employees pressured employers to grant their demands.

20. The Haymarket Riot began as a peaceful meeting at which workers for the McCormick Harvesting Machine Company in Chicago voiced their desire for an eight-hour workday. During that meeting, in Haymarket Square, someone threw a bomb, and police responded with gunfire. Rioting and several deaths resulted from the chaos that followed.

HISTORICAL THINKING ANSWERS

21. Possible responses: Not many laws protected workers until reforms were put into place. These workers generally had less education and less understanding of laws that did exist, so they did not know their rights.

22. Addams and Starr founded Hull House, dedicated to a range of social services for poor and immigrant residents. Wells used her journalistic skills to expose discrimination, formed anti-lynching societies, and co-founded the NAACP. Together, Wells and Addams worked to keep Chicago schools from segregating students based on race.

23. Answers will vary. Possible response: People benefited from rail travel because it allowed them to get places more quickly. They also benefited from the steel industry because steel enabled builders to construct stronger and taller buildings. However, railway builders and steelworkers often got hurt or were taken advantage of by employers who made them work long hours for low pay.

24. Answers will vary. Possible response: The reform of child labor practices had the biggest impact. The reforms made it possible for children to be safer and to get an education, making a better future more likely.

25. Rail lines extended outward from cities, and suburbs grew near rail stations and along the rail lines.

26. Some Californians believed that the Chinese immigrants were to blame for unemployment during the bad economy of the 1870s. Discrimination by whites against workers from Asia and the Pacific Islands was also tied to fear of unemployment.

INTERPRET GRAPHS ANSWERS STEM

27. Chicago

28. New Orleans

ANALYZE SOURCES ANSWER

29. Possible response: Americans were excited and happy about the railroad's completion. They felt patriotic about the linking of the coasts, and people displayed flags to celebrate.

CONNECT TO YOUR LIFE ANSWER

30. Paragraphs will vary but should emphasize the positive contributions of the person chosen and should make a realistic application of the person's traits to the student's own actions.

UNIT 7 RESOURCES

UNIT INTRODUCTION

UNIT TIME LINE

UNIT WRAP-UP

NATIONAL GEOGRAPHIC | CONNECTION

National Geographic Magazine Adapted Articles
- "This Land is Your Land"
- "The Native American Photography of Edward Sheriff Curtis" ONLINE

Unit 7 Inquiry: Innovate a New Solution

NG Learning Framework Activities
- Research American Species
- Write a Journal Entry

Unit 7 Formal Assessment

CHAPTER 20 RESOURCES

Available at NGLSync.Cengage.com

TEACHER RESOURCES & ASSESSMENT

Reading and Note-Taking

Vocabulary Practice

Social Studies Skills Lessons
- Reading: Synthesize
- Writing: Write an Expository Paragraph

Formal Assessment
- Chatper 20 Pretest
- Chapter 20 Tests A & B
- Section Quizzes

Chapter 20 Answer Key

ExamView®
One-time Download

STUDENT DIGITAL RESOURCES

- **eEdition** (English)
- **eEdition** (Spanish)
- **Handbooks**
- **Online Atlas**
- **American Gallery Online**
- **History Notebook**
- **American Voices (Biographies)**
- **Active History**
- **Projects for Inquiry-Based Learning**

Chapter 20 Spanish Resources are available at NGLSync.Cengage.com.

AMERICAN STORIES | **America's National Parks**

- Primary Sources
- On Your Feet: Take a Tour

NG Learning Framework:
Propose a Monument

American Voices Biography
John Muir ONLINE

SECTION 1 RESOURCES

TEDDY ROOSEVELT AND PROGRESSIVISM

LESSON 1.1
Progressives Attack Problems

- On Your Feet: Practice a Negotiation

NG Learning Framework:
Analyze a Speech

LESSON 1.2
AMERICAN VOICES
The Muckrakers

- On Your Feet: Fishbowl Activity

NG Learning Framework:
Analyze Primary and Secondary Sources

LESSON 1.3
Expanding Democracy and Reforming Government

- On Your Feet: Turn and Talk on Topic

NG Learning Framework:
Analyze the Wisconsin Idea

LESSON 1.4
Teddy Roosevelt and the Square Deal

 Yosemite National Park

NG Learning Framework:
Investigate Land Conservation

SECTION 2 RESOURCES

THE PROGRESSIVES

LESSON 2.1
Progressivism Under Taft

- On Your Feet: Team Word Webbing

NG Learning Framework:
Explore the Legacy of a Tragedy

LESSON 2.2
Wilson Continues Reform

- On Your Feet: Tell Me More

NG Learning Framework:
Analyze an Election

American Voices Biography
Woodrow Wilson ONLINE

LESSON 2.3
Modern Technology and Mass Markets

- On Your Feet: Fishbowl

NG Learning Framework:
Explore the Technology of the *Titanic*

SECTION 3 RESOURCES

WOMEN WIN NEW RIGHTS

LESSON 3.1
Women's Changing Roles

- On Your Feet: Household Invention Jigsaw

NG Learning Framework:
Write Diary Entries

LESSON 3.2
Women as Leaders

- On Your Feet: Analyze a Photograph

NG Learning Framework:
Explore Settlement Houses

LESSON 3.3
The Nineteenth Amendment

- On Your Feet: Who or What Am I?

NG Learning Framework:
Analyze Effects of Woman Suffrage

SECTION 4 RESOURCES

AMERICA ON THE WORLD STAGE

LESSON 4.1
The United States Expands

- On Your Feet: Three-Step Interview

NG Learning Framework:
Write a Magazine Article

LESSON 4.2
The Spanish-American War

- On Your Feet: Sentence Chain

NG Learning Framework:
Write a Biography

LESSON 4.3
The Filipino-American War

- Active History: Analyze Achievements of Emilio Aguinaldo

NG Learning Framework:
Analyze Perspectives

LESSON 4.4
Involvement in Latin America and Asia

- On Your Feet: Fishbowl

NG Learning Framework:
Pose and Answer Historical Questions

LESSON 4.5
GEOGRAPHY IN HISTORY
Building the Panama Canal

- On Your Feet: Become an Expert

NG Learning Framework:
Create a Public Health Brochure

CHAPTER 20 REVIEW

Strategy 1
Find Someone Who Knows

Give students copies of questions, such as the ones below. Instruct them to find a different classmate to answer each question. The student must read the question to the classmate and record the answer.

1. Who used an assembly line to make cars? *(Henry Ford)*

2. Which amendment gives Congress power to collect income tax? *(16th Amendment)*

3. Which industry did Upton Sinclair write about in *The Jungle*? *(meatpacking)*

4. What right did suffragists want? *(the right to vote)*

Use with All Lessons

Strategy 2
Write Alternative Captions

Tell students to read a lesson, and then ask them to read the captions aloud. Instruct them to find a sentence in the lesson that supports the visual and to rewrite the caption to include the information from that sentence. The visuals and extended captions can serve as reminders of content as students review a lesson.

Use with Lessons 1.3, 1.4, 2.1, 3.1, 3.3, and 4.3 *Tell students to focus on visuals that illustrate an event rather than on portraits of individuals.*

Strategy 3
Create an ABC Summary

To help them review the reading, suggest that students write important words from the lessons that begin with each letter of the alphabet. Direct them to make a chart beginning with *A* and ending with *Z* and to record words as they read the lessons. Challenge them to find one or more words for each letter, but point out that they might not find any words for a few of the letters. Then have students use their lists to summarize the main ideas of each lesson. Students can compare summaries.

Use with All Lessons *Remind students that they are not limited to Key Vocabulary words and names.*

Strategy 1
Use Flash Cards

Help students recall the important people from this chapter by limiting the list of names they need to remember. Write the list on the board. Then distribute index cards and instruct students to create a flash card for each person on the list. On one side of the card, students should write the name of the person. On the other side, they should write a fact about the person. Allow students to work in pairs. Instruct them to take turns reading a fact from one of their cards and challenging their partner to identify the person it describes.

Use with All Lessons *You might use students' cards for a team challenge. Collect the cards, and divide the group into two teams. As you read a fact, have teams alternate trying to identify the person.*

Strategy 2
Create a Summary Chart

Pair students of different reading proficiencies. Instruct the more proficient reader to read a lesson aloud, stopping after the first subheading. Have the listening partner identify two facts from the text to record on a summary chart. Repeat for the second subheading. Then have the partners use the chart to summarize the lesson.

Lesson	Subheading	Two Facts
1.1	Call for Change	
	A New Era Begins	
1.2	Abuses of Power	
	Conditions in the Meatpacking Industry	

Use with All Lessons *As students summarize the lesson, encourage them consider any additional facts that would help make a stronger summary and then add those facts to the chart.*

ENGLISH LANGUAGE LEARNERS

Strategy ❶
Use Your Own Words

Pair students at the **Emerging** and **Expanding** levels. Prompt partners to explain the meaning of Key Vocabulary words and other important content terms by using their own words, examples, visuals, and gestures. Then place students in new pairs. Partners present an explanation, example, visual, or gesture from their first grouping, and their new partners try to identify the word it represents.

Use with All Lessons *You might choose specific words and terms for students to explain, draw, or act out.*

Strategy ❷
Write a Tweet

To help students at **All Proficiencies** identify main ideas, have them read a lesson and write a tweet that explains the main idea of each subheading. Encourage students to work in pairs to compare tweets and collaborate on a final version.

Use with All Lessons *You might ask students to write a tweet for each paragraph of a lesson. Then they could use their tweets to summarize the main ideas.*

Strategy ❸
Ask Either/Or Questions

After reading a lesson, ask students either/or questions, such as those below, to reinforce meaning. Give copies of the questions to students at the **Emerging** level and have them circle the correct answer. Then have students work in pairs to compare their answers and resolve differences by consulting the text.

- Is a commissioner a [voter or a government leader]?
- Does a referendum allow voters to [propose or reject] a law?
- Did Prohibition ban the sale of [alcohol or drugs]?
- Is an archipelago a chain of [lakes or islands]?
- Did the Open Door Policy refer to [China or Hawaii]?

Use with All Lessons *You might wish to have students at the **Bridging** level write either/or questions to ask students at the **Emerging** or **Expanding** levels.*

GIFTED & TALENTED

Strategy ❶
Advertise a Product

Have students work in pairs or small groups to develop an advertisement or commercial for a product from the Progressive Era. Encourage them to choose an appropriate medium to share their work with the class.

Use with Lessons 2.3 and 3.1 *You might also suggest that students do research to find other products from the Progressive Era for their advertisements.*

Strategy ❷
Portray the Changing Roles of Women

Allow students to work individually or with partners to investigate and portray the changing roles of women in the United States from 1890 to 1920. Topics include roles at home, in the workplace, in society, and in government. Encourage students to create multimedia presentations or skits to perform for the class. Discuss how progressive reforms influenced the changes in women's roles.

Use with Lessons 3.1–3.3 *Some students might investigate and present the ways in which women's clothing styles changed during the time period.*

Pre-AP

Strategy ❶
Synthesize and Strategize

Allow students to work individually or in teams to discuss what they have learned and inferred about the effects of the Progressive Era. Instruct them to create a list of ways the progressives addressed issues that the United States or other countries may still face today. Encourage students to present strategies for addressing these modern issues.

Use with Lessons 1.3, 1.4, 2.1, 2.3, 3.1, and 4.4 *You might have students present their strategies in a town hall forum with a moderator. Encourage the presenters to answer questions from the audience.*

Strategy ❷
Deliver a Speech

Ask students to play the roles of lobbyists during the Progressive Era. Allow them to choose a group, such as progressives, muckrakers, conservationists, prohibitionists, suffragists, imperialists, or anti-imperialists. Instruct them to write a speech that represents the views of the group they chose. Then have them deliver the speech to the class.

Use with All Lessons *You might have the class play the role of Congress and discuss whether the speeches convinced them to accept the views of the lobbyist.*

CHAPTER

20

THE
PROGRESSIVE ERA
1890–1920

ESSENTIAL QUESTION
Why did the Progressive Era arise?

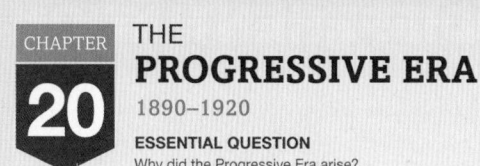

AMERICAN
STORIES America's National Parks

SECTION 1 **Teddy Roosevelt and Progressivism**
KEY VOCABULARY

commissioner	Meat Inspection Act	referendum
conservation movement	populism	Sherman Antitrust Act of 1890
direct primary election	progressivism	
initiative	Pure Food and Drug Act	

SECTION 2 **The Progressives**
KEY VOCABULARY

assembly line	income tax	reserve bank
Clayton Antitrust Act	loophole	scientific management
Federal Reserve Act		

SECTION 3 **Women Win New Rights**
KEY VOCABULARY

lobbyist	social work	teetotaler
Prohibition	suffragist	

SECTION 4 **America on the World Stage**
KEY VOCABULARY

archipelago	isthmus	Rough Riders
autonomy	lock	sphere of influence
court-martial	Open Door Policy	spoil
imperialism	Platt Amendment	yellow journalism

AMERICAN GALLERY
ONLINE Yosemite National Park

READING STRATEGY

SYNTHESIZE When you synthesize a text, you identify the most important information, look for evidence that connects the facts, and think about what you already know about the topic. Then you use the evidence, explanations, and your prior knowledge to form an overall understanding of what you have read. As you read the chapter, use a chart like this one to organize the evidence in each lesson and synthesize the information.

How did progressives address social problems?

Evidence:

↓

Supporting Explanation:

↓

Synthesis:

654 CHAPTER 20

"Much has been given us,
and much will rightfully
be expected of us."
—Theodore Roosevelt

CRITICAL VIEWING Sculptor Gutzon Borglum carved these colossal heads of (from left to right) presidents Washington, Jefferson, Theodore Roosevelt, and Lincoln into the rock of Mount Rushmore in the Black Hills of South Dakota between 1927 and 1941. Borglum chose these presidents because he believed they led the country during its most important historical periods. Based on details in the photo, what types of challenges might the sculpting team have faced during the creation of this monument?

The Progressive Era 655

INTRODUCE THE PHOTOGRAPH

Mount Rushmore

Direct students' attention to the photograph of Mount Rushmore. Ask volunteers to give their overall impression of the monument. Explain that when Gutzon Borglum accepted the offer to work on Mount Rushmore, he changed state historian Doane Robinson's vision from a sculpture of local heroes to one that memorialized four U.S. presidents. Borglum created a model and then used a process he had developed for transferring the plan to the face of the mountain. Workers used dynamite for about 90 percent of the carving. Then they worked by hand to finish the sculpture.

Borglum selected the four presidents he thought represented the most important time periods in U.S. history. Ask students to identify which president they would add to Mount Rushmore and to explain why they chose that president.

SHARE BACKGROUND

In addition to providing a colossal sculpture memorializing four presidents, Gutzon Borglum planned a hall of records. He envisioned a large room carved into the canyon behind the faces. In it would be stored important documents, such as the Declaration of Independence, the U.S. Constitution, and the Bill of Rights, for visitors to view. Congress did not approve the project, so work stopped after a small hallway had been carved.

In 1998, Borglum's daughter carried out part of her father's plan. She had a teakwood box buried in a vault in the carved hallway. The box contains 16 porcelain panels with the words of important U.S. documents on them. Other panels display the four presidents' biographies and the history of the Mount Rushmore National Memorial.

CRITICAL VIEWING Possible responses: Challenges included the danger of falling, uncomfortable working conditions, rock slides, bad weather, the task of removing tons of rock, and the amount of time required to complete the monument.

For Chapter 20 Spanish Resources, visit the Resources Menu. Chapter 20 Resources are available at NGLSync.Cengage.com.

INTRODUCE THE ESSENTIAL QUESTION

Why did the Progressive Era arise?

Four Corners Activity: Problems of the Industrial Age Encourage students to take a few minutes to reflect on what they know about the United States at the turn of the 20th century and to identify a problem the country faced during the decades surrounding the year 1900. While students are reflecting, assign each of these labels to one corner of the room: Social, Economic, Business, and Government.

Tell students to move to the corner of the room with the most appropriate label for the problem they identified. Instruct students in each corner to create a master list of the problems in their category to post in the classroom.

Explain to students that the Progressive Era was a time of reform in which the government and citizens addressed the problems facing the country. As students read the chapter, suggest that they revisit their lists of problems and identify changes or solutions that resulted from the Progressive Era.

INTRODUCE CHAPTER VOCABULARY

Word Web

As students read each lesson, encourage them to complete Word Webs for Key Vocabulary words. Have them write each word in the center circle. Explain that they should use the spokes of the circle to record examples, characteristics, and descriptive words associated with the Key Vocabulary word as they encounter it in the lesson. Model an example for students on the board using the graphic organizer below.

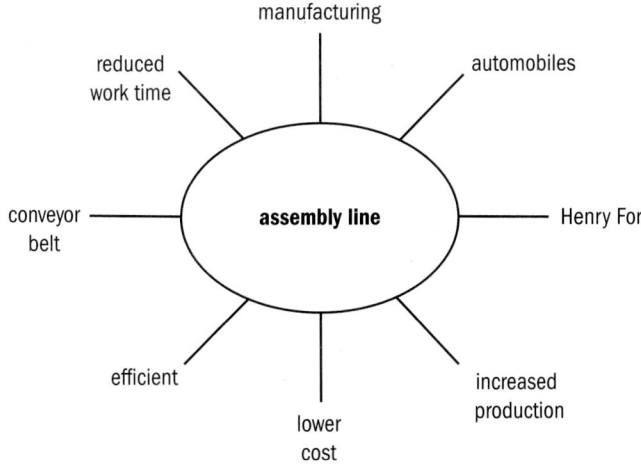

INTRODUCE THE READING STRATEGY

SYNTHESIZE

Remind students that synthesizing occurs when readers put different pieces of information together to add to their understanding of what they read. Write the following equation on the board: *evidence from the text + explanations from the text + your own knowledge of the topic = synthesis.* After students have read Lesson 1.2, work with them to complete the graphic organizer below. Then discuss any new understandings they gained by synthesizing information.

How did progressives address social problems?

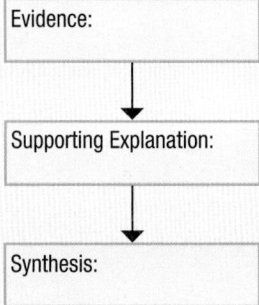

| Evidence: |
| Supporting Explanation: |
| Synthesis: |

KEY DATES FOR CHAPTER 20

1890	Sherman Antitrust Act
1898	Spanish-American War
1901	Theodore Roosevelt elected president
1906	Upton Sinclair publishes *The Jungle*
1906	Pure Food and Drug Act
1911	Triangle Waist Company fire kills 146 workers
1913	Federal Reserve Act establishes a central bank
1914	Panama Canal opens
1920	19th Amendment gives women the right to vote

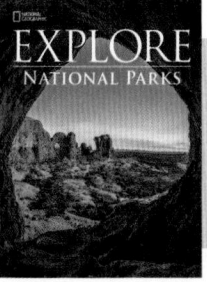

For more on public lands and monuments, see *EXPLORE NATIONAL PARKS.*

STEM

Objectives

- **Learn the history of America's national parks.**
- **Understand the role of the conservation movement in protecting wilderness areas.**
- **Determine the role of significant individuals and laws in creating national parks and monuments.**
- **Learn how the National Park Service grew to include the variety of sites it manages today.**
- **Study a primary source: excerpt of President Roosevelt's speech at the Grand Canyon.**

Critical Thinking Skills for "America's National Parks"

- Make Connections
- Draw Conclusions
- Analyze Language Use
- Form and Support Opinions
- Interpret Maps
- Identify Problems and Solutions
- Explain

Background for the Teacher

This American Story explores the history of the national parks from their beginnings in the late 19th century through today. By studying the detailed history—supplemented with an analysis of photographs, written primary sources, maps, and charts—students will understand the historical context under which the national parks were created, as well as the importance of conservation in American history.

The upcoming chapter, The Progressive Era, explores a time of reform and increased government intervention in American society. While this period is often associated with dissolving business monopolies and trusts, the fight for labor laws, and woman suffrage, one of the most lasting developments of the era was the beginning of federal support for the conservation movement. This American Story will provide an in-depth study of that movement—the successes of which are still visible to this day.

History Notebook

Encourage students to complete the American Story page for Chapter 20 in their History Notebooks as they read.

Note to the Teacher

Introduce this American Story after the class has engaged with the content in Lesson 1.4.

AMERICAN STORIES

NATIONAL GEOGRAPHIC

CRITICAL VIEWING Yellowstone National Park contains many natural wonders, including these travertine terraces. What does this photo reveal about the type of rock called travertine?

656 CHAPTER 20

AMERICA'S
NATIONAL PARKS

In a book about the American West, writer and historian Wallace Stegner called the national parks "the best idea we ever had." He continued, "Absolutely American, absolutely democratic, they reflect us at our best rather than our worst."

Yellowstone, the first national park in the world, was created in 1872. The idea of setting aside and protecting wilderness areas, however, was not new. In 1832, artist George Catlin visited South Dakota and observed threats to both the buffalo herds and the Native American groups that relied on them. In his journal, he imagined a solution to the problem. It would be "some great protecting policy of the government preserved . . . in a *magnificent park . . . a nation's park,* containing man and beast, in all the wildness and freshness of their nature's beauty!"

AN EARLY VOICE FOR PARKS

One of the strongest voices in the early national parks movement was John Muir. Born in Scotland in 1838, Muir moved to the United States with his family when he was a boy. He was an inquisitive young man with a thirst for travel and a fascination with wild places. In 1868, Muir arrived in California. There, he found his spiritual home in the Yosemite Valley, part of the Sierra Nevada mountain range. Later, he described his first walk through the remote high country: "Then it seemed to me

the Sierra should be called not the Nevada, or Snowy Range, but the Range of Light . . . the most divinely beautiful of all the mountain chains I have ever seen."

Muir traveled widely and pursued several careers, but he never stopped writing about the wilderness he loved so passionately, and especially about Yosemite. Muir once wrote, "It is easier to feel than to realize, or in any way explain, Yosemite grandeur. The magnitudes [size and extent] of the rocks and trees and streams are so delicately harmonized, they are mostly hidden." His writings attracted the attention of many influential people. Along with others, Muir lobbied tirelessly for the protection of Yosemite from grazing by herds of sheep and cattle, until Congress created Yosemite National Park in 1890. Muir's continuing efforts also lent strong support to the creation of Sequoia, Mount Rainier, Petrified Forest, and Grand Canyon national parks.

In 1892, Muir and several associates founded the Sierra Club. In his own words, the club's mission was to "do something for wildness and make the mountains glad." Muir wanted to protect Yosemite

INTRODUCE & ENGAGE

Preview Using Visuals

Point out the photograph of Yellowstone National Park. **ASK:** What words would you use to describe the image? *(exotic, open, beautiful, rocky)* Discuss with students the geography of the landscape. **ASK:** What physical features do you notice? *(There are layers of rock, mountains in the background, and maybe hot springs in the distance.)* Inform students that the image shows Yellowstone National Park—the first national park. Then tell students they are going to read an American Story about the history of the national parks and the creation of the National Park System.

Activate Prior Knowledge

Invite students to share what they know about the national parks. Examples could include the names of parks, when and why they were created, the geography of the park, or any personal experiences. Record student responses in a Word Web on the board.

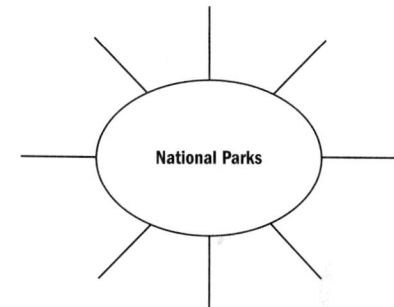

Top Ten Toss

Provide a small beanbag or soft ball that can be safely tossed. Ask students to write down questions they would like answered about the national parks. When they have finished writing questions, toss the beanbag to a student and ask that student to state a question. Record the question on the board. Then have that student toss the beanbag to someone else. Repeat the tossing and asking throughout the classroom until a list of questions has been created. Ask students as a class to choose the top 10 questions they'd like answered. After reading this American Story, review the top 10 list with the class to see if all questions were answered.

CRITICAL VIEWING Travertine appears to be a type of rock that forms in layers, and when it is weathered and eroded, the layers seem to create flat surfaces, making the terraced levels. The hot springs in the background suggest a relationship in the formation of the travertine.

Roosevelt in Africa

Theodore Roosevelt's love of the outdoors did not end with his presidency. In 1909, after declining to run for a third term, Roosevelt embarked on a year-long safari across Africa. Sponsored by the Smithsonian Institution, the safari was tasked with documenting and collecting samples from the African continent. Over the course of the expedition, Roosevelt and his party hunted, trapped, and collected just about everything imaginable, from elephants and lions to small insects. In the end, the expedition amassed more than 23,000 specimens—a number so large that it took eight years to properly catalog. While the vast majority of the specimens were hunted and killed, a small number of cheetahs, lions, and leopards were captured alive and given to the National Zoological Park. Many of the preserved specimens became part of the National Museum of Natural History, and one, the white rhinoceros, remains on display today.

Federal Lands—The Vast and the Tiny

Although the phrases "national park" and "national monument" conjure images of vast landscapes and magnificent vistas, not all federal lands fit this description. The Antiquities Act of 1906 allows the federal government to protect and preserve land for future generations. This land includes not only environmental wonders but also landmarks, structures, and objects of historical and cultural significance. Thus, alongside the breathtaking national parks of Alaska, more urbanized areas and smaller structures, such as the birthplace of the modern gay rights movement at the Stonewall Inn in New York City, John F. Kennedy's childhood home in Massachusetts, and Ford's Theater in Washington, D.C.—the site of Lincoln's assassination—are also federally protected places.

Conservation Under Obama

Although Theodore Roosevelt is the president most closely associated with the conservation movement, the president who added the greatest amount of federal territory is Barack Obama. During his tenure, through the use of the Antiquities Act, Obama established 29 national monuments and protected more than 500 million acres of land and water—more than double the amount of any previous president. These protected areas include more than half a million square miles of ocean habitat off Hawaii, three national monuments in the California desert, and, off the coast of New England, the first marine national monument in the Atlantic Ocean—the Northeast Canyons and Seamounts.

LEAVE IT AS IT IS

Theodore Roosevelt was both blunt and eloquent in his support for the protection of wilderness areas. During his 1903 tour of the western states, he spoke to a group near the rim of the Grand Canyon and made an important request.

Friends and early environmentalists Teddy Roosevelt and John Muir pose for this 1903 photo at Glacier Point in Yosemite Valley, California.

PRIMARY SOURCE

I want to ask you to do one thing in connection with [the Grand Canyon] in your own interest and in the interest of our country—to keep this great wonder of nature as it now is.

Leave it as it is. You cannot improve it. The ages have been at work on it, and man can only mar it. What you can do is to keep it for your children, your children's children, and for all who come after you, as one of the great sights which every American, if he can travel at all, should see.

—President Theodore Roosevelt, 1903

How did the resources in the Grand Canyon influence Roosevelt's request to preserve the site?

National Park from ranchers or others who would seek to turn the park's lands over for commercial use. Since then, the Sierra Club's mission has expanded greatly. Today, it is one of the world's oldest environmental organizations and works to protect wild spaces throughout the United States.

THE PARKS PRESIDENT

One fan of John Muir, President Theodore Roosevelt, did not need to be convinced that conservation was a good idea. An avid outdoorsman and hunter, Roosevelt had been involved for many years in efforts to create wilderness preserves and carefully manage natural resources such as forests, rivers, and streams.

Roosevelt became president in 1901. In 1903, he went on an extensive tour of the country, visiting

25 states in 8 weeks. He took advantage of his time in the West to explore the existing national parks. At Yosemite, local officials had planned a series of elaborate parties and dinners in the president's honor. Instead of attending any of these events, Roosevelt slipped away from the dignitaries and the journalists to spend three nights camping in the wilderness with John Muir.

Muir wasn't afraid to address the president directly. Of Roosevelt's hunting, he asked, "Mr. Roosevelt, when are you going to get beyond the boyishness of killing things?" Despite—or perhaps because of—Muir's lack of tact, the two men became firm friends. Muir later wrote of the encounter, "I had a perfectly glorious time. I never before had a more interesting . . . companion."

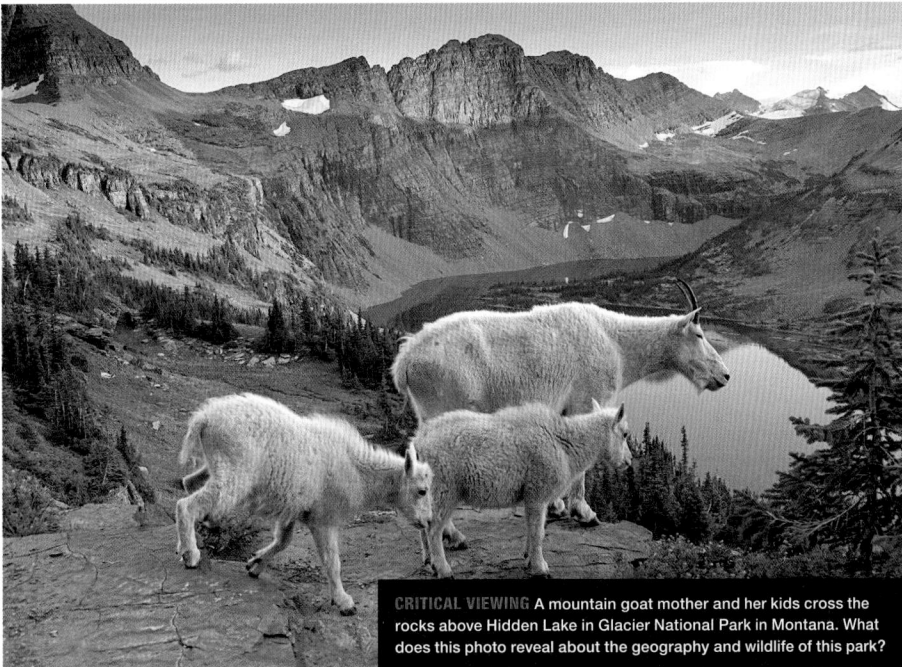

CRITICAL VIEWING A mountain goat mother and her kids cross the rocks above Hidden Lake in Glacier National Park in Montana. What does this photo reveal about the geography and wildlife of this park?

President Roosevelt emerged from Yosemite with a renewed commitment to conservation as well. After his outing with Muir, he told an audience at Stanford University in California, "There is nothing more practical than the preservation of beauty, than the preservation of anything that appeals to the higher emotions of mankind." Roosevelt turned out to be one of the national parks' most effective supporters. By the time he left office, he had created five new ones and added land to Yosemite. He also established 150 national forests, 51 federal bird reserves, 4 national game preserves, and 18 national monuments.

CONTINUED PROTECTION

In 1906, Congress established a new type of protected area. The Antiquities Act of that year made it possible for the president to create national monuments. These were pieces of public land that had "historic landmarks, historic and prehistoric structures, and other objects of historic and scientific interest."

The difficulty with the national parks and national monuments was that they were not managed by a single government agency. The national parks were part of the Department of the Interior. Some national monuments were on land owned by the War Department; others were controlled by the Department of Agriculture. Many national parks and monuments were poorly funded. "They were orphans," wrote Horace Albright, who later played an important role in creating the National Park Service. "They were anybody's business and therefore nobody's business."

MATHER AND ALBRIGHT

An unlikely hero stepped into the spotlight. Stephen Mather was not a government official. He was a businessman who had made millions of dollars selling a type of soap called Borax. In 1914, Mather sent a scathing letter to Secretary of the Interior Franklin Lane about the poor condition of roads and facilities in the national parks. Lane decided to try an unusual solution to the problem. He talked Mather into taking charge of the parks office in the Department of the Interior. To assist him, Mather brought along Horace Albright, a young law student. For both men, the job was supposed to be a one-year assignment.

The Progressive Era **659**

TEACH

Guided Discussion

1. **Analyze Language Use** Have students read the excerpt from Roosevelt's Grand Canyon speech. **ASK:** Why does Roosevelt tell people, "Leave it as it is. You cannot improve it"? *(He is advocating for preservation of the Grand Canyon, arguing that making changes to the land won't make it better in any way.)* What does he mean when he says, "The ages have been at work on it, and man can only mar it"? *(Roosevelt is stating that nature has already made the Grand Canyon beautiful and that using it for any purpose other than observation and enjoyment would destroy the beauty of the land.)*

2. **Form and Support Opinions** Have students reread the third and fourth paragraphs under the subsection The Parks President. **ASK:** Does it surprise you that Roosevelt, the conservationist, was also an avid hunter who traveled extensively to hunt animals? *(Answers will vary.)* Is it possible for a person to be both a conservationist and someone who hunts animals? *(Possible responses: No, someone who takes the life of an animal is not conserving. Yes, someone who hunts also has an interest in thinning herds to make sure their numbers are sustainable for future generations.)* How do you think Roosevelt's background as an outdoorsman influenced his position on conservation? *(Roosevelt's familiarity with nature made him more aware of its beauty, its usefulness to the country, and its fragility.)*

Draw Conclusions

What factors do conservation and historic preservation experts consider when deciding which places to protect? *(Possible responses: Some areas that have unusual natural features, such as rock formations, or uncommon animals or plants may be protected. Places where historical events happened may be chosen. Places that have resources that are vital for human survival may be a priority to protect.)*

CRITICAL VIEWING The photo illustrates the diverse geography of the park because viewers can see grassland, water, mountains, forests, and even glaciers. It also shows mountain goats as one type of wildlife living in the park.

Utah's National Parks

Five national parks have a home in Utah: Arches, Bryce Canyon, Canyonlands, Capitol Reef, and Zion. Arches National Park is noted for its more than 2,000 stone arches, including Delicate Arch, the park's largest freestanding arch. The opening beneath the arch stretches 45 feet wide and 64 feet high. Bryce Canyon National Park is home to the world's largest collection of hoodoos. Hoodoos are columns of weathered rock that are formed through erosion. Canyonlands National Park is a primitive desert wilderness of canyons and buttes formed by the Colorado River and its tributaries. Capitol Reef National Park is home to red rock canyons and cliffs, white domes of Navajo sandstone, and the Waterpocket Fold, a nearly 100-mile-long geologic monocline. A monocline is a warp or step-up in rock layers. Zion—Utah's first national park—is noted for its massive cream, pink, and red cliffs and narrow slot canyons. The park contains many archaeological sites that provide clues to the region's past. Only a few of the sites are open to the public.

NATIONAL GEOGRAPHIC PHOTOGRAPHER
Paul Nicklen

National Geographic photographer Paul Nicklen is a marine biologist as well as a photographer. In addition to capturing this image from the rocky landscape of Utah, Nicklen has documented the wildlife inhabiting Arctic ecosystems and ocean habitats—and the challenges they face for survival. Nicklen calls himself "an interpreter and a translator" because he uses the medium of photography to help people envision environmental issues and understand warnings from the scientific community.

CRITICAL VIEWING An arch is a curved structure with a connection on top—a description that perfectly matches the stone formation. It may be referred to as Delicate Arch because the arch is showing signs of continuous weathering and erosion and appears a bit fragile, as if it may crumble and fall at some point.

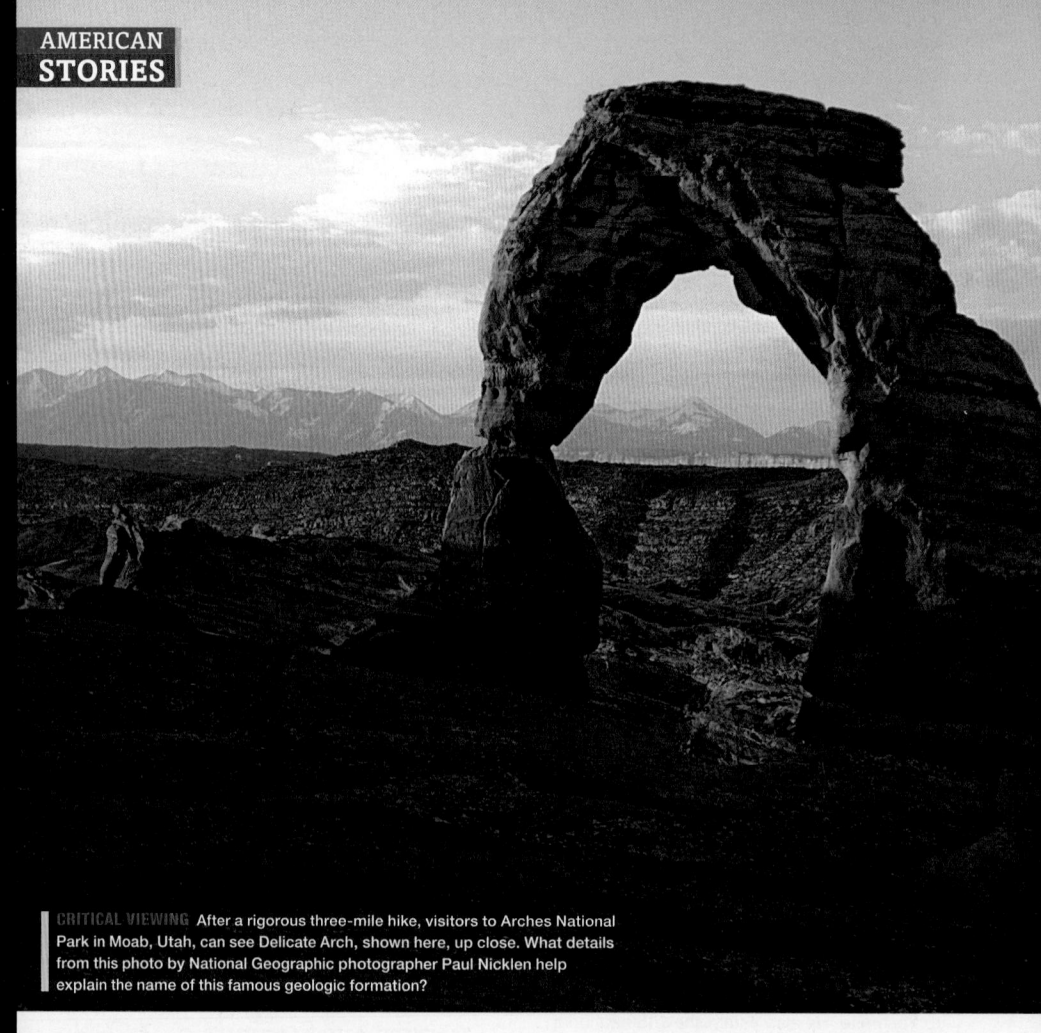

AMERICAN
STORIES

CRITICAL VIEWING After a rigorous three-mile hike, visitors to Arches National Park in Moab, Utah, can see Delicate Arch, shown here, up close. What details from this photo by National Geographic photographer Paul Nicklen help explain the name of this famous geologic formation?

Mather knew the parks needed more money, and he decided the first step would be to attract more visitors. With increased tourism would come greater attention to the national parks and, he hoped, more funding from the government. To this end, he established a marketing plan. He recruited the help of the railroads and automobile associations to publicize the national parks. Mather's campaign worked. At Yosemite, the number of visitors grew from around 15,000 in 1914 to around 33,000 in 1915.

Mather took his campaign to the next step by inviting 15 influential American businessmen,

journalists, congressmen, and politicians on a two-week tour through Sequoia National Park in California. At the end of the trip, he made his case for a single government agency to manage the national parks. "Just think of the vast areas of our land that should be preserved for the future," he told his guests. "Unless we can protect the areas currently held with a separate government agency, we may lose them to selfish interests."

PASSING THE ACT

Mather and his supporters succeeded in their goal. Congress passed the National Park Service Organic Act, which President Woodrow Wilson

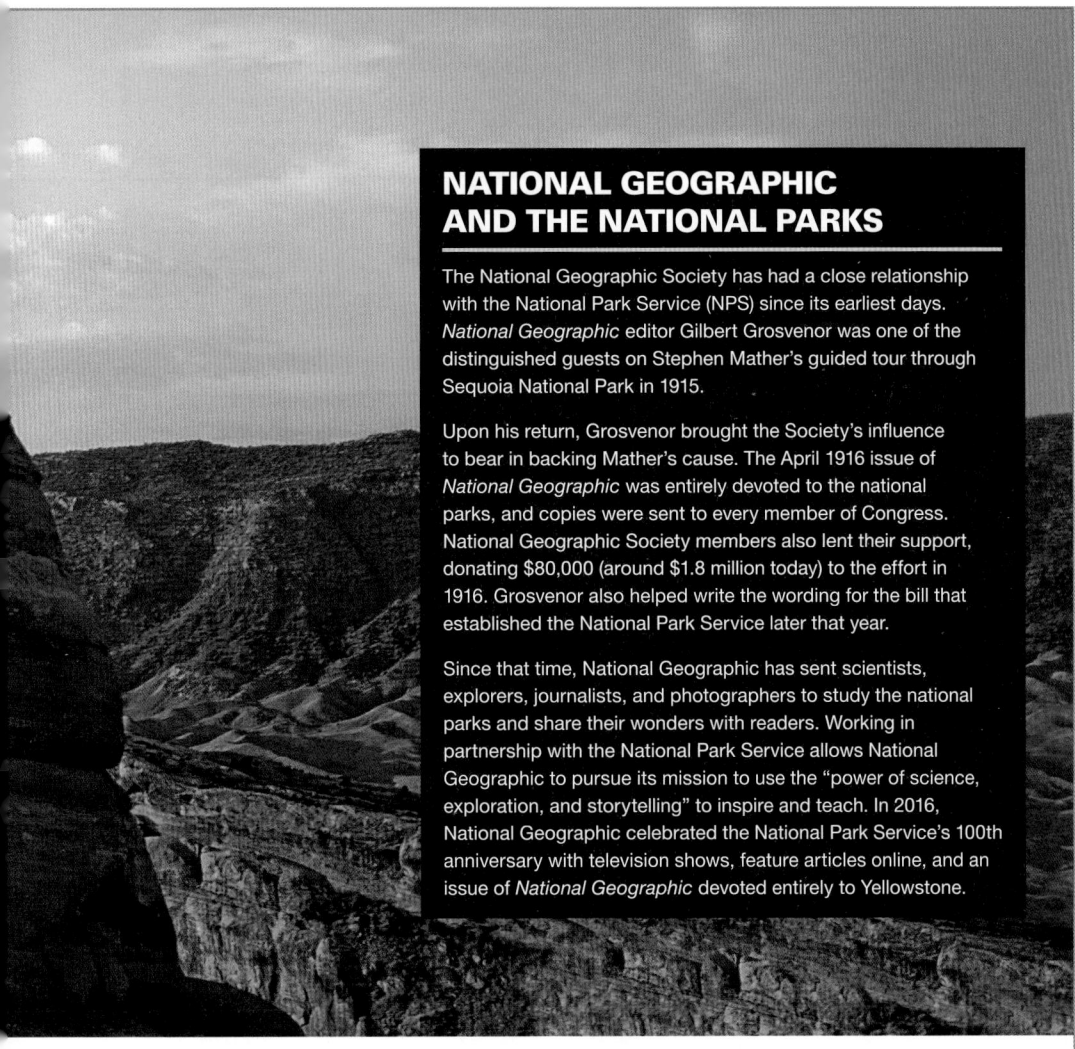

NATIONAL GEOGRAPHIC AND THE NATIONAL PARKS

The National Geographic Society has had a close relationship with the National Park Service (NPS) since its earliest days. *National Geographic* editor Gilbert Grosvenor was one of the distinguished guests on Stephen Mather's guided tour through Sequoia National Park in 1915.

Upon his return, Grosvenor brought the Society's influence to bear in backing Mather's cause. The April 1916 issue of *National Geographic* was entirely devoted to the national parks, and copies were sent to every member of Congress. National Geographic Society members also lent their support, donating $80,000 (around $1.8 million today) to the effort in 1916. Grosvenor also helped write the wording for the bill that established the National Park Service later that year.

Since that time, National Geographic has sent scientists, explorers, journalists, and photographers to study the national parks and share their wonders with readers. Working in partnership with the National Park Service allows National Geographic to pursue its mission to use the "power of science, exploration, and storytelling" to inspire and teach. In 2016, National Geographic celebrated the National Park Service's 100th anniversary with television shows, feature articles online, and an issue of *National Geographic* devoted entirely to Yellowstone.

signed on August 25, 1916. The United States now had a single agency, the National Park Service, or NPS, in charge of its precious protected lands. Stephen Mather was chosen to be its director.

Mather's "one-year contract" ended with his retirement in 1929. During his time as director, he was tireless in his efforts to bring visitors into the national parks. He delighted in the idea that people from all income levels—not just the wealthy— enjoyed the parks. According to Albright, "There could never be too many tourists for Stephen Mather. He wanted as many as possible to enjoy his 'treasures.'" Horace Albright succeeded Mather

as director of the National Park Service, continuing in the post until 1933. For his contributions to the national parks, Albright was awarded the Presidential Medal of Freedom in 1980.

Since Mather's and Albright's day, numerous national parks and monuments have been added to the list. Today, the system includes 413 national parks, monuments, battlefields, seashores, and recreation areas. Visitors can experience sites as diverse as the majestic six-million-acre Denali National Park in Alaska and Liberty Island in New York Harbor.

Active Options

On Your Feet: Take a Tour After students review the National Geographic and the National Parks feature, allow them to access printed magazines, maps, or digital resources from National Geographic featuring national parks. Place these resources in different locations throughout the classroom. Alternatively, post images of various national parks around the room. Divide the class into small groups. Have each group move throughout the classroom to examine the images and information. When finished, invite groups to discuss the similarities and differences observed between the parks, recording their notes in a Venn Diagram. Encourage groups to share their findings with the class.

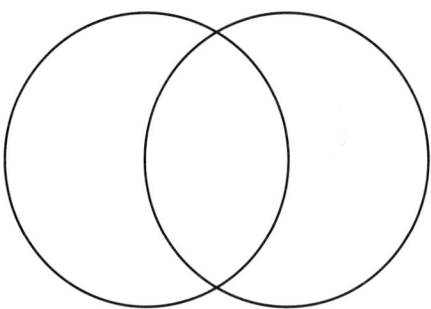

NG Learning Framework: Propose a Monument

ATTITUDE Responsibility

SKILLS Observation, Problem-Solving

Divide the class into small groups. Instruct the groups to research the Antiquities Act of 1906. In their research, students should focus on the requirements a site needs to meet in order to be designated a national monument. After groups have completed their research, prompt them to propose a site in their state that they think should become a national monument. Groups should research the site and prepare a persuasive presentation that explains how the site meets the requirements of the Antiquities Act. The presentation should utilize photographs, maps, and other visuals. Allow time for each group to present their proposal.

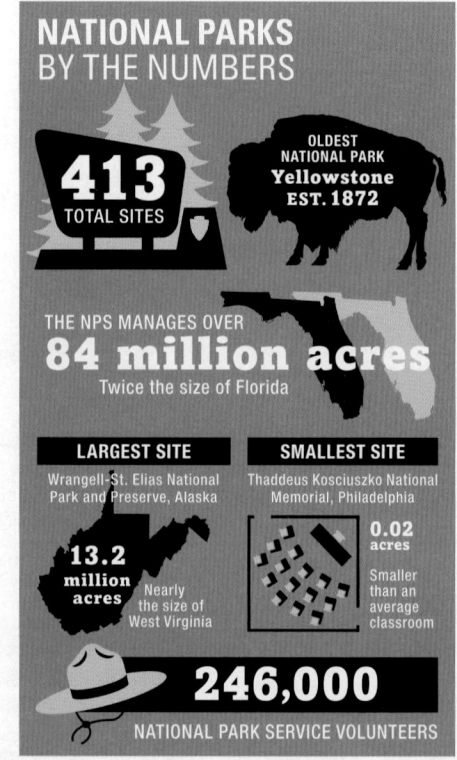

TEACH

Guided Discussion

1. **Interpret Maps** Based on the National Parks in the United States map, what conclusions can be drawn about the regional distribution of federally protected lands? *(The majority of the national parks and protected lands are in the western portion of the country, particularly California, Utah, and Alaska.)*

2. **Identify Problems and Solutions** In what ways could the national parks address the concerns of critics such as Native Americans and ranchers? *(Answers will vary. Possible response: The federal government could provide alternative grazing land for ranchers and allow Native Americans greater access to and use of the parks.)*

WRITE ABOUT HISTORY

An Opinion on the Parks This American Story explores the development of the national parks and the role of conservation in American history. To help students think more deeply about the issue, have them write a persuasive essay answering the following questions: Is it important for the government to protect land like national parks and monuments from development? Why or why not? For this essay, students should weigh both sides of the issue before settling upon their conclusion. They should consider the importance of conserving the natural environment and also consider the needs and opinions of groups such as ranchers, Native Americans, and local people. If time allows, students could conduct additional research, which might include factual information as well as opinions from critics and from proponents of federal land policies.

THINK ABOUT IT

Answers will vary. Possible response: I agree with Stegner's statement because the national parks protect and conserve land that would otherwise be used, and possibly overused, for commercial purposes.

AMERICAN STORIES

The creation of national parks has not always been popular with everyone. When Yellowstone became a national park, some Native American groups were displaced from their homes or lost the ability to hunt freely. In Yosemite, cattle and sheep ranchers bitterly resented the loss of grazing lands.

Sometimes, too, the goal of making the parks easy for visitors to explore conflicts with the need to protect wildlife from harm by humans. As in the past, today's National Park Service works to balance conservation with other human needs.

It's a difficult job, but worth every effort to keep the "best idea we ever had" safe for all generations.

THINK ABOUT IT

Do you agree with Wallace Stegner that the national parks are America's "best idea"? Explain your answer.

NATIONAL PARKS IN THE UNITED STATES

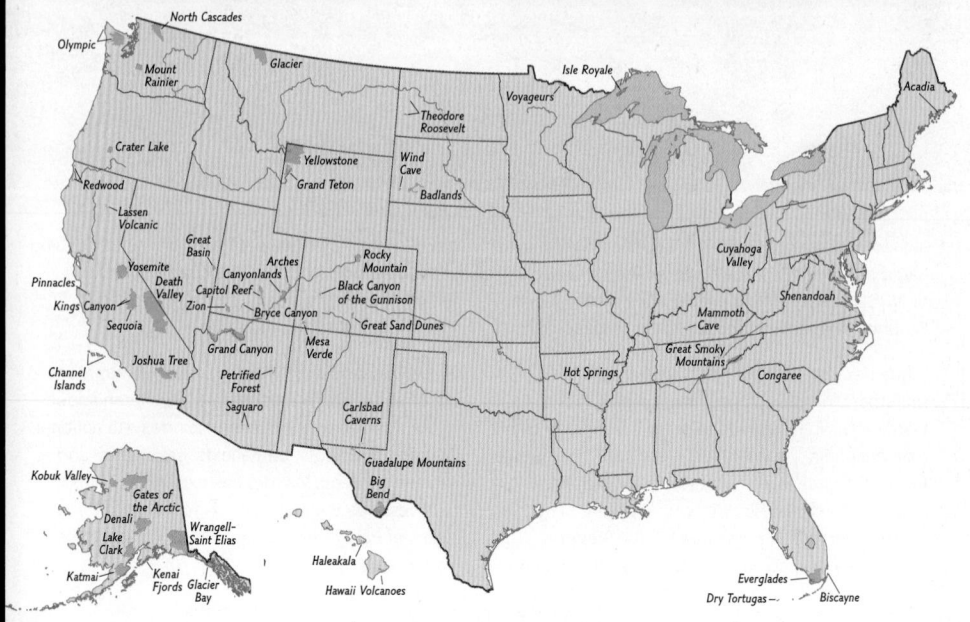

ANSEL ADAMS

In dramatic, crystal-sharp, black and white photographs, Ansel Adams captured the essence of some of America's wildest places. Born in California in 1902, Adams began to experiment with photography in 1916 after a trip to Yosemite. Before long, he was exhibiting and selling his photos at a studio called Best's, in Yosemite Valley. In 1928, he married the daughter of the studio owner, and Best's remained in the Adams family until 1971.

Although Adams traveled widely and photographed an impressive variety of subjects, Yosemite remained one of his inspirations and the scene of some of his most famous images. A strong believer in conservation, Adams sought to use his photos of Yosemite and the West to arouse people's interest in protecting wild spaces. His striking photos also helped photography gain acceptance as an art form, not just as a way to record information. Ansel Adams died in 1984.

How do you think photos like these affected people's opinions about the national parks?

Sand Dunes, Sunrise, Death Valley National Monument, California, 1948.
Photograph by Ansel Adams

These 1940s Ansel Adams photos reveal the striking geography of Sunrise Death Valley National Park (above) and Death Valley National Park (below) in California.

Rocks, Joshua Tree National Monument, California, 1942
Photograph by Ansel Adams

Striving Readers

Outline and Take Notes Assign pairs of students one of these important people from this American Story: John Muir, Theodore Roosevelt, Stephen Mather, or Horace Albright. As pairs read the text, have them take notes on their assigned person and keep this question in mind: What role did this person play in the history of the national parks? Then pairs will meet with pairs who studied a different person and share their notes so that all students have notes for all four people.

Gifted & Talented

Create an Infographic Direct students' attention to the infographic on the opposite page. Note how it uses logical design and simple comparisons to make facts more interesting and understandable. Direct students to research a national park and create an infographic that shows their findings, including facts and comparisons. Have students present their infographics to the class.

See the Chapter Planner for more strategies for differentiation.

HISTORICAL THINKING

Ask and have students answer the following questions.

1. **READING CHECK** Why were the national parks created?

2. **EXPLAIN** Why has tourism been important for the sustainability of the parks?

3. **IDENTIFY PROBLEMS AND SOLUTIONS** What problem was solved by passage of the National Park Service Organic Act?

ANSWERS

1. The national parks were created to protect land from development, preserve natural resources, safeguard wildlife, and allow access for all people to enjoy.

2. Tourism brings money to the parks, as well as attention and government funding. Conversely, if no one visited the parks, there would be less pressure to keep them funded.

3. Prior to the law, the national parks were run by multiple government agencies, which made their management difficult. The law solved the problem by putting all the national parks under a single government body.

1.1 Progressives Attack Problems

Think of the changes you'd like to see in your school. Then consider how you might make them happen. In the 1890s, Americans had ideas that would change the country. All they needed was the right leader.

MAIN IDEA Americans grew angry at the lack of government control over business and began to call for reform.

CALL FOR CHANGE

The period after the Civil War saw a sharp rise in the growth of cities. Americans attracted by the promise of factory jobs and new immigrants swelled the cities. And there was work for most everyone who arrived. A largely laissez-faire economy led to the rapid growth of business. This meant, however, that the government paid little attention to business owners' financial dealings or their treatment of workers. Bosses forced many workers to toil long hours in dangerous factories for very low wages.

This economic prosperity was repeatedly disrupted, however, by a number of economic recessions during the intense boom and bust cycles at the end of the 19th century. The country experienced a deep depression beginning in 1893. The depression occurred when a major railroad collapsed, and banks and other businesses dependent on it failed as well. By the end of 1893, about 600 banks and 15,000 businesses had closed. Early the following year, about 2.5 million people were out of work. There were no safeguards in place for helping them through the tough times. And because leaders in both the Democratic and Republican parties believed that a depression was part of the economic cycle, they did nothing to help restore the nation's economy.

Meanwhile, businesses unaffected by the depression continued to exploit, or take advantage of, their workforce. The inability—or unwillingness—of the government to change these practices sparked a rise in **populism,** the belief that common people, not the wealthy, should control their government. Remember that farmers formed the Populist Party, also called the People's Party, in 1892. The party focused on issues such as better pay and working conditions, workers' and immigrants' rights, better access to education, and an end to child labor.

In the election of 1892, the Populist Party nominated one of its members for president under the slogan "Equal rights to all; special privileges to none." The Populist candidate didn't win, but the party influenced the rise of another social movement called **progressivism**. Middle class and college-educated, progressives aligned themselves with the American workforce. They believed deeply in equality for all people and called for people and the government to work together to bring about social change.

A NEW ERA BEGINS

In 1896, Americans elected **William McKinley** as president. McKinley, who had served as governor of Ohio, undertook several progressive policies as president. For example, he worked to restore the economy, reform business practices, and open up trade with other countries. Much of his first term, however, was dominated by foreign policy and the Spanish-American War, which you'll learn about later in this chapter. A popular president, McKinley was elected to a second term in 1900. In 1901, however, while making a public appearance, McKinley was shot by an anarchist, a person who uses violence to overthrow authority. The shooter claimed he killed the president "because he was the enemy of . . . the working people."

Vice President **Theodore Roosevelt**, often called "Teddy" in the media, took over as president. Just 42 years old, he was much younger than any other president before him. He had grown up in a wealthy New York family but had spent years working on a ranch in the West. Energetic and outgoing, Roosevelt was an enthusiastic athlete, outdoorsman, and hunter. His bravery during the Spanish-American War had made him a war hero.

Roosevelt supported progressive ideas, and he looked forward to making changes as president. He especially hoped to expand U.S. power abroad and promote environmental causes. His enthusiasm spread throughout the country. Some of the most dramatic changes of the **Progressive Era** would occur during his presidency.

For his re-election campaign in 1900, McKinley chose Theodore Roosevelt as his running mate. Photos of the two appear in this campaign poster.

FOR PRESIDENT — FOR VICE PRESIDENT

WM. McKINLEY. — THEO. ROOSEVELT.

Following McKinley's death, President Roosevelt addressed Congress. He laid out a far-reaching progressive agenda that connected his own goals with McKinley's, including the relationships among big business, workers, and government.

PRIMARY SOURCE

The fundamental rule in our national life—the rule which underlies all others—is that, on the whole, and in the long run, we shall go up or down together. . . . Disaster to great business enterprises can never have its effects limited to the men at the top. It spreads throughout, and while it is bad for everybody, it is worst for those farthest down. The capitalist [business owner or investor] may be shorn [deprived] of his luxuries; but the wage-worker may be deprived of even bare necessities.

—from President Theodore Roosevelt's First Annual Address to Congress, December 3, 1901

HISTORICAL THINKING

1. **READING CHECK** What happened to many workers as a result of the depression that began in 1893?

2. **SUMMARIZE** What were some of the main beliefs and goals of populism in the 1890s?

3. **MAKE INFERENCES** How do you think both populists and progressives reacted when Theodore Roosevelt became president?

PLAN

Objective
Describe how exploitive business practices led to populism and progressivism.

Critical Thinking Skills for Lesson 1.1
- Identify Main Ideas and Details
- Monitor Comprehension
- Summarize
- Make Inferences
- Analyze Cause and Effect
- Identify Problems and Solutions

Essential Question for Chapter 20
Why did the Progressive Era arise? People wanted better working and living conditions. Lesson 1.1 explains how worker exploitation and a lack of regulations on businesses led to a call for reforms.

Background for the Teacher
The depression of 1893 had a profound effect on American workers. By 1894, the economy operated at 80 percent of capacity, and unemployment ranged between 17 and 19 percent. With husbands and fathers laid off, women and children joined the workforce in greater numbers. During the 1890s, the total number of women with jobs rose from 3.7 million to just under 5 million. The contributions of women and children were vital to most households even though their wages were far lower than those of men. By 1900, at least 18 percent of the workforce, or 1.75 million people, was children younger than 16. In the cotton mills of the South, a quarter of workers were under 15 years old, and fully half of those under 12 years old. Although 30 states had passed child labor laws by 1900, the laws were often ineffective.

Financial Literacy
To extend their knowledge and understanding about the concepts in this lesson, refer students to the Financial Literacy handbook.

Imagine a 12-Hour Workday

Point out that during the Industrial Revolution nearly 20 percent of American workers were under the age of 16. Have students imagine how their lives would be different if they had to work 10 to 12 hours a day for low wages in a factory or mine. *(Possible responses: not attending school; having no time for socializing, sports, or other leisure activities)* Tell students that Lesson 1.1 focuses on some of the social and economic issues that the progressives sought to reform, including working conditions and child labor practices.

TEACH

Guided Discussion

1. **Analyze Cause and Effect** How did the government's hands-off approach to business and labor practices affect bosses and workers? *(Businesses were unregulated and bosses could do what they wanted to make profits with little fear of punishment. As a result, many workers had to work long hours for low pay, often in dangerous conditions.)*

2. **Identify Problems and Solutions** How did President William McKinley attempt to help address the problems of American workers? *(McKinley implemented progressive policies to restore the economy and created more international trade that helped to create more jobs for people out of work. His business practice reforms were created to give workers better hours, pay, and working conditions.)*

More Information

Roosevelt's First Annual Message In his First Annual Message to Congress, Theodore Roosevelt crafted his speech to strike a balance between supporting industrialists and endorsing their critics. For example, Roosevelt stands up for industrialists, saying, "The captains of industry who have driven the railway systems across this continent … have on the whole done great good to our people. Without them the material development of which we are so justly proud could never have taken place." Later, Roosevelt shows support for reformers, saying that corporations "should be subject to proper governmental supervision, and full and accurate information as to their operations should be made public regularly at reasonable intervals." Roosevelt's evenhanded analysis of competing interests led to what later became known as his "square deal," policies that were fair to and benefited all parties.

Active Options

On Your Feet: Practice a Negotiation Divide the class into two groups. Assign one group to be business bosses and the other group to be workers. Tell groups to imagine that President McKinley has just been elected and plans to implement business reforms. Direct the boss group to record a list of reasons to retain a system where government has little oversight over business. Instruct the group of workers to create a list of reforms they want regarding working conditions in the 1880s and 1890s. Then have boss and worker groups exchange lists. Prompt each group to discuss the other side's points and identify one point on which both sides can agree, using it to start a productive negotiation between the groups. As a class, discuss the importance of understanding another person's position and looking for common ground in a dispute.

NG Learning Framework: Analyze a Speech

ATTITUDE Empowerment

SKILL Problem-Solving

Ask students to review the quote from President Roosevelt's First Annual Message to Congress in which Roosevelt acknowledges that the economic turmoil in the country affects everybody. Tell students to form their own question related to this address and to conduct research, seeking out several sources, to answer their question. Encourage students to ask and answer additional questions as part of their analysis. Allow students to share their questions and research with the class.

Striving Readers

Use Reciprocal Teaching Have partners take turns reading each paragraph of the lesson aloud. At the end of the paragraph, the reading student should ask the listening student questions about the paragraph. Students may ask their partner to state the main idea of the paragraph, identify important details that support the main idea, or summarize the paragraph in their own words. Then ask students to work together to answer the Historical Thinking questions.

Pre-AP

Connect Past and Present Challenge students to use multiple print and digital resources to research long-term effects of the progressive policies of William McKinley and Theodore Roosevelt. Remind them to assess the credibility and accuracy of sources and to paraphrase the information found in their sources. Have students report their findings on connections between the Progressive Era and today in a short essay, a slide show, or an infographic with accompanying text. Encourage students to present their findings to the class and host a class discussion.

See the Chapter Planner for more strategies for differentiation.

HISTORICAL THINKING

ANSWERS

1. Many workers lost their jobs and suffered greatly because there were no safeguards or social programs to help them.

2. One of the main beliefs of populism was that common people, not the wealthy, should control the government. Some of the main goals of populism were better wages and working conditions, workers' and immigrants' rights, better access to education, and an end to child labor.

3. Answers will vary. Possible response: Populists and progressives were excited about Theodore Roosevelt as president because he was an enthusiastic supporter of progressive ideas. He was also young and energetic and a war hero.

AMERICAN VOICES

The Muckrakers

Early 1900s

"There is filth on the floor, and it must be scraped up with the muck-rake."—Theodore Roosevelt

When President Roosevelt made this statement in a 1906 speech, he coined the term "muckraker," referring to crusading journalists who exposed corruption and appalling social and working conditions. But Roosevelt didn't entirely support the journalists' work. Fearing that newspaper publishers would just use shocking headlines to increase their sales, he emphasized that muckrakers needed to know "when to stop raking the muck."

ABUSES OF POWER

As it turned out, though, there was a lot of muck to investigate. One of the first muckrakers was Ida Tarbell, who grew up near the oil derricks and refineries of northwestern Pennsylvania in the 1850s and 1860s. She experienced firsthand the practices of John D. Rockefeller, as his Standard Oil Company moved into the region and took over its small oil businesses. Many local workers lost their jobs, including Tarbell's father.

Tarbell never forgot the impact of Rockefeller's company on her family and home. As an adult, she researched and learned about Standard Oil and the secret deals and methods for crushing the competition its president had carried out to establish his monopoly.

CRITICAL VIEWING In this 1900 political cartoon called "What a Funny Little Government," John D. Rockefeller holds the White House and Treasury Department in his hand and peers at them through a magnifying glass. Illustrator Horace Taylor has turned the Capitol Building in the background into an oil refinery, with thick smoke pouring out of its smokestacks. What does the cartoon suggest about the relationship between industries like Rockefeller's and government?

Tarbell published her findings in *The History of the Standard Oil Company*, which appeared in monthly installments in *McClure's Magazine* between November 1902 and October 1904. She concluded her series with a character study of Rockefeller in which she claimed, "Our national life is on every side distinctly poorer, uglier, meaner, for the kind of influence he exercises."

Around the time Tarbell's articles came out, another muckraker named Lincoln Steffens took on corruption in government. Steffens had recently become managing editor at *McClure's*, which now published the work of many muckrakers. He launched a series of articles, which coincided with the publication of Tarbell's. In his series, Steffens focused on government corruption in cities such as Chicago, Minneapolis, New York, and St. Louis. The articles described the deals politicians in these places struck with greedy businessmen at the expense of citizens. Steffens's dramatic narratives were popular with readers but didn't bring about much change. Eventually he became disillusioned with muckraking and its ability to achieve lasting reform.

CONDITIONS IN THE MEATPACKING INDUSTRY

Unlike Steffens, muckraker Upton Sinclair did accomplish enduring change with his writing—it just wasn't the change he'd hoped for. Sinclair investigated the working conditions in the meatpacking industry and wrote about what he

THE JUNGLE BY UPTON SINCLAIR

DOUBLEDAY, PAGE & Co NEW YORK

CRITICAL VIEWING This poster, printed in 1906, was used to advertise Upton Sinclair's novel and shows a lion standing on the head of a steer. Sinclair may have intended the title of his novel, *The Jungle*, to symbolize what he saw as the savage competition created by capitalism. With that in mind, what might the lion and steer in the poster represent?

found in his novel, *The Jungle*, published in 1906. He described the workers' long hours, low wages, and the dangerous machinery and chemicals they used, often resulting in lost fingers and limbs.

However, it was Sinclair's descriptions of the industry's unsanitary practices, sales of spoiled meat, and rats running everywhere that caught the readers' attention. They were sickened by his account of the way in which garbage and discarded animal parts were swept off the floor, ground up, and sold as "potted ham." As Sinclair said, "I aimed at the public's heart, and by accident I hit it in the stomach."

Roosevelt couldn't ignore the outcry that followed the publication of the novel. Within months, Congress passed both the Pure Food and Drug Act and the Meat Inspection Act. As Roosevelt once admitted, "The men with the muck-rakes are often indispensable to the well-being of society."

HISTORICAL THINKING

1. **READING CHECK** What was the focus of Ida Tarbell's articles?

2. **COMPARE AND CONTRAST** How were the muckraking efforts of Steffens and Sinclair similar and different?

3. **FORM AND SUPPORT OPINIONS** Do you agree with Roosevelt that muckrakers—today called investigative journalists—need to know when to stop? Explain your position.

PLAN

Objective

Explain how muckrakers used journalism to reveal corruption in government and industry.

Critical Thinking Skills for Lesson 1.2

- Identify Main Ideas and Details
- Monitor Comprehension
- Compare and Contrast
- Form and Support Opinions
- Identify
- Analyze Cause and Effect

Essential Question for Chapter 20

Why did the Progressive Era arise? The largely unchecked power of big business led to many abuses of power. Lesson 1.2 illustrates how muckraking journalists exposed corrupt political and business practices.

Background for the Teacher

Theodore Roosevelt borrowed the term *muckraker* from *Pilgrim's Progress*, the religious allegory written by John Bunyan in 1678. Roosevelt noted that in the allegory, the man with the muckrake—a device used to clean out stalls—only looked down at the filth on the floor, even when he was offered a heavenly crown. While Roosevelt was being somewhat pejorative, the term came to be seen in a positive light by many Americans because of the muckrakers' focus on social ills, fraudulent business practices, monopolies, and political corruption. Some muckrakers focused on child labor, while others tackled issues such as capital punishment, fake advertising, stock market abuses, and insurance fraud.

History Notebook

Encourage students to complete the American Voices page for Chapter 20 in their History Notebooks as they read.

INTRODUCE & ENGAGE

Discuss the Role of Investigative Journalists

Write *investigative journalist* on the board. Ask students where they've heard the term and what it means to them. **ASK:** Who are some writers or documentary filmmakers you've heard of who do investigative journalism? *(Answers will vary. Possible responses: Anderson Cooper, Katie Couric, Michael Moore)* Tell students that in this lesson they will learn about some of the very first investigative journalists in the United States—writers whose work is still admired today.

TEACH

Guided Discussion

1. **Identify** What were some of the social and economic injustices that muckrakers brought to light? *(Possible response: They exposed political corruption, underhanded business practices, and unsafe working conditions.)*

2. **Analyze Cause and Effect** What lasting reforms came about as a result of Upton Sinclair's novel *The Jungle*? *(Congress passed the Pure Food And Drug Act and the Meat Inspection Act.)*

American Voices

Political cartoons are important primary source documents that illustrate a variety of historical perspectives and provide valuable insights into the many social and political issues of an era. Political and editorial cartoonists during the Progressive Era often amplified the work of muckraking journalists by using a memorable image to convey a strong point of view at a glance. Direct students' attention to the cartoon of John D. Rockefeller by Horace Taylor, and have a volunteer read the caption. **ASK:** What point of view does the artist convey in this cartoon? *(Possible response: He portrays Rockefeller as powerful and perhaps sinister.)*

Active Options

On Your Feet: Fishbowl Activity Use a Fishbowl strategy to help students analyze *The Jungle*. Instruct students in the inside circle to discuss the intentions Sinclair had for writing the book while students in the outside circle listen. Then call on volunteers in the outside circle to summarize what they heard. Have students switch places and ask those now on the inside to discuss the effects that *The Jungle* had on the country and if the effects matched Sinclair's intent. Students in the outside circle should listen and then summarize what they heard.

NG Learning Framework: Analyze Primary and Secondary Sources

`SKILL` Communication

`KNOWLEDGE` Our Human Story

Organize students into small groups. Tell them to research primary and secondary sources about John D. Rockefeller and the Standard Oil Company. For the primary source, have students read and analyze any portion of Ida Tarbell's *The History of the Standard Oil Company*. Then direct them to find and analyze a secondary source written in response to Tarbell's exposé of John D. Rockefeller and Standard Oil. Prompt students to write a short essay about abuses of power that analyzes the primary and secondary sources and the relationship between them. Encourage students to share their essays with the class.

DIFFERENTIATE

Inclusion

Describe Details in Artwork Pair students who have visual impairments with students who do not have impairments. Ask sighted partners to describe in detail the cartoon of John D. Rockefeller and the poster for Upton Sinclair's *The Jungle*, answering any questions their partner has. Then have the pairs work together to answer the Critical Viewing questions.

Gifted & Talented

Profile a Muckraker Have students choose a muckraker not covered in this lesson, do some research, and write a short magazine profile of the person and his or her work. The profile should describe relevant biographical details from the person's life, journalistic areas of interest, and the influence of his or her muckraking work. When students are finished, encourage them to share their profiles in a class blog or read them aloud to the class.

See the Chapter Planner for more strategies for differentiation.

HISTORICAL THINKING

ANSWERS

1. Ida Tarbell's articles focused on the underhanded business practices of John D. Rockefeller and Standard Oil.

2. Steffens and Sinclair both brought negative practices to light, but Sinclair wrote about the meatpacking business, while Steffens wrote about corrupt politicians.

3. Answers will vary. Possible responses: Yes, muckrakers should stop when their reporting could do more harm than good. No, muckrakers shouldn't stop as long as they are exposing bad practices that the public should know about and are not breaking any laws.

CRITICAL VIEWING Possible response: The cartoon suggests that businessmen like Rockefeller have the upper hand in their relationship with the government, which to them is something easy to manipulate.

CRITICAL VIEWING Answers will vary. Possible response: The lion on the poster for Sinclair's book represents predatory capitalism, and the skull of the steer shows that predatory capitalists can devour weaker powers.

1.3 Expanding Democracy and Reforming Government

You may have seen or heard about groups of people calling for change in government today. But that's not a new trend. It's exactly what reformers were doing during the late 1890s.

MAIN IDEA Progressives sought to strengthen government by reducing corruption at the state and local levels and giving voters a greater voice.

EMPOWERING THE PEOPLE

As the United States emerged from economic depression around 1897, Americans looked for ways to solve the deep-rooted problems facing the country. Most progressives believed government at all levels should promote a society that benefited everyone and provide a financial "safety net" for the most vulnerable Americans. They also believed government had a responsibility to try to solve the social and economic problems caused by industrialization, including health problems in cities, unfair and dangerous work practices, and the rise of monopolies and trusts.

A key idea for progressives was giving voters a more direct voice in government. They felt that if people had more say in how the government ran the country, the elite, or powerful and wealthy, political class would have less control. Several states introduced **direct primary elections** to give voters a role in selecting candidates for

The Great Galveston Hurricane
This 1900 photo shows some of the destruction caused by a hurricane after it slammed into Galveston. The disaster occurred on September 8 when the city was filled with vacationers. A local weather forecaster drove his horse-drawn cart to the beach and advised people to move to higher ground, but his warning came too late.

important offices. In these elections, members of each political party nominate candidates by a direct vote. By 1916, direct primaries had spread across most of the country.

Progressives also supported the processes of initiatives and referendums. In an **initiative**, citizens propose a new law and force a vote on it. If the initiative receives a majority vote, it becomes law. In a **referendum**, a direct vote allows voters to accept or reject a law. Progressives believed these practices could help reduce government control and keep corrupt leaders from remaining in office. In 1898, South Dakota became the first state to adopt a statewide process for initiatives and referendums. Other states soon followed.

REFORMING THE GOVERNMENT

As urban populations grew, political corruption became widespread at the local level. As you have read, Tammany Hall was one of the best-known examples of corruption in city government. Progressives worked to clean up and improve local governments. Reform-minded mayors in the cities of Detroit, Cleveland, and Toledo pushed for safer, cleaner cities and fought political corruption.

A powerful hurricane that hit Galveston, Texas, in 1900 sparked a progressive movement that changed the structure of that city's government. The hurricane was one of the worst natural disasters in the country's history. It killed about 6,000 people and devastated the coastal city.

Concerned that Galveston would never be rebuilt under its current leaders, residents placed their hopes in a new form of government called the commission form of government, or the "Galveston Plan." The citizens of Galveston elected five **commissioners**, or government representatives, to help the city recover from the disaster. The commissioners worked together to pass laws and collect taxes. In addition, each commissioner was in charge of a specific part of the government, such as public works and public safety. One of the commissioners served as mayor, but this position had little power. The commission form of city government is widespread throughout the United States today.

Many states also elected reform-minded governors. **Robert M. La Follette**, the governor of Wisconsin from 1900 to 1906 and then a U.S. Senator until 1925, became a symbol of the Progressive Era. He established a direct primary election for the state, regulated Wisconsin's railroads, and raised taxes on corporations. Leaders such as La Follette reflected the new policies President Roosevelt sought to pass on the national level.

The "Wisconsin Idea"
Today, the idea that politicians should consult with experts in fields such as economics and business before making policy decisions is routine. But that wasn't always the case. During his two terms as governor of Wisconsin, La Follette (shown here) forged relationships with professors at the University of Wisconsin to help him confront the state's economic and social problems. This relationship was called the "Wisconsin Idea."

HISTORICAL THINKING

1. **READING CHECK** According to many progressives, what were some of the responsibilities of government?

2. **ANALYZE CAUSE AND EFFECT** How did the 1900 Galveston hurricane lead to local government reform?

3. **SYNTHESIZE** How do direct primaries, initiatives, and referendums put more political power in the hands of everyday citizens?

Objective
Discuss how progressives used the power of the voting public to bring about reforms.

Critical Thinking Skills for Lesson 1.3
- Identify Main Ideas and Details
- Monitor Comprehension
- Analyze Cause and Effect
- Synthesize
- Compare and Contrast
- Identify

Essential Question for Chapter 20
Why did the Progressive Era arise? Americans wanted government to help solve social and economic problems. Lesson 1.3 examines some ways citizens were able to gain a more direct voice in government and combat government corruption.

Background for the Teacher
The Wisconsin Idea grew out of a friendship between Robert La Follette, the governor of Wisconsin, and Charles Van Hise, president of the University of Wisconsin. The idea may have originated with Van Hise's statement in 1905, "I shall never be content until the beneficent influence of the University reaches every family of the state." Van Hise realized that one way to extend the reach of the university was through government.

To this end, Van Hise worked closely with his friend and former classmate Robert "Fighting Bob" La Follette. Together, they made the expertise of faculty members available to legislators as they deliberated on many progressive reforms, including the first workers' compensation law in the nation. Although such collaborations were unusual at the time, now it is standard practice for government officials to consult with nongovernmental experts.

Vote for Change

Lead students in a discussion about changes they would like to see in their community, and list their ideas on the board. Ask students to express which items are most important by raising their hands and voting for their favorite idea. Identify the three ideas that received the most votes, and have students vote again for the one change they believe is most likely to occur. Point out that students engaged in direct democracy by voting. Tell them that in this lesson they will learn how progressives promoted direct democracy to bring about changes. You might want to leave students' ideas on the board and return to them later in the lesson.

TEACH

Guided Discussion

1. **Compare and Contrast** How are initiatives and referendums similar and different? *(Both allow citizens to vote on an issue, but an initiative is drafted and initiated, or proposed, by unelected citizens, while a referendum is referred by elected officials and approved or denied by a direct vote.)*

2. **Identify** What was new about what came to be known as the Wisconsin Idea? *(Legislators had never consulted with academic subject-matter experts before, and the idea that their knowledge could inform government policy was a new concept.)*

More Information

Reform in Other Cities Share with students that, after Galveston, other cities also instituted reforms in the Progressive Era. In Milwaukee, Wisconsin, Mayor Daniel Hoan, a socialist, worked to improve education and formed municipally owned utilities that provided people with inexpensive water and power. In Toledo, Ohio, Mayor Samuel Jones instituted popular reforms, including an eight-hour workday for city employees and free kindergartens for children. In Cleveland, Ohio, Mayor Tom L. Johnson reduced streetcar fares to three cents and regulated public utilities. **ASK:** How did progressive politicians make ordinary people's lives better in some U.S. cities? *(Possible responses: They helped working-class people by making basic services such as public transportation, electricity, water, and sanitation available and affordable. They also provided educational opportunities and public parks.)*

Active Options

On Your Feet: Turn and Talk on Topic Organize students into four lines. Give each line the same topic sentence: Voters should have a direct voice in government. Have the first student in each line add one sentence to the topic sentence based on something the student learned in this lesson and then turn and say the sentence to the next person in line. Tell students to build a discussion on the topic as each student in the line adds another sentence. Encourage students to write their sentence to help them remember it. When students finish, have each group present its results to the class, with each student stating his or her sentence and then turning to the next person in line.

NG Learning Framework: Analyze the Wisconsin Idea

`ATTITUDE` Empowerment

`SKILL` Problem-Solving

Divide the class into small groups to further explore the reasons Robert La Follette established the Wisconsin Idea. Have students record some of the goals of the policies and take into consideration the context and time period when these policies were established. Ask students to create a proposal for solutions to the same problems that the Wisconsin Idea policies were meant to solve, basing their proposal in either the Progressive Era or the present time. Encourage students to share their solutions with the class.

DIFFERENTIATE

English Language Learners `ELD`

Use Sentence Strips Choose a paragraph from the lesson, such as the paragraph about the Galveston hurricane, and make sentence strips out of it by writing each sentence on a separate strip of paper. Read the paragraph aloud, having students at **All Proficiencies** follow along in their books. Have students close their books and give them the set of sentence strips. Students should put the strips in order and read the paragraph aloud, then summarize its meaning in their own words.

Pre-AP

Write an Editorial Instruct students to research a present-day initiative or referendum and then write an editorial either supporting or opposing it. If there are no relevant local initiatives or referendums, encourage students to research national news to find an initiative or referendum in another area. When they are done, students may present their editorials to the class or post them on a class blog.

See the Chapter Planner for more strategies for differentiation.

HISTORICAL THINKING

ANSWERS

1. Possible response: Progressives thought that the government should work to solve social and economic problems, provide a safety net for the most vulnerable, and promote a society that benefited everyone.

2. Citizens knew that an immense amount of work needed to be done to rebuild after the hurricane, so they instituted a new form of city government that included a team of representatives, called commissioners, to help Galveston rebuild swiftly.

3. Instead of the wealthy political elite deciding which candidates and laws to propose, citizens themselves can select candidates in primaries, put issues up for a vote through initiatives, and cast their vote directly on laws via referendums.

1.4 Teddy Roosevelt and the Square Deal

When you eat a hamburger or drink a glass of milk, you probably don't think of Teddy Roosevelt. But maybe you should. As president of the United States, he pushed for laws that made foods purer and safer.

MAIN IDEA As president, Theodore Roosevelt worked to control corporations, protect consumers, and conserve the environment.

Theodore Roosevelt National Park
To honor the time Roosevelt spent in the Dakota Territory, the Theodore Roosevelt National Park, shown here, was established in 1947. Roosevelt started a couple of cattle ranching operations in the badlands area of present-day North Dakota and built a home there in 1884. It was while spending time on this land that Roosevelt's conservation ideas first took root.

BUSINESS REFORM

The tremendous growth of business during the Industrial Revolution also brought an increase in inequality among some groups of people. The unfair treatment of poorly paid workers especially concerned progressives. Roosevelt wanted to find solutions that were fair to business owners, their workers, and the general public. He referred to his domestic policy as a "square deal." He meant that all sides would be treated fairly and would benefit equally. Like all progressives, Roosevelt wanted to promote the interests of those who did not share in the prosperity of the Industrial Revolution.

For decades, corporations had been allowed to grow and operate with very little government supervision. As a result, monopolies had arisen, and they were hurting the economy. Since a company with a monopoly has no competition, it can overcharge its customers, underpay its workers, produce inferior goods and services, and still be assured of a healthy profit because no other company supplies its product. To break up the monopolies, Roosevelt turned to an existing law—the **Sherman Antitrust Act of 1890**. You may remember that John D. Rockefeller transformed the Standard Oil Company into a trust so he could avoid following state laws and could buy up his competition. The Sherman Antitrust Act was the legislation that led to the end of Rockefeller's monopoly and others like it. For the most part, the end of the monopolies resulted in greater competition in prices and wages.

You have read about the journalists known as muckrakers and how one such journalist, Upton Sinclair, helped make the public aware of unsanitary practices in the meat-packing industry. Muckrakers also exposed

Booker T. Washington

Roosevelt, Washington, and Race Relations
Roosevelt was friends with African-American educator Booker T. Washington, but he did little to improve race relations. For example, in 1906, a group of African-American soldiers stationed near Brownsville, Texas, were accused of shooting a white bartender. Despite strong evidence of their innocence, Roosevelt ordered all of them to be discharged without honor. Washington pleaded with him to reconsider his decision, but Roosevelt refused.

shocking problems relating to the quality and safety of other foods and of medicines. As you know, Roosevelt pushed Congress to pass the **Pure Food and Drug Act** and the **Meat Inspection Act** after these problems had been exposed. The laws empowered the federal government to protect the quality, purity, and safety of foods and drugs.

THE CONSERVATION MOVEMENT

Roosevelt deeply loved the outdoors, and his love only grew during the two years he spent on a cattle ranch in the Dakota Territory. Riding horses, tending to livestock, hunting, and fishing had given him a great respect for the values of individualism and self-reliance. He returned to his home state of New York committed to the **conservation movement**, the idea of conserving the country's lands and wildlife—especially in the West. The conservation movement was gaining strength at the time Roosevelt became president. Conservationists wanted laws in place to protect the country's environment from wasteful practices and exploitation by agricultural, industrial, and commercial development. They were fortunate to have a president who shared their principles.

As you've read, Roosevelt worked to preserve and protect areas of unspoiled land. He created the United States Forest Service and turned its leadership over to his close friend **Gifford Pinchot** (PIN-show). Under Pinchot, the Forest Service set aside 172 million acres of land for conservation. The protected areas allowed animal and plant species to thrive and guaranteed that future generations would be able to enjoy the country's beautiful natural resources.

HISTORICAL THINKING

1. **READING CHECK** What did Roosevelt mean by the phrase "a square deal"?

2. **ANALYZE ENVIRONMENTAL CONCEPTS** Why did Roosevelt believe the ecosystems in the protected areas set aside by the Forest Service were essential to human life and to the nation's economy and culture?

3. **IDENTIFY PROBLEMS AND SOLUTIONS** How did Roosevelt and Congress use government regulations to solve problems in the business world?

Objective
Describe the impact of Theodore Roosevelt's presidency on business reform, consumer protection, and conservation.

Critical Thinking Skills for Lesson 1.4
- Identify Main Ideas and Details
- Monitor Comprehension
- Analyze Environmental Concepts
- Identify Problems and Solutions
- Make Connections
- Make Inferences

Essential Question for Chapter 20
Why did the Progressive Era arise? Monopolies and unscrupulous business practices harmed the economy as well as citizens. Lesson 1.4 explores ways that Theodore Roosevelt disrupted monopolies, provided consumer protections, and preserved wilderness areas.

Background for the Teacher
When Theodore Roosevelt traveled west he didn't know that he would also fall in love. But the beauty of the wide-open spaces, the ancient geologic features, and the abundant wildlife of the badlands captured his affection for life.

Today, Theodore Roosevelt National Park is home to large herds of bison, as well as deer, bighorn sheep, reptiles, amphibians, and birds. However, the park is best known for its landscape, evidence of 65 million years of geologic change. Erosion of the Rocky Mountains and eruptions of volcanoes throughout the West deposited layer after layer of sediment in the North Dakota badlands. Roosevelt described the landscape as "so fantastically broken in form and so bizarre in color as to seem hardly properly to belong to this earth."

History Notebook
Encourage students to complete the American Gallery page for Chapter 20 in their History Notebooks as they read.

Activate Prior Knowledge

Write the word *monopoly* on the board. **ASK:** What does the word *monopoly* mean? *(One company or person has control over a product, service, or industry.)* **ASK:** How was it possible for businesses to have a monopoly? *(Possible response: The government had a laissez-faire policy to not regulate businesses.)* Explain that in Lesson 1.4 students will learn about how President Theodore Roosevelt worked to diminish some of the negative consequences of unregulated business growth.

TEACH

Guided Discussion

1. **Make Connections** Do you think there are any companies today that could be considered monopolies? *(Answers will vary. Possible responses: Some large Internet and large media corporations seem to have little competition. Utility companies often operate as local monopolies.)*

2. **Analyze Environmental Concepts** What are some advantages and disadvantages for the U.S. economy and culture of setting aside large tracts of land as national forests? *(Answers will vary. Possible responses: Advantage: Preserving unchanged ecosystems allows generations of Americans to study and enjoy the plants and animals. Disadvantage: The land resources are protected, so economic benefits of using the resources may be limited.)*

Make Inferences

Why do you think the federal government imposed regulations specifically on businesses producing food and medicines? *(Investigative journalists had exposed appalling work conditions and dangerous food practices that could cause illness or death. Drug products are similar to foods, so the public demanded government oversight of those businesses.)*

Active Options

AMERICAN GALLERY ONLINE **Yosemite National Park** Invite students to explore the American Gallery. Have them select one of the images and do additional research to learn more about it. Ask questions that will inspire additional inquiry about the chosen gallery image, such as: Why does this image belong in this chapter? How does it aid your understanding of the Progressive Era? How does it aid your understanding of Theodore Roosevelt? What else would you like to know about the image?

NG Learning Framework: Investigate Land Conservation STEM

ATTITUDE Curiosity

KNOWLEDGE Our Living Planet

Organize students into four teams to investigate land conservation. Assign each team to research one of the following types of ecosystem services that are provided by natural systems: provisioning, regulating, cultural, or supporting. Tell each team to research what the service is, why that service is essential for our culture and economy, and how it is related to the conservation movement. Instruct the teams to synthesize their individual notes into a few sentences the group agrees upon and record them. Have the teams conclude their project by sharing their findings with the class.

English Language Learners

Use Suffixes to Expand Vocabulary Write the words *inspection* and *conservation* on the board. Explain to students at **All Proficiencies** that adding the suffixes *-ion*, *-tion*, and *-ation* changes verbs into nouns. For example, *inspect* means "to look carefully"; *inspection* means "the act of looking carefully." Ask students to tell how the words *conserve* and *conservation* are related. Then encourage them to find other words that end in *-ion*, *-tion*, or *-ation* and share their meanings with the class.

Gifted & Talented

Plan a Protected Area Have students create a plan for a new national park, national forest, or other protected area, such as a marine sanctuary. Suggest that students first conduct research to find information such as what regions have the most demand for protected public areas for recreational use, what areas are currently visited the most, or what resources are threatened and need to be protected. Instruct students to choose the location of their protected area and create a brief report, including maps or photos, explaining why they chose the area. Encourage students to share their plan with the class.

See the Chapter Planner for more strategies for differentiation.

HISTORICAL THINKING

ANSWERS

1. To Roosevelt, a "square deal" was one in which all sides—workers, business owners, and the general public—were treated fairly and benefited equally.

2. Roosevelt linked outdoor activities with individualism and self-reliance. He believed that agricultural and business interests harmed the environment and benefited a few people, while protecting wild areas helped plant and animal species survive and thrive so that future generations could enjoy them.

3. Roosevelt used existing laws such as the Sherman Antitrust Act to help dismantle monopolies, increasing competition for consumers and improving conditions for workers. He also created new laws such as the Pure Food and Drug Act and the Meat Inspection Act to protect consumers and encourage businesses to provide better, safer products.

2.1 Progressivism Under Taft

Imagine working 12 hours a day, 6 days a week, at a factory job that pays very little. The work is exhausting, and the conditions are dangerous and unsanitary. In the early 1900s, many jobs were like this—even for children.

MAIN IDEA During William Taft's presidency, progressive gains included the growth of labor unions and the adoption of the 16th and 17th amendments to the Constitution.

THE TRIANGLE FACTORY FIRE

Despite his popularity, Teddy Roosevelt decided not to run for a second full term as president in 1908. Instead he supported his Secretary of War, **William Howard Taft,** to be his successor. Taft was a well-respected conservative judge, but he pursued progressive goals when he won the election and became president. He continued Roosevelt's work by putting into action antitrust laws and breaking up monopolies. In fact, Taft filed more antitrust suits against monopolies than Roosevelt had.

By this time, some progress had been made in improving conditions for workers, but many factories remained dangerous. In 1911, a terrible tragedy occurred at the Triangle Waist Company's factory in New York City, where shirtwaists, or women's blouses, were made. Triangle was a sweatshop—a clothing factory where workers labored for long hours with little pay. When a fire broke out on the eighth floor of the building and quickly spread to the ninth and tenth floors, the workers, mostly very young immigrant women, discovered they were trapped. Some doors had been locked to prevent the workers from taking unauthorized breaks. The weak fire escape quickly collapsed under the weight of the women trying to flee. Fire trucks arrived, but their ladders could only reach as high as the sixth floor. Some workers suffocated inside the building, and others jumped to their death. Newspaper photographs showed the lifeless bodies of some of the 146 dead.

The **Triangle Waist Company factory fire** outraged the public. Many people who had not been involved in the labor movement finally

The Triangle Waist Company was located in the Asch building, which, according to its owners, was fireproof. The fire, sparked by a cigarette or tossed match, started on the eighth floor and spread rapidly. The photo shows one of the fire escapes that collapsed when the women tried to flee the fire.

A GLOBAL PERSPECTIVE Sweatshops like Triangle still exist today. This factory in the South Asian nation of Bangladesh produces clothing for export to the United States and other Western countries. What safety hazards can you identify in this photo?

recognized the value of labor unions and their fight for higher wages, more benefits, and safer working conditions. Labor unions experienced an increase in membership and growth after the fire. Nevertheless, relations between workers and company owners remained strained. In 1914, for example, miners in Ludlow, Colorado, went on strike. In response, the mine's security force and the state militia fired on the strikers and killed a number of people, including many children. The **Ludlow Massacre** showed that workers' demands would sometimes be met with violence.

TWO PROGRESSIVE AMENDMENTS

Progressives had managed to convince government to make some of the reforms they sought. Government programs cost money, however. Adding social programs meant that the government would have to raise revenue.

At the start of the 20th century, Americans did not pay federal income taxes. An **income tax** is a tax paid by employed people to the government. The tax is usually a percentage of a person's income. The higher the income, the higher the percentage the person pays. The government can use income tax revenue for any of its expenses, including the funding of social programs. To gain that stream of

money, Congress passed the **16th Amendment** to the Constitution in 1909, and it was ratified in 1913. This amendment gave Congress the power to collect taxes on money made as income.

Another amendment addressed the goal of progressives to expand democracy. The Constitution called for state legislatures to choose two people to represent the state in the U.S. Senate. The **17th Amendment**, which was ratified in 1913, changed the rules and allowed the people of each state to elect their senators by a direct vote. Taft had accomplished a great deal in his first term. He hoped to continue working for the country in a second term—but he ran up against an unexpected obstacle.

HISTORICAL THINKING

1. **READING CHECK** How did President Taft continue to build on Roosevelt's efforts?

2. **ANALYZE CAUSE AND EFFECT** In what ways did the Triangle Waist Company factory fire affect the labor movement?

3. **SYNTHESIZE** How did the 16th and 17th amendments further the aims of progressives?

PLAN

Objective
Describe progressive reforms during Taft's presidency.

Critical Thinking Skills for Lesson 2.1
- Identify Main Ideas and Details
- Monitor Comprehension
- Analyze Cause and Effect
- Synthesize
- Make Inferences
- Evaluate

Essential Question for Chapter 20
Why did the Progressive Era arise? President Theodore Roosevelt initiated progressive reforms in business and government. Lesson 2.1 discusses how progressivism continued under his successor William Howard Taft.

Background for the Teacher

The Colorado Fuel & Iron Company, owned by John D. Rockefeller, Jr., employed thousands of miners, most of whom were Italian, Greek, or Serbian immigrants. In 1913, miners went on strike to demand fair wages, an eight-hour workday, safe working conditions, and the right to live outside the company-owned town. The company responded by forcing the miners out of their homes, so the workers set up tent communities, including one at Ludlow, Colorado. Rockefeller's mining company hired guards, armed with rifles and machine guns, who carried out shooting raids against the miners.

On April 20, 1914, guards set fire to the Ludlow camp. Many of the residents, including women and children who tried to hide in a pit, died in the fire. Although changes did not happen immediately, the tragedy raised public awareness. Many historians credit the Ludlow Massacre for bringing about changes that affect workers in many industries today.

INTRODUCE & ENGAGE

Discuss Safety Measures

Ask students to identify equipment and practices that help make schools, homes, and businesses safer. *(Answers will vary. Possible responses: fire alarms, sprinkler systems, smoke detectors, carbon monoxide detectors, fire escapes, unobstructed doors, fire drills)* **ASK:** Which, if any, safety equipment and practices do you think should be required? Why? *(Possible response: Smoke detectors should be required because they can give an early warning of fire and save lives.)* Tell students that in this lesson they will learn how public outrage over a tragedy led to improvements in workplace safety.

TEACH

Guided Discussion

1. **Make Inferences** What does the information about the workers at the Triangle Waist factory indicate about the status of women and immigrants in the early 1900s? *(Answers will vary. Possible response: Most of the victims of the fire were young immigrant women. The conditions in which they worked indicates that women and immigrants were poor and did not have access to better jobs.)*

2. **Evaluate** What are some possible advantages and disadvantages of the 17th Amendment? *(Answers will vary. Possible responses: The 17th Amendment gives people a greater voice in government by allowing them to vote for the senators who represent them. However, senatorial candidates must campaign to win votes. This can be a long, costly process that involves conflict between candidates and among voters.)*

A Global Perspective

Direct students' attention to the sweatshop photo and caption. **ASK:** What details do you notice in this photo? *(Possible responses: From the big piles of cloth at each machine, it looks like an assembly line, with each worker sewing one thing—such as green sleeves. The bench seating looks uncomfortable.)* Why do you think clothing imported to Western countries is made in sweatshops like these? *(Clothing is probably cheaper to manufacture in a sweatshop in a country that does not have worker protections in place.)*

Active Options

On Your Feet: Team Word Webbing Define the word *catalyst* or have students look it up. *(a person or event that triggers an action or change)* Then organize students into groups of four to work in different parts of the classroom. Give each group a large sheet of paper with the word *catalyst* in the center. Have each group member record a specific person or event that was a catalyst for progressive change. At your signal, groups should rotate the paper, and group members should build on each other's entries. Finally, ask groups to share their catalysts and explain how each person or event was a trigger that sparked a change in society.

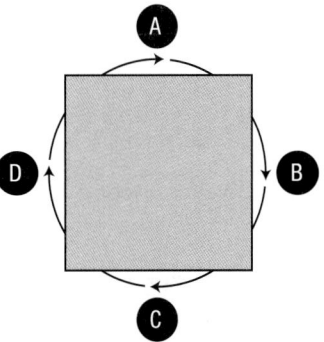

NG Learning Framework: Explore the Legacy of a Tragedy

ATTITUDE Curiosity

KNOWLEDGE Our Human Story

Invite students to research current New York City fire codes and safety regulations for factories and other places of business. Then have them explain how these precautions could have prevented the tragedy that happened at the Triangle Waist Company in New York in 1911. As a class, discuss how the legacy of that event continues to help improve conditions for workers today.

DIFFERENTIATE

Inclusion

Check Facts and Summarize Pair students with different reading proficiencies. Instruct pairs to read the first paragraph of the lesson together. Then have them close the book and write all the facts they can remember. When they have finished, tell them to open the book and check their facts. Direct them to repeat the process with the second and third paragraphs of the lesson. Finally, have students use their list of facts to write a summary of what they read.

Gifted & Talented

Discover Voices of the Past Instruct students to research primary sources from the Triangle Waist Company factory fire. Ask them to find quotes from eyewitnesses, including Secretary of Labor Frances Perkins, that reveal different perspectives on the tragedy. Have students share their quotes with the class. Then guide a class discussion about why people had different perspectives on the fire and how these eyewitness accounts influenced public opinion about the need for progressive changes.

See the Chapter Planner for more strategies for differentiation.

HISTORICAL THINKING

ANSWERS

1. President Taft continued to use antitrust laws to try to break up monopolies.

2. The fire outraged people, many of whom had not previously realized the value of labor unions, and brought about an increase in labor union membership. The unions fought to change the kinds of conditions that had led to the tragedy.

3. The 16th Amendment gave Congress the power to collect revenue by taxing incomes. The federal government could use this revenue to help pay for social programs. The 17th Amendment gave people a greater voice in government by allowing them to directly elect their U.S. senators.

A GLOBAL PERSPECTIVE Answers will vary. Possible responses: The workplace is poorly lit for sewing work and appears to be poorly ventilated. Many workers are crowded into a small space. The floor is littered with fabric, which is highly flammable and would interfere with exiting in the case of an emergency.

2.2 Wilson Continues Reform

Teddy Roosevelt enjoyed being president. So watching William Taft govern for four years was probably hard for him to take. But when Roosevelt challenged Taft in 1912, they both lost to Woodrow Wilson.

MAIN IDEA During his presidency, Woodrow Wilson fought tariffs and trusts and established the Federal Reserve System.

WILSON'S ECONOMIC CHANGES

William Taft was up for re-election as president in 1912, but he got an unwelcome surprise: Theodore Roosevelt had decided to run as well. Though they had previously been allies, Taft and Roosevelt now disagreed about the direction the country should take. A few states held primary elections for the first time, and voters tended to prefer Roosevelt. Taft, however, was the choice of most of the Republican Party delegates. After Taft won the nomination, Roosevelt decided to run as the candidate for the newly created Progressive Party, also known as the Bull Moose Party.

With the Republican vote split between Taft and Roosevelt, the Democratic candidate, New Jersey governor **Woodrow Wilson** won the election. He used the slogan "The New Freedom" to describe his domestic policies. He hoped to focus on three things: tariffs, monopolies, and banks.

Wilson pushed for economic changes that would help average Americans. He persuaded Congress to reduce the tariffs on imported goods such as wool, sugar, and cotton. The 16th Amendment had recently passed, which, as you may recall, allowed Congress to collect taxes on people's income. Wilson believed the funds raised through these taxes would offset the loss from lower tariffs.

Roosevelt and Taft had been able to prevent monopolies from forming by applying laws such as the Sherman Antitrust Act of 1890. These laws were generally vague, however, and companies had discovered **loopholes**, or unclear language that allows people to get around laws and avoid obeying them. Wilson asked Congress to put clearer and stronger laws into place. As a result,

in 1914, the **Clayton Antitrust Act** spelled out, in detail, the illegality of trusts' unlawful business practices and closed the loopholes they used.

BANKING REFORMS

Next, Wilson turned his attention to banks. The many economic panics of the previous decades convinced him that the country needed a strong central bank. It took months of negotiation, but Congress and Wilson worked out terms for the **Federal Reserve Act**. Signed into law in 1913, the act established the Federal Reserve Board. Under the board's oversight, or supervision, 12 banks, called **reserve banks**, would control the nation's flow of money. They would determine the amount of money in circulation, expand or decrease credit, and make decisions about money flow in response to changes in the economy.

While Wilson reformed the economy and the banks, other progressives came up with new ways of making businesses more efficient and improving the working environment for employees. And roads were being filled with vehicles that would revolutionize transportation.

HISTORICAL THINKING

1. **READING CHECK** What were the goals of Woodrow Wilson's "New Freedom" program?

2. **ANALYZE CAUSE AND EFFECT** What happened as a result of Roosevelt's entry into the 1912 election?

3. **IDENTIFY MAIN IDEAS AND DETAILS** What was the purpose of the Federal Reserve Board, and what were its functions?

Do what you can, with what you have, where you are.

Presidents come and go, but the Supreme Court goes on forever.

If you want to make enemies, try to change something.

THE THREE PROGRESSIVES

There is something unique and unusual about each of the presidents you have read about in this chapter.

Theodore Roosevelt
26TH PRESIDENT

- He secured the territory and right for the United States to build and administer the Panama Canal.
- His children had quite a menagerie in the White House, including a small bear, a barn owl, a hyena, and a badger, in addition to dogs, birds, and guinea pigs.
- The teddy bear is named for him.
- The Progressive Party's nickname, "Bull Moose Party," was inspired by Roosevelt's image as an outdoorsman and a tough leader.

William Taft
27TH PRESIDENT

- He was the first U.S. president to have the use of an official automobile while in office.
- He established a Children's Bureau within the Labor Department, broadened civil service protection for thousands of government workers, and added thousands of acres to protected nature reserves.
- He was the only president to also serve as Chief Justice of the Supreme Court.

Woodrow Wilson
28TH PRESIDENT

- Highly educated, Wilson had served as the president of Princeton University.
- He was the first U.S. president to hold a press conference.
- He established the official national observance of Mother's Day.
- He was the first U.S. president to cross the Atlantic Ocean while in office.

Objective
Identify ways President Wilson carried out progressive reforms.

Critical Thinking Skills for Lesson 2.2
- Identify Main Ideas and Details
- Monitor Comprehension
- Analyze Cause and Effect
- Form and Support Opinions
- Make Predictions

Essential Question for Chapter 20
Why did the Progressive Era arise? Progressive reforms continued throughout the early 1900s. Lesson 2.2 explains how President Wilson built on the work of his predecessors.

Background for the Teacher
Woodrow Wilson and Theodore Roosevelt presented an interesting contrast in personalities and styles. Wilson's campaign speeches inspired confidence through calm reasoning. His manner was that of a scholarly professor rather than a politician. Roosevelt was a colorful figure whose manner was aggressive and passionate. His references to his own strength being like that of a bull moose gave the Progressive Party its nickname. Roosevelt once delivered an entire campaign speech after having been shot in the chest. He told his audience that "it takes more than that to kill a Bull Moose."

INTRODUCE & ENGAGE

Discuss the Role of Government

Remind students that the progressives worked to improve conditions in many areas of American society. Lead a discussion about the changing role of government in confronting social and economic challenges in the Progressive Era. Create a chart on the board in which students list the challenges and the reforms they have learned about so far. After they have read Lesson 2.2, have them add economic challenges and reforms during Wilson's presidency to the chart.

TEACH

Guided Discussion

1. **Form and Support Opinions** How did President Wilson's economic changes help or hurt average Americans? Support your opinion with evidence from the text. *(Possible responses: Reducing tariffs on imported goods helped average Americans by lowering prices; hindering monopolies helped increase competition and lower consumer costs; the Federal Reserve Board would help keep the economy more steady than before.)*

2. **Make Predictions** How do you think the progressive ideas about more efficient businesses and improved working conditions would influence the growth of the American economy and communities? *(Possible responses: More efficient businesses could produce more goods and open more jobs; better working conditions might keep workers healthier; Americans could afford to live in better houses and buy more goods.)*

More Information

Reserve Banks The Federal Reserve System is a complex organization made up of three parts. (1) The Federal Reserve Board consists of seven members who supervise the system. Members are appointed by the president and approved by the Senate to serve 14-year terms. The chairperson of the board, also appointed by the president, serves a four-year term that can be renewed. (2) The 12 Federal Reserve Banks are located throughout the country to provide the services of the central bank. (3) The Federal Open Market Committee (FOMC) is in charge of making monetary policies to manage the U.S. money supply.

In 2014, Janet Yellen became the first woman to hold the position of Federal Reserve chairperson. The responsibilities of the chairperson include testifying before Congress twice a year, meeting with the secretary of the Treasury, and supervising the FOMC.

Active Options

On Your Feet: Tell Me More After students have read The Three Progressives feature, ask them to think of a question about one of the presidents that is not answered in the text. Provide time for them to research the answer, encouraging them to draw on several sources of information. Label three corners of the room with the names of the presidents. Instruct students to move to the corner that is labeled with the name of the president they researched and to take turns telling the class more about each president.

NG Learning Framework: Analyze an Election

ATTITUDE Curiosity

SKILL Communication

Organize students into three groups and assign each group one of the presidential candidates in the 1912 election—Roosevelt, Taft, or Wilson. Instruct each group to research the assigned candidate's campaign strategy and election results. What did the candidate stand for? Which groups of voters did he appeal to? Have groups share information. Then, as a class, analyze the election. Ask students what conclusions about the candidates, the election, or the issues they can draw based on their research and analysis.

DIFFERENTIATE

Striving Readers

Create a Storyboard Have students create a storyboard depicting a topic or event covered in Lesson 2.2. Tell students they may do one sketch or a series of sketches to portray the important topic or event. Assure them that they will not be judged on the quality of their drawing. Allow students to share their storyboards with the class if they choose to do so.

English Language Learners

Identify Prefixes Write the following pairs of words on the board: *clean/unclean, obey/disobey*. Ask students at the **Emerging** level to identify the prefix in each pair and explain how it changes the meaning of the word. *(The prefixes un- and dis- mean "not"; they make a word have the opposite meaning.)* Introduce the prefix *il-*, which also means "not." Then challenge students to make a list of words in Lesson 2.2 that have these prefixes. *(unwelcome, disagree, unclear, illegality, unlawful)* Ask students at the **Expanding** and **Bridging** levels to assist in defining each word and using it in a sentence.

See the Chapter Planner for more strategies for differentiation.

HISTORICAL THINKING

ANSWERS

1. The New Freedom policies focused on reducing tariffs, fighting trusts, and reforming the banking system.

2. President Taft battled former president Theodore Roosevelt for the Republican nomination. When Taft won the nomination, Roosevelt formed the Progressive Party and ran as its candidate. The Republican vote split between Taft and Roosevelt, and Democrat Woodrow Wilson won.

3. The Federal Reserve Board supervised 12 federal banks that determined the amount of money in circulation, expanded or decreased credit, and made decisions about money flow in response to changes in the economy.

Modern Technology and Mass Markets

Imagine that you're walking along a road in 1913 when suddenly several cars go chugging past you. You're fascinated. The cars are identical, and they're driven by regular working people, not the wealthy. Maybe you wouldn't mind taking a ride in one of them yourself.

MAIN IDEA New technologies and ideas that arose during the Progressive Era helped companies become more efficient and produce goods quickly.

THE MODEL T

Gasoline-powered automobiles had been around since the 1890s. But these cars were expensive to build, and their sale price was too high for most Americans. Then, in 1913, industrialist **Henry Ford** decided to use the **assembly line** system to build his cars. In this system, workers stand in place while the items to be put together move past them on a conveyor belt. The meat-packing industry had used an assembly line since the 1870s, and Ford adapted it to the production of automobiles. His Ford auto plant in Highland Park, Michigan, had conveyor belts that carried car parts ready to be assembled past workers. Each worker performed a single task and assembled the same parts over and over.

Ford chose the name "Model T" for the cars mass-produced, or manufactured in large quantities, in this manner. From the start, the time it took to build a single car was cut in half, from 12 hours to less than 6. But the repetitive nature of the work involved in assembling a Model T made many workers quit. So, in 1914, Ford raised his workers' salaries to five dollars a day, more than twice what it had been before. He also reduced their daily work hours from nine to eight. Not only did most of Ford's employees remain on the job after that, but many of them also purchased Model Ts. Because mechanization and factory production reduced labor costs and expanded production capacity, the price of the cars fell. In 1917, the Model T cost about $360, an affordable price for many people.

BUSINESS PRACTICES

Other factories and businesses also developed new practices during the Progressive Era. Some companies had tens of thousands of employees and manufacturing plants in several locations. With such large workforces, employers had to figure out new ways of managing how their employees carried out their work and making the workers more productive. Above all, employers wanted to increase industrial efficiency, or in other words, produce goods with the least amount of time and effort. Doing so would reduce production costs.

Many of the ideas for making the workplace more efficient came from an engineer named **Frederick Winslow Taylor**, who developed the idea of **scientific management**. He maintained that by carefully studying individual people at work, an employer could figure out the most effective way to do a job. Then other workers could be taught to complete the task in the same way.

Scientific management was popular with manufacturers. They discovered that, by using a strategically organized workforce, they could produce more goods for a lower price. But many workers resented it. Often the most efficient way to complete a job was through performing repetitive movements all day. Henry Ford had consulted with Taylor and used his methods when he set up the assembly lines in his Michigan auto plant.

It wasn't all about efficiency, however. Some employers tried to make the workday more pleasant for their workers. Lunchrooms, recreation areas, and bathroom facilities were put into many factories. Some employees received benefits such as a fund for retirement. Still, most Americans saw only small improvements in the workplace.

The development of electricity in the early 1900s also helped transform business and improve working conditions. The use of electric lights decreased the heat produced by gas lighting and reduced the risk of fire. By 1920, electricity powered more than half of the machines in American factories. Soon more than a third of American homes had electricity. Kerosene lamps, or lamps that burn oil for light, were quickly giving way to electric light bulbs. New electric appliances coming on the market would have a profound impact on daily life, especially for women.

Henry Ford Museum Dearborn, Michigan

The Model T was a sturdy car, manufactured from steel, leather, brass, rubber, wood, linoleum, and straw. Built to withstand America's unpaved roads, it could be purchased in gray, red, green, and blue, and later in black. The 1909 model shown here weighed 1,200 pounds and cost less than $900.

The Sinking of the Titanic

The failure to put good business practices in place sometimes cost lives in the early 20th century. In 1912, the British-built ship Royal Mail Steamer (R.M.S.) *Titanic* set sail on its maiden, or first, voyage from Southampton, England, to New York City. Said to be unsinkable, the *Titanic* struck an iceberg and plunged into the North Atlantic Ocean. Because the ship's builders had neglected to provide enough lifeboats, and its crew had not conducted lifeboat drills to prepare passengers in case of an emergency, about 1,500 people died in the disaster. The watch above had belonged to John Starr March, one of five mail clerks who died while trying to save the heavy mail bags carried by the *Titanic*.

HISTORICAL THINKING

1. **READING CHECK** How did Henry Ford revolutionize the production of automobiles?

2. **SYNTHESIZE** How did the idea of scientific management help businesses increase efficiency?

3. **MAKE INFERENCES** How do you think the availability of affordable cars changed people's lives in the early 20th century?

The Progressive Era **677**

PLAN

Objective

Describe how businesses increased efficiency and productivity during the Progressive Era.

Critical Thinking Skills for Lesson 2.3

- Identify Main Ideas and Details
- Monitor Comprehension
- Synthesize
- Make Inferences
- Identify Problems and Solutions
- Form and Support Opinions

Essential Question for Chapter 20

Why did the Progressive Era arise? In addition to social and economic reforms, the Progressive Era included changes in industry. Lesson 2.3 describes how new technologies and business practices affected people's lives.

Background for the Teacher

Frederick Winslow Taylor's innovative ideas not only revolutionized industrial productivity in the Progressive Era but also continue to influence industry today. Taylor worked in several industries, where he acquired hands-on experience as well as management skills. His methods included matching workers to the right jobs and paying them more for high productivity. Taylor gained international recognition for doubling productivity through scientific management. He died in 1915, but his scientific approach to maximizing efficiency and his incentive system for workers are still used today.

INTRODUCE & ENGAGE

Connect with the Past

Distribute index cards or slips of paper and ask students to write one word that expresses what a car symbolizes to them. Build a word wall by having students post their cards on a bulletin board. Then ask students how their lives would change if they could drive a car. Tell them that although cars have changed a lot in the last 100 years, the way people felt about cars in the early 1900s is similar to the way people feel today.

TEACH

Guided Discussion

1. **Identify Problems and Solutions** What problem did employees have with assembly-line work, and how did Ford address their concerns? *(Employees wanted to quit because the work was repetitive. Ford raised wages and reduced daily work hours so employees would stay on the job.)*

2. **Form and Support Opinions** Which workplace change described in this lesson do you think was most important to workers and why? Support your opinion with evidence from the text. *(Possible responses: Higher wages and shorter hours helped workers balance their lives and have time with their families. The assembly line was efficient and increased output but made work boring and repetitive. Better facilities and benefits improved working conditions.)*

Virtual Museum Visit

Henry Ford was an inventor and innovator, but he also was a collector. For decades, he accumulated and preserved objects he considered important in telling the story of American inventiveness. To share his artifacts, Ford created a nine-acre museum, as well as Greenfield Village—a large outdoor re-creation of America's past. It includes historic structures, such as the laboratory where Thomas Edison invented the light bulb and the workshop where the Wright brothers invented the airplane. Among the museum's exhibits are hands-on activities, including one that lets visitors experience Henry Ford's assembly line as they help build a miniature, wooden version of a Model T automobile.

Active Options

On Your Feet: Fishbowl Arrange students in two concentric circles facing inward. Provide students in the inner circle with materials to complete a task—one that requires several steps, such as folding letters and stuffing envelopes, measuring and cutting strips of paper, or rolling and banding newspapers. Instruct students in the outer circle to observe the workers and evaluate their methods. Then call on volunteers in the outer circle to explain which method was most efficient and why. Reverse roles and provide students in the inner circle with a different task. Allow students in the outer circle to evaluate and discuss the workers' efficiency. Discuss how efficiency was improved with different methods and how the "workers" felt about being observed.

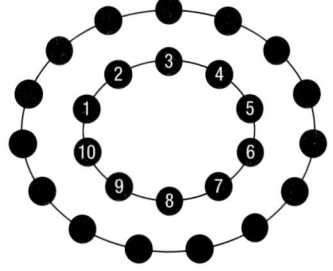

NG Learning Framework: Explore the Technology of the *Titanic*   STEM

ATTITUDE Curiosity

KNOWLEDGE Our Human Story

Allow students to work with partners or in small groups to research technological advances in shipbuilding that were used to make the *Titanic*. Encourage students to frame questions such as: What state-of-the-art technology did the ship have? Why was the ship considered unsinkable? Then instruct them to focus their research on finding answers to their questions. You might have students post their questions and answers with appropriate illustrations on a bulletin board display or class website.

DIFFERENTIATE

Inclusion

Work in Pairs Pair students who have learning disabilities with proficient readers. Instruct the proficient reader to read the subsection Business Practices aloud. After each paragraph, the reader should stop so the partners can discuss which business practices were mentioned. Instruct pairs to list the practices on an Idea Web like the one below.

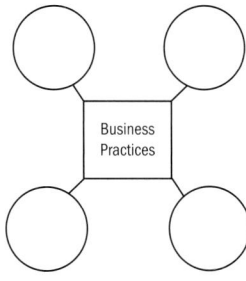

Pre-AP

Explore Effects of Mechanization Pose the following question for student research: How did increased mechanization and production during the late 19th century influence the growth of American communities? Instruct students to use multiple primary and secondary sources in print or digital form. Remind them to assess the credibility and accuracy of sources and to paraphrase the texts. Have students choose appropriate media to share the results of their research with the class.

See the Chapter Planner for more strategies for differentiation.

HISTORICAL THINKING

ANSWERS

1. Ford introduced the use of the assembly-line system, which cut production time in half. This reduced costs and increased output, which made cars available at affordable prices.

2. Scientific management increased efficiency by studying how individuals perform jobs to identify the best and quickest way for workers to complete a task. It created an organized and efficient workforce that could produce more goods in less time.

3. Answers will vary. Possible responses: People could live farther from their workplace. They could travel and see other parts of the country. They had more options for how to spend leisure time.

Women's Changing Roles

Today, more women than men attend college in the United States, and women work in every profession. Women vote in elections and hold political offices. Things were very different in the early 1900s, but change was already in the air.

MAIN IDEA The Progressive Era brought important changes to the roles of women in American society.

BREAKING MOLDS

Women began to find it easier to break from their traditional roles as mothers and homemakers during the Progressive Era for several reasons. For one thing, family size was starting to shrink. With fewer children to look after, women had more time for themselves. Thomas Edison's long-lasting light bulb brought electricity into the home. And household inventions such as the vacuum cleaner and washing machine made household chores less time-consuming. Electricity also allowed factories to produce clothing quickly and inexpensively. As a result, women could buy affordable clothes in stores rather than sew all their families' clothing themselves. These developments meant that women had more time to work outside the home.

An influential thinker and writer named **Charlotte Perkins Gilman** encouraged women to do just that and gain financial independence. If women had enough money to support themselves without relying on the income of men, she argued, they could pursue some of their own goals. Gilman published widely, sharing her ideas in several important women's publications of the day. She also spoke to women's clubs around the country.

This type of club was popular at the turn of the century. Initially, the clubs hosted cultural events and offered members a chance to socialize. But, just as groups of women had come together to discuss how they could aid the American Revolution, members of these women's clubs soon became involved in addressing the social and economic issues of their day. They opened libraries and free kindergartens for children. They worked to improve sanitation and public health services in overcrowded cities. They lobbied for better working conditions. The clubs became an important way for women to organize and carry out social reform.

The Singer Automatic

LATEST AND BEST

Absolutely the Simplest, Lightest-Running, Best-Constructed Strongest Chain-Stitch Sewing Machine ever invented. Has neither shuttle nor bobbin. No tensions to adjust. Always ready when needle is threaded.

SOLD ONLY BY **THE SINGER MANUFACTURING CO.**
OFFICES IN EVERY CITY IN THE WORLD.

Electric sewing machines, like the one in this advertisement, were among the household inventions that improved women's lives in the late 1800s. The machines allowed women to make clothing faster and more cheaply.

MAKING STRIDES

Many women in the Progressive Era took Gilman's advice. Actually, though, women had begun making strides in the workplace since the Civil War, when teaching and nursing became acceptable jobs for American women. The economic depression of 1893 brought an unexpected opportunity for other jobs. Greater numbers of women entered the workforce, taking on jobs men would not consider doing. Throughout the 1890s, women began to take on clerical work such as typing and other office tasks, and some also worked in factories. Women's wages kept many families afloat during the hard economic downturn. Even so, women made only about 60 percent of what men typically earned.

The beginning of the 20th century also witnessed more American women than ever attending and graduating from high school. Some even earned a college education but mostly in fields considered appropriate for women, such as elementary education. Women had few educational opportunities in fields such as law, medicine, and higher education, which were considered subjects only suitable for men. But a few pioneering women fought to overcome that way of thinking. Ellen Spencer Mussey and Emma Gillett had managed to become attorneys, but they knew how difficult it was for most women to study law and earn a degree in it. So, in 1898, after a woman approached Mussey about studying law with her, Mussey and Gillett decided to take action. They founded the Washington School of Law in Washington, D.C. Although the college also admitted men, its primary focus was educating women in the law. Today, it is part of American University.

Industrialization, economic growth, and urbanization increased women's chances for finding a job and securing an education. Women also asserted themselves more and more as leaders in the progressive movement.

HISTORICAL THINKING

1. **READING CHECK** Why did women begin to have more time to work outside the home during the Progressive Era?

2. **EVALUATE** In what way might Charlotte Perkins Gilman's ideas about women be considered modern?

3. **MAKE INFERENCES** Why do you think fields such as law, medicine, and higher education were not considered suitable for women around the turn of the 20th century?

Switchboard Operators
Women work the switchboard, making telephone connections for callers, in an office in 1905. The earliest switchboard operators were boys, but employers found that women were better communicators.

PLAN

Objective
Explain how and why women's roles changed during the Progressive Era.

Critical Thinking Skills for Lesson 3.1
- Identify Main Ideas and Details
- Monitor Comprehension
- Evaluate
- Make Inferences
- Compare and Contrast
- Categorize
- Evaluate

Essential Question for Chapter 20
Why did the Progressive Era arise? Women wanted more opportunities to learn and work. Lesson 3.1 discusses some of the social and technological advances that led to changes in women's roles.

Background for the Teacher
Women's clubs have been active in progressive causes for most of this country's history. In 1890, the journalist Jane Cunningham Croly formed an umbrella group, the General Federation of Women's Clubs (GFWC). Hundreds of African-American women's clubs existed, but the GFWC included only white women's clubs. A separate group, the National Association of Colored Women's Clubs (NACWC), formed in 1896. The National Council of Jewish Women formed in 1893, primarily to assist eastern European Jewish immigrants.

One of the oldest women's clubs that is still active today is the Young Women's Christian Association (YWCA), which formed in 1858, opened its first boarding house for women in 1860 in New York City, and soon expanded to provide housing and support for single women in other cities. Over time, the organization's mission evolved, addressing important social issues such as civil rights, health care, violence prevention, affordable housing, and equal pay.

INTRODUCE & ENGAGE

Preview Using Visuals

Direct students' attention to the advertisement for the sewing machine. Have them study the image and read the caption. Call on volunteers to predict what they will learn in the lesson based on the visual and the caption. At the end of the lesson, return to the advertisement and ask students to see how accurate their predictions were.

TEACH

Guided Discussion

1. **Compare and Contrast** In general, what do you think home life was like for women before and after electricity? *(Possible response: Before electricity, women had to do housework by hand, including cleaning, washing clothes, and sewing clothes. After electricity came into the home, they could use machines, such as the vacuum cleaner, washing machine, and sewing machine, for many tasks. Thomas Edison's electric light bulb allowed for working more hours and with greater ease.)*

2. **Categorize** Name some of the different kinds of issues that women's clubs addressed, and describe how the clubs addressed them. *(Possible response: Women's clubs addressed economic, social, educational, and public health issues. They also advocated for better working conditions and sanitation. In addition, they provided free kindergarten classes and opened libraries.)*

Evaluate

Guide students to consider how women's changing roles might have affected home life. **ASK:** What might men of the Progressive Era have considered advantages and disadvantages of women working outside the home? *(Answers will vary. Possible response: Advantage: Women would bring additional income to the household. Disadvantage: They could become independent and not need their husbands.)*

Active Options

On Your Feet: Household Invention Jigsaw Organize students into four "expert" groups. Assign each group an invention mentioned in this lesson: light bulb, sewing machine, washing machine, or vacuum cleaner. Instruct them to research the impact that invention had on women's lives, drawing on several sources of information. When students have finished their research, form new groups that include at least one student from each expert group. Have students share what they learned about the impact of the different inventions and then discuss changing gender roles during the Progressive Era.

NG Learning Framework: Write Diary Entries

ATTITUDE Empowerment

SKILL Communication

Have students work individually to research the life and work of one of the women who founded the Washington School of Law: Ellen Spencer Mussey or Emma Gillett. Encourage students to choose a few specific challenges and achievements and use them to write a set of diary entries. Then have students who wrote diary entries for the same person come together and arrange their entries chronologically. Each group then presents their diary entries to the class in a reader's theater format.

DIFFERENTIATE

English Language Learners

Identify Main Ideas and Details Pair students at the **Emerging** or **Expanding** level with students at the **Bridging** level and have partners take turns reading each sentence of the first paragraph of this lesson. After they finish the paragraph, have them complete a Main Idea and Details List like the one below with the paragraph's main idea and supporting details.

Main Idea:
Detail:
Detail:
Detail:

Gifted & Talented

Create a Meme Challenge students to find a quotation from one of the inventors of a technology mentioned in the lesson that conveys social commentary or philosophical content relevant to students' lives today. Have them add photographs or artwork that enhances the commentary to create a meme. Invite students to display and explain their memes to the class.

See the Chapter Planner for more strategies for differentiation.

HISTORICAL THINKING

ANSWERS

1. As women had fewer children and used more labor-saving devices, they could spend less time on childcare and housework. Electricity in homes and factories also allowed women to extend their workdays.

2. Gilman's modern views included encouraging women to work outside the home, gain financial independence, and pursue their own goals.

3. Answers will vary. Possible response: Medicine, the law, and higher education may have been considered too demanding for women, who were also expected to run the household and care for children.

3.2 Women as Leaders

When you help people in need, you show them they are not alone. Women who helped others at the beginning of the 20th century not only improved their communities but also gained political power.

> **MAIN IDEA** In the early 20th century, women's roles became key to social reform movements in the United States.

SETTLEMENT HOUSES

Community organization was a key part of achieving reform during the Progressive Era, and many of the most important leaders among these organizers were women. You have read about Jane Addams and Ellen Gates Starr, who founded Hull House in Chicago. They were pioneers in the field of **social work**, or work aimed at improving the lives of others. Hull House was a settlement house that sheltered and fed struggling immigrants and helped them settle into their new lives in the United States. Hull House also helped the working poor. Settlement houses played an important role because the populations of Chicago and other major U.S. cities had surged. The cities' mostly immigrant working-class populations suffered from poverty, overcrowding, and poor sanitation conditions.

Henry Street Settlement in New York City was founded to help ease health issues that arose as a result of these conditions. Lillian Wald, a nurse and social worker, established the settlement in 1893 to offer a free nursing service to immigrants in the city's Lower East Side neighborhood. She coined the term *public health* to refer to nursing care provided in such poor communities. As the settlement grew, Wald organized clubs, lectures, and activities there. She also set up a playground in the settlement's backyard—one of the first in the city.

On Her Rounds
A nurse from the Henry Street Settlement visits an immigrant mother and her children in the early 1900s. By 1914, a team of more than 100 nurses worked at the settlement. Wald insisted the nurses treat not only their patients' illnesses but also their social and economic problems.

By 1910, there were more than 400 settlement houses across the country, offering free services including childcare and job training. Some of the women who provided these services became influential in local government. Wald, for example, persuaded New York City's Board of Education to provide free lunches for all public school children and hire the first nurse to work at a public school. Some of the women even had an impact on the national government, working as lobbyists to pass industrial-era reforms. A **lobbyist** is someone who meets with lawmakers and tries to persuade them to support particular laws and political ideas.

TEMPERANCE WINS

As you may remember, women were the primary supporters of temperance, a movement calling for the consumption of little or no alcohol, when it first became a social issue in the early 1800s. Women continued to lead and support the movement during the rest of that century and into the next.

A reformer of the Progressive Era named **Carry A. Nation** was instrumental in the passage of an amendment to the U.S. Constitution that prohibited the sale of alcohol. Nation was a **teetotaler**, someone who does not drink alcoholic beverages. She believed alcohol was a social problem that harmed the health and well-being of Americans. Nation had witnessed the effect of excessive drinking on families, with husbands losing their jobs, beating their wives, or spending much of their wages on drink. As a result, she became a leader in the temperance movement, campaigning to ban the sale of alcoholic drinks completely. An imposing figure at almost six feet tall, Nation inspired respect.

In 1919, due in large part to the efforts of activists like Nation, the United States ratified the **18th Amendment** to the Constitution, popularly known as **Prohibition**. This legislation banned the production, sale, importation, and transportation of liquor in the United States. Household consumption of alcoholic beverages was still legal, but unless people made their own, they couldn't obtain a drink. The amendment's ratification showed that women could have a profound influence on national policy. This influence would be critical in the struggle for a woman's right to vote, which women had been demanding for many years.

Carry Nation
During her temperance rallies, Carry Nation, shown here, used a small hatchet to smash containers of alcohol. Nation and her hatchet became a symbol of the temperance movement.

HISTORICAL THINKING

1. **READING CHECK** What purpose did the settlement houses play during the Progressive Era in the United States?

2. **FORM AND SUPPORT OPINIONS** Do you think Carry Nation's methods were an effective way to combat social problems? Why or why not?

3. **SYNTHESIZE** What similar goals motivated the women of Henry Street Settlement and Carry Nation?

PLAN

Objective
Identify ways that women played key roles in bringing about progressive reforms.

Critical Thinking Skills for Lesson 3.2
- Identify Main Ideas and Details
- Monitor Comprehension
- Form and Support Opinions
- Synthesize
- Identify Problems and Solutions
- Make Connections

Essential Question for Chapter 20
Why did the Progressive Era arise? Immigration and the increasing populations of cities led to the need for more social services. Lesson 3.2 explains how women responded to the needs of immigrants and poor people.

Background for the Teacher
Carry Nation made it her mission to fight against alcohol use after suffering personal heartbreak. At age 21, she married a young physician, whose severe alcoholism left him unable to support her or their child. After leaving her husband, she returned to her family, some members of which also suffered from drinking problems. Her grandfather had a habit of sharing his morning drink of brandy with family members, including babies.

After Nation married her second husband, her religious convictions strengthened and she began to campaign against bars. She started with holding public prayers outside saloons, then escalated to throwing bricks. Bar owners and patrons opposed her efforts. Soon she was so famous for using a hatchet to destroy bars that it inspired the name of her personal newspaper, *The Smasher's Mail,* and magazine, *The Hatchet.*

INTRODUCE & ENGAGE

Discuss Getting Settled in a New Place

Tell students to imagine they have just arrived in a new school, town, or country. They have little or no money, education, or job prospects. **ASK:** What help would you need to overcome difficulties, settle in, and feel at home? Write their ideas on the board. Revisit the list after students have read Lesson 3.2, adding items based on what students learned about how women in the Progressive Era helped immigrants and others improve their lives.

TEACH

Guided Discussion

1. **Identify Problems and Solutions** What problems did many new immigrants face, and how did settlement houses address those problems? *(Possible response: Many working-class immigrants lived in poverty in crowded and unsanitary conditions. Settlement houses helped by providing health care services from nurses, other community-based services, and space for playgrounds.)*

2. **Make Connections** What are some achievements of female social workers of the Progressive Era that still exist today? *(Possible response: Present-day impacts include school nurses and free school lunches.)*

More Information

Henry Street Settlement Henry Street Settlement is still in operation, helping more than 60,000 New Yorkers each year. It provides programs and services related to employment, health and wellness, transitional and supportive housing, senior assistance, parental support, and recreation and sports. Its educational programs include early childhood education, after-school services, high school initiatives, college readiness, adult literacy, and ESL assistance. Through the Abrons Art Center, the settlment house supports performing and visual arts. Encourage interested students to investigate current programs provided by the Henry Street Settlement to see how the organization's efforts have developed over time. Have students share their findings with the class.

Active Options

On Your Feet: Analyze a Photograph Direct students' attention to the photograph of Carry Nation. Divide the class into small groups, and have each group discuss details they notice in the photograph. Prompt them to talk about what each visual detail conveys about Nation's character and mission and to record their observations. When they have finished, invite groups to present their ideas to the class. Call students' attention to any details they did not notice; for example, the hatchet pin Nation is wearing on her right lapel.

NG Learning Framework: Explore Settlement Houses

ATTITUDE Curiosity

SKILLS Collaboration, Communication

Divide the class into small groups and instruct each group to choose and investigate a settlement house that existed during the Progressive Era. Prompt them to create a newspaper article about the chosen settlement house that covers the 5Ws: *who, what, where, when,* and *why.* They may wish to use a graphic organizer to help them organize their work. Then invite students to point out the location of their chosen settlement house on a map and share their articles with the rest of the class.

DIFFERENTIATE

Inclusion

Describe Details in Photos Pair students who have visual impairments with students who do not have impairments. Ask the students without visual impairments to describe the details in both photos in this lesson. Have the partners discuss the relationship of the photos to the information in the text. Consider incorporating the resulting discussion into the Analyze a Photograph activity.

Pre-AP

Report on Prohibition Pros and Cons Have students research to find the most common reasons people at the turn of the century supported or opposed the 18th Amendment, or Prohibition. Then ask them to write a short report on their findings and share it with the class.

See the Chapter Planner for more strategies for differentiation.

HISTORICAL THINKING

ANSWERS

1. The purpose for settlement houses was to provide social services, such as food and housing, and to help immigrants get settled and the working poor live better lives. Over time, some settlement houses also provided childcare, job training, lectures, clubs, and other activities.

2. Answers will vary. Possible response: Carry Nation's methods were fairly effective because they were dramatic and memorable and drew attention to the social problems caused by alcohol consumption. Her methods attracted enough attention to get the 18th Amendment ratified.

3. Carry Nation and the women of Hull House sought to bring about social reforms that would improve people's lives, particularly the lives of women and children.

3.3 The Nineteenth Amendment

Think of the outcry if your principal denied half of the student body the right to vote in a school election. American women had been protesting and calling for the right to vote since before the Civil War. Many in the Progressive Era hoped that perhaps now their time had come.

MAIN IDEA Strong leadership and the organization of woman suffrage groups finally helped women gain the right to vote.

EARLY STRUGGLES

In 1869, the government granted women in the Wyoming Territory the right to participate in all elections. The victory was a small but important one. When Wyoming became a state in 1890, an amendment to the state constitution officially granted women voting rights. Other western states, such as Colorado, Utah, and Idaho, followed suit in 1896. Despite these gains, women understood that only an amendment to the U.S. Constitution establishing women's right to vote would guarantee their rights and protections. They continued to fight.

Do you remember reading about Susan B. Anthony and Elizabeth Cady Stanton? They were both influential suffragists. A **suffragist** (SUH-frih-jist) is someone who fights for the right to vote, particularly a woman's right to vote. Anthony's and Stanton's women's rights newspaper called *The Revolution* was small in comparison to other publications of its time, but it had a huge influence. Begun in 1868, it became the official voice of the National Woman Suffrage Association (NWSA), which Anthony and Stanton had founded in 1869. In 1890, the NWSA merged with the American Woman Suffrage Association, to form the **National American Woman Suffrage Association (NAWSA)**.

The group formed after other suffrage groups split up due to differing views over voting rights for African-American women.

Anthony became president of the NAWSA in 1892. Under her leadership, it gained the support of every women's suffrage society in the United States. State by state, the NAWSA worked to achieve women's suffrage, and the group had some success. But the suffragists wanted more.

VICTORY FOR WOMEN

In 1900, **Carrie Chapman Catt** succeeded Anthony as president of the NAWSA and continued to fight for women's suffrage at the state level. In time, though, Catt led the organization's first national campaign. Its goal was to amend the Constitution to finally guarantee suffrage for all women.

From 1905 to 1915, Catt recruited and trained political campaigners. Then, in 1917, after the United States entered World War I, the NAWSA's membership grew as a result of Catt's shrewd strategy of linking women's voting rights to the war effort. Because so many men were away fighting in the war, the government had asked women to step into jobs necessary to support the war effort. Catt and other NAWSA members argued that women's patriotism and war work should be rewarded with equal rights, including the right

to vote. The plan worked. Woodrow Wilson, the president at that time, had initially opposed voting rights for women. But the war and Catt's argument changed his mind. Calling its passage "vital to the winning of the war," President Wilson supported the **19th Amendment**, the bill that would make woman suffrage the law of the land.

Still, the road to ratification was somewhat rocky. The House of Representatives and Senate voted on the 19th Amendment in January 1918. The House approved the bill, but the Senate voted against it. Suffragists in the National Women's Party, an extension of the NAWSA, responded by campaigning to vote senators who had opposed the bill out of office. Their efforts proved successful. On August 18, 1920, the 19th Amendment was finally ratified, guaranteeing all women the right to vote under the Constitution.

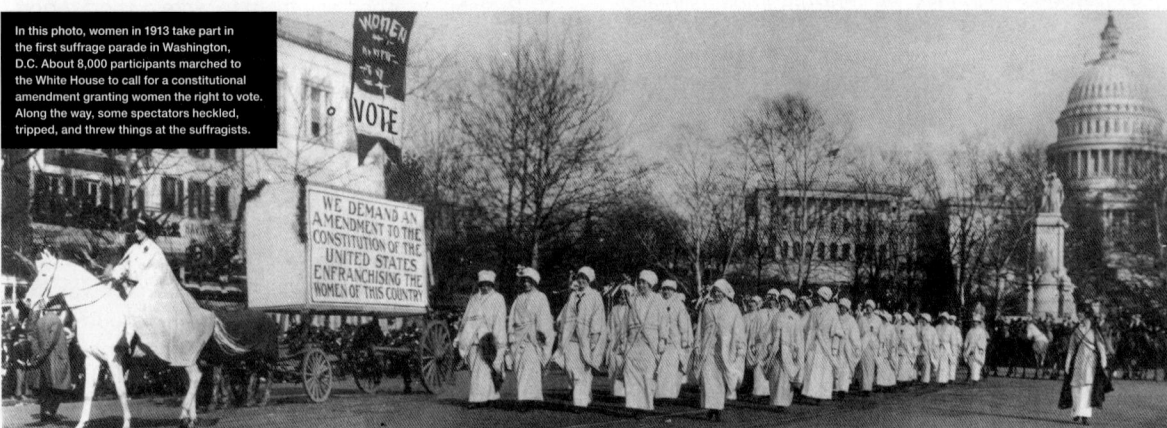

In this photo, women in 1913 take part in the first suffrage parade in Washington, D.C. About 8,000 participants marched to the White House to call for a constitutional amendment granting women the right to vote. Along the way, some spectators heckled, tripped, and threw things at the suffragists.

In 1917, Catt wrote an essay answering objections to guaranteeing women's suffrage by federal amendment. In this excerpt from her essay, Catt points out why not allowing women to vote is unreasonable.

PRIMARY SOURCE

The system which admits the unworthy to the vote provided they are men, and shuts out the worthy provided they are women, is so unjust and illogical that its perpetuation [continuation] is a sad reflection upon American thinking.

--from "Objections to the Federal Amendment," by Carrie Chapman Catt, 1917

HISTORICAL THINKING

1. **READING CHECK** What did the NAWSA seek to accomplish?

2. **SYNTHESIZE** How did the NAWSA combine some of the goals of both women's rights activists and abolitionists?

3. **ANALYZE CAUSE AND EFFECT** What led President Wilson to change his mind about women's suffrage?

PLAN

Objective

Describe the people, organizations, and events that led to the passage of the 19th Amendment.

Critical Thinking Skills for Lesson 3.3

- Identify Main Ideas and Details
- Monitor Comprehension
- Synthesize
- Analyze Cause and Effect
- Make Inferences
- Draw Conclusions
- Analyze Primary Sources

Essential Question for Chapter 20

Why did the Progressive Era arise? The Progressive Era included many social and political efforts to improve the lives of all people. Lesson 3.3 describes how a unified woman suffrage movement and strong leaders resulted in women achieving the right to vote.

Background for the Teacher

Carrie Chapman Catt does not have the same name recognition as Susan B. Anthony. However, she was the brilliant political strategist largely responsible for bringing equal voting rights to women. Catt worked tirelessly for decades, both behind the scenes and in front of crowds. As with campaigns today, communication and outreach were key. She wrote many books and pamphlets and gave hundreds of powerful speeches. She also did the hard work of raising funds and supervising people, including mobilizing 1 million volunteers. Her organizational skills and perseverance finally led to ratification of the 19th Amendment. Just before it passed, she founded and launched the League of Women Voters, which is still a respected and active organization.

Preview Using Visuals

Direct students' attention to the photograph of women marching for their right to vote. Ask volunteers to point out details that strike them. Then read the caption aloud and ask students why they think these women were heckled. Finally, ask students to compare and contrast this march with present-day marches of which they are aware.

TEACH

Guided Discussion

1. **Make Inferences** Why do you think women in many western states won the right to vote long before the 19th Amendment was passed? *(Possible responses: Pioneer women in the West were often treated as equals because husbands and wives relied on and respected each other; the West attracted independent-minded people, and western politicians were open to new ideas.)*

2. **Draw Conclusions** What was the significance of the NAWSA gaining the support of all woman suffrage groups across the country? *(A single unified organization had greater political, economic, and organizing power and a stronger voice than an assortment of smaller groups working separately.)*

Analyze Primary Sources

Share with students that Carrie Chapman Catt wrote and compiled many pamphlets and books to raise public awareness and support for woman suffrage. In one of these, *Woman Suffrage by Federal Constitutional Amendment*, Catt provides details on just which of the men who were enfranchised, or had the right to vote, she considered unworthy to vote and which women she felt were especially worthy:

> Among the enfranchised there are vast groups of totally illiterate, and others of gross ignorance, groups of men of all nations of Europe, uneducated. Among the unenfranchised are the owners of millions of dollars worth of property, college presidents and college graduates, thousands of teachers in universities, colleges and public schools, physicians, lawyers, dentists, journalists, heads of businesses, representatives of every trade and occupation and thousands of the nation's homekeepers.

ASK: How do the specifics in the quote make Catt's argument for woman suffrage harder to refute? *(Most people would not argue that an illiterate man deserves to vote but a highly educated female college president, doctor, lawyer, or business owner does not.)*

Active Options

On Your Feet: Who or What Am I? Divide the class into several small groups and assign each group one important event, person, state, or organization discussed in this lesson (e.g., Wyoming, a suffragist, *The Revolution* newspaper, the National American Woman Suffrage Association, Carrie Chapman Catt, Woodrow Wilson, the 19th Amendment). Instruct groups to come up with several clues or prepare a skit to help the other students guess who or what they are. Then have groups present their clues or skit and ask, "Who or what am I?" The rest of the students should guess until they arrive at the correct answer.

NG Learning Framework: Analyze Effects of Woman Suffrage

SKILLS Collaboration, Communication

KNOWLEDGE Our Human Story

Remind students that the Wyoming Territory passed a bill that gave women the right to vote in 1869. Ask students to work in small groups to find and analyze this bill to explore what privileges were granted, what conditions were attached, and what the long-term effects were. Have students synthesize and record their findings, and invite them to share in a class discussion.

DIFFERENTIATE

Striving Readers

Understand Main Ideas Check students' understanding of the main ideas in Lesson 3.3 by asking them to correctly complete either/or statements such as the following:

- Women in most western states were [able or unable] to vote before the 19th Amendment.
- Woodrow Wilson supported passage of the 19th Amendment [after or until] Carrie Chapman Catt linked women's rights to their war efforts.
- The 19th Amendment guaranteed voting rights to [all or some] women.

Gifted & Talented

Create and Illustrate a Time Line Have students create a paper or digital time line of the events leading up to ratification of the 19th Amendment. Because the suffragists' fight took more than 100 years, students will have to choose their starting point and also choose from many important events along the way. Instruct students to include an appropriate illustration or photo and at least one or two sentences to describe each event they include. Invite them to present their completed time lines to the class, explaining how they decided which events to include or exclude.

See the Chapter Planner for more strategies for differentiation.

HISTORICAL THINKING

ANSWERS

1. The NAWSA sought to unify all women, fighting at the state level, with the goal of amending the constitution so they would have the right to vote.

2. The NAWSA's overarching goal of enfranchising all women, regardless of race, combined the goals of abolitionists and women's rights advocates.

3. When President Wilson understood women's rights to be part of the war effort, he decided to support woman suffrage.

4.1 The United States Expands

Ever since the establishment of the 13 colonies, Americans had been on the lookout for new land to settle. Up until the late 1800s, the United States had confined its expansion within North America. But that was about to change, as Americans started to eye territory in other countries.

MAIN IDEA In the second half of the 19th century, the United States gained new territories and began to take on a larger role in world affairs.

The natural wonders of Alaska are dramatic. Wildlife like this brown bear and cub thrive among its snow-capped mountains and many lakes. Alaska also has abundant supplies of natural gas and oil. Buying Alaska was a wise purchase.

ENTERING THE WORLD STAGE

The Founders of the United States were wary of getting involved in the affairs of other countries. You may remember that, during his presidency, George Washington had advised having "as little political connection as possible" with foreign nations. And as president, Thomas Jefferson warned against engaging in "entangling alliances" with any country. Having suffered oppression under the British Empire, the Founders were suspicious of **imperialism**, a system in which a stronger nation controls weaker nations or territories.

During the Progressive Era, some American leaders agreed with the Founders. They argued that the United States should only use military force abroad to protect the freedom of its own citizens. Many progressives, on the other hand, argued that the United States was obligated to promote democracy and progress around the world.

And the nation's military was ready to carry out that mission. The U.S. Navy, in particular, grew very powerful during the Progressive Era, building the Pacific Fleet in 1907. A key figure behind the development of the navy was **Alfred Thayer Mahan**, a retired naval officer who wrote an influential book about the importance of sea power and control over sea trade. Technological advances, meanwhile, were revolutionizing warships.

As Americans watched European nations building empires in Africa and Asia, many believed the United States should also begin to expand its territory and power beyond its borders. Three main

reasons lay behind American imperialism. The first reason was economic. Industrialization had greatly increased the quantity and quality of the country's manufactured goods. Many industrialists—and farmers—were eager for new markets in which to sell their goods. They also desired the natural resources that colonies abroad might provide. The second was the desire to expand American military power. The United States wanted to establish a military presence in other parts of the world to demonstrate its strength and protect its economic interests. The third reason was ideological. Many Americans believed they should spread not only democracy but also Christianity to

CRITICAL VIEWING Queen Liliuokalani, the last queen of Hawaii, was a well-educated woman who met with European royalty and dined at the White House. She was also proud of her Hawaiian culture and loyal to her kingdom. What details in the photograph reveal her royal status?

other people. Underlying this belief was the racist assumption of the superiority of Western society and white culture.

EXPANDING THE NATION

Of course, the United States had been expanding westward for most of its history. Then in 1867, Secretary of State **William Henry Seward** arranged for the United States to purchase Alaska from Russia. At the time, Russia was struggling with war debt and eager to sell. Some Americans supported the purchase of this enormous territory. They also wanted to annex, or take possession of, Canada and considered acquiring Alaska a necessary step toward that goal. Many more Americans were critical of the purchase, however. Alaska, they claimed, was too far from the rest of the country. It was an "icebox" and, at a cost of $7.2 million, too expensive. These critics called the purchase "Seward's Folly." As Americans would discover, Alaska had abundant natural resources. The United States made a good deal.

Around this time, American economic interests were growing in the Hawaiian Islands, an **archipelago** (ahr-kuh-PEL-uh-goh), or chain of islands, that lies in the middle of the Pacific Ocean. Wealthy Americans who owned sugar plantations on the islands were gaining financial and political power there at the expense of the Hawaiian monarchy. These planters helped secure a treaty

in 1875 that established free trade between Hawaii and the United States. Then, in 1887, the United States gained the right to build a naval base at Pearl Harbor in Hawaii.

Queen Liliuokalani (lee-lee-oo-oh-kah-LAH-nee), who became Hawaii's queen in 1891, hoped to restore the power of the monarchy and maintain the islands' independence. Concerned that the queen's actions would threaten their interests, American and foreign businessmen, supported by U.S. Marines, rebelled against the queen and forced her from power. Recognizing the strategic naval importance of the Hawaiian Islands and the value of their rich agricultural lands, the U.S. government annexed the islands in 1898. Meanwhile, events in another part of the world would lead to the acquisition of yet more territory.

HISTORICAL THINKING

1. **READING CHECK** How did progressives feel about U.S. involvement in the affairs of other countries?

2. **MAKE INFERENCES** Why do you think some Americans thought that acquiring Alaska might help lead to the acquisition of Canada?

3. **SYNTHESIZE** How does the U.S. annexation of Hawaii illustrate the three main reasons behind American imperialism?

PLAN

Objective

Analyze why the United States acquired Alaska and Hawaii.

Critical Thinking Skills for Lesson 4.1

• Identify Main Ideas and Details

• Monitor Comprehension

• Make Inferences

• Synthesize

• Evaluate

• Form and Support Opinions

Essential Question for Chapter 20

Why did the Progressive Era arise? Many people felt that it was time for America to expand beyond the continental United States. Lesson 4.1 explores some of the reasons behind the U.S. acquisition of Alaska and Hawaii.

Background for the Teacher

Queen Liliuokalani was an educated and accomplished woman who stood up for her people and their rights. When a group of American businessmen who had been secretly plotting against her invaded the palace, she was forced to abdicate at gunpoint. Instead of surrendering to the provisional government of white businessmen, she surrendered to the U.S. government. Her surrender read, "I, Liliuokalani, by the grace of God yield my authority until such time as the government of the United States shall reinstate me as the constitutional sovereign of the Hawaiian islands." She believed that when President Grover Cleveland, with whom she had met and dined, learned what had happened, she would regain her throne. However, she underestimated the role that money would play, and she was arrested and tried for treason.

INTRODUCE & ENGAGE

Discuss Culture

Have students think of a cultural or family tradition that is important to them. Invite volunteers to share their thoughts. **ASK:** How would you feel if an important tradition were suddenly taken away? *(Possible responses: upset, angry, sad, lost)* Tell students they will learn about a cultural loss suffered by the people of Hawaii.

TEACH

Guided Discussion

1. **Evaluate** What does Alaska contribute to the United States? *(Alaska, purchased from Russia at a relatively low cost, has abundant natural resources that have made large contributions to the U.S. economy.)*

2. **Form and Support Opinions** Of the three main reasons behind the U.S. annexation of Hawaii, which do you think was most influential? *(Answers will vary. Possible responses: Powerful U.S. businessmen were making a lot of money on sugar plantations and other businesses and wanted to ensure that those profits continued. Hawaii was halfway across the Pacific, so it was a perfect place for a military base and for civilian and military vessels to refuel and take on supplies. Native Hawaiians were considered primitive people in need of "civilizing.")*

More Information

Native Hawaiians Tell students that when westerners first arrived on the Hawaiian Islands in 1778, the islands were home to about 800,000 Hawaiian people. Just 50 years later, 80 percent of those people had died of diseases such as smallpox, and children of the ruling families had been sent to missionary schools. **ASK:** How is what happened in Hawaii similar to what happened to Native Americans on the mainland? *(Possible response: White Americans saw the native populations of both the mainland and the islands as uncivilized beings who needed to be educated in western ways and converted to Christianity. The fact that they were not immune to smallpox and other diseases was not a concern to most Americans.)*

Active Options

On Your Feet: Three-Step Interview Have students work in pairs to conduct Three-Step Interviews about the roles William Henry Seward and Alfred Thayer Mahan played in U.S. expansion in the late 1800s. First, one student should interview the other using these questions: What did [Seward's or Mahan's] actions reveal about his beliefs regarding U.S. expansionism? What were the consequences of his actions? After the first student answers, the two reverse roles. Invite pairs to share the final results of their interview with the class.

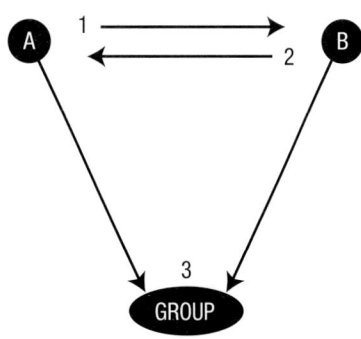

NG Learning Framework: Write a Magazine Article

ATTITUDE Curiosity

SKILL Communication

Instruct students to conduct research to find out more about the native peoples of Hawaii or Alaska. Have students use their research to write a magazine article about a few different aspects of the natives' cultures before their land became part of the United States. Tell students to add appropriate maps and illustrations to their articles. Compile the articles into a class magazine and share it in print or online.

DIFFERENTIATE

English Language Learners   ELD

Use a Term in a Sentence Pair students at the **Emerging** level with English-proficient students. Provide students with a list of words from this lesson. (You may wish to use *suspicious, influential, assumption, superiority, eager, abundant*.) First, direct pairs to find and then read the sentences aloud that use the target words. Then ask the proficient students to model the activity by making up a new sentence that uses one of the target words. Finally, pairs work together to compose a sentence for each word, ideally a sentence that is relevant to the lesson or to their lives. Invite pairs to share their sentences with the class.

Pre-AP

Research and Reenact Have students research the appeals that Queen Liliuokalani made to President Grover Cleveland to restore her to the throne. Ask pairs of students to reenact a meeting between the president and the queen in which she asks (or demands) to regain her position as queen of her people.

See the Chapter Planner for more strategies for differentiation.

HISTORICAL THINKING

ANSWERS

1. Some progressives believed the United States should avoid interfering with other countries. Others believed that Americans had a duty to spread democracy and "progress" around the world.

2. Some Americans may have believed that once the United States acquired Alaska, it would be easier to acquire the land between Alaska and the lower 48 states (Canada).

3. Hawaii occupied a strategically important location for military purposes as it is halfway across the Pacific to Asia. It was economically important to many large agricultural corporations producing sugar and other crops. Hawaii's annexation also rested on the ideological assumption of the innate superiority of white Americans.

CRITICAL VIEWING Answers will vary. Possible response: The queen's white sash, serious expression, brooch pin, large chair/throne, necklace, hair ornaments, and feathery epaulets all reveal her royal status.

4.2 The Spanish-American War

Do you believe everything you read on the Internet? You've probably learned to be skeptical of claims made on many sites. The public wasn't always so critical of the press, though. The tales told by some journalists in the 1890s might even have persuaded the United States to go to war with Spain.

MAIN IDEA Due in part to exaggerated claims reported in the press, the United States waged the Spanish-American War, which resulted in new territorial acquisitions.

"REMEMBER THE *MAINE*!"

Spain had been a major imperialist power since the late 1400s. By the end of the 1800s, Spain's colonial holdings included the Caribbean islands of Puerto Rico and Cuba, the Philippines in Southeast Asia, and several Pacific islands, including Guam.

People in the Caribbean began to call for independence toward the end of the 19th century. Around 1890, a journalist named **Luis Muñoz Rivera** became a leading voice in a movement to gain **autonomy**, or self-rule, for Puerto Rico. Success came in 1897 when Spain granted the island its autonomy. Although Spain still maintained a governor in Puerto Rico, the island's citizens were allowed to set up their own government and manage local affairs.

Cuba was not as fortunate in its goals as Puerto Rico. In 1895, **José Martí** led Cuba in a rebellion to break from Spain. Instead of granting Cuba its independence, however, Spanish troops repressed the rebels with brutal force in its early battles and killed Martí. Cuban guerrillas continued the fight.

Though the United States had not been involved in the rebellion, the American press wrote sensationalized, or exaggerated, stories about it. Publisher **William Randolph Hearst** decided to frame the story in a dramatic way designed to sell his newspapers. His reporters wrote about the

On February 17, 1898, the front page of William Randolph Hearst's newspaper, the *New York Journal and Advertiser,* announced the destruction of the U.S.S. *Maine.*

PRIMARY SOURCE

George Eugene Bryson, the Journal's special correspondent at Havana, cables [telegraphs] that it is the secret opinion of many Spaniards in the Cuban capital, that the Maine was destroyed and 258 men killed by means of marine mine or fixed torpedo. This is the opinion of several American naval authorities. The Spaniards, it is believed, arranged to have the Maine anchored over one of the harbor mines. Wires connected the mines with a . . . magazine [supply of ammunition], and it is thought the explosion was caused by sending an electric current through the wire. If this can be proven, the brutal nature of the Spaniards will be shown by the fact that they waited to spring the mine after all the men had retired for the night.

—*New York Journal and Advertiser,*
February 17, 1898

A five-foot nameplate from the wreck of the U.S.S. *Maine*

bravery of Cuban soldiers and the suffering of women and children—much of it made up. The publisher also sent American artists, including Frederic Remington, to Cuba to draw pictures of the violence occurring there. When Remington reported that the violence had been overstated, Hearst replied, "You furnish the pictures, and I'll furnish the war." Purposely exaggerating and dramatizing these events, a practice that came to be called **yellow journalism**, raked in big profits for Hearst, but it left readers with a distorted view of the truth. The term was coined as a result of a battle between Hearst and rival newspaper publisher Joseph Pulitzer over a comic strip featuring a character called "the yellow kid."

Through his coverage of the rebellion, Hearst built wide public support for Cuba. He got his biggest story in 1898, when the U.S.S. *Maine*, a naval battleship, sailed to the Cuban harbor of Havana to protect American interests there. On February 15, a mysterious explosion sank the ship, and more than 250 American sailors died. The cause of the disaster was never determined, but Hearst blamed Spain. Much like the slogan "Remember the Alamo" earlier in the century, "Remember the *Maine*!" became a rallying cry for those demanding war against Spain.

A WORLD POWER

The public outcry led the U.S. government to take action. Congress declared that Cuba should be independent and that President William McKinley should send military forces to make sure Spain obeyed. In response, Spain declared war against the United States on April 24, 1898.

The Spanish-American War was fought on several fronts. It started in the Philippines with the Battle of Manila Bay on May 1. Under Commodore **George Dewey**, the U.S. Navy easily destroyed the Spanish fleet. The war was also fought in Cuba. Future president Theodore Roosevelt played a leadership role in these battles. He was an effective recruiter and persuaded an untrained but tough group of cowboys, miners, police officers, and Native Americans to volunteer. Nicknamed the **Rough Riders**, these soldiers helped capture key locations in Cuba , including Kettle Hill. The Rough Riders also played a supporting role in the **Battle of San Juan Hill** on July 1, which led to a critical victory. Spanish troops left Cuba shortly thereafter.

Completely unprepared for an expanded war with the powerful U.S. military, Spain surrendered on July 17. Through the treaty that ended the war, the United States gained control of Puerto Rico, the Philippines, and the Pacific island of Guam. In 1901, under an agreement with Cuba known as the **Platt Amendment**, the United States agreed to withdraw from Cuba but retained the right to intervene in Cuban affairs. The United States had become a world power.

CRITICAL VIEWING In this painting, W. G. Read's *Rough Riders*, Roosevelt leads his forces in the charge on San Juan Hill. In the actual battle, Roosevelt and his men ascended the hill on foot. And although the African-American troops, the Buffalo Soldiers, did the bulk of the fighting, Roosevelt got most of the credit for the victory. What details in the painting depict Roosevelt as a heroic figure?

HISTORICAL THINKING

1. **READING CHECK** What is yellow journalism?

2. **EVALUATE** How does the newspaper article use facts and opinions to make readers conclude that Spain destroyed the *Maine*?

3. **DRAW CONCLUSIONS** Why do some people consider the Spanish-American War a "newspaper war"?

PLAN

Objective

Explain how newspaper reports played a role in starting the Spanish-American War.

Critical Thinking Skills for Lesson 4.2

- Identify Main Ideas and Details
- Monitor Comprehension
- Evaluate
- Draw Conclusions
- Form and Support Opinions
- Analyze Primary Sources

Essential Question for Chapter 20

Why did the Progressive Era arise? The United States continued to expand and acquire new territory during the Progressive Era. Lesson 4.2 explains how newspapers provoked public outcry and stirred emotions that led the United States into the Spanish-American War.

Background for the Teacher

Even before the explosion that sunk the U.S.S. *Maine*, newspaper publisher William Randolph Hearst was known for sensationalistic reporting that would later be known as "yellow journalism." In 1887, when he was only 24 years old, Hearst became the owner of the *San Francisco Examiner* thanks to funding from his father's mining fortune.

To make his newspaper turn a profit, he imitated the flashy style of his competitor and former mentor Joseph Pulitzer. Then, in 1895, Hearst purchased the *New York Journal* and began to compete directly with Pulitzer in an already competitive market. That same year, the Cuban Revolution erupted, and soon Pulitzer and Hearst were in a war for readership, exploiting whatever lurid story their reporters could devise.

Preview Terms

Write the words *yellow journalism* on the board. Then lead the class in a discussion about how media outlets try to gain a reader's attention. Ask volunteers to define the slang term *clickbait*. As students discuss *clickbait*, ask them to provide a few contemporary examples of it. Guide them to discuss the value of verifying the credibility of sources and how to distinguish fact from opinion in news media. Tell students that in this lesson they will learn about yellow journalism and how it exaggerated the truth. Explain that its sensational headlines and articles were the 19th-century equivalent of 21st-century clickbait.

TEACH

Guided Discussion

1. **Draw Conclusions** Would most Americans at the turn of the century have considered the Spanish-American War a success? *(Possible response: Yes, the war was brief, and the United States won it easily, gaining important territories in the Caribbean and Asia.)*

2. **Form and Support Opinions** Why might the United States agree to withdraw from Cuba but want to retain rights to intervene in Cuban affairs as stated in the Platt Amendment? Support your opinion with evidence from the text. *(Possible responses: Cuba is an island in the Caribbean, and it may have been strategically valuable for military reasons. American leaders may have wanted to help the Cuban people live in better conditions.)*

Analyze Primary Sources

About a month after the explosion on the U.S.S. *Maine*, a U.S. Naval Court of Inquiry concluded that the ship had been blown up by a mine, although the court did not directly blame Spain. However, much of the American public, swayed by yellow journalism, was sure that Spain was responsible and urged Congress to declare war. **ASK:** What details in the lesson excerpt from the *New York Journal and Advertiser* might lead readers to believe that Spain was responsible for the explosion? *(Readers would assume that if both "American naval authorities" and "many Spaniards" in Cuba said that a mine or torpedo destroyed the ship, then it must be true. Adding details, such as suggestions that the Spaniards ensured the ship was moored over a harbor mine, might lead readers to believe the theories were facts.)*

Active Options

On Your Feet: Sentence Chain Organize students into small groups. Tell students that they are journalists working on a story about the sinking of the U.S.S. *Maine*. Their main goal is to create a story that will sell a lot of newspapers. Tell each group their story needs a sensational headline and one sentence composed by each person in the group. Each sentence must have at least one real name, place, date, or other fact related to the sinking of the *Maine*. Encourage students to use their imaginations and make the story as compelling as possible. Prompt the groups to share their stories by standing in a line and doing a dramatic reading. Then have students vote on the news story that was the most sensational.

NG Learning Framework: Write a Biography

ATTITUDE	Curiosity
KNOWLEDGE	Our Human Story

Have students write a short biography of either the Puerto Rican journalist Luis Muñoz Rivera or the leader of the Cuban independence movement, José Martí. Instruct students to use multiple print and online resources for their research, using search terms effectively to find out about their subject's life and the role he played in his island's struggle for independence from Spain. Remind students to paraphrase their conclusions and to cite their sources using a standard format. Students may present their biographies to the class or post them in a class blog. Guide the class to discuss similarities and differences between the lives of the two leaders and the results of their respective struggles.

Striving Readers

Read and Recall Assign pairs of students to read Lesson 4.2 independently. Then, to see what they recall, ask them to discuss the lesson without consulting the text, making notes as they discuss. When they have finished their discussion, tell students to review the text and make any necessary additions or changes to their notes. They can then use their notes to review the lesson as needed.

Gifted and Talented

Create an Infographic Have students do research to learn more about the U.S. territory of Guam in the western Pacific. Then direct them to work alone or in pairs to create an infographic comparing and contrasting Guam in the late 1800s and today. Students may also include in their infographic some of the important roles Guam has played in history since the United States acquired it at the end of the Spanish-American War. Ask students to present their infographics to the class and answer other students' questions.

See the Chapter Planner for more strategies for differentiation.

HISTORICAL THINKING

ANSWERS

1. Exaggerated or sensationalized news reports are considered yellow journalism.

2. The newspaper states two facts and supports them with unnamed sources that are represented as being from both sides of the conflict. The article implies that the statements made are being investigated, further supporting the statements.

3. Sensational stories inflamed public opinion, which pushed the U.S. Congress to declare war against Spain.

CRITICAL VIEW Possible response: Theodore Roosevelt is at the center of the painting. His arm is raised, holding his sword aloft, as he leads the charge. Amid all the action—and with his horse in full gallop, frothing at the mouth—Roosevelt appears stoic, steady, and calm.

4.3 The Filipino-American War

The people of the Philippines had longed to be free of Spanish rule, and now they were. But they had merely exchanged one ruler for another. And they were more than disappointed—they were angry.

MAIN IDEA The people of the Philippines fought for independence from American rule in the Filipino-American War.

During the Filipino-American War, entire villages, like this one, were damaged or completely destroyed. Residents were often driven from their homes or imprisoned.

RESISTANCE IN THE PHILIPPINES

After more than 300 years of Spanish rule, the people of the Philippines, called Filipinos, didn't want to be controlled by another colonial power. They wanted their independence. The island nation's independence movement had grown strong during the long struggle against Spanish rule, and it now turned its full force against the United States.

Resistance leader **Emilio Aguinaldo** did not waste any time rallying his forces after the Spanish-American treaty was signed. On the night of February 4, 1899, Filipino insurrectionists, or rebels, and American troops clashed outside the capital city of Manila. The **Filipino-American War** had begun. Fierce fighting continued through the night, but by morning, the Americans had defeated the outnumbered Filipinos. Aguinaldo and his troops retreated northward into the mountains to regroup and rethink their strategy.

GUERRILLA WARFARE

Since conventional warfare against the American military had ended in defeat, the Filipinos turned to guerrilla warfare. This military tactic, which involves quick, unexpected attacks by small groups, is often effective for those fighting on their own land. The geography of the Philippines was well suited for guerrilla warfare. The country consists of thousands of islands, most with heavily forested mountains and, at that time, also with dense tropical rain forests.

The Filipino soldiers' tactics proved successful and resulted in the deaths of many American soldiers. In retaliation, the U.S. Army resorted to killing and torturing some Filipino prisoners of war. After an incident in which Filipino guerrillas massacred American troops, American general Jacob F. Smith engaged in a campaign of revenge. The violence committed by soldiers under his command was so extreme that the U.S. Army court-martialed Smith, or tried him in a military court, for his conduct and forced him to retire.

The brutality of the war strengthened an American movement against imperialist expansion. The American Anti-Imperialist League had been formed in 1898 to protest the expansion of the United States and its treatment of the Filipino people. Politicians, businesspeople, and writers joined the league to speak out against U.S. imperialism.

Mark Twain and the Filipino-American War
The famous U.S. novelist Mark Twain (shown here in a painting by Frank Larson) paid close attention to the Filipino-American War. At first he supported the war, but Twain grew dismayed by the imperialist aspirations of his government and joined the American Anti-Imperialist League.

Despite this opposition, the United States was determined to maintain its hold on the Philippines and eventually defeated the insurrectionists. The war officially came to an end in 1902, though guerrillas continued to battle American troops for a few more years. The fighting had resulted in a tremendous loss of life in the Philippines. Around 20,000 Filipino troops had been killed, and more than 200,000 civilians had died from combat wounds, disease, and starvation. On the American side, about 1,500 troops had been killed, and disease had claimed some 2,800 additional lives. The Philippines remained a U.S. territory until 1946 when the United States granted the country its independence. For a time, Filipinos were allowed to migrate freely to the United States because of their U.S. national status. As a result, many Filipinos immigrated to Hawaii around 1910 to work on its sugar plantations.

In the early 1900s, the United States continued to exert its influence in the world. But rather than acquire more territory, the nation focused on protecting its interests in Latin America and Asia.

In 1899, the Anti-Imperialist League issued its platform, or statement of beliefs, on U.S. imperialist policy. In this excerpt, the league explains why it condemns that policy.

PRIMARY SOURCE

We earnestly condemn the policy of the present National Administration in the Philippines. It seeks to extinguish the spirit of 1776 in those islands. We deplore the sacrifice of our soldiers and sailors, whose bravery deserves admiration even in an unjust war. We denounce the slaughter of the Filipinos as a needless horror. We protest against the extension of American sovereignty by Spanish methods.

—from "Platform of the American Anti-Imperialist League," 1899

HISTORICAL THINKING

1. **READING CHECK** How did the people of the Philippines react to American rule following the Spanish-American War?

2. **DRAW CONCLUSIONS** What does the Anti-Imperialist League mean when it claims that U.S. policy "seeks to extinguish the spirit of 1776" in the Philippines?

3. **MAKE INFERENCES** Why do you think the United States was so determined to hold onto the Philippines?

PLAN

Objective

Recognize the reasons that both sides had for fighting the Filipino-American War.

Critical Thinking Skills for Lesson 4.3

- Identify Main Ideas and Details
- Monitor Comprehension
- Draw Conclusions
- Make Inferences
- Analyze Cause and Effect
- Form and Support Opinions
- Make Generalizations

Essential Question for Chapter 20

Why did the Progressive Era arise? The United States gained overseas territories because of the Spanish-American War. Lesson 4.3 examines how the brutality of the Filipino-American War started a backlash against American imperialism.

Background for the Teacher

When Americans realized that the United States was fighting a colonial war against people who wanted independence, many were appalled. The Anti-Imperialist League's platform reproachfully stated, "We regret that it has become necessary in the land of Washington and Lincoln to reaffirm that all men, of whatever race or color, are entitled to life, liberty, and the pursuit of happiness." Members of the Anti-Imperialist League included people such as Jane Addams, Samuel Gompers, William James, William Jennings Bryan, Alice Thacher Post, Mark Twain, and Andrew Carnegie. One historian claims that the steel magnate Andrew Carnegie offered to purchase the Philippines for 20 million dollars, the same amount the United States had paid Spain for the islands, in order to return the country to the Filipinos and thus avoid war. President William McKinley declined the offer, and during the brutal three-year Filipino-American war that followed, the Anti-Imperialist League grew to about 30,000 members.

Discuss a Proverb

Ask students if they've heard the expression "Practice what you preach." Have a volunteer explain what it means. Invite students to give examples of situations in which they might use this phrase. Tell them that in this lesson they will see that sometimes it's difficult for governments to practice what they preach, or stay true to their ideals, especially when competing interests are involved.

TEACH

Guided Discussion

1. **Analyze Cause and Effect** Explain how U.S. imperialism led to the Filipino-American War, which in turn strengthened support for the anti-imperialist movement. *(The imperialist push to acquire more land and resources around the world led to the Filipino-American War when Filipinos rebelled against U.S. claims to the Philippines. Opposition to imperialism, including the Anti-Imperialist League, grew in response to the brutal war in which the United States tried to crush the Filipinos' desire for freedom and self-determination.)*

2. **Form and Support Opinions** Do you think the United States should have annexed the Philippines or not? Support your opinion with evidence from the text. *(Answers will vary. Possible responses: No, the United States should have respected the Filipino desire for independence. Yes, because the United States needed the Philippines to expand international trade and to have a military base in Asia. If the United States hadn't occupied the Philippines, another power would have, and that would have made the United States weaker.)*

Make Generalizations

What kind of geography is generally most advantageous for guerrilla fighters? *(Possible response: Rough terrain, especially mountainous islands with dense vegetation that is familiar to the local people, helps guerrilla fighters attack quickly and then escape.)*

Active Options

Active History: Analyze Achievements of Emilio Aguinaldo Extend the lesson by using either the PDF or Whiteboard version of the activity. These activities take a deeper look at a topic from, or related to, the lesson. Explore the activities as a class, turn them into group assignments, or even assign them individually.

NG Learning Framework: Analyze Perspectives

ATTITUDE Curiosity

SKILLS Collaboration, Communication

Organize students into three groups, each of which will advise President McKinley on a different aspect of how to handle the newly acquired Philippines. The first group will advise the president from an economic perspective, the second from a military perspective, and the third from a moral or ideological perspective. Tell each group to research the assigned perspective using print and digital sources and then prepare a memo for the president, concluding with a recommendation as to what he should do. Choose a student to play the role of president. Direct that student to call an advisory meeting and listen to each group's advice.

DIFFERENTIATE

Inclusion

Map Imperialism Pair students with learning disabilities with other students. Provide access to a world map online where partners can make digital notes, or provide a wall map with sticky notes. Have pairs mark the locations that have been discussed in Section 4 that relate to imperialism, including the United States, Spain, and Cuba. Instruct the partner with disabilities to read the lesson aloud while the other partner follows along. As they read the lesson, have students locate and record notes about places related to the lesson content.

Pre-AP

Research Soldiers' Experiences Challenge students to use digital resources to find letters from American soldiers that express differing experiences and opinions in regard to the Filipino-American War. Then have students evaluate the source material and write an essay about what they discovered. Students should address whether they think the soldiers' letters reflect their true experiences or reflect pro- or anti-imperialist propaganda. Students may then present their findings to the class, using some of the soldiers' own words.

See the Chapter Planner for more strategies for differentiation.

HISTORICAL THINKING

ANSWERS

1. The Filipinos had been struggling for independence from Spanish rule, so they were not happy to be under U.S. rule after the Spanish-American War. They clashed with American troops on their soil, and the Filipino-American War started.

2. The "spirit of 1776" refers to the ideals of freedom and self-determination that the colonists embraced when they declared independence from England. The Anti-Imperialist League meant that U.S. actions in the Philippines were crushing U.S. ideals.

3. Possible responses: The location of the Philippines, near Asia, made it militarily and economically valuable to the United States. Many Americans thought that Filipinos were primitive people incapable of self-governing themselves. Other world powers were expanding their empires, so many people thought that if the United States did not control the islands, another country would.

4.4 Involvement in Latin America and Asia

Do you know the saying, "Actions speak louder than words"? It means that people should be judged by what they do rather than what they say. As a man of action, Theodore Roosevelt practically embodied the saying. But he used another one to describe his foreign policy.

MAIN IDEA During the Progressive Era, the United States became increasingly involved in the affairs of Latin American and Asian countries.

U.S. Acquisitions and Interventions, 1867–1902

BIG STICK POLICY

President Theodore Roosevelt favored American involvement in foreign affairs. He characterized his foreign policy with the saying, "Speak softly and carry a big stick." That meant that he would "speak softly," or negotiate with a country in a calm, assured manner. But if the country did not cooperate, he might use his "big stick"—U.S. military power.

Since 1823, the United States had followed the principles of the Monroe Doctrine. According to this policy, Europe would not acquire new colonies in the Western Hemisphere. In exchange, the United States would not get involved in political affairs in Europe and would respect existing European colonies in the Western Hemisphere.

Roosevelt decided to take this policy a step further by adding the **Roosevelt Corollary** to the Monroe Doctrine. This addition asserted that, under certain circumstances, the United States had the right to intervene in the affairs of Latin American countries.

Several presidents after Roosevelt followed his lead in policing the Western Hemisphere. A revolution in the Central American country of Nicaragua in 1909 resulted in a government that the United States viewed as a threat to its economic interests. President William Taft sent in troops to dismantle this government and set up a new one—one that would be friendly to American businesses.

President Woodrow Wilson got involved in Mexico's political affairs after General Victoriano Huerta overthrew the country's elected president in 1913. Mexico had been engaged in an on-going revolution since 1899. Calling Mexico's new leaders "a government of butchers," Wilson took steps to weaken Huerta's control and overthrow him. His measures worked, but the United States became involved in Mexico's revolution until 1917, when Wilson withdrew all U.S. forces from the country.

OPEN DOOR POLICY

Meanwhile, the United States had been exerting its influence in East Asia since the mid-1800s. For centuries, Japan had adopted a policy of isolation and greatly limited trade with other countries. On July 8, 1853, four American ships under the command of Commodore **Matthew Perry** sailed into Japan's Tokyo Bay. Perry had been sent to negotiate diplomatic relations and trade between Japan and the United States. As a result, Japan opened its ports to American ships for the first time in more than 200 years.

Like Japan, China tried to resist involvement with other countries. But the 19th century was an unsettled period for China. Following a series of wars with Britain, China had been forced to remove its barriers to foreign trade in 1842. Then around 1899, several countries—primarily Britain, France, Germany, and Russia—sought to establish spheres of influence in China. A **sphere of influence** is a

claim a country makes to be the exclusive influence on another country's political or economic activities. Within China, each European power carved out a sphere of influence and controlled investment within that area.

The United States opposed these claims, fearing that the countries controlling their spheres of influence would monopolize all trade in China. As a result, the United States proposed the **Open Door Policy**. This policy called for equal trading privileges for all nations with economic interests in China. Although the nations that had carved out spheres of influence in China were not enthusiastic about this plan, they didn't openly oppose it either. So the U.S. government claimed that the powers had accepted the policy's terms and called their responses "final and definitive."

Many people in China were not happy with the flow of foreigners coming to their country. In 1900, a Chinese secret society known as the Society of the Righteous and Harmonious Fists rebelled against

the spread of Western and Japanese influence and sought to drive all foreigners out of China. Westerners called the society "Boxers" because its members carried out ritual boxing exercises. The Boxers killed foreigners and missionaries and destroyed property. An international coalition, which included American troops, was finally brought in and suppressed what would become known as the **Boxer Rebellion**. But the violent episode had exposed the unpredictable nature of increased contact with countries around the globe.

HISTORICAL THINKING

1. **READING CHECK** What was Theodore Roosevelt's big stick policy?

2. **SYNTHESIZE** How did presidents Taft and Wilson implement the Roosevelt Corollary?

3. **INTERPRET MAPS** How would you describe the location of most of the lands acquired by the United States?

Objective
Describe how U.S. foreign policy affected countries in Latin America and Asia.

Critical Thinking Skills for Lesson 4.4
- Identify Main Ideas and Details
- Monitor Comprehension
- Synthesize
- Interpret Maps
- Make Connections
- Form and Support Opinions

Essential Question for Chapter 20
Why did the Progressive Era arise? In the late 19th century, the United States became a new global power. Lesson 4.4 identifies changes in U.S. foreign policy that led to imperialist interventions in Nicaragua, Mexico, Japan, and China.

Background for the Teacher
The secret group of rebels, *I Ho Ch'uan*, known as the Boxers, had expelled Jesuit missionaries from China as early as 1747. The Boxer Rebellion gained strength as Western imperial powers flocked to China in the 19th century, often exploiting its land and people. Many of the rebels were peasants from the Shandong Province, on the northeast coast between Beijing and Shanghai. This area had suffered floods and famine, and much of its land was given to foreign businesses by the Chinese government, impoverishing ordinary people.

To regain their land and way of life, the Boxers traveled to Beijing and attacked their hierarchy of enemies on the way: foreigners, Chinese Christians, and any Chinese person working for foreigners. When the Boxers reached Beijing's foreign district, the empress dowager of the Qing dynasty, which had ruled China since 1644, backed their cause, declaring war against nations that had diplomatic ties with China. The Boxers were defeated. This defeat ended the Qing dynasty in 1911, and a new republic was established in 1912.

INTRODUCE & ENGAGE

Get in the Big Game

Ask students to think about sports teams they have been on or know about. Call on volunteers to explain the terms *benchwarmer, starting lineup,* and *power hitter.* Tell students that in this lesson they'll see how the United States continued to transform itself from a benchwarmer to a power hitter in the practice of global imperialism.

TEACH

Guided Discussion

1. **Make Connections** What reasons may have prompted President Roosevelt to add a corollary to the Monroe Doctrine? *(Possible response: Roosevelt may have extended the reach of the Monroe Doctrine because he thought the political unrest in Latin America could affect U.S. interests and he wanted to protect them. Protecting U.S. interests in Latin America did not necessarily mean involvement in the political affairs of Europe.)*

2. **Form and Support Opinions** Overall, was Roosevelt's "big stick" policy and its influence on presidents Taft and Wilson a positive or negative development in U.S. foreign policy? *(Possible responses: It was positive because leaders may have felt they could negotiate calmly. It was negative because leaders likely knew that if they did not agree with the negotiation efforts, then military action against them was very likely.)*

More Information

Commodore Perry and His Evil Ships When Commodore Matthew Perry sailed into Tokyo's harbor, some Japanese leaders wanted to send the foreigners immediately away. They referred to Perry's ships as having an "evil mien," or evil appearance, and judged their presence as a sign of bad things to come. Perry had only four ships. Japan, however, had no navy at all and so was unable to force Perry's ships to turn back. **ASK:** How did Perry's negotiations with Japan represent the policies of the "big stick" approach that were put in place by Theodore Roosevelt? *(Perry's show of superior naval force in a country with no navy of its own represented a "big stick" that showed Japanese leaders that they had little choice but to do what Perry and the U.S. government demanded.)*

Active Options

On Your Feet: Fishbowl Have one half of the class sit or stand in a close circle, facing inward. The other half of the class sits or stands facing inward in a larger circle around the first circle. Present this question: How did U.S. intervention affect Latin American and Asian countries in the 19th century? Students in the inner circle should discuss the question while those in the outer circle listen to the discussion and evaluate the points made. Then have the groups reverse roles and continue the discussion.

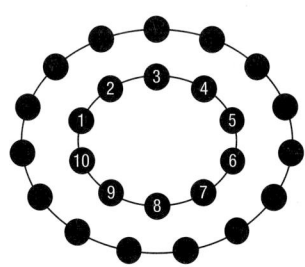

NG Learning Framework: Pose and Answer Historical Questions

ATTITUDE Curiosity

KNOWLEDGE Our Human Story

Ask students to pose questions they have about the U.S. interventions shown on the map in Lesson 4.4 that were not answered in the lesson. Allow students to work individually, in pairs, or in small groups to research answers to their questions. Instruct them to draw on several sources, which may generate additional questions to help focus their research. Provide time for groups to share their questions and answers with the class.

DIFFERENTIATE

English Language Learners   ELD

Read in Pairs Pair English language learners at the **Emerging** or **Expanding** level with English-proficient students, and have them read the lesson together. Ask pairs to pause after each paragraph and work together to state its ideas in words the English learners can understand. Encourage the English-proficient readers to help their partners use context clues to determine the meanings of unfamiliar words in the text rather than immediately supplying definitions or synonyms.

Gifted & Talented

Research and Write a Newspaper Article Tell students to imagine they are newspaper reporters covering the arrival of Commodore Perry and his gunboats in Japan in 1853. Instruct them to use a variety of online sources to research Perry's arrival. Then have students write a newspaper account from the Japanese point of view. Encourage them to share their article with the class.

See the Chapter Planner for more strategies for differentiation.

HISTORICAL THINKING

ANSWERS

1. Theodore Roosevelt believed in trying to negotiate peaceful solutions for international concerns. However, he was also willing to use the threat of military force as a "big stick" to sway negotiations in the United States' favor.

2. Both presidents intervened in the affairs of Latin American countries. President Taft sent troops to Nicaragua to overthrow that country's government and install a new one friendly to U.S. business interests. President Wilson destabilized and overthrew Mexico's elected president.

3. United States acquisitions were in Latin America, Asia, and the Pacific Ocean. These locations were strategically important for economic and military reasons and provided the United States with power and influence around the globe.

4.5 Building the Panama Canal

MAIN IDEA In the early 1900s, the United States overcame geographic challenges and built the Panama Canal to connect the Atlantic and Pacific oceans.

THE DREAM OF A CANAL

For decades, people dreamed of building a shortcut between the Atlantic and Pacific oceans: a canal across the **isthmus** of Panama, a narrow strip of land connecting North and South America. Before the Panama Canal, ships had to sail around the southern tip of South America to get from America's East Coast to the West Coast. A canal would shorten this voyage by nearly 8,000 miles.

The French had tried to build a canal, but they failed because of the geographic challenges. The canal had to be about 50 miles long, and had to cut through rugged mountains. Additionally, a nearby river caused frequent flooding in the region, landslides were common, and mosquitoes infected construction workers with diseases.

But President Theodore Roosevelt was determined to have a canal built. First, he had to acquire the land. This was a big problem, because the isthmus belonged to the country of Colombia. Colombia and other Latin American countries did not trust the United States because of the Spanish-American War. Roosevelt didn't care. In 1903, he engineered a rebellion in which Panama broke away from Colombia and established its own country. Then the United States negotiated a treaty to create the Canal Zone, a ten-mile-wide strip of land the United States could lease from Panama. That was where the canal would be built.

Once they had the land, the Americans had to overcome the same geographic obstacles that had defeated the French, but the Americans succeeded. The Panama Canal opened in 1914 and has operated continuously since. Read about these challenges and the technology Americans used to overcome each one.

The Panama Canal

map labels: ATLANTIC OCEAN; Caribbean Sea; Colón; Gatún Locks; Gatún; Center line of the canal; Gatún Lake; REPUBLIC OF PANAMA; CANAL ZONE; Alajuela Lake; Continental Divide; Culebra Cut; Culebra; Pedro Miguel Locks; Pedro Miguel; Miraflores Locks; Miraflores; Panama City; Balboa; Bay of Panama; PACIFIC OCEAN; Center line of the canal; REPUBLIC OF PANAMA; Continental Divide; 10 Miles; 10 Kilometers

GEOGRAPHIC CHALLENGE	TECHNOLOGICAL SOLUTION
MALARIA AND YELLOW FEVER	
Two dangerous diseases were widespread in Central America: malaria and yellow fever. The illnesses killed one in five workers, and no one knew what caused them.	When the chief medical officer for the project discovered mosquitoes could pass both diseases to humans, he insisted on placing screens on every building's windows. He had all standing water treated to prevent mosquito breeding. Then workers agreed to come to Panama.
DIGGING THE LOCKS	
Panama is an extremely mountainous country. The engineers decided to build the canal at the level of the mountains rather than at sea level. To do so, they needed to build **locks**. A lock is a confined section of water used to raise or lower ships.	To build the locks, workers used steam shovels, which had only recently been developed, to dig enormous holes where the locks would be. They then poured more than four million barrels of cement to form the locks.
DIGGING THE CULEBRA CUT	
The most difficult part of the canal was a 9-mile section called the Culebra Cut. It was a human-made ditch 45 feet deep and 9 miles long that would carry ships past the highest mountains.	First engineers blasted the rock loose with dynamite. Then they used huge steam shovels to lift the **spoil**, or excess dirt and rock, into waiting railroad cars. Each shovel could lift eight tons of spoil at a time. Railroad cars would carry the spoil away from the worksite.
DAMMING THE CHAGRES RIVER	
Another major geographic challenge was the Chagres River, which fed into the Canal Zone. This river was wild, and during the rainy season, it flooded the entire region.	Engineers built an earthen dam in a valley about four miles east of the Atlantic Ocean. The dam controlled the river and prevented flooding by backing up the waters of the Chagres to form Gatun Lake. Ships sailed across the lake on their way to the locks at the canal's ends.

map labels: San Francisco; NORTH AMERICA; New York; Panama Canal; SOUTH AMERICA

From New York to San Francisco:

BEFORE THE CANAL
13,000 Miles

AFTER THE CANAL
5,200 Miles

THINK LIKE A GEOGRAPHER

1. **IDENTIFY MAIN IDEAS AND DETAILS** How was the mountainous terrain of Panama a problem, and how did the engineers solve it?

2. **ANALYZE ENVIRONMENTAL CONCEPTS** How did the Chagres River benefit from being dammed during the building of the Panama Canal?

3. **MAKE INFERENCES** In 1977, President Jimmy Carter signed a treaty promising to return control of the Canal Zone to the country of Panama by the year 2000. Why do you think he might have signed this treaty?

PLAN

Objective

Explain how building the Panama Canal presented engineering and health challenges.

Critical Thinking Skills for Lesson 4.5

- Identify Main Ideas and Details
- Monitor Comprehension
- Analyze Environmental Concepts
- Make Inferences
- Identify Problems and Solutions
- Interpret Maps

Essential Question for Chapter 20

Why did the Progressive Era arise? The concept of "progress" included overcoming geographic challenges. Lesson 4.5 describes how President Roosevelt overcame many challenges to build a canal through the Panamanian isthmus.

Background for the Teacher

Building the Panama Canal was considered such a tremendous feat of progress that many human and environmental costs of the project were overlooked. Some 30,000 workers labored 10-hour days, moving up to 200 trainloads of earth each day. Many were from the West Indies and earned 10 cents an hour, half of what European and white U.S. workers made. The work was difficult and dangerous and led to nearly 6,000 worker deaths.

Much of the earth that workers removed was transported to the dam site on the Chagres River. Once the massive earthen dam was completed, the backed-up river submerged 150 square miles of land that had been a dense jungle, creating a new lake and permanently changing the environment.

INTRODUCE & ENGAGE

Take a Shortcut

Write the word *shortcut* on the board. Ask students to list as many different kinds of shortcuts as they can and to provide examples of each. *(Possible responses: crossing a park to get from one street to another, using an app to complete a task)* Tell students that since the 14th century, people had wanted to create a shortcut between the Atlantic and Pacific oceans through the isthmus of Panama. In this lesson, students will learn more about how the Panama Canal was finally built.

TEACH

STEM

Guided Discussion

1. **Identify Problems and Solutions** Transporting the Culebra Cut spoil from the work site solved one problem. What problems might it have caused, and how might those problems have been solved? *(Possible response: The spoil had to be deposited somewhere else, which could change the landscape, harm wildlife, and cause other environmental issues. However, with planning, the spoil could perhaps be used for other infrastructure projects, such as filling in areas prone to flooding or raising roads.)*

2. **Analyze Environmental Concepts** What were some of the negative ecological impacts of the technological solutions the builders of the Panama Canal used? *(Treating water to prevent mosquitoes from breeding may have contaminated the water for other uses. Digging deep ditches through the mountains involved deforestation and destruction of native habitats. Damming the river drowned plant and animal life.)*

Geography in History

Interpret Maps Instruct students to analyze and compare the information conveyed by the two maps. **ASK:** How does the geographic information conveyed by each map differ? *(The small-scale map of the continents shows how much shorter the distance is to travel by ship. The large-scale map of the canal zone conveys topographic and ecological information.)* **ASK:** How does the combined information from the two maps present a more complete view of the advantages and disadvantages of the canal? *(Possible response: The small-scale map conveys the great advantage of the shortcut and makes the isthmus of Panama look like an obvious place to build a canal; the large-scale map points out the geographic challenges and ecological drawbacks of the canal.)*

Active Options

On Your Feet: Become an Expert Label each of the corners of the room with one of the headings from the chart showing geographic challenges and technological solutions. Organize students into four groups and have each group move to a corner. Instruct group members to use information from the text and from other sources to research their topic. Then regroup students so that each new group has at least one "expert" on each topic. Have members of the new groups take turns sharing what they learned about their challenge and its solution.

NG Learning Framework: Create a Public Health Brochure

ATTITUDE Empowerment

SKILLS Problem-Solving, Communication

Challenge teams of students to research the best practices recommended for preventing malaria and yellow fever today. Based on what they learn, have students create public health brochures to inform Americans of steps they can take to avoid contracting these diseases when traveling. The information in the brochures should be brief yet compelling, combining words and artwork or images. Invite students to share their brochures and talk about similarities and differences in prevention of these diseases between the time the canal was built and today.

DIFFERENTIATE

Inclusion

Preview Maps Before reading the lesson, pair students who have learning disabilities with other students who can help them preview the maps. Encourage students to use their fingers on the distance map to trace the long path that ships had to make all the way around South America before the canal was built and compare it with the journey ships could make afterward. They may also use their fingers on the Panama Canal map to trace the route of a ship from the Atlantic Ocean, through the Gatun Locks, into Gatun Lake, and out into the Pacific Ocean. Pairs may discuss the topography and other details featured on the large-scale map.

Pre-AP

Report on a Presidential Plan Invite students to research and prepare an oral report covering the obstacles Theodore Roosevelt faced and the actions he took when the Colombian government was reluctant to provide the United States with access to the isthmus of Panama. Ask students to include insights about why Roosevelt thought he was doing the right thing at the time and how such actions might be viewed today from the standpoint of international law or individual morality.

See the Chapter Planner for more strategies for differentiation.

THINK LIKE A GEOGRAPHER

ANSWERS

1. Engineers decided to build a series of locks that raised ships because the mountains of Panama are far above sea level and digging a sea-level canal was impractical.

2. The dam controlled flooding of the river.

3. Possible response: The land was leased to the United States by Panama. The Panamanian people may have resented the American presence in their country, and Carter didn't want the resentment to turn into bloodshed.

20 REVIEW

VOCABULARY

Match the following vocabulary terms with their definitions.

1. referendum
2. autonomy
3. suffragist
4. sphere of influence
5. imperialism
6. loophole
7. initiative
8. conservation movement

a. unclear language that allows people to avoid obeying laws

b. a group of people working together to protect plants, animals, and the natural environment

c. a proposed law that citizens vote on to accept or reject

d. a law that citizens propose

e. an area of a country where another country has a great deal of power

f. a person who actively supports the right to vote, particularly a woman's right to vote

g. self-rule or independence

h. the use of power to gain control over other areas of the world

READING STRATEGY
SYNTHESIZE

If you haven't already, complete your chart by organizing the evidence in each lesson and synthesizing the information. Then answer the question.

9. What measures and strategies did progressives use to address social problems?

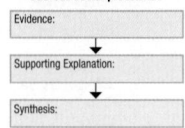

How did progressives address social problems?

Evidence:

↓

Supporting Explanation:

↓

Synthesis:

MAIN IDEAS

Answer the following questions. Support your answers with evidence from the chapter.

10. What 19th-century movement promoted equality for people of all races, genders, and sexual orientations? **LESSON 1.1**

11. Why did progressives promote primary elections, referendums, and initiatives? **LESSON 1.3**

12. How did Theodore Roosevelt help protect the environment? **LESSON 1.4**

13. How did Woodrow Wilson encourage business expansion through the Clayton Antitrust Act? **LESSON 2.2**

14. What was different about how Henry Ford ran his factories? **LESSON 2.3**

15. How did Jane Addams and Ellen Gates Star help the immigrant population of Chicago? **LESSON 3.2**

16. Who was Carrie Chapman Catt? **LESSON 3.3**

17. Why did many Americans oppose the purchase of Alaska? **LESSON 4.1**

18. How did newspaper accounts of the sinking of the U.S.S. *Maine* affect public opinion? **LESSON 4.2**

19. Why did the United States propose the Open Door Policy for China? **LESSON 4.4**

HISTORICAL THINKING

Answer the following questions. Support your answers with evidence from the chapter.

20. **COMPARE AND CONTRAST** What similar ideas about business practices did Roosevelt, Taft, and Wilson share?

21. **DRAW CONCLUSIONS** Why was the passage of the 19th Amendment so significant?

22. **SYNTHESIZE** How did increased mechanization lead to phenomenal growth in industrial efficiency?

23. **FORM AND SUPPORT OPINIONS** Do you think the pursuit of imperialist goals during the Progressive Era helped or hurt the United States? Explain your answer.

ANALYZE VISUALS

Look closely at the photograph on the right taken in 1913 at the Ford plant in Highland Park, Michigan. Then answer the questions that follow.

24. What are the workers in the plant doing?

25. What is the purpose of the tracks on the floor?

26. What issues might the workers have had as they completed this task and worked in this way all day, every day?

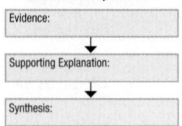

ANALYZE SOURCES

Jane Addams strongly believed women should have the right to vote. In the following excerpt from her 1915 pamphlet, "Why Women Should Vote," Addams offers one reason.

> To turn the administration of our civic affairs wholly [only] over to men may mean that the American city will continue to push forward in its commercial and industrial development, and continue to lag behind in those things which make a city healthful and beautiful. . . . If women have in any sense been responsible for the gentler side of life which softens and blurs some of its harsher conditions, may they not have a duty to perform in our American cities?

27. How does Addams use information about the traditional roles of men and women as an argument for granting women's suffrage?

CONNECT TO YOUR LIFE

28. **EXPOSITORY** News coverage of events and ideas during the Progressive Era shaped people's opinions. Think about how news is covered today. Then write a paragraph comparing the two.

TIPS

• Review the influence of newspaper coverage of the Spanish-American War and how the NAWSA used media to spread its message.

• Consider how people learn about the news today. Think about the role of the Internet and social media in spreading news.

• Write a paragraph comparing and contrasting the media of the Progressive Era with today's media. Include observations about how the speed at which news spreads affects people's opinions today.

VOCABULARY ANSWERS

1. c
2. g
3. f
4. e
5. h
6. a
7. d
8. b

READING STRATEGY ANSWER

How did progressives address social problems?

Evidence: Progressive reformers exposed social problems.

↓

Supporting Explanation: Muckrakers published books and articles about business abuses, corruption in government, and working conditions.

↓

Synthesis: Progressive reformers raised public awareness that resulted in legislation to address social problems.

9. Answers will vary. Possible response: Progressives published books and articles that exposed corruption in government and unsafe conditions in the workplace. They formed groups to work for social change. They gave speeches, marched, and lobbied to influence legislation that would address problems.

MAIN IDEAS ANSWERS

10. Progressivism promoted equality among different groups of people and called for government support of social reform.

11. Through these changes, progressives promoted a more direct voice in government for the people.

12. Roosevelt created the United States Forest Service, which set aside land for conservation.

13. The Clayton Antitrust Act strengthened legislation against monopolies. This law controlled large businesses and gave small businesses opportunities to expand and compete in the marketplace.

14. Ford implemented an assembly-line system in which workers added parts to cars moving past them in a line. This made the production of cars much faster and cheaper.

15. Addams and Starr ran Hull House, a settlement house that helped the immigrant population by offering shelter, food, and other services and resources.

16. Carrie Chapman Catt was a suffragist who linked women's voting rights to the war effort. Her argument that women's patriotic efforts in World War I should earn them the right to vote caused President Wilson to support the 19th Amendment.

17. Many Americans claimed Alaska was too far from the rest of the United States, very cold, and too expensive.

18. The media exaggerated and distorted the truth regarding the U.S.S. *Maine*, causing many people to blame Spain for the tragedy. The public started to support American intervention in Cuba's revolt against Spain.

19. The United States was not able to trade in the spheres of influence that five other countries had carved out in China. The Open Door Policy would give the United States and other countries equal trading privileges in China.

HISTORICAL THINKING ANSWERS

20. All three presidents supported antitrust laws to break up and prevent monopolies.

21. Answers will vary. Possible response: The 19th Amendment gave women the right to vote, thereby changing their status in society and opening the way for greater opportunities.

22. Increased mechanization cut production time, reduced labor costs, and expanded production.

23. Answers will vary. Possible responses: Imperialism helped the United States acquire new land, including the giant territory of Alaska and the strategically located Hawaiian Islands. The negative results of imperialism included wars that the United States fought, the lives that were lost in these wars, and the anti-American and anti-imperialist feelings provoked by U.S. actions.

ANALYZE VISUALS ANSWERS

24. Workers appear to be adding parts to a car.

25. The tracks on the floor allow the car to move to other workers who have specific tasks to complete in the car's assembly.

26. Workers may have found this work boring and repetitive. The repetitive movement may have been hard on them physically as well.

ANALYZE SOURCES ANSWER

27. Addams contrasts men's traditional role of commercial and industrial development with women's traditional responsibility for addressing life's harsh conditions to make an argument for why women should have a greater role in government policies by being able to vote.

CONNECT TO YOUR LIFE ANSWER

28. Answers will vary, but students should contrast the way news spreads today, especially via electronic media, with the way it spread during the Progressive Era, when people got most of their news from newspapers. Students should draw conclusions about how the rapid and direct spread of news today influences people's opinions.

NATIONAL GEOGRAPHIC | CONNECTION

This Land Is Your Land

BY DAVID QUAMMEN

Adapted from "This Land Is Your Land," by David Quammen, in *National Geographic*, January 2016

The year 2016 marked the 100th anniversary of one of the brightest moments in American history. In 1916, President Woodrow Wilson signed a law creating the National Park Service. Setting aside land for national parks might be the best idea America ever had. With the creation of the National Park Service, America took the preservation of our most precious resource to a higher level. There would now be a system dedicated to doing this work.

A half century before the National Park Service was born, the United States took its first step toward preserving its scenic treasures. In 1864, President Abraham Lincoln signed the Yosemite Valley Grant Act. This law placed California's Yosemite Valley and a nearby grove of giant Sequoia trees under protection. The president and Congress were persuaded to act by the efforts of private citizens. And it didn't hurt that stunning photographs of Yosemite's grandeur were presented as part of their effort.

A few years later, a 29-year-old John Muir stopped a passerby in San Francisco to ask for directions out of town. The man asked where Muir wanted to go. He answered, "Anywhere that is wild." Muir's love for the great outdoors led him to the Yosemite Valley. Later, it became the center of his conservation movement.

By 1916, only 14 parks had been created, and many were difficult for visitors to reach. Yellowstone had been set aside by federal law in 1872, making it the first national park not only in the United States, but in the world. The other U.S. parks, like Yellowstone, lay west of the Mississippi. There were also 21 national monuments. The Antiquities Act of 1906 gave the president the power to protect land not only for its natural beauty, but also for its cultural or scientific value. President Theodore Roosevelt took full advantage of this law. In his last three years in office, he created eight monuments, including the Grand Canyon in Arizona and Devils Tower in Wyoming.

Since Roosevelt's time, the list of both parks and monuments has grown dramatically. Today the NPS manages 390 areas located in 49 states, the District of Columbia, and islands in the Pacific and Caribbean. The NPS has grown to 20,000 full-time employees, and the number of yearly visits has risen from 350,000 to nearly 300 million. But this good news is also the bad news. During the busy season, bumper-to-bumper traffic causes visitor frustration and pumps damaging levels of pollution into delicate ecosystems. Today, one of the great challenges is managing crowds of eager tourists who are "loving the parks to death."

Yet it was precisely citizens' love that played a role in even the earliest stages of forming the National Park Service. The early parks in the American West had been established to protect scenic wonders. In other words, they had little economic value. Some foresaw the flood of tourists and the restaurants and hotels they would need. But few others saw any chance of making money from national parks. Not many complained when new areas were added to the national park system. Early on, the NPS found it far easier to get approval for creating new parks than it would later.

National parks were a good idea that has gotten better—and bigger. The system now includes national parks, monuments, battlefields, forts, seashores, scenic rivers, grave sites, historic landmarks, and noteworthy paths through landscape and history. It may take but one act of Congress and a presidential signature to put a park on the map, but that's just a formality. From the very beginning, private citizens have done much of the work to make it possible. The responsibility of preserving these places and their stories falls to us now, as citizens, as owners. And the work is never done.

For more from National Geographic, check out "The Native American Photography of Edward Sheriff Curtis" online.

UNIT INQUIRY: Innovate a New Solution

In this unit, you learned about a number of economic, social, and political problems Americans confronted in the late 19th and early 20th centuries. You also learned how Americans tried to solve those problems. Based on your understanding of the text, in what ways did different individuals, groups, and governments serve as problem-solvers? How did these solutions shape American identity?

ASSIGNMENT

Innovate a solution to a problem you read about in this unit. Your solution should demonstrate an understanding of the historical context of the problem and illustrate how your approach is similar to or different from the solution that was actually proposed. Be prepared to present your solution to the class.

Gather Evidence As you plan your solution, gather evidence from this unit about the cultures that came into contact with each other during this time period and about how some groups sought to achieve or maintain power over others. Also consider the ways in which some solutions led to unexpected consequences. Take notes on problems, cultures, unexpected consequences, and solutions. Use a graphic organizer like this one to help organize your thoughts.

Produce Use your notes to produce an explanation of your new solution. Write a paragraph that identifies your problem within its historical context. Then write a paragraph proposing your solution.

Review Your Paragraphs Is your writing appropriate for your audience? Do you meet the purpose of the assignment? Revise or edit as needed.

Present Choose a creative way to present your new solution to the class. Consider one of these options:

- Design a colorful brochure for a target audience advertising your new solution.

- Illustrate a poster that shows the different parts of the problem you selected and describes how your new solution would address them.

- Draw and annotate a political cartoon about the problem you select and the new solution you propose. Your cartoons might be humorous, serious, or both.

NATIONAL GEOGRAPHIC | LEARNING FRAMEWORK ACTIVITIES

Research American Species

ATTITUDE Curiosity

KNOWLEDGE Critical Species

As the United States expanded, it increased the number of unique animal and plant species within its borders. At the same time, the processes of industrialization and urbanization had a tremendous impact on many species. Research an American species and learn about its characteristics, its location, its habitat, and the ways in which it has thrived or diminished since the late 19th century. Prepare a species report that includes photos or illustrations of your species and present it to the class.

Write a Journal Entry

ATTITUDE Empowerment

SKILLS Communication, Problem-Solving

Immigrants traveling to and settling in the United States encountered a number of difficult situations. Write a journal entry in the voice of an immigrant. Include where you are emigrating from, why you have chosen to immigrate to the United States, where you are settling, what difficulties you encounter, and how you solve those problems. You might consider writing one long entry or a series of shorter entries. When you have completed your journaling, present your entry or entries to the class.

NATIONAL GEOGRAPHIC CONNECTION

Guided Discussion for "This Land is Your Land"

1. **Summarize** When and why was the National Park Service established? *(The National Park Service was founded in 1916 during President Woodrow Wilson's tenure to create a system dedicated specifically to managing lands set aside for preservation.)*

2. **Make Inferences** Author David Quammen describes Americans as "loving the parks to death." What do you think one challenge facing the National Park Service might be in coming decades? *(Answers will vary. Possible response: Given a growing population and Americans' growing interest in learning about the world around them, the National Park Service will have to make decisions about park usage and citizens' desires to engage with the parks.)*

Guided Discussion for "The Native American Photography of Edward Sheriff Curtis"

1. **Describe** What critique does Alexandra Harris put forth about the photography of Edward Sheriff Curtis? *(Answers will vary. Possible response: While Harris acknowledges the breadth and depth of his work, she argues that he reinforces a societal myth of Native Americans as a "vanishing race," static and unchanging.)*

2. **Make Generalizations** Why did Curtis embark on a decades-long project to document Native American life? *(Answers will vary. Possible response: Curtis was inspired by a Native American woman he met and photographed and later received the backing of J.P. Morgan and Theodore Roosevelt, making his project possible.)*

Assess

Use the rubric to assess each student's participation and performance.

SCORE	ASSIGNMENT	PRODUCT	PRESENTATION
3 GREAT	• Student thoroughly understands the assignment. • Student participates fully in the project process.	• Explanation is well thought out. • Explanation clearly identifies a problem and solution within a historical context. • Explanation contains all of the key elements listed in the assignment.	• Presentation is clear, concise, and logical. • Presentation does a good job of creatively presenting a solution. • Presentation engages the audience.
2 GOOD	• Student mostly understands the assignment. • Student participates fairly well in the project process.	• Explanation is fairly well thought out. • Explanation identifies a problem and solution and addresses some of the historical context. • Explanation contains most of the key elements listed in the assignment.	• Presentation is fairly clear, concise, and logical. • Presentation does an adequate job of creatively presenting a solution. • Presentation somewhat engages the audience.
1 NEEDS WORK	• Student does not understand the assignment. • Student minimally participates or does not participate in the project process.	• Explanation is not well thought out. • Explanation does not identify a problem or solution in a historical context. • Explanation contains few or none of the key elements listed in the assignment.	• Presentation is not clear, concise, or logical. • Presentation does an inadequate job of presenting a solution. • Presentation does not engage the audience.

Assess

Use the rubric to assess how each student applies the National Geographic Learning Framework.

SCORE	ASSIGNMENT	ASSIGNMENT	FINAL PRODUCTS
3 GREAT	• Report reflects **Curiosity** well. • Report explores **Critical Species** well.	• Journal entry reflects **Empowerment** well. • Journal entry demonstrates **Communication** and **Problem-Solving** well.	• Final products are engaging, creative, and well presented.
2 GOOD	• Report reflects **Curiosity**. • Report explores **Critical Species**.	• Journal entry reflects **Empowerment**. • Journal entry demonstrates **Communication** and **Problem-Solving**.	• Final products are interesting, logical, and complete.
1 NEEDS WORK	• Report does not reflect **Curiosity**. • Report does not explore **Critical Species**.	• Journal entry does not reflect **Empowerment**. • Journal entry does not demonstrate **Communication** or **Problem-Solving**.	• Final products are not creative, complete, or interesting.

Soldiers Training by William H. Johnson

After the United States entered World War II in 1941, the federal government funded the creation of patriotic works of art. For two government-sponsored exhibitions, William H. Johnson painted works that celebrated African-American participation in the war. His inspiration for *Soldiers Training* might have been based on descriptions of a company of African-American military personnel known as the Buffalo Soldiers, who trained at a desert outpost at Fort Huachuca, Arizona. Native Americans had given the name "Buffalo Soldiers" to the first black regiment, the 10th Cavalry, during the late 1800s.

When Johnson painted *Soldiers Training*, African Americans had limited opportunities in the U.S. military. They were not allowed to enlist in the Air Corps or in the Marines. They could serve in the army, but only a few units were open to them. Even when they were accepted, African Americans tended to be assigned menial duties. In the navy, for example, they could serve only as "messmen," who set up and cleared away dishes in the mess hall.

Read the following quote from Johnson aloud to the class: "In all my years of painting, I have had only one absorbing and inspired idea, and have worked toward it with unyielding zeal—to give, in simple and stark form— the story of the Negro as he has existed."

ASK: What do you think Johnson wanted to express through this painting about the story of the African American "as he has existed" in the U.S. military during World War II? *(The painting itself is simple and stark, as Johnson described his style. In it, Johnson shows an all African-American regiment with an African-American leader. No white people are present, which might have been Johnson's way of pointing out segregation. The men appear disciplined and ready for action.)*

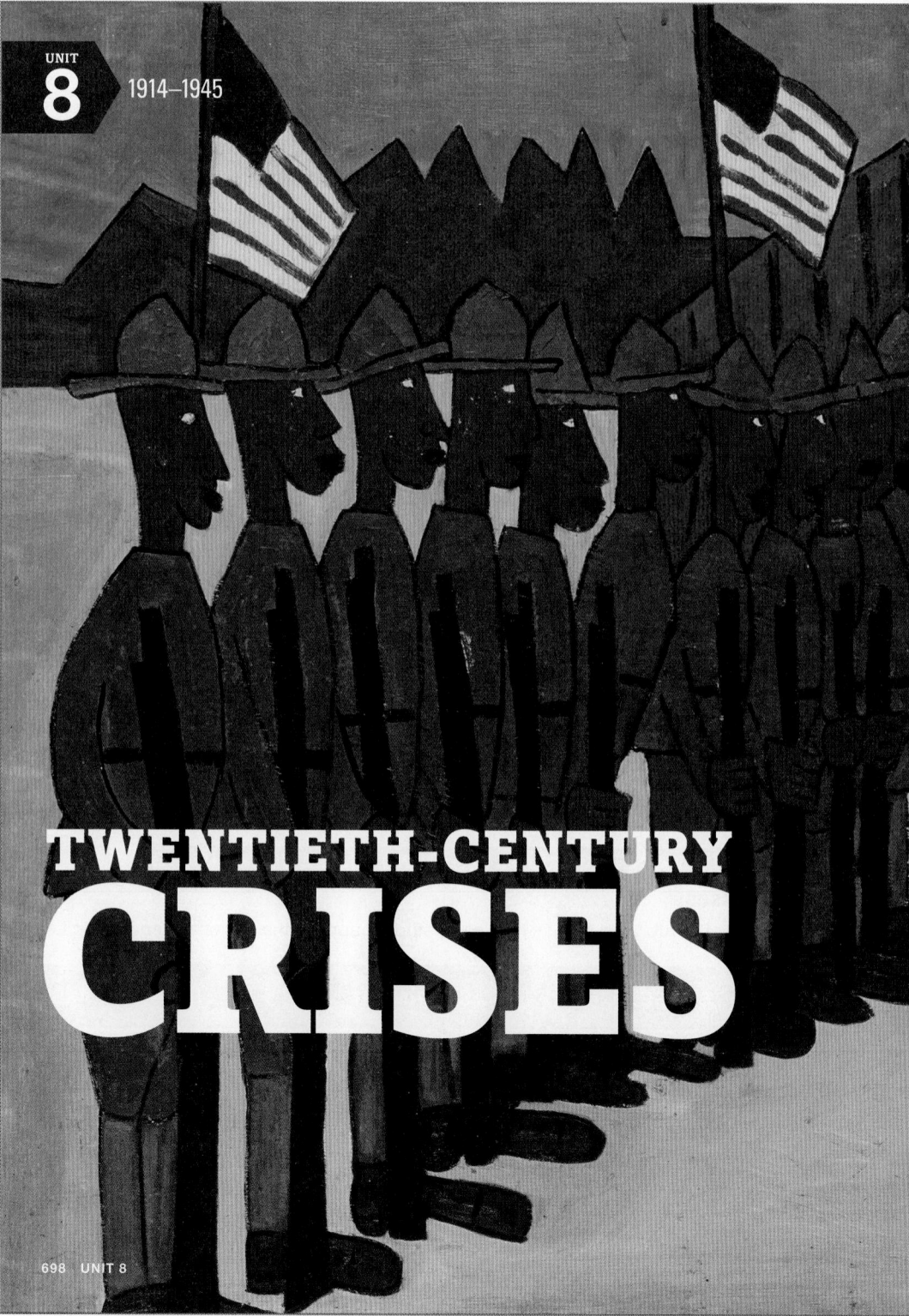

UNIT **8** 1914–1945

TWENTIETH-CENTURY CRISES

698 UNIT 8

Smithsonian American Art Museum, Washington, D.C.

The bombing of Pearl Harbor during World War II inspired two government-sponsored art exhibitions in 1942. For one exhibit, artist William H. Johnson painted scenes of African Americans involved in the war effort. *Soldiers Training* depicts an African-American unit at an army base.

CRITICAL VIEWING Some believe this painting contrasts the U.S. military's segregation policies with the patriotism of African-American soldiers. What details in the painting convey the soldiers' patriotism?

699

Virtual Museum Visit

The Smithsonian American Art Museum in Washington, D.C., features a searchable online Art + Artists database that gives users an opportunity to access visuals and textual information from the museum's massive collections. Guide students to search the Art + Artists database to locate more works by William H. Johnson. Invite them to compare and contrast the subject matter and style of *Soldiers Training* with one of the artist's earlier works from the 1930s. Have the class discuss why Johnson might have used different styles to depict different subject matter.

CRITICAL VIEWING Johnson conveys the soldiers' patriotism by showing them at attention in tight formation, holding their rifles, while three American flags wave over their heads. They look serious and proud to be U.S. soldiers.

1919 EUROPE:
The Treaty of Versailles

At the end of World War I, the Treaty of Versailles stripped Germany of several territories and gave them to Belgium, Czechoslovakia, and Poland. The terms of the treaty also forced Germany to cede the territories of Alsace and Lorraine, which it had annexed in 1871, and return them to France. Along with other restrictions, the treaty imposed limitations on the German military, capping it at 100,000 soldiers and banning German acquisition or maintenance of naval ships weighing more than 10,000 tons. The treaty also banned Germany from maintaining a submarine fleet or an air force altogether.

France, which had suffered more war damage than many other parts of Europe, pushed for even harsher terms. The "war guilt" clause in the treaty named Germany as the main aggressor in the war. It levied punishing reparations that Germany would have to pay other nations for damage inflicted during the conflict. A commission later set the reparations at $33 billion, a staggering sum that economists said could not be repaid without disrupting international finance.

Members of Germany's new democratic government deeply resented the terms of this "dictated" treaty, which would greatly undermine the German economy and national pride. Instead of resolving the international disputes that had led to World War I in Europe, the treaty undermined cooperation among nations. In the decades that followed, however, the Treaty of Versailles was amended a number of times, usually in Germany's favor. By 1938, only the territorial allocations from the original agreement remained in force. **ASK:** Why do you think the Treaty of Versailles sought to limit the number of soldiers the German army could keep on hand? *(Possible response: Europeans who had experienced German aggression during World War I hoped that the limit on soldiers would help prevent Germany from raising an army large enough to wage war or occupy foreign territories in the future.)*

UNIT 8
TWENTIETH-CENTURY CRISES

THE UNITED STATES

I WANT YOU *for the* **U.S. ARMY ENLIST NOW**

1917
The United States declares war on Germany and enters World War I.
(an Uncle Sam poster used to recruit soldiers during World War I)

1919–1920
Government officials conduct the Palmer Raids to root out suspected communists and other radicals.

1921
Italian immigrants Nicola Sacco and Bartolomeo Vanzetti are convicted of robbery and murder.

1927
Charles Lindbergh becomes the first person to fly solo nonstop across the Atlantic Ocean.
(Lindbergh's plane, the Spirit of St. Louis*)*

1929
The stock market crashes and ushers in the Great Depression.

1910

1920

THE WORLD

1914 EUROPE
War spreads throughout Europe, giving rise to World War I.

1928 AMERICAS
President Álvaro Obregón of Mexico is assassinated.

1919 EUROPE
The Treaty of Versailles, signed in France, ends World War I and imposes harsh terms on Germany.
(an original booklet from the signing of the treaty)

700 UNIT 8

1942
President Roosevelt signs an order that forces thousands of Japanese Americans to relocate to internment camps. *(1942 painting by artist Henry Sugimoto showing a Japanese American family reacting to the news about Pearl Harbor)*

1941
Japan bombs Pearl Harbor in Hawaii, which causes the United States to enter World War II.

1933
The Roosevelt administration enacts the New Deal, a series of federal programs intended to bring economic relief to Americans.

1932
Franklin Delano Roosevelt wins his first term as president.

1945
The United Nations is established. *(United Nations flag showing a map of the world)*

1940

1945

1930

1945 ASIA
Japan surrenders after the United States bombs Hiroshima and Nagasaki, and World War II comes to an end.

1939 EUROPE
World War II begins after Germany invades Poland. *(jacket worn by an inmate of a German concentration camp during World War II)*

1933 EUROPE
Adolf Hitler becomes chancellor of Germany.

1943 AFRICA
British and American forces defeat the German Army in Tunisia in North Africa. *(photo of British soldiers during the advance on Tunisia's capital, Tunis, on May 6, 1943)*

Twentieth-Century Crises **701**

HISTORICAL THINKING: DETERMINE CHRONOLOGY

Which event occurred in response to the crisis of the Great Depression?

1943 AFRICA: Allied Victory in Tunisia

The military campaign in North Africa began almost the moment Italy declared war on the Allied nations. In December 1940, Italy's first strategic move was to invade Egypt in order to gain control of the Suez Canal and Middle East oil fields. In response, British and Indian troops counterattacked and captured about 130,000 Italian soldiers.

The success of the Allied initiative prompted Adolf Hitler to send troops into Africa under the command of General Erwin Rommel. The Allied and Axis armies spent three years fighting each other across Libya and Egypt. Each side periodically gained and lost territory in a series of brutal and bloody battles. As the war dragged on, however, the German army found itself increasingly short of fuel and supplies, which hampered its ability to fight. Finally, the British Eighth Army, under the command of Lieutenant-General Bernard Montgomery, drove the Axis armies back to Tunisia.

In 1943, a new Allied offensive, Operation Torch, brought thousands of fresh American and British troops into the fight and overpowered German forces. When the Axis troops surrendered in May 1943, the Allies took about 250,000 prisoners into custody. Following victory in North Africa, the region became a base for Allied operations against Italy. **ASK:** Why do you think controlling North Africa was important to both sides? *(Answers will vary. Possible response: Both sides wanted to seize control of the Suez Canal and the Middle East oil fields.)*

HISTORICAL THINKING: DETERMINE CHRONOLOGY

Answer: The Roosevelt administration enacted the New Deal in 1933 in response to the Great Depression. The New Deal included a series of federal programs that helped bring economic relief to Americans.

UNIT 8 TWENTIETH-CENTURY CRISES

UNIT 8 RESOURCES

UNIT INTRODUCTION

UNIT TIME LINE

UNIT WRAP-UP

NATIONAL GEOGRAPHIC | CONNECTION

National Geographic Magazine Adapted Articles
- "WWI and Mapmaking at National Geographic"
- "Untold Stories of D-Day" ONLINE

Unit 8 Inquiry: Respond to a Crisis

NG Learning Framework Activities
- Research War Damage
- Share the Arts of the 1920s

Unit 8 Formal Assessment

CHAPTER 21 RESOURCES

Available at NGLSync.Cengage.com

TEACHER RESOURCES & ASSESSMENT

Reading and Note-Taking

Vocabulary Practice

Document-Based Question Template

Social Studies Skills Lessons
- Reading: Make Inferences
- Writing: Write an Expository Paragraph

Formal Assessment
- Chapter 21 Pretest
- Chapter 21 Tests A & B
- Section Quizzes

Chapter 21 Answer Key

ExamView®
  One-time Download

STUDENT DIGITAL RESOURCES

- **eEdition** (English)
- **eEdition** (Spanish)
- **Handbooks**
- **Online Atlas**
- **American Gallery Online**
- **History Notebook**
- **Active History**
- **Projects for Inquiry-Based Learning**

Chapter 21 Spanish Resources are available at NGLSync.Cengage.com.

AMERICAN STORIES | The Great War's Killer Technology

- Primary Sources
- On Your Feet: Analyze Technology's Effectiveness

NG Learning Framework:
Build a Model

SECTION 1 RESOURCES
WAR BREAKS OUT IN EUROPE

LESSON 1.1
Poised for War

- Active History: Analyze Causes of World War I

NG Learning Framework:
Create a Time Line

LESSON 1.2
A New Kind of War

- On Your Feet: T-Chart

NG Learning Framework:
Create Monologues

LESSON 1.3
America Enters the War

- On Your Feet: Inside-Outside Circle

NG Learning Framework:
Research the *Lusitania*

SECTION 2 RESOURCES
PUSHING THE GERMANS BACK

LESSON 2.1
Americans on the Western Front

 AMERICAN GALLERY ONLINE — The Great War: A Photo Essay

NG Learning Framework:
Research American Contributions

LESSON 2.2
On the Home Front

- On Your Feet: Numbered Heads

NG Learning Framework:
Write a Script

LESSON 2.3
Victory for the Allies

- On Your Feet: Roundtable Discussion

NG Learning Framework:
Create an Infographic

SECTION 3 RESOURCES
THE LEGACY OF WORLD WAR I

LESSON 3.1
Wilson's Goals

- On Your Feet: Create Live Maps

NG Learning Framework:
Debate the Treaty

LESSON 3.2
DOCUMENT-BASED QUESTION
Woodrow Wilson and World Peace

- On Your Feet: Use a Jigsaw Strategy

LESSON 3.3
Aftermath of the War

- On Your Feet: Three-Step Interview

NG Learning Framework:
Research the Influenza Epidemic

CHAPTER 21 REVIEW

Strategy ❶
Turn Headings into Outlines

To help students organize and understand lesson content, explain that headings can provide a high-level outline of the lesson. Model for students how to use the lesson title and subheadings to create a basic outline structure. Encourage students to add information to their outlines as they read.

Use with All Lessons

Strategy ❷
Sequence Events

To build understanding of the critical events in history and their relationship to one another in time, prompt students to note events in a Sequence Chain, such as the one shown. Explain to students how a completed Sequence Chain will show the multiplicity and complexity of the causes and effects of historical events.

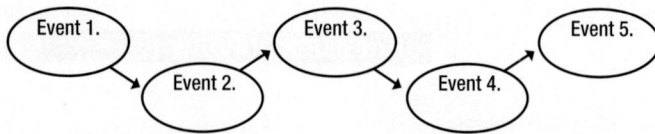

Use with All Lessons *You may suggest students use the Sequence Chain to trace the major events that led to the Great War in Lessons 1.1 and 1.3, and the events that led to the Allied victory in Lessons 2.1 and 2.3.*

Strategy ❸
Clarify Information

Students may have difficulty understanding the complicated reasons for the many social and economic upheavals in the United States after the Allied victory in World War I. To help students organize their thoughts and clarify the information in the lesson, instruct them to use a 5Ws Chart to take notes on information from each paragraph.

What?
Who?
Where?
When?
Why?

Use with Lesson 3.3

Strategy ❶
Preview and Predict

Pair visually impaired students with students who are not visually challenged. Instruct them to read the lesson title and subheadings together. Tell sighted students to describe lesson visuals in detail to help their partners understand them. Then have partners work together to write notes regarding what they think the lesson will be about. After reading, ask pairs to review their notes to see whether their predictions were confirmed.

Use with All Lessons

Strategy ❷
Use Supported Reading

Have pairs read the chapter aloud lesson by lesson. Instruct them to stop at the end of each lesson and use these sentence frames to monitor their comprehension of the text:

- This lesson is mostly about _____.
- Other topics in this lesson are _____ and _____.
- One question I have is _____.
- One of the vocabulary words is _____, and it means _____.
- One word I don't recognize is _____.

Use with All Lessons

Strategy ❶
Use Sentence Strips

Choose a key paragraph from the lesson to read aloud while students at **All Proficiencies** follow along in their books. Then tell students to close their books. Provide sentence strips of the paragraph and direct students to place the strips in order. Ask students to read their paragraphs aloud.

Use with All Lessons *You may want to ask students at the Emerging level to read the sentence strips aloud and identify meaningful words before they start placing the strips in order.*

Strategy ❷
Use Paired Reading

Pair students at the **Expanding** and **Bridging** levels to read passages from the text aloud.

1. Partner 1 reads a subsection; partner 2 retells the passage in his or her own words.

2. Partner 2 reads a different subsection; partner 1 retells it.

3. Pairs repeat the process with each subsection.

Use with All Lessons

Strategy ❸
Use Meaning Maps

Pair students at the **Emerging** level with those at the **Expanding** or **Bridging** levels. Demonstrate how to use a graphic organizer such as the Meaning Map shown here for any of the Key Vocabulary or other important words and terms in the lesson. As students work, encourage them to discuss the words and clear up any misunderstandings.

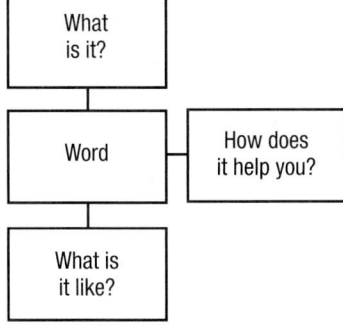

Use with All Lessons

Strategy ❶
Present a WWI Figure

Instruct students to conduct preliminary research about the experiences of various Americans during World War I, such as a pilot, an infantry soldier, a nurse, a war photographer, or a woman working on a farm or in a factory on the home front. Then have students conduct in-depth research on one such person, accessing letters, diary entries, and other primary and secondary sources. Prompt students to assume that person's identity and present themselves to the class in a theatrical performance, drawing on their research to speak and act in character.

Use with Lessons 2.1–2.3

Strategy ❷
Create a Podcast

After reading the chapter, allow students to choose one lesson to further research so they can develop a richer understanding and a point of view. Then direct them to use what they have learned to prepare an episode of a history podcast. Invite students to present their podcast live or record it and play it for the class.

Use with All Lessons

Strategy ❶
Write an Essay

Direct students to choose one of the battles shown on the maps World War I Alliances and Major Battles, 1914–1916, and Major Battles of World War I, 1917–1918. Then have them conduct research to learn more about how the battle arose, evolved, and ended. When they have completed their research, prompt students to write an essay synthesizing information from chapter maps and other sources. Ask students to share their essays with the class.

Use with Lessons 1.1 and 2.3

Strategy ❷
Form and Support a Thesis

Instruct students to form and support a thesis about why the U.S. Senate voted twice to oppose the League of Nations, an international peacekeeping organization proposed and supported by President Wilson. Direct students to conduct online research to find data in primary and secondary source materials that support their thesis. Then have students write a report that includes statistics and expert analyses supporting their thesis.

Use with Lesson 3.1

THE GREAT WAR
1914–1920

ESSENTIAL QUESTION
What did the United States gain and lose by going to war?

READING STRATEGY

MAKE INFERENCES
Inferences are conclusions or interpretations a reader makes from information that a writer does not state directly. When you make inferences, you "read between the lines" to figure out what the writer means. As you read the chapter, use a two-column chart like this one to list facts about the Great War and the inferences you draw from them.

Facts	Inferences
Many European nations formed alliances.	

"The world must be made safe for democracy."
—Woodrow Wilson

CRITICAL VIEWING American soldiers "go over the top" as they charge out of a trench to fight the Germans in 1918. What does this photo convey about battle conditions during World War I?

INTRODUCE THE PHOTOGRAPH

"Over the Top"

Direct students' attention to the photograph of American soldiers climbing out of a trench during World War I and read the sentence from Critical Viewing aloud. Explain that the high death tolls resulting from modern artillery, machine guns, and rifle fire during the Great War forced both American and German troops, as well as those from other nations, to dig trenches for protection. Tell students that the land between the opposing sides' trenches was known as "No Man's Land." When soldiers went "over the top," they charged out of their trenches across No Man's Land toward the enemy's trenches. Lines of barbed wire, not to mention enemy fire, impeded their progress. **ASK:** Why do you think going "over the top" was a daunting prospect for soldiers? *(Possible response: Soldiers had to climb the steep trench walls while wearing heavy backpacks and carrying their rifles and then face being out in the open while enemy soldiers were still safely hidden down in their own trenches.)*

Share Background

Moving across No Man's Land presented serious challenges for soldiers. Before soldiers left their trenches, armies used artillery fire to try to clear barbed wire from the surface of the ground and knock out the enemy's forward trenches and guns. Although good in theory, this approach did not always work. Both sides also used the tactic of the "creeping barrage" to provide protection for the advancing infantry. Rather than running across the field, the infantry advanced by walking closely behind a heavy line of artillery fire aimed at the enemy. This maneuver took practice to perfect, and many soldiers lost their lives to friendly fire in the process.

CRITICAL VIEWING Trenches provided some cover from enemy fire, but soldiers had to climb over the top of the trenches and cross open territory to engage enemy soldiers directly if they wanted to take their trenches. The bayonets on the end of the rifles indicate that soldiers fought in hand-to-hand combat.

For Chapter 21 Spanish Resources, visit the Resources Menu. Chapter 21 Resources are available at NGLSync.Cengage.com.

INTRODUCE THE ESSENTIAL QUESTION

What did the United States gain and lose by going to war?

Preview the Chapter: Consider Gains and Losses Discuss with students the idea that World War I resulted in both gains and losses for the United States. Preview the chapter by providing a brief description of each section and a question for students to consider, such as those shown below. After allowing time for individual thought, organize the class into three groups, one for each chapter section. Have students number off within each group. Direct groups to discuss the question so that any member of the group can report for the group. Call a number, and the student with that number answers the question for the group.

Section 1 is about the causes and consequences of World War I for Europe and the reluctant entry of the United States into the war. **ASK:** Why might the United States believe it had more to lose than to gain by entering the war?

Section 2 is about U.S. participation in the war and the war's effect on the American people and economy. **ASK:** What might Americans gain and lose by the United States going to war?

Section 3 is about how participation in World War I made the United States a world power but also resulted in economic and social problems in postwar America. **ASK:** Why might the United States have problems adjusting to peacetime and a new role in the world because of the war?

INTRODUCE CHAPTER VOCABULARY

Vocabulary Pyramids

As students read the chapter, encourage them to complete Vocabulary Pyramids for Key Vocabulary words. Tell students to make a pyramid for each word, write what they know about that word before reading, and then add to or correct the pyramid after they encounter the word in the chapter. Model an example for students on the board, using the graphic organizer below.

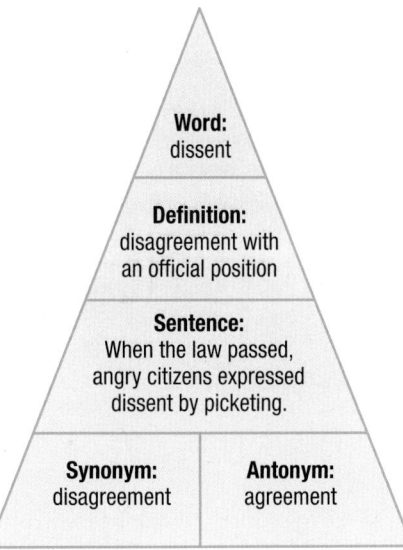

Word: dissent

Definition: disagreement with an official position

Sentence: When the law passed, angry citizens expressed dissent by picketing.

Synonym: disagreement

Antonym: agreement

INTRODUCE THE READING STRATEGY

MAKE INFERENCES
Remind students that writers state some ideas directly, but readers must figure out other ideas by making inferences. Explain that readers make inferences when they combine what they read in a text with what they already know. Read the first paragraph from Lesson 1.1 aloud. Then read the fact listed in the first column of the chart. **ASK:** Based on what we have read and what we know, what inference can we make about why European nations formed alliances? *(Answers will vary. Possible response: Given that Europe was divided by hostilities, nations worried that more wars were likely and wanted to protect themselves.)* Tell students to complete the chart with facts about the Great War and the inferences they draw from them as they read the chapter.

Facts	Inferences
Many European nations formed alliances.	

KEY DATES FOR CHAPTER 21

1914	World War I begins in Europe
1915	German submarine sinks the *Lusitania*
1917	United States declares war on Germany
1917	Russian Revolution; Russia withdraws from war
1918	Flu epidemic begins
1918	Armistice ends fighting
1919	Paris Peace Conference produces Treaty of Versailles
1920	Great Steel Strike ends

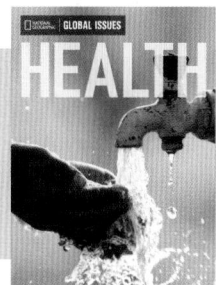

GLOBAL ISSUES

HEALTH

For more on factors that impact health, see *GLOBAL ISSUES: HEALTH.*

STEM

Objectives

- **Identify the types of weapons technology developed during World War I.**
- **Explain the significance of technological advancements during World War I.**
- **Determine the benefits and drawbacks of wartime technology.**
- **Study primary sources: photographs of World War I technologies.**

Critical Thinking Skills for "The Great War's Killer Technology"

- Make Connections
- Draw Conclusions
- Identify Problems and Solutions
- Integrate Visuals

Background for the Teacher

This American Story examines the advances in technology that came about because of World War I. Students will learn about the weapons utilized by Germany and the Allied nations during World War I, why those weapons were developed, and the benefits and drawbacks of those technologies. Photographs, diagrams, and quotations from the Germans and the Allies give readers insight into what the war was like. Use this American Story to help students understand the war's intensity and the reasons why many of its battles resulted in such a grievous loss of life.

By providing greater detail about weapons technology, such as tanks and submarines, this American Story helps explain more specifically one of the reasons why World War I was different from previous wars. Chapter 21, The Great War, discusses this topic more broadly, addressing why the war involved so many countries and the reasons it was so deadly.

History Notebook

Encourage students to complete the American Story page for Chapter 21 in their History Notebooks as they read.

Note to the Teacher

Introduce this American Story after the class has engaged with the content in Lesson 1.2.

THE GREAT WAR'S
KILLER
TECHNOLOGY

CRITICAL VIEWING An American soldier walks ahead of a British-made tank in this photograph, taken around 1918. What can you observe about tank technology from this photo, and what might it suggest about the usefulness of tanks during World War I?

The word *modern* has many positive meanings. Modern things are often new, up-to-date, and better than the older things they are replacing. However, when historians say the Great War— or World War I, as it would come to be known—was the first modern war, there's nothing positive about that. The Allies and the Germans used advances in technology to fight a more deadly war at sea, on land, and in the skies.

ON LAND: TANKS

In 1915, British navy secretary Winston Churchill wrote a letter to Prime Minister H. H. Asquith on the subject of the land war. "The question to be solved," he wrote, "is the actual getting across of 100 or 200 yards of open space and wire entanglements." In clinical terms, Churchill summed up the life-or-death problem that soldiers faced on the war's merciless battlefields. Men were dying by the thousands in charges against enemy trenches protected by machine guns and artillery.

Tanks, invented by the British, were designed to solve this problem. The first British tank, called the Mark I, fought at the Battle of the Somme in France in 1916. The Mark I proved to be unreliable—49 of the tanks were present at the battle but only 18 were able to fight. Later tank models, however, were much more effective, including the massive German 36-ton A7V tank.

Tanks were powerful weapons, but they had some weaknesses. Early tanks had a range of only 25 miles and were difficult to maneuver. They suffered frequent mechanical failures and broken tracks. Later models were more reliable, although they remained vulnerable to some types of mechanical problems. The Mark V, introduced in 1918, had a sophisticated steering system, two six-pounder guns, and four machine guns.

For the men serving inside them, tanks and submarines had many awful similarities. Both were hot, cramped, enclosed spaces. The air inside an unventilated tank was sometimes so bad that crews became sick or fainted. Tank crews could be killed by their own equipment. A light tank could become hot enough to explode its ammunition.

Armies continued to use and improve tanks well after the close of World War I. Today, the U.S. military employs several models of tanks as well as armored personnel carriers and specialized armored vehicles designed to protect against dangers such as land mines.

Mark IV Tank

Materials: 0.5-inch thick steel armor

Length: 26 feet, 5 inches

Weight: 62,600 pounds, loaded

Top speed: 4 miles per hour

Range: 35 miles

Crew: up to 8 people

Armaments: 2 QF (quick firing) 6-pounder, and three 0.303-inch machine guns

TOP VIEW

crew shown in red

exhaust silencer

engine

driver

rear gunner

gas tank

armored tread

side gunners

The Great War **705**

Consider Weapons Technology

Write *weapons technology* in the center circle of a Word Web. Ask students to think of examples of current or past weapons technology used during wars they are familiar with, and add each type of technology to the web. Prompt students to provide details about the way each type of technology works. Then tell students they will learn about technologies developed during World War I and how those technologies were used.

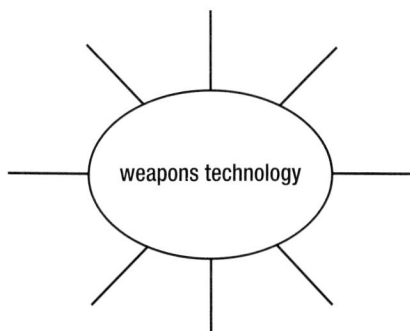

weapons technology

Preview Using Visuals

Draw students' attention to the photograph and the diagram of the tank. Ask them to make parallels between the two visuals, identifying the parts of both tanks shown. **ASK:** What can you learn about the tank from the photograph that you don't learn from the diagram? *(Possible response: The photograph shows how large the tank is within a real setting, what the steel armor looks like, and the details of the outer part of the tank, such as the armored tread.)* Prompt students to examine both the top and side views of the tank diagram, along with the labels and the crew information listed. **ASK:** Why do you think that tanks had up to eight crew members, and why were they positioned as they were? *(Possible response: The driver would be at the front, and the person beside him might be a gunner, a navigator, or someone who could drive in an emergency. Gunners were placed to fire in all directions. Crew members beside them might have helped the gunners with ammunition. The crew member near the engine might have been a mechanic.)*

CRITICAL VIEWING Possible response: The photo shows how sturdy and durable tanks are, indicating that they can withstand a lot of damage. The armored tread shows that tanks are capable of moving over difficult terrain. This made tanks useful during World War I because they could get across open space, wire entanglements, and trenches protected by enemy machine guns and artillery.

Deadly Gases

Poisonous gases like chlorine and mustard gas not only had profound physical effects on soldiers during World War I, but they also had deep psychological effects. Unlike more obvious weapons, such as guns and bombs, the presence of gas could be difficult to detect. As a result, some World War I soldiers would imagine they had been victims of gas attacks even when they had not. The mere suggestion of the presence of gas could trigger panic among troops. Compounding this fear was the very real fact that certain gases, such as phosgene, could take hours or days to have an effect, leaving a person with a false sense of security. During World War I, poison gases had such an adverse effect on soldiers' morale—not to mention their physical well-being—that many in the military considered them an "unsoldierly" weapon.

Blood Transfusions

Scientists had explored the idea of blood transfusions off and on for centuries, but it wasn't until just before and during World War I that technological advances made blood transfusions practical for the battlefield. In the early 20th century, for example, blood was transfused directly from the donor to the recipient through tubing or by splicing their blood vessels together—which meant that both parties had to be present and lie quietly during the procedure, and it was difficult to know how much blood was actually transfused. In addition, clotting blood would slow blood flow, and some recipients had bad reactions to blood from some donors.

Before the outbreak of World War I, a few doctors in the United States began matching donors and recipients based on ABO blood types, which reduced the rate of bad reactions. Other advances included extracting blood into a glass container or syringe coated with an anticoagulant, which slowed the clotting and eliminated the need for donor and recipient to be connected during a transfusion. Finally, doctors discovered that adding sodium citrate could extend the shelf life of blood to a few days, and adding dextrose could extend it to about four weeks. In this way, blood could be collected ahead of time and stored for use as needed. When the United States entered World War I, American doctors brought these advances to help treat wounded soldiers on European battlefields.

GUNS

Machine guns were invented in the late 1800s, but they first saw extensive use during World War I, which has been called the "machine gun war." Early hand-cranked machine guns, such as the Gatling gun, were used in the Civil War. In the 1880s, American inventor Hiram Maxim was the first to create the modern form of the machine gun. Maxim guns used ammunition that was fed into the weapon on a belt. Both Germany and the Allied nations used Maxim-style machine guns, to lethal effect. The guns could fire up to 600 bullets per minute.

Stationed at intervals along a trench, machine guns could mow down waves of attacking foot soldiers. According to one estimate, during one day of battle in France, German machine guns killed or injured two British soldiers for each yard of a 16-mile battlefield.

World War I also saw the development of antiaircraft guns. As the war took to the skies, land-based troops needed artillery that could aim sharply upward at airplanes. Antiaircraft guns were mounted on bases that could swivel to point in any direction and at any angle.

In addition to more nimble weapons, the Germans put their resources into building the largest guns ever seen at the time. Guns nicknamed Big Berthas could fire explosive projectiles weighing 1,785 pounds nearly 6 miles. Big Berthas weighed around 47 tons and required a crew of 240 men. They had to be shipped on special wagons or railroad cars. While terrifying, Big Berthas were huge and heavy and required a lot of effort to move. In the first two years of the war, however, they were instrumental in conquering cities in both Belgium and Russia.

GAS

The most terrifying weapon of World War I arrived not with an explosion but in chilling silence. The first major release of poison gas was made by

Nurses driving their ambulance in Pervyse, Belgium, c. 1917

HEALING TECHNOLOGIES

New weapons caused the number of casualties to skyrocket, and medical technology scrambled to catch up. The use of x-rays in medicine was still a new science in 1914, but it was quickly put to use in treating the wounded of World War I. Ambulances equipped with x-ray machines brought diagnosis and treatment to the battle zones. Marie Curie, a pioneer in x-ray science and winner of two Nobel Prizes, helped install the x-ray machines. She trained ambulance drivers, many of whom were women, to use the machines and also drove an ambulance herself.

Advancements in blood transfusions also benefited wounded soldiers. It was during this war that doctors first discovered a way to store blood successfully. As a result, soldiers could receive transfusions at hospitals near the battlefields, and many lives were saved.

the Germans in Belgium at the Second Battle of Ypres in 1915, but it was later used by both sides. Different types of gases provoked different symptoms. Some caused blindness or burned and blistered the skin. Others choked soldiers and burned their throats. All were deadly if inhaled. Some killed instantly, while others caused painful, lingering deaths. Around 1,200,000 soldiers were gassed. Of that number, more than 91,000 died.

At first there was no protection from attack by poison gas, but within a short time, both the Germans and Allies developed gas masks. These masks, which covered the entire face to protect eyes, nose, and throat, became standard equipment for soldiers on the battlefield. After the war, recognizing the horrors inflicted by the weapon, many countries signed a treaty banning the use of poison gas.

IN THE SKIES: AIRPLANES

By 1914, airplanes had come a long way from the Wright brothers' first flying machine, built only 11 years earlier. But they were still flimsy compared with today's high-tech jets. World War I fighter planes were made of canvas stretched over light wooden frames, and pilots sat exposed in open cockpits. In the hands of their daring pilots, these delicate birds were highly effective war machines.

At first, planes were used for observing and reporting enemy positions and occasionally dropping bombs. Pilots also engaged with enemy fliers in spectacular aerial fights called dogfights. In the earliest dogfights, pilots would shoot at each other with pistols. It was impossible to use a machine gun because such a weapon would have to be mounted in front of the pilot and fired forward, thus shooting into the plane's own propeller. The Germans solved this problem in 1915, when airplane designer Anthony Fokker invented a machine gun that could be synchronized with the propeller, firing bullets between the propeller's blades as it spun.

Pilots were glamorous figures, admired for their daring and bravery. But the price of this celebrity was high. In battlefield conditions, a new pilot survived between three and six weeks, on average.

AIRSHIPS

Planes, of course, remain a key part of the modern battle arsenal today. Airships, on the other hand, have largely disappeared from the skies. An airship was basically a huge balloon filled with hydrogen gas. The captain and crew controlled the ship from a cockpit suspended beneath the balloon. Airships were slow and hard to steer, but they could stay in the air for hours, allowing the crew to observe troop movements or conduct bombing raids. German airships bombed London several times.

As airplanes and other technology improved, airships quickly lost their usefulness. Hydrogen gas is very flammable, so they were vulnerable to weapon fire from ground guns or planes. Overall, airships did a better job of terrifying people on the ground with their ominous bulk than by causing real damage.

F.1 Sopwith Camel Biplane

wood frame

pilot

machine guns

fabric-covered wings

propeller

landing gear

Materials: wood frame, aluminum and fabric covers

Top speed: 117 m.p.h. at sea level

Maximum altitude: 19,000 ft.

Climb rate: 10 min. to reach 10,000 ft.

Weight: 929 lb. empty; 1,453 lb. fully loaded

Wingspan: 28 ft.

Length: 18 ft. 9 in.

Armaments: two synchronized 0.303-inch Vickers machine guns four 20-lb Cooper bombs

THE GREAT INDESTRUCTIBLE

The most successful World War I pilots—those who had shot down at least 10 enemy planes—were called "aces." American pilot Eddie Rickenbacker was one of the most dashing American aces. By the end of World War I, he had flown 300 combat hours, been in 134 air battles, and shot down 26 enemy planes. He had survived plane crashes and dogfights that left his plane riddled with bullet holes.

During World War II, Rickenbacker acted as a nonmilitary advisor and once narrowly escaped death when the plane he was riding in crashed in the Pacific Ocean. After he drifted in a lifeboat for 22 days before being rescued, the *Boston Globe* newspaper dubbed Rickenbacker "the Great Indestructible."

American Air Medal awarded for heroic action

The Great War **707**

TEACH

Guided Discussion

1. **Make Connections** How did the use of more-destructive advanced weapons in World War I lead to other technological breakthroughs? *(Possible response: With new weapons came increased numbers of casualties, which created a need for medical technology to develop quickly. To help treat wounded soldiers, scientists worked to make advancements with x-ray machines and ways to store blood.)*

2. **Draw Conclusions** What do the celebrity status and short lifespans for military pilots suggest about World War I airplane technology? *(Possible response: Airplanes were still very new, and dramatic battles in the sky must have made the pilots seem wildly courageous and brave. However, those early planes didn't protect pilots very well. They were made of materials that couldn't withstand a lot of damage, and the open cockpits left the pilots exposed.)*

The Submarine's Evolution

In the 1620s, a Dutch inventor built and tested the first submarine in England's Thames River. Constructed of a wooden frame covered by greased leather, this first submarine featured oars to propel it. By the mid-1700s, an unidentified inventor had discovered how to ballast a submarine by filling goatskin bags with water. The submarine would sink when the bags were full, and it would rise to the surface when the operator forced the water out of the bags. The submarine made its debut as a weapon of war during the American Revolution, when a submarine known as the *Turtle* launched an unsuccessful attack on a British ship. Though the attack did not go according to plan, the attempt set the stage for future wartime submarine use.

Active Options

On Your Feet: Analyze Technology's Effectiveness

Organize students into groups of three or four. Instruct each group to complete a Goal-and-Outcome Chart for one of these technologies covered in the text— On Land: Tanks; In the Skies: Airplanes, Airships; or At Sea: U-boats. Tell groups to identify the goals for the technology's use, obstacles encountered, and outcomes of its use, and to then provide a summary. Have groups present their charts to the class.

NG Learning Framework: Build a Model **STEM**

ATTITUDE Curiosity

SKILL Collaboration

Ask pairs of students to construct a model of a vessel discussed in the text that interests them, such as a tank, a biplane, or a submarine. Direct partners to conduct online research to find a specific make or style used during World War I and to use text diagrams as necessary. To construct their model, partners should first sketch a design and then determine which materials they will use to build it. Prompt students to include labels or captions. Display finished models.

WRITE ABOUT HISTORY

Express an Opinion This American Story explores the weapons technology of World War I and the soldiers, pilots, and sailors who utilized it. Ask students to imagine that they have enlisted in the U.S. military during World War I. Direct them to write a short opinion piece expressing which of the following they would prefer to operate: a tank, a plane, a submarine. Remind students to give reasons for their choice and explain why they would prefer it to the others.

THINK ABOUT IT!

Possible response: Machine guns were the most significant advancement because they made it easier to kill large numbers of the enemy and could be used from tanks and planes.

THE ULTIMATE WWI U-BOAT

In 1916, Germany started building the UA class of U-boats. Only nine of these subs entered service before the end of the war, but they were formidable fighting ships.

UA Class U-Boat

Length: 230 feet
Weight: about 1,500 tons
Speed: 15.3 knots on the surface
Range: 12,630 miles at 8 knots
Crew: 56, with room for 20 additional crewmembers

The battery engines generated explosive hydrogen gas.

Armaments:
two 5.9-inch deck guns with 1,000 rounds of ammunition

19 torpedoes

AT SEA: U-BOATS

Even though Britain had a much larger navy, better technology allowed Germany to dominate the war beneath the waves. German submarines were nicknamed U-boats because the German word for "submarine" is *unterseeboot*.

In February 1917, German leader Wilhelm II told his submarine commanders, "We will frighten the British flag off the face of the waters." U-boats were so effective at attacking Allied ships that Wilhelm's threat may have seemed quite believable. During one 4-month period in 1916, U-boats sank nearly 500 ships. By the end of the war, German subs had sunk more than 5,000 ships—that is, around one-quarter of the world's shipping tonnage.

Diesel engines allowed the U-boats to travel great distances. The subs carried torpedoes to fire underwater and had guns mounted on their decks for fighting when the boats were attacked at the surface. As the war progressed, the German Navy rushed to build U-boats with longer ranges and increased torpedo capacities. At the start of the fighting, Germany had 38 functioning subs. By the end of the war, it had 170 new U-boats at sea and 226 more under construction. In between, 203 U-boats were lost to Allied defenses, accidents, or unknown causes.

HOW TO SINK A U-BOAT

The Allies developed various technologies for countering the U-boat threat. Two of these were mines and depth charges. It is believed that during World War I, 30 U-boats were sunk by depth charges, while at least 48 were lost to mines.

A depth charge was a bomb that could be dropped into the water and rigged to detonate at a certain depth. It was shaped like a barrel, filled with high explosives, and triggered by a device that could sense the water pressure surrounding the bomb. The first effective depth charge, produced by the British Navy in 1916, could be triggered to explode as deep as 300 feet and carried nearly 300 pounds of explosives. By the end of the war, the Allies had 600-pound depth charges.

A U-boat could shrug off the shock of an individual depth charge exploding nearby because the subs' hulls were designed to survive the intense strain of water pressure at great depths. However, when an Allied ship detected a submarine, it would attack with multiple depth charges. A surface ship could send a U-boat to the bottom of the ocean if it succeeded in battering the sub with several well-placed explosions.

Mines were also explosive devices, but instead of being dropped from ships, they floated in the ocean, anchored at different depths across a certain span of water. When a submarine bumped into a mine, it triggered an explosion. Near the end of the war, the United States and Britain laid the North Sea Mine Barrage, a gigantic grid of mines to block the passage of U-boats between Scotland and Norway. The barrage used a new type of mine with long antennas that would set off the explosives when brushed by a U-boat. When completed, this deadly curtain of explosives had more than 70,000 mines, and it blocked one of the Germans' main routes to the North Atlantic.

machine guns

Up to 76 men slept in very cramped conditions.

The U-boats were armed with torpedoes.

CRITICAL VIEWING The photo above shows a German U-boat stranded on the English coast after the German surrender. The photo on the right shows the engine room of a German submarine. What do these photos reveal about wartime technology?

THE WORST PLACE TO LIVE

Living conditions aboard a U-boat were often unbearable. During World War I, submarines did not have the technology to recirculate air. Instead, during the hours that a sub cruised underwater, the air became hot, stale, smelly, and occasionally scarce. Fresh air would be restored only when the U-boat surfaced and hatches could be opened. Because the U-boats carried a limited supply of fresh water, bathing and shaving were not options. In addition, the men were at constant risk not only from enemy ships, but also from their own equipment. The battery cells that ran the U-boat's electrical systems could explode if the ventilation failed. Also, if the batteries were touched by sea water, they would create poisonous chlorine gas.

One officer who served on a World War I U-boat later recalled life aboard the vessel. He explained that space was so tight inside the sub that

whenever a torpedo had to be loaded into a forward tube, the commanding officers' cabins had to be cleared out to make room for the men and equipment coming through. Describing the crew's situation, he wrote, "The crew space had bunks for only a few of the crew—the rest slept in hammocks. . . . Since the temperature inside the boat was considerably greater than the sea outside, moisture in the air condensed on the steel hull-plates; the condensation had a very disconcerting way of dropping on a sleeping face, with every movement of the vessel. It was in reality like a damp cellar."

THINK ABOUT IT

What do you think was the most significant technological advancement of World War I? Explain your answer.

DIFFERENTIATE

Striving Readers

Main Ideas and Details Elicit from students a main idea for each of the following areas of war technology: land, air, water. Prompt students to write the main ideas and to list three details for each main idea.

Pre-AP

Investigate Women's Roles in the Great War Direct students to research how women contributed to the war effort, both in official and unofficial capacities. Suggest that students research the Army Nurse Corps, the female yeomen in the Navy, and the "hello girls" of the U.S. Army Signal Corps. Instruct students to write a report that includes visual documentation of what they have learned and then present their reports to the class.

See the Chapter Planner for more strategies for differentiation.

HISTORICAL THINKING

Ask and have students answer the following questions.

1. **READING CHECK** What new technologies were developed during World War I?

2. **IDENTIFY PROBLEMS AND SOLUTIONS** What problem on the battlefield did Winston Churchill identify, and how did tanks provide a solution?

3. **INTEGRATE VISUALS** How does the U-boat diagram support the description of conditions detailed in The Worst Place to Live subsection?

ANSWERS

1. New World War I technologies included antiaircraft guns, tanks, poison gases, depth charges, and x-rays.

2. Churchill noted the problem of soldiers dying as they crossed open battlefields. Tanks protected them by providing armored coverage, and the heavy tanks could roll over obstacles like wire.

3. It shows how small the quarters were. Readers can see how difficult it would be to move torpedoes through the tight space in a U-boat.

CRITICAL VIEWING Possible response: The photograph of the U-boat reveals how huge and awe inspiring this technology was. The photo inside the submarine reveals the complicated equipment onboard and the cramped space of an engine room.

1.1 Poised for War

When conditions are dry in the woods, one spark can set the whole forest blazing. By 1914, tensions had reached a high point in Europe. A single act would trigger war.

MAIN IDEA Alliances, nationalism, imperialism, and militarism all contributed to the outbreak of World War I.

TENSIONS IN EUROPE

In 1914, Europe was divided by hostilities, some of which had deep roots. After losing the Franco-Prussian War to Germany in 1870, France made an alliance, or an agreement of mutual support, with Russia and Great Britain. The three countries pledged to come to each other's defense if attacked. Germany, Austria-Hungary, and the Ottoman Empire had formed a similar alliance.

Nationalism, a strong belief in one's country and in its superiority to others, and imperialism fueled tensions in Europe. In the early 1900s, Austria-Hungary and Serbia competed for the **Balkan Peninsula** in southeastern Europe. Serbia, a Slavic nation, wanted to unite with other Slavs in the Balkans to form a large state. When Austria-Hungary annexed, or seized, the Slavic territories of Bosnia (BAHZ-nee-uh) and Herzegovina (HURT-zih-goh-VEE-nuh) in 1908, the Serbians were outraged. Other powers, including Germany, Great Britain, and France, competed for natural resources and colonies in Africa and Asia.

To achieve their nationalist and imperialist goals, many European countries embraced **militarism**, the belief that a government must build a strong military force and be ready to use it to defend its interests. In 1914, Germany was a major military power. Other countries scrambled to catch up. All of these factors brought Europe to the brink of war.

ASSASSINATION TRIGGERS WAR

The continent tipped over the edge on June 28, 1914, when **Archduke Franz Ferdinand** of Austria-Hungary and his wife were visiting Sarajevo (sair-uh-YAY-voh), the capital of Bosnia. As the couple toured the city in an open car, a Bosnian

Serb nationalist named Gavrilo Princip (GA-vrih-loh PRIHN-sihp) shot and killed the archduke and his wife. The assassination set the alliances in motion. Germany supported Austria-Hungary when the latter blamed Serbia for the assassination. As Serbia's ally, Russia came to that country's defense, and France pledged to support Russia. In August, Germany declared war on Russia and France. Soon Britain declared war on Germany.

Within months, war spread throughout Europe. Countries joined one of two alliances. The Central Powers were primarily made up of Germany, Austria-Hungary, and the Ottoman Empire. The principal nations belonging to the Allies were Great Britain, France, and Russia. The United States declined to take part in the war. Many Americans believed in the principles of the Progressive Era, with its faith in progress and the betterment of humanity. War was unthinkable.

Those who lived at the time of the conflict called it "the Great War" because so many nations took part in it and so many soldiers died or were wounded fighting it. When war once again arose in Europe in the 1930s, the conflict that began in 1914 would also be known as "World War I."

World War I Alliances and Major Battles, 1914–1916

The Western Front, 1914–1916

HISTORICAL THINKING

1. **READING CHECK** What is militarism?

2. **INTERPRET MAPS** What geographic advantages did the Allies have in the war?

3. **ANALYZE CAUSE AND EFFECT** Why did the assassination of Archduke Ferdinand trigger the war in Europe?

The Great War **711**

PLAN

Objective
Understand how an assassination and other factors led to war in Europe in 1914.

Critical Thinking Skills for Lesson 1.1
- Identify Main Ideas and Details
- Monitor Comprehension
- Interpret Maps
- Analyze Cause and Effect
- Make Connections
- Make Inferences

Essential Question for Chapter 21
What did the United States gain and lose by going to war? When war raged across Europe in 1914, the United States at first stayed out of the fray, recognizing little to gain. Lesson 1.1 discusses the events and factors that led to World War I.

Background for the Teacher
After the assassination of Archduke Franz Ferdinand and his wife, Austria-Hungary sent Serbia an ultimatum by which war could be avoided—one that Austria-Hungary, longing to crush Serbia, actually hoped Serbia would not accept. Because the leaders of Austria-Hungary believed that if the conditions were not met, the world would consider them justified in going to war, the list of demands was humiliating—and therefore seemed sure to be rejected. Serbia had to agree to suppress all anti-Austria-Hungary propaganda, eradicate anti-Austria-Hungary terrorist organizations, punish all military and government officials who may have aided the movement against Austria-Hungary, launch an investigation into the assassination, and include delegates from Austria-Hungary in the investigation. Surprisingly, Serbia agreed to the terms—all except one: Serbia would not include the delegates in the investigation. That was the opening Austria-Hungary wanted, and it declared war.

A Fatal Chain Reaction

Ask students if they have ever created or seen a row of falling dominoes. **ASK:** What happens when you knock over the first domino in the line? *(The first domino knocks over the next, which knocks over the next, causing all of the dominoes to fall one by one in a chain reaction.)* Explain that, much like falling dominoes, a single event set off a chain reaction of events that led to the outbreak of World War I. Tell students that in this lesson they will learn about the factors that set this fatal chain reaction in motion.

Guided Discussion

1. **Make Connections** How did nationalism and imperialism contribute to the outbreak of World War I? *(Nationalism and imperialism caused tensions as countries competed for dominance and for land. Serbia and Austria-Hungary, for example, competed for land in the Balkan Peninsula. In the spirit of nationalism, Serbia wanted to unite the Slavs in a single state, while ambitious Austria-Hungary wanted to seize land to increase its empire. This put the two countries in conflict.)*

2. **Make Inferences** Why might historians argue that World War I would have occurred without the assassination of Archduke Ferdinand and his wife? *(Possible response: Old hostilities simmered between many European nations, such as between France and Germany after the Franco-Prussian War. Some nations were eager to expand their borders at the expense of other nations. In addition, many nations were building up their military power and allying with other nations. Given the military buildup, the national ambitions, and the animosities lurking beneath the surface, another event would likely have come along to trigger war.)*

Interpret Maps

Guide students to analyze the map of alliances. **ASK:** Based on the geographic location of the countries in the Central Powers alliance, what would Germany still have access to in the event war broke out? *(Possible response: By joining forces with Austria-Hungary, Bulgaria, and the Ottoman Empire, Germany would still have access to the natural resources in Africa and Asia in the event of war.)*

Active Options

Active History: Analyze Causes of World War I Extend the lesson by using either the PDF or Whiteboard version of the activity. These activities take a deeper look at a topic from, or related to, the lesson. Explore the activities as a class, turn them into group assignments, or even assign them individually.

NG Learning Framework: Create a Time Line

ATTITUDE Curiosity

KNOWLEDGE Our Human Story

Instruct students to work in groups to create an annotated time line of events leading to the outbreak of World War I. Tell each group to select an event that they would like to learn more about, such as the formation of alliances, tensions between Serbia and Austria-Hungary, the assassination of Archduke Ferdinand and his wife, or the domino effect of the declarations of war. Ask groups to pool their research to create a single annotated time line to discuss as a class.

English Language Learners

Understand Related Words Call students' attention to the words *alliance* and *Allies*. Note the difference in meaning between the uppercase and lowercase form of *allies*. Model their pronunciation and explain that both words share the Latin root *alligare*, meaning to bind together. Pair English language learners at the **Emerging** or **Expanding** level with proficient English speakers and have them develop a list of synonyms for the words *allies* and *alliance*.

Gifted & Talented

Write a Response to the Assassination Instruct students to research the reactions of various European leaders to the assassination of Archduke Franz Ferdinand and his wife. Then prompt them to take on the role of one of the leaders and write a short response to the event in their own words. Point out that their response should reflect the perspective of the leader they chose, such as shock over and condemnation of the incident or support for the actions and ideology of the assassin. As a class, discuss the different leaders' reactions.

See the Chapter Planner for more strategies for differentiation.

ANSWERS

1. Militarism is the belief that a government needs a strong military and must be prepared to use it when necessary to defend the nation's interests.

2. Geographically, the Allied countries surrounded the countries that made up the Central Powers, which could potentially make invasions easier. Additionally, neutral countries bordered the Ottoman Empire and did not join with the Central Powers.

3. The assassination of Archduke Ferdinand triggered war in Europe because several countries felt compelled to support their allies. Germany supported Austria-Hungary and so declared war on Russia, which sided with Serbia, and on France, which sided with Russia. Great Britain, allied with Russia and France, then declared war on Germany.

1.2 A New Kind of War

The Germans had come up with a war plan and intended to end the conflict quickly. But plans don't always work out. Everyone fighting in World War I was in for a long, brutal war.

MAIN IDEA Soldiers in World War I fought on two fronts and used deadly new weaponry.

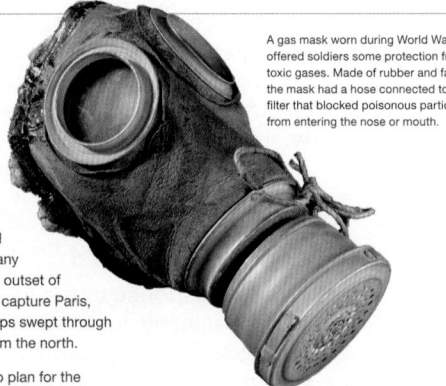

A gas mask worn during World War I offered soldiers some protection from toxic gases. Made of rubber and fabric, the mask had a hose connected to a filter that blocked poisonous particles from entering the nose or mouth.

CRITICAL VIEWING The British soldiers in this photo were temporarily blinded by a poison gas attack during a World War I battle. What details in the photo help convey their condition?

WAR ON TWO FRONTS

Germany had been preparing for war against France and Russia for years. General Alfred von Schlieffen, a German officer, had come up with a plan for such a war in 1906. According to his strategy, the German Army would attack and conquer France quickly and then march on to Russia. Germany put the strategy in motion at the outset of the war by sending its troops to capture Paris, the French capital. German troops swept through Belgium and invaded France from the north.

At first, things went according to plan for the German Army. But in September 1914, when their troops reached the Marne River—just 30 miles from Paris—the French and British armies launched a successful counterattack. The Germans were forced to retreat in what would be called the First Battle of the Marne. Schlieffen's plan had not taken into account the support of the British Army. By the end of 1914, Germany found itself fighting the war on two **fronts**, or battle lines. On the **Western Front**, Germany and the Central Powers faced off against France, Britain, and other Allies. On the **Eastern Front**, Germany and the Central Powers battled Russia along an area that would eventually stretch from the Baltic Sea to the Black Sea.

On both fronts, armies employed trench warfare, a battle strategy you might recall from the Civil War. Troops from the two alliances dug long, deep ditches into the ground that were large enough for them to hunker down in. Trenches were often lined

with boards so that the soldiers could use them as passageways. The boards also helped troops avoid potential diseases caused by sitting or standing in mud and dirty water. Soldiers could fight from the trenches and shelter there from enemy fire.

Trench warfare often resulted in staggering death tolls, as opposing armies struggled to take an enemy trench. In the July 1916 battle along the Somme River in France, fierce fighting went on for four months. During the First Battle of the Somme, the Allies managed to push the Germans back only six miles. More than a million soldiers from both sides were killed or wounded during the battle.

DEADLY TECHNOLOGY

Weapons technology made World War I deadlier than any previous war. The new and improved machine guns mounted on top of the trenches resulted in high death tolls on both sides. You

may recall that the British invented the **tank**, an armored, heavily armed vehicle with treads instead of wheels, to counter machine gun fire. Originally known as "landships," tanks could be driven right into enemy trenches.

Airplanes filled the sky for the first time in any war. Piloting a war plane was a dangerous assignment. In addition to attacks in the air, firepower from the ground could take down the planes. The **antiaircraft gun** was a heavy weapon that could be pointed to the sky to fire missiles from a metal tube or barrel. Weaponry even filled the seas when Germany used submarines, also called **U-boats**, to shoot torpedoes and sink enemy warships.

On the ground, chemical weapons terrorized soldiers. Cylinders filled with chlorine, mustard, or other types of **poison gas** were tossed and released into enemy trenches. The Germans also developed the flamethrower, which shot a stream of fire about 20 or 30 feet long through a length of pipe. Flamethrowers could only be used at short

range, but they caused panic when they were turned on soldiers in a trench. These weapons were first used by the German Army in Belgium at the 1915 Battle of Hooge. A British soldier who took part in the battle said the flamethrowers were "like a line of powerful fire hoses spraying fire instead of water across my [trench]." Just sheltering in the trenches posed a danger to troops. Many soldiers perished from exposure to cold and from illnesses contracted in the crowded, filthy, rat- and lice-infested ditches.

HISTORICAL THINKING

1. **READING CHECK** Why did Germany's plan to wage a quick, efficient war fail?

2. **MAKE INFERENCES** What can you infer about the effectiveness of trench warfare in World War I?

3. **DRAW CONCLUSIONS** What impact did new weapons technology have on the numbers of casualties suffered in the war?

PLAN

Objective
Explain how poison gas and other technologies proved deadly for World War I soldiers.

Critical Thinking Skills for Lesson 1.2
- Identify Main Ideas and Details
- Monitor Comprehension
- Make Inferences
- Draw Conclusions
- Make Generalizations

Essential Question for Chapter 21
What did the United States gain and lose by going to war? The drawn-out war and the extraordinary number of casualties eventually pulled the United States into World War I, in which many U.S. soldiers were also killed or injured. Lesson 1.2 discusses the reasons for the staggering number of dead and wounded soldiers.

Background for the Teacher
Trenches offered more than just places to hunker down during deadly machine gun fire. Trench systems allowed troops to dig in and maintain battle and support lines during long stalemates in which little territory changed hands. Eventually, trench lines ran from the Belgian coast on the English Channel to the border of Switzerland. Most trench systems consisted of two to four rows of trenches that stretched back a mile or more from the front line. Relatively perpendicular trenches connected the rows of main trenches. The connecting trenches served as communication and supply lines between the front line and the command center in the rear. A trench line was usually dug in a zigzag pattern so that the enemy could not shoot down the length of the trench. Each row was fronted by barbed wire meant to slow enemy troops that crossed the No Man's Land that separated opposing troops.

Understand the Numbers

Use comparisons to help students put the human toll of World War I into perspective. Ask students to estimate how many people they think would fill a stadium at a professional football game. *(about 75,000)* **ASK:** About how many people live in New York City—the most populous city in the United States? *(about 8.5 million)* **ASK:** How many thousands of people are in a million? *(one thousand thousands)* Point out that some wars have lasted for hundreds of years and have resulted in hundreds of thousands of people killed. Explain that World War I lasted only four years, but 9 million soldiers were killed and an additional 21 million soldiers were wounded or listed as missing. Tell students that in this lesson they will learn about why World War I was so deadly.

TEACH

Guided Discussion

1. **Make Generalizations** Why might you expect fighting a war on two fronts to be more difficult than fighting a war on a single front? *(Possible responses: Troops would be spread thinner because some would be pulled away to fight a different enemy. Logistics would be harder because military leaders would need to constantly assess how to allocate supplies and personnel.)*

2. **Draw Conclusions** Why do you think that poison gas and flamethrowers were especially terrifying to soldiers? *(Possible responses: Guns had been used in many wars, and many soldiers would have been familiar with guns at home. Poison gas and flamethrowers worked differently from anything soldiers had experienced. Both weapons could kill soldiers in a horrible way or leave them with excruciating injuries.)*

Make Inferences

Remind students that more than a million soldiers from both sides were killed or injured during the First Battle of the Somme. **ASK:** What factors likely contributed to the high number of casualties? *(Possible responses: The length of the battle—four months—and the fact that both sides were dug into trenches likely accounted for the high casualty rate. Each side must have attacked the other side's trenches many times. Each attempt would have resulted in heavy casualties as troops on the offensive emerged from their trenches.)*

Active Options

On Your Feet: T-Chart Arrange students in groups of three or four around a section of a bulletin board or a table. Provide each group with a large sheet of paper. Tell group members to construct a T-Chart comparing and contrasting fighting tactics and technologies in the Civil War with those in World War I. Prompt students to revisit the relevant chapters in the text and conduct online research if needed. When groups have finished, call on volunteers from each group to share their T-Charts with the class.

Civil War	World War I

NG Learning Framework: Create Monologues

SKILLS Collaboration, Communication

KNOWLEDGE Our Human Story

Prompt small groups of students to review the information about trench warfare in the lesson and to research the topic further. Instruct groups to use their findings to write a set of dramatic monologues that represent the experiences of different soldiers in the trenches. Encourage students to consider both the advantages and disadvantages of trench warfare when creating their monologues and to collaborate so they portray a variety of characters and perspectives. Invite groups to present their monologues to the class. As a class, compile a list of advantages and disadvantages of trench warfare based on the monologues.

DIFFERENTIATE

Inclusion

Practice Summarizing Instruct partners to work together to understand the lesson. Ask the pairs to read the first paragraph together. Then tell them to close the book and write down all the facts they can remember. When students have finished, direct them to open the book and check their facts. Encourage them to repeat the exercise with additional paragraphs.

Pre-AP

Write a News Report Prompt students to take on the role of a foreign correspondent in Paris in 1914. Direct them to conduct online research to learn more about the First Battle of the Marne. Then have them write a detailed news story, including quotes from eyewitnesses. Remind students that news reports begin with the most important information and answer the questions *Who? What? Where? When?* and *How?* Invite students to post their articles on a class blog or publish them on a school website.

See the Chapter Planner for more strategies for differentiation.

HISTORICAL THINKING

ANSWERS

1. Germany's plan for a quick war failed because German leaders did not anticipate Great Britain joining France in a counterattack on the Western Front. This meant that Germany was forced to fight a war on two fronts simultaneously, rather than one after the other.

2. The trenches did provide cover from enemy fire, but trenches were not very effective in protecting troops from tanks or poison gas. Overall, trench warfare was not a very effective strategy because it resulted in high death tolls and little gained territory.

3. The new weapons technology, such as tanks that could overrun trenches, advanced machine guns that shot hundreds of bullets a minute, and deadly poison gas, contributed to high numbers of dead and wounded soldiers.

CRITICAL VIEWING The bandages over the soldiers' eyes indicate that their eyes have been burned or otherwise damaged. Each holds onto the shoulder of the soldier in front of him to help guide him. Most of their heads are tilted downward, as if in despair.

1.3 America Enters the War

To Americans, the war in Europe seemed far away. Most didn't want to have anything to do with it. But soon the war would come a little closer and be harder to ignore.

MAIN IDEA After events led the United States to enter World War I on the side of the Allies, the nation prepared for the conflict.

MOVING TOWARD WAR

Most Americans didn't want to get involved in World War I and neither did their president, Woodrow Wilson. When the war began, Wilson made an official declaration of neutrality, urging Americans to act in "the spirit of impartiality," which meant to avoid taking sides. However, a series of events made it impossible for the United States to remain on the sidelines. The first was

the sinking of the British passenger ship *Lusitania* (loos-ih-TAY-nee-uh) by a German submarine on May 7, 1915. At least 129 Americans were among the nearly 1,200 people who drowned that day. The attack outraged Americans, and President Wilson demanded an apology from the German government. But he still refused to enter the war.

Two years later, other developments arose that finally changed Wilson's mind. British intelligence

In this U.S. government factory, women wrap rockets that will be sent to the front lines. Some of the war work women performed was repetitious, but it could also be difficult and dangerous.

The Sinking of the *Lusitania*

When the *Lusitania* set sail from New York City for England on May 1, 1915, it carried almost 2,000 passengers and ammunition for the British war effort. German submarines had begun attacking any ship suspected of carrying war supplies. On May 7, off the coast of Ireland, a German submarine torpedoed the ocean liner. Terrified passengers tried to board the ship's lifeboats, but only six were successfully launched. Within 18 minutes of the attack, the ship sank. The cork life ring shown here was recovered from the wreckage.

agents intercepted a telegram sent by the German foreign minister, Arthur Zimmermann, to Germany's ambassador in Mexico. Zimmermann proposed that Mexico join the war on the German side. In return, Zimmermann said, Mexico could regain Texas, New Mexico, and Arizona. Wilson released the **Zimmermann Telegram**, as it came to be known, through the newspapers to the American public on March 1, 1917.

On March 18, German submarines sank three U.S. ships, resulting in many deaths. Americans were infuriated, and this was the last straw for the president. On April 2, Wilson asked Congress to declare war on Germany, pledging the United States would fight for "the ultimate peace of the world and for the liberation of its peoples, the German peoples included." Congress declared war on Germany on April 6, 1917.

GEARING UP FOR WAR

Once the United States joined the Allies, the government took immediate steps to build up its military. In 1917, U.S. Army and National Guard

troops numbered only about 309,000. To increase these numbers, Congress passed the Selective Service Act in May, requiring all men between the ages of 21 and 30 to register for the draft. By the end of the war, 3.7 million American men had taken part in World War I.

The soldiers sent to fight in Europe belonged to the **American Expeditionary Forces (AEF)**. They fought under the command of General John J. Pershing, who had led troops in Cuba, Mexico, and the American West. The battle-weary Allies enthusiastically welcomed the Americans' help. Intense fighting and high casualties on both sides were taking their toll. In 1915, more than 1.4 million French soldiers had been killed or wounded fighting on the Western Front. A single battle in the French town of Verdun in 1916 claimed more than 300,000 men on both sides of the combat.

To take part in the conflict, the United States had to manufacture the machinery of war, including airplanes, guns, and ammunition. Wilson established the **War Industries Board (WIB)** to produce these supplies. Factories that had manufactured items such as cars and bicycles in peacetime converted to wartime production. The WIB oversaw manufacturing and came up with ways to make the factories more efficient.

As men left for the war, women filled many of the jobs in these factories and other workplaces. Some labor unions threw their support behind the war effort. They promised not to strike for the duration of the war or to insist that the war production factories hire only union members. Armed for battle, the United States soon sent troops to Europe.

HISTORICAL THINKING

1. **READING CHECK** What events led President Wilson to ask Congress to declare war on Germany?

2. **MAKE INFERENCES** How do you think Americans reacted when they heard about the Zimmermann Telegram?

3. **ANALYZE CAUSE AND EFFECT** How did entering World War I affect many American businesses and workers?

PLAN

Objective
Analyze why the United States entered World War I and how it readied troops and supplies.

Critical Thinking Skills for Lesson 1.3
- Identify Main Ideas and Details
- Monitor Comprehension
- Make Inferences
- Analyze Cause and Effect

Essential Question for Chapter 21
What did the United States gain and lose by going to war? The goal of neutrality slipped away as world events showed the United States what it stood to lose because of German aggression. Lesson 1.3 discusses how the *Lusitania*'s sinking and the Zimmermann Telegram drew the nation into war and how the United States instituted a draft and geared up to produce war machinery.

Background for the Teacher
Like the Germans, the British were also tangled in the intrigue of the Zimmermann Telegram. Early in the war, a British ship had cut Germany's telegraph lines in the English Channel. Consequently, Germany sometimes sent its diplomatic messages through neutral countries. Arthur Zimmermann used the U.S. Embassy in Berlin to send his coded telegram through the U.S. Embassy in Copenhagen to the German Embassy in Washington—to be sent on to the German Embassy in Mexico. When the U.S. Embassy routed the telegram through London, the British intercepted it and decoded part of it. The British knew the message would likely bring the United States into the war, but they had a dilemma—how to alert U.S. President Wilson about the message without revealing that they had cracked the German code and that they were spying on U.S. diplomatic communications. The British solved the problem by saying that they had intercepted the telegram sent from Washington to Mexico—which had been recoded in an older code and sent via a commercial telegraph company in Mexico.

Making Choices

Create a T-Chart on the board. Label the left column Oppose and the right column Support. **ASK:** Why might Americans oppose getting involved in a war on foreign soil? *(Possible responses: no immediate threat or benefit to the United States; general opposition to war; family ties to the opposing side)* List the reasons for opposition in the left column. **ASK:** What might cause reluctant people to support a war? *(Possible responses: a clear threat on the home front; a direct attack on the United States; a strong moral or human rights issue)* List the reasons for support in the right column. Tell students that public opinion regarding World War I changed when Germany seemed to be directly threatening the United States.

TEACH

Guided Discussion

1. **Make Inferences** How did the sinking of the *Lusitania* undermine President Wilson's call for Americans to act in "the spirit of impartiality"? *(At the beginning of the war, most Americans supported Wilson's call for neutrality. However, the sinking of the* Lusitania, *which resulted in the death of at least 129 Americans, angered Americans and caused many to view Germany as the aggressor in the war.)*

2. **Analyze Cause and Effect** Why was Congress's declaration of war against Germany significant for the Allies? *(In entering the war, the United States provided fresh troops, which the Allies badly needed because of high casualties, and the United States also geared up to provide planes, ammunition, and other necessary war supplies.)*

More Information

War Industries Board Tell students that the War Industries Board (WIB) had authority over many aspects of the U.S. economy—to determine which existing industries should produce which war materials, what prices they should charge, and how raw materials should be used. The WIB also emphasized standardizing products to increase efficiency. The WIB worked so well, in fact, that U.S. productivity increased by 20 percent under its policies. **ASK:** Why do you think President Wilson felt the need to establish the WIB? *(Possible response: The United States needed to gear up quickly and efficiently for war. The WIB helped ensure that the demand for war materials could be met on time and at a reasonable cost, while limiting waste and duplication of effort.)*

Active Options

On Your Feet: Inside-Outside Circle Arrange students in concentric circles facing each other. Direct each student in the outside circle to ask a question about how the United States prepared for war. Then have each student in the inside circle answer his or her partner's question. On a signal, have students on the inside circle rotate to create new partnerships and begin again. On a different signal, have students trade roles so that those in the inside circle ask questions and those in the outside circle answer questions.

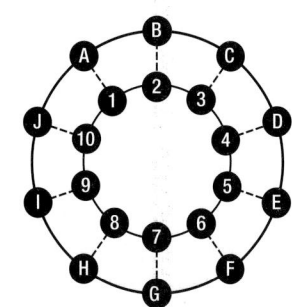

NG Learning Framework: Research the *Lusitania*

ATTITUDE Curiosity

KNOWLEDGE Our Human Story

Prompt students to work in groups to research the sinking of the *Lusitania*. Instruct students to gather information about parts of the event that interest them, such as statistics about the ship, facts about how the captain handled the crossing, details about the sinking, and reactions to the sinking. Encourage students to use diagrams, time lines, maps, and other graphics to present their findings to the class.

DIFFERENTIATE

Striving Readers

Summarize Place students in mixed-proficiency pairs. Assign each pair one or more paragraphs from the lesson. Tell students to read their assigned paragraphs and then work together to summarize each paragraph in one or two sentences. When all pairs are finished, prompt them to read their summaries in the order in which the paragraphs appear in the lesson.

Gifted & Talented

Illustrate Figurative Language Bring students' attention to the phrase "the last straw," used to describe what finally brought the United States into the Great War. Elicit that the phrase comes from the proverb "It was the last straw that broke the camel's back." Prompt students to draw a picture or use a computer graphics program to create artwork that visually represents the phrase as it is used in this lesson. Students may use any artistic style, from realistic to impressionistic to cartoon. Invite them to share their pictures with the class and explain why they chose the style and images they did.

See the Chapter Planner for more strategies for differentiation.

HISTORICAL THINKING

ANSWERS

1. The sinking of the *Lusitania* pushed Wilson closer to war, but the interception of the Zimmermann Telegram—offering Mexico the states of Texas, New Mexico, and Arizona in exchange for siding with Germany—and the German sinking of three U.S. ships in 1917 prompted him to ask for a declaration of war.

2. The Zimmermann Telegram likely angered Americans, since it encouraged Mexico to form an alliance with the Central Powers with the intent of attacking the United States in return for regaining territory from the United States.

3. In order to produce supplies needed to fight the war, factories converted to making war materials, such as airplanes and weapons. With men going overseas to fight, factories and other businesses hired women to do jobs men had typically done.

2.1 Americans on the Western Front

The Allies had looked forward to this day for almost three years. American entry into the war came later than the Allies had hoped, but they greatly welcomed the help.

MAIN IDEA The arrival of U.S. troops brought a much-needed boost to the Allied effort in the war.

BATTLING IN FRANCE

In late June 1917, the first 14,000 American troops landed in France. For several months, the soldiers of the American Expeditionary Forces (AEF) trained for combat and set up communication and supply networks. They began to take part in the fighting in October. The buildup of the AEF continued, and by 1918, millions of American troops had poured into France.

In contrast with the other Allied troops, the Americans were fresh and well fed. The U.S. soldiers brought a renewed sense of optimism to the war effort. The Americans were especially needed after Russia pulled out of the war. In March 1917, a revolution in Russia overturned its monarchy. A second revolution erupted in November, and the Bolsheviks, a party of communist extremists, took power. The

CRITICAL VIEWING American gunners of the Coastal Artillery fire a 1,400-pound shell from a U.S. Navy gun mounted on a railcar during a battle in France in September 1918. Shells shot from this large-caliber gun had a range of about 24 miles. What details in the photo convey the size and power of the gun?

Russian Revolution would usher in **communism**, a form of government in which all means of production and transportation are owned and controlled by the state. The new government declared an end to Russia's part in the war.

With the Russian withdrawal, the Germans hoped to win the war before the arrival of more American troops could reinforce the Allies. Germany quickly transferred huge numbers of its troops from the Eastern Front to the Western Front. Then, on March 21, 1918, the Germans launched an offensive attack. Over the next two months, the German Army gained ground in Belgium and France.

By May, however, millions of well-supplied American troops had arrived in France. The U.S. First Infantry Division attacked German positions in and around Cantigny (KAHN-tee-nyee) in northern France. After a brief battle, the Americans captured the town. The Germans launched a counterattack, but the Americans refused to yield. The Battle of Cantigny was the first sustained offensive the United States fought. Germany's bid for victory in the war had failed. In June, the AEF fought in battles at Belleau (BEHL-oh) Wood and Chateau-Thierry (shah-TOH TEE-uh-ree). They suffered tremendous losses but succeeded in blocking German forces that had advanced dangerously close to Paris. These victories greatly boosted the Allies' **morale**, or confidence.

ROLE OF MINORITIES AND WOMEN

American soldiers belonging to minority groups contributed to the victories on the Western Front. Thousands of African Americans volunteered to fight in World War I and served in segregated army units. Most of these soldiers provided support and were not assigned combat duties. However, several units fought alongside white soldiers in France and served with distinction. Asian Americans also chose to serve in the war

and were granted U.S. citizenship as a reward. Some Hispanic Americans from Texas and New Mexico refused to register for the draft to protest the discrimination they faced in the United States. Others, however, enlisted and fought bravely in the war in Europe.

During World War I—and for the first time in U.S. history—women were allowed to officially join the armed forces. Most of these servicewomen performed clerical work. Several hundred accompanied the AEF to France to serve as telephone operators. Women of the Army Nurse Corps treated the injured at the front, and some drove ambulances filled with wounded soldiers to hospitals behind the lines. One American nurse, **Julia C. Stimson**, arrived in France shortly after the United States entered the war. She later became head of the nursing services of the AEF.

While Americans fought overseas, men and women at home also supported the war effort. They, too, played a significant role in World War I.

Croix de Guerre
The African-American soldiers of the 369th Regiment from New York City, nicknamed the "Harlem Hellfighters," fought with the French. These soldiers were the first Americans to be awarded the French medal shown here, known as the Croix de Guerre (krwah dih GAIR), or War Cross, for gallantry.

HISTORICAL THINKING

1. **READING CHECK** Why did the Allies welcome the arrival of U.S. troops on the Western Front?

2. **DRAW CONCLUSIONS** Why did the Germans believe they could win the war after Russia pulled out?

3. **MAKE INFERENCES** Why might it have been important to African Americans and other minorities to fight in World War I?

PLAN

Objective
Examine how well-supplied and fresh American forces affected the war on the Western Front.

Critical Thinking Skills for Lesson 2.1

- Identify Main Ideas and Details
- Monitor Comprehension
- Draw Conclusions
- Make Inferences
- Analyze Cause and Effect
- Summarize

Essential Question for Chapter 21

What did the United States gain and lose by going to war? Millions of American soldiers fought side by side with Allied soldiers, leading to some decisive victories. Lesson 2.1 describes how certain groups on the home front gained opportunities, while others did not.

Background for the Teacher

Many minority soldiers who fought valiantly during World War I faced discrimination back in the United States. For example, the courageous African-American soldiers of the 369th Infantry Regiment, known as the "Harlem Hellfighters," lost more than 800 officers and soldiers on the front lines in France. One soldier of that regiment, Sergeant Henry Johnson, was severely injured fighting off a dozen Germans to save a fellow soldier. In recognition, the French awarded Johnson the Croix de Guerre. New Yorkers did welcome home the regiment with a parade, but the United States waited until long after Johnson's death to award him the Purple Heart in 1996, the Distinguished Service Cross in 2002, and the Medal of Honor, the nation's highest personal military honor, in 2015—nearly one hundred years after the war had ended.

History Notebook

Encourage students to complete the American Gallery page for Chapter 21 in their History Notebooks as they read.

Welcome Relief

Present the following scenario: New rules require that a football game begin at sunrise and continue until sunset, regardless of weather. Each team is limited to 11 players, and all players must be on the field at all times. If players are injured and cannot play, the team has to carry on with fewer players. **ASK:** What would happen to players if a team had to play all day without substitutes? *(Possible response: Team members would quickly become too tired to play effectively; morale would plummet.)* Tell students that something similar happened on the Western Front. After years of fighting, the Allies were desperate for fresh soldiers and supplies to carry on the battle. The United States' entry into the war threw weary Allied forces a lifeline.

TEACH

Guided Discussion

1. **Analyze Cause and Effect** How did the arrival of the American Expeditionary Forces impact Germany's bid for victory on the Western Front? *(The AEF's efforts in the battles of Cantigny, Belleau Wood, and Chateau-Thierry caused Germany's bid for victory to fail by preventing German troops from advancing all the way to Paris.)*

2. **Summarize** How did American servicewomen contribute to the war effort in Europe? *(Many servicewomen worked as telephone operators or in clerical positions. Army nurses treated soldiers at the front and drove ambulances to move the wounded to hospitals behind the lines.)*

More Information

Julia C. Stimson Julia C. Stimson aspired to be a doctor, but her family did not approve of the idea. Instead, she pursued a long, accomplished career in both nursing and the military. When the United States entered World War I, Stimson was serving as head of the Washington University Training School for Nursing in St. Louis, Missouri. She left her position to join the Army Nurse Corps. She was assigned as chief nurse at Base Hospital 21 in France, which was staffed by doctors and nurses from Washington University. Stimson left Hospital 21 to head the Red Cross Nursing Service before becoming the chief nurse for the American Expeditionary Forces. She received the Distinguished Service Medal for her work in France during World War I. Following the war, Stimson became the superintendent of the Army Nurse Corps, attained the rank of major and finally full colonel, and worked to recruit nurses to help during World War II.

Active Options

AMERICAN GALLERY ONLINE **The Great War: A Photo Essay** Invite students to explore the American Gallery. Have them select one of the images and do additional research to learn more about it. Ask questions that will inspire additional inquiry about the chosen gallery image, such as: What details do you see? What is the physical setting? What is happening? What purpose do the objects in the photo serve? How does the photo relate to the way the war was fought?

NG Learning Framework: Research American Contributions

ATTITUDE Curiosity

KNOWLEDGE Our Human Story

Instruct students to work in groups to use print and digital resources to learn more about one of the following American contributions on the Western Front that interests them: the U.S. First Infantry Division at the Battle of Cantigny, AEF forces at the battles of Belleau Wood and Chateau-Thierry, the 369th Infantry Regiment during the Meuse-Argonne Offensive, or the women of the Army Nurse Corps at the front and behind the lines. Prompt students to use their research to create a slide show, a group report, or other presentation. Allow time for groups to share and discuss their findings as a class.

DIFFERENTIATE

English Language Learners

Look for Cognates As they read, instruct students of **All Proficiencies** to look for words that are similar in spelling and meaning to words in their home language. For example, the words *communication, optimism, revolution,* and *communism* have cognates in Spanish: *comunicación, optimismo, revolución,* and *comunismo.* For each word they identify, prompt students to make a vocabulary card with the English word and definition on one side and the word and its definition in their home language on the other side. Encourage them to note any differences in the meanings of the two words.

Pre-AP

Analyze Cause and Effect Direct students to conduct research to learn more about how the entry of U.S. troops impacted the Great War. Tell them to gather information from a variety of sources and to take notes in a Cause-and-Effect Web or other graphic organizer. Instruct students to use their notes to write an essay analyzing the effects U.S. troops had on the war in both general and specific ways. Invite students to share their analyses with the class.

See the Chapter Planner for more strategies for differentiation.

HISTORICAL THINKING

ANSWERS

1. The Allied troops were exhausted and malnourished, so they felt relief to be joined by fresh troops who were optimistic and in better shape for fighting.

2. The Russian exit allowed Germany to move troops from the Eastern Front to the Western Front. The Germans believed that if they acted before the Americans arrived with troops and supplies, they could overwhelm the Allied forces on the Western Front, forcing them to surrender.

3. African Americans and other minorities served in the military to prove their patriotism and bravery, which they hoped would translate into civil rights gains after the war.

CRITICAL VIEWING The width and height of the gun barrel in relation to the size of the railroad car and the soldiers help convey the gun's large size. The amount of smoke conveys the gun's power.

2.2 On the Home Front

Would you be willing to make sacrifices to support a war? Many Americans during World War I were. They helped out financially and made changes in their daily lives. Some were even willing to give up a few of their liberties.

MAIN IDEA On the American home front, World War I was a time of sacrifice, patriotism, and suppressed liberties.

SUPPORTING THE WAR

As you know, the U.S. government had factories produce goods for the war after the country entered the conflict. The government also called on civilians to support the war by buying **Liberty Bonds**. Millions of Americans loaned the government money by buying these bonds. The government promised to repay the cost of a bond in 30 years. In the meantime, the buyer received annual interest on each bond at a rate of 3.5 percent.

The Allies needed food as well as financial support, so Americans were also asked to help the war effort by changing their eating habits. The Food Administration was established to oversee the country's agricultural resources. President Wilson named **Herbert Hoover** to head the agency.

Hoover urged Americans to do without meat and wheat sometimes because "wheatless days in America make sleepless nights in Germany." Many families also grew their own fruits and vegetables in what became known as "victory gardens."

To heighten support for the war and inspire patriotism, the government established the **Committee on Public Information (CPI)** to launch an extensive propaganda campaign. **Propaganda** is information used to promote a particular point of view. The committee created posters, pamphlets, billboards, and movies to influence public opinion about World War I. The posters designed by the committee used colorful graphics and thought-provoking messages to fuel hostility toward the enemy and, indeed, everything German. Hamburgers, named after a city in Germany,

The woman in this 1918 photo is Mrs. Drewry, a well-known figure in Cincinnati, Ohio, during World War I. She encouraged other women in Cincinnati to take part in the war effort and was even called their "commander in chief." Here, Mrs. Drewry uses a tractor to plow a victory garden.

came to be called "Salisbury steaks" or "liberty steaks." Schools stopped offering instruction in the German language. Unfortunately, some of this hostility was turned on German Americans. Many experienced prejudice and became the targets of suspicion, threats, and even violence.

SUPPRESSING OPPOSITION

Not all Americans supported the war. Some men expressed their **dissent**, or disagreement, with the government's decision to go to war by refusing to go themselves. These men, known as **conscientious objectors**, often cited religious reasons for not fighting. Others simply failed to register for the draft. Many German Americans and Irish Americans also opposed the war.

To ensure patriotic behavior, President Wilson and Congress enacted the **Espionage Act of 1917**. The act was designed to prevent espionage, or spying, and sabotage. **Sabotage** is action carried out to harm a nation's war effort. The government had sound reasons to be concerned about German espionage. While maintaining neutrality, the United States had supplied the Allies with ammunition and other goods in the early years of the war. In 1916, German agents had caused the explosion of a munitions depot in New Jersey. These were serious crimes, but Americans could be arrested for simply speaking out against the war.

The **Sedition Act of 1918** took these restrictions even further. The act prohibited Americans from "uttering, printing, writing, or publishing any disloyal, profane, scurrilous [insulting], or abusive language" about the government or the armed forces. Any public criticism could be considered sedition, the crime of inciting others to rebel against or overthrow government. Many Americans

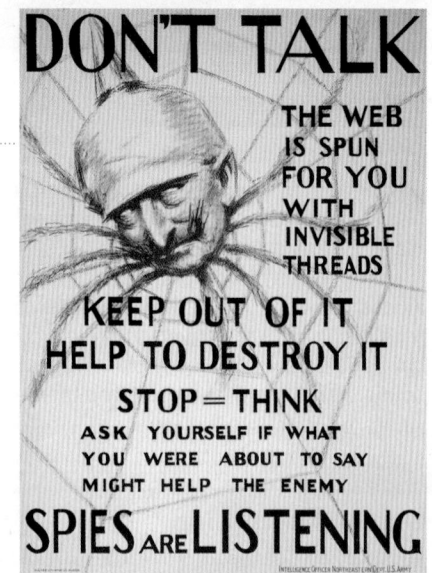

felt the act limited their **civil liberties**—individual rights, such as freedom of speech, that are protected by law. Even criticizing President Wilson could land the speaker in jail.

While life changed for everyone at home, the war continued. But the American troops were making a difference. Soon the long war would finally come to an end.

HISTORICAL THINKING

1. **READING CHECK** How did Americans at home support the war?

2. **MAKE INFERENCES** Why do you think propaganda is particularly effective during times of war?

3. **FORM AND SUPPORT OPINIONS** Do you think the U.S. government was right to restrict civil liberties during the war? Explain your answer using evidence from the text.

PLAN

Objective

Describe how Americans supported the war and how the government suppressed dissent.

Critical Thinking Skills for Lesson 2.2

- Identify Main Ideas and Details
- Monitor Comprehension
- Make Inferences
- Form and Support Opinions
- Analyze Cause and Effect
- Draw Conclusions

Essential Question for Chapter 21

What did the United States gain and lose by going to war? Entering the war changed life on the home front, both positively and negatively. Lesson 2.2 describes how Americans willingly made sacrifices for the war effort and how the government worked to promote cooperation and squash dissent.

Background for the Teacher

On the World War I home front, the federal government spread propaganda with gusto and smothered opposing views. George Creel, a former newspaperman, headed the Committee on Public Information (CPI). Creel saw his task as "the world's greatest adventure in advertising" and his goal as fusing Americans into "one white-hot mass . . . with fraternity, devotion, courage, and deathless determination." In addition to using posters, pamphlets, and movies, the CPI employed a force of 75,000 speakers, known as "Four Minute Men" because of the length of their speeches. The speakers traveled around the country promoting unity. Citizens who did not buy into the message could expect trouble. Under the Espionage Act of 1917, people could be imprisoned for 20 years for criticizing how the government conducted the war.

Financial Literacy

To extend their knowledge and understanding about the concepts in this lesson, refer students to the Financial Literacy handbook.

INTRODUCE & ENGAGE

Preview Using Visuals

Direct students' attention to the propaganda poster and read the caption. **ASK:** What does the poster suggest? *(German spies are everywhere, so be careful what you say.)* **ASK:** Why do you think the federal government was worried about average citizens unintentionally providing information that could help the Germans? *(Possible response: The government worried that German immigrants and Americans of German descent might be serving as spies. Discussing the war with neighbors or at work could result in information making its way to Germany.)* Tell students that in this lesson they will learn what steps the United States took to curb espionage.

TEACH

Guided Discussion

1. **Analyze Cause and Effect** What negative consequences resulted from the point of view expressed by the Committee on Public Information? *(The extreme anti-German sentiments expressed by the CPI caused a backlash against German Americans, resulting in their being subjected to suspicion, threats, and violence.)*

2. **Make Inferences** Why do you think some German Americans and Irish Americans opposed the war? *(Possible response: Some German Americans may have had family members still living in Germany. In addition, they may have resented the hostility created by CPI propaganda. Some Irish Americans may have also opposed the war because of negative feelings toward Great Britain.)*

Draw Conclusions

Ask students to reread the text information about the Espionage Act of 1917 and the Sedition Act of 1918. **ASK:** Why do you think someone might argue that the Sedition Act was a stronger attack on civil liberties than the Espionage Act? *(Possible response: Although both acts stipulated that a person could be arrested for speaking out against the war, the Sedition Act was much broader regarding what was considered criminal. Any criticism of the government, armed forces, or the president was a criminal offense.)*

Active Options

On Your Feet: Numbered Heads Arrange students in four groups and assign each group one of the following topics: how civilians supported the war effort; how the government worked to inspire support for the war; how and why some people opposed the war; how the government dealt with dissent. Tell students to number off within each group and then review information in the lesson about their topic. Instruct groups to discuss their topic so that any member can report for the group. Finally, call a number, and the student with that number reports for the group.

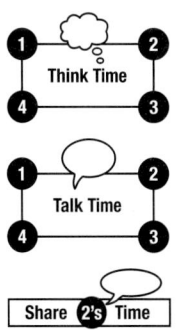

NG Learning Framework: Write a Script

SKILL Collaboration

KNOWLEDGE Our Human Story

Show students a propaganda film created during WWI. Then direct students to work in small groups to create a script for a short propaganda film to influence public opinion about the war and to spur U.S. citizens to take some kind of action in support of the war effort. Prompt students to think about dialogue, props, and tone as they create their scripts and to divide up the tasks and work as a team. Provide time for each group to act out their script for the class.

DIFFERENTIATE

Striving Readers

Read and Recall Invite students to work in pairs. First have each student read the lesson independently. After reading, pairs should meet without the book and share ideas they recall. One partner should take notes. Together, students should then review the lesson and decide what to add or change in the notes.

Gifted & Talented

Create a Poster Direct students to conduct online research to find World War I propaganda posters, including those urging citizens to buy war bonds, eat less of particular foods, and plant victory gardens. Prompt students to analyze the images, slogans, and persuasive appeals used in the posters. Then tell them to create a poster in a similar style. They may use conventional art materials or an online design program. Invite students to display their posters and explain the images, colors, and words they chose and how their choices relate to their research.

See the Chapter Planner for more strategies for differentiation.

HISTORICAL THINKING

ANSWERS

1. Many Americans bought Liberty Bonds to help pay for the war. Americans also conserved resources, changed their eating habits, and planted victory gardens so more food could go to feed U.S. soldiers.

2. Possible response: Wartime can be stressful. Propaganda persuades people to support a particular point of view. Uniting people against a common wartime enemy helps them feel like they belong to a larger community and that they are doing something powerful and useful during uncertain times.

3. Answers will vary. Possible response: The government was right to do so. Given that German agents had committed sabotage, the government had reason to worry about German spies in the United States. Curtailing civil liberties was the price to pay for national security.

2.3 Victory for the Allies

At the beginning of the war, the Germans had believed they would win it fairly quickly and easily. Now, more than four years later, a German victory was looking less and less likely. The American armed forces had tipped the balance.

MAIN IDEA In the summer and fall of 1918, the Allies gained the upper hand in World War I and forced Germany to surrender.

FINAL BATTLES

The German Army made one more offensive push in July 1918. German troops planned to attack northern France and southern Belgium, an area known as Flanders. However, to draw Allied troops away from their real target, German generals planned a misleading offensive farther south. On July 15, the push began.

However, the French Army launched a surprise counter-offensive of its own. When the Germans advanced, they ran into thousands of French and American soldiers ready to attack. The German forces soon found themselves surrounded. The confrontation that followed is called the **Second Battle of the Marne**, and it turned the tide of the war in the Allies' favor.

Major Battles of World War I, 1917–1918

Allied Powers
Central Powers
Neutral nation
★ Allied Powers victory
★ Central Powers victory
— German offensive line
— Armistice Line, November 11, 1918

After that, the Allies attacked the German forces and pushed them back. Then, in a final drive to end the war, the Allies began an operation called the **Meuse-Argonne offensive** in September. American divisions disabled the railroad tracks that brought supplies to the German Army. In October, General Pershing, now the commander of the Allied forces, led his troops to force the German Army out of the Argonne Forest in northeastern France. The bloody **Battle of Argonne Forest** took a terrible toll on both sides. German casualties rose to 100,000. French casualties totaled 70,000. In the deadliest campaign in U.S. history, American casualties reached 117,000, with 26,000 killed. But the American troops distinguished themselves in the offensive. Three African-American regiments took part, fighting alongside the French, and earned the respect of their French counterparts.

Pilots also displayed great bravery. As you have learned, American ace fighter pilot Eddie Rickenbacker was the most famous flier on the Allied side. In September 1918, at the start of the Meuse-Argonne offensive, he engaged in a fierce aerial battle with 7 German warplanes. Outmaneuvering the aircraft, he shot down 2 of them. By the end of the war, Rickenbacker was known as "the Ace of Aces."

THE WAR ENDS

After the Meuse-Argonne offensive, the war ground down to its end. Germany's hopes for victory had been replaced by fear of an Allied invasion that would force a humiliating surrender. In addition, an Allied blockade of German ports caused severe food shortages in Germany.

In early October, German leaders had asked President Wilson to arrange an **armistice**, or an end to the fighting. Following weeks of negotiation, Germany surrendered and reached a peace agreement with the Allies. The war came to an end on November 11, 1918, at 11:00 a.m.—the 11th hour of the 11th day of the 11th month. The day would come to be known as Armistice Day, or Veterans Day. Relief that day was evident. Britain's prime minister, David Lloyd George, said, "This is no time for words. Our hearts are too full of gratitude to which no tongue can give adequate expression."

The devastation of the war was overwhelming. As many as 9 million soldiers died, and another

In 2014, artists Paul Cummins and Tom Piper observed the 100th anniversary of Britain's entry into World War I with an art installation of 888,246 ceramic poppies, one for each British soldier killed in the war. Poppies grew in the battlefields of Flanders and came to represent the blood spilled in the war. Here, British prince William, his wife, Kate Middleton, and Lord Richard Dannatt visit the installation, called *Blood Swept Lands and Seas of Red*.

21 million were wounded. Millions of civilians perished from starvation and disease. The death toll, the numbers of countries involved, and the cost of the Great War exceeded that of any previous war in history. Because the bloodshed and destruction were so extreme, people called World War I "the war to end all wars." The French and the British blamed Germany for the war, and they were determined to make the country pay.

HISTORICAL THINKING

1. **READING CHECK** What happened at the Second Battle of the Marne?

2. **INTERPRET MAPS** Where were most of the battles fought between 1917 and 1918?

3. **IDENTIFY MAIN IDEAS AND DETAILS** Why did people call World War I "the war to end all wars"?

PLAN

Objective
Discuss how two key battles helped change the course of the war.

Critical Thinking Skills for Lesson 2.3
- Identify Main Ideas and Details
- Monitor Comprehension
- Interpret Maps
- Draw Conclusions

Essential Question for Chapter 21
What did the United States gain and lose by going to war? The soldiers of the American Expeditionary Forces played vital roles in securing an Allied victory in Europe, gaining respect and gratitude on the world stage. Lesson 2.3 describes how the American forces helped the Allies win the war but paid the price with many American lives.

Background for the Teacher
Eddie Rickenbacker was an unlikely flying ace. Forced to drop out of school in seventh grade to help support his family, Rickenbacker bounced from job to job, finally ending up in the automotive industry. This led to a stint as a successful race car driver. When the United States entered World War I, Rickenbacker joined the army as a driver for General Pershing's staff. He was assigned to drive Colonel William Mitchell, an advocate for air power. Mitchell arranged for Rickenbacker to attend flight school, even though he was two years past the cutoff age of 25 that the Army Air Service had set for pilots. Rickenbacker joined the 94th Aero Pursuit Squadron, the first all-American air unit to go into combat. He quickly became an ace and rose to command the squadron. By war's end, Rickenbacker led the squadron in the number of downed planes, earning him his title of "Ace of Aces."

The Legacy of War

Direct students' attention to the photograph of Prince William and his wife, Kate Middleton, at the *Blood Swept Lands and Seas of Red* art installation and read the caption aloud. **ASK:** Why do you think World War I still matters some 100 years later? *(Possible response: World War I was the first modern war and resulted in high casualties.)* Ask students to discuss the benefits of remembering the consequences of war. Tell students that Lesson 2.3 examines the Allied victory and its cost in lives.

TEACH

Guided Discussion

1. **Identify Main Ideas and Details** What contributions did the American forces make in the Meuse-Argonne offensive? *(American forces cut off supplies for the Germans by disabling railroad tracks and pushed German forces out of the Argonne Forest with the help of the French. In addition, American pilots provided aerial support.)*

2. **Draw Conclusions** Why did German leaders want an armistice? *(Faced with severe food shortages because of the Allied blockade of their ports, the Germans didn't want to be forced to surrender if the Allies invaded Germany.)*

Interpret Maps

Instruct students to compare the inset map Western Front, 1914–1916 from the beginning of the chapter with the map Major Battles of World War I, 1917–1918 in this lesson. **ASK:** What evidence indicates that the position of the Western Front changed little over the course of the war? *(Possible response: There were battles along the front in Ypres in 1914, 1915, and 1917 and in Somme in 1916 and 1918. The front also passed through the Argonne Forest in both 1914 and 1918.)*

Active Options

On Your Feet: Roundtable Discussion Instruct students to sit in groups of four around tables to discuss the following question: How did victory turn into defeat for the Germans following the United States' entry into the war? Provide each group with a large sheet of paper. Tell group members to take turns jotting down as many answers to the question as possible based on information in the lesson. When time for the activity has elapsed, call on a representative from each group to share the group's ideas with the class.

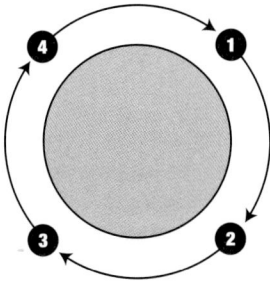

NG Learning Framework: Create an Infographic

SKILL Communication

KNOWLEDGE Our Human Story

Ask students to work in groups to create infographics presenting statistics about World War I. Encourage groups to consider not only statistics about people, such as numbers of troops and military and civilian casualties, but also statistics about types and amounts of military equipment and ammunition, food and supplies, trenches, communication systems, costs, and other aspects of the war. Prompt groups to share their infographics with the class and to discuss any differences between the statistics of different groups.

Inclusion

Analyze Visuals Provide concrete questions to help students understand both the map and the photograph; for example, What does each color represent? *(Allied, Central, and neutral countries)* Where were most of the Allied victories? *(near the France-Belgium border)* What do poppies represent? *(blood spilled and people who died in World War I)* Why did British royalty visit the art installation? *(to commemorate the millions of British casualties)* Encourage students to point to details that they don't understand, and help them frame questions about these details that other students can answer.

Gifted & Talented

Create a Social Media Profile Direct students to conduct online research to learn more about the life of Eddie Rickenbacker before, during, and after World War I. Then have students write a social media profile of Rickenbacker and some posts he might have written at different times in his life; for example, after the death of his father, after his first flying lesson, after shooting down an enemy plane, and after being featured on the cover of *Time* magazine. Invite students to share their profile and posts with the class.

See the Chapter Planner for more strategies for differentiation.

ANSWERS

1. The Germans had planned to distract the Allies with a misleading offensive farther south, but the French anticipated this plan. Thus the French and American forces were waiting for the Germans when they marched on Flanders.

2. Most of the battles between 1917 and 1918 were fought on the Western Front in northeastern France and Belgium.

3. People called World War I "the war to end all wars" because it was so devastating in terms of the number of wounded and dead soldiers and civilians, the cost, and the number of countries involved.

3.1 Wilson's Goals

Woodrow Wilson dreamed of a world with no more war and an organization of nations dedicated to keeping the peace. But the rest of the Allied leaders had other ideas.

MAIN IDEA After the war, President Wilson met with other Allied leaders to negotiate a peace treaty and present his proposal for the world.

European Borders after World War I, 1920

THE FOURTEEN POINTS

In 1918, before the war ended, President Wilson had outlined his vision for world peace in the **Fourteen Points**. The Fourteen Points consisted of principles that promoted fairness, openness, and democracy. Recognizing that secret treaties had played a major role in the outbreak of World War I, Wilson called for all future diplomacy to be carried out "frankly and in the public view." Recalling Germany's attacks against merchant ships and passenger vessels, such as the *Lusitania*, Wilson called for free navigation of the seas.

He also proposed national arms reduction, free trade among countries, and national **self-determination**. This is the idea that countries should form their own governments and borders to reflect the national origins of the people who live there. In his last point, Wilson called for the formation of a "general association of nations." This organization would provide a place for all countries to settle arguments through discussion and diplomacy rather than war.

Wilson wanted his principles to be used as the basis for peace negotiations. However, Britain and France objected to the Fourteen Points. They didn't like Wilson's interference with European policies, and his proposal didn't call for heavy penalties against Germany. The two European nations wanted to punish Germany and prevent it from waging any more wars in the future.

PRIMARY SOURCE

President Wilson delivered his Fourteen Points to Congress on January 8, 1918. Points 1–5 deal with diplomatic issues that he believed were essential to prevent further war. Point 14 calls for a peacekeeping organization.

1. Open covenants [agreements] of peace, openly arrived at, . . . [and] diplomacy shall proceed always frankly and in the public view.

2. Absolute freedom of navigation upon the seas, outside territorial waters, alike in peace and in war. . . .

3. The removal, so far as possible, of all economic barriers and the establishment of an equality of trade conditions among all the nations consenting to the peace. . . .

4. Adequate guarantees given and taken that national armaments [weaponry] will be reduced to the lowest point consistent with domestic safety.

5. A free, open-minded, and absolutely impartial adjustment of all colonial claims, based upon a strict observance of the principle that in determining all such questions of sovereignty, the interests of the populations concerned must have equal weight with the equitable [fair] claims of the government. . . .

14. A general association of nations must be formed under specific covenants for the purpose of affording mutual guarantees of political independence and territorial integrity to great and small states alike.

THE TREATY OF VERSAILLES

German leaders hoped Wilson's proposals would shape the postwar peace settlement, but they were bitterly disappointed. The terms were worked out at the Paris Peace Conference, which began in January 1919 in Versailles (vur-SY), France.

On June 28, 1919, negotiations among the Allies produced the **Treaty of Versailles**, which formally ended the war. In spite of Wilson's objections, the treaty blamed Germany for starting the war. It also called for Germany to make **reparations**, or payments, of about $33 billion to the Allies for the damages and casualties caused by the war. These terms fueled resentment in Germany that deepened in the following decades. However, Wilson achieved his main goal: the creation of an international peacekeeping organization, which would be called the **League of Nations**.

When Wilson returned to the United States, he tried to persuade the Senate to ratify the treaty. Most Republicans opposed the League of Nations, believing it would force the United States to give up too much of its sovereignty. Wilson set off on a tour in September 1919 to promote the treaty but suffered a stroke that left him partially paralyzed. He could no longer govern effectively or speak in favor of the Treaty of Versailles. The treaty came up for a vote in the Senate twice and was defeated both times. The United States would not be part of the League of Nations. Wilson died in 1924.

HISTORICAL THINKING

1. **READING CHECK** What were the Fourteen Points?

2. **MAKE INFERENCES** Why might Germany have struggled to pay the reparations demanded by the Treaty of Versailles?

3. **INTERPRET MAPS** Which nations formed in northeastern Europe on land that was part of the Russian Empire before the war?

PLAN

Objective

Identify the arguments over President Wilson's Fourteen Points and the Treaty of Versailles.

Critical Thinking Skills for Lesson 3.1

- Identify Main Ideas and Details
- Monitor Comprehension
- Make Inferences
- Interpret Maps
- Draw Conclusions
- Analyze Primary Sources

Essential Question for Chapter 21

What did the United States gain and lose by going to war? The United States gained a platform to promote world peace, but President Wilson lost his quest for a U.S. role in the League of Nations. Lesson 3.1 explores the debate over the Fourteen Points and ratification of the Treaty of Versailles.

Background for the Teacher

When Wilson asked Congress to declare war on Germany, he hoped that entering the war would serve a higher purpose than simply defending the United States. He cast the U.S. mission in terms of vindicating "the principles of peace and justice." Consequently, he hoped that the conclusion of the war would amount to more than a shift in the balance of power in Europe. He sought a "just and secure peace." Toward that end, he convened a committee called the Inquiry, a group of political and social scientists who studied Allied and American policies and drafted recommendations for a peace settlement. These recommendations became the basis for Wilson's Fourteen Points. Wilson took his plan to Europe, where he stayed for six months negotiating the Treaty of Versailles. To Wilson's surprise, France and Great Britain rejected most of the Fourteen Points, although they did support the creation of the League of Nations.

INTRODUCE & ENGAGE

Negotiating Peace

Explain to students that in a telegram to a U.S. senator, Teddy Roosevelt railed against Wilson's Fourteen Points, saying, "Let us dictate peace by the hammering guns and not chat about peace to the accompaniment of the clicking of typewriters." **ASK:** What do you think the former president meant? *(Possible response: The victors should dictate peace; it should not be decided through negotiation with the losers.)* Ask students to discuss whether they agree or disagree with Roosevelt's position, and why. Tell students that Lesson 3.1 explores the conflict over the rules for peace.

TEACH

Guided Discussion

1. **Draw Conclusions** Why do you think the Germans might have been more supportive than the British and French of using Wilson's Fourteen Points as the basis for peace negotiations? *(Possible response: Wilson's Fourteen Points didn't call for severely punishing Germany. The Germans would have been happy to escape punishment, but Britain and France objected, because they wanted the peace treaty to blame Germany for the war and make that country pay reparations.)*

2. **Make Inferences** Why might the Treaty of Versailles be seen as both a step toward and a step away from maintaining world peace? *(Possible response: On the positive side, the treaty established the League of Nations, which Wilson hoped would provide a forum for maintaining peace. On the negative side, reparations led to a deepening resentment among Germans that grew over time, and that is not conducive to peace.)*

Analyze Primary Sources

Direct students' attention to point 5 in the Primary Source feature and encourage them to revisit previous lessons. **ASK:** What connection do you see between point 5 and World War I? *(Possible response: Austria-Hungary's seizure of Bosnia and Herzegovina infuriated Serbians and may have directly led to the assassination of Archduke Franz Ferdinand. If the people of Bosnia and Herzegovina had been given a say in this change in sovereignty, World War I might not have occurred.)*

Active Options

On Your Feet: Create Live Maps Tell students to refer to the maps in Lessons 1.1 and 3.1. Then ask them to imagine that the classroom represents Europe during and after World War I. Instruct them to work together to create two live maps: one that shows Europe during the war and one that shows Europe in 1920. Direct students to represent different countries by creating signs with names of countries. Point out that their 1920 live map should include the nations created from land lost by Germany and Russia.

NG Learning Framework: Debate the Treaty

| ATTITUDE | Responsibility |
| SKILL | Problem-Solving |

Organize students into two groups. Ask them to imagine that they are U.S. senators debating ratification of the Treaty of Versailles in 1919. Assign one group to represent senators in favor of the treaty and the other to represent those opposed to the treaty. Tell the pro-treaty group to research Wilson's arguments in favor of ratification and the anti-treaty group to research the 12 reservations proposed by Senate Majority Leader Henry Cabot Lodge in opposition to the treaty. Instruct students to use their research to debate and vote as a class whether or not to pass the treaty.

DIFFERENTIATE

English Language Learners ELD

Write Sentences Pair students at the **Emerging** level with students at the **Expanding** or **Bridging** level. Ask them to identify challenging words in the lesson and to look up each in a dictionary. Then tell them to work together to write a sentence for each word that demonstrates their understanding of its meaning. You might wish to suggest the following terms: *arms reduction, self-determination, reparations, stroke,* and *paralyzed.*

Pre-AP

Write a Peace Treaty Instruct pairs of students to revisit the causes of World War I. Compile a list of causes they identify. Then prompt partners to work individually to craft their own peace treaty, addressing the causes that led to World War I. Finally, ask students to compare their finished treaties with Wilson's Fourteen Points in a class discussion.

See the Chapter Planner for more strategies for differentiation.

HISTORICAL THINKING

ANSWERS

1. The Fourteen Points were specific actions Wilson believed world leaders should take to prevent future world wars.

2. Germany may have struggled to pay the $33 billion in reparations because the nation was already dealing with the cost of a war it lost, facing food shortages, and trying to rebuild its economy.

3. Finland, Estonia, Latvia, Lithuania, and Poland formed on this land.

3.2 Woodrow Wilson and World Peace

President Woodrow Wilson dreamed of a peaceful world in which countries would settle their differences diplomatically. Admirers considered him an ambassador of peace, while detractors mocked his ideas. In time, World War I forced Wilson to adjust his thinking about how peace could best be achieved.

When Woodrow Wilson ran for re-election in 1916, his campaign featured the slogan "He kept us out of war." Wilson believed deeply in the importance of peace. He supported a policy called **moral diplomacy**, which called for reduced interference in the affairs of other countries. He also thought the United States should be an example of democracy to the world. In 1917 and 1918, Wilson delivered several speeches in which he discussed his ideals.

CRITICAL VIEWING When Woodrow Wilson first ran for president in 1912, he focused largely on domestic issues. Here, candidate Wilson delivers a campaign speech in September to supporters in New York City's Union Square, pledging to lower tariffs. He made good on this promise in his first term as president. The focus of his second term, of course, would be the war and foreign affairs. What details in the photo suggest Wilson was a forceful speaker?

DOCUMENT ONE

Primary Source: Speech
from Wilson's "Peace Without Victory" speech, January 22, 1917

In Wilson's "Peace Without Victory" speech to the U.S. Senate, the president appealed to nations on both sides of World War I to stop the fighting and negotiate a peace. In this excerpt from the speech, Wilson describes the price of victory.

CONSTRUCTED RESPONSE According to Wilson, why would peace be temporary if one side achieved victory in the war?

Victory would mean peace forced upon the loser, a victor's terms imposed upon the vanquished [defeated]. It would be accepted in humiliation, . . . at an intolerable sacrifice, and would leave a sting, a resentment, a bitter memory upon which terms of peace would rest, not permanently but only as upon quicksand. Only a peace between equals can last. Only a peace the very principle of which is equality and a common participation in a common benefit.

DOCUMENT TWO

Primary Source: Speech
from Wilson's declaration of war message to Congress, April 2, 1917

Once he determined that American involvement in the Great War was inevitable, Wilson delivered his "war message" to a special session of Congress to ask for a declaration of war against Germany. Here, he explains why he has decided to take such a serious step.

CONSTRUCTED RESPONSE What ideas and values did Wilson claim the United States would fight for in the war?

It is a fearful thing to lead this great peaceful people into war, into the most terrible and disastrous of all wars, civilization itself seeming to be in the balance. But the right is more precious than peace, and we shall fight for the things which we have always carried nearest our hearts—for democracy, for the right of those who submit to authority to have a voice in their own governments, for the rights and liberties of small nations, for a universal dominion of right . . . as shall bring peace and safety to all nations and make the world itself at last free.

DOCUMENT THREE

Primary Source: Speech
from Wilson's Fourteen Points speech, January 8, 1918

The president presented his Fourteen Points to Congress nine months after the United States entered the war. Before discussing the individual points, Wilson made the demands of the United States clear and explained what he expected to result from the war.

CONSTRUCTED RESPONSE How did Wilson envision the world after the war, and why did he characterize his view as "nothing peculiar to ourselves"?

What we demand in this war, therefore, is nothing peculiar to ourselves. It is that the world be made fit and safe to live in; and particularly that it be made safe for every peace-loving nation which, like our own, wishes to live its own life, determine its own institutions, be assured of justice and fair dealing by the other peoples of the world, as against force and selfish aggression. All the peoples of the world are in effect partners in this interest, and for our own part we see very clearly that unless justice be done to others it will not be done to us.

SYNTHESIZE & WRITE

1. **REVIEW** Review what you have learned about President Woodrow Wilson and his ideas about world peace.

2. **RECALL** On your own paper, write the main idea that Wilson expressed in each excerpt from his speeches.

3. **CONSTRUCT** Construct a topic sentence that answers this question: How did President Wilson adjust his ideas about world peace after the United States entered World War I?

4. **WRITE** Using evidence from this chapter and the documents, write an informative paragraph that supports your topic sentence in Step 3.

PLAN

Objective
Synthesize information about President Wilson's ideals about world peace from primary source documents.

Critical Thinking Skills for Lesson 3.2
- Synthesize
- Make Inferences
- Draw Conclusions
- Evaluate

Essential Question for Chapter 21
What did the United States gain and lose by going to war? Woodrow Wilson believed that in entering World War I, the United States would be fighting for democracy and world peace. Lesson 3.2 provides excerpts from Wilson's speeches in which he describes his plan for gaining a lasting world peace.

Background for the Teacher
Woodrow Wilson, as standard-bearer of world peace, appears to have drawn on several influences—his Christian upbringing, the views of his first wife, and his own belief in the right of people to determine their own government. Wilson's father, a Presbyterian minister, instilled in him a strong sense of Christian values and a mission to improve the world. His first wife, Ellen Axson, urged him to work for the poor and dispossessed, not just for political and economic reforms. By the time Wilson was elected president, he had become a progressive Democrat with a strong domestic and foreign policy agenda. Wilson fervently supported democracy by supporting nations who similarly embraced democratic ideals, but he didn't want war. However, as the Central Powers exerted tyranny and oppression throughout Europe, Wilson felt it was the duty of the United States—the very symbol of freedom and democracy—to fight to end the war and bring about peace.

INTRODUCE & ENGAGE

Prepare for the Document-Based Question

Before students start the activity, briefly preview the three documents. Remind students that a constructed response requires full explanations in complete sentences. Emphasize that students should use what they have learned about Woodrow Wilson and the United States' entry into World War I in addition to the information in the documents.

TEACH

Guided Discussion

1. **Make Inferences** How might treating a defeated nation as an equal help to ensure a lasting peace? *(Possible response: The defeated nation would be more likely to accept the victor's terms and wouldn't feel it had been treated unfairly. There would be no reason for that nation to break the peace—for instance, by taking revenge on an unjust victor.)*

2. **Draw Conclusions** Based on the last two excerpts, what role did Wilson believe he had as president of the United States? *(Possible response: Wilson believed his role as president was to lead the United States in the fight for democracy and justice and, after the war ended, to help make the world safe and just for all peace-loving nations.)*

Evaluate

After students have completed the Synthesize & Write activity, allow time for them to exchange paragraphs and read and comment on the work of their peers. Establish guidelines for comments prior to this activity so that feedback is constructive and encouraging in nature.

Active Options

On Your Feet: Use a Jigsaw Strategy Organize students into three "expert" groups and have students from each group analyze one of the documents and summarize the main ideas in their own words. Then have the members of each group count off using the letters A, B, and C. Regroup students into three new groups so that each new group has at least one member from each expert group. Have students in the new groups take turns sharing the simplified summaries they came up with in their expert groups.

DIFFERENTIATE

Striving Readers

Summarize and Respond Read each document aloud to students. Then have pairs work together to reread each document and write a brief summary. Read each Constructed Response question aloud, and make sure all students understand what they are to do. Ask volunteers to suggest responses.

Gifted & Talented

Perform a Dramatic Reading Tell students to choose one of the documents and prepare to give a dramatic reading. Instruct them to practice reading it with a partner and to encourage feedback from each other about their use of expression and gestures. Then invite students to perform their dramatic readings for the class. Lead a discussion about how the performed readings affected their understanding of Wilson's ideas.

See the Chapter Planner for more strategies for differentiation.

SYNTHESIZE & WRITE

ANSWERS

1. Answers will vary.

2. Answers will vary.

3. Answers will vary. Possible response: After the United States entered World War I, Woodrow Wilson's ideas changed to include the belief that world peace could be achieved by fighting aggressor nations in the name of "the right."

4. Answers will vary. Students' paragraphs should include their topic sentence from Step 3 and provide several details from the documents to support the sentence.

CONSTRUCTED RESPONSE

Document 1: Wilson suggested that enforced peace would create humiliation and bitterness in the defeated nation, resulting in a weak foundation going forward.

Document 2: Wilson said the United States would fight for democracy, for rights and liberties, for freedom, and for people to have a voice in their government.

Document 3: Wilson saw a fit and safe world where peace-loving nations would mirror what he believed Americans enjoyed as citizens—fairness, justice, and self-determination—and be partners with other nations to ensure these same qualities for all.

CRITICAL VIEWING Wilson is leaning forward toward the audience and pointing his finger for emphasis. He is speaking directly to them and not reading from a written speech. The serious expression on his face reflects his deep feelings about his subject.

3.3 Aftermath of the War

World War I launched the United States onto the world stage, and the country became a major global power. But the end of the war also brought social and economic challenges to the nation.

MAIN IDEA The United States became a world leader after World War I but struggled with disease, economic woes, and racial discrimination.

A WORLD POWER

In many ways, the war changed how the rest of the world regarded the United States. American forces had played a key role in defeating Germany and ending the war. And President Wilson had been a major leader in hammering out the terms of the Treaty of Versailles. His idea that the United States should engage diplomatically with other nations and promote democracy and national self-determination would influence U.S. foreign policy for the rest of the 20th century—and into the 21st.

Since the war hadn't been fought on American soil, the United States hadn't suffered as many casualties as the other Allies or the Central Powers. American dead and wounded totaled about 320,000, while those of countries such as Great Britain and France numbered in the millions. However, the United States was not spared from an epidemic, or widespread outbreak of disease, that affected much of the world. A powerful strain of **influenza**, the virus we now call "the flu," swept the country at the end of 1918. Scientists had not yet developed an effective vaccine that could treat or prevent the spread of the disease, which killed about 600,000 Americans in 1918 and 1919. By the time the influenza had run its course in 1920, it had caused about 50 million deaths worldwide.

ECONOMIC AND SOCIAL UPHEAVAL

The war's aftermath also brought economic turmoil to the United States. Many industries had to convert back to peacetime production, and inflation greatly raised prices. Soldiers returning from war discovered that jobs were few, and unemployment soared to nearly 12 percent in 1921. Wages also fell. In early 1919, labor unions staged major strikes calling for higher wages at shipyards across the country. The largest industrial strike of the year, the Great Steel Strike of 1919, involved steelworkers in the Midwest and lasted for months. Strikers called for an end to the 7-day workweek and the 12-hour workday. As many as 350,000 workers took part in the strike, but they couldn't hold out under the financial strain of being without a paycheck. In early 1920, the strike ended, having failed to achieve its goals.

Although they served their country honorably in the war, African-American soldiers returned home to face widespread segregation and discrimination. Racial tensions flared in the years following the war. There were frequent lynchings in the South. Great numbers of southern African Americans came to cities in the North in a mass movement known as the **Great Migration**. The movement began in 1910, but the stream of African Americans swelled during the war, when thousands of jobs opened up in northern industrial centers. About 500,000 African Americans moved north between 1914 and 1920.

As jobs became scarce after the war, the flood of African Americans led to confrontations with angry urban whites who feared the newcomers would compete with them for jobs. Race riots broke out in Chicago, Washington, D.C., and other U.S. cities during the summer of 1919, a period of violence and bloodshed known as "the red summer." The riot in Chicago was triggered when an African-American teenager swimming in Lake Michigan drowned after being stoned by whites. The incident touched off 5 days of violent chaos that left 38 people dead, more than 500 injured, and roughly 1,000 families homeless.

As a result of all this unrest, Americans were too focused on problems at home to embrace the country's new role as a world leader. Many wanted little to do with the outside world. In particular, they feared that foreign influences could result in the spread of communism to the United States.

This mural, located at a youth center in Chicago, is called *The Great Migration* and was completed in 1995 by artist Marcus Akinlana. It represents the continuing migration of African Americans to Chicago and other northern cities in the 1940s. The mural contrasts the farm labor of African Americans in the South (on the right) with the job opportunities in industry and entertainment available to them in the North (on the left).

HISTORICAL THINKING

1. **READING CHECK** Why did the United States emerge as a major power after World War I?

2. **SUMMARIZE** What postwar economic problems did the United States face?

3. **MAKE INFERENCES** How do you think African Americans who fought in the war reacted to the racism they encountered when they returned home?

PLAN

Objective
Recognize factors contributing to U.S. social and economic problems after World War I.

Critical Thinking Skills for Lesson 3.3
- Identify Main Ideas and Details
- Monitor Comprehension
- Summarize
- Make Inferences
- Evaluate

Essential Question for Chapter 21
What did the United States gain and lose by going to war? World War I made the United States a world leader, but its end also led to problems at home. Lesson 3.3 examines the social and economic problems the nation faced after the war.

Background for the Teacher

The influenza epidemic came not all at once but in waves. The first wave, which was mild, occurred in late spring of 1918. Most victims recovered after about three days. The second wave, which struck in the fall, was deadly, and some victims died within hours. Adults between the ages of 20 and 40 were so hard hit that the average U.S. life expectancy dropped by 10 to 12 years as the flu raged on. American troops helped spread the epidemic across the United States and around the world as they moved between training camps in the United States to the seaports and trenches of Europe and back again. Epidemiologists believe that conditions within the trenches helped create this especially deadly strain of influenza. As soldiers rotated in and out of the trenches, they provided fresh hosts for the disease. By the time the epidemic ran its course, more American military personnel had died of influenza than were killed in combat.

INTRODUCE & ENGAGE

Activate Prior Knowledge

Ask students to recall how entering World War I affected U.S. industries and workers. *(Possible response: Industries had to convert from manufacturing peacetime items to manufacturing war machinery, and workers were in demand.)* **ASK:** What effect do you think the end of the war might have on factories and workers? *(Possible response: Factories would have to convert to making peacetime goods; factories may no longer need the increased supply of workers, leaving some job seekers without jobs.)*

TEACH

Guided Discussion

1. **Make Inferences** How might World War I have contributed to the severity of the influenza outbreak of 1918? *(Possible response: The war contributed to the severity of the epidemic because infected soldiers helped spread the disease within the trenches and between countries as they moved from the home front to war zones and back again.)*

2. **Evaluate** What benefits and drawbacks did African Americans face in moving north during the Great Migration? *(Possible responses: Benefits—They might avoid lynchings. There were more factory jobs. Drawbacks—Jobs became scarce when soldiers returned home. Competition for jobs led to confrontations and violence. They might be caught up in race riots.)*

More Information

The Great Migration Direct students' attention to the mural *The Great Migration*. Tell students that this mural is located on the playground of the Elliott Donnelley Youth Center on the South Side of Chicago. In the 1920s, Chicago's Bronzeville neighborhood served as a hub of African-American homes and businesses that grew out of the Great Migration. Note that the water dividing the right and left sides of the mural is the Mississippi River. The blue river represents African Americans bringing blues music to Chicago. **ASK:** What differences do you notice between the scene on the left side of the mural and the scene on the right side? *(Possible response: The left side of the mural shows happy, excited people in fashionable suits and dresses, playing a guitar and perhaps singing, against the backdrop of a city skyline. On the right side, people are working hard in a rural setting, dressed in farm clothing, and do not appear content.)*

Active Options

On Your Feet: Three-Step Interview Tell students to choose a partner. Instruct one student to interview the other about the following question and then switch roles: What problems did the United States face in the aftermath of World War I? When time is up, invite students to share the results of their interviews with the class.

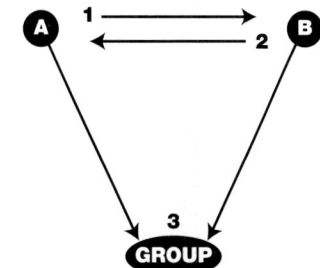

NG Learning Framework: Research the Influenza Epidemic

ATTITUDE Curiosity

SKILLS Collaboration, Communication

Instruct students to work in teams to research an aspect of the 1918–1919 influenza epidemic that interests them. Suggest that some teams collect statistics on the number of cases and deaths over the course of the epidemic and others look into such topics as how the epidemic spread, what steps the military and cities took to contain the spread, and what made the epidemic so deadly. When they have completed their research, invite teams to share what they learned in a class discussion.

DIFFERENTIATE

English Language Learners ELD

Understand Compound Words Arrange students at the **Emerging** and **Expanding** levels in mixed pairs. Bring their attention to the sentence containing the words *workweek* and *workday.* Ask students to identify the two words that make up each of these compound words. Then ask students to brainstorm and list other compound words beginning with *work-*, such as *workbench, workplace, worksheet, workout, workload, workstation,* and *workforce.* Prompt pairs to write a sentence using each compound word, assisting each other as needed.

Pre-AP

Research and Report on Impacts After they read the lesson, prompt students to write three questions they have about the impact that World War I had on the role of the United States in world affairs. The questions should seek a deeper understanding of the long-term impacts of the war. Then instruct students to conduct online research to answer their questions. Tell students to summarize their findings in a report that analyzes the impacts of the war on the international role of the United States throughout the 20th century, as well as today.

See the Chapter Planner for more strategies for differentiation.

HISTORICAL THINKING

ANSWERS

1. The United States emerged as a major power because of its role in winning the war for the Allies and in negotiating the Treaty of Versailles. In addition, Wilson's ideas about democracy and national self-determination helped shape modern U.S. foreign policy.

2. Inflation raised the prices of goods after the war, unemployment skyrocketed as soldiers returned from fighting and joined the workforce, and wages fell, leading to strikes.

3. African-American soldiers likely felt betrayed since they risked their lives for their country but were treated as second-class citizens at home. Many used protests to fight for their civil rights and push the United States to live up to its democratic ideals.

21 REVIEW

VOCABULARY

Use each of the following terms in a sentence that shows an understanding of the term's meaning.

1. militarism

   A country practicing militarism builds up its armed forces and is prepared to use them.

2. front

3. morale

4. conscientious objector

5. propaganda

6. reparations

7. sabotage

8. armistice

9. Liberty Bond

READING STRATEGY
MAKE INFERENCES

If you haven't already, complete your chart by listing facts from the chapter about the Great War and then writing the inferences you draw from each one. Then answer the question

Facts	Inferences
Many European nations formed alliances.	

10. Why do you think Americans on the home front were willing to make so many sacrifices to support the war?

MAIN IDEAS

Answer the following questions. Support your answers with evidence from the chapter.

11. Why did hostility begin to arise between Austria-Hungary and Serbia before 1914? **LESSON 1.1**

12. Describe some of the deadly new weapons used in World War I. **LESSON 1.2**

13. What position did President Woodrow Wilson take when World War I broke out? **LESSON 1.3**

14. Why did Russia withdraw from the war? **LESSON 2.1**

15. During the war, what new legislation was passed in the United States to suppress opposition? **LESSON 2.2**

16. What role did Americans play in the Meuse-Argonne offensive? **LESSON 2.3**

17. Why did Wilson want to create an international peacekeeping organization? **LESSON 3.1**

18. What event in 1918 and 1919 caused more American deaths than World War I? **LESSON 3.3**

HISTORICAL THINKING

Answer the following questions. Support your answers with evidence from the chapter.

19. **SEQUENCE EVENTS** List some of the key events that led up to the outbreak of World War I.

20. **DRAW CONCLUSIONS** What was life probably like for soldiers who fought in the trenches in World War I?

21. **MAKE PREDICTIONS** What might have happened if the United States had not entered the war?

22. **ANALYZE CAUSE AND EFFECT** Why did race riots take place in the United States after the war?

23. **FORM AND SUPPORT OPINIONS** Do you think the United States was right to take part in World War I? Explain your answer.

24. **MAKE INFERENCES** How do you think the war changed the roles of women in the United States?

INTERPRET VISUALS

Much of the propaganda created in the United States during World War I was designed to inspire patriotism and stir Americans to action. The poster below calls on men to "enlist," or join the armed forces; "plow," or provide food for the troops and the country; and "buy bonds," or help pay down the cost of the war. Study the poster, and then answer the questions that follow.

25. Whom or what does each figure in the poster represent?

26. What elements in the poster were probably meant to inspire patriotism?

ANALYZE SOURCES

When the Senate debated the Treaty of Versailles, the most divisive issue was U.S. involvement in the League of Nations. On the last day of the debate, Idaho senator William Borah delivered a long, passionate speech against the League of Nations. Read the following excerpt from his address. Then answer the question that follows.

> It imperils [endangers] . . . the very first principles of this Republic. It is in conflict with the right of our people to govern themselves free from all restraint, legal or moral, of foreign powers. I will not, I can not, give up my belief that America must, not alone for the happiness of her own people, but for the moral guidance and greater contentment of the world, be permitted to live her own life.

27. According to Borah, what American freedoms would the League of Nations imperil?

CONNECT TO YOUR LIFE

28. **EXPOSITORY** Imagine you are an American soldier or nurse who has just returned home from the war. Write a letter to a friend pointing out the social, political, and economic changes you see in the country. Discuss how these changes affect you.

   TIPS

   - Consider the political changes that took place during the war.

   - Review the social and economic challenges that developed after the war.

   - Identify who you are as the letter writer and what you did during the war. You can include your gender, race, or ethnic origin if it helps explain your experiences.

   - Tell how the country has changed and how the changes have—or haven't—affected you.

   - Use two or three vocabulary terms from the chapter in your letter.

   - Conclude the letter with a brief summary about the direction the country has taken.

VOCABULARY ANSWERS

1. A country practicing militarism builds up its armed forces and is prepared to use them.

2. Germany battled Russia along a front that stretched from the Baltic Sea to the Black Sea.

3. After the American troops arrived in France in 1917, the morale improved among the Allied troops.

4. A conscientious objector refuses to fight in a war.

5. The CPI created propaganda films to influence public opinion.

6. Britain and France wanted Germany to make reparations for the damages it caused during the war.

7. The federal government worried that foreign spies might sabotage the American war effort.

8. After years of fighting, the Allies and Central Powers agreed to an armistice and peace negotiations.

9. Americans loaned the government money for the war effort by buying Liberty Bonds.

READING STRATEGY ANSWER

Facts	Inferences
Many European nations formed alliances.	Most Americans believed the United States should side with the Allies.
Germans sent the Zimmermann Telegram and sank U.S. ships.	Most Americans saw Germany as working against the United States.
The U.S. government created propaganda.	Propaganda reinforced Americans' negative view of Germany.

10. Germany's hostile actions combined with U.S. propaganda helped Americans equate sacrifice with being patriotic.

MAIN IDEAS ANSWERS

11. Competition for the Balkan Peninsula, nationalism, and militarism caused hostility to arise between Austria-Hungary and Serbia before 1914.

12. Some of the deadly new weapons used in World War I included tanks, which were heavy armored vehicles with treads instead of tires; antiaircraft guns, which could be aimed toward the sky to fire on airplanes; U-boats, which were submersible ships; poison gas, which could be fired in canisters among enemy troops; and flamethrowers, which shot fire and were used at close range.

13. Wilson initially took the position of neutrality when the war broke out. However, he changed his mind two years later when aggressive German actions against the United States forced him to ask Congress to declare war.

14. A revolution occurred in Russia in which the Communist Party overthrew the monarchy, and the new government chose to end Russian participation in the war.

15. Wilson and Congress enacted the Sedition Act of 1918 to suppress opposition.

16. In the Meuse-Argonne offensive, American troops disabled the railroad tracks that brought supplies to the German Army, and they fought in the Battle of Argonne Forest.

17. Wilson wanted to create an international peacekeeping organization, the League of Nations, to provide a place where all countries could settle arguments through discussion and diplomacy rather than war.

18. A worldwide outbreak of influenza caused more American deaths than World War I.

HISTORICAL THINKING ANSWERS

19. Austria-Hungary annexed Bosnia and Herzegovina; Serbian Gavrilo Princip assassinated Archduke Franz Ferdinand; Austria-Hungary blamed Serbia for the assassination and declared war; Russia pledged support to Serbia; Germany declared war on Russia and France; Great Britain declared war on Germany.

20. Life in the trenches was probably terrifying and miserable. In addition to the constant danger from enemy fire, soldiers had to deal with filthy conditions, crowding, rats, and disease.

21. Answers will vary, but students should understand that Germany would have likely continued to attack civilian targets, including U.S. ships. In addition, Germany may have been able to defeat the already weakened Allies, given that Germany could divert troops from the Eastern Front after Russia's withdrawal.

22. Converting back to peacetime production levels caused inflation; there were few jobs available, causing high unemployment rates; African Americans had migrated north to fill industrial jobs left open by soldiers who went to war, but in the postwar economy job competition between angry urban whites and African Americans caused confrontation and riots.

23. Answers will vary. Students should use examples from the text to support their opinions.

24. As women worked at jobs traditionally held by men, they proved they could make contributions to businesses and industry. Some women found a purpose for their lives outside of raising a family and taking care of the home. They saw themselves differently when the men returned from the war to civilian life, and they may not have wanted to give up their jobs.

INTERPRET VISUALS ANSWERS

25. The figures are a farmer, a soldier, and a private citizen willing to buy Liberty Bonds, representing three segments of American society important to the war effort.

26. The slogan "Your Country Calls" was likely meant to inspire patriotism, and the heroic stance of the three figures—particularly the soldier—likely stirred feelings of patriotism, too.

ANALYZE SOURCES ANSWER

27. Borah suggests that joining the League of Nations would keep U.S. citizens from being able to govern themselves without being influenced by the interests and pressures of other nations.

CONNECT TO YOUR LIFE ANSWER

28. Expository letters should clearly explain the perspective of the writer and his or her opinions on the political, social, and economic changes seen in the country after returning from war, discussing how the changes affect the writer.

UNIT 8 RESOURCES

UNIT INTRODUCTION

UNIT TIME LINE

UNIT WRAP-UP

NATIONAL GEOGRAPHIC | CONNECTION

National Geographic Magazine Adapted Articles
- "WWI and Mapmaking at National Geographic"
- "Untold Stories of D-Day" ONLINE

Unit 8 Inquiry: Respond to a Crisis

NG Learning Framework Activities
- Research War Damage
- Share the Arts of the 1920s

Unit 8 Formal Assessment

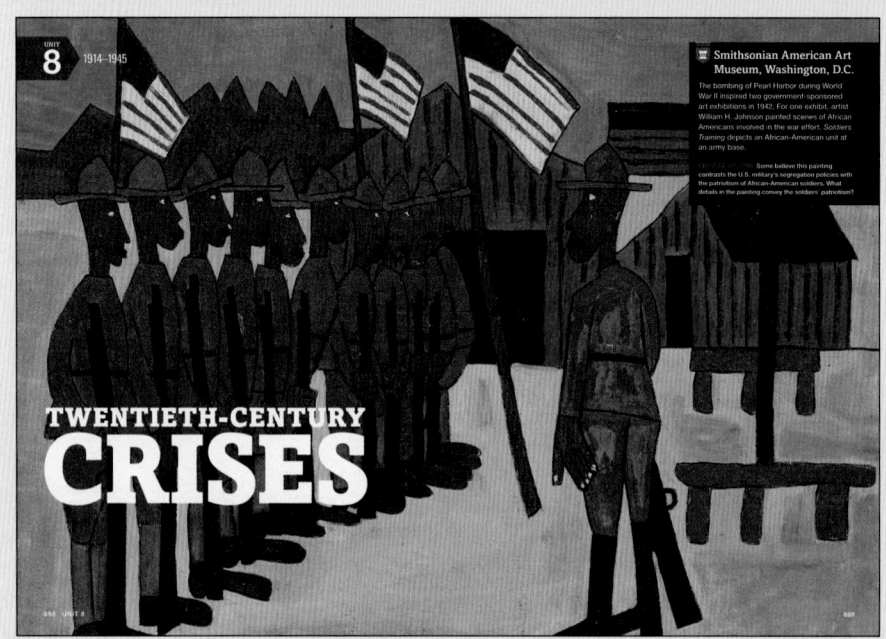

CHAPTER 22 RESOURCES

Available at NGLSync.Cengage.com

TEACHER RESOURCES & ASSESSMENT

Reading and Note-Taking

Vocabulary Practice

Document-Based Question Template

Social Studies Skills Lessons
- Reading: Draw Conclusions
- Writing: Write a Narrative

Formal Assessment
- Chapter 22 Pretest
- Chapter 22 Tests A & B
- Section Quizzes

Chapter 22 Answer Key

ExamView®
One-time Download

STUDENT DIGITAL RESOURCES

- **eEdition** (English)
- **eEdition** (Spanish)
- **Handbooks**
- **Online Atlas**
- **American Gallery Online**
- **History Notebook**
- **American Voices (Biographies)**
- **Active History**
- **Projects for Inquiry-Based Learning**

Chapter 22 Spanish Resources are available at NGLSync.Cengage.com.

- Primary Sources
- On Your Feet: Perform a Skit
- **NG Learning Framework:** Write for a Newspaper

SECTION 1 RESOURCES
RETURN TO NORMALCY

LESSON 1.1
Challenges After the War
- On Your Feet: Numbered Heads
- **NG Learning Framework:** Create a Time Line

LESSON 1.2
Prohibition
- On Your Feet: Build a Paragraph
- **NG Learning Framework:** Research Organized Crime

LESSON 1.3
Social Conflicts
- On Your Feet: Question and Answer
- **NG Learning Framework:** Create a Data Graph

SECTION 2 RESOURCES
THE JAZZ AGE

LESSON 2.1
The Consumer Economy
- ▶ The Model T
- On Your Feet: Fishbowl
- **NG Learning Framework:** Explore Planned Obsolescence

LESSON 2.2
Mass Culture
- Active History: Analyze Primary Sources
- **NG Learning Framework:** Compose a Radio News Story

LESSON 2.3
All That Jazz
- ▶ This Is Jazz
- On Your Feet: Team Questions
- **NG Learning Framework:** Learn a 1920s Dance Step

American Voices Biographies
Louis Armstrong
F. Scott Fitzgerald ONLINE

LESSON 2.4
CURATING HISTORY
National Jazz Museum
- **NG Learning Framework:** Create a Jazz Hall of Fame

SECTION 3 RESOURCES
THE HARLEM RENAISSANCE

LESSON 3.1
GEOGRAPHY IN HISTORY
The Great Migration
- **AMERICAN GALLERY ONLINE** The Great Migration
- **NG Learning Framework:** Write Journal Entries

LESSON 3.2
The Harlem Renaissance
- On Your Feet: Guess the Person or Place
- **NG Learning Framework:** Compare Two Poems

LESSON 3.3
DOCUMENT-BASED QUESTION
Writers and Artists of the Harlem Renaissance
- On Your Feet: Host a DBQ Roundtable

LESSON 3.4
AMERICAN VOICES
Zora Neale Hurston
- On Your Feet: Word Chain
- **NG Learning Framework:** Create a Blog Page

CHAPTER 22 REVIEW

Strategy ❶
Focus on Main Idea

To help students anticipate and organize content, provide modified Main Idea statements for Lessons 1.1, 1.2, and 1.3 before reading. Explain to students that these statements summarize important ideas and will be useful for helping them pay attention to what matters most in the text.

1.1 After World War I most Americans worried that life would never be normal again.

1.2 The United States passed laws to prohibit alcohol, which resulted in good and bad changes in society.

1.3 Racial tensions and discrimination against immigrants grew in the 1920s.

Use with Lessons 1.1–1.3 *Help students get in the habit of using Main Idea statements to set a purpose for reading.*

Strategy ❷
Record and Compare Facts

After reading each lesson, ask students to write three important facts that they recall about the Great Migration and the Harlem Renaissance from Lessons 3.1–3.4. Pair students to compare and check their facts and then use the facts to write a few sentences regarding what they learned about African-American life in the 1920s.

Use with Lessons 3.1–3.4

Strategy ❸
Use Reciprocal Teaching

Tell partners to take turns reading each paragraph of the lesson aloud. At the end of each paragraph, the reading student should ask the listening student questions about the paragraph. Students may ask their partners to state the main idea, identify important details that support the main idea, or summarize the paragraph in their own words. Then have students work together to answer the Historical Thinking questions.

Use with All Lessons

Strategy ❶
Clarify Text

Pair visually impaired students with sighted partners and have them listen to an audio recording of the text. Ask the visually impaired students to indicate if there are words or passages they do not understand. Instruct their partners to clarify meanings by looking up definitions, emphasizing context clues, and paraphrasing from the text.

Use with All Lessons

Strategy ❷
Monitor Comprehension

Ask inclusion students to partner read the text, taking turns reading aloud with a more proficient student. At the end of each paragraph, tell students to stop and use these sentence frames:

- This paragraph is about _____.

- One detail that stood out to me is _____.

- The word _____ means _____.

- I don't think I understand _____.

Encourage students to pose questions to their partner about what they do not understand, and ask the partner to help them locate answers in the text. Then have both students work together to answer the Critical Viewing and Historical Thinking questions.

Use with All Lessons

ENGLISH LANGUAGE LEARNERS

Strategy ①
Use Visuals to Predict Content

Direct students at the **Emerging** and **Expanding** levels to read the lesson title and examine the visuals. Then ask them to write a sentence predicting how the visuals are related to the lesson. After they finish reading the lesson, you may wish to have students review their predictions and revise them as necessary.

Use with All Lessons *Encourage students at the **Emerging** level to ask questions if they have trouble writing a prediction. You might pair students at the **Bridging** level with students at the **Emerging** and **Expanding** levels to work together on the predictions.*

Strategy ②
Pair Partners for Dictation

After reading a lesson, pair students at the **Emerging** and **Expanding** levels with students at the **Bridging** level. Direct partners to take turns explaining in their own words an important idea from the lesson. Each partner writes down the other's explanation. Then tell students to work together to revise their dictated explanations into sentences with correct spelling and accuracy.

Use with All Lessons

Strategy ③
Compose a Sentence

Pair students at **All Proficiencies** with English-proficient students and provide them with a list of important words and terms from the lesson. Then have each pair work together to compose a sentence using each word. Invite pairs to share their sentences and discuss different ways to use each word.

Use with All Lessons

GIFTED & TALENTED

Strategy ①
Create a Poster

Point out the various forms of art used in the chapter. Then have students research the art, headlines, and tag lines used in advertising for music, movies, and books in the 1920s. Ask students to create a poster in a similar style for a book they have read or a movie or performance they have seen. They may use conventional art materials or graphic design software, if available. Invite students to display their posters and explain details that are similar to 1920s advertising.

Use with Lessons 2.2–2.3 and 3.4

Strategy ②
Record a Biographical Podcast

Have students research a celebrity from the 1920s and use the information to record a podcast. Ask students to tell an engaging story about some aspect of the person's life that conveys the individual's values, struggles, or achievements. Encourage students to include relevant sound clips, and guide them in how to credit them properly. Invite students to play their podcast for the class.

Use with Lesson 2.2

Pre-AP

Strategy ①
Write an Analysis

Assign students an essay analyzing the changing attitudes of the general public toward alcohol consumption since Prohibition. Tell students to focus their research on specific ideas, events, and movements. Ask them to draw a conclusion about how attitudes have or have not changed and explain contributing factors. Encourage students to share their essays with the class.

Use with Lesson 1.2

Strategy ②
Explore the Effects of Advertising

Tell students to investigate how advertising affected consumers in the 1920s. They should include relevant data, using charts or graphs as necessary. Encourage students to use a Cause-and-Effect Chart to organize their notes and clarify the relationship between events. Convene students for a panel discussion in which they share information and draw conclusions.

Use with Lesson 2.1

ESSENTIAL QUESTION
What economic, political, and social changes
occurred in the United States after World War I?

AMERICAN
STORIES
ONLINE
The Roaring Twenties

SECTION 1 **Return to Normalcy**
KEY VOCABULARY

black market	fundamentalism	organized crime
bootlegging	immigration quota	speakeasy
dissident		

SECTION 2 **The Jazz Age**
KEY VOCABULARY

advertising	flapper	mass media
blues	improvise	newsreel
consumer	jazz	planned obsolescence
consumer economy	marketing	

SECTION 3 **The Harlem Renaissance**
KEY VOCABULARY

anthropologist	gospel music	renaissance

AMERICAN **GALLERY**
ONLINE
The Great Migration

READING STRATEGY

DRAW CONCLUSIONS

Drawing conclusions can help
you make judgments about what
you read. You analyze the facts,
make inferences and consider
your own experiences to decide
what those facts mean. Use a
graphic organizer to help you draw
conclusions about how the events
of the 1920s changed American
life and identity.

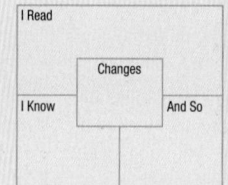

I Read

Changes

I Know   And So

"Here was a
new generation."

—F. Scott Fitzgerald,
from *This Side of Paradise*

CRITICAL VIEWING Marquees and billboards
flash as automobiles and streetcars drive
through Times Square in New York City
circa 1926. What details in this photo might
indicate changes in the American identity?

The Roaring Twenties 731

INTRODUCE THE PHOTOGRAPH

Times Square at Night

Direct students' attention to the photograph of
Times Square in New York City, circa 1926. Make
sure they understand that Times Square is a major
commercial, entertainment, and tourist hub. Explain
that at the time this photo was taken, for the first
time in U.S. history more Americans were living in
cities than on farms and leading faster-paced lives,
the middle class was expanding, and the rapid
growth of businesses and industries was making
some people very wealthy. Point out the quotation
from *This Side of Paradise*. Ask students to think
about and then discuss the possible connection
between the quotation and the photograph. Then
tell students that in this chapter they will learn about
the factors and events affecting the decade that
earned the nickname "the Roaring Twenties," an
era of high-spirited social freedoms that replaced
traditional standards and contributed to the
changing perception of American identity.

*For Chapter 22 Spanish Resources, visit the
Resources Menu. Chapter 22 Resources
are available at NGLSync.Cengage.com.*

Share Background

This Side of Paradise and *No, No, Nanette* are
examples of popular-culture perceptions of the
wealthy during the 1920s. The musical *No, No,
Nanette* focuses on the romantic exploits of Nanette,
who embraces the exuberant life of a flapper and
then later happily marries. The novel *This Side of
Paradise* takes a darker approach, centering on
Amory, an aimless, wealthy idler at Princeton who
enlists during World War I. Upon his return home, he
falls in love with a rich young woman. But when his
family fortune is lost, she breaks their engagement
and marries a wealthy man. Amory is alone at the
end, bewildered, lost, and also part of the "new
generation" called out by F. Scott Fitzgerald.

CRITICAL VIEWING Possible response: Theater
marquees suggest a market for entertainment, and
electrified advertising signs and the number of cars
parked along the street suggest that Americans
were interested in acquiring goods. How Americans
spent their free time and what they bought probably
influenced the reshaping of the American identity.

INTRODUCE THE ESSENTIAL QUESTION

What economic, political, and social changes occurred in the United States after World War I?

Three Corners Activity: United States During World War I

Label three corners of the room with one of the following: Social, Economic, Political. Divide the class into three groups and direct each group to a corner to discuss these questions:

Social: What social issues did Americans face during World War I? How might these issues be resolved following the war?

Economic: What issues affected the U.S. economy during World War I? How did the Allied victory immediately affect the U.S. economy?

Political: What might be the long-lasting effects of the propaganda campaign against Germany? How might Americans feel about foreign influences going forward?

Ask students to come to an agreement on the responses to their questions. Have each group read their questions and answers to the class. Record student answers and revisit them at the end of the chapter.

INTRODUCE CHAPTER VOCABULARY

Definition Chart

As students read the chapter, encourage them to complete a Definition Chart for Key Vocabulary words. Instruct students to list the Key Vocabulary words in the first column of their chart. Then, as they encounter each word in the chapter, tell them to write its definition in the center column and what the word means in the third column, using their own words. Model an example for students using the graphic organizer below.

Word	Definition	In My Own Words
consumer	person who buys goods or services	a customer or buyer

INTRODUCE THE READING STRATEGY

DRAW CONCLUSIONS

Remind students that drawing conclusions involves combining information that is stated directly and indirectly in a text with information that they already know to make a judgment. Work as a class to complete the graphic organizer for how one change that occurred during the 1920s transformed American life and identity. As you complete the And So section, remind students that this is the conclusion you have drawn.

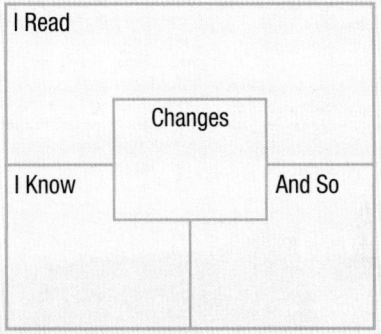

I Read

Changes

I Know   And So

KEY DATES FOR CHAPTER 22

1919	18th Amendment passed
1920	Warren G. Harding elected president
1921	Federal Highway Act
1921	Edith Wharton wins Pulitzer Prize for literature
1924	National Origins Act
1925	Alain Locke writes essay about African-American culture
1927	Scopes conviction upheld
1927	Sacco and Vanzetti executed
1927	First "talkie," *The Jazz Singer*, premieres
1929	Ernest Hemingway publishes *A Farewell to Arms*

AMERICAN STORIES ONLINE For instructional support for the online American Story "The Roaring Twenties," go to NGLSync.Cengage.com.

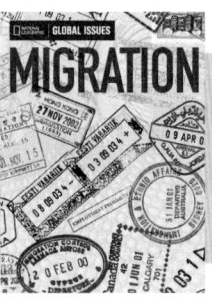

For more on immigration patterns, see *GLOBAL ISSUES: MIGRATION.*

1.1 Challenges After the War

After a tough day, you probably feel like retreating to your room and enjoying a little peace and quiet. After the suffering and hardships of World War I, most Americans wanted a return to "normalcy" and peace.

MAIN IDEA Exhausted by war, most Americans looked back with longing at the life they lived prior to World War I and hoped to return to that way of life.

THE RED SCARE

As you have read, during World War I, many Americans became increasingly suspicious of foreigners and radicals, or those who hold extreme political beliefs. These feelings were fueled largely by the federal government's propaganda campaigns promoting national pride during the war and by the Russian Revolution. After communists came to power in Russia, they were able to win a civil war within Russia, and they changed the country's name to the Union of Soviet Socialist Republics (U.S.S.R.), or the **Soviet Union.** In the United States, the end of World War I failed to disperse, or dissolve, the cloud of fear and resentment that had settled over the country.

In April 1919, a package exploded inside the home of a Georgia senator. In the following months, anarchists, people who advocate the absence of all government, mailed more bombs to prominent Americans around the country. Some bombs reached their destinations and blew windows out of houses. Some were discovered at post offices before they were detonated. Many Americans feared the bombings were part of a communist takeover plot. The incidents helped to trigger what came to be known as the **Red Scare**. Communists were called "reds" after the Soviet Red Army. The Red Scare characterized a period of near hysteria in the United States over the perceived threat from **dissidents**, people who strongly disagree politically, such as communists and anarchists.

The Election of 1920

Warren G. Harding (Republican)

Electoral Vote: 404 votes, 76%

Popular Vote: 16,151,916 votes, 60.3%

James M. Cox (Democrat)

Electoral Vote: 127 votes, 24%

Popular Vote: 9,134,074 votes, 34.1%

Eugene Debs and other candidates

Popular Vote: 1,482,467 votes, 5.6%

Socialist Eugene Debs and Parley Christensen, a Farm-Labor party candidate, won significant popular votes in Wisconsin, Minnesota, South Dakota, and Washington.

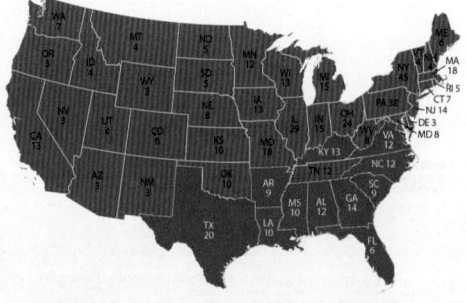

270 ELECTORAL VOTES NEEDED TO WIN

404		127
Electoral Vote: 404 votes, 76%		127 votes, 24%

60.3%	5.6%	34.1%
Popular Vote: 16,151,916 votes		9,134,074 votes

The Red Scare came to a climax in the **Palmer Raids** of late 1919 and early 1920. Under the direction of U.S. Attorney General **A. Mitchell Palmer**, federal, state, and local authorities conducted raids on numerous organizations to root out suspected communists, anarchists, and other radicals. Police officers arrested thousands of immigrants, some of whom were then deported. Many of the arrests were carried out without warrants and with little or no evidence that the individuals were traitors or that they had violent intentions.

HARDING'S ELECTION

Feelings of suspicion and alarm fostered by the Red Scare were part of a larger, more general fear felt by many Americans. Their familiar world had been torn apart by the war, and they feared it would be impossible to put it back together. The horrific accounts soldiers brought home from the war and the fear that such a conflict could happen again caused many Americans to worry that the world would never return to normal. Politicians strongly disagreed with each other, arguing over the League of Nations, the Russian Revolution, the unpopularity of President Wilson, and the collapse of the economy.

Building confidence that the United States would return to what it had been before the war became one of the biggest issues of the 1920 presidential campaign, which pitted Republican **Warren G. Harding** against Democrat James M. Cox. Harding's emphasis on a return to normality, or as he put it, "normalcy," struck a chord with Americans weary of fear, confusion, and disorder. Harding won the election by a landslide. But *normalcy* would be hard to define. The world was changing, and there would need to be a "new normal" going forward.

CRITICAL VIEWING This sheet music cover promoted Warren G. Harding's 1920 run for president during the first national election after World War I. What are the many patriotic symbols on the cover, and why do you think they were used in 1920?

HISTORICAL THINKING

1. **READING CHECK** Why were Americans so suspicious of foreigners and radicals after World War I?

2. **INTERPRET MAPS** What conclusions can you draw about political party loyalty in the United States by studying the electoral map of 1920?

3. **FORM AND SUPPORT OPINIONS** Do you think authorities who carried out the Palmer Raids went too far in their efforts to arrest suspected radicals? Support your response with evidence from the text.

PLAN

Objective

Analyze the rise of suspicion and fear in the United States after World War I.

Critical Thinking Skills for Lesson 1.1

- Identify Main Ideas and Details
- Monitor Comprehension
- Analyze Data
- Form and Support Opinions
- Draw Conclusions

Essential Question for Chapter 22

What economic, political, and social changes occurred in the United States after World War I? The end of World War I left many Americans with profound questions about the safety of their nation and way of life. Lesson 1.1 examines the rise of hysteria and backlash against foreigners and radicals in post-World War I United States.

Background for the Teacher

A. Mitchell Palmer did not start out as an opponent of civil rights. He was planning to run as a Democrat in the 1920 presidential race and wanted to establish himself firmly in the public consciousness. His prediction that a Bolshevik revolution would erupt in the United States in May 1920 foreshadowed his eponymous Palmer Raids. The raids began on November 7, 1919, when authorities descended on New York City's Union of Russian Workers and arrested 200 people. On December 21, nearly 250 radicals were arrested, among them the fiery anarchist Emma Goldman. Authorities deported many detainees to the Soviet Union. On January 2, raids in more than 30 U.S. cities rounded up thousands of suspects. The public eventually became disillusioned with Palmer and began to question his methods. When his prediction about a homegrown communist revolution came to nothing, support dwindled, bringing an end to his raids.

INTRODUCE & ENGAGE

Discuss Postwar Realities

Explain that Americans hoped that the end of World War I would mean an end to hardships and constant worries. Then remind students of, or ask them to volunteer, what they read about the uncertainties and difficulties that Americans experienced immediately following the war, such as high unemployment, inflation, strikes, the influenza epidemic, and, for many African-American soldiers and civilians, discrimination. Explain that the atmosphere in the United States would not improve for Americans as they had hoped. Then tell students that they will read about new fears and concerns that Americans would experience and how these concerns would affect the election of 1920.

TEACH

Guided Discussion

1. **Form and Support Opinions** How do you think the Palmer Raids affected how safe Americans felt? *(Possible response: The Palmer Raids resulted in the arrest of some suspected communists and anarchists, so some Americans likely felt safer from communism. Other Americans, however, may have been wary of the power wielded by Attorney General Palmer and felt less safe because some authorities violated peoples' constitutional rights.)*

2. **Draw Conclusions** Why are Eugene Debs and other independent candidates not represented on the electoral map? *(Although Debs and other independents together won more than 5 percent of the popular vote, none won any state's electoral votes.)*

More Information

The 1920 Presidential Campaign Warren G. Harding campaigned almost exclusively from the ornately designed and expansive front porch of his home in Marion, Ohio, drawing more than 500,000 visitors. James M. Cox and his running mate Franklin D. Roosevelt ran a barnstorming campaign, giving speeches in 36 states, largely throughout the North and Midwest. Campaigning in the "Solid South" was not a priority because it had voted Democratic since the end of the Civil War. The Democrats campaigned directly to the American people to find out, according to Roosevelt, "what the country is thinking." Harding already knew the answer to this question. His landslide win holds the record as the widest margin of victory in the history of U.S. presidential elections. **ASK:** What is it that Harding already knew? *(Possible response: Harding's campaign promised a return to "normalcy" because he knew many Americans were tired of feeling fearful and worried.)*

Active Options

On Your Feet: Numbered Heads Organize students into groups of four and give each member a number. Assign one of the following topics to each group: Red Scare, Palmer Raids, 1920 presidential election. Tell students to think about and discuss a response to this question: How does your group's topic demonstrate the fears and anxiety Americans were feeling after World War I? Then call a number and have the student from each group with that number report for the group. Ask groups with the same topic to report together.

NG Learning Framework: Create a Time Line

SKILL Communication

KNOWLEDGE Our Human Story

Encourage students to find out more about the troubled presidency of Warren G. Harding. After they gather information, tell them to create a time line of events that defined Harding's administration. Distribute sheets of chart paper so students can craft poster-sized time lines. Tell students to compose a brief paragraph comparing Harding's accomplishments in office with his campaign promise of a return to "normalcy" and to include the paragraph on their time lines. Ask for volunteers to share their work with the class.

DIFFERENTIATE

English Language Learners

Practice Synonyms Pair students at the **Emerging** level with students at the **Bridging** level. Instruct pairs to make a list of unfamiliar words they encounter as they read. Ask students at the **Bridging** level to write down two or three synonyms for each unfamiliar word listed. After pairs complete their lists, tell them to write one original sentence for each word they identified. If time allows, encourage pairs to share and compare their lists and sentences.

Gifted & Talented

Present an Oral Report Encourage students to conduct research to learn more about the election of 1920. Ask students to focus on a topic, such as a political candidate and his platform or campaign, an examination of the electoral vote, or divisions within the country based on regional or demographic differences. Tell students to compile information into a report that they can present orally to the class.

See the Chapter Planner for more strategies for differentiation.

HISTORICAL THINKING

ANSWERS

1. The federal government engaged in anti-German propaganda throughout the war, and radical socialists had come to power during the Russian Revolution. Mail bombings by anarchists added to Americans' fears of communism.

2. Southern states (except Tennessee) supported Cox, while all other states supported Harding. The country was clearly divided geographically over key issues.

3. Answers will vary. Possible response: The authorities went too far because they acted without warrants in some cases. Innocent immigrants were deported as a result of the Palmer Raids.

CRITICAL VIEWING Possible response: Patriotic symbols include the stars and stripes of the American flag, the American eagle, and the torch and wreath. Harding's campaign likely used these familiar symbols to appeal to Americans who were fearful of foreign influences and to reassure them of Harding's patriotism.

1.2 Prohibition

When someone tells you not to do something, do you then feel the urge to do it? That's what happened for many Americans during Prohibition. After being told they could not drink alcohol, they ignored the law and turned illegal drinking into a multimillion-dollar business.

MAIN IDEA After World War I, alcohol consumption became illegal, but anti-alcohol laws were difficult to enforce and came with unintended consequences.

THE 18TH AMENDMENT

You'll recall that anti-alcohol, or temperance, movements had been growing in the United States since the early 1800s. Women had led temperance efforts in an attempt to reduce domestic violence and abuse. Some states had banned the sale of alcohol, but members of the temperance movement sought to extend prohibition to a national level. In January 1919, they succeeded with the passage of the 18th Amendment.

The amendment prohibited the "manufacture, sale, or transportation of intoxicating liquors . . . for beverage purposes" throughout the United States. To enforce the amendment, Congress passed the **Volstead Act**, which created a new division within the Treasury Department to focus on executing the laws and gave federal agents the power to arrest violators. But enforcing Prohibition proved to be much more difficult than its advocates expected.

ENFORCING THE LAW

Although alcohol consumption decreased during Prohibition, many Americans still wanted to drink. Enforcement was spotty. In small towns and rural areas, where citizens supported the law, there was greater enforcement and obedience. But most of the people who lived in urban areas, especially the nation's largest cities, were opposed to Prohibition. As a result, urban enforcement of the law was weak, and people found creative ways to get around the Volstead Act.

Prohibition agents often wore plain clothes while searching for illegal alcohol. When they found it, they removed and disposed of the beverages. In this 1925 photo, agents empty bottles of whiskey into a sewer.

In many cities, **speakeasies**, or secret saloons and drinking halls, provided access to illegal alcohol. To enter a speakeasy, a patron had to know a special password and tell it to the guard at the door. Some speakeasies were hidden underground in basements or in tunnels, while others were concealed in hard-to-reach sections of shops and other legal businesses. Frequent police raids forced owners to change the locations of these speakeasies often.

In addition to selling alcoholic beverages, some speakeasies offered jazz music and dancing. These establishments were very popular. In one block on West 58th Street in New York City, for instance, a person could drink liquor in any of 39 clubs and speakeasies during Prohibition.

The reign of gangster Al Capone (left) came to its official end upon his conviction of tax evasion in 1931. U.S. Marshall Henry C. W. Laubenheimer (right) escorted Capone on the train that would take him to prison for his 11-year sentence.

The illegal manufacture and sale of alcohol, or **bootlegging**, was widespread. In coastal areas, rumrunners in small, fast boats dodged law enforcement to deliver alcohol from Canada or the Caribbean. Other bootleggers made their own alcohol and sold it on the **black market**, a system through which prohibited items are bought and sold illegally. Chief among these bootleggers was the crime boss of Chicago, **Al Capone**, whose income from illegal alcohol reached an estimated $60 million a year.

Capone had joined a New York gang in his youth. He followed another crime boss to Chicago, where he took charge of the operations for manufacturing and selling alcohol. Rumors claim he murdered anyone who challenged him. Capone ruled the world of Chicago gangsters from 1925 until 1931, when he was convicted on charges of income tax evasion and sentenced to prison. He was never charged with the other crimes he committed.

Prohibition did not create **organized crime**, planned illegal activities carried out by powerful leaders, but it did help strengthen it. During Prohibition, gangsters in one city frequently sought partners in other cities and states. However, the 1920s was not a decade of rising crime rates. Rather, awareness of crime as a social problem increased during Prohibition, due largely to the well-publicized activities of gangsters. One positive outcome of Prohibition was its influence in advancing recognition of alcoholism, the excessive consumption of alcoholic drinks, as a health issue. In addition, the rate of alcohol-induced diseases dropped during Prohibition and the years that followed. However, Americans realized that Prohibition was nearly impossible to enforce effectively. As the 1920s progressed, support for the 18th Amendment began to weaken.

HISTORICAL THINKING

1. **READING CHECK** What was Prohibition, and why did so many people support it?

2. **DRAW CONCLUSIONS** What specific factors made Prohibition so difficult to enforce?

3. **MAKE INFERENCES** Why do you think the U.S. government charged Al Capone with tax evasion rather than other crimes?

PLAN

Objective
Analyze the economic and social consequences of the 18th Amendment.

Critical Thinking Skills for Lesson 1.2
• Identify Main Ideas and Details
• Monitor Comprehension
• Draw Conclusions
• Make Inferences
• Analyze Cause and Effect

Essential Question for Chapter 22
What economic, political, and social changes occurred in the United States after World War I? In the aftermath of World War I, temperance leaders won their battle against the consumption of alcohol with the passage of the 18th Amendment. Lesson 1.2 discusses the social and economic effects of Prohibition in the United States.

Background for the Teacher

In spite of Prohibition, the manufacture, transport, and sale of alcohol continued, with Michigan playing a key role. The state of Michigan favored Prohibition long before the 18th Amendment went into effect because most Michiganders believed it would limit crime and bring families together. Not surprisingly, Michigan passed a statewide alcohol ban in 1916. Ironically, bootlegging developed almost immediately, with liquor coming from Ohio. When Ohio passed its own ban, smugglers turned to Canada, where liquor laws were more lax, and ferried liquor into Michigan via waterways. The main route ran from Windsor, Ontario, to Detroit, and in winter, bootleggers drove over the frozen Detroit River, pulling liquor-laden sleds behind their cars. By the time federal Prohibition began, smuggling was well under way. By some estimates, 75 percent of all alcohol smuggled into the United States during Prohibition arrived via the Detroit-Windsor Tunnel.

Preview Using Visuals

Direct students' attention to the photograph of the Prohibition agents and read the caption. **ASK:** In what way do the agents' actions appear symbolic? *(Possible response: Pouring confiscated liquor down the sewer equates liquor with sewage and was likely supposed to serve as a warning to both bootleggers and alcohol drinkers.)* Ask students to identify and discuss contemporary behaviors that are illegal yet commonplace, such as driving while texting or copyright infringement. Generate a discussion about why some illegal acts are prevalent in a culture. Then tell students that they will read about the reaction of Americans to the constitutional ban of alcohol in 1919.

TEACH

Guided Discussion

1. **Make Inferences** What attitudes might have accounted for the differences between urban and rural responses to Prohibition? *(Possible response: Urban areas, with diverse populations and attitudes, gave people easy and more socially acceptable access to alcohol—something they obviously wanted—as opposed to rural areas. There may have been an emphasis on religious teachings and conservative values in rural areas, and the consumption of alcohol may have been considered sinful to begin with.)*

2. **Analyze Cause and Effect** What lasting social changes did Prohibition bring to the public consciousness? *(Possible response: Prohibition brought greater public awareness of organized crime as a social threat and of alcoholism as both a health issue and a social problem.)*

More Information

Bootlegging The term *bootleg* dates back to the late 19th century, when midwestern settlers often used alcohol to trade with local Native American populations. The word reflected the common practice of people discreetly concealing bottles of alcohol in the opening of their boots. In the 1920s, bootlegging took on many forms, including purchase at drugstores. Using either a real or forged prescription, a person could buy "medicinal" whiskey from the drugstore to use for illegal resale.

Active Options

On Your Feet: Build a Paragraph Divide the class into three groups and provide each with the following topic sentence: Many Americans did not support the 18th Amendment. Tell each group to discuss the consequences of Prohibition and the reactions of American citizens and law enforcement to it. After students have had time to discuss, instruct groups to develop a complete paragraph in which each student supplies at least one sentence. Encourage groups to present their paragraphs with each group member reading his or her sentence aloud in the correct order.

NG Learning Framework: Research Organized Crime

ATTITUDE Curiosity

SKILL Collaboration

Organize the class into groups of four and tell each group to develop two questions that they would like answered about organized crime during Prohibition. Then tell groups to divide into two pairs who will each conduct research to answer one of the questions. Have each pair report their findings to the others in the group. Then ask group representatives to share their questions and answers with the class.

DIFFERENTIATE

English Language Learners ELD

Use Verb and Noun Forms Arrange students in mixed-proficiency pairs. Write *prohibit* and *prohibition* on the board. Explain that *prohibit* is a verb and that adding *-tion* creates the noun form. Provide students with similar verbs, such as *correct*, *pollute*, *attract*, *relate*, *operate*, and *construct*, and have them write the noun forms, guiding students in dropping the verb form's final *-e* as necessary. If time permits, direct students to work together to write an original sentence using each word in both the verb and noun form.

Pre-AP

Research and Write an Expository Essay Instruct students to conduct research using credible print and online sources to learn more about the goals of Prohibition advocates, positive and negative impacts of Prohibition, events following passage of the 18th Amendment, and the final outcome of Prohibition. Encourage students to use a Goal-and-Outcome graphic organizer as they prepare their notes and then write an expository essay about Prohibition. Invite students to share their essays with the class and answer their classmates' questions.

See the Chapter Planner for more strategies for differentiation.

HISTORICAL THINKING

ANSWERS

1. Prohibition, enacted by the 18th Amendment, made the manufacture, sale, or transportation of alcohol illegal. Those who supported Prohibition wanted to reduce domestic violence and abuse, which they saw as consequences of the consumption of alcohol.

2. Possible response: Enforcement of Prohibition was uneven because many people enjoyed drinking alcohol and found ways to obtain it through the black market and consume it privately.

3. Evidence of tax evasion was likely available through Capone's filing of fraudulent tax forms, or not filing at all, each being a federal offense. Evidence for other crimes he committed would have been difficult to obtain.

1.3 Social Conflicts

If you work hard and contribute to society, you expect to receive respect and equal treatment in return. During the 1920s, African Americans and immigrants did not receive such treatment.

MAIN IDEA In the 1920s, conflicts arose between Americans who embraced new ideas of society and those who held more traditional beliefs.

RACIAL TENSIONS

Earlier, you learned that the Great Migration brought millions of African Americans from the rural South to northern cities seeking greater equality and job opportunities. They did not face the same types of Jim Crow laws as they did in the South, but they still faced discrimination. Many had served the country during World War I. Now these African-American veterans did not have equal access to good jobs and homes. The riots of the summer of 1919 set the tone for continuing racial tensions throughout the 1920s.

In response to continued discrimination, **Marcus Garvey** formed the Universal Negro Improvement Association (UNIA), which promoted the establishment of a separate African-American society apart from the white-dominated mainstream. Born in Jamaica, Garvey immigrated to the United States in 1916. He formed the UNIA soon afterward, hoping to organize African Americans to return to Africa and settle a great nation there. He urged African Americans to be proud of their history and race.

By the middle of the 1920s, the UNIA had 700 branches in large northern cities and in the rural South, a newspaper, restaurants, factories, and grocery stores. Garvey never achieved his dreams of a separate society or an African homeland, but his efforts showed what African Americans could do if they worked together to build economic and political power.

As racial tensions rose, so did membership in the white supremacist Ku Klux Klan. The organization spread northward, particularly into the Midwest. By the early 1920s, about 4 million people had joined the organization and local chapters had been established throughout the United States. The 20th-century Klan did not target only African Americans, however. They also opposed and threatened immigrants, Catholics, Jews, and women.

IMMIGRATION RESTRICTIONS

The Klan's stance against immigrants mirrored a growing national sentiment. In 1921, Congress enacted **immigration quotas**, or limits, that capped the number of people arriving from Europe at 600,000 per year. Three years later, in 1924, the **National Origins Act** reduced annual legal immigration from Europe to about 150,000.

Religion vs. Science

In addition to contributing to the increasing distrust of immigrants, religious **fundamentalism**, or the strict belief in the literal truth of the Bible, rose in the 1920s in opposition to new scientific ideas. In the **Scopes trial**, science teacher John Scopes was accused of violating Tennessee law by teaching about the theory of evolution. The theory states that species, or types of living things, change over time.

The judge refused to let defense attorney Clarence Darrow bring scientists as witnesses. So Darrow questioned prosecutor William Jennings Bryan as a Bible expert. During the trial, Bryan became uncertain as he tried to explain his interpretation of the Bible. But the judge ordered Bryan's testimony to be struck from the record, and the jury convicted Scopes. The judge fined him $100. Although Scopes lost the trial, many Americans believed traditional religious values had lost to modern science. The decision has impacted the subjects students are allowed to learn in school.

The laws gave preference to northern Europeans and reduced quotas for southern and eastern Europeans, who were seen as "lacking the qualities" of successful American citizens. Many Americans feared the U.S. culture would be negatively impacted if too many foreigners were allowed into the country. Without basis, immigrants were viewed as likely to express radical views. All Asians, including the previously unrestricted Japanese, were denied entry. This damaged the relationship between the United States and Japan.

The **Sacco-Vanzetti case** illustrates the anti-immigrant attitude of the time. **Nicola Sacco** and **Bartolomeo Vanzetti** were Italian immigrants who had come to the United States in 1908. They were also anarchists. In 1921, they were arrested and accused of stealing the payroll at a Massachusetts shoe factory, killing a guard and a clerk in the process. Even though another man confessed to the crimes, a jury found Sacco and Vanzetti guilty. They were executed on August 23, 1927. Many believed the men had not received a fair trial because of their political beliefs and because they were immigrants.

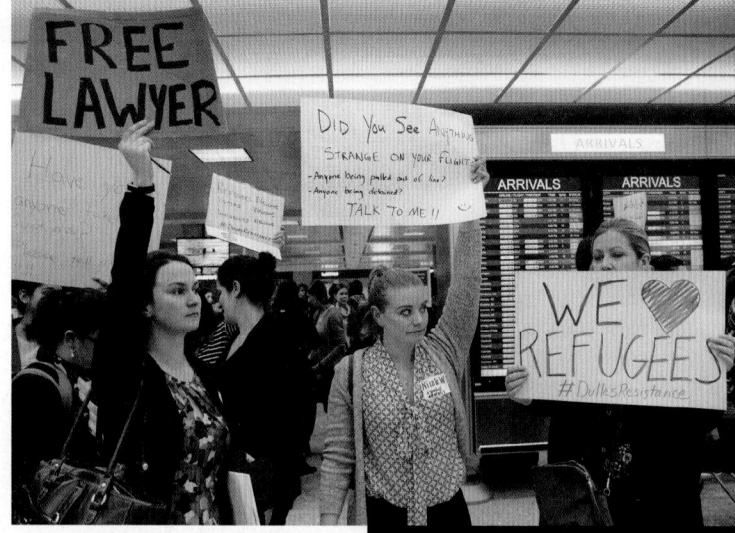

A GLOBAL PERSPECTIVE On January 27, 2017, President Donald Trump ordered that people from seven specified countries could not enter the United States. Hundreds of people were already in mid-flight from those countries to their U.S. destinations. Many were detained on arrival, causing confusion at airports. Lawyers went to airports to offer their services for free, hoping to help release people to go to their families and friends. What type of views do the lawyers shown above appear to have toward Trump's order?

HISTORICAL THINKING

1. **READING CHECK** What challenges did African Americans and immigrants face in the early 1920s?

2. **COMPARE AND CONTRAST** How were Marcus Garvey's solutions for the problem of racial discrimination different from those of other African Americans?

3. **DRAW CONCLUSIONS** Based on the evidence provided in the text, what conclusion can you draw about the verdict in the Sacco-Vanzetti case?

PLAN

Objective

Learn how racial discrimination and anti-immigration sentiment fueled tensions within American society in the 1920s.

Critical Thinking Skills for Lesson 1.3

- Identify Main Ideas and Details
- Monitor Comprehension
- Compare and Contrast
- Draw Conclusions
- Make Generalizations
- Make Inferences

Essential Question for Chapter 22

What economic, political, and social changes occurred in the United States after World War I? The growth of the Ku Klux Klan during the 1920s symbolized growing sentiment against African Americans, Catholics, Jews, and immigrants. Lesson 1.3 discusses the atmosphere of fear, anger, and suspicion in post-World War I America.

Background for the Teacher

At the trial of Sacco and Vanzetti, prosecutors focused on the men's immigrant status, anarchist views, and their avoidance of the draft during World War I, rather than present factual evidence of guilt. The men had not been identified at the time of the crime, and they weren't arrested until weeks later. At their arrest, both men were armed, but they had no link to violent crimes or the missing money. Sacco, however, had a handbill about an anarchist rally at which Vanzetti was planning to speak. After the two received death sentences, the system continued to work against them. Sacco and Vanzetti's lawyers repeatedly petitioned for a new hearing based on the lack of evidence against their clients, but the decision of whether to allow a new trial fell to the judge who had presided over the first trial. The judge turned down each new request, and legal protocol at the time did not allow the Supreme Court to intervene or reevaluate the evidence presented in criminal cases.

Create a Word Web

Write the term *civil rights* on the board and ask students to offer names, dates, words, and phrases they associate with it. Create a Word Web on the board to incorporate their suggestions. Explain to students that many people may think that civil rights activism took place only from the mid-1950s through 1968, but civil rights abuses in the United States have a long and continuing history. Tell students that in this lesson they will learn about how discrimination and restriction of civil rights affected the lives of many different groups during the 1920s.

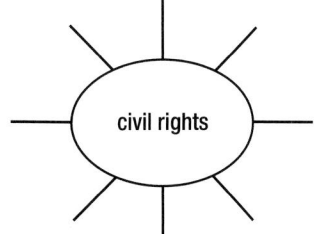

civil rights

TEACH

Guided Discussion

1. **Make Generalizations** What generalization can you make about why racial tensions did not improve even after Jim Crow laws were abolished? *(Possible response: African Americans, even those who fought during World War I, continued to be discriminated against because of fear, economic uncertainty, and long-established beliefs. Many African Americans were increasingly angry and frustrated when they experienced unfair treatment, particularly African-American veterans who were not treated with the same respect as other returning veterans.)*

2. **Make Inferences** Why do you think Clarence Darrow called the prosecuting attorney, his opponent, as a witness in the Scopes trial? *(Possible response: The judge would not allow Darrow to use scientists as witnesses, and Darrow knew that his opponent would not be able to argue effectively against evolution using only his interpretation of the Bible rather than logical, legal terms.)*

A Global Perspective

Explore the photograph and caption for this lesson with students. **ASK:** What connections do you see between the 2017 travel ban and the 1924 National Origins Act? *(Both sought to limit entry into the United States for people from specific parts of the world.)* **ASK:** What point might the lawyers be making in offering their services for free? *(Possible response: They are likely demonstrating the importance of protecting people from discrimination based solely on their nationality and that such a ban is not in keeping with American laws and values.)* Lead a class discussion about the 2017 travel ban, and ask students whether they think the ban reflected the overall attitude or mood of the country.

Active Options

On Your Feet: Question and Answer Divide the class into two teams and have each team create flash cards containing questions about Marcus Garvey, immigration quotas, or the Sacco-Vanzetti case. Tell team members to take turns calling on a member of the opposing team to answer a question. Direct students who answer incorrectly to sit down. When both teams have answered all the questions, the team with the most members left standing wins.

NG Learning Framework: Create a Data Graph

SKILL Observation

KNOWLEDGE Our Human Story

Encourage students to use current statistics on immigration to the United States to create a visual representation of the data. Direct students to conduct online research to locate information to create a pie chart, bar graph, or other graphic depiction that shows the most current estimates of the number of naturalized citizens, lawful permanent residents, temporary lawful residents, and unauthorized immigrants in the United States. Create a classroom gallery of students' completed graphs. Invite students to make statements about immigration based solely on the data represented in the graph.

DIFFERENTIATE

Striving Readers

Understand Main Ideas Check students' understanding of main ideas with either/or statements, such as the following:

• Marcus Garvey encouraged African Americans to [establish a homeland in Africa or stay in the United States] to have better lives. *(establish a homeland in Africa)*

• Immigration laws of the 1920s discriminated against [northern or southern] Europeans. *(southern)*

• A jury convicted John Scopes for teaching [fundamentalism or evolution] in a Tennessee classroom. *(evolution)*

Pre-AP

Analyze Immigration Policy Instruct students to research and report on the National Origins Act versus the 2017 ban on travelers from specific countries. Tell students to identify and analyze factors that influenced immigration policy in each era. Invite students to share their analyses with the class.

See the Chapter Planner for more strategies for differentiation.

HISTORICAL THINKING

ANSWERS

1. African Americans were discriminated against in housing, jobs, and justice and faced terror from the Ku Klux Klan. Immigrants were often treated with suspicion and faced prejudice as well.

2. Garvey thought that African Americans should separate from white society and create their own nation in Africa. Other African Americans believed they should integrate with white society or use protest and lawsuits to fight discrimination.

3. Possible response: The guilty verdict was shaped by prejudice rather than a desire for justice. A man confessed to the crime, so Sacco and Vanzetti should have been freed. Instead, they were found guilty based on their ethnicity and political beliefs.

A GLOBAL PERSPECTIVE The signs alert banned travelers that the lawyers want to help them, so the lawyers appear to oppose Trump's order. One sign reads "#DullesResistance," overtly defying the order. Even if the lawyers support Trump's order, they likely want to make sure that the travelers' rights are not violated.

2.1 The Consumer Economy

You probably don't give much thought to the colorful images on TV or on the Internet that tempt you to buy things. But in the 1920s, such messages, conveyed through print and the radio, were new to Americans.

MAIN IDEA In the 1920s, consumer spending and new technologies helped build a prosperous economy.

NEW TECHNOLOGIES

The technological advances of the 1920s changed people's lives. Americans could purchase an increasing variety of household appliances and labor-saving gadgets, such as washing machines and vacuum cleaners. Before these appliances were available, people had to hand wash dishes, scrub floors and rugs on their hands and knees, and have blocks of ice delivered regularly to their homes to keep their food cold inside ice boxes.

To make sure people knew about and wanted to buy these products, a booming advertising industry arose in the 1920s. **Advertising** is the act of presenting products and ideas to the public. Advertising is an important part of **marketing**, which is the process of promoting products or services. Companies hired marketers to determine the best way to reach specific groups of **consumers**, or those who might buy their products. They then used advertising to attract consumers and persuade them to buy. For example, Ford marketed the Model T automobile to the middle class by placing targeted advertisements in the mass media that middle-class people listened to and read. **Mass media** refers to sources of information and entertainment, such as publications, radio, and movies, meant to reach a large group of people at once.

The result of the combination of available goods, consumers, and advertising was a new **consumer economy**, an economy in which people have many choices about what to buy and in which they make purchases often. Soon consumers faced more purchasing decisions than ever before. And since the newest appliance or automobile was expensive, average consumers needed a way to

afford these items. In response, companies offered consumers the option to buy on credit, or to put a little money down and pay the rest over time.

One result of the consumer economy was that by 1927, there were more than 20 million cars on the roads. Additionally, there were more than 3 million trucks and buses. The Federal Highway Act of 1921 left road construction to the states, but it set national standards for concrete road surfaces and smaller roads to access the highways. The size of the American road network grew from 7,000 miles at the end of World War I to 50,000 miles in 1927. Gasoline taxes brought in revenues for the states, enabling them to build more roads. This led to the continued development of areas outside of the old city centers and to the greater need for consumers to buy cars to travel those distances.

SELLING A DREAM

Soon companies weren't just selling cars and household products. They were selling the idea of the American dream. At a 1923 advertising convention, speaker Helen Landon Cass advised, "Sell them their dreams. Sell them what they longed for and hoped for and almost despaired of having. After all, people . . . buy *hope*—hope of what your merchandise will do for them. Sell them this hope and you won't have to worry about selling them goods."

Women were recognized as critical members of the new consumer society. Typical advertisements for household products presented the ideal American housewife: a stylishly dressed manager of the home with plenty of leisure time and a spotless house. Brightly colored graphics caught the consumer's eye, while photographs

A full-page magazine ad boasts of the many benefits of Old Dutch cleanser. The ad appeals to the female consumer who wants to protect her family's health and save time: Old Dutch "cleans quicker" for a beautifully polished bathtub and washstand. Products like the soap Boraxine (below) came wrapped in eye-catching designs.

defined the modern, affluent American family and home. Such strategies reinforced the idea that a truly modern consumer would buy whatever the advertisement was selling, at any cost.

Advertising had another message. To stay ahead of the crowd, consumers had to replace some of the things they owned with the latest versions. This idea, which would later come to be called **planned obsolescence**, aimed at convincing consumers not to wait until an item was broken or worn out to purchase a new one. They needed to replace it when it was out of style. Buying on credit made it possible to replace previous purchases—up to a point. But advertising conveyed the message that if consumers could not afford to replace an item with cash on hand, they not only could, but should, purchase it on credit.

HISTORICAL THINKING

1. **READING CHECK** How did advertising change American culture in the 1920s?

2. **DRAW CONCLUSIONS** Why did advertisers try to persuade consumers to replace items even if they weren't broken or worn out?

3. **IDENTIFY MAIN IDEAS AND DETAILS** What factors drove the 1920s consumer economy?

PLAN

Objective

Analyze how marketing and mass media in the United States created a consumer economy.

Critical Thinking Skills for Lesson 2.1

• Identify Main Ideas and Details

• Monitor Comprehension

• Draw Conclusions

• Analyze Cause and Effect

• Analyze Visuals

Essential Question for Chapter 22

What economic, political, and social changes occurred in the United States after World War I? The 1920s introduced new products that were supposed to make Americans' lives better. Lesson 2.1 discusses how advertising connected the accumulation of products with the American dream.

Background for the Teacher

Advertising has been around almost since the development of printing, but advertising agencies came of age in the early 20th century. Advertising agencies of the 19th century focused only on positioning clients' ads in a single newspaper. In the 1920s, advertising agencies became full-service providers. A typical agency's campaign included product and marketing research, advertising slogans, ad copy and artwork development, and placement within a wide array of newspapers and magazines.

Financial Literacy

To extend their knowledge and understanding about the concepts in this lesson, refer students to the Financial Literacy handbook.

History Notebook

Encourage students to complete the Reid on the Road video series page for Chapter 22 in their History Notebooks after they view the video.

Discuss Slogans and Jingles

Ask students to volunteer slogans or jingles related to products they are familiar with, such as soft drinks, clothing, snack foods, or technology. **ASK:** Why do you think you remember these slogans and jingles? *(Possible response: It's easy to remember them because they're built around catchy tunes, rhymes, or unique taglines.)* **ASK:** What is the purpose of advertising? *(The purpose is to create messaging that makes consumers want to buy products or services.)* Guide a discussion about how students think advertising influences their buying behavior and that of present-day Americans. Then tell students that Lesson 2.1 introduces them to the expansion of advertising in the 1920s.

TEACH
Guided Discussion

1. **Analyze Cause and Effect** What future consequences might have been caused by the development of areas beyond city centers in the 1920s? *(Possible response: Development of areas beyond city centers probably led to the increased demand for and manufacture of cars. Decades later, clogged highways and pollution from car exhaust became a problem.)*

2. **Analyze Visuals** How does the appearance of the woman and child in the advertisement for Old Dutch Cleanser contribute to its overall effectiveness? *(Possible response: The mother and child appear clean, healthy, and, most importantly, happy, which is meant to create a warm, positive association in consumers' minds.)*

More Information

Radio Advertising In 1922, AT&T set up radio station WEAF to use as a toll broadcaster, meaning anyone wanting time to broadcast from the station had to pay to do so. For months there were no takers, but finally a few companies signed on. The first radio ad promoted apartments for sale in Queens, a borough of New York City. The ad proved successful, with the sale of a few apartments resulting. Before the year was out, WEAF had signed up 25 advertisers, including big names like Macy's and Metropolitan Insurance. Soon advertisers became the main funding source for radio content.

Active Options

On Your Feet: Fishbowl Divide the class in half and have one half sit in a small circle, facing inward, and the other half sit in a larger circle around them. Pose the question: How has the mass media environment changed from the 1920s to the present day? Prompt students in the inner circle to discuss this question while those in the outer circle listen and take notes to evaluate the points made. Then have groups reverse roles and continue the discussion.

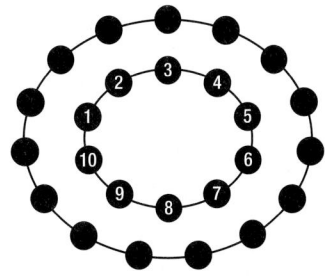

NG Learning Framework: Explore Planned Obsolescence

SKILL Collaboration

KNOWLEDGE Our Human Story

Encourage students to explore the impact of planned obsolescence and how it might be a factor in some of the products they use today. Ask students to work individually to research the planned obsolescence of such products as smartphones, music players, or tablets. Then invite groups of students to discuss the issue together and take notes. Finally, encourage groups to use their notes to present roundtable discussions on the issue for the class.

Striving Readers

Summarize Place students in pairs. Assign them one or two paragraphs to read together and summarize in one or two sentences. When all pairs are finished, have them read their summaries aloud in the order in which the material appears in the lesson.

Gifted & Talented

Present Information Graphically Bring students' attention to the paragraph about the number of cars and miles of roads in the 1920s. Challenge students to convey the information in this paragraph graphically. They could choose a simple chart or graph format, or they might create a more involved infographic. Encourage students to research additional relevant information to make their graphics more robust. Invite students to display their graphics and answer classmates' questions.

See the Chapter Planner for more strategies for differentiation.

HISTORICAL THINKING

ANSWERS

1. Advertising in the 1920s encouraged consumers to buy more products, which led to the development of a consumer economy and buying on credit.

2. Selling products was the key to success for advertisers' businesses. They needed to find a way to give consumers an urgent reason for buying a new item rather than fixing the old one. Manufacturers produced new styles and versions of their products, and advertisers convinced consumers of the importance of having the latest versions, even if they had to buy them on credit.

3. The rise of mass media and advertising, the practice of buying on credit, and new technologies that produced more consumer goods all drove the 1920s consumer economy.

2.2 Mass Culture

In the 1920s, the idea of a "celebrity" arose. Technology had made it possible for an actor, an athlete, a novelist, a pilot, or a wealthy businessperson, to be known by almost everyone in a very short time.

MAIN IDEA In the 1920s, radio and the movies changed the way that people got their information and entertainment.

CRITICAL VIEWING Charlie Chaplin didn't only star in films. He also wrote, directed, and produced them. He obtained the industry's first million-dollar contract. In *A Dog's Life* (1918), the first film he made under that contract, Chaplin plays a homeless man who rescues a dog, finds a wallet of money that some shady characters have gotten dishonestly and buried, and begins a romance with a lonely singer. What does this poster convey about the film?

UNIFYING AMERICAN CULTURE

One of the most influential new technologies of the 1920s was the radio, which became a fixture in almost every American home. By 1922, there were more than 500 radio stations in the United States. Radio played an important role in the development of mass media and advertising, as many radio programs were sponsored, or paid for, by companies that aired commercials to sell goods and services during broadcasts.

Technology also had a great impact on the movie industry. Motion picture projectors were originally developed in the early 1890s, and at first, all movies were silent. Musicians in the theater played as the film rolled, providing background music and sound effects. The film's dialogue appeared on title cards inserted between action scenes. Actors conveyed emotions with facial expressions and exaggerated movements.

Throughout the 1920s, filmmakers experimented with aligning film and sound so they occurred at the same time. At first, the technology was crude and unreliable, but in 1927, Warner Brothers studio released *The Jazz Singer*, a feature film with scenes that contained synchronized sound, or sound that aligned with the words and action in the film. Now audiences could hear the actors speak and sing.

Once the movie industry developed synchronized sound, movie fans packed the theaters to see these new "talkies." By the end of the decade, more than 80 million people went to the movies each week—more than double the number in 1922. As Americans started listening to the same popular radio programs and watching the same hit movies, a mass culture, or similar worldview based on shared experience, began to emerge.

AN ERA OF CELEBRITIES

Mass culture made it possible for athletes, entertainers, and other people of note to become celebrities. Movie actors such as **Charlie Chaplin**, Gloria Swanson, Louise Brooks, and Buster Keaton became world famous, as did the characters they played in the movies. Chaplin, **Mary Pickford**—one of the biggest stars of the 1920s—her husband, actor Douglas Fairbanks, and director D. W. Griffith started their own film company, United Artists. They sought to give actors and directors more artistic control than did the studio system, where actors were simply assigned to their films by studio bosses.

Mass culture also spread through short news and sports films that played before feature films. Called **newsreels**, they helped make heroes out of athletes such as Babe Ruth, the New York Yankee who is considered by many to be the greatest baseball player of that era, and Olympic swimming star Gertrude Ederle, who became the first woman to swim across the English Channel. Johnny Weissmuller, who won five gold medals at the 1924 and 1928 Olympics, was such a popular sports hero that he was offered the lead role as Tarzan in a Hollywood film, even though he had very little acting experience.

Aviation was also a new and exciting pursuit, and newsreels and other mass media promoted the adventures of daredevil pilots such as **Charles Lindbergh** and **Amelia Earhart**. Lindbergh was the first person to fly solo nonstop across the Atlantic Ocean. Earhart was the first person to fly across both the Atlantic and Pacific oceans, before she disappeared while attempting to circumnavigate, or travel completely around, the world.

National Baseball Hall of Fame and Museum, Cooperstown, New York

Before halls of fame for other sports began opening in the 1950s, the Baseball Hall of Fame was known simply as the "Hall of Fame," recognizing the sport as the one national pastime. New York Yankee outfielder George Herman "Babe" Ruth was one of the first five players inducted into the museum when it opened in 1936. "The Bambino," as Ruth was called—Italian for "baby"—was more than his overwhelming batting statistics. Sportswriters said that to understand Babe's effect on his fans, you had to see him play. His home runs went higher and farther than anyone else's, and he swung with a unique kind of drama. This photo from the 1930s, along with Ruth's Louisville Slugger bat, shown below, are on display at the Baseball Hall of Fame.

HISTORICAL THINKING

1. **READING CHECK** How did mass culture shape American identity in the 1920s?

2. **MAKE INFERENCES** Why do you think movie attendance increased so much by the end of the 1920s?

3. **ANALYZE CAUSE AND EFFECT** How did newsreels make celebrities out of people like Babe Ruth and Amelia Earhart?

PLAN

Objective

Analyze how communications technology contributed to a mass culture in the 1920s.

Critical Thinking Skills for Lesson 2.2

- Identify Main Ideas and Details
- Monitor Comprehension
- Make Inferences
- Analyze Cause and Effect
- Compare and Contrast
- Make Connections

Essential Question for Chapter 22

What economic, political, and social changes occurred in the United States after World War I? Radio and film, as means of entertainment for Americans, contributed to the creation of a mass culture. Lesson 2.2 discusses how this mass culture emerged and how it embraced figures in entertainment, sports, and aviation.

Background for the Teacher

The success of *The Jazz Singer* seems to have rested squarely on its inclusion of synchronized dialogue. For more than 30 years, film studios had been trying, without much success, to effectively synchronize moving pictures with sound. In 1925, Bell Labs launched the Vitaphone system, a new technology that used a single motor to power both the film projector and a turntable containing the soundtrack. The Vitaphone also featured state-of-the-art sound recording that theaters could play through newly developed loudspeakers. When *The Jazz Singer* was released, it featured only two minutes of dialogue; the rest was music and sound effects. Even so, audiences were instantly hooked. Despite lackluster critical reviews that dismissed *The Jazz Singer* as overly sentimental, the film, produced by Warner Brothers for $422,000, earned more than three times that amount by 1931, a massive profit.

INTRODUCE & ENGAGE

Preview Using Visuals

To introduce the power of media in mass culture, show photographs of a few currently popular film, television, music, and sports stars, and ask students to identify them. **ASK:** How did these people become so well known to the public? *(Possible response: Millions of people know about them because of their exposure on media platforms and on film, television, and the Internet.)* Ask students to name celebrities who interest them. Then lead a discussion in which students assess common factors that contribute to the celebrity status of the individuals they named.

TEACH

Guided Discussion

1. **Compare and Contrast** How do present-day forms of mass media compare with mass media of the 1920s? *(Possible response: The 1920s pioneered radio programs and film, media in which audiences were passive listeners or viewers. Present-day media includes online social platforms, cable and satellite television and radio, and on-demand access to films and programs, all of which require people to become more actively involved in their forms of entertainment than just buying a ticket or turning a channel. With social media especially, fans can interact with celebrities in the form of feedback and comments.)*

2. **Make Connections** How did synchronized sound contribute to the development of a mass culture in the United States? *(Possible response: People loved talkies, and attendance at movie theaters soared. As huge numbers of people watched the same movies all across the United States, they became familiar with images and story lines that collectively shaped many of their likes and dislikes.)*

Virtual Museum Visit

The National Baseball Hall of Fame and Museum opened its doors in 1939 to honor the game and the players who played it best. The museum's multimedia collection features video and audio installations, interactive computer displays, and many artifacts from the history of baseball. Access the museum's website, display the virtual tour, and find the Babe Ruth exhibit. Have students read the text and view the artifacts on display. Encourage small groups of students to explore the exhibit and create time lines of Ruth's life and career. Display students' completed time lines in the classroom.

Active Options

Active History: Analyze Primary Sources Extend the lesson by using either the PDF or Whiteboard version of the activity. These activities take a deeper look at a topic from, or related to, the lesson. Explore the activities as a class, turn them into group assignments, or even assign them individually.

NG Learning Framework: Compose a Radio News Story

| ATTITUDE | Curiosity |
| KNOWLEDGE | Our Human Story |

Direct students to learn more about the celebrity aviator Amelia Earhart. Instruct them to use a variety of resources to research Earhart's career and disappearance. Then tell students to write an original radio news story about Earhart's final flight. Invite students to read their news stories to the class or record them for individual playback.

DIFFERENTIATE

English Language Learners ELD

Create a Word Web Pair students at the **Emerging** and **Expanding** levels with students at the **Bridging** level and direct them to create a Word Web for the term *mass culture*. Tell students to reread the lesson, note words and terms that refer to mass culture, and write them on the spokes of the Word Web. Invite pairs to trade and compare their webs.

Gifted & Talented

Create a Multimedia Presentation Have students research the mass media technologies introduced in the 1920s. Then tell them to create a multimedia presentation about one technology to explain how it has affected American culture over time. Encourage students to use photographs, news headlines, audio and video clips, and other media to enhance their presentation. Invite students to share their presentation with the class.

See the Chapter Planner for more strategies for differentiation.

HISTORICAL THINKING

ANSWERS

1. Media, such as radio, film, and newsreels, brought entertainment and news about individuals' exceptional achievements to Americans across the country. Americans with diverse backgrounds began to identify with a collective set of values about society and success.

2. Audiences enjoyed "talkies" more than they did silent films. Viewers likely enjoyed hearing actors convey emotion in their speech rather than watching them portray emotions through exaggerated facial expressions and gestures.

3. Movie theaters showed audiences newsreels before a film began. The newsreels promoted the feats of sports stars and adventurers, such as Babe Ruth and pilot Amelia Earhart, and made them appear glamorous to audiences, who in turn developed a keen interest in them.

CRITICAL VIEWING Possible response: It conveys that Charlie Chaplin stars in *A Dog's Life* and that the movie studio has spent $1 million on the film. "The One and Only" conveys the star power of Charlie Chaplin.

2.3 All That Jazz

Do you listen to the music your parents listened to at your age? Probably not! As times change, music, literature, and art change as well. An exciting new form of music emerged in the 1920s, shaping the culture of that decade.

MAIN IDEA In the 1920s, a unique form of African-American music grew in popularity in the United States and Europe.

A NEW KIND OF MUSIC

The music that came to be called **jazz** began with African-American musicians in New Orleans. Jazz grew out of a number of musical styles and has fast-paced, interacting rhythms. Jazz musicians use a variety of instruments to create the sound unique to this form of music. They also **improvise**, or create and play music without rehearsing, often inventing musical styles as they play.

From its beginnings, jazz brought together black and white musicians. Though very few jazz bands of the time allowed musicians of different races to play together in public, in private they improvised together and shared techniques as they learned

this new form of music. Jazz spread northward from New Orleans to St. Louis, Kansas City, Chicago, and New York. Thanks to record players and radio, jazz quickly spread from coast to coast in the United States and to parts of Europe, especially Britain and France. With its lively rhythms and innovative sounds, jazz appealed to a younger, modern audience. It also defined the 1920s as the Jazz Age.

One of the leading early jazz musicians was **Louis** (LOO-ee) **Armstrong**. A jazz trumpeter and singer from New Orleans, Armstrong influenced and played with many musicians. One such musician was a native of Washington, D.C., **Duke Ellington.**

Singer Ma Rainey toured with her Georgia Jazz Band and recorded with Louis Armstrong, playing trumpet in this photo.

Ellington started out as a piano player at age 17. He went on to pioneer the "big-band" jazz sound that became extremely popular in the 1940s.

The popularity of jazz also helped increase the appeal of the **blues**, another African-American genre, or form, of music. Unlike upbeat jazz music, blues songs are usually about hard times. Jazz and blues singer **Gertrude "Ma" Rainey** often drew upon heartache in her own life when she sang and in lyrics she created. In tracing the history of the blues, music historians cite her as a bridge from early African-American folk music and vaudeville to the blues. Hailed as the "Mother of the Blues," Rainey and her Georgia Jazz Band performed blues and jazz music to sellout crowds in the 1920s. Rainey discovered **Bessie Smith**, a young blues artist who sang with Rainey and one of her bands. Smith became known as "Empress of the Blues" and was the highest paid African-American performer by the end of the 1920s.

LITERATURE OF THE JAZZ AGE

The Jazz Age was also a time of experimentation and achievement in literature. Two of the most popular authors in the 1920s were **F. Scott Fitzgerald** and **Ernest Hemingway**. Fitzgerald published his most famous novel, *The Great Gatsby*, in 1925. It's the story of Jay Gatsby, a troubled young man whose wealth came from bootlegging. The novel gives readers a glimpse into the lives of people caught up in the Jazz Age, including the music, parties, and excesses of the time.

Ernest Hemingway served as an ambulance driver in World War I, which greatly influenced his work. In his bestselling novels *The Sun Also Rises* (1926) and *A Farewell to Arms* (1929), Hemingway wrote about how the war affected Americans and others who had fought in it. Hemingway wrote in short, plain sentences—an innovative writing technique for which he became famous.

Women authors also gained popularity during the 1920s. **Willa Cather** grew up in Nebraska. Her frontier childhood on the Nebraska prairies influenced many of her novels, including *O Pioneers!* (1913) and *My Ántonia* (1918). **Edith Wharton** began her writing career as a poet, but she also wrote short stories, plays, and novels. In 1921, Wharton became the first woman to win the Pulitzer Prize for her novel *The Age of Innocence*.

A New Kind of Woman
American women gained more rights and freedoms in the 1920s, including the right to vote. Many young women also embraced new social freedoms. Called **flappers** by the media, they expressed the same spontaneity that jazz did, but through fashion and dance. They wore bobbed hair and a freer, shorter style of dress. The flapper in this photo is dancing to music played by the jazz band in the background.

HISTORICAL THINKING

1. **READING CHECK** What kinds of music and literature became popular in the 1920s?

2. **COMPARE AND CONTRAST** How did women's lives change in the 1920s from what they were before World War I?

3. **DRAW CONCLUSIONS** Why do you think the 1920s became known as the Jazz Age? Support your response with text evidence.

PLAN

Objective
Discuss the rise of uniquely American art forms in the 1920s.

Critical Thinking Skills for Lesson 2.3

- Identify Main Ideas and Details
- Monitor Comprehension
- Compare and Contrast
- Draw Conclusions
- Make Generalizations
- Describe
- Make Inferences

Essential Question for Chapter 22
What economic, political, and social changes occurred in the United States after World War I? The 1920s were a time of experimentation and innovation in the arts. Lesson 2.3 discusses musical and literary luminaries who shaped the Jazz Age.

Background for the Teacher
Jazz spread to Europe quickly and became a permanent fixture in music scenes. In Britain, records, radio programs, and the music industry publication *Melody Maker* introduced jazz to a public who embraced it enthusiastically. British jazz bands soon appeared, copying jazz rhythms from recordings. The French had become enthralled by the syncopated music of renowned African-American bandleader and composer James Reese Europe and his 369th Infantry band. The band's music is acknowledged as the precursor to jazz. In 1918, the band performed in several French cities. Already fascinated by Europe and his band's music, the French were captivated by jazz itself. In Germany, economic hardships following World War I delayed jazz's popularity, but by 1925, Berlin's music scene had placed jazz at its center.

History Notebook
Encourage students to complete the Reid on the Road video series page for Chapter 22 in their History Notebooks after they view the video.

Preview Vocabulary

Write the word *improvise* on the board. **ASK:** What do you think it means to improvise? *(Possible response: To improvise is to create or use something without planning or thinking about it ahead of time.)* **ASK:** In what situations might people find they need to improvise? *(Possible response: Actors sometimes improvise their lines; if you're making something and you don't have the right materials, you might come up with a substitute.)* Write students' responses underneath the word. After reading the lesson, return to students' responses. **ASK:** Why is the word *improvise* appropriate when discussing the Jazz Age? *(Possible response: To improvise implies trying something new and taking a risk, which also describes the spirit of the Jazz Age.)*

TEACH

Guided Discussion

1. **Make Generalizations** In what ways did Ma Rainey and Ernest Hemingway promote the spirit of the Jazz Age? *(The Jazz Age was a time of great artistic experimentation. Rainey popularized the African-American blues by bringing it to a new, wider audience. Hemingway's individual writing style, using short sentences and direct language, probably sounded straightforward and fresh to readers.)*

2. **Describe** How would you define and describe jazz to a friend? *(Possible response: Jazz is a combination of musical styles that uses several different instruments and alternating rhythms. Jazz is often created by the musicians spontaneously as they perform.)*

Make Inferences

Remind students that Prohibition was in effect during the Jazz Age. **ASK:** What role do you think Prohibition might have played during the Jazz Age? *(The Jazz Age was a time of taking risks in the arts and society, reflecting a general willingness to break rules, including rules prohibiting the sale and consumption of alcohol.)*

Active Options

On Your Feet: Team Questions Assign students to four teams and place each team in a different corner of the room. Tell each team to come up with four questions about the impact of the Jazz Age in the United States. Begin the discussion by having Team One ask Team Two one of its prepared questions. When Team One is satisfied with a correct answer, tell Team Two to call on Team Three to ask one of its prepared questions. Continue until all teams have asked all their questions.

NG Learning Framework: Learn a 1920s Dance Step

ATTITUDE Curiosity

SKILL Collaboration

Explain that the music of the Jazz Age inspired the invention of several new dance steps, including the Charleston and shimmy. Instruct pairs of students to search online for videos about how to perform different 1920s dances and to choose one that interests them. Allow students time to learn and rehearse the steps, using music appropriate for accompaniment. Invite volunteers to perform their Jazz Age dance for the class.

Inclusion

Use Clarifying Questions Pair special needs students with students who can read the lesson aloud and describe the photographs. Instruct students to ask clarifying questions and for their partners to provide answers and explanations, including vivid details about the clothing, hairstyles, and facial expressions of the performers in the photographs. Instruct pairs to discuss how the details in the lesson convey the social and cultural changes taking place during the Jazz Age. Then have pairs work together to answer the Historical Thinking questions.

Pre-AP

Connect History and Literature Ask students to select one of the titles mentioned in the text and conduct research to explain how the work connects to the idea of experimentation or achievement in literature. Instruct them to construct a clear topic sentence and to provide specific examples for support. Invite students to share their essays with the class.

See the Chapter Planner for more strategies for differentiation.

HISTORICAL THINKING

ANSWERS

1. Jazz and blues music became popular, as did literature from female writers and literature that reflected the effect of World War I on the lives of Americans.

2. Women gained the right to vote, female musicians and authors gained recognition, and women's hairstyles and fashions became freer and less restrictive.

3. Possible response: Jazz was a uniquely American form of music. It was sometimes improvised, which reflected the new freedoms and spontaneity of American life in the 1920s.

2.4 The National Jazz Museum in Harlem, New York City

The National Jazz Museum in Harlem is a place that stimulates hearts and minds through music. Founded in 1997, its mission is "to preserve, promote, and present jazz by inspiring knowledge, appreciation, and the celebration of jazz music locally, nationally, and internationally."

The museum achieves its mission by reaching out to diverse audiences. Its staff organizes free music education programs, hosts live performances, and presents exhibitions of musical recordings and instruments so people around the world can enjoy this uniquely American music.

"Jelly Roll's Jazz" Album
Born in 1890 in New Orleans, Jelly Roll Morton was an African-American jazz pianist and composer. Morton helped the New Orleans music scene move from the earliest forms of jazz to jazz played with an orchestra. In the 1920s and early 1930s, Morton recorded many national hits with his band, Morton's Red Hot Peppers.

In 1951, 10 years after Morton's death, the Lawson-Haggart Band paid tribute to Morton by recording some of his most famous original compositions, such as "King Porter Stomp," "Dead Man Blues," and "Kansas City Stomp," on an album called "Jelly Roll's Jazz."

"Charlie Parker with Strings" Album
Charlie "Yardbird" Parker was one of the most important and influential saxophonists and jazz players of the 1940s. His impressive career as a musician revoled around jazz-infused cities such as Kansas City, Chicago, and New York.

The album "Charlie Parker with Strings" includes recordings from the late 1940s and early 1950s. The songs feature Parker with a small group of stringed instruments and a jazz rhythm section instead of the bebop quintet with whom he typically performed and recorded.

Duke Ellington's Baby Grand
African-American pianist Duke Ellington is considered to be the greatest jazz composer and bandleader. After beginning his musical career at the age of 17, Ellington went on to compose thousands of musical scores and lead a jazz orchestra for over 50 years.

During his long career, Ellington also wrote music for movies and composed pieces for the ballet and theatre. At the height of the civil rights movement, Ellington composed the score for the 1964 show *My People*, a celebration of African-American life.

Ellington's distinctive white baby grand piano was on exhibit in the National Jazz Museum in Harlem. In 2016, several of Ellington's personal artifacts, including the piano and sheet music, were put up for auction at the museum. Photos of the collection still remain on-site.

What other instruments are commonly used by jazz musicians? Conduct online research and explore the museum's website to find out.

Charlie Parker's Saxophone
Saxophones come in many sizes. Charlie Parker played an alto sax, which is smaller than its cousin, the tenor sax. Musicians can play the same music with both instruments, but the size difference makes the voice of an alto sax naturally higher than the voice of a tenor sax. Parker used this alto sax (left) to record such hits as "Ornithology" (1946) and "Out of Nowhere" (1947).

WANN Radio Station Microphone
In 1948, WDIA in Memphis, Tennessee, became the first radio station to feature only African-American announcers. Soon, more radio stations dedicated to African-American listeners began to emerge, including WANN in Baltimore, Maryland. These stations reached the growing black, middle-class population with music and advertising.

Legendary disc jockey Hoppy Adams joined WANN founder Morris Blum in 1953 and together, they used the station's airwaves for more than just music. For example, after the assassination of Dr. Martin Luther King, Jr., Blum gave airtime to a group of teenagers who wanted to express their concerns. He frequently gave civil rights activists a voice on the station.

PLAN

Objective
Learn about African-American jazz legends and the instruments they played.

Critical Thinking Skills for Lesson 2.4
- Make Connections
- Analyze Visuals
- Evaluate
- Make Inferences

Essential Question for Chapter 22
What economic, political, and social changes occurred in the United States after World War I? Jazz emerged from 1920s' American culture and continued to grow and transform musical entertainment in the decades to come. Lesson 2.4 introduces a national museum that is dedicated to preserving and promoting jazz.

Background for the Teacher
New Orleans is the birthplace of jazz, but, according to many, no place cultivated jazz like Harlem, in New York City, now the home of the National Jazz Museum in Harlem. Loren Schoenberg, one of its directors notes: "In Harlem, in the early days of jazz, the piano was at the center of most homes, regardless of the financial stability of the household." A player piano sits near the entrance of the museum to symbolize that fact. Inside the museum, visitors can learn about jazz, attend concerts, and participate in workshops and jam sessions. One of the museum's greatest treasures is the Savory Collection. William Savory, a saxophonist and sound engineer, recorded live radio broadcasts of performances by jazz musicians between 1935 and 1941. The recordings are available through the museum's website.

History Notebook
Encourage students to complete the Curating History page for Chapter 22 in their History Notebooks as they read.

INTRODUCE & ENGAGE

Create a Music Exhibit

Engage students in a discussion about the types of music they like to listen to, and list their preferences on the board. Have students with similar musical tastes brainstorm how they would create a museum to preserve and promote that music. Encourage students to think about the items and musicians they would feature and the types of exhibits they would create to engage museum visitors. After students complete Lesson 2.4, ask them to share the ideas they had for creating their music museum. Tell students they will learn about some of the artifacts from the collections at the National Jazz Museum in Harlem.

TEACH

Guided Discussion

1. **Evaluate** Direct students to read the lesson's introduction to the National Jazz Museum in Harlem. **ASK:** To what extent do the artifacts featured in the lesson support the mission of the museum? *(Possible response: By preserving the record albums, people have access to jazz music of the 1940s and 1950s and can be inspired to appreciate jazz greats Charlie Parker and Jelly Roll Morton. Displaying and picturing the instruments that Parker and Duke Ellington played promotes knowledge of the musicians and the instruments used by a jazz band.)*

2. **Make Inferences** Why would a radio station microphone become an important artifact for the museum? *(Possible response: The radio was how music reached the general population, building a base of jazz enthusiasts. This particular microphone is from a radio station that was dedicated to African-American listeners, and in 1948 was the first station with only African-American announcers.)*

Curating History

The National Jazz Museum in Harlem's Savory Collection offers 100 hours of jazz recordings from the 1930s in a three-volume set. Captured on long-playing aluminum disks are the live radio performances and improvisation sessions of jazz artists Ella Fitzgerald, Count Basie, Fats Waller, Coleman Hawkins, and others. Access a volume from the museum's website and choose a track to play aloud. Prompt students to think about and discuss the song's mood, rhythm, and lyrics—if any. Allow time for students to explore the Savory Collection on their own and choose another piece to listen to. Ask volunteers to play the piece for the class and to offer comments on the aspects that place it in the jazz genre.

Active Option

NG Learning Framework: Create a Jazz Hall of Fame

SKILLS Communication, Collaboration

KNOWLEDGE Our Human Story

Organize students in groups of four to research and nominate jazz artists to be entered into a Jazz Hall of Fame. Group members will collaborate to choose one artist from their research, and then assemble an exhibit that may include a photo display, brief biography, audio clip, and information about the musician's achievements and contributions to jazz. Assemble the exhibits into a classroom Jazz Hall of Fame, and have each group present their exhibit to the rest of the class.

DIFFERENTIATE

Striving Readers

Analyze Figurative Language Pair striving readers with more proficient readers to help deepen their understanding of the text. Have pairs locate the following excerpts from the lesson introduction and the Charlie Parker's Saxophone caption and together determine the literal and figurative meanings of the words *hearts, cousin,* and *voice*. Ask students how these word choices affect the meaning of the following excerpts from the text:

- a place that stimulates hearts and minds through music
- Charlie Parker played an alto sax, which is smaller than its cousin
- size difference makes the voice of an alto sax naturally higher

Gifted & Talented

Write and Present a Radio Advertisement Direct students to fully explore the National Jazz Museum in Harlem's website to learn more about the organization, the museum, and the events it holds. Then ask students to write the script for a radio advertisement inviting people to come to an exhibit or to attend a specific special event. Remind students to include directions for including sounds or music in their scripts. To present the advertisement to the rest of the class, students may record the ad and play it back or perform it live.

CHARLIE PARKER'S SAXOPHONE

Answers will vary. Possible responses: Students may also know about or find more jazz instruments online, such as piano, drums, trumpet, trombone, clarinet, flute, guitar, and upright bass.

3.1 The Great Migration

MAIN IDEA A number of factors led to millions of African Americans moving from the South to cities in the North during the Great Migration.

THE PULL OF THE NORTH

As you know, the Great Migration involved the movement of about 6 million African Americans from the rural South to the urban North between 1910 and 1970. The numbers of African Americans on the move increased during World War I and World War II and significantly decreased during the Great Depression of the 1930s. During the first wave of the Great Migration, between 1910 and 1930, the African-American population in cities such as New York, Chicago, Detroit, and Cleveland grew by about 40 percent.

African Americans traveled north by bus, train, boat, and even horse-drawn carts. The arrival of these migrants transformed the culture of northern cities. It also created a new African-American urban culture. As you'll learn in this chapter, the migration resulted in a great flowering of the arts in New York City.

So what led African Americans to move north? Like all migrations, the Great Migration was the result of push-pull factors. As you may remember, push factors are the reasons that make people want to leave one place. Pull factors are the reasons that make people want to settle in a new one. During the first wave of the Great Migration, push factors included the discrimination, poverty, and fear African Americans endured in the South. Pull factors included the dream of greater equality, opportunities, and safety in the North.

PUSH FACTORS	PULL FACTORS
DISCRIMINATION	**EQUALITY**
African Americans in the South faced racial discrimination. Jim Crow laws enforced the segregation of schools, transportation, restaurants, and drinking fountains. The facilities for African Americans were inferior to those for white people. Living as second-class citizens, African Americans in the South were also regularly denied their constitutional right to vote.	African Americans had more freedom in northern cities. Segregation in the North was not widespread. African Americans could exercise their right to vote more easily. In addition, northern states passed laws guaranteeing all students an education, regardless of race. However, schools and cities in the North were often segregated, with African Americans forced to live in ghettos, or slums.
POVERTY	**OPPORTUNITY**
Few employment opportunities were available to African Americans in the rural South. The best jobs were reserved for whites, and so unemployment rates among African Americans were high. Many of those who had jobs worked as sharecroppers in a system that kept them in poverty. As a result, many African Americans lived in extremely poor conditions.	Immigration from Europe and men leaving to fight in World War I had caused labor shortages in northern factories. African-American newspapers encouraged people to move north with promises of plentiful jobs, good wages, and better living conditions. While many African Americans did find work, the higher cost of living in the North largely erased the benefit of earning a higher wage.
FEAR	**SAFETY**
African Americans in southern society were expected to regard white people as their superiors. On the other hand, whites showed African Americans little courtesy. Whites could beat and kill African Americans with little fear of punishment. All-white juries would acquit them of the crimes—even lynching.	The threat of violence against African Americans was lower in the North. Lynching was rare. Yet the threat of violence did not go away completely. As you know, in 1919, an African-American teenager was killed for swimming in the white section of a segregated beach in Chicago, which caused race riots to sweep through the country.

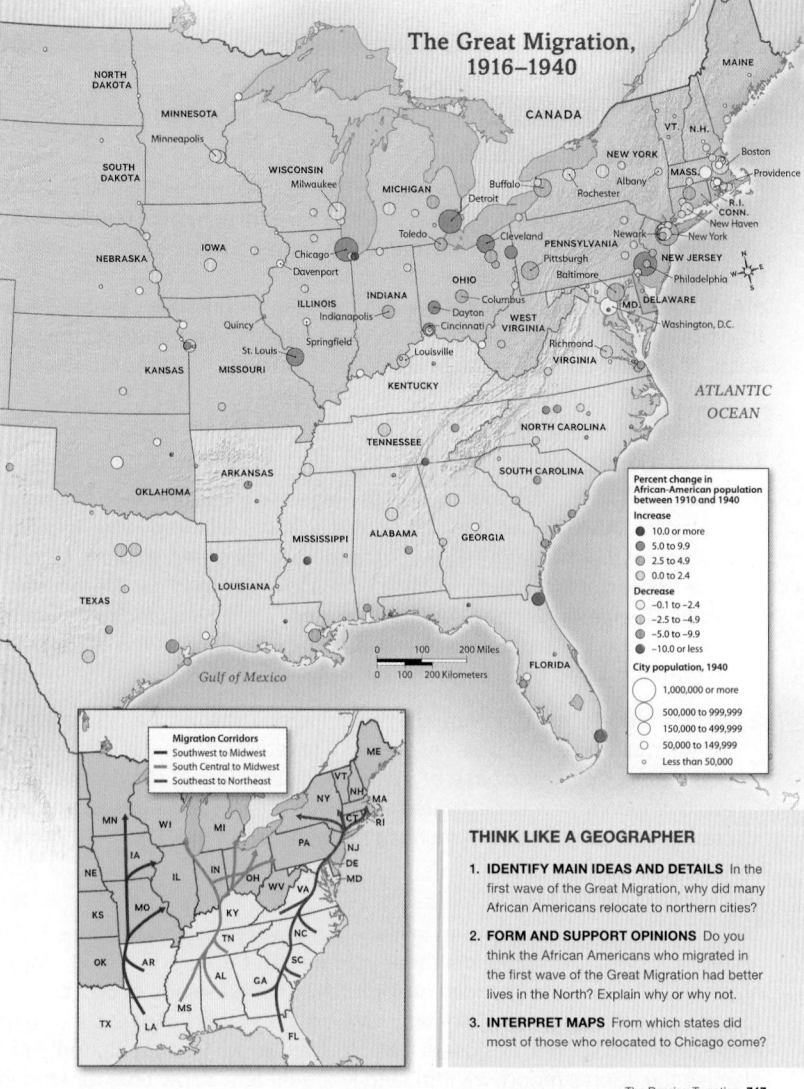

The Great Migration, 1916–1940

Percent change in African-American population between 1910 and 1940

Increase
- 10.0 or more
- 5.0 to 9.9
- 2.5 to 4.9
- 0.0 to 2.4

Decrease
- −0.1 to −2.4
- −2.5 to −4.9
- −5.0 to −9.9
- −10.0 or less

City population, 1940
- 1,000,000 or more
- 500,000 to 999,999
- 150,000 to 499,999
- 50,000 to 149,999
- Less than 50,000

Migration Corridors
- Southwest to Midwest
- South Central to Midwest
- Southeast to Northeast

THINK LIKE A GEOGRAPHER

1. **IDENTIFY MAIN IDEAS AND DETAILS** In the first wave of the Great Migration, why did many African Americans relocate to northern cities?

2. **FORM AND SUPPORT OPINIONS** Do you think the African Americans who migrated in the first wave of the Great Migration had better lives in the North? Explain why or why not.

3. **INTERPRET MAPS** From which states did most of those who relocated to Chicago come?

PLAN

Objective

Analyze factors that led to the Great Migration of African Americans to the North.

Critical Thinking Skills for Lesson 3.1

- Identify Main Ideas and Details
- Monitor Comprehension
- Form and Support Opinions
- Interpret Maps
- Evaluate
- Make Connections

Essential Question for Chapter 22

What economic, political, and social changes occurred in the United States after World War I? From 1910 to 1930, the African-American population in large northern cities grew by 40 percent. Lesson 3.1 explores the Great Migration, which transformed the culture of these cities.

Background for the Teacher

African Americans discovered that traveling north could vary widely in cost and duration of the trip. During World War I, some northern industries, desperate for workers, gave free railroad passes to African-American migrants to bring them north. Eventually, companies cut back on the free passes, which drove the cost of regular passenger fares up more than tenfold. Many families had to stop and work along the way to afford the journey, a "step migration" that could take months. Some Virginia migrants took manufacturing jobs in Richmond and Norfolk before continuing north. Families who couldn't afford to travel together even in steps often pooled their money to send one male member ahead to a city like Chicago or Philadelphia. They hoped the person would find a job and send money back home so the rest of the family could join him.

History Notebook

Encourage students to complete the American Gallery page for Chapter 22 in their History Notebooks as they read.

INTRODUCE & ENGAGE

Activate Prior Knowledge

Ask students to think of reasons why groups of people might leave their homes and most of their belongings and travel long distances to a new city or state. Encourage students to think about how people would travel, where they would go, and what they would need to start a new life. Write students' answers on the board. Then explain to them that many African Americans faced these same choices when they took part in the Great Migration between 1910 and 1930. Tell students that in this lesson they will examine many of the push-pull factors driving people to leave the South and move to the North.

TEACH

Guided Discussion

1. **Evaluate** For African-American parents with small children, what might be some of the strongest push-pull factors motivating them to move north? *(Possible response: African-American parents probably wanted their children to receive an education, guaranteed by law for all races in some northern states, and freedom from the brutal discrimination the parents had experienced in the South.)*

2. **Make Connections** Why might the Great Depression have caused the numbers of African Americans moving north to significantly decrease? *(Possible response: The Great Depression meant fewer jobs in the North and less incentive for people to move there. Also, the Depression would have made it harder for families to earn enough money to afford the move.)*

Geography in History

Interpret Maps Direct students' attention to the two maps in the lesson. **ASK:** What geographic advantages do the largest northern cities have in common? *(Most of the cities are located on water, including lakes, rivers, and the Atlantic Ocean, making them good transportation centers for industry and agriculture.)* **ASK:** What can you infer about why African Americans chose to move to these largest cities? *(Possible response: Cities like Chicago, Detroit, New York, and Philadelphia would be easy to reach and would have large industrial centers offering jobs in manufacturing, transportation, and other industries.)* **ASK:** According to the map, which state had the most cities that gained African-American population, and which state had the most cities that lost this population? *(Ohio had the most cities that gained population; Texas had the most cities that lost population.)*

Active Options

AMERICAN GALLERY ONLINE **The Great Migration** Invite students to explore the American Gallery. Ask them to choose one of the photographs or paintings and do additional research to learn more about it. Ask questions that will inspire additional inquiry about the chosen visual, such as: When and where was this photo taken? What does it show about the people making the Great Migration? What purpose was there for depicting or photographing this scene? Why does it belong in this chapter? What else would you like to know about it?

NG Learning Framework: Write Journal Entries
ATTITUDE Responsibility
KNOWLEDGE Our Human Story

Ask students to imagine they are making the Great Migration with their family. Explain that they will write in character, first-person journal entries about this experience, based on the text and additional research. Review the discrimination that African Americans faced in the South and North, as described in Push Factors and Pull Factors. Then have students research the types of discrimination families often faced when trying to leave the South and when trying to establish a new life in the North. For example, some families were arrested for "vagrancy" in an effort to stop them from leaving the South. Encourage students to recount in their entries a type of discrimination that their character either witnessed or experienced. Allow time for students to share their journals with the class.

DIFFERENTIATE

Inclusion

Describe Map Information Pair students with learning disabilities with students who are proficient readers. Ask the proficient readers to assist their partners in understanding the information presented in the maps. Instruct pairs to first read each line in each legend and then locate and describe the corresponding location on its corresponding map. Then tell students to work together to answer the Think Like a Geographer questions.

Gifted & Talented

Write a Summary Remind students of the Essential Question: What economic, political, and social changes occurred in the United States after World War I? Tell students to review the lesson and identify how the Great Migration impacted the economy, politics, and society of the United States. Then have students use the examples they identify to write a summary that answers the Essential Question. Invite students to share their summary with the class.

THINK LIKE A GEOGRAPHER

ANSWERS

1. Labor shortages in the North attracted many African Americans who sought a better life through work and education, away from the discrimination, denial of constitutional rights, and fear of attacks from whites that they experienced in the South.

2. Possible responses: Yes. They faced less discrimination and violence and had more opportunities, such as access to education and higher-paying jobs. No. The higher cost of living in the North meant they still didn't have much money, they still faced some violence and discrimination, and they were far away from friends and family.

3. Mississippi, Alabama, and Tennessee

3.2 The Harlem Renaissance

Sometimes a community can be so inspiring that it ignites creativity and new ideas. That's just what happened in a New York City neighborhood called Harlem in the 1920s.

MAIN IDEA During the Great Migration, large numbers of African Americans settled in the North, where they led a rebirth in culture and the arts.

A DIVERSITY OF TALENT

The neighborhood of Harlem, located north of Central Park in New York City, was one of the vibrant communities that emerged from the Great Migration. By the 1920s, Harlem was the thriving center for a movement of African-American arts and culture, known as the **Harlem Renaissance**. A **renaissance** is a rebirth, and the Harlem Renaissance marked a revival of African-American pride and creativity that spread across the country.

The magazine of the National Association for the Advancement of Colored People (NAACP), *The Crisis*, became a leading voice of the Harlem Renaissance. It was launched by W.E.B. DuBois in 1910. With a circulation of 100,000, *The Crisis* provided African-American authors a platform for expressing their ideas.

At an important dinner party in 1924, African-American writers and scholars met some of New York's influential white editors and critics. Before the evening ended, publications were being planned, including a special edition of the magazine *Survey Graphic* that focused on "Harlem: Mecca of the New Negro." That issue included an essay by **Alain Locke**, a Howard University professor, who urged his African-American readers to take pride in their culture.

CELEBRATING A CULTURE

The Harlem Renaissance gave African-American authors, poets, playwrights, musicians, performers, and visual artists a new stage upon which to express their creativity and identity. They sought not just acceptance, but a celebration of their achievements and what it meant to live the African-American experience.

Among the most famous of the Harlem Renaissance authors was **Langston Hughes**. He wrote plays and novels, but he is best remembered for his poetry. Hughes used the rhythms of jazz and blues in his poems to speak to African Americans throughout the country.

Many authors, including **Zora Neale Hurston**, wrote in a variety of genres. An **anthropologist**, or person who studies cultures, as well as an author, Hurston collected folktales from the Caribbean, Latin America, and the South. The novel *Their Eyes Were Watching God* (1937) is considered her masterpiece. Other major literary figures in the Harlem Renaissance included poets **Countee Cullen** and **Claude McKay**. While in his twenties, Cullen won prizes in many of America's leading literary journals for his racially themed poetry. McKay was born in Jamaica but later became an American citizen. He wrote about life in Harlem in one of his poetry collections, *Harlem Shadows*.

Music, art, and performance were also part of the Harlem Renaissance. **James Weldon Johnson** was a leading figure in the United States even before the Harlem Renaissance. He composed "Lift Every Voice and Sing," a well-known song in the genre of **gospel music**, blending biblical subjects with melodic themes similar to those of jazz. Artist **Jacob Lawrence** became known for a series of paintings, *The Migration of the Negro*, depicting African-American life during the early 20th century. **Paul Robeson** was an attorney, but racism at his firm led him to quit law and turn to acting and singing. Given respect in other nations that he did not receive at home, Robeson became an outspoken supporter of civil rights.

AN EXPLOSION·OF·CULTURE

The Harlem Renaissance occurred in part because of the diversity of those who migrated to Harlem. In the words of Alain Locke, "their greatest experience has been the finding of one another."

1 Strivers' Row was the home of W. C. Handy, writer of the iconic "St. Louis Blues."

2 Smalls Paradise featured jazz and was a haunt of Harlem Renaissance writers.

3 Liberty Hall hosted Marcus Garvey's UNIA meetings every Sunday.

5 James Weldon Johnson lived on 135th Street from 1925–1938, publishing his own and others' poetry.

4 Langston Hughes spent the last 20 years of his life in a home on 127th Street.

6 Apollo Theater Ella Fitzgerald first performed at amateur night at the Apollo.

HISTORICAL THINKING

1. **READING CHECK** What was the Harlem Renaissance?

2. **DRAW CONCLUSIONS** How did writers and artists of the Harlem Renaissance help change perceptions of American identity?

3. **INTERPRET VISUALS** What aspects of the Harlem Renaissance are represented in the illustrated map?

PLAN

Objective
Explore key figures and ideas of African-American cultural expression in 1920s Harlem.

Critical Thinking Skills for Lesson 3.2
- Identify Main Ideas and Details
- Monitor Comprehension
- Draw Conclusions
- Interpret Visuals
- Compare and Contrast
- Make Inferences
- Make Connections

Essential Question for Chapter 22
What economic, political, and social changes occurred in the United States after World War I? In the 1920s, Harlem was a focal point for African-American writers and artists. Lesson 3.2 introduces the people and ideas that shaped the Harlem Renaissance.

Background for the Teacher
In 1925, Langston Hughes seized an opportunity to make a fast connection with Vachel Lindsay, one of the most celebrated poets of his day, who happened to be dining at the hotel where Hughes was working as a busboy. During the course of Lindsay's meal, Hughes wordlessly set down three of his own poems next to the writers plate. Lindsay was initially annoyed by the intrusion, but he read the poems. When he found out that Hughes had written them, he was impressed. The following day, Lindsay was quoted in several newspapers, saying that he had discovered a wonderful young African-American poet working as a busboy. Lindsay took Hughes under his wing, and it was not long before he had introduced Hughes to a number of leading publishers. In 1926, Hughes published his first collection of poetry, *The Weary Blues*.

Improvise a Class Poem

Access a copy of Langston Hughes's eight-line poem "Dreams" and read it to the class. **ASK:** What do you think the poet is saying? *(Answers will vary. Possible response: Without something to believe in and strive for, life can be very empty.)* Write students' ideas on the board. Then have students work together to improvise a poem with a similar theme and tone, using words and phrases they provided to describe Hughes's poem. Explain that in this lesson, students will read about Langston Hughes and other figures of the Harlem Renaissance who created a community based on their hopes and dreams.

TEACH

Guided Discussion

1. **Compare and Contrast** How were the Harlem Renaissance and the Jazz Age similar to and different from one another? *(The Harlem Renaissance and the Jazz Age were both arts movements that took place during the 1920s, but the focus of the Jazz Age was music, specifically jazz and the people who played it. The Harlem Renaissance included musicians, but it centered on the ideas and artistic expression of African Americans who gathered in Harlem during the decade.)*

2. **Make Inferences** Reread the caption underneath the title of the illustration in the lesson. **ASK:** What do you think Alain Locke meant when he said, "their greatest experience has been the finding of one another"? *(Answers will vary. Possible response: Locke might have meant that the strength of the people who moved to Harlem was in their shared cultural heritage, which helped them form a tight community and lay a foundation for an artistic movement.)*

Make Connections

Explain to students that the official publication of the NAACP, *The Crisis*, founded by W.E.B. Du Bois in 1910, is still in operation today. Direct students to visit the magazine's website, and have them locate and view the publication's statement of principles. Then tell students to use the Archives link to find an issue from the 1920s and one published after the year 2000, and to read or scan some of the articles from each. **ASK:** What common themes do both the issue from the Harlem Renaissance and the 21st-century issue of the magazine convey, and how do the themes reflect the time period? *(Answers will vary. Possible response: Both issues cover a variety of topics, including social and political events, culture, leisure, interviews of important and famous African Americans, as well as advertisements aimed at the African-American community. The articles reflect current events, including riots, protests, and current cultural events.)*

Active Options

On Your Feet: Guess the Person or Place Arrange students in two teams and give each team several small slips of paper. Ask teams to write down the names of important people and places from the Harlem Renaissance. Then allow one team member to choose a slip of paper from the other team and describe or act out the person or place to his or her own team without mentioning the proper name. Encourage teams to take turns and move through their lists until all the people and places have been correctly identified.

NG Learning Framework: Compare Two Poems

ATTITUDE	Responsibility
SKILL	Observation

Prompt students to examine and write about the poetry of Countee Cullen and Claude McKay. Tell them to locate and read a few poems by each poet, choose one from each that shares a similar idea or perspective about the African-American experience, and write one or two paragraphs about the authors' message. Ask students to form a topic sentence about the message and support it with examples of language and imagery from the two poems. Ask volunteers to read the poems they chose and their paragraphs to the class.

Striving Readers

Create a Concept Cluster Write *Harlem Renaissance* in the center oval of a Concept Cluster and *literature*, *art*, and *music* in the other three ovals. Instruct students to reread the lesson and write names of people and specific examples of their art forms on the spokes. Encourage students to create additional spokes as necessary. Ask them to compare their completed Concept Clusters and revise as necessary.

Pre-AP

Research the Roots of Creativity Tell students to choose one of the writers or artists discussed in the lesson and write two questions that seek a deeper understanding of what motivated that person's creativity. Direct students to use print and online sources to research their questions. Ask them to summarize their findings in a brief report that analyzes the roots of the person's creativity and method of expression. Students may share their report by posting it online or presenting it to the class.

See the Chapter Planner for more strategies for differentiation.

ANSWERS

1. The Harlem Renaissance was a period of cultural creativity of African Americans in art, literature, and music that impacted the nation during the 1920s.

2. Possible response: Their work exposed the white majority to the thoughts and artistic expressions of African Americans, adding a layer of diversity to the American identity.

3. The map shows how close the homes and gathering places were to each other, suggesting that the figures of the Harlem Renaissance lived in a relatively small, close community, where they could find inspiration, collaboration, and safety. The map also illustrates historical landmarks relevant to the movement.

3.3 Writers and Artists of the Harlem Renaissance

Artists express themselves in music, words, and images. They show where people have been and where they are going, acknowledging the past and expressing hope for the future. Alain Locke, Zora Neale Hurston, Langston Hughes, and William H. Johnson were among the great creative influences of the Harlem Renaissance.

The term "Harlem Renaissance" did not come into use until the 1940s, but in his 1925 essay "Harlem," Alain Locke (right) called Harlem "the sign and center of the renaissance of a people." Also in 1925—a busy year for Locke—he published an anthology entitled *The New Negro*, consisting of over 40 works by African-American authors, many of them young. The anthology included writings by Locke and the two writers on the next page, Zora Neale Hurston and Langston Hughes.

CRITICAL VIEWING Locke helped to define the Harlem Renaissance by describing the Harlem neighborhood and calling attention to its best writers and artists. What does Winold Reiss's portrait convey about Locke?

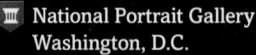
National Portrait Gallery Washington, D.C.

African-American writer and philosopher Alain Locke is pictured here in a 1925 drawing by artist Winold Reiss. Reiss contributed this portrait and similar drawings of many other Harlem Renaissance figures to an illustrated edition of Locke's *The New Negro*.

DOCUMENT ONE

Primary Source: Essay
from "How It Feels to Be Colored Me"
by Zora Neale Hurston, 1928

Zora Neale Hurston was one of the most productive writers of the Harlem Renaissance. Though largely forgotten by the time she died, Hurston was reintroduced to a younger generation by later African-American authors such as Alice Walker.

CONSTRUCTED RESPONSE What does Hurston mean when she writes that being discriminated against doesn't anger her so much as astonish her?

At certain times I have no race, I am me. When I set my hat at a certain angle and saunter down Seventh Avenue, Harlem City, feeling as snooty as the lions in front of the Forty-Second Street Library, for instance. . . . The cosmic Zora emerges. I belong to no race nor time. . . . I have no separate feeling about being an American citizen and colored. I am merely a fragment of the Great Soul that surges within the boundaries. My country, right or wrong. Sometimes, I feel discriminated against, but it does not make me angry. It merely astonishes me. How can any deny themselves the pleasure of my company?

DOCUMENT TWO

Primary Source: Painting
Soldiers Dancing by William H. Johnson, 1942-1943

Artist William H. Johnson studied in New York City in the 1920s during the height of the Harlem Renaissance. However, the movement influenced Johnson's art for the rest of his life. Characteristics of the movement in his paintings included using simple shapes and bright colors to depict scenes of racial pride.

CONSTRUCTED RESPONSE In what other ways does this painting convey racial pride?

DOCUMENT THREE

Primary Source: Essay
from "The Negro Artist and the Racial Mountain"
by Langston Hughes, 1926

Langston Hughes was one of the most important figures in the Harlem Renaissance. A playwright, novelist, and poet, he was one of the first writers to incorporate jazz rhythms into his writing.

CONSTRUCTED RESPONSE What do you think Hughes is saying about art and the African-American experience when he says, "If white people are pleased we are glad. If they are not, it doesn't matter"?

We younger Negro artists who create now intend to express our individual dark-skinned selves without fear or shame. If white people are pleased we are glad. If they are not, it doesn't matter. We know we are beautiful. And ugly too. The tom-tom cries and the tom-tom laughs. If colored people are pleased we are glad. If they are not, their displeasure doesn't matter either. We will build our temples for tomorrow, strong as we know how, and we will stand on top of the mountain, free within ourselves.

SYNTHESIZE & WRITE

1. **REVIEW** Review what you have learned about the Harlem Renaissance.

2. **RECALL** On your own paper, write the main ideas from the excerpts from Zora Neale Hurston's and Langston Hughes's essays and the painting from William H. Johnson.

3. **CONSTRUCT** Construct a topic sentence that answers this question: What cultural changes came about because of the Harlem Renaissance?

4. **WRITE** Using evidence from this chapter and the documents, write an informative paragraph that supports your topic sentence in Step 3.

PLAN

Objective
Synthesize information about African-American identity during the Harlem Renaissance from primary source documents.

Critical Thinking Skills for Lesson 3.3
- Synthesize
- Analyze Language Use
- Make Connections
- Evaluate

Essential Question for Chapter 22
What economic, political, and social changes occurred in the United States after World War I? The Harlem Renaissance revealed a wide range of talent in the African Americans who came to Harlem. They gave a voice to the African-American experience and added a layer of diversity to the cultural landscape of America. Lesson 3.3 provides examples of the artistic expression of four of Harlem's most significant artists.

Background for the Teacher
William H. Johnson (1901–1970), born in rural South Carolina, developed his artistic ability as a child by copying cartoons from local newspapers. He studied art in New York City and Paris and traveled extensively throughout Europe and North Africa before ultimately choosing to depict African-American life and culture in his paintings. He developed a flat, primitive style using a limited number of colors and simple forms. For *Soldiers Dancing*, he used ink, tempera, watercolor, and pencil to capture the vibrant tones and movements of the people and music of Harlem. Johnson said of himself, "My aim is to express in a natural way what I feel, what is in me, both rhythmically and spiritually." Many of Johnson's works are among the collection of the Smithsonian American Art Museum, which, like the National Portrait Gallery, where many of Winold Reiss's works are held, is part of the Smithsonian Institution.

INTRODUCE & ENGAGE

Prepare for the Document-Based Question

Before students start the activity, briefly preview the three documents. Remind students that a constructed response requires full explanations in complete sentences. Emphasize that students should use what they have learned about the Harlem Renaissance in addition to the information in the documents.

TEACH

Guided Discussion

1. **Analyze Language Use** What words does Zora Neale Hurston use to describe herself, and what impression of her do they create? *(Possible response: She describes herself as someone of "no race," who can "saunter down Seventh Ave," "snooty as the lions," and as "cosmic Zora" who belongs to no country but is part of the "Great Soul." The words create an impression of someone who has great self-confidence and pride and sees herself as part of the whole of society.)*

2. **Make Connections** What common theme do all three artists express through their art, and how is that theme conveyed? *(Possible response: All three artists express the theme of identity through the words and images they create, expressing new ways for African Americans to describe themselves, to have pride in who they are and what they can do, and to communicate their heritage and lives without fear or shame.)*

Evaluate

After students have completed the Synthesize & Write activity, allow time for them to exchange paragraphs and read and comment on the work of their peers. Establish guidelines for comments prior to this activity so that feedback is constructive and encouraging in nature.

Active Option

On Your Feet: Host a DBQ Roundtable Arrange students around tables in groups of four. Ask them the following question: In what ways did the Harlem Renaissance change the way African Americans viewed themselves? Instruct each student in a group to answer the question in a different way. Then ask groups to summarize their answers for the class.

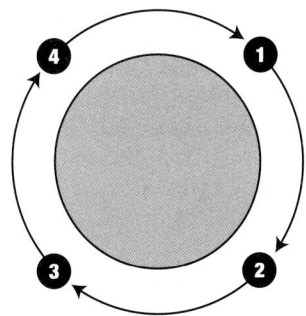

DIFFERENTIATE

English Language Learners

Simplify Complex Sentences Pair students at the **Emerging** and **Expanding** levels with students at the **Bridging** level. Read the first paragraph of the text on page 750 aloud, emphasizing punctuation and intonation to help students understand meaning. Read the paragraph again and tell students to listen and then write short, simple sentences that state the meaning. Then have pairs read the text and check their sentences.

Pre-AP

Analyze the Impact of a Harlem Renaissance Figure Direct students to use print and online sources to research the impact that one of the writers from the lesson had on African-American culture during the Harlem Renaissance. Ask students to determine how that person's influence resonates in present-day American culture. Ask volunteers to summarize their findings in an oral report to the class.

See the Chapter Planner for more strategies for differentiation.

SYNTHESIZE & WRITE

ANSWERS

1. Answers will vary.

2. Answers will vary

3. Answers will vary. Possible response: The Harlem Renaissance produced cultural changes in American music, art, literature, dance, and politics.

4. Answers will vary. Students' paragraphs should include their topic sentence from Step 3 and provide several details from the documents to support the sentence.

CONSTRUCTED RESPONSE

Document 1: Because Hurston doesn't feel separate, she is astonished when others see her as different. Instead of feeling angry when she is discriminated against, she is surprised because she expects others to enjoy her company.

Document 2: Possible response: Racial pride is conveyed through the men depicted in uniform and the stylish women out for an evening of entertainment. Johnson emphasizes the dancers' ethnic features by exaggerating their lips and depicting the women's hair in a style likely fashionable for African-American women during World War II. The overall effect portrays the subjects as elegant and distinctly African American.

Document 3: Hughes is saying that art has freed African-American artists from being limited by what white people think, so they can focus on expressing themselves.

CRITICAL VIEWING Winold Reiss calls attention to Locke's head and hands through color, shading, and detail, while the rest of the portrait appears sketched in black and white. In this way, Reiss expresses the importance of Locke's head and hands to him as a writer. Locke's face conveys the impression of someone who is serious and scholarly, with eyes slightly downcast as if he were reflecting on an idea or question.

3.4 Zora Neale Hurston 1891–1960

"I do not weep at the world—I am too busy sharpening
my oyster knife."—Zora Neale Hurston

Zora Neale Hurston brushed aside any limitations society might have placed on an African-American woman in the early 20th century. As far as she was concerned, the world was her oyster. In other words, Hurston felt that life was full of possibilities, and she could do whatever she wanted. Outgoing and charming, Hurston used her intellectual talents, sense of humor, and "gift of walking into hearts," as one friend put it, to pursue her many interests and achieve her goals.

GETTING OFF THE GROUND

Hurston very likely formed her optimistic view of the world as a child. She grew up in Eatonville, Florida, the country's first incorporated township run entirely by African Americans. Hurston's father, a former slave, served as the town's mayor several times, and her mother had a prominent teaching position in the community's two churches. Surrounded by positive African-American role models, Hurston developed into a confident young girl.

It probably helped that, as a child, Hurston rarely encountered a white person and so was never made to feel inferior. Hurston's mother encouraged her children's high spirits and urged them to "jump at de sun." Hurston later said, "We might not land on the sun, but at least we would get off the ground."

When she was 13, Hurston's happy childhood came abruptly to an end with the death of her mother. Her father remarried but then showed little interest in his daughter. Hurston spent the next few years being passed around among various family members. According to Hurston, she learned she was just "a little colored girl" while staying with her sister and brother in Jacksonville, Florida.

Zora Neale Hurston is known for her fiction writings, but she was also a published scientist. In 1928, she received a degree in Anthropology from Barnard College in New York City. After college, she researched the folklore of Haiti and Jamaica and published her findings in a book called *Mules and Men* in 1935.

The cover shown here appeared on the first edition of *Their Eyes Were Watching God*. The characters in Hurston's novel speak in dialect, which some black writers claimed reinforced white stereotypes about African Americans. Today, the book is praised for giving voice to African-American men and women.

in 1931 and published her first novel, *Jonah's Gourd Vine*, in 1934. After studying anthropology at Barnard College and Columbia University in New York City, she researched and published a collection of African-American folktales called *Mules and Men* in 1935. Hurston's most famous work, *Their Eyes Were Watching God*, followed two years later.

Her autobiography, *Dust Tracks on a Road*, came out in 1942. In this, as in most of her writing, Hurston didn't discuss the segregation, or separation of races, that was widespread at the time. Although Hurston certainly encountered discrimination in her life, she laughed it off. "How can any deny themselves the pleasure of my company?" she once said. "It's beyond me."

When she struck out on her own, Hurston had to neglect her education and work in several low-paying jobs instead. She wasn't able to return to finish high school until she was 26. To take advantage of free public schooling, the youthful-looking Hurston convinced school officials she was 16. After graduating, she spent two years at Howard University in Washington, D.C.

LANDING ON THE SUN

In 1925, Hurston moved to Harlem where she met some of the leading figures of the Harlem Renaissance, including Langston Hughes and Countee Cullen. Some of Hurston's short stories had been published in literary journals and had come to their attention. She soon became an important part of the Harlem Renaissance and often hosted parties for the movement's writers and artists. Still, Hurston sometimes stole away to her bedroom to write while a party continued in her living room.

Her hard work paid off. Over the next 10 years or so, Hurston enjoyed considerable success. In addition to writing short stories and articles, she collaborated with Hughes on the play *Mule Bone*

Most of Hurston's works were well-received but earned little money. For the rest of her life, Hurston struggled with her finances. When she died in Florida in 1960, her friends paid for her funeral but could not afford a gravestone. Hurston and her works were nearly forgotten. Then in 1973, Alice Walker, an African-American writer who had been inspired by Hurston, located the unmarked grave. Walker introduced Hurston's work to a whole new audience. She also had a gravestone erected over the burial site with the inscription "Zora Neale Hurston: A Genius of the South."

HISTORICAL THINKING

1. **READING CHECK** Why were Hurston's early years in Eatonville so happy?

2. **MAKE INFERENCES** Why do you think Hurston was not upset by the racial discrimination she encountered?

3. **EVALUATE** Based on what you have read, what words would you use to describe Hurston's personality?

PLAN

Objective

Describe the life, character, and work of Harlem Renaissance writer Zora Neale Hurston.

Critical Thinking Skills for Lesson 3.4

- Identify Main Ideas and Details
- Monitor Comprehension
- Make Inferences
- Evaluate
- Summarize

Essential Question for Chapter 22

What economic, political, and social changes occurred in the United States after World War I? The Harlem Renaissance included the work of female writers who celebrated African-American life. Lesson 3.4 discusses how Zora Neale Hurston became an important voice for African-American culture.

Background for the Teacher

Zora Neale Hurston was the most widely published African-American female writer of the Harlem Renaissance, but there were dozens of others. Gwendolyn Bennett published poems in Alaine Locke's *New Negro* and wrote an arts column for *Opportunity: Journal of Negro Life*. Nella Larsen's novels *Quicksand* and *Passing* explored the complexities of mixed-race women finding their way. Essayist and poet Jessie Fauset was the literary editor of *The Crisis* magazine and co-editor of *The Brownies' Book*, which taught African-American children about their culture. The youngest and last surviving member of the Harlem Renaissance group of artists was award-winning short story writer Dorothy West, who died in 1998.

History Notebook

Encourage students to complete the American Voices page for Chapter 22 in their History Notebooks as they read.

INTRODUCE & ENGAGE

Preview Using Visuals

Point out the opening quotation and the photograph of Zora Neale Hurston in the lesson. Explain to students that "oyster knife" is a reference to a line from one of William Shakespeare's plays: "Why then the world's mine oyster, Which I with sword will open." **ASK:** Based on the photograph and quotation, what is your impression of Hurston? *(Possible response: Based on Hurston's easy smile and clothes, she is open and friendly with a unique sense of style—a person you'd like to get to know. Her reference to a quotation from Shakespeare suggests that she is well read, and her meaning could be that she carves opportunities for herself rather than letting circumstances dictate the paths her life might take.)*

TEACH

Guided Discussion

1. **Summarize** What challenges did Hurston face as a teenager? *(Hurston's biggest challenge came at the age of 13 when her mother died, and the relatives she then lived with treated her with indifference. Fortunately, the encouragement and optimism that her mother had provided gave her the confidence to "strike out on her own," but that created more challenges because she had to work to support herself.)*

2. **Make Inferences** Why do you think Hurston didn't discuss or write about segregation in her books, including her autobiography? *(Possible response: Hurston was focused on the subject of African-American culture and may have felt that addressing the problem of segregation would have been a distraction from her research and writing.)*

American Voices

In her novels and stories, Zora Neale Hurston used the dialect and speech patterns of African Americans from the rural South and the Caribbean. She traveled to Haiti and Jamaica to document the songs, sermons, folk tales, ceremonies, customs, and superstitions that reached back to the era of slavery. She and Langston Hughes tried to preserve this rich, lyrical way of speaking in their play *Mule Bone*, which they wrote in 1930 as "the first real Negro folk comedy." They wanted to show the way many blacks felt, thought, and spoke to each other when whites weren't around. But even at the time, the play was viewed as perpetuating negative stereotypes of African Americans, and it wasn't performed until 1991 in New York City. Today, Hurston's works, including *Mule Bone,* are regarded as preserving an important form of African-American oral history.

Active Options

On Your Feet: Word Chain Have students form three lines. Hand a piece of paper to the first person in each line with one of these phrases from the text: *oyster knife; get off the ground; land on the sun.* The first student in line adds a word or phrase that relates to the original phrase. Students pass the paper from person to person, each one adding a word or phrase they associate with the previously written word or phrase. Ask a volunteer from each group to read the groups' Word Chain. Tell the rest of the class to listen for any words that were used more than once or that may not connect.

NG Learning Framework: Create a Blog Page

SKILL Communication

KNOWLEDGE Our Human Story

Ask students to work in small groups to create a blog page for Hurston in which they write from her point of view on some aspect of her life. Topics could include other artists she knew, advice to those who feel discouraged, what it was like to live in Harlem, or a scene from her childhood. Students can use the information in the lesson and their own research for the blog. Discuss with students what else the page could feature, such as links to her books, a time line of her life, a list of her publications, or photographs of life in Harlem. Invite students to share their blog pages with the class.

DIFFERENTIATE

Striving Readers

Sequence Events Arrange students in pairs and instruct them to determine the sequence of major events in Hurston's life and connect them in a Sequence Chain. Ask students to include two major personal events and three major professional events and to annotate each one with the date and important details. Invite students to share their Sequence Chain with other pairs and discuss any differences.

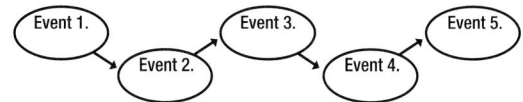

Gifted & Talented

Create an Online Interview Tell students to research Zora Neale Hurston's life beyond what is covered in the lesson. Then direct student pairs to write a series of questions and answers for an interview that they will record about Hurston's childhood, her experiences as a writer, and her impoverished later years. Ask students to decide who will role-play Hurston and the interviewer and to then conduct the interview and record it for playback on a monitor or laptop. Students could also post their interviews for viewing on a class or school web page.

See the Chapter Planner for more strategies for differentiation.

HISTORICAL THINKING

ANSWERS

1. Growing up in the country's first township run by African Americans, Hurston was happy and loved, raised by two parents who were prominent members of the community, and had successful African-American role models around her.

2. Hurston never felt inferior in any way and was probably aware that she was more intelligent and talented than most of the people she encountered during her lifetime. She was successful and happy, so while she likely felt that discrimination directed at her was wrong, she decided not to acknowledge it.

3. Answers will vary. Possible responses: *positive, confident, courageous, ambitious, talented, stylish, determined, charming, inspiring, brilliant*

VOCABULARY

Use each of the following vocabulary words in a sentence that shows an understanding of the term's meaning.

1. jazz
   Jazz was a unique form of American music that came to define the 1920s.
2. immigration quota
3. advertising
4. renaissance
5. consumer
6. dissident
7. fundamentalism
8. mass media

READING STRATEGY
DRAW CONCLUSIONS

If you haven't done so already, complete your diagram about how changes that occurred in the United States during the 1920s transformed American life and identity.

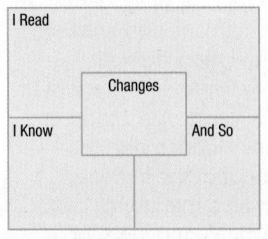

9. Identify one change that occurred during the 1920s that has had a long-lasting impact on American life, and explain why you think it has.

MAIN IDEAS

Answer the following questions. Support your answers with evidence from the chapter.

10. What was the Red Scare? **LESSON 1.1**
11. What was the Volstead Act? **LESSON 1.2**
12. How did U.S. laws reflect the prejudice many Americans had against immigrants in the early 1920s? **LESSON 1.3**
13. Why did the advertising industry grow so quickly in the 1920s? **LESSON 2.1**
14. How did new forms of entertainment help create a mass culture? **LESSON 2.2**
15. In what way was jazz a unifying factor in 1920s America? **LESSON 2.3**
16. What was one effect of the Harlem Renaissance? **LESSON 3.2**

HISTORICAL THINKING

Answer the following questions. Support your answers with evidence from the chapter.

17. **DRAW CONCLUSIONS** Why do you think Sacco and Vanzetti were accused, tried, and executed?
18. **SYNTHESIZE** How do you think the Red Scare affected the election of 1920?
19. **COMPARE AND CONTRAST** In what way did the enforcement of Prohibition in cities differ from enforcement in rural areas?
20. **MAKE INFERENCES** What conflicts might have arisen in a home where the parents, who had been raised in the late 1800s, were adjusting to life with a "flapper" daughter?
21. **FORM AND SUPPORT OPINIONS** Do you think the development of a consumer economy was positive or negative for the United States? Explain why or why not.

22. **ANALYZE CAUSE AND EFFECT** Describe how racial and ethnic tensions arose as a result of social changes in the 1920s.
23. **FORM AND SUPPORT OPINIONS** How do you think American identity changed in the 1920s? Include evidence from the chapter to support your answer.

INTERPRET VISUALS

Following World War I, fear of the communist Bolsheviks led to a period of mass hysteria in the United States. Cartoonist Sidney Joseph Greene responded to this Red Scare with a political cartoon focusing on a character, "Labor," descending a staircase. His cartoon, entitled "Step by Step," appeared in the *New York Evening Telegram* newspaper in 1919.

24. What does the cartoon imply will happen "step by step"?
25. Do you think the cartoonist has presented his genuine belief, or is he viewing it as an absurd idea? Support your answer with evidence from the cartoon and what you have learned about labor unions.

ANALYZE SOURCES

Few people portrayed the free and loose spirit of the 1920s as well as author F. Scott Fitzgerald. In his essay "My Lost City," Fitzgerald looks back at the glamour and the excesses of the time period. Read the excerpt from Fitzgerald's essay, and then answer the question.

> The uncertainties of 1920 were drowned in a steady golden roar and many of our friends had grown wealthy. But the restlessness of New York in 1927 approached hysteria. The parties were bigger . . . the pace was faster . . . the shows were broader, the buildings were higher, the morals were looser and the liquor was cheaper; but all these benefits did not really minister to much delight [make people happy].

26. What is the key point Fitzgerald is making in this quotation about the 1920s?

CONNECT TO YOUR LIFE

27. **NARRATIVE** The 1920s were a decade of great change in the United States. How has U.S. life changed in the last year or two? What change affected you the most? Identify connections you can make between this change and one that occurred in the 1920s. Write a paragraph describing these connections.

TIPS

- In a two-column chart, describe life in the 1920s on one side and your life on the other. Think about things like advertising, the consumer economy, and human rights.
- How is the information similar? Cite evidence from the text to support your ideas.
- Use two or three vocabulary terms from the chapter in your narrative.
- Conclude the narrative with a sentence that connects how the 1920s changed American life to how current events changed your life.

VOCABULARY ANSWERS

1. Jazz was a unique form of American music that came to define the 1920s.
2. In the 1920s, immigration quotas limited the number of eastern and southern Europeans allowed into the United States.
3. Advertising promotes new products and tries to persuade people to buy them.
4. Harlem became the center of a vibrant renaissance, or rebirth, in African-American arts and culture.
5. Consumers are people who buy goods and services.
6. Many Americans felt threatened by dissidents who promoted communism or anarchy and challenged the rules of democracy.
7. Fundamentalism, or the belief that what is written in the Bible is literally true, grew in some parts of the United States during the 1920s.
8. Mass media, such as print publications, television, and movies, is meant to reach a large group of people.

READING STRATEGY ANSWER

I Read
Ads placed in mass media convinced consumers to buy products and replace them with new and "better" ones.

Changes
advertisements; mass media; consumer economy; planned obsolescence

I Know
People I know buy newer models of things they already own.

And So
Advertising still influences the buying habits of U.S. consumers.

9. Answers will vary. Possible response: During the 1920s, advertisers took advantage of a consumer economy to influence what goods consumers bought. The advertising industry continues to impact American life by convincing people to buy products that will make them feel good about themselves.

MAIN IDEAS ANSWERS

10. The Red Scare was a form of mass panic among Americans who believed that communists and other radicals were plotting to incite rebellion in the United States.

11. The Volstead Act was enacted to enforce Prohibition, which made illegal the manufacture, sale, purchase, and consumption of alcohol.

12. Immigration laws in the 1920s restricted the number of immigrants overall, but they particularly targeted immigrants from southern Europe, who many Americans believed did not have the character to become good American citizens.

13. The boom in new products made advertising necessary as a marketing tool to reach consumers through print ads in national magazines and radio ads during popular radio programs.

14. Before the development of mass media, such as radio and movies, different regions in the United States did not share the same interests or concerns. By listening to the same radio programs and going to the same movies, more people began to identify with a shared, common experience, creating a mass culture.

15. Jazz music had an appeal that cut across racial lines, with people of diverse ethnic backgrounds listening and dancing to and playing jazz music.

16. Possible response: The Harlem Renaissance provided African-American writers and artists with a cultural center in New York City in which to gather and flourish.

HISTORICAL THINKING ANSWERS

17. Possible response: Sacco and Vanzetti were immigrants who promoted anarchy, so bias against them was likely very strong in spite of the lack of evidence that they had committed a crime.

18. The Red Scare was an example of why so many Americans longed to go back to a time when they were not afraid of foreign influence that would change their way of life. Harding was likely elected because he promised a return to "normalcy."

19. Many people in cities were opposed to Prohibition, so it was hard to enforce the law with a large part of the population determined to consume alcohol. People in rural areas tended to support Prohibition, making it easier to enforce the law.

20. Possible response: The parents might have held traditional values and opinions about women and struggled to accept their flapper daughter's shorter, less restrictive clothing style and freer social behavior.

21. Answers will vary. Students might support the opinion that a consumer economy was positive for the United States because Americans buying cars and spreading outward from cities boosted the country's economy through consumers' demand for goods and construction. Conversely, students might suggest that the growing importance of entertainment in Americans' lives and Americans' need to acquire products, especially those bought on credit, indicated that traditional values were not as important as acquiring status by owning things.

22. The movement of African Americans to the North led to them making social and economic gains. This threatened the established white culture, and membership in the Ku Klux Klan increased. Prejudice created fears about immigrants potentially changing the American way of life, and immigration quotas resulted.

23. Answers will vary. Students should clearly state their opinion about how American identity changed in the 1920s and support their opinions with evidence from the chapter.

INTERPRET VISUALS ANSWERS

24. The cartoon implies that each step labor takes on this path is one step closer to chaos and something even worse, as suggested by the question mark in the water.

25. Answers will vary. Students might suggest that the aim of labor unions is to organize workers to get fair treatment and pay, not to overthrow the government. The cartoonist was pointing out that the hysteria about the rise of labor unions was absurd. He exaggerated the result of strikes by showing steps leading to murder and chaos, ideas he likely hoped the reader would understand as unlikely to follow a labor strike.

ANALYZE SOURCES ANSWER

26. Answers will vary. Possible response: The excessive partying during the 1920s didn't make people happier because of the "uncertainties of 1920." Fitzgerald may have been suggesting that immediately following World War I, society and the economy hadn't yet settled into normal states.

CONNECT TO YOUR LIFE ANSWER

27. Answers will vary. Students should identify a recent change that has happened in American life that affected them and write a paragraph that makes a connection between this change and a change that happened during the 1920s. Students should cite text evidence, use at least three Key Vocabulary words, and conclude with a sentence that connects how the 1920s changed American life to how current events changed their life.

UNIT 8 RESOURCES

UNIT INTRODUCTION

UNIT TIME LINE

UNIT WRAP-UP

NATIONAL GEOGRAPHIC | CONNECTION

National Geographic Magazine Adapted Articles
- "WWI and Mapmaking at National Geographic"
- "Untold Stories of D-Day" ONLINE

Unit 8 Inquiry: Respond to a Crisis

NG Learning Framework Activities
- Research War Damage
- Share the Arts of the 1920s

Unit 8 Formal Assessment

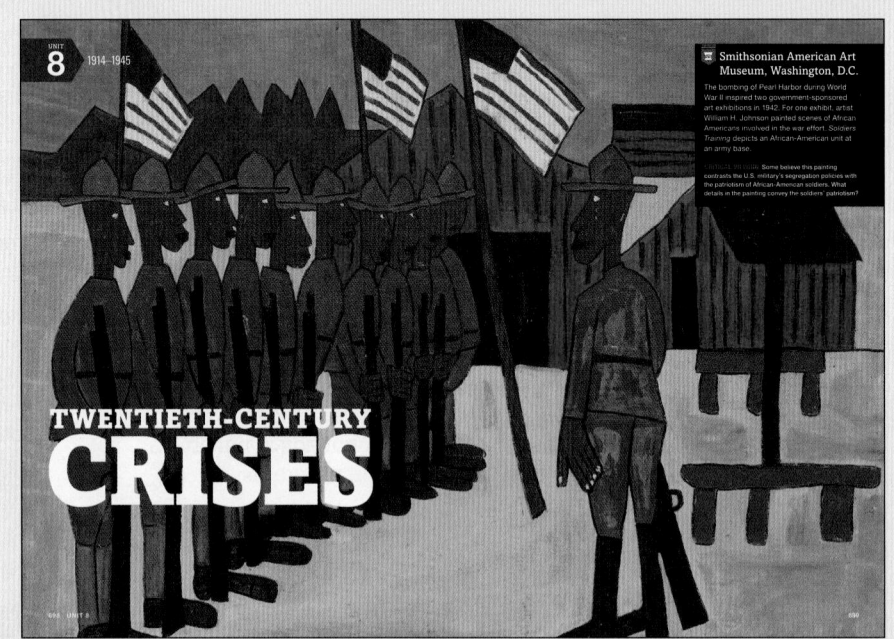

CHAPTER 23 RESOURCES

Available at NGLSync.Cengage.com

TEACHER RESOURCES & ASSESSMENT

Reading and Note-Taking

Vocabulary Practice

Social Studies Skills Lessons
- Reading: Identify Main Ideas and Details
- Writing: Write an Explanatory Paragraph

Formal Assessment
- Chapter 23 Pretest
- Chapter 23 Tests A & B
- Section Quizzes

Chapter 23 Answer Key

ExamView®
One-time Download

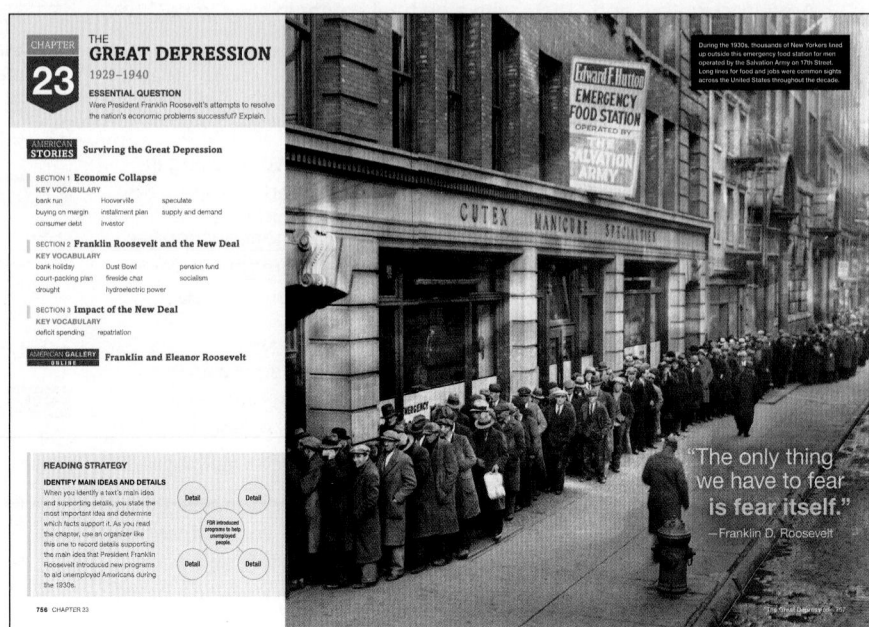

STUDENT DIGITAL RESOURCES

- **eEdition** (English)
- **eEdition** (Spanish)
- **Handbooks**

- **Online Atlas**
- **American Gallery Online**
- **History Notebook**

- **American Voices (Biographies)**
- **Active History**
- **Projects for Inquiry-Based Learning**

Chapter 23 Spanish Resources are available at NGLSync.Cengage.com.

CHAPTER 23 PLANNER

AMERICAN STORIES | Surviving the Great Depression

- Primary Sources
- On Your Feet: Rotating Discussion
- NG Learning Framework: Create a Media Gallery

SECTION 1 RESOURCES
ECONOMIC COLLAPSE

LESSON 1.1
Weaknesses in the Economy
- Active History: Graph Stock Prices
- NG Learning Framework: Explore the Power of Advertising

LESSON 1.2
Stock Market Crash
- On Your Feet: Become an Expert
- NG Learning Framework: Analyze a Stock

LESSON 1.3
Hard Times
- On Your Feet: Create a Cause-and-Effect Chain
- NG Learning Framework: Assemble a Photo Gallery

SECTION 2 RESOURCES
FRANKLIN ROOSEVELT AND THE NEW DEAL

LESSON 2.1
Franklin Roosevelt Takes Office
AMERICAN GALLERY ONLINE Franklin and Eleanor Roosevelt
- NG Learning Framework: Create a Collage
- American Voices Biographies Franklin D. Roosevelt and Eleanor Roosevelt ONLINE

LESSON 2.2
Putting People to Work
- On Your Feet: Categorize Multiple Effects
- NG Learning Framework: Research Hydroelectricity
- American Voices Biography John L. Lewis ONLINE

LESSON 2.3
The Dust Bowl
- On Your Feet: Inside-Outside Circle
- NG Learning Framework: Create an Environmental Campaign

LESSON 2.4
Social Security
- On Your Feet: Build on What You Know
- NG Learning Framework: Write an Endorsement

LESSON 2.5
The Second New Deal
- On Your Feet: Tell Me More
- NG Learning Framework: Find Local Evidence of the WPA

SECTION 3 RESOURCES
IMPACT OF THE NEW DEAL

LESSON 3.1
The New Deal's Effects on Women and Minorities
- On Your Feet: Four Corners
- NG Learning Framework: Connect Past and Present

LESSON 3.2
Legacy of the New Deal
- On Your Feet: Weigh the Pluses and Minuses
- NG Learning Framework: Showcase a Legacy

CHAPTER 23 REVIEW

Strategy ❶
Focus on Main Ideas

Tell students to locate the Main Idea statement at the beginning of each lesson. Explain that these statements summarize the important ideas of the lesson and will be useful for helping them focus on what matters most in the text. Throughout the chapter, help students get in the habit of using the Main Idea statements to set a purpose for reading.

Use with All Lessons

Strategy ❷
Sequence Events

To build understanding of the critical events in a section and their relationship to one another in time, direct students to note them in a Sequence Chain like the one shown.

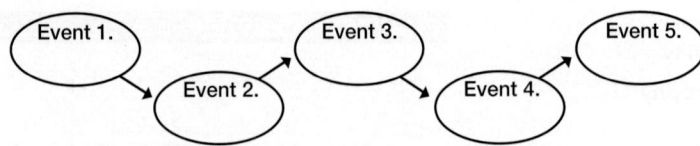

Use with Lessons 1.1–1.2, and 2.1 *Completing the graphic organizer will help students trace the sequence of events related to various aspects of the Great Depression, including events leading up to it (Lesson 1.1), the stock market crash (Lesson 1.2), and Roosevelt's election and first actions as president (Lesson 2.1).*

Strategy ❸
Preview and Review the Text

Prompt students to preview the lesson by reading the title, Main Idea statement, subheadings, and captions for art and photographs. Then ask them to write questions they have about the Great Depression that they expect to be answered in the text. After students read the lesson, direct them to work in groups to discuss what they learned and find answers to their questions.

Use with All Lessons

Strategy ❶
Modify Vocabulary Lists

Limit the number of Key Vocabulary words that students will be required to master. As they read, have students create a vocabulary card for each word in the modified list. Students may write definitions, synonyms, or examples on the back of each word card. Encourage students to refer to their vocabulary cards often as they read.

Use with All Lessons

Strategy ❷
Preview Using Maps

To help students better understand Roosevelt's landslide win and his plan to help rural areas, have students preview the maps in Lessons 2.1 and 2.2. First have students look at the legend indicating what the colors on the map The Election of 1932 represent to understand Roosevelt's decisive win. Then have them look at the legend of the map TVA Dams, 1933–1945, to understand the large multistate area impacted by dam projects. Prompt students to trace some of the rivers with a finger and then identify what the colored dot on the river represents.

Use with Lessons 2.1–2.2

ENGLISH LANGUAGE LEARNERS ELD

Strategy 1
PREP Before Reading

Encourage students at **All Proficiencies** to use the PREP strategy to prepare for reading. Write this acrostic on the board:

PREP **P**review the title.
Read Main Idea statement.
Examine visuals.
Predict what you will learn.

Use with All Lessons *Students at the **Bridging** level may help students at the **Emerging** or **Expanding** level write their predictions.*

Strategy 2
Review Transitional Words

To help students put events in chronological order and summarize what they read, write these transitional words on the board: *first, next, then, also, while, immediately, later, earlier, meanwhile, whenever, simultaneously, subsequently, during, following, before, afterward,* and *finally.* Instruct students at the **Emerging** and **Expanding** levels of proficiency to work together to write a series of sentences describing what happens in each lesson. Encourage them to use transitional words to tell about the time order of events. Have students at the **Bridging** level construct a paragraph that summarizes the material. Prompt them to use a variety of transitional words and to vary their sentence structure.

Use with All Lessons

Strategy 3
Create Word Maps

Pair students at the **Emerging** level of proficiency with those at the **Expanding** or **Bridging** level. Tell pairs to work together to identify at least three words from the lesson that they had difficulty understanding. Instruct students to create Word Maps for each word.

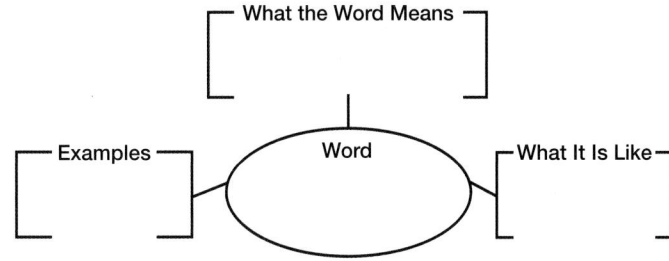

Use with All Lessons

GIFTED & TALENTED

Strategy 1
Create a Biography

Begin by asking students to select a woman or an African American mentioned in Lesson 3.1 to research and write a biography of in a comic book or graphic novel style. Encourage students to first frame questions about the historical figure and to then conduct research to answer their questions. Tell them to use both visuals and text in their biography. Prompt students to share their completed biographies with the class and answer questions.

Use with Lesson 3.1 *You may also suggest photographers Walker Evans, Arthur Rothstein, Gordon Parks, and Dorothea Lange, whose photographs appear in this chapter.*

Strategy 2
Visually Enhance a Chart

Tell students to choose one of the charts in the chapter to enhance. They could, for example, use presentation software and convey the information through bullet points. Instruct students to use noncopyrighted visuals to illustrate the programs described in the chart. Alternatively, they could use animation or make an interactive infographic. Invite students to present their charts to the class.

Use with Lessons 2.2 and 2.5

Pre-AP

Strategy 1
Extend Knowledge

Invite students to conduct research to find out more about a person, place, program, or event introduced in Chapter 23, such as rail-riders, Okies, Wall Street, hydroelectric power, erosion, fireside chats, the Social Security Act, Indian Reorganization Act, or Mexican Repatriation Program. Prompt students to present their findings in an oral report to the class or in a digital report posted on a class blog.

Use with All Lessons

Strategy 2
Write an Evaluative Essay

Explain to students that evaluative essays include a judgment, criteria for making that judgment, and evidence supporting it. Instruct students to conduct further research to evaluate the New Deal and its legacies, including the differing outcomes for particular groups, such as Hispanic, Asian, Native, and African Americans, and women and children. Students may read their essay to the class or publish it on a school blog.

Use with Lessons 3.1–3.2

THE GREAT DEPRESSION

1929–1940

ESSENTIAL QUESTION

Were President Franklin Roosevelt's attempts to resolve the nation's economic problems successful? Explain.

READING STRATEGY

IDENTIFY MAIN IDEAS AND DETAILS

When you identify a text's main idea and supporting details, you state the most important idea and determine which facts support it. As you read the chapter, use an organizer like this one to record details supporting the main idea that President Franklin Roosevelt introduced new programs to aid unemployed Americans during the 1930s.

Detail   Detail

FDR introduced programs to help unemployed people.

Detail   Detail

During the 1930s, thousands of New Yorkers lined up outside this emergency food station for men operated by the Salvation Army on 17th Street. Long lines for food and jobs were common sights across the United States throughout the decade.

Edward F. Hutton

EMERGENCY FOOD STATION

OPERATED BY

THE SALVATION ARMY

CUTEX MANICURE SPECIALTIES

"The only thing we have to fear is fear itself."

—Franklin D. Roosevelt

INTRODUCE THE PHOTOGRAPH

Feeding the Hungry

Direct students' attention to the photograph and caption. Explain that for thousands of people during the 1930s, emergency food stations like the one shown in the photo became the main source of food. People in need stood in "breadlines" to receive a free meal from the Salvation Army and other charitable institutions. **ASK:** What emotions does the photograph convey of the people waiting in line for food? *(Possible responses: One man seems to be hiding his face, so he may be embarrassed to need free food. Others have expressions of anxiety or frustration. Many look downcast.)* Then ask a volunteer to read the quotation from Franklin D. Roosevelt's inaugural address aloud. **ASK:** What message does President Roosevelt want to convey to those in need? *(Possible response: He is encouraging people not to be afraid and saying that their fear is worse than what is actually happening and paralyzing efforts to improve the economy.)*

Share Background

Places that provided food became known as "soup kitchens" because soup was often the main item on the menu. Soup was cost-effective to prepare, and it could be stretched to feed more people by adding water. It was easy to serve in a bowl or a cup, and even spoons weren't absolutely necessary to eat it. Charities that operated the soup kitchens could get meat scraps from butchers or restaurants, but obtaining fresh vegetables was far more challenging. People who were able to do so grew "charity gardens" and donated their crops to soup kitchens to help feed the hungry.

For Chapter 23 Spanish Resources, visit the Resources Menu. Chapter 23 Resources are available at NGLSync.Cengage.com.

INTRODUCE THE ESSENTIAL QUESTION

Were President Franklin Roosevelt's attempts to resolve the nation's economic problems successful? Explain.

Team Word Webbing: Facing Hard Times Ask students to brainstorm a list of problems that might result from an economic crisis. Examples might include unemployment, poverty, business closures, widespread hunger, or an increase in homelessness. Write each problem singly in the center of a sheet of paper. Divide the class into four or five teams and give each team one of the sheets of paper. Instruct teams to write down ways a president might attempt to resolve the problem. Each member should write a suggestion and then rotate the paper to add more suggestions. Ask groups to share their ideas with the class, and then post the Word Webs in the classroom. As students read the chapter, have them compare their suggestions with President Roosevelt's actions.

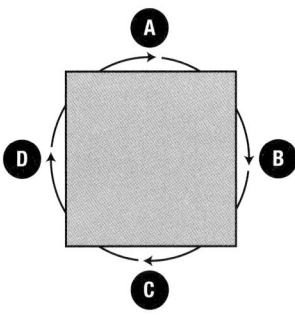

INTRODUCE CHAPTER VOCABULARY

Vocabulary Pyramids

As students read the chapter, encourage them to complete Vocabulary Pyramids for Key Vocabulary words. Tell them to make a pyramid for each word, complete what they know about each word before reading, and then add to or correct the pyramid after they encounter the word in the chapter. Model an example for students on the board, using the graphic organizer below.

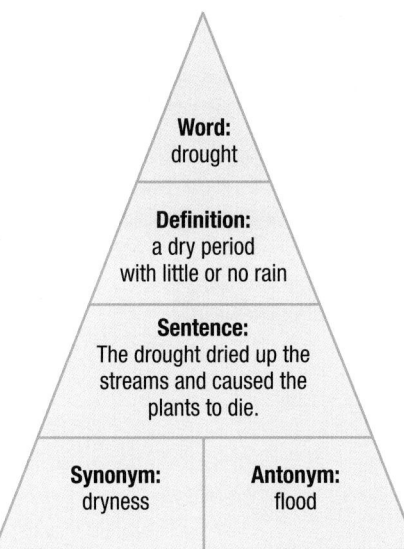

INTRODUCE THE READING STRATEGY

IDENTIFY MAIN IDEAS AND DETAILS

Remind students that identifying a main idea and determining which facts support it helps them understand the text as they read. Model by finding the main idea of the first paragraph of the subsection An Uneven Prosperity in Lesson 1.1 and adding it to a Main Idea Cluster. Then ask students to find details that support the main idea and add them to the graphic organizer. Remind students to use a Main Idea Cluster to record main ideas and details as they read the chapter.

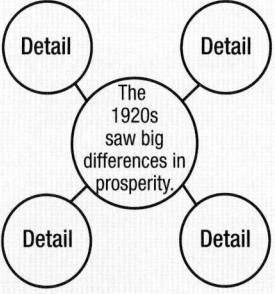

KEY DATES FOR CHAPTER 23

1929	Stock market crash
1930	Smoot-Hawley Tariff raises taxes on imports
1931	The Dust Bowl hits the Great Plains
1932	Bonus Army demands pay from government Franklin Roosevelt elected president
1933	Roosevelt introduces the New Deal
1935	Social Security becomes law
1936	Roosevelt wins re-election
1937	Court-packing plan fails

For more on climate, see *EXPLORE EXTREME WIND AND WATER*

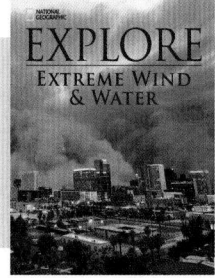

Objectives

- **Describe ways people experienced and survived the Great Depression.**
- **Learn about relief programs created by the federal government.**
- **Analyze art, photography, and literature that depict the Great Depression.**
- **Study primary sources: excerpt from *The Grapes of Wrath* and photography from *Let Us Now Praise Famous Men*.**

Critical Thinking Skills for "Surviving the Great Depression"

- Make Connections
- Draw Conclusions
- Analyze Primary Sources
- Form and Support Opinions
- Evaluate

Background for the Teacher

This American Story explores life during the Great Depression, focusing on people who migrated west, farmers, and those employed by the federal agencies that President Franklin Roosevelt established. Through the study of an engaging narrative and multiple primary sources, including photographs, paintings, and literature, students will understand how the Depression altered where and how people lived, as well as Americans' relationships with each other and the federal government.

Chapter 23, The Great Depression, discusses the economic calamities that struck the nation during the 1930s. While the chapter analyzes the underlying causes of the Great Depression and the multitude of relief and recovery programs initiated by the Roosevelt administration, this American Story provides an in-depth understanding of how people experienced—and survived—the Great Depression.

History Notebook

Encourage students to complete the American Story page for Chapter 23 in their History Notebooks as they read.

Note to the Teacher

Introduce this American Story after the class has engaged with the content in Section 2.

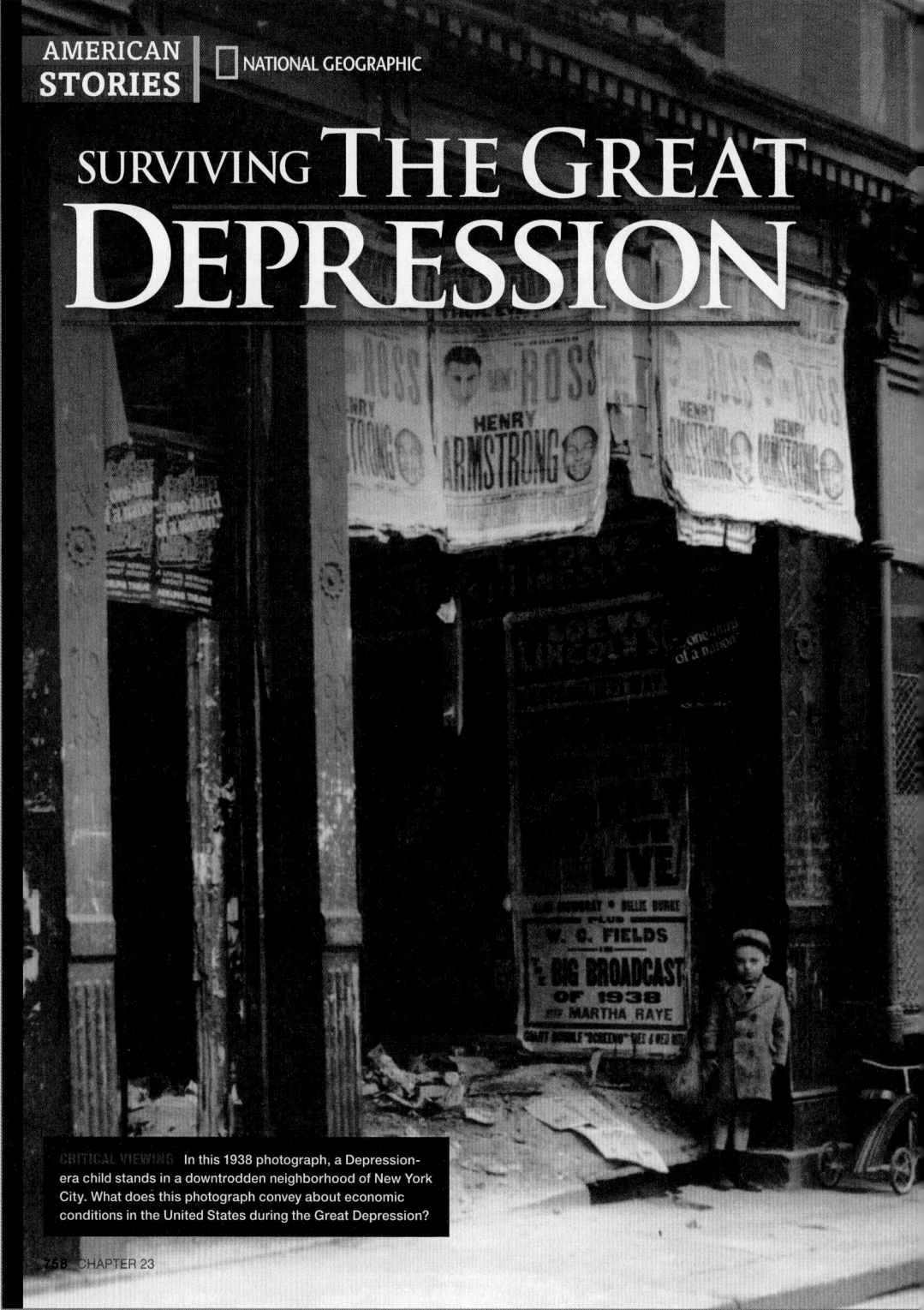

AMERICAN STORIES | NATIONAL GEOGRAPHIC

SURVIVING THE GREAT DEPRESSION

CRITICAL VIEWING In this 1938 photograph, a Depression-era child stands in a downtrodden neighborhood of New York City. What does this photograph convey about economic conditions in the United States during the Great Depression?

758 CHAPTER 23

The 1920s were nicknamed the "Roaring Twenties" for a reason: The economy was booming, and many Americans were sharing in the wealth. Millions of people had the luxury of wondering how to spend their larger incomes—perhaps on a few more trips to the movies, a radio for the house, or even a car. Then in 1929, stock prices fell suddenly and dramatically, contributing to a sharp decline in the economy. Many Americans lost their jobs—and their optimism. Between 1929 and 1933, unemployment rose from 3 percent to 25 percent of the labor force. Now people were asking a new question: How will we survive?

HEADING WEST

With little work at home, millions of people took to the roads in search of jobs during the economic downturn that became known as the Great Depression. Most headed west because they thought they had a better chance of finding a job in California. Unable to pay for a bus or train ticket, some decided to "ride the rails." That is, they illegally jumped onto freight trains to travel. Many survived by finding temporary jobs, begging, and occasionally stealing.

According to some estimates, about 2 million men, 8,000 women, and 250,000 children rode the rails during the Great Depression. Eric Sevareid, a well-known American journalist, rode the rails as a teen during the 1930s. He later described this temporary community as "a great underground world, peopled by tens of thousands of American men, women, and children, white, black, brown, and yellow."

Life on the rails was difficult and extremely dangerous. Thousands died in the act of trying to jump onto a moving train, and most suffered from injuries, hunger, and thirst. Despite the harsh conditions, however, some rail riders went on to have successful careers after the Depression.

The Great Depression **759**

INTRODUCE & ENGAGE

Consider the Impact of Economic Hardship

Remind students that during the Great Depression millions of people found themselves out of work and struggling to survive. Ask students to respond to the following questions: How might people who couldn't find jobs and had very little money have felt? Who might have been able to help people struggling financially and how? Write students' responses on the board. After reading "Surviving the Great Depression," revisit the list and ask if students would like to add to or revise any of their responses.

Find Mural Themes

Display photographs of WPA murals found in schools, post offices, libraries, and other public buildings across the United States. Photos of these murals can be found through online searches for New Deal Art or New Deal Murals. Before giving background on the works, prompt students to point out details in the murals that reveal the time period in which the artwork was created. Then ask students to categorize the murals by topic or theme and identify commonalities across the collection. After students have expressed their ideas, tell them where the different murals are displayed, and explain that they were painted during the Great Depression.

Examine Photographs of the Great Depression

Invite students to examine the black-and-white photographs found throughout this American Story and to think about what the photographs reveal about life during the Great Depression. **ASK:** Based on the photos, how do you think the Depression affected most people? *(Possible response: The Depression left people poor, often homeless, and forced people to migrate to new areas.)* Inform students that in this lesson they will learn about the role photographers played in expressing and communicating the effects of the Great Depression.

CRITICAL VIEWING The worn condition of the building and the posters suggests that the businesses are long closed, and former owners and employees have likely lost income and jobs. The dirty sidewalk and the litter also indicate that there is no promise of the businesses reopening.

BUILD BACKGROUND

The Depression Hits California

During the Great Depression, hundreds of thousands of people migrated to California in search of opportunity, but the Golden State did not prove to be an economic haven. By 1934, farm income dropped in half, wages decreased dramatically, new construction dried up, and more than 1 million people lived on public relief. This situation led to heightened tensions between business and labor, as seen during numerous clashes between growers and farm laborers and the "Bloody Thursday" strike of 1934, in which two strikers were killed and many more were injured. With the arrival of the so-called Okies, who joined the throngs of migrant farm laborers, hostilities grew as locals feared a further reduction in wages and quality of life. The Okies' tents and squalid shantytowns were not welcome neighbors.

The Federal Theatre Project

One of the more interesting WPA initiatives was the Federal Theatre Project (FTP), a program designed to provide employment for actors, directors, playwrights, designers, technicians, and others involved in the theatrical profession. The FTP staged a wide variety of productions, including modern, classic, and children's plays as well as vaudeville and dance. In order to reach a wide geographic area, the FTP toured throughout the country, often stopping in rural areas where dramatic productions were rarely seen. At its height, the FTP employed more than 12,000 people—including Orson Welles, the famed director of *Citizen Kane*, who in 1936 produced an all African-American version of *Macbeth*.

CRITICAL VIEWING The billboard reflects a time of prosperity when people could afford to travel in luxury. The sight of the men carrying their luggage as they walk down a dirt road contrasts with the billboard's image of a relaxing train ride, showing how the Great Depression had changed the travel experience and other aspects of life for many Americans.

AMERICAN STORIES

CALIFORNIA, HERE I COME!

For farmers living in the Great Plains, an environmental disaster added to the economic problems of the 1930s. Poor farming practices and a long period with little rainfall caused the soil in the region to dry out. The drought was especially severe in Texas, Oklahoma, Colorado, Kansas, and New Mexico. The dried-out soil could not support crops or livestock. Even worse, it was often swept up into the air by strong prairie winds, causing dangerous dust storms called black blizzards. In 1935, a journalist coined the term "Dust Bowl" to describe the region, and the nickname stuck.

Most farmers in the Dust Bowl remained on their land and endured the years of heat, hunger, and choking dust. About one-quarter of them, however, were forced to move in order to survive. Between 1930 and 1940, about 2.5 million people left the Great Plains. Some 300,000 of them headed for California because they believed they could find work in the fertile fields of the Golden State. This group was known as the Okies, even though most were not from Oklahoma.

Unlike the rail riders, most people who left the Dust Bowl drove, piling their possessions into cars or trucks and heading west on Route 66. American novelist John Steinbeck wrote about a fictional journey by an Okie family to California in his 1939 novel *The Grapes of Wrath*.

The trip was a days-long trial. Often short of money, the travelers would camp out by the roadside at night. To reach California, they had to cross the desert in their hot, overstuffed, and often run-down cars. By the time these migrants arrived, California looked like paradise to them.

For most, the joy of arrival did not last long, since Californians were not happy to see thousands of new farm workers in search of jobs. Some towns tried to set up blockades to prevent newcomers from crossing into the state. Okies who did make it to California found that the competition for jobs was fierce and wages were low.

Many Dust Bowl refugees found themselves living in "ditch camps," clusters of shacks set up near drainage or irrigation ditches. The camps were crowded and dirty, and families struggled to maintain their dignity and patterns of life. One social worker described a family living in the shell of an old car: "The mother . . . was trying to carry on a home life as best she could, using cupboards and tables made of old boxes, a rusty tin can as her stewpot, wash water taken out of an irrigation ditch." Eventually, the federal government stepped in to improve conditions and build better camps. For most migrants, however, true relief would come only when the Great Depression ended in the 1940s.

CRITICAL VIEWING Two men trudge down a deserted highway on their way to California, passing by a Southern Pacific railroad advertisement, in this 1937 photograph. How do the men and the billboard convey the story of the Great Depression?

BUILDING AND REBUILDING

In 1932, Franklin Roosevelt was elected president based on his promises to take strong action to end the Great Depression. One of his ideas was to put unemployed workers back on the job—working for the government. To this end, he created the Civilian Conservation Corps (CCC) in 1933 and the Works Progress Administration (WPA) in 1935. Both agencies hired workers for projects to benefit the country. CCC employees worked mainly in the nation's parks, building lodges, planting trees, maintaining roads and trails, and fighting fires. The WPA put people to work building bridges, schools, and airports; running nursery schools; and serving school lunches.

Neither agency paid well, and most of the jobs were temporary, but even a low-paying job could mean the difference between survival and starvation. One WPA laborer in North Carolina earned $18.50 every two weeks working at a printing plant. It was barely enough money to support a family with eight children, but his wife later remarked, "If it hadn't been for the WPA, I don't know what we would have done."

WPA employees lived at home and worked in their communities. Working for the CCC, in contrast, was like a combination of military boot camp and school. The CCC hired young men and brought them to camps in national parks and other federal lands. By day, the men maintained and improved natural areas, and by night many of them attended school or job training programs. Over 9 years, 57,000 men learned to read and write in CCC classes.

The WPA oversaw some job programs that targeted specific groups. The National Youth Administration (NYA), for example, employed students and helped young people find job training programs.

Two other specialized programs were the Federal Writers' Project and the Federal Arts Project. The Federal Writers' Project employed writers to create travel guides for the United States. Well-known writers who worked on the guides included Ralph Ellison, John Cheever, and Saul Bellow.

The Federal Arts Project and other government agencies hired artists to create paintings, sculptures, and other forms of art to adorn public

THE GRAPES OF WRATH

Published in 1939, John Steinbeck's novel, *The Grapes of Wrath*, introduces the Joads, a family of Dust Bowl refugees. The book is a sympathetic portrayal of a family determined to rise above desperate conditions and build a better life. One of its major themes is the power of love and generosity shared by strangers. To write the book, Steinbeck researched the real lives of Dust Bowl migrants and visited a migrant camp in California.

PRIMARY SOURCE

And here's a story you can hardly believe, but it's true, and it's funny and it's beautiful. There was a family of twelve and they were forced off the land. They had no car. They built a trailer out of junk and loaded it with their possessions. They pulled it to the side of 66 and waited. And pretty soon a sedan picked them up. Five of them rode in the sedan and seven on the trailer, and a dog on the trailer. They got to California in two jumps. The man who pulled them fed them. And that's true. But how can such courage be, and such faith in their own species? Very few things would teach such faith.

The people in flight from the terror behind—strange things happen to them, some bitterly cruel and some so beautiful that the faith is refired forever.

The Great Depression **761**

Guided Discussion

1. **Form and Support Opinions** Considering that the Depression was a devastating time in U.S. history, why do you think 20th Century-Fox decided to produce a film from John Steinbeck's novel *The Grapes of Wrath*? *(Answers will vary. Possible responses: The American public could relate to a movie about hard times during the Depression, and the movie was based on a book by an author who had researched real people and conditions in a migrant camp. The producers may have also felt the movie would have an audience because the characters in the novel were shown in a sympathetic light. The text explains that the government supported documenting life during the Depression, which this film does. The producers may have also wanted to depict a ray of hope and optimism, since the primary source indicates that the novel's major themes are love and generosity.)*

2. **Make Connections** How did the Great Depression worsen the plight of Dust Bowl farmers? *(Possible response: The lack of jobs across the nation resulting from the Depression made it difficult for farmers, who could no longer grow crops, to find work.)*

Active Options

On Your Feet: Rotating Discussion Divide the class into four teams and assign each team a corner of the room. Ask each team to prepare several questions about how the Great Depression affected people and what the government did in response to the Depression. Start the discussion by tossing a beanbag or other soft object to Team 1 and asking a question. After the members of that team answer the question, they toss the beanbag to another team while asking one of their prepared questions. Continue until all teams have exhausted their questions.

NG Learning Framework: Create a Media Gallery

SKILL Observation

KNOWLEDGE Our Human Story

Ask students to work in pairs to research photographs by Walker Evans and other Depression-era photographers, such as Dorothea Lange and Gordon Parks. Instruct pairs to create a media gallery using photographs they've viewed and selected. Students must decide on a theme for their gallery and choose and arrange the photographs accordingly. When finished, invite students to share their gallery and explain to the class the theme it expresses.

The Hoover Dam

The Hoover Dam was built to tame the Colorado River. During the spring, melting snow from the mountains caused the river to rise, which resulted in damaging floods across the region—some of which included important farmland. Engineers were hired to study the river and locate places to dam in order to store the spring runoff and release it slowly over the summer. As the population of Southern California grew, people in the region saw the dam as a way to divert water to the area for homes, businesses, and factories. Seven states, fearing California would secure much of the water for itself, met in 1922 to resolve the issue of how the water would be divided. They developed the Colorado River Compact. This agreement set the amount of water for each state, and it is still in effect today.

🏛 Virtual Museum Visit

Located near the White House, the Renwick Gallery is part of the Smithsonian American Art Museum. In 1858, William Wilson Corcoran, a prominent banker and art collector, had the Renwick Gallery designed specifically to showcase works by American artists, believing that achievements in art and culture were as important as those in industry and trade. Access the museum's website to find information on the Renwick Gallery exhibit "1934: A New Deal for Artists." Point out that the paintings *Valley Farms* by Ross Dickinson and *Apple Vendor* were both created as part of the Public Works of Art Project to depict "the American Scene." **ASK:** Which painting do you think is more effective in showing "the American Scene" and why? *(Possible responses: Apple Vendor is more effective because it shows the hard reality of the Great Depression. Valley Farms is more effective because it shows the United States as a still-vibrant country.)*

WRITE ABOUT HISTORY

Compare Historical Migrations In this American Story, students examined how the Great Depression affected people's lives, causing many to migrate west. To draw comparisons across history, instruct students to select and research another example of historical migration. Then tell students to write an essay comparing and contrasting the motivations and the experiences of people in both migrations.

RENWICK GALLERY

The painting focuses on a man trying to make a living selling apples on the street, which shows the kinds of things people did to survive the Depression.

THINK ABOUT IT

Hard times could come again, for individuals or for the nation, and it's important to understand how people can get through them.

AMERICAN STORIES

places. They commissioned many artists to create large wall paintings called murals for public buildings. These colorful works of art decorated post offices across the United States. The murals were generally patriotic and optimistic, portraying scenes of industry or agriculture. Many influential artists of the 20th century were WPA muralists early in their careers.

Some people objected to the government spending taxpayers' money to support struggling writers and artists. Harry Hopkins, the head of the WPA, replied, "They've got to eat, just like other people."

THE HOOVER DAM

Plans to dam the Colorado River had been in the works for decades before the Great Depression began. But the timing of the dam's construction could not have been better. By the time work began in 1931, thousands of unemployed workers had arrived in nearby Las Vegas hoping for a job.

Work on the Hoover Dam was hard—and sometimes terrifying. Laborers had to dig tunnels through solid rock, enduring temperatures of 140 degrees and high levels of carbon monoxide. Other workers, called "high scalers," dangled 800 feet above the ground while using heavy jackhammers to carve canyon walls. Still, many men were grateful even for dangerous, low-paying work.

Near the construction site, the government built a town called Boulder City with dormitories for single men and cottages for married men who had come with their families. A worker could pay $1.60 a day for a room and three hearty meals. The town had strict rules that sometimes frustrated the workers, but it provided a welcome shelter from even worse

🏛 Renwick Gallery, Washington, D.C.

This oil painting, entitled *Apple Vendor*, was created by American artist Barbara Stevenson around 1933 as part of a New Deal program that supported American artists during the Depression. Artists were encouraged to paint "the American Scene" and capture the look and feel of the country. How do you think the subject matter reflects the Depression?

conditions in many parts of the country. African-American, Native American, and Hispanic workers, however, had to find housing elsewhere because they were not permitted in Boulder City.

When the Hoover Dam was completed in 1935, it was the tallest dam in the world. Its construction required about 5 million barrels of cement, 45 million pounds of reinforcement steel, and 6.6 million tons of concrete. More important for the people concerned, it had employed about 21,000 workers, helping them survive some of the hardest years of the Great Depression.

THINK ABOUT IT

Why do you think it's important to remember how people survived the Great Depression?

DOCUMENTING THE DEPRESSION: WALKER EVANS

In 1935, President Franklin Roosevelt created the Resettlement Administration (RA) to help address the problems of farmers during the Great Depression. The agency was later renamed the Farm Security Administration. The RA hired American economist and photographer Roy Stryker to head up a team of photographers called the Historical Section. Their mission was to document conditions in rural areas and show Americans why the work of the RA was necessary. In Stryker's words, the group "introduced Americans to America."

One of Stryker's photographers—Walker Evans— proved to be a genius at making the introduction. His photos revealed the lives of Depression survivors in sharply defined black and white. He later became one of the most influential American photographers of the century.

Evans, born in 1903, once wanted to become a writer. By the late 1920s, however, he had turned to photography to express himself. In 1935, Roy Stryker hired Evans to photograph a community of unemployed coal miners in West Virginia. Next, Evans traveled throughout the southeastern states with his camera. He had a special interest not only in people but also in places. He photographed buildings and objects that represented people's lives and concerns, and he also captured many striking images of individuals and families.

In 1936, Evans took a break from his work for the Historical Section and traveled to Alabama with a friend, American writer James Agee. There, they documented the lives of three cotton sharecropper families struggling to make a living. Evans's photos and Agee's text appeared in a 1941 book called *Let Us Now Praise Famous Men*, which has been described as a "stunningly honest" portrayal of families confronting the challenges of the Depression. Some of the individuals featured in the book, however, were upset over how they were represented, in spite of the dignity and honesty of the photos.

After the Depression, Evans continued working as a photographer, expanding his interests to such subjects as people on the New York City subway. He died on April 10, 1975. Many prominent photographers today credit him as an inspiration for their own work.

CRITICAL VIEWING (top) Evans captured this everyday street scene in Selma, Alabama, in 1936. (bottom) Sharecropper Floyd Burroughs rests on a porch in Hale County, Alabama, in 1936, surrounded by the children of a neighboring family. Why might the people in these photographs have objected to the way they were portrayed?

The Great Depression 763

Weaknesses in the Economy

Imagine that you're a midwestern farmer in the 1920s. You keep hearing stories about how great the country is doing. But on your farm, it sure doesn't seem that way. You've lost money for five years in a row, in spite of great harvests. What has gone wrong?

MAIN IDEA The 1920s were prosperous years for many Americans, but the economy had significant weaknesses.

AN UNEVEN PROSPERITY

The "Roaring Twenties" are remembered as years of progress and plenty, but not all Americans prospered. Some people were wealthy, and the middle class lived comfortably, but many people just scraped by. While the average person's income rose, the distribution of income became more unequal. By 1929, the top 0.1 percent of Americans had a combined yearly income equal to that of the bottom 42 percent.

American farmers in particular struggled financially. Their troubles began soon after World War I ended. During the war, demand for agricultural products increased, especially overseas. Prices rose too, following the economic principle of **supply and demand**, which states that the price of a product depends on how much is available (the supply) and how much is wanted (the demand). To increase their production of crops, many farmers borrowed money to buy more land and new or better machinery. But after the war ended, the demand for U.S. agricultural products dropped

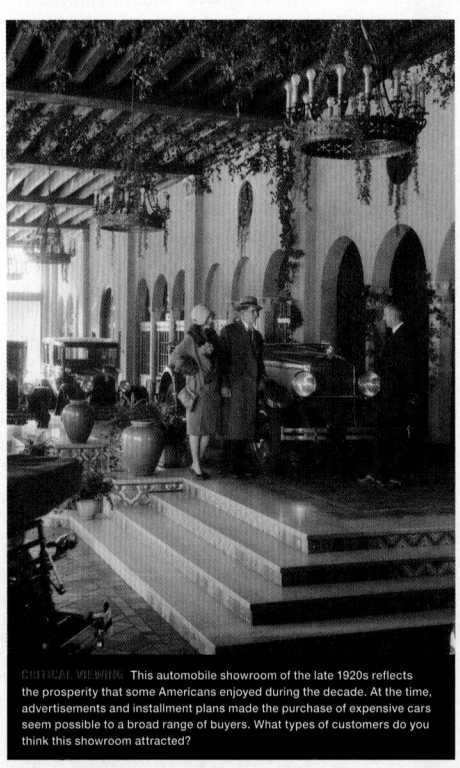

CRITICAL VIEWING This automobile showroom of the late 1920s reflects the prosperity that some Americans enjoyed during the decade. At the time, advertisements and installment plans made the purchase of expensive cars seem possible to a broad range of buyers. What types of customers do you think this showroom attracted?

as Europeans returned to farming. Prices also decreased, but production did not, resulting in surpluses throughout the 1920s. American farmers found themselves caught in a web of deep debt, low prices, and overproduction.

Other struggling industries included textiles and coal mining. Like agriculture, the textile industry had boomed during World War I. But a postwar drop in demand for textiles reduced prices by 60 percent, forcing the industry to reduce production. Textile mills closed, and many people lost their jobs. The coal industry also suffered as the nation began to use more oil, natural gas, and electrical energy. Production of bituminous coal, the most common type of coal, dropped from 144 million tons in 1929 to 75 million in 1932. Between 1920 and 1930, the price of coal dropped by more than a third.

Another disturbing trend was the high level of **consumer debt**, which is the amount of money that people have borrowed to purchase goods. During the 1920s, many Americans bought cars, appliances, and other goods on credit using an **installment plan**, which meant they made a series of partial payments over time. By 1929, according to one estimate, 75 percent of the radios and washing machines and 80 to 90 percent of the furniture sold in the United States was financed through an installment plan.

INVESTING IN THE STOCK MARKET

Despite these troubling signs, the U.S. economy boomed during the 1920s. So did the stock market, in which people called **investors** buy shares in companies in the hope of making money when they sell the shares. Investors commonly track the performance of the stock market using a stock market index, such as the **Dow Jones Industrial Average (DJIA)**, often simply referred to as "the Dow." The Dow charts the daily prices of a select number of stocks on the New York Stock Exchange, the largest market where stocks are bought and sold, and since 1971, on NASDAQ, the second-largest market. As the value of the selected stocks rises, the Dow rises too.

During the 1920s, many ordinary people began to **speculate**, or invest in stocks, hoping to make a quick profit. Some people depended on **buying on margin**, or buying a stock for a percentage of

American journalist and social historian Frederick Lewis Allen remarked on the spread of stock speculation in the late 1920s.

PRIMARY SOURCE

The speculative fever was infecting the whole country. Stories of fortunes made overnight were on everybody's lips. . . . Wives were asking their husbands why they were so slow, why they weren't getting in on all this, only to hear that their husbands had bought a hundred shares of American Linseed that very morning. Brokers' branch offices were jammed with crowds of men and women watching the shining transparency on which the moving message of the ticker tape [a device that conveys stock information] was written.

—from *Only Yesterday: An Informal History of the 1920s,* by Frederick Lewis Allen, 1931

its price and borrowing to pay for the rest. If the stock's price rises, the borrower repays the lender after selling the stock for a profit. But if the price declines, the borrower owes the lender the balance, plus interest. Between September 1922 and December 1927, the value of the Dow doubled from 100 to 200 points. Investors believed the market was on a permanent upward trend. Thousands of small business owners invested their company's working capital, the money that is typically used to cover short-term expenses, in the stock market.

HISTORICAL THINKING

1. **READING CHECK** How did the end of World War I affect American farmers?

2. **COMPARE AND CONTRAST** How are the installment plan and buying on margin similar and different? Explain your answer with evidence from the text.

3. **DRAW CONCLUSIONS** What problems might a high level of consumer debt create for a nation's economy, especially when unemployment is rising?

Objective

Identify economic problems and trends that affected Americans during the 1920s.

Critical Thinking Skills for Lesson 1.1

• Identify Main Ideas and Details
• Monitor Comprehension
• Compare and Contrast
• Draw Conclusions
• Make Predictions
• Analyze Primary Sources

Essential Question for Chapter 23

Were President Franklin Roosevelt's attempts to resolve the nation's economic problems successful? Explain. Unequal distribution of income and the stock market affected the nation's prosperity. Lesson 1.1 describes the state of the U.S. economy in the 1920s, setting the stage for political impacts and policy decisions.

Background for the Teacher

Charles Dow, an editor of *The Wall Street Journal,* and Edward Jones, a statistician, began calculating the Dow Jones Industrial Average (DJIA) in 1896. At that time, few Americans had an understanding of the stock market, so they did not invest in it. The DJIA provides a way for investors to gauge the ups and downs of the market by showing how a select group of stocks in large companies has performed during a normal trading day. Today, the 30 companies on the DJIA index include manufacturers, financial services, entertainment industries, and information technology firms. Critics contend that a sampling of 30 stocks does not provide an accurate picture of the entire market. However, many investors rely on the DJIA to identify market trends and inform their decisions.

Financial Literacy

To extend their knowledge and understanding about the concepts in this lesson, refer students to the Financial Literacy handbook.

Consider the Pros and Cons of Credit Cards

Point out that the use of credit cards, or "paying with plastic," has become a way of life in the United States. Ask students to think of one positive aspect and one negative aspect of using credit cards. Draw a T-chart on the board, and label one side Pros and the other side Cons. Invite students to add their ideas to the chart without repeating those already listed. Then ask them to summarize the pros and cons. Tell students that in this lesson they will learn about economic developments in the 1920s, such as the use of credit to purchase consumer goods, and how those developments affected the nation's economy.

TEACH

Guided Discussion

1. **Identify Main Ideas and Details** How did the economic principle of supply and demand affect U.S. industries in the 1920s? *(After World War I, the demand for agricultural products, textiles, and coal dropped, causing a decrease in prices. With lower prices for their produce, farmers struggled under debt. The textile and mining industries were forced to reduce production, so many textile workers and miners lost their jobs.)*

2. **Make Predictions** What do you think would be the likely outcome for small business owners from investing their working capital in the stock market? Why? *(Possible response: Small business owners would likely lose their companies because they are risking money needed to cover expenses by investing it in stocks that can go down as well as up.)*

Analyze Primary Sources

Direct students' attention to the Primary Source feature. Discuss the tone of Allen's writing and have students identify words or phrases that convey Americans' reactions to the booming economy of the 1920s. **ASK:** How does the excerpt from *Only Yesterday* support the main idea of the lesson? *(Possible responses: Words such as* fever, jammed, crowds, *and* shining transparency *suggest that everyday people who knew little about the stock market were jumping into something they didn't understand and were blinded to any potential negatives. The people described in the excerpt seem focused only on making a fortune speculating, paying little attention to problems in the underlying economy.)*

Active Options

Active History: Graph Stock Prices Extend the lesson by using either the PDF or Whiteboard version of the activity. These activities take a deeper look at a topic from, or related to, the lesson. Explore the activities as a class, turn them into group assignments, or even assign them individually.

NG Learning Framework: Explore the Power of Advertising

ATTITUDE Curiosity

KNOWLEDGE Our Human Story

Encourage students to explore the relationship between advertising and consumer debt. Ask them to find examples of ads for cars and appliances during the 1920s and to notice how advertisers used the installment plan as a lure to encourage consumers to buy these items. Allow students to work in pairs or small groups to create a 1920s-style ad for an expensive product that interests them, using the persuasive tactics they discovered through their research. As each pair or group presents its ad to the class, discuss how long it would take for a consumer to pay off the balance of the cost of the product. Finally, ask what tactics advertisers use today to encourage consumers to buy expensive items on credit.

English Language Learners

Create a Word Web Pair students at the **Emerging** and **Expanding** levels with students at the **Bridging** level. Direct pairs to create a Word Web with the label Economic Terms in the center oval. Tell students to take turns reading paragraphs of the lesson, writing any economic terms they encounter, such as *wealthy* and *income*, on the spokes of the Word Web.

Pre-AP

Write a Comparison-Contrast Essay Instruct students to conduct online research to learn about income inequality during the Great Depression and in recent years. Encourage students to use a Venn diagram to keep track of the similarities and differences between inequality then and now. Instruct students to use their research to write a comparison-contrast essay and to share their essays with the class.

See the Chapter Planner for more strategies for differentiation.

HISTORICAL THINKING

ANSWERS

1. After the war, demand for products dropped, but farmers continued high levels of production. This created an oversupply, which resulted in lower prices.

2. In both cases, people borrow money to purchase something they might not have the money on hand to buy. The installment plan enables people to make small payments on an expensive item, but they do not expect the value of the item to increase, and they do not intend to sell it. Buying on margin enables people to buy stock shares by borrowing some of the money needed. They expect the stock to increase in value so they can sell it at a profit.

3. A high level of consumer debt reduces the amount of money in circulation. Unemployed people cannot afford to make payments on items they bought, so retailers lose money and sell fewer goods.

CRITICAL VIEWING With the chandeliers and fancy decor, the showrooms likely attracted wealthy customers who could afford to buy automobiles. They may also have attracted people who hoped for prosperity in the future or who wanted to feel wealthy.

1.2 Stock Market Crash

Investors celebrated as the value of stocks rose to new heights in September 1929. More people rushed to buy stocks with borrowed money. Few realized that the stock market was about to crash.

MAIN IDEA After years of often reckless speculation, the stock market experienced a rapid and steep drop in stock prices on October 29, 1929, throwing the economy into a deep decline.

STOCK PRICES DRIFT LOWER

On September 3, 1929, the Dow Jones Industrial Average reached its peak of 381.17 points, having doubled in only 18 months. During the same period, the value of stocks bought on margin, or with borrowed money, had also doubled, reaching about $6.2 billion. Mostly ignored were the few experts who questioned how this rapid growth, fueled by borrowed money, could continue.

Through the rest of September and early October, stock prices varied, but they generally declined. By the last week in October, fearful investors were ready to cut their losses and sell their stock for whatever price they could get. On October 24, which became known as Black Thursday, investors traded nearly 13 million shares of stock, setting a record. In early trading, the market fell 11 percent. To help stabilize the market, several major banks and investment companies made large stock purchases, which served to raise prices. As a result, the Dow Jones Industrial Average lost only six points that day.

PANIC ON WALL STREET

Investors breathed a sigh of relief, but the worst was yet to come. By the following Monday, the market fell another 13 percent. Panic set in again, and many investors tried to sell all their shares of stock. A stock market crash—a rapid, steep decline in stock prices—occurred on **Black Tuesday**, October 29, 1929. Over the two days, the Dow dropped by 25 percent, and eventually, the stock market lost an estimated $30 billion. Thousands of investors were wiped out and had no way to repay the money they had borrowed to buy stocks. An article in the October 30, 1929,

edition of the *New York Times* described the reaction of people learning the bad news:

The crowds [gathered] about the ticker tape, like friends about the bedside of a stricken friend. There were no smiles. There were no tears either. Just the camaraderie [companionship] of fellow-sufferers. Everybody wanted to tell his neighbor how much he had lost. Nobody wanted to listen. It was too repetitious a tale.

Black Tuesday began a long, miserable period for **Wall Street**, the home of the New York Stock Exchange. Stock prices fell even lower. The Dow hit a low of 41.22 on July 8, 1932, which was a stunning 89 percent below its high of 381.17 in 1929. It would take a little more than 25 years for the Dow to rise above 381.17 once again.

The stock market crash led to the most severe depression, or period of low economic activity, in U.S. history. But the crash wasn't the only cause of the depression. Other causes included declining demand in such industries as agriculture, coal, and textiles; high levels of consumer debt; and unequal distribution of income and wealth.

HISTORICAL THINKING

1. **READING CHECK** Why is October 29, 1929, called Black Tuesday?

2. **ANALYZE CAUSE AND EFFECT** What effect did the 1929 stock market crash have on the economy of the United States?

3. **IDENTIFY PROBLEMS AND SOLUTIONS** What problems resulted from the practice of buying stocks on margin?

AMERICAN PLACES
Wall Street, Manhattan, New York City

Only about seven city blocks long, Wall Street doesn't occupy much space, but the business conducted there reaches into every corner of the world. Recognized as the financial center of the United States for more than 150 years, Wall Street has come to symbolize both financial opportunity and financial ruin. It has been a magnet, drawing immigrants to the United States, as well as a symbol of greed, arousing anger and disgust. The bronze statue *Charging Bull*, a symbol of Wall Street, was installed in front of the New York Stock Exchange in 1989 without permission. The city soon moved the statue to a nearby park. To some, the statue represents the unpredictable and sometimes dangerous nature of the stock market. Installed in 2017, the statue *Fearless Girl* faces off against the raging bull, symbolizing the power of strong women in the workplace and the nation.

PLAN

Objective
Describe the causes and effects of the 1929 stock market crash.

Critical Thinking Skills for Lesson 1.2
- Identify Main Ideas and Details
- Monitor Comprehension
- Analyze Cause and Effect
- Identify Problems and Solutions
- Make Inferences
- Analyze Language Use

Essential Question for Chapter 23
Were President Franklin Roosevelt's attempts to resolve the nation's economic problems successful? Explain. Declining industries, high consumer debt, and income inequality contributed to an economic downturn. Lesson 1.2 describes how the stock market crash added to U.S. economic problems.

Background for the Teacher

Today, the term *Wall Street* refers not only to a location in New York City but also to all financial business related to the stock market. The name dates back to the 17th century when New York was a Dutch colony called New Amsterdam. The Dutch built a wall as protection against invasions. The area along the wall, called Wall Street, became a busy trading district. Long after the wall was torn down and the colony had become the state of New York, the name *Wall Street* and its association with trading remained. In 1792, a group of 24 New York stockbrokers decided to separate their business from that of other traders. They gathered under a buttonwood tree on Wall Street and signed the Buttonwood Agreement, which created the New York Stock Exchange (NYSE). They started with only five securities, but within a few years, the NYSE was trading the stocks of hundreds of companies.

Read a Stock Table

Show students how to read a stock table from the financial pages of a newspaper. Display a table and note the name of one company and its ticker symbol—the unique combination of letters that identify it. Point out the columns that show the number of shares traded and the closing price—the value of a share of that company at the end of the previous day. Then help students interpret the net change—the increase or decrease in value of the stock during the previous trading day. Allow students to practice reading the table for other stocks. **ASK:** Why are investors interested in stock tables? *(The tables show whether their investments have increased or decreased in value.)* Tell students that in this lesson they will learn how dramatic changes in stock prices affected the nation's economy.

Guided Discussion

1. **Make Inferences** Why might investors have ignored experts who questioned the rapid growth of the stock market? *(Possible response: The history of the stock market over an 18-month period showed a steady increase. People were still making money and wanted to believe the trend would continue.)*

2. **Analyze Language Use** How does the language of the *New York Times* article provide insight into investors' feelings about the stock market crash? *(Possible response: The article compares investors' reactions to those of people gathered around a friend who is seriously ill, implying they are gathered together quietly and sadly. With the phrases* no smiles *and* no tears, *the article also conveys a sense of shock and disbelief.)*

American Places

Sculptor Arturo Di Modica created *Charging Bull* as a positive image of strength and power. He wanted the statue to boost morale in the financial district after the stock market crash of 1987. State Street Global Advisors, a financial company, commissioned sculptor Kristen Visbal to create the statue *Fearless Girl* as a celebration of female leadership and to encourage gender equality. Di Modica wanted *Fearless Girl* to be moved elsewhere because he believed it changed the positive message of *Charging Bull* into a negative threat.

Active Options

On Your Feet: Become an Expert Organize students into four "expert" groups and assign each group one of the causes of the depression that began in 1929: stock market crash, declining demand in certain industries, consumer debt, unequal distribution of income and wealth. Tell groups to study their topic and become experts on their cause. Then regroup students so that each new group has at least one member from each expert group. Allow time for the experts to present their topics and learn from one another.

NG Learning Framework: Analyze a Stock `STEM`

`ATTITUDE` Empowerment

`SKILLS` Observation, Communication

Encourage students to learn more about the stock market and research how investors can use information to help them make decisions. Ask students to work in small groups to choose one of the stocks on the Dow Jones Industrial Average and research its performance over the last year. Instruct groups to create a graph to display the increases and/or decreases in value of their stock. Post the following questions for groups to answer as they present their completed graphs to the class:

• If you had invested $1,000 in this stock one year ago, how much would it be worth today?

• Would you hold on to the stock or sell it? Why?

• How does tracking the performance of a stock help investors make decisions?

• What other factors might influence a choice of investments?

English Language Learners

Understand Multiple Meanings Pair students at the **Emerging** and **Expanding** levels and ask them to reread the lesson together, noting how the word *crash* is used as a noun and as a verb. Encourage students to use a dictionary to discover other meanings of *crash* (a loud noise, a collision, a computer crash, a crash course, crashing a party), and to write original sentences using *crash* as a noun and a verb.

Gifted & Talented

Create a Multimedia Presentation Challenge students to conduct research using print and online sources to learn more about the *Charging Bull* and *Fearless Girl* statues. Prompt students to assemble their findings into a compelling multimedia presentation, focusing on topics such as the backstory of each statue, how each was designed and constructed, and/or recent opinions and reactions to the statues. Invite students to share their presentations with the class and to answer questions from their classmates.

See the Chapter Planner for more strategies for differentiation.

ANSWERS

1. October 29, 1929, was the day the U.S. stock market crashed, causing thousands of investors to suffer severe financial losses—a life-changing event.

2. The stock market crash, by financially ruining large and small investors, deepened the nation's economic decline, leading to the worst depression in U.S. history.

3. When stock prices fell, investors who had bought stocks on margin were unable to repay the money they had borrowed. Both the investors and the lenders lost money.

1.3 Hard Times

The entire nation experienced a roller-coaster ride when the stock market crashed in 1929. One year people were prosperous, and the next they were destitute. It was a ride no one would want to take twice.

MAIN IDEA The severe depression that followed the stock market crash of 1929 spread from the United States to the rest of the world.

THE DEPRESSION SPREADS

After the stock market crashed, many banks failed. The slumping farm economy had already weakened rural banks. Now the vast sums of money lost in the stock market crash made the financial condition of urban banks even worse. Some banks ran short of money and closed. One bank failure often led to another as large numbers of depositors panicked and caused **bank runs** by trying to withdraw all their money. In 1930, banks failed at an alarming rate: 1,350 in that year alone.

In that same year, Congress passed the **Smoot-Hawley Tariff Act**. The act raised the import tax, or tariff, that the United States placed on a wide range of agricultural and manufactured goods.

Dow Jones Industrial Average, 1922–1934

This chart shows the steady climb and abrupt fall of the Dow from 1922 to 1932. Following the crash in October 1929 and through 1932, the Dow lost 89 percent of its value.

Source: Federal Reserve Bank of St. Louis

Many countries responded by passing high tariffs of their own, and worldwide trade declined markedly. The Smoot-Hawley Tariff Act's greatest export was, unfortunately, economic distress.

With the bad signs in the economy, businesses of all sizes cut back. They produced fewer goods, stopped hiring, and laid off workers. By 1932, industrial production in the United States had declined nearly by half. Ordinary people stopped spending money and cut their consumption, which in turn reduced manufacturing even more. Additional wage cuts and layoffs followed. The growing ranks of the unemployed had no money to spend, so the cycle continued to worsen. Two years into the depression, the rate of unemployment topped 20 percent. Many of the unemployed became homeless and could not even afford to buy food.

This economic downturn, called the **Great Depression**, lasted from 1929 to about 1939. From the United States, the depression spread worldwide, though its severity varied. In Canada, the depression was about as long and severe as it was in the United States. In Germany, it was slightly longer and nearly as harsh. In the United Kingdom, Sweden, and Japan, however, it was shorter and less difficult. The international economic instability also caused political instability, especially in Europe, which was still recovering from World War I.

HOOVER'S ACTIONS

Herbert Hoover, elected president in 1928, was a self-made millionaire—a mining engineer with a knack for business. But he grew up poor and was orphaned at the age of nine. His rise from poverty

shaped his views on the nature of American character and the role of government in people's lives. A strong believer in self-reliance, Hoover felt that Americans would thrive if they simply applied their own creativity and work ethic. He thought that federal aid would make Americans dependent on the government. At first, he championed the efforts of local governments, civic and religious groups, and voluntary organizations to provide help to the hungry and homeless.

But the crisis was too great for local charities to handle. Hoover eventually saw that federal action was needed. He began to provide limited financial relief to banks and other lenders, insurance companies, and railroads. Hoover also endorsed efforts to finance public works projects that were aimed at creating jobs. However, the president stuck by his belief that direct financial aid to needy people would make them permanently reliant on government handouts.

For everyday Americans, Hoover's measures were too little, too late. Joblessness and homelessness kept growing. Shantytowns, or communities of makeshift shacks, sprang up across the United States. As an insult to the president, people began to call the shantytowns **Hoovervilles**.

The Bonus Army

In 1924, Congress voted to give World War I veterans a bonus, to be paid in 1945. But with the arrival of the Great Depression, many men needed the money right away. Calling themselves the **Bonus Army**, about 15,000 veterans gathered in Washington, D.C., in 1932 to pressure Congress to pay them immediately. They set up a Hooverville near the U.S. Capitol. After a bill to allow immediate bonus payments failed in Congress, most of the veterans went home. On President Hoover's orders, federal troops, using tanks and tear gas, cleared out the remaining 2,000 to 5,000 protesters. To many Americans, this action was evidence of Hoover's uncaring treatment of needy citizens.

HISTORICAL THINKING

1. **READING CHECK** How did the depression deepen and spread after the stock market crash of 1929?

2. **IDENTIFY MAIN IDEAS AND DETAILS** How did President Hoover respond to the Great Depression?

3. **MAKE CONNECTIONS** If you were president, how would you have handled the protest of the Bonus Army, and why?

Objective

Analyze how the economic depression in the United States expanded throughout the world.

Critical Thinking Skills for Lesson 1.3

- Identify Main Ideas and Details
- Monitor Comprehension
- Make Connections
- Compare and Contrast
- Make Predictions
- Form and Support Opinions

Essential Question for Chapter 23

Were President Franklin Roosevelt's attempts to resolve the nation's economic problems successful? Explain. A president's actions can affect the nation's economy positively or negatively. Lesson 1.3 discusses how then-president Hoover dealt with the economic depression of 1929 and how it spread.

Background for the Teacher

During the 1930s, many Americans blamed President Hoover for the nation's economic woes. However, more than any previous president, Hoover used the power of the executive branch to address the situation. Congress opposed his efforts to reduce taxes, ease the banking crisis, and establish a program of public works to provide jobs. Hoover urged business leaders not to reduce wages and to keep workers employed, but industries were forced to cut payrolls and jobs in order to reduce costs.

The treatment of the Bonus Army added to Hoover's image as an unsympathetic leader, but he doesn't deserve all the blame for that incident, either. The president ordered the removal of the protesters, and he took responsibility for the tragedy that resulted. However, evidence indicates that General Douglas MacArthur, the leader in charge of the evacuation, disregarded orders and used excessive military force against the veterans and their families.

INTRODUCE & ENGAGE

Preview Using Visuals

Direct students' attention to the Dow Jones Industrial Average, 1922–1934, graph. Discuss what the graph indicates about the nation's economy and how it fits with what students have already learned. **ASK:** What effect did the plunge in the stock market have on people's lives? *(Many lost all their money.)* Then have students look at the photo of protesters at the nation's capital. **ASK:** What does this photo suggest about people's reactions to the economic crisis? *(Possible response: They are banded together on the steps of Congress, and they look as if they are not going anywhere soon, so they seem to be blaming the government or looking to the government to solve the problem.)* Tell students that in this lesson they will learn about the government's response to the economic crisis of 1929.

TEACH

Guided Discussion

1. **Compare and Contrast** How was the effect of the Smoot-Hawley Tariff Act different from the outcome Congress intended? *(Possible response: Congress intended to protect U.S. farmers and manufacturers by raising taxes on imported goods. When other countries also imposed high tariffs on imports, the effect was a decrease in world trade, which hurt everyone.)*

2. **Make Predictions** How do you think President Hoover's policies affected his chances for re-election in 1932? *(Possible response: Hoover's policies probably hurt his chances for re-election because people felt he had ignored their problems and had done little to solve the nation's economic crisis.)*

Form and Support Opinions

Ask students whether they agree or disagree with President Hoover that direct financial aid to needy people would make them permanently reliant on government handouts. Post these two signs on different sides of the classroom: Agree, Disagree. Tell students to move to the side of their choice and, within their group, discuss why they agree or disagree with Hoover. Then ask members of each side to share and support their opinions.

Active Options

On Your Feet: Create a Cause-and-Effect Chain Organize students into five groups and assign one of the following topics to each group: banks, trade, manufacturing, workers, veterans. Direct groups to reread the text and conduct additional research to determine how the Great Depression affected the people or industry they were assigned. Then have each group create and present a Cause-and-Effect Chain to share the results of their research with the class.

NG Learning Framework: Assemble a Photo Gallery

SKILL Observation

KNOWLEDGE Our Human Story

Invite students to brainstorm a list of adjectives to describe conditions during the Great Depression and list them on the board. Ask students to find Depression-era photographs in online or print sources that illustrate these adjectives. Then prompt them to assemble a photo gallery that tells the story of the Great Depression and present their gallery to the class. As a class, discuss how the photos add to students' understanding of life during the Great Depression.

DIFFERENTIATE

Striving Readers

Read and Recall Instruct students to read the lesson independently. Then arrange students in pairs, and ask them to share ideas they recall. One partner should take notes. Then have pairs review the lesson together, changing or adding to their notes.

Pre-AP

Explain Feedback Loop Instruct students to conduct research using print and online sources to learn more about how the economy worsened during the Great Depression. Direct them to take notes in a Cycle Diagram and then use their notes to write an essay explaining how the negative cycles made the economy go from bad to worse. For example, when businesses weren't selling much, they cut back production, lowered wages, and laid off workers. This led to high unemployment, which led to low consumer spending, which led to more cuts in business production and more employment.

See the Chapter Planner for more strategies for differentiation.

HISTORICAL THINKING

ANSWERS

1. After the stock market crash of 1929, banks began to fail, and businesses cut back on production and reduced their workforces. The unemployed had no money to spend, so the cycle worsened. From the United States, the depression spread around the world.

2. President Hoover initially believed that local governments, religious groups, and volunteers offered the solution. He eventually had the federal government take action, instituting programs to help businesses without providing direct aid to needy Americans.

3. Answers will vary. Possible response: I would have negotiated with the veterans and asked Congress to offer 75 percent of the bonus for payouts before the original 1945 date, because the veterans, after risking their lives for their country, deserved the payment promised to them.

2.1 Franklin Roosevelt Takes Office

Who among your friends and family is the best at solving difficult problems? In the election of 1932, voters chose a new president to solve problems that many Americans believed had no solutions.

MAIN IDEA Franklin D. Roosevelt promised strong action to address the problems of the Great Depression.

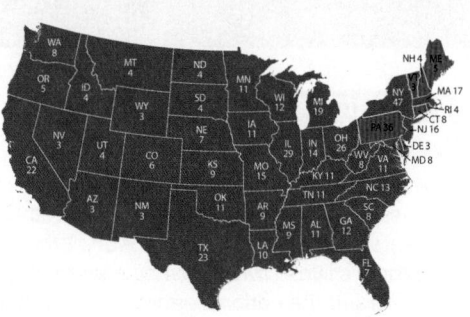

The Election of 1932

Herbert Hoover (Republican)
Electoral Vote: 59 votes, 11.1%
Popular Vote: 15,760,425 votes, 39.6%

Franklin Roosevelt (Democrat)
Electoral Vote: 472 votes, 88.9%
Popular Vote: 22,818,740 votes, 57.4%

Socialist and Other Parties
Electoral Vote: 0
Popular Vote: 1,169,367 votes, 3%

ROOSEVELT'S ELECTION

The 1932 presidential election pitted President Hoover against the Democratic governor of New York, **Franklin Delano Roosevelt (FDR)**, who would become one of the most important leaders of the 20th century.

Franklin Roosevelt was born into a wealthy New York family and was the fifth cousin of President Theodore Roosevelt, whom he greatly admired. Franklin Roosevelt attended an exclusive prep school, graduated from Harvard College, and became a lawyer. But he was never a highly committed student or lawyer. It wasn't until Roosevelt entered politics that he found his real calling in life.

After winning election to the New York State Senate in 1910, Roosevelt became known as a progressive reformer. His innate, or natural, charm and confidence as a public speaker helped spark his rapidly advancing political career. In late summer 1921, however, Roosevelt contracted poliomyelitis, a disease commonly called polio. The illness left his legs permanently paralyzed. His recovery—both personally and politically—was due partly to the hard work of his wife, Eleanor.

Franklin Roosevelt throws out the first pitch to start Game 3 of the 1932 World Series at Wrigley Field in Chicago. The Cubs-Yankees baseball game was a Midwest campaign stop for FDR, who caught the action with his son James (right) and Chicago mayor Anton Cermak (left).

Like her husband, **Eleanor Roosevelt** came from a wealthy family. A distant cousin of Franklin's, she became a lifelong champion of equal rights for women and minorities and an advocate for the underprivileged. Eleanor Roosevelt advised her husband on a wide range of social and political issues. She helped him campaign for and win the governorship of New York in 1928.

A successful governor, Franklin Roosevelt developed a national reputation for leadership. During his 1932 presidential campaign, Roosevelt offered few specific plans to address the nation's economic problems. He told voters he would expand the government's role to help those in need and to regulate the excesses of big business. Overall, he promised the people action.

American voters apparently did not require specific details. They were fed up with Hoover and the Republicans. Roosevelt won the presidential election by a large margin, and Democrats gained majorities in both the U.S. House and Senate.

THE NEW DEAL

In his inaugural speech on March 4, 1933, Roosevelt sought to boost the confidence and hope of the American people. He reassured them with these words: "This great Nation will endure as it has endured, will revive and will prosper." Roosevelt promised to experiment with new ideas to fight the Depression. His plan of action was to establish programs that would provide what became known as the "three Rs": relief, recovery, and reform. To develop his plan, called the New Deal, Roosevelt depended on a group of academic advisors known as his "brain trust." This group of university professors helped the president-elect prepare his strategy for immediate action after Inauguration Day.

Roosevelt's first move as president was to declare a **bank holiday** on March 6. This measure closed the country's banks for four days to avoid another bank run. It would keep people from withdrawing so much money that the banks might be forced into failure. After four days, only those banks judged able to succeed in the long run would reopen. Roosevelt's plan seemed to work. By March 15, the banks that reopened controlled 90 percent of U.S. banking resources. Inspired by Roosevelt's assured leadership, more people were putting money into the banks than were taking money out.

HISTORICAL THINKING

1. **READING CHECK** Why did President Roosevelt declare a bank holiday two days after taking office?

2. **IDENTIFY MAIN IDEAS AND DETAILS** During his campaign, how did Franklin Roosevelt persuade American voters to support him in the 1932 presidential election?

3. **INTERPRET MAPS** How many states did Herbert Hoover win in the presidential election of 1932, and in what region were they located?

PLAN

Objective

Learn Franklin Roosevelt's plan to end the Great Depression with relief, recovery, and reform.

Critical Thinking Skills for Lesson 2.1

- Identify Main Ideas and Details
- Monitor Comprehension
- Interpret Maps
- Synthesize
- Evaluate
- Compare and Contrast

Essential Question for Chapter 23

Were President Franklin Roosevelt's attempts to resolve the nation's economic problems successful? Explain. Roosevelt won the 1932 election by promising bold action to solve the nation's economic problems. Lesson 2.1 discusses his election and his New Deal plan to fight the Great Depression.

Background for the Teacher

Although polio left Franklin Roosevelt unable to stand or walk without assistance, he never wanted Americans to view his disability as an obstacle to the successful performance of his duties. To that end, he developed ways of getting around without calling attention to his condition. He balanced himself by using a cane and the arm of an assistant. He gave the appearance of walking by jerking his hip forward and then swinging his leg. He grasped both sides of a podium when he gave a speech. Most of the press honored FDR's request to avoid photographing him being pushed in his wheelchair or being lifted in or out of a car. Secret Service agents intentionally obstructed photographers who disregarded the request and tried to take a picture that would portray the president as incapacitated.

History Notebook

Encourage students to complete the American Gallery page for Chapter 23 in their History Notebooks as they read.

Listen to Lyrics

Tell students that presidential candidates often choose a theme song for their campaigns. Find and play a clip of the song "Happy Days Are Here Again" and explain that this song became FDR's theme. **ASK:** What message did Roosevelt want to deliver to the American people with this song? *(Possible response: He wanted to give people hope for a better future in which the troubles of the Great Depression would be behind them.)*

TEACH

Guided Discussion

1. **Synthesize** What were Franklin Roosevelt's qualifications for the presidency? *(Possible responses: He was a lawyer and a politician. He had been elected to state government offices, serving as a senator and a governor in New York. He was known as a progressive reformer. He was a good public speaker with the ability to gain the support of his listeners.)*

2. **Evaluate** How do you think the American public felt about Roosevelt's New Deal? Explain. *(Possible responses: Americans probably felt relieved and hopeful because Roosevelt's New Deal offered a definite plan for action. They were probably pleased that the new president surrounded himself with knowledgeable advisors and began immediately to address the nation's economic crisis and to provide help for its people.)*

Compare and Contrast

Instruct students to compare and contrast Herbert Hoover and Franklin Roosevelt. Provide, or allow students to choose, categories in which to compare the two men, such as background, personality, and attitudes toward government. Ask students to record their results on a chart like the one shown. **ASK:** How did the backgrounds and attitudes of these two presidents influence their ways of dealing with the Great Depression? *(Possible response: Because Hoover grew up poor and became wealthy, he believed people should help themselves and solve their own problems. Roosevelt grew up wealthy so he probably recognized that neither wealth nor poverty was always earned and believed in helping those less fortunate.)*

Categories	Hoover	Roosevelt

Active Options

AMERICAN GALLERY ONLINE **Franklin and Eleanor Roosevelt** Invite students to explore the American Gallery. Have them select one of the photos and do additional research to learn more about it. Ask questions that will inspire inquiry about the chosen photo, such as: Why does it belong in this chapter? What else would you like to know about it?

NG Learning Framework: Create a Collage

SKILL Communication

KNOWLEDGE Our Human Story

Note that during her lifetime Eleanor Roosevelt was often called "the world's most admired woman." Encourage students to find out more about the woman who redefined the role of First Lady and played a significant part in 20th-century U.S. history. Challenge them to create a collage of photos, drawings, quotations, or other items to convey Eleanor Roosevelt's accomplishments. Provide time for students to share and discuss their work.

Striving Readers

Make a Top Five Facts List Tell students to reread the information about Franklin Roosevelt, his election to the presidency, and his early days in office. Then have students write in their own words five facts they have learned. Have students work in pairs to compare lists and consolidate the facts into one final list.

Pre-AP

Profile a Presidential Advisor Prompt students to conduct preliminary research to discover who served in Roosevelt's "brain trust." Then have them choose one person to research and profile. Encourage students to use multiple print and digital sources and to cite both primary and secondary sources. The profile should elucidate the advisor's background, motivations, and goals and give specific examples of how that person advised the president. Invite volunteers to share their profiles with the class.

See the Chapter Planner for more strategies for differentiation.

HISTORICAL THINKING

ANSWERS

1. President Roosevelt declared a bank holiday to keep people from withdrawing their money, which might have brought about bank runs.

2. Roosevelt promised to take action. Although he offered few specifics, he said he would expand the government's role to directly help those in need and to regulate big business.

3. Hoover won only six states, and they were all in the Northeast.

2.2 Putting People to Work

If you couldn't afford food because you didn't have a job, what would you want the government to do? During the Depression, President Roosevelt believed the government should provide both food and jobs.

MAIN IDEA President Roosevelt acted boldly and swiftly in establishing New Deal programs and agencies to resolve the country's economic problems.

THE FIRST HUNDRED DAYS

Unlike Hoover, Roosevelt approached the nation's financial crisis by looking for ways to provide direct relief to Americans in need. Within his first few months in office, the president and his brain trust initiated 15 laws to provide money and jobs for Americans and to strengthen the economy. These laws established government programs that focused on the three Rs. Relief programs helped the jobless and hungry directly. Recovery programs were aimed at returning agriculture and industry to profitability. Reform programs sought to correct banking and investment practices that had contributed to the Depression.

Key Programs of the New Deal

Program	Description
Federal Emergency Relief Administration (FERA)	Established as a temporary measure to provide money and work to unemployed citizens through grants given to state and local agencies
Civilian Conservation Corps (CCC)	Provided conservation jobs, mostly to young single men
Public Works Administration (PWA)	Provided jobs by funding such large construction projects as roads, dams, bridges, and public buildings
Agricultural Adjustment Administration (AAA)	Designed to make agriculture profitable by paying subsidies to farmers who agreed to reduce production
National Recovery Administration (NRA)	Designed to help industries recover by establishing fair business practices that would reduce labor strikes
Federal Deposit Insurance Corporation (FDIC)	Created to insure depositors' bank accounts up to a certain amount
Tennessee Valley Authority (TVA)	Established to control flooding and provide electricity to impoverished areas along the Tennessee River and its tributaries

New Deal legislation was based on the ideas of **John Maynard Keynes**, a British economist. Keynes proposed a new approach to government spending during an economic downturn. He argued that the government should spend money to help people rather than cut spending to limit debt. Roosevelt's New Deal proposals applied this approach. With little debate, Congress passed the New Deal legislation. This period of intense lawmaking was later named the **First Hundred Days**.

THE TENNESSEE VALLEY AUTHORITY

The Great Depression hit almost everyone hard, whether they lived in large cities or rural areas. But among the most impoverished regions in the nation was the Tennessee Valley, located in Tennessee and several surrounding states. The 4 million people who lived in the region included some of the country's poorest farmers. Many lived in isolated communities that lacked doctors, good schools, paved roads, and electricity.

Geography played a role in the problems that farmers in the region faced. The Tennessee Valley forms the watershed, or drainage area, of the Tennessee River, which flows through parts of seven southern states. The river and its tributaries, which are smaller streams that flow into a larger body of water, periodically experienced severe flooding. Deforestation, the cutting down of trees, added to the problem of soil erosion in the valley. In the river itself, a series of shallow areas along its middle course made navigation difficult.

TVA Dams, 1933–1945

- ● TVA-built hydroelectric dams
- ● TVA-built flood-control dams (hydroelectric power added later)
- ◐ TVA-acquired hydroelectric dams
- ▨ TVA service area

To aid struggling farmers and others living in the Tennessee Valley, President Roosevelt established a federal agency called the **Tennessee Valley Authority (TVA)** in May 1933. Roosevelt envisioned the TVA as an agency that would combine the power of government with the initiative of private business. The TVA aimed to reduce flooding, improve river navigation, and provide electricity to the region. The agency built dams to control flooding and produce inexpensive **hydroelectric power**, or electricity generated by the energy of flowing water. Over the next decade, the TVA constructed 16 dams and hydroelectric plants along the river, providing thousands of jobs. In addition, the TVA deepened the river's channel, which helped boost shipping along the river. It replanted trees and promoted better farming methods.

The TVA brought dramatic changes to the Tennessee Valley. Its inexpensive electricity stimulated industrial development and improved standards of living in the region. Its flood control efforts were so effective that no major flood damage occurred in the Tennessee Valley until 2010, when flooding occurred along the Cumberland River, especially in the Nashville area.

The TVA is still active today. It currently provides electricity for 9 million people in parts of Alabama, Georgia, Kentucky, Mississippi, North Carolina, Tennessee, and Virginia. In addition, the artificial lakes that were created by the dams have become popular recreation areas.

HISTORICAL THINKING

1. **READING CHECK** What were the goals of the New Deal agencies and programs?

2. **IDENTIFY MAIN IDEAS AND DETAILS** How did Roosevelt and his brain trust apply the ideas of John Maynard Keynes in the first hundred days of FDR's presidency?

3. **INTERPRET MAPS** In which states did the TVA build hydroelectric dams between 1933 and 1945?

Objective

Explain how President Roosevelt established the Tennessee Valley Authority to aid the South.

Critical Thinking Skills for Lesson 2.2

- Identify Main Ideas and Details
- Monitor Comprehension
- Interpret Maps
- Interpret Charts
- Draw Conclusions

Essential Question for Chapter 23

Were President Franklin Roosevelt's attempts to resolve the nation's economic problems successful? Explain. After his election, President Roosevelt immediately began to put New Deal programs into effect. Lesson 2.2 describes the scope of the Tennessee Valley Authority (TVA)—one of Roosevelt's early accomplishments.

Background for the Teacher

The practice of measuring a president's success by judging the first hundred days in office began with Franklin Roosevelt. It has become a benchmark by which all presidents since Roosevelt have been measured. FDR's feat of 15 laws passed in 100 days is an impressive record, and it has not been matched since. However, many historians argue that this accomplishment was due not so much to Roosevelt as to the extraordinary circumstances of the times, in which Congress responded to the need to provide relief from the Great Depression. In addition, they point out, it is unfair to judge FDR's success at the hundred-day milestone since the programs did not actually affect people until later, and, in fact, new jobs developed years after the hundred-day period was over. Many historians argue that this is an arbitrary and unrealistic measure of a president's performance.

Write a Letter

Direct students' attention to the question in the introduction to the lesson. Ask students to imagine they are writing a short letter to President Roosevelt addressing this issue. **ASK:** What questions, suggestions, or complaints would you include in the letter? *(Answers will vary but may include specific or general questions, concrete ideas, pleas for help, or ideas about assigning blame.)* Write student responses on the board under the heading Dear President Roosevelt. Then tell students that they will learn about some of the New Deal programs put into place by the government to address the country's economic problems.

TEACH

Guided Discussion

1. **Interpret Charts** Which key programs of the New Deal specifically addressed Roosevelt's priority of putting people to work? *(FERA, CCC, and PWA)*

2. **Draw Conclusions** Would direct relief, including money and the creation of jobs, have solved the problems of the people in the Tennessee Valley? Explain. *(Possible response: Direct relief would have helped in the short term, but many of the problems were related to the geography of the area. The TVA was designed to reduce flooding, promote improved farming methods, and provide electricity, which helped people for years to come.)*

More Information

PWA Fact Sheet The Public Works Administration (PWA) was created in 1933 to provide jobs that would improve the nation's infrastructure. The PWA funded construction of bridges, dams, and highways. It partnered with state and local governments to improve waterworks and sewage treatment plants. Unlike work-relief programs, the PWA did not hire workers in need of relief. Instead, it helped the nation's economy by paying wages that workers then spent on goods and services, which provided money and jobs for others. When the organization ended in 1939, it had provided thousands of public works projects that are still in use today. Help students use this information to create a fact sheet about the PWA. Then invite them to choose another New Deal program and create a fact sheet to share with the class.

Active Options

On Your Feet: Categorize Multiple Effects Arrange students in small groups in separate areas of the room. Provide each group with a Cause-and-Effect Web. Tell groups to write the label TVA in the center circle of the web. Then ask them to write the effects of this program in the adjacent squares. Finally, challenge students to categorize the effects as relief, recovery, or reform. Note that some effects may belong in more than one category. Allow groups to share and discuss their work.

NG Learning Framework: Research Hydroelectricity

SKILLS Communication, Collaboration

KNOWLEDGE Our Human Story

Remind students that one of the continuing results of the TVA is providing electricity to millions of people. Pose the question: How does a dam provide electricity? Direct students to work in pairs or small groups to research hydroelectricity. Then instruct them to create a diagram, model, or other form of presentation to answer the question. Ask pairs or groups to present their work to the class.

DIFFERENTIATE

English Language Learners

Using Context Clues Pair students at the **Emerging** level of proficiency with those at the **Expanding** level. Direct them to read the lesson together, noting unfamiliar terms and the context clues and definitions that help them understand those terms. For example, *tributaries* are "smaller streams that flow into a larger body of water," *deforestation* is "the cutting down of trees," and *hydroelectric power* is "electricity generated by the energy of flowing water."

Gifted & Talented

Illustrate a Phrase Explain that the strategy of using government spending to spur the economy is sometimes called "priming the pump." Instruct students to research both the literal and metaphorical meaning of the phrase. Then challenge them to visually interpret the phrase as it relates to Roosevelt's economic stimulus plan. Have students present their visual interpretations to the class. They may then lead a class discussion about the historical and current views of using taxpayer funds to "prime the pump" and boost the economy.

See the Chapter Planner for more strategies for differentiation.

HISTORICAL THINKING

ANSWERS

1. The New Deal agencies and programs aimed to provide relief to the jobless and hungry, aid the recovery of agriculture and industry and return them to profitability, and reform financial practices to prevent another depression.

2. Roosevelt took an aggressive approach to the country's economic problems and initiated many programs to provide both direct relief and jobs for the public. Based on Keynes's ideas, he invested a huge amount of the nation's money back into the country to help pull the United States out of the Great Depression.

3. The TVA built hydroelectric dams in Tennessee, Alabama, North Carolina, and Kentucky.

2.3 The Dust Bowl

You've probably experienced a rainstorm or snowstorm that was so heavy you couldn't see very far. But can you imagine being in a storm of dust so thick you can't see your own hands?

MAIN IDEA At the height of the Great Depression, an environmental disaster in the Great Plains caused a massive migration out of the region.

ENVIRONMENTAL DISASTER

As you know, most American farmers were struggling financially even before the Great Depression, and the economic downturn caused many to lose their farms. For those living in the Great Plains, a serious environmental crisis brought disaster. For almost 20 years, the Great Plains farmers had been plowing up grasslands and planting wheat. They did not realize that the prairie's natural, deep-rooted grasses anchored the rich topsoil. Without the grasses, the soil became vulnerable to wind erosion, especially during a **drought**, or a long period with little rainfall.

In 1931, a lengthy drought hit the region. With little grass left to hold the dry soil in place, the wind carried it off. In parts of Oklahoma, Colorado, Kansas, New Mexico, and Texas, high winds picked up the dry soil and whipped it into massive dust clouds. "Black blizzards," dust storms that blocked the sunlight, engulfed whole towns. The dust destroyed crops and sickened and killed people and livestock. Following a dust storm, farmers often found their horses and cattle buried alive. The devastated region became known as the **Dust Bowl**.

MIGRATING WEST

Unable to grow crops, many Dust Bowl farmers could not pay their mortgages, and so they lost their farms. Hundreds of thousands of farmers and their families fled the region. Some remained because of pride, determination, or hope. Others stayed because they were too poor to leave.

Many Dust Bowl farmers migrated to California, where they were called "Okies," though only some were from Oklahoma. In California, most Okies experienced extreme poverty. The fortunate ones found steady but low-wage work picking fruit, boxing vegetables, and baling hay.

In response to the Dust Bowl crisis, the **Civilian Conservation Corps (CCC)** planted shelter belts, or rows of trees that serve as windbreaks and so reduce soil erosion. The federal government also educated farmers about soil conservation techniques and promoted their use.

To help farmers throughout the country, Roosevelt instituted programs to make farming more profitable. The **Agricultural Adjustment Administration (AAA)**, for example, paid farmers who agreed not to grow crops on some of their land. The AAA also established price supports, in which the government guaranteed farmers certain prices for their crops.

The drought that helped produce the Dust Bowl ended in the fall of 1939, and the region recovered in the early 1940s. But by then, an estimated 2.5 million people, both farmers and nonfarmers, had left the region.

HISTORICAL THINKING

1. **READING CHECK** What caused the environmental disaster called the Dust Bowl?

2. **IDENTIFY PROBLEMS AND SOLUTIONS** How did the CCC help solve one problem of the Dust Bowl?

3. **MAKE INFERENCES** Under what conditions could the Great Plains again become a Dust Bowl?

Documenting the Dust Bowl

A man and his son in rural Cimarron County, Oklahoma, work to raise their fence above the drifting sand of the Dust Bowl (top photograph). This photo was taken in 1936 by Arthur Rothstein, the first photographer hired by the **Farm Security Administration (FSA)** to document the lives of America's rural poor, including the Great Plains farmers. The agency wanted to use photographs to show who the New Deal programs were helping and to convey how misuse of the land led to the region's dust storms.

While some farmers battled for survival in the Dust Bowl, one-quarter of the region's population left. Many migrants hoped to find work in California, where the climate was mild and the growing season long. In 1936, FSA photographer Dorothea Lange took the photo at right of a family who left Abilene, Texas, for California, looking for farm work.

PLAN

Objective
Describe the impact of the Dust Bowl on the Great Plains during the Great Depression.

Critical Thinking Skills for Lesson 2.3
- Identify Main Ideas and Details
- Monitor Comprehension
- Identify Problems and Solutions
- Make Inferences
- Describe
- Analyze Visuals

Essential Question for Chapter 23
Were President Franklin Roosevelt's attempts to resolve the nation's economic problems successful? Explain. The Dust Bowl required a response to environmental as well as economic problems. Lesson 2.3 describes this disaster and the attempts to resolve the crisis.

Background for the Teacher

The migration of people out of the Dust Bowl region was one of the largest population shifts in U.S. history. Extreme examples include the area around Boise City, Oklahoma, which lost 40 percent of its population, and the San Joaquin Valley in California, whose population increased by about 40 percent.

Far from the utopia the migrants had hoped for, California did not provide work for farmers. Local police turned them away at the border, and groups of vigilantes sometimes beat them and burned their belongings. The Federal Security Administration built 13 camps for the migrants. Each camp housed 300 families in tents built on wood platforms. But the migrants had to work and pay for their shelter. For picking grapes or cotton, a worker received about one dollar a day. Eventually, migrant farm families assimilated into communities, but they continued to be treated as second-class citizens.

Discuss Environmental Disasters

Ask students to recall a recent environmental disaster in the United States, such as a hurricane, a flood, or a forest fire. Discuss how the disaster affected people. **ASK:** How did the government respond? *(Answers will vary. Possible responses: federal aid, temporary housing, assistance with clean up and recovery)* Tell students that in this lesson they will learn how the government responded to an environmental disaster in the midst of the Great Depression.

TEACH

Guided Discussion

1. **Describe** Using the text and photographs, describe what it must have been like to live in the Dust Bowl? *(Possible response: It must have been hard both physically and psychologically for people to cope when dust storms buried their homes and farms, and it must have felt futile—as well as back-breaking—to try to dig out fence posts and other property. After losing their livelihood, many probably felt the only option was to leave their home behind, likely a sad and overwhelming situation.)*

2. **Make Inferences** Why might some people have been opposed to Roosevelt's attempts to help farmers? *(Possible response: Paying farmers not to grow crops and guaranteeing prices for crops made food more expensive for other people.)*

Analyze Visuals

Direct students' attention to the photographs of the Dust Bowl. **ASK:** Why might it be important to document the Dust Bowl with photographs? *(Possible responses: The photographs provide a permanent record of how the Dust Bowl affected people. The photos convey the need for and effectiveness of New Deal programs. They influence public opinion about the plight of Dust Bowl farmers.)* Challenge students to write a one-word caption for each photo. Encourage them to research and study other photographs of the Dust Bowl. Provide time for students to discuss how the photos enhance their understanding of the era.

Active Options

On Your Feet: Inside-Outside Circle Remind students that in the face of an environmental disaster, such as the Dust Bowl, people must decide whether to stay in the area or leave. Give students a few minutes to think about what might motivate people to make their choice. Then arrange students in concentric circles facing each other. Those in the inside circle represent people who decide to stay. Those in the outside circle must interview them to find out their reasons. At your signal, have students reverse places. This time, those in the outside circle represent people who decide to leave. Those in the inside circle must interview them to find out their reasons. Ask each group of "reporters" to summarize the motivations of those they interviewed.

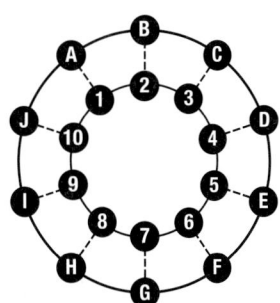

NG Learning Framework: Create an Environmental Campaign

SKILL Problem-Solving

KNOWLEDGE Our Living Planet

Divide the class into small groups. Tell groups to research the human and environmental causes of the Dust Bowl as well as the human actions and conservation practices that provided solutions. When they have completed their research, prompt groups to create a public education campaign or PSA to promote best practices to help people become good stewards of the land. For example, they could compile a dos and don'ts list, a brochure, or a radio skit or news segment. Remind students that their campaign should be engaging as well as informative. Invite groups to present their projects to the class.

Inclusion

Explore Documentary Photographs Pair students who are visually impaired with students who are not. Ask the latter to describe the Dust Bowl photographs and to read the caption explaining why the Farm Security Administration had Arthur Rothstein and Dorothea Lange take these and other documentary photos. Prompt visually impaired students to ask clarifying questions to help them understand the visuals.

Pre-AP

Write a News Report Assign students the role of 1930s journalists covering the Dust Bowl. Instruct them to conduct online research to find primary source materials regarding dust storms, life on a farm, migrating "Okies," or another aspect of the Dust Bowl that interests them. Then have them use their research to write a detailed news story, including quotes from eyewitnesses. Remind students that news reports begin with the most important information and answer the questions *Who? What? Where? When?* and *How?* Invite students to post their reports on a class blog or publish them on a school website.

See the Chapter Planner for more strategies for differentiation.

HISTORICAL THINKING

ANSWERS

1. Farmers plowed up the native prairie grasses, which held topsoil in place, to plant wheat. Drought dried out the soil, and heavy winds caused massive dust storms that eroded soil and made the land useless for agriculture.

2. The CCC planted rows of trees that acted as windbreaks to lessen soil erosion.

3. Possible response: If the measures put into place after the Dust Bowl of the 1930s were destroyed and farmers ignored conservation practices, a severe drought could cause another Dust Bowl in the Great Plains.

Social Security

Even before the Great Depression, most older Americans had only their savings and relatives to rely on for support when they could no longer work. But what if they lost their savings to a bank closure? Or their farm failed? Or they had no relatives? Whom or what could they depend on?

MAIN IDEA The New Deal introduced a pension system for elderly Americans that still exists today.

President Franklin Roosevelt is about to deliver a fireside chat in this photo from the mid-1930s. Roosevelt's fireside chats were informal radio broadcasts in which he spoke directly to the American people. He used these addresses to reassure people and inspire hope and to introduce, explain, and defend his New Deal programs. Tens of millions of Americans listened to each chat.

HELPING THE ELDERLY

The Great Depression focused more attention on the problem of poverty among older Americans. Surveys conducted in New York in 1929 and in Connecticut in 1932 showed that half of Americans 65 years of age and older lived on less than $300 per year. Even at a time when the average annual income had dropped from $2,500 per year to about $1,100 per year, this amount was alarmingly low. Clearly, something needed to be done.

President Roosevelt and his advisors proposed the **Social Security Act**, which would provide not only a pension fund for the elderly but also unemployment insurance and aid for the disabled and others in need. A **pension fund** is a pool of money used to pay retirees a certain income. To support the program, both workers and employers would pay a federal tax.

When the Social Security Act was presented to Congress, some legislators criticized it as being a step toward socialism, a system in which the government controls the economy. One critic of the plan, Oklahoma senator Thomas Gore, stated, "Isn't this plan . . . in effect to take private property for public use?" In response, supporters pointed out that every tax takes citizens' money and uses it for the public good, including tax dollars that pay for roads, schools, police and fire protection, and national defense.

Despite the criticism from opponents, Congress readily passed the Social Security Act, and President Roosevelt signed it into law on August 14, 1935. The Social Security Act is one of the New Deal programs that still benefit Americans today.

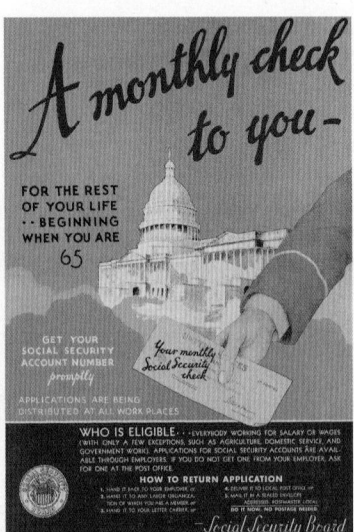

A monthly check to you—

FOR THE REST OF YOUR LIFE ·· BEGINNING WHEN YOU ARE 65

GET YOUR SOCIAL SECURITY ACCOUNT NUMBER promptly

Your monthly Social Security check

APPLICATIONS ARE BEING DISTRIBUTED AT ALL WORK PLACES

WHO IS ELIGIBLE . . .

HOW TO RETURN APPLICATION

Social Security Board

INFORMATION MAY BE OBTAINED AT ANY POST OFFICE

CRITICAL VIEWING The federal government's Social Security Board distributed posters to inform citizens about the 1935 Social Security Act. How does the poster grab the viewer's attention and make Social Security appear appealing?

ROOSEVELT'S RE-ELECTION

Although Roosevelt was a popular president, he also had critics in the run-up to the 1936 election. One vocal critic was Father Charles Coughlin, a Catholic priest who hosted a radio program that had 40 million listeners. Coughlin thought the president's reforms did not go far enough. He proposed that the government take control of the banking and energy industries. But Coughlin was removed from his radio show for expressing anti-ethnic views. Huey Long, a former governor of Louisiana who had been elected a U.S. Senator in 1932, also attacked FDR for not doing enough. He called for heavily taxing the wealthy to support programs that helped the needy. Many leaders in business, though, attacked FDR and the New Deal because they opposed increasing taxes to pay for expanding government programs.

Roosevelt's position as the front-runner in the 1936 presidential election was never really challenged, however. The Democratic Party consisted of a broad coalition, or alliance, of diverse voters, including African Americans, women, union workers, intellectuals, and southern Democrats.

The Republican Party nominated Kansas governor Alf Landon as its candidate. Landon campaigned against Roosevelt by attacking the New Deal for wasting money and by accusing the president of exercising more executive power than the Constitution allowed.

The 1936 election showed that the majority of voters approved of the president's leadership and activism. As in 1932, Roosevelt won easily; in fact, Landon got only eight electoral votes.

HISTORICAL THINKING

1. **READING CHECK** How did the Social Security Act of 1935 affect Americans' lives, and how was it funded?

2. **FORM AND SUPPORT OPINIONS** You've read the opinions of opponents and supporters of the Social Security Act. What is your opinion of the act? Give reasons for your opinion.

3. **MAKE CONNECTIONS** How do you think Americans today would respond to fireside chats given by their president?

PLAN

Objective

Learn how the New Deal provided aid for elderly Americans.

Critical Thinking Skills for Lesson 2.4

- Identify Main Ideas and Details
- Monitor Comprehension
- Form and Support Opinions
- Make Connections
- Make Generalizations
- Summarize

Essential Question for Chapter 23

Were President Franklin Roosevelt's attempts to resolve the nation's economic problems successful? Explain. While Roosevelt's policies continued to help the public, some critics felt his programs did not go far enough. Lesson 2.4 discusses the birth of Social Security and, despite the critics, Roosevelt's landslide victory in 1936.

Background for the Teacher

Social Security is part of the enduring legacy of FDR's New Deal. For more than 80 years, it has provided retirement income for the elderly and aid for people with disabilities. The cumulative effect of paying into and receiving benefits from Social Security reduced the poverty rate among senior citizens from around 50 percent in the 1930s to about 10 percent today. Without it, an estimated 43 percent of seniors would live in poverty. The rate would be higher for elderly members of minority communities. The Social Security Administration reports that about 62 million Americans currently receive Social Security benefits. Ninety percent of citizens age 65 and older depend on Social Security as a major source of their income.

INTRODUCE & ENGAGE

K-W-L Chart

Tell students that Social Security is a New Deal program that is still in effect today. Post a K-W-L Chart on the board. Ask students to share what they already know about Social Security. Record their responses, regardless of inaccuracies, in the first column of the chart. Then ask what they would like to learn about Social Security, and record those responses in the second column. Encourage students to refer to the chart as they read Lesson 2.4. They will revisit the chart later.

K What Do I Know?	W What Do I Want To Learn?	L What Did I Learn?

TEACH

Guided Discussion

1. **Make Generalizations** Why were the nation's economic problems especially hard on older people? *(Possible responses: Older people who were no longer working had little money and lived on their savings or depended on their families. The Great Depression erased people's savings and made it difficult for families to support their older relatives.)*

2. **Summarize** What were some of the major criticisms of Roosevelt's policies? *(Possible response: Some criticized Roosevelt for doing too little to solve the nation's problems. Others felt he did too much by expanding the role of government in people's lives.)*

More Information

Roosevelt's Fireside Chats Just eight days after he took office, President Roosevelt delivered the first of about 30 radio broadcasts, called "fireside chats" because of their conversational style. The radio talks made listeners feel as if the president were visiting in their homes. Roosevelt's tone of voice and easily understood explanations gave people confidence in his leadership. **ASK:** What characteristics do you think an effective public speaker needs to have? *(a clear voice, confidence, knowledge, an ability to connect with the audience)* Invite students to listen to a recording of one of FDR's fireside chats. As a class, discuss his characteristics as a speaker.

Active Options

On Your Feet: Build on What You Know Tell students to work in small groups. Direct their attention to the K-W-L Chart from the beginning of the lesson. Ask groups to discuss what they have learned about Social Security and how they would complete the third column of the chart. Then instruct them to decide whether the responses in the first column are true or false and to determine whether the lesson provided all the information they wanted to know, as noted in the second column. Invite groups to share and discuss their answers.

NG Learning Framework: Write an Endorsement

ATTITUDE Empowerment

SKILL Communication

Ask students to assume the role of voters in the 1936 presidential election. Invite them to write an endorsement for the candidate of their choice: Franklin Roosevelt or Alf Landon. Tell students to incorporate facts from the lesson or from other sources to back up their endorsements. Encourage them to share their work by holding a rally, creating posters, or writing and compiling newspaper editorials.

DIFFERENTIATE

Striving Readers

Write a Tweet As students read the lesson, direct them to pause after each paragraph and write a tweet summarizing the paragraph's main idea in their own words. Ask students to read their tweets aloud to the class one at a time, with the first student reading his or her tweet about the first paragraph, the second student reading a tweet about the second paragraph, and so forth.

Gifted & Talented

Give a Speech Tell students to reread the lesson, noting the reasons people supported or opposed the Social Security Act. Prompt them to choose which side to defend in a speech and to conduct research to gather support for their position. Instruct students to write a persuasive speech promoting their position and then give their speech to the class. After the speeches, ask the class to discuss how the viewpoints expressed are relevant to today's debates about the role of government in providing a social safety net.

See the Chapter Planner for more strategies for differentiation.

HISTORICAL THINKING

ANSWERS

1. The Social Security Act provided a pension fund for the elderly as well as unemployment insurance and aid for the disabled and others in need. It was funded by a federal tax paid by workers and employers.

2. Answers will vary. Students might mention too much government control as a reason against Social Security or using tax money for public good as a reason for it. Students should support opinions with evidence from the text.

3. Possible response: Today, people are more likely to get information from television, online, or through social media instead of radio. Across these media, they would probably respond well to informal chats rather than formal addresses given by the president.

CRITICAL VIEWING The poster is colorful and informative, and it depicts a pleasant scene. The hand delivering a check with the words *Your monthly Social Security check* grabs the viewer's attention and makes it more personal, indicating that the viewer will directly benefit.

2.5 The Second New Deal

Sometimes, instead of fighting your critics, it's smart to follow their direction. Some critics thought the New Deal didn't go far enough, so Roosevelt reached farther.

MAIN IDEA Roosevelt expanded the New Deal by introducing additional programs as he contended with the Supreme Court over his legislation.

NEW PROGRAMS

By the mid-1930s, the U.S. economy had begun to recover, but many Americans were still out of work. To boost employment and help those still in need, Roosevelt initiated a second wave of relief legislation, which formed the **Second New Deal**. The Social Security Act of 1935 was a major component of the Second New Deal. The chart on this page summarizes the Social Security Act and other key components of this new progressive legislation.

In the same year that he signed the Social Security Act, the president launched the **Works Progress Administration (WPA)**, which became one of the most famous and far-reaching pieces of New Deal legislation. During its eight-year run, the WPA employed workers who completed thousands of construction projects throughout the nation. These projects included 950 airports, 651,000 miles of highways, 124,000 bridges, 18,000 playgrounds and athletic fields, and 125,000 public buildings.

In addition to hiring workers for construction projects, the WPA also provided jobs to unemployed artists and writers through the Federal Art Project (FAP) and the Federal Writers' Project (FWP). The FAP employed as many as 10,000 artists over the course of 8 years. Artists in the FAP created nearly 2,600 murals and 18,000 sculptures, many of which still adorn public buildings throughout the nation today. FWP writers produced such works as regional guidebooks and folklore studies. Some great American authors worked for the FWP, including Richard Wright and Saul Bellow.

EXPANDING THE SUPREME COURT

Some of Roosevelt's critics believed the president had overstepped his executive power in establishing the New Deal. These critics took their complaints to the courts. In 1935, the Supreme Court declared the law that created the **National Recovery Administration (NRA)** unconstitutional, ruling that lawmaking powers assigned to the NRA belonged to Congress. The Court also ruled the Agricultural Adjustment Act (AAA) to be unconstitutional because it infringed on the regulatory authority of the state governments. These decisions angered Roosevelt and led him to make one of the biggest mistakes of his presidency.

Roosevelt worried that conservative justices on the Supreme Court might strike down other New Deal legislation, such as the Social Security Act. He felt such action would endanger his agenda and the country's recovery. But his plan to protect the New Deal from court interference met with opposition from his friends and enemies alike.

In February 1937, FDR announced a plan to reorganize the federal court system. The plan would allow up to six additional justices on the Supreme Court. Critics viewed the plan as an attempt by Roosevelt to fill the Supreme Court with his allies.

Even Roosevelt's supporters felt this scheme would weaken the judicial branch of government. Hiram Johnson, a progressive Republican and New Deal supporter, summed up the beliefs of many: "Down that road lies dictatorship." Roosevelt's **court-packing plan** failed. It turned out to be unnecessary anyway, because the Court did not oppose any other New Deal legislation.

Key Programs of the Second New Deal

Program	Description
Social Security Act	Provided income to elderly, unemployment insurance, and aid to the disabled and needy
Works Progress Administration (WPA)	Provided construction jobs and funded projects that employed artists, photographers, writers, and musicians
Wagner Act	Established the right of employees to form and join labor unions and to bargain collectively with employers
National Labor Relations Board (NLRB)	Created to resolve disputes between labor and management
National Youth Administration (NYA)	Provided educational grants, job training, and jobs to young Americans
Rural Electrification Administration	Expanded electrical service to rural homes

Smithsonian American Art Museum Washington, D.C.

Buzzing with life, a crowded tenement in the Bunker Hill neighborhood of Los Angeles is the center of Millard Sheets's oil painting *Tenement Flats* (1933–1934). The multi-staired apartments were converted from or replaced mansions abandoned during the Depression. Sheets created this painting for the Public Works of Art Project, an early art program of the WPA.

HISTORICAL THINKING

1. **READING CHECK** Why did Roosevelt introduce his court-packing plan in 1937?

2. **INTERPRET CHARTS** Review the two charts in this chapter, which summarize New Deal programs and Second New Deal programs. How did the Second New Deal expand on the original New Deal?

3. **MAKE CONNECTIONS** What products of the WPA do Americans still enjoy today?

Objective

Describe the Second New Deal and President Roosevelt's conflicts with the Supreme Court.

Critical Thinking Skills for Lesson 2.5

- Identify Main Ideas and Details
- Monitor Comprehension
- Interpret Charts
- Make Connections
- Evaluate
- Draw Conclusions

Essential Question for Chapter 23

Were President Franklin Roosevelt's attempts to resolve the nation's economic problems successful? Explain. By the mid-1930s, Roosevelt's policies had improved the economy somewhat, but unemployment remained high. Lesson 2.5 discusses how FDR attempted to resolve that problem with the Second New Deal.

Background for the Teacher

The National Recovery Administration (NRA) was a significant component to President Roosevelt's economic planning. Established to end hostile competition, the NRA encouraged business leaders in many industries to cooperate in creating codes that promoted fair competition in the workplace. The codes set a limit on the number of hours employees would work and set minimum wages to be paid to workers. They prohibited child labor and guaranteed labor unions the right to organize. In return, the government suspended antitrust laws for participating businesses. To show their support for the NRA, companies displayed the administration's blue eagle symbol with the slogan "We Do Our Part." While the NRA helped foster a positive outlook for the economy, in the end it proved unproductive. Many codes were cumbersome and illogical and favored larger businesses.

Explore Resources

Display photographs of the following kinds of WPA projects or list them on the board: a novel, a guidebook, a mural, a photograph, a sculpture, a public building, a bridge, a highway, and a playground. Ask students to suggest things that all these projects might have in common. Then tell students that each of the projects was created as a result of a New Deal program called the Works Progress Administration (WPA), and many are still in existence. **ASK:** What do these creations convey about the Great Depression era to people viewing them today? *(Answers will vary. Possible responses: These creations reflect aspects of the Great Depression such as the cultural outlook, architectural trends, technology, and priorities.)* Tell students that this lesson discusses the programs of Roosevelt's Second New Deal.

TEACH

Guided Discussion

1. **Evaluate** Which were more important: WPA construction projects or the works produced by WPA artists and writers? Explain your answer. *(Answers will vary. Possible responses: Construction projects were more important because they improved the country's transportation and recreation facilities, and some of them are still in use. Works produced by artists and writers were more important because they documented the times and have provided a lasting record of the way people lived and felt during the Great Depression.)*

2. **Draw Conclusions** How could FDR's court-packing plan have weakened the judicial branch of government? *(By appointing additional justices who favored New Deal programs, the president would be disrupting the separation of powers and influencing the Court, which should be independent from the executive branch.)*

Virtual Museum Visit

The Smithsonian American Art Museum includes a large collection of American art, which documents three centuries of American culture. The museum exhibits a wide variety of visual arts, including photography, folk art, and impressionist paintings. Its permanent "Experience America" exhibit features an extensive collection of New Deal art, including works by WPA artists. Access the museum's website and find the *Tenement Flats* painting in its collection. Share with students the additional information about Millard Sheets's work. Encourage them to explore the "Experience America" image gallery on their own and choose another work of art from the 1930s to present to the class.

Active Options

On Your Feet: Tell Me More Organize students into six groups and assign each group one of the Second New Deal programs highlighted in the chart. Instruct groups to research their program and list facts about it. When groups have compiled their lists, call out the name of a program at random. The group to whom it was assigned must stand and recite one fact about it. The rest of the class calls out "Tell me more." The procedure continues until the group runs out of facts. Then call out the name of another program and repeat the procedure until all programs have been reviewed.

NG Learning Framework: Find Local Evidence of the WPA

ATTITUDE Curiosity

KNOWLEDGE Our Human Story

Discuss the kinds of projects the WPA undertook. Then challenge students to find evidence of those projects in their local community or in their state. Direct them to find historical pictures and current photos of the project and to research some aspect of the work or its history they would like to know more about. Then tell students to write informative captions for past and present images. Instruct them to choose an appropriate medium for assembling and displaying their work.

Striving Readers

Make Lists After students read the lesson, direct pairs to create a chart showing how different groups benefited under the Second New Deal. First, tell them to draw a chart with the title Benefits of the Second New Deal and the column headings Elderly, Youth, and Artists and Writers. Instruct partners to work together to list as many details as they can about how the Second New Deal benefited each group. Invite pairs to share their lists with the class.

Gifted & Talented

Investigate New Deal Art Prompt students to gather information from a variety of primary and secondary sources to create an oral or written report about art that was created as a result of New Deal programs. Remind students to cite their sources and to quote or paraphrase as appropriate. Invite volunteers to share their reports with the class.

See the Chapter Planner for more strategies for differentiation.

HISTORICAL THINKING

ANSWERS

1. The Supreme Court had struck down some key parts of the New Deal. Roosevelt was concerned that conservative justices might invalidate more programs and delay the country's recovery. To protect his agenda, the president wanted to increase the number of justices so he could add allies to the court.

2. The Second New Deal created more jobs for a broader segment of society, created a safety net for the elderly and needy, established rights for workers, and extended rural electrification to more areas.

3. Americans still benefit from construction projects, such as airports, highways, and bridges, and enjoy artwork, including murals and sculptures, and writings produced by the WPA.

The New Deal's Effects on Women and Minorities

Eleanor Roosevelt was an outspoken and assertive woman at a time when women were expected to take a back seat to men. She asserted the right of women—and minorities—to take a front seat.

MAIN IDEA Women and minorities benefited from the New Deal but not as much as white men did.

WOMEN AND THE NEW DEAL

As you have read, Eleanor Roosevelt championed equal rights for women, and she strongly influenced her husband's policies. At her urging, women were appointed to important positions in the federal government for the first time.

Frances Perkins, a New York labor rights activist, became the first woman in American history to serve as a cabinet secretary after President Roosevelt appointed her as secretary of labor. She helped develop the Civilian Conservation Corps, the Federal Emergency Relief Administration, the Social Security Act, and the Fair Labor Standards Act. Roosevelt implemented so many of Perkins's ideas in his New Deal programs that she was later called "the architect of the New Deal." **Ellen Woodward**, a Mississippi legislator, served as director of the Women's Division of FERA. She greatly improved FERA's formerly dismal record in finding jobs for women. She also served in the WPA and on the Social Security Board.

Although women played important roles in Roosevelt's administration, the New Deal programs mostly focused on helping men find jobs. In 1938, for example, women held only 13.5 percent of the jobs in the Works Progress Administration (WPA), and they were often placed in lower-paying jobs.

In 1935, Frances Perkins (center), U.S. secretary of labor, toured the construction site of the Golden Gate Bridge in San Francisco, California. Perkins strongly promoted workplace safety and workers' rights.

MINORITIES AND THE NEW DEAL

African Americans also played more significant roles in the Roosevelt administration than they had in any previous one. FDR gathered a group of esteemed African-American leaders, known informally as the "black cabinet," to advise him on minority issues. The chair of the black cabinet was **Mary McLeod Bethune**, the founder of Bethune-Cookman College in Florida and a friend of Eleanor Roosevelt's. In 1936, FDR put her in charge of African-American affairs for the National Youth Administration. The black cabinet also included Dr. Robert Weaver, a Harvard-educated economist, and William Hastie, who became the first African-American federal judge in 1937.

The Great Depression hit African Americans especially hard. By 1932, the unemployment rate of African Americans in cities had climbed to nearly 50 percent. The WPA employed about 350,000 African-American workers per year, and the National Youth Administration helped to educate and employ more than 300,000 young African Americans.

Although many African Americans were employed through the New Deal, the Roosevelt administration failed to support important civil rights legislation. For decades, African Americans in the South had lived under the threat of lynching. In 1935, the NAACP pushed Congress to pass federal anti-lynching legislation. Roosevelt declined to back the bill, fearing he would lose the crucial support of white southern Democrats for New Deal legislation.

Mexican Americans and Mexican immigrants confronted a different threat during the Great Depression. Many Mexican immigrants had arrived in the United States during the 1920s. Most came to work on farms. They faced competition from white workers, including Dust Bowl migrants, during the Great Depression. In 1929, the federal government began a repatriation program, which deported hundreds of thousands of people of Mexican descent, including American citizens. **Repatriation** is the act of sending immigrants back to their home countries.

CRITICAL VIEWING During the 1940s, noted African-American photographer Gordon Parks took this photo of students attending a popular radio technology class at Bethune-Cookman College. What details are emphasized by the angle from which this photograph was taken?

Native Americans benefited from the appointment of John Collier, a social worker, as commissioner of Indian affairs in 1933. Collier pushed Congress to pass the **Indian Reorganization Act (IRA)** of 1934, which reduced federal control of Native American affairs and promoted self-government. The act helped Native Americans regain control of their communities, improve their schools and health services, and buy millions of acres of land for tribal use.

HISTORICAL THINKING

1. **READING CHECK** In what ways did the Roosevelt administration both help and fail women and minorities?

2. **EVALUATE** What is your assessment of President Roosevelt's reason for not supporting anti-lynching legislation?

3. **MAKE INFERENCES** Why do you think the Great Depression was especially devastating for minorities, such as African Americans and Mexican Americans?

Objective

Evaluate the positives and negatives for women and minorities under the New Deal.

Critical Thinking Skills for Lesson 3.1

- Identify Main Ideas and Details
- Monitor Comprehension
- Evaluate
- Make Inferences
- Identify
- Draw Conclusions

Essential Question for Chapter 23

Were Franklin Roosevelt's attempts to resolve the nation's economic problems successful? Explain. Roosevelt's attempts to include women and minorities in the New Deal were somewhat successful. Lesson 3.1 explains how and why these attempts fell short.

Background for the Teacher

One of 17 children born to a formerly enslaved couple, Mary McLeod Bethune personified the spirit she instilled in others. Undaunted by the inability to fulfill her goal of becoming a missionary, she opened a boarding school for African-American girls. Starting with only five students, the school expanded within two years to 250 students due to Bethune's determination and resourcefulness in raising funds. Her boarding school later merged with an all-male school and became a college that established standards that still inspire educational institutions. Through Roosevelt's appointment, Bethune became the highest-ranking African-American woman in government. She used the opportunity to serve as an advocate for women and minorities. Her roles as educator, advisor, businesswoman, writer, and leader earned her many honors, including a memorial statue in Washington, D.C.

INTRODUCE & ENGAGE

Activate Prior Knowledge

Ask students to read the introductory text above the Main Idea statement. **ASK:** How were women and minorities viewed during the New Deal era as compared with white men? *(Answers will vary. Possible response: Women were not viewed as primary breadwinners, so many New Deal programs focused on employing men—as evidenced by the large construction projects undertaken by the PWA and TVA. Minorities were probably overlooked as a group with particular concerns, and managers on New Deal projects most likely chose to hire white workers over minority workers, who already faced discrimination.)* **ASK:** How might New Deal programs have been crafted to help women and minorities? *(Possible responses: They could offer job training for those who did not have educational or job training opportunities before. They could invest in projects that utilized skills traditionally acquired by women or by people in minority communities.)*

TEACH

Guided Discussion

1. **Identify** How did Eleanor Roosevelt influence New Deal policies? *(Possible response: She urged the president to appoint women and minorities to government positions to better address the needs of those groups.)*

2. **Draw Conclusions** Why did the government deport Mexican people during the Great Depression? *(Many Mexican immigrants worked on farms. Deporting them removed competition for jobs sought by white Dust Bowl migrants.)*

More Information

Repatriation The so-called repatriation of Mexicans began in the 1920s under the Hoover administration and extended into the 1930s. Many of the almost 2 million people who were deported had been born in the United States, so they found themselves not in their home country but in a place they had never been before. The repatriation raids reflected the attitude "a Mexican is a Mexican," which included people of Mexican descent, whether or not they were U.S. citizens. For example, on a Sunday afternoon in 1931, officials surrounded La Placita Park in a Latino neighborhood of Los Angeles. They detained everyone in the park, put them on a train, and sent them to central Mexico. In 2006, the state of California issued a formal apology to its Mexican residents. A memorial in Los Angeles commemorates the 1931 event in La Placita Park.

Active Options

On Your Feet: Four Corners Post these signs in four corners of the classroom: Women, African Americans, Mexican Americans, Native Americans. Organize students into groups around each sign. Direct them to discuss the problems their assigned group faced during the Great Depression. Encourage students to become the voice of those people by preparing short speeches or posters representing their causes. Then hold a rally in which groups share their work.

NG Learning Framework: Connect Past and Present

SKILL Collaboration

KNOWLEDGE Our Human Story

Ask students to compare and contrast the repatriation of Mexicans and Mexican Americans in the 1930s with the Trump administration's plan to deport people of Mexican descent in 2017. Divide the class into two groups and assign one of the topics to each group. Prompt group members to work together to create and follow a research strategy. After groups have researched their topics, hold a class discussion in which each side presents its facts. Then have the class as a whole identify similarities and differences.

DIFFERENTIATE

English Language Learners ELD

Clarify Multiple Meaning Words Pair students at the **Expanding** and **Bridging** levels with those at the **Emerging** level. Remind students that some words have more than one meaning. Elicit multiple meanings of the word *depression* (the state of feeling sad; a place lower than its surroundings; a period of low economic activity). Instruct pairs to use context clues or a dictionary to determine the correct meaning of these words as they are used in this lesson: *depression, positions, cabinet, pass,* and *descent.*

Pre-AP

Compare Time Lines Instruct students to conduct research to learn more about the women named in the lesson and their professional accomplishments before, during, and after working in Roosevelt's administration. Then prompt students to create a time line for each woman. When they have finished, instruct students to compare the time lines of the different women to find commonalities and differences. Invite students to share their findings with the class.

See the Chapter Planner for more strategies for differentiation.

HISTORICAL THINKING

ANSWERS

1. More women and African Americans were appointed to important positions. New Deal programs provided jobs to women and African Americans. Native Americans gained more control over their own government. Still, the administration did not promote civil rights legislation and deported many people of Mexican descent.

2. Possible response: The reason—that he would lose the support of white southern Democrats—was politically realistic and practical, but it was morally disappointing.

3. African Americans and Mexican Americans experienced discrimination and poverty before the Great Depression, and when times are harder for everybody, those already struggling will struggle even more.

CRITICAL VIEWING Possible responses: The angle of the photo focuses on students' faces and the organization of the classroom, emphasizing the quality of learning. The instructor seems to be looming large, and the faces of students are all upturned and respectful.

Legacy of the New Deal

A historian called it "the only light in the darkness." A political writer describes it as "one of the greatest acts of wreckage in world history." Both people were describing the New Deal.

MAIN IDEA The New Deal affected American government and society in ways that are still evident today.

EXPANDING GOVERNMENT

By the end of the 1930s, the New Deal had lost support in Congress, and most of the programs came to an end due to a lack of funding. The New Deal was not a complete success; it had not restored the country to the prosperity of the 1920s. However, the New Deal had provided hope and relief to millions of Americans when they desperately needed it. It restored the public's confidence in the nation's future.

The New Deal also changed the nature of the federal government by expanding its power and size. The president developed legislation that Congress simply approved. The federal government became more involved in the economy by creating jobs; supporting agriculture; and regulating banking, investment, and business activities. The administration of New Deal programs required a much larger executive staff, which resulted in the hiring of many additional federal employees. Besides concentrating power in the executive branch, the New Deal made the federal government far more of a presence in the daily lives and business of Americans.

LASTING IMPACT

A number of New Deal programs continue to play a significant role in American life, though they have undergone changes over the years. For example, most Americans count on Social Security payments for at least partial financial support after retirement. Social Security also provides benefits to disabled Americans who are unable to work, to children who have lost a parent, and to husbands or wives who have lost their spouses. The federal government continues to provide farmers with price supports for crops.

Several New Deal regulatory agencies continue to operate today. The National Labor Relations Board, created by the Wagner Act, still regulates relations between unions and employers. The Federal Deposit Insurance Corporation (FDIC) guarantees bank deposits against loss. The Securities and Exchange Commission (SEC), created in 1934, still protects investors from illegal and deceptive practices.

Every day, Americans use roads, bridges, airports, and other infrastructure originally built by New Deal workers. They hike park trails and view artwork created by New Deal employees.

To this day, Americans disagree on whether the changes brought about by the New Deal have been positive or negative. As they did in the 1930s, conservatives generally object to the increased size and power of the federal government. They also oppose **deficit spending**, or spending more money than the government receives from taxes. Liberals generally believe the government should take more responsibility for citizens' welfare, business regulation, and environmental protection. The gap between the two points of view has not lessened. Rather, it has widened in recent years.

Grand Coulee Dam in Washington State was a federal relief project of the New Deal. It was designed to benefit the country in the long term as well as to help people recover from the Depression in the short term. The dam provides hydroelectric power, irrigation, and flood control and generates enough hydroelectric power to supply two cities the size of Seattle.

HISTORICAL THINKING

1. **READING CHECK** How did FDR's presidency affect the power and size of the executive branch of government?

2. **IDENTIFY MAIN IDEAS AND DETAILS** What were some successes and failures of the New Deal?

3. **FORM AND SUPPORT OPINIONS** How involved do you think the federal government should be in helping citizens, regulating business, and protecting the environment? Give reasons for your opinion.

PLAN

Objective
Describe the lasting impact of the New Deal in programs and agencies that still exist today.

Critical Thinking Skills for Lesson 3.2
- Identify Main Ideas and Details
- Monitor Comprehension
- Form and Support Opinions
- Draw Conclusions
- Compare and Contrast
- Make Connections

Essential Question for Chapter 23
Were President Franklin Roosevelt's attempts to resolve the nation's economic problems successful? Explain. Roosevelt's New Deal expanded the role of government and affected people's lives in many ways. Lesson 3.2 assesses the lasting results—positive and negative—of the New Deal programs.

Background for the Teacher
American savers and investors today still look to two institutions established during the Great Depression to support their financial health. The Federal Deposit Insurance Corporation (FDIC), formed in 1933, helped rebuild public confidence in banking after the bank failures of the early 1930s. Today, the FDIC logo on local banking institutions indicates that the government insures deposits up to $250,000. The FDIC directly manages more than 4,000 banks and ensures that they and other banks comply with laws that protect consumers. The Securities and Exchange Commission (SEC), created in 1934, helped restore confidence in the stock market after the 1929 crash. Today, the SEC monitors stock exchanges, brokers, and investment advisors. It protects investors by requiring companies and brokers to provide accurate information about businesses and securities. In this way, the SEC ensures that people have access to good knowledge about an investment before they buy or sell it.

INTRODUCE & ENGAGE

Define *Legacy*

Ask students to define the word *legacy*. *(Possible responses: money or property left to someone in a will; something that is handed down from the past; something that is outdated but still usable, such as legacy software)* Read the lesson title. **ASK:** What do you think *legacy* means in this title? *(Possible response: the lasting effects of New Deal programs on the nation)* How can you evaluate a legacy? *(Possible response: You determine whether its aftereffects are good or bad.)* Tell students that this lesson discusses different opinions about the legacy of the New Deal.

TEACH

Guided Discussion

1. **Draw Conclusions** Why would funding for New Deal programs have come to an end? *(Possible responses: Congress stopped supporting New Deal legislation, so it may not have appropriated additional funding for programs already in progress. The government may have run out of money. Congress may have felt that many programs had outlived their usefulness.)*

2. **Compare and Contrast** How do conservatives and liberals differ in their view of deficit spending? *(Possible response: Conservatives believe that government spending should not exceed revenue received from taxes, so they oppose deficit spending. Liberals believe that government should spend what is necessary to provide for citizens' welfare, even if it results in a deficit.)*

Make Connections

Direct students' attention to the photograph of the Grand Coulee Dam and read the caption aloud. Explain that the construction of the dam took eight years and required the work of thousands of men. **ASK:** How did the dam benefit the country in the short term and in the long term? *(Possible responses: In the short term, the construction of the dam provided jobs during the Great Depression, and in the long term, it continues to supply hydroelectric power to people in the region.)*

Active Options

On Your Feet: Weigh the Pluses and Minuses Divide the class into small groups and instruct group members to create a balance sheet by listing the positive and negative effects of the New Deal on a T-Chart. Invite groups to gather around a balance scale. Call on each group to demonstrate its balance sheet by placing a weight for each positive effect on one side of the balance and a weight for each negative effect on the other side. (If a balance scale is not available, have students stack same-sized books to indicate the number of positive and negative effects and then compare the height of the two stacks.) Compare the groups' demonstrations and encourage students to defend their assessments of the New Deal.

NG Learning Framework: Showcase a Legacy

SKILL Communication

KNOWLEDGE Our Human Story

Ask students to choose one legacy of the New Deal that they would like to learn more about. For example, they might choose to research a particular New Deal program, the work of one or more WPA writers or artists, or another legacy of the New Deal. Tell them to choose an appropriate method to showcase their selected legacy. For example, they might create a collage, political cartoon, speech, poem, or song to present their choice. Students might also want to work in a small group to create a short skit. Provide time for students to share their work with the class.

DIFFERENTIATE

Striving Readers

Summarize Direct students to work in pairs to read and summarize the text. Ask them to write at least three notes for each of the two sections of the lesson. Guide students to create a summary statement for each section, followed by a summary statement for the entire lesson.

Pre-AP

Compare Programs After they read the lesson, prompt students to research comparisons between the New Deal and the Affordable Care Act, which became law in 2010. Then direct them to write an essay highlighting parallels between the programs in terms of purpose, urgency, implementation, and reception. Suggest that students consider how emotions and opinions, such as hope for change or resistance to change, translated to support for or opposition to the New Deal and the ACA. Encourage students to read their essay to the class and to answer any questions.

See the Chapter Planner for more strategies for differentiation.

HISTORICAL THINKING

ANSWERS

1. During FDR's presidency, the federal government became larger by hiring many employees to manage its programs. It extended its power into many more aspects of American life than ever before.

2. The New Deal succeeded in giving people hope, providing them with relief from the Great Depression, and restoring their confidence in government. It failed to end unemployment and restore the economy to its former prosperity.

3. Answers will vary. Students might say that the government should take more responsibility in order to make people's lives better, or they may say the government should take less responsibility so that people develop independence and don't rely too much on the government.

23 REVIEW

VOCABULARY

Match the following vocabulary terms with their definitions.

1. supply and demand
2. consumer debt
3. bank run
4. speculate
5. pension fund
6. bank holiday
7. buying on margin
8. repatriation

a. a situation in which a large number of depositors withdraw their money from a bank because they fear the bank will close

b. buying stock for a small percentage of its price and borrowing to pay the rest

c. to buy and sell stocks in the hope of making a quick profit

d. a pool of money used to pay retirees a certain income

e. the act of sending immigrants back to their home country

f. a day or period of time during which banks are closed by law

g. the amount of a good or service that is available compared to the amount that people want to buy

h. the amount of money that people have borrowed to purchase goods

READING STRATEGY
IDENTIFY MAIN IDEAS AND DETAILS

If you haven't done so already, complete your graphic organizer by recording details that support the identified main idea. Then answer the question below.

9. How did President Roosevelt's New Deal help unemployed people?

MAIN IDEAS

Answer the following questions. Support your answers with evidence from the chapter.

10. What difficulties did American farmers encounter after World War I? **LESSON 1.1**

11. What happened to the stock market on Black Tuesday? **LESSON 1.2**

12. How did many business owners respond to the economic troubles at the beginning of the Great Depression? **LESSON 1.3**

13. What did Franklin Roosevelt promise voters in his 1932 campaign for president? **LESSON 2.1**

14. How long did it take FDR to push his first 15 New Deal laws through Congress? **LESSON 2.2**

15. Why did many farmers leave the Dust Bowl region and migrate westward? **LESSON 2.3**

16. What was the purpose of the Social Security Act? **LESSON 2.4**

17. Why did FDR try to increase the number of justices on the Supreme Court? **LESSON 2.5**

18. Who was Frances Perkins, and what was her role in the New Deal? **LESSON 3.1**

19. How did FDR change the office of the presidency? **LESSON 3.2**

HISTORICAL THINKING

Answer the following questions. Support your answers with evidence from the chapter.

20. **COMPARE AND CONTRAST** How did Herbert Hoover and Franklin Roosevelt differ in their ideas for dealing with the Great Depression?

21. **ANALYZE CAUSE AND EFFECT** Summarize the causes and effects of the Dust Bowl.

22. **SYNTHESIZE** How was the Roosevelt administration more inclusive—that is, open to everyone—than previous presidential administrations?

23. **FORM AND SUPPORT OPINIONS** What do you think is the most important legacy of the New Deal, and why?

INTERPRET VISUALS

This graph shows the unemployment rate from the early years of the Depression through the partial recovery achieved by 1940. Study the graph and answer the questions that follow.

U.S. Unemployment Rate, 1930–1940

Source: Bureau of Labor Statistics

24. During which years was the unemployment rate higher than 20 percent?

25. In which year was the unemployment rate highest, and how high was it?

26. About what percentage of the labor force was unemployed in 1937?

ANALYZE SOURCES

In a fireside chat on September 30, 1934, President Roosevelt responded to opponents' criticisms of the New Deal.

> To those people who say that our expenditures [costs] for public works and for other means for recovery are a waste that we cannot afford, I answer that no country, however rich, can afford the waste of its human resources. Demoralization [discouragement] caused by vast unemployment is our greatest extravagance. Morally, it is the greatest menace to our social order.

27. What effects of unemployment does the president focus on in this passage?

CONNECT TO YOUR LIFE

28. **EXPLANATORY** The Great Depression was one of the most difficult domestic struggles Americans faced in the 20th century. The government programs designed to help people were controversial. Some thought they didn't do enough, and others thought of them as "handouts" that threatened American identity. Yet some of those programs still exist and affect the lives of many Americans. Choose a New Deal program, agency, or project that exists now and write a paragraph explaining how it is important today in the lives of people you know.

TIPS

- Review the lesson on the New Deal's legacy and research the subject. Identify a New Deal program, project, or agency you think is significant in the lives of people you know.

- In a topic sentence, clearly state why the program, project, or agency matters to people you know.

- Provide supporting details that further explain the effects on people today.

- Write a concluding sentence that sums up your thoughts.

VOCABULARY ANSWERS

1. g
2. h
3. a
4. c
5. d
6. f
7. b
8. e

READING STRATEGY ANSWER

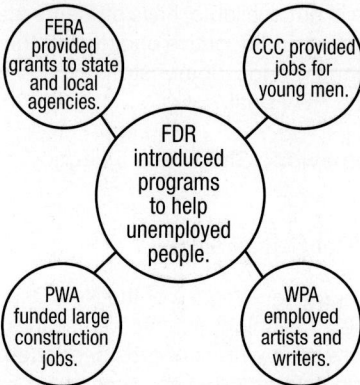

9. Roosevelt's New Deal helped unemployed people by establishing assistance programs, such as the CCC, WPA, PWA, and FERA, that created jobs, resulting in paychecks for construction work as well as for artistic creations.

MAIN IDEAS ANSWERS

10. After World War I, European farmers returned to work, decreasing demand for U.S. farm products. U.S. farmers continued a high level of production, causing a surplus of goods, which lowered prices. As a result, farmers found themselves in debt.

11. Investors realized that the downward trend of the stock market was going to continue. On Black Tuesday, people rushed to sell off their stocks, even at a loss, causing the market crash.

12. In response to economic troubles, businesses cut back on production of goods, laid off workers, and stopped hiring.

13. During his campaign for president, Roosevelt promised to take action that would expand the role of government and put regulations in place for businesses.

14. Roosevelt put in place his first 15 New Deal laws within his first hundred days in office.

15. Drought and soil erosion in the Dust Bowl ruined farmers' crops, and with no income, the farmers were unable to pay their mortgages. Many migrated west in search of work.

16. The Social Security Act provided a pension fund for the elderly as well as unemployment insurance and aid for the disabled and others in need.

17. After conservative justices ruled that parts of his New Deal program were unconstitutional, FDR believed that reorganizing the federal court system and adding different justices would prevent further interference in New Deal programs.

18. Frances Perkins was a labor rights activist whom Roosevelt appointed as secretary of labor. She was a driving force in creating several New Deal relief programs.

19. Roosevelt concentrated power in the executive branch by developing legislation that Congress simply approved. He expanded the role of the federal government in people's lives and in businesses.

HISTORICAL THINKING ANSWERS

20. Hoover believed that providing direct assistance to people would make them rely on the government, so he approved limited financial support to businesses and some public works programs with the intent of creating jobs and keeping government intervention at a minimum. Roosevelt believed that the government had responsibility for the welfare of citizens, so he provided direct aid to the needy, made efforts to regulate business, and took action to create relief programs to combat the effects of the Great Depression.

21. Farmers on the Great Plains plowed up deep-rooted grasses that held soil in place and planted shallow-rooted wheat plants. When drought hit the Great Plains, winds picked up the dry topsoil and caused dust storms that destroyed livestock, sickened people, and ruined crops. Farmers didn't have income from crops to pay their bills or mortgages, so they lost their homes. About a quarter of people in the area left to find work in the West.

22. Roosevelt's administration included women and African Americans as members of the Cabinet and implemented many of their ideas and programs to specifically help minorities.

23. Answers will vary. Students should use facts from the text to support their opinions.

INTERPRET VISUALS ANSWERS STEM

24. From part of 1931 up to 1935, the unemployment rate was at or above 20 percent.

25. In 1933 the unemployment rate peaked at 25 percent.

26. In 1937 the unemployment rate was a little less than 15 percent.

ANALYZE SOURCES ANSWER

27. Roosevelt focuses on the demoralizing effects of unemployment on human lives and abilities.

CONNECT TO YOUR LIFE ANSWER

28. Answers will vary. Students should explain how a New Deal program, agency, or project affects the lives of people today. Their paragraphs should incorporate a topic sentence, supporting details, and a concluding sentence that summarizes their ideas.

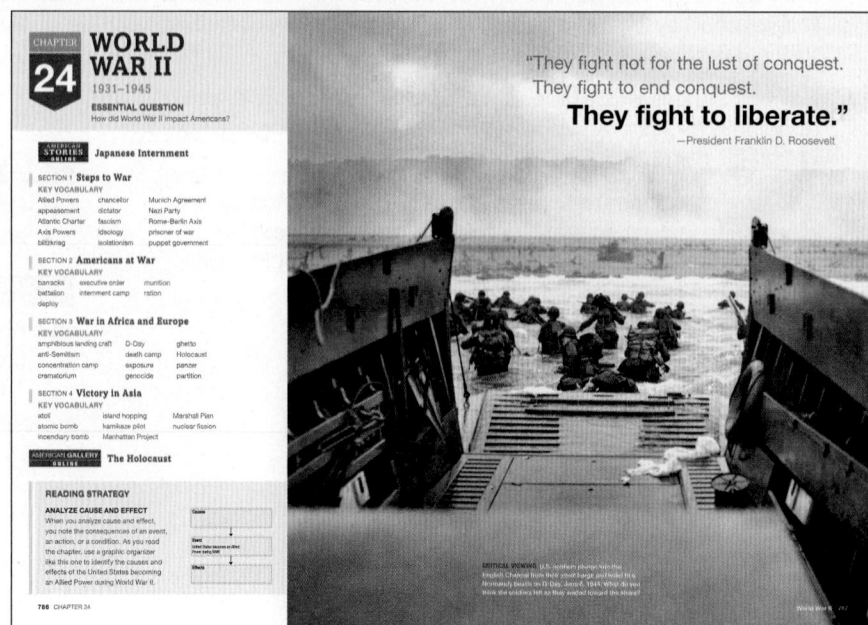

Chapter 24 Spanish Resources are available at NGLSync.Cengage.com.

AMERICAN STORIES ONLINE | **Japanese Internment**

- Primary Sources
- On Your Feet: Create a Concept Web
- **NG Learning Framework:**
  Make a Civil Liberties Time Line

SECTION 1 RESOURCES
STEPS TO WAR

LESSON 1.1
New Dictators Arise

- Active History: Compare and Contrast Fascism and Neo-Fascism
- **NG Learning Framework:**
  Prevent a Dictatorship

LESSON 1.2
Germany on the Attack

- On Your Feet: Three Corners
- **NG Learning Framework:**
  Investigate the Impact of the Neutrality Acts

LESSON 1.3
Hitler Attacks West and East

- On Your Feet: Evaluate a Speech
- **NG Learning Framework:**
  Forge a Plan for Lasting Peace

LESSON 1.4
Attack on Pearl Harbor

- On Your Feet: Analyze Roosevelt's Speech
- **NG Learning Framework:**
  Create an Annotated Time Line

LESSON 1.5
CURATING HISTORY
National Air and Space Museum, Washington, D.C.

- On Your Feet: Sort the Artifacts
- **American Voices Biography**
  Amelia Earhart ONLINE

SECTION 2 RESOURCES
AMERICANS AT WAR

LESSON 2.1
Pulling Together

- On Your Feet: Numbered Heads
- **NG Learning Framework:**
  Compose a Journal Entry

LESSON 2.2
Women in the War

- ▶ Rosie the Riveter
- On Your Feet: Word Chain
- **NG Learning Framework:**
  Hold a Panel Discussion
- **American Voices Biography**
  Rosie the Riveter ONLINE

LESSON 2.3
A Diverse War Effort

- On Your Feet: Chart Relay
- **NG Learning Framework:**
  Devise a Code

LESSON 2.4
NATIONAL GEOGRAPHIC EXPLORER
BARRINGTON IRVING, JR.
Soaring to New Heights

- On Your Feet: Brainstorm How to Start a Program
- **NG Learning Framework:**
  Propose an Expedition

LESSON 2.5
Japanese American Internment

- On Your Feet: Roundtable Writing
- **NG Learning Framework:**
  Present an Interned Japanese American

SECTION 3 RESOURCES
WAR IN AFRICA AND EUROPE

LESSON 3.1
Fighting in Africa and Italy

- On Your Feet: Create a Quiz
- **NG Learning Framework:**
  Explore Fighting a War in a Foreign Land

LESSON 3.2
The Allies Advance

- On Your Feet: One-on-One Interviews
- **NG Learning Framework:**
  Write a First-Person Account

LESSON 3.3
End of War in Europe

- On Your Feet: Create a Concept Cluster
- **NG Learning Framework:**
  Stage a Mock Conference

LESSON 3.4
The Holocaust

AMERICAN GALLERY ONLINE The Holocaust

- **NG Learning Framework:**
  Research Holocaust Stories
- **American Voices Biography**
  Elie Wiesel ONLINE

SECTION 4 RESOURCES
VICTORY IN ASIA

LESSON 4.1
War in the Pacific

- On Your Feet: Rotating Review
- **NG Learning Framework:**
  Write a Letter Home

LESSON 4.2
Island Hopping

- On Your Feet: Question and Answer
- **NG Learning Framework:**
  Compose an Expository Essay

LESSON 4.3
Final Victory

- On Your Feet: Paragraph Chain
- **NG Learning Framework:**
  Compose a Journal Entry

LESSON 4.4
Legacy of World War II

- On Your Feet: Fishbowl
- **NG Learning Framework:**
  Present a News Report

CHAPTER 24 REVIEW

Strategy ❶
Create "What Happens" Charts

Help students summarize the chapter by having them create four "What Happens" Charts, one for each of the following topics: Steps to War, Americans at War, War in Africa and Europe, Victory in Asia. Instruct students to complete each chart with relevant information as they read the lessons.

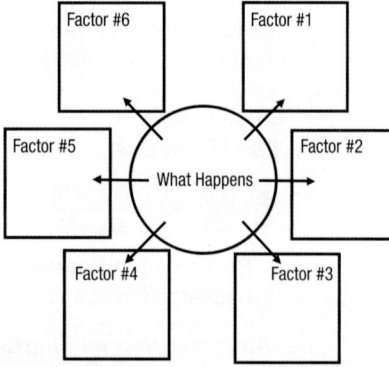

Use with All Lessons *For example, for the topic Steps to War, students may add the following events to their chart: Dictators and military leaders take power; German invasions start the war; German aggression continues, and the United States prepares to enter the war; Japan's attack on Pearl Harbor draws the United States into the war.*

Strategy ❷
Rewrite Main Ideas as Questions

Before students read a lesson, help them set a purpose for reading by rewriting the Main Idea statement as a question. Tell students to write an answer to the question after they read. Below are sample questions for Lessons 1.1 and 1.2.

1.1 What factors led to the rise of dictators and military leaders in Italy, Germany, the Soviet Union, and Japan?

1.2 How did Hitler's recapturing of areas that were once part of Germany lead to the start of World War II?

Use with All Lessons

Strategy ❸
Read and Recall

Tell students to read the lesson independently. Then instruct them to meet in pairs without the text and share ideas and facts they recall. One partner should take notes and list all the facts and ideas. Students should then review the lesson using the text and decide what to add or change in the list.

Use with All Lessons

Strategy ❶
Use Echo Reading

Point out that the Main Idea statements at the beginning of the lessons all relate to important aspects of World War II. Pair students so that there is a proficient reader in each pair. After each lesson, have the proficient partner read the Main Idea statement aloud. Have the other partner "echo" the same statement using his or her own words.

Use with All Lessons

Strategy ❷
Describe a Historical Photograph

Pair students who are visually impaired with students who are not. Ask the latter to describe the photograph in Lesson 1.1 of members of Nazi youth organizations in detail, including the people at the rally, facial expressions, and gestures. Have them answer any questions their partner may have, and encourage both to discuss the possible reasons that Nazis recruited children.

Use with Lesson 1.1 *You may wish to repeat this strategy for the historical photographs in other lessons.*

ENGLISH LANGUAGE LEARNERS

Strategy ①
Activate Prior Knowledge

Display the terms shown below in a random "splash" arrangement, and explain that the terms relate to the Japanese attack on Pearl Harbor. Ask students to discuss the terms' meanings, and then have them work in pairs to write sentences, each containing two or more of the terms listed. You may wish to pair students at the **Emerging** level with students at the **Expanding** or **Bridging** level.

Use with Lesson 1.4 *You may wish to repeat this strategy for other lessons, using Key Vocabulary words and important terms.*

Strategy ②
Use Pronunciation Keys

Preteach the meaning and pronunciation of Key Vocabulary words before each lesson. Give a brief definition or example for each word and then pronounce it slowly and clearly several times. Have students repeat after you. Then have students create a pronunciation key for each word, and remind them to refer to it. After each lesson, guide students in writing simple sentences using each word. (After Lesson 1.1 for example: In fascism, leaders use racism, nationalism, and the military to control people.) Provide sentence stems for students at the **Emerging** level. Encourage students at the **Bridging** level to develop complex sentences for each word.

Use with All Lessons

Strategy ③
Create a Word Wall

Work with students at the **Emerging** and **Expanding** levels to select three words from each lesson to display in a grouping on a Word Wall for the chapter. Choose words students are likely to encounter in other chapters, such as *territory, turmoil,* and *military*. Display and discuss each word as students encounter it during reading. Suggest that students at the **Bridging** level contribute by adding phrases or examples to each word to develop understanding.

Use with All Lessons

GIFTED & TALENTED

Strategy ①
Present a World War II Figure

Instruct students to conduct preliminary research about the experiences of various groups of people during World War II, such as Japanese Americans living in an internment camp, Japanese American soldiers, African-American pilots, Native American code talkers, female factory workers, or combat photographers. Then have students conduct in-depth research on one such person, accessing letters, diary entries, and other primary and secondary sources. Prompt students to assume that person's identity and present a theatrical performance to the class, drawing on their research to speak and act in character.

Use with Lessons 2.2–2.3 and 2.5

Strategy ②
Make a Poster

Ask students to think about ways that the U.S. government could have appealed to the different groups mentioned in the lesson to urge them to join the war effort. Have students work with a partner to create a poster aimed at a specific group to urge its members to enlist or contribute to the war effort in some way. Display completed posters in the classroom and invite students to discuss them.

Use with Lesson 2.3

Pre-AP

Strategy ①
Write a Feature Article

Instruct students to research women's contributions during World War II. Tell them to select a woman that they discovered in their research and write a feature article about her specific contribution to the war effort. Invite students to publish their articles on the school or class website or present them to the class.

Use with Lesson 2.2 *You may wish to provide examples of feature articles as models.*

Strategy ②
Report on the Roles of Native Americans

Encourage students to research the roles of Native Americans during World War II, at home and abroad, and their contributions to the war effort. Then have them develop a topic and write a report about what they learned. Students may include photographs or other visuals if they wish. Encourage them to present their reports to the class.

Use with Lesson 2.3

CHAPTER

24

WORLD WAR II

1931–1945

ESSENTIAL QUESTION
How did World War II impact Americans?

 Japanese Internment

SECTION 1 **Steps to War**
KEY VOCABULARY

Allied Powers	chancellor	Munich Agreement
appeasement	dictator	Nazi Party
Atlantic Charter	fascism	Rome-Berlin Axis
Axis Powers	ideology	prisoner of war
blitzkrieg	isolationism	puppet government

SECTION 2 **Americans at War**
KEY VOCABULARY

barracks	executive order	munition
battalion	internment camp	ration
deploy		

SECTION 3 **War in Africa and Europe**
KEY VOCABULARY

amphibious landing craft	D-Day	ghetto
anti-Semitism	death camp	Holocaust
concentration camp	exposure	panzer
crematorium	genocide	partition

SECTION 4 **Victory in Asia**
KEY VOCABULARY

atoll	island hopping	Marshall Plan
atomic bomb	kamikaze pilot	nuclear fission
incendiary bomb	Manhattan Project	

AMERICAN **GALLERY**
ONLINE **The Holocaust**

READING STRATEGY

ANALYZE CAUSE AND EFFECT
When you analyze cause and effect,
you note the consequences of an event,
an action, or a condition. As you read
the chapter, use a graphic organizer
like this one to identify the causes and
effects of the United States becoming
an Allied Power during World War II.

Causes

Event
United States becomes an Allied
Power during WWII

Effects

"They fight not for the lust of conquest.
They fight to end conquest.

They fight to liberate."

—President Franklin D. Roosevelt

CRITICAL VIEWING U.S. soldiers plunge into the
English Channel from their small barge and head to a
Normandy beach on D-Day, June 6, 1944. What do you
think the soldiers felt as they waded toward the shore?

*For Chapter 24 Spanish Resources, visit the
Resources Menu. Chapter 24 Resources
are available at NGLSync.Cengage.com.*

INTRODUCE THE PHOTOGRAPH

D-Day Landing at Normandy

Ask students to study the photograph and read
the caption. Explain that the photograph was taken
as American soldiers disembarked from a landing
craft at one of the landing points of the Normandy
invasion, commonly known as D-Day, near the end
of World War II. Use a classroom map to show the
location of Normandy, the English Channel, and
the southern coast of England. Tell students that
British, Canadian, and U.S. forces departed from
cities along the southern coast, were transported
across the English Channel by boat, and landed
on the northern coast of France in Normandy, at
beaches below German-occupied territory. Then
draw students' attention to the quotation from
President Franklin D. Roosevelt. Explain that it
refers to Adolf Hitler's conquest of much of Europe
and how combined forces from countries around
the world were fighting to free people from Hitler's
control. Tell students that in this chapter they will
learn about World War II and the impact it had on
the United States and the world.

Share Background

During the Normandy invasion, the U.S. Coast
Guard sent in correspondents and combat
photographers to document the event. Chief
Photographer's Mate Robert F. Sargent took this
photograph, titled *Into the Jaws of Death*. The
title alludes to a line from Alfred, Lord Tennyson's
narrative poem "The Charge of the Light Brigade"
(1854), about a famous battle during the Crimean
War in which outnumbered British cavalrymen
fought bravely: "Stormed at with shot and shell, /
Boldly they rode and well, / Into the jaws of Death, /
Into the mouth of hell / Rode the six hundred."
A press release accompanying the photograph
included Sargent's firsthand account of the troops
disembarking at Omaha Beach and the retreat of
the landing craft.

CRITICAL VIEWING Possible response: The soldiers
might have felt fear as they struggled through the
water and onto the heavily fortified and chaotic
beach. But they might also have felt bravely
determined to fight the enemy they faced.

INTRODUCE THE ESSENTIAL QUESTION

How did World War II impact Americans?

Four Corners Activity: War and Society This activity prompts students to think about how a war can impact different segments of society, specifically people in the armed forces, business owners and manufacturers, families, and foreign-born U.S. residents. Assign each corner of the room to one of the four segments, and ask students to count off by fours. Direct students to the corner that corresponds to their number. After students are organized in their groups, have them discuss the question provided. Then call on a volunteer from each group to summarize the group's thoughts for the class.

People in the Armed Forces What effect might a war have on people already in the armed forces?

Business Owners and Manufacturers How might businesses and manufacturers contribute to a war effort?

Families What hardships might families experience during a war?

Foreign-born U.S. Residents How might being at war with a foreign nation affect the attitude of Americans toward U.S. residents of that nationality?

INTRODUCE CHAPTER VOCABULARY

Word Webs

Have students complete a Word Web for each Key Vocabulary word as they read the chapter. Ask them to write each word in the center of an oval and then look through the chapter to find examples, characteristics, and descriptive words that may be associated with the vocabulary word. At the end of the chapter, ask students what they learned about each word. Model an example for students on the board, using a graphic organizer like the one shown.

absolute ruler
restricts civil rights
not subject to laws
Joseph Stalin in the Soviet Union
dictator
Benito Mussolini in Italy
backed by strong military
puts enemies in prison
Adolf Hitler in Nazi Germany

INTRODUCE THE READING STRATEGY

ANALYZE CAUSE AND EFFECT

Remind students that sometimes multiple causes lead to an event, such as how farming practices and a drought caused the Dust Bowl phenomenon in the Great Plains. One event could also have several effects, such as the establishment of the Tennessee Valley Authority creating thousands of jobs, providing power to industries, and promoting better farming methods. Explain that students can use a chart to show the causes and effects of events, actions, and conditions. Point out the three sections of the chart. Ask for suggestions of one possible cause and one possible effect of the United States becoming an Allied Power during World War II. Model completing the chart. Remind students to use the chart as they read the chapter.

Causes

↓

Event
United States becomes an Allied Power during WWII

↓

Effects

KEY DATES FOR CHAPTER 24

1933	Adolf Hitler becomes chancellor of Germany
September 1938	Munich Agreement
November 1938	Kristallnacht
August 1939	German-Soviet Nonaggression Pact
September 1939	World War II begins in Europe
December 1941	Japan attacks Pearl Harbor
February 1942	FDR signs Executive Order 9066
June 1944	D-Day
May 1945	Nazis surrender to Allies
August 1945	Bombing of Hiroshima and Nagasaki

AMERICAN STORIES ONLINE For instructional support for the online American Story "Japanese Internment," go to NGLSync.Cengage.com.

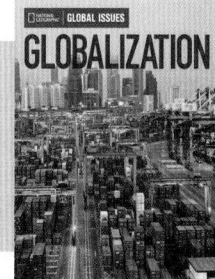

For more on the United States' involvement with other nations, see *GLOBAL ISSUES: GLOBALIZATION.*

New Dictators Arise

During times of trouble, governments often question whether their priority should be protecting citizens' freedoms or making the nation secure. Historically, security usually wins the debate. That is what happened in Europe in the 1930s.

MAIN IDEA In the 1930s, dictators and military leaders rose to power in Italy, Germany, the Soviet Union, and Japan.

At a 1933 rally in Erfurt, Germany, members of Nazi youth organizations, including Hitler Youth, salute dictator Adolf Hitler. Hitler Youth was formed in 1926 to teach young people Nazi ideas.

DICTATORS COME TO POWER

During the Great Depression, Americans focused on their own hardships, but in Europe and Asia, economic turmoil was making countries vulnerable to the rise of **dictators**. A dictator is an absolute ruler, not subject to controls within his or her government. Dictatorships would lead to an international catastrophe that has continued to affect world politics to this day.

As you know, World War I ended with the defeat of the Central Powers. The Treaty of Versailles forced Germany to accept blame for the war, give up large amounts of territory, and pay billions of dollars in reparations to the Allies. Austria-Hungary signed a similarly harsh treaty. The treaties bankrupted these nations. The Central Powers felt their punishments were unfair.

Italy and Japan had sided with the Allies and faced disappointments following the victory. Italy did not receive the territory it had been promised in return for supporting the Allies. Both countries suffered from the post-war economic turmoil that occurred worldwide. In Italy, widespread strikes and fighting split political parties. Political power in Japan began to shift to the military.

The Great Depression came as an additional blow. Across Europe, unemployment rose, and food prices skyrocketed. People grew angry, blaming their governments for these problems. The growing civil unrest and lack of strong democratic conditions gave cunning politicians an opportunity to seize power.

In Italy, a war veteran named **Benito Mussolini** used economic and social discontent to take control of the government, eventually banning all political parties but his own. Mussolini declared himself dictator in 1925. Meanwhile, the emperor of Japan, **Hirohito**, was allowing military leaders to take over the government. In Germany, a young politician named **Adolf Hitler** promised to restore the country to its pre-war greatness. In 1933, Hitler was appointed **chancellor**, a leader whose role is similar to that of a U.S. president. Soon Hitler was a dictator as well. In the Soviet Union, a high-ranking politician named **Joseph Stalin** secretly began to appoint his friends to key government positions beginning in 1922. By 1924, Stalin was dictator of the Soviet Union.

TENSIONS RISE IN EUROPE

Both Mussolini and Hitler practiced **fascism**, a political system that depends on nationalism, militarism, and racism to control a nation's population. Hitler's **ideology**, or set of beliefs, included the idea that the world was divided into superior and inferior races. With the help of his political party, the **Nazi Party**, Hitler began to blame members of ethnic groups and religions he deemed inferior, specifically Jewish people, for Germany's problems. The Nazis won public support by using propaganda, including posters and films that promoted the party's ideas for fixing the country.

Both Mussolini and Hitler desired conquest. On March 7, 1936, Hitler sent 22,000 German troops into the Rhineland, an area in western Germany that the Treaty of Versailles had placed under Allied control. The treaty stated that Germany could not keep military forces in the Rhineland, but neither Great Britain nor France took action. The invasion marked the beginning of Hitler's aggressive strategy in Europe.

Similarly, Mussolini sought to conquer more land for Italy, hoping to restore the glory of the ancient Roman Empire. On May 9, 1936, Italian forces took over the African nation of Abyssinia (now Ethiopia). Sharing a common goal, Hitler and Mussolini signed a pact of friendship in October 1936 known as the **Rome-Berlin Axis**, the alliance that established the two countries as the **Axis Powers**. The nations that would eventually band together to fight the Axis would once again be known as the **Allied Powers**.

HISTORICAL THINKING

1. **READING CHECK** What factors allowed dictators to take power in Europe?

2. **COMPARE AND CONTRAST** How were German, Italian, and Japanese objections over the treaties ending World War I similar, and how were they different?

3. **ASK AND ANSWER QUESTIONS** What questions do you have about the European dictators mentioned in this lesson, and where can you find the answers?

PLAN

Objective

Describe the rise of dictatorships during the 1920s and 1930s.

Critical Thinking Skills for Lesson 1.1

- Identify Main Ideas and Details
- Monitor Comprehension
- Compare and Contrast
- Ask and Answer Questions
- Interpret Visuals
- Analyze Cause and Effect

Essential Question for Chapter 24

How did World War II impact Americans? During the 1920s and 1930s, dictatorships emerged in nations in Europe and Asia. Lesson 1.1 examines this trend and how it contributed to the United States' involvement in World War II.

Background for the Teacher

The rise of Adolf Hitler and the Nazi Party was rapid. The Nazis used the economic downturn of the Great Depression to attract support from specific groups: the lower middle class, farmers, the unemployed, young people. This newfound support led to victory in the 1932 elections and Hitler's appointment as chancellor. Hitler took quick action to strengthen his rule and place the country under firm Nazi control. Less than a month after he took office, his regime suspended individual rights guaranteed by the constitution by giving the government the power to imprison people without a specific charge and curtailed free speech by suppressing publications. Later, the Enabling Act empowered Hitler to declare laws without the consent of the parliament. In addition, the Nazi Party forced rival political parties, local governments, educational institutions, and employers to align their efforts with Nazi goals. As a result, six months after Hitler took office, the Nazis had become the only political party in Germany, with Hitler as dictator.

INTRODUCE & ENGAGE

Determine Characteristics of a Dictatorship

Write *dictator* on the board, and discuss with students what the term means. Then ask students to brainstorm characteristics of a society under a dictatorship. Inform students that during the 1920s and 1930s, dictators took power in many countries throughout the world. **ASK:** What factors might lead a country to accept a dictatorship? *(Possible response: High unemployment and worries about national security might allow a strong individual with a compelling personality who promises economic prosperity to gain power.)* Finally, tell students that in this lesson they will examine the causes and effects of the rise of dictators in Europe and Asia.

TEACH

Guided Discussion

1. **Interpret Visuals** What details in the photograph suggest that the plan to teach Nazi ideas to young people has been successful? *(Some of the boys in the photograph are saluting and looking at Hitler with admiration. One boy appears to have ducked his head in order to get a better view. Hitler is smiling, apparently pleased with the attention and respect from the onlookers at the rally.)*

2. **Analyze Cause and Effect** How did the Treaty of Versailles contribute to the rise of dictatorships in Europe following World War I? *(Possible response: The harsh terms of the treaty bankrupted and humiliated the Central Powers. In response, nationalism rose, and fascist political candidates, such as Adolf Hitler and Benito Mussolini, gained support by convincing people that they could fix their nations' problems.)*

Identify Main Ideas and Details

Inform students that censorship, propaganda, and the control of information are key tools used by dictators to consolidate power and mislead the public about the causes of social and economic conditions. **ASK:** How did Hitler distort the causes of historical events in order to strengthen his power? *(Hitler assigned blame for Germany's economic downturn to minority groups, such as Jews, using propaganda in films and posters to promote his ideas. This argument was not about the actual causes of Germany's economic problems, but rather a method to gain support by blaming outside groups.)*

Active Options

Active History: Compare and Contrast Fascism and Neo-Fascism Extend the lesson by using either the PDF or Whiteboard version of the activity. These activities take a deeper look at a topic from, or related to, the lesson. Explore the activities as a class, turn them into group assignments, or even assign them individually.

NG Learning Framework: Prevent a Dictatorship

SKILL Problem-Solving

KNOWLEDGE Our Human Story

Ask students to think about the conditions that allowed dictators to seize power in Europe and Asia. Then ask them to consider whether the United States could ever become a dictatorship. Guide a discussion about what safeguards the United States has in place to protect against a dictatorship, such as the checks and balances among the three branches of government. Then have students work in small groups to create an educational pamphlet titled *How to Prevent Dictatorship in Your Country.* In the pamphlet, students should include five recommendations for citizens or governments to follow in order to prevent the rise of a dictatorial government. Alternatively, students could provide suggestions about how to halt an individual who is trying to establish a dictatorship. Invite groups to share their finished pamphlets. Then discuss as a class the similarities and differences among the groups' approaches.

DIFFERENTIATE

English Language Learners ELD

Identify and Record Cognates Suggest that as they read, students at **All Proficiencies** look for words that are similar in spelling and meaning to words in their home language. For example, the words *fascism, nationalism, militarism,* and *racism* have cognates in Spanish: *fascismo, nacionalismo, militarismo, racismo.* Guide students to make a vocabulary card for each cognate they identify, writing the English word and definition on one side. On the other side, have them write the word and its definition in their home language.

Pre-AP

Analyze Dictatorships Instruct students to research dictatorships from ancient Rome to the present and create a list of causes and effects of different dictatorships. Tell students to examine their list and then consider the following question: Are all dictatorships bad? Then have students write an analytical essay that answers the question, drawing on their research and including details from their list. Ask volunteers to read their analysis to the class.

See the Chapter Planner for more strategies for differentiation.

HISTORICAL THINKING

ANSWERS

1. Faltering economies, weak democratic governments, and resentment of the terms of the Treaty of Versailles allowed dictators to gain power.

2. They were similar in that their complaints included territorial disappointments and economic difficulties. They were different in that Germany lost the war, but Italy and Japan were on the winning side.

3. Answers will vary. Questions should relate to the lesson, and potential answer sources should include reputable websites, reference or textbooks, and encyclopedia articles.

Germany on the Attack

It is never easy dealing with bullies. Do you ignore them or confront them? In the 1930s, many European countries and the United States had to decide how to deal with Adolf Hitler, whom they considered a mere bully at first. But Hitler was on his way to setting a new standard for brutal tyranny.

MAIN IDEA Hitler's capture of areas that were previously part of Germany led to the start of World War II.

Hitler's Advance, 1938–1940

Map legend:
- Allied territory
- Axis powers
- Axis satellite
- Axis-controlled by 1940
- Soviet territory
- Neutral nation
- German troop movements

HITLER STAYS ON THE ATTACK

Encouraged by his military success in the Rhineland, Adolf Hitler decided to unite all German-speaking countries under his authority. He tried to bully the Austrian president into appointing Nazis to government positions. When that plan failed, Hitler ordered German troops to invade Austria on March 12, 1938. The Austrian government quickly accepted Hitler's demands.

Austria became a part of Germany that same day without any shots being fired.

Sudetenland (soo-DAY-tuhn-land), the name for a region in Czechoslovakia where many Germans lived, was next. In May 1938, Hitler ordered German troops into position along the Czechoslovakian border. His aim was to intimidate the Czech government into surrendering the region.

In response, the Czechs sent their troops to meet the German army. A fear of war spread throughout Europe.

As tensions rose in Europe, the United States enacted **isolationism**, a policy of staying out of the disputes of foreign nations. The country passed laws called **Neutrality Acts**, which banned the United States from making loans with or transporting goods to hostile countries in an effort to avoid war.

In September 1938, British Prime Minister **Neville Chamberlain** and French Premier Édouard Daladier (EHD-wahr duh-lah-dee-AY) flew to Munich, Germany, to compromise with Hitler. The meeting resulted in the **Munich Agreement**, which gave Sudetenland to Germany in return for Hitler's promise to stop invading countries. Chamberlain and Daladier's decision to sign the agreement was an act of **appeasement**, or a policy of agreeing to demands of a powerful opponent in order to avoid conflict. The Allies continued to appease Hitler to avoid another war. The men did not expect Hitler to break his promise.

In August 1939, the world was shocked to learn that sworn enemies Nazi Germany and the Soviet Union had signed an agreement. Under the **German-Soviet Nonaggression Pact**, the two countries vowed to take no military action against each other for 10 years. A secret part of the pact set the stage for a joint invasion of Poland by both countries, which occurred the following month.

EUROPE AT WAR AGAIN

The pact allowed Hitler to attack other countries without fear of retaliation from the Soviet Union. On September 1, 1939, he sent the German army, called the **Wehrmacht** (VAIR-mahkt), into Poland, where his troops introduced a new type of warfare, **blitzkrieg** (BLIHTS-kreeg) or "lightning war." This strategy involved bombarding important targets from the air and taking out railroads, landing strips, and communication lines before sending in a massive land invasion. The speed of these assaults confused enemy armies and allowed the Germans to launch more surprise attacks. As planned, Stalin's army invaded Poland

Winston Churchill addresses sailors in London in 1940, shortly before becoming Prime Minister. The sailors had just survived the destruction of their ship by German warships in Norway.

in October. The two countries quickly conquered and divided Poland. This violation of the Treaty of Versailles forced Britain and France to declare war on Germany, and **World War II** began.

In April 1940, the Wehrmacht blitzkrieg overran Denmark and Norway. Next it attacked Belgium, Holland, and Luxembourg. As a new British prime minister named **Winston Churchill** took office in May, the Wehrmacht invaded France. Hitler's army trapped British and French forces in the French port of Dunkirk, on the English Channel. The British were able to evacuate thousands of troops by sea while the Wehrmacht turned toward Paris. The French capital fell on June 14, 1940, and France surrendered on June 17. The terms of the surrender divided France. Only an area in southeastern France known as **Vichy** (VISH-ee) was left unoccupied by German troops. A free government was established there, but it quickly fell under Nazi influence. Britain now stood alone.

HISTORICAL THINKING

1. **READING CHECK** How did Great Britain become the only major Allied Power left to fight against the Axis?

2. **DETERMINE CHRONOLOGY** What German and Soviet actions led to the start of World War II?

3. **INTERPRET MAPS** On which continents had the Axis conquered countries by 1940?

World War II **791**

Objective

Analyze how German aggression led the world into war.

Critical Thinking Skills for Lesson 1.2

- Identify Main Ideas and Details
- Monitor Comprehension
- Determine Chronology
- Interpret Maps
- Form and Support Opinions
- Make Connections

Essential Question for Chapter 24

How did World War II impact Americans? Upon gaining control of Germany, Adolf Hitler led the country on an aggressive campaign of invading other nations throughout Europe. Lesson 1.2 details these events, which brought the United States closer to entering the war.

Background for the Teacher

Modern historians and politicians have sharply criticized Neville Chamberlain's decision to appease Hitler, but the realities of the time were complex. Many Britons were determined to stay out of another conflict that was emerging just decades after the horrors of World War I, and they saw appeasement as the best hope to preserve peace. Furthermore, Britain's military was stretched thin with managing colonies across the globe while at the same time countering the emerging threats in Europe and Asia. From a global perspective, it wasn't clear that Germany posed the greatest danger to world stability. Joseph Stalin sought to spread communism throughout the Soviet Union and had murdered millions of people who opposed him. Many across the West saw communism as more insidious than Nazism, so they thought that directing the full force of the British Empire against Germany was not the wisest course of action.

INTRODUCE & ENGAGE

Consider Targets and Alliances

Ask students to preview the map titled Hitler's Advance, 1938–1940, noting countries that Germany had invaded. Point out the legend. **ASK:** Based on the map, which countries might Germany invade next? *(Possible response: Sweden, Yugoslavia, Great Britain)* Which countries might pose a threat to Germany's advances? *(Great Britain and the Soviet Union)* Ask students to think about strategies that Hitler might use to further his territorial advances and how world powers might react. Then tell students that in this lesson they will read about Hitler's strategy for conquering Europe and how world powers dealt with his increasing territorial demands.

TEACH

Guided Discussion

1. **Form and Support Opinions** Was appeasement the best way to address German aggression? *(Answers will vary. Students could argue that appeasement was the best way to avoid war and was thus worth the attempt. Conversely, students could contend that there was no evidence Hitler would comply with such an agreement, so giving in to his demands set a precedent for future responses to German aggression.)*

2. **Make Connections** Why did the signing of the German-Soviet Nonaggression Pact indicate that Hitler intended to break the Munich Agreement? *(In the Munich Agreement, Hitler promised to cease territorial expansion. In making an alliance with the Soviet Union, which had the power and resources to halt Hitler's ambitions, Germany could invade and conquer any other country without consequence from the Soviets.)*

More Information

German-Soviet Nonaggression Pact The German-Soviet Nonaggression Pact stunned the world because relations between the two dictatorships had previously been tense. The benefits of the pact to the Soviets soon became clear. Without fear of interference from other nations and with world attention focused on the Germans, the Soviets took Poland, Estonia, Latvia, Lithuania, and part of Romania. They executed or sent to camps conquered army officers, government officials, intellectuals, and priests. Those who did not match the ethnic ideals of the Soviets, such as Jews and Poles, were persecuted, compelled to flee, or forced into slave labor. **ASK:** Why do you think the Soviet Union's actions during World War II are not discussed as often as those of Germany? *(Answers will vary. Students could conclude that because the Soviet Union was a U.S. ally, less attention is paid to the Soviets' atrocities.)*

Active Options

On Your Feet: Three Corners Place signs around the room that give three reasons for the outbreak of war in Europe: harshness of the Treaty of Versailles, policy of appeasement, and the German-Soviet Nonaggression Pact. Tell students to move to the sign for the reason they think was most responsible for war. Then ask groups to confer about their position and select a representative to present their position to the rest of the class.

NG Learning Framework: Investigate the Impact of the Neutrality Acts

SKILL Communication

KNOWLEDGE Our Human Story

To help students understand the changes in U.S. isolation policy toward the end of the 1930s, instruct them to use classroom and online sources to investigate the specifics of the three Neutrality Acts passed between 1935 and 1937. Encourage students to note how each act changed U.S. isolation policy and which segments of society, such as average Americans, manufacturers, and specific industries, were impacted with each new provision. Then have students discuss their findings as a class, identifying some causes and effects of the Neutrality Act.

DIFFERENTIATE

Striving Readers

Mark Up Maps Provide a printed copy of the map accompanying the lesson. Work with students to ensure they understand the legend and the original territory of the Axis Powers. Then have students circle the territories under Axis control by 1940. Bring students' attention to the arrows with dates above or below them. Then provide sentence frames for students to complete based on the map.

• Hitler invaded _____ and _____ in 1938. *(Austria; Czechoslovakia)*

• German and Soviet forces conquered and divided Poland in _____. *(1939)*

• In 1940, Germany invaded the Scandinavian countries of _____ and _____. *(Norway; Denmark)*

• Before invading France, Germany invaded Luxembourg, _____, and _____ at its western border. *(Netherlands; Belgium)*

Gifted & Talented

Analyze Historical Events Tell students to research events in Europe and Asia from 1931 to 1937 and to analyze which events affected Congress's decision to draft the Neutrality Acts. Ask students to write an analysis in which they make clear and direct connections between specific events and specific wording in the acts. Invite volunteers to present their analysis to the class by reading their paper aloud or presenting their findings in a brief oral report.

See the Chapter Planner for more strategies for differentiation.

HISTORICAL THINKING

ANSWERS

1. Hitler quickly swept through northern and western Europe, invading and conquering bordering nations. After the fall of France, only Britain was left unconquered.

2. In August 1939, Germany and the Soviet Union revealed they had signed the German-Soviet Nonaggression Pact. In September 1939, Hitler's Wehrmacht invaded Poland, and in October 1939, the Soviet Union also invaded Poland. The two countries conquered and divided Poland, a violation of the Treaty of Versailles, causing Britain and France to declare war.

3. Europe, Asia, and Africa

Hitler Attacks West and East

As the war continued, the United States found it increasingly difficult to remain neutral. Dozens of American merchant ships delivering cargo around the world were detained or sunk by both the Allies and the Axis.

MAIN IDEA Major German campaigns against Great Britain and the Soviet Union ended Hitler's string of victories.

THE BATTLE OF BRITAIN

On June 18, the day after France fell to the Nazis, Winston Churchill declared, "The Battle of France is over. The **Battle of Britain** is about to begin." Great Britain was the only Allied country left to fight Nazi Germany. The British people prepared for an invasion. The Battle of Britain mostly took place in the air. Between June and September 1940, the Luftwaffe (LOOFT-vahf-uh)—the German air force—and Britain's Royal Air Force (RAF) battled in the skies over Great Britain. Sticking to the blitzkrieg strategy, the Germans bombed strategic British cities relentlessly. Their goal was to force Britain's surrender.

British civilians suffered greatly. Hoping to keep their children safe, urban parents sent them to stay in homes in the countryside. Many children never saw their parents again. Whole neighborhoods in

CRITICAL VIEWING Stations along London's Underground, or subway system, provided shelter for many British citizens during the German bombing raids of 1940. What does the photo convey about life for Londoners during the war?

London and other cities were destroyed. Residents took cover in underground bunkers, bomb shelters, and subway stations. One of the deadlier attacks killed 1,500 Londoners in one night.

The Germans had conquered most of western Europe in fewer than two months, but they were no match for the RAF. The Royal Air Force drove the Luftwaffe into retreat before Nazi land troops could arrive. Hitler decided to turn his attention to the Soviet Union.

OPERATION BARBAROSSA

On June 21, 1941, in violation of his nonaggression pact with Stalin, Hitler ordered more than 3 million German soldiers, 3,000 tanks, and 2,500 airplanes to attack the Soviet Union. It was the largest invasion the world had ever seen. Hitler named it **Operation Barbarossa** after a medieval emperor of German-speaking people who also conquered countries in Europe. Hitler did not trust Stalin and wanted to take the Soviet Union out of the picture. He also wanted to secure oil supplies in Romania.

The Germans started off strong. The Wehrmacht captured more than 1 million **prisoners of war**, or soldiers captured by an enemy force, as they invaded the Soviet Union. But the Germans miscalculated three key factors: the number of Soviet soldiers, the weather, and the unity of

Operation Barbarossa, 1941

(map)

- Axis-controlled as of December 5, 1941
- Soviet-controlled as of December 5, 1941
- German-controlled Soviet territory as of December 5, 1941
- Areas of fierce fighting
- Neutral nation
- Front line, December 5, 1941
- German troop movements

0   100   200 miles
0 100 200 kilometers

the Allies. The Soviets quickly raised approximately 200,000 more soldiers to join the fight. The Germans found themselves unprepared for the bitterly cold Soviet winters. The Soviets, however, were well clad and trained for battle in extremely cold conditions. As the war raged on, Soviet supplies dwindled, but help was on the way.

In response to Germany's aggression, President Roosevelt pushed Congress to pass the **Lend-Lease Act** in 1941. The legislation authorized the United States to sell, lease, or lend military equipment to any country whose defense was vital to American security. The act boosted Great Britain and other allies efforts to defeat Germany. Many Americans had no desire to engage in another foreign war. They believed fighting in World War I was a mistake that should not be repeated. But Roosevelt believed Hitler must be stopped at any cost. Therefore, the United States helped arm the Soviets.

Even though the United States had not entered the war, President Roosevelt and Winston Churchill met to outline their goals for defeating Hitler. The document that resulted was called the **Atlantic Charter**. In it, they agreed not to wage any war to expand their territories and committed to help improve living conditions worldwide. They encouraged other countries to do the same. By late 1941, 26 nations had agreed to these terms. Meanwhile, Operation Barbarossa began to fail as the Soviet Union held off the German advance.

HISTORICAL THINKING

1. **READING CHECK** Why did Germany end its effort to conquer Great Britain?

2. **MAKE INFERENCES** Think about the wars Americans had fought in the past. Why do you think many Americans had no desire to engage in a war in Europe?

3. **INTERPRET MAPS** Why do you think the routes that German troops took toward Moscow and Leningrad diverge, or split?

Objective

Explain the effects of Hitler's air war with Great Britain and the invasion of the Soviet Union.

Critical Thinking Skills for Lesson 1.3

- Identify Main Ideas and Details
- Monitor Comprehension
- Make Inferences
- Interpret Maps
- Analyze Cause and Effect
- Evaluate

Essential Question for Chapter 24

How did World War II impact Americans? After the initial success of its blitzkrieg, Germany set its sights on U.S. allies Great Britain and the Soviet Union. Lesson 1.3 discusses how these campaigns brought the United States closer to entering the war.

Background for the Teacher

Hitler's goal to invade and quickly defeat Great Britain could be achieved only if the Germans first controlled the air over southern England. To counter the Luftwaffe's offense, the British rapidly mobilized a robust air defense. Most visible were the nearly 3,000 pilots of the RAF—dubbed "The Few" by Winston Churchill. The RAF was supported by a complex air defense network that utilized radar, radio, antiaircraft guns, searchlights, and barrage balloons to counter German attacks. Large ground crews maintained the fleet of aircraft, factory workers ramped up aircraft production, and tens of thousands of volunteers manned observation posts. This complex operation succeeded in defending British airspace—and at the same time drained the Luftwaffe's resources—until Hitler abandoned efforts to defeat Great Britain and end the war quickly.

Activate Prior Knowledge

Have students recall the initial success of Germany's blitzkrieg strategy at the outset of World War II. Review which nations had fallen under Nazi control and that Great Britain had not been invaded. Inform students that in this lesson they will learn about the Battle of Britain, Germany's attempt to complete its domination of Europe. Then present the class with photographs that show some of the destruction Britain suffered when Germany bombed its cities. Discuss the photographs and any prior knowledge students may have about conditions and activities in Great Britain during World War II.

TEACH

Guided Discussion

1. **Analyze Cause and Effect** What impact did Operation Barbarossa have on the course of the war? *(The invasion of the Soviet Union was more difficult than the Germans expected. The German army became bogged down in the Soviet winter, weakening Germany's war effort. The operation caused the United States to become more involved with the war through the Lend-Lease Act and the Atlantic Charter.)*

2. **Evaluate** How do you think Americans might have felt about the Lend-Lease Act? *(Possible response: Some were likely happy since it kept the United States from entering the war, but others may have disliked the fact that the United States was becoming involved at all.)*

More Information

Operation Pied Piper Code-named Operation Pied Piper, Britain's "voluntary evacuation scheme" of relocating children from industrial areas was planned before the official declaration of war in September 1939. However, parents did not always know where their children would be relocated to, how long they would be gone, and with whom they would be living. Children were sometimes evacuated hours away from their homes to rural western areas, such as Wales or Devon. While hosting of evacuees by rural residents with available rooms was technically voluntary, local billeting officers, who were responsible for placing relocated individuals, had the power to force Britons—especially those owning large estates—to house evacuees. Large homes were alternatively used as temporary schools, since education for evacuated children was required. Some children spent their formative years with foster families as far away as the United States, and some, after returning to their parents, found themselves estranged from their homeland.

Active Options

On Your Feet: Evaluate a Speech Inform students that Americans were deeply divided about becoming involved in World War II. Some, such as aviator Charles Lindbergh, argued adamantly for neutrality and isolationism. Arrange students in small groups and supply them with copies of Lindbergh's speech in Des Moines, Iowa, on September 11, 1941, or access and play video or audio versions of the speech. Have groups read or listen to the speech and take turns listing the arguments Lindbergh made for nonintervention. Then, as a class, evaluate the validity of Lindbergh's arguments.

NG Learning Framework: Forge a Plan for Lasting Peace

ATTITUDE Responsibility

SKILL Problem-Solving

Inform students that the Atlantic Charter included eight principles that President Roosevelt and Winston Churchill hoped would prevent future world conflicts. Organize students into small groups to think about the reasons international conflicts begin. Tell groups to come up with their own list of eight principles that aim to prevent future wars. Have groups share and explain their finished lists. Then provide a list of the eight principles agreed upon by Roosevelt and Churchill, and guide a class discussion to compare the Atlantic Charter list with students' lists. Conclude by having students agree on a final list of principles that they believe would contribute to a lasting world peace.

English Language Learners ELD

Use 5Ws Questions Arrange students at the **Emerging** and **Expanding** levels in mixed pairs and have them reread the lesson together, pausing after each paragraph to ask each another *who, what, when, where,* or *why* questions about what they just read. Guide students to use correct word order when forming a question. Ask students at the **Expanding** level to assist students at the **Emerging** level as needed.

Pre-AP

Form and Support a Thesis Challenge students to conduct preliminary research about the three factors that the Germans miscalculated when they launched Operation Barbarossa: the number of Soviet soldiers, the unity of the Allies, and the harsh Soviet winter. Instruct students to develop a thesis regarding what they consider the most crucial factor. Tell them to write an essay supporting their thesis, using a variety of primary and secondary source materials. Encourage students to share their essays on a class or school blog.

See the Chapter Planner for more strategies for differentiation.

HISTORICAL THINKING

ANSWERS

1. The persistence and skill of the RAF drove the Luftwaffe back. Lacking air support to invade Great Britain by land, Hitler invaded the Soviet Union instead.

2. Possible response: Many Americans were reluctant to engage in another foreign conflict because World War I had claimed large numbers of casualties and created hardships for civilians and returning soldiers, circumstances that Americans did not want to repeat.

3. The German military strategy likely involved trying to surround cities, such as Moscow, and attack them from multiple sides.

CRITICAL VIEWING The Londoners in the photograph are crowded together and sleeping, possibly having run to the Underground station in the middle of the night. They must have lived in constant fear of air attacks, always prepared to run for cover. After an attack, those underground would have felt dread for what they might find on the surface.

1.4 Attack on Pearl Harbor

Focused on the war in Europe, Americans were shocked by an early morning bombing of their homeland. Everyone was in disbelief and felt fear on December 7, 1941.

MAIN IDEA Japan's sudden attack on the U.S. Pacific fleet at Pearl Harbor, Hawaii, brought the United States into World War II.

JAPAN ON THE ATTACK

Like Germany, Japan looked beyond its borders for ways to improve its economy in the 1930s. The Chinese region of **Manchuria** was rich in resources, including oil, rubber, and lumber. Controlling this region could boost Japan's resource-hungry industries and expand the market for Japanese goods. On September 18, 1931, Japanese armed forces invaded Manchuria and installed a **puppet government**, or a set of political leaders who would follow Japan's orders. The Japanese moved into China itself and captured Beijing, Shanghai, and Nanjing. By 1937, the situation had developed into an all-out war.

In 1940, Japan announced a plan to conquer Southeast Asia and the Western Pacific by overpowering the European colonies there. Realizing their common goals of expansion, Japanese leaders met with German and Italian officials on September 27, 1940. The three countries signed the **Tripartite Pact**, an agreement to help one another achieve their goals. With the signature of its representative, Japan became part of the Axis.

By April 1941, Japan had invaded and occupied French Indochina (now Vietnam, Laos, and Cambodia). This aggression finally persuaded President Roosevelt to act. He banned the sale of

Japan in Eastern Asia, 1931–1941

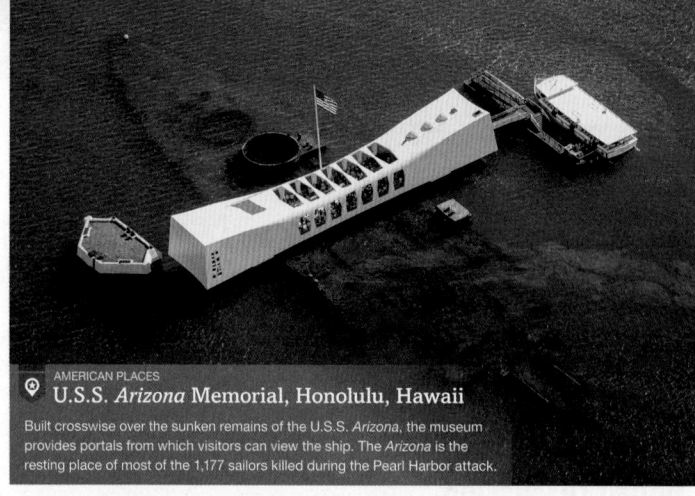

AMERICAN PLACES
U.S.S. *Arizona* Memorial, Honolulu, Hawaii

Built crosswise over the sunken remains of the U.S.S. *Arizona*, the museum provides portals from which visitors can view the ship. The *Arizona* is the resting place of most of the 1,177 sailors killed during the Pearl Harbor attack.

scrap metal and halted U.S. oil exports to Japan. He increased the size of the U.S. Navy, and moved the Navy's Pacific fleet from San Diego to **Pearl Harbor**, in Hawaii, hoping to deter Japan from moving against other nations in the region.

TARGET: PEARL HARBOR

In 1941, **Hideki Tojo** (hee-DAY-kee TOH-joh) became Prime Minister of Japan. He was an army officer who had risen through the military and political ranks. Tojo and U.S. officials tried to solve their differences diplomatically, but neither side would budge. After several months, peaceful efforts failed. Tojo was ready to act.

American politicians believed a war with Japan was likely, but they did not believe Japan would dare to attack the United States. Japan and Hawaii are separated by 4,000 miles of open ocean, and Hawaii is more than 2,000 miles from the American mainland. The distance alone made staging any attack very difficult. But the Japanese wanted to annihilate, or utterly destroy, the U.S. Pacific fleet before it could be used against them. Japan moved a fleet of aircraft carriers toward Hawaii under strict radio silence, meaning they were not to communicate with each other while steaming toward their target. Detectable radio signals could give away a ship's location.

On Sunday morning, December 7, 1941, Japanese warplanes headed for Pearl Harbor to bomb the U.S. naval base there. The battleships U.S.S. *Oklahoma* and U.S.S. *Arizona* were hit before the sailors on board could respond, and both ships quickly sank. The *Arizona* went under with more than 1,000 men trapped below decks. The surprise attack destroyed 18 American ships and more than 180 airplanes. In a famous speech he gave on December 8, 1941, President Roosevelt referred to December 7 as "a date which will live in infamy," and asked Congress for a declaration of war against Japan. The request was granted. Bound by the Tripartite Pact, both Italy and Germany declared war on the United States on December 11. The United States was now involved in World War II as an Allied Power.

HISTORICAL THINKING

1. **READING CHECK** Why did Japan invade Manchuria?

2. **INTERPRET MAPS** Geographically, what was the military strategy of the Japanese in their efforts to occupy China?

3. **IDENTIFY MAIN IDEAS AND DETAILS** Why did Japan decide to attack Pearl Harbor?

Objective

Summarize the events leading up to, and the effects of, Japan's attack on Pearl Harbor.

Critical Thinking Skills for Lesson 1.4

- Identify Main Ideas and Details
- Monitor Comprehension
- Interpret Maps
- Make Inferences
- Make Predictions

Essential Question for Chapter 24

How did World War II impact Americans? While war waged in Europe, Japan expanded its empire across Asia and the Pacific. Lesson 1.4 discusses this expansion and U.S. efforts to halt it—a conflict that formally brought the United States into World War II.

Background for the Teacher

Japan's invasion of China resulted in one of the most heinous atrocities of the 20th century: the Nanjing Massacre. After capturing the city of Nanjing, then the capital of China, Japanese troops went on a six-week rampage that resulted in the widespread rape and killing of civilians. Death tolls are disputed, but at least 100,000 Chinese people, and perhaps as many as 300,000, were killed. In addition, the Japanese army looted and burned Nanjing and neighboring towns, destroying nearly a third of all buildings. After the war, persons responsible for the acts were charged, found guilty of war crimes, and later executed. The incident still causes tension between China and Japan. In more recent times, depictions of the event in Japanese textbooks caused outrage in China and Korea, where many argued that the books glossed over the horror of the invasion.

K-W-L Chart

Provide each student with a K-W-L Chart. Guide students to brainstorm what they know about the Japanese attack on Pearl Harbor, such as its location in Hawaii, that it was a surprise attack, or that it caused the United States to declare war on Japan. Then ask students to list questions they have about the event, such as: Did U.S. ships or planes engage with the Japanese during the attack? How did Americans react to the attack? Allow time at the end of the lesson for students to add what they have learned.

K What Do I Know?	W What Do I Want To Learn?	L What Did I Learn?

TEACH

Guided Discussion

1. **Make Inferences** Why did President Roosevelt believe that economic sanctions and military buildup would halt Japanese expansion? *(Possible response: President Roosevelt believed that cutting the Japanese off from access to oil and scrap metal would deprive them of resources that they needed for use in their military buildup. The presence of U.S. forces in the Pacific was intended to pose an immediate threat to further Japanese aggression.)*

2. **Make Predictions** How do you think the attack on Pearl Harbor changed Americans' opinions about World War II? *(Possible response: Before the attack, many Americans opposed entering the war. However, after the attack upon the U.S. fleet, followed by a declaration of war by Germany and Italy, Americans' opinions likely shifted from nonintervention to a desire for retaliation.)*

American Places

The U.S.S. *Arizona* Memorial is part of the World War II Valor in the Pacific National Monument. The trip to and from the memorial is part of a 75-minute program that also includes a documentary film and time to view the memorial. Visitors can also explore the Battleship *Missouri* Memorial, the U.S.S. *Bowfin* Submarine Museum and Park, and the Pacific Aviation Museum Pearl Harbor. Access the website and video titled *Remembering the Pacific* where small groups of students can view firsthand accounts of the attack.

Active Options

On Your Feet: Analyze Roosevelt's Speech Tell students that Franklin Roosevelt's Pearl Harbor speech, one of the most impactful in American history, was addressed to a joint session of Congress and broadcast live by radio across the nation to millions of listeners. Play the entire speech for the class. Then have students form groups of four. Provide each group with a copy of the speech and a large sheet of paper. Assign each group a short excerpt and tell them to discuss its meaning and the message Roosevelt intended to convey. Have groups read their excerpts and present their explanations to the class.

NG Learning Framework: Create an Annotated Time Line

SKILL Collaboration

KNOWLEDGE Our Human Story

Prompt students to recall their earlier research about the Neutrality Acts. Then assign students to small groups to research other aspects of American foreign policy from the end of World War I until the attack on Pearl Harbor. Tell groups to choose five laws, agreements, or events that took place during the era. Then instruct group members to work together to arrange their choices on a time line with annotations explaining how each exemplifies isolationism or nonintervention. Have groups share their completed time lines with the class.

Striving Readers

Identify Facts Arrange students in pairs and guide them to conduct a round-robin activity to review what they have learned in the lesson. Ask pairs to generate facts for about three to five minutes. Then invite one student from each pair to share their facts. Write a list of facts from all pairs on the board.

Gifted & Talented

Analyze a Newsreel Instruct students to analyze a World War II newsreel featuring Pearl Harbor. Tell them to take notes about the language, images, and music used and then write one or two paragraphs about how each had an effect on the message of the newsreel. Ask volunteers to prepare segments of newsreel footage to show to the class to illustrate the effects they identified.

See the Chapter Planner for more strategies for differentiation.

HISTORICAL THINKING

ANSWERS

1. Japan wanted to boost its economy using the resources found in Manchuria, such as oil and lumber.

2. First, the Japanese invaded Manchuria to the north and set up a puppet government. Then they occupied French Indochina to the south, flanking China for an attack from multiple locations.

3. Possible response: When the Pacific Fleet moved to Hawaii, Japan saw the United States as a threat to its expansion in Asia. Japan attacked Pearl Harbor to cripple the U.S. fleet, a move likely intended to reduce the immediate threat of the United States entering the war.

1.5 National Air and Space Museum Washington, D.C.

Devoted to the subject of flight, the National Air and Space Museum features the world's largest collection of historic aircraft and spacecraft. Among its famous artifacts are the first plane to achieve flight and the first aircraft to carry a human to the moon.

More than 60,000 artifacts are housed in two separate locations. The museum on the National Mall in Washington, D.C., features an observatory and planetarium. A facility in Chantilly, Virginia, displays such artifacts as the space shuttle *Discovery*.

Royal Air Force Helmet
This brown leather flying helmet from 1941 was donated by the Royal Air Force Museum to the National Air and Space Museum. During World War II, the air forces of Great Britain and the United States coordinated their attacks on Germany. But even before entering the war, the United States helped provide training and aircraft for British soldiers learning to become Royal Air Force (RAF) pilots. This RAF flying helmet has black rubber receptacles for headphone receivers and snaps for an oxygen mask.

Flight Jacket
In World War II, American pilots wore this kind of flight jacket, known as Type A-2, which is still used by the U.S. Air Force today. This particular jacket was worn by General Claire Chennault, who led the Flying Tigers, a volunteer group of American pilots who flew for China against the Japanese in 1941 and 1942.

Chennault later became commander of the 14th Air Force in China. The insignia, or badge, of the 14th Air Force appears on the left side of the jacket. On the jacket's inside is a *blood chit*, or a message asking for assistance from anyone who may find the jacket owner injured or lost.

Why do you think the message on the inside of the jacket is in Chinese?

Aircraft Recognition Dial
During World War II, military personnel had to quickly distinguish between friendly and enemy aircraft. American soldiers studied pictorial manuals to help build their aircraft recognition skills. Some civilians in both the United States and Great Britain also received training in aircraft recognition to help spot enemy aircraft. This aircraft recognition dial from 1942 is a wheel chart that rotates to allow pictures of different aircraft to appear in the triangular window at the top. The blocks of text around the outer edge provide basic information about each type of aircraft.

Why do you think the military trained civilians to recognize enemy aircraft?

Stinson L-5 Sentinel
The Stinson L-5 Sentinel was an important type of light aircraft used in World War II. This durable, versatile plane—constructed from steel tubing and plywood covered with lacquered cotton—served many purposes. Its pilots delivered supplies and information to frontline troops, and on return trips, transported wounded soldiers to hospitals. They also took aerial photographs of enemy targets and directed artillery fire. All branches of the U.S. Armed Forces, as well as the British air force, used this plane in World War II.

The unarmed L-5, nicknamed the "Flying Jeep," had a single engine and two seats.

An Early "Computer"
A slide rule is a mechanical computer that performs mathematical calculations. Slide rules were commonly used until they were replaced by handheld electronic calculators in the 1970s. Pilots in World War II used circular slide rules, like the one shown here, as navigation aids.

World War II 797

PLAN

Objective
Identify artifacts related to aerial combat and defense in World War II.

Critical Thinking Skills for Lesson 1.5
- Make Connections
- Analyze Visuals
- Make Inferences
- Draw Conclusions

Essential Question for Chapter 24
How did World War II impact Americans? Many Americans served in the civil air defense system and in the U.S. and Allied air forces during World War II. Lesson 1.5 examines World War II artifacts related to aerial combat that are included in the National Air and Space Museum's collection.

Background for the Teacher
The National Air and Space Museum promotes the study of aviation and collects, preserves, and displays aeronautical equipment, ranging from high-tech aircraft to low-tech aviation gear, such as the Type A-2 flight jacket shown in this lesson. The Army Air Corps originally introduced the jacket in 1931. The first versions were made with silk-lined leather and designed for wear in the cramped, open cockpits of such warplanes as those used by General Claire Chennault's Flying Tigers. The jacket's reinforced pockets, tight wool cuffs, buttoned collar, and double layer of leather over the zipper helped protect the pilots against the strong winds generated in flight.

History Notebook
Encourage students to complete the Curating History page for Chapter 24 in their History Notebooks as they read.

Review Aircraft Knowledge

Discuss with students what they remember reading about aerial warfare during World War I, using the American Story "The Great War's Killer Technology" as a reference. **ASK:** What roles did airplanes play in World War I? *(Possible response: reconnaissance, combat and bombing runs, carrying mail and supplies, transporting wounded)* Tell students that in this lesson they will learn about some of the aviation equipment used in World War II and its significance in the war effort.

TEACH

Guided Discussion

1. **Make Inferences** Why do you think so many different planes were used during World War II? *(Possible response: Planes were used for purposes that required different designs; for example, some needed to have room to transport supplies or people, and some had to carry bombs and be able to maneuver during enemy fire.)*

2. **Draw Conclusions** Based on the pilot's gear and the circular slide rule, what conclusions can you draw about the jobs that pilots performed during World War II? *(Answers will vary. Possible responses: Pilots had to perform multiple tasks in order to communicate via radio, perform navigational calculations, and take aerial photographs while operating their planes. Pilots who flew noncombat missions, such as carrying supplies or moving soldiers, were as heroic and necessary as fighter pilots.)*

Curating History

The National Air and Space Museum's website offers several resources for learning about the history of U.S. air units during World War II. Help students locate the artifacts shown in this lesson and encourage them to explore the World War II aviation content on their own. Then ask them to work in pairs or small groups to find other objects that relate to the World War II aerial war in the Pacific and European theaters. Invite students to select one or two objects that particularly interest them and do further research. Instruct them to summarize their findings for the class or create a museum web page of their own to display the items and describe their importance in the war.

Active Option

On Your Feet: Sort the Artifacts Tell students to work in teams of four to examine the museum's online collection and complete two Concept Clusters like those shown below. In one cluster, ask students to identify various types of artifacts related to Allied aerial combat in World War II. In the other, ask students to identify a different class or genre of artifacts, to be determined by the team. When teams are finished, invite them to share their Concept Clusters with the class.

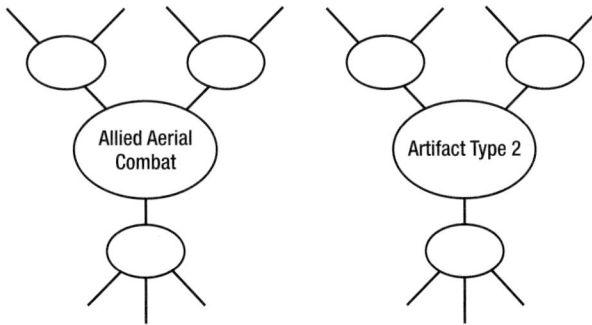

Inclusion

Clarify Text Have sighted partners work with visually impaired students, reading the text aloud. Direct the visually impaired students to indicate if there are words or passages they do not understand. Their partners can clarify meanings by repeating passages, emphasizing context clues, and paraphrasing.

Gifted & Talented

Create a Multimedia Presentation Tell students to conduct preliminary online research about the combat aircraft of World War II. Then have them choose one aircraft to research in depth, including archival photographs and newsreel footage. Encourage students to assemble their research into a compelling format using an online presentation tool. Ask volunteers to show their multimedia presentation to the class and answer their classmates' questions.

See the Chapter Planner for more strategies for differentiation.

AIRCRAFT RECOGNITION DIAL

Possible response: If civilians were trained to tell the difference between friendly and enemy planes, they could act as a large observation network to let the military know when and where enemy planes were approaching. Such advance warning might give the military time to shoot down enemy planes and give civilians time to take cover.

FLIGHT JACKET

Possible response: Probably few American pilots flying over China spoke Chinese, so if they were shot down, lost, or injured, they would have no way to communicate with the Chinese people who found them. In addition to asking for help, a message in Chinese would be a way to provide information about the pilot.

Pulling Together

The Axis was a powerful enemy. After the surprise attack on Pearl Harbor, the United States knew it would require a unified, far-reaching effort to prepare quickly for war.

MAIN IDEA The United States built up its armed forces rapidly and found ways to get the entire country behind the war effort.

BUILDING AN ARMY AND A NAVY

In a presidential address in January 1942, Franklin Roosevelt said of the war, "Powerful enemies must be out-fought and out-produced." That was the goal the United States set as it moved into 1942 determined to defeat the Axis.

The first efforts involved rebuilding the U.S. Pacific fleet and boosting the U.S. military. Some of the ships that sank in the attack on Pearl Harbor were salvaged and repaired. They sailed again to fight the Axis. The government also built new ships and expanded shipyards on both coasts.

Army Chief of Staff General **George C. Marshall** led the mobilization effort, or the act of gathering and preparing troops for war. When he took the position in 1939, the United States had only around 180,000 soldiers serving to protect 130 million citizens. When war broke out in Europe, Marshall pushed the president to supply more men. In September 1940, President Roosevelt signed the Selective Service and Training Act into law, requiring men aged 21 to 35 to register for the draft. Once war was declared, many men did not wait to be drafted. Instead, the attack on Pearl Harbor inspired them to enlist on their own. Marshall also utilized the National Guard, smaller military units charged with defending their home states, for war duty. The number of soldiers in the army increased to more than 3 million by 1942. By 1945, the total number of men serving in all military branches was more than 12 million.

Roosevelt established the **War Production Board** in January 1942 to transform U.S. factories into producers of war supplies. Automobile manufacturers began to make airplanes, ships, tanks, and weapons. War supply factories expanded. As a result, employment grew, boosting the economy and pulling the United States out of the Great Depression.

EVERYONE JOINS THE WAR EFFORT

With the War Production Board creating so many new civilian jobs, African Americans, Latinos, and women entered the workforce as never before. They filled numerous defense jobs, joining together to help defeat the Axis and bring the troops home. The government continually reminded civilians of their important roles in assisting the troops overseas. One such reminder is shown in the poster at the right.

Knowing that war required numerous resources, the government realized American citizens would need to consume less food and fewer supplies. The War Production Board implemented **rationing**, or the controlled distribution of important foods and supplies, to reserve limited resources for the war effort. Though it caused some inconvenience, rationing such items as butter and gasoline allowed American civilians to help the war effort. Price limits set by the government ensured rationed items remained affordable for everyone. Americans also contributed by planting victory gardens, as they had done during World War I. Growing vegetables, fruits, and herbs at home prevented food shortages.

CRITICAL VIEWING One of the U.S. government's poster campaigns stressed the need to conserve resources at home so more would be available for the war effort. Why might this poster have been effective in reducing the amount of gasoline used by U.S. civilians?

Fighting a war is expensive. The United States spent about $300 billion in its efforts to stop Germany and Japan. That's more than $4 trillion in today's economy. To help raise the funds, the U.S. Treasury issued war bonds. People bought a bond for $18.75, for example, with the understanding that the government would pay them back $25 in 10 years. Some Americans bought war bonds of higher denominations. Children and people from lower incomes bought war stamps for a dime. After buying a certain number of stamps, they could trade them in for a war bond.

HISTORICAL THINKING

1. **READING CHECK** How did the United States prepare for war?

2. **ANALYZE GRAPHS** According to the graph, between which years did the number of military personnel grow the most?

3. **ANALYZE CAUSE AND EFFECT** What was the effect of the war on the U.S. economy?

WORLD WAR II U.S. MILITARY BY THE NUMBERS

Profiles of U.S. Servicemen

33 MONTHS AVERAGE DURATION OF SERVICE

73% SERVED OVERSEAS WITH AN AVERAGE OF 16 MONTHS ABROAD

Military Personnel by Year

1939	ARMY 189,839 NAVY 125,202 MARINES 19,432	

ARMY · NAVY · MARINES · COAST GUARD

0 · 2 MIL · 4 MIL · 6 MIL · 8 MIL · 10 MIL · 12 MIL · 14 MIL

Total Women Serving During War

TOTAL WOMEN **358,000**

- SERVICE PILOTS 1,074
- NURSE CORPS 74,000
- ARMY 150,000
- RESERVES, OTHER BRANCHES 33,000
- NAVY 100,000

Total Minorities Serving During War (all branches)

TOTAL MINORITIES **more than 1,032,000**

- JAPANESE AMERICANS 33,000
- AFRICAN AMERICANS 901,000
- PUERTO RICANS 51,000*
- CHINESE AMERICANS 13,000
- NATIVE AMERICANS 20,000
- FILIPINO AMERICANS 12,000

* Total number of Latino servicemen unknown.

Source: National WWII Museum

PLAN

Objective

Identify ways that U.S. citizens at home prepared for and supported the war effort.

Critical Thinking Skills for Lesson 2.1

- Identify Main Ideas and Details
- Monitor Comprehension
- Analyze Graphs
- Analyze Cause and Effect
- Draw Conclusions
- Make Inferences

Essential Question for Chapter 24

How did World War II impact Americans? To fight a war on the scale of World War II, the federal government knew that it had to inspire its citizens at home, as well as its military, to contribute to the war effort. Lesson 2.1 discusses wartime military and civilian support efforts in the United States.

Background for the Teacher

The roots of the U.S. National Guard go back to the earliest days of the American colonies. Loosely formed militias had existed in the colonies for some years, and in 1636, the Massachusetts colonial legislature ordered its militias to reorganize, effectively creating three reserve units. These first three regiments—two infantry units and one engineer battalion—were the earliest form of an organized military in the United States. The dual mission of the National Guard in its early days was the same as it is today: to serve the U.S. cause when disaster strikes on home shores and to deploy to foreign shores if necessary.

Financial Literacy

To extend their knowledge and understanding about the concepts in this lesson, refer students to the Financial Literacy handbook.

INTRODUCE & ENGAGE

Discuss Wartime Sacrifices

Tell students that in times of national crisis, a government may enforce spending cuts or service cuts that affect the public. Have students consider how their lives might be different if, to help their country, they had to ration their Internet use to 15 minutes per day. Invite them to discuss how this rationing might change their day-to-day activities. Tell students that public use of many commodities was limited during World War II and that in this lesson, they will learn how World War II affected the lives of U.S. civilians at home.

TEACH

Guided Discussion

1. **Draw Conclusions** Why do you think large numbers of Americans enlisted rather than being drafted into the military after Pearl Harbor? *(Possible response: The Japanese had attacked a U.S. military base, which led to feelings of vulnerability and patriotism. These feelings likely inspired many Americans to enlist.)*

2. **Make Inferences** Why do you think the federal government sold bonds to Americans at all economic levels, even to children and low-income people without much money to spare? *(Possible responses: The government needed a lot of money, so it had to ask for everyone's help. Providing low-cost options allowed all Americans to feel they were contributing to the war effort. Interest payments on bonds also allowed all to profit from their purchase, perhaps avoiding perceptions that only the wealthy were profiting.)*

More Information

Housing U.S. Soldiers During World War I, many U.S. soldiers were sent to Europe and trained there before being deployed to fight. Conditions for trainees were rough, including enduring a harsh winter. By World War II, the nation expected better, and the Selective Training and Service Act included a promise of adequate housing. To meet the need, the U.S. Army relied heavily on mass production and assembly-line techniques originally pioneered by Henry Ford near the beginning of World War I. The leaders of construction divisions developed kits made of prefabricated materials and standardized plans for barracks with heating, showers, and latrines that could be put together in less than an hour by a crew working in an assembly line.

Active Options

On Your Feet: Numbered Heads Arrange students in groups of four and assign them numbers one to four. Ask the following question: How did Americans at home support the war effort? Tell students to think about the answer independently and then discuss it as a group. After allowing time for discussion, call a number and have the student with that number in each group report the group's response.

NG Learning Framework: Compose a Journal Entry

SKILL Communication

KNOWLEDGE Our Human Story

Remind students that children and young people were expected to contribute to the war effort along with adults. Direct students to use digital and print resources to find out how young Americans did their part. Then have them use their research findings as background for a journal entry written from the point of view of a person their own age after an ordinary day in the 1940s. Compile completed journal entries on a class website, and ask volunteers to read their entry aloud to the class.

DIFFERENTIATE

Inclusion

Explore the Infographic Allow students with disabilities to work with students who can describe the infographic accompanying the lesson in detail. Ask the partner without disabilities to read the title of each of the four sections and describe the data presented. Encourage students with disabilities to ask clarifying questions.

Pre-AP

Investigate Conservation Efforts Instruct students to gather information from a variety of sources about government-imposed rationing, conservation, and collection of items for reuse during World War II. Ask students to choose one item and write a report about the ways the government encouraged or mandated the rationing or conservation of it and how conserving the item for military use would benefit the war effort. Students should use primary and secondary sources, quoting or paraphrasing them as appropriate. Invite volunteers to share their reports with the class.

See the Chapter Planner for more strategies for differentiation.

HISTORICAL THINKING

ANSWERS

1. The United States rebuilt the Pacific Fleet and built more ships, tanks, planes, and bombs. It established a draft to build up military strength and created the War Production Board to oversee the war effort at home, including the conversion of factories to produce military equipment.

2. The number of military personnel expanded most between 1942 and 1943.

3. Increased manufacturing required by war production provided jobs for millions of workers, ended the Great Depression, and brought many new workers, such as women and African Americans, into the workforce.

CRITICAL VIEWING Answers will vary. Possible response: Hitler loomed large in the imagination of U.S. citizens, representing menace and evil that no patriotic American wanted to help in any way. Civilians were likely willing to follow government recommendations to aid in thwarting him.

Women in the War

When you feel strongly about a cause, you don't hesitate to volunteer your support. In desperate times, women answered the call and took on leadership roles at home and abroad to help win the war.

MAIN IDEA The roles and expectations of American women changed drastically during World War II.

WOMEN IN THE MILITARY

As the United States waged war, every citizen became involved. Women, especially, were needed to help keep the country war-ready. As was the case in every war in which the United States was engaged, many women joined the war effort as nurses, taking care of wounded soldiers. Early in the United States' involvement in the war, the government expanded official wartime opportunities for women.

In May 1942, Congress established the Women's Auxiliary Army Corps, later called the **Women's Army Corps (WAC)**. Volunteers who enlisted in the WACs program worked in more than 200 noncombat jobs in the United States and worldwide where U.S. soldiers were stationed.

In this 1945 photograph, WACs climb down nets in a simulation designed to mimic the escape from a damaged transport ship into lifeboats. As the war came to a close, women in non-combat military roles helped establish order in areas in Europe and the Pacific where life had been disrupted by war.

A female welder works on an escape hatch of the Bream (SS-243) submarine in a Connecticut shipyard. This photo was part of a 1943 *Life* magazine color photo essay that documented the building of submarines. Other photos featured women painting and tightening bolts.

At first, they worked tracking aircraft, in clerical jobs, or as motor pool drivers. As the war continued, they learned to break enemy codes, operate and repair radios, rig parachutes, and maintain special equipment, among many other responsibilities. By the end of the war, more than 150,000 WACs had served in the military, and more than 6,000 of them had been promoted as officers.

The U.S. Navy, too, benefited from women volunteers. Members of **Women Accepted for Volunteer Emergency Service (WAVES)** supported worldwide Navy efforts from bases in the United States. In the U.S. Air Force, women pilots served in the **Women's Airforce Service Pilots (WASP)**. These women piloted planes to deliver cargo from factories to bases, which freed thousands of male pilots to fly planes into combat.

In all, about 350,000 women enlisted in the U.S. Armed Forces during World War II. Their contributions continue to be celebrated today. On March 10, 2010, about 200 WASPs were awarded the Congressional Gold Medal for their service in World War II.

WOMEN IN THE WORKFORCE

With so many men serving in the armed forces, who was left to keep up war production in U.S. factories? The answer was women. War industries actively sought female workers to build tanks, ships, guns, and airplanes. Before the war, it was rare to find women working in factories that made weapons. In 1943, more than 310,000 women worked in the U.S. aircraft industry alone, making up 65 percent of the aircraft industry's total workforce. Industries that produced **munitions**, or military weapons, also employed large numbers of female workers.

The government honored these women in its **"Rosie the Riveter"** campaign. Rosie was an illustrated character based on a metal presser named Geraldine Doyle. Rosie's image appeared on posters everywhere during the war. She became a symbol of the power of women war workers and inspired more women to join the war effort. Women responded in large numbers. The social impact of so many women entering the workforce was strong. Many women felt they had proven that they could do any job a man could do. When the war ended, many of them hoped a wider range of career options would still be available to them.

HISTORICAL THINKING

1. **READING CHECK** Why was there an increase in the number of women working in factories during the war?

2. **EVALUATE** What evidence in the text suggests that there were still limitations to women's roles in the military?

3. **IDENTIFY MAIN IDEAS AND DETAILS** What impact did World War II have on women's expectations in the U.S. workforce?

PLAN

Objective

Describe women's roles in the military and the U.S. workforce during World War II.

Critical Thinking Skills for Lesson 2.2

- Identify Main Ideas and Details
- Monitor Comprehension
- Evaluate
- Ask and Answer Questions
- Compare and Contrast

Essential Question for Chapter 24

How did World War II impact Americans?

American women greatly contributed to the war effort in both traditional and nontraditional female roles. Lesson 2.2 discusses their contributions at home and abroad during World War II.

Background for the Teacher

WASPs were the first women in U.S. history to fly American military planes. Of the 25,000 women who applied for the program, only 1,830 were accepted, and fewer than 1,100 successfully completed the training. These women flew more than 60 million miles during the two years the program was in operation, using every type of aircraft that male pilots flew. Though they were not allowed to fly combat missions, 38 pilots and trainees were killed flying other types of missions. The WASP program was quietly disbanded in 1944. The women, who had paid their own way to go into training, had to pay their own way home again. In addition, none of them ever received military benefits.

History Notebook

Encourage students to complete the Reid on the Road video series page for Chapter 24 in their History Notebooks after they view the video.

Consider Characteristics of Female Soldiers

Create a Venn diagram on the board. Write *female soldiers* on the left, *male soldiers* on the right, and *both* in the middle. Ask students to help you complete the diagram by suggesting traits they believe describe military men, military women, or both. Remind students to be mindful of their own biases. When suggestions are biased, encourage further discussion. Tell students that Lesson 2.2 discusses the military and civilian roles women played in World War II.

TEACH

Guided Discussion

1. **Ask and Answer Questions** If you could interview a woman working in a World War II factory, what questions would you ask her, and how might she respond? *(Answers will vary. Possible response: Question: What job do you do at this factory, and how does it help the war effort? Answer: I inspect Plexiglas noses for attack bombers at an aircraft factory, making sure there are no flaws in construction. Every nose I reject means that I have kept a pilot and crew safe from an equipment failure during a combat mission.)*

2. **Compare and Contrast** What were the military job possibilities for women volunteers at the beginning and the end of the war, and how did opportunities change over time? *(Possible response: At the beginning of the war, women did mostly clerical tasks with some serving as drivers. By the end of the war, women were working higher-level jobs, breaking codes, maintaining equipment, piloting planes, and becoming officers. However, throughout the war, women were not allowed to take part in combat.)*

More Information

First African-American WAC Unit in Europe In February 1945, the 6888th Central Postal Directory Battalion became the first and only African-American Women's Army Corps unit sent to Europe during World War II. Under Major Charity Adams, the unit served in England and France, sorting and accurately addressing undelivered mail. Working three shifts a day, seven days a week, the women of the 6888th processed roughly 65,000 pieces of mail per shift. They tracked down soldiers' locations, corrected names, and censored mail, completing the task in half the time expected. While well received by civilians, the women faced racism within the military, most infamously on the troop ship as it was about to return home. Major Adams, as the highest-ranking female officer on board, was in command of white Army Nurse Corps personnel who would not accept her authority. Adams gave them 20 minutes to leave the ship or sail under her command. The captain, making a sudden appearance, supported Adams, but offered the nurses 17 minutes to leave. They all stayed.

Active Options

On Your Feet: Word Chain Have students form three lines. Hand a piece of paper to the first person in each line with one of these acronyms from the lesson: WAC, WAVES, WASP. Students pass the paper from person to person, each one adding a word or phrase they associate with the acronym. Have a volunteer from each group read from their Word Chain. Ask the rest of the class to listen for any words that were used more than once or that may not connect correctly.

NG Learning Framework: Hold a Panel Discussion

SKILL Communication

KNOWLEDGE Our Human Story

Explain that in 2015, the U.S. military granted women the right to participate in combat missions. Instruct students to use online and print resources to learn more about this decision. Ask them whether they agree or disagree with women taking part in combat missions and to compile a list of reasons for their arguments. Suggest that students hold a panel discussion to share and debate their positions, using evidence from their research to support their arguments.

English Language Learners   ELD

Explore Multiple Meanings Explain that while the word *pool* commonly refers to a small structure that holds water in which to swim, it can also refer to a group of people, as in motor pool or car pool, or a combined effort, as in pooling money or talents. Pair students at the **Emerging** level with those at the **Bridging** level. Have pairs find and read aloud the sentence in the lesson containing the word *pool.* Then have them use a dictionary to write the definition of this use of *pool,* and independently write an original sentence using the word. Ask students to share and discuss their sentences.

Gifted & Talented

Create a Poster Tell students to briefly research the Rosie the Riveter poster by J. Howard Miller as inspiration for a poster they will create. Then have students work in pairs to create a poster with a strong image and brief message aimed at involving people in a cause or organization that would benefit society, such as a conservation effort or a government or civic organization. Display students' posters in a gallery and invite pairs to explain the thoughts behind their work.

See the Chapter Planner for more strategies for differentiation.

HISTORICAL THINKING

ANSWERS

1. Production of supplies and military equipment required an overall increase in the number of people in the workforce. With so many men serving in the military, women took over vacancies and filled new jobs that supported the war effort.

2. Most women served in traditionally female occupations, such as nursing. Women were not allowed to serve in combat roles, so WAC personnel filled clerical, maintenance, and technical jobs. WASP personnel flew in noncombat roles so male pilots could be assigned to combat missions.

3. After performing factory and technical jobs, many women became confident that they could do any job a man could do, and they began to expect that there would be such opportunities after the war ended.

A Diverse War Effort

If you need help, you don't care about the race, gender, or ethnicity of the person who comes forward. American leaders found that to succeed during World War II, they had to include everyone in the effort.

MAIN IDEA African Americans, Asian Americans, Latinos, and Native Americans all played important roles in fighting World War II.

MINORITIES IN THE MILITARY

During World War II, many African Americans were conflicted about the war. They were eager to fight for democracy and freedom abroad, but they were too often denied equal rights at home. One African American named James Thompson expressed his feelings in a letter to the editor of the *Philadelphia Courier* newspaper in January 1942. He suggested that African Americans fight two battles at the same time. They could fight the Axis Powers abroad and fight for equality at home. Thompson called his idea the **Double V campaign**, as in "double victory."

In response, the editors of the newspaper had "Double V" lapel pins and stickers made to distribute to the African-American community.

The campaign took off, lifting the spirits of African Americans and encouraging them to enlist.

About 1.1 million African Americans served in separate units in all branches of the armed forces during World War II. The 92nd Infantry Division, an African-American army unit, **deployed**, or was sent, to Italy in August 1944 and captured more than 20,000 German prisoners there. The **Tuskegee Airmen** were one of the most famous World War II African-American units. Trained at Tuskegee Institute in Alabama, these 450 pilots were the first African Americans to fly missions for the Army Air Corps overseas. They defended larger bomber planes traveling to and from their missions. They lost 25 bombers during the war, far fewer bombers than other units in the air force.

The Tuskegee Airmen
In the photo at left from 1942, five Tuskegee airmen pose in front of their fighter planes at the training center in Alabama. A bronze replica of the Congressional Gold Medal is shown below. The medals were given to the soldiers at a White House ceremony in 2007 to honor their military contributions.

Asian Americans, Latinos, and Native Americans also made major contributions to the war. About 58,000 Japanese-, Chinese-, and Filipino-Americans fought for their country. Around 500,000 Mexican Americans and around 51,000 Puerto Ricans served. More precise numbers aren't known, because Latinos were counted as white people on enlistment papers.

Of the estimated 350,000 Native Americans living in the United States in 1941, as many as 44,000 saw military service during the war. Native American soldiers were involved in all areas of the conflict.

OPPORTUNITIES AT HOME

As it did for women, the war created numerous job opportunities for all minorities. More than 40,000 Native Americans left their reservations for the very first time to work in the defense industry. Many African Americans also migrated to northern cities and to California to find jobs in the defense industry. There, both groups faced discrimination. Some factories refused to hire Native Americans and African Americans, while others segregated the workers.

Witnessing this discrimination and segregation, some civil rights leaders decided to act. One activist, **A. Philip Randolph**, started planning a large march on Washington, D.C., for the summer of 1941, to protest discrimination in the workplace. Randolph put increased pressure on the government to address the issue, and it worked. President Roosevelt introduced an executive order that ended racial discrimination in the defense industry. He signed the bill on June 25, 1941, and Randolph canceled the protest.

Farms also needed more workers. Congress passed the **Bracero Program**, a plan for replacing farmers who had left to fight in the war. The word braceros means "strong armed ones" in Spanish. It included a series of agreements that opened the U.S. border to Mexican farm and transportation workers. Forty thousand workers came from Mexico to the United States in 1942. The program continued until 1964.

The Navajo Code Talkers
U.S. forces in the Asia-Pacific region sent and received messages in the Navajo language. In this 1943 photo, U.S. Marine Preston Toledo (above) dictates a message while his cousin and fellow Marine Frank Toledo writes down a message he is receiving. The cousins were Navajos. The Japanese had broken all the codes used by the American military, but in 1942, the Marine Corps began using an unbreakable code based on the Navajo language.

Navajo was a difficult language to learn, and the Japanese had no knowledge of its existence. The U.S. Marines enlisted 29 Navajo soldiers, who came to be known as "Code Talkers," to transmit messages in their language. By the end of the war, more than 375 Navajo soldiers had served their country as Code Talkers. The Japanese never broke this code.

HISTORICAL THINKING

1. **READING CHECK** What series of events led to the Double V campaign?

2. **MAKE INFERENCES** How do you think the experiences of minority groups during World War II influenced the country after the war?

3. **COMPARE AND CONTRAST** What difference do you notice between the treatment of African-American and Latino soldiers during the war?

PLAN

Objective
Summarize the contributions of diverse groups of Americans in World War II.

Critical Thinking Skills for Lesson 2.3

• Identify Main Ideas and Details

• Monitor Comprehension

• Make Inferences

• Compare and Contrast

• Draw Conclusions

Essential Question for Chapter 24
How did World War II impact Americans?
Although Americans from minority groups may have experienced discrimination at home, many supported the United States by joining the military. Lesson 2.3 discusses the contributions these groups made to the war effort.

Background for the Teacher
The NAACP and many African-American-operated newspapers had fought for the right of African Americans to become pilots in the U.S. military. The military's solution was to create separate units for African-American pilots, continuing with the tradition of segregation within the armed forces. With approval directly from President Roosevelt, the segregated Tuskegee Army Air Field opened for training purposes on July 19, 1941. The Tuskegee Airmen flew their first mission about two years later, on June 2, 1943, when they attacked an Italian island in the Mediterranean. Over the years they served, they won more than 850 military medals.

Eliminate Discrimination

Lead a class discussion about how society benefits when all of its members have equal rights and are respected and treated fairly. Students might give examples of how society benefits when all individuals have the opportunity to reach their full potential or the advantages of having a fully educated and gainfully employed citizenry. Ask volunteers to suggest ways that discrimination, which threatens equality, could be eliminated in our society. Explain to students that this lesson is about how the United States addressed discrimination in order to succeed during World War II and about the struggles of diverse groups of Americans during that time and their contributions to the war effort.

TEACH

Guided Discussion

1. **Draw Conclusions** What might you conclude about the Tuskegee Airmen, based on the information in the text? *(Possible response: The fact that the Tuskegee Airmen lost the fewest number of planes while flying dangerous missions suggests that they were some of the best pilots, regardless of race. This demonstrates that African Americans could excel at highly technical jobs if given the opportunity.)*

2. **Make Inferences** Why do you think the Bracero Program continued after World War II ended? *(Possible responses: Farm owners still wanted inexpensive labor. Bracero workers still needed income from seasonal labor in the United States.)*

More Information

A Tale of Two Protest Marches Review the information about the march A. Philip Randolph began planning for the summer of 1941. Then explain that in 1963, Martin Luther King, Jr., organized the March on Washington, a political demonstration for jobs and equality for African Americans. The march drew a crowd of 200,000 to the Lincoln Memorial, where King delivered his famous "I Have a Dream" speech and discussed his belief in a future of justice and equality for all. By the following year, public opinion had turned in King's favor, leading to passage of the Civil Rights Act of 1964, which addressed voting rights and discrimination in schools and public places. **ASK:** How were the goals and outcomes of Randolph's planned march similar to and different from those of King's March on Washington? *(Possible response: Both aimed to protest discrimination against African Americans in Washington, D.C., and both caused U.S. policy changes. Randolph's march never happened, but its planning led to Roosevelt's executive order ending discrimination in the defense industry. King's march led to much broader antidiscrimination legislation.)*

Active Options

On Your Feet: Chart Relay Organize students into teams of four. Have each team create a four-column chart with these headings: Double V Campaign, Tuskegee Airmen, Bracero Program, and Code Talkers. Direct teams to determine four facts about each topic. Then assign team members a number from one to four, with each team member taking one of the four facts. On your signal, have all number ones write their facts on the chart. Students follow in order as soon as the previous team member has finished writing. The team that completes its chart first is the winner.

NG Learning Framework: Devise a Code

SKILLS Communication, Collaboration

KNOWLEDGE New Frontiers

Encourage students to use library or online resources to learn more about the Navajo Code Talkers and codes in general. Organize students into pairs and tell them to devise a unique code of their own and to write and decode encrypted messages to one another. Then have pairs teach their code to another pair and exchange more messages.

Striving Readers

Create a Concept Cluster Display a Concept Cluster with the following in the center oval: diverse war effort. Instruct students to reread the lesson and create their own Concept Cluster by copying the one displayed and adding the names of ethnic groups in the outer ovals. Then ask students to write specific examples on the spokes stating how people from the group helped the war effort. Encourage students to create additional ovals and spokes as necessary. Then have them share and discuss their Concept Cluster with others.

Gifted & Talented

Perform an Oral History Tell students to access oral histories of the Tuskegee Airmen collected in books, university oral history collections (such as those at the Library of Congress website), and online video archives. Instruct students to select a portion of one oral history to read aloud in three or four minutes. Invite them to practice reading their selection dramatically and to perform it for the class. Discuss how the oral histories reinforce or supplement the information in the lesson.

See the Chapter Planner for more strategies for differentiation.

HISTORICAL THINKING

ANSWERS

1. Denial of rights in their own country made African Americans reluctant to enlist in the war effort. James Thompson brought attention to the situation in a letter to the *Philadelphia Courier*, urging African Americans to aid the war effort and fight for equality at the same time.

2. Possible response: After the war, many citizens understood that Americans with diverse ethnic backgrounds had made invaluable contributions to the war effort and should not be excluded from American society simply because of their race or ethnicity.

3. African-American soldiers were segregated into their own units, unlike Latino soldiers, who were considered white and integrated into white units.

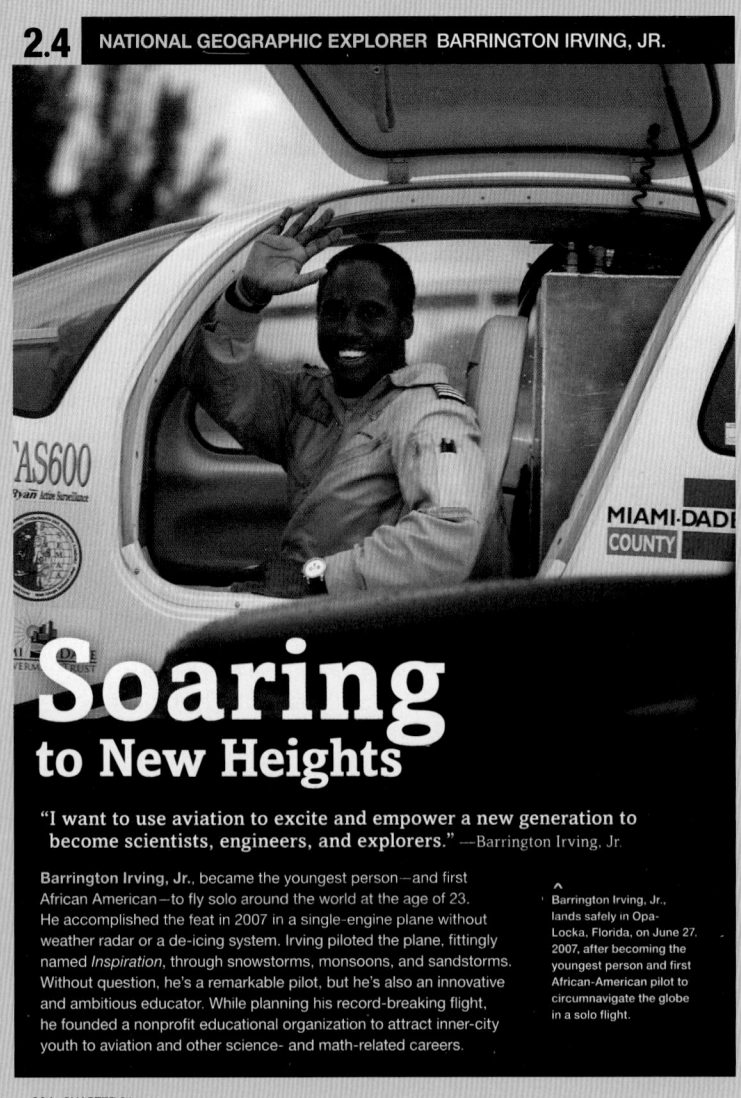

Soaring
to New Heights

"I want to use aviation to excite and empower a new generation to become scientists, engineers, and explorers." —Barrington Irving, Jr.

Barrington Irving, Jr., became the youngest person—and first African American—to fly solo around the world at the age of 23. He accomplished the feat in 2007 in a single-engine plane without weather radar or a de-icing system. Irving piloted the plane, fittingly named *Inspiration*, through snowstorms, monsoons, and sandstorms. Without question, he's a remarkable pilot, but he's also an innovative and ambitious educator. While planning his record-breaking flight, he founded a nonprofit educational organization to attract inner-city youth to aviation and other science- and math-related careers.

^
Barrington Irving, Jr., lands safely in Opa-Locka, Florida, on June 27, 2007, after becoming the youngest person and first African-American pilot to circumnavigate the globe in a solo flight.

MAIN IDEA National Geographic Explorer, pilot, and educator Barrington Irving, Jr., uses his aviation expertise to inspire young people to pursue careers in math and science.

A YOUNG PILOT

The path for Irving's entry into aviation was paved by other remarkable African-American pilots—the Tuskegee Airmen. As a young pilot, Irving met some Tuskegee Airmen who had served in World War II. "These men had fought two wars—one for their country and another for equality and respect when they got back home," says Irving. "They are my heroes."

Raised in Miami's inner city, surrounded by crime, poverty, and failing schools, Irving became interested in aviation at age 15 when a pilot asked Irving if he'd like to become a pilot. "I told him I didn't think I was smart enough," explains Irving. "But he gave me the chance to sit in the cockpit of the commercial airplane he flew, and just like that I was hooked." Irving began spending his free time at a local airport, washing planes and talking to pilots. He also practiced flying using flight simulator software at home.

Irving turned down a full football scholarship to the University of Florida and majored in aeronautical science at a community college. He also began speaking to groups of inner-city youth in Miami, sharing his passion for aviation. In 2003, his volunteer work earned him a scholarship to Florida Memorial University. While excelling academically, he earned several piloting licenses—and set a new goal.

FLYING SOLO

At the age of 20, Irving wanted to fly around the world. Although he couldn't find an aircraft company that would donate a plane, Irving persuaded companies to donate aircraft parts. Then the aircraft manufacturer Columbia began building him a plane using these donated parts.

While his plane was being built, Irving established a nonprofit educational organization in 2005 called Experience Aviation. Funded by donations and grants, Irving and his staff set up a learning center at a Miami airport where students could operate flight simulators, chart flights, and do other projects.

CRITICAL VIEWING Irving flew his single-engine Columbia 400 aircraft named *Inspiration* for three months to accomplish his goal. Based on details in this photograph, what types of physical challenges do you think Irving likely faced during his flight?

Irving's historic flight began in Florida on March 23, 2007. The trip in his newly-built plane took 97 days, and he made 26 stops. He piloted through a blinding sandstorm over Saudi Arabia and an ice storm that forced him to land on an Alaskan island with only 12 minutes of fuel left. On June 27, 2007, Irving landed before a youthful crowd in Miami.

That reception made a strong impression on Irving. "Stepping from the plane, it wasn't all the fanfare that changed my life. It was seeing so many young people watching and listening. I had no money, but I was determined to give back with my time, knowledge, and experience."

In Irving's Build and Soar program, 60 students from failing schools built an airplane from scratch in 10 weeks and watched Irving pilot the aircraft into the clouds. For his Flying Classroom initiative, Irving transformed the jet into an "exploration vehicle" and shared live data involving science, technology, engineering, math, geography, culture, and history with students in classrooms. Taking the jet on a "Journey for Knowledge" across the globe, Irving flew the plane to visit all seven continents and teach science to children around the world.

HISTORICAL THINKING

1. **READING CHECK** In what ways is Barrington Irving, Jr., a remarkable pilot and educator?

2. **MAKE CONNECTIONS** How did the Tuskegee Airmen pave the way for Irving's future?

PLAN

Objective
Describe how Barrington Irving, Jr., used his aviation experience to inspire students.

Critical Thinking Skills for Lesson 2.4
- Identify Main Ideas and Details
- Monitor Comprehension
- Make Connections
- Evaluate
- Make Inferences

Essential Question for Chapter 24
How did World War II impact Americans? The achievements of the Tuskegee Airmen continue to inspire African Americans today, including Barrington Irving, Jr. Lesson 2.4 describes how Irving uses his love of flying to influence and inspire young people.

NATIONAL GEOGRAPHIC EXPLORER
Barrington Irving, Jr.

Barrington Irving, Jr., launched his Flying Classroom program in 2014, using his plane, the *Inspiration III,* to conduct expeditions around the world and engage students by making them feel they are part of his research. Flying Classroom students study STEM subjects relevant to Irving's missions as they follow along virtually, through online videos and Irving's blog. Irving's learning adventures include investigating how eradicating a poisonous toad could help balance an ecosystem in Australia, and spending two days eating out of dumpsters in San Diego, California, to better understand issues of food waste. To date, Irving's Flying Classroom has invited students to join expeditions in 50 different nations.

History Notebook
Encourage students to complete the Explorer page for Chapter 24 in their History Notebooks as they read.

Discuss Being the First

Direct students' attention to the photographs in the lesson and tell them to read the captions. Then work with students to brainstorm a list of "firsts" they might like to do or be part of, such as be the first on Mars or be the youngest person to break a specific world record. After students have finished brainstorming, ask them to list and evaluate the steps they would need to take to achieve their goals. Explain that in this lesson, they will read about a young man who was inspired by others to set a goal and achieve a world record.

TEACH

Guided Discussion

1. **Evaluate** What types of skills did Barrington Irving, Jr., need to achieve his goals? *(Possible response: He needed computer skills to use his flight simulator software, and he needed science, math, and engineering skills to pass his aviation course work and build his plane. He had to learn to fly and know geography to help him navigate.)*

2. **Make Inferences** Why do you think that seeing so many young people greet him after his solo flight made Irving want to help others? *(Possible response: They probably reminded him of how much he had looked up to role models as a young person, and now these young people were looking at him in the same way. He may have realized that it was his turn to help and inspire young people, just as others had inspired him.)*

More Information

Build and Soar Explain that Build and Soar involves intense engagement from participating students, who work hours equivalent to a full-time job during the weeks it takes to build a plane. The success of the program has led Experience Aviation to launch the Super Car program, in which students construct a race car. Discuss with students whether they would enjoy participating in these programs. **ASK:** What other kinds of programs might give students a chance to try out careers that require STEM skills? *(Students might suggest programs that allow students to work with computer programmers, accountants, or lab technicians.)* List students' ideas on the board for use with the On Your Feet activity.

Active Options

On Your Feet: Brainstorm How to Start a Program Share the Build and Soar information with students. Write the names of four or five programs that students suggested on chart paper and place them in different stations around the room. Ask students to gather at the station with the program that most interests them. Instruct each group to consider and discuss ways they might encourage their school or local businesses to create such a STEM-related career program in their area. Tell students to record their ideas. Encourage groups to follow through by writing a letter to the school board or local businesses that might be interested in starting such a program.

NG Learning Framework: Propose an Expedition STEM

SKILL Problem-Solving

KNOWLEDGE Our Human Story

Direct students to work in small groups to devise a Flying Classroom expedition they think would be interesting, such as to a dinosaur excavation site in the United States or an endangered ecosystem in South America. Tell groups to use a map of the United States to construct a flight path from Opa-Locka, Florida, Irving's headquarters, to their chosen destination. Instruct them to calculate the number of miles Irving would have to fly to make the round-trip, describe the focus of his expedition, and list the equipment and people he would need to bring with him. Invite groups to share their proposed expedition and calculations with the class.

DIFFERENTIATE

Striving Readers

Write Summary Statements Have students work in pairs to read and summarize the text and photo captions. Tell students to write at least three notes for each of the lesson's sections. After they have completed writing notes, guide students to create a summary statement for each section and then a summary statement for the whole lesson.

Pre-AP

Map a Flight Path Instruct students to research the route that Irving took on his round-the-world flight and then create a map to show the route. Encourage them to provide additional information through annotations, photographs, or illustrations. Some students may wish to use an online presentation or animation program to better convey Irving's journey. Ask students to share their maps with the class.

See the Chapter Planner for more strategies for differentiation.

HISTORICAL THINKING

ANSWERS

1. He is remarkable because he set and achieved tremendous goals for his own gratification, including becoming a pilot, building his own plane, and flying solo around the world. He also set goals to help others, establishing nonprofit foundations to help young people around the world explore new possibilities for themselves.

2. The Tuskegee Airmen paved the way for Irving's future by fighting discrimination in the military, so they could fight for their country, and at home to gain equal rights for African Americans.

CRITICAL VIEWING Possible response: Irving flew alone in a small aircraft, so he had to deal with fatigue, boredom, and being cramped in a small space with no room to move about or exercise.

2.5 Japanese American Internment

Fear makes people do things they normally wouldn't think of doing. When a country is engaged in war, its citizens begin to imagine enemies all around them.

MAIN IDEA During World War II, the U.S. government imprisoned thousands of Japanese Americans because they shared ancestry with an enemy.

TARGETING JAPANESE AMERICANS

The bombing of Pearl Harbor caused panic and outrage among Americans. They feared Japan would strike the United States again. Rumors spread questioning the loyalty of Japanese Americans living in the country and implying they might interfere with the American war effort. Newspapers fed into the hysteria by printing dramatic headlines accusing Japanese Americans of being threats to national security. Some Italian Americans and German Americans were also targeted as "enemy aliens."

Japanese immigrants and their American-born children, who were called **Nisei** (NEE-say), were a small minority in the United States. Only about 125,000 people of Japanese ancestry lived in the states along the West Coast. More lived in Hawaii, which was a U.S. territory, not yet a state. Japanese Americans had little political power and historically had been required to live and work within their own culture. They were not in a position to fight the damaging rumors about their loyalty to their country.

As the fear of Japanese Americans grew, the U.S. government felt it must take action. In early 1942, President Roosevelt passed an **executive order**, a law issued by the president. **Executive Order 9066** forced most Japanese Americans to leave their homes on the West Coast. The government relocated them to ten **internment camps**, or detention centers, around the country. Congress and the Supreme Court quickly approved the bill, but some Americans questioned whether forced relocation violated Japanese Americans' constitutional rights.

THE INTERNMENT CAMPS

Before they were relocated in 1942, Japanese Americans were forced to report to government processing centers. They lived there until soldiers packed them into trains and sent them to their assigned camps. The families arrived at the camps with the few belongings they could carry with them. They were housed in large **barracks**, simple buildings meant to shelter many people without much privacy. Most of the barracks had no running water. Bathing facilities and toilets were located in separate buildings. Walls topped with barbed wire surrounded the camps, and armed soldiers guarded detainees from watchtowers day and night. Escape wasn't an option.

Some Nisei men in the camps volunteered to fight in the war. They were given a test to determine their loyalty to the United States. If they passed, they trained to become members of the 442nd Regimental Combat Team. As the 92nd Infantry was restricted to African Americans, the 442nd was restricted to Nisei. About 1,200 Nisei from the camps volunteered, but only 800 were accepted into the army. Those men joined the Hawaiian Nisei, who had not been sent to internment camps. Nearly 10,000 Hawaiian men volunteered for the 442nd, and 2,600 were accepted.

The 442nd fought heroically, liberating several Italian and French towns in 1944. In October 1944, a U.S. **battalion**, a large group of soldiers on a single mission, had become cut off and surrounded by the Germans in the mountains of eastern France. Called upon to rescue the soldiers, the 442nd broke through German defenses and freed 230 soldiers while losing half of their own. The unit suffered the highest casualty rate in the

Japanese American National Museum, Los Angeles

Hisako Hibi, whose painting *Laundry Room* is shown here, taught at an art school formed at the Topaz Internment Camp in Utah. Hibi painted scenes of daily life in the camp, expressing both the drabness of the camp confines and the spirit of the internees in overcoming it. Laundry facilities, like many other aspects of the camp, were communal or shared. Here, women use laundry tubs to bathe their children. Through the doorway, a row of barracks is visible. The small, dull living quarters contrasts with the liveliness and activity in the laundry room.

war. The 442nd's record in battle answered the question of Japanese Americans' loyalty to the United States.

In 1980, a congressional commission looked into the treatment of Japanese Americans during World War II. The result was the 1988 Civil Liberties Act. The act required victims of the internment camps to be paid reparations for the violation of their civil rights. Congress issued a formal apology and awarded $20,000 to each camp survivor. The investigation arose out of a resolution at the 1978 convention of the Japanese American Citizens League.

HISTORICAL THINKING

1. **READING CHECK** What was the purpose of Executive Order 9066?

2. **ANALYZE CAUSE AND EFFECT** Why did the attack on Pearl Harbor spark suspicion of Japanese Americans living on the West Coast?

3. **MAKE GENERALIZATIONS** Why do you think many Japanese American men enlisted in the armed forces after they had been sent to internment camps?

Objective

Describe the federal government's treatment of Japanese Americans during World War II.

Critical Thinking Skills for Lesson 2.5

• Identify Main Ideas and Details
• Monitor Comprehension
• Analyze Cause and Effect
• Make Generalizations
• Summarize
• Form and Support Opinions

Essential Question for Chapter 24

How did World War II impact Americans? During times of national crisis, the government sometimes exercises the right to restrict constitutional freedoms. Lesson 2.5 discusses the imprisonment of Japanese Americans by the federal government during World War II.

Background for the Teacher

Executive Order 9066 affected all people of Japanese ancestry in the United States, even though two-thirds of the 117,000 people detained were American-born citizens. Japanese Americans were first ordered to report to assembly centers near their homes, where they were forced to wait before being transported to camps. Some spent months quartered in sheds and stables at fairgrounds before a permanent internment camp was ready. At the camps, multiple families lived in barracks and were forced to eat in communal areas, disturbing their cultural norms and depriving them of privacy. Most were unable to earn a living during their internment, a further disruption of their lives. Though detainees often were told that they were interned for their own protection, it was clear to most that the guards posted around the camps pointed their guns toward the detainees rather than the outer walls.

INTRODUCE & ENGAGE

Consider How the Media Can Shape Perceptions

Ask students to think about recent major news stories and the role that print and social media play in shaping how the public perceives the information. **ASK:** How do news organizations bring an issue to the public's attention? *(Answers will vary. Possible response: News organizations use dramatic headlines and language to attract readers and viewers. On TV or online, the media sometimes repeats a story over and over again, giving it greater drama and importance than it may deserve.)* Tell students that in this lesson they will read about how media-fueled fears affected Japanese Americans during World War II.

TEACH

Guided Discussion

1. **Summarize** What happened during the 442nd Regimental Combat Team's October 1944 battle in eastern France? *(The 442nd rescued a group of soldiers who had been surrounded by Germans, and half of the 442nd's troops were killed in the process. By enlisting and serving, the men of the 442nd demonstrated their loyalty to the American cause.)*

2. **Form and Support Opinions** Do you think the apology and compensation that the federal government gave to interned Japanese Americans was appropriate? Support your opinion with evidence from the text. *(Possible response: No. They were not compensated fairly. First, the apology came many years too late. Second, $20,000 could hardly repay people for lost businesses and homes and the interruption to their lives that they suffered.)*

🏛 Virtual Museum Visit

The Japanese American National Museum is the result of the efforts, begun in 1982, of Los Angeles businesspeople and a group of veterans of the 442nd Regimental Combat Team. The veterans had previously backed an exhibit about Japanese American soldiers at the Los Angeles County Museum of Natural History. These two groups joined forces to raise funds, and 10 years later succeeded in opening the museum. Have small groups of students access the museum's website and select one of the online collections to present to the class. Instruct groups to give background information on the collection and present three or four items, explaining the significance of each.

Active Options

On Your Feet: Roundtable Writing Ask students to consider the following question: If you or members of your family were confined in an internment camp during a war, what would you do, and why? Arrange students in groups of four, and allow them a few minutes to discuss the topic. Then tell them to each write two or three sentences in response to the question, including their explanation. Ask group members to exchange and read each other's responses and discuss possible consequences of their actions.

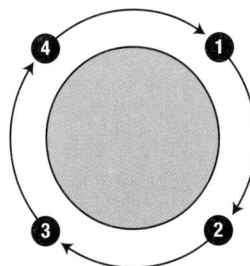

NG Learning Framework: Share an Interned Japanese American's Story

ATTITUDE Responsibility

KNOWLEDGE Our Human Story

Instruct students to use online and print resources to research and present the story of a Japanese American who was interned during World War II. Tell students to include details about the person's location before and during internment and how the person's life changed as a consequence of internment. Ask them to include a photograph of the person if available. Invite volunteers to present their subject's story to the class.

DIFFERENTIATE

English Language Learners `ELD`

Sound Out Words Before reading, preview with students at **All Proficiencies** the Key Vocabulary term *internment camp*. Point out the unusual combination of consonants in the word *internment*. Then say the word slowly, and have students repeat. Suggest that students make a word card for the term, with the definition and pronunciation hints for themselves.

Pre-AP

Write a Comparison-Contrast Essay Instruct students to conduct online research to learn about similarities and differences in the way German, Italian, and Japanese "enemy aliens" were treated in the United States during World War II. Tell students to use their research to write a comparison-contrast essay about the different treatment of the groups. When finished, ask them to share their essays with the class. Use the information to prompt a class discussion about how the diverse groups were treated and possible reasons why.

See the Chapter Planner for more strategies for differentiation.

HISTORICAL THINKING

ANSWERS

1. The executive order commanded the removal of Japanese Americans from the West Coast to internment camps in the interior of the United States, where they would be unable to engage in acts against the government.

2. The Pearl Harbor attack caused U.S. citizens to fear that Japanese Americans on the West Coast might be loyal to the Japanese and work with them to help carry out further attacks.

3. Possible response: Despite the way they were treated, they were loyal to the United States, and enlisting would demonstrate their loyalty. Their reasons for going to war were the same as any soldier who enlisted to fight the Axis.

Fighting in Africa and Italy

Assessing a situation before jumping in can be the difference between success and failure. That is why the Allies sent reconnaissance teams to find out the size and organization of the German army in France. With this new information, the Allies decided not to invade France quite yet.

MAIN IDEA As the United States joined the war in Europe, the Allies fought the Axis armies in North Africa and Italy.

CHASING THE DESERT FOX

With the United States finally involved in the war, the Allies needed to set new strategies in place. Rather than send forces immediately against German forces in Europe, Churchill and Roosevelt planned **Operation Torch**, an invasion of areas in North Africa controlled by Nazi Germany, such as Morocco, Algeria, and Tunisia. The German

presence there was small and spread out over a large distance. Overtaking them seemed like a good first task for the fresh American forces.

A German commander, Field Marshall **Erwin Rommel**, and his troops had moved into North Africa early in 1941. Rommel's ability to strike quickly, outmaneuver the enemy in the arid region, and win battles against larger Allied forces earned

The War in Europe and Africa, 1942–1943

him the nickname "the Desert Fox." His mission was to capture the **Suez Canal**, a waterway in Egypt that connects the Mediterranean and Red seas. The Allies used the canal to receive necessary oil shipments from the Middle East. They could not let Rommel have his way.

On October 23, 1942, Rommel's troops and British Allied forces collided in eastern North Africa at El Alamein (ehl ah-luh-MAYN), Egypt. Rommel had 500 tanks and about 100,000 men. **Bernard Law "Monty" Montgomery**, a British military leader and nobleman, had more than twice the number of men and tanks, as well as warplanes. After 10 days of furious combat, the Allies eventually forced Rommel to withdraw his army to Tunisia.

On November 8, 1942, American General **Dwight D. Eisenhower** and his Allied troops landed in western North Africa and successfully surrounded Rommel's troops. The Germans had no way to receive reinforcements or supplies. They surrendered on May 13, 1943. With the Nazis defeated in North Africa, the Allies planned to invade Sicily, a Mediterranean island off the

In 1942, Lieutenant General Dwight D. Eisenhower was named supreme commander of the Allied forces in North Africa and of Operation Torch. Eisenhower won the respect of the British, French, and Canadian officers and soldiers. In this photo from January 1943, Eisenhower (second from right) inspects British troops in Tunisia.

southern coast of Italy. From there, they intended to sweep up the Italian peninsula into the heart of Europe.

ALLIES ADVANCE INTO ITALY

The victory in North Africa made it much safer for the Allies to ship supplies and troops in the Mediterranean. Led by General **George S. Patton**, more than 150,000 troops, 3,000 ships, and 4,000 aircraft traveled north from Tunisia to Sicily in July 1943. Sicily's volcanoes and mountainous terrain made for difficult and fierce fighting, but by August 17, the Allies controlled the island. The British 8th Army then crossed the narrow strait between the island and mainland Italy on September 3, 1943.

Many opposing forces were at work in Italy while the Allies were fighting in Africa. Mussolini's hold on the Italian government had weakened and new, anti-fascist leaders were positioning themselves to grab power. In response to the instability, Hitler moved his troops into Italy.

On July 25, 1943, Italians successfully overthrew and arrested Mussolini. But the Allies still had to battle German troops as they made their way up the Italian peninsula. By June 1944, the Allies had reached Rome, but then they were called to fight on another front: a massive invasion of northern France. You will read about that turning point in the war in the next lesson. In April 1945, the Allies resumed battling the Nazis in Italy, but this time they had the advantage. German forces surrendered Italy on May 2.

HISTORICAL THINKING

1. **READING CHECK** What was Operation Torch?

2. **ANALYZE CAUSE AND EFFECT** What factors aided the defeat of Rommel's troops in Egypt and Tunisia?

3. **INTERPRET MAPS** Why did Allied control of North Africa make it safer to move troops and supplies on the Mediterranean Sea?

PLAN

Objective

Explain the Allied military strategy in North Africa and Italy.

Critical Thinking Skills for Lesson 3.1

- Identify Main Ideas and Details
- Monitor Comprehension
- Analyze Cause and Effect
- Interpret Maps
- Draw Conclusions
- Analyze Visuals
- Identify

Essential Question for Chapter 24

How did World War II impact Americans? Early U.S. strategies involved landing troops in North Africa. Lesson 3.1 examines the United States's early military successes and eventual conquest of Italy, setting the stage for a larger Allied invasion.

Background for the Teacher

President Roosevelt's decision to invade North Africa was met with skepticism by many in the United States. Designed to take pressure off the battered Soviets and prevent German advances in the Middle East, this campaign was initially opposed by American military leaders, who felt a more direct attack through the United Kingdom would be more effective than spreading troops across Africa. However, Winston Churchill opposed a direct attack, and memories of earlier carnage made many Britons wary of such an engagement. In the end, Roosevelt saw the benefits of Churchill's view: fighting in North Africa would both accustom Americans to the realities of war—and hopefully offer early victories—and indicate to the Germans that U.S. military strength was present on their side of the Atlantic.

INTRODUCE & ENGAGE

Where to Invade First?

Direct students' attention to the map in this lesson and have them locate Germany. Inform students that when the United States entered the war, military leaders debated the best route for U.S. troops to take to reach the heart of the Axis Powers. **ASK:** Which countries appear to have been the best places for U.S. troops to land in order to eventually invade Germany, and why? *(Possible response: The United Kingdom, North Africa, and Spain appear to have been reasonable places for troops to land because they were not controlled by the Axis Powers.)* Explain that in this lesson, students will read about strategies that U.S. military leaders used early in the war and the outcome of the decisions.

TEACH

Guided Discussion

1. **Draw Conclusions** In addition to gaining control of the Suez Canal, for what other reasons do you think Hitler moved troops into Africa? *(Morocco, Algeria, and Tunisia provided locations from which the Allies could attack Europe, so it was in Germany's interests to occupy the area. In addition, gaining control of territories could provide resources to fuel the war.)*

2. **Analyze Visuals** Based on the photograph, what attributes do you think Eisenhower was looking for in the Allied troops? *(Possible response: Based on the appearance of the men standing at attention, Eisenhower wanted his troops to be disciplined, physically fit, attentive, well ordered, and properly equipped.)*

Identify

Review with students why the Suez Canal was an important strategic location, vital for the Allies to control. **ASK:** What other waterways have been strategically important in your study of American history? *(Answers will vary. Students might point to examples such as the Rio Grande during westward expansion, Boston Harbor during the American Revolution, or the Potomac River during the Civil War.)* Guide a discussion about the role geography has played in the strategies and outcomes of the conflicts that students identify.

Active Options

On Your Feet: Create a Quiz Organize students into two teams and have each team write 10 *who, what, when, where,* and *why* questions about the movement, successes, and failures of Allied and Axis Powers in Africa and Italy. Then have teams take turns reading aloud a question and answering the question the other team asks. Review the answers as a class and have teams keep track of their number of correct answers. After all questions have been asked, the team with the most correct answers wins.

NG Learning Framework: Explore Fighting a War in a Foreign Land   STEM

ATTITUDE Curiosity

KNOWLEDGE Our Living Planet

Arrange students in small groups and ask them to brainstorm a list of challenges that members of the Allied forces likely faced in North Africa. Students might consider issues that troops and machinery could have with enduring the hot, dry climate; getting supplies and troops to front lines over unfamiliar terrain; and communicating with African people who might provide assistance. After brainstorming, direct groups to research their ideas and compile a report about how the Allies met the challenge of fighting in North Africa. Encourage students to include visuals, such as photographs, in their presentation.

DIFFERENTIATE

Striving Readers

Complete a T-Chart Instruct students to create a T-Chart, labeling the columns as follows: War in Africa and War in Europe. Tell them to write key facts as they read the lesson. If time permits, encourage students to create an additional T-Chart to note information about military leaders Rommel and Montgomery. Encourage students to compare their completed charts.

Gifted & Talented

Create an Annotated Time Line Have students create and annotate a time line of the major troop movements and battles that took place in Europe and Africa in 1942 and 1943. Students should supplement information from the text and map with research. Tell them to include dates, locations, and important people associated with the events on their time lines. Students may also include relevant photographs, political cartoons, and other art. Invite them to share their finished time lines with the class.

See the Chapter Planner for more strategies for differentiation.

HISTORICAL THINKING

ANSWERS

1. Operation Torch was the Allied invasion of North Africa. It was designed to liberate the region from Nazi control.

2. The biggest factor in Rommel's defeat was the Allies' superior troop strength, with more than twice as many troops as Germany. The Allies also had superior equipment, including tanks and aircraft.

3. Once in control of North Africa, the Allies could establish military bases on the southern coast of the Mediterranean Sea. From here they could protect shipments through the Suez Canal and prevent Nazis from launching attacks from North Africa on shipments in the Mediterranean.

3.2 The Allies Advance

Joggers talk of getting their "second wind," feeling energized about halfway through a run. During World War II, a similar feeling spread among the Allied troops between 1943 and 1944. Despite brutal combat, the Allies sensed they were winning.

MAIN IDEA Two key victories changed the course of the war in favor of the Allies.

THE BATTLE OF STALINGRAD

Though the Soviets had managed to slow Operation Barbarossa, by the end of 1941, German armies had penetrated deep into the Soviet Union. When the United States joined the war, Stalin hoped the Allies would attack the Germans in France, taking the heat off of his troops. But the Allies invaded North Africa instead. The Soviet and German armies continued battling fiercely on a front that spanned more than 2,000 miles.

The Nazis soon learned that invading such a large country was not easy. The winter of 1942 was one of the worst in history. Deep snow and blizzard conditions slowed the German advance. **Exposure**—having no shelter or protection from severe weather—killed many soldiers. The vast expanse of the front greatly delayed the delivery of supplies. These conditions wore down the German troops as they fought to take the city of Stalingrad (now called Volgograd).

The **Battle of Stalingrad** was horrific. Early on, Stalin decided that losing the city that bore his name would look terrible for him as a leader. He ordered his troops to hold it at all costs. Hitler was just as determined. He forbade his forces to retreat, even after they ran out of fuel and food. Civilians also suffered from hunger and were trapped in the ruined city. Surrounded by Soviet troops and overwhelmed by starvation and low morale, the Germans finally surrendered on February 2, 1943. Around 2 million soldiers and civilians had lost their lives in total. Despite the casualties, the Soviets had successfully defended the city and won a victory.

THE D-DAY INVASION

After the victories in Italy and the Soviet Union, the United States and Great Britain felt the war had swung to their advantage. They commanded the skies above western Europe and sailed the oceans with little fear of German submarines. Their replenished armies were strong and well-equipped. They were finally ready to invade Europe from the west.

In January 1944, General Dwight Eisenhower was appointed commander of the invasion called **Operation Overlord**. Eisenhower and other military leaders planned for thousands of American, Canadian, and British troops to land on and overwhelm the Atlantic shore of northern France. Eisenhower chose June 5, 1944, for the invasion. He assigned General **Omar Bradley** to lead the ground fighting. As Eisenhower built up his troops in southwestern England, the Allies mounted a massive deception campaign to fool the Germans into believing the Allies would strike farther north at Calais, France. The campaign involved a fictitious force headed by General Patton, spies, impersonation, fake radio transmissions, inflatable replicas of tanks and landing craft, and dummies with sound equipment parachuting into France. When the dummies landed, a mechanism triggered sounds of gunfire and grenades.

Bad weather and rough seas on June 5 delayed the operation. However, on June 6, 1944, also known as **D-Day**, approximately 160,000 Allied soldiers mainly from the United States, Great Britain, and Canada stormed beaches in northern France. The troops arrived by airplane, cargo boat,

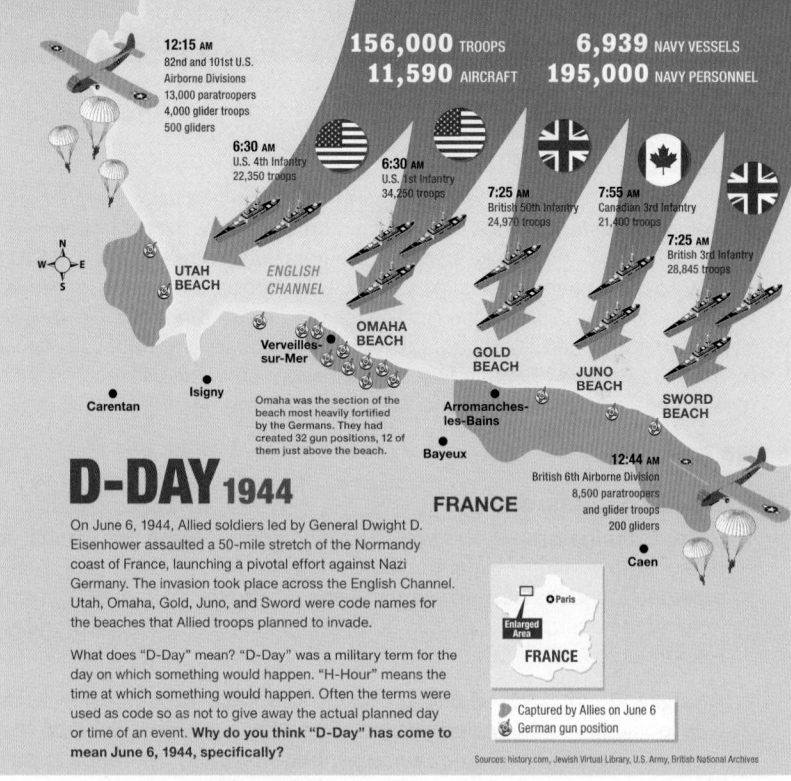

12:15 AM 82nd and 101st U.S. Airborne Divisions 13,000 paratroopers 4,000 glider troops 500 gliders

156,000 TROOPS
11,590 AIRCRAFT
6,939 NAVY VESSELS
195,000 NAVY PERSONNEL

6:30 AM U.S. 4th Infantry 22,350 troops

6:30 AM U.S. 1st Infantry 34,250 troops

7:25 AM British 50th Infantry 24,970 troops

7:55 AM Canadian 3rd Infantry 21,400 troops

7:25 AM British 3rd Infantry 28,845 troops

UTAH BEACH

ENGLISH CHANNEL

OMAHA BEACH

GOLD BEACH

JUNO BEACH

SWORD BEACH

Verveilles-sur-Mer

Carentan · Isigny

Omaha was the section of the beach most heavily fortified by the Germans. They had created 32 gun positions, 12 of them just above the beach.

Arromanches-les-Bains

Bayeux

12:44 AM British 6th Airborne Division 8,500 paratroopers and glider troops 200 gliders

Caen

D-DAY 1944

FRANCE

On June 6, 1944, Allied soldiers led by General Dwight D. Eisenhower assaulted a 50-mile stretch of the Normandy coast of France, launching a pivotal effort against Nazi Germany. The invasion took place across the English Channel. Utah, Omaha, Gold, Juno, and Sword were code names for the beaches that Allied troops planned to invade.

What does "D-Day" mean? "D-Day" was a military term for the day on which something would happen. "H-Hour" means the time at which something would happen. Often the terms were used as code so as not to give away the actual planned day or time of an event. **Why do you think "D-Day" has come to mean June 6, 1944, specifically?**

Paris

Enlarged Area
FRANCE

☐ Captured by Allies on June 6
⚓ German gun position

Sources: history.com, Jewish Virtual Library, U.S. Army, British National Archives

or **amphibious landing craft**, boats that could be used as trucks when they hit shore. During the previous night, paratroopers and gliders had landed behind German lines. The surprised Germans recovered quickly. The Allied soldiers encountered land mines and persistent gunfire. Many died that day, but they drove the Nazi army into retreat. Eisenhower's deception had worked.

More than 800,000 Allied soldiers flowed into France within two months of D-Day. By late August, Paris was free. By September, the Germans were pushed back into their own country, but they still had some fight left in them.

HISTORICAL THINKING

1. **READING CHECK** How did the Battle of Stalingrad and the D-Day invasion help turn the tide of the war to the Allies' advantage?

2. **DESCRIBE** What barriers did the Allied forces overcome as they invaded the French coast?

3. **ANALYZE CAUSE AND EFFECT** What was the effect of Eisenhower's deception campaign to fool the Germans?

Objective

Analyze how Allied victories at Stalingrad and Normandy changed the course of World War II.

Critical Thinking Skills for Lesson 3.2

- Identify Main Ideas and Details
- Monitor Comprehension
- Describe
- Analyze Cause and Effect
- Draw Conclusions
- Determine Chronology
- Interpret Visuals

Essential Question for Chapter 24

How did World War II impact Americans? With Operation Overlord, U.S. troops directly assaulted the German front in France. Lesson 3.2 examines how this invasion was planned, as well as its significance in the eventual Allied victory.

Background for the Teacher

The debate about when and if to open a second front—an invasion of western Europe by British and American troops—was one of the greatest points of tension among the Allies. Early in the war, Stalin suggested attacking Germany from both the west and the north; he wrote to Churchill in 1941 that it was the surest way to defeat Hitler. But Stalin watched the war drag on through 1942 and 1943 as millions of Soviet soldiers and civilians died in combat with Germany while American and British troops had far easier conditions in Africa. It wasn't until late 1943 that relations among the Allied leaders began to thaw, when Stalin, Churchill, and Roosevelt met in person in Tehran and agreed on the D-Day invasion. Even though tensions resumed between the United States and the Soviet Union after the war, D-Day itself is recognized throughout Russia as a pivotal moment in its history.

Preview Using Terms

Ask students if they are familiar with the term *turning point*. Encourage volunteers to share examples of the meaning. Display a Word Square and guide the class in completing it with appropriate responses. Discuss students' reasoning for designating examples and non-examples. Finally, inform students that in this lesson they will examine two events that are considered turning points of World War II.

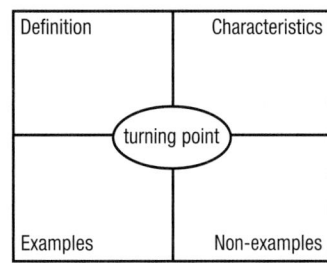

Definition	Characteristics
turning point	
Examples	Non-examples

TEACH

Guided Discussion

1. **Draw Conclusions** What do the costs and results of the Battle of Stalingrad tell us about both Hitler and Stalin? *(Both leaders were stubborn and willing to suffer enormous military and civilian casualties in order to be victorious.)*

2. **Determine Chronology** What events led up to the D-Day invasion? *(The invasion was preceded by victory at Stalingrad, the appointment of Eisenhower as commander of the invasion, the buildup of troops, the campaign of deception, and the one-day weather delay.)*

Interpret Visuals

Direct students' attention to the infographic in the lesson. Guide them in understanding the information found in the text and visuals. **ASK:** What can we infer about the different conditions and experiences of soldiers during the D-Day invasion? *(Possible response: The experiences of the soldiers varied. The plane and ship graphics show that some arrived by sea, with the dangers of slogging through water amid gunfire, while others parachuted from the air, exposed to German fire until they touched down and could seek cover. In addition, the gun position symbols on the beaches indicate that some troops, such as those landing on Omaha Beach, were met with heavy German firepower, while those landing at Gold Beach, for example, encountered less opposition.)*

Active Options

On Your Feet: One-on-One Interviews Group students into pairs, and tell both students to write three questions about the Battle of Stalingrad. Then have partners take turns posing and answering the questions. Students' questions and answers should show an understanding of material from the lesson.

NG Learning Framework: Write a First-Person Account

SKILL Communication

KNOWLEDGE Our Human Story

Have students use online resources, such as the Library of Congress's Veterans History Project, to watch or listen to interviews of soldiers who took part in the D-Day invasion. Tell students to take notes on the experiences of the soldiers. Ask volunteers to share their notes as you create a list of observations. Direct students to refer to the list as they independently write first-person accounts of the D-Day landing from the perspective of someone who participated.

DIFFERENTIATE

English Language Learners

Explore New Terms Bring students' attention to the Key Vocabulary term *amphibious landing craft* and the explanatory phrase after it. Make sure students understand that *amphibious* is an adjective, as indicated by the *-ous* ending. Place students at **All Proficiencies** in mixed pairs and ask them to write sentences using *amphibious* to modify *animal, plant, vehicle,* and *assault*. When students have finished, have pairs exchange and compare their sentences.

Gifted & Talented

Create a Photo Essay Instruct students to use online and print sources to find photographs of the D-Day invasion. Then have them create a digital photo essay using an online presentation tool. Alternatively, students might make hard copies and create a print album. Remind them to fully cite the sources of their photographs and to write a brief caption for each one, explaining how it illustrates the realities behind the D-Day invasion. Invite students to present their photo essay to the class.

See the Chapter Planner for more strategies for differentiation.

HISTORICAL THINKING

ANSWERS

1. The Battle of Stalingrad weakened and demoralized the German army. The D-Day invasion landed Allied troops in western Europe, which led to the liberation of France and a push toward Germany.

2. In addition to the challenges of landing troops and equipment by sea and air, Allied forces had to confront land mines, heavy gunfire, and fortified German positions.

3. Eisenhower's deception campaign succeeded in convincing the Germans to prepare for an invasion in the wrong area of France. As a result, they were not prepared where and when the invasion occurred.

D-DAY 1944

Because the Allied invasion of Normandy is one of the most famous military operations in American history, the general term *D-Day* has become synonymous with the invasion on June 6, 1944.

End of War in Europe

How do you know when you are beat? Surrounded by the enemy with few supplies, the Nazis had little trouble in answering this question in 1944 and 1945.

MAIN IDEA Allied forces ended the war in Europe by defeating the Germans on two fronts, and Allied leaders decided the future of Germany and the world.

BATTLE OF THE BULGE

As the Allies made their way east through France to the German border, French civilians often greeted them with flowers and celebrations. Spirits were high, but this mood wouldn't last long. In December 1944, the Germans reorganized and attacked at the German border shared with France and Belgium. The battle, known as the **Battle of the Bulge**, was the last German offensive of the war, but it surprised American and British troops.

Hitler's plan was to divide the Allied forces and capture Antwerp, a city in Belgium. He put most of his army on the operation. Some 200,000 soldiers guarded by swift German tanks called **panzers** (PAN-zurz) thundered into the forests of the Ardennes (ahr-DEHN) Mountains in northeastern France. With help from the mountain fog, the Germans forced the Allies into retreat. In an act of desperation, General George Patton, who had played a key role in driving the Germans from

northern Africa, broke through the German lines and rescued Bastogne (bah-STAWN), a town in Belgium that was vital to Allied supply and defense lines. The Germans ceased their attack. Both sides suffered tremendous losses. Germany alone lost 100,000 men.

Meanwhile, the Soviet army was sweeping west through Nazi territory, retaking the land they had controlled before the war. They recaptured Ukraine, Poland, and Lithuania. They were advancing on Germany's eastern border by August 1944. The Soviet Union's march through Eastern Europe had a resounding impact on the future of Europe. With Allied troops making their way into Germany from both sides, the war was swiftly coming to an end.

VICTORY IN EUROPE

Knowing that Hitler's chances of winning the war were dwindling, the Allied leaders decided to meet face-to-face in February 1945. President Franklin D. Roosevelt, British prime minister Winston Churchill, and Soviet premier Joseph Stalin gathered at Yalta, a small city in the south of the Soviet Union. During the **Yalta Conference**, the men discussed the future of Europe and the world. Together they planned to force Germany's surrender and to **partition**, or separate, Germany into four regions controlled by their nations and France. Their plan became known as the **Yalta Accords**. They discussed the need for an international peace-keeping organization, which would become the **United Nations (UN)**. Roosevelt and Churchill urged Stalin to allow democracy in Eastern Europe and help the Allies defeat Japan.

Franklin Roosevelt did not live to see the Allied victory, however. On April 12, 1945, he died suddenly while visiting Warm Springs, Georgia. Vice President **Harry S. Truman** became president and took charge of the U.S. role in the last stage of the war. By the end of April, Soviet troops were fighting the Nazis in the streets of Berlin, the German capital.

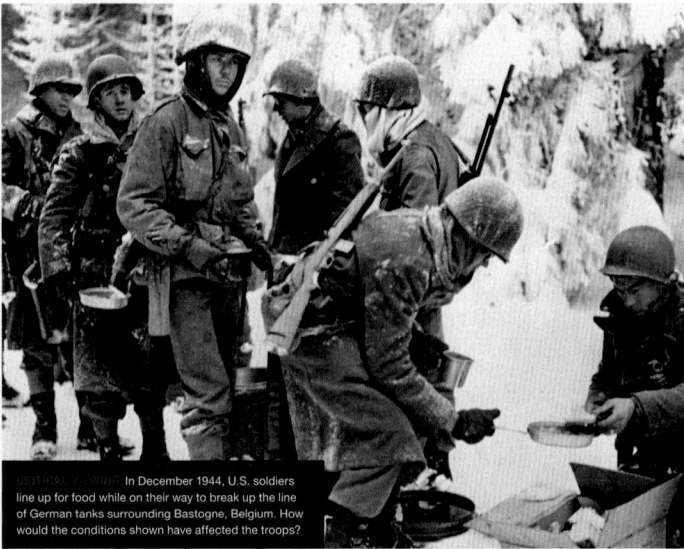

CRITICAL VIEWING In December 1944, U.S. soldiers line up for food while on their way to break up the line of German tanks surrounding Bastogne, Belgium. How would the conditions shown have affected the troops?

In February 1945, the Allied leaders known as the "Big Three" met at Yalta, a town in the Soviet Union along the Black Sea. Left to right, the leaders, seated, are Winston Churchill, Franklin Roosevelt, and Joseph Stalin. Their advisors stand at attention behind them.

Hitler knew he had lost the war. He committed suicide on April 30, 1945. The Nazis surrendered to Allied forces on May 7 and to the Soviets on May 9. In the nations that made up the Allied Powers, citizens celebrated in the streets. The war in Europe was finally over, and the Allies were victorious. Allied attention shifted to the horrifying reality of Hitler's death camps. Meanwhile, the war between the Allies and Japan continued.

HISTORICAL THINKING

1. **READING CHECK** On what two fronts did the Allies finally defeat the Nazi army?

2. **DETERMINE CHRONOLOGY** Describe the events that led to the Yalta Conference and the need for the meeting.

3. **ASK AND ANSWER QUESTIONS** What other questions do you have about the end of fighting in Europe, and how might you find the answers?

PLAN

Objective

Describe the end of the war in Europe and Allied decisions made in the Yalta Accords.

Critical Thinking Skills for Lesson 3.3

- Identify Main Ideas and Details
- Monitor Comprehension
- Determine Chronology
- Ask and Answer Questions
- Make Inferences
- Form and Support Opinions
- Compare and Contrast

Essential Question for Chapter 24

How did World War II impact Americans?
Following D-Day, the Allies closed in on Germany from the east and west. Lesson 3.3 explains how, with victory near, the Allies made decisions that would shape the postwar world.

Background for the Teacher

Although the Yalta Conference was initially praised, many critics voiced harsh opposition after President Roosevelt's death. Concessions to the Soviet Union regarding Eastern Europe, particularly Poland, generated the most controversy. Stalin promised free elections in lands once conquered by Germany and agreed to make the provisional government that he controlled in Poland more democratic. Although Roosevelt had hoped to contain the spread of communism in Eastern Europe, he and Churchill conceded that nations bordering the Soviet Union should be "friendly" to the communists. However, Stalin did not honor the Yalta Accords, and Poland and other Eastern European nations became satellites of the Soviet Union. Roosevelt and the Allies were accused of abandoning Eastern Europe to the Soviets. Poland's people—whose defense had begun the war—spent decades under Soviet control.

Predict Peace Terms

Remind students of the terms of the Treaty of Versailles, ending World War I, and other underlying causes of World War II, including alliances, a militarized Germany, and border disputes. **ASK:** As the war in Europe draws to a close, what ideas do you think Allied leaders might have to prevent future German aggression? *(Answers will vary. Possible responses: Germany giving up its military; an international peacekeeping organization; Allied occupation of Germany)* Tell students that in this lesson they will learn about the end of World War II in Europe and the decisions Allied leaders made.

TEACH

Guided Discussion

1. **Make Inferences** Why did the Battle of the Bulge surprise American and British troops? *(After the decisive victory in Normandy, the Allies likely thought the worst of the war was over and that total defeat of Germany was imminent. They had not expected Hitler to organize such an offensive in a forested area of the Ardennes Mountains, which would be more difficult to defend than the beaches of Normandy.)*

2. **Form and Support Opinions** Do you agree with the decision made at the Yalta Conference to divide Germany up into four regions controlled by the United States, Britain, the Soviet Union, and France? *(Possible response: Yes. Germany needed help to rebuild, so the Allies shared the responsibility of helping German citizens by dividing the country into four regions.)*

Compare and Contrast

Remind students that in 1941, before the United States formally joined the war, Roosevelt and Churchill forged the Atlantic Charter, an eight-point statement of principles for the postwar world. Provide students with copies of the Atlantic Charter and the Yalta Accords. Guide them to complete a Venn diagram comparing and contrasting the two agreements. Then discuss as a class whether or not the Yalta Accords lived up to the ideals of the Atlantic Charter.

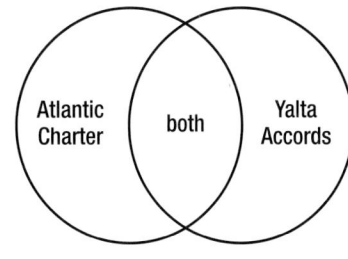

Atlantic Charter | both | Yalta Accords

Active Options

On Your Feet: Create a Concept Cluster Arrange students in groups of four, and provide each group with a large sheet of paper. Give group members a specified time to take turns contributing a word or phrase to a Concept Cluster with the following topic in the large oval: The end of World War II in Europe. When time has run out, ask volunteers from each group to share their Concept Cluster.

NG Learning Framework: Stage a Mock Conference

SKILLS Collaboration, Problem-Solving

KNOWLEDGE Our Human Story

Divide the class into three groups, and assign them to represent the United States, Great Britain, and the Soviet Union at the Yalta Conference. Have each group research their country's position going into the conference and then compile a list of five proposals upon which the country wanted agreement. Next, stage a mock conference. As each group presents proposals, the other two groups can agree, disagree, or offer counterproposals. After all proposals have been presented, list the points of agreement and discuss with the class the difficulties of foreign diplomacy.

Striving Readers

Use Supported Reading Assign pairs of students paragraphs to read aloud together. At the end of each paragraph, have students use the following sentence frames to identify what they do and do not understand:

- This paragraph is about _____.
- One fact that stood out to me was _____.
- I had trouble understanding _____, so I figured it out by _____.

Be sure all students understand the content before moving on to the next paragraph.

Pre-AP

Explain the Origin of the United Nations Tell students to access a variety of sources to create an oral or written report about the creation of the United Nations. Encourage students to use primary and secondary sources and to quote or paraphrase them as appropriate. Invite volunteers to share their reports with the class.

See the Chapter Planner for more strategies for differentiation.

HISTORICAL THINKING

ANSWERS

1. The Allies defeated Germany on its western border, at the Battle of the Bulge, and on its eastern border, when the Soviet army reclaimed land it had held before the war.

2. After General Patton's rescue of Bastogne, Hitler's forces were no longer on the attack, a clear indication that the war in Europe was coming to an end. Roosevelt, Churchill, and Stalin understood that a postwar strategy was needed, so they met at Yalta in February 1945 to discuss plans.

3. Answers will vary, but students should identify credible websites, books, and magazines as places to find additional information on the subject.

CRITICAL VIEWING Possible response: Minor tasks, let alone fighting, would have been difficult. Moving supplies and personnel through an accumulation of snow, the cold weather, and eating military rations, all without shelter, would have lowered morale and tired the troops.

3.4 The Holocaust

Hitler's hatred of Jews was not a secret. But it wasn't until the end of the war that the extent of his violence became widely known. The world would never be the same.

MAIN IDEA The Nazis killed millions of Jews and others they deemed "undesirable" during World War II.

PERSECUTION OF THE JEWS

As the Allied army marched east and the Soviet army marched west through Eastern Europe, they came upon places of unspeakable horror. They found huge compounds filled with starving people and piles of dead bodies. The Nazis had attempted to commit **genocide**, or wipe out a particular group of people through mass killing. Hitler's genocide became known as the **Holocaust**.

As you read earlier, before Adolf Hitler rose to power, he traveled through Germany making political speeches blaming the problems of the country on the Jewish people. This hatred of Jews is called **anti-Semitism**. After Hitler became Germany's chancellor, his Nazi Party began instituting national laws restricting Jewish rights. Regional and local politicians also passed anti-Semitic laws. Most of the early laws limited Jews' social lives and their ability to work. They were no longer allowed to be members of certain organizations and could no longer work in certain professions, including in the government.

In September 1935, the Nazi Party released new policies called the **Nuremberg Laws**, which stripped Jews of their German citizenship and voting rights. They were not permitted to marry non-Jewish people. Businesses fired their Jewish workers and no longer let Jewish doctors and lawyers help German people. Jewish children could no longer attend school. Then Nazi soldiers moved Jewish families to **ghettoes**, forced housing for a particular race or ethnicity, far away from their homes.

On November 7, 1938, the situation became dire for German Jews. A 17-year-old Polish Jew shot and killed a German diplomat in France. **Joseph**

Goebbels (GEH-buhlz), the Nazi propaganda minister, immediately used the assassination to whip up anti-Semitic sentiments, or feelings. On November 9, Nazis burned down synagogues and damaged Jewish homes, schools, and businesses in Germany. Around 100 people were killed that night. The incident was called **Kristallnacht** (krees-TAHL-nahkt), which means "Night of Broken Glass" in German.

Soon, many German Jews were forced to wear an armband or badge that identified their heritage and religion. The badge made it easier for Nazis and racists to humiliate and segregate the Jews. Eventually, all Jews had to wear some form of identification in Germany and in some of the countries controlled by Germany.

NAZI CONCENTRATION CAMPS

In the months following Kristallnacht, tens of thousands of Jewish men were arrested. They were transported to work camps known as **concentration camps**, where they were forced to perform hard labor. Many people died on the journey and in the camps due to starvation and disease. Eventually, entire Jewish families were sent there, as well as the Roma people, also known as gypsies; homosexuals; people with disabilities; and people who opposed the Nazis.

Some of the concentration camps had gas chambers where prisoners who could not work, pregnant women, children, and the elderly, were killed with poisonous gas. Their bodies were burned in rooms equipped with large ovens called **crematoria**. These places were called **death camps**, and they were part of a Nazi plan to kill all of Europe's Jewish people, called the

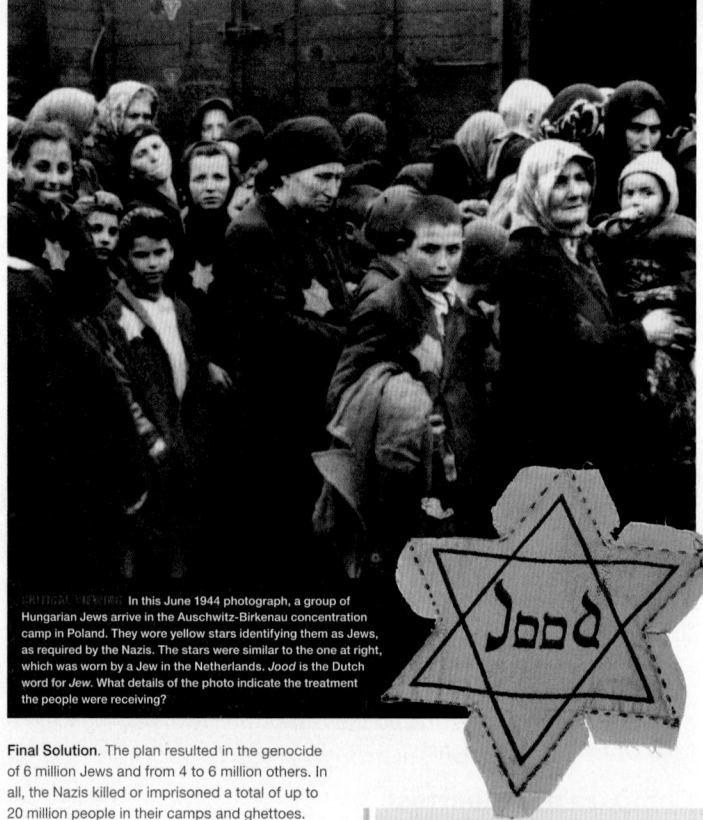

CRITICAL VIEWING In this June 1944 photograph, a group of Hungarian Jews arrive in the Auschwitz-Birkenau concentration camp in Poland. They wore yellow stars identifying them as Jews, as required by the Nazis. The stars were similar to the one at right, which was worn by a Jew in the Netherlands. *Jood* is the Dutch word for *Jew*. What details of the photo indicate the treatment the people were receiving?

Final Solution. The plan resulted in the genocide of 6 million Jews and from 4 to 6 million others. In all, the Nazis killed or imprisoned a total of up to 20 million people in their camps and ghettoes.

While Allied leaders knew about the death camps, they failed to investigate them or address them during the war. Allied warplanes flew within 35 miles of Auschwitz-Birkenau in Poland, but they didn't bomb the railroad lines the Nazis used to transport their prisoners. In the United States, immigration boards allowed few Jewish refugees entrance. The U.S. State Department claimed some of the refugees could be spies, and could pose a security risk.

HISTORICAL THINKING

1. **READING CHECK** Why did the Nazis force Jews to wear badges and armbands?

2. **MAKE CONNECTIONS** How did Joseph Goebbels exploit the death of the German diplomat in France?

3. **DESCRIBE** What did witnesses to the Kristallnacht riots see?

Objective
Summarize facts about the Holocaust and the response to it by world nations.

Critical Thinking Skills for Lesson 3.4
- Identify Main Ideas and Details
- Monitor Comprehension
- Make Connections
- Describe
- Form and Support Opinions
- Analyze Language Use

Essential Question for Chapter 24
How did World War II impact Americans? Prior to U.S. involvement in the war, Hitler implemented his Final Solution—an effort to exterminate Europe's Jews. Lesson 3.4 discusses the horrors of the Holocaust and the Allied Powers' response to ongoing atrocities.

Background for the Teacher
By 1942, the U.S. government was fully aware of Hitler's Final Solution, but it is not clear how much the American public knew. Although U.S. newspapers ran front-page stories about major events such as the Nuremberg Laws and Kristallnacht, articles about mass killings of civilians carried out by Nazi death squads were buried far below the front page, without photographs that would have made the horrors more tangible, and often without stating the ethnic identity of most victims. For example, a 1942 *New York Times* story about the Chelmno concentration camp appeared on page six, and the Allies' formal condemnation of mass murder of Jews at the end of 1942 also did not make front-page news. Stories and photos of the Nazi crimes didn't gain prominence until the final days of the war.

History Notebook
Encourage students to complete the American Gallery page for Chapter 24 in their History Notebooks as they read.

Activate Prior Knowledge

Instruct students to look at the title, photograph, and subheadings in the lesson. Then discuss with them what they know about the Holocaust and the persecution of ethnic groups and other groups of people. Ask students to be respectful of the subject and each other as they discuss. Point out that details of the Holocaust are documented in film and photographs taken by liberating troops and through records that the Germans themselves kept. Then tell students that they will read about one of the most brutal periods in history.

TEACH

Guided Discussion

1. **Form and Support Opinions** Why do you think more German people didn't stand up against Hitler's persecution of the Jews? *(Answers will vary. Possible response: Some people were looking for someone to blame for their problems, and Jews provided a target. Others were afraid of the Nazis and didn't want to risk their own lives by opposing their policies.)*

2. **Analyze Language Use** Why do you think the Nazis called their plan the "Final Solution"? *(The Nazis blamed Jews for Germany's problems, so they wanted Germans to believe that eliminating Jews would prove to be the ultimate, or final, solution to their problems. The phrase also could have been used as a euphemism for death.)*

More Information

The U.S. Holocaust Response The United States was severely criticized for its decision not to bomb the Nazi death camp at Auschwitz-Birkenau. Although the camp was within reach of Allied bombers in July 1944, U.S. leaders argued that American aircraft did not have the ability to target death camps accurately and that bombing the camp could kill thousands of prisoners and detract from attacks on military targets that could hasten Allied victory. In response, critics have argued that bombing the camp or the railroads that led to it dovetailed military goals and that the number of prisoners killed during bombings would likely have been less than the number killed at the camp in the six months before its liberation in January 1945. Western nations' refusals to accept Jewish refugees from Europe also drew criticism. U.S. refusal reflected general anti-immigrant sentiment and tight quotas on European immigrants that had been in place since the 1920s. During the war, the United States and European nations scrutinized prospective immigrants intensely for fear of spies and sabotage. The effect of immigrant restrictions resulted in allowing only 200,000 Jews entry into the United States between 1933 and 1945, a tiny fraction of those who needed shelter. Guide a discussion with students, raising questions such as the following: How can a government balance competing goals, such as winning a war and saving civilian lives? What are the benefits and drawbacks of strict immigration policies? How could the United States and other nations have done more to help Jewish refugees?

Active Options

AMERICAN GALLERY ONLINE **The Holocaust** Invite students to explore the American Gallery. Have them select one of the photographs and do additional research to learn more about it. Ask questions that will inspire additional inquiry, such as: What is it depicting? What is the significance of the object? How does the image further our understanding of the Holocaust?

NG Learning Framework: Research Holocaust Stories

ATTITUDE Responsibility

KNOWLEDGE Our Human Story

Have students research or talk to people to identify a person who lived through the Holocaust. Students might use an online resource such as the interviews conducted by the Shoah Foundation or the United States Holocaust Museum. Have students summarize for the class the experiences of the person they researched.

Inclusion

Use Clarifying Questions Pair inclusion students with students who can assist by reading the lesson to them or describing the photograph, including details about the clothing, facial expressions, and age and gender of the people. Instruct the inclusion partner to ask clarifying questions. Then tell pairs to discuss how details in the text and photograph convey what happened to Jewish people under Nazi rule. Partners may then work together to answer the Critical Viewing question.

Pre-AP

Connect History and Literature Instruct students to conduct library and online research to learn more about Holocaust memoirs, such as *Night* by Elie Wiesel, *Survival in Auschwitz* by Primo Levi, *I Am a Star* by Inge Auerbacher, and *All But My Life* by Gerda Weissmann Klein. Ask students to read one such memoir, or excerpts from it, and then write an essay about how the memoir portrays historical events. Invite students to share their essays with the class.

See the Chapter Planner for more strategies for differentiation.

HISTORICAL THINKING

ANSWERS

1. The badges and armbands allowed Nazis to readily identify and segregate Jews from non-Jewish society.

2. Since the person who shot the diplomat was Jewish, Goebbels used the murder as a way to encourage anti-Semitic beliefs and actions.

3. Witnesses saw synagogues on fire and people destroying the homes and businesses of Jewish people. Some also saw people being killed.

CRITICAL VIEWING Details such as the stars on the clothing, presence of the train, and frightened and worried facial expressions of the people indicate the persecution and harsh treatment of the Jews shown.

4.1 War in the Pacific

Even if you are on the right side of a conflict, you may not win every battle. The first year of the war in the Pacific was a great challenge for the Allies, particularly for the United States.

MAIN IDEA After the United States entered the war, Japan continued to expand its power in the Pacific through a string of victories.

EARLY JAPANESE VICTORIES

After its successful attack on Pearl Harbor, Japanese forces moved swiftly through southeastern Asia, capturing American territories and other Allied colonies in the region. For the United States, an early defeat took place within hours of the attack on Pearl Harbor. Japanese forces struck the Philippines, which had been designated a commonwealth, or territory, of the United States in 1935.

General Douglas MacArthur arrives in Melbourne, Australia, from the Philippines on March 21, 1942.

American troops, including many Filipino soldiers, were headquartered there under the command of American general **Douglas MacArthur**, but they were not yet fully prepared for battle. The Japanese air force bombed airfields, bases, harbors, and shipyards. More than 40,000 Japanese soldiers came ashore at Luzon, the largest island of the Philippines. By January 2, 1942, Japanese troops had taken Manila, the capital of the Philippines. American troops retreated to the jungles of the Bataan Peninsula, which they defended for 99 days.

In March 1942, Roosevelt ordered MacArthur to leave the Philippines. MacArthur was too valuable an officer for the United States to lose, so to avoid capture by the Japanese, he was brought to safety in Australia. He vowed to one day return to the Philippines. Still, the Filipino and American troops continued to fight, even though they suffered from starvation and disease. Meanwhile in Australia, MacArthur became supreme commander of Allied forces in the southwestern Pacific.

Finally, on April 9, 1942, the remaining 75,000 Filipino and American troops surrendered. The Japanese forced them to march without food, water, or shelter, for 60 miles to a prison camp. Those who collapsed during the ordeal were beaten, bayoneted, shot, and even beheaded by their Japanese captors. Thousands died in what became known as the **Bataan Death March**, and thousands more died in the prison camp at their destination. Many American prisoners were later transported to the Japanese main island. There, they mainly worked as slave laborers in mines. Thousands more died while traveling, crowded into the coal holds of the ships or while enslaved.

This photo, taken on June 4, 1942, shows the U.S.S. *Yorktown* moments after it was bombed by the Japanese during the Battle of Midway. It took four torpedoes and two air raids over the course of three days for the Japanese to finally capsize the boat.

AMERICAN STRATEGIES PAY OFF

Even though the news from the Pacific was not good, the United States fought on. Under the command of **Lieutenant Colonel James H. Doolittle**, American B-25 bombers attacked the Japanese mainland on April 18, 1942. Although the attack did not do much damage to the Japanese infrastructure, it was a great embarrassment to the Japanese government. Within a month, the U.S. Navy began to win some important battles.

In early May 1942, the Japanese attempted to attack air bases in the South Pacific. Instead, U.S. naval forces turned them back at the **Battle of the Coral Sea**. Between June 3 and June 6, the United States defeated Japan in the **Battle of Midway**, sinking 4 Japanese aircraft carriers, destroying about 300 enemy aircraft, and killing more than 3,000 enemy sailors. Though the Americans lost about 145 aircraft and more than 300 sailors, the Battle of Midway was a major Allied victory.

Midway Islands consist of an **atoll**, a ring-shaped coral reef that forms a series of islands. The strategic location of the atoll gave the United States and the Allies a much-needed advantage. By retaining control of Midway, the United States was in a stronger position to defend Hawaii and launch attacks on Japanese territories.

HISTORICAL THINKING

1. **READING CHECK** How successful was the war in the Pacific for the Allies immediately following the attack on Pearl Harbor?

2. **MAKE INFERENCES** Why was the attack by American bombers on April 18, 1942, a great embarrassment to the Japanese government?

3. **ANALYZE CAUSE AND EFFECT** What was the strategic effect of the U.S. victory at Midway?

PLAN

Objective
Describe U.S. challenges and successes in the Pacific in 1942.

Critical Thinking Skills for Lesson 4.1
- Identify Main Ideas and Details
- Monitor Comprehension
- Make Inferences
- Analyze Cause and Effect
- Draw Conclusions
- Analyze Data

Essential Question for Chapter 24
How did World War II impact Americans? Early in the war, U.S. forces struggled against the Japanese in the Pacific. Lesson 4.1 explores the evolving military strategies in 1942 that strengthened the position of Allied forces.

Background for the Teacher
Every year on the last Sunday of March, thousands of people gather at White Sands Missile Range in southern New Mexico to take part in the Bataan Memorial Death March. This event, in honor of American soldiers who lost their lives in the Philippines in 1942, is a challenging 26.2-mile trek through rough desert scrub. In 2017, the 28th annual commemoration drew a record 7,200 participants, including eight survivors of the original march in Bataan, one of whom walked in the reenactment. The history of Bataan has a special meaning for New Mexicans, as troops from the state played a crucial role in the 1942 battle. Soldiers from the New Mexico National Guard, the 200th Coast Artillery, were the first to fire on enemy troops. More than 1,800 New Mexicans fought at Bataan, and 829 of them died in battle or as prisoners of war.

INTRODUCE & ENGAGE

Preview Vocabulary

Write the word *atoll* on the board, and challenge students to define it. *(a reef, island, or group of islands made of coral)* Show students the location of the Midway Islands on a map. **ASK:** Why do you think this atoll is called Midway? *(It is about halfway between the mainland United States and East Asia.)* Briefly discuss why Japan and the Allies might both want to control Midway. Then tell students that in this lesson they will learn more about events in the Pacific during World War II.

TEACH   STEM

Guided Discussion

1. **Draw Conclusions** Why did the Japanese attack the Philippines in 1942? *(They were trying to capture Allied territories and colonies, and the Philippines was a U.S. commonwealth.)*

2. **Analyze Data** What was the ratio of Japanese to American casualties in the Battle of Midway? Base your calculation on the figures in the text, and express the answer as a ratio. *(The Japanese had 3,000 casualties and the Americans had 300, making the ratio of Japanese to American casualties 10:1.)*

More Information

Realities of Bataan In a cable to Washington, D.C., in late December 1942, General Douglas MacArthur exaggerated his troop strength to leaders as an "invasion force of 130,000." In reality, he commanded 22,000 American soldiers, many of whom had no combat experience, a few tens of thousands of underequipped Filipino reservists with little training, a group of pilots without aircraft, and sailors without ships. Given the reality of MacArthur's forces, it is not surprising that the Japanese were able to overcome them. Approximately 40 percent of the American military personnel captured on the Bataan Peninsula died, a much higher rate than the 3 percent who died in Axis captivity in Europe. **ASK:** How would you summarize the conditions prisoners faced during and after the march? *(Possible response: Prisoners were starved, dehydrated, tortured, murdered, and worked to death as part of the brutal Bataan ordeal.)* **ASK:** Can you recall a similar march in U.S. history? *(Possible response: This march is somewhat similar to the Trail of Tears in 1838 and 1839, when American soldiers removed the Cherokee from their homes in Georgia, encamped them, and then forced them to march to designated Indian Territory in Oklahoma. The Cherokee also received brutal treatment, and many died along the way.)*

Active Options

On Your Feet: Rotating Review Organize students into four groups, and assign each a corner of the room. Tell groups to come up with several questions about the war in the Pacific to help them review the lesson. Begin the review by having Group 1 ask a question of Group 2. Then Group 2 asks a question of Group 3, and so forth in rotation until groups ask and answer all the questions.

NG Learning Framework: Write a Letter Home

ATTITUDE Responsibility

KNOWLEDGE Our Human Story

Have students conduct online research about soldiers and other personnel who participated in the Battle of Midway. Direct them to write a letter to a friend or family member from the perspective of someone who played a role in the battle. Tell students to write in the first person and to focus on facts and details they read in the text or gathered from their source materials. Publish their finished letters on a class blog or website or in a physical album, and invite volunteers to read their letters to the class.

DIFFERENTIATE

Striving Readers

Make a List Post the following heading: Five Things I Know About the War in the Pacific. After students read the lesson, ask them to copy the heading onto a piece of paper and write five sentences about the topic. Invite volunteers to share their sentences with the class.

Gifted & Talented

Create an Illustrated Sequence Chain Tell students to create an illustrated Sequence Chain with dates, events, and visuals to show how victories and defeats played out on both sides of the war in the Pacific in 1942. Provide various Sequence Chain graphic organizers from which to choose. Instruct students to use information from the text as well as online and print sources. They might use newspaper headlines and political cartoons from 1942 to illustrate events. Ask students to color-code their Sequence Chain to distinguish Allied and Axis information. Invite them to present their completed Sequence Chain to the class.

See the Chapter Planner for more strategies for differentiation.

HISTORICAL THINKING

ANSWERS

1. Immediately after the Pearl Harbor attack, the war was not successful for the Allies because the United States lost control of the Philippines and thousands of troops to Japan.

2. Possible response: A U.S. attack on Japanese home soil was an embarrassment because the bombing caught the Japanese government unaware and unprepared to defend its home territory.

3. Gaining control of Midway gave the United States a good location from which to defend and protect Hawaii and a launching place for attacks on Japanese territories.

4.2 Island Hopping

How do you fight a war against an enemy positioned on islands scattered thousands of miles across the ocean? This was a question the U.S. military needed to answer.

MAIN IDEA The United States targeted Japanese islands in the Pacific one after the other, attacking the easiest to secure first.

ONE ISLAND AT A TIME

Island hopping was the strategy employed by the United States to gain military bases and secure many of the small islands in the Pacific. At first, U.S. troops targeted islands that were not as strongly defended by the Japanese. The U.S. military swept in and built landing strips and bases on those islands, inching U.S. military power closer and closer to Japan itself. Island hopping was made possible partly by the U.S. victory at Midway, which limited Japan's reach in the Pacific.

The **Battle of Guadalcanal** in the Solomon Islands was an early Allied victory. U.S. Marines launched the attack in August 1942, two months after the Battle of Midway. They quickly seized a Japanese air base that was under construction, but the battle itself raged for another six months. By the battle's end, only about a third of the Japanese troops who had been on the island at the peak of fighting survived. American forces lost fewer than 2,000 of the 60,000 troops deployed. After its defeat on Guadalcanal, Japan questioned its

The War in Asia, 1942–1945

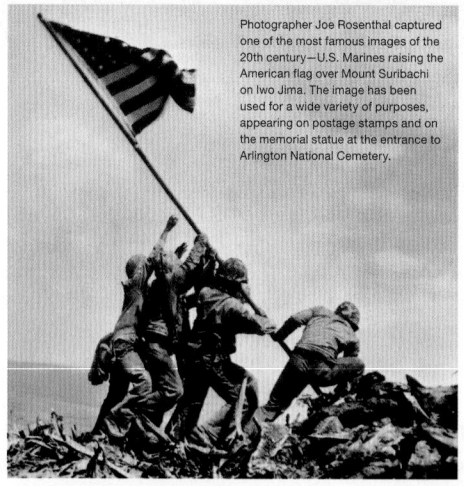

Photographer Joe Rosenthal captured one of the most famous images of the 20th century—U.S. Marines raising the American flag over Mount Suribachi on Iwo Jima. The image has been used for a wide variety of purposes, appearing on postage stamps and on the memorial statue at the entrance to Arlington National Cemetery.

ability to defeat the United States. Over the next few years, the Allies continued island hopping as Japan fought back, with mixed success.

In October 1944, American forces focused on recapturing the Philippines. The Japanese sent almost all of their remaining naval forces to the Philippines to fight against the Allies. As in the case of Midway, U.S. commanders were ready for the Japanese strategy. Some historians say the resulting clash, the **Battle of Leyte Gulf,** was not just the largest naval battle in the war but the largest naval battle ever. The U.S. 7th Fleet annihilated, or destroyed, one of the Japanese forces and drove a second into retreat. In desperation to keep the Philippines, the Japanese deployed **kamikaze pilots**. These pilots crashed their planes into Allied ships, taking their own lives as they took the lives of many Allied sailors.

The stage was set for the Allies to retake the Philippines. U.S. General Douglas MacArthur declared his triumphant return to the nation he was forced to flee more than two years earlier. By March 1945, the United States again controlled the Philippines, but at great cost. Two-thirds of the Allied soldiers MacArthur left behind in March 1942 had perished by the time he returned.

MOVING TOWARD JAPAN

On February 19, 1945, the U.S. Marines invaded the island of Iwo Jima, around 760 miles from Tokyo, Japan. Roughly 22,000 Japanese troops defended the island. They had dug miles of tunnels connecting man-made caves in which to hide. This made it difficult for the Marines to find them and resulted in fierce fighting over most of the island. By the time fighting ended in late March, the entire Japanese force had been wiped out except for around 1,000 prisoners of war. American losses were estimated at 6,000 dead and 21,000 wounded.

On March 9, 1945, the Allies brought the war to the Japanese mainland as U.S. warplanes released 2,000 tons of **incendiary bombs**, or fire bombs, on Tokyo. Fifteen square miles were set ablaze, and between 80,000 and 130,000 Japanese lives were lost. Some say it was the deadliest firestorm in recorded history.

Then, from April 1 to June 22, 1945, U.S. troops battled to capture Okinawa, a large island only 340 miles from mainland Japan. The final battle of the island-hopping campaign was also the largest. As a result of their victory there, the Allies could now use Okinawa as a base for the planned ground invasion of the Japanese home islands.

HISTORICAL THINKING

1. **READING CHECK** What was the significance of the U.S. capture of Okinawa?

2. **DETERMINE WORD MEANING** Think about how incendiary bombs affected the Japanese. What does that reveal about the meaning of the word *incendiary*?

3. **MAKE INFERENCES** What does the image of the Marines raising the flag on Iwo Jima symbolize?

PLAN

Objective

Describe U.S. military strategy in the Pacific toward the end of World War II.

Critical Thinking Skills for Lesson 4.2

- Identify Main Ideas and Details
- Monitor Comprehension
- Determine Word Meaning
- Make Inferences
- Summarize
- Interpret Maps

Essential Question for Chapter 24

How did World War II impact Americans? As the war escalated in the Pacific, U.S. and Japanese military commanders sought new battle strategies. Lesson 4.2 discusses tactics used by both sides during the war.

Background for the Teacher

The Japanese word *kamikaze* means "divine wind," a reference to a typhoon, or hurricane-strength storm, that drove away invading Mongol ships just as they were menacing the coast of Japan in 1281. During World War II, each kamikaze plane was loaded with a missile carrying more than a ton of explosive charge. Once the missile was in place, there was no way for the pilot to exit the aircraft. The pilot would fly to an altitude of about 25,000 feet and within three miles of the target. Then the pilot would engage the missile's rocket engines, accelerating the plane to a speed of about 600 miles per hour toward the target. Kamikazes were particularly deadly at Okinawa, where they killed nearly 5,000 U.S. Navy troops, the greatest number of casualties of any single naval battle.

Brainstorm Military Strategies

Display a large map of Asia and review the positions of the Japanese and Allied forces at the end of the Battle of Midway. Then ask students to suggest strategies that either side might employ next. Ask for volunteers to indicate strategies on the map, pointing out possible military targets and objectives. Then explain that this lesson describes strategies that the Allies and Japan used in the final years of the war. After completing the lesson, review students' proposed strategies and discuss whether they were used or could have been used along with actual strategies on either side.

TEACH

Guided Discussion

1. **Summarize** In 1944, how did the Japanese try to defend their control of the Philippines? *(They sent most of their fleet to fight there, and when that failed, they sent kamikaze pilots after Allied targets.)*

2. **Interpret Maps** Based on details in the map, why was the Battle of Guam in 1944 an important battle for the Allies to win? *(The Allies used Guam as a jumping-off point for the Battles of Leyte Gulf, Iwo Jima, and Okinawa.)*

More Information

The Rise of Photojournalism Direct students' attention to the photograph of U.S. Marines raising the flag at Iwo Jima. Explain that such photographs first became possible with the 1925 German invention of the 35mm Leica camera. Using film that required minimal light and created crisp negatives, this portable, single-exposure camera allowed photographers to go anywhere and shoot anything. One result was the photojournalism magazine, also from Germany, which used multiple photos and minimal written text to tell a story. In 1936, weekly *Life* magazine debuted in the United States, presenting photographs that told stories to its readers. Within five years, photojournalists were accompanying troops to all arenas of World War II, capturing photos that often told a story that the Office of War Information did not want told. Shaping information about the war in a positive light, newsreels and newspaper photos did not focus on the grim realities captured by photojournalists, and images of dead U.S. soldiers were forbidden. In September 1943, *Life* published the first photo depicting dead U.S. troops. Editors had struggled for 10 months with censors, ultimately receiving approval from President Franklin Roosevelt. The photo of three fallen soldiers on a beach in New Guinea told a heartbreaking story of the cost of war.

Active Options

On Your Feet: Question and Answer Divide the class into two teams and direct students to write five True-False statements based on information they see on the map accompanying the lesson. Provide or have teams create answer cards with "True" written on one side and "False" on the other. Then have teams take turns asking the other team a question. Tell students to answer questions by holding up the "True" or "False" side of the card. If a team's answer is not unanimous, encourage members to review the map and the lesson text and discuss to arrive at a unanimous answer. As needed, guide discussion to correct any misunderstandings. Have teams alternate asking and answering until all questions have been used.

NG Learning Framework: Compose an Expository Essay

ATTITUDE Curiosity

SKILL Communication

Direct students to work in pairs to research something they would like to know about kamikaze pilots and incendiary bombs, with each partner taking one of the topics. Tell students to use the chapter text and additional print and digital source materials to compose a brief expository essay about the topic they chose and then exchange essays with their partner. After partners read each other's essay, ask them to discuss similarities and differences between the two tactics and how they were used during World War II.

Inclusion

Preview Using a Map To help students better understand the U.S. strategy of island hopping and to prepare them for reading, direct their attention to the map. First help students understand the meaning of the colors and symbols in the legend. Then direct them to use a finger to trace and distinguish the territories held by the Japanese and the Allies. Next have them trace the lines of the Allied advances, noting the dates near each line. Encourage students to refer to the map as each location is referenced in the lesson.

Pre-AP

Present an Eyewitness Account Assign students the role of a war correspondent reporting on events in the Pacific that were described in the lesson. Ask them to select one event, research it using print and online sources, and then write an eyewitness account, describing the event as a war correspondent would have done. Students might prepare by researching archival newsreel footage of battles in the Pacific Ocean. Invite students to read their eyewitness account to the class, record it for playback as a podcast, or post it on a class or school website.

See the Chapter Planner for more strategies for differentiation.

HISTORICAL THINKING

ANSWERS

1. The Allies could use Okinawa as a base for air operations and for the planned ground invasion of the Japanese home islands.

2. *Incendiary* means more than merely "causing fire." Based on the number of Japanese people killed and the destruction caused by the bombs, *incendiary* suggests a destructive power capable of extinguishing everything in its path.

3. The image symbolizes Americans' determination to fight, the ability to triumph against powerful opponents, and Americans' pride in their country.

4.3 Final Victory

Is it acceptable to sacrifice the few to save the many? No doubt it is a difficult decision to make, but it is one sometimes required of doctors, police officers, and world leaders during conflicts.

MAIN IDEA President Truman was forced to make a decision between ordering an atomic strike on Japan or risking an invasion that might cost more than a million American lives.

THE ATOMIC BOMB

The planned U.S. invasion of Japan was referred to as "Operation Downfall." It was to be the largest amphibious operation in history, using all available combined resources of the Army, Navy, Marines, and Air Force, attacking from the sea. Massive fatalities on both sides were almost a certainty, and the lives of millions of Japanese civilians would be at risk. Battle planners estimated that hundreds of thousands of American troops could die in the invasion, even though they were almost certain to win in the long run. But President Truman had another option.

On August 9, 1945, the second atomic bomb exploded over Nagasaki, Japan. This photo shows the resulting mushroom cloud and blast wave moving out from it.

Truman and some of his advisors believed that attacking Japan with a terrible new weapon might prevent the casualties of a full-scale invasion. That weapon was the **atomic bomb**, a type of nuclear weapon whose violent explosion is triggered by **nuclear fission**, or splitting atoms. Nuclear fission releases intense heat and radioactivity. In 1940, the U.S. government had begun funding an atomic weapons program code-named the **Manhattan Project**. Over the next four years, the program's scientists worked on extracting the key materials for nuclear fission—uranium 235 and plutonium. At Los Alamos, New Mexico, **J. Robert Oppenheimer** and his team of physicists used these materials to develop the first atomic bomb.

By the time the bomb was successfully tested at Alamogordo, New Mexico, the Allied powers had already defeated Germany. In late July 1945, Japan's government rejected the Allies' demand for surrender, which threatened Japan with "prompt and utter destruction" if it refused. In the wake of Japan's refusal, Truman hoped to bring the war to a decisive end by dropping atomic bombs on one or more Japanese cities.

HIROSHIMA AND NAGASAKI

On the morning of August 6, 1945, the United States sent out the *Enola Gay,* a modified B-29 bomber that carried an atomic bomb. The target was **Hiroshima**, a military center with a population of 350,000. At 8:15 in the morning, the plane dropped the bomb, and within seconds five square miles of the city had been reduced to rubble. Some 90,000 to 166,000 people were instantly killed or died within four months from burns and radiation sickness.

Three days later, another B-29 plane dropped an atomic bomb on the city of **Nagasaki**. Again, tens of thousands of Japanese civilians died in an instant, and Nagasaki lay in ruins. On August 15, Emperor Hirohito announced that Japan would surrender to the Allied Powers. The news spread quickly and "Victory in Japan" or "V-J Day" celebrations broke out across the United States and in other Allied nations. With General MacArthur presiding over negotiations, Japan formally surrendered aboard the U.S.S. *Missouri,* anchored in Tokyo Bay, on September 2, 1945.

Ari Beser, Fulbright–National Geographic Fellow

Ari Beser's grandfather (below) flew as the radar specialist on the planes that dropped atomic bombs on Hiroshima and Nagasaki in 1945. In 2015, Beser (right) traveled to Japan to interview survivors of the bombings. Many survivors were eager to talk. They hoped that their stories would end the possibility of nuclear warfare forever. The survivors recalled the blinding flash of the bomb detonating, the heat, and the strong wind. They also recounted the physical effects of the attack, such as chronic pain, they still experience today.

HISTORICAL THINKING

1. **READING CHECK** What was the result of the Manhattan Project?

2. **FORM AND SUPPORT OPINIONS** Do you agree with President Truman's justification for dropping atomic bombs on Japan? Support your opinion with evidence from the text.

3. **IDENTIFY MAIN IDEAS AND DETAILS** Why didn't the United States use atomic weapons on Germany to end the war in Europe?

World War II **821**

PLAN

Objective

Learn how the atomic bomb brought an end to World War II.

Critical Thinking Skills for Lesson 4.3

- Identify Main Ideas and Details
- Monitor Comprehension
- Form and Support Opinions
- Ask and Answer Questions
- Summarize
- Draw Conclusions

Essential Question for Chapter 24

How did World War II impact Americans? The U.S. invasion of Japan threatened to be a long, costly battle. Lesson 4.3 discusses the U.S. decision to end the war by dropping two atomic bombs on Japan.

FULBRIGHT–NATIONAL GEOGRAPHIC FELLOW

Ari Beser

In addition to his work with survivors of atomic bombs, Ari Beser regularly blogs about survivors of the 2011 meltdown at Japan's Fukushima Daiichi Nuclear Power Plant. The disaster, the second worst in nuclear power history, occurred after an earthquake and a tsunami crippled three of the plant's reactors, leading to the release of toxic radiation. The immediate area surrounding the plant might remain unsafe for decades. Beser is quick to point out that Japan is the only nation in the world to have experienced both atomic war and a nuclear meltdown. Unlike survivors of Nagasaki and Hiroshima, Fukushima survivors find it difficult to tell their stories because the disaster happened so recently. Beser takes no sides in national conflicts but states that the overarching mission of his work is to help bring about nuclear disarmament.

INTRODUCE & ENGAGE

Activate Prior Knowledge

Brainstorm with students what they already know about the atomic bomb. Record their answers in a Concept Cluster, and then ask what questions they might want answered about the atomic bomb, such as: Why were scientists trying to make an atomic bomb? How did scientists create the atomic bomb? Why did the United States use it against Japan? After the lesson, revise the Concept Cluster to include answers to students' questions and new information students learned. For unanswered questions, guide students in conducting research to find answers.

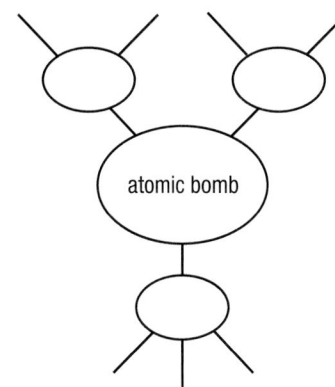

atomic bomb

TEACH

Guided Discussion

1. **Ask and Answer Questions** Imagine you are a reporter investigating the Manhattan Project. What questions would you ask, and how would you find the answers? *(Answers will vary but should include focused questions about the Manhattan Project, such as the following: Why was the project started? Why was it in New Mexico? How many bombs were built? Students might state that they would conduct online research to find answers in encyclopedia articles, government websites, and news archives.)*

2. **Summarize** What details show how the atomic bomb differed from other weapons of war? *(Possible response: In a few seconds, a single bomb could unleash enormous heat, light, and power to destroy nearly an entire city, kill thousands of people, and contaminate the area with radioactivity. No other weapon of war could do this.)*

Draw Conclusions

Discuss with students the ultimatum the United States issued to Japan in late July 1945 in which it promised "prompt and utter destruction" of Japan if it didn't surrender. **ASK:** Why do you think the Japanese refused to surrender despite the seriousness of the U.S. ultimatum? *(Possible response: The Japanese probably did not believe the threat because they had fought U.S. forces before and had not suffered "utter destruction." They didn't know about the atomic bomb and how powerful it was.)*

Active Options

On Your Feet: Paragraph Chain Organize students into four groups and give each group a sheet of chart paper. Assign the following topic sentence: After considering possible consequences and weighing his options, President Truman ordered an atomic bomb to be dropped on Hiroshima. Tell students to build a paragraph on the topic, with each group member writing a sentence on the chart paper. After students finish, have groups present their paragraphs, with students reading the sentences they contributed.

NG Learning Framework: Compose a Journal Entry

SKILL Communication

KNOWLEDGE Our Human Story, Our Living Planet

Tell students to research the immediate and long-term effects of the atomic bombs on Japan. Encourage them to locate print and digital source materials that provide details about the initial blast and the aftermath. Give students the option to explore the long-term environmental effects of the bombings, such as how radiation contaminated the air, soil, and water. Then ask students to write a journal entry from the point of view of a survivor of the blast at Hiroshima or Nagasaki that specifically refers to the atomic bombings. Remind students to use the first-person point of view and their own words to avoid plagiarism. Invite them to share their journal entries with the class.

DIFFERENTIATE

English Language Learners ELD

Use Terms to Write Sentences Pair students at the **Emerging** level with those at the **Bridging** or **Expanding** level. Review the meaning of the following terms: *atomic bomb, nuclear fission,* and *Manhattan Project.* Model composing a sentence using the three terms: Scientists who worked on the Manhattan Project developed an atomic bomb based on the energy released during nuclear fission. Then tell students to review the meaning of the following terms and take turns using multiple terms to compose original sentences: *massive, casualties, invasion, radioactivity, physicists, radiation,* and *surrender.* Invite pairs to share their sentences.

Pre-AP

Write a Report Tell students that the devastation and loss of life caused by the atomic bombs dropped on Japan prompted many organizations to oppose nuclear weapons. In 2017 the International Campaign to Abolish Nuclear Weapons (ICAN) won the Nobel Peace Prize. Instruct students to use information from several library or online sources to write a report about ICAN or about another anti–nuclear weapons group, focusing on such topics as mission and goals, outreach to the public, and achievements. Encourage students to share their reports with the class.

See the Chapter Planner for more strategies for differentiation.

HISTORICAL THINKING

ANSWERS

1. The Manhattan Project was a secret program that developed and built the atomic bombs dropped by the United States on Japan to end World War II.

2. Possible responses: Yes. Even though many Japanese died in the atomic blasts, using the bombs likely saved millions of American and Japanese lives that would have been lost in a full-scale invasion. No. Hiroshima and Nagasaki should not have been bombed because each city had a large civilian population. The United States could have bombed an unpopulated area to demonstrate the power of this new weapon.

3. The bombs weren't needed because the war in Europe was over. Germany had surrendered before the first atomic bomb was tested.

4.4 Legacy of World War II

How does a region recover from a devastating war? How can we rebuild and prevent war in the future? The Allies together sought answers to these questions as World War II ended.

MAIN IDEA After the war, the Allies put German leaders on trial for war crimes and attempted to rebuild Europe from the devastation of World War II.

THE NUREMBERG TRIALS

World War II was history's most destructive war. Total war deaths—both civilian and military—are estimated to have numbered at least 60 million people. The Soviet Union lost approximately 24 million soldiers and civilians, and China lost at least 20 million, although some estimates reach as high as 50 million. Germany lost between 6 and 8 million. American deaths totaled 418,500, of which more than 99 percent (416,800) were soldiers, airmen, and sailors.

After the war was over, the Allies decided to try Nazi leaders for war crimes. The trials were held in the German city of Nuremberg between 1945 and 1946. The charges against the defendants included crimes against peace, war crimes, and crimes against humanity.

The Holocaust was a major factor in establishing the trials. In December 1942, the Allies had issued a joint declaration that called out Germany for the mass murder of Europe's Jews. Once the war ended and the horrific brutality of Germany's work and death camps was exposed, the Allies became even more determined to see justice done. They vowed to prosecute anyone responsible for violence against civilian populations. The Trial of Major War Criminals, best-known as the **Nuremberg trials**, lasted from November 20, 1945, to October 1, 1946. All but three of the defendants received a guilty verdict. Twelve were sentenced to death, and the rest were given prison terms ranging from 10 years to life behind bars.

In later trials, 183 defendants that included Nazi government officials, military leaders, industrialists, physicians, and judges, were convicted on the same charges. Between 1946 and 1948, Japanese leaders were also charged for the Bataan Death March and other war crimes.

REBUILDING THE WORLD

The United States emerged from the war as the world's most powerful nation. In June 1947, U.S. Secretary of State George C. Marshall asked Congress to give the war-ravaged European countries billions of dollars in aid for the countries to spend as they saw fit. The resulting **Marshall Plan** was a $13 billion aid plan to ensure the recovery of Western Europe from the economic devastation caused by the war there. The United States provided most of the money by pledging

The Marshall Plan

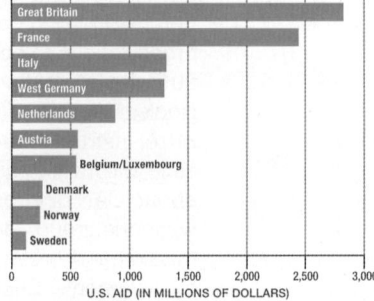

Country	U.S. AID (IN MILLIONS OF DOLLARS)
Great Britain	
France	
Italy	
West Germany	
Netherlands	
Austria	
Belgium/Luxembourg	
Denmark	
Norway	
Sweden	

0 — 500 — 1,000 — 1,500 — 2,000 — 2,500 — 3,000

Source: "The Marshall Plan: A Reality Check," by Nicholas Crafts, 2011

Italian citizens read a poster (also shown at right) that roughly translates to "American aid—wheat, coal, food, medicine— helps Italians to help themselves." The photograph was taken in 1948 at a time when Europe relied heavily on foreign aid for basic necessities.

GLI AIUTI D'AMERICA
GRANO·CARBONE·VIVERI·MEDICINALI
CI AIUTANO AD AIUTARCI DA NOI

more than 10 percent of its entire federal budget. The Marshall Plan was an important part of American and Western European policy to halt the spread of communism from the Soviet Union into the countries of Eastern Europe.

Several weeks later, 17 European nations met in Paris, France, to assess their needs under the Marshall Plan. The Soviets declined their invitation to the meeting. They did not like the idea of giving critical economic information to outsiders. They also felt that taking aid from capitalist countries might undermine the communist Soviet system. Even without Soviet participation, the Marshall Plan successfully restored economic confidence throughout Western Europe.

At the end of World War I, President Woodrow Wilson proposed an international organization to help avoid war by dealing with conflicts among members diplomatically rather than with force. The U.S. Congress failed to ratify the treaty that established this organization. After World War II ended in Europe, the nations of the world tried this

idea again. On April 25, 1945, representatives of 50 nations attended a conference in San Francisco, California, where they formed the United Nations (UN). There they agreed upon the principles of the United Nations Charter: to prevent another war through open communications and to work to guarantee basic human rights for everyone in the world.

HISTORICAL THINKING

1. **READING CHECK** What was the purpose of the Nuremberg trials?

2. **ANALYZE CAUSE AND EFFECT** How were the Marshall Plan and the creation of the UN expected to affect Europe and the rest of the world?

3. **ANALYZE GRAPHS** In total, how much money did the Marshall Plan give to former Axis powers, West Germany and Italy?

PLAN

Objective
Describe the Allies' efforts to restore Europe after World War II.

Critical Thinking Skills for Lesson 4.4
- Identify Main Ideas and Details
- Monitor Comprehension
- Analyze Cause and Effect
- Analyze Graphs
- Draw Conclusions
- Compare and Contrast
- Interpret Graphs

Essential Question for Chapter 24
How did World War II impact Americans? After the war, much of Europe lay in ruins. Lesson 4.4 discusses how the United States and its allies worked to administer justice, rebuild Europe, and establish a lasting peace.

Background for the Teacher
The three types of crimes prosecuted at the Nuremberg trials had important distinctions. Crimes against peace included actions that violated treaties and other international or regional agreements. War crimes were classified as violations of the laws and customs governing warfare, including murder or poor treatment of prisoners of war, killing of hostages, unjustified destruction of towns or cities for other than military reasons, and theft of civilian property. Crimes against humanity covered the most serious actions: extermination, deportation, or other inhumane acts against civilian populations, as well as persecution of those populations on religious, racial, or political grounds, even in cases where the offending nation's laws had not necessarily been violated.

Discuss International Aid

Write the term *international aid* on the board and challenge students to define it. *(voluntary transfer of resources from one country to another)* Then ask students to think about a recent disaster, such as a hurricane, flood, or earthquake, that took place outside the United States. **ASK:** What kinds of aid do nations often provide to another after a disaster? *(food and water, money, clothing, construction help, assistance restoring power, medical and educational materials, military personnel)* Tell students that in Lesson 4.4, they will learn how the United States helped to restore Europe after the war and establish an international peace organization.

TEACH

Guided Discussion

1. **Draw Conclusions** Why did the United States emerge after World War II as the most powerful nation in the world? *(Possible response: The United States is separated from Europe by the Atlantic Ocean and from Asia by the Pacific Ocean, so, unlike much of Europe, it had not experienced bombing or invasion. The U.S. military was strong, with bases positioned around the world as a result of the war. These factors combined with a strong economy boosted by the war effort made the United States the most powerful nation.)*

2. **Compare and Contrast** How did the American and Allied response after World War II differ from their response after World War I? *(Possible response: The Marshall Plan helped all of western Europe recover, including Italy and parts of Germany, instead of punishing the Axis Powers. The United States agreed to join the United Nations after World War II instead of rejecting it as it did its forerunner, the League of Nations, after World War I.)*

Interpret Graphs

Direct students' attention to the Marshall Plan graph. **ASK:** Why do you think Great Britain received the most aid? *(Possible response: Great Britain had been the United States' closest ally during the war, and it had experienced heavy bombing by the German Luftwaffe. The United States likely wanted to support a speedy recovery for Great Britain.)* **ASK:** What does it mean that there are no communist nations on the list? *(Possible response: Since the Soviet Union had refused capitalists' aid, countries under Soviet rule were likely compelled to refuse aid as well.)*

Active Options

On Your Feet: Fishbowl Arrange students in two concentric circles, with both circles facing inward. Ask students in the inner circle to discuss the following question: Besides prosecuting those who committed war crimes, what greater purpose did the Nuremberg trials serve? Direct students in the outer circle to listen and evaluate the discussion. After a time, have students reverse roles and continue the discussion. At the end of the activity, ask the class to summarize conclusions they have reached regarding the question.

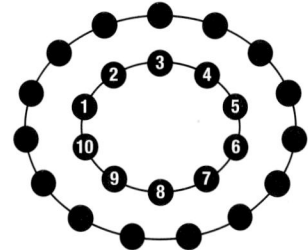

NG Learning Framework: Present a News Report

ATTITUDE Curiosity

KNOWLEDGE Our Human Story

Have students conduct online research to look more deeply into some of the specific events and people involved in the Nuremberg trials. Then ask them to write a short radio news report about a person or event that caught their interest as they researched the topic. Students may deliver their stories live or record them to play back for the class or as part of a class podcast series.

English Language Learners   ELD

Create a Word Web Pair students at the **Emerging** and **Expanding** levels with students at the **Bridging** level. Tell pairs to take turns reading sentences under the subsection The Nuremberg Trials. Instruct students to use a Word Web as they read, writing on the spokes words or terms that refer to important ideas about the trials, their purpose, and the outcome. Direct pairs to trade and compare their webs.

Gifted & Talented

Create a Biographical Profile Tell students to conduct online research to learn more about George C. Marshall in order to write a biographical profile. Instruct them to focus on Marshall's accomplishments, personality, philosophy, strategies, successes, and failures. Encourage students to include photographs, newspaper headlines, and other visuals. Invite them to share their profiles with the class.

See the Chapter Planner for more strategies for differentiation.

HISTORICAL THINKING

ANSWERS

1. Their purpose was to bring German war criminals to justice.

2. The goals of the United Nations were to decrease the chances of another war and establish basic human rights around the world. The goal of the Marshall Plan was to help rebuild Western Europe.

3. The Marshall Plan gave West Germany and Italy a combined total of about $2.75 billion in aid.

24 REVIEW

VOCABULARY

For each pair of vocabulary words, write one sentence that establishes a connection between the words.

1. ideology; fascism

   The ideology of fascism is to put nation and race before the needs of individual citizens.

2. panzer; blitzkrieg

3. anti-Semitism; genocide

4. Allied Powers; deploy

5. barracks; internment camp

6. atoll; island hopping

7. D-Day; amphibious landing craft

8. incendiary bomb; atomic bomb

READING STRATEGY
ANALYZE CAUSE AND EFFECT

If you haven't done so already, complete your chart showing the causes and effects of the United States becoming an Allied Power during World War II. List causes of the event in the top box and the effects of the event in the bottom box.

Causes

↓

Event
United States becomes an Allied Power during WWII

↓

Effects

9. How did United States involvement in World War II impact average Americans at home?

MAIN IDEAS

Answer the following questions. Support your answers with evidence from the chapter.

10. What was the significance of the Rome-Berlin Axis? **LESSON 1.1**

11. What did Winston Churchill mean when he said "The Battle of France is over. The Battle of Britain is about to begin."? **LESSON 1.3**

12. What was the Selective Service and Training Act of 1940? **LESSON 2.1**

13. How did the activities of the War Production Board help the country prepare for war? **LESSON 2.1**

14. What was the "Double V" campaign? **LESSON 2.3**

15. How did the Final Solution connect to Hitler's political ideologies? **LESSON 3.4**

16. Why did U.S. military leaders choose the strategy of island hopping to fight the Japanese? **LESSON 4.2**

17. What war strategy was replaced by the deployment of atomic weapons on Japanese cities? **LESSON 4.3**

18. What steps did the Allies take to help keep peace and rebuild after World War II? **LESSON 4.4**

HISTORICAL THINKING

Answer the following questions. Support your answers with evidence from the chapter.

19. **DETERMINE CHRONOLOGY** What military events in 1940 led to the Battle of Britain?

20. **MAKE INFERENCES** What was the appeal of the fascist movement to citizens in Italy, Germany, and Spain?

21. **SYNTHESIZE** What events and attitudes led to the establishment of internment camps for Japanese Americans during the war?

22. **ANALYZE CAUSE AND EFFECT** How did events of World War I influence the start of World War II?

23. **MAKE CONNECTIONS** How did technology affect the way World War II was fought?

24. **FORM AND SUPPORT OPINIONS** What was the most important factor in President Truman's decision to drop atomic bombs on Hiroshima and Nagasaki?

INTERPRET VISUALS

In this 1941 political cartoon by Daniel Bishop, Uncle Sam carries a cannon to the shores of England. In the background, Adolf Hitler offers a warning. Think about what you have learned about the Lend-Lease Act. Then answer the questions that follow.

Uncle: 'It Would Be Dynamite if I Didn't' — By Bishop

25. Based on the title at the top of the cartoon, what is the illustrator's view of the act?

26. Based on the cartoon and text evidence from the chapter, what was the significance of the United States offering assistance to Great Britain and other countries fighting against Nazi Germany?

ANALYZE SOURCES

Elie Wiesel was a survivor of the Auschwitz concentration camp and an author. He wrote a book about his experiences there called *Night* (1960). In this excerpt, Wiesel explains why he felt it was important to share his story with the world.

> For the survivor who chooses to testify, it is clear: his duty is to bear witness for the dead and for the living. He has no right to deprive [rob] future generations of a past that belongs to our collective memory. To forget would be not only dangerous but offensive; to forget the dead would be akin to killing them a second time.

27. Why would forgetting the victims of the Holocaust be like "killing them a second time"?

CONNECT TO YOUR LIFE

28. **NARRATIVE** In 1945, representatives of the United Nations signed a statement called a preamble that declared the new organization's purpose. In the statement, they expressed that they would like to prevent future wars, support human rights, and promote better standards of living. If you were writing a preamble for your own life, what goals would you list? Think about the kinds of personality traits you would want your friends to say you possessed. Then write four or five points that would help you demonstrate those traits.

TIPS

- Make sure your points reflect your image of yourself in terms of how you choose to act and not the outcomes you seek. A statement like "I promise to get rich" reflects outcomes. A statement like "I will fight for equality" reflects action.

- Use precise words and phrases to convey a vivid description of your traits.

- Conclude the narrative with a summary of the kind of person you would like to be.

VOCABULARY ANSWERS

1. The ideology of fascism is to put nation and race before the needs of individual citizens.

2. Hitler's blitzkrieg strategy was to rapidly unleash troops, planes, ships, and panzers in order to overwhelm a target's defenses.

3. The anti-Semitism of the Axis Powers led to the genocide of European Jews.

4. Troops deployed to North Africa by Allied Powers Great Britain and the United States successfully forced Rommel into retreat.

5. Japanese Americans detained in internment camps were housed in crowded barracks.

6. The Pacific Fleet captured islands in the Midway atoll one after another, island hopping to move closer and closer to Japan.

7. The D-Day invasion at Normandy included amphibious landing craft that carried troops from the ships onto the beaches.

8. Incendiary bombs burned much of Tokyo, and atomic bombs reduced Hiroshima and Nagasaki to rubble.

READING STRATEGY ANSWER

Causes
• German aggression in Europe
• Battle of Britain
• Attack on Pearl Harbor

↓

Event
United States becomes an Allied Power during WWII

↓

Effects
• Massive U.S. war effort
• Japanese American internment
• Allies defeat Axis Powers
• First use of atomic bomb

9. Answers will vary. Students' answers should include impacts on average Americans, such as the enlistment and drafting of American men and the hardship to their families, new job opportunities for minorities and women in the military and in jobs supporting the war effort, the internment of Japanese Americans, rationing, and loss of lives overseas.

MAIN IDEAS ANSWERS

10. The Rome-Berlin Axis was an agreement between Mussolini of Italy and Hitler of Germany that established the Axis Powers of World War II.

11. Churchill was acknowledging that since Hitler had conquered France, he would be attacking Great Britain next.

12. The Selective Service and Training Act made all American men between the ages of 26 and 35 subject to be drafted into military service.

13. The War Production Board oversaw the conversion of factories from making peacetime products, such as cars, to manufacturing planes, tanks, and other equipment and supplies needed for the war effort.

14. The "Double V" campaign urged African-American men to enlist to fight the war against Hitler, which would also be fighting inequality at home, thus gaining two victories in that one effort.

15. Hitler believed that the world contained superior and inferior races. He judged Jewish people as inferior and blamed them as the cause of Germany's problems. The Final Solution was the Nazis' plan to kill all European Jews and rid Germany of its problems.

16. The island-hopping strategy allowed U.S. troops to work their way to attacking Japan by first taking possession of islands that were less strongly defended by the Japanese.

17. The use of atomic weapons allowed the Allies to avoid staging a massive land invasion of Japan.

18. The Allies and other nations joined together to create the United Nations to prevent another war and to protect the human rights of everyone in the world. The Marshall Plan provided funds to countries in western Europe to help them rebuild.

HISTORICAL THINKING ANSWERS

19. Nazi Germany first took Poland, followed by Denmark, Norway, Belgium, the Netherlands, Luxembourg, and finally, France. This left Great Britain alone among the original Allied Powers in Europe to fight the German advance.

20. Fascists promised strong leadership in countries with economic difficulties. They convinced people that only their party could solve each country's economic and social problems.

21. The attack on Pearl Harbor, racism, fear that Japanese Americans would help Japan attack the West Coast of the United States, and ignorance about the Japanese in America led to the internment of Japanese Americans.

22. An economic depression caused in part by the reparations Germany and other countries were forced to pay for their crimes in World War I allowed dictators to rise up in several European countries.

23. Possible response: Submarines made battles possible under the surface of the water. Airplanes were fitted with guns and loaded with bombs to make air raids possible. The development and use of the atomic bomb ended the war, but there were dire consequences.

24. Possible responses: Truman wanted to save hundreds of thousands of American and Japanese lives that might be lost in an invasion of Japan. He wanted to end the war quickly. He felt that Japan would surrender when threatened with a devastating attack.

INTERPRET VISUALS ANSWERS

25. Possible response: The word *dynamite* can be used as a slang term to mean something is great or excellent, so the author is suggesting that it would be great if the United States did not lend or lease arms to Great Britain.

26. Possible response: While the arms to be supplied were intended to fight the Nazis, the United States would have no control over how a country, such as the Soviet Union, might use the arms after the war. In the cartoon, the Hitler character's dire warning about playing with dynamite suggests that the Lend-Lease Act could blow up in Uncle Sam's face if the arms were used to support aggression against countries following World War II.

ANALYZE SOURCES ANSWER

27. Possible response: Killing Holocaust victims robbed them of their lives; forgetting them would rob them again by taking away their role in history of helping future generations understand the tragedy that happened and could happen again.

CONNECT TO YOUR LIFE ANSWER

28. Answers will vary. Students should follow the tips to write a narrative that expresses their desired personality traits and lists four to five points that would help them demonstrate those traits. Students should include a vivid description of their traits that uses precise words and phrases. The narrative should conclude with a summary of the kind of person the student would like to be.

WWI and Mapmaking at National Geographic

By Becky Little

Adapted from "How World War I Launched Mapmaking at National Geographic," by Becky Little, news.nationalgeographic.com, July 16, 2014

In the summer of 1914, Americans began reading news accounts of a conflict that would be called the Great War. The conflict would draw in the United States three years later and eventually also become known as World War I. According to Robert Poole, a former executive editor of *National Geographic*, people followed the war by reading newspapers, "and maps were a very important way to make sense of these faraway places [and] strange names."

World War I broke out in Europe on July 28, 1914. The August 1914 issue of *National Geographic* was changed to include a map of "New Balkan States and Central Europe." The map featured the names of the places where fighting was most severe. The popular map boosted the organization's visibility. By year's end, membership in the National Geographic Society had grown 50 percent, to more than 336,000.

The Balkans map was ready to print on short notice because the magazine's editor, Gilbert H. Grosvenor, had commissioned it in the summer of 1913. He had anticipated heightened conflict in Europe after visiting Great Britain, France, and Russia that summer.

"He could tell that something important was happening in Europe," Poole says. "[He knew] that people needed this sort of information that they weren't getting anywhere else. There was this niche that National Geographic could fit that no one else was fitting. He began to get favorable responses not only from the public, but [also] from the White House, the Navy."

National Geographic is well known today for its maps and atlases. But the magazine did not actually create its own maps during the first 27 years of its existence. Grosvenor had commissioned outside companies to produce both the Balkans map and a 1915 follow-up map of the expanding war front. However, Grosvenor was disappointed with the quality of the initial drafts of the war-front map. Mapmaking at the outside companies also took longer than Grosvenor wanted.

To produce the maps he wanted, Grosvenor established National Geographic's map department in 1915 with a single cartographer, Albert Bumstead. The department's first map supplement was the 1918 "Map of the Western Theatre of War." It provided readers with the name and location of every town or small village that they would likely encounter in reports from the front. The secretary of the Geographic Society of France called it the most complete map of the Western Front. The map launched National Geographic's reputation for detailed mapping.

Those war years marked a turning point for the National Geographic Society—and for the cartography field. "The mapmaking became much more professional during and as a result of World War I," Poole says. "People began to associate Nat Geo with cartographic authenticity. They knew that they could go to National Geographic for reliable info."

The development of mapmaking expertise during World War I laid the foundation for the role that National Geographic would play in World War II. During the Second World War, the *New York Times* wrote that the Society's maps were "to be found at the front, in the air, in our embassies and consulates."

"National Geographic supplied the White House with maps for the White House map room," Poole says. "[President Roosevelt] would go over the maps with his chief advisers, keep track of the action, what was happening in the war, by following those maps." Later, according to Poole, the leaders of the United States, Great Britain, and the Soviet Union "were actually using a National Geographic map to decide what postwar Europe would look like."

For more from National Geographic, check out "Untold Stories of D-Day" online.

UNIT INQUIRY: Respond to a Crisis

In this unit, you learned about major crises that Americans faced in the first half of the 20th century. They confronted not only two world wars but also the worst economic depression the country had ever known. Based on your understanding of the text, in what ways did government leaders, businesses, organizations, and individual Americans respond to these crises? How did leaders, groups, and individuals work together to survive and prevail through the troubled times?

ASSIGNMENT

Choose one of the crises that you've read about in this unit, such as America's entry into World War I, the stock market crash of 1929, the Dust Bowl, or the bombing of Pearl Harbor. Consider what the ideal response of your community's government, schools, businesses, and individual citizens would be to the crisis. Outline an action plan for the various groups. Be prepared to present your action plan to the class and explain the reasons for the actions you suggest.

Gather Evidence As you consider your action plan, gather evidence from this unit about the ways Americans actually responded to the crisis you have chosen. Note the challenges that the crisis posed and how those challenges were addressed. Think about the benefits and drawbacks of the various reactions to the crisis. Use a graphic organizer like this one to help organize your evidence.

CRISIS	
CHALLENGES	RESPONSES

Produce Use your notes to create an action plan for the following groups in your community: the government, schools, businesses, and individual citizens. For each group, outline a list of actions they might take to help address the challenges posed by the crisis.

Present Choose a creative way to present your action plan to the class. Consider one of these options:

- Create an illustrated poster that shows the challenges you've identified and the actions that you propose each group take.

- Stage a debate with a classmate in which each of you present your ideas and debate the best actions to take.

- Organize teams based on the particular crisis that students chose. Hold team discussions on ways to respond to the crisis.

NATIONAL GEOGRAPHIC | LEARNING FRAMEWORK ACTIVITIES

Research War Damage

SKILLS Communication

KNOWLEDGE Our Living Planet

Besides taking the lives of many people, warfare also kills other living organisms and scars the natural environment. Environmental damage results not only from the warfare itself but also from the need to exploit natural resources to manufacture weapons and supplies. Research the environmental damage caused by World War I or World War II. You might focus on the damage in a specific area or region, such as Europe or Hiroshima, or investigate the overall environmental damage. Use your findings to prepare a multimedia presentation for the class.

Share the Arts of the 1920s

ATTITUDE Empowerment

SKILLS Collaboration, Observation

At the end of World War I, drastic changes in attitude and expression occurred in the United States. Young Americans sought something different and exciting. New developments in art, architecture, fashion, music, and literature occurred. Work in pairs or as a small group to investigate one of these forms of expression. Share examples of the art, fashion, or music of the 1920s with the class through a presentation or demonstration. Explain how the form of expression differs from those of previous generations.

NATIONAL GEOGRAPHIC CONNECTION

Guided Discussion for "WWI and Mapmaking at National Geographic"

1. **Analyze Cause and Effect** What were some results of *National Geographic*'s inclusion of the "New Balkan States and Central Europe" map in its August 1914 issue? *(Possible response: Membership in the National Geographic Society greatly expanded, National Geographic added its own in-house maps department, and the magazine won a reputation for featuring accurate and detailed maps.)*

2. **Make Inferences** Why do you think people in the United States might have been interested in having access to detailed maps of the fighting in Europe in 1914? *(Possible response: Americans had begun reading accounts of the conflict in Europe, and maps were a way to make sense of "faraway places [and] strange names." Additionally, when the United States entered the war in 1917, maps would have been a way for families to see where their soldiers were stationed or fighting.)*

Guided Discussion for "Untold Stories of D-Day"

1. **Summarize** What potential "intelligence nightmare" concerned General Dwight D. Eisenhower in the aftermath of the failed Exercise Tiger action, and how did he address the problem? *(Possible response: Eisenhower worried that U.S. soldiers captured by the Germans during Exercise Tiger might have had highly classified Allied military information that would reveal Allied plans for D-Day. He ordered Allied code breakers to monitor German communications to find out whether the Germans had information about the real D-Day operations.)*

2. **Ask and Answer Questions** Imagine that you had the chance to interview Joe Vaghi or another D-Day soldier about his experiences on Omaha Beach. What questions would you want to ask him, and how do you think he might respond? *(Answers will vary, but questions and answers should reflect details and ideas from the text about events prior to the invasion and on D-Day itself.)*

UNIT INQUIRY PROJECT RUBRIC

Assess

Use the rubric to assess each student's participation and performance.

SCORE	ASSIGNMENT	PRODUCT	PRESENTATION
3 GREAT	• Student thoroughly understands the assignment. • Student participates fully in the project process. • Student works well with team members.	• Action plan is well thought out. • Action plan offers a number of examples of the benefits and drawbacks of the selected response to the crisis. • Action plan contains all of the key elements listed in the assignment.	• Presentation is clear, concise, and logical. • Presentation does a good job of creatively representing all aspects of the action plan. • Presentation engages the audience.
2 GOOD	• Student mostly understands the assignment. • Student participates fairly well in the project process. • Student works fairly well with team members.	• Action plan is fairly well thought out. • Action plan offers at least two examples of the benefits and drawbacks of the selected response to the crisis. • Action plan contains most of the key elements listed in the assignment.	• Presentation is fairly clear, concise, and logical. • Presentation does an adequate job of creatively representing most aspects of the action plan. • Presentation somewhat engages the audience.
1 NEEDS WORK	• Student does not understand the assignment. • Student minimally participates or does not participate in the project process. • Student does not work well with team members.	• Action plan is not well thought out. • Action plan does not offer examples of the benefits and drawbacks of the selected response to the crisis. • Action plan contains few or none of the key elements listed in the assignment.	• Presentation is not clear, concise, or logical. • Presentation does an inadequate job of representing aspects of the action plan. • Presentation does not engage the audience.

NATIONAL GEOGRAPHIC LEARNING FRAMEWORK RUBRIC

Assess

Use the rubric to assess how each student applies the National Geographic Learning Framework.

SCORE	ASSIGNMENT	ASSIGNMENT	FINAL PRODUCTS
3 GREAT	• Presentation demonstrates **Communication** well. • Presentation explores **Our Living Planet** well.	• Presentation reflects **Empowerment** well. • Presentation demonstrates **Collaboration** and **Observation** well.	• Final products are engaging, creative, and well presented.
2 GOOD	• Presentation demonstrates **Communication**. • Presentation explores **Our Living Planet**.	• Presentation reflects **Empowerment**. • Presentation demonstrates **Collaboration** and **Observation**.	• Final products are interesting, logical, and complete.
1 NEEDS WORK	• Presentation does not demonstrate **Communication**. • Presentation does not explore **Our Living Planet**.	• Presentation does not reflect **Empowerment**. • Presentation does not demonstrate **Collaboration** or **Observation**.	• Final products are not creative, complete, or interesting.

Selma, Alabama, 1965

On February 1, 1965, Martin Luther King, Jr., and more than 700 other activists were arrested in Selma, Alabama, for demonstrating in support of voting rights for African Americans. While in jail, Dr. King penned a letter to the *New York Times* in which he noted that there were more African Americans locked up with him than there were listed on the voter registration roles. Dr. King's observation was an accurate reflection of a sad reality. According to a 1961 report by the Civil Rights Commission, less than one percent of voting-age African Americans in Montgomery County were registered to vote. In the 1960s, Selma was located in this county.

Then on February 18, a little more than two weeks after Dr. King's arrest, 26-year-old civil rights activist Jimmie Lee Jackson was shot and killed by Alabama state trooper James Bonard Fowler in Marion, Alabama. Jackson had been protesting the arrest of fellow activist James Orange, and his death sparked outrage. Dr. King spoke at Jackson's funeral, and in March, he led the Selma-to-Montgomery march featured in this photo. The event was both a protest against Jackson's killing and a demonstration for basic civil rights, including the right to vote.

In 2007, 42 years after Jackson was killed, 77-year-old James Fowler was finally charged with murder, although the charge was eventually reduced to manslaughter. Fowler pleaded guilty and served less than six months in jail for Jackson's death.

ASK: Why do you think the marchers decided to carry an American flag? *(Possible response: The marchers might have wanted to dramatize their belief that the United States stood for justice and freedom and that, in the end, justice would prevail.)* **ASK:** Why do you think civil rights activists focused on voting rights? *(Possible response: The United States is a democracy, which means that all citizens must have a voice in how they are governed. Without the ability to vote, citizens have little power in the country's political process.)*

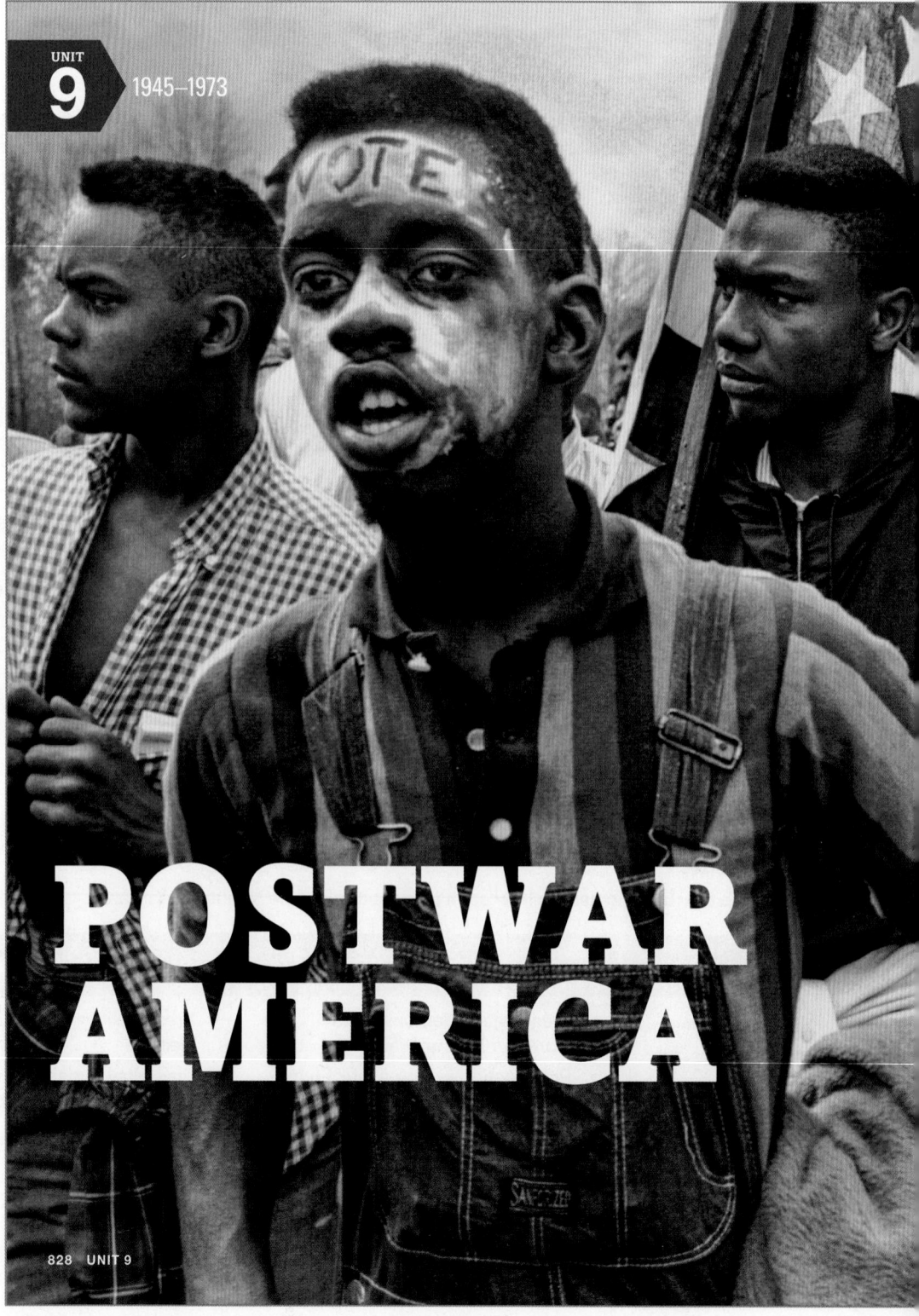

UNIT
9 1945–1973

POSTWAR AMERICA

828 UNIT 9

CRITICAL VIEWING In 1965, Selma, Alabama, was arguably the hub of civil rights activism. This photo shows protesters led by Martin Luther King, Jr., marching from Selma to Montgomery to demand voting rights for African Americans. Months later, Congress would pass the Voting Rights Act of 1965, outlawing literacy tests and other discriminatory practices used to deny minorities the right to vote. What does this photo reveal about the mood of the Selma-to-Montgomery marches and the sentiments of the marchers?

829

Bobby Simmons

The young man in the foreground of the photograph is 18-year-old Bobby Simmons. On March 25, 1965, while marching from Selma to Montgomery, Simmons rubbed a pale white sun-blocking product called zinc oxide on his face and then scratched the word *VOTE* into his forehead. A photographer captured the image, and this photograph became a symbol of the civil rights movement in general and of the voting rights campaign in particular. The Selma-to-Montgomery march was just one of many protests in which Simmons and thousands of other young people participated during the 1960s. Many observers note that young people were, in fact, the backbone of the civil rights movement.

CRITICAL VIEWING Possible response: The young man in the foreground has painted his face white and written *VOTE* across his forehead, making his sentiments about the importance of voting rights clear. The expressions on the marchers' faces show determination, concern, anger, and perhaps fear. Another young man carries an American flag, which shows the marchers still believe in their country and its promise of equal rights for all citizens.

1949 ASIA:
The People's Republic of China

In 1949, Mao Zedong ousted the leader of the opposition party, Chiang Kai-shek, and founded the communist People's Republic of China. It did not take the West long to realize that Mao's takeover of China would shift the global balance of power, giving the Soviet Union a major new eastern ally. With China providing support in the East, the Soviets were free to focus their efforts against the combined forces of the Western allies.

Mao had a very specific vision for China, and he began to change Chinese society to reflect this vision. He ordered the state to seize control of all industries and mandated that farmers organize into farming collectives. Mao was determined to create a distinctly Chinese form of communism. As a consequence, the relationship between China and the Soviet Union eventually began to erode. Mao remained a strict authoritarian leader, ruthlessly shutting down any and all opposition from inside China.

To accomplish his economic goals, Mao implemented a series of programs known collectively as the Great Leap Forward, marshaling China's labor force to increase industrial and agricultural output. The plan backfired, however, due to a combination of faulty implementation methods and unusually small harvests. The nation descended into famine, and millions starved to death. Mao eventually abandoned his Great Leap Forward, but the disaster significantly diminished his power and reputation.

ASK: What effect might the emergence of Mao as the leader of China have had on American politics and culture? *(Possible response: The United States feared communism, and Mao represented a new threat, especially in terms of an alliance between China and the Soviet Union. The United States would have viewed China as a powerful new enemy and acted accordingly.)*

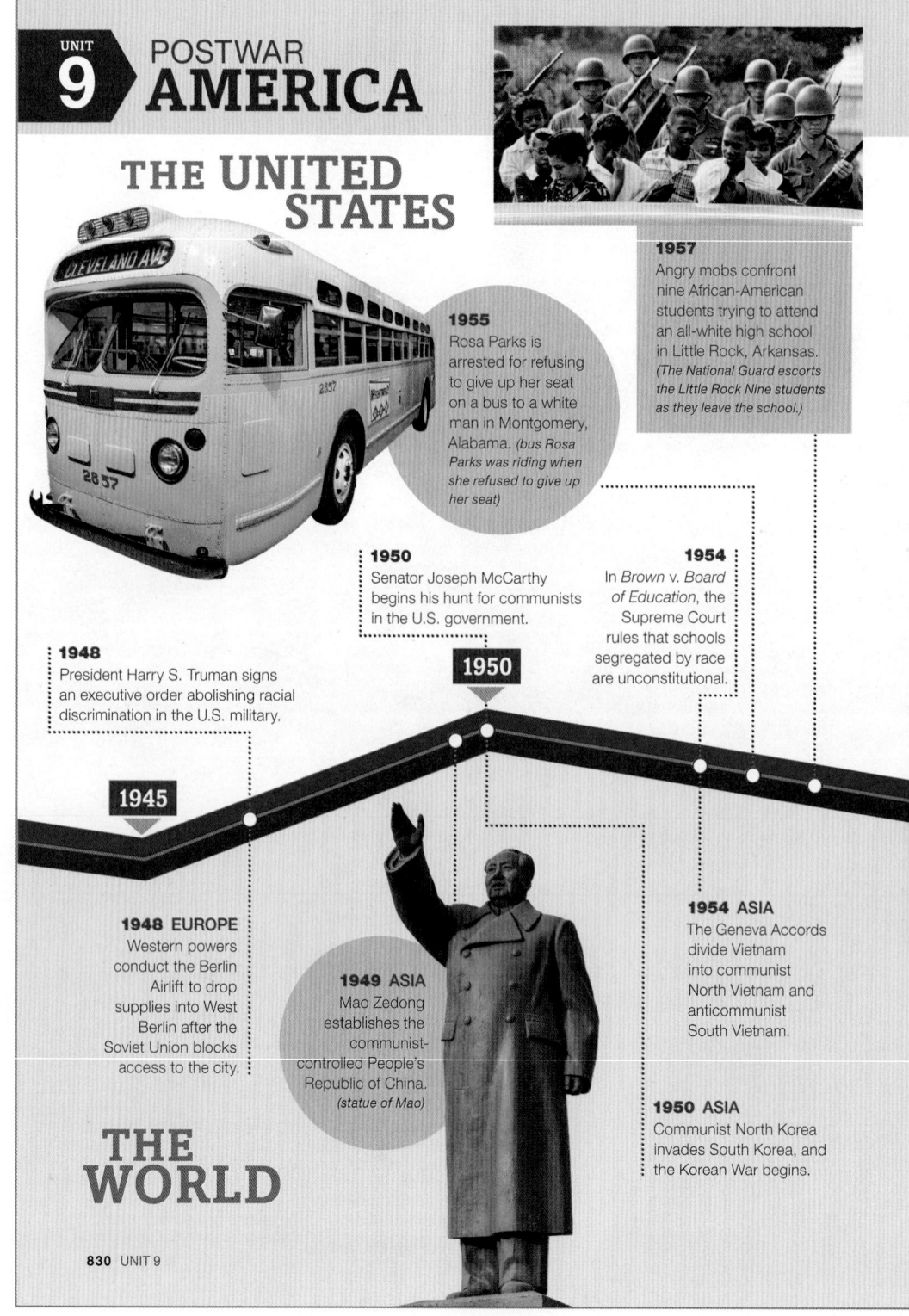

UNIT 9

POSTWAR AMERICA

THE UNITED STATES

1957
Angry mobs confront nine African-American students trying to attend an all-white high school in Little Rock, Arkansas. *(The National Guard escorts the Little Rock Nine students as they leave the school.)*

1955
Rosa Parks is arrested for refusing to give up her seat on a bus to a white man in Montgomery, Alabama. *(bus Rosa Parks was riding when she refused to give up her seat)*

1950
Senator Joseph McCarthy begins his hunt for communists in the U.S. government.

1954
In *Brown* v. *Board of Education*, the Supreme Court rules that schools segregated by race are unconstitutional.

1948
President Harry S. Truman signs an executive order abolishing racial discrimination in the U.S. military.

1950

1945

1948 EUROPE
Western powers conduct the Berlin Airlift to drop supplies into West Berlin after the Soviet Union blocks access to the city.

1949 ASIA
Mao Zedong establishes the communist-controlled People's Republic of China. *(statue of Mao)*

1954 ASIA
The Geneva Accords divide Vietnam into communist North Vietnam and anticommunist South Vietnam.

1950 ASIA
Communist North Korea invades South Korea, and the Korean War begins.

THE WORLD

830 UNIT 9

HISTORICAL THINKING: DETERMINE CHRONOLOGY

What earlier occurrence in Asia is probably related to events that took place in the United States in 1964 and in Asia in 1968?

1962
Astronaut John Glenn becomes the first American to orbit Earth.
(helmet Glenn wore when he orbited Earth)

1964
The Gulf of Tonkin Resolution gives President Lyndon Johnson the power to expand the U.S. presence in the Vietnam War. *(carrier U.S.S. Constellation involved in the Gulf of Tonkin incident)*

1968
Martin Luther King, Jr., and Robert Kennedy are assassinated.

1963
President Kennedy is assassinated.

1970

1973
Members of the American Indian Movement occupy Wounded Knee, South Dakota, to protest the conditions on reservations.

1961
President John F. Kennedy establishes the Peace Corps.

1960

1962 AMERICAS
The United States and the Soviet Union face off after the Soviets begin building missile sites in Cuba.

1975

1961 EUROPE
Communists construct a wall between East Berlin and West Berlin to prevent people from leaving East Germany.

1960 AFRICA
Seventeen African nations gain their independence.
(flag of Mauritania)

1968 ASIA
North Vietnam launches the Tet Offensive against South Vietnamese cities and military bases.
(a battle in Saigon following the Tet Offensive)

Postwar America **831**

INTRODUCE TIME LINE EVENT

1960 AFRICA:
Decolonization in Africa

The year 1960 was a pivotal time in the decolonization of the African continent. Of the 17 nations that asserted their independence that year, 14 had been ruled by France. Some African nations had already broken free of colonial rule, including Egypt in 1922, Ethiopia in 1941, Libya in 1951, and Sudan, Morocco, Tunisia, Ghana, and Guinea between 1956 and 1958. Despite this great surge of independence, not all African nations were free from outside rule by 1960. Angola and Mozambique did not become independent until 1975, and Zimbabwe not until 1980. Namibia, colonized first by Germany and later by South Africa, finally became an independent African nation in 1990.

The 20 years following 1960 became known as the golden era of African development, mostly the result of the newly independent nations spending vast sums of money to support new infrastructure. By the 1980s, however, most of the newly independent nations' economies were in decline. **ASK:** What benefits do you think the 17 African nations hoped for after gaining their independence? *(Possible response: They wanted the opportunity to build their own governments and economies and to use their national resources for their own benefit and not the benefit of a colonial nation.)*

HISTORICAL THINKING: DETERMINE CHRONOLOGY

Answer: When the 1954 Geneva Accords split Vietnam into the communist North and the anticommunist South, war between North Vietnam and South Vietnam became a likely consequence. In 1964, the Gulf of Tonkin Resolution expanded U.S. presence in that conflict. In 1968, the North Vietnamese launched the Tet Offensive, which shook American confidence that U.S. forces could win the war.

UNIT 9 RESOURCES

UNIT INTRODUCTION

UNIT TIME LINE

UNIT WRAP-UP

NATIONAL GEOGRAPHIC | CONNECTION

National Geographic Magazine Adapted Articles
• "50 Years of Wilderness"
• "Slipping the Bonds" ONLINE

Unit 9 Inquiry: Protest an Injustice

NG Learning Framework Activities
• Compile a Song Medley
• Build Models

Unit 9 Formal Assessment

CHAPTER 25 RESOURCES

Available at NGLSync.Cengage.com

TEACHER RESOURCES & ASSESSMENT

Reading and Note-Taking

Vocabulary Practice

Social Studies Skills Lessons
• Reading: Summarize
• Writing: Write an Expository Paragraph

Formal Assessment
• Chapter 25 Pretest
• Chapter 25 Tests A & B
• Section Quizzes

Chapter 25 Answer Key

ExamView®
One-time Download

"Anything you want we got right here in the U.S.A."
—Chuck Berry, "Back in the U.S.A."

STUDENT DIGITAL RESOURCES

• eEdition (English)	• Online Atlas	• Active History
• eEdition (Spanish)	• American Gallery Online	• Projects for Inquiry-Based Learning
• Handbooks	• History Notebook	

Chapter 25 Spanish Resources are available at NGLSync.Cengage.com.

AMERICAN STORIES | TV Nation

- Primary Sources
- On Your Feet: Create a TV Museum Exhibit

NG Learning Framework:
Analyze Society Through Television

SECTION 1 RESOURCES

PEACETIME ADJUSTMENTS

LESSON 1.1
A Postwar Economic Boom

- On Your Feet: Fishbowl

NG Learning Framework:
Research Executive Order 9981

LESSON 1.2
Truman's Fair Deal

- On Your Feet: Card Responses

NG Learning Framework:
Compare Elections

SECTION 2 RESOURCES

THE COLD WAR, KOREA, AND MCCARTHYISM

LESSON 2.1
The Cold War Starts

- Active History: Compare Cold War Enemies

NG Learning Framework:
Script a Documentary Film

LESSON 2.2
Communism in Asia

- On Your Feet: Tell Me More

NG Learning Framework:
Create an Annotated Time Line

LESSON 2.3
The Korean War

- On Your Feet: Sequence Chain

NG Learning Framework:
Learn About North Korea Today

LESSON 2.4
Fear of Communism

- On Your Feet: Create a Concept Web

NG Learning Framework:
Explore Perspectives

SECTION 3 RESOURCES

THE FIFTIES

LESSON 3.1
The American Dream?

- On Your Feet: Numbered Heads

NG Learning Framework:
Create an Infographic

LESSON 3.2
GEOGRAPHY IN HISTORY
The Suburbanization of America

- On Your Feet: Fishbowl

NG Learning Framework:
Design a City and Its Suburbs

LESSON 3.3
Television and Rock and Roll

- ▶ The Motown Sound

 Rock and Roll

NG Learning Framework:
Create a Multimedia Fanzine

CHAPTER 25 REVIEW

Strategy ❶
Use a K-W-L Chart

Provide each student with a K-W-L Chart. Have students brainstorm what they already know about the post-World War II era, such as the return of veterans, the Cold War, or the Korean War. Have students write these topics in the first column of the chart. Then ask them to write in the second column of the chart questions they have about each topic, such as: What happened when so many veterans returned? or Why did the Cold War start? or Why were Americans fighting in the Korean War? Remind students to complete the third column of their chart as they read each lesson in the chapter.

K What Do I Know?	W What Do I Want To Learn?	L What Did I Learn?

Use with All Lessons

Strategy ❷
Use a TASKS Approach

Help students get information from visuals by using the following TASKS strategy.

T Look for a **title** that may give the main idea.
A **Ask** yourself what the visual is trying to show.
S Determine how **symbols** are used.
K Look for a **key** or legend.
S **Summarize** what you learned.

Use with Lessons 1.2, 2.1, 2.3, and 3.2 *Suggest that students use the TASKS strategy to analyze the maps and photographs in these lessons.*

Strategy ❸
Make a Top Facts List

Tell students to reread the lesson and the captions for the lesson's visuals. Then ask them to write down three to five key facts they remember from the text. Have students work with a partner to compare their lists against the lesson for accuracy. Then encourage pairs to consolidate their two lists into one final list of key facts.

Use with All Lessons

Strategy ❶
Use Supported Reading

Have students read the chapter aloud lesson by lesson. Instruct them to stop at the end of each lesson and use these sentence frames to monitor their comprehension of the text:

- This lesson is mostly about _____.
- Other topics in this lesson are _____ and _____.
- One question I have is _____.
- One of the vocabulary words is _____, and it means _____.
- One word I don't recognize is _____.

Use with All Lessons

Strategy ❷
Build a Time Line

After students read each lesson, instruct them to identify key events of the time period immediately following World War II, and add them to a time line on the board. You can expand and extend the time line, and guide students to suggest more key events as they read each lesson in the chapter.

Use with All Lessons *For example, key events from Lesson 1.1 might include the passage of the GI Bill of Rights (1944), the invention of the portable transistor radio (1947), and the signing of Executive Order 9981, ending racial segregation in the military (1948).*

ENGLISH LANGUAGE LEARNERS

Strategy ❶
Compose Captions

Pair students at the **Emerging** and **Expanding** levels of proficiency with English-proficient students. Direct them to work together to read the chapter and then write an original caption for one photograph in each lesson of the chapter. Invite pairs to compare their captions with those written by other pairs and to revise their work as necessary.

Use with All Lessons *You can expand this activity to include the VA poster in Lesson 1.1.*

Strategy ❷
Use Visuals to Predict Content

Direct students at the **Emerging** or **Expanding** level of proficiency to read the lesson title and look at the visuals. Then ask them to write a sentence predicting how the visuals are related to the lesson. After reading, you may wish to have students verify their predictions and reword their sentences, if necessary.

Use with All Lessons *Encourage students to ask questions if they have trouble writing a prediction. You may ask students at the **Bridging** level to help students at the **Emerging** and **Expanding** levels write their predictions.*

Strategy ❸
Pair Partners for Dictation

After reading a lesson, direct students at **All Proficiencies** to think of a sentence that states an important idea from the reading. Pair students and let them take turns dictating their sentences to each other. Then ask them to work together to check the spelling and accuracy of their statements.

Use with All Lessons

GIFTED & TALENTED

Strategy ❶
Create a Gallery Walk

To help students learn more about the issues of the 1950s, instruct them to conduct online research to find resources such as 1950s song lyrics, editorial cartoons, newspaper headlines, photographs, movie posters, and quotations from important people. Encourage students to work together to group their findings by theme, such as TV's growing influence. Have them set up stations with gallery-style labels connecting the resources on display with the larger social, political, and economic issues of the decade. Students can then conduct a gallery walk of all the stations.

Use with All Lessons

Strategy ❷
Create a Graphic Biography

Tell students to conduct online research about one of the people mentioned in the chapter and create a graphic-novel-style biography. Students can include quotations from or about the individual and visuals illustrating the individual's role in the postwar period. Invite students to share their completed graphic biographies with the class and to answer questions about their work.

Use with Lessons 1.2, 2.2, 2.4, and 3.3

Pre-AP

Strategy ❶
Write a News Report

Assign students the role of a foreign correspondent covering either China's civil war or the Korean War. Instruct them to conduct research about the U.S. role in these conflicts, both in terms of the actual fighting and in the context of the Cold War, and then write a detailed news story that includes eyewitness accounts. Remind students that news reports begin with the most important information and answer the questions *Who? What? Where? When?* and *How?* Invite students to post their articles on a class or school blog.

Use with Lessons 2.2–2.3

Strategy ❷
Extend Knowledge

Invite students to conduct research about a topic or event introduced in Chapter 25. For example, students might choose the Taft-Hartley Act, the Berlin Airlift, or Levittown. Encourage them to discover little-known facts or information that might provide a different perspective on their topic. Students can present their findings to the class in an oral presentation or as a digital report on the class blog.

Use with All Lessons

THE COLD WAR AND THE AMERICAN DREAM

1945–1959

ESSENTIAL QUESTION
How did the United States change after World War II?

AMERICAN STORIES TV Nation

SECTION 1 **Peacetime Adjustments**
KEY VOCABULARY
demobilization   national health insurance
low-cost housing

SECTION 2 **The Cold War, Korea, and McCarthyism**
KEY VOCABULARY
blacklist   containment   occupation zone
bloc   McCarthyism   reunify
brinkmanship

SECTION 3 **The Fifties**
KEY VOCABULARY
baby boom   situation comedy
Frostbelt   Sunbelt

AMERICAN GALLERY
ONLINE   Rock and Roll

READING STRATEGY

SUMMARIZE

When you summarize, you restate text in your own words and shorten it by including only the most important main ideas and details. As you read this chapter, use a graphic organizer like this one to help you summarize important information about topics in the text. In the three columns, note key details. Then use your notes to write your summary about one of the topics in this chapter.

Supporting Detail	Supporting Detail	Supporting Detail
Many service members came home all at once after World War II.		
Summary		

CRITICAL VIEWING In 1953, this audience wore special glasses to watch a movie in three dimensions (3-D). Different-colored lenses created an illusion of depth in the film. Although 3-D technology had been around since the 1830s, and in movies since 1922, it became a novelty only in the 1950s when major Hollywood studios produced their first 3-D films. Do you think everyone in this audience is enjoying the 3-D effect? Explain your answer.

"Anything you want we got right here in the U.S.A."

—Chuck Berry, "Back in the U.S.A."

INTRODUCE THE PHOTOGRAPH

3-D Movies

Tell students that the first 3-D films were part of a short-lived craze during the early 1950s. As television became more popular, the movie industry needed a gimmick to attract moviegoers back into theaters. The new movies gave people something television couldn't—the feeling that objects were moving out of the screen straight at the audience. To achieve this effect, the movies were filmed with two cameras and then played on side-by-side projectors that ran the two reels—one for each eye—in sync. Audiences wore special glasses that helped combine the images from the two projected films into one 3-D movie. **ASK:** Why do you think the movie industry might have been worried about the spread of television? *(Possible response: Because people could watch a variety of programs in their own homes, they would go to theaters less often, hurting the movie industry's profits.)*

For Chapter 25 Spanish Resources, visit the Resources Menu. Chapter 25 Resources are available at NGLSync.Cengage.com.

Share Background

Although 3-D movies are still made today, they are usually reserved for action, horror, or animated productions. Their decline in the 1950s and 1960s was due to two main factors. First, 3-D movies were expensive to show in theaters. Because the films required two separate reels, the movie studios charged a rental fee for both reels, twice the fee for a regular film. Most moviegoers weren't willing to pay double the price for tickets, so many theaters rented only one of the reels, thereby destroying the 3-D effect. Second, if one of the reels ran slightly behind the other, a moviegoer's eyes and brain had to work hard to compensate for the images being out of sync. The result was often a pounding headache.

CRITICAL VIEWING Possible response: People appear to be having mixed reactions to the movie. Some appear to be enjoying it; others look apprehensive or even a bit bored; and still others may be physically uncomfortable with the visual effects of 3-D.

INTRODUCE THE ESSENTIAL QUESTION

How did the United States change after World War II?

Jigsaw Activity: Preview Content This activity will help students preview and make predictions about the topics covered in Chapter 25. Divide the class into three groups. Assign one of the section titles to each group and have them discuss what they think they will learn. Ask students to consider the following questions:

Group 1: Section 1 is about the United States returning to peacetime. What problems might Americans face as they return to a peacetime economy?

Group 2: Section 2 is about the Cold War between the United States and the Soviet Union. Why might the United States worry about the spread of communism?

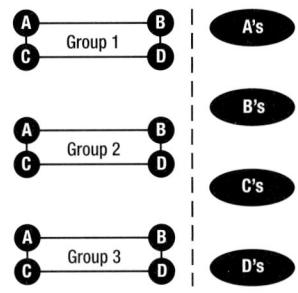

Group 3: Section 3 is about American society and culture in the 1950s. How might prosperity, television, and a growing youth culture change society?

Regroup students so each new group has at least one member from each original group. Have students share their predictions about their section so that others can learn what to expect from reading Chapter 25.

INTRODUCE CHAPTER VOCABULARY

Word Webs

As they read the chapter, have students complete Word Webs for Key Vocabulary words. Tell students to write each word in the center of an oval and look through the chapter for examples, characteristics, and descriptive words that they associate with the vocabulary word. Model an example for students on the board, using the graphic organizer below.

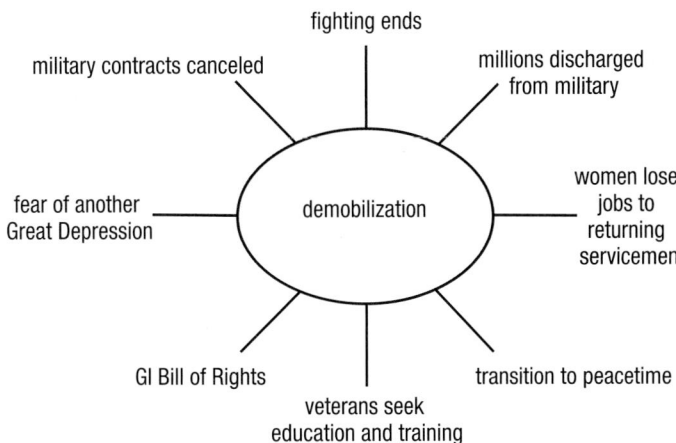

INTRODUCE THE READING STRATEGY

SUMMARIZE
Remind students that when they summarize text, they restate the main ideas and supporting details in their own words. Encourage students to use a graphic organizer to keep track of the supporting details they might include in a summary of a lesson. Complete the following graphic organizer as a class. Ask for suggestions regarding details from Lesson 1.1 and write a summary. Remind students to use the graphic organizer for the remaining lessons of the chapter.

Supporting Detail	Supporting Detail	Supporting Detail
Many service members came home all at once after World War II.		
Summary		

KEY DATES FOR CHAPTER 25

1944	Congress passes the GI Bill of Rights
1945	Allies divide Berlin into four occupation zones
1947	Congress passes the Taft-Hartley Act
1948	Allies launch Berlin Airlift to counteract Soviet blockade
1948	President Truman signs Executive Order 9981
1949	North Atlantic Treaty Organization (NATO) is formed
1949	Mao proclaims the People's Republic of China
1953	Armistice ends Korean War in a stalemate
1954	Senator McCarthy's anticommunist campaign ends
1956	President Eisenhower signs Federal-Aid Highway Act

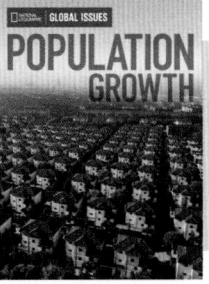

For more on factors that impact population growth, see *GLOBAL ISSUES: POPULATION GROWTH.*

STEM

Objectives

- **Analyze how television reflected and influenced American identity.**
- **Identify popular television program genres during the postwar era.**
- **Evaluate how accurately early television reflected American society.**
- **Study primary sources from early television programs and advertisements.**

Critical Thinking Skills for "TV Nation"

- Draw Conclusions
- Make Connections
- Compare and Contrast
- Identify
- Make Inferences
- Analyze Primary Sources
- Evaluate
- Analyze Cause and Effect

Background for the Teacher

This American Story examines the growth of television in the 1950s and 1960s and how the medium both reflected and influenced American identity and culture. By reading this engaging essay, filled with examples of important television programs and milestones from the era, students will understand how television shaped American society. Its entertainment and news programs provided Americans with a common cultural experience and unleashed a demand for products that helped fuel a postwar economic boom.

The upcoming chapter, The Cold War and the American Dream, analyzes the changes that took place throughout postwar American society. As American troops and personnel returned from the war in Europe and the Pacific, many yearned for a peaceful, comfortable life and found it in the sprawling suburbs. Television reinforced this idyllic image of the American dream while ignoring its darker side. This American Story chronicles the birth of the TV nation in the United States.

History Notebook

Encourage students to complete the American Story page for Chapter 25 in their History Notebooks as they read.

Note to the Teacher

Introduce this American Story after the class has engaged with the content in Lesson 3.3.

AMERICAN STORIES

NATIONAL GEOGRAPHIC

TVNATION

834 CHAPTER 25

CRITICAL VIEWING New Yorkers watch the 1953 live coronation of Queen Elizabeth on a display television in a store window. What does this photograph suggest about the availability of televisions in the early 1950s and the impact television had on society?

Today, our viewing options are almost staggering in number. We can watch content on a smartphone, tablet, laptop, or desktop computer. We can choose from cable networks, Internet streaming services, and videos posted by friends and strangers. Or we can relax in front of a flat-screen TV at home, watching a program produced by an old-fashioned broadcast network.

In the 1950s, the entertainment scene was much simpler. Sitting in front of your family's one TV set to watch one show at a time was the only option. Television had three national networks—NBC, ABC, and CBS—and color TVs were not common until the mid-1960s. Even so, families were hurrying to buy their first TVs, and the United States was becoming a TV nation.

THE 1950s: HAPPY FAMILIES

While the number of networks was small, the variety of programming was broad enough to satisfy even the pickiest viewer. You could watch comedies, dramas, Westerns, variety shows, and news programs. The situation comedy, or "sitcom," originated in the earliest days of television and remains popular today. A sitcom is a half-hour comedy show with a cast of characters that appears every week. In the 1950s, like today, many sitcoms revolved around the lives and adventures of a single family.

The sitcoms of the 1950s generally reflected both the stereotypes and dreams of some Americans. Popular shows such as *Father Knows Best, Ozzie*

The Cold War and the American Dream **835**

INTRODUCE & ENGAGE

Rate the Shows

Ask students to call out television programs or other media shows they've enjoyed watching or have heard about, and record the titles on the board. Then ask students to rate the shows, from one to four stars, and choose the top 10. Review the list with the class and identify any common themes, situations, or messages across the shows. Discuss what the shows say about American identity and culture—who we are and what we value. Tell students that this American Story will examine how television reflected and shaped American culture in the 1950s and 1960s.

Media Then and Now

Ask students to think about the various ways Americans currently watch entertainment, get news, and learn about new products. Conduct a class discussion, asking questions such as the following: How many viewing options do people presently have? What does it mean if people get news from different sources? Are there any programs almost all Americans watch? Write students' ideas on the board.

Inform students that in the 1950s, only three major television networks existed, and you could watch a show only when it aired—there were no reruns, podcasts, or YouTube videos. **ASK:** How does having only a few versus nearly unlimited entertainment options impact a society? *(Answers will vary. Possible responses: In a society with few options, people watch the same programs, which could help create a sense of shared identity and values. However, fewer people's stories are told. With nearly unlimited options, people watch different shows, which could create a fragmented national identity and sense of values. It is more likely that various people's stories are told that connect with diverse groups of people.)*

Finally, inform students that this American Story will examine how the limited television options of the 1950s and 1960s helped form a cohesive American identity.

CRITICAL VIEWING The photo of so many people crowded around the window, all staring at the television, suggests that this form of media is still a novelty and that few people own a TV set. In addition, the absorbed look on most people's faces shows the power of television to hold people's attention and potentially influence them through its programming.

Television in the American Home

The flood of televisions into American homes began as a mere trickle. In the 1940s, only the wealthy could afford TV sets—the average price was equivalent to $3,000 in present-day money, adjusted for inflation. But as the price of black-and-white sets fell in the 1950s, the number of American households owning TVs rose sharply, from 10 percent to nearly 90 percent by the end of the decade. Even in the early 2000s, television sets remained a fixture in more than 95 percent of American homes. More recently, however, TV ownership has declined for the first time, due to the increase in viewing options on smartphones, tablets, and computers. In 2015, for example, 2.6 percent of American households reported that they didn't own a television, double the number reported in 2009.

The Evolution of Westerns

Westerns were not a genre unique to television or to the 1950s. For decades, stories about the Wild West had been popular entertainment in dime novels, radio programs, and film. In fact, many of the earliest television Westerns were recycled from old Hollywood movies. The popular Hopalong Cassidy films were the basis for an equally popular weekly television series. These series and films portrayed people in the Old West as primarily white, ignoring the fact that one in four cowboys in the 1800s was an African American. The stories were often simple "good-versus-evil" episodes in which the good guy always won.

In the mid-1950s, Westerns began to change, becoming more sophisticated to appeal to adults as well as to children. Programs such as *Gunsmoke* and *Have Gun—Will Travel* featured stories with more psychologically complex characters, moral ambiguity, and greater violence. However, these new Westerns provoked an audience backlash. By the 1960s, series such as *Bonanza* offered a domestic-type Western that emphasized family relationships over gunplay and chases on horseback.

CRITICAL VIEWING Possible response: Performers would not only hear and see a live studio audience's reactions but would have the added pressure of knowing that thousands, even millions, of people were watching them live on TV. They would be judged not just on their sound but on how they looked. Any mistakes or mishaps could not be edited out or rerecorded later, as could be done with a recorded or taped session.

AMERICAN STORIES

CRITICAL VIEWING The Beatles (from left: Paul McCartney, George Harrison, John Lennon, and Ringo Starr) rehearse before performing on *The Ed Sullivan Show* in 1964. What might be challenging about playing in front of a live studio audience and a TV audience simultaneously?

and *Harriet*, and *Leave It to Beaver* portrayed the charmed lives (and minor problems) of middle- to upper-class white families in the suburbs. Mother was a housewife. Dad was a businessman who left for work every day wearing a suit and carrying a briefcase. The kids were well adjusted and witty, money was never a problem, and nobody stayed angry for long. "You know, Mom," says the young son in *Leave It to Beaver*, "when we're in a mess, you kind of make things seem not so messy." "Well," his mother replies cheerfully, "isn't that sort of what mothers are for?"

Dialogue like that is almost painfully cute to today's audiences. However, it reflects the optimistic mind-set and idealized vision of the American family common in the 1950s. Still, family sitcoms did portray some realities of life in the 1950s. Millions of people were moving to newly built suburbs, and the number of women working outside the home was much lower than it had been during World War II. On the other hand, even though people of color formed a large percentage of the U.S. population, they rarely appeared on TV. Few sitcoms featured a minority family or a single-parent household.

VARIETY SHOWS AND NEWS

Like sitcoms, variety shows were a 1950s favorite. The reigning king of the genre was Ed Sullivan, whose program debuted in 1948. *The Ed Sullivan Show* featured acts from every realm of entertainment, including opera singers, ballet dancers, acrobats, magicians, comedians, jugglers, jazz musicians, and rock stars. Elvis Presley, the Beatles, and the Rolling Stones all appeared on the *The Ed Sullivan Show*, which ran until 1971.

In the 1950s, TV was also becoming Americans' favorite way to get the news. Many journalists who had previously worked in radio made the transition to TV, including Edward R. Murrow. Murrow was much admired for the reports he had broadcast from London during World War II. He began hosting a news program on CBS called *See It Now* in 1951. In 1956, NBC launched *The Huntley-Brinkley Report*, anchored by Chet Huntley in New York City and David Brinkley in Washington, D.C. It was the first news program broadcast from two locations at the same time. News anchors such as Murrow, Huntley, and Brinkley became familiar and trusted faces night after night.

CRITICAL VIEWING A family views a Western from the comfort of their living room in the 1950s. What can you observe about the culture of the decade from this photograph?

THE CALL OF THE WEST

Possibly the most popular TV genre of the 1950s and 1960s was the Western. Heroic sheriffs and brave cowboys chased after bad guys night after night during prime time. Westerns for children, such as *The Roy Rogers Show*, dominated Saturday TV. By the end of the 1950s, 31 prime-time Westerns were appearing each week—on just three networks.

Some of the most beloved Westerns enjoyed long runs. *The Lone Ranger* aired from 1949 to 1957. Even more extraordinary, *Gunsmoke* ran for 20 years, from 1955 to 1975. Short-run Westerns also could be wildly successful. One children's five-part series about Davy Crockett, which first aired in 1954, started a regular craze. Millions of children begged for Davy Crockett shirts, blankets, toothbrushes, and lunch boxes. Backyards and playgrounds were filled with boys wearing coonskin caps just like the one Crockett wore on TV.

Westerns may have been popular because they supported the upbeat American outlook of the 1950s. In a Western, it was always easy to tell the good guys from the bad guys, and the good guys always won. Very few characters were seriously harmed or killed, even in gunfights. Justice and the law always prevailed.

TV Westerns and other programs led to a boom in television-related merchandise, like this lunch box featuring Roy Rogers.

It was a Western series that brought the first Latino characters to television. In *The Cisco Kid*, Duncan Renaldo and Leo Carrillo portrayed Cisco and Pancho, two Mexican adventurers traveling around the Southwest. The show's tone was light hearted, and much of its humor came from Pancho making mistakes with the English language. Still, the pair were portrayed as admirable characters. They regularly helped the innocent and sent villains packing. Running from 1950 to 1956, *The Cisco Kid* was also the first TV series filmed in color.

The Cold War and the American Dream **837**

TEACH

Guided Discussion

1. **Draw Conclusions** Direct students to the dialogue from the television program *Leave It to Beaver*. **ASK:** What does the dialogue suggest about the role of women in 1950s America? *(Possible response: Women were seen as the primary caregivers of the family, who would always know how to fix whatever went wrong.)*

2. **Make Connections** What types of current-day programs are equivalent to the 1950s variety show? *(Possible response: Late-night talk shows and talent shows. Late-night talk shows feature many different acts, such as musicians, artists, comedians, animal acts, and more. Talent shows also feature a variety of entertainment acts, performed by people competing for a top prize.)*

Compare and Contrast

Point out the photograph of the Beatles on *The Ed Sullivan Show*, and explain they were one of the most popular bands in the world during the 1960s. Then find a video recording of the Beatles' 1964 performance to play for the class. Before playing it, tell half the students to close their eyes and just listen to the music. Tell the other half to both watch and listen to the performance. After the recording is over, ask students from each group to share their reactions to the performance, comparing and contrasting their experiences. Finally, discuss how being able to see performers might have changed the way Americans experienced mass entertainment on broadcast media.

CRITICAL VIEWING The photograph suggests that in the culture of the 1950s, watching TV was how families spent time together. The photo also portrays families as middle-class and white, composed of a father, mother, and two or more children. The father is the only one seated in a chair, with other family members grouped around him, which suggests that he's the most important member of the family.

Minorities in Television

When minorities appeared in early television programs, which was not often, they usually played roles that reinforced mainstream stereotypes: Hispanics were typecast as bandits, African Americans played servants or provided comic relief, and Asian Americans were relegated to being houseboys or a hero's sidekick. In addition, Westerns rarely cast Native American actors. Instead, white actors donned "red face" makeup to play the roles. It wasn't until the 1970s that television began to offer minorities more complex roles and to base some series on minorities' experiences. Programs such as *Sanford and Son*, *The Jeffersons*, and *Good Times* featured African-American casts and were grounded in realistic settings. **ASK:** Why do you think television of the 1950s and 1960s provided so few opportunities for minorities? *(Possible response: During this time, segregation and prejudice were deeply ingrained in American society, and television reflected mainly a middle-class white point of view.)*

Discuss with students the status of minorities in current television programs. Ask questions such as: Do you think current programs accurately depict all members of American society? What programs do a good or bad job depicting minorities? How well do programs reflect the reality of present-day society?

Have students work in pairs to conduct online research about the power and influence of minorities and women in the entertainment industry. Ask questions such as: What positions in media companies do women or minorities hold? How many are producers or directors? Instruct pairs to find one article about the topic and then use a Main Idea and Details Chart to organize their notes. When finished, allow pairs to share their findings and discuss as a class the extent to which progress has been made since the 1950s and 1960s.

Main Ideas	Details

CRITICAL VIEWING With a main character who was both African American and a single mother, *Julia* broke two early television taboos regarding race and the ideal family structure.

THE 1960s: AN EXPANDING WORLD

The 1960s ushered in many cultural changes in the United States. The civil rights movement was gaining strength. Women, Latinos, and other minorities joined African Americans in seeking equal treatment in schools, workplaces, and society in general. Many young people began to rebel against the comfortable suburban lifestyle their parents had built. TV, as it always does, responded to the trends of the time.

African Americans had rarely appeared on-screen in the 1950s. The one notable exception was a comedy called *Amos 'n' Andy*, which, according to the NAACP, portrayed African Americans as either "clowns" or "crooks." Gradually this began to change in the 1960s. *Julia*, a comedy starring African-American actress Diahann Carroll as a widow raising her son on her own, was a hit with viewers. But the show was also criticized for skipping too lightly over real challenges faced by African Americans.

The face of television comedy also changed in 1968 when comedians Dan Rowan and Dick Martin launched a sketch comedy show called *Laugh-In*. The look of the show was a true departure from *Leave It to Beaver*'s calm suburban living room. The sets were painted in the wild colors and patterns fashionable among youth and teens in the late 1960s. The comedy was fast paced, featured a mixed-gender cast, and often poked fun at people in the news.

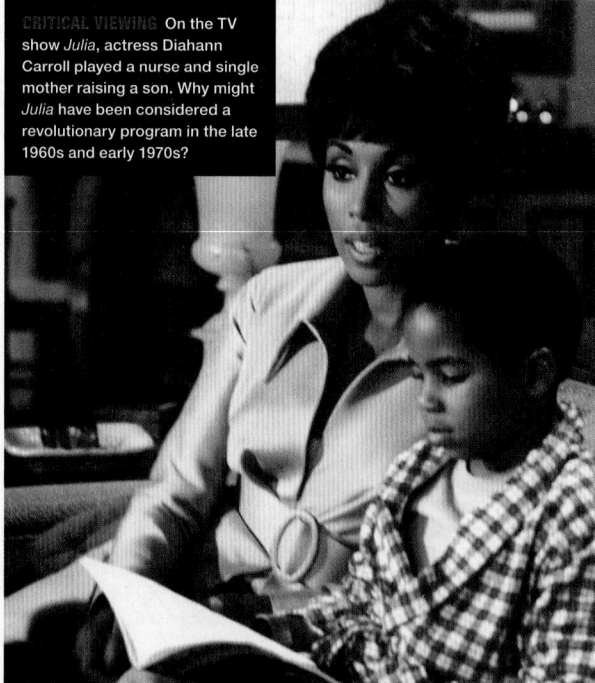

CRITICAL VIEWING On the TV show *Julia*, actress Diahann Carroll played a nurse and single mother raising a son. Why might *Julia* have been considered a revolutionary program in the late 1960s and early 1970s?

NBC pushed for increased cast diversity in the original *Star Trek* series by including characters from different cultures and giving an African-American female character, Lieutenant Uhura, a rare position of authority at the time.

Many people fondly remember the 1960s program *Star Trek*. Set in the 23rd century, the science fiction series revealed a future of harmony and equality among races, genders, and even species. The officers of the starship *Enterprise* included Lieutenant Uhura, played by African-American actress Nichelle Nichols, and Lieutenant Sulu, played by Japanese American actor George Takei.

THE MOST TRUSTED MAN IN AMERICA

News anchor Walter Cronkite was not glamorous or flashy. He had a deep, steady voice and a way of addressing viewers as if they were sitting across the table from him. His comforting presence and reputation for honesty earned him the nickname "most trusted man in America."

Cronkite served as the anchor of the *CBS Evening News* from 1962, when he helped launch the program, until 1981. From the anchor desk, he informed viewers of the most important stories of the 1960s—the highs and lows of the decade. He told the country about the assassinations of President Kennedy and Dr. Martin Luther King, Jr., and about the first moon landing.

Walter Cronkite also showed that news reporting can influence as well as inform. In 1968, according to his biographer, "Cronkite got up from his anchor desk, and flew to Vietnam, and put on a helmet and flak jacket, and interviewed anybody and everybody he could." Because Americans trusted Walter Cronkite, his "embedded reporting" from the battlefield was especially effective in bringing home the realities of war, and many were convinced by his conclusion that the war could not be won. Later, his coverage of the environment and the first Earth Day gave the environmental movement a boost.

After retiring from the *CBS Evening News*, Cronkite hosted numerous TV programs and short series for different channels and wrote several books. He died in 2009 at the age of 92.

CRITICAL VIEWING These images show Cronkite in one of his most difficult television moments: delivering the news, live, that President Kennedy had been assassinated on November 22, 1963. What do the photos reveal about Cronkite's emotional state?

Dr. Martin Luther King, Jr., a *Star Trek* fan, once told Nichols to stay with the show because Uhura was a symbol of promise for African Americans.

In the realm of current events, TV continued to be both a news reporter and a news maker. The Vietnam War became the first war to be extensively viewed on live television. Reporters filmed battles and their gory aftermath. They interviewed politicians at home and exhausted soldiers in Vietnam coping with the miseries of war. As commentator Marshall McLuhan remarked, "Television brought the brutality of war into the comfort of the living room." The shocking footage inspired many Americans to support the antiwar movement.

Another landmark moment for television news was the assassination of President John F. Kennedy in 1963. Within an hour of the president's shooting, both CBS and NBC had interrupted their programming to announce that the president had been shot. Soon after, CBS anchor Walter Cronkite, visibly upset, told the country that the president was dead. For the next four days, the networks covered the events that followed as millions of grieving viewers remained glued to their TV sets. Cameras were present when Lee Harvey Oswald, the man who killed Kennedy, was transferred from one jail building to another. Among the reporters, a man named Jack Ruby slipped close to Oswald and shot him to death on live TV.

Active Options

On Your Feet: Create a TV Museum Exhibit Divide the class into small groups. Assign each group one of the following categories: sitcoms, Westerns, variety shows, news programs, and advertising. Tell them they will create a classroom museum exhibit about 1950s and 1960s television. Instruct groups to research their category and find photographs, video clips, or other visuals to create a display of the popular shows, commercials, or news programs from the 1950s and 1960s. Remind students to include captions for their visuals. When finished, arrange each group's visuals in one area to create the classroom museum exhibit.

NG Learning Framework: Analyze Society Through Television

SKILL Communication

KNOWLEDGE Our Human Story

Direct students' attention to the last sentence of this American Story and discuss its meaning. Then organize students into groups of four. Assign each group a top-rated television program from the 1950s and 1960s, such as *Gunsmoke, I Love Lucy, The Andy Griffith Show*, or *The Beverly Hillbillies.* Instruct groups to research the premise of their show and watch clips or a complete episode. Then ask groups to prepare a presentation about their show in which they analyze the time slot in which it aired, the tone and format of the program, the trends or styles it featured, and how it reflected the American identity of the time. After all groups have presented, help the class synthesize the information from the presentations to describe the American culture of the 1950s and 1960s.

CRITICAL VIEWING The photographs show the range of emotions Cronkite experienced during this time. In the first two photos, he appears calm and professional. In the last two photos, he has removed his glasses, looks away from the camera, and then directly at the audience, showing people how deeply President Kennedy's death affected him.

Guided Discussion

1. **Identify** What factors led to the growth of advertising in the 1950s and 1960s? *(the widespread adoption of television, its ability to influence viewers' choices, and the emerging youth market)*

2. **Make Inferences** Direct students to read the information on *The Mickey Mouse Club* and study the photograph. **ASK:** Why do you think *The Mickey Mouse Club* was such a popular program? *(Possible response: The cast of children appealed to a young audience; the show had a consistent, entertaining format; it was tied to a popular cartoon character; and its wholesome messages encouraged parents to let their children watch it.)*

Analyze Primary Sources

Direct student pairs to conduct online research to find examples of television advertising during the 1950s and 1960s. Tell pairs to choose one ad and create a short presentation in which they analyze the target audience of the commercial and the technique used to sell the product. Ask students to compare and contrast the ad with commercials aired on television today.

Connect to Culture This American Story examines the role of television in the 1950s and 1960s and how it reflected and influenced American identity. To help students make connections between the American Story and their own lives, provide the following prompt: Name a television program that best reflects your own life. Ask students to write a short essay about the program, explaining why they chose it and how it reflects their lives. If students are having difficulty making a connection with a television show, allow them to choose a motion picture, song, or other media.

CRITICAL VIEWING: Both casts consist of the same characters, wear similar clothing, and have the same overall physical appearance. In the movie poster, however, the entire cast stands together in strong lighting, showing the popularity of all the characters. In the photo, the mother and father appear to be the most important characters, while the hand is not shown.

THINK ABOUT IT

Possible response: The United States became a TV nation because so many households bought television sets and began watching the programs. Television had a great impact on American culture by providing a shared experience for the country, by influencing the type of products people bought, and by shaping American values and identity.

AND ALWAYS, THE COMMERCIALS

Where there is TV, there is advertising. This was as true at the dawn of the television age as it is today. When sales of TV sets took off in the 1950s, advertisers followed. By the end of the decade, advertising took up 15 percent of airtime. More money was spent making commercials than producing the shows themselves. Like the sitcoms of the 1950s, many commercials portrayed a wealthy, happy, suburban America. Families were shown enjoying the many consumer goods that went on sale after the end of World War II.

Some advertising trends that exist today were set in those early days. Advertisers quickly recognized that children and teens were a growing and receptive audience. As a result, companies began targeting certain ads toward the youth market. Many brands also began using celebrities as on-screen spokespeople, and a few fictional "spokespeople," such as Tony the Tiger, also got their start in the 1950s.

TV advertising also made its presence known in the presidential elections in the 1950s. In the 1952 race, General Dwight D. Eisenhower's campaign produced a series of ads called "Eisenhower Answers America." Each spot showed the candidate appearing to answer questions from a variety of citizens. After the election, some people criticized these ads. They thought that selling a candidate as if he were a product hurt the dignity of the office. These criticisms were largely ignored, and campaign advertising became a mainstay on American TV.

In the 1960s, commercials once again moved with the times. In the middle of the decade, almost 50 percent of the U.S. population was younger than 25 years old. Advertisers continued their strong focus on the youth market. They noticed that many young people were rebelling against the consumer society of the 1950s, so they got creative with their approach and used humor and irony instead of images of traditional families to sell their products.

Advertising was slow to begin featuring people of color. Throughout the 1960s, most commercials featured only white actors. By the end of the decade, however, they were becoming more diverse. This movement reached a landmark moment in 1971, when Coca-Cola's "I'd Like to Buy the World a Coke" ad debuted. The spot showed young people of many races and nationalities singing a catchy jingle about living in harmony—and, of course, buying Coke. It has been called the world's most famous ad.

In many ways, the world of television and video we know today simply continues in the patterns that were first set in the 1950s. News programs are live

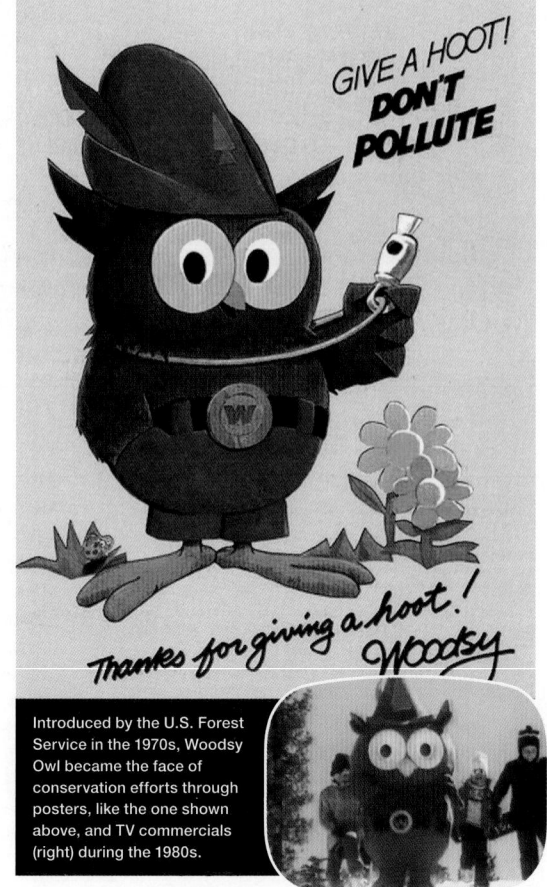

GIVE A HOOT!
DON'T POLLUTE

Thanks for giving a hoot! Woodsy

Introduced by the U.S. Forest Service in the 1970s, Woodsy Owl became the face of conservation efforts through posters, like the one shown above, and TV commercials (right) during the 1980s.

THE MAGIC OF A MOUSE

Every weekday evening from 1955 to 1959, kids across the United States took a break from their homework to tune in the family TV set to *The Mickey Mouse Club*. Considered revolutionary, this brainchild of Walt Disney himself was the first children's TV show that featured mostly child actors.

The young performers danced, sang, and entertained on the hour-long show, which also included a newsreel, a Mickey Mouse cartoon, and an ongoing drama series. Viewers were hooked. The wholesome Mouseketeers reached their audience in positive ways through songs and skits about such topics as the importance of drinking milk and bicycle safety. The show's iconic theme song emphasized its appeal to all children with lyrics that included, "Hey there, hi there, ho there, you're as welcome as can be. M-I-C-K-E-Y M-O-U-S-E." New versions of *The Mickey Mouse Club* aired in the 1970s and 1990s.

With their signature ears and labeled sweaters, the talented Mouseketeers, shown in this 1956 photo, charmed audiences from coast to coast.

CRITICAL VIEWING Compare the photograph of the original *Addams Family* TV cast with the modern movie poster. How are they similar and different?

FROM CLASSIC TV TO THE MOVIES

The appeal of many TV series from the 1950s and 1960s has lasted into the 21st century. In recent decades, movie producers have often looked back to old hit shows for inspiration. This is a short list of classic TV shows that have been made into movies:

— *Star Trek* (numerous movies, beginning in 1979 and ongoing)
— *The Addams Family* (1991)
— *The Fugitive* (1993)
— *Maverick* (1994)
— *Leave It to Beaver* (1997)
— *The Mod Squad* (1999)
— *Get Smart* (2008)
— *The Lone Ranger* (2013)
— *The Man from U.N.C.L.E.* (2015)

and utterly up-to-date, sitcoms and dramas still draw viewers during the evenings, and the three major networks still exist. On the other hand, much has changed. Many more comedies and dramas now feature a diverse cast of characters, including gay and transgender people. Major networks face powerful competition from cable channels, streaming services, and newer broadcast networks. Variety shows have largely vanished, and reality shows now entrance viewers. Many people act as their own series creators and news reporters, posting their footage on different social media platforms. But one thing remains the same: TV and video provide a mirror that reflects who Americans are and who we want to be.

THINK ABOUT IT

How did the United States become a "TV Nation," and what influence has television had on American culture?

DIFFERENTIATE

Inclusion

Predict Using Photos and Captions Pair special-needs students with proficient students. Instruct them to preview the American Story section by section, with the proficient partners describing the photographs and reading the captions. Tell students to write predictions about what they will learn in each section. After students read the lesson, encourage them to revise their statements based on what they have learned.

Gifted & Talented

Create a Multimedia Newscast Challenge students to conduct online research to find information and archival footage of news broadcasts from the 1950s and 1960s. Then have students select one broadcast and deliver it as a modern news anchor, incorporating the information, photographs, and clips they discovered. Invite students to discuss the differences and similarities between the the two broadcasts.

See the Chapter Planner for more strategies for differentiation.

HISTORICAL THINKING

Ask and have students answer the following questions.

1. **READING CHECK** Why were television sitcoms, variety shows, and Westerns so popular throughout the 1950s and 1960s?

2. **EVALUATE** How accurately did early TV programs reflect all of American society?

3. **ANALYZE CAUSE AND EFFECT** How did television programs and advertising respond to the cultural changes of the 1960s?

ANSWERS

1. Sitcoms gave people a happy vision of family life; variety shows provided different types of entertainment; and Westerns showed the good guys always winning in the end.

2. They did not reflect society accurately because early television programs depicted middle-class, white suburban families as the model.

3. Television began to show more African Americans and other minorities, while advertisers focused on humor and irony instead of images of the typical suburban family.

As World War II came to an end, Americans looked cautiously to the future. Would good times finally return, or would the country sink back into the joblessness, poverty, and despair of the Great Depression?

MAIN IDEA In the years after World War II, the United States enjoyed an economic boom and the civil rights movement gained momentum.

THE PEACETIME ECONOMY

As you have learned, World War II revitalized U.S. industry and brought an end to the Great Depression. The country enjoyed prosperity in the postwar years, but the transition from war to peace brought many challenges.

The **demobilization** of the U.S. Armed Forces following the war meant that millions of service members were discharged from the military. This huge wave of veterans returned home over a period of months, and most of them set out to find jobs. At the same time, the federal government began to cancel military contracts, which led to massive layoffs in defense-related industries. Too many applicants for too few jobs caused many Americans to fear that the Great Depression might return.

The wartime Congress had anticipated these developments, and in 1944 it had passed the Servicemen's Readjustment Act, which became known as the

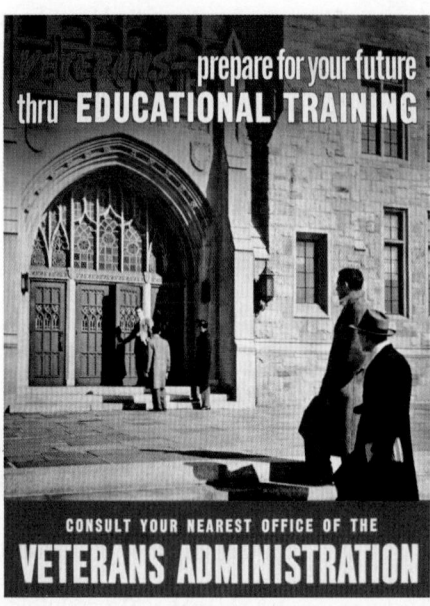

While the fighting still raged, the federal government was concerned about the veterans who were already returning from active duty and the millions who would be demobilized at the war's end. In 1943, the Office for Emergency Management created this poster advising veterans that education and training were available to them.

GI Bill of Rights. This popular bill had a profound impact on American society and on the country's economy. It fueled a nationwide construction boom by encouraging veterans to buy homes. The government provided long-term, low-interest home loans to returning GIs, including loan guarantees of up to $2,000. Further, by providing grants for college tuition, it allowed former soldiers to fulfill the dream of earning a college degree. Determined to make up for lost time, veterans formed the core of the United States' growing white-collar, or professional, workforce in the prosperous years ahead.

At the same time, many women were leaving the workforce. The war had given American women new opportunities in both military and civilian jobs. After the war, however, these gains largely disappeared, at least temporarily. Returning servicemen reclaimed jobs in offices and industries. Women were pressured to return to traditionally female roles, such as teaching, nursing, and homemaking.

At home, Americans enthusiastically embraced newly affordable consumer goods after the sacrifices of the Great Depression and World War II. Mass advertising encouraged this trend. Sales of new homes and cars soared. So did sales of home appliances such as refrigerators, washing machines, and clothes dryers. These purchases were made possible by the savings that many Americans had accumulated during the war and by the availability of easy credit.

PRESSURE FOR CIVIL RIGHTS

African Americans had played a major role in the U.S. war effort, both in the armed services and on the home front. After the war, however, they found that the country they had served faithfully still treated them as second-class citizens. Throughout the nation, African Americans faced job and housing discrimination. In the South in particular, laws mandated that blacks and whites use segregated, or separate, public services. Many felt a renewed determination to fight for their civil rights. This term refers to the fundamental rights and liberties promised to all Americans by the U.S. Constitution and its amendments.

In 1941, President Franklin Roosevelt had signed an executive order prohibiting racial discrimination in the U.S. defense industry. The armed forces, meanwhile, had remained racially segregated throughout World War II. Civil rights groups such as the NAACP and leaders like A. Philip Randolph pressured President Harry Truman to take action. Ultimately, he did so. In 1948, Truman signed **Executive Order 9981**, which abolished racial segregation in the U.S. military.

The Transistor Revolution
Measuring just three by five inches, the Zephyr 9 transistor radio sported a curved design that fit comfortably in a person's hand. The small radio and its "big" sound were made possible by the invention of the transistor, a very tiny electronic device. Radio had been losing its stars and audiences to the new medium of television throughout the 1950s, but it rebounded when the lightweight, portable transistor radios hit the market. Over the following two decades, transistor radios sold in the billions.

HISTORICAL THINKING

1. **READING CHECK** How did American consumer behavior after the war reflect the return to prosperity?

2. **MAKE INFERENCES** Why do you think President Truman decided to end segregation in the U.S. Armed Forces? Support your response with evidence from the text.

3. **SUMMARIZE** What impact did the GI Bill of Rights have on returning veterans?

INTRODUCE & ENGAGE

Connect Historical Events

Review and discuss with students the conditions returning veterans faced following World War I, such as lack of jobs, low wages, inflation, and segregation and discrimination. **ASK:** Do you think World War II veterans faced similar conditions? *(Answers will vary. Possible response: Economic conditions might have been better after World War II, since the government could learn from its previous mistakes, but racial discrimination probably remained the same.)* Tell students that in Lesson 1.1 they will learn how the government took steps to deal with peacetime problems following World War II.

TEACH

Guided Discussion

1. **Draw Conclusions** How did past experiences influence the passage of the GI Bill of Rights? *(Congress feared that demobilization might spark a return of the Great Depression if veterans were unable to find employment. To help combat this possibility, Congress passed the GI Bill of Rights to provide educational and credit assistance.)*

2. **Make Connections** In what ways were the experiences of working women similar after World War I and World War II? *(Possible response: After both wars, working women were pushed out of their jobs and back into traditional family roles to make those jobs available to returning veterans.)*

More Information

A. Philip Randolph Remind students that Randolph had threatened a massive march on Washington, D.C., which successfully pressured President Franklin Roosevelt to issue the executive order banning racial discrimination in the defense industry. Then explain that Randolph similarly pressured President Truman by threatening to launch a civil disobedience campaign. African-American youth would refuse military service if drafted unless Truman issued an executive order banning segregation in the military. **ASK:** How do you think Randolph's earlier success might have influenced Truman's response? *(Possible response: Truman knew that Roosevelt had taken Randolph's threat seriously. This may have helped convince Truman that Randolph would likely carry out his plan of civil disobedience, so Truman issued the executive order rather than face the consequences.)*

Active Options

On Your Feet: Fishbowl Arrange students in two groups. Instruct Group 1 to sit in a close circle and discuss the conditions of the peacetime economy following World War II. Direct Group 2 to form a circle around Group 1 and listen for new information. Then have groups reverse positions. Direct the new inner circle to discuss civil rights in America's postwar society. Those on the outside should listen for new information. At the end, have the class summarize the major changes that occurred in American society after the war.

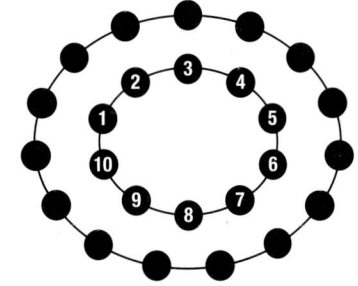

NG Learning Framework: Research Executive Order 9981

ATTITUDE Empowerment

KNOWLEDGE Our Human Story

Have students work in small groups to research the effects of Executive Order 9981. Ask students to consider such issues as how the armed forces responded, how the order changed the lives of African Americans in the military, how people in the mainstream culture reacted to the order, and how it affected other civil rights efforts in the country. When the groups have finished their research, invite them to share their findings in a class discussion about the progress of civil rights in the 1950s.

DIFFERENTIATE

English Language Learners   ELD

Understand Word Parts Bring students' attention to the paragraph containing the word *demobilization*. Ask students at **All Proficiencies** to identify the meaning of the prefix *de-* (negation or reversal) and the root word *mobilize* (to put into movement; assemble and make ready), using a dictionary if necessary. Then have students look for other words using this root *(mobile, mobility, mover)* and write an original sentence using each word.

Pre-AP

Write a Compare-Contrast Essay Ask students to conduct online research to learn more about the experiences of women and African Americans after the war. Encourage them to use a Venn Diagram to keep track of the similarities and differences between these experiences. Instruct students to use their research to write a compare-contrast essay and to share their essays with the class.

See the Chapter Planner for more strategies for differentiation.

HISTORICAL THINKING

ANSWERS

1. Encouraged by mass advertising, many Americans used their savings and credit to purchase new homes, cars, and appliances, such as refrigerators, washers, and dryers.

2. Possible responses: Pressure from civil rights leaders and groups like the NAACP likely played a major role in pushing Truman to end segregation in the armed forces. The Roosevelt administration had already banned racial discrimination in the defense industry, and Truman may have viewed this move as a logical next step. He also may have hoped that the executive order would help him win the African-American vote in the upcoming presidential election.

3. Possible response: The GI Bill of Rights had a strong impact, making it possible for many veterans to earn college degrees and to buy their own homes. The bill helped returning veterans avoid the problems World War I veterans had experienced.

1.2 Truman's Fair Deal

You've seen it happen in sports. Everyone knows which team is going to win, but then the underdog pulls off an upset. In the 1948 presidential election, Harry Truman looked like a candidate on a losing team, but he aimed confidently for a major upset at the polls.

MAIN IDEA Following a period of tensions between labor and government, Harry Truman renewed his efforts to bring about liberal domestic reforms.

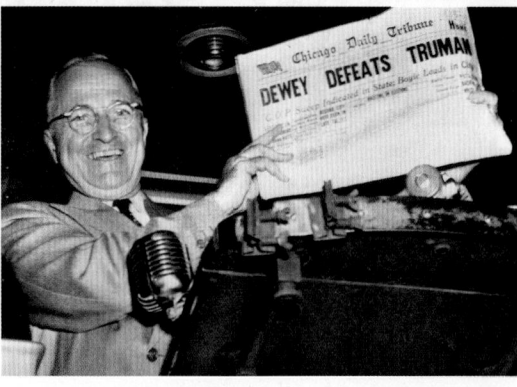

After winning the 1948 election, a laughing and triumphant President Harry S. Truman holds up the *Chicago Daily Tribune* to show off the newspaper's error in declaring his Republican rival, Thomas Dewey, the winner. Other newspapers, radio broadcasters, and even some Democrats had expected Truman to lose the election.

LABOR TENSIONS

One of the biggest problems the United States faced after World War II was inflation—that is, rising prices and a decrease in the value of money. During the war, the federal government had set price controls on many goods and services. When most of the controls were lifted in June 1946, prices shot up.

Higher prices meant a drop in workers' real income because basic purchases took up more of their paychecks. In late 1945, the United Auto Workers (UAW), a large automotive industry union, had already tackled the issue of low wages. It demanded an average pay increase of 33 cents an hour from General Motors. When the corporation refused to meet the demand, the union began a strike that

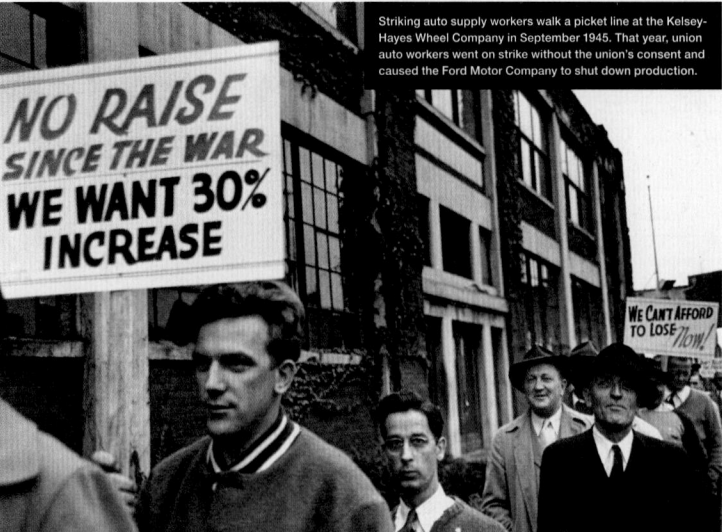

Striking auto supply workers walk a picket line at the Kelsey-Hayes Wheel Company in September 1945. That year, union auto workers went on strike without the union's consent and caused the Ford Motor Company to shut down production.

lasted 113 days. Soon, a wave of strikes hit the country. By 1946, more than 4.5 million U.S. workers had walked off their jobs, crippling entire industries.

These labor actions provoked a strong backlash against unions. In 1947, the Republican-controlled Congress passed the **Taft-Hartley Act**, which curbed the power of organized labor. It gave the president authority to impose a "cooling off" period to prevent strikes that threatened the national interest. More important, the bill made it illegal to require workers to join a union. It also encouraged states to pass "right-to-work" laws that made union organizing more difficult.

Despite the Taft-Hartley Act, union membership remained high, and the ability of unions to bargain on behalf of employees was largely unaffected. Workers in manufacturing industries enjoyed much higher wages and better benefits than they had during the Great Depression.

THE FAIR DEAL

As the presidential election of 1948 approached, few people thought Truman stood a chance of winning. His popularity was low, and he faced a strong Republican challenger, Governor Thomas Dewey of New York. Undaunted, Truman pursued a vigorous campaign of personal appearances and fiery speeches in which he laid out his policy ideas before the voters. His popularity began to climb, and on Election Day he pulled off one of the greatest upsets in American political history.

In his second term, Truman pursued an agenda of domestic reforms that he called the **Fair Deal**. The reforms included expansion of Social Security, an increase in education spending, and the creation of more **low-cost housing**—that is, housing affordable to people with lower incomes. As in his first term, Truman pushed for **national health insurance**, an insurance plan run by the government and open to any American who chose to join, but it failed to pass Congress. So did many other parts of the Fair Deal.

Truman did achieve wins in a few areas, however, including low-cost housing and an expansion of Social Security that greatly increased the number of people covered as well as the benefits they would receive. Truman also pushed for the federal minimum wage to be raised from 40 cents to 75 cents per hour, and Congress complied.

HISTORICAL THINKING

1. **READING CHECK** What events led up to the passing of the Taft-Hartley Act?

2. **DRAW CONCLUSIONS** Why do you think Fair Deal reforms might have appealed to struggling Americans? Cite evidence from the text to support your response.

3. **ANALYZE LANGUAGE USE** Why do you think Truman named his reform agenda the Fair Deal?

PLAN

Objective

Explain how Congress responded to a wave of strikes following World War II and to President Truman's attempts to institute social reforms.

Critical Thinking Skills for Lesson 1.2

- Identify Main Ideas and Details
- Monitor Comprehension
- Draw Conclusions
- Analyze Language Use
- Analyze Cause and Effect
- Summarize

Essential Question for Chapter 25

How did the United States change after World War II? Inflation and other economic problems led to strikes and the demand for federal action. Lesson 1.2 examines how Truman and the federal government responded to these challenges.

Background for the Teacher

Many factors contributed to the *Chicago Daily Tribune*'s "Dewey Defeats Truman" headline. Public opinion polls widely favored Dewey, while news commentators mocked Truman's train tour as an old-fashioned way to campaign and belittled the large crowds who greeted him. The *Tribune*'s Washington correspondent, Arthur Sears Henning, was so confident of Truman's defeat that he wrote about Dewey's victory at 9 a.m. on Election Day. However, a printers' strike forced the newspaper's staff to use typewriters to compose much of the paper, and they had to scramble to make the early-edition deadline. As a result, the *Tribune* went with Henning's prediction, even while votes were still being counted. Not only was Henning wrong, part of the main article was printed upside down!

Financial Literacy

To extend their knowledge and understanding about the concepts in this lesson, refer students to the Financial Literacy handbook.

Preview Using Visuals

Direct students' attention to the photograph of striking workers. Ask students if they have seen any strikes or picket lines where they live or in the media. **ASK:** What would make people go out on strike even when they need their jobs? *(Answers will vary. Possible responses: Their wages might be too low; working conditions might be dangerous; management might have unfair rules, such as hiring only certain people.)* Tell students that Lesson 1.2 discusses postwar labor-management tensions and Truman's efforts to institute economic reforms.

Guided Discussion

1. **Analyze Cause and Effect** How did the end of wartime price controls contribute to economic problems for average Americans? *(Possible response: When the federal government ended wartime price controls, prices increased dramatically, leading to inflation. Without a raise in pay, workers had to use more of their wages to pay for necessities, which meant they had less to buy other things they might need or want.)*

2. **Summarize** How did the Taft-Hartley Act attempt to curb the power of organized labor? *(Possible response: The act gave the president authority to require a cooling-off period to stop strikes that might harm the national interest, prohibited unions from forcing workers to become union members, and made unionizing more difficult by encouraging states to pass "right to work" laws.)*

Draw Conclusions

Why do you think Congress might have backed an expansion of Social Security, an increase in the minimum wage, and the creation of low-cost housing, but not national health insurance? *(Possible response: The expansion of Social Security, an increase in the minimum wage, and low-cost housing affected only segments of the population, generally those who were poorer and needed extra help. However, it's unlikely that Congress would have wanted the government to run a health insurance plan for the entire country. The cost would have been considered far too high.)*

Active Options

On Your Feet: Card Responses Direct half the class to write six True-False statements based on the lesson. Direct the other half to create answer cards, writing "True" on one side and "False" on the other. Tell students from the first group to take turns reading their statements. Instruct students from the second group to hold up their cards, showing either "True" or "False" in response to the statements. Have students keep track of their correct responses. Invite volunteers to modify each "False" statement into one that is true.

NG Learning Framework: Compare Elections

SKILL Collaboration

KNOWLEDGE Our Human Story

Organize students into groups to compare the presidential elections of 1948 and 2016. Instruct groups to research similarities between the two elections in terms of polling data, misreading of voter intentions, viewpoints of political experts, and final electoral and popular votes. Encourage groups to create graphic charts based on their research to compare the two elections and then share their findings with the class.

Striving Readers

Summarize Have students work in pairs to read and summarize the text. Encourage them to write at least three notes for each of the two sections of the lesson. Guide students to write a summary statement for each section and then write a summary statement for the entire lesson. Invite pairs to compare their summary statements and note similarities and differences.

Pre-AP

Report on Fair Deal Impacts After they read the lesson, have students write three questions they have about the impact of Truman's Fair Deal on the social and economic lives of Americans in the postwar period. Encourage them to conduct online research to answer their questions and then summarize their findings in a report to share with the class. Students who wish to go further may also analyze any current impacts of the Fair Deal in our society.

See the Chapter Planner for more strategies for differentiation.

ANSWERS

1. Although inflation cut into workers' earnings, companies refused to increase wages. Several unions went on strike, and other unions followed suit, which hurt entire industries. In response, Congress passed the Taft-Hartley Act to reduce the power of labor unions.

2. Possible response: The Fair Deal programs probably appealed to struggling Americans because the programs addressed their needs for affordable housing, higher wages, better Social Security coverage, and a national health care plan.

3. Possible response: The name Fair Deal might make people think of the Square Deal and New Deal programs of the past, which were also meant to help most working people. The Fair Deal tried to increase fairness in American life by helping people achieve economic and social gains.

The Cold War Starts

What do you call a war that is fought with words instead of bombs and with political strategy instead of battlefield maneuvers?

MAIN IDEA After World War II, the United States and the Soviet Union plunged into a political and diplomatic rivalry that threatened to spark a war between the two countries.

THE IRON CURTAIN

The United States and the Soviet Union had been uneasy allies in World War II. After the war, anger and suspicion grew on both sides. Soviet leaders felt that the United States cared little about the security needs of the Soviet people. American leaders increasingly viewed the Soviet Union as a warmongering force focused on expanding its communist empire.

In the summer of 1945, the United States, Great Britain, France, and the Soviet Union divided Germany into four **occupation zones**. The Soviets controlled the eastern part of Germany. The United States, Great Britain, and France each controlled an occupation zone in the west. Berlin, Germany's capital, was entirely within the Soviet occupation zone, but it was governed by a joint agency of all four nations. The Soviets controlled the eastern section of the city, or East Berlin, and the Western Allies controlled the rest, or West Berlin.

In addition to the zone it controlled in eastern Germany, the Soviet Union had gained dominance over many countries in Eastern and central Europe, including Bulgaria, Romania, Poland, and Hungary. Together with the Soviet Union, these nations came to be known as the Soviet **bloc**, or alliance. The expansion of the Soviet bloc and the resulting spread of communism worried the United States and its Western European allies.

In March 1946, former British prime minister Winston Churchill told an audience at Westminster College in Missouri that an **Iron Curtain** had descended across Europe. He was referring to the political and military barrier the Soviet Union had put in place to discourage contact between the communist Soviet bloc and the democratic countries to the west.

Amid the growing tensions, the **Cold War** began. It was a political conflict that simmered for decades, but it never heated up into full-blown warfare. It was also global: The Soviet Union sought to bring other countries under Soviet influence. In response, the United States adopted a policy of **containment**, using diplomatic and military strategies to halt the spread of communism.

To help contain communism in Europe, the United States and 11 Western European countries founded the **North Atlantic Treaty Organization (NATO)** in 1949. NATO members pledged to come to one another's aid in the event of an attack by the Soviet Union.

THE BERLIN AIRLIFT

You have read about the Marshall Plan and the role it played in rebuilding Europe after the war. It also was instrumental in the United States' containment efforts. By restoring economic confidence throughout Western Europe, it curbed the influence of local communist parties in Italy and France. The plan also increased American trade and investment in Europe, opening new markets for American goods and political ideas.

The **Berlin Airlift** was another notable postwar aid effort. In June 1948, the Soviet Union blockaded West Berlin, cutting off land access to the city. The Western Allies responded by delivering supplies such as food and fuel by air. At one point, Allied planes were landing every 45 seconds at Berlin's airport. Recognizing that the blockade had failed, the Soviets lifted it in May 1949.

In 1948, German children scrambled up a pile of rubble left from World War II to wave excitedly at a U.S. cargo plane participating in the Berlin Airlift. The United States and its allies airlifted food and other supplies to the city after the Soviets had cut off the West Berliners' access to the outside world.

Division of Europe, 1949

HISTORICAL THINKING

1. **READING CHECK** What was the Soviet bloc?

2. **INTERPRET MAPS** What do you see on the map that helps you understand why West Berlin was a source of tension between the Soviet Union and the Western Allies?

3. **IDENTIFY MAIN IDEAS AND DETAILS** How did the Marshall Plan help the United States' containment efforts?

PLAN

Objective

Describe the causes and effects of the Cold War that was waged by the United States and the Soviet Union.

Critical Thinking Skills for Lesson 2.1

- Identify Main Ideas and Details
- Monitor Comprehension
- Interpret Maps
- Evaluate
- Make Connections
- Interpret Visuals

Essential Question for Chapter 25

How did the United States change after World War II? After the war, the United States took an active role in rebuilding Europe and entered into a Cold War with the Soviet Union. Lesson 2.1 examines the beginning of the Cold War and U.S. efforts to contain communism.

Background for the Teacher

For a year, Americans dropped powdered milk, flour, medicine, food, coal, gasoline, and other goods into West Berlin to break the Soviet blockade. For the children, deliveries made by Gail Halvorsen, known as "the Candy Bomber," were always special. Halvorsen came up with the idea of dropping gum and candy into West Berlin after talking with a group of children outside the Berlin airfield. As he was about to leave, he shared his last pieces of gum with four of the children. They tore the gum into strips and passed them around so that each child could enjoy the gum's minty smell. Halvorsen, deeply moved by the gesture, realized at that moment the children hadn't tasted candy for years. He promised them he would drop more candy from his plane and waggle his wings so they would know which plane he was flying. Throughout the airlift, Halvorsen and other airmen continued to drop the "candy bombs." After the war, Halvorsen occasionally took to the sky and dropped sweets over his hometown of Salt Lake City.

Consider Hot Wars and Cold Wars

Draw a Venn diagram on the board and label one circle Hot War, the center Both, and the other circle Cold War. Tell students that World War II was a hot war, and ask them to identify some of the war's characteristics, such as battles, code-breaking, and air raids, and list them in the Hot War circle. Then inform students that after World War II, the United States entered into a cold war with the Soviet Union. Ask students to infer what the characteristics of a cold war might be, and list their reponses in the Cold War circle. Then have students identify any similarities between a hot war and a cold war and enter them in the Both section. Tell students that in Lesson 2.1 they will learn how threatening a conflict can be even without battles and air raids.

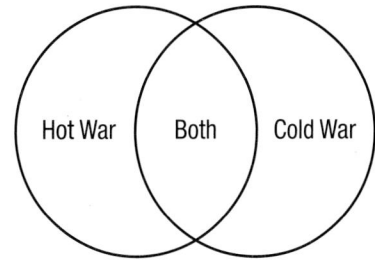
Hot War   Both   Cold War

TEACH

Guided Discussion

1. **Evaluate** Why are *Iron Curtain* and *containment* fitting terms to describe Cold War events? (*Possible response: The Soviet Union gained control over a bloc of countries in Central and Eastern Europe and then used political and military measures to limit their contact with democracies in Western Europe, in effect drawing a type of "iron curtain" around them.* Containment *refers to America's policy of preventing the spread of communism, thus containing or limiting its influence to territory it already controlled.*)

2. **Make Connections** What do you think the Soviets thought of NATO and the Marshall Plan? (*Possible response: The Soviets probably saw them both as a threat, since they expanded American influence into Europe, sought to contain Soviet expansion, and promoted ideas that clashed with communism.*)

Interpret Visuals

Direct students' attention to the photograph of the Berlin Airlift. **ASK:** How do you think people in the United States and in the Soviet Union would have interpreted this photo? (*Possible response: People in the United States might have believed that the photo proved people in West Berlin wanted American help and did not want to accept Soviet rule. The Soviets may have focused on the plane in the photo as proof of Western aggression against the Soviet bloc, since it was flying deep into East German territory.*)

Active Options

Active History: Compare Cold War Enemies Extend the lesson by using either the PDF or Whiteboard version of the activity. These activities take a deeper look at a topic in, or related to, the lesson. Explore the activities as a class, turn them into group assignments, or assign them individually.

NG Learning Framework: Script a Documentary Film

SKILLS Communication, Collaboration

KNOWLEDGE Our Human Story

Tell students to work in small groups to research the impact of the Soviet blockade and subsequent Allied airlift on the citizens of West Berlin. Have groups create a short documentary film script about the event, including specs for photographs, maps, and other visual or audio elements. When the scripts are written, have each group select a student "producer" to pitch the script to the class and answer questions. Then invite the class to vote on the script they would most like to see as a completed film.

English Language Learners

Look for Cognates Suggest that as students read they look for words similar in spelling and meaning to words in their home language. For example, the word *occupation* has a cognate in Spanish: *ocupación*. Ask students at **All Proficiencies** to make a vocabulary card for each word they identify, writing the English word and definition on one side and the word and its definition in their home language on the other.

Gifted & Talented

Illustrate a Metaphor Bring students' attention to the iron curtain metaphor coined by Winston Churchill. Have students conduct online research to find the speech in which Churchill first uses the term and write a brief explanation of what his original meaning might have been. Then invite students to draw a picture or use a computer graphics program to illustrate the metaphor and enhance its meaning, giving viewers a sense of what being behind or outside this Iron Curtain might have been like. Have students share their work with the class.

See the Chapter Planner for more strategies for differentiation.

HISTORICAL THINKING

ANSWERS

1. This term refers to the Soviet Union and the communist countries under its control in Central and Eastern Europe.

2. Possible response: West Berlin, controlled by the Allies, was located deep within East Germany, controlled by the Soviets. It prevented the Soviets from ruling all of East Germany and provided a stark contrast to the economics and politics of communism.

3. Possible response: By creating stronger economies in Western Europe, the Marshall Plan prevented local communist groups from taking over the government in countries such as France and Italy and prevented communism from expanding into other countries. It also fostered closer ties with the United States, which strengthened Western Europe against the Soviet Union.

2.2 Communism in Asia

Sometimes what works in one situation won't work in another. The U.S. policy of containment seemed to be doing a good job controlling the spread of communism in Europe. Asia, however, was a different story.

MAIN IDEA The Cold War intensified at the end of the 1940s as communism began to spread in Asia.

In Shanghai, China, a young girl glances at a huge picture of the late Chinese leader Mao Zedong, who died in 1976. To the left of the image is written "In memory of Chairman Mao's 110th birthday," which was commemorated in 2003. During his lifetime, the government produced millions of images promoting Mao's leadership.

COMMUNIST CHINA

In the late 1940s, the Cold War turned into a "hot war" in Asia. Developments in China and Korea had profound implications for the political battle that the United States and its democratic allies were waging against communist expansion.

A civil war had been raging in China since before World War II. On one side was the Nationalist Party, headed by **Chiang Kai-shek** (jee-AHNG ky-SHEHK), which relied heavily on U.S. support. On the other side was the Chinese Communist Party, whose leader was **Mao Zedong** (MOW dzuh-DUNG). When the Nationalists came to power in the 1920s, Mao recruited farmers and other rural residents to revolt against the government. Under his leadership, they joined the fighting force called the Red Army. When Chiang's forces drove the communists into a lengthy retreat, called the Long March, Mao's military strategies kept the Red Army together. Once Japan began its invasion of China during the 1930s, both Mao and Chiang turned their attention to defending the nation, putting the internal fighting on hold.

When the world war ended, the civil war began again in earnest. At first, the Nationalists seemed to have the upper hand. But in 1948, the course of the war changed. Mao's communist army, now called the People's Liberation Army (PLA), handed Chiang's forces one defeat after another. The United States sent weapons and funds to Chiang to help defeat Mao's forces, but much of this American weaponry ended up in the hands of the communists as the Nationalists retreated. By late 1949, the PLA had gained control of the entire country except for Taiwan—an island off China's southeast coast—and a few other islands. On October 1, Mao proclaimed the establishment of the **People's Republic of China.** He also declared his solidarity with the Soviet Union.

The communist takeover of China shocked many Americans. How well did the containment policy really work, they wondered, when more than 600 million people had just been "lost" to communism?

Chiang Kai-shek and other Nationalist leaders retreated to Taiwan, along with Nationalist troops and about 2 million refugees. The leaders did not admit defeat. Rather, they claimed they were still the rightful government of China.

TWO KOREAS

China wasn't the only communist threat in Asia. Communism also arose in Indochina and in Korea. Japan had annexed Korea in 1910 and had ruled it oppressively for more than three decades. With Japan's defeat in World War II, Koreans looked forward to regaining their independence. Their hopes were not met.

Two days after the bombing of Hiroshima, the Soviet Union declared war on Japan. Within days, the Soviets landed troops in the northern part of Korea. U.S. and Soviet officials arranged for Korea to be split into two occupation zones. The Soviet Union controlled the zone that lay north of the **38th parallel**—that is, the imaginary line representing 38 degrees north latitude. The United States occupied the zone south of the line.

U.S. leaders expected the division to be temporary, since both the United States and the Soviet Union had pledged to support Korea's independence. But soon the two zones began to move in different directions politically. They established separate identities as **North Korea** and **South Korea.**

In 1947, the United States handed responsibility for South Korea and Korean independence over to the United Nations. The following year, South Korea declared its independence as the Republic of Korea. The new country adopted a presidential system of government and an anticommunist stance. North Korea declared itself the Democratic People's Republic of Korea, a communist regime backed by the Soviet Union. Tensions grew between the two Koreas as their leaders made daily threats to "liberate" each other's land.

HISTORICAL THINKING

1. **READING CHECK** How did China become a communist country?

2. **SUMMARIZE** Why did Americans become disillusioned with the containment policy?

3. **MAKE PREDICTIONS** What do you think might happen in Korea after the establishment of two separate republics in 1948? Explain your response.

PLAN

Objective

Trace how communism spread to China and North Korea following World War II.

Critical Thinking Skills for Lesson 2.2

- Identify Main Ideas and Details
- Monitor Comprehension
- Summarize
- Make Predictions
- Draw Conclusions
- Make Inferences

Essential Question for Chapter 25

How did the United States change after World War II? In the early years of the Cold War, the United States saw communist forces take control of mainland China and North Korea. Lesson 2.2 explores communist expansion in Asia and the early failures of the U.S. containment policy.

Background for the Teacher

Born the son of a successful farmer, Mao Zedong rebelled against his family's traditions and left home at the age of 13 to advance his studies. Later, he served for a short time in the revolutionary army that overthrew the Qing dynasty in 1911. During this time, he learned that "political power grows out of the barrel of a gun," an idea he later made famous. After the revolution, many young people, like Mao, had little hope for advancement, since they lived in a China crippled by poverty, corruption, foreign dominance, and competing warlords, who now controlled large parts of the country.

In 1920, Mao joined a Marxist study group and soon came to believe that communism would cure China's ills. He joined the Chinese Communist Party, which eventually received support from the Soviet Union. Driven into the mountains by Chiang Kai-shek, Mao established a Soviet-type rural government. He also developed the guerrilla tactics he would use years later to defeat Chiang's forces and form the People's Republic of China.

List Causes of Civil War

Have students define the term *civil war* and recall instances of civil wars throughout history. **ASK:** What has caused civil wars to occur? *(Answers will vary. Possible responses: Issues such as slavery, religion, politics, and ethnic conflict have caused civil wars.)* Explain that China experienced a civil conflict caused by disagreements about what political system and ideology China should adopt. Then tell students that Lesson 2.2 explains how a long, intermittent civil war between Mao Zedong's communist forces and Chiang Kai-shek's nationalist forces led to the communist takeover of China.

TEACH

Guided Discussion

1. **Draw Conclusions** How might Mao's initial defeats have helped him triumph over Chiang Kai-shek? *(Possible response: By being forced into the mountains, Mao had to develop military strategies to keep the army together to fight the Japanese. When he returned to fighting Chiang's forces, Mao had spent decades refining his military tactics, which helped him defeat Chiang.)*

2. **Summarize** What chain of events led to the formation of a communist North Korea? *(Korea had been under Japanese control since 1910. After the bombing of Hiroshima, the Soviets declared war on Japan and, together with the United States, divided Korea into two occupation zones. The Soviets controlled territory north of the 38th parallel and helped northern Korea establish the Democratic People's Republic of Korea, a communist regime.)*

Make Inferences

Direct students' attention to the poster of Mao Zedong. **ASK:** Why do you think the Chinese still celebrate Mao Zedong so many years after his death? *(Possible response: Just as Americans celebrate George Washington as a founder of the United States, the Chinese probably see Mao as the founder of the People's Republic of China.)*

Active Options

On Your Feet: Tell Me More Divide the class into two groups and assign the civil war in China to one group and the Cold War history of the two Koreas to the other. Have members of each group write as many facts about their topic as they can. Then bring the class together and tell the first group to stand up. Instruct the other group to call out, "Tell me about China's civil war!" and have the standing group recite a fact. Direct the other group to call out, "Tell me more!" until the first group runs out of facts. Then have the groups reverse roles, and ask the second group to present facts about the Cold War history of the two Koreas. Keep track of which group shares the most facts.

NG Learning Framework: Create an Annotated Time Line

ATTITUDE Curiosity

KNOWLEDGE Our Human Story

Organize students into three teams and assign each team a decade: 1920s, 1930s, or 1940s. Encourage them to use the text and additional research to create a time line of Mao Zedong's rise to power during their decade. The 1920s time line should begin with Mao's introduction to Marxism; the 1940s time line should end with Mao proclaiming the People's Republic of China. Ask students to include a brief label or description for each event they list on the time line. Invite teams to combine their time lines into one complete time line and display it in the classroom.

DIFFERENTIATE

Striving Readers

Pose and Answer Questions Pair striving readers with proficient readers and ask them to reread the lesson together. Instruct them to pause after each paragraph and ask one another *who, what, when, where,* or *why* questions about what they have read. Suggest students use a 5Ws Chart to help organize their questions and answers.

Pre-AP

Create a Profile Have students conduct online research about Mao Zedong or Chiang Kai-shek to learn more about each man's background, philosophy, and actions. Challenge students to use their findings to create an online profile of one of the leaders, including background information about conditions in China at the time, photographs and maps of the civil war, and a few posts written from the leader's perspective about what he hopes to accomplish during and after the war. Invite students to read their profiles to the class or post them on the class blog or website.

See the Chapter Planner for more strategies for differentiation.

HISTORICAL THINKING

ANSWERS

1. Chiang Kai-shek and his Nationalist Party lost the long civil war with Mao Zedong and the Chinese Communist Party. After driving Chiang from the mainland to Taiwan, Mao and his followers established the communist People's Republic of China.

2. While containment seemed to be working in Europe, it could not prevent China, with its population of 600 million people, or North Korea from falling to the communists.

3. Possible responses: The two sides will probably go to war with one another because each wants to control all of Korea. There will probably be a stalemate, since both sides are backed by superpowers who don't want a war with each other.

2.3 The Korean War

It is said that war teaches geography. Until the conflict began in Korea in 1950, most Americans knew little about that distant country. Suddenly, they were reading about Korea every day in the newspapers and about the American soldiers who were risking their lives there.

MAIN IDEA U.S. forces helped repel North Korea's invasion of South Korea, but they were forced to retreat after China entered the war.

NORTH KOREA INVADES SOUTH KOREA

On June 25, 1950, troops from communist North Korea launched a massive invasion into South Korea. The North Koreans, with Soviet support, sought to forcibly **reunify**, or reunite, the two Koreas and establish communist rule over the entire Korean peninsula.

The attack put great pressure on President Truman. His administration had withdrawn American combat troops from Korea and implied that the country was not vital to the free world's security. That did not keep Truman from viewing the invasion as a clear-cut act of aggression. He also believed failure to take action might make him appear "soft" on communism.

Truman moved quickly, proposing a United Nations resolution that offered assistance to South Korea to repel the attack. A week later, without consulting Congress, Truman sent U.S. ground troops to South Korea as part of a UN military effort. In addition to American troops, soldiers and medical personnel from Australia, New Zealand, Great Britain, France, Turkey, Thailand, and 14 other countries took part.

For two months, North Korean forces pushed the UN forces back. By September, North Korea controlled all of South Korea except the southeastern corner. Then UN forces under the command of U.S. general Douglas MacArthur took the offensive. In a stroke of brilliance, MacArthur

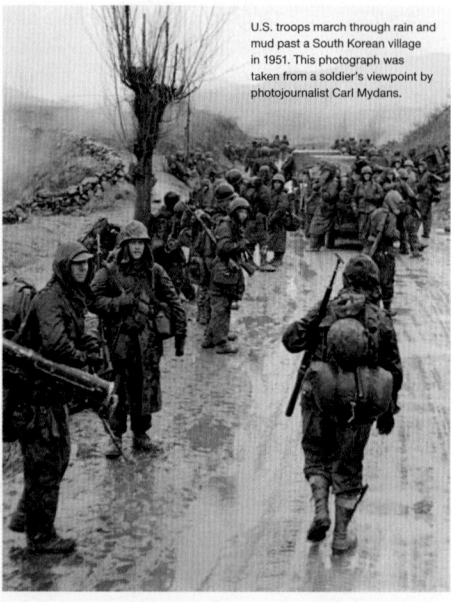

U.S. troops march through rain and mud past a South Korean village in 1951. This photograph was taken from a soldier's viewpoint by photojournalist Carl Mydans.

landed troops at **Incheon** on South Korea's west coast, deep behind enemy lines. His strategy forced the North Korean army into a hasty retreat. Within weeks, UN forces had chased the North Koreans back to the 38th parallel.

CHINA CROSSES THE YALU RIVER

Sweeping into North Korea, UN forces soon captured **Pyongyang** (pee-UHNG-YAHNG), the capital city. Ignoring warnings from China, they continued their swift northward advance. By late October, some regiments had reached the **Yalu River** on North Korea's border with China.

China responded quickly and forcefully. A large Chinese force attacked MacArthur's army and pushed it southward. After weeks of fierce fighting, American army and marine units managed to halt the Chinese advance just south of the 38th parallel. Although disaster had been avoided, Americans were shocked by what *Time* magazine described as "the worst military setback the United States has ever suffered."

Meanwhile, MacArthur and President Truman were increasingly at odds with one another. MacArthur chafed at fighting a limited war. He recommended a naval blockade of China's coast, massive bombing of its factories and power plants, and an invasion of the Chinese mainland to be led by the forces of Chiang Kai-shek. MacArthur even suggested using nuclear weapons against

North Korea. Truman worried that expanding the war would alarm the other members of the UN coalition and could even draw the Soviet Union into the conflict. In April 1951, after MacArthur had repeatedly challenged his authority, an infuriated Truman relieved the general of his command.

By June, the war had reached a stalemate. Neither side could achieve victory. Peace negotiations began in July and dragged on for two years. During this period, fighting continued along the front, and U.S. voters elected a new president: Dwight D. Eisenhower, who had commanded the Allied forces in Europe during World War II. In July 1953, North and South Korea signed an armistice that ended the hostilities but left Korea divided.

HISTORICAL THINKING

1. **READING CHECK** How did China's entry into the Korean conflict change the war for UN forces?

2. **INTERPRET MAPS** What challenges do you think Korea's terrain posed to the marines and soldiers on the ground in the Korean War?

3. **MAKE INFERENCES** Why do you think President Truman did not ask for Congress's approval before sending troops to Korea?

Objective

Analyze the causes, major events, and outcome of the Korean War, including its effects on the Cold War.

Critical Thinking Skills for Lesson 2.3

• Identify Main Ideas and Details
• Monitor Comprehension
• Interpret Maps
• Make Inferences
• Summarize
• Form and Support Opinions
• Evaluate

Essential Question for Chapter 25

How did the United States change after World War II? Although war weary, the United States aided South Korea when communist North Korea invaded. Lesson 2.3 examines the course of the Korean War and how it affected Cold War politics.

Background for the Teacher

The Korean War had serious repercussions in the United States. Many Americans, who viewed General MacArthur as a folk hero, were enraged when President Truman fired him. Citizens burned the president in effigy in cities across the nation. Letters to the White House ran approximately 21 to 1 in support of the general. On Capitol Hill, representatives placed some of the telegrams they received into the *Congressional Record*. They bore titles such as "Impeach the Imbecile" and "We Wish to Protest the Latest Outrage by the Pig in the White House." The war also increased Americans' fear of communism and possible nuclear attack. Air-raid drills became a regular part of many schools' routines as children were taught to dive under their desks and shield their eyes from an atomic blast. In New York City, school officials distributed metal tags for students to wear, stamped with their names and addresses. As one first grader explained, "If a bomb gets me in the street, people will know what my name is."

INTRODUCE & ENGAGE

Preview Using Maps

Remind students of the status of Korea following World War II. Then ask students what they know about the status of Korea today. Next, provide them with a current map of North and South Korea and draw their attention to the maps of the Korean War in this lesson. **ASK:** Which maps in the lesson best resemble the current map of Korea? *(the first and last maps)* **ASK:** What can we predict about the course of the Korean War using both the current map and the maps in the lesson? *(The Korean War ended with little change in borders, and these borders are still valid today.)* Tell students that in Lesson 2.3 they will learn about U.S. participation in the Korean War and the outcome of the fighting.

TEACH

Guided Discussion

1. **Summarize** Why did President Truman intervene in Korea? *(Although Truman did not think Korea was important to U.S. security, he committed troops to fighting the North Korean invasion because he did not want to appear "soft" on communism.)*

2. **Form and Support Opinions** Do you think the Korean War was worth fighting? Why? *(Possible responses: Yes. The war prevented North Korea from taking over South Korea and contained communism in the north. No. The war was largely a waste of human life and resources since it ended in a stalemate that left Korea divided almost exactly where it was before the war.)*

Evaluate

Direct students' attention to the *Time* magazine quote about the Korean War conflict between the United States and China as being "the worst military setback the United States has ever suffered." **ASK:** What evidence in the lesson might support this opinion? *(Answers will vary. Possible response: The map shows that U.S.-led forces had taken over almost all of Korea by November 25, 1950, and then shows the substantial territory they lost after the Chinese entered the war. The maps and text imply that MacArthur and his allies were unprepared for the Chinese forces and barely avoided a Chinese takeover of South Korea.)*

Active Options

On Your Feet: Sequence Chain Ask groups of students to trace the events in the Korean War described in the lesson by summarizing them in a Sequence Chain. When groups have completed their work, ask students from the groups to stand up and form a physical chain. As each group makes its successive link, ask a volunteer to read one event from the group's link that contributes to the chain of events in the war.

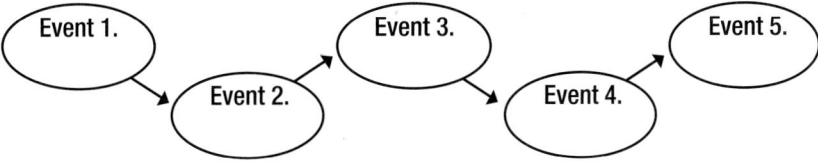

NG Learning Framework: Learn About North Korea Today

SKILL Communication

KNOWLEDGE Our Human Story

Remind students that North Korea is still a communist country and that the peninsula remains divided at the 38th parallel. Tell them to work in groups to research facts about the government of North Korea today and the threats it poses to Asia and to the world. Have groups share their findings in a class discussion about what actions—if any—the United States should take in the region. Ask students to consider the consequences of the actions they recommend not only to the peninsula but to the rest of the world.

DIFFERENTIATE

English Language Learners

Understand Figures of Speech Work with students to make sure they understand the concept of figures of speech in English. Then point out the figure of speech "appear soft" in the text. Ask students to use context clues to interpret what *soft* might mean in this instance. Finally, have students restate the figure of speech in their own words to convey its meaning. Ask them to explain why politicians would not want to "appear soft on communism."

Gifted & Talented

Research and Write a Historical Dialogue Instruct students to form a hypothesis about whether the disagreement between General MacArthur and President Truman over the Korean War was inevitable. Ask them to conduct online research about the personalities and beliefs of the two men, accessing primary and secondary sources. When students have gathered their information, challenge them to write a dialogue that might have occurred between the two leaders before Truman's final decision. Invite students to role-play their dialogues for the class.

See the Chapter Planner for more strategies for differentiation.

HISTORICAL THINKING

ANSWERS

1. China's entry into the war changed the balance of power. Chinese forces were able to push MacArthur's advancing UN forces southward across the 38th parallel. With Chinese forces in the war, the best the UN forces could do was fight to a stalemate.

2. Much of the country is mountainous, particularly in the north. This probably made troop movements difficult.

3. Possible response: Truman wanted to act quickly, and since it was a UN effort and not a war declared or waged solely by the United States, Truman may have believed he did not need Congress's approval to commit U.S. troops.

Fear of Communism

At first glance the senator from Wisconsin didn't look very intimidating. But for a short time in the 1950s, Joseph McCarthy held the country in fearful suspense with his very public search for communists in the United States.

MAIN IDEA In the late 1940s and early 1950s, fear of communism gripped citizens and government officials in the United States, leading to prosecutions of both suspected and avowed communists.

THE COMMUNIST THREAT

As the Soviet Union grew more powerful and communist regimes gained control in Eastern Europe and Asia, Americans became increasingly worried about the spread of communism. Their fears multiplied in 1949 when President Truman announced that the Soviet Union had exploded an atomic bomb. The end of the U.S. monopoly on atomic weapons raised the horrifying prospect of an all-out nuclear war.

The Soviet Union was supposedly years behind the United States in nuclear technology. How, then, had it managed to develop an atomic weapon so quickly? Some officials believed the only possible answer was espionage. Authorities soon suspected that **Julius and Ethel Rosenberg**, a husband-and-wife spy team, had provided the Soviet Union with top-secret information from the Manhattan Project. The Rosenbergs were tried, convicted, and executed. But they weren't the only Americans suspected of being communist agents.

The only two Americans executed for spying during the Cold War, Ethel and Julius Rosenberg were photographed during their trial in 1951. Later, the couple's sons worked to prove their parents' innocence. In 2016, new evidence proved their father's guilt but cast doubt on their mother's.

In the late 1930s, the U.S. House of Representatives had established the **House Un-American Activities Committee (HUAC)** to investigate Nazi propaganda in the United States. After World War II, the committee was revived as a watchdog against communist activities. In 1947, HUAC launched an investigation of the motion picture industry. The Hollywood Ten, a group of pro-communist writers and directors, refused to answer HUAC's questions about their political associations. They were sent to prison for contempt of Congress. Hollywood studio heads, caught up in the anticommunist whirlwind, put the names of those ten people and many others on a **blacklist**. Studios would not hire writers, directors, or performers who had been blacklisted.

Another person caught up in HUAC's investigation was **Alger Hiss**, a former federal government official who had served as an advisor to President Franklin Roosevelt. He was accused of stealing classified State Department documents and passing them on to a Soviet agent. Hiss was convicted and jailed for perjury, or lying under oath, sending shock waves through the nation.

During this period, the United States and the Soviet Union became locked in an arms race, a deadly serious contest to develop the most powerful weapons. It led to the development of the hydrogen bomb and to the production of rockets capable of delivering nuclear weapons to targets

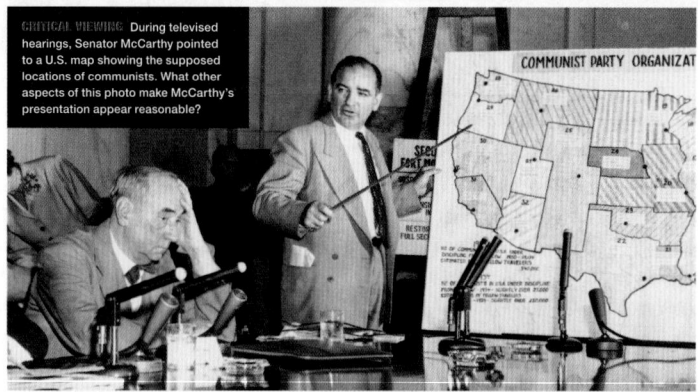

CRITICAL VIEWING During televised hearings, Senator McCarthy pointed to a U.S. map showing the supposed locations of communists. What other aspects of this photo make McCarthy's presentation appear reasonable?

COMMUNIST PARTY ORGANIZAT

thousands of miles away. Each side sought to gain advantage through **brinkmanship**, the practice of pushing interactions to the brink, or edge, of dangerous confrontation.

THE RISE AND FALL OF McCARTHY

In 1950, **Senator Joseph McCarthy** of Wisconsin began making sensational claims about communists in the federal government. In 1952, McCarthy became chairman of the Senate's Committee on Government Operations and its subcommittee on investigations. In this powerful position, he looked for "communist influence" in the State Department and other government agencies. His hearings did not uncover many communists. They did, however, ruin many careers, undermine worker morale, and make the United States look fearful in the eyes of the world. This phenomenon became known as **McCarthyism**.

One of McCarthy's biggest targets was the U.S. Army. In the spring of 1954, the Senate held nationally televised hearings on charges that a communist spy ring was operating at an Army base in New Jersey. For 36 days, the nation watched McCarthy's frightening outbursts and crude personal attacks. His popularity plummeted, and a few months later the Senate censured him for acting "contrary to senatorial ethics." McCarthyism finally came to an end.

During McCarthy's televised hearings against the U.S. Army, the senator accused one of the attorneys working with the Army's lawyer, Joseph Welch, of associating with communists. Welch uttered the now famous words that effectively ended McCarthy's career:

PRIMARY SOURCE

Until this moment, Senator, I think I never really gauged your cruelty or your recklessness. . . . Let us not assassinate this lad further, Senator. You have done enough. Have you no sense of decency?

—Attorney Joseph Welch, June 9, 1954

HISTORICAL THINKING

1. **READING CHECK** What events led to the execution of Julius and Ethel Rosenberg?

2. **SUMMARIZE** How was the rise of Joseph McCarthy related to the dominant mood of Americans at the time?

3. **FORM AND SUPPORT OPINIONS** Do you think it was right for the motion picture industry to blacklist people because of their political beliefs? Support your opinion with evidence from the text.

Objective

Discuss how the fear of communism led to the prosecution of suspected Soviet spies, blacklisting, and the rise of McCarthyism.

Critical Thinking Skills for Lesson 2.4

- Identify Main Ideas and Details
- Monitor Comprehension
- Summarize
- Form and Support Opinions
- Make Inferences
- Draw Conclusions

Essential Question for Chapter 25

How did the United States change after World War II? A climate of fear and accusations against real and suspected enemies swept across the United States in the 1950s. Lesson 2.4 examines how the fear of communism impacted U.S. society.

Background for the Teacher

Joseph McCarthy had always had a questionable relationship with the truth. While running for the U. S. Senate, he called himself "tail-gunner Joe" and claimed to have "fired more bullets than any marine in history." In reality, he had served as an intelligence officer, interviewing pilots after missions. Later, he smeared his Democratic opponent as a communist—despite a lack of proof. But it wasn't until he started worrying about his re-election that McCarthy launched his infamous anticommunist campaign. During a speech in early 1950, he claimed to have a long list of people in the federal government who were active communists. Although he never produced the list, his accusations played on the public's fears, and he won re-election. Ironically, the Republican leadership, wary of his tactics, gave him the chairmanship of the obscure Committee on Government Operations in hopes of controlling him. Instead, McCarthy used the committee as a stage for his personal anticommunist crusade.

INTRODUCE & ENGAGE

Activate Prior Knowledge

Have students recall injustices that they learned about in previous chapters. **ASK:** What are some examples of groups of people who have been targeted and mistreated because of race, religion, nationality, or political beliefs in our nation's history? *(Possible responses: Japanese American internment camps during World War II, the first Red Scare, attacks on African Americans by the Ku Klux Klan, the treatment of Native Americans during westward expansion)* After students share their ideas, explain that Lesson 2.4 examines how fear of communism led to many Americans being unjustly targeted.

TEACH

Guided Discussion

1. **Make Inferences** How could the arms race and brinkmanship have contributed to the national mood of fear during the 1950s? *(Possible response: The arms race, in which the United States and the Soviet Union competed to develop the largest arsenal of deadly weapons, increased the fear of nuclear war. Brinkmanship, where each side pushed the other to the edge of confrontation, would also have raised fears of nuclear annihilation.)*

2. **Draw Conclusions** Why did many Americans find the arrest of Alger Hiss and McCarthy's investigation of a spy ring in the U.S. Army shocking? *(Possible response: Alger Hiss had been an advisor to President Franklin Roosevelt, which meant he had access to both the president and secure information. Americans want to believe that people in the U.S. government and military are protecting the nation, not betraying it.)*

More Information

TV and the Downfall of McCarthy At the Army-McCarthy hearings, army attorney Joseph Welch was questioning McCarthy's aide Roy Cohn. McCarthy interrupted to attack a young attorney on Welch's legal team, Frederick Fisher. McCarthy accused Fisher of belonging to the National Lawyers Guild while in law school, an organization that HUAC erroneously associated with the Communist Party. Welch, enraged and saddened by the accusation, lashed out at McCarthy. Direct students to read the primary source in the lesson. **ASK:** Would Welch's words have been as effective if the hearings had not been televised? Why or why not? *(Possible response: The impact probably would not have been as great without the live coverage. People could see Welch's obvious pain and outrage, which added greater weight to his words.)* Point out that executives at ABC, which aired the hearings, hoped the live coverage would show people how misguided McCarthy was.

Active Options

On Your Feet: Create a Concept Web Arrange students in groups of four around a section of a bulletin board or a table. Provide each group with a large sheet of paper, and assign each group one of the following topics: Julius and Ethel Rosenberg, HUAC, or McCarthyism. Instruct group members to take turns adding a concept or phrase to a Concept Web about their topic. When time for the activity has elapsed, call on volunteers from each group to share their webs with the class.

NG Learning Framework: Explore Perspectives

SKILL Communication

KNOWLEDGE Our Human Story

Discuss with students how the HUAC hearings reflected the Cold War situation and the American public's mood during the 1950s. Ask students to work in groups to review the content of the lesson and write down reasons people might have had to fear communism. Then encourage each group to write an editorial either supporting or criticizing the activities of HUAC from the perspective of someone living in the 1950s. To help students understand peoples' responses to communism and nuclear war, have them compare these responses with present-day fears about extremist groups and terrorist attacks. When the groups are finished, invite them to share their editorials with the class.

DIFFERENTIATE

Inclusion

Analyze a Photo and Primary Source Pair students who are visually impaired with students who are not. Ask the latter to describe the photograph of the McCarthy hearing and to read the Primary Source feature aloud. Tell visually impaired students to ask clarifying questions. Then have pairs work together to answer the Critical Viewing question.

Pre-AP

Research Causes and Effects Have students supplement the information in the lesson by conducting research to learn more about what led HUAC to investigate the movie industry and how the investigations affected that industry. Encourage students to keep track of their findings in a Cause-and-Effect Chart. Then ask them to write an essay analyzing how the anticommunist hearings affected people in the movie industry, such as writers, producers, directors, or actors. Invite students to share their essays with the class.

See the Chapter Planner for more strategies for differentiation.

HISTORICAL THINKING

ANSWERS

1. When the Soviets exploded an atomic bomb in 1949, shocked Americans asked how they could have developed the bomb so quickly. Investigators found that the Rosenbergs had provided the Soviet Union with top-secret information about building an atomic bomb. They were tried, convicted, and executed.

2. Increasing fears of communism made Americans receptive to leaders who took a strong anticommunist stance even if they falsely accused people and agencies.

3. Answers will vary. Possible responses: No. There was no solid evidence that anyone accused had actually done anything wrong. Yes. Hollywood had a responsibility to prevent communists from using the media.

CRITICAL VIEWING Possible response: The senator is dressed in a suit and tie, holds a pointer, and appears calm and reasonable as he talks. His presentation takes place in the Senate chambers and is being televised, which also makes him appear reasonable.

3.1 The American Dream?

What is your idea of the American dream? Millions of Americans in the 1950s dreamed of earning a good wage, providing for their families, and owning a nice home and car. For some, the dream was possible.

MAIN IDEA The 1950s were a time of population shifts, social change, and—for some but not all Americans—rising prosperity and living standards.

THE AMERICAN FAMILY

During the 1950s, many different forces were at work shaping American life. These included economic prosperity, new consumer products, and shifting population patterns.

Shortly after World War II, marriage rates had spiraled upward. Birthrates had risen sharply, too, and they remained high through the 1950s and into the 1960s. This prolonged period of high birthrates came to be known as the **baby boom**.

In addition to population growth, the decade saw two significant population shifts. Seeking more space and greener, safer environments for their families, large numbers of mostly white middle-class Americans moved from cities to suburbs. Explosive suburban growth fueled booms in the housing, automobile, and construction industries. For many large cities, though, it led to declines in population, political power, and quality of life.

The other population shift was from the **Frostbelt**—the Northeast and upper Midwest regions known for their harsh winters—to the **Sunbelt**, a 15-state region stretching from coast to coast across the southern United States. The Sunbelt's low taxes, inexpensive land, and warm climate attracted businesses, especially the growing military defense, electronics, and aerospace industries. At the same time, improvements in air conditioning made hot summers more bearable. Millions migrated from the Frostbelt to the Sunbelt for the new jobs or to retire.

Not everyone was content with the trends in family life. During the war, as you have learned, many women entered the U.S. workforce for the first time. After the war ended, they were encouraged to return to the more traditional roles of wife and mother. By the end of the 1950s, however, many women were questioning the notion that their place was in the home.

THE OTHER AMERICA

Not all Americans shared in the prosperity and rising living standards of the 1950s. Despite progress due to the growing civil rights movement, African Americans continued to face widespread discrimination and segregation. Doors to advancement that were open to other Americans were closed to them.

Those doors were often closed to Americans of Mexican descent, too. The Mexican American population had soared since 1942, the year the federal government had launched the Bracero Program. As you have read, this program aimed to address a labor shortage during World War II by

Reaching 50 States

In 1959, the U.S. territories of Alaska and Hawaii were admitted to statehood, rounding out the 50 United States we celebrate today. During World War II, the United States had expanded its army and navy bases in both territories as they became important to military strategy. That importance carried over into the Cold War era. Citizens of the two territories began their statehood efforts right after the end of World War II, but it took many years for Congress to pass measures admitting Alaska and Hawaii to the Union. Alaska became the 49th state on January 3, 1959. Hawaii followed suit as the 50th state on August 21, 1959. On July 4, 1960, the 50th star was officially added to the American flag.

CRITICAL VIEWING Among the people who did not benefit from American prosperity were these young white and African-American children whose families rented poorly kept housing on the west side of Chicago in 1953. What unsafe conditions for children playing do you see in the photograph?

bringing several hundred thousand *braceros*, or manual laborers, from Mexico to the United States to plant and harvest crops. Some of the braceros chose to stay in the country illegally, prompting anger and resentment among Americans. Unfortunately, this resentment extended to Mexican Americans and legal immigrants as well.

Although President Eisenhower worked to trim government spending, he kept in place popular New Deal programs aimed at struggling Americans. These programs included Social Security and unemployment insurance. "In all those things which deal with people, be liberal," he stated. "In all those things which deal with people's money . . . be conservative."

In a groundbreaking 1962 book titled *The Other America*, author Michael Harrington challenged the widely held belief that the New Deal had almost eliminated poverty. He claimed that 40 to 50 million Americans remained poor but that they were nearly invisible to more affluent, or wealthy, Americans. Harrington called for a "comprehensive assault on poverty" through federal legislation addressing education, medical care, housing, and jobs.

HISTORICAL THINKING

1. **READING CHECK** Why might people have been tempted to leave the Frostbelt for the Sunbelt?

2. **MAKE INFERENCES** What do you think Michael Harrington meant when he stated that the poor were "invisible" to other Americans?

3. **SUMMARIZE** What are some ways in which the United States changed during the 1950s?

PLAN

Objective

Understand that while the postwar population grew, prospered, and shifted locations, some Americans were left behind.

Critical Thinking Skills for Lesson 3.1

- Identify Main Ideas and Details
- Monitor Comprehension
- Make Inferences
- Summarize
- Analyze Primary Sources
- Interpret Graphs

Essential Question for Chapter 25

How did the United States change after World War II? After the war, the birth rate soared, industries boomed, and many Americans moved to the Sunbelt. Lesson 3.1 examines the reasons behind these changes, as well as the plight of people left out of the general prosperity.

Background for the Teacher

The baby boomers did more than just increase the postwar U.S. population. This generation forever changed the demographics of the country. When baby boomers began having children of their own, they triggered another population surge—what demographers have called an "echo boom." Unlike the original baby boom, which resulted from women having many children, the echo boom resulted from the sheer number of women having children, even though they had fewer children per household. Now that baby boomers are entering retirement age, they are swelling the ranks of older Americans, a trend known as the "graying" of the U.S. population. This fact has sobering implications for social programs such as Social Security and Medicare, which are funded mainly by payroll taxes. In 2010, when the first baby boomers turned 64 and approached retirement, there were 100 working-age adults for every 21 retirement-age adults. By 2030, when the last baby boomers reach 65, that ratio will be 100 working-age adults for every 35 retirement-age adults.

Consider the American Dream

Write the term *American dream* on the board and ask students to write down or sketch on a sheet of paper what this idea suggests to them. Then have students share and compare their responses. Tell students that in this lesson they will learn about some of the postwar changes in American life that began to reshape the American dream.

TEACH

Guided Discussion

1. **Identify Main Ideas and Details** What factors kept minorities from sharing in the rising prosperity of the postwar years? *(Possible response: Segregation and discrimination kept many African Americans and Mexican Americans from advancing economically. In addition, many Mexican manual workers, who had been brought to the United States to work in the war industries, were resented for staying in the country illegally.)*

2. **Analyze Primary Sources** What do you think President Eisenhower meant when he said, "I'm conservative when it comes to money. . . . but liberal when it comes to human beings"? *(Possible response: Eisenhower believed that the government should help less fortunate Americans through programs like Social Security. At the same time, he thought the government should be mindful of the cost of these programs.)*

Interpret Graphs

Project the Birth and Marriage Rates in the Baby Boom Era (1945–1965) graph for students to view. **ASK:** How would you describe the relationship between marriage rates and birth rates immediately following World War II? *(The two rates are directly related. Marriage rates spiked, followed by a spike in birth rates.)* **ASK:** What other observations can you make about marriage rates and birth rates during the baby-boom era based on the graph? *(Possible response: Marriage rates dropped quickly after peaking, falling below the 1945 rate by the late 1940s. In contrast, birth rates fell very little until the late 1950s and did not fall to the 1945 rate until around 1965.)*

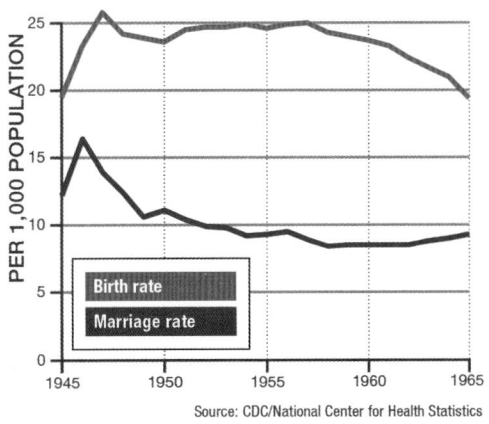

Birth and Marriage Rates in the Baby Boom Era (1945–1965)

Source: CDC/National Center for Health Statistics

Active Options

On Your Feet: Numbered Heads Arrange students in groups of four and have students count off within each group. Ask the groups to discuss what the question mark in the lesson title "The American Dream?" suggests. Direct students to find facts in the lesson that support their ideas. Then call a number and ask students with that number to summarize their group's discussion for the class.

NG Learning Framework: Create an Infographic

SKILL Communication

KNOWLEDGE Our Human Story

Divide students into three groups to research statistics about the migration of Americans from the Frostbelt to the Sunbelt in the 1950s, 1960s, and 1970s. Suggest they look for information such as the number of people who moved, what years show the highest rate of migration in their assigned decades, and which groups were most likely to migrate. Instruct students to translate their statistics into creative infographics that include charts, graphs, and maps. After they finish, invite groups to discuss their infographics with the class.

Inclusion

Explore Cultural Nicknames Ask students to research the origins of the nicknames *baby boom*, *echo boom*, *Frostbelt*, and *Sunbelt*. When did the terms first enter the language? Who coined them? Have their meanings changed over the years? Then have students think of more recent nicknames, such as *Rustbelt*, *millennials*, *Generation X*, and the *Founders*. Discuss as a class what these nicknames mean and how nicknames used in different decades can convey significant changes in American society.

Pre-AP

Write a News Profile Assign students the role of journalists reporting on "the other America." Direct them to conduct online and library research to find stories about or written by an individual who lived in "the other America" during the late 1950s. Ask students to write a profile of the person and then post their profiles on a class blog or publish them on a school website.

See the Chapter Planner for more strategies for differentiation.

HISTORICAL THINKING

ANSWERS

1. Businesses moved to the Sunbelt for its low taxes, cheaper land, warmer climate, and growing labor force. Individuals moved south for the climate, for jobs, and for retirement.

2. Possible response: Harrington meant that the poor and affluent lived separately and that the affluent didn't see or think about the nation's poor.

3. Possible response: The United States experienced a baby boom, a population shift both from cities to suburbs and from the Frostbelt to the Sunbelt, and women questioning traditional gender roles. The shift to the suburbs fueled economic growth but hurt many large cities politically and economically.

CRITICAL VIEWING Possible responses: Dangers include low porch railings on second-story balconies, steep wooden stairs, rusted and damaged trash cans, cars that might hit or injure children, and a dirt street filled with broken bricks and stones.

3.2 The Suburbanization of America

MAIN IDEA After World War II, millions of Americans moved to the suburbs, which had a significant impact on the country's economy, society, and culture.

LIVING THE AMERICAN DREAM

As you know, Congress passed the GI Bill in 1944 to help World War II veterans readjust to civilian life. The bill helped cover education costs and provided low-interest home loans to veterans. Many of the men and women who returned from the war were starting families and wanted to buy a house. Home ownership is a big part of the American dream. However, most cities couldn't keep up with the demand for housing.

As a result, veterans paid contractors to build affordable single-family houses in the suburbs. By 1950, more than 18 million people, or 1 of every 8 Americans, had moved from the cities to the suburbs. This population shift is called **suburbanization**. In addition to offering space for larger houses, suburbs often had better schools and a lower crime rate than cities. You've learned that many Americans began buying more consumer goods in the 1950s, and automobiles were at the top of the list. Cars allowed workers to travel from the suburbs to jobs in the city. Access to the suburbs became easier when President Dwight Eisenhower signed the **Federal-Aid Highway Act of 1956**. The act included the **Interstate Highway System**, which linked towns, cities, and suburbs nationwide.

In 1947, William Levitt purchased several thousand acres of farmland on New York's Long Island for the mass production of homes. Using the assembly-line system developed by Henry Ford at his automobile plants, Levitt manufactured precut building materials in his factories. Then, on the building site, each construction worker performed a single task to complete each house. Builders made as many as 180 houses in a week. Once the homes were finished, schools, parks, churches, and shopping centers were added to the neighborhoods. The Long Island Levittown, as it was called, was

completed in 1951. Levitt would go on to build several other Levittowns in the Northeast.

Suburbanization transformed the American landscape and changed American life. The mass movement had an impact on the country economically, socially, and culturally. Many of these effects continue to influence American life today.

ECONOMIC IMPACT

Suburbanization contributed to the economic boom of the 1950s. It provided jobs in several sectors, including the construction and automobile industries. However, many businesses and factories also moved from the cities to the suburbs. With fewer people and businesses remaining in cities, local governments began to have trouble funding schools, transportation, and other city services.

SOCIAL IMPACT

The suburbs provided a generally safe and clean but ultimately segregated environment. Most African Americans couldn't afford to buy a car and move to the suburbs, and those who could were often prevented from moving. Many suburban neighborhoods, including the Long Island Levittown, refused to sell to African Americans. As a result, African Americans, other minorities, and the less wealthy remained in the cities. Suburbanization forced some farmers to sell their farms. It also disrupted wildlife habitats.

CULTURAL IMPACT

Suburban residents enjoyed many conveniences they hadn't had before, including modern kitchens. But some people criticized suburban life for its homogeneity, or sameness. The houses tended to look alike, and the people living in them did many of the same things. While the men went to work in their offices, the women stayed home to cook, clean, and look after the children.

THINK LIKE A GEOGRAPHER

1. **ANALYZE CAUSE AND EFFECT** What led many people to move to the suburbs after World War II?

2. **COMPARE AND CONTRAST** How did cities and suburbs differ following suburbanization?

3. **ANALYZE ENVIRONMENTAL CONCEPTS** How did suburbanization affect rural communities?

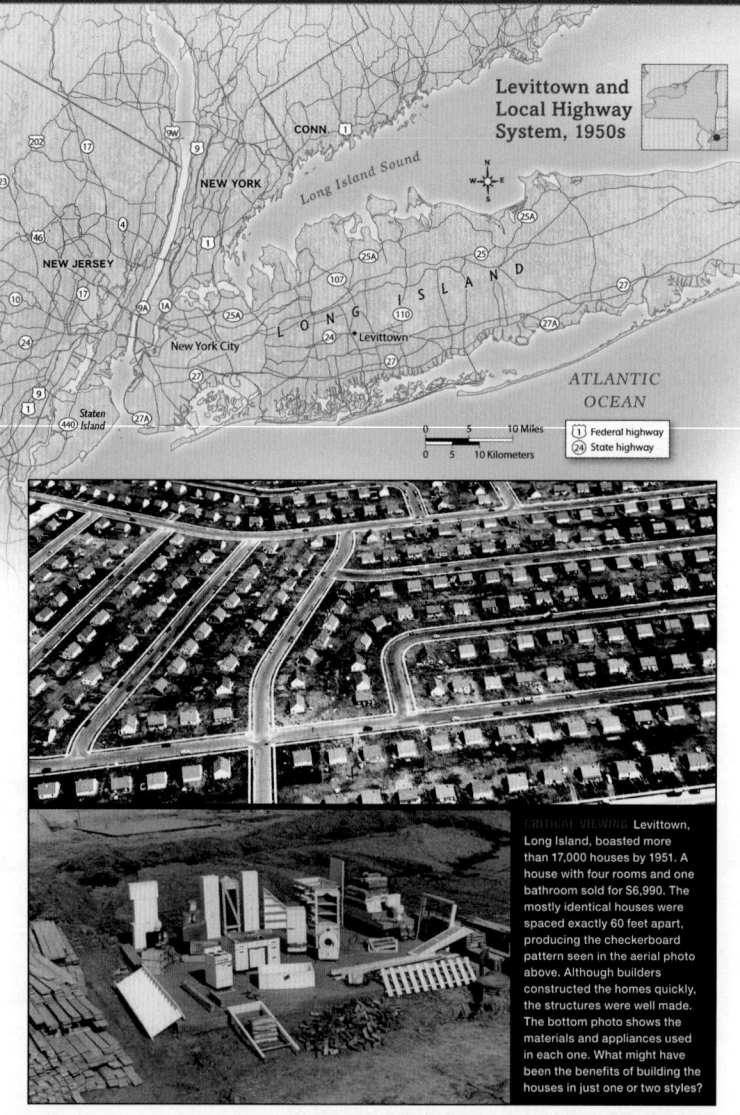

Levittown and Local Highway System, 1950s

ATLANTIC OCEAN

0   10 Miles
0 5 10 Kilometers

① Federal highway
㉔ State highway

CRITICAL VIEWING Levittown, Long Island, boasted more than 17,000 houses by 1951. A house with four rooms and one bathroom sold for $6,990. The mostly identical houses were spaced exactly 60 feet apart, producing the checkerboard pattern seen in the aerial photo above. Although builders constructed the homes quickly, the structures were well made. The bottom photo shows the materials and appliances used in each one. What might have been the benefits of building the houses in just one or two styles?

PLAN

Objective

Analyze the causes and effects of rapid suburbanization in the United States.

Critical Thinking Skills for Lesson 3.2

- Identify Main Ideas and Details
- Monitor Comprehension
- Analyze Cause and Effect
- Compare and Contrast
- Analyze Environmental Concepts
- Make Connections
- Interpret Maps

Essential Question for Chapter 25

How did the United States change after World War II? In the 1950s and 1960s, millions of people were pursuing the American dream, which included buying a home. Lesson 3.2 discusses the rapid growth of suburbs and their effects on the nation's economic, social, and cultural life.

Background for the Teacher

At the turn of the 20th century, the United States had no interstate highways and few paved roads outside of the cities. Driving any distance was an adventure that one journalist termed "the last call of the wild." Progress on roadways was slow until Dwight D. Eisenhower became president in 1952. As the supreme Allied commander during World War II, Eisenhower had been impressed with Germany's autobahn, or high-speed, multiple-lane highway. It had been a major advantage to Allied forces and their supply trucks as they pursued the German army. Eisenhower believed that a similar network of high-speed interstate roads could serve both U.S. civilian and military goals. The network would ensure safe and speedy transcontinental travel and would offer a means of rapid evacuation from target cities should there be a nuclear attack. Eisenhower's highway act authorized the building of 41,000 miles of highways, a transcontinental network that still makes commercial and private travel far safer and easier than in the past.

Compare Suburbs and Cities

Draw a Venn diagram on the board with the following labels: Suburb, Both, and City. Prompt students to suggest words or phrases they associate with suburbs, cities, or with both places, and write their suggestions in the appropriate section of the diagram. Then ask students to discuss what they think are the advantages and disadvantages of living in a suburb or a city. Explain that this lesson describes the factors that led to the rapid spread of suburbs and the flight of people from cities after World War II.

TEACH

Guided Discussion

1. **Make Connections** How did the automobile industry help increase the rate of suburbanization? *(Possible responses: More cars and roads made it easier for people to get to and from suburban areas. Developers bought land outside of cities and built homes that had become accessible and affordable. Manufacturing techniques from the automobile industry served as models for manufacturing and assembly-line construction of suburban homes, allowing suburbs to develop quickly.)*

2. **Interpret Maps** Ask students to study the map and note the location of Levittown. **ASK:** What are some of the advantages and disadvantages of Levittown's geographic location? *(Possible response: The town is situated on a network of roads, so driving to places around Long Island would be easy. It is close enough to New York City for a commute but far enough away to avoid the city's noise and pollution. However, leaving the island to drive to destinations farther north, west, or south requires going through or around New York City with its heavy traffic.)*

Geography in History

Ideas about what suburbs should look like have radically changed since the 1950s. Instead of hundreds of identical houses packed onto small lots, modern and future suburban designs include large, distinctly designed homes; community gardening areas; "smart" area-wide power systems; electric charging stations for cars; and larger yards landscaped for water management and sustainability. Designs for future suburban plans might include self-driving-car lots and community drone ports for package deliveries. In addition, urban/suburban shopping malls, hit hard by online retailing, are being repurposed as clinics, sports facilities, small business centers, and even churches. Planners envision suburbs and their cities not as separate areas but as opportunities to build an integrated, sustainable environment.

Active Options

On Your Feet: Fishbowl Direct one half of the class to sit in a circle facing inward and the other half to sit in a larger circle around them. Students on the inside discuss the following question: How do suburbs affect the environment, traffic, and diversity of businesses and people in an area? Students on the outside listen for new information. At a signal, the groups reverse their positions and continue the discussion.

NG Learning Framework: Design a City and Its Suburbs   STEM

SKILL Problem-Solving

KNOWLEDGE Our Human Story

Instruct groups of students to research online designs for future cities and suburbs in order to design their own futuristic city and suburbs. They should use math to establish a scale for their design. Encourage students to address such considerations as the ratio of open green space to developed space; transportation within and around the city; sustainable power; and the locations of schools, shopping, and public places. Students can construct a three-dimensional design using physical materials or draw plans using a software design program, if available. Invite a representative from each group to present the completed design to the class and describe some of the problems the group had to solve.

Striving Readers

Complete T-Charts Instruct students to create three T-Charts with the headings Economic Impacts, Social Impacts, and Cultural Impacts. Tell them to label the left column of each chart Positive, and the right column Negative. As they read the lesson, tell students to use their T-Charts to keep track of the positive and negative aspects of the economic, social, and cultural impacts of suburbanization. After reading, encourage students to compare their completed charts.

Gifted & Talented

Write and Record a Podcast Direct students to conduct online research about segregation in suburban areas and then write and record an informational podcast based on their findings. Encourage them to find specific studies, first-person accounts, interviews, and news coverage relating to "white flight" and practices that prevent nonwhites from buying homes in suburbs. Tell students to practice their script before they record and share it with the class.

See the Chapter Planner for more strategies for differentiation.

THINK LIKE A GEOGRAPHER

ANSWERS

1. People wanted to buy their own homes, and cities couldn't fulfill the need for more housing. With the GI Bill, many veterans could afford to buy or build homes in the suburbs. Most owned cars and newly built highways made commuting easy.

2. Cities had more low-income people, more minorities, and less money for public services and schools, but they also had diverse neighborhoods and cultures. Suburban populations had higher incomes, better public services and schools, but offered far less diversity and more limited cultural activities.

3. Developers forced some farmers to sell their land, and suburban developments reduced wildlife habitats.

CRITICAL VIEWING Possible response: It would have been cheaper and more efficient to mass-produce only a few designs. With fewer unique parts to handle, construction workers would have built homes at a record pace.

3.3 Television and Rock and Roll

Today, the average TV receives more crystal-clear channels than you can count. In the 1950s, the television experience featured a handful of channels, a sometimes wavy picture, and an antenna you had to adjust by hand. To the baby boomers and their families, it was the best entertainment ever.

MAIN IDEA In the 1950s, television emerged as a powerful medium of mass communication, and a youth culture centered on rock and roll music began to develop.

TELEVISION AND MASS CULTURE

As you have read, a mass culture arose in the United States in the 1920s. It was shaped and spread by radio and movies as well as by advertising, newspapers, and magazines. In the 1950s, television dominated American entertainment and helped transform mass culture.

In the early 1950s, television was still new. At the end of World War II, about 7,000 television sets existed in the United States. But by 1950, Americans were buying 20,000 televisions a day.

Early programming emphasized entertainment, with variety shows, quiz shows, Westerns, and **situation comedies**, such as *I Love Lucy*, in which a set cast of characters amused viewers with a funny adventure each week. The networks also aired quality dramas written by well-known authors and performed by famous stage and film actors. These programs were usually sponsored by name-brand products. Some critics have called this era the "golden age" of television.

The King of Rock and Roll
Teenage girls surround singer **Elvis Presley**, clamoring for an autograph. It was 1956—the year 21-year-old Elvis skyrocketed from a regional sensation to a national one. Girls flocked to his concerts and joined fan clubs; boys took guitar lessons and adopted his hairstyle. Admirers still call Elvis "the King."

Advertisers soon recognized television's enormous potential, and by the end of the decade advertising consumed 15 percent of television airtime. In this way, television, like radio before it, promoted the consumer society. Many economists believed that advertising contributed to prosperity by encouraging Americans to buy more goods.

The direction in which American society was heading did not sit well with all Americans. A youth rebellion that came to be known as the Beat movement took root in places such as New York City and San Francisco. Novelist **Jack Kerouac**, poet **Alan Ginsburg**, and other Beat writers criticized mass culture and the way it encouraged people to act and think alike. The Beat movement emphasized individuality and freedom of expression.

YOUTH CULTURE

Another major development in the 1950s was the rise of rock and roll music. It was deeply rooted in African-American rhythm and blues, but its influences also included country, gospel, and bluegrass music. It was characterized by a strong beat and loud singing and playing.

African-American performers such as **Chuck Berry** and **Little Richard** played leading roles in the development of rock and roll. Little Richard, in fact, proclaimed himself "the architect of rock and roll." His songs "Tutti Frutti" and "Long Tall Sally" and Berry's "Maybellene" and "Johnny B. Goode" were among the early hits that helped the genre gain broad appeal.

Rock and roll's popularity exploded with performers such as **Bill Haley**, **Elvis Presley**, and **Jerry Lee Lewis**. In 1953, Haley's "Crazy Man, Crazy" became the first rock and roll song to appear on *Billboard* magazine's pop music charts. Presley burst onto the popular music scene in 1955, and by 1956, he was a national sensation. Between 1956 and 1957, ten of his songs went to number one on the pop music chart.

Rock and roll became an important part of the youth culture emerging in the United States. This culture was rooted in the enormous prosperity and population growth that followed World War II. Unlike their parents, who had lived through desperate economic times and war, Americans

of the baby boom era were raised in relative comfort and wealth. Freed from the obligation to help support their families, many teens had money in their pockets. They bought records and listened with their friends. Nothing defined these young baby boomers more clearly than the music they shared.

In 2011, rocker Chuck Berry donated the guitar he played in his early days of touring and recording to the Smithsonian National Museum of African American History and Culture. Berry named this guitar and all his guitars for his first hit song, "Maybellene."

Chuck Berry's 1959 Gibson electric guitar

HISTORICAL THINKING

1. **READING CHECK** What kinds of programs were popular during television's "golden age"?

2. **COMPARE AND CONTRAST** What was one important difference between the youth of the 1950s and their parents?

3. **MAKE INFERENCES** Why do you think young people in the 1950s embraced rock and roll instead of the music their parents listened to?

PLAN

Objective
Assess how television and rock and roll influenced mass culture in the United States during the 1950s.

Critical Thinking Skills for Lesson 3.3
- Identify Main Ideas and Details
- Monitor Comprehension
- Compare and Contrast
- Make Inferences
- Form and Support Opinions
- Summarize

Essential Question for Chapter 25
How did the United States change after World War II? Television helped create a mass culture and consumer society in the United States, while rock and roll music spoke to the youth culture. Lesson 3.3 examines how both television and rock and roll influenced American society.

Background for the Teacher
In 1950, former disc jockey Sam Phillips opened a small recording studio in Memphis, Tennessee, with the goal of bringing African-American rhythm and blues (R&B) to a wider audience. To make ends meet, he offered his recording services to anyone who wanted to make a demonstration record. In July 1953, a young Elvis Presley paid Phillips $3.98 to record two songs as a gift for his mother. Phillips thought the young Tennessee native might be just the person to take R&B to a mainstream audience. In July 1954, Phillips released Presley's first commercial recording—up-tempo versions of Arthur "Big Boy" Crudup's "That's Alright (Mama)" and Bill Munroe's "Blue Moon of Kentucky." The record, which was a smash hit, became Presley's first step toward national and international fame.

History Notebook
Encourage students to complete the American Gallery and Reid on the Road video series pages in their History Notebooks.

Take a Poll

Write the names Chuck Berry, Little Richard, Elvis Presley, Jerry Lee Lewis, and Lucille Ball on the board. Poll the class to determine which names students recognize. Ask them to share any details they may know about these people's lives and work. Tell students that in Lesson 3.3 they will learn more about the important roles these artists played in shaping American culture in the 1950s.

TEACH

Guided Discussion

1. **Form and Support Opinions** Do you think members of the Beat movement would have agreed with the view held by some economists that television commercials served a positive function? Support your opinion with evidence from the text. *(Possible response: Those in the Beat movement would have disagreed that commercials served a positive function. They would have regarded commercials as part of the mass culture that urged people to act and think alike, rather than fostering individuality and free expression.)*

2. **Summarize** In what way was early rock and roll a blending of cultures? *(Possible response: Early rock and roll drew on African-American rhythm and blues, bluegrass, country, and gospel music. In addition, both African-American and white musicians helped make rock and roll an important part of the youth culture.)*

More Information

The Appeal of the Beat Movement Explain that members of the Beat movement associated happiness and creativity with absolute freedom. Their model was Dean Moriarty, the hero of Jack Kerouac's *On the Road*. This 1957 autobiographical novel chronicled the cross-country adventures of Kerouac and his friends, who lived very spontaneously—the exact opposite of suburban life. Have students recall what they have learned about middle-class life in the 1950s. **ASK:** Why do you think the Beat movement might have appealed to middle-class youth? *(Possible response: Middle-class life, particularly in the suburbs, appeared to be bland and uniform. People were expected to think and act like everyone else. Young people, however, might have longed for more freedom and adventure in their lives.)*

Active Options

AMERICAN GALLERY
ONLINE
Rock and Roll Invite students to explore the American Gallery. Have them select one of the images and do additional research to learn more about it. Ask questions that will inspire further inquiry about the chosen gallery image, such as: What or whom is shown in this image? What does the image tell you about early rock and roll? What does the image tell you about youth culture? What else would you like to know about it?

NG Learning Framework: Create a Multimedia Fanzine

SKILLS Communication, Collaboration

KNOWLEDGE Our Human Story

Organize students into groups, and assign each group one of the 1950s musicians discussed in the lesson. Tell students they will be creating a class multimedia fanzine dedicated to these pioneers of rock and roll. Encourage each group to collect biographical information on their musician, a list of his or her records and accomplishments, sound or video clips of the musician's recordings and interviews, and photographs of the person. Then have the groups come together to create the multimedia fanzine. Invite students to post their fanzine for other classes to enjoy.

English Language Learners

Create a Word Web Pair students at the **Emerging** and **Expanding** levels with students at the **Bridging** level. Tell pairs to take turns reading paragraphs of the lesson, noting any words or terms related to music. After each paragraph, instruct students to write the words on the spokes of a Word Web, adding more spokes if necessary. Instruct pairs to share and discuss their Word Web, which may include such terms as *rock and roll*, *rhythm and blues*, *country*, *gospel*, *bluegrass*, and *pop music chart*.

Gifted & Talented

Create a Social Media Profile Tell students to choose one of the Beat writers mentioned in this lesson and conduct online research to learn more about the person and the aspects of mass culture he was rebelling against. Then have students create a social media profile and a series of posts for that person. Posts might include reactions to events of the 1950s, excerpts from the person's work, or comments about society in general. Invite students to share their profile and posts with the class.

See the Chapter Planner for more strategies for differentiation.

HISTORICAL THINKING

ANSWERS

1. Variety shows, quiz shows, situation comedies, Westerns, and dramas

2. Possible response: Youth in the 1950s were raised in relative comfort and wealth, which enabled them to buy what they wanted. In contrast, their parents had lived through the Great Depression and World War II, which had taught them thrift and self-denial.

3. Possible response: Unlike more traditional music, rock and roll was new and exciting. It mixed cultural influences, was loud, and had a strong beat. These qualities would appeal to young people, who had time and money to spend on records and concerts.

25 REVIEW

VOCABULARY

Match the following vocabulary terms with their definitions.

1. Sunbelt
2. brinkmanship
3. demobilization
4. occupation zone
5. blacklist
6. baby boom
7. bloc
8. McCarthyism
9. containment
10. national health insurance

a. removing all or part of a nation's military from active service
b. a campaign against alleged communists in the government and other U.S. institutions
c. an extended period of elevated birthrates
d. an insurance program established by a national government to ensure that all or most citizens have access to health care
e. an alliance of countries
f. a warm, sunny region that stretches across the southern United States
g. a list of people who are forbidden to work in an industry
h. the U.S. policy of using strategic force to block the expansion of communism
i. the practice of pushing interactions to the edge of a dangerous confrontation
j. one of the four zones into which the United States, Great Britain, France, and the Soviet Union split Germany

READING STRATEGY
SUMMARIZE

If you haven't already done so, complete your graphic organizer by identifying the important information discussed in this chapter and summarize the supporting details you have collected. Then answer the question.

Supporting Detail	Supporting Detail	Supporting Detail
Many service members came home all at once after World War II.		
Summary		

11. How were returning war veterans and many American families able to achieve a kind of American dream?

MAIN IDEAS

Answer the following questions. Support your answers with evidence from the chapter.

12. What action did President Truman take in 1948 that showed his support for the civil rights of African Americans? **LESSON 1.1**

13. How did labor unions respond to inflation in the postwar years? **LESSON 1.2**

14. What was the Berlin Airlift? **LESSON 2.1**

15. Why did the 38th parallel become significant in Korea after World War II? **LESSON 2.2**

16. Why was General MacArthur's move to land U.S. troops at Incheon daring? **LESSON 2.3**

17. What were Julius and Ethel Rosenberg convicted of and executed for? **LESSON 2.4**

18. What two major population shifts occurred in the United States in the 1950s? **LESSON 3.1**

19. How did television influence mass culture during the 1950s? **LESSON 3.3**

HISTORICAL THINKING

Answer the following questions. Support your answers with evidence from the chapter.

20. **COMPARE AND CONTRAST** How did the relationship between the United States and the Soviet Union change after World War II?

21. **MAKE CONNECTIONS** What connection can you make between the Great Depression and the consumerism of the postwar period?

22. **DISTINGUISH FACT FROM OPINION** Was Senator Joseph McCarthy's claim that the U.S. government was overrun with communist spies a fact or an opinion? Use evidence from the text to support your response.

INTERPRET MAPS

This U.S. map uses colors to show population change between 1950 and 1960. Study the map and then answer the questions that follow.

23. Which Sunbelt states grew in population by more than 50 percent between 1950 and 1960?

24. Name the Sunbelt states that have coasts on either the Pacific Ocean or the Atlantic Ocean (including the Gulf of Mexico).

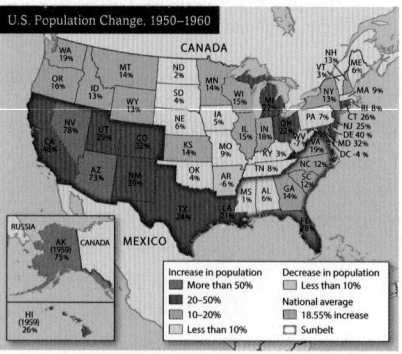

U.S. Population Change, 1950–1960

ANALYZE SOURCES

On July 26, 1948, President Truman issued Executive Order 9981, which barred segregation and discrimination in the U.S. military. Read the excerpt from the order and answer the question.

> NOW THEREFORE, by virtue of the authority vested in me as President of the United States, by the Constitution and the statutes of the United States, and as Commander in Chief of the armed services, it is hereby ordered as follows:
>
> 1. It is hereby declared to be the policy of the President that there shall be equality of treatment and opportunity for all persons in the armed services without regard to race, color, religion or national origin.

25. Why do you think the introductory section cites the president's "authority" and roles as a leader?

CONNECT TO YOUR LIFE

26. **EXPOSITORY** What are some ways in which society and popular culture in the United States have changed since the 1950s? Write a paragraph comparing the United States then and now.

TIPS

- Review the chapter and make notes about developments relating to society and popular culture.

- Use textual evidence and two or three vocabulary words from the chapter in your paragraph.

- Conclude the paragraph with a statement summarizing your ideas about changes in society and culture.

VOCABULARY ANSWERS

1. Sunbelt; f
2. brinkmanship; i
3. demobilization; a
4. occupation zone; j
5. blacklist; g
6. baby boom; c
7. bloc; e
8. McCarthyism; b
9. containment; h
10. national health insurance; d

READING STRATEGY ANSWER

Supporting Detail	Supporting Detail	Supporting Detail
Many service members came home all at once after World War II.	The GI Bill provided low-interest home loans and college tuition grants.	Savings and easy credit enabled Americans to buy consumer goods.

Summary

The GI Bill provided veterans with low-interest home loans and grants for college tuition. Easy credit and personal savings helped Americans buy consumer goods.

11. The GI Bill helped veterans achieve the American dream by providing low-interest home loans and grants for college tuition, which aided economic growth and prosperity. Easy credit and personal savings also helped Americans purchase consumer goods. In addition, jobs in construction, manufacturing, and the retail sector provided ample work opportunities.

MAIN IDEAS ANSWERS

12. Truman showed support for civil rights by signing Executive Order 9981, which abolished racial segregation in the U.S. military.

13. Labor unions responded to inflation by demanding higher wages. When their demands were not met, the unions went on strike, which brought entire industries to a halt.

14. The Berlin Airlift was the Western Allies' response to a Soviet blockade of West Berlin. The Allies delivered so many supplies by air to the people of West Berlin that the Soviets lifted their blockade within a year.

15. The 38th parallel is the line of latitude that divides the northern part of Korea from the southern part and led to the creation of two separate countries.

16. MacArthur's move was daring because Incheon was deep behind enemy lines.

17. Julius and Ethel Rosenberg were convicted and executed as spies for giving the Soviets top-secret information from the Manhattan Project, which allowed the Soviets to build an atomic bomb.

18. One shift was the movement of mostly white, middle-class families from the cities to the suburbs. The other shift was the movement of people from the Northeast and Midwest to the Sunbelt, a region that stretches coast to coast across the southern United States.

19. Television influenced mass culture through its programs and its commercials, which helped create a consumer society.

HISTORICAL THINKING ANSWERS

20. The United States and the Soviet Union had been allies in World War II. After the war, the Soviets felt that the Americans were hostile toward them, while the Americans worried that the Soviets wanted to expand their communist empire. These tensions led to the Cold War between the two superpowers.

21. During the Great Depression, Americans made sacrifices just to survive. Few people had any money to buy nonessential consumer goods. With the availability of both easy credit and inexpensive consumer goods after World War II, Americans eagerly bought all the things they previously couldn't afford or that had not been widely available.

22. McCarthy's claim that the government was overrun with communists is an opinion. McCarthy produced maps that showed supposed locations of communists and made accusations against the State Department and the U.S. Army of harboring communist agents. However, he never produced any concrete evidence to prove his accusations nor did he ever produce the lists he claimed to have of so-called communists working in the federal government and the military.

INTERPRET MAPS ANSWERS

23. Nevada, Arizona, and Florida

24. California, Texas, Louisiana, Mississippi, Alabama, Florida, Georgia, South Carolina, North Carolina, and Virginia

ANALYZE SOURCES ANSWER

25. Possible response: President Truman was making the point that he had the legal authority to order such a sweeping change without congressional approval.

CONNECT TO YOUR LIFE ANSWER

26. Answers will vary. Expository paragraphs should make clear comparisons based on evidence from the chapter and what students know about current U.S. society and popular culture, use vocabulary words from the chapter, and include a statement summarizing students' ideas about changes in American society and culture from the 1950s to now.

UNIT 9 POSTWAR AMERICA

UNIT 9 RESOURCES

UNIT INTRODUCTION

UNIT TIME LINE

UNIT WRAP-UP

NATIONAL GEOGRAPHIC | CONNECTION

National Geographic **Magazine Adapted Articles**
• "50 Years of Wilderness"
• "Slipping the Bonds" ONLINE

Unit 9 Inquiry: Protest an Injustice

NG Learning Framework Activities
• Compile a Song Medley
• Build Models

Unit 9 Formal Assessment

CHAPTER 26 RESOURCES

Available at NGLSync.Cengage.com

TEACHER RESOURCES & ASSESSMENT

Reading and Note-Taking

Vocabulary Practice

Document-Based Question Template

Social Studies Skills Lessons
• Reading: Determine Chronology
• Writing: Write an Expository Paragraph

Formal Assessment
• Chapter 26 Pretest
• Chapter 26 Tests A & B
• Section Quizzes

Chapter 26 Answer Key

ExamView®
One-time Download

STUDENT DIGITAL RESOURCES

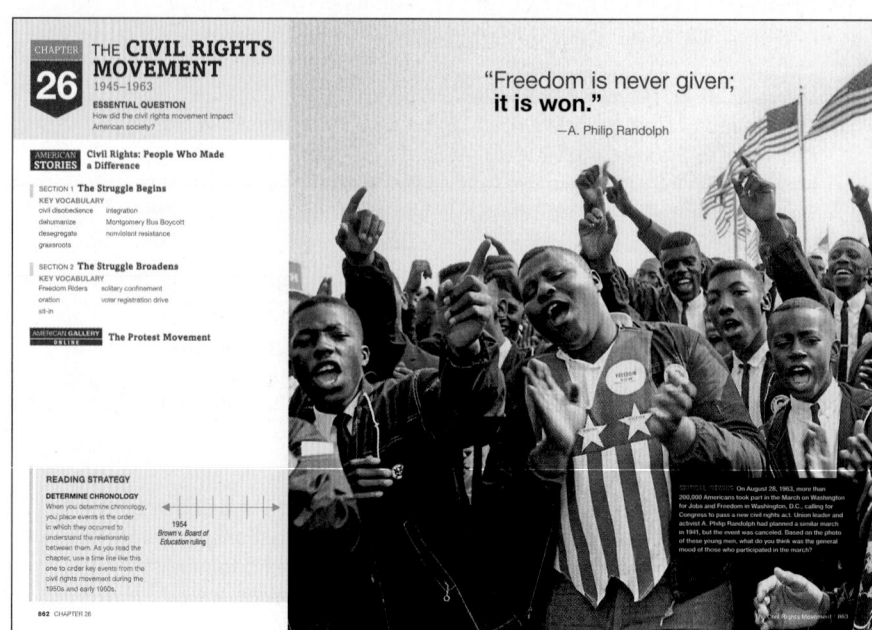

- **eEdition** (English)
- **eEdition** (Spanish)
- **Handbooks**
- **Online Atlas**
- **American Gallery Online**
- **History Notebook**
- **American Voices (Biographies)**
- **Active History**
- **Projects for Inquiry-Based Learning**

Chapter 26 Spanish Resources are available at NGLSync.Cengage.com.

AMERICAN STORIES | Civil Rights, People Who Made a Difference

- Primary Sources
- On Your Feet: Determine Problems and Solutions

NG Learning Framework:
Assemble a Photo Collage

SECTION 1 RESOURCES
THE STRUGGLE BEGINS

LESSON 1.1
Foundations of the Movement

- On Your Feet: Turn and Talk on Topic

NG Learning Framework:
Trace a Life's Work

American Voices Biography
Jackie Robinson ONLINE

LESSON 1.2
School Segregation

- On Your Feet: Define and Use Terms

NG Learning Framework:
Report on Opposing Sides

LESSON 1.3
Resistance to School Integration

- On Your Feet: Word Chain

NG Learning Framework:
Explore Reactions to the Little Rock Nine

LESSON 1.4
Women in the Movement

- On Your Feet: Question and Answer

NG Learning Framework:
Craft a Statement of Purpose

LESSON 1.5
Dr. King and Peaceful Protest

- Active History: Research Leaders in Nonviolent Resistance

NG Learning Framework:
Create a Skit

American Voices Biography
Martin Luther King, Jr. ONLINE

SECTION 2 RESOURCES
THE STRUGGLE BROADENS

LESSON 2.1
A Growing Movement

- On Your Feet: Fishbowl

NG Learning Framework:
Plan a Sing-in

American Voices Biographies
The Freedom Riders ONLINE

LESSON 2.2
Confrontation in Birmingham

- On Your Feet: Numbered Heads

NG Learning Framework:
Present an Excerpt

LESSON 2.3
The March on Washington

 AMERICAN GALLERY ONLINE The Protest Movement

NG Learning Framework:
Design a Media Plan

LESSON 2.4
DOCUMENT-BASED QUESTION
Voices of Equality

- On Your Feet: Host a DBQ Roundtable

LESSON 2.5
CURATING HISTORY
National Museum of African American History and Culture, Washington, D.C.

- On Your Feet: Sort the Artifacts

CHAPTER 26 REVIEW

Strategy ①
Understand Main Ideas

Direct students to read the Main Idea statements aloud for each lesson. Explain that these statements identify and summarize the key idea for each lesson. As students read the lessons, encourage them to find details in the text that connect to the Main Idea statements and to take notes in a Main Idea and Details List such as the one shown. Tell them this process will help them identify and remember the most important information.

Main Idea:
Detail:
Detail:
Detail:
Detail:
Detail:

Use with All Lessons

Strategy ②
Use Reciprocal Teaching

Tell partners to take turns reading each paragraph of the lesson aloud. At the end of the paragraph, the reading student should ask the listening student questions about the paragraph. Students may ask their partners to state the main idea, identify important details that support the main idea, or summarize the paragraph in their own words.

Use with All Lessons

Strategy ③
Clarify Information

Students may have difficulty understanding the many social, political, and economic factors that led to the civil rights movement. To help students organize their thoughts and clarify the information in the lesson, instruct them to take notes on the events and ideas presented in each paragraph and label each statement they write down as a social, political, or economic factor, or a combination of two or more.

Use with Lesson 1.1 *For example, after reading the first paragraph, students could write "African Americans thought black codes and Jim Crow laws were unfair," and they might label the statement social and economic.*

Strategy ①
Preview and Predict

Pair visually impaired students with students who are not visually challenged. Instruct students without disabilities to read the lesson title and subheadings and describe lesson visuals in detail. Then have partners work together to write notes regarding what they think the lesson will be about. After reading, ask pairs to review their notes to see whether their predictions were confirmed.

Use with All Lessons

Strategy ②
Use Echo Reading

Pair each inclusion student with a proficient reader. Ask the proficient reader to read the Main Idea statement at the beginning of a lesson aloud. The less proficient partner will "echo" by reading the same statement, modeling the first student. If time permits, you may wish to direct pairs to read the entire lesson in this manner, passing an imaginary microphone (or a pencil or pen representing a microphone) back and forth as students read and echo a sentence.

Use with All Lessons

ENGLISH LANGUAGE LEARNERS

Strategy ❶
Use Sentence Strips

Choose a key paragraph from the lesson to read aloud while students at **All Proficiencies** follow along in their books. Then tell them to close their books. Provide sentence strips of the paragraph and direct students to place the strips in order. Ask them to read their paragraphs aloud.

Use with All Lessons *You may wish to ask students at the* **Emerging** *level to read the sentence strips aloud and identify meaningful words before they start placing the strips in order.*

Strategy ❷
Create Word Squares

Place students in mixed pairs, such as pairing students at the **Emerging** level with those at the **Bridging** level. Tell partners to work together to identify at least three Key Vocabulary words or terms from the lesson that they have difficulty understanding. Instruct students to create a Word Square for each word or term. Then ask pairs to trade their Word Squares with another pair and ask and answer questions about the information in them.

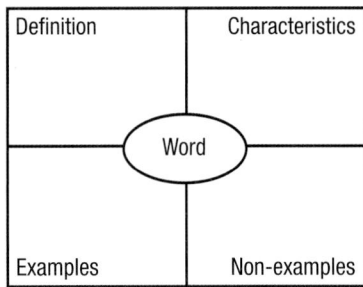

Use with All Lessons

Strategy ❸
Review Transitional Words

To help students summarize what they read and put events relating to the civil rights movement in chronological order, write these transitional words on the board: *first, next, then, also, while, immediately, later, earlier, meanwhile, whenever, simultaneously, subsequently, during, following, before, afterward,* and *finally.* Direct students at the **Emerging** and **Expanding** levels of proficiency to work together to write a series of sentences that tell what happens in each lesson. Encourage them to use a variety of transitional words and to vary their sentence structure.

Use with All Lessons *You may wish to expand the exercise by having students note transitional words as they read each lesson. For example, in Lesson 2.1, students may identify* a few years after, soon, by the summer of 1960, the following year, *and* at this time.

GIFTED & TALENTED

Strategy ❶
Live Tweet the March on Washington

Prompt students to conduct research to learn more about the speeches, music, and other activities on the National Mall on August 28, 1963. Ask them to imagine they are tweeting live from the march. Encourage them to capture not just the planned events but also the sights, sounds, and mood of the crowd. Invite students to orally present their tweets to the class and answer questions about the source materials they used.

Use with Lesson 2.3

Strategy ❷
Create a Museum Exhibit

To deepen understanding of the civil rights movement, direct students to use the chapter text and online resources to design and prepare a museum exhibit about the experiences of African Americans during the movement. Encourage students to use letters, newspaper articles, photographs, newscasts, and other primary source materials to document African-American experiences. Prompt students to display their exhibits in the classroom and present their work.

Use with All Lessons

Pre-AP

Strategy ❶
Analyze Principles of Nonviolence

Instruct students to conduct online and print research to learn more about the six principles of nonviolence promoted by Martin Luther King, Jr. Then prompt them to write a paper analyzing the principles and their historical and intellectual underpinnings. Students should conclude their analyses by stating how nonviolent principles affected the civil rights movement. Invite volunteers to share their analyses with the class.

Use with Lesson 1.5

Strategy ❷
Compare Historical and Current Events

Begin by asking students to identify recent instances of racial inequality or injustice. Then tell them to conduct online research to identify similarities and differences between issues confronting African Americans in the 1960s and today. Then direct students to write a comparison-contrast essay, and invite them to share their essays with the class.

Use with All Lessons *You may suggest that students also conduct research to discuss similarities and differences between the civil rights movement and the Black Lives Matter movement.*

THE **CIVIL RIGHTS** MOVEMENT
1945–1963

ESSENTIAL QUESTION
How did the civil rights movement impact American society?

AMERICAN STORIES Civil Rights: People Who Made a Difference

SECTION 1 The Struggle Begins
KEY VOCABULARY

civil disobedience	integration
dehumanize	Montgomery Bus Boycott
desegregate	nonviolent resistance
grassroots	

SECTION 2 The Struggle Broadens
KEY VOCABULARY

Freedom Riders	solitary confinement
oration	voter registration drive
sit-in	

AMERICAN GALLERY
ONLINE The Protest Movement

READING STRATEGY

DETERMINE CHRONOLOGY
When you determine chronology, you place events in the order in which they occurred to understand the relationship between them. As you read the chapter, use a time line like this one to order key events from the civil rights movement during the 1950s and early 1960s.

1954
Brown v. Board of Education ruling

"Freedom is never given;
it is won."

—A. Philip Randolph

CRITICAL VIEWING On August 28, 1963, more than 200,000 Americans took part in the March on Washington for Jobs and Freedom in Washington, D.C., calling for Congress to pass a new civil rights act. Union leader and activist A. Philip Randolph had planned a similar march in 1941, but the event was canceled. Based on the photo of these young men, what do you think was the general mood of those who participated in the march?

The Civil Rights Movement 863

INTRODUCE THE PHOTOGRAPH
The Right to Assemble

Direct students' attention to the photograph of the March on Washington for Jobs and Freedom. Ask students to compare the gathering shown in the photo with recent local or national public rallies or protests they are aware of, identifying ways in which the events are alike or different. Point out that the First Amendment to the U.S. Constitution protects the right to peaceful assembly. Explain that organizers of rallies, protests, and other large gatherings are usually required to obtain a permit from the local governing body. **ASK:** What might be some reasons a permit for an assembly could be refused? *(Possible response: concerns about violence or traffic problems)* Explain that the First Amendment does not protect the right to assemble in cases where there is obvious danger of a riot, extreme public disorder, interference with traffic, or any major threat to public safety.

Share Background

Eleanor Holmes Norton, later elected to Congress as the representative from Washington, D.C., worked for the organizers of the March on Washington. Some people feared that the event might descend into violence or fail to achieve anything. Flying into Washington, D.C., on the morning of the march, Norton looked down to see the largest crowd that had ever assembled on the National Mall. At that point, despite all the fearful predictions, Norton knew the March on Washington would be peaceful and would also help the movement accomplish its goals. Participants later described the mood of the marchers as determined but neither defiant nor angry. Instead, attendees retained a hopeful spirit and an overall feeling that the event would usher in positive political change for African Americans.

CRITICAL VIEWING Many of the young men appear to be joyful and excited. They may be chanting or singing, and many have arms and fingers extended, so they seem to have a feeling of solidarity.

INTRODUCE THE ESSENTIAL QUESTION

How did the civil rights movement impact American society?

Team Word Webbing Activity: The 1950s and 1960s This activity taps students' prior knowledge and thinking about some of the major issues of the U.S. civil rights movement: unfair treatment of African Americans, social and political upheaval, and methods of resistance civil rights leaders employed in their cause.

Divide the class into teams of four. Give each team a large sheet of paper, and give each team member a different color marker. Direct teams to start a Word Web, writing the topic Racial Equality at the center. On your signal, ask students to add words and phrases associated with the topic to the nearest part of the web. After a minute or two, direct teams to rotate their paper so that students can again add to the nearest part, building on their teammates' responses. When all teams have finished, lead the class to compare the finished webs and look for common and unique responses.

INTRODUCE CHAPTER VOCABULARY

Definition Chart

As they read the chapter, have students complete a Definition Chart for Key Vocabulary words. Direct them to list the Key Vocabulary words in the far left column of the chart. Then, as they encounter each word in the chapter, tell them to write the Key Vocabulary word's definition in the center column and what the word means, using their own words, in the far right column. Model an example on the board, using the graphic organizer below.

Word	Definition	In My Own Words
dehumanize	to deprive of human qualities, personality, or spirit	to treat someone as less than human

INTRODUCE THE READING STRATEGY

DETERMINE CHRONOLOGY

Remind students that when determining chronology, they are looking for more than just sequential dates. They are seeking to understand how one event led to or influenced another that came later. Explain that in this chapter, students will learn how the civil rights movement unfolded, gaining momentum over time and resulting in societal changes. Model recording information on the time line as you work through Lesson 1.1, guiding students to select only major events. Remind them to add to the time line as they read the chapter.

1954
Brown v. *Board of Education* ruling

KEY DATES FOR CHAPTER 26

1954	*Brown* v. *Board of Education* ruling
1955	Montgomery Bus Boycott
1955	Murder of Emmett Till
1957	Civil Rights Act of 1957
1960	Civil Rights Act of 1960
1960	North Carolina lunch counter sit-in
1961	CORE freedom rides begin
1963	Martin Luther King, Jr., arrested in Birmingham
1963	March on Washington
1964	Freedom Summer

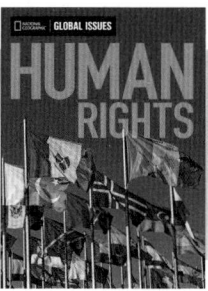

For more on the civil rights era, see *GLOBAL ISSUES: HUMAN RIGHTS.*

Objectives

- **Identify the prominent civil rights causes of the mid-20th century.**
- **Learn about different groups and people leading the struggle for civil rights.**
- **Compare civil rights leaders' goals and challenges.**
- **Study primary sources: photographs of participants in the civil rights movement.**

Critical Thinking Skills for "Civil Rights: People Who Made a Difference"

- Make Connections
- Draw Conclusions
- Make Inferences
- Compare and Contrast
- Form and Support Opinions
- Integrate Visuals
- Make Predictions

Background for the Teacher

This American Story focuses on the many civil rights struggles taking place in the United States during the mid-20th century. Through photographs, commemorative pieces, and quotations from some of the major figures of the civil rights movement, students will gain a deeper understanding of activists' experiences. Use this American Story to provide students with a more comprehensive background in what members of the movement fought for and what they endured during their struggle. Through this American Story, students will also make connections between the people profiled and how they helped shape American society today.

Chapter 26, The Civil Rights Movement, specifically focuses on African Americans' struggles for justice in the United States. This American Story addresses that facet of the movement but also the fight for Native American rights, Mexican American rights, women's rights, gay rights, and workers' rights—all of which were simultaneously taking place in the United States during the mid-20th century.

History Notebook
Encourage students to complete the American Story page for Chapter 26 in their History Notebooks as they read.

Note to the Teacher

Use this American Story as a teaser for content students will encounter in Chapter 26.

NATIONAL GEOGRAPHIC

CIVIL RIGHTS
PEOPLE WHO MADE A DIFFERENCE

When faced with injustice, what can a single person do? Senator Robert F. Kennedy had an answer to that question. In a 1966 speech, he told a group of young people, "Few will have the greatness to bend history itself, but each of us can work to change a small portion of events." The acts of individuals, he said, would add up to write the "history of this generation." Kennedy was in a position to witness the many individuals acting to fight injustice in the 1950s and 1960s. During that time, people from all walks of life joined together to fight for civil rights. This American Story profiles a few of the people whose actions helped write the history of their generation and form the world we live in today.

CRITICAL VIEWING On May 4, 1961, African-American civil rights activist and CORE leader James Farmer led 13 Freedom Riders—7 African Americans and 6 whites—from Washington, D.C., into the South on Greyhound and Trailways buses. These are the mug shots of Freedom Riders arrested in Jackson, Mississippi, that summer, including Farmer (above). They were charged for "breach of peace" and refusal to obey a police officer after attempting to use restrooms and lunch counters designated "whites only." Do you think nonviolent actions, like those of the Freedom Riders, expose injustice? Explain your reasoning.

THE FREEDOM RIDERS

Most passengers would probably find a cross-country bus trip tiring or dull. For African Americans in the South in the 1960s, it was downright dangerous. According to one witness, "Travel in the segregated South for black people was humiliating." In theory, segregation was illegal in bus stations and other facilities involved with travel between states. In practice, however, several states in the South enforced rules that separated African Americans from whites and forced them to use poorly maintained facilities.

The Congress of Racial Equality (CORE) believed the federal government was not doing enough to ensure anti-segregation laws were being followed. The group announced plans to test travel facilities in the South. CORE's national director said the goal was "to provoke the southern authorities into arresting us and thereby prod the Justice Department into enforcing the law of the land."

In May 1961, 13 "Freedom Riders" left Washington, D.C., on two buses bound for New Orleans, Louisiana. During their trip, they ignored the "white" and "colored" signs that hung by restrooms and lunch counters. Trouble erupted in Anniston, Alabama, when a white mob firebombed one of the buses. As the Freedom Riders escaped, they were attacked by the mob.

The Civil Rights Movement **865**

Discuss the Meaning of Civil Rights

Discuss with students the meaning of civil rights by first defining what *civil* means in the context of the phrase: "relating to the concerns of ordinary citizens." Ask students to think about the types of concerns that citizens might have in society. As they brainstorm, offer them categories to consider, such as voting, education, housing, and employment. On the board, list the categories in the left column of a T-Chart and write the particular concerns students suggest in the right column. Explain that in this American Story, students will learn about specific struggles relating to many of these issues.

Explore the Movement

Distribute a blank K-W-L Chart to students. Instruct them to write in the first column what they already know about the civil rights movement of the mid-20th century, including specific people or groups involved in the movement. In the second column, ask students to write questions about what they would like to learn about the movement, such as: What was the goal of the Freedom Riders? As students read the American Story, have them complete the third column of the chart, writing new or additional information they have learned about the movement from the text.

K What Do I Know?	W What Do I Want To Learn?	L What Did I Learn?

CRITICAL VIEWING Answers will vary. Possible response: Yes, I think these actions expose injustice because they show how unfairly some people were treated. The Freedom Riders were only trying to use restrooms and eat at lunch counters. They weren't doing anything violent, yet the police still arrested them.

The Freedom Riders

The Congress of Racial Equality (CORE) formed in Chicago in the early 1940s. The group, which mainly consisted of University of Chicago students, originally organized in response to segregation in the North. In Chicago, for example, members participated in nonviolent acts of civil disobedience, such as waging sit-ins at restaurants. At that time, this form of protest was a new tactic, and the group's novel approach helped establish its significance. It was not until the late 1950s that CORE became active in the South. Despite the group's nonviolent approach, the Ku Klux Klan considered CORE a threat and, at one point, voted to kill its leader, James Farmer. Though the Klan did not end up killing Farmer, other members of CORE became victims of the group's brutality.

Woodrow Wilson Mann and the Little Rock Nine

At the time of the Little Rock Nine incident, Woodrow Wilson Mann was the mayor of Little Rock, Arkansas. Though Mann did not personally support school integration, he felt the city needed to comply with the Supreme Court decision ending segregation. Mann was surprised to learn of Governor Faubus's intention to have National Guard members block Central High School's entrance to keep the African-American students out. He believed the governor ordered this act merely to appease pro-segregation politicians in the South. In response to the presence of the National Guard and the mob of protesters outside the school, Mann contacted President Dwight D. Eisenhower to request federal assistance at the building, which Eisenhower agreed to. As a result of Mann's actions, people burned crosses on his lawn. Not long after, he decided to move from Arkansas to Texas.

CRITICAL VIEWING Since the passengers look surprised and concerned, they may be looking at the angry mobs of white people who came out to attack the buses.

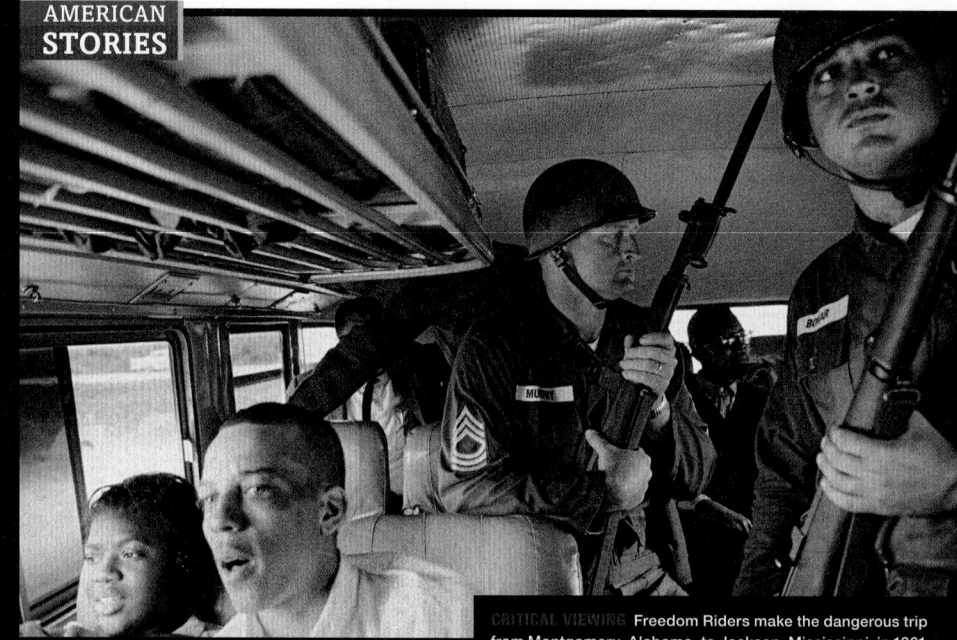

AMERICAN STORIES

CRITICAL VIEWING Freedom Riders make the dangerous trip from Montgomery, Alabama, to Jackson, Mississippi, in 1961, accompanied by armed National Guard soldiers. Based on the expressions of the passengers in this photo, what do you think they may have been observing out the bus window?

In Montgomery, Alabama, a mob attacked a church where the riders and their supporters were attending a service led by Martin Luther King, Jr. Federal troops had to be sent in to restore order.

The original CORE riders were forced to complete their trip to New Orleans by plane, but another group, the Nashville Student Movement, decided to complete the ride by bus. After more intense violence, the riders were arrested and jailed in Jackson, Mississippi. The freedom rides were far from over, though. Throughout the summer, riders continued to pour into the southern states. The media flooded the country with images of Freedom Riders being attacked and beaten by angry segregationists. Forced to act, the federal government banned interstate bus lines from using segregated bus stations.

Who were the Freedom Riders? Most were young people and many were college students. They knew they were risking arrest, beatings, and even death when they signed up to board the buses. Diane Nash, the leader of the Nashville Student Movement, was not on the bus. She was coordinating the ride from Nashville and working to recruit more riders. John Siegenthaler, who was an assistant to U.S. Attorney General Robert Kennedy, remembered trying to talk Nash out of supporting the freedom rides. "She, in a very quiet but strong way, gave me a lecture," he said. In 1962, Nash was arrested for civil rights work in Jackson, Mississippi. She continued to participate in major civil rights campaigns during the 1960s and later worked to support fairness in housing.

John Lewis was a 19-year-old member of the Nashville Student Movement, and being a Freedom Rider was not his first confrontation with segregationist law. In fact, he had already been arrested five times for protests. The son of poor farmers from Alabama, he was well acquainted with hardship and prejudice. He was arrested during the first CORE ride and spent time in prison. Lewis later took leadership roles in the civil rights movement and spoke at the March on Washington in 1963. He was elected to the U.S. House of Representatives in 1986 and continues to serve as a representative for the state of Georgia.

THE LITTLE ROCK NINE

They were called the Little Rock Nine—teenagers preparing to become the first African-American students to attend Central High School in Little Rock, Arkansas. The year was 1957, and Arkansas had been ordered by the federal government to desegregate its schools. The state, led by Governor Orval Faubus, refused. No African-American student had ever attended a white school in Arkansas.

A year earlier, it is likely that none of the students knew they would soon find themselves in the headlines. Then, sometime before the 1957 school year began, they were chosen by Arkansas civil rights leaders looking for students who had shown determination and strength of character. During the summer, they received training and counseling to help them prepare for the challenges they would encounter when they tried to attend Central High.

On the second day of school, the Little Rock Nine arrived to find troops from the Arkansas National Guard blocking the entrance. Eight of the students arrived together, driven by one of the civil rights workers, and left quickly. Elizabeth Eckford arrived on her own. For her, the day was a nightmare. She had come by bus and approached the school on foot. As she was turned away from the entrance, a mob of some 250 angry white protesters and students followed her, yelling curses and threats.

After further protests and refusals, President Eisenhower sent federal troops to take charge of the National Guardsmen and escort the teens into the school. The students' troubles were far from over, however. Every day they encountered regular harassment from a core group of segregationist students. Other students who might have been more sympathetic stayed away for fear of running into trouble themselves. Elizabeth Eckford recalled having objects thrown at her. Carlotta Walls remembered strategizing to avoid some of the abuse in the lunchroom.

After the 1957–1958 school year, Governor Faubus chose to close Arkansas high schools rather than integrate them. The schools remained closed until August 1959. That year, Carlotta Walls returned to Central High for her senior year. "I really did want that diploma," she later said, "to validate all of the [things] that I had gone through."

That year had a profound effect on the country and on the lives of the Little Rock Nine. Several followed careers in public service and continued to work for the civil rights cause. Today, Carlotta Walls LaNier is the president of the Little Rock Nine Foundation, which advocates for equal access to education. Minnijean Brown served in the Department of Work Force Diversity in the Department of the Interior during Bill Clinton's presidency. Ernest Green served as assistant secretary of the Federal Department of Labor. In 1999, all nine received the Congressional Gold Medal.

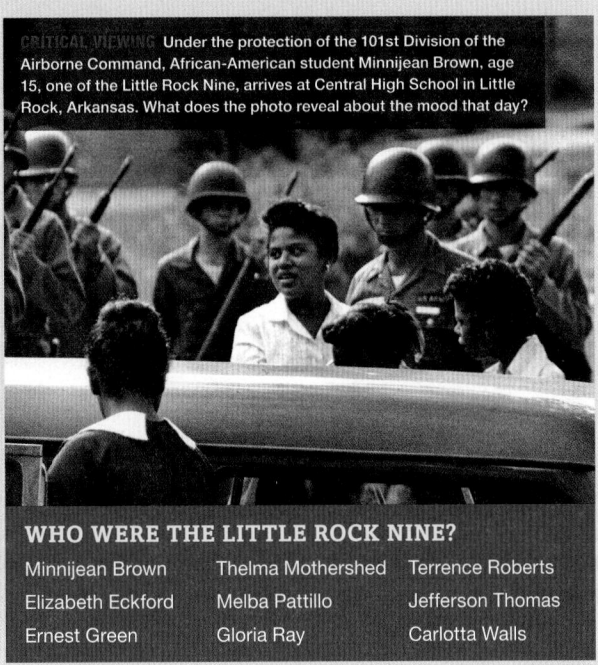

CRITICAL VIEWING Under the protection of the 101st Division of the Airborne Command, African-American student Minnijean Brown, age 15, one of the Little Rock Nine, arrives at Central High School in Little Rock, Arkansas. What does the photo reveal about the mood that day?

WHO WERE THE LITTLE ROCK NINE?

Minnijean Brown	Thelma Mothershed	Terrence Roberts
Elizabeth Eckford	Melba Pattillo	Jefferson Thomas
Ernest Green	Gloria Ray	Carlotta Walls

Guided Discussion

1. **Make Inferences** What emotions do you think the Freedom Riders felt during their trips to the South? Explain your response. *(Possible responses: They probably felt fearful because they knew people would be hostile toward them, but they probably also felt proud knowing that they were working for change that would help African Americans in the South. They may have felt angry about how they and others were treated just for doing everyday activities.)*

2. **Compare and Contrast** Point out that both the Freedom Riders and the Little Rock Nine challenged segregation. **ASK:** In what ways were the groups' experiences different and in what ways were they similar? *(Possible response: Both groups worked for desegregation, but each had a different mission. The Freedom Riders believed that not enough was being done to uphold the anti-segregation laws that existed, and they put those laws to the test by riding buses and using restrooms and lunch counters marked as "white only." The Little Rock Nine consisted of a group of selected teenagers trained to address the challenges of being the first African-American students to attend a white school after desegregation. Both groups had mobs confront and harass them, and both groups also received protection from soldiers who escorted them to safety.)*

CRITICAL VIEWING Possible response: The mood seems very tense. All of the people have serious expressions on their faces, as if they're expecting a confrontation. The girls look worried. The soldiers look stern and prepared for confrontation.

The Female Priest

Point out the reference to the National Organization for Women, and tell students that this is an organization dedicated to women's rights. Explain that in 1966, Pauli Murray and Betty Friedan both attended a conference on the status of women. While at the conference, the two women, along with a couple dozen other attendees, met privately to discuss the need for a women's organization similar to the African-American civil rights groups. Soon after that meeting, the group created the National Organization for Women.

ASK: Why do you think the women found inspiration for their organization in African-American civil rights groups? *(Possible response: They probably recognized that the civil rights groups had battled some of the same problems that women faced, such as equal opportunity to education, and they'd had success with their protest. Though it hadn't been easy, African Americans had made progress in areas like desegregation.)* **ASK:** How might Pauli Murray's prior experience with CORE and other civil rights activists have influenced her work with the National Organization for Women? *(Answers will vary. Possible response: She probably made good suggestions for how to organize events safely and effectively and about which kinds of political activities might work best. She was also probably familiar with methods for getting people involved with an organization.)*

Discuss with students how African-American women like Pauli Murray had even greater challenges to face in their lives because they had to confront both racism and sexism. Prompt students to identify some of these challenges.

CRITICAL VIEWING Possible response: He is probably emphasizing the basic unfairness of the situation: As a Mexican American, he could be drafted into the war along with young white men, but he was not granted equal educational opportunities at school.

THE EAST L.A. WALKOUTS

CRITICAL VIEWING Peter Rodriguez, a student at Wilson High School in East Los Angeles, California, addresses a student audience at a school board meeting in 1968. Why might Rodriguez be waving his draft card in this photo?

The Mexican American students who participated in the East Los Angeles Walkouts of 1968 had much in common with the Little Rock Nine. California did not have an official policy of school segregation, like the one that had existed in Arkansas. Even so, several of the city's high schools were attended primarily by Mexican Americans. Conditions in those schools were poor, and dropout rates were high. In addition, the school system discouraged Mexican American youths from seeking to go to college.

In protest, leaders from the school community organized a series of events they called "blowouts." Between March 1 and March 8, around 15,000 students walked out of 5 East Los Angeles high schools to demand a higher quality education. Several college groups also supported the blowouts. Within a week, 20,000 students in East L.A. and other parts of the city had walked out of class to support the protesters.

Eventually, the Los Angeles School Board agreed to meet most of the students' demands. The blowout organizers themselves, however, still had a struggle on their hands. On March 31, 13 of the leaders were arrested on charges of conspiracy to disturb schools and the peace. After further public protest, the 13 were released. In the end, the Los Angeles School Board, for the most part, did not follow through on its promises, claiming it did not have enough money to improve the schools. However, the East L.A. Walkouts remain an important civil rights milestone because they helped unite and focus the Mexican American community in California and the Southwest. Some of the leaders, too, made ongoing contributions to the cause of civil rights for Hispanic Americans.

THE SHOWMAN

Russell Means was a complicated figure. Many admired the Lakota Sioux for his years of activism on behalf of Native Americans. Others, including some Native Americans, disagreed with his tactics or thought he was mainly out to call attention to himself. One thing everyone agreed on: Russell Means knew how to make people notice him.

Means was born in 1939. He was an unsuccessful student and spent much of his youth wandering in the West and getting into trouble. In 1969, he found direction when he was hired by the Rosebud Sioux Tribal Council in North Dakota. In 1970, he became the national director of the American Indian Movement (AIM), an organization promoting the rights of Native Americans.

Means proceeded to lead a series of highly visible protests. In 1970, he and a group of fellow protesters took control of the Mayflower replica at Plymouth, Massachusetts, confronting several re-enactors dressed as Pilgrims. He also led a prayer vigil on the top of the presidential faces carved into Mount Rushmore, which is sacred to Native Americans. At the Little Bighorn battlefield site, Means and his group did a victory dance in honor of Custer's defeat.

In AIM's most famous protest, Means led the occupation of Wounded Knee, South Dakota. In 1890, around 350 Lakota people had been killed there by U.S. troops. In 1973, hundreds of Native Americans and white activists took over the site for 71 days, demanding the government honor treaties it

THE FEMALE PRIEST

In 1960, the dean of a medical school explained, "We do keep women out, when we can. We don't want them here." Only 6 percent of American doctors were women in the 1960s. The numbers were similarly low in other professions. Many women faced daily workplace discrimination and earned lower salaries than men, leaving them feeling powerless at home and at work.

During the 1960s, leaders emerged in a new movement to break down these barriers and establish women's rights. Women like Betty Friedan and Gloria Steinem are most often linked with the women's movement, but many others played key roles. Pauli Murray was one of them.

As an African American, Murray stood at the intersection of two civil rights movements: those of race and gender. In 1938, she tried unsuccessfully to enter the all-white University of North Carolina. In the 1940s, Murray studied law, joined CORE, and wrote poems, articles, and essays about the situation of African Americans. In the 1960s, she remained active in civil rights, working closely with Martin Luther King, Jr., and A. Philip Randolph. But she was troubled by the lack of female leadership. In 1963, she sent Randolph a letter expressing her concern about the "minor role of leadership" that women had been given.

In 1966, Murray joined with Betty Friedan and others to found the National Organization for

Women to advocate for the rights of all women. At the time of her death in 1985, the woman who had once been refused admission to the University of North Carolina held honorary degrees from Yale and Dartmouth and had become the first African-American priest in the Episcopal church.

CRITICAL VIEWING In 1977, Murray extended her extraordinary career by becoming an Episcopal priest. What types of challenges do you think female members of the clergy face today? Explain.

---

had made with Native American tribes. The event turned violent: two Native Americans were killed and a federal agent was paralyzed. Means was charged with assault, larceny, and conspiracy as a result of the Wounded Knee siege, but the case was dismissed.

In 1988, Russell Means retired from AIM after years of arguing with the movement's other leaders, who had lost trust in him. He then launched a new career that was just as visible as his previous one. In 1992, he made his debut as an actor by starring in a major Hollywood movie, *The Last of the Mohicans*. He went on to appear in more than 30 movies and TV shows and recorded music with Native American themes. He died in 2012.

AIM patch commemorating the 1973 Wounded Knee occupation

Active Options

On Your Feet: Determine Problems and Solutions
Ask groups of three or four students to complete a Problem-and-Solution Chain for one of the following subsections of the text: The Freedom Riders, The Little Rock Nine, or The East L.A. Walkouts. Tell groups to identify the problems and solutions discussed in their chosen sections, highlighting the idea that solutions sometimes lead to additional problems. Invite groups to present their finished chains to the class.

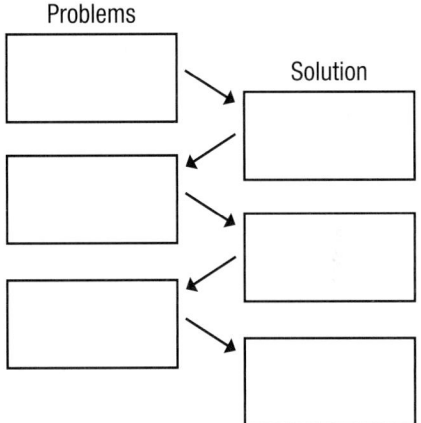

NG Learning Framework: Assemble a Photo Collage

SKILLS Observation, Communication

KNOWLEDGE Our Human Story

Ask pairs of students to assemble a photo collage of one of the civil rights events described in the American Story. For example, partners may choose to research the freedom rides, the Little Rock Nine incident, the East L.A. Walkouts, or one of the AIM protests. Tell students to find photos by conducting online research or photocopying images from a book or other print resource. Ask them to display the photos in a collage and add brief captions. Encourage pairs to present their finished collages to the class and explain why they selected the images they chose.

CRITICAL VIEWING Possible response: Women might have problems with male clergy members whose religious views favor traditional women's roles and who frown on women in leadership positions. They might also face challenges from church members who aren't used to having female clergy members.

Guided Discussion

1. **Make Connections** Why do you think Senator Robert F. Kennedy's support of the United Farm Workers union was so important to the striking workers? *(Possible response: Senator Kennedy came from a very famous and respected family, so his support probably made the workers feel encouraged in what they were doing. Also, his presence likely helped them receive greater publicity for their cause because he was not only a politician on the federal level but also the brother of the assassinated president John Kennedy.)*

2. **Form and Support Opinions** What was the greatest contribution Harvey Milk made to the LGBT community? Use details from the text to support your opinion. *(Answers will vary. Possible responses: His greatest contribution was serving on the city council, because in that position he could help establish reforms that directly affected people's lives and inspire other openly gay citizens to run for office. His greatest contribution was in challenging other gay people to embrace activism, because many people together can do more than any one person can do.)*

WRITE ABOUT HISTORY

Compose a Speech This American Story examines the various ways Americans fought for civil rights during the mid-20th century. To help students understand how those actions helped shape the world today, direct them to write a speech about civil rights. Ask students to imagine themselves as civil rights leaders during this time. Allow them to choose one of the causes the American Story discusses, such as integration, fairness in education, or LGBT rights. Then have them write a speech in support of their chosen cause. Remind students to provide reasons for their opinions and to use persuasive language in their speeches.

THINK ABOUT IT

Possible response: All of them wanted fair treatment and to have the same rights as others, whether they were gay, women, African Americans, Native Americans, or Mexican Americans. These groups faced different challenges, so their works of activism also differed. The Little Rock Nine and the students in East L.A. fought for integrated schools so they could improve their educational opportunities. Harvey Milk ran for the city council to help change laws and policies. The Freedom Riders sought to be arrested to call attention to illegal segregation policies and bring about enforcement of anti-segregation laws.

AMERICAN STORIES

Senator Robert Kennedy sits with César Chávez during a rally in Delano, California, for the United Farm Workers union. Weak and tired in this 1968 photo, Chávez had endured a 25-day hunger strike to draw attention to the farmworkers' movement.

THE PRESIDENT'S BROTHER

To some, Robert F. Kennedy may have seemed like an unlikely champion of civil rights. Born to a wealthy family, he was raised with comfort, privilege, and access to education. While he did encounter occasional discrimination because he was Catholic, his family's status shielded him from the worst effects. However, during his years of government service, Kennedy became a strong advocate for many people and groups.

In 1961, when Robert Kennedy was appointed attorney general by his brother, President John F. Kennedy, he was cautious in his support of civil rights. He asked activists not to engage in loud public protests, hoping they would accept more gradual progress toward their goals. However, he was willing to take action when necessary. He sent federal troops to protect the Freedom Riders and other protesters from violent opponents.

Over time, Kennedy abandoned his soft approach and became increasingly forceful in his support of civil rights. He helped his brother write important legislation that made racial discrimination illegal in voting and hiring. After John Kennedy was assassinated in 1963, Robert helped President Lyndon Johnson convince Congress to pass the bill into law. It became the Civil Rights Act of 1964.

Kennedy was elected to the U.S. Senate in 1964 and continued his civil rights advocacy. In 1966, he met César Chávez, founder of the United Farm Workers union, at a Senate hearing on farm labor in Delano, California. Shocked by the way the police were treating peaceful protesters, Kennedy ordered the sheriff to read the U.S. Constitution during his lunch break. His appearance drew national attention to the farmworkers' movement and energized striking workers. Kennedy returned to Delano again in 1968 to show his continued support of Chávez and the UFW movement.

THE CITY COUNCILMAN

Harvey Milk was one of the country's first openly gay elected officials. Born in New York in 1930, Milk knew he was gay before he started high school. Because the national attitude toward lesbian, gay, bisexual, and transgender, or LGBT, people at the time was mostly hostile, he kept quiet about his identity. As a young man, he probably never imagined he would someday live as an openly gay man and prominent activist for gay rights. His early career took him in many directions. He served in the U.S. Navy, taught in a public school, helped produce several Broadway shows, and worked as an investment banker. Sometime during the 1960s, he also became friends with gay activists living in the Greenwich Village neighborhood of New York City.

In 1972, Harvey Milk moved to San Francisco, California. He opened a camera shop on Castro Street, right at the center of the city's vibrant gay neighborhood. At the time, San Francisco was more tolerant of openly LGBT people than most American cities. Milk was no longer keeping his identity a secret but rather was becoming increasingly vocal about supporting gay rights. He organized Castro area businesses, which were largely LGBT-owned, into an association and coordinated events to bring more customers into the neighborhood. It did not take long for Harvey Milk to gain the nickname, the "Mayor of Castro Street."

After running unsuccessfully for city and state offices, Milk was elected to San Francisco's city council. Once in office, he advocated for many causes in addition to the protection of gay rights. He supported childcare for working mothers, community policing, and housing for low-income families, among other reforms. At a time when discrimination against the LGBT community was common, Milk was able to gather support to defeat proposed antigay laws in California.

On November 27, 1978, a former city official shot and killed Milk and San Francisco mayor, George Moscone. That night, thousands of people marched from Castro Street to City Hall. There, they held a silent candlelight vigil to honor the man who had earned the respect of people both inside and outside the gay community. As the gay rights movement continued to grow after his death, many remembered Milk's challenge to supporters: "Gay people, we will not win our rights by staying quietly in our closets. We are coming out to fight the lies, the myths, the distortions. We are coming out to tell the truths about gays, for I am tired of the conspiracy of silence, so I'm going to talk about it. And I want you to talk about it."

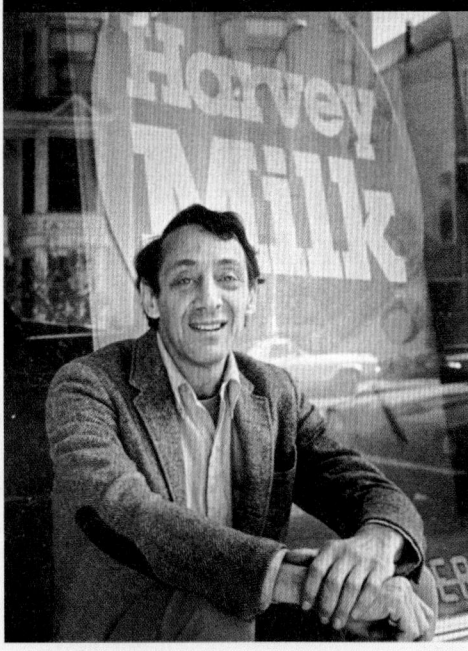

Harvey Milk sits outside of his camera shop in 1977. How does antidiscrimination legislation help members of the LGBT community enjoy the same rights as others? Do additional research on this topic, including Milk's involvement, and explain.

THINK ABOUT IT

What common goals did these "people who made a difference" share? How did their work and challenges differ?

The Civil Rights Movement **871**

DIFFERENTIATE

Inclusion

Work in Pairs Allow students with disabilities to work with partners who can read the lesson aloud to them section by section. Encourage the partner without disabilities to describe the visuals as well. Instruct pairs to work together to answer the five Critical Viewing questions. Give students the option of recording their answers rather than writing them out.

Pre-AP

Write a Newspaper Article Direct students to conduct online research to locate newspaper articles and documentaries about the Little Rock Nine or the Freedom Riders, as well as interviews with participants in or eyewitnesses to events involving those groups. Then prompt students to use their research to help them write a news account as if they were a reporter on the scene.

See the Chapter Planner for more strategies for differentiation.

HISTORICAL THINKING

Ask and have students answer the following questions.

1. **READING CHECK** What were some methods used by civil rights groups during mid-20th century protests?

2. **INTEGRATE VISUALS** How does the AIM commemorative patch's image conflict with what actually happened during AIM's protest at Wounded Knee in 1973?

3. **MAKE PREDICTIONS** Do you think protests like those described in the text will increase or decrease in the future? Explain.

ANSWERS

1. Some groups went to places they weren't allowed to go. Others staged walkouts or occupations. Some conducted strikes.

2. The patch shows a peace sign, but the protest ended in violence—with two Native Americans dead and one agent paralyzed.

3. Answers will vary. Possible response: They will increase because many people are unhappy with how they are treated by society and by authorities, and protests offer a way to be heard and perhaps bring about change.

1.1 Foundations of the Movement

When ordinary people join together to support a cause, they can make a difference. After World War II, African Americans demonstrated this fact as they tried to secure their rights guaranteed by the Constitution.

MAIN IDEA The NAACP and the Truman administration helped lay the foundation for the postwar struggle for African-American civil rights.

GRASSROOTS MOVEMENTS

Even though African Americans had made sacrifices and served the nation courageously in World War II, few shared in the postwar prosperity. As you have learned, the Jim Crow laws and black codes enforced throughout the South **dehumanized** African Americans, or treated them as though they were less than human. The laws denied them full equality and economic progress. But after fighting in a war described as a battle against the racist empires of Germany and Japan, African Americans were determined to claim their rights at home.

As a result, many African Americans worked to form equal rights movements at the **grassroots**, or community, level. Churches played an important

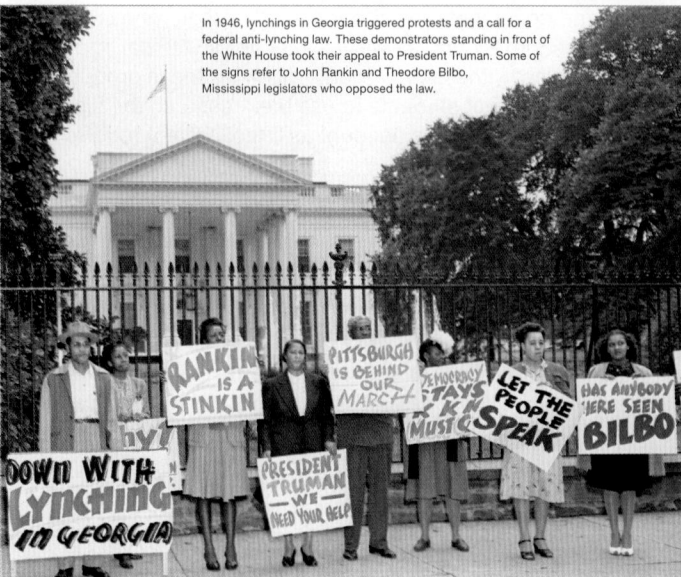

In 1946, lynchings in Georgia triggered protests and a call for a federal anti-lynching law. These demonstrators standing in front of the White House took their appeal to President Truman. Some of the signs refer to John Rankin and Theodore Bilbo, Mississippi legislators who opposed the law.

role in these movements. Church leaders stressed community support and inspired their members to work for racial justice. The NAACP, which you have read about, began as a grassroots movement. When the organization was established in 1909, it had 60 members. But by 1946, it had 600,000 members and was working to persuade Congress to pass federal anti-lynching laws. In addition, NAACP leaders, including **Walter White**, **Thurgood Marshall**, and **James Weldon Johnson**, tried lawsuits in the courts against people accused of civil rights violations.

TRUMAN AND CIVIL RIGHTS

The struggle for civil rights also received strong support at the federal level from President Harry Truman. Truman grew up in a segregated town in Missouri, and his grandparents had been slave owners. However, Truman came to recognize that everyone should be treated fairly under the law. He established the **President's Committee on Civil Rights (PCCR)** in 1946 to protect the rights of all Americans. The PCCR report, "To Secure These Rights," detailed widespread instances of discrimination and recommended what should be done to end this injustice.

In 1948, Truman also sent Congress a plan for stronger civil rights laws, the enforcement of voting rights, and federal protection against lynching. Some Republicans and many southern Democrats blocked the plan. Even many moderate Democrats, including some of the president's own aides, thought the plan went too far. They feared its passage would cost Truman votes in the South.

Liberal Democrats, on the other hand, wanted to adopt Truman's plan as the official party platform. At the 1948 Democratic Convention, **Hubert Humphrey** of Minnesota, a candidate for the Senate, urged his fellow Democrats to vote for this platform. Humphrey stated, "The time is now arrived in America for the Democratic Party to get out of the shadow of states' rights and walk forthrightly [directly] into the bright sunshine of human rights." His speech helped the liberals win a close vote. That same year, as you know, Truman abolished segregation in the U.S. military. He also banned discrimination in the hiring practices of the federal civil service. When Truman ran for president in 1948, he won the election, thanks in part to the support of African-American voters.

Jackie Robinson

From the beginning, Major League Baseball had been reserved for white players. African-American athletes played in separate leagues. All that changed when Branch Rickey, the Brooklyn Dodgers' general manager, offered Negro League player Jackie Robinson the chance to break the color barrier. Robinson was a gifted athlete who had served in World War II.

Rickey set one condition: The African-American player could not respond to the abuse he would certainly face. Robinson agreed. In April 1947, he joined the Dodgers and endured racial slurs and insults—even from his own teammates. But Robinson proved himself on the field by helping the Dodgers win six pennants and a World Series over the course of his career with the team. In time, other teams began to recruit players from minority groups.

HISTORICAL THINKING

1. **READING CHECK** How did World War II inspire African Americans to fight for their civil rights?

2. **MAKE INFERENCES** Why do you think it was important for the NAACP to fight civil rights violations in the courts?

3. **DRAW CONCLUSIONS** What did Humphrey mean when he said it was time to "get out of the shadow of states' rights"?

PLAN

Objective

Learn about the evolution of grassroots equal rights movements after World War II.

Critical Thinking Skills for Lesson 1.1

• Identify Main Ideas and Details

• Monitor Comprehension

• Make Inferences

• Draw Conclusions

• Analyze Cause and Effect

• Determine Chronology

Essential Question for Chapter 26

How did the civil rights movement impact American society? After World War II, grassroots organizations and the federal government worked to protect the rights of all Americans. Lesson 1.1 discusses President Harry Truman's contributions to the fight against racial discrimination in the United States.

Background for the Teacher

On January 15, 1947, President Truman addressed the President's Committee on Civil Rights, pointing out that neither he nor members of the committee were certain about just how far the U.S. Constitution would allow them to go in matters involving civil rights. Truman stood up for his belief that the U.S. Bill of Rights should be fully executed across the nation. Recalling racial turmoil of 1922, Truman described a time when men had "met on hills and burned crosses and worked behind sheets." He warned the committee that such times could easily come around again in the United States, adding, "I don't want to see any race discrimination. I don't want to see any religious bigotry break out in this country as it did then." He warned that in order to be truly effective, the committee's work had to begin at the grassroots level, meaning the real change would have to take place in the hearts and minds of the American people themselves.

INTRODUCE & ENGAGE

Consider Grassroots Movements

Write the term *grassroots movement* on the board. **ASK:** What do you think this term means, and what words do you associate with it? *(Answers will vary. Possible responses: a group of ordinary citizens working together to change something; protests; from the bottom up; local)* As they read the lesson, encourage students to compare their definitions with the way the term is used in the text. At the end of the lesson, revisit the student-generated list, and ask students how grassroots movements led to social change during the civil rights era. *(They got people together, organized protests, and eventually helped to get laws passed against civil rights abuses.)*

TEACH

Guided Discussion

1. **Analyze Cause and Effect** What were the long- and short-term effects of Jackie Robinson's breaking the "color barrier" in Major League Baseball? *(Short-term effects: Robinson faced insults but was allowed to play in the same league as white players. Long-term effects: Robinson helped his team win six championships and a World Series; other teams began to accept African-American players.)*

2. **Determine Chronology** What actions of President Truman's helped him win the support of African-American voters and win the 1948 presidential election? *(In 1946, Truman set up the President's Committee on Civil Rights, and he promoted a plan for stronger civil rights in 1948.)*

More Information

The Seeds of the Movement In the 1920s, the Dyer Anti-Lynching Bill was defeated in Congress. But in 1930, Walter White, the new NAACP executive secretary, began a campaign for new legislation. There were a number of lynchings in 1933, and White believed it was time to test the nation's commitment to civil rights. The NAACP's strategy was to help get a new law passed, the Costigan-Wagner Act, which would lead to federal trials for members of lynch mobs if law enforcement officers failed to act, as well as punishment for negligent officers. Unfortunately, southern opposition to the bill was strong, and Congress failed to pass it. **ASK:** In your opinion, why did it take so long for the United States to pass basic protections for African Americans? *(Students might suggest that a government composed of white people did not take the problem seriously enough or that the elected officials were more concerned about white voters than black citizens.)*

Active Options

On Your Feet: Turn and Talk on Topic Place students in three groups, and give each group the following topic sentence: Racial discrimination led African Americans to form grassroots movements demanding civil rights protections. Ask groups to build a paragraph from the topic by having each student offer one sentence. Suggest that students first discuss African Americans' participation in World War II and the unequal treatment they received upon returning home. Invite each group to present its paragraph to the class, with each group member reading his or her sentence.

NG Learning Framework: Trace a Life's Work

SKILL Collaboration

KNOWLEDGE Our Human Story

Assign small groups of students one of the following to research: Walter White, Thurgood Marshall, James Weldon Johnson, Harry Truman, Hubert Humphrey. Instruct students to conduct online research to find out how their subject's personal history, upbringing, and other factors ultimately led him to champion civil rights for African Americans. Prompt students to assign specific tasks to different group members and collaborate to create a presentation about their subject, such as a scrapbook celebrating his life, achievements, and awards. When they have finished, invite them to present their work to the class.

DIFFERENTIATE

Striving Readers

Preview and Review the Text Instruct students to preview the lesson by reading the title, Main Idea, subheadings, photograph captions, and Historical Thinking questions. Then ask them to write questions they have about the foundations of the civil rights movement that they expect to be answered in the text. After students read the lesson, tell them to work in pairs to find answers to their questions and discuss what they learned.

Gifted and Talented

Illustrate a Quotation Direct students' attention to the quote by Hubert Humphrey at the 1948 Democratic Convention. Elicit from students that Humphrey was alluding to racial segregation and other race-based injustices when he contrasted "states' rights" with "human rights." Challenge students to visually interpret the quotation in a painting, drawing, collage, or meme. Encourage them to present their work to the class.

See the Chapter Planner for more strategies for differentiation.

HISTORICAL THINKING

ANSWERS

1. When African-American soldiers came back from fighting in the war, they felt they deserved equal treatment under the law.

2. Fighting civil rights violations in the courts was important because it established legal precedent and showed the government that the Constitution covered the rights of African Americans as well as the rights of other citizens.

3. He meant that the government was wrongly putting states' rights before people's rights.

Think about the factors you and your parents might consider when deciding what school you will attend. These probably include the quality of the school and the courses it offers. Until the 1950s, the key factor in deciding what public school a student attended was his or her race.

MAIN IDEA In the 1950s, civil rights activists successfully challenged segregation in public education.

OPPOSING "SEPARATE BUT EQUAL"

As the NAACP handled civil rights lawsuits, the organization sought to overturn the doctrine of "separate but equal" established by the 1896 case *Plessy* v. *Ferguson*. Attorney Thurgood Marshall headed the NAACP's Legal Defense and Educational Fund. The fund fought inequality and segregation in educational institutions.

Marshall and his team achieved a major victory in the 1946 case *Mendez* v. *Westminster*. The court decided in favor of five Mexican American families whose children were being forced to attend schools for Mexican Americans only. With the judge's declaration that such segregation was unconstitutional, the case provided a basis for further challenges to the "separate but equal" doctrine.

In 1946, Marshall also took on the case of Heman Marion Sweatt, an African American who had applied for admission to the University of Texas School of Law. The university

Linda Brown's Activism
The young girl who became the face of the *Brown* v. *Board of Education* decision, Linda Brown, went on to become a teacher and civil rights activist. She reopened the *Brown* case in 1979, arguing that the Topeka schools remained segregated. In 1993, the court finally agreed, and three new schools were built to help integrate the city's schools.

CRITICAL VIEWING In 1953, as *Brown* v. *Board of Education* was being argued in the Supreme Court, Linda Brown continued to attend her segregated school. In this photo taken by *Life* magazine photographer Carl Iwasaki, Linda (left) and her sister Terry Lynn walk along railroad tracks on their way to the bus that would take them to their school. What possible dangers did the girls face on their walk?

denied Sweatt's application but established a new law school for African Americans to satisfy the "separate but equal" doctrine. Marshall argued the case for years. Finally, in 1950, the Supreme Court ruled in *Sweatt* v. *Painter* that the university had to admit Sweatt to the all-white law school under the terms of the 14th Amendment. As you may recall, the 14th Amendment guarantees African Americans citizenship and all its rights and privileges. The ruling in this case and others like it meant that colleges across the country were to be integrated. **Integration** is the act of allowing people of all races to participate equally in society and have equal access to the same facilities.

BROWN v. BOARD OF EDUCATION

Soon, "separate but equal" was being challenged in schools throughout the nation. By 1953, five civil rights lawsuits from different parts of the country had reached the Supreme Court. The lawsuits were combined in one case under the name *Brown* v. *Board of Education of Topeka*. The case challenged the constitutionality of segregation and inequality in public schools. Once again, NAACP lawyers took on the civil rights case. One person the lawyers represented was Reverend Oliver Brown, who was suing the Topeka, Kansas, school board. When the suit was first filed in 1950, Reverend Brown's daughter, Linda, was eight years old. His lawyers argued that Linda should not have to walk several miles to attend a segregated African-American school when an all-white school was much closer.

On May 17, 1954, the Supreme Court ruled 9–0 in favor of *Brown* v. *Board of Education*. At this time, the Chief Justice of the Supreme Court was **Earl Warren**, whom President Dwight Eisenhower had appointed the year before. Warren held more liberal views than the president. In his decision, Warren wrote, "Separate educational facilities are inherently [by their nature] unequal."

The court ordered the integration of the country's public schools "with all deliberate speed." Eisenhower kept quiet on the issue of school integration. When journalists asked for his opinion on the *Brown* decision, he replied, "The Supreme Court has spoken . . . and I will obey." Many Americans and members of Congress, however, actively opposed the decision. They would fight it for years to come.

HISTORICAL THINKING

1. **READING CHECK** What doctrine did the NAACP work to overturn?

2. **DETERMINE CHRONOLOGY** How did the Supreme Court ruling in 1950 affect the *Brown* ruling in 1954?

3. **DRAW CONCLUSIONS** Why do you think educational institutions in the early 1950s designed solely for minority groups might have been inferior to those for whites?

INTRODUCE & ENGAGE

Share What You Know

Read the lesson title aloud to students. Then post a K-W-L Chart and ask them to share what they already know about school segregation. Record their responses, including any inaccuracies, in the first column. Then ask what they would like to learn about school segregation and record their responses in the second column. Tell students to refer to the chart as they read Lesson 1.2. Encourage them to revise inaccuracies as factual statements in the last column.

K What Do I Know?	W What Do I Want To Learn?	L What Did I Learn?

TEACH

Guided Discussion

1. **Summarize** Describe Thurgood Marshall's contribution to the fight for integrated schools. *(Through the NAACP's Legal Defense and Education Fund, Marshall and his team of lawyers argued and won landmark segregation cases such as* Mendez v. Westminster, Sweatt v. Painter, *and* Brown v. Board of Education, *leading to changed policies and integrated schools.)*

2. **Evaluate** Do you agree with Earl Warren's statement that "Separate educational facilities are inherently unequal"? Explain your answer. *(Possible response: Yes, they are unequal because the fact that there is a supposed need for a separate facility indicates that one group of people is considered inherently inferior to the other.)*

Make Connections

Reread the section on *Brown* v. *Board of Education*. Prompt students to think about contemporary court cases or movements that address social and racial justice. Students could brainstorm relevant court cases or movements, or you could suggest some of the following: *Obergefell* v. *Hodges*, *Equal Employment Opportunity Commission* v. *Abercrombie & Fitch Stores*, Black Lives Matter, Occupy, #MeToo. **ASK:** At their core, what do all social justice movements have in common? *(Possible response: All social justice movements are connected by the idea of bringing about change and instituting fairness or equality for all people.)*

Active Options

On Your Feet: Define and Use Terms Have students work together in pairs. Write the terms *integration*, *segregation*, *Brown* v. *Board of Education*, and *separate but equal* on the board. Then assign one partner to define or explain each term and the other to use each term in an original sentence. Encourage them to write down their definitions and example sentences. Call on volunteers to share their work with the class.

NG Learning Framework: Report on Opposing Sides

ATTITUDE Empowerment

SKILL Collaboration

Ask students to imagine that they are news reporters covering one or more trials regarding school desegregation. Instruct them to research the arguments put forth by both sides, those supporting integration and those supporting segregation. Then prompt students to write a news article that outlines the different arguments. Encourage them to come up with an attention-grabbing headline. When writing is complete, invite students to share their articles with the class.

DIFFERENTIATE

English Language Learners

Use Prefixes Pair students at the **Emerging** level of proficiency with those at the **Expanding** level. Bring their attention to the words *unconstitutional* and *unequal*. Encourage students to use a dictionary to identify the root words (*constitutional, equal*) and how the prefix *un-* changes each word's meaning. Instruct pairs to work together to write original sentences for each word, with and without the prefix. You may encourage students to expand the exercises by writing sentences for other words (*fair, friendly, welcome*) with and without the prefix *un-*.

Gifted & Talented

Perform a Dramatic Reading Instruct students to conduct online research to find the full text of Thurgood Marshall's legal arguments in *Brown* v. *Board of Education*. Challenge them to prepare a dramatic reading of a section of the argument and then perform their reading in front of the class. Ask students to discuss how the reading affected their understanding of the power of Marshall's logic and oratory.

See the Chapter Planner for more strategies for differentiation.

HISTORICAL THINKING

ANSWERS

1. The NAACP worked to overturn the "separate but equal" doctrine established by *Plessy* v. *Ferguson*.

2. The 1950 ruling in *Sweatt* v. *Painter* forced universities to integrate. With that precedent set, the 1954 *Brown* ruling extended the *Sweatt* ruling to the nation's public elementary schools.

3. Answers will vary. Possible response: Educational institutions for minority groups were probably inferior because the state governments likely did not envision the same level of education and career opportunity for minority students and thus did not fund the minority schools as well as they did white schools.

CRITICAL VIEWING Answers will vary. Possible response: Given the Supreme Court case, many people must have known who the Brown children were, and the dangers to the two sisters in an isolated area may have included insults and threats of abduction or violence. The girls would also have to be careful to watch for trains while walking near so many tracks.

1.3 Resistance to School Integration

It's hard to change a law, but it can be even harder to change people's minds. Segregation had been practiced for so long in some places that many people could not imagine an integrated school, much less an integrated world.

MAIN IDEA Southerners and government leaders tried to prevent the integration of public schools and colleges.

Escorted by soldiers and the National Guard, nine African-American students finally attend their first full day of class at Central High School in Little Rock, Arkansas, on September 25, 1957. Troops remained at the school throughout the year.

THE LITTLE ROCK NINE

By 1956, only a few schools in the South had **desegregated**, or put an end to the separation of races. That year, about 100 southern members of Congress claimed the decision in *Brown* v. *Board of Education* was a misinterpretation of the 14th Amendment. They vowed to use "all lawful means" to resist court-ordered integration. The conflict between federal authority and states' rights erupted in 1957 in Little Rock, Arkansas, when nine African Americans were admitted to a local high school. Shortly before school began, Arkansas governor Orval Faubus announced he would use the state's National Guard to prevent the African-American students from entering the building. He claimed the measure was for the students' own safety.

On their first day of school, the students, who came to be known as the **Little Rock Nine**, were confronted by an angry mob. The students were spat on and threatened as they walked to the school before being turned away by the Arkansas National Guard. They tried to attend classes several more times in the following weeks. On September 23, President Eisenhower finally sent federal troops to escort the students to their classes and restore order. That month Eisenhower signed the **Civil Rights Act of 1957** to protect the voting rights of African Americans. The president also later signed the **Civil Rights Act of 1960**. However, both acts proved to be ineffective.

AN ONGOING BATTLE

Other states also challenged desegregation. In 1956, the Virginia legislature passed a law that would close any school that attempted to integrate. In 1958, several schools and an entire school district in Virginia were shut down to avoid integration. Parents who could afford the fees sent their children to private schools. Poor students, including many whites and African Americans, were denied any public education at all.

In 1960, officials developed a purposefully difficult test for African-American students who wished to attend white schools in New Orleans. However, a six-year-old girl named **Ruby Bridges** was one of the few students who passed the test. She gained admission to an elementary school just five blocks from her home. The Louisiana state government found a number of ways to stall and put off the

school's integration but finally had to give in. Federal marshals escorted Ruby and her mother to the school in November. The child walked past a screaming crowd of angry white parents and was led directly to the principal's office, where she spent her first day of school. Only one teacher at the school agreed to instruct Ruby. The two of them worked alone in a classroom for the entire school year. Ruby Bridges became the youngest African-American student to integrate a school in the South.

The battle over integration also continued on college campuses. In 1962, a federal court ordered the all-white University of Mississippi to admit **James Meredith**, an African-American Air Force veteran. However, when Meredith arrived on campus to register, the governor of Mississippi, Ross Barnett, blocked the entrance to the office. About a week later, U.S. marshals escorted Meredith to the registrar's office, setting off riots that ended in the deaths of two students and injured many others. Once the violence died down, Meredith was finally able to attend classes.

George Wallace had vowed to block school integration during his successful campaign for governor of Alabama in 1962. In his inaugural address, he exclaimed, "Segregation now, segregation tomorrow, segregation forever!" On June 11, 1963, Wallace kept his promise and stood in a doorway at the University of Alabama to prevent two African-American students from enrolling. In response, the U.S. government sent in National Guard troops, who forced Wallace to step aside. While schools and colleges were being desegregated, civil rights leaders also fought for equality in other public places—including buses.

HISTORICAL THINKING

1. **READING CHECK** Who were the Little Rock Nine?

2. **SUMMARIZE** How did Barnett and Wallace try to block integration on college campuses?

3. **DESCRIBE** What words would you use to describe the character of the African-American students who desegregated schools in the 1950s and 1960s?

PLAN

Objective

Learn how schools and state and local governments fought school integration.

Critical Thinking Skills for Lesson 1.3

- Identify Main Ideas and Details
- Monitor Comprehension
- Summarize
- Describe
- Draw Conclusions
- Evaluate

Essential Question for Chapter 26

How did the civil rights movement impact American society? Though integration had become law, many in the United States were slow to accept it. Lesson 1.3 discusses how some government leaders and citizens fought to preserve segregation in spite of the law.

Background for the Teacher

George Wallace, while continuing to make racist claims, ran for president in 1968 on the newly created American Independent Party ticket. He did well with some voters and ended up winning five states and 10 million votes. Four years later, he ran again. But as his 1972 bid was beginning to pick up steam, a mentally disturbed assailant shot Wallace during a campaign stop. In 1976, Wallace came back to run for president a third time, paralyzed from the assassination attempt and in a wheelchair. When Jimmy Carter won the presidency that year, Wallace took some time away from the public eye. Eventually emerging, he began to contact some of his old adversaries, including several civil rights leaders, to ask for forgiveness. One of these leaders, John Lewis, described Wallace's call as a pouring out of heart and soul.

Discuss Responses to Social Change

Tell students that in times of tremendous social change, many people may respond negatively. **ASK:** What emotional reactions do you think cause people to push back against change? *(Answers will vary. Possible responses: discomfort, fear, feelings of unfairness)* Invite volunteers to name recent or past school or community issues that may have engendered changes in policy or law. As a class, discuss the public's response to these proposed changes. Then tell students that in this lesson they will learn more about instances of resistance to school integration.

TEACH

Guided Discussion

1. **Summarize** Name some of the tactics states used to avoid federal laws demanding school integration. *(Possible response: States stalled entry of African-American students, closed schools that enrolled African-American students, allowed angry mobs to threaten incoming students, and ordered National Guard troops to restrict entry of African-American students.)*

2. **Draw Conclusions** Consider the following statement: Civil rights laws are only as effective as their overall enforcement. Using an example from the lesson, explain why you believe this statement is or isn't true. *(Possible response: The statement is true, as shown by the fact that many states continued to implement segregation in schools despite the Civil Rights Acts of 1957 and 1960.)*

Evaluate

Discuss with students the legality of a state calling on its troops to resist a federal order to integrate. **ASK:** What options might the states have had to resist the order "by all lawful means"? *(Answers will vary but may include the idea that members of Congress could have argued for states' rights in Washington, or they could have created petitions or sponsored protest marches, as civil rights activists were doing on the opposing side.)*

Active Options

On Your Feet: Word Chain Write these names from the text on three separate pieces of paper: Little Rock Nine, Ruby Bridges, James Meredith. Ask students to form three lines. Hand a piece of paper to the first person in each line. The first student in line writes a word that relates to the original name. Students pass the paper from person to person, each one adding a word or phrase they associate with the previously written word. Have a volunteer from each group read the Word Chain, and ask the rest of the class to listen for any words that were used in more than one or any that may not connect well.

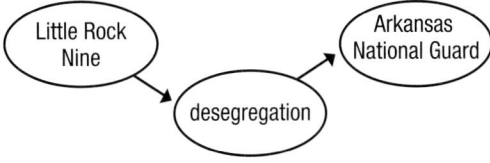

NG Learning Framework: Explore Reactions to the Little Rock Nine

SKILL Communication

KNOWLEDGE Our Human Story

Direct students to research and explore the different reactions that residents of Little Rock, Arkansas, expressed regarding the events surrounding the Little Rock Nine—toward the desegregation process as well as toward the protests and the treatment of the African-American students. Prompt students to consider why people who didn't support the protesters did nothing to stop or counteract them. Then have small groups of students use their research to write and present a skit on the topic.

Striving Readers

Create a Time Line To help students understand the resistance to the Supreme Court decision in *Brown* v. *Board of Education*, tell them to create a time line. Ask students to add notes to the time line as they read the lesson, including details such as dates, locations, and important people and events, explaining their significance. Encourage students to share their finished time lines with the class and discuss the details shown.

Pre-AP

Write a Profile Instruct students to conduct preliminary online research to learn more about the Little Rock Nine. Tell them to select one of the group to profile. The profile should include significant events in the person's life before, during, and after being denied access to Central High School. Invite students to post their profiles on a class website or blog.

See the Chapter Planner for more strategies for differentiation.

HISTORICAL THINKING

ANSWERS

1. The Little Rock Nine were a group of students who enrolled in a white high school after court-ordered desegregation. They received training from the NAACP to handle the abuse they were expected to receive when attempting to attend school.

2. They stood in the way, blocking the door so the students could not enter the building.

3. Possible response: *brave, intelligent, determined*

1.4 Women in the Movement

Do you think unjust laws should be broken? During the civil rights movement, many people did. In 1955, one woman took a stand against an unfair law by sitting down and refusing to get up.

MAIN IDEA A yearlong boycott of the bus system in Montgomery, Alabama, led to a Supreme Court decision that ordered the desegregation of the city's buses.

THE ARREST OF ROSA PARKS

On December 1, 1955, an African-American woman named **Rosa Parks** boarded a public bus in Montgomery, Alabama, prepared to break a city law. At that time, buses in Montgomery were segregated. According to a city ordinance, the first four rows were reserved for white passengers. African Americans had to pay the driver at the front of the bus and then get off to reboard at the rear. When Parks got on the bus that day, she sat in the first row behind the white section. She knew she would be asked to give up her seat to a white person if the front seats filled up.

That's just what happened. When the white section was full and more white passengers stepped aboard the bus, the driver told Parks and three other African Americans in her row to move to the back of the bus. The others gave up their seats, but Parks refused. The bus driver called the police, who arrested Parks for disobeying the ordinance. Parks worked as a seamstress, but she was also a civil rights activist and secretary of the Montgomery chapter of the NAACP. She knew that the NAACP wanted to challenge Montgomery's segregated bus law and chose to be the plaintiff in their case. As Parks said later, "The only tired I was, was tired of giving in."

In February 1956, two months after her arrest for refusing to give up her bus seat, Parks was again arrested in Alabama for violating a state law against organized boycotting. She had volunteered as a dispatcher, arranging carpool rides for bus boycotters.

MONTGOMERY BUS BOYCOTT

Parks's **civil disobedience**, or refusal to obey a law as a form of protest, energized and united Montgomery's African-American community. **Jo Ann Robinson**, the president of the city's Women's Political Council, organized a one-day boycott of Montgomery's buses. Robinson and the council had been working for at least two years to achieve bus reform, including the desegregation of Montgomery's buses.

The Murder of Emmett Till

Not all of the women involved in the civil rights movement were activists. Some, such as Mamie Till-Mobley, shown here, took personal stands against racism that commanded the nation's attention. In August 1955, Mrs. Till-Mobley's son Emmett Till was murdered by two white men in Mississippi. The men believed that the 14-year-old, who was visiting from Chicago, had flirted with a white woman. When the men were tried for the crime, an all-white jury found them not guilty.

Mrs. Till-Mobley brought Emmett's body back to Chicago. Although her son's body was horribly mutilated, Mrs. Till-Mobley insisted on having Emmett's coffin open during his funeral. "Let the people see what I've seen," she said. Photos of the funeral were published, forcing the American public to witness the impact of racism.

The **Montgomery Bus Boycott**, as it came to be called, was held on December 5, four days after Rosa Parks's arrest. The protest was such a success that Robinson, members of the NAACP, and other civil rights activists decided to continue the boycott and make it a long-term campaign. These activists joined with a group of local ministers to form the Montgomery Improvement Association (MIA). They chose **Martin Luther King, Jr.**, a 26-year-old Baptist minister and leading member of the NAACP, to be the association's president and coordinate the boycott.

Organizers believed the boycott would be successful because about 75 percent of Montgomery's bus riders were African Americans. Still, because few African Americans owned cars, they had to make some sacrifices during the boycott. Protesters walked, biked, or carpooled rather than take the bus. They also endured threats, violence, and even arrest. Boycott leaders held regular meetings to keep the participants' spirits up.

On June 5, 1956, citing the *Brown v. Board of Education* decision, a federal court finally declared segregation on buses unconstitutional. The U.S. Supreme Court upheld that decision on November 13, and soon after, a court order was delivered to Montgomery City Hall requiring the integration of the city's buses. The boycott ended on December 21. It had lasted 381 days. The boycott proved that collective action and peaceful protest could bring about social change.

HISTORICAL THINKING

1. **READING CHECK** Why was Rosa Parks arrested on December 1, 1955?

2. **DETERMINE CHRONOLOGY** What happened after Parks's first arrest?

3. **DRAW CONCLUSIONS** How did the *Brown* decision set a precedent for the federal court's ruling on the Montgomery bus ordinance?

PLAN

Objective

Describe the contributions of women in the civil rights movement.

Critical Thinking Skills for Lesson 1.4

- Identify Main Ideas and Details
- Monitor Comprehension
- Determine Chronology
- Draw Conclusions
- Analyze Cause and Effect
- Evaluate

Essential Question for Chapter 26

How did the civil rights movement impact American society? A number of women became iconic figures during the civil rights era. Lesson 1.4 discusses how women like Rosa Parks, Jo Ann Robinson, and Mamie Till-Mobley served the movement in different ways.

Background for the Teacher

In 2004, Emmett Till's family ordered the exhumation of his body from an Illinois cemetery and allowed an autopsy to be performed on the remains. Because of an Illinois state law, Till's body had to be reburied in a new coffin after the autopsy. The original coffin was housed at the cemetery. But when the Till family heard that the coffin had fallen into disrepair, they sought to acquire and refurbish it. They eventually moved the coffin to the Smithsonian Institution to be part of the Civil Rights exhibit, which opened at the National Museum of African American History and Culture in 2016. As museum visitors move through the exhibit, they learn what happened to Emmett Till in 1955. Turning a corner, they see the refurbished coffin, open to public view as it was on the day of Emmett Till's funeral in 1955.

Preview Using Visuals

Read the lesson title to students. Then direct their attention to the photographs. Prompt students to describe what they see. *(a woman being fingerprinted; a woman crying over a coffin)* **ASK:** What inferences can you make, based on details in the photographs? *(Answers will vary. Possible response: A small, well-dressed woman does not seem violent or threatening, so it seems strange to see her arrested—which makes for a powerful image. There are probably few scenes with more emotional impact than the image of a grieving mother, so the woman in that photo could help convey to the American public the pain of discrimination and violence against African Americans.)*

TEACH

Guided Discussion

1. **Analyze Cause and Effect** What were some of the short- and long-term effects of Rosa Parks's 1955 act of civil disobedience in Montgomery, Alabama? *(In the short term, Parks was arrested, and her action inspired other civil rights activists and Montgomery's greater African-American population to boycott the bus system. In the long term, the civil disobedience that started with her action eventually led to a federal court declaring bus segregation unconstitutional.)*

2. **Evaluate** Why was the Montgomery Bus Boycott so successful in changing the city's segregation policy? *(Possible response: By not riding the city buses, the African-American population deprived the bus company of some 75 percent of public transportation fares, leading to major revenue losses. Providing public transportation in Montgomery was not economically feasible without African-American ridership.)*

More Information

Rosa Parks Tell students that many myths have sprung up about Rosa Parks's act of civil disobedience on the bus. One was that she was simply a hardworking woman who refused to give up her seat because she was tired. In fact, Parks knew very well that she would be arrested for staying seated. She was even familiar with the driver, as he had kicked her off the bus once before for trying to do the very same thing. **ASK:** Why do you think people in the civil rights movement may have wanted to position Parks as a victim of her time rather than as an activist attempting to bring about change? *(Answers will vary. Possible response: They may have thought that the public would find it easier to identify with a meek, hardworking victim of systemic unfairness than with someone purposefully working against that unfairness.)*

Active Options

On Your Feet: Question and Answer Direct half the class to create True-False questions based on the lesson information. Ask the other half to create answer cards with "True" written on one side and "False" on the other. As one group asks each question aloud, students in the second group should stand and display the correct answer. When there are discrepancies, ask students to review the question and decide on the correct answer together as a class.

NG Learning Framework: Craft a Statement of Purpose

ATTITUDE Empowerment

SKILL Collaboration

Prompt students to find out more about how civil rights activists challenged social norms in such settings as schools, buses, and restaurant lunch counters. Encourage them to use information from the lesson as well as digital resources. Then ask students to imagine themselves as activists and work in small groups to craft a statement of purpose that reflects their goals in breaking down racial barriers. Invite groups to share their statements with the class.

DIFFERENTIATE

Inclusion

Interpret Photographs Pair students who are visually impaired with students who are not. Ask the latter to describe the two photographs in detail and read the captions. Then prompt students to discuss how the information in the captions adds to their understanding of women's roles in the civil rights movement.

Pre-AP

Write a Biography Direct students to write a short biography or profile of Rosa Parks using information from the chapter and additional print and digital sources. Encourage students to explore the myths surrounding Parks and compare them with the historical facts they discover through their research. Invite students to share their biographies with the class.

See the Chapter Planner for more strategies for differentiation.

HISTORICAL THINKING

ANSWERS

1. Parks was arrested for refusing to give up her bus seat so a white rider could sit.

2. After Parks's arrest, the community rallied behind her. People boycotted city buses to protest segregation.

3. The *Brown* decision stated that the "separate but equal" doctrine violated people's rights. The courts applied the doctrine from one segregated public service (schools) to another (buses).

1.5 Dr. King and Peaceful Protest

Many men and women played crucial roles in the civil rights movement.
But one person came to symbolize the cause and emerged as its leader.
That person was Dr. Martin Luther King, Jr.

MAIN IDEA Martin Luther King, Jr., with his principles of peaceful protest, became the leader of the civil rights movement.

MAN OF PEACE

Martin Luther King, Jr., grew up in Atlanta, Georgia, in a close-knit, middle-class family. His father was a minister at the Ebenezer Baptist Church. King's grandfather had also served as a pastor at the church. King entered Morehouse College in 1944 to study law and medicine. However, he eventually decided to follow in his father's and grandfather's footsteps and become a minister. His decision was influenced by Morehouse president Benjamin Mays, who also strongly supported racial equality. King went on to study at Crozer Theological Seminary in Pennsylvania and earned a doctoral degree in theology from Boston University. In Boston, King met Coretta Scott, and the pair married in 1953.

In 1954, while completing his doctoral studies, Dr. King accepted a position as pastor at Dexter Avenue Baptist Church in Montgomery, Alabama. As you know, he led Montgomery's successful bus boycott the following year. In the wake of that achievement, King, and other African-American ministers, and civil rights activists formed the **Southern Christian Leadership Conference (SCLC)**. The organization pledged to fight for racial equality using peaceful protest, or **nonviolent resistance**, and encouraged other protesters to adopt the same strategy.

Dr. King was deeply influenced by **Mohandas Gandhi**, a civil rights leader who had used nonviolent protest to help India gain independence from Great Britain in 1947. The African-American minister and his wife traveled to India in 1959 to visit political and social leaders in the country and further their understanding of Gandhi's methods. (Gandhi himself had been assassinated in 1948.)

After his trip, King became more convinced than ever in the power of nonviolent resistance. He believed the method would be an effective weapon in the fight for achieving racial equality and human dignity for all Americans.

SIX PRINCIPLES OF NONVIOLENCE

While others in the civil rights movement called for change using any means necessary—including violence—Dr. King insisted on using only peaceful methods. He knew that not responding to the insults, taunts, and violence would be hard. So King developed six principles of nonviolence to guide protesters and strengthen their resolve.

The first principle emphasizes that nonviolence requires courage. While seeming to be passive, a protester is actually being assertive spiritually, mentally, and emotionally. The second principle states that the goal of nonviolent resistance is to create understanding and community, not to

On March 22, 1956, supporters cheer as Dr. Martin Luther King, Jr., emerges from the Montgomery, Alabama, courthouse with his wife, Coretta, at his side. King had been found guilty of organizing the Montgomery Bus Boycott. The maximum penalty for the crime was $1,000 and 6 months in prison. However, because King had advocated nonviolence throughout the boycott, the judge decided to be lenient and only fine the civil rights leader $500.

humiliate opponents. According to the third principle, nonviolence seeks to defeat injustice and evil, not those who commit evil acts. The fourth principle encourages nonviolent resisters by asserting that their suffering can be liberating. The fifth principle insists that protesters must be unselfish and refuse to hate their opponents. Finally, the sixth principle teaches that nonviolent resisters should believe that justice will eventually triumph.

King called on fellow activist **James Lawson** to use these principles to conduct nonviolence training workshops for members of the SCLC. While in college in Tennessee, Lawson had organized similar workshops. Soon, protesters both inside and outside the SCLC would use nonviolent resistance to achieve their goals.

SIX PRINCIPLES OF NONVIOLENCE

1 Nonviolent resistance is assertive, not passive.

2 Its goal is to create understanding.

3 Nonviolence is directed at the evil itself, not at people.

4 Suffering for a cause can be liberating.

5 Hate is not an effective weapon against hate.

6 Justice will triumph.

HISTORICAL THINKING

1. **READING CHECK** How was King influenced by Mohandas Gandhi?

2. **MAKE INFERENCES** Why do you think workshops in nonviolent resistance were necessary to train protesters?

3. **FORM AND SUPPORT OPINIONS** Do you think nonviolent resistance can achieve better results than violent protest? Why or why not?

PLAN

Objective
Learn how Dr. Martin Luther King, Jr., became the leading voice of nonviolent resistance.

Critical Thinking Skills for Lesson 1.5
- Identify Main Ideas and Details
- Monitor Comprehension
- Make Inferences
- Form and Support Opinions
- Draw Conclusions

Essential Question for Chapter 26
How did the civil rights movement impact American society? In the 1950s, the civil rights movement promoted civil disobedience. Lesson 1.5 discusses the influence of Martin Luther King, Jr., who emphasized the importance of nonviolent resistance as a way to protest.

Background for the Teacher
One of the tactics Martin Luther King, Jr., admired most from Mohandas Gandhi's nonviolent resistance to English rule over India was the renowned 240-mile march Gandhi undertook to protest England's salt monopoly. At the time, Indian citizens were forbidden to produce or sell salt. In addition to controlling salt production and sales, the British imposed a very stiff tax on it. The lack of competition in the industry meant that ordinary Indian citizens were largely unable to afford to purchase salt, a key dietary ingredient for sustaining human life, particularly in a very warm climate like India's. Years later, Andrew Young, mayor of Atlanta and a close associate of Dr. King's, claimed that the whole civil rights movement, and perhaps especially the famous March on Washington, was an attempt to reflect the moral lessons of Mohandas Gandhi's Salt March to the sea, where Gandhi and his followers illegally collected salt themselves.

INTRODUCE & ENGAGE

Brainstorm a List

Write the term *nonviolent resistance* on the board and invite a volunteer to define it. Ask students to talk about how someone might offer strong resistance without violence through discussion and other methods. Then have them brainstorm a list of examples of nonviolent resistance, such as hunger strikes, sit-down strikes, or walkouts. Tell students that in Lesson 1.5 they will learn how the civil rights movement employed nonviolent resistance to further the cause.

TEACH

Guided Discussion

1. **Draw Conclusions** How might Dr. King's youth and college years have influenced him later in life? *(Possible response: King was from a family of ministers, which probably led to his decision to become a minister and a public speaker; the president of his college supported racial equality and civil rights, inspiring King to become a civil rights activist.)*

2. **Make Inferences** Thinking about the third principle in Dr. King's six principles of nonviolence, why is it important for nonviolent response to be directed at issues rather than at people? *(Answers will vary. Possible response: Fighting against abusive behavior instead of against the people expressing that behavior is an effective way to stay within the law, avoid violent confrontation, and limit feelings of hate, contempt, and blame. In addition, that strategy is more likely to change a person's mind than attacking that individual personally.)*

More Information

James Lawson's Nonviolence Workshops Before he taught for the SCLC, James Lawson had honed his nonviolence workshops in Nashville, Tennessee, where he had a reputation with students for being a bit more radical than other civil rights activists. His students came to the workshops believing that if they went along with Jim Crow laws, they were essentially admitting that African Americans were inferior to whites. Lawson showed them that nonviolence was actually an effective way to fight segregation. He taught them ways to react with dignity to insults and threatening situations where they were spat on or beaten. Lawson's philosophy was that a nonviolent resister had to keep up a strong and constant belief in the cause and the larger goals of the movement, remain courteous and friendly at all times, and never strike back or use insulting language toward an abuser. **ASK:** Of the six principles of nonviolence, which do you think would be most important, and why? *(Answers will vary. Possible response: Because it is vital to keep the goals of the movement in mind, the sixth principle, a belief in the long-term view that "justice will triumph," is perhaps the most important principle for anyone trying to cope directly with violent behavior.)*

Active Options

Active History: Research Leaders in Nonviolent Resistance Extend the lesson by using either the PDF or Whiteboard version of the activity. These activities take a deeper look at a topic from, or related to, the lesson. Explore the activities as a class, turn them into group assignments, or even assign them individually.

NG Learning Framework: Create a Skit
ATTITUDE Empowerment
SKILLS Collaboration, Communication

Direct students to reread the six principles of nonviolence. Then encourage them to work with a partner to choose one of the principles to bring to life in a two-character skit. Their skits should show an example of the chosen principle in action. Tell students they may write a scenario to use as the basis of an improvised scene or may script their skit completely. When students have had time to plan and practice their skits, invite each pair to present their work to the class.

DIFFERENTIATE

English Language Learners

Rephrase Principles To help students fully grasp the meaning of the six principles of nonviolence, ask pairs to rephrase each principle in their own words. Pair students at the **Emerging** level of proficiency with students at the **Expanding** or **Bridging** level. Prompt them to use a dictionary as needed to help them understand difficult or unfamiliar words.

Gifted & Talented

Create a Meme Challenge students to illustrate Dr. King's six principles of nonviolence. They can look for relevant images available for public use or create an image of their own for each principle. Direct students to use a meme-creation tool to overlay their image onto each principle. Invite them to share their memes with the class.

See the Chapter Planner for more strategies for differentiation.

HISTORICAL THINKING

ANSWERS

1. After learning about the success of Gandhi's nonviolent protests in India, King became convinced that the approach was the correct one for the U.S. civil rights movement.

2. Possible response: Workshops were necessary so that protesters were prepared for what to expect and how to respond. The opposition was known to be violent toward protesters, and protesters might be tempted to respond in kind.

3. Answers will vary. Some students might say nonviolent resistance achieves better results because it garners more sympathy from people watching on television and can protect protesters from criminal prosecution. Others might say that it's human nature to defend oneself when attacked and that the attackers need to recognize that their targets have power, too.

2.1 A Growing Movement

What would you do if a server at a fast-food restaurant refused to take your meal order but served other people? A group of students chose to wait politely for their lunch—no matter how long it took.

MAIN IDEA In the early 1960s, the call for civil rights expanded as more and more activists tried to desegregate public places.

STUDENT POWER

A few years after the Montgomery Bus Boycott, civil rights activism began to transform into a mass movement. Inspired by Dr. King's principles of nonviolent resistance, four African-American college students entered a Woolworth's store in Greensboro, North Carolina, on February 1, 1960, and sat at the lunch counter designated "For Whites Only." In the 1950s, the Supreme Court had ruled that such segregation was unconstitutional. Nevertheless, when the students ordered lunch, they were asked to leave. The students remained in their seats until the store closed, however, and came back the next day with 25 more protesters.

Reports of the protest appeared in newspapers and on television, and soon people staged sit-ins in other cities. A **sit-in** is a form of protest in which people occupy seats or floor space and refuse to leave. Besides lunch counters, activists occupied segregated churches in "pray-ins" and public swimming pools in "wade-ins." Many protesters endured abuse and were arrested, but others quickly came to take their places. By the summer of 1960, many dining establishments across the South had become desegregated—including the Greensboro lunch counter.

Encouraged by the success of the sit-ins, a group of African-American students formed the **Student Nonviolent Coordinating Committee (SNCC)**. Many of its members were frustrated with the cautious approach of the SCLC. Another organization called the **Congress of Racial Equality (CORE)**, which was founded in 1942 by **James Farmer**, had pledged to fight discrimination through nonviolent protest. The two organizations would soon work together.

FREEDOM RIDERS

In 1960, the U.S. Supreme Court had ruled in *Boynton* v. *Virginia* that the segregation of public facilities serving travelers, such as bus terminals and restrooms, was illegal. The following year, CORE decided to test that decision. In May 1961, seven African-American and six white **Freedom Riders** left Washington, D.C., on two buses bound for New Orleans, Louisiana. As they traveled from one terminal to another along the way, they ignored "white" and "colored" signs posted by restrooms, lunch counters, and waiting rooms and used whatever facilities they chose.

CORE had announced the bus rides to the press, so white segregationists were waiting at some stops to ambush and attack the riders. At this time, **John F. Kennedy** was president of the United States. In the wake of the violence, he sent U.S. marshals to protect the riders. With assistance from SNCC, CORE continued to organize freedom rides. As a result of their efforts, in September 1961, the federal government banned buses and trains traveling across state lines from using any terminal that segregated people by race.

REVIEW & ASSESS

1. **READING CHECK** How did African-American students try to desegregate a lunch counter in Greensboro, North Carolina?

2. **ANALYZE CAUSE AND EFFECT** What resulted from the Greensboro protest?

3. **MAKE INFERENCES** Why do you think CORE announced the freedom rides to the press?

Two Civil Rights Tactics

Students added two new tactics to the nonviolent struggle for civil rights: the sit-in, shown in the top photo; and the freedom ride, shown in the bottom photo. The tactics captured the attention of the American public and helped spread the civil rights movement.

Students fill the seats at this lunch counter during the Greensboro sit-in. By the sit-in's fifth day, the number of protesters exceeded 300.

Freedom Riders in Anniston, Alabama, sit beside their bus, which had been firebombed by segregationists. As the passengers fled the burning bus, the mob beat them with their fists and baseball bats.

PLAN

Objective

Learn how civil rights activism led to desegregation of lunch counters, buses, and other public facilities.

Critical Thinking Skills for Lesson 2.1

- Identify Main Ideas and Details
- Monitor Comprehension
- Analyze Cause and Effect
- Make Inferences
- Draw Conclusions
- Ask and Answer Questions

Essential Question for Chapter 26

How did the civil rights movement impact American society? As the civil rights movement expanded, nonviolent protests against segregation and other abuses spread across the United States. Lesson 2.1 examines the organizations and tactics behind this expansion.

Background for the Teacher

President Kennedy was cautious in his approach to civil rights, concentrating mainly on enforcing existing laws, such as ensuring voting rights for African Americans, rather than backing new laws. In fact, Kennedy essentially ignored the civil rights crisis for the first two years of his presidency. He knew he needed southern votes if he wanted to win a second term, and southern Democrats were opposed to expanding civil rights laws. So instead, Kennedy appointed a record number of African Americans to high-ranking positions within his administration. He also strengthened the Civil Rights Commission. He did send armed law enforcement to protect the Freedom Riders headed to Montgomery, Alabama, but even this was no guarantee of safety. In spite of repeated violent racial incidents taking place in the United States, Kennedy did not announce comprehensive new civil rights legislation until June 11, 1963.

INTRODUCE & ENGAGE

Picture a Protest

Prompt students to picture a protest based on current events they are aware of, on protests they may have witnessed, or on what they imagine a protest would look and sound like. **ASK:** What sights and sounds come to mind when you think of a protest? *(Answers will vary. Possible response: marching, signs, call-and-response chants, fighting between protesters and counterprotesters, police, shouting, singing, vandalism)* Direct students' attention to the photo of the Greensboro sit-in. **ASK:** Do you think a protest like this one could be effective? Why or why not? *(Answers will vary. Possible responses: It could be effective because it does not antagonize the opposing side; it shows the protesters to be respectful and might make people listen to their ideas. It is probably not as effective as a louder, more aggressive protest because it doesn't attract as much attention.)* Tell students that in this lesson they will learn about some nonviolent civil rights protests.

TEACH

Guided Discussion

1. **Draw Conclusions** Based on the text and what you already know, why do you think protest events and organizations often involve college students? *(Possible responses: Young people are passionate about their ideals and less willing to wait for slow change than older people. Young people attending college may have fewer work and family obligations than people with full-time jobs. A college education may help them gain a broader perspective.)*

2. **Ask and Answer Questions** Imagine that you have been invited to interview one of the Freedom Riders who went to New Orleans in May 1961. What questions would you ask this person, and how do you think he or she might answer? *(Answers will vary but should reflect ideas and information from the lesson about sit-ins, segregation, nonviolent protest, CORE, and SNCC.)*

Analyze Cause and Effect

How did the laws about transportation change because of the actions of the Freedom Riders? *(Possible response: Though racial segregation in places that served travelers had been illegal since 1960, many terminals ignored the law until the federal government placed a ban on buses crossing into any state that still had segregated facilities.)*

Active Options

On Your Feet: Fishbowl Direct half the class to sit in a small circle, facing inward, and the other half to sit in a larger circle around them. Pose this question: Why did the Freedom Riders ride into southern cities such as New Orleans and Montgomery, and what dangers did they face? Ask students in the inner circle to discuss the question as students in the outer circle listen and evaluate the points made. Then invite the groups to reverse roles and continue the discussion.

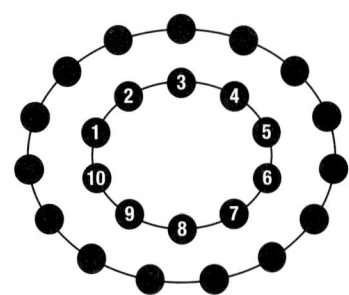

NG Learning Framework: Plan a Sing-in

ATTITUDE Empowerment

SKILL Collaboration

Review the meaning of the terms *sit-in*, *pray-in*, and *wade-in* with students. Then direct them to work together in groups of five or six to research protest songs from the civil rights era and to create a list of such songs to serve as the basis of a "sing-in." If possible, have groups learn and practice one or two protest songs from their list to present to the class.

DIFFERENTIATE

English Language Learners `ELD`

Understand Idioms Arrange students of **All Proficiencies** in pairs. Bring their attention to the idiom "in the wake of" in the last paragraph of the lesson. Guide students to look up this meaning of *wake* in a dictionary (the ripple of waves behind a ship traveling through water). Then explain the idiomatic meaning of "in the wake of" (as a result of; in the aftermath of). If time permits, introduce idioms using a different meaning of *wake* (to awaken), such as *wake-up call*, *wake up and smell the coffee*, and *wake up on the wrong side of bed*. Ask pairs to write original sentences incorporating idioms using *wake*.

Pre-AP

Research and Write an Essay Instruct students to use print and online resources to learn more about the Freedom Riders and take notes as they conduct their research. Then direct them to use their notes to write an expository essay about the goals, tactics, and experiences of the Freedom Riders and the outcome of their efforts. Ask volunteers to read their essays to the class.

See the Chapter Planner for more strategies for differentiation.

HISTORICAL THINKING

ANSWERS

1. The counter was reserved for white customers, but African-American students sat there every day and refused to leave without being served.

2. More African-American protesters showed up each day, and through their persistence, that lunch counter and many others were eventually desegregated.

3. CORE wanted the press to cover the actions to let the general public know what was happening and to attract more protesters to their cause.

Confrontation in Birmingham

In the early 1960s, Dr. Martin Luther King, Jr., claimed that "a virtual reign of terror" existed in Birmingham, Alabama. White segregationists bombed African-American homes and churches so frequently that some residents called it "Bombingham."

MAIN IDEA In 1963, peaceful protests against segregation in Birmingham, Alabama, were met with brutality by the city's police force.

THE BIRMINGHAM CAMPAIGN

Dr. Martin Luther King, Jr., had observed the successful desegregation efforts of the students who staged sit-ins and freedom rides. Using some of their tactics, King soon turned his attention to Birmingham, Alabama. In 1962, he declared that Birmingham was "by far the worst big city in race relations in the United States." For years, white segregationists in the city had committed acts of violence against African Americans, including attacks on the Freedom Riders. The segregationists had also repeatedly bombed an African-American church in Birmingham and were not punished for the crimes. Segregation laws were strictly enforced under police commissioner **Eugene "Bull" Connor**, who had ties to the Ku Klux Klan.

In April 1963, King and the SCLC began a campaign to end segregation in Birmingham. They staged sit-ins at whites-only lunch counters, organized boycotts of local businesses, and held

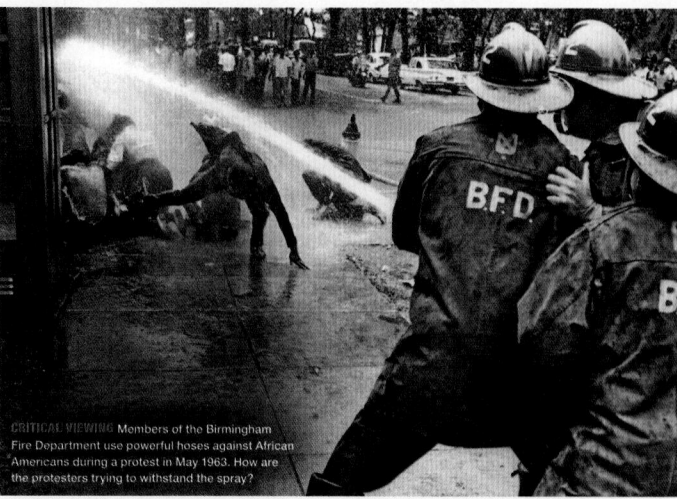

CRITICAL VIEWING Members of the Birmingham Fire Department use powerful hoses against African Americans during a protest in May 1963. How are the protesters trying to withstand the spray?

marches throughout the city. As the protests continued, more and more people took part. The police arrested and jailed many of the protesters, including Dr. King.

In response to the protests, eight white ministers from Alabama wrote a letter to the editor of the *Birmingham News* on April 12, 1963. They blamed King and other civil rights leaders for causing the chaos in their city and urged African Americans to stop supporting the demonstrations. The ministers called the protests "unwise and untimely." After King's arrest, he had been placed in a jail cell. He wrote an answer to the clergymen from his cell in what came to be known as his "**Letter from Birmingham City Jail**." In the letter, he explained the need for nonviolent resistance and defended the justice of his cause. He pointed out that those who had endured segregation had waited long enough for equal treatment in American society.

VIOLENCE IN THE CITY

King was released from jail after eight days in **solitary confinement**, or being locked in a cell alone. Meanwhile, support for the protests had decreased. Perhaps recalling the progress young people had made in the last couple of years, King recruited local students to re-energize the Birmingham campaign. On May 2, students of all ages marched through the city. Many of the protesters were arrested, but Connor also resorted to violence against them. The police and other city officials beat the demonstrators and used dogs and high-pressure fire hoses to break up the protest. However, news agencies had sent reporters to Birmingham to cover the demonstrations. The reporters captured images of children being attacked by police dogs and peaceful protesters getting knocked off their feet by the water hoses. Finally, on May 10, the campaign ended when Birmingham city leaders agreed to some of the protesters' demands. The two groups established a timetable for the desegregation of the city's public facilities.

Other events in Alabama soon took center stage. As you may recall, the state's governor, George Wallace, tried to prevent the desegregation of the University of Alabama on June 11, 1963. The governor's actions and the protests in Birmingham prompted President Kennedy to respond that evening. The president delivered a televised speech on civil rights and declared "the cries for equality" could no longer be ignored. The following week, he sent a proposal to Congress for a civil rights bill that was far stronger than those passed in 1957 and 1960. As a result of Kennedy's speech and the violent images from Birmingham, more people began to support the civil rights movement.

In his jail cell, King read the letter from the white clergymen who called for an end to the demonstrations in Birmingham and immediately wrote a response. In the excerpt below from his letter, King answers the clergymen's charge that "outsiders" incited the demonstrations.

PRIMARY SOURCES

[W]e are now confronted by a series of demonstrations by some of our Negro citizens, directed and led in part by outsiders.

—from a letter by Alabama clergy for the *Birmingham News* and *Post-Herald* newspapers, April 12, 1963

I cannot sit idly by in Atlanta and not be concerned about what happens in Birmingham. Injustice anywhere is a threat to justice everywhere.

—from "Letter from Birmingham City Jail," by Dr. Martin Luther King, Jr., April 16, 1963

HISTORICAL THINKING

1. **READING CHECK** Why did King consider Birmingham the worst big city in America on race relations?

2. **DETERMINE CHRONOLOGY** What events in Birmingham led the eight white ministers to write a letter to the local newspaper?

3. **ANALYZE CAUSE AND EFFECT** What happened as a result of Birmingham's brutal treatment of the civil rights demonstrators?

PLAN

Objective
Discuss the violent response to nonviolent civil rights protests in Birmingham, Alabama.

Critical Thinking Skills for Lesson 2.2
- Identify Main Ideas and Details
- Monitor Comprehension
- Determine Chronology
- Analyze Cause and Effect
- Analyze Primary Sources
- Make Connections

Essential Question for Chapter 26
How did the civil rights movement impact American society? Birmingham, Alabama, was known as one of the most segregated cities in the United States. Lesson 2.2 tracks how violence in this city led to major changes in civil rights law.

Background for the Teacher
In 1961, police commissioner Eugene "Bull" Connor, an avowed white supremacist, ordered Birmingham law enforcement to stay away from the bus terminal and the incoming buses bringing Freedom Riders to the city. When the buses arrived at the terminal, members of the Ku Klux Klan were lying in wait to attack the Freedom Riders. Yet despite all the turmoil in the 1960s, by 2003, Birmingham had changed greatly. Exactly 40 years after Martin Luther King, Jr., was jailed there, an African-American woman—23-year Birmingham police veteran Annetta W. Nunn—took over the position of Birmingham police chief that Connor had once held.

INTRODUCE & ENGAGE

Consider Danger and Safety

Ask students to consider the following scenario: A police officer is called to intervene when two neighbors are engaged in a heated argument. **ASK:** How should the police officer engage with the people involved in the situation? *(Answers will vary. Possible response: The police officer should behave calmly and respectfully, move to protect anyone in immediate danger, and work to de-escalate a tense situation.)* Explain that in this lesson students will learn about how police in Birmingham, Alabama, escalated the violence during times of civil unrest rather than helping defuse it.

TEACH

Guided Discussion

1. **Analyze Primary Sources** The letter by Alabama clergy casts Martin Luther King, Jr., as an "outsider" in Birmingham. Though King was not from Birmingham, why does he respond to the clergy's letter? *(Possible response: King was a leading voice for justice in the nationwide civil rights movement. He was also an African American, and the existence of segregation anywhere in the United States was a threat to African-American liberty.)*

2. **Make Connections** What role did the media play in increasing public support for the civil rights movement? *(Possible response: Images of the violence in Birmingham appearing in newspapers and on television, combined with President Kennedy's televised speech calling for racial equality, were key factors in increased public support for the movement.)*

More Information

Arrests in Birmingham In May 1963, civil rights leaders decided to use young people in the protests in Birmingham. They guessed they would need big crowds to force the city to pay attention, and they knew that many of the protesters would be jailed. However, they did not expect attack dogs and fire hoses. For some, including many children, the hoses were powerful enough to tear skin, rip off clothing, and slam people back down the street. Later, eyewitnesses claim, more than 1,500 people were jammed into Birmingham jail's holding cells, which were designed for occupancy by only 600. King himself was arrested on the charge of "parading without a permit." In response, King said in his "Letter from Birmingham City Jail" that he had no problem with an ordinance demanding a permit for a parade, but that when such an ordinance was used to shut down peaceful protest, a right protected by the First Amendment, it automatically became unjust.

Active Options

On Your Feet: Numbered Heads Have students gather in groups of four and count off within their group. Ask groups to consider, discuss, and respond to these questions: Considering what happened and what might have happened, was the choice of Birmingham for a civil rights confrontation wise? Why or why not? Then call a number and have the student from each group with that number report for the group.

NG Learning Framework: Present an Excerpt

ATTITUDE Empowerment

KNOWLEDGE Our Human Story

Encourage students to use digital resources to find, read, and discuss the complete text of King's "Letter from Birmingham City Jail." Organize students into small groups and ask them to select a portion of the letter that they find most compelling to present as a reader's theater performance. Each student in the group will read part of the selection. After groups have practiced their presentation, invite them to perform for the class.

DIFFERENTIATE

Inclusion

Analyze a Photograph Pair students who are visually impaired with students who are not. Ask the latter to describe the photograph and read the caption. Tell visually impaired students to ask clarifying questions as necessary. Then direct pairs to work together to answer the Critical Viewing question.

Gifted & Talented

Create Graphic Nonfiction Tell students to conduct online research to learn more about the eight days Martin Luther King, Jr., spent in solitary confinement in the Birmingham City Jail. Instruct students to report on their findings using the style of a graphic nonfiction book. You may provide students with examples of graphic nonfiction, such as *The 14th Dalai Lama: A Manga Biography* or *The Beats: A Graphic History*. Encourage students to use quotes from King's letter and to include some background frames showing what was happening in Alabama and throughout the United States while King was in jail. Invite students to share their completed work with the class and to answer questions.

See the Chapter Planner for more strategies for differentiation.

HISTORICAL THINKING

ANSWERS

1. Birmingham was one of the most segregated cities in the South and had long resisted integration and civil rights.

2. Massive demonstrations, which included sit-ins, boycotts, and marches, caused chaos throughout the city and prompted the ministers to write the letter.

3. The brutality and injustice shown by city officials and law enforcement only made the demonstrators more determined to continue to fight for their rights. The city's strategy failed miserably, as many more people came to support the movement after they saw the poor treatment protesters suffered there.

CRITICAL VIEWING Though the spray from the hoses is powerful enough to knock people down, the protesters are trying to stand their ground by crouching, huddling together, or crawling beneath it.

2.3 The March on Washington

There was no social media as we know it in 1963. Still, word got out about the march in Washington, D.C. Reporters had estimated that only about 25,000 people would come, but the crowds kept arriving in buses and on trains. Apparently, the message had gone viral.

MAIN IDEA In 1963, hundreds of thousands of people took part in the March on Washington, and Dr. Martin Luther King, Jr., electrified the crowd with his speech.

MARCH FOR FREEDOM

As you know, President Kennedy sent a proposal for a new civil rights bill to Congress in June 1963. The bill faced strong opposition from many legislators there, however, and wasn't making much progress. To increase support for the bill and to call attention to the high unemployment rate among African Americans, civil rights leaders planned a major rally in Washington, D.C. The demonstration was called the **March on Washington for Jobs and Freedom** and took place on August 28, 1963.

The main organizer of the event was long-time civil rights activist **Bayard Rustin**. He and A. Phillip Randolph brought together civil rights, labor, and religious organizations to support and promote the demonstration. They printed and distributed flyers and posters and coordinated buses to bring as many people as they could to the march.

Their efforts paid off. Rustin expected 100,000 people to attend the March on Washington, but more than 200,000 took part. People came from all over the country. Most were African-American, but about one-fourth of the crowd was white. Demonstrators assembled by the Washington Monument and then marched along the National Mall to the Lincoln Memorial.

As they walked, participants sang "We Shall Overcome," a gospel song that had become an anthem of the civil rights movement. Once the marchers arrived at the Lincoln Memorial, the day's program began. It featured a welcoming speech by Rustin and speeches from several civil rights leaders. Gospel singer Mahalia Jackson performed, as did folk singers Bob Dylan, Joan Baez, and the group Peter, Paul, and Mary.

"I HAVE A DREAM"

The most highly anticipated speaker of the day was Dr. Martin Luther King, Jr. Known for his eloquence, or articulate and powerful speaking, King did not disappoint. He began by referring to the march as "the greatest demonstration for freedom in the history of our nation." Then he launched into a prepared speech, pointing out that almost 100 years had passed since President Abraham Lincoln had freed enslaved people.

But as Dr. King neared the end of the speech, Mahalia Jackson called out, "Tell them about the dream, Martin!" King had spoken often about his dream of an integrated American society. During a recent speech delivered in Detroit, King had repeated the phrase, "I have a dream." Inspired by Jackson's request, he stopped reading from his notes and drew on his earlier speeches from memory. He used "I have a dream" as a constant refrain while he described his vision of a brighter future. Dr. King's "I Have a Dream" speech is considered one of the greatest **orations**, or speeches, in American history.

The March on Washington showed how strong and unified the civil rights movement had become. However, on September 15, 1963, the Ku Klux Klan detonated a bomb at the 16th Street Baptist Church in Birmingham that killed four African-American girls. The church was a center for organizing civil rights activities.

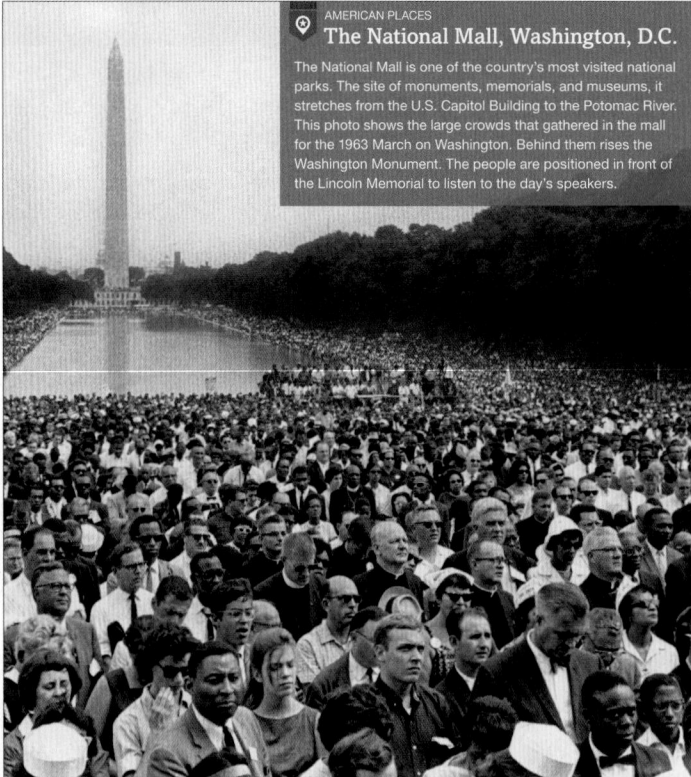

AMERICAN PLACES
The National Mall, Washington, D.C.
The National Mall is one of the country's most visited national parks. The site of monuments, memorials, and museums, it stretches from the U.S. Capitol Building to the Potomac River. This photo shows the large crowds that gathered in the mall for the 1963 March on Washington. Behind them rises the Washington Monument. The people are positioned in front of the Lincoln Memorial to listen to the day's speakers.

In 1964, SNCC and CORE launched **Freedom Summer**, a **voter registration drive** to sign up as many African-American voters in Mississippi as possible. More than 700 student volunteers from the North, many of them white, worked with civil rights groups in Mississippi to register new voters. In June, though, three of the students—two white and one black—disappeared. Their bodies were found six weeks later. They had been murdered, probably by a mob of Ku Klux Klansmen. These events demonstrated how far the country was from realizing King's dream.

HISTORICAL THINKING

1. **READING CHECK** What was the purpose of the March on Washington?

2. **DETERMINE CHRONOLOGY** What previous events might have helped swell the crowds at the March on Washington?

3. **DRAW CONCLUSIONS** What message did the people who murdered the student volunteers in Mississippi want to send?

Objective

Analyze how civil rights activists planned and carried out the massive March on Washington.

Critical Thinking Skills for Lesson 2.3

- Identify Main Ideas and Details
- Monitor Comprehension
- Determine Chronology
- Draw Conclusions
- Make Connections
- Compare and Contrast

Essential Question for Chapter 26

How did the civil rights movement impact American society? In the summer of 1963, a large-scale demonstration gave new energy to the civil rights movement. Lesson 2.3 discusses the March on Washington and its aftermath.

Background for the Teacher

Bayard Rustin was known as a brilliant peace and equal rights organizer, which made him a natural choice for the job of chief strategist for the March on Washington. Even so, Rustin had his work cut out for him, as he had less than two months to organize the event. Rustin knew that every detail of the march was important. It had to be orderly, dignified, and above all peaceful. To achieve that goal, he created a 12-page guide filled with information about where to park, which slogans to shout, and where participants could find public restrooms. During the march, thousands of helpers, dubbed "bus captains," circulated through the crowd, making sure protesters had what they needed and knew what to do. As a result, one of the largest crowds ever assembled on the National Mall remained peaceful.

History Notebook

Encourage students to complete the American Gallery page for Chapter 26 in their History Notebooks as they read.

K-W-L Chart

Provide each student with a K-W-L Chart. Guide students to brainstorm what they already know about the "I Have a Dream" speech. Then tell them to write questions they would like to answer as they study the lesson, such as How many people heard the speech? Where was the speech given? What was the purpose of the speech? Allow time at the end of the lesson for students to add what they have learned.

K What Do I Know?	W What Do I Want To Learn?	L What Did I Learn?

TEACH

Guided Discussion

1. **Make Connections** Why do you think Martin Luther King, Jr., mentioned Abraham Lincoln during his speech at the March on Washington? *(Possible response: By pointing out that African Americans were still suffering racial inequality 100 years after Lincoln had freed the slaves, King was making a distinction between a promise made and a promise kept.)*

2. **Compare and Contrast** In what ways were the events at the 16th Street Baptist Church and the events in Mississippi during Freedom Summer similar and different? *(Similarities: Young people were killed in places associated with civil rights activities, and the Ku Klux Klan was likely responsible for the deaths in both instances. Differences: Those killed at the church were four African-American girls, while those killed in Mississippi were three college students from the North who were registering African-American voters; the girls were killed by a bomb in the church, while the voting rights activists were abducted and murdered by a mob.)*

American Places

A number of America's most popular historical monuments are located within the National Mall. Some, such as the Lincoln Memorial, the Franklin Delano Roosevelt Memorial, and the Thomas Jefferson Memorial, are tributes to American presidents. There is also a monument to Martin Luther King, Jr., which was dedicated in 2011. The concept for the memorial stemmed from a line in King's "I Have a Dream" speech in which he describes despair as a mountain from which hope will be carved. The monument depicts King as a beacon of hope emerging from a huge slab of granite.

Active Options

AMERICAN GALLERY ONLINE **The Protest Movement** Invite students to explore the American Gallery. Have them select one of the photographs and do additional research to learn more about it. Ask questions that will inspire additional inquiry about the chosen photo, such as Who is shown? Where does this take place? What is happening? Who took the picture? Why was it taken? What else would you like to know about it?

NG Learning Framework: Design a Media Plan

ATTITUDE Empowerment

SKILL Problem-Solving

Encourage students to work in groups of five or six to discuss how Bayard Rustin drew on many different groups, including labor, religious, and civil rights organizations, to get the word out about the March on Washington for Jobs and Freedom. Ask students to imagine they are part of Rustin's public relations team and that they must create a media plan that will spread the word to the widest possible audience. Remind them that many technologies that are available today were not available in 1963. Invite groups to present their completed plans to the class.

DIFFERENTIATE

Striving Readers

Write Tweets As students read the lesson, direct them to pause after each paragraph and write a tweet summarizing the paragraph's main idea in their own words. When they have finished the lesson, have students take turns reading their tweets aloud to a partner one at a time. Encourage students to discuss differences in how they tweeted the same paragraph.

Pre-AP

Research and Write an Oral Report Instruct students to research, write, and present an oral report about public reactions to King's "I Have a Dream" speech. Tell students to examine the immediate reactions, reflections following King's assassination, and more recent reflections. Encourage them to explain how some of those reactions influenced specific U.S. policies regarding civil rights. Invite students to present their oral reports to the class, citing their sources and answering classmates' questions.

See the Chapter Planner for more strategies for differentiation.

HISTORICAL THINKING

ANSWERS

1. The main purpose of the march was to pressure the federal government to pass comprehensive civil rights legislation.

2. The Montgomery and Birmingham protests probably helped swell the crowds at the March on Washington.

3. The murderers wanted to send a message of terror to anyone who was considering coming to the South to promote integration and increased voting rights for African Americans, warning them to keep away.

2.4 Voices of Equality

During the civil rights movement in the 1950s and early 1960s, many African-American leaders spoke out against segregation and inequality. Through their deeds, they fought for equality. Through their words, they articulated what they envisioned for themselves, the movement, and the country. Their voices helped African Americans believe that change really was possible.

In this photo, Dr. Martin Luther King, Jr., delivers his "I Have a Dream" speech at the 1963 March on Washington from the steps of the Lincoln Memorial. The photo captures the end of his speech when he dramatically raised his arm and echoed some of the words of an old African-American spiritual, exclaiming: "Free at last! Free at last! Thank God Almighty, we are free at last!"

CRITICAL VIEWING Why do you think the organizers of the March wanted to have speeches delivered from the Lincoln Memorial?

DOCUMENT ONE

Primary Source: Interview
from a radio interview with Rosa Parks, 1992

In 1992, 37 years after Rosa Parks refused to give up her seat on a public bus in Montgomery, Alabama, she spoke to a National Public Radio interviewer about her decision. In this excerpt, Parks discusses why she kept her seat and what happened after her arrest.

CONSTRUCTED RESPONSE What took Parks by surprise after she was arrested?

[T]he more we gave in and the more we complied with that kind of treatment, the more oppressive it became. My main reason for keeping my seat was that I did not want to be mistreated. I did not have any idea at all what would be the result of my . . . arrest. I was totally surprised to know that so many others were concerned enough to stay off the buses and let it be known that we would no longer financially support the unjust treatment that we were receiving.

DOCUMENT TWO

Primary Source: Speech
from "I Have a Dream," by Dr. Martin Luther King, Jr., August 28, 1963

In this excerpt from King's speech, he describes how he believes the United States will be transformed when the country achieves racial equality.

CONSTRUCTED RESPONSE In his speech, why does King quote the line from the Declaration of Independence that begins, "We hold these truths to be self-evident"?

I have a dream that one day this nation will rise up and live out the true meaning of its creed: "We hold these truths to be self-evident, that all men are created equal."

I have a dream that my four little children will one day live in a nation where they will not be judged by the color of their skin but by the content of their character.

DOCUMENT THREE

Primary Source: Interview
from an interview with Bayard Rustin conducted for *Eyes on the Prize*, a PBS television series on the civil rights movement, 1979

Bayard Rustin, the chief organizer of the 1963 March on Washington, wanted the march to be a message that would convince Congress to support pending civil rights legislation. In this interview, Rustin explains how he thinks the members of Congress who attended the march were affected.

CONSTRUCTED RESPONSE Why did Rustin insist that the congressmen attending the march simply listen and not say a word?

There were about three hundred congressmen there, but none of them said a word. We had told them to come, but we wanted to talk with them, they were not to talk to us. And after they came and saw that it was very orderly, that there was fantastic determination, that there were all kinds of people there other than black people, they knew there was a consensus [agreement] in this country for the civil rights bill. After the March on Washington, when Kennedy called into the White House the leaders who had been resistant before the march, he made it very clear to them now he was prepared to put his weight behind the bill.

SYNTHESIZE & WRITE

1. **REVIEW** Review what you have learned about the civil rights movement of the 1950s and early 1960s and its leaders.

2. **RECALL** On your own paper, write the main idea expressed in the excerpt from King's speech and those from the interviews of Parks and Rustin.

3. **CONSTRUCT** Construct a topic sentence that answers this question: How did the leaders of the civil rights movement use their voices to help advance African-American equality?

4. **WRITE** Using evidence from this chapter and the documents, write an informative paragraph that supports your topic sentence in Step 3.

PLAN

Objective

Synthesize information about the civil rights movement from primary source documents.

Critical Thinking Skills for Lesson 2.4

• Synthesize

• Analyze Language Use

• Make Connections

• Evaluate

Essential Question for Chapter 26

How did the civil rights movement impact American society? In the 1960s, the words of civil rights leaders rallied the nation to their cause. Lesson 2.4 provides excerpts from interviews with Rosa Parks and Bayard Rustin and a speech by Martin Luther King, Jr., in which each speaks out against injustice and inequality.

Background for the Teacher

In August 1963, well-known oral historian Studs Terkel boarded the "freedom train" from Chicago to Washington, D.C. Along with about 800 other people, he and his wife headed to the March on Washington. Terkel recorded his conversations with people on the train and at the march to capture their feelings about the historic event. His interviews included one with an older African-American woman who spoke about racial prejudice in her town. When asked what she thought about the young white people traveling on the train, she said, "I think that if every white man and woman in America could get on this train and see the good fellowship, [they'd] either have a stroke or [they'd] have a change of heart." Terkel's last interviewee at the march shared this view: "My feeling is one of overwhelming gratitude, surprise, joy, pride . . . I think things in this country will never be the same."

INTRODUCE & ENGAGE

Prepare for the Document-Based Question

Before students start the activity, briefly preview the three documents. Remind students that a constructed response requires full explanations in complete sentences. Emphasize that students should use what they have learned about the civil rights movement and its leaders in addition to the information in the documents.

TEACH

Guided Discussion

1. **Analyze Language Use** Read the words by Rosa Parks and Martin Luther King, Jr. Describe the diction and tone each person uses to help communicate a message about civil rights. *(Possible response: Rosa Parks uses informal diction and a conversational tone to express her personal thoughts and feelings about her protest action and what happened afterward. Martin Luther King, Jr., uses more formal diction and a more formal tone, including a quotation from a historical document, to talk about the kind of America he hopes to see.)*

2. **Make Connections** According to Rustin's interview, how did the march help influence President Kennedy to support passage of the civil rights bill? *(Possible response: The congressmen who attended the march saw there was broad public support for the bill. That support encouraged President Kennedy to increase pressure to pass the legislation.)*

Evaluate

After students have completed the Synthesize & Write activity, allow time for them to exchange paragraphs and read and comment on the work of their peers. Establish guidelines for comments prior to this activity so that feedback is constructive and encouraging in nature.

Active Option

On Your Feet: Host a DBQ Roundtable Prompt students to reread the excerpts before they begin the activity. Organize them into groups of four for a roundtable discussion, and ask them to answer this question: In what ways did each person in the lesson become a "voice for equality"? Instruct each student around the table to answer the question in a different way. At the end, invite volunteers from each group to summarize the group's answers for the class.

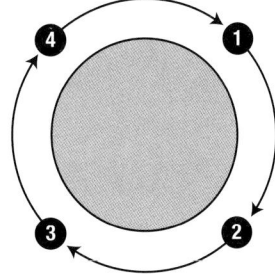

DIFFERENTIATE

Inclusion

Highlight and Summarize To help students minimize distractions, create a handout that includes the three document excerpts alone. Give a copy to each student, along with a highlighter. Tell students to highlight important words and ideas. Then have them write a summary sentence for each excerpt, using several of the words and phrases they highlighted.

Gifted & Talented

Address an Injustice Prompt students to consider a current injustice they are aware of in their school, their community, the nation, or the world. Then ask them to interview a partner about how the injustice could be addressed and what changes would need to occur to overcome the injustice. Suggest they use the excerpts featured in the lesson as inspiration for their questions and answers.

See the Chapter Planner for more strategies for differentiation.

SYNTHESIZE & WRITE

ANSWERS

1. Answers will vary.

2. Answers will vary.

3. Answers will vary. Possible response: Civil rights leaders advanced African-American equality by encouraging people to fight for their rights and by holding up the vision of a more just society.

4. Answers will vary. Possible response: Students' paragraphs should include their topic sentence from Step 3 and provide several details from the documents to support the sentence.

CONSTRUCTED RESPONSE

Document 1: She was surprised that so many people supported her cause and refused to ride Montgomery buses until their rights were respected.

Document 2: He wanted to show that the idea of basic human equality was a fundamental concept expressed in the Declaration of Independence and must apply to everyone equally, no matter their skin color.

Document 3: Rustin wanted the congressmen to listen carefully to what African Americans and others had to say rather than expressing their own opinions.

CRITICAL VIEWING Organizers probably wanted to remind people of Lincoln's emancipation of the slaves nearly 100 years earlier and to show that, even after all that time, African Americans were still fighting for equal rights and justice.

2.5 National Museum of African American History and Culture, Washington, D.C.

Open to the public in September 2016, the National Museum of African American History and Culture (NMAAHC) is the only national museum devoted exclusively to the documentation of African-American life, history, and culture. It was established by an act of Congress in 2003, following decades of efforts to promote and highlight the contributions of African Americans.

The museum has collected more than 36,000 artifacts, many of which are displayed in exhibits carefully curated around such themes as slavery, war, civil rights, photography, sports, and music. The NMAAHC is a Smithsonian museum.

Through the Lens of James Karales

From 1962 to 1964, civil rights photographer James Karales was granted remarkable access to Dr. Martin Luther King, Jr. Portraits like this one, featuring King with Rosa Parks, are some of Karales's most famous works. They tell the story of King's involvement in civil rights events, protests, and rallies, and reveal intimate family moments.

Karales took this photo at a rally at the 16th Street Baptist Church prior to its bombing on September 15, 1963. The NMAAHC has several of Karales's civil rights movement prints in its collection.

Stained Glass from 16th Street Baptist Church

On September 15, 1963, a bomb exploded at the predominantly African-American 16th Street Baptist Church in Birmingham, Alabama, as the congregation gathered for services. Four young girls—Addie Mae Collins, Denise McNair, Carole Robertson, and Cynthia Wesley—were killed by the blast. This stained glass rosette was part of the rubble.

Birmingham was plagued by violence in the 1960s. In fact, the tragedy at the church was the third bombing in the city in 11 days.

Why do you think those who violently opposed racial equality targeted African-American churches? Explain.

NAACP Hat

Roy Wilkins, an African-American civil rights activist from the 1930s to the 1970s, served as the executive secretary and director of the NAACP from 1955 to 1977. He wore this cloth hat during the 1963 March on Washington for Jobs and Freedom.

The NAACP was established in 1909 by W.E.B. Du Bois and other African-American and white leaders, including Jane Addams. The goal of the organization was to be a force for change in ending segregation and discrimination against African Americans.

Freedom Rider's Button

In 1961, many Freedom Riders who boarded buses to the South wore a button like this one as they tried to call attention to segregated public travel facilities along their journey.

March on Washington Poster

A white high school teacher named Samuel Y. Edgerton carried this poster when he attended the 1963 March on Washington to demonstrate public support for the civil rights bill proposed by President Kennedy. Edgerton had joined the NAACP in July of that year and spoken out against the segregation at a nearby school. Edgerton would become an art historian and professor at Boston University and Williams College.

WE DEMAND AN END TO POLICE BRUTALITY NOW!

Segregated Bus Station Sign

The plywood sign above hung in a segregated bus station in Birmingham, Alabama, in the 1950s. African Americans living and traveling in the South faced segregated, unpleasant, and dangerous conditions on trains and buses. Forced to sit in the backs of buses, they also suffered the humiliation of using separate restrooms, water fountains, and waiting rooms. And the threat of violence was a constant concern.

How and where else have African Americans encountered segregation throughout history? Provide examples.

PLAN

Objective
Identify artifacts relating to the civil rights movement.

Critical Thinking Skills for Lesson 2.5
- Make Connections
- Analyze Visuals
- Make Inferences

Essential Question for Chapter 26
How did the civil rights movement impact American society? The civil rights movement brought about major changes in American society. Lesson 2.5 presents and explains the significance of a sampling of artifacts included in the civil rights movement collection at the National Museum of African American History and Culture.

Background for the Teacher
Barack Obama, the nation's first African-American president, led the opening ceremony at the National Museum of African American History and Culture. He marked the occasion by ringing a church bell, a symbol of the church's central role in African-American history. The museum, which stands near the Washington Monument, presents "American history through the African American lens," with many artifacts from people's homes or personal collections. In an area called Visitor Voices, people are encouraged to record their own stories and experiences of being African-American in the United States. At the museum's opening, President Obama remarked, "It is an act of patriotism to understand where we've been."

History Notebook
Encourage students to complete the Curating History page for Chapter 26 in their History Notebooks as they read.

Discuss Family History and Memorabilia

Discuss with students how people in their own families remember significant times in family history. **ASK:** If you were putting together a museum of family artifacts or memorabilia, what would you include and why? *(Possible responses: announcements of different events, photographs, items that people made, important documents, diaries, awards or medals, clothing that might tell something important about the family's story)* Tell students that in this lesson they will read about artifacts from the civil rights movement.

Guided Discussion

1. **Make Inferences** Why might the museum have included the poster carried by Samuel Y. Edgerton? *(Possible response: The museum probably wanted to acknowledge the contributions of white people, such as Edgerton, who supported the civil rights movement by participating in marches and speaking out for equality and justice for African Americans.)*

2. **Make Connections** What do the artifacts show about the effort it took to gain equal rights for African Americans? *(Possible response: They show the cost in lives, such as the girls killed in the bombing of the Birmingham church; the different organizations that changed public policies and laws, such as the NAACP and the Freedom Riders; and many activities, such as the protests against police brutality toward African Americans. James Karales's photograph documents how civil rights leaders drew African Americans together at events such as the rally at the Baptist church.)*

Curating History

The National Museum of African American History and Culture's website offers several resources for learning more about African-American history. Access the website and help students locate the artifacts shown in this lesson. As a class, select another object from the civil rights collection, read the caption, and discuss why it would be included in the exhibit. Then encourage students to explore the collection on their own. Direct them to locate other objects that relate to the civil rights movement, and ask them to choose three to four artifacts to create their own collection. Prompt them to present their collection to the class, explaining why they selected those objects and their significance to the civil rights movement.

Active Option

On Your Feet: Sort the Artifacts Have students work in teams of four to examine the museum's online collection and complete two Concept Clusters like those shown. In one cluster, instruct students to identify various types of artifacts related to the civil rights movement in U.S. history. In the other, ask students to identify a different class or genre of artifacts, to be determined by the team. When teams are finished, invite them to share their Concept Clusters with the class.

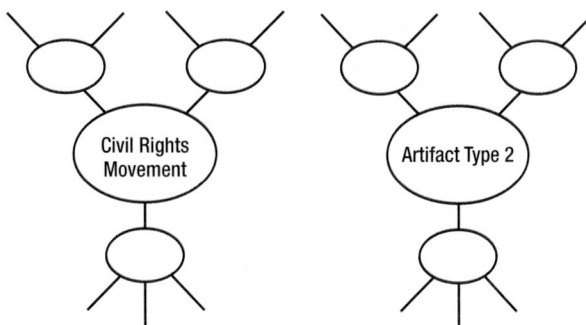

Striving Readers

Read and Recall Ask students to read the caption for each artifact independently. Then arrange students in pairs, with one partner taking notes, and direct them to cover a caption and share everything they can recall about that artifact. When they have finished, tell students to reread the caption together, identifying anything they would like to add or change in their notes. Repeat this process for each artifact.

Pre-AP

Form and Support a Thesis Challenge students to develop a thesis about why Congress established the National Museum of African American History and Culture. Direct them to conduct in-depth research to support their thesis and to learn more about how and why the museum was first envisioned and then created. Tell students to write an essay supporting their thesis, citing primary and secondary source materials and including their own analysis. Invite them to share their essays on a class or school blog.

See the Chapter Planner for more strategies for differentiation.

Answers will vary. Possible response: Churches were meeting places not only for religious and social activities but also for civil rights gatherings. By targeting churches, those who opposed racial equality signaled that no place was safe from attack and that speaking out for civil rights and against segregation would not be tolerated.

Answers will vary. Possible responses: African Americans have encountered segregation in jobs, schools, restaurants, health care, courtrooms, sports, politics, mainstream media, public swimming pools, beaches, housing, stores, and many other places. Examples include being denied service in restaurants, denied enrollment in schools, and denied the right to vote.

26 REVIEW

VOCABULARY

Use each of the following vocabulary terms in a sentence that shows an understanding of its meaning.

1. integration

   After the Supreme Court ruling, schools began the process of integration, allowing students of all races to attend.

2. desegregate

3. grassroots

4. sit-in

5. civil disobedience

6. Freedom Riders

7. oration

8. nonviolent resistance

READING STRATEGY
DETERMINE CHRONOLOGY

If you haven't done so already, complete your time line to order key events from the civil rights movement during the 1950s and early 1960s. Then answer the question.

1954
Brown v. *Board of Education* ruling

9. What subsequent events were made possible by the ruling in *Brown* v. *Board of Education*?

MAIN IDEAS

Answer the following questions. Support your answers with evidence from the chapter.

10. How did President Truman support the civil rights of African Americans? **LESSON 1.1**

11. How did the decision in *Brown* v. *Board of Education* affect schools? **LESSON 1.2**

12. What happened when James Meredith tried to register at the University of Mississippi in 1962? **LESSON 1.3**

13. What did the Montgomery Bus Boycott achieve? **LESSON 1.4**

14. What strategy did Martin Luther King, Jr., use to fight for racial equality? **LESSON 1.5**

15. Who were the Freedom Riders? **LESSON 2.1**

16. How did King try to end segregation in Birmingham in 1963? **LESSON 2.2**

17. Who made up the crowd at the 1963 March on Washington? **LESSON 2.3**

HISTORICAL THINKING

Answer the following questions. Support your answers with evidence from the chapter.

18. **COMPARE AND CONTRAST** How were the actions taken by presidents Eisenhower and Kennedy during the civil rights movement alike and different?

19. **EVALUATE** What qualities did King possess that helped him become the leader of the civil rights movement?

20. **SYNTHESIZE** How did the civil rights movement gain momentum during the 1950s and early 1960s?

21. **FORM AND SUPPORT OPINIONS** Which major event of the movement do you think had the greatest impact on helping to advance equality for African Americans? Explain your answer.

22. **MAKE INFERENCES** Why do you think the sit-ins and freedom rides energized the civil rights movement?

23. **DRAW CONCLUSIONS** What role did news outlets and reporters play in spreading the civil rights movement?

INTERPRET VISUALS

Elizabeth Eckford, the young African-American woman in the foreground of this photo taken by Will Counts, was one of the Little Rock Nine. The nine African-American students determined to integrate Central High School in Little Rock, Arkansas, on September 4, 1957, were supposed to meet that day and enter the school together. But the other students were not able to contact Eckford to let her know the plan. As a result, she endured the hostility of the white students at the school on her own.

24. How would you describe Eckford's behavior as the crowd heckles her?

25. How would you describe the face of Hazel Bryan, who is directly behind Eckford in the photo?

ANALYZE SOURCES

John Lewis has been a Georgia congressman since 1987. He was also a prominent activist during the civil rights movement. Lewis took part in lunch counter sit-ins and in the freedom rides. In the 1963 March on Washington, he delivered a forceful speech, calling on all Americans to be part of the movement.

> I appeal to all of you to get into this great revolution that is sweeping this nation. Get in and stay in the streets of every city, every village and hamlet of this nation until true freedom comes, until the revolution of 1776 is complete. We must get in this revolution and complete the revolution. For in the Delta in Mississippi, in southwest Georgia, in the Black Belt of Alabama, in Harlem, in Chicago, Detroit, Philadelphia, and all over this nation, the black masses are on the march for jobs and freedom.

26. What does Lewis mean by suggesting that the revolution of 1776 is not "complete"?

CONNECT TO YOUR LIFE

27. **EXPOSITORY** Imagine the year is 1963, and you have just taken part in the March on Washington. Write a letter to a friend describing the event and explaining how the experience has affected you.

TIPS

- Review what you have read about the march and consider what it might have been like to attend the event.

- Describe the crowds at the march and the speakers you heard, particularly Dr. Martin Luther King, Jr.

- Use two or three vocabulary words from the chapter in your letter.

- End the letter with a brief summary statement about how the march has affected you.

VOCABULARY ANSWERS

1. After the Supreme Court ruling, schools began the process of integration, allowing students of all races to attend.

2. The civil rights group wanted to desegregate buses, demanding that different races not be kept apart any longer.

3. A grassroots organization develops at the community level.

4. Students in North Carolina staged a sit-in at a lunch counter until the staff agreed to serve them.

5. Rosa Parks committed an act of civil disobedience when she refused to give up her bus seat for a white rider.

6. The Freedom Riders traveled by bus to the South to test integration laws.

7. Dr. Martin Luther King, Jr., was known for his eloquent orations.

8. Many civil rights protests used nonviolent resistance rather than rioting to bring change.

READING STRATEGY ANSWER

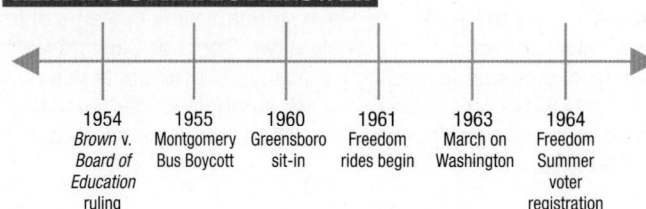

1954	1955	1960	1961	1963	1964
Brown v. *Board of Education* ruling	Montgomery Bus Boycott	Greensboro sit-in	Freedom rides begin	March on Washington	Freedom Summer voter registration

9. The court decisions following the Montgomery Bus Boycott, the lunch counter sit-in, and the freedom rides were all extensions of the *Brown* ruling that "separate but equal" was not equal.

MAIN IDEAS ANSWERS

10. Truman set up a committee to evaluate discrimination and to suggest solutions to end the injustices. He also passed legislation to enforce voting rights and protect people from lynchings.

11. The *Brown* v. *Board of Education* decision stated that separate educational facilities are unequal. Because of that decision, public schools were required to integrate.

12. When James Meredith tried to register, the governor of Mississippi physically blocked his path, and U.S. marshals had to escort Meredith to register, sparking riots.

13. The Montgomery boycott impacted the city bus system financially because most of the riders refused to take the bus, which led to the integration of the public transit system.

14. King used peaceful protests based on six principles of nonviolence: Nonviolence requires courage; nonviolent resistance creates understanding and community and does not try to humiliate its opponents; nonviolence seeks to defeat injustice and evil, not those who commit evil acts; the suffering endured by nonviolent resisters can be liberating; protesters must be unselfish and refuse to hate their opponents; nonviolent resisters believe deeply that justice will eventually triumph.

15. The Freedom Riders were a group of people of different races who traveled in buses to destinations in the South to test whether a law banning segregation in public facilities was being enforced.

16. King and others organized sit-ins, boycotts, and marches. Later, King organized Birmingham students to protest in the city.

17. Many people from all over the country congregated to show the government that a majority of Americans supported civil rights. Most were African-American, but a quarter of the crowd was white.

HISTORICAL THINKING ANSWERS

18. Both presidents signed civil rights acts. Eisenhower's were weak, however. Kennedy issued a stronger act after the Birmingham Campaign. Eisenhower did not agree with the court's decision for integration; Kennedy supported integration.

19. King was well educated, an accomplished speaker, and interested in nonviolent protests. These qualities helped him become a leader in the movement.

20. The civil rights movement gained momentum in the 1950s and 1960s through successes in defeating racist legislation. Winning the argument for school integration gave leaders the confidence to challenge other forms of segregation, such as segregation in public spaces and job discrimination.

21. Answers will vary. Possible response: I think the Birmingham Campaign had the greatest effect on securing equality for African Americans. The disturbing images of children being hosed with water and being arrested forced many Americans to take a position on civil rights, and many more people joined the movement as a result.

22. The sit-ins and freedom rides energized the movement because they were well publicized and showed regular people fighting to change society.

23. The news media reported the events and published photographs of the civil rights protests. Those reports and graphic photos swayed more people to join in later protests.

INTERPRET VISUALS ANSWERS

24. Eckford holds her head high and appears composed and dignified, though not especially happy.

25. Hazel Bryan looks angry and hateful.

ANALYZE SOURCES ANSWER

26. Possible response: The American colonies staged a revolution in 1776 to free themselves from the tyranny of the British, who would not allow the colonists basic human rights and self-governance. By referencing the "revolution of 1776," Lewis is implying that African Americans still did not enjoy the basic human rights and self-governance the colonists fought for. He means that the revolution needs to continue until those rights and that self-governance are secured for African Americans.

CONNECT TO YOUR LIFE ANSWER

27. Answers will vary. Students should incorporate what they learned in the chapter as they describe the speakers and the crowd. They should include two or three vocabulary words and conclude the letter by explaining how the march affected them personally.

Objectives

- Compare the different ways that Native American tribes relate to nature.
- Evaluate the impact of European contact on Native American tribes.
- Analyze current examples of environmental issues affecting modern Native Americans.
- Study a primary source: Constitution of the Iroquois Nations.

Critical Thinking Skills for "The First Conservationists"

- Make Connections
- Draw Conclusions
- Summarize
- Analyze Primary Sources
- Make Inferences

Background for the Teacher

This feature explores the connection between Native American cultures and the environment. Through the study of an engaging narrative, photographs, and a primary source excerpt, students will gain a nuanced understanding of the various ways Native Americans view and interact with nature and how this dynamic has changed in our modern world.

This feature comes between Chapter 26, which introduces the civil rights movement, and Chapter 27, which covers the expansion of this movement to other minorities—including Native Americans. Use the feature to help students understand the contemporary issues confronting Native Americans, as well as the historical roots of those issues.

History Notebook

Encourage students to complete the page for The First Conservationists in their History Notebooks as they read.

Note to the Teacher

Use the feature as a preview for content students will encounter in Chapter 27, Lesson 3.3, about Native American activism in the 1960s and 1970s.

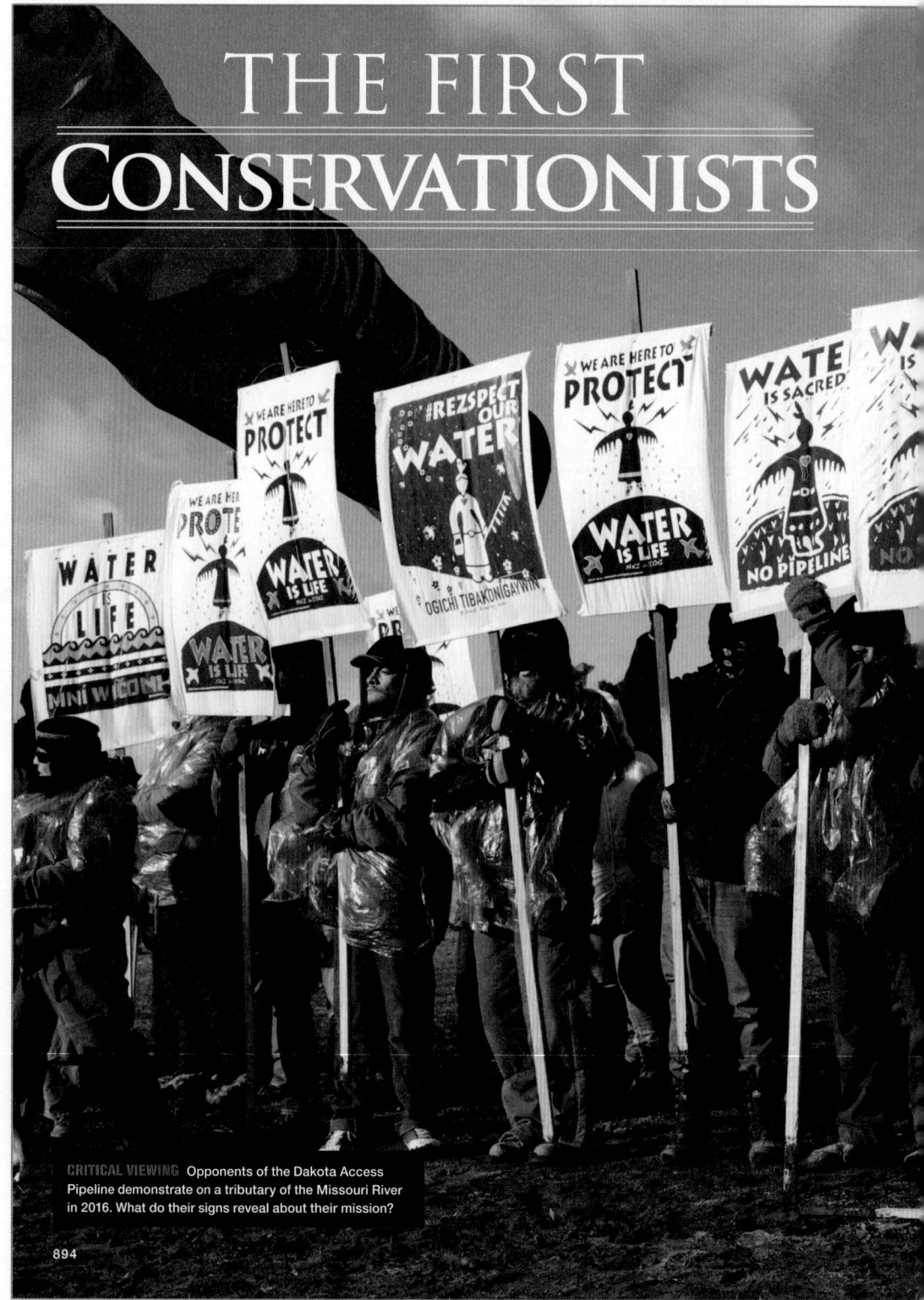

THE FIRST CONSERVATIONISTS

CRITICAL VIEWING Opponents of the Dakota Access Pipeline demonstrate on a tributary of the Missouri River in 2016. What do their signs reveal about their mission?

In 1971, an organization called Keep America Beautiful launched one of the most effective campaigns in advertising history. Billboards, magazine ads, and television commercials featured a solemn-faced man in traditional Native American clothing. As he regarded a landscape littered with garbage, a single tear trickled down his weathered cheek. The "Crying Indian" image, accompanied by such slogans as "Pollution hurts all of us," became widely recognized. The ad campaign was hugely successful in enlisting Americans to help reduce litter and fight pollution.

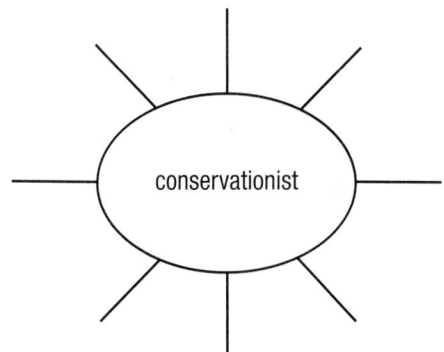

CRITICAL VIEWING What emotions do you think advertisers hoped to evoke when they chose the "Crying Indian" image for this 1970s ad campaign?

IRON EYES CODY

The story of the "Crying Indian" from the Keep America Beautiful ad campaign contains some curious twists. The craggy-faced man featured in the ads was an actor named Iron Eyes Cody. He had played Native Americans in movies since the 1920s. Sometime after the famous ad campaign, however, it was revealed that Iron Eyes Cody was not of Cherokee and Cree ancestry, as he claimed. In fact, he was a Sicilian American, born in Louisiana with the name Espera Oscar de Corti.

It would be easy to dismiss Cody as a cheap fake, but he took his pseudo-Native American identity very seriously. He married a Native American woman and adopted two Native American sons. He followed Native American practices and beliefs during his entire adult life. He also vigorously supported numerous Native American causes. In 1995, the Hollywood Native American community honored him for his work. However, some Native Americans were angered by Cody's false ancestry claims.

The "Crying Indian" image also illustrates a long-held stereotype of Native Americans as simple hunters or farmers living in harmony with nature. A common idea is that they left no trace on the environment— they were the original conservationists. While some may consider this portrayal as flattering, it may also be overly simplified. Native Americans have been using natural resources in a variety of sophisticated ways since long before the first Europeans arrived. Native American groups are as diverse as the nationalities found on any continent, and their relationships with nature reflect that diversity.

895

Access Prior Knowledge

Ask students to tell what they know about Native Americans' relationship to nature. List their responses on the board. Next, direct students' attention to the two photographs on the page. Discuss whether the photos confirm their previous ideas about Native Americans and nature or support different ideas. Inform students that in this lesson they will learn about the Native Americans' complex relationship with nature, both before and after European contact.

Tell What It Means to Be a Conservationist

Write *conservationist* in the center oval of a Word Web. Ask students to suggest words and phrases that they associate with the word *conservationist*, and add their suggestions to the Word Web. (*Students may suggest some of the following:* natural resources, caretaker, forest preserves, nature, protects for the future) Guide students to use the ideas they generated to develop a definition of *conservationist*. (*a person who protects natural resources or uses them wisely*) Then ask students to share their ideas about the importance of the conservation of natural resources.

conservationist

CRITICAL VIEWING Possible response: The protesters' signs reveal that their mission is to protect water supplies threatened by the pipeline and that their mission is closely aligned with their Native American identity.

CRITICAL VIEWING Possible response: The image of the "Crying Indian" was meant to evoke emotions such as concern and sorrow and perhaps guilt about polluting.

Defiance House

Located in southeastern Utah, Defiance House was named after a large pictograph of three warriors defiantly brandishing their weapons, which was painted on a cliff above the site. Ancient Puebloans occupied the site nearly 800 years ago, yet archaeologists say Defiance House is remarkably preserved. It is hard to reach, located at the top of a dangerous trail along a sandstone cliff, and includes ancient artifacts, such as two red bowls containing food scraps. Scientists don't know exactly why the site was abandoned, but they believe the Ancestral Puebloans eventually made their way south to the Rio Grande Valley. Modern Pueblo tribes, including the Hopi, Zuni, Acoma, and Laguna, are thought to be descendants of the ancient cliff dwellers.

The Bison (Buffalo) and the Plains Indians

The overhunting of American bison, which brought them to the brink of extinction, was the result of a combination of factors. However, central to the decline was the U.S. military's policy of encouraging people to kill as many bison as possible in an attempt to starve the Plains Indians into submission. After the Civil War, generals Philip Sheridan and William Tecumseh Sherman were put in charge of the Great Plains armies and were told to make the land habitable and safe for settlers. Both men had learned in the Civil War how effective a scorched-earth strategy could be in defeating an enemy. They soon applied similar tactics to defeat Native Americans and remove the major obstacle to westward expansion. Sheridan believed that exterminating the bison would lead to eventual victory over many Plains Indian tribes. He wrote to Sherman in October of 1868 that their goal should be to make the Indians "poor by the destruction of their stock."

As settlers flooded the region, thousands of professional and amateur hunters swarmed onto the plains, killing so many bison that the population plummeted. By the end of the 19th century, Sheridan's goal had been achieved: Only a few hundred bison remained, and the Plains Indians had been forced onto reservations.

Defiance House is a well-preserved Ancestral Puebloan cliff dwelling located in the Glen Canyon area of Utah. Used as a residence from about A.D. 1250 to 1285, it was most likely abandoned because of drought, lack of food, enemies, or land overuse.

BEFORE EUROPEAN CONTACT

The term *pre-contact* is sometimes used to refer to Native Americans before their first encounters with European explorers and settlers. Scholars believe that most pre-contact groups shared a broadly similar worldview. According to this worldview, animals, plants, and the earth itself harbored sacred spirits, and humans could ask these spirits to influence the weather, harvests, or the outcome of an upcoming battle. However, the numerous groups had widely different ways of life that varied to fit the diverse North American geography. Some groups did indeed leave little trace on the land, while others took an active role in molding the ecosystems in which they lived. Historian Louis S. Warren wrote, "To claim that Indians lived without affecting nature is akin to saying that they lived without touching anything, that they were a people without a history."

Different groups manipulated their environments in different ways to suit their needs. The Choctaw, Iroquois, and Pawnee, for example, cleared forests to create fields for farming. When those fields were no longer fertile, the tribes would abandon them and clear new land. When land was abundant, this practice could continue for a long time. But it led to deforestation and stress on local species. Certain tribes may have even caused their own downfall by overusing local resources. Some researchers believe the Ancestral Puebloans of southeastern Utah disappeared from their villages in the 13th century because they had depleted the wood in the region by burning it for fuel.

Fire was a powerful tool used by Native Americans to shape an ecosystem to their advantage. For example, some groups used fire to help create open prairies where large game animals such as bison, deer, elk, and antelope could graze. Fires were sometimes used to force animals into narrow canyons, lakes, or small areas where they could be easily hunted. Burning was also used to clear land for crops or drive out pests.

But many pre-contact groups actively practiced conservation techniques to protect game species. The Algonquian lived along the Atlantic Coast and divided hunting territories among families. Each family followed hunting practices that helped maintain the game supply. In the Pacific Northwest, some Native American tribes trapped salmon swimming up rivers to spawn. They were careful to let enough fish escape and lay their eggs so that the supply would be maintained from year to year.

896

AFTER EUROPEAN CONTACT

For years after European settlers arrived in North America, Native Americans continued their traditional ways of life. However, as groups were pushed onto reservations in the 19th century, these ways of life were disrupted. In the centuries since the first European contact, Native Americans have faced the challenge of adapting to new environments and maintaining their cultures in an ever-changing world. Today, climate change may pose one of the most severe threats to some groups, particularly in Alaska. The melting of ice and permafrost there is greatly affecting such game species as polar bear and caribou.

Native American groups remain at the forefront of conservation efforts. Many tribes are uniquely positioned to protect the wild lands they inhabit. According to one study, "many tribal lands still represent some of the largest intact habitats . . . in North America." Native American tribes control more than 81,236 square miles of land in the lower 48 states and 62,500 square miles of land in Alaska. "Much of this land is relatively undisturbed, providing a significant amount of rare and important fish and wildlife habitat," the authors of the study claim.

Examples abound of Native American tribes working to restore habitats and species. Perhaps the best-known example is the fight to restore the American bison. Historically, the bison provided a living for many Great Plains tribes and played an important role in their cultures. By 1884, as a result of overhunting, only 325 wild bison remained in the United States. Today, organizations such as the Intertribal Buffalo Council (ITBC) work to reintroduce American bison to tribal lands in South Dakota, Montana, Oklahoma, and New Mexico. As of 2017, the ITBC has 63 member tribes spread across 20 states. Those tribes, including the Lakota, Crow, Blackfeet, Ho Chunk, and Choctaw, manage a collective herd of more than 15,000 bison. Emphasizing the cultural importance of bison, the ITBC asserts, "To re-establish healthy buffalo populations on tribal lands is to re-establish hope for Indian people."

Still, like all Americans, Native Americans must balance conservation with the use of natural resources. Members of the Hoopa Valley Tribe in California, for example, have a strong belief in conservation and powerful cultural ties to the species that populate their land. At the same time, cutting and selling trees for timber is necessary for the tribe's economy. Thus, the Hoopa have developed ways to maintain a sustainable logging industry while protecting the forest habitat. Similarly, on the Great Plains, some groups harvest and sell bison meat as a healthier alternative to beef while also working to preserve the wild herds.

Occasionally, traditional practices bring tribes into conflict with environmental organizations. The Makah in Washington State had been whaling for thousands of years when they stopped in 1929, in the face of a declining whale population. In 1999, they resumed hunting, having been authorized by the International Whaling Commission to take up to four whales a year. The Makah argue that whaling is central to their culture. They also point to the Treaty of Neah Bay, signed in 1855, which granted whaling rights to the Makah in exchange for tribal

THE GREAT LAW OF PEACE

The Iroquois Confederacy was bound by a constitution that had existed for centuries before the first Europeans arrived. In pre-contact times, the constitution was passed on orally. Today, it has several names, including the Great Law of Peace.

One passage in the constitution forms the basis of an idea called seven-generation sustainability, or the seventh-generation principle. The concept is that humans should base decisions on the way they will affect the future seven generations. Today's decisions, in other words, should lead to healthy, sustainable ecosystems for many generations to come.

PRIMARY SOURCE

In all of your deliberations in the Confederate Council, in your efforts at lawmaking, in all your official acts, self-interest shall be cast into oblivion. Cast not over your shoulder behind you the warnings of the nephews and nieces should they chide you for any error or wrong you may do, but return to the way of the Great Law which is just and right. Look and listen for the welfare of the whole people and have always in view not only the present but also the coming generations, even those whose faces are yet beneath the surface of the ground—the unborn of the future Nation.

—from the Constitution of the Iroquois Nations

897

TEACH

Guided Discussion

1. **Summarize** What happened to Native American people and their cultures after contact with European colonists? *(At first, Native Americans continued their traditional ways of life. However, as more colonists arrived, tribes were forced onto reservations and lost the physical connection to their land, food sources, and many of their traditions.)*

2. **Analyze Primary Sources** How does the excerpt from the constitution of the Iroquois Confederacy convey the group's environmental values? *(The excerpt contrasts "self-interest" with the needs of "the unborn of the future Nation." From an environmental standpoint, this can be interpreted as working to ensure that the current generation does not selfishly use up natural resources but conserves them for future generations.)*

Active Options

On Your Feet: Tell Me More Divide the class into two teams, and ask each team to prepare several statements of fact about Native Americans' culture, their attitude toward the environment, and their interaction with white culture. Start the activity by asking members of one team to stand in front of the class and read one of their statements. The other team then calls out, "Tell me more!" The first team responds with more facts. After a few statements, have the teams reverse roles. Continue to alternate roles until both teams run out of facts. Keep track of which team provided the most facts.

NG Learning Framework: Write a Feature Story

ATTITUDE Empowerment
KNOWLEDGE Our Human Story

Prompt students to conduct preliminary research to learn about present-day conservation efforts involving Native Americans. You might want to encourage students to select a project spearheaded by a tribal group in your region: for example, the Sioux of the upper Midwest and Great Plains, the Iroquois in upstate New York, or the Hopi or Cochiti Pueblo in the Southwest. After students select a particular project, instruct them to collect information from a variety of print and online sources to write a feature story describing the conservation project, the project partners, and how the project relates to the Native American group's culture and values. Encourage students to share their feature stories with the class in an oral or written presentation.

Sandra Postel

National Geographic Freshwater Fellow Sandra Postel has called water "the planet's greatest gift and the source of life itself," and her work reflects this view. She oversees Change the Course, an initiative that supports projects aimed at restoring water ecosystems to their natural state. In addition to the Rio Grande project discussed in this feature, the group has worked on projects in places such as the San Joaquin Valley in California, Prickly Pear Creek in Montana, and Willow Creek in Colorado.

Black Snake Prophecy

The Lakota Sioux objected to the Dakota Access oil pipeline running under their territory for a number of cultural and spiritual reasons. Pipeline construction would disturb sacred grave sites, and some Lakota also viewed the pipeline as the fulfillment of a prophesy that a black snake would bring great harm to the land if it were allowed to go beneath nearby Lake Oahe—the proposed pipeline route. According to a lawsuit brought by the tribe, the oil pipeline "is the black slippery terror described in the Black Snake prophecy." The Lakota Sioux's lawsuit was based on the Religious Freedom Restoration Act of 1993, which prevents the government from infringing on a person's religious freedom. The Lakotas' lawyers claimed the pipeline violates this act because "the coming of the Black Snake is not without consequence in the Lakota religious worldview."

WRITE ABOUT HISTORY

Examine the Natural World This feature describes the importance of nature in the culture of many Native American tribes. To help students make a personal connection, have them think about their own relationship to nature. Prompt them with questions such as: What does nature provide you with? How do you feel when you are in nature? Then have students compose a short essay answering this question: How important is the natural world in my life? Invite students to read their essays to the class or to post them in a blog format on an approved website.

THINK ABOUT IT

Possible response: Native Americans have spearheaded many conservation efforts, such as the reintroduction of the American bison and the restoration of the Rio Grande and river habitats.

lands. Environmentalists argue that certain gray whale groups are nearly depleted, and whaling by the Makah could threaten their dwindling numbers. Some also criticize the Makah for using modern technology, in addition to traditional tools, to kill whales.

In 2000, former Tribal Council chairman Ben Johnson summed up the frustration many Native Americans feel about stereotypes that simplify Native American culture and freeze it in time. "Times change and we have to change with the times," he said. "[People] want us to be back in the primitive times. We just want to practice our culture."

THE DAKOTA ACCESS PIPELINE

From April 2016 through February 2017, an environmental protest placed the Standing Rock Sioux tribe in headlines across the country. The Sioux were fighting the construction of the last segment of the Dakota Access Pipeline (DAPL) beneath the Missouri River on land that is adjacent to the Standing Rock Reservation in North Dakota. The DAPL is a 1,170-mile-long underground pipeline built to transport oil from fields in North Dakota to southern Illinois, where it can be shipped to refineries.

The Standing Rock Sioux objected to the pipeline on both cultural and environmental grounds. They claimed its construction would disrupt sacred tribal burial sites. They also feared an oil spill would contaminate the Missouri River, the reservation's principal source of water. Protesters claimed the land through which the pipeline runs is in fact Sioux land, deeded to them in the Treaties of Fort Laramie in 1851 and 1868. Since 1851, the government has taken much of the land, but the treaties were never canceled.

In spring 2016, tribe members set up a camp on the reservation in North Dakota and publicized their mission statement: "Our goal is to peacefully and prayerfully defend our rights, and rise up as one to sustain Mother Earth and her inhabitants." Protests staged from the camp were largely peaceful, although some clashes with police did occur. Environmentalists, celebrities, and others joined the Standing Rock Sioux in their protests. Many others used donations or social media to express their

Protesters march on the Standing Rock Indian Reservation in North Dakota in 2016, attempting to halt the construction of a pipeline along the northern edge of the reservation.

support. For example, in November 2016, the rumor circulated that police officers were using Facebook check-ins to track the locations of protesters. More than 1 million people across the United States "checked in" at the Standing Rock Reservation.

On the other side of the issue, many Americans favored construction of the DAPL, which some claimed had created thousands of jobs. Several labor unions supported the pipeline for that reason. Some supporters believed transporting oil through the pipeline would be much safer than using trucks, tankers, and trains. However, experts debate the relative safety of moving oil through pipelines. A major leak discovered in 2016 in an older North Dakota pipeline added to safety concerns about the new one.

In January 2017, President Donald Trump signed an executive order to speed up the approval process for construction of the remaining section of the pipeline. In late February, police cleared demonstrators from the main protest camp. Construction was completed and oil had begun flowing through the pipeline by June 1, 2017. The Standing Rock Sioux vowed to continue their fight in the courts.

THINK ABOUT IT

In what ways have Native Americans had a positive influence on the environment?

NATIONAL GEOGRAPHIC

RESTORING THE RIO GRANDE

In September 2016, National Geographic Freshwater Fellow Sandra Postel reported that Native American tribes and Audubon New Mexico, a conservation society, were working together to restore flow to the Rio Grande. The Rio Grande is the second largest river in the Southwest. But parts of it dry up in the summer as water is diverted for irrigation and other purposes. This situation alarms water conservations like Postel. Numerous native fish and birds, including some that are threatened or endangered, depend on the Rio Grande.

Audubon New Mexico developed a plan to restore some of the river's flow. The various communities along the Rio Grande are allocated a certain amount of water from the river each year. Audubon asked Native American groups in the Middle Rio Grande Valley to transfer to Audubon a portion of the water they receive. In exchange, Audubon committed to use the water for the river's benefit and to seek funding to restore river habitats on tribal lands. The Sandia, Isleta, Santa Ana, and Cochiti Pueblos agreed, transferring over 130 million gallons of water to Audubon New Mexico. With contributions from another user, the total water donation came to more than 260 million gallons.

The water was stored in a reservoir and released at strategic locations during the summer of 2016. At the same time, the Pueblos and Audubon New Mexico worked to plant trees and restore habitats along the river's banks. Postel praised the partnership. "River by river," she wrote, "the movement of water stewardship and restoration we are working to build is growing."

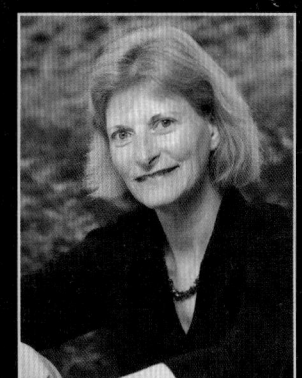

National Geographic Freshwater Fellow (2009–2015) Sandra Postel

CRITICAL VIEWING Why is cooperation among tribes and outside agencies important in restoring the Rio Grande, shown below?

899

Striving Readers

Connect Details to Main Ideas Have students work in pairs to fill out a Main Idea and Details List for each section of the feature. Elicit the kinds of details (dates, events, descriptions) that often support a main idea.

Gifted & Talented

Create a Public Service Announcement Prompt students to create a poster or short video as a public service announcement that updates the message of the "Crying Indian" television spot. Tell them that their target audience is their peers, and the message should be about an environmental issue of concern to them. Remind students to verify facts and focus their message. Invite them to share their PSA with the class.

See the Chapter Planner for more strategies for differentiation.

HISTORICAL THINKING

Ask and have students answer the following questions.

1. **READING CHECK** How did Native Americans conserve wildlife to ensure their food supply?

2. **MAKE INFERENCES** Why did the Native American community honor the "Crying Indian," despite the fact he was not a Native American?

3. **DRAW CONCLUSIONS** Why do traditional Native American practices sometimes clash with modern environmental goals?

ANSWERS

1. The Algonquian allocated different hunting grounds to different families, and when Pacific Northwest tribes trapped fish they let some go free.

2. Possible response: He held Native American beliefs, supported Native American causes, married a Native American, and adopted Native American children.

3. Possible response: Some traditional practices, such as whaling, clash with the goals of some modern environmentalists, who first and foremost seek to protect species.

CRITICAL VIEWING Possible response: What happens upstream affects what happens downstream, so all groups impacted along the Rio Grande must work together to restore the river and its wildlife habitat.

UNIT 9 RESOURCES

UNIT INTRODUCTION

UNIT TIME LINE

UNIT WRAP-UP

NATIONAL GEOGRAPHIC | CONNECTION

***National Geographic* Magazine Adapted Articles**
- "50 Years of Wilderness"
- "Slipping the Bonds" ONLINE

Unit 9 Inquiry: Protest an Injustice

NG Learning Framework Activities
- Compile a Song Medley
- Build Models

Unit 9 Formal Assessment

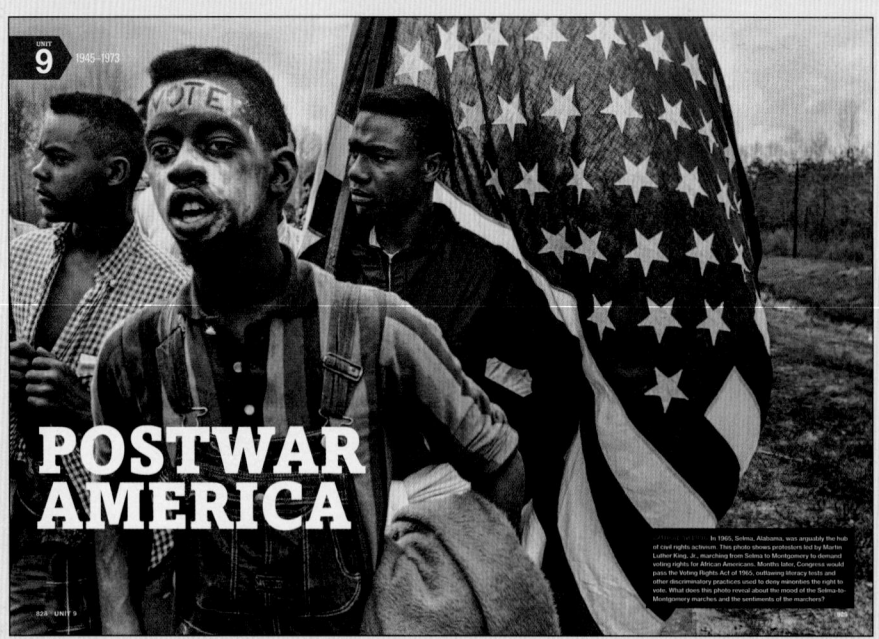

CHAPTER 27 RESOURCES

Available at NGLSync.Cengage.com

TEACHER RESOURCES & ASSESSMENT

Reading and Note-Taking

Vocabulary Practice

Social Studies Skills Lessons
- Reading: Compare and Contrast
- Writing: Write an Expository Paragraph

Formal Assessment
- Chapter 27 Pretest
- Chapter 27 Tests A & B
- Section Quizzes

Chapter 27 Answer Key

ExamView®
One-time Download

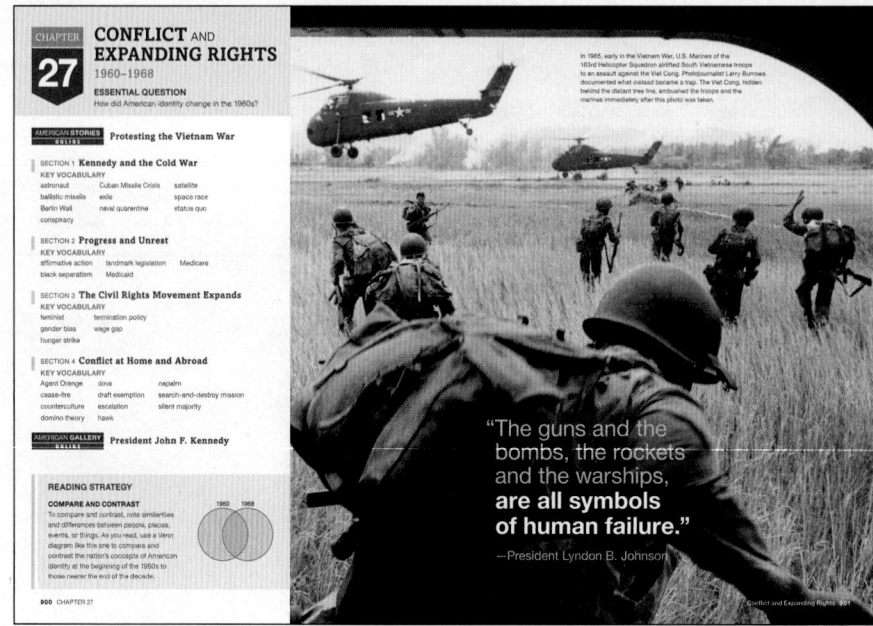

STUDENT DIGITAL RESOURCES

- **eEdition** (English)
- **eEdition** (Spanish)
- **Handbooks**
- **Online Atlas**
- **American Gallery Online**
- **History Notebook**
- **American Voices (Biographies)**
- **Active History**
- **Projects for Inquiry-Based Learning**

Chapter 27 Spanish Resources are available at NGLSync.Cengage.com.

AMERICAN STORIES ONLINE | **Protesting the Vietnam War**

- Primary Sources
- On Your Feet: Think, Pair, Share

NG Learning Framework:
Conduct a Teach-In

SECTION 1 RESOURCES

KENNEDY AND THE COLD WAR

LESSON 1.1
The New Frontier

- On Your Feet: Design a Postage Stamp

NG Learning Framework:
Coach Richard Nixon for
Televised Debates

LESSON 1.2
The Space Race

- On Your Feet: Stage a Quiz Show

NG Learning Framework:
Examine a Breakthrough

LESSON 1.3
Cold War Concerns

- On Your Feet: Think, Pair, Share

NG Learning Framework:
Resolve the Communist Threat in Cuba

LESSON 1.4
Cuban Missile Crisis

- On Your Feet: Three-Step Interview

NG Learning Framework:
Explore the 13 Days

LESSON 1.5
Kennedy's Assassination

- On Your Feet: Small-Group Brainstorming

AMERICAN GALLERY ONLINE | President John F. Kennedy

SECTION 2 RESOURCES

PROGRESS AND UNREST

LESSON 2.1
Johnson Acts on Civil Rights

- On Your Feet: Jigsaw

NG Learning Framework:
Evaluate a Supreme Court Decision

LESSON 2.2
Rising Discontent

- On Your Feet: Hold a Panel Discussion

NG Learning Framework:
Role-Play a Civil Rights Leader

American Voices Biography
Malcolm X ONLINE

LESSON 2.3
The Great Society

- On Your Feet: Jigsaw

NG Learning Framework:
Create an Infographic

SECTION 3 RESOURCES

THE CIVIL RIGHTS MOVEMENT EXPANDS

LESSON 3.1
Latinos Organize

- On Your Feet: Design a Poster

NG Learning Framework:
Create a Local Newsletter

American Voices Biography
César Chávez ONLINE

LESSON 3.2
NATIONAL GEOGRAPHIC EXPLORER
JASON DE LEÓN
Preserving Objects Left Behind by Migrants

- On Your Feet: Three-Step Interview

NG Learning Framework:
Plan a Hike

LESSON 3.3
Native American Activism

- On Your Feet: Draft Ideas for Just Compensation to Native Americans

NG Learning Framework:
Research Federal Compensation to
Native Americans

LESSON 3.4
The Women's Rights Movement

- Active History: Analyze the Wage Gap

NG Learning Framework:
Present an Argument

American Voices Biographies
Gloria Steinem and
Betty Friedan ONLINE

SECTION 4 RESOURCES

CONFLICT AT HOME AND ABROAD

LESSON 4.1
U.S. Involvement in Vietnam

- On Your Feet: Create a Time Line

NG Learning Framework:
Design a Social Media Profile

LESSON 4.2
War Strategies in Vietnam

- On Your Feet: Word Chain

NG Learning Framework:
Research the Environmental Impacts
of War

American Voices Biography
John McCain ONLINE

LESSON 4.3
The Tet Offensive

- On Your Feet: Turn and Talk on Topic

NG Learning Framework:
Compare Media Coverage

LESSON 4.4
The Counterculture

- Haight-Ashbury
- On Your Feet: Who Receives a Draft Exemption?

NG Learning Framework:
Plan a Museum Exhibition

LESSON 4.5
The Year 1968

- On Your Feet: True-False Questions

NG Learning Framework:
Create a Photo Collage

CHAPTER 27 REVIEW

Strategy ❶
Create Idea Webs

Help students summarize the chapter by having them create a "What Happens" Chart for each section: Kennedy and the Cold War, Progress and Unrest, The Civil Rights Movement Expands, Conflict at Home and Abroad. Tell students to complete each chart with relevant text information.

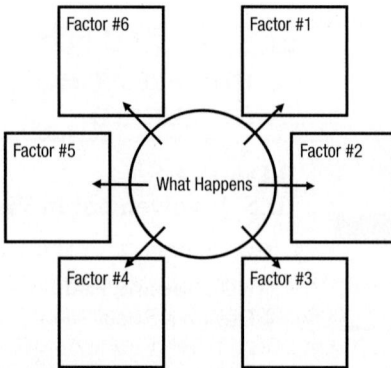

Use with All Lessons *For example, for the topic Kennedy and the Cold War, students could add Nixon-Kennedy debates; Peace Corps; space program; Bay of Pigs invasion; Berlin Wall; Kennedy's assassination.*

Strategy ❷
Turn Titles into Questions

Have students write each lesson title as a question they believe will be answered as they read. Students can write their own questions and answers, or they can work in pairs to ask and answer each other's questions.

Use with All Lessons

Strategy ❸
Ask Either/Or Questions

Monitor comprehension by asking students either/or questions such as those listed below.

- Were U.S. soldiers prepared or unprepared to fight a guerrilla war? *(unprepared)*

- Did search-and-destroy missions help or harm U.S. soldiers' efforts to win the hearts and minds of the South Vietnamese people? *(harm)*

- Was the purpose of spraying Agent Orange to eliminate dense foliage or poison communist forces? *(eliminate dense foliage)*

- Were U.S. forces welcomed or resented by the people of South Vietnam? *(resented)*

Use with Lesson 4.2 *You may wish to ask either/or questions to check comprehension of other lessons as well.*

Strategy ❶
Ask Clarifying Questions

Allow students with disabilities to work with partners who can assist them in accessing the lesson. Partners can clarify meaning by repeating passages, emphasizing context clues, paraphrasing, describing photographs, and reading captions. Encourage students to ask their partners clarifying questions. Then have pairs work together to answer the Historical Thinking questions and any Critical Viewing questions.

Use with All Lessons

Strategy ❷
Describe Details in a Portrait

Pair students who are visually impaired with students who are not. Ask the latter to describe Kadir Nelson's portrait of Shirley Chisholm, including Chisholm's posture, facial expression, coat, and size relative to the Capitol Building. Partners can record details about the portrait in a graphic organizer such as the one shown. Tell assisting students to help their partner trace the outline of Chisholm and then the Capitol to emphasize their respective sizes. Encourage pairs to discuss their overall impression of the painting and the aspects of Chisholm's personality and accomplishments that it conveys.

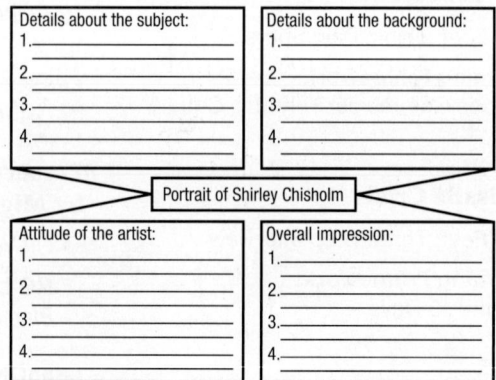

Use with Lesson 3.4

ENGLISH LANGUAGE LEARNERS

Strategy ❶
Make Word Cards

Direct students at the **Expanding** and **Bridging** levels of proficiency to make Word Cards for unfamiliar words. Tell students to write the unfamiliar word on one side of the card and illustrate or write notes about the meaning on the other side. Then place students in pairs and direct them to take turns presenting a card to their partner with the illustration/notes side face up. The partner guesses the word using the illustration or notes.

Use with All Lessons

Strategy ❷
Compose Captions

Pair students at the **Emerging** and **Expanding** levels of proficiency with students at the **Bridging** level. Tell pairs to cover the caption of the photograph or graphic element and work together to write an original caption. You may wish to invite pairs to compare their captions with those in the lesson and with those written by other pairs.

Use with All Lessons

Strategy ❸
Create a Word Web

Ask pairs of students at **All Proficiencies** to take turns reading paragraphs of the lesson, noting terms relating to Native American activism. After students read each paragraph, instruct them to write the terms on the spokes of a Word Web. When they have finished reading, tell pairs to trade and compare their work. Final Word Webs may include the following: reservations, termination policy, tribal sovereignty, tribal lands, legal rights, Wounded Knee, massacre, treaties, hunting and fishing rights.

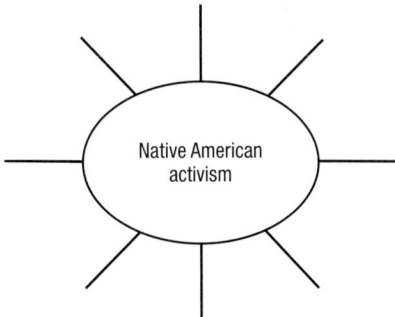

Native American activism

Use with Lesson 3.3

GIFTED & TALENTED

Strategy ❶
Teach a Class

Before beginning the chapter, allow students to choose one of the lessons and prepare to teach the content to the class. Give them a set amount of time in which to present the lesson. Suggest that students think about any visuals or activities they want to use when they teach.

Use with Lessons 2.1–2.3 and 3.1–3.4

Strategy ❷
Present an Artifact

Invite students to conduct research using a variety of print and online resources to deepen their understanding of the frictions that existed between young people who were part of the counterculture and conservative Americans. Have students choose one artifact (song, poster, clothing item, etc.) that illustrates or represents such frictions and use it as the basis of a short presentation. Allow time for students to prepare and practice before presenting to the class.

Use with Lesson 4.4

Pre-AP

Strategy ❶
Write a Report

Tell students to choose one of the groups of people discussed in the chapter who continue to fight for their civil rights, research their ongoing struggle and challenges, and write a report about the group's progress. Students may, with approval, write about a group not mentioned, such as Asian Americans, older Americans, LGBT Americans, or people with disabilities. Encourage students to use statistics, examples, and expert opinions from their research.

Use with Lessons 3.1–3.4

Strategy ❷
Analyze Effects of Television

Remind students that television brought the Vietnam War into nearly every American home. Challenge them to conduct research and write an essay about how televised coverage of politics or war has changed since the 1960s. You may suggest that students use a Cause-Effect Organizer to display the results of their research and analysis.

Use with Lessons 1.1, 1.5, and 4.3–4.4

CHAPTER 27

CONFLICT AND EXPANDING RIGHTS
1960–1968

ESSENTIAL QUESTION
How did American identity change in the 1960s?

READING STRATEGY

COMPARE AND CONTRAST
To compare and contrast, note similarities and differences between people, places, events, or things. As you read, use a Venn diagram like this one to compare and contrast the nation's concepts of American identity at the beginning of the 1960s to those nearer the end of the decade.

1960   1968

In 1965, early in the Vietnam War, U.S. Marines of the 163rd Helicopter Squadron airlifted South Vietnamese troops to an assault against the Viet Cong. Photojournalist Larry Burrows documented what instead became a trap. The Viet Cong, hidden behind the distant tree line, ambushed the troops and the marines immediately after this photo was taken.

"The guns and the bombs, the rockets and the warships, **are all symbols of human failure.**"

—President Lyndon B. Johnson

Conflict and Expanding Rights 901

INTRODUCE THE PHOTOGRAPH

Airlifting of South Vietnamese Troops

Have students study the photograph, caption, and quotation that open the chapter. Explain that the Vietnam War spanned the 1960s, a pivotal decade of social and political upheavals that led to changes in American identity. Inform students that Lyndon Johnson was the president most responsible for escalating and prolonging the conflict in Vietnam. **ASK:** How do the photograph and caption illustrate the uncertainties of war? (*Possible response: The photograph documents a seemingly successful mission—but according to the caption, moments later these soldiers were ambushed by enemy troops.*) **ASK:** In what ways are guns, bombs, rockets, and warships symbols of human failure? (*Possible response: If two sides engage in war, they have either failed to compromise and come to terms peacefully or failed to accurately understand the situation.*) Tell students that in this chapter they will examine how a country with leaders and activists who pledged peace became ensnared in a violent and prolonged conflict on foreign soil.

Share Background

Photojournalists helped shape public opinion during the Vietnam War, and their photographs continue to influence how we perceive the conflict. When many Americans think of the war today, their mental pictures are similar to the one here, of helicopters or troops slogging through water in jungles or fields, two motifs often used by photojournalists. During the war, few limits were placed on photojournalists' access to war zones, which resulted in a trove of images that conveyed the harsh realities and moral murkiness of U.S. involvement in Vietnam. Unsurprisingly, the most graphic images had the most impact. Iconic photographs of the self-immolation of a Buddhist monk, the execution of a Viet Cong suspect, and of a nine-year-old girl fleeing a napalm attack shocked Americans, and that powerful emotion played a role in turning public opinion against the conflict.

INTRODUCE THE ESSENTIAL QUESTION

How did American identity change in the 1960s?

Team Word Webbing: Elements of Identity Review the concept of American identity by inviting students to participate in a team word webbing activity. Organize students into teams of four. Provide each team with a large sheet of paper and each team member with a different colored marker. Instruct students to write the term *American Identity* in the center of the paper, and define it as "the shared beliefs by which the United States defines itself." Guide students to add examples of American identity today—such as ideas about government, family, or culture—to the part of the web nearest to them. On a signal, students should rotate the paper and then add to their teammates' responses. After the paper has rotated four times, ask a representative from each team to summarize the team's ideas.

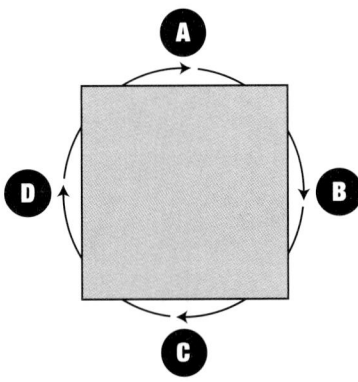

INTRODUCE CHAPTER VOCABULARY

Definition Chart

As students read the chapter, direct them to complete a Definition Chart for Key Vocabulary words. Have students list the Key Vocabulary words in the left column. Then as they encounter each word in the chapter, tell them to write the Key Vocabulary word's definition in the center column and explain the word's meaning in their own words in the right column. Model an example for students using the graphic organizer shown.

Word	Definition	In My Own Words
feminist	a person who supports the equal rights of women	A feminist thinks women are treated unfairly and should receive the same rights that men enjoy.

INTRODUCE THE READING STRATEGY

COMPARE AND CONTRAST

Remind students that Venn diagrams are used to compare and contrast two things. Display a Venn diagram and review where differences and similarities are placed. Then ask students to use a Venn diagram with labels 1960 and 1968 to organize details and attitudes about America during 1960, during 1968, and during both years (overlap). As students study Section 1 of the chapter, guide them to add details under 1960. Remind them to keep adding to their Venn diagram as they encounter new information.

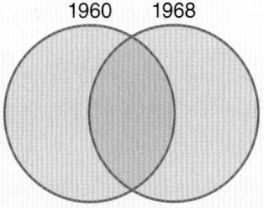

KEY DATES FOR CHAPTER 27

1960	John F. Kennedy elected president
1961	JFK pledges manned moon landing within decade
1961	JFK establishes the Peace Corps
1962	Cuban Missile Crisis
1963	JFK assassinated; Lyndon Johnson becomes president
1964	Johnson announces the Great Society program
1964	Gulf of Tonkin Resolution
1968	Tet Offensive
1968	Martin Luther King, Jr.; Robert Kennedy assassinated
1968	American Indian Movement (AIM) founded

AMERICAN STORIES ONLINE For instructional support for the online American Story "Protesting the Vietnam War," go to NGLSync.Cengage.com.

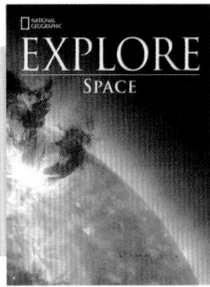

For more on the U.S. quest for a manned moon landing, see *EXPLORE SPACE.*

Sometimes, maturity and experience seem to be the most important qualities a leader can possess. At other times, a leader's youthful confidence and optimism can inspire a nation to move forward.

MAIN IDEA The 1960 presidential election was a tough, close race, but Americans looked to a new generation of leadership in John F. Kennedy.

THE 1960 ELECTION

As the November 1960 presidential election approached, Republicans nominated Eisenhower's vice president **Richard M. Nixon**, and Democrats nominated Senator John F. Kennedy of Massachusetts. Nixon campaigned on the **status quo**, or the way things were at the moment. He reminded Americans that the nation was prosperous and at peace. Kennedy took a different approach.

In his acceptance speech at the Democratic National Convention, Kennedy referred to a wealth of new opportunities awaiting the nation in the new decade, which he described as a **New Frontier**. Those opportunities included innovations in science and technology that positioned the United States for achievements in space only imagined previously. Challenges included re-energizing a sluggish economy and getting more people back to work. This New Frontier required creative problem solving and a new and forward-thinking leader. It also required an administration that shared the president's vision and confidence.

Although Kennedy did not make civil rights a campaign issue, his actions supported the civil rights movement. On October 19, 1960, Dr. Martin Luther King, Jr., was jailed for participating in a sit-in at a department store lunch counter in Atlanta. With journalists present, Kennedy phoned Dr. King's wife and offered his sympathy. His action likely won him votes, especially among African Americans.

The race between Kennedy and Nixon was extremely tight. However, Kennedy gained an advantage over Nixon when—for the first time in a presidential election—a series of debates were televised. The first debate had the greatest impact, as about 74 million Americans followed it on television or radio. On screen, Kennedy radiated confidence and charm. In contrast, Nixon appeared sweaty and nervous. The differences in their appearance had an effect on television viewers. Most of those listening on the radio thought the debate was a tie. Most who saw it on television, however, agreed that Kennedy had won. The election's popular vote was extremely close, with Kennedy defeating Nixon by fewer than 120,000 votes. But Kennedy did better in the electoral college vote, winning 303 electoral votes to Nixon's 219. As you've read, the person with the most electoral votes wins the election.

A NEW GENERATION TAKES CHARGE

As the first U.S. president born in the 20th century, Kennedy displayed optimism and confidence about the United States' future. In his inauguration speech, he declared, "the torch has been passed to a new generation of Americans—born in this century, tempered by war, disciplined by a hard and bitter peace." Kennedy's words encouraged those of his generation, who, like him, were raising young families. His words also inspired many young people who were taking part in U.S. politics for the first time.

Because Kennedy's victory had been so narrow, he needed to be cautious about pressing Congress with his proposed social reforms. Even so, Kennedy successfully persuaded Congress to support the **Alliance for Progress**, an agreement between the United States and 22 Latin American countries. The alliance was intended to win and strengthen allies in Latin America by providing foreign aid to those countries. The aid would help modernize industry and agriculture, improve the health and education of citizens, and help promote and maintain democratic governments.

On March 1, 1961, Kennedy issued an executive order establishing one of his great triumphs—the **Peace Corps**, which is still active today. A program of volunteers who work in developing countries to aid in the advancement of health, agriculture, and education, the Peace Corps showcases American idealism and know-how throughout the world. The early Peace Corps volunteers were mostly young people energized by Kennedy's call for patriotic selflessness. Kennedy's most visionary goal, however, involved a new frontier that would not be found on Earth, but in space.

During one of the four nationally televised presidential debates, Richard M. Nixon answers a journalist's question while John F. Kennedy listens. Throughout the televised debates, Nixon would look at his questioner when answering, but Kennedy seemed to be addressing the audience as he looked directly into the camera.

In 1972, the U.S. Post Office issued this 8-cent stamp to commemorate the 10th anniversary of the Peace Corps. The artist drew the stars morphing into flying birds to represent daring ideas like the Peace Corps becoming real.

HISTORICAL THINKING

1. **READING CHECK** What important role did appearances have in the first debate between Kennedy and Nixon?

2. **COMPARE AND CONTRAST** How did Nixon's and Kennedy's visions for the future of the United States differ?

3. **MAKE INFERENCES** Why do you think Kennedy emphasized the need for his generation to take up the responsibilities of governing the country?

Objective

Recap the 1960 election and John F. Kennedy's promise for a new era in U.S. politics.

Critical Thinking Skills for Lesson 1.1

- Identify Main Ideas and Details
- Monitor Comprehension
- Compare and Contrast
- Make Inferences
- Evaluate
- Make Connections
- Interpret Maps

Essential Question for Chapter 27

How did American identity change in the 1960s? At the beginning of the turbulent 1960s, the Republican traditions of the Eisenhower era gave way to new Democratic leadership, which was embraced by many young people. Lesson 1.1 examines the election of John F. Kennedy and his new vision for America.

Background for the Teacher

John F. Kennedy first became known to the American public for his service in the U.S. Navy during World War II. Kennedy commanded the patrol ship PT-109, whose mission was to stop Japanese ships from supplying their troops. In 1943, a Japanese destroyer rammed Kennedy's much smaller vessel at night, splitting it in half and killing two people. The rest of the crew went into the sea. In the darkness, Kennedy gathered the survivors to a piece of floating wreckage, pulling one injured crewmember himself. At daybreak, he led the group to swim several miles to a small island chain. After six days of searching the islands for food, water, and their comrades, the stranded crew met residents of the islands, who delivered to Kennedy's commanders a message that he had scratched into a coconut. The story, picked up by numerous media outlets, was instrumental in his early political career.

Predict Changes

Inform students that they will read about John F. Kennedy's belief that new opportunities awaited the nation. Ask them to consider what they learned in the previous chapters and what they know about the state of the nation in 1960, including issues that concerned Americans. **ASK:** What types of opportunities might have existed for the nation in 1960? *(Answers will vary. Students might mention the following: the opportunity for world peace with the establishment of the United Nations following World War II; the opportunity for equal rights for all Americans with civil rights issues brought to the forefront in the media through the efforts of Dr. Martin Luther King, Jr., Rosa Parks, and the Freedom Riders.)* Tell students that in this lesson they will learn how Kennedy's presidency represented a new frontier, or era, in American politics.

TEACH

Guided Discussion

1. **Evaluate** What do the 1960 election results suggest about whether Americans wanted to maintain Nixon's status quo or explore Kennedy's New Frontier? *(Possible response: While Nixon lost the election 303 electoral votes to 219, he lost the popular vote by fewer than 120,000 votes. This narrow margin suggests that Americans were almost evenly divided in their vision for the nation.)*

2. **Make Connections** How did the Peace Corps differ from previous opportunities for Americans to serve their country? *(Possible response: For previous generations, the main way to serve was by joining the military. The Peace Corps offered a different route of service that likely appealed to people who wanted to serve the country but were not interested in a military lifestyle.)*

Interpret Maps

Remind students that although Kennedy was generally supportive of civil rights, he did not make it a campaign issue. Then provide students with an electoral map of the 1960 presidential election. **ASK:** How does this map help support Kennedy's decision to exclude civil rights from his campaign? *(Possible response: Kennedy performed strongly in the South, where segregation was prevalent. If Kennedy had taken a firm pro-civil rights position, he likely would have lost the South and the election.)* Discuss with students if making civil rights a campaign issue could have affected the movement.

Active Options

On Your Feet: Design a Postage Stamp Have students examine the stamp created to commemorate the Peace Corps. Then provide small groups of students with poster-size sheets of paper. Tell them to design a postage stamp that depicts, without words, one of President Kennedy's accomplishments or ideas that they learned about in this lesson and create a poster of their design. When groups have finished, display the stamp designs in an exhibit. Invite students to examine each group's work and then guess which accomplishment each stamp commemorates.

NG Learning Framework: Coach Richard Nixon for Televised Debates

SKILLS Communication, Problem-Solving

KNOWLEDGE Our Human Story

Present clips from the first presidential debate of 1960 to the class. Tell students to focus on and write notes about Richard Nixon's performance. Remind them that most people who watched the debate on television judged Kennedy as the winner, while those who listened on radio believed it was a tie. Next, direct small groups of students to create a manual for Nixon to use to prepare for future televised debates. The manual should offer five tips for how he could better present himself on television, with the goal of winning the election. When finished, have groups share and discuss their tips with the class.

Striving Readers

Create a Concept Cluster Display a Concept Cluster with the term *New Frontier* in the center oval and the words *Opportunities, Challenges,* and *Requirements* in the outer three ovals. Instruct students to reread the lesson and then write specific examples of each aspect of Kennedy's New Frontier on the spokes. Encourage them to create additional spokes as necessary. Then have students share and discuss their Concept Clusters with a partner.

Pre-AP

Analyze Long-Term Impacts Tell students to work individually or in pairs to conduct online research and analyze the long-term global impact of the Peace Corps. Suggest that students use a graphic organizer such as a Cause-and-Effect Web to help organize their research. They may use a similar graphic organizer to display the results of their investigation and explain their analysis to the class.

See the Chapter Planner for more strategies for differentiation.

HISTORICAL THINKING

ANSWERS

1. Viewers who watched the debate believed Kennedy won, as he appeared confident and charming, and Nixon seemed sweaty and nervous.

2. Nixon's vision of the future included keeping the policies of the Eisenhower administration, maintaining the economy, and preserving the current peace. Kennedy saw changes on the horizon, citing new and exciting opportunities created by advances in science and technology.

3. Possible response: Kennedy likely wanted people of his generation to rally around him and support his optimistic view of the future. By calling on them to serve and participate, he probably hoped to inspire patriotism and a commitment to preserve the ideals of the nation.

1.2 The Space Race

What if you were given the opportunity of a lifetime—to try to become the first person to travel into outer space? The dangers are great and unknown. Should you risk it?

MAIN IDEA Cold War competition between the United States and the Soviet Union led both nations to expand space exploration and technology.

A NEW CHALLENGE

Three years before Kennedy's election in 1960, the United States and the Soviet Union became engaged in a new type of Cold War rivalry—one that relied more on science and less on military weapons and conflicts. Known as the **space race**, it was a competition to see which nation could make the greatest advances in space travel and technology. It started in October 1957, when the Soviets surprised the Americans by launching *Sputnik 1*. This was the world's first artificial **satellite** to orbit Earth. Any object that orbits a larger object is a satellite. For example, the moon is a satellite of Earth. Artificial satellites such as *Sputnik* were the world's first successful spacecraft.

Fearing that the Soviets might use such technology to spy on or attack the United States, Americans rushed to catch up. President Eisenhower supported increased funding for space exploration as well as for math and science education. The government created what would become the **National Aeronautics and Space Administration (NASA)** to lead this effort.

The United States launched *Explorer 1*, the first American satellite, in January 1958. This satellite carried equipment to test the level of cosmic rays hitting Earth from space. Several more *Explorer* satellites followed. In 1959, NASA chose seven men to become the first American **astronauts**, or space travelers. It would take several more years of training and experiments before the men and equipment would be ready for travel into space.

🏛 **National Air and Space Museum Washington, D.C.**

John H. Glenn, Jr., was the first American to fully orbit Earth when he flew the *Mercury Friendship 7* (above) around the globe three times. During the first orbit, the automatic control system developed a problem, but Glenn switched to a manual electric system and kept the flight going. Traveling sometimes at more than 17,000 miles per hour, he completed the orbits in just 4 hours, 55 minutes, and 23 seconds. The successful mission brought millions of people into the U.S. space industry to plan future human space flights. It also proved that the United States could compete with the Soviet Union in the space race.

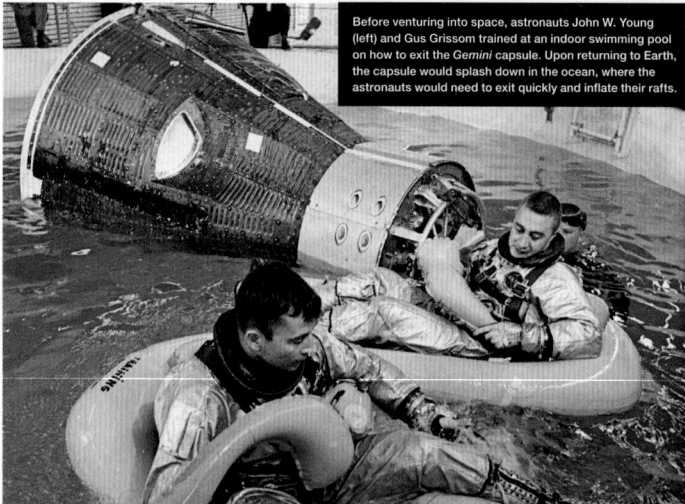

Before venturing into space, astronauts John W. Young (left) and Gus Grissom trained at an indoor swimming pool on how to exit the *Gemini* capsule. Upon returning to Earth, the capsule would splash down in the ocean, where the astronauts would need to exit quickly and inflate their rafts.

THE SPACE PROGRAM

As part of his vision for the New Frontier, President Kennedy proposed a bold expansion of the U.S. space program. In April 1961, shortly after Kennedy took office, Soviet **Yuri Gagarin** (YOO-ree guh-GAHR-ihn) became the first human in space. He orbited Earth in less than two hours. One month later, **Alan Shepard** became the first American in space. He was not able to make a full orbit around Earth, but he was able to control his spacecraft. His entire suborbital flight—a flight that doesn't complete a full orbit of Earth—lasted only 15 minutes and 22 seconds. Still, Shepard was the first American to see our entire planet from space. "What a beautiful view," he noted. That same month, on May 25, President Kennedy addressed a joint session of Congress and announced, "I believe that this nation should commit itself to achieving the goal, before this decade is out, of landing a man on the moon and returning him safely to the earth."

That July, **Gus Grissom** became the second American in space. At the end of Grissom's 15-minute suborbital flight, his capsule splashed down in the Atlantic Ocean and accidentally filled with water and sank. Grissom had to tread water and wait to be rescued. In February 1962, **John Glenn** became the first American to orbit Earth. For the rest of the 1960s, the United States and the Soviet Union continued to compete with each other in the space race. Each side hoped to "win" the contest by being the first to land a human on the moon. This competition produced many great advances in science and technology. Inventions from the space race often became part of daily life, improving everyday items such as light bulbs. It also led to new developments, such as the global positioning system (GPS).

HISTORICAL THINKING

1. **READING CHECK** Why did the United States create NASA?

2. **MAKE INFERENCES** What kind of training would be helpful to the astronauts, and why?

3. **IDENTIFY MAIN IDEAS AND DETAILS** Against which country did Americans hope to win the space race, and how?

PLAN

Objective
Summarize the causes, characteristics, and consequences of the space race.

Critical Thinking Skills for Lesson 1.2
• Identify Main Ideas and Details
• Monitor Comprehension
• Make Inferences
• Make Connections
• Form and Support Opinions

Essential Question for Chapter 27
How did American identity change in the 1960s? The Cold War between the Soviet Union and United States included the race for dominance in space. John F. Kennedy's promised exploration of the moon was at hand, and Americans had to absorb this new reality. Lesson 1.2 examines the causes and consequences of the space race, as well as the people and technology involved.

Background for the Teacher
To choose its first astronauts, NASA turned to the military, asking for a list of pilots who met strict criteria. The applicants needed flight experience, engineering training, and a college education. They also had to be younger than age 40, in excellent physical condition, and no taller than 5 feet 11 inches (in order to fit into the cramped cabin of a spacecraft). More than 500 men met the initial requirements, but many were eliminated through a process of medical exams, interviews, and psychological tests. The remaining candidates were subjected to a series of tests that included X-ray mapping of their entire bodies and monitoring their reactions to stressful space-travel conditions, including loud noises, intense pressure, heat, and vibrations. The seven who passed became America's first astronauts, and all eventually made it into space.

Create an Astronaut Profile

Tell students to imagine that they are tasked with selecting the first group of astronauts to travel into space. Ask them to use what they know about conditions in space and the work that astronauts do to brainstorm a list of attributes that candidates would likely possess and the reasons each would be necessary. Encourage students to consider physical, mental, and academic characteristics. Make a chart on which to record and display their ideas. Then tell students that in this lesson they will read about early achievements in manned space travel.

TEACH

Guided Discussion

1. **Make Connections** Remind students that the Soviet Union detonated an atomic bomb in 1949. **ASK:** How was the U.S. reaction to the Soviets' detonation of an atomic bomb similar to its reaction to the launch of *Sputnik 1*? *(Possible response: The United States viewed both events as potential military threats. Both were scientific advances that the Soviets achieved before the United States thought they were capable of doing so. As a result, the United States poured money and resources into programs in an attempt to surpass the Soviets.)*

2. **Form and Support Opinions** Do you think the United States' investment of time, effort, and money in the space race was worthwhile? *(Answers will vary. Possible responses: Yes. Beating the Soviets was important both strategically and psychologically, and the effort produced technological breakthroughs. No. Landing humans on the moon did not make the country more secure, and the money spent on the effort could have been used to address issues such as poverty and education.)*

🏛 Virtual Museum Visit

The National Air and Space Museum houses the world's largest collection of artifacts celebrating aviation, space exploration, and planetary science. Divide the class into four groups, access the museum's website, and find the online exhibition entitled "Fifty Years of Human Spaceflight." Point out the four sections of the exhibition and demonstrate how to navigate them. Assign each group to prepare a summary of one of the four sections. Summaries should explain the section's main idea and highlight at least one key item presented. Have groups share their completed summaries with the class.

Active Options

On Your Feet: Stage a Quiz Show Tell each student to write one question about the space race. Then invite two students to come to the front of the class. Explain the order in which students from the audience will ask their questions of the pair, who will "buzz in" by raising a hand or using a clicker. The student who buzzes in first and answers correctly faces a new contestant from the class. Continue the quiz show until all questions have been asked, all students have had the opportunity to participate, and one student—the winner—remains.

NG Learning Framework: Examine a Breakthrough STEM

ATTITUDE Curiosity
KNOWLEDGE New Frontiers

Remind students that as a result of the space race, many inventions became part of American life. Organize students into small groups and have each research and create a short presentation about how a modern-day consumer item, such as a smoke detector or an ear thermometer, had its roots in the space race. Presentations should explain the original use of the item and how the item's use has changed—if at all—since first being marketed to consumers. After all groups have presented, encourage students to discuss how technologies of today, such as high-capacity batteries or digital cameras, could be adapted for future uses.

Inclusion

Write Notes Allow students with disabilities to work with a partner who can read the lesson aloud to them. Encourage them to write notes as the partner without disabilities describes in detail the photographs of *Friendship 7* and the astronauts training in a swimming pool. When pairs have finished, ask them to discuss the written notes, make corrections if necessary, and then work together to answer the Historical Thinking questions.

Gifted & Talented

Create a Social Media Profile Direct students to choose one of the astronauts mentioned in this lesson and conduct online research to learn about his life and interests, his reasons for becoming an astronaut, the training he went through, and his challenges and successes. Then tell students to create a social media profile for him, and invite them to share the profile with the class.

See the Chapter Planner for more strategies for differentiation.

HISTORICAL THINKING

ANSWERS

1. The United States created NASA to fund space exploration and math and science education in order to compete with Soviet technology.

2. Answers will vary. Responses might include flight training, physical endurance training, or stress management. Students should give a reason why the training they chose would be helpful.

3. The Americans hoped to defeat the Soviet Union in the space race by developing superior technology and achieving the first landing of humans on the moon.

The year is 1959. Thousands of people have fled the island nation of Cuba following a violent revolution. Settling close by in southern Florida, many of these Cubans wonder if they will ever be able to return to their native land.

MAIN IDEA Soon after taking office, President Kennedy faced Cold War challenges in Cuba and Germany.

TROUBLE IN CUBA

In 1959, a year before Kennedy's election, rebels led by Fidel Castro had taken power in Cuba, a U.S. ally located in the Caribbean Sea only 90 miles south of Florida. Castro, a communist, helped overthrow the brutal dictator Fulgencio Batista, who had encouraged both lawful U.S. investors and criminal gangsters to finance Cuban businesses. Batista and his followers had profited from the millions of American dollars that poured into Cuba, while many working Cubans lived in poverty.

Castro was popular while he supported reforms to the corrupt government, but when he seized private and American-owned property and businesses in Cuba, thousands of Cubans fled the country. Many became **exiles**, or political outcasts, in Florida. Castro then established strong economic and political ties with the Soviet Union. Now the Soviets had an ally right in America's backyard. This foreign policy crisis was the first challenge Kennedy faced as president.

As tensions between the United States and Cuba grew, President Kennedy decided to put a secret plan into action. Developed by the Eisenhower administration, the plan called for the United States to train and equip anti-Castro exiles who would then invade Cuba and inspire Cubans to launch an anticommunist revolution. The plan's goals were to remove Castro from power and drive Soviet influence from the Western Hemisphere.

On April 17, 1961, about 1,500 exiles waded ashore at the **Bay of Pigs** on Cuba's southern coast. They hoped to land in secret and launch a surprise attack. Unfortunately, Castro's forces were waiting for them. Cuban intelligence agents in Florida had learned about the plan from gossip among Cuban exiles in Miami. Castro's troops quickly overtook the invaders. Nearly 1,200 of the attackers were captured and held prisoner for 20 months while the United States negotiated for their release.

The failed Bay of Pigs mission was a humiliating defeat for the United States. Some critics worried that the young president lacked the foreign policy experience to handle the Cold War. Kennedy reacted by approving more secret operations to undermine, or weaken, Castro's government.

TENSIONS IN BERLIN

The Soviet Union's support for Cuba increased after the Bay of Pigs invasion. Sensing weakness in the United States government's response to the Cuban crisis, Soviet leader **Nikita Khrushchev** (nih-KEE-tuh KROOSH-chehf) began to challenge Kennedy in other areas.

As you have read, when the Allies divided control of Germany after World War II, West Berlin remained part of democratic West Germany, even though it was surrounded by communist East Germany. Each day, people from communist East Berlin poured into West Berlin, seeking jobs and greater freedom. Khrushchev complained that a capitalist city in the middle of communist-controlled East Germany "stuck like a bone in the Soviet throat."

In June 1961, Kennedy met with Khrushchev. The Soviet leader threatened to limit access to West Berlin. Kennedy declared that Western military forces would defend the city at all costs. He followed up by tripling draft calls, mobilizing U.S. reserve units, and requesting more defense funding from Congress.

In August 1961, workers in East Berlin began building a wall of barbed wire and concrete along the western border of the city. Armed troops were stationed at the crossing points that divided the city. The wall stopped the flow of people leaving East Germany, and those who were caught trying to cross over the wall or tunnel under it were arrested or even shot as they fled. For many years the **Berlin Wall** stood as a symbol of the Cold War. The increasing tension between the United States and the Soviet Union soon threatened to erupt into full-blown war.

HISTORICAL THINKING

1. **READING CHECK** What was the goal of the Bay of Pigs invasion?

2. **ANALYZE CAUSE AND EFFECT** Why was the Berlin Wall constructed?

3. **COMPARE AND CONTRAST** In what way was the situation between the United States and communist Cuba different from the situation the United States faced in Berlin?

In 1961, East German soldiers stand guard as the concrete and barbed-wire Berlin Wall is constructed. The East German government built the wall to surround West Berlin and slow the steady exit of East Berliners to the West.

PLAN

Objective
Analyze how the Kennedy administration responded to Cold War incidents in Cuba and Germany.

Critical Thinking Skills for Lesson 1.3
- Identify Main Ideas and Details
- Monitor Comprehension
- Analyze Cause and Effect
- Compare and Contrast
- Determine Chronology
- Make Inferences
- Draw Conclusions

Essential Question for Chapter 27
How did American identity change in the 1960s? In the 1960s, Cold War anxiety became a defining trait of American identity. Lesson 1.3 discusses U.S. responses to communist actions in Cuba and Germany that fueled Americans' anxiety.

Background for the Teacher
The failed Bay of Pigs invasion was not the first, or the last, attempt by the United States to remove Fidel Castro from power. One of the most famous occurred in 1960 when CIA operatives attempted to assassinate the Cuban leader by poisoning his cigars. During Dwight Eisenhower's presidency, two mobsters on the FBI's Ten Most Wanted list helped the CIA try to administer poison pills to Castro. In 1963, the CIA concocted two plans that relied on Castro's love of scuba diving. One was based on explosives hidden inside a beautifully painted seashell (intended to lure Castro's attention), and the other involved contaminating his diving suit with a fungus that would produce a skin disease. Neither was fully implemented. Castro survived these and many more assassination plots; one unconfirmed account put the number at more than 600. Castro died of natural causes in 2016 at the age of 90.

INTRODUCE & ENGAGE

Preview the Photograph

Direct students' attention to the photograph of the Berlin Wall. Ask students to examine the wall and offer their observations or ask questions they may have. List their observations and questions on the board. *(Possible responses: The wall looks poorly constructed, as if built in a hurry. How long was it? What kept people from sneaking over the wall at night? Was it constantly well lit and heavily guarded?)* After students have read and discussed the lesson, revisit their comments and questions, and ask volunteers to state the answers. Students may research questions that were not answered in the lesson.

TEACH

Guided Discussion

1. **Determine Chronology** What was the order of events that led to the failed Bay of Pigs invasion? *(1. Fidel Castro gains power in Cuba. 2. Castro seizes property; Cubans flee the country. 3. Castro establishes ties with Soviets. 4. John F. Kennedy implements Eisenhower's plan to use trained Cuban exiles to overthrow Castro. 5. Castro learns of the plan. 6. Invading exiles are captured and imprisoned.)*

2. **Make Inferences** Why did communist leaders want people to stop fleeing East Berlin for West Berlin? *(Possible response: The communist system promised equality and sharply criticized Western capitalism. People fleeing East Berlin was an indication that citizens were not happy under the communist system and preferred capitalism. Communist leaders did not want that fact demonstrated through a diminishing population in East Berlin.)*

Draw Conclusions

What did West and East Berliners likely think and feel about the Berlin Wall? *(Answers will vary. Possible response: Both West and East Berliners likely understood that the Berlin Wall symbolized the divide between Western capitalism and Soviet communism, but they experienced the wall as a huge interruption to their lives. The wall suddenly cut many people off from friends, family, and jobs on the other side, likely making them angry and bitter. Those who lived near the wall probably felt intimidated by its physical presence and the guards who patrolled it. They may have also lived in constant fear of attempted escapes to the West and the violence that might follow.)*

Active Options

On Your Feet: Think, Pair, Share Give students a few minutes to think about the following question: Why were Kennedy's policies and decisions more effective in Germany than in Cuba? Have students choose a partner and talk about the question for five minutes. Then allow pairs to share and discuss their ideas with the class.

NG Learning Framework: Resolve the Communist Threat in Cuba

SKILL Problem-Solving

KNOWLEDGE Our Human Story

Organize students into small groups and ask them to reread the first two paragraphs of the lesson. Remind them that Kennedy responded to the Soviet-Cuban alliance with the failed Bay of Pigs invasion. Then provide groups with a Problem-and-Solution Plan. Instruct students to develop their own plan to resolve

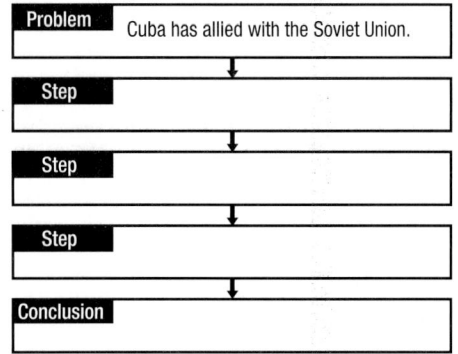

the communist threat in Cuba. Each group's plan should include at least three steps and conclude with a resolution of the situation. Invite groups to share their completed plans with the class.

DIFFERENTIATE

English Language Learners

Pose and Answer Questions Arrange students at the **Emerging** and **Expanding** levels in mixed pairs. Tell them to reread the lesson together, pausing after each paragraph to ask one another *who, what, when, where,* or *why* questions about what they have just read. Suggest that students use a 5Ws Chart to help organize their questions and answers. Ask students at the **Expanding** level to assist students at the **Emerging** level as needed.

Pre-AP

Write a News Report Assign students the role of journalists, and instruct them to conduct online research to learn more about the planning and execution of the failed Bay of Pigs mission in 1961. Suggest that they also research Castro's advance knowledge of the invasion and the CIA's failure to realize that Castro knew. Tell students to use their research to write a detailed news story, including quotes from eyewitnesses, captured prisoners, and others. Invite students to post their news reports on a class blog or publish them on a school website.

See the Chapter Planner for more strategies for differentiation.

HISTORICAL THINKING

ANSWERS

1. The invasion was intended to lead to the overthrow of Castro's government and stop the spread of communism.

2. The Berlin Wall was built to prevent people under Soviet control in East Germany from fleeing to West Berlin, a capitalist city.

3. Because Cuba is only 90 miles from the United States, the Soviet-Cuban alliance represented a direct threat to the United States. The separation of Berlin into communist and capitalist sectors did not overtly threaten the United States, but it was symbolic of the standoff between the United States and the Soviet Union during the Cold War.

1.4 Cuban Missile Crisis

If you pay attention to the news, you may find yourself worrying about your future or that of your family or community. But what if the news is so alarming that you begin to fear that the world as we know it might be coming to an end?

MAIN IDEA President Kennedy successfully faced a tense standoff with the Soviets that brought the world to the brink of nuclear war.

President Kennedy discusses strategy with General Curtis LeMay and reconnaissance, or survey, pilots who flew over Cuba to get information during the Cuban Missile Crisis. LeMay recommended a more aggressive approach than Kennedy's idea to place a naval blockade around Cuba.

SOVIET MISSILES IN CUBA

In October 1962, the world faced the most dangerous moment of the entire Cold War. It began when American spy planes discovered that the Soviets were placing ballistic missiles with nuclear warheads in Cuba. **Ballistic missiles** are rocket-powered missiles that can travel from about 620 to 3,400 miles and are guided on their ascent but fall freely on their descent. Kennedy's advisors believed that the missiles would be in place and ready to fire in a few weeks. With Cuba so close to the American mainland, such missiles could endanger the United States.

Since the Bay of Pigs invasion, Cuba had come to rely heavily on its alliance with the Soviet Union. An economic boycott of Cuba, led by the United States, was hurting the island's economy. Fearing further threats, Castro asked the Soviets for military help. At first, this aid included only defensive missiles. Then the Soviets began equipping Cuba with the offensive missiles detected by the United States— missiles capable of striking Washington, D.C., or even Chicago, Illinois. To the United States, the threat was clear.

The conflict that followed became known as the **Cuban Missile Crisis**. Kennedy met with his advisors and then ordered a **naval quarantine**, or blockade, of Cuba. The blockade prevented any ships from entering or leaving Cuba. As U.S. naval forces surrounded Cuba, the Soviets prepared to challenge them, sending their own armed ships toward the blockade.

Range of Nuclear Missiles in Cuba, October 1962

The medium-range ballistic missiles set up in Cuba by the Soviets could reach any U.S. city within about 1,000 miles. The intermediate-range missiles could reach a target of about 2,000 miles from the launch site in Cuba.

Canada
Seattle — 2,843 miles
Ottawa
USA
Chicago
New York — 1,688 miles
Denver
Washington, D.C.
Los Angeles — 1,819 miles
2,299 miles — 1,316 miles
Atlanta — 1,139 miles
751 miles
1,333 miles
Miami 234 mi.
Mexico
Mexico City
Havana
Cuba
1,103 miles

RESOLVING THE CRISIS

On October 22, 1962, Kennedy addressed the nation on television. He reported what he told the Soviets: Take away the missiles in Cuba and destroy the sites. He also warned that any missile fired from Cuba would be considered an attack on the United States by the Soviet Union and would require a military response. American forces went on full alert.

While the world watched and waited, the Soviet ships inched closer to the U.S. warships surrounding the island nation. On October 26, Khrushchev wrote to Kennedy. The Soviets would remove the missiles from Cuba, he said, if the United States guaranteed that it would never invade Cuba. Khrushchev then sent a second message in which he demanded that the United States remove the missiles it had installed in Turkey near the Soviet border. On October 27, Kennedy formally agreed to the Soviets' first offer, and Khrushchev accepted the deal. In return, the United States later quietly removed some of its old missiles from Turkey.

Khrushchev had badly misjudged how strongly the Americans would respond to the placement of missiles so close to the U.S. mainland. However, his willingness to compromise helped lead to a peaceful solution.

After a tense 13 days in October, the world avoided the threat of a nuclear war when the two countries chose to be cautious rather than reckless. That fact alone seemed to shake the leaders of both sides. In July 1963, officials installed a direct telephone link, known as the "hot line," between the White House and the Kremlin, which was the center of the Soviet government. Shortly after that, the United States and the Soviet Union joined other nations in agreeing to a **Nuclear Test-Ban Treaty**, which banned the testing of nuclear weapons in the atmosphere, in space, and under water and limited the future development of nuclear weapons.

HISTORICAL THINKING

1. **READING CHECK** What was so dangerous about the missiles U.S. spy planes discovered in Cuba in October 1962?

2. **IDENTIFY MAIN IDEAS AND DETAILS** How was the Cuban Missile Crisis resolved?

3. **INTERPRET MAPS** Examine the map in this lesson. Which cities were within striking distance of the medium-range missiles?

PLAN

Objective

Analyze the causes of the Cuban Missile Crisis and summarize its resolution.

Critical Thinking Skills for Lesson 1.4

• Identify Main Ideas and Details
• Monitor Comprehension
• Interpret Maps
• Draw Conclusions
• Form and Support Opinions
• Make Inferences

Essential Question for Chapter 27

How did American identity change in the 1960s? The Soviet Union fueled Cold War tensions by increasing its support of Cuba, the United States' communist neighbor. Lesson 1.4 explores how these tensions peaked with the Cuban Missile Crisis.

Background for the Teacher

Nikita Khrushchev's October 26 message to President Kennedy, in which he offered to remove Soviet missiles in exchange for a U.S. promise not to invade Cuba, has an interesting story behind it. The White House first learned of the offer from a reporter who was contacted by a Soviet agent, a technique known as "back channel" diplomacy because it relies on unofficial communication using intermediaries. At first Kennedy doubted the legitimacy of the offer, but later that day—which would have been late at night in Moscow—the president received a lengthy, heartfelt message from his Soviet counterpart. Worried about the possibility of nuclear holocaust, Khrushchev wrote, "Mr. President, we and you ought not now to pull on the ends of the rope in which you have tied the knot of war. . . . If there is no intention . . . to doom the world to the catastrophe of thermonuclear war, then let us not only relax the forces pulling on the end of the rope, let us take measures to untie that knot." Two days later, the crisis was over.

INTRODUCE & ENGAGE

Consider the Prospect of Nuclear War

Review the political tensions between the United States and the Soviet Union and what prompted them. Remind students that both countries at this point had nuclear weapons. Then call on volunteers to offer details about the atomic blasts that devastated Hiroshima and Nagasaki. Guide a discussion using the following questions as prompts: What circumstances would have justified the launching of a nuclear weapon? How might the United States or the Soviet Union have responded to a nuclear attack? Which cities would each likely have targeted? How might the aftermath of a nuclear exchange have affected both countries? Explain that in this lesson students will learn about a standoff between the United States and the Soviet Union in which nuclear war was a genuine possibility.

TEACH

Guided Discussion

1. **Draw Conclusions** What role did technology play in the Cuban Missile Crisis? *(Possible response: Technology played a central role because the nuclear bombs in the warheads and the ballistic missiles that carried them were fairly recent innovations. So was the spy plane that photographed and documented their existence. In addition, television played an important role, as it allowed President Kennedy to directly speak to Americans to inform them about the crisis.)*

2. **Form and Support Opinions** Which side won the nuclear standoff in Cuba? *(Answers will vary. Possible responses: The United States won because the Soviets agreed to remove their missiles from Cuba, while the United States only agreed never to invade Cuba. The Soviet Union won because it prevented capitalism from entering Cuba and achieved the removal of U.S. missiles from near its borders. Both sides won because nuclear war was prevented and millions of lives spared.)*

Make Inferences

Direct students' attention to the photograph in the lesson and ask them to read the caption. **ASK:** Why might General LeMay and others have recommended that Kennedy take an aggressive approach toward the Soviet Union? *(Possible response: The Soviets had staged missiles only 90 miles from the U.S. coast, so General LeMay likely wanted to respond with a military action, such as an invasion force.)*

Active Options

On Your Feet: Three-Step Interview Prompt pairs to interview each other using the following question: What do Kennedy's actions during the Cuban Missile Crisis tell us about his beliefs? Tell the interviewer to ask follow-up questions based on the answers provided, such as: What does Kennedy think the role of the president of the United States should be in global politics? What is Kennedy's attitude toward Khrushchev? Then direct students to reverse roles. Ask students to share their ideas from the interview with the class.

NG Learning Framework: Explore the 13 Days

ATTITUDE Responsibility

SKILL Communication

Direct small groups of students to the John F. Kennedy Presidential Library and Museum website and access the interactive exhibit "World on the Brink: JFK and the Cuban Missile Crisis." Tell groups to explore the site and write notes to answer questions such as these: What was President Kennedy willing to sacrifice for a resolution, and why? What was Chairman Khrushchev willing to sacrifice? How much did Kennedy tell the American public, and when? After groups finish their exploration, prompt them to discuss these questions: If you had the responsibility of resolving a conflict such as the Cuban Missile Crisis, how much would you be willing to compromise? How much would you or should you share with the American public during the crisis? Then have groups summarize their discussions for the class.

DIFFERENTIATE

English Language Learners ELD

Identify Antonyms Pair students at the **Emerging** level with students at the **Expanding** level. Challenge them to find antonyms in the first and last paragraphs of the lesson. *(ascent/descent; cautious/reckless)* Have students create a T-Chart for each pair of words, writing the antonyms in the top row. Direct pairs to work with a student at the **Bridging** level to write definitions in their own words below each word in the chart.

Gifted & Talented

Create an Annotated Time Line Instruct students to conduct online research to create and annotate a time line of the Cuban Missile Crisis. Encourage them to include events that led up to the crisis as well as events during the crisis itself. Tell students to include relevant news headlines, photographs, editorial cartoons, and other images. They may use an online time line tool or markers and paper. Invite students to share their finished time lines with the class.

See the Chapter Planner for more strategies for differentiation.

HISTORICAL THINKING

ANSWERS

1. The missiles were dangerous because they were offensive missiles capable of striking the United States.

2. The Soviet Union removed the missiles in exchange for the promise from the United States not to invade Cuba. The United States also later removed missiles from Turkey, located near the Soviet Union.

3. Miami and Atlanta were within range of the medium-range missiles in Cuba.

1.5 Kennedy's Assassination

It was a beautiful late fall day in Dallas, Texas. President Kennedy was visiting the city. As the president's motorcade passed by, the crowds strained to catch a glimpse of him. Suddenly, shots rang out. The country would never be the same.

MAIN IDEA President Kennedy's violent death shocked the nation and the world.

Aboard Air Force One shortly after President Kennedy's assassination, Vice President Lyndon Baines Johnson takes the oath of office with a grieving Jacqueline Kennedy beside him. U.S. District Judge Sarah T. Hughes (with her back to the camera) administers the oath.

A FATEFUL DAY IN DALLAS

After the peaceful resolution of the Cuban Missile Crisis, President Kennedy gained Americans' confidence and his popularity soared. Members of the press now treated his youth as a positive trait, calling the Kennedy administration "Camelot," a reference to the legendary kingdom where King Arthur presided over his knights of the Round Table.

In late November 1963, the president and his wife, Jacqueline, traveled to Texas on a political tour to win southern support in his upcoming re-election campaign. On November 22, the Kennedys rode in a motorcade with Governor John Connally and his wife, Nellie, through Dallas. Along the route, people waved from office buildings and cheered from the sidewalks. Even Kennedy supporters were surprised by the size of the welcoming crowds.

As the car reached Dealey Plaza, a park in downtown Dallas, gunfire came from the window of a nearby textbook warehouse. The president suddenly slumped in his seat. He had been shot in the head. President Kennedy was rushed to Parkland Hospital and pronounced dead. His assassination stunned the world.

Less than two hours after President Kennedy's assassination, **Lyndon Johnson** took the presidential oath of office aboard Air Force One before it flew back to Washington, D.C. Johnson's wife, Lady

Bird, and Jacqueline Kennedy stood by his side. As the nation mourned its fallen leader, Johnson vowed to continue the programs and policies of the Kennedy administration.

That same day, local police arrested a suspect named **Lee Harvey Oswald** after he shot and killed a Dallas police officer. Officials initially charged

On November 22, 1963, people lined the streets of Dallas, Texas, to greet President and Mrs. John F. Kennedy as they rode by in their motorcade. The Kennedys, joined by Texas Governor and Mrs. John Connally, smiled and waved at the crowds just minutes before a gunman murdered the president and wounded Connally.

Oswald only with the death of the police officer, but they considered him the prime suspect in Kennedy's assassination. On November 24, as law enforcement officers were attempting to move Oswald to a different jail location, Dallas nightclub owner Jack Ruby shot and killed him, as shown on live television. Ruby claimed he killed Oswald out of a sense of patriotism. Ruby died in prison four years later.

A NATION GRIEVES

On November 25, 1963, thousands of people gathered in Washington, D.C., for President Kennedy's funeral. Millions of others watched his funeral on television. For many of his supporters, it felt as if they were mourning the death of the hope, innocence, and idealism that Kennedy had inspired.

Some people suspected the events surrounding Kennedy's assassination were part of a larger **conspiracy**, or a plot organized by several people. President Johnson tried to reassure Americans who doubted Oswald had acted alone. The federal government immediately put together a special group led by Chief Justice of the United States Earl

Warren to investigate. The **Warren Commission** concluded that both Oswald and Ruby had acted alone. Despite this conclusion, there were still people who continued to suspect a cover-up.

Such doubts reflected the depth of shock over Kennedy's assassination. Few other events in the nation's history have produced so much shared public grief. Charming and handsome, a war hero with a glamorous wife, Kennedy represented youth and optimism. When he died, so did the dreams of many of his supporters.

HISTORICAL THINKING

1. **READING CHECK** Why were the President and First Lady traveling in Texas?

2. **COMPARE AND CONTRAST** How did the Warren Commission's conclusion about the Kennedy assassination differ from that of many Americans?

3. **MAKE GENERALIZATIONS** Why did the assassination of Kennedy cause so much grief and shock among his supporters?

Conflict and Expanding Rights **911**

PLAN

Objective

Describe the circumstances of John F. Kennedy's assassination, the events that followed, and the country's reaction.

Critical Thinking Skills for Lesson 1.5

- Identify Main Ideas and Details
- Monitor Comprehension
- Compare and Contrast
- Make Generalizations
- Make Inferences
- Form and Support Opinions
- Ask and Answer Questions

Essential Question for Chapter 27

How did American identity change in the 1960s? The Kennedy presidency lifted the country on a wave of optimism and hope. His assassination brought this feeling to an abrupt end. Lesson 1.5 examines how Kennedy's death shocked and changed the nation.

Background for the Teacher

In 2017, the federal government released 13,000 documents related to John F. Kennedy's assassination. Although no concrete evidence supporting any conspiracy theories emerged, the documents included several interesting revelations. For example, the FBI received a death threat against Lee Harvey Oswald the day before his assassination, from a man claiming to represent a "committee" to kill Oswald. Jack Ruby maintained until his death that he acted alone. The documents also contained allegations that Oswald was in contact with Cuban officials and the Russian KGB, as well as information about the Soviets' reaction to Kennedy's death. Soviet leaders seemed convinced that Kennedy's death resulted from a conspiracy among U.S. right-wing factions.

History Notebook

Encourage students to complete the American Gallery page for Chapter 27 in their History Notebooks as they read.

Preview Using Visuals

Point out the two photographs in the lesson. **ASK:** What are the similarities and differences in the tone of the two photographs and the mood of the people shown? *(Possible response: The first photograph is a vibrant image of President Kennedy's motorcade. The color and the smiling subjects, who are clearly enjoying themselves, project a cheerful and optimistic mood. The black-and-white photograph of Vice President Lyndon Johnson being sworn in as president projects a somber tone. The lack of color and the sad and stricken expressions of the subjects reflect the tragedy of the circumstances. Both photos depict onlookers witnessing a historic event.)* Explain that the photographs were taken before and after the assassination of President Kennedy—one of the defining moments of the era— and that in this lesson students will learn how the country reacted to this devastating event.

TEACH

Guided Discussion

1. **Make Inferences** Why do you think Lyndon Johnson promised to continue Kennedy's policies rather than enact new policies of his own? *(Possible response: Because Johnson had not been elected president, he might not have thought he had the country's backing to enact his personal policies. Furthermore, he may have believed that a country in mourning needed stability more than a change of direction.)*

2. **Form and Support Opinions** Why do you think conspiracy theories about John F. Kennedy's assassination have persisted for so many years? *(Possible response: The event left questions unanswered for some people because Lee Harvey Oswald was assassinated before he could face prosecution, which would likely have revealed information about his motives and actions.)*

Ask and Answer Questions

Tell pairs of students to write one or two questions they would like to answer about each of the following topics: the Kennedy assassination, Lyndon Johnson, the Warren Commission. Then review how to locate credible sources—such as books by scholars, academic websites, or primary sources—that students could use to find answers to their questions. Warn students that the Kennedy assassination is a controversial topic and much of the available information about it stems from conspiracy theories rather than facts. Finally, guide pairs to use online and text resources to find answers to their questions. When all pairs are finished, invite them to present their findings to the class.

Active Options

On Your Feet: Small-Group Brainstorming Arrange students in groups of three, and direct them to brainstorm adjectives or phrases that describe the life and presidency of John F. Kennedy, based on what they have learned from the five lessons in this section. Provide each group with a large piece of paper and have them create a visual representation of their brainstorming results. When groups have finished, arrange visuals in a gallery for the class to view and discuss.

AMERICAN **GALLERY**
ONLINE

President John F. Kennedy Invite students to explore the American Gallery. Have them select one of the images and do additional research to learn more about it. Ask questions that will inspire additional inquiry about the chosen gallery images, such as: Who is in the photo with Kennedy? When was it taken? Why is the event significant? How does the photo relate to the popular understanding of Kennedy?

DIFFERENTIATE

Striving Readers

Summarize Place students in pairs and instruct them to take turns reading paragraphs from the lesson. After reading each paragraph, students work together to summarize the paragraph in one or two sentences. When they have finished, tell them to read their summaries in the order in which the material appears in the lesson.

Pre-AP

Research a Historic Photograph Instruct students to conduct research using print and online sources to learn about the story behind the iconic photograph of Lyndon Johnson taking the oath of office. You may suggest that students read relevant excerpts from *The Years of Lyndon Johnson: The Passage of Power*, the fourth volume in a biography of Johnson by the historian Robert Caro, to discover why Jacqueline Kennedy is in a photograph taken just a few hours after her husband's assassination. Direct students to use their research to write an essay telling the story of the photo. Invite volunteers to read their essays to the class.

See the Chapter Planner for more strategies for differentiation.

HISTORICAL THINKING

ANSWERS

1. They were in Dallas on a campaign tour to win Texas's support for the president's re-election bid.

2. The Warren Commission concluded that both Oswald and Ruby acted alone. Many people, however, believed that the assassinations of Kennedy and Oswald were part of a larger conspiracy.

3. Kennedy represented a new and youthful vision and governing style. His supporters were enchanted by his family and hopeful about his ideas, and they felt an intense connection with him. His sudden and violent death created a sense of loss that fueled their grief.

2.1 Johnson Acts on Civil Rights

Voting is one of the fundamental rights and responsibilities of adult citizens in the United States. At least, it's supposed to be. But in many parts of the South, whites made it impossible for African Americans to exercise that right.

MAIN IDEA The new president supported the civil rights movement, but each step toward equality was a struggle.

THE CIVIL RIGHTS ACT OF 1964

President Johnson vowed to continue Kennedy's policies, including the late president's support of civil rights. During his short term in office, Kennedy had used federal marshals and state National Guard units to enforce existing civil rights laws. The violence against demonstrators in Birmingham had inspired Kennedy to draft a comprehensive civil rights bill, which was already in congressional committees when he was assassinated.

CRITICAL VIEWING Upon signing the Civil Rights Act of 1964, President Lyndon B. Johnson (seated) turns to shake hands with Dr. Martin Luther King, Jr., and give Dr. King the pen Johnson had used to sign the bill. Dr. King was instrumental in lobbying for passage of the bill, which was debated in the Senate for months. Others in the room include Republican and Democratic representatives who voted for the bill. How would you describe the mood captured by this photo?

Johnson, who was first elected to Congress in 1937, had been a Texas senator since 1949. He was a southern Democrat, but he championed civil rights at a time when many southern Democrats supported segregation and other Jim Crow laws. As Senate majority leader, Johnson had worked with Republicans and compromised with fellow southern Democrats to help pass the Civil Rights Act of 1957. He was determined to repeat his success with Kennedy's civil rights legislation. Johnson brought together congressional leaders with opposing interests to make sure the Civil Rights Act of 1964 passed.

The bill passed in June after Senate revisions, and President Johnson signed it into law on July 2. The act withholds funds from segregated public programs and outlaws segregation and discrimination in public places. In addition, it created the **Equal Employment Opportunity Commission (EEOC)**, an agency that monitors and protects workplace rights. The law prohibits workplace discrimination based not only on race but also on religious beliefs, national origin, and gender. As a result of the Civil Rights Act, women and minorities now have legal protection against employment discrimination.

Following the March 7, 1965, Bloody Sunday march, Dr. Martin Luther King, Jr., led a second voting rights march, which became known as Turnaround Tuesday. On March 9, Dr. King and more than 2,000 people marched across the Edmund Pettus Bridge in Selma, Alabama. Blocked by state police officers from continuing to Montgomery, the marchers knelt in prayer and then turned around, going back over the bridge.

THE VOTING RIGHTS ACT OF 1965

Even with federal law backing them, African Americans still found voter registration, or the process of signing up to vote, nearly impossible in the South. Southern states had found ways to keep African-American citizens from voting, including poll taxes, literacy tests, and even threats of physical violence. In 1965, determined African-American citizens in Selma, Alabama, began marching daily to the courthouse to register to vote. But the white sheriff repeatedly turned them away. Many were arrested and beaten.

On March 7, 1965, a day now remembered as Bloody Sunday, protesters began a 50-mile march from Selma to the state capitol building in Montgomery. Dr. Martin Luther King, Jr., and the Southern Christian Leadership Conference (SCLC) joined the protesters. They hadn't walked very far when police attacked them, sending more than 50 marchers to the hospital. They tried again and again to complete their march. People from all over the country traveled to join in the **Selma-to-Montgomery marches**. On March 25, protected by federal officials, Dr. King and 25,000 marchers arrived safely in the capital.

Spurred by President Johnson and events in Selma, Congress passed the **Voting Rights Act of 1965** on August 6. The act outlawed all obstacles that prevented African Americans from voting. This **landmark legislation**, or important and historic law, soon had an impact. By the end of 1965, as many as 250,000 African-American citizens had successfully registered to vote. Within three years, the registration rate of African Americans in the South had climbed to more than 60 percent. Even so, many activists felt the struggle for civil rights was progressing too slowly. Some were thinking of changing their strategy.

HISTORICAL THINKING

1. **READING CHECK** What was the purpose of the Selma-to-Montgomery marches?

2. **COMPARE AND CONTRAST** How were the Civil Rights Act of 1964 and the Voting Rights Act of 1965 alike and different in the ways they promoted civil rights in the United States?

3. **SYNTHESIZE** How did the Civil Rights Act of 1964 provide benefits not just to African Americans, but to other citizens as well?

PLAN

Objective

Describe how Lyndon Johnson and civil rights leaders worked to pass civil rights legislation.

Critical Thinking Skills for Lesson 2.1

- Identify Main Ideas and Details
- Monitor Comprehension
- Compare and Contrast
- Synthesize
- Make Inferences
- Make Predictions
- Determine Chronology

Essential Question for Chapter 27

How did American identity change in the 1960s? Following John F. Kennedy's assassination, Lyndon Johnson was determined to pass civil rights legislation. Lesson 2.1 discusses the peaceful marches and two landmark laws that centered on this effort.

Background for the Teacher

Alabama was, in many ways, ground zero for civil rights battles in the United States. It was the state where Rosa Parks refused to give up her bus seat and the state in which voter suppression was perhaps most glaring. While jailed in Selma, Martin Luther King, Jr., wrote a letter to the *New York Times*, and in it he remarked that there were more African Americans locked up with him than there were listed on the voter registration rolls. In some Alabama counties, no African Americans had voted in 50 years. In Selma, only 130 of 15,000 African-American citizens were registered to vote; those who tried to register were repeatedly intimidated and turned away. For example, Selma's sheriff sent photographers to take photos of voting rights protesters, which he threatened to show to their employers. Alabama's racist status quo was deeply ingrained. Selma's Edmund Pettus Bridge, which played a key role in civil rights marches, was named after a Confederate general who also served as Grand Dragon of the Ku Klux Klan.

Activate Prior Knowledge

Write the term *civil rights* on the board. Ask students what comes to their minds when they hear the term, and list their responses. They might volunteer names such as Martin Luther King, Jr., concepts such as discrimination and equality, or events such as boycotts and marches. Tell students that in this lesson they will learn about two landmark civil rights laws passed during Lyndon Johnson's administration.

TEACH

Guided Discussion

1. **Make Inferences** How did Lyndon Johnson's background prepare him to successfully promote civil rights legislation? *(Possible response: Johnson was a southerner, so his actions were met with less resistance from other southerners than if a northern president—like Kennedy—had attempted radical change. The connections and experience Johnson had gained during his 15 years in the Senate also helped him pass the laws.)*

2. **Make Predictions** How much do you think life for African Americans changed after the passage of the Civil Rights Act of 1964 and the Voting Rights Act of 1965? *(Possible response: Both acts outlawed blatant forms of discrimination such as segregated accommodations and poll taxes, allowing African Americans a more equal place in society. However, the laws likely did not instantly change racial attitudes that had been shaped by slavery or resolve other racial issues, such as disparities in business and home ownership.)*

Determine Chronology

Remind students that the passage of the Civil Rights Act of 1964 and the Voting Rights Act of 1965 represented the culmination of years of work by civil rights leaders. Provide groups of students with a large sheet of paper and have them create and caption a time line of events leading up to the passage of the two acts. Instruct groups to use their textbooks and online resources to identify and include at least three other events that contributed to the passage of these laws. Invite groups to present their completed time lines to the class, explaining their reasoning for each event they included.

Active Options

On Your Feet: Jigsaw Organize students into three "expert" groups and have each group analyze one of the following and summarize the main ideas of the topic in their own words: the Civil Rights Act of 1964, the Voting Rights Act of 1965, the laws enforced by the Equal Employment Opportunity Commission. Then have members of each expert group count off using the letters A, B, and C. Place students into three new groups, A, B, and C, so that each new group has at least one member from each expert group. Have students in each new group take turns sharing the summaries they created in their expert groups.

NG Learning Framework: Evaluate a Supreme Court Decision

ATTITUDE Responsibility

KNOWLEDGE Our Human Story

Inform students that in the 2013 case *Shelby County* v. *Holder*, the U.S. Supreme Court revisited the Voting Rights Act of 1965 and decided in a 5–4 vote to invalidate many of its key provisions. Provide small groups of students with an article about the case or with excerpts of the decision and dissent. Be sure to choose an article that explains both the rationale for the Court's decision and the dissenting opinions. Have groups complete a T-Chart with the arguments for and against overturning key provisions of the Voting Rights Act of 1965. When groups have finished, summarize the findings as a class. Then present students with some of the consequences of the decision, such as the growth of voter ID laws, and guide a discussion about whether they think that the Supreme Court made the correct decision.

Inclusion

Analyze a Photograph Pair students who are visually impaired with students who are not. Ask the latter to read the caption and describe the photograph of Johnson signing the Civil Rights Act. Encourage visually impaired students to ask clarifying questions. Then have pairs work together to answer the Critical Viewing question.

Pre-AP

Write an Analysis Essay Remind students that Johnson was able to spur Congress to pass the Civil Rights Act of 1964 and the Voting Rights Act of 1965 during a time of high racial tensions. Instruct students to conduct research and then write an essay analyzing how Johnson was able to do so. Tell them to begin by rereading the second paragraph of this lesson about Johnson's long experience in Congress.

See the Chapter Planner for more strategies for differentiation.

HISTORICAL THINKING

ANSWERS

1. Activists thought that a march including prominent citizens and a great number of people who intended to vote at the courthouse would bring attention to the fact that in the South, many African Americans were denied their right to register to vote.

2. Both were attempts to bring greater equality, but they approached the problem from different angles. The Civil Rights Act prohibited public segregation and discrimination nationwide and established the EEOC to protect employees from discrimination in the workplace. The Voting Rights Act removed obstacles to voter registration, including laws that targeted African Americans and kept them from exercising their voting rights.

3. By establishing the EEOC and prohibiting all workplace discrimination, the law helped women and other minorities.

CRITICAL VIEWING The handshake between Johnson and King and the smiles of those present suggest a congratulatory mood.

2.2 Rising Discontent

Waiting for something to change can be hard, especially if it affects your life. You might grow impatient or feel like giving up. Or you might decide to try a different strategy.

MAIN IDEA Not all civil rights leaders agreed with Dr. King's peaceful methods, and patience began to turn into tension and violence.

Three female members of the Black Panthers solemnly hold Panther flags in a photograph taken around 1968 in California. While the mainstream press mostly portrayed the Black Panthers as criminals, photographers Pirkle Jones and Ruth Marion Baruch revealed the members' humanity, concerns for family, commitment to ideals, and hope for the future.

URBAN VIOLENCE

Racial discrimination was a problem not only in the South. In the urban centers of the North and West, many African-American families lived in high-crime neighborhoods with failing schools and limited public services. In some cities, banks refused home loans to African Americans who sought to buy property outside their traditional neighborhoods. Although there were no laws prohibiting African Americans and other minorities from living wherever they wanted, such practices kept many from moving into certain areas. In addition, many people chose to stay in their neighborhoods to avoid conflicts. Yet as the civil rights movement gained strength, both supporters and opponents felt threatened, and conflicts arose anyway. Riots erupted in Los Angeles, Chicago, Detroit, and other major American cities.

While older activists believed in Dr. King's nonviolent approach, some younger African Americans believed that these methods weren't working fast enough. The **Black Power movement** arose out of their frustration. Members of this movement proclaimed pride in their African-American heritage, rejecting the importance of integration. Instead, they advocated for **black separatism**, the political and cultural division of blacks and whites.

The Nation of Islam, a religious black nationalist organization that preaches self-help, moral discipline, and black separatism, was founded in 1930 in Detroit, Michigan. The group's influence increased as the civil rights movement grew. By the late 1950s, **Malcolm X** had become one of its most forceful speakers. He preached self-defense rather than nonviolence, stating that African

Americans should protect themselves "by any means necessary." Angry members of the Nation of Islam assassinated Malcolm X after he left the group over disputes with its leader.

Malcolm X
Malcolm Little was the son of a murdered civil rights activist. When he was a boy, white supremacists burned down the family home. A wild and wayward youth, he was arrested and sentenced to prison on a burglary charge. While in prison, he learned about the Nation of Islam. After prison, he joined the Nation of Islam and changed his name to Malcolm X, dismissing the name "Little" as his slave name. His intelligence, drive, and charismatic speaking style made him the most well-known member of the Nation of Islam, eclipsing the fame of the organization's leader, Elijah Muhammad.

Members of another group, the **Black Panther Party**, saw themselves as the armed enemies of a racist "police state." Organized in Oakland, California, in 1966, the Black Panthers openly carried weapons and studied the law, strategies meant to protect themselves and their neighbors from police harassment and brutality. The Black Panthers also established many community service programs, such as health clinics, after-school enrichment classes, and free breakfasts for public school students.

THE COURTS DECIDE

Even as unrest increased, President Johnson took more steps to promote civil rights. In 1965, he signed an executive order instituting **affirmative action**, a government policy establishing racial quotas to favor groups that face discrimination. The goal of affirmative action was to improve educational and employment opportunities for all Americans. Affirmative action proved to be controversial, and it was challenged in court. In 1978, the U.S. Supreme Court ruled that affirmative action programs were constitutional but basing quotas solely on race was not.

In 1967, yet another form of racial discrimination was struck down: state bans on interracial marriage. All but nine states had enacted such

bans at some time. But most northern and western states had repealed those laws by the mid-1960s and allowed couples of different races to marry. The southern states did not. When the Lovings, an interracial couple legally married in Washington, D.C., were arrested for living together in marriage in Virginia, they appealed their case to the U.S. Supreme Court. In the matter of *Loving* v. *Virginia*, the Court agreed with the Lovings, declaring all laws against interracial marriage unconstitutional.

President Johnson's progressive plans for the nation did not end with civil rights. He also hoped to end poverty in the United States.

HISTORICAL THINKING

1. **READING CHECK** Why did some younger African Americans turn away from Dr. King's nonviolent movement?

2. **COMPARE AND CONTRAST** How was discrimination similar and different in the North and the South?

3. **IDENTIFY MAIN IDEAS AND DETAILS** How did the U.S. Supreme Court's decisions discussed in this lesson affect the civil rights of Americans?

PLAN

Objective
Explain civil rights leaders' tactics to receive rights granted by civil rights laws.

Critical Thinking Skills for Lesson 2.2
- Identify Main Ideas and Details
- Monitor Comprehension
- Compare and Contrast
- Evaluate
- Make Inferences

Essential Question for Chapter 27
How did American identity change in the 1960s? After the passage of civil rights laws, protests of racial discrimination continued throughout the country. Lesson 2.2 discusses the emergence and tactics of the Black Power movement.

Background for the Teacher
The concept of black separatism that emerged in the 1960s was not a new philosophy. Beginning in the days of slavery, some blacks and whites had argued that diverse races were forever incompatible. The African nation of Liberia was established in 1847 with the express purpose of providing a home for free blacks because many feared that living an equal life in the United States was impossible. During the early decades of the 20th century, Marcus Garvey and his followers championed the Back to Africa campaign and supported black-owned programs and businesses, asserting that white support was not needed. The separatist movement in the 1960s was different in that it was tied to a specific religion: Islam. Under the influence of Malcolm X, thousands of people converted to Islam and preached and spread the separatist ideas started hundreds of years before.

INTRODUCE & ENGAGE

Preview Using a Profile

Direct students' attention to the brief profile of Malcolm X in the lesson. Ask students to share their impression of him and their initial thoughts about how he compares with other civil rights figures they have studied. Inform students that in this lesson they will learn more about Malcolm X and how the civil rights movement evolved during the 1960s and activism increased in northern cities.

TEACH

Guided Discussion

1. **Evaluate** How does the headline of the newspaper Malcolm X holds in the photo comment on earlier civil right efforts? *(The headline "Our Freedom Can't Wait!" is critical of earlier civil rights efforts. It implies that civil rights leaders, such as Dr. Martin Luther King, Jr., have not moved quickly enough and that more aggressive steps are needed.)*

2. **Make Inferences** Why do you think the Black Panthers were generally portrayed negatively by the press? *(Possible response: Members of the party carried weapons, which alarmed people. They were also highly critical of the police, which might have caused a backlash. In addition, many members of the media were likely white and thus could not relate to the concerns and experiences of the Black Panthers.)*

More Information

Affirmative Action in Education Since their creation in 1965, affirmative action policies have remained in the news and are still controversial. In 1968, the U.S. Supreme Court mandated that school boards provide a plan to end segregated education, thus ensuring diversity within school districts. The backlash was fierce. Riots and violence erupted in some school districts that bused students across city and county lines in order to achieve diversity. In the intervening years, several white students have filed lawsuits, some of which have reached the Supreme Court, arguing that affirmative action policies discriminated against them because they were passed over for college admittance in favor of less academically qualified candidates. The issue remains relevant. In 2016, the Supreme Court narrowly upheld the affirmative action program at the University of Texas. **ASK:** How have arguments for and against affirmative action programs changed from 1968 to today? *(Possible response: In 1968, arguments for affirmative action aimed to create diversity in predominantly white schools and opportunities for previously segregated students. In recent years, some white students feel that affirmative action policies have taken opportunities away from them, a form of reverse discrimination.)*

Active Options

On Your Feet: Hold a Panel Discussion Ask volunteers to serve as moderator and panelists in a panel discussion of why and how some civil rights leaders turned away from the ideas of Dr. King. Direct students in the audience to prepare and submit questions to the moderator before the discussion. Panelists should cite multiple examples from the text in their answers and discussion of audience questions.

NG Learning Framework: Role-Play a Civil Rights Leader

ATTITUDE Responsibility

SKILLS Communication, Problem-Solving

Have students engage in a role-playing activity to compare and contrast the viewpoints of civil rights figures. Arrange students in small groups. Instruct each group to research a different civil rights leader or activist, such as Dr. King, Malcolm X, Rosa Parks, Huey Newton, and John Lewis, focusing on what that person believed was the best way to achieve equality. Then have the entire class sit in a circle. Ask questions such as the following: Do protests work? Is violence ever acceptable? What conditions are necessary for different races to live together? Allow volunteers from each group to role-play the group's assigned individual. They should answer the questions, and respond to the viewpoints of other civil rights leaders role-played by volunteers from other groups.

DIFFERENTIATE

English Language Learners

Compose a Sentence Pair students at the **Emerging** level with students at the **Bridging** level. Tell them to work together to compose a sentence using selected terms, such as *self-defense*, *police state*, *harassment*, *brutality*, and *unconstitutional*. Invite pairs to share their sentences and discuss different ways they used each term.

Pre-AP

Write a Comparison-Contrast Essay Instruct students to research and write notes about the ideology and tactics of the Black Panther organization and the Black Lives Matter movement. Encourage them to use a Venn diagram to keep track of the similarities and differences. Tell students to use their research to write a comparison-contrast essay to share with the class.

See the Chapter Planner for more strategies for differentiation.

HISTORICAL THINKING

ANSWERS

1. Some younger African Americans believed that Dr. King's techniques weren't working fast enough, so they decided to strengthen their own communities rather than demand integration. Others felt they had the right to arm and defend themselves.

2. In the South, segregation was openly practiced. In the North and West, there were no laws separating the races, but discriminatory practices, such as banks refusing home loans to African Americans who wanted to buy outside their neighborhoods, achieved the same result.

3. Court decisions upheld affirmative action policies with the goal to improve educational and employment opportunities, and the courts allowed interracial marriage.

2.3 The Great Society

Teddy Roosevelt introduced the Square Deal in 1902. Franklin Roosevelt proposed the New Deal in 1933, and Harry Truman promoted the Fair Deal in 1949. It was only a matter of time before the United States required another government program to bring about sweeping change.

MAIN IDEA In 1964, President Lyndon Johnson unveiled a new plan to address the nation's problems with poverty, health care, and education.

ATTACKING POVERTY

On May 22, 1964, President Johnson announced his sweeping new plan to improve the lives of the American people. He called it the **Great Society**, and its aim was to tackle the country's social problems: racial inequality, poverty, and lack of health care and educational opportunities.

Between the time of his announcement and the 1964 presidential election, Johnson built the foundation of his Great Society by working with Congress to pass the Civil Rights Act of 1964 and the **Economic Opportunity Act of 1964**, which established organizations that provided jobs for people living at or near the poverty level. These groups helped young people from impoverished neighborhoods gain work experience. He also created the **Office of Economic Opportunity**, a government agency that would oversee Great Society programs.

Johnson won the 1964 election in a landslide. During his State of the Union address on January 4, 1965, Johnson declared the central component of the Great Society would be the **War on Poverty**, which he had introduced in 1964.

During the 1960s, about 20 percent of the nation was living in poverty, and the rates among African Americans, Native

Americans, and Hispanics were two to three times higher than those of whites. But poverty affected white families as well, especially in rural areas of the country, such as Appalachia. **Appalachia** is a region of the Appalachian Mountains, stretching from southern New York State to northern Alabama, and it included remote and economically disadvantaged areas. Johnson's plan was to mobilize entire communities to his cause. Organizations such as the **Neighborhood Youth Corps** and the **Volunteers in Service to America (VISTA)** employed citizens in jobs that benefited their communities.

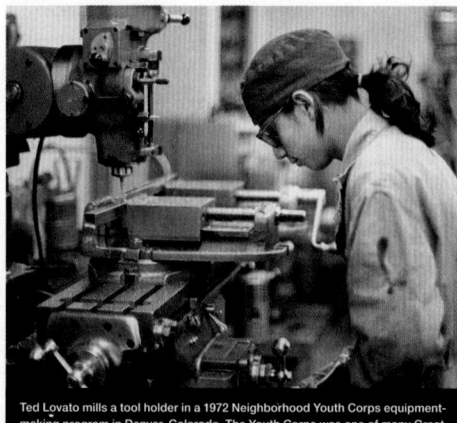

Ted Lovato mills a tool holder in a 1972 Neighborhood Youth Corps equipment-making program in Denver, Colorado. The Youth Corps was one of many Great Society programs funded by federal, state, and local governments.

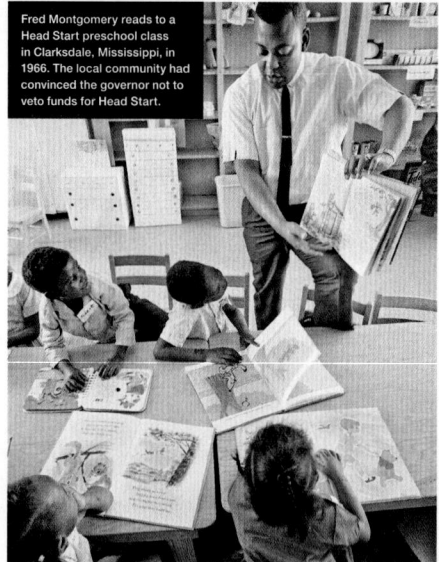

Fred Montgomery reads to a Head Start preschool class in Clarksdale, Mississippi, in 1966. The local community had convinced the governor not to veto funds for Head Start.

HUNDREDS OF NEW LAWS

Over the course of his presidency, Johnson's skill as a legislator helped him encourage Congress to pass more than 200 new Great Society bills. In addition to his efforts to fight poverty, Johnson sought to improve the nation's health care.

In 1965, Congress passed Social Security amendments that created Medicare and Medicaid. **Medicare** gave much needed government-subsidized health insurance to older Americans. More than 33 percent of Americans 65 years of age or older lived in poverty in 1960—double the percentage for the rest of the population. And of those seniors, almost half could not afford health insurance. Medicare gave them affordable access to medical care. The other program, **Medicaid**, provided health care for the poor.

Johnson also addressed the low rates of literacy, or the ability to read, and the low rates of high school graduations. In 1965, Congress passed

the **Elementary and Secondary Education Act**. The law funded elementary schools and high schools in low-income areas to improve education and lower school dropout rates. One program, **Head Start**, prepared preschool-aged children for elementary school by providing learning activities, balanced meals, medical and dental care, and supervised field trips.

HISTORICAL THINKING

1. **READING CHECK** How would you summarize President Johnson's Great Society agenda?

2. **MAKE INFERENCES** What do you think President Johnson meant when he said Americans should build a society in which "progress is the servant of our needs"?

3. **SUMMARIZE** How did the Great Society programs seek to reduce poverty in the United States?

PLAN

Objective

Explain how Great Society programs attempted to remedy U.S. social problems in the 1960s.

Critical Thinking Skills for Lesson 2.3

- Identify Main Ideas and Details
- Monitor Comprehension
- Make Inferences
- Summarize
- Make Connections
- Compare and Contrast

Essential Question for Chapter 27

How did American identity change in the 1960s? Continuing the work of earlier progressive presidents, Lyndon B. Johnson passed a sweeping set of government programs. Lesson 2.3 analyzes how these programs tackled the social problems of the 1960s.

Background for the Teacher

Lyndon Johnson's Republican opponent in the 1964 election was Barry Goldwater, a conservative Arizonan who opposed government involvement in racial integration. Goldwater's nomination marked a Republican shift toward the extreme right, and his views alienated most Americans. As a result, Johnson won the election by one of the largest margins in history. Not surprisingly, Goldwater performed well in the South, a region that had traditionally voted Democrat but had a long history of racial resentment. Goldwater's performance there inspired later Republican candidates to target disaffected white voters. Beginning with Richard Nixon's 1968 "Southern strategy," subtle support for backlash against equal rights was instrumental in the White House campaigns of Republicans for the next three decades.

Financial Literacy

To extend their knowledge and understanding about the concepts in this lesson, refer students to the Financial Literacy handbook.

INTRODUCE & ENGAGE

Thumbs Up, Thumbs Down

List some of the Great Society programs mentioned in the lesson. As you name each one, have students give a thumbs-up if they've heard of the program or a thumbs-down if not. Ask students who put their thumbs up for a program to share any details they know about it. Tell students that in this lesson they will learn more about how the Great Society attempted to combat America's social problems.

TEACH

Guided Discussion

1. **Make Connections** How did the election of 1964 affect Johnson's ability to implement the Great Society? (*Johnson won by a large margin, which indicated he had the country's backing to pursue an ambitious agenda. In addition, because of his popularity, Congress would likely cooperate.*)

2. **Make Inferences** How did the disadvantages of poverty affect the educational achievement of low-income students? (*Possible response: Many low-income students lacked adequate health and dental care, so health problems may have made it more difficult for them to learn. In addition, many younger students did not have access to preschool and other activities that stimulate early development and contribute to later success in school.*)

Compare and Contrast

Direct students' attention to the introduction, which indicates that Johnson's Great Society can be viewed as an extension of the government programs started by Theodore Roosevelt, Franklin Roosevelt, and Harry Truman. Explain that although these presidents had ambitious goals, they were not able to accomplish all they desired. **ASK:** How were the goals and outcomes of the Great Society similar to and different from those of the Square Deal, New Deal, and Fair Deal? (*Possible response: All four programs had the same philosophy and goal: to use federal resources to directly improve people's lives. However, the Great Society included more efforts to address racial issues than previous programs. In addition, Medicare and Medicaid established government health insurance, something Franklin D. Roosevelt and Harry Truman had attempted but were unable to do.*)

Active Options

On Your Feet: Jigsaw Organize students into four "expert" groups and assign each group one of the following topics: racial inequality, poverty, health care, education. Instruct each group to identify a few bills or Great Society programs that addressed their assigned topic. Then tell students to choose one of the programs and research whether it is still in use today and, if so, whether and how it has evolved. Then have members of each expert group count off using the letters A, B, C, and D. Place students into four new groups, A, B, C, and D, so that each new group has at least one member from each expert group. Have students in each new group take turns sharing what they learned in their expert groups.

NG Learning Framework: Create an Infographic

SKILL Communication

KNOWLEDGE Our Human Story

Direct groups of students to create an infographic that shows how the Great Society tackled America's problems. Tell students to organize their infographic around the four social problems that the Great Society addressed: racial inequality, poverty, health care, and education. Instruct students to use their research from the Jigsaw activity and to conduct additional research, if necessary. Advise them to include images, graphs, charts, and text to help convey the information. Students might want to create digital infographics that include video or audio clips. Have groups present and explain their completed infographics to the class.

DIFFERENTIATE

Striving Readers

Connect Details to a Main Idea Instruct students to work in pairs to complete a Main Idea and Details List for each subsection of the lesson. Guide students to identify the main idea and then the details (facts, dates, events, reasons) that support it. Have pairs share and discuss their completed list with other pairs and revise their list if necessary.

Main Idea:
Detail:
Detail:
Detail:

Gifted & Talented

Perform an Excerpt from a Speech Direct students to locate online and read the entire text of President Johnson's Great Society speech. Then have them choose an excerpt from the speech that they think applies to present-day society. Invite students to perform their excerpt in front of the class and explain why the excerpt is still relevant today.

See the Chapter Planner for more strategies for differentiation.

HISTORICAL THINKING

ANSWERS

1. The Great Society attempted to end racial discrimination, combat poverty, improve access to education, and expand health care coverage for the poor and elderly.

2. Johnson meant that progress should not be feared. Rather, it should be used to better society and move the country forward.

3. The Great Society attempted to combat a wide variety of problems that contributed to poverty, such as unemployment, inadequate education, and lack of access to health care.

Latinos Organize

Momentum and motivation often build over time, especially when they are leading to successes. Latinos had been working to combat discrimination since the 1920s, and they continued their fight in the decades that followed.

MAIN IDEA Latinos and Hispanics in the United States remained committed to their quest for civil rights and against discrimination and poor wages during the 1960s.

MEXICAN AMERICANS CONTINUE THEIR FIGHT

As early as the 1920s, Mexican Americans had organized to address discrimination. Formed in 1929, the **League of United Latin American Citizens (LULAC)** was one such organization. In 1945, LULAC sued a segregated California school system for discriminating against Latino children. LULAC also protested the 1948 **Longoria incident**, in which Felix Longoria, a Mexican American soldier killed in action during World War II, was denied a wake by a funeral home owner because Longoria was a Latino. In 1947, postwar events like these helped launch another Mexican American organization called the **Unity League**, which campaigned against discrimination in housing, education, and employment.

In the 1950s, most Mexicans and Mexican Americans, or **Chicanos**, in the United States lived in California and states in the Southwest. Many were employed as migrant workers on huge farms owned by large corporations, and they labored for low pay and no benefits. An entire family might make 20 cents for 2 hours of backbreaking work. The makeshift housing for migrant workers was crowded and often lacked electricity or running water. The companies that owned the farms prohibited unions, so the workers had no collective voice to demand higher wages and better conditions.

In 1962, two political activists, **César Chávez** and **Dolores Huerta**, formed the National Farm Workers Association, which later became a full-fledged union, the **United Farm Workers (UFW)**. Influenced by the nonviolent methods of

Dr. Martin Luther King, Jr., Chávez and Huerta led peaceful strikes, marches, boycotts, and **hunger strikes**, in which they protested by refusing to eat, in order to win rights and better wages for migrant workers. In 1965, they joined forces with Filipino American grape laborers to start a boycott to protest conditions in California's Central Valley vineyards. The effort was particularly effective.

I Am Somebody

Together We Are Strong

CRITICAL VIEWING The farmworker portrayed in this poster represents one of the many migrant workers who joined Huerta and Chávez in laying the groundwork for the current union, United Farm Workers of America. What do you think is the main message of this poster, and why?

UFW workers crisscrossed the country urging consumers not to buy California grapes. Soon millions of Americans supported the boycott. The boycott ended in 1970, when public pressure forced California's large farming companies to agree to higher wages for migrant workers and to acknowledge that farmworkers had the right to unionize.

CHALLENGES FOR OTHER HISPANIC GROUPS

Hispanic groups from the Caribbean also faced challenges in the United States. Inhabitants of Puerto Rico, for example, sometimes experienced severe poverty. Puerto Ricans had become American citizens beginning in 1917 after being residents of a U.S. territory for almost 20 years. The lure of jobs and the open immigration policies between Puerto Rico and the United States encouraged thousands to migrate to the mainland.

By the mid-1960s, about 1 million Puerto Ricans lived on the mainland. Most lived in big cities, such as New York, Philadelphia, and Chicago. Even in their new homes, many Puerto Ricans still dealt with poverty, unemployment, unsafe neighborhoods, and discrimination. They formed political groups to fight for their civil rights. They pressed for equal access to jobs and education as well as greater federal economic aid to Puerto Rico.

As you have read, the communist takeover of Cuba in 1959 caused many Cubans to immigrate to the United States. About 500,000 of them flew to the United States before Castro ceased all flights there in 1973. Most Cuban immigrants in the United States settled in Florida, mainly in Miami. Many started successful businesses, though some still faced discrimination. Cuban Americans are known for their political activism, fighting for political change both in the United States and in Cuba.

In 1973, Dolores Huerta and César Chávez shared the podium at the founding convention of the United Farm Workers union. By this time, the UFW had 50,000 dues-paying members, for whom it negotiated union contracts with grape growers, established a hiring hall, and furnished a health clinic.

Latino or Hispanic?

Though the two words are often used interchangeably, *Latino* and *Hispanic* have different meanings. *Hispanic* describes people who are from Spanish-speaking cultures or have Spanish-speaking ancestry. *Latino* (or *Latina*) describes someone exclusively of Latin American origin, including Brazilians, who speak Portuguese, not Spanish. So, while Brazilians are considered Latinos, it would be inaccurate to refer to them as Hispanics. And while people from Spain are Hispanics, they are not Latinos.

HISTORICAL THINKING

1. **READING CHECK** Why are César Chávez and Dolores Huerta significant figures in American history?

2. **IDENTIFY MAIN IDEAS AND DETAILS** Why did so many Cubans immigrate to the United States starting in 1959?

3. **ANALYZE CAUSE AND EFFECT** How might the Latino and African-American civil rights movements have influenced each other?

PLAN

Objective

Describe how and why Latinos began to organize and demand civil rights.

Critical Thinking Skills for Lesson 3.1

• Identify Main Ideas and Details

• Monitor Comprehension

• Analyze Cause and Effect

• Make Inferences

• Draw Conclusions

Essential Question for Chapter 27

How did American identity change in the 1960s? Throughout the 1960s, nonwhite groups and their supporters pressed for all Americans to have access to the American dream and for a more inclusive American identity. Lesson 3.1 explains how Latinos opposed discrimination and organized for equality.

Background for the Teacher

As leader of the United Farm Workers, César Chávez was willing to risk his own life and health to bring better lives to his members without using violence. The embodiment of this philosophy was the hunger strike, a technique he employed multiple times. In 1968, Chávez subsisted on only water for 25 days, and in 1972 he repeated the strike, this time for 24 days. In 1988, his most famous hunger strike—known as the Fast for Life—lasted 36 days. Chávez was 61 years old, and during the ordeal he lost 33 pounds and suffered from a fever, vomiting, and cramps. At the end of his fast, Chávez lowered himself into a rocking chair and listened to a Catholic Mass, during which he ate a piece of bread—his first food in more than a month. Later, others vowed to continue the fast, including notable Americans Jesse Jackson, Edward James Olmos, Danny Glover, and Whoopi Goldberg.

INTRODUCE & ENGAGE

Adjust for Inflation

Write the following on the board: 20 cents for 2 hours of work. Explain that this was the pay rate that supported an entire family of Latino farm laborers in the 1950s. Guide students to use CPI inflation figures to convert the number to today's currency. *(approximately $1 per hour)* Lead a discussion about how a family with two wage earners might support itself based on such a wage. Then inform students that in this lesson they will examine how farmworkers and other groups pressed for better wages and equal rights.

TEACH

Guided Discussion

1. **Make Inferences** Why do you think United Farm Workers representatives had to travel across the nation in the 1960s to make Americans aware of conditions affecting Mexican and Chicano farmworkers? *(Possible response: The farmworkers were clustered in California and the Southwest, invisible to people in other parts of the country. The workers' conditions might not have been easily observed because the work took place on large-scale farms isolated from the general population.)*

2. **Draw Conclusions** Why do you think people from Puerto Rico and Cuba moved mostly to large cities on the East Coast? *(Possible response: New York, Boston, and especially Miami are coastal cities close to Cuba and Puerto Rico. Those cities likely had established ethnic communities to welcome newcomers and help them adjust to daily life there, find work, and navigate city services such as public transportation.)*

More Information

Dolores Huerta, Activist After witnessing many children of farmworkers going hungry during her career as a teacher, Dolores Huerta became an activist for the rights of farmworkers and Hispanics. Often disparagingly referred to as César Chávez's sidekick, Huerta was his equal in their efforts and was the principal force behind the national grape boycotts of the 1960s. It was Huerta's slogan "Sí se puede" that became the rallying cry of the movement. Barack Obama adopted the English translation, "Yes we can," as the campaign slogan for his run for the presidency in 2008. In 1975, Huerta was largely responsible for legislation that allowed farmworkers to unionize and, thus, bargain for better wages and conditions. Huerta's activism continued in the following decades, ultimately focusing on women's issues and the election of Hispanics to political office in the 2000s. Having received many honors for her contributions over the years, including the Eleanor Roosevelt Human Rights Award in 1998, Huerta received the nation's highest civilian award in 2012—the Presidential Medal of Freedom.

Active Options

On Your Feet: Design a Poster Encourage students to use knowledge from the lesson to create a poster promoting Latino civil rights. They should first examine the poster in this lesson and then plan and make rough sketches of their own posters. Remind students to make sure the poster has a clear message and goal. Hang completed posters around the classroom and invite students to get up and examine and discuss their classmates' work.

NG Learning Framework: Create a Local Newsletter

ATTITUDE Responsibility

SKILL Communication

Tell students to select one of the groups discussed in this lesson, such as Mexican American farmworkers, Puerto Ricans living in New York City, or Cubans in Miami, and to imagine they are members of that community during the 1950s and 1960s. Arrange students in small groups and instruct them to create a newsletter for the community in which they imagine themselves. Students should use information from the chapter and additional sources to write news stories, editorials, advertisements, and other content from the group's perspective that would be relevant to the community at that time. Have groups publish their newsletters in print or electronically and share them with the class.

DIFFERENTIATE

Striving Readers

Make a List of Facts After students read the lesson, post the following topic on the board: The Latino Struggle for Equality. Ask students to copy the posted heading onto a piece of paper and list five facts about the topic that they learned in the lesson. Then arrange students in pairs and tell them to verify the facts using the text and combine their facts into one list. Invite pairs to exchange and discuss their lists.

Gifted & Talented

Create an Annotated Chart Have students create an annotated chart to document the main events in the struggle for Latino civil rights. Ask them to include key information such as dates, locations, and individuals. Encourage students to use the lesson as well as find newspaper headlines, photographs, or political cartoons to illustrate each event. Invite students to display their completed charts in the classroom.

See the Chapter Planner for more strategies for differentiation.

HISTORICAL THINKING

ANSWERS

1. Huerta and Chávez were civil rights activists who formed the United Farm Workers union to negotiate fair pay and benefits for migrant farmers in the United States.

2. Many Cubans immigrated to the United States to escape Fidel Castro's communist government.

3. Both groups likely borrowed tactics from each other, including organizing political groups, using legal measures, engaging in nonviolent, high-profile protests, and continually pressing for rights.

CRITICAL VIEWING The illustrated farmworker points to "UFW" with one hand and extends the other hand holding a piece of fruit, conveying the message that the efforts of UFW members bring food to the country.

Preserving Objects
Left Behind by Migrants

"Migrants are some of the most optimistic, resilient, inspirational people I've ever met." —Jason De León

Why pick up trash in the desert? Anthropologist Jason De León searches parched lands along the U.S.-Mexico border for things people have thrown away. But the tattered backpacks, old shoes, and other dropped items aren't trash. They're traces of human lives. Using science and storytelling, De León is shining a spotlight on Mexican migrants and their struggles and giving them a voice.

∧
De León collaborated with artist Amanda Krugliak on *State of Exception*, a wall of discarded backpacks left by Mexican migrants trying to cross into the United States through the Sonoran Desert.

MAIN IDEA Anthropologist Jason De León studies and preserves the objects left behind by people crossing the U.S.-Mexico border.

ANTHROPOLOGY AND IMMIGRATION

Some anthropologists study cultures in remote locations or in the distant past. Jason De León, a National Geographic Explorer and professor of anthropology at the University of Michigan, focuses on people. He studies the lives of undocumented migrants crossing the border from Mexico into the United States—people at the center of a major debate today.

De León's interest in the topic of immigration goes back to his childhood. Growing up in the United States near the Mexican border, he could watch migrants swimming across the Rio Grande from Mexico. De León's own grandparents were born in Mexico, and his mother came from the Philippines. "Being raised on the border in a bicultural household with a long immigration history makes me very attuned to issues of cultural identity and discrimination," he says.

CROSSING THE BORDER

To learn more about Mexican migrants, De León founded the Undocumented Migration Project (UMP). The UMP team works toward a deeper understanding of immigration by studying the lives of those who cross the border. In the desert, the team gathers artifacts. "We inventory survival-based items, like water bottles, food wrappers, and first-aid supplies, as well as very personal belongings, such as letters, baby photos, Bibles, and rosaries," De León explains.

The team also conducts personal interviews with undocumented migrants and the people whose lives they affect, such as law enforcement officers, human traffickers who smuggle migrants into the country, and U.S. citizens living near the border. Together, the objects and the stories help De León and the UMP team create a picture of the complex migrant experience.

One of De León's goals is to challenge the stereotypes tied to immigrants from Latin America. He believes everyone should have the opportunity to view undocumented migrants as individuals, each with his or her own story. De León also

Jason De León, shown here in front of a section of the U.S.-Mexico border wall, is a 2017 MacArthur Fellow and "genius" grant recipient for his work with migrants.

feels it is important for Americans to understand immigration from multiple perspectives. In 2015, De León published the book *Land of Open Graves*, in which he illustrated the lives of migrants in vivid, often heartbreaking detail. Additionally, he helped create an exhibit called *State of Exception/Estado de excepción* (see photo, left) featuring some of the objects he and his team have found, along with photos and stories. The exhibit has been shown at universities throughout the country.

De León's work places today's undocumented migrants in the larger context of American history. He compares people's present-day trek from Mexico into the United States to the journey pioneers made on the Oregon Trail. Surely, as they pushed westward, they left cast-off objects behind on the trail. Considering how people have moved from location to location throughout history in search of a better life, De León poses an important question: "If you only had a backpack to carry, what would you bring with you?"

HISTORICAL THINKING

1. **READING CHECK** What does the Undocumented Migration Project do?

2. **FORM AND SUPPORT OPINIONS** Do you agree with De León that learning about undocumented migrants helps us understand American history as a whole? Explain.

PLAN

Objective
Learn how Jason De León preserves the stories of migrants who cross the U.S.-Mexico border.

Critical Thinking Skills for Lesson 3.2
- Identify Main Ideas and Details
- Monitor Comprehension
- Form and Support Opinions
- Make Connections
- Analyze Visuals

Essential Question for Chapter 27
How did American identity change in the 1960s? The stories of migrants coming to the United States from around the globe have continually shaped the collective image of Americans. Lesson 3.2 describes how National Geographic Explorer Jason De León reveals insights into the lives of undocumented migrants who cross the U.S.-Mexico border through the items they leave behind in the desert.

NATIONAL GEOGRAPHIC EXPLORER
Jason De León

Jason De León tells the stories of migrants who cross the border and those who die trying. With increased U.S. border security near border cities, migrants have been trying to enter the country through the deadly Sonoran Desert. Those who do not make it may succumb to heatstroke, dehydration, or sometimes attacks by robbers or the border patrol. Since many migrants travel without identification, De León and his team use forensics to try to identify the bodies and determine cause of death. In De León's book *The Land of Open Graves: Living and Dying on the Migrant Trail,* he focuses on these anonymous migrants, hoping to encourage a deeper examination of U.S. immigration policies.

History Notebook
Encourage students to complete the Explorer page for Chapter 27 in their History Notebooks as they read.

INTRODUCE & ENGAGE

Deduce from Details

Direct students' attention to the photograph of backpacks and the caption. Explain to students that they will be reading about Jason De León, who has spent years examining migrants' abandoned backpacks to learn about the people who left them behind. Ask them to imagine they have left their backpacks in a public place. Guide a discussion about the contents of their backpacks and what the contents might reveal about them as individuals. Or bring in a backpack and have the class discuss its contents.

TEACH

STEM

Guided Discussion

1. **Make Connections** How did Jason De León's early experiences affect his choice of career? *(Possible response: He grew up seeing migrants crossing the Rio Grande, his own grandparents came from Mexico, and his mother came from the Philippines. These experiences made him sympathetic to migrants, a feeling that probably led him to choose a career examining their lives.)*

2. **Analyze Visuals** What might the backpacks symbolize in De León's exhibit? *(Answers will vary. Possible responses: They symbolize the hopes of each person who tried to reach the United States; people who might have died in the desert or turned back; the recurring story of immigrants leaving everything behind to find a better life; the efforts of the United States to stop migrants from crossing the border.)*

More Information

Migrants and the Oregon Trail Jason De León is similar to another preserver of migrant history, Ezra Meeker, an Oregon Trail pioneer. Like De León, Meeker viewed a migration, in this case the Oregon Trail migration, in the broader context of U.S. history. Fearful that the historical importance of the trail was fading from the public mind, Meeker set off in 1906 in a covered wagon to retrace his original journey taken 54 years earlier. Along the way, he stopped to give lectures about the history of the trail and installed his homemade "Meeker Markers" at important pioneer landmarks, such as Fort Laramie in Wyoming. The fort became known as Camp Sacrifice because of all the supplies and items abandoned there, including 20,000 pounds of bacon left outside its walls by Gold Rush pioneers in 1849. Meeker completed several crossings of the trail by car, by train, and finally, at the age of 94, by airplane. Like De León's exhibits and books, Meeker's work helped preserve the stories of migrants as part of U.S. history.

Active Options

On Your Feet: Three-Step Interview Arrange students in pairs and ask them to interview each other to answer the following question: If you had to leave your home immediately and could carry only a backpack, what would you bring with you? After sufficient time, instruct students to reverse roles. Once finished, each student shares the answers given by the person he or she interviewed. Discuss as a class which items nearly everyone mentioned and which items were left out that might have been important.

NG Learning Framework: Plan a Hike

SKILL Problem-Solving

KNOWLEDGE Our Human Story

Organize students into small groups and tell them to imagine preparing for a three-day hike through the Sonoran Desert on the Mexican side of the U.S.-Mexico border. Encourage them to conduct online research to plan a hike and download maps of the desert and information about the terrain, climate, and hazards, such as poisonous snakes or plants. Students will need to solve such problems as the best time of year to make the hike, how many miles they might safely cover each day, what they should wear, how much food and water they should bring, what first aid supplies they should include, and so on. Instruct each group to present their plans to the class. Encourage students to discuss what conditions migrants crossing the Sonoran Desert in summer might face.

DIFFERENTIATE

Inclusion

Describe Details in Photographs Pair students who are visually impaired with students who are not. Ask the latter to describe the two photographs in detail, answering any questions their partner may have. If time permits, have pairs work together to read the lesson and answer the Historical Thinking questions.

Gifted & Talented

Create a Multimedia Presentation Instruct students to conduct research using print and online sources to learn more about the life and work of Jason De León. Have them find written, audio, video, and photographic materials and assemble their findings into a compelling multimedia presentation that provides insight into what motivates De León in his work. Invite students to share their presentations with the class and to answer questions from their classmates.

See the Chapter Planner for more strategies for differentiation.

HISTORICAL THINKING

ANSWERS

1. The Undocumented Migrant Project tries to uncover the stories of undocumented individuals who have crossed or tried to cross the U.S.-Mexico border. De León gathers their cast-off belongings and interviews the people to bring their stories to the public's attention.

2. Answers will vary. Students should clearly state their opinion and provide details to support their statements. Possible responses: Yes. These latest migrants to the United States are simply doing the same thing that every wave of migrants has done. They are leaving their old lives behind to build new, better lives in the United States. No. These migrants are entering the country illegally, and their stories will not help us understand U.S. history. Unlike legal migrants, they cannot become American citizens.

3.3 Native American Activism

Native Americans living on reservations in the United States in 1970 had to be tough. Many families lived in shacks with no running water or electricity. Outbreaks of disease, such as pneumonia and strep throat, were common in the communities. But there was hope to turn things around.

MAIN IDEA Native American activists fought to improve conditions for their people in the 1960s and 1970s.

The Occupation of Alcatraz Island
In 1969, young people were photographed as they explored the abandoned prison on Alcatraz Island in San Francisco Bay. They were part of a group of Native Americans who had organized an occupation of the island, where they hoped the government would let them establish a Native American education and cultural center. Although the government denied their request, the occupation grew. It lasted 18 months and drew support and extensive publicity for the Native American rights movement.

CHALLENGES FACING NATIVE AMERICANS

While other minority groups slowly gained rights in the mid-20th century, Native Americans remained one of the most impoverished minorities in the United States. In 1970, 40 percent of Native Americans lived in poverty, and their unemployment rate was 10 times higher than the national average.

Most reservations were recognized as independent governments within the United States, with their own court systems, school districts, and tax laws. But since the reservations depended on U.S. resources, many government policies still applied. This system did not allow tribal governments to fully control their own affairs.

The Indian Reorganization Act (IRA)—Roosevelt's New Deal policy enacted in 1934—gave Native Americans more power to govern themselves and their lands. But in 1953, President Eisenhower reversed IRA policies and promoted an "Indian Termination and Relocation Policy," also known as the **termination policy**.

In 1953, Congress also passed Public Law 280, which transferred federal and tribal oversight of civil and criminal justice to five state governments. The Indian Relocation Act of 1956 encouraged Native Americans to leave their reservations and sell off the land. This plan was presented to Native Americans as a way to improve their lives by becoming integrated into the larger American society and having better access to jobs. As a result, 109 tribes voted in favor of the policy.

In reality, the policy was a way for the government to persuade Native Americans to forfeit, or give up, federal recognition, aid, services, and protection, as well as their reservation land. Most tribes remained impoverished after the policy took effect. Many hundreds of thousands of people left the reservations and moved to cities through a federal relocation program that promised to help them find jobs and affordable housing. About 33 percent of them returned to their reservations, though, as the government's promises fell through.

In 1961, the **National Congress of American Indians (NCAI)** held a conference in Chicago. More than 60 tribes came together to write the **Declaration of Indian Purpose**. The document proposed how to preserve Native American cultures and demanded greater tribal sovereignty, or self-government. It also called for a greater tribal voice in federal Native American programs.

THE AMERICAN INDIAN MOVEMENT

Native American activism increased during the 1960s. In the spirit of the civil rights movement, tribes and nations pressed their demands with demonstrations and lawsuits. In 1968, a group of Ojibwe (oh-JIHB-way) in Minnesota, led by **Dennis Banks** and George Mitchell, founded the **American Indian Movement (AIM)**. The group's purpose was to help impoverished Native Americans in cities. Soon the focus expanded to include the return of tribal lands, the protection of legal rights, and the elimination of poverty on reservations.

AIM organized and participated in a number of protests. In 1973, AIM joined the armed takeover of **Wounded Knee**, South Dakota, on the site of a massacre of Native American women and children by the U.S. Army in 1890. The occupation was a protest against conditions on reservations and government policies toward Native Americans.

Several lawsuits filed in the 1970s attempted to take back Native American rights that had been promised by the federal government in past treaties. Tribes filed other lawsuits to regain (or be paid for) lands that had been taken from them. They also fought to keep guaranteed hunting and fishing rights on land they had been forced to give up as well as on their reservations.

HISTORICAL THINKING

1. **READING CHECK** How did the goals of the American Indian Movement change over time?

2. **IDENTIFY MAIN IDEAS AND DETAILS** What major issues did Native American organizations address during the 1960s, and what actions did they take?

3. **COMPARE AND CONTRAST** How did the termination policy enacted in the 1950s contrast with the Indian Reorganization Act of 1934?

Objective

Analyze how and why Native Americans organized in the 1960s.

Critical Thinking Skills for Lesson 3.3

- Identify Main Ideas and Details
- Monitor Comprehension
- Compare and Contrast
- Synthesize
- Evaluate

Essential Question for Chapter 27

How did American identity change in the 1960s? During the era of civil rights movements, Native Americans, the country's first Americans, were arguably the most marginalized minority in the country. Lesson 3.3 looks at the efforts of Native Americans to maintain their cultural identity, improve their conditions, and force the federal government to follow through on its promises.

Background for the Teacher

At 71 days, the Wounded Knee protest was the longest-lasting civil disorder in U.S. history. It began the evening of February 27, 1973, when 200 Oglala Lakota activists and members of the American Indian Movement (AIM) took over the small town in the Pine Ridge Reservation. They demanded the federal government live up to its treaties of the 19th and early 20th centuries. Within hours, law enforcement besieged the town. For weeks, U.S. Marshals, the FBI, and National Guard traded fire with the occupiers and eventually cut off their electricity, water, and food supplies. On day 50, an occupier was shot (and later died) trying to pick up food that a sympathetic pilot had dropped into the town. This incident helped spur negotiations to end the standoff, and on May 28, the occupiers officially surrendered. Today, conditions on the Pine Ridge Reservation remain harsh, as the region has been plagued with grinding poverty and unemployment.

Review Treatment of Native Americans

Ask students to recall what they have learned about how the federal government has treated Native Americans throughout U.S. history. List their recollections on the board, including the names of events or places, specific laws, and the names of tribes and famous leaders. **ASK:** Based on what you already know, what reasons might Native Americans have had for starting their own civil rights movement in the 1960s? *(Possible response: Native Americans had suffered poor treatment by the federal government, which had taken their lands and isolated them from American society.)* Inform students that in this lesson they will examine how and why Native Americans pressed for equality.

TEACH

Guided Discussion

1. **Synthesize** How would you characterize the historical relationship between the federal government and Native American tribes up to 1960? *(Possible response: Dating back to the colonial era, the relationship has been characterized by distrust, broken promises, and unfair treatment. President Eisenhower's termination policy continued this pattern. Like other minorities, Native Americans have had to fight to receive full benefits of citizenship—rights that are guaranteed under the U.S. Constitution.)*

2. **Compare and Contrast** How was the Native American civil rights movement similar to and different from the African-American civil rights movement? *(Possible response: Both movements used similar techniques, including organization, protests, and court cases. Native Americans, however, were protesting different conditions. African Americans living in the same cities as whites were segregated by neighborhoods and schools and discriminated against in employment. Native Americans were isolated from white populations within reservations and exploited by the federal government.)*

Evaluate

What were the possible benefits and drawbacks of the occupation of Alcatraz and the takeover of Wounded Knee? *(Possible response: Occupation brought overlooked Native American issues to the attention of the public. However, because these acts were illegal, protesters faced confrontation with law enforcement officers, possible jail time, and possible public backlash against Native American causes.)*

Active Options

On Your Feet: Draft Ideas for Just Compensation to Native Americans Arrange students in small groups. Provide each student with a copy of the Concluding Statement from the Declaration of Indian Purpose, found at Education Resources Information Center (ERIC), document ED030518. Tell students to read the Concluding Statement and work within their groups to draft ideas for how the federal government could offer just compensation to Native Americans based on what is stated in the document. Have groups share their ideas with the class.

NG Learning Framework: Research Federal Compensation to Native Americans

ATTITUDE Responsibility

SKILL Observation

Tell students to conduct online research to learn how and under what circumstances the federal government has paid compensation to Native American tribes from 1960 to the present. Ask them to explain what the federal government paid in money or land and why payment was made. Students' findings might include federal payouts of $940 million in 2015 for services performed by tribes and $492 million in 2016 in settlement of lawsuits claiming that the federal government had not honored trust agreements dating to the 1800s. Ask volunteers to present their findings to the class. Use the information to generate a discussion about the manner in which the federal government has honored agreements with Native American tribes in the 20th and 21st centuries. Encourage students to compare their findings with their ideas for just compensation from the On Your Feet activity.

English Language Learners

Sound Out Words Before reading, preview with students at **All Proficiencies** words they may have difficulty pronouncing, such as *access, forfeit, sovereignty, massacre,* and *guaranteed.* Say each word slowly, and have students repeat. Provide pronunciation pointers, such as /k/ followed by /s/ in *access,* and the silent *e* in *forfeit.* Tell students to make a card for each word, including a definition and pronunciation hints.

Pre-AP

Write a Cause-and-Effect Essay Instruct students to conduct research in order to discover why Native Americans are among the most impoverished people in the United States and then write an essay based on their findings. Encourage students to use a Cause-and-Effect Chart to keep track of information they gather. Remind them to use only unbiased sources, to cite their sources, and to quote or paraphrase to avoid plagiarism. Invite volunteers to share their essays with the class.

See the Chapter Planner for more strategies for differentiation.

HISTORICAL THINKING

ANSWERS

1. AIM was initially formed to aid impoverished Native Americans within cities. But the group's mission expanded to include the protection of tribal lands, the promotion of Native American culture, and the elimination of poverty on reservations.

2. The groups sought to end poverty among Native Americans, gain tribal self-government and self-sufficiency, regain tribal lands, preserve Native American culture, and reverse federal government policies they believed were unfair to Native Americans. They took actions such as forming groups, protesting, staging occupations, and filing lawsuits.

3. The Indian Reorganization Act of 1934 gave Native Americans more power to govern themselves. The termination policy aimed to push Native Americans into leaving reservations and integrating themselves into mainstream American society, rather than governing themselves on reservations.

The Women's Rights Movement

People have often been kept from pursuing a dream career just because it wasn't a job that a man or a woman was expected to do. Until recently in some states, women, especially married women, couldn't own property or take out a loan, simply because of their gender.

MAIN IDEA In the 1960s, American women fought to change attitudes and laws that denied them their full range of rights.

ORGANIZING FOR CHANGE

By the 1960s, women still made less money than men who were working the same job, and laws still limited women from selling property and signing certain contracts. Even though more women than ever were attending college and planning careers in the 1950s, American society presumed most women would abandon their ambitions once they married. They were expected to take on traditional roles as homemakers and stay-at-home mothers, roles many found to be unfulfilling. Increasingly, women began to speak out for equal rights.

In 1966, **Betty Friedan**, an author who wrote about the growing frustration of American women, and 48 other women and men founded the **National Organization for Women (NOW)** to fight for

women's rights. NOW focused mainly on job equality and eliminating the **wage gap**, or the difference in pay between women and men in similar jobs. Members pressured Congress to pass laws that would allow more women to buy and sell property. Other organizations soon formed to address the issues of minority women. Women and men who supported this movement were (and still are) called **feminists**.

In 1971, Friedan joined feminists **Gloria Steinem**, **Bella Abzug**, and **Shirley Chisholm** in founding the **National Women's Political Caucus**. The organization's main purpose has been to increase women's participation in the political process. Steinem became the founder of *Ms.*, a feminist magazine. Abzug and Chisholm served in Congress, representing districts in New York State.

At a news conference in 1971, members of the National Women's Political Caucus, Congresswoman Bella Abzug (standing), and from left, Gloria Steinem, Congresswoman Shirley Chisholm, and Betty Friedan, announced their goal to have women make up half of the delegates to the 1972 presidential conventions.

Shirley Chisholm
This modern, stylized oil portrait is a tribute to Shirley Chisholm. Painted by Kadir Nelson, it is exhibited in the U.S. Capitol Building, where Chisholm served seven terms in the House of Representatives. As a woman, as an African American, and as a feminist, Shirley Chisholm was a pioneer. In 1968, she became the first African-American woman elected to the U.S. Congress, where she worked on the House Committee on Veterans' Affairs and the powerful Rules Committee and was a founding member of the Congressional Black Caucus. In 1972, Chisholm became the first African-American politician from a major party to run for president. After her political career, she taught at Mount Holyoke College. When she died in 2005 at the age of 80, a local NAACP official said, "She was our Moses that opened the Red Sea for us."

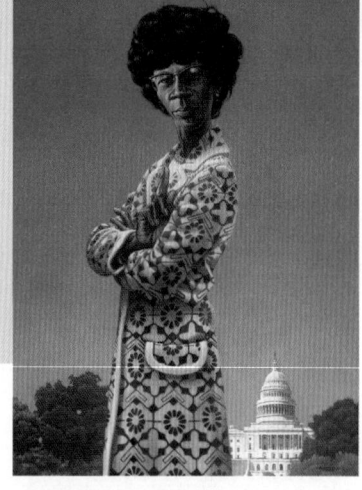

BATTLES FOR WOMEN'S RIGHTS

Feminists promoted the **Equal Rights Amendment (ERA)**, which demanded that equal treatment under the law, regardless of gender, be written into the U.S. Constitution. The amendment was originally proposed in 1923, only three years after American women won the right to vote, but it had been stalled for decades. In the late 1960s, feminists brought it back to Congress.

After the Senate passed the bill in 1972, the amendment needed 38 states to ratify it. Within a year, 30 states had done so. But opposition arose, led by antifeminist **Phyllis Schlafly**, who believed the ERA would overturn protections women already had. Male-dominated state legislatures began voting against the bill. In the end, the ERA missed ratification by only three states.

Knowing that most Americans supported the amendment, feminists continued their battle. They fought for a woman's right to serve in the military, and they set up shelters for women experiencing abuse at home. They won the passage of an education law in 1972 that established **Title IX**, which prohibited **gender bias**, or the preference of one gender over the other, in federally funded schools. Thanks to Title IX, public schools began promoting female sports teams in addition to male athletics. Women and girls became eligible for academic and athletic scholarships that had once only been available to men. NOW and other

organizations successfully lobbied Congress to get legislation passed and changed American attitudes toward women's rights.

In 1973, feminists won another battle for women's rights. In the landmark Supreme Court case *Roe* v. *Wade*, the court ruled that women have the right to choose to end a pregnancy—a ruling that remains controversial today. This decision supported a woman's right to make personal choices in her life, including to choose when and if to have children.

HISTORICAL THINKING

1. **READING CHECK** What change to the U.S. Constitution did the ERA propose?

2. **COMPARE AND CONTRAST** In what ways did the high hopes that educated women had in the early 1960s contrast with the expectations American society had for women?

3. **FORM AND SUPPORT OPINIONS** Beginning in the late 1960s, feminists brought about a number of changes in women's rights. Which change discussed in this lesson do you think is most important today, and why?

PLAN

Objective

Describe obstacles that women have attempted to overcome to achieve equality.

Critical Thinking Skills for Lesson 3.4

• Identify Main Ideas and Details

• Monitor Comprehension

• Compare and Contrast

• Form and Support Opinions

• Draw Conclusions

• Summarize

Essential Question for Chapter 27

How did American identity change in the 1960s? American women had a history of being treated as second-class citizens. In the 1960s, they demanded equality according to the law. Lesson 3.4 discusses the mobilization of women and their attempt to reshape the norms of American society.

Background for the Teacher

Betty Friedan is credited with reigniting the women's rights movement with the publication of her 1963 groundbreaking book *The Feminine Mystique*. While working for *Good Housekeeping* magazine, Friedan wrote an article about a malady plaguing suburban women. This "problem that has no name" was characterized by depression and a sense of guilt, because many women, Friedan asserted, secretly felt unhappy living what appeared to be perfect middle-class lives. Friedan expanded on this idea in her book, which argued that society had convinced women that their role was to be subservient to their husbands, creating a generation of housewives who were simultaneously frustrated at being denied their true ambitions and so bored that they were ineffective in their domestic roles. Friedan urged women to demand equality at home and in the workplace. *The Feminine Mystique* became a massive bestseller and led to an explosion of feminist activism.

Consider Social Barriers

Remind students that previous lessons have focused on the attempts by African Americans, Latinos, and Native Americans to expand their civil rights. Then inform students that this lesson will look at women's efforts to achieve equality. **ASK:** What social barriers of the 1960s do you think might have been denying women their full rights? *(Possible responses: inequality in pay; limited employment opportunities; the idea that women should stay in the home)* List responses on the board to revisit and discuss at the conclusion of the lesson.

TEACH

Guided Discussion

1. **Draw Conclusions** Why do you think NOW focused its main efforts on job equality for women and eliminating the wage gap? *(Possible response: While NOW was concerned about women having the right to break out of the traditional roles of wife, mother, and homemaker, it was a social issue that was unlikely to be made into law. A law protecting equal pay, however, would have been straightforward and enforceable. Examining employees' job descriptions and pay rates would have revealed wage gaps between men and women, and adjustments would likely have been necessary. Eliminating the wage gap would have immediately increased most women's wages and helped improve their lives.)*

2. **Summarize** How did Title IX change education? *(Possible response: The law brought greater diversity and equality to public schools, because young women were now eligible to have the same academic and athletic opportunities as young men.)*

More Information

Shirley Chisholm Call students' attention to the painting of Shirley Chisholm. Point out that the artist, Kadir Nelson, didn't depict Chisholm realistically or photographically. Instead he created a bold and provocative painting to try to convey her essence and legacy. Chisholm was known as "Fighting Shirley," and she is quoted as saying she had "no intention of just sitting quietly and observing." These traits are echoed in the brash brocade coat, large horn-rim glasses, and confident posture that the artist depicted, as well as in the painting's perspective, which shows Chisholm towering over the U.S. Capitol. **ASK:** How can paintings like this one tell us more about the subject than a photograph might? *(Possible response: Artists are able to accentuate certain characteristics of their subjects to make a point about them. For example, by showing Shirley Chisholm as larger than the Capitol Building, the artist emphasizes her historical importance as a woman in Congress.)*

Active Options

Active History: Analyze the Wage Gap Extend the lesson by using either the PDF or Whiteboard version of the activity. These activities take a deeper look at a topic from, or related to, the lesson. Explore the activities as a class, turn them into group assignments, or even assign them individually.

NG Learning Framework: Present an Argument

ATTITUDE Responsibility

KNOWLEDGE Our Human Story

Inform students that many of the laws and court decisions discussed in this lesson remain controversial. Divide the class into six groups and assign each group one of the three following topics so that two groups are covering each topic: the Equal Rights Amendment, Title IX, and the Supreme Court's ruling in *Roe* v. *Wade*. Direct one group to research arguments for the topic, and the other group to research arguments against it. Have all groups present their findings. Finally, engage the class in a discussion to examine the similarities and differences among the arguments and to evaluate which arguments they found most convincing.

DIFFERENTIATE

Striving Readers

Create a Word Square Direct students to write the word *controversial* in the center oval of a Word Square. Have them consult a dictionary and write the definition and characteristics in the upper quadrants. Then tell them to review the lesson text to find examples and non-examples and write them in the lower quadrants. You may then wish to lead a class discussion on the complexities of the word, including aspects of the women's rights movement that some argued against.

Gifted & Talented

Create a Podcast Tell students to conduct online research about one of the feminists mentioned in the lesson and then write a script for a podcast. Encourage them to establish a clear point of view for the content so that the podcast is informative and entertaining. After students write and rehearse their podcast, have them record it on a phone or other device and then upload it to an approved school website for access and playback.

See the Chapter Planner for more strategies for differentiation.

HISTORICAL THINKING

ANSWERS

1. The ERA would have added a law specifically requiring equal treatment for all, regardless of gender.

2. Many educated women wanted to have a meaningful career and earn as much money as men for the same work. However, society expected women to get married, stay home, and raise children.

3. Answers will vary. Possible responses: Title IX has affected the lives of talented female athletes who might not have been able to attend college without a scholarship, such as those that were available to talented male athletes. The *Roe* v. *Wade* ruling gave women the right to make the decision to end a pregnancy, which can impact all aspects of a woman's life, including employment, choice of housing, and ability to relocate.

U.S. Involvement in Vietnam

In the summer of 1964, American news outlets reported that U.S. ships had been fired on off the coast of North Vietnam. At the time, most Americans were unaware of how much this event on the other side of the world would affect the United States and hundreds of thousands of lives.

MAIN IDEA The United States' military involvement in Vietnam increased dramatically after a crisis in the Gulf of Tonkin.

Marines of the Seventh Regiment march past U.S. tanks while heading to their outpost in South Vietnam. They were among the first 3,500 U.S. forces to arrive in Vietnam in 1965. By the end of that year, 200,000 American service members were stationed there.

EARLY U.S. INVOLVEMENT

In the 1800s, Vietnam was a Southeast Asian country rich in fertile land. France had colonized Vietnam as part of French Indochina and profited from its rice and rubber plantations. Many Vietnamese yearned for their country to be independent again. In the 1930s, communist activist **Ho Chi Minh** began to organize an independence movement within Vietnam.

During World War II, Japanese forces occupied Vietnam. Ho Chi Minh and his followers assisted the Allied Powers in undermining the Japanese

Indochina, 1964

efforts. After the war, Ho Chi Minh thought the Western nations would reward their efforts by recognizing an independent Vietnam. Instead, fearing Ho Chi Minh would establish a communist government, the Allies backed French efforts to reclaim colonial control over Vietnam. This sparked a revolution for independence, led by Ho Chi Minh.

Even with U.S. backing, the French could not defeat the Vietnamese fighters. After losing a decisive battle to Ho's forces in 1954, France seemed ready to give up the colony. But by this time, the **domino theory** was driving U.S. policy in Asia. This was the belief that if one Asian country fell to communism, the rest would soon follow, like dominoes falling in line. China and North Korea had already fallen to communism. American officials were determined not to let Vietnam follow suit.

After Ho defeated the French, a peace agreement negotiated in Geneva, Switzerland, temporarily divided Vietnam in half at the 17th parallel. Called the **Geneva Accords**, the plan established that Ho and the communists would govern the northern part of the country while the U.S.-backed **Ngo Dinh Diem** (ungh-oh dihn zih-EHM), led the new Republic of Vietnam in the southern part. Corruption was common in Diem's government, and, though he claimed to embrace democracy, he was a dictatorial leader. Many South Vietnamese opposed him. Soon a civil war erupted in the south between Diem's government and rebel fighters the Americans called **Viet Cong**. The Viet Cong, or VC, received funding and support from Ho Chi Minh. Throughout the presidencies of Eisenhower

and Kennedy, the United States gradually increased its financial and military support for Diem, who was murdered just a few weeks before Kennedy's assassination.

THE GULF OF TONKIN INCIDENT

Like President Kennedy before him, President Johnson also believed in the domino theory. Rather than taking the chance that Vietnam might reunify under communist Ho Chi Minh, Johnson continued U.S. support for the unstable nation of South Vietnam and the string of new leaders who came into and fell out of power after Diem's death. This support included increasing the presence of the U.S. military in the region.

On August 4, 1964, reports emerged that North Vietnamese forces had attacked American ships in the Gulf of Tonkin. Although these reports later proved flawed and inaccurate, they spurred Congress into hasty action. The **Gulf of Tonkin Resolution** granted President Johnson the power

to respond to the assault with whatever force he deemed necessary. In other words, it gave Johnson the power to wage war. Johnson began a gradual military **escalation**, or increase, in South Vietnam. General **William Westmoreland** led U.S. forces in the region. As the need for troops rose, so did the number of young men drafted into the military.

HISTORICAL THINKING

1. **READING CHECK** Why did the United States refuse to support Ho Chi Minh's fight for an independent Vietnam?

2. **COMPARE AND CONTRAST** How did the newly formed countries of North Vietnam and South Vietnam differ politically?

3. **INTERPRET MAPS** What two countries were part of Indochina other than Vietnam?

PLAN

Objective

Explain how the United States became involved in Vietnam and describe the early years of the war.

Critical Thinking Skills for Lesson 4.1

- Identify Main Ideas and Details
- Monitor Comprehension
- Compare and Contrast
- Interpret Maps
- Form and Support Opinions
- Synthesize
- Make Connections

Essential Question for Chapter 27

How did American identity change in the 1960s? For many Americans, the Vietnam War became the defining foreign policy event of the second half of the 20th century. Lesson 4.1 discusses the beginnings of this conflict, which consumed the United States in an unending debate about an apparently unending war.

Background for the Teacher

More than half a century after its occurrence, the Gulf of Tonkin incident remains controversial. The night of August 4, 1964, the American destroyer U.S.S. *Maddox* and several other American ships moved out to sea off the coast of North Vietnam after receiving warning of a North Vietnamese attack. For the next three hours, amid storms and high waves, the *Maddox* and another ship reported spotting enemies in all directions (sometimes only briefly), torpedo wakes, and enemy lights. In response, the *Maddox* fired close to 400 shells and depth charges. Almost immediately, military leaders concluded the sightings likely were phantom attacks—the result of sonar errors. Regardless, amid the confusion and despite misgivings of officers on the scene, U.S. forces were ordered to launch retaliatory strikes for the alleged North Vietnamese attacks. The Gulf of Tonkin Resolution was passed three days later.

INTRODUCE & ENGAGE

K-W-L Chart

Provide each student with a K-W-L Chart. Have students add what they know about the Vietnam War. Then ask them to write questions that they would like to answer as they study the topic. Because this topic covers five lessons, allow time at the end of each lesson for students to add what they have learned and any new questions they have.

K What Do I Know?	W What Do I Want To Learn?	L What Did I Learn?

TEACH

Guided Discussion

1. **Form and Support Opinions** Was the domino theory an accurate way to understand political events in Asia? *(Answers will vary. Possible responses: Yes. China and North Korea had already become communist, apparently proving the theory. No. The domino theory viewed every country in Asia as essentially the same, ignoring the specific conditions that made nations more or less likely to become communist.)*

2. **Synthesize** What options did Lyndon Johnson have other than supporting Ngo Dinh Diem in Vietnam? *(Possible response: Johnson could have negotiated with Ho Chi Minh, withdrawn from the country completely, or attempted to help rebuild South Vietnam, as the United States had done in Western Europe.)*

Make Connections

Help students recall details of the outbreak of the Korean War. **ASK:** How were the events leading up to the Vietnam War similar to events in Korea? *(Both countries were occupied during World War II and later divided. In both cases, one half became communist and the other was backed by U.S. forces. In each instance, a civil war broke out, which eventually drew in the United States. Finally, in both conflicts, Congress never voted to approve the war. With the Korean War, authorization came through the United Nations, and with Vietnam, total military involvement came about via the Gulf of Tonkin Resolution.)*

Active Options

On Your Feet: Create a Time Line Have students work in small groups to create a time line of the events that led the United States to send forces to Vietnam. When groups have completed their time lines, call on volunteers to explain how each event led to the eventual military involvement of the United States in the Vietnam War.

NG Learning Framework: Design a Social Media Profile

SKILL Communication

KNOWLEDGE Our Human Story

Instruct students to create a social media profile for Ho Chi Minh, using information from the chapter and additional print and digital source materials. Encourage them to explore the leader's motivations, life, and relationship with the United States. Profiles could include elements common to social media, such as personal posts, a list of friends, favorites, and life milestones. Have students share their finished profiles with the class or post them on a class website or blog.

DIFFERENTIATE

English Language Learners ELD

Use Word Maps Bring students' attention to the words *flawed*, *inaccurate*, and *spurred* in the last paragraph. Pair students at the **Emerging** and **Expanding** levels with proficient English speakers and have each partner make a Word Map for each word. Direct partners to trade Word Maps, review them, and then write an original sentence using each word. Have students at **All Proficiencies** discuss how the Word Maps help them understand the main idea of the subsection.

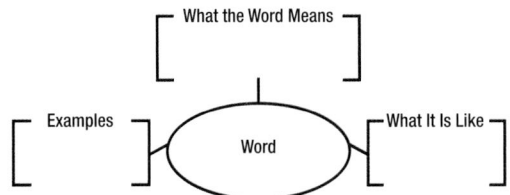

Pre-AP

Analyze Causes Instruct students to research details of the Gulf of Tonkin incident and the resulting resolution by Congress. Tell them to reference multiple online and print sources and use what they learn to write an essay analyzing how and why the United States became involved in the Vietnam War. Invite volunteers to read their essays to the class or share them on a class blog or website.

See the Chapter Planner for more strategies for differentiation.

HISTORICAL THINKING

ANSWERS

1. The United States feared Ho Chi Minh would establish a communist government.

2. North Vietnam was communist, while South Vietnam, backed by the United States, was supposedly democratic.

3. Laos and Cambodia

War Strategies in Vietnam

As the war heated up, more and more young American men were drafted and sent halfway across the world to fight in the rice paddies and jungles of Vietnam. The letters they sent home painted a grim picture for the young men still waiting to be drafted.

MAIN IDEA Fighting an unpopular war on unfamiliar terrain proved difficult for U.S. troops in Vietnam.

FIGHTING A GUERRILLA WAR

American forces faced many obstacles in carrying out their mission. Fighting in Vietnam was very different from most World War II battles. The Viet Cong engaged in guerrilla warfare much as the Continental Army did during the American Revolution. They fought in small groups, hid in the dense vegetation, and carried out sneak attacks to catch their enemies off guard. Most U.S. soldiers had not been trained for such fighting.

The landscape of Vietnam was well suited to the tactics of guerrilla warfare. There were few cities or paved roads. American soldiers often had to march through miles of thick jungles and wade through waist-deep swamps. It was easy for the enemy to set traps for them. The Viet Cong dug miles of underground tunnels to move men and supplies undetected. They also used a long trail, called the **Ho Chi Minh Trail**, that ran from North Vietnam to Saigon, the capital of South Vietnam.

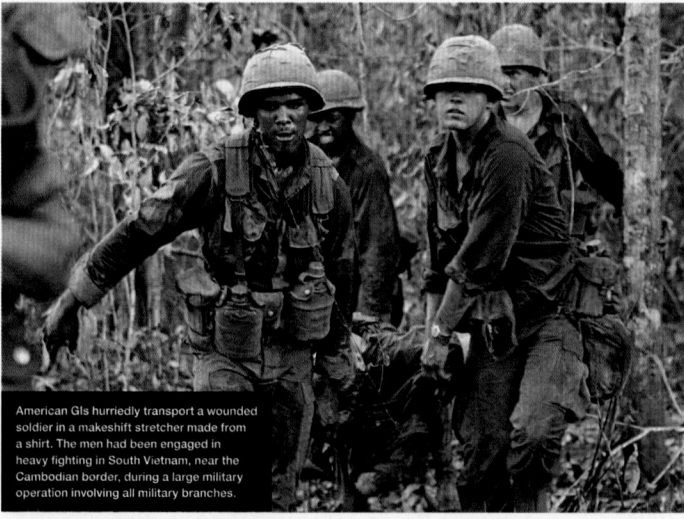

American GIs hurriedly transport a wounded soldier in a makeshift stretcher made from a shirt. The men had been engaged in heavy fighting in South Vietnam, near the Cambodian border, during a large military operation involving all military branches.

Agent Orange Flag
An American veteran donated a flag communicating an anti-Agent Orange message to the Peace Village in Hanoi, Vietnam. The Peace Village was built in 1991 to provide a home, education, and medical care for children who suffer from the effects of dioxin poisoning. Dioxin is the dangerous chemical contaminant present in Agent Orange, which was used during the Vietnam War.

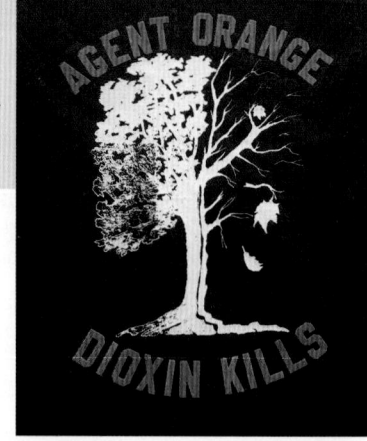

It ran along the western border of both nations and even extended into the neighboring countries of Laos and Cambodia.

The unstable and still corrupt government of South Vietnam complicated American efforts. Many South Vietnamese disliked their government. They wanted to determine their own future and resented U.S. interference. That's why many South Vietnamese aided the rebels. U.S. troops often found it difficult to tell whether civilians were friends or foes.

ESCALATING MISSIONS

Knowing the United States did not have the full support of the South Vietnamese people, the American military adopted a strategy to "win the hearts and minds" of the population. They hoped that convincing the South Vietnamese of the United States' good intentions would persuade them to join the fight against North Vietnamese communists. Winning hearts and minds was easier to discuss than to achieve, however, especially when U.S. military actions often spoke much louder than words.

Resentment against American forces grew as the United States expanded the use of **search-and-destroy missions**. This tactic cleared out entire villages suspected of aiding the enemy, destroying all the homes and crops as people fled. Many civilians were injured or killed in such operations, increasing the distrust and outright rage of the South Vietnamese.

Some of the weapons used in search-and-destroy missions caused long-lasting damage to the environment. **Napalm**, a type of gelled gasoline, burned thousands of homes and miles of jungle. Other weapons, such as the chemical **Agent Orange**, were used to kill off vegetation. The

United States military hoped that by destroying miles of forestland, they could end the Viet Cong's ability to hide in the dense jungles and ambush U.S. troops.

Agent Orange left the environment unusable for years. It poisoned water supplies, killing off livestock and leading to long-lasting health problems in humans. It has even been shown to cause high rates of unusual birth defects in the children of people exposed to it. Many American soldiers who handled Agent Orange suffered from severe health problems after the war. Given all of these conditions, it is not hard to understand why Americans found winning the hearts and minds of the South Vietnamese to be a difficult mission.

HISTORICAL THINKING

1. **READING CHECK** What was the main fighting tactic of the Viet Cong?

2. **DRAW CONCLUSIONS** What was the purpose of search-and-destroy missions?

3. **ANALYZE CAUSE AND EFFECT** Why did the U.S. military use Agent Orange, and what were the long-term effects of that strategy?

Objective

Describe the war strategies used in Vietnam and the difficulties U.S. troops experienced.

Critical Thinking Skills for Lesson 4.2

- Identify Main Ideas and Details
- Monitor Comprehension
- Draw Conclusions
- Analyze Cause and Effect
- Form and Support Opinions
- Integrate Visuals

Essential Question for Chapter 27

How did American identity change in the 1960s? Following victory in World War II, military superiority was inseparable from America's self-image. Lesson 4.2 examines how this image began to fracture as conditions in Vietnam proved to be more difficult than expected.

Background for the Teacher

The Viet Cong army consisted of main and local forces. Main forces were full-time professional soldiers accustomed to large, wide-ranging battles and the use of machine guns, rocket-propelled grenades, and mortars. Local forces operated exclusively in their own territories and were usually made up of inexperienced, idealistic teens or young people who joined under duress. They generally received a minimal amount of training, which included political instruction to solidify their ideological goals. Their abilities as guerrilla fighters, however, made up for the lack of military training and sophisticated weapons. Skilled improvisers, they constructed and set homemade bombs assembled from scavenged scrap materials and explosives taken from dud U.S. bombs that had landed in and around villages. Locals' weapons also included punji traps, which were pits or areas lined with sharp wooden spikes covered with urine, feces, or other contaminating substances. Victims suffered deep wounds and could develop serious infections.

Consider the Purpose of a Strategy

Ask volunteers to define the word *strategy*, and write their definitions on the board. *(Possible responses: a plan intended to achieve a specific goal; a scheme; a military operation)* Prompt students to offer examples of strategies they have used to achieve a goal in their lives or when playing a game, and encourage them to explain what they did if they discovered that their strategy was not working as planned. Then tell students that they will read about strategies that U.S. and North Vietnamese forces used against each other, with different degrees of success.

TEACH

Guided Discussion

1. **Identify Main Ideas and Details** What evidence does the text present to suggest that many South Vietnamese supported the Viet Cong rather than U.S. forces? *(The Ho Chi Minh Trail was maintained through South Vietnam even though it served as a supply line for the Viet Cong, indicating that some residents supported the Viet Cong; the need for U.S. efforts to "win the hearts and minds" of the South Vietnamese indicates that many South Vietnamese did not support the presence of the U.S. military.)*

2. **Form and Support Opinions** What might have made the "hearts and minds" strategy more effective? *(Possible response: The strategy might have been more successful if the United States had ceased its search-and-destroy missions, which leveled local villages and killed civilians.)*

Integrate Visuals

How does information in the photograph and caption reflect the difficulties American troops faced while fighting in Vietnam? *(Possible response: The photo shows the dense jungle, which made finding the enemy difficult. The makeshift stretcher suggests that the troops had to improvise a way to carry a wounded soldier because the terrain in that area made a helicopter evacuation impossible.)*

Active Options

On Your Feet: Word Chain Write these terms on three separate pieces of paper: *guerilla warfare*, *search-and-destroy mission*, *Agent Orange*. Have students form three lines. Hand a term to the first person in each line. That student adds a word to the paper that relates to the original term and passes it down the line for each student to add another related word or phrase. Invite a volunteer from each group to read the completed word chain. Ask the class to listen for words that were used in more than one list or that may not connect.

NG Learning Framework: Research the Environmental Impacts of War `STEM`

`SKILL` Communication

`KNOWLEDGE` Our Living Planet, Critical Species

Remind students that in addition to affecting human lives, wars often have a devastating impact on the environment. Organize students into small groups, and tell them to research and create a visual presentation to demonstrate the environmental impact of military strategies used during the Vietnam War. Encourage students to include statistics, photographs, maps, charts, or other graphic elements. Students might use software, if available, to create a digital presentation. Combine the groups' presentations into an exhibit for the class to tour. Invite constructive criticism about the presentations.

Striving Readers

Read and Recall Have students read the lesson independently, and then arrange them in pairs. Instruct partners to take turns sharing ideas they recall from the lesson without referring to the text, while the other partner writes notes. Then tell pairs to review the lesson and revise their notes, if necessary.

Gifted & Talented

Analyze Soldiers' Letters Tell students to conduct online research to find 8 to 10 excerpts from letters written home by U.S. soldiers in Vietnam and print them for inclusion in a binder. Ask students to analyze and categorize the content (such as informational, personal, political) and tone (such as optimistic, sarcastic, sad, angry, resigned, matter-of-fact, etc.) and write notes about the specific details that support their assessment. Then instruct students to write an essay in which they use details from the excerpts to explain the range of thoughts and feelings of U.S. soldiers while serving in Vietnam. Invite volunteers to share their binders and essays or read selected excerpts aloud to the class.

See the Chapter Planner for more strategies for differentiation.

HISTORICAL THINKING

ANSWERS

1. The Viet Cong used guerrilla warfare, which involved small groups of soldiers, sneak attacks, and hiding in the dense vegetation.

2. Search-and-destroy missions were aimed at finding enemies hiding in villages.

3. Agent Orange was used to kill plants in the dense jungles, making it easier to locate enemy fighters. However, it proved to be highly toxic, destroyed the environment, led to birth defects, and caused health problems in U.S. soldiers.

4.3 The Tet Offensive

Often in wartime, enemy forces cease fighting during major holidays. As people throughout both North and South Vietnam prepared to celebrate the Lunar New Year, or Tet, in January 1968, one side saw the holiday as a perfect opportunity to catch its enemy off guard.

> **MAIN IDEA** After a surprise attack by enemy forces, many Americans began to question the U.S. mission in Vietnam.

COMMUNIST ATTACKS ON THE TET HOLIDAY

Tet, or the Lunar New Year, is the biggest holiday of the year in Vietnam. In 1968, the holiday fell on January 30. Hoping to catch the American and South Vietnamese forces off guard, Ho Chi Minh and the North Vietnamese planned a coordinated attack on a large number of key sites throughout South Vietnam. They would launch the **Tet Offensive** against South Vietnamese cities and military bases just as everyone was expecting a traditional **cease-fire**, or the brief suspension of hostilities. They prepared for the attack by smuggling weapons deep into the south as they distracted U.S. forces by staging some attacks closer to the border between the two nations.

The North Vietnamese hoped that a successful attack might slow U.S. military efforts and possibly even force American leaders into peace talks to end the conflict. The attack did, indeed, catch the Americans and their allies off guard. The North Vietnamese seized several towns and even threatened the U.S. embassy in Saigon for a short time.

Soon, however, the American and South Vietnamese forces rallied. After several weeks of fighting, they had reclaimed almost all the areas that had fallen in the initial attack. From a military standpoint, the Tet Offensive did not meet North Vietnam's goals. However, the attack clearly showed that the communist forces were not as close to surrender as many American leaders had thought. The conflict promised to drag on for a long time.

TURNING AGAINST THE WAR

From the time President Johnson escalated U.S. military involvement, teams of television reporters had been stationed, or embedded, with the troops. They filed stories from the very midst of the fighting, bringing the war's blood and violence right into American homes, usually at the dinner hour. Many Americans were horrified by what they saw. In late 1967 and early 1968, they had been

Battles of the Tet Offensive, 1968

Legend:
- ★ Major battle
- ◻ U.S. military base
- — Demilitarized zone (DMZ)

NORTH VIETNAM — Quang Tri, Hue, Khe Sanh
Da Nang, Hoi An
Quang Ngai
LAOS
THAILAND
Kontum, Pleiku, Qui Nhon
SOUTH VIETNAM
Ban Me Thuot
Nha Trang
Cam Ranh Bay
CAMBODIA
Phnom Penh
Bien Hoa
Saigon, Ben Tre
Vinh Long, Can Tho
Mekong River Delta
Gulf of Thailand
South China Sea

0   50   100 Miles
0   50   100 Kilometers

assured by U.S. military and political leaders that the communists were nearly defeated and the war would be over soon. The sheer scale of the Tet Offensive made that promise seem like a lie. After the Tet Offensive, many more Americans began to turn against the war. They began to doubt if the United States should be involved or questioned the way in which the United States was fighting the war.

Not long after the Tet Offensive, an incident occurred that reinforced many people's worst fears about war. In March 1968, a group of U.S. soldiers murdered more than 500 innocent men, women, and children in the village of My Lai (MEE LY). The troops involved claimed it had been a search-and-destroy mission gone horribly wrong. When the shocking details of the **My Lai massacre** became known, even more people questioned the purpose of the war. They feared it was turning young American soldiers into cold-blooded killers.

Even President Johnson decided the U.S. strategy was not working as planned. In February, as the offensive ended, General Westmoreland asked for more than 200,000 additional soldiers. He compared the offensive to the Battle of the Bulge in World War II, which you have read about. Johnson refused and sent only 13,500 troops. He then announced that he would not run for a second full term as president.

> ### HISTORICAL THINKING
>
> 1. **READING CHECK** Why did the North Vietnamese choose to attack on the Tet holiday?
>
> 2. **INTERPRET MAPS** What was the most likely route used by the North Vietnamese to supply weapons necessary to fight in and around Saigon?
>
> 3. **DISTINGUISH FACT AND OPINION** U.S. military leaders saw the Tet Offensive as a failure for the communists, while many American civilians saw it as a victory for the communists. Which opinion is supported by the facts?

American troops of the Ninth Division sit atop their tank as it rides through a Saigon street destroyed during the May, or Mini-Tet, Offensive in 1968.

PLAN

Objective

Evaluate the impact of the Tet Offensive on the course of the Vietnam War.

Critical Thinking Skills for Lesson 4.3

- Identify Main Ideas and Details
- Monitor Comprehension
- Interpret Maps
- Distinguish Fact and Opinion
- Analyze Cause and Effect
- Evaluate

Essential Question for Chapter 27

How did American identity change in the 1960s? As the Vietnam War dragged on, more Americans began to question its purpose as well as the truthfulness of political and military leaders. Lesson 4.3 discusses how the Tet Offensive affected the course of the war and reinforced Americans' suspicions.

Background for the Teacher

The horrific events at My Lai were followed by a cover-up. Members of Charlie Company, the unit responsible, reported that 128 Viet Cong had been killed during the mission. However, the evidence did not fit their story. Only three weapons were captured from the village, an unusually small number for more than 100 Viet Cong. The men also reported that about 20 civilians were killed, when in fact the number was more than 500. A year passed before a young helicopter gunner from another unit wrote to Congress and military officials describing civilian deaths at My Lai. His reports led to an official inquiry in which the U.S. Army gathered 26,000 pages of testimony from 403 witnesses and recommended charging dozens of the men of Charlie Company with crimes that included murder, rape, and mutilation. Few charges were actually filed, and just 13 men were charged. Only one, Lt. William Calley, was tried. He was convicted of multiple crimes in 1971. In 1974, a judge overturned the conviction, making Lt. Calley a free man.

Think Like a General

Tell students to imagine they are generals in the U.S. Army during the Vietnam War. **ASK:** What do you think defines victory in a battle or war? *(Possible responses: One side gains control of an area or position or inflicts more damage. One side makes the enemy give up.)* Remind students that the Vietnam War was less straightforward than other U.S. conflicts, and sometimes the normal rules did not apply. **ASK:** Is it possible for a battle to be both a victory and defeat? *(Possible response: Yes. An army might achieve a set goal, but the victory might be considered a defeat if it does not justify the costs of the battle, including lives lost.)* Tell students that they will read about the Tet Offensive, considered a victory and a defeat for both sides, and how it further complicated U.S. efforts in Vietnam.

TEACH

Guided Discussion

1. **Analyze Cause and Effect** What was the strategic impact of the Tet Offensive? *(The communists' surprise attack succeeded in catching U.S. forces off guard, but the ultimate goal was to bring about negotiations to end the war. Instead, U.S. forces recovered from the enemy offensive and reclaimed most of the territory they lost. No peace talks resulted, and the conflict continued.)*

2. **Evaluate** Why do you think President Johnson responded to General Westmoreland's request for 200,000 troops with only 13,500? *(Possible response: Johnson likely realized that the war was going badly, and sending a great number of additional troops would not guarantee a victory. Sending no additional troops might have looked like an admission of defeat, so sending a fraction of the number, while prolonging the conflict, would result in putting fewer troops at risk.)*

Interpret Maps

Direct students' attention to the map. Tell them to locate the Ho Chi Minh Trail and the borders of countries. Remind students that the North Vietnamese used the trail to bring weapons and supplies into South Vietnam. **ASK:** About how far did North Vietnamese suppliers have to travel on the Ho Chi Minh Trail to get supplies from the border of Laos and Cambodia to Saigon? Direct students to use the map scale and give the answer in both miles and kilometers. *(approximately 356 miles/572 kilometers)*

Active Options

On Your Feet: Turn and Talk on Topic Organize students into small groups, and give each group the following topic sentence: The Tet Offensive was a turning point in the Vietnam War. Tell groups to build a paragraph on the topic by having each member contribute one sentence. Suggest that groups first discuss events leading up to and following the offensive and their effects on the war. Tell students to collaborate on a concluding sentence. After groups finish, invite each one to present its paragraph to the class, with each student reading his or her contribution aloud. The last student can also read the conclusion.

NG Learning Framework: Compare Media Coverage

SKILLS Observation, Communication

KNOWLEDGE Our Human Story

Remind students that media coverage during World War II generally portrayed war efforts in a positive way, emphasizing successes and patriotism. Have groups of students use online sources to research the media coverage of the Vietnam War. Ask them to compile their findings and then write a report in which they draw conclusions about the tone of the coverage, the information and images shown, and the message conveyed. Be sure students examine primary sources such as television news reports and newspaper articles. After volunteers share their reports, engage the class in a discussion about the similarities and differences in the coverage of the two wars.

Inclusion

Read Map Details Bring students' attention to the map and help them locate North Vietnam, the Demilitarized Zone, South Vietnam, Laos, and Cambodia. Ask pairs to work together to trace the Ho Chi Minh Trail. Guide students to understand that Laos and Cambodia helped to maintain the trail, indicating their sympathy with communist North Vietnam. Tell partners to use the legend to locate the U.S. military base at Cam Ranh Bay on the coast and note its proximity to Nha Trang, where one of the Tet battles was fought. Then have partners work together to answer the Historical Thinking questions.

Pre-AP

Form and Support a Thesis Instruct students to use print and online sources to investigate the My Lai massacre and the trial of Lt. William Calley. Tell them to examine the evidence as presented in the media and during the trial and then support an opinion about the verdict. Caution students to use credible, unbiased sources as they compile details about the massacre. Finally, direct them to write an essay supporting their thesis and to cite their sources. Invite students to share their essays with the class.

See the Chapter Planner for more strategies for differentiation.

HISTORICAL THINKING

ANSWERS

1. The North Vietnamese attacked on Tet because they knew U.S. forces would be expecting the traditional holiday cease-fire.

2. The North Vietnamese most likely transported weapons to Saigon via the Ho Chi Minh Trail.

3. Accept all reasonable answers. Students should show an understanding that although the U.S. forces ultimately took back the communists' territorial gains during the offensive, the communists won a victory by proving their strength and ability to organize and successfully execute a surprise attack.

4.4 The Counterculture

As President Johnson sits in the White House, he can hear protesters shouting outside: "Hey, hey, LBJ! How many kids did you kill today?" More and more people are angry about the Vietnam War and blame the president. How could everything have gone so wrong?

MAIN IDEA As the conflict in Vietnam dragged on, many young Americans became politically active and joined the antiwar movement.

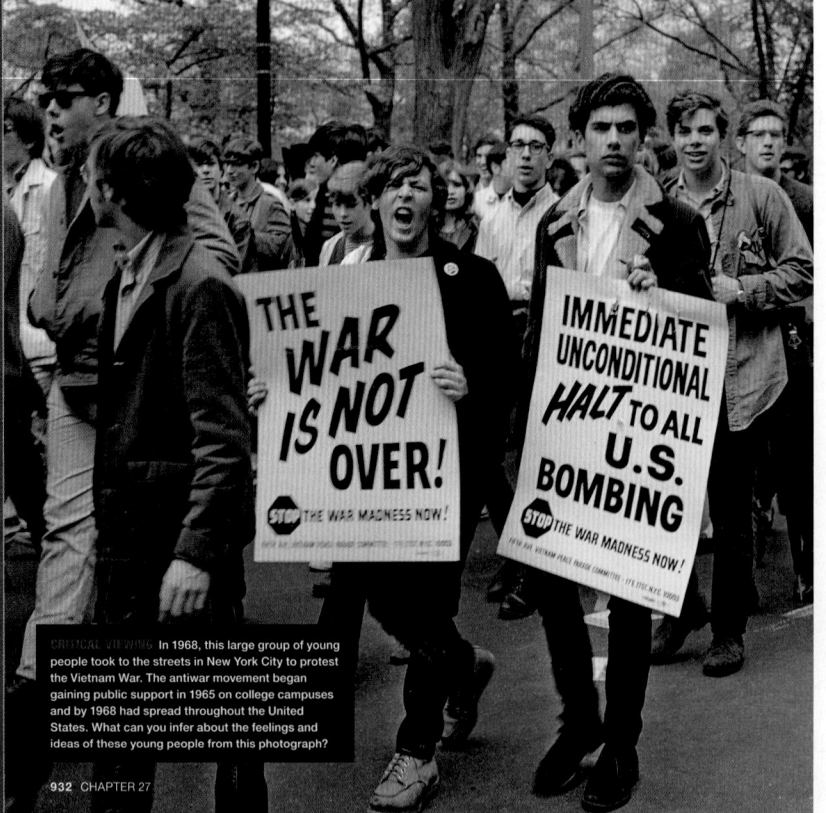

CRITICAL VIEWING In 1968, this large group of young people took to the streets in New York City to protest the Vietnam War. The antiwar movement began gaining public support in 1965 on college campuses and by 1968 had spread throughout the United States. What can you infer about the feelings and ideas of these young people from this photograph?

THE ANTIWAR MOVEMENT

By the time of the Tet Offensive, many groups had begun protesting the U.S. role in Vietnam. A diverse group of people opposed the war, but the most vocal tended to be students, civil rights leaders, writers, teachers, the clergy, and mothers.

Many protesters focused on the military draft. They argued it was unfair to force young men to fight in an unjust war. Others raised questions about the fairness of the draft system. The government allowed **draft exemptions**, or being excluded from military service, for various reasons. The system favored those wealthy enough to afford to go to college or to pay lawyers to find loopholes in the system. This meant that a higher percentage of poor and powerless men were drafted. Some young men left the United States and went to countries that allowed them to stay and avoid being returned to the United States to be drafted.

War protests were part of broader trends in youth culture. Throughout the 1960s, younger Americans had been embracing what some adults viewed as ever more radical hairstyles, fashion, and behavior. For example, men began to wear their hair long and grow facial hair, a big change from the clean-cut styles of the 1950s. Women dressed up less often and wore blue jeans more.

Some youthful behavior could be quite dangerous, such as the increased use of illegal drugs. By the late 1960s, a **counterculture** had emerged. Young people began to reject the consumerism and social expectations of their parents, focusing instead on "turning on" (taking drugs), "tuning in" (to new ideas about the individual and society), and "dropping out" (ignoring or not participating in the mainstream culture).

Music had become one of the biggest influences on youth culture, and baby boomers dominated the market for record sales. Noting this trend, record companies produced more youth-oriented music. Originally, rock and roll lyrics were mostly about cars, falling in and out of love, and other teenage concerns. But as the 1960s progressed, the lyrics grew more serious and controversial, even contributing to the growing war protest movement. Rock bands now sang about antiwar sentiments, social justice, or, in many cases, drug use.

A COUNTRY DIVIDED

By 1967, the country was divided politically between **doves**, or those who opposed the war, and **hawks**, or those who supported it. Hawks accused doves of being unpatriotic. Many doves countered that the United States weakened its own values by fighting an unjust war. Prior to the Tet Offensive, hawks outnumbered doves by a large percentage.

However, the doves had gained a valuable ally in April 1967 when Dr. Martin Luther King, Jr., gave a speech opposing the war. Dr. King said that the war was unjust, and its high cost was taking funding from programs that could help Americans here at home. He urged American leaders to stop the bombings, declare a cease-fire, and work toward a peaceful resolution to the conflict.

Then, in the months after the Tet Offensive, polls showed that a majority of Americans considered the war to have been a mistake. As you have read, before the offensive, Americans had been told that the war would soon come to a successful conclusion. The images of the Tet Offensive they saw on TV told them otherwise. From that point on, the percentage of Americans who opposed the war continued to increase as the conflict dragged on.

As support for the war decreased, many soldiers returning from Vietnam found the nation's anger and distrust directed at them. Most Vietnam veterans served honorably and to the best of their ability under difficult circumstances. Yet, unlike in World War II, when returning soldiers received a hero's welcome, some Vietnam veterans experienced poor treatment from civilians opposed to the war. Many returning veterans joined the antiwar movement.

HISTORICAL THINKING

1. **READING CHECK** Why was the military draft a focus of antiwar protests?

2. **DRAW CONCLUSIONS** Why do you think so many of the members of the counterculture were against the war in Vietnam?

3. **COMPARE AND CONTRAST** What is the difference between a hawk and a dove?

PLAN

Objective

Describe the antiwar movement and how it exposed divisions among Americans.

Critical Thinking Skills for Lesson 4.4

- Identify Main Ideas and Details
- Monitor Comprehension
- Draw Conclusions
- Compare and Contrast
- Form and Support Opinions
- Make Connections
- Make Generalizations

Essential Question for Chapter 27

How did American identity change in the 1960s? The movement against the Vietnam War gained supporters as Americans increasingly soured on the conflict. Lesson 4.4 discusses the growth of the counterculture movement and the societal divisions that emerged.

Background for the Teacher

Eligible U.S. residents are not drafted during times of peace or even necessarily during times of war, but males aged 18–25 (U.S. citizens and immigrants, including those without documentation) are required by law to register. During the Vietnam War, the Selective Service System conducted the draft via a lottery in which capsules containing birth dates were drawn from a glass jar. In the December 1969 drawing, those born between 1944 and 1950 were eligible and likely watched the televised lottery anxiously. The first capsule held the date September 14, which became lottery number one. Young men with that birth date were the first to be called for service in 1970. June 8 was pulled last, as number 366, and eligible draftees with that birth date probably celebrated.

History Notebook

Encourage students to complete the Reid on the Road video series page for Chapter 27 in their History Notebooks after they view the video.

Discuss the Reasons for a Counterculture

Write *counterculture* on the board. Ask students to break down the term and define it. *(a set of values that oppose the dominant or prevailing values of a society)* **ASK:** Why might members of a society oppose its prevailing values? *(Possible response: They aren't satisfied that established values are healthy, or they believe that authorities are not acting in the best interests of society.)* What characteristics or activities might describe members of a counterculture? *(Possible response: Their style and attitudes are different from average members of society. They make their own rules and probably protest aspects of society or government that they disagree with.)* Tell students that in this lesson they will learn about the growth of the counterculture in the 1960s and its connection to the Vietnam War.

TEACH

Guided Discussion

1. **Form and Support Opinions** Why do you think that the Vietnam War was met with more protest than earlier wars, such as World War II? *(Possible response: The United States entered World War II after being attacked, people felt patriotic and wanted to help, and men and women from all economic and social levels participated. U.S. involvement in Vietnam drew criticism as an illegal and unwinnable war, and many wealthy and connected young men received draft exemptions. In addition, Americans were more aware of the realities of the war through news articles and film footage.)*

2. **Make Connections** How could public opinion alter the course of a war? *(Possible response: In a democracy, lawmakers are elected and responsible to their constituents. If politicians continue to support a war that voters disapprove, voters will elect new leaders who may decide to change the course of the war.)*

Make Generalizations

Remind students that the counterculture was a rejection of the values of the 1950s, including consumerism, clearly defined gender roles, and mainstream culture. Ask students to think about and list the attitudes, interests, goals, and other characteristics that define their generation. Then discuss with them whether these characteristics counter their parents' values or whether they value the same things. **ASK:** Why might a generation reject the values of the previous generation? *(Answers will vary. Possible response: Young people naturally want to establish their own identities. Rejecting the values of previous generations is a way to do that.)*

Active Options

On Your Feet: Who Receives a Draft Exemption? Have students research the demographics of young men who served in Vietnam. Direct them to concentrate on who received draft exemptions and who were sent overseas. Then organize students into small groups and provide each with a set of index cards. Groups should write a short description of a demographically unique young man on each card, such as *22-year-old white male who attends Harvard.* Place completed cards in a container, then pull them out one at a time and read each description to the class. As you read each card, call on volunteers to explain the likelihood of that person serving overseas and why they think as they do.

NG Learning Framework: Plan a Museum Exhibition

SKILLS Communication, Collaboration

KNOWLEDGE Our Human Story

Organize students into small groups and have them research and create a museum-style exhibition related to the 1960s counterculture, with each group contributing an exhibit. Group exhibits should focus on a topic such as music, films, books, fashion, hairstyles, gender roles, or attitudes toward the government. Each exhibit should include items (or photographs of them) that represent the topic. Encourage students to add audio and video recordings. Have groups provide a description of each exhibit and how it relates to 1960s counterculture. Allow time for students to tour and discuss other groups' exhibitions.

DIFFERENTIATE

Striving Readers

Use Compound Words Pair students and bring their attention to the two words that make up the word *counterculture.* Ask them to brainstorm and write other words beginning with *counter-* *(counteract, counterclockwise, counterpart).* Then have them brainstorm words ending in *-culture* or *-cultural (monoculture, multicultural, agriculture).* Ask students to state the meaning of *counter* (against) and *culture* (set of values or practices). Instruct them to write their own definition of *counterculture* and compare it with a dictionary definition.

Gifted & Talented

Perform a Protest Song Direct student pairs to conduct online research to read about Vietnam War protest songs and then select a song or verse to perform. Suggest they listen to recordings by artists such as Phil Ochs, Jimmy Cliff, Nina Simone, Tom Paxton, Bob Dylan, and Pete Seeger, as well as others. Tell students to access the full lyrics in order to rehearse a verse that is appropriate for the classroom before they perform it for the class. After the performance, encourage the pairs to lead a discussion about how the song reflects the mood of the 1960s.

See the Chapter Planner for more strategies for differentiation.

HISTORICAL THINKING

ANSWERS

1. Protesters believed that once drafted, young men with low social standing were more likely to serve, while those of social power and wealth received an exemption.

2. Possible responses: Many members of the counterculture were eligible for the draft and did not want to go to Vietnam. The counterculture rejected the mainstream culture in general, and its members opposed the government and ideas like consumerism, capitalism, and waging war.

3. A hawk supports war, and a dove does not.

CRITICAL VIEWING The serious and angry expressions on the two men carrying signs suggest a strong opposition, perhaps based on eligibility for the draft. The signs indicate that the protesters believe the war is senseless and should be ended immediately.

4.5 The Year 1968

In 1968, U.S. achievements were often overshadowed by painful events. While some Americans experienced those events, others learned of them through vivid news reports and images. Americans often wondered if the country could survive such a terrible year.

MAIN IDEA During 1968, the United States was marked by many crises—over civil rights, war, poverty, and politics—that reshaped the nation and its future.

THE DEATH OF DR. KING
The year 1968 was one of the most eventful and chaotic of the 20th century. It started with the Tet Offensive in Vietnam and only seemed to worsen from there. The struggles dividing the United States all seemed to collide at once, some in tragic fashion.

In addition to speaking out in support of civil rights and against the war, Dr. Martin Luther King, Jr., increasingly focused his attention on helping poor Americans of all races from all regions. He traveled to northern cities to organize for change where people faced poverty and housing discrimination, obstacles to living healthy and successful lives.

Taken just seconds after Martin Luther King, Jr., was assassinated, this photograph shows Andrew Young and other civil rights leaders on the balcony of the Lorraine Motel in Memphis, Tennessee. They are standing near Dr. King's body and pointing toward the assailant as he runs away.

On June 6, 1968, Americans awoke to the grim news of Senator Robert F. Kennedy's death on the front pages of the country's newspapers, including the *San Francisco Chronicle*. Kennedy's assassin, Sirhan Sirhan, is believed to have been motivated by his resentment of some of Kennedy's foreign policy views.

King also spoke out for the rights of workers who were underpaid and mistreated. In early April, he traveled to Memphis, Tennessee, to support a garbage workers' strike. On the evening of April 4, as Dr. King stood on his hotel balcony, a sniper's bullet took his life. It would be months before law enforcement caught his murderer. Rage over Dr. King's assassination sparked violent rioting in some cities.

A CHAOTIC DEMOCRATIC CONVENTION
Shortly before Dr. King's murder, on March 31, President Johnson announced he would not run for re-election. Evidence of the strengthening antiwar movement had come on March 12, when antiwar candidate Senator **Eugene McCarthy** won the New Hampshire Democratic primary election, winning 20 out of the 24 delegates to the upcoming National Democratic Convention. Many people thought this threatened Johnson's chances of winning the general election in November. Johnson said he wanted to focus the remainder of his time in office on ending the war. This move left open the opportunity for new leadership over a deeply divided country.

Even with McCarthy's early primary win, many people hoped that **Robert Kennedy**, President Kennedy's brother, would win the Democratic nomination. Kennedy was a progressive candidate who supported civil rights and social justice, and many voters hoped he would continue the legacy of his fallen brother. However, only two months after Dr. King's death, the nation was shocked once again when Robert Kennedy was shot by a gunman on June 5, 1968, just after winning the California primary. He died a day later.

The Democratic Party was deeply divided when it gathered in Chicago to hold its national convention in August. Outside, antiwar protesters clashed with police. As the Democrats selected Vice President **Hubert Humphrey** as their presidential nominee, news crews were showing live images of chaos and shocking police brutality outside. To many television viewers, the convention reflected how out of control the country had become under Democratic Party leadership. To the counterculture, the doves, and civil rights' supporters, it represented a defeat.

These events provided an opportunity for the Republicans. They nominated former vice president Richard M. Nixon, who claimed to have a secret plan for ending the war that would result in "peace with honor." Nixon won the election with a narrow majority of the popular vote but a wide majority of the electoral college. He promised to stand up for the "**silent majority**" of Americans—those who quietly supported the government and who didn't protest.

HISTORICAL THINKING

1. **READING CHECK** Why was Dr. King in Memphis in April 1968?

2. **MAKE INFERENCES** Why do you think President Johnson decided not to run for re-election in 1968?

3. **ANALYZE CAUSE AND EFFECT** How did the events of the 1968 Democratic Convention help the Republicans?

Objective
Explain how two assassinations and the presidential election of 1968 changed America.

Critical Thinking Skills for Lesson 4.5
- Identify Main Ideas and Details
- Monitor Comprehension
- Make Inferences
- Analyze Cause and Effect
- Draw Conclusions

Essential Question for Chapter 27
How did American identity change in the 1960s? The events of 1968 upended the political order and changed the course of the civil rights movement. Lesson 4.5 discusses how assassinations and political turmoil set the stage for a new presidency and a reshaping of American identity.

Background for the Teacher
Dr. Martin Luther King, Jr., and Robert Kennedy were well known to each other. When Kennedy was attorney general, King was a thorn in his side, continuously pressing the administration to take a firmer stand on civil rights by protecting protesters against angry mobs and enforcing rulings that promised integration. After Kennedy became a senator, the goals of the two icons began to converge as both became passionate critics of the Vietnam War. Kennedy learned of King's death while campaigning. In a speech in front of a mostly black audience in Indianapolis, many of whom had not heard the sad news, he urged the crowd not to resort to violence, but instead to emulate Dr. King, "to comprehend, and replace that violence, that stain of bloodshed that has spread across our land, with an effort to understand, compassion, and love." Two months later, Kennedy was assassinated.

INTRODUCE & ENGAGE

What Makes a Landmark Year?

Remind students that they learned about a landmark legislation earlier in the chapter. **ASK:** What does the word *landmark* mean? *(Possible responses: important, historic, significant, marking a turning point)* As a class, develop a definition for a landmark year. Then ask students to decide which has been a landmark year in their lives and to make a list of events supporting their decision. Invite volunteers to share their responses. Then inform students that 1968 is considered to be a landmark year in American history. Based on the class definition, have students make predictions about events during 1968.

TEACH

Guided Discussion

1. **Draw Conclusions** What might be some reasons the assassination of Dr. Martin Luther King, Jr., sparked rioting, despite the fact that he was an advocate for peace? *(Possible response: Some people were probably furious that a champion for peace was taken in a violent manner and resorted to violence themselves. Some may have believed that Dr. King's peaceful methods were falling short and new tactics were necessary.)*

2. **Make Inferences** What types of people probably made up Richard Nixon's "silent majority"? *(Possible response: older people who opposed protesting, veterans of World War II who thought the military needed to be respected, conservatives who worried about maintaining law and order, people who were not interested in politics)*

More Information

Election of 1968 Remind students that the Democrats had difficulty uniting the party for the election of 1968. Eugene McCarthy's promise to end the Vietnam War was supported by students and young people but rejected by Democrats who urged the party to follow the policies of Lyndon Johnson. After Johnson announced he would not run, Vice President Hubert Humphrey entered the race. Due to his late entry, Humphrey did not run in any primaries, instead wooing delegates at the party's convention in Chicago, a move that outraged McCarthy supporters and those who had supported Robert Kennedy. The conflicts fractured the party in the election. Third-party candidate Alabama governor George Wallace, a segregationist, ran as an independent, championing states' rights and criticizing the civil rights movement. Project a map of the results of the 1968 election showing both the electoral and popular vote results. **ASK:** Do you think a more unified Democratic Party would have won the election? *(Answers will vary. Possible responses: No. A more unified party still would have lost the South, which was vital. Yes. The popular vote was very close, so if a unified message had won them slightly more support, the Democrats might have defeated Richard Nixon.)*

Active Options

On Your Feet: True-False Questions Write a series of true-false questions related to the year 1968. Establish one side of the room as "True" and another side as "False." Ask questions and have students move to the side of the room that represents their answer. Discuss any misunderstandings or controversies.

NG Learning Framework: Create a Photo Collage

ATTITUDE Curiosity

KNOWLEDGE Our Human Story

Direct students' attention to the photograph and front-page newspaper reproduction and explain how they represent two of the major events of 1968. Organize students into small groups and instruct them to use the text and online resources to make a list of 8 to 10 major events that took place during 1968. Then guide students to create a collage of photographs that represent the events they chose. Tell groups to organize their photographs in some way, such as chronologically, categorically, or thematically. Display finished collages around the room or in a digital gallery, and encourage students to offer comments about how each is organized.

DIFFERENTIATE

English Language Learners `ELD`

Understand Plural Forms Remind students that most plurals in English are formed by adding *-s* or *-es*, but not always. Bring students' attention to the word *crises* in the Main Idea statement. Elicit the singular form, *crisis*. Then ask students to infer the plural forms of the words *oasis, emphasis, analysis, thesis, axis,* and *diagnosis.* You might then ask them to complete a Meaning Map for each word.

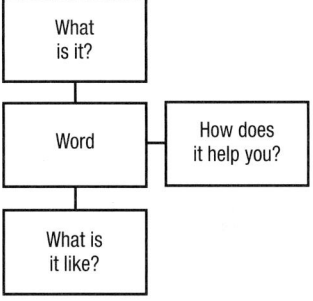

```
┌──────────┐
│  What    │
│  is it?  │
└──────────┘
     │
┌──────────┐      ┌──────────────┐
│  Word    │──────│  How does    │
│          │      │  it help you?│
└──────────┘      └──────────────┘
     │
┌──────────┐
│  What is │
│  it like?│
└──────────┘
```

Pre-AP

Connect Past and Present Instruct students to identify a social or political issue from 1968 that is a concern in present-day society, such as poverty, antiwar sentiment, police brutality, or the idea of a "silent majority." Challenge students to conduct research to find out how the issue arose in the 1960s and how it has played out in recent years at local, state, or national levels. Tell them to use their research to write a report on the persistence of the issue in the United States. Invite students to share their reports with the class.

See the Chapter Planner for more strategies for differentiation.

HISTORICAL THINKING

ANSWERS

1. Dr. King was in Memphis to support a garbage workers' strike.

2. Possible response: Johnson thought he would lose because of his growing unpopularity due to his administration's inability to end the Vietnam War.

3. The Democratic Party disagreed about issues and its nominee, which made winning the election difficult. Furthermore, the chaos at the convention made the Democrats appear out of control, which made the Republicans a better choice to many people.

27 REVIEW

VOCABULARY

Use each of the following terms in a sentence that shows an understanding of the term's meaning.

1. satellite

   Explorer 1 was the first satellite successfully launched into space by the United States.

2. gender bias
3. naval quarantine
4. domino theory
5. escalation
6. hawk
7. counterculture
8. Medicare
9. feminist

READING STRATEGY
COMPARE AND CONTRAST

If you haven't already, complete your graphic organizer by noting similarities and differences in the United States between 1960 and 1968. Then answer the question.

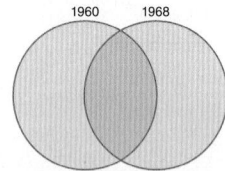

10. How did our concept of the American identity change during the 1960s, and how did it remain the same?

MAIN IDEAS

Answer the following questions. Support your answers with evidence from the chapter.

11. What impact did the first presidential debate have on the 1960 election? **LESSON 1.1**
12. What structure became a symbol of the Cold War? **LESSON 1.3**

13. What crisis brought the United States and the Soviet Union to the brink of nuclear war in 1962? **LESSON 1.4**
14. In what ways did President Johnson show his commitment to civil rights? **LESSON 2.1**
15. How were the goals of the Black Power movement different from those of earlier civil rights activists? **LESSON 2.2**
16. In what ways was President Johnson's Great Society program successful? **LESSON 2.3**
17. What issues did politically active Latino groups confront during the civil rights era? **LESSON 3.1**
18. How did the Indian Relocation Act of 1956 affect Native Americans? **LESSON 3.3**
19. What inequalities between men and women did women want to change in the 1960s and 1970s? **LESSON 3.4**
20. What power did the Gulf of Tonkin Resolution give to the U.S. president? **LESSON 4.1**
21. What was the significance of the 1968 Tet Offensive in Vietnam? **LESSON 4.3**

HISTORICAL THINKING

Answer the following questions. Support your answers with evidence from the chapter.

22. **MAKE CONNECTIONS** How did the Cold War competition affect the expansion of technology in daily life?
23. **ANALYZE CAUSE AND EFFECT** How did the domino theory affect President Johnson's foreign policy in Asia?
24. **DESCRIBE** What event at the 1968 Democratic Convention helped Nixon's campaign?
25. **FORM AND SUPPORT OPINIONS** Some historians claim 1968 was the most pivotal year in 20th-century U.S. history. Do you agree with this assessment? Explain your answer.

INTERPRET VISUALS

In a 1965 political cartoon, Paul Conrad contrasted two ongoing conflicts being fought in very different locations. Although those two struggles had little in common, one purpose they shared was to enable a group of people to experience free and equal representation. Look closely at the political cartoon featuring a U.S. soldier who holds a letter. Then answer the questions that follow.

26. Where is the soldier in this cartoon, and why is he there?
27. Why do you think the soldier in this cartoon looks so upset?
28. What is the significance of the cartoon's title, "A Letter from the Front"?

A Letter From the Front

ANALYZE SOURCES

On March 31, 1968, President Johnson addressed the nation to announce that he would not seek re-election. Read the following excerpt from the speech and then answer the question.

> Tonight I want to speak to you of peace in Vietnam and Southeast Asia.
>
> No other question so preoccupies our people. No other dream so absorbs the 250 million human beings who live in that part of the world. With America's sons in the fields far away, with America's future under challenge right here at home . . . I do not believe that I should devote an hour or a day of my time to any personal partisan causes or to any duties other than the awesome duties of this office—the Presidency of your country. Accordingly, I shall not seek, and I will not accept, the nomination of my party for another term as your President.

29. According to this speech, what was Johnson's main reason for not running for re-election?

CONNECT TO YOUR LIFE

30. **EXPOSITORY** Events of the 1960s challenged Americans as they confronted a war that seemed, to many, both immoral and unwinnable. In addition, a counterculture emerged that defied many basic ideas about what made the United States a great nation. Of the challenges that face our nation today, which one do you think is most difficult to solve? Write a paragraph about it in which you explain your answer.

TIPS

- Review the chapter and write down the similarities you notice between life then and life now.
- List five challenges that face our nation today, and rank them in order of importance. Choose the challenge you ranked highest to share and explain.
- Use at least two vocabulary words from the chapter in your response.
- Conclude your paragraph by summarizing your thoughts in one final statement.

VOCABULARY ANSWERS

1. *Explorer 1* was the first satellite successfully launched into space by the United States.
2. Title IX prohibited federally funded schools from engaging in gender bias, such as promoting only male sports teams.
3. The naval quarantine ordered by President Kennedy prevented ships from entering or leaving Cuba.
4. The domino theory claimed that if one country in Asia fell to communism, others would eventually follow.
5. The Gulf of Tonkin Resolution led to the escalation of U.S. military forces and to more young men being drafted.
6. Hawks supported the Vietnam War and believed that doing so demonstrated their patriotism.
7. The 1960s counterculture rejected society's expectations and rules and developed new fashions, lifestyles, and music.
8. Medicare ensures that seniors have access to health care.
9. A feminist believes in and works toward equal rights for women.

READING STRATEGY ANSWER

1960 ⟷ 1968

- optimistic
- support government
- traditional morals

(overlap)
- fight for equal rights
- against communism

- pessimistic
- question government
- changing morals

10. Possible response: In the early 1960s, Americans believed that the United States was headed in the right direction morally and technologically and were optimistic about the future. By the end of the decade, however, many Americans questioned the government's morality in waging war in Vietnam. Most Americans still believed in the ideals of the nation's founding—especially promoting equal rights—but not all Americans agreed on how best to express those ideals.

MAIN IDEAS ANSWERS

11. Many people who voted for John Kennedy may have watched the televised debate and been swayed in his favor by his charming and confident appearance, especially when compared with Richard Nixon's nervous and sweaty performance.

12. The Berlin Wall became a symbol of the Cold War.

13. In 1962, the Cuban Missile Crisis brought the United States and the Soviet Union to the brink of nuclear war.

14. Johnson worked with Congress to ensure the passing of the Civil Rights Act of 1964, which included the creation of the Equal Employment Opportunity Commission (EEOC), and pushed for the passing of the Voting Rights Act of 1965.

15. Frustrated by the lack of change promised by civil rights legislation, members of the Black Power movement rejected the ideas of integration and nonviolence employed by earlier activists. Instead, they called for black separatism. Malcolm X, a leader of the Nation of Islam organization, advocated self-defense using any means necessary.

16. Successes of Johnson's Great Society included the War on Poverty; passage of the Economic Opportunity Act; and creating the Job Corps, Neighborhood Youth Corps, and VISTA, all aimed at lifting minority youth from poverty. The Great Society also made advances in health care and health security, creating Medicare and Medicaid. Education was another priority, and the Elementary and Secondary Education Act helped low-income schools and created Head Start.

17. Major issues for Mexicans and Mexican Americans were the horrible conditions and low wages for migrant workers. Puerto Ricans faced poverty and discrimination in American cities. Cuban Americans became politically active to work against Castro's communist government in Cuba.

18. The Indian Relocation Act of 1956, implemented as part of President Eisenhower's termination policy, was a law that robbed Native Americans of federal benefits, support, and recognition by promising to integrate them into American society if they left their reservations and sold their land. One-third of those who relocated to cities returned to their reservations, and the circumstances of most tribes did not improve.

19. The major inequalities that women wanted to change included the female-male wage gap, limits on women buying and selling property, the right to control whether and when to have children, and unequal representation in politics and government.

20. The Gulf of Tonkin Resolution gave President Johnson the power to respond to North Vietnamese acts in the Gulf of Tonkin with whatever he believed to be an appropriate amount of force.

21. The surprise Tet Offensive showed Americans that the war was not nearing an end and the North Vietnamese were not being defeated. It led many Americans who had supported the war to question whether the war was winnable or whether the United States should even be involved in Vietnam.

HISTORICAL THINKING ANSWERS

22. Cold War competition between the United States and the Soviet Union led to the space race, which expanded science and technology and resulted in products and processes that people would use every day.

23. According to the domino theory, if one Asian nation became communist, all would follow. Thus, Johnson increased involvement in Vietnam in order to prevent the spread of communism.

24. Protesters outside the convention clashed with police, and the violent images shown on television were interpreted by viewers as weak Democratic leadership of the nation. Nixon's promise to restore order and support the silent majority—those who did not protest—struck a chord with voters.

25. Answers will vary but should reflect information covered in the text. Students who agree might point to the events that happened in 1968 and how they impacted society and government. Others might argue that years covered earlier in the text, such as those spanning U.S. involvement in World War II (1941 through 1945), had a larger impact on U.S. history.

INTERPRET VISUALS ANSWERS

26. He is in South Vietnam, fighting in the war against communist North Vietnam.

27. Possible response: The African-American soldier might be upset because he has just read about the marches in Selma, where many African Americans were beaten as they tried to register to vote. He may feel he is fighting in the wrong war. Instead of fighting communists in South Vietnam, the battles that concern him and his family are civil right struggles in the United States.

28. The term *front* refers to the front line in a battle. The title suggests that the biggest and most important battle African Americans were fighting at the time was not in South Vietnam, but in places like Alabama, where African Americans were struggling for their civil rights.

ANALYZE SOURCES ANSWER

29. Because of the pressing issues of the Vietnam War, Johnson felt he should spend the rest of his term focused on ending the war rather than on campaigning for re-election.

CONNECT TO YOUR LIFE ANSWER

30. Answers will vary. Students should write a paragraph in which they explain which modern challenge they feel is most difficult to solve, include at least two Key Vocabulary words from the chapter, and conclude with a final statement that summarizes their thoughts.

50 Years of Wilderness

By Elizabeth Kolbert

Adapted from "50 Years of Wilderness," by Elizabeth Kolbert, in *National Geographic*, September 2014

Fred Lavigne is looking for a tree. It's a beautifully clear day with a deep blue sky. Though the calendar says early spring, several feet of snow still cover the ground in the Sandwich Range Wilderness in New Hampshire.

We're surrounded by trees: towering spruces, scraggly beeches, maples, oaks, and birches. But Lavigne, a logger and outdoorsman, is looking for one tree in particular. We've left the trail behind, and he's navigating the steep terrain by memory, on snowshoes. Finally, he finds what he's been searching for: a red pine with a wide gash right at eye level. Plucking a coarse black hair from the frozen sap, Lavigne says that the gash was made by bears as a form of communication. (Though what they're telling each other no one's quite sure.) We spend several more hours snowshoeing through the forest and do not come across any other human footprints.

The Sandwich Range Wilderness isn't big—just 55 square miles—and it's not remote. Some 70 million people, including my own family, live within a day's drive. But for precisely these reasons, it's a good place to reflect on the legacy of the Wilderness Act. As I follow Lavigne through the woods, I wonder what explains our enduring attachment to wilderness and what that term even means today.

The Wilderness Act was signed into law by President Lyndon Johnson on September 3, 1964. But to understand the origin of the act, you have to go back to the 1930s. During the Great Depression, the federal government put tens of thousands of Americans to work in national parks and forests, clearing trails, erecting shelters, and building roads. The new highways opened up the parks to millions more visitors.

But the very success of these efforts troubled many conservationists, who worried that the country's most majestic landscapes were being turned into roadside attractions. A group of them formed the Wilderness

Society to defend the national parks and forests against overuse, and their first mission statement condemned the roadbuilding "craze." They worked to persuade Congress to specify tracts of land as roadless wilderness.

The resulting Wilderness Act created a new category of federal lands, off-limits to commercial ventures like logging and new mines. Humans could explore, but not with mechanized vehicles. The statute, or law, defined wilderness as "an area where the earth and its community of life are untrammeled [unrestricted] by man, where man himself is a visitor who does not remain." The 1964 act set aside 54 wilderness areas, a number that has increased to more than 750. Few of these areas are wild in any rigorous [strict] sense, however. Nearly all have at some point been logged, grazed, farmed, or otherwise altered by humans.

Today, global warming is altering even the most remote wilderness areas. In Alaska, sea ice is disappearing, permafrost [frozen soil] is thawing, and woody plants are invading the tundra. With widespread climate changes, the Wilderness Act has become even more important. Many species are on the move, following the changing climate. Plants and animals that find their routes blocked by cities or highways are likely to be in trouble. Wilderness areas, which allow for freer movement, may provide the best hope for new plant and animal communities to form.

Ecologist Peter Landres explains, "These big pieces [of land] are needed to let ecological and evolutionary processes play out. So if I'm an animal and I don't like it here, I can move over there. Yes, wilderness is affected by climate change, but it's exactly because our world is now so dominated by people that it's so important to have places where we let nature be."

For more from National Geographic, check out "Slipping the Bonds" online.

UNIT INQUIRY: Protest an Injustice

In this unit, you learned about the social, political, and economic injustices that African Americans, Latinos, Native Americans, and women faced in the postwar period. You also learned how they protested these injustices. Based on your understanding of the text, what kinds of methods did protesters use to bring attention to their causes and gain support for reforms? Which protest methods, or combination of methods, proved effective in bringing about change?

ASSIGNMENT

Identify a social, political, or economic injustice that you learned about in this unit. Devise a plan to protest the injustice, and prepare support materials designed to inspire and persuade people to remedy the injustice. Be prepared to present your plan and support materials to the class.

Gather Evidence As you plan your protest, gather evidence from this unit about the methods that African Americans, Latinos, Native Americans, and women used to draw attention to the problems they faced and to promote the reforms they sought. Think about how these protests were organized and carried out. Use a graphic organizer like this one to help develop your plan.

Produce Use your notes to write a detailed description of your protest plan. Then prepare support materials, such as a flyer, protest sign, poster, video, press release, chant, or online post, to publicize and promote your protest.

Present Choose a creative way to present your protest plan and support materials to the class. Consider one of these options:

- Create a video that publicizes your planned protest. In the video, explain the injustice you are protesting and present your demands. Provide information that will encourage others to join your protest.

- Design a flyer and protest sign that convey your message. Give your group a name and create a catchy slogan that might appear on a bumper sticker. Display the materials in your classroom.

- Work with a partner to stage a TV interview in which a "reporter" stops you as you carry a protest sign in a demonstration. Give detailed answers to the reporter's questions.

Protest Plan

Who is protesting, and **who** is the intended audience?
What is the issue, and **what** reforms are sought?
What form will the protest take?
Where will the protest occur?
When will it occur?
Why is this issue important?
How will you publicize and promote the protest?

NATIONAL GEOGRAPHIC | LEARNING FRAMEWORK ACTIVITIES

Compile a Song Medley

ATTITUDE Responsibility
SKILLS Communication

Protest songs performed and recorded by such American musicians as Bob Dylan, Joan Baez, and Sam Cooke became popular during the 1960s and 1970s. Research the protest songs of the period and compile a medley of songs to share with the class. Write and present an introduction to the medley, identifying the song titles, the recording artists, and the issues presented in each of the songs. As an alternative, you might compose and perform an original protest song of your own.

Build Models

SKILLS Observation, Collaboration
KNOWLEDGE New Frontiers

The space race began in the late 1950s with the launching of crewless satellites by the Soviet Union and United States. *Sputnik 1* was the Soviets' first successful Earth satellite, and *Explorer 1* was the Americans' satellite. Using simple materials, work with a partner to build models of these two satellites. Prepare a placard that provides identifying information and compares the two spacecraft, focusing on their design, purpose, and results. Display the models and placard in your classroom.

NATIONAL GEOGRAPHIC CONNECTION

Guided Discussion for "50 Years of Wilderness"

1. **Identify Problems and Solutions** According to this author, what is the role of humans in destroying and preserving wilderness spaces? *(Answers will vary. Possible response: Because humans have been responsible for much of the habitat loss for animals in designated wilderness areas, they are now responsible for solving the problems they caused. The designation of roadless wilderness spaces is a good example of a solution.)*

2. **Analyze Cause and Effect** What programs designed in the 1930s helped bring about the Wilderness Act of 1964? *(Possible response: During the Great Depression, the federal government hired thousands of Americans to work in the national parks, assigning them tasks such as clearing paths and building roads to increase tourism. But eventually these efforts caused problems such as overuse of resources and loss of wildlife habitat. The Wilderness Act created protected wilderness spaces to prevent further destruction.)*

Guided Discussion for "Slipping the Bonds"

1. **Compare and Contrast** In what ways was the early Soviet space program similar to and different from the U.S. space program? *(Both programs had multiple successes and failures. Initially, the Soviet program was more advanced than the U.S. program, and the Soviets were able to send a man into space in the first craft to orbit Earth; the United States launched a similar manned flight a month later. The U.S. space program began to advance beyond the Soviet program in the mid-1960s; and by the end of the 1960s, the United States had become the first nation to send human beings to the moon.)*

2. **Draw Conclusions** What made Apollo 11 the boldest of all the space missions to that point? *(Apollo 11 required more complex technology and more powerful launching rockets. The mission was also a launch into the unknown, as no one knew for certain whether the astronauts would be able to survive the trip through space, land on the moon, and return safely to Earth.)*

UNIT INQUIRY PROJECT RUBRIC

Assess

Use the rubric to assess each student's participation and performance.

SCORE	ASSIGNMENT	PRODUCT	PRESENTATION
3 GREAT	• Student thoroughly understands the assignment. • Student participates fully in the project process. • Student works well with team members.	• Plan and support materials are well thought out. • Plan and support materials are persuasive and use examples. • Plan and support materials contain all of the key elements listed in the assignment.	• Presentation is clear, concise, and logical. • Presentation does a good job of creatively laying out and supporting the plan. • Presentation engages the audience.
2 GOOD	• Student mostly understands the assignment. • Student participates fairly well in the project process. • Student works fairly well with team members.	• Plan and support materials are fairly well thought out. • Plan and support materials are somewhat persuasive and use at least two examples. • Plan and support materials contain most of the key elements listed in the assignment.	• Presentation is fairly clear, concise, and logical. • Presentation does an adequate job of laying out and supporting the plan. • Presentation somewhat engages the audience.
1 NEEDS WORK	• Student does not understand the assignment. • Student minimally participates or does not participate in the project process. • Student does not work well with team members.	• Plan and support materials are not well thought out. • Plan and support materials are not persuasive and do not include examples. • Plan and support materials contain few or none of the key elements listed in the assignment.	• Presentation is not clear, concise, or logical. • Presentation does an inadequate job of laying out and supporting the plan. • Presentation does not engage the audience.

NATIONAL GEOGRAPHIC LEARNING FRAMEWORK RUBRIC

Assess

Use the rubric to assess how each student applies the National Geographic Learning Framework.

SCORE	ASSIGNMENT	ASSIGNMENT	FINAL PRODUCTS
3 GREAT	• Song medley reflects **Responsibility** well. • Song medley demonstrates **Communication** well.	• Models demonstrate **Observation** and **Collaboration** well. • Models explore **New Frontiers** well.	• Final products are engaging, creative, and well presented.
2 GOOD	• Song medley reflects **Responsibility**. • Song medley demonstrates **Communication**.	• Models demonstrate **Observation** and **Collaboration**. • Models explore **New Frontiers**.	• Final products are interesting, logical, and complete.
1 NEEDS WORK	• Song medley does not reflect **Responsibility**. • Song medley does not demonstrate **Communication**.	• Models do not demonstrate **Observation** and **Collaboration**. • Models do not explore **New Frontiers**.	• Final products are not creative, complete, or interesting.

INTRODUCE THE PHOTOGRAPH

The American Flag of Faces

The Statue of Liberty–Ellis Island Foundation, Inc. launched The American Flag of Faces website on April 1, 2009, and the interactive exhibit opened to museum visitors soon after. Visitors to the exhibit can click on each photograph to enlarge it. They can also use a search engine to locate images of specific people and families. With a contribution to the foundation, anyone can submit personal photographs, either through digital upload or through regular mail, and the photographs then appear on both the museum exhibit and the foundation's website. Donations support the foundation's ongoing work to restore, preserve, and protect the Statue of Liberty and Ellis Island. There is no deadline for submission. The exhibit is always evolving and growing, so each day brings a new reflection of the American people.

Direct students' attention to the photograph. **ASK:** What are some of the things you notice about the faces? *(Possible response: The faces represent people of different genders, ages, races, and ethnicities.)* **ASK:** In what way does this exhibit reflect both artistic and historical achievement? *(Answers will vary. Possible response: The exhibit is an artistic achievement because of its original design and its attractive colors and imagery. It is a historical achievement because the faces represent the immigrant history not only of each person but also of the United States as a whole.)*

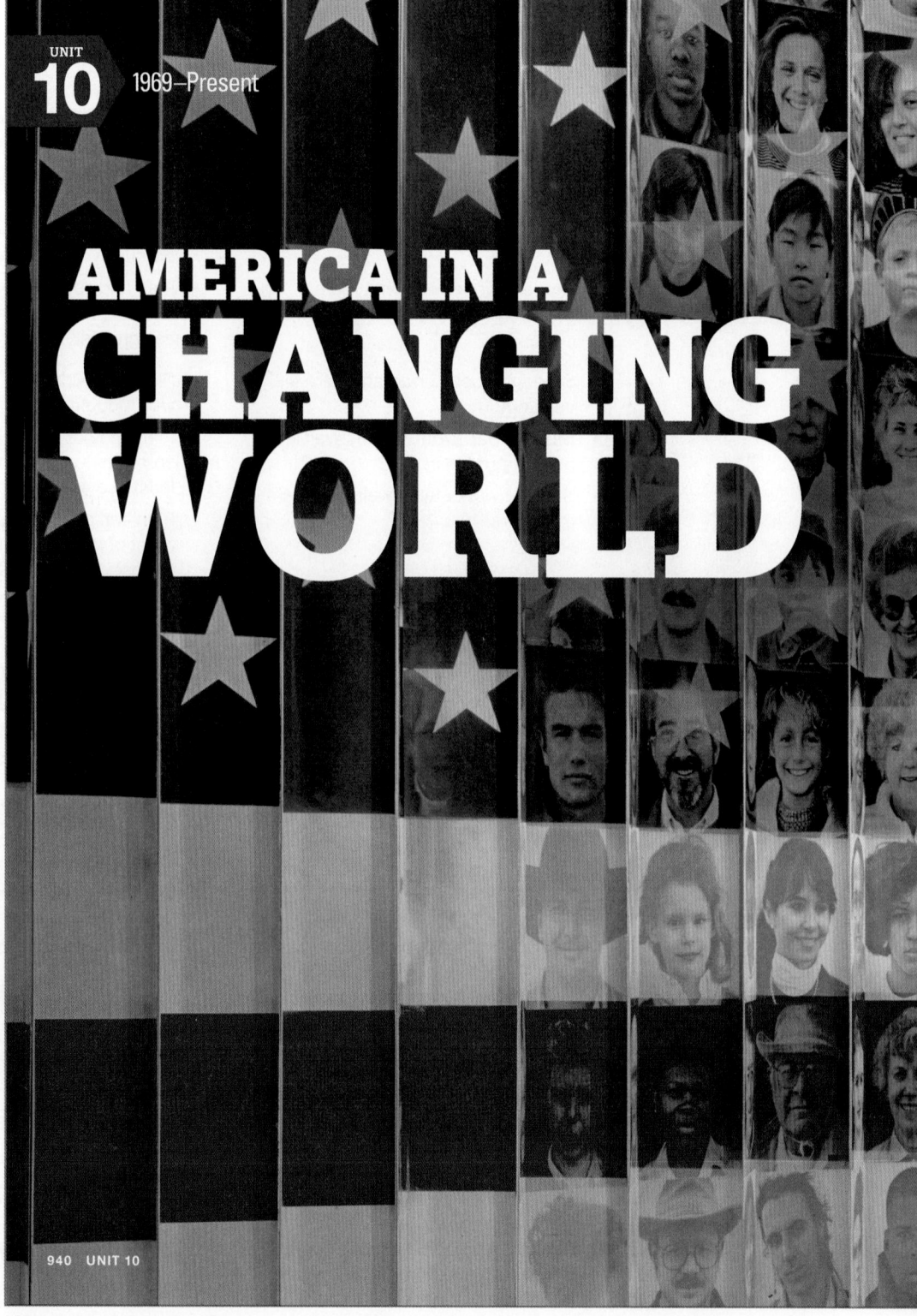

UNIT
10   1969–Present

AMERICA IN A CHANGING WORLD

940   UNIT 10

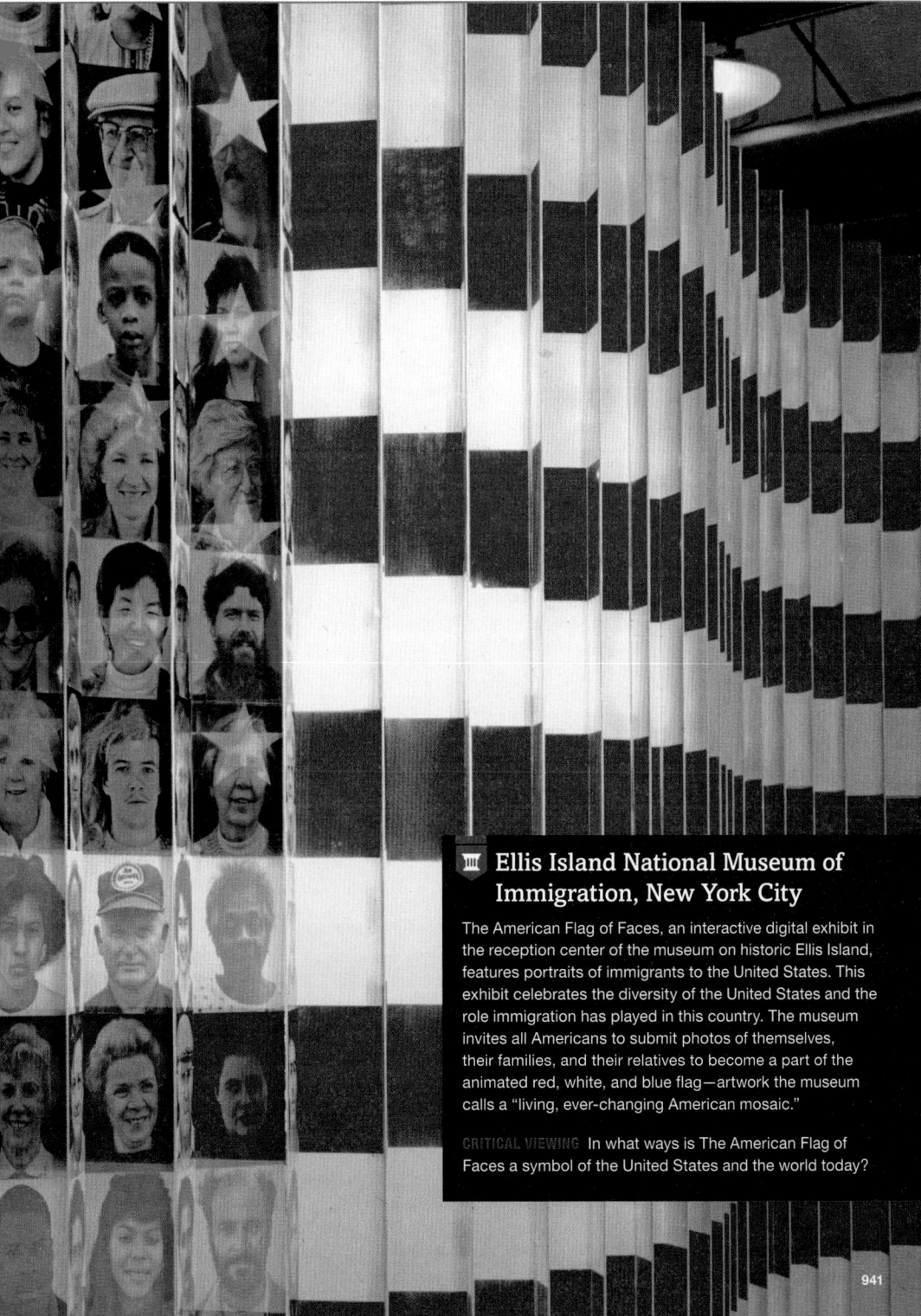

Ellis Island National Museum of Immigration, New York City

The American Flag of Faces, an interactive digital exhibit in the reception center of the museum on historic Ellis Island, features portraits of immigrants to the United States. This exhibit celebrates the diversity of the United States and the role immigration has played in this country. The museum invites all Americans to submit photos of themselves, their families, and their relatives to become a part of the animated red, white, and blue flag—artwork the museum calls a "living, ever-changing American mosaic."

CRITICAL VIEWING In what ways is The American Flag of Faces a symbol of the United States and the world today?

Virtual Museum Visit

The Ellis Island National Museum of Immigration is housed in the main building of what was once a processing center for new immigrants to the United States. Today, only tourists and museum employees arrive at Ellis Island, transported on ferries operated by Statue Cruises, the one ferry line sanctioned by the National Park Service. Ferries leave either from New York City's Battery Park or from New Jersey's Liberty State Park. The museum's exhibits are self-guided and offer visitors a range of artifacts, videos, oral histories, and more. The exhibit "Journeys: The Peopling of America, 1550s–1890" chronicles the arrival of the earliest immigrants, while "The Journey: New Eras of Immigration" documents U.S. immigration from 1954 to the present. Together, the exhibits show the broad spectrum of U.S. immigration before the processing center opened in 1892 and after it closed in 1954.

CRITICAL VIEWING As visitors to Ellis Island submit photographs of themselves and their families to The American Flag of Faces, the exhibit continues to reflect the wide diversity of the United States' population, showing we are a nation of immigrants.

1979 ASIA:
Iran Hostage Crisis

The Iran hostage crisis plagued Jimmy Carter in the last two years of his presidency, but he never stopped trying to negotiate for the hostages' release. In May 1980, the Carter administration persuaded U.S. allies to join with the United States in a strict trade embargo against Iran. Although the embargo imposed harsh conditions on the Iranian people, it was not enough to weaken Iranian resolve. The hostage crisis continued to drag on for months. In mid-August, Iran formed a new government, and the United States renewed its efforts to pursue more favorable diplomatic relations.

Then in September 1980, neighboring Iraq invaded Iran, which resulted in a brutal war between the two nations. Faced with the continued embargo and waning international support, Iran soon realized it would have little or no backing from other countries in its war with Iraq unless it gave up the U.S. hostages. U.S.-Iranian diplomatic negotiations intensified, and on January 20, 1981, the same day President Ronald Reagan took office, Iran released the hostages. In the public's eyes, Carter left office a weak, ineffectual president, while Reagan was widely credited as successfully concluding the crisis.

ASK: Why do you think the Carter administration believed an embargo against Iran might solve the hostage crisis? *(Answers will vary. Possible responses: The Carter administration might have thought the sanctions would cause so much hardship for the Iranian people they would overthrow their government. The administration might have thought the embargo would destabilize the government enough to make Iran release the hostages.)* **ASK:** Why did the hostage crisis lead to a loss of international support for Iran? *(Possible response: Taking hostages violates basic international civil and human rights. In addition, other nations might have feared that Iran would take their citizens hostage as well.)*

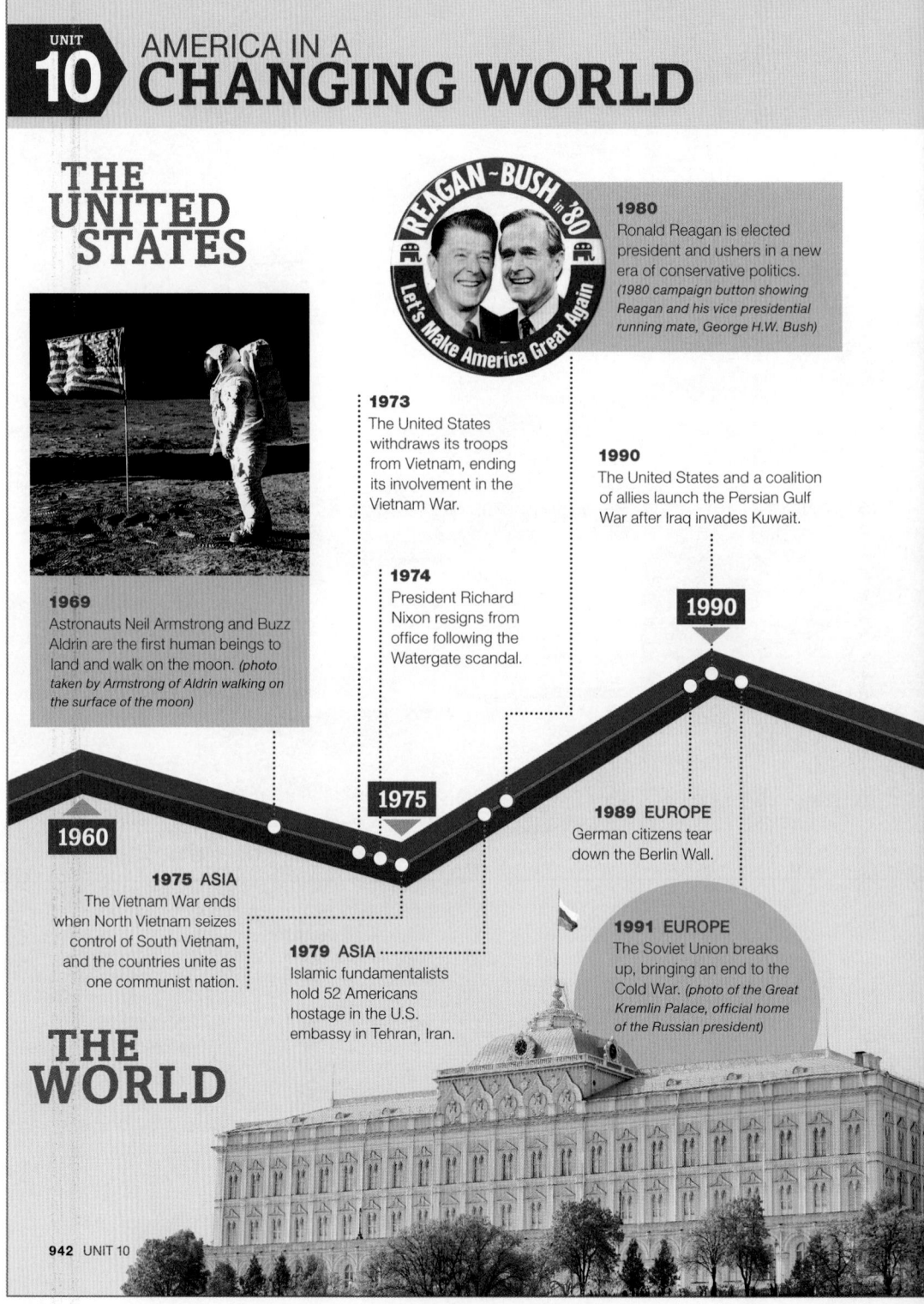

UNIT 10 AMERICA IN A CHANGING WORLD

THE UNITED STATES

1980
Ronald Reagan is elected president and ushers in a new era of conservative politics. *(1980 campaign button showing Reagan and his vice presidential running mate, George H.W. Bush)*

1973
The United States withdraws its troops from Vietnam, ending its involvement in the Vietnam War.

1990
The United States and a coalition of allies launch the Persian Gulf War after Iraq invades Kuwait.

1969
Astronauts Neil Armstrong and Buzz Aldrin are the first human beings to land and walk on the moon. *(photo taken by Armstrong of Aldrin walking on the surface of the moon)*

1974
President Richard Nixon resigns from office following the Watergate scandal.

1990

1975

1960

1989 EUROPE
German citizens tear down the Berlin Wall.

1975 ASIA
The Vietnam War ends when North Vietnam seizes control of South Vietnam, and the countries unite as one communist nation.

1979 ASIA
Islamic fundamentalists hold 52 Americans hostage in the U.S. embassy in Tehran, Iran.

1991 EUROPE
The Soviet Union breaks up, bringing an end to the Cold War. *(photo of the Great Kremlin Palace, official home of the Russian president)*

THE WORLD

942 UNIT 10

HISTORICAL THINKING: DETERMINE CHRONOLOGY

Choose an event on this time line and explain how it impacted the world.

2001
On September 11, al Qaeda terrorists carry out attacks that result in the deaths of more than 3,000 people in New York City, Washington, D.C., and Pennsylvania. *(Alan Wallace, a firefighter from nearby Fort Myer, was on duty at the Pentagon fire station on 9/11 and wore this coat as he helped Pentagon workers escape after a plane hit the building.)*

2016
Republican candidate Donald Trump defeats Democratic candidate Hillary Clinton in the 2016 presidential election. *(campaign posters of both candidates)*

2017
President Trump pulls the United States out of the Paris Agreement, an international pact to slow global warming.

2008
Voters elect Barack Obama as the nation's first African-American president.

2007
The Great Recession begins, which leads to widespread unemployment and a collapse in housing prices.

2000

2020

2015 EUROPE
The Islamic State in Iraq and Syria (ISIS) takes responsibility for a series of attacks in Paris, France, that kills about 130 people.

2008 AMERICAS
Fidel Castro resigns after leading Cuba for 49 years, and his brother Raúl succeeds him.

1994 AFRICA
South Africa holds its first democratic elections, and Nelson Mandela becomes the country's first black president. *(Mandela featured on South African paper money)*

2011 AFRICA
An uprising against the government in Egypt forces the country's president, Hosni Mubarak, from power. *(Egyptians celebrating the president's overthrow in Cairo's Tahrir Square)*

SOUTH AFRICAN RESERVE BANK
ONE HUNDRED RAND
100 100

America in a Changing World **943**

INTRODUCE TIME LINE EVENT

2011 AFRICA:
Mubarak Forced from Power

Early in his administration, Egypt's president, Hosni Mubarak, improved Egypt's relations with other Arab nations and sought stronger ties with the United States. But internal unrest was simmering under the surface in the country. Many Egyptians lived in poverty, with no hope of improving their lives. In the decades leading up to the 2011 protests, political repression, fraudulent elections, and corruption only increased. Citizens began to push for democratic reforms, including open elections, which the country had not seen since 1950.

Finally, in January 2011, the majority of Egyptians, particularly the young people, had had enough. Thousands of protesters filled the streets of Cairo, Egypt's capital, and demanded that Mubarak resign. During the demonstration, police snipers opened fire, killing 850 protesters. After Mubarak was ousted, he was tried for ordering the police action and was sentenced to life imprisonment. But in 2014, an Egyptian court dismissed the charges against him, citing the long delay in filing the original indictment in 2011.

ASK: Why do you think the lack of free and open elections might lead Egyptian protesters to demand that Mubarak resign? *(Possible response: Without free and open elections, the will of the voters cannot be expressed, allowing those in power to rule as long as they like and do whatever they like.)*

HISTORICAL THINKING: DETERMINE CHRONOLOGY

Answers will vary. Possible response: When Iraq invaded Kuwait in 1990, the United States and some of its allies launched the Persian Gulf War, which affected the economies of many countries around the world.

UNIT 10 RESOURCES

UNIT INTRODUCTION

UNIT TIME LINE

UNIT WRAP-UP

NATIONAL GEOGRAPHIC | **CONNECTION**

National Geographic Magazine
Adapted Articles
• "Changing Faces"
• "The Drones Come Home" ONLINE

Unit 10 Inquiry: Negotiate a Political Compromise

NG Learning Framework Activities
• Create a Comic Strip
• Debate the Effects of Environmental Regulations

Unit 10 Formal Assessment

CHAPTER 28 RESOURCES

Available at NGLSync.Cengage.com

TEACHER RESOURCES & ASSESSMENT

Reading and Note-Taking

Vocabulary Practice

Social Studies Skills Lessons
• Reading: Identify Problems and Solutions
• Writing: Write an Argument

Formal Assessment
• Chapter 28 Pretest
• Chapter 28 Tests A & B
• Section Quizzes

Chapter 28 Answer Key

ExamView®
One-time Download

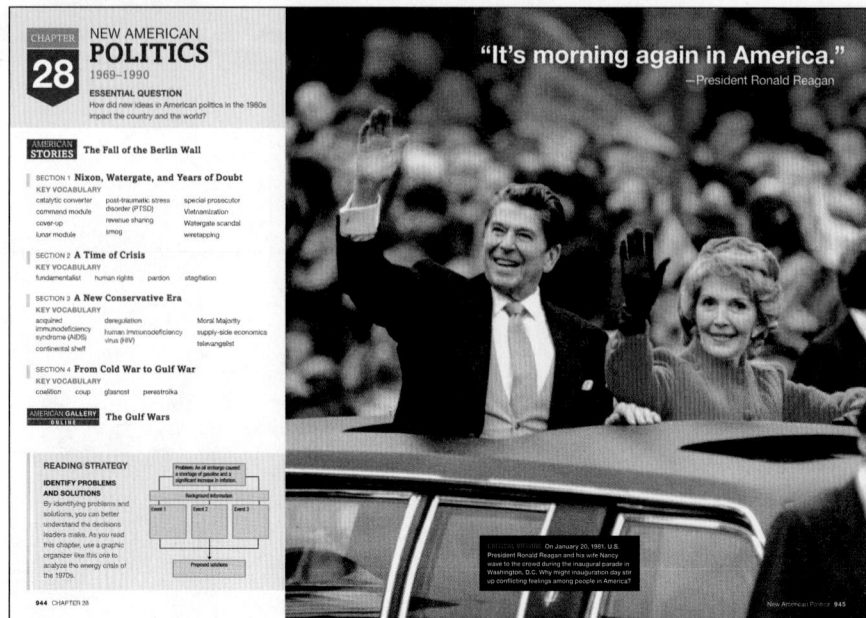

STUDENT DIGITAL RESOURCES

• **eEdition** (English)	• **Online Atlas**	• **American Voices (Biographies)**
• **eEdition** (Spanish)	• **American Gallery Online**	• **Active History**
• **Handbooks**	• **History Notebook**	• **Projects for Inquiry-Based Learning**

Chapter 28 Spanish Resources are available at NGLSync.Cengage.com.

AMERICAN STORIES | The Fall of the Berlin Wall

- Primary Sources
- On Your Feet: Compare Leaders
- **NG Learning Framework:** Draw a Map of Berlin

SECTION 1 RESOURCES

NIXON, WATERGATE, AND YEARS OF DOUBT

LESSON 1.1
Nixon and Vietnam

- On Your Feet: Sequence Chain
- **NG Learning Framework:** Write a Persuasive Speech

LESSON 1.2
Governing a Divided Nation

- On Your Feet: Roundtable Discussion
- **NG Learning Framework:** Write a Presidential Address

LESSON 1.3
Earth and Space

- On Your Feet: Three-Step Interview
- **NG Learning Framework:** Create an Apollo 11 Booklet

American Voices Biography
Rachel Carson ONLINE

LESSON 1.4
Cleaner Air and Water

- Active History: Research Local Habitat Preservation Efforts
- **NG Learning Framework:** Create a Diagram

LESSON 1.5
The Watergate Scandal

- On Your Feet: Goal and Outcome
- **NG Learning Framework:** Think Like a Journalist

SECTION 2 RESOURCES

A TIME OF CRISIS

LESSON 2.1
Ford and Carter

- On Your Feet: Time Line
- **NG Learning Framework:** Create an Inflation Graph

LESSON 2.2
Carter's Foreign Policy

- On Your Feet: Debate the Decision
- **NG Learning Framework:** Research the Camp David Accords

SECTION 3 RESOURCES

A NEW CONSERVATIVE ERA

LESSON 3.1
Reagan's Victory in 1980

- On Your Feet: Question and Answer
- **NG Learning Framework:** Build a Slide Show

American Voices Biography
Sandra Day O'Connor ONLINE

LESSON 3.2
AMERICAN VOICES
Ronald Wilson Reagan

- On Your Feet: Numbered Heads
- **NG Learning Framework:** Analyze the Great Communicator

American Voices Biography
Ronald Reagan ONLINE

LESSON 3.3
A Changing Nation

- On Your Feet: View a Clip
- **NG Learning Framework:** Research Gay Rights

LESSON 3.4
Deregulation and Defense

- On Your Feet: Roundtable Discussion
- **NG Learning Framework:** Draw a Diagram of SDI

SECTION 4 RESOURCES

FROM COLD WAR TO GULF WAR

LESSON 4.1
The End of the Cold War

- On Your Feet: 5Ws Chart
- **NG Learning Framework:** Write an Opinion Piece

LESSON 4.2
War in the Middle East

AMERICAN GALLERY ONLINE   The Gulf Wars

- **NG Learning Framework:** Present a News Report

American Voices Biographies
George H.W. Bush and George W. Bush ONLINE

CHAPTER 28 REVIEW

Strategy ❶
Read and Recall

Arrange students in mixed-proficiency pairs and tell them to first read the lesson independently. Then guide pairs to share all the facts and ideas they recall, as one partner takes notes. When students are done, instruct them to review the lesson, discussing what to add or change in the notes.

Use with All Lessons

Strategy ❷
Use a Word Splash

Display the words below in a random "splash" arrangement. Tell students the words relate to the Watergate scandal. Ask students to talk about what the words bring to mind, and then have them work in pairs and write sentences, using two of the words in each sentence.

Use with Lesson 1.5 *You might pair each student with a more proficient reader and ask them to combine their sentences to form a paragraph about the Watergate scandal. Tell partners to revise the sentences so that the paragraph makes sense and supports the ideas in the lesson.*

Strategy ❸
Use Reciprocal Teaching

Instruct partners to take turns reading each paragraph of the lesson aloud. At the end of the paragraph, the reading student should ask the listening student questions about the paragraph. Students may ask their partners to state the main idea of the paragraph, identify important details that support the main idea, or summarize the paragraph in their own words.

Use with All Lessons

Strategy ❶
Use Supported Reading

Prompt pairs of students to read the chapter aloud lesson by lesson. Instruct them to stop at the end of each lesson and use these sentence frames to monitor their comprehension of the text.

- This lesson is mostly about _____.
- Other topics in this lesson are _____.
- One question I have about the lesson is _____.
- One word I do not recognize is _____.
- I don't think I understand _____.

Guide students through portions of text they do not understand. Be sure all students understand a lesson before moving on to the next one.

Use with All Lessons

Strategy ❷
Use Maps to Support Text

To help orient students to the period from the Cold War to the Gulf War, guide them in using the map in Lesson 4.1 titled Breakup of the Soviet Union, 1991. Instruct students to use a finger to trace the line indicating territory held by the Soviet Union during the Cold War. Then tell students to point to and count each of the colored areas that represent new nations that came into existence at the end of the Cold War.

Use with Lessons 4.1–4.2 *For Lesson 4.2, bring students' attention to the map titled Middle East, 1990–91. Tell them to point to Kuwait and to note its proximity to Saudi Arabia, a U.S. ally.*

ENGLISH LANGUAGE LEARNERS

Strategy ❶
Use Paired Reading

Pair students at the **Expanding** and **Bridging** levels of proficiency. Direct them to take turns reading and retelling passages from the text aloud in the following manner.

1. Partner 1 reads a passage; Partner 2 retells the passage in his or her own words.
2. Partner 2 reads a different passage; Partner 1 retells it.
3. Pairs repeat the process, switching roles.

Use with All Lessons

Strategy ❷
Use a Main Idea Cluster

Pair students at the **Emerging** and **Expanding** levels of proficiency with students at the **Bridging** level. Direct pairs to use a Main Idea Cluster to check their understanding of the lesson. Tell partners to take turns reading a section of the lesson. Then have them work together to record the main idea and four details that support the idea. Instruct pairs to trade and compare clusters with other pairs.

Use with All Lessons

Strategy ❸
Review Transitional Words

To help students understand and express cause and effect relationships presented in the chapter, write words and phrases such as these on the board: *therefore, consequently, because of, as a result, the reason for,* and *hence.* Direct pairs of students at the **Emerging** and **Expanding** levels of proficiency to work together to identify cause and effect relationships in the lesson and write a sentence about each. Encourage them to use some of the supplied words in their sentences.

Use with All Lessons

GIFTED & TALENTED

Strategy ❶
Create a Gallery Walk

To help students gain a fuller understanding of the late 20th century, instruct them to locate online resources such as editorial cartoons, newspaper headlines, photographs, protest posters, song lyrics, and quotations from key individuals. Prompt students to group their findings by medium or theme and to set up stations around the classroom. Each station should include gallery-style signage that makes connections between the artistic expressions on display and the larger social, political, and economic realities of the time period. Then conduct a gallery walk, inviting students to stop at each station.

Use with All Lessons

Strategy ❷
Present a Documentary

Invite students to watch segments of the Ken Burns and Lynn Novick documentary *The Vietnam War* that relate to anti-war protests, the Pentagon Papers, or the U.S. withdrawal. Instruct students to present one of the segments of the documentary and develop questions for the entire class to discuss regarding the segment.

Use with Lesson 1.1

Pre-AP
Strategy ❶
Write a Letter to the Editor

Prompt students to research a current environmental issue, ideally one that affects their community or region, and to write a letter to the editor about it. Tell them to reference the Clean Air, Clean Water, or Endangered Species Act, if relevant. Students may read their letters to the class, post them on a class blog, or print and display them on a classroom bulletin board. You may also encourage students to send their letters to local newspapers.

Use with Lessons 1.3–1.4

Strategy ❷
Extend Knowledge

Direct students to conduct research to learn more about a person, event, or topic introduced in Chapter 28. For example, they could research Nixon's visit to China, the first moon landings, the first Earth Day, the Watergate scandal, Carter's Middle East peace agreement, or the gay rights movement. Invite students to present their findings in an oral report or in a digital report posted on a class blog.

Use with All Lessons

NEW AMERICAN
POLITICS
1969–1990

28

ESSENTIAL QUESTION
How did new ideas in American politics in the 1980s impact the country and the world?

AMERICAN STORIES The Fall of the Berlin Wall

SECTION 1 **Nixon, Watergate, and Years of Doubt**
KEY VOCABULARY

catalytic converter	post-traumatic stress disorder (PTSD)	special prosecutor
command module	revenue sharing	Vietnamization
cover-up	smog	Watergate scandal
lunar module		wiretapping

SECTION 2 **A Time of Crisis**
KEY VOCABULARY

fundamentalist	human rights	pardon	stagflation

SECTION 3 **A New Conservative Era**
KEY VOCABULARY

acquired immunodeficiency syndrome (AIDS)	deregulation	Moral Majority
	human immunodeficiency virus (HIV)	supply-side economics
continental shelf		televangelist

SECTION 4 **From Cold War to Gulf War**
KEY VOCABULARY

coalition	coup	glasnost	perestroika

AMERICAN GALLERY
ONLINE The Gulf Wars

READING STRATEGY

IDENTIFY PROBLEMS AND SOLUTIONS
By identifying problems and solutions, you can better understand the decisions leaders make. As you read this chapter, use a graphic organizer like this one to analyze the energy crisis of the 1970s.

> **"It's morning again in America."**
> —President Ronald Reagan

CRITICAL VIEWING On January 20, 1981, U.S. President Ronald Reagan and his wife Nancy wave to the crowd during the inaugural parade in Washington, D.C. Why might inauguration day stir up conflicting feelings among people in America?

INTRODUCE THE PHOTOGRAPH

Reagan's Inauguration Day

Direct students' attention to the photograph of President Ronald Reagan's inaugural parade that opens the chapter. Point out that Reagan's wife, Nancy, is standing next to him. Explain that during a president's inaugural parade, the president and vice president travel down Pennsylvania Avenue to the White House. Following them are marching bands, floats, and other groups that take part in the procession. During his inaugural ceremony, the first staged on the West Front of the U.S. Capitol, Ronald Reagan placed his hand on a worn family Bible and repeated the oath of office as read by Chief Justice Warren Burger. In his inaugural speech, Reagan declared his priorities— strengthening the economy and shrinking the federal government—and proclaimed his optimism for the future of the United States. Tell students that in this chapter they will learn about the presidencies during the 1980s and the effects those presidencies had on the country and the world.

For Chapter 28 Spanish Resources, visit the Resources Menu. Chapter 28 Resources are available at NGLSync.Cengage.com.

Share Background

The inaugural parade is just one of many activities that take place on Inauguration Day. Other activities typically include such events as a morning worship service, a procession to the Capitol with the president and president-elect, swearing-in ceremonies for the new president and vice president, an inaugural address, the official departure of the outgoing president, and a luncheon and ball. Some of these events have taken place since the country's beginning, while others did not become part of the schedule until the 20th century.

CRITICAL VIEWING Possible response: Those who voted for the new president would likely be happy. But those who voted for the candidates who did not win might still have feelings of patriotism about the ceremonial and peaceful transition of power even if they do not want to celebrate the individual who was elected.

INTRODUCE THE ESSENTIAL QUESTION

How did new ideas in American politics in the 1980s impact the country and the world?

Numbered Heads Activity: Government Policies This activity gets students thinking about some of the issues the president must consider as the country's leader. Divide the class into four groups and have each student in a group number off. Assign each group one of these topics: the economy, foreign policy, defense, domestic policy. Ask these questions:

Group 1: What are some issues the president must take into account when developing economic policies?

Group 2: How might world events influence a president's foreign policy?

Group 3: What are some different approaches a president might take toward defense of the country?

Group 4: In what ways does a president's domestic policy affect ordinary Americans?

Tell the group members to think individually about the question and assigned topic. Then instruct them to participate in a group discussion of the question and topic. After the discussion, call out a number and ask each group member with that number to report on the group's discussion.

INTRODUCE CHAPTER VOCABULARY

Word Webs

Instruct students to complete a Word Web for Key Vocabulary words as they read the chapter. Ask them to write each word in the center of an oval. Prompt them to look through the chapter to find examples, characteristics, and descriptive words that may be associated with the vocabulary word. At the end of the chapter, ask students what they learned about each word.

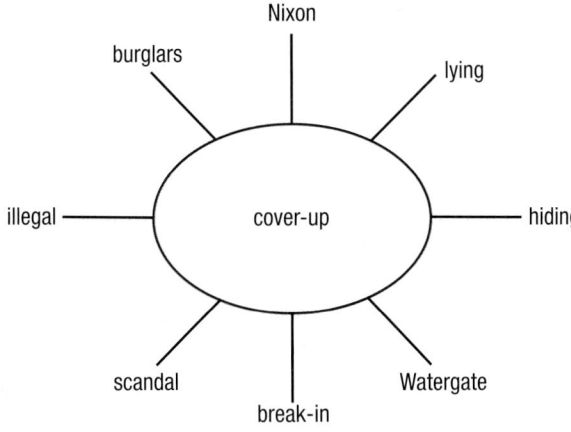

INTRODUCE THE READING STRATEGY

IDENTIFY PROBLEMS AND SOLUTIONS
Remind students that when identifying problems and solutions, it is useful to keep track of the events that caused or contributed to the problem. Sometimes a solution to one problem can actually be the cause of another problem. Preview the Problem-and-Solution Diagram. Point out the different sections: Problem, Background information, Events, and Proposed solutions. Remind students to make use of the graphic organizer as they read the chapter.

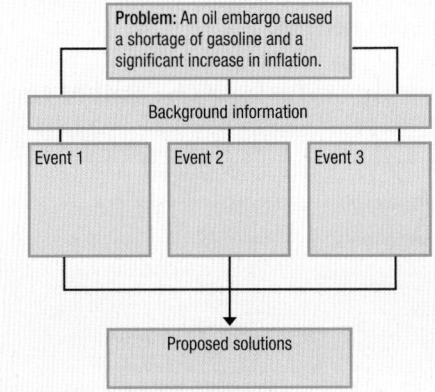

KEY DATES FOR CHAPTER 28

1969	Apollo 11 moon landing
1971	26th Amendment is ratified
1973	United States withdraws from Vietnam
1974	President Richard Nixon resigns
1978	Camp David Accords
1979	Iranians take Americans hostage
1980	Ronald Reagan elected president
1986	Iran-Contra Affair
1988	George H.W. Bush elected president
1991	Persian Gulf War

For more on challenges relating to energy resources, see *GLOBAL ISSUES: ENERGY RESOURCES.*

STEM

Objectives

- **Learn the history behind the division of East Berlin and West Berlin.**
- **Identify the reasons for the construction and destruction of the Berlin Wall.**
- **Analyze the conditions that drove people to escape East Berlin.**
- **Examine the significance of the Berlin Wall throughout the world.**
- **Study a primary source: excerpt of a speech by President Ronald Reagan.**

Critical Thinking Skills for "The Fall of the Berlin Wall"

- Make Connections
- Draw Conclusions
- Analyze Language Use
- Analyze Primary Sources
- Evaluate

Background for the Teacher

This American Story addresses the fall of the Berlin Wall in 1989. Photographs highlight the transformation of the wall over time and the protections put in place to ensure its effectiveness. Quotations from German citizens and an excerpt of a speech by President Reagan convey the strong emotions the wall evoked. Use this American Story to provide students with a greater understanding of the major social and political changes that took place during the 1980s.

This chapter, New American Politics, explores the transformation the United States underwent during the latter half of the 20th century. This American Story highlights one of the most significant events to take place during this time—and one that also marked a major progression in the relationship between the United States and the Soviet Union.

History Notebook

Encourage students to complete the American Story page for Chapter 28 in their History Notebooks as they read.

Note to the Teacher

Introduce this American Story after the class has engaged with the content in Lesson 4.1.

AMERICAN STORIES
NATIONAL GEOGRAPHIC

CRITICAL VIEWING On November 10, 1989, people were once again permitted to move between East and West Berlin. Berliners flocked to the Berlin Wall, celebrating and chanting, "Tor auf!" (Open the gate!) What does this photo reveal about the feelings of Berliners during the fall of the wall?

946 CHAPTER 28

THE FALL OF THE
BERLIN WALL

Although it was hundreds of miles from the ocean, West Berlin was an island, surrounded by a human-made barrier. In early 1945, after World War II, the triumphant Allies had divided Germany into two parts. The eastern half of the country was occupied by the Soviet Union, while the western half was split into zones overseen by the United States, Great Britain, and France. The capital, Berlin, was similarly divided, even though it was well within the Soviet occupation zone.

New American Politics 947

Determine a Border Wall's Purpose

Tell students to consider some of the purposes that walls like the one in Berlin serve. Ask them to think of one-word descriptions that identify these purposes, and list the words on the board. After the class has finished making suggestions, discuss the words listed. Ask students to determine whether the words are mainly positive or negative and to summarize what the descriptions reflect about people's perceptions of walls.

Consider the Consequences

Discuss with students what might happen if there were a wall built in the middle of their school and they had to spend the school day only in their half of the school. Guide them to think about and discuss the following questions:

• What might be some of the consequences of the wall?

• What would you do if you needed to get to the other half of the school?

• How would you communicate with students and teachers on the other side of the wall?

• What would be different on each side? What would be the same?

• Would there be different leadership, sports teams, and student government on each side?

Tell students that in this American Story they will learn about the rise and fall of the Berlin Wall and how the wall affected not only Germany but also the rest of the world.

CRITICAL VIEWING Possible response: It looks like a lot of people wanted to see the wall come down. They seem happy, enthusiastic, and curious to climb up on top of it. There seems to be a feeling of solidarity, as people on top help others climb up.

Berlin Crisis of 1961

In January 1961, Nikita Khrushchev demanded that the United States and its allies vacate West Berlin, asserting that all of Berlin was technically within the Soviet zone. Later that summer, Khrushchev again expressed his desire to President Kennedy to reunite Germany under communist control, threatening to cut off all Western access to West Berlin if the United States and its allies did not comply. They refused.

Not long after, Khrushchev abruptly made the decision to close off access between East Berlin and West Berlin and build a wall. At first Kennedy thought this signaled an end to tensions between the countries. But within just a few days of the wall's completion, Soviet and East German police and soldiers began harassing U.S. forces and diplomats at checkpoints as they tried to cross into East Berlin. During one particularly tense situation in October, Soviet and U.S. tanks sat facing each other at a checkpoint, ready to do battle, before things finally calmed down. Tensions grew so great between the Soviet Union and the United States during this period that Kennedy actually considered the possibility of a nuclear strike against the Soviets.

Television and the Great Escape

The tunnels that East Berlin citizens used to flee to West Berlin became such a subject of intrigue in the West that one U.S. television network paid a group of diggers to let them film a tunnel excavation and escape. To keep the dig a secret, only a few people were made aware of the agreement between the network and the diggers. In December 1962, the network broadcast the 90-minute documentary, *The Tunnel*, featuring both the tunnel's creation and the dramatic escape of more than two dozen people. Though the documentary won several awards, the broadcast angered members of the Kennedy administration, who feared it might further damage relations with the Soviets.

BUILDING THE WALL

In 1949, the United States, Great Britain, and France merged their occupation zones to create the Federal Republic of Germany, which was commonly known as West Germany. In response, the Soviet Union decreed the eastern half of Germany to be an independent entity as well. Its official name was the German Democratic Republic, but it was popularly called East Germany. Although hopes for a national reunification lingered, Germany was now partitioned into two countries. West Berlin remained a capitalist, western European city deep within the Soviet realm of influence. As Soviet leader Nikita Khrushchev described it, the city was "stuck like a bone in the Soviet throat."

At first, residents of East and West Berlin could travel freely between the halves of the city for jobs, shopping, and entertainment, or to visit with friends and family. To the growing embarrassment of Soviet and East German authorities, a steady flood of refugees crossed from East Germany to West Berlin to escape the repressive conditions in the communist East. By 1961, about 3 million people had fled from East to West Germany. Many of them were young, educated, skilled workers and professionals. In 1961, the numbers peaked, with more than 18,000 people leaving East Germany in the first 12 days of August.

AN IMPASSABLE WALL

The Berlin Wall was a system of concrete walls and other fencing that separated West Berlin from East Berlin and adjacent parts of East Germany. A restricted zone prevented most East Berliners from getting near the wall that marked West Berlin's border. Guards with orders to shoot on sight staffed watchtowers and patrolled the zone at all hours. Despite these obstacles, more than 5,000 East Germans managed to cross the barrier and escape into West Berlin from 1961 to 1989, including about 600 border guards. Some escapees found a way to climb over the barrier. More dramatic escape plans included crawling through tunnels and sewers, smashing through weaker parts of the barrier with vehicles, and flying over the border in a hot air balloon.

Death strip: A strip covered with soft sand revealed the footprints of anyone trying to escape.

Guard road: A concrete path allowed guards to patrol without leaving misleading footprints.

Fencing: Climbing this barbed-wire signal fence tripped an alarm.

Tank traps: Angled steel was used to prevent an escape with a car or truck.

Checkpoint: Guards checked the papers of people wishing to pass through the wall to prevent East Germans from escaping into West Germany.

TUNNEL 57

A wall, an abandoned bakery, and students with shovels. That's what it took to dig a tunnel under the Berlin Wall in 1964, through which 57 people escaped. Tunneling was only one of many plans used to secretly move from East to West Germany, and frankly, it wasn't that successful. Over 30 years, only about 300 people escaped through tunnels, which were hard to dig and were oftentimes discovered before they could be used.

But civil engineering student Joachim Neumann, who had himself escaped to West Germany using a borrowed passport, spearheaded a tunneling success. His first attempt to tunnel under the wall failed when the East German secret police, the Stasi, learned of his tunnel and arrested many of those attempting to escape. But Neumann wasn't ready to give up. He found an old bakery in West Germany and started tunneling from the bakery to the East German side of the wall. Neumann and several other students spent 5 months digging under a city street, the Berlin Wall, an alarm-equipped signal fence, and the "death strip," a no-man's-land area complete with guard towers, floodlights, and steel spikes. Their tunnel came up on the East German side in an outhouse behind an apartment building.

CRITICAL VIEWING A woman scrambles through Tunnel 57 to reach West Berlin in October 1964. What inferences can you make about her life in East Berlin based on what you observe in this photo?

On October 3, 1964, the tunnel was finally ready. Friends and family members of the tunnel diggers gathered at the East German apartment building and whispered the code word "Tokyo" to gain access to the escape route. Fifty-seven people crawled and slithered underground more than the length of a football field to the freedom of West Germany. Neumann's tunnel was discovered by East German police and closed on October 4. However, in the two days it was open, Tunnel 57 became the most successful escape path in the history of the Berlin Wall.

For Khrushchev, enough was enough. He gave the East German government permission to build a barrier that would stop the outpouring. Within two weeks, the Berlin Wall was constructed. The initial barrier consisted of barbed wire fencing. It gradually developed into a series of intimidating concrete walls and electric fencing in a border zone patrolled by armed guards and attack dogs.

In the United States, reaction to the building of the wall was mixed. Some felt the United States and its allies should destroy the wall immediately. President Kennedy did not like the wall, but he recognized that it solved a problem. The flow of people defecting—or permanently leaving—from East Germany caused tension between the Soviet Union and the United States. "It's not a very nice solution," he privately told his aides, "but a wall is a . . . lot better than a war."

For the United States, the Berlin Wall was a public relations advantage during the Cold War. It served as evidence to the world that citizens had to be forced to stay in a Soviet-dominated country. At the same time, it made West Berlin a symbol of the personal freedoms denied to individuals under communism. For many Berliner families, the construction of the wall had tragic results. With travel between the halves of the city completely shut down for citizens, some families had members trapped on the wrong side of the wall. Parents were separated from children and husbands from wives for nearly 30 years. One former East Berliner later recalled how he felt when the wall was built: "I was 14 when the Wall went up. So for me, it meant that I was stranded behind the wall and that I couldn't get out anymore. I couldn't move. I couldn't make my own decisions."

TEACH

Guided Discussion

1. **Analyze Language Use** What did Nikita Khrushchev mean when he described West Berlin as "stuck like a bone in the Soviet throat"? *(Possible response: West Berlin was under Western control, while East Berlin was under Soviet control. But West Berlin was actually still within the Soviet occupation zone, so it must have irritated Khrushchev—like when something is stuck in a person's throat and can't be dislodged—that it was not under Soviet control.)*

2. **Draw Conclusions** Why did people fleeing East Berlin into West Berlin cause tension between the United States and the Soviet Union? *(The United States was one of the countries occupying West Berlin at the time. People escaping from East Berlin to West Berlin served as a reminder to the Soviets—and the rest of the world—that people would rather live in a capitalist-controlled area than a communist-controlled area.)*

CRITICAL VIEWING Possible response: Crawling through the tunnels seems like it was a terrible experience. The opening looks small and difficult to maneuver through. If people were willing to undertake this scary, uncomfortable ordeal to get out of East Berlin, then their lives there must have been extremely unpleasant.

Active Options

On Your Feet: Compare Leaders Organize students into groups of three or four. Instruct each group to complete a T-Chart comparing the influences that Soviet leaders Nikita Khrushchev and Mikhail Gorbachev had on the Berlin Wall. As part of their comparison, groups should also address the men's general approaches to leadership. After groups have completed their charts, invite them to share their comparisons with the class and discuss who they thought was a better leader.

NG Learning Framework: Draw a Map of Berlin

Instruct partners to draw a map showing East Berlin and West Berlin and the location of the Berlin Wall along the border between the two. Ask students to indicate on their maps the approximate locations of different checkpoints along the wall and include brief facts about the wall. Tell them to conduct online research to locate images and other helpful information for completing their maps. After students have finished, invite partners to present their maps to the class.

WRITE ABOUT HISTORY

Compose a Letter to a Family Member This American Story describes the destruction of the Berlin Wall and the events leading up to it. To help students visualize what life might have been like during the division of Berlin, prompt them to write a letter from the perspective of someone living in East Berlin. Ask students to imagine they are living there after the construction of the Berlin Wall and are writing a letter to a family member in West Berlin. In the letter, students should describe conditions in East Berlin after the wall's construction and explain how it will affect their relationship with their family members in West Berlin. Encourage students to use details from the American Story to help them compose their letters.

CRITICAL VIEWING Possible response: People today talk about building walls to separate people, just like the Berlin Wall once did in Germany. While the Berlin Wall was intended to keep people in, walls discussed today are more often intended to keep people out. The history of the Berlin Wall shows what can happen as a result of a wall being built.

THINK ABOUT IT

Possible response: Events in other countries matter to the United States because they often affect the stability of the rest of the world. The fall of the Berlin Wall, for example, led to better relationships among Germany, the United States, and other countries in Europe.

AMERICAN STORIES

THE FALL OF THE WALL

By 1989, the political situation had changed enormously. Soviet leader Mikhail Gorbachev had instituted several reforms in an effort to improve the country's failing economy. He allowed elections for many political offices within the Soviet Union and loosened control over countries that the Soviet Union had previously dominated. Several countries, such as Poland and Hungary, replaced their old, Soviet-dominated governments. East Germany would not be far behind.

In October 1989, Gorbachev visited East Berlin and was greeted by crowds who were restless for a change in their government. Wanting his support, they cried out, "[Gorbachev], help us!" In the month following his visit, East Germans expressed their anger in demonstrations throughout the country. At the same time, a new portal for freedom had opened for East Germans. They could pose as tourists in Hungary, where they were allowed to travel, and then cross the border into Austria.

On November 9, 1989, the East Berlin authorities announced that at midnight they would open the gates in the Berlin Wall. Citizens on both sides would be free to cross the borders between East and West Germany at will. By the time midnight arrived, the streets near the wall were filled with Berliners celebrating and shouting, "Open the gate!" What followed has been described by one witness as "the greatest street party in the history of the world." More than 2 million people from East Berlin flooded into West Berlin. Young people explored a city they had never seen before, while their elders rediscovered places that were once familiar to them. All generations shared in the joy of the moment. Amid

"TEAR DOWN THIS WALL"

On June 12, 1987, President Ronald Reagan was scheduled to give a speech in West Berlin as part of a celebration marking the founding of Berlin 750 years earlier. The speech would be delivered in front of the Brandenburg Gate, a monument built in the late 1700s by the Prussian king Frederick William II. The gate was an important symbol of both Berlin's history and its division. It was located in East Berlin inside the restricted zone of the Berlin Wall, so that it could not be reached from either side.

In April, a young speechwriter named Peter Robinson had been assigned to write the president's speech for the occasion. Using strong language, Robinson crafted a speech that bluntly implored Gorbachev to get rid of the Berlin Wall. Some members of the State Department worried that the lines about tearing down the wall might offend the Soviet leader Mikhail Gorbachev. Reagan himself, however, liked the lines. As he was being driven to the Berlin Wall to make the speech, Reagan confided to an aide, "The boys at State are going to kill me, but it's the right thing to do." It was another two years before the Berlin Wall actually came down, but Reagan's speech is remembered as a landmark moment in the progress toward reunifying Germany.

PRIMARY SOURCE

We welcome change and openness; for we believe that freedom and security go together, that the advance of human liberty can only strengthen the cause of world peace. There is one sign the Soviets can make that would be unmistakable, that would advance dramatically the cause of freedom and peace. General Secretary Gorbachev, if you seek peace, if you seek prosperity for the Soviet Union and Eastern Europe, if you seek liberalization, come here to this gate. Mr. Gorbachev, open this gate. Mr. Gorbachev, tear down this wall!

the celebrations, a young woman named Angela Merkel crossed over into West Berlin and called her aunt in Hamburg, West Germany. After that night, she would become active in politics, and in 2005 she took office as chancellor, the highest government post in the reunified Germany.

Once the gates were open, elated Berliners determined the entire wall must come down. Unwilling to wait for official demolition crews, people began chipping away at it with hammers, picks, and whatever tools they could gather.

CRITICAL VIEWING (left) A mother and daughter stand at the foot of the half-ruined Berlin Wall looking at an East Berlin watchtower. (right) Parts of the Berlin Wall are prominently featured at the Newseum in Washington, D.C. How is the history of the Berlin Wall relevant today?

These "wall woodpeckers" continued to remove chunks of cement even as heavy construction equipment moved in to tear down the Berlin Wall. In 1990, East Germany, West Germany, the United States, Great Britain, France, and the Soviet Union signed the Treaty on the Final Settlement with Respect to Germany. When the treaty went into effect on March 15, 1991, the reunion of Germany was complete and official.

Today, the Berlin Wall is memorialized in various places throughout the city. The official memorial has been installed in a section of the former "death strip," where many people were killed while attempting to escape. The site features original sections of the wall that were left standing and informational displays about the wall's history. A few other Berlin Wall sections remain in different parts of the city. One section was transformed after the wall fell. It became a gallery that features about 100 large paintings created directly on the wall by various artists. The murals were painted on the side of the wall that had

been protected by soldiers and was therefore, understandably, untouched. The west side of the wall had been covered with graffiti and political slogans by the West Berliners who hated the separation it symbolized.

In the United States, Americans eagerly viewed scenes of joyous Berliners celebrating and tearing into the wall with sledgehammers. Many sympathized with the Berliners' desire for reunification and freedom. The event quickly came to symbolize the end of the Cold War and of the nuclear threat that had hovered in the background during those decades. The United States had first opened diplomatic relations with West Germany in 1955. In 1991, it allied itself with the reunified Germany. Today, the two countries maintain close ties as allies and strong trading partners.

THINK ABOUT IT

Why do important events abroad, such as the building and removal of the Berlin Wall, matter to the United States?

New American Politics **951**

Inclusion

Describe Lesson Photographs Pair students who are visually impaired with students who are not. Ask the latter to describe the photographs and read the captions. Tell visually impaired students to ask clarifying questions as necessary. Then have partners work together to answer the Critical Viewing questions.

Gifted & Talented

Write a Film Treatment Tell students that the fall of the Berlin Wall is full of compelling characters and dramatic moments. Instruct them to conduct research using online and print sources to access eyewitness accounts of what happened in November 1989. Then have students write a short synopsis for a documentary or narrative film. They may choose to focus on one character or incident or take a wider view. Invite students to read their treatments to the class.

See the Chapter Planner for more strategies for differentiation.

HISTORICAL THINKING

Ask and have students answer the following questions.

1. **READING CHECK** How did people react when the gates opened between East Berlin and West Berlin?

2. **ANALYZE PRIMARY SOURCES** Why do you think President Reagan thought Gorbachev might tear down the wall?

3. **EVALUATE** How effective was the wall at stopping people from leaving East Berlin?

ANSWERS

1. Two million people crossed into West Berlin. They were happy. Some began tearing down the wall themselves because they didn't want to wait for demolition crews.

2. Gorbachev had brought reforms in the Soviet Union. Reagan probably thought he might agree to similar reforms in East Berlin.

3. Answers will vary. Possible response: It was fairly effective, because only about 5,000 people escaped between 1961 and 1989. Three million people had left East Germany before the wall was constructed.

1.1 Nixon and Vietnam

How would you feel about being drafted to fight in a war you didn't believe in? That's the situation many 18-year-old American males faced during most of the Vietnam War years.

MAIN IDEA President Nixon expanded the war in Vietnam before finally withdrawing American troops in 1973, but the war continued until North Vietnam took control of South Vietnam in 1975.

VIETNAMIZATION

During his presidential campaign, Richard Nixon declared that he had a "secret plan" to end the Vietnam War. After taking office in 1969, he announced a military strategy he called **Vietnamization**. It involved slowly withdrawing U.S. troops as the South Vietnamese took over more of the fighting. However, Nixon's plan actually began an escalation of the war. For example, he began bombing communist supply lines in the neutral country of Cambodia. These supply lines ran through thick jungles just over South Vietnam's western border. Nixon tried to hide the attacks from the American public because he knew the escalation of the war would incite more protests.

On April 30, 1970, Nixon publicly announced another plan. This time he wanted to send U.S. ground troops to Cambodia to finish destroying military supply lines there. Nixon's announcement provoked massive anti-war protests on college campuses across the nation.

During a large protest at **Kent State University** in Ohio, students set fire to an army training building on campus. The governor of Ohio sent National Guard troops to maintain order. On May 4, 1970, guardsmen and protesters clashed. Several guardsmen shot their rifles directly into the crowd, killing four students and wounding nine others. Some of the students shot were not even involved in the protest. They had merely been walking across campus, headed to their next class.

The F-4 Vietnam patch (left) was given to war pilots who had flown 200 missions. The U.S. Air Force Aviator patch (below) shows an eagle holding a missile.

Post-Traumatic Stress Disorder

A number of veterans returning from service in Vietnam were suffering from **post-traumatic stress disorder (PTSD)**, a condition that had been called "shell-shock" in World War I and "battle fatigue" in World War II. Marked by flashbacks—sudden, vivid memories of terrifying events—anger-management problems, and sleeping disorders, PTSD is long-lasting and difficult to treat. Veterans who were not adequately treated for the condition often self-medicated with drugs or alcohol. Some even took their own lives. For them, the war never really ended.

A 14-year-old girl reacts to the shooting of a student by National Guard troops at Kent State University on May 4, 1970, during an anti-war protest. This photograph became a powerful symbol of Americans' pain over the Vietnam War.

The Kent State shootings horrified Americans and weakened the public's faith in the government. Public trust suffered another blow when the media published portions of the Pentagon Papers in 1971. The papers were a secret Department of Defense study of U.S. military involvement in Vietnam. A researcher who worked on the study leaked the documents to the press. The Pentagon Papers proved that government officials had lied to the public about the progress of the war.

WITHDRAWAL FROM VIETNAM

As the Vietnam War became increasingly unpopular, Nixon increased efforts to negotiate a peace settlement. In January 1973, representatives from the United States, North and South Vietnam, and the Vietcong reached an agreement to end all combat. The terms of the agreement included the complete withdrawal of U.S. troops by March. In exchange, the North Vietnamese would release American prisoners of war (POWs), and North and South Vietnam would cease combat.

These terms were not kept, however. After the bulk of U.S. troops withdrew, the North Vietnamese invaded South Vietnam, taking complete control by April 30, 1975. In the last days before South Vietnam's capital city of Saigon fell, thousands of remaining Americans and U.S. allies fled the country. North and South Vietnam then reunited as one communist nation.

The long war to prevent the spread of communism had failed. In the end, some 58,000 Americans and more than 2 million Vietnamese died in the conflict. The war influenced the ratification of the **26th Amendment**, which lowered the voting age to 18. It also led to passage of the **War Powers Act**, which limited the president's ability to wage a war without Congressional approval. In January 1973, two months before the last U.S. troops left Vietnam, the U.S. military discontinued the draft and moved to an all-volunteer army.

HISTORICAL THINKING

1. **READING CHECK** What was Vietnamization?

2. **ANALYZE CAUSE AND EFFECT** Why did the Vietnam War incite so much public opposition?

3. **DRAW CONCLUSIONS** Why do you think the Vietnam War helped promote the ratification of the 26th Amendment?

Objective

Analyze President Richard Nixon's role in escalating the Vietnam War.

Critical Thinking Skills for Lesson 1.1

- Identify Main Ideas and Details
- Monitor Comprehension
- Analyze Cause and Effect
- Draw Conclusions
- Form and Support Opinions
- Explain
- Determine Word Meaning

Essential Question for Chapter 28

How did new ideas in American politics in the 1980s impact the country and the world?

Opposition to the Vietnam War had been growing in the United States since the mid-1960s. Lesson 1.1 discusses President Nixon's role in continuing the war in Vietnam and describes the discord the war created at home.

Background for the Teacher

Because of the tragedy that unfolded in May 1970, the Kent State University protest became one of the more infamous antiwar demonstrations to take place during the Vietnam War. But antiwar protests in the United States had begun to gain momentum long before that. In April 1967, Martin Luther King, Jr., helped lead a protest in New York City, where, at Riverside Church, he delivered an antiwar speech to an audience of 3,000 people. Less than two weeks later, King helped lead about 100,000 marchers to the United Nations during another protest. In October 1967, an antiwar demonstration in Washington, D.C., drew about 100,000 protesters. They eventually marched to the Pentagon, where hundreds of them were arrested. These ongoing protests reflected a general weariness with the war. Kent State served as yet another flash point for these feelings.

Preview Using a Map

Display a map showing Vietnam and Cambodia and point out the two countries. Explain that, as part of this lesson, students will learn about how the United States involved Cambodia in a bombing campaign during the Vietnam War. **ASK:** Why might it have been easy for Cambodia to become involved in the war? *(It shares a border with Vietnam, so troops, civilians, and supplies might have easily passed from one country to the other.)* **ASK:** Why do you think the American public might be upset about the United States bringing another country into the war? *(Possible response: A larger war would likely mean more U.S. casualties, rising costs, and a longer conflict.)*

TEACH

Guided Discussion

1. **Form and Support Opinions** Do you think the events at Kent State influenced the debate over ending the Vietnam War? Explain your response. *(Possible response: Yes. I think the events made people more likely to support ending the war. Students wouldn't have been protesting at Kent State if it hadn't been for the war, so in a way, the war had now claimed the lives of some American civilians as well as soldiers.)*

2. **Explain** How did the peace agreement negotiated between the United States and Vietnam differ from what actually happened after the U.S. withdrawal from Vietnam? *(According to the peace agreement, North and South Vietnam would stop fighting upon the withdrawal of the United States. In actuality, North Vietnam invaded South Vietnam as soon as most of the U.S. troops left.)*

Determine Word Meaning

Direct students to the Vietnamization subsection. Read the sentence "A researcher who worked on the study leaked the documents to the press." **ASK:** What does the word *leaked* mean in this sentence? *(It means the researcher secretly released the documents.)*

Then direct students to the Withdrawal from Vietnam subsection. Read the sentence "In the last days before South Vietnam's capital city of Saigon fell, thousands of remaining Americans and U.S. allies fled the country." **ASK:** What does the word *fell* mean in this sentence? *(It means Saigon was defeated and taken over by the North Vietnamese.)*

Active Options

On Your Feet: Sequence Chain Ask students to form small groups of three or four. Instruct each group to complete a Sequence Chain detailing the major events described in the text. After the groups have completed their Sequence Chains, ask each one to present and summarize its events to the class. Then, as a class, discuss any differences between the groups' Sequence Chains and the reasons why some groups may have included events that others did not.

NG Learning Framework: Write a Persuasive Speech

ATTITUDE Responsibility

SKILLS Communication, Problem-Solving

Ask students to imagine they are politicians during the Vietnam War. Instruct them to write a short persuasive speech in which they argue for or against the passage of either the 26th Amendment or the War Powers Act. Students should include reasons for their support of or opposition to the piece of legislation and should incorporate details from the text. Invite them to present their speeches to the class.

Striving Readers

Record and Compare Facts After they read each section, ask students to write at least three facts they can recall. Allow pairs to compare and check their facts and combine them into one list. If the classroom dynamic is amenable, suggest a competition among pairs about which can produce the longest list.

Gifted & Talented

Review a Film Instruct students to watch *The Post* or another film about the Pentagon Papers and take notes about the obstacles that the *Washington Post* overcame in order to publish the information. Tell students to use their notes to write a review in which they explain how the film deepened their understanding of why Daniel Ellsberg took great risks to leak the top-secret document and why the *Washington Post* took great risks to publish it. Invite students to read their reviews to the class. You may then wish to lead a discussion about how contemporary films can make historical events relevant to a new generation.

See the Chapter Planner for more strategies for differentiation.

ANSWERS

1. Vietnamization was President Nixon's plan to slowly remove U.S. troops from Vietnam and allow the South Vietnamese troops to take over fighting the war.

2. Possible response: Many Americans were opposed to the war because young men were being drafted to fight and perhaps die in a faraway country. In addition, the government was secretive about it. For example, Nixon didn't tell people about bombing Cambodia at first because he knew they wouldn't approve. The release of the Pentagon Papers only caused more distrust among the public.

3. Possible response: Many believed that if citizens could be drafted at the age of 18, then they should also be able to vote.

1.2 Governing a Divided Nation

For years, American officials had refused to even recognize China's communist government. So President Nixon's visit to the country in 1972 made quite a statement. As he toured the Great Wall of China with communist guides, he hoped other nations were watching closely.

MAIN IDEA President Nixon generally took a moderate approach to domestic policy and a flexible, realistic approach to foreign policy.

During his historic visit to China in February 1972, President Nixon inspects an honor guard of Chinese soldiers along with Chinese Premier Zhou Enlai (left). The establishment of relations with China was a major foreign policy achievement.

STRIKING A BALANCE AT HOME

On domestic issues, President Nixon tried to find a political balance. He knew that the Democrats, who controlled both houses of Congress, would oppose a conservative course of action. The Senate, for example, rejected two of his conservative choices for Supreme Court justices. As a result, Nixon appointed four moderate judges to the Supreme Court.

Nixon supported certain programs promoted by the Democrats that provided government aid to needy families. But he took a conservative approach to implementing the programs. He believed it would be better for state governments, not the federal government, to control the programs' funds. To accomplish this, he promoted **revenue sharing**, which involves distributing a portion of federal tax money directly to state and local governments. The state or local governments then decide which programs to support and how much money to allocate.

In his first years in office, Nixon faced a series of economic problems. The United States had experienced an economic boom during the 1960s. But government debt from the Vietnam War and rising energy prices took their toll. By 1970, the unemployment rate had risen to 6 percent, and the economy had slowed down. Nixon's administration also struggled to halt or slow rapid inflation, or the rising prices of goods and services. To address these problems, Nixon put in place tax cuts and limits on increases in wages and prices.

PRIMARY SOURCE

In his campaign for the presidency, Richard Nixon expressed a conservative outlook on the high crime rates and civic unrest in the United States. He promised to restore law and order to the nation. In his presidential nomination speech, he described a nation torn apart.

As we look at America, we see cities enveloped in smoke and flame. We hear sirens in the night. We see Americans dying on distant battlefields abroad. We see Americans hating each other; fighting each other; killing each other at home. And as we see and hear these things, millions of Americans cry out in anguish. Did we come all this way for this?

—from Richard Nixon's presidential nomination speech, August 8, 1968

FOREIGN POLICY

Nixon adopted a flexible, realistic approach in dealing with foreign countries. To help guide foreign policy, he relied on his national security advisor, later his secretary of state, **Henry Kissinger**.

Both Nixon and Kissinger saw an opportunity to improve the U.S. economy by establishing a diplomatic and trade relationship with the People's Republic of China. On February 21, 1972, Nixon became the first American president to visit the communist country. He left with a promise from China's leaders for more open trade and cultural exchanges. Nixon used China's promise to bargain with the Soviet Union. China and the Soviet Union had a tense relationship, and Nixon knew the Soviets feared an alliance between China and the United States. The U.S. agreement with China made the Soviet Union more eager to negotiate with the United States. Three months after his trip to China, Nixon visited Moscow. Soviet leaders agreed to work with the United States to slow the arms race and open up trade. The two countries signed the first **Strategic Arms Limitation Treaty (SALT I)**, which limited each nation's number of nuclear missiles. Nixon also agreed to a trade deal, selling farming equipment and grain to the Soviet Union. The Moscow meetings eased tensions between the Soviet Union and the United States.

In October 1973, the powerful **Organization of Petroleum Exporting Countries (OPEC)** instituted an embargo on oil exports to the United States. Still in existence today, OPEC is a multinational organization that influences global policies and prices for gasoline and oil. In the early 1970s, OPEC wanted to punish the United States for backing Israel in a short war between Israel and a few OPEC member nations in the Middle East. Because the United States relied heavily on foreign oil imports, the embargo added to the nation's already high inflation. Americans had to reduce their energy use and wait in long lines to buy gasoline for their cars. The embargo ended in April 1974, but oil prices continued to rise.

HISTORICAL THINKING

1. **READING CHECK** How did revenue sharing give power back to states?

2. **IDENTIFY PROBLEMS AND SOLUTIONS** How did Nixon use foreign policy to help solve domestic economic problems?

3. **ANALYZE CAUSE AND EFFECT** What effect did Nixon's visit to China have on U.S. relations with the Soviet Union?

New American Politics 955

PLAN

Objective
Learn about the difficulties President Nixon faced regarding domestic and foreign policy.

Critical Thinking Skills for Lesson 1.2
- Identify Main Ideas and Details
- Monitor Comprehension
- Identify Problems and Solutions
- Analyze Cause and Effect
- Analyze Primary Sources
- Evaluate
- Analyze Visuals

Essential Question for Chapter 28
How did new ideas in American politics in the 1980s impact the country and the world?
Richard Nixon's presidency marked a change in foreign policy from previous administrations. Lesson 1.2 focuses on Nixon's approach toward trade with China and the Soviet Union.

Background for the Teacher
President Nixon's trips to China and the Soviet Union in 1972 not only improved the United States' relations with the two countries but also served as an opportunity to persuade both to limit their aid to North Vietnam. As communist countries, China and the Soviet Union had provided significant military and economic assistance to North Vietnam during the war. According to the CIA, they had contributed most of North Vietnam's aid—and the amount had steadily increased. By demonstrating that the United States was improving relations with China and the Soviet Union, Nixon wanted North Vietnam to experience a sense of isolation from other communist nations. Nixon hoped that the isolation, in turn, might put pressure on the North Vietnamese to negotiate with the United States for an end to the Vietnam War.

Discuss China

To help students prepare for the lesson, ask them to share what they already know about China. Suggest that they consider topics such as its geographical location, its history and culture, and its political system. Write their responses on the board. Explain that in this lesson students will learn about a trip President Nixon took to China in the early 1970s and how it affected the U.S.-China relationship.

TEACH

Guided Discussion

1. **Analyze Primary Sources** What effect do you think Nixon wanted his nomination acceptance speech to have on Americans? Explain your response. *(Possible response: He might have wanted to use fear to intimidate Americans. If he reminded people of how bad things were, then voters might see him as the solution to the problems.)*

2. **Evaluate** Why was OPEC able to create so much turmoil in this country by instituting an oil embargo on exports to the United States? Use details from the text to support your response. *(Americans used a great deal of oil and gasoline, which is made from oil, to power cars as well as factories, and the United States depended largely on oil supplied by foreign countries. By banding together, the oil-producing countries could shut down the supply of foreign oil reaching the United States.)*

Analyze Visuals

Direct students' attention to the photograph of President Nixon's 1972 visit to China. Give them time to look over the details. Then read the caption aloud. **ASK:** Based on what you see in the photo, how would you describe the reception President Nixon received in China? *(Possible response: The reception appears to have been well organized, serious, and ceremonial.)* **ASK:** Why do you think Nixon was given this kind of reception? *(Possible response: Because this was the first time a U.S. president had visited China, the Chinese wanted to greet him with the utmost formality and probably wanted to impress the United States and other Western nations with the scope of the display.)*

Active Options

On Your Feet: Roundtable Discussion Divide the class into groups of four. Ask the groups to conduct a roundtable discussion in which each group member mentions a different problem that Richard Nixon faced as president. After individuals have responded, prompt groups to discuss which problem they think was the most challenging and why. Then invite all groups to share their thoughts with the class.

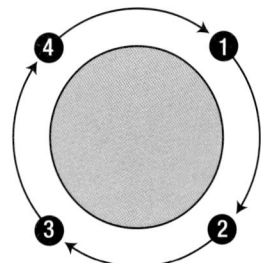

NG Learning Framework: Write a Presidential Address

SKILL Communication

KNOWLEDGE Our Human Story

Ask students to write a presidential address from the perspective of President Nixon. In the address, they should explain to the American public the purpose for the president's trips to China and the Soviet Union, what he accomplished during his visits, and how he now feels about future relations with the countries. After students have finished writing, invite them to present their addresses to the class.

Striving Readers

Complete Sentence Frames Before students read the lesson, provide them with the sentence frames below. Place students in mixed-proficiency pairs and instruct them to take turns reading paragraphs of the lesson, using what they read to complete these sentence frames.

- Nixon appointed four _____ Supreme Court justices. *(moderate)*

- During Nixon's first year in office, the unemployment rate _____ and the economy _____. *(rose; slowed)*

- Nixon used a closer relationship with China to make the _____ more willing to negotiate with the United States. *(Soviets)*

- In the Strategic Arms Limitation Treaty, the United States and the Soviet Union both agreed to _____. *(limit the number of nuclear missiles)*

Pre-AP

Form and Support a Thesis Remind students that Nixon often spoke about crime and urban unrest. Instruct them to conduct research into Nixon's "law and order" language in his nomination acceptance speech and develop a thesis about whether the language was racially coded or not. Then have students conduct further research to support their thesis and write an essay, citing source material and giving their own analysis. Invite students to share their essays on a class blog.

See the Chapter Planner for more strategies for differentiation.

HISTORICAL THINKING

ANSWERS

1. States received money from the federal government and decided which local programs they would fund.

2. Nixon opened up trade with both China and the Soviet Union, expanding markets for U.S. goods.

3. Nixon's visit to China helped improve U.S. relations with the Soviet Union. The Soviets were afraid the United States and China might become too close, so they were more willing to work with the United States after the visit, opening up trade and signing an arms agreement not long after.

Earth and Space

As technological advances carried humans farther into space, American astronauts saw Earth from a different perspective. Their reports and photos helped many Americans see the extraordinary beauty of our world—and made them want to protect it.

MAIN IDEA In the late 1960s and early 1970s, the United States explored space and took steps to solve environmental problems on Earth.

CRITICAL VIEWING On July 20, 1969, Apollo 11 mission commander Neil Armstrong took this photograph of astronaut Buzz Aldrin on the surface of the moon. You can see Armstrong's reflection in the visor of Aldrin's helmet. What does this photo convey about what it is like to walk on the moon?

MEN ON THE MOON

As you've read, President John F. Kennedy set the goal of sending American astronauts to the moon in a speech he made in 1961. On July 16, 1969, during Nixon's presidency, Kennedy's dream was realized when the **Apollo 11** mission landed the first two humans on the moon. Apollo 11 included a **lunar module**, the part of the spacecraft that landed on the moon, and a **command module**, the part that housed the crew and returned to Earth. Astronauts **Neil Armstrong** and **Buzz Aldrin** landed the lunar module, called the *Eagle*, while **Michael Collins** remained in orbit around the moon in the command module, called *Columbia*. Television and radio stations broadcast Armstrong's words as he stepped onto the moon: "That's one small step for [a] man, one giant leap for mankind."

Five more Apollo missions sent astronauts to Earth's moon between 1969 and 1972. Scientists collected rocks and soil samples and determined no life existed on the moon. NASA later shifted its focus and began working with other nations on space projects. One result was the International Space Station, a large spacecraft that has been orbiting Earth since it was launched in 1998. Scientists live on the station for months at a time and conduct experiments on a variety of topics. Besides maintaining the space station, NASA also has launched small, unmanned spacecraft equipped with cameras to explore Mars, Jupiter, and other places in the solar system.

CARING FOR EARTH

Photos of Earth from space inspired many Americans to support the environmental movement, which developed during the 1960s and 1970s. American marine biologist **Rachel Carson** drew public attention to environmental pollution with her book *Silent Spring*, published in 1962. Carson described how DDT, a commonly used pesticide, poisoned birds and contaminated human food sources. Then in 1969, a massive oil spill off the coast of Santa Barbara, California, opened many people's eyes to the potentially harmful effects of underwater oil drilling. The oil spill inspired U.S. Senator Gaylord Nelson of Wisconsin to organize the first **Earth Day**, a nationwide celebration focusing attention on environmental issues. Held on April 22, 1970, the

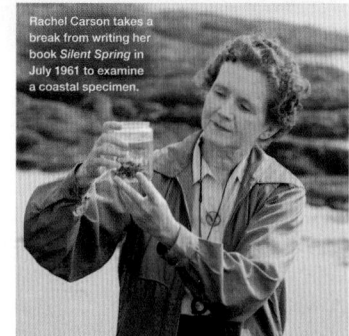

Rachel Carson takes a break from writing her book *Silent Spring* in July 1961 to examine a coastal specimen.

event drew about 20 million Americans, who rallied in the streets, attended teach-ins, and cleaned up parks. Earth Day became an annual event, held each year on April 22.

As Americans demanded action on environmental problems, Congress and the president responded with new laws—and a new agency. The **Clean Air Act** of 1970 focused on reducing the air pollution caused by vehicles and factories. The **Clean Water Act,** passed in 1972, set aside federal money to clean up polluted rivers and lakes. The 1973 **Endangered Species Act** provided protection for rare plants and animals. In 1970, President Nixon created a new agency, the **Environmental Protection Agency (EPA),** dedicated to enforcing environmental laws. In the next lesson, you'll read about some effects of these laws.

HISTORICAL THINKING

1. **READING CHECK** What actions did the federal government take in the 1970s to address environmental concerns?

2. **DETERMINE WORD MEANINGS** In your own words, explain the meaning of Armstrong's quote: "That's one small step for [a] man, one giant leap for mankind."

3. **MAKE CONNECTIONS** What environmental issues would you want to receive attention on the next Earth Day? Explain why.

PLAN

Objective
Analyze how Americans ventured into space and addressed problems on Earth.

Critical Thinking Skills for Lesson 1.3
- Identify Main Ideas and Details
- Monitor Comprehension
- Determine Word Meanings
- Make Connections
- Analyze Cause and Effect
- Draw Conclusions
- Make Inferences

Essential Question for Chapter 28
How did new ideas in American politics in the 1980s impact the country and the world?
In the 1960s and 1970s, the space race and environmental concerns captured the attention of the American people. Lesson 1.3 discusses the country's first trip to the moon and the steps the United States took to address environmental problems in response to public pressure.

Background for the Teacher
When Senator Gaylord Nelson first established Earth Day in 1970, his goal was to harness the energy of the antiwar movement and apply it to environmental activism. Nelson, a Democrat, invited a Republican congressman to cochair the event with him. They successfully brought together environmentalists representing various interests, such as wilderness conservation, wildlife preservation, clean water, and clean air. The event ultimately led to the establishment of the Environmental Protection Agency (EPA) eight months later, along with new pieces of legislation. Beginning in 1990, Earth Day celebrations expanded throughout the world, and in 1995, Nelson received the Presidential Medal of Freedom as the event's founder. Today, more than a billion people celebrate Earth Day, making it the world's largest secular observance.

INTRODUCE & ENGAGE

Identify Environmental Threats

Ask students to identify some current environmental threats to the planet. If necessary, suggest some general topics for discussion, such as landfill issues, extensive use of fossil fuels, or water contamination. **ASK:** What problems can these environmental threats lead to? *(Answers will vary. Possible responses: Burning fossil fuels pollutes the air, which can make asthma and other medical conditions worse. Throwing garbage away instead of recycling results in more land given up to landfills, and waste from landfills can contaminate local water supplies.)*

TEACH

STEM

Guided Discussion

1. **Analyze Cause and Effect** What effect do you think the moon landing had on Americans' perceptions of the United States? *(Possible response: People were proud of the United States for being the first country to get to the moon. People also were optimistic about the country's future as a result of the moon landing.)*

2. **Draw Conclusions** According to the text, scientists used samples from the moon to conclude that no life existed there. How might they have been able to determine this by studying the samples? *(Possible response: They might have looked for the presence of water in the samples. If the samples didn't show any past or present evidence of water, then the scientists might have concluded that life didn't exist on the moon.)*

Make Inferences

Direct students' attention to the photograph of Rachel Carson. Tell them to focus on the specimen Carson is holding. Ask a volunteer to read the caption aloud. **ASK:** Given Carson's background, what can you infer about why she was studying the specimen and what she might have been looking for? *(Possible response: She wanted to make sure the specimen was normal and healthy. She might have also been looking for pollutants in the water.)*

Active Options

On Your Feet: Three-Step Interview Ask students to decide which of the following events they think had the greatest impact on the environmental movement of the 1960s and 1970s: the publication of *Silent Spring,* the founding of Earth Day, or the establishment of the EPA. Give students time to review the text to make their decisions. Then tell them to form pairs. Ask one partner to interview the other to learn which event that partner chose and why. Then have the two switch roles. After pairs have completed their interviews, invite partners to explain each other's decision to the class.

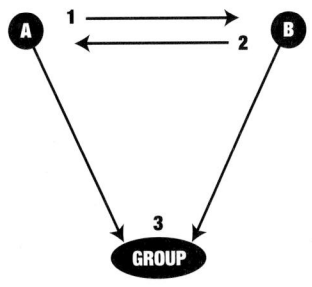

NG Learning Framework: Create an Apollo 11 Booklet

ATTITUDE Curiosity

KNOWLEDGE New Frontiers

Instruct students to conduct online research on objects used or acquired during the Apollo 11 mission. Prompt them to select objects that interest them, such as the meals the astronauts ate, the suits they wore, the instruments they used, or the samples they collected on the moon. Students should assemble six to eight photographs of the objects and compile them in a booklet. Ask students to label each photo with a description of the object, why it was important, and any facts about the object they find curious or surprising, such as why it had the characteristics it did. Invite students to present their booklets to the class.

DIFFERENTIATE

Inclusion

Use Clarifying Questions Encourage students with disabilities to work with partners who can read the lesson aloud to them and describe in detail the photographs of Neil Armstrong and Rachel Carson, including each person's clothing, facial expression, and surroundings. Prompt both partners to ask and answer clarifying questions. Challenge students to discuss how the details in the photos convey differences between the moon and Earth. Then have partners work together to answer the Critical Viewing question.

Pre-AP

Write a Biographical Sketch Instruct students to choose one of the astronauts or environmentalists mentioned in the lesson. Then have them conduct research in order to write a biographical sketch of that person. Encourage students to quote or paraphrase primary and secondary sources in their sketches. Invite them to post the sketches online or read them to the class.

See the Chapter Planner for more strategies for differentiation.

HISTORICAL THINKING

ANSWERS

1. The government established the Environmental Protection Agency (EPA) and passed legislation to clean up the air and water and to protect endangered species.

2. Possible response: He meant that even though he personally took just one small step onto the moon, the moon landing itself was a major accomplishment for humanity.

3. Answers will vary. Possible response: Since extreme weather is getting more common, that issue should be addressed. It might spur people to come up with ideas for dealing with increased threats of flooding or other weather-related problems.

CRITICAL VIEWING Possible response: The moon's surface looks pretty uneven, so walking must be challenging, especially with the astronauts' bulky protective gear. The empty landscape and the cumbersome equipment required for humans' survival probably makes the experience feel alienating and unsettling.

1.4 Cleaner Air and Water

Perhaps you've seen recent photos of people in Beijing, China, wearing masks to protect their lungs from the city's polluted air. Environmental laws passed during the 1970s are helping the United States avoid a similar situation.

MAIN IDEA In the 1970s, federal, state, and local governments took steps to reduce air and water pollution in the United States.

A CLEANER LOS ANGELES

Los Angeles, California, is a prime example of the air pollution problems that have plagued the United States. By the 1970s, the city had some of the worst air quality in the country. The air reached unhealthy pollution levels more than 200 days per year, contributing to breathing problems, heart disease, and other illnesses—and sometimes causing death.

Los Angeles became famous for a type of air pollution called **smog**, which can develop when sunlight reacts with chemicals in the air. The chemicals may come from a number of sources, including car exhaust and emissions from factories, power plants, and oil refineries. Car exhaust was a major contributor to Los Angeles's air pollution. As the population grew, the city and its suburbs spread over a great distance. Most residents relied on cars, rather than mass transit, to get around. The geography of the Los Angeles area also contributed to the problem. Mountains partly surround the area, creating a basin that traps smog over the city.

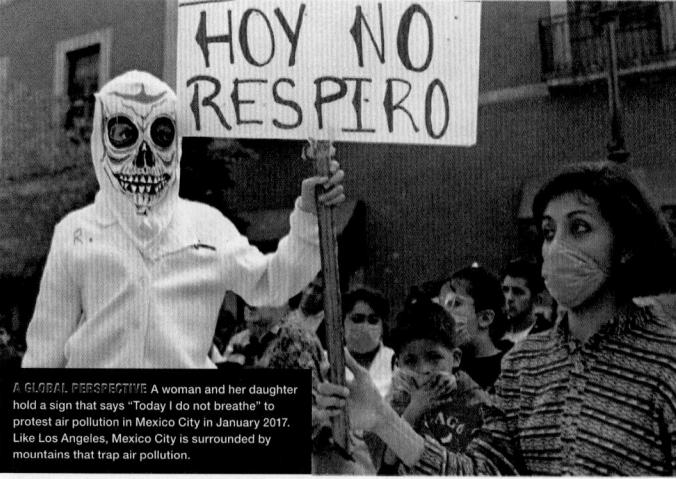

A GLOBAL PERSPECTIVE A woman and her daughter hold a sign that says "Today I do not breathe" to protest air pollution in Mexico City in January 2017. Like Los Angeles, Mexico City is surrounded by mountains that trap air pollution.

Although smog remains a problem in Los Angeles, air quality in the city has improved dramatically due to actions taken in the 1970s. The Clean Air Act of 1970 and the creation of the EPA were key factors in the reduction of air pollution in Los Angeles and other cities. A state agency, the California Air Resources Board, helped implement the Clean Air Act.

Federal and California legislators also passed laws requiring gas stations to seal hoses and storage tanks to prevent harmful chemicals from leaking. In addition, scientists developed the **catalytic converter**, a device installed on the underside of automobiles to scrub pollutants from car exhaust before it is released into the air.

Three Mile Island
In 1979, an accident at the nuclear power station at Three Mile Island in Pennsylvania posed a temporary threat to air quality in the region. A partial meltdown of the reactor's core resulted in the release of a small amount of radioactive gases into the atmosphere. Although no one was harmed, the accident increased public opposition to nuclear power.

A CLEANER LAKE ERIE

Just as the Clean Air Act improved the nation's air quality, the Clean Water Act of 1972 had a major impact on U.S. water quality. Besides funding the cleanup of polluted rivers and lakes, the Clean Water Act set federal standards for water quality and made it illegal to dump pollutants into waterways. The **Safe Drinking Water Act** of 1974 established additional standards for drinking water drawn from reservoirs and wells.

The severe pollution of Lake Erie, one of the Great Lakes, helped inspire the passage of the Clean Water Act of 1972. For many years, industrial waste, urban sewage, and fertilizers and pesticides from farms had flowed into the lake. These pollutants stimulated the growth of algae, a water plant. The algae reduced the oxygen content in the water, killing off fish and other aquatic life. By the late 1960s, Lake Erie was so polluted that scientists described it as a "dead lake."

In 1969, the Cuyahoga River, which flows through Cleveland, Ohio, into Lake Erie, caught fire. Industrial pollutants floating on its surface ignited and burned. The river had caught fire many times before, but this time it became the subject of a national news magazine article. The Cuyahoga river fire became a dramatic symbol of the nation's mounting environmental problems.

The "dead" lake and the burning river motivated the federal government and local officials to take action. Cleveland's mayor, Carl Stokes, sought federal aid to improve the city's sewer system and to clean up its waterways. Agencies from the U.S. and Canadian governments worked to clean up Lake Erie. Within decades, the lake was again safe for fishing and swimming. However, algae growth in the lake must be continually monitored.

HISTORICAL THINKING

1. **READING CHECK** How did geography contribute to Los Angeles's smog problem?

2. **IDENTIFY PROBLEMS AND SOLUTIONS** What steps were taken to combat air and water pollution in the 1970s?

3. **MAKE CONNECTIONS** How does population growth contribute to environmental problems such as polluted water and air?

PLAN

Objective
Learn about the U.S. environmental disasters that led to new legislation.

Critical Thinking Skills for Lesson 1.4
- Identify Main Ideas and Details
- Monitor Comprehension
- Identify Problems and Solutions
- Make Connections
- Analyze Language Use
- Evaluate

Essential Question for Chapter 28
How did new ideas in American politics in the 1980s impact the country and the world? During the 1970s, environmental problems in the United States showed the need for new policies and legislation. Lesson 1.4 details environmental topics such as Los Angeles smog and "dead" Lake Erie and the actions that resulted from those problems.

Background for the Teacher
Though the Cuyahoga River fire in June 1969 was what ultimately drew attention to the river's pollution—and the pollution of U.S. waterways in general—it was not the worst of the dozen or so fires that had already taken place on that river. In fact, local papers hardly covered the event. The fire was put out in such a relatively short period of time that no one even managed to take a photograph of it. Nonetheless, the event underscored the rampant pollution of rivers throughout the country, which that had become the dumping grounds for industrial waste due to a lack of regulation. Many people tolerated this pollution because they considered it an unfortunate but unavoidable side effect of business and employment. But that attitude finally began to change in the 1960s, largely because of events like the Cuyahoga River fire.

Complete a K-W-L Chart

Provide each student with a K-W-L Chart. Encourage students to consider what they already know about steps the federal government took to decrease pollution in the early 1970s, reminding them to think about what they read in the previous lesson. Tell students to list this information in the first column of the chart. Next, ask students to identify additional information they would like to learn about this topic and list it in the second column of the chart. Finally, allow time at the end of the lesson for students to complete the chart with what they have learned.

K What Do I Know?	W What Do I Want To Learn?	L What Did I Learn?
The federal government passed legislation to protect the air and water.	Was the legislation effective?	

TEACH

Guided Discussion

1. **Analyze Language Use** If water itself is not a living thing, why do scientists sometimes refer to a lake as "dead"? *(A lake is referred to as "dead" when it is so polluted that nothing can live in it.)*

2. **Evaluate** Was the legislation passed in the 1970s effective in decreasing pollution? Support your response with evidence from the text. *(Possible response: Yes. The air quality in Los Angeles has gotten much better, largely as a result of the Clean Air Act, and the Clean Water Act enabled the cleanup of Lake Erie, which, as a result, eventually became safe for swimming and fishing again.)*

A Global Perspective

Explore the photograph and caption with students. **ASK:** Why do you think the daughter in the photo is wearing a skull mask? *(Possible response: By wearing a skull mask, she's making a statement that the air pollution in Mexico City is deadly.)* Conduct a class discussion about how protesters around the world often use different kinds of visuals, such as signs or costumes, to make a point about a subject. Prompt students to discuss why visuals such as these are an effective method for communicating ideas.

Active Options

Active History: Research Local Habitat Preservation Efforts Extend the lesson by using either the PDF or Whiteboard version of the activity. These activities take a deeper look at a topic from, or related to, the lesson. Explore the activities as a class, turn them into group assignments, or even assign them individually.

NG Learning Framework: Create a Diagram

SKILLS Observation, Collaboration

KNOWLEDGE Our Living Planet

Tell partners to create a diagram that shows what happens when a lake suffers an overgrowth of algae. First, as a class, review the process, describing how contaminants get into a lake, how they stimulate the growth of algae, and how this affects the lake's inhabitants. Then prompt pairs to create their own diagram on paper, showing what happens at each step. In addition to using this lesson as a resource, students may also conduct online research as necessary. Invite pairs to present their finished diagrams to the class.

DIFFERENTIATE

English Language Learners ELD

Understand Portmanteau Words Bring students' attention to the word *smog*. Explain to students at **All Proficiencies** that this is an example of a portmanteau word, a combination of two other words. In this case, the two words are *smoke* and *fog*. Tell students that they can often figure out the meaning of such words by considering one or both of the original words. Direct pairs of students to make a list of portmanteau words they know and the two words they are made from. If necessary, suggest words, such as *brunch* (*breakfast + lunch*), *ginormous* (*giant + enormous*), *emoticon* (*emotion + icon*), and *infomercial* (*information + commercial*). Invite pairs to share their lists and create one master list of portmanteau words.

Pre-AP

Report on Impacts After they read the lesson, tell students to conduct online research to find out how the Safe Drinking Water Act has affected their community, state, or region. Then prompt them to summarize their findings in a report that analyzes the impact of the act and its continuing effects today.

See the Chapter Planner for more strategies for differentiation.

HISTORICAL THINKING

ANSWERS

1. Mountains surround part of the city, forming a basin, and smog gets trapped inside.

2. The federal government passed the Clean Air Act, the Clean Water Act, and the Safe Drinking Water Act. It also established the EPA. Scientists developed catalytic converters to reduce pollution from cars, sewer systems were improved, and laws made it illegal to dump pollutants into waterways.

3. Larger populations result in more factories and more people driving cars. More cars release greater amounts of exhaust into the air, and factories may also add to air pollution. Growing populations also lead to an increase in sewage and perhaps greater quantities of fertilizers and pesticides as well—all of which may end up in lakes, rivers, and groundwater.

1.5 The Watergate Scandal

On June 17, 1972, the night security guard on duty at the Watergate complex in Washington, D.C., was making his rounds when he noticed a piece of tape that prevented a door from locking. His discovery would bring down the President of the United States.

MAIN IDEA President Nixon's extreme efforts to get re-elected led to his resignation from office.

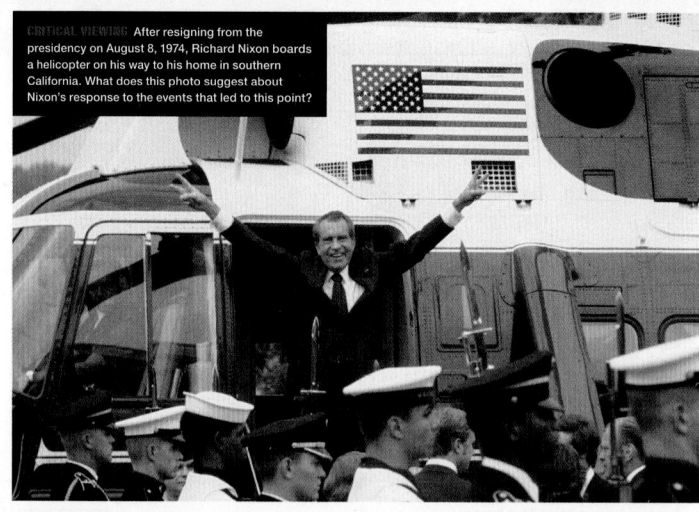

CRITICAL VIEWING After resigning from the presidency on August 8, 1974, Richard Nixon boards a helicopter on his way to his home in southern California. What does this photo suggest about Nixon's response to the events that led to this point?

WATERGATE BREAK-IN

Near the end of his first term in office, President Nixon seemed to be in an excellent position to win re-election. Yet he was worried about the election. Though he was leading in the polls, he wanted to ensure a landslide victory. To achieve this goal, some of his supporters formed a group in 1971 called the **Committee to Re-Elect the President (CRP)**, later mockingly nicknamed CREEP. Over the next year, CRP members leaked unflattering and sometimes false information about potential Democratic candidates to the press.

On June 17, 1972, police arrested five men for breaking into the Democratic National Headquarters at the Watergate complex in Washington, D.C.

One of the men was the security director for CRP. The men were trying to install listening devices on telephones so they could spy on Democratic Party leaders. Hiding a device on a telephone in order to secretly listen to conversations is called **wiretapping**. President Nixon was quick to claim that he and his administration had nothing to do with the Watergate break-in. Few people paid attention to the crime after his statement.

In July 1972, the Democrats chose South Dakota Senator **George McGovern** as their presidential candidate. McGovern was not as well known or experienced as Nixon, and he staunchly opposed the Vietnam War. Nixon won the election with the landslide he desired.

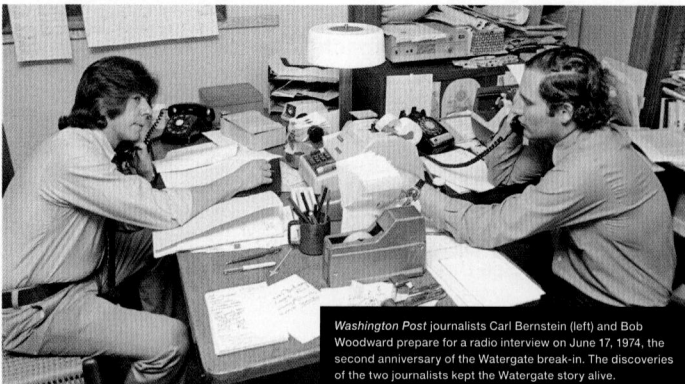

Washington Post journalists Carl Bernstein (left) and Bob Woodward prepare for a radio interview on June 17, 1974, the second anniversary of the Watergate break-in. The discoveries of the two journalists kept the Watergate story alive.

NIXON'S RESIGNATION

In his second term, Nixon faced the crisis that became known as the **Watergate scandal**. In April 1973, the Watergate burglars tried to plead guilty to minor charges of theft and wiretapping in order to avoid a public trial. The judge refused to accept their pleas because he suspected a **cover-up**, or an attempt to hide the truth. In the trial that followed, some of the burglars admitted that White House officials were involved in planning the break-in. These confessions, combined with explosive articles published in the *Washington Post* by reporters **Bob Woodward** and **Carl Bernstein**, turned the story of a small break-in into front-page news.

To handle the case, the U.S. Attorney General named a **special prosecutor**, or a private lawyer appointed to investigate and perhaps prosecute a legal case when there is a conflict of interest for the usual prosecuting attorney. The Senate also held investigative hearings. The prosecutor and the Senate hearings uncovered 69 people who had either helped to plan the break-in or tried to cover up its true purpose. Most of the people were close to the president. But Nixon denied involvement.

When evidence emerged that Nixon had secretly recorded his White House conversations, investigators demanded the tapes. At first Nixon provided transcripts, or typed versions of the conversations, which had been edited. When the tapes were finally turned over, they confirmed that Nixon had tried to cover up the burglary and block the investigation into it. The House Judiciary Committee presented the House of Representatives with charges of obstruction of justice and abuse of power. However, before the House could impeach, or formally charge, Nixon, he resigned. On August 8, 1974, he became the first president to do so.

HISTORICAL THINKING

1. **READING CHECK** What events led to President Nixon's resignation?

2. **MAKE INFERENCES** What do you think would have happened to Nixon had he not resigned?

3. **DRAW CONCLUSIONS** Why did it take officials so long to uncover Nixon's involvement in the Watergate scandal?

PLAN

Objective

Discover how the Watergate scandal ultimately forced President Nixon to resign.

Critical Thinking Skills for Lesson 1.5

- Identify Main Ideas and Details
- Monitor Comprehension
- Make Inferences
- Draw Conclusions
- Make Connections
- Describe

Essential Question for Chapter 28

How did new ideas in American politics in the 1980s impact the country and the world?
Upheaval during President Nixon's presidency created unease for Americans. Lesson 1.5 reveals the events of the Watergate scandal and the price President Nixon paid for his involvement.

Background for the Teacher

Perhaps the most intriguing aspect of the Watergate scandal was the secret identity of one of the *Washington Post*'s sources of information. Known only as "Deep Throat" at the time, the source turned out to be high-ranking FBI official W. Mark Felt. As the head of the Watergate burglary investigation, Felt suspected the White House was trying to compromise the bureau. For example, the White House insisted that its lawyers be present for every interview the FBI conducted with members of the Nixon administration and the Committee to Re-Elect the President (CRP). By publicly leaking the investigation's details, Felt thought he could put pressure on the Nixon administration. He funneled information from the bureau's reports to Bob Woodward and Carl Bernstein and provided them with leads. For more than three decades, the journalists kept their source's identity a secret until Felt finally revealed himself as "Deep Throat."

Explore the Lesson Title

Lead a class discussion about the word *scandal*. **ASK:** If something is called a scandal, what does that mean? *(Possible response: It means it's shocking and usually involves some kind of immoral or unethical behavior.)* Explain that this lesson discusses a scandal in which President Nixon was involved during the early 1970s. **ASK:** How might a president's involvement in a scandal make it even more shocking? *(Answers will vary. Possible response: As leader of the country, a president is generally held to a higher standard than ordinary citizens, so the public expects more from someone serving in that office. When a president is involved in a scandal, it affects the public's perception even more negatively.)*

TEACH

Guided Discussion

1. **Make Connections** What role did the press play in the Watergate scandal? *(Two Washington Post reporters, Bob Woodward and Carl Bernstein, ran several articles about the break-in, which helped keep the public's attention focused on the event.)*

2. **Describe** What was Nixon's initial response to requests that he release his secret tape recordings? *(He provided transcripts of the recordings rather than the recordings themselves, which allowed him to edit out the parts that revealed his involvement.)*

Draw Conclusions

Point out to students that the investigator of the Watergate scandal was a special prosecutor, a private lawyer assigned to the case by the U.S. attorney general to avoid a conflict of interest. **ASK:** How might a special prosecutor better avoid a conflict of interest than a government lawyer? *(Possible response: A special prosecutor would more likely be impartial to the case, while a government lawyer might feel loyalty to the president. The attorney general wanted the special prosecutor to be objective.)*

Active Options

On Your Feet: Goal and Outcome Ask students to break into groups of three or four and complete a Goal-and-Outcome graphic organizer. Supply them with this sentence to write in the Goal section: Nixon wanted to win re-election by a landslide. Then have students list the major events that took place as a result of this goal. They should next identify the final outcome of these events. Afterward, hold a class discussion to contrast Nixon's goal with the ultimate outcome.

NG Learning Framework: Think Like a Journalist

SKILL Communication

KNOWLEDGE Our Human Story

Encourage students to explore how reporters evaluate whether or not to publish a story. Ask them to imagine themselves in the role of a reporter or an editor who receives a tip about a potentially scandalous story involving the president of the United States. Have them meet in small groups to discuss these questions: What would they want to know before writing or publishing the story? What facts or circumstances would lead them to trust the source? What questions would they ask? Invite groups to summarize their discussions for the class.

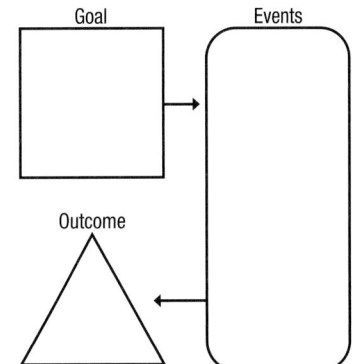

English Language Learners ELD

Use a Term in a Sentence Pair students at the **Emerging** level of proficiency with students at the **Expanding** or **Bridging** level. Instruct pairs to work together to compose a sentence using selected words and terms from the lesson. Invite pairs to share their sentences and discuss different ways to use each word or term. Suggest the following words: *unflattering, wiretapping, scandal, cover-up, confessions, prosecutor.*

Gifted & Talented

Create an Infographic Tell students that all three branches of government played roles in the Watergate scandal. Challenge them to conduct online research to learn more about the roles of the executive, legislative, and judicial branches in the scandal, from cover-up to investigation to resolution. Instruct students to use words and images to convey the roles in an infographic. Invite volunteers to post their infographics online or on a class bulletin board.

See the Chapter Planner for more strategies for differentiation.

HISTORICAL THINKING

ANSWERS

1. Five men broke into the Democratic National Headquarters to wiretap phones, trying to help the president get re-elected. Secret tapes revealed that Nixon knew about it. Nixon faced impeachment but resigned before that could happen.

2. He probably would have been impeached by Congress.

3. The men who broke in tried to avoid a public trial, but the judge wouldn't accept their plea deals. After the case went to trial, the men revealed the White House's involvement. The U.S. attorney general appointed a special prosecutor to investigate the case, and that investigation finally uncovered Nixon's secret tapes—which showed Nixon knew about the plot.

CRITICAL VIEWING Possible response: He's smiling and doesn't seem bothered by the events—or he wishes to portray himself in that light. Nixon might have even been relieved that he could resign instead of being impeached.

2.1 Ford and Carter

You know the age-old advice that the best way to deal with someone who has wronged you is to forgive and forget. But would Americans be able to take that approach to the president who gave them the Watergate scandal?

MAIN IDEA Presidents Ford and Carter both struggled to improve the nation's ailing economy.

FORD BECOMES PRESIDENT

One day after President Nixon resigned on August 8, 1974, Vice President **Gerald R. Ford** became president. Ford was an experienced politician who had been a Congressional representative from Michigan for 25 years before serving in the White House. Over that time, he had gained the reputation of being honest and fair.

Ford was the first vice president who had not been elected to that office. Nixon's first vice president, Spiro Agnew, resigned in 1973 after pleading guilty to charges of income tax evasion. The **25th Amendment** allowed the president to name a replacement. Adopted in 1967 in the aftermath of the Kennedy assassination, this amendment clarified the process for replacing a vice president who dies, resigns, or is removed from office. It also provides a way for the vice president and Congress to remove a president they deem unfit to serve.

In September 1974, about a month after taking office, President Ford formally forgave Nixon of all crimes he "may have committed" during the Watergate scandal. The **pardon** was controversial. Ford had previously promised the American people that Nixon would pay for any wrongdoing for which he was convicted. But Ford changed his mind, hoping that forgiveness would allow the country to move forward and forget the Watergate scandal. Instead, many Americans criticized his decision, and he lost their support.

As president, Ford inherited a weak and worsening economy. Years of high unemployment and slow growth had caused the economy to stagnate, or come to a standstill. At the same time, the cost of goods and services remained high. This combination of stagnation and high inflation was named **stagflation**. Ford proposed increasing taxes and limiting government spending, but Congress refused to support this plan.

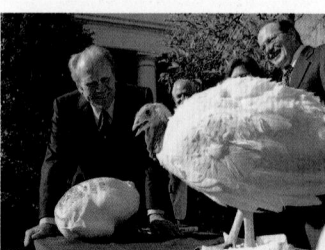

Pardoning the Turkey
Who started the Thanksgiving Day tradition of the president pardoning a turkey so that it would not be killed for dinner? In 1863, Abraham Lincoln saved a turkey that was intended for his family's Thanksgiving dinner because his son had grown fond of the bird, but modern mythology names Harry Truman as the first president to start the yearly tradition. As it turns out, there is no evidence to support this claim, although Truman and other presidents, including Gerald Ford (shown above), posed with birds sent for the White House festivities. The official annual tradition began with George H.W. Bush. Since 1989, every sitting president has annually and publicly pardoned a gobbler.

Traditionally, the sitting president invites the incoming president to the White House to discuss the transition. In this photo, President-elect Jimmy Carter, left, meets with President Ford in November 1976.

CARTER IS ELECTED

In the presidential election of 1976, President Ford ran against Democrat **Jimmy Carter**, a former governor of Georgia. Carter promised to bring honesty back to the White House and called for an end to secrecy in government. "I'll never tell you a lie," he told voters. On November 2, 1976, Carter narrowly defeated Ford by a margin of 57 electoral votes. As the nation's 39th president, Carter inherited the nation's economic woes from Nixon and Ford. He also inherited an energy crisis.

As you've read, members of OPEC placed an embargo on oil shipments to the United States in 1973. The embargo caused gasoline shortages and long lines at gas stations. When Carter took office four years later, the United States was still dependent on OPEC for its oil. The situation grew worse in December 1979, when OPEC nations doubled the price of their oil from 1976 rates. Inflation in the United States continued to climb, in part because of the price hike. Consumers had less money to spend on other goods and services.

Carter proposed a new U.S. energy program to reduce the country's dependence on foreign oil. The program combined energy conservation, investment in oil production in the United States, and research into other forms of energy, such as nuclear, solar, and wind power. But Congress failed to pass Carter's energy program. In fact, Carter had so much difficulty working with Congress that little progress was made on either the economy or the energy crisis during his presidency.

HISTORICAL THINKING

1. **READING CHECK** What economic problems did President Ford inherit?

2. **ANALYZE CAUSE AND EFFECT** How did the OPEC oil embargo affect the U.S. economy in the 1970s?

3. **MAKE INFERENCES** Why did Jimmy Carter make honesty a highlight of his 1976 presidential campaign?

PLAN

Objective

Learn about economic and energy challenges during the Ford and Carter administrations.

Critical Thinking Skills for Lesson 2.1

- Identify Main Ideas and Details
- Monitor Comprehension
- Analyze Cause and Effect
- Make Inferences
- Form and Support Opinions
- Identify Problems and Solutions
- Evaluate

Essential Question for Chapter 28

How did new ideas in American politics in the 1980s impact the country and the world? As the 1980s approached, the U.S. economy worsened. Lesson 2.1 explores the attempts of the Ford and Carter administrations to improve the economy and solve the energy crisis.

Background for the Teacher

To demonstrate his commitment to alternative energy sources, President Jimmy Carter installed 32 solar panels on the White House roof in 1979. The purpose of the panels was to provide energy for heating water in the White House. During the dedication ceremony in June of that year, Carter speculated about the fate of the panels. Though he predicted they would still be technically functional in the year 2000, Carter also wondered what would become of them a generation later—whether they would be "a museum piece" or "a small part of one of the greatest and most exciting adventures ever undertaken by the American people." Fewer than 10 years later, President Ronald Reagan had the panels removed, though some are now on display at the Jimmy Carter Presidential Library and Museum and the Smithsonian's National Museum of American History.

Preview Vocabulary

Write the word *stagflation* on the board. Explain that *stagflation* is a portmanteau word, made by combining the words *stagnation* and *inflation*. **ASK:** What does *stagnation* mean? *(Possible responses: not growing or changing; becoming foul from standing still)* **ASK:** What does *inflation* mean? *(Possible responses: expansion like a balloon; a rise in prices such that money is worth less and can buy fewer goods)* Explain that *stagflation* is an economic term that describes a period in which prices are rising but the economy is not growing. Tell students that in this lesson they will learn about the economic challenges that the administrations of Gerald R. Ford and Jimmy Carter faced.

TEACH

Guided Discussion

1. **Form and Support Opinions** Do you agree with President Ford's decision to pardon Richard Nixon? Support your opinion. *(Possible responses: No. Nixon had lied about his involvement in the Watergate scandal and tried to cover it up. He should have been impeached and, if warranted, convicted. Yes. Nixon's involvement in the cover-up could have resulted in impeachment and conviction. Either process would likely have occupied Congress for months and brought shame to the presidency.)*

2. **Identify Problems and Solutions** What solutions to different problems did Ford and Carter suggest that Congress rejected? *(Ford suggested raising taxes and cutting spending to stimulate the economy and reduce inflation. Carter proposed transforming the energy program to avoid gas shortages and high oil prices.)*

Evaluate

Give students time to consider President Carter's energy program. **ASK:** Do you think Carter's plan was a reasonable one? Explain. *(Answers will vary. Possible response: Yes. Using other forms of energy, such as solar, would have reduced Americans' reliance on gas and oil and would have been better for the environment. Also, moving toward domestic oil production would have provided a cheaper product for citizens.)*

Active Options

On Your Feet: Time Line Arrange students into groups of three or four. Tell each group to create an annotated time line that includes details and dates of the following events: OPEC places an oil embargo on the United States; Ford becomes president; Ford pardons Nixon; Carter is elected president; OPEC doubles the price of oil. Once students have completed their time

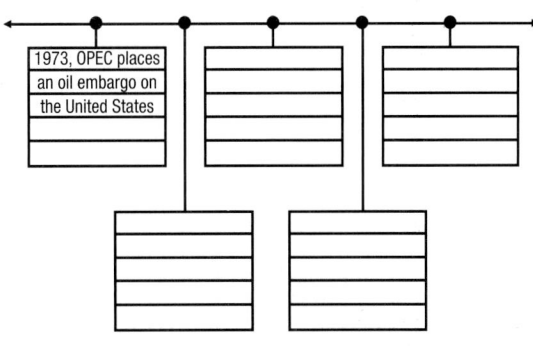

1973, OPEC places an oil embargo on the United States

lines, encourage them to draw conclusions about the periods between events, such as between the start of Ford's presidency and his pardoning of Nixon. Invite groups to share their conclusions with the class.

NG Learning Framework: Create an Inflation Graph STEM

SKILLS Observation, Collaboration

KNOWLEDGE Our Human Story

Tell students to work with a partner to create a graph that shows inflation rates between 1970 and 1979. Allow students to conduct research to gather information for their graphs and tell them to cite their sources. Pairs may choose to create either a bar graph or a line graph but should ensure that the graph shows each year of the decade and the corresponding rates of inflation. When partners have finished, invite them to display their graphs. As a class, discuss what the graphs show.

English Language Learners ELD

Understand Multiple Meaning Words
Pair students at the **Emerging** and **Expanding** levels of proficiency and ask them to reread the lesson, noting how the word *pardon* is used as a noun (in the third paragraph) and as a verb (under the turkey photograph). Ask partners to write a definition of the word using context clues. Then instruct them to write original sentences using *pardon* as a noun and a verb. You may also mention the phrase *pardon me* as a polite way of interrupting, apologizing, or disagreeing.

Pre-AP

Connect Past and Present Instruct students to conduct online research to learn more about Jimmy Carter's energy policies, including his push for renewable energy and for U.S. energy independence. Tell students to use their research to write a report to compare and contrast Carter's energy policies and current U.S. energy policies. Invite students to share their reports with the class.

See the Chapter Planner for more strategies for differentiation.

HISTORICAL THINKING

ANSWERS

1. Unemployment and inflation were high and economic growth was at a standstill.

2. The embargo caused gas shortages, so people had to wait in long lines to buy gas. The rising price of gas and oil led to inflation, and consumers who spent more on gas had less to spend on other goods.

3. Possible response: After the dishonesty of the Nixon administration, Carter thought it was important to help Americans believe they could once again trust the president.

2.2 Carter's Foreign Policy

When you think about the rights you enjoy in a democracy, which right is most important to you? Perhaps it's your right to express your own ideas, or wear the kind of clothes you like. For many people around the world, more basic rights might be most important—like the right to have food and water.

MAIN IDEA President Carter focused his foreign policy on promoting human rights and peace.

HUMAN RIGHTS AND PEACE

As a deeply religious man, President Carter strongly believed in the importance of **human rights**, which are rights that most nations recognize as belonging to all humans. They include the rights to food, housing, and education as well as political rights. One of Carter's main goals as president was to promote human rights—and peace—throughout the world.

To protest human rights violations, Carter cut off federal aid to dictatorships in Chile and Nicaragua. He encouraged the governments of Argentina and Brazil to make democratic reforms. Carter's critics pointed out, however, that he allowed continued U.S. support for **Ferdinand Marcos**, the president of the Philippines. Although he had originally been elected by a majority, Marcos ruled as a dictator from 1972 to 1981.

On November 4, 1979, Iranian militants captured 52 Americans, blindfolded them, and paraded them in front of television cameras.

To improve relations with Central America, Carter began the process of returning the Panama Canal Zone to Panama in 1977. The United States had controlled the area since the canal opened in 1914. Panamanians had staged many protests over the years, demanding that the United States give the land back. Carter believed returning the land would help promote peace in the region.

Carter also negotiated an extension of the SALT I Treaty with the Soviet Union. Called **SALT II**, the agreement set limits on the number of nuclear weapons each country could own. However, Carter himself withdrew SALT II from Senate consideration after the Soviet Union invaded Afghanistan in December 1979.

TRIUMPH AND TRAGEDY IN THE MIDDLE EAST

Carter's greatest peacemaking efforts focused on Israel's relationship with its Arab neighbors. Since its founding in 1948, Israel had fought four wars with Egypt and Syria. The most recent war had ended in 1973, and Carter hoped to prevent another one.

In August 1978, Carter invited Egyptian President **Anwar Sadat** (AHN-war suh-DAHT) and Israeli Prime Minister **Menachem Begin** (muh-NAH-kuhm BAY-gihn) to meet for peace talks in the United States at Camp David, the presidential retreat in Maryland. As a result, Egypt agreed to recognize Israel as a country, and Israel agreed to return land taken from Egypt in a war. Begin and Sadat formally signed the **Camp David Accords** at the White House on September 17, 1978. They were jointly awarded the 1978 Nobel Peace Prize for their efforts.

President Carter had little time to celebrate. In January 1979, Islamic **fundamentalists** overthrew the shah, or king, of Iran. A fundamentalist believes in the strict, literal interpretation of religious documents and doctrine. When the shah, a strong American ally, developed cancer, Carter allowed

CRITICAL VIEWING In 1978, Egyptian President Anwar Sadat (left), President Carter (center), and Israeli Prime Minister Menachem Begin (right) celebrate the signing of a treaty that ended 31 years of war between Egypt and Israel. What does the photo convey about the feelings of the three leaders?

him to come to the United States for medical treatment. Angry fundamentalists took over the U.S. embassy in Tehran, Iran's capital. In what became known as the **Iran hostage crisis**, they held 52 Americans hostage there for more than a year, demanding that the shah be returned to Iran for trial. Carter refused.

Diplomats from around the world tried to persuade the fundamentalists to release the hostages. President Carter tried, unsuccessfully, to negotiate with Iran through the United Nations. Finally, in April 1980, Carter ordered a secret military mission to rescue the American hostages. The mission was a disastrous failure, resulting in the deaths of eight American soldiers. Carter faced the 1980 presidential election with a tarnished reputation as a leader.

HISTORICAL THINKING

1. **READING CHECK** How did President Carter promote human rights around the world?

2. **FORM AND SUPPORT OPINIONS** Do you think human rights should be a focus of American foreign policy? Why or why not?

3. **EVALUATE** How would you evaluate President Carter's leadership in the Iran hostage crisis?

Objective

Analyze President Carter's attempts to protect human rights and support global stability.

Critical Thinking Skills for Lesson 2.2

- Identify Main Ideas and Details
- Monitor Comprehension
- Form and Support Opinions
- Evaluate
- Make Inferences
- Interpret Visuals
- Draw Conclusions

Essential Question for Chapter 28

How did new ideas in American politics in the 1980s impact the country and the world?
President Carter placed a new emphasis on human rights as a basis for foreign policy. Lesson 2.2 discusses his efforts to redefine relationships with other nations, to broker peace deals in the Middle East, and to negotiate the release of American hostages in Iran.

Background for the Teacher

To free the American hostages, the Carter administration conducted complicated behind-the-scenes negotiations with the captors. When the militants first seized the hostages, the U.S. government froze billions of dollars' worth of Iranian assets held in American banks. Then, late in 1980, Iran and Iraq went to war, and Iran needed money. So during the negotiations, the United States agreed to release the assets in exchange for the hostages. But the Iranians would not speak directly with the Americans, so Algerians served as an intermediary. All communications had to be translated into English, French, and Persian. Because the assets were scattered in banks throughout the world, Carter and his staff had to work with multiple countries to arrange their release. As a result, the negotiations process moved slowly, and Americans' frustration with it grew.

Examine Human Rights

As a class, discuss some examples of human rights and how they can be protected. On the board, create a Classification Chart with the following heads: Food, Housing, Education, and Political Rights. Ask students to suggest ways a country can ensure that it fulfills each of these rights for its citizens. Write their suggestions in the respective boxes. Then explain that in this lesson students will learn about President Jimmy Carter's efforts to promote human rights throughout the world.

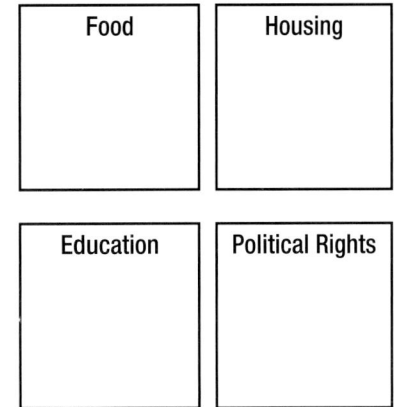

Food	Housing
Education	Political Rights

TEACH

Guided Discussion

1. **Make Inferences** Why might President Carter have wanted to establish peace between Israel and Egypt? *(Possible response: In less than three decades, Israel had been at war multiple times with Egypt, and the most recent war had ended not long before Carter became president.)*

2. **Interpret Visuals** What effect might the Iranian militants have been seeking by showing the blindfolded hostages on television? *(Possible response: They wanted to humiliate the hostages and embarrass the United States. They also wanted to show their own people and the world at large that they were in control. They may also have wanted to outrage the American public enough that people would pressure the government to bargain.)*

Draw Conclusions

Allow students time to review details about the SALT II agreement. **ASK:** What might have been the reason President Carter withdrew SALT II from Senate consideration after the Soviet Union's invasion of Afghanistan? *(Possible response: Carter might not have wanted to enter into an agreement with a country that had just invaded another country, or he might have been reluctant to limit the number of nuclear weapons the United States had at a time when the Soviet Union was demonstrating aggression.)*

Active Options

On Your Feet: Debate the Decision Divide the class into two groups. Prompt students to imagine they are advisors to President Carter during the Iran hostage crisis and must determine whether or not to take military action to release the hostages. Tell one group to argue for military action and the other group to argue against it. Then hold a class debate to allow the two sides to make their case. Remind students to be respectful of each other during the debate and to encourage everyone in the group to speak.

NG Learning Framework: Research the Camp David Accords

SKILLS Collaboration, Problem-Solving

KNOWLEDGE Our Human Story

Encourage students to learn more about the Camp David Accords. Divide the class into small groups, and tell them to conduct online or library research on the parties involved, the issues at stake, and the reasons why the accords were so important. Groups might identify one specific problem the accords were trying to solve and research it in more depth. Instruct groups to use their findings to create a poster or slide show to present to the class.

DIFFERENTIATE

Striving Readers

Complete T-Charts Instruct students to create a T-Chart with one column labeled Accomplishments and the other labeled Failures. Tell them to jot down key facts about each of Carter's foreign policy accomplishments and failures as they read the lesson. After reading, encourage students to compare their completed charts with one another, noting any differences.

Gifted & Talented

Illustrate a Phrase Challenge students to visually interpret the meaning of "human rights" through a painting, drawing, collage, or video montage. Instruct them to conduct online research to gather information and examples. As students work on their visual interpretation, you may suggest that they concentrate on one or two categories of human rights, such as social, economic, cultural, political, or civic. Encourage students to present their finished work to the class.

See the Chapter Planner for more strategies for differentiation.

HISTORICAL THINKING

ANSWERS

1. Carter cut off U.S. aid to some dictatorships and encouraged democratic reforms in other countries, returned the Panama Canal Zone to Panama, and helped negotiate peace talks between Egypt and Israel.

2. Answers will vary. Possible response: Yes, it should be a part of foreign policy because we should support the same values around the world that we do at home.

3. Answers will vary. Possible response: President Carter was in a difficult position and tried to do his best. Carter might have been reluctant to return the shah to Iran because he thought the shah might be abused or executed. He tried to negotiate with Iran before taking military action. It's sad that people died during the rescue mission, but most rescue attempts unfortunately involve this risk.

CRITICAL VIEWING They all look happy. They're smiling and joining hands together, which suggests they are proud of their achievement and feel they are in solidarity with one another.

3.1 Reagan's Victory in 1980

It's often said that Americans vote with their pocketbooks. In the 1980 presidential election, they chose Ronald Reagan to improve the nation's economy.

MAIN IDEA The election of Ronald Reagan marked the beginning of a new era of conservative politics in the United States.

THE 1980 ELECTION

The presidential campaign of 1980 took place during the Iran hostage crisis. Carter's outlook for re-election was not promising. Many Americans viewed him as a weak leader because of his handling of the crisis. In addition, Americans were upset that inflation was still high.

Carter's Republican opponent was **Ronald Reagan**, a former movie actor and a popular two-term governor of California. Reagan was a conservative and believed in low taxes, limited government regulation, a strong military, and traditional social values. Known as the "Great Communicator," Reagan had a knack for connecting with an audience. When cameras were aimed at him, he spoke directly to the viewers and won them over with his charm. During the presidential debates, he asked Americans, "Are you better off than you were four years ago?" He suggested they vote for Carter if they were better off and vote for him if they were not.

Reagan won the election with 51 percent of the popular vote. Because his support

Presidential candidate Ronald Reagan campaigns in Columbia, South Carolina, in October 1989 with his wife, Nancy, and Senator Strom Thurmond (right) of South Carolina. In his campaign, Reagan reassured voters with his view that America's best days were still to come.

was distributed throughout the nation, he won more than 90 percent of the electoral vote. On January 20, 1981, the day of Reagan's inauguration, Iran released the American hostages in Tehran.

REAGAN'S FIRST TERM

Reagan's first actions as president were aimed at improving the economy. He based his economic policy on a theory called **supply-side economics**, which holds that increased production (the "supply") of goods and services creates economic growth. According to the theory, tax cuts and **deregulation**, or loosening government restrictions, help businesses expand and increase production. This economic policy became known as "Reaganomics."

Reagan's presidency was soon interrupted by violence. On March 30, 1981, a mentally ill citizen named John Hinckley, Jr., attempted to assassinate Reagan. Hinckley fired several shots as the president was leaving a Washington, D.C., hotel, hitting Reagan's press secretary James Brady, a police officer, and a Secret Service agent. The last bullet bounced off the president's car and hit Reagan in the chest. Everyone survived the attack, though Brady was seriously injured. Hinckley was placed in a psychiatric institution.

On August 3, 1981, nearly 13,000 members of the Professional Air Traffic Controllers Organization (PATCO) went on strike for higher wages. Air traffic controllers are federal employees who direct airplanes as they take off and land. Federal law, however, prohibited such employees from striking. Reagan ordered the strikers to return to work or be fired. Most of the controllers maintained their strike, and they lost their jobs. Commercial air travel was cut back until new controllers could be hired and trained. Despite the transportation disruption, Reagan's response was seen by many as a show of strength. In the long-term, his actions weakened the power of organized labor.

Before the end of Reagan's first year in office, the country sank into a recession. This economic slowdown deepened in 1982. As huge military-spending increases raised the national debt, the unemployment rate hit almost 11 percent. To address the problem, Reagan approved a tax increase. The economy picked up by early 1983 and continued to grow.

In November 1984, Reagan won re-election in a landslide victory over former vice president **Walter Mondale** and his running mate, **Geraldine Ferraro**. A U.S. representative from New York, Ferraro was the first female vice-presidential candidate of a major political party.

Striking air traffic controllers picket outside a terminal at La Guardia Airport in New York City on August 5, 1981. This photo shows the strikers shortly before President Reagan fired them.

HISTORICAL THINKING

1. **READING CHECK** What was Ronald Reagan's political philosophy?

2. **EVALUATE** Why was Reagan's decision to fire striking PATCO union members significant for his presidency?

3. **ASK AND ANSWER QUESTIONS** What questions could you ask to better understand supply-side economics, and where might you find the answers?

PLAN

Objective

Understand Ronald Reagan's conservative principles regarding the economy, labor, and the national debt.

Critical Thinking Skills for Lesson 3.1

- Identify Main Ideas and Details
- Monitor Comprehension
- Evaluate
- Ask and Answer Questions
- Summarize
- Make Connections

Essential Question for Chapter 28

How did new ideas in American politics in the 1980s impact the country and the world?
President Ronald Reagan ushered in a new period of conservative policies. Lesson 3.1 explores the ideas behind "Reaganomics," Reagan's early struggles, and the rebound of the economy.

Background for the Teacher

The attempt on President Reagan's life had both short- and long-term effects. When Reagan was hit, he didn't realize he was bleeding until after his limousine had fled the scene with him inside. He walked into the hospital, where doctors discovered he had a pierced lung. Reagan underwent a two-hour surgery to remove the bullet and recovered.

However, Reagan's press secretary, James Brady, was shot above his left eye, sustaining brain damage that left him partially paralyzed. Brady and his wife began working with Handgun Control, Inc., later renamed the Brady Campaign to Prevent Gun Violence. They pushed for passage of a bill requiring background checks and waiting periods on handgun purchases from federally licensed dealers. The bill passed in 1993.

Financial Literacy

To extend their knowledge and understanding about the concepts in this lesson, refer students to the Financial Literacy handbook.

INTRODUCE & ENGAGE

Activate Prior Knowledge

Ask students to think about what they know about the United States just before Ronald Reagan took office in 1981. They should consider issues such as inflation, economic growth, and the hostage crisis. Draw or project on the board a graphic organizer like the one shown. Use the organizer to record student suggestions about events and issues. Then ask them to imagine that they could have voted in 1980. Prompt them to summarize the state of the country at that time and to tell what they would think about as they decided how to vote.

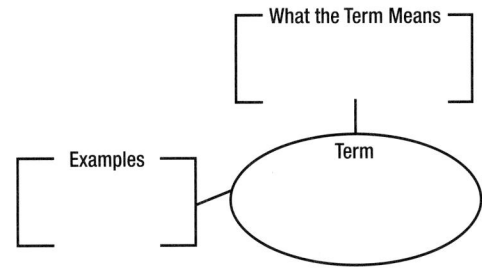

State of the Country in 1980		
Inflation	Economic Growth	Hostage Crisis
Summary		

TEACH

Guided Discussion

1. **Summarize** In what ways was Ronald Reagan's first year in office particularly challenging? *(John Hinckley, Jr., attempted to assassinate Reagan just a couple of months after he took office. A few months later, about 13,000 air traffic controllers went on strike. Then, toward the end of Reagan's first year, the economy fell into recession.)*

2. **Evaluate** Did Reagan's response to the recession in 1982 reflect the principles of his economic theory, known as "Reaganomics"? Explain. *(No. Instead of cutting taxes, which was one principle of his economic theory, Reagan raised taxes. The economy improved as a result.)*

Make Connections

Prompt students to identify two events that took place on January 20, 1981. *(Ronald Reagan was inaugurated as president, and Iran released the American hostages.)* **ASK:** What effect do you think the release of the hostages had on the public's perception of Reagan, despite his lack of involvement with it? *(Possible response: It made him popular with people right away. Even if he wasn't involved with the release, the fact that it took place on his inauguration day gave the impression that he was. People would always remember that.)*

Active Options

On Your Feet: Question and Answer Divide the class into two groups in separate parts of the room. Tell one group to write True-False questions based on information in Lesson 3.1. Tell the other group to create answer cards with "True" written on one side and "False" on the other. As students in the first group read each of their questions aloud, one by one, students in the second group should stand and display the correct answer to each question. When discrepancies occur, review the question and discuss which answer is correct.

NG Learning Framework: Build a Slide Show

ATTITUDE Curiosity

SKILLS Communication, Collaboration

Invite students to learn more about Ronald Reagan by working in pairs to build a slide show about his professional life. Tell partners to use slide show software to assemble photos into a presentation about Reagan at various points in his career, such as his time as an actor, a governor, and a president. Encourage students to include any facts that particularly interest them. As pairs display their slide shows to the class, tell one partner to summarize what each photo shows while the other partner advances the slides.

DIFFERENTIATE

English Language Learners   ELD

Use Word Maps Pair students at the **Emerging** level of proficiency with students at the **Expanding** or **Bridging** level. Instruct them to complete Word Maps to better understand the vocabulary terms *supply-side economics* and *deregulation*. Direct pairs to trade Word Maps with other pairs and note similarities and differences.

```
         ┌─ What the Term Means ─┐


┌─ Examples ─┐        ╭─────────╮
            │  Term  │
            ╰─────────╯
```

Gifted & Talented

Create a Political Cartoon To help students more fully understand the air traffic controllers' strike, direct them to conduct online research about some of the issues: working conditions, workers' demands, potential logistical problems caused by a strike, prohibitions against striking, and public opinion. Then prompt students to create a political cartoon supporting or opposing the strike. Encourage them to present their cartoon to the class, explaining symbolism as necessary and answering any questions.

See the Chapter Planner for more strategies for differentiation.

HISTORICAL THINKING

ANSWERS

1. Reagan believed in low taxes and limited government regulation. He promoted conservative values and a strong military.

2. Firing PATCO union members made Reagan appear strong, and the firings weakened the strength of organized labor.

3. Answers will vary. Possible response: I'd ask how tax cuts and deregulation lead to increased production. I'd also ask how a business's increased production then causes economic growth. Is it because people buy more things? To find my answers, I'd either do research online or read a book on economics.

3.2 Ronald Wilson Reagan 1911–2004

"My philosophy of life is that if we make up our mind what we are going to make of our lives, then work hard toward that goal, we never lose."—Ronald Reagan

Ronald Reagan didn't always believe he could achieve his goals. He admitted to lacking confidence and suffering feelings of inferiority when he was a child. To bolster his self-image, Reagan's mother encouraged him to recite a passage for a dramatic society she belonged to. The enthusiastic applause that followed his performance "was music," Reagan recalled. It was a life-changing experience. Soon he would tackle his goals with the optimism for which he would become famous.

FROM DIXON TO HOLLYWOOD

Reagan's early insecurity may have stemmed from an unsettled early childhood. His father frequently moved his family from place to place. As a result, it was hard for the young Reagan to make friends. Finally, in 1920, the family settled in Dixon, Illinois. During high school, Reagan played football, acted in the drama club, and served as student body president. In many ways, these activities foreshadowed the course his life would take.

After graduating from college in 1932, Reagan worked as a sports announcer on the radio. Five years later, he took a screen test for Warner Brothers and subsequently signed a contract with the movie studio. Over the next 20 years, Reagan appeared in more than 50 films. One of his best-known movies is the 1940 film *Knute Rockne, All American*, in which he played University of Notre Dame football player George Gipp. Reagan married actress Jane Wyman that same year. The couple divorced in 1948, and Reagan married another actress, Nancy Davis, in 1952.

CRITICAL VIEWING Reagan strikes a pose on a football field as George Gipp in *Knute Rockne, All American*. The film tells the true story of Rockne, the University of Notre Dame's football coach in the early 1900s, and Gipp, the team's first star player. Gipp developed pneumonia in 1920 and died at the age of 25. In the film, Reagan delivers his most famous on-screen line, "win one for the Gipper," as his character lies on his deathbed. After the movie became a hit, Reagan was often called "the Gipper." How might Reagan's experience as an actor have helped him as a politician?

In this photo, Reagan delivers a speech in Florida during his first successful bid for the presidency in 1980. Reagan used the slogan, "Let's Make America Great Again," during the campaign. When he ran for re-election in 1984, he developed an effective television ad using the phrase "It's morning again in America," which promised a bright future for the country.

ONTO THE POLITICAL STAGE

As an actor, Reagan closely followed the investigations into communist activities in the entertainment industry during the 1940s and 1950s and became a firm anticommunist. Once a supporter of Franklin Roosevelt's New Deal, Reagan's political views became increasingly conservative. He began to speak publicly in favor of business and lashed out against the wastefulness and excessive regulations of government. Reagan emerged as a national political figure in 1964 when he delivered a well-received speech in support of Republican presidential candidate Barry Goldwater. The speech helped Reagan secure the first of his two terms as governor of California in 1966.

After two failed bids to become the Republican presidential nominee, Reagan won the nomination and the presidency in 1980. A popular president, he was known for his sense of humor. As the oldest person at that time ever elected to the presidency, for instance, Reagan joked: "Thomas Jefferson once said, 'We should never judge a president by his age, only by his works.' And ever since he told me that, I stopped worrying."

After they left the White House, Ronald and Nancy Reagan returned to California. In 1994, the former president revealed that he had Alzheimer's disease, which causes progressive mental deterioration. With characteristic optimism he wrote, "I now begin the journey that will lead me into the sunset of my life. I know that for America there will always be a bright dawn ahead." Reagan died 10 years later.

HISTORICAL THINKING

1. **READING CHECK** How did Reagan's early interests reflect the course of his career?

2. **IDENTIFY MAIN IDEAS AND DETAILS** How had Reagan's political views changed by the 1950s?

3. **MAKE INFERENCES** What did Reagan mean when he wrote that "there will always be a bright dawn ahead" for America?

Objective

Learn about Ronald Reagan's early life and his path to politics.

Critical Thinking Skills for Lesson 3.2

- Identify Main Ideas and Details
- Monitor Comprehension
- Make Inferences
- Make Connections
- Evaluate

Essential Question for Chapter 28

How did new ideas in American politics in the 1980s impact the country and the world? With the 1980 presidential election, Ronald Reagan emerged as a new voice for the Republican Party. Lesson 3.2 discusses the opportunities and influences that shaped Ronald Reagan's rise from sports announcer to Hollywood actor and eventually to U.S. president.

Background for the Teacher

In 1932, Ronald Reagan suffered a double defeat. His fiancée broke off their engagement, and he was turned down for a manager's position at a department store. Looking for a new start, Reagan decided to look for work in the emerging radio industry and landed a job as a sports announcer, first at WOC in Davenport, Iowa, and then at WHO in Des Moines. His dramatic style of coverage made him popular with radio listeners, so the 22-year-old was earning $100 a month, a significant salary during the Great Depression. Reagan later decided to try the movie business. In 1937 he traveled to Los Angeles, supposedly to cover the Chicago Cubs spring training for WHO but in reality to break into acting. Ironically, Reagan owed his future career in Hollywood not to a lucky break but to two early failures that changed the direction of his life.

History Notebook

Encourage students to complete the American Voices page for Chapter 28 in their History Notebooks as they read.

INTRODUCE & ENGAGE

Preview Using Visuals

Discuss with students what they know about Ronald Reagan, such as his career as an actor or that he was the 40th U.S. president. Then direct their attention to the opening quotation and the two photographs of Reagan. **ASK:** How do the photos appear to illustrate Reagan's words? (*Possible response: The first photo shows him as a young man in a football pose. He seems focused and projects confidence. The second photo shows him as an older man delivering a speech. The two photos illustrate his comments about determination and achieving what you want.*) Tell students that in this lesson they will learn more about Reagan's life and guiding principles.

TEACH

Guided Discussion

1. **Make Connections** How did mass media help Ronald Reagan build his reputation as an effective communicator throughout his life? (*Possible response: Working as a sports announcer in radio provided Reagan with experience in using his voice effectively, and his appealing personality helped to convey information clearly to an audience.*)

2. **Evaluate** How does the text convey Reagan's optimism and determination to succeed? (*Possible response: He never let failure keep him from his goals. He used drama and sports to overcome his shyness. Even when he failed twice to get the presidential nomination, he kept trying until he won. When diagnosed with Alzheimer's disease, he accepted his condition and maintained an optimistic point of view.*)

American Voices

On January 28, 1986, after the *Challenger* space shuttle disaster, President Reagan delivered what is now one of his most famous speeches. A young White House speechwriter, Peggy Noonan, was given only a few hours to craft the words Reagan would say to a grieving nation. Reagan wanted the speech to honor the astronauts and to reassure the schoolchildren who had witnessed the tragedy that "life does go on and you don't back up and quit some worthwhile endeavor because of tragedy." Noonan ended the speech with a quote from a World War II poem, "High Flight," expressing the thought that the astronauts had "slipped the surly bonds of earth" and "touched the face of God." Reagan recognized the poem, and although he was not sure of its appropriateness for the occasion, he delivered the lines with an actor's skill. Praise for the speech soon poured in, with friends and critics alike saying how moved they were by Reagan's sincerity.

Active Options

On Your Feet: Numbered Heads Arrange students in groups of four and have them number off within each group. Write the lesson's opening quotation by Reagan on the board. Tell students to think about the quote and discuss their response to the following question: Do you agree or disagree with this quotation? Instruct students to explain their response, citing specific examples from the text, their own experience, and other sources. After sufficient time, call out a number and have students with that number report for their group.

NG Learning Framework: Analyze the Great Communicator

SKILL Observation

KNOWLEDGE Our Human Story

Instruct students to work in small groups to analyze what made Ronald Reagan such an effective communicator. Direct them to conduct online research for articles that analyze his abilities as a speaker, and encourage them to view video clips of his major speeches, such as his address to the nation after the *Challenger* tragedy. Tell groups to rate Reagan in terms of his use of language, dramatic phrasing and pauses, body language, and volume and tone. When groups have finished, ask them to present their analyses to the class.

DIFFERENTIATE

Inclusion

Analyze Photographs Pair students who are visually impaired with students who are not. Ask the latter to describe the photographs of Ronald Reagan as a young actor portraying a football player and as a presidential candidate and to read the captions. Tell visually impaired students to ask clarifying questions as necessary. Have partners work together to answer the Introduce & Engage and Critical Viewing questions.

Pre-AP

Write an Obituary Tell students that an obituary presents biographical information about a person's life and character. Instruct them to supplement the information in the lesson with information from multiple online and print sources to write an obituary for Ronald Reagan, quoting or paraphrasing historians and other experts. Invite volunteers to share the obituary with the class.

See the Chapter Planner for more strategies for differentiation.

HISTORICAL THINKING

ANSWERS

1. His early interests in the drama club, in sports, and in leadership roles foreshadowed his career in acting, sports announcing, and politics.

2. He had been a supporter of Franklin Roosevelt's New Deal, but by the 1950s, he had become a conservative Republican who was strongly anticommunist, favored big business, and was critical of federal government regulations.

3. Answers will vary. Possible response: Reagan probably meant that the nation would always overcome whatever difficulties it faced and renew itself.

CRITICAL VIEWING Answers will vary. Possible response: As an actor, he would have learned how to memorize and deliver speeches, connect with an audience, be comfortable in front of a camera or under scrutiny, and understand the importance of image and appearance. All these qualities would have helped him as a politician.

3.3 A Changing Nation

In the 1980s, the conservative movement gained power as Ronald Reagan—a true believer in smaller government, lower taxes, and traditional values—took over the White House. But the values of conservatives often clashed with those of other groups.

MAIN IDEA Both the conservative movement and the gay rights movement became vocal forces in American society in the 1980s.

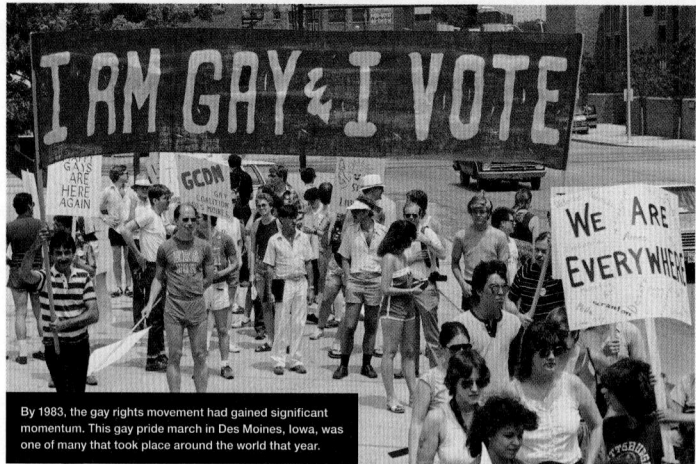

By 1983, the gay rights movement had gained significant momentum. This gay pride march in Des Moines, Iowa, was one of many that took place around the world that year.

THE CONSERVATIVE MOVEMENT

As you've read, millions of Americans moved from the Frostbelt to the Sunbelt in the 1950s. The Sunbelt states had long been more conservative than the Frostbelt states, and many of these migrants were attracted to the region's conservatism, or conservative political philosophy. They were drawn to the Republican Party because of its positions on taxes and national security.

California, however, was more politically diverse than most Sunbelt states. While its major coastal cities were politically liberal, California's rural and suburban regions, such as Orange County, became strongholds of conservatism. Both Ronald Reagan and Richard Nixon were California politicians before becoming president. Outside the Sunbelt, many states experienced a similar urban versus rural and suburban split in political orientation.

The social changes taking place in American society since the 1960s alarmed many conservatives. The number of single-parent households rose as divorce became more common. Drug abuse became more widespread. Conservatives claimed that American society was losing its moral compass.

The conservative movement included Christian fundamentalists, people who believed in strict adherence to the Bible. **Televangelists**, preachers who use television shows to spread their beliefs, encouraged their viewers to uphold what they believed to be traditional family values. Some televangelists, such as **Reverend Jerry Falwell** and **Reverend Billy Graham**, became deeply involved in politics. In 1979, Falwell formed a political group called the **Moral Majority**. The group supported prayer and religious teachings in public schools. It helped elect religious conservatives to local, state, and national offices.

Reverend Billy Graham addresses a crowd at Pilot Field in Buffalo, New York, in August 1988. Members of more than 600 churches gathered at Pilot Field, now known as Coca-Cola Field, to hear the televangelist speak.

THE GAY RIGHTS MOVEMENT

Though it often faced conservative opposition, the gay rights movement became more prominent during the 1970s and 1980s. The movement began in earnest in the late 1960s, when gay people began to fight back publicly against social discrimination and harassment. In many places, it was not only socially unacceptable but also illegal to be gay. As the gay rights movement grew, more gay people "came out," or openly acknowledged their orientation. They staged protests calling for an end to discrimination in employment, housing, and other areas of life. In 1977, San Francisco city supervisor **Harvey Milk** became the first openly gay person to be elected to public office in the United States. In the 1990s, the term **LGBT**, an acronym for "lesbian, gay, bisexual, and transgender," emerged as an alternate name covering distinct groups within the gay community.

During the 1980s, a public health crisis struck the world. An alarming number of people began dying of an unidentified disease that made their bodies unable to fight infections. In the United States, most of the first victims were gay men. Scientists learned the disease is caused by a virus, which they named the **human immunodeficiency virus (HIV)**. This is also the name of the first stage of the disease. The last stage is called **acquired immunodeficiency syndrome (AIDS)**, but not all people with HIV advance to the AIDS stage. HIV/AIDS quickly spread beyond the gay community to affect other groups of people. The initial lack of information about HIV/AIDS caused panic in the country.

Once scientists discovered that HIV was transmitted through bodily fluids, programs arose worldwide to educate people on prevention methods. Unfortunately, millions of people have died from HIV/AIDS. No cure exists, but scientists have developed medicines to help infected people manage the disease.

HISTORICAL THINKING

1. **READING CHECK** What parts of the country were conservative strongholds in the 1980s?

2. **MAKE GENERALIZATIONS** Why might many conservatives oppose the gay rights movement?

3. **IDENTIFY PROBLEMS AND SOLUTIONS** What action was taken to prevent the spread of HIV/AIDS?

PLAN

Objective

Trace the rise of the conservative and the gay rights movements during the 1980s.

Critical Thinking Skills for Lesson 3.3

- Identify Main Ideas and Details
- Monitor Comprehension
- Make Generalizations
- Identify Problems and Solutions
- Make Inferences
- Draw Conclusions
- Determine Word Meaning

Essential Question for Chapter 28

How did new ideas in American politics in the 1980s impact the country and the world? The 1980s revealed a great disparity in Americans' social and political attitudes. Lesson 3.3 examines the rise of both conservatism, including Christian fundamentalists, and the gay rights movement.

Background for the Teacher

In the 1980s, an unexpected alliance formed between the gay community and one particular televangelist after a scandal rocked the entire televangelism community. Jim Bakker, who owned an assortment of Christian businesses with his wife, Tammy Faye Bakker, went to jail after defrauding churchgoers and overselling shares in Heritage USA, a Christian amusement park and resort they owned. Tammy Faye avoided indictment and afterward divorced her husband.

At the time of the controversy, the spread of HIV/AIDS was escalating. Contrary to the conservative views of most televangelists, Tammy Faye sympathized with the gay community's suffering and went on to become an unlikely advocate, showing compassion for those who had contracted the disease. The gay community, in turn, remained by Tammy Faye's side after her family's scandal. The allegiance between these two unlikely allies remained strong for years.

Examine Political Platforms

Draw a T-Chart on the board, labeling the left column Conservative Platform and the right column Liberal Platform. Ask students to identify some of the values or beliefs that typically make up the conservative and liberal political platforms. If necessary, provide topics for them to consider, such as the environment, business, labor, family structures, and social programs. Write their responses in the T-Chart. Explain to students that in this lesson they will be exploring aspects of the conservative movement in the 1980s. After reading the lesson, revisit the T-Chart and ask students to suggest any additions or changes.

TEACH

Guided Discussion

1. **Make Inferences** Why do you think members of the Moral Majority wanted to elect religious conservatives to political offices? *(Possible response: They wanted to elect people who would support their values and promote legislation and governance that reflected those values.)*

2. **Draw Conclusions** Why might it have taken so long for scientists to determine what caused AIDS and how it was transmitted? *(Possible responses: First, scientists had to discover the virus that caused it, figure out how the patients with HIV/AIDS were similar, and establish relationships between infected patients to figure out how the virus passed between them. Because the disease was at first mostly found within the gay community, some researchers and funding organizations, including the government, might not have considered it a crucial public health issue.)*

Determine Word Meaning

Direct students to the Gay Rights Movement subsection. Read the sentence "Scientists learned the disease is caused by a virus, which they named the human immunodeficiency virus (HIV)." Remind students that the HIV/AIDS disease causes people's bodies to become unable to fight infections. **ASK:** Given the effect the disease has on the body, what do you think *immunodeficiency* means? *(It means the immune system is inadequate and isn't as strong as it should be.)*

Active Options

On Your Feet: View a Clip Show a video clip of a televangelist such as the Reverend Jerry Falwell or the Reverend Billy Graham addressing a crowd. After students view the clip, organize them into groups of three or four. Instruct the groups to discuss how the clip relates to the information they read in the lesson. Encourage students to discuss the effectiveness of the televangelist's speaking techniques and the reasons why he might draw large groups of followers. After the discussion, invite groups to share their thoughts with the class.

NG Learning Framework: Research Gay Rights

ATTITUDE Curiosity

KNOWLEDGE Our Human Story

Encourage students to conduct online research on an aspect of the gay rights movement that interests them. For example, they might focus on an issue such as current gay marriage laws in the United States or the inclusion of transgender actors in the entertainment industry, or they might focus on an individual, such as Harvey Milk and his role as an openly gay city supervisor in San Francisco during the 1970s. Once they complete their research, tell them to develop a short oral presentation sharing their findings. Some might want to include visuals, such as graphs or photos. Invite students to give their presentation for the class.

DIFFERENTIATE

Striving Readers

Connect Details to Main Ideas Direct students to work in pairs to complete a Main Idea and Details List for each subsection of the lesson. Remind students of the kinds of details (facts, dates, events, descriptions) that often support a main idea. Encourage pairs to share their lists with other pairs when they have finished.

Main Idea:
Detail:
Detail:
Detail:
Detail:
Detail:

Pre-AP

Write a Comparison-Contrast Essay Prompt students to conduct online research to find out more about the urban/rural political split in the 1980s. Encourage them to use a Venn diagram to keep track of the similarities and differences between the political, social, religious, and economic views of the majority of people living in urban or rural areas. Then tell students to use their research to write a comparison-contrast essay. When they have finished, invite them to share their essays with the class.

See the Chapter Planner for more strategies for differentiation.

HISTORICAL THINKING

ANSWERS

1. The Sunbelt states, including some parts of California in particular, were more conservative than the Frostbelt states. In general, rural and suburban parts of the country were more conservative.

2. Conservatives have more traditional ideas about what is socially acceptable, and many follow strict religious guidelines that do not approve of homosexuality.

3. Worldwide programs focused on educating people on how HIV/AIDS is spread and how to prevent getting it or passing it to others.

3.4 Deregulation and Defense

Do you ever feel that your school has too many rules? President Reagan felt that way about government regulations—and so he began getting rid of them.

MAIN IDEA President Reagan loosened regulations on businesses and increased spending on defense.

DEREGULATION

President Reagan strongly believed that too many government regulations, including environmental regulations, hurt businesses by increasing costs. He thought these costs were stifling the economy.

Reagan appointed Colorado legislator Anne Gorsuch from Colorado to head the Environmental Protection Agency (EPA) and James G. Watt, a former assistant to the Secretary of the Interior, to lead the Department of the Interior. Gorsuch slashed the EPA's budget by 25 percent and abolished many EPA regulations. Watt handed over huge areas of federal land to coal mining companies. He also opened up the U.S. **continental shelf**—the submerged, relatively shallow land surrounding a continent and extending into the ocean—to oil drilling. Environmentalists strongly opposed the actions of both officials. Gorsuch and Watt were forced to resign in 1983, and in the following years, Congress renewed and strengthened various environmental laws.

Reagan also eased rules on the savings and loan industry. Experts argue that this action led to a crisis in the late 1980s and 1990s after savings and loan associations lent money to people who could not pay it back. Many of the companies failed. Taxpayers ended up paying billions of dollars as the government reimbursed depositors at the failed companies.

Reagan cut funding for such social programs as food stamps and school lunches but kept popular programs that benefited the middle class, such as Medicare and Social Security. When experts announced Social Security funds were running low in 1983, Reagan gathered economists to solve the funding problem.

BUILDING UP DEFENSE

While Reagan reduced the size and power of the federal government through deregulation, he increased it by building up the military. A strong anticommunist, Reagan wanted to bolster the nation's defense to challenge the Soviet Union, which he called "the Evil Empire." Between 1980 and 1985, he doubled the military's budget. As you have read, Reagan approved a tax increase to pay for the increased military spending.

In 1983, the Reagan administration proposed development of a defense system called the **Strategic Defense Initiative (SDI)**, which the press dubbed "Star Wars." SDI was a system of satellites that would be launched into space to defend the United States by intercepting attacking missiles in flight. Once operational, SDI would give the United States a military advantage over the Soviet Union. Critics argued that the system was too expensive, required too much energy, and depended on technology not yet invented. The initiative was abandoned after experts determined the system would raise tensions between the United States and the Soviet Union.

In 1986, midway through his second term, Reagan faced a major political scandal called the **Iran-Contra Affair**. Because of concerns about the possible spread of communism in Central America, the Reagan administration provided military aid to a militia group called the Contras, who were fighting the leftist government in Nicaragua. In 1984, Congress passed a law banning aid to the Contras. However, the White House secretly continued to fund the group, in violation of the law.

The scandal also involved Iran because the Reagan administration was secretly selling weapons to Iran in the hopes of securing the

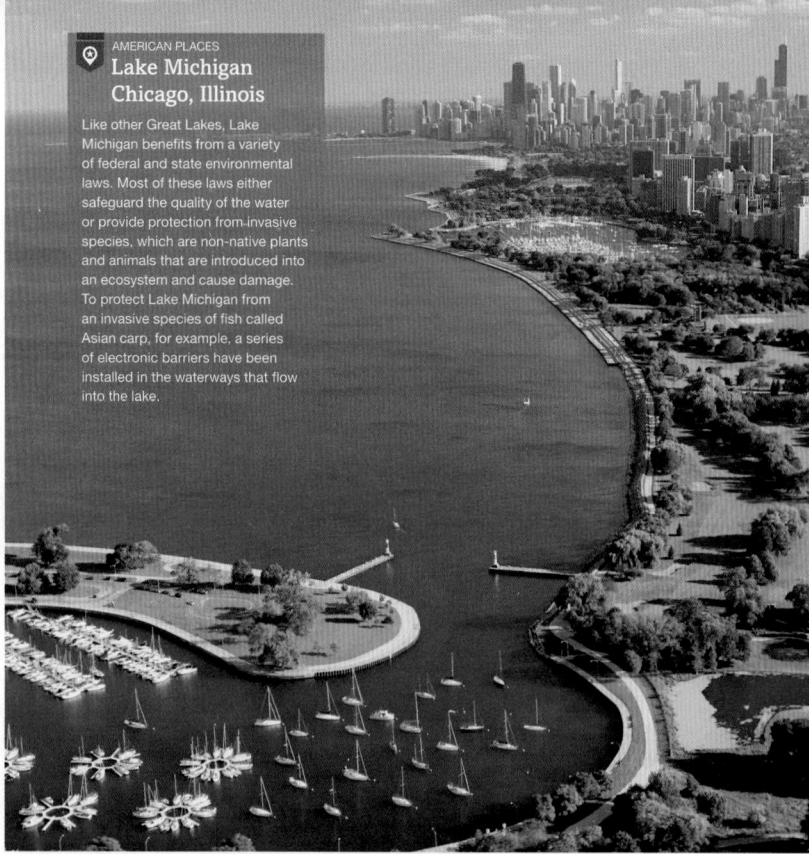

release of American hostages in Lebanon. Besides being illegal, these sales contradicted the U.S. government's stated policy of refusing to negotiate with terrorists. A portion of the money gained from these arms sales was given to the Contras.

After several investigations of the scandal, a number of members of Reagan's administration were charged and convicted of crimes. Reagan himself was never charged, but his reputation was temporarily tarnished.

HISTORICAL THINKING

1. **READING CHECK** Why did President Reagan abolish many government regulations?

2. **DRAW CONCLUSIONS** How did Reagan's anticommunism influence his foreign policy?

3. **EVALUATE** What were the pros and cons of the Strategic Defense Initiative?

Objective
Explore President Reagan's policies on the environment, social programs, and defense.

Critical Thinking Skills for Lesson 3.4
- Identify Main Ideas and Details
- Monitor Comprehension
- Draw Conclusions
- Evaluate
- Make Inferences
- Form and Support Opinions

Essential Question for Chapter 28
How did new ideas in American politics in the 1980s impact the country and the world?
Reagan's presidency resulted in a rollback of some types of funding and a growth in others. Lesson 3.4 details the changes Reagan made to environmental and business regulations and defense spending and his involvement in the Iran-Contra Affair.

Background for the Teacher
The Iran-Contra Affair first came to light when a Lebanese newspaper exposed the U.S. sale of weapons to Iran in exchange for the release of hostages in Lebanon. President Reagan at first denied the charges but later amended his statement by claiming the weapons sale was unrelated to the hostage exchange. It was not until the U.S. attorney general realized that more than half of the $30 million payment for the arms was missing that the full story emerged. A member of the National Security Council, Lieutenant Colonel Oliver North, testified that he had diverted the missing funds to the Contras. North was fired and convicted for his role in the exchange, but his conviction was later overturned. After becoming president, George H.W. Bush pardoned six other people involved in the scandal.

Discuss Deregulation and Defense

Guide students to think about the ways rules and regulations benefit people, keep them safe, and promote harmony. Then guide a discussion about the drawbacks of regulations. Remind students that *deregulation* means loosening government restrictions. **ASK:** What are some situations in which you think there are too many rules and restrictions, and why do you think so? *(Answers will vary. Possible response: There are too many rules in school about dress codes, tardiness, and talking in class, because students end up worrying more about rules than about learning.)* Next help students consider the benefits and drawbacks of a strong military. **ASK:** In what situations might the build up of defense be a drawback? *(Possible response: When two groups are moving toward conflict, the build up of defense by one group could increase tensions between them.)* Tell students that in this lesson they will learn about Reagan's policies regarding regulations and defense.

TEACH

Guided Discussion

1. **Make Inferences** Why do you think President Reagan continued funding Medicare and Social Security while cutting funding for food stamps and school lunches? *(Possible response: He was more concerned about the middle class and didn't want to lose their votes by cutting programs important to them.)*

2. **Form and Support Opinions** Do you think it was right that members of Reagan's administration were convicted for their roles in the Iran-Contra Affair and the president was not? Explain your response. *(Answers will vary. Possible responses: No. The White House broke the law twice by funding the Contras and by selling weapons to Iran. Reagan should have been convicted as well, because as the president, he had to know what was happening and probably approved it. Yes. Those who were convicted were guilty of the crimes. Congress did not impeach Reagan, so he did not face charges and a trial that could have clearly defined his role. Without this process, Reagan's guilt was not established.)*

🛡 American Places

Every year, the Chicago Yacht Club's Race to Mackinac, also known as "the Mac," takes place on Lake Michigan—the lake featured in the lesson's photograph. Beginning at the Chicago Lighthouse, the race continues northeast to Mackinac Island, Michigan. The first official Race to Mackinac was in 1898, and the event has occurred every year since 1921, making it the oldest freshwater sailing race in the world. Covering a total of 333 miles, the race is also the world's longest annual freshwater sailing competition. Each summer, people travel from all over the world to face the surprisingly difficult conditions that sailing on Lake Michigan offers.

Active Options

On Your Feet: Roundtable Discussion Divide students into groups of four. Tell the groups to conduct roundtable discussions in which each member of the group shares an example of a funding cut, an increase in spending, or an act of deregulation made by President Reagan or members of his administration. After everyone has had a chance to contribute and groups have exhausted their ideas, invite them to share with the class their thoughts about the administration's actions.

NG Learning Framework: Draw a Diagram of SDI

ATTITUDE Curiosity

SKILL Collaboration

Encourage students to learn more about the Strategic Defense Initiative (SDI) by conducting online research to locate reference materials and then work with a partner to draw a diagram of the SDI. Diagrams should include enough detail to illustrate how the system was intended to work. Invite pairs to present their finished diagrams to the class.

English Language Learners

Look for Cognates Suggest that as students read they look for words that are similar in spelling and meaning to words in their home language. For example, the words *deregulate, military, satellite, arms,* and *scandal* have cognates in Spanish: *desregular, militar, satélite, armas,* and *escándalo.* For each word they identify, tell students of **All Proficiencies** to make a vocabulary card with the English word and definition on one side. On the other side, they write the word and its definition in their home language.

Gifted & Talented

Create a Cause-and-Impact Presentation Direct students to conduct online research to learn more about a particular invasive species in Lake Michigan or in their home region. Instruct them to take notes on the origin of that species, its environmental and economic impacts, and any measures taken to lessen those impacts. Tell students to compile their research into a multimedia presentation, and invite them to share it with the class.

See the Chapter Planner for more strategies for differentiation.

HISTORICAL THINKING

ANSWERS

1. Reagan thought that abolishing certain regulations would help businesses and the economy grow because it would cut costs for businesses.

2. Reagan's administration illegally provided military aid to a militia group in Nicaragua called the Contras to help them fight the country's leftist government. To raise money to fund the anticommunist Contras, the Reagan administration secretly sold arms to Iran.

3. As proposed, the SDI would have allowed missiles to be intercepted by satellites, protecting the United States from an attack by the Soviet Union. But the SDI was also costly, needed too much energy, and relied on technology that didn't yet exist.

4.1 The End of the Cold War

For more than 45 years, the Cold War cast a dark cloud over the lives of Americans. It led Americans to build bomb shelters in backyards and practice nuclear attack drills in schools. No one imagined the war would end quickly once Soviets got a taste of democracy.

MAIN IDEA The Cold War ended with the breakup of the Soviet Union and the collapse of communist regimes in Eastern Europe between 1989 and 1991.

CHANGES IN THE SOVIET UNION

During Reagan's second term in office, in 1985, **Mikhail Gorbachev** (mih-KAY-uhl GOHR-buh-chawf) became leader of the Soviet Union. Gorbachev inherited serious domestic problems, including a stagnant economy and an inefficient government. He proposed a political program called **perestroika** (pair-ih-STROY-kuh), which means "restructuring." Perestroika called for reducing government control of the economy and taking steps toward democracy. At the same time, Gorbachev introduced a policy called **glasnost** (GLAS-nawst), which means "openness." Under glasnost, freedom of the press was expanded and criticism of the Soviet government was allowed.

Gorbachev also promoted better relations with the United States. In 1987, Reagan and Gorbachev signed the Intermediate-Range Nuclear Forces Treaty (INF), which called for both nations to eliminate their intermediate-range and medium-range nuclear missiles. The agreement eased tension between the two countries, but Reagan still spoke out against communism. During a visit to West Germany in 1987, the president stood in front of the Berlin Wall and challenged Gorbachev to "tear down this wall."

In November 1988, Reagan's vice president **George H.W. Bush** was elected president. As a former ambassador to the United Nations and director of the CIA, Bush had experience in foreign affairs. He continued the work of improving relations with the Soviet Union.

Breakup of the Soviet Union, 1991

ARCTIC OCEAN

Border of the former Soviet Union
Countries within the black border were part of the Soviet Union before its breakup in 1991.

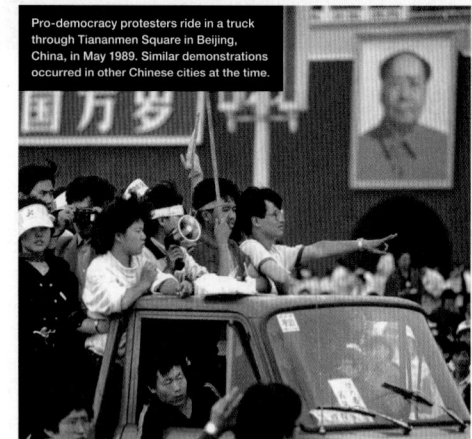

Pro-democracy protesters ride in a truck through Tiananmen Square in Beijing, China, in May 1989. Similar demonstrations occurred in other Chinese cities at the time.

GLOBAL CHANGES

Gorbachev not only introduced democratic reforms in the Soviet Union, he also encouraged reforms in the communist nations of Eastern Europe. Throughout the summer of 1989, citizens in these countries staged peaceful protests demanding democracy. In Poland, voters elected a democratic government in August. The communist governments in Hungary and Czechoslovakia fell in early fall. In November came East Germany, where journalists photographed crowds of people tearing down the Berlin Wall. In 1990, East Germany and West Germany reunited.

Gorbachev's democratic reforms had some unintended consequences. The republics that made up the Soviet Union, except for Russia, pushed to become independent nations. Then in August 1991, a group of loyal communists staged a **coup** (KOO), or government overthrow, and arrested Gorbachev. After three days of protests by Soviet citizens, the coup leaders surrendered. Even though the coup had failed, Gorbachev had lost power. On December 25, 1991, he resigned and was replaced by **Boris Yeltsin**. The next day, a joint declaration by the leaders of the Soviet republics announced the breakup of the Soviet Union. Each of the 15 former Soviet republics became an independent nation. In February 1992, President Bush and President Yeltsin of the Soviet Union announced the end of the Cold War.

Meanwhile, in China, a push for democratic reform did not succeed. In May 1989, nearly a million protesters gathered in a huge public space in Beijing called **Tiananmen Square**. For three weeks, they called for communist leaders to resign and for a new democratic government. By June 4, the Chinese government had sent troops and tanks into the square to end the protests. At least 300 people were killed that day and thousands were injured. The Bush administration denounced, or spoke out against, the attack and started an arms embargo against China.

HISTORICAL THINKING

1. **READING CHECK** What were glasnost and perestroika?

2. **MAKE GENERALIZATIONS** What does the rapid breakup of the Soviet Union indicate about life under Soviet control?

3. **ANALYZE CAUSE AND EFFECT** Why did citizens in so many Eastern European countries decide to revolt against communism in 1989?

PLAN

Objective

Analyze the changing political landscape in the Soviet Union and Eastern Europe in the 1980s.

Critical Thinking Skills for Lesson 4.1

- Identify Main Ideas and Details
- Monitor Comprehension
- Make Generalizations
- Analyze Cause and Effect
- Interpret Maps
- Compare and Contrast
- Evaluate

Essential Question for Chapter 28

How did new ideas in American politics in the 1980s impact the country and the world? In the 1980s, improved U.S.-Soviet relations led to reforms that had far-ranging effects. Lesson 4.1 details the breakup of the Soviet Union and the end of communist regimes in Eastern Europe.

Background for the Teacher

Though Mikhail Gorbachev's reforms had made him quite popular in the West, they had a very different effect at home. In fact, the reforms that Gorbachev instituted in the Soviet Union eventually worked against him. For example, freedom of the press, which Gorbachev expanded under glasnost, enabled newspapers to criticize him openly, and the economic reforms he introduced led to a destabilizing crisis in the economy. Gorbachev was woefully unprepared for criticism from within the Soviet Union. In 1991, his own chief of staff and the head of the KGB, among others, staged a coup while Gorbachev and his wife were on vacation.

Despite the upheaval during his administration, Gorbachev again decided to run for president in the mid-1990s, against Boris Yeltsin. During the campaign, Gorbachev was publicly mocked. In the end, he received less than 1 percent of the vote.

Preview Using the Map

Draw students' attention to the black lines on the map that outline the former Soviet Union. **ASK:** What does the black outline on this map represent? *(It shows all the territory that used to be part of the Soviet Union.)* **ASK:** What is the largest country on the map? *(Russia)* As a class, discuss how much territory both Russia and the countries that used to be part of the Soviet Union cover. Tell students that in this lesson they will learn how this once massive country broke apart and what the consequences were.

TEACH

Guided Discussion

1. **Interpret Maps** How does the map help you understand the scale of the Soviet Union's breakup? *(Possible response: It shows that the breakup affected many countries over a vast area.)*

2. **Compare and Contrast** How did the outcome of protests in China differ from the outcome of protests in Eastern Europe? *(In Eastern Europe, peaceful protests ushered in an era of democratic reforms. In China, the government sent in troops to break up the protests. Hundreds of people died, and thousands were injured. In the end, democratic reforms didn't take hold as they did in Eastern Europe.)*

Evaluate

Allow students to review the information about Mikhail Gorbachev's reforms in the Soviet Union and his encouragement of reforms elsewhere. **ASK:** How effective was Gorbachev at helping to spread democracy throughout the Soviet Union and other countries? Use evidence from the text to support your response. *(Possible response: Gorbachev was fairly effective. His perestroika program helped promote democracy. Also, many Eastern European countries, such as Poland, Hungary, Czechoslovakia, and East Germany, became democracies after Gorbachev encouraged similar reforms there.)*

Active Options

On Your Feet: 5Ws Chart Assign students to groups of three or four. Tell the groups to move to different parts of the room and create and complete a 5Ws Chart on Mikhail Gorbachev and his reforms. Groups should detail what major reforms Gorbachev instituted and why and note where and when reforms took place. Once groups have completed their charts, ask volunteers to summarize their group's findings for the class.

Who?	_____
What?	_____
Where?	_____
When?	_____
Why?	_____
	_____
	_____

NG Learning Framework: Write an Opinion Piece

SKILL Communication

KNOWLEDGE Our Human Story

Direct students to write an opinion piece on one of these topics: Gorbachev's reforms, the signing of the INF Treaty, or the protests in Tiananmen Square. Allow students to conduct additional research on their selected topic using online or library sources. In their opinion pieces, students should clearly state their opinion and support their ideas with evidence from the text or their research. Once students have finished their writing, invite them to read their opinion piece to the class.

Inclusion

Use Supported Reading Tell pairs of students to take turns reading paragraphs of the lesson aloud. At the end of each paragraph, have students use the following sentence frames to identify what they do and do not understand.

• This paragraph is about _____.

• One fact that stood out to me was _____.

• I had trouble understanding _____, so I figured it out by _____.

Be sure all students understand the content before moving on to the next paragraph.

Pre-AP

Analyze a Breakup Instruct students to find out more about what happened after the Soviet Union broke up, develop a topic, and write an essay. Tell them to choose one of the 15 former Soviet republics and trace economic and political developments in that nation since it gained independence, including such issues as wealth inequality and the fairness of elections. Students should conclude their essay by stating whether they think life in that nation is on the whole better or worse than under Soviet rule. Invite volunteers to read their essays to the class, or have students share them on a class blog or website.

See the Chapter Planner for more strategies for differentiation.

HISTORICAL THINKING

ANSWERS

1. Glasnost was a policy Gorbachev instituted that translates to "openness." It meant that the press would have greater freedom and that citizens could criticize the Soviet government. Perestroika, or "restructuring," was another of Gorbachev's initiatives. Under perestroika, the government would have less control of the economy and move toward democracy.

2. Possible response: It indicates that life wasn't very pleasant for the citizens. If they had been happy under Soviet control, they would have wanted to remain part of the Soviet Union.

3. Gorbachev had encouraged communist countries in Eastern Europe to follow his lead, and that helped citizens of those countries feel free to protest.

4.2 War in the Middle East

Handling foreign relations can be like fighting forest fires. As soon as one fire is put out, another one starts somewhere else. After declaring the end of the Cold War, President George H.W. Bush had to fight another fire.

MAIN IDEA President Bush faced the challenges of rising national debt and major conflict in the Middle East.

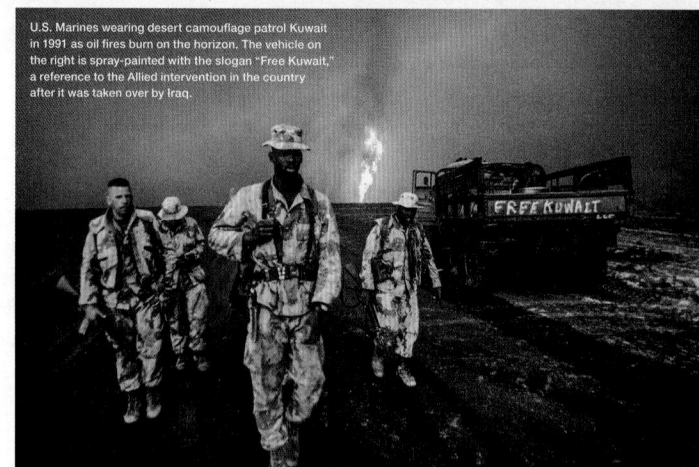

U.S. Marines wearing desert camouflage patrol Kuwait in 1991 as oil fires burn on the horizon. The vehicle on the right is spray-painted with the slogan "Free Kuwait," a reference to the Allied intervention in the country after it was taken over by Iraq.

BUSH'S DOMESTIC POLICIES

As you have read, George H.W. Bush won the 1988 presidential election. His bid for the office was bolstered by President Reagan's popularity and the lessening of tensions in the world. His campaign promise that he would not raise taxes also swayed voters to his side. This pledge turned out to be a problem, however, after Bush became president. The national debt continued to increase in the first two years of his presidency. In 1990, Bush had no choice but to introduce new taxes and cut government spending to keep the deficit under control.

With little money to spend on domestic programs, Bush promoted education reform and volunteerism. One significant law he signed was the **Americans with Disabilities Act (ADA)**. Bush said, "I am going to do whatever it takes to make sure the disabled are included in the mainstream." The new law made it illegal for employers to discriminate against disabled people. It also ensured that people with disabilities would have access to places of business, public facilities, and transportation. Although some conservatives opposed

the law, claiming it was too expensive and yet another example of government overregulation, it gained widespread public support. Under Bush, the federal government also began to fund AIDS research with the goal of finding a cure.

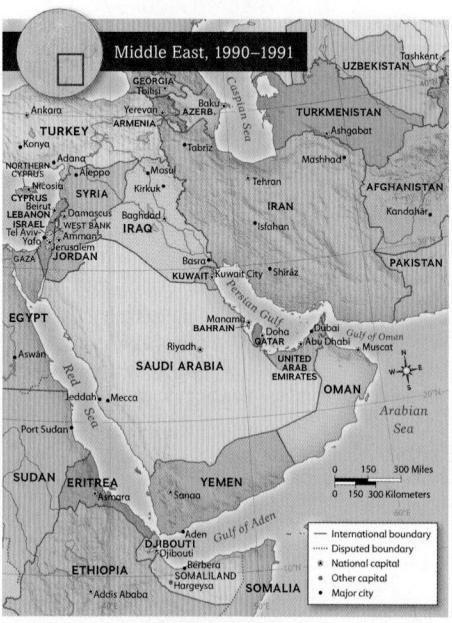

Middle East, 1990–1991

THE PERSIAN GULF WAR

As the Cold War ended, tensions increased between two dictatorships in the Middle East, Iran and Iraq. Religious leader **Ruhollah Khomeini** (roo-HOH-luh koh-MAY-nee) headed Iran's Islamic government, and the brutal dictator **Saddam Hussein** (sah-DAHM hoo-SAYN) ruled Iraq. Hussein invaded Iran in 1980, beginning a war that would last until 1988. The war ended with neither country gaining any territory.

In August 1990, Hussein declared peace with Iran and then invaded the neighboring country of **Kuwait**. He claimed that oil companies from Kuwait had taken oil that belonged to Iraq. But experts believe he invaded the country to gain its oil reserves, since he needed money to pay off his expensive war with Iran. The invasion posed a major threat to Kuwait's neighbor and U.S. ally, Saudi Arabia, which was also the world's largest oil producer. In response to the invasion, the United Nations threatened military action unless Hussein left Kuwait. Hussein refused.

With help from the United Nations, President Bush put together a **coalition**, or a group of nations that join together for a common purpose. The coalition contributed 700,000 troops, with Americans

numbering 540,000. The coalition's goal was to drive the Iraqis out of Kuwait. The short war that followed is officially known as the **Persian Gulf War**. It began on January 16, 1991, with a U.S.-led air campaign called **Operation Desert Storm**. The war lasted 42 days, thanks, in part, to modern military technology. This war saw the first use of weaponry controlled by microcomputers and enhanced by digital guidance systems and laser technology. Saddam's forces were driven from Kuwait in defeat. Bush decided not to pursue Saddam or remove him from office, believing that the coalition would not support an occupation of Baghdad, Iraq's capital.

HISTORICAL THINKING

1. **READING CHECK** What was the cause and the result of the Persian Gulf War?

2. **IDENTIFY PROBLEMS AND SOLUTIONS** How did President Bush respond to the growing national deficit?

3. **FORM AND SUPPORT OPINIONS** What is your opinion of conservatives' objections to the Americans with Disabilities Act?

PLAN

Objective

Learn how President George H.W. Bush addressed the national debt, domestic programs, and the Middle East.

Critical Thinking Skills for Lesson 4.2

- Identify Main Ideas and Details
- Monitor Comprehension
- Identify Problems and Solutions
- Form and Support Opinions
- Interpret Maps
- Make Connections
- Make Inferences

Essential Question for Chapter 28

How did new ideas in American politics in the 1980s impact the country and the world? In the late 1980s, President Bush faced domestic and international challenges. Lesson 4.2 discusses measures Bush took to rein in the national debt, to offer help to disabled people, and to stem Iraqi aggression against Kuwait.

Background for the Teacher

Saddam Hussein ruled with an iron fist. The dictator's name or image appeared everywhere—in mosques, airports, and people's homes. Known for his cruelty and his ego, Hussein threatened people with death if they criticized or mocked him. Hundreds of thousands of Iraqi citizens died while waging his wars or suffering his attacks. During the war with Iran alone, more than 200,000 Iraqi citizens died. The year that war ended, Hussein ordered a poison gas attack on an Iraqi village when he thought its inhabitants were disloyal to him. Thousands died or were injured in the attack. Through it all, Hussein's ego remained intact. Despite being driven out of Kuwait, for example, he never admitted defeat.

History Notebook

Encourage students to complete the American Gallery page for Chapter 28 in their History Notebooks as they read.

INTRODUCE & ENGAGE

View a Clip

Provide an opportunity for students to watch a video clip of George H.W. Bush's famous "no new taxes" speech during the Republican National Convention in 1988. Explain that in the speech, Bush was trying to set himself apart from the Democratic Party nominee for the presidency, Michael Dukakis. **ASK:** How do the audience members react to Bush's statement about not raising taxes? *(They applaud with approval.)* **ASK:** What image was Bush trying to project by saying this? *(He wanted to give the impression that, no matter what, he would never raise taxes and that he would remain firm on his stance.)* Tell students that in this lesson they will learn about the economic challenges Bush faced after making his pledge not to raise taxes.

TEACH

Guided Discussion

1. **Interpret Maps** Based on details you notice on the lesson's map, why would it have been easy for Iraqi forces to overrun Kuwait? *(Possible response: Kuwait is right next to Iraq, so it would have been easy for the Iraqis to storm over the border. Also, Kuwait is a much smaller country than Iraq, so Iraq could easily overpower it.)*

2. **Make Connections** How does the war between Iran and Iraq relate to Saddam Hussein's later invasion of Kuwait? *(After what turned out to be an expensive war with Iran with little to show for it, Iraq needed money. Experts think Hussein wanted to gain access to the oil reserves in Kuwait so that he could sell the oil.)*

Make Inferences

Tell students to review the details about Iraq's invasion of Kuwait and President Bush's response to it. **ASK:** Why do you think the United States was so concerned about Iraq's invasion of Kuwait? *(Saudi Arabia, a U.S. ally, shares a border with Kuwait and produces most of the world's oil supply. The United States feared that the invasion might spill over into Saudi Arabia and threaten the U.S. oil supply.)*

Active Options

AMERICAN GALLERY ONLINE **The Gulf Wars** Invite students to explore the American Gallery. Have them select one of the photos and do additional research to learn more about it. Ask questions that will inspire additional inquiry about the chosen photo, such as: What is happening in the photo? Where was it taken? Who is featured in the photo? What does it help you to understand? How does it relate to information in the text? What else would you like to know about it?

NG Learning Framework: Present a News Report

SKILLS Communication, Collaboration

KNOWLEDGE Our Human Story

Encourage students to learn more about the Persian Gulf War by researching and presenting a news report on it. Tell them to work in teams of two or three to identify a specific aspect of the war they would like to learn more about and then conduct online research to gather information. Remind teams to include specific facts in their news report, such as important dates, countries, leaders, events, and turning points, and to consider how best to divide tasks among teammates. When teams have finished writing, invite them to present their news report to the class.

DIFFERENTIATE

English Language Learners ELD

Hunt for Financial Terms Pair students at the **Emerging** and **Expanding** levels of proficiency with students at the **Bridging** level. Tell students to hunt for terms that relate to money as they take turns reading paragraphs of the lesson. Direct partners to keep a running list of the financial terms they find. When pairs finish reading, encourage them to trade and compare their lists, looking up unfamiliar words in a dictionary. Final lists may include: *taxes, national debt, spending, deficit, fund, money,* and *expensive.*

Gifted & Talented

Interview a Veteran Tell students to conduct online research to learn about experiences of Gulf War veterans. Instruct them to write questions for a radio or television interview with a veteran in order to learn about the person's role in the war and their thoughts and feelings about it. Students may write answers to their questions based on their research, or they may conduct a real interview with a veteran. Direct them to work with a partner to perform the interview live or to tape it, edit it, and make it available to classmates online.

See the Chapter Planner for more strategies for differentiation.

HISTORICAL THINKING

ANSWERS

1. Iraq's dictator, Saddam Hussein, invaded Kuwait for oil reserves. President Bush assembled a coalition of countries to drive Hussein's forces out of Kuwait. The resulting war lasted just 42 days and successfully drove the Iraqis out of the country.

2. Bush raised taxes and cut spending.

3. Answers will vary. Possible response: Conservatives should not have objected to the act. It's an example of reasonable regulation, not overregulation, because its intent was to make sure everyone has the same opportunities or access to places.

28 REVIEW

VOCABULARY

For each pair of vocabulary terms, write one sentence that explains the connection between the two terms.

1. command module; lunar module

   In 1969, Apollo 11's command module remained in orbit around the moon as its lunar module landed on the moon.

2. Watergate scandal; cover-up

3. catalytic converter; smog

4. HIV; AIDS

5. deregulation; continental shelf

6. stagflation; supply-side economics

7. Moral Majority; televangelist

8. perestroika; glasnost

READING STRATEGY
IDENTIFY PROBLEMS AND SOLUTIONS

If you haven't already done so, complete your chart by identifying events and proposed solutions in the energy crisis of the 1970s. Then answer the question below.

9. How did the energy crisis shape American politics during the 1970s?

MAIN IDEAS

Answer the following questions. Support your answers with evidence from the chapter.

10. How did the Nixon administration respond to environmental problems in the 1970s? **LESSON 1.3**

11. What role did newspaper reporters Bob Woodward and Carl Bernstein play in the Watergate scandal? **LESSON 1.5**

12. What is the purpose of the 25th Amendment? **LESSON 2.1**

13. How did President Carter promote peace in the Middle East? **LESSON 2.2**

14. What conservative policies did President Reagan enact? **LESSON 3.1**

15. What effect did the Moral Majority have on American government in the 1980s? **LESSON 3.3**

16. What was the Iran-Contra Affair? **LESSON 3.4**

17. How did the Cold War end? **LESSON 4.1**

18. What were the provisions of the Americans with Disabilities Act that improved the lives of the disabled? **LESSON 4.2**

HISTORICAL THINKING

Answer the following questions. Support your answers with evidence from the chapter.

19. **DETERMINE CHRONOLOGY** What events led to the collapse of the Soviet Union in 1991?

20. **COMPARE AND CONTRAST** How did the policies of Republican presidents Richard Nixon and Ronald Reagan differ?

21. **ANALYZE CAUSE AND EFFECT** Why did Reagan's increased military spending lead to a tax increase?

22. **DRAW CONCLUSIONS** How do you think Americans reacted to the Watergate scandal?

23. **IDENTIFY PROBLEMS AND SOLUTIONS** What problems did the Vietnam War cause in the United States?

24. **FORM AND SUPPORT OPINIONS** What was the more serious problem facing the United States in the 1970s: stagflation or pollution? Explain your answer.

INTERPRET GRAPHS

As you have read in Lesson 2.1, stagflation arose in the mid-1970s, caused by rising inflation paired with a slow, stagnant economy and a decrease in employment. Study the graph at right. Then answer the following questions.

25. What happened to the unemployment rate a year after inflation began to rise in 1972?

26. What happened to the unemployment rate a year after inflation began to decrease in 1974?

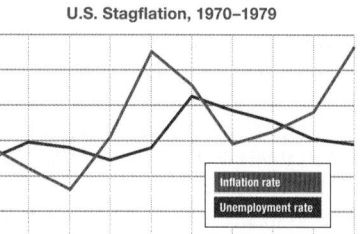

U.S. Stagflation, 1970–1979

Source: U.S. Bureau of Labor Statistics

ANALYZE SOURCES

Ronald Reagan easily won the 1980 presidential election, bringing a wave of conservatism to the Oval Office and the nation. This excerpt from his inaugural speech highlights the economic problems he planned to address.

> Idle industries have cast workers into unemployment, human misery, and personal indignity. Those who do work are denied a fair return for their labor by a tax system which penalizes successful achievement and keeps us from maintaining full productivity.
>
> The economic ills we suffer . . . will not go away in days, weeks, or months, but they will go away . . . because we as Americans have the capacity now, as we've had in the past, to do whatever needs to be done to preserve this last and greatest bastion [stronghold] of freedom.
>
> — from Ronald Reagan's First Inaugural Address, January 20, 1981

27. How does this excerpt reflect Reagan's conservative philosophy?

CONNECT TO YOUR LIFE

28. **ARGUMENT** Reread the excerpt from President Reagan's first inaugural address at left. If you were writing your own inaugural address today, what problem would you focus on, and what solution would you offer? Prepare a short persuasive speech on the subject.

TIPS

- Choose one major problem in the United States today. Research the problem and solutions that have been proposed, using appropriate sources.

- Begin your speech by introducing the problem and the solution you've chosen.

- Elaborate on your solution and explain why you chose it.

- Conclude your speech with a promise or an inspirational thought.

VOCABULARY ANSWERS

1. In 1969, Apollo 11's command module remained in orbit around the moon as its lunar module landed on the moon.

2. When Nixon's cover-up of the Watergate scandal was made public, he resigned.

3. The invention of the catalytic converter for cars helped reduce smog in Los Angeles.

4. The human immunodeficiency virus, or HIV, causes AIDS.

5. In the 1980s, deregulation led to oil drilling along the continental shelf.

6. President Reagan tried to overcome stagflation by promoting supply-side economics.

7. The Moral Majority was a political action group founded by a televangelist.

8. Perestroika and glasnost were two major reforms made by Mikhail Gorbachev in the Soviet Union.

READING STRATEGY ANSWER

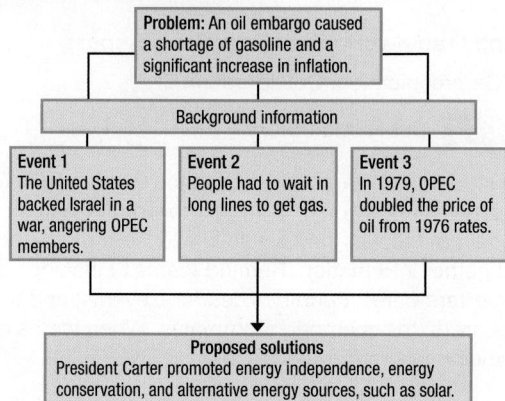

9. Americans were angry about the gas shortages and the high costs of gasoline caused by an embargo and OPEC's price increase. Politicians had to address these issues. Carter, for example, proposed consuming less energy in general, relying on domestic sources of energy, and using new energy sources.

MAIN IDEAS ANSWERS

10. The Nixon administration passed acts to protect the nation's air, water, and endangered species. It also established the EPA.

11. Bernstein and Woodward wrote articles for the *Washington Post* that kept the public focused on the Watergate burglary, turning it into front-page news.

12. The 25th Amendment allows the president to name a new vice president if necessary. It also allows for the vice president and Congress to remove an unfit president.

13. Carter negotiated a peace deal between Israel and Egypt as part of the Camp David Accords.

14. Reagan deregulated industries and cut taxes. He also increased defense spending.

15. The Moral Majority helped elect religious conservatives to national, state, and local offices throughout the country.

16. The Iran-Contra Affair was a scandal that occurred during Reagan's presidency. The United States secretly sold weapons to Iran and sent part of the profits to the Contras, an anticommunist group that was fighting against the leftist Nicaraguan government.

17. Mikhail Gorbachev and Ronald Reagan signed a treaty agreeing to eliminate certain nuclear weapons. Gorbachev also promoted the Soviet Union's transition to a democracy. Eastern European countries then began to demand democratic reforms as well. The Soviet Union eventually split up, ending the Cold War.

18. The ADA ensured that employers couldn't discriminate against disabled people. It also ensured that disabled people had access to businesses, public facilities, and transportation.

HISTORICAL THINKING ANSWERS

19. Gorbachev instituted a move toward democracy in the Soviet Union and established better relations with the United States. Eastern European countries also began moving toward democratic systems of government. Then republics within the Soviet Union demanded independence. A coup took place in the Soviet Union, and Gorbachev lost power. Boris Yeltsin eventually took over and announced the end of the Soviet Union.

20. Nixon created environmental legislation, such as the Clean Air Act, the Clean Water Act, and the Safe Drinking Water Act. He also created the Environmental Protection Agency (EPA). Reagan believed government was too big and that there were too many regulations, especially regarding the environment. He appointed someone to head the EPA who was not a supporter of environmental responsibility and who weakened the agency.

21. The increase in military spending created a deficit. Reagan had to raise taxes to address the deficit.

22. Possible response: Having a president who had committed a crime and lied about it made many Americans distrust the government.

23. Many Americans protested the war, and sometimes the protests became violent. Also, many families lost relatives who fought in the war.

24. Answers will vary. Possible response: I think stagflation was worse because inflation was high throughout the 1970s. But by the early 1970s, many pieces of environmental regulation had already been passed, so the problems were being addressed.

INTERPRET GRAPHS ANSWERS

25. The graph shows that after dropping slightly in 1973, the unemployment rate began to rise again until 1975.

26. The unemployment rate began to fall steadily.

ANALYZE SOURCES ANSWER

27. Possible response: Reagan cites taxes as the cause of unemployment, asserting that the tax system penalizes success.

CONNECT TO YOUR LIFE ANSWER

28. Answers will vary. Students should address an issue that affects the United States today. They should begin the speech by introducing the topic they are speaking about and the solution they are proposing. Students should then explain more about their solution and end their speech with a promise or an inspirational thought.

UNIT 10 RESOURCES

UNIT INTRODUCTION

UNIT TIME LINE

UNIT WRAP-UP

NATIONAL GEOGRAPHIC | CONNECTION

National Geographic Magazine Adapted Articles
- "Changing Faces"
- "The Drones Come Home" ONLINE

Unit 10 Inquiry: Negotiate a Political Compromise

NG Learning Framework Activities
- Create a Comic Strip
- Debate the Effects of Environmental Regulations

Unit 10 Formal Assessment

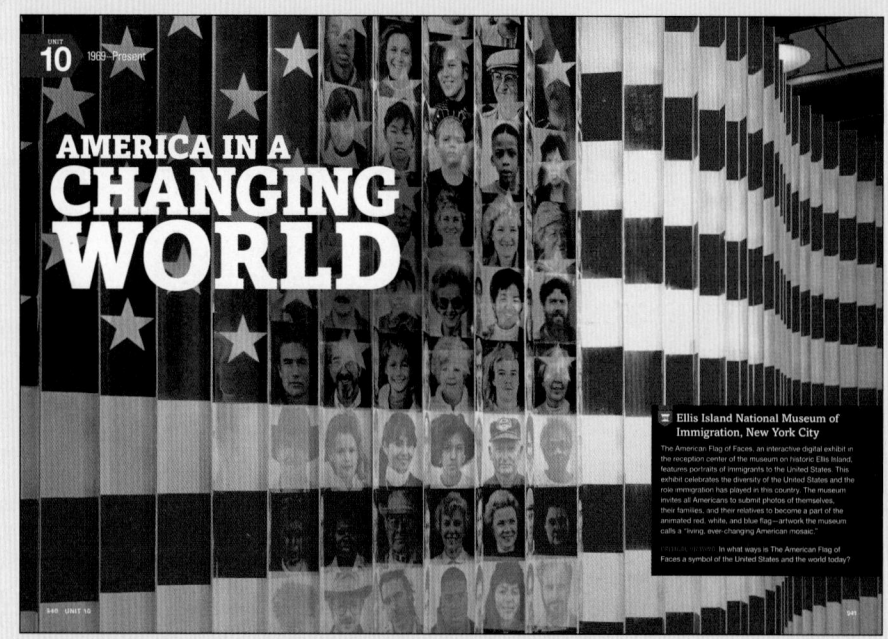

CHAPTER 29 RESOURCES

Available at NGLSync.Cengage.com.

TEACHER RESOURCES & ASSESSMENT

Reading and Note-Taking

Vocabulary Practice

Document-Based Question Template

Social Studies Skills Lessons
- Reading: Form and Support Opinions
- Writing: Write an Expository Paragraph

Formal Assessment
- Chapter 29 Pretest
- Chapter 29 Tests A & B
- Section Quizzes

Chapter 29 Answer Key

ExamView®
One-time Download

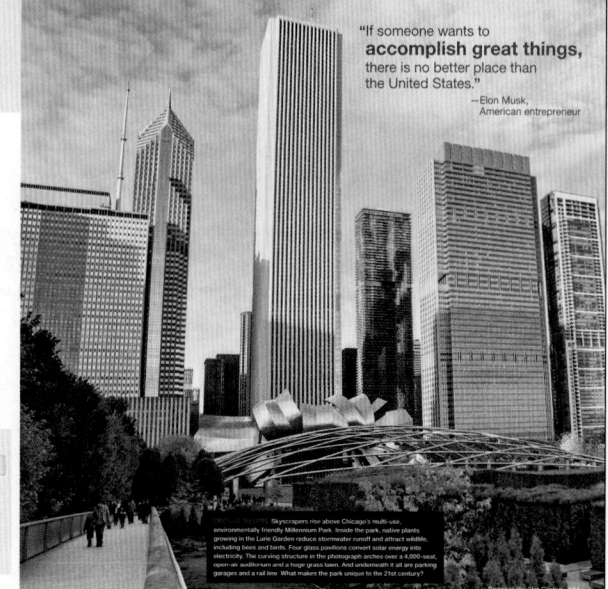

STUDENT DIGITAL RESOURCES

- eEdition (English)
- eEdition (Spanish)
- Handbooks

- Online Atlas
- American Gallery Online
- History Notebook

- American Voices (Biographies)
- Active History
- Projects for Inquiry-Based Learning

Chapter 29 Spanish Resources are available at NGLSync.Cengage.com.

AMERICAN STORIES ONLINE | **The Refugee Crisis**

- Primary Sources
- On Your Feet: Inside-Outside Circle

NG Learning Framework:
Present a Refugee's Experience

SECTION 1 RESOURCES

CHALLENGES IN THE 1990s

LESSON 1.1
Reform Under Clinton

- On Your Feet: Host a Quiz Show

NG Learning Framework:
Write a Letter to the Editor

LESSON 1.2
Crises and Responses

- On Your Feet: Inside-Outside Circle

NG Learning Framework:
Create a Time Line

LESSON 1.3
The Contested Election of 2000

- On Your Feet: Four Corners

NG Learning Framework:
Debate the Supreme Court Decision

SECTION 2 RESOURCES

CRISES AND RESPONSES

LESSON 2.1
September 11, 2001

AMERICAN GALLERY ONLINE The Attacks of September 11, 2001

NG Learning Framework:
Create a Museum Guide

LESSON 2.2
GEOLOGY IN HISTORY
How Geology Affects Flooding

- On Your Feet: Fishbowl

NG Learning Framework:
Investigate Current Flood Protection in New Orleans

LESSON 2.3
NATIONAL GEOGRAPHIC EXPLORER
CAROLINE GERDES
Preserving New Orleans Through Oral Histories

- On Your Feet: Roundtable

NG Learning Framework:
Create a Digital Oral History Book

SECTION 3 RESOURCES

A HISTORIC ELECTION

LESSON 3.1
The Election of Barack Obama

- On Your Feet: Team Word Webbing

NG Learning Framework:
Write a News Profile

LESSON 3.2
Recovery and Reform

- On Your Feet: Jigsaw

NG Learning Framework:
Create a Political Ad

LESSON 3.3
DOCUMENT-BASED QUESTION
Serving Others

- On Your Feet: Think, Pair, Share

SECTION 4 RESOURCES

RAPID CHANGES IN THE 21ST CENTURY

LESSON 4.1
From Computers to Social Media

- ▶ Internet Research
- Active History: Evaluate the Impact of Technology

NG Learning Framework:
Research Technological Innovations

American Voices Biographies
Bill Gates and
Steve Jobs ONLINE

LESSON 4.2
CURATING HISTORY
Computer History Museum, Mountain View, California

- On Your Feet: Sort the Artifacts

LESSON 4.3
Challenges of Globalization

- On Your Feet: Fishbowl

NG Learning Framework:
Graph the Immigrant Population

LESSON 4.4
The Election of 2016

- ▶ The Statue of Liberty
- On Your Feet: Hold a Roundtable Discussion

NG Learning Framework:
Grade Donald Trump's First Year in Office

LESSON 4.5
Climate Change and Energy Choices

- On Your Feet: Word Chain

NG Learning Framework:
Evaluate Arguments

CHAPTER 29 REVIEW

Strategy ❶
Sequence Events

To build understanding of the critical events and their relationship to one another in time, encourage students to note them in a Sequence Chain like the one shown. Arrange students in pairs and have them tell their partner about each event, why it is important, and how it leads to the next event in the chain.

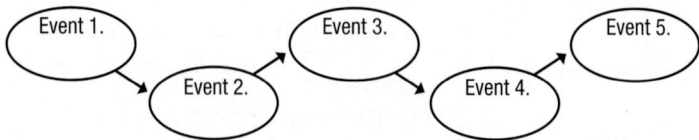

Use with Lessons 1.1–1.3, 2.2, and 3.1 *Suggest that students use a Sequence Chain to trace the events leading to the following: the Republican Revolution (1.1), the government shutdown (1.2), the contested election of 2000 (1.3), the flooding in New Orleans after Hurricane Katrina (2.2), and the election of the nation's first African-American president (3.1).*

Strategy ❷
Analyze Main Ideas

Direct students to first read each Main Idea statement aloud. Then, as students read the lesson, encourage them to make notes about details they find in the text that connect to the Main Idea statement. Tell them this process will help them identify and remember the most important information.

Use with All Lessons

Strategy ❸
Turn Headings into Outlines

Explain that headings can provide a high-level outline of the lesson. Model for students how to use the lesson title and titles of subsections to create a basic outline structure. Encourage students to add supporting details to their outlines as they read.

Use with All Lessons

Strategy ❶
Record Facts

Pair students with a proficient reader. Instruct them to read the lesson aloud paragraph by paragraph, taking turns listening and reading. After each paragraph, both students write at least one fact they recall. Tell partners to compare and check their facts and then combine their facts into one longer list. Invite pairs to compare their lists and revise them if necessary.

Use with All Lessons

Strategy ❷
Describe Details in Photographs

Pair students who are visually impaired with students who are not. Ask the latter to describe the photographs and read the captions in each lesson. Tell visually impaired students to ask clarifying questions as necessary. Then have pairs work together to answer Critical Viewing questions.

Use with All Lessons

ENGLISH LANGUAGE LEARNERS ELD

Strategy 1
Use Definition Maps

Pair students at the **Emerging** level with those at the **Expanding** and **Bridging** levels. Provide pairs with a Definition Map to complete as they encounter unfamiliar words or terms in the lesson. Encourage partners to discuss the words and terms and clear up any misunderstandings. Invite pairs to compare their responses with those of other pairs and discuss any differences.

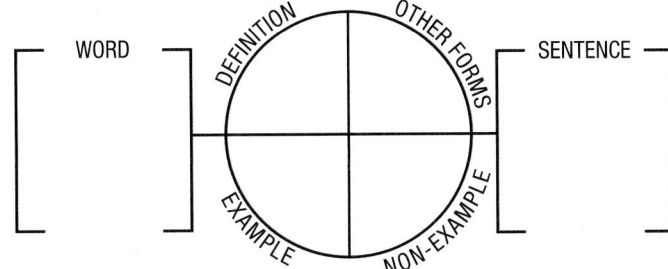

Use with All Lessons

Strategy 2
PREP Before Reading

Encourage students at **All Proficiencies** to use the PREP strategy to prepare for reading. Write this acrostic on the board:

> **PREP** **P**review the title.
> **R**ead Main Idea statement.
> **E**xamine visuals.
> **P**redict what you will learn.

Use with All Lessons *Encourage students at the **Emerging** level to ask questions if they have trouble writing a prediction. Students at the **Bridging** level could help students at the **Emerging** and **Expanding** levels write their predictions.*

Strategy 3
Use Paired Reading

Pair students at the **Expanding** and **Bridging** levels, and direct them to read passages from the text aloud.

1. Partner 1 reads a passage; Partner 2 retells the passage in his or her own words.
2. Partner 2 reads a different passage; Partner 1 retells it.
3. Pairs repeat the process, switching roles.

Use with All Lessons

GIFTED & TALENTED

Strategy 1
Perform an Oral History

Have students access interviews with survivors of Hurricane Katrina. One source is the Narrating Katrina Through Oral History collection, available on the Hurricane Digital Memory Bank website. Challenge students to choose a compelling excerpt recorded by an evacuee, first responder, or other person who experienced the devastation of Katrina, rehearse the excerpt, and perform it. Then lead a discussion about how the oral histories reinforce or supplement the information in the lesson.

Use with Lesson 2.2 or 2.3

Strategy 2
Design an Infographic

Guide students to conduct additional research into key events in the development of the computer. Tell them to use their research to create an infographic that shows the history and impact of computers and related technology. Remind them to include important dates and powerful visuals. Invite students to present their infographics to the class. Encourage comments from the class.

Use with Lesson 4.1

Pre-AP

Strategy 1
Write an Editorial

Encourage students to conduct research and then write an editorial that supports universal health care or the Affordable Care Act (ACA) or recommends a different approach. Challenge them to find present-day statistics and opinions regarding health care costs and insurance coverage. You may wish to create a display of editorials or encourage students to submit their editorials to local newspapers.

Use with Lessons 1.1 and 3.2

Strategy 2
Write an Alternate History Narrative

Instruct students to write an alternate history narrative starting with the turning point of the 2000 election. Tell them to imagine that the Florida recount proceeded and Al Gore became president. Challenge students to research Gore's ideas and consider how U.S. military engagements and environmental policies might have unfolded differently under his administration. Invite students to read their narrative to the class. Then discuss with students what they learned by exploring alternate outcomes.

Use with Lesson 1.3

BRIDGE TO THE
21st CENTURY
1992–Present

ESSENTIAL QUESTION
How has the United States responded to crises in the early years of the 21st century?

READING STRATEGY

FORM AND SUPPORT OPINIONS
You often form opinions while reading, and thinking through these opinions can help you understand historical events. As you read this chapter, decide what you think is the greatest challenge the United States has faced so far in the 21st century. Use a graphic organizer like this one to write your opinion and record your reasons to support it.

Opinion
Supporting Statement:
Supporting Statement:
Supporting Statement:
Supporting Statement:
Supporting Statement:

"If someone wants to **accomplish great things,** there is no better place than the United States."

—Elon Musk, American entrepreneur

CRITICAL VIEWING Skyscrapers rise above Chicago's multi-use, environmentally friendly Millennium Park. Inside the park, native plants growing in the Lurie Garden reduce stormwater runoff and attract wildlife, including bees and birds. Four glass pavilions convert solar energy into electricity. The curving structure in the photograph arches over a 4,000-seat, open-air auditorium and a huge grass lawn. And underneath it all are parking garages and a rail line. What makes the park unique to the 21st century?

For Chapter 29 Spanish Resources, visit the Resources Menu. Chapter 29 Resources are available at NGLSync.Cengage.com.

INTRODUCE THE PHOTOGRAPH

Millennium Park

Read the caption aloud and have students study the photograph of Millennium Park. Point out the surrounding skyscrapers, the pedestrian bridge, and other features of the park, such as the pavilions. **ASK:** What is the advantage of a park that includes a garden, an open-air auditorium, and a large grass lawn? *(Possible response: The park would draw a wider range of people, including those who enjoy gardens, those who like to attend outdoor performances, and those who want to play or picnic in the grassy area.)* **ASK:** Why might the fact that the park is built over a transportation center and is in a highly developed urban area contribute to its popularity? *(Possible response: The ability to walk, drive, or take a train to the park makes it easy for many people to reach it, including those living in the surrounding suburbs and tourists visiting the city.)*

Share Background

Chicago's Millennium Park is the product of an ambitious urban renewal effort. The park sits on a site once dominated by railroad tracks and parking lots. In 1997, Mayor Richard M. Daley suggested transforming the area into an outdoor music venue and park. Over time, the project came to reflect Chicago's unique history. The Jay Pritzker Pavilion—the arching stainless steel network in the foreground—includes a sound system that matches the quality of an indoor concert hall. The Lurie Garden pays tribute to Chicago's transition from flat marshland to a major city, now a leader in green urban development. The 15-foot-high "shoulder" hedge, which encloses two sides of the garden, pays homage to poet Carl Sandburg, who dubbed Chicago the "City of Big Shoulders."

CRITICAL VIEWING The stainless steel sculptures and arching steel beams visually set the park apart from 19th- and 20th-century public spaces, and the outdoor sound system and solar technology firmly set the park in the 21st century.

INTRODUCE THE ESSENTIAL QUESTION

How has the United States responded to crises in the early years of the 21st century?

Four Corners: Responses to Crises This activity encourages students to consider crises that the United States faced in the early 21st century. Post one of the following questions in each corner of the classroom:

1. How might a president's response to scandals or foreign or domestic crises affect a presidency?

2. How might a nation respond to events such as a deadly terrorist attack or a natural disaster?

3. What might voters want in a president during war or crises? How might political opposition affect a president's efforts at reform?

4. What social and economic issues might divide a nation? How might political responses to them impact a country or the world?

Ask students to count off by fours, and arrange groups by number in each corner of the room. Assign each group a question and tell students to discuss their assigned questions for a short time. Then ask one member of each group to summarize the group's ideas for the class.

INTRODUCE CHAPTER VOCABULARY

Vocabulary Pyramids

As they read the chapter, have students complete Vocabulary Pyramids for Key Vocabulary words. Tell students to make a pyramid for each word, fill in what they know about the word before reading, and then add to or correct the pyramid after they encounter the word in the chapter. Model an example for students on the board, using the graphic organizer shown.

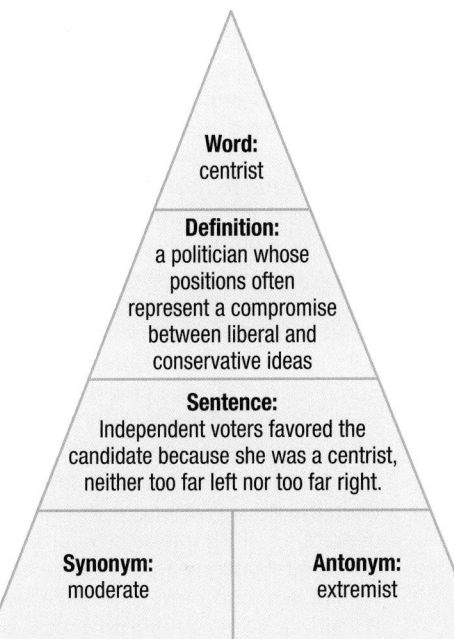

Word: centrist

Definition: a politician whose positions often represent a compromise between liberal and conservative ideas

Sentence: Independent voters favored the candidate because she was a centrist, neither too far left nor too far right.

Synonym: moderate

Antonym: extremist

INTRODUCE THE READING STRATEGY

FORM AND SUPPORT OPINIONS

Remind students that keeping track of the evidence that supports particular opinions will help them evaluate which opinion has the best supporting evidence. Model completing a graphic organizer like the one shown. Ask students to give an opinion, based on what they have read in previous chapters or what they know, about what might be one of the greatest challenges the United States has faced in the 21st century. Complete the top row of the graphic organizer. Then have students suggest supporting statements for that opinion.

Opinion
Supporting Statement:
Supporting Statement:
Supporting Statement:
Supporting Statement:
Supporting Statement:

KEY DATES FOR CHAPTER 29

1992	Bill Clinton elected president
1992	North American Free Trade Agreement (NAFTA) signed
1995	Oklahoma City bombing
2000	George W. Bush wins contested presidential election
2001	Terrorists attack World Trade Center and Pentagon
2003	Iraq War begins
2005	Hurricane Katrina batters the Gulf Coast
2008	Barack Obama elected president
2010	Affordable Care Act (ACA) becomes law
2016	Donald Trump elected president

 For instructional support for the online American Story "The Refugee Crisis," go to NGLSync.Cengage.com.

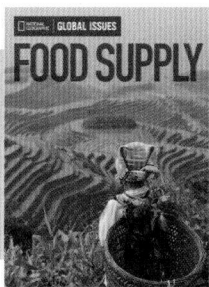

For more on feeding the world, see *GLOBAL ISSUES: FOOD SUPPLY.*

1.1 Reform Under Clinton

The Republicans and Democrats have dominated American elections for so long it's easy to forget that other parties can mount a presidential run. What happens when a third-party candidate presents a real challenge at the polls?

MAIN IDEA President Bill Clinton enacted measures to lower the budget deficit and faced diplomatic challenges abroad.

CLINTON'S DOMESTIC AGENDA

At first, President George H.W. Bush seemed poised to win a second term. He had an 83 percent job approval rating in March 1991. But as the 1992 election approached, he grew vulnerable. He had broken his promise of "no new taxes." The federal budget deficit was high, and the nation was in another recession, a period of declining economic activity. A third-party candidate, businessman **H. Ross Perot**, entered the race. Because his views were conservative, Perot had the potential to draw Republican voters.

The Democrats nominated Arkansas governor **Bill Clinton**, who considered himself a "new Democrat." Clinton was a **centrist**, which means his positions often represented compromises between liberal and conservative ideas. This proved to be a successful strategy. Clinton won the presidential election with 43 percent of the popular vote to Bush's 37.4 percent. Perot received 18.9 percent. Clinton dominated in the electoral college, winning 370 votes to Bush's 168. Perot did not win any electoral votes.

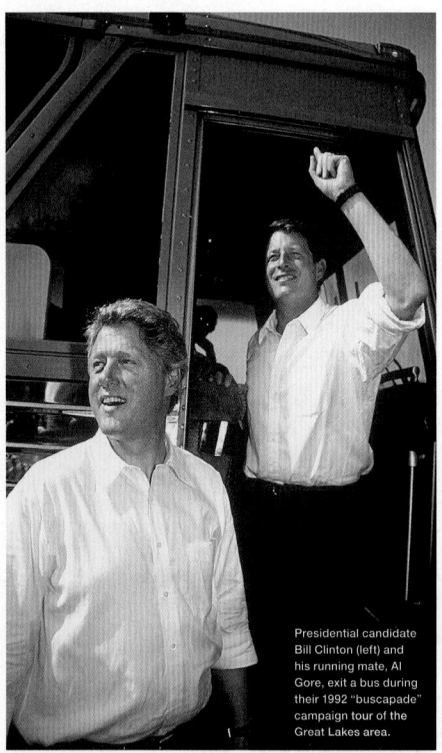

Presidential candidate Bill Clinton (left) and his running mate, Al Gore, exit a bus during their 1992 "buscapade" campaign tour of the Great Lakes area.

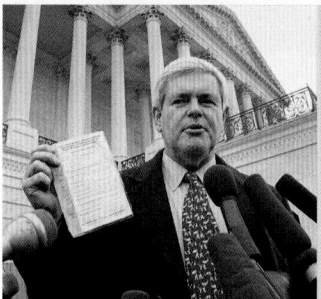

During his campaign, Clinton promised to end the recession. In August 1993, he persuaded Congress to pass tax increases and spending cuts in order to lower the federal budget deficit. In 1993, Clinton signed the controversial **North American Free Trade Agreement (NAFTA)** with Canada and Mexico, which reduced trade barriers among the three countries. Supporters claimed NAFTA would improve the economy by boosting trade. Critics believed it favored corporations over most citizens, family farms, and local governments.

Clinton met with less success in his efforts to institute a universal health care system. He named his wife, **Hillary Clinton**, to lead a health care reform group. Mrs. Clinton was a respected lawyer and an advocate for children and education. Conservatives, insurance companies, and the American Medical Association opposed the plan for universal coverage—a single health care system that would cover all Americans. The proposal failed to pass Congress.

CLINTON AND THE WORLD

Internationally, Clinton faced several challenges. The breakup of the Soviet Union and the Soviet bloc caused unrest in parts of Eastern Europe. War broke out in the Balkans, a region that was once part of Yugoslavia. Three ethnic groups—the Serbs, Croats, and Bosnians—each sought independence and control of the area. Clinton tried military means to end the violence, but he limited the U.S. commitment. Both the UN and Congress resisted requests for more military action. Critics complained that Clinton "muddled through" the crisis.

In September 1993, Clinton invited Israeli prime minister **Yitzhak Rabin** (yiht-SAHK rah-BEEN) and **Palestine Liberation Organization (PLO)** leader **Yassir Arafat** (YAH-sur AIR-uh-faht) to meet in Washington in hopes of easing high tensions between the Israelis and Palestinians. While there, Israeli and Palestinian representatives signed the Oslo Accord, granting limited self-rule for Palestinians in Gaza and the West Bank while promising withdrawal of Israeli troops from those areas.

On the domestic front, Clinton faced energized Republican opposition during the 1994 midterm elections, led by Representative **Newt Gingrich**. Gingrich's "Contract with America" promised tax cuts, welfare reform, and other typically Republican policies. Republicans won control of both houses of Congress in what one journalist called "the most consequential nonpresidential election of the 20th century."

HISTORICAL THINKING

1. **READING CHECK** What effect did H. Ross Perot's candidacy have on the outcome of the 1992 election?

2. **IDENTIFY PROBLEMS AND SOLUTIONS** What was one domestic problem President Clinton faced, and how did he try to solve it?

3. **MAKE INFERENCES** Why might the 1994 elections have been the "most consequential nonpresidential election of the 20th century"?

Objective
Examine Bill Clinton's 1992 election and how he responded to problems at home and abroad.

Critical Thinking Skills for Lesson 1.1
- Identify Main Ideas and Details
- Monitor Comprehension
- Identify Problems and Solutions
- Make Inferences
- Form and Support Opinions
- Evaluate

Essential Question for Chapter 29
How has the United States responded to crises in the early years of the 21st century? President Clinton faced economic problems at home and conflicts abroad. Lesson 1.1 shows his responses to a growing recession and war in the Balkans.

Background for the Teacher
H. Ross Perot's 1992 presidential campaign was unique in several ways. First, the Texas billionaire launched his campaign while a guest on a cable news program. During the program, Perot said that he would run for president if his supporters filed petitions to get him on the ballot in all 50 states, which they eventually did. Second, he spent $65 million of his own money to help finance much of his presidential campaign. Third, rather than travel around the country delivering speeches and holding rallies, Perot bought 30-minute television commercials. He used the time to lecture voters on the economy, particularly the federal deficit. As Perot began to slip in the polls, he suddenly withdrew from the race, only to re-enter 10 weeks later; but his campaign never recovered. Finally, despite his start-and-stop record, Perot still garnered the highest percentage of the popular vote of any third-party candidate since Teddy Roosevelt, who ran as a progressive in 1912.

The Political Spectrum

Draw on the board a horizontal line with an arrowhead on each end. Label the right arrowhead Conservative and the left arrowhead Liberal. Put a mark in the center and label it Centrist. Remind students that, to varying degrees, Republicans tend to be more conservative, while Democrats tend to be more liberal. Independents, voters who identify with neither party, often fall in the middle. **ASK:** What advantage might a candidate who falls in the middle of this spectrum have with voters? *(Possible response: The candidate might pick up votes from independents as well as from more liberal Republicans and more conservative Democrats.)* Tell students that in this lesson they will learn how Bill Clinton, a centrist Democrat, won the 1992 presidential election.

Guided Discussion

1. **Form and Support Opinions** Do you think President Clinton experienced more success dealing with the crisis in the Balkans or handling tensions between the Israelis and Palestinians in the Middle East? Support your opinion with evidence from the lesson. *(Possible response: Clinton was more successful in dealing with the Middle East, since he was able to get the Israelis and Palestinians to sign the Oslo Accord. In the Balkans, he only authorized a limited military response to the violence, causing critics to argue that he simply "muddled through.")*

2. **Evaluate** Direct students' attention to the feature on the Republican Revolution. **ASK:** Why might conservative talk radio have been a powerful tool in spreading the message of the Republican Revolution? *(Possible response: Unlike traditional news programs or newspapers, conservative talk radio presented only one side of an argument. This made it easier to sway the opinion of listeners.)*

More Information

Opposition to Health Care Reform The American Medical Association (AMA) and the Health Insurance Association of America (HIAA) both regarded Clinton's health care plan as too much federal control of the health care industry. The AMA cited concerns that the federal government would limit patients' and physicians' choices, control private doctors' fees and expenditures, and create "Federal control of medical education and the physician work force." The HIAA objected to federal limits on insurance premiums, requirements that employers must purchase health insurance, and "a possible tax on high-end insurance." Critics of the AMA and HIAA pointed out that both organizations had used similar arguments against Medicare and Medicaid yet now supported these federal plans.

Active Options

On Your Feet: Host a Quiz Show Ask each student to write one question based on the text about the 1992 presidential election or Clinton's first term as president. Then bring groups of five students to the front of the class to be panelists in a quiz show. Ask for volunteers to alternate as hosts. Instruct hosts to pose students' questions to the panelists, keeping track of questions that stump the panel. Review the answers to the questions as a class.

NG Learning Framework: Write a Letter to the Editor

SKILL Communication

KNOWLEDGE Our Human Story

Arrange students into small groups. Have each group select a topic from the lesson that they would like to know more about, such as the 1992 presidential election, Clinton's economic policies, plans for universal health care, U.S. involvement in the Balkans, the Middle East peace process, or the Republican Revolution. Direct groups to research the topic and then use the information to draft a letter to the editor, taking a stand on an issue related to the topic and supporting their stand with facts and sound reasoning. Have groups share their letters with the class.

English Language Learners ELD

Understand and Use Idioms Arrange students at **All Proficiencies** in mixed pairs. Bring their attention to the idiom "broken his promise" in the first paragraph, and elicit its meaning (not doing what was promised). Ask pairs to brainstorm other English idioms using the word *break* or provide them with the following: break the law, break a habit, break a record, break someone's heart, break the ice. Instruct students to discuss the meaning of the idioms and then write original sentences incorporating them.

Gifted & Talented

Illustrate a Centrist Direct students to conduct online research to find specific examples of conservative and liberal positions that Clinton held during his presidency. Then have them create an illustration, in any style, from realistic to cartoon, that conveys how Clinton leaned left and right at different times. Invite volunteers to post their illustrations on a class website or blog or display them in the classroom. Guide a discussion about the pros and cons of being a centrist.

See the Chapter Planner for more strategies for differentiation.

ANSWERS

1. As a businessman with conservative views, Perot cut into the Republican vote, taking 18.9 percent of the popular vote. Had he not been in the race, some of those votes would likely have gone to Bush, possibly resulting in a Republican victory.

2. Possible responses: Clinton faced the problem of lowering the federal budget deficit. To solve the problem, he convinced Congress to pass a tax hike and to cut spending. Clinton faced the problem of the recession. To address that problem, he signed NAFTA with Mexico and Canada, which was designed to boost the economy by lowering trade barriers.

3. Possible response: The 1994 elections gave control of both houses of Congress to the Republicans for the first time in 40 years. This potentially gave conservatives more influence over government than they had had in four decades.

1.2 Crises and Responses

What happens when the federal government shuts down? National parks close their gates, important medical research halts, and individuals have nowhere to turn for help with Social Security. Voters become very angry at those they hold responsible.

MAIN IDEA Re-elected in 1996, Clinton oversaw a healthy economy, helped resolve conflict in the Balkans, and remained president despite being impeached.

CHALLENGES AT HOME AND ABROAD

On April 19, 1995, the United States was shaken by a deadly terrorist attack. A former U.S. soldier, Timothy McVeigh, set off a car bomb next to the **Alfred P. Murrah Federal Building** in Oklahoma City, Oklahoma. The blast nearly destroyed the building, killing 168 people and injuring more than 500. McVeigh and his accomplice, Terry Nichols, were right-wing radicals who justified the attack as an act of self-defense against an oppressive government. After arrest and trial, Nichols was sentenced to life in prison. McVeigh was executed.

In that same year, Clinton again turned his attention to Europe and the international crisis in the Balkans. The conflict had escalated, but the Bosnian and Croat forces won their first victory over the Serbs in years. Clinton, who was previously accused of weak leadership in this crisis, sent representatives to the region to discuss peace. In November 1995, leaders of Bosnia, Serbia, and Croatia met with American and European representatives outside Dayton, Ohio. There, they worked out a peace plan. To enforce it, the United States and 25 other nations would send troops to the Balkans. In a speech, Clinton outlined the political and humanitarian reasons to send 20,000 troops. Congress agreed, and polls showed that Americans had greater confidence in Clinton.

During the dedication of the Oklahoma City National Memorial, an honor guard faces the field of memorial chairs that represent the 168 people who lost their lives in the bombing of the federal building.

Clinton's approval ratings also grew after Republicans forced a **government shutdown** that closed federal facilities. The country had a divided government. That is, one party controlled the presidency and the other controlled Congress. In November 1995, budget negotiations between Clinton and the Republican-controlled Congress failed. Clinton vetoed the budget Congress had passed. With no budget, the government could not pay its employees or its bills, so federal offices and agencies had to close. After five days, both sides agreed to end the shutdown and continue negotiations. Clinton was willing to compromise, but many Americans saw the Republicans as stubbornly demanding their budget, which included tax cuts and limits to Medicare growth.

A second government shutdown lasted 21 days, during which most federal employees stopped receiving paychecks. Republicans in Congress finally gave in, accepting a budget similar to the one they had originally rejected. Voters were angry and frustrated.

RE-ELECTION AND IMPEACHMENT

In the 1996 election, Senator Bob Dole ran as the Republican candidate. Clinton won the election with 49 percent of the vote to Dole's 41 percent. H. Ross Perot ran again, receiving 8 percent of the vote. Republicans kept control of Congress, so Clinton again faced a divided government. Still, he entered his second term with a strong economy, which would produce budget surpluses from 1998 to 2001.

But scandal plagued Clinton's second term. Questions were raised about some financial deals Clinton and his wife had made. In 1998, independent counsel Kenneth Starr began investigating these deals but found no evidence they were illegal. Then he began pursuing tips that Clinton had had a romantic relationship with a young White House intern. Clinton denied the

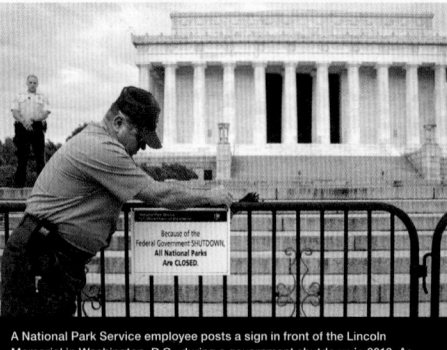

A National Park Service employee posts a sign in front of the Lincoln Memorial in Washington, D.C., during a government shutdown in 2013. As during the 1995 shutdown, many federal facilities, including national parks, were closed because Congress failed to pass a funding bill.

relationship. Eventually, investigators found solid evidence. Clinton apologized to the nation and his family. Based on Starr's report, the House approved impeachment against Clinton for perjury and obstruction of justice. In 1999, the Senate acquitted him, and his approval ratings remained high.

In 1999, Clinton again faced challenges in the Balkans. Serbian forces were conducting mass killings of ethnic Albanians in the Serbian province of Kosovo. Clinton and other world leaders worked with NATO to authorize a bombing campaign against Serbia that led to UN intervention in Kosovo's government. In 2008, Kosovo became independent. Clinton's leadership in dealing with Kosovo enhanced his reputation in foreign affairs.

HISTORICAL THINKING

1. **READING CHECK** What two events in 1995 helped improve President Clinton's approval ratings?

2. **CAUSE AND EFFECT** What was the principal cause of the government shutdowns?

3. **FORM AND SUPPORT OPINIONS** Do you think Clinton's decision to participate in a bombing campaign against Serbia was necessary? Support your opinion.

PLAN

Objective

Explore President Clinton's popularity amid impeachment and domestic and foreign crises.

Critical Thinking Skills for Lesson 1.2

- Identify Main Ideas and Details
- Monitor Comprehension
- Analyze Cause and Effect
- Form and Support Opinions
- Make Connections

Essential Question for Chapter 29

How has the United States responded to crises in the early years of the 21st century? President Clinton faced many challenges in his second term. Lesson 1.2 explores his response to domestic terrorism, the Balkans crisis, and impeachment.

Background for the Teacher

On April 19, 1995, Timothy McVeigh parked an explosive-stuffed rental truck in front of the Alfred P. Murrah Federal Building. As he walked to his getaway car, he triggered the timed fuses. Many assumed the resulting explosion was the act of Middle Eastern terrorists—but this was quickly disproved. Within the rubble, investigators found the truck's rear axle, which included the vehicle identification number. This enabled the FBI to locate where the truck had been rented from and to get a description of the man who had rented it. Agents put together a composite drawing of the suspect that enabled an employee at the hotel where McVeigh had been staying to identify him. When the FBI went to arrest McVeigh, they found he was already in custody. Less than two hours after the bombing, an Oklahoma state trooper had pulled McVeigh over for a missing license plate. The trooper had arrested him only after discovering a concealed weapon in the car.

INTRODUCE & ENGAGE

Shutting Down

Discuss with students what might happen if a store owner ran out of money for the business. *(Students might suggest that the store would have to close until the owner could find money to operate by securing a loan or finding investors.)* Explain that something similar happened to the U.S. government in the 1990s when Congress and the president couldn't agree on a federal budget. Tell students that in this lesson they will explore this and other problems Bill Clinton faced during his second term as president.

TEACH

Guided Discussion

1. **Analyze Cause and Effect** What chain of events led to Bill Clinton's impeachment? *(Possible response: Independent prosecutor Ken Starr began investigating some of the Clinton's financial dealings. While Starr failed to find evidence of illegal activities, he did uncover rumors and evidence that Bill Clinton had been involved with a young White House intern. Clinton lied when he denied the accusation under oath, leading to his impeachment for perjury and obstruction of justice.)*

2. **Make Connections** In what ways were the Balkans a continuing problem for President Clinton? *(Possible response: Clinton helped broker a peace plan between Bosnia, Serbia, and Croatia in 1995. The United States joined 25 other nations in sending troops to the Balkans to enforce the plan. Nevertheless, in 1999, Serbian forces carried out mass killings of ethnic Albanians in Kosovo, leading Clinton to work with the United Nations and other world leaders to launch a bombing campaign against Serbia.)*

More Information

Oklahoma City National Memorial Direct students' attention to the photograph of the Oklahoma City National Memorial. Point out the 9:01 on the large "gate of time" behind the reflecting pool. Tell students that the gate is paired with another gate on which 9:03 is etched. The times represent the moments before and after the explosion. **ASK:** Why do you think the designers of the memorial chose to include the times on the gates? *(Possible response: The numbers remind visitors how quickly lives can be lost or changed forever.)*

Active Options

On Your Feet: Inside-Outside Circle Arrange students in concentric circles facing each other. Tell students in the outside circle to ask students in the inside circle a question about the lesson. After students answer, have the outside circle rotate one position to the right to create new pairings. After five questions, tell students to switch circles and continue asking and answering questions.

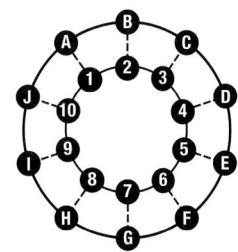

NG Learning Framework: Create a Time Line

SKILL Communication

KNOWLEDGE Our Human Story

Have students work in groups to create an annotated time line of the Balkans conflict and U.S. involvement from 1991 through 1999. Tell groups to conduct research to collect information for annotations and to provide historical context for the different events in the conflict. Encourage students to include the names of major leaders on both sides, the main ethnic groups involved, and the main locations where the fighting occurred. Invite groups to share their completed time lines with the class and discuss how and why U.S. interest in the conflict grew over the years.

DIFFERENTIATE

Striving Readers

Create a Concept Cluster Instruct students to read the Main Idea statement, and point out that it contains three topics. Provide students with three Concept Clusters, and have them write the topics in the center circles. Tell them to reread the lesson and write details (facts, dates, events, reasons) relating to each topic on the spokes. Encourage students to create additional spokes as necessary. Then have them share their work, and discuss similarities and differences among clusters.

Pre-AP

Analyze Causes and Effects Tell students to choose one of the topics covered in the lesson and investigate the topic's causes and effects by conducting online research and gathering information from a variety of unbiased sources. Encourage students to use a Cause-and-Effect Chart to organize the information they find. Then have them write an essay presenting their topic and analyzing its causes and effects. Invite students to share their analyses with the class.

See the Chapter Planner for more strategies for differentiation.

HISTORICAL THINKING

ANSWERS

1. Clinton's position with voters was strengthened by his leadership in gaining a peace agreement in the Balkans and by the government shutdown, for which many voters blamed the Republicans in Congress.

2. Possible response: The Republican-held Congress refused to compromise during budget negotiations. This caused Clinton to veto the budget passed by Congress. Without a budget, the government had to shut down two separate times because of a lack of money to pay its commitments.

3. Possible responses: Yes. The bombing campaign forced an end to the attacks and led the UN to intervene in Kosovo. No. The bombing added to the misery of civilians caught in the fighting. Clinton should have found a more peaceful solution.

The Contested Election of 2000

You run for class president and lose by one vote out of hundreds.

Then you learn that some of your supporters had problems voting.

What's your next move?

MAIN IDEA The election of 2000 was so close that it had to be settled by a controversial Supreme Court decision, leading to an even more divided nation.

BUSH v. GORE

As the 2000 election approached, the economy was booming and the federal budget had a surplus. Running on Clinton's economic and foreign policy successes, Vice President **Albert (Al) Gore** won the Democratic nomination. The Republicans ran Texas governor **George W. Bush**, son of former president George H.W. Bush, as their candidate.

Bush promised tax cuts, saying he could make up the resulting lost revenue with more efficient government. Gore argued that only the wealthiest Americans would benefit from Bush's tax cuts. On foreign policy, Bush favored the views of the **neoconservatives**, who believed the United States should assert its military power to promote its interests and overthrow anti-American

governments. Gore claimed these were Cold War ideas and no longer relevant. He advocated a foreign policy that focused more on diplomacy.

The close election ultimately hinged on who would win Florida's 25 electoral votes. In the final popular vote count, Bush led by only about 600 votes out of about 6 million. With such a close tally, Florida law required a recount, which showed Bush's lead as 327 votes.

During that first recount, officials discovered that some punch card ballots were incorrectly punched. A small fragment of paper, called a "chad," was still attached where many of the holes were meant to be. Voting machines may have failed to count votes with these "hanging chads." So the Florida Supreme Court ordered a recount

by hand of ballots from several counties. Officials had to examine each card by hand and assign it a vote, if possible. Bush appealed to the U.S. Supreme Court, asking that the recount be halted. In *Bush* v. *Gore*, the Court reversed the Florida recount order, awarding Bush the presidency.

Many people believe that **Ralph Nader**, the Green Party candidate in 2000, played a part in Gore's loss. He received only 2.74 percent of the popular vote, but his votes in New Hampshire and Florida suggest that had he not run, Gore would have won those states and, presumably, the election. Nader's supporters argued that if Nader hadn't run, they might not have voted for Gore anyway.

A DIVIDED NATION

Bush v. *Gore* divided the nation even more. The justices who made the decision to stop the recount had all been appointed by Republican presidents. Bush had lost the national popular vote, so he came into office without widespread support. Many hoped he would try to bring the nation together, but instead, he issued a divisive executive order creating the Office of Faith-Based and Community Initiatives. The order provided funds for church-affiliated schools, an action that many Americans felt violated the Constitution's First Amendment. This move represented the beginning of Bush's plan to increase the power of the presidency through executive action.

After the hard-fought 2000 election, divisions among Americans were symbolized by the "red state–blue state" pattern on electoral maps. Before 2000, mapmakers had used various colors to show which way the states voted. But after 2000, states with Democratic majorities were colored blue, and states with Republican majorities were colored red. The red-blue symbolism has become part of American politics, though many people think it creates an oversimplified view.

Bush kept his promise to cut taxes, successfully pushing $1.35 trillion in cuts through Congress in 2001 and $350 billion more in 2003. These tax cuts reduced government revenue, erased the budget surpluses, and created deficits, all of which contributed to recessions in 2002 and 2008. However, disagreements over taxes and policies were overshadowed in 2001 by an event that horrified and briefly unified the nation.

On November 8, the day after the 2000 election, Texas governor and presidential candidate George W. Bush walked out of the governor's mansion to meet with reporters for a news conference in Austin, Texas. The U.S. Supreme Court upheld Bush's election to the presidency on December 12.

The Election of 2000

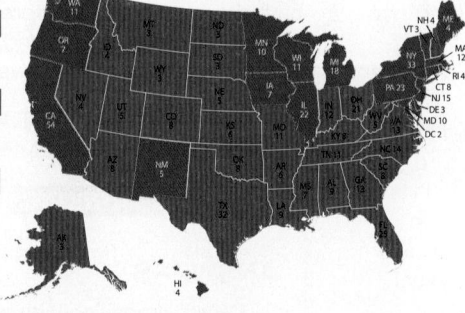

Albert (Al) Gore (Democrat)

Electoral Vote: 266 votes, 49.4%
Popular Vote: 50,992,335 votes, 48.4%

George W. Bush (Republican)

Electoral Vote: 271 votes, 50.4%
Popular Vote: 50,455,156 votes, 47.9%

Ralph Nader (Green)

Popular Vote: 2,882,738 votes, 2.7%

HISTORICAL THINKING

1. **READING CHECK** What were the two main issues on which the candidates differed during the 2000 presidential election?

2. **INTERPRET MAPS** Examine the 2000 election map. Why would Gore have won the election if he had won Florida?

3. **MAKE INFERENCES** Why did the Florida Supreme Court rule that the problem ballots had to be recounted by hand?

PLAN

Objective
Understand the outcome and impact of the 2000 presidential election.

Critical Thinking Skills for Lesson 1.3
- Identify Main Ideas and Details
- Monitor Comprehension
- Interpret Maps
- Make Inferences
- Summarize
- Analyze Language Use

Essential Question for Chapter 29
How has the United States responded to crises in the early years of the 21st century? The U.S. Supreme Court ended up deciding the outcome of the 2000 presidential race. Lesson 1.3 explores George W. Bush's controversial election and his policies.

Background for the Teacher
Election night was confusing for the media and the candidates alike. By early evening on the East Coast, it was clear that victory was riding on Florida's 25 electoral votes. Around 8 p.m. EST, the Associated Press and a number of television networks projected that Al Gore would win Florida and likely the presidency. Trusting the exit polls, CBS news anchor Dan Rather confidently declared, "If we call a state, you can take it to the bank." But by 10 p.m., CBS and other networks were scrambling to retract their projections as Bush appeared to pull ahead. Around 2 a.m., many networks issued a new Florida projection declaring Bush the winner. Trusting the projections, Gore called Bush to concede. However, by the time Gore was ready to officially concede, he and the networks realized that the Florida race was too close to call. He phoned Bush again, this time to "un-concede," and the hand-counting of ballots began.

Counting Votes

Pose the following questions to students: Should every vote count in an election? What should election officials do if ballots marked by voters are unclear? Which is more important: trying to determine which candidate voters meant to vote for or settling the outcome of an election in a timely manner? After discussing students' opinions, tell the class that this is the dilemma that the United States faced in the 2000 presidential election.

Guided Discussion

1. **Make Inferences** Why did critics of Ralph Nader's third-party presidential candidacy think he cost Al Gore the election in 2000? *(Possible response: They assumed that the people who voted for Nader would have voted for Gore had Nader not run. This would have made a difference in close contests in states like New Hampshire and Florida.)*

2. **Summarize** How did George W. Bush's presidency further divide the nation? *(Many Americans were troubled that the U.S. Supreme Court voted to halt the recount in Florida, resulting in the candidate who had lost the popular vote being awarded the presidency. Once elected, Bush further divided the nation by pushing faith-based initiatives that some Americans felt violated the First Amendment.)*

Analyze Language Use

Why might the term "red and blue states" create an oversimplified view of U.S. politics? *(Possible response: This term gives the impression that people within every state have a shared point of view, which is not accurate. Florida, for example, is categorized as red even though Bush won there by only a few hundred votes. In addition, not every red or blue state has the same issues. Voters in New Mexico, for instance, might have very different concerns from voters in Maine.)*

Active Options

On Your Feet: Four Corners Divide students into four groups and have them move to different corners of the classroom. Ask each group to address the following question: In the 2000 election, do you think it was an advantage or disadvantage for Al Gore to be associated with Bill Clinton and for George W. Bush to be associated with his father? Why? Encourage students to consider the question individually and then discuss their responses as a group. Suggest that they think about how Clinton and the elder Bush affected public opinion. Suggest that one person in the group record answers. Then invite the recorders to read their group's responses.

NG Learning Framework: Debate the Supreme Court Decision

ATTITUDE Empowerment

SKILL Problem-Solving

Invite students to re-examine the views they expressed during the Introduce & Engage activity. Have them work in groups to collect additional facts and opinions about the Supreme Court decision that awarded the election in Florida to Bush. Ask for volunteers to form two debate teams, and assign one team to argue in favor of the court decision and one team to argue against it. After teams debate, ask the class to vote on which side made the better case.

Inclusion

Interpret an Election Map Allow students with disabilities to work with a partner who can describe the map and read aloud the information about each candidate's share of electoral votes and the popular vote. Encourage students to ask and answer clarifying questions. When pairs have finished reading the lesson, you may wish to have them work together to answer the Historical Thinking question about the map.

Gifted & Talented

Tweet *Bush* v. *Gore* Instruct students to conduct online research to learn more about the crucial events between the closing of polls after the 2000 election and the Supreme Court decision. Have students imagine they are news reporters covering those events. Tell them to create a Twitter handle, profile, and hashtags and then compose a series of tweets conveying the news as it happens. Invite students to display their tweets on a poster or class website.

See the Chapter Planner for more strategies for differentiation.

ANSWERS

1. The candidates differed on the economy and foreign affairs. Bush promised tax cuts, but Gore believed those cuts mainly benefited the wealthiest Americans. Bush supported a neoconservative foreign policy based on using military might to get what the United States needed and overthrowing anti-American governments. Gore rejected that approach as outdated and instead favored a focus on diplomacy.

2. Adding 25 electoral votes to Gore's tally and subtracting them from Bush's would have given Gore more than enough to become president.

3. Incompletely punched card ballots created hanging chads that might be misread by mechanical vote-counting machines. Only by examining each ballot individually and determining the intended vote, if possible, could election judges establish an accurate count.

Most of us feel relaxed, even happy, when we spend time in parks, theaters, and restaurants. When terrorists strike, their goal is to make people feel afraid and tense in everyday places such as these, often through violent acts.

MAIN IDEA On September 11, 2001, terrorists staged a massive attack on New York City and Washington, D.C., leading President Bush to initiate a "war on terror."

ATTACKS ON NEW YORK AND WASHINGTON

On September 11, 2001, terrorists crashed two hijacked airplanes into the two 110-story buildings known as the twin towers of New York City's World Trade Center. Others from the same group crashed another plane into the Pentagon in Washington, D.C. Hijackers had captured a fourth plane and diverted it toward Washington, D.C., but the passengers fought back, causing the plane to crash in a Pennsylvania field instead of into its intended target. The terrorist group **al Qaeda** and its leader, **Osama bin Laden**, had planned the attacks.

Almost two weeks after the collapse of the World Trade Center, rescue workers confronted the enormity of their task as they sifted through the rubble, looking for the thousands of people still missing.

Terrorism is the use of threats and violence against civilians as a way of achieving political goals. Terrorists commonly stage attacks in crowded public locations, hoping to spread fear and force political change. Many terrorist groups that follow a radical fundamentalist form of Islam profess hatred toward the United States and other Western countries. Al Qaeda is one of these groups.

September 11 (9/11) was not the first attack on the World Trade Center. On February 26, 1993, terrorists detonated a car bomb in the center's underground garage, killing six and injuring more than a thousand. In the deadlier 9/11 attacks, the twin towers collapsed with many people trapped inside. Clouds of debris billowed through the streets as frightened people fled. Many **first responders**, the people such as firefighters and police officers who are first on the scene in an emergency, died when the buildings fell. Others contracted fatal illnesses from the resulting toxic dust. The death toll was more than 2,750 people in New York City, more than 180 at the Pentagon, and 40 in the Pennsylvania plane crash.

RESPONDING TO TERRORISM

The attacks of 9/11 brought Americans together in sorrow and anger, and at first, President Bush maintained that unity. Some of his actions re-established the rift, however. In October 2001, he signed the **Patriot Act** into law. The act gave the government broad powers to fight terrorism, including expanded abilities to search people's phone, email, and financial records without a court order. Many Americans feared these powers came at the price of civil liberties. A year later, Congress established the **Department of Homeland Security (DHS)**.

Sparked by 9/11, Bush's war on terror began by unleashing air strikes and troops on Afghanistan, where the extremist Islamic **Taliban** government harbored al Qaeda and Osama bin Laden. The Taliban fell, but American forces remained in the country to support the Afghan government and counter antigovernment forces. Some Afghans resented the presence of Americans, especially when innocent Afghan civilians were killed as different factions within the country attacked the U.S. troops.

AMERICAN PLACES
The Pentagon, Washington, D.C.

The Pentagon is the headquarters of the Department of Defense and houses the offices of the U.S. Army, Navy, Air Force, and Marines. It was built after President Franklin D. Roosevelt asked for a central headquarters for the War Department following Germany's invasion of the Soviet Union in 1941. The five-sided shape echoes the design of various U.S. forts, including Fort Sumter. On September 11, 2001, a hijacked passenger jet crashed into one of its walls at more than 500 miles per hour. Next to the Pentagon is the National 9/11 Pentagon Memorial, which consists of a steel bench for each of the 184 people killed in the attack.

Bush next targeted Iraq, insisting it had ties to al Qaeda and possessed **weapons of mass destruction (WMD)**. Iraqi president Saddam Hussein accepted UN demands for inspections, which revealed no WMD, but Bush continued to press for war despite opposition from the international community and many Americans. In 2003, the United States and Great Britain launched an offensive against Iraq, and in three weeks they controlled the country. U.S. leaders had no detailed plans for the occupation, however, and Iraqi **insurgents**, or rebels, attacked U.S. forces. By 2008, almost 4,000 U.S. troops had been killed and many more wounded. No WMD were found.

In 2004, Bush narrowly won re-election against Democrat John Kerry. But the Iraq war dragged on, and revelations that Iraqi prisoners were being tortured created a scandal. Bush's poll numbers declined steeply. Then, in 2005, a massive hurricane struck the Gulf Coast.

HISTORICAL THINKING

1. **READING CHECK** Why did President Bush send U.S. forces to Afghanistan and Iraq?

2. **ANALYZE CAUSE AND EFFECT** What events contributed to President Bush's falling popularity in the years after the 9/11 attacks?

3. **FORM AND SUPPORT OPINIONS** What alternatives to invading Iraq might President Bush have chosen? Support your opinion.

PLAN

Objective
Analyze the effects of the 9/11 terrorist attacks and the resulting U.S. foreign and domestic policies.

Critical Thinking Skills for Lesson 2.1
- Identify Main Ideas and Details
- Monitor Comprehension
- Analyze Cause and Effect
- Form and Support Opinions
- Make Connections

Essential Question for Chapter 29
How has the United States responded to crises in the early years of the 21st century? The 9/11 terrorist attacks resulted in a U.S. war on terror. Lesson 2.1 examines the attacks and how pursuing al Qaeda led to controversial policies and wars in Afghanistan and Iraq.

Background for the Teacher
The first hint of trouble surfaced on the morning of September 11, 2001, a little more than 13 minutes after American Flight 11 took off from Boston headed for Los Angeles. Ordered to climb to 35,000 feet by ground control, the airplane didn't respond. Shortly thereafter, someone in the cockpit turned off the transponder, making it more difficult to track the plane. Still able to hear onboard communications, the controller quickly realized that Flight 11 had been hijacked. The same controller was also tracking United Flight 175. Sometime around 8:47, someone on Flight 175 changed the transponder code two times, leading the controller to suspect another hijacking. By this time, Flight 11 had already struck the World Trade Center's north tower. At 9:03, Flight 175 struck the south tower.

History Notebook
Encourage students to complete the American Gallery page for Chapter 29 in their History Notebooks as they read.

Terrorist Motives

Ask students to consider what terrorists hope to achieve by striking civilian targets. List their ideas on the board. Briefly discuss some of the motives, such as instilling fear in citizens, inflicting economic damage, or causing political unrest. Tell students that this lesson examines the effects of terrorist attacks on the United States on September 11, 2001.

TEACH

Guided Discussion

1. **Make Connections** What message might the attackers have intended to send by targeting New York City and Washington, D.C.? *(Possible response: New York is the center of the U.S. economy, while Washington is the center of the nation's government and military power. By targeting these cities, the attackers might have wanted to show that the United States was vulnerable despite its global economic and military power.)*

2. **Form and Support Opinions** Do you think the need to combat terrorism justifies the Patriot Act's expansion of the government's search powers? Support your opinion. *(Possible responses: Yes. Preventing terrorist attacks like 9/11 requires the government to collect evidence, such as phone records, emails, and financial records, against possible terrorists. No. The protection of individual civil liberties is fundamental to the country, and no threat is worth eroding them.)*

American Places

The National 9/11 Pentagon Memorial, consisting of 184 benches, is located on the side of the Pentagon struck by Flight 77. The benches facing the building honor the 125 individuals killed inside. The benches facing the open sky honor the 59 passengers who died on the airplane. Each bench contains the person's name, age, and location at the time of the crash. The benches are arranged along a time line according to the birth dates of the victims, beginning with the youngest, 3-year-old Dana Falkenberg, and ending with the oldest, 71-year-old John D. Yamnicky, Sr., a retired Navy captain. In the evening, a reflecting pool under each bench lights up in memory of those lost. The memorial is bordered by the Age Wall, the height of which increases from 3 to 71 inches to match the age line of the benches.

Active Options

AMERICAN GALLERY ONLINE **The Attacks of September 11, 2001** Invite students to explore the American Gallery. Have them select one of the images and do additional research to learn more about it. Ask questions that will inspire additional inquiry about the chosen gallery image, such as: What or whom does it show? Where is this? What is happening? Why does it belong in this chapter? What else would you like to know about it?

NG Learning Framework: Create a Museum Guide

SKILL Communication

KNOWLEDGE Our Human Story

Arrange students in groups to create print, digital, or audio museum guides to support existing online exhibitions found on the website for the National September 11 Memorial & Museum. Have each group explore the exhibitions and select one to support with a guide. Instruct groups to create introductions and background information about their exhibition, describe the pieces in the collection, and pose questions for viewers to consider while viewing the exhibition. Encourage groups to share their guides with the class.

DIFFERENTIATE

Striving Readers

Pose and Answer Questions Have students work in pairs to read the lesson paragraph by paragraph. Instruct them to pause after each paragraph and ask one another *who*, *what*, *when*, *where*, or *why* questions about what they have just read. Suggest that students use a 5Ws Chart to help organize their questions and answers.

Pre-AP

Write a News Report Assign students the role of New York City journalists on September 11, 2001. Instruct them to conduct online research to learn more about what happened on that day and then write a detailed news story. Encourage students to incorporate the words of a number of eyewitnesses, including people their own age. Remind students that news reports begin with the most important information and answer the questions *Who? What? When? Where? Why?* and *How?* Invite students to post their articles on a class blog or publish them on a school website.

See the Chapter Planner for more strategies for differentiation.

HISTORICAL THINKING

ANSWERS

1. President Bush sent troops to Afghanistan in the wake of the 9/11 attacks because the country's Taliban government harbored Osama bin Laden and al Qaeda. He went to war in Iraq because he believed Iraq had weapons of mass destruction and ties to al Qaeda.

2. The war in Iraq hurt Bush's popularity since no weapons of mass destruction were found and the torture of Iraqi prisoners outraged some people. Many Americans also disliked Bush's approval of the Patriot Act, which they believed weakened civil liberties.

3. Possible response: President Bush should have used economic or diplomatic pressure instead of military force against Iraq. The UN inspectors did not find WMD nor did U.S. troops after the invasion. The war produced more trouble for the United States and dragged on for years.

2.2 How Geology Affects Flooding

MAIN IDEA The geology of New Orleans made the city especially vulnerable to Hurricane Katrina.

By Andrés Ruzo, **National Geographic Explorer**

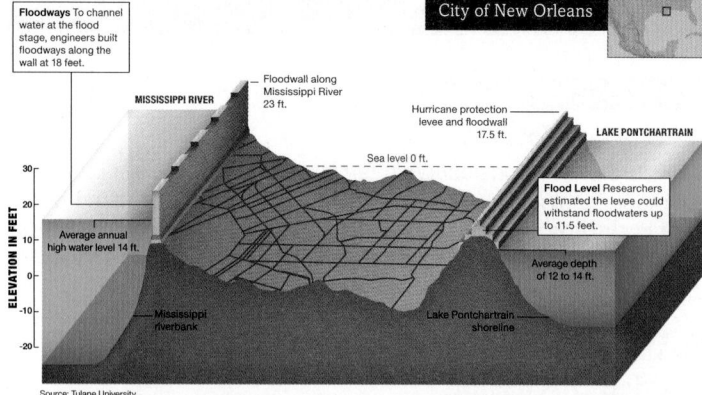

City of New Orleans

Floodways To channel water at the flood stage, engineers built floodways along the wall at 18 feet.

MISSISSIPPI RIVER

Floodwall along Mississippi River 23 ft.

Hurricane protection levee and floodwall 17.5 ft.

LAKE PONTCHARTRAIN

Sea level 0 ft.

Flood Level Researchers estimated the levee could withstand floodwaters up to 11.5 feet.

Average annual high water level 14 ft.

Average depth of 12 to 14 ft.

ELEVATION IN FEET

30 20 10 0 -10 -20

Mississippi riverbank

Lake Pontchartrain shoreline

Source: Tulane University

A BRUTAL STORM

The storm that came to be known as Hurricane Katrina battered the Gulf Coast on August 29, 2005, and was one of the deadliest hurricanes in U.S. history. It resulted in nearly 2,000 deaths and displaced hundreds of thousands of people from their homes. Katrina also caused an estimated $100 billion in damage, making it the nation's costliest natural disaster. The slow response of President Bush and government agencies to come to the aid of those affected by the storm in New Orleans, Louisiana, compounded Katrina's impact. Stranded in their homes and in shelters, many people in the city waited desperately for help. The president's failure to deal efficiently with the emergency greatly hurt his reputation.

As it happened, New Orleans was spared a direct hit by the storm. The city didn't experience the extreme winds and heavy rain that other places in the region endured. Nevertheless, New Orleans sustained more deaths and damage than any other location in Katrina's path. This destruction was caused by floodwaters. On August 29, 20 percent of the city had flooded. By the next day, about 80 percent was underwater.

IMPACT ON NEW ORLEANS

So what caused the terrible flooding in New Orleans? The answer lies, in part, with the city's geology. New Orleans is situated between Lake Pontchartrain (PAHN-shuh-trayn) and the Mississippi River. Over thousands of years,

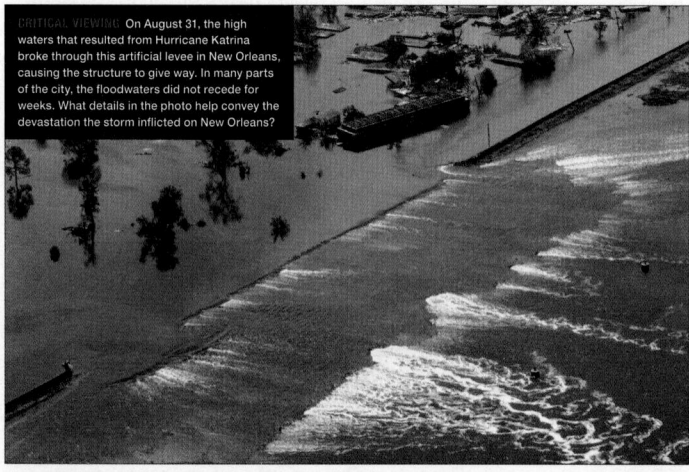

CRITICAL VIEWING On August 31, the high waters that resulted from Hurricane Katrina broke through this artificial levee in New Orleans, causing the structure to give way. In many parts of the city, the floodwaters did not recede for weeks. What details in the photo help convey the devastation the storm inflicted on New Orleans?

natural **levees**, or ridges of earth that run along the sides of a stream or river, had built up around the area as the Mississippi overflowed and deposited soil along its edges. In time, this process created higher ground on the riverbank. In 1718, New Orleans was founded on this natural high ground to protect the city from being flooded by the Mississippi.

As New Orleans grew, however, some of the surrounding swamps and wetlands were drained to provide more land. But while the original city lies about 17 feet above sea level, the newer areas are about 6 feet below sea level. Floodwaters can easily flow into the low-lying areas of New Orleans. To help prevent floods, engineers developed a system of pumps to remove the water and canals to channel it out. In the 20th century, they also built artificial levees to hold back the waters of Lake Pontchartrain and the Mississippi. As a result, roughly half of New Orleans sits below sea level in a sort of bowl, surrounded by these levees. Any water entering the bowl would be hard to drain.

That's just what happened when Hurricane Katrina struck. The storm dumped 10 inches of rain on New Orleans and created a **storm surge**, or an abnormal rise of the water level, in Lake Pontchartrain. This surge caused the lake to rise 30 feet in some places. The sheer volume of water overwhelmed many of the lake's levees.

Floodwaters breached, or broke through, the levees and spilled over them. Water also seeped into the soil beneath some of the levees, washing sections of them away. Most of the original city experienced relatively little flooding. However, other parts flooded so badly that people tried to escape the high waters by climbing onto the roofs of their homes.

It is likely that another major hurricane will hit New Orleans in the future. Since Katrina, engineers have repaired the levees and improved the structures' ability to hold back floodwaters. For example, engineers have increased the height of some of the levees and topped them with rock or concrete to prevent erosion by waves. But protecting New Orleans from the next big hurricane needs to be an ongoing process. Experts warn that the city is going to keep sinking below sea level. In some ways, geology is working against keeping New Orleans dry.

THINK LIKE A GEOLOGIST

1. **IDENTIFY MAIN IDEAS AND DETAILS** What steps did engineers take to try to prevent New Orleans from flooding before Hurricane Katrina?

2. **ANALYZE CAUSE AND EFFECT** Why did the geology of New Orleans lead to flooding in some parts of the city and not others?

PLAN

Objective
Explain how New Orleans' geology contributed to flooding following Hurricane Katrina.

Critical Thinking Skills for Lesson 2.2
- Identify Main Ideas and Details
- Monitor Comprehension
- Analyze Cause and Effect
- Analyze Visuals
- Identify

Essential Question for Chapter 29
How has the United States responded to crises in the early years of the 21st century? In 2005, a storm surge from Hurricane Katrina flooded New Orleans. Lesson 2.2 discusses how geology and human engineering made New Orleans vulnerable to devastating floods.

NATIONAL GEOGRAPHIC EXPLORER
Andrés Ruzo

Andrés Ruzo is familiar with water, whether it's the Boiling River of the Amazon or the marshlands of New Orleans. A geoscientist, author, conservationist, and educator, Ruzo aims to unite environmental responsibility with economic prosperity. To further this goal, he focuses primarily on understanding the geology of geothermal systems, not only for conservation purposes but also for their potential as an energy source. Ruzo lived in Peru, Nicaragua, and the United States while growing up and currently has active projects in all three countries. As founder and director of the Boiling River Project in the Amazon, he seeks to protect this geothermal river system by combining academic study, conservation economics, and native Amazonian knowledge of the area.

INTRODUCE & ENGAGE

Access Prior Knowledge

Ask students to recall flood disasters that have struck the United States, such as the flooding caused by Hurricane Harvey in August 2017. Invite students to describe photographs or live footage they saw in the media showing the floodwaters' effect on lives, houses, equipment, and other property. Then ask students to compare what they saw with what they see in the photograph of New Orleans in the lesson. Discuss their responses. Explain that this lesson describes why massive flooding occurred in New Orleans even though Hurricane Katrina did not directly hit the city.

TEACH   **STEM**

Guided Discussion

1. **Analyze Visuals** Ask students to study the infographic, City of New Orleans. **ASK:** What assumptions did engineers likely make when they built the levees and floodwalls? *(Possible response: Engineers assumed that levees with different heights would be adequate to prevent flooding from the Mississippi River and Lake Pontchartrain. They also assumed that no storm surge would exceed 11.5 feet above the lake and 23 feet above the river.)*

2. **Identify** What geological factors make it difficult to protect New Orleans from future flooding? *(New Orleans is built in the shape of a bowl, with parts of it below sea level, which makes it difficult to drain water from the lowest points. Low-lying parts of New Orleans continue to sink farther below sea level, making it harder to keep water out.)*

◆ Geography in History

Analyze Visuals Have students study the infographic of New Orleans. Ask them to identify the high and low points of the land, the height of the levees relative to sea level, and the bodies of water on either side of the city. **ASK:** Why might the levees on the Mississippi River be higher than the levees on Lake Pontchartrain? *(Possible response: The level of the river rises and falls depending on how much rain occurs upstream. The level of the lake probably doesn't change as much.)* **ASK:** Why did only part of New Orleans experience devastating flooding from Hurricane Katrina? *(Possible response: The section near Lake Pontchartrain lies below sea level. Floodwaters would have filled that section first.)* **ASK:** Why did it take so long for the floodwaters to recede? *(Possible response: So much of the city is below sea level that it would take a long time for the water to drain out.)*

Active Options

On Your Feet: Fishbowl Arrange half the class sitting in a circle, facing inward, with the rest of the class sitting in a larger circle around them. Have students on the inside discuss the following questions: How did humans affect the geology of New Orleans? What were the consequences to the city? Students on the outside listen to the discussion and evaluate points made. Then the groups reverse roles and continue the discussion.

NG Learning Framework: Investigate Current Flood Protection in New Orleans

SKILL Observation

KNOWLEDGE Our Living Planet

Direct students to work in small groups to investigate whether New Orleans is safer since Hurricane Katrina and to prepare a written report of their findings. Encourage groups to conduct online research to learn what measures have been taken to improve flood control in the city since 2005 and what problems still remain. Remind students to investigate flood protection for both the Mississippi River and Lake Pontchartrain. Encourage them to include visual data in the form of photographs, charts, or graphs to enhance their report. When groups have finished writing their reports, ask for volunteers to present their reports to the class.

DIFFERENTIATE

Inclusion

Analyze Visuals Guide students to understand the infographic with prompts such as the following: What do the blue, green, and brown colors represent? *(water, surface of New Orleans, land under the city)* What bodies of water is New Orleans between? *(Mississippi River and Lake Pontchartrain)* What keeps the water out of the city? *(floodwalls and levees)* How high could the water rise before flooding the city? *(17.5 feet by the lake and 23 feet on the river)*

Gifted & Talented

Create a Multimedia Presentation Have students conduct research to discover what is being done to protect New Orleans from hurricanes and rising sea levels. Encourage them to assemble their findings into a multimedia presentation that includes maps, photographs, news headlines, video clips, and other materials. Invite students to share their presentations with the class. Encourage students to discuss whether it is possible to adequately protect the city from hurricanes and floods, given its geology and geography.

See the Chapter Planner for more strategies for differentiation.

THINK LIKE A GEOLOGIST

ANSWERS

1. Engineers developed a combination of pumps and canals to remove and channel water out of the low-lying areas. They also built levees and floodwalls to keep out water from Lake Pontchartrain and the Mississippi River.

2. Part of the city was built on higher ground, which helped protect that part from flooding. However, the rest of the city was built below sea level on drained swampland and wetlands, leaving it vulnerable to flooding and storm surges.

CRITICAL VIEWING Possible response: The photograph shows a large break in the levee, and waves indicate that floodwaters were still rushing in. The ground was completely flooded, with the water level up to the roofs of buildings and halfway up the height of tall trees. The buildings shown, as well as elsewhere below sea level, would have been uninhabitable and roads impassable until after the waters receded.

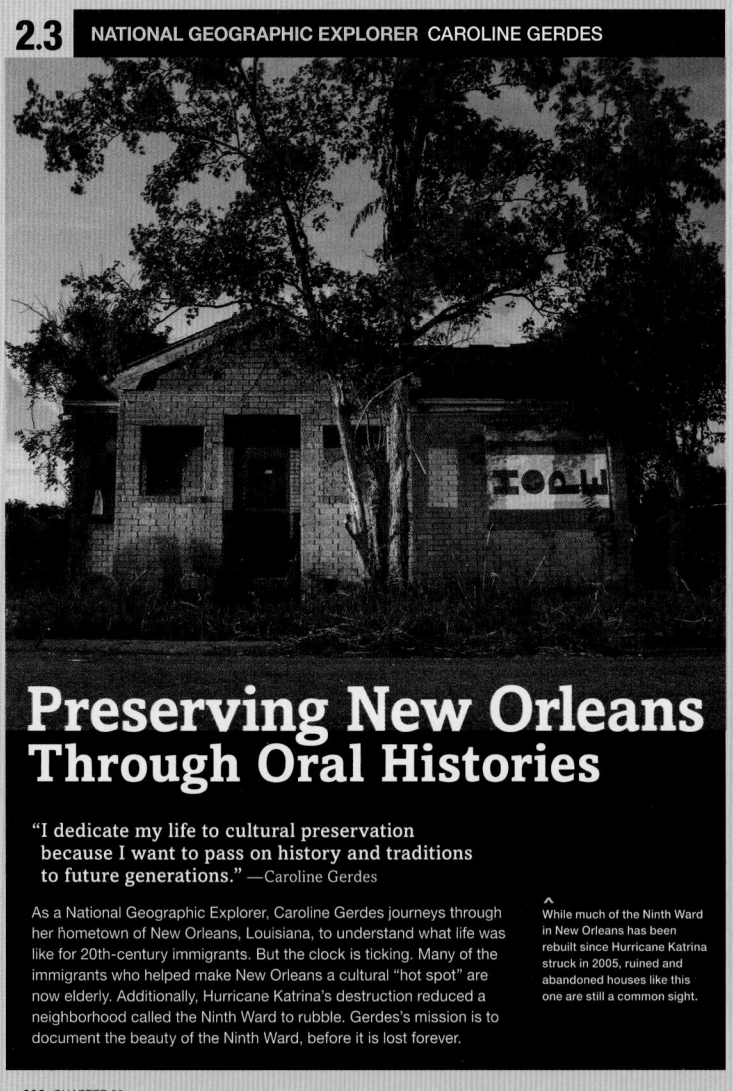

Preserving New Orleans
Through Oral Histories

"I dedicate my life to cultural preservation because I want to pass on history and traditions to future generations." —Caroline Gerdes

As a National Geographic Explorer, Caroline Gerdes journeys through her hometown of New Orleans, Louisiana, to understand what life was like for 20th-century immigrants. But the clock is ticking. Many of the immigrants who helped make New Orleans a cultural "hot spot" are now elderly. Additionally, Hurricane Katrina's destruction reduced a neighborhood called the Ninth Ward to rubble. Gerdes's mission is to document the beauty of the Ninth Ward, before it is lost forever.

^ While much of the Ninth Ward in New Orleans has been rebuilt since Hurricane Katrina struck in 2005, ruined and abandoned houses like this one are still a common sight.

MAIN IDEA National Geographic Explorer Caroline Gerdes captures the oral histories of a generation of New Orleans residents.

Journalist and oral historian Caroline Gerdes was born and raised in the greater New Orleans area. In 2005, Hurricane Katrina struck the city. Gerdes was just 15 years old. Her family evacuated their home, which was miraculously left standing. But most other residents were not so lucky, including her grandmother, who was able to salvage little after the disaster. In all, more than 1,400 people in Louisiana were killed in Hurricane Katrina. Most of them were elderly, and many of them drowned.

Hurricane Katrina did more than take lives. It destroyed homes, businesses, restaurants, and schools—whole communities. The place it hit the hardest was the Lower Ninth Ward. That's where Gerdes's father and paternal grandparents had grown up. As a child, Gerdes listened to her grandmother's stories about the Italian market, her uncle's jazz club, and other incredible places in her community. Those places are no longer standing— they exist only in memories now.

Living through Hurricane Katrina helped shape Caroline Gerdes as a person. "I am a writer and an explorer, in many ways because of Katrina. At a young age, I learned that we are shaped by our experiences, and we don't always have a choice in what we can take with us. But, upon closer inspection, we can find something in the bleakest of places and make it beautiful again."

That's just what Gerdes set out to do. In a partnership with National Geographic, she conducted an oral history project in the Ninth Ward to capture the feel of the area. She couldn't take photographs to show what the area once was—that time had come and gone. But many of the immigrants who had created the Lower Ninth Ward, shaping its history, culture, and communities, still lived there.

The Lower Ninth Ward was the subject of many news reports during and after Hurricane Katrina, so it is best known for the destruction it endured. However, this area was culturally rich for decades before Katrina, and Gerdes set out to explore that richness. She spoke with many people who shared stories about the community's history—both the

Caroline Gerdes discusses her book, *An Oral History of the New Orleans Ninth Ward*, at the National Geographic Society in Washington, D.C., in 2017.

bad events and the good. She learned about immigrant settlements, jazz music, food, faith, the Great Depression, Prohibition, desegregation, and, of course, hurricanes.

The Ninth Ward was made up of immigrant populations—French, Sicilian, African-American, Hispanic, Jewish, German, Irish, and many others. Overflowing with culture, it was a community full of life. After Katrina, it became lifeless and desolate. "The Lower Ninth Ward . . . has never regained its pre-Katrina population," Gerdes explains. "In addition to fractured streets, many homes remain abandoned. Nature has taken over. Trees envelop flood-worn homes." But the people of New Orleans are resilient. And while the Ninth Ward may no longer be the thriving cultural hub it was before Katrina, life is returning to New Orleans.

Gerdes's book, *An Oral History of the New Orleans Ninth Ward*, was published in April 2017.

HISTORICAL THINKING

1. **READING CHECK** Why is Gerdes concerned about capturing the oral history of the Ninth Ward?

2. **MAKE INFERENCES** How can a natural event impact the culture of a region?

3. **SYNTHESIZE** If you could take an oral history from anyone, who would it be? Explain your choice and what you would hope to learn.

PLAN

Objective

Describe Caroline Gerdes's use of oral histories to preserve the legacy of New Orleans' Lower Ninth Ward.

Critical Thinking Skills for Lesson 2.3

- Identify Main Ideas and Details
- Monitor Comprehension
- Make Inferences
- Synthesize
- Summarize

Essential Question for Chapter 29

How has the United States responded to crises in the early years of the 21st century? During Hurricane Katrina, flooding destroyed New Orleans' Lower Ninth Ward. Lesson 2.3 describes how National Geographic Explorer Caroline Gerdes documented life in the neighborhood to preserve its history.

NATIONAL GEOGRAPHIC EXPLORER
Caroline Gerdes

In 2012, Caroline Gerdes received a National Geographic Young Explorers grant to fund her oral history project. To conduct her interviews, Gerdes, along with photographer Robert Giglio, canvassed southeastern Louisiana, where many Ninth Ward residents had moved after Katrina. In the Introduction to her book, Gerdes states: "I spent the rest of the year blogging for National Geographic, writing a report, transcribing interviews, creating video, editing photos and multimedia, [and] researching and reading about New Orleans history." Her first interview and her inspiration to preserve the cultural history of New Orleans was her grandmother, whose battle with dementia made completing the work more urgent.

History Notebook

Encourage students to complete the Explorer page for Chapter 29 in their History Notebooks as they read.

Discuss Family Stories

Ask students whether they have heard older relatives tell stories about events, people, or places from their pasts. Explain that these are oral histories and that when they are repeated or recorded, they are being preserved. Invite students to tell a story—appropriate for the classroom—that they have heard from a relative that recounts a place or activity from years ago. After a few students have shared stories, explain that in this lesson they will read about a young woman who collected peoples' stories to preserve the rich cultural history of New Orleans' Ninth Ward, destroyed by flooding caused by Hurricane Katrina.

TEACH

Guided Discussion

1. **Make Inferences** What do you think Gerdes meant when she said, "We can find something in the bleakest of places and make it beautiful again"? *(Possible response: She was probably referring to the Ninth Ward after Hurricane Katrina as the "bleakest of places" and the oral histories as a way to "make it beautiful again." Telling stories passes on the richness and culture of the ward.)*

2. **Summarize** What were some of the factors that made the Ninth Ward so unique? *(Possible response: It was made up of a diverse ethnic, racial, and immigrant population, it was relatively poor but had a vibrant culture, and it had endured a series of major economic and social changes along with flooding disasters.)*

More Information

Ninth Ward Oral Histories The interviews in Gerdes's book, *An Oral History of the New Orleans Ninth Ward*, include memories of street vendors selling their wares and the struggle to integrate the Ninth Ward school system. Former resident Charles Capdepon remembered the "Roman Candy Man," who sold a kind of pink taffy from his decorated wagon, pulled by a mule. Other residents recalled the vegetable vendor who would push his cart through the streets, singing out what was for sale that day. Added to that voice were the sounds of ice cream trucks, milk trucks, and organ grinders, creating a chorus of entrepreneurship. Leona Tate recalled her role as part of the McDonogh Three, when she and two other girls were chosen to integrate the first grade in public school McDonogh 19. The girls, selected for their ability to remain calm under pressure, went on to integrate three other schools. Such stories make Gerdes hope that new generations coming to the Ninth Ward will respect its tenants and honor its cultural past.

Active Options

On Your Feet: Roundtable Arrange students in groups of four. Hand each group a sheet of paper with the question: What location in or aspect of your neighborhood could be preserved in an oral history? The first student in each group writes an answer, reads it aloud, and passes the paper clockwise to the next student. The paper should circulate several times. Then students discuss their responses and add details that might be included in an oral history.

NG Learning Framework: Create a Digital Oral History Book `STEM`

`SKILLS` Communication, Collaboration

`KNOWLEDGE` Our Human Story

Have small groups brainstorm a focus for entries they will write or record for a digital oral history book. Students might choose a focus such as a family tradition, a significant event in their lives, or a profile of a relative. Tell students to discuss how they might organize, illustrate, and compile the book as a single digital collection for a class or school website or as an electronic presentation. Direct students to research the subject, write notes, and plan before they begin. They should write or record their oral histories as first-person accounts and submit them in acceptable formats as text files or audio or video recordings. Assign or ask for volunteers to guide others in compiling and publishing the groups' digital collection of oral histories. Invite volunteers to present their oral histories to the class.

English Language Learners

Expand Vocabulary Pair students at the **Emerging** level with those at the **Bridging** or **Expanding** level. Bring students' attention to the following words and phrases: *clock is ticking*, *hot spot*, *salvage*, *elderly*, and *memories*. Have partners take turns reading the words and phrases in context and explaining the meanings. Then challenge students to compose an original sentence for each. Invite pairs to share their sentences by reading them aloud.

Pre-AP

Compare and Contrast Interviews Direct students to read a number of interviews from Gerdes's book. Ask them to choose two or more interviews to present to the class. Students should discuss the similarities and differences between the interviewees, as well as how the neighborhood shaped their lives.

See the Chapter Planner for more strategies for differentiation.

HISTORICAL THINKING

ANSWERS

1. Hurricane Katrina destroyed much of the property and culture of the Ninth Ward, so Gerdes wants to preserve the ward's history by talking to older people who remember it best.

2. Natural events can take human lives, destroy a region's historic properties, and force residents to move elsewhere, all of which would impact the region's culture. Without traditional places to gather and without its talented people, a region would have a hard time maintaining or recovering its culture.

3. Answers will vary. Students might take an oral history of a relative, a neighbor, a famous person, or someone else important to them or about whom they are curious. They might say they want to know about the person's childhood, life-shaping events, advice to pass on, or the legacy the person would like to leave.

The Election of Barack Obama

American children are often told that anyone can grow up to be president. All of the first 43 U.S. presidents, however, were white males. That trend was broken in 2008.

MAIN IDEA In the eventful year 2008, the United States slipped deeper into recession, and Barack Obama was elected as the country's first African-American president.

President Barack Obama and First Lady Michelle Obama smile and wave at the people lining the route of the traditional Inaugural Parade in Washington, D.C. Held on January 20, 2009, the inauguration of the 44th president of the United States was attended by about 1.8 million people.

A HISTORIC CAMPAIGN

The year 2008 opened on a pessimistic note in the United States. The unpopular war in Iraq was dragging into its sixth year, and a recession was pulling down the economy. These factors gave Democrats an advantage in the approaching presidential election.

A two-way race for the Democratic nomination developed between former First Lady and New York senator Hillary Clinton and Illinois senator **Barack Obama**. Clinton, the wife of former president Bill Clinton, was the early favorite. She faced many obstacles, however, including anger over her vote in the Senate in favor of the U.S. invasion of Iraq.

Obama was relatively unknown at the start of the campaign, but he soon won a large and enthusiastic following. An inspiring speaker, he offered a message of hope and change that struck a chord with many voters. Unlike Clinton, he had opposed the war in Iraq from the beginning. And unlike any major presidential candidate before him, he was biracial. His mother was white, and his father was African, born in Kenya. The race was very close, but Obama emerged as the Democratic nominee. He chose Delaware senator Joe Biden as his running mate.

In the Republican primary elections, Senator John McCain, a former prisoner of war during the Vietnam War, pulled away from seven other candidates to win his party's nomination. For his running mate, McCain selected the governor of Alaska, Sarah Palin.

THE GREAT RECESSION

As Obama and McCain squared off, the recession that had begun in late 2007 worsened dramatically. The **Great Recession**, as it came to be known, developed into the nation's worst economic downturn since the Great Depression. In large part, the recession was rooted in the housing market. In the years immediately leading up to the crisis, more people wanted to buy houses, which caused home prices to rise sharply. The belief that they would keep rising had fueled speculation, or risky investing in the hope of making big profits. Banks had put themselves in danger by making large numbers of **subprime** home loans—that is, loans to borrowers with poor credit ratings.

Other economic issues, some of which had been developing for decades, contributed to the Great Recession. Lenders had been making increasing use of certain risky financial practices, for example. In addition, consumers were taking on greater debt, but their wages had failed to increase for several years.

By 2007, large numbers of homeowners discovered that they could not afford their mortgage payments. To make matters worse, the market had cooled and home prices were dropping. People were forced to sell their houses for less than what they had paid in the first place. As **loan defaults**, or failures to repay mortgages, increased, the economy fell into chaos. Many small banks failed, and other industries took severe hits. Shrinking revenues pushed some states to the brink of bankruptcy. Millions of Americans lost their jobs, their homes, and their savings.

To prevent the country's biggest banks from failing, Congress passed the Emergency Economic Stabilization Act (EESA) in 2008. This legislation provided the U.S. Secretary of the Treasury up to $700 billion to buy risky mortgages and other potentially poor investments from banks and other financial institutions, saving them from collapse.

On the campaign trail, Barack Obama impressed many voters with his focused, confident response to the economic crisis. At the same time, many blamed the Republicans for the Great Recession because they were the party in power during the buildup and the crash. Obama won the election with 53% of the popular vote and 365 electoral votes, becoming the first African-American president in the country's history.

HISTORICAL THINKING

1. **READING CHECK** How did Hillary Clinton and Barack Obama differ in their positions on the war in Iraq?

2. **IDENTIFY PROBLEMS AND SOLUTIONS** What problem did the Emergency Economic Stabilization Act address, and how?

3. **ANALYZE LANGUAGE USE** What are the root and prefix of the word *subprime*, and what do they mean?

Objective

Analyze the historic election of Barack Obama and the Great Recession.

Critical Thinking Skills for Lesson 3.1

- Identify Main Ideas and Details
- Monitor Comprehension
- Identify Problems and Solutions
- Analyze Language Use
- Analyze Cause and Effect
- Form and Support Opinions
- Make Connections

Essential Question for Chapter 29

How has the United States responded to crises in the early years of the 21st century? Barack Obama inherited an economy in crisis. Lesson 3.1 explores the 2008 election and the causes and consequences of the Great Recession.

Background for the Teacher

Among the risky financial practices that led to the Great Recession was the bundling of mortgage loans—including subprime loans—into packages that could be sold to investors around the globe. Investors regarded the U.S. real estate market as one of the most stable in the world, so individuals and nations bought millions of dollars' worth of these mortgage bundles. However, they didn't realize that many of the loans were too risky and would fail. As homeowners began to default on their loans, investors' mortgage bundles began losing value until they became virtually worthless. This bankrupted many companies and even some nations, such as Iceland, and severely crippled other countries—especially Portugal, Spain, and Greece—making it the worst global financial failure since the Great Depression.

INTRODUCE & ENGAGE

Activate Prior Knowledge

Ask students what they know about the Great Depression. *(Possible response: It was the world's longest and deepest economic downturn, resulting from the stock market crash in October 1929.)* Invite them to name some of the causes and effects of the Great Depression that they learned about in earlier lessons. Use a Cause-and-Effect Chart to record their responses. Then tell students that in this lesson they will read about the Great Recession, a more recent major economic downturn. After completing the lesson, review the chart and compare the Great Depression with the Great Recession.

TEACH

Guided Discussion

1. **Analyze Cause and Effect** How did risky financial practices contribute to the Great Recession? *(Possible response: During the housing boom, banks made large numbers of subprime loans, allowing individuals to buy homes with loans they could not pay back. Soon, many borrowers began defaulting on these home loans. This caused a ripple effect in the economy: housing prices dropped, banks failed, states went into bankruptcy, and many Americans lost their jobs and savings.)*

2. **Form and Support Opinions** How might the Great Recession have helped Barack Obama win the 2008 presidential election? Support your opinion with evidence from the text. *(Possible response: Obama offered a message of hope and change at a time when many Americans were suffering financially. He also seemed focused and confident when discussing the economy. Since many voters blamed the Republicans for the Great Recession, Obama's message and confidence were appealing.)*

Make Connections

Tell students that between the middle of 2006 and the middle of 2009, housing prices fell about 30 percent on average. At about the same time, the net worth of U.S. households and nonprofit organizations fell by almost $15 trillion. **ASK:** How might these two statistics be related when it comes to U.S. households and nonprofits? *(Possible response: For many Americans, the value of their home accounts for much of their net worth. Thus, if the value of their home declines or if they lose their home, their net worth decreases. When individuals face financial difficulties, they have less money available to contribute to nonprofit organizations, so the net worth of those organizations also falls.)*

Active Options

On Your Feet: Team Word Webbing Invite students to gather in small groups, and provide each group with a sheet of chart paper. Give each student a different colored marker. Ask students to create a Word Web to brainstorm words and phrases they associate with the term *Great Recession*. Each student should add to the part of the web closest to him or her. After a minute, signal to the groups to rotate their paper and have students again add to the nearest part.

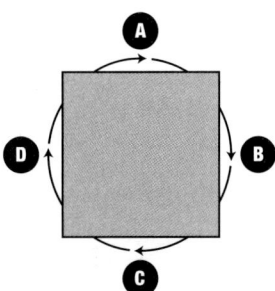

NG Learning Framework: Write a News Profile

ATTITUDE Curiosity

KNOWLEDGE Our Human Story

Tell students to imagine they are reporters covering Barack Obama's 2008 presidential campaign. Instruct them to work in groups to write a short video script or print profile about Obama, using information from the lesson and additional print and digital sources. Encourage students to include information about his background, political positions, and why he appealed to such a wide range of voters. Remind them to quote and paraphrase the conclusions of others, avoiding plagiarism and following a standard format for citations. Invite groups to share their profiles with the class.

DIFFERENTIATE

Striving Readers

Understand Cause and Effect Provide pairs of students with a Cause-and-Effect Chart, and instruct them to label the chart The Great Recession. Then tell them to reread that section of the lesson, noting specific causes and effects of the Great Recession. Invite pairs to share their completed charts with other pairs and discuss any differences.

Pre-AP

Compare Financial Crises Prompt students to conduct online research to learn more about the causes of the Great Recession and the Great Depression. Encourage them to use a Venn diagram to keep track of the similarities and differences between the two financial crises. Tell students that there may be some general similarities (speculation), but differences within those similarities (stock speculation vs. housing speculation). Instruct them to use their research to write a compare-contrast essay and to share their essays with the class.

See the Chapter Planner for more strategies for differentiation.

HISTORICAL THINKING

ANSWERS

1. Clinton had voted in favor of the U.S. invasion of Iraq, while Obama had opposed the war from the outset.

2. The Emergency Economic Stabilization Act was aimed at preventing the largest banks and financial institutions from collapsing. To accomplish this, the act provided up to $700 billion to the U.S. Treasury to buy risky mortgages and investments from these banks and institutions.

3. The prefix *sub* usually means "below" or "under," and the root *prime* usually means "of the highest quality or value." Thus, *subprime* means "below the highest quality" or "undervalued."

Recovery and Reform

The president is sometimes called "the captain of the ship of state." President Barack Obama became captain at a time when the ship seemed in danger of sinking.

MAIN IDEA After taking office as president, Barack Obama focused on pulling the country out of a recession and reforming the health care system.

RECOVERING FROM THE RECESSION

Barack Obama inherited the worst economy since Franklin D. Roosevelt took office in 1933. Obama's priority was to lead the country out of the crippling recession that had begun more than a year earlier. As the Democratic president, Obama could expect cooperation from Congress because his party had gained firm control of both the House of Representatives and the Senate.

Just days after Obama's inauguration, House Democrats introduced a major bill aimed at stimulating the economy. Although every House Republican voted against it, the bill passed easily. Two weeks later, the bill made it through the Senate. Three Republicans and two independents joined all the Democratic senators in voting yes. On February 17, 2009, Obama signed the bill into law as the **American Recovery and Reinvestment Act (ARRA)**.

Totaling $787 billion, this **economic stimulus** package was the largest in U.S. history. It sought to save existing jobs, create new ones, and encourage long-term economic growth. In addition to authorizing tax cuts, it included payments to states and localities to help fund community programs, an increase in infrastructure projects such as the construction of roads and schools, and funds to enhance energy independence.

By summer 2009, the recession had officially ended. Recovery, however, was slow. Millions of Americans remained unemployed or under-employed. In fact, the unemployment level climbed for several more months to 10 percent before slowly beginning to drop in early 2010. By late 2015, unemployment had reached its pre-recession level of 5 percent.

HEALTH CARE REFORM

Another of President Obama's priorities was health care reform. In a speech to Congress in September 2009, he pointed out that more than 30 million Americans lacked health insurance. He spoke of the devastating cost of health care and the waste within the medical system and accused insurance companies of unethical practices.

In November, a sweeping health care reform bill squeaked through the House of Representatives. Then, on December 24, the Senate approved a significantly different version of the bill. Congressional Republicans fiercely opposed it, but the determined efforts of House Speaker Nancy Pelosi and President Obama kept it alive.

Finally, in March 2010, the House passed the Senate version of the bill, and Obama signed the **Patient Protection and Affordable Care Act (ACA)** into law. It came to be known as **Obamacare**. Its aim was to broaden health insurance coverage by making it more affordable and easier to obtain through online exchanges, or marketplaces. The government also provided subsidies, or money to help people pay for insurance. The ACA sought to end discriminatory insurance practices such as denial of coverage for preexisting conditions and limits on how much a policy would pay in a lifetime. To help low-income citizens, states were given the option to apply for federal grants to expand Medicaid.

Early in Obama's presidency, a conservative populist movement arose to oppose the new president and his progressive agenda. It was known as the **Tea Party**, a connection with the patriots of the Revolutionary era. Its members were united in their belief that the American

The American Recovery and Reinvestment Act (ARRA)

Infrastructure projects funded by the ARRA included bridge repairs and expansions, like the one shown below. Signs erected alongside these projects identified the ARRA as their financial source. A primary goal of the ARRA was to jump-start the economy and save or create 3.5 million jobs. Toward that goal, about 65 percent of the act's appropriations were spent investing in activities that would stimulate the economy. The remaining amount went to tax cuts. The pie chart at right shows the major categories Congress chose to fund.

Major Categories Funded by the ARRA

- Education and Training $105.9 billion
- Infrastructure and Science $120.0 billion
- Law enforcement, oversight, and other programs $7.8 billion
- Health $14.2 billion
- Helping Americans most severely hit by the economic crisis $24.3 billion
- Energy $37.5 billion

An infrastructure project near Warsaw, Kentucky, 2009

people were victims of excessive taxation and too much government intervention. The Tea Party objected to the amount of money the government was spending to fight the recession. It supported stronger controls over immigration and objected to reforms to the health care system. Most Tea Party members were Republicans.

Energized by the fast-growing movement, Republicans made historic gains in the 2010 midterm elections. They gained 6 seats in the Senate and took control of the House by gaining 63 seats there. The federal government was once again divided.

HISTORICAL THINKING

1. **READING CHECK** What was the biggest challenge facing Barack Obama when he took office as president?

2. **IDENTIFY PROBLEMS AND SOLUTIONS** What were some of the problems that President Obama hoped to solve through the reform of health care?

3. **ANALYZE DATA** Which two categories in the pie chart received the most funding, and why do you think they were given that much?

PLAN

Objective

Analyze how Barack Obama sought to end an economic recession and reform health care and why the Tea Party resisted his efforts.

Critical Thinking Skills for Lesson 3.2

- Identify Main Ideas and Details
- Monitor Comprehension
- Identify Problems and Solutions
- Analyze Data
- Evaluate

Essential Question for Chapter 29

How has the United States responded to crises in the early years of the 21st century? Barack Obama pushed major reforms through Congress during his first term. Lesson 3.2 examines the American Recovery and Reinvestment Act and the Patient Protection and Affordable Care Act.

Background for the Teacher

In 2010, the *New York Times* and CBS News conducted a survey to better understand the Tea Party. The name references an American Revolution connection and the populist slogan "Taxed Enough, Already." The data showed the movement was largely made of white men older than 45 who were self-described conservatives and tended to vote Republican. Around 40 percent of this group believed that the country needed a third party. What tied them together was anger about the direction the country was headed and a deep antipathy toward President Obama. Many also believed he was raising taxes and bringing the country toward socialism. Thirty percent were not even sure that Obama had been born in the United States—a false idea promoted by some on the right, including future president Donald Trump.

Financial Literacy

To extend their knowledge and understanding about the concepts in this lesson, refer students to the Financial Literacy handbook.

INTRODUCE & ENGAGE

The Role of Government

Pose the following scenario to students: the U.S. economy is in crisis, health care costs are rising quickly, and many Americans cannot afford health insurance. **ASK:** What role do you think the government should play in addressing these problems? *(Answers will vary. Encourage students to consider the pros and cons of government intervention in the economy and health care.)* Tell students that this lesson examines the efforts of the Obama administration to intervene and how the Tea Party movement responded.

TEACH

Guided Discussion

1. **Identify Problems and Solutions** How did the American Recovery and Reinvestment Act (ARRA) try to address the problems facing the economy? *(Possible response: Because of the housing crisis, the economy had ground to a halt: businesses weren't hiring, states were going bankrupt, and people were losing their homes and their jobs. The ARRA put a huge amount of money into the economy to try to create and save jobs through tax cuts and by giving funds to states and local communities for infrastructure and energy programs, for example.)*

2. **Evaluate** Why was the rise of the Tea Party movement a problem for the Obama presidency? Support your reasoning with text evidence. *(Possible response: The Tea Party opposed the stimulus measures and health care reforms that Obama and the Democrats pushed through Congress. In the 2010 midterm elections, the Tea Party helped Republicans take back the House and gain seats in the Senate. The Obama administration no longer had a supportive Congress to help push through Democratic reforms.)*

More Information

Stimulating the Economy Tell students that economists disagree on how best to stimulate a struggling economy. Some studies suggest that providing tax cuts to families and businesses and giving direct aid to states for Medicaid and other assistance programs for low-income households have a more immediate effect than providing federal aid for infrastructure and other projects. Lower-income households tend to spend assistance money quickly, which provides an immediate stimulus to the economy. **ASK:** Why might low-income families spend their assistance money quickly during economic recessions? *(Possible response: They are less likely to have financial reserves or be able to borrow money during economic downturns, and they need the money for immediate necessities.)*

Active Options

On Your Feet: Jigsaw Arrange students evenly into groups and assign each group one of the following topics: American Recovery and Reinvestment Act, Patient Protection and Affordable Care Act, Tea Party. Groups will research their topics to find key facts about each one and become "experts." Guide students to make use of consumer or news websites, where the facts are usually written in easily understood language. Regroup students so that each new group has at least one member from each expert group. Invite experts to report on their assigned topic.

NG Learning Framework: Create a Political Ad

SKILL Communication

KNOWLEDGE Our Human Story

Have students work in small groups to create a political advertisement for or against the Obama administration's economic stimulus or health care reform act. Encourage them to use information from the lesson and outside resources to plan their advertisements, which should include clear arguments. Invite groups to share their advertisements with the class. When finished, have the class vote on which ads were most persuasive.

DIFFERENTIATE

English Language Learners ELD

Create Word Squares Pair students at the **Emerging** or **Expanding** level with students at the **Bridging** level. Bring their attention to the sentence containing the words *unemployed* and *underemployed*. Elicit the meaning of the prefixes *un-* ("not") and *under-* ("insufficiently"). Ask pairs to complete a Word Square for each word, with students at the **Bridging** level providing assistance and aiding in using a dictionary, if needed. If time permits, you may wish to provide other words that could take these prefixes, such as *funded* and *skilled*, and direct students to complete Word Squares for them as well.

Pre-AP

Evaluate the ARRA Instruct students to conduct online research to evaluate the effectiveness of the American Recovery and Reinvestment Act (ARRA). Have students find and analyze the Congressional Budget Office's report about the impact of the stimulus package and compare it to information and opinions they locate in newspaper articles and op-ed pieces. Prompt them to consider whether the sources they find exhibit any particular slant and how that bias might color the article or op-ed piece. Then ask them to summarize their findings for the class, explaining whether the ARRA was successful and whether it had a lasting impact.

See the Chapter Planner for more strategies for differentiation.

HISTORICAL THINKING

ANSWERS

1. The country was in the middle of a devastating economic recession.

2. More than 30 million Americans did not have health insurance, health care was very expensive, and insurance companies could discriminate against groups of people. Such discrimination included denying coverage for those with preexisting medical conditions and limiting how much in insurance payments people could receive in a lifetime.

3. The two biggest categories of funding were (1) infrastructure and science and (2) education and training. Infrastructure and science projects may require immediate workers for repairs or to address technical or scientific issues. Education and training prepare people for future jobs.

3.3 Serving Others

We often look to our leaders to bring about positive change. In turn, leaders sometimes remind us that every citizen can make a difference through public service. In his 1961 inaugural address, President John F. Kennedy famously made this request to Americans: "Ask not what your country can do for you—ask what you can do for your country."

In different words but with the same intention, American leaders have reminded citizens of the rewards that come with helping others. President Barack Obama was one of the many government and civilian leaders who continued this tradition of encouraging Americans to become involved in community service.

CRITICAL VIEWING A Houston, Texas, SWAT officer carries a mother and her baby to safety after rescuing them from their flooded home. In 2017, civilians and officers took to the streets to help people caught by the drenching rains and high winds of Hurricane Harvey. Describe the dangers visible in this photograph.

DOCUMENT ONE

Primary Source: Speech
from President Barack Obama's inaugural address,
January 20, 2009

In his inaugural address, Obama spoke of Americans who embody "the spirit of service" through their "willingness to find meaning in something greater than themselves." This spirit, he continued, "must inhabit us all."

CONSTRUCTED RESPONSE
What does President Obama suggest about the types of people who can perform public service?

For as much as government can do, and must do, it is ultimately the faith and determination of the American people upon which this nation relies. It is the kindness to take in a stranger when the levees break, the selflessness of workers who would rather cut their hours than see a friend lose their job which sees us through our darkest hours. It is the firefighter's courage to storm a stairway filled with smoke, but also a parent's willingness to nurture a child that finally decides our fate.

DOCUMENT TWO

Primary Source: Speech
from First Lady Laura Bush's address to the Global Literacy
Conference in New York, September 18, 2006

Laura Bush was a teacher and school librarian before she met and married George W. Bush. As First Lady, she strongly supported literacy programs not only within the United States but also throughout the world. She also established the Laura Bush Foundation for America's Libraries to help the neediest school libraries.

CONSTRUCTED RESPONSE
Why does Laura Bush encourage her audience to teach by example?

Investing in literacy and education helps governments meet their fundamental obligations, by improving opportunities for children and families, by strengthening their economies, and by keeping their citizens in good health. . . . Today, as we discuss how to improve educational opportunities around the world, it's important to remember that we're all teachers. A person who's never stood by a blackboard still teaches by example. By demonstrating our commitment to literacy, we can let millions of people know that reading and writing are important, and we can help build a healthier, more prosperous, and more hopeful world.

DOCUMENT THREE

Primary Source: Interview
from The Gathering's interview with former NBA star
David Robinson, May 19, 2005

After a stellar career with the San Antonio Spurs, David Robinson retired from basketball in 2003. He and his wife then founded the Carver Academy, a K–12 school serving a poor inner-city area of San Antonio, Texas.

CONSTRUCTED RESPONSE
Why does Robinson think that children should be taught to use their talents to serve other people?

Why can't we teach [children] that the most important thing they can ever do with their lives is to use their talents to serve other people? There are plenty of role models out there who have done just that. George Washington Carver, the African-American botanist whom we named the academy after, helped farmers produce a wide range of crops through his inventions, thereby promoting better health and sound nutrition for all Americans.

SYNTHESIZE & WRITE

1. **REVIEW** Review what you have learned about volunteerism and serving others.

2. **RECALL** On your own paper, write down the main idea presented in each document and in the photograph.

3. **CONSTRUCT** Construct a topic sentence that answers this question: Why is it important to serve others?

4. **WRITE** Write a paragraph that supports the statement in step 3. Use evidence from the documents to support your statement.

PLAN

Objective
Synthesize information about public service from primary source documents.

Critical Thinking Skills for Lesson 3.3
- Synthesize
- Summarize
- Form and Support Opinions
- Evaluate

Essential Question for Chapter 29
How has the United States responded to crises in the early years of the 21st century? There is a long-held American tradition to respond to natural and human-made crises by helping one another. In Lesson 3.3, Barack Obama, Laura Bush, and David Robinson emphasize that serving others as a matter of course benefits society in far-reaching ways.

Background for the Teacher
In 2009, with support from their parents, grade-schoolers Carter and Olivia Ries founded the nonprofit organization One More Generation (OMG). Their mission originally was to help save all endangered species for one more generation and beyond, but they soon extended their service to people, such as helping the homeless and children in shelters. Part of their mission became inspiring and supporting other young people to serve. To do so, the brother and sister started We've Got You Covered, a youth empowerment division of OMG. As they explain, "[The division] is designed to ignite a spark in youth everywhere and to help them find ways they, too, can get involved in what moves them to make a difference." Young people can submit their ideas to the OMG website and receive help, advice, and encouragement from the OMG founders and board members.

INTRODUCE & ENGAGE

Prepare for the Document-Based Question

Before students start the activity, briefly preview the three documents. Remind students that a constructed response requires full explanations in complete sentences. Emphasize that students should use what they have learned about government, civilian leaders, and community service in addition to the information in the documents.

TEACH

Guided Discussion

1. **Summarize** In what ways are the three speakers leading by example? *(Possible response: The three speakers took action to make a difference, providing examples for others to follow. President Obama was serving the nation as president at the time of his speech; Laura Bush established a foundation to help instead of just talking about the importance of literacy; David Robinson founded Carver Academy to help inner-city students rather than merely pointing out that they lacked educational opportunities.)*

2. **Form and Support Opinions** Do you believe that individuals can make a difference through public service, or do you think the government alone should be responsible for the welfare of the public? *(Possible response: I think individuals can make a difference by taking action to help others reach both immediate and far-reaching goals, such as what David Robinson does with his academy. I also think that the government has a responsibility in situations such as disasters like Hurricane Harvey to send trained rescue workers to help people in need. People who want to help but are not trained could put their lives and others' at risk.)*

Evaluate

After students have completed the Synthesize & Write activity, allow time for them to exchange paragraphs and read and comment on the work of their peers. Establish guidelines for comments prior to this activity so that feedback is constructive and encouraging in nature.

Active Option

On Your Feet: Think, Pair, Share Ask students to reread the three quotations. Then organize students into pairs and give them a few minutes to think about the following question: When you serve others, how might you be helping yourself as well? After pairs have had sufficient time to discuss their responses, invite them to share their thoughts with the class. Encourage a class discussion about ways that people can serve others regardless of their age, abilities, location, or circumstances and what benefits service might have for the one providing it.

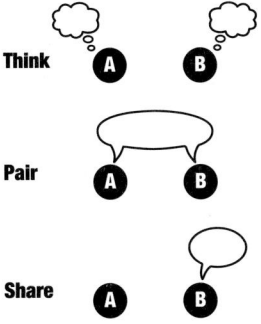

DIFFERENTIATE

Striving Readers

Summarize Read each document aloud to students. Then have them work in pairs to reread the documents and summarize them. After students complete a summary for a document, read the Constructed Response question aloud and make sure they understand it before they respond. You may wish to have pairs work together to respond to the Synthesize & Write questions.

Gifted & Talented

Create a Graphic Biography Tell students to select one of the individuals behind the primary source documents and create a short biography in the style of a comic book or graphic novel. Prompt them to conduct research that focuses on how and why the person sought to serve others. Students might include primary or secondary quotations or visuals illustrating the individual's personality, goals, actions, and ideas. Encourage them to share their completed graphic biography with the class and answer questions.

See the Chapter Planner for more strategies for differentiation.

SYNTHESIZE & WRITE

ANSWERS

1. Answers will vary.

2. Answers will vary.

3. Answers will vary. Possible response: It is important to serve others because in doing so, we can use our talents to help build a stronger, better life for everyone.

4. Answers will vary. Students' paragraphs should include their topic sentence from Step 3 and provide several details from the documents to support the sentence.

CONSTRUCTED RESPONSE

Document 1: President Obama suggests that anyone—volunteers, workers, parents—can and should always help others through acts of kindness. He implies that when parents nurture their children, they may be performing the ultimate service to their community by creating a concerned and caring citizen.

Document 2: Having been a teacher, Laura Bush understands that children are influenced by what they see others do. When adults show their dedication to literacy by stressing its importance to children and reading themselves, children will embrace reading and writing, become better educated, and pass along the importance of literacy to future generations.

Document 3: David Robinson believes that teaching children to use their talents to serve others can improve life for people in unpredictable ways.

CRITICAL VIEWING Possible response: The roads are underwater and impassable, and the floodwaters could contain hazards that might damage the boat, injure people, or knock them off their feet. The water might be contaminated with waste and carry diseases.

4.1 From Computers to Social Media

Website, search engine, blog, social media, unfriend. You won't find any of these terms in a dictionary published before 1990. The explosion of new tech terms since that year reflects the tremendous speed at which the world has been changing.

MAIN IDEA The invention of the computer, the creation of the Internet, and the birth of social media led to major changes in American work and society.

DEVELOPMENT OF THE COMPUTER

Along with radio and television, the computer ranks as one of the most significant electronic inventions of the 20th century. Computers have transformed the way people learn, work, shop, interact with one another, and spend their free time.

One of the earliest general-purpose electronic digital computers was built during World War II by a team at the University of Pennsylvania. This enormous and enormously complex machine was known as ENIAC, or Electronic Numerical Integrator and Computer. It measured about 130 feet in length and used 18,000 vacuum tubes to control its electric current. Its main function was to calculate the paths that bombs would follow after they were launched.

The 1947 invention of the transistor, a little device that regulates and switches electrical current, allowed for the production of computers that were smaller, faster, more accurate, and more energy efficient. Another key development was the invention of the integrated circuit (IC), or computer chip, in the late 1950s. An IC packed numerous transistors onto a small surface.

By the late 1970s, several companies, including Apple, Inc., had begun selling computers for home use. These devices came to be known as personal computers (PCs). International Business Machines (IBM), the world's largest computer manufacturer, entered the PC market in 1981. As people learned how useful PCs could be, sales began to skyrocket and prices dropped, making the machines more affordable for the average family.

THE INTERNET AND SOCIAL MEDIA

In the late 1950s and early 1960s, some government agencies and large companies began to create networks of computers that could share information with one another. One of the first general-purpose networks was the U.S. Department of Defense's ARPANET, which was first used in 1969. Within a few years, computer engineers had worked out ways to connect networks to one another. The expanding "network of networks" came to be known as the **Internet**.

In the late 1980s and early 1990s, a British computer scientist named Tim Berners-Lee led the development of a system that allowed sites or documents to be identified by individual addresses. That made it possible to link sites to one another in the way we are used to seeing today. The result was the **World Wide Web**. Usage of the web expanded rapidly after the introduction of Mosaic, a free, user-friendly browser developed at the University of Illinois. A **browser** is a computer program that helps users navigate the Internet.

After becoming available to the general public in 1991, the Internet exploded in popularity. People eagerly took to email and online shopping. Computer programs called search engines provided easy and instant access to a world of information. The Internet's impact on society increased dramatically in the early 2000s with the birth of **social media**. This term refers to services, such as Twitter, Facebook, and Instagram, that enable people to interact on electronic devices.

Groups and individuals use social media to express their opinions as well as to share personal news. As a result, issues of privacy and free speech have arisen. Social media companies and the government are grappling with questions about what types of speech on the Internet are protected when they cause personal offense or even harm. The framers of the First Amendment could never have imagined the conflicts between allowing free speech and defending against online bullying, for example.

Like computer technology, mobile telephone technology advanced rapidly after World War II. The introduction of cell phones—handheld mobile phones that use cellular network technology—in the mid-1980s meant that people could make and receive phone calls from any location. The communication revolution took another leap forward in the early 1990s with the emergence of smartphones. These devices combine the features of a cell phone with those of a handheld computer. By 2017, more than three-quarters of Americans owned a smartphone.

Smithsonian American Art Museum, Washington, D.C.

Nam June Paik, a Korean American video artist, created the work above, titled *Electronic Superhighway*, in 1995. It consists of 336 television monitors displaying scenes from across the United States and from famous films that took place in specific states. Paik has taken the centuries-old idea of a map and presented it in a new way for an audience that lives in a tightly networked world. His creation is a virtual experience of driving across the country on its superhighways.

HISTORICAL THINKING

1. **READING CHECK** Why is the Internet described as a "network of networks"?
2. **ANALYZE CAUSE AND EFFECT** How did changes in electronic technology affect American society?
3. **FORM AND SUPPORT OPINIONS** Do you think the effects of social media on society are mostly positive or mostly negative? Support your opinion with evidence from the text and from your own experiences.

1000 CHAPTER 29

PLAN

Objective
Describe the development of computers, the Internet, and social media and their impact on American society.

Critical Thinking Skills for Lesson 4.1
- Identify Main Ideas and Details
- Monitor Comprehension
- Analyze Cause and Effect
- Form and Support Opinions
- Make Connections

Essential Question for Chapter 29
How has the United States responded to crises in the early years of the 21st century? The ways that people use technology have helped reshape human interactions in the 21st century. Lesson 4.1 examines the development of computers and the Internet and the civil liberties issues they raise.

Background for the Teacher
Science fiction sometimes offers glimpses into the future. In the 1946 short story "A Logic Named Joe," writer Will F. Jenkins foretold the modern era of personal computers and the Internet in his tale of interconnected "logics." Each logic, resembling a television with a keyboard, connects to a "tank" that stores huge amounts of data, which provides families with access to information and entertainment. All is well until a rogue machine dubbed Joe decides to provide unfettered access to all of the tank's data to anyone who asks for it. Soon—in details that reflect the modern dangers of the information age—the network is dispensing instructions on topics such as how to poison your wife, make counterfeit money, and access the private information of others.

History Notebook
Encourage students to complete the Reid on the Road video series page for Chapter 29 in their History Notebooks after they view the video.

INTRODUCE & ENGAGE

Brainstorm a List

Ask students to think about the impact of computers, smartphones, and social media on their lives. Draw a T-Chart on the board, like the one shown. Prompt students to brainstorm technologies and list them by whether they have made people's lives easier or more difficult. Then guide a discussion to elicit specific ways that technologies have impacted students' lives. Explain that in this lesson students will learn about the development of various technologies and how they have changed the ways people live and work.

Easier	More Difficult

TEACH

Guided Discussion

1. **Form and Support Opinions** Which invention—the radio, television, or computer—do you think had the biggest impact on the 20th century? *(Answers will vary. Students should provide evidence to support their claims. Possible response: Computers had the biggest impact because they fundamentally changed how people communicate, and they provide almost unlimited access to information.)*

2. **Make Connections** Why was Tim Berners-Lee's work important to the way we use computers and social media today? *(Possible response: He developed the system to identify sites by individual addresses and link them to one another. This breakthrough made it possible for people to go online and access and share information, communicate with family and friends, be entertained, shop, and work.)*

Virtual Museum Visit

In 2009, the Smithsonian American Art Museum acquired the complete archive of Nam June Paik's writings, research materials, and other creative records, making it a center for Paik scholarship. Access the museum's website and navigate to the *Electronic Superhighway: Continental U.S., Alaska, Hawaii*. Zoom in on sections of the installation and discuss Paik's use of different colored lights to remind viewers that the states have unique identities. Inform students that Paik used television and audio clips to suggest the influence of media on our perceptions of the United States. Ask them to explore other works by Paik on the site and share their impressions with the class.

Active Options

Active History: Evaluate the Impact of Technology Extend the lesson by using either the PDF or Whiteboard version of the activity. These activities take a deeper look at a topic from, or related to, the lesson. Explore the activities as a class, turn them into group assignments, or even assign them individually.

NG Learning Framework: Research Technological Innovations `STEM`

`ATTITUDE` Curiosity

`KNOWLEDGE` New Frontiers

Organize students into groups. Tell each group to research a current technical innovation that has improved electronic devices, Internet performance, or social media platforms. Encourage students to create a summary describing the innovation and to explain why it is important. Then have groups predict what future developments might occur in electronic devices, the Internet, or social media and their potential impact on people's lives. Invite groups to share their findings and predictions with the class.

DIFFERENTIATE

English Language Learners

Create a Word Web Pair students at the **Emerging** and **Expanding** levels with students at the **Bridging** level. Tell pairs to take turns reading paragraphs of the lesson, noting any terms relating to technology. After each paragraph, instruct students to write those terms on the spokes of a Word Web, adding more spokes if necessary. When pairs have finished reading, ask them to trade and compare their work with other pairs. Final Word Webs could include *electronic*, *digital*, *integrated circuit*, *computer chip*, *Internet*, *browser*, *social media*, and *smartphone*.

Gifted & Talented

Illustrate a Metaphor Remind students that a metaphor is an implied comparison between two dissimilar things. Point out that *electronic superhighway* is a metaphor that Nam June Paik interpreted with an array of monitors. Challenge students to interpret a metaphor related to technology, such as *the cloud*, *data stream*, or *data mining*, by creating art to represent it. Students may use conventional art materials or an online design program, if available. Invite them to display their art and answer their classmates' questions about it.

See the Chapter Planner for more strategies for differentiation.

HISTORICAL THINKING

ANSWERS

1. The Internet is considered a network of networks because it links multiple networks rather than just individual computers in a series.

2. Changes in electronic technology made computers smaller, faster, and more powerful and put personal computers in the hands of individuals. This changed the way people work, shop, learn, play, and communicate.

3. Answers will vary but should show strong, clear reasoning. Students who view social media as mostly positive might mention how it enables people to share their lives and ideas in real time with friends and family anywhere in the world. Students who focus on negative effects might mention issues such as cyberbullying and offensive speech.

4.2 Computer History Museum
Mountain View, California

The Computer History Museum is aptly located in California's Silicon Valley—the home of Apple, Google, and other major technology corporations. In its multimedia exhibitions, the museum tells the stories of the companies, people, and equipment that make up computer history.

Museum visitors can play computer games, experiment with coding, and view demonstrations. The museum also offers extensive online exhibits. How does the equipment shown on these pages compare with the digital devices you use in your home and classroom today?

First Mouse

In 1961, American engineer and inventor Doug Engelbart came up with a new idea for a tool to move a cursor on a computer screen. He envisioned a simple, handheld mechanical device with a pair of small wheels, one turning horizontally and one vertically when moved across a tabletop. Bill English, the lead engineer of Engelbart's research team at Stanford Research Institute, built the first prototype of a mouse, shown here, in 1964. But it wasn't until the 1980s that the mouse came into general use. Today, it's considered an essential tool for interacting with computers.

Inventor Doug Engelbart cannot recall who named the mouse. He says, "It just looked like a mouse with a tail, and we all called it that."

Apple I

Electronics engineer and Apple Computer co-founder Steve Wozniak, or "Woz," showed the first Apple I prototype to the Homebrew Computer Club in 1976. Interested members got a blank printed circuit board, some parts, and a 16-page assembly manual. Wozniak showed them how to assemble the computers and add a keyboard, display screen, and power supply. When a store in Mountain View, California, ordered 100 assembled Apple I computers, Wozniak and his friend Steve Jobs sold some personal possessions to pay for parts and began small-scale production to fill the order. The early computers were sold for $666.66—and that was the start of Apple Computer.

Research the functionality of the Apple I (shown here) and compare it to today's computers. How has computer technology evolved?

Kenbak-1

In 1986, the Computer Museum in Boston held a contest to answer the question "What was the first PC?" Judges decided that the first personal computer was the Kenbak-1, which was introduced in 1971. Working in his garage, American computer engineer John Blankenbaker designed and built the machine.

The Kenbak-1 had switches for entering input and lights to display output. Blankenbaker intended his invention to be educational, introducing the user to computer programming. But at a cost of $750 each, only 40 of the computers were sold.

The Kenbak-1 offered 256 bytes of memory—or about 1,000 words. How does that compare with the memory of today's computers?

The Lisa

Along with some huge successes, Apple has had a few failures. In 1983, the company released the Lisa, the first commercial personal computer featuring a graphic user interface. Instead of typing commands to operate the Lisa, a person used a mouse to direct a cursor and to click on windows, icons, and menus. Slow and expensive, the Lisa sold poorly. Apple introduced the less costly Lisa 2, shown here, in 1984. But it faced stiff competition from a computer called the Macintosh, also released by Apple that year.

PLAN

Objective
Identify artifacts related to the development of computers.

Critical Thinking Skills for Lesson 4.2
- Analyze Visuals
- Make Connections
- Draw Conclusions
- Make Inferences

Essential Question for Chapter 29
How has the United States responded to crises in the early years of the 21st century? With the technology boom in the 21st century, advances in computers have profoundly changed the way people learn and communicate. Lesson 4.2 presents several artifacts from the early years of computer development.

Background for the Teacher
The Computer History Museum's mission is explained by board chairman Leonard J. Shustek: "We are living through [a] time of transition, from there being no computers anywhere to there being computers in everything we touch. . . . We owe it to the future to preserve the artifacts and stories of how that happened." The museum, which started out in Boston, was primarily a place for technology insiders. Then in 1996, the growing collection of tech hardware, trinkets, and other materials moved to its new home in Mountain View and became available to the general public. Curators usually wait for a decade before deciding which items deserve a place in the exhibits, letting time indicate whether and how something new impacts computer technology.

History Notebook
Encourage students to complete the Curating History page for Chapter 29 in their History Notebooks as they read.

INTRODUCE & ENGAGE

Going Back to the Future

Discuss with students the first computer-related devices they remember using. List the devices, what they could do, and which ones are still sold. **ASK:** How do the devices you use today compare with the first ones you used? *(Answers will vary. Most students will probably be using a mobile device, notepad, or laptop computer, which will have more memory, computing power, and functions than their first devices. Students may state that today's devices are smaller, more attractively designed, and come in a variety of models.)* Then discuss with students why someone might want to keep outdated devices. Tell them that in this lesson they will learn about some of the early computer artifacts that people have preserved and the significance of each one to the development of computers.

TEACH

Guided Discussion

1. **Draw Conclusions** What does the design of each device reveal about its intended customer? *(Possible response: The Apple I's open board design seems geared toward early computer science enthusiasts or people who used computers as a hobby and had experience with electronics. The Kenbak-1, with its switches and buttons, likely targeted customers who wanted to learn programming. The Lisa, with its built-in monitor, was probably aimed at average customers and students who wanted to create art and graphics in addition to text.)*

2. **Make Inferences** Why do you think it took more than 20 years for the mouse to become a popular tool for the computer? *(Possible response: Computer design didn't develop a graphic interface with icons and menus to click until the 1980s, when a tool was needed to access these features.)*

Curating History

The Computer History Museum website offers several resources for learning more about how the modern computer and its accessories developed, about the people involved in computer history, and about how students can participate in online events and workshops. Help students locate the artifacts shown in this lesson and encourage them to explore the museum's web pages on their own. Then ask them to work in pairs or in small groups to locate other objects that relate to the history of computers. Invite them to select one or two objects that particularly interest them and do further research. Tell students to summarize their findings for the class or create a museum web page of their own to display the items and describe their importance to the development of modern computers.

Active Option

On Your Feet: Sort the Artifacts Have students work in teams of four or five to examine the museum's online collections and complete two Concept Clusters like those shown. In one cluster, students should identify various types of artifacts related to the development of computer monitors. In the other, students should identify artifacts in a different class or genre determined by the team. When teams are finished, have them share their Concept Clusters with the class.

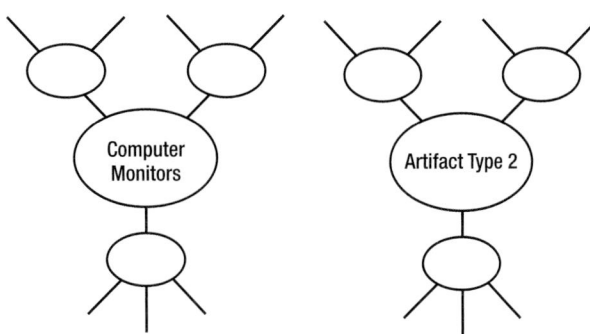

DIFFERENTIATE

Inclusion

Work in Pairs Allow students with disabilities to work with a partner who can read the lesson aloud to them and describe the visuals as well. Have pairs work together to answer the questions about the Apple I and Kenbak-1. Give students the option of recording their answers rather than writing them.

Pre-AP

Extend Knowledge Challenge students to conduct online research to learn more about the Computer History Museum, including the people behind the museum and how and why it came about. Tell students to organize their findings in a 5Ws Chart and use their notes to write a report. Invite volunteers to present their reports to the class.

See the Chapter Planner for more strategies for differentiation.

CURATING HISTORY

Answers will vary. Students should include such differences as size, shape, presence of a monitor or screen, versatility, number of apps and functions, computing power, memory storage, ease of use, processing speed, voice commands, and interconnections with other devices and the Internet.

APPLE I

Answers will vary. Possible response: Computer technology has evolved far past the Apple I. Hobbyists assembled and tinkered with this early model in addition to playing games and developing programs. It was a stand-alone machine with nowhere near the capabilities and computing power of present-day networked computers. Innovations and advances in computer chips, RAM development, batteries, screens, apps and other functions, and software have enabled computers to become small and powerful.

KENBAK-1

Answers will vary. Students may know that today's computers can store huge amounts of information in megabytes, gigabytes, and even terabytes. If the Kenbak-1 could store 1,000 words, modern computers and smartphones can store the equivalent of millions of words, plus graphics, videos, games, movies, and more.

4.3 Challenges of Globalization

Despite its massive continents, vast oceans, and billions of people, our planet sometimes feels like a small world. Rapid shipping and instant communication make distant countries seem like they're just next door. But is this always a good thing?

MAIN IDEA Globalization has brought profound changes and ignited fierce debate about its pros and cons for the United States.

THE IMPACT OF GLOBALIZATION

One of the most powerful forces affecting the United States in the 21st century is **globalization**. This term refers to the fast and free flow of people, resources, goods, services, information, technology, and ideas across national borders.

Globalization is not a new trend. It was at work in the 15th century when the urge to colonize and explore swept Europe. But the pace of globalization has greatly increased in recent decades, due to several factors. One is the revolution in communication. Computers, the Internet, and cell phones make it far easier for people around the world to share information rapidly.

Another factor is the revolution in transportation. Transportation technology has advanced quickly since the mid-20th century, transforming the movement of people and goods around the world. High-speed rail lines now crisscross Japan, China, and Western Europe. Between 1970 and 2015, annual global air travel grew from 310 million passengers to 3.44 billion. With advances in shipping technology, goods, too, travel more cheaply, efficiently, and in higher volumes. Huge container ships and barges have increased the oceangoing commercial traffic.

A third factor is the growth of **free trade**, or the reduction or elimination of trade barriers, such as tariffs. This expansion has occurred through the creation of free trade zones such as the **European Union**, which facilitates trade among European member nations, and the North American Free Trade Agreement (NAFTA) zone that spans Mexico, Canada, and the United States. The **World Trade Organization** has also worked toward freer trade among its member countries, which account for roughly 90 percent of all world trade.

Most economists agree that free trade's benefits outweigh its drawbacks. NAFTA, for example, has increased trade between the United States and Mexico, enabling Americans to buy inexpensive goods and American businesses to invest in Mexican businesses. But not all Americans have benefited. Under NAFTA, some manufacturing jobs have moved from the United States and Canada to Mexico, where labor costs are lower.

The most challenging aspect of globalization, however, may be that it has enabled groups like al Qaeda to spread terrorism on a larger scale. As a result, the pursuit of terrorists has also become global. For example, during President Obama's administration, the search continued for Osama bin Laden, who planned the 9/11 terrorist bombings. In 2011, the U.S. military found the al Qaeda leader in Pakistan and killed him.

THE IMMIGRATION DEBATE

Migration and immigration are important aspects of globalization. Migration is the movement of people from one place to another. Immigration is the movement of people from one country to another. As you know, push-pull factors drive such movement. Push factors such as war, persecution, unstable governments, natural disasters, lack of jobs, and poverty cause people to leave their homes. Pull factors, which attract people to a country, include plentiful jobs, a good education, freedom, and the chance to build a better life.

In recent decades, immigration has again become the subject of heated debate in the United States. The number of unauthorized immigrants entering the country rose sharply toward the end of the 20th century. Many came from Mexico and Central America, including children sent by their parents to escape dangerous conditions in their homelands.

Critics argued that these immigrants took jobs away from Americans, increased crime rates, and burdened social services. Some studies suggest that these arguments have little basis in fact. Immigrants are often employed in low-paying service jobs and farm work, which are jobs that employers have trouble filling. Nevertheless, some people called for greater border security and government efforts to deport unauthorized immigrants. On the other hand, some Americans advocated offering these immigrants a legal path to earning citizenship.

During the 2010s, immigration growth leveled off. According to 2013 figures, of about 41 million immigrants living in the United States, 24.2 million were employed. Thirty percent of those people worked in management, professional, and related occupations, while the remaining 70 percent worked in service jobs, sales, office support, production, transportation, outdoor jobs, and maintenance. In 2012, unauthorized immigrants in the United States were estimated to be about 11.4 million, a small drop from the previous year.

Throughout the 2010s, the intense debates over immigration continued, and no single response was supported by a majority of people. In 2016, one candidate mobilized voters over concerns about unauthorized immigrants and won the Republican presidential nomination.

HISTORICAL THINKING

1. **READING CHECK** What are three main causes of the acceleration of globalization?

2. **MAKE PREDICTIONS** Do you think the trend toward globalization will continue? Support your prediction with facts from the text and your own knowledge or experience.

3. **MAKE CONNECTIONS** Immigration from Mexico dropped during the Great Recession. What do you think explains this drop?

CRITICAL VIEWING National Geographic photographer Kirsten Luce framed the moment a group of women and children from Central America were apprehended just after crossing the Rio Grande into Texas. Each year, thousands of women and children ask for entry to the United States. What do the details in this photo suggest about their journey?

PLAN

Objective

Evaluate the impact of globalization and immigration issues on American society.

Critical Thinking Skills for Lesson 4.3

- Identify Main Ideas and Details
- Monitor Comprehension
- Make Predictions
- Make Connections
- Draw Conclusions

Essential Question for Chapter 29

How has the United States responded to crises in the early years of the 21st century? In the 21st century, globalization has profoundly impacted the United States. Lesson 4.3 examines issues of globalization, free trade, and immigration.

NATIONAL GEOGRAPHIC PHOTOGRAPHER
Kirsten Luce

National Geographic photographer Kirsten Luce has spent years documenting life on both sides of the U.S.-Mexico border, beginning as a staff photographer for the *Monitor*, a local newspaper in the border town of McAllen, Texas. Through her photography, Luce hopes "to contribute to a dialogue on the current immigration system." By maintaining a good relationship with law enforcement agencies along the border, she has been able to document illegal crossings and photograph stash houses where smugglers keep immigrants before they bring them into the United States. Luce took the photograph in this lesson in 2014 while working closely with local law enforcement. She notes that in one night, they intercepted three groups of women and children crossing the border.

List Pros and Cons

Write *Globalization*, *Free Trade*, and *Immigration* on the board, and ask students to define the terms in their own words. Provide clarification if necessary. Invite students to call out positive and negative words or phrases associated with the three topics. List their responses under the headings Pros and Cons for each topic. After students have finished reading the lesson, revisit the lists, and ask them if they would revise any of their original pros and cons.

TEACH

Guided Discussion

1. **Make Connections** Based on information in the lesson, what connection might globalization have to your life? *(Answers will vary. Students might discuss foreign-made goods they buy, jobs in their communities that were shipped overseas, or major items, such as electronics and appliances, that are cheaper because they are made overseas.)*

2. **Draw Conclusions** What do some studies show is the impact of unauthorized immigrants on the U.S. job market? *(Possible response: People claim unauthorized immigrants compete with Americans for jobs. However, studies show they often fill low-paying, less desirable jobs in the service or farming industry that most Americans don't want. Thus, they seem to provide needed services without competing with most Americans.)*

More Information

Free Trade Agreements Explain that free trade agreements are a controversial issue in U.S. politics, particularly for voters in communities where manufacturing jobs have been shifted to foreign locations. These voters see ending free trade agreements as keeping more jobs at home. However, the issue is far more complicated than that. Many economists argue that ending free trade agreements would have an overall negative impact on consumers, businesses, and the economy. For example, consumers would likely see an increase in the cost of imported goods or U.S.-made goods that rely on the global supply chain. This would mean that families would need to spend a greater portion of their incomes on essential items such as food, housing, automobiles, and clothing. At the same time, farmers and businesses that export goods would see their profits decline as tariffs increased or markets shrank. **ASK:** How do you think the government should respond when economic policies harm some Americans while helping others? *(Answers will vary. Possible response: The government should set policies that benefit the most people while providing assistance for those who are negatively affected.)*

Active Options

On Your Feet: Fishbowl Arrange students in an inner and outer circle, both facing the center. Ask students in the inner circle to discuss the following question: How has globalization impacted the United States? Have the students in the outer circle write notes on the discussion. Then tell students to switch places, and ask students in the inner circle to discuss the following question: How can globalization be used positively and negatively in the world? Afterward, have the class summarize their main conclusions.

NG Learning Framework: Graph the Immigrant Population

SKILL Communication

KNOWLEDGE Our Human Story

Tell students to work in groups to create a statistical portrait of the immigrant population in the United States. Encourage them to collect statistical data related to such things as the size of the authorized and unauthorized immigrant populations, countries or regions of origin, education and income levels, languages spoken, and length of time in the United States. Tell groups to create graphs and charts to display their data. Use the completed graphs and charts to hold a class discussion on the impact of immigration on American society.

Striving Readers

Complete a T-Chart Instruct students to create a T-Chart to better understand why some people leave their home countries. They should label the first column Push Factors and the second column Pull Factors and then jot down the factors as they read the lesson. After they finish reading, students may add other push and pull factors they know. Encourage them to compare their completed charts.

Pre-AP

Investigate Paths for Permanent Residency Direct students to research the different paths that immigrants can take to become permanent residents of the United States. Invite them to give a presentation on the challenges and benefits of each path, including how many years each path takes and what costs may be involved in the process.

See the Chapter Planner for more strategies for differentiation.

HISTORICAL THINKING

ANSWERS

1. The revolution in communication, the ease of transportation, and the growth of free trade have accelerated globalization.

2. Answers will vary. Possible responses: Yes. I think the trend will continue because of advances in transportation and communication. Also, globalization bolsters free trade, which is now central to the economy. No. I think globalization will not continue, because it harms a nation's industries and makes it harder for the nation's citizens to find jobs.

3. Possible response: Plentiful jobs are a major pull factor for immigration. During the recession, fewer jobs were available in the United States, thereby slowing immigration.

CRITICAL VIEWING Possible response: The presence of children, the lack of belongings and provisions, and the fact that the people are traveling at night indicate that they are desperate, likely left their homes hurriedly and without preparation, and are using darkness to hide from authorities.

4.4 The Election of 2016

Two historic candidates ran for president in 2016. One had no political experience and had never run for any elected office. The other was a woman. The election and its outcome exposed a severely divided nation.

MAIN IDEA Presidential candidate Donald Trump's campaign promise to "Make America Great Again" attracted enough voters to secure him the electoral vote and the presidency.

A POPULIST PREVAILS

Recall that a populist is someone who claims to represent the concerns of ordinary people. You have read about such populists as William Jennings Bryan and H. Ross Perot, who both staged unsuccessful presidential campaigns. **Donald Trump**, the controversial Republican candidate, ran a populist campaign in which he promised to use his business expertise to solve the nation's problems. But unlike previous populists, he won the 2016 presidential election, defeating Democrat Hillary Clinton.

Clinton was a former U.S. senator from New York who had also served as President Obama's secretary of state. She was the wife of former president Bill Clinton. Trump was a wealthy real estate developer and host of a popular television reality show. He had no political experience but had long been extremely outspoken in his views. As his running mate, Trump chose **Mike Pence**, the conservative governor of Indiana. Clinton's running mate was Tim Kaine, a senator from Virginia.

Trump's populist campaign rallies won the support of traditional Republicans and a number of independent voters. His ultra-nationalistic message, which strongly emphasized the superiority of the United States over all other nations, included promises to build a wall along the entire length of the border with Mexico, deport

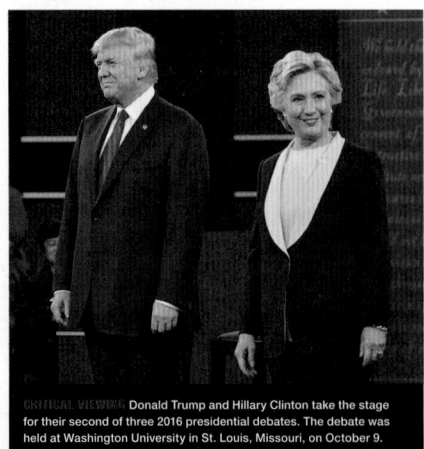

CRITICAL VIEWING Donald Trump and Hillary Clinton take the stage for their second of three 2016 presidential debates. The debate was held at Washington University in St. Louis, Missouri, on October 9. The backdrop shows part of the Declaration of Independence. What do the candidates' expressions and body language convey in this photo?

undocumented immigrants, and ban foreign Muslims from entering the United States. He pledged to repeal the Affordable Care Act, put an end to NAFTA, and withdraw from a nuclear treaty with Iran. Trump also promised a swift end to international terrorism.

In the election, Trump won a narrow majority of voters in a number of **swing states**, or states where the election might go to either party. In the end, even though 3 million more Americans cast their votes for Clinton, Trump won the electoral vote 306 to 232.

In 2017, the March for Science took place on Earth Day, April 22, in cities throughout the United States. The march was organized in response to President Trump's promise that the United States would withdraw from international climate accords. In this photo, **Bill Nye**, the host of a children's television show about science, leads marchers.

THE EARLY TRUMP PRESIDENCY

Trump began his presidency by issuing a number of executive orders, including a controversial directive banning people from seven specified, primarily Muslim, nations from entering the United States. The order was issued and began to be enforced as many travelers were already on their way to the United States, causing massive confusion at airports. Federal courts initially blocked this order, stating it was unconstitutional. Parts of the ban were reinstated, and the government issued new versions of the ban in 2017. These were contested in federal courts.

Building on his campaign promises, Trump ordered the construction of a border wall with Mexico. But Congress approved only a small fraction of the funds needed. He also ordered a sharp increase in the number of **Immigration and Customs Enforcement (ICE)** agents, thus raising the deportation rate of undocumented immigrants. As of September 2017, his promised repeal of the Affordable Care Act had failed in Congress.

On the international front, Trump ended the **Trans-Pacific Partnership (TPP)**, a trade agreement

with Asia. Although Trump had threatened to leave NAFTA, he decided it was better to try renegotiating it. Perhaps his most controversial claim was that he would withdraw the United States from international agreements on climate. This, along with his pledge to promote the use of coal and other fossil fuels, as opposed to the Obama administration's support of increased wind and solar power, put the United States at odds with many of its allies. Trump argued that NAFTA and climate accords cost U.S. jobs, but many experts believed that these agreements actually created new employment.

HISTORICAL THINKING

1. **READING CHECK** What role did swing states play in the election of 2016?

2. **MAKE INFERENCES** Why do you think Donald Trump appealed to so many independent voters?

3. **SUMMARIZE** How would you summarize Trump's presidency through the first part of 2017?

Objective

Assess the central issues in the 2016 election and Donald Trump's first year in office.

Critical Thinking Skills for Lesson 4.4

- Identify Main Ideas and Details
- Monitor Comprehension
- Make Inferences
- Summarize
- Draw Conclusions
- Make Connections

Essential Question for Chapter 29

How has the United States responded to crises in the early years of the 21st century? The 2016 election revealed deep divides among U.S. voters. Lesson 4.4 examines Donald Trump's populist message as a presidential candidate and his first year as the 45th president of the United States.

Background for the Teacher

Thousands of scientists, students, educators, and concerned citizens attended the 2017 March for Science in Washington, D.C. In some 600 other cities in the United States and around the world, thousands more gathered in support of science. Scientists are generally reluctant to express political opinions. However, faced with the Trump administration rejecting climate science, promising to roll back environmental regulations, and threatening to slash funding for scientific research and government agencies like the National Institutes of Health, many felt it was time to take a public stand. Organizers of the march challenged attendees to keep up the momentum by contacting their elected officials and contributing to citizen science projects in the week following the event.

History Notebook

Encourage students to complete the Election 2016 and the Reid on the Road video series pages for Chapter 29 in their History Notebooks.

Discuss Divisions Among Voters

Guide a discussion about the kinds of issues that might divide voters in a presidential election. **ASK:** If voters are unhappy with the direction they see the country heading, why might they be drawn to a candidate with no political experience? *(Answers will vary. Possible response: They might believe that such a candidate will offer better solutions than just politics as usual.)* Tell students that in this lesson they will learn about the factors that contributed to the outcome of the 2016 presidential election.

TEACH

Guided Discussion

1. **Draw Conclusions** Why can the 2016 presidential election be viewed as historic? *(Possible response: The election pitted the first female nominee from a major party against a businessman and reality TV star with no political experience, who ran a populist campaign and promised major policy changes. In the end, Donald Trump became the first modern populist to win the presidency, even though he lost the popular vote by 3 million.)*

2. **Make Connections** How might Donald Trump's promise to withdraw the United States from the international climate accords be related to his support for coal and fossil fuels? *(Possible response: Coal and fossil fuels are considered contributors to climate change. Consequently, supporting increased use of either would be inconsistent with supporting the international climate accords.)*

More Information

The Rural-Urban Split The 2016 presidential election reaffirmed that the United States is severely divided not only by race, gender, and education but also by geography. Hillary Clinton bested Trump in urban areas, while Trump swept the rural ones. Researchers who examine the growing divide between rural and urban Americans note distrust on both sides. Rural residents often view city dwellers as either professional elites or as undeserving poor. City dwellers, on the other hand, often characterize rural inhabitants as less educated and behind the times. Economics widens the gulf. The very things that fuel the urban areas—immigration, globalization, and foreign trade—worry voters in rural areas, who often feel ignored in the modern economy. **ASK:** How might a rural-urban split help a candidate win an electoral victory even if the candidate loses the nationwide popular vote? *(Possible response: By winning the rural vote in more states overall, a candidate would gain more electoral votes. The other candidate could win in more states with a larger urban population, such as California or New York, and gain more popular votes but fail to win enough electoral college votes.)*

Active Options

On Your Feet: Hold a Roundtable Discussion Arrange students in groups of four. Ask them to discuss the following questions: In what ways did Donald Trump's campaign and early presidency promise a new direction for the country? Why might this have proved divisive to the nation? Instruct roundtable groups to discuss the answers among themselves and then share their ideas with the class.

NG Learning Framework: Grade Donald Trump's First Year in Office

SKILL Observation

KNOWLEDGE Our Human Story

As a class, brainstorm a list of indicators of a successful presidency, such as delivering on campaign promises, pleasing supporters, uniting the nation, pushing meaningful legislation through Congress, and making the country safer. Then have students work in groups to research Donald Trump's first year in office. In their research, have them examine how well Trump performed in each of the listed indicators. Ask groups to assign a letter grade for each and to explain their reasoning. Finally, have groups share their grades and discuss similarities and differences in their points of view.

Inclusion

Identify New Words Pair special needs students with students at a higher proficiency level. Have them reread the lesson. Then ask students to identify three words from the lesson that were unfamiliar to them before they read the lesson. Prompt them to use a Two-Column Chart to record each word and its meaning.

Gifted & Talented

Debate Science Activism Direct students' attention to the photograph of and caption about the March for Science on April 22, 2017. Invite them to conduct online research to find out why scientists attended or stayed away from the march. Then ask students to stage a debate about whether scientists should or should not engage in public activism. What might be the impact on people's view of scientists and science in general? Encourage students to quote primary sources and specific examples in their debate. Have the class vote on which side presented the stronger argument.

See the Chapter Planner for more strategies for differentiation.

HISTORICAL THINKING

ANSWERS

1. A narrow majority of voters in a number of swing states cast votes for Trump, securing the electoral victory for him.

2. Possible response: Independents do not vote along party lines. Thus, they may have voted for Trump because he was an outsider and expressed their frustration over specific issues, such as immigration, trade, and the war on terror.

3. Trump failed to push through the repeal of the Affordable Care Act and received little funding for his border wall. But he did issue many executive orders, including a travel ban on several countries, an increase in the number of ICE agents, withdrawal from the Trans-Pacific Partnership and the international climate accords, and a renegotiation of NAFTA.

CRITICAL VIEWING The candidates are smiling pleasantly at the audience and appear comfortable being on a stage. They appear uncomfortable with each other, as indicated by their stiff stances with faces turned away from each other.

4.5 Climate Change and Energy Choices

For decades, scientists made predictions about the effects of rising global temperatures. Many of these predictions are now coming true. Climate change is a reality, and it is having a major impact on our planet.

MAIN IDEA Two of the biggest issues facing the United States in the 21st century are how to address climate change and how to achieve greater energy independence.

WARMING TEMPERATURES

In the 19th century, scientists began to study what we now call the **greenhouse effect**. It works like this: Carbon dioxide, methane, ozone, and other greenhouse gases in Earth's atmosphere allow sunlight to pass through, but they trap heat radiated back from Earth's surface. This trapping warms the lower atmosphere. Scientists established that burning carbon-based fossil fuels, such as coal, oil, and natural gas, intensifies the greenhouse effect.

Scientific monitoring that began in the mid-20th century shows that the concentration of carbon dioxide in the atmosphere has increased dramatically. Ocean and air temperatures are rising. The vast ice sheets that cover Antarctica and Greenland are shrinking, and the sea ice in the Arctic Ocean is melting, causing sea levels to rise.

The great majority of climate scientists agree that human activity is driving **climate change**. Some in the minority argue that this warming is part of a natural cycle and is not caused by humans. Others have expressed doubt as to whether warming is occurring at all.

In 1988, as concern about global warming grew, the United Nations and the World Meteorological Organization created the **Intergovernmental Panel on Climate Change (IPCC)**. The panel's mission was to assess and report on climate science findings to help world leaders set climate policies.

Muir Glacier, 1980

Muir Glacier, 2003

These photos show the melting of Muir Glacier in Alaska over the course of two decades. Because of climate change, the glacier has retreated more than a mile, revealing the once hidden mountaintop behind it.

In California, the Sacramento Municipal Utility District deactivated the poorly performing Rancho Seco nuclear power plant (shown in the background) in 1989. In its place, the district built a solar power facility that delivers clean energy to several buildings in downtown Sacramento.

In 2015, President Obama and the U.S. Environmental Protection Agency unveiled the **Clean Power Plan**. It established nationwide standards aimed at greatly reducing carbon dioxide emissions from power plants. The following year, the United States joined nearly 200 other countries in signing an ambitious climate treaty called the Paris Agreement. In doing so, the United States committed itself to substantially reducing greenhouse gas emissions. In 2017, however, President Trump stated his intention to pull the United States out of the Paris Agreement. Even so, many American companies, states, and cities claimed that they would continue to pursue the goal of reducing harmful emissions.

ENERGY CHOICES FOR THE FUTURE

How will the United States meet its huge energy demands in the future? This question has been hotly debated as worries about climate change and U.S. dependence on oil from foreign countries have grown. In recent decades, use of **alternative energy** sources such as solar and wind power has grown significantly. Nevertheless, the country is still primarily powered by oil, coal, and natural gas.

A controversial technology called hydraulic fracturing, or fracking, has greatly increased U.S. natural gas output since the late 1990s. It uses tremendous amounts of water, can contaminate groundwater with toxic chemicals, and can cause earthquakes. Nuclear energy is controversial, too, because accidents and natural disasters can lead to the release of harmful radiation.

Improving energy efficiency is another strategy for reducing energy dependence and combating climate change. Energy-efficient cars, buildings, and factories help reduce the amount of carbon dioxide released into the atmosphere.

Climate change poses one of the greatest threats humanity has ever faced. As evidence and awareness of the danger has increased, governments and private companies have stepped up their efforts to solve the problem. The eventual solution may come through cooperation not only among businesses and governments, but also among individual citizens.

HISTORICAL THINKING

1. **READING CHECK** What is the connection between fossil fuels and climate change?

2. **ANALYZE LANGUAGE USE** Why are greenhouse gases called by that name?

3. **MAKE INFERENCES** Why are rising sea levels a cause for concern?

Objective

Examine the challenges of climate change and adopting alternative energy sources.

Critical Thinking Skills for Lesson 4.5

- Identify Main Ideas and Details
- Monitor Comprehension
- Analyze Language Use
- Make Inferences
- Draw Conclusions
- Integrate Visuals

Essential Question for Chapter 29

How has the United States responded to crises in the early years of the 21st century? Climate change is a global problem that will affect every nation. Lesson 4.5 examines the scientific evidence and U.S. response regarding this crisis.

Background for the Teacher

While small mountain glaciers like Muir are melting at the fastest rate, the large glaciers in Greenland and Antarctica pose the biggest threats to rising sea levels. If the vast ice sheets in Greenland continue to melt, they have the potential to raise sea levels by 20 feet—submerging many islands and coastal regions around the world. Scientists are closely monitoring Greenland's glaciers, aided by satellite imagery and on-the-ground observations. They have learned that multiple factors, many related to climate change, are contributing to the island's loss of ice. For example, warming ocean waters melt Greenland's glaciers from the bottom. On top of its ice sheets, warmer air temperatures are allowing algae and microbes to grow, while winds deposit ash and soot carried from the world's wildfires and factories. As the surface of the ice becomes darker, it absorbs more of the sun's energy, which speeds up the rate of melting. The loss of ice from both the top and bottom worries many scientists.

K-W-L Chart

In the first column of a K-W-L Chart, tell students to write what they know or have heard about climate change. Brainstorm with them what they would like to know about the topic, such as how much of a problem it is, what can be done about it, and so on. Guide them to write their questions in the second column. After students finish the lesson, ask them to write what they have learned in the last column. Discuss with students whether their understanding or opinion about the topic has changed.

K What Do I Know?	W What Do I Want To Learn?	L What Did I Learn?

TEACH

Guided Discussion

1. **Draw Conclusions** How do President Trump's views about the Paris climate agreement compare with those of other world leaders? *(Possible response: Given that almost 200 nations signed the agreement, it appears that Trump disagrees with the views of most world leaders.)*

2. **Make Inferences** Why might the eventual solution to climate change require cooperation among businesses, governments, and citizens? *(Possible response: Reversing climate change will require businesses to invest in alternative energy sources that do not produce greenhouse gases, require governments to work together to pass and enforce regulations that reduce carbon emissions, and require citizens to purchase and use energy-efficient products.)*

Integrate Visuals

Point out the photographs of Muir Glacier in Alaska and discuss the differences between them. **ASK:** What do scientists think is causing the ice to melt? *(The increased concentration of carbon dioxide in the air has led to rising air and water temperatures.)* Direct students' attention to the dates on the photographs. **ASK:** If the current rate of melting continues, what is likely to happen in another two decades? *(Possible response: The glacier is likely to disappear altogether.)*

Active Options

On Your Feet: Word Chain Write these terms on separate pieces of paper: *greenhouse gases, climate change, alternative energy*. Arrange students in three lines. Hand a term to the first person in each line. Instruct that student to add a word or term that relates to the original term, based on information from the lesson. Tell students to pass the paper from person to person in line, each one adding a term associated with the previous one. Ask a volunteer from each line to read the word chain. Direct the rest of the class to listen for terms used in more than one chain or those that may not connect with the original term.

NG Learning Framework: Evaluate Arguments   STEM

SKILL Communication

KNOWLEDGE Our Living Planet

Instruct students to work in groups to find articles that present various views on climate change, such as if climate change can be reversed. Have each group select one article to evaluate for accuracy and objectivity. Encourage groups to consider the following questions: Is the article based on up-to-date information? Are the explanations and arguments supported by factual evidence? Can the assertions be verified in other reputable sources? Are opinions clearly stated as opinions and not facts? Have groups share their evaluations with the class, discuss which views best fit the evidence, and identify questions that might remain unanswered.

English Language Learners ELD

Read in Pairs Pair students at the **Emerging** or **Expanding** level with native English speakers and have them read the lesson together. Instruct native speakers to point out context clues to help their partners understand the meanings of unfamiliar terms and simplify sentence construction that may be confusing. Encourage students at the **Emerging** or **Expanding** level to restate the main idea of various paragraphs in their own words.

Gifted & Talented

Explain Paired Photographs Challenge students to conduct online research to find pairs of photographs of glaciers similar to the ones of Muir Glacier in this lesson. You may suggest resources such as the NASA Images of Change gallery or the Repeat Photography Project of the U.S. Geological Survey. Instruct students to choose one pair of photographs to research in detail in order to explain to the class what changes over time are illustrated, how those changes impact plant and animal life, and whether the changes are likely due to climate change. Invite students to present the photographs and information about them to the class.

See the Chapter Planner for more strategies for differentiation.

ANSWERS

1. Burning fossil fuels releases carbon dioxide, a greenhouse gas. Carbon dioxide traps solar heat that radiates back from Earth's surface. As carbon dioxide levels build up, the greenhouse effect causes the atmosphere to trap more heat, making Earth warmer.

2. Possible response: Students may know or can look up the fact that greenhouses trap heat inside their structures, just as certain gases trap heat inside Earth's atmosphere.

3. Possible response: Many coastal areas and islands in the world could become flooded or submerged, threatening the lives and homes of millions of people.

29 REVIEW

VOCABULARY

Use each of the following vocabulary words in a sentence that shows an understanding of its meaning.

1. centrist

   President Bill Clinton ran as a centrist who adopted both liberal and conservative ideas.

2. government shutdown

3. neoconservative

4. first responder

5. insurgent

6. economic stimulus

7. free trade

8. globalization

9. Internet

10. alternative energy

READING STRATEGY
FORM AND SUPPORT OPINIONS

If you haven't already done so, complete your graphic organizer by writing an opinion and listing your reasons. Then answer the question.

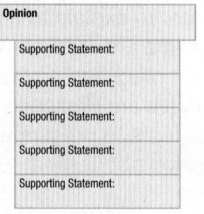

Opinion
Supporting Statement:
Supporting Statement:
Supporting Statement:
Supporting Statement:
Supporting Statement:

11. What is the greatest challenge the United States has faced during the period from 1992 to the present? Summarize your reasons.

MAIN IDEAS

Answer the following questions. Support your answers with evidence from the chapter.

12. What was one major challenge facing President Bill Clinton during his first term, and how did he confront that challenge? **LESSON 1.1**

13. How did President Clinton's responses to the government shutdown and the crisis in Kosovo affect his reputation and popularity? **LESSON 1.2**

14. What events led to the U.S. Supreme Court deciding the 2000 presidential election? **LESSON 1.3**

15. How did President George W. Bush respond to the September 11 terrorist attacks? **LESSON 2.1**

16. What was the outcome of the 2008 presidential election, and why was it historic? **LESSON 3.1**

17. What action did President Obama and Congress take to try to end the recession shortly after Obama took office? **LESSON 3.2**

18. What key developments in the 1940s and 1950s led to computers that were much smaller, faster, and more accurate than ENIAC? **LESSON 4.1**

19. How have advances in technology contributed to globalization? **LESSON 4.3**

20. What changes in the late 20th and early 21st centuries increased the controversy about immigration to the United States? **LESSON 4.3**

21. What changes did Donald Trump promise to make to U.S. policies? **LESSON 4.4**

22. What is the Paris Agreement, and why is it important? **LESSON 4.5**

HISTORICAL THINKING

Answer the following questions. Support your answers with evidence from the chapter.

23. **IDENTIFY PROBLEMS AND SOLUTIONS** Choose one major problem a president has faced in the 21st century. What solutions did the president attempt, and how successful were they?

24. **COMPARE AND CONTRAST** In what ways are the Clinton and Bush tax policies—and their results—similar and different?

25. **DRAW CONCLUSIONS** What are some ways in which globalization has brought about changes to the United States?

26. **FORM AND SUPPORT OPINIONS** Do you think the United States should be taking stronger action to promote the use of renewable energy? Why or why not?

INTERPRET VISUALS

Study the graph below, which shows how the percentage of people without health insurance in the United States changed between 1990 and 2015. Then answer the questions that follow.

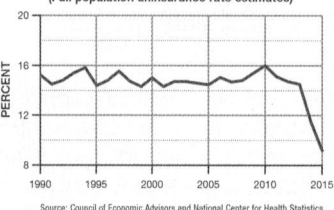

Health Insurance in the United States
(Full population uninsurance rate estimates)

Source: Council of Economic Advisors and National Center for Health Statistics

27. According to the graph, approximately what percentage of people in the United States did not have health insurance in 2010?

28. How did the percentage of uninsured people change after 2010, the year that the Affordable Care Act became law?

ANALYZE SOURCES

Barack Obama delivered his farewell speech as president on January 10, 2017. While handing the nation's leadership over to Donald Trump, Obama summed up the American identity in these words.

For 240 years, our nation's call to citizenship has given work and purpose to each new generation. It's what led patriots to choose republic over tyranny, pioneers to trek west, slaves to brave that makeshift railroad to freedom. It's what pulled immigrants and refugees across oceans and the Rio Grande. It's what pushed women to reach for the ballot. It's what powered workers to organize. It's why GIs gave their lives at Omaha Beach and Iwo Jima; Iraq and Afghanistan—and why men and women from Selma to Stonewall were prepared to give theirs as well. So that's what we mean when we say America is exceptional. Not that our nation has been flawless from the start, but that we have shown the capacity to change, and make life better for those who follow.

29. According to President Obama, what qualities make the United States exceptional?

CONNECT TO YOUR LIFE

30. **EXPOSITORY** Review what you learned about the 21st century in this chapter. Think about how you would define the American identity today. Write a paragraph connecting what you have learned to your own experiences.

TIPS

• Review the chapter and make notes about how American society has changed in the 21st century as a result of globalization, technology, and other forces.

• Use textual evidence and two or three vocabulary words from the chapter in your paragraph.

• Conclude the paragraph with a summary of your definition of the American identity.

VOCABULARY ANSWERS

1. President Bill Clinton ran as a centrist who adopted both liberal and conservative ideas.

2. The president and Congress agreed on a budget and avoided a government shutdown.

3. The new conservatives, or neoconservatives, urged more assertive military actions around the world.

4. First responders quickly help people during a disaster or attack.

5. American troops in Iraq faced insurgents who rebelled against the invasion of their country.

6. An economic stimulus can help get the economy growing.

7. Free trade takes place when trading partners drop barriers, such as tariffs.

8. Globalization allows people, goods, services, information, technology, and ideas to flow freely across national borders.

9. The Internet connects computers together in a vast network.

10. Solar power is a form of alternative energy.

READING STRATEGY ANSWER

Opinion
Terrorism is the greatest challenge facing the United States.
Supporting Statement: The underground garage of the World Trade Center was car-bombed in 1993.
Supporting Statement: The Alfred P. Murrah Federal Building in Oklahoma City was car-bombed in 1995.
Supporting Statement: Al Qaeda attacked the World Trade Center and the Pentagon in 2001.
Supporting Statement: The U.S. response to 9/11 led to war in Afghanistan.
Supporting Statement: The U.S. response to 9/11 contributed to the invasion of Iraq.

11. Possible response: The United States has experienced several terrorist attacks, including the 1993 attack on the World Trade Center, the 1995 bombing of the Alfred P. Murrah Federal Building, and the attacks of September 11, 2001. The United States has tried to prevent future attacks while fighting wars in Afghanistan and in Iraq.

MAIN IDEAS ANSWERS

12. Health care reform was a major domestic issue facing Clinton in the early years of his presidency. He appointed his wife, Hillary, to lead a health care reform group and worked to present a bill to Congress for universal health care, but his proposal failed to pass.

13. Clinton's responses to the government shutdown and to the crisis in Kosovo improved both his reputation and his popularity. Voters saw him as willing to compromise, while the Republicans seemed to rigidly support only their own measures. Clinton's military action in Kosovo reversed his reputation as being indecisive in foreign affairs because it ended the violence and mass killing in that region.

14. The election hinged on the results from Florida, but the vote count in the state was so close that it triggered an automatic recount, which showed Bush as the winner. Ballot problems caused the Gore campaign to ask for a further recount, but the Bush campaign appealed to the Supreme Court to block it. When the Supreme Court agreed, Bush's victory was upheld.

15. President Bush responded to the September 11 attacks by sending forces to Afghanistan, the country that harbored bin Laden and al Qaeda; pushing through passage of the Patriot Act; establishing the Department of Homeland Security; and initiating a war with Iraq, which he mistakenly believed had ties to al Qaeda and possessed weapons of mass destruction.

16. Barack Obama defeated John McCain. This outcome was historic because it was the first time in U.S. history that an African American had been elected president.

17. Congress passed the American Recovery and Reinvestment Act, and Obama signed it into law.

18. The invention of the transistor and the integrated circuit, or computer chip, decreased the size of computers and improved their performance.

19. Computers, cell phones, and the Internet have made it easier to communicate globally. Advances in transportation technology, such as high-speed rail lines, and advances in shipping technology have made it easier to move people and goods.

20. An increase in unauthorized immigrants from Central America and Mexico occurred toward the end of the 20th century. Critics argued that the people coming in were taking jobs away from American workers at a time when many manufacturing jobs were leaving the country because of NAFTA.

21. Donald Trump promised to use his business expertise to solve problems and "Make America Great Again." He also promised to build a wall between the United States and Mexico, deport undocumented immigrants, ban foreign Muslims from entering the United States, swiftly end international terrorism, pull out of the Iran nuclear treaty, repeal the Affordable Care Act, and withdraw from NAFTA, the TPP, and international climate agreements.

22. The Paris Agreement is a climate treaty signed by 200 nations aimed at fighting global warming by reducing greenhouse gas emissions. It is important because climate change is causing many effects in the world, including rising sea levels.

HISTORICAL THINKING ANSWERS

23. Answers will vary. Possible response: President Bush's actions against terrorism after the 9/11 attacks had mixed results. Bush's attack on the al Qaeda sanctuary of Afghanistan was effective and decisive. However, starting the war in Iraq was a mistake; it alienated the world community, and the weapons of mass destruction were never found. In addition, the Patriot Act gave the government too much power and compromised civil liberties.

24. Both tax policies were aimed at jump-starting the economy. Clinton's policy was to raise taxes in order to lower the federal budget deficit and bring the country out of recession. In contrast, Bush's tax cuts reduced government revenues, wiped out Clinton's budget surpluses, and contributed to a recession.

25. Possible response: Globalization has caused some U.S. manufacturing jobs to be relocated to countries where labor is cheaper, has led to trade deals like NAFTA, and has increased the availability of cheaper goods to consumers.

26. Possible responses: Yes. The increased use of renewable energy is an important step in combating climate change. No. The country is heavily dependent on oil, natural gas, and coal. Strongly promoting renewable energy would be too costly and might cause the loss of jobs in the fossil fuel industry.

INTERPRET VISUALS ANSWERS

27. 16 percent

28. The percentage of uninsured people dropped sharply after 2010.

ANALYZE SOURCES ANSWER

29. Possible response: Obama believes the capacity for change and the desire to make life better are qualities that make the United States exceptional.

CONNECT TO YOUR LIFE ANSWER

30. Answers will vary. Students should follow the tips indicated to write a response. Paragraphs should make a clear connection to students' own lives and experiences. Students should also use text evidence and vocabulary words from the chapter and include a summary of how they define the American identity.

NATIONAL GEOGRAPHIC | CONNECTION

Changing Faces

By Lise Funderburg

Adapted from "Changing Faces," by Lise Funderburg,
in *National Geographic*, October 2013

What is it about the faces on this page that we find so intriguing? Is it simply that their features disrupt our expectations? We're not used to seeing those eyes with that hair, that nose above those lips. Out in the world, the more curious (or less polite) among us might approach, asking, "Where are you from?" or "What are you?" We wonder because what we see says a lot about our country's past, present, and future.

The U.S. Census Bureau has collected detailed data on multiracial people only since 2000. In that year, it first allowed respondents to check more than one race, and 6.8 million people chose to do so. Ten years later, the number jumped by 32 percent. The multiple-race option is a step toward fixing a categorization system that is both wrong and essential. It is wrong because geneticists have demonstrated that race has no biological basis. However, it is essential because the tracking of race is used both to enforce antidiscrimination laws and to identify health issues specific to certain populations.

The Census Bureau is aware that its racial categorization system is flawed. Indeed, for most multiple-race Americans, identity is influenced by politics, religion, and geography, as well as by how the person believes the answer will be used. "I just say I'm brown," McKenzi McPherson, 9, says. "And I think, why do you want to know?" Maximillian Sugiura, 29, says he responds with whatever ethnicity provides a situational advantage. Loyalties figure in, too. Yudah Holman, 29, self-identifies as half Thai and half black, but marks Asian on forms and puts Thai first "because my mother raised me, so I'm really proud of being Thai."

Sandra Williams, 46, grew up at a time when the nation still turned on a black-white axis. The 1960 census depicted a country that was 99 percent black or white. When Williams was born 6 years later to parents of mixed black and white ancestry, 17 states still had laws against interracial marriage. To link her own fair skin and hair to her white ancestry, Williams says, would have been seen by blacks as a rejection. And so she checks black on the census.

Tracey Williams Bautista says her seven-year-old son identifies himself as black when he's with her, his African-American parent. When he's with his father, he'll say Mexican. "We call him a Blaxican," she jokes. Black relatives warn Williams about the one-drop rule, the long-standing practice of seeing anyone with a trace of black "blood" as black.

Certainly, race still matters in this country, despite claims that the election of Barack Obama heralded a post-racial world. We may be a pluralist nation by 2060, when the Census Bureau predicts that non-Hispanic whites will no longer be the majority. But head counts don't guarantee opportunity or wipe out the legacy of past discrimination. Whites, on average, have twice the income and six times the wealth of blacks and Hispanics.

When people ask Celeste Seda, 26, what she is, she lets them guess before she explains her Dominican-Korean background. The attention she gets for her unusual looks can be both flattering and exhausting. "It's a gift and a curse," Seda says.

It's also, for the rest of us, an opportunity. If we can't slot people into familiar categories, perhaps we'll be forced to reconsider who is us and who is them. Perhaps we'll be less stingy about who we feel connected to as we increasingly come across people whose faces seem to speak the line from Walt Whitman's poem "Song of Myself":

"I am large, I contain multitudes."

For more from National Geographic, check out "The Drones Come Home" online.

UNIT INQUIRY: Negotiate a Political Compromise

In this unit, you learned about the ongoing and growing divisions between conservatives and liberals, Republicans and Democrats. You also learned about leaders who attempted to bridge the divisions and negotiate agreements on important issues. Based on your understanding of the text, what are the issues that the Republican Party and Democratic Party disagree on? Do they agree on *any* points?

ASSIGNMENT

Identify three political issues that divide the Democratic Party from the Republican Party. You could choose from such issues as government spending, government regulations on businesses and other organizations, energy policy, immigration, and health care. Examine the positions of both sides on the three issues. Develop a political compromise, or agreement, by writing position statements on these issues that you think both sides could agree to.

Gather Evidence As you plan your position statements, gather evidence from this unit about the opposing ideas of the two sides. State each side's point of view on the three issues you've identified. If necessary, conduct additional research. Use a graphic organizer like this one to organize your notes.

Political Positions		
Issue	Democratic Party	Republican Party

Produce Use your notes to develop a political compromise that the two sides might accept. For each issue, create a position statement in which both sides give up something their party could bear to let go.

Present Choose a creative way to present your political compromise to the class. Consider one of these options:

- Play the role of an independent political candidate who can bridge the divide between the two sides. Give a campaign speech in which you present your positions.

- Work with a partner to stage a dialogue between a Democrat and a Republican in which they reach the compromise you've developed.

- Write a letter to your state representative or senator outlining your ideas for political compromise. Share your letter with the class.

NATIONAL GEOGRAPHIC | LEARNING FRAMEWORK ACTIVITIES

Create a Comic Strip

SKILLS Problem-Solving, Communication
KNOWLEDGE Our Human Story

Imagine a natural event or a power outage that makes it impossible to use cell phones, tablets, and computers for a week. Team up with a partner or a small group and create a comic strip in which you portray how the loss of cell phones, tablets, and computers affects you, your friends, and your family. Think about the positive as well as the negative effects. Portray in the comic strip how you would overcome any challenges or how you would make the most out of any benefits presented by the disruption. Share your comic strip with the class, and discuss whether people have become overly dependent on electronic devices in the 21st century.

Debate the Effects of Environmental Regulations

ATTITUDE Responsibility
KNOWLEDGE Our Living Planet

Prepare an argument in response to the following question: Does helping the environment harm or benefit the U.S. economy? Review what you've learned about environmental regulations and how businesses and governments have tried to minimize climate change. Then conduct online research about the Clean Power Plan of 2015 and the Paris Agreement of 2016 and how these acts have affected the U.S. and global economies. Present your argument to the class and hold a debate about the positive and negative effects of regulations on the economy.

Guided Discussion for "Changing Faces"

1. **Evaluate** Why might it be considered rude or overly curious to ask a multiracial person such questions as Where are you from? or What are you? *(Possible responses: These questions are based only on appearance or accent and tend to point out "otherness" or differences between people. The questions generalize and make assumptions about the importance of race and place of origin instead of taking the whole person into account.)*

2. **Explain** Why does the author describe the U.S. Census Bureau's categorization system as "both wrong and essential"? *(Possible response: The author describes the categorization system as wrong because racial identity has no biological basis but is instead shaped by politics, religion, history, and geography. The categorization system is essential because tracking race is used to enforce antidiscrimination laws and to identify health issues among certain populations.)*

Guided Discussion for "The Drones Come Home"

1. **Identify** In addition to military personnel, what other groups of people use drones? *(Possible responses: law enforcement, weather and climate information services, aviation firms, tracking services trying to locate lost people and animals, science researchers, natural disaster prediction services, hobbyists)*

2. **Make Inferences** Why do you think privacy advocates, including the ACLU, have concerns about persistent surveillance? *(Answers will vary. Possible response: Law enforcement agencies might choose persistent surveillance as a tool to monitor U.S. citizens, which could lead to violations of the Fourth Amendment.)*

Assess

Use the rubric to assess each student's participation and performance.

SCORE	ASSIGNMENT	PRODUCT	PRESENTATION
3 GREAT	• Student thoroughly understands the assignment. • Student participates fully in the project process. • Student works well with partner.	• Agreement is well thought out. • Agreement offers a number of examples of the issues facing both political parties. • Agreement contains all of the key elements listed in the assignment.	• Presentation is clear, concise, and logical. • Presentation does a good job of creatively representing both sides. • Presentation engages the audience.
2 GOOD	• Student mostly understands the assignment. • Student participates fairly well in the project process. • Student works fairly well with partner.	• Agreement is fairly well thought out. • Agreement offers at least two examples of the issues facing both political parties. • Agreement contains most of the key elements listed in the assignment.	• Presentation is fairly clear, concise, and logical. • Presentation does an adequate job of creatively representing both sides. • Presentation somewhat engages the audience.
1 NEEDS WORK	• Student does not understand the assignment. • Student minimally participates or does not participate in the project process. • Student does not work well with partner.	• Agreement is not well thought out. • Agreement does not offer examples of the issues facing both political parties. • Agreement contains few or none of the key elements listed in the assignment.	• Presentation is not clear, concise, or logical. • Presentation does an inadequate job representing both sides. • Presentation does not engage the audience.

Assess

Use the rubric to assess how each student applies the National Geographic Learning Framework.

SCORE	ASSIGNMENT	ASSIGNMENT	FINAL PRODUCTS
3 GREAT	• Comic strip demonstrates **Problem-Solving** and **Communication** well. • Comic strip explores **Our Human Story** well.	• Argument reflects **Responsibility** well. • Argument explores **Our Living Planet** well.	• Final products are engaging, creative, and well presented.
2 GOOD	• Comic strip reflects **Problem-Solving** and **Communication**. • Comic strip explores **Our Human Story**.	• Argument reflects **Responsibility**. • Argument explores **Our Living Planet**.	• Final products are interesting, logical, and complete.
1 NEEDS WORK	• Comic strip does not reflect **Problem-Solving** or **Communication**. • Comic strip does not explore **Our Human Story**.	• Argument does not reflect **Responsibility**. • Argument does not explore **Our Living Planet**.	• Final products are not creative, complete, or interesting.

Objective

- **Demonstrate understanding of demographic shifts in the U.S. population from 1800 to 2010.**
- **Describe and display graphically how shifts in the U.S. population have affected American identity.**

Critical Thinking Skills for "Why Study U.S. History?"

- Make Connections
- Draw Conclusions
- Analyze Data
- Summarize

Background for the Teacher

On these pages, Fred Hiebert, Archaeologist-in-Residence, National Geographic, invites students to look at the changing American identity as shown in a series of graphs related to immigration, population shift, education, and women in the workforce. Use these graphs as an example of how statistics can demonstrate important changes in the U.S. population and can illustrate traits about Americans over several decades.

Collect and Describe Class Statistics

Ask students to think about numerical data that could describe the population of their class, such as numbers of students broken down by participation in extracurricular activities, ethnicity, pet ownership, dominant hand, and so on. Create a chart titled Class Categories, and record students' suggestions. Then ask a volunteer to poll the class for each category and record the totals under each one. Guide students in representing the totals as percentages of the population of the class.

ASK: Based on the data in the chart, what factual statements can you make about the composition of this class? *(Students' statements should accurately reflect the data displayed on the chart. For example: Four percent of the class is Native American, and 29 percent is Hispanic. Only 8 percent of the class is left-handed. There is an almost even distribution of dog and cat ownership among students, with 47 percent having cats, and 45 percent having dogs.)* **ASK:** How do the statistics in the chart create an understanding of the class identity? Of your own identity? Guide a discussion about the two types of identity, and then encourage students to keep this activity in mind as they read the feature, which provides a statistical look at the U.S. population over two centuries.

WHY STUDY U.S. HISTORY?

Looking Ahead

Now that you've explored centuries of American history, you might wonder: How does it all add up? Take a look at the graphics on these pages—they'll give you a good idea of the United States today and how you fit into the larger picture of your country.

Fred Hiebert
Archaeologist-in-Residence,
National Geographic Society

MOVING TO CITIES RURAL AND URBAN POPULATION

1800 RURAL
93.9%

2010 RURAL
19.3%

URBAN
80.7%

Source: U.S. Census Bureau

MOVING TO THE UNITED STATES TOTAL FOREIGN-BORN POPULATION

1870 5.6 million

= 1 MILLION PEOPLE

2016 40 million

1014

RISING EDUCATION LEVELS

Check out how education expectations have changed over the last century.

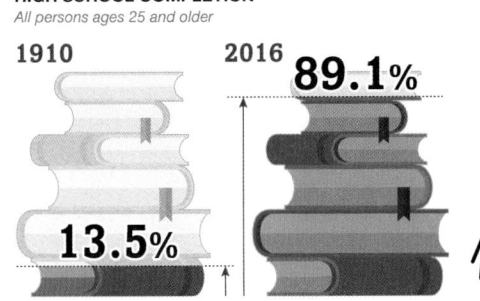

HIGH SCHOOL COMPLETION
All persons ages 25 and older

1910 — 13.5%
2016 — 89.1%

BACHELOR'S DEGREE OR HIGHER
All persons ages 25 and older

1910 — 2.7%
2016 — 33.4%

Source: National Center for Education Statistics

URBAN 6.1%

WORKING WOMEN
EMPLOYED POPULATION
All persons ages 25 to 34

1975 — 100%
2016

Men: 84.9% — 83.7%

The gap is closing.

Women — 70.4%

80%
60%
40%
20%
0%

Source: U.S. Census Bureau

FOREIGN-BORN POPULATION

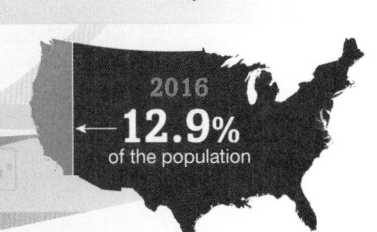

1870 ← 14.4% of the population

2016 ← 12.9% of the population

49.3% of women ages 25–34 were employed in 1975

Source: U.S. Census Bureau

Think About It

1. Which major historical events or trends that you've studied were likely to have impacted the data represented in the Moving to Cities graph? Explain why.

2. Identify a data set in this lesson that has affected you or your relatives. What connections can you make between the information on these pages and your American identity?

Guided Discussion

1. **Analyze Data** Why did the percentage of the foreign-born population decrease, even though the total foreign-born population increased? *(The total number of foreign-born individuals represented a smaller portion of the total population in 2016 than in 1870.)*

2. **Summarize** Choose one data set and summarize what it shows about the U.S. population. *(Answers will vary. Possible response: Between 1910 and 2016, the percentage of people older than 25 who completed high school increased by 75.6 percent, which shows the growing importance and availability of education.)*

Active Option

NG Learning Framework: Create a Statistics Display

ATTITUDE Curiosity

SKILLS Observation, Communication

Direct students to the U.S. Census website. Tell them to collect statistics that interest them about the U.S. population from 2000 and 2010, analyze the data, and draw a conclusion about why it changed. Then prompt students to create a graphic that displays the data, including a statement that explains their analysis. Invite students to present their displays to the class.

DIFFERENTIATE

Inclusion

Analyze Data Sets Pair proficient readers with students who have difficulty reading the statistics in the data sets. Prompt proficient readers to help their partners understand the labels and what each element represents. Then ask inclusion students to explain what each graphic conveys about the U.S. population.

Pre-AP

Interpret and Recast Data Sets Have students research the historical factors behind one of the data sets. Then challenge students to recast the data set in a different way. For example, students might use circle charts to emphasize percentages. Invite them to present their graphic and findings to the class.

Think About It

1. Answers will vary. Students might mention trends such as industrialization, immigration, transportation improvements, mechanization of farming, and urban job opportunities.

2. Answers will vary. Students should make a clear connection between the data set they choose and their own or their family's identity.

STUDENT REFERENCES

This famous Civil War battlefield in Gettysburg, Pennsylvania is a peaceful place today.

More Information

Drafting the Declaration The Declaration of Independence with which we are familiar today was not, in fact, Thomas Jefferson's original draft. After meeting with the committee several times, Jefferson spent two and a half weeks writing. He rose before dawn each day, sat down at his personally designed desk, set his quill pen to paper, wrote, and often ripped up drafts that did not satisfy him.

Once he was satisfied, Jefferson showed his draft of the Declaration to both Benjamin Franklin and John Adams. They were delighted and suggested only minor revisions. On June 28, 1776, Jefferson submitted the draft to the Continental Congress. Delegates debated it for days and had many criticisms. The most controversial passage offered a fierce condemnation of slavery, in which Jefferson accused the king of "wag[ing] cruel war against human nature itself, violating it's [sic] most sacred rights of life & liberty in the persons of a distant people who never offended him, captivating & carrying them into slavery." However, delegates from Georgia and Southern Carolina objected to the passage—because their economies were heavily reliant on the slave trade—and it was removed. In the end, about a quarter of the submitted text was cut out.

CITIZENSHIP
HANDBOOK

This Citizenship Handbook will help you take a detailed look at our two most important documents: the Declaration of Independence and the U.S. Constitution, which contains the Bill of Rights. The handbook includes notes to help you understand the formal language and difficult concepts contained in the more than 225-year-old documents. At the end of the handbook, you will learn about citizenship and the rights and responsibilities that come along with it. You will also find out how you can build and practice citizenship skills.

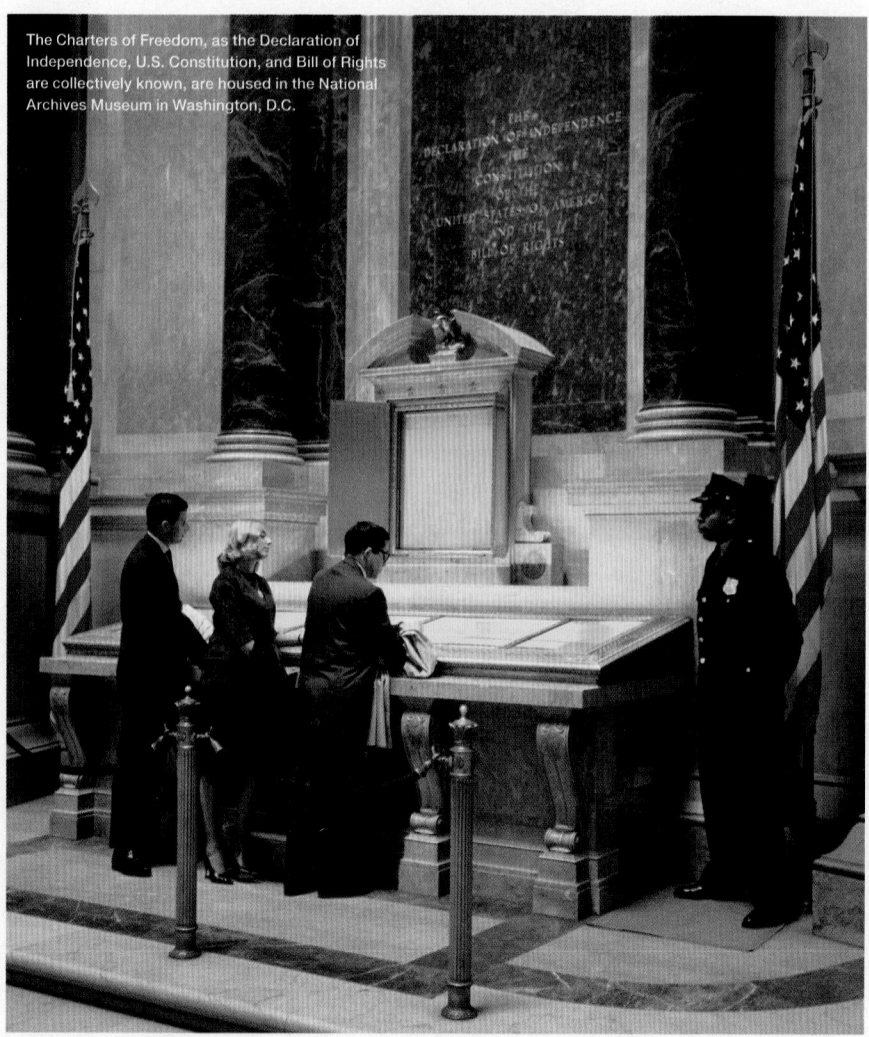

The Charters of Freedom, as the Declaration of Independence, U.S. Constitution, and Bill of Rights are collectively known, are housed in the National Archives Museum in Washington, D.C.

DECLARATION OF INDEPENDENCE

Introduction

The American colonists wrote the Declaration of Independence in 1776 to call for their separation and independence from Britain. During the first half of the 1700s, the colonists had lived in relative isolation from British authority and largely governed themselves. They modeled their colonial governments on Parliament, Britain's legislative body, by forming elected assemblies similar to the House of Commons. Unlike the British legislature, however, elected officials in the assemblies lived in the areas they represented. The colonists believed that representatives who lived among the people who elected them would better understand local interests and needs. They had no representatives in Parliament and sometimes resented what they felt to be unfair treatment by Britain.

GROWING RESENTMENT

The colonists' resentment grew after they fought alongside the British in the French and Indian War. The Americans had joined the fight so that they could expand their settlements westward into Native American territory. After Britain won the war against the French in 1763, however, the British government issued a proclamation stating that colonists could not settle west of the Appalachian Mountains. To make matters worse, British king George III charged a series of taxes against the colonists to help pay for the war. The king believed that the role of a colony was to support the mother country—in this case, Britain.

Crying "No taxation without representation," the colonists protested against the British legislation. As tensions rose, violence erupted in 1770 with the Boston Massacre, resulting in the deaths of five colonists at the hands of British soldiers. Three years later, colonists demonstrated their anger over a law on the sale of tea by staging the Boston Tea Party in Boston Harbor. A group of colonists boarded British ships and threw more than 300 crates of tea overboard.

Finally, in 1775, feelings on both sides reached the boiling point. After British troops learned that the colonists had stored weapons in Concord, Massachusetts, the troops marched to the town. Colonial militiamen rushed to face down the British soldiers in nearby Lexington. Shots rang out at what would later be called the first battle of the American Revolution.

DECLARING INDEPENDENCE

Colonial delegates to the two Continental Congresses met in Philadelphia in 1774 and 1775. Some delegates called for the colonies to separate completely from Britain. While the 1775 Congress debated the issue, a committee was formed to write an official document to declare independence from Britain. The committee included Thomas Jefferson, John Adams, and Benjamin Franklin, three of America's Founding Fathers.

Jefferson became the principal author of the Declaration of Independence. Like many American colonists, Jefferson had been deeply influenced by the Enlightenment, a movement that spread from Britain to the colonies in the 1700s. Enlightenment thinkers, such as John Locke, claimed that humans were born free and equal and that a leader could rule only with the consent of the people.

Inspired by the Enlightenment philosophy of unalienable, or natural, rights, Jefferson called for "Life, Liberty, and the Pursuit of Happiness" in the Declaration. These unalienable rights, he insisted, could not be taken away. Jefferson also drew on the principles of freedom contained in the Magna Carta as he wrote the document. On July 4, 1776, the delegates to the Continental Congress adopted the Declaration of Independence. In 1782, more than six years after the first shots were fired, the American Revolution officially ended. The American colonists had fought for and won their freedom and independence from Britain.

Citizenship Handbook **R3**

Guided Discussion

1. **Make Inferences** Study the photograph and its caption. What do you think the term *charters* means? *(Possible response: a written document that defines people's rights)* What can you infer about these three documents, based on the title Charters of Freedom? *(Possible response: These documents define the basic freedoms and rights given to all United States citizens.)*

2. **Analyze Cause and Effect** What events contributed to the growing resentment between the colonies and Britain, which eventually led to the writing of the Declaration of Independence? *(Possible response: Events such as the Proclamation of 1763, increased taxation, the Boston Massacre, the Boston Tea Party, and the armed confrontation in Lexington contributed to colonists' growing resentment and provided the foundation for the writing of the* Declaration of Independence.*)*

More Information

News Travels Slowly With the signing of the Declaration of Independence on July 4, 1776, the colonies formally declared independence from Britain. However, it took some time for the new United States—and the world—to learn about that decision. Unlike today, with nearly instantaneous, digital communication, most people in 1776 received their information from newspapers, printed broadsides, and public readings. News generally traveled slowly.

People living in Philadelphia learned of independence quickly because the text of the Declaration was published in local papers on July 6. Four days later, word reached New York City; two weeks later, Boston got the news. On July 20, the Declaration was published in Virginia, the largest colony and the home of Jefferson. It wasn't until August 2 that South Carolina learned the news—almost a full month after the event.

It took even longer for this monumental announcement to appear overseas. Britain learned of its colonies' attempted separation in mid-August. The news reached other parts of Europe over the next several months.

THE DECLARATION OF INDEPENDENCE

IN CONGRESS, JULY 4, 1776

The Declaration begins by explaining why the colonists want to break away from Britain and become independent. The Founding Fathers believed it was important to explain why they wanted to take this step.

The unanimous Declaration of the thirteen united States of America, When in the Course of human events, it becomes necessary for one people to dissolve the political bands which have connected them with another, and to assume among the powers of the earth, the separate and equal station to which the Laws of Nature and of Nature's God entitle them, a decent respect to the opinions of mankind requires that they should declare the causes which impel them to the separation.

The American colonists believed people are born equal and have rights that should be kept safe by the government. The Declaration explains that government is necessary to make sure people keep their natural rights; for example, the right to life, liberty, and the pursuit of happiness.

Once a government takes such rights away, the people must work to change or overthrow the government.

Such action is taken very seriously but is necessary because of King George's treatment of the colonies.

We hold these truths to be self-evident, that all men are created equal, that they are endowed by their Creator with certain unalienable Rights, that among these are Life, Liberty and the pursuit of Happiness.—That to secure these rights, Governments are instituted among Men, deriving their just powers from the consent of the governed, —That whenever any Form of Government becomes destructive of these ends, it is the Right of the People to alter or to abolish it, and to institute new Government, laying its foundation on such principles and organizing its powers in such form, as to them shall seem most likely to effect their Safety and Happiness. Prudence, indeed, will dictate that Governments long established should not be changed for light and transient causes; and accordingly all experience hath shown, that mankind are more disposed to suffer, while evils are sufferable, than to right themselves by abolishing the forms to which they are accustomed. But when a long train of abuses and usurpations, pursuing invariably the same Object evinces a design to reduce them under absolute Despotism, it is their right, it is their duty, to throw off such Government, and to provide new Guards for their future security.—Such has been the patient sufferance of these Colonies; and such is now the necessity which constrains them to alter their former Systems of Government. The history of the present King of Great Britain is a history of repeated injuries and usurpations, all having in direct object the establishment of an absolute Tyranny over these States. To prove this, let Facts be submitted to a candid world.

The Declaration goes on to explain exactly what King George has done. This section is commonly referred to as the list of grievances.

The king has refused to approve laws that people need.

He has refused his Assent to Laws, the most wholesome and necessary for the public good.

He has forbidden his Governors to pass Laws of immediate and pressing importance, unless suspended in their operation till his Assent should be obtained; and when so suspended, he has utterly neglected to attend to them. He has refused to pass other Laws for the accommodation of large districts of people, unless those people would relinquish the right of Representation in the Legislature, a right inestimable to them and formidable to tyrants only.

> Laws are needed, but the king has failed to approve or disapprove them, so no new laws can be put into effect. He has claimed that unless people in the colonies give up the right to have representatives in their own government in America, he will not pass laws those people need.

He has called together legislative bodies at places unusual, uncomfortable, and distant from the depository of their public Records, for the sole purpose of fatiguing them into compliance with his measures.

He has dissolved Representative Houses repeatedly, for opposing with manly firmness his invasions on the rights of the people.

> The king has put an end to lawmaking bodies that opposed laws representatives believed were harmful to people's rights.

He has refused for a long time, after such dissolutions, to cause others to be elected; whereby the Legislative powers, incapable of Annihilation, have returned to the People at large for their exercise; the State remaining in the mean time exposed to all the dangers of invasion from without, and convulsions within.

> After the legislatures were dismissed, some colonies had no laws to protect them.

He has endeavored to prevent the population of these States; for that purpose obstructing the Laws for Naturalization of Foreigners; refusing to pass others to encourage their migrations hither, and raising the conditions of new Appropriations of Lands.

He has obstructed the Administration of Justice, by refusing his Assent to Laws for establishing Judiciary powers.

He has made Judges dependent on his Will alone, for the tenure of their offices, and the amount and payment of their salaries.

> Judges have been appointed who favor the king's interests.

He has erected a multitude of New Offices, and sent hither swarms of Officers to harass our people, and eat out their substance.

He has kept among us, in times of peace, Standing Armies without the Consent of our legislatures.

> The king has sent soldiers to America, without the agreement of its lawmakers. He has made his soldiers more powerful than the colonists.

He has affected to render the Military independent of and superior to the Civil power.

Guided Discussion

1. **Analyze Language Use** What words or phrases in the Declaration of Independence suggest that Jefferson believed his argument was universal—not just applicable to the United States? *(Phrases such as "unalienable rights" imply that they are universal. Also, in the second paragraph, Jefferson uses terms such as "Governments" and "their," rather than "Britain" and "colonists." This suggests his argument could be applied to other nations.)*

2. **Make Connections** How might the phrase "all men are created equal" have a different meaning now than in 1776? *(In 1776, full equality did not apply to women, African Americans, or even white men without property. Today, however, all these groups have the same rights.)*

More Information

The Declaration Heard 'Round the World The Declaration of Independence was meant, in part, as a biting criticism of the British monarchy, but its impact was felt across Europe and the world. At the time of its publication, most European countries were ruled by absolute monarchs, who wielded complete power. Thus, a document that denied the legitimacy of such a government was not warmly received.

In Austria, news of the Declaration was heavily censored, and the empress was outraged when a newspaper described the American Revolution as a clash between monarchy and self-rule rather than as an unlawful rebellion. In Russia, the colonists were described in print as "rebels" rather than "revolutionaries" or "freedom fighters." The British government published a response to the Declaration that forcibly argued against the document's reasoning. Other countries, however, received news of the revolution more positively. For example, the people of Belgium, a country under the control of Austria, closely followed news of the Declaration, and by 1787, they had begun their own movement for independence.

DECLARATION OF INDEPENDENCE

The king has allowed others to pass and enforce new laws in the colonies.

He has combined with others to subject us to a jurisdiction foreign to our constitution, and unacknowledged by our laws; giving his Assent to their Acts of pretended Legislation:

For Quartering large bodies of armed troops among us:

For protecting them, by a mock Trial, from punishment for any Murders which they should commit on the Inhabitants of these States:

For example:
- making sure that soldiers who kill colonists are given a fake trial and not held accountable for murder;
- stopping American trade with other countries;
- taxing without permission;
- often refusing the right of trial by jury;
- sending colonists far away to be tried in courts for things they have not done;
- abolishing laws made by the colonies;
- stopping lawmaking groups in America and declaring that only the British government can make laws for people in America.

For cutting off our Trade with all parts of the world:

For imposing Taxes on us without our Consent:

For depriving us in many cases, of the benefits of Trial by Jury:

For transporting us beyond Seas to be tried for pretended offences

For abolishing the free System of English Laws in a neighboring Province, establishing therein an Arbitrary government, and enlarging its Boundaries so as to render it at once an example and fit instrument for introducing the same absolute rule into these Colonies:

For taking away our Charters, abolishing our most valuable Laws, and altering fundamentally the Forms of our Governments:

For suspending our own Legislatures, and declaring themselves invested with power to legislate for us in all cases whatsoever.

The colonists claim that the king has essentially given up ("abdicated") his power to govern in America—because he refuses to protect America and has started a war against the colonies.

He has abdicated Government here, by declaring us out of his Protection and waging War against us.

He has plundered our seas, ravaged our Coasts, burnt our towns, and destroyed the lives of our people.

In a way that has almost never been seen before, the king is now sending soldiers from other countries to harm and kill Americans.

He is at this time transporting large Armies of foreign Mercenaries to complete the works of death, desolation and tyranny, already begun with circumstances of Cruelty & perfidy scarcely paralleled in the most barbarous ages, and totally unworthy the Head of a civilized nation.

DECLARATION OF INDEPENDENCE

He has constrained our fellow Citizens taken Captive on the high Seas to bear Arms against their Country, to become the executioners of their friends and Brethren, or to fall themselves by their Hands.

He has excited domestic insurrections amongst us, and has endeavored to bring on the inhabitants of our frontiers, the merciless Indian Savages, whose known rule of warfare, is an undistinguished destruction of all ages, sexes and conditions.

He has encouraged conflict among Americans and incited Native Americans to attack the colonists.

In every stage of these Oppressions We have Petitioned for Redress in the most humble terms: Our repeated Petitions have been answered only by repeated injury. A Prince whose character is thus marked by every act which may define a Tyrant, is unfit to be the ruler of a free people.

We have repeatedly and unsuccessfully made formal requests for this behavior to stop. The king has become cruel and oppressive.

Nor have We been wanting in attentions to our British brethren. We have warned them from time to time of attempts by their legislature to extend an unwarrantable jurisdiction over us. We have reminded them of the circumstances of our emigration and settlement here. We have appealed to their native justice and magnanimity, and we have conjured them by the ties of our common kindred to disavow these usurpations, which, would inevitably interrupt our connections and correspondence. They too have been deaf to the voice of justice and of consanguinity. We must, therefore, acquiesce in the necessity, which denounces our Separation, and hold them, as we hold the rest of mankind, Enemies in War, in Peace Friends.

We have appealed to the British people, pointing out the injustice of our treatment and our close ties to them ("consanguinity"), but they have ignored us. So we have no choice but to consider them our enemies.

We, therefore, the Representatives of the united States of America, in General Congress, Assembled, appealing to the Supreme Judge of the world for the rectitude of our intentions, do, in the Name, and by Authority of the good People of these Colonies, solemnly publish and declare, That these United Colonies are, and of Right ought to be Free and Independent States; that they are Absolved from all Allegiance to the British Crown, and that all political connection between them and the State of Great Britain, is and ought to be totally dissolved; and that as Free and Independent States, they have full Power to levy War, conclude Peace, contract Alliances, establish Commerce, and to do all other Acts and Things which Independent States may of right do. And for the support of this Declaration, with a firm reliance on the protection of divine Providence, we mutually pledge to each other our Lives, our Fortunes and our sacred Honor.

For all of these reasons, we declare that the United Colonies are free and independent states with no further allegiance to Britain. Because we are free, we can declare war, declare peace, make agreements to work with other countries, establish commerce, and participate in all other activities allowed by independent states.

Guided Discussion

1. **Form and Support Opinions** The Declaration states that the colonists had made repeated requests of the king to address various injustices but with no results. In your opinion, how important was it to the argument for independence that the Declaration include this fact? Support your opinion. *(Possible response: Including this fact strengthened the Declaration's argument that the colonies should be free and independent. Without it, someone reading the document may not have understood the lengths to which the colonists had already gone to try to resolve issues and may therefore have decided that the "declaration" was premature or unnecessary.)*

2. **Make Predictions** How do you think the Declaration of Independence was viewed by various people across the colonies and in Britain? *(Possible response: Various groups probably had different responses to the document. People who opposed the king's treatment of the colonies likely supported it. However, colonists who benefited financially from trade with Britain, or perhaps members of the British government, may have opposed the ideas put forth in the Declaration.)*

More Information

The People's House According to Article I, Section 2.1, members of the House of Representatives are to be chosen by "the People." While this phrasing may seem obvious today, at the time of the nation's founding, this was the only part of the legislative branch in which the people had a direct say. As students will read in Section 3.1, senators originally were selected by state legislatures, not the people. This exclusion can be said to extend to the judicial branch, for Supreme Court justices are appointed by the president (with congressional approval; see Article II, Section 2.2). Similarly, although the people can vote for president, the official choice comes from the electoral college (Article II, Sections 1.1–1.4).

To make the House of Representatives the part of government most responsive to the people's needs, the bar for becoming a representative was set purposely low: It has the least restrictive qualifications in terms of age and citizenship. In addition, representatives stand for reelection more frequently than do senators or the president, making it easier for citizens to exert influence.

Writing about the House of Representatives, James Madison noted, "Under these reasonable limitations, the door of this part of the federal government is open to merit of every description, whether native or adoptive, whether young or old, and without regard to poverty or wealth, or to any particular profession of religious faith."

CONSTITUTION OF THE UNITED STATES

Introduction

In 1787, after much debate, delegates at the Constitutional Convention in Philadelphia, known as the Framers, signed the U.S. Constitution, which became the supreme law of the land in the United States. Considering the size and complexity of the United States today and its position as a world power, the U.S. Constitution is relatively simple. It consists of a Preamble, 7 articles, and currently 27 amendments, based on the 7 key principles discussed below. About the simplicity of the Constitution, John Adams wrote, "Our Constitution was made only for a moral and religious People. It is wholly inadequate to the government of any other."

1. Popular Sovereignty This principle addresses the idea that people together create a social contract in which they agree to be governed.

2. Republicanism In a republic, citizens have the power and authority to make decisions as to how they are governed. The citizens elect representatives, and the representatives then have the power to make and enforce laws.

3. Federalism A government operating under federalism features a strong central government, but states do not lose all rights and power. The federal government holds some powers, which are enumerated, or listed, powers. The states have other powers, which are reserved, or unwritten, powers. And some powers are concurrent powers, which means that they may be practiced by both the federal government and the state governments.

4. Separation of Powers To reduce the potential for abuse of power, the government was divided into three branches: the legislative branch (made up of the Senate and the House of Representatives), which makes the laws; the executive branch (led by the president), which enforces the laws; and the judicial branch (made up of the U.S. Supreme Court and additional federal courts), which interprets the laws.

5. Checks and Balances Each branch of the government provides a check for the others, which means that it can limit the power of those branches. Such checks provide a balance among the three branches. For example, while the legislative branch can make laws, the judicial branch interprets them and decides if those laws are constitutional. And while the president can veto a law made by Congress, Congress can override a presidential veto.

6. Limited Government A strong central power was important to those who developed the Constitution. Still, the Framers believed the strong central government should not be allowed to abuse its power by providing particular rights to some groups or taking away rights from others. This principle of government seeks to protect rights by limiting the power of the central government.

7. Individual Rights Amendments, or articles added to the Constitution, have become part of the U.S. Constitution over the years. The first 10 amendments, known as the Bill of Rights, were added in 1791. These amendments address many individual rights, such as freedom of religion, freedom of speech, and the right to trial by jury. The Bill of Rights was added to the Constitution to ensure that all states would accept and ratify this new plan for government.

THE CONSTITUTION

Preamble We the People of the United States, in Order to form a more perfect Union, establish Justice, insure domestic Tranquility, provide for the common defense, promote the general Welfare, and secure the Blessings of Liberty to ourselves and our Posterity, do ordain and establish this Constitution for the United States of America.

Article I Legislative Branch

SECTION 1: CONGRESS

All legislative Powers herein granted shall be vested in a Congress of the United States, which shall consist of a Senate and House of Representatives.

SECTION 2: THE HOUSE OF REPRESENTATIVES

1 The House of Representatives shall be composed of Members chosen every second Year by the People of the several States, and the Electors in each State shall have the Qualifications requisite for Electors of the most numerous Branch of the State Legislature.

2 No Person shall be a Representative who shall not have attained to the Age of twenty five Years, and been seven Years a Citizen of the United States, and who shall not, when elected, be an Inhabitant of that State in which he shall be chosen.

3 *Representatives and direct Taxes shall be apportioned among the several States which may be included within this Union, according to their respective Numbers, which shall be determined by adding to the whole Number of free Persons, including those bound to Service for a Term of Years, and excluding Indians not taxed, three fifths of all other Persons.* The actual Enumeration shall be made within three Years after the first Meeting of the Congress of the United States, and within every subsequent Term of ten Years, in such Manner as they shall by Law direct. The Number of Representatives shall not exceed one for every thirty Thousand, but each State shall have at Least one Representative; and until such enumeration shall be made, the State of New Hampshire shall be entitled to choose three, Massachusetts eight, Rhode-Island and Providence Plantations one, Connecticut five, New-York six, New Jersey four, Pennsylvania eight, Delaware one, Maryland six, Virginia ten, North Carolina five, South Carolina five, and Georgia three.

4 When vacancies happen in the Representation from any State, the Executive Authority thereof shall issue Writs of Election to fill such Vacancies.

5 The House of Representatives shall choose their Speaker and other Officers; and shall have the sole Power of Impeachment.

NOTE Boldfaced headings, section numbers, margin notes, and questions have been inserted to help you understand and interpret this complex document. Passages that are no longer part of the Constitution have been printed in italic type.

PREAMBLE
UNDERSTANDING THE CONSTITUTION The phrase "We the People" begins the Preamble to the Constitution. The Preamble states the "why" and the "how" of Americans' agreement to be governed. The Preamble also states that the Constitution will define the government and that the document will be a social contract.

ARTICLE I
UNDERSTANDING THE CONSTITUTION Section 2 The House of Representatives provides one of the most direct ways in which citizens can participate in the political process. People can communicate with representatives by mail, email, and phone, and by visiting the lawmakers' offices.

UNDERSTANDING THE CONSTITUTION 2.3 Each state can have one representative for every 30,000 people in the state. The phrase "their respective Numbers" refers to the states' populations. Today every state has a population greater than 30,000, but the Constitution made sure that states with fewer people had a representative. The Constitution indicates the initial numbers of representatives for each of the original 13 states.

HISTORICAL THINKING In 2.3, the italicized phrase "three fifths of all other persons" refers to enslaved people. Why do you think slaves were not counted in the same way as free persons?

UNDERSTANDING THE CONSTITUTION 2.5 The Speaker presides over sessions of Congress, but the Constitution says nothing about what the Speaker or other officers will do.

Guided Discussion

1. **Synthesize** What steps did the Framers take to limit the powers of the federal government? *(Possible response: The Framers enumerated the powers of the federal government—that is, they spelled out those powers precisely. In addition, principles such as separation of powers and checks and balances were meant to ensure that no one branch of the government could hold too much power.)*

2. **Draw Conclusions** In what ways did the Constitution attempt to fix the problems that the Framers saw in the British form of government? *(Possible response: The idea that government is a "social contract," in which citizens agree to be governed, is different from the way in which the British monarchy functioned. In addition, the various methods used to limit the power of the president represent an attempt to prevent a British king-like figure from taking power.)*

HISTORICAL THINKING

ANSWER

Enslaved people were considered property, not citizens. Thus, they could not vote, nor did they pay taxes. However, southern states wanted them included in their population so that they would have more representation. The "three fifths of all other persons" phrasing is a compromise reached by the Framers.

More Information

Power of the Purse The issue of taxation was important to the Framers, and they addressed it in the Constitution. In the years leading up to the American Revolution, the cry "no taxation without representation" was a crucial rallying point for colonists. It referred to the British government levying taxes on the colonists without their input—a practice that colonists interpreted as a violation of their rights as British citizens.

Article I, Section 7.1, addresses the "power of the purse"—the ability to levy taxes and spend revenue. The Framers debated who should have this authority. In Britain, the king had power over spending decisions, but the Framers were adamant that in the United States, the people should be in control of public financing. Thus, the president was unanimously disqualified for the role. Some argued that the Senate should take this responsibility. However, because its makeup favored small states, and thus their interests, it, too, was given limited power. As a result, all taxation and spending decisions would begin in the House, as it was the chamber that more clearly reflected the wishes of the people.

HISTORICAL THINKING

ANSWER

Doing so prevents the House alone from removing the president from office.

ANSWER

Without this process in place, if a president was seriously threatening the nation, the only way of removing him or her would be by force.

CONSTITUTION OF THE UNITED STATES

UNDERSTANDING THE CONSTITUTION 3.1 The Constitution originally provided for the election of senators by the state legislatures, but the 17th Amendment changed that in 1913 with the election of senators by voters.

UNDERSTANDING THE CONSTITUTION 3.2 The terms of senators are staggered. One class of senators begins their term in an even-numbered year, the next class begins two years later, and the third class begins two years after that.

HISTORICAL THINKING In the previous section, the Constitution states the House has the power of impeachment, and in 3.6, it says the Senate tries impeachments. Why do you think the Constitution separates these powers?

HISTORICAL THINKING Only two U.S. presidents have been impeached: Andrew Johnson in 1868 and William Clinton in 1998, but neither was convicted by the Senate. Why do you think impeachment is part of the Constitution?

Visitors with tickets could observe President Andrew Johnson's impeachment trial from the gallery of the Senate. Each ticket was valid for one day in March through May 1868, indicated by the ticket's color.

UNDERSTANDING THE CONSTITUTION 4.2 In 1933, the 20th Amendment changed the starting date for meetings of Congress to January 3.

SECTION 3: THE SENATE

1 The Senate of the United States shall be composed of two Senators from each State, chosen by the Legislature thereof, for six Years; and each Senator shall have one Vote.

2 Immediately after they shall be assembled in Consequence of the first Election, they shall be divided as equally as may be into three Classes. The Seats of the Senators of the first Class shall be vacated at the Expiration of the second Year, of the second Class at the Expiration of the fourth Year, and of the third Class at the Expiration of the sixth Year, so that one third may be chosen every second Year; and if Vacancies happen by Resignation, or otherwise, during the Recess of the Legislature of any State, the Executive thereof may make temporary Appointments until the next Meeting of the Legislature, which shall then fill such Vacancies.

3 No Person shall be a Senator who shall not have attained to the Age of thirty Years, and been nine Years a Citizen of the United States, and who shall not, when elected, be an Inhabitant of that State for which he shall be chosen.

4 The Vice President of the United States shall be President of the Senate, but shall have no Vote, unless they be equally divided.

5 The Senate shall choose their other Officers, and also a President pro tempore, in the Absence of the Vice President, or when he shall exercise the Office of President of the United States.

6 The Senate shall have the sole Power to try all Impeachments. When sitting for that Purpose, they shall be on Oath or Affirmation. When the President of the United States is tried, the Chief Justice shall preside: And no Person shall be convicted without the Concurrence of two thirds of the Members present.

7 Judgment in Cases of Impeachment shall not extend further than to removal from Office, and disqualification to hold and enjoy any Office of honor, Trust or Profit under the United States: but the Party convicted shall nevertheless be liable and subject to Indictment, Trial, Judgment and Punishment, according to Law.

SECTION 4: CONGRESSIONAL ELECTIONS

1 The Times, Places and Manner of holding Elections for Senators and Representatives, shall be prescribed in each State by the Legislature thereof; but the Congress may at any time by Law make or alter such Regulations, except as to the Places of choosing Senators.

2 *The Congress shall assemble at least once in every Year, and such Meeting shall be on the first Monday in December, unless they shall by Law appoint a different Day.*

CONSTITUTION OF THE UNITED STATES

SECTION 5: RULES

1 Each House shall be the Judge of the Elections, Returns and Qualifications of its own Members, and a Majority of each shall constitute a Quorum to do Business; but a smaller Number may adjourn from day to day, and may be authorized to compel the Attendance of absent Members, in such Manner, and under such Penalties as each House may provide.

2 Each House may determine the Rules of its Proceedings, punish its Members for disorderly Behavior, and, with the Concurrence of two thirds, expel a Member.

3 Each House shall keep a Journal of its Proceedings, and from time to time publish the same, excepting such Parts as may in their Judgment require Secrecy; and the Yeas and Nays of the Members of either House on any question shall, at the Desire of one fifth of those Present, be entered on the Journal.

4 Neither House, during the Session of Congress, shall, without the Consent of the other, adjourn for more than three days, nor to any other Place than that in which the two Houses shall be sitting.

SECTION 6: PAY AND EXPENSES

1 The Senators and Representatives shall receive a Compensation for their Services, to be ascertained by Law, and paid out of the Treasury of the United States. They shall in all Cases, except Treason, Felony and Breach of the Peace, be privileged from Arrest during their Attendance at the Session of their respective Houses, and in going to and returning from the same; and for any Speech or Debate in either House, they shall not be questioned in any other Place.

2 No Senator or Representative shall, during the Time for which he was elected, be appointed to any civil Office under the Authority of the United States, which shall have been created, or the Emoluments whereof shall have been increased during such time; and no Person holding any Office under the United States, shall be a Member of either House during his Continuance in Office.

SECTION 7: PASSING LAWS

1 All Bills for raising Revenue shall originate in the House of Representatives; but the Senate may propose or concur with Amendments as on other Bills.

2 Every Bill which shall have passed the House of Representatives and the Senate, shall, before it become a Law, be presented to the President of the United States; If he approve he shall sign it, but if not he shall return it, with his Objections to that House in which it shall have originated, who shall enter the Objections at large on their Journal, and proceed to reconsider it. If after such Reconsideration two thirds of that House shall agree to pass the Bill, it shall be sent, together with

UNDERSTANDING THE CONSTITUTION Section 5

This section calls for a "journal" of each house's proceedings. These proceedings include debates, bills introduced, laws passed, and a record of how each member voted on each bill introduced. Debates were recorded in writing in the House and Senate *Journals* until 1873. Since then, debates have been recorded in the *Congressional Record*.

UNDERSTANDING THE CONSTITUTION 7.2

How a Bill Becomes a Law in Congress

A A representative in either the House or Senate introduces a bill. A citizen may bring the idea for a bill to the attention of a representative.

B The bill is debated, and revisions may be made.

C A committee irons out any differences if the House and Senate pass different versions of the bill.

D If both houses accept the compromises, Congress sends the bill to the president.

E The president either signs the bill—and it becomes law—or vetoes the bill. Congress can override the veto with a vote of two-thirds of the members present in each house, making the bill become a law.

Citizenship Handbook **R11**

Guided Discussion

1. Identify What happens when the voting on a bill in the Senate results in a tie? *(The vice president acts as the president of the Senate and can vote to break a tie.)*

2. Form and Support Opinions Remember that giving each state two senators, regardless of population, was a compromise made between big and small states during the writing of the Constitution. Therefore, a densely populated state such as California has the same number of senators today as a sparsely populated state such as Wyoming. Do you think this provision in the Constitution is fair? Support your opinion with evidence from the text. *(Answers will vary. Students may note that larger states—and thus the majority of the people—are not given a proportional voice concerning the Senate's decisions. On the other hand, students may argue that smaller states and their concerns would be ignored if not for the makeup of the Senate.)*

More Information

Suspension of *Habeus Corpus* *Habeus corpus*, a foundational part of American law that originated in England, was designed to protect people from illegal imprisonment. A writ of *habeus corpus* requires law enforcement to give legal justification for a person's detainment, such as the specific law that the person broke. If no justification can be given, the person must be released.

Article I, Section 9.2, gives the government the ability to suspend *habeus corpus* in times of rebellion or to protect public safety during an invasion. The suspension allows law enforcement to imprison people without having a specific legal reason. This section of the Constitution has been invoked on a few occasions. During the Civil War, for example, President Lincoln suspended *habeus corpus* in Maryland to silence protestors, crack down on riots, and prevent the movement of Confederate troops. In 1871, President Grant suspended *habeus corpus* across South Carolina to combat the violence being perpetrated by the Ku Klux Klan. In recent years, suspension has been rare. However, following the terrorist attacks of September 11, 2001, Congress passed—and the president signed—a law banning detainees at the American naval base in Guantanamo Bay, Cuba, from invoking this right, thus allowing for their prolonged imprisonment.

HISTORICAL THINKING

ANSWER

Although Congress can raise and support armies, the president is the commander in chief of the armed forces.

ANSWER

Different states' money could have different values, and it would be necessary to convert in order for the people of different states to do business with one another.

CONSTITUTION OF THE UNITED STATES

UNDERSTANDING THE CONSTITUTION Section 8 Section 8 provides a list of 17 specific powers given to Congress and empowers it "to make all laws" necessary to support those functions. Additionally, the first paragraph of the section empowers Congress to provide for the "general welfare" of the nation. However, the Constitution includes little detail on how some of these powers should be carried out.

HISTORICAL THINKING How does the Constitution balance the power of Congress to raise and support armies?

UNDERSTANDING THE CONSTITUTION 8.3 Regulating commerce with foreign nations means controlling imports and exports to provide maximum benefit for U.S. businesses and consumers. Regulating commerce between states means maintaining a common market among the states, with no restrictions. Remember that at the time the Constitution was written, Native Americans traded fur and other items with U.S. citizens.

HISTORICAL THINKING What problems might arise if the United States did not have a common coinage?

the Objections, to the other House, by which it shall likewise be reconsidered, and if approved by two thirds of that House, it shall become a Law. But in all such Cases the Votes of both Houses shall be determined by yeas and Nays, and the Names of the Persons voting for and against the Bill shall be entered on the Journal of each House respectively. If any Bill shall not be returned by the President within ten Days (Sundays excepted) after it shall have been presented to him, the Same shall be a Law, in like Manner as if he had signed it, unless the Congress by their Adjournment prevent its Return, in which Case it shall not be a Law.

3 Every Order, Resolution, or Vote to which the Concurrence of the Senate and House of Representatives may be necessary (except on a question of Adjournment) shall be presented to the President of the United States; and before the Same shall take Effect, shall be approved by him, or being disapproved by him, shall be re-passed by two thirds of the Senate and House of Representatives, according to the Rules and Limitations prescribed in the Case of a Bill.

SECTION 8: POWERS OF CONGRESS

1 The Congress shall have Power To lay and collect Taxes, Duties, Imposts and Excises, to pay the Debts and provide for the common Defense and general Welfare of the United States; but all Duties, Imposts and Excises shall be uniform throughout the United States;

2 To borrow Money on the credit of the United States;

3 To regulate Commerce with foreign Nations, and among the several States, and with the Indian Tribes;

4 To establish an uniform Rule of Naturalization, and uniform Laws on the subject of Bankruptcies throughout the United States;

5 To coin Money, regulate the Value thereof, and of foreign Coin, and fix the Standard of Weights and Measures;

6 To provide for the Punishment of counterfeiting the Securities and current Coin of the United States;

7 To establish Post Offices and post Roads;

8 To promote the Progress of Science and useful Arts, by securing for limited Times to Authors and Inventors the exclusive Right to their respective Writings and Discoveries;

9 To constitute Tribunals inferior to the supreme Court;

10 To define and punish Piracies and Felonies committed on the high Seas, and Offences against the Law of Nations;

11 To declare War, grant Letters of Marque and Reprisal, and make Rules concerning Captures on Land and Water;

CONSTITUTION OF THE UNITED STATES

12 To raise and support Armies, but no Appropriation of Money to that Use shall be for a longer Term than two Years;

13 To provide and maintain a Navy; To make Rules for the Government and Regulation of the land and naval Forces;

14 To provide for calling forth the Militia to execute the Laws of the Union, suppress Insurrections and repel Invasions;

15 To provide for organizing, arming, and disciplining, the Militia, and for governing such Part of them as may be employed in the Service of the United States, reserving to the States respectively, the Appointment of the Officers, and the Authority of training the Militia according to the discipline prescribed by Congress;

16 To exercise exclusive Legislation in all Cases whatsoever, over such District (not exceeding ten Miles square) as may, by Cession of particular States, and the Acceptance of Congress, become the Seat of the Government of the United States, and to exercise like Authority over all Places purchased by the Consent of the Legislature of the State in which the Same shall be, for the Erection of Forts, Magazines, Arsenals, dock-Yards, and other needful Buildings;—And

17 To make all Laws which shall be necessary and proper for carrying into Execution the foregoing Powers, and all other Powers vested by this Constitution in the Government of the United States, or in any Department or Officer thereof.

SECTION 9: RESTRICTIONS ON CONGRESS

1 *The Migration or Importation of such Persons as any of the States now existing shall think proper to admit, shall not be prohibited by the Congress prior to the Year one thousand eight hundred and eight, but a Tax or duty may be imposed on such Importation, not exceeding ten dollars for each Person.*

2 The Privilege of the Writ of Habeas Corpus shall not be suspended, unless when in Cases of Rebellion or Invasion the public Safety may require it.

3 No Bill of Attainder or ex post facto Law shall be passed.

4 *No Capitation, or other direct, Tax shall be laid, unless in Proportion to the Census or Enumeration herein before directed to be taken.*

5 No Tax or Duty shall be laid on Articles exported from any State.

6 No Preference shall be given by any Regulation of Commerce or Revenue to the Ports of one State over those of another: nor shall Vessels bound to, or from, one State, be obliged to enter, clear, or pay Duties in another.

UNDERSTANDING THE CONSTITUTION Section 9 Section 9 lists specific areas in which Congress may not legislate. These include laws governing the importation of slaves—a provision made obsolete with the abolition of slavery (9.1); holding a person without charging him or her with a crime (9.2); passing an act that declares a specific person guilty of a crime ("bill of attainder") (9.3); and making an action illegal after it has been committed ("ex post facto") (9.3).

UNDERSTANDING THE CONSTITUTION 9.4 A "capitation tax" is a tax charged on an individual.

UNDERSTANDING THE CONSTITUTION 9.6 Congress cannot pass laws that favor commerce in one state over that of another. For example, Congress cannot pass a law requiring shipping to go through a particular state's port.

Guided Discussion

1. **Categorize** The Constitution ensures that the states make up a "common market," a group that promotes free trade and the easy movement of workers and money among its members—in this case, the states. What provisions in Article I, Sections 8 and 9, refer to a common market? *(Possible responses: All taxes and duties are the same for each state; a common currency is used; laws cover bankruptcies uniformly; states may not tax goods sent to other states; and ports must be treated equally.)*

2. **Draw Conclusions** Why do you think the Constitution has a specific provision for establishing post offices and post roads? *(Possible response: At the time of the writing of the Constitution, sending letters through the mail was the primary form of communication. Thus, for the country to operate properly, a functioning postal system had to be established.)*

More Information

The Electoral College Article II of the Constitution includes the establishment of the electoral college, an institution that has been controversial since the nation's beginnings. Originally, the electoral college functioned as a mechanism to allow citizens to vote, but with the safeguard of having knowledgeable electors make the final decision about who would actually serve as the chief executive. At the same time, the electoral college was closely linked to slavery. At the time of its creation, most Americans lived in the North. Thus, an election by popular vote alone would guarantee free states a firm grip on the presidency. However, the Three-Fifths Compromise counted a fraction of enslaved people (who could not vote) when determining representation in the House of Representatives. Thus, by using the number of representatives in its determination of electors, the electoral college gave southern states a voice in deciding the presidency that was disproportionate to what their voting population warranted.

In modern times, the electoral college has remained controversial. Although electors now—with rare exceptions—follow the wishes of the voting public, and although the Three-Fifths Compromise is gone, critics argue that the electoral college makes some people's votes more important than others. Thus, in states where votes tend to be close in presidential elections—such as Iowa or New Hampshire—a person's vote is far more important than those in more politically polarized larger states such as California or Alabama. In addition, the elections of 2000 and 2016, in which the winner of the electoral college lost the popular vote, heightened calls to reform the system.

HISTORICAL THINKING

ANSWER

Each of its subsections prohibits states from doing things the Confederacy did after its formation.

ANSWER

Answers will vary. Students may argue that electoral votes prevent a small number of large states from deciding an election. On the other hand, it could be argued that the president represents the entire population and not states, so direct voting is more representative.

CONSTITUTION OF THE UNITED STATES

7 No Money shall be drawn from the Treasury, but in Consequence of Appropriations made by Law; and a regular Statement and Account of the Receipts and Expenditures of all public Money shall be published from time to time.

8 No Title of Nobility shall be granted by the United States: And no Person holding any Office of Profit or Trust under them, shall, without the Consent of the Congress, accept of any present, Emolument, Office, or Title, of any kind whatever, from any King, Prince, or foreign State.

UNDERSTANDING THE CONSTITUTION Section 10 Section 10 sets out actions that the states are not permitted to take on their own: for example, entering into a treaty, coining money, or passing laws that interfere with contracts.

HISTORICAL THINKING How can Section 10 be used to prove that the secession of the southern states was unconstitutional?

SECTION 10: LIMITING THE AUTHORITY OF STATES

1 No State shall enter into any Treaty, Alliance, or Confederation; grant Letters of Marque and Reprisal; coin Money; emit Bills of Credit; make any Thing but gold and silver Coin a Tender in Payment of Debts; pass any Bill of Attainder, ex post facto Law, or Law impairing the Obligation of Contracts, or grant any Title of Nobility.

2 No State shall, without the Consent of the Congress, lay any Imposts or Duties on Imports or Exports, except what may be absolutely necessary for executing its inspection Laws: and the net Produce of all Duties and Imposts, laid by any State on Imports or Exports, shall be for the Use of the Treasury of the United States; and all such Laws shall be subject to the Revision and Control of the Congress.

ARTICLE II
UNDERSTANDING THE CONSTITUTION Section 1 Section 1 describes a detailed process for choosing the president. This process was replaced in 1804 by another detailed in the 12th Amendment.

UNDERSTANDING THE CONSTITUTION 1.2 Each state determines how its electors are chosen, but all follow the same principle. Voters cast their ballots for a ticket consisting of a president and a vice president. In most states, whoever wins the most votes in the state wins all that state's electoral votes.

HISTORICAL THINKING Some Americans believe voters should directly elect the president. Do you agree or disagree? Explain.

3 No State shall, without the Consent of Congress, lay any Duty of Tonnage, keep Troops, or Ships of War in time of Peace, enter into any Agreement or Compact with another State, or with a foreign Power, or engage in War, unless actually invaded, or in such imminent Danger as will not admit of delay.

Article II The Executive Branch
SECTION 1: ELECTING THE PRESIDENT

1 The executive Power shall be vested in a President of the United States of America. He shall hold his Office during the Term of four Years, and, together with the Vice President, chosen for the same Term, be elected, as follows

2 Each State shall appoint, in such Manner as the Legislature thereof may direct, a Number of Electors, equal to the whole Number of Senators and Representatives to which the State may be entitled in the Congress: but no Senator or Representative, or Person holding an Office of Trust or Profit under the United States, shall be appointed an Elector.

CONSTITUTION OF THE UNITED STATES

3 *The Electors shall meet in their respective States, and vote by Ballot for two Persons, of whom one at least shall not be an Inhabitant of the same State with themselves. And they shall make a List of all the Persons voted for, and of the Number of Votes for each; which List they shall sign and certify, and transmit sealed to the Seat of the Government of the United States, directed to the President of the Senate. The President of the Senate shall, in the Presence of the Senate and House of Representatives, open all the Certificates, and the Votes shall then be counted. The Person having the greatest Number of Votes shall be the President, if such Number be a Majority of the whole Number of Electors appointed; and if there be more than one who have such Majority, and have an equal Number of Votes, then the House of Representatives shall immediately choose by Ballot one of them for President; and if no Person have a Majority, then from the five highest on the List the said House shall in like Manner choose the President. But in choosing the President, the Votes shall be taken by States, the Representation from each State having one Vote; A quorum for this Purpose shall consist of a Member or Members from two thirds of the States, and a Majority of all the States shall be necessary to a Choice. In every Case, after the Choice of the President, the Person having the greatest Number of Votes of the Electors shall be the Vice President. But if there should remain two or more who have equal Votes, the Senate shall choose from them by Ballot the Vice President.*

4 The Congress may determine the Time of choosing the Electors, and the Day on which they shall give their Votes; which Day shall be the same throughout the United States.

5 No Person except a natural born Citizen, or a Citizen of the United States, at the time of the Adoption of this Constitution, shall be eligible to the Office of President; neither shall any Person be eligible to that Office who shall not have attained to the Age of thirty five Years, and been fourteen Years a Resident within the United States.

6 *In Case of the Removal of the President from Office, or of his Death, Resignation, or Inability to discharge the Powers and Duties of the said Office, the Same shall devolve on the Vice President, and the Congress may by Law provide for the Case of Removal, Death, Resignation or Inability, both of the President and Vice President, declaring what Officer shall then act as President, and such Officer shall act accordingly, until the Disability be removed, or a President shall be elected.*

7 The President shall, at stated Times, receive for his Services, a Compensation, which shall neither be increased nor diminished during the Period for which he shall have been elected, and he shall not receive within that Period any other Emolument from the United States, or any of them.

UNDERSTANDING THE CONSTITUTION 1.3 The italicized text refers to how vice presidents were originally elected. Voters cast ballots for presidential candidates, and the one who came in second became vice president. Today, a presidential candidate selects a running mate, and voters cast a single vote for the entire ticket.

Both houses of Congress convene each year in the House chamber to hear the president's State of the Union address. In this photo, Congress listens as President Barack Obama delivers his 2016 address.

Guided Discussion

1. **Make Inferences** Why do you think Section 1.3 of Article II was changed? *(Possible response: Originally, after votes were counted, the person with the most electoral votes became president and the runner-up vice president. However, these two people often disagreed with one another, making working together difficult. Thus, the provision was changed.)*

2. **Compare and Contrast** How do the requirements for a president differ from the requirements for a representative or a senator? *(Possible response: The requirements for a president are more stringent; a president must be at least 35 years old and a natural-born citizen. Senators and representatives can be younger and are not required to have been born in the United States.)*

More Information

The Constitution and the Court The Constitution has surprisingly little to say about the makeup and specific power of the Supreme Court. Today, the Court consists of eight associate justices and one Chief Justice, but that has not always been the case. As the Constitution is not specific about the number of justices, several laws over time have addressed this issue. The Judiciary Act of 1789 called for five associate justices and one Chief Justice. Later, Congress passed various laws changing the number, which varied from as many as ten to as few as five. In 1869, another Judiciary Act set the number at nine—a standard kept ever since.

The most important job of the Court is determining whether laws and presidential actions are in line with the Constitution. However, this responsibility—known as judicial review—is not explicitly granted in the Constitution. Alexander Hamilton and James Madison argued that the Court should take the role of interpreter of the Constitution. However, others, including Thomas Jefferson, were convinced that judicial review would make the Court too powerful and argued that all three branches should have equal say over constitutionality. It wasn't until 1803 that the argument was settled in *Marbury* v. *Madison*. In this case, the Court affirmed its responsibility for judicial review when Chief Justice John Marshall wrote, "It is empathetically the province and duty of the judicial department to say what the law is."

HISTORICAL THINKING

ANSWER

Examples include occasions such as George W. Bush's address concerning the U.S. response to the terrorist attacks of September 11, given on September 21, 2001.

CONSTITUTION OF THE UNITED STATES

UNDERSTANDING THE CONSTITUTION 1.8 Every president has taken the same oath of office, saying these exact words at the inauguration.

UNDERSTANDING THE CONSTITUTION Section 2 Section 2 outlines the president's authority. Among other duties, the president is commander in chief of the armed forces, has the power to make treaties, and can appoint ambassadors and Supreme Court justices. However, the treaties and appointments are subject to approval by the Senate.

HISTORICAL THINKING On what "extraordinary occasions" might a president wish to address both houses of Congress?

UNDERSTANDING THE CONSTITUTION Section 4 In the phrase "high crimes and misdemeanors," the word *high* does not mean "more serious" but rather refers to highly placed public officials.

8 Before he enter on the Execution of his Office, he shall take the following Oath or Affirmation:—"I do solemnly swear (or affirm) that I will faithfully execute the Office of President of the United States, and will to the best of my Ability, preserve, protect and defend the Constitution of the United States."

SECTION 2: EXECUTIVE POWERS

1 The President shall be Commander in Chief of the Army and Navy of the United States, and of the Militia of the several States, when called into the actual Service of the United States; he may require the Opinion, in writing, of the principal Officer in each of the executive Departments, upon any Subject relating to the Duties of their respective Offices, and he shall have Power to grant Reprieves and Pardons for Offences against the United States, except in Cases of Impeachment.

2 He shall have Power, by and with the Advice and Consent of the Senate, to make Treaties, provided two thirds of the Senators present concur; and he shall nominate, and by and with the Advice and Consent of the Senate, shall appoint Ambassadors, other public Ministers and Consuls, Judges of the supreme Court, and all other Officers of the United States, whose Appointments are not herein otherwise provided for, and which shall be established by Law: but the Congress may by Law vest the Appointment of such inferior Officers, as they think proper, in the President alone, in the Courts of Law, or in the Heads of Departments.

3 The President shall have Power to fill up all Vacancies that may happen during the Recess of the Senate, by granting Commissions which shall expire at the End of their next Session.

SECTION 3: THE PRESIDENT AND CONGRESS

He shall from time to time give to the Congress Information of the State of the Union, and recommend to their Consideration such Measures as he shall judge necessary and expedient; he may, on extraordinary Occasions, convene both Houses, or either of them, and in Case of Disagreement between them, with Respect to the Time of Adjournment, he may adjourn them to such Time as he shall think proper; he shall receive Ambassadors and other public Ministers; he shall take Care that the Laws be faithfully executed, and shall Commission all the Officers of the United States.

SECTION 4: IMPEACHMENT

The President, Vice President and all civil Officers of the United States, shall be removed from Office on Impeachment for, and Conviction of, Treason, Bribery, or other high Crimes and Misdemeanors.

CONSTITUTION OF THE UNITED STATES

Article III The Judiciary Branch

SECTION 1: SUPREME COURT AND LOWER COURTS

The judicial Power of the United States, shall be vested in one supreme Court, and in such inferior Courts as the Congress may from time to time ordain and establish. The Judges, both of the supreme and inferior Courts, shall hold their Offices during good Behavior, and shall, at stated Times, receive for their Services, a Compensation, which shall not be diminished during their Continuance in Office.

The Supreme Court justices posed for this photo in 2017. In the top row, from left to right, are Elena Kagan, Samuel Alito, Jr., Sonia Sotomayor, and Neil Gorsuch. In the bottom row, from left to right, are Ruth Bader Ginsburg, Anthony Kennedy, John Roberts, Jr. (chief justice), Clarence Thomas, and Stephen Breyer.

SECTION 2: AUTHORITY OF THE SUPREME COURT

1 The judicial Power shall extend to all Cases, in Law and Equity, arising under this Constitution, the Laws of the United States, and Treaties made, or which shall be made, under their Authority;—to all Cases affecting Ambassadors, other public Ministers and Consuls;—to all Cases of admiralty and maritime Jurisdiction;—to Controversies to which the United States shall be a Party;—*to Controversies between two or more States;—between a State and Citizens of another State;—between Citizens of different States;—between Citizens of the same State claiming Lands under Grants of different States, and between a State, or the Citizens thereof, and foreign States, Citizens or Subjects.*

2 In all Cases affecting Ambassadors, other public Ministers and Consuls, and those in which a State shall be Party, the supreme Court shall have original Jurisdiction. In all the other Cases before mentioned, the supreme Court shall have appellate Jurisdiction, both as to Law and Fact, with such Exceptions, and under such Regulations as the Congress shall make.

3 The Trial of all Crimes, except in Cases of Impeachment, shall be by Jury; and such Trial shall be held in the State where the said Crimes shall have been committed; but when not committed within any State, the Trial shall be at such Place or Places as the Congress may by Law have directed.

SECTION 3: TREASON

1 Treason against the United States, shall consist only in levying War against them, or in adhering to their Enemies, giving them Aid and Comfort. No Person shall be convicted of Treason unless on the Testimony of two Witnesses to the same overt Act, or on Confession in open Court.

2 The Congress shall have Power to declare the Punishment of Treason, but no Attainder of Treason shall work Corruption of Blood, or Forfeiture except during the Life of the Person attainted.

ARTICLE III
UNDERSTANDING THE CONSTITUTION 2.1 The italicized portion of this section was changed in 1795 by the 11th Amendment, which states that the Judicial Department does not have jurisdiction in matters between states or between a foreign country and a U.S. state.

UNDERSTANDING THE CONSTITUTION 2.2 When the Supreme Court serves as an appeals court, it reviews decisions made by lower courts.

UNDERSTANDING THE CONSTITUTION Section 3 Treason is the only crime specifically defined in the Constitution. Between 1954 and 2016, one person was charged with treason for collaborating in the production of propaganda videos for the terrorist group al-Qaeda.

Citizenship Handbook **R17**

Guided Discussion

1. **Form and Support Opinions** Why do you think the Framers required two-thirds of senators to approve treaties rather than the simple majority needed to pass laws? *(Possible response: Since treaties concern important foreign policy questions, which impact the entire country, the Framers wanted to ensure that these decisions had widespread support and could not pass without bipartisanship.)*

2. **Make Predictions** Remember that the president can do some things without the Senate's approval—for example, command the army and navy, ask opinions of the departments, grant pardons, and make recess appointments. What potential problems could arise from a president's being given these unilateral powers? *(Answers will vary. Possible response: A president might make unpopular and even dangerous decisions, claiming that they fell under one or more of these categories.)*

More Information

Religion and the Constitution The only overt mention of religion in the original, unamended Constitution is found in Article VI, Section 3. This portion, known as the no religious test clause, forbids requiring federal office holders to be of a specific religion to serve. Thus, anyone—Muslim, Jew, Christian, Sikh, or follower of any other belief—theoretically could be elected to Congress or become president. The Framers inserted this provision because they believed that singling out certain religions would inevitably lead to discrimination, and they believed that religious requirements might prohibit some of the best people from serving the national interests.

However, in the nation's early days, this clause did not apply to state officeholders. Every state required local officeholders to be Christian; in some cases, only Protestants could hold office. This interpretation lasted until 1961 when, in the case *Torcaso* v. *Watkins*, the Supreme Court ruled that all religious tests—even at the local level—were unconstitutional.

HISTORICAL THINKING

ANSWER

Forming a state within an existing state could make the nation unmanageably complex.

CONSTITUTION OF THE UNITED STATES

ARTICLE IV
UNDERSTANDING THE CONSTITUTION Section 1 "Full faith and credit" means that states agree to respect and honor each other's laws and documents.

UNDERSTANDING THE CONSTITUTION 2.3 The text in italics is known as the fugitive slave clause, which barred people who had escaped slavery in the South from living as free people in northern states. It became obsolete with the abolition of slavery.

HISTORICAL THINKING Why do you think the Framers felt the Constitution needed to place limits on the formation of a state within an existing one?

UNDERSTANDING THE CONSTITUTION Section 4 Here the Constitution commits the U.S. government to protecting the people of a state from attack by a foreign government, but also from violence originating within the United States, or "domestic violence."

Article IV States and Citizens

SECTION 1: MUTUAL RESPECT AMONG STATES

Full Faith and Credit shall be given in each State to the public Acts, Records, and judicial Proceedings of every other State. And the Congress may by general Laws prescribe the Manner in which such Acts, Records and Proceedings shall be proved, and the Effect thereof.

SECTION 2: CITIZENS OF STATES AND OF THE UNITED STATES

1 The Citizens of each State shall be entitled to all Privileges and Immunities of Citizens in the several States.

2 A Person charged in any State with Treason, Felony, or other Crime, who shall flee from Justice, and be found in another State, shall on Demand of the executive Authority of the State from which he fled, be delivered up, to be removed to the State having Jurisdiction of the Crime.

3 *No Person held to Service or Labor in one State, under the Laws thereof, escaping into another, shall, in Consequence of any Law or Regulation therein, be discharged from such Service or Labor, but shall be delivered up on Claim of the Party to whom such Service or Labor may be due.*

SECTION 3: NEW STATES

1 New States may be admitted by the Congress into this Union; but no new State shall be formed or erected within the Jurisdiction of any other State; nor any State be formed by the Junction of two or more States, or Parts of States, without the Consent of the Legislatures of the States concerned as well as of the Congress.

2 The Congress shall have Power to dispose of and make all needful Rules and Regulations respecting the Territory or other Property belonging to the United States; and nothing in this Constitution shall be so construed as to Prejudice any Claims of the United States, or of any particular State.

SECTION 4: PROTECTION OF STATES BY THE UNITED STATES

The United States shall guarantee to every State in this Union a Republican Form of Government, and shall protect each of them against Invasion; and on Application of the Legislature, or of the Executive (when the Legislature cannot be convened), against domestic Violence.

CONSTITUTION OF THE UNITED STATES

Article V Amending the Constitution

1 The Congress, whenever two thirds of both Houses shall deem it necessary, shall propose Amendments to this Constitution, or, on the Application of the Legislatures of two thirds of the several States, shall call a Convention for proposing Amendments, which, in either Case, shall be valid to all Intents and Purposes, as Part of this Constitution, when ratified by the Legislatures of three fourths of the several States, or by Conventions in three fourths thereof, as the one or the other Mode of Ratification may be proposed by the Congress; **2** Provided that no Amendment which may be made prior to the Year One thousand eight hundred and eight shall in any Manner affect the first and fourth Clauses in the Ninth Section of the first Article; and that no State, without its Consent, shall be deprived of its equal Suffrage in the Senate.

Article VI The Supreme Law of the Land

1 All Debts contracted and Engagements entered into, before the Adoption of this Constitution, shall be as valid against the United States under this Constitution, as under the Confederation.

2 This Constitution, and the Laws of the United States which shall be made in Pursuance thereof; and all Treaties made, or which shall be made, under the Authority of the United States, shall be the supreme Law of the Land; and the Judges in every State shall be bound thereby, any Thing in the Constitution or Laws of any State to the Contrary notwithstanding.

3 The Senators and Representatives before mentioned, and the Members of the several State Legislatures, and all executive and judicial Officers, both of the United States and of the several States, shall be bound by Oath or Affirmation, to support this Constitution; but no religious Test shall ever be required as a Qualification to any Office or public Trust under the United States.

ARTICLE V
UNDERSTANDING THE CONSTITUTION Article 5
This article describes the process for amending the Constitution but states that the first and fourth clauses in Article 1's ninth section cannot be amended before 1808. Remember that these clauses refer to the importation of slaves and to a tax charged on an individual.

ARTICLE VI
UNDERSTANDING THE CONSTITUTION Article 6
This article states that all judges and legislators must uphold and be bound by the Constitution, the supreme law of the land. When any state law or part of a law conflicts with the Constitution or federal laws and treaties, the federal law is the one that must be followed. This concept was important to keep the states of the new nation united in their dealings with each other, with foreign powers, and with the federal government.

HISTORICAL THINKING What might happen if a state established laws that contradicted those in the Constitution?

Today, "the people" referred to in the Constitution includes all adult U.S. citizens.

Guided Discussion

1. **Synthesize** Imagine that a person commits a crime in Texas and flees to New Mexico. What part of the Constitution addresses this situation? *(Article IV, Section 2.3)* According to the Constitution, what must New Mexico do with that fugitive? *(The government of New Mexico must return the fugitive to California.)*

2. **Make Inferences** Article IV, Section 2.3, addresses the situation of fugitive slaves, but the words *slave* and *slavery* are not used anywhere in the original Constitution. Why do you think the Framers avoided putting the word *slave* and *slavery* in the Constitution? *(Possible response: They might have purposely avoided the words because they realized that slavery contradicted many of the goals of the nation's founding.)* Why do you think references to slavery existed in the Constitution at all? *(Possible response: At the time of its writing, slavery was an important part of the economy in many states. If the Constitution had prohibited—or perhaps even ignored—slavery, those states may have refused to approve it.)*

HISTORICAL THINKING

ANSWER

Such a law would likely be challenged in court and ultimately found to be unconstitutional.

More Information

The Stubborn "Rogue's Island" Rhode Island's reluctance to ratify the Constitution stemmed from its citizens' fear that a strong central government would become too powerful, stifling Rhode Island's tradition of individualism, self-reliance, and abolitionism. Members of the colony's ruling rural party were so opposed to becoming part of the United States, in fact, that they refused to send delegates to the Philadelphia Convention of 1787.

The Framers wanted each state to hold its own local conventions to debate the ratification of the Constitution. However, from 1787 to 1790, the leaders of Rhode Island refused to do so. Instead, they put the choice to popular vote, allowing the citizens to choose for themselves. The results were overwhelming: Rhode Islanders voted to reject the Constitution by a vote of 2,708 to 243. It wasn't until eight months after George Washington's inauguration that a local convention was finally called. Even so, it took two attempts and the narrowest vote of any state (34 to 32) for Rhode Island to join the United States.

HISTORICAL THINKING

ANSWER

The question asks for an opinion, but students should see that all the states are committed to the same constitutional principles.

CONSTITUTION OF THE UNITED STATES

Article VII
UNDERSTANDING THE CONSTITUTION Article 7
On June 21, 1788, New Hampshire became the 9th state to ratify the Constitution and make it the law of the United States. The Framers clearly stated in Article 7 that the Constitution required the approval of only 9 states, not the 13 then in existence. However, the Framers wanted each state to ratify the Constitution through a state convention. They knew the new nation's survival depended on the populous and wealthy states of Virginia and New York, which were slow to ratify. After lengthy debates, first Virginia and then New York gave approval, becoming the 11th and 12th states to ratify the Constitution. But Rhode Island was the main roadblock to unanimous approval. It officially joined the United States only after being told the state would be treated like a foreign government if it did not.

HISTORICAL THINKING Do you think your state would ratify the Constitution today? Why or why not?

Article VII Ratification

The Ratification of the Conventions of nine States, shall be sufficient for the Establishment of this Constitution between the States so ratifying the Same.

[Here appears some text noting corrections that were made on the original copy of the document.]

Done in Convention by the Unanimous Consent of the States present the Seventeenth Day of September in the Year of our Lord one thousand seven hundred and Eighty seven and of the Independence of the United States of America the Twelfth In witness whereof We have hereunto subscribed our Names,

G°. Washington
President and deputy from Virginia

Massachusetts
Nathaniel Gorham
Rufus King

New York
Alexander Hamilton

Delaware
George Read
Gunning Bedford, Jr.
John Dickinson
Richard Bassett
Jacob Broom

Virginia
John Blair
James Madison, Jr.

Pennsylvania
Benjamin Franklin
Thomas Mifflin
Robert Morris
George Clymer
Thomas Fitzsimons
Jared Ingersoll
James Wilson
Gouverneur Morris

New Hampshire
John Langdon
Nicholas Gilman

New Jersey
William Livingston
David Brearley
William Paterson
Jonathan Dayton

Connecticut
William Samuel Johnson
Roger Sherman

North Carolina
William Blount
Richard Dobbs Spaight
Hugh Williamson

South Carolina
John Rutledge
Charles Cotesworth Pinckney
Charles Pinckney
Pierce Butler

Maryland
James McHenry
Daniel of St. Thomas Jenifer
Daniel Carroll

Georgia
William Few
Abraham Baldwin

THE BILL OF RIGHTS AND AMENDMENTS 11–27

Introduction

Individual rights are fundamental to liberty. As you've read, the Magna Carta influenced the Declaration of Independence, but it also helped inspire the Bill of Rights. The people who came to America from Britain had enjoyed the freedoms granted to them under both the Magna Carta and the English Bill of Rights. They believed they were entitled to these rights when they settled their colonies. After the American Revolution, the new country's leaders wanted citizens' individual freedoms to become law. In 1787, Thomas Jefferson wrote to James Madison, "[A] bill of rights is what the people are entitled to against every government on earth, general or particular, and what no just government should refuse."

As a result, a list of basic citizenship rights became a permanent part of the Constitution. The following is a transcription of the first 10 amendments to the Constitution in their original form: the Bill of Rights. As you'll see, over time, more amendments were added to the Constitution to address issues that arose as the nation grew and changed.

The Preamble to the Bill of Rights

Congress of the United States begun and held at the City of New York, on Wednesday the fourth of March, one thousand seven hundred and eighty nine.

THE Conventions of a number of the States, having at the time of their adopting the Constitution, expressed a desire, in order to prevent misconstruction or abuse of its powers, that further declaratory and restrictive clauses should be added: And as extending the ground of public confidence in the Government, will best ensure the beneficient ends of its institution.

RESOLVED by the Senate and House of Representatives of the United States of America, in Congress assembled, two thirds of both Houses concurring, that the following Articles be proposed to the Legislatures of the several States, as amendments to the Constitution of the United States, all, or any of which Articles, when ratified by three fourths of the said Legislatures, to be valid to all intents and purposes, as part of the said Constitution; viz.

UNDERSTANDING THE PREAMBLE *Viz* is Latin for "that is to say" or "namely."

More Information

Bills of Rights Over the years, nations as diverse as South Africa, the Philippines, Canada, France, and India have incorporated a bill, charter, or declaration of rights into their constitutions. Often, these documents protect many of the same freedoms guaranteed by the U.S. Bill of Rights—speech, assembly, and religion, or the freedom from unlawful imprisonment. Like the Bill of Rights, which includes a prohibition on forcing citizens to quarter soldiers, these documents can also address other more specific concerns of a nation's citizens.

For example, India's Fundamental Rights (Article III of its constitution) guarantees citizens the freedom to practice any professions they choose and prohibits a form of discrimination called "untouchability." South Africa's Bill of Rights protects the rights of citizens to form and join labor unions. In France, the Declaration of the Rights of Man and the Citizen, written in 1789, specifically prohibited certain actions that the monarchy had taken before the French Revolution. **ASK:** Why might people forming a new government consider a specific list of protected rights to be important? *(Possible responses: People forming a new government might have recent memories of times when their rights, or the rights of others, were violated; also, they might not want to assume that everyone who leads the government will share their opinions.)*

More Information

Miranda Rights In the decision *Miranda* v. *Arizona* (1966), the Supreme Court considered four cases in which people had been convicted of crimes on the basis, or partial basis, of their own confessions. In some cases, people had been interrogated several times, or over many days, and at no time had anyone told them of their right to remain silent. The Court debated whether, given the stress and isolation of the interrogations these people experienced, they might have been "compelled" to be witnesses against themselves, in violation of Amendment 5. The Court concluded that "without proper safeguards, the . . . inherently compelling pressures" of being interrogated could "compel" people to speak, when otherwise they would not. To prevent this issue, persons being arrested must be informed of their rights. In 2000, the Supreme Court upheld this decision.

Students may recognize the Miranda Warning (named for Ernesto Miranda, the plaintiff in the case cited above) from popular culture. Display its text on the board or distribute copies to the class: "You have the right to remain silent. Anything you say can and will be used against you as evidence in a court of law. You have the right to an attorney. If you cannot afford an attorney, one will be appointed for you. Do you understand these rights as they have been read to you?" Discuss with students whether this warning is an effective way to protect people from incriminating themselves. **ASK:** What is the importance of the warning's final sentence to people under arrest? *(Possible response: If people cannot understand these rights—perhaps because they cannot speak the language, or are stressed and confused—then they cannot effectively protect themselves.)*

HISTORICAL THINKING

ANSWER

Freedom of religion is one of the most basic principles on which our country was formed.

ANSWER

Answers will vary. Students might think about why the Framers would have included this as one of the 10 most important rights.

AMENDMENTS

UNDERSTANDING AMENDMENT 1 The determination to protect religious freedom arose in part from Thomas Jefferson's 1786 Statute for Religious Freedom, which he composed for Virginia's legislature. In his statute, Jefferson called for religious liberty and the separation of church and state.

HISTORICAL THINKING Why do you think the Framers insisted there should be "no law respecting an establishment of religion"?

UNDERSTANDING AMENDMENT 2 This amendment has been hotly debated for decades. Many Americans believe the amendment grants them the right to possess guns. Others think gun ownership should be controlled.

HISTORICAL THINKING Do you think the Framers intended to grant all Americans the right to own guns or just those in militias? Explain your ideas.

UNDERSTANDING AMENDMENT 3 This amendment stemmed from the colonists' experience during the American Revolution. Back then, British soldiers could come into colonists' homes and demand food and shelter. This isn't an issue anymore.

ARTICLES in addition to, and Amendment of the Constitution of the United States of America, proposed by Congress, and ratified by the Legislatures of the several States, pursuant to the fifth Article of the original Constitution.

Amendment 1 (1791)

Congress shall make no law respecting an establishment of religion, or prohibiting the free exercise thereof; or abridging the freedom of speech, or of the press; or the right of the people peaceably to assemble, and to petition the Government for a redress of grievances.

Amendment 2 (1791)

A well regulated Militia, being necessary to the security of a free State, the right of the people to keep and bear Arms, shall not be infringed.

Amendment 3 (1791)

No Soldier shall, in time of peace be quartered in any house, without the consent of the Owner, nor in time of war, but in a manner to be prescribed by law.

Amendment 4 (1791)

The right of the people to be secure in their persons, houses, papers, and effects, against unreasonable searches and seizures, shall not be violated, and no Warrants shall issue, but upon probable cause, supported by Oath or affirmation, and particularly describing the place to be searched, and the persons or things to be seized.

AMENDMENTS

Amendment 5 (1791)

No person shall be held to answer for a capital, or otherwise infamous crime, unless on a presentment or indictment of a Grand Jury, except in cases arising in the land or naval forces, or in the Militia, when in actual service in time of War or public danger; nor shall any person be subject for the same offence to be twice put in jeopardy of life or limb; nor shall be compelled in any criminal case to be a witness against himself, nor be deprived of life, liberty, or property, without due process of law; nor shall private property be taken for public use, without just compensation.

Amendment 6 (1791)

In all criminal prosecutions, the accused shall enjoy the right to a speedy and public trial, by an impartial jury of the State and district wherein the crime shall have been committed, which district shall have been previously ascertained by law, and to be informed of the nature and cause of the accusation; to be confronted with the witnesses against him; to have compulsory process for obtaining witnesses in his favor, and to have the Assistance of Counsel for his defence.

Amendment 7 (1791)

In Suits at common law, where the value in controversy shall exceed twenty dollars, the right of trial by jury shall be preserved, and no fact tried by a jury, shall be otherwise re-examined in any Court of the United States, than according to the rules of the common law.

Amendment 8 (1791)

Excessive bail shall not be required, nor excessive fines imposed, nor cruel and unusual punishments inflicted.

Amendment 9 (1791)

The enumeration in the Constitution, of certain rights, shall not be construed to deny or disparage others retained by the people.

Amendment 10 (1791)

The powers not delegated to the United States by the Constitution, nor prohibited by it to the States, are reserved to the States respectively, or to the people.

UNDERSTANDING AMENDMENTS 4–6 These three amendments protect people who are suspected of a crime or being tried for one.

- Amendment 4 says that police must have a good reason ("probable cause") before they can seize, or take someone's possessions.
- Amendment 5 means that a person has the right to remain silent when charged with a crime. The amendment is the basis for the Miranda rights warning, which requires police to tell those they arrest their rights.
- Amendment 6 guarantees those accused of a crime to a speedy and public trial.

UNDERSTANDING AMENDMENT 7 This amendment provides the right to a trial by jury. Common law is unwritten law created by judges that apply to all people.

UNDERSTANDING AMENDMENT 8 This amendment proclaims that no punishment should be "excessive" or "cruel and unusual." In other words, the harshness of the punishment should match the seriousness of the crime.

HISTORICAL THINKING How might this amendment be used to either justify or oppose the death penalty as punishment for a crime?

UNDERSTANDING AMENDMENTS 9 and 10 Amendment 9 promises that other rights not stated in the Bill of Rights, such as the right to travel freely, are still covered. Amendment 10 says each state has the power to make laws that are not covered by the Constitution, including laws about starting a business.

Guided Discussion

1. **Make Generalizations** What do the liberties enumerated in Amendment 1 have in common? *(Possible response: They protect people's right to have and express opinions without fearing punishment from their government.)*

2. **Draw Conclusions** What kinds of searches would be permitted under Amendment 4, and why would those searches be permitted? *(A search is permitted when the police or government officials have gotten a warrant based on probable cause and have clearly established where they are looking and what they are looking for. Some searches might be permitted so that police and government officials can investigate actual crimes without violating peoples' rights.)*

HISTORICAL THINKING

ANSWER

Answers will vary. Students may argue that while the amendment prohibits "cruel" punishments, it does not specifically prohibit the death penalty, so it is justified as a punishment; students may also offer evidence that lifetime imprisonment or other punishments would be crueler. Other students may offer evidence that the death penalty qualifies as cruel, even if it isn't "unusual," and therefore it should be prohibited.

More Information

The 2000 Presidential Election The race between Republican George W. Bush and Democrat Al Gore was a close one in many states, with one candidate or the other holding a lead of just a few thousand—or even a few hundred—votes. Bush only needed Florida's electors to win, and he initially had enough of a lead in that state that Gore conceded. As vote counting continued, however, Bush's Florida lead shrank to fewer than 600 votes and then to fewer than 400. Gore took back his earlier concession. Over the next several weeks, election officials in Florida held recounts and examined whether issues with some of Florida's ballots might have affected the totals.

Eventually, the Florida Supreme Court called for a manual recount, which the Bush campaign appealed. In the decision of *Bush* v. *Gore*, the United States Supreme Court overturned the recount decision, which meant that Bush's narrow Florida victory stood. As a result, Bush won the electoral college by a single vote and became the nation's 44th president. He had lost the popular vote by about half a million votes. **ASK:** Why do you think an election like this one prompts people to challenge the role of the electoral college in presidential elections? *(Possible response: When the electoral college makes an election decision that seems to go against the decision made by voters, people may question whether their votes really count or even whether the electoral college is necessary.)*

HISTORICAL THINKING

ANSWER

Answers will vary. Responses may be consistent with each student's answer to the previous question on popular election of the president.

AMENDMENTS

UNDERSTANDING AMENDMENT 11 According to this amendment, the United States has no power in lawsuits against individual states.

UNDERSTANDING AMENDMENT 12 This amendment established the electoral college, which decides who the president and vice president will be. The electoral college was challenged in 2000 and 2016, when the candidates who won the popular vote (Al Gore in 2000 and Hillary Clinton in 2016) lost the elections to George W. Bush and Donald Trump, respectively.

HISTORICAL THINKING Do you think presidential elections should be decided by the electoral college? Explain why or why not.

Amendment 11 (1798)

[**Note:** Article 3, Section 2, of the Constitution was modified by the 11th Amendment.]

The Judicial power of the United States shall not be construed to extend to any suit in law or equity, commenced or prosecuted against one of the United States by Citizens of another State, or by Citizens or Subjects of any Foreign State.

Amendment 12 (1804)

[**Note:** Part of Article 2, Section 1, of the Constitution was replaced by the 12th Amendment.]

The Electors shall meet in their respective states and vote by ballot for President and Vice-President, one of whom, at least, shall not be an inhabitant of the same state with themselves; they shall name in their ballots the person voted for as President, and in distinct ballots the person voted for as Vice-President, and they shall make distinct lists of all persons voted for as President, and of all persons voted for as Vice-President, and of the number of votes for each, which lists they shall sign and certify, and transmit sealed to the seat of the government of the United States, directed to the President of the Senate; —the President of the Senate shall, in the presence of the Senate and House of Representatives, open all the certificates and the votes shall then be counted; —The person having the greatest number of votes for President, shall be the President, if such number be a majority of the whole number of Electors appointed; and if no person have such majority, then from the persons having the highest numbers not exceeding three on the list of those voted for as President, the House of Representatives shall choose immediately, by ballot, the President. But in choosing the President, the votes shall be taken by states, the representation from each state having one vote; a quorum for this purpose shall consist of a member or members from two-thirds of the states, and a majority of all the states shall be necessary to a choice. *And if the House of Representatives shall not choose a President whenever the right of choice shall devolve upon them, before the fourth day of March next following, then the Vice-President shall act as President, as in case of the death or other constitutional disability of the President.* The person having the greatest number of votes as Vice-President, shall be the Vice-President, if such number be a majority of the whole number of Electors appointed, and if no person have a majority, then from the two highest numbers on the list, the Senate shall choose the Vice-President; a quorum for the purpose shall consist of two-thirds of the whole number of Senators, and a majority of the whole number shall be necessary to a choice. But no person constitutionally ineligible to the office of President shall be eligible to that of Vice-President of the United States.

AMENDMENTS

Amendment 13 (1865)

[Note: A portion of Article 4, Section 2, of the Constitution was superseded by the 13th Amendment.]

SECTION 1: Neither slavery nor involuntary servitude, except as a punishment for crime whereof the party shall have been duly convicted, shall exist within the United States, or any place subject to their jurisdiction.

SECTION 2: Congress shall have power to enforce this article by appropriate legislation.

Amendment 14 (1868)

[Note: Article 1, Section 2, of the Constitution was modified by Section 2 of the 14th Amendment.]

SECTION 1: All persons born or naturalized in the United States, and subject to the jurisdiction thereof, are citizens of the United States and of the State wherein they reside. No State shall make or enforce any law which shall abridge the privileges or immunities of citizens of the United States; nor shall any State deprive any person of life, liberty, or property, without due process of law; nor deny to any person within its jurisdiction the equal protection of the laws.

SECTION 2: Representatives shall be apportioned among the several States according to their respective numbers, counting the whole number of persons in each State, excluding Indians not taxed. But when the right to vote at any election for the choice of electors for President and Vice-President of the United States, Representatives in Congress, the Executive and Judicial officers of a State, or the members of the *Legislature thereof, is denied to any of the male inhabitants of such State, being twenty-one years of age, and citizens of the United States,* or in any way abridged, except for participation in rebellion, or other crime, the basis of representation therein shall be reduced in the proportion which the number of such male citizens shall bear to the whole number of male citizens twenty-one years of age in such State.

SECTION 3: No person shall be a Senator or Representative in Congress, or elector of President and Vice-President, or hold any office, civil or military, under the United States, or under any State, who, having previously taken an oath, as a member of Congress, or as an officer of the United States, or as a member of any State legislature, or as an executive or judicial officer of any State, to support the Constitution of the United States, shall have engaged in insurrection or rebellion against the same, or given aid or comfort to the enemies thereof. But Congress may by a vote of two-thirds of each House, remove such disability.

UNDERSTANDING AMENDMENT 14 Section 1 This section defines citizenship and ensures that all citizens enjoy the same rights and the same protections by the law.

UNDERSTANDING AMENDMENT 14 Section 2 This section overrides the Three-Fifths Compromise in Article I. As a result of this amendment, each citizen is counted as a whole person—except Native Americans.

UNDERSTANDING AMENDMENT 14 Sections 3 and 4 These sections of the amendment refer to those who supported or fought for the Confederacy.

Citizenship Handbook **R25**

Guided Discussion

1. **Make Inferences** What do Sections 1 and 2 of Amendment 14 suggest about the authors' points of view on citizenship and voting rights? *(Possible response: These sections suggest that the authors did not consider voting rights to be an automatic right of citizenship, since Section 1 grants citizenship to "all persons born or naturalized in the United States" and Section 2 limits voting rights to men 21 years of age or older.)*

2. **Analyze Language Use** Section 3 of Amendment 14 is directed at people who "shall have engaged in insurrection or rebellion against the same [the United States], or given aid or comfort to the enemies thereof." Note the date of this amendment and consider what you know about American history. To whom does this description most likely refer? *(It most likely refers to people who had fought for the Confederacy in the Civil War or who otherwise had supported the Confederacy.)*

More Information

The Equal Rights Amendment Three years after Amendment 19 granted women the right to vote, former suffrage activist Alice Paul introduced a potential Amendment 20 to Congress, one that would grant equal rights in all areas to women who were citizens of the United States. The Equal Rights Amendment, or ERA, did not pass in 1923; it languished in committee in the House, appearing at each session but never getting approval. Finally, in 1970, Representative Martha Griffiths petitioned to have the ERA brought out for House approval. It won House approval in 1971 and Senate approval the following year. The ERA faced strong public and political opposition, however; and although a majority of states (35) ratified it, it did not reach the number needed to pass (38). Had it passed, it would have become Amendment 27. The effort to pass the ERA has not disappeared: In 2011, members of the House and Senate again introduced the amendment to Congress for consideration.

ASK: Do you think that a new constitutional amendment would be an effective way to achieve widespread equal rights for all people? *(Answers will vary. Students should support their opinions with evidence from history, their own experience, and their understanding of existing constitutional amendments.)*

HISTORICAL THINKING

ANSWER

Reconstruction was a process of bringing southern states back into the Union, but they had to follow new rules regarding the rights of former slaves. These amendments were passed during the process, and they outlined these new rights.

AMENDMENTS

UNDERSTANDING AMENDMENT 15 As a result of this amendment, African-American men were granted voting rights. No woman of any race or color could vote. Unfortunately, even after this amendment was passed, some states passed laws that required taxes, tests, and other unfair requirements for people to be permitted to vote.

HISTORICAL THINKING Why do you think the 13th, 14th, and 15th amendments are sometimes referred to as the "Reconstruction amendments"?

SECTION 4: The validity of the public debt of the United States, authorized by law, including debts incurred for payment of pensions and bounties for services in suppressing insurrection or rebellion, shall not be questioned. But neither the United States nor any State shall assume or pay any debt or obligation incurred in aid of insurrection or rebellion against the United States, or any claim for the loss or emancipation of any slave; but all such debts, obligations and claims shall be held illegal and void.

SECTION 5: The Congress shall have the power to enforce, by appropriate legislation, the provisions of this article.

Amendment 15 (1870)

SECTION 1: The right of citizens of the United States to vote shall not be denied or abridged by the United States or by any State on account of race, color, or previous condition of servitude—

SECTION 2: The Congress shall have the power to enforce this article by appropriate legislation.

Amendment 16 (1913)

[**Note:** Article 1, Section 9, of the Constitution was modified by the 16th Amendment.]

The Congress shall have power to lay and collect taxes on incomes, from whatever source derived, without apportionment among the several States, and without regard to any census or enumeration.

In this illustration, a group of men who helped bring about the 15th Amendment, including Abraham Lincoln, Hiram Revels, and Frederick Douglass, watch as President Ulysses S. Grant signs the amendment.

AMENDMENTS

Amendment 17 (1913)

[Note: Article 1, Section 3, of the Constitution was modified by the 17th Amendment.]

The Senate of the United States shall be composed of two Senators from each State, elected by the people thereof, for six years; and each Senator shall have one vote. The electors in each State shall have the qualifications requisite for electors of the most numerous branch of the State legislatures.

When vacancies happen in the representation of any State in the Senate, the executive authority of such State shall issue writs of election to fill such vacancies: Provided, That the legislature of any State may empower the executive thereof to make temporary appointments until the people fill the vacancies by election as the legislature may direct.

This amendment shall not be so construed as to affect the election or term of any Senator chosen before it becomes valid as part of the Constitution.

Amendment 18 (1919)

Repealed by the 21st Amendment.

SECTION 1: *After one year from the ratification of this article the manufacture, sale, or transportation of intoxicating liquors within, the importation thereof into, or the exportation thereof from the United States and all territory subject to the jurisdiction thereof for beverage purposes is hereby prohibited.*

SECTION 2: *The Congress and the several States shall have concurrent power to enforce this article by appropriate legislation.*

SECTION 3: *This article shall be inoperative unless it shall have been ratified as an amendment to the Constitution by the legislatures of the several States, as provided in the Constitution, within seven years from the date of the submission hereof to the States by the Congress.*

Amendment 19 (1920)

The right of citizens of the United States to vote shall not be denied or abridged by the United States or by any State on account of sex.

Congress shall have power to enforce this article by appropriate legislation.

UNDERSTANDING AMENDMENT 18 Known as the Prohibition Amendment, the 18th Amendment was repealed only 14 years later, in 1933, by the 21st Amendment. Alcohol was associated with social problems including abuse of women and children.

HISTORICAL THINKING Why do you think the 18th Amendment was repealed?

Federal agents pour a barrel filled with beer down a sewer during Prohibition.

UNDERSTANDING AMENDMENT 19 With the passage of the 19th Amendment, all women received the right to vote in all states. Prior to ratification of this amendment, a number of states already permitted women to vote.

HISTORICAL THINKING Why was it important to add an amendment to the Constitution granting women voting rights and not just leave the matter to individual states?

Citizenship Handbook **R27**

Guided Discussion

1. **Analyze Language Use** Why might the authors of Amendment 19 have wanted to reflect the language of Amendment 15 so closely? *(Possible response: The clear, concise language of Amendment 15 granted voting rights to all African Americans—as well as to people of any other race—without any qualifications or limitations. The authors of Amendment 19 may have wanted to make it clear that women were being granted the exact same rights, so they used nearly identical language.)*

2. **Analyze Visuals** Describe the illustration related to Amendment 15. What do the images that surround the central image suggest about the illustrator's thoughts on the results of the amendment? *(Possible response: The images show African Americans serving in the military, working on farms, attending school, and waiting to vote. These images suggest that having the right to vote will open opportunities to African Americans in all areas of society.)*

HISTORICAL THINKING

ANSWER

Possible response: Prohibition was difficult to enforce, meant that a sector of the economy could not operate, and went against the idea that people should make decisions for themselves on the use of alcohol.

ANSWER

It was the only way to ensure that every woman in the United States would have the right to vote.

More Information

Presidential Term Limits Students may be surprised to learn that the two-term limit on presidencies was only tradition, not law, prior to 1951. Like several other presidential traditions—such as the form of address "Mr. President" or the wording and public delivery of the inaugural oath of office—it began with George Washington's presidential administration. As Washington's second term came to a close, many people pressured him to continue in the office. Some encouraged it even after his retirement. Although he had been unanimously elected to both of his terms, Washington had never been eager for the position. Additionally, he felt that the rise of political parties meant that he would no longer have the full support of the people.

This precedent held until the election of 1940. President Franklin D. Roosevelt also claimed reluctance to serve more than two terms, but he felt that the looming international crisis—the Second World War—justified his run for reelection. By a constitutional coincidence, in addition to inspiring Amendment 22 with his four-term presidency, Roosevelt was also the first president to be inaugurated under the requirements outlined by Amendment 20.

ASK: What might be some of the advantages and disadvantages of having a president serve more than two terms during a crisis? *(Answers will vary. Possible advantages: The president could ensure that helpful policies and strategies continue; people might be reassured by the stability of having the same leadership. Possible disadvantages: The public might lose out on a leader who would have more effective crisis policies; it might make an unethical president less careful about keeping the nation out of crisis.)*

HISTORICAL THINKING

ANSWER

There is little reason to compromise, since the lame duck will not be able to help other lawmakers in the future.

AMENDMENTS

UNDERSTANDING AMENDMENT 20 This amendment is often called the "Lame Duck Amendment." In government, a lame duck is an elected official whose term in office is about to end. So, for instance, a president who has already served two terms is a lame duck. Officials who have not won re-election are also considered lame ducks.

HISTORICAL THINKING Why do you think it is more difficult for so-called lame-duck officials to enact legislation?

Amendment 20 (1933)

[**Note:** Article 1, Section 4, of the Constitution was modified by Section 2 of the 20th Amendment. In addition, a portion of the 12th Amendment was superseded by Section 3.]

SECTION 1: The terms of the President and the Vice President shall end at noon on the 20th day of January, and the terms of Senators and Representatives at noon on the 3d day of January, of the years in which such terms would have ended if this article had not been ratified; and the terms of their successors shall then begin.

SECTION 2: The Congress shall assemble at least once in every year, and such meeting shall begin at noon on the 3d day of January, unless they shall by law appoint a different day.

SECTION 3: If, at the time fixed for the beginning of the term of the President, the President elect shall have died, the Vice President elect shall become President. If a President shall not have been chosen before the time fixed for the beginning of his term, or if the President elect shall have failed to qualify, then the Vice President elect shall act as President until a President shall have qualified; and the Congress may by law provide for the case wherein neither a President elect nor a Vice President elect shall have qualified, declaring who shall then act as President, or the manner in which one who is to act shall be selected, and such person shall act accordingly until a President or Vice President shall have qualified.

SECTION 4: The Congress may by law provide for the case of the death of any of the persons from whom the House of Representatives may choose a President whenever the right of choice shall have devolved upon them, and for the case of the death of any of the persons from whom the Senate may choose a Vice President whenever the right of choice shall have devolved upon them.

SECTION 5: Sections 1 and 2 shall take effect on the 15th day of October following the ratification of this article.

SECTION 6: This article shall be inoperative unless it shall have been ratified as an amendment to the Constitution by the legislatures of three-fourths of the several States within seven years from the date of its submission.

AMENDMENTS

Amendment 21 (1933)

SECTION 1: The eighteenth article of amendment to the Constitution of the United States is hereby repealed.

SECTION 2: The transportation or importation into any State, Territory, or possession of the United States for delivery or use therein of intoxicating liquors, in violation of the laws thereof, is hereby prohibited.

SECTION 3: This article shall be inoperative unless it shall have been ratified as an amendment to the Constitution by conventions in the several States, as provided in the Constitution, within seven years from the date of the submission hereof to the States by the Congress.

Amendment 22 (1951)

SECTION 1: No person shall be elected to the office of the President more than twice, and no person who has held the office of President, or acted as President, for more than two years of a term to which some other person was elected President shall be elected to the office of the President more than once. But this Article shall not apply to any person holding the office of President when this Article was proposed by the Congress, and shall not prevent any person who may be holding the office of President, or acting as President, during the term within which this Article becomes operative from holding the office of President or acting as President during the remainder of such term.

SECTION 2: This article shall be inoperative unless it shall have been ratified as an amendment to the Constitution by the legislatures of three-fourths of the several States within seven years from the date of its submission to the States by the Congress.

UNDERSTANDING AMENDMENT 21 This amendment repealed the 18th Amendment and ended Prohibition.

UNDERSTANDING AMENDMENT 22 Franklin D. Roosevelt served three terms as president of the United States and was elected to a fourth term shortly before he died in 1945. All presidents before Roosevelt served two terms. Within months of Roosevelt's death, Republicans in Congress presented the 22nd Amendment for consideration.

HISTORICAL THINKING Do you think the U.S. president should be limited to serving two terms? Why or why not?

Guided Discussion

1. **Identify Problems and Solutions** Why is a "lame duck" session, or a time difference between Election Day and the start of a new term, necessary? *(Possible response: New presidents, senators, and representatives need time to prepare themselves to take office. They cannot do so fully before the election, since they might not win. As a result, there needs to be some period of time in which the officials they will replace remain in office.)*

2. **Form and Support Opinions** From a modern perspective, do Amendments 18 and 20 seem consistent with the other amendments to the Constitution? Explain how the interpretation of these amendments may have changed over time. *(Answers will vary. Some students may note that other amendments also deal with individual rights or prohibit specific actions, making the amendments consistent. Other students may argue that the amendments are inconsistent because they regulate people's private and business activities, while the other amendments deal mostly with people's rights and activities related to the government.)*

HISTORICAL THINKING

ANSWER

Answers will vary, but reasons for it might include that one person cannot have too much power; reasons against might include that it limits continuity of policies.

More Information

Washington, D.C.'s Statehood Movement

Amendment 23 gave residents of the nation's capital a say in choosing the president and vice president, but they have not stopped fighting for full representation in Congress. Organizations supporting full statehood, such as the New Columbia Statehood Commission, have pushed to reclassify the district's residential areas and have the district admitted to the Union as the 51st state. Opponents to statehood argue that the move would drastically shift the balance of power in Congress, for the district is heavily Democratic.

In 2016, a referendum calling for a congressional petition for D.C.'s statehood passed with a large majority—79 percent of the vote. This meant that the mayor could then petition Congress for admission, on the grounds that the voters have approved a state constitution drafted and made available for citizens to review. If admitted, the new state would be called New Columbia. **ASK:** In your opinion, would full statehood for the residents of the District of Columbia be a good idea? (*Answers will vary. Students should support their opinions with substantial evidence and reasoning.*)

HISTORICAL THINKING

ANSWER

Possible response: A poll tax likely deterred many less-well-off voters and so led to the election of more candidates who favored the well-off; since the poll tax prevented many African-American citizens from voting, it might have led to the election of officials who did not work to protect African Americans' civil rights and interests.

AMENDMENTS

UNDERSTANDING AMENDMENT 23 Although the District of Columbia is the official seat of the U.S. government, it is a federal territory, not a state, and has only a nonvoting representative in Congress. Washington, D.C., began as a very small community. However, by 1960, more than 760,000 people who paid federal taxes and could be drafted to serve in the military lived in the District. The states ratified Amendment 23 in 1961 to give the residents of the District the right to have their votes counted in the presidential elections.

UNDERSTANDING AMENDMENT 24 This amendment abolished poll taxes, election fees charged by states to keep low-income and mostly African-American citizens from voting. The amendment was passed in response to the demands of the civil rights movement of the 1960s, which condemned the poll tax.

HISTORICAL THINKING What impact did the poll tax probably have on election results?

Amendment 23 (1961)

SECTION 1: The District constituting the seat of Government of the United States shall appoint in such manner as the Congress may direct:

A number of electors of President and Vice President equal to the whole number of Senators and Representatives in Congress to which the District would be entitled if it were a State, but in no event more than the least populous State; they shall be in addition to those appointed by the States, but they shall be considered, for the purposes of the election of President and Vice President, to be electors appointed by a State; and they shall meet in the District and perform such duties as provided by the twelfth article of amendment.

SECTION 2: The Congress shall have power to enforce this article by appropriate legislation.

Amendment 24 (1964)

SECTION 1: The right of citizens of the United States to vote in any primary or other election for President or Vice President, for electors for President or Vice President, or for Senator or Representative in Congress, shall not be denied or abridged by the United States or any State by reason of failure to pay any poll tax or other tax.

SECTION 2: The Congress shall have power to enforce this article by appropriate legislation.

AMENDMENTS

Amendment 25 (1967)

[Note: Article 2, Section 1, of the Constitution was affected by the 25th Amendment.]

SECTION 1: In case of the removal of the President from office or of his death or resignation, the Vice President shall become President.

SECTION 2: Whenever there is a vacancy in the office of the Vice President, the President shall nominate a Vice President who shall take office upon confirmation by a majority vote of both Houses of Congress.

SECTION 3: Whenever the President transmits to the President pro tempore of the Senate and the Speaker of the House of Representatives his written declaration that he is unable to discharge the powers and duties of his office, and until he transmits to them a written declaration to the contrary, such powers and duties shall be discharged by the Vice President as Acting President.

SECTION 4: Whenever the Vice President and a majority of either the principal officers of the executive departments or of such other body as Congress may by law provide, transmit to the President pro tempore of the Senate and the Speaker of the House of Representatives their written declaration that the President is unable to discharge the powers and duties of his office, the Vice President shall immediately assume the powers and duties of the office as Acting President.

Thereafter, when the President transmits to the President pro tempore of the Senate and the Speaker of the House of Representatives his written declaration that no inability exists, he shall resume the powers and duties of his office unless the Vice President and a majority of either the principal officers of the executive department or of such other body as Congress may by law provide, transmit within four days to the President pro tempore of the Senate and the Speaker of the House of Representatives their written declaration that the President is unable to discharge the powers and duties of his office. Thereupon Congress shall decide the issue, assembling within forty-eight hours for that purpose if not in session. If the Congress, within twenty-one days after receipt of the latter written declaration, or, if Congress is not in session, within twenty-one days after Congress is required to assemble, determines by two-thirds vote of both Houses that the President is unable to discharge the powers and duties of his office, the Vice President shall continue to discharge the same as Acting President; otherwise, the President shall resume the powers and duties of his office.

UNDERSTANDING AMENDMENT 25 The 25th Amendment was ratified in 1967 to set up procedures to follow if a president becomes disabled while in office. It was proposed after the assassination of President John F. Kennedy in 1963. Following his death, some people began to wonder what would have happened if he'd survived the shooting but been unable to govern. This amendment provides for an orderly transfer of power.

HISTORICAL THINKING Why is there a plan of succession for the presidency?

Guided Discussion

1. **Evaluate** Why might civil rights activists have considered a constitutional amendment the most effective way to influence the government and address the issue of poll taxes? *(Possible response: An amendment would apply to all states at once, but only three-fourths of the states would have to ratify it, so it could become the law of the land even if a few states objected.)*

2. **Make Connections** In what ways do amendments prompted by specific historical events, such as Amendment 25, illustrate the importance of amendments to the political process and an effective Constitution? *(Possible response: Such amendments illustrate how the amendment process allows the Constitution to change to reflect and address changing situations and new possibilities.)*

HISTORICAL THINKING

ANSWER

Possible response: Having a predetermined succession of the presidency works to limit power struggles and to prevent people from taking advantage of a president's death or disability to further their own purposes.

More Information

Amendment 27 The most recent amendment to the Constitution was actually one of the first to be written. In 1789, James Madison suggested 12 amendments to the Constitution—but only 10 of them were approved and ratified. This amendment, which would give the people a way to vote on any pay raises Congress might try to give itself, was one of the two that failed. Because it did not expire, however, states could choose to ratify it at any time. In fact, over the next 200 years the states of Ohio and Wyoming did just that, almost 100 years apart.

The lost amendment gained new publicity and support when a college student in Texas argued for its approval in the early 1980s. Ten years later, and more than 200 years after Madison proposed it, Amendment 27 finally went into effect. **ASK:** Why might Madison have thought it important to give voters a chance to respond when Congress wants to give itself a pay raise? *(Possible response: Madison might have thought that since congressional salaries are paid by tax dollars, voters should be able to show that they approve or disapprove of how those dollars are being spent.)*

HISTORICAL THINKING

ANSWER

Possible response: People might have argued that a person should have the right to influence, through voting, a policy that so directly affected him or her.

AMENDMENTS

President Richard Nixon signs the 26th Amendment in 1971. Looking on are members of the youth choir Young Americans.

UNDERSTANDING AMENDMENT 26 The voting age had been 21 since 1868. However, while the United States fought the Vietnam War in the 1960s and 1970s, people began to question why 18-year-old men could be drafted to serve in the military but could not vote. As a result, the 26th Amendment was passed by Congress and ratified by the states on July 1, 1971.

Through the progressive expansion of voting rights, the Constitution has provided ever-increasing opportunities for citizens to participate in the political process.

HISTORICAL THINKING Why do you think many Americans questioned the fairness of denying voting rights to 18-year-olds, especially to those who could be drafted to go to war?

Amendment 26 (1971)

[**Note:** Amendment 14, Section 2, of the Constitution was modified by Section 1 of the 26th Amendment.]

SECTION 1: The right of citizens of the United States, who are eighteen years of age or older, to vote shall not be denied or abridged by the United States or by any State on account of age.

SECTION 2: The Congress shall have power to enforce this article by appropriate legislation.

Amendment 27 (1992)

No law, varying the compensation for the services of the Senators and Representatives, shall take effect, until an election of Representatives shall have intervened.

Citizenship and You

Imagine your parents have given you the right to play a computer game during your free time. To keep enjoying this right, you have some responsibilities. You're responsible for having your homework and chores done before you play the game. You're responsible for using the computer according to your family's or school's rules. Similarly, our responsibilities as citizens balance the rights we receive as citizens. Let's take a closer look at the whats, whys, and hows of **citizenship**—being a full member of a country in exchange for certain responsibilities.

AS DEFINED BY THE FRAMERS

As you have observed by studying the U.S. Constitution and Bill of Rights, privileges and rights like citizenship and voting have been contested, reshaped, and amended over time. We started with the freedoms outlined by the Framers, but many contributions have been made throughout history by Americans who have worked to expand our rights. These include the civil rights of individuals and minorities, the right to participate in government, the right to speak freely, the right to a fair trial, and many others. The efforts of those activists have helped us move forward in our continuing struggle to become a more perfect union—a struggle that continues today.

A COUNTRY WITHOUT RULES?

Picture this: You arrive at school on the first day of classes, but no schedules are available for the students. Nobody knows the school rules. Teachers and office workers can't answer any questions, and no one has been assigned a locker. Everything is completely disorganized and confusing.

This is similar to what would happen in a government without clear rules—or laws—that define the rights and responsibilities of its citizens. Order, organization, equality, and safety would all suffer without these laws. Is it fair that a government makes the laws that define the rights and responsibilities of a nation? In essence, a democratic government IS the people of its nation. The people who serve in the government and make its laws are elected by people across the country. So, these lawmakers represent the people of that country.

In the United States, we work to be *good citizens* by obeying laws, *participatory citizens* by voting and serving on juries, and *socially-just citizens* by standing up for the rights of others. Read on to learn more about the rights and responsibilities of citizenship.

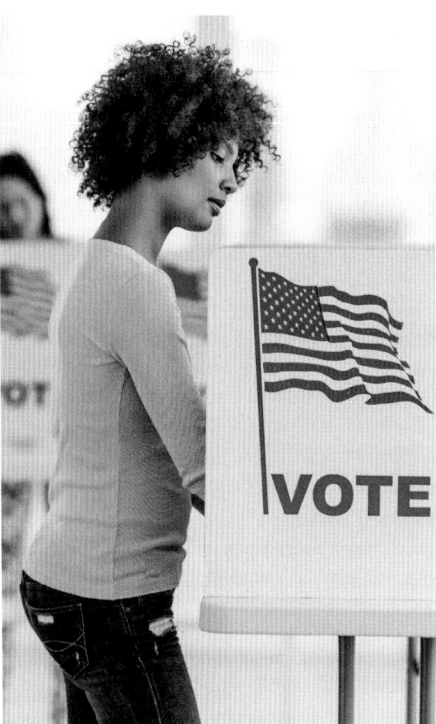

While you might not be old enough to vote in the United States, you have many other rights, and as you'll see, those rights come with responsibilities.

THINK ABOUT IT

SUMMARIZE How have the rights and responsibilities of U.S. citizens been defined and changed over time?

Guided Discussion

1. **Make Connections** The text compares a nation without laws to a school that has no clear organization or order. What other kinds of relationships or situations are similar to the relationship between citizens and their nations? Explain how they are similar. *(Answers will vary. Possible response: Members of a sports team are expected to follow codes of conduct and rules for the privilege of playing.)*

2. **Form and Support Opinions** Is obeying the law always a requirement for being a good citizen? Support your opinion with examples from history or your own experience. *(Answers will vary, but students should support their opinions with sound reasoning and examples from experience or history. For example, Rosa Parks could be viewed as an example of a person who disobeyed an unjust law; yet, it would be difficult to decide from her actions that she was not a good citizen.)*

THINK ABOUT IT

Possible response: Rights and responsibilities have expanded as society has increasingly recognized the many different ways in which people contribute.

More Information

First Amendment Cases Point out to students that the text's example of "shouting 'fire' in a crowded theater" comes directly from a decision by the United States Supreme Court. In the case of *Schenck* v. *United States* (1919), the defendant, Charles T. Schenck, had been convicted of espionage for distributing a leaflet that discouraged people from obeying the draft during World War I. The court ruled that while "ordinarily" the First Amendment would protect someone's right to oppose a military draft, in wartime such activity could "create a clear and present danger." "The most stringent protection of free speech," Justice Oliver Wendell Holmes, Jr. wrote, "would not protect a man in falsely shouting fire in a theatre and causing a panic." With this reasoning, the Court upheld Schenck's conviction.

Many other landmark Supreme Court cases have outlined the specific limits and protections of the First Amendment. For example, in *Tinker* v. *Des Moines Independent Community School District* (1969), the Court extended First Amendment protection to students expressing political opinions in schools unless the school officials could prove that the expression violated other students' rights or interfered with the educational process. **ASK:** Why do you think the Supreme Court allows for the restriction of free speech when such speech poses significant danger? *(Possible response: The Supreme Court must balance defending the Constitution with preserving peoples' safety and general order.)*

The Rights and Responsibilities of Citizens

In the United States, citizens have many rights, regardless of whether they were born here or came here from another country. Knowing their rights helps citizens understand the responsibilities they have to balance and support their rights. Rights are simple: they are established in the U.S. Constitution and Bill of Rights. Responsibilities are pretty simple, too. Mostly they consist of simply doing what is right and showing good character. As you read, think about specific actions you might take to be a good, participatory, and socially-just citizen.

BECOMING A CITIZEN

Some residents of the United States are citizens because they were born in the country. Others came from foreign countries to legally enter and live in the United States. They worked to become citizens through an immigration process called **naturalization**. People becoming naturalized citizens work hard to learn the laws, rights, and responsibilities of American citizenship. They take a citizenship test and are sworn in as citizens during a naturalization ceremony. Immigrants enhance the diversity of the United States and have contributed greatly throughout history. It is a proud day when they become U.S. citizens who can enjoy the rights of citizens listed below.

Rights of Citizens
Right to freedom of religion
Right to freedom of speech
Right to freedom of the press
Right to assemble
Right to trial by jury (in specific types of cases)
Right to vote
Right to buy and sell property
Right to freely travel across the country and to leave and return to the country

LIMITS ON RIGHTS

By now, you're probably pretty familiar with the basic rights of citizens as guaranteed in the Constitution. It's worth noting there are limitations that apply to some of these rights. Some of these restrictions were built into the laws that established the rights. Others have come into being because of cases that have come before the Supreme Court and tested various rights. For example, it's true that as stated in the First Amendment to the U.S. Constitution, people have the right to free speech—to say what they are thinking without fear of the government punishing them for expressing their thoughts or ideas. But this freedom of speech is not absolute. For example, suppose someone shouted "Fire!" in a movie theater or crowded shopping mall when there actually was no fire. That person would not be protected by the right to free speech, as his or her clearly intentional "speech" could cause harm to others.

CIVIC RESPONSIBILITIES

U.S. citizens have two different types of responsibilities: civic and personal. **Civic responsibilities** include voting, paying taxes, and serving on juries. **Personal responsibilities** include respecting others, helping in the community, standing up for others, and staying informed about issues.

If people didn't exercise their civic responsibilities, rights would not exist. In the United States, for example, many people take for granted their right to vote and don't bother to vote at all. Perhaps they don't consider the fact that the right to vote is a privilege that doesn't exist in all countries. People in many countries do not have the opportunity to elect officials who will represent them and make decisions that determine how everyone will be governed.

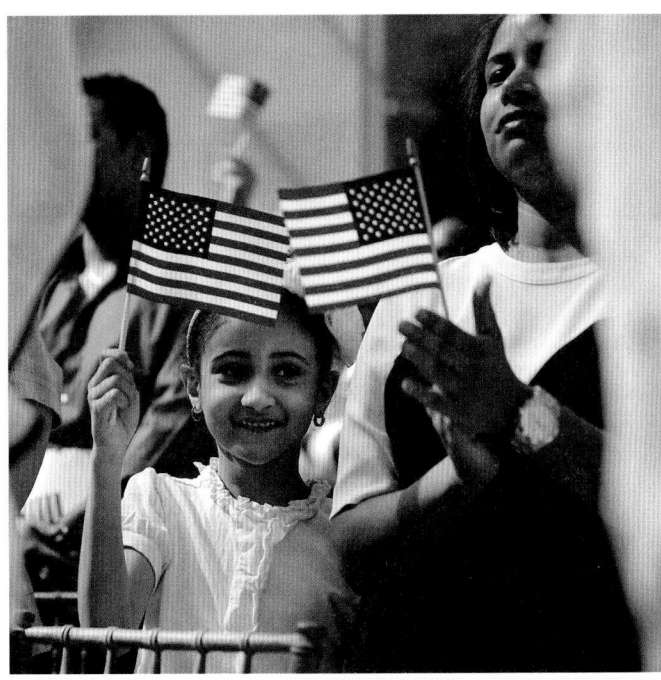

A six-year old stands in proud support as her mother receives her citizenship. This naturalization ceremony took place in 2014 in the Metropolitan Museum of Art in New York City.

Guided Discussion

1. **Make Predictions** What are some of the consequences of uninformed voting? *(Possible responses: People might elect unqualified or dishonest officials; they might fail to vote for someone who best represents their political beliefs; they might contribute to the implementation of laws or policies with which they disagree or that might even be harmful to people.)*

2. **Make Connections** Why might it be important for young people to participate in citizenship activities even when they are not yet old enough to vote? *(Possible response: The opportunity to practice becoming informed, to take on civic and personal responsibilities, and to observe the political process will make young people more effective voters and citizens when they do reach voting age.)*

THINK ABOUT IT

Taking on responsibility for oneself lessens the need for government control over individuals' actions and so increases the options for how government can work.

Because people in the United States have the right to vote, they have a corresponding responsibility to exercise that right. They are also responsible for being informed voters. Voters have an obligation to use reliable sources to learn about candidates who are running for office. Voters must determine the similarities and differences between the candidates' positions on issues and use evidence to analyze the credibility of their claims. Similarly, voters have the same obligation to inform themselves about new laws before casting votes in favor of or against them.

How can a young person exercise civic responsibilities related to voting if he or she is not old enough to vote? You can participate in mock elections or student government elections in your school. You can create posters and pamphlets to encourage adults to vote, or volunteer to help with a candidate's campaign. Remember, the decisions of voters impact people of every age.

PERSONAL RESPONSIBILITIES

When you think of your personal responsibilities as a citizen, consider the choices you make in terms of your actions. Being a responsible citizen means behaving in ways that are right, moral, and just, and acting in a way that benefits you and those around you. Considering the rights of all people, not just the rights of a select few, will help you be a personally responsible citizen.

Citizens have many personal responsibilities, such as being open-minded, respecting the opinions of others, and showing respect for the beliefs and individuality of people with different backgrounds. People of any age can take on personal responsibilities by doing community service projects, standing up for the rights of others, and respecting all people regardless of ethnicity, nationality, gender identity, sexual orientation, or beliefs. Living up to these personal responsibilities helps citizens contribute to an environment of respect and caring.

THINK ABOUT IT

EXPLAIN How does a democracy depend on people fulfilling their civic and personal responsibilities?

More Information

National History Day The last of the text's suggested citizenship projects is participation in National History Day. National History Day, despite its name, is not a holiday, or even a single day; rather, it is a national competition in which students present in-depth reports on the history-related theme announced for that year. Students initially compete in their local regions, with winners going on to the state level. Winners of the state competitions advance to the nationals event.

The approximately 500,000 students who participate each year craft papers, documentaries, online presentations, artistic performances, or exhibits that engage with the announced theme. Thorough and hands-on research practices, such as interviews and relevant travel, are strongly encouraged. **ASK:** Do you think a project like this one is a good way to participate in the democratic process? Why or why not? *(Answers will vary. Students may argue that it is a good way to participate because it will improve understanding of historical events, which helps students become more informed citizens. Other students may argue that it is not a good way to participate because it does not focus directly on the democratic process.)*

Building and Practicing Citizenship Skills

Building citizenship skills is like building muscle. It takes hard work and repetition, but the rewards pay off for everyone. Some citizenship skills, such as helping raise voter participation, will require you to seek out specific opportunities. Others, such as refusing to tolerate bullying, can be exercised whenever appropriate situations arise. Citizenship affords many rights and requires many responsibilities. Enjoying these rights and responsibilities is the reward of being a good citizen.

The following chart includes ways you can build and apply citizenship skills and become an active participant in our democracy. Study the chart and check out the Active Citizenship for the Environment Activities in this program's online resources. Then brainstorm more ways you can be a good, participatory, socially-just citizen.

THINK ABOUT IT

DESCRIBE What citizenship project would you be interested in undertaking, and how would you carry it out?

Citizenship in Action

Responsibilities	Citizenship Projects: Ways to Take Action
Become informed.	• Read books and articles from reliable sources. • Attend, watch, or read transcripts of debates and speeches. • Watch broadcast journalists on reliable cable and digital sources. • Ask questions of others who are well informed.
Make decisions based on facts.	• Think about whether you are acting on emotion or fact. • Use reliable sources to evaluate statements you hear and read. • Check reliable sources to see if others' statements are accurate.
Listen to the opinions of others. Discuss differences of opinion in a kind and civil manner.	• When friends or acquaintances express opinions that differ from yours, explain why you disagree, if you do. • Use appropriate language and remain calm as you discuss opinions. If the other person refuses to be calm or civil, end the conversation and walk away.
Respect the value of individuals. Respect differences among people.	• Enjoy the differences among people. • Make friends with people who are different from you. • Volunteer in your community to interact with and help others.
Stand up for rights of others. Work to stop bullying.	• Do not stand by silently when someone is being bullied. Speak up. If you do not feel safe, immediately seek the help of an adult. • Write articles and blog posts about the importance of stopping the act of bullying. Develop or participate in an antibullying program.
Volunteer in your community.	• Determine how your skills and interests could help someone else. • Talk with your parents, teachers, and friends to learn what types of volunteer services your community needs. • Make volunteering a regular part of your life. You could consider serving food to the homeless, collecting clothing or canned goods to help a local shelter, cleaning or restoring a local park or playground, or tutoring students who are struggling with their school work.

Responsibilities	Citizenship Projects: Ways to Take Action
Express political opinions.	• Write a letter or an email to a newspaper editor about an issue that concerns you. • Use clear and concise language. Edit your letter carefully.
Obey the law.	• Become familiar with the laws in your state, city, and town that apply to people your age.
Pay taxes.	• Read more about your local and state taxes, and what the revenue is used for. • Recognize that you are already paying sales taxes when you purchase many items.
Lobby for change.	• Form a lobbying committee with other students to influence legislation or public policy. • Establish a goal for your lobbying campaign. • Identify whom to lobby. (Who are the people who can help you accomplish your goal?) • Find information and statistics to support your goal. • Get public support for your cause. You might consider gathering signatures on a petition or creating flyers to publicize your campaign. • Present your case to the appropriate individuals.
Accept responsibility for your actions.	• If someone asks about a mistake you have made, tell the truth. • Ask what you might do to make up for the mistake.
Participate in the democratic process.	• Ask a teacher to organize a trip to a local courtroom to see the law in action. • Contact a local political candidate whose ideas you support to see how you might help with his or her campaign. • Plan and/or participate in mock elections, student government elections, and student government meetings. • With the help of a parent or teacher, seek opportunities to participate in a naturalization ceremony. • Research how you and your classmates can participate in National History Day at a state or national level.

One way of practicing citizenship is by volunteering.

Citizenship Handbook **R37**

Guided Discussion

1. **Ask and Answer Questions** One responsibility noted in the chart is the responsibility to pay taxes. What kinds of questions might a citizen have about taxes, and how could he or she find answers for them? *(Possible responses: How much of my income goes to pay taxes? What kinds of taxes do I need to pay? What things are paid for by my taxes? How do current taxes compare with taxes in the past? People could find these answers by researching online or contacting an organization such as the IRS.)*

2. **Draw Conclusions** Think about what the chart says regarding the responsibility of citizens to be informed and to use reliable sources. Why might a free press be such an important element of American society? *(Possible response: Without a free press, citizens would have a much harder time accessing the reliable, unbiased information they need to participate responsibly in the political process.)*

THINK ABOUT IT

Answers will vary, but students should give a clear picture of what their project would be like, with some details.

GLOSSARY

A

abolition n. (a-buh-LIH-shuhn) the act of putting an end to something, such as slavery (page 349)

abolitionist n. (a-buh-LIH-shuhn-ihst) a person who wants to end slavery (page 446)

acquired immunodeficiency syndrome (AIDS) n. (uh-KWYRD ih-MYOO-noh-dih-FIH-shun-see SIHN-drohm) the final stage of a disease caused by a virus that attacks the system in the human body that fights off illnesses (page 971)

advertising n. (AD-vuhr-ty-zhing) the act of presenting products and ideas to the public (page 738)

affirmative action n. (uh-FUR-muh-tihv AK-shuhn) a government policy that institutes racial quotas to favor groups that suffer from discrimination (page 915)

African diaspora n. (A-frih-kuhn DY-as-poh-rah) the removal of Africans from their homelands to the Americas (page 74)

Agent Orange n. (AY-juhnt OR-ihnj) a potent herbicide used to kill vegetation (page 929)

agrarian adj. (ah-GRAR-ee-ehn) related to agriculture or farming (page 366)

Agricultural Revolution n. (AHG-rih-kuhl-chuhr-uhl REV-oh-luh-shuhn) the transition in human history from hunting and gathering food to planting crops and raising animals (page 9)

Alien and Sedition Acts n. (AY-lee-uhn AND sih-DIH-shun AKTS) a series of four laws passed to keep certain groups from immigrating to the United States; the laws gave the government power to expel aliens living in the United States and targeted U.S. citizens who criticized the U.S. government (page 293)

alliance n. (ah-LY-ans) an agreement between nations to fight each other's enemies or otherwise collaborate; a partnership (page 111)

Allied Powers n. (AHL-ayhd POHW-uhrs) Several countries, including France and Great Britain, working together to oppose the Axis Powers of Germany, Italy, and Japan during World War II (page 789)

alternative energy n. (awl-TUR-nuh-tihv EH-nur-jee) electricity or power that is created from a source that will not run out, such as wind or solar power (page 1009)

amendment n. (uh-MEND-muhnt) a formal change to a law, usually referring to a formal change to the U.S. Constitution (page 263)

American System n. (uh-MAIR-uh-kuhn SIHS-tuhm) a policy of promoting the U.S. industrial system through the use of tariffs, federal subsidies to build roads and other public works, and a national bank to control currency (page 342)

Americanization n. (uh-mair-uh-kan-ih-ZAY-shuhn) the act of teaching immigrants and Native Americans the mainstream culture and language of the United States with the expectation that they will adapt to and embrace it (page 598)

amphibious landing craft n. (am-FIH-bee-uhs LAN-ding KRAFT) boats used to convey soldiers and equipment from the sea to the shore during military attacks (page 811)

Anaconda Plan n. (a-nuh-KAHN-duh PLAN) a military strategy during the Civil War in which the North planned to set up a blockade around the southern coast to ruin the South's economy and secure ports on the Mississippi River; much as a huge snake, like an anaconda, crushes its prey (page 504)

anarchist n. (AHN-ark-ist) a person who advocates lawlessness and the absence of all government (page 650)

annex v. (a-NEX) to add (page 391)

antebellum adj. (an-tih-BEH-luhm) before the American Civil War (page 340)

anthropologist n. (an-thruh-PAH-luh-jist) a person who studies cultures (page 748)

antiaircraft gun n. (AN-ty-AIR-kraft GUHN) a piece of heavy artillery modified so that it can be pointed skyward at enemy planes (page 713)

antifederalist n. (an-tee-FEH-duh-ruh-list) a person who opposed the U.S. Constitution of 1787 because of its emphasis on a strong national government (page 262)

anti-Semitism n. (AN-tee SEHM-ih-tih-zuhm) discrimination, prejudice, and hostility against the Jewish people (page 814)

appeasement n. (uh-PEEZ-muhnt) a policy of making political compromises in order to avoid conflict (page 791)

apprentice n. (ah-PREHN-tis) a person who learns a craft or trade by working with a skilled member of that craft or trade (page 129)

arable adj. (AIR-ah-bl) able to grow crops; fertile (page 140)

archipelago n. (ahr-kuh-PEL-uh-goh) a chain of islands (page 685)

armistice n. (AHR-muh-stuhss) an agreement between opposing sides in a conflict to stop fighting (page 721)

arson n. (AR-son) the purposeful burning of buildings illegally (page 560)

Articles of Confederation n. (AHR-TIH-kuhls UHV kuhn-feh-duh-RAY-shuhn) a set of laws adopted by the United States in 1777 that established each state in the union as a republic, replaced by the Constitution in 1789 (page 222)

artillery n. (ahr-TIH-luh-ree) large guns that can fire over a long distance (page 203)

artisan n. (AR-tih-san) a person skilled at making things by hand (page 136)

assassinate v. (uh-SA-suh-nayt) to murder for political reasons (page 538)

assembly line n. (uh-SEHM-blee LYN) a system in which workers stand in place as work passes from operation to operation in a direct line until a product is assembled (page 676)

assimilate v. (ah-SIM-ih-late) to adopt the culture or way of life of the nation in which one currently lives; to become absorbed in a culture or country (pages 368, 433)

astronaut n. (AS-truh-nawt) a person who is trained to travel in space (page 904)

asylum n. (uh-SY-luhm) a hospital dedicated to treating the mentally ill (page 441)

Atlantic Charter n. (aht-LAHN-tick CHAHR-tuhr) a charter that lists eight principles for a better world, composed during a meeting between President Franklin Roosevelt and British Prime Minister Winston Churchill in 1941 (page 793)

atoll n. (A-tawl) a ring-shaped reef, island, or series of islands formed from coral (page 817)

atomic bomb n. (uh-TAH-mihk BAHM) a type of nuclear bomb whose violent explosion is triggered by splitting atoms, which releases intense heat and radioactivity (page 821)

attorney general n. (uh-TUR-NEE JEN-ruhl) a member of the president's Cabinet, whose primary role is to represent the United States before the Supreme Court (page 281)

autonomy n. (aw-TAH-nuh-mee) self-rule (page 686)

Axis Powers n. (ACK-sihs POHW-uhrs) Germany, Italy, and Japan, which formed an alliance together at the start of World War II (page 789)

B

baby boom n. (BAY-bee BOOM) a significant increase in the birthrate (page 854)

backcountry n. (BAK-kuhn-tree) the western part of the Southern Colonies just east of the Appalachian Mountains (page 134)

ballistic missile n. (buh-LIHS-tihk MIH-suhl) a nuclear weapon that is propelled by a rocket and guided using a GPS system (page 908)

banish v. (BA-nish) to send away as punishment, usually without hope of return (page 101)

bank holiday n. (BANGK HAH-luh-day) a day or period of time when banks are closed by government order (page 771)

bank run n. (BANGK RUHN) an event in which many customers panic and rush to withdraw their money from a bank at the same time (page 768)

barrack n. (BAIR-uhk) a building or group of buildings used to house large numbers of people (page 806)

battalion n. (buh-TAL-yuhn) a large group of military troops (page 806)

bayonet n. (BAY-uh-nuht) a sharp blade attached to the end of a rifle (page 228)

bedrock n. (BEHD-rahk) solid rock that lies under loose soil (page 636)

GLOSSARY

Bering Land Bridge *n.* (BARE-ingh LAND BRIJ) a piece of land between Alaska and Siberia that was above sea level 13,000 years ago and allowed early humans to cross into North America (page 6)

Berlin Wall *n.* (buhr-LIHN WAWL) a concrete and barbed wire wall that surrounded the democratic West Berlin, built by the communist East Berlin to prevent citizens of East Berlin from moving to the democratic city (page 907)

Bessemer process *n.* (BEH-seh-mur PRAH-sehs) a steel manufacturing process that involves blowing air into molten iron to remove impurities, which results in a stronger metal (page 624)

Bill of Rights *n.* (BIHL UHV RITES) the first 10 amendments to the U.S. Constitution; a list of guarantees to which every person in a country is entitled (page 263)

black codes *n.* (BLAK KOHDZ) laws passed by southern states immediately after the Civil War for controlling African Americans and limiting their rights; repealed by Reconstruction in 1866 (page 554)

black market *n.* (BLAK MAHR-khut) a system through which prohibited goods are bought and sold illegally (page 735)

black peonage *n.* (BLAK PE-eh-nij) economic slavery that tied African Americans to sharecropping landlords' lands (page 559)

black separatism *n.* (BLAK SEH-puh-ruh-ti-zuhm) the political and cultural division of blacks and whites within a society (page 914)

blacklist *v.* (BLAK-lihst) to put one or more people on a list indicating they are to be shunned or punished (page 852)

blight *n.* (BLYT) a fungus or an insect that causes plants to dry up and die (page 432)

blitzkrieg *n.* (BLIHTS-kreeg) a war strategy performed swiftly that involves bombarding transportation and communication targets from the air before starting a land invasion (page 791)

bloc *n.* (BLOK) a group that is formed to support a common interest or purpose (page 846)

blockade *v.* (blah-KAYD) to block ships from entering or leaving a harbor (page 228)

blues *n.* (BLOOZ) a style of music originating among African-American musicians that tells stories about hard times and heartache (page 743)

bluff *n.* (BLUHF) a cliff (page 528)

bonanza farm *n.* (buh-NAN-zuh FAHRM) an enormous farm established by an investor who runs it for profit (page 586)

bond *n.* (BAHND) a certificate offered for sale to the public with the promise that the government will pay the money back at a later date (page 524)

boom-and-bust cycle *n.* (BOOM AND BUHST SY-kuhl) a series of periods of economic growth followed by sudden economic downturns (page 627)

boomtown *n.* (BOOM-town) a town that experiences a great population increase in only a short time period (page 418)

bootlegging *n.* (BOOT-lehg-ihng) illegally making, transporting, or supplying alcohol (page 735)

border state *n.* (BOR-dur STAYT) at the time of the Civil War, a state that bordered both Union and Confederate states, namely Maryland, Kentucky, Delaware, Missouri, and West Virginia (page 489)

Boston Massacre *n.* (BAWS-tuhn MA-sih-kur) the 1779 incident in which British soldiers fired on locals who had been taunting them (page 188)

Boston Tea Party *n.* (BAWS-tuhn TEE PAR-tee) the 1773 incident in which the Sons of Liberty boarded British ships and dumped their cargo in protest of British taxes on the colonists (page 191)

boycott *n.* (BOY-kaht) a form of protest that involves refusing to purchase goods or services (page 183)

bribery *n.* (BRY-buh-ree) offers of money or privileges to those in power in exchange for political favors (page 564)

brinkmanship *n.* (BRIHNGK-muhn-ship) the practice of pushing a conflict to the edge of violence without getting into a war, usually as a tactic to gain a favorable outcome (page 853)

browser *n.* (BROW-zur) a computer application that is used to view websites (page 1000)

burgeon *v.* (BUR-jehn) to grow quickly (page 146)

buying on margin *n.* (BY-ihng AWN MAHR-juhn) buying a stock by paying a small amount of what it is worth and borrowing the rest of the money to pay for it (page 765)

C

Cabinet *n.* (KAB-niht) the heads of the departments that assist the U.S. president (page 279)

Californio *n.* (kal-uh-FOWR-nee-oh) a resident of California who was of Spanish or Mexican descent and lived there before the gold rush (page 417)

capitalism *n.* (KAP-ih-tuh-lih-zuhm) an economic system in which private individuals, as opposed to the government, own and profit from businesses (page 627)

caravan *n.* (KARE-uh-van) a group of people and animals traveling together, usually for trade (page 42)

caravel *n.* (KEHR-ah-vehl) a small, fast ship used by Spanish and Portuguese explorers (page 40)

cash crop *n.* (KASH KRAHP) a crop grown for sale rather than for use by farmers (page 132)

casualty *n.* (KAH-zhuhl-tee) a dead or injured person (page 540)

catalytic converter *n.* (ka-tuh-LIH-tihk kuhn-VUR-tur) a part of a vehicle's exhaust system that changes harmful gases from the vehicle into less harmful or harmless gases (page 959)

cattle drive *n.* (KA-tuhl DRYV) the process of moving a herd of cows and steers from one place to another, usually from ranch to railroad hub (page 584)

cavalry *n.* (KA-vuhl-ree) army troops who fight on horseback (page 491)

cease-fire *n.* (SEEHS FY-ur) a military order to end fighting (page 930)

cede *v.* (SEED) to give up (page 288)

centrist *n.* (SEHN-trihst) a person who holds politically moderate views (page 982)

chancellor *n.* (CHAN-suh-lur) a leader in some European countries whose role is similar to that of the U.S. president (page 789)

charter *n.* (CHAHR-tuhr) a written grant establishing an institution and detailing members' rights and privileges (page 92)

chattel slavery *n.* (CHA-tuhl SLAY-veh-ree) a system in which enslaved people have no human rights and are classified as goods (page 72)

checks and balances *n.* (CHEKS AND BAH-luhn-suhz) the system established by the U.S. Constitution that gives each of the branches of government the power to limit the power of the other two (page 258)

Chief Justice *n.* (CHEEF JUH-stuhs) the head of the judicial branch of the government; presides over the Supreme Court (page 281)

chiefdom *n.* (CHEEF-duhm) a large community of people ruled by a chief (page 9)

child labor *n.* (CHYLD LAY-bur) the practice of hiring children to perform paid work, often in dangerous conditions and for low wages (page 647)

Chinese Exclusion Act *n.* (chy-NEEZ ihk-SKLOO-zhuhn AKT) an 1882 law prohibiting Chinese workers from immigrating to the United States for a 10-year period (page 640)

circumnavigate *v.* (sur-cuhm-NAV-ih-gayt) to travel completely around Earth (page 62)

citizenship *n.* (SIH-tuh-zuhn-ship) the condition of having the opportunities and duties of citizens (page R32)

civic responsibility *n.* (SIH-vihk rih-spawn-suh-BIHL-uh-tee) responsibility that is either required or essential that people perform, such as voting, paying taxes, and serving on juries (page R34)

civil disobedience *n.* (SIH-vuhl dihs-uh-BEE-dee-uhnts) the nonviolent disobeying of laws as a form of protest (page 878)

civil liberty *n.* (SIH-vuhl LIH-bur-tee) individual rights protected by law from government interference (page 719)

Civil Rights Act of 1866 *n.* (SIH-vuhl RITES AKT UHV 1866) a bill granting full equality and citizenship to "every race and color" (page 554)

civilian *n.* (suh-VIHL-yuhn) a person who is not in the military (page 497)

civilization *n.* (sih-vuhl-ih-ZAY-shun) a society with a highly developed culture and technology (page 24)

GLOSSARY

Clayton Antitrust Act *n.* (KLAY-tuhn an-tee-TRUHST AKT) a 1914 law that described the illegality of trusts' unlawful business practices and closed the loopholes they used (page 674)

climate change *n.* (KLY-muht CHAYNJ) changes in Earth's weather patterns (page 1008)

coalition *n.* (koh-uh-LIH-shuhn) an alliance of people, parties, or states focused on a common goal (page 977)

collective bargaining *n.* (kuh-LEHK-tihv BAHR-guhn-ihng) a negotiation carried out by a labor union with an employer to try to improve wages, working conditions, and hours (page 648)

Columbian Exchange *n.* (kuh-LUM-bee-uhn ehks-CHAYNJ) the exchange of plants, animals, microbes, people, and ideas between Europe and the Americas following Columbus's first voyage to the Western Hemisphere (page 70)

command module *n.* (kuh-MAND MAH-jool) the main part of a space vehicle that carries the crew, main supplies, and equipment to return to Earth (page 957)

commerce clause *n.* (KAH-murs KLAWZ) a provision in Article 1 of the U.S. Constitution granting Congress the power to make laws concerning foreign trade as well as trade among the states and with Native American nations (page 261)

commissioner *n.* (kuh-MIH-shuh-nur) a government representative (page 669)

committee of correspondence *n.* (kuh-MIH-tee UHV KAWR-uh-spahn-dunts) in the Revolutionary era, a group of colonists whose duty it was to spread news about protests against the British (page 191)

commodity *n.* (kuh-MAH-duh-tee) a trade good (page 142)

common market *n.* (KAH-muhn MAHR-kuht) a group of countries or states that allows the members to trade freely among themselves (page 261)

common school *n.* (KAH-muhn SKOOL) a colonial elementary school (page 129)

common school movement *n.* (KAH-muhn SKOOL MOOV-muhnt) an educational reform movement in the 1830s that promoted free public schools funded by property taxes and managed by local governments (page 441)

communism *n.* (KAHM-yuh-nih-zuhm) a form of government in which all the means of production and transportation are owned by the state (page 717)

Compromise of 1877 *n.* (KAHM-pruh-myz UHV 1877) a deal in which Democrats agreed to make Rutherford B. Hayes president if Republicans ended Reconstruction and pulled federal troops out of the South (page 565)

concentration camp *n.* (kahnt-suhn-TRAY-shuhn KAMP) a place where prisoners of war or members of persecuted minorities are confined; in World War II, the camps where Jews and others were held and murdered by the Nazis (page 814)

Conestoga wagon *n.* (kah-nuh-STOH-guh WA-guhn) a kind of wagon, made by German settlers in North America, that could carry heavy loads (page 143)

confederacy *n.* (kon-FED-ur-uh-see) an agreement among several groups, states, or governments to protect and support one another in battle or other endeavors (page 111)

Confederacy *n.* (kon-FED-ur-uh-see) the 11 southern states that seceded from the Union to form their own nation, the Confederate States of America (page 474)

conformity *n.* (kuhn-FAWR-mih-tee) an obedience to a set of beliefs (page 144)

conquistador *n.* (kon-KEE-stuh-dohr) a Spanish conqueror who sought gold and other riches in the Americas (page 56)

conscientious objector *n.* (KAHN-shee-ehnt-shuhs ahb-JEHK-tur) a person who refuses to fight in a war, often for religious reasons (page 719)

Conscription Act *n.* (kuhn-SKRIHP-shuhn AKT) a law instituted by the Union in 1863 stating that men between the ages of 20 and 45 years of age were liable to be drafted into the military but they could pay $300 to avoid service (page 522)

conservation movement *n.* (kahn-sur-VAY-shuhn MOOV-muhnt) a movement to promote the protection of natural resources and wildlife (page 671)

conspiracy *n.* (kuhn-SPIHR-uh-see) a secret plan to harm or commit an illegal act (page 911)

constitution *n.* (kahn-stuh-TOO-shuhn) a document that organizes a government and states its powers (page 250)

constitutionalism *n.* (kahn-stuh-TOO-shuh-nuh-lih-zuhm) the concept of governing based on a constitution (page 251)

consumer *n.* (kuhn-SOO-mur) a person who buys a product or service (page 738)

consumer debt *n.* (kuhn-SOO-mur DEHT) the amount of money people have borrowed to purchase goods (page 765)

consumer economy *n.* (kuhn-SOO-mur ih-KAH-nuh-mee) an economy in which people make purchases often and have many choices about what products to buy (page 738)

containment *n.* (kuhn-TAYN-muhnt) a U.S. security policy during the Cold War in which diplomatic and military action was used to stop the Soviet Union from spreading communism (page 847)

contiguous *adj.* (kuhn-TIH-gyuh-wuhs) connected (page 413)

Continental Army *n.* (kahn-tuh-NEHN-tuhl AHR-mee) the American army formed in 1775 by the Second Continental Congress and led by General George Washington (page 203)

Continental Divide *n.* (kahn-tuh-NEHN-tuhl duh-VYD) the high point in the Rocky Mountains that divides the watersheds of the Atlantic and Pacific oceans (page 395)

continental shelf *n.* (kahn-tuh-NEHN-tuhl SHELF) a relatively shallow area of land under the ocean water that extends outward from a continent before a steep drop-off into the open ocean (page 972)

convert *v.* (kuhn-VERT) to persuade to change one's beliefs; often refers to a change in religion (page 43)

cooperative *n.* (koh-AH-pruh-tihv) a group of farmers or others who combine their money to purchase needed products and services (page 591)

Copperhead *n.* (KAH-pur-hed) a negative nickname for Democrats who opposed emancipation of enslaved people and the draft (page 562)

corporation *n.* (kor-puh-RAY-shuhn) a company or group that acts legally as a single unit to run a business (page 626)

corruption *n.* (kuh-RUHP-shuhn) dishonesty, unlawfulness (page 564)

cotton gin *n.* (KAH-tuhn JIHN) a machine that separates the cotton seeds and hulls from the cotton boll (tuft of cotton) (page 338)

counterattack *n.* (KOWN-tur uh-TAK) an attack made in response to a previous attack (page 227)

counterculture *n.* (KOWN-tur-KUHL-chur) a movement in the 1960s that promoted a way of life that was in opposition to American society's established rules and behavior (page 933)

coup *n.* (KOO) an illegal overthrow of the government (page 975)

court-martial *v.* (KORT-mahr-shuhl) to try a member of the armed services accused of offenses against military law (page 688)

court-packing plan *n.* (KORT PA-king PLAN) President Franklin Roosevelt's controversial plan to increase the number of justices on the Supreme Court from nine to fifteen and to add six justices who shared his progressive views (page 779)

cover-up *n.* (KUH-vur UHP) an attempt to hide the truth from the public (page 961)

craft union *n.* (KRAFT YOON-yuhn) a labor union that advocates for workers' rights and protections, whose members are specialized skilled workers or craftsmen (page 443)

credit *n.* (KREH-diht) the privilege of purchasing something or borrowing money and paying the money back over time (page 254)

creditor *n.* (KREH-dih-tur) a person to whom a debt is owed (page 590)

crematorium *n.* (kree-muh-TOR-ee-uhm) a furnace or oven used to burn human or animal remains; in World War II, the ovens used by Nazis to burn their victims' bodies (page 814)

Crittenden Plan *n.* (KRIHT-uhn-duhn PLAN) a proposal that stated the federal government would have no power to abolish slavery in the states where it already existed; it reestablished and extended the Missouri Compromise line to the Pacific Ocean (page 476)

Cuban Missile Crisis *n.* (KYOO-buhn MIH-suhl CRY-suhs) a political showdown in 1962 between the United States and the Soviet Union caused by the presence of nuclear weapons in Cuba (page 908)

Currency Act *n.* (KUR-uhn-see AKT) the British law that regulated paper money in the American colonies (page 181)

customs *n.* (KUH-stuhmz) the taxes placed on imported and exported goods (page 319)

D

D-Day *n.* (DEE DAY) the day, June 6, 1944, in World War II when Allied forces invaded northern France by landing on beaches at Normandy (page 810)

death camp *n.* (DEHTH KAMP) a camp where Jews and others were held and murdered by the Nazis during World War II (page 814)

Declaration of Independence *n.* (deh-kluh-RAY-shun UHV ihn-duh-PEHN-duhns) the document declaring U.S. independence from Great Britain, adopted July 4, 1776 (page 208)

defect *v.* (dih-FEKT) to break away (page 564)

defensive war *n.* (dih-FEHN-sihv WOR) a war to protect one's own land, on familiar ground, from outside attackers (page 222)

deficit spending *n.* (DEH-fuh-suht SPEHND-ihng) a practice in which the government spends more money than it receives from taxes (page 783)

dehumanize *v.* (dee-HYOO-mahn-ize) to treat people as if they are not human beings (page 872)

delegate *n.* (DEH-lih-guht) a person chosen or elected to represent a group of people (page 256)

demobilization *n.* (dih-moh-buh-ly-ZAY-shuhn) the release of soldiers from military duty (page 842)

democratic republic *n.* (deh-muh-KRA-tihk RE-puhb-lik) an independent country ruled by its citizens through elections and other forms of voting (page R32)

deploy *v.* (dih-PLOY) to send into military action (page 802)

depression *n.* (dee-PREH-shuhn) a period of slow economic activity when many people are without work (page 375)

deregulation *n.* (dee-reh-gyuh-LAY-shun) the removal of laws or regulations governing a particular industry (page 966)

desegregate *v.* (dee-SEH-grih-GAYT) to end a policy that forces the separation of groups of people in public spaces (page 877)

desert *v.* (dih-ZURT) to run away from the army or another branch of the military to avoid military service (page 231)

dictator *n.* (DIHK-tay-tur) a leader who rules with absolute power (page 789)

diplomat *n.* (DIH-pluh-mat) a person sent to another nation to represent his or her country's interests (page 409)

direct primary election *n.* (duh-REKT PRY-mair-ee ih-LEK-shuhn) an election in which members of a political party nominate candidates by a direct vote (page 668)

dissent *n.* (dih-SEHNT) a disagreement with the government's official opinion (page 719)

dissenter *n.* (dih-SEHN-tur) a person who disagrees with a majority belief or position (page 100)

dissident *n.* (DIH-suh-duhnt) a person who strongly disagrees with official policy (page 732)

diversity *n.* (duh-VUR-suh-tee) a wide variety (page 143)

doctrine *n.* (DAHK-truhn) a principle or set of beliefs accepted by a group (page 109)

doctrine of nullification *n.* (DAHK-truhn UHV nuh-luh-fuh-KAY-shuhn) a doctrine that said a state could nullify, or reject, a federal law they felt was unconstitutional, held by some southern politicians before the Civil War (page 366)

domestic service *n.* (duh-MEHS-tihk SUR-vuhs) housework in another person's home, performed as a job (page 433)

domesticate *v.* (duh-MEHS-tih-kayt) to raise plants and animals for human benefit and consumption (page 27)

domestication *n.* (duh-mehs-TIH-kay-shuhn) the practice of raising animals and growing plants for human benefit (page 9)

domino theory *n.* (DAH-muh-noh THEER-ee) an idea during the Cold War that countries that neighbor communist countries are more likely to fall to communism (page 926)

dove *n.* (DUHV) a person who opposes war (page 933)

draft *n.* (DRAFT) a mandatory term of military service (page 522)

draft exemption *n.* (DRAFT ihg-ZEHM-shuhn) a reason to exclude a citizen from performing involuntary military service (page 933)

Dred Scott decision *n.* (DRED SKAHWT dih-SIH-zhuhn) a Supreme Court decision that African Americans held no rights as citizens and that the Missouri Compromise of 1820 was unconstitutional; Dred Scott, the escaped slave at the center of the case, was returned to slavery (page 468)

drought *n.* (DROWT) a prolonged period with little or no rainfall (page 774)

drumlin *n.* (DRUHM-luhn) a smooth-sloped hill made of glacial sediments (page 204)

dual sovereignty *n.* (DOO-uhl SAH-vuh-ruhn-tee) the concept that state governments have certain powers the federal government cannot overrule (page 257)

Dust Bowl *n.* (DUHST BOHL) a region of the Great Plains, including parts of Oklahoma, Colorado, Kansas, New Mexico, and Texas, that suffered from severe drought, soil erosion, and dust storms during the 1930s (page 774)

duty *n.* (DOO-tee) a tax on imports (page 181)

E

earthworks *n.* (URTH-wurks) human-made land modifications (page 204)

economic activity *n.* (eh-kuh-NAH-mihk ak-TIH-vuh-tee) actions that involve the production, distribution, and consumption of goods and services (page 114)

economic stimulus *n.* (eh-kuh-NAH-mihk STIHM-yuh-luhs) a measure aimed at promoting and enabling financial recovery and growth (page 996)

Electoral College *n.* (ee-lehk-TAWR-uhl KAH-lihj) the group that elects the U.S. president; each state receives as many electors as it has congressional representatives and senators combined (page 258)

emancipation *n.* (ih-man-suh-PAY-shuhn) the ending of slavery (page 446)

Emancipation Proclamation *n.* (ih-man-suh-PAY-shuhn prah-kluh-MAY-shuhn) an 1863 document issued by Abraham Lincoln that freed all slaves living in Confederate-held territory during the American Civil War (page 517)

embargo *n.* (ihm-BAHR-goh) a law that restricts commerce with one or more nations (page 319)

Embargo Act of 1807 *n.* (ihm-BAHR-goh AKT UHV 1807) a federal legislation that stopped all foreign imports from entering American harbors (page 319)

emigrate *v.* (EH-muh-grayt) to move away from a country in order to live in another (page 430)

encomienda *n.* (en-coe-mee-AYN-dah) a system in Spain's American colonies in which wealthy settlers were given plots of land and allowed to enslave the people who lived there (page 66)

Enlightenment *n.* (ihn-LY-tuhn-muhnt) an intellectual movement that emphasized the use of reason to examine previously accepted beliefs (page 149)

enlist *v.* (ehn-LIST) to join (page 520)

entrepreneur *n.* (ehn-treh-preh-NEUR) a person who starts, manages, and is responsible for a business (page 583)

envoy *n.* (AHN-voy) an ambassador (page 292)

escalation *n.* (ehs-kuh-LAY-shuhn) an increase of intensity, as during war (page 927)

espionage *n.* (EH-spee-uh-nahj) the practice of spying to obtain information (page 232)

evacuate *v.* (ih-VA-kyoo-wayt) to leave a location, usually for one's own protection (page 488)

evangelize *v.* (ih-VAN-juh-lyz) to spread one's religious beliefs through public speaking and personal witness (page 438)

executive branch *n.* (ihg-ZEH-kyuh-tihv BRANCH) the section of the U.S. government headed by the president; responsible for enforcing the law (page 258)

executive order *n.* (ihg-ZEH-kyuh-tihv OR-dur) a directive, or command, issued by a president, that has the force of law (page 806)

exemption *n.* (ihg-ZEHMP-shuhn) a release from obligations (page 522)

exile *n.* (EHG-zyl) a person who is a political outcast (page 906)

exodus *n.* (EHK-suh-duhs) a mass departure (page 395)

exoduster *n.* (EHK-suh-duhs-tur) one of the thousands of African Americans who migrated to the midwestern plains from the post-Civil-War South to start a new life (page 586)

expertise *n.* (ehk-spur-TEEZ) an expert knowledge or skill (page 241)

exposure *n.* (ihk-SPOH-zhur) having no shelter or protection from severe weather or cold temperatures (page 810)

F

factory system *n.* (FAK-tuh-ree SIHS-tuhm) a method of production in which large crews of people perform work in one location (page 328)

famine *n.* (FA-muhn) an extreme lack of crops or food causing widespread hunger (page 432)

Farmers' Alliance *n.* (FAHR-murz ah-LY-ans) one of several organizations founded in the 1880s to advance political and economic concerns of farmers; similar to the Grange but more political (page 591)

fascism *n.* (FA-shih-zuhm) a political movement based on extreme nationalism, militarism, and racism promoting the superiority of a particular people over all others (page 789)

federal *adj.* (FEH-duh-ruhl) relating to a government where power is shared between the central, national government and that of states or provinces (page 250)

federal marshal *n.* (FEH-duh-ruhl MAHR-shuhl) a law enforcement officer who works for the United States government (page 463)

Federal Reserve Act *n.* (FEH-duh-ruhl rih-ZURV AKT) the 1913 law that established the Federal Reserve Board that oversaw 12 reserve banks; the banks would control the nation's flow of money (page 674)

federalism *n.* (FEH-duh-ruh-lih-zuhm) the support of a government where power is shared between the central, national government and that of states or provinces (page 257)

federalist *n.* (FEH-duh-ruh-lihst) a person who supported the U.S. Constitution of 1787 as it was written during the process of ratification (page 262)

feminist *n.* (FEH-muh-nihst) people who practice the idea that women are equal to men socially and politically (page 924)

feudalism *n.* (FEW-dahl-izm) a political and social system in which a vassal receives protection from a lord in exchange for obedience and service (page 36)

15th Amendment *n.* (15th uh-MEND-muhnt) an amendment to the Constitution that says that federal and state governments cannot restrict the right to vote because of race, color, or previous condition of servitude (page 562)

financier *n.* (fih-nuhn-SIHR) a person who lends or manages money for a business or undertaking (page 229)

fireside chat *n.* (FY-ur-syd CHAT) one of a series of radio broadcasts that President Franklin Roosevelt made to the nation throughout his presidency (page 777)

First Continental Congress *n.* (FURST kahn-tuh-NEHN-tuhl KAHN-gruhs) the 1774 meeting of representatives from all American colonies to decide on a response to the Intolerable Acts (page 195)

first responder *n.* (FURST rih-SPAHND-ur) a person such as an emergency medical worker or police officer who provides rapid assistance at the scene of an accident or crime (page 989)

flapper *n.* (FLA-pur) a young woman in the 1920s who embraced a freer style of dress and the use of cosmetics (page 743)

flotilla *n.* (flo-TIHL-ah) a small fleet (page 528)

fortification *n.* (fawr-tuh-fuh-KAY-shuhn) a structure built to protect a place from attack (page 227)

forty-niner *n.* (for-tee-NY-nur) one of the thousands of prospective miners who traveled to California seeking gold in 1849 (page 417)

framers *n.* (FRAYM-urz) delegates to the 1787 Constitutional Convention who helped shape the content and structure of the U.S. Constitution (page 257)

free silver movement *n.* (FREE SIHL-vur MOOV-mehnt) a late-19th-century economic movement that promoted a monetary system based on silver in addition to gold (page 591)

free trade *n.* (FREE TRAYD) a form of international trade that has few or no restrictions (page 1004)

Freedmen's Bureau *n.* (FREED-muhns BYOOR-oh) the Bureau of Refugees, Freedmen, and Abandoned Lands, created by Congress in 1865 to help former slaves, as well as poor white southerners (page 553)

Freedom Riders *n.* (FREE-duhm RY-durz) interracial groups who participated in bus trips through the South to protest and call attention to segregation (page 882)

French Revolution *n.* (FRENCH re-vuh-LOO-shuhn) the 1789 rebellion against the French monarchy that sought to put an end to upper-class privilege and demanded equality for the lower classes (page 289)

front *n.* (FRUHNT) a battle line between armies (page 712)

Frostbelt *n.* (FRAHST-behlt) the north-central and northeastern regions of the United States, which have cold winters (page 854)

fugitive slave clause *n.* (FYOO-juh-tihv SLAYV KLAWZ) a provision in Article 4 of the U.S. Constitution that prevented free states from emancipating enslaved workers who had escaped from their masters in other states (page 260)

Fundamental Orders of Connecticut *n.* (fuhn-duh-MEHN-tahl AWR-duhr UHV kuh-NEH-tih-kuht) a founding document of the Connecticut colony that listed 11 laws and stood as the framework for governing the colony (page 101)

fundamentalism *n.* (fuhn-duh-MEHN-tah-lih-zuhm) a movement that promoted the idea that every word of the Bible was the literal truth (page 736)

fundamentalist *n.* (fuhn-duh-MEHN-tuh-lihst) a person who believes in strict or literal adherance to a belief system (page 965)

G

Gadsden Purchase *n.* (GADZ-duhn PUHR-chuhs) a sale of land in 1853 from Mexico to the United States that established the current U.S. southwestern border (page 413)

galleon *n.* (GAL-eeahn) a large sailing ship used especially by the Spanish in the 16th and 17th centuries (page 62)

garrison *n.* (GAIR-uh-suhn) a defense force of soldiers (page 477)

gender bias *n.* (JEHN-dur BY-uhs) the preference for one gender over another (page 925)

genocide *n.* (JEH-nuh-syd) the deliberate murder of a large number of people belonging to a specific racial, cultural, or political group (page 814)

geographic perspective *n.* (jee-uh-GRA-fihk pur-SPEHK-tihv) the examination of how geography affects people and culture (page 34)

geology *n.* (jee-AH-luh-jee) the study of the processes that shape Earth's rocks and landforms (page 204)

Gettysburg Address *n* (GEH-teez-burg uh-DREHS) an 1863 speech delivered by President Lincoln to commemorate the loss of life at the Battle of Gettysburg and to dedicate a military cemetery (page 529)

ghetto *n.* (GEH-toh) forced housing for a particular race or ethnicity (page 814)

Ghost Dance *n.* (GOHST DANTS) a Native-American religious movement based on a dance ritual meant to communicate with the dead and bring an end to white control of the West; began in the 1870s (page 598)

ghost town *n.* (GOHST TOWN) an abandoned town that has fallen into ruin (page 583)

Gilded Age *n.* (GIHL-duhd AJ) the last three decades of the 19th century, characterized by greed and corruption (page 628)

glacial period *n.* (GLAY-shuhl PEER-ee-uhd) a period of time in history during which huge sheets of ice covered much of Earth (page 5)

glasnost *n.* (GLAS-nawst) a government policy of open communication in the former Soviet Union (page 974)

globalization *n.* (gloh-buh-luh-ZAY-shuhn) the faster and freer flow of people, resources, goods, and ideas across national borders (page 1004)

gold standard *n.* (GOLD STAN-durd) a monetary policy requiring that the government can print only an amount of money equal to the total value of its gold reserves (page 591)

gospel music *n.* (GAH-spuhl MYOO-zik) music that combines biblical subject matter and melodic themes similar to jazz songs (page 748)

government shutdown *n.* (GUH-vur-muhnt SHUHT-down) a time when the executive branch of the government has to close federal government offices and federal government services because of a failure to pass funding legislation for these offices or services (page 985)

GLOSSARY

Grange *n.* (GRAYNJ) a U.S. farmers' organization founded in 1867 to provide social and economic support to agricultural families (page 590)

grassroots *adj.* (GRAS-roots) organized by ordinary people, who do not have money or power, to bring about change (page 872)

Great Awakening *n.* (GRAYT uh-WAY-kuhn-ing) a series of Protestant religious revivals that swept across the American colonies (page 148)

Great Migration *n.* (GRAYT my-GRAY-shuhn) the mass movement of African Americans who left the South for cities in the North, beginning in 1910 (page 727)

greenhouse effect *n.* (GREEN-hows uh-FEHKT) the warming of Earth's surface caused when greenhouse gas emissions trap the sun's heat (page 1008)

grievance *n.* (GREE-vuhnts) an objection or reason to complain (page 181)

gristmill *n.* (GRIHST-mihl) a building that houses machinery for grinding grain (page 140)

guerrilla *adj.* (guh-RIH-luh) relating to an independent military group that uses methods such as sneak attacks and sabotage (page 237)

gunboat *n.* (GUHN-boht) a small, fast ship carrying mounted guns (page 508)

H

habeus corpus *n.* (HA-be-as COR-pus) the right of an arrested person to be brought before a judge before going to jail (page 523)

hacienda *n.* (hah-see-EHN-dah) a large plantation in a Spanish-speaking colony (page 66)

hawk *n.* (HAWK) a person who supports war (page 933)

heretic *n.* (HAIR-uh-tihk) a person who holds beliefs different from the teachings of the Catholic Church (page 61)

Hessians *n.* (HEH-shuhnz) German soldiers hired by the British to fight during the American Revolution (page 206)

hierarchy *n.* (HY-uh-rahr-kee) the classification of a group of people according to ability or to economic, social, or professional standing (page 36)

Holocaust *n.* (HOH-luh-cawst) the mass slaughter by the Nazis of six million Jews and others during World War II (page 814)

Homestead Act *n.* (HOHM-stehd AKT) an act that started a program of public land grants to small farmers (page 541)

Hooverville *n.* (HOO-vur-vil) a makeshift village for homeless Americans with shelters made of cardboard, scrap metal, or other cheap and available materials, built during the Great Depression and named after President Herbert Hoover (page 769)

human geography *n.* (HYOO-muhn jee-AH-gruh-fee) the study of how people and their cultures are affected by physical geography and how human activities affect the environment (page 34)

human immunodeficiency virus (HIV) *n.* (HYOO-muhn ih-MYOO-noh-dih-FIH-shun-see VY-ruhs) a virus that attacks the system in the human body that fights off illnesses (page 971)

human right *n.* (HYOO-muhn RYT) a basic right that most societies believe should be given to all people (page 964)

humanism *n.* (HYOO-muh-nih-zhum) a movement that focuses on the importance of the individual (page 39)

hunger strike *n.* (HUNG-gur STRYK) the act of refusing to eat as a protest to show disapproval or disagreement (page 918)

hunter-gatherer *n.* (HUHN-tuhr GAHTH-ur-ur) a human who hunts animals and gathers wild plants to eat (page 7)

hydraulic mining *n.* (hy-DRAW-lik MY-nihng) a system of mining in which pressurized water is used to remove topsoil and gravel, which are then processed to draw out precious metals (page 583)

hydroelectric power *n.* (hy-droh-ih-LEHK-trihk POHW-uhr) a source of electricity created by flowing water that turns turbines, which generate power (page 773)

I

ice age *n.* (AISS AJ) a period of time in history during which huge sheets of ice covered much of Earth (page 5)

ideology *n.* (I-dee-AH-luh-jee) a belief system that guides a political or social plan (page 789)

immigrate *v.* (IH-muh-grayt) to permanently move to another country (page 430)

immigration quota *n.* (ih-muh-GRAY-shuhn KWOH-tuh) a limit on the number of people that are allowed to emigrate from certain countries (page 736)

immunity *n.* (ih-MYOO-nih-tee) a protection against disease, either natural or induced by vaccination (page 70)

impeachment *n.* (ihm-PEECH-muhnt) the official charge of a president with misconduct while in office (page 555)

imperialism *n.* (ihm-PIHR-ee-uh-lih-zuhm) a governmental system in which a stronger nation controls weaker nations or territories (page 684)

implied power *n.* (ihm-PLYD POW-ur) a power not explicitly stated in the Constitution (page 343)

impressment *n.* (ihm-PRESS-muhnt) the act of forcing men into military or naval service (page 319)

improvise *v.* (IHM-pruh-vyz) to create and play music without rehearsing it, often making up the musical lines on the spot (page 742)

inauguration *n.* (uh-NAW-gyuh-ray-shun) the ceremony that marks the beginning of a presidency (page 279)

incendiary bomb *n.* (ihn-SEHN-dee-ehr-ee BAHM) a bomb that is designed to start fires (page 819)

income tax *n.* (IHN-kuhm TAKS) a tax on the income of an individual (page 673)

incumbent *n.* (ihn-KUHM-buhnt) the person currently in office; the incumbent president is the current president (page 306)

indentured servant *n.* (ihn-DEHN-churd SUR-vuhnt) a person under contract to work, usually without pay, in exchange for free passage to the colonies (page 93)

Indian Removal Act *n.* (IHN-dee-uhn rih-MOO-vuhl AKT) a law that ended the U.S. government's earlier policy of respecting the rights of Native Americans to remain on their land (page 368)

Indian Territory *n.* (IHN-dee-uhn TAIR-uh-tawr-ee) the area of land in present-day Oklahoma and parts of Kansas and Nebraska to which Native Americans were forced to migrate (page 368)

indigo *n.* (IHN-dih-goh) a plant that produces a blue dye for cloth (page 132)

individualism *n.* (ihn-duh-VIHJ-wuh-lih-zuhm) self-reliant independence (page 390)

Industrial Revolution *n.* (ihn-DUH-stree-uhl rev-oh-LUH-shuhn) an era in which widespread production by machinery replaced goods made by hand (page 328)

industrialist *n.* (ihn-DUH-stree-uh-lihst) a person who owns and runs an industry (page 591)

infantry *n.* (IHN-fuhn-tree) foot soldiers (page 491)

inflation *n.* (ihn-FLAY-shuhn) a decrease in the value of money that causes an increase in the price of goods and services (page 374)

influenza *n.* (ihn-floo-EHN-zuh) an acute and highly contagious illness commonly called "the flu" (page 726)

initiative *n.* (ih-NIH-shuh-tihv) a process by which regular citizens propose a law and require that fellow citizens vote on it (page 669)

installment plan *n.* (ihn-STAWL-muhnt PLAN) a plan for purchasing goods by making a series of partial payments over a set time period (page 765)

institution *n.* (ihn-stuh-TOO-shuhn) an established and accepted practice in a society or culture (page 74)

insurgent *n.* (ihn-SUR-juhnt) a rebel or revolutionary (page 989)

insurrection *n.* (ihn-suh-REK-shun) a rebellion (page 410)

integration *n.* (ihn-tuh-GRAY-shuhn) the act of allowing the free association of people of different races or ethnicities (page 875)

interchangeable part *n.* (ihn-tur-CHAYN-juh-buhl PAHRT) parts of a mechanism that can be substituted one for another (page 330)

Internet *n.* (IHN-tur-neht) the electronic network that allows computers to communicate (page 1000)

internment camp *n.* (ihn-TURN-muhnt KAMP) a prison camp to hold enemy aliens and other prisoners of war during wartime (page 806)

interstate slave trade *n.* (IHN-tur-stayt SLAYV TRAYD) the buying and selling of slaves within the United States (page 339)

Intolerable Acts *n.* (ihn-TAHL-ruh-buhl AKTS) the British laws passed to punish the people of Boston after the Boston Tea Party; also called the Coercive Acts (page 194)

GLOSSARY

investor *n.* (ihn-VEH-stuhr) a person who buys shares of a company with the intent of making a profit when he or she sells the stock shares (page 765)

ironclad ship *n.* (I-urn-klahd SHIP) a ship armored with iron plates to protect it from cannon fire (page 495)

Iroquois League *n.* (EER-uh-koy leeg) the confederation of five Iroquois-speaking nations: the Mohawk, Oneida, Onondaga, Cayuga, and Seneca; later joined by the Tuscarora (page 29)

irrigation *n.* (eer-uh-GAY-shun) the supply of water to fields using human-made systems (page 24)

island hopping *n.* (I-luhnd HAH-pihng) a strategy that involves capturing and setting up military bases on island groups one island at a time (page 818)

isolationism *n.* (I-soh-LAY-shuh-nih-zuhm) a policy in which a nation stays out of the affairs of other nations (page 791)

isthmus *n.* (IHS-muhs) a narrow strip of land that connects two larger landmasses and separates two bodies of water (page 692)

J

Jacksonian democracy *n.* (jak-SOH-nee-uhn dih-MAH-kruh-see) a political movement that celebrated the common man and defended the will of the people, named for President Andrew Jackson (page 362)

jazz *n.* (JAZ) a style of music originating among African-American musicians that contains lively rhythms, sounds from a variety of instruments, and improvisation (page 742)

Jim Crow laws *n.* (JIHM KROH LAWZ) laws created in the 1880s by southern politicians to take away the rights of African Americans (page 640)

joint-stock company *n.* (JOYNT STAHK KUHM-puh-nee) a company whose shareholders own stock in the company (page 92)

judicial branch *n.* (joo-DIH-shehl BRANCH) the section of the U.S. government that includes the courts and legal system, led by the Supreme Court; responsible for interpreting the law (page 258)

judicial review *n.* (joo-DIH-shuhl rih-VYOO) the power to invalidate any law the Supreme Court deems unconstitutional, even if it has been passed by Congress and signed into law by the president (page 310)

Judiciary Act of 1801 *n.* (joo-DIH-shee-air-ee AKT UHV 1801) the federal legislation that reduced the number of justices on the Supreme Court from 6 to 5 (page 310)

jurisdiction *n.* (jur-uhs-DIHK-shuhn) the authority to enforce laws within a given area (page 538)

K

kamikaze pilot *n.* (kah-mih-KAH-zee PI-luht) one of a group of Japanese suicide bomber pilots who crashed their planes, loaded with explosives, into American ships during World War II (page 819)

kayak *n.* (KAI-yak) a canoe with a light frame and a small opening on top in which to sit (page 26)

King Philip's War *n.* (KING FIH-luhps WOR) a violent conflict between Native Americans and English colonists from New England, who were aided by Native American allies (page 106)

Know-Nothing Party *n.* (NOH NUH-thing PAHR-tee) a political party formed in the 1850s to oppose immigration, also called the American Party (page 436)

Ku Klux Klan *n.* (KOO KLUHKS KLAN) the group whose purpose was to maintain the social and political power of white people (page 560)

L

labor union *n.* (LAY-bur YOON-yuhn) a voluntary association of workers that uses its power to negotiate better working conditions (page 442)

laissez faire *n.* (leh-say FAIR) an economic policy in which a government lets businesses operate without much regulation; laissez-faire means "allow to" in French (page 627)

landmark legislation *n.* (lahnd-MARK lehj-iss-LAY-shun) an important and historic law (page 913)

League of Nations *n.* (LEEG UHV NAY-shuhnz) an international peacekeeping organization proposed by President Woodrow Wilson after World War I (page 723)

Legal Tender Act *n.* (LEE-guhl TEHN-dur AKT) an act that replaced the notes of individual banks with a unified national currency (page 524)

legislative branch *n.* (LEH-jeh-slay-tihv BRANCH) the section of the U.S. government led by Congress; responsible for making the law (page 258)

levee *n.* (LEH-vee) a ridge of earth that runs along the sides of a stream or river (page 991)

levy *v.* (LEH-vee) to require the payment of a tax (page 105)

libel *n.* (LY-buhl) the publishing of lies (page 152)

Liberal Republicans *n.* (LIH-buh-ruhl rih-PUH-blih-kuhnz) a group during the 1870s that believed the government had become too large and too powerful (page 564)

Liberty Bond *n.* (LIH-bur-tee BAHND) a government bond sold to individuals to help support U.S. involvement in World War I (page 718)

literacy *n.* (LIH-tur-uh-see) the ability to read and write (page 559)

literacy test *n.* (LIH-tur-uh-see TEST) test of one's ability to read and write (page 565)

loan default *n.* (LOHN dih-FAWLT) a failure to repay a loan (page 995)

lobbyist *n.* (LAH-bee-ihst) a person who tries to persuade lawmakers to support particular laws and political ideas (page 681)

lock *n.* (LAHK) a confined section of water used to raise or lower ships (page 693)

lode *n.* (LOHD) a large deposit of ore, such as silver or gold (page 582)

Long Walk *n.* (LONG WAWK) the 300-mile forced walk of the Navajo from their homeland to a reservation at Bosque Redondo, New Mexico; imposed by the U.S. government in 1864 (page 596)

loophole *n.* (LOOP-hohl) unclear language that allows people to get around laws and avoid obeying them (page 674)

loose interpretation *n.* (LOOS ihn-tur-pruh-TAY-shuhn) an understanding of the Constitution as one that gives Congress and the president broad powers (page 286)

Louisiana Purchase *n.* (lu-ee-zee-A-nuh PUR-chuhs) a treaty between France and the United States in which a large area of land between the Mississippi River and the Rocky Mountains was purchased (page 313)

low-cost housing *n.* (LOH KAWST HOW-zingh) housing that is affordable to people with low incomes (page 845)

Loyalist *n.* (LOY-uh-lihst) an American colonist who supported Britain during the American Revolution (page 198)

lunar module *n.* (LOO-nuhr MAH-jool) a part of a space vehicle meant to carry astronauts from the command module to the surface of the moon and back to the command module (page 957)

lynch *v.* (LINCH) to hang someone illegally by mob action (page 560)

M

Manhattan Project *n.* (man-HA-tuhn PRAH-jehkt) the code name for the U.S. government-funded atomic weapons program during the 1940s (page 821)

manifest destiny *n.* (MAN-uh-fehst DEHS-tuh-nee) the idea that the United States had the right and the obligation to expand its territory across North America to the Pacific Ocean (page 391)

manor system *n.* (MA-nur SIHS-tuhm) an economic system in which peasants are bound to a lord and work his land, or manor, in exchange for food and shelter (page 37)

margin *n.* (MAHR-juhn) the amount by which something is won or lost (page 403)

market revolution *n.* (MAHR-kuht rev-uh-LOO-shun) the transition from a pre-industrial economy to a market-oriented, capitalist economy (page 328)

marketing *n.* (MAHR-kuh-ting) the process of promoting products or services (page 738)

Marshall Plan *n.* (MAHR-shuhl PLAN) an aid plan to help European countries rebuild and recover economically after World War II (page 822)

mass culture *n.* (MAS KUHL-chur) the set of popular values and ideas that arise from widespread access to media, music, art, and other entertainment (page 628)

mass media *n.* (MAS MEE-dee-uh) the sources of information and entertainment that reach large groups of people at the same time (page 738)

matrilineal *adj.* (ma-truh-LIN-ee-uhl) relating to descendants traced through the mother (page 29)

Mayflower Compact *n.* (MAY-flow-uhr KAHM-pakt) a shipboard contract signed by the Pilgrims on the *Mayflower* before they landed in North America, binding them to abide by their own laws and establish a civil society (page 100)

McCarthyism *n.* (muh-KAHR-thee-ih-zuhm) the practice of accusing people of being traitors to their country without offering proof (page 853)

Meat Inspection Act *n.* (MEET ihn-SPEHK-shuhn AKT) a 1906 law that sought to ensure the purity and safety of meat (page 671)

Medicaid *n.* (MEH-dih-kayd) a U.S. government program started in 1965 that gives medical insurance to impoverished people (page 917)

Medicare *n.* (MEH-dih-kair) a U.S. government program started in 1965 that gives medical insurance to older people (page 917)

megafauna *n.* (MEH-guh-faw-nuh) the large animals of a particular area in the world or a particular time in history (page 6)

mercantilism *n.* (MUHR-kuhn-teel-ih-zuhm) an economic policy that gives a country sole ownership of the trade occurring in its colonies (page 52)

mercenary *n.* (MUR-suh-nair-ee) a soldier who is paid to fight for a country other than his or her own (page 222)

mestizo *n.* (mes-TEE-zoh) a person who has mixed Spanish and Native American ancestry (page 66)

Middle Passage *n.* (MIH-duhl PA-sihj) the long trip across the Atlantic Ocean by which enslaved Africans were brought to the Americas; the second leg of the triangular trade route (page 73)

midwife *n.* (MIHD-wyf) a person who is trained to help deliver babies (page 146)

migrant worker *n.* (MY-gruhnt WUR-kur) a laborer who moves from one job to another as needed; usually a farm laborer (page 586)

migrate *v.* (MY-grayt) to move from one place to another (page 27)

militarism *n.* (MIH-luh-tuh-rih-zuhm) the belief that a government must create a strong military and be prepared to use it to achieve the country's goals (page 710)

militia *n.* (muh-LIH-shuh) military force made up of local citizens to help protect their town, land, or nation (page 178)

minuteman *n.* (MIH-nuht-man) an American colonial militia member who was ready to join in combat at a moment's notice (page 196)

mission *n.* (MIH-shuhn) a Christian church settlement established to convert native peoples (page 66)

missionary *n.* (MIH-shuh-nair-ee) a person who tries to spread Christianity to others (page 53)

Missouri Compromise *n.* (mih-ZUR-ee KAHM-pruh-myz) an agreement that stated the people of Missouri could own slaves and be admitted to the Union along with Maine, a free state (page 344)

mobilize *v.* (MOH-buh-lyz) to organize and prepare troops for war (page 490)

monopoly *n.* (muh-NAH-puh-lee) the complete and exclusive control of an industry by one company (page 343)

Monroe Doctrine *n.* (muhn-ROH DAHK-truhn) an approach to foreign policy that stated the American continents were no longer under European influence (page 345)

Montgomery Bus Boycott *n.* (mahnt-GUH-muh-ree BUHS BOY-kaht) a mass protest, sparked by the arrest of Rosa Parks, against the racial segregation practices of the public bus system in Montgomery, Alabama (page 879)

moral diplomacy *n.* (MOR-uhl duh-PLOH-muh-see) the concept that the United States should drastically reduce its intervention in the affairs of other countries (page 724)

Moral Majority *n.* (MOR-uhl muh-JOR-uh-tee) a politically conservative group formed by the Reverend Jerry Falwell, a televangelist, in 1979 (page 970)

morale *n.* (muh-RAL) the amount of confidence or enthusiasm felt by a group of people (page 717)

morphine *n.* (MOR-feen) a powerful painkiller (page 534)

mortality *n.* (mor-TAH-luh-tee) the death rate (page 495)

mountain men *n.* (MOWN-tuhn MEHN) the American fur trappers and explorers who began to explore and move west (page 390)

Munich Agreement *n.* (MYOO-nihk uh-GREE-muhnt) an agreement Hitler made with the rulers of Great Britain, France, and Italy, declaring that Germany had the right to seize the Sudetenland, a portion of Czechoslovakia (page 791)

munitions *n.* (myoo-NIH-shuhns) military weapons (page 801)

mutual aid society *n.* (MYOO-chuh-wuhl AYD suh-SY-uh-tee) an organization formed by members of a particular group to provide economic and other assistance to each other (page 631)

N

napalm *n.* (NAY-pahlm) a thick flammable, jellylike substance used in bombs to cause and spread fires (page 929)

national debt *n.* (NA-shuh-nuhl DEHT) the amount of money a government owes to all its creditors, including to other nations and to companies from which it purchases goods and services (page 282)

national health insurance *n.* (NA-shuh-nuhl HELTH ihn-SHUR-uhns) an insurance plan run by the government and open to anyone to join (page 845)

nationalism *n.* (NA-shuh-nuh-lih-zuhm) the concept of loyalty and devotion to one's nation (page 342)

nativist *n.* (NAY-tih-vihst) a person who believes native-born people should be favored more than immigrants (page 436)

natural resource *n.* (NACH-uh-ruhl REE-sawrs) a material or substance found in nature that can be used to sustain a society or exploited for economic gain, such as minerals, water, or living things (page 114)

natural rights *n.* (NACH-uh-ruhl RYTS) rights such as life or liberty that a person is born with (page 149)

naturalization *n.* (NACH-uh-ruh-lih-ZAY-shuhn) the process of becoming a U.S. citizen for people who are not native-born citizens (page R32)

naval quarantine *n.* (NAY-vuhl KWAWR-uhn-teen) a blockade imposed on the ports of another country (page 908)

navigation *n.* (nav-ih-GAY-shuhn) the science of finding position and planning routes, often used in relation to seafaring (page 40)

Navigation Acts *n.* (nav-ih-GAY-shuhn AKTS) a series of laws passed by the English Parliament to protect English shipping by restricting the transport of goods to and from the English colonies (page 125)

Nazi Party *n.* (NAHT-see PAHR-tee) a political party led by Adolf Hitler that used force to exert complete control over Germany from 1933 to 1945 (page 789)

neoconservative *n.* (nee-oh-kuhn-SUR-vuh-tihv) a person who strongly supports a free-market economy and believes the United States should actively promote its ideals around the world (page 986)

neutrality *n.* (noo-TRA-luh-tee) the refusal to take sides or become involved (page 111)

newsreel *n.* (NOOZ-reel) a short news or sports film that plays before a feature film (page 741)

nonviolent resistance *n.* (nahn-VI-uh-luhnt rih-ZIHS-tuhns) a practice of using civil disobedience, noncooperation, and other means of peaceful protest to achieve social change (page 880)

Northwest Ordinance of 1787 *n.* (nawrth-WEHST AWR-duh-nuhns UHV 1787) a legislation adopted by Congress to establish stricter control over the government of the Northwest Territory (page 252)

Northwest Passage *n.* (nawrth-WEHST PA-sihj) a passage by water between the Atlantic and Pacific oceans along the northern coast of North America (page 60)

nuclear fission *n.* (NOO-klee-ur FIH-shuhn) the splitting of atoms that causes a release of energy (page 821)

O

oasis *n.* (oh-AY-sihs) a fertile place with water in a desert (page 42)

occupation zone *n.* (AH-kyoo-pay-shuhn ZOHN) an area of a country in which a foreign military takes control (page 846)

GLOSSARY

Open Door Policy *n.* (OH-puhn DOHR PAH-luh-see) the late 19th century and early 20th century policy calling for equal trading privileges for all nations with economic interests in China (page 691)

oration *n.* (uh-RAY-shuhn) a formal speech (page 886)

ordinance *n.* (AWR-duh-nuhns) an official law, decree, or directive (page 252)

Ordinance of 1785 *n.* (AWR-duh-nuhns UHV 1785) a federal law that set up a system to allow settlers to purchase land in the undeveloped West (page 252)

organized crime *n.* (AWR-guh-nyzd KRYM) planned illegal activities that are carried out by powerful criminals (page 735)

overhead *n.* (oh-vur-HEHD) the cost of doing business (page 647)

overseer *n.* (OH-vur-see-ur) a supervisor (page 134)

P

Pacific Railway Acts *n.* (puh-SIH-fihk RAYL-way AKTS) two acts passed in the 1860s that gave two companies the contracts to construct a transcontinental railroad (page 620)

pacifist *n.* (PA-suh-fihst) a person who stands against war and violence (page 239)

Panic of 1837 *n.* (PA-nihk UHV 1837) the widespread fear of a failing economy that caused the beginning of a U.S. economic recession that lasted until 1840 (page 375)

Panic of 1873 *n.* (PA-nihk UHV 1873) an economic crisis triggered by bank and railroad failures (page 565)

panzer *n.* (PAN-zur) a thickly armored German tank with impressive firepower used during World War II (page 812)

parallel *n.* (PAIR-uh-lehl) a line of latitude (page 413)

pardon *n.* (PAHR-duhn) a release from legal punishment (page 962)

Parliament *n.* (PAHR-luh-muhnt) the legislative body of England, and, later, Great Britain (page 150)

partition *v.* (pahr-TIH-shuhn) to divide a whole into parts (page 813)

passive resistance *n.* (PA-sihv rih-ZIHS-tuhns) a nonviolent refusal to obey authority and laws (page 341)

patent *n.* (PA-tuhnt) a document that gives the bearer exclusive rights to make and sell an invention (page 624)

Patriot *n.* (PAY-tree-uht) an American colonist who supported the right of the American colonies to govern themselves (page 198)

pension fund *n.* (PEHN-shuhn FUHND) a pool of money used to pay people a small, established income after they retire (page 776)

perestroika *n.* (pair-ih-STROY-kuh) a government policy of economic and political reform in the former Soviet Union (page 974)

persecute *v.* (PUR-seh-kyoot) to punish, particularly because of beliefs or background (page 61)

personal responsibility *n.* (PURS-uh-nuhl rih-SPAWN-suh-BIHL-uh-tee) responsibility that is not required but that contributes to a more civil society, such as respecting and standing up for others' rights, helping in the community, and staying informed (page R34)

philanthropist *n.* (fuh-LAN-thruh-pihst) someone who actively promotes human welfare (page 496)

philanthropy *n.* (fuh-LAN-thruh-pee) the financial support of a worthy or charitable cause (page 627)

physical geography *n.* (FIH-zih-kuhl jee-AH-gruh-fee) the study of Earth's exterior physical features (page 34)

Piedmont *n.* (PEED-mont) a relatively flat area between the Appalachian Mountains and the coastal plain (page 134)

pilgrimage *n.* (PILL-gruhm-ij) a religious journey (page 45)

pioneer *n.* (py-uh-NIHR) a settler moving to a new and unfamiliar land (page 392)

placer mining *n.* (PLAH-sur MY-nihng) a system of mining in which individual miners find gold nuggets in riverbeds, usually by panning (page 583)

planned obsolescence *n.* (PLAND abh-suh-LES-uhns) the idea that people should plan to replace an item before it is broken or worn out (page 739)

plantation *n.* (plan-TAY-shuhn) a large farm; on southern plantations, slaves worked to grow and harvest crops (page 66)

Platt Amendment *n.* (PLAHT uh-MEND-muhnt) a 1901 amendment to military legislation establishing the conditions by which the United States would withdraw from Cuba after the Spanish-American War but retain the right to intervene in Cuban affairs (page 687)

Pleistocene epoch *n.* (PLEIS-toh-seen EH-puhk) a period in the history of Earth in which large animals and plants existed and glaciers covered Earth (page 5)

poison gas *n.* (POY-zuhn GAS) a chemical released into the air that causes harm or death (page 713)

political machine *n.* (poh-LIH-tih-kuhl muh-SHEEN) a party organization that ran big cities, ruled by strong and often corrupt leaders who offered favors to members in exchange for votes and other support (page 634)

poll tax *n.* (POHL TAKS) a fee charged when people register to vote (page 563)

poll watcher *n.* (POHL WAH-chur) a person assigned to a polling place to guard against voting irregularities (page 643)

pontoon *n.* (pahn-TOON) a portable, cylindrical float used to build a temporary bridge (page 511)

popular sovereignty *n.* (PAH-pyuh-lur SAHV-run-tee) the idea that the residents of a region or nation decide an issue by voting (page 466)

populism *n.* (PAH-pyuh-lih-zuhm) the belief that common people, not the wealthy, should control their government (page 665)

populist *n.* (PAH-pyuh-lihst) a politician who claims to represent the concerns of ordinary people (page 591)

posse *n.* (PAH-see) a group organized by a sheriff to hunt down criminals or fugitives (page 583)

post-traumatic stress disorder (PTSD) *n.* (POHST truh-MAH-tihk STREHS dihs-AWR-dur) a condition brought on by injury or psychological trauma (page 952)

potlatch *n.* (PAHT-lach) a gift-giving ceremony practiced by the Kwakiutl and Haida Native American tribes (page 26)

power base *n.* (POW-ur BAYS) an area or group of people providing the biggest influence over a political candidate (page 286)

prairie *n.* (PRAIR-ee) a vast area of flat land covered with tall plants (page 586)

precedent *n.* (PREH-suh-duhnt) a prior event or decision that serves as an example for events or decisions that follow (page 278)

prejudice *n.* (PREH-juh-duhs) a broad judgment about a group of people not based on reason or fact (page 436)

Presidential Reconstruction *n.* (preh-zuh-DEN-shuhl ree-kuhn-STRUHK-shuhn) a policy that stated Confederate states must ratify the 13th Amendment and create new governments with new constitutions before they could rejoin the Union (page 552)

presidio *n.* (prih-SIH-dee-oh) a military post or settlement (page 398)

printing press *n.* (PRIHN-ting PREHS) an invention that used movable metal type to print pages (page 39)

prisoner of war *n.* (PRIH-zuhn-ur UHV WOR) a soldier captured by an enemy force (page 793)

privateer *n.* (PRY-vah-teer) an armed but privately owned ship that acts under the authority of a government to participate in warfare; or a sailor on such a ship (page 62)

Proclamation of 1763 *n.* (prah-kluh-MAY-shuhn UHV 1763) a law requiring colonists to stay east of a line drawn on a map along the crest of the Appalachian Mountains (page 178)

profit *n.* (PRAH-fuht) the amount of money left for a business after expenses are deducted (page 40)

progressivism *n.* (pruh-GREH-sih-vih-zuhm) a social movement that believes in equality for all people and calls for people and the government to work together to bring about social change (page 665)

Prohibition *n.* (proh-uh-BIH-shuhn) the 18th Amendment to the Constitution banning the production, sale, importation, and transportation of liquor in the United States (page 681)

propaganda *n.* (prah-puh-GAN-duh) information spread to influence people's opinions or advance an organization's or party's ideas (page 718)

prophet *n.* (PRAH-fuht) someone who is believed to deliver messages from God or some other divine source (page 321)

proprietor *n.* (pruh-PRY-uh-tuhr) a person with ownership of a colony, including the right to manage and distribute land and to establish government (page 112)

prospector *n.* (PRAH-spek-tur) a person who searches in the earth for valuable resources, such as gems or precious metals (page 416)

Protestant *n.* (PRAH-teh-stant) a follower of the Reformation in Christianity (page 39)

provision *n.* (pruh-VIH-zhuhn) a legal condition that anticipates future needs (page 244)

provisions *n.* (pruh-VIH-zhuhnz) the supplies of food, water, and other items needed for a journey (page 124)

proviso *n.* (pruh-VY-zoh) a condition attached to a legal document or legislation (page 413)

puppet government *n.* (PUH-puht GUH-vur-muhnt) a government that appears to have authority but is controlled by another power (page 794)

Pure Food and Drug Act *n.* (PYOOR FOOD AND DRUHG AKT) a 1906 law that empowered the federal government to protect the quality, purity, and safety of foods and drugs (page 671)

push-pull factor *n.* (PUSH PUL FAK-tur) a reason why people immigrate, such as lack of economic opportunity or freedom in one country and the promise of a better life in another (page 430)

Q

quarantine *v.* (KWAWR-uhn-teen) to keep infected people away from those who have not yet contracted a disease (page 527)

Quartering Act *n.* (KWAWR-tuh-ring AKT) one of several British laws that required American colonists to provide housing and food for British soldiers stationed in North America (page 178)

quinine *n.* (KWHY-nyn) a substance made from the bark of a tree that is an effective remedy for malaria (page 71)

R

racism *n.* (RAY-sih-zuhm) the belief that one race is better than others (page 464)

radical *n.* (RA-dih-kuhl) a person who supports complete social or political change (page 289)

Radical Reconstruction *n.* (RA-dih-kuhl ree-kuhn-STRUHK-shuhn) the name given to the Republicans' plan in passing the Reconstruction Acts of 1867 (page 554)

rancho *n.* (RAN-choh) land granted by Mexico to settlers in the form of large estates in what is now California (page 415)

ratify *v.* (RA-tuh-fy) to approve formally, by vote (page 250)

rationing *v.* (RA-shuh-nihng) the controlled distribution of important food or supplies (page 799)

rations *n.* (RA-shuhnz) supplied food (page 527)

raw material *n.* (RAW muh-TIHR-ee-uhl) the basic substances and elements used to make products (page 114)

reaper *n.* (REE-pur) a machine that cuts stalks of wheat or oats (page 331)

recession *n.* (rih-SEH-shuhn) an economic downturn (page 590)

Reconstruction *n.* (ree-kuhn-STRUHK-shuhn) the effort to rebuild and reunite the United States following the Civil War (page 538)

Reconstruction Acts of 1867 *n.* (ree-kuhn-STRUHK-shuhn AKTS UHV 1867) acts that put the Republican Congress in charge of Reconstruction instead of the president (page 554)

referendum *n.* (reh-fuh-REN-duhm) the practice of submitting a law directly to voters to accept or reject the law (page 669)

refugee *n.* (REH-fyoo-jee) a person who flees to another country to escape danger or persecution (page 630)

reinforcements *n.* (ree-uhn-FAWRS-muhnts) more soldiers and supplies sent to help military troops engage in warfare (page 224)

religious freedom *n.* (rih-LIH-juhs FREE-duhm) the right to practice the religion of one's choosing without government interference (page 126)

renaissance *n.* (reh-nuh-SAHNTS) a rebirth or revival of interest in the arts or academics (page 748)

rendezvous *n.* (RAHN-deh-voo) a temporary market where trappers met to trade and socialize (page 390)

reparations *n.* (reh-puh-RAY-shunz) the money paid to compensate for damages in war (page 723)

repatriation *n.* (ree-PAY-tree-ay-shuhn) the act of returning or being returned to the country of one's origin or citizenship (page 781)

repeal *v.* (rih-PEEL) to cancel or nullify, especially a law (page 183)

republic *n.* (RE-puhb-lik) a form of government in which the people elect representatives to speak for them and enact laws based on their needs (page 222)

republican motherhood *n.* (rih-PUH-blih-kuhn MUH-thur-hud) the idea that women should raise their children to be good citizens who participate in the government (page 348)

Republican Party *n.* (rih-PUH-blih-kuhn PAHR-tee) a political party founded in 1854 by antislavery leaders (page 468)

republicanism *n.* (rih-PUH-blih-kuh-nih-zuhm) a government in which people choose representatives to make their laws (page 244)

reservation *n.* (reh-zur-VAY-shuhn) an area of land in the United States that is kept specifically for Native Americans to live on (page 592)

reserve bank *n.* (rih-ZURV BAYNK) a bank that, under the Federal Reserve Board's supervision, controls the nation's flow of money (page 674)

reunify *v.* (ree-YOO-nuh-fy) to bring something that split apart back together again (page 850)

revenue *n.* (REH-vuh-noo) income; money that is received (page 180)

revenue sharing *n.* (REH-vuh-noo SHAIR-ing) a method of distributing federal tax revenue to state and local governments (page 954)

revival meeting *n.* (rih-VY-vuhl MEE-ting) an informal religious gathering meant to inspire people to join the faith, often held outdoors or in tents (page 438)

robber baron *n.* (RAHB-ur BA-ruhn) an industrial leader known for cutthroat tactics against workers and competitors (page 649)

Rome-Berlin Axis *n.* (ROHM burh-LIHN ACK-sihs) an agreement formed between Germany and Italy in 1936 (page 789)

Rough Riders *n.* (RUHF RY-durz) the untrained but tough group of cowboys, miners, police officers, and Native Americans who volunteered to be soldiers under the command of Theodore Roosevelt in the Spanish-American War (page 687)

royal colony *n.* (ROY-uhl KAH-luh-nee) a colony ruled by a monarch through an appointed governor (page 112)

S

sabotage *n.* (SA-buh-tahzh) the action of harming, interfering with, or destroying something (page 719)

salutary neglect *n.* (SAL-yuh-tair-ee nih-GLEKT) the policy of the British government to not strictly enforce its colonial policies (page 151)

salvation *n.* (sal-VAY-shuhn) the act of being forgiven for wrongdoings or sins (page 148)

satellite *n.* (SA-tuh-lyt) an object that moves around a larger object (page 904)

scab *n.* (SKAB) a person willing to cross union lines to work during a strike (page 651)

scapegoat *n.* (SKAYP-goht) an individual or group blamed for the mistakes or faults of others (page 523)

scientific management *n.* (sy-uhn-TIH-fihk MA-nihj-muhnt) the process of studying individual people at work to determine the most efficient, most cost-effective way to do a job (page 677)

scurvy *n.* (SCUR-vee) a disease linked to malnutrition and a diet lacking in fruits and vegetables (page 527)

search-and-destroy mission *n.* (SUHRCH AND dih-STROY MIH-shuhn) a method used by the U.S. military to empty and wreck entire villages that may have provided help to the enemy (page 929)

secede *v.* (seh-SEED) to formally withdraw from a nation or organization in order to become independent (page 474)

secession *n.* (seh-SEHSH-ehn) the act of formally withdrawing from an organization, a nation, or any other group in order to be independent (page 367)

Second Continental Congress *n.* (SEHK-und kahn-tuh-NEHN-tuhl KAHN-gruhs) a group of leaders of the American colonies who met to address the problem of British tyranny, declared independence in 1776, and led the United States through the American Revolution (page 203)

Second Great Awakening *n.* (SEHK-und GRAYT uh-WAYK-ning) an American Protestant movement based on revival meetings and a direct and emotional relationship with God (page 438)

sectionalism *n.* (SEHK-shnuh-lih-zuhm) a loyalty to whichever section or region of the country one was from, rather than to the nation as a whole (page 344)

sedition *n.* (sih-DIH-shuhn) the act of provoking rebellion (page 293)

segregation *n.* (seh-grih-GAY-shuhn) the separation of people based on race (page 465)

self-determination *n.* (SELF dih-tur-muh-NAY-shuhn) the idea that countries should form their own governments and borders to reflect the national origins of the people who live there (page 722)

self-governance *n.* (SELF GUH-vur-nuhnts) the control of one's own affairs; the control of community affairs and laws by those who live there rather than by an outside ruler or monarch (page 105)

self-reliance *n.* (SELF rih-LY-uhns) individual independence developed through practical skills and education (page 644)

Seneca Falls Convention *n.* (SEH-nih-kuh FAWLS kuhn-VEHN-shuhn) an 1848 women's rights convention organized by Elizabeth Cady Stanton and Lucretia Mott in Seneca Falls, New York (page 450)

separation of powers *n.* (seh-puh-RAY-shuhn UHV POW-urs) the division of governmental power among the three branches of U.S. government: the executive branch, the judicial branch, and the legislative branch (page 258)

separatist *n.* (SEH-prah-tihst) a person in the 16th and 17th centuries who wished to leave the Church of England (page 100)

serf *n.* (SURF) a person who lived and worked on the private land of a landowner such as a noble or medieval lord (page 37)

servitude *n.* (SUR-vuh-tood) the state of being enslaved (page 538)

settlement house *n.* (SEH-tuhl-muhnt HOWS) a place that provides assistance to poor and immigrant residents of a community (page 635)

sharecropping *n.* (SHAIR-krahp-ing) an agricultural system in which a farmer raises crops for a landowner in return for part of the money made from selling the crops (page 559)

Shays's Rebellion *n.* (SHAYZ rih-BEL-yuhn) the 1786–1787 uprising of Massachusetts farmers in protest of high taxes (page 255)

Sherman Antitrust Act of 1890 *n.* (SHUR-muhn an-tee-TRUHST AKT UHV 1890) a federal statute passed to prohibit monopolies (page 670)

siege *n.* (SEEJ) a tactic in which a military force surrounds a city in an attempt to take control of it (page 401)

silent majority *n.* (SY-luhnt muh-JOR-uh-tee) a term used by Richard Nixon in the late 1960s to describe a large group of moderate voters who did not publicly express their political opinions (page 935)

sit-in *n.* (SIT IN) an organized protest where people sit down and refuse to leave (page 882)

situation comedy *n.* (sih-chuh-WAY-shuhn KAH-muh-dee) a weekly series that features a familiar setting and a group of characters who face amusing problems (page 858)

skirmish *n.* (SKUR-mish) a small, short-lasting battle (page 231)

skyscraper *n.* (SKY-skray-pur) a very tall building (page 636)

slash-and-burn agriculture *n.* (SLASH AND BURN A-grih-kuhl-chur) a method of clearing fields for planting that involves cutting and setting fire to existing trees and plants (page 29)

slave importation clause *n.* (SLAYVE ihm-pohr-TAY-shuhn KLAWZ) a provision in Article 1 of the U.S. Constitution that established that the United States would not consider prohibiting the international slave trade in the United States until 1808 (page 260)

slavery *n.* (SLAY-veh-ree) a social system in which human beings take complete control of others (page 72)

slogan *n.* (SLOH-guhn) a catchy phrase meant to attract and keep attention (page 362)

smallpox *n.* (SMAWL-poks) a deadly virus that causes a high fever and small blisters on the skin (page 56)

smog *n.* (SMAHG) a type of air pollution that develops when sunlight reacts with chemicals from such sources as car exhaust and factory emissions (page 958)

smuggle *v.* (SMUH-guhl) to import or export goods illegally (page 125)

Social Gospel *n.* (SOH-shuhl GAH-spuhl) a Protestant religious movement that stressed the importance of churches to become involved with social issues and reform (page 634)

social justice *n.* (SOH-shuhl JUH-stuhs) the fair distribution of opportunities and privileges, including racial equality (page 557)

social media *n.* (SOH-shuhl MEE-dee-uh) electronic media that allow people to communicate and form online communities (page 1001)

social work *n.* (SOH-shuhl WURK) work aimed at improving the lives of others (page 680)

socialism *n.* (SOH-shuh-lih-zuhm) an economic system in which the government controls economic resources, which are publicly owned (page 776)

solitary confinement *n.* (SAHL-it-tar-ee cuhn-FINE-ment) a form of punishment, isolating a prisoner from contact with other people (page 885)

Sons of Liberty *n.* (SUHNS UHV LIH-bur-tee) the groups of merchants, shopkeepers, and craftsmen who successfully opposed the Stamp Act by establishing networks to boycott British goods (page 183)

sovereign *adj.* (SAH-vuh-ruhn) having the right to self-rule or independent government (page 250)

space race *n.* (SPAYSS RAYSS) the competition between the United States and the Soviet Union to be the first to travel outside Earth's atmosphere (page 904)

speakeasy *n.* (SPEEK-ee-zee) an illegal drinking club where people secretly gathered in the evenings during Prohibition (page 735)

special prosecutor *n.* (SPEH-shuhl PRAH-sih-kyoo-tur) a private attorney or official appointed by the court to investigate or bring legal action against a party when the regular prosecutor is unable or has a conflict of interest with the accused (page 961)

speculate *v.* (SPEH-kyuh-layt) the act of buying stocks with the hope of selling and making a profit, while taking the risk of a loss (page 765)

sphere of influence *n.* (SFEER UHV IHN-floo-ents) a claim a country makes to be the exclusive influence on another country's political or economic activities (page 690)

spiritual *n.* (SPIHR-ih-chuh-wuhl) a religious song based on scripture and biblical figures in the Bible, first sung by enslaved people in the South (page 341)

spoil *n.* (SPOY-uhl) excess dirt and rock from a construction site (page 693)

spoils system *n.* (SPOY-uhlz SIHS-tuhm) the practice of rewarding political backers with government jobs (page 365)

stagflation *n.* (stag-FLAY-shuhn) an economic condition in which stagnation, or slow economic growth, is accompanied by inflation, or rising prices (page 962)

stalemate *n.* (STAYL-mayt) a situation in which neither side in a conflict is able to win (page 516)

Stamp Act *n.* (STAMP AKT) the British law requiring colonists to purchase a stamp for official documents and published papers (page 182)

standard time *n.* (STAN-durd TYM) the uniform division of time among locations that lie roughly on the same line of longitude, establishing time zones (page 621)

states' rights *n.* (STAYTS RITES) the concept that individual states have rights that the federal government cannot violate (page 293)

status quo *n.* (STA-tuhs KWOH) the existing state of a situation (page 902)

statute *n.* (STA-choot) a formal, written law (page 267)

steamboat *n.* (STEEM-boht) a boat outfitted with steam boiler engines to power the paddle wheels that propel it forward (page 331)

steel *n.* (STEEL) a hard metal made from a mixture of iron and carbon (page 624)

steerage *n.* (STEER-ehg) the inferior section of a ship housing passengers who pay the lowest fare for the journey (page 430)

steppe *n.* (STEP) a vast, grassy plain (page 42)

stockyard *n.* (STAHK-yard) an enormous outdoor corral in which animals are penned until they can be slaughtered (page 584)

Stono Rebellion *n.* (STOH-noh rih-BEL-yuhn) a 1739 revolt by enslaved Africans against their owners (page 137)

storm surge *n.* (STAWRM SUHRJ) an abnormal rise of water generated by a storm, over and above the predicted tides, and pushed toward the shore by storm winds (page 991)

streetcar *n.* (STREET-kahr) a vehicle on rails set in city streets that can transport many passengers at once, like a train (page 634)

strict interpretation *n.* (STRIHKT ihn-tur-pruh-TAY-shuhn) an understanding of the Constitution as one in which the Constitution is strictly followed as it was written (page 286)

strike *n.* (STRYK) a work stoppage in order to force an employer to comply with demands (page 328)

subprime *adj.* (SUHB-prym) describes a type of home loan issued to buyers with poor credit history (page 995)

subsidy *n.* (SUHB-suh-dee) government funds for improvements or support of commerce (page 342)

subsistence farming *n.* (suhb-SIHS-tuhnts FAHR-ming) the practice of producing enough food for a farmer and his family but not enough to sell for profit (page 123)

suburb *n.* (SUH-burb) a residential area on the edge of a city or town (page 634)

suburbanization *n.* (suh-bur-buh-nuh-ZAY-shuhn) a population shift from cities to outlying communities (page 856)

suffrage *n.* (SUH-frihj) the right to vote (page 451)

suffragist *n.* (SUHF-rih-jihst) a person who supports and fights for the right to vote, particularly a woman's right to vote (page 682)

Sugar Act *n.* (SHU-gur AKT) the British law that lowered the duty on molasses to cut out smuggling so that the British would get the revenue (page 181)

Sunbelt *n.* (SUHN-behlt) the southern and southwestern regions of the United States, which have mild winters (page 854)

supply and demand *n.* (suh-PLY AND dih-MAND) an economic principle that states that the price of something depends on how much is available, the supply, and how much is wanted, the demand (page 764)

supply-side economics *n.* (suh-PLY SYD eh-kuh-NAH-mihks) a financial theory that promotes lowering tax rates for businesses and investors in the hope of boosting production and trade (page 966)

Supreme Court *n.* (soo-PREEM KORT) the highest court in the United States (page 258)

surplus *n.* (SUR-plus) the amount left over; an excess (page 587)

sweatshop *n.* (SWEHT-shahp) a factory that pays low wages, provides crowded, unsafe conditions, and requires long work hours (page 647)

swing state *n.* (SWIHNG STAYT) a state in which voters are evenly divided between parties, making it difficult to predict which candidate will gain the state's electoral votes (page 1006)

T

tank *n.* (TANGK) an armored, heavily armed vehicle that uses treads instead of wheels (page 713)

tariff *n.* (TAIR-uhf) a tax on imports and exports (page 282)

Tariff of Abominations *n.* (TAIR-uhf UHV uh-bah-muh-NAY-shuhns) the term used by southerners to refer to the Tariff of 1828 because it stirred feelings of disgust and hatred (page 366)

Tea Act *n.* (TEE AKT) the British law stating that only the East India Company was allowed to sell tea to the American colonists (page 191)

teetotaler *n.* (TEE-toh-tuh-lur) a person who does not drink alcoholic beverages (page 681)

telegraph *n.* (TEHL-uh-graf) a machine that sends messages long distances by sending electrical pulses in code over electrical wires (page 331)

televangelist *n.* (teh-lih-VAN-juh-lihst) a religious leader who shares Christian teachings on a regularly scheduled television broadcast (page 970)

temperance movement *n.* (TEHM-pur-uhns MOOV-mehnt) a 19th-century reform movement that encouraged the reduction or elimination of alcoholic beverage consumption (page 438)

tenement *n.* (TEH-nuh-muhnt) a quickly constructed apartment building; usually refers to a crowded urban dwelling for immigrants and the poor (page 630)

tepee *n.* (TEE-pee) a cone-shaped tent made of bison hides (page 27)

termination policy *n.* (tur-muh-NAY-shuhn PAH-luh-see) a policy enacted under President Eisenhower that removed Native Americans from reservations, while the government ended the limited sovereignty of individual tribes and nations (page 922)

terrain *n.* (tuh-RAYN) the physical features of the land (page 204)

textile *n.* (TEHKS-ty-uhl) the cloth and clothing made from cotton and other raw materials (page 328)

Three-Fifths Compromise *n.* (THREE FIFTHS KAHM-pruh-myz) the agreement that determined that only three-fifths of the total population of enslaved persons in a state would be counted for purposes of taxation and representation (page 260)

tolerance *n.* (TAH-luh-runts) the acceptance of others (page 144)

total war *n.* (TOH-tuhl WOR) a war in which all rules and laws of war are ignored and all resources are used for defeating the enemy (page 530)

Townshend Acts *n.* (TOWN-sehnd AKTS) a set of British laws that placed duties on tea, glass, paper, lead, and paint; required colonists to purchase from Britain (page 186)

trading post *n.* (TRAYD-ing POHST) a small settlement established for the purpose of exchanging goods (page 155)

Trail of Tears *n.* (TRAYL UHV TEHRS) the route the Cherokees and other Native Americans took during their forced migration from the southeast United States to Oklahoma (page 373)

traitor *n.* (TRAY-tohr) a person who betrays his or her own people, nation, or cause (page 99)

trans-Saharan *adj.* (tran-suh-HAHR-uhn) across the Sahara (page 42)

transcendentalism *n.* (tran-sehn-DEHN-tuh-li-zuhm) an intellectual and social movement of the 1830s and 1840s that called for rising above society's expectations (page 444)

transcontinental railroad *n.* (tranz-kahn-tuh-NEHN-tuhl RAYL-rohd) a railroad that runs across a continent (page 620)

treason *n.* (TREE-zuhn) the crime of aiding the enemy of one's nation or plotting to overthrow one's nation; the act of being disloyal to one's nation (page 367)

treaty *n.* (TREE-tee) a peace agreement (page 158)

Treaty of Greenville *n.* (TREE-tee UHV GREEN-vihl) a treaty between the United States and a number of Native American nations in which the Native American nations gave up their lands in present-day Ohio and Indiana to the United Sates (page 288)

Treaty of Paris of 1783 *n.* (TREE-tee UHV PAIR-uhs UHV 1783) the binding agreement between Britain and the United States in which Britain acknowledged American independence, and the initial borders of the United States were determined (page 244)

Treaty of Versailles *n.* (TREE-tee UHV vur-SY) the treaty that officially brought World War I to a close (page 723)

trench warfare *n.* (TREHNCH WOR-fair) a battle strategy that uses a system of ditches to give soldiers a protected place from which to fire during battle (page 495)

triangular trade *n.* (try-ANG-gyuh-lur TRAYD) a transatlantic trade network formed by Europe, West Africa, and the Americas (page 73)

tributary *n.* (TRIH-byoo-tair-ee) a creek, stream, or river that flows into a larger river or other body of water (page 112)

GLOSSARY

truce *n.* (TROOS) an agreement to stop fighting (page 371)

trust *n.* (TRUHST) a group of corporations managed, but not directly owned, by a board (page 627)

tundra *n.* (TUHN-druh) the flat treeless land found in arctic and subarctic regions (page 26)

tyranny *n.* (TEER-uh-nee) unjust rule by an absolute ruler (page 181)

U

U-boat *n.* (YOO BOHT) a German submarine (page 713)

unalienable right *n.* (uhn-AY-lee-uhn-ah-buhl RITE) a right that cannot be taken away (page 208)

unconstitutional *adj.* (uhn-KAHNT-stuh-too-shnuhl) an idea or law that goes against the principles of the U.S. Constitution (page 310)

Underground Railroad *n.* (uhn-dur-GROWND RAYL-rohd) a network of people who worked together to help African Americans escape from slavery from the southern United States to the northern states or to Canada before the Civil War (page 447)

Unionist *n.* (YOON-yuh-nihst) a member of the Constitutional Union Party (page 472)

unorganized territory *n.* (uhn-AWR-guh-nyzd TAIR-uh-tawr-ee) lands governed by the federal government but not belonging to any state (page 345)

urbanization *n.* (ur-buh-nuh-ZAY-shuhn) a process in which economic, industrial, and population patterns shifted from rural areas to cities (page 634)

V

vassal *n.* (VA-suhl) in the medieval European feudal system, a person, usually a lesser nobleman, who received land and protection from a feudal lord in exchange for obedience and service (page 36)

veteran *n.* (VEH-tuh-ruhn) a person who has served in the military (page 534)

veto *v.* (VEE-toh) to formally reject a decision or proposal made by a legislature (page 375)

viceroy *n.* (VYSE-roy) a governor of Spain's colonies in the Americas who represented the Spanish king and queen (page 58)

viceroyalty *n.* (vyse-ROHY-uhl-tee) a territory governed by a viceroy (page 58)

Vietnamization *n.* (vee-eht-nuh-muh-ZAY-shun) a military strategy that allowed for the gradual replacement of U.S. troops with South Vietnamese troops during the Vietnam War (page 952)

voter registration drive *n.* (VOH-tur reh-juh-STRAY-shuhn DRYV) an effort by groups or government to sign up as many eligible voters in a targeted area as possible (page 887)

voting rights *n.* (VOHT-ing RITES) the laws that tell who can vote and when; the civil right to vote (page 362)

W

wage economy *n.* (WAYJ ih-KAH-nuh-mee) an economy in which people are paid for their work (page 559)

wage gap *n.* (WAYJ GAP) the difference in pay between men and women who perform similar jobs; men usually earn more than women (page 924)

wagon train *n.* (WA-guhn TRAYN) a large group of covered wagons that traveled together across the North American continent as American pioneers moved westward (page 396)

War Hawk *n.* (WOR HAWK) a person who approved of and encouraged war; an American who favored war with Great Britain in 1812 (page 321)

War of 1812 *n.* (WOR UHV 1812) the war against Great Britain that James Madison declared (page 322)

Watergate scandal *n.* (WAH-tur-gayt SKAN-duhl) a break-in at the Democratic National Headquarters in the Watergate complex in Washington, D.C., in 1972 by burglars associated with President Richard Nixon's re-election committee (page 961)

watershed *n.* (WAH-tuhr-shed) an area of land that includes a particular river or lake and all the bodies of water that flow into it (page 64)

weapon of mass destruction (WMD) *n.* (WEH-puhn UHV MAS dih-STRUHK-shuhn) weapons that use nuclear, chemical, or biological substances to harm large numbers of people (page 989)

Whig Party *n.* (WIHG PAHR-tee) a political party formed to oppose the policies of Andrew Jackson, who the party believed had exceeded his power as president (page 376)

Whiskey Rebellion *n.* (HWIH-skee rih-BEL-yuhn) a series of violent protests among farmers in western Pennsylvania against a tax on whiskey (page 289)

wiretapping *n.* (WY-urh-tap-ihng) the act of placing a device on a telephone in order to secretly listen to conversations (page 960)

World Wide Web *n.* (WURLD WYD WEHB) the system that allows Internet sites to be identified by addresses, linked to each other, and located by search engines (page 1000)

writ *n.* (RIHT) a legal document (page 310)

writ of assistance *n.* (RIHT UHV uh-SIHS-tuhns) a legal document giving authorities the right to enter and search a home or business (page 186)

X

XYZ Affair *n.* (X Y Z uh-FAIR) the meeting with French agents after France began seizing American ships in the late 18th century in an effort to prevent U.S. trade with Britain (page 293)

Y

yellow fever *n.* (YEH-loh FEE-vur) an often fatal disease carried by mosquitoes in tropical climates (page 312)

yellow journalism *n.* (YEH-loh JUR-nuh-lih-zuhm) a type of news reporting that exaggerates and dramatizes events, presenting readers with distorted views of the truth, in order to sell newspapers (page 687)

Z

Zimmermann Telegram *n.* (ZIH-mur-muhn TEH-luh-gram) secret German telegram sent to the German ambassador in Mexico, proposing that Mexico join World War I on the German side (page 715)

ACADEMIC VOCABULARY

abomination *n.* (uh-bah-muh-NAY-shuhn) a thing worthy of hatred or disgust (page 366)

acclaim *n.* (uh-KLAYM) enthusiastic praise (page 285)

acquisition *n.* (a-kwuh-ZIH-shuhn) the act of obtaining something as one's own; an item obtained (page 37)

affluent *adj.* (A-floo-uhnt) wealthy, prosperous (page 855)

allegory *n.* (A-luh-gor-ee) a story told through symbols, in which the characters and other story elements represent human actions and emotions (page 444)

allocate *v.* (A-luh-kayt) to divide and give out for a specific purpose (page 954)

annihilate *v.* (uh-NY-uh-layt) to destroy totally (page 795)

ardent *adj.* (AHR-duhnt) very eager; passionate (page 282)

arduous *adj.* (AHR-juh-wuhs) difficult; requiring great effort to achieve (page 395)

arid *adj.* (AIR-uhd) extremely dry (as a desert) (page 24)

atrocity *n.* (uh-TRAH-suh-tee) an extremely brutal, cruel act (page 593)

consensus *n.* (kuhn-SEHNT-suhs) general agreement, harmony (page 889)

covenant *n.* (KUH-vuh-nuhnt) an agreement or promise between two parties (page 179)

debilitating *adj.* (di-BIH-luh-tayt-ing) harming the strength or power of someone or something; making effective action impossible (page 647)

derogatory *adj.* (dih-RAH-guh-tor-ee) degrading or unflattering; meant to cast someone or something in a negative light (page 641)

destitute *adj.* (DEHS-tuh-toot) lacking wealth or resources; impoverished (page 768)

disperse *v.* (dih-SPURS) to scatter and spread widely (page 586)

divisive *adj.* (duh-VY-sihv) causing angry dissent and disunity (page 462)

dumbfounded *adj.* (DUHM-fownd-uhd) at a loss for words (page 58)

elite *n.* (ih-LEET) a person or group that is superior in wealth, intellect, education, or athletic ability (page 668)

eloquence *n.* (EH-luh-kwuhnts) an elegant, articulate speaking ability (page 886)

encompass *v.* (ihn-KUHM-puhs) to form a circle around; to surround; to include (page 559)

evade *v.* (ih-VAYD) to avoid capture or to avoid giving a straight, truthful answer (page 596)

evasion *n.* (ih-VAY-zhuhn) the act of avoiding discovery or punishment, usually by stealth (page 735)

exploit *v.* (EHK-sployt) to make use of, often for one's own gain at the expense of another person or of a resource (page 665)

fertile *adj.* (FUR-tuhl) capable of growing plants (page 24)

fervor *n.* (FUR-vur) an intense feeling (page 439)

forfeit *v.* (FOR-fuht) to give up, often as a result of a loss or the imposition of a fine (page 922)

formidable *adj.* (FOR-mih-duh-buhl) awe inspiring, usually in a menacing way (page 223)

forthrightly *adv.* (FORTH-ryt-lee) directly, honestly (page 873)

iconography *n.* (ai-kuh-NAH-gruh-fee) the representative objects or symbols of a culture or religion (page 131)

impartiality *n.* (ihm-PAR-shee-al-ih-tee) neutrality; fairness (page 714)

indispensable *adj.* (ihn-dih-SPENT-suh-buhl) necessary; cannot be done without (page 103)

inherently *adv.* (ihn-HAIR-uhnt-lee) essentially, naturally (page 875)

intervene *v.* (ihn-tur-VEEN) to interfere, usually to force or prevent an action (page 397)

intimidate *v.* (ihn-TIH-muh-dayt) to use threats, usually to make someone do one's bidding (page 371)

knack *n.* (NAK) a person's natural talent or skill (page 768)

legacy *n.* (LEH-guh-see) a body of knowledge or accomplishment from the past (page 250)

lenient *adj.* (LEE-nee-uhnt) tolerant; easygoing (page 552)

lethal *adj.* (LEE-thuhl) deadly (page 647)

manor *n.* (MA-nur) an estate, or the central house on an estate (page 64)

martyr *n.* (MAHR-tur) a person who sacrifices his or her life or something of great value for the good of a cause (page 469)

mechanized *adj.* (MEH-kuh-nyzd) carried out entirely or in part with machines (page 328)

militant *adj.* (MIHL-uh-tuhnt) combative and aggressive; acting as one fighting a war (page 467)

monetary *adj.* (MAH-nuh-tair-ee) taking the form of money (page 303)

nullify *v.* (NUH-luh-fy) to negate, especially in legal terms (page 366)

offensive *n.* (uh-FENT-sihv) the fighting initiated by one side in a war (page 231)

orthodox *adj.* (OR-thuh-dahks) following a strict religious doctrine (page 101)

parcel *n.* (PAHR-suhl) a plot or designated area of land (page 598)

pardon *v.* (PAHR-duhn) to forgive or excuse (page 552)

philosophy *n.* (fuh-LAH-suh-fee) the basic beliefs of a person or group (page 39)

poised *adj.* (POYZD) ready for something to happen (page 982)

prestigious *adj.* (preh-STIH-juhs) having a reputation of quality, esteem, and respect (page 362)

prominent *adj.* (PRAH-muh-nuhnt) widely known (page 971)

prosperous *adj.* (PRAHS-pur-uhs) economically successful (page 842)

prosthetic *n.* (prahs-THEH-tihk) an artificial limb or body part (page 494)

rehabilitate *v.* (ree-uh-BIH-luh-tayt) to restore to previous health or reputation (page 441)

replenish *v.* (rih-PLEH-nish) to fill up again (page 495)

retaliation *n.* (rih-ta-lee-AY-shuhn) the act of getting revenge or working against someone because he or she has harmed you (page 791)

rhetoric *n.* (REH-tuh-rihk) the way words are used to express an idea, usually to persuade (page 562)

sentiment *n.* (SEHN-tuh-muhnt) an attitude based on feelings (page 815)

shrapnel *n.* (SHRAP-nuhl) the sharp pieces of an exploded shell or cannonball (page 172)

specimen *n.* (SPE-suh-muhn) one example of something from nature, such as a certain plant, animal, or mineral (page 300)

sphere *n.* (SFEER) an area defining one's function or authority (page 328)

suborbital *adj.* (suhb-OR-buh-tuhl) less than one complete circling of an object or body around another; less than a complete circular path (page 905)

survey *n.* (sur-VAY) a measurement to establish land boundaries (page 252)

susceptible *adj.* (suh-SEHP-tuh-buhl) open to being affected or influenced by something (page 527)

synchronize *v.* (SING-kruh-nyz) to cause to occur at the same time (page 740)

tenure *n.* (TEHN-yur) the act of holding something of value, such as land or an important position, or the term during which such a thing is held (page 555)

turmoil *n.* (TUR-moyl) confusion; upheaval (page 727)

undermine *v.* (UHN-dur-myn) to weaken (page 906)

unethical *adj.* (uhn-EH-thih-kuhl) morally wrong (page 996)

usher *v.* (UH-shur) to bring in something new (page 717)

valor *n.* (VA-lur) the quality of great courage or bravery (page 520)

vigorous *adj.* (VIH-guh-ruhs) done with energy or with force (page 845)

GLOSARIO

A

abolición *s.* acto de poner fin a algo, como la esclavitud (página 349)

abolicionista *s.* persona que quería que la esclavitud terminara (página 446)

abolir la segregación *v.* terminar con una política que obliga a la separación de las personas en espacios públicos (página 877)

abstemio *s.* persona que no consume bebidas alcohólicas (página 681)

acatamiento *s.* obediencia a un conjunto de creencias (página 144)

acción afirmativa *s.* política gubernamental que estableces cuotas raciales para favorecer a los grupos que han sufrido discriminación (página 915)

acero *s.* metal muy resistente hecho a partir de una mezcla de hierro y carbono (página 624)

acreedor *s.* persona a quien se le adeuda un préstamo (página 590)

actividad económica *s.* operaciones de producción, distribución y consumo de bienes y servicios (página 114)

Acuerdos de Múnich *s.* un acuerdo que Hitler hizo con los líderes de Gran Bretaña, Francia e Italia, declarando que Alemania tenía derecho a anexarse los Sudetes, una parte de Checoslovaquia (página 791)

afluente *s.* arroyo, riachuelo o río que desemboca en un río más grande o en otra masa de agua (página 112)

agente federal (marshal) *s.* agente federal (marshal) s. agente del orden público que trabaja para el gobierno de los Estados Unidos (página 463)

Agente Naranja *s.* un potente herbicida, usado para exterminar la vegetación (página 929)

agrario(a) *adj.* relativo al campo o la agricultura (página 366)

agricultura de subsistencia *s.* modo de producir suficientes alimentos para el granjero y su familia, pero no para la venta (página 123)

agricultura de tala y quema *s.* método de despejar los campos para sembrar cultivos que consiste en cortar y quemar los árboles y las plantas existentes (página 29)

aislacionismo *s.* política en la que una nación se mantiene lejos de los asuntos de otras naciones (página 791)

alfabetizar *s.* enseñar a leer y escribir (página 559)

alianza *s.* acuerdo entre naciones para luchar en contra de los enemigos de cada una o para colaborar entre ellas; pacto (página 111)

Alianza de Agricultores *s.* una de las muchas organizaciones fundadas en la década de 1880 para promover los intereses políticos y económicos de los agricultores; similar a La Granja, pero con un perfil más político (página 591)

alistarse *v.* unirse a la milicia (página 520)

alocución *s.* discurso formal (página 886)

americanización *s.* proceso de inducción dirigido a los inmigrantes e indígenas norteamericanos para que aprendan la cultura y lengua convencionales de los Estados Unidos con el objetivo de que se adapten y acojan a este país (página 598)

anarquista *s.* persona que defiende la anarquía y, por lo tanto, la ausencia de todo gobierno (página 650)

anexar *v.* agregar (página 391)

antifederalista *s.* persona que se oponía a la Constitución de EE. UU. de 1787 porque el énfasis de esta era un gobierno nacional poderoso (página 262)

antisemitismo *s.* discriminación, prejuicio y hostilidad contra el pueblo judío (página 814)

antropólogo *s.* persona que estudia las culturas (página 748)

apaciguamiento *s.* política de hacer concesiones políticas para evitar los conflictos (página 791)

aparcería *s.* sistema agrícola en donde los jornaleros levantan la cosecha de un terrateniente a cambio de recibir una parte de la venta de dichas cosechas (página 559)

aprendiz *s.* persona que aprende un arte u oficio manual trabajando junto a un experto en ese arte u oficio (página 129)

arancel *s.* impuesto a las importaciones y exportaciones (página 282)

arancel de aduana *s.* impuesto a las importaciones (página 181)

arancel de las abominaciones *s.* término usado por los sureños para referirse al arancel de 1828 porque lo consideraban odioso y opresivo (página 366)

archipiélago *s.* conjunto de islas en una misma zona marina (página 685)

armas de destrucción masiva *s.* armas que usan sustancias nucleares, químicas o biológicas para dañar a un gran número de personas (página 989)

armisticio *s.* un acuerdo entre los lados opuestos de un conflicto para dejar de pelear (página 721)

arreo *s.* proceso de conducir el ganado de un lugar a otro, comúnmente der un rancho a una estación ferroviaria (página 584)

artesano *s.* persona que realiza a mano objetos con gran destreza (página 136)

Artículos de la Confederación *s.* conjunto de leyes adoptado por los Estados Unidos en 1777, que establecía cada estado de la Unión como una república, reemplazado por la Constitución en 1789 (página 222)

artillería *s.* cañones y armas largas que disparan a gran distancia (página 203)

asimilar *v.* adoptar la cultura o forma de vida de la nación donde se vive; integrarse por completo a una cultura o a un país (páginas 368, 433)

astronauta *s.* persona entrenada para viajar al espacio (página 904)

Asunto XYZ *s.* reunión con agentes franceses luego de que Francia comenzara a capturar barcos estadounidenses para prevenir el comercio entre EE. UU. y Gran Bretaña (página 293)

atolón *s.* arrecife o conjunto de islas coralinas en forma de anillo (página 817)

autodeterminación *s.* la idea de que cada país debe tener sus propios gobiernos y fronteras para reflejar los orígenes nacionales del pueblo que allí vive (página 722)

autonomía *s.* control de sus propios asuntos por parte de uno mismo; control de los asuntos y leyes de una comunidad por parte de aquellos que viven en ella y no por parte de un monarca o gobernante ajeno (página 105)

autónomo *s.* gobernado por sí mismo (página 686)

autosuficiencia *s.* independencia individual obtenida a través de destrezas prácticas con base en la educación (página 644)

B

baby boom *s.* un incremento significativo en la tasa de natalidad (página 854)

baja *s.* persona muerta o herida en combate (página 540)

banco de la reserva *s.* uno de los bancos que supervisa la Junta de la Reserva Federal, y controla el flujo de dinero en los Estados Unidos (página 674)

bar clandestino *s.* un local ilegal donde las personas se reunían en secreto para consumir alcohol durante la Prohibición (página 735)

barco de vapor *s.* barco equipado con calderas de vapor que impulsaban ruedas giratorias para hacerlo navegar (página 331)

barraca *s.* construcción usada para albergar a un gran número de personas (página 806)

base de poder *s.* zona o grupo de personas que provee la mayor influencia sobre un candidato político (página 286)

batallón *s.* amplio grupo de tropas militares (página 806)

bayoneta *s.* cuchillo afilado que se une a la boca de un fusil (página 228)

Bimetalismo *s.* movimiento económico que surgió a finales del siglo XIX para promover un sistema monetario basado en la plata además del oro (página 591)

Blitzkrieg *s.* estrategia de guerra ejecutada de forma rápida que implica bombardear desde el aire objetivos de comunicaciones y transporte, antes de comenzar la invasión por tierra (página 791)

bloque *s.* un grupo que se forma para apoyar un interés o propósito común (página 846)

bloquear *v.* cortar la entrada o salida de barcos de una bahía (página 228)

blues *s.* un estilo musical que se originó entre los músicos afroamericanos, que cuenta historias sobre tiempos difíciles y penas (página 743)

boicot *s.* forma de protesta que rechaza la compra de bienes o servicios (página 183)

boicot de autobuses de Montgomery *s.* una protesta masiva contra las prácticas de segregación racial en el sistema de autobuses públicos en Montgomery, Alabama, que estalló con el arresto de Rosa Parks (página 879)

bomba atómica *s.* un tipo de bomba cuya violenta explosión es provocada por la división de los átomos, lo cual libera un intenso calor y radioactividad (página 821)

bomba incendiaria *s.* una bomba diseñada para iniciar incendios (página 819)

bono *s.* bono s. certificado puesto a la venta al público por el gobierno con la promesa de pagar esa cantidad en una fecha posterior (página 524)

Bonos de la Libertad *s.* bonos del gobierno que fueron vendidos a individuos para apoyar la participación de los Estados Unidos en la Primera Guerra Mundial (página 718)

C

caballería *s.* tropas de un ejército que luchan montadas a caballo (página 491)

Cabeza de Cobre *s.* apodo peyorativo para designar a los miembros del Partido Demócrata que en los estados de la Unión se oponían a la emancipación de los esclavos y al reclutamiento (página 562)

cabildero *s.* persona que intenta persuadir a los legisladores para que apoyen ciertas leyes y proyectos políticos (página 681)

cacicazgo *s.* comunidad de personas regida por un cacique o jefe (página 9)

californio *s.* residente de California de descendencia española o mexicana y que vivía allí antes de la fiebre del oro (página 417)

cambio climático *s.* un cambio en los patrones climáticos de la Tierra (página 1008)

Camino de Lágrimas *s.* ruta que los cheroquis y otras tribus norteamericanas tomaron durante su migración forzada desde el sureste de los Estados Unidos hacia Oklahoma (página 373)

campaña de registro de votantes *s.* esfuerzo de grupos o del gobierno por inscribir a todos los votantes posibles en un área determinada (página 887)

campo de concentración *s* un lugar donde confinar a los prisioneros de guerra o miembros de minorías perseguidas; durante la Segunda Guerra Mundial, fueron los campos en que judíos y otros prisioneros fueron recluidos y asesinados por los nazis (página 814)

campo de exterminio *s.* un campo donde judíos y otros fueron recluidos y asesinados por los nazis durante la Segunda Guerra Mundial (página 814)

campo de internamiento *s.* campo de prisioneros para mantener a los soldados enemigos u otros prisioneros de guerra durante la contienda (página 806)

canciller *s.* un líder que en algunos países europeos juega un papel similar al del presidente en los Estados Unidos (página 789)

cañón antiaéreo *s.* una pieza de artillería pesada, modificada para apuntar a los aviones enemigos (página 713)

cañonero *s.* embarcación rápida y pequeña que llevaba cañones (página 508)

capataz *s.* supervisor (página 134)

capitalismo *s.* sistema económico donde las entidades privadas, por oposición al gobierno, son propietarias de negocios que administran con fines de lucro (página 627)

carabela *s.* barco pequeño y rápido usado por los exploradores españoles y portugueses (página 40)

caravana *s.* grupo de personas y animales que viajan juntos, usualmente para comerciar (página 42)

caravana *s.* grupo grande de carretas cubiertas, una detrás de otra, donde viajaban los pioneros a través de Norteamérica hacia el Oeste (página 396)

carrera espacial *s.* la competencia entre los Estados Unidos y la Unión Soviética para ser los primeros en viajar al espacio fuera de la atmósfera terrestre (página 904)

carreta Conestoga *s.* tipo de carreta diseñada por colonos alemanes en Norteamérica para llevar cargas pesadas (página 143)

Carta del Atlántico *s.* un documento que enlista ocho principios para un mundo mejor, redactado durante la reunión entre el presidente Franklin Roosevelt y el primer ministro británico Winston Churchill en 1941 (página 793)

casa de asistencia *s.* lugar donde se proporciona ayuda a los inmigrates y a las personas más necesitadas de una comunidad (página 635)

caso Dred Scott *s.* decisión de la Corte Suprema que dictaminó que los afroamericanos no tenían derechos como ciudadanos y que invalidó el Compromiso de Missouri de 1820; Dred Scott, el esclavo en cuestión, fue devuelto a la esclavitud (página 468)

cateador *s.* persona que busca en la tierra recursos minerales valiosos, especialmente piedras y metales preciosos (página 416)

cazador-recolector *s.* ser humano que cazaba animales y recolectaba plantas silvestres para su alimentación (página 7)

ceder *v.* renunciar (página 288)

cédula real *s.* título por escrito que concede el establecimiento de una institución y que detalla derechos y privilegios de los miembros (página 92)

centrista *s.* una persona que profesa visiones políticas moderadas (página 982)

cese al fuego *s.* la orden militar de terminar la lucha (página 930)

charlainformal *s.* una de las transmisiones radiales que el presidente Roosevelt hizo para dirigirse a la nación durante su presidencia (página 777)

chivo expiatorio *s.* individuo o grupo culpado por los errores o las faltas de otros (página 523)

ciclo de auge y depresión *s.* serie de periodos de crecimiento económico seguidos de repentinas crisis económicas (página 627)

cierre de la Administración *s.* cuando la rama ejecutiva del gobierno tiene que cerrar las oficinas y los servicios del gobierno federal debido a que la legislatura no ha aprobado la financiación para estas oficinas o servicios (página 985)

circunnavegar *v.* viajar por completo alrededor de la Tierra (página 62)

ciudad en auge *s.* ciudad cuya población aumenta repetinamente y en grandes cantidades (página 418)

ciudadanía *s.* la condición de tener los derechos y deberes de los ciudadanos (página R32)

civil *s.* persona que no es militar (página 497)

civilización *s.* sociedad con una cultura y una tecnología muy desarrolladas (página 24)

cláusula *s.* condición adjunta a un documento legal o ley (página 413)

cláusula de comercio *s.* disposición del Artículo 1 de la Constitución de EE. UU., que otorga al Congreso el poder de hacer leyes con respecto al comercio internacional, entre estados y con las naciones indígenas (página 261)

cláusula de esclavo fugitivo *s.* disposición del Artículo 4 de la Constitución de EE. UU., que prohíbe a los estados libres la liberación de trabajadores esclavos que se hayan escapado de sus amos en otros estados (página 260)

cláusula de importación de esclavos *s.* disposición del Artículo 1 de la Constitución de EE. UU., que establece que los Estados Unidos no considerará prohibir el comercio internacional de esclavos en el país hasta 1808 (página 260)

clientelismo *s.* práctica que recompensa a los partidarios políticos con puestos en el gobierno (página 365)

coalición *s.* una alianza de personas, partidos o estados dedicados a un objetivo común (página 977)

códigos negros *s.* leyes aprobadas por los estados sureños inmediatamente después de la Guerra Civil para controlar y limitar los derechos de los afroamericanos; fueron revocadas durante la Reconstrucción en 1866 (página 554)

Colegio electoral *s.* grupo que elige al presidente de los EE. UU.; cada estado tiene un número de electores igual al número de sus representantes y senadores en el Congreso (página 258)

colonia real *s.* colonia gobernada por un monarca a través de un gobernador designado (página 112)

comedia costumbrista *s.* programa semanal que muestra a una familia o a un grupo de personajes que enfrenta problemas divertidos (página 858)

comercio de esclavos interestatal *s.* la compra y venta de esclavos dentro de los Estados Unidos (página 339)

comercio triangular *s.* red transatlántica de comercio formada por Europa, África Occidental y las Américas (página 73)

comisionado *s.* representante de un gobierno (página 669)

comité de correspondencia *s.* en la época de la independencia, grupo de colonos cuyo deber era hacer correr la voz para la organización de protestas contra los británicos (página 191)

comité de vigilancia *n.* grupo armado y comandado por un alguacil para capturar criminales o fugitivos (página 583)

Compra de Gadsden *s.* venta de tierras de México a los Estados Unidos en 1853, que estableció la frontera suroeste actual de los EE. UU. (página 413)

Compra de Louisiana *s.* tratado entre Francia y los Estados Unidos, por el cual fue comprada una gran extensión de tierras entre el río Mississippi y las montañas Rocosas (página 313)

comprar a préstamo *v.* comprar algo pagando una pequeña cantidad de lo que vale y pedir prestado el resto del dinero para irlo pagando (página 765)

Compromiso de 1877 *s.* acuerdo mediante el cual el Partido Demócrata se comprometió a reconocer a Rutherford B. Hayes como presidente a cambio de que los Republicanos concluyeran la Reconstrucción y retiraran a las tropas federales del Sur (página 565)

Compromiso de las tres quintas partes *s.* acuerdo en el cual se determinó que solo tres quintas partes de la población total de esclavos en un estado se tomarían en cuenta para objetivos de impuestos y representación (3/5) (página 260)

Compromiso de Missouri *s.* acuerdo que estableció que Missouri podía tener esclavos y a su vez ser admitido a la Unión junto con Maine, un estado libre (página 344)

comunismo *s.* una forma de gobierno en la que todos los medios de producción y transporte son del estado (página 717)

comunitario *a.* esfuerzo organizativo de la gente común, de base, que no tiene dinero ni poder, pero son capaces de lograr un cambio (página 872)

confederación *s.* acuerdo entre varios grupos, estados o gobiernos para protegerse y apoyarse unos a otros en batallas u otros emprendimientos (página 111)

Confederación *s.* los 11 estados que se separaron de la Unión para formar su propia nación: los Estados Confederados de América (página 474)

confinamiento en solitario *s.* una forma de castigo que consiste en aislar al preso del contacto con otras personas (página 885)

conquista de isla-en-isla *s.* una estrategia que implicó capturar y establecer campamentos militares en las islas, una por una (página 818)

conquistador *s.* explorador español que buscaba oro y otras riquezas en las Américas (página 56)

conspiración *s.* un plan secreto para dañar o cometer un acto ilegal (página 911)

constitución *s.* documento que organiza los poderes de un gobierno y los estados (página 250)

constitucionalismo *s.* sistema de gobernar basándose en una constitución (página 251)

consumidor *s.* persona que compra un producto o servicio (página 738)

contención *s.* política de seguridad norteamericana durante la Guerra Fría, en la que la acción diplomática y militar se usaba para impedir que la Unión Soviética difundiera el comunismo (página 847)

contiguo *adj.* junto a algo (página 413)

contraataque *s.* ataque en respuesta a un ataque previo (página 227)

contrabandear *v.* importar y exportar productos de manera ilegal (página 125)

contrabando *s.* fabricación, transporte o suministro ilegal (página 735)

contracultura *s.* un movimiento que en los 60 promovió un modo de vida que era lo opuesto a las reglas y conductas establecidas en la sociedad norteamericana (página 933)

contrato colectivo *s.* negociación llevada a cabo entre un sindicato y un empleador y que tiene por finalidad elevar los salarios y mejorar las condiciones laborales (página 648)

Convención de Seneca Falls *s.* convención por los derechos de la mujer, organizada por Elizabeth Cady Stanton y Lucretia Mott en Seneca Falls, Nueva York, en 1848 (página 450)

conventillo *s.* edificio de apartamentos construido de prisa; comúnmente se refiere a una vivienda urbana en donde los inmigrantes y los más necesitados viven temporalmente en condiciones de hacinamiento (página 630)

convertidor catalítico *s.* una parte del sistema de escape de un vehículo que cambia los gases nocivos en gases menos dañinos o inofensivos (página 959)

convertir *v.* persuadir a alguien para que cambie sus creencias; generalmente se refiere a un cambio de religión (página 43)

cooperativa *s.* grupo de agricultores o de otros trabajadores que se forma para adquirir productos y servicios mediante la contribución económica de cada miembro (página 591)

corporación *s.* compañía o grupo empresarial que opera legalmente como una sola entidad para administrar un negocio (página 626)

corral *s.* área protegida de gran tamaño en donde se encierra el ganado hasta que esté listo para su sacrificio (página 584)

corrupción *s.* deshonestidad, ilegalidad (página 564)

corsario *s.* buque mercante privado autorizado por un gobierno para perseguir a las embarcaciones enemigas siguiendo las leyes de guerra, o un marinero a bordo ese tipo de barco (página 62)

Corte Suprema *s.* la corte o tribunal más alto de justicia en EE. UU. (página 258)

crédito *s.* privilegio para comprar algo o pedir prestado dinero, devolviendo el dinero con el tiempo (página 254)

crematorio *s.* un horno usado para quemar restos humanos o animales; durante la Segunda Guerra Mundial, los Nazis los usaron para quemar los cuerpos de sus víctimas (página 814)

crimen organizado *s.* actividades ilegales planeadas y llevadas a cabo por criminales poderosos (página 735)

Crisis de los Misiles *s.* una confrontación política que tuvo lugar en 1962 entre los Estados Unidos y la Unión Soviética, causada por la presencia de armas nucleares en Cuba (página 908)

cuarentena *v.* acción de mantener aislados a quienes han contraído alguna enfermedad de aquellas personas que aún no han sido infectadas (página 527)

cuarentena naval *s.* un bloqueo impuesto a los puertos de otro país (página 908)

cuenca *s.* área de tierra que incluye un río o lago en particular y todos los cuerpos de agua que afluyen al mismo (página 64)

cultivable *adj.* apto para cultivos; fértil (página 140)

cultivo comercial *s.* cultivo plantado para la venta y no para el consumo del granjero (página 132)

cultura de masas *s.* conjunto de valores e ideas populares que surge a partir del amplio acceso a los medios de comunicación, a la música, al arte y a otras formas de entretenimiento (página 628)

cuota de refugiados *s.* un límite en el número de personas a las que se le permite emigrar desde ciertos países (página 736)

D

Danza de los Espíritus *s.* movimiento religioso impulsado por los nativos amerindios y basado en una danza ritual cuyo fin era comunicarse con los muertos y lograr el fin del dominio blanco en el Oeste; comenzó en la década de 1870 (página 598)

de alto riesgo (préstamos hipotecarios) *a.* un tipo de préstamo hipotecario concedido a compradores con un pobre historial crediticio (página 995)

Decimoquinta Enmienda *s.* una enmienda efectuada a la Constitución de los Estados Unidos de América, que establece que los gobiernos federal y estatal no pueden limitar el derecho al voto en virtud de la raza, el color de la piel o por una condición previa de esclavitud (página 562)

Declaración de Derechos *s.* las diez primeras enmiendas a la Constitución de EE. UU.; lista de garantías a las que tienen derecho todas las personas del país (página 263)

GLOSARIO

Declaración de Independencia *s.* documento que declara la independencia de los Estados Unidos de Gran Bretaña, emitido el 4 de julio de 1776 (página 208)

déficit presupuestario *s.* una práctica en que el gobierno gasta más dinero del que recibe por los impuestos (página 783)

delegado *s.* persona elegida para representar a un grupo de personas (página 256)

democracia jacksoniana *s.* movimiento político que honraba al hombre común y defendía la voluntad del pueblo; su nombre deriva de Andrew Jackson (página 362)

depresión *s.* período de baja actividad económica, cuando muchas personas se quedan sin trabajo (página 375)

derecho al voto *s.* ley que establece quién puede votar y cuándo; derecho civil a votar (página 362)

derecho estatal *s.* concepto de que los estados individuales tienen derechos que el gobierno federal no puede violar (página 293)

derecho humano *s.* derecho básico que la mayoría de las sociedades cree que debe garantizarse a todas las personas (página 964)

derecho inalienable *s.* derecho que no se puede quitar (página 208)

derechos civiles *s.* derechos individuales, que la ley protege de la interferencia gubernamental (página 719)

derechos naturales *s.* derechos de una persona desde su nacimiento, como a la vida o a la libertad (página 149)

derogar *v.* cancelar o revocar, especialmente una ley (página 183)

desertar *v.* abandonar una obligación o causa (página 564)

desertar *v.* huir del ejército o de otra fuerza armada para evitar el servicio militar (página 231)

deshumanizar *v.* tratar a las personas como si no fueran seres humanos (página 872)

desmotadora de algodón *s.* máquina que separa las fibras de algodón de sus semillas y vainas (página 338)

desmovilización *s.* la liberación de los soldados de su deber militar (página 842)

desobediencia civil *s.* desobediencia no violenta de las leyes como una forma de protesta (página 878)

desplegar *v.* enviar en misión militar (página 802)

desregulación *s.* la eliminación de leyes o reglamentos que rigen una industria en particular (página 966)

desterrar *v.* expulsar a alguien de un territorio como castigo, generalmente sin la esperanza de regresar (página 101)

destino manifiesto *s.* idea de que los Estados Unidos tenían el derecho y la obligación de expandir su territorio a través de Norteamérica hacia el océano Pacífico (página 391)

deuda del consumidor *s.* la cantidad de dinero que se ha pedido prestada para comprar bienes (página 765)

deuda nacional *s.* cantidad de dinero que un país debe a todos sus acreedores, que incluyen otros países y compañías a las que compra bienes y servicios (página 282)

Día D *s.* el día 6 de junio de 1944, cuando las fuerzas aliadas invadieron el norte de Francia y desembarcaron en las playas de Normandía (página 810)

diáspora africana *s.* el traslado de africanos de su lugar natal a las Américas (página 74)

dictador *s.* un líder que gobierna con el poder absoluto (página 789)

difamación *s.* publicación con la intención de desacreditar (página 152)

diferencia salarial *s.* la diferencia de salario entre hombres y mujeres que realizan trabajos similares; los hombres usualmente ganan más que las mujeres (página 924)

diplomacia moral *s.* el concepto de que los Estados Unidos debían reducir drásticamente su intervención en los asuntos de otros países (página 724)

diplomático *s.* persona enviada a otro país para representar los intereses del suyo propio (página 409)

dique *s.* cresta de tierra que corre a lo largo de los lados de un arroyo o río (página 991)

Discurso de Gettysburg *s.* discurso pronunciado en 1863 por el presidente Lincoln para conmemorar a los caídos en la Batalla de Gettysburg, y para instaurar un cementerio militar en ese sitio (página 529)

disenso *s.* desacuerdo con la opinión oficial del gobierno (página 719)

disidente *s.* persona que se separa de la creencia u opinión de la mayoría (página 100)

disidente *s.* persona que se opone firmemente a la política oficial (página 732)

disposición *s.* condición legal que anticipa necesidades futuras, o para evitar un mal (página 244)

diversidad *s.* amplia variedad (página 143)

dividir/división *v./ s.* dividir un conjunto en varias partes (página 813)

divisoria continental *s.* punto alto en las montañas Rocosas que marca la divisoria de aguas, o vertientes hidrográficas, que van a los océanos Atlántico y Pacífico (página 395)

doble soberanía *s.* sistema en el cual los gobiernos de los estados tienen ciertos poderes que el gobierno federal no puede desautorizar (página 257)

doctrina *s.* conjunto de ideas o creencias aceptadas por un grupo (página 109)

doctrina de anulación *s.* doctrina que decía que un estado podía anular o rechazar una ley federal si creía que era inconstitucional, apoyada por un político sureño antes de la Guerra Civil (página 366)

Doctrina Monroe *s.* enfoque de política exterior que expresaba que las Américas ya no estaban bajo el influjo europeo (página 345)

domesticación *s.* práctica de criar animales y cultivar plantas para el beneficio humano (página 9)

domesticar *v.* cultivar plantas y criar animales para que sean útiles a los seres humanos (página 27)

drumlin *s.* montículo pequeño de laderas lisas formado por sedimientos glaciares; también llamado "cresta de una colina" (página 204)

Dust Bowl *s.* una región de las Grandes Llanuras, que incluye partes de Oklahoma, Colorado, Kansas, Nuevo México y Texas, y que sufrió una severa sequía, erosión del suelo y tormentas de polvo durante los años 30 (página 774)

E

economía asalariada *s.* economía donde se remunera a los trabajadores (página 559)

economía de consumo *s.* una economía en que la gente compra frecuentemente y tienen muchas opciones de productos para comprar (página 738)

economía de la oferta *s.* una teoría financiera que promueve la reducción de impuestos para las empresas y los inversores con la esperanza de impulsar la producción y el comercio (página 966)

efecto invernadero *s.* el calentamiento de la superficie de la Tierra causado cuando las emisiones de gases de efecto invernadero atrapan el calor del sol (página 1008)

Eje Roma-Berlín *s.* un acuerdo entre Alemania e Italia, firmado en 1936 (página 789)

Ejército Continental *s.* ejército norteamericano formado en 1775 en el Segundo Congreso Continental y liderado por el general George Washington (página 203)

el Eje *s.* Alianza de Alemania, Italia y Japón durante la Segunda Guerra Mundial (página 789)

elección primaria directa *s.* elección donde los militantes de un partido político nominan a sus candidatos por medio del voto directo (página 668)

emancipación *s.* fin de la esclavitud (página 446)

embarcaciones de desembarco anfibio *s.* botes o barcazas usadas para transportar soldados y equipamiento militar desde el mar a la costa durante ataques militares (página 811)

embargo *s.* ley que limita o prohíbe el comercio con una o más naciones (página 319)

emigrar *v.* irse de un país para vivir en otro (página 430)

empleados de emergencia *s.* una persona (por ejemplo, un trabajador médico de emergencia o un oficial de policía) que proporciona asistencia urgente en caso de accidente o delito (página 989)

emprendedor *s.* persona que inicia, administra y es responsable de un negocio (página 583)

en ejercicio *adj.* persona que ocupa el cargo en el presente; el presidente en ejercicio es el presidente actual (página 306)

encomienda *s.* sistema de España en sus colonias en América, en el cual colonos ricos recibían terrenos y se les permitía esclavizar a las personas que allí vivían (página 66)

encubrimiento *s.* un intento de esconder la verdad al público (página 961)

energía alternativa *s.* electricidad o energía que se crea a partir de una fuente que no se agotará, como la energía eólica o solar (página 1009)

energía hidroeléctrica *s.* una fuente de electricidad creada por el flujo del agua que mueve turbinas generadoras (página 773)

enmienda *s.* cambio oficial a una ley, generalmente con respecto a un cambio oficial a la Constitución de EE. UU. (página 263)

Enmienda Platt *s.* enmienda hecha en 1901 a la legislación militar y en donde se establecían las condiciones para que los Estados Unidos se retirara de Cuba al cabo de la Guerra Hispanoamericana, pero sin que por ello perdiera su derecho a seguir interviniendo en los asuntos de ese país caribeño (página 687)

enviado *n.* embajador (página 292)

Era Dorada *s.* época que abarca las últimas tres décadas del siglo XIX, caracterizada por la codicia y la corrupción (página 628)

escalada *s.* un incremento de intensidad, como en la guerra (página 927)

escándalo de Watergate *s.* una intrusión en la Sede Nacional Demócrata del complejo Watergate en Washington, D.C., en 1972 por ladrones asociados con el comité de reelección del presidente Richard Nixon (página 961)

escaramuza *s.* lucha de corta duración (página 231)

esclavitud *s.* sistema social en el cual unas personas toman control total sobre otras (página 72)

esclavitud como propiedad personal *s.* sistema según el cual las personas esclavizadas no tienen ningún derecho humano y se clasifican como bienes (página 72)

esclusas *s.* sección reducida de agua que se usa para subir o bajar barcos. (página 693)

escombros *s.* exceso de tierra y rocas (página 693)

escorbuto *s.* enfermedad vinculada a la malnutrición y a una dieta carente de frutas y verduras (página 527)

escuela común (common school) *s.* nombre que se le daba a la escuela primaria en las colonias (página 129)

eslogan *s.* frase breve y fácil de recordar hecha para atraer y llamar la atención (página 362)

especular *v.* acto de comprar acciones con la esperanza de venderlas y obtener beneficios, mientras se corre el riesgo de una pérdida (página 765)

espionaje *s.* práctica de espiar para obtener información (página 232)

espiritual *s.* canto religioso basado en figuras bíblicas y de las escrituras de la Biblia cristiana, cantado por primera vez por los esclavos del Sur (página 341)

esquirol *s.* persona dispuesta a ignorar las disposiciones sindicales para trabajar durante una huelga (página 651)

estado decisivo *s.* un estado en el cual los votantes están divididos equitativamente entre los partidos, lo que hace difícil predecir qué candidato ganará los votos electorales del estado (página 1006)

estado fronterizo *s.* estado, durante la Guerra Civil, que limitaba tanto con los estados de la Unión como con los estados Confederados, específicamente Maryland, Kentucky, Delaware, Missouri y Virginia Occidental (página 489)

estancamiento *s.* situación en la que ninguna de las partes de un conflicto tiene posibilidad de ganar (página 516)

estanflación *s.* una condición económica en la que el estancamiento o el lento crecimiento económico va acompañado de inflación o aumento de los precios (página 962)

estatuto *s.* ley oficial escrita (página 267)

estepa *s.* planicie amplia y cubierta de hierbas (página 42)

estímulo económico *s.* una medida destinada a promover y permitir la recuperación financiera y el crecimiento (página 996)

evacuar *v.* dejar un lugar, generalmente para evitar el peligro (página 488)

Evangelio social *s.* movimiento religioso protestante que hizo hincapié en la importancia de que las iglesias se involucraran más en los asuntos sociales y en la reforma (página 634)

evangelizar *v.* predicar las creencias de una religión mediante charlas públicas y testimonios personales (página 438)

examen de lectoescritura *s.* prueba aplicada para evaluar la capacidad de alguien para leer y escribir (página 565)

excedente *s.* cantidad sobrante, exceso de algo (página 587)

exención *s.* librar de obligaciones a alguien (página 522)

exención de servicio *s.* una razón para excluir a un ciudadano de realizar un servicio militar en contra de su voluntad (página 933)

exiliado *s.* una persona que es un marginado político (página 906)

éxodo *s.* salida masiva de personas (página 395)

exoduster *s.* uno de los miles de afroamericanos sureños que migraron hacia las planicies del Medio Oeste al término de la Guerra de Secesión en la esperanza de comenzar una nueva vida (página 586)

expandirse *v.* extenderse; aumentar de manera rápida (página 146)

expuestos a congelación *s.* permanecer en temperaturas muy frías o clima severo sin protección (página 810)

F

factor de expulsión o atracción *s.* razón por la cual las personas migran, por ejemplo, por falta de oportunidades económicas o de libertad en un país y la promesa de una vida mejor en otro país (página 430)

fascismo *s.* movimiento político, basado en el nacionalismo extremo, el militarismo y el racismo, que promueve la superioridad de cierto pueblo sobre los otros (página 789)

federal *adj.* gobierno en el cual el poder es compartido entre el gobierno nacional central y el de los estados o provincias (página 250)

federalismo *s.* apoyo al gobierno en el cual el poder es compartido entre el gobierno nacional central y los estados o provincias (página 257)

federalista *s.* persona que apoyaba la Constitución de EE. UU. de 1787 según se redactó durante el proceso de ratificación (página 262)

feminista *s.* persona que practica la idea de que las mujeres son política y socialmente iguales a los hombres (página 924)

feriado bancario *s.* un día o periodo de tiempo en que los bancos cierran por disposición gubernamental (página 771)

ferrocarril transcontinental *s.* ferrocarril que opera a lo largo de un continente (página 620)

feudalismo *s.* sistema político y social en el que un vasallo recibe protección de un señor feudal a cambio de prestarle obediencia y servicio (página 36)

fiebre amarilla *s.* enfermedad, con frecuencia mortal, transmitida por mosquitos en climas tropicales (página 312)

filantropía *s.* apoyo financiero a favor de una causa noble y caritativa (página 627)

filántropo(a) *s.* persona que promueve activamente el bienestar de los demás (página 496)

financista *s.* persona que presta o maneja dinero para un negocio u emprendimiento (página 229)

fiscal especial *s.* un abogado privado o funcionario designado por el tribunal para investigar o entablar acciones legales contra una parte cuando el fiscal ordinario no puede o tiene un conflicto de intereses con la parte acusada de un delito (página 961)

fiscal general *s.* miembro del Gabinete del presidente, cuyo papel principal es representar a los EE. UU. ante la Corte Suprema (página 281)

fisión nuclear *s.* la separación de los átomos, que provoca una liberación de energía (página 821)

flapper *s.* mujer joven que en los años 20 asumía un estilo más libre de vestir y maquillarse (página 743)

flotilla *s.* flota pequeña o compuesta de buques de menor calado (página 528)

fondo de pensiones *s.* un fondo monetario usado para pagar a las personas un ingreso pequeño y estable luego que se retiren (página 776)

GLOSARIO

fortificación *s.* estructura construida para proteger un lugar de un ataque (página 227)

forty-niner **(buscador de oro)** *s.* uno de los miles de futuros mineros que viajaron a California a buscar oro en 1849 (página 417)

Framers **(autores de la Constitución)** *s.* término histórico para los delegados en la Convención Constitucional de 1787, quienes ayudaron a crear y redactar la Constitución de los Estados Unidos (página 256)

frente *s.* una línea de batalla entre ejércitos (página 712)

Frostbelt *s.* regiones del norte y noreste de Estados Unidos que tienen inviernos muy fríos (página 854)

fuga de depósitos *s.* momento en el que muchos clientes se asustan y corren a retirar su dinero de un banco al mismo tiempo (página 768)

fundamentalismo *s.* un movimiento que promueve la idea de que cada palabra de la Biblia es una verdad literal (página 736)

fundamentalista *s.* Una persona que cree en la adhesión estricta o literal a un sistema de creencias (página 965)

G

Gabinete *s.* los jefes de los departamentos que asisten al presidente de los EE. UU. (página 279)

galeón *s.* buque de vela grande usado especialmente por los españoles en los siglos XVI y XVII (página 62)

ganancia *s.* cantidad de dinero que sobra en un negocio después de descontar los gastos (página 40)

gas venenoso *s* un producto químico dispersado en el aire, que causa daño o muerte (página 713)

gastos corrientes *s.* el costo de operar un negocio (página 647)

genocidio *s.* asesinato deliberado de un gran número de personas que pertenecen a una raza específica o a un determinado grupo cultural o político (página 814)

geografía física *s.* estudio de las características físicas externas de la Tierra (página 34)

geografía humana *s.* estudio de la influencia que tiene la geografía física sobre las personas y su cultura, así como de los efectos que producen las actividades humanas sobre el medio ambiente (página 34)

geología *s.* estudio de los cambios que formaron las rocas y los accidentes geográficos de la Tierra (página 204)

gestión científica *s.* proceso que busca estudiar a los trabajadores para determinar la manera más eficiente y rentable de hacer un trabajo (página 677)

Glaciación *s.* período en la historia durante el cual inmensas capas de hielo cubrían gran parte de la superficie terrestre (página 5)

glásnost *s.* una política gubernamental de transparencia comunicativa en la antigua Unión Soviética (página 974)

globalización *s.* el flujo más rápido y más libre de personas, recursos, bienes e ideas a través de las fronteras nacionales (página 1004)

gobierno títere *s.* gobierno que parece tener autoridad pero en realidad es controlado por otro poder (página 794)

golpe *s.* el derrocamiento ilegal de un gobierno (página 975)

Gran Despertar *s.* serie de avivamientos religiosos protestantes que se extendieron por las colonias en Norteamérica (página 148)

Gran Migración Negra *s.* movimiento masivo de afroamericanos que abandonaron el Sur y emigraron a las ciudades del norte a principios de 1910 (página 727)

granja de bonanza *s.* granja de gran tamaño propiedad de un inversionista, quien la administra para obtener ganancias (página 586)

guarnición *s.* tropa de defensa (página 477)

Guerra de 1812 *s.* guerra contra Gran Bretaña declarada por James Madison (página 322)

guerra de trincheras *s.* estrategia de guerra que usa un sistema de zanjas de protección desde donde los soldados disparan durante la batalla (página 495)

guerra defensiva *s.* guerra para proteger su propio país de ataques extranjeros, luchada en tierras conocidas (página 222)

Guerra del rey Philip *s.* conflicto violento entre indígenas americanos y colonos ingleses de Nueva Inglaterra, ayudados estos últimos por indígenas aliados (página 106)

guerra sin cuartel *s.* guerra en la cual se ignoran todos los convenios bélicos y se usan todos los recursos para vencer al enemigo (página 530)

guerrillero(a) *adj.* que usa tácticas de ataque encubiertas y sabotajes (página 237)

gueto *s.* alojamiento obligatorio para una determinada raza o etnia (página 814)

H

hábeas corpus *s.* derecho de una persona arrestada para comparecer ante un juez antes de ser encarcelada (página 523)

hacienda *s.* plantación grande en una colonia española (página 66)

halcón *s.* una persona que apoya la guerra (página 933)

Halcón de Guerra *s.* persona partidaria de la guerra; estadounidense que estaba a favor de la guerra contra Gran Bretaña en 1812 (página 321)

hambruna *s.* escasez extrema de cultivos o alimentos, que causa hambre generalizada (página 432)

hereje *s.* persona que tiene creencias diferentes a las enseñanzas de la Iglesia Católica (página 61)

Hessians **(hesianos)** *s.* soldados alemanes contratados por los británicos para luchar durante la Guerra de Independencia (página 206)

Hijos de la Libertad *s.* grupos de mercaderes, comerciantes y artesanos que se organizaron con éxito para rechazar la Ley del Timbre mediante el boicot a los productos británicos (página 183)

historia oral *s.* entrevista grabada con una persona cuyas experiencias y recuerdos tienen un significado histórico (página R38)

Holocausto *s.* la matanza masiva por parte de los nazis de seis millones de judíos y otros durante la Segunda Guerra Mundial (página 814)

hombres de montaña *s.* cazadores y comerciantes de pieles conocidos como tramperos que contribuyeron con la exploración del Oeste (página 390)

Hooverville *s.* grupo de viviendas improvisadas para dar albergue a gente sin techo, hechas con restos de cartón, placas metálicas u otros materiales baratos, que se construyeron durante la Gran Depresión y fueron bautizadas con el nombre del presidente Herbert Hoover (página 769)

horario estándar *s.* división uniforme del tiempo entre lugares que se encuentran aproximadamente en la misma línea de longitud, estableciendo así zonas horarias (página 621)

huelga *s.* huelga s. interrupción del trabajo para forzar a un empleador a cumplir con ciertas demandas (página 328)

huelga de hambre *s.* el acto de negarse a comer como protesta para mostrar desaprobación o desacuerdo (página 918)

humanismo *s.* movimiento basado en la importancia del individuo (página 39)

I

ideología *s.* sistema de creencias que guía un plan social o político (página 789)

Ilustración *s.* movimiento intelectual caracterizado por el uso de la razón para revisar creencias aceptadas anteriormente (página 149)

imperialismo *s.* sistema político mediante el cual un país más poderoso controla a países o territorios más débiles (página 684)

imponer *v.* requerir el pago de un impuesto (página 105)

imprenta *s.* invención que usaba letras móviles de metal para imprimir páginas (página 39)

improvisar *v.* crear o ejecutar música sin ensayarla previamente, a menudo inventándola en el acto (página 742)

impuesto electoral *s.* cuota impuesta a los ciudadanos al registrarse en el padrón electoral (página 563)

impuesto sobre la renta *s.* impuesto que grava los ingresos de cada contribuyente (página 673)

incendio intencional *s.* incendio ilegal provocado de manera deliberada en contra de propiedades y edificios (página 560)

GLOSARIO

inconstitucional *adj.* idea o ley que va en contra de los principios de la Constitución de los EE. UU. (página 310)

incumplimientos de pago *s.* una falla en el pago de un préstamo (página 995)

independizarse *v.* separarse oficialmente de una nación u organización para hacerse independiente (página 474)

indiferencia saludable *s.* política del gobierno británico que evitaba que sus leyes en las colonias se cumplieran estrictamente (página 151)

índigo *s.* planta que produce un tinte azul para teñir telas (página 132)

individualismo *s.* independencia autosuficiente (página 390)

industrial *s.* propietario que administra una compañía industrial (página 591)

infantería *s.* tropas de soldados a pie (página 491)

inflación *s.* disminución en el valor de una moneda que causa el aumento en el precio de bienes y servicios (página 374)

influenza *s.* una grave enfermedad, altamente contagiosa, comúnmente llamada "gripe" (página 726)

ingreso *s.* recaudación de dinero; dinero que se recibe (página 180)

iniciativa *s.* proceso por medio del cual los ciudadanos proponen una ley y es necesario que los demás ciudadanos emitan su voto al respecto (página 669)

inmigrar *v.* llegar a vivir a un país de manera permanente (página 430)

inmunidad *s.* protección contra una enfermedad, ya sea natural o provocada por vacunación (página 70)

institución *s.* práctica establecida y aceptada en una sociedad o una cultura (página 74)

insurgente *s.* un rebelde o revolucionario (página 989)

insurrección *s.* rebelión (página 410)

integración *s.* el acto de permitir la asociación libre de personas de diferentes razas o etnias (página 875)

intercambio colombino *s.* intercambio de plantas, animales, microbios, personas e ideas entre Europa y las Américas después del primer viaje de Colón al Hemisferio Occidental (página 70)

Internet *s.* la red electrónica que permite comunicarse a los ordenadores (página 1000)

interpretación estricta *s.* un entendimiento de la Constitución en el cual la Constitución debe ser seguida estrictamente como fue redactada (página 286)

interpretación flexible *s.* un entendimiento de la Constitución que le da al Congreso y al presidente amplios poderes (página 286)

inversor *s.* persona que compra parte de una compañía con la intención de obtener beneficios al vender su parte de acciones (página 765)

ironclad (barco blindado) *s.* barco revestido con planchas de hierro para protegerlo del fuego de los cañones (página 495)

irrigación *s.* suministro de agua a los campos mediante el uso de sistemas hechos por el hombre (página 24)

istmo *s.* franja estrecha de tierra que conecta dos masas de tierra más grandes y separa dos cuerpos de agua (página 692)

J

jazz *s.* un estilo musical que se originó entre los músicos afroamericanos, que contiene ritmos animados, sonidos de una variedad de instrumentos e improvisaciones (página 742)

jerarquía *s.* clasificación de un grupo de personas de acuerdo con su capacidad o con su posición económica, social o profesional (página 36)

Jinetes Duros *s.* grupo de vaqueros, mineros, oficiales de policía e indígenas norteamericanos que, aunque no contaban con entrenamiento militar, eran considerados muy rudos, y participaron de manera voluntaria en la guerra hispanoamericana bajo el mando de Theodore Roosevelt (página 687)

Juicio Político *s.* acusación formal para destituir a un presidente en funciones a causa de malos manejos en su administración (página 555)

jurisdicción *s.* poder o autoridad concedida a alguien para aplicar la ley en determinado territorio (página 538)

justicia social *s.* régimen caracterizado por una justa distribución de las oportunidades y los privilegios, incluyendo la igualdad racial (página 557)

juzgar ante una corte marcial *v.* juzgar a un miembro de las fuerzas armadas que ha sido acusado de haber violado la ley militar (página 688)

K

kayak *s.* canoa con un armazón liviano y con una pequeña abertura superior para sentarse (página 26)

Ku Klux Klan *s.* grupo clandestino cuyo propósito era mantener el poder social y político de la comunidad blanca en los Estados Unidos (página 560)

L

La Granja *s.* organización fundada en 1867 por agricultores estadounidenses para proporcionar apoyo social y económico a las familias dedicadas a la agricultura (página 590)

laissez faire *s.* política económica aplicada por el gobierno para permitirles a las empresas operar sin muchas regulaciones; laissez-fairesignifica "dejar hacer" en francés (página 627)

La Larga Marcha *s.* marcha forzosa que los navajos debieron emprender desde su lugar de origen hasta una reservación en Bosque Redondo, Nuevo México, a 300 millas (482.8 km) de distancia; fue impuesta por el gobierno de los Estados Unidos en 1864 (página 596)

leal a Gran Bretaña *s.* colono que apoyaba a Gran Bretaña en la Guerra de Independencia (página 198)

lecho de roca *s.* roca sólida que se localiza debajo del suelo (página 636)

legislación histórica *s.* ley importante e histórica (página 913)

Ley Clayton Antimonopolio *s.* ley de 1914 que describía la ilegalidad de las prácticas comerciales de los monopolios, y buscaba llenar los vacíos legales de que solían aprovecharse esos monopolios (página 674)

Ley de Alimentos y Fármacos No Adulterados *s.* ley de 1906 que le otorgaba mayor poder al gobierno federal para que protegiera la calidad, pureza y sanidad de los alimentos y los fármacos (página 671)

Ley de Alojamiento *s.* una de varias leyes británicas que exigía a los colonos proporcionar vivienda y comida a los soldados británicos en Norteamérica (página 178)

Ley de Asentamientos Rurales (Ley de Homstead) *s.* ley que impulsó un programa para otorgar tierras públicas a pequeños agricultores (página 541)

Ley de Conscripción *s.* ley promulgada en 1863 por la Unión mediante la cual se estipulaba que todos los hombres de entre 20 y 45 años de edad podrían ser reclutados en el ejército, pero también podían pagar $300 dólares para evitar el servicio militar (página 522)

Ley de Derechos Civiles de 1866 *s.* proyecto de ley que les otorgaba plena igualdad y ciudadanía a los estadounidenses de "cualquier color y raza" (página 554)

Ley de Desalojo de los Indígenas *s.* ley que terminó con una ley anterior de los EE. UU. que respetaba los derechos de los indígenas norteamericanos a permanecer en sus tierras (página 368)

Ley de Embargo de 1807 *s.* legislación federal que prohibió la entrada de todas las importaciones extranjeras a los puertos estadounidenses (página 319)

Ley de Exclusión China *s.* ley que, en 1882, prohibía la inmigración de trabajadores chinos a los Estados Unidos durante un periodo de diez años (página 640)

Ley de Inspección de Productos Cárnicos *s.* ley de 1906 que pretendía asegurar la pureza y sanidad de la carne (página 671)

Ley de Judicatura de 1801 *s.* legislación federal que redujo de 6 a 5 la cantidad de jueces de la Corte Suprema (página 310)

Ley de la Moneda *s.* ley británica que regulaba el papel moneda en las colonias de Norteamérica (página 181)

Ley de la Reserva Federal *s.* ley de 1913 mediante la cual se creó la Junta de la Reserva Federal, que supervisaría las operaciones de otros doce bancos de reserva; todos ellos controlarían el flujo de dinero en los Estados Unidos (página 674)

Ley del Azúcar *s.* ley británica que rebajaba el arancel de aduana a la melaza importada para disminuir su contrabando, y así los británicos recibían las ganancias (página 181)

GLOSARIO

Ley del Té *s.* ley británica que otorgaba a la Compañía Británica de las Indias Orientales el monopolio de la venta del té en las colonias (página 191)

Ley del Timbre *s.* ley británica que exigía a los colonos la compra de un timbre para documentos oficiales y materiales impresos (página 182)

Ley Seca *s.* decimoctava enmienda hecha a la Constitución de Estados Unidos para prohibir la producción, venta, importación y transportación de bebidas alcohólicas dentro del territorio nacional (página 681)

Ley Sherman Antimonopolio de 1890 *s.* estatuto federal aprobado para prohibir la formación de monopolios (página 670)

Ley sobre Moneda de Curso Legal *s.* ley que reemplazó los billetes emitidos por los bancos privados con una moneda unificada a nivel nacional (página 524)

Leyes de Extranjería y Sedición *s.* serie de cuatro leyes aprobadas para prevenir que ciertos grupos inmigraran a los Estados Unidos; las leyes dieron al gobierno el poder para expulsar extranjeros que vivían en el país y perseguir a ciudadanos estadounidenses críticos del gobierno (página 293)

Leyes de Jim Crow *s.* leyes promovidas en la década de 1880 por políticos sureños con la intención de privar de sus derechos a los ciudadanos afroamericanos (página 640)

Leyes de Navegación *s.* leyes aprobadas por el Parlamento inglés para proteger las compañías navieras inglesas al restringir el transporte de bienes desde y hacia las colonias inglesas (página 125)

Leyes de Townshend *s.* grupo de leyes británicas que imponían aranceles de aduana a las importaciones de té, vidrio, papel, plomo y pintura; los colonos tenían que comprar estos productos a Gran Bretaña (página 186)

Leyes del Tren del Pacífico *s.* dos leyes promulgadas en la década de 1860 por medio de las cuales se le otorgaron a dos compañías los contratos para la construcción de una vía ferroviaria transcontinental (página 620)

Leyes Intolerables *s.* leyes británicas aprobadas para castigar a la gente de Boston después del Motín del Té; llamadas también Leyes Coercitivas (página 194)

Leyes para la Reconstrucción de 1867 *s.* leyes que le otorgaban al Congreso Republicano el poder necesario para llevar a cabo la Reconstrucción, por encima del Presidente (página 554)

libertad de religión *s.* derecho a practicar la religión que uno desee sin intervención del gobierno (página 126)

libre comercio *s.* una forma de comercio internacional que tiene pocas o ninguna restricción (página 1004)

Liga de las Naciones *s.* organización internacional pacificadora, propuesta por el presidente Woodrow Wilson después de la Primera Guerra Mundial (página 723)

Liga Iroquesa *s.* confederación compuesta por cinco naciones de habla iroquesa: los mohawk, los oneida, los onondaga, los cayuga y los seneca; más tarde se sumaron los tuscarora (página 29)

linchar *v.* ejecución ilegal por parte de una turba (página 560)

línea de ensamblaje *s.* sistema en el cual cada trabajador se coloca en determinado lugar, y el proceso de producción pasa de una función a otra, en línea recta, hasta que un producto se ensambla por completo (página 676)

los Aliados *s.* grupo de países, incluyendo a Francia y Gran Bretaña, que colaboraron para oponerse a los países del llamado Eje (Alemania, Italia y Japón) durante la Segunda Guerra Mundial (página 789)

M

macartismo *s.* la práctica de acusar a personas de ser traidores a su país sin ofrecer pruebas (página 853)

madres republicanas (Republican Motherhood) *s.* término histórico que describía la idea de que las mujeres debían educar a sus hijos como buenos ciudadanos participantes del gobierno (página 348)

magnate ladrón *s.* líder industrial conocido por sus tácticas despiadadas en contra de los trabajadores y sus competidores (página 649)

magnicidio *v.* el asesinato de una persona muy importante por su cargo o poder (página 538)

maquinaria política *s.* organización partidista que gobernaba grandes ciudades, y era dirigida por líderes fuertes, y a menudo corruptos, que ofrecían favores a los miembros de dicha organización a cambio de votos y otros apoyos (página 634)

marejada *s.* un aumento anormal del nivel del mar generado por una tormenta, por encima de las mareas pronosticadas, y empujada hacia la costa por los vientos de la tormenta (página 991)

margen *s.* la cantidad de diferencia por la que se gana o se pierde algo (página 403)

Masacre de Boston *s.* incidente en 1779, en el cual soldados británicos dispararon contra personas locales que los estaban insultando (página 188)

materia prima *s.* materia o sustancia básica necesaria para la fabricación de un producto (página 114)

matrilineal *adj.* relacionado con los descendientes que provienen de la madre (página 29)

Mayoría Moral *s.* un grupo político conservador formado por el reverendo Jerry Falwell, un tele-evangelista, en 1979 (página 970)

mayoría silenciosa *s.* un término usado por Richard Nixon a finales de los 60 para describir a un amplio grupo de votantes moderados que no expresaban públicamente sus opiniones (página 935)

Medicaid *s.* programa gubernamental norteamericano iniciado en 1965 para proporcionar un seguro médico a las personas de bajos ingresos (página 917)

Medicare *s.* programa gubernamental norteamericano iniciado en 1965, que proporciona un seguro médico a las personas mayores (página 917)

medios de comunicación masiva *s.* fuentes de información o entretenimiento que llegan a una gran cantidad de personas al mismo tiempo (página 738)

megafauna *s.* animales gigantescos, o muy grandes, que habitan un área particular o que vivieron en un período histórico determinado (página 6)

mercado común *s.* grupo de países o estados que permite que sus miembros comercien libremente entre ellos (página 261)

mercado negro *s.* un sistema a través del cual mercancías prohibidas se venden y compran ilegalmente (página 735)

mercadotecnia *s.* proceso de promover productos o servicios (página 738)

mercancía *s.* bien comerciable (página 142)

mercantilismo *s.* política económica que le da a un país la propiedad exclusiva del comercio en sus colonias (página 52)

mercenario *s.* soldado al que se le paga para luchar por un país que no es el suyo (página 222)

mestizo *s.* persona que tiene ascendencia mixta española e indígena americana (página 66)

migrar *v.* mudarse de un lugar a otro (página 27)

milicia *s.* fuerza militar compuesta por ciudadanos civiles locales con el fin de proteger su pueblo, tierra o nación (página 178)

miliciano *s.* miembro de la milicia colonial que estaba dispuesto a luchar en cualquier momento (página 196)

militarismo *s.* creencia en que un gobierno debe crear un ejército fuerte y estar preparado para usarlo para alcanzar los objetivos nacionales (página 710)

minería aluvial *s.* sistema minero en donde gambusinos o buscadores de oro intentan encontrar pepitas de oro en el lecho de los ríos, comúnmente mediante cribas (página 583)

minería hidráulica *s.* sistema minero en donde se usa agua a presión para remover la parte superior del suelo y la grava, los cuales se procesan después para extraer metales preciosos (página 583)

misil balístico *s.* un arma nuclear que es propulsada por un cohete y guiada con un sistema de GPS (página 908)

misión *s.* asentamiento de una iglesia cristiana establecida para convertir a las personas indígenas (página 66)

misionero *s.* persona que se esfuerza por divulgar el cristianismo a los demás (página 53)

GLOSARIO

módulo de mando *s.* la parte principal de un vehículo espacial que lleva a la tripulación, los suministros principales y el equipo de regreso a la Tierra (página 957)

módulo lunar *s.* la parte de un vehículo espacial que debe transportar a los astronautas del módulo de mando a la superficie lunar, y de regreso al módulo de mando (página 957)

molino harinero *s.* pieza donde estaba la maquinaria que molía los granos (página 140)

monopolio *s.* el control total y exclusivo de una industria por parte de una sola compañía (página 343)

moral *s.* el nivel de confianza o entusiasmo que siente un grupo de personas (página 717)

morfina *s.* potente analgésico (página 534)

mortalidad *s.* tasa de muertes (página 495)

Motín del Té *s.* incidente en 1773, en el cual los Hijos de la Libertad subieron a bordo de barcos británicos y botaron al mar los cargamentos de té en protesta por los impuestos británicos a los colonos (página 191)

movilizar *v.* organizar y preparar tropas para la guerra (página 490)

movimiento conservacionista *s.* movimiento que promueve la protección de los recursos naturales y de la fauna salvaje (página 671)

movimiento de escuelas comunes (common schools) *s.* movimiento de reforma a la educación en la década de 1830 para promover escuelas públicas gratuitas financiadas por la recolección de impuestos a la propiedad y manejadas por los gobiernos locales (página 441)

movimiento por la moderación *s.* movimiento de reforma del siglo XIX que buscaba reducir o eliminar el consumo de bebidas alcohólicas (página 438)

municiones *s.* proyectiles militares (página 801)

Muro de Berlín *s.* un muro de concreto y alambre de espino que rodeaba la democrática Berlín oeste, y que fue construido por los comunistas de Berlin Este, para prevenir que sus ciudadanos se fugaran a la parte democrática de la ciudad (página 907)

música gospel *s.* música que combina los temas bíblicos y un estilo musical semejante a las canciones de jazz (página 748)

N

nacionalismo *s.* concepto de lealtad y devoción al país de uno (página 342)

napalm *s.* una sustancia gelatinosa, altamente inflamable, usada en las bombas para provocar y propagar incendios (página 929)

nativist (antiinmigrante) *s.* término histórico para aquella persona que creía que los nacidos en un lugar debían tener más privilegios que los inmigrantes (página 436)

naturalización *s.* el proceso de convertirse en ciudadano estadounidense para quienes no son ciudadanos nativos (página R32)

navegación *s.* ciencia que consiste en determinar la ubicación de un barco y en planificar rutas, a menudo usado para referirse a los viajes por mar (página 40)

navegador *s.* un programa de ordenador que se usa para ver sitios web (página 1000)

neoconservador *s.* una persona que apoya firmemente una economía de libre mercado y cree que Estados Unidos debería promover activamente sus ideales en todo el mundo (página 986)

neutralidad *s.* negativa a tomar parte en un conflicto entre otros (página 111)

noticiero cinematográfico *s.* corto noticioso o deportivo que se proyecta antes de una película (página 741)

O

oasis *s.* lugar fértil con agua en un desierto (página 42)

objetor de conciencia *s.* una persona que se niega a pelear en una guerra, a menudo por razones religiosas (página 719)

observador electoral *s.* persona asignada a una casilla electoral con el fin de detectar cualquier irregularidad en el proceso electoral (página 643)

obsolescencia programada *s.* la idea de que las personas deben planear reemplazar un objeto antes de que éste se rompa o se gaste (página 739)

oferta y demanda *s.* un principio económico que establece que el precio de algo depende de cuánto haya disponible (la oferta) y cuán deseado sea (la demanda) (página 764)

Oficina de Libertos *s.* Oficina para Refugiados, Hombres Libres y Tierras Abandonadas, creada por el Congreso en 1865 para brindar ayuda a los afroamericanos que habían sido esclavos, así como a los sureños blancos más pobres (página 553)

orden de asistencia *s.* documento legal que daba a las autoridades el derecho de entrar y registrar una casa o negocio (página 186)

orden ejecutiva *s.* directiva o mandato de un presidente que tiene la fuerza legal (página 806)

orden judicial *s.* documento legal (página 310)

ordenanza *s.* mandato, decreto o ley oficial (página 252)

Ordenanza de 1785 *s.* Ordenanza de 1785 *s.* ley federal que creó un sistema que permitía a los colonos comprar tierras en el oeste (página 252)

Ordenanza del Noroeste de 1787 *s.* legislación adoptada por el Congreso para establecer un control más estricto sobre el gobierno del Territorio del Noroeste (página 252)

Órdenes Fundamentales de Connecticut *s.* acta de fundación de la colonia de Connecticut que establecía 11 leyes y fue el marco de gobierno de la colonia (página 101)

P

pacifista *s.* una persona que se opone a la guerra (página 933)

pacifista *s.* persona que se resiste a la guerra y a la violencia (página 239)

Pacto del *Mayflower* *s.* documento que firmaron los peregrinos a bordo del Mayflower antes de llegar a Norteamérica, que los vinculaba a obedecer sus propias leyes y establecer una sociedad civil (página 100)

Pánico de 1837 *s.* episodio de temor por una caída de la economía, que causó el comienzo de una recesión económica en los EE. UU. hasta 1840 (página 375)

Pánico de 1873 *s.* crisis económica desencadenada por la quiebra de algunos bancos y empresas ferroviarias (página 565)

panzer *s.* tanque alemán fuertemente armado con un impresionante poder de fuego, usado durante la Segunda Guerra Mundial (página 812)

paralelo *s.* línea de latitud (página 413)

Parlamento *s.* cámara legislativa de Inglaterra, y después de Gran Bretaña (página 150)

partera *s.* persona entrenada para atender partos (página 146)

partes intercambiables *s.* partes de un mecanismo que pueden ser sustituidas unas por otras (página 330)

Partido de los Know-Nothing *s.* partido político que se formó alrededor de 1850 para oponerse a la inmigración, y cuyos miembros secretos contestaban "no sé nada" (know nothing) a cualquier pregunta; también se llamó American Party (página 436)

Partido de los Whigs *s.* partido político que se opuso a las políticas de Andrew Jackson, de quien consideraban que tenía demasiado poder (página 376)

Partido Nazi *s.* partido político comandado por Adolf Hitler, que usó la fuerza para ejercer un control absoluto sobre Alemania de 1933 a 1945 (página 789)

Partido Republicano *s.* partido político fundado en 1845 por líderes antiesclavistas (página 468)

pasaje medio *s.* el largo viaje a través del océano Atlántico durante el cual los africanos esclavizados eran llevados a las Américas; segunda etapa de la ruta del comercio triangular (página 73)

Pasajeros de la Libertad *s.* grupos interraciales que participaron en las caravanas de autobuses por todo el Sur para protestar contra la segregación (página 882)

paso del noroeste *s.* canal entre los océanos Atlántico y Pacífico a lo largo de la costa norte de América del Norte (página 60)

patente *s.* documento que le concede a su poseedor el derecho exclusivo de fabricar y vender un invento (página 624)

patriota *s.* colono que apoyaba el derecho de las colonias en Norteamérica a gobernarse a sí mismas (página 198)

GLOSARIO

patrón oro *s.* política monetaria que le exige al gobierno emitir exclusivamente una cantidad de dinero equivalente al valor total de sus reservas en oro (página 591)

perdón *s.* una liberación del castigo legal (página 962)

peregrinación *s.* viaje religioso (página 45)

perestroika *s.* una política gubernamental de reforma política y económica en la antigua Unión Soviética (página 974)

pericia *s.* conocimiento de una ciencia o habilidad (página 241)

periodismo amarillista *s.* forma de reportar las noticias que exagera y dramatiza los eventos, ofreciéndoles a los lectores una perspectiva distorsionada de la realidad, con el ánimo de vender más ejemplares (página 687)

perseguir *v.* castigar, en particular debido a creencias o antecedentes (página 61)

perspectiva geográfica *s.* examen de la influencia que tiene la geografía sobre las personas y su cultura (página 34)

pesos y contrapesos *n.* sistema establecido en la Constitución de EE. UU. que da a cada una de las ramas del gobierno el poder para controlar a las otras dos (página 258)

Piedmont *s.* región relativamente plana entre los montes Apalaches y la llanura costera (página 134)

piloto kamikaze *s.* pilotos suicida de los bombarderos japoneses que estrellaban su avión cargado con explosivos contra los barcos norteamericanos durante la Segunda Guerra Mundial (página 819)

pinchar las líneas telefonicas *v.* colocar un aparato en un teléfono para escuchar en secreto las conversaciones (página 960)

pionero *s.* colono que va a una tierra nueva y desconocida (página 392)

plaga *s.* hongos o insectos que causan que las plantas se sequen y mueran (página 432)

Plan Anaconda *s.* estrategia militar durante la Guerra Civil, en la cual el Norte planeó un bloqueo alrededor de las costas sureñas para arruinar la economía del Sur y tomar los puertos en el Mississippi; al igual que una enorme serpiente, como la anaconda, estrangula a su presa (página 504)

plan de "empaquetamiento de la Corte" *s.* un controversial plan del presidente Franklin Roosevelt para incrementar el número de jueces de la Suprema Corte de 9 a 15, añadiendo seis jueces que compartieran sus visiones progresistas (página 779)

Plan de Crittenden *s.* propuesta que establecía que el gobierno federal no tuviera poderes para abolir la esclavitud en los estados donde ya existía; reestablecía y extendía el límite del Compromiso de Missouri hasta el océano Pacífico (página 476)

plan de pagos *s.* un plan para comprar algo haciendo una serie de pagos parciales durante un periodo determinado (página 765)

Plan Marshall *s.* un plan para ayudar a los países europeos a reconstruir y recuperarse económicamente después de la Segunda Guerra Mundial (página 822)

plantación *s.* granja grande; en las plantaciones del Sur, los esclavos trabajaban plantando y cosechando cultivos (página 66)

plataforma continental *s.* un área de tierra relativamente poco profunda bajo el océano que se extiende hacia afuera desde un continente antes de una caída abrupta en el océano abierto (página 972)

Pleistoceno *s.* período en la historia de la Tierra durante el cual existieron animales y plantas gigantescos, y grandes extensiones de tierra se cubrieron de hielo (página 5)

poder ejecutivo *s.* rama del gobierno de EE. UU. presidida por el presidente; responsable de que se cumpla la ley (página 258)

poder implícito *s.* poder que no está explícito en la Constitución (página 343)

poder judicial *s.* rama del gobierno de EE. UU., que incluye las cortes o tribunales y el sistema legal, presidida por la Corte Suprema; responsable de interpretar las leyes (página 258)

poder legislativo *s.* rama del gobierno de EE. UU. presidida por el Congreso; responsable de hacer las leyes (página 258)

Política de Puertas Abiertas *s.* política impulsada a finales del siglo XIX y principios del XX para exigir igualdad de privilegios comerciales para todos los países que tuvieran intereses económicos con China (página 691)

política de riesgo calculado *s.* la práctica de llevar un conflicto hasta el borde de la violencia sin caer en una guerra, usualmente una táctica para obtener un resultado favorable (página 853)

política de terminación *s.* una política promulgada por el presidente Eisenhower que sacaba a los indígenas americanos de las reservas, al mismo tiempo que el gobierno terminaba con la soberanía de las naciones y tribus individuales (página 922)

política de tierra arrasada *s.* un método usado por el ejército norteamericano para vaciar y destruir pueblos completos que podrían haber proporcionado ayuda al enemigo (página 929)

poner en la lista negra *v.* poner una o más personas en una lista indicando que deben ser rechazadas o castigadas (página 852)

pontón *s.* flotador cilíndrico portable, que se usaba para construir un puente temporal (página 511)

populismo *s.* posición política que afirma que el control del gobierno debe recaer en la gente común y corriente, y no en los miembros de la élite (página 665)

populista *s.* político que asegura representar los intereses de los ciudadanos comunes y corrientes (página 591)

potlatch *s.* ceremonia de entrega de obsequios practicada por las tribus indígenas norteamericanas kwakiutl y haida (página 26)

pradera *s.* extensa área territorial cubierta de plantas altas (página 586)

prebélico *adj.* anterior a la Guerra Civil de los Estados Unidos (página 340)

precedente *s.* suceso anterior o resolución que sirve de ejemplo para sucesos o resoluciones futuras (página 278)

preferencia de género *s* preferencia por un género sobre otro (página 925)

prejuicio *s.* juicio generalizado acerca de un grupo de personas que no está basado en razones o hechos (página 436)

presidente de la Corte Suprema *s.* jefe máximo del poder judicial del gobierno; preside la Corte Suprema (página 281)

presidio *s.* puesto o asentamiento militar (página 398)

Primer Congreso Continental *s.* reunión en 1774 de los representantes de todas las colonias norteamericanas para dar una respuesta a las Leyes Intolerables (página 195)

prisionero de guerra *s.* soldado capturado por una fuerza enemiga (página 793)

Procedimiento Bessemer *s.* proceso de fabricación de acero que implica soplar aire en hierro fundido para eliminar impurezas, gracias a lo cual es posible producir un metal más fuerte (página 624)

Proclamación de 1763 *s.* ley que establecía que los colonos debían mantenerse al este de una línea dibujada en un mapa, a lo largo de la cima de los montes Apalaches (página 178)

Proclamación de Emancipación *s.* documento de 1863, emitido por Abraham Lincoln, que abolió la esclavitud en los estados gobernados por la Confederación durante la Guerra Civil de los Estados Unidos (página 517)

profeta *s.* alguien de quien se cree que trae mensajes de Dios o de cualquier otra fuente divina (página 321)

progresismo *s.* movimiento social que cree en la igualdad para todas las personas, e invita a los ciudadanos y al gobierno a trabajar todos juntos para lograr un cambio social (página 665)

propaganda *s.* información difundida para influenciar las opiniones de las personas o promover la ideas de un partido o una organización (página 718)

propietario *s.* dueño de una colonia, que tenía el derecho a manejar y distribuir tierras y a establecer un gobierno (página 112)

protestante *s.* seguidor de la Reforma en el cristianismo (página 39)

provisiones *s.* conjunto de alimentos, agua y otras cosas reservadas para un viaje (página 124)

Proyecto Manhattan *s.* el nombre en clave del programa atómico financiado por el gobierno norteamericano durante los años 40 (página 821)

psiquiátrico *s.* hospital o clínica donde se trata a los enfermos mentales (página 441)

publicidad *s.* el acto de presentar productos e ideas al público (página 738)

pueblo fantasma *s.* pueblo abandonado que ha quedado en ruinas (página 583)

puente de Beringia *s.* territorio entre Alaska y Siberia que se encontraba por encima del nivel del mar hace unos 13,000 años, lo que permitió el paso a grupos humanos que migraban hacia Norteamérica (página 6)

puesto comercial *s.* pequeño asentamiento establecido con el propósito de intercambiar bienes (página 155)

Q

quinina *s.* sustancia hecha de la corteza de un árbol que es un remedio eficaz contra la malaria (página 71)

R

ración *s.* porción de comida suministrada (página 527)

racionamiento *s.* distribución controlada de la comida u otros suministros (página 799)

racismo *s.* creencia de que una raza es mejor que otras (página 464)

radical *n.* persona partidaria de cambios sociales o políticos extremos (página 289)

rancho *s.* terreno cedido por México a los colonos, en forma de grandes fincas, en lo que hoy es California (página 415)

rascacielos *s.* edificio muy alto (página 636)

ratificar *v.* aprobar formalmente mediante el voto (página 250)

Rebelión de Shays *s.* revuelta de los granjeros de Massachusetts en protesta por los altos impuestos, ocurrida entre 1786 y 1787 (página 255)

rebelión del Stono *s.* revuelta de esclavos africanos en contra de sus dueños ocurrida en 1793 (página 137)

Rebelión del Whiskey *s.* serie de protestas violentas de los granjeros del oeste de Pennsylvania contra un impuesto al whiskey (página 289)

recesión *s.* grave desaceleración económica (página 590)

reclamación *s.* objeción o motivo para quejarse (página 181)

reclutamiento forzoso *s.* acto que obliga a los hombres a prestar el servicio militar o naval (página 522)

reclutamiento forzoso *s.* acto que obliga a los hombres a prestar el servicio militar o naval (página 319)

Reconstrucción *s.* etapa posterior a la Guerra de Secesión caracterizada por el anhelo de reunificar a los Estados Unidos de América (página 538)

Reconstrucción Presidencial *s.* política impulsada para obligar a los estados confederados a ratificar la Decimotercera Enmienda y a formar nuevos gobiernos, regidos por nuevas constituciones, como condición para poder reintegrarse a la Unión (página 552)

Reconstrucción Radical *s.* nombre dado al plan del Partido Republicano que buscaba aprobar las Leyes de Reconstrucción de 1867 (página 554)

recurso natural *s.* material o sustancia que se encuentra en la naturaleza que se usa para mantener una sociedad o para ser explotado con fines económicos, como minerales, agua o seres vivos (página 114)

redes sociales *s.* medios electrónicos que permiten a las personas comunicarse y formar comunidades online (página 1001)

redistribución de ingresos *s.* un método para distribuir los ingresos de los impuestos federales a los estados y gobiernos locales (página 954)

referendo *s.* práctica democrática que consiste en someter una ley directamente a los votantes para que la aprueben o rechacen (página 669)

refuerzos *s.* más soldados y suministros que se envían para ayudar a las tropas en batalla (página 224)

refugiado *s.* persona que huye a otro país para escapar de un peligro o una persecución (página 630)

regionalismo *s.* lealtad a cualquier sección o región del país de donde una persona es, en vez de a la nación como tal (página 344)

renacimiento *s.* acción de renacer o despertar un interés renovado por las artes o temas académicos (página 748)

rendezvous *s.* mercado temporal donde los tramperos y cazadores se encontraban para comerciar y socializar (página 390)

reparaciones de guerra *s.* el dinero que se paga para compensar los daños de guerra (página 723)

repatriación *s.* regreso o retorno al país de origen o ciudadanía (página 781)

república *s.* forma de gobierno en la cual la gente elige a sus representantes para hablar por ellos y aprobar leyes según sus necesidades (página 222)

república democrática *s.* un país independiente gobernado por sus ciudadanos a través de elecciones y otras formas de votación (página R32)

republicanismo *s.* gobierno en el que la gente elige a sus representantes para crear las leyes (página 244)

Republicanos liberales *s.* grupo durante la década de 1870 que pretendía contrarrestar el creciente tamaño y poderío del gobierno (página 564)

reserva *s.* área territorial dentro de los Estados Unidos destinada específicamente para que los indígenas norteamericanos vivan allí (página 592)

resistencia no violenta *s.* el uso de la desobediencia civil, la no cooperación y otras formas de protesta pacífica para conseguir el cambio social (página 880)

resistencia pasiva *s.* negativa no violenta a obedecer a la autoridad y las leyes (página 341)

responsabilidad cívica *s.* responsabilidad que es obligatoria o esencial para las personas, como votar,

pagar impuestos y servir en jurados (página R34)

responsabilidad personal *s.* responsabilidad que no es obligatoria pero que contribuye a una sociedad más civilizada, como respetar y defender los derechos de los demás, ayudar a la comunidad y mantenerse informado (página R34)

reunificar *v.* juntar de nuevo algo que había sido separado (página 850)

reunión de reavivamiento *s.* reunión religiosa informal que buscaba avivar la fe en la religión del grupo, y que generalmente se hacía en carpas o al aire libre (página 438)

revisión judicial *s.* poder de la Corte Suprema para invalidar cualquier ley que considere inconstitucional, incluso si fue aprobada por el Congreso o firmada por el presidente (página 310)

revolución del mercado *s.* transición de una economía preindustrial a una economía capitalista, o sea orientada hacia el mercado (página 328)

Revolución francesa *s.* rebelión de 1789 contra la monarquía francesa que buscó poner fin al privilegio de las clases altas y demandó igualdad para las clases más bajas (página 289)

Revolución industrial *n.* época en que la producción de bienes hechos con máquinas reemplazó de manera generalizada a los productos hechos a mano (página 328)

Revolución neolítica *s.* transición, en la historia de la humanidad, de una forma de vida basada en la caza y recolección a una forma productora agrícola y ganadera (página 9)

risco *s.* peñasco (página 528)

S

sabotaje *s.* acción de dañar, interferir con o destruir algo (página 719)

salvación *s.* acto de ser perdonado por pecados o faltas cometidas (página 148)

satélite *s.* un objeto que se mueve alrededor de otro mayor (página 904)

secesión *s.* acto de separación formal de una nación o de un territorio para ser independiente (página 367)

sedición *s.* alzamiento contra la autoridad (página 293)

segadora *s.* máquina que corta las plantas de trigo y avena (página 331)

segregación *s.* separación de las personas de acuerdo a su raza (página 465)

Segundo Congreso Continental *s.* grupo de líderes de las colonias norteamericanas que se reunieron para tratar el tema de la tiranía británica, declarar la independencia en 1776 y conducir la Guerra de Independencia hasta formar los Estados Unidos (página 203)

Segundo Gran Despertar *s.* movimiento protestante estadounidense basado en las reuniones de reavivamiento y en una relación directa y emocional con Dios (página 438)

GLOSARIO

seguro nacional de salud *s.* un plan de seguro médico dirigido por el gobierno y abierto a cualquiera que desee sumarse (página 845)

sentada *s.* una protesta organizada donde la gente se sienta en el suelo y se niega a abandonar el sitio (página 882)

separación de poderes *s.* división de poderes gubernamentales entre las tres ramas del gobierno de los EE. UU.: el poder ejecutivo, el poder judicial y el poder legislativo (página 258)

separatismo negro *s.* la división política y cultural de los negros y blancos dentro de una sociedad (página 914)

separatista *s.* persona que quería dejar la Iglesia de Inglaterra (página 100)

sequía *s.* periodo prolongado con poca o ninguna lluvia (página 774)

servicio doméstico *s.* trabajo o tareas del hogar que hace una o varias personas en la casa de otro (página 433)

servidumbre *s.* estado o condición de siervo o esclavo (página 538)

servidumbre negra *s.* esclavitud de tipo económico que condenaba a los trabajadores afroamericanos a permanecer como aparceros de los terratenientes (página 559)

siervo *s.* persona que vivía y trabajaba en la tierra perteneciente a un noble o a un señor feudal (página 37)

sindicato de oficio *s.* sindicato que defiende los derechos y protecciones de los trabajadores, cuyos miembros se especializan en el mismo oficio de quienes defienden (página 443)

sindicato de trabajadores *s.* asociación voluntaria de trabajadores que usa su poder para negociar condiciones mejores de trabajo (página 442)

Síndrome de Inmunodeficiencia Adquirida (SIDA) *s.* la etapa final de una enfermedad causada por un virus que ataca el sistema del cuerpo humano que combate las enfermedades (página 971)

sirviente ligado por contrato *s.* persona obligada por contrato a trabajar, generalmente sin paga, a cambio de un boleto gratis a las colonias (página 93)

Sistema americano (American System) *s.* política para promover el sistema industrial de los EE. UU. mediante aranceles, subsidios federales para construir carreteras y otras obras públicas y un banco nacional para controlar la moneda (página 342)

sistema de fábrica *n.* método de producción en el que grandes grupos de operarios trabajaban en un solo lugar (página 328)

sistema de señorío *s.* sistema económico en el cual los campesinos están vinculados a un señor feudal y trabajan su tierra, o señorío, a cambio de comida y vivienda (página 37)

sitio *s.* táctica militar durante la cual las tropas de soldados rodean una ciudad para intentar apoderarse de ella (página 401)

smog *s.* un tipo de contaminación atmosférica que se desarrolla cuando la luz solar reacciona con los productos químicos de fuentes tales como los escapes de los automóviles y las emisiones de las fábricas (página 958)

soberanía popular *s.* idea de que los residentes de una región o país deciden sobre un tema mediante el voto (página 466)

soberano *adj.* que posee la autoridad para gobernarse o que es un gobierno independiente (página 250)

soborno *s.* dádiva en dinero o en privilegios que se da subrepticiamente a funcionarios a cambio de favores políticos (página 564)

socialismo *s.* sistema económico en que el gobierno controla los recursos económicos, que son de propiedad colectiva (página 776)

sociedad de ayuda mutua *s.* organización formada por miembros de un determinado grupo para apoyarse mutuamente con recursos económicos u otro tipo de asistencia (página 631)

sociedad fiduciaria *s.* grupo de corporaciones administrado por un consejo, sin que éste sea el propietario directo (página 627)

sociedad por acciones *s.* compañía cuyos accionistas poseen acciones en la propia compañía (página 92)

status quo *s.* el estado existente de una situación (página 902)

subsidio *s.* fondo del gobierno para mejoras y apoyo al comercio (página 342)

suburbanización *s.* asentamiento de la población de las ciudades en comunidades de la periferia (página 856)

suburbio *s.* área residencial que se localiza en los límites de una ciudad o de un pueblo (página 634)

sufragio *s.* derecho al voto (página 451)

sufragista *s.* persona que apoya la lucha por el derecho a votar y ser votado, especialmente en beneficio del derecho de las mujeres a participar en los procesos electorales (página 682)

sumergible *s.* un submarino alemán (página 713)

Sunbelt *s.* regiones del sur o suroeste de Estados unidos que tienen invierno cálidos (página 854)

sweatshop *s.* tipo de fábrica en donde se pagan salarios muy bajos, en condiciones de hacinamiento e inseguridad, y donde las jornadas laborales son extenuantes (página 647)

T

tanque *s.* un vehículo blindado y fuertemente armado, que usa bandas de rodaje en vez de ruedas (página 713)

tasa de aduana *s.* impuesto sobre bienes importados y exportados (página 319)

tele-evangelista *s.* líder religioso que comparte enseñanzas cristianas en una emisión televisiva con horario regular (página 970)

telégrafo *s.* máquina que envía mensajes a grandes distancias mediante señales eléctricas en código a través de cables eléctricos (página 331)

telegrama Zimmermann *s.* telegrama secreto que los alemanes enviaron al embajador alemán en México, proponiéndole que México se sumara a la Primera Guerra Mundial del lado alemán (página 715)

teoría del dominó *s.* una idea de la Guerra Fría que sostenía que los países cercanos a un vecino comunista son más propensos a adoptar ese régimen (página 926)

tercera clase *s.* término histórico para la sección inferior de un barco en la que viajaban los que pagaban el boleto más barato (página 430)

terraplén *s.* movimiento de tierra hecho por el hombre, que se levanta como defensa (página 204)

terreno *s.* características físicas de la tierra (página 204)

Territorio Indígena *s.* área de tierra, en lo que hoy es Oklahoma y parte de Kansas y Nebraska, a la cual fueron obligados a migrar los indígenas norteamericanos (página 368)

territorio no organizado *s.* tierras bajo el gobierno federal pero que no le pertenecían a ningún estado (página 345)

textil *s.* tela o tejido hecho de algodón u otras materias primas (página 328)

tierras fronterizas *(backcountry)* *s.* la zona oeste de las Colonias del Sur justo al este de los montes Apalaches (página 134)

tipi *s.* tienda de campaña que tiene forma de cono y que está hecha con pieles de búfalo (página 27)

tiranía *s.* abuso de poder injusto por parte de un gobernante absoluto (página 181)

tolerancia *s.* aceptación de otros (página 144)

toma de posesión *s.* ceremonia que marca el comienzo de una presidencia (página 279)

trabajador migratorio *s.* trabajador que se desplaza de un empleo a otro según sea necesario; por lo general, se trata de trabajadores agrícolas (página 586)

trabajo infantil *s.* contratación de niños para realizar algún tipo de trabajo, a menudo en condiciones peligrosas y con salarios muy bajos (página 647)

trabajo social *s.* trabajo cuyo propósito es mejorar las condiciones de vida de otras personas (página 680)

traición *s.* delito cometido por ayudar al enemigo o planear un derrocamiento; la falta de lealtad a su propia nación (página 367)

traidor *s.* persona que traiciona a su propia gente, nación o causa (página 99)

transahariano *adj.* que cruza el Sahara (página 42)

tranvía *s.* vehículo sobre rieles que recorre las avenidas de una ciudad y puede transportar a muchos pasajeros en un solo viaje, como un tren (página 634)

GLOSARIO

trascendentalismo *s.* movimiento intelectual y social en las décadas de 1830 y 1840 que pedía ir más allá de lo que la sociedad esperaba de cada uno (página 444)

Trastorno de Estrés Postraumático *s.* un síndrome provocado por una herida o trauma psicológico (página 952)

tratado *s.* acuerdo de paz (página 158)

Tratado de Greenville *s.* tratado entre los Estados Unidos y varias naciones indígenas en el cual las naciones indígenas cedieron sus tierras a los Estados Unidos, en lo que hoy es Ohio e Indiana (página 288)

Tratado de París de 1783 *s.* Tratado de París de 1783 acuerdo entre Gran Bretaña y los Estados Unidos, en el cual Gran Bretaña reconoce la independencia de sus colonias en Norteamérica y se determinan los límites iniciales de los Estados Unidos (página 244)

Tratado de Versailles *s.* el tratado que acabó oficialmente con la Primera Guerra Mundial (página 723)

tregua *s.* acuerdo para dejar de luchar (página 371)

Tren Clandestino *s.* red de personas que trabajaron juntas para ayudar a los afroamericanos a escapar de la esclavitud en los estados sureños de los EE. UU. hacia los estados del Norte y Canadá antes de la Guerra Civil (página 447)

tundra *s.* terreno plano y sin árboles de las regiones ártica y subártica (página 26)

U

unionista *s.* miembro del Partido de la Unión Constitucional (página 472)

urbanización *s.* proceso mediante el cual los patrones de tipo económico, industrial y social pasaron de las zonas rurales a las ciudades (página 634)

V

vacío legal *s.* lenguaje poco claro que les permite a ciertas personas burlar las leyes y no obedecerlas (página 674)

vasallo *s.* en el sistema feudal medieval europeo, era una persona, usualmente un noble de menor rango, que recibía tierras y protección de un señor feudal a cambio de prestarle obediencia y servicio (página 36)

veta *s.* rico depósito de minerales, como plata u oro (página 582)

vetar *v.* rechazar oficialmente una decisión o propuesta dictada por el poder legislativo (página 375)

veterano *s.* persona que sirvió al ejército (página 534)

vietnamización *s.* estrategia militar que permitió el reemplazo gradual de las tropas estadounidenses con tropas sudvietnamitas durante la Guerra de Vietnam (página 952)

virreinato *s.* territorio gobernado por un virrey (página 58)

virrey *s.* gobernador de las colonias españolas en las Américas que representaba al Rey y la Reina de España (página 58)

viruela *s.* virus mortal que causa fiebre alta y pequeñas ampollas en la piel (página 56)

virus de la inmunodeficiencia humana (VIH) *s.* un virus que ataca el sistema del cuerpo humano que combate las enfermedades (página 971)

vivienda de bajo costo *s.* viviendas que pueden ser pagadas por personas con bajos ingresos (página 845)

W

World Wide Web *s.* el sistema que permite que los sitios de Internet sean identificados por direcciones, vinculados entre sí y localizados mediante búsquedasel sistema (página 1000)

Z

zona de influencia *s.* declaración hecha por un país para tener influencia exclusiva en las actividades políticas o económicas de otro país (página 690)

zona de ocupación *s.* área de un país en la que un ejército extranjero tiene el control (página 846)

VOCABULARIO ACADÉMICO

a punto de *a.* listo para que algo suceda (página 982)

abarcar *v.* formar un círculo en torno a algo; redondear; incluir (página 559)

abominable *a.* digno de odio o malestar (página 366)

aclamación *s.* elogio entusiasta (página 285)

activista *a.* combativo y determinado; que actúa como si combatiera en una guerra (página 467)

adquisición *s.* acción de obtener algo en calidad de propiedad; artículo obtenido por alguien (página 37)

agitación *s.* confusión, turbulencia (página 727)

alegoría *s.* historia contada a través de símbolos, en la cual los personajes y otros elementos narrativos representan acciones y emociones humanas (página 444)

aniquilar *v.* destruir totalmente (página 795)

ardiente *a.* quien se muestra muy ansioso o apasionado en el objetivo de realizar su deseo (página 282)

arduo *a.* difícil; que requiere de un gran esfuerzo para poder lograrse (página 395)

árido *a.* extremadamente seco (como un desierto) (página 24)

asignar *v.* dividir y repartir con un fin específico (página 954)

atrocidad *s.* acto extremadamente brutal o cruel (página 593)

consenso *s.* acuerdo general, armonía (página 889)

dar lugar *v.* traer algo nuevo (página 717)

delimitación *s.* acción mediante la cual se miden y establecen los límites entre dos o más áreas territoriales (página 252)

despectivo *a.* degradar o despreciar algo o a alguien; siempre con la intención de rebajar a alguien o a algo (página 641)

directamente *adv.* francamente, honestamente (página 873)

dispersar *v.* esparcir y desplegar a todo lo largo y ancho (página 586)

divisivo *a.* que causa disenso y desunión con ánimo de discordia (página 462)

élite *s.* persona o grupo que se considera superior en términos de riqueza, intelecto, educación o, incluso, en capacidades atléticas (página 668)

elocuencia *s.* capacidad de hablar de manera elegante y articulada (página 886)

espécimen *s.* muestra de alguna criatura o parte de la naturaleza, tal como una planta, un animal o un mineral (página 300)

evadir *v.* evitar ser capturado o eludir la obligación de dar una respuesta directa y verdadera (página 596)

evasión *s.* el acto de evitar ser descubierto o castigado, usualmente con sigilo (página 735)

explotar *v.* aprovecharse de personas o recursos, por lo general con fines de lucro (página 665)

fértil *a.* capaz de dar vida, como parir crías o hacer crecer plantas (página 24)

fervor *s.* sentimiento o celo muy intenso hacia algo, generalmente espiritual (página 439)

filosofía *s.* conjunto de creencias argumentadas por una persona o por un grupo (página 39)

formidable *a.* asombroso, generalmente de manera temible (página 223)

habilidad *s.* talento natural o destreza que tiene una persona (página 768)

iconografía *s.* objetos o símbolos representativos de una cultura o religión (página 131)

imparcialidad *s.* neutralidad, equidad (página 714)

indigente *a.* carente de riqueza o recursos; empobrecido (página 768)

indispensable *a.* necesario; algo de lo que no se puede prescindir (página 103)

indulgente *a.* tolerante; comprensible (página 552)

inherentemente *adv.* esencialmente, naturalmente (página 875)

inhibidor *a.* capaz de aminorar la fuerza o el poder de alguien o de algo; que cuenta con una acción efectiva en términos negativos (página 647)

inmoral *a.* moralmente equivocado (página 996)

intervenir *v.* interferir, generalmente para provocar o prevenir una acción (página 397)

intimidar *v.* servirse de amenazas, por lo general para obligar a alguien a hacer lo que se le exige (página 371)

legado *s.* conjunto de conocimientos o realizaciones transmitido de una generación a otra (página 250)

letal *a.* mortal (página 647)

mártir *s.* persona que sacrifica su vida o algo de gran valor en beneficio de una causa superior (página 469)

mecanizado *a.* que ha sido realizado íntegra o parcialmente por máquinas (página 328)

metralla *s.* conjunto de pedazos filosos lanzados por un proyectil, una granada o, incluso, por una bala de cañón (página 172)

monetario *a.* que tiene, representa o asume la forma del dinero (página 303)

nulificar *v.* eliminar o negar, especialmente en términos legales anular algo (página 366)

ofensiva *s.* lucha iniciada por uno de los bandos que participan en una guerra o disputa (bélica, política, personal e, incluso, deportiva) (página 231)

ortodoxo *a.* que sigue una doctrina religiosa de manera estricta (página 101)

pacto *s.* acuerdo o promesa que negocian dos o más partes en conflicto (página 179)

parcela *s.* terreno o cierta área delimitada de tierra (página 598)

perdonar *v.* eximir, excusar a otra persona de alguna culpa por voluntad propia (página 552)

perplejo *a.* quien se queda de pronto sin palabras para expresar sus ideas o emociones (página 58)

prestigioso *a.* que cuenta con una reputación de calidad, estima y respeto (página 362)

prominente *s.* ampliamente conocido (página 971)

próspero *a.* que tiene éxito económico (página 842)

prótesis *s.* miembro, extremidad o parte artificial del cuerpo humano (página 494)

pudiente *a.* rico, próspero (página 855)

quinta *s.* finca o casa principal de una hacienda (página 64)

rehabilitar *v.* restaurar la salud o la reputación original (página 441)

rellenar *v.* volver a poner todo el contenido que originalmente tenía algo (página 495)

renunciar *v.* rendirse, a menudo como resultado de una derrota o la imposición de una multa (página 922)

represalia *s.* el acto de de vengarse o de actuar en contra de alguien porque te ha perjudicado (página 791)

retórica *s.* manera de usar las palabras para expresar una idea, comúnmente para persuadir (página 562)

sentimiento *s.* una actitud basada en emociones (página 815)

sincronizar *v.* hacer que ocurran al mismo tiempo (página 740)

soberanía *s.* área donde se puede ejercer a plenitud la función o la autoridad de una entidad (página 328)

socavar *v.* debilitar (página 906)

suborbital *a.* menos de un círculo completo de un objeto o cuerpo alrededor de otro; menos que un recorrido circular completo (página 905)

susceptible *a.* capaz de percibir la acción o intención de otra persona (página 527)

tenencia *s.* acción de ostentar algo valioso, como un terreno o una posición relevante, o el período durante el cual dicho cargo u objeto es ostentado (página 555)

valentía *s.* tener gran valor, coraje o voluntad para enfrentar cualquier obstáculo (página 520)

vigoroso *a.* hecho con energía o con fuerza (página 845)

ACKNOWLEDGMENTS

NATIONAL GEOGRAPHIC LEARNING | CENGAGE

National Geographic Learning gratefully acknowledges the contributions of the following National Geographic Explorers and affiliates to our program:

Jason DeLeon, National Geographic Explorer
Ken Garrett, National Geographic Photographer
Caroline Gerdes, National Geographic Explorer
Fredrik Hiebert, National Geographic Archaeologist-in-Residence
Barrington Irving, Jr., National Geographic Explorer
Kathryn Keane, Vice President, National Geographic Exhibitions
John Kelly, National Geographic Explorer
William Kelso, National Geographic Explorer
William Parkinson, National Geographic Explorer
Robert Reid, National Geographic Digital Nomad
Andrés Ruzo, National Geographic Explorer
Pardis Sabeti, National Geographic Explorer
Joel Sartore, National Geographic Photographer
Donald Slater, National Geographic Explorer

Photographic Credits

T2 ©NASA. T3 (bl) Mark Thiessen/National Geographic Creative. (c) Mary Lynne Ashley Photography/National Geographic Learning. (br) National Geographic Creative. T4 (tl) Marcie Goodale/National Geographic Learning. (tr) Brian Nelson/National Geographic Learning. (cl) ©Kenneth Garrett Photography. (cr) Robert Reid/National Geographic Creative. (bl) KMK/National Geographic Creative. (br) Andrés Ruzo/National Geographic Creative. T5 (tl) ©Jason DeLeón. (tcl) ©George Ohrstrom. (tcr) ©Taylor Mickal. (tr) Robert Sullivan/Getty Images. (cl) ©David Kilper/WUSTL. (ccl) ©Ira Block/National Geographic Creative. (ccr) Robert Reid/National Geographic. (cr) ©Chiun-Kai Shih/National Geographic Creative. (bl) JOEL SARTORE/National Geographic Creative. (br) ©Khiem DoBa. T7 (tr) Cory Richards/National Geographic Creative. T8 KMK/National Geographic Learning. T9 ©George Ohrstrom/Kenneth Garrett Photography. T10 (tr) Robert Reid/National Geographic Creative. (bl) Marcie Goodale/National Geographic Learning. T11 Rebecca Hale/National Geographic Creative. T12 National Geographic Learning. T14 Mary Lynne Ashley Photography/National Geographic Learning. T26 RALPH LEE HOPKINS/National Geographic Creative T27 The Departure of the Mayflower for England in 1621, 1941 (oil on canvas)/Wyeth, Newell Convers (1882–1945)/Private Collection/Bridgeman Images. T28–T29 (spread) Washington Crossing the Delaware River, 25th December 1776, 1851 (oil on canvas) (copy of an original painted in 1848)/Leutze, Emanuel Gottlieb (1816–68)/Metropolitan Museum of Art, New York, USA/Bridgeman Images. T30–T31 (spread) ©Ken Garrett Photography. T32–T33 (spread) Barney Burstein/Getty Images. T34–T35 (spread) Jennifer Counter/Moment/Getty Images. T36–T37 (spread) PhotoQuest/Archive Photos/Getty Images. T38 Smithsonian American Art Museum, Washington, DC/Art Resource, NY. T40–T41 (spread) Bruce Davidson/Magnum Photos. T42–T43 (spread) Library of Congress, Prints & Photographs Division, LC-DIG-highsm-12456. T45 ©AFP PHOTO/Robert Sullivan/Getty Images. T46 aimintang/Getty Images. T47 Erik Sampers/Getty Images. 0–1 (spread) RozanneHakala/ Getty Images. 1 (tl) Mark Thiessen/National Geographic Creative. 2 Fred Hiebert. 3 (tl) ©National Postal Museum/Smithsonian. (br) Mark Summers/ National Geographic Learning. 4 (bg) Daniel Gomes Lacerda/EyeEm/Getty Images. 6 ©Levi Stroud/Michigan News. 7 ©National Museum of the American Indian, Smithsonian Institution (6/8904). Photo by NMAI Photo Services. 8 (tr) Nicolle Rager Fuller, National Science Foundation. (cr) Philippe Psaila/Science Source. (c) Daniel Gomes Lacerda/EyeEm/Getty Images. 9 IRA BLOCK/National Geographic Creative. 10 (tr) Werner Forman/Getty Images. (cl) Marilyn Angel Wynn/Getty Images. (c) Marilyn Angel Wynn/Getty Images. (bc1) IRA BLOCK/National Geographic Creative. (bc2) Werner Forman/Getty Images. 11 (tr) ©National Museum of the American Indian, Smithsonian Institution 5/4385. (cr) Heritage Image Partnership Ltd/Alamy Stock Photo. (cl) Aldo Tutino/Art Resource, NY. (bl) Bryan Mullennix/Getty Images. (br) Mask with antlers, 1400–1600 (wood & bone)/Mississippian culture (c. 800–1500)/DIRK BAKKER PHOTOGRAPHY/Private Collection/Bridgeman Images. 12–13 (spread) RALPH LEE HOPKINS/National Geographic Creative. 14 (tr) Victor R. Boswell, Jr./National Geographic Creative. (tl) Simon Dannhauer/ Shutterstock. com. (br) WernerForman/Getty Images. 15 (tl) Inca mask (gold with red & green paint), Peruvian School/MuseoArqueologia, Lima, Peru/ Photo Boltin Picture Library/The Bridgeman Art Library. (cr) akg-images/ The Image Works. (bl) Fine Art Images/Fine Art Images/Superstock. 16–17 (spread) Danita Delimont/Alamy Stock Photo. 18–19 (spread) ©Macy Davco. 20 ©Ken Stanback/500px. 21 kenneth-cheung/Getty Images. 22 (tr) ©Mark Malijan Photography. (b) ©Mark Malijan Photography. 23 Werner Forman/ Getty Images. 24 Werner Forman Archive/Bridgeman Images. 26 George H. H. Huey/age fotostock. 28 Tony Linck/Tony Linck/Superstock. 30 IRA BLOCK/National Geographic Creative. (tr) IRA BLOCK/National Geographic Creative. 31 ©David Kilper/WUSTL. 32–33 (spread) ©National Museum of the American Indian, Smithsonian Institution 9/7850 & 9/7851. 32 (bc) National Museum of the American Indian, Smithsonian Institution 20/2175. 33 ©National Museum of the American Indian, Smithsonian Institution 14/9624. 34 (c) Werner Forman/Getty Images. (bl) Smithsonian American Art Museum, Washington, DC/Art Resource, NY. (br) Werner Forman/Universal Image Group/Getty Images. 37

Bettmann/ Getty Images. 38 J. Paul Getty Museum, Los Angeles, USA/Bridgeman Images. 41 Chris Lawrence/Alamy Stock Photo. 43 ©Trevor Cole/500px. 44 ©JaumeCusidó/500px. 46 BibliothequeNationale de France/National Geographic Creative. 47 Abraham Cresques/Getty Images. 50–51 (spread) The Columbus Foundation. 52 James L. Stanfield/National Geographic Creative. 53 AP Images/Elaine Thompson. 54 Alfredo DagliOrti/The Art Archive at Art Resource, NY. 55 ©The New York Public Library Digital Collections. 56 Museum of Fine Arts, Houston, Texas, USA/Gift of Alfred C. Glassell, Jr./Bridgeman Images. 57 Private Collection/Bridgeman Images. 58 George H. H. Huey/AlamyStockPhoto. 61 Cleveland Museum of Art, OH, USA/Bridgeman Images. 62 National Portrait Gallery/National Portrait Gallery. 63 Interfoto/Interfoto. 65 (t) MARKLEY BOYER/National Geographic. (c) Robert Clark/National Geographic Creative. 67 Spring Images/Alamy Stock Photo. 68 Damon Winter/The New York Times/Redux. 69 (tr) George Musil/Getty Images. 71 National Geographic Learning. 72 Library of Congress. 75 (t) Elsa Hahne for Whitney Plantation. (bl) ©British Library, London, UK/British Library Board. All Rights Reserved/Bridgeman Images. 78 JON FOSTER/National Geographic Creative. 80–81 (spread) Bridgeman Images. 82 (tr) Robert Clark/National Geographic Creative. (cl) bpk, Berlin/Art Resource, NY. (b) ClaudineVM/Getty Images. 83 (tl) ViewStock/AGE Fotostock. (cr) The Trustees of the British Museum/Art Resource, NY. (br) Science & Society Picture Library/Getty Images. 84–85 (spread) Joe Raedle/Getty Images News/Getty Images. 86 Photo Researchers, Inc/Alamy Stock Photo. 87 The Trustees of the British Museum/Art Resource, NY. 88 Anna Pomaville/Getty Images. 89 Peter Newark American Pictures/Bridgeman Images. 90 Mark Thiessen/National Geographic Creative. 91 The Trustees of the British Museum/Art Resource, NY. 92 Cameron Davidson/Getty Images. 93 (c) Pocahontas, c. 1852 (oil on canvas)/ Sully, Thomas (1783–1872)/VIRGINIA HISTORICAL SOCIETY/Virginia Historical Society, Richmond, Virginia, USA/Bridgeman Images. (tl) Pocahontas (c. 1595–1617) 1616 (oil on canvas)/English School, (17th century)/PETER NEWARK'S PICTURES/Private Collection/Bridgeman Images. (tr) W. LANGDON KIHN/National Geographic Creative. 94 (t) ©Historic Jamestowne. (bl) Robert Clark/National Geographic Creative. 95 (tr) Robert Clark/National Geographic Creative. (tl) ©Historic Jamestowne. (b) ©Historic Jamestowne. 96 IRA BLOCK/National Geographic Creative. 97 Art Resource, NY. 99 The Burning of Jamestown, 1676, illustration from 'Colonies and Nation' by Woodrow Wilson, pub. in Harper's Magazine, 1901 (litho)/Pyle, Howard (1853–1911) (after)/Private Collection/Bridgeman Images. 100 ©Pilgrim Hall Museum. 101 ROBERT SISSON/National Geographic Creative. 102 Bridgeman Images. 103 Kean Collection/Getty Images. 104 T. J. Kirkpatrick/Getty Images News/Getty Images. 107 (tl) North Wind Picture Archives/Alamy Stock Photo. (tr) H. S. Photos/Alamy Stock Photo. (b) H. S. Photos/Alamy Stock photo. 109 US Capitol. 111 CPC Collection/Alamy Stock photo. 113 (t) Kevin Fleming/Corbis/VCG/Getty Images. (cl) Richard Ellis/Alamy Stock Photo. 117 AP Images/BRUCE PARKER. 117 The Washington Post/Getty Images. 120–121 (spread) Jon Bilous/Shutterstock.com. 122 ReinhardDirscherl/Alamy Stock Photo. 123 Science & Society Picture Library/Getty Images. 125 Blackbeard the pirate (coloured engraving)/English School, (19th century)/PETER NEWARK'S PICTURES/Private Collection/Bridgeman Images. 127 Ralph Earl Gentleman with Attendant, 1785–88 Oil on canvas 30 . x 25 . in. Courtesy of the New Britain Museum of American Art Harriet Russell Stanley Fund 1948. 6. 128 Joseph Sohm/Getty Images. 129 Bettmann/Getty Images. 130 (t) ©Nathan Hamilton. (inset) ©Donald Slater. 131 ©Donald Slater. 133 ©Courtesy, Georgia Archives, Vanishing Georgia Collection, sap093. 135 zrfphoto/Getty Images. 136 Bill Grant/Alamy Stock Photo. 137 ©Division of Culture & the Arts, National Museum of American History, Behring Center, Smithsonian Institution. 138 OlaudahEquiano alias GustavusVassa, a slave, 1789 (mezzotint)/BRITISH LIBRARY/British Library, London, UK/ Bridgeman Images. 142 ©The Metropolitan Museum of Art. Image source: Art Resource, NY. 143 ©JC Shamrock/500px. 145 Quaker Meeting (oil on canvas), English School, (18th–19th century)/Museum of Fine Arts, Boston, Massachusetts, USA/Bequest of Maxim Karolik/The Bridgeman Art Library. (bl) czarny_bez/Getty Images. (br) Warming pan, probably from Boston, 1780–90 (brass & maple or birch)/American School, (18th century)/HISTORIC NEW ENGLAND/Historic New England, Boston, Massachusetts, USA/Bridgeman Images. 149 George Whitefield preaching, Collet, John (c. 1725–80)/Private Collection/The Bridgeman Art Library. 150 Heritage Image Partnership Ltd/Alamy Stock Photo. 151 Portrait of King James II, c. 1690 (oil on canvas)/English School, (17th century)/National Portrait Gallery, London, UK/Bridgeman Images. 152 Bettmann/Getty Images. 153 (tl) Bettmann/Getty Images. (cl) ©The New York Times. 156 Ball-Headed Tomahawk Club (wood and brass), American School/Ashmolean Museum, University of Oxford, UK/Bridgeman Images. 157 AKG Images. 159 Pontiac (1720–69) 1763 (oil on canvas), Stanley, John Mix (1814–72)/Private Collection/Peter Newark American Pictures/The Bridgeman Art Library. 162 (tl) Philip Straub/National Geographic Creative. (tr) Robert Clark/ National Geographic Creative. 164–165 (spread) Washington Crossing the Delaware River, 25th December 1776, 1851 (oil on canvas) (copy of an original painted in 1848), Leutze, Emanuel Gottlieb (1816–68)/Metropolitan Museum of Art, New York, USA/The Bridgeman Art Library. 166 (t) Joseph Sohm; Visions of America/Corbis. (cl) Don Troiani/Corbis. (b) Mike Randolph/Masterfile/Corbis. 167 (tr) Fraser Hall/robertharding/Corbis. (br) Gianni DagliOrti/Corbis. 168–169 (spread) Kenneth Garrett. 170 Richard Freeda/Aurora Photos. 171 Richard Freeda/Aurora Photos. 172–173 (spread) AP Images/Ric Tapia. 174 National Postal Museum, Smithsonian. 174 KevorkDjansezian/Getty Images News/Getty Images. 175 (cl) Ken Cedeno/Corbis. (bl) HALSTEAD; DIRCK/Corbis. (cr) Tim Sloan/AFP/Getty Images. (br) Apollo 11 Commander Neil Armstrong/NASA Kennedy Space Center (NASA-KSC)/National Aeronautics and Space Administration (NASA). 176–177 (spread) ©National Musuem of American History. 177 ©National Musuem of American History. 178 North Wind Picture Archives/The Image Works. 179 Library of Congress Geography and Map Division Washington, D.

Civil War Archive/Bridgeman Images. **442** Library of Congress. **443** ©The Metropolitan Museum of Art. Image source: Art Resource, NY. **445** Tomas Abad/Alamy Stock Photo. **446** Esclave/Photo Gerald Bloncourt/Bridgeman Images. **447** MPI/Getty Images. **448** Fotosearch/Getty Images. **450** Library of Congress/Getty Images. **451** Library of Congress/Getty Images. **454** JIM RICHARDSON/National Geographic. **456–457** (spread) Jennifer Counter/Moment/Getty Images. **458** (tl) Schomburg Center, NYPL/Art Resource, NY. (tr) ©National Museum of American History, Political History. (bc) Pictorial Press Ltd/Alamy Stock Photo. **459** (tr) ©National Museum of American History Smithsonian. (cl) ©Chicago History Museum. (bc) John Stevenson/ Getty Images. **460–461** (spread) DamirFrkovic/Masterfile. **464** (bl) National Portrait Gallery, Smithsonian Institution/Art Resource, NY. (br) Schomburg Center, NYPL/Art Resource, NY. **465** Iberfoto/Superstock. **467** John Brown, 1859 (colourlitho), Balling, Ole Peter Hansen (1823–1906)/Private Collection/Peter Newark American Pictures/Bridgeman Images. **468** Pictorial Press Ltd/Alamy Stock Photo. **469** ©Kenneth Garret Photography. **470** Abraham Lincoln and Stephen A. Douglas debating at Charleston, Illinois on 18th September 1858, 1918 (oil on canvas), Root, Robert Marshall (1863–1937)/Private Collection/ Bridgeman Images. **471** Niday Picture Library/Alamy Stock Photo. **472** Niday Picture Library/Alamy Stock Photo. **474** Everett Collection Inc/Alamy Stock Photo. **475** Abraham Lincoln (1809–65) 1860 (b/w photo), Hesler, Alexander (1823–95)/Private Collection/ Peter Newark American Pictures/Bridgeman Images. **477** Charles Phelps Cushing/ClassicStock/Getty Images. **480–481** (spread) ©Kenneth Garrett Photography. **482** The Library of Congress. **483** ©Armed Forces History Division, National Museum of American History, Smithsonian Institution. **484** The Library of Congress. **484** (b) ©Armed Forces History Division, National Museum of American History, Smithsonian Institution. **485** (tl) Smithsonian American Art Museum, Washington, DC/Art Resource, NY. (b) ©Historical Society of Carroll County. **487** ©The Library of Congress. **489** ©Jason Demek/500px. **490** Library of Congress, Prints & Photographs Division, Reproduction number LC-DIG-cwpb-04402 (digital file from original neg.)LC-B8172-0001 (b&w film neg.). **491** (tl) ©Chicago Historical Society. (tr) ©Confederate Memorial Hall Museum, New Orleans. **492** (bl) ©Confederate Memorial Hall Museum. (br) ©Confederate Memorial Hall Museum. **493** (t) ©Confederate Memorial Hall Museum. (b) ©Confederate Memeorial Hall Museum. **494** Wellcome Images/Science Source. **495** Science & Society Picture Library/Getty Images. **496** ©Clara Barton National Historic Site/National Parks Service. **497** Fotosearch/Getty Images. **498** ©George Ohrstrom II. **499** ©Kenneth Garrett Photography. **500** ©Kenneth Garret Photography. **501** ©Kenneth Garret Photography. **502** ©Kenneth Garret Photography. **503** ©Kenneth Garret Photography. National Geographic Learning. **508** Library of Congress, Prints & Photographs Division, LC-DIG-cwpb-07310. **509** Library of Congress, Prints & Photographs Division, LC-DIG-ppmsca-31277. **513** Library of Congress, Prints & Photographs Division, LC-DIG-stereo-1s02987. **514–515** (spread) ©Kenneth Garrett Photography. **516** Library of Congress, Prints & Photographs Division, LC-DIG-cwpb-04351. **518** The Art Institute of Chicago, IL, USA/Major Acquisitions Centennial Endowment/Bridgeman Images. **519** Smithsonian American Art Museum, Washington, DC/Art Resource, NY. **521** B Christopher/Alamy Stock Photo. **523** The Everett Collection. **525** LynseyAddario/Getty Reportage. **526** Library of Congress, Prints & Photographs Division, LC-DIG-ppmsca-33993. **529** Library of Congress, Prints & Photographs Division, LC-B8184-7964-A. **531** Ian Dagnall/Alamy Stock Photo. **532** Library of Congress, Prints & Photographs Division, LC-DIG-ds-03106. **535** TOM LOVELL/National Geographic Creative. **536–537** (spread) ©Kenneth Garrett Photography. **539** Chicago History Museum, USA/Bridgeman Images. **543** Library of Congress, Prints & Photographs Division, LC-DIG-pga-03898. **544–545** (spread) Kenneth Garrett Photography. **546** Hulton Archive/Staff/Getty Images. **548** Library of Congress. **549** (tr) SSPL/Science Museum/Art Resource, NY. (br) Library of Congress. **550** (t) Sunday morning in Virginia, 1877 (oil on canvas)/Homer, Winslow (1836–1910)/CINCINNATI ART MUSEUM/Cincinnati Art Museum, Ohio, USA/Bridgeman Images. (b) National Archives Washington DC/The Art Archive at Art Resource, NY. **551** ©Collection of the Massachusettes Historical Society. **553** Victor Cardoner/Moment Open/ Getty Images. **555** Bettmann/Getty Images. **557** Library of Congress Prints and Photographs Division Washington, D. C. **558** Angus Osborn/Getty Images. **560** MPI/Getty Images. **561** (tl) Everett Collection Historical/Alamy Stock photo. (cr) Universal Images Group/Art Resource, NY. **562** ©National Parks Service. **563** Library of Congress Prints and Photographs Division Washington, D. C. **564** The Rush from the New York Stock Exchange on September 18, 1873, from 'A History of the Last Quarter Century' by E. Benjamin Andrews, published in Scribner's Magazine, July 1895 (oil on canvas), Pyle, Howard (1853–1911)/Delaware Art Museum, Wilmington, USA/The Bridgeman Art Library. **567** MPI/Getty Images. **568** Library of Congress, Prints and Photographs Division, LC-DIG-ppmsca-23855. **570–571** (spread) PhotoQuest/Archive Photos/Getty Images. **572** (cl) George H. H. Huey/Alamy Stock Photo. (cl) Atlaspix/Alamy Stock Photo. (br) AP Images/ JOEL PAGE. **573** (tl) National Park Service, Statue of Liberty National Monument and Ellis Island. (tr) ©National Museum of American History, Political History. (bl) DEA/A. DAGLI ORTI/Getty Images. (br) Michael Nicholson/Getty Images. **574–575** (spread) CHRIS JOHNS/National Geographic Creative. **576–577** (spread) JOEL SARTORE/National Geographic Creative. **578** The Buffalo Hunt (colourlitho)/Catlin, George (1796–1872)/Private Collection/ Bridgeman Images. **579** (tr) Hulton Archive/ Getty Images. (b) William Hornaday and Bison c. 1905. **580** ©Division of Culture & the Arts, National Museum of American History, Behring Center, Smithsonian Institution. **581** ©Sean Beckett/500px. **582–583** (spread) Pete Ryan/Getty Images. **584** Tar_Design/Shutterstock. com. **585** Christie's Images/Bridgeman Images; Art © T. H. Benton and R. P. Benton Testamentary Trusts/UMB Bank Trustee/Licensed by VAGA, New York, NY. **587** PhotoQuest/Getty Images. **588** National Geographic Learning. **589** Bettmann/Getty Images. **590** Library of Congress Prints and Photographs Division Washington, D. C. **593** Library of Congress

Prints and Photographs Division Washington, D. C. **594** Canton, Kansas/ National Geographic. **595** (t) Joel Sartore/National Geographic Creative. (b) JOEL SARTORE/National Geographic Creative. **597** Photo Researchers, Inc/ Alamy Stock Photo. **599** (t) ©National Museum of the American Indian/ Smithsonian Institution. (b) ©National Museum of the American Indian/ Smithsonian Institution. **602** Dan Westergren/National Geographic. **604–605** (spread) Richard T. Nowitz/ Corbis Documentary/Getty Images. **606** Christian Heeb/Prisma/SuperStock. **607** (tl) Christian Heeb/Prisma/SuperStock. (br) ©Chad Coppess/South Dakota Department of Tourism. **608** (t) Philip Scalia/ Alamy Stock Photo. (cl) Stillman Rogers/Alamy Stock Photo. **609** WILLIAM ALBERT ALLARD/ National Geographic Creative. **610–611** (spread) iofoto,2009/Used under license from Shutterstock.com. **612–613** (spread) The Library of Congress. **613** ©NPS. **614–615** (spread) Fotosearch/Getty Images. **615** Photo by Scott Dunn/Getty Images. **616** Time Life Pictures/Getty Images. **616** Justin Sullivan/Getty Images. **617** ©Ben Lee. **618** (tr) Statue of Liberty National Monument, National Park Service. (bl) ©Holt-Atherton Special Collections, University of the Pacific Library. **619** ©Holt-Atherton Special Collections, University of the Pacific Library. **622–623** (spread) Danita Delimont/Getty Images. **624** SSPL/Getty Images. **625** The Wright Brothers testing an early plane at Kitty Hawk, North Carolina (sepia photo), American Photographer, (20th century)/Private Collection/The Stapleton Collection/Bridgeman Images. **626** ©Ana Gómez/500px. **627** (tl) Underwood Archives/Getty Images. (tr) Hulton Archive/Getty Images. **628** ©Chicago Historical Society. **629** ©Chicago Historical Society. **631** ©Jordan J. Lloyd/Dynamichrome. **632** (tl) ©Lower East Side Tenement Museum. (c) National Geographic Learning. (br) ©Lower East Side Tenement Museum. **633** (tl) ©Lower East Side Tenement Museum. (cr) National Geographic Learning. **633** ©Lower East Side Tenement Museum. **635** Fotosearch/Getty Images. **636** Patti McConville/Alamy Stock Photo. **637** johnkellerman/iStock/Getty Images. **638** Jacob A. Riis/Getty Images. **640** ©New York Times Archive. **641** ©Missouri History Museum. **643** Library of Congress, Prints and Photographs Division [LC-USZC2-1058]. **644** Bettmann/ Getty Images. **645** (tl) Bettmann/Getty Images. (tr) Chicago History Museum/ Getty Images. **646** Library of Congress Prints and Photographs Division Washington[LC-D401-11590]. **648** ©ACUA—Archives of The Catholic University of America. **649** Everett Collection Inc/Alamy Stock Photo. **650** ©Chicago Historical Society. **651** ©Chicago Historical Society. **644–645** (spread) ©Johnnie Welborn,Jr./500px. **656** Jim Brandenburg/Minden Pictures. **658** The Library of Congress. **659** Danita Delimont/Getty Images. **660–661** (spread) PAUL NICKLEN/National Geographic Creative. **663** (tr) ©The Ansel Adams Publishing Rights Trust. 76. 577. 40. (b) ©The Ansel Adams Publishing Rights Trust. 84. 92. 156. **664** Photo Researchers, Inc/Alamy Stock Photo. **666** Photo 12/Getty Images. **667** Everett Collection Historical/ Alamy Stock Photo. **668** Library of Congress Prints and photographic Division[LC-USZ62-56439]. **669** Library of Congress/Getty Images. **670** Archive Pics/Alamy Stock Photo. **671** DOMINIQUE BRAUD/ANIMALS ANIMALS/ EARTH SCENES/National Geographic Creative. **672** National Archives. **673** AP Images/Casillas/REX Shutterstock.com. **675** Marcelo Baez/Shannon Associates/National Geographic Learning. **676** From the Collections of The Henry Ford. **677** AP Images/J. SCOTT APPLEWHITE. **678** North Wind Picture Archives/Alamy Stock Photo. **679** FPG/Getty Images. **680** Bettmann/Getty Images. **681** American Stock Archive/Getty Images. **682–683** (spread) American Stock Archive/Getty Images. **684** Haeckel collection/ullsteinbild/Premium Archive/Getty Images. **685** ©David Silverman/500px. **686** Armed Forces History, Division of History of Technology, National Museum of American History. **687** Theodore Roosevelt leading the 'Rough Riders' during the Spanish-American War, detail of a painting by W. G. Road, 1898 (colourlitho)/American School, (19th century)/PETER NEWARK'S PICTURES/Private Collection/ Bridgeman Images. **688** National Portrait Gallery, Smithsonian Institution/ Art Resource, NY. **689** Library of Congress/Getty Images. **693** FransLanting/ National Geographic Creative. **695** From the Collections of The Henry Ford. Gift of Ford Motor Company. **696** Archive Photos/Getty Images. **698–699** (spread) Smithsonian American Art Museum, Washington, DC/Art Resource, NY. **700** (cl) The Library of Congress. (tr) National Air and Space Museum, Smithsonian Institution. (b) Popperfoto/Getty Images. **701** (tl) ©Japanese American National Museum. (cr) Leonard Zhukovsky/ Shutterstock.com. (bl) ©United States Holocaust Memorial Museum. (b) IWM/Getty Images/Getty Images. **702–703** (spread) American infantry in WWI leaving their trench to advance against the Germans, 1918 (b/w photo)/American Photographer, (20th century)/PETER NEWARK'S PICTURES/Private Collection/Bridgeman Images. **704** Hulton Archive/ Getty Images. **706** IWM/Getty Images/Getty Images. **707** (tr) Jim Tannick/ Getty Images. (br) National Air and Space Museum. **709** (cl) Library of Congress, Prints & Photographs Division, LC-USZ62-93699. (cr) Everett Collection/AGE Fotostock. **712** Science & Society Picture Library/Getty Images. **713** UniversalImagesGroup/Getty Images. **714** Library of Congress/ National Geographic Learning. **716** US Army Signal Corps/Getty Images. **717** Collection of the Smithsonian National Museum of African American History and Culture, Gift of Gina R. McVey, grand daughter. **718** Cincinnati Museum Center/Getty Images. **719** Library of Congress, Prints & Photographs Division, LC-USZC4-2793. **721** WPA Pool/ Getty Images. **724** Library of Congress/Getty Images. **726–727** (spread) ©Marcus Akinlana. **729** Library of Congress/Prints & Photographs Division, LC-USZC4-7817. **730–731** (spread) Edwin Levick/Getty Images. **733** Sheridan Libraries/Levy/Gado/Getty Images. **734** Niday Picture Library/ Alamy Stock Photo. **735** SUETONE Emilio/AGE Fotostock. **737** REUTERS/ Mike Theiler. **739** The Advertising Archives/Alamy Stock Photo. **740** SilverScreen/Alamy Stock Photo. **741** (t) Glasshouse Images/Alamy Stock Photo. (c) ©Milo Stewart Jr./ National Baseball Hall of Fame and Museum. **742** Pictorial Press Ltd/Alamy Stock Photo. **743** Sueddeutsche Zeitung Photo/Alamy Stock Photo. **744** National Geographic Learning. **745** (tl) (bl) ©Smithsonian National Museum of American History. (cr) Jemal Countess/ Getty Images. **750** National Portrait Gallery, Smithsonian Institution/Art Resource, NY. **751** ©Smithsonian

American Art Museum, Washington, DC/ Art Resource, NY. **752** The Everett Collection. **753** INTERFOTO/Alamy Stock Photo. **755** ©Sidney Joseph Greene/ Newman Libary, CUNY. **756–757** (spread) Bettmann/Getty Images. **758–759** (spread) AKG Images. **760** Library of Congress, Prints & Photographs Division [LC-USZC4-8174]. **762** Smithsonian American Art Museum, Washington, DC/ Art Resource, NY. 1(c) AKG Images. (b) Library of Congress, Prints & Photographs Division, LC-DIG-fsa-8a44522. **761** SilverScreen/Alamy Stock Photo. **764** ClassicStock/Alamy Stock Photo. **767** quietbits/Shutterstock.com. **769** The Library of Congress—Prints & Photographs Division, LC-USZ62-31111. **770** Bettmann/Getty Images. **775** (t) Library of Congress, Prints & Photographs Division, Reproduction number LC-DIG-ppmsca-31916. (br) Dorothea Lange/ Getty Images. **776** GraphicaArtis/Getty Images. **777** MPI/Getty Images. **779** Smithsonian American Art Museum, Washington, DC/Art Resource, NY. **780** AP Images. **781** Everett Collection Inc/Alamy Stock Photo. **782–783** (spread) Spring Images/Alamy Stock Photo. **786–787** (spread) Education Images/UIG/ Getty Images. **788** Chronicle/Alamy Stock Photo. **791** Popperfoto/Getty Images. **792** Hulton Deutsch/Getty Images. **795** Danita Delimont/Getty Images. **796** (t) ©Smithsonian National Air and Space Museum. (b) Image by Plane Facts, Inc., National Air and Space Museum, Smithsonian Institution. **797** ©Smithsonian National Air and Space Museum. **799** Hulton Archive/Getty Images. **800** Bettmann/Getty Images. **801** Bernard Hoffman/Getty Images. **802** (bl) Afro Newspaper/ Gado/Getty Images. (br) ©National Museum of the US Airforce. **803** Everett Collection Inc/Alamy Stock Photo. **804** Robert Sullivan/AFP/Getty Images. **805** AP Images/Alan Diaz. **807** ©Japanese American National Museum. **809** Keystone-France/Getty Images. **812** Photo 12/Getty Images. **813** U.S. GOV'T GSA : ROOSEVELT, FRANKLIN D. LIBRARY/National Geographic Stock. **814** (t) Galerie Bilderwelt/Getty Images. (cr) ©United States Holocaust Memorial Museum Collection, Gift of Evelyn Levy Paswell. **816** AP Images. **817** Official U.S. Navy Photograph, now in the collections of the U.S. National Archives. **819** AP Images/JOE ROSENTHAL. **820** Galerie Bilderwelt/Getty Images. **821** (tr) ©Courtesy of the Beser family. (cr) ©Courtesy of the Beser family. **823** (tr) De Agostini Picture Library/Getty Images. (tc) Keystone-France/Getty Images. **826** adoc-photos/Getty Images. **828–829** (spread) Bruce Davidson/Magnum Photos. **830** (tl) Ian Dagnall/ Alamy Stock Photo. (tr) ©Bettmann/Getty Images. (b) wanderworldimages/ Alamy Stock Photo. **831** (tl) ©National Air and Space Museum. (tr) Bettmann/Getty Images. (bl) Aleksandar Milosavljevic/Alamy Stock Photo. (br) Bettmann/Getty Images. **832–833** (spread) Bettmann/Getty Images. **834–835** (spread) Bettmann/Getty Images. **836** Mirrorpix/Courtesy The Everett Collection. **837** (t) ClassicStock/ Alamy Stock Photo. (cr) ©Smithsonian National Museum of American History. **838** (tr) 20thCentFox/Courtesy The Everett Collection. (br) CBS Photo Archive/ Getty Images. **839** (tr) CBS Photo Archive/Getty Images. (tcr) CBS Photo Archive/Getty Images. (cr) CBS Photo Archive/Getty Images. (br) CBS Photo Archive/Getty Images. **840** (tr) Nature and Science/Alamy Stock Photo. (br) National Archives. **841** (tr) (cl) The Everett Collection. (c) Paramount/ Courtesy The Everett Collection. **842** war posters/Alamy Stock Photo. **843** (tr) Skim New Media Limited/Alamy Stock Photo. **844** William C. Shrout/ Getty Images. **845** Bettmann/Getty Images. **847** Bettmann/Getty Images. **848** Claro Cortes/ Reuters. **850** Carl Mydans/Getty Images. **852** NYPL/ Science Source/Getty Images. **853** Bettmann/Contributer/Getty Images. **855** AP Images/Nap. **857** (c) Ewing Galloway/Alamy Stock Photo. (bl) Tony Linck/Getty Images. **858** Bettmann/Getty Images. **859** ©Collection of the Smithsonian National Museum of African American History and Culture, Donation of Charles E. Berry; ©Gibson Brands, LLC. **862–863** (spread) Bruce Davidson/Magnum Photos. **864–865** (spread) The Washington Post/Getty Images. **866** Bruce Davidson/Magnum Photos. **867** A. Y. Owen/Getty Images. **868** ©Los Angeles Public Library. **869** (cr) AP Images. (br) ©Minnesota Historical Society. **870** Michael Rougier/Getty Images. **871** Bettmann/Getty Images. **872** Bettmann/ Getty Images. **873** JOHN LENT/AP Images. **874** Carl Iwasaki/Getty Images. **875** AP Images/TOM LEININGER. **876** Burt Glinn/Magnum Photos. **878** Underwood Archives/Getty Images. **879** AP Images/Anonymous. **881** AP Images/GENE HERRICK. **883** (t) Bruce Roberts/Getty Images. (b) Bettmann/ Getty Images. **884** AP Images/BILL HUDSON. **887** Bruce Davidson/Magnum Photos. **888** ©Bob Adelman. **890** (bl) Collection of the Smithsonian National Museum of African American History and Culture, Gift of Samuel Y. Edgerton, 2013.187.4. (cr) Collection of the Smithsonian National Museum of African American History and Culture, Gift of the Family of Rev. Norman C. "Jim" Jimerson and Melva Brooks Jimerson, 2013.138a–c. **891** (tl) Collection of the Smithsonian National Museum of African American History and Culture, 2012.107.10. (cr) Collection of the Smithsonian National Museum of African American History and Culture, Gift from Dawn Simon Spears and Alvin Spears, Sr., 2011.159.3.25. (cl) Collection of the Smithsonian National Museum of African American History and Culture, 2012.107.10. (b) Collection of the Smithsonian National Museum of African American History and Culture, Gift of University of Mary Washington, Fredericksburg, VA in honor of Dr. James Farmer, 2011.130. **893** Bettmann/Getty Images. **894–895** (spread) Terray Sylvester/Redux Photo. **895** Everett Collection Inc/Alamy Stock Photo. **896** MICHAEL MELFORD/National Geographic Creative. **898** Alyssa Schukar/The New York Times/Redux. **899** Mark Thiessen/National Geographic Creative. **899** Robert Alexander/Getty Images. **900–901** (spread) Larry Burrows/Getty Images. **902** Paul Schutzer/Getty Images. **903** ©Smithsonian National Postal Museum. **904** ©National Air and Space Museum. **905** Bettmann/Getty Images. **906–907** (spread) Keystone-France/ Getty Images. **909** Charles Phelps Cushing/ ClassicStock/Getty Images. **910** Bettmann/Getty Images. **911** UniversalImagesGroup/Getty Images. **912** Bettmann/Getty Images. **913** Bettmann/Getty Images. **914** AP Images/ Anonymous. **915** ©Pirkle Jones/UC Santa Cruz. **916** ©Denver Post/Getty Images. **917** AP Images/Charles Kelly. **918** ©Graphic Arts Group, San Francisco/Center for the Study of Political Graphics; "Yo Soy Alguien" poster image is the intellectual property of the UFW and is used with permission of the United Farm Workers of America. **919** Bob Fitch photography archive, © Stanford University Libraries. **920** ©Richard Barnes. **921** ©Jason DeLeón. **923** Bettmann/Getty Images. **924** AP Images/ Charles Gorry. **925** ©Collection of the U.S. House of Representatives. **927** Paul Schutzer/Getty Images. **928** Bettmann/Getty Images. **929** Thomas White/ REUTERS. **931** tim page/Getty Images. **932** Harvey Silver/Getty Images. **934** Joseph Louw/Getty Images. **936** (tr) ©San Francisco Chronicle/ Polaris. **937** Conrad cartoons are used with permission of the Conrad Estate. **938** MICHAEL MELFORD/National Geographic Creative. **940–941** (spread) Library of Congress, Prints & Photographs Division, LC-DIG-highsm-12456. **942** (tl) Courtesy of NASA. (tc) ©Smithsonian National Museum of American History. (b) Evgeniya Anikienko/Shutterstock.com. **943** (tl) EQRoy/Shutterstock.com. (tr) Leonard Zhukovsky/Shutterstock.com. (cl) ©2014 The Washington Post/ Getty Images. (bl) Jonny White/Alamy Stock Photo. (cr) ©Ron Haviv/VII. **944–945** (spread) David Hume Kennerly/Getty Images. **946–947** (spread) Agencja Fotograficzna Caro/Alamy Stock Photo. **948** Keystone/Getty Images. **949** AKG Images. **951** (l) mauritius images GmbH/Alamy Stock Photo. (r) Rolf Adlercreutz/Alamy Stock Photo. **952** (c) PJF Military Collection/Alamy Stock Photo. (br) Stuart Lutz/Gado/Getty Images. **953** John Filo/Getty Images. **955** Historical/Getty Images. **957** Alfred Eisenstaedt/Getty Images. **958** Edgard Garrido/Reuters. **959** Bloomberg/Getty Images. **960** Waring Abbott/Getty Images. **961** Bettmann/ Getty Images. **962** Smith Collection/Gado/Getty Images. **963** AP Images/ Benjamin E. "gene" Forte. **964** Bettmann/Getty Images. **965** ©Tel Or Beni/ GPO/Getty Images. Getty Images/Getty Images. **966** MPI/Getty Images. **967** Yvonne Hemsey/Getty Images. **968** Entertainment Pictures/Alamy Stock Photo. **969** Robert R. McElroy/Getty Images. **970** Joe Traver/Getty Images. **971** Bettmann/Getty Images. **973** Panoramic Images/ Getty Images. **975** Bobby Yip/Reuters. **977** Wally McNamee/Corbis Premium Historical/Getty Images. **980–981** (spread) Richard Ellis/AGE Fotostock. **982** Visions of America/Getty Images. **983** AP Images/J. Scott Aplewhite. **984** JM/ BM/AA/ REUTERS. **985** AP Images/Carolyn Kaster. **986** Robert King/Getty Images. **987** AP Images/ERIC DRAPER. **988** POOL Old/REUTERS. **989** Universal Images Group North America LLC/DeAgostini/Alamy Stock Photo. **990** REUTERS/Marc Serota. **992** REUTERS/Carlos Barria. **993** ©Taylor Mickal. **994** Pool/Getty Images. **997** AP Images/ Ed Reinke. **998** AP Images/David J. Phillip. **1001** The Smithsonian American Art Msueum, Gift of the artist ©Nam June Paik Estate. **1003** ©Mark Richards, Computer History Museum. (br) ©Mark Richards/Zuma Press/Alamy. **1005** ©Kirsten Luce. **1006** MANDEL NGAN/Getty Images. **1007** Aaron Bernstein/Reuters. **1008** Bruce Molnia/U.S. Geological Survey. **1009** Roger Ressmeyer/Corbis/VCG/Getty Images. **1012** Martin Schoeller/National Geographic Creative. **1014** Mark Thiessen/National Geographic Creative. **R0–R1** (spread) GREG DALE/ National Geographic Creative. **R2** Bettmann/Getty Images. **R10** Bygone Collection/Alamy Stock Photo. **R15** SAUL LOEB/Getty Images. **R17** ©REUTERS/Jonathan Ernst **R19** National Archives. **R26** Library of Congress, Prints & Photographs Division, LC-DIG-pga-03453. **R27** Library of Congress, Prints & Photographs Division, LC-USZ62-123257. **R32** Bettmann/Getty Images. **R33** Tetra Images/ Shutterstock.com. **R35** Spencer Platt/Getty Images. **R37** Hill Street Studios/ Eric Raptosh/Getty Images.

Text Credits

Pg. 885 "Letter from Birmingham City Jail," by Dr. Martin Luther King Jr. April 16, 1963. Reprinted by arrangement with The Heirs to the Estate of Martin Luther King Jr., c/o Writers House as agent for the proprietor New Nork, NY. ©1963 Dr. Martin Luther King Jr. ©Renewed 1991 Loretta Scott King.

Pg. 886, 889 "I Have a Dream," by Dr. Martin Luther King Jr. Reprinted by arrangement with The Heirs to the Estate of Martin Luther King Jr., c/o Writers House as agent for the proprietor New Nork, NY. ©1963 Martin Luther King Jr. ©Renewed 1991 Coretta Scott King.

Illustration Credits

Unless otherwise indicated, all illustrations are created by Lachina and all maps are created by Mapping Specialists.